American Beech	369
American Elm	1034
Bald Cypress	996
Bitternut Hickory	184
Black Gum	680
Bur Oak	821
Catalpa	193
Chinese Chestnut	190
Chinese Pistache	749
Dawn Redwood	662
Fraxinus pennsylvanica/ Green A	393
Freeman's maple	45
Ginkgo	406
Hackberry	203
Japanese Zelkova	1106
Katsura Tree	207
Lacebark/Chinese Elm	1041
Large leaf linden	1018
Little leaf linden	1020
London Plane Tree	752
Mimosa	83
Northern Red Oak	835
Norway Maple	40
Overcup Oak	820
Pecan	154
Persian Parrotia	695
Pin Oak	826
Post Oak	837
Red Maple	44
River Birch	126
Sawtooth Oak	812
Shumard Oak	829
Silver Maple	50
Sourwood	692
Southern red oak	816
Sugar Maple	53
Sweetgum	568
Thornless Honeylocust	408
Tulip Poplar	572
Umbrella Magnolia	617
Upright English Oak	833
Upright European Hornbeam	178
Water Oak	826
Weeping Willow	922
White Oak	814
Willow Oak	830
Winged Elm	1037

of

ape Plants

Scientific Name	Common Name	Number
Callicarpa americana	American Beautyberry	159
Clematis armandii	Armand's clematis	236
Vinca major	Big Periwinkle	1090
Aesculus parviflora	Bottlebrush Buckeye	75
Koelreuteria bipinnata	Bougainvillea Goldenrain Tree	534
Ajuga reptans	Bugleflower	
Spiraea x bumalda	Bumald Spirea	956
Euonymus alatus	Burning Bush	354
X Fatshedera lizei	Bush Ivy	375
Buddleia davidii	Butterfly-bush	144
Pyrus calleryana	Callery Bradford Pear	806
Gelsemium sempervirens	Carolina yellow Jessamine	403
Aspidistra elatior	Cast-iron Plant	112
Vitex agnus-castus	Chastetree	1091
Cornus kousa	Chinese Dogwood	260
Chionanthus retusus	Chinese Graybeard	229
Hamamelis mollis	Chinese Witchhazel	419
Ficus pumila	Climbing Fig	377
Ficus carica	Common fig	377
Trachelospermum jasminoides	Confederate Jasmine	1027
Cornus mas	Cornelian Cherry Dogwood	268
Lagerstroemia indica	Crape Myrtle	538
Liriope spicata	Creeping Lilyturf	599
Bignonia capreolata	Crossvine	694
Hemerocallis spp.	Daylilies	197
Fothergilla gardenii	Dwarf Fothergilla	385
Cercis canadensis	Eastern Redbud	208
Hedera helix	English Ivy	425
Akebia quinata	Fiveleaf Akebia	81
Cornus florida	Flowering Dogwood	253
Forsythia x intermedia	Forsythia	379
Chionanthus virginicus	Fringetree	227
Koelreuteria paniculata	Goldenrain Tree	533
Corylus avellana 'Contorta'	Henry Lauder's walking stick	279
Prunus subhirtella	Higan Cherry	790
Cyrtomium falcatum	Holly Fern	311
Hosta	Hosta	
Prunus serrulata	Japanese Cherry	789
Acer palmatum	Japanese Maple	27
Styrax japonica	Japanese snowbell	973
Pachysandra terminalis	Japanese Spurge	694
Stewartia pseudocamelia	Japanese stewwartia	971
Wisteria floribunda	Japanese Wisteria	1098
Viburnum carlesii	Koreanspice Viburnum	1060
Rosa banksiae	Lady Banks Rose	910
Helleborus orientalis	Lenten Rose	107
Liriope muscari	Lilyturf	
Gordonia lasianthus	Loblolly Bay	391
Ophiopogon japonicus	Monkeygrass	
Hydrangea quercifolia	Oakleaf Hydrangea	446
Hydrangea paniculata	Panicle Hydrangea	442
Acer griseum	Paperbark maple	19
Rhododendron canescens	Piedmont Azalea	854
Aesculus pavia	Red Buckeye	77
Rosmarinus officianalis	Rosemary	918
Hibiscus syriacus	Rose-of-Sharon	427
Viburnum sargentii	Sargent viburnum	1084
Magnolia x soulangiana	Saucer Magnolia	611

Manual of
Woody Landscape Plants

Their Identification, Ornamental Characteristics, Culture, Propagation and Uses

11st 4

Amelanchier sp.	Serviceberry	471
Hydrangea arborescens	Smooth Hydrangea	435
Magnolia stellata	Star Magnolia	616
Clethera alnifolia	Summersweet clethera	239
Magnolia virginiana	Sweetbay	618
Sarcococca hookeriana var. humilis	Sweetbox	935
Calycanthus floridus	Sweetshrub; carolina allspice	166
Malus hupehensis	tea crabapple	644
Spirea thunbergii	Thunberg's spirea	963
Acer buergerianum	Trident maple	13
Clematis virginiana	Virgin's Bower	238
Ardisia japonica	Whitecap Marlberry	107
Jasminum nudiflorum	Winter Jasmine	497
Ilex verticillata	Winterberry	467
Euonymus fortunei	Wintercreeper	359
Trachelospermum asiaticum	Yellow star jasmine	1028
Prunus x yedoensis	Yoshino Cherry	793

RONNIE DIRR

American Arborvitae	Thuja occidentalis	1009
Arizona Cypress	Cupressus arizona	307
Chinese Fir	Cunninghamia lanceolata	303
David Viburnum	Viburnum davidii	1064
Dwarf Alberta Spruce	Picea glauca	716
Hetz Juniper	Juniperus chinensis "Hetzi"	504
Hinoki Cypress	Chamaecyparis obtusa	218
Japanese Andromeda	Pieris japonica	722
Japanese False Cypress	Chamaecyparis pisifera	220
Leatherleaf Mahonia	Mohonia bealei	627
Lusterleaf or Magnolialeaf Holly	Ilex latifolia	481
Mt. Laurel	Kalmia latifolia	526
Oriental Artorvitae	Thuja orientalis	1011
Pfitzer's Juniper	Juniperus chinensis "Pfitzeriana"	504
Scarlet Firethorn	Pyracantha coccinea	803
Western Arborvitae	Thuja pliccata	1013

Champaign, Illinois

The plants on the back cover represent six of the more than fifty cultivars introduced by the author through the University of Georgia Plant Introduction Program.

Inquiries should be addressed to:

Stipes Publishing L.L.C.
P.O. Box 526
Champaign, Illinois 61824

Library of Congress Cataloging in Publication Data

Dirr, Michael A.
      Manual of Woody Landscape Plants
      Their Identification, Ornamental Characteristics, Culture, Propagation and Uses
      Fifth Edition

Summary: A reference guide to the identification and culture of over 1,600 species and over 7,800 cultivars of woody landscape plants. Includes bibliography, common name and scientific indexes.

            1. Woody Landscape Plants. 2. Plant Identification. 3. Plant Culture.
            4. Plant Propagation.

Library of Congress Catalog Card Number: 98-61065

ISBN 0-87563-795-7

04   20 19 18 17 16 15 14

To The Dirr Family.

The Journey has been a Joy.

ACKNOWLEDGMENTS

To the great plantsmen who provided the inspiration, information, and new plants through exploration, breeding, serendipity, lectures, and literature.

To Hillary Barber who typed, edited, and attempted to keep the author in bounds.

To Vickie Waters-Oldham who maintained the integrity of my research program and provided the warm smile which translated to, "You will soon have the *Manual* completed."

To Bob Watts, Publisher, who believes that the author should know, not the corporate editor.

To Bonnie, my wonderful wife, for all the great times together: hiking Isle au Haut in Maine; Joyce Kilmer, North Carolina; Rabun Bald, Georgia; Hoh Rain Forest, Washington; and for loving plants and me. Also, her terrific pen-and-ink drawings to make the *Manual* more meaningful and aesthetic.

The Greatest Admiration.

PREFACE TO THE FIFTH EDITION

At times I pondered whether this latest version of the *Manual* would make its way to press. Obviously it has, for in the pages to be turned reside the fruits of my activities. In a meaningful and spiritual way, the *Manual* and I are enmeshed so seamlessly that it is difficult to tell where Dirr starts and the Manual picks up. Indeed, they weigh about the same. The words are more than ink on paper. They articulate and extoll biological organisms that I lovingly term *Woody Landscape Plants*.

The Fifth Edition is rich with new cultivars, some so fresh as yet to have made their way into nursery production. The nursery industry is cognizant of the essentiality of new plants to increase market share. Larger nurseries have established plant testing and introduction programs under their corporate umbrellas. In many respects the industry has become more business oriented. Plant patents and trademarks are an integral part of the process. Something akin to 396 plant patents were granted in 1997 with 20 to 25% of those woody. Since 1930, when the Plant Patent Act was established, 9,700 patents were granted through 1996. New plants are rolling off the assembly line faster than anyone can evaluate. I have tried to make the *Manual* as up-to-date as rationally feasible. Please write or call with information on plants that escaped my purview.

The years since the Fourth Edition have witnessed remarkable growth of gardening, the nursery industry, and supporting activities (Home & Gardening Television, radio gardening shows, CD-ROMs, books, periodicals, botanical gardens, and arboreta). Gardening, in whatever form practiced, provides positive emotional and spiritual experiences that are available nowhere else. For most of us, lack of time is the greatest frustration. We go to work in the dark, and return in same. Perhaps the garden offers the mini-sanctuary where we can reflect on the craziness that, at times, appears to control our lives. A garden is indeed the forum for creativity, reflection, repose, and spirituality.

Since the publication of the Fourth Edition (1990), the horticultural world lost several of its greatest ambassadors and scholars: Dr. J.C. Raulston, North Carolina State University, Dr. John Pair, Kansas State University, Mr. Benny Simpson, Texas A&M University, Mr. Lynn Lowrey, Texas, and Mr. David Leach, North Madison, Ohio, who provided our gardens with new woody and herbaceous introductions. Too many wonderful plantsmen, too soon taken from their gardens, work, and families.

The preface to the Fourth Edition mentioned the 46th year of a satisfying life. Nothing has changed except for the better and the fact I am 54. Students whom I trained early in my career are sending their children to college. Has the time evaporated that quickly?

Obviously, my academic career is in the waning years. I was profoundly influenced by the wisdom of Liberty Hyde Bailey who thoughtfully advocated training one's self for 25 years, working for 25 years, and doing what one pleased for 25 years. I am slightly behind schedule for the third leg of the journey but hope to quickly catch up.

My best in life, gardening, and wherever the garden path takes the reader.

Enjoy the Manual.

Michael A. Dirr
Athens, Georgia
July, 1998

INTRODUCTION TO THE USE OF THE MANUAL

Each plant type (taxon) is discussed in a defined sequence and usually accompanied by a line drawing and identification characteristics related to leaf, bud, and stem. Certain plants are discussed under the heading RELATED SPECIES. This approach was taken to avoid repetition and at the same time allow for a significantly greater number of plant discussions. However, not all plants discussed under RELATED SPECIES are perfect taxonomic "fits."

The plant's scientific (with pronunciation), common, and family names are the first items treated under each description. After the family name has been listed for a particular genus it is usually omitted for the other species within the genus. The latin names are as accurate and current as are feasible. Also included are the authority names, i.e., the individual who first and/or correctly named the plant. Readers requested this inclusion. For those botanical purists, I discovered by cross-checking scientific name authorities, that there is not homogeneity of authorship for all plants.

Since 1990, three major taxonomic tomes on wild and cultivated plants were published. They are *The New Royal Horticultural Society Dictionary of Gardening* (1992); *A Synonymized Checklist of the Vascular Flora of the United States, Canada, and Greenland* (1994); and *A Catalog of Cultivated Woody Plants of the Southeastern United States* (1994). Unfortunately, the three references do not always agree relative to the universal scientific name for a cultivated plant. For example, *Stewartia* species' treatments are messy. Plants that gardeners knew as *Acanthopanax sieboldianus* (now *Eleutherococcus sieboldianus*), *Feijoa sellowiana* (now *Acca sellowiana*), and *Kalopanax pictus* (now *Kalopanax septemlobus*) should have been maintained intact. I have included the new(er) name changes but most often only in a parenthetical way. *The International Code for Nomenclature of Cultivated Plants* was revised in 1995. This was followed, although there are several gaps in my presentation(s). Common names are essentially offered to the reader based on usage in everyday horticultural and gardening publications. In several cases, my decision almost equated with a roll-of-the-dice when picking an everyday name.

Common names are a constant source of confusion and embarrassment. I have attempted, in most cases, to use the common name which is widely spoken. Certain plants might have 3 to 5 common names and they are usually included after the "accepted" common name. Common names should be written in lower case unless part of the name is proper and then the first letter of only the proper term is capitalized. For example, sugar maple would be written with lower case letters while Japanese maple would be written with the capital J. This is the accepted method for writing common names in scientific circles and should be familiar to the student. In this text, and many others, common names are written with capital first letters. This was done to set the name off from the rest of the sentence and make it more evident to the reader. Actually in modern horticultural writings the capitalized common name predominates.

The family name was included so that the reader could begin to see the common floral or fruit bonds which exist among genera which are dissimilar to each other in vegetative (leaf, bud, stem, habit) characters. For example, Kentucky Coffeetree does not appear similar or related to Redbud but the similarity of fruits should imply a familial relationship.

The use of SIZE delineations is a moot question and almost any description can be challenged due to the great variation which is to be found in a native population compared to a landscape population. I have attempted to estimate sizes which might be attained under "normal" landscape situations and, in many instances, have listed maximum heights and national champion sizes so that the reader might get a feel for the differences. Plants can be maintained at various heights and widths by proper pruning. If a plant is listed as 25 feet in height and one only has space for a 20 foot specimen this is no reason to avoid using the tree. There are simply too many variables which affect the size of a tree or shrub. Plants which appear gnarled and dwarfed on high mountain tops where the soil is dry, rocky, and the exposure windy and cold, may grow to be gentle giants in the moist, fertile, well-drained soils of the valley below. Do not attempt to evaluate the size of a tree in one individual's yard with that in another's even though both may be of the same age. The conditions under which they are growing may be very different.

HARDINESS ratings are risky business since many factors other than low temperatures affect plant survival in a specific area. The hardiness zones mentioned in this book follow the 1990 edition (1 to 11 Zones) of the U.S. Hardiness Zone Map compiled by the U. S. Department of Agriculture. A picture of the map is presented. Each zone includes 10°F increments and is split into an *a* and *b* Zone with the lower temperature occurring in the *a* Zone.

USDA Hardiness Zones

Zone 1	—	below	-50°F
Zone 2	—	-50 to	-40°F
Zone 3	—	-40 to	-30°F
Zone 4	—	-30 to	-20°F
Zone 5	—	-20 to	-10°F
Zone 6	—	-10 to	0°F
Zone 7	—	0 to	10°F
Zone 8	—	10 to	20°F
Zone 9	—	20 to	30°F
Zone 10	—	30 to	40°F
Zone 11	—	above	40°F

Hardiness ratings are meant only as a guide and should not be looked upon as a limiting factor in plant use. Large bodies of water, well-drained soil, wind protection, and adequate moisture will help to increase plant survival. Many plants such as forsythia are limitedly flower bud hardy but quite shoot hardy. Plants, such as *Abelia* × *grandiflora*, are best considered weakly shoot hardy and are often killed to the ground in central Illinois but, as with herbaceous perennials, develop new shoots and will make an attractive show during the growing season since flowers are produced on new wood.

Hardiness is a dual-edged sword for heat, like cold, can limit successful growth of certain plants. Unfortunately, heat tolerance has not been studied to any degree. *Acer platanoides*, Norway Maple, languishes in the heat of Zone 7 and 8. The same is true for most firs, spruces, and white-barked birches. The reasons for their lack of adaptability are unknown but rest assured heat stress, high night temperatures, and/or perhaps lack of sufficient chilling to satisfy bud rest, contribute to plant decline. The American Horticultural Society via the leadership of Dr. Marc Cathey has published a heat adaptability map. I secured a copy, studied same, and believe the concept is meritorious. It will take a terrific amount of time to assign the woody plants in this *Manual* to the best-suited heat zones. In some respects this has been accomplished by assigning southern limits to most of the taxa. There is no guarantee that a species which performs well in Boston or Cincinnati will do likewise in Atlanta or Orlando. The hardiness zone ratings have been expanded to include the most suitable range for the culture of a specific plant.

Another hardiness factor relates to a particular plant species' or cultivar's ability to acclimate (develop cold hardiness) early in autumn thus avoiding early freezes and, conversely, maintain this cold hardiness into spring to avoid late spring freezes. For many plants the process (rates) of cold acclimation and deacclimation are possibly more important in plant performance and survival than absolute low temperature tolerances in mid-winter. Several examples serve to highlight the phenomena. *Lagerstroemia indica*, Common Crapemyrtle, acclimates slowly and can be seriously injured by early fall freezes. Although late to show leaf development (April) in Zone 7b, April freezes have devastated newly emerging leaves and killed the cambium. In fact, in leaf Crapemyrtle has almost no tolerance to below 32°F temperatures. *Hydrangea macrophylla* is early leafing (March) in Zone 7b and is seriously damaged by late freezes. Since flower buds are formed on the previous year's stems, flowering is reduced or rendered null and void.

In many instances, I have offered a ballpark estimate of flower bud or plant low temperature tolerance. These predictions are based on extensive observations, the literature, and laboratory cold hardiness determinations that Dr. Orville M. Lindstrom and I have conducted on many taxa. Use these as a guide and not absolute values. One should never allow hardiness ratings to solely determine whether he/she will use a specific plant. Since plants have not been known to read what is written about them in terms of hardiness, they often surprise and grow outside of their listed range of adaptability.

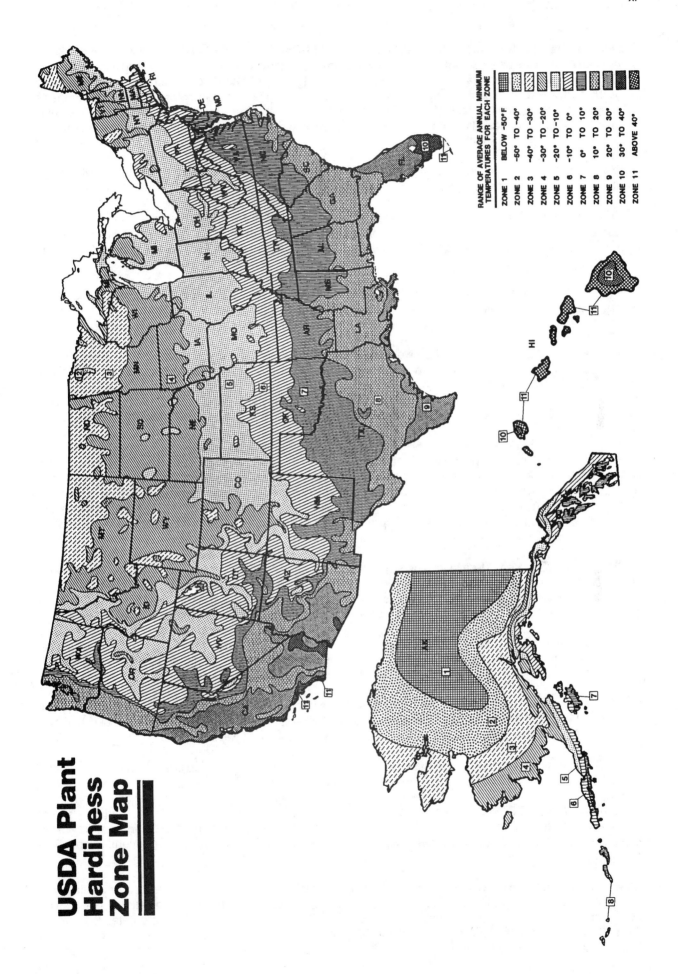

USDA Plant Hardiness Zone Map

RANGE OF AVERAGE ANNUAL MINIMUM
TEMPERATURES FOR EACH ZONE

ZONE 1   BELOW −50°F
ZONE 2   −50° TO −40°
ZONE 3   −40° TO −30°
ZONE 4   −30° TO −20°
ZONE 5   −20° TO −10°
ZONE 6   −10° TO 0°
ZONE 7   0° TO 10°
ZONE 8   10° TO 20°
ZONE 9   20° TO 30°
ZONE 10   30° TO 40°
ZONE 11   ABOVE 40°

The effects of lack of chill hours (defined as hours below 45°) are often evident after a mild winter in the South (Zone 7 to 9). Cultivars derived from northern provenances (seed sources) require more chilling than those from southern sources. 'October Glory' Red Maple does not fully leaf out until mid-May in a mild winter in Zone 7b while the native Red Maples are in full leaf by late April. Flowering is also impacted with a number of the *H. × intermedia* cultivars, most notably 'Arnold Promise', flowering in March in Athens, and late January–February in Boston. Although this has little to do with cold hardiness, the fact that plants do not experience sufficient cold (chill) profoundly affects expected plant performance.

HABIT as used in this book should supply the reader with a mental picture of the ultimate form or outline of the plant and should prove useful to landscape architecture and design students.

RATE of growth refers to the vertical increase in growth unless specified differently. Rate, as is true for size, is influenced by numerous variables such as soil, drainage, water, fertility, light, exposure, ad infinitum. The designation *slow* means the plant grows 12″ or less per year; *medium* refers to 13 to 24″ of growth per year; and *fast* to 25″ or greater.

TEXTURE refers to the appearance of the plant in foliage and without foliage. A plant that is fine in leaf may be extremely coarse without foliage. Best landscape effects are achieved when similar textures are blended. For example, a planting of catalpa next to a weeping willow is a definite contrast of textures.

The BARK and STEM color and texture were included so that the reader could develop an appreciation for these ornamental characters. Too often they are overlooked and omitted as integral parts of the plant's aesthetic qualities. Considering that most deciduous trees and shrubs are devoid of foliage for six months in the northern states, it behooves gardeners and designers to use trees and shrubs with good bark character. To my way of thinking trees like *Acer griseum*, *Stewartia* spp., and *Ulmus parvifolia* are more beautiful without foliage.

LEAF COLOR refers to the shade of green of trees in spring–summer as well as the colors attained in fall. Again, nutritional and soil factors partially influence the degree of greenness and to a lesser extent the quality of fall color. Fall color is very strongly genetically controlled. The maximum expression of fall coloration is realized when environmental conditions and plant genotypes are in synchrony. This means that no matter how perfect the environmental conditions, *Acer negundo* will not have red fall color! The genes for same are essentially lacking in the Boxelder. However, provide the perfect environment to 'October Glory' and the red fall color is maximized.

FLOWERS are discussed in terms of color, size, fragrance, period of effectiveness (based on my observations in central Illinois, Boston, and Athens-Atlanta, GA), and the type of inflorescence. Some plants bear monoecious flowers (both sexes on same plant) while others are dioecious (sexes separate). This has profound implications if one is interested in fruit production. It does no good to buy 5 female *Ilex opaca*, American Holly, unless a male plant accompanies them. The male is necessary for pollination and subsequent fruit set. A good rule of thumb to apply to flowering as treated in this book is to add (3)4(5) weeks to Georgia dates to equate them with central Illinois-Boston and reverse the procedure for Illinois-Boston dates to bring them into harmony with Athens-Atlanta. Unless dates are specified as Georgian, they refer to central Illinois-Boston.

FRUIT discussion covers the type of fruit for each particular plant (i.e., whether it is a drupe, pome, berry); the size and color; period of effectiveness; persistence; and ornamental value. Fruits are one of the most cherished attributes of many trees and shrubs, particularly for fall–winter color and wildlife food.

The CULTURE section discusses the ease of transplanting, soil, light, pruning, pollution tolerance, and other factors which govern the successful growth of a particular plant type.

DISEASES AND INSECTS is a listing of problems encountered with various plant types. If a particular insect or disease is a significant problem it is usually discussed in some detail. Surprisingly most plants require limited maintenance. Ask yourself how often you have sprayed for insects or diseases on your ornamental plants. The necessary trend into the new millennium is toward low maintenance, low chemical input plants.

LANDSCAPE VALUE is an arbitrary judgement on my part as to the best location or use for a particular plant in the landscape. Plants can be tailored to specific locations by pruning and other manipulations. The "pigeon holing" of plants is by far the worst crime one can commit. Certain plants are used for celebrated locations in the landscape and have become stereotyped. Blue Colorado Spruce or a White Birch are common occurrences in the front yard. Yews and many junipers are often reserved for foundation plantings. The effective use of a particular plant requires a thorough knowledge of all the factors discussed under that plant. It does no good to use a plant that has lovely flower and fruit qualities in wet soils if it is not adapted to this condition.

CULTIVARS are important (essential) components of the modern landscape and have been selected for growth habit, flower, fruit, pollution tolerance and myriad other factors. I have attempted to list the more common and recent introductions which are worthy of landscape consideration. Almost every juniper which is now sold is a cultivar which has been selected for good foliage and/or growth habit. The same could be said for many plants and you will note that many cultivar names are probably more familiar to you than the species. Readers might note the more liberal inclusion of trademark names in this edition. Cultivar names cannot be trademarked, so plants must travel with trademark (Red Sunset®) and cultivar ('Franksred') names. A registered trademark is written with a superscript ^{R} and a circle ® while ™ in superscript can be attached by any individual to a name to protect the commercial application of that name to said plant. The registered trademark is registered with the Office of Trademarks and Patents, Washington, DC. Trademarking has escalated into a nonsensical and confusing practice by plantsmen and the nursery industry. Plum Delight® loropetalum of one nursery is also Pizzazz™ of another; Goldflame honeysuckle, *Lonicera × heckrottii*, for marketing purposes has been renamed Pink Lemonade™, Mardi Gras™, and 'Summergold'. Product identity for consumers of horticultural products is already confusing, this new tact takes it to the nightmare level.

PROPAGATION section lists the most effective methods of seed and vegetative reproduction. One of my research interests is in the area of propagation and much of the information in this section is based on actual experience. This section continues to expand with each edition and often includes references for the individual requiring additional information.

RELATED SPECIES section discusses plant types which are similar to the species in many characters but differ in a few areas such as size, flower, or fruit color. Also included are those plants which are of negligible importance in the landscape but are worth considering if native to a particular area. Other plants discussed include plants which are limitedly known and available but may have excellent landscape potential.

ADDITIONAL NOTES is a potpourri of facts, trivia, or minutia related to the use of plant parts for food, fiber, and man's enjoyment. In actuality, it provides a venue for information that simply will not fit anywhere else.

NATIVE HABITAT discusses the natural distribution or range of a particular plant type. The introduction or cultivation date is the earliest record of the plants. Many people have questioned the authenticity of the dates. I did not make them up, only recorded them based on the literature. History fibs, so do not suffer anxiety attacks if my date varies from yours.

PLANT MORPHOLOGY

In order to successfully identify woody plants it is necessary for an individual to have a keen awareness (working knowledge) of taxonomic terminology and concise mental pictures of leaf, bud, stem, flower and fruit morphology. The glossary in the back of the text capably defines the terminology. This section is devoted to line drawings of woody plant morphological characters which will aid in the identification of various plant types. Definitions and examples are also included.

LEAF MORPHOLOGY

ANGIOSPERM LEAF TYPES

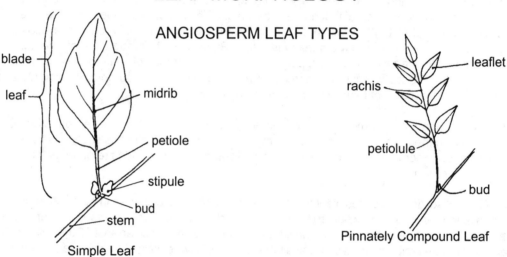

Simple Leaf

Pinnately Compound Leaf

The position of the bud determines whether the leaf is simple or compound. In this case the bud is located in the axil of a single leaf and the stem, therefore, the leaf is classified as simple. Ex: *Acer* (primarily), *Betula, Cornus, Fagus, Quercus, Ulmus.*

In this case the bud is located in the axil of a structure with more than one leaf (leaflet) attached, therefore, the leaf is termed compound. Compound leaves are composed of anywhere from three (*Acer griseum*) to 400 to 1500 leaf-like structures in the case of *Albizia julibrissin.*

OTHER TYPES OF COMPOUND LEAVES

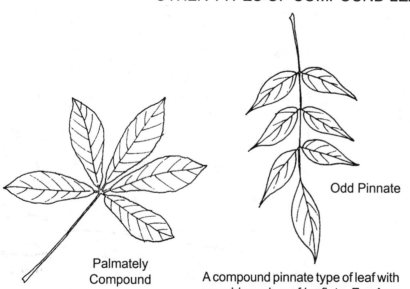

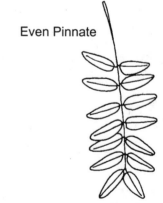

Even Pinnate

Palmately Compound

Odd Pinnate

In this situation each leaflet is attached to a common point. Ex: *Aesculus, Acanthopanax, Akebia quinata, Parthenocissus quinquefolia.*

A compound pinnate type of leaf with an odd number of leaflets. Ex: *Acer negundo* has 3 to 5 leaflets; *Cladrastis kentukea* has 7 to 9 leaflets; *Fraxinus americana* has 5 to 9 leaflets; *Rhus glabra* has 11 to 31 leaflets.

A compound pinnate type of leaf with an even number of leaflets. Ex: *Gleditsia, Caragana, Pistacia chinensis, Sapindus drummondii.*

Bipinnately Compound

Bipinnately compound leaves are twice divided. What was considered the leaflet of the pinnately compound leaf is now another leaf-bearing axis to which additional leaflets are attached. The new leaf bearing axes are referred to as pinnae. Each pinna has a certain number of leaflets. Ex: *Albizia, Aralia* (bi- and tripinnately compound), *Gleditsia* (in certain instances), *Gymnocladus*.

Tripinnately Compound

Tripinnately compound leaves are thrice divided with the leaflet of the bipinnately compound leaf becoming a stalk to which leaflets are attached. Ex: *Nandina domestica*.

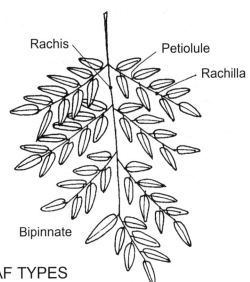

Rachis Petiolule Rachilla

Bipinnate

GYMNOSPERM LEAF TYPES

Cone-bearing or naked seeded plants often display different leaf types than those associated with angiosperm plants. Not all conifers (or cone-bearers) have evergreen foliage (several exceptions include *Taxodium, Metasequoia, Larix,* and *Pseudolarix*.)

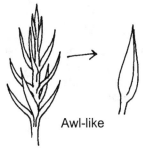

Awl-like

The needles (leaves) are shaped like an awl. They are usually very sharp to the touch. Many *Juniperus* (Junipers) exhibit awl-shaped foliage. This character is manifested in juvenile forms of juniper, however, there are many species and cultivars (*Juniperus communis, J. procumbens, J. chinensis* 'Pyramidalis' to name a few) which possess the awl-like or needle foliage in youth and old age.

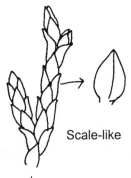

Scale-like

Scale-like foliage overlaps like the shingles on a roof or the scales on a fish. This type of foliage is relatively soft to the touch. *Calocedrus, Chamaecyparis, Cupressus, Thuja,* and many *Juniperus* species exhibit this type of foliage.

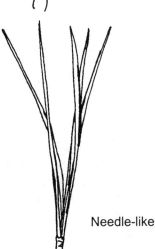

Needle-like

Needle-like foliage is typical of several evergreen genera and species. The drawing depicts the foliage of a 5-needled pine. In the genus *Pinus* the leaves (needles) are usually contained in fascicles of 2, 3, 2 and 3, or 5. Other species such as *Abies, Cedrus, Picea, Pseudotsuga,* and *Taxus* have the needles borne singly or in clusters along the stem. The needles may be relatively flat (2-sided) or angular (often quadrangular) in cross-section. See the respective genera for a detailed discussion of their leaf morphology.

ARRANGEMENT OF LEAVES

Many vegetative keys employ the arrangement of leaves and buds as a basis for separation. Arrangement simply means the position of a leaf or bud in reference to another leaf or bud along the stem. The use of the four categories by the student allows him/her to categorize plants into groups and assists in eliminating many plants from consideration in the process of positive identification.

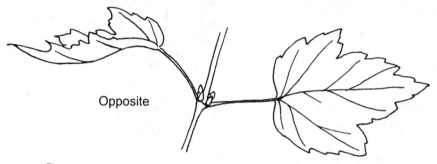

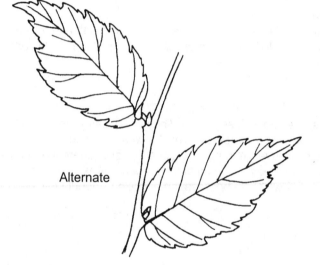

Opposite

Leaves and buds directly across from each other on the stem. Ex: *Acer, Aesculus, Cornus* (most), *Deutzia, Evodia, Fraxinus, Lonicera, Phellodendron, Viburnum.*

Alternate

Leaves and buds are spaced in alternating fashion along the axis of the stem and seldom, if ever, are seated directly across from each other. Ex: *Betula, Carya, Celtis, Cercis, Fagus, Gleditsia, Gymnocladus, Juglans, Quercus, Robinia, Ulmus.*

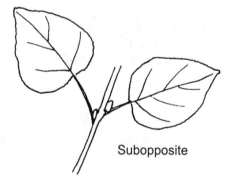

Subopposite

Subopposite refers to a condition where the leaves and buds are not spaced sufficiently far apart to be considered alternate nor are they perfectly opposite, hence, the term subopposite. Ex: *Cercidiphyllum japonicum, Chionanthus retusus, Chionanthus virginicus, Rhamnus cathartica.*

Whorled

Whorled refers to a condition when three buds and leaves (or more) are present at a node. Often, the more rapid the growth the more pronounced the whorled condition. Ex: *Catalpa, Cephalanthus occidentalis, Hydrangea paniculata* 'Grandiflora', *Nerium oleander.*

TYPES OF VENATION

Pinnate. The leaf has a prominent central vein (often termed the midrib) which extends from the base, where the petiole attaches to the blade, to the apex of the leaf. If the interveinal areas were removed the overall effect would be that of a fishbone. Pinnate venation occurs in the leaves of many plant types. The Elm (*Ulmus*) and Oak (*Quercus*) are classic examples.

Elm
Pinnate

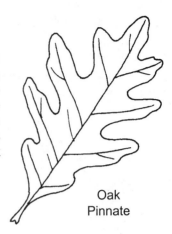

Oak
Pinnate

sinus

lobe

Palmate

Palmate. There are several main veins all of approximately equal size which extend from the base of the leaf to the apex of the lobe or margin of leaf. Ex: *Acer, Cercis, Platanus*.

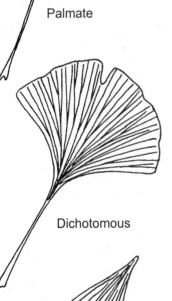

Dichotomous. A very limited type of venation, the most familiar representative of which is *Ginkgo biloba*. The basal veins extend for a distance and then branch forming a "Y" type pattern.

Dichotomous

Parallel

Parallel. Typical of many monocotyledonous plants. The veins run essentially parallel to each other along the long axis of the leaf. Ex: *Danae, Ruscus*.

LEAF SHAPES

The tremendous quantity of terminology related to leaf shapes can be confusing. Association of the following pictures with the terms will help to alleviate the burden of strict terminology. This also applies to leaf bases, margins, and apices.

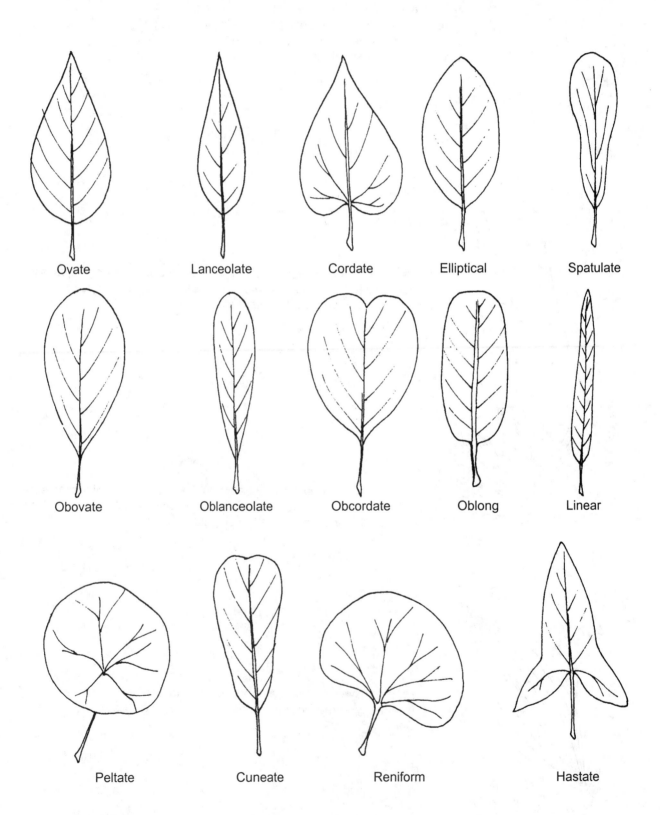

Ovate	Lanceolate	Cordate	Elliptical	Spatulate
Obovate	Oblanceolate	Obcordate	Oblong	Linear
Peltate	Cuneate	Reniform	Hastate	

LEAF BASES, MARGINS, APICES

BASES	MARGINS	APICES
Cuneate	Entire	Acuminate
Acute	Serrate	Acute
Rounded	Serrulate	Obtuse
Cordate	Doubly-Serrate	Truncate
Oblique	Dentate	Emarginate
Sagittate	Crenate	Obcordate
Hastate	Incised	Mucronate
Truncate	Sinuate	Cuspidate
Auriculate	Undulate	
	Lobed	

STEM AND BUD MORPHOLOGY

Deciduous woody plant identification in winter must be based on stem, bud and bark characters. Buds and stems offer the principal means of identification.

The shape, size, color, and texture of *buds* offer interesting identification characters. The large, sticky, mahogany brown bud of *Aesculus hippocastanum*, Common Horsechestnut, contrasts with the pubescent, soft-textured bud of *Magnolia × soulangiana*, Saucer Magnolia.

Leaf Scars often provide distinguishing identification characters. Both the shape and vascular bundle arrangement are often used to separate plants. *Fraxinus americana*, White Ash, can be separated from *F. pennsylvanica*, Green Ash, on the basis of leaf scar shape. The leaf scar of White Ash usually possesses a notch while the leaf scar of Green Ash is straight across. The leaf scar of *Aesculus pavia*, Red Buckeye, is flat across the top while that of *A. parviflora*, Bottlebrush Buckeye, is indented.

Lenticels are produced through the action of the cork cambium. Essentially they are lip-shaped structures composed of rather corky cells. Possibly they function in gas exchange between the atmosphere and the intercellular areas of the plant tissues. Lenticels are beneficial for identification as they possess different colors and sizes. *Rhamnus frangula*, Glossy Buckthorn, has whitish, rectangular, vertically arranged lenticels which offer a valid and consistent identification character. *Prunus*, cherry, species have elongated horizontal lenticels.

Bud Scales by their size, color, shape or markings offer good characters for identification. The scales of *Ostrya virginiana*, American Hophornbeam, are striately marked while those of *Carpinus caroliniana*, American Hornbeam, are smooth.

Terminal Bud Scale Scar is the place where the previous year's bud scales were attached. As the buds open and expand in Spring the scales abscise and leave a distinct scar around the stem. This scar can be useful for gauging the amount of linear growth in a particular season or over a number of seasons. The distance from the scar to the new terminal bud which is set in late summer and early fall represents the growth for that season.

Pith is a very valuable plant tissue for separating closely related plants. Pith is derived from a primary meristem and is usually vestigial. The color and texture of pith can often be used for separating similar plant types. Forsythia types can be separated by the texture and arrangement of the pith. Several closely related *Cornus* species can be identified by pith color [*C. amomum* (brown) from *C. sanguinea* (white)].

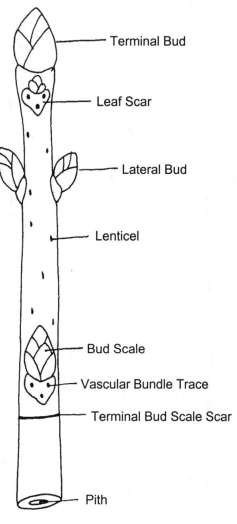

- Terminal Bud
- Leaf Scar
- Lateral Bud
- Lenticel
- Bud Scale
- Vascular Bundle Trace
- Terminal Bud Scale Scar
- Pith

SEVERAL TYPES OF PITH COMMON TO WOODY PLANTS

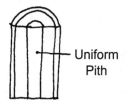

Uniform Pith

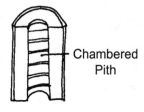

Chambered Pith

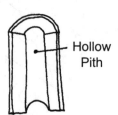

Hollow Pith

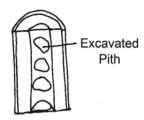

Excavated Pith

BUD TYPES FREQUENTLY FOUND IN WOODY PLANTS

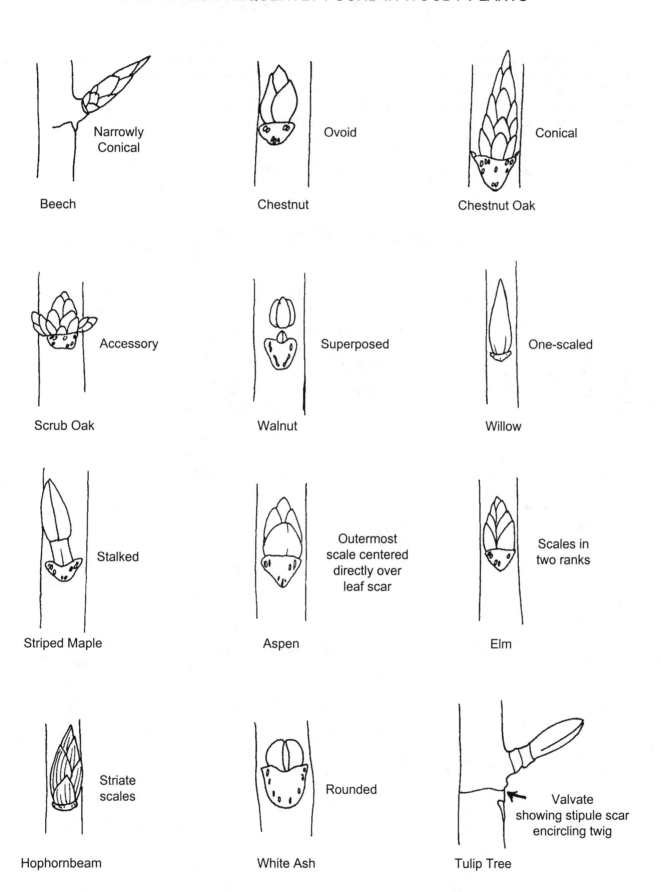

Narrowly Conical

Beech

Ovoid

Chestnut

Conical

Chestnut Oak

Accessory

Scrub Oak

Superposed

Walnut

One-scaled

Willow

Stalked

Striped Maple

Outermost scale centered directly over leaf scar

Aspen

Scales in two ranks

Elm

Striate scales

Hophornbeam

Rounded

White Ash

Valvate showing stipule scar encircling twig

Tulip Tree

FLORAL MORPHOLOGY

Flowers are important components of most botanical keys and the positive identification of various plants is based on some aspect of floral morphology. This approach is acceptable but only allows for positive identification a short period of the year (the flowering periods of most woody plants would average seven to fourteen days). The homeowner, nurseryman, student, and interested plantsman often wish or are required to identify plants the year-round and the use of features other than flowers is a must. If there is significant doubt about a certain plant the most logical approach is to wait for flowers and then consult a reputable text such as Rehder's, Bailey's, Bean's, or Krüssmann's great taxonomic works.

The following diagrams are representative of a "typical" angiosperm flower. There are numerous variations in flower shape but the reproductive parts, i.e., stamens (male, staminate) and pistils (female, pistillate) are essentially similar.

SIMPLE FLOWER STRUCTURE

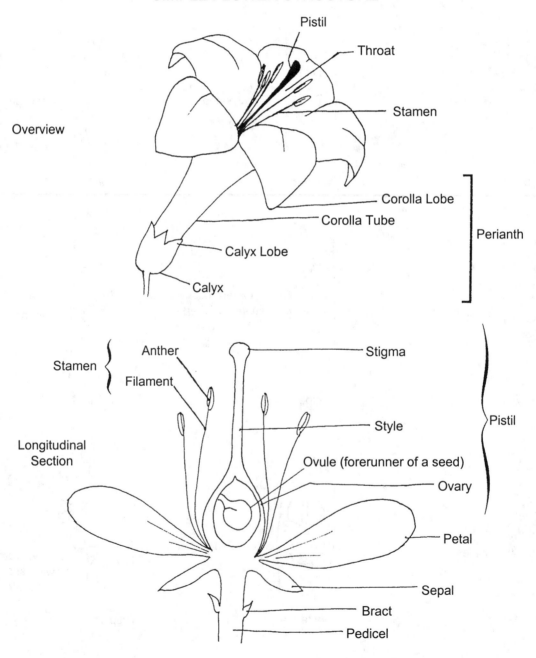

Flowers which have all the parts (sepals, petals, stamens, and a pistil or pistils) are termed *complete*. *Incomplete* flowers lack one or more whorls of floral parts such as the petals. *Imperfect* flowers lack either stamens or pistils. *Perfect* flowers have both stamens and pistils. *Monoecious* means that staminate and pistillate flowers are present on the same plant but in different structures (*Betula, Carpinus, Carya, Fagus, Ostrya, Quercus,*). *Dioecious* means the staminate and pistillate flowers are borne on different plants (*Cercidiphyllum, Gymnocladus dioicus, Ilex,* and *Lindera*). *Polygamo-monoecious* refers to a condition where perfect, pistillate, and staminate flowers occur on the same tree. *Polygamo-dioecious* implies perfect and pistillate flowers on the same plant or perfect and staminate flowers. Several woody plants which show polygamous characters include *Chionanthus, Fraxinus, Gleditsia, Morus, Osmanthus.*

INFLORESCENCES

Flowers are borne on structures which are referred to as inflorescences. An inflorescence is a collection of individual flowers arranged in some specific fashion. The following are some of the representative types found in both woody and herbaceous plants.

Spike. Individual flowers are sessile on the elongated axis (peduncle). The male flower of *Alnus, Betula, Carpinus, Carya, Populus, Quercus,* and *Salix* are spikes with a special name termed catkin or ament (Indeterminate). Indeterminate inflorescences continue to elongate as the flowers open with the uppermost opening last.

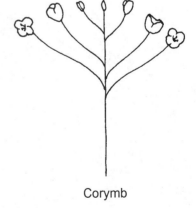

Spike

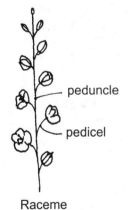

peduncle

pedicel

Raceme

Raceme. In the simplest terms it is a modification of a spike with the individual flowers stalked (on a pedicel). *Clethra, Itea, Laburnum,* and *Wisteria* possess racemose flowers (Indeterminate).

Corymb. An indeterminate (can continue to elongate) inflorescence in which the individual flowers are attached at different points along the peduncle. The outer flowers open first. *Iberis, Malus,* and *Prunus* show corymb inflorescences.

Corymb

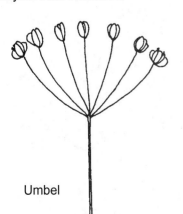

Umbel

Umbel. An indeterminate inflorescence in which the pedicels of the individual flowers radiate from about the same place at the top of the peduncle. Flowers open from outside in. *Aralia,* × *Fatshedera, Fatsia,* and *Hedera helix,* are examples.

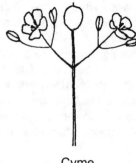

Cyme. A determinate, flat or convex inflorescence, the central or inner flowers opening first. *Cornus*, *Viburnum* (many) are examples.

Cyme

Panicle. An indeterminate inflorescence with repeated branching. Panicles can be made up of many racemes, spikes, corymbs, or umbels. Racemose-panicles are found in *Koelreuteria*, *Pieris*; spikose-panicles in corn; corymbose-panicles in *Pyracantha*; umbellose-panicles in *Aralia*.

Panicle (of Racemes)

Solitary. Indicates a single flower with a pedicel attached to the stem. *Calycanthus*, *Kerria*, *Magnolia* and many other woody plant flowers fall into this category.

Solitary

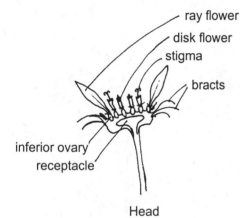

ray flower
disk flower
stigma
bracts

inferior ovary
receptacle

Head. The typical inflorescence of the family Asteraceae (Compositae). Made up of ray (sterile) and disk (fertile) flowers which are arranged on a flattened receptacle. *Baccharis* is an example.

Head

A *spadix* is a specialized type of inflorescence typical of many tropical plants. The showy part is the bract or spathe while the spike-like structure which is partially surrounded by the spathe bears the fertile flowers. Examples include: *Anthurium*, *Caladium*, *Calla*, *Philodendron*, *Spathiphyllum*.

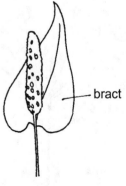

bract

Spadix

FRUIT MORPHOLOGY

The longitudinal section of the "typical" flower offers a representative view of the ovary. The ovary is the forerunner of the fruit and is defined as an unripened fruit. The ovary is composed of carpel(s) which are highly modified leaf-like structures which inclose ovules (forerunner of seeds). An ovary may be composed of one carpel (simple fruit) or two or more carpels (compound fruit). Fruits are very important considerations in woody landscape plants for they offer good ornamental assets (color, texture) and positive identification features through late summer, into fall, and often persist until spring of the year following maturation. Fruits of many woody plants are essentially foodstuffs for birds, bears, squirrels and the forest community. The fruits of *Ilex* (Holly) are often colorful for a long period of time while fruits of *Prunus* (Cherry), some *Malus* (Flowering Crabapples), and several *Crataegus* (Hawthorns) persist briefly after ripening (2 to 4 weeks).

The following classification scheme for fruits along with their definitions and line drawings should afford an idea of the diversity of fruit types which are manifested by woody or herbaceous plants.

I. SIMPLE FRUITS

    A. Dry Fruits

        1. *Indehiscent fruits* (not splitting open at maturity)

            a. *Achene* — one-seeded fruit with seed attached at only one place to the pericarp. Pericarp is very close-fitting and does not split open, at least along regular established lines. Examples: *Calycanthus*, *Chimonanthus*, *Rosa*.

            b. *Caryopsis* — similar to an achene but the pericarp is adherent to the seed, the two often being indistinguishable (seed coat is inseparable from the pericarp). Examples: Corn, Wheat.

            c. *Samara* — usually one-seeded (not always) with a membranous wing which develops from the pericarp. Examples: *Acer*, *Fraxinus*, *Ulmus*.

            d. *Nut* — a bony, hard, one-seeded fruit. The pericarp is bony throughout. Examples: *Castanea*, *Corylus*, *Quercus*.

            e. *Utricle* — similar to an achene but the ovary wall is relatively thin and inflated so it fits only loosely around the seed. Examples: Goosefoot, Pigweed.

            f. *Nutlet* — diminutive of nut. Examples: *Betula*, *Carpinus*, *Ostrya*.

        2. *Dehiscent fruits* (splitting open when mature)

            a. *Legume* (*Pod*) — composed of one carpel and opens along two sutures; characteristic of most members of the Fabaceae (Leguminosae); contains several to many seeds. Examples: *Albizia*, *Cercis*, *Gleditsia*, *Gymnocladus*, *Laburnum*, *Robinia*.

            b. *Follicle* — composed of one carpel but splits open at maturity along one suture exposing several to many seeds. Examples: *Spiraea*, individual fruits of *Magnolia*.

            c. *Capsule* — many-seeded fruits formed from more than one carpel. The carpels are united. Loculicidal Capsule opens along midrib; Septicidal Capsule divides through the partitions. Examples: *Deutzia*, *Forsythia*, *Philadelphus*, *Rhododendron*, *Syringa*.

            d. *Silique* — composed of two carpels which separate at maturity, leaving a thin partition between. Example: Mustard family.

            e. *Silicle* — a short, broad silique. Examples: Shepherd's Purse, Peppergrass.

            f. *Pyxis* — type of capsule which opens around a horizontal ring, the top of fruit falling away like a lid. Example: Purslane.

B. Fleshy Fruits

1. *Berry* — the entire pericarp (exocarp, endocarp, mesocarp) is fleshy. Examples: Tomato, Date, Banana, *Lonicera*, *Vaccinium* (Blueberry, Cranberry).

   a. *Hesperidium* — a berry with a leathery rind. Examples: *Poncirus*, Lemon, Grapefruit.

   b. *Pepo* — a berry with a hard rind and fleshy inner matrix. Examples: Watermelon, Squash, Pumpkin.

2. *Drupe* — the pericarp is clearly differentiated into three layers; exocarp is the epidermis; middle layer, the mesocarp, is fleshy; and the inner layer, the endocarp, is stony. Examples: *Ilex, Prunus* (Cherry, Peach, Plum), *Sassafras, Viburnum*, and numerous other woody ornamental plants.

3. *Pome* — the pericarp is surrounded by the floral tube (hypanthium) which becomes fleshy and tasty. Examples: *Malus* (Apple), *Pyrus* (Pear), *Cydonia* and *Chaenomeles* (Quince).

II. AGGREGATE FRUITS

Develop from a single flower which contains many pistils. Several to many fruitlets are massed on one receptacle. Examples: *Fragaria* (strawberry)—aggregate of achenes; *Liriodendron*—aggregate of samaras; *Maclura*—aggregate of drupes; *Magnolia*—aggregate of follicles; *Rubus* (raspberry)—aggregate of drupes.

III. MULTIPLE FRUITS

Consists of several flowers which are more or less united into one mass. Example: *Morus* (mulberry).

FRUIT TYPES

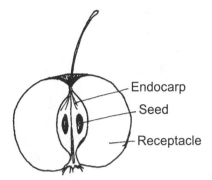

Endocarp
Seed
Receptacle

POME
(*Malus, Pyrus,
Chaenomeles*)

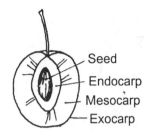

Seed
Endocarp
Mesocarp
Exocarp

DRUPE
(*Prunus, Viburnum,
Celtis, Sassafras*)

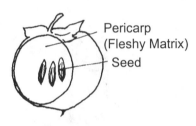

Pericarp
(Fleshy Matrix)
Seed

BERRY
(*Asimina, Diospyros,
Lonicera*)

SAMARA
(*Ulmus*)

SCHIZOCARP
(*Acer*)

SAMARA
(*Fraxinus*)

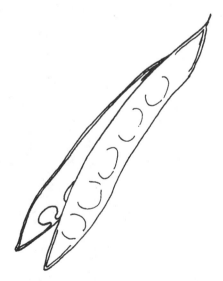

LEGUME (POD)
(*Robinia, Cercis,
Gleditsia*)

CAPSULES
(*Kalmia, Forsythia,
Rhododendron*)

ACORN
(*Quercus*)

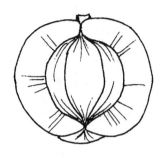

NUT WITH DEHISCENT HUSK
(*Carya*)

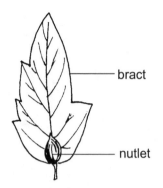

NUTLET
(*Carpinus*)

bract

nutlet

CONE
(*Tsuga, Pinus, Abies*)

AGGREGATE OF SAMARAS
(*Liriodendron*)

MULTIPLE FRUIT
OF SMALL DRUPES
(*Morus*)

STROBILE:
WINGED NUTLET
(*Betula*)

AGGREGATE OF FOLLICLES
(*Magnolia*)

THE USE OF KEYS FOR IDENTIFYING WOODY PLANTS

A key is, in essence, an artificial contrivance which outlines specific morphological features in an organized manner that allows the identifier (user) to eventually arrive at a specific plant or at least reach a point where he/she can consult other references for further separatory information. The information in many keys is geared to flower and fruit morphology; however, keys have been constructed from leaf, stem, bud, root, plant habit, anatomical traits and about any other feature be it macro- or micro-scopic.

Technology that involves DNA fingerprinting, Amplified Fragment Length Polymorphism (AFLP) and Restriction Fragment Length Polymorphism (RFLP), has permitted the separation of cultivars by assessing differences in DNA banding patterns. Also, various gene sequencing protocols are used to determine the differences in DNA base pairs that constitute the gene or part of the gene of a given protein. The differences in these nitrogenous base pairs (adenine, guanine, cytosine, thymine) when compared across species permit the determination of the degree of species' integrity. Dr. Donglin Zhang, one of my recent Ph.D. students, used the rbc*L* chloroplast gene to determine the legitimacy of seven *Cephalotaxus* species. He reduced the seven extant species to three and in those cases there were only 6 and 8 base pair differences of *C. fortunei* and *C. oliveri*, respectively, from *C. harringtonia*. For another example, the number of nucleotide substitutions in the rbc*L* gene of *Cornus* taxa varied from 5 base substitutions between *C. mas* and *C. officinalis* to 52 base substitutions between *C. canadensis* and *C. mas*. Genomic data banks are available to check the status of various genera and species. Molecular biology has invaded the herbarium cabinets of traditional taxonomists. However, traditional taxonomy will always be important in pragmatic horticulture.

A key is an aide to plant identification but far from the sole answer as many individuals would lead one to believe. Plants are variable entities! They may be in flower an average of only 7 to 14 days. The leaves of deciduous trees and shrubs, in the northern climes, are present, at most, 5 to 7 months. Bud and stem colors change drastically from fall through winter and into spring. A key that includes all season features is the utopian necessity but does not exist. Keys are often based on one or two morphological traits which suffice for a single time period. Gardening enthusiasts and those who work in horticultural related businesses must be able to identify plants throughout the seasons. I have seen more mixed up landscape plantings of birch, witchhazel, and honeysuckle simply because the buyer and seller could not distinguish between and among the various species. The Illinois campus was a monument to this problem for pink and white flowering honeysuckles were mixed unintentionally in hedges; Japanese and Mentor Barberries confused in the same planting; and Gray and European White Birch in total chaos. These examples are not isolated for I have seen foul-ups like this in many landscape situations. The moral is that plants must be learned by the characteristics which will permit separation in any season.

A key is a supplement and should not be used as the sole mode for teaching and/or learning plants. Innumerable times I have heard people say they can always "key" the plant out. Yet when I asked them to define several of the simple terms used in keys they were boggled. The successful use of a key demands a specific level of horticultural and botanical expertise. Considerable practice, patience, taxonomic vocabulary, and a more knowledgeable plant person (who can tell you if the answer is correct) are the necessary prerequisites. If one makes the wrong choice in the dichotomy of the key, he/she is hopelessly lost.

Too often keys attempt to simplify and reduce morphological characters to a paradigm. Maples are often construed as having the "typical" five-lobed leaves when; in fact, the genus *Acer* possesses species with trifoliate, compound pinnate, simple pinnate, simple palmate, deciduous, and evergreen leaves. The same is true for oaks where one gets the impression that White and Bur Oak leaves are characteristic of the genus. If one looks at enough oaks he/she quickly finds this more the exception than the rule.

A typical woody plant key for several *Cornus*, dogwood, species might be constructed like the following:

A. Leaves alternate. . . . . *C. alternifolia*

A. Leaves opposite.

    B. Flowers and fruits in open cymes or panicles, pith white, buff or brown.

        C. Fruits cream colored, inflorescence paniculate, pith buff. . . . . *C. racemosa*

    C. Fruits cream or bluish, inflorescence cymose, pith white or brown.

        D. Fruits and pith white. . . . . *C. sericea*

        D. Fruits porcelain-blue or bluish white, pith brown. . . . . *C. amomum*

  B. Flowers sessile in compact umbels, true flowers surrounded by conspicuous, white, petal-like bracts.

    C. Bracts emarginate (indented). . . . . *C. florida*

    C. Bracts acuminate (long pointed). . . . . *C. kousa*

A key starts with a general categorization (alternate versus opposite) and gradually works to the smallest component. The above example is geared to 6 dogwood species and shows the pathway of least resistance for "keying out a plant." One would note that the leaves are opposite or alternate. If alternate, the plant in question is *C. alternifolia*. The opposite branch offers 5 possibilities which can be separated without great difficulty assuming stem, floral and fruit structures can be examined.

The following references offer valuable "keys" for distinguishing among plants. See bibliography for complete citation.

Apgar, Austin C. *Ornamental Shrubs of the United States and Trees of the Northern United States.*

Bailey, L.H. *Manual of Cultivated Plants.*

Blackburn, Benjamin. *Trees and Shrubs in Eastern North America.*

Core, Earl L., and Nelle P. Ammons. *Woody Plants in Winter.*

Curtis, Ralph W., et al. *Vegetative Keys to Common Ornamental Woody Plants.*

Duncan, Wilbur H. and Marion B. Duncan. *Trees of the Southeastern United States.*

Godfrey, Robert K. *Trees, Shrubs, and Woody Vines of Northern Florida and Adjacent Georgia and Alabama.*

Gray, Asa. *Gray's Manual of Botany* (revised by M.C. Fernald).

Harlow, William M. *Fruit Key and Twig Key.*

Rehder, Alfred. *Manual of Cultivated Trees and Shrubs.*

Sargent, Charles S. *Manual of the Trees of North America.* Vol. I and II.

Swanson, Robert E. *A Field Guide to the Trees and Shrubs of the Southern Appalachians.*

Trelease, William. *Winter Botany.*

Vietel, Arthur T. *Trees, Shrubs and Vines.*

CLASSIFICATION AND NOMENCLATURE OF PLANTS

I. METHODS AND RATIONALES FOR NAMING AND CLASSIFYING PLANTS

A. According to use

   Edible—tree, shrub, vine, small fruits, vegetables
   Drugs or spices
   Ornamental—considered non edible but aesthetic
   Timber—forestry

   Problem with this criterion is tremendous overlap in use. Within edible crops, confusion over the difference between vegetable and fruit, i.e., tomato called a vegetable but is botanically a berry. Between edibles and ornamentals, some edibles are used as ornamentals, i.e., *Amelanchier* spp. (juneberry, downy service-berry), *Asimina* (pawpaw), *Vaccinium* spp. (blueberry), and others.

B. Growth habit or physiological characteristics (descriptive nomenclature)

   Herbaceous—fleshy, soft tissue, dies to ground in winter
   Woody—maintains above-ground woody parts
       vine—twining, clasping or self-clinging growth habit
       tree—woody plant with single central axis, 6 feet or more from ground
       shrub—woody plant with several stems branched from ground

   Deciduous—leafless part of year
   Evergreen—leaves all year
   Semievergreen—holds leaves most of the year, generally into winter

   Annual—one year to complete life cycle, seed to seed then plant dies
   Biennial—two years to complete life cycle, seed to seed then plant dies
   Perennial—plant grows indefinitely from year to year

   Hardy—withstand low winter temperatures
   Tender—harmed by low temperatures, most annuals

   Problem with this system is that plant characteristics may change with environment or culture. For example, a hardy plant in one location may be tender elsewhere. *Lantana camara*, Lantana, in Florida and south Texas is a perennial weed; semi-hardy in Georgia and annual in Massachusetts.

C. Descriptive system—An early "scientific" method of naming plants was to use a complex and cumbersome descriptive system. Examples illustrate the cumbersome nature and difficulty with descriptive nomenclature.

   Examples: 1. Japanese maple, *Acer palmatum* Thunb.
                   was
           "Acer orientalis, hederae folio"

           2. Carnation, *Dianthus caryophyllus* L.
                   was
           "Dianthus floribus solitariis, squamis calycinis subovatis brevissimus, corollis crenatis"

D. Use of common names. Common names can be confusing and inaccurate. Why?

   1. Many different English names have been assigned to the same plant.

   2. Difficult to impossible to ascertain which of many English names for a given plant may have been employed first.

3. Common names are of little use in identification since no treatments of the world flora are based on them. Common names provide no use for ID.

4. English names may indicate no close affinities at all.

   Example: True oaks are associated with the genus *Quercus*; however, Tanbark Oak is a *Lithocarpus*, Poison Oak is a *Rhus*, Silk Oak is a *Grevillea*, Jerusalem Oak is a *Chenopodium*, She Oak is a *Casuarina*.

5. Usually the use of a particular common name is restricted to the people of a given region or language. Limited internationally. Example: *Liriodendron tulipifera* is called Tuliptree in the North and Yellow Poplar in the South although these distinctions are not always 100%.

6. In absence of ordered system, common name proliferation occurs.

   Carpinus caroliniana
   American Hornbeam (accepted common name)
   Blue Beech
   Musclewood
   Water Beech
   Ironwood

   Rhododendron canescens
   Piedmont Azalea (accepted common name)
   Wild Honeysuckle

   Nymphaea alba, European White Waterlily
   a. 15 English common names
   b. 44 French
   c. 105 German
   d. 81 Dutch

E. Scientific Names—Binomial Nomenclature

Binomial nomenclature, which evolved from the Linnean system, is now the international language for naming plants. Latinized name is made up of two parts—the generic term and the specific epithet—which forms a binomial called the species. The author citation, i.e., individual who first and correctly named the plant, is included with the species name in scientific writing but not everyday horticulture or garden use.

WHY USE THE BINOMIAL SYSTEM?

The method used today is the accepted international language of scientifically naming plants. As such, the method brings some degree of order to the process of naming plants (compared to descriptive or common names) by assigning a universal name throughout the world to a given plant, providing a basis for identification and taxonomic affinities.

Latinized name is composed of 2 parts: the generic term
                                     the specific epithet

Together, these 2 parts form a binomial called the species name.

The complete scientific name must actually include a third term—the name of the person(s) who named the plant, called the author citation. Author citation is seldom utilized in everyday horticulture and garden writing.

Acer palmatum Thunb., Japanese Maple, named by Swedish botanist Thunberg (1743—1822).

II. HORTICULTURAL AND BOTANICAL PLANT CLASSIFICATION TERMINOLOGY

A. Accepted Taxonomic Units:

>Kingdom
>>Division
>>>Class
>>>>Order
>>>>>Family
>>>>>>Genus
>>>>>>>Species
>>>>>>>>Variety or subspecies
>>>>>>>>>Cultivar
>>>>>>>>>>Forma

The first four categories (kingdom, division, class, and order) have little significance in everyday horticulture and gardening. The crux of understanding and utilizing taxonomy to develop realistic plant affinities and relationships starts with the family and reaches a crescendo with cultivar.

B. Other Botanical And Horticultural Terms With Useful Ties to Nomenclature Include:

>Graft chimera
>>Intergeneric hybrid
>>>Interspecific hybrid
>>>>Intraspecific hybrid
>>>>>F_1 hybrid
>>>>>>F_1 hybrid series
>>>>>>>Line, strain, race
>>>>>>>>Clone
>>>>>>>>>Grex
>>>>>>>>>>Trademarks

A. Accepted Taxonomic Units

1. FAMILY

a. An assemblage of genera (can be single genus) that rather closely or uniformly resemble each other in general appearance and technical characters.

Families of higher plants are separated from one another by characteristics inherent in their reproductive structures (flower, fruit, seed).

b. Characteristics:
inflorescence type
ovary position
placentation type
pistil and carpel number
ovule type
embryology
anther number and position
disposition of sexes (monoecious and dioecious)

c. Size of a family

Varies from a single genus to 100 and more.

Examples of families with a single member:
Cercidiphyllaceae—*Cercidiphyllum japonicum*
Eucommiaceae—*Eucommia ulmoides*
Ginkgoaceae—*Ginkgo biloba*

Examples of families with numerous genera:
Rosaceae—possesses about 100 widely distributed genera of herbs, shrubs, and trees
Asteraceae (formerly Compositae)—950 genera

Family name always ends in . . . ACEAE, and is capitalized but not italicized.

Example: Rosaceae
Ulmaceae
Aceraceae

2.   GENUS: A more or less closely related and definable group of plants comprising one or more species.

A Genus is a category whose components (i.e. species) have more characters in common with each other than they do with components of other genera within the same family.

Similarity of flowers and fruits is the most widely used feature although roots, stems, buds, and leaves are used.

GENERIC name is always capitalized and italicized.

Example: *Rosa*
Ulmus
Acer

The plural of genus is genera.

3.   SPECIES: Most important unit in classification with many definitions depending on authority.

G.H.M. Lawrence: "Botanists of every generation have attempted to answer this question, one for which there may be no single answer."

L.H. Bailey: "A kind of plant or animal distinct from other kinds in *marked or essential features* that has *good characters* of *identification*, and may be assumed to represent in nature a *continuing succession* of individuals from generation to generation."

Bailey then goes to note that the term is *incapable of exact definition* for nature is not laid out in formal lines.

Actually the species term is a concept, the product of each individual's judgement.

The author defines a species as a group of individuals that adhere to the essential identification characteristics but display sufficient variation so as not to be categorized as replicas of one another. This species variation can be described by a bell-shaped curve. The plural of species is species. The term is sometimes abbreviated to sp. (singular) and spp. (plural).

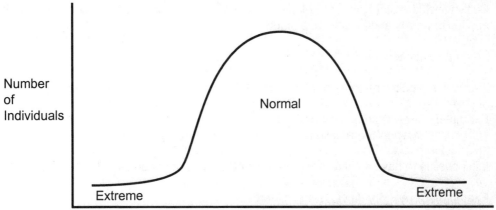

Distribution of characteristics within the concept of a species. For example, leaf shape, bud size and color, bark texture, fruit size, flower color, growth habit.

Writing a species: Generic term is treated as previously discussed. Specific epithet is lower case and italicized.

Acer saccharum Marsh.

Author citation, Humphrey Marshall (US 1722-1801)

genus   specific epithet

species

4. VARIETY or SUBSPECIES (BOTANICAL SENSE): A group or class of plants subordinate to a species. The term is assigned to individuals displaying rather marked differences in nature. The differences are inheritable and reproduce true-to-type in succeeding generations.

    Example: *Gleditsia triacanthos* var. *inermis*, Thornless Common Honeylocust.

    The variety is essentially thornless and when grown from seed produces 90% thorn-free offspring.

    a. Geographic distribution. Usually a variety has a distinct geographical niche.

        Example: *Acer saccharum*, Sugar Maple, extends from Canada to north Georgia and west to Minnesota and Oklahoma. The variety *nigrum* occurs in Iowa and drier Midwest locations, i.e., western part of the range.

    b. Variety is abbreviated var.; the plural is varieties.
        Subspecies is abbreviated subsp. and also ssp.; the plural is subspecies.

5. CULTIVAR: Horticulturally, this is the most important unit of classification.

    a. Definition: An assemblage of cultivated plants which is clearly distinguished by any characters (morphological, physiological, cytological, chemical, or others) and which when reproduced (sexually or asexually) retains its distinguishing characteristic(s).

        Examples: *Cedrus deodara*
                    Cedrus deodara 'Kingsville'

        'Kingsville' looks like the species except it is more cold hardy.

        Cercis canadensis
        Cercis canadensis 'Forest Pansy'

        'Forest Pansy' has maroon leaves that fade to green.

    b.   Cultivar includes seed produced plants that are homogeneous for one or more characteristics. This applies to woody and herbaceous plants.

    c.   Writing a cultivar name.

       Terms in the cultivar name are always capitalized and included in single quotes.

       Example: *Acer rubrum* 'October Glory'
                     Magnolia grandiflora 'Bracken's Brown Beauty'

       It is possible to have a cultivar of a botanical variety or subspecies.

       Example: *Cornus florida* var. *rubra* 'Cherokee Chief'

6.   FORMA: Designates plant variation that occurs sporadically and randomly throughout the population of a native plant species. The variation is usually manifested in flower and fruit colors but extends to foliage and growth habit characteristics. The trait is usually unstable (unreproducible) through sexual reproduction (seed) and must be reproduced vegetatively by cuttings, grafting/budding or tissue culture.

      Examples: *Lindera benzoin* forma *rubra*—the red-flowered form of the typical yellow-flowered Spicebush
                   Ilex opaca forma *xanthocarpa*—the yellow-fruited form of the typical red-fruited American Holly
                   Fagus sylvatica forma *pendula*—includes the weeping forms of the European Beech

      The term forma is often abbreviated to f. and appears in front of the actual term, i.e, f. *xanthocarpa*. The term is always italicized and lower case. The forma name can never stand alone and must be included with the species or variety name. The plural of forma is formae.

B.   Other Botanical and Horticultural Terms with Useful Ties to Nomenclature

   1.   GRAFT CHIMERA: Is little known in everyday horticulture but refers to a plant derived from the union of two distinct cells or tissues each contributed by a different plant (taxon). The new plant (shoot) arises in callus tissue that occurs at the graft or bud union. The cells are not arranged in a defined pattern in the meristematic area and give rise to plant parts (leaves, flowers and fruits) on the same plant that reflect the characteristics of each parent.

      The inclusion of a large + (plus) sign in front of the generic name indicates graft chimera. The most famous example is:

      + *Laburnocytisus adamii*—the product of *Cytisus purpureus* and *Laburnum anagyroides*. The parent plant produces yellow and purple flowers as well as intermediate colors.

      Graft chimeras must be reproduced vegetatively and choice of cutting/scion material is important to maintain intermediate characteristics.

   2.   SEED PRODUCED TAXA: Unfortunately most seed-produced cultivars are not discussed in general botany or taxonomy courses. However, their importance is paramount to commercial horticulture. Most vegetables, annuals and some herbaceous perennials are offered as seed-derived cultivars. A limited number of woody plant cultivars are produced through seeds.

      A cultivar is so defined by the *International Code of Nomenclature for Cultivated Plants* (1995) so that if a single phenotypic trait is maintained through sexual reproduction then the cultivar term can be applied.

      Examples: *Malus sargentii* 'Rose Glow' is a seed-produced Flowering Crabapple with colorful rose fruit.
                   Acer ginnala 'Flame' is a seed-produced Amur Maple with orange-red fall color.

a. F₁ hybrids—are created by crossing two specifically created and maintained inbred lines to produce seedling populations consistent in their characteristics (flower size, color, etc.) which ideally should be as uniform as if they were propagated vegetatively. Petunia, Marigold, Pansy, Salvia, and Impatiens cultivars fall in this category. A designation would read: *Petunia × hybrida* 'White Cascade'.

b. F₁ hybrid series—implies a series of distinct lines distinguished usually only by flower color.

Example: *Impatiens walleriana* Super Elfin Series consists of 18 lines all with similar low spreading growth habit *but* with flowers in 18 different shades.

3. INTERGENERIC HYBRID: Result of hybridization between two genera. Although not common, intergeneric hybrids occur and occasionally result in a unique and important plant.

Example: × *Cupressocyparis leylandii*—Leyland Cypress

Chance intergeneric hybrid between *Cupressus macrocarpa* and *Chamaecyparis nootkatensis*

Always written with a large multiplication sign in front of the generic term.

4. INTERSPECIFIC HYBRID: Controlled or chance hybridization between two related species.

Example: *Hamamelis mollis* × *Hamamelis japonica* resulted in *Hamamelis × intermedia* from which numerous cultivars have been selected. In this case the small multiplication sign is placed in front of the specific epithet.

5. INTRASPECIFIC HYBRID: Generally controlled cross between members of the same species with unique traits (flower color) that when sexually combined produce uniform offspring.

Examples: *Petunia × hybrida* white form times *Petunia × hybrida* red form results in pink flower color. *Petunia × hybrida* 'Pink Beauty'

6. LINE, STRAIN, RACE: Refers to genetically pure (more or less) groups of plants with defined characteristics(s) that permit separation from another group. Line is the preferred term and each line if named can be termed a cultivar.

7. CLONE: Important non-taxonomic unit that refers to a single plant with unique characteristics that when reproduced vegetatively carries these same characteristics both genetically and phenotypically (what you see).

A clone is often thought of as a cultivar but is nothing taxonomically until given a fancy name which according to the *Code of Nomenclature for Cultivated Plants* since 1959 must be a non-latinized name.

Example: An upright-columnar Sugar Maple, *Acer saccharum*, reproduced vegetatively is a clone but when given the name 'Steeple' becomes a cultivar. *Acer saccharum* 'Steeple'

Not all cultivars are clones. See (2) *Seed produced taxa*. However, most woody cultivars started as clonal units.

8. GREX: Refers to the progeny (offspring) produced from the crossing of two or more species. The grex name umbrellas all the plants produced from the crosses and serves as a useful guide to the character traits of the individual progeny.

Example: All progeny resulting from crosses between *Ilex opaca* and *Ilex cassine* (reciprocal crosses also) are termed *Ilex × attenuata* with × *attenuata* the grex name.

From these hybrids such cultivars as 'Foster's #2', 'Savannah', and 'East Palatka' have been selected.

When seedling populations are grown from *Ilex × attenuata* segregation occurs with some progeny resembling *I. opaca*, some *I. cassine*, and others in-between.

9. TRADEMARK NAMES: Present day plant commerce has focused on protection of new introductions so that the name(s) cannot be used for any other plant or product. If someone other that the discoverer (namer) wishes to grow and market a trademarked plant, a licensing and royalty agreement must be consummated. Trademark names have no taxonomic validity and so a nonsense cultivar name must be developed. Anyone who shows continued use of a specific name for a plant (product) and places a ™ in superscript behind the name has a sole right to that name. A registered trademark is signified by ® in superscript. This means that the name was registered with The Office of Patent and Trademarks in Washington, D.C.

> Examples: *Ulmus parvifolia* Alleé® ('Emer II')
> *Betula nigra* Dura-Heat™ ('BNMTF')

REFERENCES:

Bailey, L. H. 1933. *How Plants Get Their Names*. Macmillan Co., NY.

Greuter, W., F. R. Barrie, H. M. Burdet, W. G. Chaloner, V. Demoulin, D. L. Hawksworth, P. M. Jørgensen, D. H. Nicolson, P. C. Silva, and P. Trehane (editorial committee). 1994. *International Code of Botanical Nomenclature*. Koeltz Scientific Books. Königstein, Germany.

Jones, S. B. and A. E. Luchsinger. 1986. *Plant Systematics*. McGraw-Hill, NY.

Lawrence, G. H. M. 1951. *Taxonomy of Vascular Plants*. Macmillan Co., NY.

Trehane, P., C. D. Brickell, B. R. Baum, W. L. A. Hetterscheid, A. C. Leslie, J. McNeill, S. A. Spongberg, and F. Vrugtman (editorial committee). 1995. *International Code of Nomenclature for Cultivated Plants*. Quarterjack Publ. Wimborne, UK. 175 p.

Woodland, D. 1997. *Contemporary Plant Systematics.* Andrews Univ. Press. Berren Springs, MI.

Abelia × grandiflora (André) Rehd. — Glossy Abelia

(á-bē′li-á gran-di-flō′rá)

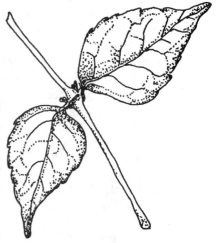

FAMILY: Caprifoliaceae

LEAVES: Opposite, simple, ovate, 1/2 to 1 1/2″ long, half as wide, acute, rounded or cuneate at base, dentate, lustrous dark green above, turning bronze-red in winter, paler beneath and glabrous, except bearded near base of midrib; petiole—1/8″ long.

BUDS: Small, ovoid, with about 2 pairs of rather loose scales.

STEM: Young-pubescent, reddish purple to reddish brown, fine textured appearance; older stem-exfoliating and split to expose light inner bark, bark peeling in string-like threads, leaf scars connected by a stipular line.

SIZE: 3 to 6′ high by 3 to 6′ wide; usually at the low end of the range in northern areas; have seen 8′ high plants in the South.

HARDINESS: Zone 5 as a herbaceous perennial but best in Zone 6 to 9, −5 to −10°F appears to coincide with stem kill, flowers often evident in November–December in Zone 7.

HABIT: Often a spreading, dense, rounded, multi-stemmed shrub with arching branches; in the North is often killed back to ground or snow line and quickly grows back into a rather dense small shrub; at times somewhat loose in outline; may be leggy and require pruning to develop a full constitution.

RATE: Medium to fast.

TEXTURE: Medium-fine in all seasons.

LEAF COLOR: Lustrous dark green in summer, bronze-green to bronze-red to bronze-purple in late fall and into winter; in North shows semi-evergreen tendency and leaves hold late into fall or early winter; in the South leaves persist through winter; one of first shrubs to produce new leaves; on Georgia campus abundant new foliage was evident in early March.

FLOWERS: White-flushed pink, funnel-shaped, 3/4 to 1″ long and one-half as wide, throat 5-lobed, slightly fragrant, 2 to 5 together in leafy panicles at end of lateral branches, 3/4″ long sepals (2 to 5 per flower, usually 5) develop a rose to purplish tinge and persist for months, sepals often most colorful in late summer, fall and early winter carrying themselves into spring; May–June through frost; flowers on new growth of season; usually profuse, prolific flowering plant but does not produce an overwhelming display like forsythia; great for summer and fall floral effect but seldom considered for this lovely seasonal trait; a butterfly plant.

FRUIT: One-seeded, leathery achene with no ornamental value; have never seen a stray seedling and suspect the plant may be essentially sterile; in fact, I have not observed a single fruit.

CULTURE: Easily grown, transplant balled and burlapped or from containers; prefers acid, well-drained, moist, soil; Texas literature reports extreme chlorosis in high pH soils; full sun up to half shade; often damaged in severe winters and proper siting is necessary; will require pruning of dead wood in North; shade tolerance is greater than the literature indicates; plants under red maples made a respectable show although less dense and with decreased flowering compared to plants in full sun.

DISEASES AND INSECTS: None serious but leaf spots, mildew and root rots have been reported, aphids are a problem on soft, succulent growth.

LANDSCAPE VALUE: Excellent for textural effects, handsome in flower, often used as a bank cover, mass or facing plant; used as a hedge in southern areas; combines well with broadleaf evergreens; safest when used in Zone 6 and south; receiving greater attention in the 1990's and along with the newer cultivars will remain a positive factor in contemporary landscapes; requires no chemical inputs to keep it in relatively pristine condition.

CULTIVARS:

'Compacta'—Difficult to quantify taxonomically but produced by several major southern nurseries and advertised as growing 3 to 4′ high and wide with pinkish white flowers; have observed in Houston area and leaves appeared about the same size and color as the species.

Confetti™—Is a variegated branch sport of 'Sherwoodii' introduced by Flowerwood Nursery in Mobile, AL. The cream-margined leaves turn rose in winter. The habit will be similar to 'Sherwood' but smaller. Produces white flowers with no trace of pink and the flowers are quite showy. The cultivar withstands sun or partial shade and will prove an outstanding massing or ground-cover plant. In the Dirr garden has not shown great vigor and has declined with time. I had great aspirations for the plant. Will grow 1 1/2 to 2′ high, with a greater spread.

'Dwarf Purple'—Lavender-pink flowers are produced continuously from June until frost; lustrous dark green leaves turn rich reddish purple in autumn and retain most of the leaves until late winter; forms a low growing dense 2 1/2′ high plant; a plant in my possession appears to be nothing more than 'Edward Goucher'.

'Francis Mason'—Produces copper colored young shoots that mature to yellow or yellow-green with a richer marginal yellow border. The color fades in the heat of the summer; plants in my garden lose most of their effect by mid to late summer. If new shoots continue to develop, the color is maintained. Foliage can look particularly tired, sick, worn out in the dead of winter. This form is somewhat less vigorous than the species, but my three plants grew 5 feet high and were quite leggy. Can be rejuvenated by late winter pruning. When nursery-grown under high nutrition and high water status, it is quite spectacular. Originated as a branch sport in the 1950's at Mason's Nurseries in New Zealand, it also sports to produce various colored shoots that have received clonal names. In my travels I have seen plants in the 6 to 8′ high range.

'Golden Glow'—A form with golden yellow foliage and white flowers, leaf has a more uniform yellow margin than 'Francis Mason'.

'John Creech'—Listed as a sister seedling of 'Edward Goucher'; I see minimal morphological similarities; foliage is lustrous dark green; flowers are white and shaped more like *A.* × *grandiflora*; sepals number 4 to 5 rather than the 2 associated with 'Edward Goucher'; I witnessed 'John Creech' next to *A.* × *grandiflora* at Live Oak Gardens, New Iberia, LA during the October 1996 Southern Region IPPS meeting, under proper nutrition and water, the plant was dense, upright-mounded with lustrous dark green foliage, *A.* × *grandiflora* grew much more loose, lax, and sprawly; apparently 'John Creech' does not throw the reversion (long shoots) of 'Sherwoodii' and would make a more uniform massing plant.

'Little Richard'—A sport of 'Sherwoodii' with lustrous dark green leaves, prolific white flowers, and more dense growth; matures into a dense, compact mound 2 1/2 to 3′ high and wide; it holds its leaves through winter if maintained under high fertility; Currin reported no foliar or stem damage at 2°F; selected by Richard Currin, Currin's Nursery, Willow Springs, NC.

'Prostrata'—Is a low-growing, broad-spreading selection that averages 1 1/2 to 2′ high. Plants I have observed turned bronze-purple winter leaf color; however, California literature reports the cultivar becoming partially deciduous even in the mildest climates. This cultivar was patented (No. 1431).

'Really Pink'—Difficult to assess status of this cultivar but described by Sabuco as having clear pink flowers and remaining evergreen to −10 to −15°F.

'Sherwoodii' ('Sherwood')—More dense and compact in habit, leaves smaller and more refined than those of species, 3 to 3 1/2′ high and 4 to 4 1/2′ wide, occasional reversions to the species should be removed; 'Nana' may be synonymous; plants on the Georgia campus are quite lovely, do not become as ragged as *A.* × *grandiflora*; in winter the small leaves turn purple-green; good plant for massing in sun or partial shade.

'Sunrise'—Leaf margins are distinct gold with a green center; more vigorous than Confetti™, will probably grow 3′ or higher at maturity; based on early evaluations by the author it is a plant with great commercial merit; discovered as a branch sport of *A.* × *grandiflora* at Taylor's Nursery, Raleigh, NC; will occasionally develop green shoots that must be removed; Pat McCracken has widely promoted the plant with the royalty proceeds earmarked for the J.C. Raulston Arboretum at NCSU.

PROPAGATION: Softwood cuttings root readily; I have rooted this plant with 100% success any time foliage was present using 1000 ppm IBA; cuttings collected in November rooted well; seeds should be sown when ripe.

MAINTENANCE CONSIDERATIONS: Trouble-free, easy to maintain plant requiring occasional pruning to keep it well coiffured; hard pruning in late winter is recommended to rejuvenate old plants; plants will flower the same year after pruning.

ADDITIONAL NOTES: The hardiest hybrid and most free-flowering of the abelias; best reserved for eastern and southern gardens. Result of a cross between *A. chinensis* × *A. uniflora*. Originated in Italy possibly before 1866 but supposedly not introduced until 1886. See Dirr, *NMPRO* 13(3):14–15, 71–72 (1997) for an overview of *Abelia* taxa. Also an earlier article in *Nursery Manager*, February 1994.

RELATED SPECIES:

Abelia chinensis R. Br., (ȧbē′li-ȧ chi-nen′sis), Chinese Abelia, is a 5 to 7′ high upright spreading, oval-rounded ʹdeciduous shrub. The young branches are covered with reddish tomentum; with maturity becoming glabrous and gray brown; the 3/4 to 1 1/2″ long leaves are dark green, lighter green beneath, with serrate margins; flowers are white, fragrant, two or more per cluster, appearing (June) July to September; 5 sepals

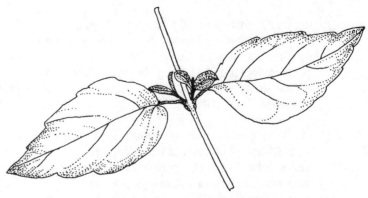

that remain green for a period before turning rose. One of the parents of *A.* × *grandiflora*. Flowers on new growth of the season. Excellent for butterflies. I had this plant for a time and never got excited but many of my cohorts have extolled its virtues for summer flowering and attracting butterflies. I have rooted the plant from cuttings collected in fall at the Brooklyn Botanic Garden with the same procedure as described under *A.* × *grandiflora*. China. Introduced 1844. Zone (6)7 to 9.

The Morton Arboretum, Lisle, IL (Zone 5) reported that the species is killed to the ground yearly but develops new shoots often to 5′ high during the growing season. Seeds germinate without pretreatment.

Abelia 'Edward Goucher' is a hybrid between *A.* × *grandiflora* and *A. schumannii* and tends to be intermediate in habit between the parents. The leaves tend toward *A.* × *grandiflora* while the darker-colored lavender-pink to purple-pink flowers reflect the influence of *A. schumannii* (Gräbn.) Rehd.; leaves are often borne in whorls; often confused with *A.* × *grandiflora* when not in flower but leaves are not as lustrous or dark green and the leaf surface is "bumpy"; sepals often in two's and stems more brown than red and covered with a fine pubescence; average 5′ by 5′ at maturity; flowers from May–June until frost; resulted from a cross made at the Glenn Dale Plant Introduction Center by Edward Goucher in 1911; best reserved for Zone 6 to 9; showier in flower than *A.* × *grandiflora* but unfortunately less hardy, probably 5 to 10°F less so. At –3°F was severely injured but grew back. Other taxa including 'Dwarf', 'Dwarf Pink', and 'Dwarf Purple' that I have collected, when flowered in the greenhouse, appear nothing more than 'Edward Goucher' renames. Perhaps growth habit and size will be different.

Abelia floribunda Decne., (ȧbē′li-ȧ flôr-i-bun′dȧ), Mexican Abelia, is an evergreen shrub, 5 to 8′(10′) tall, with 1/2 to 1 1/2″ long, lustrous dark green leaves; the trumpet-shaped flowers are 1 1/2 to 2″ long, 1″ across at the mouth, cherry-red in bud, perhaps with a tinge of magenta-red when open; have observed as a wall (espalier) shrub at Mount Usher Garden in Ireland; appears to be our best source of genetic material for flower color and size; plan to cross with *A. chinensis*; flower buds formed the year prior to flowering and occur several together on short branches along the previous year's growth; flowers in summer in California, but also in full flower in January on occasion; California literature reports severe damage at 20°F; described by Gerd Krüssmann as the most beautiful of the genus, the plant that Smith College provided was grown from seed collected around Oaxaca, Mexico. Mexico. Zone 8 and 9.

Abeliophyllum distichum Nak. — Korean Abelialeaf or White Forsythia
(ȧ-bē-li-o-fīl′um dis′ti-kum)

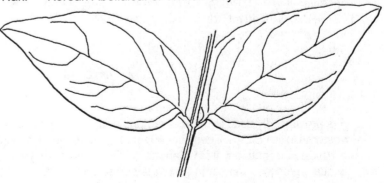

FAMILY: Oleaceae
LEAVES: Opposite, simple, entire, 2 to 3 1/2″ long, one half as wide, spreading in two ranks, ovate to elliptic-ovate, acute, broad-cuneate or rounded at base, entire, appressed pilose on both sides, medium green to dark green; petiole—1/12 to 1/5″ long.

BUDS: Imbricate, brown, small, 1/10″ long, 3-exposed scales, glabrous, form 45° angle with stem; flower buds exposed, purplish, small, evident through winter months, borne in terminal racemose panicle.

STEM: Slender, light brown to tan, glabrous, 4-sided, with prominent ridges on vigorous stems; second year stems develop a shreddy, stringy condition; pith—white, finely chambered through nodes and internodes.

SIZE: 3 to 5′ by 3 to 4′ (perhaps wider); have seen 6 to 8′ high and wide plants. 6′ high at Minnesota Landscape Arboretum.

HARDINESS: Zone 5 to 8, can grow in Zone 4; reports from the University of Minnesota Landscape Arboretum (-25 to -30°F) indicated the flower buds may be injured in a severe winter but are more dependable than *Forsythia × intermedia* types.

HABIT: Multi-stemmed (often straggly) small shrub of rounded outline developing arching branches; at times rather ragged looking and disheveled.

RATE: Depending on situation will range from slow to fast; has the ability to produce long trailing branches in a single season.

TEXTURE: Medium in leaf, perhaps medium-coarse in winter.

LEAF COLOR: Medium to dark green in summer; no significant change in fall although muted yellow-brown to muted purple have developed on occasion.

FLOWERS: Perfect, white or faintly tinged pink, 4-petaled, 3/8 to 5/8″ across, fragrant, borne in 1/2 to 1 1/2″ long axillary racemes in March–April

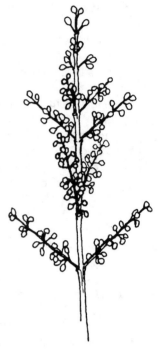

Inflorescence

before the leaves; entire inflorescence occurs at end of shoots and would be classified as a racemose panicle; often in full flower by late February in the Athens area.

FRUIT: Two-celled compressed rounded capsule which is winged all around; similar to an elm fruit; not ornamental.

CULTURE: Easily transplanted; adapted to many soils preferably those that are well-drained; proper siting is important; acid or alkaline conditions; full sun or very light shade; renew frequently by heavy pruning immediately after flowering; plants in half shade have flowered respectably.

DISEASES AND INSECTS: None serious.

LANDSCAPE VALUE: Provides early spring color to an otherwise dull landscape; since the flowers are borne along the leafless stems they make quite a show; makes a nice companion shrub to forsythia; best if set off by a dark green background; more suitable than forsythia for plains states but not as showy.

CULTIVARS: A uniformly colored pink form has apparently been named 'Rosea' ('Roseum'). At the Arnold Arboretum the species and 'Rosea' were growing in close proximity and the pink coloration was significantly potent to justify designation from the white flowers of the species.

PROPAGATION: Easily rooted from softwood cuttings; in England it is propagated by cuttings of half-ripened wood taken in July, and treated with IBA or IAA; bottom heat may be helpful; seeds should be sown when ripe.

MAINTENANCE CONSIDERATIONS: Have observed old, overgrown plants that looked like a tangle of vines and brush; needs to be renewal pruned every 3 to 4 years; prune to 6 to 12″ from ground in late winter, ideally after flowering.

ADDITIONAL NOTES: Certainly not the best of the deciduous shrubs but early flowering enough that it avoids competition from better plants; often ragged and straggly in habit and needs to be rejuvenated; have observed it in full flower at Bernheim Arboretum, Clermont, KY, after exposure to approximately -18°F.

NATIVE HABITAT: Central Korea. Introduced 1924.

Abies Mill. — Fir
FAMILY: Pinaceae

Firs are limitedly used in midwestern and southern landscapes but often appear in the northeastern and northwestern United States. There are 40 to 50 species found in Europe, northern Africa, temperate Asia and on the American continent from Canada to Guatemala. In youth they are mostly conical and extremely symmetrical in outline, and some types may grow over 200′.

MORPHOLOGICAL CHARACTERISTICS

Monoecious trees, evergreen, habit symmetrically pyramidal, or narrow-conical while young, or with age becoming large forest trees; trunk simple, rarely forked; bark usually smooth, thin on young trees, often thick and furrowed at the base on old trees; branchlets smooth, or grooved in a few species; winter-buds usually resinous; leaves spirally inserted, often spreading in 2 ranks (pectinate), linear or linear-lanceolate, entire, sessile, contracted above the base, on falling leaving a circular scar, usually flattened and grooved above, in most species with 2 white or pale stomatic bands and keeled beneath, rarely with stomata above, rarely 4-sided and with stomata on all 4 sides, rounded and variously notched or pointed at the apex; female flowers in cones composed of numerous scales, each with two ovules adaxially at the base and subtended by a narrow exserted or included bract; scales falling at maturity from the persistent axis; seeds ovoid or oblong; wing large and thick; cotyledons 4 to 10.

GROWTH CHARACTERISTICS

The firs would be considered slow-growing landscape plants especially when planted outside of their native habitats. It is safe to generalize that the majority of species are conical to pyramidal, almost spirelike, in outline. From this aspect they are somewhat difficult to work into the small, residential landscape. There are many cultivars among the various species including prostrate, compact, pendulous, contorted, fastigiate, yellow-foliaged, and blue-foliaged types. These cultivars fall in the novelty category and are difficult to find in the landscape trade; however, they do add different textures, colors and shapes not available from the fir species.

CULTURE

Firs require moist, well-drained, acid soil and high atmospheric moisture coupled with cooler temperatures. The hot, dry summers which occur in the Midwest and South tend to limit their landscape usefulness. Firs are not suited for city plantings and do not tolerate air pollution. Transplanting is best accomplished in the spring using balled and burlapped specimens or small container-grown plants. Pruning should be kept to a minimum for when older branches are removed new growth seldom develops and, consequently, the trees become ragged and unkempt. They are most appropriately sited in full sun but light shade is also acceptable.

DISEASES AND INSECTS

Firs do not seem to be extensively troubled with disease and insect pests. At least this was true for firs which I have seen in landscape plantings. Needle and twig blight, leaf cast, rusts, cankers, shoestring root rot, wood decay, balsam twig aphid, bagworm, caterpillars, spruce spider mite, scale, balsam woolly adelgid, spruce budworm and dwarf mistletoe (plant parasite) have been listed as problems.

PROPAGATION

Seed is the principal means of propagation. Dormancy of fir seed appears to be both physical and physiological in nature. There is considerable variation between seed lots in degree of dormancy. Part of this variability in dormancy is attributable to time of collection, methods of processing, seed cleaning, and storage. Seed is typically stratified under cool, moist conditions at 34° to 41°F for 14 to 28 days.

Cuttings have been rooted but the percentages were low and this approach is not practical on a commercial basis. The cultivars are usually grafted and some type of a side graft is most appropriate.

LANDSCAPE USE

Abies balsamea and *Abies fraseri*, which are grown for Christmas trees, only do well in colder climates. Their stiff, rigid habit and specific cultural requirements place a restriction on extensive use. They are best employed in groupings, near large buildings, as specimens and screens.

SELECTED SPECIES

Based on observations I have made at various arboreta and in landscape plantings around the Midwest and East, the following firs would be my first choice.

Abies cilicica	Cilician Fir
Abies concolor	White Fir
Abies homolepis	Nikko Fir
Abies procera	Noble Fir

Other firs which are worthwhile include:

Abies alba	Silver Fir
Abies balsamea	Balsam Fir
Abies cephalonica	Greek Fir
Abies firma	Momi Fir
Abies fraseri	Fraser Fir
Abies grandis	Giant Fir
Abies holophylla	Manchurian Fir
Abies koreana	Korean Fir
Abies lasiocarpa	Subalpine or Alpine Fir
Abies mariesii	Maries Fir
Abies nordmanniana	Nordmann Fir
Abies veitchii	Veitch Fir

SELECTED LITERATURE: A fine review, "Silver firs in cultivation, a survey of the species," by John Horsman appeared in *The Plantsman* 6(2):64–100 (1984). Also, Paul Cappiello, *Nursery Management and Production* 11(8):14, 73–76 (1995) discusses fir species with merit for cold climate landscapes.

Abies alba Mill. — Silver Fir, European Silver Fir

LEAVES: Spreading horizontally along branches, 1/2 to 1 1/4″ long, 1/16 to 1/12″ wide, notched at the blunt to rounded apex, lustrous dark green above, with 2 white bands of stomata below.
BUDS: Winter buds are not resinous.
STEM: Gray brown, pubescent when young.

Abies alba, (ā′bēz al′bà), Silver Fir, is a frequent occurrence throughout Scotland where 100′ high trees are as common as kudzu in Georgia. Truly noble, conical evergreens, they grace the slopes and valleys of many Scottish gardens. This species tolerates more shade than the typical fir species but requires heavier, moister soils and atmospheres. At Dawyk Arboretum and Kildrummy Castle Gardens, Scotland, I was literally mesmerized by the stature and size of the specimens. Cappiello described a 20-year-old plant on the UMaine (Orono) campus that was 18′ high. Obviously growth is slow. I harken back to my early foraging days in Spring Grove, Cincinnati, OH, where a grouping of Weeping Silver Fir ('Pendula') survived the atrocities of the midwestern climate. These same trees (1998) are extant and in reasonably good shape. The cones of the species are quite large, 4 1/2 to 6″ long, 1 1/2 to 2″ wide, initially green maturing to brown with exserted and reflexed bracts. Rehder reported that the species was not performing well in the eastern states, and the paucity of specimens throughout the colder areas of the United States supports this contention. Central and southern Europe. Long cultivated. Zone 4 to 6(7).

Abies balsamea (L.) Mill. — Balsam Fir, Balm of Gilead.
(ā′bēz bâl-sām′ē-à)

LEAVES: Variable, 5/8 to 1″ long, 1/20 to 1/16″ wide, horizontally arranged in 2 lateral sets with a V-shaped parting between, apex slightly notched, upper surface shining dark green with interrupted lines of stomata towards the tip, lower surface with 2 gray bands of stomata, typical balsam odor.
BUDS: Small, ovoid or globular, resinous and seemingly varnished, brownish.
STEM: Smooth, covered with fine, soft grayish hairs.

SIZE: 45 to 75′ in height by 20 to 25′ in spread; national champion is 100′ by 45′ in Fairfield, PA.
HARDINESS: Zone 3 to 5(6), suitable in higher elevations of the Southeast.
HABIT: Stiff in habit, symmetrically pyramidal or narrow-conical when young before losing its pyramidal habit with age.
RATE: Slow.
TEXTURE: Medium.
BARK: Dull green, later with grayish areas, smooth except for numerous raised resin blisters; eventually breaking up into small reddish brown, irregular scaly plates, 1/2″ thick.
LEAF COLOR: Lustrous dark green with white stomatic bands below.

FLOWERS: Male—catkin-like, yellow, developing from the underside of the leaf axil.

FRUIT: Cone, dark violet when young, 2 to 4″ long, turning gray-brown and resinous at maturity; soon after the ripening of the seeds the scales fall off, leaving only the central axis.

CULTURE: Shallow rooted, readily transplanted balled and burlapped; adaptable to cold climates and there makes its best growth; prefers well-drained, acid, moist soil, however, in the wild it often forms pure stands in swamps but does best in association with spruce on ground which is better drained; it also grows on higher ground and is found in dwarfed, matted, pure stands, or entangled with Black Spruce, *Picea mariana*, near the windswept summits of mountains where great extremes in temperature occur. More shade tolerant than other firs but will not withstand polluted areas.

DISEASES AND INSECTS: Troubled by spruce budworm, woolly adelgid and several canker diseases; see general *Abies* discussion.

LANDSCAPE VALUE: Used mainly as a specimen tree and popular as a Christmas tree. Does not hold its needles very long in a dry house and for this reason is not as desirable as the pines. In youth it looks good but under hot, dry conditions may lose the older needles and become open and unkempt.

CULTIVARS: Many named selections, few of which are available in commerce.

> f. *hudsonia*—I see this form always listed as 'Hudsonia', a rather cute, compact, 1 to 2′ high broad mound with numerous short branches; needles radially arranged, dark green above, silvery beneath, about 1/2″ long, never bears cones, found in White Mountains of New Hampshire.

> 'Nana'—Possibly the same thing as f. *hudsonia*, dwarf globose with dark green needles, whitish stomatic lines on underside.

> For cultivars of this species and other conifers I highly recommend the reference *Conifers: The Illustrated Encyclopedia* 1996. Timber Press. Great photographs and sufficient captioned text by van Gelderen and van Hoey Smith to realize that experts have assembled the treatise.

PROPAGATION: A brief stratification period of 15 to 30 days in moist medium at 34 to 41°F is recommended.

ADDITIONAL NOTES: I have seen this species growing in the barren rock on Cadillac Mountain in Maine; the resin from this tree was used to mount thin specimens under slides but has now been supplanted by other materials. More salt tolerant than I would have believed. Have observed along the coast of Maine with its needlely boughs thrust seaward, yet with no significant needle burn evident. Often mixed with *P. glauca* and *P. rubens* in Maine.

NATIVE HABITAT: Native over a wide part of North America, especially in the higher altitudes from Labrador to Alberta to Pennsylvania. Cultivated 1696.

Abies cilicica (Antoine & Kotschy) Carr. — Cilician Fir

LEAVES: Spreading upward and forward, 3/4 to 1 1/4″ long, 1/12 to 1/10″ wide, on weaker branches outward and upward forming a V-shaped depression, rounded or acute and slightly 2-notched at apex, shining bright green above, with narrow whitish bands beneath.

Abies cilicica, (ā′bēz si-li′see-kȧ), Cilician Fir, has thrived for many years in Spring Grove, Cincinnati, OH where the largest plants have now exceed 70′ high. They are distinctly columnar-spirelike, varying very little from base to apex in width. The foliage from a distance is more gray-green than the normal dark green of most firs. The species has survived in the heavy clay soils and –25°F temperatures and deserves consideration at least in the midwestern states. Cones 6 to 10″ long, 2 to 2 1/2″ wide, cylindric and reddish brown. Asia Minor, Syria. In the wild often grows in association with Cedar-of-Lebanon on calcareous, limestone-based rocky soils with hot dry summers and mild rainy winters. Has produced stray seedlings in the surrounding woods in Spring Grove. Introduced 1855. Zone 5 to 6.

Abies concolor (Gordon & Glend.) Lindl. ex Hildebr. — White (Concolor) Fir
(ā′bēz kon′kul-ēr)

LEAVES: Curving outwards and upwards or almost vertically arranged on the stems, 1 1/2 to 2 1/2″ long and 1/12 to 1/10″ wide, flattened, glaucous on both surfaces, apex short-pointed or rounded, upper surface slightly convex, not grooved, with faint lines of stomata, lower surface with 2 faint bands of stomata separated by a green band, both sides more or less bluish green.

BUDS: Large, broadly conical, blunt, covered with resin which conceals the scales, light brown.

STEM: First year, glabrous or minutely downy, yellowish green; second year, grayish or silvery.

SIZE: 30 to 50′ in height by 15 to 30′ in spread; can grow to 100′ or more; national champion (var. *concolor* Dougl. ex Forbes) is 94′ by 48′ in Uinta National Forest, UT; var. *lowiana* (Gord.) Lemm., California White or Sierra Fir, is widely distributed in the Sierra Nevada of western North America, national champion is 178′ by 28′ in Deschutes National Forest, ID.

HARDINESS: Zone 4 to 7.

HABIT: Conical and branched to the base, the branches on the upper half of the tree tend to point upward, the lower horizontal or deflected downward, creating a rather rigid, stiff appearance in the landscape.

RATE: Slow to medium; one authority reported that this species will grow 50 to 60′ in 30 to 60 years.

TEXTURE: Medium.

BARK: Smooth on young stems except for resin blisters; 4 to 7″ thick on old trunks, ashy gray and divided by deep irregular furrows into thick, horny, flattened ridges.

LEAF COLOR: Bluish or grayish green with pale bluish bands beneath; new growth a light rich green or bluish green; on some forms a silvery blue; significant variation in seed-grown material.

FLOWERS: Inconspicuous, monoecious; staminate—red or red-violet.

FRUIT: Cones are stalked, cylindrical, 3 to 6″ long, 1 1/2 to 1 3/4″ wide, pale green before maturity often with a purplish bloom, finally brown.

CULTURE: The best fir for the Midwest and East; transplant balled and burlapped; while withstanding heat, drought and cold equally well, it prefers and makes best growth on deep, rich, moist, well-drained gravelly or sandy-loam soils; dislikes heavy clay. This species requires less moisture than other western firs and can exist on dry, thin layers of partially decomposed granite or nearly barren rocks. Although full sun is preferable, it will tolerate light shade. Root system, according to some authorities, is shallow and wide spreading while others indicated there is a tap root; seems to hold its needles better than any other fir; a 30-year-old specimen at my former Illinois residence attested to this; a degree more tolerant of city conditions than other fir species.

DISEASES AND INSECTS: None serious.

LANDSCAPE VALUE: Because of its growth habit and softer effect it could well replace the spruces in the landscape; beautiful foliage, especially those trees with bluish needles.

CULTIVARS: There are at least 20 cultivars that I have run across in the literature and possibly more.

　'Candicans'—Large bright silver-blue needles on a narrow upright tree.

　'Compacta'—Irregularly dwarf compact shrub with bright blue 1 to 1 1/2″ long needles.

　'Dwarf Globe'—A 3′ high dwarf with bluish green, densely set needles.

　'Gable's Weeping'—Slow growing, mounding plant with drooping branches.

　'Violacea' (f. *violacea*)—Offers silver blue needles of great beauty; from a distance might be mistaken for one of the silvery-blue forms of *Picea pungens* var. *glauca*; I can still see (20 years later) a handsome specimen in the meadow by Bussey Brook at the Arnold Arboretum; although this form is usually grafted, apparently similar forms occur in nature and seed-beds.

PROPAGATION: Seed shows variability in its chilling requirements; a period of 30 days in moist medium at 41°F is recommended; cuttings taken in early December failed to root without treatment but rooted 50% after treatment with 100 ppm IBA/24 hour soak; in another study, cuttings taken in early December rooted 73% with the above treatment but did not root at all without treatment; in another study, cuttings taken in late January rooted 76% in eight months without treatment, and 100% after treatment with 8000 ppm IBA talc; in other work, cuttings rooted best when taken in March and treated with 100 ppm IBA for 24 hours. Cultivars are usually grafted on seedling understock.

NATIVE HABIT: Colorado to southern California, northern Mexico and New Mexico. Introduced 1872.

Abies firma Sieb. & Zucc. — Momi Fir, Japanese Fir

LEAVES: Arranged in a comb-like pectinate fashion, to 1 1/2″ long, broadest at about the middle, sharply two-pointed at apex on young plants, becoming obtuse or emarginate on older plants, dark green above and furrowed with a few stomatal lines near the apex, lighter green beneath with 2 gray-green bands; of the firs described herein this one is quickly identifiable by the sharp prickly apex.

Abies firma, (ā′bēz fir′mȧ), Momi Fir, has been praised for heat tolerance among firs and indeed is growing in the Mobile, AL, Athens, GA, and Raleigh, NC areas. The plants I have observed were significantly short of spectacular. A plant in the University's Botanical Gardens grew 8 to 10′ high in 12 years. The needles have a notch at their tip and are extremely sharp to the touch. In 1992, a mysterious "Dixie Fir" appeared in the Georgia market promising new horizons for the Christmas tree industry. After considerable checking and the acquisition of a plant, I was convinced the miracle "Fir" was nothing more or less than *Abies firma*. As I pen the above, there is no longer mention of the miracle "Fir." Sargent considered it the most beautiful of Japanese firs, in which country it can grow 120 to 150′. Most widely distributed fir in Japan and is found in dry and moist sites. Under cultivation, 40 to 50′ is more realistic, but I have seen nothing approaching this size. Might be worth trying by the conifer collector. Cones 3 1/2 to 5″ long by 1 1/2 to 2″ wide, brown. Introduced 1861. Zone 6 to 9.

Abies fraseri (Pursh) Poir. — Fraser Fir, Southern Balsam Fir, Southern Fir
(ā′bēz frā′zer-ī)

LEAVES: Crowded, directed forward, pectinate below, 1/2 to 1″ long, 1/24″ broad, entire or emarginate at apex, flat, grooved, shining dark green above, with stomates above near apex, with 2 broad silvery bands of 8 to 12 stomatic lines beneath.
STEMS: Gray or pale yellowish brown, in the first winter reddish brown, very resinous.

SIZE: 30 to 40′ in height by 20 to 25′ in spread; occasionally to 70′ high; national champion is 94′ by 58′ at High Hampton Inn, Cashiers, NC.
HARDINESS: Zone 4 to 7, suitable in higher elevations of Southeast (2000′ and above).
HABIT: Pyramidal, with horizontal, stiff branches, opening up with age.
RATE: Slow.
TEXTURE: Medium.
LEAF COLOR: Shining dark green with stomata above near the apex and two broad silvery bands of 8 to 12 stomatic lines beneath; Cappiello (UMaine) noted the needle fragrance was significantly less than that of *A. balsamea*.
FLOWERS: Monoecious.
FRUIT: Cones ovoid or cylindrical, 1 1/2 to 2 1/2″ long and 1 to 1 1/4″ broad, purple when young becoming tan-brown; bracts much protruded and bent downwards so as to hide the scales, the exserted bracts provide a distinguishing feature between this and *A. balsamea*.
CULTURE: Transplants well when root pruned, does better in dry situations than *Abies balsamea* but prefers a moist, well-drained loam and sun or partial shade.
LANDSCAPE VALUE: Excellent evergreen in the right climate; like Balsam suffers in hot, dry weather; Fraser has become a favored Christmas tree in the southern highlands and North Carolina State University has an active research program with the species; truly a beautiful Christmas and ornamental tree; in recent years Bonnie and I have utilized this species for the family Christmas tree; with proper attention to water needs, Fraser Fir holds up reasonably well over its 10- to 14-day house visit; a 1993 report noted 2500 North Carolina growers planted 30,000 acres of Fraser Fir, where planting on 4′ by 4′ spacing produces about 2,700 trees per acre. Fraser Fir has been designated the Cadillac of Christmas Trees.
CULTIVARS:
　'Klein's Nest' (have seen spelled 'Kline's Nest')—Dense compact form with semi-erect branches with short dark green needles and small purple cones, to 30″ high.
　'Prostrata'—Slow-growing, spreading, mounded, can grow 4 to 5′ high by 12 to 14′ wide, needles like the species; originated in East Boxford, MA, 1916; probably more than one clone in cultivation.
PROPAGATION: Seed, again actual recommendations vary somewhat but a cold period of 15 to 30 days would probably be somewhat beneficial. See Dirr and Heuser (1987) for an overview of cutting propagation. North Carolina State researchers have successfully rooted cuttings [*HortScience* 20: 1065–1067 (1985)] but I do not know of any Christmas tree growers who have extended the results to the production of clonal material. See *Amer. Nurseryman* 181(5):54–58, 60–67 (1995) for a detailed discussion of propagation.
ADDITIONAL NOTES: In 1993, during a mini-trek through the southern Appalachians, I saw *Abies fraseri* on Clingman's Dome, decimated by Balsam Woolly Adelgid. Many trees were dead and the eerie aura was one of a lost legacy. The National Park Service was attempting to control the pest.
　　Certainly one of the more beautiful sights my wife and I experienced was a large Fraser Fir Christmas tree farm near Lake Glenville, NC. The trees, in orderly ribbon-like rows appeared to be marching down the slopes.
NATIVE HABITAT: Native to the mountains of West Virginia, North Carolina, and Tennessee at altitudes of 3000 to 6000′. Introduced 1811.

Abies homolepis Sieb. & Zucc. — Nikko Fir

LEAVES: Needles form almost a solid cushion without the distinct pectinate arrangement, glossy dark green above, 2 white bands below, 1/3 to 1 1/8″ long, slight notch at rather flat apex; the lowest leaves are the largest and spread horizontally, each succeeding rank is smaller and more erect producing a narrow or scarcely perceptible V-shaped opening at the top.

Abies homolepis, (ā′bēz hō-mō-lep′us), Nikko Fir, is a tree of great formal beauty that has prospered in Bernheim Arboretum, Clermont, KY. The tree is densely clothed with branches to the base and forms a rather fat pyramid, not as narrow and loose as some firs. Probably will grow 30 to 50′ under cultivation but grows 100 to 130′ in its native Japan. Cones cylindrical, 4 to 5″ long, green in youth and pale brown when mature. Have seen photos of almost ruby-red young female cones that age to bluish purple. For midwestern and eastern states, it is worth trying. Don Shadow, Winchester, TN, has several seedling survivors that have withstood the heat and drought. One, in particular, is a broad, dark green pyramid of exceptional beauty. 'Prostrata', a spreading form, has long, shiny, olive-green needles with silver on the reverse. Introduced 1861. Zone 4 to 6(7).

Abies koreana Wils. — Korean Fir

LEAVES: Thickly set on stem, 1/2 to 3/4″ long, 1/16 to 1/12″ wide, notched or rounded at apex which is the broadest point of needle, dark green above, two whitish bands below divided by a thin green midrib.

Abies koreana, (ā′bēz kôr-ē-ā′na), Korean Fir, is a slow growing, rather small-statured, 15 to 30′ high, compact tree. Most notable characteristic is the rich violet-purple, some would argue blue, 2 to 3″ long, 1″ wide cones that occur on 3 to 5′ high plants. Appears slightly more heat tolerant than many firs but still best in cold climates. 'Aurea' has golden needles, spreading irregular habit. 'Horstmann's Silberlocke' is a handsome, irregular branching form with the needles curling up and revealing the bright silver lower surface. 'Prostrata' ['Prostrate Beauty'(?)] is a reasonably common, rich green, low growing type. Quite a number of selected forms that enjoy reasonable success in commerce. Counted 19 cultivars in the *Conifers* reference, several that are staggeringly beautiful. Korea. Introduced 1908. Zone 5 to 6(7).

Abies lasiocarpa (Hook.) Nutt. — Rocky Mountain Fir, Alpine Fir, Subalpine Fir

LEAVES: Much crowded and directed forward and upward, 1 to 1 1/2″ long, acute or rounded at apex, rarely emarginate, pale bluish green, stomatiferous above and slightly grooved, with silvery-gray stomatal bands below.

Abies lasiocarpa, (ā′bēz lā-si-ō-kär′pà), Rocky Mountain Fir, is a large, 100 to 160′ high tree with grayish or chalk-white bark. National champion is 125′ by 26′ in Olympic National Park, Washington. Cones are oblong-cylindric, 2 to 4″ long and dark purple. 'Compacta' produces short stiff gray-blue needles on a compact pyramid, 6′ by 3′ in 10 years. 'Glauca' is a rich silver-blue needle form, habit is pyramidal. 'Glauca Compacta' is a dwarf pyramid with silver-blue congested foliage. In general it is not well suited to culture in the East and Midwest but I have seen variety *arizonica* which is a smaller, rich blue-green pyramid and has a thick corky creamy white bark. The needles of the variety are distinctly emarginate, pectinate, and whiter beneath. Forms a narrow pyramid. Found at high altitudes in northern Arizona and New Mexico. In July, 1995 while visiting Mt. Rainier and hiking the trail to Mt. Dege (7000′ elevation), I marveled at the Rocky Mountain Firs that dotted either side of the ridge. Tall, narrow, almost spire-like in habit, the trees are able to resist limb breakage from the snow. Foliage color, although described as bluish green, was variable. I wish that firs were adapted to the Southeast, but only for a fleeting second, for each geographical nook and cranny of the United States houses unique flora. It is better and more noble to enjoy and savor than to covet. Introduced 1901. Zone 5 to 6(7). The species from Alaska to Oregon, Utah and northern New Mexico. Introduced 1863.

Abies nordmanniana (Steven) Spach. — Nordmann Fir, Caucasian Fir

LEAVES: Directed forward and densely covering the branches, 3/4 to 1 1/2″ long, 1/16 to 1/12″ wide, apex rounded and notched, lustrous dark green above, midrib sunken, 2 white bands below.

Abies nordmanniana, (ā′bēz nôrd-man-ē-ā′nȧ), Nordmann Fir, is perhaps the handsomest of the firs. Stately, elegant with almost black green needles it may grow 40 to 60′ under cultivation but in the wild grows to 200′. Many old +100′ specimens exist in England. Cones are 5 to 6″ long, 1 3/4 to 2″ wide, cylindrical or tapered to apex, reddish brown, with prominent exserted bracts. 'Golden Spreader' cropped up in several gardens during a 1994 garden tour to England and Wales. A genuine conversation piece with striking golden yellow needles on a 3 to 4′ high and wide shrubby framework. Will cook without protection in the eastern United States. 'Pendula' has weeping branches and is a rather curious but not aesthetic sight. 'Prostrata' is a slow growing form with a trailing habit. Occasionally, good specimens appear in Zone 7. Caucasus, Asia Minor. Introduced 1848. Zone 4 to 6.

Abies procera Rehd. — Noble Fir
(ā′bēz prō′ser-ȧ)

LEAVES: Crowded above, the lower ranks spreading outward, those of the middle rank much shorter, appressed to the branchlet, curving upwards near the base, pectinate below and curved, 1 to 1 1/2″ long, 1/16″ wide, scarcely broadened, rounded or slightly notched at apex, grooved, bluish green, stomatiferous above, with narrow pale bands below.
BUDS: Roundish, resinous, surrounded at base by a collar of long pointed scales free at the tips.
STEM: In youth covered with a reddish brown minute pubescence.

SIZE: 50 to 100′ under landscape conditions, 180 to 270′ in height in native stands; Co-national champions are 238′ by 41′ at Gifford Pinchot National Forest, Washington and 272′ by 49′ at Mt. St. Helens National Monument, Washington.
HARDINESS: Zone 5 to 6(7).
HABIT: Symmetrically pyramidal or narrow; conical in youth; mature trees develop a long, clear, columnar trunk, with an essentially dome-like crown.
RATE: Slow to medium, will reach 75′+ in 30 to 60 years; trees 100 to 120 years of age are commonly 90 to 120′ in height.
TEXTURE: Medium.
BARK: Gray and smooth for many years, with prominent resin blisters; eventually dark gray, often tinged with purple and broken up into thin, nearly rectangular plates separated by deep fissures on old trunks; bark about 1 to 2″ thick; this is thin in comparison to other trees and specimens are often ruined by fire.
LEAF COLOR: Bluish green, stomatiferous above with narrow pale bands below.
FLOWERS: Inconspicuous, monoecious.
FRUIT: A large, cylindrical cone, 6 to 10″ long by approximately 2 to 3″ broad, green before maturity, finally turning purplish brown.
CULTURE: Readily transplanted balled and burlapped if properly root pruned, prefers a moist, deep, cool, well-drained soil, sun or partial shade and dislikes high pH soils as well as windy conditions; good growth is also made on thin rocky soils if provided with an abundance of moisture.
DISEASES AND INSECTS: Damaged by the spruce budworm, woolly adelgid and several canker diseases.
LANDSCAPE VALUE: Can be used as a specimen tree, however, best adapted in its native habitat.
CULTIVARS: Have seen 7 to 8 cultivars listed in the literature.
  'Aurea' ('Sherwoodii')—Foliage suffused with golden yellow on the outer needles, tree form, discovered as a chance seedling at Sherwood Nurseries, Portland, OR.
  'Glauca'—Extremely glaucous foliage and a liberal cone bearer, becomes a reasonably large tree with time; also 'Glauca Prostrata' is offered in commerce.
PROPAGATION: Stratified and non-stratified seeds gave good germination percentages.
NATIVE HABITAT: Native to the Cascade Mountains of Washington, Oregon and the Siskiyou Mountains of California. Western United States. Introduced 1830.

Abies veitchii Lindl. — Veitch Fir
(ā′bēz vetch′ē-ī)

LEAVES: One half to (+)1″ long and about 1/16″ wide, flattened, gradually tapering to the base, apex truncate, notched; upper surface dark green, shining, grooved; lower surfaces with 2 conspicuously broad white bands of stomata.
BUDS: Small, nearly globular, resinous, grayish brown.
STEM: Green, reddish brown to brown, more or less clothed with short pubescence.

SIZE: 50 to 75′ high by 25 to 35′ in spread.
HARDINESS: Zone 3 to 6.
HABIT: A broadly pyramidal tree with horizontal, spreading branches.
RATE: Slow to medium; one authority reported 20 to 50′ in height after 20 to 30 years.
TEXTURE: Medium.
LEAF COLOR: Lustrous dark green above with prominent, chalky-white bands below.
FLOWERS: Inconspicuous, monoecious.
FRUIT: Cones are sessile, cylindrical, 2 to 3″ long, 1 1/4″ broad and bluish purple when young, becoming brown.
CULTURE: Transplants well balled and burlapped if properly root pruned; prefers moist, well-drained soils; sun or partial shade; dislikes high pH soils; supposedly performs acceptably in semi-urban conditions.
DISEASES AND INSECTS: As is the case with most firs it is troubled by the spruce budworm, woolly adelgid and several canker diseases.
LANDSCAPE VALUE: Because of its extremely hardy nature and handsome foliage it should be considered more often for a specimen tree.
PROPAGATION: There appears to be a significant increase in germination percentage with stratified versus non-stratified seeds; stratify in a moist medium for 15 to 30 days at 41°F; cuttings taken in late December rooted 60% with 8000 ppm IBA-talc; not at all without treatment; rooting of winter cuttings has also been improved by IBA, 40 ppm soak for 24 hours.
NATIVE HABITAT: Central and southern Japan. Introduced 1865.

Acanthopanax sieboldianus Mak. [new name is now *Eleutherococcus sieboldianus* (Mak.) Koidz.] — Fiveleaf Aralia
(à-kan-thō-pā′naks sē-bōl-dē-ā′nus)

FAMILY: Araliaceae
LEAVES: Alternate, palmately compound, partly fascicled on short spurs, leaflets 5 to 7, subsessile, obovate to oblong-obovate, 1 to 2 1/2″ long, 1/3 to 1″ wide, acute, cuneate, crenate-serrate, rich bright green, glabrous; petiole—1 to 3″ long.
BUDS: Solitary, sessile, conical-ovoid with about 3 exposed scales.
STEM: Light brown, warty, with 1 (usually) or 2 slender arching prickles beneath each narrow leaf-scar; pith—solid, ample, white; leaf scars narrowly crescent shaped or U-shaped, somewhat raised.

SIZE: 8 to 10′ by 8 to 10′
HARDINESS: Zone 4 to 8.
HABIT: Erect, upright-growing deciduous shrub with arching stems which gradually flop over to form a rounded outline; can be maintained in a more upright fashion with proper pruning.
RATE: Medium to fast in good soil; grows remarkably fast under less-than-ideal conditions.
TEXTURE: Medium in all seasons.
LEAF COLOR: Rich bright green, leafing out by late March—early April in Athens and holding late into fall; I have observed a full complement of leaves as late as mid-November; fall color is not consistent, at best some degree of yellow.
FLOWERS: Unisexual, usually dioecious, small, greenish white to greenish yellow, borne in a spherical umbel, 3/4 to 1″ diameter, which terminates a 2 to 4″ long slender stalk, arises from cluster of leaves on one-year-old wood, May–June.
FRUIT: Sparingly produced in cultivation, 1/4″ wide, 2 to 5-seeded black berry; Bailey noted only the pistillate form was in cultivation and produced no fruit for lack of a suitable pollinator; perhaps other members of the genus can act as pollinators.

CULTURE: Readily transplanted and cultured; adapts to unfavorable conditions; prefers well-drained soil, acid or alkaline, sand to clay, full sun to heavy shade, withstands heavy pruning, tolerates polluted conditions.

DISEASES AND INSECTS: Nothing serious although a leaf spot has been reported.

LANDSCAPE VALUE: Tremendous plant for cities; have seen this plant performing magnificently under the worst conditions; quite tolerant of dry soils; makes a good screen or barrier; tends to sucker and may need to be restrained; will withstand considerable shade or full sun.

CULTIVARS:

'Variegatus'—A handsome form, the leaves bordered creamy white; will grow 6 to 8′ high and wide; although listed at the previous landscape size, everything I have observed in gardens, even old specimens, were smaller in the 4 to 5′ range. Bean considered it one of the daintiest of variegated shrubs; I first saw this plant at the Oxford Botanic Garden, England, and was quite taken with its handsome variegation pattern; this plant would make an excellent focal point in a shady shrub border; appears less drought/sun tolerant than the species.

PROPAGATION: Seed requires a warm:cold treatment and 6 months warm:3 months cold should suffice; easily rooted from softwood cuttings; root cuttings and division also work; August-collected cuttings rooted 93% when treated with 8000 ppm IBA + Thiram and placed under mist.

NATIVE HABITAT: Japan. Cultivated 1859.

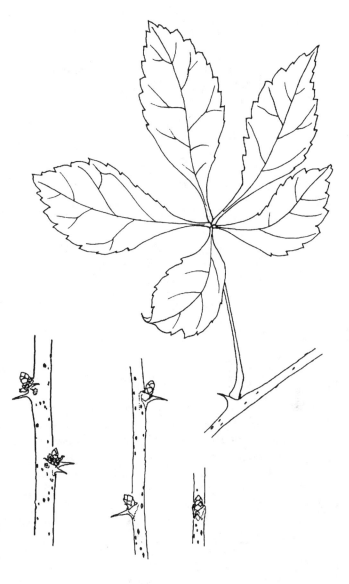

RELATED SPECIES:

Acanthopanax henryi (Oliv.) Harms (now *Eleutherococcus henryi* Oliv.), (ȧ-kan-thō-pā′naks hen′ri-ī), Henry's Aralia, is a sturdy, upright, strongly multi-stemmed shrub growing 8 to 10′; the dull dark green, rough-surfaced leaves hold late into fall; greenish flowers give way to inky-black, 3/8″ long fruits in 1 1/2 to 2″ diameter umbels, fruits persist for a time and are rather attractive. This species fruits commonly in cultivation. 'Nana' grows about 1/2 to 2/3 the size of the species and forms a solid, impenetrable thicket of upright, multi-spined, grayish stems. China. 1901. Zone 5 to 7.

ADDITIONAL NOTES: None of these plants will supersede the viburnums for ornamental qualities but where pollution tolerant, low-maintenance plants are needed they may have a place; they make superb barrier plants because of nodal spines. About 30 species native to southeastern and western China.

Acer buergerianum Miq. — Trident Maple
(ā′sẽr bẽr-jẽr-ē-ā′num)

FAMILY: Aceraceae

LEAVES: Opposite, simple, 3-lobed, 1 1/2 to 3 1/2″ high and wide, 3 nerved at base and rounded or broad-cuneate, lobes triangular, acute and pointing forward, entire or slightly and irregularly serrate primarily toward apex of lobes, pubescent while young, soon glabrous, very lustrous dark green; on certain trees lobes widely spreading and sinuses deeply cut, often evident on young seedlings; petiole—about as long as blade.

BUDS: Imbricate, terminal—1/4″ long, rich brown, 4-angled, pyramid-shaped, pubescent on edge of scales, scales sharply acute; laterals—smaller, somewhat appressed, otherwise similar.

STEM: Slender, pubescent, gray-brown, small lenticels, pith—solid, greenish white; second-year stems becoming darker brown and lose pubescence.

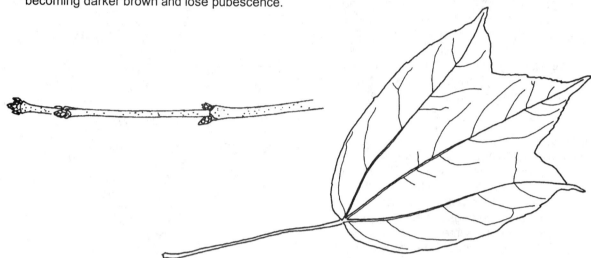

SIZE: 20 to 30′ perhaps to 30 to 35′; spread approaches height; can reach 40 feet high; Roy Lancaster noted that it can grow to 100′ in China.

HARDINESS: Zone 5 to 8(9); in September 1994 I visited with Buddy Hubbuch, horticulturist, Bernheim Arboretum, Clermont, KY, who showed me a grove of Trident Maple that was severely injured by -24°F in January 1994; trees were not killed and regrowth had developed from major branches, obviously severe young and intermediate stem damage as well as cambial damage on major trunks had occurred; in the 1990 edition I speculated on cold hardiness between -15 and -25°F; appears -20°F and warmer are most appropriate.

HABIT: Distinctly oval-rounded to rounded outline; very lovely small tree; tendency toward multiple and low branching unless trained to a single stem; greatly variable from seed as row-run seedlings are all over the growth habit map.

RATE: Slow to medium, over time would be considered a slow grower.

BARK: On 2 to 3″ diameter trunks becomes gray-brown-orange and develops an exfoliating, platy, scaly character; pretty bark that adds winter interest.

LEAF COLOR: New growth often rich bronze to purple maturing to glossy dark green in summer, changing to yellow, orange and red in fall; colors later than many maples (late October–early November); can be very good but is often variable; trees in Mt. Auburn Cemetery, Cambridge, Mass turned a lovely combination of yellow to red; a 30′ tree on the Georgia campus colors a rich rose to red; a new selection Streetwise® produces reddish purple fall coloration.

FLOWERS: Greenish yellow, borne in downy umbel-like corymbs with the leaves in March (often in Athens), April–May; scarcely noticeable.

FRUIT: Samara, 3/4 to 1″ long, the wings 1/4″ wide, parallel or connivent, mature in October–November; fruit set is often so heavy that trees do not carry a full complement of foliage and appear less-than-pristine in late summer-early fall.

CULTURE: Transplants readily but best moved balled and burlapped before budbreak in winter or early spring; well-drained, acid soil; displays good drought resistance; full sun; has received plaudits from many plantsmen; may suffer breakage in severe ice and snow storms; have moved it in full leaf successfully.

DISEASES AND INSECTS: None serious, see *A. saccharinum* for listing of maple problems.

LANDSCAPE VALUE: Very handsome small patio, lawn, or street tree; might work well in planter boxes; definitely should be used more extensively; makes a good bonsai specimen; in Japan it is widely planted as a street tree; reports on quality of fall coloration are somewhat contradictory; significant variation does occur; the late Professor Clancy Lewis, Michigan State, described a tree on campus which turned a good red with some purple; reports from Morton Arboretum, Chicago, IL, note that it can be used in that area with proper siting.

CULTIVARS: Dwarf and variegated forms exist; seedlings and cultivars utilized extensively for bonsai; anyone interested in specifics should read J.D. Vertrees, *Japanese Maples*, Timber Press.

Streetwise®—A vigorous grower with lustrous dark green foliage that turns burgundy red in autumn; bark exfoliates at an early age, more upright in habit than typical seedlings and can be more readily trained to a single stem (leader), introduced by Tree Introductions, Inc., Athens, GA.

PROPAGATION: Seed, 3 months at 41°F works well; cuttings from mature trees are difficult to root but cuttings taken from 2-year-old seedlings rooted 75 to 95% depending on treatment (nothing, 10000 ppm NAA, 3000 or 8000 ppm IBA talc); cuttings collected in late June rooted 60% when treated with 20000 ppm IBA talc, fine sand, intermittent mist.

ADDITIONAL NOTES: I have noticed great variation in the leaves with some accurately depicted by the drawing while others show a rounded-lobing pattern with deeper-cut sinuses; variety *trinerve* (Siesmeyr) Rehd. has spreading lateral lobes; margins of all lobes coarsely toothed and underside of leaf glaucous; this variety is considered a juvenile form.

Acer is comprised of probably 120 to 150 species, evergreen or deciduous, fruit 2, 1-seeded samaras fused at their ovaries to form a schizocarp.

One of the most exciting advances in *Acer* research is the breeding work of Dr. Susan Wiegrefe, University of Minnesota, with typically compatible species and rather wide crosses. Although seed set was minimal she managed to successfully cross *A. cissifolium* × *A. henryi* and has a seedling to show for this work. Also produced seed from *A. griseum* × *A. triflorum*. See *Newsletter of Landscape Development Center* 5(1):14–18 (1995) for complete discussion. Van Gelderen et al., *Maples of the World*. 1994. Timber Press should be consulted for additional information about the *Acer* species. The authors list 20 cultivars, none of which are in significant production in the United States. The book *is* a terrific reference and should be in the library of true *Acer* aficionados.

NATIVE HABIT: China. Cultivated 1890.

Acer campestre L. — Hedge Maple, Field Maple
(ā′sĕr kam-pes′trē)

FAMILY: Aceraceae

LEAVES: Opposite, simple, 2 to 4″ long and wide, pubescent beneath, 3 to 5 rounded, entire lobes, sometimes denticulate, deep dark green; petiole—to 4″ long, when detached yields a milky sap.

BUDS: Terminal—imbricate, 1/8 to 1/4″ long, grayish brown to brownish black, tips of scales often pubescent and chaffy; laterals—appressed, smaller.

STEM: Slender, glabrous, light brown, somewhat lustrous, lenticelled; second year stems gray-brown, more prominently lenticelled; stems often develop corky fissures; pith—solid, white.

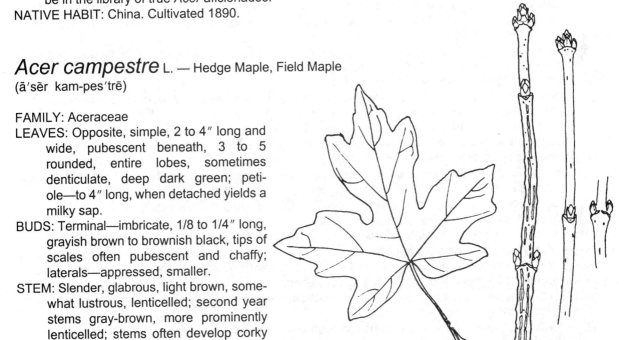

SIZE: 25 to 35′(45′), occasionally 70 to 75′; spread would be comparable to height, especially on specimens 30 to 35′ high.

HARDINESS: Zone (4)5 to 8.

HABIT: Usually rounded and dense, often branched to the ground making grass culture difficult; some trees display a pyramidal-oval outline; can be easily limbed up.

RATE: Slow, 10 to 14′ over a 10 to 15 year period; can be pushed in the nursery and may average 2′ per year in youth.

TEXTURE: Medium in all seasons.

BARK: Gray-black, lightly ridged-and-furrowed, resembles bark of Norway Maple.

LEAF COLOR: Handsome dark green in summer changing to yellow-green or yellow in fall; does not color consistently in Midwest or South but trees in the Arnold Arboretum colored a lovely yellow; one of the latest trees to color developing along with Norway Maple in late October–early November and remaining effective for a long period; a tree on the Georgia Campus has colored bright yellow on several occasions.

FLOWERS: Few, green, initially in erect corymbs, May, ineffective.

FRUIT: Samara, 1 1/4 to 1 3/4″ long, 1/3 to 1/2″ wide, nutlet often pubescent, wings horizontally spreading, forming a 180° angle from wing to wing.

CULTURE: Readily transplanted; extremely adaptable; prefers rich, well-drained soil but performs admirably in high pH soils; also does well in acid situations (pH 5.5 and above); tolerant of dry soils and compaction; air pollution tolerant; full sun or light shade; withstands severe pruning.

DISEASES AND INSECTS: None serious.

LANDSCAPE VALUE: Excellent small lawn specimen, street tree in residential areas and perhaps cities, good under utility lines because of low height; can be pruned into hedges and is often used for this in Europe; probably the best maple for dry, alkaline soils; have observed trees in the Salt Lake City, UT area which were 30 to 40′ high and wide with a full complement of healthy foliage in October.

CULTIVARS:

‘Compactum’ (‘Nanum’ in *Maples of the World*)—A dwarf, multi-stemmed shrub of very close, compact growth, 2 to 4′(6′) high and usually broader than high; very effective and handsome dwarf shrub; have noticed some tip dieback as a result of low temperatures; apparently not as hardy as the species; develops a good yellow fall color under proper environmental conditions; at Hilliers, the cultivar has been grafted onto a standard (species) to produce a rather novel small “broomy” tree; have attempted to root softwood cuttings but with no success; Arnold Arboretum experienced 68% rooting on August cuttings treated with 8000 ppm IBA-talc; found in 1874.

‘Eastleigh Weeping’—Pendulous habit; raised in Eastleigh nursery of Hilliers & Sons.

‘Fastigiatum’—Upright form with corky branches, leaves 5-lobed, hairy beneath, found in the wild about 1930; to my knowledge not present in commerce.

‘Leprechaun’—Know little of this oval-rounded, densely branched form but it appears more uniform than typical seedling material. Nice specimen at Spring Grove, Cincinnati, OH that is now (1997) about 20′ by 15′.

‘Postelense’—Leaves golden yellow when young gradually changing to green, interesting in spring but losing the yellow color with the advent of warm weather; have seen at Kew gardens in May–June and the effect was potent.

‘Pulverulentum’—A form with cream flecked and spotted leaves, quite striking on close inspection but does not appear to be a stable variegation.

Queen Elizabeth™—Small to medium sized tree, 35′ by 30′, rounded with a flat top, more vigorous than the species, branches at 45° angle, leaves darker green and larger than the species, fall color yellowish; included in tests at Milliken Arboretum, Spartanburg, SC and has proved quite adaptable with a uniform oval-rounded outline and dense canopy of foliage, has set abundant seeds on several occasions, more than normal on a Hedge Maple; may not be perfectly cold hardy in Zone 5; introduced by J. Frank Schmidt and Sons, Boring, OR. Queen Elizabeth is the trademark name, ‘Evelyn’ the cultivar name, plant patent 4392.

‘Schwerinii’—Leaves purple when unfolding, finally turning green; not spectacular, have seen in England.

PROPAGATION: Seed requires a warm/cold period for germination, 68 to 86°F for 30 days followed by 36 to 40°F for 90 to 180 days; I have raised many seedlings following this procedure; soaking seeds in warm water followed by 3 months at 41°F has a positive effect; softwood cuttings collected on June 4, treated with 8000 ppm IBA-talc, placed under mist with bottom heat rooted 79%; timing appeared to be critical; cultivars are grafted or budded.

MAINTENANCE CONSIDERATIONS: Surprisingly durable small maple that is not common in American gardens; essentially pest and disease free; will take considerable pruning and is a familiar inhabitant of the hedge rows encountered along English roads.

ADDITIONAL NOTES: A variable species and at least 4 varieties/subspecies are recognized: *austriacum*, *hebecarpum*, *leiocarpon*, and *tauricum*; interestingly *Maples of the World* recognizes no varieties/subspecies; appears to be significant variation in degree of leaf lobing and pubescence; used as a hedge in Europe and some of the famous hedges at Schönbrunn, near Vienna, form perpendicular walls 35′ high.

NATIVE HABIT: Widespread in Europe, Near East and Africa. Introduced in colonial times to the United States.

Acer carpinifolium Sieb. & Zucc. — Hornbeam Maple

LEAVES: Opposite, simple, ovate-oblong, 3 to 5″ long, one-half as wide, long acuminate, subcordate to truncate, doubly serrate, glabrous or nearly so at maturity, dark green; petiole—1/2″ long.

BUDS: Terminal—imbricate, 1/8 to 3/16″ long, ovoid, 4-sided, lustrous blood red, edge of scales light brown, pubescent at collar where petiole abscised; laterals—1/2 size of terminal.

STEM: Slender, lustrous gray-green-brown, slightly lenticelled, glabrous, angular.

Acer carpinifolium, (ā′sĕr kär-pīn′i-fō-lē-um), Hornbeam Maple, may have the most appropriate common name of any maple. The leaves are atypical for maple, resembling in shape and character those of *Carpinus caroliniana*. The dark green leaves change to rich gold and brown in autumn. Habit is often vase shaped, multistemmed and round headed. Landscape size would range from 20 to 25′ although most that I have seen were smaller than this. In Japan, it is described as growing to 50′. Bark is smooth and gray. The greenish flowers (May) are borne in short glabrous racemes and the 3/4″ long samaras diverge at a right or obtuse angle. Prefers a moist, well-drained soil and some shade. I would surmise that in the wild this tree exists as an understory plant. Can be rooted from August cuttings using 8000 ppm IBA talc. 'Esveld Select' develops a fastigiate growth habit. Japan. Introduced 1881. Zone (4)5 to 7.

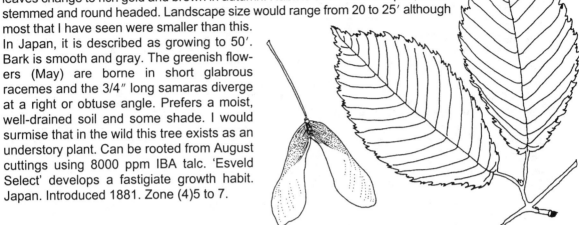

Acer cissifolium (Sieb. & Zucc.) K. Koch — Ivy-leaved Maple

LEAVES: Opposite, trifoliate, each leaflet 1 1/2 to 3″ long, ovate or obovate to elliptic, long acuminate, cuneate, medium green above, glabrous, whitish tufts in axils of veins below, prominent mucronate, Zelkova-like serrations, terminal leaflet stalked, petiolule about 1″ long, laterals 1/2″ long; petiole—3 to 4″ long, reddish purple.

BUDS: Terminal—reddish purple, 3/16″ long, valvate, pubescent, lower part of bud glabrous, lustrous; laterals—similar, 1/2 as long, appressed.

STEM: First year—slender, reddish purple, prominently pubescent; second year—gray-brown with an onion skin effect.

Acer cissifolium, (ā′sĕr sis-i-fō′lē-um), Ivy-leaved Maple, is extremely rare in cultivation but certainly worthy of consideration. Young trees are upright-oval in outline but with age may become distinctly mushroom-like and broad spreading at least with open-grown specimens. My original description is based on the now deceased magnificent specimen on The Ohio State University campus. Subsequent evaluations, particularly young specimens, reflect an oval to rounded outline. Ultimate height and spread range from 20 to 30′. The medium green foliage changes to yellow and red in fall although I have not seen good color on the trees I've observed. Flowers are born in 2 to 4″ long slender racemes; the samaras are 1″ long and diverge at an angle of 60° or less. Fruit set may be abundant but the percentage of solid seed is low. Cuttings of this species can be readily rooted. Cuttings collected in mid-August, treated with 8000 ppm IBA talc rooted 100%; those that were wounded had heavier root systems. The branches are intricate and low slung, often growing parallel with the ground but still twisting and turning in elegant fashion. The smooth, slightly dimpled gray bark is an added feature. Prefers well-drained, moist, acid soil and a partially shaded location although plants I have seen in full sun were performing well. The species is supposedly allied to *Acer negundo* but this is like allying a Rolls Royce with a Pinto; the only similarity being trifoliate leaves in the case of the trees, with 4 wheels in the case of the cars. A close relation that I have seen at the Morris Arboretum and Bernheim Arboretum is *Acer henryi* Pax but that species is larger and the leaflets are often entire to slightly serrated. *Acer henryi* is listed as *A. cissifolium* subsp. *henryi* (Pax) E. Murray and indeed branches of both taxa side-by-side are not easy to differentiate. One major difference is cold hardiness with ssp. *henryi* surviving -24°F without injury while *A. cissifolium* was killed to the main trunk. Also the new growth on ssp. *henryi* is red. I saw the two taxa in close proximity at Bernheim Arboretum in September, 1994. It appears that ssp. *henryi* might prove a worthy choice for colder portions of the Midwest and Northeast. *Acer cissifolium* is native to Japan. Introduced 1875. Subspecies *henryi* is native to central China. Introduced 1903. *Maples of the World* treats these two taxa as distinct species.

Acer diabolicum Bl. ex Koch — Devil Maple, Horned Maple

LEAVES: Opposite, simple, 5-lobed, 4 to 6″ across, with broad-ovate short-acuminate coarsely and remotely dentate lobes, extremely silky-pubescent in youth, at maturity the veins below densely so, interveinal areas less so, dark green; petiole—1 3/4 to 2″ long, pubescent, with milky sap.

STEM: Young—whitish and pubescent, finally glabrous and red-brown.

Acer diabolicum, (ā′sēr dī-à-bol′i-kum), Devil Maple, is not well known in American gardens and is seldom seen in European gardens but is certainly a handsome tree, possibly best reserved for the collector. The habit is rounded with ultimate landscape size approximately 20 to 30′. A tree has prospered in the Arnold Arboretum for years. In my mind, the most recognizable trait is the thick bristly nutlet of the samara. The wings are upright or spreading, 1 1/4 to 1 3/4″ long; fruits occur on a 1/2 to 2″ long stalk; dioecious: yellow flowers before the leaves, male fascicled on pendulous, pilose pedicels, sepals connate; female flowers in several-flowered racemes, with sepals and petals distinct and of equal length. Species appears adaptable but has not been tested extensively. 'Purpurascens' offers emerging purple-red leaves, flowers and fruits; the color is lost with maturity. Harris, *The Plantsman* 83(5):35–58, stated that it is simply the male tree with attractive red flowers. Have seen the male form in flower and it is slightly short of spectacular. A handsome specimen resides in Bernheim Arboretum that has withstood -24°F. Mountains of Japan. Cultivated 1850. Zone 5 to 7.

Acer ginnala Maxim. [now *A. tataricum* L. ssp. *ginnala* (Maxim.) Wesm.] — Amur Maple
(ā′sēr gi-nā′là)

LEAVES: Opposite, simple, 1 1/2 to 3″ long, 3-lobed, middle lobe is much longer than the 2 lateral lobes, doubly serrate, glabrous above and below, dark green and lustrous above, light green beneath; petiole—1/2 to 1 3/4″ long.
BUDS: Small, 1/8″ long, imbricate, reddish brown or lighter, glabrous.
STEM: Glabrous, slender, gray-brown; gray, rougher and striped on older branches.
FRUIT: Samaras hang on late into fall; wings virtually parallel; persistent into spring.

SIZE: 15 to 18′, possibly to 25′ in height, spread equal to or exceeding height, especially multi-stemmed specimens.
HARDINESS: Zone 3 to 8; does not perform as well in Zone 7 and 8 as it does further north.
HABIT: Multi-stemmed large shrub or small tree often of rounded outline; shape is variable and can be successfully tailored to specific landscape requirements by pruning.
RATE: Over a period of 10 to 20 years the growth in height would average 12 to 20′; however, in extreme youth can be induced into rapid growth by optimum fertilizer and moisture.
TEXTURE: Medium-fine in leaf; medium in winter.
BARK: Grayish brown on older branches; smooth with darker striations like serviceberry.
LEAF COLOR: Handsome glossy dark green in summer changing to shades of yellow and red in fall; does not fall color consistently; best coloration is seen in full sun situations; extreme variation in fall coloration and selections should be made for this trait; one of the first trees to leaf out, often in full leaf by late March in Athens, GA.
FLOWERS: Yellowish white, fragrant as the leaves unfurl in April to May, borne in small (1 to 1 1/2″ diameter) panicles; one of the few maples with fragrant flowers.
FRUIT: Samara, 3/4 to 1″ long, wings nearly parallel, red to brown, variable in coloration but there are several good red fruiting types available; red color most vibrant in June–July; fruits ripen September–October.
CULTURE: Very easy to transplant; quite adaptable to wide range of soils and pH ranges; performs best in moist, well-drained soil; withstands heavy pruning; can be successfully grown as a container plant; full sun or light shade.
DISEASES AND INSECTS: Relatively free of problems although can be affected by several of the pests listed under Silver Maple; *Verticillium* has been a problem on 'Compactum' and 'Flame'.

LANDSCAPE VALUE: Small specimen, patio tree, screen, grouping, massing, corners or blank walls of large buildings; very popular maple in East and Midwest; certainly one of the hardiest; seems to do better in shade than many maples; tends toward multi-stemmed character and this would limit street tree use; one of the better maples for above-ground container use; the previous use was spawned by a planting in Tulsa, OK where multi-stemmed 10 to 12′ high and wide plants were utilized in raised (2′ off pavement) planters; it was late October and the yellow fall coloring leaves and branch structure were reflected in the glass of a neighboring office building; I still utilize the slides in my classes and quietly anticipate the positive responses from the students.

CULTIVARS:

'Compactum' ('Bailey Compact')—Supposedly more dense and compact than 'Durand Dwarf' but based on limited observations this does not appear true; shows vigorous growth and may reach 5 to 6′ and larger; leaves are lustrous dark green, about the size of the species, and color a good red-purple in fall; leaves 1/4 developed by early March in my garden; full flower by mid-April; wonderfully fragrant and certainly a worthy garden plant. Plants in my garden made over 2′ of growth in a single season and had to be cut back to maintain compactness; in 10 years in the Dirr garden the plant was 12′ high and 20′ wide, densely branched and serves as an effective barrier. Introduced by J.V. Bailey Nursery, Newport, MN. I am sorry to report the cultivar's demise in 1993 to the front-end loader of a Kubota.

'Durand Dwarf'—Dwarf, shrubby type, branches more dense than 'Compactum'; will grow 3 to 5′ high with a similar or greater spread; have seen a 15′ high densely twiggy plant labeled as 'Durand Dwarf'; leaves are about 1/2 the size of the species; summer leaf color lighter green than 'Compactum'; fall color is often poor but can range from yellow to bronze, orange and red; colors early (early October); easily rooted from cuttings; originated from a witches' broom before 1955 in Durand Eastman Park, Rochester, NY; seedlings I grew from this form were as vigorous as the species.

'Embers'—Excellent bright red fruits and fall color, introduced in 1990 by Bailey Nurseries, Inc., St. Paul, MN, 15 to 20′ high, 15′ wide.

'Emerald Elf'—Compact, rounded, slow growing, 5 to 6′ by 5 to 6′, glossy green foliage turning scarlet to purple in autumn.

'Flame'—Dense shrub or small tree with red fruits and fiery red fall color; several nurserymen have indicated that this selection is superior to seedlings of the species; 'Flame' is seed grown and should be somewhat variable in fall and fruit color; has performed extremely well in trials at Spartanburg, SC.

'Red Fruit'—A collective term for types whose fruit color a brilliant red; Minnesota Landscape Arboretum has a clone whose fruits turn a good red; based on observations in 1976 the tree fruits so heavily that vegetative growth is somewhat reduced. 'Red Wing' is included here (Introduced by McKay Nursery in Wisconsin).

Red Rhapsody™ ('Mandy')—Improvement on species, lustrous dark green leaves, brilliant red fall color; 15 to 20′ when multi-stemmed; 30′ high as a single stemmed tree. Monrovia introduction.

var. *semenovii* [now listed as *A. tataricum* ssp. *semenovii* (Reg. & Herd) Pax.]—An interesting shrubby type (10 to 15′) with smaller, more graceful, deeper cut lobes; would make an effective screen or barrier; leaves are lustrous dark green in summer turning red-purple in fall; it is a geographical form found farther to the west, in Turkestan. I have seen spelling with a "w" and "v" although more references have "v" than "w".

'Summer Splendor'—Described as having bright red fruits but produces fewer fruits.

PROPAGATION: Seed—stratify at 68 to 86°F for 30 to 60 days followed by 41°F for 150+ days, or light scarification and then stratification for 90 days at 41°F; 3 to 4 months at 41°F also induces good germination; softwood cuttings collected in June rooted 90% in peat:perlite under mist with 1000 ppm IBA treatment; one of the easiest maples to root from cuttings; success can be variable and timing is critical—generally the earlier the better for maximum rooting.

ADDITIONAL NOTES: This species is closely allied to *A. tataricum* but differs principally in the shape of the leaf. The new nomenclature is presented above. Logically, *A. tataricum* should be reduced to the subspecies category because it is so minimally important in modern horticulture. *Acer ginnala* is known, grown and used; *A. tataricum* seldom, if ever.

NATIVE HABITAT: Central and northern China, Manchuria and Japan. Introduced 1860.

Acer griseum (Franch.) Pax — Paperbark Maple
(ā′sēr gris′ē-um)

LEAVES: Opposite, trifoliate, 3 to 6′ long, each leaflet elliptic to ovate-oblong, 2 to 2 1/2″ long, half as wide, apex acute, base cuneate, middle leaflet short-stalked, coarsely toothed; lateral leaflets almost sessile, not as

toothed, lower surface distinctly pubescent especially on the veins, dark
bluish green above, pale green to
glaucous beneath; petiole—distinctly
pubescent, 2 to 3″ long.

BUDS: Imbricate, brownish black, 1/8 to
1/4″ long, sharply pointed, reminiscent of Sugar Maple buds except for
size and color; distinctly pubescent at
base of bud, almost a collar of hairs
surrounds the terminals and laterals.

STEM: Fine branches, pubescent at first,
rich brown; stems develop exfoliating
character during their second and
third year which becomes more pronounced with age; bark color varies
but is usually a cinnamon brown; leaf
scars are surrounded by tufts of
hairs; pith—white, solid, becoming
brown on older stems.

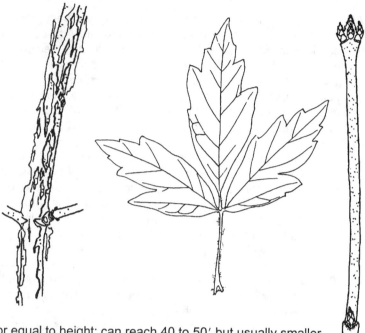

SIZE: 20 to 30′ in height; spread one-half or equal to height; can reach 40 to 50′ but usually smaller
under cultivation.

HARDINESS: Zone 5 to 7(8); not as happy in the South but performs reasonably well. I continue to
jockey with the hardiness zones and believe Athens-Atlanta (now 7b) is at the southern limit for
good growth; northern Illinois in a broad arc to southern New Hampshire for a northern limit;
certainly a "doer" in the Pacific Northwest.

HABIT: Upright-oval, oval or rounded; usually favoring the latter two descriptions; the splendid specimens on
the University of Illinois campus are extremely variable but tend toward the oval-rounded habit; the
specimens at the Arnold Arboretum offer age and, with age, *Acer griseum* assumes a dignity unmatched
by other trees; a trip to view the Arnold's magnificent specimens is justified in any season; the oldest
specimen in the United States exists in the Arnold Arboretum (91 years as of this publication date);
specimens in Europe tend to be rounded to broad spreading.

RATE: Slow, 6 to 12″ per year over a 10 to 15 year period.

TEXTURE: Medium-fine in leaf and winter habit.

BARK: Young stems rich brown to reddish brown; older wood (1/2″ diameter or greater) a beautiful cinnamon
or red-brown as the bark exfoliates to expose these colors; second year wood usually starts to exfoliate,
thus the exquisite bark character develops at a very young age; old trunks lose some of the exfoliating
character but retain the rich brown colors; significant variation in degree of flakiness, and if a young tree
does not exhibit a striking exfoliating character, this will carry into maturity; verbal descriptions cannot do
justice to this ornamental asset and only after one has been privileged to view the bark first hand can he
or she fully appreciate the character; snow acts as a perfect foil for the bark and accentuates its qualities.

LEAF COLOR: Flat dark to bluish green in summer changing to bronze, russet-red or red in fall; fall color can
be spectacular but in seven years at Illinois I never once witnessed anything but muted green-red-brown
colors; however, while on sabbatical leave at the Arnold Arboretum I was fortunate enough to have seen
spectacular red coloration; in Georgia fall color is a muted red; *Acer griseum* is the last of the trifoliate
maples [*A. mandshuricum, A. maximowiczianum* (*A. nikoense*), *A. triflorum*] to color and may hold some
leaves into early November as far north as Boston.

FLOWERS: Few or solitary, greenish, on pendulous, 1″ long, pubescent peduncles.

FRUIT: Samara, 1 to 1 1/2″ long, pubescent, woody nutlet, wings diverge at a 60 to 90° angle.

CULTURE: Transplant balled and burlapped or as a container-grown plant in spring; adaptable to varied soils;
prefers well-drained and moist but performs well in clay soils; pH adaptable; full sun although all trifoliates
withstand partial shade and still produce respectable fall color.

DISEASES AND INSECTS: None serious.

LANDSCAPE VALUE: In the 1990 edition, this category was absent through author error, but 1000 or so
comments from readers admonished me properly; without question Paperback Maple is a *specimen* tree,
truly existing on its own merits; have seen it used in groupings (Hidcote), in a tree-shrub border (Bodnant),
as a single woodland edge tree (University Botanical Garden), and all were right; in fact the last was
moved about five times, finally to the north side of a native tree stand, provided well-drained soil, mulched,
and supplementally watered; tree has prospered and elicits more questions than any plant in the garden;
nobility of character, great seasonal deportment, and unrivaled aesthetic qualities.

CULTIVARS: Whether this is the place to discuss hybrids of *Acer maximowiczianum* (*A. nikoense*) and *Acer griseum* is a moot point. I suspect that within the next five years named clones, i.e., cultivars will be available in commerce. I have heard stories of as many as four different selections being evaluated. Mr. Al Fordham, former propagator, Arnold Arboretum, had a 30 to 40′ high magnificent specimen in his Westwood, MA garden. The Arnold Arboretum harbors a smaller but no less outstanding specimen along Meadow Road. Also the Dirr garden is home to a splendid 20′ high prototype. Why the excitement? Hybrid vigor, excellent heat tolerance, superb rich blue-green, pest-free summer foliage, late developing (November), spectacular orange-red fall color, and cinnamon-stick, flaking bark may make the hybrid an everyday garden tree. Girard Nursery, Geneva, OH, provided my initial tree and I believe is still selling the Girard form. Phil King, Greenwood Propagation, Hebron, IL, has successfully rooted the clone. Trials at Georgia using May 12 cuttings, 10000 ppm KIBA, 3 perlite:1 peat, intermittent mist, provided 50 percent rooting.

Buds are brownish black and resemble those of *A. griseum* in most characteristics. The lighter blue-green leaves are less toothed and lobed than *A. griseum*, and more closely resemble *A. maximowiczianum*. The growth rate is phenomenal and, in Zone 7b, has outstripped *Acer griseum* 2 to 3:1. As the reader can sense, I am excited about the potential for this hybrid. It brings the best of *A. griseum* and *A. maximowiczianum* to the garden.

'Cinnamon Flake' is a selection made by Dr. Sid Waxman, former Professor, University of Connecticut. It has darker green foliage, tighter, finer flaking bark than Gingerbread™, and grafts onto *Acer saccharum*. Gingerbread™ ('Ginzam') is the name given to one selection, possibly the Girard form. Lake County Nursery, Perry, OH, named and introduced it.

PROPAGATION: Difficult, the biggest problem is poor seed quality; seeds are often void as is true for the other trifoliate maples; fruits we collected had 1% and 8% viable seeds; seeds will germinate after 90 days stratification at 41°F in moist peat; however, the fruit wall is so tough the root radical cannot penetrate and will spiral around within the structure; after stratification, I have removed the embryos and the majority continued to grow; commercial production of this species involves fall planting and waiting for two years for germination to begin; see Stimart, *HortScience* 16:341–343 (1981) "Factors regulating germination of trifoliate maple seeds"; Don Allen, F. W. Schumacher, Sandwich, MA, provides a hot water treatment (180°F), followed by a 24 hour soak; the sound seeds sink, hollow float; this is a quick way to assess seed quality; I have conducted many experiments with cuttings and of two or three thousand mature woody cuttings have had one root; Brotzman, *Proc. Intl. Plant Prop. Soc.* 30:342–345 (1980), showed strong clonal differences in rooting among trees of *Acer griseum*; with 6 clones, rooting ranged from 17 to 80% using June collected cuttings from semi- to mature trees, wounding, treating with 2% IBA, mist.

It is well documented that cuttings taken from seedlings will root with relative ease [*Proc. Intl. Plant Prop. Soc.* 34:570–573 (1984)] and some nurserymen produce them this way; by continually cutting the young seedlings back juvenility is maintained; even when rooted the cuttings should not be disturbed until they have gone through a dormant period. The basic recipe: Seedling stockblock, pruned in March (Rhode Island) to induce long shoots, 3rd week in June (timing is critical; wood can't be too hard or soft), sand, 8″ long cutting, tip removed with only 1 pair of leaves remaining, 8000 ppm IBA-talc, 3″ deep in medium, mist, fungicide applied regularly, rooting takes place in 8 to 10 weeks, lifted with a spading fork, average 60% rooting. Rooted cuttings are potted in 2 1/2″ clay pots in soil:peat:sand and placed pot to pot in the greenhouse to reroot. Plants syringed and given bottom heat until mid-October. Pots moved to deep pit house, covered with 1/2″ peat moss and watered in. Maintained at minimum 28°F during winter. When shoots emerge in spring (June) plants are planted in outdoor beds under 50% shade. After 3 years they are sold for lining out material or transplanted to field. We have budded *Acer griseum* on *Acer saccharum* in August with about 40% success: the budded-stock was dug, brought into the greenhouse and grew 18 to 30″ the first three months; I know of one commercial grower who produces *Acer griseum* by grafting on *Acer saccharum*; I am a degree skittish about long term prospects because of possible incompatibilities. See also *Proc. Intl. Plant Prop. Soc.* 19:346–349 (1969) and Dirr and Heuser, *The Reference Manual of Woody Plant Propagation*, for more details. Perhaps, the propagation literature will never stop materializing. Etiolation, stem banding, IBA, and catechol were tested for efficacy. Best rooting occurred with etiolation (41%) and etiolation plus banding (37%). See *HortScience* 25:200–202 (1980).

ADDITIONAL NOTES: *Acer griseum* is more evident in commerce; not inexpensive but worth the expenditure; I grew some seedlings of *A. griseum* and one showed intermediate characteristics between the maternal parent and Sugar Maple; it is definitely a hybrid and shows tremendous vigor, slightly fissured bark, trifoliate and simple leaves and beautiful red fall color. Might be reasonable to assume that all trifoliate maples will hybridize with each other.

NATIVE HABITAT: Central China. Introduced by Veitch in 1901.

RELATED SPECIES: Three closely allied species, all with magnificent ornamental attributes, are presented here for the purposes of comparison and appreciation.

Acer mandshuricum Maxim. — Manchurian Maple
LEAVES: Opposite, trifoliate, terminal leaflet 3 to 5″ long, 1 to 1 1/4″ wide, lanceolate, pointed, saw-toothed, glabrous except on midrib and larger veins; lateral leaflets shorter with a 1/4″ long petiolule, terminal petiolule 1/2 to 1″ long, medium to dark green above, glaucous beneath; petiole—glabrous, reddish, 2 to 6″ long.
BUDS: Imbricate, brownish black, glabrous; terminal—3/8″ long, angled; laterals—smaller, 1/4″ long, appressed, angled; slight spiral hook to the buds.
STEM: Slender, 1st year somewhat lustrous brown, glabrous, covered with numerous, elongated vertical lenticels; 2nd year becoming gray-brown with slight vertical fissuring.
BARK: Smooth, gray, somewhat beech-like, and maintaining this character into old age.

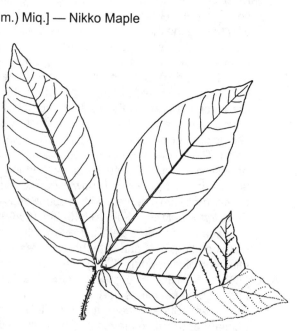

Acer mandshuricum, (ā′sĕr mand-shör′i-kum), Manchurian Maple, is a fantastic small tree that develops an upright-spreading crown. Height approaches 30 to 40′ and spread slightly less. The insect and disease-free foliage turns a magnificent rose-red to red in early October. It is one of the earliest of all maples to develop fall color. Norway Maple is totally green while Manchurian is in full spectacle. Fruits glabrous, wings spreading at a right or obtuse angle, the nutlets thick and reticulate, samara averaging 1 to 1 1/2″ in length. A beautiful, small specimen tree that is worth the effort to procure. The most magnificent specimens I have observed are at the Arnold Arboretum and Smith College Botanic Garden. During my 1978–79 sabbatical at the Arnold, I watched the fall color peak by October 5 to 7 and the leaves completely abscise by October 10 to 12. Rare in cultivation but may become more available through the efforts of Don Allen, F. W. Schumacher, Sandwich, MA, and Mark Krautmann, Heritage Seedlings, Salem, OR. Small (7′) plant has performed well in Dirr garden and produced rose-red fall coloration. Native to Manchuria, Korea. Cultivated 1904. Zone 4 to 7.

Acer maximowiczianum Miq. [formerly _A. nikoense_ (Maxim.) Miq.] — Nikko Maple
LEAVES: Opposite, trifoliate, leaflets ovate to elliptic-oblong, 2 to 5″ long, middle—short stalked, lateral ones subsessile, acute, obtusely dentate or nearly entire, medium green above, villous-pubescent beneath; petiole—1 to 1 1/2″ long, densely pilose.
BUDS: Imbricate, pyramid-shaped.
STEM: Slender, angled, brownish, prominently lenticelled, with pilose pubescence near end of stem; glabrous the 2nd year.

Acer maximowiczianum, (ā′sĕr max-im-ō-wix-ē-ā′num), Nikko Maple, is a lovely, slow-growing, vase-shaped, round-headed, 20 to 30′ high tree. Although slow growing, it is interesting throughout the seasons and would make a fine specimen for the small property. The leaves are bronzy when emerging, changing to medium green in summer and finally glorious yellow, red and purple in fall. The fall color is not as brilliant as the other three trifoliates at least as I observed them at the Arnold. The fall color peaks in mid-October in Boston. Some trees develop a muted, subdued red. Bark is, like *A. mandshuricum*, a handsome smooth gray to grayish brown. Flowers are yellow, 1/2″ diameter, produced usually 3 together on drooping pedicels, 3/4″ long, May.

Fruit is a thick, densely pubescent samara, 1 to 2″ long; the upright wings curved inward or spreading at a right angle. This species seems to prefer a well-drained, loamy, moist, slightly acid soil. Seven-year-old trees were 8 to 12′ high and 5″ in diameter at Wooster, OH. A 30-year-old specimen at the Morton Arboretum was 32′ high, while older specimens of *A. griseum* were considerably smaller. I have seen it performing well in the vicinity of Louisville, KY, and Cincinnati, OH. Truly a beautiful tree but, like *Acer griseum*, the fruits are often devoid of solid seed and germination is a two year process. Native to Japan, central China, now quite rare in its native haunts. Introduced 1881. Zone (4)5 to 7. Slightly more cold hardy than *A. griseum*.

Acer triflorum Komar. — Three-flower Maple
(ā′sĕr trī-flō′rum)

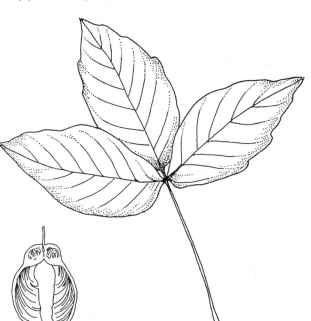

LEAVES: Opposite, trifoliate, leaflets ovate-lanceolate, dark green, 2 to 3″ long, 1″ wide, irregularly serrate, acuminate, leaf bases uneven, some cuneate or rounded, scattered pubescence above, veins pubescent beneath, especially mid-vein with long hispid hairs, margins of leaves with prominent hairs; basal leaflets short-stalked, terminal leaflet with a 1/4 to 1/2″ stalk; petiole—2 to 3″ long, pubescent.

BUDS: Imbricate, brownish black, scales tipped with short, whitish pubescence, 1/8 to 1/4″ long, resemble *Acer griseum* buds; distinct pilose pubescence at nodes around base of buds.

STEM: Slender, brown, angled, abundant small lenticels, pilose pubescent at apex; 2nd and 3rd year stems brownish, exfoliating.

SIZE: 20 to 30′ in height, comparable spread; may grow to 45′ in the wild.

HARDINESS: Zone 5 to 7; there is a specimen at the Minnesota Landscape Arboretum which might indicate Zone 4 hardiness.

HABIT: Small, upright-spreading tree of rather delicate proportions; the few open grown trees I have observed were full, dense and round-headed while those in more confined areas developed an upright-spreading outline.

RATE: Slow in the landscape.

TEXTURE: Medium through the seasons.

BARK: Outstanding; on young stems weakly exfoliating, while mature bark is ash-brown to almost golden amber, loose, and vertically fissured; the exfoliation is not as pronounced as with *Acer griseum*.

LEAF COLOR: Dark green changing to rich yellow and reds in fall; overall effect is orange and based on Arnold Arboretum observations is truly beautiful; also rose-red to red; third of trifoliates to color.

FLOWERS: In clusters of 3, terminating short, 2-leaved shoots; hence, common name Threeflower Maple

FRUIT: Samara, wings 1 to 1 1/4″ long, 3/8 to 5/8″ wide, spreading at an angle of 120°; nutlets are thick, prominently pubescent; fruit-stalk hairy, about 5/8″ long; fruits reminiscent of *Acer griseum* but are more hairy.

CULTURE: Transplant balled and burlapped or from a container; prefers acid, moist, well-drained soil; English reference indicated that a plant growing in chalk (limestone) collapsed and died; in early stages should be kept moist and adequately fertilized.

DISEASES AND INSECTS: None serious.

LANDSCAPE VALUE: Simply an outstanding small specimen maple, lovely foliage, exquisite bark and small habit contribute to the overall landscape effectiveness; would make a fine lawn specimen, focal tree in border planting, or perhaps small street tree; uses for good trees are endless.

PROPAGATION: Seed—same difficulty as with *A. griseum*; requires warm-cold; takes two years in nature; can be grafted on other trifoliates; Brotzman [*Proc. Intl. Plant Prop. Soc.* 30:342–345 (1980)] achieved 58% rooting with June collected cuttings treated with 2% IBA talc, silica sand, poly house.

ADDITIONAL NOTES: One of my favorites; the bark and fall color cannot be adequately described in words; not easy to propagate and obtain, but a real treasure for the discriminating gardener; the Arnold Arboretum has some fine specimens and all seem to color a bit differently which is related to seedling variation; Gary Koller has an excellent article on the species in *Horticulture* 57(10):32–35 (1979).

NATIVE HABIT: Manchuria and Korea. Introduced 1923.

Acer macrophyllum Pursh — Oregon Maple, Bigleaf Maple
(ā'sĕr mak-rō-fil'um)

FAMILY: Aceraceae

LEAVES: Opposite, simple, 8 to 12″ across, often bigger and deeply cut on vigorous shoots, glossy dark green above, pale beneath, 3 to 5 toothed lobes, the middle lobe mostly 3-lobed; petiole—10 to 12″ long, yields a milky sap when detached.

BUDS: Rounded with overlapping scales.

STEM: Young twigs glabrous, green to reddish brown.

SIZE: 45 to 75′ tall, occasionally reaching 100′, one half to equal this in spread, usually smaller under cultivation; trunk diameter reaching 3 to 4′; national champion is 101′ by 90′ in Clotsop County, OR.

HARDINESS: Zones 5 to 7 (to 9 in West).

HABIT: Young trees with erect branches, becoming more rounded at maturity, often categorized as broad oval to rounded.

RATE: Slow to medium.

TEXTURE: Coarse in summer and winter.

BARK: Gray to reddish brown, furrowed with small flattened platelets.

LEAF COLOR: Young emerging leaves are often reddish bronze, maturing to glossy dark green, changing to yellow-orange in fall.

FLOWERS: Yellow, fragrant, produced in 4 to 8″ long nodding racemes appearing with the leaves in April–May; each flower is approximately 1/3″ across.

FRUIT: Samara, approximately 1 1/2″ long, nutlet covered with brown pubescence, wings nearly glabrous, forming a 60″ angle from wing to wing.

CULTURE: Prefers cool moist environment such as that in its native Pacific Northwest; invasive root system that can break walks and drives; mentioned as adapting well to summer drought in southern California.

LANDSCAPE VALUE: Too many superior maples in the Midwest and East but perhaps worthy of consideration in the West; have seen at Morris Arboretum in Pennsylvania and the tree appeared prosperous; perhaps too coarse because of large leaves for the average landscape; recommended for planting natural areas in its range.

CULTIVARS: An upright form is in cultivation and I have seen such a plant at the Hillier Arboretum; not the most aesthetic or dignified of fastigiate plants.

'Seattle Sentinel'—A 1992 introduction from the Center for Urban Horticulture, Washington Park Arboretum, Seattle, WA, discovered in 1951 by Brian Mulligan, original tree 60′ by 15′, unusually fastigiate, reminiscent of Lombardy Poplar, considered more drought tolerant than columnar forms of *Acer rubrum*, *Acer platanoides*, *Acer saccharum*, and *Carpinus betulus*; same foliar and floral characteristics as the species.

ADDITIONAL NOTES: Have seen in the Portland, Oregon and Seattle, Washington areas where the tree is quite common. Seems to pop up in fence rows and waste areas not unlike Norway Maple in the midwestern and northeastern states.

NATIVE HABITAT: Alaska to southern California. Introduced 1812.

Acer miyabei Maxim. — Miyabe Maple

LEAVES: Opposite, simple, 4 to 6″ wide, 3 to 5″ high, mostly 5-lobed, each lobe with prominent indentations, long acuminate, cordate, flat to semi-lustrous dark green above, lower surface olive-green, pubescent, prominently so on veins, tufts of hairs in axils; petiole—4 to 7″ long, pubescent, with milky sap.

BUDS: Terminal imbricate, 1/8 to 3/16″ long, brownish, bud scales edged with fine pubescence; laterals similar but smaller and hidden by petiole bases.

STEM: Lustrous brown, angled, glabrous.

BARK: Grayish, scaly but in long strips.

Acer miyabei, (ā'sēr mi-ya'bē-ī), Miyabe Maple, is an upright-oval to rounded small tree growing 30 to 40', either open or densely branched. The habit is quite lovely and may remind one of the outlines of *Acer campestre* or *Acer buergerianum*. The leaves stay green into October and then turn rapidly to pale yellow and fall soon thereafter. The flowers are greenish yellow, borne in slender-stalked, 10- to 15-flowered pyramidal corymbs in May. The wings of the fruits horizontally spreading, the nutlet silky-hairy, averaging 1 3/4 to 2" in length. Culturally the species prefers moist, well-drained soils probably on the acid side. Several specimens are doing quite well in the Morton Arboretum where the soil could best be described as a clay loam. Propagation has been a problem as vegetative and seed attempts have met with limited success. Fall planting or 3 months cold stratification will overcome dormancy. Percent over-

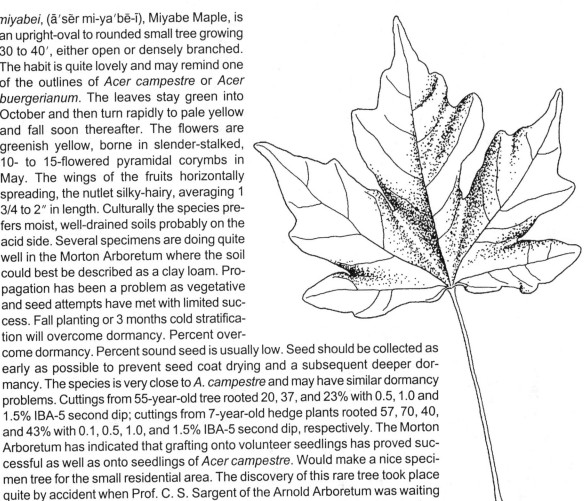

come dormancy. Percent sound seed is usually low. Seed should be collected as early as possible to prevent seed coat drying and a subsequent deeper dormancy. The species is very close to *A. campestre* and may have similar dormancy problems. Cuttings from 55-year-old tree rooted 20, 37, and 23% with 0.5, 1.0 and 1.5% IBA-5 second dip; cuttings from 7-year-old hedge plants rooted 57, 70, 40, and 43% with 0.1, 0.5, 1.0, and 1.5% IBA-5 second dip, respectively. The Morton Arboretum has indicated that grafting onto volunteer seedlings has proved successful as well as onto seedlings of *Acer campestre*. Would make a nice specimen tree for the small residential area. The discovery of this rare tree took place quite by accident when Prof. C. S. Sargent of the Arnold Arboretum was waiting for a train at Iwanigawa, a railroad junction in Yezo, Japan. He had some time before the train arrived and, as any good plantsman, strolled out of the town to a small grove of trees. In this grove, occupying a piece of low ground on the borders of a small stream was *A. miyabei* covered with fruit. The only commercial cultivar that I know is State Street™ ('Morton'), a 40' by 25', upright oval form with dark green foliage turning yellow in fall. Schmidt Nursery called it a turbo-charged, more cold hardy alternative to *A. campestre*. Handsome corky bark, fast growth and ascending branch habit. Listed as Zone 4 adaptable. The species is hardy to Zone 4 and I have seen a specimen doing quite well at the Minnesota Landscape Arboretum where winter temperatures may drop to -30°F. Japan. Introduced 1892.

Acer negundo L. — Boxelder, Ash-leaved Maple
(ā'sēr ne-goon'dō)

LEAVES: Opposite, pinnately compound, 3 to 5 (7 to 9) leaflets, ovate or lance-oblong, 2 to 4" long, coarsely serrate or terminal one lobed, bright green above, glabrous, lighter green beneath and slightly pubescent or eventually glabrous; petiole—2 to 3" long.
BUDS: 1/4" long, greenish or reddish scales covered with silky hairs, two scales often split exposing inner, more pubescent scales.
STEM: Green to reddish brown, often covered with a waxy whitish bloom that can be rubbed off, glabrous; leaf scars encircle twig and meet at a sharp angle; malodorous when bruised; pith—large, white, solid.

SIZE: 30 to 50' in height, can reach 70', but this is the exception; spread variable but usually equal to or greater than height; national champion is 110' by 127' in Washtenaw, WI.
HARDINESS: Zone 3 to 9.
HABIT: Usually rounded to broad-rounded in outline, branches develop irregularly to support the uneven crown; often a small "alley cat" tree with multi-stemmed character and ragged appearance.

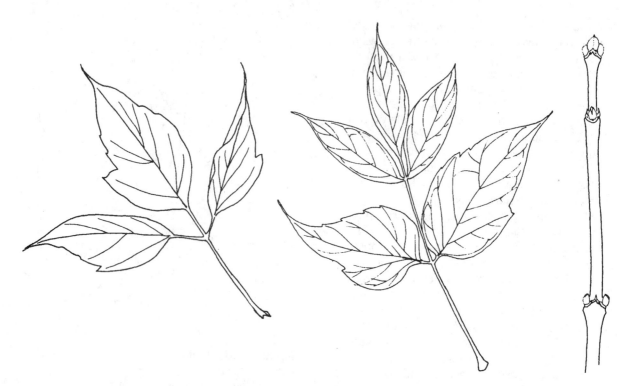

RATE: Fast, extremely so when young, the wood is weak and will break up in ice and wind, can grow 15 to 20′ in a 4 to 6 year period.

TEXTURE: Owing to ragged habit, the tree is coarse in all seasons; perhaps a degree unfair and the best forms grade to medium.

BARK COLOR: Gray-brown, slightly ridged and furrowed.

LEAF COLOR: Light green on the upper surface and grayish green below in summer, foliage turns yellow-green to brown in fall; usually of no ornamental consequence; along with *Acer mandshuricum* one of the earliest maples to develop fall color.

FLOWERS: Dioecious, yellowish green, March to April, male flowers born in corymbs; female in slender pendulous racemes and usually in great quantity; not ornamentally effective but worth avoiding the female forms if the tree has to be used.

FRUIT: Samara, maturing in September or October, usually profusely borne, yellowish green maturing to ash-brown, persisting into winter, the pair forming an angle of 60° or less, 1 to 1 1/2″ long, virtually every seed is sound.

CULTURE: Easy to transplant, actually native to stream banks, lakes, borders of swamps but performs well out of its native habitat in poor, wet or dry soils and cold climates; pH adaptable; full sun; a necessary tree under difficult conditions where few other species will survive; usually a short-lived tree.

DISEASES AND INSECTS: Described under Silver Maple; boxelder bugs make nice pets. Did the reader realize that *Leptocoris* (*Boisea*) *trivittatus* is one of the most common household pests in the United States and is usually found wherever boxelders are grown. The adults emit a foul odor, stain fabric, and may cause severe asthmatic reactions. They migrate in the fall so be on the lookout for the orange and black bugs.

LANDSCAPE VALUE: Extensive use is limited due to lack of ornamental assets; however, has been used in Great Plains and Southwest; falls in same category as *Ulmus pumila*, *Ailanthus altissima*, and *Morus alba*; *Journal of Arboriculture* 16(12): 309 (1990) reported this species was, along with American elm, the highest ranked for overall pruning and removal urgency; the cultivars have some landscape merit and in European gardens are used as focal points because of the strong foliage colors; many times these variegated forms are pruned in late winter to encourage vigorous, highly colored shoots; variegated forms, especially those with marginal patterns, tend to revert to the green, although albino shoots are also thrown; careful attention to pruning is necessary.

CULTIVARS: When traveling through Europe, the variegated forms of Boxelder are everywhere in evidence. They can be particularly striking and for that reason are treated here in detail.

'Auratum'—The leaflets entirely yellow; in proper climate will retain this color into fall; Bean considered it one of the best golden colored trees; have seen in Europe where the plant may be cut back in winter to force long shoots that provide vivid yellow leaf color; used as a filler in shrub borders to provide color.

'Aureo-marginatum' ('Aureo-variegatum')—The late Dr. J. C. Raulston, North Carolina State Univ., in 1987 led a group of Southeasterners, including the author, through Germany, and to my delight we chanced upon an experiment station that had a handsome tree with yellow-bordered leaves. Up close and personal the leaves were rather striking, but better used at a theme park. The tree was 15 to 20′ tall. A male.

'Baron'—Selection from Morden Arboretum, Canada, male, free of seed, grows 35 to 50′ high, 30 to 35′ wide, upright oval habit, a Canadian Ornamental Plant Foundation introduction from Morden Research Station.

'Elegans'—Have seen small plants at Bressingham Gardens and the leaves are edged with a handsome irregular yellow margin; the plant does not appear as vigorous as 'Aureo-marginatum', however, the two could be synonymous.

'Flamingo'—A rather curious form with brilliant pink new shoots that age to green with a white border. The color is best in cool weather and plants should be cut back in late winter to encourage vigorous new extension growth. I have seen the plant used in English gardens and it is most effective from May–June. Late in the season the pink color occurs in the new growth and is not as vibrant. Older leaves are quite similar to 'Variegatum' and this form could be a branch sport of same; originated in Holland. Listed as 20′ by 15′; have read 30 to 40′ by 30′. A male.

'Odessanum'—Strong-growing selection with bright orange-yellow new foliage fading to light green in the heat of summer.

'Sensation'—More controlled, slower growth and improved branch structure than species, medium green summer foliage, brilliant red in fall, rounded habit, 30′ by 25′, Zone 2 to 7, a 1989 Schmidt introduction. Performance in Southeast has been less than satisfactory.

'Variegatum'—A common form with irregular white margined leaves; I consider it one of the most effective of variegated small trees; a female clone and the fruits are variegated like the leaves; will revert to green or produce albino leaves; must be carefully pruned; originated as a branch sport in the nursery of M. Fromant at Toulouse, France in 1845; best in Zone 5 to 7.

'Wells Golden'—From New Zealand . . . I blame Don Shadow for this spectral pollution; on April 21, 1994 a group of interested plantsmen gazed at a row of golden boxelders; the entire population was purchased and planted in Spartanburg, SC; who said plants are not golden? Could this be the same as 'Kelly's Gold'?

Several geographical varieties exist including var. *californicum* Wesm. with pubescent leaves and stems and var. *violaceum* Vaeg. with purplish or violet branches covered with a glaucous bloom and the male tree with pink tassel-like flowers; also var. *texanum* Pax. with 3 leaflets and pale tomentose branches and var. *mexicanum* Kuntze with 3 leaflets, and densely pubescent young stems are listed. The above may or may not be discrete taxonomic units, for one perusal of the species distribution map indicates that many varieties (subspecies) could be established.

PROPAGATION: In general a 2 to 3 month treatment at 40°F is necessary; however, pretreatment of seeds for 2 weeks by soaking in cold water or mechanical rupture of pericarp are recommended before stratification; cuttings will root readily and for the cultivars this may be the preferred route; softwood material treated with 8000 ppm IBA in talc rooted readily when taken as late as mid-September.

MAINTENANCE CONSIDERATIONS: Not the neatest tree and certainly should not be used if better trees are available. Female trees are actually ugly because fruits hang like dirty light brown socks through fall and early winter. The various colored foliage types can be rather cheerful but in the South (Zones 7 and 8) require special siting under pines or some form of partial shade. At the University's Botanical Garden, a small tree of 'Variegatum' always developed leaf burn in summer; also 'Wells Golden' lost all its color by mid-June in Zone 7b and some leaves were burned.

ADDITIONAL NOTES: Not my favorite tree but kind of pleasant when exposing its yellow-green flowers in early spring before most trees have even awakened; found along streams and rivers; will withstand periodic flooding; probably the most aggressive of the maples in maintaining itself in unfavorable sites; can become a noxious weed.

NATIVE HABITAT: Virtually the entire United States, southern Canada, and into Mexico. Cultivated 1688.

Acer palmatum Thunb. — Japanese Maple
(ā′sĕr pal-mā′tum)

LEAVES: Opposite, simple, 2 to 5″ long and wide, deeply 5- to 7- to 9-lobed, lobes being lance-ovate to lance-oblong in shape, acuminate, subcordate, doubly serrate, glabrous and bright green beneath; color varies depending on cultivar, generally dark green on species; petiole—3/4 to 2″ long, glabrous.

BUDS: Tend toward valvate character, small, green or red, hidden by base of petiole, frequently double terminal buds; margin of leaf scar much elevated forming flaring collar around bud; remind one of Easter eggs sitting in grass; buds essentially hidden by base of petiole.

STEM: Glabrous, slender, usually green to red, often with a glaucous bloom, tremendous variation in stem coloration with green-leaf types green to reddish purple, red-leaf types often bright red to blood red to reddish purple; exceptions arise and certainly 'Sango Kaku' with coral red stems and green leaves is a prominent aberration.

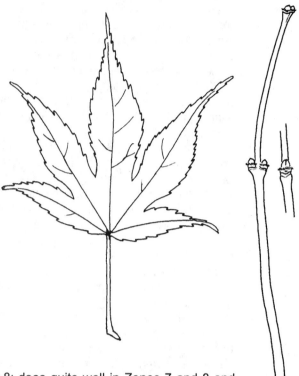

SIZE: 15 to 25′ in height, spread equal to or greater than height; great variation in this species due to large number of cultivars which are common in commerce; many of the *dissectum* types only reach 6 to 8′ and become quite mound-like in shape; the species can reach 40 to 50′ in the wild state; magnificent specimens along the East Coast from Boston to Washington that approach 40 to 50′.

HARDINESS: Depending on cultivar, Zones 5 and 6 to 8; does quite well in Zones 7 and 8 and provides excellent fall color in November; since the last edition I have taken a more broad, encompassing evaluation of the species' adaptability; my plant materials in crime colleague, Dr. Paul Cappiello, formerly at the University of Maine, Orono, and I visit and correspond regularly; no *Acer palmatum* seedlings or cultivars survive in Orono (–30°F), however, Mr. Roger Luce, Newburgh, ME, south of Bangor, has several seedlings in his nursery/garden; from the southern perspective, *Acer palmatum* is a terrific garden plant if selected for adaptability and sited correctly; I have visited garden centers in coastal Georgia (Zone 8b) that offer 5 to 10 different selections; Post Properties, Inc., Atlanta, uses with confidence the green leaf species, 'Bloodgood', 'Oshio beni', 'Seiryu', and variety *dissectum* 'Viridis' and 'Tamukeyama'; in the Dirr garden var. *dissectum* 'Waterfall', 'Tamukeyama', normal red leaf types 'Bloodgood', 'Moonfire', and green seedlings perform admirably; a selection I made from green leaf seedlings at the University's Botanical Garden shows terrific vigor and heat tolerance; a few Georgia growers are now producing 'Glowing Embers', so named because the leaves develop orange red-purple fall coloration in mid to late November in Athens.

HABIT: Species tends towards a rounded to broad-rounded character, often the branches assume a layered effect similar to Flowering Dogwood; the plant can be grown as a single-stemmed small tree or large multi-stemmed shrub; perhaps the greatest ornamental attributes are exposed in the latter situation.

RATE: Over many years a slow grower but in youth will tend toward the medium rate; about 10 to 15′ over a 10 year period.

TEXTURE: Fine to medium-fine in leaf depending on the cultivar; of similar texture during winter.

BARK: Young stems vary from green to polished or bloomy reddish purple and red; older branches assume a gray cast; handsome for bark character but often not considered for this feature due to over-shadowing by excellent foliage.

LEAF COLOR: Leaves emerge early, the species is green in summer, becoming yellow, bronze, orange, purple or red in the fall; many of the var. *atropurpureum* types turn a magnificent red in fall; leaves hold late and are often present into November; interesting Japanese study of native and nursery grown trees in shade versus sun; plants in shade flushed earlier in spring, shed leaves later, and developed yellow autumn color (red in sun); one of the *best* scientific papers assessing red-purple leaf color retention or loss at high night temperatures appeared in *J. Amer. Soc. Hort. Sci.* 115: 135–140 (1990). *Acer palmatum* 'Bloodgood' grown at 57, 64, 72, or 79°F produced 51% greater growth in a 6 to 8 week period compared with warmer night temperatures. Ultimately, growth decreased 7, 19 and 32% from the 57°F treatment as night temperatures increased to 64, 72, and 79°F, respectively. Leaf redness index values at 57 or 64°F were 2 to 7 tones greater than those at 72 and 79°F.

FLOWERS: Small, red to purple, May–June (April in Athens), borne in stalked umbels (possibly corymbs), quite attractive on close inspection, emerging with the new leaves of the season, arching-pendulous, the reddish flowers are more evident on the green leaf types.

FRUIT: Samara, 1/2 to 3/4″ long, wings 1/4 to 3/8″ wide, much incurved, the pair forming a broad arch; wings often turning a good red especially those of the var. *atropurpureum* series; ripen in September– October.

CULTURE: Transplant balled and burlapped or as a container plant into moist, high organic matter, well-drained soil; protect from sweeping winds and late spring frosts for the young foliage is sensitive to cold; tends to leaf out early and many nurserymen and gardeners have lost a year's growth or the entire plant to frost; ideally provide dappled shade; if too much the plants grow slowly and the purple types become more green (still lovely though); too little they may literally cook in the summer sun; provide supplemental moisture and mulch.

I have been amazed at Japanese maple performance in Zones 7 and 8. Certainly some specimens fry in the heat and during the summers of 1988, 1993, and 1995, three of our worst drought periods, young plants that were not provided supplemental water turned up their toes (roots) and died. Minimal attention will reward the gardener manyfold. If the plants are adequately cared for in the early years of establishment, then they appear to cope more efficiently with stresses imposed in later years.

DISEASES AND INSECTS: Actually surprisingly few; have had a real problem with rooted cuttings in plastic houses that leafed out early. The high humidity promoted *Botrytis* infection which literally killed 80 fine specimens in about three days. A recent paper, *Plant Disease* 77: 197–198 (1993), reported canker on young propagated *A. palmatum* caused by *Colletotrichum acutatum*.

LANDSCAPE VALUE: Probably one of the most flexible maple species as far as landscape uses; magnificent specimen, accent plant, shrub border, grouping, bonsai; definitely lends an artistic and aristocratic touch; considering the tremendous heat in the South I am amazed at the number of choice specimens; even in full sun the plant does reasonably well; the purple-leaf forms appear to lose the pronounced color earlier in the growing season; there are a number of Japanese Maples, including 'Dissectum Atropurpureum' types, in the Athens-Atlanta area and most have prospered.

CULTIVARS: In the previous edition many cultivars were included; here I have included a selected few and recommend that anyone serious about cultivars consult the 2nd edition (1987) of J. D. Vertrees magnificent reference, *Japanese Maples*, Timber Press, Portland, OR; most of those presented herein are available in commerce. Other sources of reasonable cultivar information are the many generalist and specialist nurseries who offer *Acer palmatum*. Secure catalogs and cross-check cultivar descriptions for the most prevalently listed. Use this as a baseline for selection and in your later, more adventuresome moments . . . speculate. A word of economic advice . . . buy small plants and enjoy their formative years. I recently (1997) purchased 32 different grafted forms, all small, but with the promise of greatness. Counted 158 cultivars of *A. palmatum* and 28 cultivars of var. *dissectum* in Stanley and Sons, Boring, OR 1997–98 catalog.

The classification of the various *Acer palmatum* cultivars is a taxonomic nightmare and several artificially contrived categories have been created.

Index of Garden Plants by Mark Griffiths lists . . .

a) Palmatum group	d) Linearilobum group
b) Elegans group	e) Variegated cultivars
c) Dissectum group	

Japanese Maples, Michael and Janet Kristick, 155 Mockingbird Road, Wellsville, PA list . . .

Upright growing types	Dwarf types
Dissectum form	Variegated group
Deeply divided leaves	Unusual feature group
Linearilobum group	

Kristick's combined offerings of cultivars in the above groups total 157.

NON-DISSECTED TYPES:

var. *atropurpureum* ('Atropurpureum')—Leaves reddish purple, 5- to 7(9)-lobed, color usually fades with maturity and summer heat, excellent in spring and fall for red coloration; seedlings produced from seeds of the type are variable in leaf coloration; the better red-leaved seedlings generally command a superior price; several plants in the University Botanical Garden are somewhat disappointing since the purplish red spring leaf color only persists into June before turning green; if one wants superior foliage color then choose a good cultivar. Have grown many red leaf seedlings over my career and have witnessed nothing that rivals a worthy 'Bloodgood'.

'Bloodgood'—Based on my observations over the years, perhaps the best for deep reddish purple leaf color retention; have seen good color in summer in the Boston area, a slow-growing, small round-headed tree probably maturing in the 15 to 20′ range; excellent red fall color; the leaves ranging from 4″ long to 5″ wide; also has beautiful red fruits; commonly propagated from cuttings and one of the easier to root and overwinter cultivars; possibly the most cold hardy reddish purple form as I witnessed it standing after about −29°F in Williamstown, MA; other observers have formed the same opinion about Bloodgood's cold hardiness; possibly originated at Bloodgood Nursery, Long Island, NY; definitely more than one clone in the trade; it is possible to order 'Bloodgood' from three different sources and receive three different plants.

'Burgundy Lace'—Growing next door to 'Bloodgood' at the Arnold Arboretum but does not hold the reddish purple color as well; turns purple-bronze-green in summer, the sinuses are cut almost to the point of attachment of the blade to the petiole and each lobe is finely serrated and cut along the margins; leaves average 4″ long by 3 1/2″ wide; usually a small tree about 10 to 12′ high and 12 to 15′ wide; another good form for American gardens.

'Butterfly'—One of the older garden tested variegated forms with emerging leaves green with pink margins, maturing to gray green with cream-colored variegation and variable rose-red to red purple in fall; habit is upright, vase shaped, 12 to 15′ high, 6 to 8′ wide, relatively slow growing.

'Crimson Prince'—Selected seedling of 'Bloodgood', bright red summer foliage, scarlet in fall, resistant to summer leaf scorch, more cold hardy than 'Bloodgood', Princeton Nursery introduction.

'Emperor I' (II)—Large leaf like 'Bloodgood', red leaf with more blue pigment like Purpleleaf Plum, holds color in heat, leafs out 12 to 14 days later than 'Bloodgood' which helps avoid spring frost damage, grows rapidly, 'Emperor I' at same age will be one nursery grade larger than 'Bloodgood', from Don Schmidt Nursery, Boring, OR.

Fascination® ('Vandermossuper')—From Schmidt Nursery, upright spreading form becoming rounded with age, large deep green, long ribbon-like lobed leaves turn orange in fall, 16′ by 16′.

'Glowing Embers'—A selection I made from seedlings at the University Botanical Garden, exceedingly vigorous, small dark green, 2 to 3″ long and wide leaves turn orange-red-purple in fall and die off like embers; heat tolerance is significantly better than average green seedlings; Bennett's Nursery, Alma, GA, reported this the fastest growing, most heat tolerant clone; several Georgia growers are producing the selection; fall colors were just developing on November 29, 1994 in Athens.

'Moonfire'—A relatively new introduction from the Red Maple Nursery, Media, PA, an excellent purple-red leaf form that holds color during the summer and will not bronze like many var. *atropurpureum* forms; (5)7-lobed leaves turn crimson in fall, leaf size ranges from 3 to 5″ in length and about 4 1/2″ wide; habit is upright in youth gradually broadening with maturity, will grow about 15′ high; not as red leaf color retentive as 'Bloodgood' in Dirr garden.

'Oshio Beni'—The new growth emerges a vibrant orange-red to red but unfortunately loses the color in late spring–early summer, becoming bronze to greenish red; fall color is rich scarlet; the 7-lobed leaves average 3″ long and 3 to 4″ wide, margins are finely serrate like the species; will grow 15 to 20′ and develops a spreading habit.

'Osakazuki'—An old cultivar with 7 evenly serrated lobes, bright green leaves that turn a rich crimson in the fall, considered one of the best for autumnal coloration; becomes a round-topped 15 to 20′ high tree at maturity; small tree in Dirr garden is starting to strut its fall plumage.

'Red Sentinel'—"Witches' broom" of 'Bloodgood', 8′ by 5′ in 5 years, holds dark red foliage all summer, from Ken Twombly, Monroe, CT.

'Sango Kaku' ('Senkaki')—A common cultivar and often praised for the brilliant coral fall and winter color of the young stems; the color is striking but as the branches mature the color is lost and only the first and second year growth show rich coloration; 5- to 7-lobed leaves with doubly serrate margins, leaves about 2″ long by 2 1/2″ wide, new leaves are reddish tinged, become medium green in summer and finally yellow gold with light red overtones in fall; habit is upright with numerous smaller "twiggy" stems; will grow 20 to 25′ high by 18 to 22′ wide; some stem dieback often evident on plants in Zones 7 and 8; does not appear as heat tolerant as some of the other cultivars discussed herein.

'Scolopendrifolium'—Quite a handsome green, 5-lobed leaf form with the lobes cut to the point of attachment, each lobe only 1/4 to 1/2″ wide with irregularly toothed margins; entire leaf about 3″ long by 4″ wide; yellow fall color; leaf effect is quite digitate or finger-like; strong growing form to 15′ developing a rounded canopy at maturity.

'Scolopendrifolium Rubrum'—As above but not as vigorous, more bushy growing 6 to 8′ high; reddish purple new leaves turn bronzy red-green in summer and reddish in fall; handsome form and appears adapted to Zone 8.

'Trompenburg'—Leaves 7- to 9-lobed, 2 to 3 1/4″ high and 3 1/2 to 5″ across, sinuses cut to within 1/2″ of petiole, petiole 3/4 to 1 1/2″ long, on each oblong-ovate lobe the edges roll under almost forming a tube, foliage is deep purple red and persists into summer when they change to deep reddish green, fall color is red to crimson, upright growing as a young tree, becoming more broad spreading with age, 13 to 16′ high, 10 to 13′ wide at maturity.

DISSECTUM GROUP ('Dissectum', var. *dissectum*): Perhaps the most refined of all maples, the 7, 9, or 11 lobes are cut to the point of attachment with each lobe in turn finely cut and each division toothed. The cultivars vary in the fineness of the cutting as well as color. Seedlings are remarkable for variation in foliage but generally show the cut leaf characteristics.

var. *dissectum atropurpureum* ('Dissectum Atropurpureum')—Leaves deep red, a compact, slow-growing shrub of mounded, pendulous outline; usually growing 6 to 8′ but I have seen plants in the 10 to 12′ category; the entire plant appearing as a mound of rich, purple-red, ferny foliage; the color fading to purple-green or green with time and in fall turning glorious burnt orange that implies the plant is on fire; perhaps the most magnificent aspect of the plant is the twisted, contorted branching pattern; it is an architectural masterpiece that only a higher being could create; these forms set fruit and the resultant seedlings will yield plants of different colors and degrees of ferniness.

'Crimson Queen'—New growth bright crimson-red which Vertrees states persists throughout the entire growing season; plants I have seen in the South lose the color and become more bronze-green to red; fall color is in the scarlet range; this is a strong growing 7- to 9- to 11-lobed form that is popular in commerce; will eventually grow 8 to 10′ by 12′; develops handsome cascading branches.

'Ever Red'—Interesting 7-lobed form of var. *dissectum atropurpureum* with the newly emerging leaves covered with fine silky pubescence, pubescence soon fades and the deep purple-red color becomes prominent; does not hold the color as prominently as 'Crimson Queen' and fades to purple-bronze and bronze-green in the heat of the summer; fall color is bright red; vigorous form with cascading, pendulous growth habit and old specimens 15′ are known; apparently many plants sold as 'Ever Red' are in fact something else; 'Everdark' ('Ebony') has darker red foliage.

'Filigree'—A handsome yellow-green, 7-lobed var. *dissectum* type that is overlain with minute dots and flecks of pale cream and gold; leaves turn a rich golden in fall; this cultivar is romantically delicate and provides a bright element in shady locations; forms a rounded cascading 6′ by 9′ mound.

'Flavescens'—Weeping, haystack to rounded form, lace leaf with light yellow-green leaves turn yellow-orange in fall, 6 to 8′ high and 8′ wide.

'Garnet'—I grew this var. *dissectum atropurpureum* form in my Illinois garden where the rich gemstone garnet color faded to a purple-green; when grown in shade the leaf maintains a greenish cast but develops the garnet color in sun; a vigorous form that will grow 10′ high; leaves are slightly more coarse than most var. *dissectum atropurpureum* types; fall color is a good red; common in commerce and one of the more available types; a recent addition to the Georgia Dirr garden and performance has been exceptional.

'Inaba Shidare'—Leaves up to 6″ long and wide, usually 4″, 7-lobed with each lobe tapering at each end to less than 1/16″ wide, widening to 1″ or so in the middle, petiole 1 to 2″ long, purple-red in spring and hold their color reasonably well in heat, tips may scorch in high heat and drought, red to crimson fall color, sturdy and more vigorous than many var. *dissectum* types; branching slightly more rigid, probably 8 to 10′ at maturity, faster growing than many red dissectums as much as 20 to 30%, considered one of the more cold hardy dissectums and survived −24°F, also known as 'Red Select'. Known in Japan since mid-1800's.

'Ornatum'—An old var. *dissectum atropurpureum* cultivar that I have kind of grown up with; the new leaves are more bronze-red than 'Garnet' and 'Ever Red' and during summer turn largely green; fall color is often an excellent crimson-red; 7-lobed leaves are finely dissected and delicate; grows 6′ by 9′ or more; has lost popularity due to better colored foliaged types but still reasonably common.

'Red Dragon'—Bright cherry red new growth, maintains good color in heat, resistant to leaf scorch, from New Zealand; one Georgia grower reported it the best for red leaf color retention.

'Red Filigree Lace'—A relatively new form of var. *dissectum atropurpureum* with deep purple-red or maroon leaf color that is retained into summer and then turns rich crimson in fall; 7-lobed leaves that are more finely dissected than other cultivars presented here, leaves are 2 to 3″ long and 3 to 3 1/4″ wide; typical habit of the Dissectum group, but not as fast as 'Crimson Queen' and 'Garnet'.

'Seiryu'—An upright vase-shaped form, atypical for the *dissectum* group; rich green summer foliage turning brilliant gold, orange to orange red in fall, probably mature at 10 to 15′ high, 8 to 10′ wide.

'Sherwood Flame'—A spreading, almost broad rounded form with burgundy summer foliage that changes to shades of red in fall, 13′ by 16′, more resistant to fading in heat of summer, selected by Will Curtis, Sherwood, OR.

'Tamukeyama'—Mr. Don Shadow, Winchester, TN considers this the best of the purple dissected group; the 7- to 9-lobed leaves are not as finely dissected as 'Crimson Queen', 'Red Filigree Lace', or 'Ever Red'; leaves average 3 to 3 3/4″ long and 4 to 4 1/2″ wide; the young foliage is deep crimson-red and matures to purple-red and holds quite well; an old cultivar that according to Vertrees was listed as early as 1710; 50- to 100-year-old plants are 13′ high.

'Viridis'—This is probably a catch-all term for all green leaf dissected types; 'Viride' is occasionally listed in nursery catalogs; the leaves vary from 7- to 9-lobed with the usual dissections; fall color is yellow-gold to red; in my travels I have observed beautiful green leaf dissected forms; they have a place in almost any garden.

'Waterfall'—Considered the best green leaf dissected form with 7 to 9 multi-dissected lobes; leaves are larger than typical 'Viridis' types ranging from 3 to 5″ long, 3 to 5″ wide; the rich green foliage holds up well in Zone 7 and 8 heat; fall color is golden with reddish suffusions; I have a plant and it is truly a beautiful form; will grow 10′ high and 12 to 14′ wide.

Many variegated foliage cultivars are described but are limitedly available to the general gardening public and must be sought from specialty producers. Vertrees' wonderful book is a must for anyone interested in Japanese Maples. One's eyes are opened to an entirely new adventure in gardening.

PROPAGATION: Based on the literature I have reviewed, a book could be written on *Acer palmatum* propagation. See Dirr and Heuser, 1987, and also James Wells, "How to propagate Japanese Maples," *American Nurseryman* 151(9):14, 117–120 (1980). In general, seed should be collected when green or red before it dries on the tree; it can be planted directly and should germinate the following spring; dried seed should be soaked in water at 110°F for 2 days followed by stratification; dried seed from Japan when pretreated in a "normal" manner germinated over a 5 year period; seed that is collected green/red, cleaned, dusted with fungicide, stratified in moist peat for 90 to 150 days at 40°F and sown should germinate. Many cultivars are grafted but choice of understock is important. Softwood cuttings are rooted by taking 6 to 8″ lengths (smaller on less vigorous cultivars), wounding, applying high IBA (10000 to 20000 ppm); placing in peat:perlite under mist; when rooted they should be left undisturbed until they have gone through a dormant period or transferred to supplemental light and induced into growth; I have rooted softwood cuttings that were collected in July, wounded, treated with 10000 ppm IBA quick dip, placed in peat:perlite under mist; roots developed only from wounded area; rooting took 2 months. Anyone serious about Japanese Maple propagation should consult *The Reference Manual of Woody Plant Propagation* for detailed information.

NATIVE HABITAT: *Acer palmatum* is native to Japan, China, Korea. Introduced to England in 1820. Long cultivated by the Japanese.

RELATED SPECIES:

Acer circinatum Pursh — Oregon Vine Maple
LEAVES: Opposite, simple, (5)7- to 9(11)-lobed, 3 to 5″ long and wide, almost circular in general outline, but heart shaped at the base, lobes unequal or doubly toothed, glabrous, pale to medium green above, petiole—1 to 1 1/2″ long.

Acer circinatum, (ā′sĕr sĕr-sin-ā′tum), Oregon Vine Maple, grows commonly as a large multistemmed tree in the 10 to 20′ range. National champion is 46′ by 35′ in Tillamook County, OR. I have seen numerous specimens in Oregon, Washington, and British Columbia area and they are predominantly shrubby and start to develop a tinge of fall color in August—early September. Fall color is variable, ranging from yellow-orange to red, the new spring growth is reddish tinged. The reddish purple sepals subtend small dull white petals and make a

handsome display against the conspicuous crimson bud scales. Red fruits about 1 1/2″ long with the wings spreading horizontally, develop in late spring. Found in moist woods, along streambanks from British Columbia south to northern California. It appears to perform reasonably well in drier situations but will develop earlier fall coloration. 'Glen-Del' is a branch sport with 5, finger-like lobes, the center lobe the longest, margins are essentially entire unlike 'Monroe' which is serrated, tight-growing compact plant.'Monroe' has deeply cut leaves like *A. japonicum* 'Aconitifolium'. 'Little Gem' is a compact roundish shrub with smaller leaves than the species. Roy Lancaster mentioned that both 'Monroe' and the species provide excellent fall color in the dryness of his English garden. See *The Garden* 119: 534–535 (1994).During a July, 1995 trek to the Pacific Northwest, I witnessed the species in the shadiest of shady habitats. Almost universally shrubby, the largest specimen was plus 20′ high in the Hoh Rain Forest, Olympia National Park. Introduced 1826. Zone 5 to 6 on East Coast. I tried to grow a plant in my Illinois garden but was unsuccessful.

Acer japonicum Thunb. — Fullmoon Maple
LEAVES: Opposite, simple, roundish, 3 to 6″ across, 7- to 11-lobed, lobes ovate to lanceolate, long pointed, sharply and irregularly toothed, sinuses often shallow, cordate, rich green, tuft of whitish pubescence at end of downy leaf stalk on upper side, underside with whitish hairs on veins and in their axils; petiole—1 to 1 1/2″ long, pubescent when young.
BUDS: Similar to *A. palmatum* in every way, bud is valvate, lustrous red; collars flare and produce "nest" effect, collars are fringed with hairs.
STEM: 1st year—slender, glabrous, reddish green, angled, slightly bloomy, smooth, nodes flattened (similar to *Cercidiphyllum*); pith—white, solid; 2nd year—marked color change— becoming brown, lightly fissured; sharp demarcation between current and last season's growth; pith—whitish to tan.

Acer japonicum, (ā′sĕr jȧ-pon′i-kum), Fullmoon Maple, grows 20 to 30′ in height with a comparable or larger spread (supposedly can reach 40 to 50′ in the wild). Leaves are an extremely handsome soft green changing to rich yellow and crimson in fall. Purplish red, 1/2″ diameter flowers are produced in April before the leaves on long stalked nodding corymbs. Fruit is 1″ long and wings range from nearly horizontal to forming an obtuse angle. Culture is similar to *Acer palmatum*. Japan. Zone 5 to 7. Not common in southern gardens, in fact, as I pen this not a single plant comes to mind in the Athens-Atlanta area. The following cultivars are probably more common than the species in gardens and include:

'Aconitifolium'—Lobes extend to 1/2 or 1/4″ of the end of petiole, each lobe (9 to 11) being again divided and sharply toothed; magnificent crimson fall color; rounded bushy habit to 8 to 10′ in height; one of the most beautiful of all fall coloring shrubs. *Maples of the World* lists size to 50′. Everything I observed in cultivation is wee small.

'Aureum'—Leaves golden yellow and effective during the summer; reaching 10 to 20′ in height with a comparable spread; literally lights up a garden; have seen listed as a selection of *Acer shirasawanum* which is probably where it belongs. *Acer shirasawanum* Koidz. has 11- to 13-lobed leaves, generally 2 1/2 by 2 1/2″ high and wide. Although 'Aureum' is included under *A. shirasawanum* and listed as a shrub, I have seen 15 to 20′ high specimens in Europe with distinct arborescent habit.

'Green Cascade'—Vigorous, weeping, with deeply cut lacy foliage and marvelous orange red fall color. Leaves similar to 'Aconitifolium' though smaller. Wright Nursery, Canby, OR introduction.

'Itaya'—Leaves larger than the species with good yellow fall color, name applied to cultivars of

Acer shirasawanum

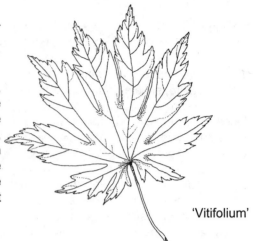

other *Acer* species, considered close to the species if not the same.

'Junihitoe'—Leaves smaller than the species, 2 to 3″ across, 11-lobed, orange fall color.

'Vitifolium'—Excellent type because of the rich purple, crimson, orange, and yellow fall colors, leaves are large, up to 6″ long and wide and of grape-like shape; beautiful plant at Longwood Gardens, that, in fall color, is a garden, to 20′(40′); have seen this labeled as 'Aconitifolium' but the leaves are not as deeply cut, usually about one-half the distance from lobe tip to petiole, and does not develop the vibrant red color of 'Aconitifolium'.

'Vitifolium'

Acer oliverianum Pax.

LEAVES: Opposite, simple, 2 to 4″(5″) long and wide, 5-lobed, truncate or subcordate, lobes ovate, caudate-acuminate, finely serrate, middle lobe with 5 to 8 pairs of lateral veins, finely reticulate, lustrous medium green above, lustrous and glabrous beneath; petiole—2 to 3″ long.

BUDS: Essentially valvate, ovoid, almost triangular in outline, glabrous, glossy reddish purple, about 1/4″ long and wide, presents a squat appearance when nestled against the stem.

STEM: Medium, terete, glabrous, lustrous purple to green, often covered with a waxy bloom.

Acer oliverianum, (ā′sĕr ol-i-vēr-ē-ā′num), is a relatively unknown small (15 to 25′) maple with characteristics similar to *A. palmatum*. The fall colors are rich shades of orange and red. I was first introduced to the tree at the old USDA Bamboo Station in Savannah, GA where the plant has prospered for many years. The habit is upright-spreading with the more or less horizontal branching of *A. palmatum*. The most impressive aspect is the tremendous heat tolerance since Savannah is in Zone 8. The tree grows in sandy soil and is perhaps more drought tolerant than *A. palmatum*. The 1 to 1 1/4″ long fruits have nearly horizontal (subhorizontal) wings while those of *A. palmatum* are more incurved. A few Georgia nurserymen have started to grow the species and the tree may prove a valuable addition to Zones 8 and possibly 9. Have grown the tree in the Dirr garden and although handsome in summer foliage neither fall color nor general performance (vigor) match the better *Acer palmatum* forms. Fall color has emulated that of sweetgum with yellow, orange, and red present on the tree. In fact, the leaves look like those of *Liquidambar styraciflua*. Seeds collected in fall, sown in peat:sand medium in flats, left outside, germinated the following spring. Central China. Introduced 1901. Zone 7 to 9.

Acer pseudosieboldianum (Pax.) Komar. — Purplebloom Maple, Korean Maple

LEAVES: Similar to *Acer japonicum*; 9- to 11-lobed, 4 to 6″ across, doubly- serrate lobes, lustrous dark green above, pubescent beneath; petiole—1 to 2″ long.

BUDS: Similar to *A. japonicum*; silky, rusty brown hairs are evident at point where bud attaches to stem.

STEM: Red to reddish purple, glabrous.

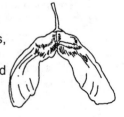

Acer pseudosieboldianum, (ā'sēr sö-do-sē-bōl-dē-
ā'num), is a lovely small (15 to 25') tree
similar to *A. japonicum* and *A. sieboldianum*
and rather difficult to differentiate from unless
detailed characteristics are applied. Leaves of
A. sieboldianum are smaller, 7- to 9-lobed.
Habit is more upright and stiff. E. H. Wilson
noted that in its native Manchuria and Korea
it assumes wonderful tints of orange, scarlet
and crimson. As I viewed it in the Arnold
Arboretum during the fall of 1978 the colors
approximated a green-brown haze. A freeze
effectively eliminated the possibility of good
fall color. Flowers are composed of reddish
purple sepals and creamy petals, usually
opening before the leaves. Samara 1 1/4"
long, divergent, brown to purple. Have added
a few interesting facts about this species to
my vocabulary since the last edition. Thrives
in Maine for at Orono trees have become
almost naturalized in one part of the campus.
Dr. Cappiello reported excellent fall color.
Have seen the trees and believe the species

is a fine *Acer palmatum* substitute for Zone 4 and 5 conditions. Mr. Dennis Mareb, Windy Hill Nursery,
Great Barrington, MA, reports excellent winter hardiness in western Massachusetts. With selection for
quality growth habit and fall color this would serve as a worthy substitute in climes where winter lows drop
below –20°F. Cultivated 1903. Zone 4 to 7.

Acer sieboldianum Miq. — Siebold Maple

Acer sieboldianum, (ā'sēr sē-bōl-dē-
ā'num), is similar to the previous
but differs in the small yellow
flowers (purple on *A. pseudosieboldianum*) and pubescence of
the leaves and stems. The dark
green leaves are 3 to 4" high
and wide, 7- to 9(11)-lobed. The
pubescence is a constant character. Samaras range from 1/2
to 4/5" long, ascending, and glabrescent. Fall color is yellow-
orange and had started to develop by Oct. 16, 1978 at the
Arnold. A report from the Morton
Arboretum, Lisle, IL, listed the
fall color as intense red. Unfortunately the same freeze (Oct.
23) that eliminated the fall color
of *A. pseudosieboldianum* also
eliminated this species. Grows
20 to 30' high and wide in outline. Japan. Cultivated 1880.
Zone 5 to 7.

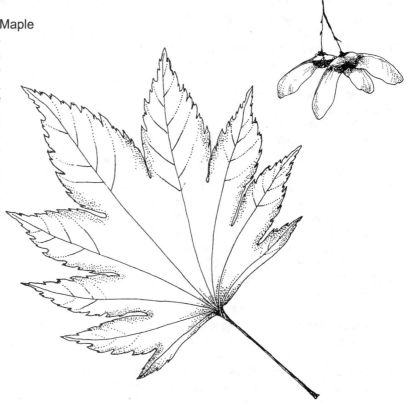

ADDITIONAL NOTES: These maples are outstanding landscape plants; almost a guaranteed success in any
landscape if sited and cultured properly; the cultivars of *A. palmatum* have become a passion for many
gardeners.

Acer pensylvanicum L. — Striped Maple, also called Moosewood, Whistlewood, Snake Bark Maple, Goose Foot Maple

(ā′sĕr pen-sil-vā′ni-kum)

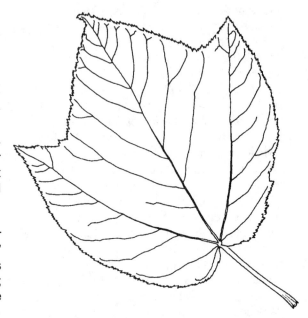

LEAVES: Opposite, simple, roundish obovate, 3-lobed at apex, 5 to 8″ long and wide, subcordate, the lobes pointing forward, acuminate, cordate, serrulate, bright green, ferrugineous-pubescent beneath when young, finally glabrous; petiole—1 to 3″ long, rufous pubescent when young, finally glabrous or nearly so.

BUDS: Glabrous, 1/3 to 1/2″ long, blunt, 2 scales, valvate; terminal—almost 1/2″ long, much longer than the lateral buds, covered by 2 thick, bright red, spatulate, boat-shaped prominently keeled scales, inner scales green; stalk—about 1/12″ long, red, glossy.

STEM: Smooth, stout, green changing to red or reddish brown; lenticels few; leaf scars "U" shaped, almost encircling twigs, older stems eventually becoming green striped with white; very handsome for this characteristic; snake bark term is derived from this trait.

SIZE: 15 to 20′ in height but can grow to 30′ or more in the wild, spread is less than or equal to height; national champion is 77′ by 28′ in Bailey Arboretum, Nassau County, NY.

HARDINESS: Zone 3 to 7 in higher elevations of southern Appalachians.

HABIT: Large shrub or small tree with a short trunk and ascending and arching branches that form a broad but very uneven, flat-topped to rounded crown.

RATE: Slow under cultivation, medium or greater in native haunts.

TEXTURE: Medium-coarse in leaf, medium in winter.

BARK: Young stems greenish brown or reddish; young branches (1/2″ or greater) are green and conspicuously marked by long, vertical, greenish white stripes, hence, the name Striped Maple; old trunks lose the pronounced striping.

LEAF COLOR: Pinkish tinged when unfolding, bright green at maturity; apparently a great concentration of yellow pigments is present in the leaves; leaves change to vibrant yellow in autumn; in North Georgia the species only occurs on the highest peaks and is unbelievably spectacular in mid-October when in fall color; have had students collect leaves during this time and bring them back to Athens for positive identification; if the students notice, then the pigmentation must be sensational.

FLOWERS: Dioecious, yellow to yellow-green, May, produced on pendulous, slender 4 to 6″ long racemes, each 5-petaled flower is 1/3″ diameter; studies have shown that flowers are primarily dioecious with a ratio of 81 male:15 female, but 4% of the population monoecious [see *Bull. Torrey Botanical Club* 106(3): 222–227]. Another study, *Amer. J. Bot.* 70(6): 916–924 (1983), reported essentially the same thing for this species and *A. spicatum*. Also bees were mentioned as the principal vectors for pollen transfer. I bring these studies up for on cultivated trees minimal sound seeds are produced.

FRUIT: Samara, about 1/2 to 1″ long, wings spreading at a wide angle, born on a 1″ long pedicel on a 4 to 6″ long raceme.

CULTURE: Does not proliferate under cultivation, prefers partially shaded woods; well-drained, cool, moist, slightly acidic soils; in native range exists as an understory plant which provides an index of its shade tolerance; have seen on rocky mountainsides in Georgia and Massachusetts growing in the most inhospitable of situations; not amenable to culture where heat and drought are common denominators.

DISEASES AND INSECTS: See Silver Maple discussion.

LANDSCAPE VALUE: Very inadequate lawn specimen but for naturalizing purposes has possibilities; fall color and bark are lovely and for that reason worth considering if proper cultural conditions can be supplied.

CULTIVARS:

‘Erythrocladum’—Young stems turn a bright coral-red after leaf fall; had only read about this form until viewing it first hand in Boston and England; spectacular coral-pink-red stems with white striations that literally glow in winter; introduced by Späth's nursery in 1904; unfortunately has been difficult to propagate.

'Silver Vein'—Listed as a hybrid between 'Erythrocladum' × Forrest's form of *A davidii*; cross made by Peter Douwsma at Hilliers Nursery in 1961, notable for silver striations on the bark which persist as branches enlarge, spreading habit like *A. davidii* with 3-lobed leaves of *A. pensylvanicum*.

'White Tigress'—For ease of presentation I include it here although technically considered *Acer davidii* × *A. tegmentosum*; leaves large and 3-lobed, green bark with pronounced white striations; considered more heat tolerant and, indeed, I have seen a plant in full sun at Don Shadow's, Winchester, TN; he considers it the most heat tolerant snake bark; Tim Brotzman, Madison, OH introduction; a small plant in the Dirr garden sited in shade has contracted tip borers and canker; a plant in Spring Grove, Cincinnati, OH is unabashedly thriving.

PROPAGATION: Seed, 41°F for 90 to 120 days; I have tried cuttings with no success; *Acer capillipes* and *A. tegmentosum* have been rooted with good success [see *Proc. Intl. Plant Prop. Soc.* 30:342 (1980)]; seed of the above and following species that I have collected was void of embryos; this could relate to the lack of a suitable male for pollination.

MAINTENANCE CONSIDERATIONS: Although lovely trees because of bark and fall color, they offer little in the way of urban toughness; bark is thin and subject to mower and weed-eater damage; plants appear canker susceptible under stress; I can never remember seeing a prospering snakebark maple under adverse conditions; reserve for cooler climates, moist, well-drained soil and perhaps partial shade.

NATIVE HABITAT: Nova Scotia to Minnesota, south to northern Georgia. Introduced 1755.

RELATED SPECIES: *Acer pensylvanicum* is the only snakebark maple native to North America. There are about 14 asiatic maple species with similar floral and bark characteristics. They are discussed here in encapsulated form. None is widely available in commerce. I have observed all species in my travels and have attempted here to highlight the differences.

Acer capillipes Maxim.

LEAVES: Opposite, simple, 4 to 7″ long, 3 to 5″ wide, 3(5)-lobed, lobes triangular, the lateral lobes much shorter, acuminate, cordate, prominently serrate from apex to base, dark green, glabrous above and below; gummy substances in axils of veins; petiole—1 1/2 to 2 1/2″ long, glabrous, channeled above, reddish.

BUDS: Similar to *A. pensylvanicum*.

STEM: Greenish purple to reddish purple, with white striations, terete, glabrous.

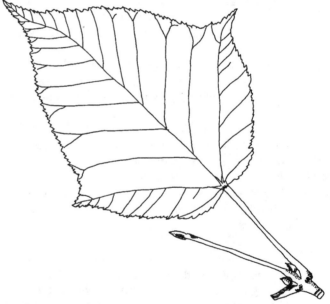

Acer capillipes, (ā′sēr ka-pil′i-pēz), is a small (30 to 35′ high) round-headed tree that often branches close to the ground. The young leaves are reddish and upon maturity turn dark green. Fall color may be yellow to red but trees I have observed were injured by a freeze before turning. On November 20, 1994 in the University's Botanical Garden the leaves had developed a muted bronze, red, brown . . . nothing to get excited about. Young branches are greenish to reddish brown with whitish stripes; the bark eventually becomes grayish brown and ridged and furrowed. Very handsome small tree and the most beautiful specimen in this country is located at the Arnold Arboretum. The greenish white, 1/3″ diameter flowers occur in slender 2 1/2 to 4″ long pendulous racemes. The samara is 3/4″ long and the wings form a 120° to 180° angle. Japan. Introduced 1892. Zone 5 to 7. This is probably the most heat tolerant of the Snakebark maples and has performed reasonably well in Athens in a shady setting with supplemental irrigation. Tree is now 20 to 25′ high.

Acer davidii Franch. — David Maple

LEAVES: Opposite, simple, ovate to ovate-oblong, 3 to 6″ long, 1 1/2 to 2 1/2″ wide, acuminate, subcordate or rounded at base, with a central midrib and no prominent lobes like most snakebark species; leaves of young seedlings are often lobed; unequally crenate-serrulate, green beneath andrufous-villous on veins when young, finally glabrous or nearly so, lustrous dark green; petiole—3/4 to 2″ long.

BUDS AND STEM: Similar to *A. capillipes*, younger branches green or purplish red becoming striped with white.

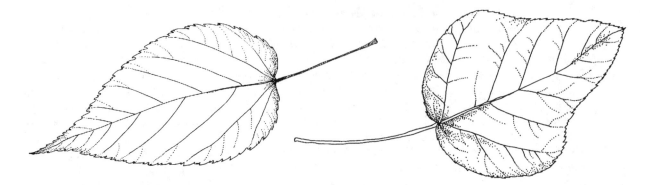

Acer davidii, (ā′sē r dā-vid′ē-ī), David Maple, is seldom seen in cultivation outside botanical gardens and arboreta. I have observed only small trees although the species can grow 30 to 50′. The mature leaves, being unlobed, are easily distinguished from most other species. The yellowish flowers (May) are borne in slender, pendulous, 2 to 3″ long racemes; the female on longer inflorescences than the males. The 1 1/4″ long glabrous fruits spread horizontally. Apparently there are different forms of the species in cultivation. Common in English gardens and certainly a stellar performer there. Is not as well adjusted to United States conditions except in the Pacific Northwest. In late June 1997 I visited Camellia Forest Nursery, Chapel Hill, NC where Dr. Cliff Parks showed me self sown seedlings by the hundreds. All were in some degree of shade and were thriving with neglect. 'Ernest Wilson' is a small compact tree with lustrous dark green, triangular-shaped, essentially unlobed leaves; bark is green with white stripes. 'George Forrest' is a medium sized, more open growing form with attractive dark green, triangular-shaped, 3-lobed leaves; the young stems are rhubarb red and later become red with white stripes; have seen at Edinburgh Botanic Garden; larger growing and more vigorous than typical for the species. Central China. Introduced 1879 and 1902. Zone 5 to 7 in cool mountain regions.

Acer rufinerve Sieb. & Zucc. — Redvein Maple

LEAVES: Opposite, simple, 2 1/2 to 5″(6″) across, 3-lobed to obscurely 5-lobed, truncate or cordate (also rounded), terminal lobe triangular, larger than the laterals, margins finely and irregularly doubly toothed, dark green above, glabrous, lower pale with reddish down on veins; petiole—1 to 2″ long, pubescent in youth.

BUDS: Similar to *A. pensylvanicum*.

STEM: The young stems are extremely glaucous (bluish white) which separates it from *A. pensylvanicum*, *A. capillipes*, and *A. hersii*.

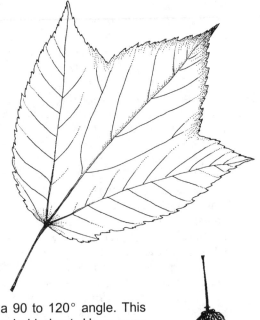

Acer rufinerve, (ā′sēr rū-fi-nĕr′vē), Redvein Maple, can grow 30 to 35′ but seldom attains that size in the United States. The dark green leaves may turn yellow-orange to red in fall. The pale green flowers are borne in 3″ long erect rusty brown pubescent racemes in May. The 3/4″ long samaras are covered with reddish brown pubescence which falls away at maturity; the wings spread to form a 90 to 120° angle. This species can be grown in full sun but partial shade is probably best. Have seen limitedly in cultivation in the United States and the trees were never overwhelming. 'Albolimbatum' is a handsome cultivar with white splashed and marbled leaves, the entire variegation pattern quite irregular. Green stems show good white striation pattern. Have only seen the plant at Edinburgh Botanic Garden and on every visit always make the journey to view this most handsome foliaged maple. 'Winter Gold' offers bright, golden yellow winter bark which changes to yellow-green in spring and summer; smaller in habit but otherwise similar to the species; 4-year-old tree is 6.5′ high, 2′ wide, hardy to Zone 5, selected from open pollinated seedlings by Peter Douwsma in Olinda, Victoria, Australia. The species is described as the most common of the snakebarks in cultivation by *Maples of the World*. It is quite similar to *A. tegmentosum* and *A. davidii* subsp. *grosseri*. Japan in mountain forests to 8000′. Introduced 1879. Zone 5 to 7.

Acer tegmentosum Maxim. — Manchustriped Maple

LEAVES: Opposite, simple, 3- to 5-lobed, 4 to 6″ high and wide, pale to rich green above, paler (glaucous) beneath, glabrous, margin finely and uniformly serrate, acuminate, cordate; petiole—1 to 3″ long, glabrous, with a groove at the point of attachment.

BUDS: Similar to *A. capillipes*.

STEM: Rich green to greenish purple, glabrous, bloomy; 2nd year develop a vertical white fissured pattern, becomes more prominent with time.

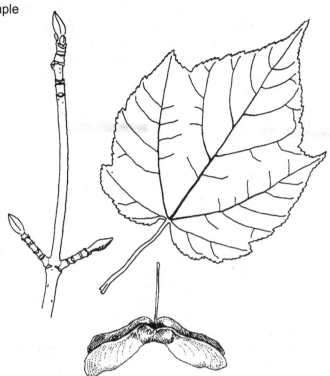

Acer tegmentosum, (ā′sēr teg-men-tō′sum), Manchustriped Maple, is a small oval to rounded tree reaching 20 to 30′ in height. Most of the trees I have observed in cultivation had 5-lobed leaves although the literature states unlobed to 3- and 5-lobed. The lateral lobes are much smaller than the terminal lobes. May leaf out too early in spring and be injured by late spring frosts. The pale green leaves may turn golden yellow in fall. Yellowish green flowers occur in 3 to 4″ long pendulous racemes. The samaras are 1 1/4″ long and form a wide angle or are nearly horizontal. Fine specimens are located at the Rowe and Arnold Arboreta. Based on rather incomplete information about the "Snakebarks" I would opt for this species for general garden purposes, although *Acer capillipes* seems well adapted. Similar to *A. rufinerve*, but leafs out early in spring and flowers at least 4 weeks earlier. Camellia Forest Nursery, Chapel Hill, NC, has hybridized this × *A. davidii* with the resultant progeny exceedingly vigorous. Manchuria, Korea, Russia. Introduced 1892. Zone 4 to 7.

ADDITIONAL NOTES: The striped maples are not easy to distinguish especially in winter dress. Even leaves do not provide totally reliable features and with certain species separation is dictated by the "bloom" (wax) on the stems. They will never become commonplace in American gardens. It is certainly invigorating to stumble upon a specimen for the unusual bark is both beautiful and a reliable giveaway as to relative identification. Many snakebark species are known and quite similar in general characteristics. In my travels through European gardens, it became evident that my knowledge of the striped bark maples was, at best, superficial. The following are listed for the collector to pursue: *A. crataegifolium* Sieb. & Zucc. (has performed well in North Carolina), *A. forrestii* Diels [now *A. pectinatum* subsp. *forrestii* (Diels) Murray], *A. grosseri* Pax. [now *A. davidii* subsp. *grosseri* (Pax.) de Jong], *A. micranthum* Sieb. & Zucc., *A. pectinatum* Wall. ex Pax., and *A. tschonoskii* Maxim. All of the snakebarks have stalked valuate buds which allows the snakeophile to choose a great key and proceed with caution. My working knowledge of the breadth of the species in the snakebark grex has been severely limited by the opportunity to study them in living collections. In late March,

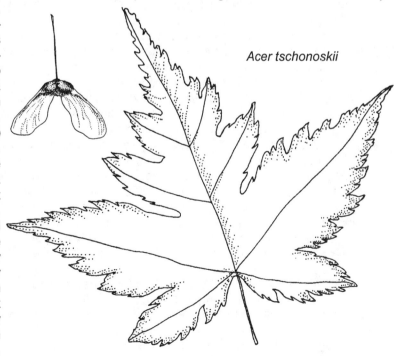

Acer tschonoskii

1995, I witnessed a large collection of snakebark maples at Branklyn Gardens, Perth, Scotland and attempted to delineate among species. For the most part, it is virtually impossible to identify young specimens in winter dress. Several specimens of *Acer rufinerve* in the Garden were quite different in stem coloration; one green with white striations; the other reddish with white striations; and the keys say bark distinctively white striped on green, not reddish.

Acer platanoides L. — Norway Maple
(ā′sēr plat-an-oi′dēz)

LEAVES: Opposite, simple, 4 to 7″ across and high, 5-lobed, lobes sharp pointed (acuminate), subcordate, remotely dentate, lustrous dark green above, lustrous beneath often with hairs in axils of veins; milky sap is visible when petiole is removed from stem; petiole—3 to 4″ long.

BUDS: Terminal—imbricate, 1/4 to 3/8″ long, ovoid-rounded, scales plump, fleshy, lustrous, greenish maroon to maroon, essentially glabrous except for pubescence at edge of scales, 6 to 8 scaled, two accessory buds 1/3 to 1/2 size, usually with 2 evident scales; terminal when cut in cross section will exude milky sap if slight pressure is applied; lateral—1/8″ long, often appressed, 2 to 3 scaled, greenish to maroon.

STEM: Stout, smooth, glabrous, lustrous olive brown, lenticelled, leaf scars meet to form a sharp angle; 2nd year stems lose luster, become more gray-brown; pith—solid, white.

SIZE: 40 to 50′ in height occasionally over 90′, usually spread is 2/3's or equal to height; national champion is 137′ by 116′ in New Paltz, NY.

HARDINESS: Zone 4 to 7, seldom grown in Zone 7b at least with any success, bark split may be common under Zone 4 conditions.

HABIT: Rounded, symmetrical crown, usually with very dense foliage and shallow root system which limits successful turf culture.

RATE: Medium, 10 to 12′ in 5 to 8 years, 30′ in 20 years, 45′ in 40 years, 60′ in 60 years.

TEXTURE: Medium-coarse in summer and winter.

BARK: Grayish black with ridges and shallow furrows that form a rather interesting textural effect.

LEAF COLOR: Dark green in summer; sometimes changing to handsome yellow in fall; leaves hold late and color toward the end of October and into November; when fall color is maximally expressed it is the rival of *Betula lenta*, Sweet Birch.

FLOWERS: Perfect, yellow or greenish yellow, each flower 1/3″ diameter, April before the leaves, produced in erect, many-flowered corymbs; quite effective in the early spring landscape; one of the most floriferous maples; the entire tree a thing of great beauty.

FRUIT: Samara, maturing in September–October; samaras wide spreading, each 1 1/2 to 2″ long, glabrous, with virtually horizontally spreading wings.

CULTURE: Easy to transplant; well adapted to extremes in soils, will withstand sand, clay, acid to calcareous soils, seems to withstand hot, dry conditions better than Sugar Maple; tolerates polluted atmosphere, especially those containing ozone and sulfur dioxide; intolerant of 2,4-D; in the South (Zone 7 and higher) the warm summer nights retard growth, trees simply are not as vigorous as in northern latitudes; 'Crimson King' has been planted numerous times and usually disappears over time; the species grew 8.3″ per year over a 10 year period in Kansas tests; more resistant to leaf scorch than *A. rubrum* and its cultivars but very poor fall color.

DISEASES AND INSECTS: *Verticillium* wilt, anthracnose, tar spot caused serious defoliation in several upstate New York communities, some leaf scorch; some cities are skittish about the long-term prospects for this tree.

LANDSCAPE VALUE: Over-used and probably over-rated tree; the species and several of the cultivars, especially 'Crimson King', are overplanted; has been used as lawn, street and park tree; should be given considerable room for it does cover large areas; often creates many problems along streets; the cultivars offer the greatest hope for the landscape; still in the top 5 shade trees as far as numbers produced annually; a major West Coast liner producer lists 18 different Norway Maple types in 1995 catalog, Santamour and McArdle, *J. Arboriculture* 8:241 (1982) listed 89 *valid* cultivars; species has escaped and in pockets is out-competing the native flora; I remember an early November drive from Swarthmore College to Longwood Gardens, PA and Norway Maple was everywhere in evidence in the local woodlands with the bright yellow leaves still persisting.

CULTIVARS: As mentioned under LANDSCAPE VALUE, cultivarism is rampant. For many of the European selections see Bean, Hillier, Krüssmann, and van Gelderen et al.

'Alberta Park'—Straight, vigorous grower that forms a beautiful proportional head with width 25% less than the height; not narrow like 'Emerald Queen'; no frost cracking in certain locations where all other varieties have; excellent tough green foliage.

'Almira'—Small (20 to 25'), globe shaped, round-headed, and twiggy; discovered on a street in Cleveland, OH.

'Aureo-marginatum'—Leaves with three deep, long-pointed lobes, margined with yellow.

'Cavalier'—Very compact with rounded habit, almost a large globe; 30 to 35' tall.

'Charles F. Irish' ('Chas. F. Irish')—More rounded in outline, akin to species, 50 to 60' high.

'Cleveland'—Upright oval to oval-rounded, not as wide spreading as species, dense dark green foliage, excellent golden yellow fall color, coarsely branched, 6.4' high and 2.7' wide after 4 years; considered one of the best Norway cultivars for urban plantings, 40 to 50' high by 30 to 40' wide.

'Columnare'—In my mind no one has ever adequately described the differences between this and 'Erectum'; I offer the following based on a great deal of observation; 'Columnare' is an old cultivar having been raised in the nursery of Simon-Louis at Plantieres, France in 1855; the dark green leaves are smaller and shallower lobed than the species; the habit is that of a fat column with branches that spread at a 60 to 90° angle from a central trunk; height approximates 60'; spread 15 to 20'.

'Crimson King'—Rich maroon leaf color throughout the growing season; probably the most vigorous of all persistent red leaved forms; could be called a horticultural exclamation point in the landscape; grew 19' by 16' in 10 years; originated as a seedling of 'Schwedleri' in 1937 in Belgium and put into commerce in the United States around 1948; the flowers are maroon-yellow; slower growing than 'Schwedleri'; 40 to 50' by 35 to 45'; grew 5.2" per year over a 10 year period in Wichita tests; will grow 40' to 50' in 25 to 30 years under good conditions; slow growing and poorly adapted especially in the Southeast; plant patent 735, selected by Barbier & Co., Orleans, France.

'Crimson Sentry'—A dense, broad-columnar form, dark purple foliage in spring and summer; a bud sport of 'Crimson King'; slower growing than 'Crimson King', 25' by 15'; plant patent 3258 (1975).

'Deborah'—Originally selected in Canada and introduced in 1978 by Holmlund Nursery, Gresham, OR; brilliant red new growth, wrinkled margins, eventually changing to dark green; orange-yellow fall color; seedling of 'Schwedleri'; rounded to broad rounded outline; like 'Schwedleri' but with a straight leader, 50' by 45'; plant patent 4944.

'Dissectum'—One of the many cut-leaf forms, leaves finely cut, margins crinkled, small bushy tree; put into commerce about 1845; other cultivars with unusual leaf lobing patterns include 'Cucullatum' (absolutely abominable) and 'Palmatifidum'; others exist.

'Drummondi'—Light green leaves edged with white, supposedly the best of its class, 23' high and 13.9' wide after 10 years; reverts and must be pruned; common in Europe, develops a rounded outline, probably 30 to 40' and as wide.

Easy Street™ ('Ezeste')—Pyramidal outline, faster growing and slightly wider than 'Columnare' from which it was derived as a bud sport, dark green summer foliage, yellow in fall, 40' high by 20' wide.

Emerald Lustre™ ('Pond' is cultivar name)—Vigorous, prolific branching as a young tree, good branching structure, rounded habit, new leaves with a reddish tinge, glossy deep green foliage with wavy margin; better branching than 'Emerald Queen'; plant patent 4837, 45' high by 40' wide.

'Emerald Queen'—Ascending branches, oval-rounded outline, rapid grower, dark green leaves, similar to 'Summershade'; fall color is bright yellow; 26' high and 20.7' wide after twenty years; one of the best Norway cultivars for urban plantings, 50' by 40' at landscape maturity, possibly the most widely used Norway cultivar; introduced 1962.

'Erectum'—Columnar with short lateral branches; the Lombardy poplar of Norway maples, not particularly appealing in the nakedness of winter, discovered in a cemetery in Rochester, NY.

'Faasen's Black'—Lustrous purplish brown leaves, folded upwards at the margins, young leaves not wrinkled, red fall color under the proper environmental conditions, put into commerce about 1936; I asked a nurseryman how to tell this cultivar from 'Crimson King' and he said that after a rain 'Faasen's Black' would hold the water in the rim formed by the upfolded margins; 'Crimson King' did not; there was never any mention of color differences. I have compared 'Faasen's Black' to 'Crimson

King' and, indeed, the leaf differences are as manifest as described; originated from same seedlings of 'Schwedleri' as 'Crimson King'.

'Fairview'—A seedling of 'Crimson King' with reddish purple new growth that matures to bronze, narrower and more upright than 'Deborah' and 'Schwedleri'; upright oval in habit, 45' high by 35' wide.

'Globosum'—Dense, formal globe habit only growing to a height of 15 to 18'; usually grafted or budded at 6 to 7' height; similar to 'Almira' but slower growing and smaller; 5' high and 5' wide after 4 years; provides a lovely lollipop effect in the landscape.

'Goldsworth Purple'—Light reddish brown when young becoming deep, dull, blackish purple fading with the heat of summer; young leaves wrinkled; grows 40 to 50'; not as red as 'Crimson King'; put into commerce about 1949.

'Greenlace'—Interesting form with a deeply cut, lace-like leaf; upright branching habit (50'); fast growing; discovered as a seedling and introduced about 1968 by Schmidt Nursery, OR.

'Jade Glen'—Similar to species, supposedly rapid growing and extremely sturdy, produces a more open rounded canopy, dark green summer foliage, yellow in fall, 40 to 50' by 40 to 50', Schmidt introduction.

'Laciniatum'—Smaller and more twiggy tree than the type, of more erect, narrow habit; leaves tapering and wedge-shaped at base, the lobes ending in long, often curved claw-like appendages; the oldest of named varieties (1683); grows 30 to 35' high.

Lamis Crystal® ('Lamis')—Vigorous straight trunk; better branching than 'Emerald Luster' with a lighter colored leaf tip; selected by Bailey Nursery, 50 to 60' high by 50 to 60' wide.

'Lorbergii'—Leaves palmately divided to base of leaf but tips ascending from plane of leaf; a dense, rounded, very slow growing tree with a central leader; 60 to 70', 1881.

Medallion™ ('Medzan')—Broad oval rounded, dense compact branching, thick lustrous dark green leaves, turn red and gold in autumn, 45' by 35 to 40'.

'Olmsted'—Upright, similar to 'Columnare', grows 35' to 45' high, 20 to 25' wide, selected in Rochester, NY, introduced in 1955.

'Oregon Pride'—Cutleaf form with waxy dark green leaves, gold-bronze fall color, fast growing with a heavy crown, broadly oval, 40 to 50' high.

Parkway™—Broader form of 'Columnare' (probably 'Erectum'), maintaining a strong central leader, essentially oval in outline with dense dark green summer foliage, 40' by 25'; cultivar name is 'Columnarbroad'.

'Princeton Gold'—Leaves emerge bright yellow, color diminishes with the heat of summer, oval-rounded in habit, 35' high by 30' wide, has crisped significantly in the heat of Zone 7b, plant patent 6727.

'Royal Red'—Similar to 'Crimson King' but slower growing, supposedly better maroon color; supposedly hardier than 'Crimson King' but there is an underlying suspicion that the two are in fact the same tree . . . only the names are different; averaged 2.6″ per year over a 10 year period in Wichita tests; severe leaf scorch and borers, 40' high by 30' wide.

'Schwedleri'—Common older form with purplish red spring foliage changing to dark green in early summer, wider spreading than most selections, slightly hardier than 'Crimson King'; 17.5' high and 21' wide after 10 years; parent of 'Crimson King' and 'Deborah'; cultivated since at least 1869. Averaged 5.3″ per year over a 10 year period and developed severe leaf scorch, 40 to 60' high and wide.

'Stand Fast'—Very dwarf, sparingly branched, leaves small, dark green, ruffled and clustered at the ends of branches; 47-year-old tree only 30″ high; have seen at Longwood Gardens, a curiosity at best, discovered in 1932 by Elsie Lundquist of Kennett Square, PA.

'Summershade'—Rapid growing, heat resistant and broadly oval to rounded in habit, maintains a single leader; the foliage is more leathery than the other varieties and retained later in the fall; 12' high and 10.6' wide after 4 years; at maturity almost rounded in outline; ranked extremely high in the Shade Tree Evaluation Trials conducted at Wooster, OH. Averaged 10.4″ of growth per year over a 10 year period; proved the most vigorous of Norway maples in Dr. Pair's tests, produced less scorch than either Sugar or Red Maple, but did not develop appreciable fall color; 42' by 40'; plant patent 1748; derived as an open-pollinated seedling of 'Erectum'.

'Superform'—Rapid growing with straight trunk and heavy dark green foliage, broad oval to rounded outline, 22.6' high and 21' wide after 10 years; 50' by 45' at maturity, good hardiness, introduced in 1968, a seedling selection of 'Erectum'.

'Walderseei'—White interveinal areas; have seen at Edinburgh Botanic Garden and the tree literally grabs the passerby; would "cook" in heat of summer in United States; 25 to 30' high.

PROPAGATION: Seed, 41°F for 90 to 120 days in moist peat or other media; cultivars are budded on seedling understocks; species can be rooted from softwood cuttings collected in mid-June, treated with 8000 ppm IBA talc, placed under intermittent mist with bottom heat [*Proc. Intl. Plant Prop. Soc.* 29: 345–347 (1979)].

ADDITIONAL NOTES: A very popular maple and probably will continue to be in demand; often the bark splits on the species and cultivars on the south or southwest side of the trunk where the sun warms the bark and then sudden low temperatures cause contraction and splitting occurs; often termed "frost cracks." Interesting and thoughtful reading in *J. Arboriculture* 16: 291–296 (1990) titled "History and range of Norway maple." One of the supposed reasons for its widespread planting is that after American elm was obliterated by Dutch elm disease, Norway maple was one of the few available replacements. Norway maple is not without problems and horticulturists, urban foresters, and landscape architects have moved away from the species to *Acer rubrum* and cultivars. I "see" the tree in the South (Zones 7b and 8) occasionally and it simply languishes.

NATIVE HABITAT: Continental Europe, where it is widely spread in a wild state from Norway southwards; also has escaped from cultivation in United States. Introduced about 1756.

Acer pseudoplatanus L. — Planetree Maple; also called Sycamore Maple
(ā′sĕr sö-dō-plat′a-nus)

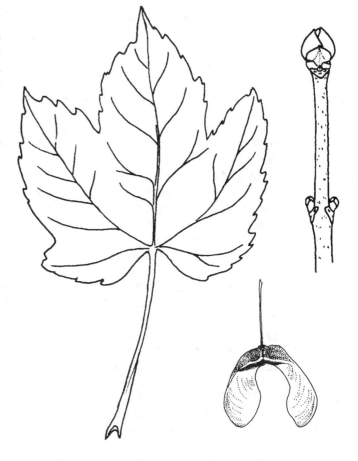

LEAVES: Opposite, simple, 3 to 6″ across, 3- to 5-lobed, lobes ovate, coarsely crenate serrate, veins impressed, cordate, dark green and glabrous above, greenish white beneath, sometimes pubescent on veins, leaf is leathery; petiole—2 to 3 1/2″ long.

BUDS: Terminal large, greenish, slightly pointed, imbricate, glabrous, 1/4 to 1/3″ long, only single buds above leaf scar; buds similar to Norway, but remain green through winter; lateral buds smaller than terminal.

STEM: Glabrous, gray-brown, dull, lenticelled, slightly 4-sided, leaf scars do not meet as is the case in Norway Maple.

SIZE: 40 to 60′ in height under most landscape conditions but specimens of over 100′ are known, spread two-third's of, or equal to height; impressive trees in England and continental Europe where it thrives in the cooler climate.

HARDINESS: Zone 4 to 7, not suited to the South, has not performed well at Morton Arboretum, Lisle, IL.

HABIT: Tree with upright, spreading branches forming an oval to rounded outline; can become a massive tree with maturity.

RATE: Medium, 10 to 12′ in 5 to 8 years.

TEXTURE: Medium in leaf and winter.

BARK: Grayish, reddish brown to orangish; flaking into irregular, rectangular scales, exposing orangish brown inner bark.

LEAF COLOR: Dark green in summer; fall color a dingy brown or possibly with a tinge of yellow.

FLOWERS: Perfect, yellowish green, May, born in upright panicles, 2 to 4″(6″) long; flowers are borne after the leaves and become pendulous as the fruits develop.

FRUIT: Samara, maturing in September–October, each samara 1 1/4 to 2″ long, forming angle of about 60°.

CULTURE: Transplant balled and burlapped in spring; very adaptable to soil types, preferably well-drained; tolerates high lime to acid conditions and exposed sites; will withstand the full force of salt-laden winds in exposed places near the sea; often listed as a salt tolerant species and has been used extensively in the Netherlands; full sun or light shade; abundant throughout Europe, almost weed-like.

DISEASES AND INSECTS: Cankers, subject to considerable dead wood and requires ample maintenance for that reason; in Pacific Northwest anthracnose, caused by *Apiognomonia ventia*, kills leaves and stems, also occurs on East Coast with *Gnomonia* species the causal fungus.

LANDSCAPE VALUE: Probably too many better maples for this species to ever assume any popular status in American gardens; where conditions warrant (exposed, saline environment) it might be used to good advantage; in evidence everywhere in Europe; actually makes a magnificent tree; have seen 80 to 100′ high specimens in England.

CULTIVARS: Too numerous to expound upon but a few of the more "outstanding" that have crossed my path are included here. Counted about 70 cultivars in the van Gelderen, de Jong, and Oterboom Maple book.

'Atropurpureum' ('Spaethii', 'Purpureum')—Leaves dark green above, rich purple beneath, samaras dark purplish red, a rather pretty form and reasonably common in the United States, especially handsome when the leaves are backlighted; will come partially true-to-type from seed, aphids love it, produces large quantities of fruit, vigorous, has grown 26′ high and 25′ wide after 10 years in Oregon tests; mature size 70 to 80′ high; introduced in 1883 through Späth's nurseries; grew 11.3″ per year over a 9 year period in Kansas tests, developed severe leaf scorch, sunscald, and high borer infestations.

'Brilliantissimum'—A real show stopper as the new leaves unfold shrimp pink and later to pale cream to yellow-green and finally off-green; slow growing round-headed tree; I was in Hidcote Garden, England, on a miserable rainy May day and this plant was the first thing that caught my eye; widely used in European gardens, would have to be sited in some shade in the United States; usually grafted on a standard; will reach 15 to 20′ high.

'Erectum'—An upright form, rather wide, compared to many erect types, not particularly outstanding, 50 to 60′.

'Erythrocarpum' (f. *erythrocarpum*)—Form with red samara wings, rather effective, reportedly wild in the Alps of Bavaria, have seen this form or something similar at Stourhead in England, the bright red wings are effective in June, red petioles, grows 60 to 75′ high.

'Leopoldii'—A form with yellowish pink and purple stained leaves; originated about 1860; there seems to be some confusion about this cultivar for plants that I have seen did not color pink or purple but were distinctly white and green, the variegation pattern almost resembling that of a marble cake; other forms of the same character are 'Nizetii', 'Simon Louis Frères', and 'Tricolor'. I have chased the 'Marble Cake' variegated forms around botanical gardens and books with little success. The labels only confuse me. Large tree 50 to 60′ high.

'Prinz Handjéry'—I first saw this at the Arnold Arboretum and identified it as 'Brilliantissimum'. The label indicated I was incorrect. The new foliage is a rich shrimp pink; the literature says yellow above, purple beneath. It is a slow growing bushy tree but more open than 'Brilliantissimum'; purple lower leaf surface distinguishes it from 'Brilliantissimum' which is green below.

f. *variegatum*—Bean applies this term to any form with yellowish or yellowish white blotched and/or striped leaves. These variegated forms are often derived from seed and thus would show some variation in degree of variegation. The trees appear amazingly vigorous and specimens 80 to 90′ are known.

'Worley'—Leaves soft yellow-green at first then yellow and finally pale green with reddish petioles; raised in Germany and introduced into cultivation about 1893; 35 to 45′ high; often spelled 'Worleei', have counted eight different spellings.

PROPAGATION: Seed, 41°F for 90 plus days in moist peat; cultivars are budded onto seedlings.

ADDITIONAL NOTES: Old world tree, cannot compete with American or Asiatic species for fall color; considerable number along the New England coast especially Cape Cod and coastal Rhode Island.

NATIVE HABITAT: Europe, especially mountainous regions, western Asia. Cultivated for centuries.

Acer rubrum L. — Red Maple, Scarlet Maple, Swamp Maple
(ā′sĕr rū′brum)

LEAVES: Opposite, simple, 2 to 4″(5″) long and wide, 3 although often 5-lobed, triangular ovate lobes and sinuses are irregularly toothed (in Silver Maple the sinuses are entire), medium to dark green above, grayish to silvery beneaths with hairy veins, new growth and petioles often red; petiole—2 to 4″ long.

BUDS: Imbricate, red to green, blunt and several scaled, 1/16 to 1/8″ long with rounded bud scales (Silver Maple scales are slightly pointed); flower buds in clusters often encircling nodes, flower buds spherical, edge of scales finely pubescent.

STEM: Glabrous, lenticelled, green-red-brown; when crushed does not have rank odor; usually green becoming red as winter progresses.

FLOWER: Flowers are borne with petals; Silver Maple flowers without them.

BARK: Young—smooth, light gray; old—dark gray and rough, scaly and/or ridged and furrowed.

SIZE: 40 to 60′ in height, but occasionally reaches 100 to 120′ in the wild; spread less than or equal to height; co-national champions are 179′ by 120′ in St. Clair County, MI and 135′ by 88′ in Great Smoky Mountains National Park, TN.

HARDINESS: Zone 3b to 9, best to select Red Maples for a specific area that have been grown from seed collected there; ample evidence to suggest provenance is important for hardiness. See Dirr and Lindstrom, *Amer. Nurseryman* 169(1):47–55 (1989). Dr. Lindstrom and I have conducted considerable cold hardiness research with *Acer rubrum* (*HortScience* 24:818–820, 1989) with the conclusion that red maples from southern provinces are not extremely cold hardy. The largest problem is the inability to develop cold hardiness early in fall and the ability to deacclimate early in spring. These patterns set the trees up for early fall and late spring freezes. Considerable data are available on Red Maple cultivar cold hardiness and I have integrated same into the descriptions.

HABIT: In youth often pyramidal or elliptical, developing ascending branches which result in an irregular, ovoid or rounded crown; variable over its range and the numerous cultivars reflect the degree of variation.

RATE: Medium to fast; 10 to 12′ in 5 to 7 years.

TEXTURE: Medium-fine to medium in leaf; medium in winter.

BARK: Soft gray or gray-brown; see above.

LEAF COLOR: Emerging leaves are reddish tinged gradually changing medium to dark green above with a distinct gray cast beneath; fall color varies from greenish yellow to yellow to brilliant red; Red Maple does not always have brilliant red fall color and unscrupulous plantsmen who offer seedling trees and guarantee red fall color are frauding the public; the onslaught of red fall colored cultivars has changed the buying patterns of knowledgeable gardeners; nurserymen have told me that it is difficult to sell anything but a guaranteed red fall colored clone; interestingly, the upper Midwest, New England, and middle Atlantic states are imbued with the species in its myriad forms and fall colors; there is nothing wrong with a seedling Red Maple, however, one should realize that variation is inherent in virtually all characteristics; in the Southeast, particularly the Piedmont and Coastal Plain, Red Maple is abundant but bright red fall coloring plants are seldom evident. Sibley et al., *J. Environ. Hort.* 13:51–53 (1995) evaluated 9 *A. rubrum* cultivars, 3 *A.* × *freemanii* cultivars, and *A. rubrum* seedlings for growth and fall color growing at Camp Hill, AL (Zone 7). Data indicated 'Autumn Blaze', 'Autumn Flame', 'Fairview Flame', and 'October Glory' were superior while 'Karpick' and 'Northwood' were inferior selections for the Southeast.

FLOWERS: Red, rarely yellowish; March into April, in dense clusters before the leaves, each flower on a reddish pedicel at first quite short but lengthening as the flower and fruit develop; the stigmas and styles as well as the small petals are the showy part of the flower; I have seen trees which are predominantly pistillate, largely staminate or monoecious; all are showy; the male does not have the intense red color compared to the female; on the Georgia campus some trees are in flower in January, others February, and others early March; great spread of flowering times; since the 1990 edition I have assessed the peculiar sexual preferences of this species—actually quite kinky for in a given population of seedlings staminate, pistillate, monoecious, and monoecious with hermaphrodite (bisexual) flowers occur; an interesting anecdote concerns male trees in a 25-tree plantation on the Georgia campus that grow much faster than their seed bearing sisters; my supposition . . . so much stored carbohydrate is required for fruit formation that vegetative growth is reduced; observations of even age stands show this to be valid; most of the superior red fall coloring cultivars are female except for the recent introductions from the U.S. National Arboretum.

FRUIT: Samara, often but not always reddish maturing to brown; on slender drooping pedicels 2 to 3″ long, wings 3/4 to 1″ long, 1/4 to 1/2″ wide, spreading at a narrow to about a 60° angle, maturing May–June.

CULTURE: Transplants readily as a small specimen bare root, or balled and burlapped in larger sizes, move when dormant although summer digging is now common; very tolerant of soils, however, prefers slightly acid, moist conditions; tolerant of ozone and intermediately tolerant of sulfur dioxide; occurs naturally in low, wet areas and is often one of the first trees to color in the fall; shows chlorosis in high pH soils, in the past this was thought to be due to iron deficiency, however, research has shown that manganese is the causal agent; not particularly urban tolerant, although planted in ever-increasing numbers in cities; averaged 11″ per year in Wichita tests over a 9 year period; tremendous variation in growth rates from seedling material, considerable leaf scorch; newer growth data from Auburn University's excellent shade tree evaluation tests showed over an 11 year period the species (seedlings) averaged 1.9′/year, 'Armstrong'—2.2′, 'Autumn Flame'—1.4′, 'Bowhall'—1.7′, 'Red Sunset'—1.6′, 'Gerling'—1.6′, 'Karpick'—2.5′, Scarlet Sentinel™—2.1′, 'Schlesingeri'—2.4′, and 'Tilford'—1.5′.

DISEASES AND INSECTS: Leaf hoppers will cause considerable damage, also borer that attacks young terminals and a petiole borer.

LANDSCAPE VALUE: Excellent specimen tree for lawn, park or street; does not tolerate heavily polluted areas; does not grow as fast as *Acer saccharinum*, Silver Maple, however, is much preferable because of cleaner foliage, stronger wood, and better fall color; Red Maple is the light that brightens the fall color sky throughout the northern, midwestern, and northeastern states; the fall color can be so dazzling and combined with a backdrop of *Pinus strobus* paints a picture that no master could duplicate; the only thing consistent about Red Maple fall coloration is the inconsistency from tree to tree; some remain almost green or at best yellow-green, others bright yellow, others flaming orange or red. In the 1970's many budded trees of *A. rubrum* began to decline for no apparent reason. Nurserymen and researchers determined that the problem was a graft incompatibility and developed a system of own-root production that eliminated the decline. Now most cultivars are on their own roots, either via cutting or tissue culture.

CULTIVARS: New introductions seem to cascade like rain drops and it is difficult to assess their worthiness. Since the 1990 edition another 20 cultivars have surfaced. See Santamour and McArdle, *J. Arboriculture* 8:110–112 (1982), for the more obscure cultivars. Several of the cultivars included herein are selections of *A. × freemanii* (*A. rubrum* × *A. saccharinum*). Their affinity is shown with the *A. × freemanii* listed after the name.

'Ablaze'—Rounded crown, fall color brilliant red, foliage held late into the fall.

'Armstrong' (*A. × freemanii*)—Fastigiate (50 to 70′ by 15′) with tree gradually spreading out a degree but still distinctly upright, beautiful silver-gray bark, faster grower than upright Sugar or Norway; essentially female; fall color is often poor although I have seen trees with good orange-red fall color if environmental conditions are ideal; fast grower, 15.4′ high and 4.5′ wide after 4 years; leaf is more Silver Maple than Red Maple like, distinctly 5-lobed with rather deeply cut sinuses and silvery underside, extremely long petioles and leaves tend to droop; has performed quite well in Zone 7 but fall color is at best an inadequate yellow-orange; problems have surfaced on this cultivar most prominently a dieback (trunk will turn black) that has been linked to glyphostate and/or *Phytophthora*, selected by Newton Armstrong, Windsor, OH in 1947.

'Armstrong Two' ('Armstrong II') (*A. × freemanii*)—Better fall color than 'Armstrong', has more dense form and more tightly ascending branches, selected in 1960 from a planting of 'Armstrong'; based on what I see in the trade, 'Armstrong' is predominant; side by side comparison of this and 'Armstrong' at Bernheim Arboretum gave 'Armstrong' the nod for habit, general appearance.

Autumn Blaze® (*A. × freemanii*)—Deeply 5-lobed resembling Silver Maple, rich green leaves with excellent orange-red fall color that persists later than many cultivars, dense oval-rounded head with ascending branch structure and central leader, rapid growth and Zone 4 hardiness, may be more drought tolerant than true *Acer rubrum* cultivars, fall color is excellent orange-red to red and in Zone 7b it is among the best of all Red and hybrid Red Maples for fall color; Hasselkus, University of Wisconsin, stated it grew 4 times as fast as the species; southern tree producers have noted that it grows almost too fast; definitely does not develop the tight head of October Glory® and Red Sunset®; proved more resistant to leafhopper injury than *A. rubrum*, October Glory®, and Red Sunset® [*J. Environ. Hort.* 11: 101–106 (1993)]; plant patent 4864; selected by Glenn Jeffers, Fostoria, OH in late 1960's, 50′ by 40′, possibly larger at maturity.

Autumn Fantasy™ (*A. × freemanii*)—Upright-oval, with 5-lobed leaves more closely resembling Silver than Red Maple, attractive crimson fall color, original tree from central Illinois, introduced by Bill Wandell, Discov-tree, Oquawka, IL, cultivar name 'DTR 102', 50′ by 40′, good fall color in Zone 8.

'Autumn Flame'—Handsome selection, eventually forming a rounded outline (to 60'), excellent and early red fall color, smaller leaves that color earlier than the species; grew 21' high and 24' wide after 10 years; severely injured during the horrendous winter of 1976–77 in the Chicago area, trees as large as 5″ diameter were killed, 80 to 90% loss of fall planted stock was reported, has slipped somewhat in popularity especially with all the new introductions; grew 1'1″ per year in Wichita tests over a 10 year period; colored early and developed considerable leaf scorch; in Athens has colored 3 to 4 weeks ahead of October Glory®, uniquely different in the almost broad-rounded outline at a young age, small 3-lobed leaves and exceptionally early fall color; peaked October 16, 1993 and October 21, 1994 in Athens, a male but I have not verified this; plant patent 2377, introduced 1964.

'Autumn Glory'—Upright tree with oval spreading crown; selected for exceptional red fall color; doubtfully being produced in commerce; plant patent 2431; introduced about 1967 by Davey Tree, Kent, OH.

'Autumn Radiance'—Dense oval form, green summer foliage turning brilliant orange-red in fall. Zone 4.

'Autumn Spire'—Broad columnar form with consistent red fall color, showy red, male (seedless) flowers in spring; 50' by 25', considered Zone 3 to 6, introduced by University of Minnesota, plant patent 7803, from a seed source near Grand Rapids, MN, 24-year-old tree was 30' by 10', reported as coloring earlier and better than other *A. rubrum* cultivars in Oregon. See *J. Environ. Hort.* 11: 147–148 (1993).

'Bowhall'—Upright form with a symmetrical, narrow pyramidal-columnar head; good yellowish-red fall color; I have equated this cultivar with 'Columnare', but erroneously so; although literature says good red fall color, I have seen yellow-orange with some red in midveins; 50' by 15'; in some quarters this is equated with 'Scanlon', may be confused in trade, introduced in 1948 by the Cole Nursery Co., Circleville, OH; also reported as Scanlon introduction in 1951; I have seen this form in Oregon and it is indeed narrow and upright, some nurseries list it as 40' by 10', material in some East Coast plantings is anything but. Have observed severe Lindane spray damage on young leaves at 2# active/100 gallon. Also have been informed that an additive to spray mixes to keep nozzles from clogging has caused foliar necrosis.

'Brandywine'—Moderately columnar crown, leaves 4 1/2″ long and 4 1/2″ wide, pronounced autumn red leaf color that turns brilliant purple-red as the days shorten, frequently 14 days of effective peak red color, good potato leaf hopper resistance, male, 25' high and 12' wide after 12 years, Dr. A. M. Townsend, U.S. National Arboretum, introduction. Zone 4 to 8, result of cross between October Glory® × 'Autumn Flame'.

Burgundy Belle®—Compact, oval-rounded crown, extremely uniform in outline, parent tree is 45' by 35'; summer foliage medium to dark green; in late September (Midwest) foliage develops intense red maturing to burgundy; fall color is long persistent; withstood -28 to -32°F without injury; parent tree grows in northeast Kansas; cultivar name is 'Magnificent Magenta'; 1995 introduction by Heritage Trees, Jacksonville, IL.

Celebration™ (*A.* × *freemanii*)—Upright habit, uniform growth and strong crotch angles; dense foliage starts to color in early October with a cast of red turning to gold in mid to late October; introduced by Lake County Nursery, Perry, OH; mature tree 45' high and 20 to 25' wide; leaves similar to Silver Maple; fall color is yellowish green in Madison, WI; listed as male; cultivar name is 'Celzam'; plant patent 7279; introduced about 1980.

'Columnare'—A very handsome, narrow columnar-pyramidal form that is a degree slower growing and more compact than 'Armstrong' but to me preferable because of darker green foliage and excellent orange to deep red fall color; grew 12.5' high and 3.6' wide after 4 years; predominantly male; leaves are 3-lobed with rounded leaf bases and shallow lobes toward the apex; pictured in Garden and Forest, 1894, at which time it was 80' high.

'Cream Lace'—Narrow cream colored margin, 3-lobed, crow's foot shaped leaf.

'Cumberland'—Moderate globe-shaped crown with dense dark green foliage that turns brilliant red in autumn, original selection was 34' high and 15' wide after 20 years in sod culture, selected in 1986 by Dr. A. M. Townsend from open pollinated seedlings derived from a Norris, TN provenance, leaves average 4″ long, 4 1/2″ wide, spring leaf, flower and fruit color are red, good tolerance to potato leaf hopper, Zone (4) 5 to 8 adaptability and has fall colored well in Tennessee, Georgia and Alabama, U.S. National Arboretum introduction.

'Curtis'—Moderately ovate, reddish green new growth, soon green, red in autumn, female, 40' by 30', introduced 1949.

'Davey Red'—Thick tough dark green foliage, excellent red fall color, compact upright growth, cold hardy (Zone 3), 50 to 60' high, introduced by Davey Tree, Kent, OH. 'Davey' is described as upright growing, medium size leaves, yellow fall color, offered by Brotzman's Nursery, Madison, OH. I trust this latter description.

DJ 1-69—Selected in Connecticut by Richard Jaynes and Earl Cully for perfect branching habit, brilliant scarlet fall color, cold hardiness (-28°F), first tree to turn color, will be patented and trademarked; write Heritage Trees, Inc., RR #5, Jacksonville, IL 62650 for details.

'Doric'—Upright form, not to the degree of 'Armstrong', female, selected by Ed Scanlon, branches at 30° angle, ascend to two third's the height of the tree, leathery glossy leaves turn red in fall, doubtfully in commerce; in September 1994 and again in June 1997 I saw a 20- to 25-year-old specimen at Bernheim with tight columnar habit and outstanding foliage, appeared superior to 'Armstrong'.

variety *drummondii*—The southern version of Red Maple, Louisiana Nursery lists three forms, 'Live Oak Form', 'Louisiana Red', and 'San Felipe', all selected for various red shades of the samaras; leaves of variety are coriaceous, white beneath.

'Edna Davis'—Selected from the garden of Mrs. Edna Davis in Athens, GA for broad-pyramidal habit, 3-lobed dark green summer leaves, excellent late October orange-red to red fall color, and good heat tolerance, appears to be a form of variety *drummondii*, parent tree 35 to 40' by 25', a female, Zone 6 to probably 8b, as a young nursery grown tree not as dense and full headed as October Glory®; see *Nursery Manager* 7(5): 43 (1991) for specifics.

'Embers'—A tree with narrow habit in youth maturing to a rounded outline, lustrous green summer foliage turns consistent bright red in fall, vigorous and hardy, female, 50' by 30'.

'Excelsior'—Pyramidal to teardrop shape, upsweeping branches can be observed early in life, fall color orange-red, 35 to 40', Zone 4.

Fairview Flame®—Oval rounded crown, supposedly excellent red to scarlet fall color, 48' by 35', Zone 4 to 8(9), McGill introduction, good fall color in Auburn University tests.

Firedance® ('Landsburg')—Medium size tree with good branch structure, early brilliant red fall color, oval-rounded outline, 50' by 30–40', selection by Roger Landsburg, Brainerd, MN, Zone 3 to 6, plant patent 6977, Bailey Nursery introduction.

'Florida Flame'—Red fall color on a sustained basis, seedling selection by Bob Burns, Trailridge Nursery, Florida from a local seed source, resistant to leaf spots.

'Gerling'—Small broad pyramidal form, eventually becoming rounded, densely branched, yellow to red fall color, red flowers, no fruits observed, mature height listed as 40 to 60', 11 years in Auburn tests was 22' by 13', Scanlon introduction around 1956.

'Globosum'—Compact, dwarf form with scarlet flowers; have not observed this cultivar in cultivation.

'Karpick'—Dense narrow form, 40 to 50' tall, by 20' wide, distinct red twigs and green foliage turning yellow or red in fall, Schichtel introduction in 1974, named after Frank E. Karpick, former city forester of Buffalo, NY, 33' by 10' in 11 years, male.

'Lee's Red' (*A.* × *freemanii*)—Brilliant red fall color, foliage not as deeply divided as that of Silver Maple, successful in Minnesota, selected by Sheridan Nurseries.

'Marmo' (*A.* × *freemanii*)—A selection from the Morton Arboretum, habit is distinctly broad-columnar, the leaves start to color in mid-September (Lisle, IL) with red dominating and green patches interspersed, color lasts for 2 to 4 weeks and is outstanding, the leaves are intermediate between the parents, the wood is considered moderately tough, 60-year-old specimen is 70' by 35 to 40', leaves 5-lobed with sinuses toothed 2/3 the depth of the sinuses, and more closely resembles Silver than Red Maple, flowers staminate. Zone 4.

'Morgan' (*A.* × *freemanii*)—One of the fastest growing red maples, habit open, oval rounded, brilliant orange-red to red fall color, colors well in mild climates, supposedly brightest of all red maples, pistillate flowers, 'Indian Summer' is United States name; hardier than the typical cultivars, valid as Zone 4, selected at Morgan Arboretum, MacDonald College, Quebec, 45 to 50' by 40', not as good as October Glory® and Red Sunset® in South.

'New World'—According to Denny Townsend, US National Arboretum, the habit is initially upright, then arching and weeps in the upper reaches, parent tree is 31' high and 15' wide, orange-red fall color, excellent cold hardiness to –30°F, high potato leaf hopper resistance, probably best for northern areas.

Northfire™ ('Olson')—Oval habit with good branching structure, brilliant red fall color ahead of Firedance™, 50' by 30 to 40', selected by Roger Landsburg, Brainerd, MN, introduced by Bailey Nursery, Zone 3 to 5.

Northwood®—Rounded-oval crown with branches ascending at a 45° angle, dark green summer foliage; good orange-red fall color and adaptability to the rigors of the Minnesota climate. Selected from a native seedling population near Floodwood, MN by Dr. Leon Snyder, and introduced by the University of Minnesota. In Spring Grove, Cincinnati, OH, turns yellow-orange-red; definitely not as effective for fall color in the southern states, some indication that growth habit is rather irregular and unruly, plant patent 5053, 50' by 35', introduced 1980.

'October Brilliance'—Excellent red fall color, well shaped tight crown, delayed leaf emergence in spring, reduces chance of frost injury, 40' by 30', Zone 5 to 7.

Octoberfest®—Listed as a strong grower with bright deep red fall color, survived -30°F, 50 to 60' high, from Many Oaks Nursery, Bagdad, KY, listed in 1995 Moller's Nursery Catalog.

October Glory®—Good oval-rounded (40 to 50') form but tends to hold its lustrous dark green leaves late and the intensity of the brilliant orange to red fall color may be impaired by early freezes; can be spectacular when right; grew 11' high and 6.4' wide after 4 years; suffered in extreme winter of 1976–77 in the Midwest. Superb for fall coloration in the South and has been better than 'Red Sunset' in Zone 7b–8. Both are excellent but with 'October Glory' the red color is more intense and has lasted into mid-November in my garden. I watched closely the development of fall color in 1988 and witnessed red to orange-red to a dying ember red. The colors changed with time and weather conditions. This form and 'Red Sunset' are the dominant selections in the market place. This is a female form and wings of the fruits are reddish tinged. The patent (1961) has expired but the name is trademarked. Introduced in 1961 by Princeton Nursery. Possibly the most impressive aspect of 'October Glory' is the ability to develop excellent red fall color in latitudes were environmental conditions are not "perfect" for expressions of maximum color. Averaged 1'1" per year in Wichita tests over a 10 year period; developed good fall color late in the season that persisted for 3 to 4 weeks.

'Red Rocket'—Columnar outline, fiery red fall color, hence, the name, parent tree is 35' high and 8' wide, high potato leaf hopper resistence, will survive into Zone 3, derived from a northern Minnesota provenance, US National Arboretum introduction.

'Red Skin' (Schichtel)—A rounded form characterized by large thick foliage and early reddish maroon fall color, 40' by 40', Zone 4.

Red Sunset®—One of the best Red Maple cultivars, excellent orange to red fall color, colors before 'October Glory', lovely pyramidal to rounded outline; 13.6' high and 7.8' wide after 4 years; one of the highest rated trees in Ohio Shade Tree Evaluation tests; came through the 1976–77 (-20 to -25°F) winter as the only unscathed patented Red Maple now superseded in cold hardiness by Northwood® and other primarily Minnesota-based introductions; considered the best by many nurserymen and landscape designers; 'Franksred' is the cultivar name, Red Sunset the trademark name; ultimately 45 to 50' by 35 to 40'; a female. Grew 1'1" in Wichita tests in 9 years; develops good branch angles, bright red fall color, but still showed some leaf scorch, introduced in 1966 by J. Frank Schmidt and Son, Boring, OR.

'Red Vase'—Upright spreading, vase-shaped outline, good red and yellow fall coloration, Zone 4, selected by Neil Millane, Connecticut, plant patent 4202.

RK 1-75—Almost an October Glory® habit at a young age, large dark green leaves turn brilliant scarlet-red in fall, withstood -30°F without injury, will be patented and trademarked, original seed source from southern Illinois, near Mt. Vernon; Heritage Tree introduction, Jacksonville, IL.

'Scanlon'—Forms a compact conical crown of dense branches with central leader, colors rich orange-red in fall; Scanlon introduction and patent 1722 (1958), no longer common in cultivation, but occasionally found in arboreta, not an unworthy selection and may be the same as 'Bowhall', probably 40' by 15', have seen at Mt. Auburn, Cambridge, MA, a handsome columnar tree, denser than 'Armstrong'.

'Scarlet Knight'—Oval-rounded habit, 5-lobed, medium green leaves, superb late developing, long persistent fall color, often holding into late November in Athens, consistent Ac*red* fall color in the heat of Zone 7b. Dirr introduction.

Scarlet Sentinel™ (*A.* × *freemanii*)—(Schichtel Nursery, NY). According to the literature, columnar, fast-growing, good rich green leaves, yellow-orange to orange-red fall color, leaves 5-lobed, closely resembling Silver Maple, flowers pistillate, probably the fastest-growing upright maple, bark smooth and shiny; my observations indicate that this form is anything but upright, more toward broad columnar to oval-rounded, have seen at Spring Grove in Cincinnati, 'Scarsen' is cultivar name, Scarlet Sentinel the trademark, 45' by 25', has not fall colored well in Athens, plant patent 3109, discovered in Ashtabula, OH by George Schichtel.

'Schlesingeri'—Introduced for superior rich red to reddish purple fall color, forms a large (60 to 70') upright spreading rounded crown at maturity; the earliest Red Maple and for that matter shade tree to color; by September 15, 1978 at the Arnold Arboretum it had developed full coloration, color holds for a long time (20 to 30 days); female; 12.6' high and 6.9' wide after 4 years; largely fallen out of favor since the introduction of the "better" fall coloring, smaller types; still a magnificent tree; some of the material in today's market does not appear similar to the Arnold Arboretum's fine specimen, discovered by C.S. Sargent of the Arnold Arboretum on the grounds of a Mr. Schlesinger; an old cultivar dating back to the 1880's.

'Shade King'—Upright oval head, well branched in first year; leaves dark green, fall color orange to red, slightly serrated, Zone 4, 50' by 40', Handy Nursery introduction, OR.

'Silhouette'—A Bill Wandell introduction about which I can find no information; may be an *A.* × *freemanii* type.

'Somerset'—Moderate ovate crown, leaves 4″ long, 4 1/2″ wide, red autumn color later than 'Sun Valley', 23′ high and 11′ wide after 12 years, good potato leaf hopper resistance, male, result of cross between October Glory® and 'Autumn Flame', Dr. A. M. Townsend made the original crosses in 1982; Zone 4 to 8.

'Summer Red'—Produces brilliant new reddish purple young shoots, fall color is yellow, beautiful in spring growth, a Head-Lee Nursery introduction, Seneca, SC.

'Sun Valley'—Ovate crown with 4″ long and 4″ wide leaves that turn brilliant red in fall, 21′ high and 10′ wide after 12 growing seasons, good resistance to potato leaf hopper, male; a cross between Red Sunset® and 'Autumn Flame', crosses made in 1982 by Dr. A. M. Townsend, U.S. National Arboretum, Zone 4 to 7.

'Tennessee Blaze'—Listed as a hardy form with distinctive fall color that changes from yellow to scarlet; 40 to 55′ high; from Beaver Creek Nursery, Knoxville, TN.

'Tilford'—Globe headed, uniform in shape, vigorous, red to yellow fall color, 35′ by 35′; averaged 9″ per year over a 7 year period; developed leaf scorch and high borer infestations; in Auburn tests averaged 1.5′ per year over 11 years, 22′ by 10.5′ in this time frame, red, orange, yellow fall color, may grow 40 to 60′ high and appears more oval rounded than globe headed.

'Variegatum'—Leaves variegated; have seen one specimen of a marbled white variegated leaf type that was a rather weak grower; the new growth was reddish pink owing to the normal red pigment coupled with the white areas; seemingly a grex name for cream, yellow splotched leaves.

'V.J. Drake'—Selected for the pattern of fall coloration with the outside of the leaf coloring a deep red and this color progressing toward the green middle, plant patent 3542 (1974).

'Woodlands'—A selection of var. *drummondii* from Hines Nursery, Houston, TX for good red fall color in the Southwest.

PROPAGATION: Seeds mature in early summer and will germinate without pretreatment although stratification for 60 to 75 days at 41°F or a cold water soak for 2 to 5 days will hasten and unify germination; softwood cuttings can be rooted readily and considerable work has been undertaken with the various cultivars; the idea being to put these maples on their own roots and avoid the incompatibility problems; over the years my students and I have propagated many red maples from cuttings. A few hints follow: use healthy stock plants, preferably firm wooded, mature leaved cuttings, single or multiple node, 5000 ppm IBA in 50% alcohol or similar concentration of KIBA, peat:perlite, mist that is applied evenly and without fail, and cuttings should root in 3 to 5 weeks. For detailed information see Dirr and Heuser, *The Reference Manual of Woody Plant Propagation*. Also tissue culture is a common avenue of vegetative propagation.

ADDITIONAL NOTES: The cultivars should be used in preference to seedling stock if consistent, good red fall color is desired; Red Maple is definitely a candidate for regional selection; a good fall coloring selection from a mature population is needed in the southern states; Red Maple has been called a cosmopolitan species because of its adaptability to swamps, bottomlands, mixed forest situations, and rocky uplands; the late winter–early spring flowers are attractive and forewarn that spring is just "around the corner."

Acer rubrum and cultivars are dominating the modern shade tree markets. The only limitation is the inadequate adaptability in high pH, dry soils and windswept sites. Literature has increased at a phenomenal pace and I refer the reader to "*Acer rubrum* cultivars for the South," *J. Arboriculture* 16: 25–29 (1990) where 'Autumn Flame', 'Bowhall', 'Gerling', and 'Tilford' are rated high for consistent fall coloration. The authors' evaluations are certainly not in line with mine or other observers.

Several interesting papers relative to *Acer* × *freemanii* and cultivars that offer worthwhile background and technical data [*American Nurseryman* 168(18): 40 (1989) and *J. Arboriculture* 19: 195–200 (1993)]. Also Kim Krahl et al., *J. Environ. Hort.* 11: 89–92 (1993) utilized DNA amplifications for the separation of 18 *Acer rubrum*, *A. saccharinum* and *A.* × *freemanii* hybrids. Ruter et al., *Proc. SNA Research Conf.* 42 (1997) discusses in some detail growth of 31 *Acer rubrum* taxa at Blairsville, Athens, and Tifton, GA. 'Alapaha', one of Dr. Ruter's selections from Florida was the fastest growing at Tifton. In general, October Glory® grew as fast as any, averaging over 31″/year at both Tifton and Athens. No fall color assessments were provided.

NATIVE HABITAT: Newfoundland to Florida west to Minnesota, Oklahoma and Texas. Introduced 1860.

Acer saccharinum L. — Silver Maple, also called Soft, White, River Maple
(ā′sĕr sak-kär-ī′num)

LEAVES: Opposite, simple, 3 to 6″ across, 5-lobed, with deeply and doubly acuminate lobes, the middle often 3-lobed, bright to medium green above, silvery white beneath and pubescent when young; petiole—3 to 5″ long.

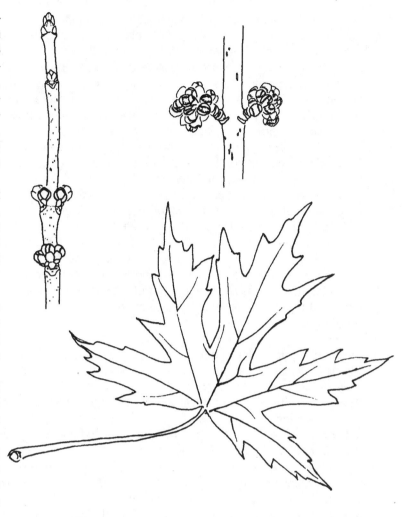

BUDS: Vegetative—imbricate, flattened, ovoid, 2 outer scales form a "V" shaped notch, appressed, 1/8 to 3/16″ long, lustrous red or reddish brown on outside of scales, edges fringed with short pubescence; flower—imbricate, globose, accessory, often in dense, compact, corymb-like clusters, 1/8 to 3/16″ high, margins of scales prominently fringed.

STEM: Similar to Red Maple except with rank odor when bruised, moderate, terete, lustrous red to brown, glabrous, slender vertical lenticels; pith—solid, white; 2nd year stem becoming gray.

SIZE: 50 to 70′ in height and can grow 100 to 120′; spread is usually about 2/3's the height; national champion is 61′ by 82′ in Polk County, IA.

HARDINESS: Zone 3 to 9, although native in Zones 8 and 9, I have yet to see a quality specimen in a landscape setting.

HABIT: Upright with strong spreading branches forming an oval to rounded crown with pendulous branchlets which turn up at the ends.

RATE: Fast, 10 to 12′ in 4 to 5 years from a small newly planted tree is not unreasonable, unfortunately with fast growth comes a weak-wooded tree, often will break up in wind, ice, and snow storms; fastest growing American maple species.

TEXTURE: Medium in leaf, but coarse in winter; may appear somewhat disheveled in winter.

BARK: On young branches (1″ or more) color is an interesting gray or gray-brown and can be mistaken for the bark of *Acer rubrum*; however, the color is usually darker (or with a tinge of red) compared to that of *Acer rubrum*; with maturity becomes ridged and furrowed, scaly, gray to gray-brown.

LEAF COLOR: Bright to medium green above, gray or silver beneath in summer; fall color is usually a green-yellow-brown combination; a tinge of red is evident with certain trees during the fall but this is the exception rather than the rule, some of the red fall color may be attributable to hybridization with *A. rubrum*.

FLOWERS: Monoecious, predominantly staminate or pistillate; greenish yellow to red, without petals, opening before *Acer rubrum*, usually in early to mid-March; borne in dense clusters similar to Red Maple, some trees are as showy as Red Maple, female showier than male.

FRUIT: Samara, not ornamentally important, wings spreading at an 80 to 90° angle, subhorizontal, each samara 1 1/3 to 2 1/3″ long, matures in late May–June, one of the largest fruited maples.

CULTURE: Of the easiest culture, transplants well bare root or balled and burlapped; tolerant of wide variety of soils but achieves maximum size in moist soils along stream banks and in deep, moist soiled woods; prefers slightly acid soil; will cause sidewalks to buckle and drain tiles to clog because of vigorous, gross feeding root systems; one of the best trees for poor soils where few other species will survive and for these areas should be considered.

DISEASES AND INSECTS: Anthracnose (in rainy seasons may be serious on Sugar, Silver, Sycamore Maples and Boxelder), leaf spot (purple eye), tar spot, bacterial leaf spot, leaf blister, powdery mildew, *Verticillium* wilt (Silver, Norway, Red and Sugar are most affected), bleeding canker, basal canker, *Nectria* canker, *Ganoderma* rot, sapstreak, trunk decay, forest tent caterpillar, green striped maple worm, maple leaf cutter, Japanese leafhopper, leaf hopper, leaf stalk borer, petiole borers, bladder-gall mite, ocellate leaf gall,

Norway Maple aphid, boxelder bug, maple phenacoccus, cottony maple scale (Silver Maple is tremendously susceptible), other scales (terrapin, gloomy, and Japanese), flat-headed borers, Sugar Maple borer, pidgeon tremex, leopard moth borer, metallic borer, twig pruner, carpenter worm, whitefly and nematodes; maples are obviously susceptible to a wide range of insect and disease problems; several physiological problems include scorch where the margins of the leaves become necrotic and brown due to limited water supply; this often occurs on newly planted trees and in areas where there is limited growing area (planter boxes, narrow tree lawns, sidewalk plantings); Red and Silver Maple also show extensive manganese chlorosis in calcareous or high pH soils and should be grown in acid soils.

LANDSCAPE VALUE: The use of this tree should be tempered as it becomes a liability with age; possibility for rugged conditions or where someone desires fast shade; there are far too many superior trees to warrant extensive use of this species; in its native habitat along streams it withstands several weeks of complete inundation but cultivated trees will do well in dry soils; the English consider the Silver Maple a tree of great beauty in habit and foliage; I saw magnificent specimens in Europe, some approaching 100′ in height; although I would never plant a Silver Maple, there are places and times that perhaps warrant a tree of this ilk; in the Arnold Arboretum along Meadow Road a 100′ high, century old specimen resides; many trees throughout the Arnold have come and gone while this survived; ample room for selection and I see several new cultivars; reflecting on my visits to Maine where along the Stillwater and Penobscot Rivers, Silver Maples were everywhere in evidence; many horticulturists speculate that the *Acer* × *freemanii* selections might supersede *A. saccharinum* in harsh sites where *Acer rubrum* would languish.

CULTIVARS:

'Blair'—Stronger branching pattern than the species, yellow fall color, 50 to 70′ high, Zone 4.

'Borns Graciosa'—Extreme cut leaf form, possibly the most dissected of all the cutleaf forms, relatively strong growing to 30′ high.

'Elegant'—Appears in English literature and is listed as an upright form, considered *A.* × *freemanii* in parentage.

'Laciniatum'—A catch-all term (grex) for plants whose leaves are more deeply divided than the type; 'Beebe' and 'Wieri' are categorized here.

'Lochstead'—Leaves small, extremely deeply lobed, the lobes thread-like, parent tree 79′ by 40′ with pendulous branch tips, discovered in 1990 by Norman Stewart, Blacksville, New Brunswick, hardy to Zone 2b.

'Lutescens'—New leaves orangish yellow in color turning yellowish green at maturity. Fall color is yellow. Introduced before 1883.

'Northline'—A Morden, Manitoba introduction with wide branching habit and slower growth than the species, adaptable to the prairie regions, Zone 3 to 7, listed as 60 to 80′ by 40 to 45′, good hardiness and branch strength, open-pollinated seedling in 1970.

'Pyramidale'—A type of broadly columnar habit, maintaining central leader, 70′ high, 40′ wide.

'Silver Cloud'—Upright oval form with narrower branch angles and compact crown compared to 'Northline', selected in Canada, hardy to Zone 3.

'Silver Queen'—More upright oval-rounded habit, fruitless, and leaves are bright green above with silvery lower surface, yellow fall color, becoming more common in commerce; 50′ by 40′; averaged 2′7″ per year in Wichita tests over a 10 year period; although listed as seedless, trees did produce some fruits; has performed well in Spartanburg, SC.

'Skinner'—A cut-leaf form with bright green foliage and a pyramidal outline; lateral branches more slender and horizontal, also listed as 'Skinneri'; originated as a chance seedling in the J.H. Skinner Nursery, Topeka, KS.

'Wieri'—Branches pendulous, leaf lobes narrow and sharply toothed; discovered in 1873 by D.B. Wier; now listed as 'Laciniatum Wieri'.

PROPAGATION: Seed has no dormancy and germinates immediately after maturing; seedlings grow in every idle piece of ground and gradually overtake an area; cuttings have been taken in November and rooted with 84% efficiency; softwood cuttings root readily; treat like Red Maple.

ADDITIONAL NOTES: This species has been and will continue to be overplanted; it is one of the nurseryman's biggest moneymakers because of fast growth and ease of culture; responds well to heavy fertilization and watering; with selection a better class of Silver Maples will enter the marketplace; like Red Maple, seed source selection is important to insure cold hardiness.

NATIVE HABITAT: Quebec to Florida, to Minnesota, Nebraska, Kansas, Oklahoma, and Louisiana. Introduced 1725.

Acer saccharum Marshall — Sugar Maple; often called Rock Maple or Hard Maple
(ā'sẽr sak-kär'um)

LEAVES: Opposite, simple, 3 to 6″ long and across, 3- to 5-lobed, acuminate, cordate, slightly coarsely toothed with narrow and deep sinuses; variable but generally dark green, glabrous or pubescent, often pale green to gray-green below; petiole—(1 1/2″) 2 to 3″ (4 1/2″) long.

BUDS: Terminal—imbricate, 3/16 to 1/4″ long and sharp pointed, cone-shaped, gray-brown, glabrous or hairy at apex; axillary buds 1/2 as long as terminal, hairs are found at upper edge of leaf scar and are brown in color.

STEM: Brown, often lustrous, glabrous, angled, lenticels are small and not as conspicuous as those of Black Maple.

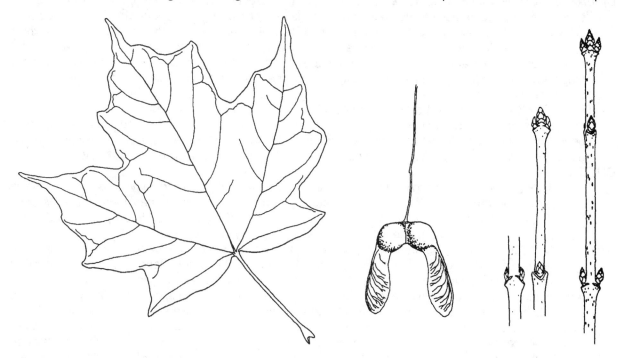

SIZE: A landscape size of 60 to 75′ is often attained; potential to 100 to 120′ in height; the spread is variable but usually about 2/3′s the height although some specimens show a rounded character; national champion is 87′ by 100′ in Kingston, NH.

HARDINESS: Zone 4 to 8.

HABIT: Upright-oval to rounded; usually quite dense in foliage.

RATE: Slow, possibly medium in youth; the size of one recorded specimen was 23′ in 28 years and 62′ in 128 years; obviously this indicates that Sugar Maple is of slow growth; however, has grown 23′ high and 23′ wide in ten years in Oregon tests; *Journal of Arboriculture* 16: 231–235 (1990) presented worthwhile information on growth rate of *Acer platanoides*, *A. saccharinum*, and *A. saccharum* using more than 3000 trees in the study in Rochester and Syracuse, NY. Silver maples were the tallest of the three, however, the average mature height for all three species was 75 to 80′. Average height of Sugar Maple was greater than Norway Maple for trees up to 28″ diameter.

TEXTURE: Medium in leaf and winter; I have seen delicately branched specimens of a distinct upright-oval character which appeared fine in winter character.

BARK: Young trees develop a smooth, gray-brown bark; with age the bark becomes deeply furrowed, with long irregular thick plates or ridges, sometimes quite scaly; bark is tremendously variable on this species; some trees from a distance remind one of a Shagbark Hickory.

LEAF COLOR: Usually a medium to dark green in summer (not as dark as Norway or Black Maple); changing to brilliant yellow, burnt orange and limited red tones in autumn; there is great variation in fall color among members of this species; the New England types seem to show more orange and red than the southern Indiana, Ohio, and Illinois group which develops a beautiful golden yellow; cultivated trees in Georgia develop good fall coloration; magnificent in the fall even in 7b–8a, colors persist on selected trees into late November in the Athens area; with the newer, heat tolerant cultivars there is much more latitude for successful use in Zones 7–8.

FLOWERS: Perfect, staminate or pistillate, apetalous, 5-sepals, campanulate, 1/5 to 1/4″ wide, greenish yellow, borne on 1 to 3″ long pendulous hairy pedicels in subsessile corymbs; stamens exserted in the staminate flower, before the leaves in April; attractive in a subtle way.

FRUIT: Samara, glabrous, 1 to 1 3/4″ long, somewhat horseshoe-shaped with nearly parallel or slightly divergent wings, maturing September–October; often devoid of sound seed.

CULTURE: Transplant balled and burlapped; prefers well-drained, moderately moist, fertile soil; pH-no preference although a slightly acid soil seems to result in greater growth; does not perform well in tight, compacted situations such as planter boxes, small tree lawns or other restricted growing areas; not extremely air pollution tolerant; tolerates shade and is often seen on the forest floor under a canopy of leaves gradually developing and assuming its place in the climax forest; susceptible to salt.

DISEASES AND INSECTS: Leaf scorch (a physiological disorder) can be a serious problem caused by excessive drought; *Verticillium* wilt; in the early sixties many New England Sugar Maples were declining or dying and the cause was unknown; this "Maple Decline" was attributed to drought conditions which persisted in the fifties and affected the overall vigor of the trees and made them more susceptible to insect and disease attacks; apparently, the problem has subsided for the noticeable decline has ceased; pear thrips have been a problem in the Northeast in recent years, see *Tree Physiology* 9: 401–413 (1991) for details on the insect.

LANDSCAPE VALUE: One of the best of the larger shade and lawn trees; excellent for lawn, park, golf course, possibly as street tree where tree lawns are extensive; definitely not for crowded and polluted conditions; beautiful fall color and pleasing growth habit, suffers from extended heat and if used in the South should be located away from stressful sites, 'Legacy' has been used successfully in downtown Atlanta.

CULTIVARS:

Adirondak®—Compact ascending branching structure with tightly layered leaves, overall outline is pyramidal, dark green foliage turns golden orange two weeks later than most Sugar Maples, supposedly more drought resistant than typical species, 75 to 90′ by 25 to 30′; listed as Zone 3, 'Adirzam' is the cultivar name, introduced by Lake County Nursery, Perry, OH.

Appollo™ ('Barrett Cole')—Symmetrical, narrow, tight-columnar shape, 25′ high and 10′ wide after 30-years in an urban environment, dense branching and short internode length, dark green summer foliage, yellowish orange to red in autumn, Zone 4 to 7, Schmidt Nursery introduction.

'Arrowhead'—Upright, pyramidal head with a strong leader and dense branching, large dark green leaves, yellow to orange fall color 60′ tall by 30′ wide; Schichtel, Orchard Park, NY, introduction.

'Bonfire'—Polished medium green, 5″ long by 5″ wide leaves which supposedly turn brilliant carmine red in fall, canopy broad oval, vigorous grower and appears to be a fast growing cultivar, exhibits good heat tolerance and resistance to leaf hopper; I have not observed good fall color on this form, the best to date was yellow-orange; fall color in the Midwest has not been good; 50′ by 40′, included in Milliken Arboretum, Spartanburg, SC where it has grown satisfactorily but not developed good fall color, defoliated by early November in Spartanburg which is earlier than other Sugar Maples, have been sent photographs by Princeton Nursery that depicted good reddish fall color; Minnesota evaluations showed it a vigorous grower, oval crown, irregular branching, with fall color inferior to other cultivars, have seen size estimations of 65′ by 50′, plant patent 3817, introduced circa 1965.

Caddo—An epithet without botanical merit to describe a disjunct population of *Acer saccharum* from Oklahoma; I was fortunate to travel with Steve Bieberich, Clinton, OK, John Barbour, Bold Spring Nursery, Monroe, GA, and Mike Glenn, Select Trees, Athens, GA to Red Rocks Canyon State Park, Hinton, OK to see the tree in its natural state. Trees in landscapes around Hinton and Clinton, OK were compact, some in the 30 to possibly 50′ range, with leathery, deeply lobed, dark green leaves, the trees are extremely heat and drought tolerant, fall color is variable and borders on spectacular on certain trees; the late Dr. John Pair, Kansas State University, has shown me slides of a magnificent red fall colored specimen; I suspect several worthy introductions will emerge from this western extreme of *Acer saccharum*. I planted several Caddo seedlings in my Georgia test plots. All died and the cause is unknown. Possibility that excessive moisture (at times) and heavy wet soils might limit success in parts of the eastern United States. Appears to be a good form for Plains States.

'Cary'—Slow-growing form, shorter and more compact than the species; foliage dense, one-half size of species, long-lasting; habit narrow bell-shaped; plant patent 2581 (1965).

'Commemoration'—Vigorous, fast-growing oval-rounded 50′ by 35′ tree with dense canopy, calipers well at an early age, moderately spreading crown; heavy textured glossy dark green leaves abundant throughout the crown, resistant to leaf tatter, fall color deep yellow-orange-red occurring 10 to 14 days earlier than species, a Bill Wandell introduction; like 'Legacy' has performed well in Zone 7b, fall color is yellow-orange, peak fall color in early November (Spartanburg, SC), one of the fastest growing cultivars, plant patent 5079.

Crescendo™ ('Morton')—Thick dark green foliage, superb orange-red fall color, excellent heat and drought tolerance, planted in 1960s at Morton Arboretum, Lisle, IL, parent tree 25 to 30′ high with a broad-oval head, derived from a western seed source, perhaps Illinois, good grower in nursery, similar to Green Mountain® in shape, Keith Warren, horticulturist, Schmidt Nursery, considers this a worthy addition.

'Endowment'—Columnar, compact cylindrical head, rapid growth, scorch free dark green summer foliage, orange-red fall color, 50′ by 20′, most reports list fall color as yellow, plant patent 4654, Siebenthaler introduction, slow growing in Zone 7b, but with outstanding orange-red fall color.

Fairview™—Sturdy broad-oval tree growing 50′ by 40′, leaves emerald green, changing to yellow and orange in fall, supposedly calipers faster than other cultivars, has not performed well or fall colored in Zones 7b–8a, in 1996, fall color was birch yellow.

Fall Fiesta™—Upright rounded habit, 50 to 70′ high, 50′ wide, fast growing compared to other Sugar Maple selections, summer foliage is thick, leathery, glossy green, fall colors are yellow, orange, and red, foliage is resistant to leaf tatter, selected from a seedling population in Oregon, Zone 4 to 7, Bailey Nursery introduction.

'Globosum'—Round headed form, 20-year-old plant being 10′ by 10′, good yellow fall color; not common; my knowledge of this clone, probably more than one, was scant but in recent years have seen specimens in the 20 to 25′ range, extremely dense branches and foliage, not a total landscape abomination and the excellent yellow to orange fall color is a worthwhile attribute; Mr. Theodore Klein (89-years-young), Crestwood, KY, who I had the pleasure of meeting in January 1994, introduced several forms ('Shawnee', 'Natchez') that are more compact and oval in outline than the typical 'Globosum'; two fine specimens are housed in Bernheim Arboretum, both are derived from witches' brooms discovered in Oldham County, KY; the 20-year-old plants in Bernheim are still compact and dense.

'Goldspire'—Densely columnar, leathery dark green foliage, highly resistant to scorch, rich bright yellow-orange fall color, 40′ by 15 to 20′; a Princeton introduction, plant patent 2917 (1969), supposedly a hybrid between 'Temple's Upright' and 'Newton Sentry'.

'Greencolumn'—Form of *A. nigrum* selected by Bill Heard of Des Moines, Iowa. Found growing in a stand in the central part of the state; selected for upright, columnar shape, maintains a central leader, 65′ high, 25′ wide; leaves yellow-orange in fall; hardy in Zone 4, worthwhile trying in Zone 3; displays visible characteristics and functional qualities that indicate successful performance in the Midwest, plant patent 3722.

Green Mountain®—Dark green leathery foliage with good scorch resistance; supposedly orange to scarlet in fall but reports from Midwest indicate yellow and from Pacific Northwest yellow-red; upright oval crown; supposed hybrid of *Acer saccharum* and *Acer nigrum*; quite heat tolerant and performs better than species in dry restricted growing areas; 7.2′ and 5′ wide after 4 years. 70′ high by 45′ wide; Princeton Introduction. Averaged 1′1″ growth per year over a 10 year period in Wichita tests; developed severe leaf scorch, fall color is yellow-orange in South, inferior to 'Legacy' and 'Commemoration', plant patent 2339.

Johnnycake™ ('Jocazam')—Uniform pyramidal crown, large rich green leaves, orange-red fall color, vigorous grower, 65′ by 40′.

'Lanco Columnar'—Broad columnar form, resists summer scorch and frost crack, excellent fall color, plant patent 4654 (1981).

'Legacy'—Crown heavier with better distribution of leaves throughout; glossy dark green leaves thicker with heavy wax; approximately 1.5 times thicker than species, no leaf tatter, good yellow-orange fall color; has proven superior in South; leaves are dark green and tatter-free into late October on Georgia campus trees; appears to be the best of the newer, drought resistant cultivars; as previously mentioned this is a winner in Zones 6 to 8 and has also performed well in Minnesota where the fall color was orange-red, leaves hold late, some into winter, with fall color starting in early November and fading by late November; excellent tight oval head as a young tree; has substance as a 1 1/2 to 3″ diameter tree; can appear somewhat "butter-ball" shaped because of density; Wandell introduction, plant patent 4979, 50′ by 35′.

'Majesty' ('Flax Mill Majesty')—Fast growing, symmetrically ovoid, large thick dark green leaves turning red-orange in fall, free from frost crack and sun scald, thick branching structure, perhaps 2 to 3 times the branch number of the species, 60 to 80′ by 40 to 50′, has withstood –38°F, performed well in Minnesota with excellent orange to red fall color, plant patent 5273. Flax Mill Nursery Inc., Cambridge, NY.

'Millane's Dwarf'—Unusual, slow growing dwarf tree, 2 to 3″ of growth per year, egg-shaped outline, specimen plant, 8′ high and 3′ wide in 15 years.

'Moraine' (See 'Wright Brothers')

Mountain Park™—Uniform branching as a young tree, mildew resistant foliage that develops excellent orange-red fall color, 50 to 75′ high, Zone 3, Moller Nursery introduction.

'Newton Sentry' ('Columnare')—Found by the entrance to Newton Cemetery, Newton, MA and introduced by F.L. Temple, a Cambridge, MA nurseryman around 1885–86; Temple described the original tree as 30′ high and only 2.5′ in diameter at the top; the leaves leathery, thick and dark green; in 1983 the original tree was 50′ high, 14′ wide, with a 16″ caliper; it is the most upright of all maples and presents a rather harsh winter silhouette; generally it does not maintain a single central leader above 6′ from the ground, the major and minor branches are laden with short stubby branchlets, fall color is yellow-orange like the species.

'Seneca Chief'—Narrow tree with oval crown; dense branching; fall color orange to yellow, 50′ by 20′, Schichtel Nursery introduction.

'Skybound'—Upright, tight almost oval crown, excellent yellow-orange fall color, introduced by Synnesvedt Nursery, Illinois.

'Slavin's Upright'—Upright form with strongly ascending branches, considered an *A. nigrum* type.

Steeple™—Narrow, symmetrically oval growth habit, heat and drought resistant, dark green summer foliage, yellow-orange fall color, 45′ by 20′ after 26 years; the parent tree is in Athens, GA and was selected by Michael Dirr and introduced through Athena Trees, Inc.; nonsense cultivar name is 'Astis'.

'Summer Proof'—Vigorous spreading form; heat tolerant and does not suffer from windburn.

'Sweet Shadow'—Leaves deeply cut, each lobe also cut, medium green, yellow to orange fall color, most trees I have seen were rounded, although literature says oval to vase-shaped; have seen this cultivar at a number of locations throughout the Midwest and East, appears to be adaptable; grows quite vigorously, growing in Minnesota and Maine campus, hardy to at least −30°F, plant patent 2139 (1962), 45′ by 35′.

'Temple's Upright' ('Monumentale')—Often confused with 'Newton Sentry' but maintaining a central leader well into the crown, the major branches ascending and absence of short stubby lateral branchlets; the outline is distinctively elliptical and the branches ascend and gently curve upwards; a 98-year-old tree in the Arnold Arboretum was 60′ high, 17′ wide with a 16″ diameter.

'Wright Brothers'—Broad cone-shaped head, brilliant fall color of mottled gold, pink, orange and scarlet; rapid growth rate, calipers at approximately twice the rate per year as seedling *A. saccharum*, non frost cracking, resistant to scorch, hardy to −25°F, 50 to 75′, Zone 3, introduced by The Siebenthaler Nursery, plant patent 4534, formerly called 'Moraine'.

PROPAGATION: Seed should be stratified in moist medium for 60 to 90 days at 41°F; take note that seeds are often hollow, i.e., fruits form but no seed inside the nutlet (pericarp), need to run a cut test (pruners, knife) and open up 10 seeds, then another subset, etc., to obtain representative sample; one can *collect* the fruits all day and *never* have a viable seed; cuttings collected in early June and treated with 1000 ppm IBA-talc rooted 57%; not considered easy to root from cuttings; all cultivars are budded on seedling understocks.

ADDITIONAL NOTES: *Acer saccharum* is an outstanding native tree, unexcelled for fall color; sap is boiled down to make maple syrup; a trip to a sugar camp in February or March is a unique experience; takes about 40 gallons of sap to make a gallon of syrup; trees are being selected with the highest possible sugar content; 'Sweet' Sugar Maple with 4% sap (twice norm) was developed at The Ohio State University, apparently it is seed produced; wood makes great furniture and bird's eye maple is much cherished; also used to mellow (filter) Jack Daniels Whiskey, Lynchburg, TN as the alcohol is passed through sugar maple charcoal.

Sugar Maple is not easy to taxonomically pidgeon-hole and several varieties/ subspecies exist and are treated under related species. Most of the inadequately defined taxa occur in the Southeast and Southwest. An excellent practical discussion by Benny Simpson and Billy Hipp, "Maples of the Southwest," *American Nurseryman* 177(5): 26–35 (1993) should be consulted by anyone who wants to understand the taxonomic relationships. In brief, the authors ascribed 8, possibly 9, maples to the Southwest including:

A. barbatum (*A. floridanum*)—Southern (Florida) Sugar Maple
A. glabrum—Rocky Mountain Maple
A. grandidentatum—Bigtooth or Western Sugar Maple
A. leucoderme—Chalkbark Maple
A. negundo—Boxelder
A. nigrum—Black Maple
A. rubrum—Red Maple
A. saccharinum—Silver Maple
and possibly *A. saccharum*—Sugar Maple

Also, other references ascribe subspecies or variety status to *barbatum*, *leucoderme*, *grandidentatum*, and *nigrum*. Ideally do not become frozen with fear relative to the "correct" name. I know no recent deaths from taxonomic poisoning.

Simpson and Hipp studied chlorosis resistance of these various maples and recommended the Caddo strain and certain provenances of the Bigtooth Maple for high pH soils.

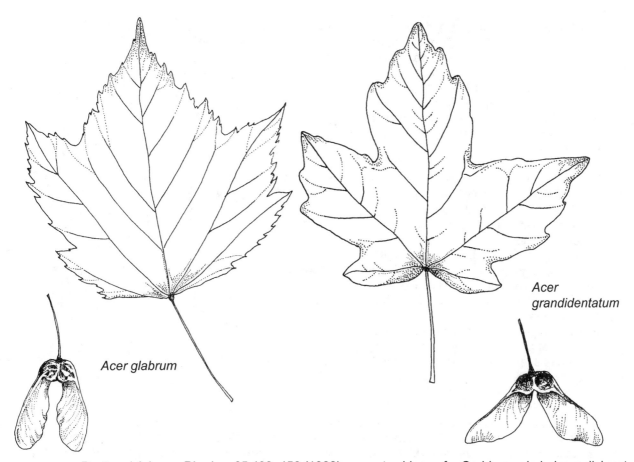

Acer glabrum

Acer
grandidentatum

Dent and Adams, *Rhodora* 85:439–456 (1982) present evidence for Caddo maple being a disjunct of *Acer saccharum* subsp. *saccharum*.

Studies by Dr. John Pair at the Horticulture Research Center, Kansas State University, Wichita, showed large differences in stress (heat and drought) of Sugar Maple taxa. 'Legacy' and 'Commemoration' were the most scorch- and tatter-free of the 10 types tested, with the exception of Caddo sugar maple seedlings that represent a disjunct *Acer saccharum* population from the Red Rocks Canyon in Caddo County near Hinton, OK.

On a 0 to 9 scale, with 9 representing no scorch (browning of margins), 'Legacy' scored 8.6, 'Commemoration'—7.3, 'Green Mountain'—4.4 (50 percent of leaves were scorched) and Caddo seedlings—8.8.

The leaf tatter (tearing of leaves caused by wind and unknown factors) test rated percentage of total leaf area affected. The findings: 'Legacy'— 3.2, 'Commemoration'—8.0, 'Green Mountain'—22.0, and Caddo—6.8. There were no statistical differences among 'Legacy', 'Commemoration' and Caddo.

Growth rates for all sugar maple types were 12' to 19' from 1983 to 1990; Caddo grew 18.5', 'Commemoration'—16', 'Green Mountain'—14.5', and 'Legacy'—14'.

In 1982, Santamour and McArdle published a checklist of cultivated *Acer saccharum* taxa, *J. Arboriculture* 8:164–167. This should be consulted for the odd cultivar not included herein. Also, van Gelderen et al., *Maples of the World*, list additional cultivars.

NATIVE HABITAT: Eastern Canada to Georgia, Alabama, Mississippi and Texas. Introduced 1753.

RELATED SPECIES:

Acer barbatum Michx. — Florida Maple, Southern Sugar Maple
LEAVES: Opposite, simple, 3 to 6″ high, 3 to 6″ wide, 3- to 5-lobed, lobes not as finger-like as *A. leucoderme*, sinuses more deeply cut in U or V shapes, base truncate to slightly subcordate, dark green above, glabrous above except for a few hairs where petiole joins blade; glaucous beneath and consistently hairy, more so on veins; petiole—3/4 to 3″ long, glabrous or pubescent.
BUDS: Similar to *A. leucoderme*, possibly plumper.
STEM: Slender, reddish brown with vertical lenticels, glabrous at maturity.

Acer barbatum (*A. floridanum*), (ā′sĕr bär-bā′ tum), Florida Maple, Southern Sugar Maple, is mentioned here because of its possible use as a Sugar Maple substitute in the South. It is essentially smaller in all parts compared to *A. saccharum* and occurs as a small spreading, 20 to 25′ high understory tree from Virginia to Florida, Louisiana, southeastern Missouri, Arkansas, and eastern Oklahoma and Texas. It is usually found along streams and swamps in both the Piedmont and Coastal Plain. If planted in the same area as *A. saccharum*, it normally flowers about two weeks earlier and colors two weeks later. The 3/4 to 1 1/4″ long fruits have an angle of 60 to 70°. The autumnal fall coloration is usually yellow and not as vibrant as the northern form. Some botanists list this as a subspecies or variety of *Acer saccharum*. Bill Inabinet, Bold Spring Nursery, Monroe, GA said it is not a nurseryman's tree . . . meaning it does not form a good head without considerable pruning. I have observed trees in several nurseries and the rankness and variation in growth were phenomenal. Fall color is not always as good as advertised but I have seen glowing yellow to reasonable orange with a red suffusion. Fall color was peaking on nursery grown trees at Piedmont, SC on November 15–25, 1994.

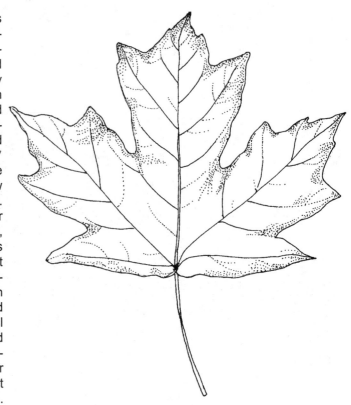

Also the size listed above in no way reflects the possibilities for this species for near Nacogdoches, TX trees in the 50 to 60′ range were common. Duncan and Duncan, 1988, *Trees of the Southeastern United States* lists size to 100′ high with 3′ trunk diameter. National champion is 100′ by 64′ in Jasper County, GA. Also, leaves often persist into and through winter on young trees. Many observations indicate this is common to *A. barbatum*, less so with *A. leucoderme*. Zone (6)7 to 9.

Acer leucoderme Small — Chalkbark Maple, Whitebark Maple

LEAVES: Opposite, simple, 3- to 5-lobed, 1 1/2 to 4″ high, 1″ to 3 1/2″ wide, lobes long acuminate, sinus shallow, base subcordate to cordate, medium green above, lighter green below, pubescent, consistently pubescent on herbarium specimens; petiole—1 to 3″ long, glabrous.

*One of the key ways I have found to separate this from *A. barbatum* is that the leaves are green on both sides, while *A. barbatum* is glaucous (gray-green) below.

BUDS: Similar to Sugar Maple but smaller with short silky pubescence at edges of bud scales.

STEM: Fine, reddish brown, with vertical lenticels, essentially glabrous.

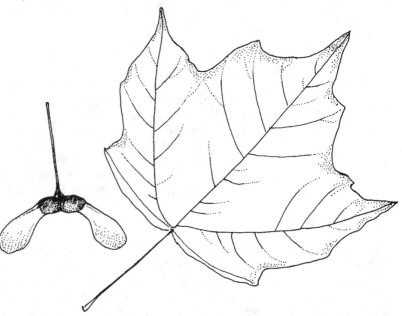

Acer leucoderme, (ā′sēr lū-kō-dēr′mē), Chalkbark or Whitebark Maple, is another southern variation of Sugar Maple. It is quite similar to *A. barbatum* but is supposedly more pubescent on the underside of the leaf. I have studied herbarium specimens and would say that the two are quite difficult to separate (see under LEAVES). The 1 to 1 1/4″ long samara wings of the fruits spread at a wider angle (50 to 60°) than those of *A. saccharum* and *A. barbatum*. *Acer leucoderme* is found in drier, upland woods in the Piedmont from

North Carolina to Georgia, panhandle of Florida, Louisiana, eastern Oklahoma and Texas. It occurs as an understory species and matures at about 25 to 30′. Co-national champions are 57′ by 36′ and 49′ by 35′ both in Sumter National Forest, SC. In the Georgia Botanical Garden, numerous specimens occur and in fall put on a dazzling show that rivals *Acer saccharum*. Trees are often multi-stemmed. Trees vary from yellow-orange to deep red. Several nurserymen are growing this species and hopefully it will be "accepted" by the landscape designers and public. It is smaller in all parts compared to Sugar Maple and displays good dry soil tolerance. In nursery production, side-by-side plantings of *A. barbatum* and *A. leucoderme* show the former is larger in all its parts, faster growing and could be a better commercial item. Unfortunately the variation is tremendous and next to *A. saccharum* 'Legacy' and 'Commemoration' neither species will compete. May be listed as a subspecies of *A. saccharum*. Zone 5 to 9.

Acer nigrum Michx. f. — Black Maple
LEAVES: Opposite, simple, 3 to 6″ wide, 3- to 5-lobed, deeply cordate with closed sinus, lobes acute, sides of blade drooping, dull dark green above, yellow-green beneath, pubescent; petiole—3 to 5″ long, usually pubescent, often enlarged at base, stipules present.
BUDS: Imbricate, pubescent, much more so than Sugar Maple, tend to be plumper than Sugar Maple buds and gray-dust-brown in color; 2 axillary buds at terminal, 1/2 to 3/4's as long as terminal.
STEM: Straw colored with prominent lenticels; much more so than Sugar Maple.

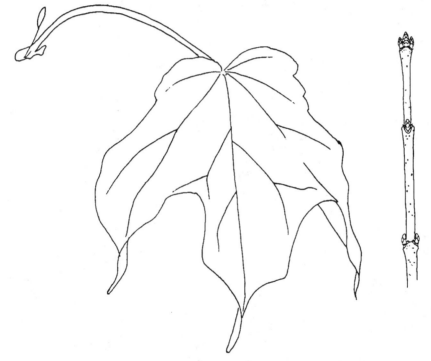

Acer nigrum, (ā′sĕr nī′grum), Black Maple, is extremely similar to *A. saccharum* and is often difficult to differentiate. The principal differences are the drooping lateral leaf lobes, the stipules that are present at the base of the petiole, the more pubescent underside of the leaf and the yellow fall color. Growth habit and size are similar to *A. saccharum*. National champion is 118′ by 127′ in Allegan County, MI. Perhaps the most important difference is the supposed greater heat and drought tolerance of Black compared to Sugar Maple. At times I have trouble accepting this because in the Midwest, plants of both grow side by side and appear equally satisfied. Black Maple is found further west in Minnesota, Iowa, Kansas and Arkansas, although one range map showed distribution from New England, south to North Georgia, Alabama, and Arkansas. Selections from these western populations might exhibit greater drought tolerance. Grew 4″ per year over a 9 year period in Wichita tests; large bare-root trees did not establish well and developed some leaf scorch. 'Greencolumn', listed under *A. saccharum*, is a Black Maple selection from Iowa. Black Maple should never be slighted for it is equal to Sugar Maple in ornamental characteristics and perhaps superior in tolerance to hostile growing conditions. Pair et al. presented quantitative data for selected Sugar Maple taxa from 1983 to 1990. *Acer nigrum* seedlings were the slowest growing plants in terms of height and caliper. Also leaf tatter rating as percent of total leaf area was much higher than expected at 16 percent compared to Caddo, 'Commemoration', and 'Legacy' at 6.8, 8.0, and 3.2, respectively. In Dr. Pair's 1996 report, seedlings of *A. nigrum* developed significant leaf spotting, curling, and tatter. Fall color was the worst of the 10 taxa tested.

Graves, *HortScience* 79: 1292–1294 (1994), reported that Sugar Maple seedlings and Black Maple seedlings on 10-, 26- and 42-day irrigation intervals grew at different rates with the former producing greater dry weight on 10-day intervals. Black Maple had a greater capacity to withstand drought at the decreased irrigation frequencies. The authors noted the relatively slow growth of Black Maple compared to Sugar Maple.

Most researchers and plantsmen have intuitively concluded that Black Maple would prove "better" than Sugar Maple for more drought stressed environments. Based on the above studies, a superior selection of Sugar Maple appears preferable to seedling grown Black Maple. In the main, this is the situation in nursery production.

The yellow fall color needs no apologies. Quebec and New England to New York, West Virginia, and Kentucky, west to South Dakota, Iowa, Kansas, and Arkansas. Introduced 1812. Zone 4 to 8.

Acer spicatum Lam. — Mountain Maple
(ā′sĕr spi-kā′tum)

LEAVES: Opposite, simple, 3-lobed or sometimes slightly 5-lobed, 2 to 5″ long and wide, lobes ovate, acuminate, coarsely and irregularly serrate, cordate at base, dark yellowish green and smooth above, paler beneath and covered with a short grayish down.

BUDS: Usually less than 1/4″ long, stalked, pointed, red but dull with minute, appressed, grayish hairs, 2 visible scales (valvate).

STEM: Young stems grayish pubescent, developing purplish red, or often greenish on one side, minutely pubescent with short, appressed, grayish hairs, particularly about the nodes and toward the apex; leaf scars are narrowly crescent shaped.

SIZE: Variable, but 10 to 30′ in height and width over its native range, common at higher elevations in the southern Appalachians and usually shrubby or low-branched, the largest I have observed was about 25′ high; national champion is 58′ by 31′ in Houghton County, MI.

HARDINESS: Zone 3 to 7 at high elevations.

HABIT: Shrub or small, short trunked tree of bushy appearance.

RATE: Slow to medium.

TEXTURE: Medium.

BARK: Thin, brownish or grayish brown, smooth, eventually becoming slightly furrowed or warty.

LEAF COLOR: Dark yellowish green in summer, changing to yellow, orange and red in fall.

FLOWERS: Small, perfect, greenish yellow, borne in erect, 3 to 6″ long racemes in June, each flower on a slender stalk about 1/2″ long.

FRUIT: Samara, wings diverge at an acute or right angle, essentially glabrous at maturity, about 1″ long, nutlet 1/2″ long, apparently apomixis is important in the development of sound seed.

CULTURE: Transplant balled and burlapped; actually not well adapted to civilization and prefers cool, shady, acid, moist situations similar to where it is found in the wild.

DISEASES AND INSECTS: None serious.

LANDSCAPE VALUE: Limited; however, if native worth leaving; have observed it on the highest mountains in Georgia peeking its little head out of a mixed understory; leaves among native maples are unmistakable.

PROPAGATION: Seed requires 90 to 120 days at 41°F.

NATIVE HABITAT: Labrador to Saskatchewan, south to northern Georgia and Iowa. Introduced 1750.

Acer tataricum L. — Tatarian Maple
(ā′sẽr tȧ-tär′i-kum)

LEAVES: Opposite, simple, 2 to 4″ long, usually unlobed, irregularly double serrate, bright to medium green above, often pubescent when young on veins beneath; on adult trees leaves are essentially unlobed, on young trees or vigorous shoots leaves may be 3- to 5-lobed and resemble *Acer ginnala*; often very difficult to separate these two maples; petiole—3/4 to 2″ long.

BUDS: Imbricate, small, 1/8 to 1/4″ long, reddish brown to brownish black, glabrous to slightly hairy.

STEM: Slender, glabrous, reddish brown to brown, angular, dotted with numerous lenticels.

SIZE: 15 to 20′ in height with a comparable spread; can grow to 30′ in height.

HARDINESS: Zone 3 to 8, seldom seen in Zone 7 to 8 and like *Acer ginnala*, best reserved for cooler climates; reports from University of Alberta, Canada, indicate *A. tataricum* is not as hardy as *A. ginnala*.

HABIT: A large multi-stemmed shrub of bushy habit or a small, rounded to wide spreading tree; have seen handsome tree specimens.

RATE: Slow to medium.

TEXTURE: Medium in foliage and in winter habit.

LEAF COLOR: Medium green in summer; yellow, red and reddish brown in fall; very variable; leaves fall earlier than those of *Acer ginnala*.

FLOWERS: Greenish white, appearing with the leaves in April–May, borne in upright 2 to 3″ long and wide panicles; not overwhelmingly ornamental but a definite asset in the landscape.

FRUIT: Samara, 3/4 to 1″ long, wings almost parallel, red, variable in intensity of color, July–August, effective 3 or more weeks before turning brown, fruit on some trees is green to brown.

CULTURE: Transplant balled and burlapped, tolerant of adverse conditions including drought; similar to *Acer ginnala*; averaged 10″ per year in Wichita tests over a 9 year period; may prove more alkaline soil tolerant than *A. ginnala*.

DISEASES AND INSECTS: None particularly serious.

LANDSCAPE VALUE: Handsome small specimen tree for the limited residential landscape, street tree use, perhaps planter boxes, groupings; could be used more than is currently being practiced; Michigan State and Ohio State campuses and Missouri Botanical Garden have handsome specimens.

CULTIVARS:
'Rubrum'—Leaves color a blood red in the fall.

PROPAGATION: Seed, 41°F for 90 to 180 days; cuttings collected in mid-August rooted 77% when treated with 10,000 ppm IBA talc.

ADDITIONAL NOTES: Nice small tree with landscape attributes similar to *Acer ginnala*; not common in commerce and probably never will be owing to pronounced similarity to *A. ginnala*; *Index of Garden Plants* by Griffiths reduces *A. ginnala* to a subspecies of *A. tataricum*, certainly the two are morphologically similar but *Acer ginnala* and the various cultivars are better landscape plants.

NATIVE HABITAT: Southeast Europe, western Asia, in sunny dry situations, often as forest undergrowth, rarely as solitary tree. Introduced 1759.

Acer truncatum Bunge — Purpleblow Maple, Shantung Maple
(ā′sẽr trun-kā′tum)

LEAVES: Opposite, simple, 3 to 5″ wide, not as high, 5(7)-lobed, each lobe ovate to triangular in shape, two basal lobes drawn out, often truncate at base, lobes acuminate, dark green above, paler beneath, glabrous except at point of attachment to petiole where axillary tufts of pubescence occur; petiole—2 to 4″ long, glabrous, contains milky sap.

BUDS: Terminal—imbricate, plump, reddish brown, 4-sided, 1/4″ high, essentially glabrous, tips of upper scales with pubescence, resembles Norway Maple bud; laterals—much smaller.

STEM: Moderate, lustrous reddish brown, glabrous, slightly lenticelled, leaf scars meet at a point like Norway.

SIZE: 20 to 25′(30′) in height with a spread slightly less than or equal to height.

HARDINESS: Zone 4 to 8, will withstand −20 to −25°F (Zone 4), successful at Morton Arboretum and Minnesota Landscape Arboretum; also University of Maine is blessed with a handsome specimen that survived −30°F and below; University of Minnesota lists adaptability to Zone 3b.

HABIT: Small, round-headed tree of neat outline with a regular branching pattern; often densely branched and foliaged.

RATE: Slow.

TEXTURE: Medium in all seasons.

BARK: Often tinged with purple when young; older branches assuming a gray-brown color; mature trunks rough and fissured.

LEAF COLOR: Reddish purple when emerging (very beautiful) gradually changing to dark glossy green in summer; fall color, as observed at the National and Arnold Arboreta, was an excellent combination of yellow-orange-red; some trees glistening yellow-orange; a small tree in the Dirr garden develops muted yellow-orange.

FLOWERS: Greenish yellow, 1/3 to 1/2″ diameter, each on a slender stalk 1/2″ long, borne in erect branching, 3″ diameter corymbs in May, can be spectacular, much akin to flowers of *A. platanoides*.

FRUIT: Samara, 1 1/4 to 1 1/2″ long, forming an angle of about 90°, wings may spread obtusely.

CULTURE: A relatively hardy tree which thrives under conditions similar to those required for *Acer griseum*; I have seen many specimens and they appeared vigorous and healthy in the Midwest, East, and the Middle Atlantic States; averaged 1′4″ per year over a 9 year period and developed purplish fall color and purplish fruits; a Chinese study concluded that the species was extremely drought tolerant.

DISEASES AND INSECTS: None particularly serious, tar spot has been reported.

LANDSCAPE VALUE: A very lovely small maple with potential for street or residential areas; do not know why the tree is not better known; appears to have potential for urban areas; resistant to leaf scorch and may prove a valuable addition to the list of urban trees; I have a small plant in my garden and am encouraged by performance in Zone 7, 8. Dr. John Pair, Kansas State, has championed this fine tree because of heat and drought tolerance; his article in *Proc. Intl. Plant Prop. Soc.* 36:403–408 (1988) presents an ornamental and propagational overview.

CULTIVARS: No commercial straight species cultivars but evaluation work at Wichita, KS by Dr. Pair indicated significant variation in cold hardiness, borer damage, growth and fall color with clones from Ames, IA, Michigan State University, and Morton Arboretum proving superior. See 1996 Woody Ornamental Evaluations, Report of Progress 770. Wichita Horticulture Research Center. Kansas State.

Norwegian Sunset™ ('Keithsform')—An upright oval outline with good branch structure and uniform canopy structure, glossy dark green foliage turns yellow-orange to red in fall, exhibits more heat and drought tolerance than typical Norway, 35′ by 25′, hardy to −25°F, hybrid between *Acer truncatum* and *A. platanoides*; has performed well in Zone 7b in Spartanburg, SC; based on side-by-side evaluations of this and Pacific Sunset™, I would opt for the latter; a 1989 Schmidt introduction, plant patent 7529.

Pacific Sunset™ ('Warrenred')—An upright spreading, rounded crown form with finer branch structure than 'Norwegian Sunset', 30′ by 25′, very glossy dark green summer foliage colors, bright yellow-orange to red in fall, colors a little earlier than 'Norwegian Sunset', *Acer truncatum* × *A. platanoides* hybrid, hardy to −25°F, a 1989 Schmidt introduction, plant patent 7433, as mentioned appears to be the bests small landscape tree of the two, colors yellow-orange in autumn in Zone 7b.

PROPAGATION: 30 to 60 days cold moist stratification produced 85% or higher germination; Pair (1996) reported that seed have a short stratification period and often germinate after 32 days of chilling. Sometimes soaking overnight and chilling for only two weeks can break dormancy. June cuttings from a 10-year-old tree rooted 71 and 79% after treatment with 1000 and 5000 ppm IBA solution, respectively. T-budding (wood removed) in August (Kansas) has been successful. *Acer truncatum* and *A. t.* subsp. *mayrii* are monoecious but male and female flowers do not open at the same time; hence, most seeds are void of embryos; Dr. Paul Cappiello, University of Maine, mentioned that he found a small number of sound seeds on the lone campus tree.

ADDITIONAL NOTES: As the breadth of my observations increases, I question the lack of commonality of the species; the obvious answer lies in lack of cultivars and promotion; the everyday requirement for small trees is significant; expect to see *A. truncatum* gain landscape momentum in the next 5 to 10 years.

NATIVE HABITAT: Northern China. Also Russia, Japan, Korea, Manchuria. Introduced 1881.

RELATED SPECIES: The nomenclature of *A. mono* is frighteningly confusing and I am not absolutely sure how to treat it so will stay with the previous edition's format. Hillier Manual treats it as a species *A. mono* Maxim., Griffiths as *A. mono* Maxim., with *mayrii* (Schwerin) Nak. as a variety; and Meyer et al. place it in synonymy with *A. truncatum*. In *Maples of the World* van Gelderen et al. treat *A. mono* as a species with *mayrii* a variety.

Acer truncatum subsp. *mono* Murray — Painted Maple

LEAVES: Opposite, simple, 5(7)-lobed, 3 to 6″ across, each lobe tapering to a long, narrow acuminate apex, entire, truncate or cordate, dark green above, lighter beneath, pubescent on veins; petiole—2 to 4″ long, pubescent, milky sap at base.

BUDS: Terminal— imbricate, ovoid, 4 to 6 scaled, 3/16 to 1/4″ long, weakly 4-sided, deep purplish red with a luster, edges of scale finely pubescent, apex of bud silky pubescent.

STEM: Slender, glabrous, reddish brown to purple, no prominent lenticels.

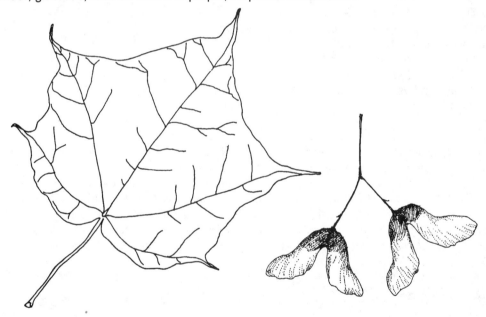

Acer truncatum subsp. *mono*, (ā′sēr trun-kā′tum mon-ō), Painted Maple, is a lovely small to medium sized landscape tree. The habit is somewhat vase-shaped with the branches forming a dome-like crown at maturity (30 to 40′). The dark green leaves may turn yellow orange in fall but on trees that I observed the leaves died off green because of early freezes. The greenish yellow flowers appear in 2 to 3″ long corymbose racemes in April–May. The samaras are 3/4 to 1 1/4″ long and spread at right angles to almost horizontally. The bark is Japanese Maple-like, smooth, gray, broken only by irregular, shallow, longitudinal fissures. This is one of the most beautiful trees in the Arnold Arboretum and as one walks along the Meadow Road this beautiful mushroom-headed tree looms on the horizon directly in front of the Japanese maples. Although similar to *A. truncatum* it differs in the larger leaves, more uniform habit and smoother bark. Other closely related taxa include *Acer cappadocicum* and *A. truncatum* subsp. *mayrii*, both of which have milky sap. The unfolding leaves of subsp. *mayrii* are a rich bronze and extremely attractive. During my 1991 sabbatical at the Arnold Arboretum, I tried again to make sense of subsp. *mayrii* compared to subsp. *mono* and *A. truncatum*. The new flowers and young leaves of subsp. *mayrii* were emerging on

4-26, significantly ahead of the other taxa listed. The yellowish flowers reminded of Norway Maple. Leaves of subsp. *mayrii* are mostly 5-lobed, almost round, thin textured, green on both surfaces, and glabrous. China, Manchuria and Korea. Introduced 1880. Zone (4) 5 to 8.

Acer cappadocicum Gled. — Coliseum Maple, Caucasian Maple

LEAVES: Opposite, simple, 5- to 7-lobed, 3 to 6″ across, cordate at base, lobes triangular-ovate, long acuminate, entire, rich green and finely reticulate beneath with axillary tufts of hairs; petiole—2 to 4″ long, milky sap at base of petiole.

STEM: Remains green the second and third years, smooth and gray thereafter.

Acer cappadocicum, (ā′sĕr kap-a-dō′sē-kum), Coliseum Maple, is virtually unknown in commercial horticulture and in many respects could be confused with *Acer truncatum* and subspecies *mono* and *mayrii*. A principal difference is that in subsp. *mono* the second year stems become gray-brown and wrinkled or fissured. The habit is rounded and landscape size approximates 25 to 30′. European literature describes the tree as stately and growing 80 to 100′ high. What I experienced were smaller trees. The yellow flowers occur with the leaves in 2″ long glabrous corymbs. The samara ranges from 1 1/4 to 1 3/4″ long and the wings spread at a wide angle. Tree appears quite adaptable and might be considered for more culturally difficult sites. 'Aureum' is a rather handsome yellow leaf form that emerges yellow, changes to green in summer and finally yellow in autumn. This form is quite common in European gardens and I have seen a specimen in Winchester, TN that was thriving. 'Rubrum' offers blackish red unfolding leaves that gradually change to green although the young tips of branches still maintain a reddish coloration. In England, this form has grown over 70′ high. In addition, several varieties are known which differ in leaf characteristics, primarily size and lobing. Caucasus and western Asia to Himalayas. Introduced 1838. Zone 5 to 7.

Actinidia arguta (Sieb. & Zucc.) Planch. ex Miq. — Bower Actinidia, Tara Vine
(ak-ti-nid′i-à är-gū′tà)

FAMILY: Actinidiaceae

LEAVES: Alternate, simple, broad-ovate to elliptic, 3 to 5″(6″) long, abruptly acuminate, rounded to subcordate at base, rarely cuneate, setosely and sharply serrate, lustrous dark green above, green beneath and usually setose on midrib; petiole—1 1/2 to 3″ long, sometimes setose, reddish purple.

BUDS: Small, concealed in the thickened cortex above the leaf scar, the end bud lacking.

STEM: Stout, brownish, heavily lenticelled (vertical), glabrous; pith—brown, lamellate; leaf scars raised with single bundle trace (looks like an eyeball).

SIZE: 25 to 30′ in height but seems to be limited only by the structure to which it is attached, supposedly growing to the tops of trees in its native lands.

HARDINESS: Zone 3 to 7b, often described as the hardy kiwi.

HABIT: Vigorous, high climbing, twining vine which requires support.

RATE: Fast, can grow 20′ in 2 to 3 years time.

TEXTURE: Medium in leaf; medium-coarse in winter; actually the tangled, jumbled thicket of winter stems would be considered coarse by most observers.

LEAF COLOR: Lustrous dark green in summer, petioles often with reddish tinge; fall coloration is yellowish green, leaves hold late and seldom show any change; beautiful, disease-free foliage.

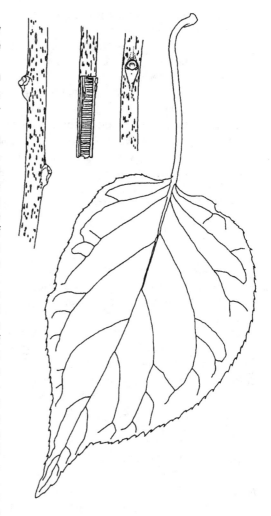

FLOWERS: Polygamo-dioecious, delicately fragrant, whitish or greenish white, 3 or more together in axils of leaves, each about 4/5″ across, and 1/2 to 3/4″ long; sepals green, ovate-oblong, blunt; waxy petals orbicular, white tinged with green, very concave and incurving giving the flowers a globular shape; numerous dark purple anthers; ovary with a short, stout style, at the top of which about 20 stigmas radiate like the spokes of a wheel; May–June, essentially hidden by the foliage, bee pollinated and one male can pollinate up to 8 females.

FRUIT: A greenish yellow, 1 to 1 1/4″ long by 3/4″ wide ellipsoidal berry with lime green flesh, chocolate-colored seeds; fruits have been described as possessing flavors ranging from insipid (unripe) to pleasant (?) to that of strawberries, melons, gooseberries and bananas; I sampled a ripe fruit at Fred and Mary Ann McGourty's in mid-October, 1984 and was, what's the term, pleasantly surprised by the mild mixed flavor; the species is effectively dioecious and a male must accompany the female for best fruit set; has received considerable attention in recent years as an edible landscape plant and a partial substitute for *Actinidia deliciosa* (*A. chinensis*), True Kiwi, in cold climates; advantages of *A. arguta* fruits include the hairless nature, no peeling, high vitamin C (10 times higher than oranges), as much potassium as a 6″ long banana, high in fiber, low in calories and sodium free; two mature vines (male and female) may produce up to 10 gallons of fruit per year; fruits can be stored up to 16 weeks in the refrigerator; any fruiting plant with so many virtues must be looked upon with great skepticism; yes, and fat-free potato chips are as good as the type that leave grease stains on clothes . . . do I believe this!?

CULTURE: Like most rampant vines easy to transplant; usually container grown; this is probably the most vigorous of the *Actinidia* species; will tolerate any type soil but best sited in infertile soil to reduce rapid growth; full sun or partial shade; needs considerable pruning and this can be accomplished about any time of year; probably one of the most adaptable vines; for best fruit production, each winter the stems should be cut back to 8 to 10 buds, in the Department of Horticulture's edible fruit test plots, this species is thriving in rock hard clay and spreading faster than crabgrass, interestingly, *Actinidia deliciosa* was killed to the ground while *A. arguta* prospered.

DISEASES AND INSECTS: None serious.

LANDSCAPE VALUE: Good vine for quick cover but can rapidly overgrow its boundaries; the foliage is excellent and for problem areas where few other vines will grow *Actinidia arguta* could be used; has possibilities for home garden use especially in cold climates.

CULTIVARS:

'Ananasnaja'—A cold hardy form that is available in modern day commerce, sweet pineapple fruit to 1″ diameter, have seen this cultivar listed as a possible hybrid of *A. arguta* × *A. kolomikta*.

'Issai'—A hermaphroditic (perfect flowered) selection and no male is necessary for fruit set, flowers and fruits as a young plant, fruits up to 1 1/2″ long, smooth skinned, sweet.

'Purpurea' (*A. purpurea*)—Produces purple fruit.

Other cultivars include '119-40B'—bisexual clone; '125-40'—prolific bearer of high quality fruit (USDA introduction); 'Akin #3'—rounded, larger fruit than 'Ananasnaja'; 'Chico 74-62'—long cylindrical fruit, smooth skinned, sweet, less productive than 'Ananasnaja', but larger fruited; 'Geneva #1'—high quality fruit and exceptional cold tolerance; 'Geneva #2'—heavy bearing; 'Langer'—highest quality clone for Northwest; also various unnamed male and female clones have been described.

Several vendors for edible landscape plants and particularly *Actinidia* taxa include Burnt Ridge Nursery and Orchards, Onalaska, WA; Northwoods Nursery, Molalla, OR; and Edible Landscaping, Afton, VA.

PROPAGATION: All species can be propagated by seed; stratification for 3 months at 41°F in a moist medium is recommended, but *A. kolomikta* has shown a double dormancy and requires a warm plus cold stratification; tremendous amount of cutting research especially on *A. deliciosa* (see Dirr and Heuser); softwood and hardwood cuttings have been successful; June–July cuttings, slightly firm, 3000 to 5000 ppm IBA-solution, peat:perlite, and mist would be a good starting point; there are literally hundreds of recipes for success; generally rooting percentages will fall in the 50 to 80% category; for some strange reason entire papers are devoted to the propagation of *Actinidia* species; perhaps the best for the lay person is Philip McMillan Browse *The Plantsman* 6(3): 167–180. "Some notes on Actinidias and their propagation." Also a tissue culture paper in *HortScience* 27:443–445 (1992) describes the successful regeneration of *Actinidia deliciosa* 'Hayward'.

NATIVE HABITAT: Japan, Korea, Manchuria. Cultivated 1874.

RELATED SPECIES:

Actinidia deliciosa C.S. Liang & A.R. Ferguson (formerly *A. chinensis*) — Chinese Gooseberry or Kiwi Fruit

LEAVES: Alternate, simple, orbicular or oval, 3 to 5″(7″) long, cordate at base, rounded, emarginate or on vigorous shoots acuminate, crenate-serrulate, newly emerging leaves purplish gradually changing to dark green, densely pubescent at first, finally slightly hairy above and densely tomentose beneath with reddish hairs on veins; petiole—1 1/2 to 3″ long, densely covered with reddish hairs.

STEM: Thick, brown, with shaggy brown hairs; pith—whitish to yellowish and solid.

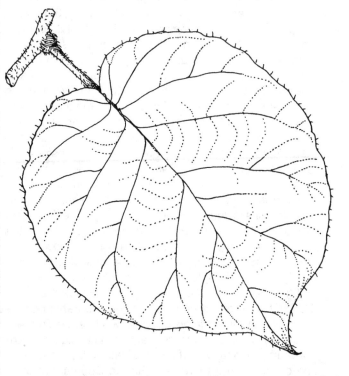

Actinidia deliciosa, (ak-ti-nid′i-à dē-lis-i-ō′så), Chinese Gooseberry, has received considerable attention in recent years for fruit production. The foliage is attractive and the 1 1/2″ diameter, creamy-white fragrant flowers are produced in April– May on short branches from year-old wood. The plant is functionally dioecious and male and female plants are necessary for good fruit set. Seed grown plants take 4 to 7 years to flower and fruit. The fruit is an elongated, 1 to 2″ long, hairy, brownish green, edible berry. The fruit in the produce section of the grocery store that you have no earthly idea of its identity is probably Kiwi. Requires well-drained, moderately moist, acid soil; full sun or partial shade; no significant pest problems. Makes a good cover for a fence, trellis, arbor or pergola. Rapid growth rate and coarse-textured, luxuriant foliage are principle landscape assets. Late spring frosts may injure foliage. It is used in Europe as a wall and arbor cover. Many cultivars, probably the most famous in the United States is 'Hayward' ('Chico Hayward')(female) and 'Chico Male'. 'Hayward' constitutes more than 98% of commercial plantings in New Zealand. Other cultivars include: 'Abbott'—a low chill, less than 200 hour, male that serves as a pollinator for 'Elmwood', with twice the size of store fruit (up to 9 ounces each); 'Blake'—smaller fruit than 'Hayward' but ripens one month before; 'Dexter'—an early maturing, low chill cultivar; 'Saanichton' (1 1/2″) like 'Hayward' but has fruited on Vancouver Island where 'Hayward' has frozen out; and 'Vincent'—originating in coastal southern California; important New Zealand cultivars encompass: 'Abbott'/'Allison', probably the same clone with two names, early flowering, heavy bearing, medium size oblong fruit is covered with dense long coarse hairs; 'Bruno'—early flowering, elongated cylindrical fruit covered with dense, short, bristly hairs, heavy bearing; 'Gracie'—elongated fruit with more width and substance than 'Bruno'; 'Monty'—late flowering, prolific, oblong shape; 'Tomuri'—male, one of the most widely employed pollinizers; various selections are usually grafted onto seedling rootstocks. Cuttings, root cuttings and budding are also used. Seeds germinate maximally when removed from flesh, stored at 40°F for 2 weeks, then provided alternating 68°F day/50°F night temperatures for 2 to 3 weeks. The same effect can be achieved by soaking seeds in gibberellic acid at concentrations to 5000 ppm for 20 hours. Has been promoted as a potential fruit crop in the Southeast with marginal success. Sixty-eight percent of the Kiwi crop is produced in New Zealand with the United States producing 12%. Interestingly, the New Zealanders consume 5% of the production, while the United States consumes 12%. New Zealand has accomplished miracles with this plant and is responsible for the common name Kiwi and popularizing the plant worldwide. National Geographic (May 1987) presented a fine article with numerous potential trivial pursuit questions and answers. For example, an average 100-acre New Zealand dairy farm earns $30,000 U.S. yearly; the same acreage in Kiwis can bring in $1,000,000 U.S.; plants may grow as much as 8″ in 24 hours; and a fine white wine, often mistaken for a Riesling is made; the crop is now worth $40,000,000 annually in the United States. See *New Zealand J. Botany* 24:183–184 (1986) for discussion of nomenclature change. China. Introduced 1900. Zone 8 to 9.

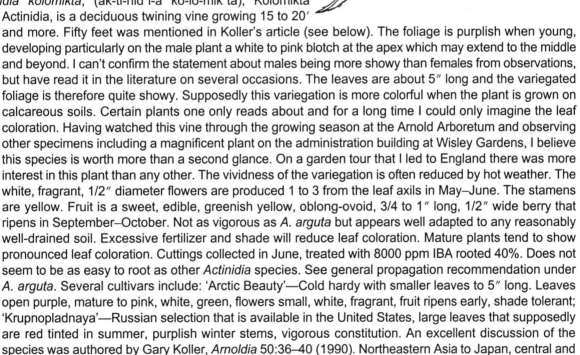

Actinidia kolomikta (Rupr. & Maxim.) Maxim. — Kolomikta Actinidia
LEAVES: Alternate, simple, broad-ovate, 3 to 6″ long, 3 to 4″
    wide, cordate, acuminate, sharply and uniformly serrate,
    6 to 8 vein pairs, glabrous, dark green and/or brushed
    with pink or white towards their apices, slightly pubes-
    cent on veins beneath; petiole—1 to 1 1/2″ long, essen-
    tially glabrous.
BUDS: Perhaps superposed with one imbedded in leaf scar
    and the other small and globose.
STEM: Rich brown, glabrous, prominently lenticelled, nodes
    appear swollen; pith—rich brown, finely chambered.

Actinidia kolomikta, (ak-ti-nid′i-à kō-lō-mik′tà), Kolomikta
    Actinidia, is a deciduous twining vine growing 15 to 20′
and more. Fifty feet was mentioned in Koller's article (see below). The foliage is purplish when young, developing particularly on the male plant a white to pink blotch at the apex which may extend to the middle and beyond. I can't confirm the statement about males being more showy than females from observations, but have read it in the literature on several occasions. The leaves are about 5″ long and the variegated foliage is therefore quite showy. Supposedly this variegation is more colorful when the plant is grown on calcareous soils. Certain plants one only reads about and for a long time I could only imagine the leaf coloration. Having watched this vine through the growing season at the Arnold Arboretum and observing other specimens including a magnificent plant on the administration building at Wisley Gardens, I believe this species is worth more than a second glance. On a garden tour that I led to England there was more interest in this plant than any other. The vividness of the variegation is often reduced by hot weather. The white, fragrant, 1/2″ diameter flowers are produced 1 to 3 from the leaf axils in May–June. The stamens are yellow. Fruit is a sweet, edible, greenish yellow, oblong-ovoid, 3/4 to 1″ long, 1/2″ wide berry that ripens in September–October. Not as vigorous as *A. arguta* but appears well adapted to any reasonably well-drained soil. Excessive fertilizer and shade will reduce leaf coloration. Mature plants tend to show pronounced leaf coloration. Cuttings collected in June, treated with 8000 ppm IBA rooted 40%. Does not seem to be as easy to root as other *Actinidia* species. See general propagation recommendation under *A. arguta*. Several cultivars include: 'Arctic Beauty'—Cold hardy with smaller leaves to 5″ long. Leaves open purple, mature to pink, white, green, flowers small, white, fragrant, fruit ripens early, shade tolerant; 'Krupnopladnaya'—Russian selection that is available in the United States, large leaves that supposedly are red tinted in summer, purplish winter stems, vigorous constitution. An excellent discussion of the species was authored by Gary Koller, *Arnoldia* 50:36–40 (1990). Northeastern Asia to Japan, central and western China. Introduced about 1855. Zone 4 to 8(?). Actually, this species is listed as hardy to -45°F.

Actinidia polygama (Sieb. & Zucc.) Maxim. — Silver-vine
LEAVES: Alternate, simple, broad-ovate to ovate, oblong, 3 to 6″ long, acuminate, rounded or subcordate at
    base, appressed serrate, usually setose on the veins beneath, on male plants the upper half or almost
    the whole leaf silver white or yellowish; petiole—bristly.

Actinidia polygama, (ak-ti-nid′i-à pō-lig′à-mà), Silver-vine, is probably the weakest grower of the *Actinidia* group.
    It may grow 15′ but is definitely not as vigorous as *A. arguta*. The 3 to 5″ long leaves of staminate plants

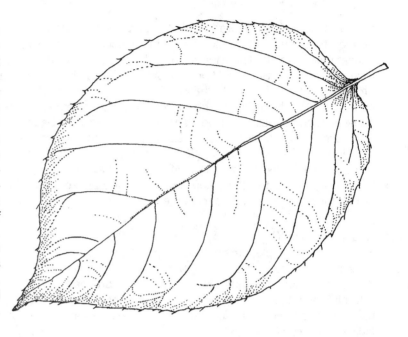

are marked with a silver-white to yellowish color. Cats apparently are attracted to this plant and will maul the foliage. The leaves of female plants are a duller green than *A. arguta*. The flowers are white, 1/2 to 3/4″ across, 1 to 3 together, anthers yellow, fragrant, June–July; the fruit is an edible 1″ long, greenish yellow berry of little ornamental significance. Have seen reference to '418-77B', a self fruitful clone with edible fruit. Differs from previous species in the solid, white pith. Roots readily from softwood cuttings. Native to Manchuria, Japan and central China. Introduced 1861. Zone 4 to 7.

ADDITIONAL NOTES: An interesting group of vines but seldom used in modern landscaping; their adaptability to difficult situations should make them more popular; the difference in foliage colors between male and female plants is a rarity among dioecious plants. Do not be disappointed if young plants of *A. kolomikta* and *A. polygama* do not develop the pronounced leaf coloration; the juvenile nature and high nutrition appear to suppress color formation; an excellent article on the *Actinidia* species appeared in *The Plantsman* 6(3):167–180 (1984) by Philip McMillan Browse.

Adina rubella Hance — Chinese Buttonbush

FAMILY: Rubiaceae
LEAVES: Opposite, simple, elliptic-ovate, to 1 to 2″ long, one half as wide, acute, rounded, entire, lustrous dark green above, paler and pubescent on veins beneath; petiole—virtually absent, subsessile.
STEM: Slender, reddish brown, pubescent.

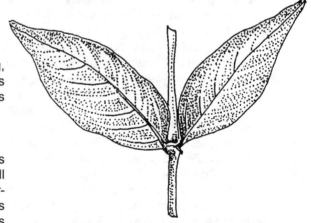

Adina rubella, (a-dī′nȧ rū-bel′ȧ), Chinese Buttonbush, is a handsome lustrous dark green foliaged small shrub that is essentially unknown in American gardens. One lone planting on the Georgia campus has served as a favorite test plant that almost all visitors have been asked to identify. The reader can guess the results. The habit is upright spreading, about 8 to 10′ at maturity. I have seen the species in Bernheim Arboretum, Clermont, KY, where it was prospering. In northern latitudes it is a dieback shrub. White, slightly fragrant flowers occur in 1/2 to 3/4″ diameter rounded heads in June–July to October in Athens. In Lee's *Forest Botany of China* (1935), the flower color is listed as purple. Fruit is two valved, dehiscent, many seeded capsule. Although not overwhelming, they are curiously interesting and remind of the more common buttonbush, *Cephalanthus occidentalis*. Requires nothing more than well-drained soil. Partial shade appears to serve it best. Have become enamored with this superb foliage shrub that could be utilized for masses and groupings in shady environments. The magnificent foliage was still present on December 21, 1994 on campus plants. At Bernheim Arboretum plants subjected to –24°F died back to the ground but produced 3 to 4′ of new growth by late September. I suspect –5 to –10°F represents the limit of stem cold hardiness. The species is easy to root from May (Athens) softwood, 1000 or 5000 ppm KIBA, peat-perlite medium, mist, with 11% rooting in 24 days. Shows micronutrient deficiency quickly so provide macro and micro elements after rooting. Appears to tolerate dry shade which would endear it to many landscape designers and gardeners. Southern China at altitudes of 100 to 1100′. Zone 6 to 9.

Aesculus californica (Spach) Nutt. — California Buckeye

FAMILY: Hippocastanaceae

LEAVES: Opposite, compound palmate, 5 (4 to 7) leaflets, each 3 to 6″ long, elliptic-oblong to lance-oblong, acuminate, narrowed or rounded at the base, sharply serrate, glabrous, lustrous dark green above; petiole—3 to 4″ long; petiolules—1/2 to 1″ long.

BUDS: Imbricate, lance-shaped, pointed at tip, dark brown, quite sticky, probably more so than *A. hippocastanum*.

STEM: Stout, gray-brown to reddish when young, glabrous, with age becoming lighter.

BARK: Essentially smooth and light to pale silver, reminding of American Beech bark; have seen native trees in California and the silvery-gray bark color really stands out.

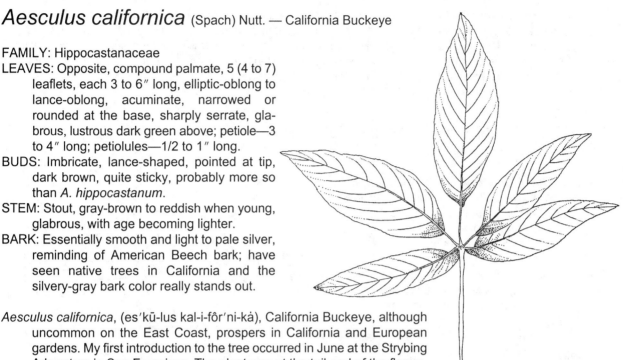

Aesculus californica, (es′kū-lus kal-i-fôr′ni-kȧ), California Buckeye, although uncommon on the East Coast, prospers in California and European gardens. My first introduction to the tree occurred in June at the Strybing Arboretum in San Francisco. The plant was at the tail-end of the flowering season but still spectacular. The habit is broad globose to rounded with a regular, symmetrical branching structure (15 to 20′ tall). National champion is 48′ by 78′ in Walnut Creek, CA. The lustrous dark green foliage is striking. It occurs naturally on dry soils in canyons and gullies and drops its leaves in July–August but if given ample moisture will hold them into fall. Interestingly, the tree does well in England with the cooler climate and moist atmospheric conditions. I circled a buckeye for 20 minutes at the Bath Botanic Garden, Bath, England, before admitting I did not know its identity. The label said *A. californica*! Flowers are primarily white but may be pink, fragrant, and occur in 4 to 8″ long, 2 to 3″ wide, bottlebrush-shaped panicles. The stamens extend beyond the petals and provide a feathery texture. The 2 to 3″ long pear shaped, smooth capsule contains 1 to 2, 1 1/2 to 2″ wide pale orange-brown seeds. The most beautiful flowering specimens I have observed are housed at Knightshayes Court, Somerset, England. On a late June day, the floral display was spectacular. One particular tree had pinkish white flowers the others essentially white. I suspect there is room for floral selection. The late Dr. J.C. Raulston, North Carolina State University Arboretum, has been able to grow the species successfully in Raleigh. However, during the extemely hot and dry summer of 1995, the NCSU Arboretum specimen had defoliated. The high night temperatures and humidity may wreak havoc. I have observed the two specimens at the NCSU Arboretum and with consistency they shed leaves in summer. More of a collector plant on the East Coast. Seed will germinate without pretreatment and, like all *Aesculus* seeds, dry and shrivel rapidly. Plant after collection in beds or deep containers. Generally buckeyes develop a long taproot as a seedling. See McMillan Browse and Leiser, *The Plantsman* 4:54–57 (1982), for a detailed analysis of the species. See Wright, *The Plantsman* 6:228–247 (1985), for "*Aesculus* in the Garden." California. Introduced 1855. Zone (6)7 to 8(?).

Aesculus chinensis Bunge — Chinese Buckeye, Horsechestnut

LEAVES: Opposite, palmately compound, (5)7 leaflets, 5 to 8″ long, about 1/3 as wide, narrow oblong to obovate, cuneate, finely serrate, glossy dark green, glabrous beneath except sparingly hairy on the veins; petiolules— 1/6 to 5/8″ long.

Aesculus chinensis, (es′kū-lus chi-nen′sis), Chinese Horsechestnut, is a species I have coveted for years and all procurement efforts have gone awry. A plant at the Arnold Arboretum labeled as such proved to be *A. pavia* and, in European gardens, *A. turbinata* has been identified as *A. chinensis*. The habit is rounded with landscape size in the 30 to 40′ range. Lancaster, *The Garden* 105:122 (1980), described 60 to 70′ high trees with "Slender tapering cylindrical panicles, up to 16″ long, leaning out or gently ascending from the shoot tips. The white petals were exceeded by the stamens, and the overall effect of some hundreds of inflorescences was staggering." The description is enough to make me faint. The fruit averages 2″ diameter and is truncate or slightly indented at the top, subglobose, rough on the exterior but not spiny. The seed is 3/4 to 1″ across with the hilum covering one-half of it. Considered more drought tolerant than other horsechestnuts but prefers moist, well-drained soil in sun or partial shade. Foliage may be injured by late spring frosts. Northern China. Introduced 1912. Zone 5 to 7.

Aesculus glabra Willd. — Ohio Buckeye, also called Fetid Buckeye
(es′kū-lus glā′brȧ)

LEAVES: Opposite, palmately compound, 5 leaflets, rarely 7, elliptic to obovate, 3 to 6″ long, 1 to 2 1/4″ wide, acuminate, cuneate, finely serrate, pubescent beneath when young, nearly glabrous at maturity, medium to dark green; petiole—approximately 3 to 6″ long.

BUDS: Imbricate, ovoid, sessile, terminal—2/3″ long, brown, with prominently keeled scales, hairy on margins, lateral buds smaller.

STEM: Stout, pubescent at first becoming glabrous, ash-gray to red-brown with disagreeable odor when bruised.

BARK: Ashy gray, thick, deeply fissured and plated, scaly.

SIZE: Usually in the range of 20 to 40′ in height with a similar spread although can grown to 80′; national champion is 148′ by 48′ in Liberty, KY.

HARDINESS: Zone 4 to 7.

HABIT: Rounded to broad-rounded in outline, usually low branched with the branches bending down toward the ground and then arching back up at the ends; actually quite handsome in foliage; very dense and therefore difficult to grow grass under; as my Ohio Buckeye observation file expands, I see many trees with a pyramidal-rounded to oval-rounded habit, particularly in youth.

RATE: Medium, 7 to 10′ over a 6 to 8 year period.

TEXTURE: Medium-coarse in leaf; coarse in winter.

BARK: Ashy-gray, rather corky-warty, and on the older trunks much furrowed and scaly.

LEAF COLOR: Bright green when unfolding (very handsome) changing to dark green in summer; one of the first trees to leaf out (often late March–early April) and also one of the first to defoliate in fall; fall color is often yellow but at times develops a brilliant orange-red to reddish brown, best termed a pumpkin-orange.

FLOWERS: Perfect, greenish yellow, 1″ long, 4 petaled, borne in early to mid-May in 4 to 7″ long by 2 to 3″ wide terminal panicles; not overwhelming but handsome when viewed close-up, flowers occur with foliage and tend to get lost in the shuffle.

FRUIT: Capsule, light brown, dehiscent, 1 to 2″ long, broadly obovoid, with a prickly (echinate) cover similar to Common Horsechestnut; the seeds (buckeyes) are usually borne solitary; no childhood is complete without a pocketful of buckeyes! The seeds are poisonous but nonetheless often eaten by hungry squirrels; only American buckeye with a prickly fruit, although the closely related *A. arguta* is often spiny.

CULTURE: Transplant balled and burlapped into moist, deep, well-drained, slightly acid soil; tends to develop leaf scorch and prematurely drops leaves in hot, droughty situations; found native in bottomlands along banks of rivers and creeks; full sun or partial shade; prune in early spring.

DISEASES AND INSECTS: Leaf blotch is very serious on this species and *A. hippocastanum*; the leaves develop discolored spots which gradually change to brown; powdery mildew is also a problem and some trees appear gray in color; other problems include leaf spot, wood rot, anthracnose, canker, walnut scale, comstock mealybug, white-marked tussock moth, Japanese beetle, bagworm, flat-headed borer; if a problem occurs, and it is likely to be on the two species mentioned above, consult your extension agent for proper diagnosis and control measures; another significant problem is leaf scorch which is physiological in nature; the margins of leaves become brown and curled; trees located in tight planting areas are especially susceptible although it has been noted as occurring on selected trees even in moist years.

LANDSCAPE VALUE: I value this species as a good native tree best left in the wild or natural setting; a good tree for parks and large areas; definitely not recommended for streets or the small residential landscape;

when selecting a tree many factors should be considered and I believe the messiness and lack of ornamental attributes limit extensive use; I have seen trees planted in narrow (3 to 4′ wide) tree lawns completely defoliated by late August; I still remember my Dad pointing out the tree on our squirrel hunting trips in southern Ohio; my main interest was collecting pocketfuls of shiny brown seeds; the squirrels probably wondered who was more squirrelly.

CULTIVARS:

var. *nana*—Woodlanders, Aiken, SC has a dwarf shrubby form that flowers at a young age and comes true to type from seed, makes a rather handsome small rounded bush; Bob McCartney related that this variety is native in and around Douglas County, GA; flowers at a young age and produces fruits as an isolated specimen at Woodlanders, must be self fertile; grows 4 to 5′(6′) high and wide; flowers in early April (Aiken, SC); have grown for several years in the Dirr garden; early leafing and flowering; fruits ripen in August; extremely spiny, 1/2 to 3/4″ capsule; seed black.

PROPAGATION: Seed should be stratified in a moist medium for 120 days at 41°F; *Aesculus* seed should be collected as soon as capsules show a tendency toward dehiscence; it is often a race with the hungry squirrels to see who wins; much of stored material is fats and lipids and the seeds degenerate rapidly; best to sow in fall and cover to a depth equal to the seed's height; cultivars are usually grafted onto *A. hippocastanum*, *A. glabra*, or *A. flava*.

NATIVE HABITAT: Pennsylvania to Nebraska, Kansas and Alabama. Cultivated 1809.

RELATED SPECIES:

Aesculus arguta Buckley [probably more correctly *A. glabra* var. *arguta* (Buckley) Robinson] — Texas Buckeye

LEAVES: Opposite, compound palmate, 7 to 9(11) leaflets, each leaflet 2 to 5″ long, 1/2 to 1 1/4″(2″) wide, lanceolate to obovate-lanceolate, deeply and doubly serrate with obtuse teeth, glabrous at maturity, medium green; petiole—as long as leaflet.

Aesculus arguta, (es′kū-lus är-gū′tà), Texas Buckeye, is a small tree (15 to 20′) or more commonly a low shrub of rather ungainly proportions. National champion is 30′ by 24′ in Harper, TX. In general, it is similar to the above but smaller in all parts. Flowers are listed as cream colored but are actually yellow-green and often with larger inflorescences than typical *A. glabra*. Has been listed as a variety by some botanists. Leaflets are narrower than Ohio Buckeye and usually 7 to 9 per leaf. Although native to east Texas the species can be grown as far north as Boston and I know of an established specimen at Mt. Airy Arboretum, Cincinnati that withstood -25°F. The Mt. Airy tree is 20′ high and has set many fruits. East Arkansas, eastern Missouri westward to east Texas. 1909. Zone 4 to 8.

Aesculus flava Sol. (*Aesculus octandra* Marsh.) — Yellow Buckeye

LEAVES: Opposite, compound palmate, generally 5 leaflets, each 4 to 6″ long, oblong-obovate or narrow elliptic, acuminate, cuneate, finely serrate, dark green above, yellow green and pubescent beneath when young, essentially glabrous and glaucous below at maturity; petiole—3 to 4″ long.

Aesculus flava (*A. octandra*), (es′kū-lus flā′và), Yellow Buckeye, is, to me, the most beautiful of the large growing North American *Aesculus*. The upright-oval to slightly spreading crown often reaches 60 to 75′ in height. National champion is 136′ by 53′ at Gaber Mountain Trail, Great Smoky Mountains National Park, TN. The dark green leaves (5-leaflets) may turn a pumpkin color in fall and do not appear to be as troubled by foliar diseases as *A. glabra*. The bark is a rather curious combination of gray and brown with large, flat, smooth plates and scales comprising old trunks. The yellow (tinge of green) flowers are borne in erect 6 to 7″ long by 2 to 3″ wide panicles in May. The fruit is smooth, pear-shaped, 2 to 3″ long capsule

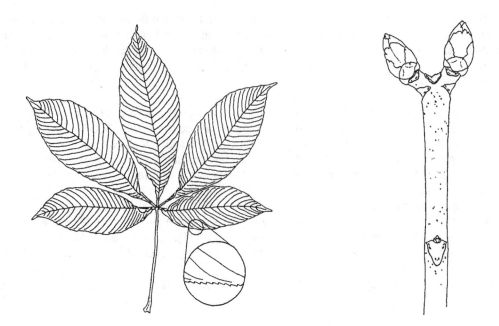

usually containing two brown seeds. There are magnificent trees in Sosebee Cove, North Georgia that ascend fully 90′. The most beautiful trees in cultivation that I have seen are housed at Spring Grove, Cincinnati, OH. Many of these trees range from 60 to 80′ in size. Prefers a deep, moist, well-drained root run. A very handsome buckeye and preferable to the Ohio Buckeye for general landscape situations. Abundant in southern Appalachians to 6000′ elevation. Quite common in mixed deciduous woods from riverbottoms to mountain tops. I could look at this tree forever. Pennsylvania to Tennessee, northern Alabama, and northern Georgia, west to Ohio and Illinois. Introduced 1764. Zone 4 to 8.

Aesculus × hybrida DC., represents a group of hybrids between *A. flava* and *A. pavia*. The flowers are yellow-red to reddish; the red trait being inherited from *A. pavia*. These hybrids also have glands as well as hairs on the margins of the petals which is indicative of *A. pavia*. I have seen many trees with yellowish red flowers, sometimes labeled as *A. flava*; others as *A. × hybrida*. Fortunately or unfortunately, there are a significant number of *Aesculus* hybrids many with *A. pavia* as one parent. The taxonomy is not exactly clear-cut but described hybrids of various buckeyes include:

> *A. × arnoldiana* Sarg. [(*A. glabra* × *A. flava*) × *A. pavia*]
> *A. × bushii* Schneid. (*A. glabra* × *A. pavia*)
> *A. × dupontii* Sarg. [*A. flava* × (*A. pavia* × *A. sylvatica*)]
> *A. × marilandica* Booth. (*A. glabra* × *A. flava*)
> *A. × mutabilis* (Spach) Schelle. (*A. pavia* × *A. sylvatica*)
> *A. × neglecta* Lindl. (*A. × glaucescens* Sarg.) (*A. flava* × *A. sylvatica*)
> *A. × woerlitzensis* Koehne (*A. × hybrida* × *A. sylvatica*)

The range of flower color is extreme and it is very difficult to accurately categorize them. The Minnesota Landscape Arboretum has given one of these hybrids a cultivar name *A. × arnoldiana* 'Autumn Splendor'. Now considered a cultivar of *A. glabra*. This cultivar maintains dark green summer leaf color while changing to brilliant maroon-red in fall. The foliage has been scorch resistant in the northern states. Flowers are yellow-green and open in late April in Winchester, TN. See *HortScience* 24:180–181 (1989) for complete description of 'Autumn Splendor'.

ADDITIONAL NOTES: Buckeyes are beautiful trees when properly grown. I delight in an early spring walk in the woods when the leaves of buckeyes are unfurling their rich green to deep purple-green leaves.

Aesculus hippocastanum L. — Common Horsechestnut, European Horsechestnut
(es′kū-lus hip-ō-kas-tā′num)

LEAVES: Opposite, palmately compound, 7 leaflets, sometimes 5, each leaflet obovate, 4 to 10″ long, 2 to 5″ wide, acuminate, cuneate, obtusely double serrate, rusty tomentose near base beneath when young, dark green at maturity; petiolules absent-blade present to point of attachment; petiole—3 to 5″ long.

BUDS: Imbricate, ovoid, large, 1/2 to 3/4″ long, dark reddish brown, varnished with sticky gum, glabrous.

STEM: Stout, reddish yellow to grayish brown, glabrous or slightly finely-downy.

BARK: Dark gray to brown becoming shallowly fissured into irregular plate-like scales resembling bark of apple trees.

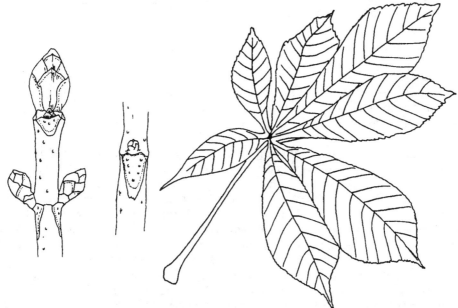

SIZE: 50 to 75′ in height, will usually develop a 40 to 70′ spread, can grow to 100′ or larger.

HARDINESS: Zone 4 to 7 and possibly 8 although does not perform well in Athens, GA.

HABIT: Upright-oval to rounded in outline, making a very striking specimen especially as the new leaves emerge.

RATE: Medium, 12 to 14′ over a 6 to 8 year period.

TEXTURE: Medium to coarse in leaf; definitely coarse in winter.

BARK: Dark gray to brown, on old trunks becoming platy, exfoliating, and exposing orangish brown inner bark.

LEAF COLOR: Light yellow green when unfolding, changing to dark green at maturity; fall color is often a poor yellow and often the leaves develop a brown color; have seen trees in Europe with reasonably good yellow fall color; one of the earliest trees to leaf out but still later than *A. glabra*.

FLOWERS: Perfect, each flower with 4 or 5 petals, white with a blotch of color at the base which starts yellow and ends reddish; flowers borne in 5 to 12″ long and 2 to 5″ wide terminal panicles in early to mid-May; very showy and, at one time, much over-planted in the eastern states for that reason.

FRUIT: Light brown, spiny, dehiscent, 2 to 2 1/4″ diameter capsule containing one, sometimes two blackish seeds; matures in September–October.

CULTURE: Transplant balled and burlapped into moist, well-drained soil; full sun or light shade; pH adaptable; prune in early spring; avoid extremely dry situations.

DISEASES AND INSECTS: See under Ohio Buckeye.

LANDSCAPE VALUE: Park, arboretum, campus, commercial grounds, golf courses and other large areas—not for small residential properties; abundant through the eastern states, virtually every campus has a horsechestnut; the blotch and mildew limit extensive use; widely used in Europe; gardens such as Versailles, Schwetzingen and many English parks are well endowed with this species; at its best, which is often in European cities and gardens, a tree that attracts and demands attention; on our European garden tours this tree, especially in flower, elicits more responses than any other.

CULTIVARS:

'Baumannii'—Double white flowers, no fruits, flowers last longer than the type, the best of the garden forms, handsome and impressive in flower; discovered by A.N. Baumann near Geneva; occurred as a branch sport on a tree in the garden of Mons. Duval around 1820; specimens in the 80 to 100′ high range are relatively common in England.

There are other cultivars with white and yellow variegation as well as cutleaf, compact, fastigiate, and weeping types. Most are to be avoided except for the fanatical collector. I have observed many of the variegated leaf types in European gardens and some are rather handsome. Doubtfully would they prosper in the United States. At the Trompenburg Arboretum, Rotterdam, Mr. J.R.P. van Hoey Smith has assembled a terrific collection of *A. hippocastanum* cultivars. His head gardener delighted in quizzing me on their exact identification. In brief . . . he won.

PROPAGATION: Cultivars are grafted on the species; seeds require 3 to 4 months at 41°F.

ADDITIONAL NOTES: A cherished plant in European countries but not so much in the United States; my wife and I sat on a bench in Hyde Park, London, and watched boys collect the nuts as if they were nuggets; boys play a game of "conkers" ; in addition they make great ammunition, and provide food for squirrels and deer.

NATIVE HABITAT: Greece and Albania in the mountainous, uninhabited wilds, and large groves in Bulgaria; introduced 1576; once thought to be native to India.

RELATED SPECIES:

Aesculus × **carnea** Hayne. — Red Horsechestnut

LEAVES: Opposite, palmately compound, usually only 5 leaflets, leaflets subsessile or short-stalked, obovate, 3 to 6″ long, acute, cuneate, doubly serrate, leathery, lustrous dark green above, nearly glabrous below; petiole—2 1/2 to 4″ long.

Aesculus × *carnea*, (es′kū-lus kär′nē-à), Red Horsechestnut, resulted from a cross between *A. pavia* and *A. hippocastanum*. Little is known of the origin of the hybrid except that it probably occurred in Germany. It is one of the most popular trees in England and in May the rose-red flowers are spectacular. The flowers are borne on a 6 to 8″ high and 3 to 4″ wide panicle. The globose, 1 1/2″ diameter capsules are slightly prickly. The species comes true-to-type from seed which is unusual for most hybrids. The theory behind this quirk is unraveled here. The original *A.* × *carnea* was probably a diploid with 40 chromosomes, as in the parents. At some stage, spontaneous doubling took place thus resulting in an 80 chromosome complement. There are reports that *A.* × *carnea* does and does not breed true. This could be explained if, assuming the doubling took place on the original tree, scions or seeds were collected and distributed. Some would be of the 40 chromosome complement; others the 80. It is illogical to assume this spontaneous doubling took place in every bud and consequently the above rationale.

   Aesculus × *carnea* makes a splendid rounded to broad-rounded 30 to 40′ tree in our country. In Europe, the species is listed as growing 60 to 80′ although I saw no trees of that magnitude and Red Horsechestnut was everywhere in evidence. The lustrous dark green leaves are composed of 5, occasionally 7, leaflets. The leaflets are smaller than those of *A. hippocastanum*. The buds are not quite as large or as sticky as *A. hippocastanum*. 'Briotii' has deeper red colored and larger (to 10″ long) panicles. There are several yellow-variegated forms as well as a pendulous type but these are uncommon. 'Briotii' originated in 1858 from seed grown at Trianon in France. Madison, Wisconsin indicated that young trees were severely injured or killed during the severe 1976 to 77 winter. Minnesota Landscape Arboretum mentioned that a tree north of St. Paul has flowered for a number of years. *Aesculus* × *carnea* is not as susceptible to blotch and mildew as *A. hippocastanum*. In October, I was walking along a street in Salt Lake City, Utah and noticed *A.* × *carnea* interplanted in a tree lawn with *A. hippocastanum*. The foliage of the latter was paper-bag brown while *A.* × *carnea* was lush lustrous dark green. A pronounced difference in growth habit was evident with *A.* × *carnea* rounded and *A. hippocastanum* upright-oval. 'O'Neill' was included in the last edition with a note about the double-flowered nature. I found out through correspondence that it was not double-flowered as advertised. I have since observed the plant in flower at the Strybing Arboretum in San Francisco and the flowers are a fine red, better than 'Briotii', and occur in 10 to 12″ long panicles. To my knowledge, Weston Nurseries, Hopkinton, MA is the only eastern source for the plant. Another rather recent introduction is 'Fort McNair', selected on the grounds of Fort McNair, Washington, DC for its good foliage and pink flowers with yellow throats. As lovely as *A.* × *carnea* is, the fungal disease is still a possibility and I have seen trees that were less than pristine. *A.* × *carnea* 'Briotii' was originally described in *Revue Horticale* 50:370 (1878).

Aesculus × **plantierensis** André, (es′kū-lus plan-ti-er-en′sis), is the result of a backcross of *A.* × *carnea* × *A. hippocastanum*. Flowers are a soft pink or red with a yellow throat, panicles to 12″ long. The tree does not set fruit and the fact that it is a triploid explains this sterility. Raised in the nursery of Simon-Louis Frères, at Plantières, near Metz, France. Has been placed as a cultivar of *A.* × *carnea* by Griffiths. A lovely plant has established a niche in the Arnold Arboretum's great *Aesculus* collection and a plant also resides in Athens.

Aesculus indica (Wallich ex Cambess.) Hook. — Indian Horsechestnut

LEAVES: Opposite, compound palmate, (5)7(9) leaflets, short stalked, obovate-lanceolate, 6 to 10″(12″) long, finely serrate, glabrous, lustrous dark green above and with a distinct undulating margin.

BUDS: Imbricate, gray-brown.

STEM: Stout, gray-green to green-brown.

Aesculus indica, (es′kū-lus in′di-kà), Indian Horsechestnut, is perhaps the finest of the genus for foliage and flower effect. In the United States, maximum cultural success would be realized in the Pacific Northwest. My fondest recollections are derived from yearly June visits to Kew Gardens, where several spectacular 50 to 60′ high specimens line the entrance walk. The habit is best described as oval-rounded but there is a classic, undefinable dignity inherent in this species that sets it apart from the more pedestrian *A. hippocastanum*. The summer foliage is a lustrous dark green and in fall may develop salmon to orange-red colors. The flowers occur in 12 to 16″ long, 4 to 5″ wide erect cylindrical panicles and are as close to awe-inspiring as an *Aesculus* can get. Each 4-petaled flower is about 1″ long, white, with the upper two petals blotched yellow and red at base, the lower shorter pair pale rose. The stamens protrude about 3/4″ beyond the petals. The overall flower effect is pink to pinkish rose. Fruit is a 2 to 3″ rounded roughened (not spiny) capsule. Prefers moist soil, full sun and an even cool climate. Tremendous park and large estate, or commercial grounds tree. 'Sydney Pearce' has deeper pink flowers in tighter panicles that are freely borne. I have seen the tree at Kew and only wish I could grow it. Northwestern Himalayas. Introduced 1851. Zone 7? Probably, best adapted to the San Francisco area in a coastal sweep to Victoria and Vancouver, British Columbia.

Aesculus parviflora Walter. — Bottlebrush Buckeye
(es′kū-lus pär-vi-flō′rà)

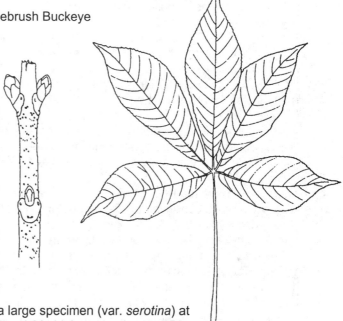

LEAVES: Opposite, palmately compound, 5 to 7 leaflets, nearly sessile, elliptic to oblong-obovate, 3 to 8″ long, 1 1/4 to 4″ wide, acuminate, crenate-serrulate, medium to dark green above, grayish and pubescent beneath; petiole—3 to 5″ long.

BUDS: Weakly imbricate, usually with 4 exposed scales, terminals 1/4 to 1/3″ long, laterals smaller, scales minutely pubescent and glaucous, gray-brown, covered with wax to the degree of appearing white.

STEM: Stout, gray-brown, with raised light brown lenticels; leaf scar half encircling bud, vascular bundle traces forming a face-like image, usually 3 to 6 in number.

SIZE: 8 to 12′ in height, spreading to 8 to 15′; a large specimen (var. *serotina*) at the Arnold Arboretum ranges between 15 and 20′ high; a specimen at Birr Castle, Ireland, is 15′ by 27′; at High Hampton, Cashiers, NC, 18′ by 40′; all the above appear to have developed from a single mother plant; national champion is 14′ by 20′ at Virginia Beach, VA.

HARDINESS: Zone 4 to 8(9); the Zone 9 is a stretch particularly with the new boundaries of the 1990 USDA Hardiness Zone Map; grows contentedly on the Maine campus where it has withstood −31°F; at the University of Minnesota Landscape Arboretum it is listed as borderline.

HABIT: Wide-spreading, suckering, multi-stemmed shrub with many upright, slender branches; often with an irregular, spreading almost stratified appearance; excellent form and texture in the branching structure; have not seen other plants competing under this buckeye, either through shade, root or alleleopathic effects, no (minimal) seedlings of other plants grow under Bottlebrush Buckeye.

RATE: Slow on old wood but shoots which develop from the base will grow 2 to 4′ in a single season.

TEXTURE: Medium-coarse in summer and winter.

LEAF COLOR: Medium to dark green in summer, turning yellow-green to yellow in fall; foliage is little troubled by diseases which afflict *A. glabra* and *A. hippocastanum*; have observed excellent bright yellow color on plants; expression of good fall color appears to be strongly dependent on ideal environmental conditions; the yellow fall color has been consistently outstanding on plants in Zone 7; on the Georgia campus and in my garden, the bright yellow has been a pleasing addition to the autumn landscape.

FLOWERS: White with 4 petals, 1/2″ long, stamens thread-like and pinkish white, standing out an inch from the petals, anthers red; produced June–July on cylindrical 8 to 12″ long and 2 to 4″ wide panicles; outstanding in flower; there are few summer flowering plants which can rival this species; many flowers in the same inflorescence are male, others perfect; I wait with anxious anticipation for the plant to flower in my garden which it normally does from early to mid-June; in my mind, it is one of the handsomest of all native southeastern flowering shrubs; inflorescence length is terrifically variable with some as long as 18″, in the Dirr garden at least two distinct flowering forms are evident, one with panicles fattest at the base, conical-pyramidal, with the flowers opening from the base to the apex; the other with flowers in cylindrical, bottlebrush-like inflorescences, all flowers opening more or less at the same time, about 2 to 3 weeks later than the first mentioned form; this latter form may be var. *serotina* but I cannot taxonomically separate the two; indeed the flowering period is extended from early to mid-June into early July; have successfully rooted the latter form and will add more plants to the garden; most of the flowers on an inflorescence are male with the perfect flowers appearing toward the apical end of the inflorescence, the stigma is creamy white and slightly curved.

FRUIT: Dehiscent, 1 to 3″ long, pear-shaped, light brown smooth capsule; seeds a polished light brown; have not noticed abundant fruit set in northern states possibly because of shortness of growing season; in more southerly areas significant fruit set often occurs, ripen in late September to early October (Athens), collect seeds as capsules start to dehisce (open) along suture lines.

CULTURE: Transplant balled and burlapped or from a container in early spring into a moist, well-drained soil that has been adequately prepared with organic matter; prefers acid soil but is adaptable; full sun or partial shade; in fact, seems to proliferate in shade; pruning is seldom necessary; can be rejuvenated by pruning to ground.

DISEASES AND INSECTS: None serious compared to Ohio Buckeye and Common Horsechestnut; have observed mites on container grown plants, generally no problems of note on plants under reasonable garden culture.

LANDSCAPE VALUE: Excellent plant for massing, clumping or placing in shrub borders; actually a handsome specimen plant; very effective when used under shade trees and in other shady areas; W.J. Bean noted, "No better plant could be recommended as a lawn shrub"; even if it never flowered it would be a superb shrub for foliage effect; a full grown, broad spreading specimen appears to be flowing across the landscape; perhaps the greatest planting anywhere in the world is located at Bernheim Arboretum, Clermont, KY; will proliferate in the shade of Green Ash and flower superbly.

CULTIVARS:

'Rogers'—Selection made by J.C. McDaniel of the University of Illinois from seedlings he grew from seed of var. *serotina* collected at Missouri Botanical Garden; it is named for Dr. Rogers in whose yard it grows in Urbana, IL; flowers later than the species and variety; inflorescences fully 18 to 30″ long, very striking; in the early editions it was stated that this selection did not sucker as profusely as the species; this is not true for in recent years I noticed considerable basal suckering; variety *serotina* and 'Rogers' are actually larger growing than the typical species, as I write this the mind wanders to the Arnold Arboretum where an immense specimen of variety *serotina* approaches 20′ high.

var. *serotina* Rehd.—Flowers 2 to 3 weeks later than the species; leaflets supposedly less pubescent than species; Alabama, introduced 1919.

PROPAGATION: Seed should be planted as soon as it is collected and should never be allowed to dry out; in our program seeds are harvested (Sept.–Oct.) as soon as ripe, planted about 1″ deep in pine bark in 3 gallon containers, covered with wire mesh; a carrot-like root appears within one month, with a barely perceptible shoot; the following spring, shoot growth commences. In early October 1994, I collected over 100 seeds, planted them outside in raised wooden frames filled with amended, well-drained soil. Germination was excellent and by September, 1995 plants averaged 2 to 3′ high. Several cultural observations were evident: uniform moisture throughout the hot, dry summer of 1995 and 3 split applications of 10-10-10 granular promoted superb growth. Plants were not sprayed for insects and diseases. Root cuttings, 2 1/2 to 3″ long, buried in sand in a cool place in December and then set in the field in spring produced plants; May collected softwood cuttings from shoots which had developed from roots were treated with 0, 1000, 10000, and 20000 ppm IBA/50 percent alcohol; the cuttings were placed in peat:perlite under mist; the respective rooting percentages were 70, 80, 20 and 10 for various treatments; the 10000 and 20000 treatments resulted in premature defoliation and death; for more details see Burd and Dirr, 1977, Bottlebrush Buckeye: Ornamental Characteristics and Propagation, *The Plant Propagator* 23(4):6–8; Dick Bir, North Carolina State University, has rooted the species in high percentages (over 90%) by collecting cuttings within the first month after vegetative bud break, and dipping for one-second in 5000 ppm IBA-alcohol. The early rooted cuttings produced a growth flush and responded to fertilizer and water. See *American Nurseryman* 181(10):42–47 (1995). *Proc. Intl. Plant Prop. Soc.* 43:470–473 (1993) described efficient cutting propagation utilizing fog. In brief, softwood, early June to early July (Chicago), single node, leaf surface reduced 1/3 to 1/2, fungicide, about 1500 ppm IBA + 750 ppm NAA, perlite:peat medium, rooting in 10 to 20 days, about 70% rooting.

NATIVE HABITAT: *Aesculus parviflora* ranges from South Carolina, Georgia to Alabama and Florida. Introduced 1785.

RELATED SPECIES:

Aesculus pavia L. — Red Buckeye
LEAVES: Opposite, palmately compound, 5(7) leaflets, short stalked, oblong-obovate or narrow elliptic, 3 to 6″ long, acuminate, cuneate, irregularly and often double serrate, glabrous or slightly pubescent beneath, often lustrous dark green; petiole—2 to 5″ long.
BUDS: Terminal—imbricate, large, 1/3 to 1/2″ long, brownish, glabrous, laterals—much smaller than terminal.
STEM: Stout, olive-brown in color with raised light brown lenticels; leaf scars triangular to shield-shape with "V" arrangement of leaf traces.

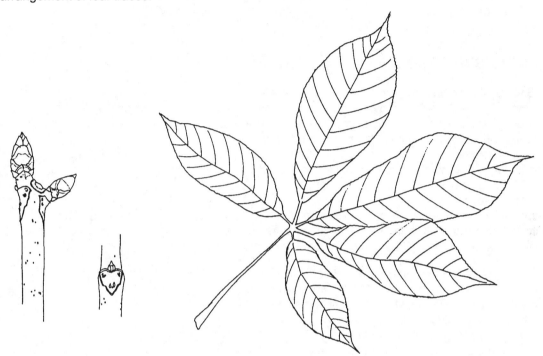

Aesculus pavia, (es′kū-lus pā′vē-à), Red Buckeye, is a small clump-forming, round-topped shrub or small tree reaching 10 to 20′ in height under cultivation and spreading that much or more; can grow 30 to 36′ in the wild; co-national champions are 64′ by 52′ in Kalamazoo County, MI and 58′ by 48′ in Roanoke, VA; handsome lustrous dark green foliage with no appreciable fall color; in Athens leaves have emerged in late February–early March long before oaks, hickories and maples have shown signs of green life; flowers in 4 to 8″ long, 1 1/2 to 3″ wide panicles, each flower 1 1/2″ long, with the 4 to 5 petals glandular at the margins, stamens about length of petals, April–May; fruit a subglobose to ovoid, smooth, dehiscent, 1 1/2 to 2 1/3″ diameter capsule with 1 to 2 lustrous brown seeds, ripening in October; handsome small tree in flower; flowers well in rather dense shade but becomes open; best in full sun; is not prone to severe mildew of *A. hippocastanum* but may contract blotch; best to provide a moist, well-drained soil; ideally site in partial shade for plants hold leaves longer and in better condition; loses its leaves early, often by late September; 'Atrosanquinea' has deeper red flowers and 'Humilis' is a low or even prostrate shrub with red flowers in small panicles. Native from Virginia to Florida, Louisiana and Texas. Introduced 1711. Zone 4 to 8. A 1995 Pennsylvania Horticultural Society Gold Medal Winner. There are a number of other red or yellow-red flowered species that are similar to *Aesculus pavia* in certain features.

It is fair to say that the variation in the species is tremendous as it extends from coastal North Carolina to the Edwards Plateau of Texas. I have seen seedling beds of *A. pavia* with both yellow and red flowers. Interestingly 2- to 3-year-old plants will flower. Wyatt and Harden, *Brittonia* 9:147–171, 173–195 (1957), mentioned that populations of *A. pavia* from the Edwards Plateau of Texas are uniformly yellow-flowered but otherwise similar to typical red-flowered plants. Wyatt and Lodwick, *Brittonia* 33:39–51 (1981), indicate sufficient differences that the yellow- flowered population is *A. p.* var. *flavescens*; the red types *A. p.* var. *pavia*. Plants of typical *A. pavia* have red, tubular flowers with exserted stamens and are effectively pollinated by ruby-throated hummingbirds. Plants of var. *flavescens* have yellow, campanulate flowers with included stamens that can be pollinated effectively by large bees.

Aesculus splendens Sarg. is listed by Rehder as a distinct species and several horticulturists feel strongly about its authenticity. Perhaps the most striking difference is the dense pubescence on the underside of the leaflets that persists until leaf fall. The few plants I have observed had scarlet flowers compared to the red of *A. pavia*. Exists as a 10 to 15′ high shrub or small tree. Hardin and Griffiths include it with *A. pavia*. Alabama to Mississippi and Louisiana. Introduced 1911. Zone (5)6 to 9.

I checked herbarium specimens of *A. discolor* var. *mollis*, *A. pavia*, and *A. sylvatica*. I could see no consistent difference in leaf characteristics except that *A. sylvatica* is more glabrous and generally has yellow-green flowers. *Aesculus sylvatica* was listed as growing as tall as 30′. *Aesculus pavia* varies from pubescent on the midvein on the underside of the leaf to soft velvety pubescent. I did not find a completely glabrous specimen of *A. pavia*. Size notations on *A. pavia* ranged from 5 to 10′ to 25′. *A. discolor* var. *mollis* has a dense velvety pubescence on the underside of the leaflets, but is otherwise similar to *A. pavia*. It would be difficult for the amateur (me) to distinguish between the pubescent forms of *A. pavia* and *A. d.* var. *mollis*. Again, *A. d.* var. *mollis* has been merged into *A. pavia*.

Aesculus sylvatica Bartr. — Painted Buckeye

LEAVES: Opposite, compound palmate, 5 leaflets, each 4 to 6″ long, 1 1/2 to 2 1/2″ wide, ovate to obovate, tapering at apex and base, finely and often doubly serrate, dark green, pubescent in youth finally glabrous or hairy on margins below petiole; petiole—3 1/2 to 8″ long.

BUDS: Similar to *A. pavia*; imbricate, reddish brown, 3/8 to 1/2″ long, glabrous, tips of scales mucronate.

STEM: Stout, terete, smooth, light gray-brown, glabrous; leaf scars shield shaped, large in relation to stem diameter. Similar to *A. pavia*; it is quite difficult to separate *A. sylvatica* and *A. pavia* by bud and stem characteristics.

Aesculus sylvatica, (es′kū-lus sil-vat′i-kà), Painted Buckeye, has become a cherished horticultural friend since my arrival in Georgia. The plant is abundant in moist woods in the piedmont of Georgia, existing as a (6 to 15′ tall) shrub or small tree in the understory. Brown and Kirkman mention that 60′ high trees were documented along the Oconee River in Georgia. Duncan and Duncan cite height to 50′. Never have I observed anything over 20′. The leaves emerge in late March–early April in the Athens area and vary from green to a reddish purple. The flowers (bisexual and male) occur together in a 4 to 8″ long, narrow to broad-oblong to pyramidal panicle during April–May. The panicle is often broader than that of *A. pavia*. Flower color is tremendously variable and ranges from yellow-green, yellow, pink to red, often pink, touches of red and yellow green in the same inflorescence. The reddish color is thought to result from hybridization with *A. pavia*. The stamens are shorter than the lateral petals and there are no glands on the petals and pedicels. Fruit set has been minimal on plants in the University Botanical Garden. The leathery, 3-valved, smooth, 1 to 2″ thick capsule contains 1 to 3 shiny dark brown seeds. Prefers a moist, humusy soil in partial shade and makes an excellent naturalizing plant. Found mixed with beech, maple, oak and hickory in the Botanical Garden often on gentle slopes. See dePamphilis and Neufield, *Canadian Journal of Botany* 67:2161–2167 (1989) "Phenology and Ecophysiology of *Aesculus sylvatica*, a Vernal Understory Tree." Virginia to Georgia, west to Tennessee and Alabama. Introduced 1905. Zone 6 to 9.

Aesculus turbinata Bl. — Japanese Horsechestnut

LEAVES: Opposite, palmately compound, (3)5 to 7 leaflets, 8 to 14″ long, obovate, acuminate, cuneate, crenate serrate, dark green; axillary tufts of hairs and/or pubescent veins; petiole—5 to 10″ long.

Aesculus turbinata, (es′kū-lus tēr-bi-nā′tà), Japanese Horsechestnut, is a large tree, 80 to 100′, with stiff branching and coarse-textured, large leaves. For many years I admired the plant in the Arnold Arboretum's collection and thought it might serve as a replacement for *A. hippocastanum* because of leaf blotch (anthracnose) resistance. I have since observed leaves that did not differ from *A. hippocastanum* in degree of infection. The white flowers occur in 6 to 10″ long panicles in May–June (Boston). Fruits are 2″ wide, broad pear-shaped and rough on the exterior but usually with spines. Seed about 1 to 1 1/3″ wide, with the hilum covering nearly half the surface. A plant for the collector. Japan. Introduced before 1880. Zone 5 to 7.

Aesculus turbinata

Ailanthus altissima (Mill.) Swingle — Tree of Heaven
(ā-lan′thus al-tis′i-mȧ)

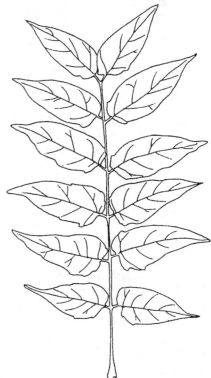

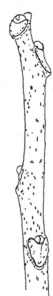

FAMILY: Simaroubaceae

LEAVES: Alternate, pinnately compound, 18 to 24″ long, leaflets—13 to 25, stalked, lance-ovate, 3 to 5″ long, usually truncate at base, finely ciliate, with 2 to 4 coarse teeth near base, dark green, glabrous and glaucescent beneath; petiolules—1/4 to 3/4″ long.

BUDS: Terminal—absent; lateral—relatively small, 1/6″ or less long, half spherical, reddish brown, downy; scales—thick, the 2 opposite lateral scales generally alone showing.

STEM: Stout, yellowish to reddish brown, covered with very short fine velvety down or smooth; rather rank-smelling when crushed; older stems often shedding the epidermis in the form of a thin skin and exposing very fine, light longitudinal striations; pith—wide, light brown.

SIZE: 40 to 60′ in height with an extremely variable spread, but often 2/3's to equal the height.

HARDINESS: Zone 4 to 8; not as prevalent in South.

HABIT: Upright, spreading, open and coarse with large chubby branches.

RATE: Fast, 3 to 5′ and more in a single season.

TEXTURE: Coarse throughout the year.

BARK: Grayish, slightly roughened with fine light colored longitudinal streaks in striking contrast to the darker background.

LEAF COLOR: Newly emerging leaves bronze-purple finally dark green in summer, no fall color.

FLOWERS: Dioecious, although some trees with both sexes; yellow-green, borne in 8 to 16″ long panicles in early to mid-June; male flowers of vile odor; females odorless; effect is often lost because flowers are masked by the foliage; of course no one of sound mind will use the plant for flower effect.

FRUIT: Samara, 1 1/2″ long, 1/2″ wide, thin, flat, narrow-oblong, tapering at both ends with one seed in the center; slight twist to fruit; yellow-green to orange-red, effective in late summer, finally changing to brown and persisting through winter; some plants with good red fruit.

CULTURE: Without a doubt probably the most adaptable and pollution tolerant tree available; withstands the soot, grime and pollution of cities better than other species.

DISEASES AND INSECTS: *Verticillium* wilt, shoestring root rot, leaf spots, twig blight and cankers have been reported; *Verticillium* is the most destructive of these pests; none are particularly serious.

LANDSCAPE VALUE: For most landscape conditions it has *no* value as there are too many trees of superior quality; for impossible conditions this tree has a place; selections could be made for good habit, strong wood, better foliage which would make the tree more satisfactory; I once talked with a highway landscape architect who tried to buy *Ailanthus* for use along polluted highways but could not find an adequate supply; I always knew a specialist growing *Ailanthus* could make money! An update on the money potential of *Ailanthus* is in order; in January, 1982 I received a letter from a gentleman who grew *Ailanthus*, advertised in a local paper and did not sell one; he should have grown *Acer griseum*.

CULTIVARS:

'Erythrocarpa'—Pistillate type, with dark green leaves and red fruit.

'Metro'—Handsome confined crown, a male, Wandell introduction.

'Pendulifolia'—Branches erect as in the type but the longer leaves hang downward, rather than being horizontally disposed as in the species; have attempted to locate this form to date without success.

'Aucubifolia' and 'Tricolor' are described in *Dendroflora* 26:3–5 (1989).

PROPAGATION: Seed which I have worked with required no pre-treatment although 60 days in moist medium at 41°F is a recommendation; root pieces will work.

ADDITIONAL NOTES: Abundant *Ailanthus* literature has appeared almost like *Ailanthus* suckers and sprouts. There is considerable interest in what makes *Ailanthus* tick. Perhaps the most vocal opponent of the tree was Peter Feret, *J. Arboriculture* 11:361–368 (1985). He stated, ". . . In all the *Ailanthus* seedlings I handled during the course of seed source trials, I never found one without leaf glands, and never saw growth forms or phenological mutants of redeeming horticultural utility. I do not recommend *Ailanthus* as an urban tree, as a species for short rotation biomass production or as a substitute for pines or junipers on droughty sites. When it comes to pollution, I would prefer to search for new plant varieties for those sites than to encumber them with a tree species having as many disadvantageous traits as has *Ailanthus*." Another author posed the question, "Arboreal riffraff or ultimate tree?" For avid readers see Pam and Bassuk, *J. Environmental Horticulture* 4:1–4 (1986), "Establishment and Distribution of *Ailanthus altissima* in the Urban Environment." The authors attributed the species' survival in urban sites to the presence of simple rope-like lateral roots. Same authors, *J. Environmental Horticulture* 3:158–162 (1985) assessed growth under different soil types and degrees of compaction. Seedlings, although reduced in growth under compacted conditions, continued to grow throughout experimental period. Graves, Dana and Joly, *J. Environmental Horticulture* 7:79–82 (1989) assessed root zone temperatures and seedling growth. Reported that plants were adversely affected at 86°F and 97°F.

NATIVE HABITAT: China, naturalized over much of the United States. Introduced 1784.

RELATED SPECIES:

Picrasma ailanthoides (Bunge) Planch., formerly *P. quassioides* (Hamilt.) Benn. — India Quassiawood

FAMILY: Simaroubaceae

LEAVES: Alternate, compound pinnate, 10 to 14″ long, 9 to 15 leaflets, each 1 3/4 to 4″ long, subsessile, ovate to oblong-ovate, acuminate, broad cuneate or nearly rounded at the oblique base, crenate serrate, lustrous dark green above, lighter beneath and glabrous except on midrib when young.

BUDS: Terminal—naked, rich brown, pubescent, unique posturing of buds remind of hands folded in prayer.

STEM: Coarse, reddish brown, marked by conspicuous lenticels.

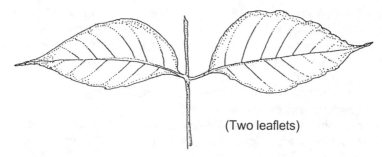

(Two leaflets)

Picrasma ailanthoides, (pi-kraz′må å-lan-thoy′dēz), India Quassiawood, is virtually unknown in American gardens and exists in perhaps only a handful of arboreta. The tree develops a rounded outline, eventually growing 20 to 40′ high. The rich green summer foliage may turn orange and red in fall. The 1/3″ diameter green perfect flowers occur in 6 to 8″ long, loose corymbs. The red, pea-sized obovoid berry ripens with the calyx still attached. There is a tree in the Arnold Arboretum which indicates a Zone 6 hardiness rating. The most unique identification feature is the terminal naked bud with two fuzzy brown pubescent primordia slightly clasped like hands in prayer. The tree might hold a future for urban conditions but has never been adequately tested. Distributed in the wild over a wide area from Japan, Korea, through China to the Himalayas. Introduced 1890.

Akebia quinata Houtt. — Fiveleaf Akebia
(å-kē′bē-å kwi-nā′tå)

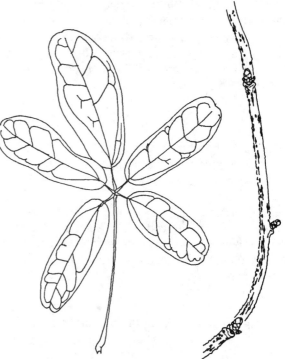

FAMILY: Lardizabalaceae

LEAVES: Alternate, palmately compound, 5 leaflets (sometimes 3 or 4), obovate or elliptic to oblong-obovate, 1 1/2 to 3″ long, emarginate, rounded or broad cuneate at base, bluish green above, glaucous beneath; petiolules—1/2″ long.

BUDS: Imbricate, glabrous, small, sessile, ovate, with 10 to 12 mucronate scales.

STEM: Slender, rounded, green becoming brown, glabrous, heavily lenticelled, leaf scars with 6 or more traces in a broken ellipse, half elliptic, much raised.

SIZE: 20 to 40′, essentially restricted by the structure upon which it grows.

HARDINESS: Zone (4)5 to 8, deciduous in northern climates, more evergreen in warm; at Illinois I noticed the plants kept some basal foliage in winter; at Georgia is completely deciduous; literature seems to indicate one thing, the plant does another.

HABIT: Twining vine or a rampant ground cover.

RATE: Fast

TEXTURE: Medium-fine, a little rougher in winter.

LEAF COLOR: New leaves are tinged purplish and mature to a handsome blue-green; leaves die off green with a hard freeze; have never observed fall color; leafs out by early to mid-March in Georgia, foliage present until December.

FLOWERS: Polygamo-monoecious, pistillate are chocolate-purple, 2 to 5 together, staminate, lighter rosy purple, borne in the same pendent axillary raceme, the pistillate at the ends (outside) and about 1″ diameter, composed of 3 rather fleshy concave showy sepals, the staminate at the end (middle) of the raceme, about 1/4″ across, fragrant and uniquely attractive on close inspection; flowers appear with leaves in late March–early April and can be lost among the foliage; not spectacular from afar; ratio of pistillate to male flowers was 0.74 to 4.66 on 196 plants sampled from 16 sites; cross pollination was necessary for fruit set in artificial pollination studies.

FRUIT: Fleshy, 2 1/4 to 4″ long, fattened sausage-shaped pod of purple-violet color and covered with a waxy bloom, inside is a central pulpy whitish core with numerous imbedded blackish seeds; ripens in

September–October; for best fruit set hand pollination has been suggested but I have observed fruit set at the Arnold Arboretum without any man-made influences; it could be that the plant is self-sterile or male flowers do not open at the same time the gummy stigmatic surface is receptive; the late Dr. J.C. Raulston assembled a tremendous collection of species and cultivars of *Akebia* at the North Carolina State Arboretum which are displayed on a pergola at the entrance to the garden; in late October I observed abundant fruit set, more so than on any other plants, that might suggest cross fertility or vines that open over a staggered period; fruits are supposedly edible.

CULTURE: Transplant from container, extremely fast to establish; adaptable to drought and moisture, sun or shade, displays excellent landscape toughness, major problem is vigor for it can consume a piece of landscape real estate in short order.

DISEASES AND INSECTS: None serious.

LANDSCAPE VALUE: Excellent fast cover but seldom seen in typical landscape situations; good choice for trellises, arbors, pergolas, fences and other structures, will require pruning to keep it in bounds; has assumed weed proportions in some gardens, need to monitor its spread.

CULTIVARS:

'Alba'—Quite a departure from the species, this form offers white flowers and white fruits. 'Shirobana' may be the same as 'Alba' and is listed as having white flowers with exceptional fragrance.

'Rosea'—More lavender or light purple than pink; much lighter colored compared to species.

'Variegata'—Produces pale pink flowers and white variegated foliage.

PROPAGATION: Softwood cuttings will root readily, use 1000 to 3000 ppm IBA-solution; division is also a possibility; seed requires a cold moist stratification for one month, possibly as long as 10 weeks, although 30% germination occurred with freshly sown seed. Worthwhile propagation article by Philip McMillan Browse, *International Dendrological Society Yearbook* 1986/1987 pages 57–67.

NATIVE HABITAT: Central China to Korea and Japan. Introduced 1845.

RELATED SPECIES

Akebia × ***pentaphylla*** Mak., (à-kē′bē-à pen-tà-fil′à), is a hybrid between *A. quinata* and *A. trifoliata* with 3 to 5 leaflets, intermediate in characteristics between the two parents, flowers slightly fragrant, have read references that state between 4 to 7 leaflets. This cross has been reconstituted under controlled conditions.

Akebia trifoliata (Thunb.) Koidz. — Three-leaflet Akebia

LEAVES: Alternate, compound palmate, 3-leaflets, each 1 1/2 to 4″ long, broad ovate to ovate, emarginate, rounded or truncate at base, undulate or irregularly and shallowly lobed, sometimes entire, bluish green above, glaucescent or greenish beneath, the leaflets stalked with the terminal leaflet stalk three times those of the laterals.

Akebia trifoliata, (à-kē′bē-à trī-fō-li-ā′tà), Three-leaflet Akebia, is seldom seen in American gardens but is a worthy twining climber, possibly less cold-hardy than *A. quinata*. The flowers are similar to *A. quinata* with the 3/4 to 1″ diameter pistillate maroon-red, non-fragrant flowers and the pale purple, smaller (1/4″) numerous stamens on short 1 1/2″ long pedicels, March–April. The sausage-shaped, 3 to 5″ long, 1 1/2 to 2 1/2″ diameter pale violet (to dark bluish purple) pod, with dense tiny white spots, ripens in fall and splits from the base to reveal rows of black seeds embedded in the white pulp. Same general landscape uses as *A. quinata*. Not quite as vigorous or high climbing. Central China to Japan. Introduced before 1890. Zone 5 to 8.

(Leaflet)

Alangium platanifolium Harms

FAMILY: Alangiaceae

LEAVES: Alternate, simple, roundish to broad ovate, 4 to 8″ long, almost as wide, with (2)3 to 5(7) prominent lobes toward the apex, entire, dark green above with scattered pubescence, lower surface with pale pubescence; petiole—1 to 3″ long.

BUDS: Large, hairy, reddish, prominent in winter.

STEM: Uniquely zig-zag, light brown, slightly pubescent, usually unbranched.

Alangium platanifolium, (à-lan-gē′um plat-à-ni-fō′li-um), has found a crevice in the *Manual* in which to hide. My first introduction to this 6 to 10′ high, vase-shaped, unbranched caned shrub occurred in March 1996 at the Missouri Botanic Garden. In its native China, the habit may be tree-like but every plant I have witnessed is shrub-like. The large dark green leaves are attractive and turn yellow in fall. The flower is cream-yellow and one of the more bizarre manifestations of a reproductive structure imaginable. Flowers occur on new growth of the season in June in Zone 7b. Fruit is a 1/2″ long, egg-shaped thinly fleshy drupe containing a bony endocarp. Grow as a woodland plant in moist, organic, well-drained soil. A collector's item to be sure. Japan, China. Introduced 1879. Zone 7 to 8(9).

Albizia julibrissin Durazz. — Albizia, also called Silk-tree and Mimosa

(al-biz′i-à jū-li-bri′sin)

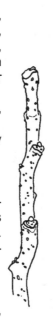

FAMILY: Fabaceae

LEAVES: Alternate, bipinnately compound, to 20″ long, with 10 to 25 pinnae, each with 40 to 60 leaflets, leaflets falcate, oblong, very oblique, 1/4 to 1/2″ long, dark green, ciliate and sometimes pubescent on midribs below, often does not leaf out until late May or early June.

BUDS: Terminal absent, laterals with 2 to 3 scales, small, rounded, brownish.

STEM: Slender, greenish, gray brown at maturity, heavily lenticelled, glabrous, angled.

SIZE: 20 to 35′ in height; spread similar or greater.

HARDINESS: Zone 6 to 9, based on considerable observation and laboratory hardiness testing, temperatures below –5°F for any period of time will result in injury.

HABIT: Vase-shaped, often multi-stemmed, broad-spreading, forming a flat-topped crown.

RATE: Fast.

TEXTURE: Fine in leaf; medium in winter.

BARK: On larger branches and trunks relatively smooth, gray-brown.

LEAF COLOR: Late to leaf out, dark green at maturity, no fall color as leaves die off green when killed by frost.

FLOWERS: Light to deep pink, fragrant, the numerous thread-like, 1″ or more long pink stamens create a brush-like effect; flowers borne in slender-peduncled heads in May, June, July, and August.

FRUIT: Pod, 5 to 7″ long, 1″ wide, light straw to gray-brown, thin, September–October, and persisting into winter and often until the following spring, usually becoming uglier with age.

CULTURE: Transplants readily, extremely adaptable, will withstand drought, high pH and soil salinity; withstands excessive wind; flowers best in full sun.

DISEASES AND INSECTS: Unfortunately very susceptible to a vascular wilt disease (*Fusarium*); this disease seems to be widespread and numerous plants in the South show evidence of infection; often killed to ground and develops shoots from roots creating a mass of suckers; webworm can be highly destructive, leaf spot and rust.

LANDSCAPE VALUE: Not a quality plant because of insect and disease problems; sets prodigious quantities of fruits and effectively seeds itself in waste and road-side situations; foliage and flowers provide a tropical effect; unless a wilt-immune clone is found I would avoid using the species; many people relate to this tree because of handsome summer flowers and would purchase/utilize the plant if it was commonly available; Dr. Frank Santamour, U.S. National Arboretum, has bred and screened 7600 seedlings and selected three wilt and nematode resistant clones that have prospered in my Georgia tests, one has a reddish-maroon foliage cast and deep rose-pink flowers, the foliage color is evident even in the heat and stress of Georgia summer, to date no plants have been released. See *Plant Disease* 70:249–251 (1986).

CULTIVARS:

'Charlotte' and 'Tryon'—Wilt resistant clones, introduced in 1949–50, but documented reports indicate *Fusarium* has infected them; doubtfully available in commerce.

'E.H. Wilson' ('Rosea')—Whether or not these two are synonyms is a moot question but they (it) show increased hardiness to perhaps -15°F; in early July 1991 plants were in full flower at the Arnold Arboretum.

'Flame'—Deep rose-flowered form offered by LandArts, Monroe, GA, their source was L.E. Cook, Visalia, CA.

'Union'—Another wilt resistant clone, little is known about the degree of resistance, not widely tested, introduced 1979.

PROPAGATION: Seed dormancy is due to a hard seed coat and acid scarification for 30 minutes permits germination to ensue; root cuttings collected in spring will produce shoots which can be easily rooted. See Fordham, *Proc. Intl. Plant Prop. Soc.* 16:190–193 (1966).

ADDITIONAL NOTES: Very popular throughout the southern states; its day of reckoning has come due to the wilt disease; as one drives along Interstate 75 through Tennessee and Georgia, *A. julibrissin* is everywhere in evidence; many plants survive only as root sprouts, because the main portion of the tree has been killed by the disease. Have read recent reports from China that mention 24% mortality of the trees in Jwan City, Shandong Province, China. Also, a *Fusicoccum* canker has damaged 40% of young trees in the city. A virus that induced chlorotic leaf stipling symptoms has been reported from Arkansas. See *Phytopathology* 77:935–940 (1987).

NATIVE HABITAT: Iran to central China. Introduced 1745.

Aleurites fordii Hemsl. — Tung-oil Tree

FAMILY: Euphorbiaceae

LEAVES: Alternate, simple, evergreen (defoliates in frost), variable shape from unlobed, broad-ovate to 3- to 5-lobed, 4 to 10″ long and wide, short acuminate, cordate, lustrous dark green, glabrous, palmately veined; petiole—2 to 5″ long, milky sap when broken.

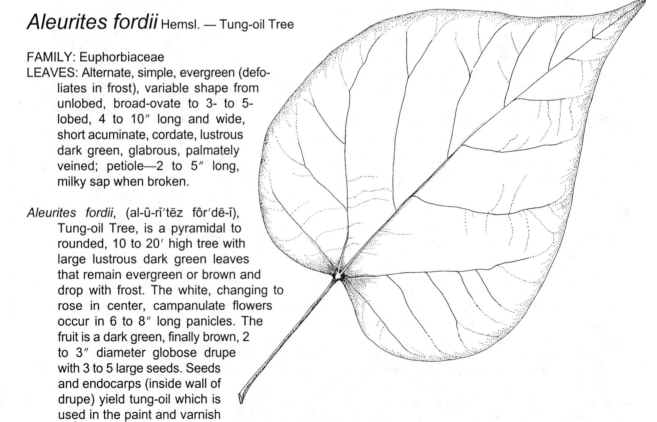

Aleurites fordii, (al-ū-rī′tēz fôr′dē-ī), Tung-oil Tree, is a pyramidal to rounded, 10 to 20′ high tree with large lustrous dark green leaves that remain evergreen or brown and drop with frost. The white, changing to rose in center, campanulate flowers occur in 6 to 8″ long panicles. The fruit is a dark green, finally brown, 2 to 3″ diameter globose drupe with 3 to 5 large seeds. Seeds and endocarps (inside wall of drupe) yield tung-oil which is used in the paint and varnish industry. Seeds and leaves are also poisonous. I have only observed the tree in South Georgia, Florida, and Louisiana. Appears to prosper with neglect. Flowers are quite handsome. Middle Asia. Zone 8 to 10.

Alnus glutinosa (L.) Gaertn. — Common Alder, also called Black or European Alder
(al′nus glū-ti-nō′så)

FAMILY: Betulaceae

LEAVES: Alternate, simple, 2 to 4″ long, 3 to 4″ wide, oval or orbicular to suborbicular, rounded or emarginate at apex, usually broad cuneate, very gummy when young, coarsely and doubly serrate, dark green, glabrous above, axillary tufts beneath, 6 to 8 vein pairs; petiole—1/2 to 1″ long.

BUDS: Stalked, 1/4 to 1/2″ long, reddish or reddish purple, appearing valvate.

STEM: Glabrous, green-brown, finally brown, pith—small, three sided, continuous.

FRUIT: Nutlet, borne in persistent 1/3 to 2/3″ long ovoid strobile, on 1/2 to 1″ long peduncles; the long peduncle permits separation from *A. incana.*

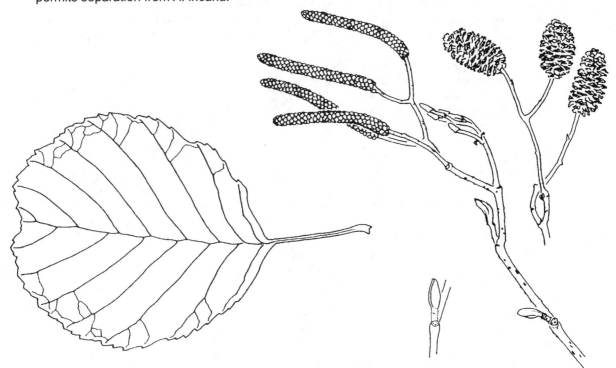

SIZE: 40 to 60′ in height with a spread of 20 to 40′, can grow to 90 to 100′, often shrubby in inhospitable situations; national champion is 76′ by 41′ in Davenport, IA.

HARDINESS: Zone 4 to 7.

HABIT: Often weak pyramidal to narrow pyramidal outline and at other times developing an ovoid or oblong head of irregular proportions; small trees show a pyramidal habit; often grown multi-stemmed and, in fact, has more ornamental appeal when cultured in this fashion.

RATE: Fast in youth, tends to slow down when abundant flowering and fruiting occur, although will average 24 to 30″ per year over a 20 year period; the wood is not as weak and brittle as *Acer saccharinum*, Silver Maple.

TEXTURE: Medium in leaf and in winter.

BARK: Young bark is often a lustrous gray-green or greenish brown and changes to polished brown with age.

LEAF COLOR: Dark glossy green in summer, fall color does not occur as the leaves abscise green or brown; I have read British literature which reported that fall color may be a good yellow; the foliage is extremely handsome.

FLOWERS: Monoecious, reddish brown male flowers in 2 to 4″ long catkins, 3 to 5 together; rather handsome but seldom noticed by most individuals; purplish females borne in a distinct egg-shaped strobile, March.

FRUIT: A small winged nutlet borne in a persistent 1/3 to 2/3″ long egg-shaped woody strobile; maturing in October–November and shed when strobile opens; strobile persists brown through late fall and winter.

CULTURE: Transplants readily; prefers moist or wet soil but performs well in dry soils; full sun or partial shade; seems to be tolerant of acid or slightly alkaline soils; prune in winter or early spring; if used along waterways will seed in along the banks and eventually cover large areas; I have seen the species growing submerged in the water; for extremely wet areas the tree has distinct possibilities; a nitrogen fixing species; does not perform well in the heat of the South; German studies showed that the species is a tremendous pioneer or nurse crop on bogs and land fill sites.

DISEASES AND INSECTS: Powdery mildew attacks the female strobili but this is rarely serious, cankers can be a problem, leaf rust—rarely serious, woolly alder aphid, alder flea beetle, alder lace bug, leaf miner, sawfly, and tent caterpillar; have seen a few serious tent caterpillar infestations.

LANDSCAPE VALUE: Perhaps for difficult, wet sites such as those encountered along highways, in parks and other large areas; does well in infertile areas and has the ability to fix atmospheric nitrogen; widely used throughout Europe; have seen its roots submerged yet plants appear to thrive; to my mind a better plant than many willows and poplars but not as popular (no pun intended); as a biomass source the alders would make good choices; of 35 species, 33 have been reported to fix nitrogen.

CULTIVARS:

'Aurea'—Leaves golden yellow, fading to green with time, quite handsome in May–June especially as seen in the English landscape; would probably succeed in more northern locations in the United States; not a vigorous grower; introduced around 1860.

'Charles Howlett'—Variously shaped and variegated leaves, yellow to orange streaked bark, slightly less vigorous than the species; discovered in Chandler's Ford, Hampshire, England in 1982.

'Imperialis'—A form with deeply and finely cut light green leaves; much more prominently incised than 'Laciniata', the sinuses cut more than halfway to the midrib; it is fair to say that in youth the tree is ungainly but I have observed several handsome specimens in England that inspire me to try one in my garden; behind the Spread Eagle Hotel in Midhurst, England are several beautiful specimens; almost like a weeping willow in texture but branches are not as weeping, quite wispy, elegant and refined, seems to improve with age.

'Laciniata'—Leaves cut and lobed but not to the degree of 'Imperialis'; lobes not prominently serrated and almost triangular in outline; a vigorous form growing 50 to 70' high; in existence probably before 1819.

'Pyramidalis' ('Fastigiata')—Good looking form of upright columnar habit, 40 to 50', resembling Lombardy Popular; definitely should be used more extensively; occasionally seen in midwestern arboreta but not common in commerce; might make a suitable substitute for *Populus nigra* 'Italica'.

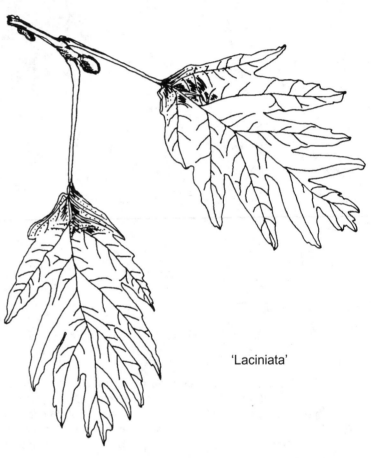

'Laciniata'

PROPAGATION: The following applies to all the alders discussed herein. Seed requires a cold period and 3 months at 41°F or fall sowing should suffice; seeds are similar to birch and have a low survival rate; strobiles should be collected as they begin to change from green to brown; there is some indication that fresh seed will germinate without a cold treatment; I participate in the Royal Horticultural Society seed exchange and experiment with new genera every year; seed (as dry as hay) were sown in early March (no pretreatment) and started to germinate in 7 days; once the seed are dried then moist-cold stratification supposedly becomes necessary; information on cutting propagation is scant but June and July collected cuttings treated with 8000 ppm IBA have been rooted at a 20 to 40% rate; cultivars are usually grafted onto the species.

ADDITIONAL NOTES: See Ashburner, *The Plantsman* 86:170–188 (1986) "*Alnus*—A Survey." This article provides a practical discussion of the performance and garden merits of the genus.

NATIVE HABITAT: *Alnus glutinosa* is indigenous to Europe (including Britain), western Asia and northern Africa; long cultivated; escaped from cultivation in the United States and is frequently observed forming pure stands along waterways. Several botanical varieties and formae are described in Griffiths and represent the variation over the wide native range.

RELATED SPECIES:

Alnus cordata Desf. — Italian Alder

LEAVES: Alternate, simple, 2 to 4″ long, 3/4 to as much in width, broad-ovate to roundish, abruptly acuminate, cordate at base, finely serrate, glabrous above, lustrous dark green, lighter beneath with brownish tufts in axils of veins; petiole—1/2 to 1 1/2″ long, slender, glabrous.

FRUIT: Large, egg-shaped, 1 to 1 1/4″ long, 5/8 to 3/4″ wide, erect, woody strobile, often occurring in 3's; persistent and offering a consistent identification feature; the largest fruit of the cultivated alders.

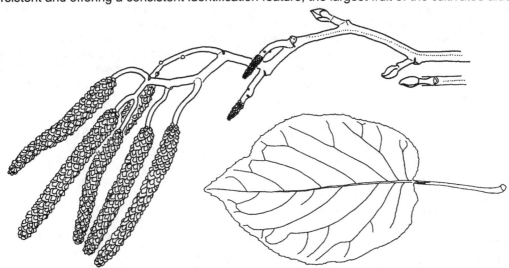

Alnus cordata, (al′nus kôr-dã′tà), Italian Alder, forms a 30 to 50′(70′) high pyramidal to pyramidal rounded tree. Resembles to a degree Littleleaf Linden in outline. In many respects, from a distance, it resembles the Common Pear in appearance. Bark is a glistening brown in youth. Thrives in infertile, dry, high pH soils but is most at home near water. Perhaps the most beautiful of the alders for landscape use but little known and grown. Have seen it thriving in Midwest. A superb tree as seen in Europe and the neat pyramidal-oblong outline, handsome foliage and cultural adaptability justify greater consideration in the United States. Trees in Urbana, IL, survived -20°F. In the world of *Alnus*, this may be the finest for street and urban use. Great trees in the city of Bath, England. In Italian tests, *Alnus cordata* proved the most resistant to simulated acid rain. 'Purpurea' produces purple brown emerging leaves that age to green. 'Sipkes' was discovered in a seedling population of *A. cordata*. It has large, glossy, dark green leaves and uniform, vigorous growth habit. Forms an upright-oval crown. Will grow 50 to 60′ high. See *Dendroflora* 25:4–6 (1988). Corsica and southern Italy. 1820. Zone 5 to 7.

Alnus incana (L.) Moench. — White or Gray Alder

LEAVES: Alternate, simple, 2 to 4″ long, 1 1/4 to 2 1/4″ wide, ovate, oval or obovate, apex acute, base rounded or cuneate, double serrate and usually slightly lobulate, dull green above, impressed veins, grayish beneath, 9 to 12 vein pairs; petiole—1/2 to 1″ long, pubescent.

BUDS: Distinctly stalked, 1/4 to 1/2″ long, reddish, more or less whitened with fine down, slightly sticky within.

STEM: Slender, finely downy or glabrous, grayish brown, hairy towards tips especially of fruiting twigs.

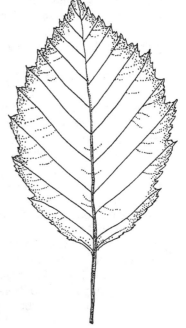

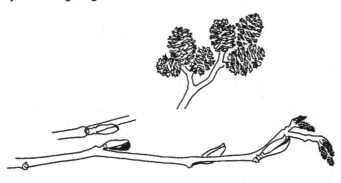

Alnus incana, (al'nus in-kā'nȧ), White or Gray Alder, is a large pyramidal-oval tree 40 to 60'(100') in height with dull dark green foliage. Next to *Alnus glutinosa* the commonest of the alders and is useful for planting in cold (Zone 2), wet places. It is closely allied to *Alnus rugosa* and, at one time, the Speckled Alder was listed as *Alnus incana* var. *americana* Regel. There are several cultivars *of Alnus incana* which are more common in the landscape than the species:

'Aurea'—Leaves are yellow, young stems are reddish yellow and remain so throughout the winter, young catkins orangish; have seen in England during September and the yellow leaf color is essentially past but the orange male catkins are quite distinct.

'Laciniata'—The handsomest of the many cut-leaved types with the blade divided into 6 or 8 pairs of lobes reaching 2/3's or more of the way to the midrib, leaves light green.

'Pendula'—A fine form with pendulous branches and gray-green leaves; leaves are actually dark green above, gray-green below; the branches decidedly pendulous and the entire tree quite attractive; large specimen in the Palmengarten, Frankfurt, West Germany, that makes the trip justifiable. This species can be distinguished from *A. glutinosa* by the shape and color of the leaves. Europe and the Caucasus; long cultivated in Europe; not common in America. Zone 2 to 6.

Alnus rugosa (Duroi) Spreng. — Speckled Alder

LEAVES: Alternate, simple, 2 to 4 1/2" long, ovate, acute or obtuse, rounded to cuneate, with a row of 2 distinctly different-sized teeth along the margin, dull dark green, glabrous, and somewhat wrinkled on the upper surface, paler and covered with rusty red hairs below; petiole—short, stout, smooth, white dotted.

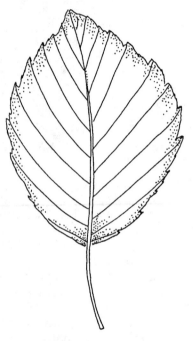

Alnus rugosa, (al'nus rū-gōs'ȧ), Speckled Alder, is usually a coarse shrub or small tree ranging from 15 to 25' tall. National champion is 66' by 56' in St. Clair County, MI. It occurs in a broad band across Canada into North Dakota south to West Virginia and Virginia. I first saw the species along the Concord River in Minuteman National Park in Concord, MA . . . or did I? There seems to be much confusion between this and *A. serrulata*. Both grow in similar moist habitats and their native ranges overlap. A key difference is the more even serrations of *A. serrulata*. *Alnus rugosa* has distinct 1/6 to 1/3" long whitish lenticels on the stems; hence, the name Speckled Alder. The erect 1/2" long catkins occur in clusters of 4 to 10. For moist areas along ponds and streambanks it is a possibility. Cultivated 1769. Zone 3 to 6.

Alnus serrulata (Ait.) Willd. — Tag or Hazel Alder

LEAVES: Alternate, simple, 2 to 4" long, 1 1/4 to 2 1/2" wide, ovate or obovate, acute, cuneate, with uniform fine teeth along the margin, dark green and glabrous above, paler and pubescent beneath especially on the veins, with 8 to 12 vein pairs; petiole—smooth, about 1" long.

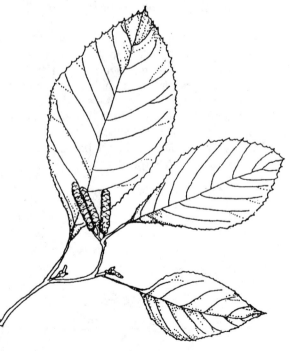

Alnus serrulata, (al'nus ser-ū-lā'tȧ), Tag Alder, is closely allied to *A. rugosa*, differing chiefly in its leaves, which are usually broadest above the middle and have the margins set with fine, nearly regular teeth. The habit is strongly multi-stemmed and suckering, the bark a shiny gray-brown. Size ranges from 6 to 10' to 20' and the species, like willow, can colonize moist soil areas to the detriment of other plants. Four national champions are listed, all about 30' by 20'. The 1/2" long, 1/4" wide oval cone-shaped fruit persists through the winter months. The fruits are smaller than those of *A. rugosa*. The male catkins occur in groups of 3 to 5. Neither this nor *A. rugosa* will take the nursery industry by storm. In fact, I do not know of a nurseryman that grows either. Abundant in southern states along streams and lakes. In my mind there is little difference between this and the above species. Very beautiful in February–March when the yellow-brown catkins are waving in the early spring breezes. Maine south to Florida and Louisiana. Zone (4)5 to 9.

ADDITIONAL NOTES: None of the alder species mentioned here are widely cultivated in the United States. They make excellent plants for use along stream banks and in poor soil areas. There is considerable interest in their potential for biomass and subsequent energy production. Interestingly, *Alnus* has been tissue culture propagated by researchers at the University of Minnesota. In early spring, as their elongating yellow-brown catkins sway with the warm breezes, they provide interesting color to an otherwise drab landscape.

Alnus rhombifolia Nutt., White Alder, grows 50 to 60′ high and has been used as a street tree in the West. National champion is 70′ by 48′ in Nezperce National Forest, ID. The lustrous, dark green leaves average 2 to 4″ long and are finely doubly serrate. Zone 6.

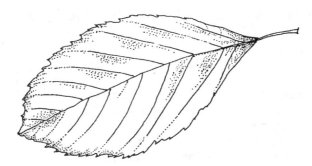

Alnus rubra Bong., Red or Oregon Alder, a West Coast species, makes a 60 to 75′(100′) high tree with gray-white bark and reddish buds and male catkins. National champion is 104′ by 49′ in Clatsop County, OR. The 3 to 7″ long, dark green leaves are strongly toothed or lightly lobed and have revolute margins. Found from Alaska to California. Used as a nurse and short term tree. Susceptible to wind throw with age and size. Also a favorite host for the tent caterpillars. Zone 6.

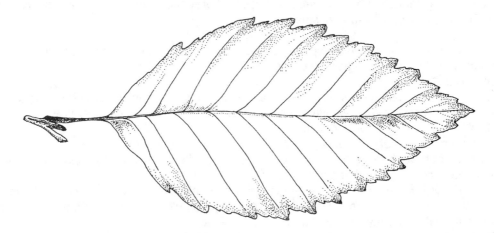

The West is endowed with other alder species including: *A. sinuata* (Reg.) Rydb., Sitka Alder, a shrub or small tree to 30′. Co-national champions are 30′ by 39′ and 37′ by 29′ on Maury Island, King County, WA. Alaska to California. Zone 2; *A. oblongifolia* Torr., Arizona Alder, tree 50 to 60′. National champion is 129′ by 50′ in Cibola National Forest, NM. Arizona to California. Zone 8; and *A. tenuifolia* Nutt., Thinleaf or Mountain Alder, a shrub-tree, 20 to 30′ high. National champion is 71′ by 39′ in Umatila National Forest, WA. British Columbia to California. Zone 2. Although beyond the scope of this book, their mention provides an idea of the diversity and distribution of the genus. Elias, *Trees of North America*, provides excellent coverage of the genus.

Three species: *A. maritima* (Marsh.) Muhlenb., Seaside Alder, national champion is 24′ by 12′ in Lake Accotink, Springfield, VA; *A. nepalensis* D. Don, Nepal Alder; and *A. nitida* (Spach) Endl. flower in autumn; all others with or before the leaves. Supposedly several taxa, *A. viridis* (Chaix) DC. subsp. *crispa*

(Ait.) Turrill (national champion is 28′ by 12′ in Marquette, MI) and *A. rugosa,* burn so hot they melt stoves. *Alnus crispa* (Ait.) Pursh, Mountain or Green Alder, has been keyed by the author on top of Rabun Bald, Georgia's second highest mountain. It is a shrubby, almost decumbent shrub. And finally, 33 of 35 *Alnus* species have been shown to fix atmospheric nitrogen. To observe alders inhabiting and colonizing the most inhospitable sites is to infer that they can adjust and thrive due to inherent genetic advantage(s). The *Alnus* species could serve to stabilize the soil, improve fertility and act as a nurse crop until other woody species become established. Alders have never been a significant factor in American tree or shrub planting and are not, to my knowledge, offered by the major shade tree liner producers.

Two Japanese species, *A. japonica* (Thunb.) Steud., Japanese Alder, with 2 to 4″ long, lustrous, dark, green leaves, 60 to 75′ high stature, Zone 4 and *A. hirsuta* (Spach) Rupr., Manchurian Alder, 50′, 2 to 5″ long, dull, dark, gray-green leaves, Zone 3, have crossed the author's path on several occasions. *Alnus japonica* has beautiful foliage, much more so than *A. hirsuta*, and should be worthy of trialing.

Amelanchier arborea (Michx. f.) Fern. — Downy Serviceberry also called Juneberry, Shadbush, Servicetree or Sarvis-tree
(am-e-lang′kē-ēr är-bō′rē-ȧ)

FAMILY: Rosaceae

LEAVES: Alternate, simple, generally obovate, less often ovate, elliptic or oblong, 1 to 3″ long, 1/2 to 1 3/4″ wide, acute or acuminate, usually cordate at base, sharply serrate nearly or quite at base, when young densely tomentose beneath, less so above, tomentum usually partly persistent, when unfolding grayish pubescent, medium to dark green at maturity; petiole—3/8 to 1 1/4″ (1 1/2″).

BUDS: Terminal—present, 5 to 7 scaled, laterals of similar size, 1/3 to 1/2″ long, imbricate, narrowly ovate to conical, sharp pointed, greenish yellow, more or less tinged with reddish purple, glabrous or with white silky hairs at apex and edges of scales, mostly appressed; tend to show a slight spiraling; color is highly variable from green to maroon.

STEM: Slender, olive-green to red-brown often covered with a gray skin, generally smooth, glabrous, with slight taste of bitter almonds; pith—green, small.

SIZE: 15 to 25′ in height with a variable spread; can grown to 40′ but this is rare under cultivation; national champion is 60′ by 53′ in Burkes Garden, VA.

HARDINESS: Zone 4 to 9.

HABIT: Multi-stemmed large shrub or small tree with a rounded crown of many small branches; often dissipates in old age to a rounded form; beautiful in winter dress with an understated elegance.

RATE: Medium, 9 to 10′ in 5 to 8 year period.

TEXTURE: Medium-fine in leaf; medium in winter.

BARK: Grayish, smooth but streaked with longitudinal fissures, often with a reddish cast, very ornamental; in extreme age becoming ridged and furrowed and scaly.

LEAF COLOR: Grayish tomentose when emerging and gradually changing to a medium to dark green in summer; fall color can vary from yellow to apricot-orange to dull, deep dusty red; one of our finest small trees for fall coloration; may color and drop early in the fall.

FLOWERS: Perfect, white, borne in pendulous racemes, 2 to 4″ long, mid to late March (early April) in Athens, GA, mid to late April in Boston, MA, about the time the leaves are emerging and about 1/2 normal size; effective for 4 to 7 days depending on weather; very ornamental but briefly persistent; weakly malodorous.

FRUIT: Berry-like pome, orange-shaped, 1/4 to 1/3″ diameter, changing from green to red and finally to purplish black, bloomy, slightly sweetish, and birds love them; ripens in June; actually matures over a 3 to 4 week period and must be picked before birds clean the plant; ripe fruits are better than highbush blueberries; I have had serviceberry pie and it ranks in the first order of desserts.

CULTURE: Transplant balled and burlapped or container grown plants into moist, well-drained, acid soil; will tolerate full sun or partial shade; in the wild commonly found along borders of woodlands, streambanks and fence rows in open country, although also occurs on hillsides and mountain slopes where conditions are drier; from my own observation I would expect the amelanchiers to perform well in many types of soils; not particularly pollution tolerant; rarely require pruning; not reliable under high stress conditions.

DISEASES AND INSECTS: Rust (cedar serviceberry rust, comparable to cedar apple and hawthorn rusts), witches' broom caused by a fungus, leaf blight, fire blight, powdery mildews, fruit rot, leaf miner, borers, pear leaf blister mite, pear slug sawfly and willow scurfy scale. Have observed reasonable amount of leaf spot (*Entomosporium* species) which disfigures leaves and causes early defoliation; many of the newer cultivars are free of any serious insects and diseases; over the years I have been advised that fireblight was a problem; interestingly in 1988, the Athens–Atlanta area suffered the worst fireblight on pears, apples and other rosaceous plants in my 10 years in the area; serviceberries on campus and at the Botanical Garden were essentially free of infestation; a local nurseryman had fireblight on 'Cumulus' but this could have been related to the high nutritional status of the plants.

LANDSCAPE VALUE: Very pleasing in a naturalistic planting and probably used to best advantage there; blends in well on the edges of woodlands, near ponds and streambanks; blends into shrub borders especially with evergreen background; serviceberries are now used in all facets of landscaping but their most effective use is as described above.

CULTIVARS: In the third (1983) edition no selections were listed except under *A. alnifolia* and *A. laevis* and these were of no significance in the Midwest, East, and South. In the recent years the entire scene has changed with many new introductions and a few older ones that are being offered in commerce. They are presented here in alphabetical order with the suspected parentage. Unfortunately, *Amelanchier* taxonomy is not clear and I have pieced the information together and will be pleased to entertain other observations and ideas.

'Autumn Brilliance'—An *A.* × *grandiflora* selection. Plant patent 5717. Bill Wandell, Oquawka, IL has introduced a number of excellent shade tree selections as well as the amelanchier with the poetic name 'Autumn Brilliance'. It will reach 20 to 25′ at maturity. White flowers, edible fruits, clean summer foliage, persistent leaves and brilliant red fall color are notable attributes. Light gray bark, attractive in winter; grows faster and will produce a 6 to 8′ high heavily branched plant from an 18 to 24″ liner in 3 years. Hardy to -35°F. In our Georgia trials, this along with 'Ballerina' and 'Princess Diana', have proven the best of the parade. Fall color on *all* amelanchiers is variable from year to year. Also, the above mentioned cultivars are more leaf spot (*Entomosporium*) resistant.

'Autumn Sunset'—A particularly fine form of *A.* × *grandiflora*. I selected it in 1986 from seedling plants on the University of Georgia campus, Athens. The habit is rounded with a strong single trunk. The plant's flowers and summer foliage are typical of *A.* × *grandiflora*, and the principal attributes are superior leaf retention and rich, pumpkin-orange fall color. Fall color in the Athens area develops from late October to mid-November and is consistent from year to year. 'Autumn Sunset' displays excellent heat and drought tolerance and did not drop a leaf in the worst drought of the century (1986). The plant was probably grown from a southern seed provenance. Hardiness tests indicate it will tolerate -24°F or lower. I suspect its mature landscape size will average 20 to 25′.

'Ballerina'—A selection of *A.* × *grandiflora* made by the Experiment Station at Boskoop, Netherlands, from plants sent as *A. ovalis* by Hillier and Sons, Winchester, England. It is an upright shrub or small tree with spreading branches. The young leaves are broad elliptic, finely saw-toothed, 2 to 3″ long and 1 1/4 to 1 1/2″ wide, bronze-colored, essentially without pubescence. They turn glossy dark green in summer and finally purple-bronze in fall. The pure white flowers average 1 to 1 1/8″ in diameter and occur 6 to 8 together in a 3 to 5″ long fleecy raceme that is more or less pendent. The 3/8 to 1/2″ diameter fruit is bright red, turning purplish black when ripe. It is tender and sweet. This selection will grow 15 to 20′ high and is hardy in Zone 4. One source indicated this is a hybrid with *A. laevis* and the other parent unknown. Named in 1980. Several American nurseries are growing this selection; the fall color is brick-red in the Southeast; has been a genuine success in Zone 7b, superb, large, sweet, juicy fruits, excellent leaf spot resistance, essentially free of fire blight.

'Cole' ('Cole's Select')—A designation I will use for lack of a better name. Dr. Ed Hasselkus, now retired, University of Wisconsin, mentioned that this selection of *A.* × *grandiflora* has exceptional red fall color. The Cole Nursery Co., Circleville, OH grew, but did not name it. At least one nursery in the United States (Briggs Nursery, Olympia, WA) has the plant and will be producing it through tissue culture. Have read recent evaluations that the habit is spreading and the fall color is excellent orange-red; thicker, glossier foliage than many serviceberries resulting in improved summer appearance; upright-spreading growth habit, 20′ by 15′.

'Cumulus'—An introduction from Princeton Nurseries, Princeton, NJ. According to Dr. Hasselkus, this is a selection of *A. laevis*. It grows 20 to 30′ high, 15 to 20′ wide, and is hardy in Zone 4. It has fleecy white flowers in spring and bright yellowish to orange-scarlet fall color. Plants I have observed displayed a distinct upright-oval outline in youth, which would make this form useful for street tree plantings or where lateral branch spread must be restricted. Unfortunately, 'Cumulus' has been grafted or budded in the past, and several plants I have observed had suckers developing from the rootstock. Supposedly less prone to suckers than other forms. Fire blight was devastating during the 1988 growing season in the southeastern United States. Plant patent 3092.

'Forest Prince'—*A.* × *grandiflora* selection with clean, healthy summer foliage and good orange-red fall color; pure white flowers offer a billowy appearance, opening over the length of the stems instead of at the tip; a Klehm Nursery introduction.

'Jackie'—Listed as a sweet fruit producing selection; have not observed this clone.

'Lustre'—Excellent shiny green summer foliage changing to orange and red in fall, Carlton Nursery, OR introduction.

'Majestic'—New, exceptionally vigorous grower, large clean disease resistant foliage is red when emerging maturing to dark green then rich scarlet in autumn; large pure white flowers in April, 20 to 25', plant patent 7203, Moller Nursery introduction.

'Prince Charles'—An *A. laevis* form that flowers ahead of the leaves, thus offering a prominent display. The bronzy red new foliage matures to a pleasant green and develops orange-red fall color. Again, the 3/8″ diameter fruits are edible. In fact, during a serviceberry taste test, this along with 'Ballerina' rated tops by the author. This is an upright form (probably maturing about 25' by 15'), selected from a number of *A. laevis* that Mr. Watson and Dr. Ed Hasselkus were evaluating. The final selection was a plant growing in the University of Wisconsin Arboretum. Plant patent 6039.

'Prince William'—Probably a hybrid, with *A. canadensis* as one parent. The habit is shrubby, like that of a typical *A. canadensis*, with landscape size approximating 8' or possibly taller by 6' wide. The emerging leaves are reddish tinged (suggesting *A. laevis* parentage) developing a rich glossy green and finally an orange-red in fall. The sweet edible fruit averages about 1/2″ in diameter. Plants may flower the second year out of tissue culture. This form was selected in the Madison, WI area and is hardy to -25 to -30°F. Plant patent 6040.

'Princess Diana'—A selection of *A.* × *grandiflora* from the garden of Tom Watson's parents in Milwaukee, WI. Abundant white flowers, clean foliage, 3/8″ diameter edible fruits and outstanding red fall color (appearing in early October in Cambridge, WI), provide superlative ornamental traits. The habit can be multi- or single-stemmed; plants from tissue culture develop the multi-stemmed habit. Watson estimates 25' by 15 to 20' for the mature landscape size. Plants will flower in their third year out of tissue culture. I have seen photographs of fall color and found a triple take necessary to assure myself that the color was as good as the print. This form is hardy to at least -35°F. Report from Galen Gates, Chicago Botanic Garden, indicates this form has not fall colored as well as the original plant. At Bold Spring Nursery, Monroe, GA, this was the most leaf spot free serviceberry in 1991 when leaves were cascading like raindrops from *A. laevis* and others. Plant patent 6041.

'R.J. Hilton'—A selection of *A. laevis* from Canada, numerous accessions were collected from the wild and evaluated at the University of Guelph Arboretum, this form is tree-like with excellent flower, foliage and fruit. See *HortScience* 29:1, 43 (1994).

Rainbow Pillar® ('Glenn's Upright')—A reasonably tight upright form with bright, white flowers and mixed mottled, bright rainbow of yellow, orange, red fall color; supposedly will reach 25' high, a small plant in Georgia tests appears more shrubby, foliage is mildew resistant, recommended as screen and hedge because of upright, multi-branched habit, introduced by Herman Losely and Son, Perry, OH.

'Robin Hill'—Grows 20 to 30' high by 12 to 15' wide, and is hardy in Zone 4. It is another *A.* × *grandiflora* form, but the pink color resides in the buds and fades as the flowers unfurl. The color is intense in cool weather but fades rapidly if the weather is hot and dry at flowering time, yellow to red fall color, good tree form.

'Rubescens'—Grows 20 to 25' tall and is hardy in Zone 4. It is another *A.* × *grandiflora* form, which arose as a seedling in Seneca Park, Rochester, NY. It has been in cultivation since 1920. The flowers are purplish pink in bud and open to a light pink. In my forays through the Arnold Arboretum, I chanced upon this most handsome form. With the renewed interest in amelanchiers, enterprising nurserymen should resurrect this clone. In England, this form is described as developing excellent autumn color.

'Silver Fountain'—A weeping form with branches that arch to the ground, have seen the plant at Theodore Klein's Crestwood, KY arboretum; large somewhat rounded in outline, described as a large snowball in flower.

'Snowcloud'—An *A. laevis* form, a narrow, upright tree with branches spreading at a wide angle, overall texture-delicate, airy and graceful; large white flowers, showy, sweet, purplish black fruits suitable for pies and jellies, blue-green summer foliage, coppery orange fall color, 20 to 25' high, 15 to 20' wide, plant patent 7203, Princeton Nursery introduction.

'Spring Glory' ('Sprizam')—Believe in a former life this may have been named 'Springtime'/'Springtyme'; a compact, 8 to 10' tall selection of *A. canadensis*; provides a graceful column of white flowers; supposedly has brilliant fall color of golden amber and orange; introduced by Lake County Nursery, Perry, OH.

'Strata'—A form of *A.* × *grandiflora* selected by Dr. Hasselkus because of its strong horizontal branching. Produces abundant white flowers. It is in the University of Wisconsin Arboretum and was originally bought as a seedling from Tures and Sons Nursery in Kingston, IL. The fall color is said to have "tinges of orange."

Tradition® ('Trazam')—A strong tree form with a central leader and excellent branching habit, showy white flowers, heavy fruiting, fall color a blaze of orange and red; grows to 25′ tall by 15′ wide; listed as *A. canadensis*, but is probably a selection of one of the other species, Lake County Nursery introduction.

'White Pillar'—Tight columnar habit, late flowering, dark green leaves, orange-red fall color, 20 to 30′ high, selected by Peter E. Costich, Long Island, NY.

PROPAGATION: Cold stratification for seed of most species is recommended; 90 to 120 days at 41°F in moist medium would suffice; tissue culture has opened the floodgates for new introductions and Knight Hollow Nursery (Dr. Deborah McCown), Madison, WI and Briggs Nursery (Mr. Bruce Briggs), Olympia, WA, have been successful. For specific tissue culture recipes see Dirr and Heuser, 1987. In the past I have had miserable success with cuttings, but have listened to many people and have developed a reasonably safe procedure. Timing is important and cuttings should be taken when the growth extension has ceased, the end leaf is maturing and the stem tissue is firming. In my experiences, 3000 to 10000 ppm KIBA-quick dip has produced good results; May 12, 1988 cuttings of 'Autumn Sunset', 10000 ppm KIBA quick dip, peat:perlite, mist resulted in 72% rooting; results have been as high as 96%; leave cuttings in the bed or rooting cells, take through an overwintering period and sell preferably as 2-year-old liners; overwintering losses can be a problem especially if cuttings are transplanted immediately after rooting.

NATIVE HABITAT: Maine to Iowa, south to northern Florida and Louisiana. Introduced about 1746.

RELATED SPECIES:

Amelanchier alnifolia (Nutt.) Nutt. — Saskatoon Serviceberry

LEAVES: Alternate, simple, 1 to 2 1/2″ long, 1 to 1 1/2″ wide, broad-oval to suborbicular, rounded to slightly indented at apex, rounded to heart-shaped at base, sharply and coarsely toothed especially on the upper one-half of the margins, pale to dark green above, paler beneath, glabrous; petiole—1/2 to 1″ long, pubescent or glabrous.

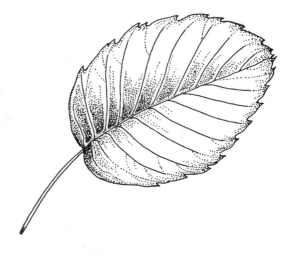

BUDS: Imbricate, ovoid, sharp pointed, 1/4 to 3/8″ long, 5 to 7 visible scales, reddish brown and glabrous on outer surface, silver hairs protruding from underside, appressed half their length.

STEM: Moderate, slightly angled, rich brown, epidermal layer gray and peeling, odor of almond extract when bruised; pith—green, solid.

Amelanchier alnifolia, (am-e-lang′kē-ēr al-ni-fō′lē-à), Saskatoon Serviceberry, deserves mention because of its development for commercial fruit production. It is closely allied to *A. florida* (now *A. alnifolia* var. *semi-integrifolia*) and much confused with that species. It is distinguished by the smaller flowers (3/4″ diameter) and the thicker, rounder leaves. It is also smaller in habit but according to the literature ranges from 3 to 18′ in height. National champion is 42′ by 43′ in Beacon Rock State Park, WA. All forms I have grown or observed in Illinois and Georgia have been 6 to 10′ high, multi-stemmed shrubs. This may seem like a strong statement, but this species and the cultivars have been ravaged by leaf spot in the eastern and southern United States. The 1/3 to 1/2″ diameter berries are bluish purple when ripe (June–July), juicy and edible. Prairie Indians mixed it with buffalo meat and fat to make pemmican, their principal winter food. It tolerates harsh climates and alkaline soil. 'Altaglow' produces excellent fall colors; 'Honeywood' produces excellent fruit; 'Regent' is a compact (4 to 6′ by 4 to 8′) shrub with excellent foliage and extra sweet fruit; 'Smokey' is a large-fruited form with excellent flavor; 'Success' produces an abundance of fruit; 'Northline', 'Parkwood', 'Pembina' and 'Theissen' are also excellent fruit producing selections. Native to Great Plains from Manitoba and Saskatchewan to Nebraska. Cultivated 1918. Zone 4 to 5. Not well adapted to Zone 6 to 8 of eastern United States.

Amelanchier alnifolia var. ***semi-integrifolia*** (Hook.) C. Hitchc. (*A. florida* Lindl.) — Pacific Serviceberry

LEAVES: Alternate, simple, broad-oval to ovate, 3/4 to 1 1/2″ long, truncate or subcordate at base, coarsely and sharply toothed above the middle, rarely below, quite glabrous or slightly floccose-tomentose at first.

BUDS: Ovoid to ellipsoidal, acute or acuminate, dark chestnut brown, glabrous or puberulous, 1/4 to 3/4″ long, scales of the inner ranks ovate, acute, brightly colored, coated with pale silky hairs.

STEM: Slender, pubescent when they first appear, bright red-brown and usually glabrous during their first season, darker second year, ultimately dark gray-brown.

BARK: Light brown, slightly tinged with red, smooth or slightly fissured.

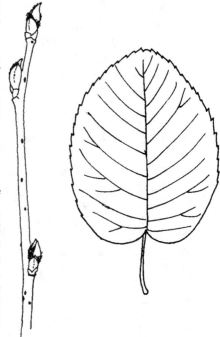

Amelanchier alnifolia var. *semi-integrifolia*, (am-e-lang′kē-ēr al-ni-fō′ lē-á sem-ĭ-in-teg-ri-fō′li-á), Pacific Serviceberry, is a shrub of erect stems to 10′ or more high or a small tree; flowers are white, about 3/4 to 1 1/4″ across, borne 5 to 15 together in erect racemes; fruit purplish black, juicy and edible although the birds do not seem to bother it like the fruit of other species. There was a specimen on the Illinois campus and the flowers never compared with *A. arborea*, *A.* × *grandiflora*, or *A. laevis*. In fact they paled by comparison. Also, the fruits often dried on the plant like raisins. Fresh fruits were not tasty. Southern Alaska to Idaho and northern California. Introduced 1826. Zone 2 to 5.

Amelanchier asiatica (Sieb. & Zucc.) Walp. — Asian Serviceberry

LEAVES: Alternate, simple, 1 1/2 to 3″ long, ovate to elliptic-oblong, acute, rounded to subcordate at the base, finely serrate along the margin, densely woolly when young, dark green.

Amelanchier asiatica, (am-e-lang′kē-ēr ā-shi-at′i-ká), Asian Serviceberry, is a tree of very graceful form growing from 15 to 25′(40′) high; flowers are white, fragrant, and borne about 2 to 3 weeks after *A. arborea* when the leaves are about full size; fruit is purple-black, edible, about 1/3″ diameter. Winter buds are a very deep red and quite different in that respect from most of our native types. Although described as possessing orange-red fall color, the potential is not realized to any degree. Native to China, Korea, and Japan. Zone 5.

Amelanchier canadensis (L.) Medik. — Shadblow Serviceberry, Thicket Serviceberry

LEAVES: Alternate, simple, elliptic to oblong, 1 1/2 to 2 1/2″ long, 1/2 to 1 1/4″ wide, rounded, rarely cordate, finely and uniformly toothed, sometimes entire near base, woolly when young ultimately becoming glabrous, medium to dark green.

BUDS: Imbricate, slender, conical, 1/4 to 3/8″ long, 5 to 7-scaled, greenish to reddish purple, some pubescence often evident under edges of scales, outside of scales glabrous.

STEM: Slender, brown with gray onion-skin effect, glabrous, small lenticels; pith—solid, green, small.

HABIT: Upright, suckering, tightly multi-stemmed shrub; distinctly different in habit from *A. arborea* and *A. laevis* with which it is often confused.

Amelanchier canadensis, (am-e-lang′kē-ēr kan-a-den′sis), Shadblow Serviceberry, is often confused with *A. arborea* and, in fact, the two are used interchangeably in the nursery trade. *Amelanchier canadensis* as now understood is a shrub with erect stems, spreading by means of sucker growths from the base, 6 to 20′ tall, occurring in bogs and swamps from Maine to South Carolina along the coast; the white flowers are borne in erect, compact, 2 to 3″ long racemes in late March on the Georgia Campus and the petals are more distinctly and uniformly obovate than in *A. arborea* or *A. laevis* and somewhat shorter, 3/5″ long; fruit is black, juicy and sweet. This species flowers about one week after *A. arborea*. The fall color is often yellow and gold but I have seen specimens with sprinklings of orange and red. In Bernheim Arboretum, *A. canadensis* had developed excellent orange-red fall color by 9-27-94. By far, the best serviceberry in the collection. Zone 3 to 7(8).

Amelanchier* × *grandiflora Rehd., (am-e-lang′kē-ēr gran-di-flō′rà), Apple Serviceberry, is a hybrid between *A. arborea* × *A. laevis* with young leaves purplish and pubescent. The flowers are larger, on longer, slender racemes, tinged pink in bud. Kartesz merges this into synonymy with *A. laevis*. This is the progenitor species of several important landscape cultivars that are listed under *A. arborea*. Cultivated since 1870. Zone 4 to 9.

Amelanchier laevis Wiegand — Allegheny Serviceberry
LEAVES: Alternate, simple, elliptic-ovate to ovate-oblong, 1 1/4 to 3″ long, short acuminate, subcordate or rounded at base, quite glabrous and purplish when young, dark green at maturity.
BUDS: Imbricate, similar to *A. arborea*, usually 1/2″ long, green tinged with red, the inner scales lanceolate, bright red above the middle, ciliate with silky white hairs.
STEM: Slender, glabrous, reddish brown 1st year, dull grayish brown in their second season.

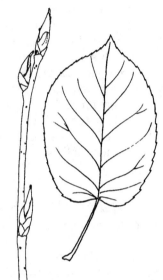

Amelanchier laevis, (am-e-lang′kē-ēr lē′vis), Allegheny Serviceberry, is closely allied to *A. arborea* but differs by reason of the bronzy color of the unfolding leaves and their lack of pubescence as well as the almost glabrous pedicels and peduncle of the inflorescence. The fruit is black and sweet. The fruits were preferred by the American Indians. Many birds and animals are also extremely fond of them. Have observed in the Georgia and North Carolina mountains in full flower in late March to mid-April on rocky soils. Landscape size 15 to 25′(40′); co-national champions are 78′ by 47′ and 73′ by 38′ in Great Smoky Mountains National Park. The leaves are a distinct purple bronze and the flowers occur in nodding, fleecy, to 4″ long panicles. In Europe, a closely related species, if not the same, is described as *A. lamarckii* F.G. Schröd. Bean suggests it is possibly a hybrid with *A. canadensis*, along with *A. laevis*, as the parents. He further suggests that it might be a microspecies and is, therefore, effectively apomictic. Apomixis has been described as occurring in *A. laevis*. See Campbell et al., "Apomixis in *Amelanchier laevis*, shadbush." *Amer. J. Bot.* 1397–1403 (1985). It has naturalized in England, Netherlands, and Germany. I have seen the plant in relative abundance in the Netherlands and Germany and have sampled the fruits. They are sweet, edible, 3/8″ across and rich purple-black at maturity. I noticed a great number used in large containers in German cities. Native from Newfoundland to Georgia and Alabama, west to Michigan and Kansas. In Georgia has been free of fireblight and produced an orange-red to brick-red fall color. Cultivated 1870. Zone 4 to 8(9).

Amelanchier stolonifera Wiegand, (am-e-lang′kē-ēr stō-lon-if′ēr-à), Running Serviceberry, is a small 4 to 6′ high stoloniferous shrub which forms small thickets of stiff, erect stems; flowers are white; fruit is purplish black, glaucous, sweet, juicy and of good flavor, ripening in July. Native from Newfoundland and Maine

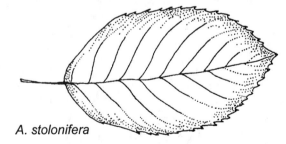

A. stolonifera

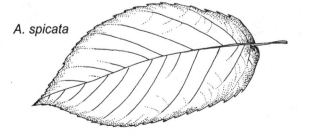

A. spicata

to Virginia in non-calcareous soils. Introduced 1883. Zone 4. A number of small, suckering species including *A. humilis* Wiegand, *A. obovalis* (Michx.) Ashe, *A. spicata* (Lam.) K. Koch, and *A. bartramiana* (Tausch) Roem. All are native to the eastern United States but of no great merit for commercial horticulture.

ADDITIONAL NOTES: The *Amelanchier* species as a group make excellent landscape plants. They offer four season interest and excellent edible fruit. To my mind and stomach, a serviceberry pie is the rival of the best blueberry pie. The serviceberries are difficult to separate and are confused in the nursery profession. Unless flowers and developing leaves are present it is impossible to accurately separate *A. arborea, A. canadensis, A. laevis,* and *A.* × *grandiflora. Amelanchier arborea* is native to the Piedmont woods of Georgia and is one of the first shrubs/trees to flower. Considering the wide-spread range of adaptability of the *Amelanchier* species, it is surprising they are not more commonly used.

For a more detailed account of *Amelanchier* species, see Dirr, *American Nurseryman* 166(5): 66–83 (1987). *Amelanchier* taxonomy is fraught with difficulty and certainly not clear-cut. It is reasonably fair to state that what one orders and receives is not necessarily the same in the world of serviceberries. Although many nursery catalogs list *A. canadensis,* in fact, what is sold is *A. arborea, A.* × *grandiflora,* and *A. laevis.* In recent works (Elias), I noticed *A. laevis* was listed as a synonym of *A. arborea.* I doubt if many people would agree with this. *Amelanchier lamarckii* mentioned under *A. laevis* has been thoroughly discussed in European literature (see W.J. Bean, Eight Edition, Supplement). The belief is that *A. lamarckii* originated from eastern North American material, either *A. laevis* or *A.* × *grandiflora.* I have seen it in Dutch and German gardens and the rich bronze-red (coppery red) new growth and profusion of flowers are quite spectacular. Several United States nurseries who imported stock from Europe report that the dark green leaves turn outstanding orange to red in autumn. Also, the leaves are significantly resistant to leaf drop. The species is possibly reproduced true-to-type through apomixis. This would explain the uniformity that is observed and described on European material. Two worthwhile readings are Jones, "American species of *Amelanchier,*" *Illinois Biological Monograph* 20:1–126 (1946), and Robertson, "Genera of Rosaceae–*Amelanchier,*" *J. Arnold Arboretum* 55:633–640 (1974).

Amorpha fruticosa L. — Indigobush Amorpha, also called Bastard Indigo
(à-môr′fà frū-ti-kō′sà)

FAMILY: Fabaceae
LEAVES: Alternate, pinnately compound, 13 to 33 leaflets, oval or elliptic, 1/2 to 1 1/2″ long, 1/4 to 1/2″ wide, mucronate at apex, rounded at ends, finely pubescent or glabrate; short thread-like stipule at base of each leaflet and transparent dots on the blade, bright green.
BUDS: Imbricate, often superposed, essentially glabrous, appressed, brownish gray.
STEM: Gray to brown, slender, often looks dead.

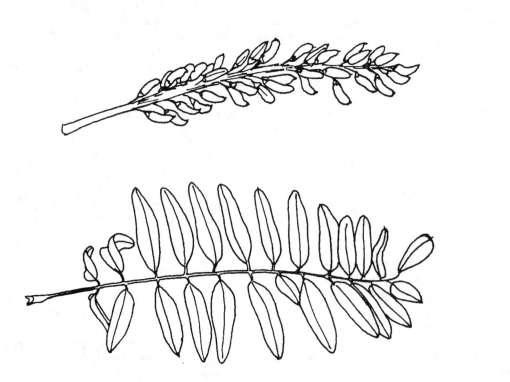

SIZE: Variable, 6 to 20′ tall with a 5 to 15′ spread; a planting on the Illinois campus was about 12′ tall and 8 to 10′ wide.

HARDINESS: Zone 4 to 9.

HABIT: Ungainly deciduous shrub developing a leggy character with the bulk of the foliage on the upper 1/3 of the plant.

RATE: Medium in youth.

TEXTURE: Medium in foliage, coarse in winter.

LEAF COLOR: Bright green in summer, slightly yellowish in fall; late leafing shrub, early hard freeze turns foliage brown.

FLOWERS: Perfect, purplish blue with orange anthers, each flower 1/3″ long, June, borne in 3 to 6″ long upright spikes; flowers are not extremely showy but the colors are unusual.

FRUIT: Small, 1/3″ long, warty, kidney-shaped pod; persistent into winter and offers a good identification feature.

CULTURE: Transplants readily; does extremely well in poor, dry, sandy soils; pH adaptable; full sun; prune in late winter or early spring to keep the plant looking somewhat neat; Russian work reported the species was resistant to fumes, drought and saline conditions.

DISEASES AND INSECTS: Plants may be completely defoliated by the uredinal stage of the rust, *Uropyxis amorphae*; other problems include leaf spots, powdery mildew and twig canker; I have also observed a gall forming insect which causes a swelling of the spent inflorescences; inside the gall is a small larva similar to those found in galls of oaks.

LANDSCAPE VALUE: Not a great deal of worth attached to this plant; perhaps for poor soil areas where few plants will survive; spreads easily by seeds and can become a noxious weed; interestingly many horticultural forms are listed but I have never seen one in gardens or nurseries.

CULTIVARS:

‘Albiflora’—White flowers.

‘Coerulea’—Pale blue flowers.

‘Crispa’—Leaflets crinkled.

‘Dark Lance’—Rich green globular plant with purple (violet) flowers (petals) that subtend golden brown (yellow-orange) filaments, grew 14′ by 6 1/2′ in 6 years, selection from the wild by Mr. Benny J. Simpson, Zone 5 to 9. See *HortScience* 24:713–714 (1989).

‘Lewisii’—Large flowers.

‘Pendula’—Prostrate or pendulous branches.

PROPAGATION: Seed has an impermeable coat and dormant embryo; light acid scarification for 5 to 8 minutes in sulfuric acid followed by cold stratification is recommended; cold stratification may not be necessary based on some research results I have read; softwood cuttings can be rooted; untreated softwoods from 1, 2 and 5-year-old plants rooted 89, 88 and 89%, respectively; division, especially of *A. brachycarpa*, *A. canescens*, and *A. nana*, is effective; one researcher reported that July cuttings treated with 480 ppm Ethrel and placed in peat:perlite rooted well.

NATIVE HABITAT: Connecticut to Minnesota, south to Louisiana and Florida. Introduced 1724.

RELATED SPECIES:

Amorpha brachycarpa Palmer, (à-môr′fà brak-i-kär′pà), is a small dense, rather fine-textured shrub growing about 3′ high and wide. The purple flowers are borne in 1 to 2″ long cylindrical, terminal panicles during July. Full flower on July 2, 1991 at the Arnold Arboretum. Not common in cultivation but a lovely addition to the summer garden. This species has been reduced to synonymy with *A. canescens* according to Kartesz. Interestingly, the two species appear eminently identifiable as discrete units, at least as I observed them in gardens. The Arnold Arboretum has probably the best collection of *Amorpha* species in North America. I consider this the best of the species for garden use. Missouri. Introduced 1920. Zone 5 to 6. *Amorpha nana* Nutt. non Sims., Fragrant False Indigo, is similar but differs in having 13 to 19 leaflets compared to 21 to 45 for the above. It also occurs over a wider range from Manitoba and Saskatchewan to Iowa and New Mexico. Introduced 1811. Zone 2 to 6.

Amorpha canescens Pursh — Leadplant Amorpha

LEAVES: Alternate, compound pinnate, with 15 to 45 leaflets, entire leaf curved and 2 to 5″ long, each leaflet 1/3 to 1″ long, elliptic to oblong-lanceolate, acute or obtuse, rounded at base, densely grayish pubescent on upper and lower surfaces.

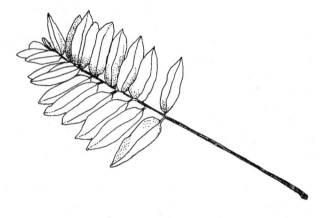

Amorpha canescens, (à-môr′fà kà-nes′enz), Lead-plant Amorpha, grows 2 to 4′ high and spreads 4 to 5′. The habit is broad, rounded and flat-topped. The foliage is an interesting gray-green in summer and can be used for contrast. Flowers (blue-violet) are similar to the above species. Flowering completed by July 2, 1991 at the Arnold Arboretum. Should be used as an herbaceous perennial, accent plant, or useful in rock gardens. Can be propagated by cuttings; seed should be treated similar to *A. fruticosa*. Native from Michigan and Saskatchewan to Indiana, Texas and northern Mexico. Introduced 1812. Zone 2 to 6.

Ampelopsis brevipedunculata (Maxim.) Trautv. — Porcelain Ampelopsis
(am-pe-lop′sis brev-i-ped-unk-ū-lā′tà)

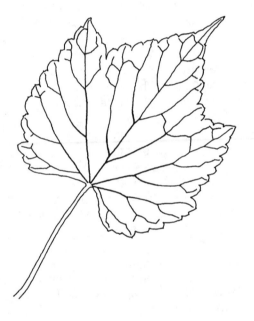

FAMILY: Vitaceae

LEAVES: Alternate, simple, 2 1/2 to 5″ long and wide, broad-ovate, acuminate, cordate, 3- rarely 5-lobed, the lateral lobes broadly triangular-ovate, spreading, coarsely serrate, pilose beneath, dark green above with short pubescence, bristly hairy beneath; hairy petioles as long as blade or slightly shorter.

BUDS: Subglobose, solitary though collaterally branched in development, sessile, with 2 or 3 scales, brownish.

STEM: Hairy when young, angled or nearly terete, brownish; pith—continuous, white.

SIZE: 10 to 15 to 25′ and more.

HARDINESS: Zone 4 to 8.

HABIT: Vigorous vine clinging by tendrils; not as dense as some vines, but certainly vigorous.

RATE: Fast, can grow 15 to 20′ in a single season; however, this is the exception.

TEXTURE: Medium-coarse in leaf and winter.

LEAF COLOR: Dark green in summer, not much different in fall; no appreciable fall coloration.

FLOWERS: Perfect, greenish, unimportant; borne in long stalked cymes in June, July, and August; flowers on new growth of season so can be cut to ground in late winter to maintain control and will still produce flowers and fruits the same season.

FRUIT: Berry, 1/4 to 1/3″ diameter, yellow to pale lilac and finally amethyst purple to bright blue; often all colors are present in the same infructescence; effective in September and October.

CULTURE: Easily transplanted, adaptable to many soils except those that are permanently wet; best fruiting occurs in full sun; requires adequate support for climbing; plants should be sited where the root growth can be restricted, for under this condition, fruiting is optimized.

DISEASES AND INSECTS: Some of the problems which are common to *Parthenocissus* could prove troublesome on *Ampelopsis* species; Japanese beetles are a genuine problem.

LANDSCAPE VALUE: Another vine which is rarely visible in the landscape; the fruit is extremely handsome and is probably unrivaled by any other woody plant in vitality of color; could be effectively integrated into a landscape by growing on a fence or over a rock pile; rapid cover for unsightly objects and valuable for that reason; unfortunately, Japanese beetles love the foliage and can render a green vine a missing object in short order; one authority calls the fruits an amethyst blue color, which the more I observe rings true.

CULTIVARS:

   ‘Citrulloides’—Leaves deeply incised, 5-lobed, with typical green flowers and bluish fruits.

'Elegans'—A rather interesting type with slightly smaller leaves, variegated with white; greenish white and tinged pinkish when young; not as vigorous as species and would be a good choice for locations where the species is too aggressive; handsome; supposedly comes true-to-type from seed; introduced before 1847.

var. *maximowiczii* (Reg.) Rehd.—Leaves more deeply lobed, 3 to 5 lobes, interesting for textural difference compared to species; I planted this variety on a drain spout at my Illinois home and in a single growing season it started to grow in the window; vigorous to a fault.

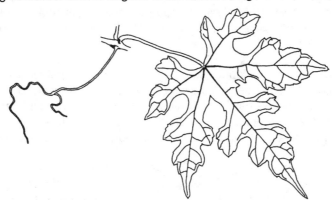

PROPAGATION: All species are easily rooted from leafy cuttings of firm growth taken in June, July and August; *A. brevipedunculata* cuttings taken in early summer, untreated, and planted in sand rooted 90 percent in 30 days under mist; doubtful if a hormone treatment is needed to improve rooting; seed when cleaned and sown will germinate in rather irrational percentages; a 30-day or longer cold period may improve germination; and, in our studies, seeds proved easy to germinate when removed from pulp and cold stratified for 3 months.

NATIVE HABITAT : China, Korea, Japan and the Russian Far East. Cultivated 1870.

RELATED SPECIES:

Ampelopsis aconitifolia Bunge, (am-pe-lop′sis ak-on-ĭt-i-fō′li-ȧ), Monks Hood Vine, is a slender luxuriant vine with delicate, deep glossy green, 3- to 5-foliate leaves. The vine grows 15 to 25′ and can develop as much as 12 to 15′ of linear growth in a single season. The flowers are perfect, greenish, August, borne in cymes. The fruits are dull orange or yellow, sometimes bluish before maturity, 1/4″ diameter, effective in September and October. Valued for delicate foliage; offers variation in texture; can be used on fences, rock piles, walls and other structures. Native to northern China. Zone 4 to 7.

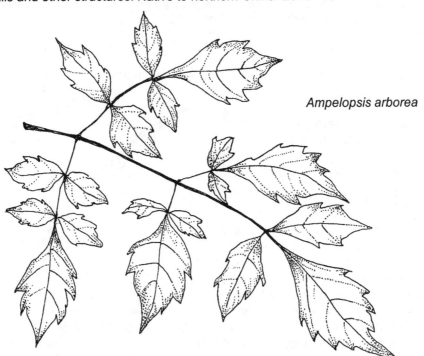

Ampelopsis arborea

Ampelopsis arborea (L.) Koehne, (am-pe-lop′sis är-bō′rē-à), Pepper Vine, is a common occurrence in the southern United States and is considered by many to be a pernicious pest. The bipinnately compound, 4 to 8″ long leaves are composed of numerous 1/2 to 1 1/4″ long, broad-ovate or rhombic-ovate to obovate leaflets, apex acute to acuminate, broad-cuneate to rounded at base, terminal leaflet stalked, lateral ones short-stalked to subsessile, coarsely toothed, dark green. The young slender somewhat angular stems are purplish and glabrous or nearly so. The 1/3″ diameter berries are dark purple at maturity but go through the same color transitions as *A. brevipedunculata*. The species is particularly rampant and is seldom cultivated. My first introduction came at the Atlanta Botanical Garden where it smothered a chain-link fence. Quite beautiful in fruit. Virginia to Missouri, Florida, Texas, and Mexico. Introduced 1700. Zone 7 to 9.

Ampelopsis humulifolia Bunge, (am-pe-lop′sis hū-mū-li-fō′li-à), Hops Ampelopsis, is a climbing, shrubby vine with lustrous bright green 3- to 5-lobed foliage with rounded sinuses resembling that of *Vitis* (true grape) in shape and texture. This species has been confused with *A. brevipedunculata*, but differs in the thicker, firmer leaves which are whitish beneath. The fruit is not borne profusely. The color ranges from pale yellow, changing partly or wholly to pale blue. Native to northern China. Introduced 1868. Zone 5.

ADDITIONAL NOTES: I remember learning *A. brevipedunculata* in my plant materials courses at Ohio State in 1963 and did not see it again until the fall of 1975 when several students, who were involved in a fruit collecting project, brought in several clusters. Having not seen the plant for 12 years, I hesitated to immediately identify it, but the fruit color struck a mental note which I translated to *A. brevipedunculata*. The moral is that once one sees the fruit, he/she never forgets which plant to associate it.

Andrachne colchica Fisch. & C.A. Mey. — Andrachne

FAMILY: Euphorbiaceae
LEAVES: Alternate, simple, 1/4 to 3/4″ long, one half as wide, ovate, obtuse, rounded at base, entire, thin with margins thickened, rich green, glabrous.

Andrachne colchica, (an-drac′nē kol′chi-kà), Andrachne, is a wispy 2 to 3′ high shrub with rich green foliage that would serve as a filler or facer plant in a shrub border. The plant is most interesting as a hardy member of the Euphorbiaceae family and my initial introduction came during sabbatical at the Arnold Arboretum where this rather unknown shrub labored in relative obscurity. Flowers (yellow-green) and fruits are not showy. Appears to almost thrive with neglect but would require full sun. August cuttings can be rooted. Asia Minor. Introduced before 1990. Zone 5 to 7.

Andromeda polifolia L. — Bog-rosemary, Marsh Andromeda

FAMILY: Ericaceae
LEAVES: Alternate, simple, evergreen, linear-oblong, 1 to 1 1/2″ long, 1/8 to 1/3″ wide but appearing narrower because of the recurved entire margins, apex sharp tipped, blue green to dark green above, glaucous or slightly tomentose beneath.

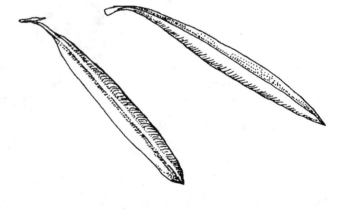

Andromeda polifolia, (an-drom′e-dà pol-i-fō′li-à), Bog-rosemary, is an extremely interesting, slow growing (1 to 2′ high by 2 to 3′ wide) evergreen shrub with creeping rootstocks and upright limitedly branched stems. The foliage is stiff, leathery textured and deep dark green. The flowers are perfect, white tinged pink, 1/4″ long, urn-shaped; borne in May at the end of the shoots in 2- to 8-flowered umbels. The fruit is a capsule. The species requires a peaty or sandy soil which is constantly moist and cool; full sun or light shade; best to move it as a container grown plant; in the wild it is most commonly found in peat or sphagnum bogs. A very lovely and interesting plant for edging or naturalized conditions but very exacting as to culture. Not very common in the trade but I have seen it offered in several garden centers as well as through mail order firms. I attempted to grow a compact form of the species in Illinois but with meager success. I planted it in pure peat and provided sufficient water. No doubt, the high summer heat and humidity were not to its liking. Found in colder parts of northern hemisphere and significant variation must occur over such diverse terrain. Various epithets such as 'Nana', 'Compacta', 'Compacta Alba', 'Grandiflora Compacta', and 'Congesta' have been applied to compact forms. *Andromeda glaucophylla* Link. is similar with linear leaves, tomentulose beneath, and short erect pubescence on the lower surface. Flowers are borne on shorter pedicels than *A. polifolia*. Newfoundland and Labrador to Manitoba, south to New Jersey, Indiana and Minnesota. Cultivated 1829. Zone 2 to 6. *Andromeda polifolia* is native to north and central Europe, northern Asia, North America south to New York and Idaho. Cultivated 1786. Zone 2 to 6 (higher elevations in the South).

Aralia spinosa L. — Devils-walkingstick or Hercules-club
(à-rā′li-à spī-nō′sà)

FAMILY: Araliaceae
LEAVES: Alternate, bi- to tri-pinnately compound, 32 to 64″ long, rachis with scattered prickles, leaflets ovate, 2 to 4″ long, 1/2 to 2/3's as wide, acuminate, serrate, dark green to blue green, glaucous and nearly glabrous beneath, sessile, 7 to 13 per pinna; petiole—to 10″ long; entire leaf presents a tropical effect.
BUDS: Ovoid-conical, solitary, with few scales.
STEM: Stout, gray-straw colored, glabrous, with prickles; leaf scars fully half encircling stem, bundle traces 15 in a single series; pith—large, pale white.

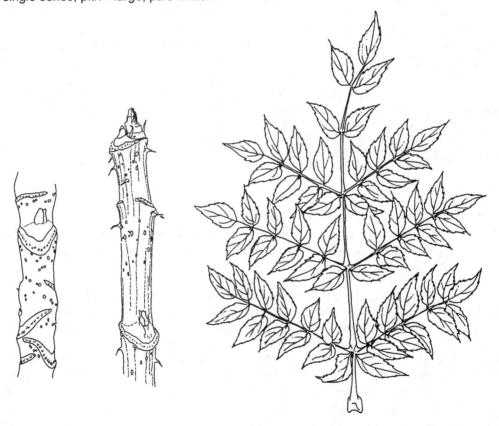

SIZE: 10 to 20′ in height although can grow to 30 to 40′, spreading to infinity; national champion is 60′ by 35′ in Great Smoky Mountains National Park.
HARDINESS: Zone 4 to 9.
HABIT: Large, few-stemmed shrub or small tree with stout, coarse branches forming an obovate outline; often renews itself by developing shoots from the base and forms a dense thicket of impenetrable branches; I have seen a large planting like this in Mt. Airy Arboretum, Cincinnati, OH, and the overall effect is quite

handsome (soft-textured) in summer with the compound foliage; however, in winter the planting is extremely coarse.

RATE: Slow to medium on old wood, but fast on shoots which develop from roots.

TEXTURE: Medium, possibly medium-fine in leaf; appearing coarse in winter.

LEAF COLOR: Medium to dark green, at times blue-green, sometimes lustrous, changing to subdued yellow-green and yellow; an occasional leaf turns purple; have seen in recent years reasonable yellow to purple fall coloration on selected plants, never consistent across the species.

FLOWERS: Perfect, maybe unisexual, small, 1/8″ across, 5-petaled, whitish, produced from July to August in large 12 to 18″ diameter pubescent umbellose-panicles at the end of the branches; interestingly handsome in flower; akin to a lacy veil over the top of the plant; flowers last for a long time but the July to early September flowering period refers to the periods of time in which individuals in a given geographic area will flower; during my sabbatical I monitored flowers from late July to early September at the Arnold Arboretum.

FRUIT: Drupe, purple-black, 1/4″ long and wide, with 3 to 5 seed-like stones (hard endocarp), late August into October, produced in great quantities and are either eaten by birds or fall soon after ripening; the infructescence turns a pinkish red and is attractive for several months in late summer through early fall.

CULTURE: Easy to transplant, performs best in well-drained, moist, fertile soils, but also grows in dry, rocky or heavy soils; best in full sun or partial shade; pH tolerant as will do well under acid or slightly alkaline conditions; does well under city conditions; it has been noted that this plant "thrives with neglect"; the freedom with which it develops new shoots from roots can create a maintenance problem and this should be considered when siting the plant.

DISEASES AND INSECTS: None serious.

LANDSCAPE VALUE: Somewhat of a novelty plant because of large leaves and clubby stems; possibly could be used in the shrub border or out-of-the-way areas; worthwhile for rugged areas and seems to prosper in sun or shade; Swarthmore College used the plant next to a campus building in an area surrounded by walks; the textural quality of foliage and stems against the building were superb.

PROPAGATION: Seed, 41°F for 60 to 90 days will generally overcome the dormancy of this species; however, other species have double dormancy (seed coat and embryo); possible to dig young shoots which develop from the roots and use these as propagules; root cuttings.

ADDITIONAL NOTES: Common throughout the Southeast and Bonnie and I comment often as we drive the highways and byways about the showy summer flowers. They are effective for two months in their transition from green to cream, and into fruit development.

NATIVE HABITAT: Southern Pennsylvania and southern Indiana and eastern Iowa to Florida and east Texas. Introduced 1688.

RELATED SPECIES:

Aralia elata (Miq.) Seem. — Japanese Angelica-tree

LEAVES: Alternate, bipinnately compound, 16 to 32″ long, up to 40″ long, leaflets ovate or elliptic ovate to narrow ovate, 2 to 5″ long, acuminate, serrate with broad teeth, dark green above and glaucescent beneath, 5 to 9 leaflets per pinna.

Aralia elata, (à-rā′li-à ē-lā′tà), Japanese Angelica-tree (Japanese Aralia), is similar to the above species but differs in its larger size (20 to 30′); the more pubescent underside of the leaflets; and greater hardiness [Zone (3)4, Minnesota Landscape Arboretum reports this hardy at Chanhassen where *A. spinosa* is not]. The plants I have seen in the United States and Europe appeared extremely similar to *A. spinosa*. Here is a situation where it is difficult to tell the "player" without a scorecard. Upon close examination the pubescence differences seem to hold up and the veins run to the end of the serrations on *A. elata* and anastomose in *A. spinosa*; the stems are not as spiny as *A. spinosa*. A thornless form has been selected in China. 'Aureovariegata' has leaflets edged with an irregular border of golden-yellow, a most beautiful form but a weak grower; 'Pyramidalis' is an upright form with smaller leaflets than the species; 'Variegata' offers an irregular creamy white border along the margin of the leaflet. 'Albovariegata', with white margined leaflets is described; how different from the commercial 'Variegata', I do not know. 'Silver Umbrella'—Noted this in Dr. Raulston's North Carolina State University Arboretum newsletter; no description of the leaf but is probably a silver to creamy edged variegated form; listed as growing 10′ by 6′. I saw several cultivars at Treasures of Tenbury in England and Mr. John Treasure, the owner, bemoaned the fact that they were so slow growing and provided limited amounts of bud wood. He purchased his plants from Holland and noted they commanded a premium price. Most of the variegated forms are produced in Dutch nurseries. Perhaps the best specimen of 'Variegata' I have seen resides at Wisley in the walled garden. About 15′ high now and the subtle (not harsh) variegation, artistic, elegant leaf texture and branch architecture can make a disbeliever into a convert. Dr. Raulston has flowered the variegated form in Raleigh. A small plant of 'Variegata' in the Dirr garden flowered in June 1994, 1996, and 1997, unfortunately most of the leaves defoliated by early October. Also, 'Variegata' is grafted on the species or *A. spinosa* so unwanted suckers develop and must be removed. Be vigilant! Japan, Korea, Manchuria, and Russian Far East. Introduced 1830.

Araucaria araucana (Molina) K. Koch — Monkey Puzzle, Chilean Pine

FAMILY: Araucariaceae
LEAVES: Evergreen, spirally arranged, radially spreading, essentially 2-ranked, ovate-lanceolate, spiny pointed stiff leaves, 1 to 2″ long, 1/2 to 1″ wide, slightly concave above, lustrous dark green on both sides, persisting alive for 10 to 15 years and then indefinitely when dead; needles densely packed about 24 to an inch of stem, pungent when bruised.
HABIT: Unique and easily identifiable because of stiff, gaunt, rather scary growth habit; belongs in a horror movie (Adams Family Garden Show); branches are produced in tiers (whorls of 5 to 7), are minimally branched and protrude horizontally for a distance from the center of the trunk and then ascend in a gentle arch skyward.

Araucaria araucana, (ar-â-kā′ri-à ar-â-kā′nà), Monkey Puzzle, was essentially unknown to this author until observed in European gardens. Surprisingly hardy (Zone 7) and a report indicated the plant had been grown in Knoxville, TN. Probably better adapted to the West Coast but for novelty purposes worth a try in the coastal southeastern region. A large tree, 50 to 80′ with a pyramidal-oval outline at maturity; the lower limbs are often lost creating a slender bole and a crown restricted to the upper 1/2 to 1/3 of the tree. Essentially dioecious and the male flowers occur in 3 to 5″ long cylindrical catkins; female in 5 to 8″ thick pineapple-shaped cones that take two years to mature. I saw a cone in California and decided that there were no rakes strong enough to compete. The conical seeds are 1 1/2″ long by 3/4″ wide. Certainly an imposing specimen, especially in English gardens. Quite difficult to utilize in garden-making and should be used as a single specimen or perhaps in widely spaced groupings. Soil should be cool and moist. Seems to prosper in cooler, continental climates. A Georgia gardener and nurseryman, Willis Harden, has grown the plant in his Commerce garden with less than outstanding success. Many cultivars (10 or more) are described in the literature and might prove of worth to the collector. *Araucaria heterophylla* (Salisb.) Franco., Norfolk Island Pine, is suitable for Zone 10 to 11 conditions and is quite common in Hawaii. It has received wide favor as a houseplant. Makes a rather attractive plant were adapted. Chile, Argentina. Introduced 1795.

Arbutus unedo L. — Strawberry Tree
(är-bū′tus ū′nē-dō)

FAMILY: Ericaceae
LEAVES: Alternate, evergreen, narrowly oval to obovate, 2 to 4″ long, 1/2 to 3/4″ wide, acute, cuneate, serrate, lustrous dark green above, glabrous; petiole—1/4″ long, glandular, red.

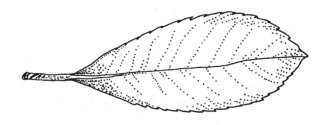

SIZE: 15 to 30′ with a similar habit; at best 10 to 15′ in cultivation in the Southeast.
HARDINESS: Zone 7 to 9; doubtful in Zone 9 of the southeastern United States, acceptable on West Coast.
HABIT: A small shrub in the southeastern United States but in Europe a large shrub or round-headed small tree, have seen in abundance in Ireland, almost always shrubby.
RATE: Slow.
TEXTURE: Medium fine throughout the season.
BARK: The bark on *A. unedo* is gray-brown and fissured. Reminds of *Kalmia latifolia* bark. Handsome beyond description on *A. menziesii* and *A.* × *andrachnoides* with rich reddish brown coloration and shredding

fibrous texture; becomes twisted (spiraled) and gnarled with age, certainly one of the most beautiful features of these species.

LEAF COLOR: Lustrous dark green, perhaps slight off-green in winter in the Southeast.

FLOWERS: Perfect, urn-shaped like blueberry, about 1/4″ long, white to pinkish, in 2″ long and wide panicles from October–December; not spectacular in flower but certainly alluring; have seen in flower in early December in Aiken, SC; also a recent planting on the Georgia campus has provided a baseline for evaluation; actually flowers initiate by late September and in 1995 a stray flower or two was evident in early January, for fall-winter effect the plant has merit.

FRUIT: A 3/4″ diameter, sub-globose, orange-red, berry-like, granular surfaced drupe with mealy flesh; supposedly edible but bland; ripens the year following flowering; have seen flowers and ripe fruits present at the same time; the fruit is striking; superb fruit set on a campus plant and in 1994 the warm fall promoted fruit ripening immediately after flowering; I noticed the brilliant colored fruits on a walk and by the time I returned the next week with camera in tow, fruits were gone; do birds eat the fruits? Also, the plant appears self-fruitful based on quantity of fruits on an isolated plant.

CULTURE: Observations indicate the plant is easy to grow and in California it grows well in dry (once established) and moist, well-drained garden soils; apparently also quite salt-tolerant, sun or shade.

DISEASES AND INSECTS: None serious

LANDSCAPE VALUE: Handsome out-of-season plant for the discriminating gardener, certainly an eye catcher in a shrub border where the off-season flowers and normal-season fruits dominate.

CULTIVARS:

'Compacta'—Slower growing, deep green form that does not flower as heavily as the species; contorted branching structure, picturesque and probably no bigger than 5′ after 8 to 10 years; have seen reports in literature that note this form flowers and fruits continuously; a plant in the University's Botanical Garden mirrors the previous description, survived 4°F in 1994 without injury, almost perpetual winter flowering but have not noticed fruit set, beautiful lustrous bronzy green new growth that matures to lustrous dark green, holds good color during the winter; late freeze in early March 1996 injured the plant.

'Elfin King'—A common compact form that bears abundant flowers and fruits; am most impressed with this small bushy form that will probably mature between 5 and 10′.

'Quercifolia'—Appears in European literature but I have not come across the plant in gardens; dark green dissected leaves with reddish veins; flowers and fruits like the species.

'Rubra' (f. *rubra*)—Rich dark pink flowers, slightly less vigorous and hardy than species; Bean describes it as virtually lost to cultivation.

NATIVE HABITAT: Southwestern Ireland where it attains greatest proportions to the Mediterranean region. Cultivated for centuries.

RELATED SPECIES:

Arbutus andrachne L. — Madrone

LEAVES: Alternate, simple, evergreen, 2 to 4″ long, 1 to 2″ wide, oval to oblong, obtuse, lustrous dark green above, paler and glabrous below, toothed on young and vigorous shoots, but entire when mature; petiole—1/2 to 1″ long.

STEM: Glabrous which separates it from the glandular-hairy nature of *A. unedo*.

Arbutus andrachne, (är-bū′tus an-drac′nē), Madrone, is a 10 to 20′ evergreen shrub with the ornamental traits of *A. unedo*. The white flowers appear in March–April in pubescent 2 to 4″ long and wide panicles. The globose 1/2″ diameter orange-red fruit is much smoother than that of *A. unedo*. Native of southeastern Europe, Asia Minor. Introduced 1724. Possible Zone 7, best in 8 to 9.

Arbutus* × *andrachnoides Link., (är-bū′tus an-drac-noy′dēz), is a hybrid between *A. unedo* and *A. andrachne* that is more common in cultivation than the latter parent; it is strongly intermediate in characteristics. A fine 30′ high specimen exists at Bodnant Garden, Wales and on every garden tour receives more attention than any other plant. The 1 1/2 to 4″ long, oval, oblong, elliptic to lanceolate, finely serrate leaves are dark green above, lighter and pubescent below. Flowers are white to ivory colored and fruits are seldom produced. The rich reddish brown branches literally grab even the most passive of passers-by. The sun enriches the intensity of the bark color. A most handsome tree probably reserved for more even, cool climates than the United States. The Bodnant tree is spectacular but has lost a limb or two and is showing some of its 100 years of earthiness. Kew Gardens has a magnificent specimen. For as wonderful as the plant is, it is still uncommon. 'Marima' was discovered in San Francisco, considered an *A.* × *andrach-noides* selection with shredding bark yielding an orange-red inner bark color. Found wild in Greece and was hybridized in England around 1800.

Arbutus menziesii Pursh — Pacific Madrone, Madrone

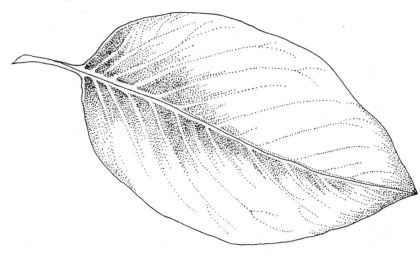

LEAVES: Alternate, simple, evergreen, 2 to 6″ long, 1 to 3″ wide, oval, serrated on vigorous shoots, entire with maturity, lustrous dark green above, glaucous to whitish beneath; petiole—1/2 to 1 1/4″ long.

Arbutus menziesii, (är-bū′tus men-zēz′ē-ī), Pacific Madrone or Madrone, is a beautiful tree with striking cinnamon (red-brown) colored bark. The bark peels until becoming perfectly clean, smooth and colored. Additionally, the trunks are uniquely shaped adding great architecture to the formula. Cultivated trees range from 20 to 50′, although it grows 75 to 100′ in the native habitat. National champion is 96′ by 113′ in Humboldt County, CA. The greenish white, 1/4″ long flowers occur in 3 to 9″ long, up to 6″ wide terminal panicles in May. The flowers are not overwhelming but are followed by 1/3″ diameter red fruits that color in fall and persist into winter. Considered difficult to transplant and should be moved as a small seedling or container plant. Prefers well-drained, dryish soils. Excessive soil moisture, especially through modern lawn irrigation systems may prove lethal. May prove messy in the garden for like *Magnolia grandiflora* is often dropping parts of its anatomy. Found on dry bluffs or ridges in infertile soil, often near salt water. Native from British Columbia to the San Francisco area. Introduced 1827. Zone 7. Have seen hardiness listed as Zone 5 to 9 but seriously doubt the validity of same. Have observed many plants, the most notable on Vancouver Island, British Columbia.

Arctostaphylos uva-ursi (L.) A. Gray. — Bearberry, also called Kinnikinick, Mealberry, Hog Cranberry, Sandberry, Mountain Box, Bear's Grape

(ärk-tō-staf′i-los ū-vȧ-ēr′si)

FAMILY: Ericaceae

LEAVES: Alternate, simple, obovate or obovate-oblong, 1/4 to 1 1/4″ long, 1/4 to 1/2″ wide, cuneate, revolute, glabrous, lustrous dark green above, lighter beneath; petiole—1/4″ long.

BUDS: Solitary, sessile, ovoid with about 3 exposed scales.

STEM: Minutely tomentulose-viscid, becoming glabrate; leaf scars small, crescent-shaped, bundle trace one; older branches covered with papery, reddish to ashy exfoliating bark.

SIZE: 6 to 12″ in height by 2 to 4′ in width, spreading to infinity.

HARDINESS: Zone 2 to 5 or 6; have seen in Zone 8.

HABIT: Low growing, glossy leaved evergreen ground cover forming broad, thick mats; single plant may cover an area 15′ in diameter; native colonies on Cape Cod appear to be derived from a single plant, against the whitish dunes, a colony appears like a round dark green tarpaulin.

RATE: Slow.

TEXTURE: Fine.

LEAF COLOR: Glossy bright green to dark green in summer, bronze to reddish in fall and winter; the foliage effect is unique and quite different from most ground covers.

FLOWERS: Perfect, white tinged pink, small (1/6 to 1/4″ long), urn-shaped, April to May, borne in nodding racemes; dainty and beautiful.

FRUIT: Fleshy drupe, lustrous bright red, 1/4 to 1/3″ diameter, late July through August and persisting; beautiful on close inspection.

CULTURE: One of the more interesting species as far as cultural requirements; difficult to transplant and container-grown plants or large mats of plants should be used; although found in diverse soils and habitats it does best in poor, sandy, infertile soils; full sun or partial shade; pH 4.5 to 5.5 is preferable; exhibits good salt tolerance (I have seen the plant growing right next to beach grass on the beaches of Cape Cod); set plants 12 to 24″ apart; pruning is seldom necessary; never fertilize.

DISEASES AND INSECTS: Black mildew, leaf galls and rust have been reported; in recent years have noticed a leaf type gall that disfigures the plant; use resistant cultivars.

LANDSCAPE VALUE: Outstanding ground cover for that different effect; has been called "the prettiest, sturdiest, and most reliable ground cover"; good bed preparation for this one plant alone is worth the effort; used with greater frequency in northeastern states but still not a common occurrence.

CULTIVARS:

'Alaska'—Compact flat growing form with small, round, dark green leaves.

'Anchor Bay'—Glossy dark green, oblong leaves, dense mat-forming ground cover.

'Big Bear'—Large, shiny dark green leaves and large red fruits, reddish winter leaf color.

'Emerald Carpet'—Probably a hybrid; dark green, 3/4″ long leaves on a 10 to 18″ high, 3 to 6′ wide groundcover, reddish bronze in winter, pink flowers, tolerates shade better than most cultivars.

'Massachusetts'—Small, dark green leaved, flat growing form with good resistance to leaf spot and leaf gall, abundant pinkish white flowers followed by red fruits, originated from Massachusetts seed grown in Oregon by Bob Tichnor; one of the best and most widely grown selections.

'Microphylla'—Tiny leaf form with bonsai potential; for the collector.

'Pacific Mist'—Gray green leaves, pale pink flowers, grows 2 to 3′ high, 4 to 6′ wide, probably a hybrid.

'Point Reyes'—Dark green leaves closely spaced on the stems, reasonable heat and drought tolerance.

'Radiant'—Leaves lighter green and more widely spaced than 'Point Reyes'; bears abundant bright red fruit that persists into winter.

'Rax'—A prostrate form with leaves smaller than the type; original clone was discovered in eastern Austria, put into commerce by Zwijnenburg, Boskoop.

'Selected Form'—From Mitsch Nursery, Oregon, small leaf form, resistant to leaf gall, good grower; may now be named 'Thymifolia'.

'Tilden Park'—Dark green closely set oval foliage on a 2 to 3″ high by 2 to 3′ wide plant.

'Tom's Point'—Low, dense, uniform habit, glossy dark green leaves, showy flowers, abundant red fruit, see *HortScience* 30:445 (1995).

'Vancouver Jade'—Introduction from University of British Columbia Botanical Garden, lustrous dark green summer foliage, good deep red winter color, resistance to leaf spot, flowers white with pink tinge, red fruits like those of species.

'Wood's Red'—Large, bright red fruits on a compact form, small dark green leaves turn reddish in winter; pink flowers; an American clone that received the Award of Merit from the Royal Horticultural Society.

PROPAGATION: Seeds have impermeable seed coats and dormant embryos; acid scarification for 3 to 6 hours followed by 2 to 3 months of warm and 2 to 3 months of cold stratification resulted in 30 to 60% germination; nursery practice involves 2 to 5 hours in acid followed by summer planting with germination taking place the following spring; at one time, based on the literature, I reported that cuttings were somewhat difficult to root; based on my work and the new work of others I would say this is not true; cuttings collected July 28 and treated with IBA rooted 80% in sand:peat under mist; October and December cuttings treated essentially as above rooted 70% to 80% in about 6 weeks; see Dirr and Heuser 1987 for specifics.

ADDITIONAL NOTES: Although considered to be a strong acidophile by gardeners, it is equally at home on limestone and siliceous rock and is a vigorous colonizer of exposed, sandy soils; there are magnificent colonies on Cape Cod that thrive in the most infertile sand; the "emerald carpet" of ground covers; have seen in Aiken, SC where the plant was prospering; certainly would not recommend for wholesale use in the Southeast, but for small areas may be worth a try.

NATIVE HABITAT: Circumboreal covering Europe, Asia, North America, south to Virginia, northern California. Cultivated 1800.

Ardisia japonica (Thunb.) Bl. — Japanese Ardisia, Marlberry

FAMILY: Myrsinaceae

LEAVES: Alternate, simple, evergreen, crowded at end of stems and appearing whorled, elliptic-oval, 1 1/2 to 3 1/2″ long, 3/4 to 1 1/2″ wide, tapered at both ends, sharply serrate, glabrous except on midrib, lustrous dark green; petiole—1/4″ long, puberulous.

Ardisia japonica, (är-diz′i-à jà-pon′i-kà), Japanese Ardisia, is a magnificent, bold-textured 8 to 12″(16″) high evergreen ground cover that to a degree resembles *Helleborus orientalis* in leaf texture but is not as coarse. The dark green leaves are leathery. The white to pale pink, 1/2″ diameter, star-shaped, 5 narrow, ovate-petaled flowers are borne in 2 to 6, rarely many-flowered racemes (forming a panicle) in July–August. Have observed a few flowers in October in Louisiana. The rounded 1/4″ diameter, red drupes mature in September–October and persist. Culturally, an acid, organic, moist, well-drained soil is best. It spreads rapidly and forms a solid ground cover. Prefers partial to full shade and is an ideal choice for woodsy, shaded situations. Callaway Gardens, Pine Mountain, GA, has beautiful plantings and this is where I first came to appreciate this species' potential for ground cover use in the South. On many occasions I have been queried about the landscape worthiness of this species. The aesthetic compliments are of the highest caliber yet I question quality and stability of performance in the average garden setting. After 10 to 12 years, all the variegated forms in my garden have been killed. Only the green type remains and invariably the foliage is destroyed. The foliage apparently acclimates (develops cold hardiness) slowly and deacclimates (loses cold hardiness) quickly. On March 13, 1993 19°F was recorded in Athens and the *Ardisia* leaves were killed; on January 19, 1994, 7°F was the low and as my field notes state . . . "leaves were flattened as were the stems." A walk outside on the twelfth day of February corroborated the above comments. For the collector, perhaps acceptable; for the landscaper who may be accosted at some later date, another evergreen ground cover should be used. Propagation is easiest by division. Have rooted stem cuttings that were collected in late February, in fact, have found the various cultivars easy to root. Apparently variable in degree of hardiness; probably best in Zone 8 and 9 although it is mentioned as being hardy in Zone 5 and 6. Hardiness has never been well defined and until Dr. Raulston provided me with several plants, my observational experience was limited. During the difficult winter (–3°F) of 1983–84 in Athens plants were killed to the ground but came back from the roots. The variegated forms were less cold hardy than the green leaf types. Raulston noted that the variegated forms die back to the ground at about 15°F but will regrow from the roots. Plants are protected on the north side of my home and were injured in the relatively mild winter of 1986–87. The foliage may not harden quickly in the fall and an early freeze induces injury. Many forms exist including those with varying degrees of variegation. 'Chirimen' may be the hardiest selection. They are beautiful plants probably best reserved for shady protected areas in moist, loose soil. Japan, China. Introduced about 1830.

CULTIVARS:

'Amanogawa'—Leaves with a large gold splash in the center.

'Beniyuki'—Leaves irregularly shaped and notched—wide bands (more than 1/2″ wide) of white on edges.

'Chiyoda'—Leaves irregularly shaped and notched—thin bands (less than 1/4″ wide) of white on edges.

'Eco Hardy Marlberry'—Hardy form from Don Jacobs, Eco Gardens, Decatur, GA.

'Hakuokan'—One of the largest and most vigorous cultivars—heavily variegated white on edges.

'Hinode'—A large and vigorous plant with broad band of yellow variegation in the center of leaves; have seen spelling as 'Hinadi'.

'Hinotsukasa'—Irregular rounded "teeth" on margins of leaf. Main blade green but "teeth" often (not always) white. From distance has a "dotted" look.

'Hoshiami'—Attractive deep green leaves with cream edges.

'Ito-Fukurin'—An elegant, subtle cultivar—light silvery-gray leaves with a very thin margin of white outlining each leaf.

'Matsu-Shima'—Stems pink, waxy dark green leaves with creamy center, margins deeply toothed and frilled; also listed as 'Matsushima'.

'Nishiki'—Gold and pink variegated leaves; more accurately rosy pink leaf margin turns a handsome yellow with age, also listed as 'Hokan Nishiki'.

'Variegata'—Several southern United States nurseries are producing a creamy white variegated leaf form that supposedly grows 10 to 15″ high; might be a rename.

RELATED SPECIES:

Ardisia crenata Sims. — Coralberry
LEAVES: Alternate, simple, evergreen,
to 8″ long, oblanceolate to elliptic-
lanceolate, crenate-undulate, lustrous dark green.

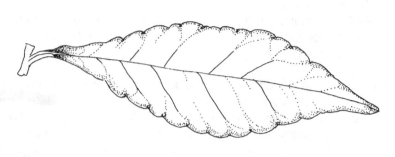

Ardisia crenata, (är-diz′i-à krē -nā′tà),
Coralberry, is truly a Zone 8b to 9
plant, at least in the Southeast. I
have tried it several times in the
garden and it is *always* killed to
the root apices. Forms an evergreen shrub 2 to 4′(6′) high. Flowers white to pink and the bright red fruits
follow and persist into winter. Requires well-drained, acid soil and at least partial shade. Nematodes are
a problem. Nice color touch in the winter garden. 'Alba' is a white- fruited form; 'Crinkle Leaf' has crinkled
foliage; and 'Variegata' has green, yellow, and white splashed leaves.

Aristolochia macrophylla Lam. (formerly *A. durior* Hill) — Dutchman's Pipe

FAMILY: Aristolochiaceae
LEAVES: Alternate, simple, 4 to 10″(12″) long,
almost as wide, heart- or kidney-shaped,
pointed or obtuse, entire, dark green and
glabrous above, pale green and pubescent beneath, finally glabrous; petiole—1
to 3″ long.
BUDS: Superposed, 3, one above the other,
appear to be enclosed in stem tissue,
upper largest, greenish, glabrous.
STEM: Green, glabrous, nodes swollen, leaf
scars form a horse-shoe crescent around
buds; pith—white, greater than 1/2 the
diameter of the stem.

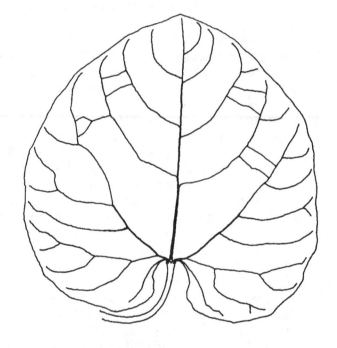

Aristolochia macrophylla, (a-ris-tō-lō′ki-à mak-
rō-fil′à), Dutchman's Pipe, will never
make the best seller list but in bygone
days was a staple for screening front
porches. I have seen many sunscreens
fashioned from a trellis covered with
Dutchman's Pipe. It is a vigorous, climbing,
twining vine that can grow 20 to 30′. Given the appropriate arbor, trellis, pergola or pillar, it will cover the
structure in a single season. The large leaves form a solid screen and are certainly more attractive than
bamboo curtains and related tack. The unusual flowers by virtue of their shape give rise to the common
name. They occur 1 or 2 together from the axils of the leaves in May or June. They are yellow-green and
glabrous on the outside; at the mouth the perianth tube (1 to 1 1/2″ long) contracts to a small orifice,
spreading into 3-lobed, smooth, brownish purple limb 3/4″ across. The fruit is a 6-ribbed, 2 to 3″ long
capsule. Appears to thrive in about any soil as long as it is moist and well-drained. Leaves may wilt under
droughty conditions. Will withstand full sun or partial shade. Propagate by division or July cuttings. A
rooting compound should be used. For best germination, seeds should be stratified for 3 months at 40°F
or sown in fall. Some botanists have placed the species in the genus *Isotrema*. Something akin to 300
species. *Aristolochia californica* Torr., *A. littoralis* L. Parodi (*A. elegans* Mast.), *A. gigantea* Mart. & Zucc.,
and *A. manshuriensis* Komar. are offered by several American nurseries. They vary in size of leaf and
flowers as well as flower color. Relatively common along Blue Ridge Parkway from Cherokee to Asheville,
NC. Pennsylvania to Georgia, west to Kansas. Introduced 1783 by John Bartram. Zone 4 to 8.

Aronia arbutifolia (L.) Pers. — Red Chokeberry
(à-rō'ni-à âr-bū-ti-fō'li-à)

FAMILY: Rosaceae

LEAVES: Alternate, simple, elliptic to oblong or obovate, 1 1/2 to 3 1/2″ long, 1/2 to 3/4″ wide, acute or abruptly acuminate, the margins set with even, black-tipped teeth, the upper surface lustrous dark green with dark glands along the midrib, lower with permanent gray tomentum; petiole—1/3″ long, pubescent.

BUDS: Imbricate, 1/4 to 3/8″ long, usually 5-scaled, green tinged red, often completely red, glabrous, scales somewhat fleshy, often mistaken for an *Amelanchier*.

STEM: Slender, brownish, tomentose.

FRUIT: Bright red pome that persists into winter.

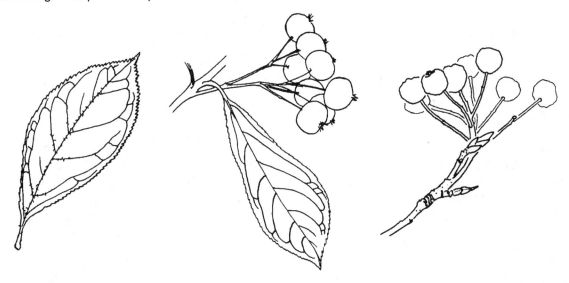

SIZE: 6 to 10′ in height by 3 to 5′ in spread, or wider than high at maturity; quite variable, suckers and forms a colony.

HARDINESS: Zone 4 to 9.

HABIT: Distinctly upright, spreading-suckering, multi-stemmed shrub, somewhat open and round topped; shrub tends to become leggy with age as the majority of the foliage is present on the upper 1/2 to 1/3 of the plant; breeding and selection for good habit, foliage and fruit could result in a superior landscape plant.

RATE: Slow, at least the case with the growth of plants I have recorded in the Midwest; in good soil will grow faster; suckers from roots can grow 2 to 3′ in a season.

TEXTURE: Medium in leaf; medium-coarse in winter although good fruit quality tends to minimize the ragged habit.

LEAF COLOR: Lustrous deep green above, grayish tomentose beneath in summer, changing to red, rich crimson or reddish purple in fall; color is not consistent on row-run seedlings.

FLOWERS: Perfect, white or slightly reddish (anthers), about 1/3″ diameter; flowers early to mid-April in Athens, May in most Zone 5 areas; borne in 9- to 20-flowered, 1 to 1 1/2″ diameter grayish, tomentose corymbs; not overwhelming.

FRUIT: Pome, 1/4″ diameter, rounded, bright red; September through November and later; fruits are firm and glossy into January in Midwest, borne in great abundance along the stems; called Chokeberry because of the astringent taste, even the birds do not like it.

CULTURE: Finely fibrous root system, transplants well, prefers soil with adequate drainage but seems well adapted to many soil types, even poor soils; seems to tolerate both wet and dry soils; full sun or half shade, however, best fruit production occurs in full sun; tends to sucker.

DISEASES AND INSECTS: Leaf spots, twig and fruit blight results in gray, powdery mold over affected plant parts, round-headed apple borer; none serious.

LANDSCAPE VALUE: Border, massing, groups; very effective fruit character in the fall; the most useful way to compensate for the leggy character is to mass this species; extremely effective when used in this manner; almost a sea of red in fall and winter; might be a good choice for highway use because of adaptability and brilliant fruit display; a large mass on the Georgia campus which is now reaching fruiting maturity has been spectacular.

CULTIVARS:
> 'Brilliantissima'—Having observed this form in greater numbers I am giving it a first class rating. It is superior to the species because of the almost waxy, lustrous dark green leaves that turn brilliant scarlet in fall, the more abundant flowers and the glossier, larger, more abundant red fruit. In fall color it is equal and perhaps superior to *Euonymus alatus*. I have had excellent success (80%) rooting it from softwood (June) cuttings using 4000 ppm IBA quick dip, peat:perlite, mist; plants continued to grow after rooting. This cultivar grows 6 to 8′(10′) and forms a suckering colony not unlike that of the species; can be propagated by division; can become unruly, large and unkempt, ideally prune to maintain density of colony.
>
> 'Erecta'—An upright form that as I studied it at the Arnold appeared to show hybrid characteristics between *A. arbutifolia* and *A. melanocarpa* var. *elata*; upright in habit and not as beautiful as the two species or the above cultivar; fruit not as colorful as the species.

PROPAGATION: Seeds, stratify in moist peat for 90 days at 33 to 41°F; cuttings, softwood root readily; untreated cuttings taken in early summer rooted 92% in six weeks in sand medium; best results obtained when the basal cut was made 1/2″ below a node; division is also a practical way to increase the plant in small numbers; nothing more than a sharp spade and steel-toed boots work wonders.

NATIVE HABITAT: Massachusetts to Florida, west to Minnesota, Ohio, Arkansas and Texas. Introduced 1700.

RELATED SPECIES:

Aronia melanocarpa (Michx.) Elliott — Black Chokeberry
LEAVES: Alternate, simple, 1 to 3″ long, 3/4 to 2″ wide, obovate, abruptly acuminate, or obtusish, finely and regularly serrate, lustrous dark green above with dark glands on the midrib, lower surface light green, entire leaf glabrous; petiole—1/4″ or less.

Aronia melanocarpa, (à-rō′ni-à mel-an-ō-kâr′pà), Black Chokeberry, is similar to *A. arbutifolia* except the leaves and stems are glabrous and the fruit is blackish purple. This species grows 3 to 5′(10′) and tends to sucker profusely thus forming large colonies. Again, a very adaptable species for I have seen it growing in low wet areas in the Chicago area and on dry, sandy hillsides in Wisconsin. Good shrub for wetland reclamation plantings. Fall color can be a good wine red and the purplish black, 1/3 to 1/2″ diameter fruits are also handsome. Propagation is as described under *A. arbutifolia*. Variety *elata* is considered superior for landscape use and I would agree with this assessment. I have seen plants of var. *elata* 10 to 12′ high although it is usually smaller. It has larger leaves, flowers and fruits (up to 1/2″ diameter). It was listed in "The Top Ten-Plus-One-Shrubs for Minnesota," *Minnesota Horticulturist* 106(6):152–154. June–July. 1978. 'Autumn Magic' is a more compact version of the species with a brilliant mixture of red and purple autumn foliage and purple-black fruits; Iroquois Beauty™ ('Morton') is a dwarf, 2 to 3′ high form with the same flowers, fruits and foliage characteristics as the species, selected at the Morton Arboretum and introduced by the Chicagoland Grows® Program; 'Viking' has glossy deep green foliage, brilliant red fall color, large black edible fruits, grows 3 to 6′ high, 6 to 8′ wide. Extracurricular reading introduced me to Hardin, *Bull. Torr. Bot. Club* 100:178–184 (1973), "The Enigmatic Chokeberries." According to Hardin true *A. melanocarpa* does not develop autumn fall color which means that the respectable fall coloring forms have *A. arbutifolia* in their makeup. Also the hybrid progeny can "breed" true through apomixis, this leading to unique populations. Nova Scotia to Florida, west to Michigan, introduced about 1700. Zone 3 to 8(9). Very diverse over its range and also forming natural hybrids with *A. arbutifolia*.

Aronia × **prunifolia** (Schneid.) Gräbn., (à-rō′ni-à prū-ni-fō′li-à), Purple-fruited Chokeberry, is similar to *A. melanocarpa* except it is larger (12′). The fall color is good wine-red or purplish red. The flowers are white, about 1/2″ across borne in terminal corymbs in late April through early May. The fruit is a lustrous, 1/3″ diameter, purplish black drupe that may abscise after the first frost. According to Rehder, this species is intermediate between *A. arbutifolia* and *A. melanocarpa*, but is not a hybrid. Current thinking, with which I concur, has it that *A.* × *prunifolia* is a hybrid species. Native from Nova Scotia to Florida, west to Indiana. Cultivated 1800. Zone 4 to 7(8).

Asimina triloba (L.) Dunal — Common Pawpaw, Custard Apple
(à-sim′i-nà trī -lō′bà)

FAMILY: Annonaceae

LEAVES: Alternate, simple, 6 to 12″ long, one-half as wide, obovate-oblong, apex short acuminate, base uniformly tapering, entire, medium to dark green, glabrous above at maturity with pubescence on veins of lower surface; petiole—1/3″ long.

BUDS: Terminal—naked, 1/3 to 1/2″ long, larger than laterals, pubescent, dark brown; lateral—naked, obliquely superposed; flower buds—pubescent, globose to rounded, 2 to 3 scaled, 1/4″ diameter.

STEM: Essentially glabrous at maturity, brown, with fetid odor when broken; pith—continuous, white, with firmer greenish diaphragms at intervals in second year's growth.

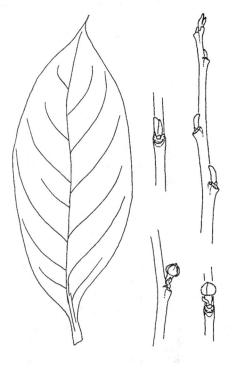

SIZE: 15 to 20′ high and wide; will grow 30 to 40′ in height in favorable locations; more often a suckering, spreading colony; national champion is 60′ by 30′ in Newton County, MS.

HARDINESS: Zone 5 to 8.

HABIT: Multi-stemmed shrub or small tree with short trunk and spreading branches forming a dense pyramidal or round-topped head; tends to sucker and forms rather loose colonies in the wild; presents a semi-tropical appearance.

RATE: Medium as a small tree.

TEXTURE: Medium-coarse in leaf and in winter habit; the summer foliage tends to droop and presents the tree with an overall sleepy (lazy) appearance; easily recognizable by this feature.

BARK: Dark brown with grayish areas when young; becoming rough and slightly scaly with maturity.

LEAF COLOR: Medium to dark green above, paler green beneath in summer changing to yellow or yellow-green in fall; have observed brilliant yellow fall color on selected trees.

FLOWERS: Lurid purple, 1 to 2″ across; early to mid-May in Zone 5; borne singly; there are six petals, the outer three much larger than the inner three; flowers before or as leaves are developing on thick, often recurved, downy, 1/2 to 3/4″ long pedicels; not particularly showy but interesting; seldom seen by the uninitiated.

FRUIT: Edible, bloomy, greenish yellow berry finally turning brownish black, 2 to 5″ long, of many shapes—sometimes elongated, at other times rounded, has a taste similar to a banana with a custard consistency, usually containing 2 to 3 almost 1″ long dark brown flattish to bean-shaped seeds.

CULTURE: Somewhat difficult to transplant and should be moved as a small (3 to 6′) balled and burlapped or container grown plant; prefers moist, fertile, deep, slightly acid soils; does well in full sun; have seen extensive groves of Pawpaw along Sugar Creek (Turkey Run State Park, IN) growing in very dense shade; however, the trees were of open, straggly habit; in the southern Appalachians, tree is common in rich hardwood forests and riverbottoms, almost universally as an understory tree.

DISEASES AND INSECTS: None serious.

LANDSCAPE VALUE: Interesting native tree which could be used for naturalizing in moist, deep soils along streams; the fruits have a sweet, banana-like flavor and are eaten by man and animal; interesting species but its landscape uses are limited; have seen at the edges of woodlands where it provided a rather striking pose; will never replace Bradford Pear but has a place in specific situations.

CULTIVARS: Not readily available but three of the best include 'Davis', 'Overleese', and 'Sunflower'; these forms bear 3 to 6″ long fruits that average between 5 and 12 ounces each; 'Overleese' may produce fruits that weigh one pound or more. Louisiana Nursery, Opelousas, LA offers 'Mitchell' (large fruit, excellent quality), 'Sweet Alice', 'Triple Cross #1' (fruits to 8 ounces), and 'Wilson' (flavorful, sweet, yellow, medium size fruit).

PROPAGATION: Seeds possess a dormant embryo and possibly an impermeable seed coat and should be stratified in a moist medium for 60 days at 41°F; germination may be erratic, cultivars are budded onto seedling understock.

ADDITIONAL NOTES: Animals (especially racoons) seem to relish the fruits; the epithet *triloba* refers to the 3-lobed calyx. The fruit has a fragrant aroma and a custard-like texture of a banana and the taste of a banana-pear; excellent source of Vitamins A and C; high in unsaturated fats, proteins, carbohydrates, richer than apples, peaches or grapes in K,P,Mg,S; also good balance of amino acids. See Callaway, *HortScience* 27:90,191 (1992) for a discussion of commercialization. Also, Peterson, *Acta Horticulturae* 290:567–600 (1990), and Callaway and Callaway, *Arnoldia* 21–29 (Fall, 1992).

NATIVE HABITAT: New York to Florida, west to Nebraska and Texas. Introduced 1736.

RELATED SPECIES:

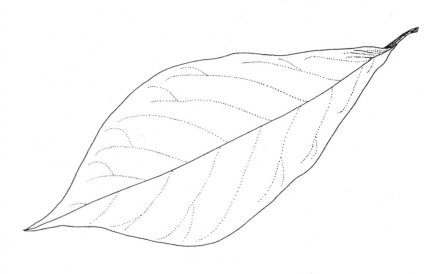

Asimina parviflora (Michx.) Dunal, (à-sim′i-nà pär-vi-flō′rà), Dwarf Pawpaw, is a reasonably common 6 to 8′ high shrub of the Piedmont and Coastal Plain from Virginia to Mississippi and east Texas. National champion is 24′ by 17′ in Lake Jem County Park, FL. The dark green, 4 to 8″ long leaves, up to 4″ wide, are covered with a rusty pubescence beneath. The brownish purple to greenish purple flowers average 1/2 to 3/4″ wide and occur before the leaves in April in Georgia. The fruit is small compared to *A. triloba*, averaging 1/2 to 1 1/2″(2 1/2″) long and about 1/2″ wide, seeds are about 1/2″ wide. Often found in sandy or dry woods. I have observed the plant on several occasions in the Athens area. Not very striking but a worthwhile naturalizing plant. Zone 7 to 9.

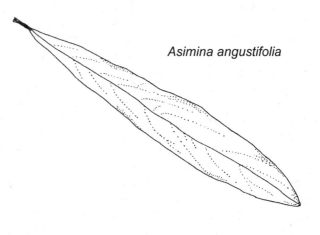

Asimina angustifolia

Asimina incana (Bartr.) Exell (*A. speciosa* Nash.), (à-sim′i-nà in-kā′nà), Flag Pawpaw, an unknown but beautiful species is included out of respect for a former student, Mr. Mark Callahan, Hazelhurst, GA who consistently baffled me with unusual quiz material. The 1 1/2 to 2″ diameter white outer petals surround the inner cream or yellow ones and appear in March to June depending on location. The oval fruits range from 1 3/4 to 3″ long and contain 1/2″ long seeds. The habit is typically shrubby, 4 to 5′ high with dark gray bark. Found in the sandhills from southeastern Georgia to northeastern Florida. Other rare southeastern *Asimina* species including *A. angustifolia* Raf. with showy white flowers and *A. obovata* (Willd.) Nash. with up to 6″ diameter flowers are native to the sandhills of the Coastal Plain. Woodlanders, Inc., Aiken, SC offers these rare plants. Probably only cold hardy in Zones 8 and 9.

Aspidistra elatior Bl. — Cast-iron Plant, Bar-room Plant
(as-pi-dis′trà ē-lā′ti-ôr)

FAMILY: Liliaceae

LEAVES: Evergreen, long ovate, parallel venation, blade 12 to 18″ long, dark green, entire, glabrous, acute apex; petiole—8 to 12″ long.

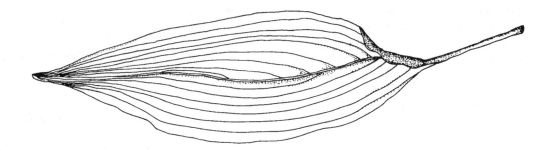

SIZE: 1 1/2 to 2′ high, 2 to 3′ wide.

HARDINESS: Zone 7 to 9, injured at 0°F, portion of the leaves turned brown, literally killed to the ground at −3°F in Athens; Zone 7 is probably over-optimistic unless the plant is protected.

HABIT: Upright clumps of evergreen foliage that develop from rhizomes.

RATE: Slow.

TEXTURE: Coarse.

LEAF COLOR: Lustrous dark green; wonderful contrast with lighter foliage colors; old brown leaves need to be removed in spring or entire plant cut to ground.

FLOWER: Purple, insignificant; occur underground and are only appreciated by moles.

CULTURE: Easily grown, provided a few simple rules are followed; prefers *full to partial* shade; deep, rich, well-drained soil; should be sheltered from winter winds; displays excellent drought tolerance.

DISEASES AND INSECTS: None serious; scale has been mentioned.

LANDSCAPE VALUE: Excellent for low light areas; good plant for textural contrast; at the Georgia Botanical Garden it is planted under a ramp and receives limited light yet is a tremendous performer; can be used in containers, as an edging along walks, in masses or for accent; also makes a good indoor plant.

CULTIVARS:

'Akebono'—White variegation on margin, much better than the striped form.

'Variegata'—Leaves have alternate stripes of green and white in varied widths; will lose pronounced variegation if grown in high fertility soil; quite attractive and does add interesting color; less hardy than the species. Other selections include 'Milky Way' with white spots on leaf surface; 'Variegata Ashei'—leaf centers flushed white with age; and 'Variegata Exotica' with parchment whitish variegations.

PROPAGATION: Division of established clumps.

ADDITIONAL NOTES: Does well in Coastal, Piedmont and lower South; called Bar-room Plant because of its ability to thrive under spittoonish conditions.

NATIVE HABITAT: Himalayas, China, Japan.

Aucuba japonica Thunb. — Japanese Aucuba, Spotted Laurel
(â-kū′bà jà-pon′i-kà)

FAMILY: Cornaceae

LEAVES: Opposite, simple, leathery, elliptic-ovate to elliptic-lanceolate, 3 to 8″ long, 1 1/2 to 3″ wide, acute to acuminate, broad cuneate at base, entire to remotely coarsely dentate toward the apex, glabrous, lustrous dark green above, lighter beneath; petiole—1/2 to 2″ long.

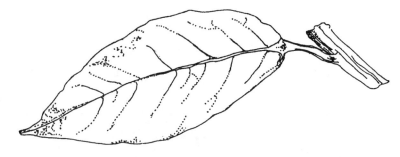

BUDS: Terminal (flower)—1/2 to 3/4″ long, conical, imbricate, slightly pubescent; lateral—brown, small, 1/32″ long, nestled in notch of leaf scar.

STEM: Stout, 1/4 to 3/8″ diameter, rounded, green, glabrous, leaf scars shield shape, connected by transverse stipular scar, 3 bundle traces; pith—white, solid, ample; fetid odor when bruised, box-elder-like.

SIZE: Usually ranges from 6 to 10′ in height, slightly less in spread; can grow to 15′.

HARDINESS: Zone 7 to 10, possibly 6, prefers warmer temperatures and in northern climates is used as indoor plant; hardy to 0 to −5°F.

HABIT: Densely upright-rounded to rounded shrub consisting of a thicket of erect or arching, limitedly branched shoots; always a rather neat and tidy evergreen shrub.

RATE: Slow, can easily be forced into more rapid growth with water and fertilizer.

TEXTURE: Medium, although medium-coarse could be easily argued.

LEAF COLOR: Dark lustrous green throughout the seasons; needs to be sited in shade, at least in South, for younger leaves when exposed to hot sun will blacken.

FLOWERS: Dioecious, purple, male flowers borne in upright, terminal, 2 to 4 1/2″ long, cymose panicles, individual flowers 1/3″ wide, with 4, occasionally 5 petals; female in shorter inflorescences from the axils of the leaves; March–April; in Athens flowers in mid to late March.

FRUIT: An ellipsoidal, 1/2″ long, scarlet, one-seeded, berry-like drupe; matures in October and November and persists through the following spring; quite handsome but often hidden by the foliage; anywhere from 1 to 5 present in leaf axil.

CULTURE: Easily transplanted, most plants are container-grown and present no transplanting problem; prefers well-drained, moist, high organic matter soils; must be sited in shade; has been known to grow under beeches, lindens and horsechestnuts where grass will not grow; tolerates polluted conditions extremely well; winter shade is also required for the leaves may become sickly green.

DISEASES AND INSECTS: In the last edition I reported no serious problems but in recent years have witnessed considerable stem dieback, at times just an occasional branch, others half the plant; *Sclerotium raulsoni* may be the causal agent for it girdles the stems.

LANDSCAPE VALUE: Used extensively in the South under the canopy of large trees and in ground cover plantings to break up the monotony of the sea of green; used in foundation plantings especially on the north and east side of homes; the variegated types add a touch of brightness to dark corners; also nice in groupings; remains quite dense even in heavy shade; in Ireland the various Aucubas are as common as goldenrod in the United States.

CULTIVARS: Many cultivars have been selected over the centuries and their nomenclature is somewhat confused. Have walked many blocks of variegated Aucubas only to be confused. Variation in degree of variegation from clonally propagated material means chimeras (branch sports) are a common occurrence. The following represent some of the more common types.

var. *borealis*—Compact small leaved form surviving 4°F in 1994; found along high snowfall line along sea of Japan on Honshu. Collected by U.S. National Arboretum.

'Crassifolia'—A male form with large, leathery, dark green leaves; 'Macrophylla' is similar but female.

'Crotonifolia'—Large leaves are finely speckled with yellow; separate authorities list the sex as male and female.

'Fructo Albo'—Leaves white variegated, the fruits pinkish cream, female.

'Gold Spot'—Gold spots throughout the leaf surface, may be another variant of 'Variegata'.

'Golden King'—Broadly golden variegated, male.

'Goldieana'—Solid gold splash in the center of the dark green leaves.

var. *himalaica*—Arguably a distinct species and treated as such, *A. himalaica* Hook. by Griffiths; leaves narrow, lanceolate, glossy dark green, flowers white, fruit orange, native to eastern Himalayas, Sikkim. Zone 6(?), have seen size listed as 6 to 10′.

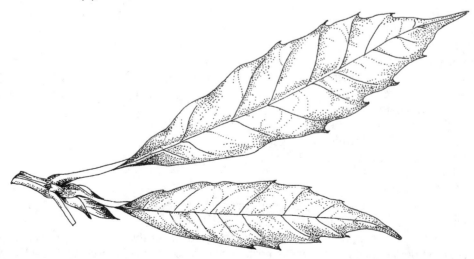

'Limbata'—Thickish leaves with intense yellowish green margins, leaves have coarse ascending serrations, young stems yellowish green, very similar to 'Sulphur'.

'Longifolia' (var. *longifolia*)—A catch-all name for narrow leaved forms; many have been introduced into cultivation; some male, others female; true 'Longifolia' is female; leaves may be 5″ long, only 1/4″ wide and faintly toothed; 'Augustifolia' ('Angustata') is male.

'Maculata'—Leaves blotched yellowish white, male.

'Mr. Goldstrike'—Leaves heavily splashed with bold gold markings, much more intense than common gold dust plant, male.

'Nana'—Compact form, one-half the size of species, growth habit more erect and female selections bear more abundant fruit; also better display since the fruits are borne above the foliage; probably several 'Nana' clones in commerce; 'Nana Cuspidata' has more variegation; perhaps the same as 'Variegata Nana' (female).

'Nana Rotundifolia'—Compact habit, roundish, toothed toward apex, almost unspeckled leaves, female.

'Picturata'—The leaves with a distinct solid yellow blotch in their middle and surrounded by smaller yellow flecks, appear to be unstable, original was a male, 'Bicolor', 'Elegans' and 'Elegantissima' belong here.

'Rozannie'—Flowers perfect, producing large bright red fruits in the absence of a male, forms a spreading compact shrub about 3′ high, leaves lustrous dark green, broad elliptic with a few coarse teeth near the apex, have grown in the garden for a number of years and although impressed by characteristics, it may be excessively slow for commercial production, supposedly fruits more freely when cross-pollinated.

'Salicifolia'—A green-leaved form with narrow, serrated leaves, a female.

'Serratifolia'—A rather handsome clone with large teeth along the margin; may also be listed as 'Dentata'.

'Sulphur'—Wide, golden yellow edges with dark green centers, leaves serrated, female, the same as 'Sulphurea Marginata', an old cultivar dating from 1800's.

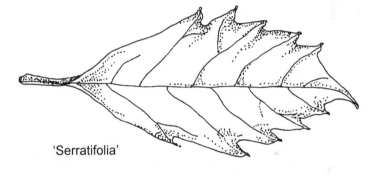

'Serratifolia'

'Variegata'—The true Gold Dust Plant, introduced ahead of the species in 1783 from Japan by John Graeffer; this is the yellow-flecked form and is female; there are numerous variegated types—some are stable and others revert back to the green condition of the species.

'Wisley Nana'—Compact, well formed, self-fruitful form; could this be the same as 'Rozannie'?

PROPAGATION: Interestingly, I can find no information on seed propagation and on several occasions have attempted to germinate seeds without success. George Thomas, a former student conducted a mini-study using March collected seeds with fruit coat removed. Seeds soaked in 0.05% (500 ppm) solution of GA for 24 hours germinated 78%; all other treatments 24% or less. Cuttings root easily, about any time of the year; I have had 100% success by treating cuttings with 3000 ppm IBA-quick dip; cuttings should be firm.

ADDITIONAL NOTES: Certainly a popular landscape plant from Zone 7 south; an attempt could be made to straighten out some of the cultivar confusion. In recent years, popularity in the South has declined most probably related to the devastating freeze of 1983–84 when the leaves were knocked from many plants. Generally, stem tissue was not killed and regrowth was slow. In 1989, I see more 'Variegata' still alive and it appears slightly hardier than the species or other cultivars. *Aucuba chinensis* Benth., Chinese Aucuba, is a shrub to 10′ with matt green above, blue-green beneath, up to 8″ long leaves. Woodlanders describes the leaves as slightly gold-flecked. The same as *A. omeiensis* Fang.? Inheritance appears to be maternal (chloroplastic DNA) and all seedlings from variegated plants produced variegated leaves. Patterns of spots and their shape and size were variable. The ratio of female:male seedlings was 3:1, and indication of cytoplasmic inheritance. A vigorous green leaved female seedling was named 'Copdock Seedling'. See *The Plantsman* 11:244–245 (1990). Interesting research study *HortScience* 26:1485–1488 (1991) showed *Aucuba japonica* 'Variegata' to be a shade obligate taxon that performed best with exposure to less than or equal to 47% of full sunlight.

NATIVE HABITAT: Japan. Variegated form was introduced in 1783; the green form in 1861.

Baccharis halimifolia L. — Groundsel-bush

FAMILY: Asteraceae
LEAVES: Alternate, simple, semi-evergreen to deciduous, obovate to oblong, 1 to 3″ long, 1/4 to 1 1/2″ wide,
acute, cuneate, coarsely toothed, upper leaves may be entire, both surfaces resinous-dotted, bright to
gray-green; petiole—1/8 to 1/4″ long.

Baccharis halimifolia, (bak′à-ris   ha-li-mi-fō′li-à), Groundsel-bush, is a handsome, unusual, native, multi-
stemmed, semi-evergreen to deciduous shrub with soft gray-green to rich green leaves. The habit is
distinctly oval to rounded. Makes a good mass or filler plant in difficult soil areas. Common along the coast
of Georgia (quite salt tolerant) where in late summer and fall the white fruits appear as a froth over the top
of the plants. Flowers are dioecious and are not particularly showy. The actual white color is the silky hairs
on the pappus of the pistillate flowers much like the dandelion. The plant grows 5 to 12′ high (national
champion is 21′ tall by 20′ wide, Nahunta, GA) and is cold hardy to Boston. In many inland areas in
Georgia it has naturalized. The landscape jury is still deliberating the merits of the species for general
garden use. I have watched the species move inland and at an old landfill site near Atlanta, it has
colonized more prevalently than any other species. The opportunity for selection is evident and 'White
Caps' a compact upright form, 5 to 6′ high, bluish foliage, heavy fruit producing selection was introduced
by Kurt Bluemel. The most aesthetic aspect of the species is the "cottony" fruits that persist, at least in
Georgia, into November–December. Cold hardiness has been listed to −20°F, but this usually translates
to stem kill. The Morton Arboretum, Lisle, IL has grown the species for many years with winter kill a matter
of course. Plants regenerate to as much as 7′ in a single season and flower and fruit in September–October. Seed germinates without pretreatment. Ideally, in colder climates treat the species as an
herbaceous perennial. Grows in the most impoverished of soils and is common along the coast near salt
marshes and ditches. Shows significant salt tolerance. Considered a noxious weed in Australia.
Massachusetts to Florida and Texas. Introduced 1683. Zone 5 to 9.

Other species offered in commerce include: *Baccharis glomerulifera* Pers., Southern Groundsel-
bush, with leathery light green leaves and brilliant white fruits in November, 3 to 10′ high, southeastern
United States, Zone 7 to 10; *Baccharis neglecta* Britt. (formerly *B. angustifolia*) with glossy narrow leaves
and dull white fruits, Nebraska to Texas and northern Mexico, Zone 4; and the evergreen *Baccharis
pilularis* DC, Dwarf Chapparal-broom, with lustrous green foliage, 12 to 20″ high; 'Centennial' is a low,
prostrate, evergreen form, 2′ high and over 10′ wide in 4 years, with numerous compact branches at the
base completely covering the ground, foliage is dark green except in dry season when it becomes light
green, has survived temperatures of 14°F to 113°F, result of controlled cross between *Baccharis
sarothroides* and *B. pilularis*. *Baccharis pilularis* is native to California coast. The species is one of the best
ground covers for California high desert conditions. See *HortScience* 19: 403 (1984). 'Pigeon Point' is a
fast-growing form with larger lighter green leaves, 3′ by 12′; 'Twin Peaks' grows 2 to 2 1/2′ high, 6′ wide,
described as a fire-retardant, deer-resistant, drought tolerant, mounding ground cover.

Berberis candidula Schneid. — Paleleaf Barberry
(bĕr′bĕr-is kan-did′ū-lå)

FAMILY: Berberidaceae

LEAVES: Alternate, simple, evergreen, 3 to 9 at a node, 1 to 2″ long and 1/2″ wide, oblong or narrowly oval, leathery, spiny-margined, edges of leaves recurved under, lustrous dark green above, glaucous white beneath, glabrous, cuneate, acute with spine-like apex; petiole—1/16″ or smaller.

BUDS: Loosely aggregated scales arise in center of leaves, nondescript.

STEM: Light brown, glabrous, angled, zig-zag, 3-pronounced spines, each about 1/2″ long at node; pith—white, solid.

SIZE: 2 to 4′ in height, spreading to 5′.

HARDINESS: Zone (5)6 to 8; –10°F or below will take the leaves off.

HABIT: Low-growing, dense, evergreen shrub of hemispherical habit with branches rigidly arching and covered with three-pronged spines.

RATE: Slow.

TEXTURE: Medium-fine in all seasons.

LEAF COLOR: Dark glossy green above, whitish below in summer; mature leaves may develop bronze to wine red tint in fall and winter.

FLOWERS: Perfect, bright yellow, 5/8″ diameter, borne singly on a 1/2″ long pedicel in May–June; very dainty and appealing; unfortunately, lost among the foliage.

FRUIT: True berry, purplish, bloomy, 1/2″ long, August–September.

CULTURE: Transplants readily; prefers moist, well-drained, slightly acid soils; full sun or light shade; withstands pruning well; fertilize in spring.

DISEASES AND INSECTS: Nothing exceptionally serious.

LANDSCAPE VALUE: Very handsome and beautiful plant for rock gardens; used in Europe in groupings or masses; could be used as a ground cover.

PROPAGATION: This discussion applies to barberries in general: I have rooted cuttings using 1000 ppm IBA/50% alcohol (KIBA is better than the acid), peat:perlite, under mist with 90% or greater efficiency; barberries, in general, can be rooted from softwood cuttings; excessive moisture in the rooting bench is problematic and as soon as cuttings are rooted misting should be curtailed; I have rooted many different barberry species and cultivars utilizing the technique described above; the literature is full of "how to's" related to rooting barberry; I think it is probably more important how the cuttings are handled at the end of the cycle than the beginning; the deciduous types should be rooted from June through August while the evergreen types can be done at this time but also are amenable to September–October collection and sticking with rooting occurring 6 to 8 weeks later. Seeds should be removed from the pulp and sown in the fall with normal winter temperatures satisfying the cold-stratification period or placed in a moist medium and provided 3 months at 41°F and sown in flats in the greenhouse; damping off of seedlings can be a problem and fungicidal treatments may be appropriate; barberries have a high percentage (90 to 99%) of sound seed.

NATIVE HABITAT: *Berberis candidula* is native to central China. Introduced 1894.

RELATED SPECIES:

Berberis × chenaultii Ahrendt, (bĕr′bĕr-is she-nōw′ē-ī), Chenault Barberry, is a hybrid that is probably the equal of *B. julianae* for cold hardiness. The plant grows 3 to 4′ high (8′ high plant at Wisley) and slightly greater in spread. The lustrous dark green leaves turn a rich bronze-red with the onset of cold weather. Flowers and fruits are sparse compared to *B. julianae*. *Berberis × chenaultii* resulted from crosses between *B. gagnepainii* and *B. verruculosa*, and several selections were named. At least 14 cultivars have been selected and introduced. It is questionable whether one is buying the species or the named selections. The original crosses were made by Chenault of Orleans, France, around 1933. *Berberis × hybrido-gagnepainii* Sur. is probably the more correct name. Zone 5 to 8.

Berberis × frikartii Schneid. ex Van de Laar, (bĕr′bĕr-is frik-är′tē-ī), Frikart's Barberry, is a hybrid between *B. candidula* and *B. verruculosa*. The type was first raised by Frikart of Stäfa, Switzerland around 1928. Mr. H. van de Laar in 1972 applied the grex name to these hybrids. The current 8 clones show hybrid vigor and differ from their parents in supposed lighter green leaves. I have seen 'Amstelveen' and 'Telstar' in England and am hard pressed to tell them from the parental species. 'Telstar' formed a 4′ high, flat-topped clump in 5 years at Kew. 'Amstelveen' is slightly less vigorous.

Berberis gagnepainii Schneid., (bĕr′bĕr-is gag-ne-pān′ē-ī), Black Barberry, serves as a parent for several of the hybrids but is doubtfully available commercially in this country. The plant ranges between 3 1/2 and 5′ in height and is usually higher than wide at maturity. The glossy, dark green, 1 1/4 to 4″ long leaves are the largest of the evergreen species mentioned here. *B. gagnepainii* has not proven hardy where winter temperatures range from –5 to –15°F.

Berberis* × *gladwynensis 'William Penn', (bĕr′bĕr-is glad-win-en′sis), was introduced by the Henry Foundation of Gladwyne, PA. Its habit is dense and mounded, and plants mature at about four feet. The foliage is a lustrous dark green and turns a beautiful bronze in winter. Bright yellow flowers appear in April–May. The foliage may be the handsomest of any evergreen barberry. Unfortunately, the plant is not well-known. It is represented in only a limited number of arboreta. This selection has picked up steam (1997) and is now being produced by major container growers. The parents are *B. verruculosa* and *B. gagnepainii*. Hardiness is suspect, and temperatures below –10° will probably eliminate it from the land-scape. I saw a planting killed to the ground in Mt. Airy Arboretum after exposure to –17°F. One reference reported that this plant was hardy to –25 to –30°F but I don't believe it and neither does the plant. Continuous snow cover may permit survival at lower temperatures.

Berberis julianae Schneid. — Wintergreen Barberry

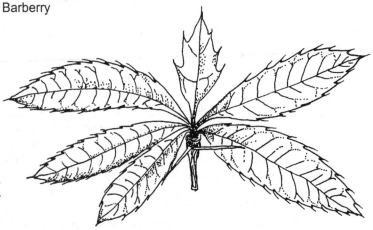

LEAVES: Alternate, simple, evergreen, narrow-elliptic to lanceolate or oblan-ceolate, 2 to 3″ long, 1/3 to 3/4″ wide, spiny-serrate, lustrous dark green above, much paler and indistinctly veined beneath, rigidly coriaceous, often 5 leaves at a node; petiole—1/3 to 5/8″ long.

STEM: Slightly angled, yellowish when young, light yellowish gray or yellowish brown the second year, spines rigid, 3-parted, 1/2 to 1 1/4″ long; the inner bark and wood is yellow.

Berberis julianae, (bĕr′bĕr-is jū-lē-ā′nȧ), Wintergreen Barberry, is probably the hardiest of the evergreen barberries, although I have observed considerable leaf burning and abscission after exposure to temperatures of –6°F. Desiccating winds play a role in the browning and leaf drop observed on this species in northern states. On the University of Georgia campus in Athens, the leaves are retained through winter but may bronze. The species forms a 6 to 8′(10′) mound of dense branches and foliage when properly maintained. Bean mentioned a 10′ high by 12′ wide "luxuriant rounded mass of foliage." It is almost impenetrable to students, children and dogs; for that reason, it makes a good barrier or hedge. The lustrous dark green foliage is handsome throughout the growing season. Abundant yellow flowers (mid to late March, Athens) are followed by glaucous bluish black, 1/3″ long oval fruits that persist into fall. 'Nana' appears to be a good cultivar but is seldom available commercially. It grows about half the size of the species and forms a solid mound. Several southern nurseries have started to grow the plant for it makes an effective mass planting on commercial properties. 'Spring Glory' (also sold as 'Webberi', 'Webb') is a selection with brilliant coloration to the new shoot growth; leaves and stems are tinted red to bronze-red. Mr. Don Shadow, Winchester, TN, first pointed out the plant to me. Based on initial observations it is superior to the species and will prove a worthy landscape plant with time. Pruning tends to ruin the plant and throughout the Southeast, especially on campuses, it is reduced to a 30 to 42″ high hedge. The lower branches lose their foliage with time and plants become open and ratty. Ideally, let the plant go and develop the naturally dense rounded habit or cut to within 6 to 12″ of the ground and allow for complete rejuvenation. Central China. Introduced 1900. Zone (5)6 to 8.

Berberis sanguinea (now *B. panlanensis* Ahrendt), (bĕr′bĕr-is san-gwin′ē-à), Red-pedicel Barberry, and **B. sargentiana** Schneid., (bĕr′bĕr-is sär-jen-tē-ā′nà), Sargent Barberry, deserve mention because of their fine evergreen foliage, yellow flowers, and red maturing to black fruit. Both are dense in habit growing 6 to 9′ high and 6′ wide. I have seen them used in Zones 6 to 8 and feel they are worthy of consideration. *Berberis sargentiana* continues to fascinate me for I never see it in commerce only in botanical gardens and arboreta yet, according to Bean, it was described as the only evergreen barberry known to be hardy at the Arnold Arboretum. I did not locate it during sabbatical. In most respects, it is like *B. julianae*, except the leaves are larger, 1 1/2 to 5″ long, 1/2 to 1 1/4″ wide, dark green (without prominent luster of *B. julianae*), the stems are rounded (*B. julianae* are angled) and the fruit is a 1/3″ long, egg-shaped, black berry. Supposedly, the new growth is reddish while that of *B. julianae* is not. I have seen numerous *B. julianae* seedlings (apparently) and some have rich yellow green, bronze to bronze-red new growth. Both are native to China.

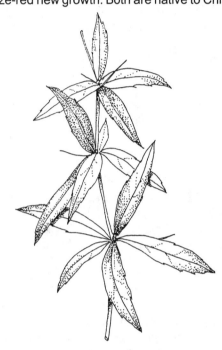

Berberis triacanthophora Fedde — Threespine Barberry
LEAVES: Alternate, simple, evergreen, linear to oblanceolate, 1 to 2″ long, 1/8″(1/2″) wide, with 1 to 5 setose teeth on each margin, bright green above, glaucous or glaucescent beneath.
STEM: Three-parted, 5/8″ long spine at each node.

Berberis triacanthophora, (bĕr′bĕr-is trī-à-kan-thof′o-rà), Threespine Barberry, differs from the previous evergreen species in that the flowers are pale yellow or whitish, tinged red outside, producing a pink effect overall. Fruit is bluish black, slightly bloomy, 1/3″ diameter. The plant matures at three to five feet and tends to be more open than other evergreen species. The foliage is bright green above, somewhat glaucous on the underside and some leaves turn reddish purple in winter. Spines are 3-parted and vicious. I had one plant in my garden and was never impressed by its performance. Griffiths lists it as *Berberis × wisleyensis* Ahrendt. Central China. Introduced 1907. Zone 5 to 8.

Berberis verruculosa Hemsl. & Wils. — Warty Barberry
LEAVES: Alternate, simple, evergreen, 1/2 to 1 1/2″ long, elliptic or ovate to ovate-lanceolate, tapering at both ends, leathery, margins recurved and remotely spiny-toothed, glabrous, lustrous dark green above, glaucous beneath, leaves arranged in clusters along the stems.
STEM: Rounded, light brown, covered with tiny dark brown excrescences which give the bark a rough surface; spines are slender, 3-parted, 1/2 to 3/4″ long.

Berberis verruculosa, (bĕr′bĕr-is vĕr-uk-ū-lō′sà), Warty Barberry, grows 3 to 6′ and forms a dense evergreen shrub. Leaves are small and lustrous dark green above, whitish beneath and remain green, become purplish green or rich mahogany in winter. The flowers are golden yellow, 5/8 to 3/4″ diameter. Fruit is violet-black, bloomy, 1/3″ long, ovoid or pyriform berry. Closely related to *B. candidula*. Although listed as hardy in Zone 5, it was severely injured above the snowline during the winter of 1975–76 in Illinois and the lowest recorded temperature was –8°F. *Berberis candidula* growing next to it was not affected. It is similar to and often confused with *B. candidula*. Based on my experience with the two species, the following differences seem relatively constant. The leaves of warty barberry are not as white on their underside, although this characteristic appears less than absolute, and the stems are covered with tiny, wart-like excrescences. Height may approach 3 to 6′ compared to 3′ for *B. candidula*. 'Apricot Queen' produces bronze new growth and apricot-yellow flowers. 'Compacta' has been listed, but I have not seen the plant in cultivation. Western China. Introduced 1904. Zone 5 to 7.

ADDITIONAL NOTES: I could ramble for pages over the various species of evergreen barberries. They can be among the handsomest of landscape plants when properly groomed. The reciprocal is also true. In traveling through European gardens I noticed an abundance of evergreen barberries of great foliage and floral beauty. On the West Coast especially in the San Francisco area I observed a number of the same species. Some of the best include: *B. darwinii* Hook., Darwin Barberry; *B. empetrifolia* Lam., Crow Barberry; *B. linearifolia* Philippi, Jasperbells Barberry, and *B. × stenophylla* Lindl., Rosemary Barberry. These species house great numbers of cultivars differing in flower color and growth habit. In flower, the species and cultivars are spectacular. I cannot remember viewing a specimen of these barberries in the eastern United States.

Berberis koreana Palib. — Korean Barberry
(bĕr′bĕr-is kôr-ē-ā′nȧ)

LEAVES: Alternate, simple, obovate or elliptic, 1 to 3″ long, rounded at apex, cuneate at base, rather densely spinulose-serrulate, reticulate beneath, medium to dark green above, strongly veined beneath; petiole—1/4 to 1/2″ long.

STEM: Moderate, reddish to purple-brown, bloomy, grooved, glabrous, with 1 to 5 spines, usually 3, each spine flattened and nearly 1/4″ wide.

SIZE: Rather dense shrub growing 4 to 6′(8′) high and usually slightly less in spread.

HARDINESS: Zone 3 to 7.

HABIT: Multi-stemmed oval to haystack-shaped plant of rather dense constitution; however, it does sucker from the roots and at times becomes quite unruly in its growth habit; will form large, clump-type colonies.

RATE: Medium.

TEXTURE: Medium in all seasons; this species has larger foliage than most barberries.

STEM COLOR: Young shoots are reddish and bloomy.

LEAF COLOR: Medium to dark green in summer changing to deep reddish purple in the fall; often spectacular and holding late (November).

FLOWERS: Perfect, yellow, 1/4″ diameter, each flower on a 1/2″ long pedicel, borne in drooping, 3 to 4″ long, up to 20-flowered racemes in early to mid-May in Boston; borne after foliage has matured but still quite showy, perhaps the handsomest of the deciduous barberries for flower although I know plantsmen who will argue this contention.

FRUIT: True berry, bright red, covered to varying degrees with a waxy bloom, egg-shaped, 1/4 to 3/8″ long, effective through fall and into winter.

CULTURE: Easy to transplant; will tolerate about any soil except those that are permanently wet; full sun or light shade; prune anytime; extremely cold hardy.

DISEASES AND INSECTS: Discussed under *B. thunbergii*; usually very few problems.

LANDSCAPE VALUE: A worthwhile barberry for foliage, flower, and fruit: makes an excellent barrier plant and I have seen it used in mass plantings with a degree of success; presents an impenetrable barrier to unwanted neighbors; best in northern gardens.

CULTIVARS:
'Red Tears'—Leaves rich reddish purple, arching branches, 6′ high, rich red fruits in 4″ long clusters.

PROPAGATION: Softwood cuttings of young growth collected in May or June and treated with 1000 ppm IBA rooted readily; most barberry species have internal dormancy and require cold stratification to stimulate germination; a period of 60 to 90 days at 41°F is suitable for this species.

NATIVE HABITAT: Korea. Introduced 1905.

RELATED SPECIES:

Berberis gilgiana Fedde — Wildfire Barberry
LEAVES: Alternate, simple, elliptic or elliptic-obovate to oblong, 1 to 2″ long, acute, attenuate at base, remotely serrate, dull green above, either glabrous or slightly pubescent, gray-green below.

STEM: Grooved, usually 3-parted spines, although also single-spined, 1/4 to 1″ long.

Berberis gilgiana, (bĕr′bĕr-is gil-jē-a′nȧ), Wildfire Barberry, has excellent garden potential, but very few people know the plant. A mature specimen may be 6 to 8′ high and densely branched to form a rounded outline. The rich green foliage is attractive throughout the growing season and changes to beautiful shades of yellow, orange and red in fall. The bright yellow flowers are borne in spike-like, pendulous, 2 to 3″ long racemes in May. They are followed by wine red to reddish, 1/3″ long, ovoid fruits that persist into fall. This is an extremely attractive barberry at least worthy of trial by nurserymen. The species is hardy to -15°F and possibly lower. North and Central China. Introduced 1910. Zone 5 to 7.

Berberis vulgaris L. — Common Barberry
LEAVES: Alternate, simple, oval or obovate, 1 to 2″(3″) long, obtuse,
    rarely acutish, finely toothed, thin, dull green.
STEM: Yellow, 3-parted spines.

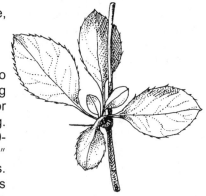

Berberis vulgaris, (bĕr′bĕr-is vul-gā′ris), Common Barberry, grows 6 to
    10′ high producing a mass of stems; erect at the base, branching
    and spreading outwards at the top into a graceful, arching or
    pendulous form. The foliage is dull green, about 1 to 2″ long.
    Flowers are yellow and borne in 2 to 3″ long, pendulous, up to 20-
    flowered racemes in May. Fruit is a bright red or purple, 1/3 to 1/2″
    long, egg-shaped berry which becomes effective in fall and persists.
    W.J. Bean is manifest in his praise of this shrub but in America it is
    a significant problem for it has escaped from cultivation and serves
    as the alternate host for the wheat rust, *Puccinia graminis*. In some states the laws require the destruction
    of Common Barberry on this account. A hybrid, *B.* × *ottawaensis* Schneid. (*B. thunbergii* × *B. vulgaris*),
    is common in Europe and Canada. It is a vigorous shrub, the most common form being 'Purpurea' with
    purplish leaves. Native to Europe, North Africa and temperate Asia. Long cultivated. Zone 3 to 6.

Berberis × *mentorensis* H. Schultz & Horvath ex L.M. Ames — Mentor Barberry; result of cross
    between *B. julianae* and *B. thunbergii*.
(bĕr′bĕr-is men-tor-en′sis)

LEAVES: Alternate, simple, elliptic-ovate, 1 to 2″ long, subcoriaceous, sparingly spinulose-toothed toward apex
    or entire, very dark green, pale beneath; tends to be semi-evergreen or hold leaves late in fall.
BUDS: Small and scaly, usually 6 pointed scales borne on spurs which is true for most barberries.
STEM: Glabrous, usually three-spined, grooved, inner bark and wood yellow as is true for all barberries; 3-
    spined on older branches, young stems often have only a single spine.

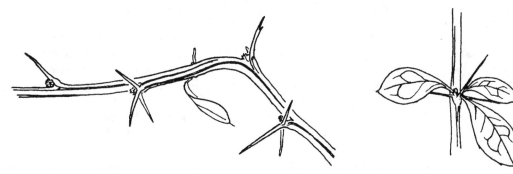

SIZE: 5′ in height by 5′ to 7′ in spread; have seen specimens 5 to 7′ high and 10 to 12′ wide.
HARDINESS: Zone 5 to 8; does not seem as prosperous in the South (Zone 7) yet both parents are adapted.
HABIT: Upright, stiff, with many slender stems, becoming bushy with age, very regular and rounded in outline.
RATE: Medium to fast, good rapid-growing hedge plant.
TEXTURE: Medium in foliage, medium in winter.
LEAF COLOR: Dark green, leathery in nature; often developing yellow-orange-red late in fall; have observed
    leaves as late as December 5 in Boston, MA; a California reference noted it is evergreen to −5°F but in
    my 18 years in Athens (the lowest temperature was −3°F and one winter temperatures did not drop below
    18°F) it has always become deciduous.
FLOWERS: Yellow, usually April–May, not as showy as other species but still attractive; flowers in mid to late
    March in Athens, GA; somewhat offensive to the olfactory senses.
FRUIT: Until 1991, I had never observed fruit on this hybrid and assumed it was sterile; possibly a triploid?; one
    parent is bright red-fruited; the other bluish black; at the Arnold Arboretum red fruits were produced.
CULTURE: Easily transplanted, very adaptable; full sun to 1/2 shade situations; well-drained soil is preferable.
DISEASES AND INSECTS: None serious, although *Verticillium* wilt has been reported; see under *B. thunbergii*.
LANDSCAPE VALUE: Excellent hedge plant because of uniform growth rate; makes an excellent barrier plant
    because of thorny nature of stems; can be used for massing, shrub border and foundation plant; possibly

the best of the barberries for hedging in the Midwest and East; makes a beautiful dense, mounded shrub if left to its own genetic code and not that of the pruning shears.

PROPAGATION: Roots readily and one report mentioned that cuttings collected in early August and treated with 8000 ppm IBA rooted 100% by late September.

ADDITIONAL NOTES: Result of breeding work of M. Horvath, Mentor, OH. Introduced 1942. Although considered quite hardy, severe top damage occurred during the winters of 1976–77, 77–78 when temperatures dropped to –25°F in the midwestern states.

Berberis thunbergii DC. — Japanese Barberry
(bĕr′bĕr-is thun-bĕr′jē-ī)

LEAVES: Alternate, simple, obovate to spatulate-oblong, 1/2 to 1 1/4″ long, obtuse, rarely acute, sometimes spine-tipped, narrowed at base into a petiole—1/12 to 1/2″ long, quite entire, bright green above, glaucescent beneath, leaves borne in clusters along the branches.

BUDS: Small, ovoid, solitary, sessile, about 6 pointed scales born on spurs.

STEM: Reddish brown, angled or grooved, glabrous, single spine, 1/2″ long (usually), does not always hold true.

SIZE: 3 to 6′ by 4 to 7′; Bean mentions plants 8′ high and 15′ wide.

HARDINESS: Zone 4 to 8; not as robust in heat of Zone 8 but performs reasonably well.

HABIT: Much-branched, very dense rounded shrub usually broader than tall at maturity.

RATE: Medium.

TEXTURE: Medium fine to medium in leaf, medium to coarse in winter; tends to attract leaves, papers, cans and bottles due to dense, multi-stemmed habit; I have personally looked upon this shrub as a winter garbage can because of this ability; truly requires a spring cleaning.

LEAF COLOR: Bright green in summer changing to orange, scarlet, and reddish purple in the fall; usually quite variable in fall color; one of first shrubs to leaf out in spring; this is true for most of the deciduous barberries.

FLOWERS: Perfect, yellow, 1/3 to 1/2″ across, borne on a 1/2″ long pedicel, April–May, solitary or 2 to 4 in umbellate clusters, actually not showy for individual flowers are small and borne under the foliage.

FRUIT: Bright red, 1/3″ long, ellipsoidal berry, October and persisting into winter; excellent winter effect and should be considered more often for its fruits.

CULTURE: Easily transplanted as a container plant; extremely adaptable, withstands dry conditions; will not withstand extremely moist conditions; best in full sun; tolerates urban conditions better than many shrubs.

DISEASES AND INSECTS: Bacterial leaf spot, anthracnose, root rots, rusts (Japanese Barberry is not susceptible), wilt, mosaic, barberry aphid, barberry webworm, scale, and northern root-knot nematode; usually barberries are little-troubled under ordinary landscape conditions.

LANDSCAPE VALUE: Hedge, barrier, groupings; the cultivars offer different foliage colors and forms and therefore other landscape possibilities; the compact dwarfish forms are used in masses, 'Crimson Pygmy' is probably the largest selling barberry in the world; some of the colored foliage types like 'Rose Glow' provide variety in shrub and perennial borders; in my Georgia garden, barberry has been shut out with the exception of 'Rose Glow'; with the plethora of new cultivars perhaps an attitude adjustment is in order.

CULTIVARS: In the last edition (1990), I commented about the number of new cultivars (10 to 15) that had been introduced and actively promoted since the 1983 edition. Well, another 10 or so have appeared since the 1990 edition. The old descriptions are intact with an embellishment here and there; the new included to the degree I know them.

PURPLE LEAF TYPES:
  var. *atropurpurea*—The foliage assumes reddish or purplish shades. There is extreme variation among seed-grown progeny, and selections have been made for superior red-purple coloration. The history of this plant is interesting—the original plant arose in the nursery of Renault in Orleans, France, about 1913, but it was not distributed until 1926. At first, the plant was propagated vegetatively, but it was later discovered that it would come relatively true-to-type from seed. Many nurserymen still grow it from seed and rogue the off-color seedlings. The red-purple foliage becomes more greenish if the plants are sited in shade. This is true of the various named selections of var. *atropurpurea*. The yellow

flowers are tinged with purple, but the fruits are the same bright red as those of the species. Generally grows about the same size as the species. Fall color is often rich red to reddish purple.

var. *atropurpurea* Angel Wings™—Interesting variation on 'Golden Ring' with a more prominent golden leaf margin that persists into the summer and fall; a vigorous grower and should mature between 5 to 6′ high; the reddish purple new leaf color becomes purple-bronze in the heat of summer; first leaves are often spotted rose, green, and red-purple, eventually turning reddish purple with the golden leaf margin; introduced by Bill Ford, Johnson Nursery, Ellijay, GA.

var. *atropurpurea* 'Bagatelle'—A compact form like 'Crimson Pygmy' except the leaves are slightly glossier, considered slower growing, more compact (16″ high) and with smaller leaves (1″ long); a most beautiful selection with vivid red-purple leaves; Mr. Adrian Bloom, Bressingham Gardens, England, mentioned that a 30″ high plant in his garden was 15- years-old; every time I see this selection the garden juices start to flow; a few nurseries in the United States have this form but it is not commercially available on a wide-spread basis; originated at Van Klavern, Boskoop and introduced in 1971; supposedly a hybrid between 'Kobold' and 'Atropurpurea Nana'.

var. *atropurpurea* Burgundy Carousel™ ('Bailtwo')—Summer and fall foliage burgundy-purple, spreading growth habit, 3′ by 4 to 5′, foliage larger than typical var. *atropurpurea*, Bailey Nursery introduction, has performed well in Georgia tests (Zone 7b), slightly slower growing than Ruby Carousel™, holds deep red-purple leaf color in the heat of the South.

var. *atropurpurea* Cherry Bomb™ ('Monomb')—The foliage color is similar to 'Crimson Pygmy' but the growth habit is intermediate between var. *atropurpurea* and 'Crimson Pygmy', more open branching habit, larger foliage, 3 to 4′ high and wide, Monrovia introduction.

var. *atropurpurea* 'Concorde'—Extremely slow-growing, compact habit, probably 2′ by 3′, small deep red-purple leaves that hold color in heat; in Georgia trials, this maintained deeper color than 'Crimson Pygmy' and Royal Burgundy™; superior to 'Crimson Pygmy' but not as well-known and slightly slower growing; introduced by Wavecrest Nursery, Michigan.

var. *atropurpurea* 'Crimson Giant'—A large-leaved, reddish purple form that holds color into the summer.

var. *atropurpurea* 'Crimson Pygmy'—This is the most popular Japanese Barberry selection. This low, dense plant grows 1 1/2 to 2′ tall and 2 1/2 to 3′ wide. The reddish purple foliage color is best when the plant is grown in full sun. The plant was raised by Van Eyck in Boskoop, Holland, in 1942. Unfortunately, it has been sold under the names 'Little Gem', 'Little Beauty', 'Little Favorite' and 'Atropurpurea Nana'. It is an excellent landscape plant from Chicago, IL, to Atlanta, GA, and can be used for a multitude of purposes. A 12-year-old plant may be 2′ high and 5′ wide.

var. *atropurpurea* 'Crimson Velvet'—Fuchsia new foliage that deepens to smokey maroon, the color holding throughout the growing season, vigorous grower, fall color is a good red, similar to var. *atropurpurea* in size and habit; leaves are larger and more leathery than var. *atropurpurea*; has performed well in the South; at Tifton, GA, Dr. John Ruter reported it remained crimson throughout the canopy until the middle of September; likewise at Athens, GA; has grown twice as fast as Burgundy Carousel™ and Ruby Carousel™; introduced by Lake County Nursery, Perry, OH.

var. *atropurpurea* 'Dart's Red Lady'—Large, dark purple-black leaves, good autumn color, semi-spreading habit; have seen in Mr. Adrian Bloom's great garden and was impressed by intensity of foliage color; have seen in September at Sissinghurst and although the purple was distinct it was not as vibrant as in the spring.

var. *atropurpurea* 'Erecta'—It is similar to var. *atropurpurea*, except that its habit is more upright, burgundy foliage, brilliant red berries, makes an excellent upright thorny hedge. It was found at Marshall Nurseries, Arlington, NE in a block of two-year seedlings; also listed as 'Marshall Upright', 'Marshall's Upright' and 'Marshall's Red'.

var. *atropurpurea* 'Golden Ring' ('Golden Rim' in Europe may be the same thing?)—This is a reddish purple leaf form similar to the variety in growth habit but with a green or yellow-green border around the margin of each leaf. The effect is not noticeable except on close inspection.

var. *atropurpurea* 'Harlequin'—New foliage a mottle of pink, cream and purple; forms a tight, rather compact shrub about 4′ high, a Dutch introduction.

var. *atropurpurea* 'Helmond Pillar'—Distinct upright form reminiscent of 'Erecta' but narrower and with reddish purple leaves, leaf color fades in heat of summer, good red autumn color, reasonably common in English gardens, probably grows 4 to 5′ by 2′ wide, narrower at base than top.

var. *atropurpurea* 'Intermedia'—This cultivar was selected from a group of seedling 'Crimson Pygmy' plants at Zelenka Evergreen Nursery Inc., Grand Haven, MI; it grows much faster than 'Crimson Pygmy', with good reddish purple foliage; its mature size averages about three feet; good looking plant.

var. *atropurpurea* 'Limeglow'—Similar to 'Rose Glow' in habit, but with green and yellow variegation, from Flowerwood Nursery, Mobile, AL.

var. *atropurpurea* 'Pink Queen'—Young foliage nearly red like 'Rose Glow', later leaves more brown with pink-red, gray and white specks and stripes, turns good red in fall, probably 4' by 4 to 6' wide, has also been listed as 'Atropurpurea Rosea'.

var. *atropurpurea* 'Red Bird'—This is a selection made by Willis Nursery Co., Inc., Ottawa, KS, prior to 1959; it has better color and larger leaves and is more compact than var. *atropurpurea*.

var. *atropurpurea* 'Red Chief'—Vivid reddish purple new foliage that becomes green-purple-brown with maturity, leaves 1 1/2″ long by 1/2″ wide, stems also bright reddish purple, orange-red to orange-purple fall color, grows 6' by 8'.

var. *atropurpurea* 'Red Pillar'—Red to reddish purple leaves, good orange-red fall color, dense upright column at maturity, 4 to 5' by 1 1/2 to 2'.

var. *atropurpurea* 'Rose Glow'—Spaargen & Sons of Holland raised this selection about 1957. The new foliage is rose-pink, mottled with deeper red-purple splotches. The colors gradually mature to a deep reddish purple. The ultimate size is about 5 to 6'. I have grown 'Rose Glow' in Urbana, IL, and Athens, GA, with excellent success. First leaves are purple, the new shoots that follow produce the characteristic mottled color. Has become extremely popular in the South. A good form.

var. *atropurpurea* Royal Burgundy™ ('Gentry Cultivar', have seen spelled Royal Burgandy™)—The color is a much richer burgundy than 'Crimson Pygmy', new spring foliage beads water droplets like a freshly waxed car, small velvety leaf holds the deep burgundy color throughout summer, changing to black-red in autumn, forms a low-mounding shrub smaller than 'Crimson Pygmy' but similar in growth habit, selected in 1989 by Leo Gentry, Sr.; plant patent 1461; in Georgia tests has grown faster than 'Crimson Pygmy' and retains deeper red-purple leaf color.

var. *atropurpurea* 'Royal Cloak'—Described by Heronswood Nursery, Kingston, WA, as looking like a purple smoketree from a distance, large deep red-purple leaves, compact mounded habit, 4' high.

var. *atropurpurea* Ruby Carousel™ ('Bailone')—Summer and fall foliage burgundy-purple, low rounded habit, 3 to 3 1/2' by 3 1/2', selected for good red foliage color and uniform habit, Bailey Nursery introduction, good red-purple leaf color retained in heat of Zone 7b.

var. *atropurpurea* 'Sheridan's Red'—A single observation at the Royal Botanic Garden, Hamilton, Ontario, Canada, is sufficient reason for including this selection. The leaves are larger and more leathery than those of var. *atropurpurea*, and were a vivid red-purple in mid-August.

GREEN, YELLOW, VARIEGATED LEAF TYPES:

'Aurea'—This plant is a definite knockout if one is looking for contrast. The leaves are a vivid yellow and hold this color except in shade, where they become yellow-green. Surprisingly, the yellow foliage does not seem to burn or scorch, even in southern landscapes. 'Aurea' is a dense, relatively slow-growing shrub, eventually reaching a height of 3 to 4' (5 to 6' is possible). Apparently it does not flower or fruit heavily.

Bonanza Gold™ ('Bogozam')—Dwarf golden foliaged barberry that does not "burn," may grow 18″ by 36″ in 10 years, needs full sun for maximum expression of color, flowers are described as pink in bud opening white, if this is true it is a first for me, fruits are bright red, plant patent 8215, Lake County Nursery introduction, growing in Zones 7 and 8 with relative impunity, 'Aurea Nana' appears to be a rename to circumvent paying royalties on the trademarked plant.

'Carpetbagger'—Low-growing, green leaves, maximum height 2', yellow flowers, red autumn color.

Emerald Carousel™ ('Tara')—Interesting hybrid between *B. thunbergii* and *B. koreana*, deep green summer foliage develops outstanding early, long retentive, red to reddish purple fall color, rounded with arching branches, grows 4 to 5' high, 4 to 5' wide, listed as Zone 4 to 6 but with *B. thunbergii* genes may be adapted further south, Bailey Nursery introduction; to date has not exhibited great vigor in Georgia trials; interestingly, this cultivar is extremely susceptible to deer browsing in our Georgia trials, while the red-leaved forms Burgundy Carousel™, Ruby Carousel™, 'Crimson Velvet', 'Concorde', 'Crimson Pygmy', and 'Gentry's Royal Burgundy' were not affected; I speculate that Emerald Carousel™, a hybrid between *B. koreana* and *B. thunbergii*, is susceptible to deer browsing because of the hybrid parentage.

'Emerald Pygmy'—Dwarf form with deep blue-green leaves that become fiery orange-red in fall, makes a good low hedge.

'Erecta'—A fine selection seldom available commercially, it was introduced by Horvath after five generations of selections for upright habit. This cultivar grows 4 to 5' high and 8 to 10' wide, but only after a great many years. Each branch is distinctly upright, and very few laterals are produced. The fall color varies from yellow, orange to red and can be truly spectacular. 'Erecta' was patented by Cole Nursery Co., Painesville, OH, in 1936. Another name applied to this clone is 'Truehedge Columnberry'.

'Globe'—This patented selection has also been listed as 'Nana' and 'Compacta'. The habit is that of a globe. Mature height ranges from 2 to 3', with a spread about twice the height. The foliage is a uniform dark green and may be reddish in fall.

Gold Nugget™ ('Monler')—Orange new growth maturing to golden yellow foliage, more sun tolerant than other golden barberries, compact-mounded habit, 15″ by 24″, Monrovia introduction.

'Green Carpet'—Light green, oval to rounded leaves turn good yellow-orange-red in fall, develops a spreading growth habit, 3′ by 5′, a Dutch introduction.

'Green Ornament'—Good dark green, 1/2 to 1 1/4″, rounded-elliptic foliage on an upright ascending shrub that will average 5′ by 3′ at landscape maturity, a free-fruiting form with glossy red fruits, fall color brownish yellow.

'Kelleriis'—A compact 4 to 5′ by 4 to 5′ form with medium green foliage that is speckled and splashed with white variegation on the new shoots, variegation persists into fall, a Dutch introduction.

'Kobold'— Introduced by Van Klavern of Boskoop, Holland, around 1960. Its habit is similar to that of a compact Japanese Holly or boxwood, and in summer offers a visual substitute. The new foliage is rich green, becoming lustrous dark green with maturity. In fall, it is off-yellow, with perhaps a tinge of red. Flowers and fruits are sparsely produced. This selection grows 2 to 2 1/2′ at maturity and forms a perfect mound without pruning. It is tremendous addition to the list of landscape barberries. Have read about a form called 'Dwarf Green' that sounds suspiciously like 'Kobold'.

Lustre Green™ ('Anderson')—Rounded and compact, 2 to 3′ high and wide, glossy green summer foliage, yellow, orange and red in fall, abundant bright red berries persist into winter, discovered in Carlton Plants seedling crop in 1989 by propagation manager Mike Anderson, introduced by Carlton Plants, Dayton, OR.

'Minor'—It was grown from seed collected at the Arnold Arboretum in 1892. The leaves, flowers and fruits are smaller than those of the species. The habit is dense, rounded and compact, reaching a height of 3 1/2 to 5′.

'Pow-wow'—Compact grower, yellowish foliage as I viewed the plant in March 1996 in an English nursery, the description said young shoots reddish yellow, aging creamy-white-yellow, to my knowledge unknown in the United States.

'Silver Beauty'—A sprawly grower with variegated green and white foliage; not uniform in variegation patterns; does not appear to possess the vigor of the species; also listed as 'Argenteo-marginata'.

'Silver Mile'—Deep burgundy-red foliage suffused with irregular gray splotches and splashes, not spectacular, will grow 4 to 5′ high, possibly greater at maturity, acceptable in Zones 7 and 8.

'Sparkle'—The plants, even when young, have arching horizontal branches and maintain a dense constitution into old age. The plant grows 3 to 4′ high and slightly wider at maturity. The glossy, rich dark green, almost leathery foliage turns a fluorescent reddish orange in fall. Abundant yellow flowers are followed by persistent bright red fruits. Did not do particularly well in my Georgia garden but have seen handsome specimens in Cincinnati, Chicago, and western Massachusetts. Introduced by Synnesvedt Nursery, IL.

Sunsation™ ('Monry')—Compact, upright, vase-shaped habit, 3 to 4′ high, to 4′ wide, green new growth with gold hues, matures to brilliant gold, discovered by Henry Eiler, Litchfield, IL in the mid-1980s, introduced by Monrovia Nursery Co.

'Thornless'—Because most barberries carry thorns, this one is somewhat of a novelty. The habit is globe-like, with a mature size of about 4 by 6′, also listed as 'Inermis'.

'Variegata'—There are several variegated forms mentioned in the literature, and it is questionable how different they are. This cultivar originated as a chance seedling among 20,000 plants in the nurseries of Alex Toth, Madison, OH. The leaves are predominantly green with spots, splotches, or dots of white, light gray and yellow. Have seen an 'Aureo-marginata' described that has green, yellow, pink new leaves and pink stems; grew 3′ by 4′ in 6 years.

'Vermillion'—Dense, compact form, 3 to 3 1/2′ high, green summer foliage turning vermillion red in fall.

ADDITIONAL NOTES: Amazing . . . the only way to describe the proliferation of Japanese Barberry cultivars. When I came to Georgia in 1979, very few Japanese barberries were grown in commercial nurseries. With the expansion of markets into the northern states, the Georgia and southeastern growers have increased the barberry product mix. Without question, the Japanese Barberry cultivars are first rate plants for color and durability.

Years past I germinated seeds of 'Kobold' that were collected from the Arnold Arboretum's plant. In the vicinity were the various color and growth forms, so cross pollination was insured. The little population showed considerable variation in leaf color and vigor. The population was not grown to maturity. I suspect many of the new cultivars are derived from open-pollinated seedlings. Barberries are self-fertile and copious fruits may be set on isolated plants. Also, cross pollination is effectively engineered by bumble bees.

A final note concerns the tremendous number of *Berberis* species, something like 450 worldwide. My treatment is sparse compared to the number available. In the Pacific Northwest, some of the specialty nurseries are offering rare and unusual species.

NATIVE HABITAT: Japan. Introduced about 1864.

Betula lenta L. — Sweet Birch, also called Black or Cherry Birch
(bet′ū-là len′tà)

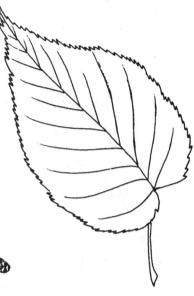

FAMILY: Betulaceae

LEAVES: Alternate, simple, ovate or ovate-oblong, 2 1/2 to 6″ long, 1 1/2 to 3 1/2″ wide, acuminate, mostly cordate, serrated, often doubly, glossy dark green and glabrous above, paler beneath and hairy on veins, 10 to 13 vein pairs; petiole—1/2 to 1″ long, pubescent.

BUDS: Imbricate, conical, sharp-pointed, reddish brown, divergent, terminal—absent on long shoots; buds on short spurs—terminal.

STEM: Slender, light reddish brown, glabrous, shining, with strong wintergreen flavor when chewed or smelled, short spur-like lateral shoots abundant, bearing 2 leaves each season.

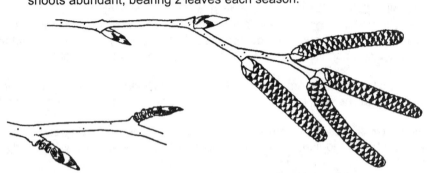

SIZE: Possibly 40 to 55′ in height in a landscape situation with a spread of 35 to 45′; in the wild may reach 70 to 80′ in height; national champion is 78′ by 80′, New Boston, NH.

HARDINESS: Zone 3 to cool mountain areas of Georgia and Alabama.

HABIT: Pyramidal and dense in youth forming an irregular, rounded, sometimes wide-spreading crown at maturity.

RATE: Medium, 20′ over a 20 year period.

TEXTURE: Medium in leaf and winter.

BARK COLOR: Glistening reddish brown to almost black on young trees, reminds of wild black cherry, *Prunus serotina* bark, with prominent horizontal lenticels; on mature trees brownish black and breaking up into large, thin, irregular, scaly plates.

LEAF COLOR: Lustrous dark green in summer changing to golden yellow; exhibits the best fall color of the commonly cultivated birches especially in Midwest (among *B. nigra*, *B. papyrifera*, *B. pendula*, and *B. populifolia*).

FLOWERS: Monoecious, staminate catkins, 2 to 3″ long; the male flowers on birches are apparent on the tree during the winter as they are formed during summer and fall of the year prior to flowering; the pistillate flowers are enclosed in the bud and are borne upright while the male catkins are pendulous; the birches flower in April before the leaves; they possess a hidden beauty which is lost to most people because they have never examined or considered the birches as flowering species; on *B. lenta*—male 3 to 4″ long, female 1/2 to 1″ long.

FRUIT: Small winged nutlet, occurring in a 3/4 to 1 1/3″ long, 3/5″ wide strobile.

CULTURE: Reaches its best development in deep, rich, moist, slightly acid, well-drained soils; however, is often found on rocky, drier sites; has performed reasonably well on the heavy soils of the Midwest.

DISEASES AND INSECTS: Birches are subject to many problems and the following list is applicable to this and the species which follow unless otherwise noted; leaf spots, leaf blisters, leaf rust, canker (black, paper, sweet and yellow birches are particularly affected), dieback, wood-decay, and mildew are the most commonly noted pathogens; insects include aphids, witch-hazel leaf gall aphid, birch skeletonizer, leaf miner (gray, paper, white are very susceptible), bronze birch borer and seed mite gall.

LANDSCAPE VALUE: Makes an excellent tree for parks, naturalized areas, does not have the white bark often synonymous with birches and for this reason is often shunned; Dr. Wyman mentions it is the best of the birches for fall color; based on midwestern and eastern observations, I would agree; resistant to bronze birch borer.

PROPAGATION: Birch seeds have low viability, but produce numerous nutlets (1/2 to 1 million) per pound; germination is facilitated by exposure to light, never plant seeds too deeply; one month cold stratification will compensate for light treatment; over the years I have germinated seeds of many birch species all with ease by simply sowing on milled sphagnum or commercial seed mix, no cover, under mist, with 14 to 21(28) days for germination to occur. Many cultivars are grafted but cuttings and tissue culture are now being used more effectively. See Dirr and Heuser, 1987.

ADDITIONAL NOTES: Approximately 40 species of birches are found in the temperate regions of the world with the United States and Asia housing the largest numbers. Birches are among the first species to colonize abandoned fields, roadside cuts and spoiled land. In the United States, *Betula papyrifera* and *B. populifolia* are obvious colonizers, but as common are *B. lenta* and *B. alleghaniensis* that inhabit every highway cut in the southern Appalachians.

NATIVE HABITAT: Maine to Alabama, west to Ohio. Introduced 1759.

RELATED SPECIES:

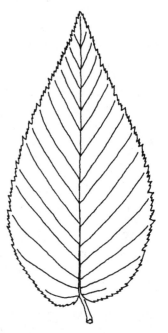

Betula alleghaniensis Britt. (*B. lutea* Michx.) — Yellow Birch
LEAVES: Alternate, simple, ovate to oblong-ovate, 3 to 5″ long, 1/2 as wide, pointed at tip, rounded or heart-shaped at base with pale hairs on the veins above and below, nearly glabrous at maturity, double-toothed, at the end of vigorous shoots often pubescent below, with 9 to 11 pairs of veins, dull dark green above; petiole—1/2 to 1″ long, slender.
BUDS: Imbricate, appressed at least along the lower part of the stem, often hairy.
STEM: Slender, dull-light yellowish brown, exhibiting the faint odor and taste of wintergreen, bark has a bitter taste.
CATKINS: Fruiting catkins 1 to 1 1/2″ long, 3/4″ thick, erect, short-stalked or subsessile, fatter than those of *B. lenta*; back of scales are pubescent, those of *B. lenta* are not or sparingly so.

Betula alleghaniensis, (bet′ū-là al-le-ghe′ni-en′sis), Yellow Birch, is similar to *B. lenta* but grows 60 to 75′ and occasionally 100′ in height. National champion is 76′ by 91′, Deer Isle, ME. The leaves are dull dark green above, pale yellow-green beneath in summer changing to yellow in fall. Bark on young stems and branches is yellowish or bronze and produces thin papery shreds, gradually changing to reddish brown and breaking into large, ragged edged, grayish to blackish brown plates. It prefers moist, cool soils and cool summer temperatures as it does not perform well in hot, dry climates. An important lumber tree as the wood is used extensively for cabinets, furniture, flooring and doors. In my mental travels, the spectacular round-headed form of *B. alleghaniensis* in golden autumn robes at the Arnold Arboretum is forever imbedded in the brain cells. I did notice a small amount of leaf miner on the species but relative to *B. populifolia* and other species, it was insignificant. This and *B. lenta* have pleasing winter texture and color with uniform branching and glistening, yellow-brown to red-brown stems and branches. In North Georgia, western North Carolina, and along the Blue Ridge Parkway the species is abundant. Native to Newfoundland to Manitoba, south to high peaks of Georgia and Tennessee. Cultivated 1800. Zone 3 to 7, only in higher elevations in South.

ADDITIONAL NOTES: Rather difficult to separate these two species; often found together especially in the Appalachian range to North Georgia. They are beautiful in fall color and valuable for lumber but their lack of white bark precludes their ever becoming popular landscape species. Oil of wintergreen can be distilled from the stem and bark of these species.

Betula nigra L. — River Birch, also termed Red Birch
(bet′ū-là nī′grà)

LEAVES: Alternate, simple, 1 1/2 to 3 1/2″ long, 3/4 to 2 1/2″ wide, rhombic-ovate, sharp-pointed, base wedge-shaped, doubly serrate, or shallowly lobed, lustrous medium to dark green above, glaucous beneath with 7 to 9 pairs of impressed veins; petiole—1/4 to 1/2″ long, downy.
BUDS: Imbricate, small, about 1/4″ long, light chestnut brown, sometimes pubescent, more or less appressed.
STEM: Pubescent at first, later essentially glabrous, reddish brown, with warty excrescences.
BARK: Young trunks and branches thin, shining, cream, salmon, orange-brown, light reddish brown to cinnamon-brown, peeling freely; older trunks, dark reddish brown to grayish brown, deeply furrowed, broken into irregular plate-like scales.

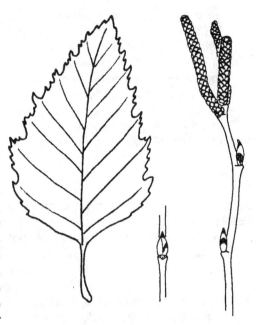

SIZE: 40 to 70' and may reach 90' in height; spread 40 to 60';
    national champion is 111' by 96' in Lamar County, AL.

HARDINESS: Zone 3b to 9.

HABIT: Pyramidal to oval-headed in youth, often rounded in outline
    at maturity; the trunk is usually divided into several large
    arching branches close to the ground; the tree is more
    handsome when grown as a multi-stemmed specimen.

RATE: Medium to fast, over a 20 year period can be expected to
    grow 30 to 40'.

BARK: On branches 2" or greater diameter, exfoliating into
    papery sheets and plates, exposing the inner bark which is
    colored gray-brown, salmon-brown, cinnamon-brown to
    reddish brown; various authors list the color as salmon-pink
    but this is stretching the fact; there is tremendous variability
    in bark color among trees; most River Birch are seedling-
    grown so differences in bark and other characteristics are
    the rule and not the exception; the biological world is
    composed of shades of gray and not black and white; there
    simply are no stereotypes in the species category; one
    cannot unequivocally say that all River Birch (or any other
    species) will have the same leaf, bark, or fall color; it is folly to think like this in relation to biological
    systems; old bark of River Birch becomes brown and develops a ridged-and-furrowed character.

LEAF COLOR: Lustrous medium to dark green in summer changing to yellow in fall and soon dropping; the fall
    color on River Birch is seldom effective; the previous phrase requires a mini-disclaimer for in the South
    where falls are long and pleasant, the leaves of River Birch often turn a soft, pleasing, butter yellow; in
    fact, on those special occasions, I realize that the earlier *Manual* descriptions of fall color had fallen short
    of reality.

FLOWERS: Male in 2 to 3" long, slender dark brown catkins.

FRUIT: Small nutlet, born in a 1 to 1 1/2" long, 1/2" thick cylindric, pendulous catkin, ripens and sheds seed
    in spring.

CULTURE: Transplants well and is often container- and field-grown; best adapted to moist soils and is usually
    found in the wild along stream banks and in swampy bottomlands which are periodically flooded; will
    survive in drier soils although reaches its maximum development in moist, fertile areas; prefers an acid
    soil (6.5 or below) for chlorosis will develop in high pH situations. In early March I was putting a rope swing
    over our creek and had to cut a branch from this species; the end of the branch actually produced a
    steady stream of sap. Moral: don't prune this birch and other birches until summer. They are "bleeders"
    and should not be cut when the sap is flowing.

        Several additional cultural comments are worth mentioning; this is certainly the most adaptable birch
    species for North-South landscapes; the heat tolerance is legendary, however, it is not drought tolerant
    and in dry years will shed interior leaves in response to lack of moisture; in extremely wet years leaf spot
    is problematic and leads to at least partial early defoliation; neither problem is lethal and represents, at
    most, only a chink in the biological armor of one of the great native birches.

        Ranney et al., *Tree Physiology* 8:351–360 (1991), reported that *Betula platyphylla* var. *japonica*
    'Whitespire' was better adapted to dry sites than *B. maximowicziana*, *B. nigra*, *B. papyrifera*, *B. pendula*,
    and *B. populifolia*. In my opinion, this is a situation where laboratory results bear little resemblance to what
    happens in the real world. Assess *B. nigra* next to *B. platyphylla* var. *japonica* 'Whitespire' in the southern
    nursery or garden. *Betula nigra* appears healthy, 'Whitespire' sickly.

DISEASES AND INSECTS: Probably the most trouble-free birch, but in moist years I have noticed significant
    leaf spot that may cause premature defoliation of older (interior) leaves; most important, the species is
    bronze birch borer resistant, perhaps immune; resistance is based on the lack of rhododendrol, a
    chemical borer attractant that is present in white-barked species; aphids are common, particularly on soft,
    succulent growth.

LANDSCAPE VALUE: Very handsome specimen tree for estates, parks, golf courses, campuses and other
    large areas; particularly well-suited to areas which are wet a portion of the year yet may be quite dry in
    the summer and fall; handsome for bark character and should receive wider landscape use as it becomes
    better known; the iron chlorosis on high pH soils has been extremely common in the Midwest, for this
    reason I would test the soil and make sure it read pH 6.5 or below before planting River Birch; River Birch

is being planted more widely in the South; on the University of Georgia campus it is used effectively in a multiplicity of situations; the most widely distributed birch in the United States and definitely the best choice for hot climates.

CULTIVARS:

Dura-Heat™ ('BNMTF', also previously known as 'Moonshine')—Glossy dark olive green leaves, leaves smaller than those of species, good yellow fall color, aphid resistance, closely spaced nodes, from Moon Nursery, Loganville, GA; Tree Introductions, Inc., Athens, GA has trademarked the name; I am impressed with the closely spaced leaves and seemingly greater leaf spot resistance, probably will be smaller than Heritage® and the species; bark exfoliates early and is whitish; an exciting new introduction; in laboratory cold hardiness tests as hardy as Heritage®, possibly more so.

Fox Valley™ ('Little King')—Discovered and originally introduced in late 1970's by Jim King, Oswego, IL and recently (1991) popularized through the Chicagoland Grows® program; exhibits dense, compact, oval-rounded growth habit with branches to the ground, glossy medium green foliage is densely borne, exfoliating bark like the species makes a pleasing winter effect, 10′ high and 12′ wide after 15 to 20 years, will prove useful as a shrub mass along water courses and in perpetually moist soils; apparently leaf miner has occurred on this selection as the *Chicago Botanic Garden Plant Evaluation Notes*, Issue 2(1991) mentioned the use of Orthene to control the problem; the plant has yet to flower; Zone 7b growers have succeeded with this cultivar and it is appearing in southern landscapes.

'Graceful Arms'—Large, spreading, semi-weeping form found in Wisconsin by Darrell Kromm and Tom Dilatush, first offering made spring 1997 catalog, Brotzman's Nursery, Inc., Madison, OH.

Head-Lee Selection—Dark green leaf, more leathery than typical, foliage holds into fall, minimal leaf spot, has not yet been released, appears to be a valuable addition to the current cultivar matrix.

Heritage® ('Cully', listed as improved Heritage, plant patent 4409)—A patented selection introduced by Mr. Earl Cully, Heritage Trees, Inc., Rural Route 5, Jacksonville, IL; this introduction has earned a place in the birch hall of fame; it is commonly grown and superior to the run-of-the-mill seedlings, generally produced through tissue culture and rooted cuttings; tremendous vigor and side-by-side comparisons in a southern nursery show Heritage® outgrowing the seedlings by 50%, leaves are larger, glossier dark green and less prone to leaf spot; fall color, like the species, is variable but has developed excellent yellow in the Athens area; does not match that of *B. lenta*, but what does?; the bark starts to exfoliate on young trunks (1 to 2″ in diameter) and opens to a white to salmon-white on young stems eventually darkening to salmon-brown as the tree ages; the bark is in every way superior to row-run seedlings and I have walked many nursery rows and literally marveled at the fine coloration; is cold hardy to at least –40°F and is extremely well-adapted to the heat of Zone 8; interestingly, side-by-side comparisons of Heritage® and 'Whitespire' in a local nursery indicate Heritage® is superior in every characteristic; Earl has selected a specimen of Heritage® that grows in the late J.C. Raulston's North Carolina State University Arboretum (now J.C. Raulston Arboretum); the bark is creamier and holds the coloration longer than typical Heritage®; some speculation that this is a branch sport (chimera); tissue culture labs are producing the Improved Heritage®.

'Suwanee'—Leaves more lustrous and larger than the species, bark salmon-white, exfoliating, introduced by Bob Byrnes, Trail Ridge Nursery, see *Proc. Fla. State Hort. Soc.* 98:308–309 (1985).

Tecumseh Compact™—A rounded shrubby form with graceful, semi-arching branches, Studebaker Nursery introduction, found as a seedling in Wisconsin, cinnamon-colored exfoliating bark, leaves similar to species in size and coloration, estimated to grow one-half as high as species, although I have read size of 10 to 12′ high and wide.

PROPAGATION: I have had good success with softwood cuttings treated with 1000 ppm IBA/50% alcohol (KIBA in water may be better) and placed in peat:perlite under mist; over the years I have rooted many cuttings and found one common denominator: any period of dryness on the leaf surface insures failure; after cuttings root, they will produce a flush of growth especially if a light application of liquid fertilizer is applied; also birch, particularly *B. nigra*, is responsive to extended photoperiod and will continue to grow; seed ripens in the spring and should be direct sown.

ADDITIONAL NOTES: A worthwhile paper, "Checklists of Cultivars in *Betula* (birch)," appeared in *J. Arboriculture* 15: 170–176, (1989) and provided updated and necessary information on birch cultivar nomenclature.

NATIVE HABITAT: Massachusetts to Florida west to Minnesota and Kansas; restricted to stream banks and other moist places. Cultivated 1736.

Betula papyrifera Marsh. — Paper Birch, also called Canoe or White Birch
(bet′ū-là pap-i-rif′ẽr-à)

LEAVES: Alternate, simple, ovate to narrow ovate, 2 to 4″ (5 1/2″) long, 2/3's as wide, acuminate, rounded or sometimes wedge-shaped, coarsely and doubly serrate, glabrous and dark green above, pubescent on veins beneath, 3 to 7 pairs of lateral veins; peti-ole—about 1″ long, pubescent.

BUDS: Imbricate, 1/4 to 1/2″ long, ovate, pointed, divergent, brown-black, lustrous, scales downy on margin.

STEM: Smooth or somewhat hairy, reddish brown, young stem—lightly glandular.

BARK: Trunk and older branches chalky white, peeling or easily separated into thin paper-like layers.

SIZE: 50 to 70′ in height with a spread equal to one-half to two-third's the height; may reach 90 to 120′ in height; national champion is 107′ by 76′ in Cheboygan County, MI.

HARDINESS: Zone 2 to 6(7).

HABIT: Loosely pyramidal in youth developing an irregular, oval to rounded crown at maturity; usually maintaining its branches close to the ground unless limbed up; handsome as a single or multi-stemmed specimen.

RATE: Medium to fast, over a 10 to 20 year period averaging 1 1/2 to 2′ of growth per year.

TEXTURE: Medium in leaf and in winter habit.

BARK: Thin, smooth, reddish brown on young branches, becoming creamy white in the third to fourth year, perhaps the whitest of all birches; peels freely to expose a reddish orange inner bark; old trunks become marked with black; in general the bark stays whiter longer than that of *B. pendula*.

LEAF COLOR: Usually dark green in summer changing to yellow in fall; I rate this second to *Betula lenta* for excellence of fall color; this is one of the trees that contribute to the magnificent fall color spectacle in our northern forests.

FLOWERS: Staminate, brown, 2 to 4″ long, usually born in 2's or 3's; female in erect, 1 to 1 1/4″ long, greenish catkins.

FRUIT: Small nutlet, borne on a 1 to 1 1/2″ long, pendulous catkin.

CULTURE: Transplants readily as balled-and-burlapped specimen; best adapted to colder climates; adapted to a wide variety of soils; does best on well-drained, acid, moist, sandy or silty loams; full sun; not a particularly tough tree and should not be used in difficult, polluted areas; based on Midwest observations much more tolerant to high pH soils than *B. nigra*.

DISEASES AND INSECTS: Much more resistant to bronze birch borer than *B. pendula*. Miller et al., *J. Amer. Soc. Hort. Sci.* 116:580–584 (1991), reported *B. papyrifera* was superior to *B. pendula* in height and borer resistance at age 12 years from seed.

LANDSCAPE VALUE: Handsome for bark and fall color attributes; good in parks, estates and large area plantings; splendid in winter when framed against evergreens.

CULTIVARS:

'Chickadee'—A striking, narrow columnar-conical selection with exceptionally white bark, from Canada, if the photograph I viewed is realistic then this is a fine birch.

Snowy™—Attractive white bark, deep green foliage, grows 3 to 6′ per year, proved highly resistant to bronze birch borer in 15 years of testing, originated at Michigan State University, East Lansing, MI, a multi-clonal seedling cultivar.

PROPAGATION: Seed requires no cold period but when exposed to 9 plus hours of light per 24 hour period germinated 30%; 2 to 3 months of cold at 41°F will compensate for light; nursery practice involves fall sowing with germination occurring in spring; this applies to all birch species presented here except *B. nigra*; there is considerable interest in accelerated growth of birches especially *B. papyrifera* and *B. pendula*; Krizek, *Proc. Intl. Plant Prop. Soc.* 22:390–395 (1972), reported that *B. papyrifera* would produce white bark in 2 rather than 3 years; it is more responsive to light than *B. pendula*; optimum seedling growth requires 77°F day/65°F night; long days (16 hr); good air movement and adequate moisture and nutrition.

Cuttings can be rooted with significant attention to detail; an English report (*Proc. Intl. Plant Prop. Soc.* 18:67–68) indicated that 6 to 8″ long cuttings collected on August 18 and September 1, treated with 2000 ppm IBA-quick dip rooted well; also 8000 ppm IBA-talc gave 100% rooting; best not to disturb rooted cuttings but allow them to go through natural dormancy cycle and pot them during their spring flush; I have had poor success rooting this species.

ADDITIONAL NOTES: The bark has been used for utensils, canoes, and wigwam covers. After fire, Paper Birch often seeds large areas where mineral soil was exposed; and especially on moist sites it forms nearly pure stands. There is evidence that this species, at least in the Midwest, is a much better landscape species than *B. pendula*. Although susceptible to the borer, especially stressed trees, it seems to perform better than the European White Birch.

NATIVE HABITAT: Greenland, Labrador to British Columbia, Alaska and Washington south to Pennsylvania, Michigan, Nebraska, and Montana. It is the most widely East-West distributed of all North American birches. Introduced 1750.

RELATED SPECIES: There are many varieties of *B. papyrifera* described but their separation is fraught with difficulty. These geographical variants are probably only of significant interest to the botanist and forester. I am afraid nurserymen have paid little attention to seed source. In *American Forests* 102(1):(1996), "National Register of Big Trees," seven varieties are listed.

Betula pendula Roth. — European White, Silver, Warty and Common Birch (formerly listed as *B. alba* L. and *B. verrucosa* Ehrh.)

(bet′ū-lȧ pen′du-lȧ)

LEAVES: Alternate, simple, broadly ovate, sometimes rhomboidal to diamond-shaped, 1 to 3″ long, 3/4 to 1 1/2″ wide, slenderly tapered at apex, broadly wedge-shaped or truncate at base, doubly serrate, glabrous, lustrous dark green, dotted with glands on both surfaces; petiole—1/2 to 3/4″ long.

BUDS: Imbricate, curved, pointed, brownish black.

STEM: Glabrous, resinous-glandular (results in warty appearance), brown, smoother than paper or gray.

BARK: Whitish, does not peel (exfoliate) to degree of Paper Birch; with age trunk becomes black with relatively small amount of white bark showing.

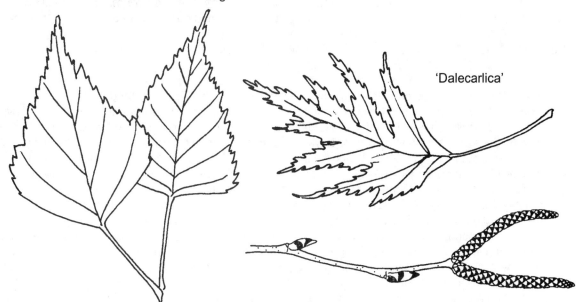

'Dalecarlica'

SIZE: 40 to 50′ in height with a spread one-half to two-third's the height, may reach 80 to 100′ or more in the wild.

HARDINESS: Zone 2 to 6(7).

HABIT: Gracefully pyramidal in youth, developing an oval pyramidal to oval outline with time while maintaining the graceful pendulous branching habit; sometimes rounded in outline, trees in Europe are more upright in branching habit and their bark is at best dirty gray-white.

RATE: Medium to fast, growing 30 to 40′ over a 20 year period.

TEXTURE: Medium-fine in leaf; medium in winter habit.

BARK: Brownish in youth (1 to 1 1/2″ diameter) changing to white on larger branches and with time developing black fissured areas.

LEAF COLOR: Glossy dark green in summer often changing to a poor yellow or yellow green; leafs out early in spring; seems to hold the green leaves later into fall than the other species; have seen excellent fall color in Michigan and New England; not as pronounced yellow fall color as that of *B. papyrifera*.

FLOWERS: Staminate, 1 1/2 to 3 1/2″ long, usually in 2's, sometimes singly or in 3's.

FRUIT: Small nutlet, produced in 3/4 to 1 1/4″ long by 1/3″ wide, cylindrical catkins, shed in fall.

CULTURE: Transplants readily; should be moved in spring; does best in moist, well-drained, sandy or loamy soil but will tolerate wet or dry soils; more pH tolerant than *B. nigra*; should be pruned in summer or fall as pruning in late winter or early spring causes the tree to "bleed" excessively.

DISEASES AND INSECTS: See under *B. lenta*; leaf miner and bronze birch borer are serious pests; I do not recommend European White Birch because of the borer; it can be controlled but most people wait until considerable injury has occurred and then it is too late to save the tree; the top is infected first; if one has specimen trees a regular spray program is a worthwhile investment; birch leaf miner adults overwinter in soil and emerge as leaves expand and lay eggs in leaf, appearance correlates with crabapple and lilac flower; yellow sticky bands and Orthene work well.

LANDSCAPE VALUE: At one time a very popular tree gracing the front or back yard of one out of three homes in parts of Midwest; still widely sold by many nurserymen and, unfortunately, purchased by the uninitiated; tree has been extensively used for lawns, parks, and cemeteries; if a suitable white-barked alternative can be found it should be planted; reflecting on recent trips through the East and Midwest I see less of this species and more of *B. nigra* and Heritage®; the birch borer has become such a horrendous pest that it renders successful long term culture almost impossible; interestingly, Santamour and McArdle, *J. Arboriculture* 15: 170–176 (1989), speculate that no white-barked selections of Asiatic origin will prove resistant to borers.

CULTIVARS:

Avalanche® ('Avalzam')—I did not know where to place this new introduction so I arbitrarily put it here with *B. pendula*. Observed and introduced by Lake County Nursery, original trees were imported from Japan by Storrs and Harrison Nursery, Painesville, OH over 60 years ago, original tree(s) still extant, great resistance to bronze birch borer, vigorous grower, lustrous thick rich green leaves, bark is light tan, adding pinkish traces, finally exfoliating to white, grows 50′ high, 30 to 40′ wide, oval to rounded outline.

'Barossa Wintergreen'—A sport of a tree at Tanunda, Australia that arose in 1978, lacks winter dormancy, resulting in evergreen foliage, active growth and production of male catkins during winter, leaves are glabrous with a serrate margin, habit is pendulous, see *Plant Varieties Journal* 3(4):19–20 (1990).

'Birkalensis' (Also spelled 'Bircalensis')—Each leaf has 3 or 4 acute lobes on each margin that reach halfway to the middle, tree is columnar in habit, found in Finland.

'Burgundy Wine'—Dark purple leaves, excellent white bark, older trees spreading with semi-pendulous branches, 40′ by 30′, developed by Richard Bush, Canby, OR.

var. *crispa* (f. *crispa*)—Has been confused with 'Dalecarlica' but the leaves are more regularly and less deeply cut; often listed as 'Laciniata'; found wild in several localities in Scandinavia.

'Dalecarlica'—A very distinct tree, branches and leaves pendulous; the whole tree very elegant; the leaves are lobed to within 1/8 to 1/4″ of the midrib, the lobes lanceolate, coarsely toothed with long slender points, ends of basal lobes curving backward; the most common form in cultivation. Bean in the 1988 supplement stated that the plant in commerce described as 'Dalecarlica' is actually 'Laciniata'; the leaves of 'Laciniata' are supposedly 2″ long and those of 'Dalecarlica' about 3″; in the United States the plant I know as 'Dalecarlica' fits the 3″ leaf characteristic.

'Elegans'—Branches hanging almost perpendicularly, leader erect; a mop; originated at Bonamy's Nursery, Toulouse, France about 1866.

'Fastigiata'—Branches erect, of columnar habit, resembling a Lombardy Poplar; there is a recorded specimen in England that measures 95′ high; holds foliage later than other cultivars; actually this is a rather ugly upright cultivar and the bark appears to turn darker faster than the species; the habit is never very uniform for in winter the upright branches look like bundles of sticks tied together, branches are incurved, leaves normal; my observational powers may be diminishing, however, this cultivar appears more borer resistant based on longevity in various collections and campuses.

'Golden Cloud'—Introduced by Bressingham Gardens in England for "the gleaming" bark of the Silver (White) Birch, and in late spring reddish shoots emerge, unfolding as bright golden leaves; the leaves become deeper gold in the summer in sun, less intense in partial shade; fall color is yellow; leaves normal; growth rate is similar to the species and white bark should develop in 2 to 3 years; have seen in Mr. Adrian Bloom's garden and the leaves are a distinct golden yellow; would probably burn in heat of midwestern and eastern United States; I suspect it will perform best in a cool continental climate; has not held the yellow-gold leaf color in English summers.

'Gracilis'—A small tree without a central leader (15 to 20'), with finely cut leaves and drooping branches; stems are produced in clusters like elongated witches' brooms, almost ponytail-like, leaves finer and more deeply lobed than 'Dalecarlica'.

'Laciniata'—Arguably genuine or a myth, Santamour and McArdle provide legitimate taxonomic status, leaves deeply incised, less so than 'Dalecarlica', thick female catkins, long pendulous twigs, upright growth habit with only extremities of the branches pendulous, winter buds are sharp-pointed compared to the blunt and rounded buds of 'Dalecarlica', slower growing than species, 40' by 20'.

'Obelisk'—Found in northern France in 1956 and put into commerce by P.L.M. van der Bom, upright like 'Fastigiata' with a narrower crown and whiter bark, strong straight ascending branches, leaves normal.

Purple Rain™ ('Monte')—New foliage displays lustrous vivid purple color that is retained through the season, a lovely contrast of purple foliage and white bark, leaves normal, tissue culture is being used to produce the plants, a Monrovia introduction; realistically, most of the purple leaf types lose the color in the heat of summer, I suspect this is no different.

'Purpurea'—Leaves deep reddish purple gradually losing the strong color with the coming of summer; I have never been pleased with the landscape performance of this cultivar, lacks vigor and the purple leaf color fades in the heat of the summer; sounds wonderful in catalog descriptions but acts as a borer magnet and is not worth spending money for; named clones include 'Purple Splendor' (plant patent 2107) and 'Scarlet Glory', leaves normal. 'Burgundy Wine' is listed as a superb purple leaf form that grows 60' high. Also, 'Dark Prince' produces dark purple leaves on a somewhat pendulous tree, leaves contrast beautifully with white bark, considered superior to 'Purpurea'. Santamour crossed *B. populifolia* × *B. pendula* 'Purpurea' and the hybrid progeny segregated 168 green and 97 purple seedlings in the cotyledon stage. Hattemer et al., *Silvae-Genetica* 39:45–50 (1990), reported that a single, fully dominant gene responsible for purple pigmentation in *B. pendula* was identified.

Rocky Mountain Splendor™ ('Rockimon')—A broadly pyramidal to oval tree with medium green summer foliage that turns yellow in fall, has white bark, cold hardy in Rocky Mountain states, 45' by 30', considered a hybrid between *B. pendula* and *B. occidentalis* Hook., -30 to -40°F hardiness, a 1989 Schmidt introduction; plant patent 6192; trials in Spartanburg, SC indicated this selection was less than satisfactory for Zone 7 to 8.

'Tristis'—A clone similar to 'Elegans' developing a central leader, the side branches extending and arching, forming a tall ovate crown, leaves normal, bark reasonable white.

'Trost Dwarf' (Often listed as 'Trost's Dwarf')—Too many people have gotten excited about a rather inferior witches' broom-like compact shrubby form of the species; actually there has been a great deal of promotion behind the plant that could have been better spent behind a good form of *Fothergilla gardenii*; the habit is best described as "bushy," probably 3 to 4' high and wide after 8 to 10 years; the rich green leaves are almost thread-like; perhaps a good collector's item but doubtfully for mainstream American gardens; has not performed as well in landscapes as it has on paper; discovered in 1976 by Dieter Trost at Southern Oregon Nurseries, Medford, OR; registered and described in *AABGA Bulletin* 19(3):86–94.

'Youngii'—Branches are slender and perfectly pendulous, without a leading stem; best to graft on a standard; have seen this cultivar at several gardens and it always reminded me of a fat mop head; however, a plant at Bodnant Gardens, Wales, had been trained so the branches grew horizontally for a distance and were then allowed to weep; this specimen was truly spectacular; have also seen it staked until a 10 to 12' high leader developed and then allowed to weep; leaves normal; originated in England about 1873.

PROPAGATION: Seed will germinate with proper light treatment or 2 to 3 months of stratification at 41°F will compensate; cuttings treated with 50 ppm IBA for 32 hours rooted 25%; cultivars are grafted on seedling understock.

NATIVE HABITAT: Europe (including Britain), especially high altitudes and parts of northern Asia. Long cultivated.

RELATED SPECIES: The descriptions of *B. platyphylla* Sukachev var. *japonica* (Miq.) Hara and var. *szechuanica* (Schneid.) Rehd. are presented as they appear in the fourth edition with the following additions since new facts concerning their bronze borer resistance have come to light. Both varieties have been reported to contract the borer. The University of Wisconsin seed source of var. *japonica* shows good resistance. See Dirr, *Weeds, Trees, and Turf* 20(2):51, 54 (1981), for more details. The key differences between the two varieties are that var. *japonica* has thinner leaves that abscise earlier, finer and less warty stems, less tolerance to wet soils, and better leaf miner resistance. Santamour and McArdle do not recognize var. *szechuanica* in *J. Arboriculture* 15:170–176 (1989). In fact, they relate the plants sold as var. *szechuanica* by Evergreen Nursery Co., Sturgeon Bay, WI were of uncertain origin and resembled *B. populifolia*. At the University of Illinois, I had the various *B. platyphylla* varieties in field trials and *neither* looked like

B. populifolia. At the January, 1995 Iowa Nursery and Landscape Association meeting, Roy Klehm, Klehm Nursery, Arlington Heights, IL, addressed the birch issue by relating that only 'Whitespire' derived from the best tree at the University of Wisconsin Arboretum was borer resistant. This selection had been reproduced through tissue culture. Name of original Wisconsin selection is 'Whitespire Senior'. Most people who have grown the true 'Whitespire' realize that it is not the panacea for white-barked birches. Bark on *all* trees that I have seen did not measure up to the best *Betula papyrifera* seedlings.

Betula platyphylla, (bet′ū-là   plat-i-fil′à), Asian White Birch, is probably represented in cultivation by the varieties *japonica* and *szechuanica*. Dr. Ed. Hasselkus, retired, University of Wisconsin, mentioned that while other birches, especially *B. pendula*, were dying out in the U. of W. Landscape Arboretum this birch continued to thrive. Variety *japonica* would be the preferred tree under landscape conditions for it is rather large (85′), with thin, spreading branches and pure white bark on the trunk. Under landscape conditions the tree would grow 40 to 50′. When I last viewed the Wisconsin trees, they were 25 to 30′ with a relaxed, pyramidal habit and a dominant central leader. The leaves are about 1 1/2 to 3″ long, glossy dark green and shaped somewhat like those of *B. pendula* but differ by virtue of being broader with axillary tufts beneath, more numerous veins and usually single toothing. Bean noted that in England it thrives well in cultivation. Native to Japan and the Okhotsk peninsula. Cultivated since 1887. Zone 4 to 7. In the 1990 edition, I mentioned that perhaps the species (varieties) will prove better than *B. pendula*. This statement may still be true but in recent years tremendous borer damage has appeared. During my 1991 sabbatical at the Arnold Arboretum, several *B. platyphylla* var. *japonica* had been riddled by borers. The variety *szechuanica* is more open and wide-spreading than the above but according to Bean a rather graceless tree, with a silvery white bark. The leaves are thick, blue-green, and remain on the tree longer than other birches.

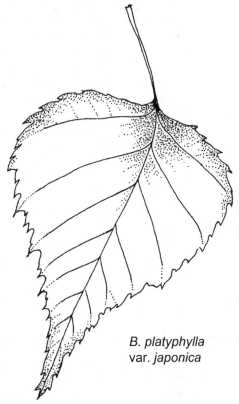

B. platyphylla
var. *japonica*

'Fargo' is a new narrow columnar introduction from North Dakota State University, 10-year-old tree is 30′ tall and 8.25′ wide, to date has been resistant to bronze birch borer. 'Fargo' is in the process of being patented and growers need to contact NDSU. See *HortScience* 32:1304–1305 (1997). *Betula platyphylla* var. *szechuanica* 'Purpurea'—I had never heard of this selection until paging through a Studebaker (1988–89) nursery catalog; the new leaves are described as deep purple and contrast with the white bark, leaves mature to purple-green. Is it, in fact, a purple leaf *B. pendula* type? Intriguing how things come full circle since I discussed this birch with one of the sales representatives from Studebaker's. The plant was registered as 'Crimson Frost' on June 18, 1994 by Tom Pinney, Jr., Evergreen Nursery Company. The original tree was selected in 1985 from progeny of the cross *B. platyphylla* var. *szechuanica* and *B. pendula* 'Purpurea' made in 1978. At 15 years of age, the tree was 45′ high and 35′ wide; leaves are deep crimson and glossy, fall color is crimson to bright red, orange-red, orange-yellow, retaining colors up to one month; bark is white with cinnamon tones and exfoliating; considered hardy to (4b)5 to 6; introduced to nursery trade in 1989 and described in *American Nurseryman* 175(5):44 (1992). It is propagated through tissue culture. The species is native to western China. Introduced 1872. Zone 5 to 6.

Without becoming excessively repetitive, let me warn the gardener and nurseryman that both *B. platyphylla* var. *japonica* and *B.p.* var. *szechuanica* are susceptible to borer. Only 'Whitespire' from the original selection by Dr. Hasselkus, University of Wisconsin, is borer-free. In a 1989 telephone conversation, he reiterated the original introduction was borer-free. Unfortunately, many trees have been sold as 'Whitespire' that were actually grown from seed from the original tree. Be sure that the trees you buy were produced by tissue culture or cuttings from the original. The tree is not totally resistant to leaf miner but is less susceptible than *B. papyrifera*. Hasselkus feels that the tree's resistance to borer can be related to the tree's heat tolerance which means it is under less stress in hot climates and thus better able to resist infestation. 'Whitespire' has survived −30°F at Madison and after 27 years was 33′ high and 14′ wide with a distinctive spire-like form. It is fine-textured in stem and foliage and the glossy dark green leaves turn yellow in fall. The chalky white, non-exfoliating bark is marked with black triangles at the base of lateral branches. The original seed was collected by John L. Creech of the U.S. Plant Introduction Station in 1951 from a single tree in an open field above Shibuyu Onsen at 5000′ in the Yatsugatake Mountains. Dr. Hasselkus planted 5 trees from these seeds and selected the one with the best developed white bark and habit. Tom Pinney in an October 15, 1986 'Whitespire' birch update reported that seedling trees of 'Whitespire' under stress did contract the borer. He emphasized that plants in good vigor were more resistant. 'Whitespire' seedlings in Zone 7 to 8 nurseries have not looked as inspiring as Dura-Heat™ or Heritage® River Birch. Time will tell, but to date I have not been as impressed with 'Whitespire' in the South as some literature leads one to believe. Early reports from Oklahoma State University indicated the high heat tolerance. Over the past 8 years, the plants I see look tired and less-than-thrifty; leaves actually curl and appear wilted; this may be related to high heat. Also, the bark, even on developing trees, is an ugly dirty gray. Most Atlanta–Athens area growers could not sell (actually give away) the trees and bulldozed entire blocks. For Zone (4)5 through 6, the tree is acceptable. For the warmer areas, Zone 7 and south, opt for *B. nigra* and cultivars.

ADDITIONAL NOTES: Other birches are more suitable for the Midwest and should be used in preference to *B. pendula*. When purchasing a "white" birch make sure of the scientific name, for any birch with white bark is a "white" birch. Santamour, *American Nurseryman* 156(11):61 (1982), presented interesting data relative to which white-barked birches are least susceptible to borer. The trees were surveyed in their tenth year in the Washington, DC area. The borer attacks started in the fifth growing season with borer populations remaining extremely high until the survey. *Betula papyrifera* grew slowly but 84% of the trees survived; *B. pendula* showed variable borer susceptibility depending on seed source. Survival varied from 15% to 75%. *Betula platyphylla* var. *japonica* from five seed sources showed 1 out of 127 trees alive and the lone survivor was also infested. Interestingly, this variety was the most adaptable and fastest growing *but* the most susceptible. Santamour suggests that the concept of plants under stress being more susceptible to borer might be reexamined. *Betula populifolia* survived 75% and shows some borer resistance.

Betula populifolia Marsh. — Gray Birch, also called Old Field Birch, White Birch, Poverty Birch, and Poplar Birch
(bet′ū-là pop-ū-li-fō′li-à)

LEAVES: Alternate, simple, 2 to 3 1/2″ long, 1 1/2 to 2 1/4″ wide, triangular-ovate or deltoid, long acuminate, truncate at base, coarsely or doubly serrate, glutinous when young, lustrous dark green above, glabrous, 6 to 9 vein pairs; petiole—3/4 to 1″ long, dotted with black glands.

BUDS: Imbricate, 1/4″ or less in length, brownish, smooth, somewhat resinous, ovate, pointed, divergent; scales finely downy on margin.

STEM: Slender, bright reddish brown or grayish, roughened by warty resinous exudations, glabrous.

BARK: Dull chalky white (older branches), close, not peeling, with distinct dark triangular patches below insertion of branches.

MALE CATKIN: Borne singly at end of branches, 2 to 3 1/2″ long; most effective way to separate this species from other cultivated birches.

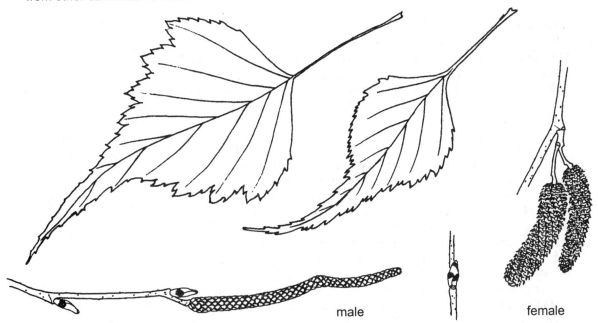

male   female

SIZE: 20 to 40′ in height with 30′ representing an average size; spread is about 10 to 20′; national champion is 68′ by 50′ in Parkton, MD.

HARDINESS: Zone 3 to 6 (7).

HABIT: Narrow, irregularly open, conical crown with slender branches ending in fine stems that are often pendulous; usually a multi-stemmed tree in the wild but can be grown single-stemmed; has a tendency to develop shoots from the roots and often forms thickets; one of the smallest of the birches and usually short-lived (15 to 25 years).

RATE: Medium to fast, averaging 2′ per year over a 10 to 15 year period; often forms pure stands in cut-over or burned forest lands in a very short time.

TEXTURE: Medium-fine in leaf; medium in winter habit.

BARK: Thin, smooth, reddish brown on young trunks becoming chalky white with prominent, triangular black patches below the bases of the branches; loses color quickly, becoming dirty gray, does not peel readily.

LEAF COLOR: Dark glossy green in summer changing to yellow in fall; leafs out early and provides a nice touch of "spring green."

FLOWERS: Staminate, 2 to 3 1/2″ long, catkin borne singly at the end of the branches, rarely in 2's.

FRUIT: Small nutlet, borne in 3/4 to 1 1/4″ long by 1/4″ diameter, cylindrical catkins.

CULTURE: Transplant balled-and-burlapped in spring; relishes the poorest of sterile soils; will grow on sandy, rocky, gravelly sites and also heavier soils; tolerates wet and dry conditions; full sun, intolerant of competition and this should be considered if it is used in the landscape; will develop chlorosis in extremely high pH soils.

DISEASES AND INSECTS: Leaf miner, cankers, more resistant to bronze birch borer; leaf miner as I have seen it in New England, can literally turn a green tree into a Kraft (brown) bag; certainly not worth trying to control, on the other hand no need to use the plant in the contrived landscape and ask for problems.

LANDSCAPE VALUE: Good for naturalizing, possibly could be used in poor soils along highways and other difficult sites; the ability to quickly seed an area as well as develop shoots from roots (suckering) is valuable in developing rough sites where few plants will survive.

PROPAGATION: Cuttings taken in July treated with 50 ppm IBA for 6 hours rooted 30%; seed—cold stratification for 60 to 90 days or light during the germination treatment will break the dormancy.

ADDITIONAL NOTES: Commercially of limited value but serves in nature as a nurse plant for more valuable seedlings.

NATIVE HABITAT: Nova Scotia and Ontario to Delaware. Introduced 1780.

OTHER BIRCHES OF POSSIBLE LANDSCAPE INTEREST

The previous species were afforded considerable attention because they are the most common in cultivation or the wild in the eastern half of North America. There are about 40 species distributed in North America, Europe and Asia; most are essentially northern in their distribution. The following are species that have crossed my path or created a sensation because of some advertised trait like bronze birch borer resistance.

Betula albo-sinensis Burk. — Chinese Paper Birch, Chinese Red Birch

LEAVES: Alternate, simple, ovate to ovate-oblong, 2 to 3″ long, 1 to 1 1/2″ wide, acuminate, rounded or sometimes subcordate, doubly serrate and often slightly lobulate, dark green above, light green and glandular below, with 10 to 14 vein pairs that may be silky hairy or glabrous; petiole—1/4 to 3/4″ long, 1/3″ wide, sparingly silky or glabrous.

Betula albo-sinensis, (bet′ū-là al′bō-sī-nen′sis), Chinese Paper Birch, is a little known and grown species with an exquisite bark character rivaled by few trees. E.H. Wilson in his *Aristocrats of the Trees* noted, "The bark is singularly lovely, being a rich orange-red or orange-brown and peels off in sheets, each no thicker than fine tissue paper, and each successive layer is clothed with a white glaucous bloom." Foliage is dark yellow-green in summer changing to yellow in fall. The habit is rounded and size in a landscape situation would range from 40 to 60′ although it can grow 80 to 90′. The variety *septentrionalis* Schneid. is similar but differs in the up to 5″ long, oblong-ovate rather than ovate leaves, distinctly glandular young shoots, silky hairs on veins beneath and prominent axillary tufts of hair. I have seen the species at Vineland Station, Ontario, Canada.

The tree was about 25′ tall and the bark had a distinct orangish cast but the exfoliating character was not evident. It was my privilege to view a mature, 40 to 45′ high and 40 to 50′ wide specimen on the Isle of Mainau in the Lake of Constance, Germany. The trunk and major branches of this impressive specimen were covered with lichens but the younger branches showed the "orange-brown, orange to yellowish orange and orange-gray." Common in European gardens, seldom seen in American. Without question this species ranks among the most beautiful of all birches. At Edinburgh Botanic Garden and Hillier Arboretum, splendid specimens are evident. The first time one sees the well-developed bark, it is hands-on. Cannot resist the temptation to tear, pull, rub and whatever else one's hands can do. In European literature, 'Fascination' with attractive bark and 'Hergest' as fast-growing are listed. Western China. Zone 5 to 6. Introduced 1908. The species was introduced in 1910. Zone 5 to 6. Central and western China.

Betula apoiensis Nak.
LEAVES: Alternate, simple, 3/4 to 1 1/2″ long, ovate to ovate orbicular, acute, irregular dentate, dark green, silky pubescent below.

Betula apoiensis, (bet′ū-là à-pō-ē-en′sis), was introduced to me by Gary Koller during the 1991 sabbatical at the Arnold Arboretum. The species is reminiscent of a pygmy tree, and the Arnold plants were 6 to 8′ high. Could be used in mini-groupings in a border for accent. Bark was not particularly attractive, young stems are bronze, fall color clear golden yellow. May contract birch borer. Northern Japan. Zone 4 to 6?

Betula davurica Pall. — Dahurian Birch, Asian Black Birch
LEAVES: Alternate, simple, 2 to 4″ long, 1 1/2 to 3″ wide, rhombic-ovate, acute or acuminate, cuneate, unequally dentate-serrate, dark green and glabrous above, gland-dotted beneath, 6 to 8 vein pairs, pubescent on veins below; petiole—1/4 to 1/2″ long.
STEM: Resinous, pilose when young, finally dark gray with white glands.

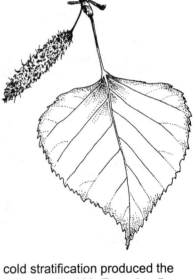

Betula davurica, (bet′ū-là dà-vūr′i-kà), Dahurian Birch, is used on the East Coast to a small degree. The species grows 40 to 50′ in height and has rather wide and spreading branches. A 72-year-old tree at the Arnold was 35′ by 40′. The summer foliage is dark green changing to yellow in fall. The bark is not unlike that of *B. nigra*, River Birch, exfoliating in curly flakes of warm brown to reddish brown. An adequate description of the bark is difficult for the flakes appear to puff out from the trunk rather than curl off in papery flakes and sheets like *B. nigra*. Most trees I have observed were small and appeared to lack significant vigor, lacks graceful arching branches and twininess of *B. nigra*. Tolerates dry, infertile soils better than *B. nigra*. Unfortunately, it is borer susceptible. Three months cold stratification produced the best seed germination. Native to Manchuria, northern China, and Korea. Introduced 1883. Zone 4 to 5.

Betula ermanii Cham. — Erman Birch
LEAVES: Alternate, simple, 2 to 4″ long, 1 1/2 to 2 1/2″ wide, triangular-ovate, acuminate, truncate or subcordate, unequally coarsely serrate, dark green, usually glandular beneath or pubescent on veins, 7 to 11 vein pairs; petiole—1/4 to 1 1/2″ long, warty.

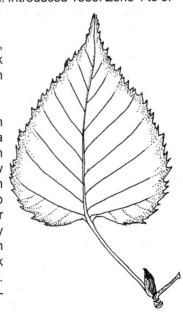

Betula ermanii, (bet′ū-là er-man′ē-ī), Erman Birch, is a pyramidal-oval tree in youth said to grow to 100′. The few trees I have seen possessed a creamy or pinkish white, peeling bark that was the rival of any birch species. The bark comes off in large papery sheets. Mr. Don Shadow reported that it did not perform well in his nursery (Zone 7). Seldom seen in cultivation in the eastern United States and the reasons are linked to lack of heat tolerance and borer susceptibility. This is a spectacular species for bark effect and the cream-pink bark is blushed with a waxy bloom. Probably acceptable in the Pacific Northwest. 'Blush' is a Dutch selection with pinkish cream bark, the name obviously refers to the bark color. 'Holland' is also listed for a plant grown in the Netherlands as *B. ermanii*. Three months cold stratification produced good seed germination. Northeast Asia, Japan. Cultivated 1880. Zone 5 to 6.

Betula grossa Sieb. & Zucc. — Japanese Cherry Birch
LEAVES: Alternate, simple, 2 to 4″ long, one-half as wide,
    ovate to oblong-ovate, acuminate, subcordate at
    base, coarsely double-toothed, glandular beneath,
    with 10 to 15 vein pairs with silky pubescence, lus-
    trous dark green; petiole—1/2 to 1″ long, silky.

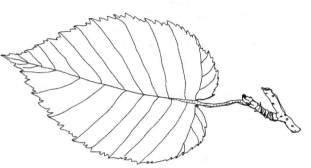

Betula grossa, (bet′ū-là grō′sà), Japanese Cherry Birch,
    reminds of *B. lenta* and *B. alleghaniensis* with its
    aromatic wintergreen stems. The lustrous dark
    green leaves turn a good yellow in fall. The beauti-
ful, rich, polished, reddish brown, cherry-like bark is especially handsome. The Arnold Arboretum had a
lovely specimen of pyramidal outline about 25′ high. In 1991, a small amount of leaf miner damage was
evident on the Arnold's tree. Japan. Introduced 1896. Zone (4)5 to 6.

Betula maximowicziana Reg. — Monarch Birch
LEAVES: Alternate, simple, broad-ovate, 3 to 6″ long, 3/4 as wide, acute to
    acuminate, deeply cordate at base, doubly serrate, pubescent on
    young trees, nearly glabrous on old trees, with 10 to 12 pairs of veins,
    dark green; petiole—1 to 1 1/2″ long.

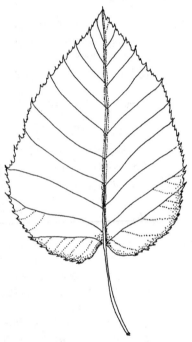

Betula maximowicziana, (bet′ū-là max-im-ō-wix-ē-ā′nà), Monarch Birch, has
    attained heights of 100′ or more in its native habitat of Japan, however,
    experimental plantings in arboreta in the United States have indicated
    that it will generally be closer to 45 to 50′. The habit is roundish and of
    a mop-like nature. Leaves on seedlings and young trees are densely
    pubescent and purple-veined on the lower surface. The foliage is dark
    green in summer changing to yellow in fall. The leaves and catkins
    (male 4 to 5″ long; fruiting 2 to 2 1/2″ long by 1/3″ wide, 2 to 4 together)
    are the largest of all known hardy birches. The young branches are
    reddish brown eventually becoming gray or whitish and the bark splits
    into long, broad, thin sheets which cling to the tree in shaggy masses.
    I have seen trees labeled as *B. maximowicziana* at the Holden
    Arboretum, Mentor, OH and they were truly beautiful; however, the
    older bark was a uniform white, the leaves were small (about the size
    of *B. papyrifera*) and the leaf bases were not cordate as is supposedly
    typical. Significant advantages of this birch are the supposed complete
resistance to bronze birch borer and, unlike other birches, the tolerance to urban environments. According
to Cole Nursery Co., Circleville, OH, this species grows about 33% faster than *B. pendula* or *B. papyrifera*.
The very confusing aspect of the Monarch Birch is the fact that what we (horticulturists) are calling *B. m.*
does not fit the taxonomic description. Drs. P.C. Kozel and R.C. Smith had an interesting article in *Horticulture* 54(1):36 (1975), "The Monarch Birch," from which much of the above information was abstracted.
Since the 1983 edition, it has been documented that the Holden and Cole trees were not Monarch. See
Santamour and Meyer, *American Nurseryman* 145(12):7. I have seen several trees of the "real thing" and
they bore no resemblance to what is in the trade as Monarch. A few comments follow: I chased the tree all
over Winkworth Arboretum in England and was disappointed with what I discovered. The habit was
pyramidal-oval and the bark rather unglamourous dirty gray-brown. In fact, I saw no evidence of white even
on the younger branches. The bark did not exfoliate in shaggy masses and was rather smooth in
appearance. This shagginess could be a variable trait. The leaves and male catkins were the largest I have
seen on a birch. At the Arnold Arboretum, several recently planted *B. maximowicziana* specimens have
a distinct pyramidal habit and reasonably good white bark. Also, the leaves turned a good yellow in
October. I believe these were from wild-collected seed when Drs. Spongberg and Weaver were in Japan.
If they prove leaf miner and bronze birch borer resistant perhaps someone should consider vegetative
propagation. At least one of the Arnold trees has been infected with borer so what appeared a sure thing,
i.e., resistant, is anything but. Also, a small amount of leaf miner was evident. Again the hype relative to the
greatness of Monarch Birch far out-distanced the reality of any real testing and evaluation. The leaves are
so large that they form a layer (carpet) over the ground in autumn. Fall color is actually quite a handsome
yellow. Probably good only in cooler climates and Don Shadow reported poor growth at his nursery in
Winchester, TN. From discussions with nurserymen, the true Monarch is not very cold hardy. It perished
at -20°F in Illinois field tests. Native to northern Japan. Introduced 1888. Zone 5 to 6.

Betula nana L. — Dwarf Birch
LEAVES: Alternate, simple, rounded or occasionally broader than long, 1/4 to 1/2″ diameter, round-toothed, lustrous dark green above, net-veined below, glabrous, 2 to 4 vein pairs; petiole—1/12″ or less with a fringed stipule on each side.

Betula nana, (bet′ū-là nã′nà), Dwarf Birch, is a neatly rounded, 2 to 4′ high and wide shrub with lustrous dark green, orbicular, 1/4 to 1/2″ wide, conspicuously round-toothed leaves. This is a very dainty shrub that is both beautiful and provides a challenge for one's plant material friends. It is found in the northern latitudes of Europe and North America in moist habitats. Among the shrubby birches it is distinguished by its round-toothed, orbicular leaves and the absence of warts or glands on the stems. Cultivated 1789. Zone 2.

B. glandulifera   B. pumila

Other shrubby species that may be of interest but are generally larger than *B. nana* include *B. glandulifera* (Reg.) Butler, *B. glandulosa* Michx., *B. humilis* Schrank., and *B. pumila* L.

Betula occidentalis Hook. non Sarg. (formerly *B. fontinalis* Sarg.) — Water Birch, American Red Birch
LEAVES: Alternate, simple, 1 to 2″ long, 3/4 to 1 1/2″ wide, glandular, broad-ovate, rounded or slightly heart-shaped, pointed, double-serrate, dull dark green and slightly hairy above, paler and glabrous below, 3 to 5 vein pairs; petiole—1/4 to 1/2″ long, at first hairy, finally glabrous.

Betula occidentalis, (bet′ū-là ok-si-den-tā′lis), Water Birch, is a handsome, small (20 to 30′), shrubby tree with close reddish brown bark. I first made its acquaintance on a trip to Salt Lake City. It is a rather graceful tree with slender spreading and pendulous branches. I do not know of plants east of the Mississippi. National champion is 53′ by 42′ in Wallowa County, OR. This is one of the parents of Rocky Mountain Splendor™. Native from Alaska to Oregon and through Rocky Mountains to Colorado. Introduced 1874. Zone 4 to 6.

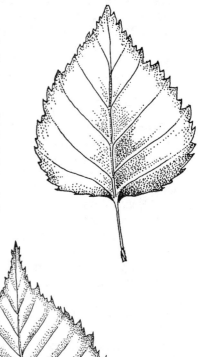

Betula schmidtii Reg. — Schmidt Birch
LEAVES: Alternate, simple, 1 1/2 to 3″ long, 1 to 1 3/4″ wide, ovate, slender-pointed, rounded or wide cuneate at base, finely and irregularly serrate, 9 to 11 vein pairs, dark green above, hairy on veins below; petiole—1/2 to 3/4″ long, hairy.

Betula schmidtii, (bet′ū-là schmid′tē-ī), Schmidt Birch, is a rather unusual species noted for its wood which is too heavy to float in water. The tree makes a fine ornamental with excellent summer foliage followed by golden yellow fall color. The brownish black bark falls off in small, irregular-shaped plates. There is a fine specimen at the Arnold Arboretum. In cultivation it forms a neat rounded outline and will grow 20 to 40′ high, although in the wild it is reported growing 60 to 100′. Japan, Korea and Manchuria. Introduced 1896. Zone 5 to 6.

Betula uber (Ashe) Fern. (also listed as *B. lenta* subsp. *uber*), (bet′ū-là ū′bĕr), Roundleaf Birch, is mentioned here only because of an October visit to the Arnold Arboretum where a small tree fluoresced yellow. I never gave the species a second thought for landscape use since it was discovered as a remnant population in Virginia and a significant stir developed over its taxonomic status. Only known from a single stand about 0.6 mile long and 0.06 mile wide growing in the flood plain of Cherry Creek, Smyth County, VA. It is allied to *B. lenta*, but is smaller in all its parts. National champion is 49′ by 15′ in Jefferson National Forest, VA. Zone (5)6 to 7.

Betula utilis D. Don var. **jacquemontii** (Spach) Winkl. — Whitebarked Himalayan Birch
LEAVES: Alternate, simple, ovate, 2 to 3″ long, rounded or slightly
cuneate at base, double-serrate, dark green above, glandular
below, pubescent on veins, with 7 to 9 vein pairs; petiole—1/2 to
1″ long.

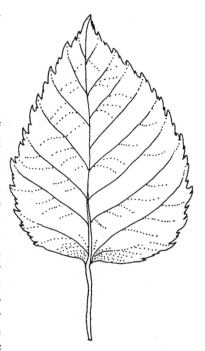

Betula utilis var. jacquemontii, (formerly B. jacquemontii Spach), (bet′ū-
là ū′ti-lis jak'mont-ē-ī), Whitebarked Himalayan Birch, is an
enigma in the world of white-barked birches. In its finest form, the
bark is a beautiful cream-white and probably the most striking of
all the white-barked birches. I attended a nursery conference at
Pershore Horticultural College, England, in 1989 and listened to
the speakers question the authenticity of what is being offered in
the trade as this species. The literature is equally fun to wade
through since Krüssmann, Bean, Rehder, et al. have slightly
different views. Bean remarks that the bark is not always white and
may be pale-colored, ochre-cream, ochre-brown or light pinkish
brown. The whitest barked trees I have seen in European gardens
were labeled B. jacquemontii or B. utilis. Betula utilis is highly
variable like B. jacquemontii and houses B. jacquemontii as a
variety. Ashburner and Shilling, "Betula utilis and its varieties," The
Plantsman 7(2):116–125 (1985), give B. jacquemontii variety
status. They state that B. jacquemontii occurs in the western
Himalayas, has whiter bark and fewer veins. Betula utilis var. utilis
has browner bark and more vein pairs (10 to 14). I was wandering through Edinburgh Botanic Garden,
Scotland and chanced upon a young planting (10 to 15′ high) of what I thought was B. jacquemontii. Bark
was beautiful white on some seedlings and polished brown on others. All were labeled as B. utilis. Next
time I will count vein pairs.

Betula utilis var. jacquemontii is being grown by several West Coast growers and shipped into the
Midwest and East. Dr. J.C. Raulston made a case for the use of var. jacquemontii in the Southeast based
on evaluations at North Carolina State University. Also, he suggested grafting it on B. nigra which would
improve adaptability to moist and wet soils. My experiences indicate otherwise for in my travels and
consulting, both borer damage (extensive) and severe Japanese beetle damage were prominent. Ranney
and Walgenbach, J. Environ. Hort. 10:177–180 (1992), assessed feeding preferences of Japanese beetle
for birch, cherry and crabapple. Of the 9 birch taxa, 8 had no significant injury, while B. utilis var.
jacquemontii had 16% injury (16% of leaf tissue was destroyed). At one garden, the owner removed an
entire grove because of the Japanese beetle frailties described. Also, the plant has been in cultivation a
long time, and I have yet to see a mature tree anywhere in the East. I believe growers and gardeners need
to adjust their antennae to make sure they are getting the best reception (information).

Without question, in its best form which appears to occur in European gardens, particularly
Edinburgh Botanic Garden, it is one of the most beautiful trees on the planet. The habit is typically
pyramidal-oval with dark green leaves and, on the best form, milky white bark. Cuttings have been rooted
successfully (90%) in July, 1000 to 3000 ppm IBA-talk, mist.

Two perhaps worthwhile hybrids of great beauty include 'Grayswood Ghost' at the Garden of the
Royal Horticultural Society at Wisley with superb foliage and white bark and 'Jermyns', introduced by
Hillier Nursery, England, with striking white bark on young stems, peeling orange-brown or coppery on
larger branches and the trunk. 'Inverleith' produces snow white bark and grows at the Royal Botanic
Garden, Edinburgh. 'Kashmir White' resulted from seeds collected at 10,000′ in Kashmir by Roy
Lancaster, the bark is snow white even on young plants, good dark green foliage. Also listed by several
West Coast nurseries is Betula utilis var. utilis 'Yunnan' with rich polished mahogany bark similar to
Prunus serrula, white splashes appear in the bark providing rich contrast to the dark bark. At one time this
"species" showed promise for borer resistance but recent reports indicate it is susceptible. The adaptability
range is probably Zones 5 to 6.

There is abundant literature on the birches and to sift through it all is akin to sieving the sand on the
beaches of the world. There is considerable confusion regarding the various white-barked birches. If you
have a desire to confuse a botanist hand him or her a handful of birch leaves and run. See Richard
Weaver's, "The Ornamental Birches," Arnoldia 38(4):117–131 (1978), and Santamour and McArdle,
"Checklist of Cultivars in Betula (Birch)," J. Arboriculture 15(7):170–176 (1989).

Bignonia capreolata L. [*Anisostichus capreolatus* (L.) Bureau.] — Crossvine, Quartervine
(big-nō′ni-à kap-rē-ō-lā′tà)

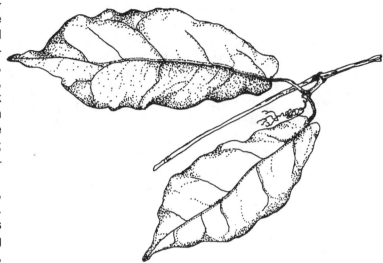

FAMILY: Bignoniaceae

LEAVES: Opposite, semi-evergreen to ever-green, trifoliate, leaflets 2, stalked, the rachis ending in a branched tendril clinging by small disks, leaflets oblong-ovate to oblong-lanceolate, 2 to 6″ long, 1/2 to 2″ wide, obtusely acuminate, cordate, entire, glabrous, lustrous dark green in summer changing to reddish purple in winter; underside of leaf more pronounced purple than upper surface; petiole—about 1/2″ long; petiolules—curved, 1/2 to 3/4″ long.

BUDS: Imbricate, reddish purple, 1/8″ long, glabrous, diverge at 45° angle to stem.

STEM: Squarish, reddish purple, glabrous on young stems, with brown spotting on mature first year stem; pith—solid, cross-shaped.

SIZE: Depending on structure, will climb 30 to 50′, usually less, with delight have watched this vine across the Southeast and cataloged 70′ high plants.

HARDINESS: Zone 6 to 9, possibly 5.

HABIT: Semi-evergreen to evergreen self-clinging and twining vine climbing by tendrils; will cover trees or often snakes along the ground; this species and the author have developed a mutual admiration society (can vines admire); on my jogging trail there are two notable specimens that have essentially overtaken the trees (sweetgums) to which they have become attached, one is 20′, the other is 15′, both are dense, full vines in their full sun exposure; for best growth and flowering the plant should be sited in sun, however, it performs admirably in partial shade.

RATE: Fast.

TEXTURE: Medium.

LEAF COLOR: Dark green in summer, developing reddish purple cast in cold weather; foliage is not dense and does not make a solid cover like many vines unless provided with sufficient sun.

FLOWERS: Perfect, brown to brownish orange or brownish red to orange and orange-red on the outside; the typical wild form that I commonly see is reddish brown with yellow to orangish inside, each flower shaped like a trumpet to broad funnelform-campanulate, 1 1/2 to 2″ long, 3/4 to 1 1/2″ wide at the end of the 5-lobed corolla, borne 2 to 5 together in short-stalked cymes, interesting mocha fragrance on the wild type, flowers open in mid-April in Athens with an effective 3 to 4 week period; curiously attractive, yet effective because of the large numbers of flowers; superb flower colors and delightful fragrance should endear this vine to more gardeners; a native plant on the Dirr property, it flowered late April–early May, 1993, and mid-April 1994; interestingly, I do not see any significant reblooming during the summer on the typical brownish red forms; however, an orange-flowered selection ('Jekyll') I made from a wild population on Jekyll Island, GA will produce flowers sporadically through the growing season; additionally, hybrids between this and *Campsis radicans* would prove extremely exciting, one of the many projects slated for my retirement.

FRUIT: Slender, compressed, 4 to 7″ long capsule, green initially, finally brown, seeds winged.

CULTURE: Typically container-grown, prefers moist, well-drained soils, will grow in heavy shade but best flowering is achieved in full sun; have observed plants that were covered with water for 2 to 4 weeks in March–April and still flourished; inherently tough plant; needs to be pruned and trained under cultivation.

DISEASES AND INSECTS: None serious.

LANDSCAPE VALUE: Handsome foliage and flowers are principal ornamental features; in the wild is often thin and sparse-flowering; excellent for covering a fence or trellis; should be more widely used; actually allowed 'Jekyll' to climb the screen on our porch, wonderful to have the leaves peeking into my private life.

CULTIVARS:

'Atrosanguinea'—Flowers dark red-purple; leaves narrower and longer than species; the plant I have grown as 'Atrosanguinea' is more orange-red than purple-red and the flowers are more narrow trumpet-shaped than the species; interestingly, the color inside is similar to the outside.

'Jekyll'—Enjoy riding my bike particularly on Jekyll Island and on a late March day in 1993 a handsome orange-flowered form was in full glory, needless to state the bicycle careened into the vegetation, the body was flying, the senses tingling, and the plant worth the bodily damage, no lawsuits were filed; vigorous, with foliage like the species, but flowers smaller and not as wide, rich orange on the outside and yellow on the inside of the corolla, not fragrant, has been propagated and distributed to Georgia growers; has possibilities, feedback has been terrific, Bob and Bill Head, Seneca, SC, mentioned that 'Jekyll' was the most evergreen and cold tolerant selection.

'Shalimar Red'—Fast-growing, to 40′, repeat flowering, red form.

'Tangerine Beauty'—Is indeed as the name implies; introduced over 50 years ago and reintroduced and promoted by J.C. Raulston; vigorous and similar to the species except for the ruby-tangerine flowers that are produced in copious quantities; a plant in our evaluation trials has been spectacular and the photographs J.C. has shown over the years will tantalize even the moribund gardener; interestingly this form does not have the floral fragrance of the species; flowers sporadically into summer.

Ample opportunity exists for continued selection and improvement. A soft yellow to deep yellow form would be a great addition. The idea of growing open-pollinated seedling populations has merit. Have heard of a burgundy-rose flowering selection.

PROPAGATION: Seed requires no pretreatment; cuttings root readily when taken in June and July; I have lifted plants that were trailing on the ground and noticed an abundance of roots all along the vine; this is a good indication that the plant is easily rooted; the literature and this author surmised what is written above about cutting propagation, the truth is that cuttings root in high percentages but do so slowly, in our work 1000 to 3000 KIBA was beneficial, cuttings form a callus at the base and roots emerge from this area with the process taking 8 to 10 weeks; there is room for improvement, particularly in the speed of rooting.

ADDITIONAL NOTES: The vine climbs by tendrils but the tendrils are subtended by small disks that allow the plant to cement itself to wood and masonry structures; will readily climb a tree or porous concrete and brick; on trail walks that I have led at the University's Botanical Garden people frequently ask about the identity of the *Bignonia*; apparently very few people are familiar with it; the common name, Crossvine, is derived from appearance of the pith of the stem in cross section.

NATIVE HABITAT: Maryland, Virginia and southern Illinois to Florida and Louisiana. Cultivated 1653.

Broussonetia papyrifera (L.) L'Hér. ex Vent. — Paper Mulberry, Tapa-cloth Tree
(broo-so-nesh′ē-a   pap-i-rif′ēr-à)

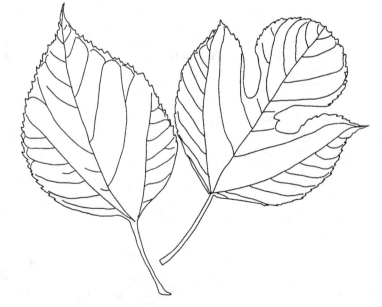

FAMILY: Moraceae

LEAVES: Alternate, occasionally opposite, simple, ovate, 3 1/2 to 8″ long, almost as wide, acuminate, broad cuneate to cordate at base, coarsely dentate, on young plants often deeply lobed, dull green and scabrous above, soft-pubescent beneath; petiole—1 1/4 to 4″ long, sap milky.

BUDS: Moderate, conical, solitary, sessile, outer scale longitudinally striped, grayish brown, appear similar to "dunce" caps.

STEM: Stout, coarse, gray-green, finally gray-brown, thickly downy, almost to the point of being hispid, covered with prominent orange-brown lenticels; pith—large, white, with a green diaphragm at each node.

SIZE: 40 to 50′ in height with a comparable or greater spread; usually smaller under cultivation; national champion is 75′ by 55′ in Flamingo Tropical Gardens, Fort Lauderdale, FL.

HARDINESS: Zone 6 to 10; what is the definition of hardiness?; to me it translates to the plant's ability to survive (without significant injury) and consistently complete the biological reproductive processes, i.e., flowering and fruiting; well, this definition leaves much to be desired from the gardener's viewpoint; in Chicago/Lisle, IL the species is consistently killed to the ground, resprouts but never flowers; well, one mild winter the shoots were not injured and it flowered and fruited; is it hardy?—depends on your definition; is it garden worthy?—No.

  With that, I might add that a tree, albeit a small (+15′) specimen, has flowered and fruited at the Arnold Arboretum; interestingly in the South where the species is a weed and 30 to 40′ high trees are common, I have yet to see a fruiting tree.

HABIT: Tree with wide-spreading branches forming a broad-rounded crown; usually low branched; often shrubby and forming colonies in waste areas, tends to sucker profusely and can assume weed-like proportions if not controlled.

RATE: Fast, 20 to 30′ over a 6 to 8 year period; a genuine weed.

TEXTURE: Medium-coarse in all seasons.

BARK: Gray-brown, shallowly ridged-and-furrowed on large trunks; often assuming the appearance of kneaded bread; there are magnificent old specimens at Colonial Williamsburg with well-developed trunks and interesting bark.

LEAF COLOR: A rather innocuous dull green changing to yellow-green in fall; fall color is not great but trees can be readily spotted because of the mottle of yellow-green that is produced; seems as if one leaf turns all yellow, another stays green and the pattern is repeated over the entire tree; leaves of vigorous shoots are often highly lobed while those on mature specimens show little lobing.

FLOWERS: Dioecious, male borne in cylindrical, often curly, woolly, 1 1/2 to 3″ long and 1/4″ wide, yellowish catkins; female flowers in a ball-like, 1/2″ diameter head; May in North, early April in Athens.

FRUIT: Red, 3/4″ diameter, aggregate of drupes; September, have seen fruits on a tree at Brooklyn Botanic Garden in late September; most plants in Athens are apparently male for I have never seen a single fruit; as many times as I have seen the fruit the color has never been red but orange-red; kind of reminds of the brain-like texture of *Maclura pomifera* fruits.

CULTURE: Easy to grow; thrives in any soil; does well in dirt and grime of cities; tolerates heat and drought; highly alkaline soils; full sun.

DISEASES AND INSECTS: Canker, root rot, dieback, leaf spot, root knot nematode.

LANDSCAPE VALUE: Once planted for ornament; sometimes used as a street tree, casts heavy shade and will send up shoots from the roots; W.J. Bean mentions that this tree can make a nice street specimen; have seen at Colonial Williamsburg where it is used rather effectively, at least in a historical context; a weed in the South.

CULTIVARS:

  'Aurea'—Don Shadow found this rather curious form with rich yellow leaves, the color most pronounced in spring and fading with the heat of the summer; the plant is growing in Don's Dad's garden in Winchester, TN.

  'Cucullata'—A male tree with curious leaves whose margins are curled upwards, so as to give the leaf the shape of a boat.

  'Laciniata'—A dwarfish clone with the leaf reduced to a stalk and the three main veins, ends of which have a small, narrow, variously shaped blade.

  'Variegata'—A yellow-green splashed leaf variant that Bob McCartney found in Gainesville, GA; unfortunately, not stable and most of Bob's tree in Aiken, SC is now green.

PROPAGATION: Softwood cuttings collected in July and August of short shoots with a heel attached will root readily; root cuttings would also work quite well; seed requires no pretreatment; three months cold produced good germination but no control was included to determine whether the cold enhanced germination.

ADDITIONAL NOTES: Interesting tree which is closely allied to the mulberries (*Morus*) but is less woody. The common name is derived from the use of the bark for paper, and in the Polynesian islands for the fiber, which is made into a cloth.

NATIVE HABITAT: China, Japan. Cultivated 1750. Occasionally naturalized from New York to Florida and Missouri.

Buddleia davidii Franch. — Butterfly-bush, Summer Lilac
(bud′lē-ȧ dā-vid′ē-ī)

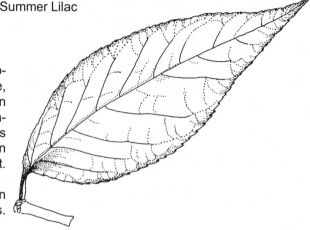

FAMILY: Loganiaceae

LEAVES: Opposite, simple, ovate-lanceolate to lanceolate, 4 to 10″ long, 1 to 3″ wide, acuminate,
cuneate, closely serrate or serrulate, gray-green
to dark green above and glabrous, white-tomentose beneath, leaf color among cultivars varies
significantly and this should be considered when
reading the above description; petiole—very short.

BUDS: Naked, 2-scaled, pubescent, grayish green.

STEM: Stout, prominently angled, 4- to 6- to 8-sided, in
youth covered with pubescence, finally glabrous.

SIZE: Large shrub, 10 to 15′ high, but usually ranging from 5 to 10′; quite tender and frequently killed back to
the ground in northern areas.

HARDINESS: In Chicago, IL, and Orono, ME an herbaceous perennial if not killed outright; in Atlanta, GA a
large rather unkempt woody shrub; can be grown in Zones 5 through 9.

HABIT: Rather succulent caned, large, arching shrub; in many respects better pruned to the ground in spring
since it flowers on new growth of the season; habit is variable and most often rounded in outline; even the
compact types like the Nanho series reach 6 to 8′(10′) high unless restrained; in the Dirr garden, butterfly-
bushes receive lots of play, on occasion plants were pruned to 12 to 18″ of the ground, at other times
untouched with only a tip prune here and there; several observations—unpruned plants produce flowers
sooner in the growing season than heavily pruned plants; foliage persists in the South in mild winters and
is attractive in the shades of gray and green.

RATE: Fast, when cut to ground in spring will easily reach 5 to 8′ high by fall.

TEXTURE: Medium throughout the seasons.

LEAF COLOR: Overall effect is a gray-green to blue-green; rather subdued but serves as a handsome
accompaniment to other more obtrusive foliaged shrubs; leaves appear late in spring and hold late in fall;
in Athens during mild winters (+10°F or above) some foliage persists; no fall color.

FLOWERS: Perfect, usually lavender, lilac to purple, orange at the mouth, 4-petaled, each flower 1/4 to 1/3″
wide, delightfully fragrant, borne in 4 to 10″(18 to 30″) long upright or nodding panicles; June (Athens)
through frost on new growth; cut off old inflorescences and plant will bloom all summer; peak period in
July–August on Cape Cod; in full flower in Camden, ME in early September.

FRUIT: Two-valved, septicidal, 1/4 to 1/3″ long, brown capsule; not ornamentally important; the entire dried
infructescence might be used in arrangements; best to remove the spent flowers before they go to fruit;
tends to seed freely and may become weed-like.

CULTURE: Easily transplanted, almost weed-like in its ability to survive; prefers well-drained, moist, fertile soils;
full sun; prune before growth ensues in spring; the more vigorous the growth the larger the flower panicles;
in Europe the plant has become an "urban dweller" and grows from loose mortar joints and sidewalk cracks,
amazingly durable plant; Bean reported it is now thoroughly naturalized in waste areas in the south of
England and established itself on bombed sites in London after World War II; Lancaster, *Travels in China*,
mentioned that in a wild state it seeds with the same abandon as in Britain, seedlings sprouting in the most
unlikely places except in the forest shade; Jeff Gillman assessed the species' lime requirements and
indeed discovered that 4 pounds per cubic yard increased growth and floral quality over no lime additions
or 8 and 16 pounds per cubic yard; the study was conducted with 'Royal Red' in containers.

DISEASES AND INSECTS: In the last edition, I was excessively kind to this species by stating that there were
no serious pests; from experience and observation, mites can be problematic especially when plants are
drought stressed; if kept vigorous the problem is minimized; also, nematodes are serious particularly in the
sandy soils of the Coastal Plain; a student also mentioned to me that individuals may be prone to a contact
dermatitis when working around the plants, I have had no problems, but it is something to be cognizant
about; various viruses including alfalfa and cucumber mosaic have been isolated from *Buddleia davidii*.

LANDSCAPE VALUE: Valued for summer flowering; makes a fine addition to the shrub or perennial border; have
seen it used in mass with good success; fine for cut-flower use but flowers do not last long, about two good
days in a vase when fresh cut; inflorescences vary from 4 to 30″ in length; attracts butterflies in profusion.
Since arriving in Georgia this plant has become a mainstay in our garden and deserves consideration by
all gardeners. Attracts an amazing array of butterflies and bees. Numerous new or resurrected older

cultivars have become available. In early October, 'Nanho Purple' was still flowering prolifically in Ithaca, NY. The planting was most effective since a large mass had been allowed to drift through the Cornell Plantations. In Athens, flowers continue into November if new growth is promoted by pruning, fertilizer and water. Have noticed flowering pretty much shuts down when night temperatures reach 40 to 45°F.

CULTIVARS: Numerous, for every stray seedling has the potential to be the next greatest cultivar. Many forms are similar in color, size, fragrance, etc., and it would make sense to assemble a list of the top 5 to 10. Nurserymen cannot grow and retailers cannot sell the matrix of butterfly-bush cultivars. Be leery of the reliability of cultivar names. A horticulturist at one arboretum mentioned that their collection was less than accurate. I do not know the answer but would like to evaluate a complete collection of cultivars for garden attributes. One of my Ph.D. students, Jeff Gillman, is working toward the above stated objective. With over 70 taxa collected, and 45 *B. davidii* types, the project has escalated to significant proportions. The cultivars described below are based on the literature and our observations over the past two summers. I might add that every visitor who experiences this collection becomes enthused. One Georgia nurseryman said his firm was growing 10 different types. After assessing our collection, he took home another 27 types. Like candy, difficult to resist.

I have had wonderful experiences studying our butterfly-bush collection. The colors vary by the light of day and time of year. Colors are deeper in cool weather and inflorescences longer. The first produced panicles of the season are the largest. Fragrance is difficult to assess and Bonnie and I have tried. We utilized low, medium, and high fragrance ratings. The following are favorites, grouped by color, although as I have learned there are very few castaway butterfly-bushes. Virtually all have intrinsic beauty and at least one quality trait.

White
'Nanho Alba' ('Nanho White')
'Peace'
'White Bouquet'
B. fallowiana 'Alba' (for silver foliage)

Lavender, blue, or combination
'Bonnie'
'Deep Lavender'
'Empire Blue'
'Moonshadow'

Pink, Rose, Mauve
'Summer Beauty'
'Summer Rose' ('Raspberry Wine')
'Pink Delight'

Purple, Violet, Magenta, "Red"
'Black Knight'
'Dubonnet'
'Potter's Purple'
'Royal Red'

Yellow
'Honeycomb'

To determine similarity of flowers and foliage, cut inflorescences and shoots of *different named types*, exhibiting seemingly similar characteristics, are meshed together, with the flowers of one inflorescence actually intermixed with those of another, when the colors are so similar that those (flowers) of plant A cannot be separated from plant B (more than one observer), then do we provide the synonyms or related types described below. Growth habit differences are also evaluated. 'Royal Red' has come to us as 'Black Knight', 'Burgundy', 'Purple Prince', and 'Red Plume' (mixed-up for sure). Based on our experiences, if the gardener desires specific true-to-type flower colors, wait until the plant is flowering before buying.

'African Queen'—Dark violet, fragrant, panicles 7 to 9″ long.

'Amplissima'—Large mauve panicle.

'Black Knight'—Very deep violet to dark purple, vigorous grower, 8 to 10′ high, may be slightly hardier than other clones, panicles 6 to 8″ long, introduced about 1959.

'Bonnie'—Pretty light lavender with orange eye flowers, 8 to 12″ long inflorescences, sweet fragrance, vigorous-growing to 10′ by 10′, large dark gray-green leaves, silvery beneath, named after my wife.

'Border Beauty'—Deep lilac-purple (crimson-purple) flowers, heavy-flowering, strongly branched, a lower growing form, about 2/3's the size of the species; a plant labeled as such at Wisley was compact but with rose-purple, 6 to 8″ long inflorescences; the plant in out tests matches up with 'Dubonnet'.

'Burgundy'—Fragrant, magenta-red panicles, large shrub, appears similar to 'Royal Red', cross referencing with true 'Royal Red' indicates the plant received as 'Burgundy' is in fact 'Royal Red', listed by Hines Nursery as 'Burgundy'.

'Charming'—Pink flowers in 6 to 8″(12″) long panicles, each flower with an orange throat, upright and strong-growing, 7′ by 6′ in two years, blue-green foliage.

'Cornwall Blue'—True lavender-violet flowers, gray foliage, in Georgia trials this is the same as 'Lochinch'.

'Darent Valley'—A name I saw at Wisley, plant was not in flower, no literature to substantiate.

'Darkness'—Wide-spreading arching habit and deep blue to purple-blue flowers.

'Dartmoor'—Large-growing (10′) form with magenta flowers in multi-branched inflorescences, known since 1971, rather impressive floral display, discovered near Yelverton on Dartmoor, flower color is more mauve-purple on plants in our collection, inflorescences are multi-branched and large.

'Deep Lavender'—Deep lavender-lilac with an orange eye, each floret heavily ruffled and fringed, profuse-flowering, discovered in an old nursery and introduced by Carroll Gardens, Westminster, MD.

'Dubonnet'—Dark purple flowers, each flower with a light orange throat, strong upright grower, panicles 6 to 10″(14 to 18″) long; although described as such in the literature the typical 'Dubonnet' in the United States has medium violet-purple flowers with an orange eye; an early-flowering form; dark blue-green foliage; 7′ by 9′ in two years; the clone is obviously terribly confused in commerce; 'Princeton Purple' and 'Border Beauty' that we tested were the same as 'Dubonnet'. My best concept of 'Dubonnet' is violet-purple flowers, sweet fragrance, large dark gray-green leaves, upright-rounded, vigorous habit, one of the best garden types.

'Ellen's Blue'—Deeply saturated blue flowers, bright orange eye, pleasing fragrance, grayish silver leaves, a seedling of 'Lochinch', according to Heronswood a selection by Ellen Hornig, and named for her.

'Empire Blue'—According to the literature, rich violet-blue flowers with orange eye, panicles 6 to 12″(18″) long, somewhat upright habit, silvery green foliage, strong grower, well-branched, 6 to 10′ high; again the forms I have observed have lavender-blue (more bluish) coloration with an orange eye, flowers on the plant in our evaluation tests are often in the 12″ long category, lovely fragrance, more loose and open habit, now 10′ high in the Dirr garden.

'Fascination' ('Fascinating')—Broad panicles of vivid lilac-pink, 8 to 12″ in summer, 14 to 18″ possible, one report noted up to 32″ long, 2 to 3″ wide, very strong grower, saw a 12 to 14′ high plant at Wisley, low fragrance, inflorescence not as full as many cultivars because petals are bent forward and cupped rather than flat-faced.

'Flaming Violet'—Flowers to 10″ long, violet-purple, fragrant, dark blue-green foliage, pretty form, but not well-known in commerce.

'Fortune'—Long cylindrical panicles (up to 16″), medium purple flowers each with a yellow to orange eye, prolific-flowering, introduced 1936; our 'Fortune' has rich medium purple, 6 to 8″ long inflorescences, oval-rounded habit, 8′ high.

'Fromow's Purple'—Deep purple-violet in handsome long panicles.

'Glasnevin Blue'—Early evaluations in my garden indicate handsome smallish gray-green leaves, light lavender-blue flower, inflorescences smaller about 6″, and more compact habit, a young plant has been quite spreading; considered a *B. fallowiana* selection, probably a hybrid with *B. davidii*; in Georgia trials a weak grower and 'Bonnie', 'Empire Blue', and 'Moonshadow' are superior.

'Golden Sovereign'—Chimera (sport) of 'Empire Blue' with random gold variegation ranging from slight to almost entirely golden leaves, discovered and propagated in 1991 by Peter G. Addison.

'Harlequin'—A rather handsome form with cream-variegated leaves, the new leaves yellow, aging white, flowers reddish purple, not as vigorous and smaller than 'Royal Red' of which it is a sport, growth habit is almost rounded, 6 to 8′ by 6 to 8′, extremely susceptible to mites and many growers have discontinued growing it.

'Hever Castle' [*B. × pikei* = (*B. alternifolia* × *B. crispa* or *B. caryopteridifolia*)]—Shrub to 5′ high, open, with gray-green leaves, fragrant, mauve-pink, orange-throated flowers in up to 12″ long panicles, flowers interrupted along the length of the inflorescence, somewhat weak grower, inferior to better *B. davidii* types.

'Honeycomb'—Surprise yellow-flowered addition to the Georgia evaluations; in June 1995, I purchased two butterfly-bushes, 'E.H. Wilson' and 'Ile de France', at Crathes Castle Garden, Scotland; neither were in flower and the transported cuttings flowered in 1996 with 'Ile de France' matching its floral description and 'E.H. Wilson' (supposedly lavender) flowering yellow with deeper orange eye; plants of the latter were distributed to Georgia growers with considerable positive feedback concerning growth, flower color, and quality of foliage; vigorous grower of *B. × weyeriana* parentage, with medium green foliage, definitely different than 'Sungold' and 'Moonlight'; in fact, side-by-side comparisons of 'Honeycomb' and 'Sungold' indicate the former is consistently superior for the grower and gardener; individual flowers are larger, sweet fragrance; close examination of the flower buds indicates that 'Moonlight' is deep lavender, 'Sungold' light lavender, and 'Honeycomb' cream-yellow; has flowered, along with 'Sungold' and 'Moonlight' the latest of all *Buddleia* taxa in our trials with flowers still present on November 23, 1997.

'Ile de France'—Dark violet flowers with a yellow-orange throat, 4 to 8″ long summer panicles, described as having panicles to 28″ long, a well-branched shrub, 10′ high, 7 1/2′ by 7′ in 2 years, flowers not as dark as 'Dubonnet' or 'Potter's Purple', blue-green foliage, introduced about 1930.

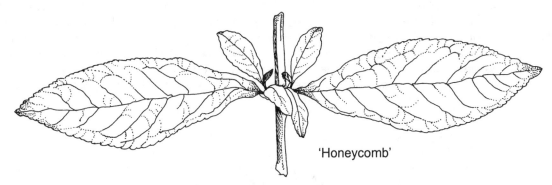

'Honeycomb'

'Lochinch' (a hybrid between *B. fallowiana* × *B. davidii*)—A more vigorous, large-growing form with sweetly scented, lavender-blue flowers, each with a large orange eye that occur in 12″ long panicles. I first spied the plant at Wakehurst Place in West Sussex, England. Will grow 12 to 15′ high and as wide. Cut to ground to rejuvenate and will flower on new growth of the season. Leaves are 8 to 10″ long, gray-green above and silvery-gray below; should be adaptable to Zones 6 to 8. The above description was derived from the plant mentioned at Wakehurst; unfortunately, this is not the true 'Lochinch' which I now have growing in the garden and test plots. The genuine article has smaller gray-green leaves (upper and lower surfaces), 5 to 6″ long, light lavender-violet inflorescences, and a more restrained growth habit, maturing around 6 to 8′, the entire plant is covered in white, tomentose pubescence, creating a more silvery effect than the average *B. davidii* forms.

var. *magnifica* (Wils.) Rehd. & Wils.—Bluish purple with reflexed petals, parent of *B.* × *weyeriana* along with *B. globosa*.

'Mary's White'—Received in our shop as *B. yunnanensis* 'Alba', after 2 years evaluation it was apparent that it was a *B. davidii* type, grew 7 1/2′ tall by 6 1/2′ wide in 2 years, leaves narrower than typical *B. davidii* types, leaves blue-green, flowers white, profuse, inflorescence 8 to 9″ long, one of the best

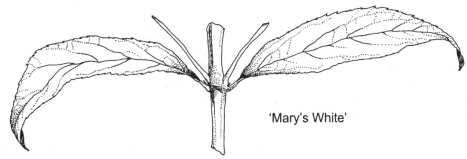

'Mary's White'

and most consistent white flowering forms in our tests, reported cold hardy to Hopkinton, MA, named after Mary Hayes, grandmother of Dr. Jeff Gillman, now assistant professor, Department of Horticulture, University of Minnesota, St. Paul, MN.

'Masquerade'—Sport of 'Harlequin' with broad cream-white band, slightly stronger growing, magenta red flower of typical 'Harlequin' and 'Royal Red' the progenitor cultivar; patented by Notcutts, England.

'Miss Ellen'—Rich, robust blue-green foliage that looks as good in October as May–June, highly fragrant flowers, vibrant violet-purple with an orange eye, individual flowers somewhat cupped rather than flat faced, inflorescences average (4″)6 to 8″(10″) in length, plant in my garden appears more restrained (compact) than most cultivars, 7 1/2′ by 7 1/2′ in 2 years, Steve Thomas introduction, Greene Hill Nursery, Waverly, AL, one of the more promising new introductions.

'Moonshadow'—Small dark blue-green leaves, lilac-purple buds, soft lavender flowers in 4 to 6″ long panicles, more white towards center of flower, grows 3 1/2′ by 4′, open, spreading habit, will make a handsome addition to the shrub and perennial borders, seedling of 'Nanho Blue'.

'Nanho Alba'—Compact full dense form with haystack habit, slender blue-green leaves and low to medium fragrant white flowers, in Georgia trials one of the best whites, inflorescences larger (8 to 12″) than typical Nanho types, larger leaves, profusion of flowers cover the 6 to 8′ high and 5 to 6′wide framework, an excellent white for the smaller garden.

'Nanho Blue'—Mauve-blue flowers, 4 to 6″ long panicles, low fragrance, small gray-green leaves, compact grower, have seen 8′ high.

'Nanho Purple'—Magenta-purple flowers, high fragrance, spreading dwarf habit about 5′ high, small blue-green foliage, hybrid between *B. d.* var. *nanhoensis* and *B. d.* 'Royal Red', have grown 'Nanho Blue' and 'Nanho Purple' with 'Nanho Blue' reaching 8′ and 'Nanho Purple' about 6′, leaves and flowers are smaller than typical *B. davidii* types; var. *nanhoensis* (see above) is a botanical taxon that grows about 5′ high and occurs naturally in central China, possibly the other Nanho selections in cultivation have genes of *B. davidii*; 'Nanho Purple' is the smallest of the Nanho types; the parentage of 'Nanho Purple' is purported to be var. *nanhoensis* × 'Royal Red', backcrossed to 'Royal Red'; line drawing shows the narrow, slender leaves, the largest 2 1/2 to 3″ long, 1/2″ wide, dull dark blue-green, finely serrate, silver-white on lower surface.

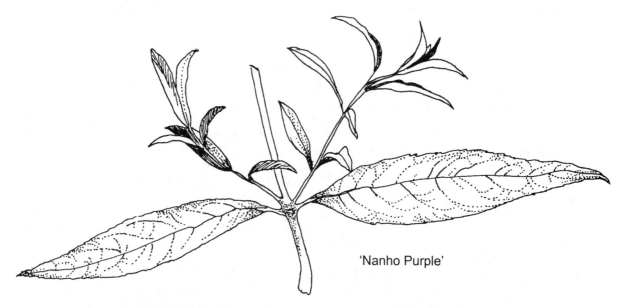

'Nanho Purple'

var. *nanhoensis* (Chitt) Rehd.—Have not seen the true variety in cultivation; listed as elegant, slender-branched, with long narrow leaves and cylindrical panicles of mauve flowers, introduced 1914 by Reginald Farrer from Kansu, China.

'Niche's Choice'—Unusually long panicles of rich purple, fragrant flowers, vigorous grower, 6 to 8′ high by 5 to 6′ wide, an introduction of unknown origin from Niche Gardens, Chapel Hill, NC.

'Opera'—Strong-growing form with deep purple-red flowers, almost fuchsia-colored, 1 to 2′ long panicles; our Georgia plant has lavender-purple, low fragrance flowers in 8 to 10″ (20″) long panicles, grew 6′ high and 4′ wide by mid-August of first growing season, blue-green summer foliage.

'Orchid Beauty'—Less vigorous than the species with mauve flowers (lavender-blue), fragrant.

'Ornamental White'—Large white flowers on a 30 to 36″ high and wide shrub.

'Peace'—Arching habit, 2/3's the size of species, white flowers with orange throat, medium fragrance, 6 to 14″ long panicles, handsome large-flowered form, terrific in our tests, one of the best whites for foliage and flower, in my mind superior to 'White Profusion'.

Petite Indigo™ (var. *nanhoensis* type)—Lilac-blue flowers in 4 to 6″ long inflorescences, small gray-green leaves on a compact, much-branched shrub, 6′ high and greater with age, in our tests 8′ by 7′ in 2 years, Monrovia Nursery introduction.

Petite Plum™ (var. *nanhoensis* type)—Light purple, medium fragrance flowers with an orange eye, foliage darker green and larger than above and longer persistent, 6′ high, 8′ by 6′ in our tests in 2 years, Monrovia introduction.

'Pink Charmer'—8 to 10″(16″), rose-pink (lavender-pink) panicles, in our tests 9′ by 7′ in 2 years, large leaves, upright-oval, strong vertical shoots.

'Pink Charming'—8′ by 8′ in 2 years, upright-arching-rounded, light lavender-blue, moderately fragrant flowers, large 6 to 10″(14″) panicles, flat blue-green leaves.

'Pink Delight'—A Dutch introduction with true pink, fragrant (low to medium) flowers, panicles 6 to 12″(18″) long, gray-green leaves, compact growth habit, have seen in England and the flower color is excellent, added a plant to the garden and have been ecstatic about the rich pink flower color and large size inflorescences, compact growth habit (5′ by 5′ in 2 years) could be a misnomer, I suspect 8′ and more; this has become the most popular pink form in the trade, parentage rather convoluted with 'Fascination', 'Nanho Alba', and 'West Hill' involved.

'Pink Pearl'—Pale lilac-pink flowers with soft yellow eye borne in dense panicles.

'Potter's Purple'—Robust rounded habit, 5.4′ by 5.6′ in 1 1/2 growing seasons, large dark green foliage, 5 to 8″(12″) long, deep purple-budded flowers open to bluish purple, low to moderate fragrance.

'Princeton Purple'—Broad cone-shaped trusses of medium blue-purple that open from bottom to the top at the same time, densely branched shrub, 6 to 8' high, loaded with side buds, in our trials this is the same as 'Dubonnet'.

'Purple Prince'—Rich magenta-red, fragrant (low to medium) flowers on an 8 to 10' high shrub, large blue-green leaves, very similar to 'Royal Red', inflorescences 6 to 14" long.

'Raspberry Wine'—Dusky deep mauve flowers in large, full panicles, each floret ruffled with a deep gold center, 6 to 8' high, introduced by Carroll Gardens, appears the same as 'Summer Rose'.

'Red Plume'—Rich, velvety reddish violet, 8 to 10' high and 8 to 10' wide, color strongly resembles 'Royal Red'; small plant in Georgia tests matches with 'Royal Red' for flower color.

'Rice Creek'—Lavender flowers, root hardy in Minnesota, introduced by Betty Ann Addison and Harvey Buchite.

'Royal Red'—Rich purple-red flowers on up to (6 to 12")20" long panicles, considered the best "red" form, first saw in England and was taken with the color and size of the flowers, strong upright-growing shrub easily to 10' and more, 8 1/2' by 8' in 2 years, have grown this in the garden and appreciate the great vigor, floral bounty and fragrance, introduced 1941; apparently many renames or cultivars so close florally that separation is neigh impossible; 'Burgundy', 'Purple Prince', and 'Red Plume' are similar.

'Salicifolia'—Leaves and panicles narrow, no flower color given.

'Santana'—Sport of 'Royal Red', found in a nursery in Knaresborough, England; irregular gold margins with green center, flowers rich magenta-red of the parent plant; see *The Garden* 122(11):769 (1997).

'Snow Bank'—Pure white flowers.

'Summer Beauty'—Saw this in late September, 1994 at Bernheim Arboretum and asked Buddy Hubbuch for cuttings of this most beautiful true rose-flowered form, with silver leaves, habit is more restrained and compact, 5 to 6' high, have shared this with growers and the universal acclaim indicates this is one of the most beautiful of all pink-rose forms; two years of field and garden data reflect the appeal of this cultivar to both grower and gardener; universally visitors ask the identity and remark about the beautiful deep rose flower color; may not be as cold hardy or vigorous as some cultivars.

'Summer Rose'—Large 8 to 12"(18") long inflorescences of iridescent mauve-rose, inflorescences are consistently larger even in the heat of summer, excellent fragrance, large robust, densely foliaged, dark blue-green foliaged shrub, 8 to 10' high, 7' by 7' in 2 years, can't find in literature, original cuttings were mixed, in my top five *B. davidii* types, may be the same as 'Raspberry Wine'.

'Variegata'—May be a catchall category for variegated foliage types, have seen at Glasnevin, Ireland, larger leaves than Harlequin; variegated leaves occur occasionally as chimeras (branch sports).

var. *veitchiana* (Veitch) Rehd.—Lavender flowers in large panicles.

'Violet Message'—Medium violet flowers with a light yellow eye, multi-branched panicles, 8' high plant, from Netherlands via Dan Hinckley, Heronswood.

'West Hill'—Pale lavender with orange eye, fragrant flowers in arching panicles on a medium size, spreading shrub, leaves are white tomentose below.

'White Bouquet'—White fragrant flowers with an orange (yellowish) throat in 8 to 12" long panicles, inflorescences broad-conical, narrow gray-green leaves, introduced 1942.

'White Cloud'—Pure white flowers with yellow eye in 8 to 10" long dense panicles, grows 10' high.

'White Delight'—White flowers.

'White Harlequin'—Variegated foliage like 'Harlequin' but with white flower panicles.

'White Profusion'—White, low to medium fragrant flowers with yellow eyes, in 6 to 8"(16") long panicles, 6 to 10' high shrub, foliage light green, leaves narrow compared to 'White Bouquet' and 'Nanho Alba', upright growing habit, in my experience becoming somewhat open with age, although common in the trade certainly not the best white for 'Nanho Alba', 'Peace', and 'White Bouquet' are superior, 7.8' by 7' in 2 years.

'Windy Hill'—Cold hardy, purple-flowered form with narrow delicate blue-green leaves, selected by Dennis Mareb, Windy Hill Nursery, Great Barrington, MA, originated as a spontaneous seedling, the only butterfly-bush that consistently regenerates year in year out, of all the butterfly-bush cultivars that Mr. Mareb has attempted to grow in the vicinity of Great Barrington, MA (-25 to $-30°$F winter lows) this has been the only truly cold hardy form, regrowth strong, probably 5 to 8' in a single season.

'Wine'—Rich burgundy flowers, listed in 1997 Flowerwood Nursery catalog, another moniker for 'Royal Red'?

PROPAGATION: Seed requires no pretreatment; cuttings collected from May–June through August root readily; winter hardwood cuttings can be rooted; I have used 1000 to 3000 ppm KIBA quick dip; once rooted, remove cuttings from the bench or turn off mist; they deteriorate rapidly with excess moisture; fertilize cuttings with water soluble nitrogen fertilizer or slow release and/or place under extended photoperiod; buds will break in 2 to 3 weeks and the shoot elongation will be rapid.

ADDITIONAL NOTES: An amazing plant for many aesthetic reasons and also for its tenacity; in England it grows out of mortar joints in walls and buildings; in Edinburgh, Scotland, Dr. Armitage and I were returning from the Botanic Garden and as we peered out of the bus window, a rubble-strewn lot inhabited with stray *Buddleia* seedlings of every hue and color gazed back at us; Al and I witnessed cultivar city at its most promising but the driver (bus) would not allow us to jump from the coach; actually the species becomes or assumes weed status in Europe; kind of hard to accept? Butterfly-bush mania is a serious disease and to some degree I have been infected. There are about 100 species worldwide and I have seen about 10. A few notes are provided to whet the reader's appetite. Realistically, most of these have no place in the average American garden because of the significant quantity of excellent *B. davidii* forms. Several might be used in breeding to increase the color range and plant habit.

NATIVE HABITAT: China. Cultivated 1890.

RELATED SPECIES:

Buddleia alternifolia Maxim. — Alternate-leaf Butterfly-bush
LEAVES: Alternate, simple, lanceolate, 1 1/2 to 4″ long, 1/4 to 1/2″ wide, narrowed toward the acute or obtusish apex, cuneate, entire, dull dark green above, with grayish white scurfy tomentum beneath; petiole—about 1/8″ long.

Buddleia alternifolia, (bud′lē-à   al-ter-ni-fō′li-à), Alternate-leaf Butterfly-bush, is a large shrub or small tree that grows 10 to 20′ in height. The habit is lax and long pendulous shoots flay their supple arms in the slightest breeze. The dull dark green leaves take on a gray cast from a distance and provide interesting foliage color. The bright lilac-purple flowers appear in dense clusters in June from the axils of the previous season's wood. The flowers are fragrant but not to the degree of many *B. davidii* cultivars. Prefers loose loamy soil and a sunny position. Has been likened to a gracious, small-leaved, weeping willow when not in flower and a sheer waterfall of soft purple when it is. I have had more difficulty rooting this from softwood cuttings than the *B. davidii* cultivars. 'Argentea' has appressed silky hairs which give the leaves a silvery sheen. This is a most handsome form and preferable to the species. Flowers 7 to 10 days ahead of the species. Great for foliage color and texture in a border. This is the hardiest of the butterfly bushes, and the first to flower. Remember, this species flowers on last year's wood so prune *after* flowering. In our heavy, wet Georgia soils it has not persisted. In fact, several replantings have died while *B. davidii* in the same location prospers. Native to northwestern China. Introduced 1914. Zone 5 to 7.

Buddleia asiatica Lour., (bud′lē-à   ã-shi-at′i-kà), with 3 to 6″ long, 1 to 1 1/2″ wide, narrow, lustrous dark green, finely serrated leaves, fragrant white flowers, and large shrub stature was outplanted in our trials. Leaf underside is silver-white and young stems are covered with silver-white indumentum. Although listed as evergreen (Griffiths), it was anything but and was killed outright. Our 1996 planting was killed at about 15°F. Exceptionally vigorous and small rooted cuttings grew 8′ in a single season. At 22°F, the plant was killed on November 18, 1997. It had yet to flower. Eastern Asia. Zone 9(?).

Buddleia colvilei Hook f. & Thoms., (bud′lē-à kol-vil′ē-ī), is a shrub or small tree, 10 to 15′ high. The magnificent aspect of the species is the large, campanulate, up to 1″ diameter, rose, purple to crimson-maroon flowers. Flowers occur in pendulous panicles to 8″ long, on previous season's wood. It was in flower at Glasnevin, Dublin, Ireland and my first thought was what a terrific source for new genes. Have seen 15′ high plants at Edinburgh Botanic Garden. 'Kewensis' has rich red flowers. I brought a small plant of the species from Arduaine Garden, Scotland and it flowered pink in the greenhouse. Did not survive outside. Himalayas. Zone 8 to 10 on West Coast. Has not survived in Georgia trials. Heat and cold have eliminated several plants.

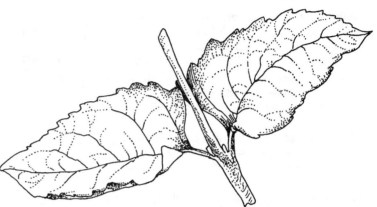

Buddleia crispa Benth., (bud′lē-à kris′pà), grows 8 to 10′(15′) high with beautiful gray-green, almost silvery leaves. The fragrant lavender-lilac, orange-throated, 1/3 to 2/3″ diameter flowers are borne in 4 to 5″ long and wide panicles. Flowers more or less continuously from July onward on new growth. I saw the plant for the first time in late June 1994 at Kew Gardens and was more impressed with the foliage than the flower. The 2 to 5″ long, 3/4 to 1 1/2″ wide, gray-green leaves, silver below, are lanceolate, strongly toothed and heavily pubescent on both surfaces; petiole 1/4 to 1″ long. Our plant has smaller leaves and is more broad-ovate in outline with a semi-cordate to truncate leaf base. Variety *farreri* is probably the most common form in cultivation and may be smaller growing than the species. The plant in the Georgia trials is slow-growing and no more than 2′ by 3′ in a single growing season. There is a 15′ high and 15′ wide plant at Wisley. Himalayas. Zone 7b to 8.

Buddleia fallowiana Balf. f., (bud′lē-à fal-ōw-ē-ā′nà), is a parent of 'Loch-inch', with 2 to 4″ long, dull blue-green leaves, white-felted below and on stems, robust grower, 10 to 15′ high ('Alba' has grown 4′ by 5′ in 2 seasons), terminal thryse-type, 6 to 8″ long inflorescence, white to lavender orange-throated, slightly fragrant flowers, each lobe crenate, spreading. Variety *alba* 'Sabourin' produces white flowers with orange eye. 'Alba' is great for silvery summer foliage, withstands the heat and cold of Zone 7, and has become a favorite of visitors to our test plots. The silver-gray foliage and compact growth habit bode well for everyday garden use. The above listed species is as handsome in foliage as flower. Many herbaceous perennial fanatics wax eloquently about the silver and gray foliage of *Stachys* and *Artemisia*, most of which turn to canned mush in southern summers. Why not consider the *B. fallowiana* types for possible foliage color and contrast? Might treat as annual foliage plants. Western China. Zone (7)8.

Buddleia globosa Hope — Orange Butterfly-bush, Orange Ball Tree
LEAVES: Alternate, simple, deciduous to semi-evergreen, elliptic-ovate to lanceolate, 3 to 8″ long, about 1/4 to 1/3 as wide, acuminate, cuneate, crenate, lustrous dark green, rugose and glabrous above, covered with light brown pubescence below; petiole—1/4″ long.

Buddleia globosa, (bud′lē-à glō-bō′sà), Orange Butterfly-bush, is a robust 10 to 15′ high and wide semi-evergreen to deciduous shrub of rather open gaunt habit. The bright yellow, fragrant, 3/4 to 7/8″ diameter, rounded flowers occur 8 to 10 together in a terminal 6 to 8″ long and wide panicle in opposite pairs, each flower on a 1 to 1 1/2″ long pedicel. Flowers in June in England and probably early to mid-May in the Athens area. Flowers on previous season's wood and should not be pruned until *after* flowering. Actually a striking shrub in flower and certainly worthy of consideration by Zone 8 and 9 gardeners. Prefers a loamy, well-drained, moist soil and ample sunlight. One of the parents of the *B.* × *weyeriana* hybrids. 'Lemon Ball' is later-flowering than the species with lemon-yellow flowers. Repeatedly died in the Georgia trials (Zone 7b). Chile, Peru, Argentina. Introduced 1774. Zone 7 to 9.

Buddleia lindleyana Fortune

LEAVES: Opposite, simple, deciduous, semi-evergreen, evergreen, ovate to oblong-lanceolate, 2 to 4″ long, half or less wide, acuminate, cuneate to broad cuneate, remotely denticulate to entire, shiny dark green above, pale gray-green below, impressed veins; petiole—1/8 to 1/4″ long.

BUDS: Small, 1/8″ long, light gray-brown, dusted with short pubescence.

STEM: Distinctly quadrangular, greenish purple, short pubescent; older stems shiny brown, pubescent, with obvious wings at each of the 4-sided stems; pith—white.

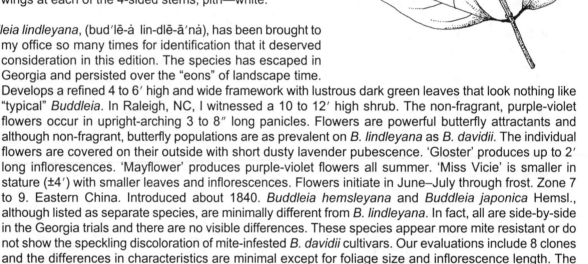

Buddleia lindleyana, (bud′lē-à lin-dlē-ā′nȧ), has been brought to my office so many times for identification that it deserved consideration in this edition. The species has escaped in Georgia and persisted over the "eons" of landscape time.

Develops a refined 4 to 6′ high and wide framework with lustrous dark green leaves that look nothing like "typical" *Buddleia*. In Raleigh, NC, I witnessed a 10 to 12′ high shrub. The non-fragrant, purple-violet flowers occur in upright-arching 3 to 8″ long panicles. Flowers are powerful butterfly attractants and although non-fragrant, butterfly populations are as prevalent on *B. lindleyana* as *B. davidii*. The individual flowers are covered on their outside with short dusty lavender pubescence. 'Gloster' produces up to 2′ long inflorescences. 'Mayflower' produces purple-violet flowers all summer. 'Miss Vicie' is smaller in stature (±4′) with smaller leaves and inflorescences. Flowers initiate in June–July through frost. Zone 7 to 9. Eastern China. Introduced about 1840. *Buddleia hemsleyana* and *Buddleia japonica* Hemsl., although listed as separate species, are minimally different from *B. lindleyana*. In fact, all are side-by-side in the Georgia trials and there are no visible differences. These species appear more mite resistant or do not show the speckling discoloration of mite-infested *B. davidii* cultivars. Our evaluations include 8 clones and the differences in characteristics are minimal except for foliage size and inflorescence length. The indeterminate paniculate inflorescence continues to elongate and seemingly flowers "forever." Flowers are formed on new growth so pruning to remove spent flowers and tidying the plant results in more flowers. Extremely easy to root from cuttings.

Buddleia salvifolia (L.) Lam., (bud′lē-à sal-vi-fō′li-à), South African Sage Wood, is a surprisingly cold hardy

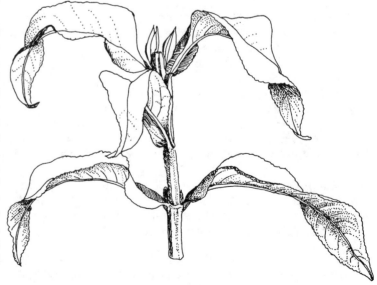

upright oval to haystack-shaped species with 2 to 4″(5″) long, lanceolate, undulating-surfaced, sage-textured and colored (gray-green), round-toothed leaves. Leaves are rugose, reticulate below, and covered with white (gray-brown on veins) tomentum. The stems are quadrangular and brownish tomentose. The single plant in the Georgia trials has grown 7′ high and 5′ wide in 2 years. The pale lavender-lilac flowers open on the previous year's wood. They are minimally fragrant and not particularly showy. Might be a useful foliage plant in a border or container. All visitors to our trials have become enamored with the foliage. South Africa. Introduced 1873. Zone 7.

Buddleia × ***weyeriana*** Weyer, (bud'lē-ȧ wāy-ēr-i-ā'nȧ), represents hybrids between *B. globosa* × *B. davidii* var. *magnifica* by Mr. Van de Weyer in 1914 in Dorset, England. This is superior to *B. globosa* for general adaptability and is offered in the United States, especially the form 'Sungold' ('Sun Gold'), a sport of 'Golden Glow', with yellow-orange, fragrant flowers, flowers occur in interrupted patterns along the length of the inflorescence rather than in a continuum like most *B. davidii* types. This has been one of the worst performers in the Athens area, however, on the Olympic Peninsula, Washington, plants were robust and large-flowered. Due to the nature of the parents, the flower colors in the seedlings can be quite variable. 'Golden Glow' is a strong-growing form with pale yellowish orange flowers with a trace of lilac (from *B. davidii*). 'Moonlight' has cream-yellow flowers with a trace of lilac-pink and a dark orange throat. 'Elstead Hybrid' produces pale apricot flowers with a brown throat. Hardier and more adaptable than *B. globosa*. My technical understanding of this hybrid was minimal until recently. Having grown 'Sungold' and watched nursery colleagues do the same, the knowledge base has increased. In leaf and habit the effect is very much *B. davidii*. The flowers are not really in 3/4″ diameter heads like *B. globosa* but irregularly and loosely distributed along the peduncle of the inflorescence. The inflorescences are not as full as the typical *B. davidii* types. In the heat of the Southeast, the flowers appear to brown quickly and are not as vibrant, robust or floriferous as the *B. davidii* types. For color effect it is worth considering. In our Georgia trials 'Sungold' was always the laggard although one plant is 8′ by 8′ in 2 years. In 1995, I purchased several *Buddleia* taxa at the Crathes Castle and Garden, Scotland, plant center. 'E.H. Wilson' is a lavender-purple type and I wanted the name and plant for the garden. When it flowered, the color was golden yellow, so obviously the plant I purchased was not 'E.H. Wilson'. The clone has been christened 'Honeycomb' (see under *B. davidii*). Plants were given to a few producers and all commented on the larger flowers, better foliage, and more vigorous constitution compared to 'Sungold'. Variety *wilsonii* is described as having delicate pink panicles, narrow leaves, and large individual flowers with reflexed margins to the lobes.

ADDITIONAL NOTES: Many botanical varieties of *B. davidii* are spread over central and western China. Most of the garden varieties descended from seed Wilson collected in Hupeh and Szechuan during the years 1900–1908. There are many other *Buddleia* species but none, to my mind, are as effective as the types described above for American gardens. See Maunder, *The Plantsman* 9(2):64–80 (1987), for a discussion of the tender *Buddleia* species.

Buxus microphylla Sieb. & Zucc. [now *B. sinica* (Rehd. & Wils.) M. Cheng var. *insularis* (Nakai) M. Cheng]— Littleleaf Box or Boxwood
(buk′sus mī-krō-fil′ȧ)

FAMILY: Buxaceae

LEAVES: Opposite, simple, evergreen, obovate to lance-obovate, 1/3 to 1″ long, 1/6 to 1/3″ wide, rounded or emarginate, cuneate, entire, usually medium green often turning yellowish brown in winter.

BUDS: Small, solitary, sessile, ovoid with 1 to 2 pairs of visible, scarcely specialized scales.

STEM: Slender, green, flat, grooved between each pair of leaves, stems appear sharply quadrangular, glabrous.

SIZE: 3 to 4′ in height by 3 to 4′ in spread, report from Minnesota noted 6′ high plant, this size is amazing because of northern latitude.

HARDINESS: Zone 6 to 9, although some cultivars of the variety *koreana* will grow in Zone 4.

HABIT: Evergreen, much-branched, compact, dense, rounded or broad-rounded shrub.

RATE: Slow.

TEXTURE: Medium-fine in all seasons.

LEAF COLOR: Medium green in summer changing to repulsive yellow-green-brown in winter.

FLOWERS: Apetalous, in axillary or terminal clusters consisting of a terminal pistillate flower and several staminate flowers, March–April; not showy but fragrant; bees are quite active when this species is in flower.

FRUIT: Three-celled capsule, each valve 2-horned, seeds shining black.

CULTURE: Transplant balled-and-burlapped or from a container into well-drained soil; responds well to mulching with peat or leaf mold for roots require cool moist conditions; full sun or light to moderate shade; protect from drying winds and severe low temperatures; often necessary to shade newly transplanted plants from summer sun; boxwood should not be cultivated around since it is a surface rooter; in the South partial shade is preferable, although plants, especially of the variety *japonica*, appear to prosper in full sun.

DISEASES AND INSECTS: Canker, blight, leaf spots, root rot, winter injury and sun scald (physiological injury), mealybugs, scales, boxwood psyllid, boxwood leaf miner, giant hornet, boxwood webworm, nematodes and boxwood mite; most of these problems are more prevalent on *Buxus sempervirens*; root rot (*Phytophthora*) is a problem in inadequately drained soils and is usually manifested by an off-color to the foliage.

LANDSCAPE VALUE: Excellent as hedge plant, for foundations, edging situations, parterres, formal gardens; too often pruned into a green meatball and allowed to haunt a foundation planting; if used properly boxwood can be a superb plant, this species and in particular the better cultivars have been utilized for every imaginable landscape purpose, a particular planting in downtown Philadelphia was a broad mass all pruned to a uniform height forming a tall ground cover.

CULTIVARS: Considerable confusion relative to parental status of the following cultivars. I attempted to place them in the proper category based on the literature and observations. Griffiths treats four varieties—*insularis* (Nak.) Hatsusima, *japonica* (Muell-Arg) Rehd. & Wils., *koreana* Nak., and *sinica* Rehd. & Wils. Unfortunately, his placement of cultivars within the varieties does not agree with the American literature and nursery naming. I have left the taxonomic designations as per the 1990 edition but listed Griffiths at the end of each description.

'Compacta'—Small, dense, slow-growing form with excellent dark green foliage; 47-year-old plant is 1' by 4'.

'Curly Locks'—Have seen this rather unusual twisted branched form in Georgia on occasion; can be espaliered on walls, fences, etc.; makes a dense mound of yellow-green foliage, 3 by 4' high; supposedly a sport of 'Compacta'.

'Green Beauty' (var. *japonica* form)—Compact habit and glossy dark green foliage color; less hardy than 'Winter Gem', considered hardy to -10°F; holds color in cold weather and is greener than var. *japonica* in the heat of the summer; var. *sinica* in Griffiths.

'Green Pillow'—Similar to 'Compacta' except the leaves are twice as large, deep dull green, 1' by 1 1/2'.

'Hanlim'—Selection for good hardiness and persistent green foliage in winter, selected from about 60,000 seedlings, introduced 1990.

var. *japonica*—Sometimes listed as a species but doubtfully so; have seen plants labeled as *B. japonica* but could not be sure if they were correct; 3 to 6' high loose rounded shrub, stems glabrous, winged; leaves 1/3 to 1" long, and often as broad, rounded or notched at apex, cuneate at base, lustrous dark green; flowers (occur at terminals) more freely than the species; better adapted to Southeast; heat and nematode resistant; early leafing often by late March in Athens; new growth may be injured by late spring frosts; on a mid-February day Bob Hoffman, Fairweather Gardens, and I were touring the Founder's Garden on the Georgia campus and I pointed out the lustrous dark green leaf planting 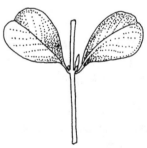 of var. *japonica*, 14 paces away was a parterre garden with off-color, orangish bronze *Buxus sempervirens*; moral—we attempt historically correct plantings at the expense of pragmatism. Japan. Introduced 1860. Zone 6 to 9.

'Kingsville Dwarf' (var. *japonica* form)—Compact and slow-growing form selected by Mr. Henry Hohman, Kingsville, MD, tiny leaves 1/5 to 1/4" long, used in bonsai, will revert.

var. *koreana* Nak.—Extremely hardy geographical variety of the species; the foliage turns yellowish brown in the winter; leaves 1/2 to 3/4" long, obovate to elliptic-oblong, margins inrolled, venation scarcely visible in upper surface, young stems and petioles hairy; somewhat loose and open in habit and twice as wide as high at maturity; grows 2 to 2 1/2' high; the best choice for northern areas; has survived some miserable winters (-20 to -25°F); Zone 4; probably correctly *B. sinica* (Rehd. and Wils.) M. Cheng var. *insularis* (Nak.) M. Cheng.

'Morris Midget' (var. *japonica* form)—Low-mounded, slow-growing, 1' by 1 1/2' after many years, yellow-green notched leaves; var. *sinica* Griffiths.

'National'—Derived from var. *japonica*, selected for upright habit, faster growth, lustrous foliage, leaves 1" long by 5/8" wide, oval, have seen it in one Georgia nursery and was not impressed, excessive leaf discoloration in January, 15' by 15' in 35 years.

'Pincushion' (var. *koreana* form)—Low-mounded, 1 1/2' by 2' with light green foliage that turns bronze in winter, hardy form, leaves rounded ovate, 1/3" long.

'Richardii' (var. *japonica* form)—Darker green, larger leaves notched at apex, more vigorous to 6' and hardy to 0°F; var. *sinica* Griffiths.

var. *sinica*—Although not exactly sure of the status of this variety, I present it for the reader since var. *koreana* and var. *japonica* are common in commerce; the former in the North, the latter in the South; the Chinese Box grows 3 to 18' in its native habitat; the 3/4 to 1 1/4" long, ovate to obovate, lustrous green leaves have visible venation on the upper surface (unlike var. *koreana*), emarginate at apex with petiole and basal midrib puberulous. Introduced about 1900. Zone 6 to 9.

'Sunnyside' ('Sunnyside Largeleaf') (considered a form of var. *japonica*)—A large leaf form with good winter hardiness, remains green with a slight bronze cast during the winter; had a plant in my Georgia garden and was not impressed by performance; developed bronze-yellow-green winter color even in Zone 7b; will grow 6' by 6'; var. *koreana* Griffiths.

'Tall Boy' (var. *koreana* form)—Loose upright to rounded form, 4 by 5', medium green foliage, becoming bronze-brown in winter.

'Tide Hill'—Cultivar of the var. *koreana* with green foliage all winter, shiny lanceolate leaves; 20-year-old plant is 15" by 5'.

'Winter Beauty'—Good mounded form, 3' by 4', with dark green foliage; have seen in a windswept nursery situation in northern Illinois and the foliage was a coppery green, no broadleaf evergreen maintains "normal" leaf color under those conditions; a seedling selection of *B. microphylla* var. *koreana*.

'Winter Gem' (var. *koreana* form)—Apparently quite comparable to 'Wintergreen' with all the traits of that cultivar although described in another catalog as having rich deep velvety green foliage; grows 2' high; might be a rename, listed in 1989 Monrovia catalog.

'Wintergreen' (var. *koreana* form)—The original introduction constituted more than one clone and multiple plants were released by Scarff Nursery Co., New Carlisle, OH; today the plant I see labeled as 'Wintergreen' is quite uniform and suspect the best form has been selected and propagated over the years; this is a handsome light green, small-leaved form that performs superbly in colder climates; at the Chicago Botanic Garden, Glencoe, IL, considerable use has been made of this fine selection for low hedges and the like; in warmer climates where other forms can be grown it is probably not preferable; listed as 5' by 5' but in northern landscapes usually 3 to 4' by 3 to 4'.

var. *koreana* × *B. sempervirens* hybrids

A handsome and valuable group of boxwoods with the hardiness and compactness of var. *koreana* and the good leaf color of *B. sempervirens*. Introduced by Sheridan Nursery Co., Oakville, Ontario, Canada, the plants have found application in northern landscapes and are now widely grown. Resulted from open-pollinated plants grown row-to-row at Oakville Nursery in the 1960's. Sheridan Nursery selected 60 seedlings from the many thousands. In 1966, they chose three for release in the early 70's. Have observed all selections at Royal Botanic Garden, Hamilton, Ontario, in December and was impressed by retention of dark green color. The following are selections from this cross:

Chicagoland Green® ('Glencoe')—I have no face-to-leaf knowledge of this taxon, however, LeDuc et al., *Landscape Plant News* 7(4):9–10 (1996), reported this as a hybrid between *B. sempervirens* × *B. koreana* that held the best winter color among 'Winter Gem', 'Green Mountain', 'Green Velvet', and 'Green Beauty' at Manhattan and Wichita, KS in 1995–96 where temperatures dropped to -13 and -10°F, respectively, with dry desiccating winds throughout the winter; reported as faster growing than 'Green Velvet'; compact-spreading habit 2 to 3' high.

'Green Gem'—A green mound, actually described by introducer as a perfect round ball, hardier than var. *koreana* 'Winter Beauty', slow-growing, requires little pruning, deep green foliage through winter, 2 by 2'; roots easily and makes a salable plant faster than *B. m.* var. *koreana*; also, sets very little fruit compared to var. *koreana*; in Georgia trials has been extremely slow.

'Green Ice'—Described as super hardy and deep green all winter; blue-green flush in spring reflects strong *B. sempervirens* parentage although listed as a hybrid; glossy deep green summer foliage remains so in the hardest of winters; grows 3' by 3'; PPAF, Conard-Pyle introduction.

'Green Mountain'—Forms a perfect wide pyramidal oval, is the most upright of this group of hybrids, small dark green leaves, excellent for hedging, 5' by 3', considerable bronzing in Wichita, KS tests.

'Green Mound'—Forms an attractive mound of dark green foliage, grows 3' by 3'.

'Green Velvet'—Rounded, full-bodied, slow-growing with small dark green leaves similar to 'Green Gem', 4' by 4', second best winter color in Wichita, KS tests.

A postscript to the above is in order for in 1991, the latter 3 forms were placed in the Georgia test plots in heavy clay soil, in full sun and with maximum exposure to winter winds; all discolored with 'Green Velvet' turning orange-bronze-green, the others remaining green but still off color; however, by April they are fully green, and remain so until December; I believe these are worthy plants and if properly sited will prove outstanding; in late January 1997, I assessed winter color and 'Green Velvet' and 'Green Mountain' were dark green with a slight bronze hue; in July, 1994 at Williamstown, MA, Neils Oleson showed me a long border of 'Green Mountain' that had survived −30°F without injury; previously in Williamstown, MA, I had recorded the same cultivar surviving −22°F in 1990.

PROPAGATION: Seed apparently requires a cold period of 1 to 3 months to facilitate good germination although seed will germinate without pretreatment. Cuttings root readily anytime of year; have had good success with 1000 to 3000 ppm KIBA, quick dip, peat:perlite, mist or poly-tent; abundant literature on boxwood cutting propagation; see Dirr and Heuser, 1987; a qualification is necessary relative to rooting readily, in actuality they will root but in our work the 'Green Velvet' et al. series has taken 12 weeks; ideally take cuttings after the growth has hardened in summer.

ADDITIONAL NOTES: A new reference on boxwood by Lynn Batsdorf should be consulted for the latest nomenclatural changes. See reference under *Buxus sempervirens* cultivars.

NATIVE HABITAT: Japan, Introduced 1860.

RELATED SPECIES:

Buxus harlandii Hance., (buk′sus har-lan′dē-ī), Harland Boxwood, is occasionally seen in southern landscapes (Zone 8 to 9) and is something of a mystery as to exact identity. The form in cultivation is probably a clone from *B. microphylla* var. *sinica*. The leathery lustrous dark green evergreen 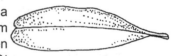 leaves are 1 1/2″ long, distinctly obovate, emarginate at apex on a 2 to 3′ high and wide, mounded shrub. A plant in the Dirr garden is now 6′ high and 6′ wide. Appears more resistant to the pests that beset *B. sempervirens*. I have grown a plant for 10 years and it has performed admirably but during the −3°F (1985) winter in Athens, the leaves were killed. Interestingly, Bean says the leaves are only 1/4″ wide but a ruler indicated the leaves on the Harland Clone in my garden were greater than 1/2″ wide at the widest point. Krüssmann mentioned that *B. harlandii* cultivated in German nurseries is probably a form of *B. microphylla* var. *japonica*. Perhaps it is a hybrid.

Buxus sempervirens L. — Common Box or Boxwood
(buk′sus sem-pēr-vī′renz)

LEAVES: Opposite, simple, evergreen, elliptic or ovate to oblong, 1/2 to 1″ long, about 1/2 as wide, obtuse or emarginate at apex, dark green above, light or yellowish green beneath, and usually lustrous on both sides; midvein on lower side wide and cream to yellowish; petiole—short and minutely hairy.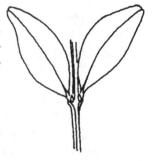

STEM: Somewhat angled (squarish) but not like *Buxus microphylla*, minutely hairy.

SIZE: 15 to 20′ in height with an equal or greater spread; can grow to 30′ but this size is rarely attained; actually makes a handsome small tree.

HARDINESS: Zone 5 to 6 depending on cultivar, to 8.

HABIT: Dense, multi-branched evergreen shrub of rounded or broad-rounded outline that holds its foliage to the ground; old, overgrown specimens in Spring Grove Cemetery, Cincinnati, OH, with 4 to 6″ diameter trunks were cut back to 1 to 2′ from the ground, developed new shoots and filled in nicely; however, the new growth is extremely sensitive to winter injury; have seen tremendous winter damage that occurred when box was pruned too late in season (August); apparently tissue never hardened properly and was literally blitzed by low temperatures.

RATE: Slow, but faster than *B. microphylla*.

TEXTURE: Medium-fine in all seasons.

LEAF COLOR: Lustrous dark green above, light or yellowish green below in all seasons; I was drinking a toddy when the lustrous dark green was penned; on occasion this is true but generally the new growth emerges a flat bluish gray-green and darkens with maturity; generally easy to differentiate between *B. microphylla* types for their new foliage is particularly waxy, glossy and light green; the new foliage of both species is terrifically sensitive to late spring frosts; will discolor in severe winters in the face of desiccating winds.

FLOWERS: Creamy yellow, in clusters developing from leaf axils, without petals, the female flower often terminal in the cluster, the male subterminal, the male with 4 sepals and 4 stamens that are longer than the sepals; female with 6 sepals and a 3-loculed ovary, flowers occur in April–May and are fragrant.

FRUIT: A 1/3″ long, 3-horned dehiscent capsule, each valve containing 2 lustrous seeds.

CULTURE: Easily transplanted; similar to *B. microphylla* except does best from Boston to North Georgia; this species has prospered in climates that do not have extremes of summer heat or winter cold; prune in late winter; appears quite adaptable; prefers limestone soils, pH 6 and greater; in a controlled study, 'Suffruticosa' grown in various lime amended media outgrew the non lime amended treatment.

DISEASES AND INSECTS: See under *B. microphylla*.

LANDSCAPE VALUE: Excellent specimen and is used extensively in East and South; good for hedges, massing, topiary work, formal gardens; might be called the "aristocrat" of the hedging plants.

CULTIVARS: There are numerous cultivars and anyone contemplating boxwood gardening should visit the U.S. National, Arnold, and J.C. Raulston Arboreta which have rather extensive collections. In my mind most cultivars are almost indistinguishable and once they are put to the shears no one can reliably separate them. There is an American Boxwood Society, P.O. Box 85, Boyce, VA 22620, that "Boxophiles" should consider joining if all other societies are full. A valuable reference on Boxwood taxonomy and culture is *Boxwood Handbook, A Practical Guide to Knowing and Growing Boxwood*, by Lynn R. Batdorf (1995), available from the Boxwood Society for $15.00.

'Angustifolia'—Tree-like in habit with leaves 1 to 1 1/4″ long, 'Longifolia' may belong here, 14′ by 12′ in 30 years.

'Arborescens'—Upright, irregular form, dark green foliage, 6′ by 3′, leaves quite large, this form or something very close surfaces in my travels, termed True Tree Boxwood, 20′ by 15′ in 40 years.

'Argenteo-variegata'—Leaves variegated with white.

'Aurea-pendula'—Large shrub, small tree with weeping branches, leaves splashed and flecked creamy yellow, 7′ by 6′ in 25 years.

'Aureo-variegata'—Leaves variegated with yellow.

'Bass'—Medium-sized, densely branched form with slightly larger foliage than 'Inglis' and the dark green color is retained through winter.

'Bullata' (also known as 'Latifolia Bullata')—Low-growing form with short blunt leaves that are decidedly dark green, 8′ by 10′.

'Elegantissima'—A rather pretty cream-margined form that I have seen used with good taste at Callaway Gardens; in dappled pine shade it presented a rather peaceful repose nestled among the bright vivid Kurume azaleas; not as vigorous as the species but certainly not docile either, probably 5 to 8′ by 5 to 8′ in 15 years; may revert and green branches should be removed; has been a reliable performer in the Dirr garden but is quite slow growing, 9′ by 1 to 1 1/2′ in 20 years.

'Graham Blandy'—Striking, narrow upright outline, very columnar, good hedging plant for tight spaces; 9′ by 1 1/2′ in 20 years; introduced from Blandy Experimental Farm in Virginia.

'Handsworthiensis'—Wide, strong-growing, upright form with dark green foliage; makes a good hedging plant, 15′ by 20′ at maturity.

'Hermann von Schrenk'—Medium green leaves, 8′ high, received highest rating from Midwest Boxwood Society.

'Inglis'—Hardy form, densely pyramidal in habit with good dark green foliage in winter; supposedly hardy to -20°F, 7′ by 6′ in 20 years.

'Myrtifolia'—Low-growing form, 4 to 5′ tall; leaves 1/3 to 3/4″ long and 1/3″ wide.

'Newport Blue'—Foliage is bluish green, habit is densely rounded; 14-year-old plant is 18″ by 3′, grows 3 to 5″ per year; selected in 1940's by Boulevard Nurseries, RI.

'Northern Beauty'—A form that survived the terrible winters of 1976–77, 77–78 with no foliage burn.

'Northern Find'—Hardy form selected from a group of plants at Cookville, Ontario, Canada, where it withstood temperatures of -30°F; doubtfully hardy to this temperature.

'Northland'—Hardy form from central New York state; 14-year-old plant is 4′ by 5′ with dark green foliage all winter.

'Pendula'—Form with pendulous branchlets that grows into a small tree, 5 1/2′ by 5′ in 30 years.

'Pullman'—Selected by W.A.P. Pullman, Chicago, IL, for incredible vigor and hardiness (-20°F); starts growth in mid-May and is not injured by late freezes; rounded, dense habit and will probably grow to about 6' in height, listed as 3' by 4'.

'Rosmarinifolia'—Low shrub with leaves 1/6 to 1/4" wide, about the smallest of any cultivar.

'Rotundifolia'—Rich bright green rounded leaves, oval-compact habit, 4' by 3', 10' by 9' in 20 years.

'Suffruticosa'—Dense, compact, slow-growing form ideal for edging; leaves quite fragrant and considered the least susceptible to box leaf miner; susceptible to nematodes; 150-year-old plants are about 3' high; this is a centuries old boxwood that is considered the standard or "True Edging" Boxwood; it can be kept a few inches high or will grow 4 to 5' after many years; if left alone it reminds of clouds fused together; leaves obovate-rounded, 1/3 to 3/4" long.

'Vardar Valley'—In the previous edition I commented on the beauty of this low-growing, flat-topped, mounded form, 2 to 3' by 4 to 5', excellent dark blue-green foliage; unfortunately, over the years it has been brow-beaten by the cold weather and even in Cincinnati was severely injured at -25°F while *B. microphylla* var. *koreana* was not injured; based on more recent observations, about -15°F (Zone 5) coincides with some injury; we have used a few plants in the Betty Johnson horticultural garden and they lacked vigor possibly because of nematodes; all developed bronze leaf condition and were removed; brought from Romania in 1935, introduced 1957.

'Variegata'—Catchall term, have seen leaves described as edged with ivory, with cream, with gold, with creamy yellow, with nice variegation, with irregular yellow blotches, merrily edged with cream; all from different sources but with the same name.

'Welleri'—Dense, broad form, 13-year-old plant is 3' by 5' and green throughout the winter; this is a good form and does well in the Midwest; originated in Michigan.

'Zehrung'—Robust dark green foliage form with a columnar growth habit.

PROPAGATION: Cuttings root readily; I use 1000 ppm IBA/50% alcohol and achieve excellent results; seeds need no pretreatment although a slight chilling will unify germination.

ADDITIONAL NOTES: Wood is of a hard, bony consistency and good for carving. The foliage has a distinctly malodorous fragrance. Boxwood through the years has been associated with formal gardens. Boxwood parterres and hedges can be seen in many of the great gardens of Europe and America. W.J. Bean put it so straightforwardly when he noted that boxwood was among the most useful of garden plants but not the most beautiful. An excellent practical article on boxwood was penned by Flint, *Horticulture* 65(3):50–59 (1987); also good reading is Creech, *American Nurseryman* 162(2):36, 39–41 (1985).

Common Box is truly a beautiful plant and is a staple of many southeastern formal gardens. Colonial Williamsburg, especially around the Governor's Mansion, offers wonderful examples of formal boxwood use. Unfortunately, culture is not without some difficulty and in the lower South, nematodes and root rot, especially in heavy clay soils, contribute to decline over time. On the Georgia campus, in a rather handsome formal boxwood garden, plants were declining badly. The entire planting was removed, soil sterilized, and new plants installed. After 12 years most plants are still vigorous although a few are developing the characteristic discoloration. The old plants had developed the bronze-yellow to orange color, started to thin out and drop leaves and lacked vigor. These are tell-tale signs that something needs to be adjusted. The root knot nematode's tell-tale symptoms are manifested by stunted roots with a bunchy dark appearance.

NATIVE HABITAT: Southern Europe, northern Africa, western Asia. Long cultivated and steeped in legend and lore. First described by Linnaeus in 1753.

Callicarpa japonica Thunb. — Japanese Beautyberry
(kal-i-kär′pȧ jȧ-pon′i-kȧ)

FAMILY: Verbenaceae

LEAVES: Opposite, simple, elliptic to ovate-lanceolate, 2 to 5" long, 1 1/2 to 2" wide, long acuminate, cuneate, serrulate, medium blue-green with yellowish glands beneath, nearly glabrous; petiole—1/6 to 1/3" long.

BUDS: Small, superposed, light gray-brown, often distinctly stalked or the uppermost developing the first season, round or fusiform-oblong, naked, or the smaller appearing to have two nearly valvate scales.

STEM: Round, slender, gray-buff, pubescent, with a purplish tinge when young, glabrous at maturity.

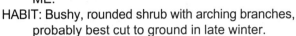

SIZE: 4 to 6′ in height by 4 to 6′ in spread; have seen plants 8 to 10′ high.

HARDINESS: Zone 5 to 8; –5 to –10°F will usually result in stem dieback, only root hardy at the Morton Arboretum, killed outright in Orono, ME.

HABIT: Bushy, rounded shrub with arching branches, probably best cut to ground in late winter.

RATE: Fast.

TEXTURE: Medium in all seasons.

LEAF COLOR: Medium blue-green in summer becoming faintly yellowish to purplish in fall; sometimes almost pinkish lavender fall color.

FLOWERS: Perfect, pink or white, appear lavender, July (Boston), many flowered cymes from axil of leaf, 1 to 1 1/2″ across, not showy, occur on new growth of the season from June to August (Athens), each flower tubular or campanulate with 4 teeth, corolla 4-lobed with 4 exserted stamens.

FRUIT: Berry-like drupe, 1/6 to 1/5″ across, violet to metallic purple; borne in rather loose 1 to 1 1/2″ diameter cymes; effective in October and longer for about 2 weeks after the leaves fall off; doubtfully as showy or as abundant as *C. americana*, *C. dichotoma*, or *C. bodinieri*; some will argue this and I have observed excellent fruit on *C. japonica* in arboreta where other seedlings or species were present; I grew this species in Georgia and it never fruited like *C. dichotoma* (which see); also *C. dichotoma* fruits consistently from year-to-year without other seedlings or species for possible cross-pollination; a group of *C. japonica* seedlings at the University's Botanical Garden have been spectacular in October through early December, perhaps cross pollination among the seedlings promoted heavy fruit set, also *Callicarpa bodinieri* 'Profusion' and *C. americana* are in close proximity; this group of *C. japonica* is sited under Loblolly Pines and has consistently produced the outstanding fruit, the other *Callicarpa* taxa mentioned also fruit heavily in the pine shade environment; have read a reference that stated beautyberries fruit more heavily when outcrossed by other seedlings or clones.

CULTURE: Readily transplanted from containers; well-drained soil; full sun or light shade; prune to within 4 to 6 to 18″ of the ground every spring as the flowers are produced on new growth; avoid excess fertility, plants *do not have* to be pruned to the ground, if in good condition simply remove dead limbs (always a few) and allow nature to take its course, plants can look ratty with age and a good approach is to rejuvenate through pruning.

DISEASES AND INSECTS: Leaf spots, black mold, and various stem diseases, none of these are serious.

LANDSCAPE VALUE: Most effective when planted in groups in the shrub border; actually makes a pleasant foliage mass and certainly the brilliant fruits demand attention in the autumn garden; the fruit is very attractive and unusual in color among woody plants; best to treat as an herbaceous perennial in northern areas.

CULTIVARS:

'Heavy Berry'—Extremely fruitful clone.

'Leucocarpa'—White fruits, good looking plant, not readily available in commerce, certainly less offensive in color than the species; leaves of this form are lighter green than the species.

var. *luxurians*—Large fruit clusters but not as cold hardy as the species.

var. *taquetii*—Narrower and smaller leaves, tiny lavender-purple fruits.

PROPAGATION: Softwood cuttings root readily in sand under mist, in fact, all *Callicarpa* root readily from softwood cuttings, roots will form in 7 to 14 days; seeds require cold, moist stratification.

NATIVE HABITAT: Japan. Introduced 1845.

RELATED SPECIES:

Callicarpa americana L. — American Beautyberry

LEAVES: Opposite, simple, elliptic-ovate to ovate-oblong, 3 1/2 to 6″ long, 1/2 as wide, acuminate, cuneate, crenate serrate, medium green and pubescent above, tomentose and glandular below; petiole—1/2 to 1″ long.

STEM: Four-sided or subterete, covered with dense, tomentose, light brown pubescence.

Callicarpa americana, (kal-i-kär′på à-mer-i-kā′nà), American Beauty-berry or French Mulberry, is a rather coarse, 3 to 8′(10′) high, loose, open shrub that is found throughout the Southeast. The 3 1/2 to 6″(8″) long, extremely pubescent, anemic medium green leaves are the largest and coarsest of the species discussed here. The light lavender-pink flowers are borne in axillary cymes on new growth from June into August (Athens). The 1/4″ diameter, violet to magenta fruits are produced in profusion. The nodes of the stems are literally encircled by the fruit clusters. Fruit ripening proceeds over a long time period. Makes a good shrub for naturalizing or massing. Have seen it used under pine trees with excellent effect. Denser and more fruitful in sun. Does better with ample root moisture. When overgrown cut back as described under *C. japonica*. Variety *lactea* is white-fruited. Considerable variation in fruit coloration and opportunities exist for selection. At the University's Botanical Garden the white-fruited form grows next to a light lavender-fruited form. I suspect the seedling populations from these forms would yield interesting progeny. 'Lactea' also has white flowers and my observations indicate the lighter colored the fruit the lighter the flower color. This could be a worthwhile selection criteria for segregating seedling populations. 'Russell Montgomery' is a white-fruited form supposedly more attractive than 'Lactea'. Dr. Kim Krahl, former graduate student, found that cleaned seed provided 90 days cold moist stratification,

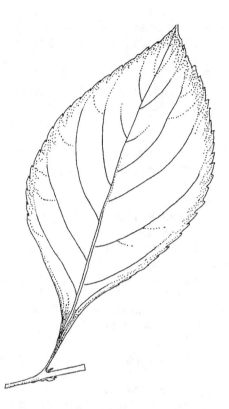

germinated in high percentages. I suspect fruits that remain on the plant into December have received sufficient cold to the degree that seeds have self-stratified in the pulpy matrix. In the past, seeds have germinated without pretreatment. There is also interest in this species for cut branches because of the magnificent fruit colors. Southwest Maryland to North Carolina, Arkansas, south to Mexico and the West Indies. Zone (6)7 to 11.

Callicarpa bodinieri Lév. — Bodinier Beautyberry
LEAVES: Opposite, simple, narrow oval or lanceolate, 2 to 5″ long, 1 to 2 1/4″ wide, acuminate, cuneate, denticulate or dentate, dull dark blue-green above and slightly pubescent, distinctly so beneath, particularly on veins; petiole—1/5 to 1/2″ long.

Callicarpa bodinieri, (kal-i-kär′på bō-din-i-er′ī), Bodinier Beautyberry, is rarely cultivated in American gardens, but the British consider it the finest species for their gardens. The shrub reaches 6 to 10′ at maturity and has erect-arching branches much more distinct than *C. americana* or *C. dichotoma* in this character. Flowers are lilac and occur in 1 to 1 1/2″ diameter cymes on new growth of the season, but flowers of seedling plants vary from lavender to rich purple. The 1/8 to 1/6″ diameter fruit is a glossy bluish lilac and a white-fruited form also exists. The fruits of this species are borne in a fashion similar to *C. japonica* and in my opinion do not make the best

show. The infructescences of both species are loose and the fruits do not seem to persist as well as *C. americana* or *C. dichotoma*. *Callicarpa japonica* can be distinguished from *C. bodinieri* by its narrower glabrous leaves and glabrous inflorescences. Variety *giraldii* (Hesse ex Rehd.) Rehd. is glabrous above and less pubescent beneath. 'Profusion' (a Dutch selection) is a more fruitful form with 1/6″ wide violet fruits that occur 30 to 40 together per infructescence. Abundant fruits even on young plants. New leaves bronze-purple and turn a pinkish purple in fall. This has performed well in the Athens area and is superior to run-of-the-litter *C. japonica* for quantity and quality of fruit. Plants are upright-arching, fully 10′ high. Szechuan, Hupeh, Shensi provinces of China. Introduced 1887. Zone 6 to 8.

Callicarpa dichotoma (Lour.) K. Koch — Purple Beautyberry
LEAVES: Opposite, simple, elliptic to obovate, 1
to 3″ long, 1/2 as wide, acuminate, cuneate,
coarsely serrate except at apex and base,
bright medium green, glabrous above, glandular and sparingly pubescent beneath;
petiole—1/8″ long.

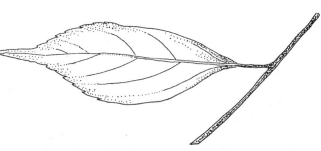

Callicarpa dichotoma, (kal-i-kär′pȧ dī-kot′ō-mȧ),
Purple Beautyberry, is the most graceful and
refined of the species. The species grows 3
to 4′(6′) high with a slightly greater spread. The long slender branches arch and touch the ground at their
tips. The bright medium green leaves are borne in one plane along the stem rather than radiating, as is
true for *C. bodinieri* and *C. japonica*. The small, pinkish lavender, 3/4″ diameter cymes are borne on stalks
above the foliage from June to August (Athens). The 1/8 to 1/6″ diameter, lilac-violet fruits are perfectly
displayed, with the foliage acting as a foil. A white-fruited form, var. *albifructus*, is also quite attractive.
Fruits are colorful by early to mid-September in Athens. I had a plant of *C. dichotoma* by the driveway that
was raised at Illinois from seed which I received from Smith College Botanic Garden. Three plants resulted
and the one I brought south proved to be a bountiful fruitier without the presence of other plants for cross-
pollination. In fruit, it drew much comment with the ultimate being, "What is it?" I took several rooted
cuttings to a regional American Rhododendron Society meeting and after presenting a slide lecture on this
and other plants the Society auctioned off the rooted cuttings for $7.00 each. I have grown or observed
all the species listed herein and consider *C. dichotoma* the best garden form. Additional comments are
warranted since the plant in my garden has been removed for newer items. The species is the hardiest
of those mentioned herein with stem dieback at Orono, ME. Also, 'Albifructus' ('Albescens', var. *albifructus*) grows larger than the species and one specimen at the University's Botanical Garden was 8′ high.
The white fruits discolor (brown) much sooner than the magenta fruits. 'Early Amethyst' produces
prodigious quantities of small, lilac fruits, graceful arching habit, 3 to 4′ high and wide. 'Issai' fruits heavily
as a young plant. A small plant in the evaluation plots bore a heavy crop of fruits in 1996 and in 1997 with
ripening fruits evident by mid-August. Like the other species this is an easy plant to grow. Eastern and
central China, Japan. Introduced 1857. Zone 5 to 8.

ADDITIONAL NOTES: There are few fruiting shrubs that can compete with the beautyberries in September–
October when they are at their fruiting best. When used in mass the effect is spectacular. Should be
treated as herbaceous perennials in most northern gardens. Other species have surfaced in recent years
but it is doubtful whether they can nudge the current crop of good to excellent garden species from their
perches. Something akin to 140 species of *Callicarpa* occur worldwide. *Callicarpa acuminata* Roxb. (8′
high with small, shiny, very dark purple fruits); *C. cathyana* Chang (mauve-purple fruits); *C. kwantungensis*
Chun (white flowers, 10″ leaves); *C. mollis* Sieb. & Zucc. (dull purple fruits); *C. pedunculata* R. Br. (purple
to dark violet fruits, long persistent); *C. pedunculata* 'Alba' (white-fruited); *C. pilosissima* Maxim. (large
leaves like *Hydrangea sargentiana* and lavender flowers); *C. rubella* Lindl. (pink flowers and rose-red
purple fruits); *C. shikokiana* Makino (lavender flowers with yellow stamens in 2″ diameter cymes, dark pink
aging to dark purple fruits); and *C. tosaensis* Makino (Yukushima, Japan) are mentioned.

Callistemon citrinus (Curtis) Skeels (*C. lanceolatus* DC.) — Lemon Bottlebrush
(kal-i-stē′mon si-trī′nus)

FAMILY: Myrtaceae
LEAVES: Alternate, simple, evergreen, lanceolate, 1 to 3″(4″) long,
1/8 to 3/4″ wide, acute, entire, reddish when young, finally bright
green, midrib and axillary veins elevated.

SIZE: 10 to 15′ high and wide, when pruned and staked 20 to 25′.
HARDINESS: Zone 8b to 11; have witnessed severe damage at 11°F
along the Georgia coast in 1983–84, no preconditioning occurred
ahead of the low temperatures.

HABIT: Large shrub or small tree with almost needle-like, evergreen foliage and rather graceful branches.
RATE: Medium to fast.
TEXTURE: Fine throughout the seasons.
LEAF COLOR: Coppery new growth, then lustrous bright to dark green in summer, discolors a degree (mauve to purple-green) in winter, foliage lemon scented if crushed.
FLOWERS: Perfect, axillary in bottlebrush-like pseudo-terminal spikes, 5 petals and 5 sepals, numerous stamens and the anthers and filaments the showy parts of the flower, longer than petals, bright crimson, borne in 4 to 5″ long, 2 to 2 1/2″ wide inflorescences, extremely showy, have seen flowers in December, March and summer during visits to Orlando; have read West Coast references that report flowers are produced in cycles; a few Florida references point to spring flowering, when flowers appear on the new growth of the season; good hummingbird attractant.
FRUITS: Woody, globose, 1/4″ capsules that persist on the branches, appear as small fat buttons along the stem and can remain for several years.
CULTURE: Transplant from containers, water regularly during early years of establishment, dry to moist, well-drained soil, chlorosis can be problematic, full sun, requires protection in more northern locations, often used as a container plant and must be protected in a cool house during winter, provide ample fertilizer in split applications over the growing season, displays moderate salt tolerance.
DISEASE AND INSECTS: Mites, scales, nematodes, witches' broom.
LANDSCAPE VALUE: Freestanding shrub, screens, grouping, masses and containers, beautiful for flower effect, has been used in hedges, of the *Callistemon* species this is the most heat, cold and soil tolerant.
CULTIVARS:
   'Burning Bush'—Compact rounded habit, 4′, dark green narrow pointed leaves, red flowers.
   'Compacta'—Grows 4′ by 4′, with smaller red flowers.
   'Hannah Ray'—Bright orange-red flowers, semi-weeping habit, 4′.
   'Jeffersii'—Stiff branching, narrow short leaves, red-purple flowers fade to lavender, 6′ by 4′. 'Mauve Mist' may be the same.
   'Little John'—Compact bushy hybrid, 3′ high, 5′ wide, blue-green narrow leaves, soft pubescent new growth, blood red flowers in spring into summer.
   'Splendens' (var. *splendens* Stapf.)—Flowers bright crimson, stamens 1 1/2 to 2″ long, flowers heavily as a young plant, raised from Australian seed at Kew Gardens.
PROPAGATION: Seeds germinate without pretreatment and grow off rapidly; about 6 years past, I received seeds of 4 *Callistemon* species and all germinated; the plants were outplanted and survived 4°F with some shoot dieback, all regrew and I eagerly await the first flowers; disappointingly all appear to be genetically and phenotypically the same and are consistently injured by cold.
NATIVE HABITAT: From the coasts of Australia, New South Wales, Victoria, and Queensland. Introduced 1788.

RELATED SPECIES: Without question the various species are difficult to separate as young plants. In fact the four species grown from Wisley seed mentioned above are virtually identical. In February 1995, I examined leaves and stems of the seed-grown plants and was unable to differentiate between and among them.

Callistemon linearis DC., (kal-i-stē′mon lin′ē-ēr-us), Narrow-leaved Bottlebrush, is a 6 to 8′(15′) high and 5′ wide shrub with linear leaves up to 5″ long and 1/10″ wide, grooved on the upper surface. Inflorescence 4 to 5″ long, 2″ wide, crimson stamens, gold anthers. New South Wales. Zone 9 to 10.

Callistemon rigidus R. Br., (kal-i-stē′mon rij′i-dus), Stiff Bottlebrush, is a small to medium shrub to 8′, perhaps to 15′, with 10′ spread, leaves gray-green (occasionally purplish), linear to linear-lanceolate, up to 6″ long, 1/4″ wide, sharp pointed, not grooved. Inflorescences 3 to 4″ long, 1/2 to 1″ wide, filaments dark red, anthers dark brown, spring and summer. Considered one of the hardier species. Not as graceful as other species. Quite drought tolerant. New South Wales, Queensland. Zone (8)9 to 11.

Callistemon salignus (Sm.) DC., (kal-i-stē′mon sȧ-līg′nus), is a large shrub or small tree to 20 to 25′ high, with new growth bright pink to copper, willow-shaped, 2 to 3″ long mature leaves, green-white, light yellow to pink flowers in 1 1/2 to 3″ long clusters, and papery white bark. Variety *viridiflora* has green-yellow flowers. Australia. Zone 9 to 10.

Callistemon sieberi DC., (kal-i-stē′mon sī-bir′-ī), Alpine Bottlebrush, is a spreading loose arching shrub usually in the 6 to 10′ range under cultivation, to 15′ in the wild. Leaves linear, thick, 1/2 to 1″ long, 1/10″ wide, closely packed along the stems, glossy dark green. The cream to yellow (light yellow) flowers appear in 1 to 6″ long, 3/4 to 11/4″ wide inflorescences. Have seen this in flower at Lanhydrock in the southwest of England during June. Appears the most cold hardy of the species described herein. Mountains of southeastern Australia. Zone 7 to 9.

Callistemon speciosus (Sims) DC., (kal-i-stē′mon spē-si-ō′sus), has deep red flowers, dense dark green foliage, leaves turn purple in winter. Australia. Zone 9 to 10.

Callistemon viminalis (Sol. ex Gaertn.) G. Don ex Loud., (kal-i-stē′mon vim-i-nal′is), Weeping Bottlebrush, is a round headed, 20 to 25′ by 20 to 25′ weeping tree that produces bright red, 2 to 8″ long, 1 to 2 1/2″ wide inflorescences. The lanceolate, light green leaves average 1 to 2 1/2″(6″) long, 1/5 to 2/5″ wide. The habit is particularly graceful and several notable plants at Disney's Magic Kingdom, Orlando, FL have been appreciated by millions. Flowers normally appear spring (May–July) but I have seen flowers in December (Orlando). 'Captain Cook' is a compact form, 4′ high and wide, deep crimson flowers. 'McCaskillii' is dense, vigorous with better flower color and form. 'Red Cascade' has pendulous branches and rose-red flowers in abundance, 20 to 25′ high, 15′ wide. Australia. Probably the least cold hardy and only suitable for Zone 9 to 11.

Calluna vulgaris (L.) Hull — Scotch Heather
(ka-lū′nȧ vul-gā′ris)

FAMILY: Ericaceae
LEAVES: Opposite, simple, evergreen, scale-like, 4-ranked, giving a squarish shape to the shoot, sessile, keeled, oblong-ovate, 1/25 to 1/8″ long, sagittate at base, puberulous or nearly glabrous, closely packed, appearing almost scale-like.
BUDS: Small, solitary, sessile, angularly globose, with about 3 scales.
STEM: Very slender, terete; pith—very small, roundish, continuous.

SIZE: 4 to 24″(30″) in height; spread 2′ or more.
HARDINESS: Zone 4 to 6(7); some winterkill depending on cultivar in Orono, ME; survival might be a function of snow cover.
HABIT: Upright branching, small evergreen ground cover with dense, leafy ascending branches forming thick mats; old plants become unkempt and need an occasional pruning to keep them respectable.
RATE: Slow.
TEXTURE: Fine in all seasons.
LEAF COLOR: Medium green in summer; winter color varies from green to bronze; cultivars may be silver, yellow to red.
FLOWERS: Perfect, rosy to purplish pink, urn-shaped sepals showy part of 1/4″ long flower, 4-lobed corolla; borne in 1 to 12″ long racemes in July–September; exquisite, dainty, refined plants especially when in flower; bees are especially fond of the flowers and the honey they give is regarded as special quality.
   Calluna is a long day plant judging from the time it flowers. Research, *Acta Horticulturae* 205:219–224 (1987), showed the critical photoperiod for flowering was between 12–16 hours. Also temperatures in excess of 57°F, applied during initiation and development, encouraged flowering and increased the number of flowers produced.
FRUIT: Four-valved, 1/10″ long capsule, October, not ornamental.
CULTURE: Move as a container-grown plant in spring; prefers acid (pH 6 or less), sandy, organic, moist, perfectly drained soils; avoid sweeping winds as plants are very susceptible to drying; full sun or partial shade, however, plants do not flower as profusely in shade; prefers low fertility soils, otherwise become ratty looking; do not over fertilize, prune in early spring before new growth starts; do not cultivate soil around plants; mulch and water during dry periods; Raulston reported a 20 to 25% loss per year in the Raleigh, NC area.
DISEASES AND INSECTS: Japanese beetle, two-spotted mite, oyster shell scale, *Rhizoctonia* spp.
LANDSCAPE VALUE: Good ground cover plant, edging, rock garden; excellent flowers and foliage put this plant at the top of my ground cover list; fastidious as to soil requirements and attention to cultural details

is necessary; realistically, because of soil requirements, this will never become a mass-market commercial ground cover like ivy, liriope, vinca, pachysandra, and wintercreeper; I have watched a number of plants die probably from excessive care and definitely too much water.

CULTIVARS: Where does it stop?! In the 1990 edition I mentioned a report that stated there were 663 heather cultivars with 338 in private gardens. Griffiths reported over 1000 cultivars. All of this is amazing because *Calluna vulgaris* is a monotypic species and the variants have arisen within the genetic boundaries of one species. The species is beautiful in flower and foliage. During my Illinois days, many seedlings were raised and planted in peat-amended medium. Their performance was exemplary and, by rooting cuttings, plants were distributed to gardening friends. Since it is hopeless to list cultivars and do any sort of justice, I refer the reader to the following literature:

Chapple, F.J. 1952. *The Heather Garden*. W.H. and L. Collingridge LTD. London. Covers *Calluna*, *Daboecia* and *Erica* with numerous cultivar descriptions.

Knight, F.P. 1976. *Heaths and Heathers*. Wisley Handbook No. 3. RHS. Woking, Surrey, England.

Metheny, D. 1991. *Hardy Heather Species*. Frontier Publishing. Seaside, Oregon. Fine book featuring author's 55 years of experience cultivating heather. Related genera also featured.

Proudley, B. and V. Proudley. 1983. *Heathers in Color*. Blandford Press. Dorset, England. Significant color of good quality which adds to the book's pleasure. Includes *Calluna*, *Daboecia* and *Erica* with descriptions of cultivars.

Underhill, T.L. 1971. *Heaths and Heathers*. David and Charles. Newton Abbot, England. Newer and more detailed concerning cultivar descriptions. Thirty-three pages of *Calluna vulgaris* cultivars presented. I counted 27 cultivars with the 'alba' prefix; many were synonyms but it affords some idea of possible similar selections. Appears to be the most complete.

van de Laar, Harry. 1975. *The Heather Garden*. Collins. London.

A group of heathers that I knew nothing about is terminal Bud-Flowering Heathers. The flowers remain closed, go unpollinated and do not set fruit. They retain their color well into winter. Apparently they were known in Holland in the 1920's and 1930's. In 1972 five cultivars were introduced from Holland and more recently three from Germany. See *The Garden* 119(11):543 (1994) for specifics.

PROPAGATION: Seed should be sown on peat moss; there is no dormancy and germination takes place in 2 to 3 weeks; I have raised many *Calluna* plants this way; softwood cuttings treated with 1000 ppm IBA quick dip, rooted in 2 to 3 weeks in a peat:perlite medium under mist.

ADDITIONAL NOTES: The moors of northern England and hills of Scotland are covered by the heathers and heaths (*Erica cinerea*) and become beautiful in late summer and autumn. *Calluna vulgaris* was everywhere in evidence in the Yorkshire Dales National Park, England. Bonnie, Katie, Matt, Susy and I picnicked among the heather on an early August day, the flowers just starting to show pink, the sky a rich blue, the clouds drifting across the countryside. Wonderful memories!

Over the years of visiting European gardens, I have returned to the United States with a much greater appreciation for this species and its garden uses. Perhaps the finest display occurs in Mr. Adrian Bloom's garden, Foggy Bottom, at Bressingham. He has skillfully integrated heathers, heaths, conifers, deciduous shrubs, small trees to produce unbelievable summer and even more striking winter combinations. Certainly a garden worth visiting. Several notable collections of heathers and heaths include Wisley and Edinburgh Botanic Garden. Wisley holds a large collection as does Bells Cherrybank Garden in Perth, Scotland. The latter is new but well-designed and focused on *Calluna*, *Erica*, *Daboecia*, et al. My colleague, Al Armitage, and I visited the garden in March and June, 1996. We were overwhelmed by the flower and foliage colors of *Erica* and *Calluna*.

A good nursery source for *Calluna* and *Erica* is Rock Spray Nursery, P.O. Box 693, Truro, MA, 02666-0693. I counted 46 different heathers and about 10 heaths.

NATIVE HABITAT: *Calluna vulgaris* is found in Europe, Asia Minor, and has naturalized in northeastern North America. Cultivated for centuries.

Calocedrus decurrens (Torr.) Florin. (formerly *Libocedrus decurrens* Torr.) — California
Incensecedar
(kal-ō-sed′rus de-kēr′enz)

FAMILY: Cupressaceae

LEAVES: In 4's, closely pressed, equal in size, oblong-obovate, apex finely pointed and free, narrowing to base, lustrous dark green; on ultimate branches about 1/4″ long; on main shoots about 1/2″ long, lateral pair boat-shaped, almost wholly ensheathing the facial pairs; glandular, emitting an aromatic odor when crushed.

STEM: Branchlets flattened, terminating in dense, fan-like sprays in which the ultimate branches point forward at an acute angle.

SIZE: 30 to 50′ high by 8 to 10′ wide; can grow to 125 to 150′ high in the wild; national champion is 152′ by 49′ in Marble Mountains Wilderness, CA.

HARDINESS: Zone 5 to 8.

HABIT: Stiff or narrowly columnar in youth, very regular in outline, with a distinct formal character even in old age; a beautiful conifer that is often confused with arborvitae; the typical form in cultivation is 'Columnaris' or at least a seed derived form that is essentially narrow-columnar; Longwood Gardens has one of the better plantings of this form in the eastern states; in Athens, and throughout the Southeast, is a form with an oval-oblong head; one large 70 to 80′ specimen has a 25′ to 30′ spread; van Gelderen and van Hoey Smith in *Conifers* mention that plants in the northern part of the range are more columnar than those further south.

RATE: Slow-medium, in proper soil and atmosphere may grow 50 to 70′ after 30 to 50 years, have read estimates of 2′ per year once established.

TEXTURE: Medium.

BARK: Thin, smooth, and grayish green or scaly and tinged with red on young stems; on old trunks—thick (3 to 8″), yellowish brown to cinnamon-red, fibrous, deeply and irregularly furrowed.

LEAF COLOR: Shiny dark green on both surfaces, borne in vertical sprays; holds color well in winter months, pungently fragrant in warm weather.

FLOWERS: Monoecious, male-oblong with 12 to 16 decussate stamens.

FRUIT: Cones flattened, 3/4 to 1″ long, 1/4 to 1/3″ wide at base, tapered, yellowish brown to reddish brown when ripe in early autumn, remaining on the tree until spring, lowest pair of cone-scales half as long as the others, seeds 1/3″ long, awl-shaped, with a large wing on one side, a small one on the other, shape reminds of a duck's bill, 6 scales, rarely 8.

CULTURE: Prefers moist, well-drained, fertile soil; full sun or light shade; not tolerant of smoggy or wind-swept conditions; shows good adaptability to different soil types; may be somewhat difficult to transplant; once established quite drought and heat tolerant; also will tolerate poor soils.

DISEASES AND INSECTS: A heart rot caused by *Polyporus amarus* is this tree's most destructive single enemy; other conspicuous, but seldom damaging, diseases are a brooming *Gymnosporangium* rust and a leafy mistletoe; Incensecedar scale is reported.

LANDSCAPE VALUE: Handsome specimen for large areas and formal plantings; not used enough; the plant that your neighbor will wonder about; the plant does quite well in the South and one 70 to 80′ high specimen in Athens attests to its tolerance of heat and drought; very formal and should probably be restricted to that style of landscaping; Longwood Gardens has a fine grove all of which are distinctly columnar; also performing well on Oklahoma State Campus, Stillwater, OK.

CULTIVARS:

'Aureovariegata'—A rather interesting yellow-variegated form; the size of the yellow variegation varying from a small spot to an entire spray; first saw this at the Parc Floral, Orleans, France and was genuinely dazzled (also blinded).

'Berrima Gold'—A broad columnar form with yellow-green summer foliage turning rich golden orange in winter.

'Compacta'—Rich green, dwarf globe, matures around 6′ high, grows 2 to 4″ per year.

'Maupin Glow'—Interesting columnar, bright yellow form that does not sunburn, original plant was 15′ high, grows 6 to 12″ per year.

Several other cultivars, 'Compacta', 'Depressa', 'Glauca', 'Intricata', 'Pillar', and 'Riet' are listed but I have not seen them in gardens or commerce.

PROPAGATION: Propagated by seed, which requires a stratification period of about 8 weeks at 32 to 40°F for good germination; I have had poor success trying to grow this species; cuttings are difficult and in the last edition I mentioned no success; in January 1996 cuttings collected from a 30′ high tree in Spring Grove treated with 5000 ppm KNAA rooted 60%; all other treatments (KIBA, control) were failures; I followed the results of Nicholson, *The Plant Propagator* 30(1):5–6 (1984), where mid-November cuttings, 75°F bottom heat, poly tent, 50 to 60°F air temperature, obtained 92, 66, 58 and 8% rooting with 2500 ppm NAA dip, 2500 ppm NAA + 2500 ppm IBA dip, 200 ppm IBA-24 hour soak, and control (0), respectively; can be grafted on *Thuja occidentalis*.

ADDITIONAL NOTES: Have seen the plant in abundance in Portland, OR area, appears better adapted and more vibrant. Interestingly, it has performed quite well in the heat of Zone 7. Might be worth additional testing in Midwest and South.

NATIVE HABITAT: Western United States from Oregon to Nevada and lower California. Introduced 1853.

Calycanthus floridus L. — Common Sweetshrub, also called Carolina Allspice, Strawberry-shrub, Bubby Blossom, Sweet Bubby, Sweet Bettie, Spicebush.
(kal-i-kan'thus flôr'i-dus)

FAMILY: Calycanthaceae

LEAVES: Opposite, simple, broad-ovate, ovate or elliptic to narrow-elliptic, 2 to 5″(6″) long, acute or acuminate, rarely obtuse, cuneate or rounded at base, entire, dark green and slightly rough to the touch above or smooth, grayish green and densely pubescent beneath; petiole—1/3″ long.

BUDS: Superposed in a single bud-like aggregate, sessile, round or oblong, brown hairy, without evident scales, the end bud lacking; buds concealed by base of petiole.

STEM: Aromatic when bruised, stout, glabrous, gray-brown, compressed at the nodes appearing angled; leaf scars—horseshoe or U-shaped, raised, 3 bundle traces; pith—relatively large, somewhat 6-sided, white, continuous.

SIZE: 6 to 9′ in height by 6 to 12′ in spread.

HARDINESS: Zone 4 to 9; have seen it injured in Zone 4; –15 to –20°F is the break point; appears to be room for movement into Zone 4; at Orono, ME plants have been injured after –30°F but have regenerated; Cappiello in his Maine *Woody Landscape Plant Cold-Hardiness Ratings* listed the species as suffering occasional tip dieback; Morton Arboretum mentioned that it freezes back to some extent but generally flowers freely from early June to early July; flowers occur on short shoots from the leaf axils along the entire stem length, i.e., where buds are present; even if shoot tips are winter killed, the potential for good flowering is excellent.

HABIT: Dense, bushy, rounded or broad rounded shrub of regular outline; is often straggly and unkempt in the wild; the plant is unbelievably forlorn in its native haunts under the forest canopy; with sun and reasonable culture, it makes a handsome shrub.

RATE: Slow to medium.

TEXTURE: Medium in leaf and in winter.

LEAF COLOR: Dark green in summer, on some clones lustrous, yellowish in fall, but usually not outstanding; leaves persist late (November); have observed quite excellent fall color, definitely varies from year-to-year, perhaps I have been unkind in my assessment of fall color, the three cultivars 'Athens', 'Edith Wilder', and 'Michael Lindsey' developed brilliant yellows in November of 1993, 1994, 1995, 1996, and 1997 with the latter two clones the best.

FLOWERS: Perfect, dark reddish brown, maroon to almost red, up to 2″ across when fully open, very fruity fragrance, May and flowering sporadically into June and July, borne singly from the leaf axil; flowers on current season's growth and wood of previous season; sepals and petals numerous and similar (tepals); in our garden it may be in flower by early April, usually mid-April and have buds still opening as late as early May; flowers before leaves emerge, with leaves, and sporadically on new growth of the season; floral fragrance appears at its best when flowers are 1/2 to 3/4 open and the air is warm; remember that most sweetshrubs grown from seed are not fragrant, sometimes actually vinegar-scented, buy when plants are in flower; Bonnie and I, during our forays around the garden, noticed that the scent is always best in the evening.

FRUIT: Urn-shaped, leathery, wrinkled, brown receptacle, 2 to 3″ long, 1 to 1 1/2″ wide, somewhat capsule-like at maturity and enclosing many one-seeded, rich brown, 1/3 to 1/2″ long achenes, September–October and persisting through winter.

CULTURE: Easily transplanted, adaptable to many soils, preferably a deep, moist loam; shade or sun, but does not grow as tall in sun as in shaded places; prune after flowering; adapts to acid and alkaline soils.

DISEASES AND INSECTS: Very resistant shrub.

LANDSCAPE VALUE: Worthwhile plant for every garden, especially welcome in the shrub border or around an outdoor living area where the sweet strawberry-banana-pineapple scent can permeate the entire area; great variation in flower odor and it is best to smell before buying; this is a trouble-free plant that can be meshed into any garden setting.

CULTIVARS: A yellow-flowered form exists but is not well-known; supposedly Henry Hohman, Kingsville, MD, had the plant; Callaway Gardens, Gene Cline, Canton, GA and Jane Symmes, Madison, GA have the plant but its origin is lost to antiquity; I have a plant provided by Mrs. Symmes and it has tremendous fragrance—as good as I have ever experienced on any sweetshrub; the foliage is lustrous dark green and the habit dense and mounded; in the third edition I mentioned naming the shrub after my oldest daughter, Katherine; someone decided this was not kosher and named it 'Athens' so the plant with these two names is actually one and the same; the plant has brought great delight to our garden and home and virtually every garden could make use of such a plant; cut branches (from April to May) are frequently brought into the house and provide a heady fragrance; in the 1983 edition, I mentioned only 50% success with rooting, since that time better techniques have evolved that insure 80% or greater success; they include: firm wooded cuttings (as late as August), peat:perlite, mist, 10000 ppm KIBA (water soluble) and 10000 ppm IBA-alcohol produced 93 and 82% rooting, respectively; in the past with soft cuttings, alcohol has injured the stem tissue; in this study the wood was quite firm and more resistant to alcohol. In 1988 trials, 3000 and 5000 ppm KIBA from early June and early July cuttings produced 77 and 87% rooting, respectively. I was told that this cultivar reproduced partially true-to-type from seed but have found this not true with populations I grew. Seeds were collected from an isolated plant in my garden, hence, no cross-pollination, and in 3 years flowered the typical reddish-maroon-brown color of the species. Most were fragrant but even some seedlings exhibited no delightful fragrance.

McDaniel, *American Nurseryman* 140(10):48,50,52 (1974), reported that the Tingle Nursery Co., Pittsfield, MD in the 1950's offered 'Mrs. Henry's Variety', a yellow-flowered form than Mrs. J. Norman Henry collected in Alabama. This form may still be extant at the Henry Foundation, Gladwyne, PA.

'Edith Wilder'—A form that I first witnessed at Mrs. Gertrude Wister's garden in Swarthmore, PA. It has the typical deep brown-maroon-red flower of the species and excellent fragrance; Scott Arboretum provided a plant and it has flourished in the garden, leaves are flat dark green, more rounded than 'Athens' and 'Michael Lindsey', excellent yellow fall color, reddish brown flowers exhibit exceptional sweet fragrance, large-growing form to 10′. McDaniel mentioned an unnamed fragrant clone that grew in Dr. Wister's garden in Swarthmore, the unnamed clone was collected around 1919 by Mrs. Arthur Hoyt Scott, this I suspect is the current 'Edith Wilder'.

'Katherine'—See 'Athens' above.

'Luslawice'—Flowers lighter than the type, rose madder, described as madder-lake deep color; have seen photos described in *Rocznik Dendrologiczny* 42:107–108 (1994).

'Margarita'—A yellow-flowered, fragrant selection named after Margarita Cline, Canton, GA.

'Michael Lindsey'—Selected and introduced by Allen Bush, Holbrook Farm and Nursery (no longer in business), Fletcher, NC, named by Allen after the new baby boy of one of his staff members, the habit is dense, compact and rounded in outline, plant will mature between 6 and 8′(10′), the reddish brown flowers are absolutely fruity with fragrance, the elliptical-ovate leaves are lustrous dark green and have a bullate consistency almost like the leaves of spinach, beautiful yellow to golden yellow fall color, little doubt that this will be the standard by which other introductions will be measured, plant grew 5′ by 5′ in 10 years, draws rave reviews in the Dirr garden.

'Purpureus'—A form with purplish leaves, I have not seen this clone, listed by some as a *C. fertilis* selection.

'Towe'—Selection by Clarence Towe, Walhalla, SC for yellow flower color; unfortunately, the flowers are not fragrant; large lustrous dark green leaves that develop lovely yellow autumn color; will probably mature around 8 to 10′, a robust grower.

'Urbana'—A selection by the late great plantsman Professor J.C. McDaniel, University of Illinois, for sweet fragrance and the typical species flower color; during my years at the University of Illinois, I never saw (smelled) this selection although Professor McDaniel took me under his considerable wing and shared virtually everything, this is one we missed; would love to obtain a plant, is there anyone who has the plant? Raised from seed of 'Edith Wilder'.

My love for sweetshrub is common knowledge and in 1997 two lustrous dark green leaved, fragrant reddish brown flowered forms were provided by Fred Spicer, Willowwood Arboretum and Barry Palevitz, Department of Botany, University of Georgia. Both clones are happily ensconced in the Dirr garden.

PROPAGATION: I have collected seeds in December and sown them immediately with good results; they could have naturally stratified outside; 3 months at 41°F is recommended; I collected seeds just as the urn-shaped receptacle was changing from green to brown (August); the seed coats could be easily broken with the fingernail, these seeds (achenes) germinated 90% 3 weeks after planting; in follow-up work I collected the receptacles when they were brown and withered, extracted the seed which at this time had bullet-hard seed coats; out of 75 seeds planted, one germinated; my guess is that the dormancy of *Calycanthus* is probably due to the seed coat and not strict internal embryo dormancy. July-collected cuttings rooted 90% in sand in 60 days when treated with 8000 ppm IBA talc; however, I have seen reports of only 30% success at this same time; I have rooted softwood cuttings with poor success using 1000 or 3000 ppm IBA-quick dip; the alcohol seems to cause the leaves to defoliate ahead of cuttings treated with talc; see report under cultivars for best cutting procedure; many commercial growers reported miserable rooting results; on June 11, 1994, my technician Vickie Waters-Oldham and I collected cuttings of 'Athens', 'Edith Wilder' and 'Michael Lindsey' from firm wooded shoots, 5000 ppm KIBA, 3 perlite:1 peat, mist with 56, 20 and 57% rooting by 8-26-94; any time extremely softwood cuttings were used, rooting was minimal to zero; the need for gray brown color and a woody stem is important; even cuttings rooted in August when transferred to extended photoperiod (60 watt bulb) broke dormancy and continued to grow in the greenhouse; these guaranteed fragrant forms will have a place in the market for years to come so propagators might as well learn how to increase numbers.

ADDITIONAL NOTES: All parts and particularly the wood when dry exude a camphor-like fragrance. Supposedly the bark was used as a substitute for cinnamon.

NATIVE HABITAT: Virginia to Florida. Introduced 1726.

RELATED SPECIES: Based on my studies I am not sure there are related species at least among the eastern types. They should all be included under the above species. Meyer et al. (1994) reduced them into synonymy with *C. floridus*. *Calycanthus fertilis* Walter, Pale Sweetshrub, supposedly has less pubescent leaves and purple to red-brown flowers with minimal to no scent. Great quantities of fruit are set. *Calycanthus mohrii* (Small) Pollard., Mohr Sweetshrub, is similar to *C. fertilis* with broad ovate leaves and rounded or heart-shaped leaf bases. I have looked at *C. floridus* native populations in the Southeast and can find the characteristics of all three species in any one population. *Calycanthus occidentalis* Hook and Arn., California Sweetshrub, is similar to the above but has larger parts (leaves up to 8″ long) and exposed leaf buds. The California Sweetshrub is more common in English gardens. It is more vigorous and I have seen 12 to 15′ high plants. The flower color is lighter (more red) and the fragrance is minimal and, based on actual nose

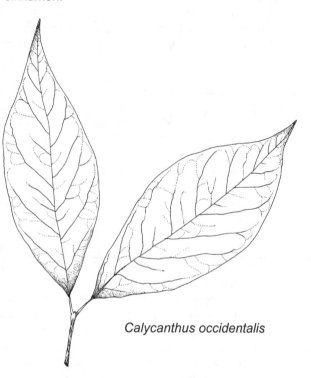

Calycanthus occidentalis

tests, not at all pleasant. Where the fragrant type eastern species can be grown this should not be considered. California species is considered hardy in Zone (6)7. I have not seen a single specimen on the East Coast, i.e., Maine to Florida.

Musgrave, *The New Plantsman*, pp 40–47, March (1996), provides an account of Calycanthaceae in the wild and cultivation. This English account lists only two cultivars, 'Purpureus' and 'Walter Nanus'.

Sinocalycanthus chinensis Cheng and Chang, (sī-nō-kal-i-kan′thus chi-nen′sis), Chinese Sweetshrub, is a relative new comer to North America. Nomenclature is in a state of flux with *Calycanthus chinensis* Cheng and Chang occasionally listed. In my opinion, having grown both in the Dirr garden, *Calycanthus* and *Sinocalycanthus* are unique, distinct genera. Dr. Raulston at NCSU Arboretum (now J.C. Raulston Arboretum) had one of the first plants to flower in the United States. The plant was about 5′ (will grow 6 to 9′) high with large (6 to 10″ long, up to 6″ wide) glossy dark green leaves. The 2 1/2 to 3″ diameter, nodding flowers are white, sometimes tinged pink on the outer tepals, the inner smaller with pale yellow to white at base with maroon markings. Flowers for about one month in mid to late spring. A 3 to 4′ plant in our garden flowered in May, 1997. Flowers are beautiful but have no fragrance. The large leaves appear tired by late summer–fall. May need extra soil moisture, some shade and wind protection. Certainly a unique plant but doubtfully as garden worthy as *Calycanthus floridus*. A hybrid between this and the native *C. floridus* was produced at the J.C. Raulston Arboretum. It flowered in 1996 and from all accounts was spectacular. Probably will be more adaptable and cold hardy than *S. chinensis*. I crossed *Calycanthus floridus* 'Athens' with *Sinocalycanthus chinensis* in 1997 with one fruit maturing. Stay tuned for the next edition. Eastern China. Zone (6)7 to 8.

Camellia japonica L. — Japanese Camellia
(kȧ-mēl′i-ȧ jȧ-pon′i-kȧ)

FAMILY: Theaceae

LEAVES: Alternate, simple, evergreen, ovate to elliptic, 2 to 4″ long, abruptly acuminate, cuneate, serrate, each serration tipped with a black gland, lustrous dark green above, glabrous, firm, leathery, almost plastic texture, underside with black gland-like dots; petiole—1/4″ long.

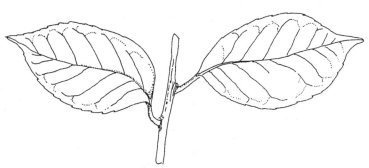

BUDS: Flower—imbricate, green, pubescent on upper portion, rounded-conical, 3/4″ long, 1/2″ wide; vegetative—imbricate, green, glabrous, angular-conical, 1/4 to 3/8″ long, both buds may be present at same node.

STEM: Moderate, rich brown, covered with blackish lenticels, glabrous; pith—white, spongy; leaf scars—crescent-shaped to nearly elliptical; one bundle trace.

SIZE: 10 to 15′ (20 to 25′), 6 to 10′ wide.

HARDINESS: Zone 7 to 9; in Athens-Atlanta area numerous plants were killed at -3°F during the 1983–84, 84–85 winters; the plants never really acclimated (cold hardened) and when the cold arrived plants succumbed, with proper hardening the best of the cold hardy selections should survive Zone 6 (0 to -10°F) with protection; work at Clemson, *The Camellia Journal* 44(3):30–31 (1989), indicated that excessive fertilization and irrigation applied after spring growth may predispose plants to greater cold injury; late pruning (September, October, and November) also predisposed plants to greater winter kill.

HABIT: Usually a dense pyramid of lustrous dark green foliage; some forms more open than others and a bit more graceful; have also seen forms that are columnar-pyramidal; in general rather stiff, stodgy and formal.

RATE: Slow.

TEXTURE: Medium to medium-coarse.

LEAF COLOR: New growth generally shiny rich green, lustrous dark green at maturity and through the seasons; if sited in full sun some discoloration may occur in winter; this is not, however, absolute.

FLOWERS: Perfect, non-fragrant except for a few cultivars, axillary, solitary, rarely 2 to 3 together, 5 to 7 petals in the species to numerous petals in the doubles, 3 to 5″(6″) across; white, pink, rose, red, about every conceivable combination; some flowers are variegated; may open from November through April in the Athens, GA area; entire floral structure drops intact rather than isolated, sporadic petals; cold is their biggest enemy and turns the flowers to brown mush; beautiful when unadulterated by the weather; over 2000 (3000) cultivars that vary in form, color and markings; very difficult to assess the best forms and the local garden center and nursery are the best sources for what will grow locally and perform successfully.

FRUIT: Rather unusual loculicidal woody capsule that houses 1 to 3 seeds; seeds are brown, subglobose or angular and about 1″ long, ripen in fall.

CULTURE: Easily transplanted from containers; prefer moist, acid, well-drained, high organic matter soils; plants in high pH soils do not prosper; best to mulch since root system is not particularly deep; should be sited in partial shade; too much shade or sun results in depressed flowering; pine shade appears ideal for successful culture; have balled plants in a nursery and most of the root system was in confined area around the trunk; prune anytime but most logically after flowering; cold is a limiting factor in Zones 7 and 8; plants are often grown in conservatories in the northern states.

Gibbing is the process of applying gibberellic acid to induce early and large flowers. The vegetative (leaf) bud next to the flower bud is twisted out. A drop of gibberellic acid solution is placed in the old bud cup. Growth activity (flower bud swelling) is often evident in 2 weeks. If the treatment is made in September, early-flowering cultivars may open in 30 days, late cultivars may take 60 to 90 days.

DISEASES AND INSECTS: Spot disease on leaves, black mold on leaves and stems, leaf gall, leaf spot, flower blight, stem cankers, root rot, leaf blight, virus induced flower and leaf variegation, tea scale (serious pest in South), Florida red scale, numerous other scales, Eriophyid mites, mealy bugs, weevils, Fuller rose beetle, thrips, spotted cut worm, numerous other insects, root-nema; physiological disorders include bud drop, chlorosis, oedema, sunburn, salt injury.

LANDSCAPE VALUE: A cherished plant in southern gardens but the devastating freeze of 1983–84 and 84–85 killed old venerable specimens with 12 to 16″ trunk diameters. On the Georgia campus a few survived, many were killed to the ground and resprouted, and others perished. The flowers are beautiful and a shrub in full regalia is an object of great beauty. Unfortunately, with flowers opening from November–December to April in the Athens area, many times the petals are turned brown from the cold. I suspect anything below 32°F for a time will cause some petal deterioration. I *had* seen entire collections of nothing but *Camellia japonica* without much feeling for placement and design considerations. The plant is experiencing a rebirth and being used in borders, mixed plantings and as an accent or focal point in protected courtyards or against walls. Careful siting in Zone 7 is a must. Also choose the cultivars based on cold hardiness since this dictates whether the plant will survive.

CULTIVARS: Numerous (over 2000), in fact, confused to the point of hopelessness; professional and amateurs have bred, selected, and introduced new cultivars, any attempt at a list would be superfluous so I will recommend that interested parties join the American Camellia Society.

'Adolphe Audusson'—Dark red or variegated, large, semi-double, mid-season.
'Altheaflora'—Dark crimson, semi-double.
'Are-jishi'—Light red, medium, full peony.
'Betty Sheffield Supreme'—White with rose fringe, double, mid to late season.
'Chandleri Elegans'—Pink with white center, large, anemone form, early-flowering.
'Chojo-Haku'—White, single, fall blooming.
'Christine Lee'—Red with yellow stamens, rose form.
'Greensboro Red'—Light red, semi-double, vigorous.
'Hagoromo'—Dark red, single form.
'Jacks'—Medium red, formal.
'Kumagai'—Dark red, single form.
'Latifolia'—Red and white, semi-double.
'Mathothiana Rubra'—Red with purplish cast, double, mid to late season.
'Mathothiana Supreme'—Red and white variegated, large, double.
'Mrs. Charles Cobb'—Dark red, semi-double, mid-season.
'Ozeki'—Red, single form.
'Park Hill Tomorrow'—Light pink deepening at petal edges, semi-double, early to mid-season.
'Pope Pius IX'—Cherry red, double; compact, upright growth habit.
'Rose Dawn'—Rose-pink, double, early to mid-season.
'Shiro Tama'—White, single.
'Showa-No-Hikari'—Red or variegated, single.
'Tenko'—Soft pink, slightly fragrant.
'Tojo Haku'—White, single.
'White by the Gate'—White, medium, double, mid to late season.
'Willie Hite'—Light pink with shaded petals, semi-double.
'Yuki-Komachi'—Deep rose-pink, large glossy leaves.

Mr. Gerald Smith, former Extension Specialist, University of Georgia, and gardener, provided a list of some of the hardier types. (See Univ. of Georgia Cooperative Extension Bulletin #813, *Camellia Culture for Home Gardeners*.) They include:

'Bernice Boddy'—Light pink, semi-double, very cold hardy flower buds.
'Debutante'—Light pink, early-flowering, peony form, complete double.
'Flame'—Red, semi-double, very cold hardy flower buds, late season.
'Governor Mouton'—Red and white variegated flowers, cold hardy buds.
'Kumasaka'—Dark pink, cold hardy, incomplete double, late season.
'Lady Clare'—Dark pink, large, semi-double, above average cold hardiness.
'Lady Vansittart'—Variable colors on same plant from semi-double, white, pink to red, shiny dark green pointed leaves, above average cold hardiness.
'Magnoliaeflora'—Light pink, cold hardy, semi-double, compact plant.
'Pink Perfection'—Pink, formal double, early to mid-season.
'Rev. John C. Drayton'—Carmine-rose, semi-double, late season.
'White Empress'—White, early, above average hardiness, incomplete double.

Additional Cold Hardy Forms as listed by Ackerman who bred for cold tolerant camellias during his U.S. National Arboretum career [see Ackerman, "Camellia cultivars that have withstood the test of time in the Washington, DC area," *The Camellia Journal* (50)4:22 (1995)]:

'Aunt Jetty'—Red, medium, peony form, non-variegated form of 'Governor Mouton'.
*'Bernice Boddy'—Light pink, medium, semi-double.
'Betty Sette'—Pink, medium, formal-double, late season.
'Blood of China'—Red, medium, semi-double also listed as peony.
'Bob Hope'—Red.
'C.M. Wilson'—Light pink, sport of 'Elegans'.
'Daikagura'—Red and white variegated, peony form, early season.
'Donckelarii'—Variegated, semi-double.
'Dr. Tinsley'—Pink, medium, semi-double.
'Elegans' ('Chandleri')—Pink.
'Fire 'n Ice'—Bright red, medium to large, semi-double to rose-double, late season.
*'Flame'—Red, semi-double.
'Flame Variegated'—Red and white variegated, semi-double.
'Frost Queen'—White, large, semi-double.
'Glen 40'—Red
*'Governor Mouton'—Red and white variegated, medium, peony form also listed as semi-double peony, considered very hardy suffering no stem or leaf injury at -5° F.
'Herme'—Pink with irregular white borders, semi-double.
'Ice Follies'—Bright pink, medium to large, semi-double, late season.
'Jarvis Red'—Red
*'Kumasaka'—Red or pink, medium to large, semi-double also listed as rose form double.
'Kumasaka Variegated'—Red and white variegated, medium to large, semi-double also listed as rose form double.
*'Lady Clare'—Pink, semi-double.
*'Lady Vansittart Red'—Red, semi-double.
'Lady Vansittart Variegated'—Variegated, semi-double.
'Leucantha'—White, semi-double.
'Marie Bracey'—Pink.
'Mathotiana'—Red, rose form, double.
'Paulette Goddard'—Red or rose pink, medium, rose form, most winter tolerant according to Ray Bond, "Winter tolerant Camellias," *The Camellia Journal* (50)4:2–3 (1995), suffered no stem or leaf injury at -5° F.
*'Pink Perfection'—Pink, formal-double.
'Professor Charles S. Sargent'—Red, medium, peony form, mid-season.
'Purity'—White, rose form double.
*'Rev. John C. Drayton'—Semi-double peony.
'R.L. Wheeler'—Deep pink, large, semi-double.
'Sharon Elizabeth'—Fall blooming.
'Spring Frill'—Bright iridescent pink, large, rose-double, late season.
'Tricolor' (Siebold)—Red and white variegated, semi-double.
'Tricolor' (Siebold) Red'—Red, semi-double.
'Ville de Nantes'—Semi-double.
*'White Empress'—White, semi-double.
'White Queen'—White.

*Plants with an asterisk appear in Smith's and Ackerman's lists.

PROPAGATION: Seed requires no pretreatment if taken from the capsules and planted immediately; if seed dry out they should be covered with hot water (190°F) and allowed to imbibe for about 24 hours; after this time they can be placed in seed flats. Cuttings are best collected from May to September and in the fall, about November; cuttings should be taken from the current season's growth just below the fifth node; 3000 to 8000 ppm IBA is effective; sand and peat or peat and perlite, mist or poly-tent are the other important ingredients. West Coast and southern propagators reported good success from July–August cuttings from clean, container-grown stock plants. Camellias are also grafted and air-layered.

NATIVE HABITAT: China, Japan. Cultivated 1742.

RELATED SPECIES: In a manual such as this it is impossible to do justice to *Camellia*. About 250 species of *Camellia* are reported and numerous hybrids have been constructed by passionate amateur and professional breeders. The possibilities for floral improvement are limitless. From a cold hardiness standpoint, Dr. William Ackerman, U.S. National Arboretum and Dr. Clifford R. Parks, University of North Carolina, Chapel Hill have provided the greatest number of new cultivars.

Camellia oleifera Abel — Tea-oil Camellia

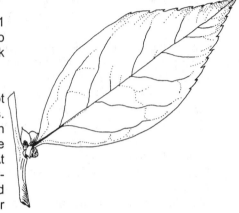

LEAVES: Alternate, simple, evergreen, 1 to 3″(5″) long, 3/4 to 1 1/4″ wide, broad elliptic or oblanceolate to obovate, acute to acuminate, cuneate or obtuse, serrate, leathery, lustrous dark green, glabrous; petiole—short, hairy.

Camellia oleifera, (kȧ-mēl′i-ȧ ō-lē-if′ĕr-ȧ), Tea-oil Camellia, is not well-known in cultivation but is one of the hardiest camellias. In most respects it is similar to *C. sasanqua* and has been hybridized with that species. The 2 to 2 1/2″ wide, white flowers appear in the leaf axils from October to January. At the J.C. Raulston Arboretum, I have seen the species (hybrids) in flower in October. Interestingly, these plants had survived –9°F, were 12 to 15′ high and vigorous. Flower color was variable white to pink, possibly because of the hybrid parentage. The leaves of *C. sasanqua* are thinner (not as leathery), smaller, and blunter pointed. Virtually unknown to me until "discovering" a splendid plant at the U.S. National Arboretum. This plant survived –10°F on several occasions and possessed handsome rich, almost buff-cinnamon brown bark. This plant was the progenitor cold hardy breeding line for Dr. Ackerman's hybrids. The plant was recently given the name 'Lu Shan Snow' and has been released by the U.S. National. *Exobasidium* leaf gall is a problem and seedlings were susceptible to *Cylindrocladium crotalariae*. In China, the species is cultivated for the seeds which are processed for oil, hence, the common name. China. Zone 6 to 9.

Ackerman Hybrids: Parentage *C. oleifera*, *C. hiemalis*, and/or *C. sasanqua*, characteristics include October–November flowering; plants I have grown and seen do not have the best growth habit, often a degree irregular. See *HortScience* 26:1432–1433 (1991) for detailed descriptions of 'Winter Rose', 'Snow Flurry', and 'Polar Ice'; *HortScience* 27:855–856 (1992) for 'Winter's Charm', 'Winter's Hope', and 'Winter's Star'; *HortScience* 16:690 (1981) for 'Frost Prince' and 'Frost Princess'; I should emphasize that these selections do not compete in any way, shape or form with the better *C. japonica* and *C. sasanqua* forms. Their use lies in more northerly areas where the dream of growing camellias, prior to this group, was just that.

'Frost Prince'—Flowers deep pink, 3 to 3 1/2″ across, single to semi-double, October to November, up to 6 weeks, petals fall separately, upright habit with spreading branchlets drooping at extremities.

'Frost Princess'—Flowers lavender-pink, about 3″ across, semi-double to anemone form, late October to late November flowering period, plant habit more spreading and branchlets more pendulous than 'Frost Prince'.

'Polar Ice'—Flowers white, 3 to 3 1/2″ wide, anemone form, 12 petals, many petaloids, October to November flower (Maryland), petals fall separately at senescence, more upright grower than 'Snow Flurry' and 'Winter's Rose', 5 1/2′ in 10 years.

'Snow Flurry'—Flowers white, peony form, 12 petals, 18 petaloids, October to November, up to 7 weeks, petals fall separately, spreading-arching growth habit, branchlets drooping, 6′ tall in 11 years.

'Winter's Beauty'—Newest release, rich pink semi-double to peony form flowers open from early fall to Thanksgiving, has shown outstanding cold hardiness.

'Winter's Charm'—Flowers lavender pink, 3 1/2″ diameter, peony form, 14 petals, 14 petaloids, October through November for up to 6 weeks, petals fall separately, 6 1/4′ by 4 1/4′ after 10 years.

'Winter's Hope'—Flowers white, 4″ across, semi-double, 12 petals, October to November for up to 5 weeks, petals fall separately, 8′ by 8′ in 12 years.

'Winter's Interlude'—Flowers lavender-pink, anemone form, late October, upright habit, excellent cold hardiness.

'Winter's Rose'—Flowers shell pink, 2″ diameter, formal double, 28 petals, October to November for up to 6 weeks, petals fall separately, slow-growing with moderately spreading branches and drooping branchlets, 4′ in 9 years.

'Winter's Star'—Flowers red-purple, 3 1/2″ wide, single, 6-petaled, October to November for up to 6 weeks, petals fall separately, 7′ by 5 1/4′ in 12 years, upright grower.

'Winter's Waterlily'—Flowers white, formal double, late-flowering, upright grower.

Ackerman *C. oleifera* × *C. japonica*—These hybrids are hardy to about –10°F, flower buds to 10°F, flower in winter–spring:

'Pink Icicle'—Flowers clear shell pink, large, peony-form, yellow stamens, compact upright-growing shrub.

'Spring Frill'—Flowers iridescent pink, semi-double, petals ruffled and frilled.

Ackerman Heat Tolerant Camellias—These hybrids are suitable for Zone 8 to 10(11), supposed grew in full sun in Miami, FL and performed well:

'Sunworshipper' (*C. hongkongensis* × *C. rusticana*)—Flowers bright rose-red, double, spring, upright habit, new foliage dark red purple, dark green at maturity.

'Two Marthas' (*C. sasanqua* × *C. kissii*)—Flowers bright rose-pink, semi-double, open October–November, upright habit.

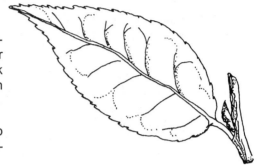

Camellia sasanqua Thunb. — Sasanqua Camellia
LEAVES: Similar to *C. japonica* but smaller, obovate or narrowly oval, 1 1/2 to 3″ long, 1/3 to 1/2 as wide, acute or with broad cusp to 1/12″ long, cuneate, lustrous dark green, hairy on midrib above and below, rounded teeth on the margin; petiole—pubescent.
BUDS: Similar, one-half size of *C. japonica*, pubescent.
STEM: Slender, compared to *C. japonica*, often reddish to purplish when young, finally brown, covered with prominent pubescence.

Camellia sasanqua, (kȧ-mēl′i-ȧ sa-san′kwȧ), Sasanqua Camellia, tends to be smaller, 6 to 10′(15′) high, and more refined than *C. japonica*. It, too, forms a densely branched, evergreen, pyramidal to oval-rounded outline. The leaves are a lustrous dark green and considerably smaller than those of *C. japonica*. The flowers (6 to 8 petals) are usually smaller (2 to 3″ diameter) and more open than *C. japonica* but no less diverse in color, or degree of doubleness. They open ahead of *C. japonica* and range from September into December in the Athens area. Petals abscise individually rather than as a floral tube like *C. japonica*. This species has the same basic cultural requirements as *C. japonica* but is considered less hardy. As a group will be more severely injured by cold than *C. japonica*. I have observed specimens in full sun that were quite healthy. After the two devastating winters of 1976–77 and 1977–78 almost all the *C. sasanqua* were eliminated from the camellia collection at the U.S. National Arboretum (Zone 7) whereas many *C. japonica* survived. Based on 1983–84, 84–85 freeze damage in Athens, this species survived better than *C. japonica*. Large flowering specimens in 1987 and 1988 were of this species which indicated better freeze survival or subsequent regrowth than *C. japonica*. The plant is more refined and more lax and open than *C. japonica* and is more attractive from a landscape point of view. A very easy way to tell *C. japonica* from *C. sasanqua* is by the pubescent stems of the latter. Exobasidium leaf gall is a problem and all cultivars and seedlings were susceptible to *Cylindrocladium crotalariae*. China, Japan. Introduced 1811. Zone 7 to 9.

Cultivars include:

'Bonanza'—Deep red, large, semi-peony form.

'Carolina Moonmist'—Cold hardy hybrid of *C. sasanqua* × *C. oleifera* with large pink to rose flowers, best sited in partial shade, hardy to Zone 6, hybridized by Dr. Fred Cochran, NCSU, introduced by J.C. Raulston Arboretum.

'Cleopatra'—Pink, semi-double; vigorous grower.

'Daydream'—White edged deep rose, single large flowers; somewhat columnar in habit.

'Hana Jiman'—White edged with pink, large, semi-double.

'Jean May'—Shell pink, semi-double to double, large.

'Maiden's Blush'—Blush pink.

'Martha's Dream'—Pink budded and edged petals on a white almost carnation-like textured flower, 3″ across, introduced by the late Cecil Hill, Homer, GA and named after his wife Martha, an absolutely beautiful selection.

'Midnight Lover'—Deep red; as described by Camellia Forest Nursery, the deepest red of *C. sasanqua* they have seen; vigorous and erect grower.

'Mine-No-Yuki'—White, double, large, sets buds heavily; spreading, loose habit.

'Mist Maiden'—Possibly of worth because of excellent cold hardiness, not injured over last 19 years in Athens area, 3″ diameter, lavender-pink single flowers on a robust, 12 to 15′ high shrub, might prove worthy as a breeding line, certainly Zone 6 adaptable.

'Northern Lights'—White with pink margins; free-flowering; vigorous and erect grower.

'Pink Butterfly'—Bright pink, single, very large; early to mid-season (October–November); vigorous grower.
'Pink Goddess'—Pale pink, large, cup-shaped flowers; fine foliage texture.
'Pink Snow'—Light pink, semi-double, large, more vigorous than 'Mine-No-Yuki', does not bud as quickly.
'Setsugekka'—White, semi-double, large ruffled petals.
'Shishigashira'—Rose and red, semi-double, opening throughout fall and winter; compact habit.
'Sparkling Burgundy'—Ruby rose overlaid with lavender sheen, peony-form.
'Swan Lake'—White.
'Usi Bene'—Salmon pink, semi-double; semi-dwarf, compact habit.
'Wm. Lanier Hunt'—Medium red, peony-form; mid-season (October–early November); vigorous grower.
'Yuletide'—Red flower with yellow stamens, single form; upright habit; lustrous dark green foliage.

Camellia sinensis (L.) Kuntze. — Tea
LEAVES: Alternate, simple, evergreen, elliptic, 2 to 4 1/2″ long, 1/3 as wide, obtuse to broad obtuse, cuneate, serrate, lustrous dark green above, light green beneath; petiole—short.

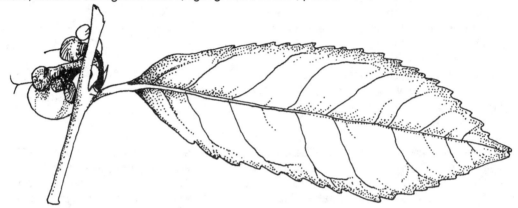

Camellia sinensis, (kȧ-mēl′i-ȧ sī-nen′sis), Tea, is one of the great, unsung treasures of the *Camellia* world for use in Zone 6 to 9 gardens. It is distinguishably hardier than the previous *Camellia* species and makes a fine 4 to 6′(10′) high and wide evergreen shrub especially adapted to shady environments. The 1 to 1 1/2″ diameter, fragrant, 7 to 8 petaled, white, yellow-stamened flowers open in September–October (Athens) and continue into November and on occasion early December, usually 1 to 3 produced from the leaf axils on 1/2″ long pedicels; unfortunately, flowers are hidden by the leaves and do not jump out like those of the brethren above. The fruit is a 3/4″ long shiny capsule with 1 or 2 seeds that matures the year after flowering. The plant is not particular about soil or exposure and will perform quite well in full sun. It also displays high heat and drought tolerance and could prove a valuable plant for southeastern conditions. A pink form 'Rosea'('Rubra') is known. The flowers are light pink but the new growth is rich reddish purple. The species is easily maintained and I prune the two plants in the garden on a regular basis. Scale is listed as a problem but to date has not developed. Good plant for massing and grouping in semi-shade to rather heavy shade. Appears amazingly drought tolerant once established. Considerably more cold hardy than given credit in the everyday literature. I have propagated June, July–August firm wooded cuttings with great success (80 to 90%) although rooting may take 8 weeks. Seeds are desiccation sensitive and remain viable for one year at 41°F and 40 to 45% relative humidity. Fresh seeds contain 40% moisture and germination is 100%. At 28% moisture content, germination is reduced to 46%. Seed moisture level of 30% correlated with 86% germination. This is the plant from which tea is made and many cultivars exist. Over 3000 genotypes (clones) are known. Next time you read the tea leaves, reflect on the beauty of this double-duty plant. Native to China and cultivated for centuries by the Chinese. Zone 6 to 9.

ADDITIONAL NOTES: Almost any discussion of camellias is superfluous because of the staggering number of hybrids and cultivars that stream into the market place. The American Camellia Society told me that over 30,000 cultivars of Camellias had been named and introduced.

Camellias will grow on even the casual gardener and when in full fall–winter regalia their beauty is unrivaled. Bonnie and I have sprinkled, almost liberally, many *C. sasanqua* cultivars in the shady nooks and crannies of the garden. It is easy to envision how a gardener could become a Camellia-addict. The only known antidote—severe cold.

I would like to suggest membership in the American Camellia Society, 1 Massee Lane, Fort Valley, GA, 31030 (912-967-2358). The Society maintains a lovely garden and has one of the largest collections of camellias in the United States. Membership is still $20.00 which is a great bargain.

Campsis radicans (L.) Seem. — Common Trumpetcreeper, Trumpet Vine
(kamp′sis rad′i-kanz)

FAMILY: Bignoniaceae

LEAVES: Opposite, pinnately compound, 6 to 15″ long, (7)9 to 11 leaflets, short-stalked, elliptic to ovate-oblong, each leaflet 3/4 to 4″ long, 1/4 to 2″ wide, coarsely and angularly toothed, with a long acuminate apex, lustrous dark green above, glabrous, pubescent beneath especially on veins, veins impressed.

BUDS: Small, mostly solitary, sessile, triangular, compressed, with 2 or 3 pairs of exposed scales.

STEM: Light brown, glabrous, aerial rootlets develop between nodes; leaf scar—crater-like depression with one bundle trace, bud sits on top of leaf scar, leaf scars connected by hairy ridge; pith—solid, pale brown.

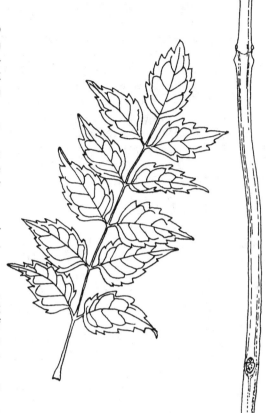

SIZE: 30 to 40′ high, actually will scramble and climb over everything in its path, essentially limited by size of structure.

HARDINESS: Zone 4 to 9.

HABIT: Rampant, deciduous, clinging (root-like holdfasts), strangling vine; at its best on fenceposts for when it reaches the top of the post it forms an immense whorl of stems; makes the post appear as if it is about to fly; needs frequent pruning; suckers profusely and forms impenetrable colonies.

RATE: Fast; keep your legs moving when in the vicinity of this plant.

TEXTURE: Medium in summer, coarse in winter.

LEAF COLOR: Lustrous dark green changing to yellow-green in fall and not effective; late leafing, as late as early May in Athens.

FLOWERS: Perfect, corolla rich orange and scarlet, trumpet-shaped, 2 1/2 to 3″ long, 1 1/2″ wide at mouth with triangular teeth, borne 4 to 12 together in terminal cymes from June (Athens) to September; flowers on new growth of the season; tremendous variation in flower color from orange to red in Southeast; the corolla sometimes darker spotted on the outside.

FRUIT: A 3 to 5″ long, 3/4″ wide capsule; each loaded with numerous flattened seeds with 2 large transparent wings.

CULTURE: If you cannot grow this, give up gardening; grows in any soil and also prospers in sidewalk cracks; extremely rampant in rich soil; best to prune back to a few buds in spring; if the developing fruits are removed the plant will flower even more heavily into late summer.

DISEASES AND INSECTS: Blight, leaf spots, powdery mildew, plant hoppers, scale and whitefly occur but are not serious enough to warrant controls.

LANDSCAPE VALUE: Good for screening, covering rock piles, have seen it used tastefully over trellises and lath structures; good pruning is a necessity to keep it in bounds; amazingly salt tolerant; all over Cape Cod, MA growing in sandy infertile soils; probably a worthy plant in hostile environments.

CULTIVARS:

'Apricot'—From the Arnold Arboretum's collection; much like 'Flava', perhaps more apricot-yellow, but may be the same.

'Crimson Trumpet'—A strong-growing form with pure glowing red (velvet red) flowers without any trace of orange; corolla is not as widely flaring as many wild types; not a bad selection but larger flowered, clearer red forms are available in the wild.

'Flava' (var. *flava*)—Handsome form with yellow, perhaps orange-yellow flowers; this is a particularly handsome form and in my mind preferable to the species; corolla tube is fatter and not as long extended as species type, also wider at the mouth where the corolla lobes spread/reflex; one of the most beautiful specimens I have seen is found in Mr. Airy Arboretum, Cincinnati, OH; easily rooted from cuttings; cultivated 1842.

'Judy'—Like 'Flava'; from Coastal Plain of eastern North Carolina.

'Praecox'—Flowers red, appearing in June; I have seen many forms in the South that approach red to scarlet; the midwestern type appears to have more orange.

University Hybrids—Currently an unnamed group of selections that resulted from an undergraduate research project by Ms. Holly Scoggins. Holly crossed *C. radicans* 'Oconee' (large flowered, almost pure red form I selected from Oconee County, GA), *C. radicans* 'Flava', and *C. grandiflora*. Container-grown plants were forced in the greenhouse (1992), crosses made and mature fruits harvested. Seedlings started to flower in 1993 with the greatest percentage in 1994. The F_1 generation has yielded exciting, large yellow to red-flowered plants beyond our wildest imaginations. To date, a yellow-flowered form with orange striping inside the corolla and a uniformly ruby-flowered form with flowers like 'Mme Galen' are the most garden worthy. The color range has been kaleidoscopic. Kind of provides an inkling of the power of plant breeding and subsequent plant improvement.

PROPAGATION: Seeds germinate more uniformly when given 2 months at 41°F or fall sown; in Holly's work fresh seeds germinated upon sowing; softwood cuttings (June–July) root readily and root cuttings work well; in fact it is hard to get rid of this plant because of its propensity to sucker from root pieces.

NATIVE HABITAT: Pennsylvania to Missouri, Florida and Texas. Introduced 1640.

RELATED SPECIES:

Campsis grandiflora (Thunb.) Schum., (kamp′sis gran-di-flō′rà), Chinese Trumpetcreeper, grows 15 to 25′ and is similar to *C. radicans* in most foliage respects. Does not develop the abundant and prominent root-like hold fasts of *C. radicans*. The deep orange and red corolla is widely trumpet-shaped, 2 to 3″ long and wide with 5, broad-rounded lobes. Flowers on the single plant I received from Dr. Raulston are muddy apricot-orange with yellowish interior and orangish stripes. I suspect, like *C. radicans*, the flower color is highly variable. This particular form was utilized as one of the parents in the University Hybrids. The influence of flower size, shape, rounded corolla lobes and striping is evident in the progeny. Flowers on new growth with 6 to 12 flowers per pendulous panicle. Has flowered in June (Athens). Does not appear to repeat bloom like *C. radicans*. The leaflets (7 or 9) are glabrous, 1 1/2 to 3″ long, 1/2 as wide, long-pointed, and coarsely toothed. The inflorescence paniculate and the flowers are longer than *C. radicans*. Not as vigorous as *C. radicans*. 'Morning Calm' was introduced by the J.C. Raulston Arboretum. I believe it is the same form described above. Native to Japan, China. Introduced 1800. Zone (6)7 to 9.

Campsis* × *tagliabuana (Vis.) Rehd., (kamp′sis tag-lē-a-bwa′nà), is a hybrid between *C. grandiflora* × *C. radicans* and is intermediate in characteristics. The first plant to be identified as a hybrid arose in the nursery of the Tagliabue brothers near Milan. Many forms were distributed by French nurseries; the finest and most common being 'Mme. Galen' which was put into commerce in 1889. It makes a spectacular show in flower and is superior and hardier than *C. grandiflora*. Flowers are orange, 3″ long, 3″ wide, the *C. grandiflora* parentage strongly evident. Have observed slightly different color forms and suspect more than one clone is floating in the trade. 'Coccinea' with brilliant red flowers is described. I grew an open-pollinated population of 'Mme Galen' seedlings and all were inferior to the original. Have seen in coastal Georgia where it prospers in the summer heat; an indefatigable flowerer. Zone 5, probably best in 6 to 9.

ADDITIONAL NOTES: The common name is appropriately derived. A genetic engineer should transfer the genes from *C. radicans* to some of the more temperamental ornamental plants. Abundant interest in the *Campsis* taxa because of user-friendly nature and the fact that they attract hummingbirds. In the Sunday newspaper supplements this vine (*C. radicans*) is often sold as the Hummingbird Vine. Shows one the power of good marketing. Over the years, I have been less than kind to *C. radicans* but have learned from nurserymen in the Southwest that this genus will survive, actually thrive, in high pH, alkaline, dry soils once established. It has the landscape ubiquity that is foreign to many vines. It is also a tremendous weed that one report noted occurred in 33 to 38% of the cotton fields in the Mississippi Delta region.

Caragana arborescens Lam. — Siberian Peashrub
(kãr-à-gā′nà är-bō-res′enz)

FAMILY: Fabaceae

LEAVES: Alternate, evenly pinnately compound, 1 1/2 to 3″ long, 8 to 12 leaflets, each leaflet obovate to elliptic-oblong, 1/2 to 1″ long, rounded at apex and acuminate, pubescent when young, later glabrescent, bright green, stipules linear, spine tipped, developing into a pair of stiff 1/4″ spines at each node, this is more prevalent on wild rather than cultivated specimens.

BUDS: Weakly imbricate, light brown in color; scales—chaffy in nature.

STEM: Green in color, remaining so for several years, angled from the nodes, with pale, horizontal lenticels, usually of scurfy appearance.

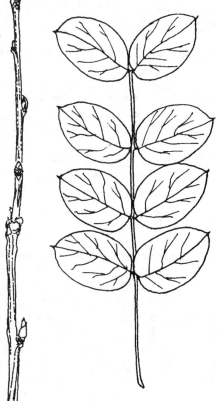

SIZE: 15 to 20′ in height with a spread of 12 to 18′.

HARDINESS: Zone 2 to 7.

HABIT: Erect, oval shrub, often taller than broad with moderate, sparse branches; have observed broad-rounded multi-stemmed forms; can also be grown as a tree; branches may be so erect as to create a fastigiate appearance.

RATE: Medium to fast.

TEXTURE: Medium in summer, coarse in winter.

LEAF COLOR: Light bright green in summer; briefly yellow-green in fall.

FLOWERS: Perfect, bright yellow, 1/2 to 1″ long, early to mid-May on previous year's wood when the leaves are 2/3's to fully developed; borne singly or up to 4 in fascicles.

FRUIT: A cylindrical pencil-shaped narrow pod, 1 1/2 to 2″ long, yellow-green changing to brown, with 3 to 5 seeds, matures July–August, makes popping sound as pod opens.

CULTURE: Very easy to grow; extremely cold hardy and able to tolerate poor soils, drought, alkalinity, salt as well as sweeping winds; an extremely adaptable but limitedly ornamental plant; nitrogen fixing.

DISEASES AND INSECTS: Nothing too serious although leaf-hoppers can disfigure young growth.

LANDSCAPE VALUE: Good for hedge, screen, windbreak where growing conditions are difficult; I would not recommend it for wholesale use.

CULTIVARS:

'Lorbergii'—Leaflets (10 to 14) reduced to linear proportions, each 1/4 to 3/4″ long, 1/25 to 1/12″ wide; flowers are also narrower; has an overall ferny appearance; not bad for textural quality; saw it at one nursery identified as *Robinia pseudoacacia* 'Lorbergii'—close, but no cigar; found in Lorberg's Nursery, Germany and introduced around 1906.

'Nana'—A dwarf, rather stunted form with stiff contorted branches; similar in leaf and flower to the species upon which it is grafted; Arnold Arboretum has a nice specimen; 17-year-old plant may be 6′ high and 3′ wide.

'Pendula'—Stiffly weeping form that when grafted on a standard makes a rather pleasant ornamental; several plants at Niagara Falls, Canadian side are beautiful; leaves and flowers as in the species.

'Plume'—A fine-textured form to 5′ high with loose billowing masses of foliage on pendulous branches.

'Sutherland'—An upright form that would be effective for screening; have seen it at Minnesota Landscape Arboretum and was quite impressed.

'Tidy'—Foliage like 'Lorbergii' on an upright-spreading habit.

'Walker'—Much like 'Lorbergii' in leaf character but strongly weeping; arose from a cross between 'Lorbergii' and 'Pendula' at Morden Research Station, Canada.

Several other cultivars are described but I have not observed them in commerce.

PROPAGATION: Apparently seed dormancy is shallow and/or caused by an impermeable seed coat; stratification for 15 days at 41°F or longer is recommended; cold water and preferably hot water (180°F) 24 hour soaks have induced 80% plus germination; a light acid scarification (5 minutes) would probably be effective or simply plant in fall and let nature take its course. 'Nana', 'Lorbergii', 'Pendula', and the species have been rooted at 80% levels when collected in May, June, July and treated with 3000 to 8000 ppm IBA-talc; the weeping type is usually grafted on a standard to produce a rather handsome small tree.

NATIVE HABITAT: *Caragana arborescens* is found in Siberia, Mongolia. Introduced 1752.

RELATED SPECIES: There are many *Caragana* species but it is doubtful that any will ever become extremely popular. The two best collections I have seen are at the Arnold and Minnesota Landscape Arboreta. Minnesota has a particularly large collection. Most of the following remarks are based on evaluations of those collections.

Caragana aurantiaca Koehne, (kăr-à-gā′nà â-ran-ti-ā′kà), Dwarf Peashrub, is a small (4′ high), graceful shrub that is armed with triple-spines. The dark green leaves, 4 leaflets, and solitary orange-yellow flowers which hang from the underside of the stem in a long row, 3 to 4 to the inch, make it particularly attractive. Siberia to Afghanistan and Turkestan. Cultivated 1850, lost and reintroduced 1887. Zone 4.

Caragana frutex (L.) K. Koch, (kăr-à-gā′nà frū′teks), Russian Peashrub, is an upright, unarmed, suckering shrub growing 6 to 9′ high. There are 4, stalked, closely spaced, 1/4 to 1″ long, dark green leaflets per leaf which distinguishes this from *C. pygmaea* and the other species treated here. The bright yellow, 1″ long, 1- to 3-clustered flowers appear in May–June. 'Globosa' is a diminutive, globe-shaped form growing 3′ high and wide. Considered more resistant to insect attacks than other species. See *Proc. Intl. Plant Prop. Soc.* 40:629 (1990). Southern Russia to Turkestan and Siberia. Introduced 1752. Zone (2)3.

Caragana maximowicziana Komar., (kăr-à-gā′nà max-im-ō-wix-ē-ā′nà), Maximowicz Peashrub, is a low-spreading, spiny form with 4 to 6, grass to blue-green leaflets. Size ranges from 3 to 6′ high and 1 1/2 to 2 times as wide. It has bright yellow, 1″ long flowers and is a rather pretty alternative to barberries for barrier planting. Western Szechuan and Kansu, China and eastern Tibet. Introduced by E.H. Wilson in 1910. Zone 2.

Caragana microphylla Lam., (kăr-à-gā′nà mī-krō-fil′à), Littleleaf Caragana, grows 6 to 10′ high with a greater spread and has 12 to 18, 1/8 to 1/3″ long, dull grayish green, oval to obovate leaflets. The light yellow, 3/4″ long flowers are produced during May and June. Minnesota Landscape Arboretum lists cultivar 'Tidy' that description-wise sounds very much like the species. See under *C. arborescens* cultivars. Siberia, northern China. Introduced 1789. Zone 2.

Caragana pygmaea (L.) DC., (kăr-à-gā′nà pig-mē′à), Pygmy Peashrub, is similar to *C. aurantiaca* and along with that species is considered the prettiest of the peashrubs. My field notes say only interesting, wispy form. Apparently it is very tolerant of dry, alkaline soils. There are 4, 1/2″ long, dark green leaflets per leaf. The 1″ long yellow flowers are produced in May–June. Grows about 2 1/2′ high, 1 1/2 to 2 times this in spread. Northwest China, Siberia. Introduced 1751. Zone 3.

Caragana sinica (Buchoz) Rehd., (kăr-à-gā′nà sin′-i-ka), Chinese Peashrub, is a spiny 5′ by 8′ shrub of rather pretty nature. There are 4 large, 1 1/2 by 3/4″ on young plants, 1/4 to 3/4″ long on mature growth, glossy dark green leaflets per leaf. The 1 1/4″ long reddish yellow flowers were the first to open among all the peashrubs in the Arnold Arboretum collection, starting to show color on May 1. The bruised bark smells like anise. Northern China. Introduced 1773. Zone 5.

ADDITIONAL NOTES: As a group the *Caragana* species are little-used or known in American gardens. Their bright green foliage and pretty yellow flowers are certainly attractive. As a group, they display good dry soil tolerance and would be excellent choices for containers, dry banks, cuts and fills along highways. Some sucker which would make them ideal candidates for holding soil. Most species develop some sort of spines in the wild but under cultivation these are reduced or absent from certain species, particularly *C. arborescens* and *C. frutex*, upon which I have not seen spines. There are about 80 species in eastern Europe and central Asia.

Carpinus betulus L. — European Hornbeam, Common Hornbeam
(kăr-pī′nus bet′ū-lus)

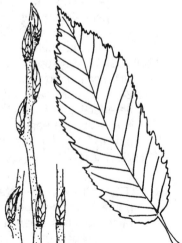

FAMILY: Betulaceae

LEAVES: Alternate, simple, ovate to ovate-oblong, 2 1/2 to 5″ long, 1 to 2″ wide, short pointed at apex, cordate or rounded at base, similar to *Carpinus caroliniana* except leaf of thicker texture, sharply and doubly serrate, 10 to 14 (12 to 18) vein pairs, veins more impressed above; petiole—1/4 to 1/2″ long.

BUDS: Imbricate, angular-conical, usually appressed, brownish to reddish, curl around stem, scales with soft pubescence, 1/4 to 1/3″ long.

STEM: Glabrous, olive-brown, prominently lenticelled.

BARK: Smooth, steel gray, fluted, presenting muscle character of *C. caroliniana*.

SIZE: 40 to 60′ in height by 30 to 40′(60′) in spread; can grow as wide as high; potentially can reach 70 to 80′ in height.

HARDINESS: Zone (4)5 to 7, have seen respectable plants in Zone 7b/8a, not considered perfectly hardy in Chicago area.

HABIT: Pyramidal to rounded in youth, oval-rounded to rounded at maturity.

RATE: Slow to medium, about 10′ over a 10 year period, perhaps slightly faster; Ford, *Secrest Arboretum Notes*, Spring, 1984, mentioned rates of 16 to 20″ per year over a 7 year period in Wooster, OH, definitely faster than the 10′ in 10 years if provided ample moisture and fertilizer.

TEXTURE: Medium-fine in leaf and winter habit; exquisitely tailored in winter with the slender branches dapperly arranged around the main leader.

BARK: Usually on old wood a handsome slate gray and the wood is beautifully fluted; akin to muscle-wood.

LEAF COLOR: Dark green in summer changing to yellow or yellowish green in fall; the summer foliage is usually very clean, i.e., no evidence of insect or disease damage; fall colors quite late.

FLOWERS: Monoecious; male—not preformed as in *Betula*, nor ornamentally important, the male catkins, 1 1/2″ long; female—1 1/2 to 3″ long, furnished with large conspicuous 3-lobed bracts, the middle lobe 1 to 1 1/2″ long, up to 2″ across, often toothed, borne in April, bracts produced in pairs and face each other.

FRUIT: Nut(let), ribbed, 1/4″ long, borne at the base of the above described bract, maturing September–October.

CULTURE: Transplant as a small balled-and-burlapped or container-grown tree in spring; tolerant of wide range of soil conditions—light to heavy, acid to alkaline, but prefers well-drained situations; performs best in full sun but will tolerate light to moderate shade; pruning is seldom required although this species withstands heavy pruning; partially tolerant of difficult conditions.

DISEASES AND INSECTS: None serious, in fact, unusually free of problems which lead to extensive maintenance; have noticed some leaf miner and dieback in Spring Grove, Cincinnati, OH.

LANDSCAPE VALUE: One of the very finest landscape trees; excellent for screens, hedges, groupings, around large buildings, in malls, planter boxes; withstands pruning as well as or better than European Beech; a choice specimen with an air of aloofness unmatched by any plant; the many excellent cultivars are probably preferable to the species for landscape situations; widely used in England for hedges; in the 1990 edition I termed the tree "small," well it is not and large plants particularly at the Arnold Arboretum reflect this fact; at Oxford Botanic Garden, England, an 80′ tree makes one a believer; the plant, particularly 'Fastigiata' is showing up with great regularity in the Athens-Atlanta region.

CULTIVARS: There are several cultivars that offer excellent color, texture and form. Unfortunately, several of the upright types are often confused in the trade. New cultivars are originating in Europe and slowly making their way to America.

'Asplenifolia'—Leaves deeply and regularly double-toothed, the primary teeth large enough to be called lobes, not as pronounced as *Fagus sylvatica* 'Asplenifolia'.

'Columnaris'—A densely branched and foliaged, spire-like, slow-growing tree, usually maintaining a central leader; Bean noted that this cultivar developed an egg-shaped outline with time; however, the few trees I have seen were distinctly columnar; Wyman noted that 'Columnaris' has been confused in American gardens with 'Fastigiata', it is possible that 'Globosa' is confused with this form.

'Fastigiata'—The most common cultivar in cultivation; however, somewhat of a misnomer, because the plant develops an oval-vase shape, with distinct fan-ribbed branches, and may grow 30 to 40′(50′) tall and 20 to 30′ wide; it does not develop a central leader, and the foliage is more uniformly distributed along the branches than on 'Columnaris' and 'Globosa', where the foliage is concentrated at the perimeter of the branches; trees with a habit similar to 'Fastigiata' occur in the wild in France and Germany; based on the tremendous variation in fastigiate types, it is obvious that there is confusion among upright-growing cultivars or that more than one fastigiate clone is in the trade; this cultivar grew 25′ high and 14′ wide after 10 years in Oregon tests; very highly rated (7th) in the Ohio Shade Tree Evaluation Tests; serves as an effective screen in winter because of the dense, compact, close-knit nature of the ascending branches; introduced before 1883.

'Franz Fontaine'—Several southern growers, Don Shadow being most prominent, have this unique, fastigiate (even into old age) form in production; I have only seen small plants; if true to description will be a wonderful plant for restricted growing areas; current season's growth curves inward toward the central leader; 30 to 35′ by 15 to 18′.

'Globosa'—Rounded and globose in outline with no central trunk; the foliage is borne toward the perimeter of the branches; distinct when compared to 'Columnaris' and 'Fastigiata' and could, like them, serve as a screen even in winter because of the close-knit branches; slow-growing and at maturity may reach 15 to 20′ in height.

var. *horizontalis* or 'Horizontalis'—A flat-topped form supposedly similar to *Crataegus crusgalli* (Cockspur Hawthorn) in outline.

'Incisa'—Similar to 'Asplenifolia' but differs by virtue of smaller and shorter leaves, which are coarsely and irregularly toothed with only about six pairs of veins.

'Monument'—Pyramidal-shaped form from Italy.

'Pendula'—As I have seen the clone, a shrubby grower with weakly pendant branches; there is a clone listed by Bean as 'Pendula Dervaesii' which is more elegant than 'Pendula'; in 1988 I saw a 30 to 40′ high, 60′ wide specimen probably of the latter at Sezincote Gardens in England; I believe the plant would be a welcome addition to American gardens; striking and singularly dominating; see Dirr, *American Nurseryman* 170(8):146 (1989); several plants have been passed around as the "true" weeping form but are anything but; a selection termed 'Vienna Weeping' is growing in Spring Grove and as a young plant appears to have the same qualities as the Sezincote form; during a 1992 garden tour that Allan Armitage and I were leading to the southwest of England, the plant center at Savill Gardens in Great Windsor Park was literally overflowing with the true weeping form for 13 pounds sterling, 95 pence; to this day, I kick (verbally) myself for not at least trying to bring one home; Weston Nurseries, Hopkinton, MA and Manor View Farm, Monkton, MD have the genuine article; before 1873.

The 'Vienna Weeping' was brought to the United States by the late tree guru, Ed Scanlon, North Olmsted, OH, who discovered it during a vacation in Vienna. The original plant grew (perhaps is growing) on the grounds of the Hapsburg Palace where it was planted by the Emperor Franz Josef in 1885. This was reported in *Trees* magazine April–May (1959). Apparently, Mr. Scanlon obtained scions, for in *Trees*, Jan.–March (1975), a 6-year-old tree was planted in North Olmsted, OH. Offered by Handy Nursery, Portland, OR.

'Pinoccheo'—Narrow, strong-growing form; original plant was 20′ by 5′; from Arborvillage, Holt, MO.

'Purpurea'—The new foliage is purplish but rapidly fades to the dark green of the species; I have seen the cultivar in mid-May, and the only purple evident was on the immature shoots.

var. *quercifolia* or 'Quercifolia'—The leaves are somewhat oak-like in shape; before 1783.

'Rogów'—Of seedling origin from Poland; parent tree is 8 1/4′ high, 21 1/2′ wide and about 30-years-old; schematics presented in the original description show it to be a broad umbrella-like head with a short handle; described in *Rocznik Dendrologiczny* 42:63–70 (1994).

University of Georgia Selections—Over 20 years ago, Mr. Will Corley, Research Horticulturist, Griffin Experiment Station, Griffin, GA, lined out seedlings from U.S. National Arboretum collection trips; two proved superior and will be named and introduced; one (Columnar Form) is 24′ high, 8 to 10′ wide and uniformly columnar; the other is broader (Oval Form) but still oval in outline with exceptionally thick, dark green leaves; Will has 5-year-old plants on their own roots and the Oval Form is dense, well-branched and better looking than 'Fastigiata'; the Columnar Form is not as dense at a comparable age.

'Variegata'—Krüssmann lists both a white ('Albo-variegata') and this form—an irregular yellow patched and marked form; before 1770; 'Punctata' with white spotted leaves is also described.

PROPAGATION: The best prescriptions for handling seed vary so several are presented here. Dormancy may be caused by conditions in the embryo and endosperm and stratification for 28 days at 68°F followed by 87 to 98 days at 41°F is recommended; seed should be collected green and sown if germination is expected the first spring; seed should be collected as wings are turning yellow and are still pliable; drying allows hard seed coat to develop and if this happens a warm followed by cold period is needed; seed that has not become hard-walled can be germinated if stratified for 3 to 4 months at 41°F. The best information on cuttings is derived from Cesarini, *Proc. Intl. Plant Prop. Soc.* 21:380–382 (1971):

1. Select healthy, vigorous stock plants. Cuttings should be six to eight inches long and wounded.
2. Cuttings should be taken about the time the last leaf reaches mature size and the last bud has not fully developed. This would probably coincide with the month of July.
3. Many rooting mediums were tested; however, the best was a mixture of perlite and peat moss.
4. Hormone concentrations must be high. 3000 ppm and 8000 ppm are not sufficiently high and a concentration of 2% IBA (20,000 parts per million) was required to successfully root *Carpinus betulus* 'Fastigiata'.
5. After rooting, the cuttings require a dormancy period. Placing them at a temperature of 32°F during the winter months satisfied the dormancy requirements, and, when budbreak ensued in March or April, the rooted cuttings were transplanted to containers.

Other work I have read corroborates Cesarini's findings. Cultivars are usually grafted onto seedlings of the species. Etiolation has increased the rooting potential of the species. See *Proc. Intl. Plant Prop. Soc.* 34:543–550 (1984) for specifics.

Perhaps an addendum is justified since my research technician Ms. Vickie Waters-Oldham and I have proceeded even further down the propagation path. Firm cuttings, May 31, 1994 (Griffin, GA), 10000 ppm KIBA, 3 perlite:1 peat medium, intermittent mist, produced 50% rooting in 8 weeks; after rooting cuttings are lightly fertilized (Osmocote 18-6-12) and placed under extended photoperiod with almost 80% bud break being induced, cuttings are hardened off outside starting in late September and overwintered. 'Pendula' has also been rooted and overwintered with similar success.

ADDITIONAL NOTES: Minimum seed bearing age is between 10 and 30 years. To date I have had poor success with seed propagation. The wood is extremely hard, heavy, and tough. Cogs, axils, and spokes were made of hornbeam. It is used extensively in English and continental Europe for hedges and allées. There are many fine specimens of this species and the cultivars in Cave Hill Cemetery, Louisville, KY, and Spring Grove Cemetery, Cincinnati, OH. Perhaps the most spectacular specimens of the species are located in Lexington Cemetery, Lexington, KY, although the Arnold Arboretum has several magnificent specimens, one a 50′ high, oval-rounded, central leadered tree; another a superlative low-branched, wide-spreading form of broad-rounded proportions. Has performed well in Athens and Griffin, GA. Beavers appear to love the tree and, in test plots at Griffin, chewed this species while ignoring *Zelkova*, *Prunus*, *Ilex*, and × *Cupressocyparis*. Tremendous influx of papers on *Carpinus* and the closely related *Ostrya* appeared in *The Plantsman*. The reader is referred to 7(3):173–191 (1985), 7(4):205–212 (1986), 7(4):212–216 (1986), and 8(2):112–117 (1986). More information than this book can present but excellent discussions of species and cultivars.

NATIVE HABITAT: Europe, Asia Minor, southeast of England. Long cultivated.

Carpinus caroliniana Walter — American Hornbeam, also called Blue Beech, Ironwood, Musclewood, and Water Beech.
(kär-pī′nus ka-ro-lin-i-ā′nȧ)

LEAVES: Alternate, simple, 2 1/2 to 5″ long, 1 to 2″ wide, ovate-oblong, acuminate, rounded or heart-shaped, sharply and doubly serrate, glabrous, dark green, often lustrous, 10 to 14 vein pairs, pilose on veins beneath and with axillary tufts of hair, veins seldom forking at ends; petiole—1/4 to 1/2″ long, pubescent.

BUDS: Imbricate, small, 1/6 to 1/4″ long, 12, 4-ranked scales, narrowly ovate to oblong, pointed, reddish-brown-black, more or less hairy, especially buds containing staminate catkins, terminal bud absent; scales—often downy on edges, frequently with woolly patch of down on tip.

STEM: Slender, dark red-brown, shining, smooth or often somewhat hairy; pith—pale, continuous.

BARK: Smooth, thin, dark bluish gray, close fitting, sinewy, fluted with smooth, rounded, longitudinal ridges; wood—heavy and hard.

FRUIT: Small, ribbed, seed-like nutlet enclosed by a veiny, irregular 3-lobed bract, about 1″ long.

SIZE: 20 to 30′ in height and as wide, often smaller but with the potential to reach 40 to 50′; 65′ high by 66′ wide tree reported from Milton, NY; 68′ high by 42′ wide in Spring Grove, Cincinnati, OH; national champion 69′ by 56′ in Ulster County, NY.

HARDINESS: Zone 3b to 9.

HABIT: Small to medium, multi-stemmed, bushy shrub or single-stemmed tree with a wide-spreading, flat or round-topped (often irregular) crown; some plants are quite uniform.

RATE: Slow, averaging 8 to 10′ over a 10 year period; will grow faster with uniform moisture and fertility.

TEXTURE: Medium in leaf and winter.

BARK COLOR: On older branches develops a slate gray, smooth, irregularly fluted appearance; the overall appearance is comparable to the flexed biceps and forearm muscles and, hence, the name Musclewood.

LEAF COLOR: Dark green, often lustrous, in summer changing to yellow, orange, red and reddish purple in the fall; have seen trees of good yellow and others orange-red; considerable fall color variation exists; drops its leaves ahead of *Carpinus betulus*, actually an opportunity for selecting superior fall coloring clones.

FLOWERS: Monoecious; male—1 to 1 1/2″ long; female—2 to 4″ long; the bracts 3-lobed, 1 to 1 1/2″ long, the middle lobe the widest (1″ diameter), toothed.

FRUIT: A nut(let), borne at base of 1 to 1 1/2″ long, 3-lobed bract; the middle largest and almost 1″ high; entire infructescence 2 to 4″ long.

CULTURE: Somewhat difficult to transplant and should be moved balled-and-burlapped or from a container in winter to early spring; performs best in deep, rich, moist, slightly acid soils although will grow in drier sites; does well in heavy shade and is often found as an understory plant in forests; I have observed this species in many landscape situations and believe it is much more adaptable than ever given credit; has prospered in calcareous soils of Illinois without evidence of chlorosis; has been used in shopping mall island plantings in Georgia and performed reasonably well; in the 1990 edition I mentioned it did not withstand pruning as well as *C. betulus*, recent discoveries indicate that *C. caroliniana* is readily prunable/pleachable and will serve as a hedge, screen, formal element; William Paca Gardens, Annapolis, MD has used the plant effectively.

DISEASES AND INSECTS: Leaf spots, cankers, twig blight, maple *Phenococcus* scale, none of which are significantly serious although of late I have seen considerable dieback which appeared to be caused by canker; two-lined chestnut borer has attacked and killed stressed trees of *C. caroliniana* and *C. betulus*, see *J. Arboriculture* 16:236–239 (1990).

LANDSCAPE VALUE: Best in naturalized situation; interesting native tree often seen in the woods and inappropriately called "beech" by the uninitiated; does well in moist soils and will tolerate periodic flooding; might be worth a longer look in man-made landscapes.

CULTIVARS:

Palisade™ ('Ccsqu')—A broad upright selection with strongly ascending branches; 2 to 1 height to width ratio; have seen the parent tree and was impressed by habit and good dark green foliage; respectable yellow fall color; introduced by Tree Introductions, Inc., P.O. Box 5014, Athens, GA 30604.

'Pyramidalis'—The tree is supposedly V-shaped with a rounded top; a tree in the Arnold Arboretum at 43 years of age was 40′ tall and 33′ in spread; as I viewed it not too different from the species.

PROPAGATION: Seed, moist stratification at 68 to 86°F for 60 days followed by 41°F for 60 days; see *HortScience* 14:621–622 (1979) for good information on seed germination; in short, authors found that green seeds collected in early September germinated 24% the following spring; those collected in late September germinated less than 1%; stratification for 15 and 18 weeks increased germination to 43 and 58%, respectively. Cuttings have been rooted but the process is slow and unreliable.

ADDITIONAL NOTES: Quite a handsome native tree, usually found as an understory plant along rivers and streams throughout its native range where it withstands periodic flooding. This tree has a lot to offer our landscapes in subtle beauty. See Dirr, "The hornbeams—choice plants for American gardens," *American Nurseryman* 148(10):10–11, 46, 48, 50, 52 (1978), for more detailed information.

NATIVE HABITAT: Nova Scotia to Minnesota, south to Florida and Texas. Introduced 1812.

RELATED SPECIES: There are a number of other species that one only sees in arboreta, botanical gardens and private plant collections. The following remarks are based on my observations.

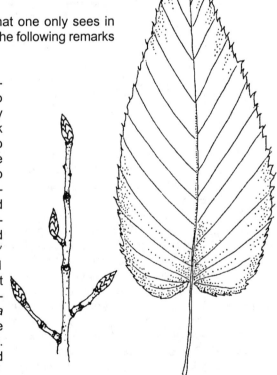

Carpinus cordata Bl., (kär-pī′nus kôr-dā′tà), Heartleaf Hornbeam, is a rather large-leaved (2 1/2 to 5 1/2″ long, 1 1/2 to 1 3/4″ wide) species; the leaf bases of which are deeply heart-shaped and give rise to the specific epithet. The dark green leaves (15 to 20 vein pairs) show no propensity to develop fall color. The habit is rounded and landscape size ranges from 20 to 30′ although the species can grow 40 to 50′ in the wild. The Arnold and Morton Arboreta have specimens that have grown slowly over the years. A 52-year-old tree in the Morton was 13′ by 14′. The bark is totally different from the above species being slightly furrowed and scaly. The ovoid, rich brown winter buds are about 5/8″ long. The fruits are borne in cigar-shaped, 3 to 5″ long, 1 1/2″ wide catkins; the bracts closely overlapping, each bract folded and partially covering the nut; the entire infructescence reminding of *Ostrya virginiana*. *Carpinus japonica* has a similar fruiting structure. One of the most handsome examples of *C. cordata* resides in Bernheim Arboretum. Northeast Asia, north and west China, Japan. Introduced 1879. Zone (4)5 to 6.

Carpinus japonica Bl., (kär-pī′nus jȧ-pon′i-kȧ),
Japanese Hornbeam, is a small tree seldom
growing more than 20 to 30′ in this country.
The wide-spreading branches radiate like
the ribs on a fan and the species can be
identified by this feature. The ovate to oblong, 2 to 4 1/2″ long, 3/4 to 1 3/4″ wide,
acuminate, weakly cordate to rounded (a
feature that separates it from *C. cordata*),
doubly toothed, 20 to 24 vein-paired, deeply
impressed dark green leaves do not color
appreciably in the fall although the literature

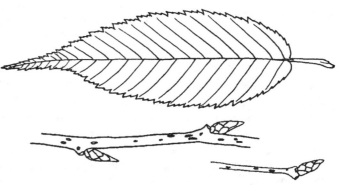

mentions red. The fruits are similar to those of *C. cordata* but shorter (2 to 2 1/2″ long). The bark is
shallowly furrowed and scaly. The foliage is handsome and for this reason alone it is worth planting. John
Barbour, Bold Spring Nursery, Monroe, GA and Select Trees, Athens, GA have grown this species and
it never lived up to the superior billing. Leaves appear tired (bedraggled) by late summer–early fall and
never develop noticeable fall color. The literature has been kinder to the species than the reality of its
performance warrants. Japan. Introduced 1879. Zone (4)5 to 7.

Carpinus orientalis Mill., (kär-pī′nus ôr-i-en-tā′lis), Oriental Hornbeam, exists as a large shrub or small tree
(20 to 25′) with an overall U-shaped branching pattern. The small, glossy dark green leaves are 1 to 2″
long and 1/2 to 1″ wide. Again they do not color well
in the fall although the literature says red. The bracts
of this species are unlobed which separates it from *C.
betulus* and *C. caroliniana*. The bark is similar, on a
micro-scale, to *C. betulus* and *C. caroliniana*. The
main branches and stems are twisted, presenting an

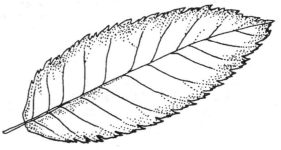

interesting winter branch structure. In Wooster, OH, trees averaged 14 to 20″ in height per year over a
7 year period. Southeast Europe, Asia Minor. Introduced 1739. Zone 5 to 6(7).

Other species that the intrepid hornbeam lover might want to track down include: *C. coreana* Nak.; *C.
fangiana* Hu.; *C. henryana* Winkler; *C. laxiflora* (Sieb. & Zucc.) Bl., Loose-flower Hornbeam (appropriately
named); *C. mollicoma* Hu.; *C. omeiensis* Hu & Fang; *C. polyneura* Franch.; *C. × schuschuensis* Winkler; *C.
tschonoskii* Maxim., Yeddo Hornbeam; *C. turczaninovii* Hance; and *C. viminea* Wall. ex Lindl. There is a
pendulous form of *C. laxiflora* that is rather elegant. In Zone 7b, *C. laxiflora* has not performed well.

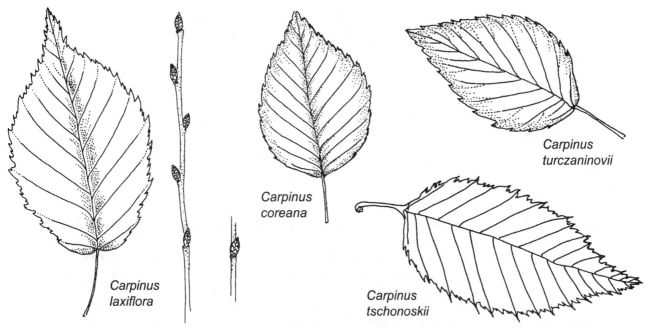

*Carpinus
turczaninovii*

*Carpinus
coreana*

*Carpinus
laxiflora*

*Carpinus
tschonoskii*

Carya Nutt. — Hickory, Pecan, Bitternut
FAMILY: Juglandaceae

The hickories are treated as a group rather than individual entities because of their limited use in normal landscape situations. Although extremely beautiful and aesthetic native trees, they develop large taproots and are difficult to transplant. Most are large trees reaching 60′ or more and may drop leaves, stems, or fruits. Their size and limited ornamental assets, as well as the difficulty in transplanting, limit extensive landscape use. Arguably, they offer the most beautiful yellow to gold fall color of any tree. Color persists for an extended period of time. The nuts of several species are edible and utilized extensively by man and animal. The production of pecan, *Carya illinoinensis*, is a large commercial business and research and breeding continues on this most important crop.

The flowers are monoecious with the male borne in drooping 3-branched catkins; the female in few-flowered terminal spikes, developing with the leaves in April into early May. The fruits are bony, hard-shelled nuts encased in a 4-valved "husk" (involucre?) often splitting away but in some species persisting. They usually ripen in October and drop from the trees. The seeds are either bitter or sweet. In the wild, seed dissemination is largely through squirrels who bury them in the forest floor as a food reserve. The hickories are typically American trees and the following are some of the more common.

ADDITIONAL NOTES: *Carya* exhibit embryo dormancy and should be stratified in a moist medium at 33 to 40°F for 30 to 150 days. Prior to the cold treatment nuts should be soaked in water at room temperature for 2 to 4 days with 1 or 2 water changes per day. Typically in our work, *C. glabra*, *C. tomentosa*, and *C. ovata* are fall planted in 3-gallon containers in a bark medium, covered with a screen and placed outside over winter. Germination takes place in spring with a pronounced tap root and minimal shoot growth evident the first year. Cultivars are budded or grafted on seedling understocks. Pecan grafting is an art and science and for detailed information see Dirr and Heuser, 1987. Although seldom rooted from cuttings success is achievable with attention-to-detail. Young shoots of 20-year-old 'Colby' pecan were etiolated for 20 days, detached on June 25, treated with 0, 2500 or 5000 ppm IBA dip for 10 seconds, sand, intermittent mist, with 18, 66 and 96% rooting, respectively.

Carya cordiformis (Wang.) K. Koch— Bitternut Hickory, Swamp Hickory

LEAVES: Alternate, pinnately compound, 6 to 10″(15″) long, composed of 7, sometimes 5 or 9, leaflets, each 3 to 6″ long, 3/4 to 2 1/2″ wide, ovate to lanceolate, acuminate, sharply serrate, light green and glabrous above, pubescent below on midrib and veins; petiole and rachis pubescent.

BUDS: Valvate scales, strikingly sulfur-yellow; terminal bud—1/2 to 3/4″ long, flattened, obliquely blunt pointed, scurfy-pubescent; lateral buds—more or less 4-angled, much smaller than the terminal.

STEM: Stout, buff, gray or reddish, smooth or slightly downy toward apex; pith—brown, solid.

Carya cordiformis, (kä′ri-à kôr-di-fôr′mis), Bitternut Hickory, can grow to 50 to 75′ in height and larger. National champion is 134′ by 91′ at Lake Accotink, VA. Professor J.C. McDaniel, University of Illinois, first introduced me to this species and pointed out the striking sulphur yellow buds that permit distinction from other *Carya* species. It is usually a slender tree with rather irregular, cylindrical crown of stiff ascending branches, often widest at the top. Supposedly the fastest growing of the hickories. Bark is gray to brown and shallowly furrowed. Fruit suborbicular, 1 1/4″ long, 4-winged. Seeds are bitter and squirrels tend to ignore them. Native from Quebec to Minnesota, south to Florida and Louisiana. Introduced 1689. Zone 4 to 9.

Carya glabra (Mill.) Sweet. — Pignut Hickory

LEAVES: Alternate, pinnately compound, 5 to 7 leaflets, usually 5, entire leaf 8 to 12″ long, each leaflet 3 to 6 1/2″ long, 1 to 2″ wide, the terminal leaflets largest, the lowest pair about 1/3 the size; terminal obovate, basal ovate-lanceolate, sharply toothed, dark yellowish green, glabrous above, except on midrib and veins beneath.

BARK: On young trees smooth, gray-brown, eventually developing rounded ridges, forming an irregular diamond-shaped pattern.

Carya glabra, (kā′ri-à glā′brà), Pignut Hickory, reaches 50 to 60′ in height with a spread of 25 to 35′ although can grow to 100′. National champion is 95′ by 55′ in Green Ridge State Forest, Flintstone, MD. It has a tapering trunk and a regular, rather open, oval head of slender, contorted branches. Found along hillsides and ridges in well-drained to dry, fairly rich soils. Nuts are subglobose, 3/4 to 1 1/4″ diameter. Seeds are bitter and astringent although there are references that state sweet. From Ohio childhood experiences I remember an astringent taste. Could it be that my third grade powers of identification (taste) were not fully developed? Certainly beautiful in rich golden yellow fall color. No other tree rivals it in late October–early November on the Georgia campus. In this author's opinion—an absolutely beautiful tree particularly in autumn. I have tried to buy small seedlings with minimal good fortune. In 1995, purchased *Carya ovata* seedling liners and the root was literally a carrot. Tap roots were immense. Transplanted into 15-gallon containers with about 60% mortality. The same result would probably occur with *C. glabra*. *Carya glabra* is an important timber tree and the strong, hard wood is used for tool handles and fuel. Native from Maine to Ontario, south to Florida, Alabama and Mississippi. Introduced 1750. Zone 4 to 9.

Carya illinoinensis (Wang.) K. Koch. — Pecan

LEAVES: Alternate, pinnately compound, 12 to 20″ long, 9, 11 to 17 leaflets, each leaflet 4 to 7″ long, 1 to 3″ wide, short-stalked, lustrous dark green, oblong-lanceolate, usually falcate, serrate or doubly serrate, glandular and tomentose when young, becoming glabrous; petiole—glabrous or pubescent.

BUDS: Valvate, 1/4 to 1/3″ long, dark brown, pubescent, ovoid, apex pointed, looks like a small roasted almond.

STEM: Stout, olive-brown, pubescent, leaf scar indented and partially surrounding bud.

Carya illinoinensis, (kā′ri-à il-in-oyn-en′sis), Pecan, will grow 70 to 100′ in height with a spread of 40 to 75′ and can reach 150′. National champion is 118′ by 159′ in Weatherford, TX. Largest of the hickories, tall and straight with a uniform, symmetrical, broadly oval crown. Extremely difficult to transplant as it develops a long taproot. On a 6′ tree the taproot may extend 4′ or more. Prefers deep, moist, well-drained soil. The best hickory for fruits and many cultivars have been selected for outstanding fruiting characters. Bark is brown-black and with age becomes somewhat scaly. Makes an interesting ornamental in the Midwest but does not bear liberal quantities of fruit. Abundant in South and trees are often low-branched and wide-spreading. This seems to be especially true of trees in orchard and cultivated situations. Pecans are a major horticultural crop in the Southeast and Southwest. For landscape purposes it is not a good tree because of insect and disease problems. Also the tree produces a high level of litter, especially in late summer and fall when infected leaves and maturing nuts start to abscise. Georgia has an excellent pecan research program that has served as the foundation for the industry. Many excellent publications on pecan culture are available from the Georgia Cooperative Extension Service. "Insect pests and diseases of the Pecan," USDA ARM-S-5 (1979) describes the biology of 40 insects and diseases that affect pecan. Dr. Darrel Sparks, Department of Horticulture, University of Georgia, published the definitive book on pecans. It is available through the author. Native from Iowa to Indiana to Alabama, Texas and Mexico. Follows the river basins very closely. Introduced 1760. Zone 5 to 9.

Carya laciniosa (Michx. f.) Loud. — Shellbark Hickory

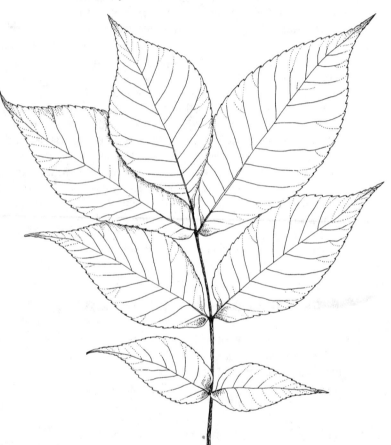

LEAVES: Alternate, pinnately compound, 10 to 24″ long, 7 leaflets, rarely 5 to 9, 4 to 10″ long, oblong-lanceolate, acuminate, serrate, dark yellow-green, pubescent beneath; petiolule and rachis pubescent or glabrous, often persistent during winter. Similar to *C. ovata* in bud, stem and bark characteristics; leaflets do not have hairs at tip of teeth like those of *C. ovata*; stem is often orange-brown (pubescence) in color; oval fruit is somewhat larger (2″), 1/4″ husk, lacking wings, and nut is 4- to 6-ribbed versus 4-ribbed nut of *C. ovata*.

Carya laciniosa, (kā′ri-à là-sin-i-ō′sà), Shellbark Hickory, Big Shellbark Hickory, King Nut Hickory, reaches 60 to 80′ in height or greater and forms a high branching tree with a straight slender trunk and narrow oblong crown of small spreading branches, the lower drooping, the upper ascending. National champion is 139′ by 80′ in Greenup, KY. The seed is sweet and edible. In many respects similar to *C. ovata* except it does not grow as large and tends to inhabit wet bottomlands, even those which are covered with water for a time. Possesses the interesting "shaggy" bark similar to *C. ovata*. Excellent lumber quality, used for tool handles, implements, furniture and construction timbers. Native from New York to Iowa, south to Tennessee and Oklahoma on deep, moist, fertile soils of floodplains and bottomlands. Introduced 1800. Zone 5 to 8.

Carya ovata (Mill.) K. Koch. — Shagbark Hickory

LEAVES: Alternate, pinnately compound, 8 to 14″ long, 5 leaflets, rarely 7, 4 to 6″ long, 1/2 to 2 1/2″ wide, elliptic to oblong-lanceolate, acuminate, serrate and densely ciliate, pubescent and glandular below when young, finally glabrous, deep yellow-green.
BUDS: Imbricate, terminal—1/2 to 1″ long, broadly ovate, rather blunt-pointed, brown, with 2 to 4 visible, overlapping, pubescent, loose fitting scales.

STEM: Stout, somewhat downy or smooth and shining, reddish brown to light gray; lenticels—numerous, pale, conspicuous, longitudinally elongated.

BARK: On old trunks shagging characteristically into long flat plates which are free at the base or both ends; usually more pronounced than Shellbark with plates more recurved.

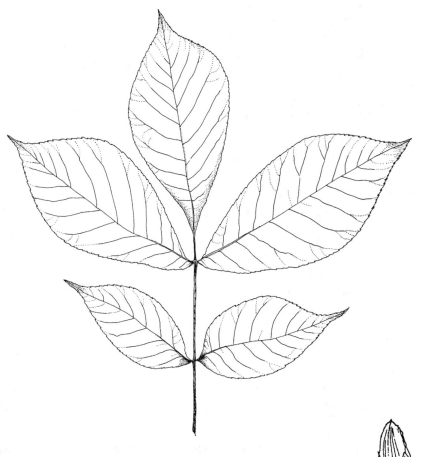

Carya ovata, (kā′ri-ȧ ō-vā′tȧ), Shagbark Hickory, is a large tree reaching 60 to 80′ in height but can grow to 100 to 120′. Co-national champions are 153′ by 56′ in Sumter National Forest, SC and 132′ by 109′ in Todd County, KY. Usually develops a straight, cylindrical trunk with an oblong crown of ascending and descending branches (similar to *C. laciniosa*). The foliage is a deep yellow-green in summer and changes to rich yellow and golden brown tones in fall (this is also true for *C. laciniosa*). Leaves when bruised or crushed have the faint aroma of apples. Fruit is nearly round, 1 to 1 1/2″ diameter, shell angled, thick (1/4 to 3/8″ diameter), splitting at base. The seed is edible and quite sweet. As a boy I collected bags full of these nuts. The trees always grew on the lower slopes and in well-drained alluvial soils of southern Ohio. Prefers rich and well-drained loams, but is adaptable to a wide range of soils. Is found on both drier upland slopes and deep well-drained soils in lowlands and valleys. Seedlings of this hickory develop a large and remarkably deep taproot which may penetrate downward 2 to 3′ the first season with a corresponding top growth of only a few inches. This is typical of many hickories. The bark is gray to brown and breaks up in thin plates which are free at the end and attached at the middle; the overall effect is a "shaggy" character and, hence, the name Shagbark Hickory. Certainly, along with *C. laciniosa*, one of the most beautiful and easily identifiable of all eastern North American hardwoods. What could taste better than Hickory smoked hams and bacon? Try some hickory chips in your next barbecue outing. Native from Quebec to Minnesota, south to Georgia and Texas. Cultivated 1629. Zone 4 to 8.

Carya tomentosa Nutt. — Mockernut Hickory, White Hickory

LEAVES: Alternate, compound pinnate, 6 to 12″ long, 7 to 9 leaflets, the upper pair 5 to 9″ long, 3 to 5″ wide; the lower pair two third's that size, oblong to oblong-lanceolate, acuminate, serrate, dark yellow-green above, densely pubescent and glandular below, fragrant when bruised; petiole and rachis tomentose.

Carya tomentosa, (kā′ri-ȧ tō-men-tō′sȧ), Mockernut Hickory or White Hickory, develops a narrow to broadly rounded outline and trees may average 50 to 60′ in height, although trees over 100′ are known. National champion is 156′ by 70′ in Humphreys County, MS. Bark, unlike *C. laciniosa* and *C. ovata*, is dark gray, thin, with shallow furrows and narrow flat ridges forming a net-like, diamond pattern. The tree is found on ridges, dry hills and slopes but grows best in moist, well-drained soil. In the 1990 edition, I mentioned that the tree was not common in the Athens area. The truth is that either I could not separate it from *C. glabra* which is everywhere or had my head in the clouds. The species *now* appears with frequency in dry woods and is mixed with *C. glabra*. The larger and greater leaflet numbers and the distinct pubescence on the stems and leaf provide easy separation from *C. glabra*. Fall color is a deep golden yellow to golden brown and long persistent. The fruit is rounded to elliptical, 1 to 1 1/2″ long, angled, with a 1/4 to 1/3″ thick husk splitting to the base. Seed is edible. If native, like

other hickories, do not destroy. To find one in commerce would be difficult. Massachusetts to Ontario and Nebraska, south to Florida and Texas. Introduced 1766. Zone 4 to 9.

ADDITIONAL NOTES: Other species of lesser importance that occasionally rear their heads for identification include: *C. aquatica* (Michx. f.) Nutt., Water Hickory, 7 to 13 leaflets, to 4 1/2″ long; *C. myristiciformis* (Michx. f.) Nutt., Nutmeg Hickory, 5 to 11 leaflets, silvery beneath, terminal 3 to 5″ long, lower pairs narrower, smaller; and *C. pallida* (Ashe) Engl. and Gräbn., Sand Hickory, 7 to 9 leaflets, to 4 1/2″ long, silver gray scales and hairy beneath.

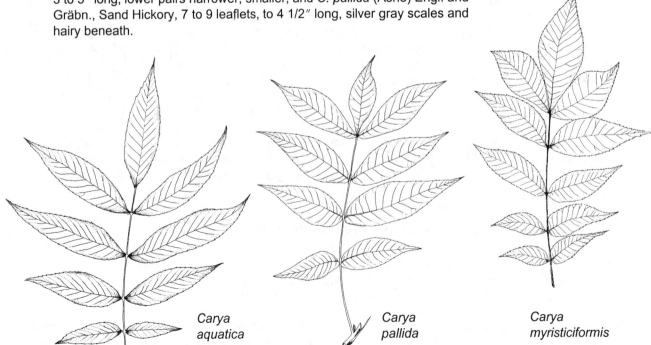

Carya aquatica

Carya pallida

Carya myristiciformis

Caryopteris × *clandonensis* A. Simmonds ex Rehd. — Bluebeard, Blue-spirea, Blue-mist Shrub

FAMILY: Verbenaceae
LEAVES: Opposite, simple, ovate, 1 to 2″ long, 1/2 to 1 1/4″ wide, acute, rounded, entire or with full teeth, dull blue-green above, silvery tomentose beneath; petiole—about 1/4″ long, pubescent.
STEM: Slender, 4-sided, pubescent, grayish green, nodes flattened.

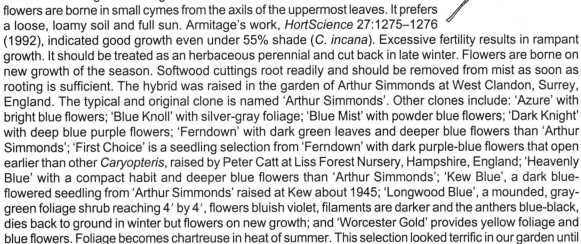

Caryopteris × *clandonensis*, (kar-i-op′tēr-is klàn-dō-nen′sis), Blue-spirea, is a low (2′ to 3′), mounded, almost herbaceous shrub that graces the late summer garden with lovely bright blue flowers. This species is the result of a cross between *C. incana* × *C. mongholica* Bunge. and is the most common form in cultivation. The flowers are borne in small cymes from the axils of the uppermost leaves. It prefers a loose, loamy soil and full sun. Armitage's work, *HortScience* 27:1275–1276 (1992), indicated good growth even under 55% shade (*C. incana*). Excessive fertility results in rampant growth. It should be treated as an herbaceous perennial and cut back in late winter. Flowers are borne on new growth of the season. Softwood cuttings root readily and should be removed from mist as soon as rooting is sufficient. The hybrid was raised in the garden of Arthur Simmonds at West Clandon, Surrey, England. The typical and original clone is named 'Arthur Simmonds'. Other clones include: 'Azure' with bright blue flowers; 'Blue Knoll' with silver-gray foliage; 'Blue Mist' with powder blue flowers; 'Dark Knight' with deep blue purple flowers; 'Ferndown' with dark green leaves and deeper blue flowers than 'Arthur Simmonds'; 'First Choice' is a seedling selection from 'Ferndown' with dark purple-blue flowers that open earlier than other *Caryopteris*, raised by Peter Catt at Liss Forest Nursery, Hampshire, England; 'Heavenly Blue' with a compact habit and deeper blue flowers than 'Arthur Simmonds'; 'Kew Blue', a dark blue-flowered seedling from 'Arthur Simmonds' raised at Kew about 1945; 'Longwood Blue', a mounded, gray-green foliage shrub reaching 4′ by 4′, flowers bluish violet, filaments are darker and the anthers blue-black, dies back to ground in winter but flowers on new growth; and 'Worcester Gold' provides yellow foliage and blue flowers. Foliage becomes chartreuse in heat of summer. This selection looked terrific in our garden until about late July 1994 then the foliage melted out, possibly due to the rainiest year in decades. See *Plantsman* 11(1):15–19 (1989) for discussion of cultivars. Zone 6 to 9.

RELATED SPECIES:

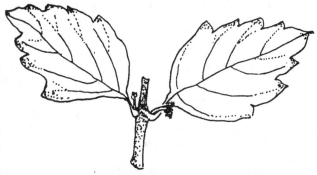

Caryopteris incana (Thunb.) Miq., (kar-i-op′tēr-is in-kā′nà), Common Bluebeard, grows 3 to 5′ and is rather loose and open. The leaves are coarsely toothed, almost lobed, 1 to 3″ long, 1/2 to 1 1/2″ wide, dull green and pubescent above, silvery pubescent beneath. The bright violet-blue fragrant flowers occur in hemispherical cymes from the axils of the uppermost leaves and literally encircle the stem. Has proven spectacular in Dr. Armitage's cut flower tests at Georgia. Much showier than the *C.* × *clandonensis* types but not as cold hardy. 'Blue Billows' is a low compact trailer with dense lavender-blue flowers throughout September–October. Longwood Gardens has a large planting of this cultivar and reported it was killed to the ground in the severe winter of 1976–77 but grew and flowered the next season. 'Candida' is a white-flowered form. Japan to northwestern China. Introduced 1844. Zone 7. Can be grown further north when treated as an herbaceous perennial.

ADDITIONAL NOTES: The *Caryopteris* make lovely garden shrubs. Their leaves, stems and flowers are pleasantly scented. Their late flowering period makes them valuable garden plants. Given a well-drained, loose soil and a sunny position they will prosper for years. I have grown *C.* × *clandonensis* for years and treat the plant with minimal maintenance, yet it responds with numerous light blue flowers from July to late August. I always cut the plant back in late winter and provide a handful of granular 10-10-10 fertilizer at the base. On occasion I have literally pulled plants out of the ground for relocation. Roots are sparse and stringy but I have never lost a plant after transplanting. Since flowers occur on new growth of the season nothing is lost by vigorous pruning early in the season. My observations indicate that the plant will fruit itself out of flowering much like *Hibiscus syriacus*. When the flower production is slowing in August, a feather pruning to induce new shoot growth will increase flower production. Worthwhile plant for massing in dry, sunny situations or for a filler in a low border where the gray-green foliage color provides an interesting diversion.

Castanea mollissima Bl. — Chinese Chestnut
(kas-tā′ne-à mol-lis′i-mà)

FAMILY: Fagaceae

LEAVES: Alternate, simple, 3 to 6″(8″) long, 2 to 3 1/2″ wide, elliptic-oblong to oblong-lanceolate, acuminate, cuneate at base, teeth triangular or aristate, lustrous dark green above, whitish tomentose or green and soft-pubescent beneath at least on veins; petiole—1/4 to 1/2″ long, usually hairy.

BUDS: Two to 3 scales weakly overlapping, gray-brown, pubescent, 1/4″ long, ovoid.

STEM: Pubescent with long spreading hairs, olive-brown, prominent lenticels; pith—star-shaped, 4- to 5-sided; bark on second and third year stems is cherry-like in appearance.

SIZE: 40 to 60′ in height with an equal spread.

HARDINESS: Zone 4 to 8.

HABIT: Rounded in youth, developing a rounded to broad-rounded outline at maturity, usually low-branched.

RATE: Slow to medium, 4 to 7′ over a 3 to 4 year period.

TEXTURE: Medium throughout the seasons.

BARK: Gray-brown to brown and strongly ridged-and-furrowed.

LEAF COLOR: Reddish upon unfolding, changing to a lustrous dark green in summer culminating with shades of yellow and bronze in fall; can be handsome and often long persistent.

FLOWERS: Pale yellow or creamy, of heavy, unpleasant odor, monoecious, staminate in erect cylindrical catkins, pistillate on the lower part of the upper staminate catkins, usually 3 female in a prickly symmetrical involucre, borne in a 4 to 5″(8″) long and wide panicle in June (late May, Athens).

FRUIT: Nut, 1 to 4 enclosed in a prickly involucre which splits at maturity into 2 to 4 valves, fruits are edible and relished by man and animals, seed-grown trees often produce fruit after 4 to 5 years, involucre ranges from 2 to 3 1/2″ wide and is covered with dense slender spines (i.e., prickly involucre), nuts rich chestnut brown in color, 3/4 to 1 1/2″ across.

CULTURE: Easily transplanted when young (5 to 6′); prefer acid (pH to 5.5 to 6.5), well-drained, loamy soil; full sun; does well in hot, dry climates; responds well to fertilization; actually a very tough and seemingly durable tree that I have observed under a host of differing environmental conditions; actually might fall in the ornamental tree category of requiring minimal attention although nut production is not without problems.

DISEASES AND INSECTS: Blight (discussed under *C. dentata*), twig canker of asiatic chestnuts, weevils which damage the roots, oriental chestnut gall wasp is a devastating insect, this species is *not* immune to chestnut blight but resistant.

LANDSCAPE VALUE: Best as a replacement for the American Chestnut; valued for fruits; in previous editions I mentioned the possibility of street tree use but have seen too many instances of prickly burrs littering the ground, the fruits' prickly covers are a real nuisance and fall over an extended period of time making quick cleanup a somewhat dubious process.

PROPAGATION: Seed should be stratified under cool moist conditions for 60 to 90 days or fall planted; seeds deteriorate rapidly and should not be allowed to dry out; cuttings taken from young trees have been rooted; cultivars are budded.

ADDITIONAL NOTES: Interesting story relative to one man's love for the chestnut that may prove of interest to the reader. The Dunstan Hybrid chestnuts have been under development since the 1950's. Dr. Robert Dunstan of North Carolina grafted an apparent blight-free American strain onto *Castanea crenata* Sieb. & Zucc., Japanese Chestnut.

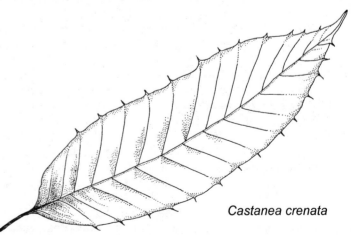

Castanea crenata

When it flowered he crossed it with Chinese Chestnut. Using progeny from this cross he backcrossed it to the American parent. The resulting F$_2$ generation was moved to Alachua, FL where there are now 50 mature trees, none with blight despite attempts to induce fungal cankers by inoculation. Several superior trees have been grafted. They produce straight trunks, with heavy crops of sweet nuts, supposedly superior to Chinese Chestnut. Trees bear in 3 to 5 years. Write Chestnut Hill Nursery, Route 1, Box 341, Alachua, FL, 32615.

NATIVE HABITAT: Northern China, Korea. Introduced 1853 and 1903.

RELATED SPECIES:

Castanea dentata (Marshall) Borkh. — American Chestnut
LEAVES: Alternate, simple, oblong-lanceolate, 5 to 8″(11″) long, 1 3/4 to 2″(3″) wide with cuneate base and long-pointed tips, numerous coarse, sharp pointed serrations, glandular, lustrous dark green above, glabrous at maturity on both surfaces; petiole—about 1/2″ long.
BUDS AND STEM: Glabrous, chestnut brown.

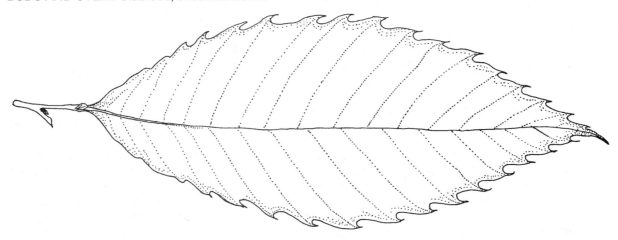

Castanea dentata, (kas-tā′ne-à den-tā′tà), American Chestnut, was once native from southern Maine to Michigan, south to Alabama and Mississippi. This tree was the queen of eastern American forest trees but now is reduced to a memory. About 1904 a blight, *Cryphonectria parasitica* (*Endothia parasitica*), was introduced along the East Coast (New York) and spread like wildfire through the forests. In the 50 years since the pathogen's introduction it spread through the entire native range. All that remains are isolated stump and root sprouts which developed after the parent tree was killed. Shoots that regenerate from roots may reach 20 to 25′ high and are then attacked by the fungus. The tree reached heights of 100′ and developed massive, wide-spreading branches, and a deep broad-rounded crown. Co-national champions are 106′ by 101′ in Cicero, WA and 86′ by 111′ in Carson, WA. The flowers are similar to those of *C. mollissima* however the fruits (bur globose, 2 to 3″ diameter, dense slender spines, with 2 to 3 nuts) are reported as being much sweeter and more flavorful than the asiatic species although I know people who do not agree. Cultivated 1800. Zone 4 to 8.

Castanea pumila (L.) Miller — Allegheny Chinkapin
LEAVES: Alternate, simple, elliptic-oblong or oblong-obovate, 3 to 5″ long, 1 1/2 to 2″ wide, acute, rounded or broadly cuneate at the base, coarsely serrate, the teeth reduced to bristles, dark green above, whitish and hairy below; petiole—1/4 to 1/2″ long, hairy, flattened on upper surface.

Castanea pumila, (kas-tā′ne-à pū′mi-là), Allegheny Chinkapin, has entered my plant life since moving south and makes, as I have seen it, a small shrub that could be used for naturalizing and providing food for wildlife. It can grow 20 to 25′ high but most often forms a 6 to 10′ high shrub. National champion is 55′

by 60′ in Putman County, FL. The fruit is about 1 1/2″ wide with normally a single (occasionally 2), 3/4 to 1″ long, dark brown, sweet, edible nut. The involucre is quite prickly. Resistant to chestnut blight. The species occurs in drier woodlands from Pennsylvania to Florida and west to Oklahoma and Texas. Introduced 1699. Zone 5 to 9.

A closely related species, *Castanea alnifolia* Nutt., Bush or Trailing Chinkapin, is a suckering shrub to 3′ high. National champion is 50′ by 30′ in Hampstead County, AR. The oblong to elliptic, 2 to 6″ long leaves are lustrous dark green above, initially tomentose beneath with shallow, bristle-tipped teeth. The prickly involucre is covered with short stout spines and houses a single nut. Georgia to Florida and Louisiana. Cultivated 1906. Zone 6 to 9.

Castanea alnifolia

Castanea sativa Mill. — Sweet, Spanish or European Chestnut
LEAVES: Alternate, simple, oblong-lanceolate, 4 1/2 to 9″ long, 2 to 3 1/2″ wide, acute or short acuminate, broad cuneate, rounded or subcordate at base, coarsely serrate, covered with a soft pubescence when developing, lustrous dark green above, glabrous on both surfaces at maturity; petiole—1/2 to 1″ long.

Castanea sativa, (kas-tā′ne-à sa-tī′và), Sweet, Spanish or European Chestnut, is not used in this country to any degree but is widespread in Europe, especially England. It is a magnificent, impressive, enormous (80 to 100′) tree that is found in parks and gardens. The rich brown bark is deeply furrowed and the ridges and furrows spiral around the trunk. On my first visit to England, this tree seemed to stand out above all others. It is an excellent choice for dry, rather sandy soils of acid persuasion. Many cultivars have been selected for fruiting characteristics and variegated, purple and cut-leaf forms have been selected for ornament. The 1 3/4 to 3″ diameter involucre is covered with dense, slender spines and houses 1 to 5(7), 3/4 to 1 1/4″ diameter nuts. Although I have not seen the plant in the eastern United States, it might be worth trying, especially the garden forms. The variegated forms 'Albo-marginata' with creamy white margins and 'Aureo-marginata' with yellowish margins are quite striking. They grow slower than the species. At Petworth House in West Sussex, there existed several magnificent old specimens that were devastated by the terrible hurricane force winds of October 16, 1987. The trunks were fully 12′ in diameter. The species is susceptible to chestnut blight and is restricted in the United States. Southern Europe, western Asia, northern Africa. Long cultivated. Zone 5 to 7.

Catalpa speciosa (Warder ex Barney) Engelm. — Northern
Catalpa, also called Western Catalpa or Hardy Catalpa.
(kà-tal′pà spē-si-ō′sà)

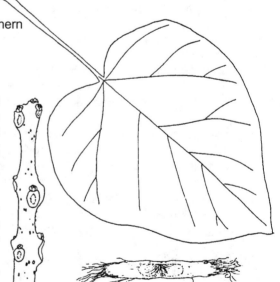

FAMILY: Bignoniaceae
LEAVES: Whorled or opposite, simple, ovate to ovate-oblong, 6 to 12″ long, 3 to 8″ wide, long acuminate, truncate to cordate, entire or with 1 to 2 lobes, medium green and glabrous above, densely pubescent beneath, scentless; petiole—4 to 6″ long.
BUDS: Terminal—absent; lateral—small, hemispherical, 1/12″ high; scales—brown, loosely overlapping.
STEM: Stout, smooth or slightly short-downy, reddish to yellowish brown; lenticels large, numerous; leaf scars— round to elliptical with depressed center; bundle traces— conspicuous, raised, forming a closed ring; pith—solid, white.
FRUIT: Capsule, 8 to 20″ long, 1/2 to 3/4″ wide, wall thick, seeds fringed, persisting into late fall and winter.

SIZE: 40 to 60′ in height with a spread of 20 to 40′ but sometimes reaching 100′ or more in the wild; co-national champions are 107′ by 85′ on State Capitol Grounds, Lansing, MI and 86′ by 79′ in Walla Walla, WA.

HARDINESS: Zone 4 to 8(9).

HABIT: Tree with a narrow, open, irregular, oval crown; can be quite striking in winter with bold rugged outline.

RATE: Medium to fast, 15′ over 7 to 8 year period.

BARK: Grayish brown on old trunks usually exhibiting a ridged-and-furrowed character although some trees exhibit a thick, scaly bark.

LEAF COLOR: Medium green although there is some variation in leaf color, some leaves are a bright green in summer, fall color a poor yellow-green to brownish, often falling before turning.

FLOWERS: Perfect, corolla white, 2″ long and wide, the tube bell-shaped, the lobes spreading and frilled at the margin, the lower one with yellow spots and ridges as in *C. bignonioides*, but less freely spotted with purple, borne in May–June, in large upright terminal panicles, 4 to 8″ long, full flower June 11, 1991 in Boston, noticed a slight fragrance.

FRUIT: Capsule, thick walled, green changing to brown, pendulous, 8 to 20″ long, 1/2 to 3/4″ wide, persisting through winter, contains numerous fringed seeds.

CULTURE: Transplant balled-and-burlapped as a small tree; very tolerant of different soil conditions but prefers deep, moist, fertile soil; withstands wet or dry and alkaline conditions; sun or partial shade; withstands extremely hot, dry environments.

DISEASES AND INSECTS: Leaf spots, powdery mildew, *Verticillium* wilt, twig blight, root rot, comstock mealybug, catalpa midge and catalpa sphinx; have not observed any *Catalpa* succumbing to insects and diseases.

LANDSCAPE VALUE: Limited value in the residential landscape because of coarseness; has a place in difficult areas but the use of this and the following species should be tempered.

PROPAGATION: Seeds germinate readily without pretreatment; cuttings of root pieces taken in December can be used for most species.

ADDITIONAL NOTES: Catalpa wood is usually quite brittle and frequently small branches are broken off in wind and ice storms. The wood in contact with the ground is extremely resistant to rot and has been used for railroad ties.

NATIVE HABITAT: Southern Illinois and Indiana to western Tennessee and northern Arkansas. Cultivated 1754.

RELATED SPECIES:

Catalpa bignonioides Walter — Southern Catalpa, also called Common Catalpa, Eastern Catalpa, Indian Cigar and Indian Bean.

LEAVES: Whorled or opposite, simple, 4 to 8″(10″) long, 3 to 8″ wide, apex abruptly acuminate, base truncate to subcordate, medium to dark green and nearly glabrous above, paler green and slightly pubescent beneath, especially on veins, of unpleasant odor when crushed; petiole—4 to 6″ long. Similar to *C. speciosa* except on veins, of smaller size and rounded habit. Flowers two weeks later than *C. speciosa* and has a thinner walled fruit. End of seeds are tufted versus fringed of *C. speciosa*.

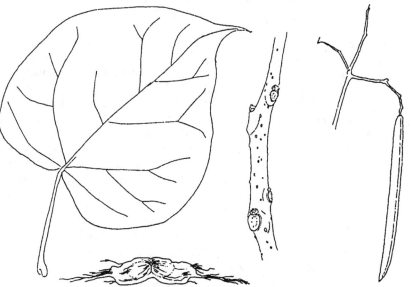

Catalpa bignonioides, (kȧ-tal′pȧ big-nō-ni-oy′dēz), Southern Catalpa, is smaller than *C. speciosa* reaching heights of 30 to 40′(60′) with an equal or greater spread. National champion is 69′ by 71′ in Palestine, TX. It is broadly rounded in outline with an irregular crown composed of short, crooked branches. Flowers are white with 2 ridges and 2 rows of yellow spots and numerous purple spots on the tube and lower lobe, borne in broad, pyramidal panicles, 8 to 10″ long and wide, mid to late May, Athens, GA, mid to late June in Boston, about two weeks after *C. speciosa*. Fruit is a 6 to 15″ long capsule. 'Aurea' has leaves of a rich yellow which, in England, does not become dull or green during the summer. 'Nana' is an old (1850), dwarf, bushy form of French origin that is grafted on a standard to produce a mushroom or globe, this form rarely if ever flowers. Other cultivars are known but to my knowledge not available in commerce. Georgia, Florida, Alabama, Mississippi and possibly Louisiana. Introduced 1726. Zone 5 to 9.

Catalpa bungei C.A. Mey., (kȧ-tal′pȧ bun′gē-ī), is a small, bushy, pyramidal to round-headed, 20 to 30′ high tree that has been confused with *C. bignonioides* 'Nana'. Its leaves vary from 2 to 7″ long and 1 1/2 to 4 1/2″ wide; petiole—1 to 3 1/2″ long. They are dark green, ovate, sometimes entire, but often scalloped with 1 to 6 large teeth on each side, mostly on the lower one-half of the leaf, glabrous at maturity. This species is rare in cultivation but there is one at the Arnold Arboretum which adheres closely to the above leaf description. The 1 to 1 1/2″ long flowers are rose-pink to white, with purple and yellow markings inside, and are borne in a 3- to 12-flowered corymb (raceme?). The capsular fruit ranges from 12 to 20″ long. Northern China. Cultivated 1877. Zone 5 to 8(?).

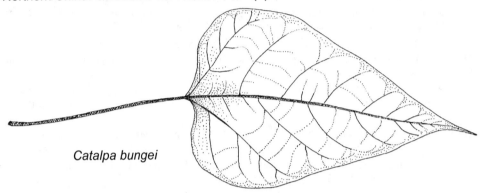

Catalpa bungei

Catalpa × erubescens Carr., (kȧ-tal′pȧ e-rū-bes′enz), represents a group of hybrids between *C. bignonioides* and *C. ovata*. The hybrid has occurred at different times and places around the world resulting in several named clones. The best known form was raised by J.C. Teas at Bayville, IN around 1874 from seed of *C. ovata*. The unfolding leaves are purplish, broad-ovate or slightly 3-lobed, cordate, up to 10 to 12″ long, and pubescent beneath. The white flowers are smaller than *C. bignonioides* but more numerous and stained with yellow and minutely spotted with purple. In 'Purpurea' the emerging shoots are black-purple and gradually change to dark green, the petiole retaining the purple coloration. It is speculated that this clone was raised in the Meehan Nurseries, Germantown, PA before 1886. 'Purpurea' is rather handsome in spring when the blackish purple shoots are emerging. I have seen plants at Kew Gardens and the Arnold Arboretum. 'Victoria' is a double-flowered, sterile form, produces no fruit, found at Queen Victoria Park, Niagra Falls, Canada. Zone 5 to 8?

Catalpa fargesii Bur., (kȧ-tal′pȧ far-jēs′ē-ī), Farges Catalpa, is mentioned here because of the unusual 1 1/2″ wide, rosy-pink to purple, with yellow and purple-brown dotted, 1 1/4″ long flowers (June), produced 7 to 15 together in corymbs. I have seen this plant at the Arnold Arboretum and in flower it is lovely. Capsules are slender and range from 12 to 18″ long. The tree is open and not particularly attractive. It would be a good candidate for hybridization work. Will mature between 40 to 50′ high in cultivation. Leaves are dark green, 3 to 6″ long, elliptic-ovate to deltoid-cordate, acuminate, subcordate to truncate or cuneate, entire or with 1 to 2 lobes, sparse pubescence above, densely so beneath. Forma *duclouxii* (Dode) Gilmour, has 1 1/2″ long, purple flowers and up to 32″ long capsules. This forma was in full flower in late June 1994 at Bath Botanic Garden, England and bordered on spectacular. Flowers appear before the leaves or as the leaves are emerging. Western China. Cultivated 1900. Zone (5)6 to 8.

Catalpa ovata G. Don., (kȧ-tal′pȧ ō-vā′tȧ), Chinese Catalpa, is similar to other species except the 8 to 12″ fruit is often thinner, less than 1/3″ wide. The 4 to 10″ long, entire or lobed leaves are glabrous, almost completely so. Seeds are smaller than *C. speciosa* and *C. bignonioides* and exhibit the fringed character of *C. speciosa*. *Catalpa ovata* is only mentioned here because of the long, thin (1/3″ diameter) fruits. Flowers are yellowish white in 4 to 10″ high narrow pyramidal panicles and not as effective as *C. speciosa* or *C. bignonioides*. In the last edition I mentioned seedlings that I had grown of this species. In a single growing season some flowered and by the second all produced flow-

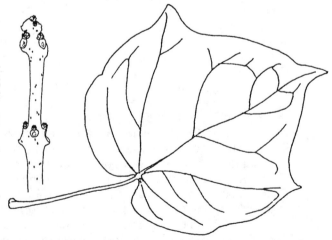

ers. There is a notable specimen on the Smith College Campus. China. Introduced 1849. Zone 5 to 8.

Ceanothus americanus L. — New Jersey Tea, also called Redroot, Wild Snowball, Mountain Sweet

(sē-à-nō'thus à-mer-i-kān'us)

FAMILY: Rhamnaceae

LEAVES: Alternate, simple, ovate to obovate, 2 to 3″ long, 3/4 to 2″ wide, acute or acuminate, irregularly serrulate, dark green at maturity, with 3 conspicuous veins, pubescent or nearly glabrous beneath; petiole—1/4 to 1/2″ long.

BUDS: Sessile, ovoid, with several glabrate, stipular scales of which the lowest only are distinct.

STEM: Rounded, rather slender, more or less puberulent, green or brownish; leaf scars—small, half-round, somewhat raised; 1 transverse bundle trace, more or less evidently compound, sometimes distinctly 3; stipules small, persistent or leaving narrow scars; pith—relatively large, white, continuous.

SIZE: 3 to 4′ high by 3 to 5′ in width.

HARDINESS: Zone 4 to 8, probably the hardiest of the *Ceanothus*.

HABIT: Low, broad, compact shrub with rounded top and slender upright branches; plants I have seen were quite low and dense.

RATE: Slow to medium.

TEXTURE: Medium in all seasons.

LEAF COLOR: Dark green in summer, perhaps yellow to tan in fall.

FLOWERS: Perfect, white, odorless, less than 1/8″ diameter, borne in 1 to 2″ long corymbose panicles at the ends of the stems in June and July.

FRUIT: Similar to a capsule, dry, triangular, 1/5 to 1/4″ wide, separating into 3 compartments at maturity, not showy.

CULTURE: Supposedly somewhat difficult to transplant; prefers light, well-drained soil; tolerates dryness; full sun or shade; found on dry banks along highways throughout East; fixes atmospheric nitrogen; growing on a dry hillside in the University's Botanical Garden.

DISEASES AND INSECTS: Leaf spots and powdery mildew are two minor problems.

LANDSCAPE VALUE: This species is a parent of many of the hybrids which are used extensively in Europe and the West Coast; may have a place in difficult areas.

PROPAGATION: Seed dormancy occurs in most *Ceanothus* species; germination has been induced by a hot water soak, a period of cold stratification, or both; seed should be stratified in a moist medium for periods of 30 to 90 days at 34 to 41°F; cuttings, especially softwood, root readily when collected in summer; treatment with IBA will hasten and improve rooting to a degree.

ADDITIONAL NOTES: The New Jersey Tea is a rather handsome plant. I have seen it in flower along highways in the mountains of New York in late June and early July and it makes a rather pretty show. It is an extremely adaptable species and, in the wild, occurs in sandy woods, dry prairies, and mixed deciduous forest communities. It can withstand inhospitable conditions due to presence of massive, woody, deep red colored roots. The robust, gnarled roots may reach diameters of 6 to 8″.

NATIVE HABITAT: Canada to Manitoba, Nebraska, Texas and South Carolina. Introduced 1713.

RELATED SPECIES:

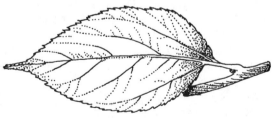

Ceanothus ovatus Desf., (sē-à-nō'thus o-va'tus), Inland Ceanothus, grows 2 to 3′ high and is quite dense in foliage. This species is considered superior to *C. americanus* because of its growth habit and the dry capsules which turn bright red in July and August. The flowers are white and minimally showy. The summer foliage is a shiny green while fall coloration is of no consequence. The oval-lanceolate to oblong-elliptic leaves have small gland-tipped teeth. Leaves range from 1 to 2 1/2″ long. Best reserved for out of the way areas and naturalizing. Native from New England to Nebraska, Colorado and Texas. Cultivated 1830. Zone 4 to 6.

Ceanothus* × *pallidus Lindl. (*C.* × *delilianus* × *C. ovatus*), (sē-à-nō'thus pal'lid-us), deserves perhaps more attention than it was provided in the 1990 edition. I have seen plants of various cultivars in the United States and Europe and was impressed by the dainty habit and soft pink flowers. In general the habit is broad mounded, 2 to 3′ high, with broad oval shiny green leaves. The soft pink flowers occur in dense conical inflorescences on new growth of the season in June (Boston). 'Roseus' was injured at −6°F but grew back and flowered the same season. This form originated in France before 1830. Also included herein are: 'Ceres' with lilac-pink flowers; 'Marie Simon' (perhaps same as 'Roseus') with soft pink flowers; 'Perle Rose' with soft carmine-pink to strawberry-pink flowers; and 'Plenus' with pink buds opening to white, double flowers.

ADDITIONAL NOTES: The *Ceanothus* number about 50 species with numerous hybrids and cultivars, leaves are opposite or alternate. The alternate group with different vein patterns, evergreen or deciduous, flowers white, rose into blue. Most are too tender or ill-adapted for the Midwest, East, and South. I brought one of the blue-flowered hybrids from California to Georgia. The leaves abscised for no apparent reason, grew back, then abscised again. The high humidity may be its downfall. I have seen many of the West Coast species on the side of a mountain growing in sandy, rocky soil under dry atmospheric conditions. On the other hand, many of the *Ceanothus* hybrids appear to prosper in England. One particular hybrid group, *C. × delilianus* Spach., French Hybrid Ceanothus, a cross between the tender blue-flowered *C. coeruleus* Lagasca, of Mexico and *C. americanus* has given rise to beautiful blue-flowered forms. One of the most beautiful blue forms is 'Gloire de Versailles' which I saw in several English gardens. This and the blue poppy, *Meconopsis* species, are real show stoppers.

A more complete discussion is warranted but unrealistic in light of non-performance except for the West Coast of the United States. Most of the species and hybrids are listed as Zone 7 and 8. I do not believe the central cultural issue is cold-tolerance, rather excessive rain, humidity and wet soils in the Southeast. Even West Coast references (see *Sunset Western Garden Book*) note that the species and hybrids are short-lived (5 to 10 years) in the garden. Plants are native to drier habitats and, when grown in gardens, succumb particularly to root rot caused by excessive irrigation. For a worthy list of species and cultivars see *Sunset* (1995).

A final thought takes the author and the reader to Edinburgh Botanic Garden almost 16 years past where the first rich blue *Ceanothus* stopped me in my tracks. The camera nearly imploded. This form is listed as 'Edinburgh' and is almost justification for traveling to Scotland.

Cedrus atlantica (Endl.) Manetti ex Carr. — Atlas Cedar
(sē′drus ăt-lăn′t -kă)

FAMILY: Pinaceae

IDENTIFICATION FEATURES: Closely related to *C. libani*, distinguished by the taller crown, less densely arranged branchlets, the bluish or dark green leaves which are mostly as thick as broad, the smaller cones (2 to 3″ long) and the smaller seeds (1/2″ long).

SIZE: 40 to 60′ high by 30 to 40′ wide but can grow to 120′ in height by 90 to 100′ spread; trees over 100′ are relatively common in England.

HARDINESS: Zone 6 to 9; this and Deodar are the least cold hardy of the cedars; have seen in New Bedford and Cape Cod, MA; Spring Grove, Cincinnati, OH has tried this and 'Glauca Pendula' but the winters of −20°F and lower eliminated the plants; the breakpoint for winter survival appears to be −5 to −10°F.

HABIT: In youth and early maturity the form is stiff with an erect leader and the overall shape is pyramidal; unfortunately, open and gaunt in youth and not as preferable to the customer on first inspection compared to *C. deodara* but a superior plant over time; in age it assumes a flat-topped habit with horizontally spreading branches; extremely picturesque and interesting tree, its beauty perhaps unmatched by any other conifer.

RATE: Slow (fast when young).

TEXTURE: Medium.

LEAF COLOR: Bluish green, varying in color from light green to almost silvery blue.

FLOWERS: Monoecious, male cones very densely set, erect, finger-shaped, 2 to 3″ long, 1/2 to 5/8″ wide, shedding clouds of yellow pollen in fall; usually more numerous on the lower portion of the tree (the above description applies to the other cedars); female borne in stout, erect cones, greenish to purplish initially, usually in the upper parts of the tree.

FRUIT: Cones rather short, long persistent, upright on upperside of branches, often 2 1/4 to 4″ long, 1 3/4 to 2″ wide, requiring two years to mature; glaucous green while developing, finally brown.

CULTURE: Difficult to transplant and should be moved as a container or balled and burlapped plant; prefers a well-drained, moist, deep, loamy soil but will tolerate sandy, clay soils if there is no stagnant moisture;

sun or partial shade; needs shelter from strong, sweeping winds; preferably acid soil although withstands alkaline soils; does reasonably well in the heat of the South (Zone 7).

DISEASES AND INSECTS: Tip blight, root rots, black scale and Deodar weevil.

LANDSCAPE VALUE: A handsome specimen tree, particularly striking when fully mature; the cedars should never be considered for anything but specimen use; when they are surrounded by ample turf and allowed to develop naturally they have no garden rivals; not used enough in the South were *C. deodara* dominates because of its fuller, denser habit and faster growth in youth; unfortunately, *C. deodara* will often die back starting at the top of the plant; to be sure, magnificent specimens of *C. deodara* can be found throughout the Southeast, Southwest, and West.

CULTIVARS:

'Argentea'—Perhaps the best of the bluish needle forms, the whole tree is a beautiful pale silver-gray-blue color.

'Aurea'—A rather stiff form with yellowish needles, not as robust as the species, 'Aurea Robusta' has golden yellow foliage, central leader.

'Fastigiata'—An upright form with good blue-green needles; have seen at Morris Arboretum, Philadelphia, PA and Bedgebury Pinetum, Goudhurst, Kent, England; good looking plant; unfortunately, something is lost in translation with this cultivar since it will never develop the grandiose outline of the species.

'Glauca' (f. *glauca* by Bean)—Might well be listed as a true variety comparable to *Picea pungens* var. *glauca* as bluish forms can be selected from seedling populations; usually the foliage colors range from very blue to green in a given population; beautiful plant; there is a +80-year-old plant on the Georgia campus that evokes considerable comment.

'Glauca Pendula'—Weeping form with bluish foliage; the branches cascade like water over rocks; must be staked to develop a strong leader; truly a beautiful clone; have seen in many gardens and each is slightly different due to training, pruning and staking in the early years.

PROPAGATION: Seeds of *Cedrus* exhibit little or no dormancy; however, prechilling or cold stratification at 37 to 41°F for 14 days has been recommended.

ADDITIONAL NOTES: Closely related to *C. libani* from which it differs in the shoots always being downy and the cones do not taper above the middle so much. Bean noted that *C. atlantica* was thriving splendidly in various parts of the British Isles. At Kew Gardens, on dry, hot soil it grows more quickly and withstands London pollution better than *C. libani* or *C. deodara*.

About 10 years past, a former student Dan Paterson, gave me a *Cedrus atlantica* 'Glauca'. After several tip prunings it has filled in and hovers around 15' high. From our porch, the rich blue-green foliage is the first landscape element to attract the eyes. Unfortunately, it is growing in a 2' wide strip between the pool and fence. Great siting? I should have paid attention to the above statement about *only* specimen tree status. However, on the flip side 10 years of beauty and perhaps more can justify its placement.

The taxonomic status of *C. atlantica* now reduces it to a subspecies, i.e., subsp. *atlantica* (Endl.) Battand. & Trabut of *C. libani*. Doubtfully, will this be assimilated into American garden parlance.

NATIVE HABITAT: Algeria and Morocco on the Atlas Mountains. Introduced before 1840.

Cedrus deodara (D. Don) G. Don. — Deodar Cedar, Himalayan Cedar
(sē′drus dē-ō-där′à)

LEAVES: One to 1 1/2″ long (occasionally 2″), needle-like, on current season's growth extension singly and spirally, 15 to 20 per whorl, dark green, glaucous or silvery, sharply pointed.

BUDS: Minute, ovoid, with brown scales which remain on the shoots after the appearance of young leaves.

STEM: Long stems bearing scattered leaves and short, spur-like stems with whorled leaves; stems usually clothed with a grayish down; silvery, glaucous appearance.

SIZE: 40 to 70' after 30 to 40 years; supposedly can grow 150 to 200' high with a spread of 150'.

HARDINESS: Zone 7 to 8(9); references state hardy to –12°F, but this is generally not true, less cold hardy than *C. libani* and *C. atlantica*.

HABIT: Broadly pyramidal when young with gracefully pendulous branches; becoming wide-spreading and flat-topped in old age; the most graceful cedar especially in youth, also more dense and full as a young plant.

RATE: Medium, grows about 2' in a year when young.

TEXTURE: Fine, especially in youth.

LEAF COLOR: Light blue or grayish green, sometimes silvery in color.

FLOWERS: As described under *C. atlantica*.

FRUIT: Cones solitary to two together on short branchlets, ovoid or oblong ovoid, 3 to 4″(5″) long by approximately 3″ broad; apex rounded, bluish, bloomy when young turning reddish brown at maturity.

CULTURE: If root pruned, transplants easily; prefers a well-drained and somewhat dry, sunny location and protection from sweeping winds; often container-grown to avoid transplanting difficulties.

DISEASES AND INSECTS: Tops die back because of canker(?), weevil, and/or cold.

LANDSCAPE VALUE: Excellent specimen evergreen because of extremely graceful and pendulous habit; in the last edition I mentioned planting 3 in my garden; 2 are dead because of cold and poor root systems (produced from cuttings); for a shorter term investment than the other cedars, it is acceptable; although the most widely planted *Cedrus* in the southeastern United States it seldom reaches the proportions seen in European gardens; a 40 to 50′ high specimen would be an anomaly; I see many plants with top dieback and general decline; the end user should be cognizant that 10 to 20 years may represent the species' useful garden life.

CULTIVARS: I was somewhat remiss for not listing more cultivars in previous editions and considered expanding the lists of the three *Cedrus* species treated herein. However, upon reflection, common sense took command and said . . . practice restraint. Many excellent conifer books, including van Hoey Smith and van Gelderen; Bean; den Ouden and Boom; Welch; and Krüssmann, have noteworthy lists. I counted 33 named forms of *C. deodara* alone in Krüssmann. Also many specialist evergreen nurseries have quite extensive lists. Iseli Nursery, Boring, OR, a wholesale producer of quality evergreens (plants in general) lists (1989 catalog) 19 forms of *C. deodara*, 13 of which are not listed in Krüssmann. In the 1994 Iseli catalog the list of offerings was reduced to 7 *C. deodara*, 4 *C. atlantica*, and 3 *C. libani*; interestingly 10 of the 14 offerings were new since the 1989 catalog; provides some idea of the ephemeral nature of the cultivar explosion as well as their staying power in everyday commerce.

    Apparently, the quest for more cold hardy cultivars (see below) continues and seeds collected from Paktia Province, Afghanistan have yielded 'Eisregen', 'Karl Fuchs', and 'Polar Winter'. Most of these selections have bright blue-green needles.

'Kashmir'—Hardy form, silvery blue-green foliage, survived rapid temperature drop of 25°F below zero; repeated trials in Illinois have met with failure; one of my University of Illinois colleagues and I were determined to grow this form and tried it in every imaginable microclimate except the greenhouse and all attempts met with winter kill and the lowest temperature experienced was −20°F; doubtfully much better than −5°F cold tolerance.

'Kingsville'—Similar to above, possibly hardier than 'Kashmir' but again met with the same fate as above.

'Shalimar'—An introduction by the Arnold Arboretum that displays good blue-green needle color and excellent hardiness in vicinity of Boston, MA; this, to date, is the hardiest cultivar; grown from seed collected in a garden by that name in Srinigar in the Kashmir region of India in 1964; reports indicated growth of 9 to 15′ in 10 years from a cutting; has shown needle damage in severe winters but vastly superior to 'Kingsville' and 'Kashmir'; Don Shadow indicated it had survived at least −15°F in his Winchester, TN nursery; Nicholson, *The Plant Propagator* 30(1):5–6 (1984), took 'Shalimar' cuttings in mid-November (Boston), sand:perlite, 75°F bottom heat, poly tent in 50 to 60°F greenhouse, evaluated cuttings in April with 67% rooting from 5000 ppm IBA 5-second dip and 50% from 10,000 ppm dip.

PROPAGATION: Seed as described for *C. atlantica*; it should be noted that seed is oily and deteriorates quickly on drying; see Fordham, *Arnoldia* 37:46–47 (1977), for more details. Cuttings can be rooted and should be collected in October and later, treated with at least 8000 ppm IBA, given bottom heat and placed in a poly tent; rooting with various cultivars and the species ranged from 64 to 90%; cultivars of various species are often grafted on *C. deodara* because it has the most fibrous and compact root system; Belgian work confirmed the suitability of *C. deodara* as the universal rootstock for *C. atlantica*, *C. libani*, and *C. deodara* cultivars; side grafts from December to February and maintained under glass at 62°F were best.

NATIVE HABITAT: Western Himalayas from Afghanistan to Western Nepal. Introduced 1831.

Cedrus libani A. Rich. — Cedar of Lebanon
(sē′drus lib′an-ī)

LEAVES: 30 to 40 per spur, 3/4 to 1 1/2″ long, needle-like, stiff, quadrilaterally compressed, pointed at apex, dark or bright green, often lustrous.

STEM: Branchlets very numerous, densely arranged, spreading in a horizontal plane, short, glabrous or irregularly pubescent.

SIZE: 40 to 60′ after 40 to 70 years but can grow 75 to 120′ in height by 80 to 100′ spread.

HARDINESS: Zone 5 to 7.

HABIT: A stately tree with a thick, massive trunk and very wide-spreading branches, the lower ones sweeping the ground; pyramidal when young; superb in mature outline with horizontally disposed branches and a flat-topped crown.

RATE: Slow.

TEXTURE: Medium.

BARK: Gray-brown to brown forming a pebble-like appearance (warty protuberances) on old trunks; this applies to all the cedars.

LEAF COLOR: Dark or bright green.

FLOWERS: As previously described, yellow-brown, erect male catkins; pistillate purplish.

FRUIT: Cones stalked, solitary, upright, barrel-shaped, 3 to 5″ long by 2 to 2 1/2″ across, impressed at the apex, sometimes resinous, requiring two years to mature, purple-brown in color.

CULTURE: Somewhat difficult to transplant; a good, deep, well-drained loam; open, sunny, spacious location; intolerant of shade; needs a pollution-free, dry atmosphere; at the species level the hardiest type; variety *stenocoma* has withstood −15 to −25°F temperatures in the Cincinnati area, but did suffer some dieback and needle burn.

DISEASES AND INSECTS: None serious.

LANDSCAPE VALUE: A specimen tree of unrivaled distinction, uniting the grand with the picturesque; the dark green foliage, stiff habit, and rigidly upright cones give this tree a popular interest; somewhat stiff in youth becoming more picturesque with age.

CULTIVARS:

'Argentea'—Could be listed as a true variety; leaves of a very glaucous (silvery blue) hue; supposedly is found wild in the Cilician stands.

var. *brevifolia* (Hook. f.) Meikle—Cyprus Cedar, is generally smaller in all its parts compared to *C. libani*; the needles range from 1/4 to 1/2″ long, the cones are smaller and ultimate size (height) averages about 40′; cones at an earlier age.

'Pendula'—Handsome form with gracefully pendulous branches; often grafted high to produce a small weeping tree.

'Sargentii'—A dwarf 3 to 5′ high mound with numerous horizontal branches and long dark green needles.

var. *stenocoma*—Extremely hardy form and more stiff and rigid than the species; specimens on the Purdue campus, West Lafayette, IN, Spring Grove, Cincinnati, OH, and several handsome plants at the Arnold Arboretum attest to this; apparently raised from seeds collected in Cilician Taurus; preferred choice for cold climates; has survived −24°F with needle loss but regrowth was complete.

PROPAGATION: Seed, see under *C. atlantica*; cuttings taken in November rooted 30% in sand:peat without treatment; the most difficult cedar to root from cuttings.

ADDITIONAL NOTES: All the *Cedrus* are exquisite, lovely trees but C. *libani* has received the most notoriety, and justifiably so. There are disagreements as to the exact taxonomic status of the various cedars. Some botanists regard them all as geographical forms of one species. One botanist divided them into four subspecies. No matter how they are allied taxonomically they offer incomparable beauty among the large conifers. The U.S. National Arboretum, Washington, DC has a notable collection of *Cedrus* as does Longwood Gardens.

NATIVE HABITAT: Asia Minor, best known for its historic stands in Lebanon, but attaining maximum size in the Cilician Taurus, Turkey. Further west it occurs in scattered locales as far as the Aegean. Introduced in colonial times.

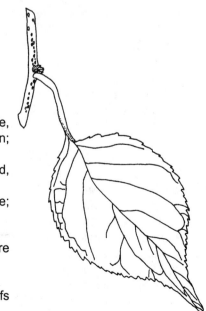

Celastrus scandens L. — American Bittersweet
(sē-las′trus skan′denz)

FAMILY: Celastraceae

LEAVES Alternate, simple, ovate to oblong-ovate, 2 to 4″ long, acuminate, broad cuneate at base, serrulate, glabrous, lustrous dark green; petiole—1/4 to 1″ long.

BUDS: Brownish, small, sessile, solitary, sub-globose, with about 6, hard, mucronate scales, glabrous.

STEM: Brown to tan, lenticels scarcely noticeable; one bundle trace; pith—solid, white.

SIZE: Often listed as 20′ but seems to continue growing as long as there is something to climb upon.

HARDINESS: Zone 3 to 8.

HABIT: Vigorous, deciduous, twining vine or vine-like shrub which engulfs every fence in sight.

RATE: Fast, can kill shrubs or small trees as it girdles the stems.

TEXTURE: Medium in leaf; medium-coarse in winter.

LEAF COLOR: Deep glossy green in summer; greenish yellow to yellow in fall.

FLOWERS: Polygamo-dioecious, primarily dioecious, yellowish white, not showy, borne in 2 to 4″ long, terminal panicles, May–June.

FRUIT: Three-lobed capsule, 1/3″ across, yellow orange on the inside, with crimson seeds; ripens in October and is extensively collected and sold for dried flower arrangements.

CULTURE: Most nurserymen sell it as a small container plant; the problem occurs because the sexes are never labeled; in this respect, it is like holly for without the male, fruit set will be nonexistent; quite easy to grow as it withstands about any soil condition including those that are dry; pH adaptable; full sun for best fruiting; probably best to locate in a poor soil site as it will quickly overgrow its bounds when placed in good soil.

DISEASES AND INSECTS: Leaf spots, powdery mildews, crown gall, stem canker, *Euonymus* scale, aphids, and two-marked treehopper.

LANDSCAPE VALUE: Little, except in rough areas; could be allowed to scramble over rock piles, fences, old trees and the like; the fruit is handsome and is always welcome in arrangements.

CULTIVARS: Although it makes sense to segregate plants by sex, I have not noticed this occurring in American commerce. Have seen 'Indian Maiden' (female) and 'Indian Brave' (male) described in the literature. These two cultivars are offered by Midwest Groundcovers, St. Charles, IL.

PROPAGATION: Seeds have a dormant embryo and require after-ripening for germination; there is some evidence that the seed coat may have an inhibiting effect upon germination; seeds or dried fruits should be stratified in moist sand or peat for 2 to 6 months at 41°F; softwood cuttings root readily in sand without treatment, but rooting may be hastened or improved by treatment; cuttings collected in early August, treated with 8000 ppm IBA-talc rooted 83%; softwood cuttings of all species when collected in July and treated with IBA root readily.

ADDITIONAL NOTES: About 30 species are known in Africa, America, Asia, Australia, and Pacific. Flowers are largely pale green, cream to white and not particularly effective. The capsular fruits are showy upon opening when the inside of the capsule (often yellow) and the fleshy orange to red aril become visible. Unfortunately, *C. orbiculatus* has become a serious weed in the New England States. The two species have also hybridized and identification may not be clear cut.

NATIVE HABITAT: Canada to South Dakota and New Mexico. Introduces 1736.

RELATED SPECIES:

Celastrus loeseneri Rehd. & Wils., (sē-las′trus lō-sen′ēr-ī), Loesener Bittersweet, is similar to *C. orbiculatus* but differs in its thinner, rounder leaves and lamellate pith. I have seen this plant at several gardens and was not sure of how it differed from the Oriental Bittersweet. It can grow to 20′. The greenish white flowers are produced in axillary cymes. The 1/3″ diameter fruits open to expose a yellow inner capsule and a red seed. Central China. Introduced 1907. Zone 4 to 8(?).

Celastrus orbiculatus Thunb. — Chinese Bittersweet

LEAVES: Alternate, simple, obovate to orbicular, 2 to 5″ long, almost as wide, acute or acuminate, cuneate, crenate-serrate, lustrous rich green, glabrous; petiole—1/3 to 1″ long.

STEM: Light brown, rounded; pith—solid, white.

Celastrus orbiculatus, (sē-las′trus ôr-bik-ū-lā′tus), Chinese Bittersweet, is similar to the above but tends to be more rampant. The fruits are in axillary cymes which permits separation from *C. scandens*. Handsome in fruit but has become a rather noxious weed in the northeastern United States. It has escaped from cultivation and is particularly abundant along roadsides in some parts of New England. Have also seen it in the southern Appalachians. Often developing a good yellow fall color. Will grow 20 to 30′ high and develop a shrub-like constitution with long spraying shoots. Japan, China. Introduced 1870. Zone 4, possibly best in 5 to 7.

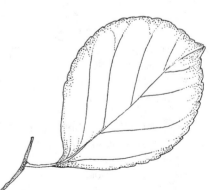

Celtis occidentalis L. — Common Hackberry
(sel'tis ok-si-den-tā'lis)

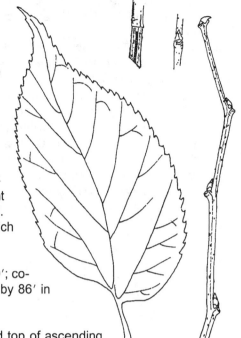

FAMILY: Ulmaceae

LEAVES: Alternate, simple, ovate to oblong-ovate, 2 to 5″ long, acute to acuminate, oblique and rounded or broad-cuneate at base, serrate except at base, bright green and usually smooth, dull light to medium green above, paler below and glabrous or slightly hairy on veins; petiole—1/2 to 3/4″ long.

BUDS: Small, imbricate, 1/4″ long or less, downy, chestnut brown, ovate, sharp pointed, flattened, appressed; terminal—absent.

STEM: Slender, somewhat zig-zag, light olive-brown, prominently lenticelled, more or less shining, more or less downy; wood of stem light greenish yellow when moistened; pith—white, finely chambered.

BARK: Trunk and older limbs with narrow corky projecting ridges which are sometimes reduced to wart-like projections.

SIZE: 40 to 60′ in height with a nearly equal spread, can grow to 100′; co-national champions are 94′ by 85′ in Mason City, IL and 87′ by 86′ in Lafayette County, MO.

HARDINESS: Zone 3 to 9.

HABIT: In youth weakly pyramidal; in old age the crown is a broad top of ascending arching branches, often with drooping branchlets; not unlike the American Elm in outline; however, by no means as aesthetic.

RATE: Medium to fast, 20 to 30′ over a 10 to 15 year period.

TEXTURE: Medium-coarse in leaf and in winter.

BARK: Grayish with characteristic corky warts or ridges, later somewhat scaly.

LEAF COLOR: Dull light to medium green in summer; yellow or yellow-green fall color, not impressive.

FLOWERS: Polygamo-monoecious, staminate ones in fascicles toward base; the perfect and pistillate flowers above; solitary in the axils of the leaves; April–May with the emerging leaves.

FRUIT: Fleshy, yellow, orange-red to dark purple rounded drupe, 1/3″ diameter, borne on a 1 to 2″ long pedicel, ripening in September and October, often persistent for several weeks; flavored like dates and relished by birds and wildlife; one hard seed which if bitten into will shatter teeth.

CULTURE: Easily transplanted bare root as a small tree or balled-and-burlapped in larger sizes; prefers rich, moist soils, but grows in dry, heavy or sandy, rocky soils; withstands acid or alkaline conditions; moderately wet or very dry areas; tolerates wind; full sun; withstands dirt and grime of cities.

DISEASES AND INSECTS: Leaf spots, witches' broom, powdery mildew, *Gonoderma* rot, hackberry nipple-gall, mourning-cloak butterfly and several scales are troublesome; personally I find the witches' broom often caused by an *Eriophyid* mite and the powdery mildew fungus, *Sphaerotheca phytophylla*, particularly offensive for trees are often totally disfigured by broom-like clusters of abnormal branch growth; some trees show resistance and should be propagated vegetatively to avoid this problem; the nipple gall is another serious problem as the leaves are often disfigured by these bullet-like appendages.

LANDSCAPE VALUE: Good tree for plains and prairie states because it performs admirably under adverse conditions; good for park and large area use; has the innate ability to grow in dry soils and under windy conditions; have observed some beautiful hackberries that need to be vegetatively propagated; Roy Klehm, Klehm Nursery, South Barrington, IL, has taken the bull by the horns and introduced several worthy selections.

CULTIVARS:

'Chicagoland'—Develops a single upright leader, a 15-year-old tree was 26′ high and 14′ wide, a chance seedling selected by Roy Klehm, South Barrington, IL.

'Delta'—Selected from a native stand near the south shore of Lake Manitoba, Canada, upright oval growth habit.

'Prairie Pride'—Selected by Bill Wandell; the foliage is thick, leathery, lustrous dark green and as a small tree develops a nice uniform, compact oval crown; does not develop witches' broom and has lighter than usual fruit crops; young trees under cultivation show rapid upright growth and few spur branches; tree was initially somewhat difficult to propagate but is now being produced in commercial quantities. Plant Patent 3771 (1975).

'Windy City'—Another Klehm selection with upright-spreading habit, attractive foliage and healthy growth rate.

PROPAGATION: Seed should be stratified for 60 to 90 days at 41°F in moist medium; this is a general recommendation for all species; cuttings have been rooted but the percentages were low; cultivars are budded.

ADDITIONAL NOTES: *Celtis occidentalis* is immune to Dutch elm disease. Best growth occurs in rich bottomlands of the Ohio River where trees in the original forest grew to be 5′ in diameter and 100′ high, living 150 to 200 years. The name Hackberry is a corruption of the Scottish Hagberry which in Britain was the Bird Cherry (*Prunus avium*). Other hackberry species, *C. australis* L., Mediterranean Hackberry, and *C. sinensis* Pers., Japanese Hackberry, are occasionally encountered on the West Coast and the latter shows up in slide lectures as the next great shade tree (it has leathery lustrous dark green foliage). There is a pendulous selection of *C. sinensis*. Realistically, I have never seen a notable specimen on the East Coast. Probably the greatest hope for significant use of *Celtis* species resides with selections of *C. laevigata* and *C. occidentalis*. Approximately 70 species of *Celtis* have been described with a limited number suitable for garden and commercial consideration.

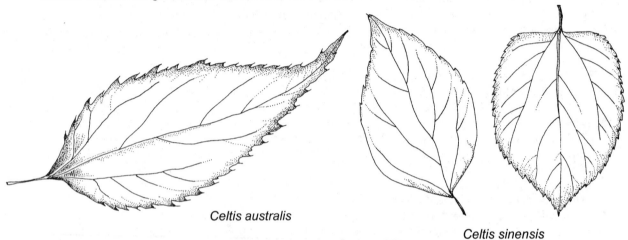

Celtis australis

Celtis sinensis

NATIVE HABITAT: I have seen the Common Hackberry in about every imaginable situation—in flood plains, open fields, along roadsides and in fence rows. Quebec to Manitoba, south to North Carolina, Alabama, Georgia and Oklahoma. Cultivated 1636.

RELATED SPECIES:

Celtis jessoensis Koidz. — Jesso Hackberry

LEAVES: Alternate, simple, ovate, 2 to 3 1/2″ long, acute, rounded, oblique, to subcordate, strongly serrated, almost dentate to base, lustrous dark green above, glaucous and pubescent on veins beneath; petiole—about 1/2″ long, pubescent.

BUDS: Imbricate, appressed, 1/8″ long, reddish brown, scales vari-colored, perhaps pubescent at edges.

STEM: Slender, brown, zig-zag, pubescent, dotted with gray-brown lenticels; second year gray-green; end of stem terminates in woody petiole base like *Eucommia*; pith—does not show chambers.

Celtis jessoensis, (sel′tis jez-ō-en′sis), Jesso Hackberry, will not ring anyone's plant material bell simply because it is so uncommon. My good friend Gary Koller introduced this species to me during my 1978–79 sabbatical at the Arnold Arboretum and after one year of almost everyday evaluation I think it has a genuine place in the landscape. The Arnold has several plants that are upright-spreading, 50 to 60′(70′) high. The leaves are the best dark green (perhaps not as pristine as *C. sinensis*) of any hackberry I have observed and completely free of nipple gall. Also no "witches' broom" was present. The Jesso Hackberries are planted next to the other hackberries, and the elms and zelkovas are within throwing distance; so if serious insect or disease maladies were associated with the species they should have been present. The bark is a smooth gray not unlike that of *Cladrastis kentukea* or beech. Korea, Japan. Introduced 1892 into the Arnold Arboretum and the trees mentioned were derived from this accession. Zone 5 to 7.

Celtis laevigata Willd. — Sugar Hackberry, Sugarberry
LEAVES: Alternate, simple, oblong-lanceolate, sometimes ovate, 2 to 4″ long, 1 1/4″ wide, long-acuminate and usually falcate, broad-cuneate or rounded at base, entire or sometimes with a few teeth, dark green above, slightly paler beneath, glabrous, thin; petiole—1/2 to 3/4″ long. Similar to *C. occidentalis* in bud and stem characteristics. Bark is generally smooth and devoid of wart-like projections, although I have seen them on this species.

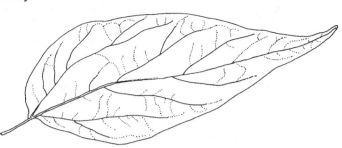

Celtis laevigata, (sel′tis lev-i-gā′tà or lē-vi-gā′tà), Sugar Hackberry, is also known as the Sugarberry, Southern Hackberry or Mississippi Hackberry. The tree can grow from 60 to 80′ in height with a similar spread. The habit is rounded to broad rounded with spreading, often pendulous branches. This tree is used in the South on streets, parks, and large areas; have seen a great number used as street trees in Savannah, GA. Resistant to witches' broom. The fruit is orange-red to blue-black, very sweet and juicy, and relished by birds. The common name is derived from the sweet taste of the fruits. Many of our best urban or compact soil tolerant trees inhabit flood plain environments. Sugar Hackberry occurs in low wet areas such as floodplains, bottomlands and sloughs, generally in clay soils. In Urbana, IL there were a number used around a downtown shopping mall that showed tremendous variation in foliage and habit. I believe Bill Wandell's 'All Seasons' Sugarberry was selected from one of these. 'All Seasons' has an excellent well-balanced crown, full and fine-textured, small lustrous green leaves that turn good yellow in fall, heavy interior leaf population, smooth American Beech-like bark, excellent growth under adverse city conditions and cold hardiness to -25°F. Although advertised with such gusto, the tree has proven not as spectacular in real world performance. Estimated size 40′ by 25′. Plant Patent 4989 in 1983. Another selection is a purported cross between *C. laevigata* × *C. occidentalis* called 'Magnifica' and introduced by Princeton Nursery. It does not develop witches' broom, is drought resistant, salt tolerant and withstands low oxygen tensions. Plant Patent 2795 (1990). Southern horticulturists need to work with this tree since many have been planted as street trees in the South and ample opportunity exists for superior introductions. For years I have admired the splendid sugarberries in Savannah, GA and in 1994 asked Don Gardner, City Urban Forester, to send budwood to Schmidt Nursery. The selection from a distance, is indistinguishable from American Beech with smooth silver-gray bark, upright arching to horizontally disposed branches and clean foliage. Native from southern Indiana, Illinois to Texas and Florida. Cultivated 1811. Zone 5 to 9.

Cephalanthus occidentalis L. — Buttonbush, Button-willow, Honey Bells

FAMILY: Rubiaceae
LEAVES: Opposite or whorled, deciduous to evergreen (extreme southern part of range), simple, ovate to elliptic-lanceolate, 2 to 6″ long, about half as wide, acuminate, cuneate, entire, lustrous bright to dark green above, lighter and glabrous or somewhat pubescent beneath; petiole—1/4 to 3/4″ long.

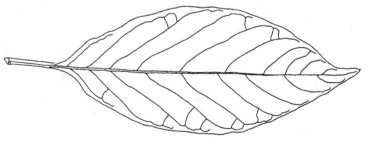

BUDS: Terminal—absent; laterals—solitary, sessile, conical, in depressed areas above the leaf scars, often superposed.
STEM: Moderate to stout, coarse, slightly pubescent or glabrous, weakly 4-sided, dirty gray brown to shining olive, prominent vertical lenticels; 2- to 3-year-old stems take on a reddish brown color and develop prominent fissures at the lenticels; ellipsoidal leaf scar with C-shaped bundle traces; scars connected by a line as in *Campsis radicans*; pith—light brown, solid.
FRUIT: Rounded mass of nutlets persisting through winter.

Cephalanthus occidentalis, (sef-à-lan′thus ok-si-den-tā′lis), Buttonbush, is a rounded 3 to 6′ high, occasionally 10 to 15′ shrub (southern part of range), of rather loose, gangling proportions. National champion is 20′ by 15′ in Buttonwillow, CA. The winter texture is quite coarse; however, the glossy summer foliage lends a medium texture. Leaves emerge late in spring and the plant looks dead until mid-May. The flowers are creamy white, crowded in globular heads, without the projecting styles, 1 to 1 1/4″ across, on peduncles 1 to 2 1/2″ long in June, July, August. The fruit is a nutlet and the compound structure is present throughout winter. Culturally, Buttonbush is best adapted to moist situations, and in cultivation is averse to dryness. Probably best reserved for wet areas in a naturalized situation. Have seen it growing in water; seems to prosper in such habitats. The glossy foliage is quite attractive and the late flower is interesting. Have seen it in full flower on the Outer Banks of North Carolina in mid-June and in swamps outside Greenfield, MA on July 12. Flowers over a long time frame. Easily propagated by softwood and hardwood cuttings. Softwood cuttings taken in late July and early August rooted 100% in sand:peat in one month without treatment. Seeds will germinate promptly without pretreatment. Native from New Brunswick to Florida, west to southern Minnesota, Nebraska, Oklahoma, southern New Mexico, Arizona and central California; also occurring in Cuba, Mexico and eastern Asia. Introduced 1735. Zone 5 to 11.

Cephalotaxus harringtonia (Forbes) Koch. — Japanese Plum Yew, Cow's Tail Pine
(sef-à-lō-tak′sus hăr-ing-tōn-i-a)

FAMILY: Cephalotaxaceae

LEAVES: Linear, evergreen, spirally arranged in 2 planes, forming a distinct V-shaped trough, 3/4 to 1 3/4″(2″) long, 1/8″ wide, abruptly pointed, lustrous dark green above, with 2 grayish bands beneath, each with about 15 rows of stomata. The description fits the species and in certain cases var. *drupacea*. Under cultivars, a more detailed description of needle characteristics is presented.

BUDS: Male and female in uniquely different shaped structures; male—globose, rounded, on a short stalk, opening and shedding pollen in February–March (Athens); female—conical-ovoid on a thick stalk, containing multiple ovules.

STEM: Relatively stout, lighter green than needles, sometimes bronze tinged in winter, with distinct ridges and furrows evident where each needle attaches to the stem, glabrous.

SIZE: Variable, from a spreading 5 to 10′ evergreen shrub to a 20 to 30′ high small tree; the former predominant in the eastern United States; since becoming more familiar with the species, I have seen everything from 12 to 18″ high and wide and spreading forms to tree-like specimens.

HARDINESS: Zone (5)6 to 9; amazing heat tolerance and should be the *Taxus* substitute for the South.

HABIT: Spreading evergreen shrub under normal landscape conditions; usually wider than high at maturity.

RATE: Slow.

TEXTURE: Medium-fine throughout the seasons.

BARK: Rich gray-brown to red-brown on old trunks, exfoliating in strips.

LEAF COLOR: Lustrous dark green throughout the seasons, holds good color in winter unless sited in wind-swept, sunny locations.

FLOWERS: Dioecious, male composed of 4 to 6 stamens, enclosed in a bract and arranged in clusters of small rounded heads on the growth of the previous season, opening February–March (Athens); female composed of pairs of carpels in a mass of scales borne on underside of stems.

FRUIT: Actually a naked seed, obovoid in shape, 1 to 1 1/4″ long, 3/4″ wide, on a 1/4 to 1/2″ long peduncle, turns a brown (olive to reddish brown) color at maturity.

CULTURE: Easily transplanted as a container-grown plant, root system is white and rather fleshy like that of *Taxus*; requires moist well-drained soil but once established will tolerate drought; have seen plants in full sun in virtual pure sand in Savannah, GA and was amazed at their quality; locate in shade but will tolerate full sun; one of the best needle evergreens for use in shade and heat in the South; has proven deer proof and will survive when *Taxus* will perish.

DISEASES AND INSECTS: None serious, although have seen some mite damage.

LANDSCAPE VALUE: Potential has not even been tapped for southeastern gardens; a superb and shade tolerant aristocratic evergreen for groupings, masses and accents; slow-growing which frightens those who design with a juniper mentality, but the rewards over time are abundant; in 1994 the low-growing forms were promoted through the Georgia Gold Medal Program and the supply of nursery stock was reduced to minimal quantities; exciting to watch a plant take off and this plant has become known at the gardener and professional levels; my prediction is for it to substitute for many of the low-growing junipers and hollies.

CULTIVARS: More than anyone thought possible . . . the best article is by Kim Tripp, *American Nurseryman* 180(9):28–37 (1994). Kim's comments are meshed with mine in the cultivar descriptions.

var. *drupacea* (Sieb. & Zucc.) Koidz.—Often listed as a species but current thinking places it in the varietal category. Needles are generally shorter and plants I have seen were more bushy and spreading. The above abbreviated account appeared in the 1990 edition and represented my then less than thimble-full of knowledge. Since that time, I, along with graduate students Donglin Zhang (PhD) and Andrea Southworth (MS), have cascaded into the abyss searching for and accumulating knowledge and plants. Donglin assembled 45 different *Cephalotaxus* taxa. Three forms labeled as var. *drupacea* were dramatically different. Donglin ran thin layer chromatography and found different chemical constituents (alkaloids in this case) for each. The fascinating aspect of this saga is that one was literally tree-like with a central leader, another spreading with 2″ long needles and a V-shaped arrangement of the needles along the stem, and the third with shorter needles that radiate in a bottlebrush-like fashion around the stem.

The literature lists var. *drupacea* as a large shrub or bushy tree with drooping branches, 3/4 to 2″ long needles, in a strong V-shaped arrangement and 3/4 to 1 1/4″ long olive-green seeds. A 12′ high var. *drupacea* I studied and photographed at Hillier Arboretum, England was multi-stemmed and the foliage was almost like the *C. fortunei* growing next to it, i.e., 2″ long needles with almost planar disposition.

Part of Donglin's work was to establish as complete a collection as possible to assess over time the horticultural taxonomy, botanical idiosyncracies, and garden merits. A listing of 16 distinct taxa in the collection follows: *C. harringtonia*, *C. h.* 'Duke Gardens', *C. h.* 'Fastigiata', *C. h.* 'Goodyear', *C. h.* var. *koreana*, *C. h.* 'McCorkle', *C. h.* var. *nana*, *C. h.* 'Prostrata', *C. h.* 'Ridge Spring', *C. h.* var. *wilsoniana*, *C. fortunei*, *C. f.* var. *alpina*, *C. f.* 'Grandis', *C. f.* 'Prostrate Spreader', *C. oliveri*, *C. sinensis*. Our plan is to preserve this germplasm and have established a trial planting at the Horticulture Department's testing area. Also, a collection will be provided to County Line Nursery, Byron, GA, for germplasm preservation. I have starred those clones that have commercial potential. Perhaps the most pragmatic aspect of Donglin's work is the discovery of one beautiful clone that grew ten times the rate of 'Duke Gardens'.

*'Duke Gardens'—A handsome 2 to 3′ tall and 3 to 4′ wide form that originated as a branch sport of 'Fastigiata' at Duke Gardens in Durham, NC; has all the desirable characteristics of a gracefully spreading yew; Kim lists size as 3 to 5′ high and wide; 8 years ago I saw the original plant at Duke Gardens and was impressed by its lustrous deep green foliage color even in full sun; in late September, 1994, Buddy Hubbuch, Horticulturist, Bernheim Arboretum, showed me 'Duke Gardens' that survived –24°F in January 1994 with some snow cover, the plant was in remarkably good condition; the needles radiate around the stem in a bottlebrush-like fashion and occur in a planar configuration on the same shoot; a female form.

'Fastigiata'—A rotund columnar form that will grow 10′ tall and 6 to 8′ wide; the up to 2″ long leaves are black-green and spirally arranged on the stem but instead of appearing 2-ranked like the species are arranged in a bottlebrush-like fashion and present a rather unusual textural quality; Raulston mentioned that this is an old Japanese clone (more probably Korean) that was introduced in 1830 by Dr. von Siebold to Ghent, Belgium, from Japan; 20- to 25-year-old plant at North Carolina State was 7′ high and wide. The origin, i.e., seed derived or chimeral (branch sport), is lost to the ages. However, I see this form producing numerous branch reversions that may have served as the progenitor material for the spreading, shrubby types ('Duke Gardens' is one example). At Edinburgh Botanic Garden, a 15 to 18′ high and wide specimen is peppered with branch reversions. Bonnie and I visited an old Monastery in Conyers, GA and out of 10 'Fastigiata' plants, three had produced branch reversions; one large revision looked much like 'Duke Gardens'. Kim mentions a 'Fastigiata Aurea' with gold margined needles.

'Fritz Huber'—Have seen at North Carolina State, a smaller form to 2′ high and wider at maturity, shorter needles than 'Prostrata', perhaps too slow for commerce, mentioned as more sun tolerant by Yucca Do Nursery, Waller, TX.

*'Gnome'—As seen at Hillier a virtual rounded mass of dense stems and needles, supposedly originated as a branch sport of 'Fastigiata', possibly too slow-growing for everyday commerce, a larger specimen under a shade tree at Hillier's was 2′ by 3′ and reminded of a yew, *Taxus*.

'Korean Gold'—The new foliage emerges uniform yellow-gold and darkens as it ages until indistinguish-able from 'Fastigiata', Tripp mentioned it was introduced into the United States in the early 1980's by Barry Yinger of Brookside Gardens. Other names include 'Ogon'.

'Mary Fleming'—In 1983 several seedling were purchased by Yucca Do Nursery from Will Fleming; these young plants were found in his mother's garden in New York; all have distinctly different forms; however, this one is quite unique in that the needles are extremely recurved.

'Nana'—Occasionally seen but doubtfully is the same shrub that Rehder mentioned as 6′ high, spreading by suckers with upright, ascending stems. Creech, *American Nurseryman* Jan. 15 (1986), reports that var. *nana* grows along the Sea of Japan on the coast of Honshu and is found in the dense conifer forests of Hokkaido; develops a low shrubby rounded habit at maturity; needles are shorter, narrower and finer textured than other *C. harringtonia*; branches are closely spaced and ascend to a 45 to 60° angle from the ground, mature between 4 to 6′ high and wide.

*'Prostrata'—At best a topophytic form propagated from a lateral, horizontal shoot; 2 to 3′ high, 2 to 3′ in width, have seen the plant in Dutch gardens; considerable clarification is necessary here for 'Prostrata' (sometimes var. *prostrata*) is a greatly variable entity; plants that best match the description have distichously arranged needles (almost planar) about 3/4 to 1 3/4″ long, about 1/8″ wide, the form that fits this description is a female, in 8 years the plant is about 18″ high and 4 to 5′ wide; the long shoots cascade over a stone wall; Tripp mentions a 'Prostrata' clone that grows 2 to 4′ high and 20 to 30′ wide at maturity.

PROPAGATION: Seed germination is inadequately defined and certainly unattainable in the literature. Donglin Zhang and I purchased seeds of *C. fortunei* and *C. harringtonia* var. *drupacea*. Various stratification treatments indicated that three months cold produced 33% germination. However, seeds provided this plus warm stratification (summer) plus another cold period (winter) germinated over 50%.

Before the 1990 edition, I could find no reliable references and suspect it should be handled like *Taxus*; cuttings are rooted commercially and usually taken in winter months, treated with a rooting compound and left alone for 3 to 4 months; one report said rooting compound did not help; patience is the key factor; I have rooted a few cuttings but have found that it is one plant that will not hurry; after transplanting, plants do not grow off fast; probably takes two years from a rooted cutting to produce a one-gallon salable plant.

New developments since the 1990 edition are rather exciting and deserve mention. First tissue culture [see *HortScience* 29:120–122 (1994)] has proved successful utilizing somatic embryos derived from embryo tissue. The only negative with this is the uncertainty of the propagules. One of the researchers, Dr. John Frett, University of Delaware, sent me a plant for examination. It is much more shrub/tree-like than typical. Without knowing the provenance (source) of the seed, it is difficult to predict the final disposition of the mature plant.

Ms. Andrea Southworth initiated a timing study utilizing a low-growing clone ('Duke Gardens') on campus. Cuttings were collected from September to August, 0 or 1000 ppm KIBA-5 second dip, 75 perlite:25 peat medium, mist and evaluated for percentage rooting, number and length of roots. Best rooting occurred in December, January, and February cuttings; 88, 90, 78%; 9, 10, 7 roots/cutting; and 25, 38, 13 centimeters root length/rooted cutting, respectively, with KIBA treatment. Rooting averaged 86% for untreated cuttings in April–May–June with an average of 4.3 roots per cutting. All other times were significantly less. See *HortScience* 31:222–223 (1996).

ADDITIONAL NOTES: Not the easiest genus to separate into identifiable species and at times the reader will come across *C. fortunei*, *C. harringtonia*, *C. drupacea*, et al. I did once attempt to develop reliable methods of separation in Cambridge Botanic Garden's collection but decided that life was too short for such frustration. Recent rbcL gene sequencing by Dr. Donglin Zhang, University of Maine, indicates that of the cultivated taxa only *C. harringtonia*, *C. fortunei*, and *C. oliveri* are distinct. *Cephalotaxus drupacea*, *C. sinensis*, *C. koreana*, and *C. wilsoniana* are not valid species.

NATIVE HABITAT: Japan, where it is distributed in the mountains from Kyushu to northern Honshu in moist, semi-shaded environments. Introduced 1830.

RELATED SPECIES:

Cephalotaxus fortunei Hook., (sef-à-lō-tak′sus fôr-tū′nē-ī), Chinese Plum Yew, Fortune's Plum Yew, is a small tree or large shrub, 15 to 20′ high, with horizontally extending, slightly pendulous branches. The habit is rather open and, doubtfully, will the species become important in commerce. The lustrous dark green needles are 2 to 3 1/2″ long, 1/5″ wide, with 2 silver-white stomatiferous bands beneath. The seed is 1 to 1 1/2″ long, oval, olive green ripening purple-brown. The reddish brown bark peels off in large flakes leaving pale brown markings. Bob McCartney, Woodlanders, showed me a fruiting specimen in Aiken, SC that fit the above description to the letter. 'Prostrate Spreader' is a wide-spreading, large-needled shrub introduced by Hillier Nursery. Eastern and central China. Introduced 1849. Zone 7 to 9.

Cercidiphyllum japonicum Sieb. & Zucc. — Katsuratree
(sẽr-si-di-fil´um jȧ-pon´i-kum)

FAMILY: Cercidiphyllaceae

LEAVES: Opposite or subopposite, simple, 2 to 4″ long and as wide, suborbicular to broad ovate, obtusish, cordate at base, crenate-serrate, dark bluish green above, glaucescent beneath; leaf resembles redbud, purplish when unfolding; petiole—3/4 to 1 1/2″ long

BUDS: Two scales, not overlapping, reddish, 1/16 to 1/8″ long, appressed, glabrous, angular; terminal—absent.

STEM: Slender, swollen at nodes, brownish, glabrous; second year at each node 2 short "spur-type" growths develop that bear the male or female flowers and a single leaf.

SIZE: 40 to 60′ in height and can reach 100′ in the wild; I have seen 40 to 50′ high trees with a 20 to 30′ spread and other trees of the same size with a spread equal to and in some cases greater than the height.

HARDINESS: Zone 4 to 8; several beautiful trees on the Georgia campus, as well as on the Maine campus, provide an index of adaptability.

HABIT: Pyramidal in youth, full and dense even as a young tree; greatly variable with maturity, some trees maintaining pyramidal habit, others wide-spreading; literature has ascribed a more upright habit to male trees, more spreading to female, but I find this inconsistent with actual observations.

RATE: Medium to fast; once established about 14′ over a 5 to 7 year period and about 40′ over 20 years.

TEXTURE: Medium-fine in leaf; medium in winter habit.

BARK: Brown, slightly shaggy on old trunks with the ends loose; limitedly reminiscent of Shagbark Hickory bark; very handsome and quite refined compared to Hickory.

LEAF COLOR: New leaves emerge a beautiful reddish purple and gradually change to bluish green in summer; fall color varies from yellow to apricot with the emphasis on the yellow, often a soft apricot-orange fall color develops; leaf is shaped like a *Cercis* (Redbud) leaf, hence, the generic name *Cercidiphyllum*; have seen magnificent apricot fall color on trees in New England but never the red or scarlet that some literature ascribes to this tree; tends to be early leafing; should be in full fall color by mid-October; the senescing (fall coloring) leaves give off a delightful spicy cinnamon/brown sugar odor, several students liken the odor to cotton candy.

FLOWERS: Dioecious, male consists of a minute calyx and an indefinite number of stamens; pistillate of four green, fringed sepals, and four to six carpels; open from late March to early April before the leaves; not showy.

FRUIT: Small, 1/2 to 3/4″ long dehiscent pods; borne 2 to 4 together on a short stalk (spur); pods should be collected in October before they split; seeds are paper thin and winged.

CULTURE: Somewhat difficult to transplant; move as a balled-and-burlapped or container-grown plant in early spring; soil should be rich, moist and well-drained; pH adaptable although seems to fall color better on acid soils; full sun; an effort should be made to provide supplemental watering during hot, dry periods during the initial time of establishment.

DISEASES AND INSECTS: None serious; sun scald and bark splitting may occur.

LANDSCAPE VALUE: Possibly a street tree but requires ample moisture in early years of establishment; excellent for residential properties, parks, golf courses, commercial areas; one of my favorite trees, overwhelming in overall attractiveness; if I could use only one tree this would be my first tree; I do not mind admitting to a few biases and for that reason have included a list of places where I have seen choice to magnificent specimens, they include: off the town square in Amherst, MA (a wow specimen, now 117-years-old), Arnold Arboretum, Callaway Gardens, Depauw, Hunnewell Estate, Michigan State, Morris Arboretum (what a specimen!), Morton Arboretum, Purdue, Regis College, Smith College, Spring Grove Cemetery, Stockbridge, MA, University of Georgia, University of Illinois, University of Maine, University of Massachusetts; and the planting at Regis consists of numerous seedling trees lining either side of a long semicircular drive and in the fall it is absolutely unbelievable; worth first class airfare to see the spectacle.

CULTIVARS:

'Aureum'—New foliage purplish, then light green, finally bright yellow; from Piroche Plants.

'Heronswood Globe'—A dwarf, perfect globe-shaped form; smaller (15′) and refined, ideal for the small garden; saw at Wilkerson Mill Garden, Palmetto, GA; handsome small stature, tight branching, a perfect fit for gardens where the species would devour; from Heronswood Nursery, Kingston, WA.

'Pendula'—Forms a mound of gracefully weeping branches which looks like blue-green water cascading over rocks; Spring Grove, Cave Hill Cemetery, Bernheim and Holden Arboreta have sizable specimens; it appears this cultivar will grow 15 to perhaps 25′; it is a fast-growing form; the plant in Spring Grove is 18′ high, 30′ wide after 19 years; I have tried unsuccessfully to root cuttings and now realize it must be grafted onto seedling understock; this form was discovered in a seedling population by Mr. Theodore Klein, Crestwood, KY; has tentatively been christened 'Amazing Grace' by Robert Hill of The Louisville Courier Journal.

There is another pendulous clone of larger size; Gary Koller showed me a photograph of a large weeping form that probably topped 50′; it, too, was beautiful; *C. magnificum* 'Pendulum' is now offered in commerce in the United States; I suspect it is larger growing than *C. j.* 'Pendula'; the leaves are slightly larger and the branches do not appear to weep as strongly at an early age as *C. j.* 'Pendula'; this latter form has become reasonably common in commerce; it is more upright in habit with a dominant central leader and cascading secondary branches; as a young tree it is more open than 'Pendula'; successfully growing in the Lyle E. Littlefield Ornamentals Trial Garden, Orono, ME.

PROPAGATION: Seed requires no pretreatment and can be sown when mature; have produced 3 to 5′ high and branched plants in a single growing season by sowing seed in flats in the greenhouse in November, keeping the seedlings growing under lights through winter, transplanting them to containers in spring and fertilizing and watering them regularly; capsules dehisce at maturity (October–November) but are held upright on branches and the small seeds remain imbedded (some) in the fruits; have collected fruits in mid-February (Cincinnati) and late April (Northampton, MA) with sufficient viable seeds that with direct sowing produced 3′ high trees by September; fun plant to work with for a plant propagation class; have rooted softwood cuttings from seedlings with 100% success but have not been able to root cuttings from mature trees; cultivars are top-grafted to produce small weeping trees.

ADDITIONAL NOTES: What more can I say . . . See Spongberg, *J. Arnold Arboretum* 60:367–376 (1979). Spongberg makes a case for two distinct species, *C. magnificum* and *C. japonicum*. Since the 1983 edition I have been subjected to the var. *magnificum* Nak. (Nak.) or, by some authorities, species *magnificum*. Apparently this taxonomic unit is restricted to Japan and does not grow as large as *C. japonicum*. The distinguishing features are the larger leaf, more rounded shape and more cordate base. The seeds are slightly larger and winged at both ends (compared to one end of *C. japonicum*). Also the bark remains smoother much longer. The typical form is actually var. *sinense* Rehd. & Wils. which occurs in China and tends to be more tree-like. Wilson described trees of var. *sinense* up to 130′ high and exceeding in height and girth all other deciduous, non-coniferous trees from China.

NATIVE HABITAT: China, Japan. Introduced 1865.

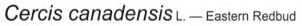

Cercis canadensis L. — Eastern Redbud
(sẽr′sis kan-a-den′sis)

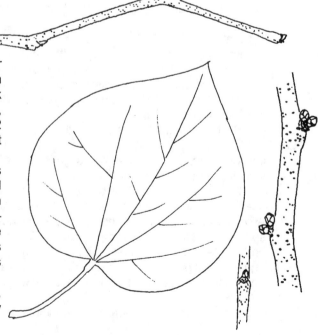

FAMILY: Fabaceae

LEAVES: Alternate, simple, broad-ovate to suborbicular (broadly heart-shaped), 3 to 5″ high and wide, often wider than long, acute, cordate, entire, lustrous dark green, base with 5 to 9 prominent, radiating veins, pubescent to glabrous beneath; petiole—1 1/2 to 2 1/2″ long with conspicuous swelling (pulvinus) just below blade.

BUDS: Terminal—absent; laterals—small, 1/8″ or less long, blunt, blackish red, somewhat flattened and appressed, one or more superposed buds often present, the uppermost the largest; bud scales—overlap, somewhat hairy on edges, about 2 visible to a leaf bud, several to a flower bud; flower buds larger (1/4″ long) and more rounded than leaf buds and often clustered at each node.

STEM: Slender, glabrous, dark reddish brown to black, zig-zag; pith—especially of older growth generally with reddish longitudinal streaks.

SIZE: 20 to 30′ in height by 25 to 35′ in spread; national champion is 44′ by 33′ in Memphis, TN.

HARDINESS: Zone 4 to 9; can be grown in Minneapolis, MN vicinity (Zone 3b); seed source selection is essential for reliably cold hardy trees; have observed small trees in Orono, ME.

HABIT: Usually a small tree with the trunk divided close to the ground forming a spreading, flat-topped to rounded crown, very handsome with its gracefully ascending branches, "a native tree with a touch of class."

RATE: Medium, 7 to 10′ in 5 to 6 years, actually faster with ample moisture and fertilizer in the production phase.

TEXTURE: Medium-coarse in leaf; medium in winter.

BARK: Older bark black or brownish black usually with orangish inner bark peaking through; develops scaly condition with age; not often considered as a tree with interesting bark but it does possess ornamental value.

LEAF COLOR: New growth when emerging is a reddish purple and gradually changes to a dark, often somewhat lustrous green in summer; fall color is usually yellow-green but can be an excellent yellow; leaves appear tired by late summer and are often spotted, off-color, or on the ground; this coupled with the excess fruit production and natural browning of the pods can produce a rather "scary" plant.

FLOWERS: Perfect, reddish purple in bud, opening to a rosy pink with a purplish tinge, 1/2″ long on a 1/2″ long pedicel; open in March–April and are effective for 2 to 3 weeks; borne 4 to 8 together, fascicled or racemose; often flowers are produced on old trunks 4 to 8″ in diameter; flowers at a young age, 4 to 6 years.

FRUIT: True pod (legume), brown-brownish black, 2 to 3″ long, 1/2″ wide, October; reddish to green before maturity; may look a tad untidy with heavy fruit set; fruits often persist through the winter.

CULTURE: Transplant balled-and-burlapped or container-grown as a young tree in spring or fall into moist, well-drained, deep soils; however, does exceedingly well in many soil types except permanently wet ones; adaptable to acid or alkaline soils; full sun or light shade; keep vigorous by regular watering and fertilization; redbud suffers dramatically from excessive stress be it lack of water, excessive moisture, mechanical injury, et al.; a weakened tree is more susceptible to canker and *Verticillium*; Dr. G. Randy Johnson, formerly at the U.S. National Arboretum, was breeding for canker resistant redbuds; he noted essentially no resistance in *C. canadensis*.

DISEASES AND INSECTS: Canker is the most destructive disease of redbud and can cause many stems to die, leaf spots and *Verticillium* wilt are other disease problems; tree hoppers, caterpillars, scales and leafhoppers can also cause damage; *Xylaria polymorpha* root rot may play a role in the decline of urban trees.

LANDSCAPE VALUE: Effective as a single specimen, in groupings, in the shrub border, especially nice in woodland and naturalized type situations; one of my favorite eastern United States native plants; the cultivars are much preferable to row-run seedlings and should be given preferential status for garden use.

CULTIVARS:

'Alba' (var. *alba*)—White flowers; comes true-to-type from seed; look for absence of purplish pigment in the young seedling leaves; from abundant personal experience germinating and growing populations of 'Alba' (var. *alba*), I know it does not come true-to-type . . . all seedlings flowered pink to rose-magenta; if two different white-flowered plants (different clones) are isolated from the typical species then cross fertilization occurs and the resulting population should be predominantly white; easy to tell since white-flowered seedlings lack any trace of anthocyanin pigment and the new growth is yellow-green; several nurserymen have told me 'Alba' is less cold hardy than 'Royal White', although Hayman reported no damage to 'Alba' at -24°F in Bernheim Arboretum.

'Appalachian Red'—Supposedly close to red but the plant in my possession has deep red-purple buds that open to bright (neon) pink, habit akin to the species, striking in flower but not *red*.

'Covey'—Weeping form, contorted stem with shoots arching to produce an umbrella-shaped crown; vegetative characteristics, flowers and fruits are similar to the species; original, +30-year-old plant is 5′ high and 8.25′ wide with a 5″ trunk diameter; the original plant was purchased as a seedling in a pot about 1965 on a return trip from Florida to New York; grown in the garden of Connie Covey, Westfield, NY; propagated and patented by Tim Brotzman, Madison, OH, Zone 5 to 7.

'Dwarf White'—An 8 to 10′ high small tree that produces abundant white flowers; Raulston reported 7′ tall after 10 years at NCSU Arboretum (now J.C. Raulston Arboretum).

'Flame'—A rather interesting double rose-pink form that I believe is rather attractive; flowers are atypical as stamens are petaloid; may prove offensive as does not fit the definition of a redbud; may be called 'Plena'; seldom sets fruit; vigorous grower as seen at Bold Spring Nursery, Monroe, GA; less cold hardy and was killed to ground after -24°F at Bernheim Arboretum; found in the wild in Illinois in 1905.

'Forest Pansy'—A very handsome purple leaf type, the new foliage emerges a screaming, shimmering red-purple and changes to a more subdued color as the season progresses; one of my favorites for colored foliage and I do not rate too many purple leaf plants among my top 1000; have monitored hardiness over the past 5 years and found it not to be hardy much below -10°F; plants survived the extreme lows of the 1976–77 (-20 to -25°F) winter but did not leaf out after the winter of 1977–78 when the low was only -10°F but the average minimum for December through February was 10° lower than the normal; established plants were wiped out in Mt. Airy and Spring Grove, Cincinnati,

OH; it is growing successfully in the Dirr garden but loses the intense color by late May–June when it becomes almost dark green; flowers are more rose-purple than the species and open a little later; new hardiness information is unexplainable but after ‑24°F at Bernheim Arboretum during the 1994 winter, there was no damage; found in a seedling block at Forest Nursery, McMinnville, TN, in 1947.

subspecies (variety) *mexicana* (Rose) Murray—A botanical entity that reproduces relatively true-to-type from seed. As I have seen it a shrubby form, 5 to 12′ high, with small 2 to 3″ diameter, orbicular, shiny, medium green leaves and wavy margins. Flowers are similar in color to the species. There is significant variation in the taxon and Raulston reported leaf sizes from 1 to 6″ diameter. In my test plots, the single plant of subsp. *mexicana* has large leaves to 5″ diameter, large stature and minimally glossy and undulating margined leaves. Eighty eight percent rooting of cuttings taken 4 weeks after budbreak, treated with 2% KIBA. Maximum seed germination of 95% after 62 minutes acid scarification and 35 days cold moist stratification. See *HortScience* 25:196–198 (1990) and 27:313–316 (1992). Probably hardy in Zone 6 to 9. In my opinion, will never become a commercial entity. Have observed significant winter injury in Zone 7b, apparently dehardens early in spring (winter) and late spring freezes wreak havoc.

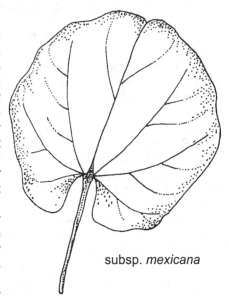

subsp. *mexicana*

'Northland Strain'—A cold hardy, seed-produced cultivar that grew for years at the Horticulture Farm, University of Minnesota, and was formally introduced by the U. of M. Landscape Arboretum.

'Pinkbud'—A pure, bright true pink flower; discovered wild on an estate near Kansas City.

'Royal White'—A selection made by Professor J.C. McDaniel of the University of Illinois, Department of Horticulture, for outstanding and abundant white flowers; the parent tree is located in Bluffs, IL; probably the most cold-hardy form; flowers larger than var. *alba* and open slightly earlier; grew in the tree lawn in front of the house next to Professor McDaniel's.

'Rubye Atkinson'—Flowers pure pink; in the 1990 edition I speculated that this cultivar was a *Cercis canadensis* subspecies *texensis* form; based on the single tree at the Griffin Experiment Station, this is not the case; the flowers are a lovely pink and extremely effective in the early spring landscape; does not appear to be as vigorous as the typical species, flowers are also smaller.

'Silver Cloud'—A variegated form, the leaves splotched, blotched and speckled with creamy white; best grown in some shade; leaves show tremendous variegation pattern; less floriferous; chimera is unstable and branch reversions to green may occur; uninjured at ‑24°F; introduced by Theodore Klein, Crestwood, KY.

'Tennessee Pink'—True clear pink flowers; excellent plant habit; selected by Hidden Hollow Nursery; offered by Fairweather Gardens, Greenwich, NJ; 1997 release.

subspecies (variety) *texensis* (Wats.) Murray—Another variable entity from the western portion of the range, found in Texas, Oklahoma and Mexico. On the best forms, 'Oklahoma' (rosy magenta) and 'Texas White' (milk white), the leaves are leathery lustrous green with undulating margins. The stems are thicker and more rigid than typical *C. canadensis* and the older trees tend toward a more compact, broad-rounded outline. Mature landscape size will range from 15 to 25′ high and wide. National champion is 30′ by 33′ in Dallas County, TX. Adaptable in Zone 6 to 9. 'Oklahoma' was killed in Urbana, IL after exposure to ‑20°F, although *Verticillium* wilt could have been a conspirator in its demise. 'Oklahoma' was discovered in the spring of 1964 in the Arbuckle Mountains of Oklahoma, named and released by Warren and Son Nursery, Oklahoma City. 'Texas White' originated as a chance seedling at the old Germany Nursery, Fort Worth, TX, during late 60's or early 70's.

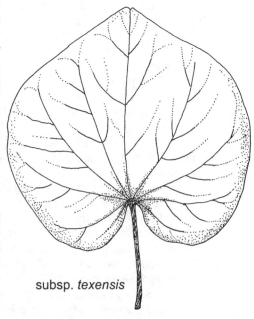

subsp. *texensis*

'Traveller'—A broad mound with semi-arching branches, 5′ high by 5 to 12′ wide, exceptionally glossy dark green leaves, new leaves rich copper-red, rose-pink flowers, have observed one plant and indeed it is beautiful, Zone 6 to 8(9), discovered as a seedling by Dan Hosage, Jr., Madrone Nursery, San Marcos, TX, will be patented, a selection of var. *texensis*.

'Withers Pink Charm'—Flowers soft pink without the purplish tint of the species; have seen at Bernheim Arboretum; buds rich bright pink, opening to pink flowers; uninjured at -24°F; discovered by D.D. Withers in mountains of Virginia about 1930.

PROPAGATION: Seeds have hard, impermeable seedcoats and internal dormancy; scarification in concentrated sulfuric acid for 30 minutes followed by 5 to 8 weeks of cold (41°F), moist stratification is recommended; see Frett and Dirr, *The Plant Propagator* 25(2):4–6 (1979), for more details on seed propagation; cultivars are budded on seedling understock, the budding is not easy and significant skill and know-how are required; in nurseries, I have noticed significant suckering from the understock which often portends problems; also recent tissue culture breakthroughs mean that the cultivars will now be on their own roots; see *Plant Cell Reports* 7:148–150 (1988) and *J. Environmental Horticulture* 8:177–179 (1990) for tissue culture details.

Redbuds flower quickly from seed particularly if "pushed" with water and fertilizer. In 1990 seeds were collected from 'Alba', 'Oklahoma', 'Rubye Atkinson', and the species, all growing in close proximity at Griffin, GA. My hope, with the abundant cross pollination by the bees, was to produce a pink form with leathery leaves. In spring of 1992 seedlings were planted in the field, several seedlings flowered in 1993 and all flowered in 1994. Seedlings of 'Oklahoma' were consistently deep rose-magenta color with leathery, undulating surfaced, lustrous dark green leaves. No 'Alba' seedlings flowered white. I flagged four potential keepers, but by the end of 1995 decided none were worthy and the bulldozer moved in.

ADDITIONAL NOTES: Redbud, like Flowering Dogwood, occurs over an extended range and plants grown from southern seed sources (Florida, Georgia) are not cold hardy in northern areas. Seed should be collected from local or regional sources. An interesting paper, *Ecology* 63:962–971 (1982), discusses cold acclimation, dormancy, genetic variation, geographic variation, growth, hardiness, morphological variation, photoperiod effects, and xeric modification of redbud from 13 geographic locations. Interestingly, the Minnesota Landscape Arboretum is growing seedlings from one tree that has prospered at the University's Horticultural Research Center with the offspring showing the hardiness of the parent. Redbud cold hardiness is always debated but in my travels trees crop up that survived -30°F. At Williamstown, MA a number of trees were evident on the Williams College Campus. It makes sense to utilize these plants, like the Minnesota tree, as seed sources. Also, redbud grows at Orono, ME. The redbud is a breath of fresh air after a long winter. In my opinion one of our most beautiful native trees.

NATIVE HABITAT: New Jersey to northern Florida, west to Missouri and Texas and northern Mexico. Cultivated 1641.

RELATED SPECIES: No one was more fervent about promoting redbuds than Dr. J.C. Raulston, North Carolina State University Arboretum (now J.C. Raulston Arboretum), and his superlative treatise was published in the *Arboretum Newsletter* No. 14 July (1986). Nine pages of single spaced type provide as great a synopsis as one could hope to locate. Additionally Raulston brought to the Arboretum a virtual complete collection of species and cultivars. See also *American Nurseryman* 171(5):39–51 (1990).

Cercis chinensis Bunge. — Chinese Redbud
LEAVES: Alternate, simple, heart-shaped, 3 to 5″ long and wide, deeply cordate, lustrous dark green above, glabrous, leathery, very difficult to separate this species from *C. canadensis*.

Cercis chinensis, (sĕr′sis chi-nen′sis), Chinese Redbud, is usually a small, erect, multi-stemmed shrub less than 10′ in height. Flowers are rosy purple about the same time (slightly ahead) as *C. canadensis* and about 3/4″ long; pods distinctly taper-pointed and 3 1/2 to 5″ long. Very handsome and showy in flower. Does particularly well in the South where I have seen 15′ specimens that dazzle the eye in March–April when the erect branches are clothed with vivid rosy purple

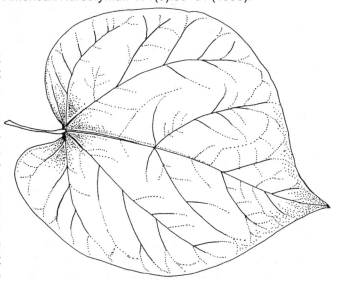

flowers. Actually more showy than *C. canadensis*. 'Alba' is a milky white-flowered form that is particularly attractive. 'Avondale' produces a profusion of deep rose-purple flowers, is more tree-like and has heavier textured dark green leaves. The quantity of flower buds set each year is far superior to row-run seedlings. This selection can also be rooted from cuttings. Originated in the suburb of Avondale, Auckland, New Zealand and propagated and promoted by Duncan and Davies, New Plymouth, New Zealand. The U.S. National Arboretum has a lavender-flowered, fruitless form that was 5 1/2' after 8 years. Also the late Dr. Dan Egolf hybridized *C. chinensis* × *C. canadensis*, the resultant progeny with two-toned pink/white flowers and large shrub habit. Native to central China. Introduced before 1850. Zone 6 to 9. Consistently killed to the ground at Spring Grove and Bernheim after exposure to -20°F or lower.

Cercis chingii Chun, (sĕr'sis ching'ē-ĭ), was given to me by Dr. Raulston. In ten years it has developed into a rather sprawling shrub 10' by 8'. The ultimate height may approximate 10 to 15'. The dark green leaves average 4″ across and become tatty by summer's end. The large pink flowers are the first to open of all the redbuds described herein. Dr. J.C. Raulston's original *Newsletter* description is reproduced in full:

The most exciting and rarest plant in our collection. Grown from an accession of seed received from China in 1984, planted out to the arboretum bed in the spring of 1985, and our first few flowers were produced this spring. As far as I can determine it is not in cultivation in either Europe or the United States at this point. We grew 4 seedlings and sent one each to the Arnold Arboretum and the U.S. National Arboretum, and planted two in the arboretum. Both our plants flowered about 7 to 10 days before the eastern redbud and seemed pinker in color—but that needs another look next spring when we should have excellent flowering on much larger plants. At first I thought it might be simply another Chinese name applied to *C. chinensis* (as often happens with a variety of material I've received from there—e.g. *Cryptomeria japonica* is usually cited in Chinese seed lists as *C. fortunei*) but the plant is quite distinctly different with much more vigorous growth (some 4 to 5' whips last year, and that much more growth this year looks likely) and already a more tree-like form. An unusual feature I've never noted on any of our other redbud species are large stipule-like growths at the base of leaves about 1/4 to 3/4″ in diameter (very prominent on one plant, much less so on the other). I will be very anxious to see the flowering next spring, and particularly anxious to have seed produced so we can begin to distribute the plant elsewhere to test potential adaptability and use. What a thrill it was to daily watch the flower buds expand and realize it was possibly the first time for this species to flower in the western world!

Cercis gigantea Cheng, (sĕr'sis jĭ-gan-tē'à), Giant Redbud, is possibly nothing more than an anomaly and doubtfully will become and important landscape tree. The glossy dark green leaves are 6 to 8″ across and the habit rounded with arching branches. At J.C. Raulston Arboretum, it grew 17' in 6 years. Dr. Johnson reported almost complete kill at -5°F in the winter of 1994 at the U.S. National Arboretum. China. Zone 7 to 8.

Cercis occidentalis Torr. & A. Gray, (sĕr'sis ok-si-den-tā'lis), Western Redbud, California Redbud, is a small tree with 1 to 3″ diameter, blue-green, notched to round tip leaves and pink to magenta flowers. I have seen the species growing on dry slopes in the California wine country. Appeared extremely variable in habit. Do not know of a single plant on the East Coast. National champion is 29' by 35' in Santa Rosa, CA. Arizona, Utah, Nevada, California and Oregon. Cultivated 1886. Zone 7 to 9, 10 on West Coast.

Cercis racemosa Oliver, (sēr′sis ra-se-mō′sà), Chain-flowered Redbud, is unique by virtue of the muddy (silver) rose-purple flowers produced 20 to 40 in 2 to 4″ long racemes. The effect is akin to wisteria. Habit is rounded with landscape size around 20 to 25′ high. I had high hopes for the species but the flower color is not as vivid as the other species listed and –5°F in 1994 (U.S. National Arboretum) resulted in complete flower bud kill and significant stem injury. Central China. Introduced 1907. Zone 7 to 9.

Cercis siliquastrum L., (sēr′sis sil′ik-as-trum), Judas-tree, Mediterranean Redbud, is the redbud of England and continental Europe. Generally a small tree, 15 to 25′ high, it can reach 40′. The 2 to 4″ high, up to 5″ wide leaves are rich bronze-reddish purple upon emergence changing to matt dark green. The leaf surface is characteristically undulating. The pale rose to magenta flowers occur 3 to 6 per cluster. The flowers and leaves are often present together for a long time, whereas the *C. canadensis* completes, or almost so, flowering before leaves mature. Southern Europe, Western Asia. Cultivated since ancient times. Zone (6)7 to 8.

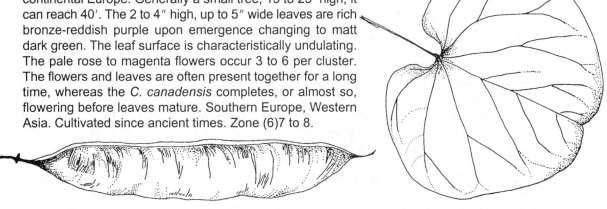

Cercis yunnanensis Hu & Cheng, (sēr′sis yū-na-nen′sis), Yunnan Redbud, is similar to *C. chinensis* and Raulston speculates that it is an ecotypic variant that was assigned species status. The habit is shrub-like, upright-vase-shape, 10 to 15′ high. Flowers are rose-magenta and there is also a white-flowered form. The latter has been a great performer in my Georgia garden. Quite resistant to canker. Easy to root from cuttings. The following information was provided courtesy of Mrs. Ruth Dix, Horticulturist, U.S. National Arboretum, Washington, DC. Cuttings of *C. yunnanensis* and *C. chingii* collected May 27, 1992, Woods Rooting Compound (19:1 = 500 ppm IBA + 250 ppm NAA), sand, mist, with 90 to 95% rooting in 4 to 6 weeks. Repeated on June 25, 1992, 0.4% IBA talc, 100% rooting in 4 weeks. Survived –5°F (1994) without flower bud or stem injury. 'Celestial Plum'—similar to *Cercis chinensis*, but it forms a small multi-trunked tree or large shrub, flowers are deep plum-purple, introduced by J.C. Raulston Arboretum. China. Zone 6 to 8.

ADDITIONAL NOTES: Redbud, as the reader can surmise, is one of my favorite trees. If a redbud only lived 7 years, it is still inherently more artistic, aesthetic and American than Bradford Pear. Dr. J.C. Raulston literally promoted *Cercis* species to the gardeners and nurserymen of America. A redbud will fit into the fabric of almost any garden. Four different types are included in the Dirr garden and as this is being written the first signs of color are evident on *Cercis chinensis* 'Avondale'. In my heart, I know that spring is close and the joy and excitement of a new gardening season looms on the horizon.

Chaenomeles speciosa (Sweet) Nak. — Common Floweringquince
(kē-nom′e-lēz spē-si-ō′sà)

FAMILY: Rosaceae
LEAVES: Alternate, simple, ovate to oblong, 1 1/2 to 3 1/2″ long, acute, cuneate, sharply serrate, lustrous dark green above, glabrous, stipules large and conspicuous on current season's growth, up to 1 1/2″ diameter, rounded, toothed.
BUDS: Similar to *C. japonica*, usually larger.
STEM: Slender, brownish, often slightly pubescent.
GROWTH HABIT: More upright in habit than *C. japonica*; 6 to 10′ in height.

SIZE: 6 to 10′ in height, spread 6 to 10′ or greater; quite variable and may be smaller due to hybridization with *Chaenomeles japonica*.
HARDINESS: Zone 4 to 8(9); no cultivars have proven hardy at the Minnesota Landscape Arboretum where lows reach –30°F; in Orono, ME flower buds are killed regularly but vegetative tissues are uninjured.

HABIT: A shrub of rounded outline, broad-spreading with tangled and dense twiggy mass of more or less spiny branches; some forms are more erect while others are quite rambling, variable in habit.

RATE: Medium.

TEXTURE: Medium in leaf; coarse in winter; collects leaves, bottles and trash in the twiggy network; rates highly as a "garbage can" shrub; over-rated plant, primarily because of flowers.

LEAF COLOR: Bronzy red when unfolding gradually changing to glossy dark green; fall color is nonexistent.

FLOWER: Five petaled, perfect, 40 to 60 stamens, scarlet to red in the type varying to pink and white, single to double; borne solitary or 2 to 4 per cluster on old wood; each flower 1 1/2 to 1 3/4″ diameter, very showy; January–February–March in South; April further north; before leaves; flower buds can be killed when a freeze eliminates the expanding flower buds; usually in full flower in the North when the leaves are about one-half mature; peak month(s) in Athens are late February into March; used extensively for cut branches and particularly popular for flower show competitions.

FRUIT: Pome, apple-shaped, 2 to 2 1/2″ long and wide, yellowish green often with a reddish blush, fragrant, speckled with small dots (glands), ripening in October; fruits are quite bitter (sour) when eaten raw but when cooked are used for preserves and jellies.

CULTURE: Transplant balled-and-burlapped or from a container; adaptable to a wide range of soil conditions; performs well in dry situations; full sun or partial shade with best flowering in sun; develops chlorosis on high pH soils; renewal pruning either by eliminating the older branches or simply cutting the whole plant to within 6″ of the ground will result in more spectacular flower; prune after flowering.

DISEASES AND INSECTS: Leaf spots result in premature defoliation, abundant rainfall in the spring and early summer can cause 50 to 75% defoliation by July; there are other problems (scale, mite) but none of an epidemic nature; aphids are prevalent on young stems and foliage.

LANDSCAPE VALUE: Excellent for flower effect when fully realized; range of flower colors is tremendous going from orange, reddish orange, scarlet, carmine, turkey red and white; there was a planting on the Illinois campus which in full flower was beautiful, however, during the rest of the year (50 to 51 weeks) the planting was intolerable; often used for hedge (makes a good barrier), shrub border, massing, grouping; I evaluate this species and its many cultivars as a single season plant (flower) and have discovered too many superior (multi-season) plants to justify using this extensively in the landscape; unfortunately, it will continue to be widely sold because many people are only interested in flowers when in essence, this feature is the most short-lived of all ornamental attributes; frequent in old residences throughout the Midwest, East, and South, particularly the orange-red forms; has staying power and like *Nandina* almost unkillable.

CULTIVARS: Abundant; Wyman noted that the Arnold Arboretum was growing 150 forms; most appropriate to check with the local nurseryman and note the color he has available; white, pink and scarlet tend to be the most commonly available colors; during sabbatical I evaluated the *Chaenomeles* collection at the Arnold and was left with the feeling that the differences between and among many of the cultivars were so minute as to be meaningless. I have included a few here that the nurseryman or homeowner might consider and are often available in everyday commerce.

'Apple Blossom'—An old cultivar with large 2″ diameter pink blushed flowers, saw it several years back in flower (May 20, 1993) at the Heritage Plantation, Sandwich, MA, still a pretty form.

'Cameo'—One of the best double forms with fluffy, peachy pink (apricot pink) flowers borne in profusion, flowers later, generally with the leaves, appears more resistant to leaf blight, probably 4 to 5′ high and wide at maturity, leaves bright, vivid, refreshing green, the *only* floweringquince in the Dirr garden. Mr. Don Shadow found and propagated a white-flowered sport.

'Contorta'—Offered by several nurseries, stems and leaves twisted, white flowers.

'Crimson and Gold'—Brilliant deep red flowers with showy yellow anthers on a dense spreading shrub.

'Hollandia'—Vibrant red, 2″ diameter flowers with rich yellow stamens on a tall, irregular shrub, flowers in spring and sporadically thereafter.

'Jet Trail'—A white-flowered sport of 'Texas Scarlet' with the qualities of the parent, 3′ high, wide-spreading.

'Knap Hill Scarlet'—Orange-red, profuse flowers on a compact 5 to 6′ high shrub, deep green leaves persist until frost, a *C.* × *superba* form.

'Mandarin'—Orange-flowered vigorous clone.

'Minerva'—Cherry red flowers on a compact, low-growing shrub.

'Nivalis'—Upright form of vigorous constitution with pure white flowers.

'Orange Delight'—Deep orange flowers on a low-spreading, 2 to 3′ high shrub, have seen size estimates of 4 to 5′ high; probably *C. japonica* clone.

'Red Chief'—Double, bright red flowers, compact habit.

'Rowallane'—Only included because of the large orange flowers on a large mounding shrub, have visited the great garden of Rowallane and felt compelled to include this clone after seeing the original(?) plant.

'Scarff's Red'—Red flowers, almost thornless, upright form, 4 to 5′ high.

'Spitfire'—A vivid red-flowered form of upright habit.

'Texas Scarlet'—Many consider this the best tomato red-flowered form because of its spreading habit and profuse flowers that are borne on a rather compact spreading plant, 2 to 3 1/2′ high.

'Toyo-Nishiki'—Upright grower with pink, white, red and combination colored flowers on the same branch, very pretty, has shown greater susceptibility to fireblight than others, 6 to 10′ high, proven one of the most cold hardy clones at the Morten Arboretum.

PROPAGATION: Cuttings collected in August, dipped in 1000 ppm IBA solution rooted 100% in peat:perlite medium under mist; softwood cuttings collected as growth is firming in late May–early July root in high percentages; seed requires 2 to 3 months at 41°F.

ADDITIONAL NOTES: Often flowers sporadically late into spring and again in fall may show some color; interesting but not overwhelming.

NATIVE HABITAT: China, cultivated in Japan. Introduced before 1800.

RELATED SPECIES:

Chaenomeles japonica (Thunb.) Spach. — Japanese Floweringquince

LEAVES: Alternate, simple, broad-ovate to obovate, 1 to 2″ long, obtuse or acutish, coarsely crenate-serrate, lustrous dark green, glabrous; stipules large on young shoots, ovate or broadly heart-shaped, 1/4 to 3/4″ wide.

BUDS: Imbricate, solitary, sessile, round-ovoid, with few exposed scales, brown.

STEM: Slender, dark gray to brown, glabrous, sometimes spiny.

GROWTH HABIT: Low-growing, densely branched shrub to 3′.

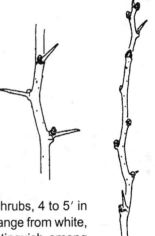

Chaenomeles japonica, (kē-nom′e-lēz jà-pon′i-kà), Japanese Floweringquince, forms an interlacing network of thorny stems in a wide-spreading, usually 2 to 3′ high framework. Flowers orange-red, scarlet or blood red on year-old wood; each flower about 1 1/2″ across, early to mid-April (before *C. speciosa* at least as observed in central Illinois). Fruit is a greenish yellow, fragrant, 1 1/2″ diameter pome, late September to October. A ratty shrub whose use should be tempered by astute judgment; not as ornamental as *C. speciosa*. *Chaenomeles* × *superba* Frahm (Rehd.) represents a hybrid species between *C. japonica* × *C. speciosa*. Usually they are low-spreading shrubs, 4 to 5′ in height; most characters are intermediate between the parents. Flower colors range from white, pink, crimson to shades of orange and orange-scarlet. Quite difficult to distinguish among various *C.* × *superba* forms and *C. speciosa* forms. Russian work showed *C. japonica* was the most winter hardy and resistant to late spring frosts; *C. cathayensis* (Hemsl.) Schneid. the least. Fruits of *C. japonica* contain 3 to 5% organic acids (hence, tartness) and 111 to 134 milligrams ascorbic acid (Vitamin C)/100 grams. Native of Japan. Cultivated 1874. Zone 5 to 8.

Cydonia oblonga Mill. — Quince, Common Quince

FAMILY: Rosaceae

LEAVES: Alternate, simple, ovate-elliptic, 2 to 4″ long, acute, subcordate, entire, deep green above, woolly pubescent beneath, large stipules; petiole—1/3 to 2/3″ long, tomentose.

STEM: Pubescent, finally glabrous, brown, not spiny.

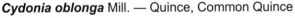

Cydonia oblonga, (sī-dō′ni-à ob-long-à), Quince, is a large multi-stemmed shrub growing 15 to 20′ high. It will never become a common landscape plant but over the years many readers asked me the difference between this and *Chaenomeles* species. Leaves and fruits are the easiest way to separate the two genera. Flowers are 5-petaled, 20-stamened, 1 1/2 to 2″ diameter, white to soft pink, often blush pink at the ends of the petals. Flowers in April–May. Fruits are fragrant, yellow, many seeded pomes, tapering to the point of attachment (pyriform) and averaging 3 1/2 to 4 1/2″ long, slightly less in width. They are utilized as ammunition and my mom made jelly from the two immense plants that grew in our Cincinnati homeplace. My memories of the two plants are still vivid because they served as goal posts for my neighbor, Bill Brannock, and myself. Any kick remotely close to sailing over the leafy outstretched branches constituted a successful attempt. Requires nothing more than well-drained soil and full sun. The plant proved unkillable in my Dad's garden and certainly we tried to break as many limbs as possible. Several cultivars listed by American nurseries include: 'Jumbo' with large white-fleshed fruit; 'Orange' with medium-sized, rounded, orange-yellow fleshed fruit; 'Pineapple' with large, golden yellow white-fleshed fruit with a pineapple-like flavor; and 'Smyrna' with pink flowers and large, rounded-oblong fruits with a lemon skin. Central Asia. Cultivated since ancient times. Zone 5 to 7(8).

Chamaecyparis Spach. — Falsecypress
FAMILY: Cupressaceae

At one time I would have said that the falsecypress might as well be omitted from midwestern and southern landscapes but the more I travel the more convinced I become that many of the cultivars are suitable for these regions. *Chamaecyparis* is generally considered the least important of the smaller evergreens used in contemporary landscaping. They appear frequently on the East and West Coast in cooler, more humid regions. All, except *C. thyoides* of eastern North America, are native of the lands bordering the Pacific Ocean, two in western North America and the other three in Formosa and Japan. With the exception of *C. formosensis* all the species are hardy. Cultivars of *C. obtusa* and *C. pisifera* are most common in the United States trade although *C. lawsoniana* has yielded many cultivars that are used extensively in European gardens. The leaves of seedling and juvenile plants are very distinct from those of adult trees, being needle-like or awl-shaped, up to 1/3″ long and spreading. Formerly plants with these features were placed in the genus *Retinospora*, but this genus is no longer recognized. It is interesting to note that some juvenile forms of more recent origin, having produced neither cones nor reversion shoots, still cannot be placed with certainty, either as to species or even to genus. It is easy to confuse *Thuja* with *Chamaecyparis*, however, the cones differ and the lateral leaves nearly cover the facial in the former, whereas in the latter, the facial leaves are more exposed.

MORPHOLOGICAL CHARACTERISTICS

Monoecious trees, pyramidal, leading shoots nodding; branchlets mostly frond-like, usually flattened; leaves opposite, scale-like (awl-shaped only in the juvenile state), ovate to rhombic, pointed or obtuse; flowers borne terminally on lateral branchlets; male flowers ovoid or oblong, yellow, rarely red, often conspicuous by their large number, stamens with 2 to 4 anther-cells; female flowers small, globular, less conspicuous; cones globose, short-stalked, solitary, ripening the first season (except *C. nootkatensis*, cones of which ripen in the second year); scales 6 to 8 (seldom 4, or 10 to 12), peltate, pointed or bossed in the middle; seeds (1)2, rarely up to 5 per scale, slightly compressed; wings broad, thin, cotyledons 2.

GROWTH CHARACTERISTICS

The *Chamaecyparis* species are large pyramidal, almost columnar trees with pendulous branches at the tips. All but *C. thyoides* can regularly grow to over 100 feet in native stands; however, they are generally (about 50%) smaller under landscape conditions and can be maintained at suitable heights by proper pruning. The species are seldom in evidence in landscape plantings but many of the cultivars are excellent and offer diversity of form, color and texture.

CULTURE

Falsecypress does best in full sun in rich, moist, well-drained soil. They thrive in a cool, moist atmosphere where they are protected from drying winds. *Chamaecyparis thyoides* is found in fresh-water swamps and bogs, wet depressions, and along stream banks, obviously withstanding less than perfect drainage, and holding promise for expanded use in North American gardens because of its tremendous wet soil tolerance. *Chamaecyparis obtusa* and *C. pisifera* types seem best adapted to the Midwest and South. Fall or spring transplanting with a ball of soil or as a container plant are satisfactory. Pruning is best accomplished in spring although branches can be removed about anytime.

DISEASES AND INSECTS

Falsecypress is relatively free of serious problems although blight (*Phomopsis juniperovora*), witches' broom, spindle burl gall, root rot and other minor insect pests have been noted.

PROPAGATION

Seed germination is usually low, due in part to poor seed quality, and also to various factors of embryo dormancy. In general, 2 to 3 months at 41°F is advisable. See specific recommendations under each species. Softwood or hardwood cuttings are the principal means of propagation although a few difficult to root types may be grafted. "The propagation of *Chamaecyparis*," *The Plantsman* 9(1):39–41 (1987), provides a worthwhile overview of cutting and grafting.

LANDSCAPE USE

Falsecypress can be used for about any landscape situation if the proper cultivar is chosen. They make good hedges, screens, foundations, and border plants. Some of the cultivars make strong accent or specimen plants and their use should be tempered so as not to detract from the total landscape. If not properly cared for the species will become ratty, open, and sorrowful looking. As a genus, this is relatively unimportant when compared to *Thuja*, *Juniperus*, and *Taxus*; for few plants are used in contemporary midwestern and southern landscapes.

SELECTED CULTIVARS

For inexplicable reasons I counted cultivars that were listed as available by major and specialty growers in their 1994 and 1995 catalogs. Here goes: *C. lawsoniana*—35, *C. nootkatensis*—10, *C. obtusa*—83, *C. pisifera*— 57, and *C. thyoides*—13. Pretty scary?! The following cultivars are recommended for general use. Most of these are available in the trade.

C. nootkatensis 'Pendula'
C. obtusa 'Filicoides'
C. obtusa 'Nana'
C. obtusa 'Nana Gracilis'
C. pisifera 'Boulevard'

C. pisifera 'Filifera'
C. pisifera 'Filifera Aurea'
C. pisifera 'Plumosa' and types
C. pisifera 'Squarrosa' and types

Chamaecyparis lawsoniana (Murray) Parl. — Lawson Falsecypress, Port Orford Cedar, Oregon Cedar
(kam-e-sip′a-ris la-so-ni-a′na)

LEAVES: Closely pressed, arranged in opposite pairs marked with indistinct white streaks on the undersurface; the lateral pair keel-shaped, 1/16 to 1/12″ long, slightly overlapping on the facial pair, which are rhomboidal and much smaller, about 1/20″ long, often glandular pitted, those on the main axis oblong, unequal; the lateral pair 1/4″, the facial pair 1/5″ long, with short or long spreading points.
STEM: Flattened, frond-like, arranged in a horizontal plane; entire spray deep green to glaucous green and not developing the prominent whitish markings on the underside.

SIZE: Almost impossible to estimate landscape size but 40 to 60′ high under landscape conditions is reasonable; can grow 140 to 180′ high and greater in the wild; national champion is 239′ by 39′ in Siskiyou National Forest, OR.
HARDINESS: Zone 5 to 7, possibly 8; does not thrive in excessive heat; serious winter kill in Orono, ME.
HABIT: A pyramidal to conical tree with massive, buttressed trunk and short ascending branches, drooping at the tips and ending in flat sprays.
RATE: Medium.
TEXTURE: Medium.
BARK: Silvery brown to reddish brown, fibrous, divided into thick, rounded ridges separated by deep irregular furrows, 6 to 10″ thick on old trees.
LEAF COLOR: Glaucous green to deep green above.
FLOWERS: Monoecious, staminate—crimson; pistillate—steely blue.
FRUIT: Cones numerous, globose, 1/3″ across, at first bluish green, afterwards reddish brown, bloomy; scales 8, with thin, pointed, reflexed bosses, each with 2 to 4 seeds; seeds oblong, appressed, glossy brown, broadly winged.
CULTURE: Transplant balled-and-burlapped if root-pruned or from containers; prefers well-drained, moist soil; full sun or partial shade; shelter from winds; supposedly does not like chalky soils; in South inadequate drainage and high night temperatures spell doom.

DISEASES AND INSECTS: Until recently it was thought this tree to be insect and disease-free, but there is a fungus, *Phytophthora lateralis*, which is devastating the species; it does its main damage by rotting the root system, which in turn kills the tree, see *Plant Disease* 73:791–794 (1989).

LANDSCAPE VALUE: A very handsome specimen with beautiful foliage and graceful habit for gardens and plantations where it can be grown; has numerous variations for form and color.

CULTIVARS: The number of selections staggers even the most ardent plantsman. For some unknown reason, I have never gotten excited with the species and the cultivars. In recent years, I have mellowed and now appreciate how truly stately and elegant the larger forms can be especially as viewed in European gardens. Many dwarf forms exist and are available from specialist nurseries. I have not seen outstanding, in most cases even mediocre, specimens in the eastern United States. Practicality points toward *C. obtusa*, *C. pisifera*, and *C. thyoides* for the eastern United States. Krüssmann in *Manual of Cultivated Conifers* lists 238 cultivars of *C. lawsoniana*.

PROPAGATION: Germination of Falsecypress seed is characteristically low, due in part to poor seed quality, and also to various degrees of embryo dormancy. Sound, unstratified seeds of *C. lawsoniana* have germinated completely on moist paper in less than 28 days at diurnally alternating temperatures of 86°F for 8 hours and 68°F for 16 hours with light during the warm periods. However, in Britain, presowing stratification has yielded the most consistent results. Stratification for 60 to 90 days at 41°F is recommended. This species is easily propagated by cuttings taken in fall. Cuttings taken in October and placed untreated in sand:peat rooted 90% or more. Untreated cuttings taken in January rooted equally well but more slowly. IBA treatments will hasten rooting.

ADDITIONAL NOTES: This species performs best where there is an abundance of soil and atmospheric moisture although it is less exacting in this respect than Redwood, *Sequoia sempervirens*, and frequently occurs on rather high, dry, sandy ridges which are often 30 to 40 miles inland. Bedgebury Pinetum, Kent, England holds the English national collection of *C. lawsoniana*. It was a sight to behold simply because of sheer numbers of cultivars varying in needle colors.

NATIVE HABITAT: Southwestern Oregon and isolated parts of northwestern California. Introduced 1854.

Chamaecyparis obtusa (Sieb. & Zucc.) Endl. — Hinoki Falsecypress
(kam-e-sip′à-ris ob-tū′sà)

LEAVES: Closely pressed, of 2 sizes, the lateral pair much the larger, boat-shaped, 1/12″ long, blunt at the apex or with a minute point; the smaller pairs about 1/24″ long, triangular, with a thickened apex, all prominently lined beneath with white X-shaped markings produced by a coating of wax along the margin, dark green above.

STEM: Flattened, slightly drooping at the tips.

SIZE: 50 to 75′ in height with a 10 to 20′ spread, to 120′ in the wild.

HARDINESS: Zone 5 to 8; some cultivars are being grown in Athens, GA; no doubt over generous in the 1990 edition relative to Zone 4 cold hardiness; cultivars vary in degree of cold tolerance, but anything less than −20°F will probably induce some injury; Cappiello and Littlefield tested at least 12 cultivars at Orono, ME with all exhibiting some cold injury and several complete kill.

HABIT: A tall, slender pyramid with spreading branches and drooping, frond-like branchlets.

RATE: Medium (25′ in 20 years).

TEXTURE: Medium.

BARK: Reddish brown, shed in long narrow strips.

LEAF COLOR: Shining dark green above, whitish markings beneath.

FLOWERS: Monoecious, staminate—yellow, pistillate—solitary.

FRUIT: Cones short-stalked, solitary, globose, 1/3 up to 3/8″ across, orange-brown; scales 8, rarely 10, depressed on the back and with a small mucro; seeds 2 to 5 on each scale, convex or nearly triangular on both margins, often with 2 glands, wings narrow, membranous.

CULTURE: Supposedly somewhat difficult to transplant but most of the cultivars are container-grown and move without great difficulty as is true with most *Chamaecyparis*; this species prefers a moist, well-drained soil and moderately humid atmosphere in a sunny, protected (from wind) area; according to an English reference the species and its cultivars thrive in moist, neutral soils and in those that have decidedly acid tendencies; from my own observations I would have to rank the cultivars of this species about the best suited for landscape use.

LANDSCAPE VALUE: Useful as a specimen; dwarf forms valuable for rock gardens and that different landscape touch; dark green foliage is particularly handsome; several forms have performed well on the Georgia campus, in fact a branch reversion of 'Nana Gracilis' was 25′ high and showed no foliage browning or discoloration; plants I rooted from this reversion have performed admirably; would I recommend *C. obtusa* and cultivars for wholesale landscape use . . . not unless I wanted to go broke replacing plants and placating clients.

CULTIVARS:

'Crippsii'—Broad pyramid, branches spreading, branchlets broadly frond-like, tops decurving, rich golden yellow, changing to green within plant, yellowish at ends of sprays, large tree, have observed 50′ specimens on Cape Cod.

'Filicoides'—A bush or small tree of open, irregular habit, branches long and straggly, clothed with dense pendulous clusters of fern-spray, green foliage.

'Nana'—Very slow-growing type to about 3′ in height and slightly broader, a 90-year-old specimen was 20″ high and 25″ wide; often confused with the following cultivar.

'Nana Gracilis'—Has thick dark green foliage; grows slowly to a height of about 6′ and has a spread of 3 to 4′; makes a pyramidal bush; fine form.

It is hopeless to list all the cultivars of this species. Many are so close in morphological features that as small plants it is impossible to distinguish among them. I have seen the fine dwarf conifer collection at the Arnold Arboretum and was thoroughly impressed by the many types of falsecypress. Mr. Al Fordham, the former propagator at the Arnold, showed me some seedlings of Hinoki Falsecypress which had been grown from seed collected from a dwarf clone. The variation was endless and the possibilities for introducing more dwarf forms existed. I also saw a large seedling population which was grown from a yellow foliaged form of *C. pisifera*. Again, there were many different types for some had yellow foliage, some blue or bluish green, others had juvenile needles while some showed adult foliage. The bottom line is that production of new and different cultivars of falsecypress is about as simple as sowing seed. The new *Conifers* book by van Gelderen and van Hoey Smith has wonderful photos of many of the cultivars.

PROPAGATION: Considerable variation in cutting rootability among different cultivars of this species; cuttings of the species and the cultivars 'Nana', 'Compacta', 'Lycopodioides', 'Filicoides', 'Gracilis', and 'Magnifica' were taken eleven times between late September and late January; the average percentage of rooting of untreated cuttings was 41%; rooting of cuttings treated with 50 to 100 ppm IBA/18 to 24 hours soak, or 8000 ppm IBA-talc was 96%; cutting wood was collected from current season's growth although 2- and 3-year-old wood also rooted; untreated cuttings rooted equally well when taken from September through January.

NATIVE HABITAT: Japan and Formosa. Introduced 1861.

RELATED SPECIES:

Chamaecyparis nootkatensis (D. Don) Spach. — Nootka Falsecypress, Alaska-cedar, Yellow-cypress
LEAVES: Closely appressed, spreading on vigorous shoots, pointed, keeled or rounded on the back, 1/8 to 1/4″ long, usually not glandular, gray-green to bluish green, color similar on upper and lower surfaces.
STEM: Branchlets usually pendulous, rounded or quadrangular, often in vertical planes on upper part of tree.

Chamaecyparis nootkatensis, (kam-e-sip′à-ris noot-ka-ten′sis), Nootka Falsecypress, is a medium-sized tree reaching 60 to 90′(120′) in the wild but one-half of that under cultivation. The crown is conical and composed of numerous drooping branches with long, pendulous, flattened sprays. The leaves are a dark bluish green or grayish green. The leaves do not possess white markings on the underside and are rank-smelling when bruised or rubbed. Branchlets are often quadrangular. Cones 1/3 to 1/2″ across, globose, glaucous, with 4(6) scales furnished with a triangular pointed boss, ripen in second year. This species does best where both soil and atmospheric moisture are abundant. Not seen in cultivation too extensively compared to *C. obtusa*, *C. pisifera*, and their clones. There is a rather attractive pendulous form, 'Pendula', that has become increasingly common in the eastern United States. Beautiful, graceful, elegantly arranged, pendulous branches and rich green foliage. I have stood on the sideline and watched with a less-than-careful eye as the species continued to gain ground in the landscape competition. Although not well-known compared to *C. obtusa* and *C. pisifera* it is definitely more cold hardy and adaptable than given credit. In Maine, 'Pendula' has withstood -30°F without injury. About 8 cultivars are commercially available in the United States, most offered by West Coast vendors. Handsome plants of the species and 'Pendula' in Boston, MA, also 'Pendula' at Williamstown, MA. Considerable dieback in native stands in southeast Alaska. Native from coastal Alaska to Washington; the Cascades to Oregon. Introduced 1853. Zone 4 to 7(8).

Chamaecyparis pisifera (Sieb. & Zucc.) Endl. — Sawara or Japanese Falsecypress
(kam-e-sip′à-ris pī-sif′ĕr-à)

LEAVES: Appressed, long pointed, ovate-lanceolate, 1/12 to 1/8″ long, with slightly spreading tips, obscurely glandular, dark green above, with whitish lines beneath; branchlets flattened, 2-ranked and arranged in horizontal planes.

CONE: Smallest of species presented herein with exception of *C. thyoides*, about 1/4″ long and wide, with 6 to 8 scales with hardened wavy, deeply sunken center (center of each scale).

SIZE: 50 to 70′ in height by 10 to 20′ in width, grows to 120′ in the wild.

HARDINESS: Zone 4 to 8; specimens at the Morton Arboretum, Lisle, IL, where the species actually seeds naturally, Orono, ME, Williamstown, MA, Athens, GA, and Spartanburg, SC provide a baseline of adaptability; second to *C. nootkatensis* in degree of cold adaptability.

HABIT: A pyramidal tree with a loose open habit and numerous branchlets thickly covered with slender feathery sprays, elegant particularly in youth.

RATE: Medium.

TEXTURE: Medium.

BARK: Rather smooth, reddish brown, peeling off in thin strips, extremely handsome.

LEAF COLOR: Dark green above with whitish lines beneath.

FLOWERS: Monoecious, small, inconspicuous.

FRUIT: Cones crowded, short-stalked, globose, 1/6 to 1/4″ across, yellowish brown; scales 6 to 8, soft-woody, upper side wrinkled, the middle depressed, with a small mucro at the depression; seeds 1 to 2, ovoid, bulbous on both sides, glandular; wing broad, membranous, notched above and below.

CULTURE: Moist, loamy, well-drained; humid climate; sunny, open conditions; prefers lime-free soils.

LANDSCAPE VALUE: Handsome when small but may lose its beauty with old age as the lower branches die; the chief advantage lies in the many cultivars which have a place in various parts of the landscape, especially in rock gardens or as accent plants.

CULTIVARS:

'Boulevard' ('Squarrosa Cyano-viridis')—Foliage is needle-like, silvery blue-green in summer and grayish blue in winter; up to 10′(15 to 20′) high and rather narrow-pyramidal; reasonably heat-tolerant; 20′ specimen on the Georgia campus is 15′ wide, attracts considerable attention, unfortunately, numerous brown needles are retained in the interior.

'Filifera'—Has drooping stringy branches and forms a dense mound, usually no higher than 6 to 8′ after 10 to 15 years although can become quite large; very fine-textured, a lovely and different accent plant; displays reasonable heat tolerance to at least Zone 7b.

'Filifera Aurea'—Similar to above with yellow foliage; striking, rather obtrusive especially in winter; 15 to 20′; acceptable and adaptable in the heat of Zone 7b.

'Plumosa'—Foliage is very soft-textured, almost feathery in constitution; large plant 30 to 50′; tree-like; like the species in habit and size.

'Plumosa Aurea'—Soft, feathery golden yellow foliage; retains considerable color throughout the summer and ranks among the best in this respect; slower than above but easily 20 to 30′ high; acceptable in Zone 7b.

'Squarrosa'—Foliage is almost needle-like, very feathery, definitely not flat and frond-like; soft gray-green foliage; large plant, 30 to 40′.

'Squarrosa Minima'—Fluffy, dense, gray-green foliage; slow-growing globe form to 30″.

PROPAGATION: Cuttings should be taken in October, November, and December, treated with 1000 ppm IBA and placed in sand:peat; there are other manipulations which can be performed to increase rootability but the above should work for most clones.

ADDITIONAL NOTES: Four more or less distinct foliage classes are distinguishable, each harboring a number of cultivars. Logically, one should attempt to assess the foliage category for an unknown cultivar and then proceed with the detective work. The categories include:

1. *Normal*: Foliage is similar to the species and cultivars vary in color and/or habit.
2. *Filifera* (Threadleaf Falsecypress): The main branchlets become stringy and cord-like without the typical flattened sprays of the normal group. The silver markings on the underside of the foliage are not detectable. The most common forms in cultivation are 'Filifera' (green) and 'Filifera Aurea', a rather ghastly golden-yellow form that can grow 15 to 20′ high. In my worst dreams, the large specimen by the waterfall at Longwood Gardens always surfaces. 'Filifera', the green form, can grow

40 to 50'. 'Filifera Nana' is a handsome dwarf green form that is preferable to its large relative. Occasionally a 'Filifera Aurea Nana' is listed but the ultimate size is unknown to this author. Plants I have seen appear more compact and rounded than 'Filifera Aurea'. 'Golden Mop' is a true compact yellow-foliaged form that is sold in the United States. This selection holds up relatively well in the heat of Zone 7. Dudley Nursery, Inc., Thomson, GA reports this one of the easier golden foliage forms that can be grown in containers.

3. *Plumosa* (Plume Falsecypress): In most respects like the species but more airy and ferny in texture because the opposite awl-shaped leaves stand out at a 45° angle to the stem. Even though the leaves are awl-shaped they are soft to the touch unlike many junipers with a common form. Grows into a good size, 20 to 30' high (potentially larger) tree under cultivation. The silver markings are distinguishable on the underside of the sprays. On the Illinois and Georgia campuses, 'Plumosa' has survived (notice I did not say prospered) for many years. 'Plumosa Aurea', as mentioned under cultivars, is common in the trade. Plants over 60' high have been recorded.

4. *Squarrosa* (Moss Falsecypress): Has the feel of a soft fluffy stuffed animal and serves as a substitute pacifier for adult gardeners who are embarrassed to carry their furry bears. Foliage shows a more juvenile condition than plumosa types. Foliage is dense, silvery glaucous blue and borne on rather billowy branches; the entire plant becoming irregularly fluffy. Needles are about 1/4" long, narrow, flat, glaucous on both surfaces and stand out 45 to 90° from the stem. 'Boulevard' as described above, is one of the most common. 'Squarrosa Pygmaea' is a cuddly, soft blue foliaged globe that provides sparkle to a rock garden. This clone is quite common and tends to produce reversion shoots which should be removed. 'Squarrosa' is a large plant and many fine specimens occur in New England, especially Cape Cod where 30 to 40' is the norm. Arnold Arboretum houses a 60' high specimen.

Perhaps southern gardeners have missed the landscape boat by not experimenting with the cultivars of *C. obtusa* and *C. pisifera*. I suspect that the high summer night temperatures (+65°F) may contribute to their slower growth in the South. A neighbor has a number of *C. p.* 'Boulevard' that were 3' high in 1979, 8' in 1989, and dead in 1995. A campus plant in full sun and compacted soil grew even less. This same plant appeared to develop more brown dead needles toward the interior. Interestingly, I always query the students about the correct identification of 'Boulevard'. Most have no idea where to start with identification because keys were not written for juvenile foliage forms.

NATIVE HABITAT: Japan. Introduced 1861.

Chamaecyparis thyoides (L.) BSP. — Atlantic Whitecedar or Whitecedar Falsecypress
(kam-e-sip'à-ris thī-oi'dēz)

LEAVES: Bluish green, glaucous green, to bright green, 1/10 to 1/12" long, lateral pairs boat-shaped with sharp-pointed, spreading tips, facial pairs closely pressed, ovate-triangular, short-pointed, flat or keeled; most of the green to bluish leaves are marked on the back with a resinous gland; leaves turn brown the second year but may persist for several years.

STEM: Branchlets slender, rather irregularly arranged (not flattened), spreading, not decurving, very thin; spray orientation dependent on cultivar with some highly irregular, others somewhat flattened.

SIZE: 40 to 50' high, 10 to 20' wide; can grow 75' and larger; national champion is 88' by 42' in Brewton, AL.

HARDINESS: Zone 4 to 8(9).

HABIT: A slender column in youth, forming a narrow, spire-like crown at maturity devoid of branches for 1/2 to 3/4's of its length.

RATE: Medium (25' in 20 years), depending on seed provenance (source), rates may approach fast, a few selections are growing as fast as Leyland Cypress.

TEXTURE: Medium.

BARK: Thin, on old trunks 3/4 to 1" thick, ashy gray to reddish brown, beautiful, ridged-and-furrowed, intricately irregular.

LEAF COLOR: Green to bluish green turning brown the second year, but persistent for several years; since 1995, we have been collecting germplasm from the length and breadth of the range; the northern accessions are consistently blue-green to bluish, the southern (GA, FL, MS, AL) consistently green; many forms develop an off-color (bronze, brown, etc.) with the advent of cold weather; our research has us on the trail of forms with year-round blue or green foliage.

FLOWERS: Monoecious, small, staminate red or yellow and abundant; pistillate green, few.

FRUIT: Cones on small branchlets, globose, small, 1/4″ across, green to bluish purple, bloomy; scales 4 to 5, rarely 6, acute often with a reflexed base; seeds 1 or 2 on each scale, oblong; wing narrow, as broad as the seed.

CULTURE: In the wild, characteristic of fresh-water swamps and bogs, wet depressions, or stream banks, and is rarely found except on such sites; extensive pure stands are the rule, occurring on shallow-peat covered soils underlain with sand; under cultivation it is best to provide a moist, sandy soil; have observed in dry soils under cultivation; prefers full sun and cannot compete with hardwood species.

DISEASES AND INSECTS: None serious.

LANDSCAPE VALUE: Useful on low lands and boggy sites where it is native; performs well in garden situations; seldom seen in the everyday landscape but significant interest in the species and cultivars for wetland reclamation and general garden use; from a southeastern perspective probably the best choice but seldom available except from specialist nurseries.

CULTIVARS: Over the past few years I have bumped into a few of the compact cultivars. Probably will never replace juniper but worth the effort for the true gardener. In late 1995, I initiated a *C. thyoides* germplasm accession project and now have 50 different clones. The 1990 edition of the *Manual* listed only two. The nursery industry is extremely enthused about the use of this native conifer to bring biodiversity to the upright needle evergreen screening and hedging syndrome. Currently × *Cupressocyparis leylandii*, *Thuja occidentalis*, *T. plicata*, and several upright *Juniperus* taxa are the principal components. All the accessions are listed but only the more commercially available discussed in any detail. Write if you have material to share. Our plant material door swings both ways.

'AA 102284'—Fast-growing, soft-textured, scale-like foliage, needles closely appressed, blue-green (more green than blue), slight silvery markings, irregular flattened sprays.

'AA 129681'—Moderate- to fast-growing, soft-textured, scale-like foliage, rich green-blue, prominent silvery markings.

'AA 13047'—Slower growing than the above, soft-textured, scale-like foliage, bluish, silvery markings on both surfaces.

'Andelyensis'—Compact, slow-growing, broad pyramidal form to 10′, always with several main branches at the top, i.e., never a clear central leader; bright blue-green in summer turning purplish green in winter, aromatic when bruised, produces abundant cones.

'Andelyensis Meth Dwarf'—A compact conical form, gray-green foliage.

'Andelyensis Nana'—Smaller than above, broader across the top.

'Aqua-velva'—Blue foliage form from Weston Nursery, Hopkinton, MA.

'Atrovirens'—Foliage pure dark green, no trace of blue, known before 1852, have been unable to locate this in commerce.

'Aurea'—Bright yellow summer foliage, bronze yellow in winter, densely conical to 15′.

'Blue Broom'—Soft lacy bluish foliage.

'Blue Sport'—Blue foliage, soft-textured, can be pruned and maintained as a compact shrub or will develop large upright habit, absolutely beautiful.

'Compacta'—Perhaps a catch-all term for slow-growing types. Received one form from Okefenokee Growers that was rich green, soft scale-like foliage, needles slightly separated from stem, oval-mounded, with abundant cones on a 2′ high plant. Also have seen photographs of an old, rather contorted, irregular dwarfish form.

'Compacta Glauca'—Compact conical form with bluish foliage, our plant has scale-like, soft-textured needles, silvery markings on both sides, handsome foliage.

'Conica'—'Andelyensis' mutation, 10 to 12″ in 10 years, needles in 3's, all needle-like, blue-green, somewhat brownish in winter, developed by Konijn about 1940 in Reejwijk, Holland, similar to 'Top Point'.

Dodd Form—Seedlings from Tom Dodd Nurseries, Semmes, AL with green, scale-like foliage with needles free at apices and conical, tree-like habit, similar to var. *henryae* (which see).

'Ericoides'—Appearing more and more in everyday commerce, a juvenile form with blue-green, spreading needle-like leaves, resembling *Erica* in disposition, turning bronze to reddish purple in winter, grows 4 to 5′ high, have read estimates to 30′, have seen a 20′ high specimen in Statesboro, GA, have grown this for a number of years with significant ambivalence, but visitors always ask its identity. Also sold under the name 'Red Star', which is a different taxon based on my evaluations.

Georgia Form—Dr. John Ruter of our Department (Tifton, GA) collected this green, scale-like foliage form in Taylor County, GA. It is tree-like in growth habit. Foliage has remained green during winter in the Dirr garden. Similar to var. *henryae* in foliage.

'Glauca'—Graceful, cone shape, compact habit, silver-blue-green foliage, young plants are anything but cone-shaped and grow almost akin to a blue Pfitzer juniper.

'Glauca Pendula'—Gracefully nodding branches, rich blue foliage, relatively dense habit, probably 15 to 25′ at maturity, described by Tony Avent, Plant Delights, and those who have seen the plant in his garden as one of the most beautiful conifers.

'Heatherbun'—Compact mounding globe, soft blue-green in summer, plum color in winter, listed as 6 to 10′ by 4 to 5′, but based on our evaluations probably smaller than 'Ericoides'.

var. *henryae*—Generally not accepted as a distinct taxonomic unit but embraces plants in the southern part of the range, perhaps Florida to Mississippi; we have acquired four different accessions from FL, AL, MS, and GA and all have rich green, scale-like foliage with needles free at tips, no silvery markings on either surface; Yucca-Do Nursery, Waller, TX noted that the tree is dense-branching with foliage to the ground.

'Hopkinton'—Selected by Weston Nursery for narrow habit, rapid growth and aromatic blue-gray needles, produces numerous cones; might be worth using in moist areas where other Falsecypress, Leyland Cypress, upright junipers, and yews would suffer.

'Hoveyi'—Contorted form, slender habit, branch tips cockscomb-like, crowded.

'Little Jamie'—Dark green (gray-green) summer foliage, purple-brown (plum) winter color, forms a narrow cone to 4′ high, grows slower than 'Andelyensis' but otherwise similar.

Maine Selection—Found this form growing in heavy shade on the University of Maine campus, blue-green, soft-textured foliage on a rather loose and open 10 to 12′ high plant; Dr. Paul Cappiello told me it was derived from native Maine *C. thyoides*.

'Meth Dwarf'—Similar to 'Andelyensis' but soft foliage texture, blue-green, silver markings on both surfaces, with more juvenile foliage (not much), although adult foliage still predominated, reddish green winter foliage, upright conical-pyramidal growth habit.

Mobile Bay Form—Collected by Coach Vincent Dooley, Athletic Director, University of Georgia, along Mobile Bay; rich green, scale-like foliage, tree type, similar to var. *henryae*.

'Nana'—Dwarf form, globose, very small, needles all blue-green. 1842.

Okefenokee Seedlings—Mixture of tree types all with rich green summer foliage.

'Purple Heather'—Similar to 'Heatherbun', if not the same.

'Pygmaea'—Dwarf, cushion-form habit, blue-green, branches spreading along the ground, scale-like leaves, tightly appressed, marked with bluish lines. Smallest dwarf form, 1867.

'Pyramidata'—Dwarf, small, narrow columnar form, short and densely branched, 1867.

'Raraflora'—Upright form, 10 to 12′ high, feathery, bluish green foliage.

Raulston Form—A more upright, slender conical form (more open than most) with light gray-blue-green, soft-textured foliage, needles free at tips, silvery markings on both sides, fast-growing, from J.C. Raulston Arboretum.

'Red Star'—Compact, dense, columnar growth habit, blue-green summer foliage, plum-purple in winter, will grow 15 to 25′, witnessed three 20 to 25′ specimens in late February near Sandersville, GA.

'Rubicon'—see 'Red Star'.

'Shiva' ('Fanfare')—A pretty feathery blue-green foliage form (brownish in winter) that was 5′ high and 4′ wide at 10 years, forms a feathery pyramid and maintains a central leader, sterile to date, found by Dr. Rekhe at Woods Hole, MA, some thinking this may be a *C. pisifera* form, has contracted root rot under container culture.

'Tom's Blue'—Foliage nearly as blue as some of the bluer *Cupressus* selections, tree form, saw listed in J.C. Raulston Arboretum Newsletter #2, Winter 1998, p. 3.

'Top Point'—Soft glaucous green, needle-like foliage, 1/4″ long, in 3's, 2 silvery bands on either side of midrib on lower surface, broad conical habit, grows slowly, one plant in our possession provided minimal inspiration.

'Variegata'—Foliage with bright gold splotches and flecks, conical habit, probably 10′ or more, have two similar accessions under test, both brown (gold foliage) in heat of Zone 7b, probably needs dappled shade, possibly better in North.

'Webb #1' ('Emily')—Rich green, soft-textured, scale-like, tightly appressed foliage with no glaucous bands on a dense, conical framework; late February cuttings are now (September 1997) 36″ high in 3-gallon containers; one of two selected from the seed orchard; primarily selected for density, rich green color and lack of bronzing.

'Webb #2' (Rachel')—Akin to #1 only broader in outline, needles more free at tips, no silvery markings, slightly darker green than #1, invariably visitors ask the identity of these clones; they do stand out, 24″ of growth from February cuttings in one growing season, slower than 'Webb #1'.

'Webb Gold'—A yellow-gold (almost cream-yellow) foliage seedling that the Webbs selected, soft-textured, scale-like foliage, apices looser than Webb 1 or 2, slower growing than the other Webb forms, parent plant was about 6′ high.

PROPAGATION: Seeds require cold moist stratification for 90 days. Supposedly somewhat difficult to root from cuttings but cuttings taken in mid-November and treated with 125 ppm IBA/24 hour soak rooted 96% in sand:peat in 6 months; cuttings taken in mid-December and placed in sand:peat rooted 14% without treatment and 70% with 8000 ppm IBA-talc; Hinesley et al., *HortScience* 29:217–219 (1994), proved categorically that the species was easy to root; of the 50 clones that we collected, all have rooted readily in 6 weeks, summer and winter (best), using 3000 to 5000 ppm KIBA, 3 perlite:1 peat medium, intermittent mist; bottom heat (70°F) accelerates rooting in cold weather.

ADDITIONAL NOTES: Quite an interesting species because of its adaptability to wet, boggy sites. Not a good competitor in the wild and it avoids competition by growing in these wet habitats. I have seen considerable stands in Massachusetts. Perhaps one of the most beautiful sites is the White Cedar Swamp in the Cape Cod National Seashore where an interpretive trail walk leads one through a native stand. In my travels, I see the plant with increasing frequency. With selection the plant will become more popular. Have added 10 to 15 selected seedlings to the Dirr garden and am ecstatic about performance in a semi-shaded location. Plants grew 1 to 2′ per year when watered and fertilized. "Identification of the heath-leaved cypress," *Baileya* 23(2):57–67 (1989), is worthwhile reading for *C. thyoides* aficionados. Wood anatomy studies proved 'Ericoides' was a *C. thyoides* selection. 'Ericoides' has had 13 published name combinations. This is no dwarf conifer since it can grow to 30′ high.

NATIVE HABITAT: Eastern United States in swamps, along the Atlantic coast from Maine to Florida, to Alabama and Mississippi. Introduced 1727.

Chamaedaphne calyculata (L.) Moench. — Leatherleaf

FAMILY: Ericaceae
LEAVES: Alternate, simple, evergreen, 1/2 to 2″ long, half as wide, elliptic or obovate to oblong or lanceolate, acute or obtuse, shallowly serrate toward apex, revolute, dull green, slightly scaly above, densely scaly beneath; petiole—short.

Chamaedaphne calyculata, (kam-e-daf′nē kȧ-lik′ū-la′tȧ), Leatherleaf, is an evergreen shrub of sparse, open habit with rather thin, wiry branches. Size is variable, anywhere between 2 and 5′. The leaves have a brownish green color. The small, 1/4″ long, white, urn-shaped flowers occur in 1 1/2 to 5″ long terminal racemes in April–June. The fruit is a 1/6″ diameter, dehiscent capsule containing small seeds. I have seen the plant in Connecticut, Massachusetts and Maine where it always inhabited boggy wet areas. Perhaps a worthwhile plant for naturalizing in wet areas and wetlands mitigation. Site in a semi-shaded environment. 'Nana' is smaller, generally 12 to 18″ high, forming a dwarf, dense thicket. 'Verdant' forms a thicket-like ground cover to 20″ high, shiny evergreen foliage, white flowers similar to blueberry appear terminally in May, useful for wet areas, discovered by Richard Lighty from the New Jersey Pine Barrens, Burlington County in 1985, introduced by Mt. Cuba, Greenville, DE, Zone 3 to 8 adaptability. Easily rooted from cuttings or grown from seeds. Northern Europe, northern Asia, in North America south to Georgia, Illinois and British Columbia. Cultivated 1748. Zone 3 to 5(6).

Chilopsis linearis (Cav.) Sweet — Desert-willow

FAMILY: Bignoniaceae
LEAVES: Opposite, simple, linear to linear-lanceolate, 6 to 12″ long, 1/4 to 1/2″ wide, entire, narrowed at ends, rich green, glabrous; petiole—short to sessile.
BUDS: Imbricate, rusty pubescent.

Chilopsis linearis, (chē′lop-sis lin′ē-ēr-is), Desert-willow, is a large shrub or small tree of rather loose gangly proportions. Grows 15 to 25′ high, 10 to 15′ wide. National champion is 68′ by 48′ in Gila County, AZ. In Texas, where I have seen specimens, they were always loose and open. The rich green summer foliage develops no appreciable fall colors. Flowers occur on new growth of the season in June through August. One to 1 1/2″ long and wide, funnelform-campanulate, with 2 upper and 3 lower lobes, range in color from white, pink, rose, lavender with purple markings inside and are sweetly fragrant. The fruit is a 6 to 12″ long, 1/4″ wide, 2-valved capsule with winged seeds that are fringed at the ends. Develops twisted trunks and shaggy bark. Leaves tend to drop early and the long stringy fruits persist through winter. Requires well-drained, dry soils. Cannot withstand heavy, wet soils. Roots rope-like and thick. Pretty for summer foliage texture and flower display. Have seen at Stephen F. Austin University, Nacogdoches, TX and was less than enthralled. Have not seen a viable specimen on the East Coast. 'Alpine' is an ascending shrub, tending toward tree habit, leaves 5″ long, 3/4″ wide, corolla tube is bicolor, top two lips are white, bottom three amaranth with a white border; 'Burgundy' has burgundy colored flowers; 'Marfa Lace' is a shrub 25 to 30′ high, leaves 4 1/2″ long, 1/3″ wide, semi-double, blush pink-rose flowers occurring in terminal panicles, flowers late May and early June, then intermittently through September (El Paso, TX); 'Regal' produces pale lavender flowers with a large lower lip of deep burgundy; 'Tejas' has habit similar to 'Marfa Lace', leaves 4″ by 1/3″, corolla and top two lips uniformly rose-pink, bottom three lips amaranth bordered with rose-pink. Southern California to Texas, south to Mexico. Cultivated before 1800. Zone 7 to 9.

RELATED SPECIES:

× ***Chitalpa tashkentensis*** Elias & Wisura, (chi-tal′på tåsh-ken′ten-sis), is the grex name for crosses between *Catalpa bignonioides* and *Chilopsis linearis*. The initial crosses were made in the USSR and reported about 1964. For years I grew a plant in my Georgia garden and finally removed it because of tremendous mildew susceptibility. The plant grew vigorously and approached 15′ high in 5 to 6 years. The habit was shrubby, loose, and open. The lavender flowers were pretty but as a whole the hybrid did not measure up to the better deciduous shrubs. The hybrid is sterile and fruits were never set on the single Dirr garden plant. 'Pink Dawn' has light pink flowers with a pale yellow throat and 'Morning Cloud' white to pale pink flowers with rich purple streaks in the corolla throat, 25 to 30′, branches more weeping than 'Pink Dawn'. Zone 6 to 9.

Chimonanthus praecox (L.) Link. — Fragrant Wintersweet
(ky′mo-nan′thus prē′koks)

FAMILY: Calycanthaceae

LEAVES: Opposite, simple, elliptic-ovate to ovate-lanceolate, 2 1/2 to 6″(8″) long, acuminate, rounded or cuneate at base, entire, glabrous, lustrous dark green, rough to the touch above, almost like sandpaper; petiole—1/4 to 1/2″ long.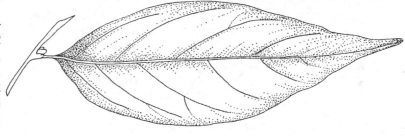

BUDS: Flower—imbricate, greenish brown, glabrous, appearing as stalked globes, 1/4 to 3/8″ long and wide, opening in December–January; vegetative—small, 1/8″ long, imbricate, green-brown, borne at 45° angle to stem, glabrous.

STEM: Somewhat squarish, stout, glabrous, shiny gray-brown, prominently covered with orangish brown lenticels, compressed at nodes, when bruised does not have the strong odor of *Calycanthus*, actually rather stinky; pith—white, solid, ample.

SIZE: 10 to 15′ high and 8 to 12′ wide in South, less in North to Philadelphia where the winters may regulate size, a 5′ high plant was growing at Long Hill, Beverley, MA, I was told that the plant flowered, at the Isle of Mainau, Germany, a gigantic specimen approximated 15′ by 18′.

HARDINESS: Zone (6)7 to 9.

HABIT: Large multi-stemmed shrub usually with fountain-like outline; with age becomes quite leggy and ragged; can be pruned to within 6 to 12″ of the ground in late winter and will rejuvenate.

RATE: Considered slow.

TEXTURE: Medium to coarse.

LEAF COLOR: Lustrous dark green changing to yellow-green in fall; does not overwhelm one in fall but the combination of yellow and green leaves is rather handsome, i.e., does not have to apologize for its fall performance; have observed old foliage in early January in Athens, GA; emerging leaves are quite frost sensitive, have noticed this particularly true on 'Mangetsu'.

FLOWERS: Perfect, fragrant, cupped, transparent yellow on outside grading to purple in the middle, each flower 3/4 to 1″ across, composed of numerous tepals (petals and sepals are indistinguishable), borne singly on leafless branches in the axils of the previous summer's wood; opening over a long period of time depending on the mildness of the winter; often from December to January–February in the Athens-Atlanta, GA areas; a few flowers still present in early March; may be injured by cold in more northern gardens; wonderfully fragrant when all goes right.

FRUIT: One to 2″ long, urn-shaped receptacle, 5 to 8 shining brown fruits (achenes) are held within this structure, each achene about 3/8 to 1/2″ long, somewhat bean-shaped, not ornamental, fruit set apparent by April, can be collected, harvested and sown by late May, fruits will persist through winter.

CULTURE: Easily transplanted from containers; adaptable to varied soils, needs good drainage; prune out old canes after flowering; full sun or partial shade.

DISEASES AND INSECTS: None serious.

LANDSCAPE VALUE: In the southern states, it makes a prized winter flowering shrub; it appears that some protection (a courtyard, wall) prevents excessive flower bud damage; can be used in a shrub border but is best employed along walks and entrances to buildings; the fragrance is the principal ornamental characteristic; cut branches may be brought inside and used in floral arrangements; flowers were fully open in January, 1982 when 0°F temperatures and 4″ of snow graced the Athens area, surprisingly the flowers held up reasonably well although some injury occurred; my flower dates over the past 18 years indicate that mid-January is peak flowering period; flowers are never overwhelming but when backlighted by the sun almost sparkle.

CULTIVARS: To my knowledge the following cultivars are not common in this country; however, they are worth listing. There is need for a compact form of the species.

    var. *concolor*—Pure yellow flowers, otherwise like the species, I purchased several plants and look forward to their flowers, however, suspect this taxon is the same as 'Mangetsu'/'Lutea', have seen flower color listed as pale yellow with excellent fragrance.

    'Grandiflorus'—Flowers purer yellow and more showy than the species; may reach 1 3/4″ diameter but are not as fragrant; the leaves may be larger and the overall habit larger.

    'Luteus' ('Mangetsu')—In the 1990 edition, I mentioned a pure golden yellow form without any trace of purple; the bright yellow petals are not transparent. I have one small plant that put out one flower in 6 years. In fact, my field notes say late January, 1984, pure golden yellow. Outstanding though it was, I wait for a second. The plant has been shuffled throughout my garden but appears less than satisfied. Seedlings I grew from campus plants at the same age are 6 to 8′ tall. The above is almost verbatim from the 1990 edition and not much has changed, the same plant is about 3′ high, is injured by late spring frosts on a yearly basis and has now been relegated to the recycling center. Good discussion of 'Mangetsu' by Creech appears in the *American Nurseryman* 160(12):70–71 (1984).

PROPAGATION: Seeds will germinate readily if collected in late May or June when the receptacles are changing from green to brown; at this stage the seed coat (actually pericarp wall) is quite soft and can be broken with a fingernail; if seeds are allowed to dry out and the seed coat becomes hard, germination is reduced to less than 5% compared to 90 plus percent for the soft seeds. Collected fruits in mid-February 1995, pericarp walls (coats) were as hard as bullets, soaked fruits for 48 hours, planted, with irregular but good germination in 14 days; this suggests that the dormancy in the embryo is very shallow or is simply related to the thickness (hardness) and imperviousness of the fruit wall; if water is imbibed then germination can proceed. Cuttings are described as difficult to root but my experiences at Georgia have led me to believe this is not the case; cuttings were collected in late July from a mature, 15′ high shrub; they were given a 3000 ppm IBA quick dip and placed in peat:perlite under mist; the wood was quite hard and growth had stopped by the time the cuttings were taken; 70% of the cuttings developed strong root systems and 3 made it through winter; I suspect that cuttings taken from rejuvenated shrubs would root in higher percentages than old wood cuttings.

ADDITIONAL NOTES: See Dirr, *American Nurseryman* 154(8):9, 40, 42 (1981), for detailed information. Raulston gave me *Chimonanthus nitens* Oliver, which appears to be rank-growing like its cousin but not as tall. The leaves are lustrous dark green, glabrous and 3 to 4″ long, 1 1/2″ wide, flowers are white, 3/4″ diameter, borne in the axils of the leaves, weakly fragrant. China. Zone 6 to 8. *Chimonanthus yunnanensis* W.W. Sm. with dull yellow flowers; *C. zhejiangensis* with evergreen leaves and soft yellow fragrant flowers; and *C. grammatus* are also described. These species offer interest for the collector but will not replace *C. praecox*.

NATIVE HABITAT: China. Introduced 1766.

Chionanthus virginicus L. — White Fringetree, Grancy Gray-beard, Old-man's-beard
(kī-ō-nan'thus vĕr-jin'i-kus)

FAMILY: Oleaceae

LEAVES: Opposite or subopposite, simple, narrow-elliptic to oblong or obovate-oblong, 3 to 8″ long, 1/2 as wide, acute or acuminate, cuneate, entire, medium to dark green and often lustrous above, paler and pubescent at least on veins beneath, usually becoming glabrate; petiole—1/2 to 1″ long, downy.

BUDS: Terminal—present, ovoid with keeled scales, acute, 1/8″ long, green to brown, 3 pairs of sharp-pointed keeled scales, angled appearance when looked upon from apical end.

STEM: Rather stout, green to buff to brown, glabrous or pubescent when young, slightly squarish, epidermis peeling to give onion-skin effect; have looked at many *C. virginicus* and some have quite hairy almost to-mentose stems, others gla-brous; have also noticed stem color is a rich dark purple-brown on certain plants and the color per-sists into late summer–fall.

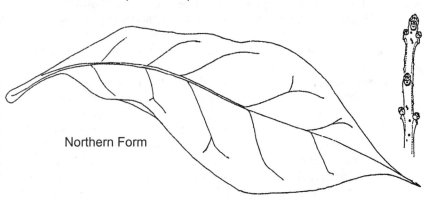

Northern Form

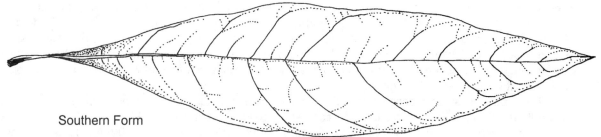

Southern Form

SIZE: In the wild may reach 25 to 30′ with an equal spread but under landscape conditions is often a shrub or small tree 12 to 20′ with an equal spread; co-national champions are 41′ by 31′ in Telford Spring County Park, FL and 32′ by 35′ at Mt. Vernon, Fairfax County, VA.

HARDINESS: Zone 4 to 9.

HABIT: Large shrub or small tree with a spreading, rather open habit; often wider than high; the range of shapes is as variable as the stem characteristics—some open and straggly, others bushy and robust, others tree-like.

RATE: Slow, under ideal conditions possibly 8 to 10′ in 10 years but plants I have observed in the Midwest averaged only about 4 to 6″ per year over a five year period; a 13-year-old plant in my garden is 15′ high.

TEXTURE: Medium-coarse in leaf, fine in flower, medium in winter.

BARK: Gray, smooth on young branches; finally slightly ridged-and-furrowed.

LEAF COLOR: Late to leaf out, often not until mid-May or later in Urbana, IL and Boston, MA; medium to dark green, sometimes lustrous, in summer; fall coloring is usually yellowish green-brown but can range from a bright to golden yellow; have observed good yellow on selected specimens.

FLOWER: Dioecious or polygamo-dioecious, white, slightly fragrant, males more effective than females because of longer petals, 4 petals, 2 stamens, each petal 3/4 to 1 1/4″ long, 1/16 to 1/12″ wide, borne in 6 to 8″(10″) long and wide, fine, fleecy, soft-textured panicles in May (early to mid in Athens) to early June just as leaves are expanding to point of complete development, on previous season's wood; one of our more handsome native plants in flower; each flower stalk of the panicle bears 3 flowers and emerges from the axil of a 1 to 1 1/2″ long, leaf-like bract; bracts persist until fruits ripen.

FRUIT: Dark blue, bloomy, fleshy egg-shaped drupe, 1/2 to 2/3″ long, effective in August–September; interesting but often overlooked because the fruits are partially hidden by the foliage; birds relish them; invariably ripen by mid-August in Athens.

CULTURE: Transplant balled-and-burlapped or as a container-grown plant in spring; supposedly difficult to move although several nurserymen I have talked with indicated they have had no problems; prefers deep, moist, fertile, acid soils but is extremely adaptable; full sun to partial shade; pruning is rarely required; in the wild is most commonly found along stream banks or the borders of swamps.

DISEASES AND INSECTS: None serious, occasionally scale, borer, perhaps ash borer, has been reported, leaf spots, powdery mildew, and canker; Don Shadow mentioned that borers were a problem.

LANDSCAPE VALUE: Very beautiful specimen shrub, excellent in groups, borders, near large buildings; outstanding in flower; will do well in cities as it is quite air pollution tolerant; I would like to make a case for this as the national shrub for even dogwood does not carry itself with such refinement, dignity and class when in flower; possibly not considered sufficiently hardy but is prospering in Orono, ME, Manchester, NH, and Chicago, IL. In fact, the Manchester specimen by the Art Museum will perpetually linger in my memory as one of the largest specimens I have observed. On a chilly October day, Peter Kidd, Phil Caldwell and I perused every Manchesterian nook and cranny for unusual plants. I look forward to returning. Becoming more available in commerce and several mail-order firms offer the plant.

CULTIVARS: Although the plant is difficult to propagate vegetatively the Dutch have grafted selected forms onto *Fraxinus ornus* and *F. excelsior*. Doubtfully, will the plants be long lived. I saw Dutch grafted stock in a Georgia nursery and was impressed by the large leathery dark green leaves but also noticed the suckering ash understock.

'Floyd'—The only American named clone that I know; named by Professor J.C. McDaniel, *Proc. Intl. Plant. Prop. Soc.* 19:377–378 (1969) for upright growth habit, neater large flower panicles; predominately male, but with some perfect flowers since a light smattering of fruit is produced; doubtfully in commerce.

The possibilities for selections are endless and a particularly fine lustrous dark green, narrow-leaved seedling in my garden resists every propagation attempt. A correlation appears to exist between leaf width and petal diameter: the wider the leaf the wider the petal and conversely. Two- to three-year-old plants may flower and I purchased two such plants for our garden. This is an indication that juvenility is lost at an early age which may correspond to miserable rooting results even with young seedlings.

At a 1993 meeting in Thomson, GA, where I gave a lecture, a lady approached me and mentioned that she knew of red- and pink-flowered forms. Needless to relate, I had abnormal heart palpitations. Arrangements were made to propagate the forms, seedlings were purchased, letters and phone calls executed, but to this day I await the first scion. Why did she bring it up in the first place? In Nicholson's excellent article, *Arnoldia* 50(4):24–31 (1990), he reported a rose-colored form was found in Virginia, also similar variants were observed in other parts of the United States. One of these days I will find such a plant and share it with my fellow gardeners.

There appears significant consistent difference between the southern or Florida type (*C. henryi*) and the northern types. The southern type has narrower, more lustrous dark green leaves, and appears more uniform in a seedling population. Superior Trees, Lee, FL supplied me with 100 seedlings and their uniformity was remarkable.

PROPAGATION: Seed possesses a double dormancy and requires a warm period of 3 to 5 months, during which a root unit is made while the shoot remains dormant; then cold temperature at 41°F for one or more months overcomes the shoot dormancy; if sown in fall outside, seed germinates the second spring; first year seedlings do not put on much shoot extension; Dr. John Frett, one of my former graduate students, now at the University of Delaware, has extracted embryos from August collected seed and incubated them on a gibberellic acid:nutrient solution; these embryos greened up and produced both shoots and roots; based on John's work the dormancy is fairly complex and appears to involve a hard, bony endocarp that must be broken down, inhibitors in the endosperm and then a dormancy in the shoot portion of the embryo. A detailed seed germination study showed that removal of the pericarp including the hard exocarp, 6-hour 1000 ppm GA_3 soak resulted in 83% germination in 15 weeks at 77°F. The authors showed (more or less) that the shoots did not require cold (41°F for 30 and 60 days) to initiate growth. See *American Nurseryman* 176(4):127–129 (1992) for more specifics. Until 1987, I had never rooted cuttings and have taken wood from 3-year-old seedlings which should still be juvenile. Alcohol quick dips result in rapid deterioration of cuttings and talc preparations appear to be necessary. I suspect that cuttings taken from rejuvenated shrubs would root in higher percentages than old wood cuttings. Peter Del Tridici and I set up an elaborate rooting experiment at the Arnold with different rooting compounds and concentrations. Nothing worked on *C. virginicus* but some rooting did occur on *C. retusus*. *Chionanthus retusus* has essentially the same seed requirements (perhaps shorter) as *C. virginicus* but it can be rooted from cuttings. I know of one Tennessee nurseryman who is rooting *C. retusus* in commercial quantities. A Tennessee report noted that cuttings of *C. retusus* should be taken as they harden, wound, 8000 ppm IBA talc with early July and mid-July cuttings rooting 85 and 95%, respectively. Over the years, I have used 10000 ppm KIBA on early June *C. retusus* cuttings, peat:perlite, mist, 8 to 10 week period, with 40 to 50% success. Have rooted *C. virginicus* in low percentages at the same time from a six-year-old plant using same procedure with perlite medium. Rooting took 12 to 14 weeks and several cuttings were successfully overwintered. One is now 10′ high and flowering in our garden.

ADDITIONAL NOTES: I could ramble for pages but suggest the insatiable "Chionanthus-phile" read Fagan and Dirr, *American Nurseryman* 152(7):14–15, 114–117 (1980). Considered by the British to be one of the finest American plants introduced into their gardens. Although native to the Southeast, it is perfectly hardy in Maine and Minnesota. In the wild is found in a variety of habitats including upland hardwood or pine forests, rock outcrops, savannas, flatwoods and shrub bogs.

NATIVE HABITAT: Southern New Jersey to Florida and Texas. Introduced 1736.

RELATED SPECIES:

Chionanthus pygmaeus Small, (kī-ō-nan'thus pig-mē'us), Dwarf Fringetree, is a dwarf form (3 to 6′ high) from the sandy soils of central Florida that flowers with the same intensity and character as *C. virginicus* yet on a smaller framework. I have seen plants in Aiken, SC about 3 to 4′ high literally dripping with large fleecy, white panicles in mid to late April. Fruits are about twice the size of those of *C. virginicus*. Leaves are leathery lustrous dark green. This is an endangered species and as such will be difficult to obtain across state lines. As I view it, the ornamental potential is great and perhaps will be exploited in the future. Florida. Zone (5)6 to 9. Has survived -13°F.

Chionanthus retusus Lindl. & Paxt. — Chinese Fringetree

LEAVES: Opposite, subopposite, narrow-elliptic to oblong or obovate-oblong and on some forms almost rounded, 3 to 8″ long, one-half as wide, acute or acuminate, cuneate, entire or serrate, lustrous dark green, either thick and leathery or rather thin, usually glabrous at maturity; petiole—1/2 to 1″ long.

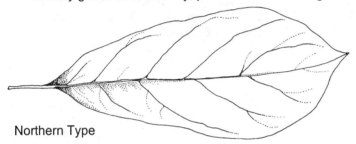

Northern Type

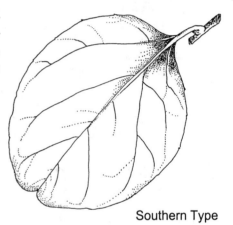

Southern Type

Chionanthus retusus, (kī-ō-nan'thus rē-tu'sus), Chinese Fringetree, is a large multi-stemmed shrub in cultivation but can be grown as a small tree. Usually reaches 15 to 25′ in height but may grow 30 to 40′ in the wild. The outline is spreading, rounded. The gray bark may be peeling or tightly ridged-and-furrowed. The leaves are leathery, often smaller than those of *C. virginicus*, and lustrous. The flowers are snow white, May–June (late April–early May in Athens), produced in erect, 2 to 3″ high and 2 to 4″ wide, cymose panicles, terminating young shoots of the year. It tends to be alternate in flowering abundance, although I have not noticed this tendency on plants in the Athens area. Fruit is an ellipsoidal, 1/2″ long, dark blue drupe which ripens in September through October. The flowers, fruits and foliage are highly ornamental but the fruit will only occur on female plants. Another asset is the handsome gray-brown bark which offers another season of interest. Quite variable in leaf characteristics and two distinct forms are commonly seen in cultivation in the United States. One is a tree with a distinct trunk and large, dark, rather dull green leaves; the other a shrubby form (15′) with rounded to oval-rounded, thickish, lustrous dark green leaves that persist into early December in Athens. The latter is a wide-spreading, rounded shrub with long shoot extensions. The bark is a polished light brown and may exfoliate in papery curls. In the literature I occasionally see reference to var. *serrulatus* (Hayata) Koidz. which appears to be nothing more than the seedling (juvenile) version with serrate leaves, a trait that is lost with maturity. I have grown seedlings and, indeed, they often have a serrate leaf margin. *Chionanthus retusus* is perhaps even more effective in flower than *C. virginicus* since the flowers occur at the ends of the new shoot extension. Prospers in the heat of the South and when finished flowering maintains a handsome dark green posture. On occasion, fall color has been soft yellow, generally in late November to early December (Athens). Leaves are extremely frost resistant. One traveler in China compared it in flower to a dome of soft, fleecy snow. Pair reported excellent growth and heat tolerance in Wichita, KS tests. Cold hardiness is less than *C. virginicus* and anything below -15°F will result in stem kill. At -24°F, *C. retusus* was killed to the ground but did resprout; *C. virginicus* was not injured. The finest tree in the country, perhaps the world, is located at the Arnold Arboretum. Nicholson's *Arnoldia* article points out the great variation in the species. It is mandated reading for all my friends who insist var. *serrulatus* is a legitimate taxon. As a final entry, I would make mention of seeds of the Arnold tree that were planted in the fall of 1995 and germinated in 1997. Seventy serrated leaf seedlings from an entire leaf mature tree. China, Korea, Japan. Introduced 1845. Zone (5)6 to 8.

Choisya ternata HBK. — Mexican-orange

FAMILY: Rutaceae
LEAVES: Opposite, generally trifoliate, evergreen, 3 to 6″ long, each sessile leaflet oblong to obovate, 1 1/2 to 3″ long, about as wide, rounded, cuneate, entire, lustrous rich green, glabrous, when crushed emitting a pungent odor; petiole (rachis)—1 to 2″ long.

Choisya ternata, (choiz′ē-à těr-nā ′tà), Mexican-orange, is a superb, densely rounded, evergreen shrub that ranges from 6 to 8′ high and wide. For the adventuresome gardener where winter temperatures seldom drop below 5 to 10°F it is worthy of trial. The fragrant, white flowers, each 1 to 1 1/4″ wide, occur in 3- to 6-flowered corymbs at the end of the shoots. I have seen the plant in flower in May and June in England but it will flower sporadically into winter. Requires a well-drained, acid, moist soil in partial shade to full sun. No doubt high night temperatures especially in the South will prove problematic. Used as a specimen evergreen shrub and is one of the handsomest. 'Aztec Pearl' (*C. arizonica* × *C. ternata*) is a compact shrub with lustrous rich green, narrow leaves and fragrant, white-pink flushed flowers that open over an extended period [see *The Plantsman* 13:21–26 (1991)]. 'Sundance' was introduced by Bressingham Gardens, England for its golden foliage that is richest on the young growth but persists throughout the seasons, also produces the fragrant, white flowers. This cultivar originated as a branch sport of the species and grows about one-half the rate. Mexico. Introduced 1866. Zone 7 to 9.

Cinnamomum camphora (L.) Sieb. — Camphor Tree
(sin-à-mō′mum kam-for′à)

FAMILY: Lauraceae
LEAVES: Alternate, simple, evergreen, oval, ovate-lanceolate or obovate, 3 to 4″ long, 1 1/2 to 3″ wide, acuminate, cuneate, entire, lustrous dark green and glabrous, glaucous beneath, fragrant when bruised, coriaceous, 3 to 4 vein pairs, the lower prominent and creating a palmate-like impression; petiole—3/4 to 1 1/4″ long.

SIZE: 40 to 60′ by 40 to 60′, can grow to 100′; national champion is 67′ by 103′ in Darby, FL.
HARDINESS: Zone 9 to 11; 11°F killed 42″ diameter trees at Sea Island, GA.
HABIT: In youth a uniformly branched, round headed evergreen tree of great beauty; at maturity similar but with wide-spreading branches; very elegant in general architecture.
RATE: Fast.
TEXTURE: Medium throughout the seasons.
BARK: Gray-brown, ridged-and-furrowed, rather clean and attractive.
LEAF COLOR: New growth bronze-red and quite attractive, maturing to lustrous dark green, will discolor (yellow-green) in exposed windy locations during cold weather; drops old leaves in late winter/early spring.
FLOWERS: Perfect, fragrant, greenish white, 1/6″ wide, and produced in axillary, stalked, 2 to 3″ long panicles in May.
FRUIT: A blackish, 1/3″ diameter, rounded drupe that is often borne in great abundance and becomes a nuisance especially in trafficked areas; not really showy since it blends with foliage.
CULTURE: Move as a young container or balled-and-burlapped tree; will make up quickly into a handsome specimen; acid, sandy, or clay loam soil; will tolerate dry conditions once established; sun to partial shade.
DISEASES AND INSECTS: Root rot, *Verticillium* wilt; have not noticed any problems in the Southeast.

LANDSCAPE VALUE: Handsome tree that is fast-growing and suitable for warm (20°F and above) climates; lovely shade tree but messy because of fruits; is a surface rooter and will compete with other plants; have seen a small stump sprout in Atlanta that dies back virtually every winter; best in coastal Georgia and south; has escaped from cultivation in Florida.

CULTIVARS:

'Majestic Beauty'—To this author's knowledge the first clone to be named, more uniform habit, larger richer green foliage than the species, a Monrovia introduction.

PROPAGATION: Collect fruits in fall, remove pulpy outer coating, sow outside and germination occurs in spring.

NATIVE HABITAT: Japan, China, Formosa. Introduced 1727.

Cistus laurifolius L. — Laurel Rock Rose

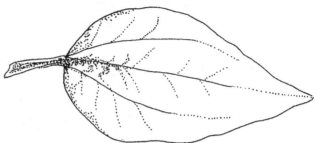

FAMILY: Cistaceae

LEAVES: Opposite, simple, evergreen, oval-oblong, 1 1/2 to 3″ long, 3/4 to 1 1/2″ wide, long taper pointed, rounded, dark green and glabrous above, gray tomentose below, sticky on both surfaces; petiole—1/2 to 3/4″ long, hairy, the bases of each leaf meeting and clasping the stem.

Cistus laurifolius, (sis'tus lâr-i-fō'lē-us), Laurel Rock Rose, was a plant I wrestled with to see whether it would find a place in this *Manual*. Obviously the plant won. I have never seen a *Cistus* in the East or South, but have fallen in love (can a man do this?) with the various species from my European visits. As per usual when the word "never" is used an exception eventually rears its ugly head. Bob McCartney, Woodlanders, Aiken, SC, is particularly fond of showing me a "patch" of *Cistus* in a pine shade environment. Will it sell in everyday commerce? Doubtfully. The following description is somewhat general to purposely provide an overview. They are evergreen shrubs with entire, opposite leaves that are usually fragrant when crushed. Most grow 1 to 3′ to 6′ high and form irregular mounds. Their real beauty resides in the 5-petaled, 2 to 3″(4″) wide flowers of white, pink, and reddish shades, often with a deeper colored spot at the base of the petal. Flowers occur in great profusion in June and July(August). I can say I never met a Rock Rose that was not attractive. Ideally, full sun in a well-drained, reasonably dry situation is ideal. Transplant as container-grown plants since they do not move readily bare root. Plants are native to the Mediterranean region and will, no doubt, suffer in the humidity of the Southeast. The hardiest and most available species include: *C. × corbariensis* Pourr., a 1 1/2′ high form with 1 1/2″ diameter, white flowers with a yellow spot at the base of the petal and with *C. laurifolius* the most hardy; *C. ladanifer* L., Gum Rock Rose, a 4 to 5′ high shrub with sticky stems and leaves and 3 to 4″ diameter, white, red-brown spotted flowers; *C. laurifolius* is a 3 to 6′ high shrub with sticky stems and leaves and 2 to 3″ diameter, white, yellow-spotted, fragrant flowers, later than the above species from June to August; this is probably the hardiest species and small seedlings in my garden were fine at 23°F; will probably take 0 to 10°F with little damage; *C. × purpureus* Lam., Orchidspot Rock Rose, is common in European gardens as a 1 1/2 to 3′ mounded shrub with 2 to 3″ wide, reddish purple to lavender-pink flowers with a dark red, basal spot. These species are best adapted along the West Coast and areas with a Mediterranean climate. It never hurts to roll the dice when gardening and these plants are deserving. Seeds of *C. laurifolius* received in a seed exchange from The Royal Horticultural Society germinated immediately after sowing. Cuttings supposedly root without difficulty but I suspect with their Mediterranean heritage, the moisture should be minimized.

Cladrastis kentukea (Dum.-Cours.) Rudd [*C. lutea* (Michx. f.) K. Koch.] — American Yellowwood, Virgilia

(klà-dras'tis ken-tuk'ē-à)

FAMILY: Fabaceae

LEAVES: Alternate, odd-pinnately compound, (5)7 to 9(11) leaflets, entire leaf 8 to 12″ long, each leaflet 2 to 3″ long, elliptic to ovate, acute, broad cuneate, glabrous, bright green, terminal the largest (4″ by 2 1/2″), basal smaller to 1 1/2″ long; petiole—enlarged at base, enclosing bud.

BUDS: Terminal—absent; laterals—naked, superposed, the uppermost the largest and generally alone developing, flattened, closely packed together to form a pointed, bud-like, hairy brownish "cone," generally less than 1/4″ long, nearly surrounded by the leaf scar.

STEM: Slender, more or less zig-zag, smooth, bright reddish brown, often bloomy, odor and taste resembling that of a raw pea or bean.

BARK: Thin, gray to light brown, resembling bark of beech, beautiful and remaining so into old age.

SIZE: 30 to 50′ in height with a spread of 40 to 55′; national champion is 72′ by 73′ in Cincinnati, OH.

HARDINESS: Zone 4 to 8; has proven hardy at Minnesota Landscape Arboretum and University of Maine.

HABIT: Usually a low branching tree with a broad, rounded crown of delicate branches.

RATE: Medium, 9 to 12′ over an 8 to 10 year period, will grow considerably faster with adequate water and fertilizer.

TEXTURE: Medium in foliage and winter; very handsome in foliage because of the bright green color of the leaves.

BARK: On older branches and trunks very smooth, gray and beech-like in overall appearance and texture; called Yellowwood because the heartwood is yellowish.

LEAF COLOR: Opening bright yellowish green gradually changing to bright green in summer; very prominent in a landscape when compared to the dark green of maples, oaks, or ashes; fall color may be a yellow to golden yellow; I have been most impressed with the soft yellow fall color on trees in the South.

FLOWERS: Perfect, white, fragrant, 1 to 1 1/4″ long; borne in 8 to 14″ long, 4 to 6″ wide at base, pendulous, terminal panicles in May to early June (late April to early May in Athens); tends to produce the greatest abundance of flowers in alternate years or every third year; flowers when 12 to 18′ tall; bees really frequent the flower for nectar; in full flower the tree appears to be dripping with white rain; I grew a tree from seed that is now 17-years-old and has not flowered.

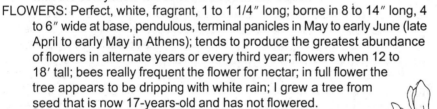

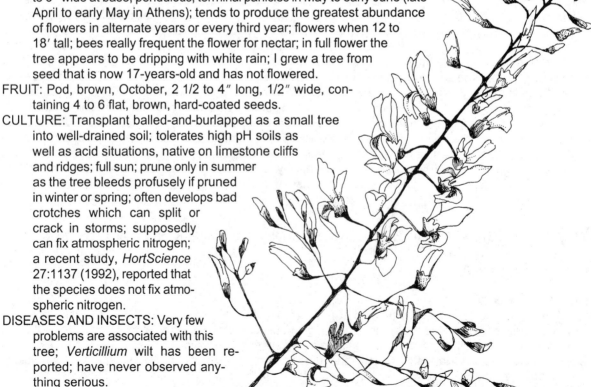

FRUIT: Pod, brown, October, 2 1/2 to 4″ long, 1/2″ wide, containing 4 to 6 flat, brown, hard-coated seeds.

CULTURE: Transplant balled-and-burlapped as a small tree into well-drained soil; tolerates high pH soils as well as acid situations, native on limestone cliffs and ridges; full sun; prune only in summer as the tree bleeds profusely if pruned in winter or spring; often develops bad crotches which can split or crack in storms; supposedly can fix atmospheric nitrogen; a recent study, *HortScience* 27:1137 (1992), reported that the species does not fix atmospheric nitrogen.

DISEASES AND INSECTS: Very few problems are associated with this tree; *Verticillium* wilt has been reported; have never observed anything serious.

LANDSCAPE VALUE: Excellent tree for flowers and foliage; the medium size and spreading habit make it a choice shade tree for smaller properties; can be used as a single specimen or in groupings; there are beautiful specimens located on the University of Illinois campus, Spring Grove Cemetery, and the Arnold Arboretum; does not appear quite as prosperous in Zone 7b but a 30' high specimen on the Georgia campus has flowered heavily over the years; another Dirr favorite that I cherish more with each passing year, the 17-year-old seedling is about 20' high and although it has never flowered it brings great presence to the garden because of the rich green foliage, surprisingly beautiful yellow fall color, and winter bark; the rachises (leaf axis) persist after the leaflets abscise adding yet another twist to the tree's character.

CULTIVARS:

'Rosea'—A beautiful pink-flowered form that has been distributed by the Arnold Arboretum to several nurseries; original plant was located on grounds of Perkins Institute for the Blind, Watertown, MA; its origin is unclear; flowered in our garden April 1994, heavily in 1997, and was a pleasing pink; flowers were quite fragrant; 'Perkins Pink' is proposed as the new name in *Proc. Intl. Plant Prop. Soc.* 46:578 (1996); the author noted that the light pink flowers appear in pendulous, terminal, 10 to 15" long panicles in early June (Boston); some seedlings grown from seeds collected from the original tree flowered pink.

PROPAGATION: Seed dormancy is supposedly caused by an impermeable seed coat and to a lesser degree by conditions in the embryo; scarify with sulfuric acid for 30 to 60 minutes plus mild stratification in moist sand or peat for 90 days at 41°F; root cuttings taken in December are an alternative method of propagation; see Frett and Dirr, *The Plant Propagator* 25(2):4–6 (1979), for a thorough insight into seed propagation of *Cladrastis*; based on that work embryo dormancy is not the limiting factor for seeds provided 0, 30, 60 and 120 minutes acid treatment germinated, 5, 41, 92 and 96%, respectively; simply a hard seed coat that must be rendered permeable; I collected seeds of 'Rosea' in late August 1997, soaked for 24 hours, sowed and within two weeks respectable germination occurred; interestingly this tree was self-pollinated and I hope the off-spring yield deeper pink or rose flowers.

ADDITIONAL NOTES: Common name is derived from the appearance of the freshly cut heartwood which is yellow; hence, yellowwood. Interestingly it is quite hardy and has flowered in the Minneapolis-St. Paul, MN area and at the University of Maine, Orono, where winter temperatures may range from -25 to -30°F. One report noted that new leaves may be injured by late spring frosts. In spring 1990 a late spring frost devastated many plants in the Dirr garden and all the new growth of our yellowwood was killed but regrowth was complete. A pleasant history was penned by Susan Sand, *American Horticulturist* 71(4):35–38 (1992), and makes worthwhile reading. An excellent article on yellowwood is by Robertson, *Arnoldia* 36(3):137–150 (1977).

NATIVE HABITAT: North Carolina to Kentucky and Tennessee, nowhere very common; reference books show it scattered in Indiana, Illinois, Georgia, Alabama, Mississippi, Arkansas, Missouri, Oklahoma. Generally occurs in rich well-drained limestone soils in river valleys, slopes and ridges along streams. Introduced 1812.

RELATED SPECIES:

Cladrastis platycarpa (Maxim.) Mak. — Japanese Yellowwood

LEAVES: Alternate, compound pinnate, 8 to 10" long, 11 to 15 leaflets, each obliquely ovate, acuminate, cuneate to rounded, 1 1/2 to 4" long, 1 to 1 1/2" wide, dark green above, glabrous except on midrib and petiole; a small stipule is at the base of the petiolule of each leaflet.

Cladrastis platycarpa, (klà-dras'tis pla-ti-kâr'pà), Japanese Yellowwood, is a rather handsome, small (20 to 40'), rounded tree with white, pea-like flowers produced in 4 to 6" high and 2 1/2 to 4" wide panicles. The 2" long by 1/2" wide pod is tapered at both ends and winged all around. There is a nice specimen in the Arnold Arboretum that flowers after *C. kentukea*. Japan. Introduced 1919. Zone 5 to 7. Killed outright at Orono, ME.

Cladrastis sinensis Hemsl., (klà-dras'tis sī-nen'sis), Chinese Yellowwood, grows 30 to 50' high and wide. The compound pinnate leaves are composed of 9 to 13(17) leaflets, each 3 to 5" long and 1 to 1 1/2" wide, obtuse or acute, rounded at base, bright green and glabrous above, rusty pubescent on midrib and petiole below. The blush white to pinkish, 1/2" long, fragrant flowers occur in July in 12" by 9", erect, terminal, pyramidal panicles. The calyx of each flower is covered with rusty pubescence. Pod is 2 to 3" long, 1/2" wide, flattened and smooth. This is an exciting tree and I saw it for the first time at Rowallane, Northern Ireland. From a distance, it looked like *C. kentukea*. It is being grown in the Pacific Northwest and now Southeast. Unfortunately, at -24°F the cultivar 'China Rose' (pink-flowered) was killed below the snowline. Probably best in Zones 6 and 7 although there are no baseline trees for evaluation. Recent literature indicated the species may not be at all adaptable to the eastern United States. Profile of the species by Lancaster in *The Garden* 364–366, July 1990. Western and Central China. Introduced 1901. Zone 5 to 7(8)?

Clematis × *jackmanii* T. Moore — Jackman Clematis
(klem′à-tis jak′man-ī or jak′man-ē-ī)

FAMILY: Ranunculaceae

LEAVES: Opposite, pinnately compound, the upper ones often simple, 2 to 4 1/2″ long, leaflets ovate, acute, cordate, entire, usually slightly pubescent beneath.

BUDS: Rather small, ovoid or flattened, sessile, solitary, with 1 to 3 pairs of exposed somewhat hairy scales.

STEM: Slender, light brown, ridged, with the 6 primary ridges prominent; pith—angular or star-shaped, white, continuous with thin firmer diaphragms at the nodes.

SIZE: 5 to 6 to 18′ on the appropriate structure.

HARDINESS: Zone 4 to 8(9).

HABIT: A vine whose stems twine around objects while the leaves clasp or fold over any object.

RATE: Fast, 5 to 10′ in a single season.

TEXTURE: Medium in summer.

LEAF COLOR: Bright green to blue-green in summer, no fall color of any consequence.

FLOWERS: Perfect, violet-purple, 4 to 7″ diameter, 4 to 6 showy sepals, each 2 to 2 1/2″ long, June (May in Athens) to frost; usually borne solitary or in 3-flowered cymes.

FRUIT: Achene, with a 1 to 2″ long, persistent style which is clothed with long, silky hairs.

CULTURE: Attention to detail is important; the adage a warm top and cool bottom apply; transplant as a container-grown plant in spring into light, loamy, moderately moist, well-drained soil (cool root environment); soil should be mulched; avoid extremely hot, sunny area; place the plant so it receives some shade during the day; higher pH soils 6 to 7.5 are often recommended as being optimum but personally I do not think it makes much difference if the pH is 4.5; avoid extremely wet conditions; I have seen clematis growing on mailboxes, posts and other structures where they are often trampled and abused; tougher than given credit!

DISEASES AND INSECTS: Leaf spot and stem rot can be a serious problem, black blister beetle, clematis borer, mites, whiteflies, scales and root-knot nematodes.

LANDSCAPE VALUE: Does not fit the absolute requirements of a woody plant but to omit these beautiful vines would be somewhat of an injustice to the reader; excellent for trellises, fences, rock walls; any structure around which the stems and petioles twine is a good support; very beautiful in flower and many of the large-flowered hybrids are worth experimenting with; the small-flowered species and large-flowered cultivars are all deserving of a place in the garden; every garden can house a clematis. On an English garden tour I visited a nursery, Treasures of Tenbury, a large clematis grower, and the owner, Mr. John Treasure, had a display garden that was open to the public; he demonstrated many different ways that clematis could be used and had them scrambling over shrubs, evergreens, up trees, on walls, ad infinitum. I have copied his approach with some success and allowed a plant to clamber over an *Itea virginica*. The effect is striking and the *Itea* has problems with its identity.

CULTIVARS: I have attempted to bring some order to the treatment of cultivars; they are divided by groups.

Florida Group—Origin married to *C. florida* Thunb.; most of the hybrids have semi-double to double flowers; they flower in late spring on previous year's wood and are not pruned until after flowering is complete.

'Bell of Woking'—Pale mauve, double.

'Duchess of Edinburgh'—Large double, rosette-like, white with green shading, scented.

'Kathleen Dunford'—Semi-double rosy purple flowers.

Jackman Group—Probably the most popular group of hybrids in American gardens; this group includes *C.* × *jackmanii* raised in 1858 at Jackman and Sons of Woking, Surrey, England and varieties raised later using it as one of the parents; this group flowers on new growth in July and August with some varieties flowering until frost. Stems can be cut back hard as buds swell; their stems may also be cut back within 4 to 6″ of origin, thus allowing a larger framework to develop.

'Comtesse de Bouchard'—Medium size flowers of soft satiny pink with a slight overlap of lavender, yellow stamens, vigorous and free-flowering, June–August.

'Crimson Star'—Vigorous, floriferous red form.

'Gipsy Queen'—Rich violet-purple, large, star-shaped flowers.

'Hagley Hybrid'—Shell pink flowers with chocolate brown anthers, free-flowering.

jackmanii 'Alba'—Large 4 to 5″ diameter, single, white flowers with a bluish tinge around the margin of each sepal.

jackmanii 'Rubra'—Flowers are deep red; sometimes double on old wood.

jackmanii 'Superba'—Improved form of *jackmanii* with rich violet-purple, 5″ diameter flowers.

'Madame Baron Veillard'—Lilac-rose, 4 1/2 to 6″ across, vigorous grower.

'Madame Edouard Andre'—Rich crimson with yellow stamens and pointed sepals, very free-flowering.

'Mrs. Cholmondeley'—Sparse-flowering with pale blue, 6″ diameter flowers.

'Perle d'Azur'—Sky blue flowers, vigorous.

'Star of India'—Reddish plum with a red bar.

'Victoria'—4 to 5″ diameter, light blue flowers, vigorous and free-flowering.

Lanuginosa Group—The lovely hybrids included here have *C. lanuginosa* Lindl. as one parent. Many of the cultivars will flower in June if a proportion of the previous year's growth is left. If cut back to within 2 to 4′ of the ground each spring, new shoots will grow quickly and more abundant bloom can be expected later. Some within the group produce double flowers on old and single on new wood.

'Beauty of Worcester'—Deep blue with white stamens, double on old, single on young wood.

'Candida'—Off-white with white centers, large flowers.

'Crimson King'—Double crimson flowers from old wood, single from new, free-flowering, large-flowered, less vigorous in growth than many.

'Elsa Spath'—Profuse, intense blue flowers, darker towards the center.

'Fairy Queen'—Flesh pink, with bright central bars, large flowers.

'Henryi'—Magnificent, large, 4 to 5″ diameter, white flowers with dark stamens, free-flowering, flowers on old wood in June and again in late summer on new.

'King Edward VII'—Large, orchid flowers with deep mauve bar in center.

'King George V'—Flesh pink, each sepal with a dark central bar.

'Lady Northcliffe'—Deep lavender blue with white stamens, 5 to 6″ diameter.

'Lord Neville'—Rich deep blue with wavy-margined sepals, flowers on old wood in June and later on new growth.

'Maureen'—Velvety royal purple.

'Nelly Moser'—Large, pale mauve-pink flowers with a deep pink bar in the center of each sepal, very free-flowering, one of the most popular.

'Prins Hendrik'—Azure blue, pointed sepals.

'Ramona'—Large, lavender-blue flowers with dark anthers, excellent for June flower on old wood.

'Violet Charm'—Rich violet.

'W.E. Gladstone'—Large, silky lavender, purple anthers, vigorous and free-flowering.

'William Kennett'—Lavender-blue with dark stamens, margins of sepals crinkled.

Patens Group—Derived from *C. patens* Morr & Decne. Flowers typically on previous year's wood; some varieties produce sparse smaller flowers in late summer. Prune dead and broken growth in spring. After flowering, a portion of old shoots should be cut back severely to encourage them to break, thus producing flowering wood for the following spring.

'Barbara Dibley'—Large, rich rosy violet flowers with deeper bars.

'Barbara Jackman'—Deep violet, striped deep carmine, May–June, again in September.

'Bees Jubilee'—Mauve pink with carmine bars and pink stamens.

'Daniel Deronda'—Large, violet-blue, paler at center with creamy stamens, often double.

'Gillian Blades'—Pure white.

'Kathleen Wheeler'—Plummy mauve.

'Lasurstern'—Deep lavender-blue, with conspicuous, white stamens and broad, tapering, wavy margined sepals.

'Lincoln Star'—Bright red with pale edges to sepals and maroon stamens.

'Marcel Moser'—Mauve with a deep carmine bar, sepals tapered.

'Marie Boisselot'—Large, pure white with cream stamens and broad, rounded, overlapping sepals, vigorous and free-flowering.

'Miss Bateman'—Medium-sized, white flowers with a cushion of chocolate stamens.

'Mrs. N. Thompson'—Deep violet with a scarlet bar, pointed sepals.

'Percy Picton'—Very large flowers of rosy purple.

'The President'—Large (6″), deep violet flowers with pointed sepals.

'Vyvyan Pennell'—Deep violet-blue suffused purple and carmine in the center, fully double, May through June, single flowers in autumn.

Viticella Group—Derived from *C. viticella* L. This is essentially a summer flowering group and can be pruned back hard in spring. If greater height is desired it is possible to retain a lower woody framework and reduce the previous season's growth to within 6″ of their origins on the more permanent woody framework. In essence, this group may be treated similar to the Jackman Group.

'Ascotiensis'—Bright blue with long pointed sepals, very floriferous.

'Duchess of Sutherland'—Petunia red with a darker bar on each tapered sepal, often double.

'Ernest Markham'—Glowing red-violet flowers with a velvety sheen, sepals rounded, 3 to 4″ diameter flowers.

'Huldine'—Pearly white, the pointed sepals with a mauve bar on the reverse, vigorous and free-flowering, 3 to 4″ diameter.

'Lady Betty Balfour'—Large, rich blue-violet flowers with yellow stamens, vigorous late-flowering form.

'Madame Julia Correvon'—Deep wine red.

'Margot Koster'—Small, rosy pink flowers in abundance.

'Mrs. Spencer Castle'—Large, pale heliotrope, sometimes double, May and June and again in fall.

'Venosa Violacea'—Violet-blue.

'Ville de Lyon'—Bright carmine red, deeper crimson on edges of sepals, golden stamens, 4″ diameter.

PROPAGATION: Seeds have dormant embryos and stratification for 60 to 90 days at 33 to 40°F is recommended. I have a feeling that embryos may not be fully developed or possible inhibitors exist in the fruit coat that slow germination. Seeds of *C. terniflora* (*C. maximowicziana*) were collected in November, sown directly in flats in a warm greenhouse and germinated 3 1/2 months later. The warm temperatures facilitate the development of the embryo to a point where it will germinate. *Clematis orientalis* and *C. tangutica* received in the Wisley Seed Exchange germinated 3 weeks after planting. Over the years, I have germinated many species and have not observed an absolute cold requirement for any. Cuttings, summer, single internode with cuts between the nodes have given good results with large-flowered types; see Evison, "Propagation of *Clematis*," *Proc. Intl. Plant Prop. Soc.* 27:436–440 (1977), for an excellent discussion of the subject.

ADDITIONAL NOTES: Five excellent reference books on *Clematis* are suggested:

Burras, J.K. (editor). 1995. *Manual of Climbers and Wall Plants*. MacMillan Press Ltd., London.

Evison, Raymond J. 1991. *Making the Most of Clematis*, 2nd Edition. Floraprint Ltd., Nottingham, England.

Grey-Wilson, Christopher and Victoria Matthews. 1997. *Gardening with Climbers*. Timber Press, Portland, Oregon.

Lloyd, Christopher. 1977. *Clematis*. William Collins Sons and Co. Ltd, London. Probably the best reference with color plates showing hybrid and species characteristics. Also excellent descriptions. Possibly being revised as I write this.

Markham, Ernest. 1935. *Clematis*. Charles Scribner, NY. Excellent treatment of species.

Taylor, Jane. 1987. *Climbing Plants*. Kew Gardening Guide.

I wrestle with the significant urge to allow *Clematis* discussions more knowledgeable than myself. Unfortunately, I cannot let go and perhaps by the 6th edition where the *Manual* is simply overburdened with material will I relent. *Clematis* taxa are magnificent flowering vines and herbaceous perennials with unbelievable flower shapes, colors and fragrances. About 200 species are described with innumerable hybrids and cultivars. Utilize the references provided above or seek out knowledgeable growers. The species types that follow are also superb garden plants, simply not as large in flower, but elegant in their unique way.

OTHER *CLEMATIS* SPECIES AND CULTIVARS

Clematis armandii Franch. — Armand Clematis

LEAVES: Opposite, compound pinnate, 3 leaflets, evergreen, each leaflet 3 to 6″ long, 1 to 1 1/2″ wide, lustrous dark green, prominently 3-veined, oblong-lanceolate to ovate, acute, rounded or slightly heart-shaped at base, glabrous.

Clematis armandii, (klem′à-tis är-man′dē-ī), Armand Clematis, would be a beautiful plant if it did not flower. A fast-growing vine that quickly covers a fence, trellis or similar structure. Have seen plants draped over trees that were 20′ high and 30′ wide. The large, glossy green, leathery leaves provide a handsome foil for the white, fragrant flowers that appear in March–May. Have monitored its flowering sequence in the Athens, GA area. It often starts in mid-March and is finished by mid-April. Individual flowers are 2 to 2 1/2″ in diameter with 4 to 7 sepals and occur in panicles on the previous season's growth. Have seen it used tastefully at Callaway Gardens, Pine Mountain, GA. 'Apple Blossom' has broad sepals of white shaded pink, especially on the reverse side; the unfolding leaves are a bronzy-green. 'Farquhariana' has pink flowers. 'Snowdrift' has pure white flowers. Central and western China. Introduced 1900 by E.H. Wilson. Can be grown from Zone 7 south. In 1981, -5°F killed the plant to the ground in exposed locations.

Clematis montana Buch.-Ham ex DC., (klem'à-tis mon-tā'nà), Anemone Clematis, is a vigorous, almost rampant, white- to pink-flowering species. The 2 to 2 1/2″ diameter, 4- rarely 5-sepaled flowers occur singly on a glabrous, 2 to 5″ long pedicel in May–June. Makes a great plant for covering walls, rock piles, and arbors. Will grow 20 to 30′. 'Alexander' has creamy white, sweetly scented flowers; 'Elizabeth' has large, slightly fragrant soft pink flowers in May and June; 'Grandiflora' is a strong-growing Chinese form that produces an abundance of 2 1/2 to 3″ diameter, white flowers; var. *rubens* is a rosy red-flowered, vigorous, hardy form that was introduced by Wilson in 1900, the flowers appear later than those of the species, easy to root from cuttings; 'Superba' offers deep pink flowers; 'Tetrarose' is a vigorous tetraploid with purplish pink, 3″ diameter flowers, the foliage has a bronzish cast; var. *wilsonii* has larger (3″), white flowers and flowers in July and August. Himalayas, central and western China. Introduced 1831. Zone 5 to 7.

Clematis orientalis L., (klem'à-tis ôr-i-en-tā'lis), Oriental Clematis, is a more restrained, perhaps 10 to 20′ high, clematis that offers delightful, slightly fragrant, 1 1/2 to 2″ diameter, yellow flowers in August and September. The flowers occur singly on 2 to 4″ long pedicels and produce a 3″ diameter tuft of glistening, feathery achenes. Fruits are in various stages of development while flowers continue to open. Similar to *C. tangutica* but more delicate. *Clematis tangutica* is larger flowered and has pubescent stems and flower stalks. See *The Plantsman* 7(4):192–204 (1986) for an excellent discussion of these and related species. Iran to Himalayas. Introduced 1731. Zone (5)6 to 9.

Clematis tangutica (Maxim.) Korsh., (klem'à-tis tan-gū'ti-kà), Golden Clematis, has bright yellow, 3 to 4″ diameter, campanulate to lantern-shaped flowers, June–July, borne solitary. The seed heads are silky. Often handsomest of yellow-flowered *Clematis*. 'Bill MacKenzie' is vigorous and large-flowered with rich yellow, thick-textured sepals. Mongolia to northwestern China. Introduced 1890. Zone 5 to 7.

Clematis terniflora DC. (formerly *C. maximowicziana* Franch. & Savat. and *C. paniculata* Gmel.) — Sweetautumn Clematis

LEAVES: Opposite, pinnately compound, 3 to 5 leaflets, 1 to 4″ long, acute, subcordate or rounded at base, entire or sometimes lobed, glabrous, dark blue-green, often suffused with a gray mottle.

BUDS: Small, with 1 to 3 pairs of rather hairy scales.

STEM: Straw colored, 12- to 18-ridged; ridges are actually vascular bundles; pith—white.

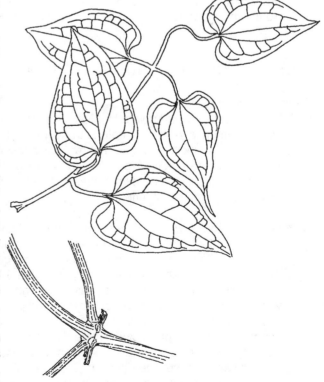

Clematis terniflora, (klem'à-tis tĕr-ni-flō'rà), Sweet-autumn Clematis, is a rampant, rampaging vine which engulfs every structure in sight. Will grow 10 to 20′ high. The flowers are white, 1 1/4″ across, fragrant, 4 sepals, August into September and October, borne in many flowered axillary and terminal panicles; quite literally make the whole plant look like a new fallen snow. Probably the easiest *Clematis* to grow as it seems to thrive with neglect. Flowers in late August–early September in our Georgia garden. Extremely vigorous to the point of viciousness. Has become a significant weed in our garden and after eradicating the original plant years ago, am still encountering stray seedlings. Also, root system is fleshy and deep. Once this plant gains a foot-hold, removal is difficult. Soft fragrance is delightful and I have allowed the plant to scramble over crape myrtles, sedums and baptisias. Japan. Introduced 1864. Zone 5 to 8(9).

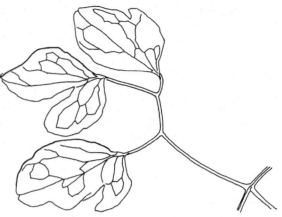

Clematis texensis Buckl., (klem′à-tis   teks-en′sis), Scarlet Clematis, has carmine or bright scarlet flowers, urn-shaped, narrowed at the mouth, about 1″ long and 3/4″ wide, June–July through until frost, solitary and nodding. 'Duchess of Albany' is a pink-flowered form with more spreading sepals than the species. 'Countess of Onslow', 'Etiole Rose', and 'Gravetye Beauty' belong here. 'Major' has 1 1/4″ long, scarlet outside, pale yellow to white interior, thick-textured sepals. The species does not propagate readily from cuttings. Scandent subshrub, 6 to 10′. Texas. Introduced 1878. Zone 4 to 7(8).

Clematis virginiana L., (klem′à-tis vĕr-jin-e-ā′nà), Virginsbower, is a handsome vine growing 12 to 20′ with bright green summer foliage. The flowers are whitish with 4, rarely 5, sepals (supposedly this is a dioecious species with staminate flowers showy white, pistillate more dull); borne in 3 to 6″ long axillary leafy panicles in July through September. Good vine for native situations; other types are more effective in flower. Native from Nova Scotia to Manitoba, south to Georgia and Kansas. Introduced 1720. Zone 4 to 8.

Clematis vitalba L., (klem′à-tis vī-tal′bà), Traveler's Joy or Old Man's Beard, has greenish white, 1″ diameter, almond scented flowers in July through September which are borne in axillary and terminal 3 to 5″ long panicles. Common name comes from the fact the flowers are slightly fragrant and odor proves refreshing to the traveler on a hot summer's day. Vigorous and aggressive, 20 to 40′(100′); vicious weed in New Zealand where it is killing the native vegetation. Europe, northern Africa. Introduced 1820. Zone 4 to 6(7).

Clematis viticella L., (klem′à-tis vī-ti-sel′là), Italian Clematis, has purple, rosy purple or violet, 1 to 2″ diameter, 4-sepaled flowers which are born in June through August singly or in 2's or 3's. The flowers are extremely dainty and hang bell-like from slender stalks. Grows to 10′. Cultivars include: 'Abundance' with delicately veined flowers of soft purple; 'Alba Luxurians' with white flowers, tinted mauve, dark purple anthers; 'Kermesina' with deep purple-wine red flowers; 'Nana' a dwarf form about 3′ high; 'Plena' with double, purple flowers, an old clone; 'Royal Velours' with velvety purple flowers; 'Rubra' an old red-flowered form. Southern Europe to western Asia. Introduced 1578. Zone 5 to 7.

Clerodendrum trichotomum Thunb. — Harlequin Glorybower

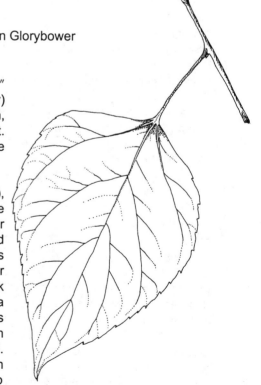

FAMILY: Verbenaceae
LEAVES: Opposite, simple, ovate to elliptic, 4 to 9″ long, 2 to 5″ wide, acuminate, broad cuneate to truncate, entire (usually) or sparsely toothed, dark green above, pubescent beneath, malodorous when bruised; petiole—1 to 4″ long, pubescent.
STEM: Coarse, green, finally brown, pubescent, soft, with pith like a *Sambucus*, nodes flattened.

Clerodendrum trichotomum, (klē-rō-den′drum   trī-kō-tō′mum), Harlequin Glorybower, missed the first three editions of the *Manual* but finally was brought on board in the fourth. Over the years, my feelings toward this plant have ebbed and flowed like the tide. In flower and fruit it is delightful but at its worst has the appearance of an overturned Dempster Dumpster. The habit, even in Zone 7, is that of a dieback shrub probably seldom growing more than 10′. It can form a small 15′(20′) tree but needs some assistance since suckers will develop. I have seen it as far north as the Brooklyn Botanic Garden but there it was an herbaceous perennial. The dark green leaves die off green. Flowers occur late, often July (mid to late July into August, Boston) and continue into fall while the fruits are developing. It is not uncommon to find flowers and developed fruits at the same time. Individual flowers are fragrant, white, 1 to 1 1/2″ wide, tubular at the base and spreading into 5 narrow oblong lobes at the mouth. Flowers occur in long stalked cymes from the upper leaves, the inflorescence averaging 6 to 9″ across. The reddish, leathery, 1/2″ long, 5 angled and 5-lobed calyx subtends a pea-sized (1/4″ diameter), bright blue drupe that is actually spectacular on close inspection. Prefers moist, well-drained soil in full sun but I have seen plants in partial shade, albeit open in habit, with decent flower and fruit. Definitely requires supplemental moisture in drought periods. I grew the plant for 4 years and never saw a flower or fruit and chucked it. Should be used in a shrub border or other area where it can blend with the woodwork until it does something. My treatment is not particularly kind and although I read tributes about the greatness of this plant I challenge the reader to send me a photograph of a choice specimen in the 15 to 20′ range. Over the past 4 to 5 years, a specimen at the University's Botanical Garden reached 12′ high and wide, produced copious flowers and fruits, then in the winter of 1994, after 4°F, lost about 60% of its superstructure. One thing is absolute, when the gardening public sees the plant with flowers and fruits present at the same time, there is an instant love affair and eagerness to buy. As the above discussion indicates, forewarned is forearmed. During my 1991 sabbatical at the Arnold, variety *fargesii* (Dode) Rehd. crossed my path. This is hardier, shrubbier (possibly from dieback), glabrous and free-fruiting. Has flowered heavily in our Georgia trials. 'Variegata' has yellowish-margined leaves, leaves also irregularly streaked, not totally stable. Species and the variety are easily rooted from June–July softwood cuttings, 1000 ppm KIBA, 3 perlite:1 peat, mist. Eastern China, Japan. Cultivated 1880. Zone (6)7 to 9.

Clethra alnifolia L. — Summersweet Clethra, Sweet Pepperbush
(klē′thrȧ al-ni-fō′li-ȧ)

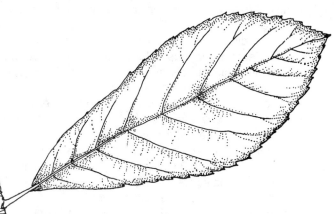

FAMILY: Clethraceae
LEAVES: Alternate, simple, obovate-oblong, 1 1/2 to 4″ long, 3/4 to 2″ wide, acute to short acuminate, cuneate, sharply serrate, usually entire toward base, glabrous or nearly so on both sides, often woolly tomentose below, particularly on the southern forms, with 6 to 10 pairs of veins, lustrous medium to dark green above; petiole—1/8 to 3/4″ long, pubescent.
BUDS: Small, loosely scaled, solitary, sessile, ovoid, pubescent, brown.
STEM: Brown, pubescent, rounded or obscurely 3-sided; pith—light brown, continuous.

SIZE: 4 to 8′(12′) high and 4 to 6′(10′) wide, apt to be variable because of soil effects, larger in moist soil; often wider than high at maturity because of suckering colonizing nature; in Rhode Island I measured an 18′ high plant.
HARDINESS: Zone 4 to 9.
HABIT: Oval, round-topped, erect, dense leafy shrub, often suckering to form broad colonies.
RATE: Slow to medium.
TEXTURE: Medium in all seasons.
LEAF COLOR: Late to leaf out in spring; lustrous medium to deep green in summer; pale yellow to rich golden brown in fall; fall color develops about mid-October, early to mid-November (Athens), and can persist for 3 to 4 weeks.
FLOWERS: Perfect, white, 5-petaled, delightfully fragrant, 1/3″ across, July into August, effective 4 to 6 weeks, borne on current season's growth in 2 to 6″ long, 3/4″ wide, upright racemes or panicles; racemes often develop under the terminal raceme, resulting in a racemose panicle (thyrse); for effectiveness of flower

the multi-flowered forms are preferred; inflorescences may reach 8 to 12″ long on some forms; lovely to look at but even lovelier to smell; the bees constantly hover about; flower buds are prominent on 'Fern Valley Pink' by late May (Athens) and flowers open in June; a selection by Tom Clark, Fern Valley Farms, flowers in October ('Fern Valley Late Sweet'); in native populations I observed on Cape Cod, individual plants will have set fruits while others are coming into flower; the opportunity for selection is phenomenal and since the 1990 edition the number of cultivars has exploded.

FRUIT: Dry, 3-valved, dehiscent, subglobose, pubescent, 1/8″ diameter capsule, persisting through winter and offering a good identification characteristic; collect entire infructescence in late fall, dry inside and shake out small dust-like seeds; in January 1995 I collected the entire infructescence of 'Hummingbird', crushed them, sowed entire contents on a seed mix under mist and within 4 weeks had a grass-like stand of seedlings.

CULTURE: Transplant balled-and-burlapped or as a container-grown plant into moist, acid soil which has been supplemented with organic matter; grows naturally in wet places; partial shade or full sun; salty conditions of seashore; I have found this plant easy to grow; this is one of my favorite shrubs and the more I work with it the greater my appreciation for its user-friendly nature; plants sited under *Quercus falcata*, Southern Red Oak, have flowered reasonably well (on occasion supplemental water is necessary); small one-gallon plants were 3 to 4′ high in a single growing season; performs admirably in English gardens and two tremendous plantings at Sissinghurst and Savill Gardens are magnificent.

DISEASES AND INSECTS: Tremendously pest-free although mite damage occurs in dry seasons, cupping and crinkling of the terminal leaves on young plants in the summer indicates the presence of Eriophyid mites.

LANDSCAPE VALUE: Excellent for summer flower and fragrance, shrub border, good plant for shade and wet areas; I would like to see this plant used more in contemporary landscapes; the foliage is very handsome and the overall winter habit is clean; does not have the dirty habits of *Weigela* and *Lonicera*; the fragrance is tremendous; fall color is a worthwhile attribute; certainly one of the best native shrubs for summer color and fragrance; appears to make great bee pasture; on a fine September day, Bonnie and I were shopping at L.L. Bean, Freeport, ME and planted by their water feature at the entrance was a grouping of *Clethra alnifolia*; I got so excited I almost fell in taking photographs; L.L. Bean is a terrific company plus they know their plants.

CULTIVARS: Tremendous number of garden worthy selections have entered the marketplace; in the 1990 edition, three cultivars were listed, the number exceeds 15 in this edition; if a retailer says he/she cannot find *Clethra* tell them Dirr said it is one of the easiest plants to grow at the commercial and garden levels and excuses will not be tolerated. For rather detailed discussions of *Clethra* species please see Dirr, *Nursery Manager* 10(11):14,16,18,20–21 (1994), *Arnoldia* 51(3):18–21 (1991), and Bir, *American Nurseryman* 175(3):51–59 (1992).

White Flowered Selections

'Anne Bidwell'—Grown by Mrs. John Bidwell, Cotuit, MA from seed purchased from F. W. Schumacher, Sandwich, MA. The inflorescences are multi-branched, tightly clustered and irregular in shape. They average 4 to 6″ high and 3 to 5″ wide. The flowers are not as elegant as those of the species. Additionally, this was the latest flowering clone in the Arnold Arboretum's collection. The flowers opened in mid to late August. Habit is more compact (4 to 6′ high) than the species and the leaves lustrous dark green.

Arnold Arboretum Selection (no cultivar name provided)—Propagated by the author during the 1991 sabbatical. This particular colony (accession #23139-A) is about 6 to 8′ high, 36′ wide and 40′ long, densely foliated with numerous terminal and axillary inflorescences. It grew in the shade of the *Carya* collection and was full and dense with abundant flowers. Not preferable to 'Hummingbird' and 'Compacta' but certainly an improvement on the typical species. In Georgia trials this is one of the best forms of the typical species types.

'Chattanooga'—I met this cultivar at the Southern Plants Conference in September of 1993. After a visit to the new Tennessee Aquarium, I toured the contiguous landscape which utilizes primarily native species. The *Clethra* in question had 8″ long fruit clusters. Permission was granted by the horticulturist to take cuttings and second generation cuttings are developing the elongated inflorescences. They are sturdy and have only a slight crook to the axis. The habit is upright-oval, densely dark green foliaged with landscape maturity around 6′, possibly to 8′. Handsome selection and is now available in commerce.

'Compacta' ('Nana')—Arrived from Vincent Simeone, a former student, who is currently assistant director at Planting Fields Arboretum. Considerable correspondence caught up with the introducer, Mr. Tom Dilatush. The original seedling germinated in Tom's brother's vegetable garden carried there in leaf-mold collected from the New Jersey pine barrens and applied as a mulch and later worked into the soil. The plant was given to Mike Johnson, Summer Hill Nursery, Madison, CT. Mr. Johnson has propagated and grown the plant and it has found a measure of commercial success in the Northeast. 'Compacta' grows 3 to 4′ high and produces lustrous dark green foliage and terminal and axillary inflorescences (racemose-panicle). Although not as black-green as 'Hummingbird', this is a superb choice particularly for the middle Atlantic and New England States and has performed well in Zone 7b.

'Creel's Calico'—Introduced by Michael Creel of South Carolina. The leaves are flecked, speckled, spotted and banded with cream to white variegation. At maturity, the leaves are lustrous dark green with pure white variegation. My initial reaction to the selection was not exactly enthusiastic. Small rooted cuttings transplanted to one-gallon containers grew 2′ in a single season and lost most of the variegation. However, the new leaves of the next growing season were uniformly variegated. When taking cutting wood, only select the most variegated shoots. Flowers are multi-branched and up to 6″ long. I suspect this cultivar will mature between 3 and 4′. The original plant was a stoloniferous colony about 3′ high.

'Fern Valley Late Sweet'—Mr. Tom Clark, Fern Valley Farms, Yadkinville, NC discovered this in a population of seedlings at his nursery. Tom's description had this clethraphile in absolute ecstasy. The framework (5 to 6′) is almost columnar and covered with small dark green leaves. Multiple racemes emerge from the shoots and are held upright. The inflorescences are 4 to 6″ long (up to 10 to 12″), exceedingly fragrant and do not show color until mid-September with full flower in October (near Winston-Salem, NC). The racemes are more conical, i.e., fattest at base tapering to the apex. The cultivar flowered in my possession during September–October, 1995. Minimal fruits are set possibly because of late flower date and/or lack of suitable pollinators. Is not as full and dense as other selections.

'Hummingbird'—Certainly one of the finest compact, deciduous shrubs available to gardeners. Although known for years, only recently has it been recognized for its merits. In 1994, it received the Pennsylvania Horticultural Society Gold Medal Award and was selected by the Ohio Nurseryman's Association as one of the recommended plants for 1994. In 1996, it received the prestigious Georgia Gold Medal Award. The irony is that the plant was selected in the South and introduced by Mr. Fred Galle, formerly of Callaway Gardens, Pine Mountain, GA. He planted it along Hummingbird Lake at Callaway Gardens and the location reflects its name. Numerous *stories* have described the origin of this clone; the above is fact. 'Hummingbird' grows 30 to 40″ high, spreads vigorously by rhizomes and forms large colonies. The lustrous black-green leaves are 1 to 2 1/2″ long and are narrower than those of the species. Fall color in our garden is golden yellow. The inflorescences range from 4 to 6″ long and open earlier than the species. The inflorescences (early June) on plants in the Dirr garden were fully 6 to 7″ long and were borne at the end of the shoots as well as from leaf axils below. The effect was spectacular and the flowers literally smothered the foliage. Surprisingly, reports from western Massachusetts and Orono, ME indicate cold hardiness in the range of -30°F. This is a superb plant that, hopefully, will be forever linked to a great horticulturist, Mr. Fred Galle. In a perusal of 1994–95 nursery catalogs, 12 vendors were discovered for this cultivar. 'Hummingbird' was registered in 1991. See *HortScience* 26:475 (1991).

'Nova Scotia'—Collected by my friend, Mr. Ray Fielding, Pleasantville, Nova Scotia from the wild. Represents the northernmost portion of the range.

'Paniculata'—An enigma and what is offered as such in the trade is anybody's guess. The typical literature describes this taxon with larger and multi-branched (paniculate) inflorescences. The clone I witnessed in flower produced only racemose inflorescences. The foliage is a lustrous dark green and has been consistent on the various plants I have seen labeled as 'Paniculata'. Landscape height ranges to 8′. The clone was introduced in England around 1770 and I have no doubt that what masquerades today as 'Paniculata' is not a descendent from the original. Tom Dilatush reported 10% paniculate, 90% racemose types from a native population in Ocean County, NJ.

'September Beauty'—Late-flowering form, 10 to 14 days after the species, lustrous dark green foliage, more compact grower, selected from New Jersey pine barrens, introduced by Princeton Nursery.

var. *tomentosa*—Has been botanically treated as a separate species, *Clethra tomentosa* Lam., but is now lumped into *Clethra alnifolia*. Pubescence alone is a fluid characteristic that creates significant consternation and frustration when used to delineate species. Herbarium specimens of the *tomentosa* type show gradations in degree of hairiness. I have collected several *tomentosa* clones, one with silver-gray felt on the underside; another with more pubescence than the species but not enough to justify a distinct species. There are garden differences worth noting. The individual flowers are larger, up to 1/2″ across. The inflorescences open (in Athens) later than the northern clones like 'Anne Bidwell', 'Paniculata', and 'Rosea'. The leaves emerge fully 2 to 3 weeks ahead of the northern types and are the last to drop their leaves in fall. I suspect the true *tomentosa* types are also less cold hardy. The leaves are more mite resistant, possibly because of the dense pubescence on the leaf underside. Woodlanders, Aiken, SC, has a more compact clone with multi-branched inflorescences, dark green upper surface leaves and silver-grey beneath. This particular form is worthy of commercial production. Seeds of 'Fern Valley Pink' and var. *tomentosa* produced pubescent seedlings all with prominent woolly tomentum on the underside of mature leaves. Mr. Robert McCartney in 1997 discovered a 14″ long inflorescence type in north Florida which will be introduced through Woodlander's, Aiken, SC.

Pink Flowered Selections: The two standard pink-flowered types 'Pink Spires' and 'Rosea' (introduced circa 1906) are either confused, the same, or distinctly unique clones. Ask any knowledgeable plantsperson about distinctions and the answers will be different. In 1991, I collected 'Pink Spires' and 'Rosea' from the Arnold's collections and could see no color differences. 'Rosea' in the heat of Athens may fade to pinkish white. Inflorescences of both forms average 3.5 to 4″ long and open about one week later than the species. True 'Pink Spires', selected by a Dutch nurseryman, is described as pinker than 'Rosea'. Both clones are upright, 6 to 10′ high and rather open. The summer foliage is lustrous dark green. Currently, I have two sources of 'Rosea', two of 'Pink Spires' plus the next three pink clones growing in Athens. Perhaps, the truth will eventually be known. In the summer of 1995, I assessed the above clones in side-by-side comparisons and witnessed nothing that could be construed as significant horticultural differences. Also, 'Hokie Pink' (which see) is not greatly different from 'Rosea' and 'Pink Spires'.

'Fern Valley Pink'—Has the potential to satisfy several generations of gardeners who desire light pink flowers and superb fragrance. My first plant came in winter, was potted and forced in the greenhouse. The deep pink buds opened to pinkish white, exceedingly fragrant flowers, borne in 8 to 10″(12″) long inflorescences. The inflorescence is so long it hangs down then turns up as it continues to elongate (indeterminate). The leaves are glossy but lighter green than the other pink-flowered forms. Also, the leaves are larger and surfaces slightly cupped and undulating rather than flat. Fall color is a soft yellow and develops in mid to late November in the Athens area. I suspect ultimate size about 4 to 6′ and to date 4′ high plants are fully clothed to the ground with foliage. This selection was discovered in eastern North Carolina and introduced by Mr. Tom Clark. This selection is the first to flower in our garden, usually in early to mid-June.

'Hokie Pink'—According to Mr. Jim Monroe, the introducer, Greenbriar Farms, WV, offers good pink flowers on a more compact, dense foliaged framework than 'Rosea'. Jim discovered the clone at the Virginia Tech Arboretum, Blacksburg, VA and utilized the team's nickname, Hokies, to provide the unusual name. In leaf, 'Hokie Pink' and 'Ruby Spice' appear similar although close inspection reveals more lustrous dark green leaves on 'Ruby Spice'. Flowers on plants in the Dirr garden were disappointing and were not distinguishable from 'Rosea'. In fact, 'Hokie Pink' has developed into a tall, rather open shrub.

'Pink Spires'—Buds pink to rose, open to soft pink and do not fade to white, upright-growing, easily to 8′ or more, lustrous dark green foliage.

'Rosea'—Flower buds pink; flowers at first pinkish fading to pinkish white, glossy dark green leaves, beautiful form; I have grown this for 10 years in Georgia, the flower color does not fade any worse in the South than the North; good plant for partial shade; introduced 1906.

'Ruby Spice'—In the early stages often listed as 'Connecticut Pink' and 'Connecticut Rose'. Discovered by Andy Brand at Broken Arrow Nursery in 1992 as a branch sport in a group of 'Pink Spires'. Dr. Richard Jaynes, Broken Arrow Nursery, 13 Broken Arrow Road, Hamden, CT, 06518, described the sport as deeper pink than typical for 'Pink Spires'. Dick supplied me with several small plants, one of which perished; the other now the proud parent of hundreds of rooted cuttings. The foliage color is lustrous dark green. Hopefully, 'Ruby Spice' will not grow as large as 'Pink Spires', although this appears to be the case based on 4 years growth in the Dirr garden. In early August, 1994, Dick sent me an inflorescence and slide of 'Ruby Spice' and 'Pink Spires'. 'Ruby Spice' is rich rose throughout the petals and holds the color to petal senescence. This color breakthrough is exciting and could lead to continued color enhancement through breeding or open-pollinated seedling selection. In this author's opinion, this will prove to be an outstanding garden plant. The inflorescence averages 3.5 to 4″ long and, in general, is shorter than 'Rosea'.

Head-Lee Nursery, Seneca, SC, told me at the 1994 Southern Nurseryman's Association trade show in Atlanta that they have a yellow-streaked, stable variegated form and a slightly deeper form of 'Rosea'. I suspect that many individuals and nurserymen are assessing and capitalizing on the variation within the species. Also, Mr. Simeone sent photographs of a deep pink-flowered form that holds its color as the flowers age. Plants of this clone are being evaluated in my Georgia trials and flowered deeper pink than 'Rosea' but not as deep as 'Ruby Spice'.

Seedling populations of 'Hummingbird' have yielded more compact (less sprawly), large-flowered clones, two of which have been selected and may possibly be introduced. Also, seedlings of 'Ruby Spice' are in their second year and will flower in 1998. The rich bronzy red new growth portends the potential for deeper red-flowered forms.

Dr. John Ruter, a colleague at the University's Tifton Station, discovered a variegated form, the leaves bordered with white; to date this form has remained stable. John also discovered a larger flowered form of variety *tomentosa* from Turner County, GA.

PROPAGATION: Cuttings taken in summer root readily in sand and peat without treatment but treatments may hasten rooting; have rooted the species and cultivars by taking softwood cuttings, 1000 ppm KIBA, sand or peat:perlite, under mist; the cuttings will root in 4 weeks at 90 to 100%; seed can be sown when ripe and requires no stratification. Easy to grow and fills a one-gallon container in a single growing season. Cuttings often continue to grow under mist. Even butter soft cuttings root readily. My experiences indicate that the firmer the wood the slower and more difficult to root.

ADDITIONAL NOTES: The late flowering is an asset to the summer garden. The preferred species is *C. alnifolia* because of its availability and adaptability. All seem to prefer moist, acid, organic soils. *Clethra pringlei* S. Wats. an evergreen species from Mexico, has frozen out in Athens and Tifton, GA. It was touted as a great addition to the *Clethra* family.

NATIVE HABITAT: Maine to Florida to coastal Texas. Introduced 1731.

RELATED SPECIES:

Clethra acuminata Michx. — Cinnamon Clethra

LEAVES: Alternate, simple, ovate-elliptic or elliptic to elliptic-oblong, 3 to 8″ long, acuminate, broad cuneate or rounded, serrulate, dark green above, pubescent below; petiole—1/4 to 1 1/4″ long.

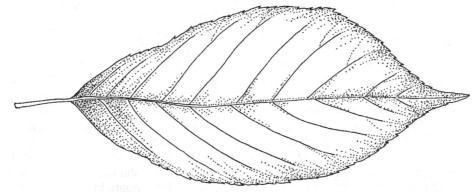

Clethra acuminata, (klē′thrȧ a-kū-mi-nā′tȧ), Cinnamon Clethra, Mountain Pepperbush, is a medium-sized, often suckering shrub or a small tree of rather gaunt proportions. Its landscape size would approximate 8 to 12′ but in the wild it can reach 15 to 20′. National champions are 33′ by 12′ and 29′ by 10′ in Great Smoky Mountains National Park, NC. The dark green, 3 to 6″(8″) leaves are toothed toward the apex. Fall color is a beautiful yellow. The white, slightly fragrant flowers are borne in 3 to 8″ long, solitary, cylindrical terminal racemes in July. Like *Clethra alnifolia* the terminal raceme may be subtended by axillary racemes producing a racemose panicle (thryse), although I have yet to see this on plants in the wild. Flowers open after *C. barbinervis*. Also they attract butterflies. The bark can be a beautiful polished cinnamon brown color but I have seen every imaginable combination of brown, with trunks often showing an exfoliating character. In the wild, it grows on rather dry, rocky, gravelly mountain sides. Seeds germinate without pretreatment and softwood cuttings root readily. Bir mentioned that 2500 ppm IBA in alcohol produced excellent rooting of late softwood-early green wood cuttings. Common on Brasstown and Rabun Balds in North Georgia where it grows on rocky soils. The plants have cinnamon brown, exfoliating, scaly bark. Selections could be made for superior characteristics. Have seen the species all over the southern Appalachians particularly in North Georgia, Tennessee, and North Carolina. Have included a plant in the garden and for general use it is not preferable to *C. alnifolia* (at least in Zone 7) principally because of drought susceptibility and lack of floral quality and fragrance. In our garden *C. acuminata* was planted next to *C. alnifolia* 'Hummingbird'; the former has died while the later is unfazed. Dick Bir's superb article provides the virtues and vices of this wonderful native species [see *American Nurseryman* 175(8):51–59 (1992)]. Head-Lee Nursery, Seneca, SC introduced 'Old Spice', a more fragrant form. Found in the mountains from Virginia to West Virginia to Georgia and Alabama. Introduced 1806. Zone 5 to 8, best in 6 and 7.

Clethra barbinervis Sieb. & Zucc. — Japanese Clethra
LEAVES: Alternate, simple, oval or obovate, 2 to 5″(6″) long, 1 to 2 1/4″ wide,
acuminate, cuneate, sharply serrate, lustrous dark green and glabrous above,
at maturity pubescent on veins below; petiole—1/4 to 3/4″ long.

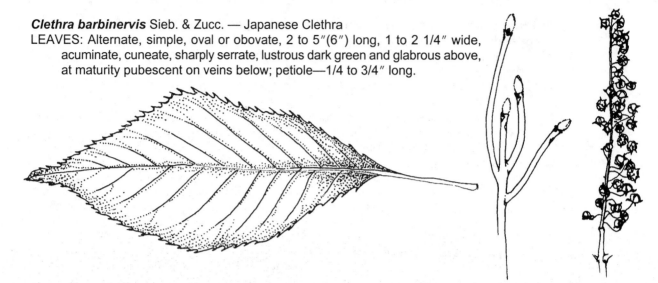

Clethra barbinervis, (klē′thrȧ bär-bi-nēr′vis), Japanese Clethra, is a beautiful large shrub or small tree (10 to
20′ high) that is seldom seen in cultivation in the United States. A notable specimen at the Arnold
Arboretum is about 18′ high. The leaves are dark green and tend to be clustered at the end of the branch,
presenting a whorled appearance. Fall color may develop bronze-red to maroon but is usually not
spectacular. The slightly fragrant, white, 1/3″ diameter flowers are borne in 4 to 6″ long, terminal,
racemose panicles from July to August. Has flowered the first and second weeks of July in Athens.
Usually the flowers are lightly fragrant at best, however, one form from Earthshade Nursery, Warne, NC
produces 6 to 8″ long, 2″ wide at base, tapering to apex, inflorescences with significant fragrance. The
bark is a beautiful, smooth, polished, gray, rich brown to cinnamon brown and may display an exfoliating
character. In many respects the best forms remind of *Stewartia pseudocamellia*. The bark is the most
beautiful aspect of this plant. Seeds germinate without pretreatment and softwood cuttings can be rooted.
Like *C. alnifolia* the softer the cutting the faster and greater the rooting. Use 1000 to 3000 ppm KIBA quick
dip. I had rooted a cutting at Illinois and included the plant in my garden. It survived the disastrous
1976–77 (-20°F) winter with slight stem dieback and grew back to produce a beautiful plant. Tends to be
fast-growing in youth if given ample moisture and fertility. This applies to all the *Clethra* treated here. I
know of one nurseryman who considers the bark of this species more beautiful than that of *Stewartia
pseudocamellia* or *S. koreana*. There is great variation among individuals and the Barnes Arboretum,
Pennsylvania, has three of the best plants on the East Coast. Not particularly content with the heat and
drought of Zone 7 and 8, but seemingly more so than *C. acuminata*. Site in moist, organic-laden, well-
drained soils in partial shade. A hybrid between *Clethra barbinervis* and *C. fargesii* has larger dark green
leaves, bronze-maroon fall color, and compact habit, 5 to 6′ high. Japan. Introduced 1870. Zone 5 to 7.

Clethra tomentosa Lam., (klē′thrȧ tō-men-tō′sȧ), Woolly Summersweet,
is similar to *C. alnifolia* but differs in the downy stems, 1 1/2 to 4″
long, 1/2 to 2″ wide, obovate, serrated on terminal half leaves with
their thick, pale tomentum, 7 to 10 vein pairs, and larger (1/2″
diameter), white, fragrant flowers borne in 4 to 6″ long woolly
racemes. Usually grows 6 to 8′. Sometimes regarded as a variety of
C. alnifolia. See the discussion under cultivars of *C. alnifolia*. I used
to question the validity of this taxon in the species context but I *see*
many exceptions to the general *C. alnifolia* rule that renders it
worthy of botanical classification. North Carolina to Florida and
Alabama. Introduced 1731. Zone 7 to 9.

The reader probably drifted into verbal numbness after wading
through *C. alnifolia*, *C. acuminata*, and *C. barbinervis*. However, there are
several additional species worth mentioning that have garden merit. Most
are tender but might prove valuable for breeding.

Clethra arborea Ait., (klē′thrȧ är-bō′rē-ȧ), Lily-of-the-Valley Tree, is occasionally grown on the West Coast.
Large (to 6″ long), evergreen, deep green leaves and large clusters of 1/3″ diameter, pure white, cup-
shaped, fragrant flowers appear in summer. Madeira Islands. Introduced 1784. Zone 9 to 10.

Clethra delavayi Franch., (klē′thra͡ del-a͡′vāy-ī), is a medium-sized small tree or large shrub with up to 6″ long leaves and 10″ long solitary racemes of white to cream. Emerging buds are reddish. Western China. Introduced 1913. Listed as Zone 5 but doubtful, probably 7.

Clethra fargesii Franch., (klē′thra͡ far-jēs′ē-ī), is a 6 to 10′ high shrub with dark green, nearly glabrous leaves and fragrant, white flowers borne in 5 to 7″ long, racemose panicles. Requires partial shade. Central China. Introduced 1913. Zone 5 to 7(8).

Clethra monostachya Rehd. & Wils., (klē′thra͡ mōn-ō-sta′kē-a͡), is a large, erect, dense shrub to 15′ with 4 to 6″ long, dark green leaves and fragrant, pure white flowers borne in 6 to 8″ long, terminal racemes. A plant at the Arnold Arboretum produced 8″ long flowers in July–August, 1991. Western China. Introduced 1903. Zone 6 to 7.

Clethra pringlei S. Wats., (klē′thra͡ prin-glē′ī), with long, cinnamon-scented, white flowers, is a large evergreen shrub member of the genus from Mexico which to date has not performed well in the Southeast. Has been killed back in Georgia at 0 to 5°F. Zone 7 to 9(10).

Cocculus carolinus (L.) DC. — Carolina Moonseed, Coral Beads, Snailseed

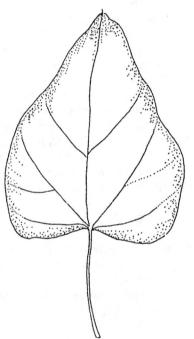

FAMILY: Menispermaceae
LEAVES: Alternate, simple, orbicular to triangular-ovate, 2 to 4″ long, 3- to 7-veined, rounded and mucronate at apex, rounded to subcordate at base, entire or often obscurely lobed, lustrous deep green and glabrous above, covered with pale pubescence below; petiole—1 1/2 to 4″ long.

Cocculus carolinus, (kok′ū-lus ka-ro-lī′nus), Carolina Moonseed, is virtually unknown in gardens except when planted by the birds. Flowers are dioecious, greenish white, male in short panicles, female in racemes. In October and November, one notices abundant red fruits dangling from odd shrubs. I had never seen the plant until arriving in Georgia. It is a reasonably vigorous twining vine that nests in shrubs or any structure that is available. The fruits are often seen hanging from shrubs and small trees like Christmas ornaments. The plant will grow 10 to 14′ and appears to do this in one season as it largely dies back some distance. Flowers are inconspicuous but the bright red, 1/4″ diameter drupes are borne in 2 to 4″ long racemes and start to manifest themselves in September through November. I have seen plants in heavy shade and full sun fruiting with equal fervor. Quite adaptable to soils. Virginia to Illinois and Kansas to Florida and Texas. Introduced 1732. Zone 6 to 9.

Colutea arborescens L. — Common Bladder-senna
(ko-lū′tē-a͡ är-bō-res′enz)

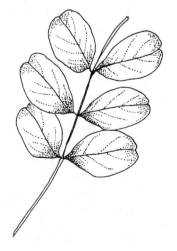

FAMILY: Fabaceae
LEAVES: Compound, odd-pinnate, 3 to 6″ long, 9 to 13 leaflets, each leaflet 1/2 to 1″ long, elliptic to obovate, usually emarginate to mucronate, entire, bright green, membranous with fairly distinct venation.
BUDS: Small, usually superposed and the upper promptly developing into slender branches, with 2 to 4 visible scales or leaves, appressed-pubescent.
STEM: Moderate, terete except for shortly decurrent lines from the nodes; leaf scars—alternate, broadly crescent-shaped, much elevated; bundle traces 1 or 3 or the middle one divided; stipules persistent on the sides of the leaf cushion; pith—moderate, rounded, continuous.

SIZE: 6 to 8′ high and about as wide at maturity, may grow larger (12′).

HARDINESS: Zone 5 to 7; freezes back to ground at the Morton Arboretum, in summer regrows to 4′ and flowers on new growth.

HABIT: Strong-growing shrub of bushy habit; becomes leggy at base.

RATE: Medium to fast.

TEXTURE: Medium in leaf; possibly medium-coarse in winter.

LEAF COLOR: Bright green in summer; fall color is not effective.

FLOWERS: Yellow, 3/4″ long, pea-shaped, the standard with red markings; (May)June through July; borne in 6- to 8-flowered, 1 1/2 to 4″ long racemes; produced on current season's growth; very pretty flowers.

FRUIT: Inflated and bladder-like pod, 3″ long and 1 to 1 1/2″ wide; greenish to slightly reddish near the base; maturing July through September; rather interesting but drying soon after maturing and assuming the dirty brown socks posture.

CULTURE: Root system is sparingly branched and plants should be grown in and transplanted from containers; easily grown in almost any soil except waterlogged; prefers full sun; prune back to old wood in winter; tends to show some dieback and is not the tidiest shrub.

DISEASES AND INSECTS: None serious.

LANDSCAPE VALUE: Most authorities consider this species too coarse and weedy for the home landscape; because of its adaptability, it could be successfully used in poor soil areas where more ornamental shrubs would not grow; I have seen the species and 'Bullata' in July at the Arnold Arboretum; at this time their foliage was in immaculate condition and they were the match of any other shrub for summer foliage effect.

CULTIVARS:

'Bullata'—A dwarf form of dense habit whose 5 to 7 leaflets are small, rounded and somewhat bullate; probably about 1/3 to 1/2 the size of the species at maturity; not the handsomest plant.

'Copper Beauty'—Orange-yellow flowers, strongly tinted reddish brown pods.

'Crispa'—A low-growing form with leaves wavy on the margins.

PROPAGATION: Seeds have a hard seed coat and should be scarified in concentrated sulfuric acid for 30 to 60 minutes; steeping seeds in hot water (190°F) for 24 hours also works; half-ripened cuttings collected in early November (England) rooted 29% without treatment, failed to respond to NAA but rooted 73% after treatment with 100 ppm IBA/18 hr.

ADDITIONAL NOTES: Only *Koelreuteria* and *Staphylea* among hardy woody plants have similar fruits. The fruits explode when squeezed. W.J. Bean noted, "Its accommodating nature had made it, perhaps, despised in gardens." *Colutea* will never supersede forsythia, or for that matter any shrub, in gardens.

NATIVE HABITAT: Mediterranean region and southeastern Europe. Introduced 1570.

RELATED SPECIES:

Colutea × media Willd., (ko-lū′tē-à mē′di-à), is a hybrid between *C. arborescens* and *C. orientalis* Mill. with bluish green foliage. Each leaf is composed of 11 to 13, obovate, 3/4 to 1″ long leaflets. Flowers show evidence of *C. orientalis* for they are brownish red to a coppery hue and quite attractive. The 3″ long inflated pod often turns solid lime green, pink or bronze, reddish or reddish purple. There is a nice specimen at the Arnold Arboretum. Koller, *Proc. Intl. Plant Prop. Soc.* 32:598 (1982), described several interesting facets of the plant's behavior. Matures into a 6 to 10′ high rounded shrub that is hardy to 10°F. Peak flowering occurs in mid-May (Boston) with scattered blossoms throughout summer. Colors range from the typical yellow to those with blends or tints of copper, pink or reddish brown. Originated before 1790; given the name *C. × media* in 1809, where it was cultivated in the Botanic Garden of Berlin. Zone 5 to 7.

Comptonia peregrina (L.) Coult. — Sweetfern
(komp-tō′ni-à per-e-grī′nà)

FAMILY: Myricaceae

LEAVES: Alternate, simple, linear-oblong, deeply pinnatifid with roundish-ovate, oblique, often mucronulate lobes, 2 to 4 1/2″ long and 1/3 to 5/8″ wide, pubescent, fragrant; looks somewhat like a fern frond; hence, the name Sweetfern; pale green when emerging, eventually dark green, often lustrous; petiole—1/8 to 1/4″ long.

BUDS: Globular, minute, solitary, sessile, with 2 or about 4 exposed scales, hairy; pistillate catkins crowded at the ends of the stems, 1/4″ long, cylindrical, pale brown, hairy.

STEM: Young stems green or yellowish or reddish brown and covered with resin dots, older stems yellowish brown with shining surface, somewhat hairy, oldest are reddish purple or coppery brown.

SIZE: 2 to 4' high and can spread 4 to 8', actually indefinite for it suckers profusely.

HARDINESS: Zone 2 to 5 or 6.

HABIT: Deciduous shrub with slender, often erect branches developing a broad, flat-topped to rounded outline as it spreads and colonizes.

RATE: Slow to medium.

TEXTURE: Medium-fine in leaf and no worse than medium in winter; the interesting fern-like foliage gives the plant a gentle, woodsy, graceful appearance.

LEAF COLOR: Dark green, almost lustrous, in summer; falls green or greenish brown in autumn.

FLOWERS: Monoecious (usually), staminate—3 to 4, usually 4, stamens, borne in cylindric catkins; pistillate—ovary surrounded with 8 persistent bracts at the base, borne in globose-ovoid catkins, April or early May, not showy, of yellow-green color.

FRUIT: Nutlet, 1/5″ long, olive-brown, borne in a distinct burr-like cluster of bracts.

CULTURE: Not the easiest plant to move; people have suggested digging large pieces of sod and, hopefully, getting sufficient roots to effect establishment. Work has sown that Sweetfern can be container-grown and successfully transplanted from containers. See *Proc. Intl. Plant Prop. Soc.* 24:364–366 (1974). Sweetfern does best in peaty, sandy, sterile, acid soils. Some authorities indicated moist soils are beneficial, however, I have seen this plant in New England growing all over cuts and fills along highways. Sweetfern has the ability to fix its own nitrogen and this partially explains the adaptability to poor, infertile soils; full sun or partial shade.

DISEASES AND INSECTS: Nothing serious.

LANDSCAPE VALUE: Interesting plant with aromatic foliage and stems; can be used for highways and other waste areas where the soil is sandy, infertile and somewhat dry; might be used in naturalistic landscaping where typical "ornamentals" tend to languish; a nice novelty plant for the collector.

PROPAGATION: Cuttings taken from mature wood rooted poorly. Cuttings taken from juvenile growth rooted readily when treated with 3000 ppm IBA and placed under mist. Best to collect juvenile stems 3″ or less in length. The principal method of propagation is by root pieces which are dug in late winter or early spring before growth starts. The root pieces should be 4″ long if 1/16″ in diameter and 2″ long if 3/8 to 1/2″ in diameter. The medium should be fine sand and Sphagnum peat. The cuttings should be horizontally placed at a 1/2″ depth and will develop shoots and additional roots. As the new juvenile shoots develop they can be collected for cutting wood. Seed propagation has met with limited success but Del Tredici and Torrey, *Botanical Gazette* 137(3):262–268 (1976), showed that seeds treated with 500 ppm gibberellic acid (GA_3) germinated 20%, those scarified and then treated with GA_3 germinated 80%; their paper is interesting and should be obtained by anyone who is serious about seed propagation of this species.

ADDITIONAL NOTES: Similar to *Myrica* but differs in the monoecious flowers and fern frond-type leaves. I had the plant in my Illinois garden and it was performing fantastically. I planted it in a peat:soil mixture. For best growth an acid soil appears mandatory. It is a nitrogen-fixing species and forms nodules in association with an Actinomycete fungus which is quite different from the *Rhizobium*-induced nodules on many leguminous plants.

NATIVE HABITAT: Nova Scotia to Manitoba, south to North Carolina; found primarily on sandy, gravelly, infertile soils; abundant along roadsides in New England, New York, Pennsylvania. Introduced 1714.

Cornus alba L. — Tatarian Dogwood

(kôr′nus al′bà)

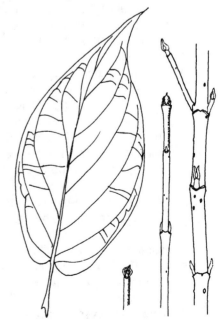

FAMILY: Cornaceae

LEAVES: Opposite, simple, ovate to elliptic, 2 to 4 1/2″ long, 1/2 as wide, acute to acuminate, usually rounded at base, entire, rugose, and often somewhat bullate above and dark green, glaucous beneath, with 5 to 6 pairs of veins; petiole—1/3 to 1″ long.

BUDS: Appressed, valvate, pubescent, deep red-brown-black in color.

STEM: Slender, hairy initially, finally glabrous; lenticels prominent, long oval, vertical, beautiful deep red (variable) in winter; pith—white, solid, ample.

FRUIT: Drupe, white or slightly bluish, stone higher than broad, flattened at each end.

SIZE: 8 to 10' in height, spread is variable ranging from 5 to 10'.

HARDINESS: Zone 3 to 7 but performing poorly in South, possibly because of canker susceptibility; have not observed a planting that thrives in Zone 7 and 8.

HABIT: Usually distinctly erect in youth, arching somewhat with age; the long branches sparsely branched creating an open, loose appearance; the lack of lateral bud development along the shoots is interesting; the branching (when it occurs) appears at the tops of the shoots; suckers forming large colonies.

RATE: Fast.

TEXTURE: Medium in leaf, medium in winter although the rich red winter stems reduce the bold harshness of the erect ascending stems.

STEM COLOR: In winter the stems change to a blood red color; the summer color is strongly greenish with a tinge of red; the color transformation can be correlated with the short, cool days of fall and the abscission of foliage which coincides quite well with the initiation of red coloration; the oldest canes should be removed as the young stems develop the most vivid reds.

LEAF COLOR: Soft yellow-green in early spring gradually changing to lustrous dark green; fall color is often a good reddish purple, however, some plants exhibit very limited coloration.

FLOWERS: Perfect, yellowish white, May–June, after the leaves have matured, in 1 1/2 to 2″ diameter, flat-topped cymes, effective 7 to 10 days; the flowers are not overwhelmingly effective; sporadic flowering may occur into the summer months.

FRUIT: Drupe, whitish or slightly blue-tinted, about 3/8″ across, June to July, interesting but not long persistent; the stone (endocarp and seed) higher than wide, flattened at each end; the fruit has ornamental appeal but is little recognized by most gardeners; in fact, a question to the most knowledgeable of gardeners concerning the fruit colors of the "red-stemmed" dogwoods (*C. alba*, *C. baileyi* Coult. & W.H. Evans, *C. sericea*) would probably yield an "I do not know" response.

CULTURE: Fibrous rooted, easy to transplant; offered bare root and in containers; adapted to varied soil conditions but prefers a moist, well-drained situation; sun or partial shade; quite vigorous and is apt to overgrow neighboring shrubs; prune 1/3 of old wood every year or cut to within 6 to 12″ of the ground in late winter; new growth of the season has the most brilliant winter stem color.

DISEASES AND INSECTS: Crown canker, flower and leaf blight, leaf spots, powdery mildews, twig blights, root rots, borers (at least seven kinds), dogwood club-gall, leaf miner, scales, and other lesser insects; the borers can be serious especially on stressed, weak-growing trees.

LANDSCAPE VALUE: Difficult to use as a single specimen plant, best in shrub border, especially in large masses along roadsides, ponds and other large display areas; definitely adds color to the winter landscape; probably does not spread as rapidly as *C. sericea* and, hence, more desirable for the home landscape; the red-stemmed dogwoods are difficult to separate by winter characteristics especially as small plants and one is never absolute as to which species he/she is purchasing; use with discretion for this species is a strong focal point in the landscape and may actually detract from the other plant materials; tremendous interest in winter gardening in Europe and the trend has crossed the Atlantic; have seen wonderful examples at Mr. Adrian Bloom's garden at Bressingham; this plant, more specifically the cultivars, make a tremendous show; in fact Mr. Bloom has written a splendid book *Winter Garden Glory*, Harper Collins, London (1993), in which the photographs establish the mood and the word pictures move one to think about winter gardening.

CULTIVARS:

'Alleman's Compact'—Compact habit, 5 to 6′ high; rich green trouble-free foliage; red stems in winter; considered Zone 3, possible substitute for 'Isanti' which is more susceptible to leaf spot.

'Argenteo-marginata' ('Elegantissima')—Leaves with an irregular creamy-white margin, the center a subdued grayish green; winter stems red; there is considerable confusion related to this cultivar and nurserymen often list it as *C. elegantissima* thus relegating it to species status which is incorrect; this is a rather pretty form and if used correctly adds a nice color touch to gardens, especially in shady areas; 'Variegata' (which may not be the correct name) is a distinctly different form with creamy white margins and dark green centers, and it is also more vigorous than 'Argenteo-marginata'; side-by-side there is a distinct difference in leaf coloration but I do not believe anyone in the United States has bothered to separate the two cultivars in commerce; generally about 6 to 8′ high.

'Atrosanguinea'—Dwarf with crimson stems.

'Aurea'—The leaves are suffused with soft yellow; have seen in England where it looked fine; in the heat of our country I do not know how it would hold up; fall color is a striking birch yellow; stems are red in winter.

'Behnschii'—Leaves variegated red and white.

'Bloodgood'—J.C. Raulston reported showiest red stem color of any selection in NCSU Arboretum (now J.C. Raulston Arboretum) trials; from garden of Dr. Tom Krenitsky in Chapel Hill, NC.

'Bud's Yellow'—A yellow-stemmed form from a seedling population of *C. alba* made by Boughen Nurseries, Saskatchewan; clean summer foliage, yellow fall color; appears resistant to canker that can devastate *C. sericea* 'Flaviramea'; 6 to 8' by 5 to 6'; plants I saw in Hillier Nursery, England were wider than tall; a recent report indicates the cultivar may not be as canker resistant as originally thought.

'Gouchaultii'—The leaf margin is yellow and rose, the center of the leaf green and rose; becoming partly white on the margin; *Hillier's Manual* suggested that there is no difference between this cultivar and 'Spaethii', at least among the plants in cultivation; 'Gouchaultii' is more vigorous with more silvery variegation compared to 'Spaethii'; stems dark blood red in winter; 6 to 8' high at landscape maturity.

Ivory Halo™('Bailhalo')—Compact selection of 'Argenteo-marginata' with green center and whitish marginal leaf variegation; red stems in winter; finer textured, more compact, rounded form, 5 to 6' by 5 to 6'; plant patent 8722; Bailey Nursery introduction.

'Kesselringii'—The stems turn dark brownish purple (purplish black) in winter; grows 6 to 9'; not overwhelming.

'Siberian Pearls'—Profusion of white flowers, followed by white fruits that turn blue with age; stems are deep red in winter; have seen in English nurseries; considered Zone 3.

'Sibirica'—The stems are bright coral red and the fruit is a bluish color; this cultivar is often offered in the trade but what is being sold is anyone's guess; 'Sibirica' differs from the species in the two characteristics mentioned above as well as having more rounded leaves with a short apex and a less vigorous nature; the bright stem color is best on stems of the current season's growth and this should be kept in mind during pruning; I saw several plants at the Arnold Arboretum, labeled 'Sibirica', and each was different from the other; there was a rather weak-growing shrub by the pond at the foot of the lilac collection that adhered to the "true" description of 'Sibirica'; a clone called 'Westonbirt' is listed but according to W.J. Bean does not differ from "true" 'Sibirica'; in Griffiths, 'Westonbirt' is described as dark coral pink-stemmed; Lake County Nursery, Perry, OH lists 'Sibirica Bloodgood' with bright coral red stems, more vivid than other "red-stemmed" dogwoods, growing 6 to 9' by 5 to 6'; also under Lake County's banner are Sibirica Red Gnome™ a compact, low-growing, 3 to 4' high, 4 to 5' wide selection with bright red stems, this is listed as a selection of 'Sibirica Bloodgood'; 'Sibirica Ruby' with bright ruby red stems, 6' by 5', upright-rounded habit; and 'Sibirica Variegata' with larger leaves than 'Argenteo-marginata', leaves with a somewhat stunted appearance, more gray-green in middle with narrow white margins.

'Spaethii'—The foliage is strongly bordered with yellow; less vigorous than 'Gouchaultii'; I have seen this used in the hedge collection at the Royal Botanic Gardens, Hamilton, Ontario, in August, and would rate it the brightest yellow of any hardy, yellow-leaved type; this clone maintains the bright yellow color throughout the summer and does not show any signs of scorch; the story goes that the cultivar originated on a stem of the species, on which was grafted a white-variegated scion; the scion died and just beneath the point of union a yellow-variegated shoot developed; it could be that some callus formation had taken place before the scion died and the resultant yellow-foliaged form was, in fact, a graft-chimera; there is some indication in the literature that 'Aurea' and 'Spaethii' are the same plant but the plants I have seen labeled as each differ by the characteristics described.

PROPAGATION: Seed should be treated like *C. sericea*; most nursery production is by cuttings; I have seen nursery operations where the long stems are cut into 8 to 10" cuttings in fall or winter and directly stuck into the field; softwood and hardwood cuttings root readily any time of year; use 1000 ppm IBA-dip on June–July cuttings; one of the easiest dogwoods to root.

ADDITIONAL NOTES: Good choice for winter color especially in the northern states where shades of brown dominate; for a rather humorous look at "red-stemmed" dogwoods see Dirr, "In search of the elusive red-stemmed dogwood," *American Horticulturist* 56(2):18–21 (1977).

NATIVE HABITAT: Siberia to Manchuria and northern Korea. Introduced 1741.

Cornus alternifolia L. — Pagoda Dogwood
(kôr′nus al-ter-ni-fō′li-ȧ)

LEAVES: Alternate, but crowded near ends of twigs, appearing as if whorled, simple, elliptic-ovate, 2 to 5" long, 1 to 2 1/2" wide, acuminate, cuneate, entire, nearly glabrous above, medium to dark green, glaucescent beneath and appressed pubescent, with 5 to 6 pairs of veins; petiole—1 to 2" long.

BUDS: Flower—1/4" long, reddish, purplish, essentially glabrous at base, pubescent toward tip, valvate, terminally born; vegetative—minute, valvate, minutely hairy.

STEM: Slender, usually greenish to reddish or purplish to dark purplish brown, shiny, somewhat bloomy and glabrous; pith—white.

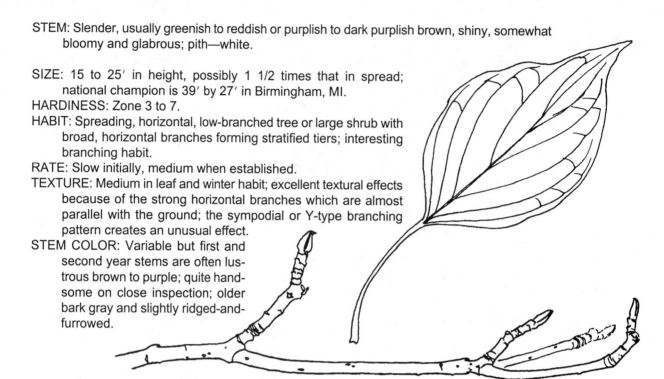

SIZE: 15 to 25′ in height, possibly 1 1/2 times that in spread; national champion is 39′ by 27′ in Birmingham, MI.

HARDINESS: Zone 3 to 7.

HABIT: Spreading, horizontal, low-branched tree or large shrub with broad, horizontal branches forming stratified tiers; interesting branching habit.

RATE: Slow initially, medium when established.

TEXTURE: Medium in leaf and winter habit; excellent textural effects because of the strong horizontal branches which are almost parallel with the ground; the sympodial or Y-type branching pattern creates an unusual effect.

STEM COLOR: Variable but first and second year stems are often lustrous brown to purple; quite handsome on close inspection; older bark gray and slightly ridged-and-furrowed.

LEAF COLOR: Medium to dark green, fall color can develop reddish purple; usually not developing outstanding fall color.

FLOWERS: Yellowish white, sickeningly fragrant, effective 7 to 10 days, May to early June; borne in 1 1/2 to 2 1/2″ diameter, flat-topped, upright cymes; the flowers are not eye catching but are sufficiently showy to be of ornamental value in the late spring landscape.

FRUIT: Drupe, bluish black, bloomy, 1/4 to 1/3″ across; July–August; not long-persisting; the fruit stalk turning a pinkish red; fruit changing from green to red to blue-black at maturity; quite handsome.

CULTURE: Fibrous, spreading root system, transplants best as young plant; requires moist, acid, well-drained soil; seems to do best in a partially shaded situation although I have observed plants in full sun which appeared quite prosperous; does best in colder climates; keeping the root zone moist, acid, and cool is the key to success.

DISEASES AND INSECTS: Leaf spot, twig blight or canker are problems; have heard and read about the twig blight/canker that kills branches and entire trees, at Williamstown, MA, Niels Oleson said when trees reach 3 to 4″ diameter a canker invades and kills the plants; it is safe to say that few large specimens are present in everyday landscapes.

LANDSCAPE VALUE: Possibly for naturalizing, where horizontal characteristics are needed, shrub border, where sharp vertical architectural lines are present; interesting dogwood, little used for it has rough competition from *Cornus florida*.

CULTIVARS:

'Argentea'—Leaves variegated with white; tends toward shrubby habit; a very pretty variegated form with leaves smaller than the species; although introduced before 1900 in the United States it is not common in American gardens; I have observed it in many European gardens; really stands out in a crowd; does not grow as large as *C. controversa* 'Variegata', perhaps 15′.

Other cultivars: 'Corallina', 'Ochrocarpa', 'Umbraculifera', and 'Virescens' are described in *The New RHS Dictionary of Gardening*. I have not observed them in the United States.

PROPAGATION: Seed requires a variable period of warm (2 to 5 months) followed by 2 to 3 months of cold; at Illinois I had some success with softwood cuttings but the percentage was low; during sabbatical I had 100% success; cuttings should be rooted and allowed to overwinter and break bud before potting; this is true for many dogwoods, especially tree types.

ADDITIONAL NOTES: I am not absolutely convinced that I absorbed the true beauty of this species until late summer of 1997 when, on vacation in Maine, Bonnie and I would surprise the tree during our frequent walks. The whorled branch development literally jumps from the surrounding vegetation and grabs one by the nape of the neck. The fruits, particularly the stalks, are beautiful. Certainly a wonderful native plant and perhaps best reserved for that hallowed niche.

NATIVE HABITAT: New Brunswick to Minnesota south to Georgia and Alabama. Introduced 1760.

RELATED SPECIES:

Cornus controversa Hemsl., (kôr′nus kon-trō-ver′sȧ), Giant Dogwood, is a strikingly picturesque, horizontally branched, wide-spreading tree reaching 30 to 45′ under cultivation but up to 60′ in the wild. The 1/2″ wide, creamy white flowers are borne in 3 to 7″ diameter, flat-topped cymes in May–June. The 1/4″ diameter fruit progresses from a reddish to purple or blue-black color in August–September. The dark green leaves range from 3 to 6″ long and 2 to 3″ wide with a 1 to 2″ long petiole. They have 6 to 8, sometimes 9, vein pairs. In fall, the leaves may turn purple but I have not noticed good fall coloration on this species. Seeds require 5 months warm followed by 3 months cold. Softwood cuttings root readily and should not be disturbed after rooting. I collected cuttings on August 24, treated them with 8000 ppm IBA-quick dip, sand:perlite and in 8 weeks had 100% rooting with unbelievably profuse root systems. 'June Snow' is rounded with layered branching in horizontal tiers, dark green leaves turn orange to red in fall, white flowers, 1/4″ diameter, blue-black fruits, 30′ high, 40′ wide, Zone 5. 'Variegata' has an irregular, creamy white border, the leaves being long, narrow and lanceolate, usually less than 1 1/2″ wide, and often unequally sided and somewhat deformed; again this cultivar is evident in many English gardens. It is more vigorous than *C. alternifolia* 'Variegata' and makes a more stunning sight. Certainly one of the handsomest trees in cultivation resides in the Bath Botanic Garden, England. Two of the most notable American specimens of the species are located at the Arnold (30 to 35′ high) and Secrest Arboreta (45′ by 48′). Raulston reported it was the fastest (3 to 5′ per year) of all dogwoods at Raleigh, NC. Has been used as a street tree in Swarthmore, PA. Safe to say that promotion of this species for "tough" situations was unrealistic for it is neither heat nor drought tolerant. Morton Arboretum reported that considerable dieback occurs, presumably from disease(s). Japan, China. Introduced 1880. Zone 5 to 7, possibly hardy in 4.

Cornus amomum Mill. —Silky Dogwood
(kôr′nus ȧ-mō′mum)

LEAVES: Opposite, simple, elliptic-ovate or ellip-
    tic, 2 to 4″ long, 1 to 2 1/4″ wide, short
    acuminate, usually rounded at base, medium to
    dark green and nearly glabrous above, glaucous
    beneath and with grayish white or brownish hairs on
    the veins, 4 to 7 vein pairs; petiole—1/3 to 2/3″
    long, pubescent.
BUDS: Flower—terminally borne, hairy, valvate, nearly
    sessile, relatively small; vegetative—valvate,
    appressed, pubescent, small.
STEM: Slender, purplish, rarely greenish, appressed
    pubescence especially on younger branches,
    second year wood showing distinct fissuring pattern;
    pith—brown, solid.

SIZE: 6 to 10′ in height by 6 to 10′ in spread, have observed 15′
    high specimens.
HARDINESS: Zone 4 to 8.
HABIT: Rounded, multi-stemmed shrub usually twiggy and round-topped in youth,
    becoming open with age; often straggly, unkempt and without ornamental appeal.
RATE: Medium (possibly fast).
TEXTURE: Medium in foliage; medium-coarse in winter.
STEM COLOR: Young branches reddish purple, sometimes greenish; older wood is brownish purple and
    develops brown fissured areas.
LEAF COLOR: Medium to dark green in summer; fall color is often green to brown although reddish purple is
    a possibility; have seen purple fall coloration but it was not spectacular.
FLOWERS: Yellowish white, not fragrant, May–June, 7 to 10 days, borne in upright, 1 1/2 to 2 1/2″ diameter,
    flat-topped, slightly villous cymes.
FRUIT: Drupe, 1/4″ across, bluish often with white blotches, almost porcelain blue, rather attractive;
    unfortunately, persisting only a brief time in August, for the birds and other forces of nature quickly ravage
    the fruits; have seen a few shrubs that were absolutely beautiful.

CULTURE: Native in low woods, along streams and borders of swamps over much of the eastern United States; fibrous rooted, easily transplanted; quite adaptable but prefers moist, partially shaded situations although it performs well in full sun and with less than optimum moisture.

DISEASES AND INSECTS: Scale may present a problem, see under *C. alba*; generally nothing serious.

LANDSCAPE VALUE: Possibly massing, shrub borders, naturalizing, in moist and wet soils where many shrubs do not grow well; probably too coarse and with limited ornamental assets to ever become a common landscape shrub but, like all plants, in the proper setting it has a place; in full sun in the University's Botanical Garden a plant has gown 10' by 15', also several campus plantings have excelled in rather heavy, wet soils.

PROPAGATION: Seed, 90 to 120 days at 41°F will break the dormancy; cuttings, softwood, taken in July rooted well without hormonal treatment; rooting can be enhanced with IBA treatment, probably 1000 to 3000 ppm IBA best; June (Georgia) cuttings, peat:perlite, 3000 ppm KIBA, mist, rooted 100% in 4 weeks.

NATIVE HABITAT: Massachusetts to Georgia, west to New York and Tennessee. Introduced 1658.

RELATED SPECIES: There are a number of related taxa that show minimal differences but have been listed as species and varieties by various authorities. They are included here so the reader can practice splitting taxonomic hairs and become sufficiently insane to warrant government subsidies. My treatment is probably no clearer than the myriad taxonomic references I read. Almost appears that lumping is in order.

Cornus asperifolia Michx., (kôr′nus as-per-i-fō′li-à), Roughleaf Dogwood, and the variety *drummondii* (C.A. Mey) Coulter & W.H. Evans are more or less pubescent cousins of *C. amomum*. I have seen *C. asperifolia* in Kansas and identified it as *C. amomum*. It can grow to 15' in height and sometimes makes a small tree. Flowers and fruits are similar to *C. amomum* although fruit is usually white. Pith is white on 2-year-old stems. The leaves of var. *drummondii* are hairy above (rough to the touch) with thicker, softer pubescence below and about 5 vein pairs. Ontario to Florida, west to Iowa, Kansas and Texas. Cultivated 1836. Zone 4 to 8(9).

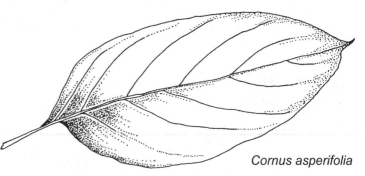

Cornus asperifolia

Cornus foemina Mill., (kôr′nus fem′i-nà), Swamp Dogwood or Stiff Dogwood, could be mistaken for *C. amomum*, except that on *C. foemina* the young and old stems remain reddish purple longer and the pith is white. Both species inhabit similar niches in the wild. Swamp Dogwood is larger, 20 to 25' high, the leaves 1 to 4″ long, grayish to dark green and smooth above. Flat-topped, white cymes range from 1 to 3″ across. Fruits are blue, oval-rounded, 1/4″ diameter. I have seen shrub and tree versions and believe that in the latter form this species would make a worthy small street, container, urban space tree. Saw a wonderful selection at Mr. Charles Webb's garden in Lee, FL. Virginia to Missouri, Florida and Texas. Introduced 1785. Zone 6 to 9.

Cornus obliqua Raf., (kôr′nus ō-blē′kwà), Pale Dogwood, is similar to *C. amomum* but is usually more loosely branched and the stems are purple to yellowish red. It grows in wet soils. Leaves are oval-elliptic to oblong, 2 to 3″ long, dark green, dull gray-white with brown-red pubescent veins below. White flowers occur in up to 2″ diameter, flat-topped cymes and are followed by bluish white fruits. Quebec, Minnesota, and Kansas, southern Pennsylvania, Illinois and Missouri. Cultivated 1888. Zone 3 to 7.

Cornus canadensis L. — Bunchberry, Dwarf Cornel, Creeping Dogwood
(kôr′nus kan-a-den′sis)

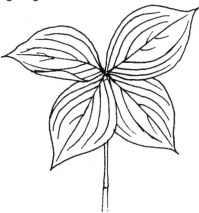

LEAVES: Opposite, appearing whorled at top of stem, oval to lanceolate,
1 to 2″(3″) long, acute, glabrous or slightly appressed-pubescent,
glossy dark green, 2 to 3 vein pairs.

SIZE: 3 to 9″ high, wide-spreading but in a slow fashion.
HARDINESS: Zone 2 to 6; best in cold climates.
HABIT: Beautiful deciduous ground cover, in favorable areas forming a
carpet-like mat.
RATE: Slow.
TEXTURE: Medium-fine in all seasons.
LEAF COLOR: Lustrous dark green in summer changing to red and
vinous red in fall.
FLOWERS: Fertile flowers greenish white in terminal umbel, not showy; bracts 4 to 6, 1/2 to 1″ long, white,
appearing from May through July; very striking in flower.
FRUIT: Scarlet, berry-like drupe, 1/4″ diameter, ripening in August and later, persisting quite late or until eaten
by the birds, again very lovely, occurs in a showy, 3/4 to 1″ diameter infructescence at end of shoot.
CULTURE: Sod cut from established plantings is probably the best mode of transplanting; container-grown
plants are acceptable; requires moist, acid soil rich in organic matter; prefers a cool atmosphere; partial
or full shade; needs frequent watering until well-established; mulching with acid material such as peat
moss or pine needles is recommended.
DISEASES AND INSECTS: None serious.
LANDSCAPE VALUE: Probably one of our most beautiful native ground covers; fastidious as to culture but
worth the effort; excellent under pines, broadleaf evergreens and other acid-requiring plants.
CULTIVARS:
'Downeaster'—Selected from a full sun situation in gravel-sand soil from the Blueberry Barrens, Jonesboro, ME; over a 5 to 6 year evaluation period, proved most sun and drought tolerant of 30 clones
evaluated; introduced by Paul Cappiello, University of Maine; Dr. Allen Barker, UMASS, reported this
clone was easy to grow in a garden setting.
PROPAGATION: Moving pieces of sod is the most practical way; seeds require a warm plus cold stratification
period; one report noted 60 minutes of acid followed by 60 to 90 days of cold resulted in high germination;
clean seed, 1 hour acid scarification followed by 90 to 120 days cold, moist stratification at 41°F; multiple
node cuttings with one node below surface of medium, fog; leave in fog until rizome breaks come through
medium; 3000 ppm KIBA, cuttings taken in April, produce finished quarts by end of growing season.
ADDITIONAL NOTES: The species takes me back to my graduate days at UMASS, Amherst, MA, where I saw
for the first time the plant in the wild; many years later Bonnie and I were tromping through Maine where
the plant is everywhere in evidence particularly in Down East, ME; the lowbush blueberry growers
consider it a weed . . . one man's wildflower is another's weed . . . or reciprocally.
NATIVE HABITAT: Southern Greenland to Alaska, south to Maryland, west to South Dakota, New Mexico, and
California; found at high altitudes in cool, moist woods, and on hummocks in bogs.

Cornus florida L. — Flowering Dogwood
(kôr′nus flôr′i-dà)

LEAVES: Opposite, simple, oval or ovate, 3 to 6″ long, 1 1/2 to 3″ wide, abruptly acuminate, broad cuneate to
rounded at base, nearly glabrous and dark green above (not as dark as *C. kousa*), glaucous beneath and
usually only pubescent on the veins, with 6 to 7 vein pairs; petiole—1/4 to 3/4″ long.
BUDS: Flower—usually at end of stem, globose, biscuit-shaped, flattened, valvate, covered by 2 large silky
appressed pubescent outer scales, another 2 inner scales at 90° angles to the outer two, these four
scales becoming the showy white bracts; vegetative—small, valvate, slender, almost hidden by raised leaf
scar; leaf scars—usually completely encircling stem.
STEM: Slender, green to purple, sometimes bloomy, pubescent when young, finally glabrous.
BARK: Broken into small squarish and rectangular, grayish brown to blackish blocks, the entire effect
reminiscent of an alligator's back, great characteristic particularly in winter.

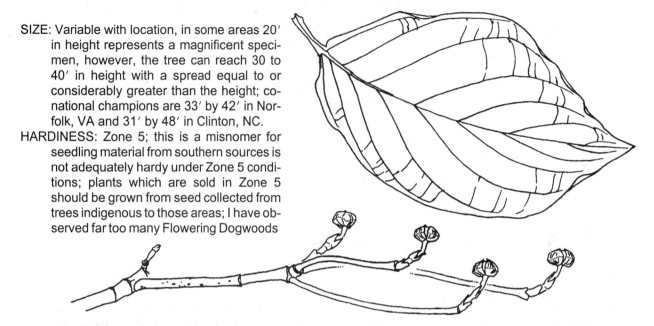

SIZE: Variable with location, in some areas 20′ in height represents a magnificent specimen, however, the tree can reach 30 to 40′ in height with a spread equal to or considerably greater than the height; conational champions are 33′ by 42′ in Norfolk, VA and 31′ by 48′ in Clinton, NC.

HARDINESS: Zone 5; this is a misnomer for seedling material from southern sources is not adequately hardy under Zone 5 conditions; plants which are sold in Zone 5 should be grown from seed collected from trees indigenous to those areas; I have observed far too many Flowering Dogwoods in the Midwest with minimal flower production principally caused by lack of flower bud hardiness; if possible, always ask the nurserymen where the trees are grown and this, in turn, will save considerable disappointment when in 3 to 5 years time the trees show limited flowering; grows into Zone 9; over the past 8 years, a great number of *C. florida* have crossed my path and I believe there is hope for a "reliable" Zone 4 clone; at Orono, ME *Cornus florida* has never been successfully grown on the University of Maine campus, however, in Williamstown, MA both on the Williams College campus and in several private gardens, specimen quality flowering trees have survived –25 to –30°F; Spring Grove, Cincinnati, OH has introduced a new patented dogwood, Spring Grove, that has performed admirably at temperatures as low as –25°F.

HABIT: Shrub (seldom) or small, low-branched tree with horizontally spreading lines, layered effect, usually with a flat-topped crown and often wider than high at maturity; excellent plant for winter habit, very unique.

RATE: Slow upon transplanting, gradually assuming a medium rate.

TEXTURE: Medium in foliage; medium or fine in winter; the soft gray to purple young stems silhouetted against snowy or evergreen backgrounds are as handsome as the flowers (almost).

STEM COLOR: Young stems are often reddish purple, gradually turning grayish; older wood (3 to 4″ diameter) becomes scaly-blocky (grayish brown) and develops an "alligator" hide appearance.

LEAF COLOR: A handsome bronze-green to yellow-green when unfolding, usually a good dark green in summer, fall color is a consistent red to reddish purple; one of the most consistent trees for excellent fall color; tremendous variation from seedling-grown material in all characteristics (habit, fall color, flower); one of the first trees to fall color especially when stressed; fall color is usually long persistent.

FLOWERS: True flowers are greenish yellow and not showy, each 1/4″ across, in a crowded 1/2 to 3/4″ wide head; showy parts of inflorescences are the 4 white bracts which are obovate or emarginate, about 2″ long, the entire involucre (bracts) 3 to 4″ across, occur in April to May, effective for 10 to 14 days (perhaps longer) depending on the weather; true flowers are borne in short stalked cymes (umbels?) and are subtended by the handsome bracts; normally in full regalia in early to mid-April (Athens, GA); flowers open before leaves and often are present to some degree as leaves develop.

FRUIT: Drupe, glossy red, 1/3 to 1/2″ long, ovoid, 3 to 4 or more in a "cluster," ripening in September to October and can persist into December; birds seem to devour them or they often simply abscise after ripening; tremendous variation in fruit retention; have seen fruits as late as early February in Athens; 43 bird species have been reported to eat the fruits and buds.

CULTURE: Even as a small tree (3 to 4′) move balled-and-burlapped or container-grown; provide an acid, well-drained soil with sufficient organic matter; mulch to maintain a cool, moist soil; place in partial shade although full sun is acceptable; this particular species grows wild over the eastern United States and if you have ever witnessed a woodland dotted in flower, the reason for its popularity becomes evident; trees planted in poorly drained soils and open areas where summer water is limited invariably decline and die; not pollution tolerant; it is essential to minimize stress, i.e., heat, drought, cold, for this predisposes the trees to insect and disease attacks; good cultural practices translate to healthy trees.

DISEASES AND INSECTS: It seems that every time I pick up a trade publication there is an article on Flowering Dogwood insects or diseases; there is no question that this species is susceptible to a number of troublesome pests including borer and various petal and leaf spots; a recent scientific paper concluded that the more stressed the tree the more likely it is to become infested with borer; an article on Dogwood diseases by Lambe and Justis, *Ornamentals Northwest*, June–July (1978), lists many *C. florida* diseases; this is worth obtaining; the old axiom in the North was never plant a dogwood in a hot, dry site but in the South I have seen trees in full sun, in acid, clay soil doing splendidly; the summers of 1980, 81, 87, 88, 90, 93, and 97 were exceptionally dry and although newly planted dogwoods declined, established trees fared reasonably well. A prominent leaf and stem anthracnose, *Discula* spp., has weakened and/or killed many dogwoods in the Middle Atlantic and New England states. Was also discovered in North Georgia on native dogwoods but has not been found to any degree in the Athens-Atlanta area. Several state and federal agencies are working on the disease. The symptoms include small, purple-rimmed leaf spots or large tan blotches that may enlarge and kill the entire leaf; infected leaves may cling to stems after normal leaf fall; twigs may die back several inches and all the way to the main stem; epicormic (water sprouts) often form up and down the main stem and on major branches; these also become infected and die; bracts may also be infected if rainy conditions prevail during flowering: trees are often killed 2 to 3 years after the first attack; disease discovered in late 1970's; by 1986 discovered in nine northeastern states and as far south as West Virginia; in 1987 found in northern Georgia; several fungicides are reasonably effective for controlling the disease; since the 1990 edition numerous publications have been produced relating to the disease; *Discula destructiva*, is a cool weather fungus and the incidence of the disease relates to moisture, cool weather, and obviously the presence of *C. florida*; plants in shade, in the native understory, particularly at higher elevations in the Southeast and up the coast into New England, have been infected; trees in greater light (foliage dries quickly), with good air movement, in nurseries under good cultural practices have not been significantly affected.

A detailed description of the fungus is presented by Redlin, *Mycologia* 83:633–642 (1991). Santamour and McArdle, *Plant Disease* 73:590–591 (1989), tested seedlings from 20 provenances of *C. florida* and reported no host genetic barriers to the continued expansion of the geographic range of *Discula*. Not everyone agrees with this assessment and I have walked the *Cornus florida* cultivar test plots at Rutgers with Dr. Elwin Orton, breeder of the *C. florida* × *C. kousa* Stellar® series, and he pointed out differences in degree of resistance among *C. florida* cultivars. Daughtrey et al. discuss cause and control of *Discula* in *J. Arboriculture* 14:159–164 (1988), where they recommend Daconil 2787 and Manzate 200 applied at 10-day intervals during leaf expansion to reduce incidence.

Possibly the most troublesome report I read comes from Britton, *Plant Disease* 77:1026–1028 (1993), where fruits of *C. florida* were collected from infected trees and shown to be infected in the pulp and seed itself which means long distance dispersal of the disease is facilitated by birds and animals.

In Florida, a leaf blight manifested in rapidly enlarging brown spots with gray-green borders developed after heavy rains; disease was caused by *Phytophthora nicoteanae* var. *parasitica*; see *Plant Disease* 71:555–556 (1987).

Pseudomonas syringae, a bacterial disease, has been reported on *C. florida* in the Pacific Northwest; see *Plant Disease* 71:412–415 (1987).

Several other disease and insect problems to consider are the spot anthracnose (*Elsinoe corni*) of bracts and leaves; this is more unsightly than anything and appears more prevalent in wet years.

Cankers on *C. florida* are caused by several fungal species; a recent report, *Plant Disease* 75:886–889 (1991), reported canker development in preinoculated non drought-stressed and preinoculation drought stressed wounded container-grown plants by *Lasiodiplodia theobranae*. Drought stressed trees developed larger cankers than non drought-stressed plants. In this study *no cankers* developed on any uninoculated trees.

To emphasize the differences in disease susceptibility among cultivars, Windham and Freeland's article, *Tennessee Farm and Home Science* 155:25–31 (1990), is presented; in field trials with 10 cultivars, canker was greatest in 'Purple Glory' while 'Barton', 'Cherokee Princess', 'First Lady', and 'Rubra' were free; spot anthracnose was more severe on 'Barton' and 'Cloud 9' while 'Cherokee Princess', 'First Lady', 'Fragrant Cloud', 'Purple Glory', and 'Springtime' were either highly resistant or resistant; 'Plena' ('Pluribracteata') appeared to be immune.

Possibly the most serious insect pest is dogwood borer (*Synantheda scitula*) which devastates trees; the borers attack stressed trees and several detailed studies confirmed this; the highest infestation levels are in urban trees (60%) where stresses are the greatest, 7% in nursery-grown trees and 1% in forest habitat trees; see *J. Entomological Science* 25:481–485 (1990) for specifics. Plastic tree wrap increased the number of borers in dogwood by providing a favorable environment for the larvae; see *J. Arboriculture* 17:29–31 (1991).

In 1995 powdery mildew, *Microsphaeria* spp., has caused problems and reduced growth of nursery trees in Tennessee. An evaluation of 19 cultivars reflected various degrees of resistance with 'Cherokee Brave' the most resistant and 'Spring Time' and 'Pygmy' with the next lowest infection. The other 16 taxa were infected with 25 to 100% mildew. See Windham, *Proc. SNA Res. Conf.* 41:197–199 (1996). The mildew problem is significant and rarely do I see a landscape or native dogwood that does not have a measure of infection. In some cases it is so heavy that growth is reduced and flower bud set is diminished. Perhaps the mildew will abate with time and changing weather patterns. I know dogwood growers who are extremely concerned about the problem.

LANDSCAPE VALUE: The aristocrat of native flowering trees, often overplanted but never becomes obnoxious as is the case with forsythia, deutzia, and spirea; a plant with four-season character (excellent flower, summer and fall foliage, fruit, and winter habit); excellent as a specimen, near a patio, corners of houses and larger buildings, parks, groupings; especially effective against dark evergreen or dark building material backgrounds where the flowers are accentuated, as is the branching habit in winter; has the quality of flowering before the leaves and consequently vegetative competition is minimized.

CULTIVARS:

The selections are numerous and to select the best may be like rolling the dice . . . one takes his/her chances. To minimize chance, I talked with John Pair (and read his publications), Wichita, KS, Don Shadow, Winchester, TN and used my eyes. Many new cultivars have been introduced since the 1990 edition and Santamour and McArdle, *J. Arboriculture* 11(1):29–36 (1985), offer a cultivar checklist of the large-bracted dogwoods.

'Abundance'—Probably same as 'Cloud 9'.

'American Beauty Red'—Attractive foliage and pretty, deep red flowers.

'Andy Hart'—Compact pink.

'Apple Blossom'—Light pink flowers shading to white in the center, from New Canaan, CT.

'Ascending'—Listed, but no botanical information available.

'Autumn Gold'—Seedling selection by Mr. Don Shadow, Winchester, TN for golden orange winter stem color, yellow fall color, white bracts and red fruits; I have seen the plant and it is beautiful.

'Barton'—A large, white-flowered form with overlapping bracts that flowers heavily as a young plant and is well-suited for culture in Zone 6 through 8; this cultivar has performed extremely well at the University's Botanical Garden, certainly one of the better cultivars for the Southeast, susceptible to spot anthracnose, resistant to canker, selected by Marvin Barton, Birmingham, AL in 1956.

'Belmont Pink'—Flowers (bracts) blush pink, found and named by Henry Hicks, Long Island, NY, about 1930, apparently no longer in cultivation.

'Big Bouquet'—Especially heavy and consistently large, pure white bracts on a compact plant, introduced by Vermeulen Nursery, Neshanic Station, NJ.

'Big Giant'—Large white flowers.

'Big Girl'—Large white flowers.

'Bonnie'—A selection from Louisiana State University with 6″ diameter white flowers and showy red fruits.

'Cherokee Brave'—Vigorous grower, reddish pink (burgundy) flowers with a white center, introduced by the late Hubert Nicholson, Commercial Nursery, Decherd, TN, resistant to mildew.

'Cherokee Chief'—Flowers rich ruby-red and new growth reddish; bracts may develop a spotting, has been serious in Athens area; one of the most popular red-bracted forms, introduced by Ike Hawkersmith, Winchester, TN.

Cherokee Daybreak™—Leaves green and margined in white and hold color without scorching in hot weather, turn pink to deep red in fall, vigorous, upright in habit, white bracts, Commercial Nursery introduction, plant patent 6320.

'Cherokee Maiden'—Derived from seeds collected from Cookson Hills, OK; selected from 125 seedlings for its superior winter hardiness, flowered after –22°F in Wichita, KS, same as 'Ozark Spring'.

'Cherokee Princess'—White with large bracts to 5″ across, early-flowering, heavy-flowering every year, virtually every evaluation places this among the best of the *C. florida* cultivars, Don Shadow calls it the *best*; Pair, Kansas State, reported good hardiness and the best flowering of clones tested at Wichita, KS over 3 seasons, full bract development in Wichita averaged only 38%, compared to 65% for KS 75-66 , which is now called 'Ozark Spring'; also in evaluations at Crossville, TN showed high resistance to spot anthracnose and canker, with individual bracts over 2″ long, introduced by J.C. Higden, Mayfield, KY, have read that Hawkersmith and Sons, Tullahoma, TN was the introducer.

Cherokee Sunset™—Pinkish red-tipped new growth, matures to green with a broad irregular margin of yellow that will not burn in the heat of summer, fall color ranges from pink through red to purple, the bracts are a good red, excellent vigor and resistance to anthracnose, performed well in Athens, Commercial Nursery introduction, Decherd, TN, plant patent 6305.

'Cloud 9'—Slow-growing with showy white overlapping bracts, profusely flowering when young, spreading habit, considered one of the best and Pair rated it one of the most cold hardy, this has been a solid performer in the Southeast, susceptible to spot anthracnose, resistant to canker, Chase Nursery, Chase, AL.

'Compacta'—Dwarf plant reaching 4′ tall in 8 to 10 years.

'De Kalb Red'—Semi-dwarf habit, bracts wine red, named for De Kalb Nursery, Norristown, PA.

'Fastigiata'—Maintains upright habit only while young; have seen a large specimen at Bernheim Arboretum and the branches were fairly erect although some of the outer branches were starting to spread, white bracts, originated at Arnold Arboretum.

'Fayetteville Columnar'—Slow-growing, not particularly columnar, information derived from a 4-10-90 letter by Dick Bir, NCSU, Fletcher, NC.

'First Lady'—Variegated yellow and green foliage, a bit difficult to work into the common landscape, more vigorous than 'Welchii' and does not tend to "burn," but loses most of its variegation in Zone 7b, white flowers, resistant to spot anthracnose and canker.

'Fragrant Cloud'—White flowers, profuse, similar to 'Cloud 9', slightly fragrant, described as gardenia and honeysuckle fragrance, moderately resistant to spot anthracnose and canker.

'Geronimo'—Red barked selection.

'Gigantea'—Large-flowered form, flower bracts 6″ from tip-to-tip, found on Long Island.

'Green Glow'—Listed as fastest growing of all dogwoods, upright, tight and compact, single white, heavy-flowering, leaves with interesting light green blotches surrounded by darker green margin, red and pink fall color, 15′ by 10′, mutation of 'Welchii', I doubt the fastest growing accolade.

'Golden Nugget'—Bronzy gold-margined leaves more vigorous than 'Welchii', white bracts.

'Hillenmeyer'—Outstanding early blooming white-bracted form.

'Hohman's Gold'—Variegated golden yellow and green foliage that turns deep red in fall; fall color is spectacular, yellowish areas lighter red (almost rose) than green areas.

'Imperial White'—Large, white bracts, "flower" diameter to 6″, from Raleigh, NC area.

'Junior Miss'—A rather attractive, large-flowered form, the outer portion of the bracts a deep pink grading to whitish in the center; grew next to 'Cherokee Chief' in the University's Botanical Garden and made the latter pale by comparison; it also contracted no bract spotting (anthracnose) while 'Cherokee Chief' was heavily infected, resistant to canker; 'Welch's Junior Miss' is the often used name.

'Magnifica'—Flower bracts white, about 4″ from tip-to-tip, from Long Island.

'Mary Ellen'—Flowers double, white.

'Miss Marion'—Double-bracted form selected by Bill Craven, Twisted Oaks Nursery, Waynesboro, GA.

'Moon'—Form with unusually large bracts; very floriferous.

'Multibracteata'—Double form.

'Mystery'—Bracts white with reddish spots; compact habit, 14′ by 12′, resists drought, dark green foliage.

'New Hampshire'—Hardy, white-bracted clone from Atkinson, NH; gave a talk in New Hampshire several years back and we had a lively discussion on whether this tree still existed; consensus was no!

'October Glory'—A selected strain of own-rooted pink dogwood with brilliant red fall color, a Princeton introduction.

'Ozark Spring'—Introduced by Dr. John Pair, Kansas State, for excellent flower bud hardiness, white bracts, in a 3 year evaluation, 65% of buds developed fully, also this had the best appearance (condition) rating, formerly KS 75-66, survived -22 to -24°F in laboratory cold hardiness tests.

'Pendula'—Weeping form with stiffly pendulous branches and white flowers; may come true-to-type from seed; original clone was raised in Meehan's nursery, Philadelphia before 1880; not a particularly attractive weeping form; in my estimation there are several weeping forms in the trade.

'Pink Autumn'—Bronze-red new growth, variegated leaf, red flowers.

'Pink Flame'—Bracts pink, selected from a sport of *C. florida* var. *rubra*, leaves green in center, cream-white on outside, with pink margins showing yellow coloration in late months, introduced by Mel Wills, Fairview, OR.

'Pink Sachet'—Similar to 'Cherokee Chief' but with pronounced fragrance to flowers resembling gardenia, honeysuckle and sweetshrub, from Raleigh, NC area.

'Plena'—Double white form, catch-all term for double types.

f. *pluribracteata* Rehd. ('Pluribracteata')—A "double" form with 7 to 8 large bracts and many aborted smaller ones, this to my aesthetic senses is one of the better "double flowering" dogwoods, flowers later than the species, flowers have greater staying power and are not ugly like certain double-flowered plants, leaves are large, robust, lustrous dark green and turn excellent red-purple in fall, Tennessee evaluation test listed this as *immune* (exceptionally strong word for a scientist to use) to spot anthracnose and moderately resistant to canker.

'Poinsett'—Compact, vigorous-growing form; yellow berries in center of red fall leaves gives this cultivar its name, introduced by Pete Girard, Geneva, OH.

'Prairie Pink'—Light pink blush flowers, cold hardy.

'President Ford'—A fast-growing, multi-colored yellow and green form; the foliage of which remains effective until after 3 or 4 killing frosts, discovered at Verkade's Nursery, Wayne, NJ in 1968.

var. *pringlei*—The white bracts are usually fused at the tips and resemble Chinese Lanterns, from Sierre Madre, Mexico.

'Prosser' ('Prosser Red')—Bracts dark red, slow to flower, found in the wild on the Prosser Property, near Knoxville, TN.

'Purple Glory'—A purple-leaved form that holds this color through the growing season; in October the leaf color is a dark, almost black-purple; dark red flowers, moderately resistant to spot anthracnose, susceptible to canker, plant patent 4627, Boyd Nursery introduction.

var. *pygmaea* or 'Pygmaea'—Considerable confusion exists within this taxon; there are several (many?) dwarf clones in cultivation; essentially they are rounded to globose and have excellent dark green foliage; some flower, others do not; degree of dwarfness varies for one plant at Longwood Gardens is a good 6 to 8' high; not a bad plant for effect; white bracts.

'Rainbow'—Variegated deep yellow and green; turns carmine red in fall, white bracts in spring, 20' by 20', found by A. Mazzilli, Canton, OH, a chimera of a stump sprout.

Red Beauty®—Semi-dwarf, dark green leaves, densely branched, symmetrical habit, bright red floral bracts, has not overwhelmed in the Dirr garden, bract color is not as deep as described, Rutgers introduction, plant patent 8214.

'Red Cloud'—Bracts pink, leaves with crinkled margins.

'Red Giant'—Bracts red with white tips.

'Reddy'—Flowers and leaves red.

'Redleaf'—Bracts red, leaves remain reddish year-round.

'Rich-red'—Red-flowered form.

'Roberts Pink'—A vigorous-growing pink dogwood for the deep South, from Louisiana.

'Rose Valley'—With light pink bracts.

'Royal Red'—New foliage opens blood red, turns red in fall; flowers are deep red and very large, a splendid tree at the Arnold Arboretum was misidentified by this author as 'Cherokee Chief' until I checked the label, the color was terrific, on May 3, 1991 it was in full flower and was still strikingly effective on May 13, from Winchester, TN area.

var. *rubra* André ('Rubra')—Pink to pinkish red flowers, considerable variation in color; the history of this variety is not clear but it was apparently first discovered in Virginia; it is a beautiful plant when properly grown; the flowers are not as cold hardy as the white form (at least those from northern sources); during the winter of 1976–77 and 77–78 when the outer bracts of many of the white trees were injured, the entire flower (4 bracts) was killed on the pink form; tends to open a few days later than the typical white form; Dr. Pair corroborates my evaluations of flower bud hardiness for in the Wichita, KS tests var. *rubra* averaged only 4% full bract development, moderately susceptible to spot anthracnose, resistant to canker.

'Salicifolia' ('Boyd's Willowleaf')—Whether these two names are synonymous is a moot question; 'Salicifolia' is a small, mounded tree, the leaves being very narrow and willow-shaped, it has a rather fine texture and to my knowledge does not flower, observed many years past at Bernheim, for the collector.

'September Dog'—Flowers in September, rather than spring, flower buds begin to develop in August but instead of entering dormancy, continue to mature and flower, no fruits are formed.

Spring Grove™—Large white bracts (5" diameter), often 2 to 3 terminal flower buds, heavy fruit set, medium green leaves turn reddish purple in fall, parent plant 22' by 32' at 45 years of age, survived –26°F, originated as a seedling at Spring Grove, Cincinnati.

'Spring Song'—Deep rose red flowers, originated in New Canaan, CT.

'Springtime'—Selection from Spring Grove, Cincinnati, large white overlapping bracts, 5" across tip-to-tip, one of the very beautiful forms, Kansas tests showed it to be minimally wood and flower bud hardy, resistant to spot anthracnose, moderately resistant to canker, selected in 1957 by the late E.C. Kern, Wyoming, OH.

'Steele's Fastigiate'—Upright branching form with darker green foliage and larger flowers than typical.

'Sterling Silver'—Non-burning, cream-margined selection with white bracts, introduced by Don Shadow.

'Stokes Pink'—Pink bracts, on a medium size upright tree, good in warm climates.

'Sweet Charlotte'—As yet an undefined selection.

'Sweetwater Red'—Deep red flowers and reddish foliage, good red-purple fall color, faster growing and more upright than 'Rubra', 20' by 15', selected in 1954 by Howell Nursery, Knoxville, TN.

'Tricolor'—White bracts, leaves with white irregular margin, flushed rose-pink, turning purple in fall with rose-red margins.

subsp. *urbiniana* (Rose) Rickett (same as var. *pringlei*?)—Leaves with bluish cast, pink petioles, exceptionally large white flowers and red fruits, bracts fused at their tips in Chinese Lantern shape, seed collected from Nuevo Leon, Mexico, 4000′ altitude, Zone 7 to 9?

'Variegata'—White- and green-variegated leaves, white bracts.

'Weaver's White'—Large white bracts, unique foliage, does well in deep South, stronger and larger foliage, numerous flowers.

'Welchii'—Leaves are a combination of green, creamy white and pink; stands out in a crowd; definite clashing of color; best in partial shade; spectacular rose red to red-purple fall color; white bracts.

'Welch's Bay Beauty'—Particularly handsome white double form with flowers like *Gardenia*; 7 sets of whorled bracts, 4.5 to 5.5″ diameter, performs better in South, holds leaves longer and develops good autumn color, 20′; probably not as hardy as 'Pluribracteata'; found in Alabama.

'White Bouquet'—Heavy and consistent display of large pure white bracts on a compact plant.

'White Cloud'—Numerous creamy white flowers especially when plant is very young.

'White Giant'—Large white bracts.

'Williams Red'—A deep rose red-flowering form for the deep South.

'Willsii'—Leaves gray-green with white margins; leaves somewhat puckered.

Wonderberry®—Vigorous, large, leathery dark green leaves, each white bract has a spot of red at tip, heavy crops of large tubular bright red fruits, up to 3/4″ long, Rutgers introduction, plant patent 8213.

'World's Fair'—Bracts white, produced at an early age, stocky trunk, large diameter limbs, drought resistant, reasonably good flower bud hardiness.

f. *xanthocarpa* Rehd. ('Xanthocarpa')—Yellow-fruited form; again several clones in cultivation; the stems show no trace of red pigment and I suspect the fall color would be yellowish, although 'Poinsett' counters this supposition.

PROPAGATION: Seed, dormant embryo, 90 to 120 days at 41°F. Major seedling producers clean the fruits of pulp, sow in fall, with germination in spring. Dogwood seedlings do not tolerate excess moisture. Cuttings, softwood, collected immediately after the flowering period ended, rooted readily in three weeks; softwood cuttings collected in June rooted 56% in sand under mist, when treated with 10000 ppm IBA, quick dip, after 8 weeks; this same clone rooted 93% in peat:perlite under mist in 10 weeks with the same hormonal treatment; apparently, the acidity of the medium influenced the degree of rooting since other factors were constant. Also see Savella, "Propagating pink dogwoods from rooted cuttings," *Proc. Intl. Plant Prop. Soc.* 30:405–406 (1980). One of the most important aspects is to allow the rooted cuttings to go through a dormant period and when growth ensues then pot them. Most trees are produced by budding which is accomplished in the summer utilizing seedling understock. Considerable emphasis on tissue culture propagation of *C. florida*, *C. kousa*, their hybrids, and *C. nuttallii*. How many plants are actually produced is unknown. Two references that might prove valuable to propagators are R.N. Trigiano et al., "Micropropagation of dogwoods (*Cornus* spp.)," p.81–90, Y.P.S. Bajaj (ed.), *Biotechnology in Agriculture and Forestry*, vol 20 (1992), Springer-Verlag, Berlin; and *HortScience* 29:1355–1356 (1994) which describes the micropropagation of Pacific Dogwood, *C. nuttallii*.

ADDITIONAL NOTES: A most important ornamental tree in commercial nursery production. Millions of seedlings and budded trees are produced every year. For the gardener, the heavy budded, large bracted cultivars are worth considering. For producers, a paper by Badenhop and Glosgow, *J. Environmental Horticulture* 3(2):49–52 (1985), discusses a production system and costs for propagating dogwoods from softwood cuttings. They estimated a cost of $0.34 per rooted cutting and reported growers in the future will be producing part of their dogwood crop by cuttings.

An excellent Extension publication, *A Guide to the Commercial Propagation of Dogwoods* by Coartney, Lukham and Smeal, 1988, Virginia Tech, Blacksburg, VA, is available. Covers all facets of seed, cutting, budding production.

NATIVE HABITAT: Massachusetts to Florida, west to Ontario, Texas and Mexico. Cultivated 1731.

RELATED SPECIES:

Cornus nuttallii Aud. — Pacific Dogwood
LEAVES: Alternate, simple, elliptic-ovate to obovate, 3 to 5″ long, 1 1/2 to 3″ wide, short acuminate, broad cuneate, dark green, appressed pilose when young, at maturity only beneath or glabrous, 5 to 6 vein pairs; petiole—1/4 to 1/2″ long.

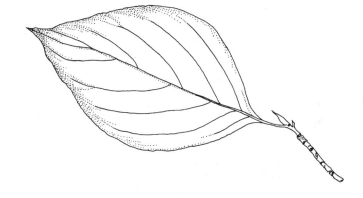

Cornus nuttallii, (kôr′nus nū-tal′ē-ī), Pacific Dogwood, is the West Coast edition of *C. florida* and is a beautiful tree in its own right. The principal difference resides in the flower; the true flowers purple and green, crowded into a dense 3/4″ diameter head; these are surrounded by 4 to 8, usually 6, showy bracts; each bract is oval to obovate, pointed and ranges from 1 1/2 to 3″ long and 1 to 2″ wide; creamy white then white or flushed with pink; the true flowers are not enclosed by the bracts as in *C. florida* and are subject to the vagaries of weather. Fruit is an orange to red, ellipsoidal, 1/3″ long drupe. This is a beautiful dogwood in flower but it does not appear suited to the eastern United States. Susceptible to *Discula* spp., anthracnose, which was reported in 1979 in Washington. 'Corigo Giant' is larger growing and flowered than the species, bracts up to 8″ across, overlapping, with large, heavy-textured, green leaves and wonderful fall color; 'Goldspot' has leaves that are splashed, spotted and mottled with creamy yellow markings and the white bracts are larger than the species. 'Eddie's White Wonder' is the result of a cross between *C. florida* and *C. nuttallii*; it is supposedly better adapted to East Coast conditions than *C. nuttallii* but has not proven that suitable; a large East Coast mail-order nursery firm who specializes in unusual woody plants has dropped this cultivar from its list; the flowers resemble *C. nuttallii* in that the overwintering flowers are not enclosed by the bracts. See *Kew Magazine* 8:71–78 (1991) for a synopsis of *C. nuttallii* in cultivation. Cultivars not described herein include: 'Ascona', 'Colrigo Wonder', 'Monarch', 'North Star', 'Ormonde', 'Pilgrim', and 'Portlemouth'.

I have observed 'Eddie's White Wonder' at the Arnold Arboretum where it was marginally subsistent owing to cold and the uncovered flower buds which appear much more cold susceptible. There is a fine plant at J.C. Raulston Arboretum that could get one excited. It has a distinct upright habit without the layered appearance of *C. florida*. I am skittish about cold hardiness and Dr. Elwin Orton, Rutgers University, reported that *C. nuttallii* flowers "blasted" in Zone 6 (USDA, -10 to 0°F) and plants were not vegetatively hardy. He also mentioned that the flower buds of 'Eddie's White Wonder' were subject to desiccation and/or winterkill in central New Jersey, and floral display was poor. Hybrids between *C. nuttallii* and *C. florida* have resembled *C. nuttallii* and were only marginally winter hardy. Also, as trees increase in caliper, bark split is common on the south and/or southwest side. Hybrids of *C. nuttallii* and *C. kousa* are typically upright in habit with naked flower buds and the usual "blasting" in winter. Vegetatively, plants are more cold hardy than *C. nuttallii* and *C. florida* hybrids but still exhibit bark split. See *Proc. Intl. Plant Prop. Soc.* 35:655–661 (1985) for more details. *Cornus nuttallii* is native from British Columbia to southern California. Introduced 1835. Zone 7 to 9(10) on West Coast.

Cornus kousa (Buerger ex Miq.) Hance — Kousa Dogwood
(kôr′nus koo′så)

LEAVES: Opposite, simple, elliptic-ovate, 2 to 4″ long, 3/4 to 1 3/4″ wide, acuminate, cuneate, dark green above, glaucous and appressed pilose beneath with large axillary fulvous tufts of hairs; petiole—1/4 to 1/2″ long.

BUDS: Flower—Formed at end of stem, fattened and globose at base with 2 valvate silky appressed pubescent bud scales forming a sharp apex; vegetative—valvate, appressed, brownish black, usually longer than those of *C. florida*.

STEM: Slender, light tan with tinges of purple and green, essentially glabrous.

BARK: Exfoliating with age and forming a mottled mosaic of gray, tan and rich brown.

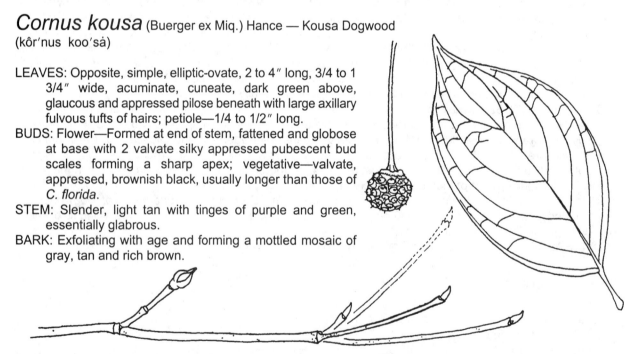

SIZE: About 20 to 30′ in height with an equal spread; can be smaller or larger depending on the area of the country.

HARDINESS: Zone 5 to 8; at one time no one thought this plant could be grown in the South; Callaway Gardens disproved that; flower buds are definitely more cold hardy than those of *C. florida*; should be given a Zone 4b designation; based on numerous evaluations over the years this species is consistently more cold hardy than *C. florida*, however, the winter of 1994 skewed the data, in the Williamstown and Great Barrington, MA areas, reports and visual evidence showed *C. florida* survived, while *C. kousa* was severely injured, the differences might have been related to preconditioning but I doubt it; no legitimate answers for this one except keep your eyes open and write to me.

HABIT: In youth, vase-shaped in habit, with age, forming a rounded appearance with distinct stratified branching pattern; very strong horizontal lines are evident in old age.

RATE: Slow, possibly medium in early stages of growth.

TEXTURE: Medium in leaf and winter character; very handsome in the winter because of horizontal branching character.

BARK COLOR: Older wood often develops multi-colored gray-tan-rich brown areas due to exfoliating nature of the bark.

LEAF COLOR: Dark green, almost blue-green, in summer; foliage changing to reddish purple or scarlet in fall, persisting for 3 to 5 weeks, significant variation in intensity of fall color, leaves of some plants more lustrous than those of others.

FLOWERS: The true flowers are small and inconspicuous and are produced in a 5/8″ diameter, rounded umbel on an upright, 2″ long peduncle that originates from short lateral spurs at the end of a small 2- to 4-leaved twig; the creamy white bracts are the showy part of the inflorescence and are borne in June (mid-May, Athens), approximately 2 to 3 weeks after those of *Cornus florida*; the 4 bracts are taper-pointed, 1 to 2″ long, 1/4 to 3/4″ wide; the flowers, being stalked, are raised above the foliage creating a milky way effect along the horizontal branches; the bracts persist for up to 6 weeks and longer; in the aging process they often become pinkish. Tremendous interest in a pure pink or rose-bracted form but most start white and age to pink; in late June of 1988 at Bodnant Gardens, Wales, I saw a deep rose-pink bracted *C. kousa*; I suspect that the cooler temperatures contribute to more intense rose-pink; have seen more trees in Europe with good pinkish bract color than in the United States; in June 1994 at Savill Gardens, Great Windsor Park, England, 'Satomi' with rich pink bract color was in full flower; may not be as colorful in the heat of the United States; also masquerades under different names like 'Rosabella'.

FRUIT: Drupe, pinkish red to red, borne in a 1/2 to 1″ diameter, globose syncarp (resembles a raspberry in appearance); borne on a 2 to 2 1/2″ long, pendulous stalk; late August through October; edible but somewhat mealy; very effective, a tree with heavy fruit is beautiful.

CULTURE: Transplant balled-and-burlapped or container-grown specimen; considered more difficult to grow than *C. florida* but this is doubtful; fastidious for acid, well-drained soil; well worth the extra cultural efforts needed to successfully grow this plant; requires a relatively sunny location, but still flowers abundantly in light to moderate shade; more drought resistant than *C. florida*.

DISEASES AND INSECTS: None serious, some borer damage reported; resistant to many of the problems that beset *C. florida*, particularly the *Discula destructiva* mentioned under *C. florida*; Holmes and Hibben, *J. Arboriculture* 15:290–291 (1989), reported incidence of *Discula* on *C. kousa* where overhead watering was employed, in an adjacent area with no overhead irrigation *C. florida* was infected, but not *C. kousa*; Smith, *Plant Disease* 78:100 (1994), reported *Discula destructiva* incidence in Connecticut on *C. florida* × *C. kousa* Constellation® and Stellar Pink® along the margins and midribs, severity was not mentioned.

LANDSCAPE VALUE: Handsome small specimen tree or shrub, excellent near large buildings or blank walls, tends to break up harshness with horizontal structure, works well in shrub border or in a foundation planting at the corner of the house; the horizontal lines break up the vertical lines and make the home appear larger; difficult to overuse this plant; the flowers appear in May–June when there is often a paucity of color; perhaps the finest specimens in the United States are located at Longwood Gardens; these 30′ high and 40′ wide trees are low-branched with rather massive trunks, the bark of which has developed the exfoliating characteristics to the maximum; in my travels to Longwood I have seen the plants in flower, fruit, fall color and winter bark and can say that if I had to choose between the best Flowering Dogwood for my garden or one of Longwood's Kousa Dogwoods, I would opt for the latter.

CULTIVARS: It is worth noting that *C. kousa* is variable from seed and I have seen selected seedling populations with immense bracts (3″ long) and fruits (1 to 2″ across); some of these may find their way into the trade in the future.

'Aget'—Large, long-lasting bracts remain to September.

'Akabana'—Has pink bracts; 'Akabana' is the Japanese word for "red flower," which is applied to all pink-flowering kousas; best bract color expressed in light shade and cooler climates; there is some question as to whether this cultivar is distinct from 'Satomi', 'Rosabella' and 'New Red'.

'Amber'—Multi-colored, irregular variegation on small leaves; a slow, open grower; selected by Handy Nursery Co., Portland, OR.

var. *angustata*—Narrow, evergreen leaves (not evergreen or fully hardy in Zone 6 and colder), foliage droops in fall and winter, evergreen but quite shabby in winter as leaves discolor and are wind burned even in Zone 7b, but it is *evergreen*; leaves actually assume purple-red-green coloration in winter, flowers and fruits like the species, provide semi-shade and wind protection, Zone 7 to 9, reports from Texas indicate respectable heat tolerance, choice 20′ by 20′ specimen at Atlanta Botanical Garden. Introduced from China in 1980 by T.R. Dudley of the U.S. National Arboretum. Dr. Frank S. Santamour, Jr. and Dudley proposed to elevate this plant to a separate species, perhaps *C. omeiensis*?

var. *angustata* Prodigy™ ('Ticrn')—New evergreen selection with improved winter foliage color, heavy flower and uniform growth habit; introduced by Tree Introductions, Inc., P.O. Box 5014, Athens, GA 30604.

'Autumn Rose'—Bracts open light green, maturing to soft white, yellow to lime green foliage in spring, light green wavy leaves in summer, fall foliage a metamorphosis of many shades of pink to light red, small upright tree, discovered by Glenda Schmoyer, sister of Gary and Mark Handy.

'Avalanche'—Flowered after -30°F in Crestwood, KY.

'Baby Splash'—A very dwarf tree with small green- and white-variegated leaves; selected by Handy Nursery Co.

'Beni Fuji'—The darkest red of all *C. kousa* cultivars, the dark pink-red bracts are narrow, produced in massive quantities, much deeper red than 'Satomi'.

'Big Apple'—A large spreading tree with heavy-textured, dark green leaves and very large, 1 1/4 to 1 1/2″ diameter fruit, bracts about 5 1/2″ across, hardy to -5°F, a Polly Hill introduction.

'Blue Shadow'—Dark blue-green foliage, reddish in fall, typical flowers and fruits, some white bracts present at fruit ripening, a large-growing form to 30′ high and wide, a Polly Hill introduction.

'Bodnant'—A *chinensis* type cultivar.

'Bon Fire'—Tricolored, variegated foliage (gold, light and dark green), fall color is multi-colored like a bonfire.

'Bush's Pink'—Pink bracts that hold their color well; color resembles that of *C. florida* 'Rubra'; leaves are tinged with crimson; arose as a chance seedling at Richard Bush's Nursery, Canby, OR.

'Camden'—Selected by Mark Stavish, Eastern Plant Specialties, Georgetown, ME, for its abundant flowers and fruits and long flowering period (until fall).

'Cedar Ridge Select'—White bracts turn red at the end of the bloom period; selected by M. Wingle, Cedar Ridge Nursery, Quakertown, PA.

'China Girl'—Early-flowering form, 18 to 24″ high plants set buds, typical flower shape, has very large bracts, good fall color and large fruit; selected in Holland.

var. *chinensis*—According to Wyman and Bean there is not much botanical difference between this form and the species, however, under cultivation the variety grows more freely and the flowers are larger than those of any form; it can grow to 30′; the bracts range from 1 1/2 to 2 1/2″ long, 3/4 to 1″ wide; the fruits as described by E.H. Wilson are sweet and edible; I have sampled the fruits of this variety and the species and can honestly say I prefer Snicker's Bars; the bracts start off a soft green and gradually change to white; certainly one of the most beautiful of all flowering trees; arguably a confused entity and for some clarification please see 'Milky Way'; introduced by E.H. Wilson from Hupeh, China in 1907.

'Doubloon'—Tall, more slender habit, dark green leaves, has more bracts in each cluster than typical, selected by William Devine, Kennedyville, MD in the early 1970's.

'Dr. Bump'—Shrubby habit, precocious and heavy blooming, bark has a flaky appearance.

'Dwarf Pink'—Narrow, light pink bracts, initial habit is upright, fairly vigorous if grafted or budded, should be on own roots to maintain dwarfness, 8′ by 6′, Japanese origin, introduced to the United States by Barry Yinger, Hines Nursery, CA and Carl Hahn, Brookside Gardens, Wheaton, MD.

'Ed Mezitt'—New growth purple, leaves remain bronze until through flowering, maturing dark green, orange-red in fall, bracts overlap, 2 1/2″ across, 3/4 to 1″ diameter fruits, 20′ high and wide, selected in 1970's from open pollinated seeds of *C. kousa* × *C. kousa* var. *chinensis*, named after the late Ed Mezitt, Weston Nurseries, Hopkinton, MA who introduced many great plants, including PJM rhododendrons, into American gardens, original plant named 'Terrace'.

'Elizabeth Lustgarten'—Distinct weeping tendency to upper branches, forms graceful rounded crown, leading branches weep 2′ from highest point of curve, 7′ high and 4 to 5′ wide after 12 years, selected by Jim Cross from seedlings grown by Baier Lustgarten, at Lustgarten Nurseries, Middle Island, NY, likely a sister plant of 'Lustgarten Weeping'.

'Elmwood Weeper'—A weeper selected by William Devine, may be the same as 'Weaver's Weeping'.

'Endurance'—Long lasting flowers; selected by Weston Nurseries Inc., Hopkinton, MA.

'Fanfare'—Fastigiate habit, rapid-growing, hardy to -20°F; patented by Polly Wakefield, Milton, MA, in 1973, plant patent 3296.

'Gay Head'—Tree of medium size, bracts of different sizes and curved or ruffled, 4 3/4″ by 5 1/4″, fruits 1 to 1 1/4″ diameter, hardy to -5°F; a Polly Hill introduction.

'Girard's Nana'—A dwarf form, 3′ in 8 years, heavy bloomer, selected by Girard's Nursery, Ohio; name invalid because it was in the Latin form after January 1, 1959.

'Gold Cup'—Leaves are slightly concave with a gold center.

'Gold Star'—Foliage splashed with broad central band of gold through spring and summer, will revert to green as is true for many plants with the center variegation, supposedly reddish stems that set off the foliage, bracts are white, I have seen the plant on several occasions and it is quite handsome but appears slow-growing; introduced from Japan by Barry Yinger, Hines Nursery, CA and Carl Hahn, Brookside Gardens, Wheaton, MD; a superior selection.

'Greensleeves'—Wavy, dark green leaves, bracts stay green, symmetrical branching, a fast grower; selected by Polly Wakefield.

'Heart Throb'—Large, red-bracted form, each flower almost 4″ wide, color described as deep red like that of 'Cherokee Chief', forms a wide, rounded head, 20 to 30′ by 20 to 30′, Don Schmidt Nursery, Boring, OR introduction.

'Highland'—Precocious, a very prolific bloomer, flower bracts are creamy white, offered by Girard's Nursery.

'Julian'—Bracts curved up at tips, 1.2″ diameter fruit, excellent fall color; selected by Polly Hill.

'July Jubilee'—Offered by Mellingers Inc., North Lima, OH in 1991.

'Kirkpatrick's Weeping'—Has a more upright habit than other weepers, branches are pendulous.

'Kordes'—Broad, overlapping bracts, a heavy bloomer, selected by Kordes Jungpflanzen, Bilsen, Germany.

'Little Beauty'—Dense habit, typical flowers, red-purple fall color, introduced by NCSU Arboretum (now J.C. Raulston Arboretum) in 1993, seedling from wild collected Korean seed, 3′ high and quite dense in 6 years, sister seedlings were 8 to 15′ high.

'Luce'—Named by Paul Cappiello after Roger Luce, Newburgh, ME who selected cold hardy seedlings and continued until a reliably cold hardy form was found, survived at -30°F, no other *C. kousa* has.

'Lustgarten Weeping'—Another weeping form; the late Jim Cross, Environmentals, Long Island, told me that this was a beautiful specimen because the flowers are positioned along the weeping stems so that they are directly in view; 12-year-old plant was 10′ wide and 2 to 3′ high; all branches arch over 12 to 15″ above ground; needs to be grafted on a standard to produce a small weeping tree; selected by Jim Cross while visiting Baier Lustgarten Nurseries in New York; likely a sister plant to 'Elizabeth Lustgarten'.

'Madame Butterfly I'—An extremely floriferous plant with flowers borne on long pedicels and bracts turning vertical about the midpoint of their length, giving the appearance of butterflies on the branches, 20′ high after 14 years; selected by David Leach, North Madison, OH.

'Madame Butterfly II'—An apparent second plant with the same name, has very large bracts; given to the U.S. National Arboretum (N.A. 59560) by Peter Chappell in England.

'Marble'—Variegated foliage; introduced by Cedar Ridge Nursery.

'Milky Way'—Cultivar of var. *chinensis* with very floriferous habit; I have witnessed this specimen at Mill Creek Valley Park, Youngstown, OH, and was amazed at the flower and fruit production compared to the species, this was a very broad, bushy form suitable for the small landscape; this may be a commercially manufactured name for the variety; nevertheless it appears more floriferous than the species and for that reason deserves to be mentioned; abundant confusion about the true nature of 'Milky Way' that Dr. Orton straightened out:

> In the 1960's, Wayside Gardens had a field of several thousand seedlings of *C. kousa*, which were grown from seed obtained from many different plants. The seedlings in this field were evaluated for floral characteristics, with primary emphasis on larger floral bracts and precocious flowering. About 15 plants that Mr. Silvieus said were truly outstanding in these characteristics were selected and transplanted to the corner of a field at the 100 acre production nursery Wayside Gardens maintained at Perry, Ohio. These selected plants constituted the "stock block" from which scionwood was taken for use in propagating plants of 'Milky Way' by budding.
>
> Thus, an "original" 'Milky Way' plant traces to any one of approximately fifteen different seedlings resulting from seed collected from many open-pollinated plants. Present day "seedlings of 'Milky Way'" would thus be open-pollinated seedling propagules of any one of those approximately 15 original open-pollinated (self-sterile) seedlings, and one would expect them to be highly variable.
>
> So, what is the purpose of this story? Two conclusions are worthy of note. First, the original plant material distributed under the name *C. kousa* var. *chinensis* 'Milky Way' was not a single clonal cultivar; rather, it was a

mixture of approximately 15 different clones, the parent plants of which were selected on the basis of floral traits.

Second, even a listing of "Seedlings of 'Milky Way'" apparently has market appeal today. This is strong testimony to the power, or value, of name recognition. Clearly, this is why many plant introductions have been patented in recent years with absurd, or nonsensical, cultivar names and trademarked under a second, and more potentially appealing, name. A registered trademark, if properly used, can be renewed every 10 years; this allows the plant originator (inventor) to earn revenue as a result of name recognition long after the 17 years [now 20] of protection provided by a plant patent runs out. 'Milky Way' was not patented or trademarked, but the fact that open-pollinated seedlings of the original mixture of approximately 15 different clones have sales appeal clearly illustrates the importance of name recognition of plant material within the nursery industry.

'Milky Way Select'—A selected seedling of 'Milky Way' introduced by Knight Hollow Nursery Inc., Middleton, WI.

'Moonbeam'—Flowers 7 to 8″ in diameter, on long peduncles inclined so blooms are visible at eye level; plant hardy to -20°F; 15 to 25′ high; selected and patented by Polly Wakefield.

'Moonlight'—Large bracts equal in size to those of 'Moonbeam' but not as floppy; a Polly Wakefield selection.

'National'—Large creamy white bracts on a vigorous vase-shaped tree, fruits are larger than normal, up to 1 to 1 1/2″ wide, 25 to 30′ by 20′.

'Nell Monk'—Large broad bracts overlap at their edges, extremely floriferous, grown from seed collected at Nymans, England in 1968 and registered in 1987.

'New Red'—See 'Satomi'.

'Pollywood'—Large, late-flowering tree, long-lasting flowers; selected by Polly Hill.

'Prolific'—White-flowered bracts in June, slightly hardier than *C. florida*; selected by Grootendorst and Sons, Boskoop, Holland in 1968.

'Radiant Rose'—Pink bracts; stems and leaves develop interesting red coloration; in autumn leaves turn rich red; to 25′; may be the same as 'Satomi'.

Raulston Selection—An evergreen form grown from seed of *C. kousa* that was wild collected by the late J.C. Raulston; to date no name has been applied.

'Repeat'—Has a second bloom period in late summer; selected by Richard Bush's Nursery.

'Repeat Bloomer'—Produces large white bracts over an extended time; selected by J.G. Marano Jr., Doylestown, PA.

'Rochester'—Large showy bracts, a vigorous grower; introduced by Hoogendorn Nursery Inc., Newport, RI.

'Rosabella'—A fine rose pink bract form that was offered through Wayside Gardens; the same as 'Satomi'.

'Rubra'—Selected by Henry J. Hohman, Kingsville Nursery, Kingsville, MD (circa 1950) but never listed in the nursery's catalogs.

'Satomi'—Listed more times in nursery catalogs than any cultivar outside of 'Milky Way'; in England it was a respectable rose pink, however, has not been as vibrant in the United States; various nurseries listed the bract color as red, rich pink, pink to red, carmine red, "red," deep pink, bright rose red, either they are all correct by virtue of growing the plant in different geographical areas and varying cultural conditions or nobody has seen it flower and decided to pick a color; same as 'Rosabella'.

'Schmetterling'—White bracts; selected by C. Esveld, Boskoop, Holland.

'Select'—Large bracts and fruits, large lustrous dark green flat-planar leaves, vigorous grower; selected from a seedling block at Select Trees, Inc., Oconee County, GA.

'Silver Cup'—White bracts curve upward to form an open silver cup; drought resistant; a Polly Wakefield selection.

'Silverstar'—Plant has upright arching, vase-shaped growth habit; smooth exfoliating bark; hardy to -20°F; selected and patented by Polly Wakefield in 1972, plant patent 3261.

'Snowbird'—Sturdy, compact form, grows 10′ in 25 years, bracts and fruits somewhat small; a Polly Hill selection.

'Snowboy'—The gray-green leaf has a creamy white, narrow to moderate margin with occasional splashes of yellow throughout the leaf; again, not a particularly stable form and not particularly vigorous, pretty in leaf particularly in the shade of pines, very slow-growing, foliage may scorch in full sun; introduced from Japan by Barry Yinger, Hines Nursery, CA and Carl Hahn, Brookside Gardens, Wheaton, MD.

'Snow Flake'—A selection of the var. *chinensis* type.

'Southern Cross'—Cream-white bracts, dense green foliage, vivid red in autumn, more restrained growth habit, 10 to 12′ high, from New Zealand.

'Speciosa'—Dark green leaves curling slightly at margins impart an interesting bicolor effect, large white bracts; selected by J. Blaauw & Co., Lincroft, NJ in the 1950's.

'Spinners'—A var. *chinensis* type.

'Square Dance'—Upright growth habit with flowers most visible from above, bracts 4 3/4″ across, fruits 1 1/4″ diameter, good fall color; hardy to −5°F; a Polly Hill selection named by Pamela Harper for its overlapping bracts which form a square pattern.

'Steeple'—Upright habit, somewhat fastigiate, glossy deep green foliage, good fall color; selected by Polly Hill.

'Summer Games'—Variegated foliage; selected by Weston Nurseries.

'Summer Majesty'—Abundant white bracts flushed with pink as the mature, effective up to 8 weeks, larger growing selection, 20 to 25′ high; selected by Mitsch Nursery, Aurora, OR and named by Diane Fincham.

'Summer Stars'—Bracts hang on up to 6 weeks after the initiation of flowering; the fruits supposedly develop with the bracts still present; dark green foliage changes to reddish purple in fall, not as good as the advertising; moderate vase shape, 25′ by 18′; have always seen Princeton Nurseries name attached to this cultivar but recently read where Peter Costitch was the introducer, plant patent 3090 in 1972.

'Sunsplash'—Bright yellow- and green-variegated foliage, slow-growing, good fall color.

'Temple Jewel'—Lightly variegated foliage of green, gold and light pink, color bold on new growth, older foliage reverts to green with a light green edge, white bracts, red fruits, dense habit, 20 to 30′; selected by Brotzman's Nursery, Madison, OH.

'Ticknor's Choice'—Bracts start out light green, turning white and then reverting to green; orange, red and pink fall color; selected by Dr. Robert L. Ticknor, retired, North Willamette Research & Extension Center Station, Aurora, OR.

'Trinity Star'—New growth is mottled pink, green and white, a heavy flowerer, moderate growth rate, develops a flat top; 12′ by 12′; a Handy Nursery Co. selection.

'Triple Crown'—Small plant with a dainty habit, may bloom in clusters of three, floriferous, hardy to −20°F; patented by Polly Wakefield in 1973, plant patent 3387.

'Twinkle'—Habit upright, compact, flowers with 6 to 9 bracts, wine red fall color; patented by Polly Wakefield in 1973, plant patent 3386.

'Variegata'—There is probably more than one variegated form in cultivation; the one plant I have seen at the Arnold Arboretum is rather unstable and the white marked leaves may revert to green; report from Boston in *Proc. Intl. Plant Prop. Soc.* 46:578 (1996) reported this form has same vigor as *C. kousa*, variegation is good in sun or shade, and fall color is excellent with cream edges turning rosy pink.

'Victory'—Similar to 'Madame Butterfly', bracts are curved upward in cup form, floriferous; selected by Jon Arnow, Alpine Distributors, Fairfield, CT.

'Weaver's Weeping'—Exceptionally heavy flower display on strongly weeping branches.

'Weisse Fontane'—White bracts, weeping; selected by C. Esveld, Boskoop, Holland.

'Wilton'—Flower bracts more persistent than typical; originally named 'Wiltoni'; introduced by Hoogendorn Nursery.

'Wolf Eyes'—Prominent white-margined leaves on a compact spreading plant, less susceptible to burning than most variegated dogwoods, outstanding pink to red fall color, slower growing, more shrubby, parent plant 6′ high and 6′ wide, does best in partial shade, have seen this at Manor View Farm, the introducer, Monkton, MD, and was impressed by the quality and apparent stability of the variegation; originated as a branch sport at Manor View Farm, Monkton, MD.

'Xanthocarpa'—Yellow-fruited form; originated in Holland before 1960.

PROPAGATION: Cuttings, somewhat more difficult to root than *C. florida* but various investigators have been able to achieve 50% success from softwood cuttings treated with IBA; from my own experience, softwood cuttings collected in June rooted 50% with 10000 ppm IBA-quick dip when placed in peat:perlite under mist after 12 weeks; all cuttings had callused and possibly would have rooted with increasing time; best not to disturb cuttings after rooting; seed is easily germinated and requires 3 months at 41°F.

ADDITIONAL NOTES: Dr. Elwin Orton, Rutgers University, has conducted outstanding work in woody ornamental plant breeding with *Ilex* and *Cornus*. I present information relative to crosses between *C. florida*, *C. kousa*, and *C. nuttallii*. For full article see *Proc. Intl. Plant Prop. Soc.* 35:655–661 (1985). Dr. Orton's goals were increased vigor, borer resistance, pink bracts perhaps on *C. kousa*. The best of his crosses produced six clones of *C. kousa* × *C. florida*. Four are intermediate in floral display and anthesis (flower opening) with the upright habit (in youth) of *C. kousa*. Three have white bracts; one soft pink bracts. The fifth clone resembles *C. florida* with a low-spreading habit of growth and floral display sufficiently early to overlap plants of *C. florida*. The bracts of all are intermediate in shape to those of the parents. Interestingly, the floral bracts do not enclose the true flowers as tightly as either parent. Many are more vigorous than the parents, i.e., display hybrid vigor and are highly resistant to dogwood borer. Vegetatively they have been winter hardy at New Brunswick, NJ although some floral bract injury has occurred following a severe winter.

These hybrids are known as the Stellar® series and have been patented, trademarked and DNA fingerprinted. Their introduction was fortuitous as it coincided with the emergence of the dogwood anthracnose, *Discula distructiva*, that injured or killed numerous *C. florida*. The Stellar® series is highly resistant but there has been one report of *Discula* infection on leaves of Constellation® and Stellar Pink® [*Plant Disease* 78:100 (1994)]. I have visited Dr. Orton and observed the parent plants at Rutgers. They are vigorous, essentially sterile, clean foliaged trees.

The habit on young trees is more open and flower bud set is not as heavy as the better forms of *C. florida*. All cultivars flowered sporadically after 3 years in Georgia field tests. Leaves are dark green in summer, heat resistant and turn reddish purple in fall. Cold hardiness has not been tested to any degree but a report from Louisville, KY by Mike Hayman noted that young trees exposed to −22°F flowered, but the same plants showed some wood (stem) dieback at −30°F.

The following descriptions are taken from Orton, *Proc. Intl. Plant Prop. Soc.* 43:487–490 (1993). Plant descriptions appear based on time of flower from earliest to latest.

Cornus 'Rutlan', PP 7732, Ruth Ellen®—Plants of Ruth Ellen® are similar to plants of *C. florida*. They are low and spreading rather than upright as with young plants of *C. kousa*. At 19 years, the original seedling was 18′ tall, had a uniform spread of 22′, and was densely branched close to the ground. The period of floral display of Ruth Ellen® slightly overlaps the last day or two of the floral display of most plants of *C. florida*. At the peak of the floral display, the trees are brilliant white in appearance and very showy even from a distance.

Cornus 'Rutfan', PP 7206, Stardust®—Plants of this cultivar are similar to the *C. florida* parent as the general form is low and horizontal but they are much smaller than plants of Ruth Ellen®. The plants are heavily branched to the ground like a hedge. At 19 years, the original seedling was 11′ tall with a uniform spread of 19′. The floral display of Stardust® typically starts one day later than that of Ruth Ellen®. The white floral bracts of Stardust® are obovate with an acute tip. The bracts are distinctly separate and do not overlap. Although plants of this cultivar are low and densely foliaged, evidence of infection by *Discula* has not been observed.

Cornus 'Rutcan', PP 7210, Constellation®—Plants of Constellation® are erect in habit and much more vigorous than plants of *C. kousa*, but do not exhibit the vase-shaped habit typical of young plants of *C. kousa*; that is, the plants branch low and are uniformly wide from base to top. The floral display commences two days after that of Ruth Ellen®, and is quite spectacular even when viewed from a distance. At 19 years, the original seedling was 21′ tall and 17′ wide. The white floral bracts are obovate with an acute tip. Both the inner and outer (lower) floral bracts are separate with no overlap and are significantly longer than are the floral bracts of Stardust®.

Cornus 'Rutdan', PP 7204, Celestial™ (formerly Galaxy)—This hybrid is vigorous and erect in habit, exhibiting a uniform width rather than the vase-shape of young plants of *C. kousa*. The floral display commences four to five days after that of Ruth Ellen®. The expanded floral bracts are white with a tinge of green and form a small cup early in the season. However, the bracts flatten and become pure white in a few days. Bracts are obovate to nearly rounded with an acute tip and a base broadly tapered. Margins of adjacent bracts often touch but do not overlap. At 19 years, the original seedling was 17′ tall and 14′ wide.

Cornus 'Rutban', PP 7205, Aurora®—Plants of Aurora® are very vigorous, erect in habit, and uniformly wide throughout. They are also very floriferous. The period of floral display is about the same as that of Celestial™. The floral bracts are white and provide a heavily textured, velvety appearance, and become creamy white as they age. They are nearly rounded to obovate with a broad, tapering base and an acute tip. The margins of the basal one-third of adjacent bracts typically overlap. At 19 years, the original seedling measured 18′ tall and 18′ wide.

Cornus 'Rutgan', PP 7207, Stellar Pink®—Plants of Stellar Pink® are very vigorous and erect in habit. They branch low and are uniformly wide throughout, as opposed to the vase-shaped habit typical of young plants of *C. kousa*. The period of floral display of the bracts is similar to that of Celestial™ and Aurora®. The rounded, overlapping bracts are a soft pink in color and have a nice textured appearance. From a distance, the pink bracts are not as showy as the dark red bracts of good clones of *C. florida*. However, they provide a very attractive display when viewed more closely. At 19 years, the original seedling was 20′ tall and 19′ wide.

For purposes of comparison, 26-year-old plants of *C. florida* 'Springtime' and 'Sweetwater' in the Rutgers performance trial measured 10′ tall by 16′ wide and 12′ tall by 19′ wide, respectively.

The six hybrids of the Stellar® series listed above represent Rutgers University's answer to "dogwood decline." New intra- and inter-specific hybrids of the large bracted dogwoods will be introduced from Rutgers University in the succeeding years.

Orton also mentions that the *C. kousa* genetic base from the original introductions was so narrow that plants show inbreeding depression, i.e., reduced vigor, rounded compact habit of growth, spindly branches and small leaves. Seed should be collected from open pollinated seedlings rather than a single isolated clone.

NATIVE HABITAT: Japan, Korea, China. Introduced 1875.

RELATED SPECIES:

Cornus capitata Wallich., (kôr′nus kap-i-ta′tà), Bentham's Cornel, is a large evergreen shrub or small tree of exceptional beauty in flower and fruit. Supposedly plants can reach 50′ high, but those that I have seen were in the 10 to 20′ range. At Blarney Castle, Ireland, a small plant produced heavy flowers, cream-yellow, perched like butterflies arching upward at their middle forming a cup-like composite of the obovate to oblanceolate bracts (June). On a March visit, the same plant was heavy with 1″ diameter, scarlet, rounded to strawberry-shaped, fleshy fruits. The color reminded of the fruits of *Arbutus unedo*. A small plant in my garden has been consistently thrashed by the Zone 7b winters. 'Mountain Moon' is the first named selection of the species. Introduced via Piroche Plants, British Columbia; a small plant in my possession looks like the species. Introduced 1825. China, Himalayas. Probably best on West Coast in Zone 8 and 9. Also, relatively new to the United States is *Cornus omeiensis* an evergreen species with coppery red new growth, glossy green leaves, that turn reddish purple in winter and creamy white bracts in June. Summer Passion™ is the name given to a clone introduced by Piroche Plants, Pitt Meadows, British Columbia. One nurseryman thought it similar to *C. kousa* var. *angustata*. Zone 8 to 9.

Cornus kousa × ***Cornus capitata*** hybrids

Another unknown dogwood until a June 1992 visit to Hillier Arboretum where 'Norman Hadden' was in full flower and the cream-white bracts were aging to pink. The tree was 20 to 25′ high and wide with gracefully arching branches that positioned the flowers so they looked at the passers by (do flowers look?). The bracts are taper-pointed and the bark exfoliates like *C. kousa* while the leaves are at least semi-persistent owing to the *C. capitata* influence. Hardiness and disease resistance are unknown in the United States. Also from similar parentage is 'Porlock', a small, spreading tree that arose in the garden of Norman Hadden, West Porlock, Somerset, England. Probably Zone (6)7 to 8.

Cornus macrophylla Wallich. — Bigleaf Dogwood

LEAVES: Opposite, simple, ovate to elliptic-ovate, 4 to 7″ long, 2 to 3 1/2″ wide, acuminate, rounded at base, dark green above and slightly rough, grayish green beneath with appressed pubescence, 6 to 8 vein pairs; petiole—1/4 to 1 1/2″ long.

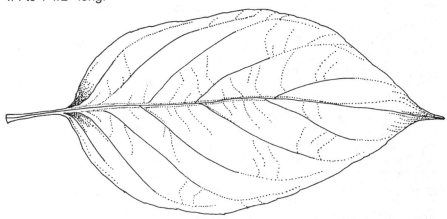

Cornus macrophylla, (kôr′nus mak-rō-fil′á), Bigleaf Dogwood, is virtually unknown in the United States but might be worth a close inspection. It is a small tree of essentially rounded outline that will grow 25 to 35′ high. Based on observations at the Arnold Arboretum, this tree might have possibilities in dry soils and could perhaps be adapted to street tree or large outdoor container use. The large, 4 to 6″ diameter, cymose-like panicles of yellowish white flowers occur in July and August at a time when precious few other trees show any color. The 1/4″ diameter, globose fruits color reddish purple and at maturity are blackish purple. In most respects the fruits are similar to *C. alternifolia*. The bark is a relatively smooth gray with maturity becoming gray-brown and shallowly ridged-and-furrowed. Interestingly it roots readily from softwood cuttings; July 28 cuttings produced tremendous root systems (100% rooting) when treated with 4000 ppm IBA-quick dip and placed in sand:perlite under mist. Gary Koller, Arnold Arboretum, believes this tree could be a valuable addition to the list of urban trees. Himalayas, China, Japan. Introduced 1827. Zone 5 to 7.

Cornus mas L. — Corneliancherry Dogwood
(kôr′nus más)

LEAVES: Opposite, simple, ovate to elliptic, 2 to 4″ long, 3/4 to 1 1/2″ wide, acute to acuminate, broad-cuneate at base, appressed-pilose on both sides, dark green above, with 3 to 5 pairs of veins; petiole—about 1/4″ long.
BUDS: Flower—borne in axillary position, appear stalked, valvate, globose, without sharp apex, yellow-green-brown in color, appressed pubescence; vegetative—valvate, more divergent than other dogwood vegetative buds, greenish with silky appressed pubescence.
STEM: Slender, angled on young stems, usually red above, green below, branches minutely appressed-pilose; pith—white, solid.

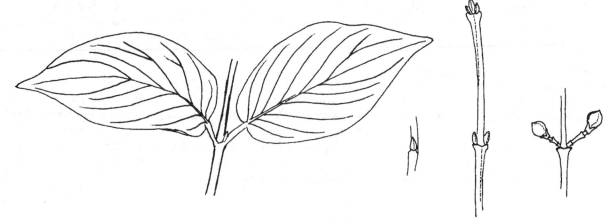

SIZE: 20 to 25′ in height by 15 to 20′ in width, from edition to edition I change my mind relative to size, plants wider than high occur, several large plants by the Georgia Tennis Stadium are now 20′ high and 15′ wide, although not given great credence by this author for general performance in the South, there are 4 or 5 gigantic specimens on the Georgia campus that have withstood the test of time.
HARDINESS: Zone 4 to 7(8); generally not as robust in the South and flowers do not appear as large or vivid.
HABIT: Large multi-stemmed shrub or small tree of oval-rounded outline, usually branching to the ground making successful grass culture impossible; it is possible to remove the lower branches and the result is a small tree of rounded habit; excellent way to use this plant; may sucker profusely.
RATE: Medium.
TEXTURE: Medium in foliage and in winter habit.
BARK: Exfoliating, scaly and flaky, often gray-brown to rich brown, rather attractive, not as showy as that of *C. officinalis*.
LEAF COLOR: Dark green, often somewhat glossy, attractive summer foliage; fall color can be purplish red, usually very poor fall color, often the leaves abscise green late in fall.
FLOWERS: Yellow, March (open mid-February in Athens), effective for three weeks or longer, borne in short stalked umbels before the leaves from the axils of the previous season's wood; each flower about 1/6″ diameter; each umbel about 3/4″ diameter, enclosed before opening in four downy boat-shaped bracts; very effective in the early spring landscape for it receives little competition from other flowering shrubs.
FRUIT: Oblong drupe, 5/8″ long and about 1/2″ wide, bright cherry red, July, often partially hidden by the foliage; the fruits are used for syrup and preserves; I have observed specimens with fruit more abundantly

borne than that often found on sour cherry trees; selections have been made for both flower and fruit production; although edible, one must be hungry.

CULTURE: Transplants well when young, move balled-and-burlapped; adaptable as far as soil types and pH are concerned, but prefers rich, well-drained soil; sun or partial shade; I would rate this the most durable of the larger dogwood types for midwestern and eastern conditions.

DISEASES AND INSECTS: None serious, actually a very pest-free plant.

LANDSCAPE VALUE: Shrub border, hedge, screen, foundation planting, around large buildings; optimum effect is achieved if the plant has a dark green or red background so the early, yellow flowers are accentuated; this species is not used enough in the modern landscape; makes an excellent small tree and should be used this way more often.

CULTIVARS:

'Alba'—White-fruited form.

'Aurea'—A rather striking golden foliaged form that is relatively common in English botanical gardens; colorful in June when it literally glows; the color diminishes with the heat of summer; no injury at −30°F, Orono, ME.

'Aureo-elegantissima' ('Elegantissima')—Leaves yellow or with an unequal border of yellow, others tinged with pink; have seen at Hillier Arboretum; rather colorful in June, settles down to yellow-green in summer; weak grower; 'Tricolor' is probably synonymous; introduced before 1872.

'Flava' (var. *flava*)—A yellow-fruited form; the fruits bigger and sweeter than those of the species and ripen ahead of typical species; large, vigorous shrub, 20′ high; no injury at −30°F; have had good (100%) success rooting this clone from August 8 (Boston) collected cuttings, treating with 3000 ppm IBA-quick dip.

'Golden Glory'—An upright, abundant flowered form introduced by the Synnesvedt Nursery Company of Illinois; it has been a good plant for Chicago and the northern Midwest where the choice of early-flowering shrubs is limited; have reports of some cold damage at −20 to −25°F from the Midwest; Cappiello, UMaine, reported complete kill at −30°F.

'Nana'—A compact dwarfish form with closely spaced nodes; could be used for hedging; I have seen several versions of these and view them as curiosities.

'Redstone'—Registered May 16, 1991 by the Arnold Arboretum; selected because of its wide area of adaptation, for its disease and insect resistance, for its longevity, and for its heavy fruit production; this is a seed-produced cultivar and some variation will occur; introduced from National Plant Materials Center, Beltsville, MD.

'Spring Glow'—A bright yellow-flowered form with leathery dark green foliage and lower chill requirement; Raulston reported it the best of six clones tested in Raleigh; should be a good selection for Zone 7 to 8 where the typical species, although vegetatively vigorous, does not flower as profusely as further north; a 2-year-old, 2 1/2′ tall plant was killed to the roots at −30°F (Maine).

'Spring Sun' (formerly 'Spring Grove')—Exceptional leathery lustrous dark green leaves, tree-like form, broad rounded outline and non-suckering habit, abundant bright yellow flowers; from Spring Grove, Cincinnati, OH.

'Variegata'—Leaf margins of irregular creamy white; overall effect if quite striking; largest specimen I have observed is in Bath Botanic Garden, Bath, England, and is a stunner; might have a difficult time in the heat of the South.

In addition to the aforementioned plants, several nurserymen have mentioned upright-growing forms that to date have no cultivar names. 'Pyramidalis'—Narrowly upright, slightly vase-shaped form that appears to be much slower growing than the species (Krüssmann). *Hillier's Manual* (1991) lists 'Hillier's Upright' with a broadly upright habit and 'Macrocarpa' with larger fruit. Bean and Krüssmann list yellowish, purplish, and white-fruited clones.

PROPAGATION: Seed should be stratified in moist medium for 120 days at 68 to 86°F followed by 30 to 120 days at 34 to 56°F; cuttings, softwood, treated with IBA root in high percentages; my successes have not been great but I have rooted the species using June–July cutting wood; Tom Tracz, former undergraduate student of mine, at Elite Growers (18 Sequoia, Hawthorn Woods, IL 60047) propagated 'Golden Glory' from mid to late June using 6 to 8″ long cuttings, 2,000 ppm Woods Rooting Compound, sand and mist; rooting takes six to eight weeks and at its best averages 90 to 95%; Tracz cautioned against excessive heat, water-logged medium, and the use of any fertilizer.

ADDITIONAL NOTES: *Cornus mas* was one of the first shrubs (way ahead of Forsythia) to flower in the Midwest and Northeast; it would have a difficult time competing with the late April and May flowering trees and shrubs but flowering when it does, it is a star; the classic case of being in the right place at the right time.

NATIVE HABITAT: Central and southern Europe and western Asia. Found in dry deciduous forests and brushlands. Cultivated since ancient times.

RELATED SPECIES:

Cornus chinensis Wangerin, (kôr′nus chī-nen′sis), is similar to *C. officinalis* but differs in the whitish pubescence on the underside of the leaves and from both *C. officinalis* and *C. mas* by the long, tapered sepals and black fruits. The flowers are sulfur yellow and more numerous than *C. mas* and the trunk is smooth and palm-like. The leaves can become quite large and can grow to one foot. Central and southern China. Introduced 1950 by Frank Kingdon Ward. Not too hardy. Zone 9.

Cornus officinalis Sieb. & Zucc., (kôr′nus o-fis-i-nā′lis), Japanese Cornel Dogwood, is similar to *C. mas* except, according to the literature, in the dense, rusty colored patches of down in the axils of the veins on the lower surface and the more open habit. It may have more vein pairs (5 to 7). Although not common in arboreta or gardens the Secrest Arboretum has grown a number of plants since 1929. One 46-year-old tree was 22′ high and 35′ wide. Plants there survived temperatures of –20°F. The following comparisons between the two species are based on close scrutinization over the past 20 years. Axillary tufts of brown down do occur on leaves of *Cornus officinalis* but this is not consistent from tree to tree. The bark of *C. officinalis* is much more showy with rich gray, brown and orange colors on the same trunk. *Cornus officinalis* flowers about one week ahead of *C. mas* but the fruits ripen considerably later, usually in September. Fruits of *C. officinalis* are more insipid. Winter buds of *C. officinalis* are covered with rusty brown pubescent. The overall flower effect is superior to *C. mas* and a tree in full flower on a March–April day is a thing of great beauty. The species has performed remarkably well in Athens and adheres to the characteristics outlined above. Almost always opens a consistent 7 to 14 days ahead of *C. mas*. In fact, full flower dates on a plant at the Botanical Garden were recorded February 22, 1992, March 12, 1993, February 26, 1994; no *C. mas* were in flower. Don Shadow has a handsome selection with heavy flowers and excellent bark that was in full flower on February 23, 1994, Winchester, TN. Also saw a clone in a British Columbia garden listed as 'Issai Minari', implying flowering at a young age. 'Kintoki' is smaller growing and heavy-flowering. A plant I viewed in late March 1996 at Wisley Garden, England triggered a "jump the turnstile" response. I have had poor success rooting this species from softwood cuttings (20%). Japan, Korea. Cultivated 1877. Zone 5 to 8.

Cornus racemosa Lam. — Gray Dogwood
(kôr′nus ra-se-mō′så)

LEAVES: Opposite, simple, narrow-elliptic to ovate-lanceolate, 2 to 4″ long, one-half as wide, long acuminate, cuneate, 3 to 4 vein pairs, dark almost gray-green, appressed-pubescent or nearly smooth, glaucous beneath; petiole—1/2 to 3/4″ long.

BUDS: Flower—terminally borne, more plump than vegetative buds, slightly appressed hairy; vegetative—valvate, very small in relation to flower buds, almost hidden by leaf scar.

STEM: Slender, young stems—somewhat angled, tan to reddish brown, essentially glabrous; older stems—decidedly gray; pith—small, white to brown, usually light brown.

FRUIT: Pedicels remain red into late fall and early winter.

SIZE: 10 to 15′ in height by 10 to 15′ in width; actually it is difficult to define the spread of this shrub for it suckers profusely from the roots and forms a large colony extending in all directions from the original plant; this should be considered when employing this plant in the home landscape for it often oversteps its boundaries; national champion is 38′ by 24′ in Oakland, MI.

HARDINESS: Zone 3b to 8.

HABIT: Strongly multi-stemmed, erect-growing, suckering shrub with short, spreading branches toward apex of stems; forms a colony because of suckering nature; occasionally grown as a standard, i.e., small tree; I believe this is a great approach but buyers need to be aware of the suckering problem.

RATE: Slow from old wood, however, shoots which develop from roots grow very fast (3 to 5′ in a season).

TEXTURE: Medium-fine in leaf; medium in winter, almost as interesting and valuable in winter as in the foliage periods.

STEM COLOR: Three-year-old wood or greater is a distinct gray and quite attractive; the first and second year stems are a light reddish brown and form an interesting contrast; the inflorescences are reddish pink and are effective into December; the total winter character is valuable in the landscape.

LEAF COLOR: Dull gray-green to dark green in summer foliage, assuming purplish red tones in fall; fall color is usually not spectacular; could be some worthwhile selections made for fall coloration.

FLOWER: Whitish, late May to early June, borne in 2″ diameter, cymose panicles which terminate almost every stem, effective for 7 to 10 days.

FRUIT: Drupe, white, bluish white, 1/4″ diameter; August into September; effective but inconsistently persistent; actually its greatest ornamental effect is evident after the fruits have fallen when the reddish pink pedicels and peduncle are fully exposed; over 100 birds supposedly savor the fruits.

CULTURE: Fibrous rooted, transplants well; very adaptable, supposedly will withstand wet or dry soils; full shade or sun; however, like many plants grows best in a moist, well-drained situation; performs admirably in the Midwest and East under the most trying of conditions; have observed it in heavy shade along the banks of streams.

DISEASES AND INSECTS: None serious.

LANDSCAPE VALUE: Border, groups, masses, near large buildings, naturalizing, possibly for poor soil areas, excellent fall and winter characteristics.

CULTIVARS:

    Counties of Ohio™—A series of Gray Dogwood introduced by Lake County Nursery. Selections include: Geauga™ ('Geazam'), 8 to 10′ by 4′, black-green leaves, mahogany red new growth; Mahoning™ ('Mahzam'), 10′ by 10′, strong grower, stoloniferous; and Muskingum™ ('Muszam'), 2′ by 4′, low-mounded, gray-green foliage turns brick red in fall. Apparently, additional cultivars are forthcoming.

    'Slavinii' ('Slavin's Dwarf')—Dwarf form with slightly twisted leaves, the nodes closely spaced, 2 to 3′ high with a greater spread due to its suckering nature.

    I have seen a creamy white-variegated leaf sport at a Chicago nursery that might have been a handsome introduction.

PROPAGATION: Seed, possesses hard endocarp and dormant embryo, needs 60 days at fluctuating temperatures of 68 to 86°F followed by 120 days at 41°F in sand or peat. Other pretreatment includes H_2SO_4 for 2 hours plus 120 days stratification at 41°F. Cuttings, softwood rooted 100% in sand in 37 days after treatment with NAA, 1000 ppm talc, and only 8% without treatment; cuttings rooted 66% with 80 ppm IBA dip, and much less without treatment.

NATIVE HABITAT: Maine to Ontario and Minnesota, south to Georgia and Nebraska. Introduced 1758.

Cornus sanguinea L. — Bloodtwig Dogwood, Common Dogwood
(kôr′nus san-gwin′ē-à)

LEAVES: Opposite, simple, broad-elliptic to ovate, 1 1/2 to 3″(4″) long, 3/4 to 1 3/4″ wide, acuminate, rounded or broad-cuneate at base, dark green above, villous on both sides, more densely so and lighter green beneath, with 3 to 5 pairs of veins; petiole—1/8 to 3/4″ long.

BUDS: Flower—terminally borne, pubescent with grayish silky hairs, fatter than vegetative buds which are valvate, appressed, coated with gray, silky, appressed pubescence.

STEM: Slender, appressed hairy, usually purple or dark blood red, often greenish on lower side; older branches greenish gray in color; pith—white.

SIZE: 6 to 15′ in height, with spread ranging from 6 to 15′, variable.

HARDINESS: Zone 4 to 7.

HABIT: A large, unkempt, sloppily dressed, spreading, round-topped, multi-stemmed shrub of a dense, twiggy nature; suckers freely from roots and forms a colony much like *C. racemosa*.

RATE: Slow to medium on old wood, fast on shoots which develop from roots.

TEXTURE: My opinion is somewhat biased, but I would rate it coarse in all seasons; very difficult to blend into the landscape; a proverbial "sore thumb" plant.

STEM COLOR: I have never understood the name bloodtwig for the stems are usually more green than blood red; often the stem portion exposed to the sun is red and the rest is green; Bean noted that the name is derived from its fall color and not the young bark; there is considerable variation in habit and stem color.

LEAF COLOR: Dull dark green in summer changing to blood red autumnal color according to many authorities; this shrub has never shown good fall color as I have observed it and is usually a sickly greenish purple.

FLOWERS: Dull white, of fetid odor, profusely produced in late May to early June in 1 1/2 to 2″ diameter, flat-topped, pubescent cymes, effective 7 to 10 days, the total effect of the flowers is somewhat reduced by the abundant foliage.

FRUIT: Drupe, 1/4″ across, shining purplish black, August–September, almost unnoticeable for they blend in with the dark green foliage.

CULTURE: Fibrous rooted, easily transplanted, very adaptable, supposedly tolerates lime better than other dogwoods; sun or partial shade; needs frequent pruning to keep it clean (presentable).

DISEASES AND INSECTS: None serious.

LANDSCAPE VALUE: Possibly shrub border, massing, screening; definitely not for specimen use or the small residential landscape; too large and clumsy, tends to look out of place with age.

CULTIVARS:

‘Atrosanguinea’—Branches of a deep red color.

‘Midwinter Fire’—Possibly the same as ‘Winter Flame’, if not, very close; red-stemmed at the base grading to orange and yellow toward the tips of the branches; need to cut back in late winter to encourage vigorous shoot growth for coloration is greatest on one-year stems; 8 to 10′ high and greater.

‘Variegata’—Leaves mottled with yellowish white; apparently a number of variegated forms have been in cultivation at various times but are not spectacular.

‘Viridissima’—A rather attractive form with yellowish green winter stems; best color occurs on current year’s growth; Arnold Arboretum had several attractive plants.

‘Winter Flame’ (synonym ‘Winter Beauty’)—Similar to ‘Midwinter Fire’ and I first saw it in Mr. Adrian Bloom’s wonderful garden; stems are fiery orange-yellow at the base and grade to pink and red at the tips, also develops golden yellow fall color; 8 to 10′ high and greater.

PROPAGATION: Cuttings taken in late June rooted 44% without treatment, and 68% in three weeks after treatment with 30 ppm IBA, 12 hour soak; seeds require warm (3 to 5 months) followed by cold (3 months) periods.

NATIVE HABITAT: Europe. Long cultivated.

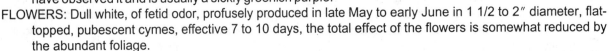

Cornus sericea L. (Formerly *C. stolonifera* Michx. f.) — Redosier Dogwood
(kôr′nus ser-ē′sē-à)

LEAVES: Opposite, simple, ovate to oblong-lanceolate, 2 to 5″ long, 1 to 2 1/2″ wide, acuminate, rounded at base, medium to dark green above, glaucous beneath, with about five pairs of veins; petiole—1/2 to 1″ long.

BUDS: Flower—terminally borne, valvate, hairy, silky-appressed pubescence; vegetative—valvate, appressed, elongated, essentially no difference between this species and *C. alba*.

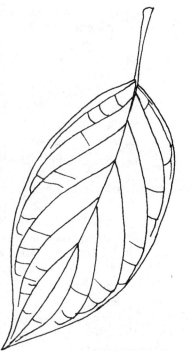

STEM: Slender, upright, bright red to dark blood red, appressed pubescence on younger stems; lenticels similar to *C. alba* except fewer per internode; pith—white, large.

FRUIT: Drupe, white, globose; stone as broad as high or slightly broader, rounded at base.

SIZE: 7 to 9′ in height spreading to 10′ or more; national champion is 26′ by 15′ in White Bird, ID.

HARDINESS: Zone 2 to 7; not performing well in Zone 7b, tolerates neither heat nor humidity, lacks vigor and succumbs to apparent canker.

HABIT: Loose, broad-spreading, rounded, multi-stemmed shrub with horizontal branches at base; freely stoloniferous as it spreads by underground stems.

RATE: Fast, quite vigorous.

TEXTURE: Medium in leaf and in winter.

STEM COLOR: Red, various authorities list the stem color as dark blood red, dark purplish red, brilliant red; very handsome and eye appealing in a winter setting especially with a sprinkling of snow to set off the stem color.

LEAF COLOR: Medium to dark green in summer; purplish to reddish in the fall, fall color is variable but can be an excellent reddish purple.

FLOWERS: Dull white, borne in 1 1/2 to 2 1/2″ diameter, flat-topped cymes in late May to early June, flowers are adequate but not overwhelming; flowering sporadically through summer.

FRUIT: Drupe, 1/3″ diameter, white, borne in August–September, briefly effective; have observed several extremely fruitful specimens with large infructescences of milky white fruit.

CULTURE: Fibrous rooted, easily moved bare root, containerized, or balled-and-burlapped; extremely adaptable to wide range of soil and climatic conditions; does best in moist soil and is often observed in the wild in wet, swampy situations.

DISEASES AND INSECTS: There is a twig blight (canker) which can wreak havoc on this species and the cultivars; leaf spot caused by *Septoria cornicola* is particularly serious in wet weather on 'Kelseyi', 'Flaviramea', et al.; scale can be a problem and I have noticed a wealth of bagworms.

LANDSCAPE VALUE: Excellent for massing in large areas, along highways, parks, golf courses; interesting stem color makes it suitable for shrub border use in residential landscapes; can be an effective bank cover for it holds soil quite well; beautiful when framed by snow, great plant for the winter garden especially mixed or contrasted with various needle evergreens.

CULTIVARS:

'Allemans'—Compact, 6′ high, rich green foliage, stays clean all summer, red stems in winter; listed also as 'Alleman Compact' under *C. alba*.

f. *baileyi* ('Baileyi')—Treated as a species in the 1990 edition, but at best a variety or forma. Grown by Midwest nurserymen for years. Grows 6 to 9′ high and wide, rich green leaves turn reddish purple in fall, white flowers are followed by bluish fruits, with reddish winter stem color. Debatable if nurserymen or academics could identify this taxon from a winter branch.

'Cardinal'—A good bright red (cherry red) stemmed form released by Minnesota Landscape Arboretum; Dr. Pellett brought many wild collected provenances to Minnesota for various research activities and hybridized them selecting 'Cardinal' as a superior seedling; reasonably resistant to leaf spot; stem color is not good in Zone 7 and as seen in Winchester, TN on February 22, 1994 color was yellowish, perhaps with a trace of orange; grows 8 to 10′ by 8 to 10′; introduced 1987.

var. *coloradensis*—This variety has smaller leaves, brownish stems and bluish white fruits; it ranges from the Yukon and Manitoba to New Mexico and California.

var. *coloradensis* 'Cheyenne'—Good selection for blood red stem color; shows growth habit of the species but does not grow as tall.

'Flaviramea'—Form with yellow stems, often inflicted with canker, nonetheless widely sold and planted; should be used with taste for a small planting

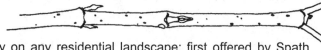

goes a long way on any residential landscape; first offered by Spath Nursery, Germany, 1899/1900, who received it from the Arnold Arboretum; also listed as Golden-twig Dogwood and 'Lutea'.

'Isanti'—Compact form with bright red stem color; shorter internodes which make for a denser plant; does contract considerable leaf spot in wet weather; grows 5 to 6′ high; Minnesota Landscape Arboretum introduction.

'Kelseyi'—Low-growing, neat, compact form, 24 to 30″ in height; nice facing plant in the shrub border to hide the "leggy" shrubs in the background; stems less colorful than the species; quite susceptible to leaf spot; fall color not as good as species.

'Nitida'—Stems are green, leaves glossy green, the winter stems a pea green color; habit more vigorous and upright than 'Flaviramea'.

'Silver and Gold'—A 1987 introduction from Mt. Cuba Center, Delaware that occurred as a branch sport from *C. s.* 'Flaviramea'; the leaves have a creamy, irregular border around the margin and the variegation pattern is stable; the stem color is yellow.

'Sunshine' (*C. s.* var. *occidentalis*)—A large 10 to 12′ high shrub with a general pale yellow or chartreuse foliar glow; leaves are variable in variegation and may be all of one hue (yellow) or have yellow margins and an irregular green center, more rarely they are creamy white-margined with a central green blotch; leaves on young shoots average 4 to 6″ long and 2 to 2 1/2″ wide; stem coloration is red; introduced by University of Washington Arboretum and described in the *Bulletin* 47(2):24 (1986); the Arboretum received the cuttings from Mr. G.W. Nadermann, Oakville, WA in 1941; apparently occurred as a branch sport in the wild.

'White Gold' ('White Spot')—Leaves edged with gold turning cream-white, stems are bright gold; have seen only in England.

PROPAGATION: Seed should be stratified for 60 to 90 days at 41°F. I have rooted cuttings with 90% success any time leaves were present by treating the cuttings with 1000 ppm IBA-quick dip. Hardwood cuttings placed in the field in late winter also give 90 to 100% success without treatment.

ADDITIONAL NOTES: Nurserymen tend to sell *C. alba* and *C. sericea* as red-stemmed dogwoods. The homeowner is at the mercy of the garden center operator or nurseryman and the differences in growth habit and stem color in old age are different enough to warrant correct labeling by the seller.

NATIVE HABITAT: Newfoundland to Manitoba, south to Virginia, Kentucky and Nebraska. Depending on one's viewpoint, the range covers most of the United States. In the West, the species is found in high mountain areas. On Mt. Lemon, outside of Tucson, AZ, I found the species in a stream side setting at about 4000 to 4500′ elevation. Cultivated 1656.

Cornus walteri Wangerin — Walter Dogwood

LEAVES: Opposite, simple, oval, 2 to 4 1/2″ long, 1 1/4 to 2″ wide, tapered at both ends, slender pointed, dark green above with fine appressed hairs, more abundant on lower surface, 3 to 5 vein pairs; petiole—to 1″ long.

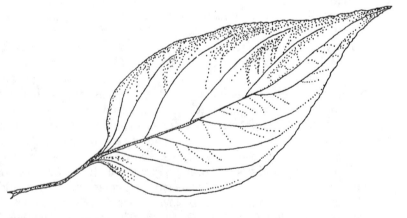

Cornus walteri, (kôr′nus wâl′ter-ī), Walter Dogwood, is a rather unusual dogwood with true alligator-hide bark and a tree-type stature. I have seen the species at two gardens in the United States and came away with the feeling that it is a meritorious plant deserving of wider use. It can grow 30 to 40′ high and wide. The 3/8″ diameter, white flowers are produced in 2 to 3″ diameter, corymbose cymes in June. The 1/4″ diameter, globose, black fruit matures in August– September. Cuttings do not root as readily as those of *C. macrophylla*. Seed requires a warm/cold period possibly as much as 4 months of each phase. A related species, *C. coreana* Wangerin, Korean Dogwood, is a larger (50 to 60′) tree with similar flower and fruit characteristics. The bark is perhaps more blocky. The Arnold had a large specimen and the Secrest Arboretum lays claim to the biggest plant that I know of in this country. Korea. Introduced 1918. Zone 5. *Cornus walteri* is native to central China. Introduced 1907. Zone 5.

Corokia cotoneaster Raoul. — Wire Netting Bush

FAMILY: Cornaceae
LEAVES: Alternate, simple, evergreen, orbicular, 1/2 to 1″ long, almost as wide, dark maroon-green to bronze and glabrous above, white tomentose below.
STEM: Thin, uniquely contorted and intertwined, white pubescent when young, black with maturity.

Corokia cotoneaster, (kôr-ō-kē′à kō-tō-nē-as′tēr), Wire Netting Bush, is a curious novelty shrub with most artistic branching. The plant is sparsely foliaged which only accentuates the contorted, bent and intertwined branches. Grows 5 to 8′ high and wide. Had a plant in Athens for two years and for no logical reason, it perished. The yellow, 1/2″ diameter, star-shaped flowers open in May–June. Fruit is a 1/4 to 1/3″ diameter, oblong to rounded, orange drupe. A most interesting shrub that is cold hardy in Zone 7b but may require perfect drainage. Displays excellent salt tolerance. Bean mentioned that it required protection from wind even in the English climate. He also referred to a plant at Castlewellan in Northern Ireland that was 8′ high and 60′ in circumference. A useful analogy to visualize the plant is to imagine barbwire rolled into rather messy tangles. Neat plant for the collector. Occasionally grown on the West Coast. New Zealand. Introduced 1875. Zone 7 to 9.

RELATED SPECIES:

Corokia* × *virgata (Turrill) Metcalfe., (kôr-ō-kē′à vēr-gā′tà), a hybrid between *C. buddlejoides* Cunn. and *C. cotoneaster*, is a slightly larger shrub with more upright habit. The branches are twisted but not to the degree of *C. cotoneaster*. Leaves are sparse, glossy dark green, white beneath, 1/4 to 1 3/4″ long, 1/8 to 2/3″ wide. Flowers yellow in May. Fruit is an orange-yellow, egg-shaped, 1/4″ long berry. New Zealand. Introduced 1907. Zone 7 to 9.

Corylopsis glabrescens Franch. & Savat. (*C. gotoana* Mak.) — Fragrant Winterhazel
(kôr-i-lop′sis glā-bres′enz)

FAMILY: Hamamelidaceae
LEAVES: Alternate, simple, ovate, 2 to 4″ long, 1 1/4 to 3″ wide, acuminate, cordate to subcordate, sinuate-dentate with bristle-like teeth, teeth turn down from margins of leaf, dark green, glaucescent beneath and sparingly silky on the veins or sometimes slightly pubescent when young, thin, 7 to 11 vein pairs; petiole—1/2 to 1″ long, slender.
BUDS: Rather large, sessile, solitary or finally short-stalked and collaterally branched, directly in the axil, fusiform or ovoid, with about 3 glabrous scales, greenish brown, brown to reddish brown.
STEM: Rounded, zig-zag, moderate or slender, brown, mostly glabrescent; pith—small, angular, continuous.

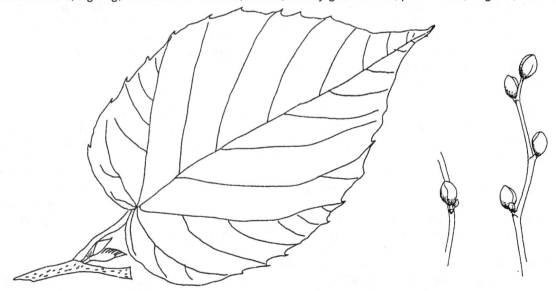

SIZE: 8 to 15′ in height with a similar spread; can be grown as a small tree.
HARDINESS: Zone 5 to 8; the hardiest of the *Corylopsis* and possibly the best choice for northern gardens.

HABIT: A wide-spreading, dense, somewhat flat-topped, rounded, multi-stemmed shrub.

RATE: Slow to medium.

TEXTURE: Medium in leaf; possibly medium to medium-coarse in winter.

LEAF COLOR: Dark green above, glaucescent beneath in summer; fall color varies from yellow-green to clear gold, often the leaves remain green late and are killed by a freeze.

FLOWERS: Perfect, pale yellow, fragrant, borne in 1 to 1 1/2″ long, pendulous racemes; bracts boat-shaped, silky inside; flower stalk glabrous; flowering in April before the leaves develop.

FRUIT: Two-valved, dehiscent capsule, about 1/4″ across, not ornamental; seeds black.

CULTURE: Transplant container-grown or balled-and-burlapped plants into moist, acid, preferably well-drained soil which has been amended with peat moss or leaf mold; full sun or light shade; should be sheltered as they flower early and are susceptible to late spring frosts; this is especially true in the Midwest and South where invariably there is a warm period in March and the buds of many plants swell and often open only to succumb to the early April freeze; pruning should be accomplished after the flowers pass, plants flower in early March in Athens, GA; lost a plant in my garden to a leaky outdoor faucet, plant does not tolerate wet feet!

DISEASES AND INSECTS: As is true with many members of the Hamamelidaceae, this genus is free of significant problems.

LANDSCAPE VALUE: Good plant for early spring flower color and fragrance; could be successfully integrated into the shrub border; worthwhile considering if a protected area is available in the garden; over the years I have grown very fond of the *Corylopsis* species; in full flower they are as beautiful as any plant that could grace a garden; probably best used against an evergreen background; the Swarthmore College campus, Arnold Arboretum and Longwood Gardens probably have the best collections on the Eastern Seaboard; have seen plants injured at Morton and Dawes Arboreta after the 1976–77 winter when temperatures dropped -20 to -25°F; this included flower buds and stem tissue; *Corylopsis* does reasonably well in the South; the J.C. Raulston Arboretum, Raleigh, and Callaway Gardens have specimens.

CULTIVARS:

'March Jewel'—A genetic dwarf with a low-spreading habit, grew 1 1/2′ by 5′ in 10 years; free-flowering and opens earlier than the species; from Camellia Forest Nursery, Chapel Hill, NC; listed as a *C. gotoana* selection.

PROPAGATION: Seeds are difficult and require an extended 5 month/3 month:warm/cold period; softwood cuttings root readily and I have collected cuttings throughout June, July and August, provided a 1000 ppm IBA-quick dip and achieved 90 to 100% success; the root systems are profuse but the cuttings, in my experience, resist moving and should be allowed to go through a dormancy cycle; when new growth ensues they can be transplanted; this approach appears to be true for many of the Hamamelidaceae; see Verstage, "Propagation of *Corylopsis*," *Proc. Intl. Plant Prop. Soc.* 29:204–205 (1979).

ADDITIONAL NOTES: Somewhat similar to *Hamamelis* and *Parrotia*, its hardy allies, but differing in the flower morphology. The raceme on which the flowers are borne is really a short branch. At the base are a few thin, membranous, bract-like organs, which are not accompanied by flowers, but from the axils of which a leaf is developed after the flowers farther along the raceme have developed. Occasionally *C. gotoana* is mentioned as perhaps the best garden species. The literature is not clear as to the exact taxonomic status and often lists *C. gotoana* as a synonym for *C. glabrescens*. Ohwi, *Flora of Japan*, mentions that the stamens of *C. gotoana* are nearly as long as the petals; those of *C. glabrescens* half as long. Also the leaf teeth of *C. gotoana* are shorter than those of *C. glabrescens*, but these characteristics according to Morley and Chao are not sufficient to warrant species status. Happy hunting! Both are native to Japan and based on Ohwi's account occur in similar habitats.

NATIVE HABITAT: Japan. Introduced 1905.

RELATED SPECIES: There is a certain commonality about the Winterhazels and if one can identify a particular species then he/she can identify the others at least to the generic level; their taxonomy is somewhat confused and I recommend the following article for additional reading: Li, "The cultivated *Corylopsis*," *Morris Arboretum Bulletin* 13(4):63–68 (1963). To illustrate the degree of uncertainty about what constitutes a *Corylopsis* species, I have read estimates of 30, 20, 7 . . . Personally, I have become so frustrated trying to straighten them out in my own mind that the lower number is probably realistic. During my 1991 sabbatical at the Arnold Arboretum, I journeyed from species to species and simply could not assess constant characteristics of identification from taxon to taxon. Certainly, when forgiven by the vagaries of late winter–early spring, they bring a magnificent presence to the landscape.

Corylopsis pauciflora Sieb. & Zucc. — Buttercup Winterhazel

LEAVES: Alternate, simple, ovate to broad-ovate, 1 1/2 to 3″ long, 1 to 2″ wide, acute, obliquely cordate to subcordate, with a few bristle-like teeth, glabrous and bright green above, silky on veins below, 7 to 9 vein pairs; petiole—1/3 to 3/4″ long, slender.

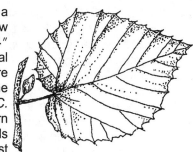

Corylopsis pauciflora, (kôr-i-lop′sis pâ-si-flō′rà), Buttercup Winterhazel, is a small (4 to 6′) shrub of spreading habit with fragrant primrose yellow flowers, about 3/4″ diameter, produced 2, sometimes 5 on 1 to 1 1/4″ long inflorescences. I have seen this species at the U.S. National Arboretum, Washington, DC, Arnold Arboretum, and Swarthmore College and was quite impressed with the floral display as well as the overall daintiness of the entire shrub compared to *C. glabrescens*, *C. spicata*, and *C. willmottiae*. This would be a good choice for modern gardens. Flowers about mid to late April in vicinity of Boston, MA. Needs to be protected from incessant wind, full sun and high pH soils. Best suited to a woodland setting. Japan and Taiwan. Introduced 1862. Zone 6 to 8.

Corylopsis platypetala Rehd. & Wils.
LEAVES: Alternate, simple, ovate or broad-ovate to elliptic, 2 to 4″(5″) long, short acuminate, cordate or subcordate, sinuate-dentate with bristle-like teeth, glabrous and dark green above, glaucous beneath; petiole—slightly glandular.

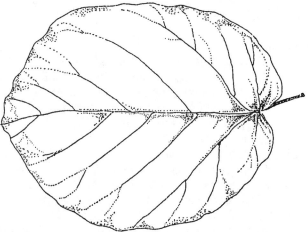

Corylopsis platypetala, (kôr-i-lop′sis plat-i-pet′àl-à), grows 8 to 10′ and larger under cultivation with specimens as large as 20′ high and 10′ wide being reported. Its leaves develop a glaucous, waxy bloom when grown in full sun. The fragrant, pale yellow flowers are borne in 8- to 20-flowered, 1 to 2″ long racemes. At Longwood Gardens a 12 to 15′ high specimen produces deep yellow flowers later than the other species. I have observed it in full flower on April 9. This is a very ornamental species and is allied to *C. willmottiae* from which it differs by some minute floral characteristic. Now listed as *C. sinensis* var. *calvescens*. It was introduced by E.H. Wilson in 1907 from Hupeh, China where it is a common shrub growing in thickets and along margins of woods. Zone 6 to 8.

Corylopsis spicata Sieb. & Zucc. — Spike Winterhazel
LEAVES: Alternate, simple, orbicular-ovate or orbicular-obovate, 2 to 4″ long, 2 to 3″ wide, abruptly short acuminate, obliquely cordate to rounded, sinuate-denticulate with bristle-like teeth, new growth purplish, later dull dark to blue green, glaucous and downy beneath, 6 to 8 vein pairs; petiole—1/2 to 1″ long, woolly.

Corylopsis spicata, (kôr-i-lop′sis spī-kā′tà), Spike Winterhazel, is a wide-spreading, 4 to 6′(10′) high shrub that forms a rather attractive mass of crooked, flexible branches at maturity. I have seen specimens twice as wide as high and in flower they were spectacular. The yellow, fragrant flowers occur 6 to 12 together on a 1 to 2″ long, pendulous raceme in April (mid-March, Athens). The stamens with pink filaments; anthers brown, purple or red. The emerging leaves are a rich vinous purple and eventually change to bluish green. This is one of the most beautiful of the *Corylopsis* and ranks at the top of my list as an early-flowering shrub. Two 50-year-old plants in the Morris Arboretum were 8′ high and 12′ wide. A floriferous hybrid between *C. spicata* and *C. pauciflora* is in cultivation. The species is native to the mountains of Japan. Introduced 1863. Zone 5 to 8.

Corylopsis willmottiae Rehd. & Wils. — Willmott Winterhazel
LEAVES: Alternate, simple, oval or obovate, 2 to 4″ long, short acuminate, subcordate or truncate, sinuate-dentate with mucronate teeth, bright green and glabrous above, rather glaucous and downy below, especially on the veins, 7 to 10 vein pairs; petiole—1/4 to 3/4″ long, glabrous or slightly pubescent.

Corylopsis willmottiae, (kôr-i-lop′sis wil-mot′i-ē), Willmott Winterhazel, is seldom seen in cultivation in the United States. It is a rather large, 6 to 12′ high shrub with glabrous, brown stems that are dotted with numerous lenticels. The winter buds are pale shining green and stalked. The fragrant flowers are soft greenish yellow and borne in 2 to 3″ long, pendulous racemes. 'Spring Purple' has plum purple young shoots that eventually change to green. Raised and introduced by Hillier Nursery. Now correctly *C. sinensis* var. *sinensis*. This species was discovered and introduced by E.H. Wilson in 1908 from western China in Sikang province. Zone 6 to 7.

ADDITIONAL NOTES: I have stayed with the older taxonomy but Morley and Chao, *J. Arnold Arboretum* 58:382–415 (1977), place *C. platypetala* under *C. sinensis* var. *calvescens*; *C. willmottiae* is included with *C. sinensis* var. *sinensis*; and 'Spring Purple' becomes a cultivar of *C. sinensis* var. *sinensis*. The authors reduced the 33 species that had been described to 7. Wow! I noticed that most nurseries have switched to the newer nomenclature, however, not all have adhered to the changes. What I knew as *C. veitchiana* Bean is now lumped into *C. sinensis* var. *calvescens* (as is *C. platypetala*). Morley and Chao treat this as forma *veitchiana*, the leaves being glabrous below and the exserted anthers brownish red. This is generally listed as a 5 to 6′ high, rounded shrub with primrose yellow flowers and reddish anthers on 1 to 2″ long inflorescences. I have seen *C. veitchiana*, at least so labeled, approaching 10′ high. A lovely selection called 'Winterthur' grows 5 to 6′ high and 10 to 12′ wide, with fragrant, yellow flowers in April. To my knowledge this cultivar has not been assigned to any species and is probably a hybrid. Selection from Winterthur Garden, Delaware.

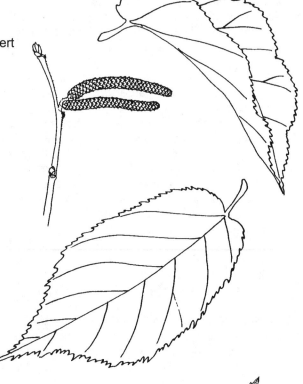

Corylus americana Marsh. — American Filbert
(kôr′i-lus à-mer-i-kā′nà)

FAMILY: Betulaceae

LEAVES: Alternate, simple, 2 1/2 to 6″ long, 1 1/2 to 2 1/2″ wide, broad-ovate to broad-elliptic, apex short-acuminate, heart-shaped or rounded at base, sparingly pubescent and dark green above, soft pubescent beneath; petiole—about 1/2″ long, glandular hairy.

BUDS: Imbricate, globose, gray, pubescent, 1/6 to 1/4″ long, greenish brown to purplish.

STEM: Young branches glandular-pubescent, brown; pith— continuous, 3-sided, pale or brown.

FRUIT: Involucre downy, deeply cut and toothed, about twice as long as the 1/2″ long, slightly flattened nut, usually tightly enclosing it, deeply and irregularly lobed.

SIZE: Listed as 8 to 10′ by many authorities but usually grows larger, 15 to 18′, spread approximately 2/3's the height; national champion is 34′ by 24′ in Oakland County, MI.

HARDINESS: Zone 4 to 9.

HABIT: Strongly multi-stemmed shrub forming a rounded top with a leggy or open base, often with wide-spreading rather straight stems branched toward their extremities.

RATE: Medium to fast.

TEXTURE: Medium-coarse in summer and winter, this is also true for the types treated under the related species category.

LEAF COLOR: Dark green in summer, muddy yellow-green in fall, sometimes with a reddish tint, usually of negligible importance, on occasion a respectable bronze-red on plants at the University's Botanical Garden.

FLOWERS: Monoecious; male—in catkins, 1 1/2 to 3″ long, yellowish brown, quite showy in early spring (March); female—inconspicuous, the stigma and style barely protruding out of the bud, color is a rich red; male catkins have opened as early as February 1 in Athens.

FRUIT: Nut, 1/2″ long, set in an involucre nearly twice its length, involucre is downy and deeply notched, maturing in September–October.

CULTURE: Transplant balled-and-burlapped or as a container-grown plant into well-drained, loamy soil; pH adaptable; full sun or light shade; prune anytime; tends to sucker from the roots and must often be thinned out to maintain a respectable appearance.

DISEASES AND INSECTS: Blight, crown gall, black knot, apple mosaic virus in *C. avellana*, leaf spots, Japanese leafhopper, caterpillar, scales; I have not

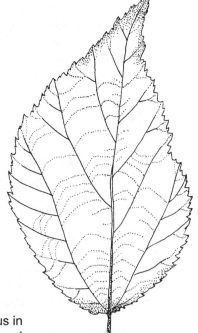

noticed extensive problems with *Corylus* although nurserymen have indicated that *Corylus avellana* 'Contorta' is affected by a blight (*Anisogramma anomala*) which injures leaves and branches.

LANDSCAPE VALUE: The American Hazel is best reserved for naturalizing and other nonformal areas; the European Filbert and especially the cultivars might lend themselves to selected landscape situations; the species are too large for contemporary landscapes.

CULTIVARS: Hybrids between *C. americana* and *C. avellana* include: 'Bixby', 'Buchanan', 'Potomac', and 'Reed'. These selections combine the best characteristics of both species and carry greater hardiness than *C. avellana*.

PROPAGATION: Seed, three months cold stratification or fall plant; softwood cuttings of *C. avellana* and *C. maxima* var. *purpurea* have been rooted but percentages were low; I have never had any success with *C. maxima* var. *purpurea*; have tried *C. avellana* 'Contorta' with no success; logically if 'Contorta' were put on its own roots the suckering experienced with grafted forms would not be a problem, considerable use of stooling, an old propagation trick where the plant is pruned to induce multiple shoots, sawdust or other organic material is pulled around shoots which eventually root and are severed from the parent plant in the dormant season; tissue culture has been successful [see *HortScience* 30:120–123 (1995)]. See Dirr and Heuser 1987 for a good overview of *Corylus* propagation.

ADDITIONAL NOTES: All shrubby filberts should be used with restraint in the landscape; probably not good choices for small properties; squirrels love the nuts.

NATIVE HABITAT: New England to Saskatchewan and south to Florida, often found in moist and dry areas, along fencerows, and at the edge of woodlands. Introduced 1798.

RELATED SPECIES:

Corylus avellana L. — European Filbert, Cobnut
LEAVES: Alternate, simple, 2 to 4″ long, 1 1/2 to 3″ wide, suborbicular to broad ovate, abruptly acuminate, cordate, double serrate and often slightly lobulate, slightly pubescent above, dark green, pubescent beneath, particularly on nerves; petiole—1/4 to 1/2″ long, glandular hairy.

BUDS: Imbricate, ovoid-rounded, glabrescent with ciliate scales, 1/6 to 1/3″ long, green to brown.

STEM: Glandular-pubescent, brownish.

FRUIT: Involucre shorter or only slightly longer than nut.

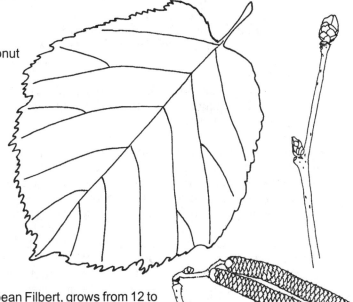

Corylus avellana, (kôr′i-lus a-vel-lā′na̍), European Filbert, grows from 12 to 20′ in height, can be a small tree, but usually forms a dense thicket of erect stems and develops extensive shoots from the roots. Nut is 3/4″ long, set in an involucre about as long as the nut, the margins are cut into shallow, often toothed lobes. Native to Europe, western Asia, and northern Africa. Prized for its nuts in European countries; this is one of the species that is grown for nut production. I never realized how much research is being conducted on this species including breeding, culture, propagation and disease control. Oregon is the major center for filbert production in the United States. In the early 1980's, I visited the Portland area and witnessed the filbert orchards for the first time. The ground is clean cultivated under the trees and apparently when the nuts fall are "vacuumed." Like many horticulture crops, *C. avellana* is home to numerous cultivars chosen for all manner of characteristics. Probably the best review is by S.A. Mehlenbacher, *Acta Horticulturae* No. 290:789–836 (1990). Zone 4 to 8.

CULTIVARS:
'Aurea'—A yellow-leaved and rather weak-growing form; have seen at Wisley, color does not persist.
'Contorta'—8 to 10′(15′), stems curled and twisted, quite an attraction when properly grown, often called Harry Lauder's Walkingstick; discovered about 1863 at Frocester, Gloucestershire, England in a hedgerow; leaves also twisted, best for winter effect; male catkins open later than those of species; have never seen fruits on this form until 1996 when a reader sent a photo of a plant with fruit, a rare occurrence to be sure; almost always grafted on the species and the understock suckers result in maintenance nightmares; more stooling now being practiced (see previous entry); in 1995 on a visit to Crathes Castle Garden, Scotland, I witnessed a 20′ specimen.

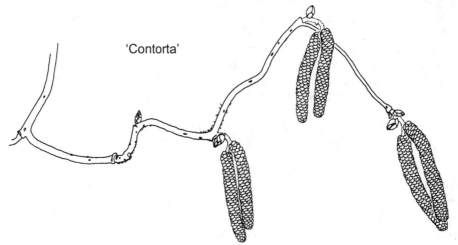

'Contorta'

'Fusco-rubra'—A purple leaf form; the purple not as dark as that of *C. maxima* var. *purpurea*; have seen at Holden and Arnold Arboreta and, from a distance, was hard pressed to separate from *C. m.* var. *purpurea*; will grow 15′ high.

'Heterophylla'—A form with smaller leaves than the species, the leaves being lobed about one-third of the distance to the midrib, each lobe triangular and sharply toothed; also listed as 'Laciniata'; finally tracked the plant in Munich Botanic Garden, not sensational.

'Pendula'—Rather interesting form with distinctly weeping branches; if grafted on a standard it forms a broad inverted soup-bowl head; there is a shrubby form at the Arnold Arboretum approximately 8′ high and 16′ wide.

'Rote Zeller'—Purple leaves and pendulous, pink, worm-like catkins in spring; foliage ages to bronze-green in summer; grows 15 to 18′ high; how different from 'Fusco-rubra' and *C. maxima* var. *purpurea* is unknown.

Corylus cornuta Marsh., (kôr′i-lus kôr-nu′tà), Beaked Filbert, is included here because of its interesting beaked fruits. It is a smaller (4 to 8′ high and wide), more refined shrub than the others. The leaves range from 1 1/2 to 4 1/2″ long and 1 to 3″ wide. The unopened male catkin is 1/2 to 1″ long and the nut only about 1/2″ long. The involucre (husk) that covers the nut is extended, forms a slender beak 1 to 1 1/2″ beyond the nut. Hybrids between *C. cornuta* and *C. avellana* called filazels produce large, early maturing nuts. 'Manoka' and 'Peoaka', from Canadian breeder J.U. Gellatly, are two of the best. Quebec to Saskatchewan south to Missouri and Georgia. Introduced 1745. Zone 4 to 8.

Corylus maxima Mill. 'Purpurea' [var. *purpurea* (Loud.) Rehd.] — Purple Giant Filbert

LEAVES: Similar to *Corylus avellana* except leaves (2 to 5″ long, 1 1/2 to 4″ wide, petiole—1/4 to 1/2″ long, glandular) dark purple in spring fading to green in summer; buds and catkins retain purplish cast; involucre and young fruits are also purplish.

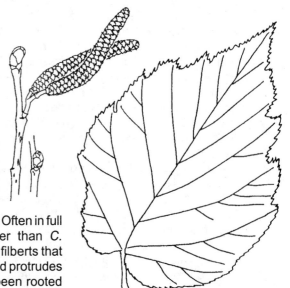

Corylus maxima Mill. 'Purpurea' (var. *purpurea*), (kôr′i-lus maks′i-mà pĕr-pū′re-à), Purple Giant Filbert is a large shrub reaching 15 to 20′ in height, with leaves of a dark purple gradually fading to dark green during the summer months. Can be grown from Zone 4 to 8 but in the South the leaves quickly change to green, usually by early June. Often in full leaf by mid-April in Athens. This variety flowers later than *C. americana* or *C. avellana*. The species is a parent of the filberts that are grown in English orchards. The involucre encloses and protrudes beyond the nut distinguishing it from *C. avellana*. Has been rooted using 4000 ppm IBA talc, 3 peat: 1 sand medium with 64% rooting after 6 months. Species is native to southeastern Europe, Western Asia. Long cultivated.

Corylus colurna L. — Turkish Filbert or Hazel
(kôr′i-lus ko-lur′nà)

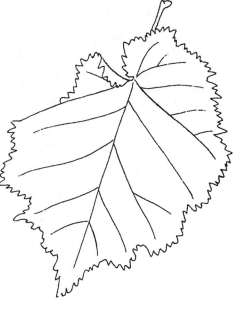

LEAVES: Alternate, simple, broadly ovate to obovate, 2 1/2 to 6″ long, acuminate, cordate, doubly serrate or crenate-serrate, sometimes lobulate, nearly glabrous above, pubescent on veins beneath; petiole—1/2 to 1″ long.

BUDS: Large (1/3″ long), softly pubescent, green-tinged brown.

STEM: Glandular-pubescent, gray-brown, coarse, with fissures up and down the stem, becoming more pronounced in second year.

SIZE: 40 to 50′ in height with a spread of 1/3 to 2/3's the height, can grow to 70 to 80′.

HARDINESS: Zone 4 to 7; injured at −30°F in Orono, ME.

HABIT: Broad pyramidal, very stately and handsome in form, usually with a short trunk and the bottom branches touching the ground.

RATE: Medium, 35′ over a 20 year period; 50′ in 50 years.

TEXTURE: Medium in leaf and winter.

BARK: Pale brown to gray-brown, older bark develops a flaky character and as scales fall off a brown or orange-brown bark is exposed.

LEAF COLOR: Dark green in summer, potentially yellow to purple in autumn but seldom handsome, drops yellow-green; have seen considerable variation in degree of greenness and texture of leaf with some extremely leathery; the summer foliage is very handsome and seems to be free of insect and disease problems.

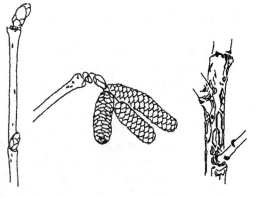

FLOWERS: Monoecious; male—in catkins, 2 to 3″ long; female—inconspicuous as only the two free styles protrude from the bud scale; tree with flowers of little ornamental appeal but the catkins in early spring (March) can be rather handsome.

FRUIT: Nut, 1/2 to 5/8″ diameter, the involucre about 1 1/2 to 2″ long, nuts are closely grouped 3 or more together; involucre deeply incised, fimbriated, twice the length of the nut, covered with a fine pubescence mixed with gland-tipped bristles; September–October.

CULTURE: Thrives in hot summers and cold winters; tolerant of adverse conditions; a well-drained, loamy soil is preferable; pH adaptable; full sun; actually a very excellent tree but little known and grown; supposedly somewhat difficult to propagate; somewhat difficult to transplant and needs supplemental watering the first few summers until it re-establishes; once established, the tree is quite drought tolerant.

DISEASES AND INSECTS: None serious.

LANDSCAPE VALUE: Excellent formal character, possibly for lawns, street tree use, also city conditions, where maples exhibit scorch this tree is still green and vigorous; little used and under-appreciated tree in the United States; occasionally found in arboreta and campus settings; always distinct because of unique outline, heavy-textured leaves, fruit and bark; difficult to locate in commerce but worth the hunt; has not performed well in Wichita, KS tests; highly rated for street tree use in Germany.

PROPAGATION: Most of the shrubby *Corylus* require 2 to 6 months of cold temperature before germination will occur; also warm alternated with cold stratifications are recommended; cuttings of the shrubby species can be rooted but are difficult; I have never had good luck; in general cuttings should be taken in June, July or August and treated with a high IBA level (10,000 ppm); *C. maxima* 'Purpurea' has been rooted 100% from late July cuttings using 10,000 ppm IBA; 'Contorta' has also been rooted 60% using similar procedures; 'Contorta' and 'Purpurea' are grafted on seedling understocks and the suckers from the understock often overgrow the scion.

ADDITIONAL NOTES: For an entire career I have wished the best for this tree but have never seen it materialize in everyday commerce. A rather interesting hybrid between *C. avellana* and *C. colurna* is *C.* × *colurnoides* Schneid., with the common name Trazel.

NATIVE HABITAT: Southeast Europe, western Asia. Introduced 1582.

Cotinus coggygria Scop. — Common Smoketree or Smokebush
(kō-ti′nus ko-gīg′ri-à)

FAMILY: Anacardiaceae

LEAVES: Alternate, simple, oval to obovate, 1 1/2 to 3 1/2″ long, rounded or slightly emarginate at apex, entire, glabrous, well-marked with parallel veins, bluish green; petiole—1/2 to 1 1/2″ long.

BUDS: Small, 1/16″ long, solitary, sessile, with several imbricate, dark red-brown scales, acute.

STEM: Stout, brown or purplish, bloomy, with numerous small lenticels, glabrous; leaf scars—not lobed, deep bloomy purple color around the leaf scars; pith—orange-brown, solid, when crushed emitting strong odor.

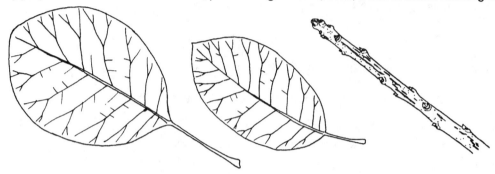

SIZE: 10 to 15′ in height by 10 to 15′ spread.

HARDINESS: Zone 4, preferably 5 to 8; at Orono, ME the purple leaf types 'Nordine', 'Royal Purple', and 'Velvet Cloak' have suffered regular stem dieback while the green leaf types were not injured.

HABIT: Upright, spreading, loose and open, often wider than high, multi-stemmed shrub; when pruned develops very long slender shoots creating a straggly, unkempt appearance.

RATE: Medium.

TEXTURE: Medium in leaf; coarse in winter.

LEAF COLOR: Late leafing, late April–early May in Athens; medium blue-green in summer and yellow-red-purple in fall; fall color is often poorly developed but at times is spectacular especially on cultivars.

FLOWERS: The flower is rather ineffective for each 5-petaled yellowish flower is about 1/3″ in diameter and sparsely borne; in June (May, Athens) the real show occurs as a result of the hairs (pubescence) on the pedicels and peduncle of the large 6 to 8″ long and wide panicle; the hairs often pass through several color changes but at their best are a smoky pink; they are effective from June into August–September; the purple-leaved types have purplish hairs; in the South (Zone 7 and 8), the effect is not as long persistent as in cooler climates.

FRUIT: A rather small 1/4″ wide, kidney-shaped, dry, reticulate drupe.

CULTURE: Transplant from a container; adaptable to widely divergent soils and pH ranges; dry and rocky soils; prefers well-drained loam and sunny exposure.

DISEASES AND INSECTS: None of serious magnitude, however, rusts, leafspot, leaf rollers and San Jose scale can attack this species; *Verticillium* can be a problem.

LANDSCAPE VALUE: Good in shrub border, possibly in masses or groupings; not for single specimen use but usually employed in that fashion for an accent or a striking focal point; have seen it used in many European gardens in such a fashion; often the purple-leaf types are cut to the ground in late winter to force vigorous shoot growth which is more colorful than the normal shoot extensions.

CULTIVARS: Several interesting purple leaf and flower forms; of special note is 'Velvet Cloak'. Dr. Kim Tripp produced a great article on *Cotinus* in *Arnoldia* 54(2):20–30 (1994). I have meshed my material with Kim's.

    'Black Velvet'—Dark purple foliage and abundant floral "smoke"; selected from a block of purple leaf seedlings; introduced by Steve Campbell, Sebastopol, CA.

    'Cooke's Purple'—Attractive purple smoky inflorescences.

    'Daydream'—Floriferous form with dense, ovoid, heavily produced, fluffy inflorescences that mature a rich brownish pink, green leaves; this is one of the handsomest of the cultivars and its habit is rather dense, flowers later, inflorescences persist longer; always one of my favorite cultivars; a 20-year-old plant at the Arnold Arboretum was more than 15′ high; selected at Newport Nurseries, MI.

    'Flame'—Selected for its brilliant orange-red fall coloration; inflorescences pink; considered a hybrid between *C. coggygria* and *C. obovatus*; grows larger than *C. coggygria*; introduced by Hillier Nursery, England.

'Foliis Purpureis'—Leaves purplish when young, later purplish green to green, inflorescence usually pinkish; one of many clones with similar characteristics; name may not be taxonomically correct.

'Grace'—From a cross (*C. coggygria* 'Velvet Cloak' × *C. obovatus*) made in summer of 1978 by Peter Dummer of Hillier Nurseries; interestingly seeds were acid scarified for 3 hours and planted with germination occurring in 12 days. No cold stratification was given. The hybrids are known as the Dummer Hybrids. 'Grace' was named after Mr. Dummer's wife and has a massive pink flower panicle, 14″ high by 11″ wide; leaves are 4 to 6″ long, 3″ wide, with a 2″ long petiole, light red when young, darkening to blue-green with age; turns red, orange, and yellow in fall; will probably mature about 20′. Received an Award of Merit from the Royal Horticultural Society in 1983. See *The Plantsman* 6(2):125–126 (1984) for the complete description. I had the good fortune to meet Mr. Dummer during a June visit to Hillier. He showed me the entire propagation operation and even gave me a plant of 'Grace'. Very kind and generous man and, as with most true gardeners, an unstated mutual respect developed.

'Nordine'—A selection made at the Morton Arboretum, Lisle, IL and supposedly resembling 'Royal Purple' in leaf color; leaves hold purplish red color well into summer, fall foliage yellow to orange-yellow; hardiest of purple-leaved smoke bushes; see comments under HARDINESS above.

'Notcutt's Variety'—As I saw it at the Oxford Botanic Garden a dark maroon-purple leaved form; the color strikingly rich and almost impossible to properly photograph (at least for me); the inflorescence purplish pink; this has also been listed as 'Foliis Purpureis Notcutt's Variety' and 'Rubrifolius'.

'Pendulus'—A form with pendulous branches; cultivated before 1885, possibly no longer in cultivation.

'Pink Champagne'—Somewhat like 'Daydream'; new growth bronzy purple maturing to green; feathery compact pink inflorescences; 6 to 8′ high, possibly larger with age.

'Purple Supreme'—Purple inflorescences age to purplish pink, rich purple foliage supposedly through the summer; 8 to 10′ high; a Sjulin Nursery introduction, Iowa.

'Purpureus' (f. *purpureus*)—Leaves green; inflorescences in some shade of purplish pink.

'Red Beauty'—Bright red-purple initially, dark red at maturity; well-branched, broad habit, strong grower; originated in the Netherlands.

'Royal Purple'—Foliage comes out rich maroon-red and darkens to almost purplish red or black; leaves are darker purple than 'Notcutt's Variety'; makes a reasonably compact plant; the inflorescences are also purplish red; the darkest purple-leaved cultivar and the color does not fade; rich red-purple fall color; less cold hardy than 'Nordine'; raised at Boskoop, Holland.

'Velvet Cloak'—Handsome, dark purple-leaved form maintaining good color through most of the summer; fall color is often spectacular reddish purple; colleagues and I have debated whether this is the same as 'Royal Purple', some say yes, others no; John Barbour, a Georgia nurseryman, and I say they are the same, anyone with absolute evidence please write; introduced by former Cole Nursery Co., Circleville, OH.

PROPAGATION: I have seen seedling populations of *C. coggygria* that showed an interesting mixture of green and purple leaf forms; apparently the seed had been collected from a purple-leaved form; seed requires 30 to 60 minutes of acid followed by 3 months at 41°F; nursery practice involves fall sowing with germination occurring in spring; cuttings are not the easiest thing to root but June–July cuttings root 80% or greater when treated with 10000 to 20000 ppm IBA; cuttings should be overwintered in flats or beds and not disturbed until growth ensues in spring; Kelly and Foret, *Proc. Intl. Plant Prop. Soc.* 27:445–448 (1977), showed that cuttings of *C. coggygria* rooted best in early June with 86% compared to 33% when collected on July 24; a 1425 ppm IBA + 1425 ppm NAA + 50 ppm boron quick dip improved rooting percentage and quality; I have had 80 to 100% success with softwood (June) cuttings treated with 1000 ppm IBA-quick dip, peat: perlite, mist.

NATIVE HABITAT: Southern Europe to central China and Himalaya. Cultivated 1656.

RELATED SPECIES:

Cotinus obovatus Raf. — American Smoketree, Chittamwood

LEAVES: Alternate, simple, entire, obovate to elliptic-obovate, 2 to 5″ long, 1/2 as wide, rounded to emarginate at apex, cuneate at base, bluish to dark green, silky pubescent beneath when young; petiole—1/2 to 1 1/2″ long. Similar to *C. coggygria* except leaf-scars lobed, stems orangish and usually an upright tree or shrub to 30 feet; the leaf scar lobing is a variable and unreliable characteristic in spite of what the keys say.

Cotinus obovatus, (kō-ti′nus ob-ō-vā′tus), American Smoketree, Chittamwood, is a large, upright shrub or small, oval-rounded to round-headed tree growing 20 to 30′ high. Co-national champions are 39′ by 38′ in West Lafayette, IN and 32′ by 43′ in Hamilton County, OH. The bluish to dark green leaves turn a

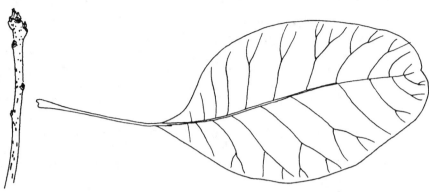

magnificent yellow, orange, amber, red and reddish purple in the fall. In fact, it may be the best of all American shrub/trees for intensity of color. In observing this tree through the Midwest, East, and South, I am amazed at the beauty and consistency of the excellent fall color. It was my good fortune to spend several days in October, 1981, with Mr. Don Shadow, Shadow Nurseries, Winchester, TN. Don took me to the mountains near Winchester where I saw *C. obovatus* in its fall splendor. There were shrub and tree forms, but all were various shades of the colors mentioned previously. The bark is also a beautiful gray to gray-brown and mature trunks become scaly reminding of the scales of a fish. Don is rooting the plant from softwood cuttings and apparently timing is quite important if success is to be experienced. One of the first things I mentioned to Don is that someone should be making selection for fall colors. Don had a twinkle in his eye so the question had already been answered. In Snyder's *Trees and Shrubs for Northern Gardens*, cultivar 'Red Leaf' is described as having especially good fall color. Interestingly the flowers are dioecious with the male being showier than the female. Panicles range from 6 to 10″ long and three-quarter's as wide. Flowers are greenish and open during late April–early May in Athens. Fruit production is sparse. Will grow in the same situations as *C. coggygria* and is particularly well-adapted to limestone soils for this is where it occurs in the wild. During the Civil War, it was almost lost because of its use for a yellow to orange dye. Found in restricted localities in Tennessee, Alabama, and the Edwards Plateau of Texas where it reaches its greatest numbers. Introduced 1882. Zone 4 to 8.

ADDITIONAL NOTES: Two excellent articles that cover a multitude of *C. obovatus* virtues include Koller and Shadow, *American Nurseryman* 159(9):155–161 (1984) and *Arnoldia* 44(2):17–22. Propagation as reported in the latter article consists of taking cuttings just before new season's growth hardens, pinching off soft tips, using 8000 ppm IBA talc or quick dip, suitable medium, 47% shade cloth, 15 second mist every 15 minutes, making sure cuttings are not overwatered for they deteriorate quickly; reduce mist as soon as cuttings root which may be as fast as 16 days to 4 to 6 weeks.

There is a great specimen at the Arnold Arboretum that exceeds 30 to 35′ in height. Fall color is magnificent reddish purple and the multiple trunks are richly sculpted with the scaly bark. For about 10 years, a plant has graced our garden and gets better with age. Fall colors hover in the yellow-amber-orange range, *never* red as with the Arnold's specimen. Certainly, as mentioned in the general description, superior selections should be introduced. Recent (1998) report of Asian Ambrosia beetle damage to this species.

Cotoneaster apiculatus Rehd. & Wils. — Cranberry Cotoneaster
(kō-tō-nē-as′tēr ā-pik-ū-la′tus)

FAMILY: Rosaceae

LEAVES: Alternate, simple, suborbicular to orbicular-ovate, 1/4 to 3/4″ long and wide, apiculate, occasionally rounded or even notched, glabrous at maturity or only slightly ciliate, lustrous dark green above, glabrous, lower surface slightly pubescent, undulating margin; petiole—1/4″ long.

BUDS: Similar to *C. lucida* except smaller.

STEM: Reddish purple with appressed pubescence; older stems gray-brown and ragged in appearance; when bruised or broken, stems emit a distinct maraschino cherry odor; this smell is more distinct on the low-growing types.

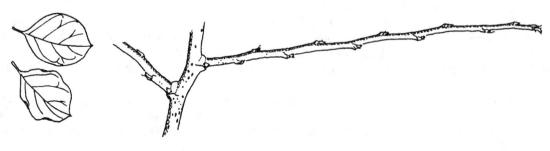

SIZE: 3′ in height by 3 to 6′ in spread.

HARDINESS: Zone 4 to 7; best in colder climates.

HABIT: Low, wide-spreading shrub with stiff branching pattern, young shoots growing herringbone fashion from the older ones; tends to mound upon itself forming dense, impenetrable tangles where leaves, bottles, and paper penetrate but rakes cannot enter; somewhat of a "garbage can" shrub but useful because of good foliage and fruit.

RATE: Slow, growth can be accelerated in youth with optimum watering and fertilization, will cover an area fairly fast.

TEXTURE: Fine in leaf, but often coarse in winter because of its "pack-rat" ability to store many unwanted articles.

LEAF COLOR: Dark glossy green, extremely handsome for its summer foliage effect; changing to good bronzy red or purplish tones in fall and holding its fall color often into late November.

FLOWERS: Perfect, pinkish, late May to early June, solitary, small, not ornamentally overwhelming but attractive.

FRUIT: Pome, 1/4 to 1/3″ diameter, rounded, cranberry red, August through September (October–November), borne singly, quite attractive for this feature alone, often heavy fruiting.

CULTURE: Transplant from a container; almost all low-growing cotoneasters are container-grown; prefers moist, well-drained soil but will grow in about any situation except those that are permanently wet; light sandy soil and heavy clays are acceptable; acid or alkaline, in fact does extremely well in high pH soils; withstands considerable drought once established; in Czechoslovakian tests detached leaves of various Cotoneasters displayed relatively good drought resistance; displays medium to high soil salt tolerance.

DISEASES AND INSECTS: Mites, in dry situations, can render this species brown, hawthorn lace bug, fireblight occasionally presents a problem, in French tests, artificial inoculations with *Erwinia amylovora* showed that *all* 50 taxa tested were susceptible, with the best resistance in 'Streib's Fiddling', 'Excellenz', and *C. horizontalis*; least resistance in *C. dammeri*, *C. salicifolius*, and *C.* × *watereri*; scale and pear slug on some species and cultivars.

LANDSCAPE VALUE: Effective as bank cover, foundation plant, near wall where branches can hang over, facer plant in shrub border, ground or large area cover, used around campuses a great deal; have seen it used with *Myrica pensylvanica* and the combination is beautiful in summer foliage; probably overused by landscape architects and nurserymen especially in Midwest but, nonetheless, a valuable landscape plant which offers good foliage and fruit; can present a maintenance problem for it is difficult to clean leaves and trash out of the interior of the plant; was surprised to see this species performing so well in the Salt Lake City-Provo, UT areas; on Brigham Young's campus the plants were much more heavily fruited than I had ever noticed in the Midwest and East; observed significant winter kill in Midwest after exposure to –20°F during winter of 1976–77; does not perform well in heat of Zone 7 to 8; rated the most popular *Cotoneaster* in a 1989 *American Nurseryman* survey.

CULTIVARS:

'Blackburn'—A more refined and compact form; has appeared in a few Midwest nurseries.

PROPAGATION: Seeds should be scarified in acid for 60 minutes and then provided 60 plus days at 41°F; seeds have a hard endocarp; the degree of hardness varies among species and consequently the time of acid treatment should vary; see *Contrib. Boyce Thompson Inst.* 6:323–338 (1934) for detailed information on seed germination; in general softwood cuttings of all cotoneasters root readily if treated with 1000 to 3000 ppm IBA-quick dip and placed in peat:perlite or sand under mist; from my experiences it is doubtful if there is a species or cultivar that cannot be rooted with some measure of success; many of the ground cover types like the above, *C. dammeri* and cultivars frequently root where the prostrate stems touch moist soil.

NATIVE HABITAT: Western China. Introduced 1910.

RELATED SPECIES:

Cotoneaster adpressus Bois. — Creeping Cotoneaster

LEAVES: Alternate, simple, broadly ovate or obovate, 1/4 to 5/8″ long, acute or obtusish, mucronate, lustrous dark green and glabrous on both surfaces except with a few scattered hairs beneath, wavy margined, somewhat scoop-shaped; petiole—1/2″ long; leaf much like *C. apiculatus* perhaps more undulating; plants I have seen have lustrous dark green leaves but some literature says dull green.

Cotoneaster adpressus, (kō-tō-nē-as′tēr ad-pres′us), Creeping Cotoneaster, is a very dwarf, close-growing, compact, rigidly branching, 1 to 1 1/2′ high shrub, spreading 4 to 6′ and rooting where branches touch the soil. The leaves are glossy dark green; flowers are solitary or in pairs, white tipped rose; fruit is a pome, 1/4 to 1/3″ diameter, dark red. Regarded by some authorities as a variety of *C. horizontalis*. This is a beautiful cotoneaster rivaling or surpassing *C. apiculatus* for fruit effect. More common in East than Midwest. Variety *praecox* is a more vigorous form growing to 3′ high and 6′ wide; the leaves (1/2 to 1″ long) and red fruits (1/3 to 1/2″ long) are larger. Even with the above described differences I find it difficult to separate the variety and species and both of these from *C. apiculatus*. The leaves of *C. adpressus* and the variety have a rather undulating surface that is quite distinct. A cultivar that masquerades under the name 'Little Gem' or 'Tom Thumb' is known. It forms a dense, closely branched, broad-spreading mound of lustrous dark green leaves and is a beautiful plant but its exact affinity is unknown. In the last edition of this work it was listed with *C. horizontalis* but is probably more properly placed here. Another cultivar called 'Boer' out of Holland looks promising because of the large red fruits that color early and remain on the plant into winter. Western China. Introduced 1896; the variety cultivated 1905. Zone 4b to 7.

Cotoneaster dammeri Schneid. — Bearberry Cotoneaster
(kō-tō-nē-as′tĕr dam′er-ī)

LEAVES: Alternate, simple, evergreen, elliptic to elliptic-oblong, acutish or obtusish, mucronulate, rarely emarginate, cuneate, 3/4 to 1 1/4″ long, 1/4 to 5/8″ wide, glabrous and lustrous dark green above, glaucescent and slightly reticulate beneath, strigose pubescent at first, soon glabrous, 4 to 6 vein pairs; petiole—1/4″ long; semi-evergreen to evergreen in protected areas; usually tardily evergreen in exposed locations; leaves assuming a purplish tinge in late fall and winter.
BUDS: Like all cotoneaster—similar; see under *C. lucidus*.
STEM: Relatively fine, quite pubescent when young, changing to reddish brown at maturity.

SIZE: 1 to 1 1/2′ in height, spread 6′ and more due to ability to root freely where branches contact soil, can grow to 3′ high.
HARDINESS: Zone 5 to 7(8); severely injured at –30°F.
HABIT: Very low, prostrate, evergreen to semi-evergreen shrub with slender, creeping stems keeping close to the ground; will cover a large area in a short period of time; branches root readily when in contact with the soil; becomes wild, woolly and ragged with age; requires pruning to keep it pristine.
RATE: Fast.
TEXTURE: Fine in all seasons.
LEAF COLOR: Lustrous dark green in summer and fall; assuming a dull dark green to reddish purple color in winter.
FLOWERS: White, 5-petaled, 1/3 to 1/2″ diameter, solitary or in pairs, borne in (late April, Athens) late May, not overwhelming.
FRUIT: Pome, 1/4″ wide, globose or top-shaped, usually with 5 nutlets, bright red, late summer; good for color, however, usually sparsely produced.
CULTURE: Transplants well from containers; adaptable but prefers well-drained soil; occurs wild on heaths (peaty areas) and rocky ground; one of the easiest cotoneasters to grow.
DISEASES AND INSECTS: Subject to usual problems; I have noticed great quantities of aphids on this plant; in the South has not been as fireblight susceptible as some species; highly susceptible to hawthorn lace bug and plantings seldom persist more than 5 years.
LANDSCAPE VALUE: The species and cultivars are among the best evergreen ground covers; excellent on banks, gentle slopes, masses, shrub border, low facing shrub, foundation and as a possible espaliered effect; the solid carpet of glossy green is difficult to duplicate with other ground covers; extremely fast-growing and can cover an area faster than *C. apiculatus* or *C. adpressus*; has picked up steam in the southeastern nursery and landscape trades and is really the only cotoneaster of commercial consequence; can be directly rooted in the container and will become a 12 to 18″ high, well-branched, salable plant in a single growing season; used extensively on banks and for large area cover; unfortunately, does not hold up over time and can become ratty in 3 to 5 years; for the past 5 to 7 years was utilized in large quantities in Athens-Atlanta landscapes but has fallen from favor because of less than stellar performance; does not age gracefully; great for quick landscape fix, not a permanent solution.
CULTIVARS:
Canadian Creeper™ ('Moner')—Grows 6″ high with graceful, weeping habit, white flowers, red fruits; Monrovia 1995 introduction.
'Coral Beauty' ('Royal Beauty', 'Pink Beauty')—Excellent free-fruiting form with coral red fruits, rich glossy evergreen foliage, 1′ by 3 to 6′; certainly does not rival *C. apiculatus* or *C. adpressus* for fruit effect

but is slightly superior to 'Skogholm'; I have seen many patches of this and it grows taller than 1', often 2 to 2 1/2'; a good quick fix and possibly more handsome than 'Skogholm'; more commonly listed as 'Royal Beauty' in commerce; 'Royal Carpet' is also similar.

'Eichholz'—Perhaps a hybrid between *C. dammeri* and *C. microphyllus* var. *colcheatus*; grows 10 to 12" high, 8 to 10' wide, small (1/2 to 3/4" long) bright green leaves assume yellow to orange red color in autumn, carmine red fruits; 'Oakwood' is a popular name.

'Lowfast'—Supposedly extremely hardy with good dark glossy green foliage; abundant glossy red fruits; 12" high.

'Major'—A more vigorous selection with leaves 1 to 1 1/2" long, some leaves turning yellow-orange with the onset of cold weather; more winter hardy than species.

'Mooncreeper' ('Moon Creeper')—A low-growing, mat-forming selection with lustrous dark green foliage; becoming more common in the Southeast, have grown in Athens, excellent foliage.

var. *radicans*—Virtually unknown in the United States but a particularly good low-growing form and, as I have seen it, will doubtfully grow more than 4 to 6" high; leaves about 1/2" long and more rounded than 'Coral Beauty' and 'Skogholm', petiole 1/5 to 3/5" long; 'Major' is apparently confused with this type; var. *radicans* is quite common in English gardens where it makes a fine lustrous dark green carpet, long persistent red fruit.

'Skogholm'—An extremely vigorous form with prostrate or serpentine branches; will grow 1 1/2 to 3' high; a two-year-old plant may be 3' across and can spread several feet each year; it is not a free-fruiting form; used this cultivar extensively in my Illinois garden; really covers an area fast; tends to send up vertical shoots which should be cut off to maintain ground cover effect; 'Skogholm' was raised in Sweden and put into commerce about 1950.

'Streib's Findling'—First saw in 1987 in the Bundesgartenschau in Dusseldorf, Germany, later to discover that the flat-growing, 4 to 6" high, dull dark blue-green leaf form was first raised in Germany; foliage is not quite as lustrous as other cultivars and is probably no longer than 1/2"; produces white flowers and red fruits but their relative abundance is unknown.

PROPAGATION: Cuttings, anytime during the growing season, treat with 1000 ppm IBA, quick dip, peat:perlite, mist, 100% rooting; perhaps the easiest *Cotoneaster* to root.

NATIVE HABITAT: Central China. Introduced 1900.

RELATED SPECIES: There are two sections of cotoneasters, those with pinkish, upright petals called Cotoneaster and those with white, spreading, more or less orbicular petals called Chaenopetalum. *Cotoneaster adpressus*, *C. apiculatus*, *C. divaricatus*, *C. horizontalis*, and *C. lucidus* belong to Cotoneaster; the others treated herein are of the section Chaenopetalum.

Cotoneaster congestus Bak. — Pyrenees Cotoneaster
LEAVES: Alternate, simple, evergreen to semi-evergreen, oval or obovate, about 1/3" long, 1/3" wide, obtuse, cuneate, dull dark green above, whitish beneath at first, becoming glabrous; petiole—1/12" long, slender, nearly glabrous.

STEM: Pubescent when young, glabrous at maturity.

Cotoneaster congestus, (kō-tō-nē-as'tēr kon-jes'tus), Pyrenees Cotoneaster, is not well known but appears to warrant consideration. It is an evergreen shrub of low, compact, dense outline, 1 1/2 to 2 1/2' high and wide. The branches, instead of spreading, are decurved and the whole shrub forms a compact, rounded mass resembling a small haystack. The leaves are dull green (effect is blue-green) above and do not assume the glossiness of the previous species. The 1/4" diameter flowers are pinkish white. The bright red, rounded, 1/4 to 1/3" diameter fruits are attractive. It makes a handsome small evergreen for the rock garden, or for small borders where it will not be overrun by more aggressive shrubs. 'Likiang' is described as slow-growing with arching branches to 3' high, small pink flowers and red fruits. Himalayas. Introduced 1868. Zone 6 to 7.

Cotoneaster conspicuus Marq. — Wintergreen Cotoneaster
LEAVES: Alternate, simple, evergreen to semi-evergreen, ovate, oval and oblanceolate to linear-obovate, 1/6 to 1/4" long, 1/12 to 1/4" wide, obtuse and often mucronulate at apex, shining black-green and glabrous above, gray and pubescent below.

STEM: Pubescent at maturity.

Cotoneaster conspicuus, (kō-tō-nē-as'tēr kon-spik'ū-us), Wintergreen Cotoneaster, is an evergreen shrub of variable habit, usually prostrate or spreading, 3 to 4' high but in some forms growing to 8' tall or more. At

Wisley, saw an 8′ by 10′ dense shrub with abundant fruits. The glossy dark green leaves are extremely small, and the underside of the leaf is gray and woolly. The white flowers range from 3/8 to 1/2″ diameter. The bright, shining, dark red-purple, globose to obovoid fruit averages 3/8″ in diameter. It is considered one of the better fruiting shrubs because the fruits are not attractive to birds and usually persist throughout the winter. Variety *decorus* ('Decorus'), Necklace Cotoneaster, is a relatively prostrate form (12 to 15″) with short, rigid branches, silvery foliage and abundant fruits. At Wisley, the plant labeled as *decorus* was 5′ high and more green than silver. In Europe, several named selections include: 'Highlight', 'Flameburst', 'Red Glory', 'Red Pearl', and 'Tiny Tim'. I have not seen them in the United States. Western China. Introduced 1925. Zone 6 to 7.

Cotoneaster microphyllus Wallich ex Lindl. — Little-leaf Cotoneaster
LEAVES: Alternate, simple, evergreen, obovate to obovate-oblong, 1/4 to 1/2″ long, half or less wide, obtuse, rarely acutish or emarginate, cuneate, lustrous dark green above, densely woolly below.
STEM: Pubescent when young.

Cotoneaster microphyllus, (kō-tō-nē-as′tēr mī-krō-fil′us), Little-leaf Cotoneaster, is an evergreen shrub of low-spreading or even prostrate habit, rarely more than 2 to 3′ high. The 1/4 to 1/2″ long, glossy deep green leaves create a light, airy texture; the leaves are grayish and woolly beneath. The 1/3″ diameter, white flowers are followed by 1/4″ diameter, rounded, scarlet red fruits. This species is closely allied to *C. congestus* and *C. conspicuus*. Himalayas. Introduced 1824. Zone 5 to 7. Several varieties and cultivars have been selected:
> var. *colcheatus*—This form is more prostrate and compact in habit with broader, brighter green leaves; now listed as *C. cashmiriensis* Klotz.
> 'Cooperi'—Small, dense mound with tiny leaves.
> 'Emerald Spray'—This selection displays a distinctive spreading, arching, dense growth habit; the leaves are glossy emerald green; flowers are white and the red fruit is about 1/3″ in diameter; in areas of high humidity this cultivar is quite susceptible to fireblight.
> 'Teulon Porter'—Prostrate form with amoeba-like spread, forming a large circle as the shoots radiate from the center; white flowers, red fruits.
> var. *thymifolius* (Lindl.) Koehne ('Thymifolius')—A dwarf or prostrate shrub, with numerous, rigid branches; the shining deep green leaves are narrower than in the species and are made to appear more so by the curling under of the margins; now listed as *C. linearifolius* (Klotz.) Klotz.

ADDITIONAL NOTES: The above three cotoneasters are susceptible to fireblight and their use should be tempered in the South. Generally, the three species flower about mid-April in Athens, mid-May Boston. Truly, if these were adaptable landscape species their presence would be known. Alas, they are not in the first or second order of landscape shrubs for most of the United States.

Cotoneaster divaricatus Rehd. & Wils. — Spreading Cotoneaster
(kō-tō-nē-as′tēr di-vãr-i-kā′tus)

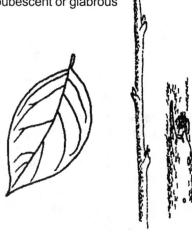

LEAVES: Alternate, simple, elliptic or broad-elliptic, acute at ends or rounded at apex, 1/3 to 1″ long, 1/4 to 5/8″ wide, lustrous dark green above, lighter and slightly pubescent or glabrous beneath, 3 to 4 vein pairs; petiole—about 1/12″ long.
BUDS: Similar to other cotoneasters.
STEM: Slender, purple, appressed pubescent, older stems becoming dark brown.

SIZE: 5 to 6′ in height with a comparable or larger spread (6 to 8′).
HARDINESS: Zone 4 to 7; growing on the Georgia campus but not a happy camper.
HABIT: Spreading, multi-stemmed shrub of rounded outline, outer branches are long, slender, and tend to droop creating a fine appearance.
RATE: Medium to fast.
TEXTURE: Fine in leaf; medium-fine in winter; tremendous textural asset in the shrub border.

LEAF COLOR: Dark glossy green, unexcelled for summer leaf color; fall color can be outstanding with the leaves changing to fluorescent yellow-red-purple combinations which persist for 4 to 6 weeks.

FLOWERS: Rose, solitary or in three's, late May to early June, not spectacular, somewhat masked by the foliage.

FRUIT: Pome, 1/3″ long and 1/4″ wide, egg-shaped, red to dark red, early September through November; one of the handsomest in fruit of the Chinese cotoneasters but not overwhelming from long distances.

CULTURE: Same as described for *C. lucidus*.

DISEASES AND INSECTS: One of the most desirable, ornamental, and trouble-free of the cotoneasters, although susceptible to the typical problems which beset them.

LANDSCAPE VALUE: Multi-faceted shrub, can be successfully used in foundation plantings, hedges, groups, borders, masses; blends well with other plants; foliage is unrivaled in summer and fall; integrates well with broadleaf evergreens.

PROPAGATION: Seed, as described for *C. apiculatus*; cuttings, softwood collected in early June, dipped in 1000 ppm IBA solution, rooted 90% in three months in sand under mist (personal experience); another worker reported 100% rooting in six weeks with untreated cuttings collected in early July.

ADDITIONAL NOTES: Always one of my favorite medium-sized cotoneasters in the Midwest and East; have one plant on the Georgia campus that has plugged along for years; not well-adapted to the heat; appears less prone to mites and fireblight than many cotoneasters.

NATIVE HABITAT: Central and western China. Introduced 1907.

Cotoneaster horizontalis Decne. — Rockspray or Rock Cotoneaster
(kō-tō-nē-as′tĕr hôr-i-zon-tā′lis)

LEAVES: Alternate, simple, suborbicular to broad-elliptic, 1/5 to 1/2″ long, about three-fourth's as wide, acute at ends and mucronate at the apex, lustrous dark green, glabrous above, sparingly strigose-pubescent beneath; petiole—1/12″ long, strigose-pubescent; leaf blade lies flat and does not have the undulating character of *C. apiculatus* or *C. adpressus*.

STEM: The interesting fishbone pattern in which the branches are borne provides a distinct identification feature (see drawing).

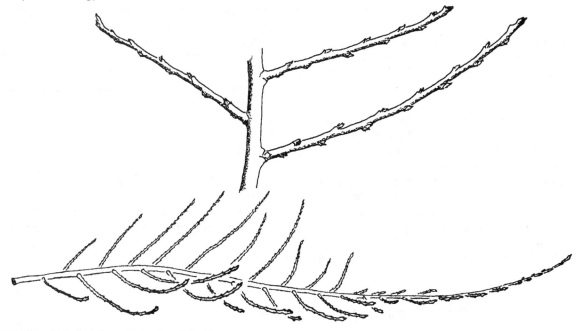

SIZE: 2 to 3′ in height, spreading 5 to 8′.

HARDINESS: Zone 5 to 7; some damage after -20°F during winter of 1976–77; best no further south than Zone 7; had a rather large planting on the Georgia campus that succumbed to mites and lace bug.

HABIT: Usually a low, flat, dense shrub with horizontally spreading branches; the branches almost form tiers and create a very unusual layered effect; often used against walls in England where the plant easily grows 6 to 10′ high.

RATE: Slow to medium.

TEXTURE: Fine in leaf, possibly medium when defoliated although the branch detail does contribute to a rather fine winter character.

LEAF COLOR: Excellent glossy dark green in summer changing to reddish purple combinations in fall; leaves hold late, often into late November.

FLOWERS: Perfect, pink, rather small (1/4″ diameter), borne in mid to late May and into early June; single or 2 together, subsessile; flowers are very small but when present in great quantity make a nice show; the bees seem to like the flowers as I was almost stung collecting cuttings from a particularly handsome plant at the Holden Arboretum, Mentor, OH.

FRUIT: Small pome, bright red, 1/5 to 1/4″ diameter; effective in late August through October; not as showy as *C. apiculatus* and *C. adpressus*, but borne in sufficient numbers to be considered showy.

CULTURE: Same as described for *C. lucidus*; this species is deciduous or semi-evergreen to almost evergreen depending on location; in northern locations it would tend toward the former, in southern towards the latter; I have seen the plant in March at Bernheim Arboretum, Clermont, KY, completely evergreen; in Georgia the plant is tardily deciduous.

DISEASES AND INSECTS: Same as discussed under *C. lucidus*.

LANDSCAPE VALUE: Nice ground cover plant; I have seen it used by gradually descending steps and it fit in very well; would work as bank cover, in masses or groupings; used for espalier, especially on walls.

CULTIVARS:
    'Ascendens'—Upright growth; leaves 1/2 to 3/5″ long, ovate, acuminate; crimson fruit.

    'Dart's Deputation'—Clear bright red fruit.

    'Dart's Splendid'—Profuse brilliant red fruit.

    'Hessei'—Considered a hybrid between *C. horizontalis* and *C. adpressus* var. *praecox*; irregularly branched deciduous shrub with decurving branches; small 1/4 to 3/5″ long, round or broad elliptic, lustrous dark green leaves; pinkish red flowers in May–June; globose, 1/4″ wide, red fruits with 2 to 3 nutlets; has been in the Midwest for a time and is being pushed by a plant evaluation program in the Chicago, IL area; originated by H.A. Hesse, Weener, West Germany before 1933.

    'Perpusillus'—A very prostrate form with leaves about 1/2″ long; 1′ by 5 to 7′; a handsome clone; I grew this form in my Illinois garden; it is definitely more prostrate than the species and the lustrous dark green leaves are handsome; unfortunately, it is one of the most susceptible to fireblight; see Davis and Peterson, "Susceptibility of Cotoneasters to Fireblight," *J. Arboriculture* May (1976); may be considered a variety.

    'Robustus'—A clone I observed at the Morton Arboretum, Lisle, IL; considerably more upright (3′ high) and vigorous than the species; a free-fruiting form; listed as *C. hjelmquistii* Flinck & Hylmö.

    'Saxatilis'—More compact than the species with distinct "fish bone" branching pattern; quite prostrate with smaller leaves; sparse fruiting; introduced by Hesse of Germany in 1950.

    'Variegatus'—Leaves are edged with white; turn rose red in autumn; considered one of the daintiest of variegated shrubs; from my experience, it is certainly one of the slowest growing; 2 to 3′ high, 5 to 8′ wide; large specimens in Europe;

    'Wilsonii'—The one plant I saw appeared similar to 'Robusta'.

    Two named hybrids, 'Gracia' and 'Valkenburg', resulted from crosses of *C. horizontalis* × *C. salicifolius* var. *floccosus*. 'Valkenburg' is supposed to have some value as a semi-evergreen ground cover. Neither of these cultivars fruit.

PROPAGATION: Seed, scarify in concentrated sulfuric acid for 90 to 180 minutes, followed by stratification at 41°F in moist medium for 90 to 120 days. Cuttings collected in June, July, and August root readily.

ADDITIONAL NOTES: Perhaps the best of the low-growing types; lovely foliage and intriguing habit; widely used in England where it seems to grow with abandon; not as cold hardy and popular as *C. apiculatus* in the United States.

NATIVE HABITAT: Western China. Introduced about 1880.

Cotoneaster lucidus Schldl. — Hedge Cotoneaster
(kō-tō-nē-as′tēr lū′si-dus)

LEAVES: Alternate, simple, elliptic-ovate to oblong-ovate, 3/4 to 2 1/2″ long, 1/2 to 1″ wide, acute, rarely acuminate, broad-cuneate, slightly pubescent above at first, lustrous dark green, sparingly pubescent beneath, more densely on the veins, finally often nearly glabrous; petiole—1/8 to 1/5″ long, pubescent.

BUDS: Weakly imbricate, 2 outer bud scales parted and exposing the hairy interior, brown to pale gray in color, usually appressed.

STEM: Slender, buff or light brown, often peeling creating an onion-skin effect.

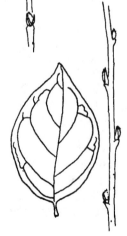

SIZE: 6 to 10′ high and as wide.
HARDINESS: Zone 4 to 7.
HABIT: Erect, round-topped shrub with slender, spreading branches, usually taller than broad.
RATE: Medium.
TEXTURE: Medium in leaf; depending on whether the plant is left unpruned or made into a hedge, medium to coarse, respectively, in winter.
LEAF COLOR: Lustrous dark green in summer; yellow to red combinations in fall; actually very effective but little praised for its fall coloration.
FLOWERS: Pinkish white, rather small and ineffective, mid to late May; borne in 2- to 5-flowered cymes.
FRUIT: Berry-like pome, black, globose, 1/3 to 1/2″ diameter, with 3 or 4 nutlets, September and persisting.
CULTURE: In general cotoneasters have sparse root systems and should be moved balled-and-burlapped or preferably as a container plant; they prefer well-drained, loose, fertile soil with adequate moisture but do quite well in dry, poor soils; tolerant of wind; pH adaptable; somewhat tolerant of seaside conditions; prune almost anytime; once established they are very vigorous, strong-growing landscape plants; full sun or light shade.
DISEASES AND INSECTS: Leaf spots, canker, fire blight, hawthorn lace bug, scales, spider mites, cotoneaster webworm, sinuate pear tree borer, and pear leaf blister mite.
LANDSCAPE VALUE: Primarily used as a hedge because of upright branching habit; excellent for screens or groupings because of handsome foliage; tends to be overused as a hedge; often plants are stereotyped as to landscape use and this plant has been relegated to the status of hedge plant.
PROPAGATION: Seed should be scarified in concentrated sulfuric acid for 5 to 20 minutes followed by cold stratification in moist peat at 40°F for 30 to 90 days. Cuttings rooted well when taken in early July; reports that this species can be difficult to root from cuttings.
NATIVE HABITAT: Siberia and other parts of northern Asia. Cultivated 1840.

RELATED SPECIES:

Cotoneaster acutifolius Turcz., (kō-tō-nē-as′tēr à-kū-tī-fō′li-us), Peking Cotoneaster, is confused with *C. lucidus* in the trade. The principal difference is in the foliage which is dull green, not shining and more hairy. Bean considers this an inferior cotoneaster and possibly a poor form of *C. lucidus*. Native to Mongolia, northern and western China and the eastern Himalayas. Introduced 1883. Zone 4 to 7.

Cotoneaster multiflorus Bunge. — Many-flowered Cotoneaster
(kō-tō-nē-as′tēr mul-ti-flō′rus)

LEAVES: Alternate, simple, broad-ovate to ovate, 3/4 to 2 1/2″ long, 1/2 to 1 1/2″ wide, acute to obtuse, rounded or broad cuneate at base, bluish green above, at first tomentose beneath, soon glabrous; petiole—1/4 to 1/2″ long.
BUDS: Similar to other cotoneasters.
STEM: Purple when young, to reddish green and finally gray; slightly pubescent to glabrous.

SIZE: 8 to 12′ and greater in height (17′ high specimens on Illinois campus) and 12 to 15′ in spread.
HARDINESS: Zone 4 to 7.
HABIT: Upright, spreading, weeping or mounded at maturity with long arching branches forming a fountain much like *Spiraea* × *vanhouttei*, Vanhoutte Spirea.
RATE: Medium; once well-established develops very rapidly.
TEXTURE: Medium-fine in foliage; medium-coarse in winter; looks a bit naked in the winter landscape and is difficult to conceal due to large size.
LEAF COLOR: Soft gray-green when unfolding, changing to gray or blue-green in mature leaf; fall color not much different or with a hint of yellow; summer foliage is different which adds unusual contrasting color to the normal green complement of most shrubs.
FLOWERS: White, each flower about 1/2″ diameter, early to mid-May, abundantly produced in 3 to 12 or more flowered corymbs, unpleasantly scented; very spectacular in flower as the flowers are borne upright along the stem on slender peduncles and effectively use the gray-green foliage as a background for accentuation of their beauty; could be mistaken for *Spiraea* × *vanhouttei* but is most definitely a superior plant.

FRUIT: Berry-like pome, 1/3″ diameter, red, late August holding into early October, borne in great quantities; appears with the foliage and falls before leaf abscission, so the total ornamental effect is somewhat masked; very beautiful in full fruit; I rate this the best flowering and fruiting shrub of the large, deciduous cotoneaster group.

CULTURE: Supposedly somewhat difficult to transplant; should be root pruned to develop good, fibrous root system; probably well-adapted to container production at least in small sizes; strongly prefers well-drained soil, sunny, airy location and no standing water.

DISEASES AND INSECTS: Comparing the cotoneasters on the Illinois campus, this species was the most trouble-free and exhibited abundant growth every year; I have not observed the fireblight or mite problem which have occurred frequently on *C. apiculatus*, although fireblight has been reported as troublesome; German research reported high fireblight susceptibility, also true for var. *calocarpus*.

LANDSCAPE VALUE: Requires room to spread, shrub border, massing, parks, golf courses, almost any public area because of low maintenance aspect; there were several large (16 to 18′) specimens on the Illinois campus which were bountiful in flower and fruit, unfortunately, I was never able to successfully propagate them from cuttings.

CULTIVARS:

var. *calocarpus* Rehd. & Wils.—Leaves longer and narrower than the type; fruits larger and more numerous; W.J. Bean termed this variety "a singularly beautiful fruit bearing shrub."

PROPAGATION: Seed should be treated as described under *C. apiculatus*. Cuttings, collected in June by this author, treated with 1000 ppm IBA solution, placed in sand under mist yielded 1% rooted cuttings; according to an Illinois nurseryman, *C. multiflorus* roots readily from June-collected softwood cuttings.

NATIVE HABITAT: Western China. Introduced 1900.

RELATED SPECIES:

Cotoneaster racemiflorus (Desf.) Booth ex Bosse var. **soongoricus** (Req. & Herd.) Schneid., (kō-tō-nē-as′tĕr rā-sem-i-flō′rus soon-gôr′i-kus), Sungari Redbead Cotoneaster, is similar in form, but slightly hardier (Zone 4), with bluer foliage and great abundance of pink (rose) fruits. In cultivation it has proven to be a graceful and exceptionally free-fruiting shrub, thriving in dry, sandy soil. This taxon is little known and used, but definitely should be brought to the gardener's eye. An asset in any garden while the liability shrubs (forsythia, deutzia, mock-orange) continue to be overplanted. Native of central Asia, introduced by E.H. Wilson, the great plant explorer. Introduced 1910. Zone 4 to 7.

Cotoneaster salicifolius Franch. — Willowleaf Cotoneaster
(kō-tō-nē-as′tĕr sal-is-i-fō′li-us)

LEAVES: Alternate, simple, evergreen, oval-oblong to ovate-lanceolate, 1 1/2 to 3 1/2″ long, 1/3 to 3/4″ wide, lustrous dark green, rugose and glabrous above, gray tomentose below, 5 to 12 prominent impressed vein pairs; leaves of species and most cultivars assume a purplish tinge in winter.

SIZE: 10 to 15′ high, not as wide-spreading.

HARDINESS: Zone 6 to 7.

HABIT: Large evergreen shrub of spreading, arching habit, will become leggy at base unless pruned.

RATE: Medium.

TEXTURE: Medium through the seasons.

LEAF COLOR: Lustrous dark green during the growing season, may develop a suffusion of plum purple during the winter months; appears to be red to purple pigment in the leaves of the low-growing types which may, in fact, be hybrids with *C. dammeri*.

FLOWERS: Individual flowers small, white, borne in woolly, 2″ diameter, flat-topped corymbs, May–June; floral effect is not really potent due to leaf competition; flowers generally stinky.

FRUIT: Bright red, 1/5 to 1/4″ wide, subglobose, with 2 or 3 nutlets, often persisting through winter.

CULTURE: Move as a container plant; best in moist, well-drained, acid soil or approaching neutral pH soil; sun or partial shade; may be tougher than given credit and should be tested, especially in the upper southern states, for relative worth.

DISEASES AND INSECTS: As described under *C. lucidus*; I keep looking for significant fireblight infestations but, to date, have not observed same.

LANDSCAPE VALUE: Large evergreen shrub valued for fruits especially in European gardens; perhaps more important as a parent in some of the larger fruited or lower growing, ground cover types.

CULTIVARS:

'Autumn Fire' ('Herbstfeuer')—A good, rather lax-growing, evergreen ground cover; it grows 2 to 3' high; the 1 1/2 to 2 1/4" long leaves are extremely glossy and leathery; scarlet fruits contrast nicely with the foliage and persist into winter; the leaves assume a reddish purple tinge in the winter months; at one time this was considered of hybrid origin but is now placed under *C. salicifolius*.

'Emerald Carpet'—More compact, tighter habit and smaller foliage than the species; white flowers, red fruits; a Monrovia introduction.

var. *floccosus* Rehd. & Wils.—Probably more common in cultivation and is semi-evergreen in the North; the lustrous dark green leaves are smaller (3/4 to 2 1/2" long); the flowers in smaller corymbs (to 1" diameter); the fruits wider (1/4" diameter) than *C. salicifolius*; it is a very graceful variety; *C. salicifolius* is a variable species and has given rise to seedlings of diverse growth habit.

'Gnom' ('Gnome')—Low-growing, 8 to 12" high, evergreen ground cover; leaves 1" long, lance-shaped, lustrous dark green above, floccose-tomentose beneath; fruit light red in dense clusters; have watched this form at Wisley over the years and am really impressed by low-growing nature.

'Parkteppich'—A good looking evergreen ground cover usually taller than 'Autumn Fire'; unfortunately, like that cultivar, never proved hardy in our Illinois garden; leaves 1" long, 1/3" wide.

'Repens' ('Repandens')—Some references say this cultivar does not exist but I have seen it enough to be positive it does; this is a good, low-growing, evergreen to semi-evergreen form with 1 to 1 1/4" long, lustrous dark green foliage and small red fruits; I have observed it being used in the Cincinnati, OH area with considerable success; depending on the degree of snow cover and severity of temperatures it ranges from evergreen to semi-evergreen; I do not doubt that this is the situation with most of these ground cover types; it also goes under the names 'Avondrood' and 'Dortmund'; foliage becomes reddish purple in winter; have seen cultivars 'HQ' and 'Green Carpet' described from East Coast nurseries, both are low-growing forms.

'Saldam'—Similar to 'Autumn Fire' but leaves remain green through winter.

'Scarlet Leader'—Excellent, low-growing, ground-hugging, glossy dark green ground cover; this cultivar was planted on a steep bank at the University's Botanical Garden and in one complete growing season formed a solid mat; witnessed no mites or fireblight in the early years; have used it in my garden where it grew 2 to 3' high and 6 to 8' wide; develops a red-purple winter leaf color; definitely grows larger than the literature ascribes; unfortunately, like *C. dammeri* cultivars looks good early on, becoming less attractive with age.

ADDITIONAL NOTES: A good review article on the ground cover cotoneasters appeared in *Dendroflora* No. 3:20–27 (1966); much of the information included here was extracted from the article. I was sent a branch of *C. salicifolius* by a lady who wanted to know which viburnum she had in her garden.

NATIVE HABITAT: Western China. Introduced 1908.

RELATED SPECIES:

Cotoneaster lacteus W.W. Sm. (formerly *C. parneyi* Poss.) — Parney Cotoneaster

LEAVES: Alternate, simple, evergreen, 1 1/4 to 2 1/4" long, 3/4 to 1 1/4" wide, obovate or broadly oval, obtuse and mucronate, rounded or broad cuneate, coriaceous, dark green above, whitish tomentose beneath, veins impressed, 6 to 9 prominent vein pairs.

Cotoneaster lacteus, (kō-tō-nē-as'tēr lak'tē-us), Parney Cotoneaster, is a 6 to 10' high evergreen shrub that has prospered on the Georgia campus despite record cold and drought and a tremendous fireblight epidemic. For those reasons it is worthy of inclusion. The white flowers (off-scented) occur in 2 to 3" wide corymbs in mid-May in Athens. Again, like *C. salicifolius*, the effect is not overwhelming. The 3/10" long, 1/8" wide, red fruits (with 2 nutlets) are handsome and persist through winter. Will never take the place of evergreen holly in the Southeast but offers different texture and form. Have observed several large plantings on the Georgia campus and Atlanta Botanical Garden. All have flourished without any special attention. The red fruits are particularly attractive against the dark green leaves. The loose, lax, upright-spreading, shrub-like habit is also elegant. Good plant for shrub border, grouping or massing. Has prospered in full sun and partial shade situations. High degree of resistance to hawthorn lace bug. See *J. Environmental Horticulture* 10:99–101 (1992) and *Environmental Entomology* 16:365–367 (1987). Resistance predicated on lower leaf surface pubescence. Western China. Introduced 1930. Zone 6 to 8.

ADDITIONAL NOTES: *Cotoneaster* contains 70 or more species and according to some authors multiple hundreds. In my travels, I came across outstanding fruiting specimens of *C. frigidus* Wallich ex Lindl., *C. roseus* Edgew, *C.* × *watereri* Exell., and others. Then I slap myself into reality by asking the pragmatic question, "Why are they not grown in the United States to any degree?" The question is rhetorical. Insects, disease (fireblight), lack of cold hardiness, and short landscape half-life. In England, *C. frigidus* grows 20 to 30′ high. During our garden tours I have quizzed travelers as to the generic identity. Few even try because the American perception of a *Cotoneaster* is always that of a ground cover shrub. In fruit the various *C. frigidus* and *C.* × *watereri* types are beautiful.

Major cotoneaster collections in Europe include National Botanic Garden, Salaspils, Latvia with 120 taxa and Dr. Bertil Hylmo's collection of around 300 taxa in Bjuv, Sweden. His collection is termed a "Cotoneasteretum." Many of the scientific names from these collections do not appear in the more up-to-date horticultural literature. The learning curve never plateaus! My supposition is that *Cotoneaster* produces apomictic seeds and thus genetically uniform off-spring that sustain themselves as micro-species. *Crataegus* falls in the same category.

Two excellent nurseries on the West Coast: Forest Farm, 990 Tetherow Rd., Williams, OR, 97544-9599 and Heronswood Nursery, Ltd., 7530 288th ST. NE, Kingston, WA, 98346, offer the widest array of unusual cotoneasters of any United States nurseries. Also, both have splendid litanies of other genera and species that far outdistance the treatment in this *Manual*. Quality from both nurseries has been excellent.

Crataegus crusgalli L. — Cockspur Hawthorn
(krȧ-tē′gus krus-gā′li)

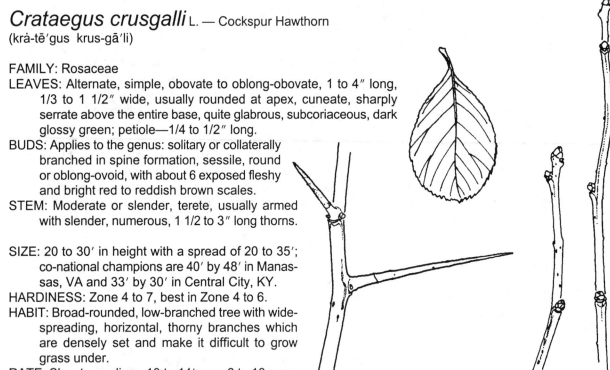

FAMILY: Rosaceae

LEAVES: Alternate, simple, obovate to oblong-obovate, 1 to 4″ long, 1/3 to 1 1/2″ wide, usually rounded at apex, cuneate, sharply serrate above the entire base, quite glabrous, subcoriaceous, dark glossy green; petiole—1/4 to 1/2″ long.

BUDS: Applies to the genus: solitary or collaterally branched in spine formation, sessile, round or oblong-ovoid, with about 6 exposed fleshy and bright red to reddish brown scales.

STEM: Moderate or slender, terete, usually armed with slender, numerous, 1 1/2 to 3″ long thorns.

SIZE: 20 to 30′ in height with a spread of 20 to 35′; co-national champions are 40′ by 48′ in Manassas, VA and 33′ by 30′ in Central City, KY.

HARDINESS: Zone 4 to 7, best in Zone 4 to 6.

HABIT: Broad-rounded, low-branched tree with wide-spreading, horizontal, thorny branches which are densely set and make it difficult to grow grass under.

RATE: Slow to medium, 10 to 14′ over 6 to 10 years.

TEXTURE: Medium-fine in leaf; medium in winter.

LEAF COLOR: Lustrous dark green in summer; bronze-red to purplish red in fall.

FLOWERS: Perfect, 1/2 to 2/3″ diameter, white, of disagreeable odor, May, effective for 7 to 10 days, borne in 2 to 3″ diameter, flat corymbs, flowers with 10 stamens, pink anthers, usually 2 styles.

FRUIT: Pome-like drupe, deep red, 3/8 to 1/2″ diameter; ripening in late September–October and persisting into late fall.

CULTURE: Transplant balled-and-burlapped in early spring as a small tree; tolerant of many soils but they should be well-drained; pH adaptable, however, I have noticed a few trees with chlorosis; full sun; tolerates soot and grime of cities; prune in winter or early spring; most bareroot liners and small trees show delayed bud break and need to be "sweated" into leaf, lay plants down, cover with a moist packing material until they break bud, temperatures should be in the 40 to 50° range.

DISEASES AND INSECTS: Fireblight, leaf blight, rusts (at least 9 species attack hawthorns), leaf spots, powdery mildews, scab, aphids, borers, western tent caterpillar, apple leaf blotch miner, lace bugs, leaf rollers, apple and thorn skeletonizer, plant hopper, scales and two spotted mite. Hawthorns, though lovely ornamentals, are severely affected by pests; the cedar hawthorn rust has been extremely bad as has the leaf blotch miner especially on *C. crusgalli*; the rust can affect the leaves, stems and fruits; I have seen it on all species treated here except *C.* × *lavallei*.

LANDSCAPE VALUE: Single specimen, groupings, screens, barrier plant, hedges; on the Illinois campus this species was effectively used around large buildings and softened the strong vertical lines; extensive use around residences must be tempered with the knowledge that the 2″ long thorns can seriously injure small children; in fact, I would not use this hawthorn in the landscape where small children are apt to play.

CULTIVARS:

var. *inermis*—Thornless type with the good features of the species; I had three under evaluation and found them to be vigorous and attractive trees; flowers and fruits similar to the species; have seen Crusader™ ('Cruzam') listed which is nothing more than a rename for var. *inermis*.

'Hooks'—A densely foliaged, round-headed form, 15 to 20′ high and wide, with disease resistant dark green foliage, white flowers, 3/8 to 1/2″ diameter red fruits, fewer thorns than species; have seen it listed as a hybrid between *C. crusgalli* and *C. prunifolium*.

'Splendens'—How different from the species, I am unsure, but listed by Forest Farm as a small, wide-spreading tree with glossy dark green foliage that turns purplish red in fall, white flowers and long lasting fruit.

PROPAGATION: Seed should be immersed in acid for 2 to 3 hours (seed should be dry) then warm stratified at 70 to 77°F for 120 days followed by 135 days at 41°F; other species do not have the bony endocarp and require only the warm-cold treatment; selected clones are budded on seedling understock.

ADDITIONAL NOTE: Only a few birds like the fruits of *Crataegus* and, consequently, they remain effective for a long time.

NATIVE HABITAT: Quebec to North Carolina and Kansas. Introduced 1656.

RELATED SPECIES:

Crataegus punctata Jacq., (krà-tē′gus punk-tā′tà), Thicket Hawthorn, grows 20 to 35′ high and is usually wider than tall at maturity. National champion is 38′ by 38′ in Canaan Valley Park, WV. The leaves are dull grayish green in summer. Flowers are white, fruit is dull red, 3/4″ diameter, ripening in October and falling soon after. Listed as quite susceptible to rust. Quebec to Ontario, Illinois to Georgia. Introduced 1716. Zone 4 to 7.

'Aurea' (f. *aurea*)—Yellow fruits and could be considered a forma as it has been found in the wild.

var. *inermis* ('Ohio Pioneer')—An essentially thornless type selected from a tree at the Secrest Arboretum, Wooster, OH, with good vigor, growth, and fruiting characteristics. I have seen the parent tree in flower and it is quite spectacular. This tree was found growing in the Secrest Arboretum nursery in 1962. At 10 years of age it had developed only three small thorns. The abundant white flowers are followed by dark red fruits in September or October. It is commercially available.

Crataegus laevigata (Poir.) DC. (*C. oxyacantha* L.) — English Hawthorn

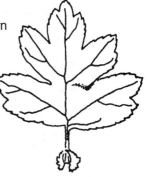

LEAVES: Alternate, simple, broad-ovate or obovate, 1/2 to 2 1/2″ long, 2/3's as wide, with 3 to 5 broad serrulate, obtuse or acutish lobes, lobes rounded or pointed, cuneate, glabrous, dark green; petiole—1/4 to 3/4″ long, slender.

Crataegus laevigata, (krà-tē′gus lē-vi-gā′tà), English Hawthorn, is a shrubby, low-branched, round-topped tree with a close, dense head of stiff, zig-zag, ascending, thorny (to 1″ long) branches reaching 15 to 20′ in height and 12 to 20′ in spread. The foliage is a deep dark green in summer, and does not color appreciably in fall. Flowers are white, with 20 stamens, anthers red, 2 or 3 styles, 5/8″ diameter, mid-May, borne in 5- to 12-flowered corymbs. Fruit is scarlet, 1/4 to 1/2″ long, ripening in September and October. The cultivars offer the greatest diversity in the landscape and include:

var. *aurea*—Fruit bright yellow.

'Autumn Glory'—Good growth habit, glossy green foliage, single white flowers and giant red fruit; however, probably a Zone 5 plant; susceptible to hawthorn leaf rust, very susceptible to fireblight; 15 to 18′ by 20′.

'Crimson Cloud'—A selection by Princeton Nurseries with good red, single flowers and resistance to the leaf blight which is so troublesome to 'Paul's Scarlet'; each flower has a white, star-shaped area in the center; glossy red fruits; supposedly does well under city conditions; I was unduly harsh on this tree having seen only young plants that were not impressive in flower; since 1983 I have observed a number of good sized specimens with excellent flower; 25′ by 18′.

'Paul's Scarlet' ('Paulii')—Flowers double, red, with a tinge of rose, lightening with opening; the most showy of all the hawthorns; arose as a branch sport about 1858 on a tree of the double pink var. *rosea-plena*; it was propagated by Mr. Paul who showed it at the International Horticultural Exhibition in 1866 under the name 'Paul's New Double Scarlet Hawthorn'; unfortunately, tremendously susceptible to hawthorn leaf spot or blight, *Entomosporium maculatum*, which in wet seasons may cause the tree to defoliate by July; in full flower a beautiful sight; 22' by 20'.

var. *plena* ('Plena')—Flowers double, white, with few fruits; Purdue University had several trees and they were attractive in flower.

var. *rosea* ('Rosea')—Flowers light rose, single; occurring frequently in the wild.

var. *rosea-plena* ('Rosea Flore Plena')—Flowers light rose, double.

var. *rubra*—A good fruiting form with 3/8″ diameter, bright red fruits; flowers single, white.

NATIVE HABITAT: *C. laevigata* is native to Europe, northern Africa. Long cultivated. Zone 4 to 7.

RELATED SPECIES: A hybrid, *C. × mordenensis* Boom., resulted from crosses between *C. laevigata* 'Paul's Scarlet' and *C. succulenta* at Morden Experimental Station, Manitoba, Canada. 'Toba' is a selection with double, white, fragrant flowers that age to pink. The dark green leaves are larger than *C. laevigata* with 2 to 4 lobes. The few plants I saw in Ohio were not very healthy and appeared to suffer from the same problem as 'Paul's Scarlet'. This form and others were selected for their high degree of resistance to rust. There is also a graft incompatibility problem that may explain the reason for the decline. 'Snowbird' is a double, white-flowered form that originated as an open pollinated seedling of 'Toba'; considered to be hardier than 'Toba'. 'Toba' is relatively common in the trade but doubtfully superior to *C. crusgalli* or *C. phaenopyrum*. Grows 20' by 20' with an upright-rounded outline. Fruit is red, 3/8″ long. 'Snowbird' and 'Toba' have been growing at the Milliken Arboretum, Spartanburg, SC and are terribly infected with diseases. Neither is a reliable performer in Zone 7 and 8 and are only suitable for colder climates. In these same evaluations the *best* hawthorn has been 'Winter King' followed by *C. phaenopyrum* and *C. × lavallei*.

Crataegus × lavallei Henriq. ex Lav. — Lavalle Hawthorn

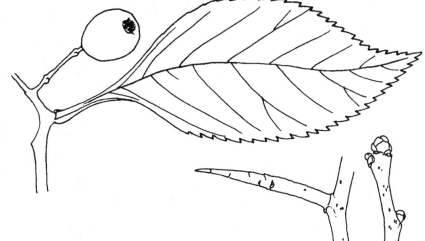

LEAVES: Alternate, simple, elliptic to oblong-obovate, 2 to 4″ long, 1 to 2 1/2″ wide, acute, cuneate, unequally serrate from below the middle, slightly pubescent above when young, finally glabrous and lustrous dark green, pubescent beneath, especially on veins; petiole—1/4 to 3/4″ long.

STEM: Greenish, glabrous, glaucous, usually without the numerous prominent thorns of *C. crusgalli* or *C. phaenopyrum*.

Crataegus × lavallei, (krȧ-tē′gus la-vāl′ē-ī), Lavalle Hawthorn, is a hybrid between *C. stipulacea* Loud. (*C. mexicana*) and *C. crusgalli*. It is a small, dense, oval-headed to rounded tree growing 15 to 30' tall, about 2/3's as wide. In England, 20' by 20', almost perfectly rounded specimens occur. The foliage is a lustrous dark green in summer followed by bronzy or coppery red colors in fall. Flowers are white, 3/4″ diameter, 20 stamens, 1 to 3 styles, late May; borne in 3″ diameter, erect corymbs. Fruit is a brick red to orange-red speckled with brown, 5/8 to 3/4″ diameter, pome-like drupe which ripens in November and persists into winter. I have seen many specimens and most exhibited a one-sided habit. They are not the most uniform-growing trees. Is used a great deal in European countries. This hybrid species arose at several gardens and was first described in 1880. Three years later Carriere published an account of a similar hawthorn, *C. carrierei*, and his clone is often designated 'Carrierei' but incorrectly so. Listed as *C. × carrierei* in some gardens. 'Lavalle' is quite free of rust and appears as adaptable as any hawthorn. Zone 4 to 7.

Crataegus mollis (Torr. & A. Gray) Scheele. — Downy Hawthorn

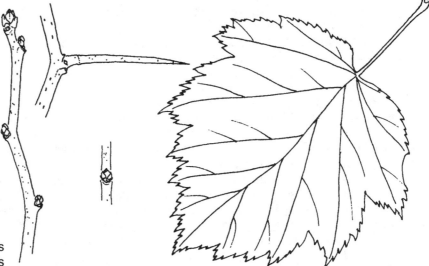

LEAVES: Alternate, simple, broad ovate, 2 to 4″ long and almost as broad, sharply and doubly serrate and with 4 to 5 pairs of short and acute lobes, medium green, densely pubescent beneath at first, later chiefly on the veins; petiole—1 to 2″ long.

STEM: Moderate, thorns to 2″ long, curved, stout or absent; older branches turn a grayish cast.

Crataegus mollis, (krȧ-tē′gus mol′lis), Downy Hawthorn, is a rounded to wide-spreading tree, reaching 20 to 30′ in height, with varying degrees of thorniness. National champion is 52′ by 62′ in Grosse Ile, MI. The branches take on a gray cast and are quite different from most hawthorns. The young leaves are very downy when unfolding and gradually change to a flat medium green in summer and can turn yellow to bronze to bronze-red in fall. Flowers are white, 1″ diameter, 20 stamens, pale yellow anthers, 4 to 5 styles, malodorous, early May (one of the earliest flowering hawthorns), borne in 3 to 4″ diameter corymbs. Fruit is red, 1/2 to 1″ diameter, subglobose, ripening in late August and September and falling soon after. Good native trees but extremely variable; not for the modern landscape as there are too many superior species and cultivars. Leaves are often so badly infected by rust that the entire plant appears to be suffering from the measles. Have seen fruit drop so heavy, the ground appeared to be covered with red marbles. Actually attractive, but for the purist, quite messy. Southern Ontario to Virginia, west to South Dakota and Kansas. Cultivated 1683. Zone 3 to 6.

Crataegus monogyna Jacq. — Singleseed Hawthorn

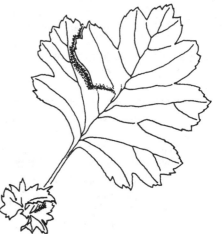

LEAVES: Similar to *C. laevigata* but more deeply 3- to 7-lobed, lobes more narrow and acute with only a few teeth at the apex, usually larger and of a rich polished green color.

FLOWERS AND FRUITS: The name Singleseed is derived from the fact that the fruit has a single stone; the flower a single style; *C. laevigata* has 2 to 3 styles and 2 nutlets (stones).

THORNS: *Crataegus monogyna* is more formidably armed than *C. laevigata*. The species is abundant throughout the English countryside and the fabled hedges that line virtually every roadway are composed principally of *C. monogyna* but also *C. laevigata*.

Crataegus monogyna, (krȧ-tē′gus mon-ō-jī′nȧ), Singleseed Hawthorn, is a round-headed, densely branched tree with slightly pendulous branches and moderate thorny character which grows to 20 to 30′ high. National champion is 37′ by 58′ at Mount Vernon, WA. The summer foliage is a rich, polished green. Flowers are white, 5/8″ diameter, mid to late May, borne in corymbs. Bean calls the odor the sweetest of open-air perfumes. Fruit is red, 3/8″ diameter, one-seeded (hence the name Singleseed), effective in September and October. The species is seldom seen in American gardens with the exception of 'Stricta', an upright form. Unfortunately, the species and cultivars are susceptible to leaf diseases and I have noticed an abundance of mites on 'Stricta'. Cultivars include:

'Biflora' (Glastonbury Thorn)—Flowers in mild seasons in mid-winter, producing the rest of the flowers in May; this cultivar has much tradition; Joseph of Arimathea, after the crucifixion of Christ, went to England to found Christianity; at Glastonbury he prayed a miracle might be performed so that the people would be convinced of his divine mission; when he thrust his staff into the ground, it immediately burst into leaf and flower, although it was then Christmas day; this is the basis for the name Glastonbury Thorn.

'Flexuosa'—Slow-growing form with twisted corkscrew branches; have seen but doubt its commercial appeal because of slow growth.

'Inermis Compacta' ('Pygmaea')—A rather curious, compact, thornless, mushroom-headed form; have seen at a few gardens; interesting.

'Laciniata'—Leaves deeply cut and the lobes irregularly toothed; probably many forms of this type since it occurs in the wild at irregular intervals.

'Pendula'—Form with pendulous branches.

'Semperflorens'—Form with small, 1/2 to 1″ long leaves and slender branches; flowers continuously or at intervals from May until August; dwarf, shrubby habit and very slow-growing.

'Stricta'—A form with upright branches and narrow habit resembling in the best form Lombardy Poplar; apparently several upright clones have been introduced at various times; in the United States I have observed what appeared to be more than one clone; some distinctly upright, others fatter in their middle; very susceptible to fireblight, leaf diseases and mites.

ADDITIONAL NOTES: With such an extended range, many varieties and selections have been designated. As lovely as the species and cultivars appear in European gardens, their performance is the antithesis of that in the United States. I always thought 'Stricta' had promise for areas where lateral space to spread was limited. Unfortunately, the leaves dehisce by July–August due to fungal problems. As mentioned under *C. laevigata*, the American species are superior performers over most of the United States.

NATIVE HABITAT: Europe, northern Africa, western Asia. Long cultivated. Zone 4 to 7.

Crataegus nitida (Engelm.) Sarg. — Glossy Hawthorn

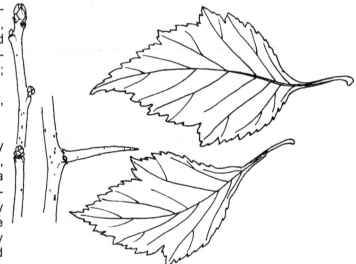

LEAVES: Alternate, simple, elliptic to oblong-obovate, 1 to 3″ long, one-half as wide, acuminate, cuneate, coarsely serrate and often slightly lobed, dark green and lustrous above, paler below, glabrous; petiole—1/2″ long.

STEM: Slender with thorns to 2″ long, straight, often thorns minimal or absent.

Crataegus nitida, (krà-tē′gus nit′i-dà), Glossy Hawthorn, grows to 30′ and forms a dense, rounded outline. Is listed by Griffiths as a hybrid between *C. viridis* × *C. crusgalli*. National champion is 22′ by 36′ at University of Washington Arboretum, Seattle. The foliage is lustrous dark green (extremely shiny) in summer and turns orangish to red in the fall. Flowers are white, small, mid to late May, borne in 1 to 2″ diameter corymbs. Fruit is dull red, 3/8 to 5/8″ diameter, ripening in October–November and persisting into spring. In my opinion a very handsome hawthorn. This species is similar to *C. viridis*, Green Hawthorn. Illinois to Missouri and Arkansas. Introduced 1883. Zone 4 to 6.

Crataegus phaenopyrum (L. f.) Medik. — Washington Hawthorn

LEAVES: Alternate, simple, broad to triangular-ovate, 1 to 3″ long, 3/4 to 2 1/4″ wide, acute, truncate or subcordate, sharply serrate and 3- to 5-lobed, dark green and lustrous above, paler beneath; petiole—about 1″ long.

STEM: Brown, slender, with very slender, 1 to 3″ long thorns.

Crataegus phaenopyrum, (krà-tē′gus fē-nō-pī′rum), Washington Hawthorn, grows to 25 to 30′ high with a 20 to 25′ spread. Three trees are tri-national champions with sizes

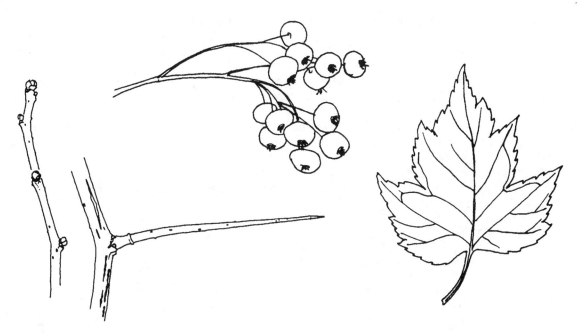

of 33′ by 39′, 36′ by 38′, and 30′ by 32′. The overall effect is a broadly oval to rounded, dense, thorny tree. The foliage is a reddish purple when unfolding gradually changing to lustrous dark green at maturity; fall color varies from orange to scarlet through purplish; flowers are white, 20 stamens, pink anthers, 2 to 5 styles, 1/2″ diameter, not badly scented compared to *C. mollis* and *C. crusgalli*, early June, effective for 7 to 10 days (the last of the cultivated hawthorns to flower); borne in many flowered terminal and axillary corymbs. Fruit is bright glossy red, 1/4″ diameter, coloring in September and October and persisting all winter. Excellent single specimen plant, screen, near buildings, streets, borders, hedges. This species is often grown as a tree or shrub form and is designated as such in nursery catalogs. In the South, hawthorns are not widely planted in the landscape but on the University of Georgia campus this species has been outstanding for fruit display. Many people remark about the attractive fruit and want to know the plant's identity. The thorns present a problem and the tree should not be used in high traffic areas. Cultivars include:

'Clark'—Heavy fruiting clone.

'Fastigiata'—Columnar type with flowers and fruits smaller than the species.

'Manbeck Select'—Improved tree form.

Princeton Sentry™—Vigorous, almost thornless, upright branching selection that can be grown single-trunked for street tree use; broadly columnar, 30′ by 20′; introduced by Princeton Nursery in 1986.

'Vaughn' (*C. crusgalli* × *C. phaenopyrum*)—Excellent for the abundance of glossy fruit it produces; have observed tremendous rust on leaves, stems and fruits; probably 15 to 20′ by 15 to 20′.

NATIVE HABITAT: Virginia to Alabama and Missouri. Introduced 1738. Zone 4 to 8; not as vigorous in the South.

OTHER HAWTHORNS

Crataegus succulenta (Link) Schräd. — Fleshy Hawthorn

LEAVES: Alternate, simple, broad elliptic to obovate, 2 to 3″ long, 1 1/4 to 2 1/2″ wide, acute or short acuminate, cuneate, coarsely and doubly serrate, lustrous dark green above, glabrous below at maturity, veins parallel in 4 to 7 pairs.

STEM: Purplish brown with 1 1/2 to 2″ long thorns, prominently borne.

Crataegus succulenta, (krȧ-tē′gus suk-ū-len′tȧ), Fleshy Hawthorn, is a heavy fruiter producing bright red, 3/8 to 1/2″ diameter, pome-like drupes in September and October. I remember this tree from my woody plant materials courses at Ohio State and can still picture the heavy fruit crops on a tree that I walked past on my way to the botany building. National champion is 21′ by 30′ at Pipestem State Park, WV. The fall color is a good purple-red. Does not seem to be common and in many respects (foliage, flower white, 3/4″ across, produced in rounded 3″ or greater corymbs, 15 to 20 stamens, pink anthers, 2 to 3 styles, fruit) is similar to *C. crusgalli*. Charles S. Sargent considered it one of the 6 best hawthorns in America and that is quite a tribute considering the great number which are native. Quite close to this in biological affinity and occasionally listed in the Midwest as a good hawthorn is var. *macracantha* (Lodd.) Eggl. with white to yellowish flowers, 10 stamens and 1/3″ to slightly larger, soft red fruit. Quebec and Ontario to Massachusetts and Illinois. Cultivated 1830. Zone 4 to 6.

Crataegus viridis L. — Green Hawthorn
LEAVES: Alternate, simple, oblong-ovate to elliptic, 1 1/2 to 3 1/2″ long, 3/4 to 2 1/2″ wide, acute or acuminate, cuneate, serrate, the terminal portion shallowly lobed, lustrous dark green above, glabrous below except for pubescence in axils of veins; petiole—1/2 to 1 1/2″ long.
STEM: Glabrous, gray-brown, thorns up to 1 1/2″ long but often absent; older stems silver-gray and finally a large caliper trunk exfoliating to expose orange-brown inner bark.

Crataegus viridis, (krȧ-tē′gus vir′i-dis), Green Hawthorn, is a rounded, sharply thorny, spreading, dense tree growing 20 to 35′ high and wide. National champion is 40′ by 45′ in Marlinton, WV. The foliage is a lustrous medium green in summer and can change to purple and scarlet in the fall. Flowers are white, 20 stamens, pale yellow anthers, 2 to 5 styles, 3/4″ diameter, mid-May, borne in 2″ diameter corymbs. The fruits are bright red, 1/4 to 1/3″ diameter, coloring in September–October and persisting.

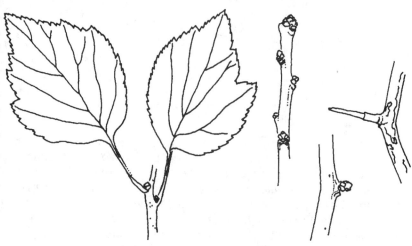

'Winter King'—Selection with lovely rounded habit, almost vase-shaped branching structure and distinct gray-green bloomy stems. The fruits are larger (1/2″ diameter) than the species and a good red. Fruits persist into winter and are among the handsomest of all hawthorns. Introduced by the Simpson Nursery Co., Vincennes, IN in 1955. Could be a hybrid as it does not match the characteristics of the species. Less susceptible to rust than other hawthorns but I have seen the fruits badly infected when the leaves showed very little infection. This and *C. phaenopyrum* are the two most outstanding hawthorns for landscape use. Has proven outstanding in Zone 7b. Will probably mature around 20 to 25′ high, with a greater spread.
NATIVE HABITAT: Maryland and Virginia to Illinois, Iowa, Texas and Florida. Cultivated 1827. Zone 4 to 7.

Crataegus species — Mayhaw
Selected species in the Southeast are affectionately termed Mayhaw and are grown for their reddish (some blue-purple) fruits which are processed into jellies, et al. The jelly is a rich rose red, jewel-like agar with a slight tangy taste. As a group, the species have perhaps little to offer the everyday landscape but are worth considering for fringe areas of the garden. The taxonomy is extremely muddled and one reference lists over 100, another lists 35, species for the Southeast. Approximately 1000 species of *Crataegus* have been proposed as legitimate. The reasons for lack of consistency include apomixis, polyploidy, and aneuploidy which results in unusual chromosome numbers that may be perpetuated via apomixis. The species occur in many habitats from river bottoms, wet depressions to sandy scrub oak-pine woods to thin soils of rock outcrops. They are an extremely important food source for wildlife and particularly birds who disseminate them widely. The principal species I see in the wild, in cultivation, and perhaps legitimately described include: *Crataegus aestivalis* (Walt.) T. & G., May Haw; *C. flabellata* (Bose)

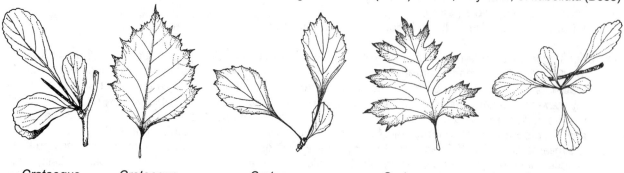

Crataegus aestivalis   *Crataegus flabellata*   *Crataegus flava*   *Crataegus marshallii*   *Crataegus spathulata*

K. Koch, Fanleaf Hawthorn; *C. flava* Ait., Southern Haw; *C. marshallii* Eggl., Parsley Hawthorn; *C. spathulata* Michx., Spathulate Haw, Littlehip Haw; and *C. uniflora* Muenchh., Dwarf Haw, One-flower Hawthorn. *Crataegus spathulata* has beautiful exfoliating bark in gray, orange, and brown. The fruits of *C. spathulata* are red, relatively small and from a distance remind of a deciduous holly. I have been fooled more than once. Virtually all species fall in the 20 to 30′ high size range. In fact, checking the *National Register for Champion Trees*, all but *C. uniflora* (18′ high) were over 20′ high with comparable spreads.

Possibly the best review paper is "Mayhaws: Trees of Pomological and Ornamental Interest," *HortScience* 25:246, 375 (1990). The three major species cited as important in the Mayhaw pomological complex include *C. aestivalis*, *C. opaca* Hook. & Arn., and *C. rufula* Sarg. Bush et al., *Proc. SNA Res. Conf.* 36:113–115 (1991), provide background about commercial production of *C. opaca* in Louisiana and list 12 cultivars.

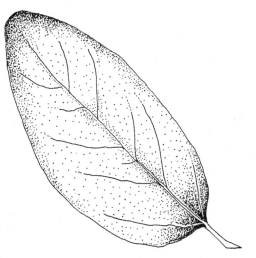

Crataegus opaca   *Crataegus rufula*

All Mayhaws are susceptible to quince rust, *Gymnosporangium clavipes*, which affects fruits. Also, leaf miners, mealy bugs, and scale may be problematic.

Croton alabamensis E.A. Sm. — Alabama Croton

FAMILY: Euphorbiaceae
LEAVES: Alternate, simple, semi-evergreen to deciduous, elliptical, 2 to 4″ long, 1/2 to 1 1/2″ wide, obtuse, cuneate to rounded, entire, medium green with silver scales above, silvery and shiny beneath, banana-apple odor when bruised; petiole—1/4 to 1/2″ long.
STEM: Silver, aging to light brown, young stems covered with scales; pith—solid, green.

Croton alabamensis, (krō′ton al-ab-am-en′sis), Alabama Croton, is one of those rare plants that surfaces every millennium and plantspeople like myself feel we have been touched by the second coming. In truth the shrub is somewhat open—flopsy and mopsy style. A plant in the University's Botanical Garden is 6 to 8′ high but grows in heavy deciduous shade. The rich apple green leaves, silver below, smell like fresh sliced apples. Some liken the odor to banana oil. The older leaves turn brilliant orange in the fall. Flowers are yellow-green and appear in 1 to 1 1/2″ racemes during March–April (Athens). Fruit is a drupe. Provide semi-shade and moist, well-drained, organic matter-laden root run. For consideration in the native and collector's gardens. Mt. Airy Arboretum had a specimen that persisted for years until -20°F and lower during the mid-1970's. This species was discovered by Dr. E. A. Smith in 1877 on dry limestone bluffs of the Cahaba River near Pratt's Ferry in Bibb County, Alabama. It has also been found on the shale cliffs of the Black Warrior River above Tuscaloosa, Alabama. November cuttings, 3000 ppm IBA-talc, sand, mist, rooted 77% after 28 days. Worth including in the garden to stump your gardening friends. Alabama. Zone 6 to 8.

Cryptomeria japonica D. Don. — Japanese Cryptomeria, Japanese Cedar
(krip-tō-mē′ri-à jà-pon′i-kà)

FAMILY: Taxodiaceae
LEAVES: Evergreen, spirally arranged, persisting 4 to 5 years, awl-shaped, 4-angled, 1/4 to 3/4″ long, the first leaves of the year shorter than the later ones, curving inwards, sometimes slightly twisted, pointed forwards, keeled on both surfaces, margins entire, apex tapering to a blunt point, base spreading and clasping the shoot, stomata on each surface, bright green to blush green.
STEM: Green, glabrous; the branchlets spreading or drooping, eventually deciduous.

SIZE: 50 to 60′ high by 20 to 30′ wide; can grow 100′ and greater.
HARDINESS: Zone 5 to 6; hardy to Boston, MA and south to Zone 8.
HABIT: A pyramidal or conical tree with a stout trunk and erect, wide-spreading branches with numerous branchlets; relatively graceful in habit.

RATE: Medium, can grow 50 to 60′ after 30 to 40 years; in the lower Midwest (Cincinnati) trees are much slower growing.

TEXTURE: Medium.

BARK: Reddish brown peeling off in long strips; beautiful bark.

LEAF COLOR: Bright green to bluish green in summer; during the winter the needles take on a bronzy hue (brown if in windy locations), becoming green again in spring.

FLOWERS: Monoecious, inconspicuous.

FRUIT: Cones are terminal, globular, 1/2 to 1″ broad, dark brown, composed of 20 to 30 scales, each with 3 to 5 seeds.

CULTURE: Easy to grow; prefers a rich and deep, light, permeable, acid soil with abundant moisture; open, sunny location, shelter from high winds, will tolerate light shade.

DISEASES AND INSECTS: Leaf blight and leaf spot, have noticed a branch dieback, particularly in Southeast; the species and cultivars have been touted as possible Leyland Cypress alternatives; increased use particularly in the Southeast has unearthed several troublesome fungi that initiate a tip dieback; *Pestalotia* sp. and *Phyllosticta* sp. have been isolated from dead shoot tips and branches; problems have occurred in container and field nurseries; the species may not be the panacea that many people thought.

LANDSCAPE VALUE: An accommodating tree, graceful, stately and handsome; useful as a specimen or for avenues; a fine evergreen, when properly grown as pretty as any conifer; some thinking that this may serve as a useful alternative to Leyland Cypress, particularly in the Southeast; my observations indicate there is no perfect *Cryptomeria* anymore than a perfect × *Cupressocyparis*; 'Yoshino' is being touted and widely grown as the selection of choice; I see many small, sometimes large, dead branches on older trees; these have been shown to our former plant pathologist who was unable to isolate a fungus and simply said was the nature of the tree; I am not so sure!? Dr. Jean Williams-Woodward, Georgia's new plant pathologist attributes some of the shoot tip dieback to *Pestalotia* and *Phyllosticta* organisms as mentioned previously.

CULTIVARS: Have seen references made to 100's of cultivars; counted 24 in the catalogs I checked; *Dendroflora* 24:9–36 (1987) reported that 90 taxa are in cultivation. *Conifers, The Illustrated Encyclopedia*, 1996, Timber Press, features color photographs of 46 cultivars, many of which are not treated in other references. Checking a photo of 'Black Dragon' against plants labeled as such in the United States indicates serious nomenclatural confusion. Tripp, *American Nurseryman* 178(7):26–39 (1993), presented an excellent discussion relative to history, culture, propagation and cultivars. It should be required reading for *Cryptophiles*. Kim lists her top ten: 'Ben Franklin', 'Black Dragon', 'Elegans', 'Elegans Aurea', 'Elegans Nana', 'Globosa Nana', 'Gracilis', 'Lobbii', 'Sekkan-sugi', and 'Yellow Twig'.

The hunt is ongoing for tree-like, relatively fast-growing forms that hold good green color in winter. I have several clones from Ted Stephens, Nurseries Caroliniana, Gilbert Nursery, Chesnee, SC and other sources that are being evaluated.

'Ben Franklin'—Much like the species in vigor and overall traits, deep green needles, rapid growth, sun or partial shade, salt tolerant, should be utilized in place of seedling material, 30 to 40′, many reports indicate this is a superior selection for retaining good green winter color; has discolored in winter in Philadelphia area; selected by North Carolina nurseryman, Benjamin Franklin Copeland.

'Black Dragon'—Compact, extremely dark green-needled form, somewhat irregular-pyramidal, sets abundant male cones; interestingly cuttings show differential habits and growth rates.

'Compacta'—Compact, narrowly conical tree to 45′ high, needles short, stiff and bluish green, good looking form, 'Lobbii Compacta' is sometimes applied to this form.

'Elegans'—Juvenile form of tall bushy habit, 9 to 15′(30′), the soft, feathery, 1/2 to 1″ long, green summer foliage turns brownish red in winter, fluffy looking juvenile foliage, less hardy than species, kind of unusual for foliage effect, have seen large plants in Europe.

'Elegans Aurea'—Yellowish needles in summer that turn green in winter.

'Elegans Compacta' ('Elegans Nana')—As above but flattened, globose, compact and slow-growing, more broad-mounded than anything; 3 to 6′ high; needles bluish green becoming purplish tinged in winter.

'Elegans Variegata'—Cream new needles that mature green.

'Globosa Nana'—This neat, dense, dome-shaped form grows 2 to 3′ high and 2 1/2 to 3 1/2′ wide in 10 to 15 years, may mature between 4 and 8′; the bluish green adult needles assume a rusty red color in winter.

'Green Grizzly'—Holds green coloration in winter better than typical, about 2/3's as large with more compact habit, introduced by Gilbert Nursery, Chesnee, SC, has bronzed in Georgia trials.

'Gyokuryu'—Dense broad pyramid; needles shorter and darker green than species, hold color in winter; darkest green of all clones at Atlanta Botanical Garden when viewed on January 26, 1997; this may be synonymous with 'Black Dragon' but 'Gyokuryu' is more vigorous without the abundant male cones.

'Jindai'—Reasonably slow-growing dense broad-conical form, handsome clone.

'Lobbii'—Considerable confusion in my mind relative to correct identity; plants I have seen labeled as 'Lobbii' were probably 'Yoshino'; true 'Lobbii' is an upright pyramidal-columnar form with denser and less pendulous branching than species, needles are longer and deeper green, and may bronze in cold weather, 30 to 40′, displays excellent disease resistance.

'Lycopodioides'—A rather curious, loose-growing, evergreen shrub, the branches long, slender and snake-like; a novelty item.

'Radicans'—Rather pretty glaucous blue-green form, tree-like habit, saw at Head-Lee Nursery, Seneca, SC.

'Sekkan-sugi' ('Sekkan')—Vigorous grower with yellow-green new growth that fades to green in the heat of summer, maintains a pyramidal-conical habit, a local nurseryman, John Barbour, has successfully grown this form, 20′ in 10 years.

'Taisho Tama'—Compact pyramidal form with good green winter color when observed in January 1997 at the Atlanta Botanical Garden.

'Vilmoriniana'—Compact, 1 to 2′ high mound of dense foliage; good collector's item or rock garden plant.

'Winter Mint'—Vigorous rather open form with rich green summer needles that maintain respectable winter color, plants were rich green on the late January 1997 day I evaluated them at the Atlanta Botanical Garden, many of the dwarf forms were muddy bronze or worse; from Head-Lee Nursery, Seneca, SC.

'Yoshino'—Handsome form like the species with rich bright blue-green summer foliage that becomes slightly bronze-green in cold weather, grows fast and develops a handsome form without extensive pruning, 30 to 40′, is now being grown by southern nurserymen, in February 1996 plants in local nurseries looked like brown toast, I have a strong suspicion that many of the plants offered as 'Yoshino' are otherwise.

PROPAGATION: Seed germination is usually quite poor; the seed should be soaked in cold water (32°F) for about 12 hours, then put moist into plastic bags and stored at 34°F for 60 to 90 days before sowing; bags should be left open for adequate aeration; 3 months warm followed by 3 months cold supposedly results in good germination; cuttings taken in summer and fall will root, although slowly; the older literature reports effective treatments of 40 to 80 ppm IBA soak for 24 hours; based on some work I did at Illinois it is probably best to collect cuttings in November (have also done it in August); treat with 10,000 ppm IBA-quick dip, place in peat:perlite, under a poly tent; rooting took place 2 or 3 months later but was generally good with large numbers of thick white roots; recent studies, *Proc. Intl. Plant Prop. Soc.* 43:404–407 (1993) and *HortScience* 29:1532–1535 (1994), reported best rooting with semi-hardwood (November) and hardwood (January) cuttings (87%) treated with 3000 ppm or greater IBA in 50% isopropanol, 2-second dip. These studies are convoluted because of cutting sampling positions, i.e., first-order laterals, distal halves, proximal halves, or tips. One needs to read the paper particularly the *HortScience* version which has a diagram. A former student Mark Griffith, Griffith Propagation Nursery, Watkinsville, GA, 30677 takes larger (thicker) cuttings with significant improved rooting over small thin cuttings. In our shop, cuttings of 'Gyokuryu', 'Taisho Tama', and 'Winter Mint' collected January 25, 1997, 3000 ppm KIBA, peat:perlite, bottom heat (70°F), mist, rooted 100, 87.5, and 87.5%, respectively, in 8 weeks.

ADDITIONAL NOTES: A lovely conifer where it can be grown. With proper cultivar selection the plant could be used in almost any landscape. The U.S. National Arboretum has a grove/grouping by the entrance to the bonsai exhibit that creates the Japanese mood; apparently the species is widely planted in Japan around temples. It is the major lumber tree in Japan.

A questionable species, *C. fortunei* Billain ex Otto & Dietz, is reduced to *C. japonica* var. *sinensis* Miq. in Sieb. & Zucc. I see little difference in this and the species. There is a specimen at the J.C. Raulston Arboretum that is rich green needled and quite vigorous but the same could be said for many specimens labeled as *C. japonica*. A specimen I received from Ted Stephens has longer, more lax needles and grows significantly faster than *C. japonica*. In fact, Ted gave me a non winter discoloring form of *C. japonica* at the same time. Both were shifted to larger containers and maintained in the greenhouse. In five months, *C. fortunei* added 3′ of new growth; *C. japonica* 6″.

NATIVE HABITAT: China and Japan, and was originally discovered in the former country in 1701 by James Cunningham, and by Kaempfer in Japan in 1692. Introduced into America 1861.

Cunninghamia lanceolata (Lamb.) Hook. f. — Common Chinafir   *Chinese Fir*
(kun-ing-ham′i-à lan-sē-ō-lā′tà)

FAMILY: Taxodiaceae

LEAVES: Evergreen, spirally arranged, those on the main axis standing out from all around the stem, those on the underside of the branches turning upwards by a basal twist so that all appear to spring from the sides and surface of the shoot; persisting 5 or more years and remaining dry and dead on the branches for several years more; lanceolate, curving backwards, 1 to 2 3/4″ long, 1/16 to 1/8″ wide at the base, green or glaucous green, margins finely toothed, apex a long slender point; stomata in a broad band on each side of the midrib on the undersurface.

SIZE: 30 to 75′ in height, 10 to 30′ wide; 150′ in native haunts. *large*
HARDINESS: Zone (6)7 to 9; is growing at the Secrest Arboretum, Wooster, OH, where temperatures drop to −20°F; tips of branches are killed every winter.
HABIT: Pyramidal with slightly pendulous branches, giving the appearance of an exotic-looking tree; often rather ragged.
RATE: Slow to medium; supposedly can grow 20 to 30′ after 15 years.
TEXTURE: Medium-fine.
BARK: Brown, scaling off in long irregular strips, exposing the reddish inner bark.
LEAF COLOR: Bright medium green or glaucous to bluish green; often discoloring in cold weather, more or less bronze-green.
FLOWERS: Monoecious; male flowers in terminal clusters; female flowers terminal.
FRUIT: Cones usually several together, rarely solitary, globose, ovoid, 1 1/2″ broad.
CULTURE: Prefers moist, acid, well-drained soils; not very hardy; grows best in open spaces shaded by trees and protected from windswept sites.
DISEASES AND INSECTS: None serious.
LANDSCAPE VALUE: Only of value in the warmer parts of the country; possibly used as a specimen or mass planting; in youth reasonably attractive but becoming "seedy" with age as the old dead needles cling to the branches; common in the South and I have seen 60′ high trees; in most landscapes seems out of place.
CULTIVARS:
   'Chason's Gift'—More compact, conical-pyramidal than typical species types, glossy dark green foliage, original tree 40′ high and 15-years-old, roots readily from early winter cuttings, unique because it develops a strong central leader as a young plant, introduced by Johnson's Nursery, Willard, NC, see *American Nurseryman* 180(1):174 (1994) for specifics.
   'Glauca'—Leaves with a conspicuous glaucous bloom, attractive when young, perhaps more cold hardy than the species. *blue cast*
PROPAGATION: Cuttings can be rooted and November appears to be the best time; probably any time in winter would be successful; high hormone treatments, 8000 ppm IBA and above are recommended; a poly-tent and bottom heat are advisable; the cuttings may retain the growth characteristics of the branch from which they were collected; if from a lateral shoot they grow laterally (plagiotropic); if from a vertical they grow upright (orthotropic); in propagation circles this is called topophysis.
ADDITIONAL NOTES: Highly prized tree in China and, next to bamboo, is the most useful for all around work. The wood is light, soft, fragrant, pale yellow or almost white, easily worked, durable, and used for housebuilding, indoor carpentry, masts, planking, box-making, and largely for coffins. The wood is very rot resistant in contact with the soil. In the wild, under forest conditions, it develops a long, straight, mast-like trunk, 80 to 150′ high, clear of branches for half its height. It has the ability when cut to produce sprouts from roots and revegetate an area. Watched a 30′ specimen being cut to the ground and 3 years later it had resprouted to 10′.
NATIVE HABITAT: Central and southern China. Introduced 1804.

× *Cupressocyparis leylandii* (Dallim. & A.B. Jackson) Dallim. — Leyland Cypress
(kū-pres-ō-si′pa-ris lā-lan′dē-ī)

FAMILY: Cupressaceae (Intergeneric hybrid between *Cupressus macrocarpa* and *Chamaecyparis nootkatensis*).
LEAVES: Very similar to those of *C. nootkatensis* but less odorous when bruised, branchlets flattened or somewhat quadrangular, see cultivars for specific foliage traits.

SIZE: 60 to 70′ under landscape conditions; can grow over 100′; spread 1/5 to 1/8 the height or less.
HARDINESS: Zone 6 to 10.
HABIT: Magnificent, noble, needle evergreen forming a columnar to pyramidal outline.
RATE: Fast, easily 3′ a year in youth, 100′ in 60 years.
TEXTURE: Fine, feathery foliage contributes to the gracefulness of the species.
BARK: Reddish brown, scaly.
LEAF COLOR: Bluish green on the type, upper and lower side of sprays of the same color; holds good color during winter.
FRUIT: Cone 1/2 to 3/4″ diameter, 8 scales, with about 5 seeds per scale, each scale with a prominent boss.
CULTURE: Transplants readily from a container; should not be field-grown as roots are somewhat stringy and plants are difficult to ball and burlap; many southern nurserymen are successfully digging the tree with

mechanical tree diggers; adaptable to extremes of soil, but requires adequate drainage; acid or calcareous; withstands salt spray; even on "poor" sites plants from cuttings have grown 48′ in 16 years; requires full sun, definitely thins out in shady environments and/or does not grow as fast.

DISEASES AND INSECTS: Since the last edition several problems have surfaced, no doubt reflective of the burgeoning use of the various cultivars. Bagworms are a universal problem and Leyland Cypress attracts its share; recognition of the problem and immediate removal of the bags defuse the situation. The most significant problems are fungal and cankers caused by *Seiridium cardinale*, *S. unicorne*, and *S. cupressi* have been identified. In North Carolina, *S. unicorne* has caused canker and twig dieback. Symptoms include gray discoloration at point of infection, resin oozing from cracks in the bark, dark brown to purplish patches on the bark, sunken cankers with raised margins, and yellow to brown discoloration of the foliage above the canker.

Dieback caused by *Botryosphaeria dothidea* is observed on trees within the first several years in the landscape. Disease is manifested as a dead leader or major side branch. A slightly sunken canker with a conspicuous crack along the margin is evident. This disease is most often associated with plant stress.

Root rot may occur in extremely wet soils and on young liner stock. *Phytophthora* spp. are the causal agent(s). In general, with good drainage, this is not a problem.

LANDSCAPE VALUE: In the 1983 edition I looked into the crystal ball and predicted the tree would become popular in the Southeast; in a sense its acceptance has snowballed not simply as an ornamental evergreen but also as a Christmas tree; production is now in the hundreds of thousands; from the gardener's perspective the plant should be purchased in a 1-, 3-, or 7-gallon container; plants in containers are not as dense as field-grown(soil) material but will fill in quickly without pruning once installed in the landscape; my neighbor and I planted one-gallon plants 4′ apart and in 2 years had 6 to 7′ plants that were touching at the base; the plant's growth rate is truly amazing; no matter what the literature states the plant grows faster in reasonably fertile, moist, well-drained soil compared to the extremes on either side; the plant can be pruned almost indefinitely to maintain a certain shape (plasticity); excellent for quick screens, groupings, hedges; possibly not a long term landscape investment (10 to 20 years) but it gets where it is going in a hurry and provides functional service; interestingly the Christmas tree growers sell this for much more than Virginia Pine yet it makes a salable tree in a shorter period of time; many cultivars have been introduced and here I attempt to present an understandable profile of their characteristics based on observation and the literature.

CULTIVARS:

'Castlewellan Gold' ('Castlewellan')—Rather handsome golden yellow foliage form that is not quite as bright as *Thuja orientalis* 'Aurea Nana'; in cool European climates the color persists through the summer but in Georgia is best in fall, winter and early spring, becoming light green, but handsomely so, in summer; I collected a branch February 18, 1989 to check intensity of color and was not impressed by the gold color but prior to this temperatures were in the 70's which may account for minimal coloration; I grew a plant for three years and the vigor is exceptional; unfortunately, the color is not as potent in hot weather; origin is interesting since a coning branch broke off *Cupressus macrocarpa* 'Lutea', Forest Park, Castlewellan, County Down, Ireland; a tree of the golden needle form of *Chamaecyparis nootkatensis* grew nearby, the seeds were sown with the hope that hybridization might have occurred and one seedling proved such and was propagated; the clone was put into commerce around 1970; foliage is not quite as flat (planar) as the typical form ('Haggerston Grey') in cultivation; original tree grew 26′ high in 16 years.

'Contorta'—A legitimate clone? . . . new growth shows a slight twist, appears to straighten itself out with time, vigorous grower, foliage color like 'Haggerston Grey', have observed this form on several occasions, be forewarned it is not contorted to the degree of *Corylus avellana* 'Contorta'.

Emerald Isle™ ('Moncal')—Bright green foliage in flat sprays, denser branching than the typical form, listed as 20 to 25′ by 6 to 8′, no doubt larger with time, reported as canker resistant, a 1992 Monrovia Nursery introduction, original plants came from Britain, I have not observed this clone in Georgia.

'Golconda'—An introduction that I know very little about; golden needles and a compact pyramidal outline; an improvement on 'Castlewellan Gold' for the intensity of yellow-gold pigmentation, one small plant has held excellent golden yellow foliage color during the winter of 1989, cursory evaluations on a 6′ plant at the J.C. Raulston Arboretum, Raleigh, NC, indicate much brighter and persistent foliage color than 'Castlewellan Gold', a branch sport of 'Haggerston Grey'.

'Gold Cup'—Bright golden yellow new growth, holds color well, especially in winter.

'Gold Nugget'—A relatively compact, erect pyramidal form with golden yellow foliage, considered inferior to 'Gold Rider'.

'Gold Rider'—Branchlets (sprays) are yellow with green tips in winter, changing to deeper yellow with dark yellow margins in summer, originated as a branch sport of 'Leighton Green' in the Netherlands and released there in 1986, in Australian evaluations the plant grew 1.9′/year, 'Leighton Green'—2.4′, and 'Castlewellan Gold'—2.3′, the branchlets are more planar in arrangement than 'Castlewellan Gold', have seen 'Gold Rider' in England in June where it was distinctly more golden yellow than 'Castlewellan Gold', small plants in our trials under 55% shade held good yellow coloration, raised and introduced by A. Vergeer, Boskoop.

'Green Spire'—Narrow columnar, very dense, with rich green foliage, branchlets spaced irregularly and at varying angles to stem, directed forward on an even plane, central leader often poorly developed, raised in 1888 (clone 1) at Haggerston Castle.

'Haggerston Grey'—More open than 'Leighton Green'; the green foliage with a slight pale gray cast, branchlets arising and lying in 2 planes at right angle, frequently in opposite and decussate pairs, the smallest branchlets often in tufts; raised in 1888 (clone 2); differs from 'Leighton Green' in the decidedly irregular lateral branches, flat and frond-like in 'Leighton Green'.

'Harlequin'—A silvery variegated form that arose from a branch sport of 'Haggerston Grey'; it develops multiple leaders and is not so pretty in variegation pattern as 'Silver Dust'; described about 1975.

'Hillspire'— Described as a large, narrow pyramidal tree with bright green foliage; I have never seen this form listed except in 1989 Iseli Nursery Catalog; could it be another name for 'Green Spire'?

'Hyde Hall'—Dwarf, slow-growing form that arose as a witches' broom on a plant in Essex, England; rather narrow flame-shaped in outline with dark green, soft, semi-juvenile foliage like a miniature *Chamaecyparis lawsoniana* 'Erecta', photograph I observed indicates a 6′ high plant about 18″ wide.

Irish Mint™—Lighter green foliage and superior root system than typical; almost appears the same as 'Castlewellan', offered by Flowerwood Nursery.

'Jubilee'—Another variegated branch sport with irregular yellow sprays, not as handsome as 'Silver Dust'.

'Leighton Green'—Tall, columnar form with central leader and rich green foliage, branchlets and their divisions in one plane recalling those of the pollen parent, *Chamaecyparis nootkatensis*; consistent cone bearer; raised in 1911 (clone 11); in actuality there is little difference in foliage color between this and 'Haggerston Grey'.

'Naylor's Blue'—The most glaucous foliaged of the cultivars; the bluish green foliage most noticeably glaucous in winter; more loosely branched and open; raised in 1911 (clone 10), available in United States; I have grown this in my garden and find it the most distinctive of the green or blue-green foliage forms; needles are distinctly blue-green, branching is more loose and irregular and the plant is not as upright and narrow as 'Haggerston Grey' or 'Leighton Green'; it is being produced in southern nurseries; is slower growing than the other types.

'New Ornament'—Very irregular habit with contorted branches, appears similar to 'Contorta', a selection termed 'Picturesque' is quite similar.

'Robinson's Gold'—Foliage arranged like 'Leighton Green' perhaps brighter yellow when young; bronze-yellow in spring, gradually turning lemon-green and gold-yellow; fast-growing but more compact and densely branched and conical than 'Leighton Green'; original plant 25′ by 10′ in 20 years; found in 1962 by George Robinson in Belvoir Park, Belfast, Northern Ireland, it was a self-sown seedling; always fascinating how plants "find" their way into cultivation.

'Rostrevor'—Similar to 'Leighton Green' but leading shoots with more widely spaced branches and denser foliage, vigorous grower.

'Silver Dust'—Although described as a branch sport of 'Leighton Green' I have genuine difficulty making the habit and needle characteristics fit; the green foliage is splotched, streaked and splashed with creamy white; from a distance, it is difficult to separate it from the typical forms; appears to grow slightly slower than 'Haggerston Grey' or 'Leighton Green' but based on plant performance in the Dirr garden will grow 2′ per year; in rooting studies this rooted faster and in higher percentages than other cultivars; 'Leighton Green' is more difficult to root than other cultivars; taxonomically I am not sure of exact status but is a rather handsome subdued variegated conifer for Zone 6 to 9; have observed prosperous plants in Savannah, GA area, made an effort to compare 'Silver Dust' branches to the literature and what I know as 'Haggerston Grey' and 'Leighton Green'; 'Silver Dust' coincides more closely with 'Haggerston Grey'; cones are green, cream, and mixed.

'Stapehill Hybrid' ('Stapehill 21') (*Cupressus macrocarpa* × *Chamaecyparis lawsoniana*)—Similar to 'Leighton Green' in appearance with darker blue-green heavily textured foliage, the undersides of the sprays blue-gray-green, young stems yellow-green, later orange-brown, finally brown tinted purple; 2 clones, 20 and 21, 21 better of the two, both over 50′ high in 40 years; developed in the Barthelemy Nursery, Stapehill, Winborne, Dorset, England in 1940; not common in the United States.

PROPAGATION: The 1983 edition went overboard on propagation information; in recent years numerous studies have been published and tell of success in summer, fall and winter; from our experience, February–March cuttings with brown wood, 5000 to 8000 ppm IBA-50% alcohol quick dip, 3 perlite:1 peat, mist with bottom heat or a wire frame that is covered with plastic and 2 layers of 50% shade cloth, cuttings are syringed twice a day, rooting will occur in 6 to 10 weeks and should approach 80%; a local nurseryman sticks cuttings in summer, about 10,000 ppm IBA and has excellent success; Whalley, *Proc. Intl. Plant Prop. Soc.* 29:190–197 (1979), presented strong evidence for taking cuttings in February; 'Haggerston Grey', 'Leighton Green', and 'Stapehill' rooted 87, 70, 99%, respectively, when treated with 3000 ppm IBA-talc, peat and sand, mist, 68°F medium temperature; cuttings collected in May, August, September *always* rooted in lower percentages sometimes 50% less. See Dirr and Frett, *HortScience* 18(2):204–205 (1983) and Dirr and Heuser, 1987. Less than successful attempt at micropropagation *Proc. Intl. Plant Prop. Soc.* 39:285–290 (1990); also cutting propagation of × *Cupressocyparis* and *Cupressus*, *Proc. Intl. Plant Prop. Soc.* 39:154–160 (1989).

ADDITIONAL NOTES: The cross first originated at the estate of Mr. Naylor, Leighton Hall, Welshpool, Wales in 1888 (6 seedlings) and again in 1911 (2 seedlings planted at Leighton Hall); also in a garden at Ferndown, Dorset in 1940 (2 seedlings). The six seedlings were taken by C.J. Leyland, and planted on his property, Haggerston Castle, Northumberland, in 1892–93. Five of the original plants still existed in 1970 and are the parents by asexual propagation of × *C. leylandii*, Clones 1 to 5. The derivation of the clonal names is evident from the brief history presented here.

My fascination with this conifer continues in this edition. As I drive through the Southeast and particularly Georgia, it is everywhere in evidence. Like all things overdone, the plant will lose its luster. I feel some of my academic colleagues have written the plant off a degree hastily. One or possibly two cultivars have been extensively planted. Are some of the others (see under CULTIVARS) perhaps resistant to the disease(s) mentioned? Dick Bir, North Carolina State, gave Bonnie and I a Leyland about 18 years ago that is now 40′ high. It has neither bump nor bruise. A screen of Leylands between our place and the neighbor has prospered for 10 years with only an occasional dead branch.

The salt tolerance is legendary and Leyland withstands saline conditions better than virtually any conifer. Soil and spray-applied NaCl did not injure container-grown Leyland Cypress. Soil salt application reduced dry weight (growth). Leyland does not accumulate high levels of Na or Cl compared to salt susceptible plants. See *J. Environmental Hort.* 8:154–155 for details. Another salt tolerance study, *The Plantsman* 9(2):110–127 (1987), describes wind and salt tolerance in the British Isles. In short, 'Leighton Green' and 'Rostrevor' were most tolerant; × *C. notabilis* and × *C. ovensii* most susceptible.

Two other × *Cupressocyparis* species, × *C.-notabilis* Mitch., and × *C. ovensii* Mitch. have been described. × *Cupressocyparis notabilis* Mitch., Noble Cypress, Alice Holt Cypress, was grown from seed collected in 1956 from a specimen of *Cupressus arizonica* var. *glabra* growing at Leighton Hall, Montgomeryshire. It develops a broader, more open crown than × *C. leylandii*. The branchlets are ascending, flattened, blue-green, bipinnate. Cones rounded, 1/2 to 3/4″ diameter, bloomy, with 4 to 8 scales. Will grow 60′ and higher. In a little over 20 years grew 41′ high. Parentage is *Cupressus arizonica* var. *glabra* × *Chamaecyparis nootkatensis*.

The other hybrid, × *Cupressocyparis ovensii* Mitch. (*Cupressus lusitanica* × *Chamaecyparis nootkatensis*) has bluish green sprays that are finely dissected. Cones globose, about 1/3″ diameter, glaucous ripening violet, 4 to 6 scales. This is a vigorous form slightly more open than typical × *C. leylandii*. The hybrid exhibits a strong influence of the Nootka parent and produces large flattened sprays of drooping, dark glaucous green foliage. In approximately 20 years the plant grew 35′ high. Out of 13 clones in the Georgia trials, × *C. ovensii* has grown the fastest, averaging 3 feet/year over a 6 year period. Raised by Howard Ovens at Tan-y-Cae, Dyfed, Wales, from seeds collected at Westonbirt Arboretum in 1961. Grew about 35′ high in 15 to 18 years at Westonbirt.

Cupressus arizonica Green. — Arizona Cypress, Smooth Cypress
(kū-prēs′us ar-i-zon′ic-à)

FAMILY: Cupressaceae

LEAVES: Evergreen scales closely overlapping, scale-like, flattened to branchlet, and superposed in 4 rows, about 1/16″ long, acutely pointed, pale green to gray-green, occasionally blue-green; the overall effect is like a braided bullwhip and since the scales are pressed against the stem the foliage is soft-textured.

BRANCHLETS: Irregularly arranged, not planar as in most *Chamaecyparis* species, the final divisions 1/20″ wide and quadrangular in cross section.

BARK: Handsome red, brown, olive, gray, smooth, peeling in flakes, on mature trees dark brown, ridged-and-furrowed and fibrous.

SIZE: 40 to 50′ high by 25 to 30′ wide; national champion var. *arizonica* is 93′ by 48′ in Santa Catalina Mountains, AZ; var. *glabra* is 70′ by 48′ in Tonto National Forest, AZ.

HARDINESS: Zone 7 to 9.

HABIT: Rather handsome graceful pyramid with fine-textured foliage.

RATE: Medium.

TEXTURE: Fine.

BARK: Interesting especially on middle-aged trees, shiny, red to brown bark exfoliates in scales.

LEAF COLOR: Green, gray-green to blue-green.

FLOWERS: Monoecious, with male in small oblong cones, yellowish in color; female in a subglobose cone.

FRUIT: Globose cone with 6 to 8 flat or slightly depressed scales, each contracted into a short mucro (point), 1 to 1 1/4″ wide, scales are peltate which separates them from arborvitae; their size separates them from *Chamaecyparis*.

CULTURE: Transplant as a container-grown specimen; all species prefer hot, dry conditions, well-drained soil, full sun (thin out significantly with competition).

DISEASES AND INSECTS: In the proper environment generally trouble-free; in the Southeast subject to canker (*Seiridium cardinale*) and are not long lived; *Diplodia pinea* causes canker on *Cupressus sempervirens*.

LANDSCAPE VALUE: Excellent specimen, windbreak, tall screen; interestingly at one time widely grown in Southeast and odd trees may be seen; have seen seedlings in abundance on dry, abandoned slopes around Athens; suspect the species is best reserved for the Southwest and West; will never compete with × *Cupressocyparis leylandii* in the Southeast.

CULTIVARS: To be honest, I never developed a passion for the genus but see a great influx of blue-foliaged cultivars that means someone is paying attention. A worthy assumption is that if the genus was persistently adaptable to the Southeast then worthy specimens would have withstood the test of time. In short, this is not the case. If infatuated with the species and cultivars, temper the infection with the reality of the above verbiage. The State and Federal Forestry Services established *Cupressus* plantings at the University's Whitehall Plantation. I spent an afternoon walking the residuals and did not see a single plant worth propagating. The blue-foliaged forms have cash and carry appeal. For a short term landscape investment, they are acceptable.

‘Blue Ice’—Powdery gray-blue, silver-blue to icy blue foliage, mahogany red stems, and conical-pyramidal outline have served to popularize this form that was first introduced by Richard Ware in New Zealand in the 1960's; has withstood −5°F; see *American Nurseryman* 181(4):106 (1994) for complete description.

‘Blue Pyramid’—Gray-blue to powder blue foliage, symmetrical pyramid, reddish brown scaly bark, 20 to 25′ high, 10 to 12′ wide; from New Zealand.

‘Carolina Sapphire’—A rather loose, airy, broad pyramid of silver-blue; apparently introduced by Clemson University and has slowly traveled around the Southeast.

‘Glauca’—Embraces blue foliage forms; several slightly different clones in the trade.

‘Limelight’—Light yellow to lime green foliage throughout the year; narrow conical outline and compact habit due to the acutely angled, slightly arching, vertical branches and short inter branchlet spacing; similar to the more narrow forms of *C. arizonica* var. *glabra*; see *Plant Varieties Journal* 4:3, 22 (1991).

‘Silver Smoke’—Silver-gray foliage, upright symmetrical pyramid, reddish bark peels with age, slow-growing, 10 to 12′ high.

PROPAGATION: Seeds require cold moist stratification for one month; cuttings have not been easy to root for this author and excessive moisture induced rapid decline; I suspect the ventilated polytent method (warm bottom, cool top) would work best; November to December may be the best months to collect cuttings, use 2000 to 5000 ppm IBA; the best information indicates early winter cuttings, 90% perlite:10% peat, 62°F bottom heat in outdoor beds, intermittent mist; *C. glabra* ‘Blue Pyramid’ rooted best with 8000 ppm IBA dip, even better with 6000 ppm IBA + 6000 ppm NAA; *C. macrocarpa* ‘Donard's Gold’ 6000 ppm IBA-dip; *C. sempervirens* ‘Glauca’ 8000 ppm IBA-dip; see *Proc. Intl. Plant Prop. Soc.* 39:154–160 (1989).

NATIVE HABITAT: Central and southern Arizona. Introduced 1887.

RELATED SPECIES: It is fair to state that the *Cupressus* are difficult to identify. The species that is often listed as *C. glabra* (which is a dense, bushy tree with a spreading crown and has gray to blue leaves) is often sold as *C. arizonica* and for 10 years I have been trying to determine the identity of a 35 to 40′ specimen on the Georgia campus that, unfortunately, has never coned. Some authorities consider *C. glabra* a variety of *C. arizonica*. The legitimate taxonomy of *C. arizonica* and *C. glabra* is fluid and seemingly no two authorities agree. Griffiths lists *C. arizonica* var. *arizonica* with thick, fibrous, coarsely shredding, gray-brown bark, needles dull gray-green with no resinous exudations and var. *glabra* (Sudw.) Little, Smooth Arizona Cypress, with smooth bark always exfoliating in papery layers, purple to red, needles bright blue-green with obvious resin glands. Most of the cultivars appear to be selected from var. *glabra*.

Cupressus macrocarpa Hartw. ex Gordon, (kū-prēs′us ma-kro-câr′pȧ), Monterey Cypress, is an artistic, horizontally branching, often flat-topped tree in its native environs of the Monterey peninsula in California. The trees are genuinely beautiful. Habit is narrow and pyramidal in youth becoming picturesque with age. Plants grow 30 to 40′(50′). Have read British references that refer to 100′ high plants. National champion is 106′ by 111′ in Pascadera County, CA. In 1991, Allan Armitage and I visited Emo Court and Powerscourt Gardens in Ireland. The *Cupressus macrocarpa* were massive. In California, nothing I have observed matched the Irish specimens. The needles are a rich dark green and as handsome as any in the genus. The 8- to 14-scaled cones are 1 to 1 1/3″ wide, grouped 1 to 2 together on short, thick stalks. Unfortunately, the species is tremendously susceptible to a canker (*Seiridium cardinale*, often listed as *Coryneum* canker) that has killed many trees, especially those planted away from the coast. In San Francisco's Golden Gate Park, I witnessed numerous trees dying and being removed. The species displays excellent salt tolerance. It is one of the parents of × *Cupressocyparis leylandii* and I wonder when the same disease will manifest itself on the intergeneric hybrid (see comments under DISEASES AND INSECTS). Numerous cultivars of *C. macrocarpa* have been selected over the years. The golden needled forms are more prevalent in Europe and are best reserved for cool climates. 'Donard Gold', 'Golden Cone', and 'Goldcrest' are three yellow to golden needle forms that have crossed my path. 'Contorta' is sold in the United States and becomes broad upright in habit with bright green twisted new foliage. Introduced 1838. Zone 7 to 9. Not for high humidity areas of the southeastern states.

Cupressus sempervirens L., (kū-prēs′us sem-pēr-vī′renz), Italian Cypress, has always been an enigma to me. The plant in its familiar cultivated form is a narrow column, which has crossed my path numerous times. The species has dark green foliage and horizontal branches. Apparently three selections dominate the cultivated market and include: 'Roylei' with bright green needles and stiff upright habit, 'Stricta' a narrow-columnar form with green foliage, and 'Glauca' ('Stricta Glauca') with genuine rich blue-green foliage and columnar habit. All look like exclamation points and their use needs to be restrained. 'Swane's Golden', also spelled 'Swain's Gold', is a slow-growing, narrow columnar form with golden green foliage throughout the year; grows like 'Skyrocket' juniper. The selections can grow 20 to 30′ and higher. I have seen 'Stricta' used in Charleston, SC where it was relatively prosperous. Several 40 to 50′ high specimens grow on Jekyll Island, GA, although a tad disheveled. Southern Europe and western Asia. Zone 7 to 9.

Cycas revoluta Thunb. — Sago Palm

FAMILY: Cycadaceae
LEAVES: In a pseudowhorl on the unbranched trunk, each leaf 4 to 5′ long, with fern-like pinnae, up to 6″ by 1/4″, leaves leathery, hard, lustrous dark green above, paler and minutely pubescent below, each pinna held at 45 to 60° angle to rachis, gracefully incurved; midvein—sunken, yellow-green.

Cycas revoluta, (sī′kas rev-o-lu′tȧ), Sago Palm, is encountered in coastal landscapes from South Carolina to Texas and the West Coast. The plant grows 4 to 6′(8′) high and wide. Although single-stemmed, eventually plants form side shoots (offsets) that create a multi-stemmed effect. The magnificent foliage is the principal asset. Plants require well-drained soil and hold best foliage color with some shade protection. Makes a lovely accent in a border or shady nook. Might lend itself to large container use. Plants are dioecious with males in a woolly cone structure, females borne as naked ovules in a loosely arranged mass of modified leaves, each bearing the seeds along its margin. Seeds ovoid, 2 to 2 1/2″ long, hard-shelled with a fleshy outer covering. Southern Japan. Zone 8 (with protection) to 11. In the mid-1980's, 11°F along Georgia's coast defoliated most of the *C. revoluta*, but did not kill the stems and regrowth was almost universal.

Cyrilla racemiflora L. — Swamp Cyrilla, Leatherwood
(sī-ril′ȧ rȧ-sem-i-flō′rȧ)

FAMILY: Cyrillaceae
LEAVES: Alternate, simple, evergreen, semi-evergreen or deciduous (North), oblong or oblanceolate, 1 1/2 to 4″ long, 1/2 to 1 1/4″ wide, obtuse, cuneate, lustrous dark green above, bright green and reticulate beneath, glabrous; petiole—1/4″ long.

BUDS: Small, 1/16 to 1/12″ long, deltoid, sitting directly above and flat across the leaf scar.

STEM: Moderate, gray-brown, glabrous, raised ridges from center of base of leaf scar giving stem angled appearance; shield-shaped leaf scar with what appears to be a single bud scar.

SIZE: Usually 10 to 15′ high and wide, but can grow 25 to 35′; national champion is 58′ by 28′ in Washington County, FL.

HARDINESS: Zone (5)6 to 11; have seen at Louisville, KY, Mentor, OH, and Boston, MA; is distinctly deciduous in cold climates and may be killed back in extremely cold winters.

HABIT: Large shrub or small tree; usually a rather sprawling/spreading rounded shrub of great beauty; develops a stout, eccentric trunk from which numerous, wide-spreading branches arise; branches contorted and twisted.

RATE: Medium.

TEXTURE: Medium.

LEAF COLOR: Lustrous rich green holding late in fall and eventually turning orange and scarlet; the beautiful foliage is sufficient reason to use this shrub; in deep South may hold leaves into the following season; has been evergreen in mild seasons in our garden.

FLOWERS: Perfect, white, fragrant, 5-petaled, 1/5″ across, in slender 3 to 6″ long and 1/2 to 3/4″ wide racemes that appear in a horizontal whorl at the base of the current season's growth; flowers quite showy and rather light and airy in texture; June–July; flowers late June–early July in our garden; supposedly good bee pasture, but a Florida publication lists "purple brood" (brood may die) as a potential problem.

FRUIT: A 1/2″ long, roundish, 2-celled, loculicidally dehiscent capsule, matures in August–September, persists into winter; rather interesting.

CULTURE: Not well-documented but prefers a high organic matter, moist, acid, well-drained soil; full sun to partial shade; in the wild found in swamps; actually once established appears difficult to kill; have removed the large specimen from the garden and eight years later have shoots developing from root pieces.

DISEASES AND INSECTS: None serious.

LANDSCAPE VALUE: Simply a beautiful shrub for foliage and flowers; can be successfully grown from Zone 6 south; have seen it used by the edge of a lake with great success; seems to belong in a naturalistic setting; a good shrub border plant in the home landscape; does not compete well with other species; used in a large bed in front of the house and many people ask me why it is there; there is no good reason except that I like it; have pruned the lower branches and suckers to expose rather handsome smooth brown bark; the contorted, twisted spiraled stems are beautiful; needs room to expand.

CULTIVARS: Unnamed selection by John Ruter carries cream-green new growth that matures to green, it is beautiful when the new leaves emerge.

PROPAGATION: Seeds can be directly sown; root cuttings will work; August cuttings treated with 10,000 ppm IBA rooted 100%; over the years I have rooted the plant many times; firm-wooded cuttings from June into September can be easily rooted.

NATIVE HABITAT: In its broadest sense a single species ranging from Virginia to Florida, also West Indies and eastern South America. Introduced 1767.

RELATED SPECIES:

Cyrilla arida Small, (sī-ril′à ār′id-à), is another interesting species with small, evergreen leaves, dense, white flowers, and rather wispy habit. Woodlanders, Aiken, SC has grown this in the garden in Aiken. Requires well-drained soil. Central Florida. It makes a rather handsome shrub for Zone 8 to 9.

Cyrilla arida

Cyrilla parvifolia Raf., (sī-ril′à pär-vi-fō′li-à), Small Cyrilla, is a Florida to Louisiana native with smaller leaves, 3/4 to 1 1/2″ long, 1/4 to 1/2″ wide, and 1 to 3″ long floral racemes. Although not common in commerce, Woodlanders, Aiken, SC has offered the plant. Might be a better choice for the small garden, but foliage, as I have observed it, is sparse and not as handsome as big sister's. Also, listed as *C. racemiflora* var. *parvifolia*.

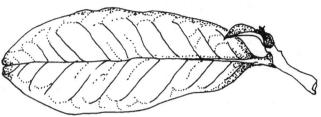

Cliftonia monophylla (Lam.) Sarg., (klif-tōn′ē-a̍ mon-ō-fil′a̍), Buckwheat-tree or Titi, is similar to the above and is found in the same locations in the wild. It forms a medium-sized [6 to 12′(18′) high], evergreen shrub. The lustrous dark green, evergreen leaves are 1 to 2″ long. The white or rose, fragrant flowers are borne in 1 1/2 to 2 1/2″ long and 5/8″ wide racemes in March–April. The ovoid, indehiscent, 3- to 4-winged fruit looks like a buckwheat fruit; hence, the common name. Has the same cultural requirements as *Cyrilla*. The foliage is beautiful and the fragrant flowers a fine asset. In the Coastal plain, this and *Cyrilla* make great bee pasture and are a source of "Titi" honey. Have seen it in Canton, GA where temperatures as low as −16°F have occurred. I took 5 cuttings from a plant in my garden in July; treated them with 3000 ppm IBA; had 80% rooting by October; no wound; rooting takes 2 to 3 months. An unnamed compact form with leaves one-third the size of the species and with closely spaced nodes is known. Georgia to Florida and Louisiana. Introduced 1806. Zone 7 to 9, perhaps 6.

ADDITIONAL NOTES: These species are highly unusual but worthy landscape plants, especially in native situations. Their foliage effect alone is sufficient reason for using them. Flowers are more spectacular on *Cyrilla*. Since flowers occur at different times, both can be effective. Bonnie and I were returning home from St. Simons in early February and were driving to Georgia Southern University, Statesboro, to visit our son Matthew. *All* along Route 80 were abundant stands of *Cliftonia* in full flower. The inflorescences were often compound racemose panicles and frequent photographic stops opened my mind to the beauty of this species.

Cyrtomium falcatum Presl. — Japanese Holly-fern

FAMILY: Polypodiaceae
LEAVES: Evergreen, 1 to 2′ long, leaflets holly-like with prominent serrations, lustrous dark green above, 1 to 2″ long, one-half as wide, leathery, underside of leaf developing numerous sori (spore clusters) in summer–fall.

Cyrtomium falcatum, (sĕr-tō′mi-um fal-kā′tum), Japanese Holly-fern, is reserved strictly for the southern United States and is one of those plants that northerners drool over the first time they see it. At the first meeting, it takes awhile for the fact to sink in that one is looking at a true fern. The lustrous dark green leaves form a lovely 1 to 2′ high and wide mound. As the young fiddle heads unroll (early to mid-April) the entire frond assumes an attractive yellow-green color before maturing to dark green. The plant tolerates partial to heavy shade and is ideal for the moist site on the north side of a structure. Prefers moist, well-drained, high organic matter soils. There are no serious insect or disease problems. 'Compactum' has shorter leaves than the species and 'Rochfordianum' has more incised leaflets that produce a finer texture than the species. Restricted to Zone 8 (10 to 20°F) and warmer conditions. Grew this for a number of years but lost foliage in late April to a freak freeze as the young fronds were developing; also lost all plants at −3°F during the 1983–84 winter. China, Malaysia, Taiwan, India, Africa, Hawaii.

Cytisus scoparius (L.) Link. — Scotch or Common Broom
(sī′ti′sus skō-pā′ri-us)

FAMILY: Fabaceae
LEAVES: Alternate, 3-foliate, obovate or lanceolate, 1/4 to 5/8″ long, sparingly appressed pubescent, the upper leaves reduced to 1 leaflet, bright to medium green.
BUDS: Small, solitary, sessile, round-ovoid, with about 4, often indistinct scales.
STEM: Slender, finely granular, green, almost winged on the ridges; bright green in summer and winter; pith—small, roundish, continuous.

SIZE: 5 to 6′ when open-grown, larger when used in shrub borders and tight situations; spread is equal to or considerably greater than height.

HARDINESS: Zone 5 to 8.

HABIT: An arching, broad rounded, deciduous shrub with very erect, slender, grass green stems and twigs; can become ratty in appearance.

TEXTURE: Medium-fine if kept in bounds during summer; similar texture in winter.

STEM COLOR: Distinctly angled stems of grass green color, very attractive in winter; young stems maintain green color, older stems become gray-brown; several studies have demonstrated that the green stems are important sites of photosynthesis and contribute to the plant's aggressive nature.

LEAF COLOR: Light to medium green in summer; fall color of no consequence.

FLOWERS: Perfect, glowing yellow, 1″ long and 4/5″ across, May–June (mid to late April in Athens), profusely borne along the stems on old wood either singly or in two's.

FRUIT: 1 1/2 to 2″ long pod, hairy along the margins, not ornamental.

CULTURE: Supposedly does not transplant well but I have had good success with container-grown material; prefers sandy, infertile soils which are somewhat on the dry side; full sun to partial shade in the South; pH adaptable; relatively easy to grow; tends to seed itself in; old plants may die out but new ones always seem to be coming along; cut back old overgrown plants, but not into the oldest, largest stems; prune after flowering.

DISEASES AND INSECTS: Leaf spot and blight can kill the plants; small irregular spots first appear on the leaf blades, enlarge rapidly, and cause a blotch or blight.

LANDSCAPE VALUE: Very good plant for poor soils; has been used for stabilizing sandy right-of-ways along eastern highways; I have seen it used in Massachusetts along highways and it made an effective cover; yields a fantastic splash of color when in flower; a Midwest nurseryman told me the plant rarely lasts more than 5 years; I witnessed tremendous injury after winter of 1977–78 when the low temperatures reached –8°F but the mean low temperature for December, January, February was 10° below normal; in general *Cytisus* will seed and can establish fairly large colonies; does quite well in South, where it often seeds in waste areas.

On our yearly garden tours to England the first plants our guests ask about are broom and gorse (*Ulex*); everyone is in the twilight zone from the flight but after boarding the bus outside Gatwick and seeing the repeated dashes of bright yellow along the M23 (motorway) the inevitable question surfaces . . . what is that plant? My colleague and I proceed to tell them and explain how the plant is often used in English gardens for May–June color; in many gardens a single plant is spotted among ground covers or heathers and literally erupts in a floral volcano; there is a tendency in the United States to use the plant in masses especially for color splashes along highways; several years past a Georgia Department of Transportation official called me and wanted to know where to locate 700 yellow brooms for a highway interchange; I had no answer but the GDOT official persisted for the plants were installed and are certainly attractive in flower.

CULTIVARS: The brooms are not popular landscape plants in the United States but in Europe they appear everywhere. The color range is rather fantastic moving from white to yellow to red with all combinations and permutations in the flower. The Dutch are breeding brooms and have introduced a number of fine forms. Several years past at the International Garden Festival in Liverpool, England, I visited the Dutch exhibit where they had displayed several of their new broom hybrids. 'Boskoop Ruby' with rich garnet flowers was one of the best, yet I have not seen it in English or American gardens or literature. Maybe too many selections are available; certainly many too similar to warrant naming (actually end up being named), that fall by the commercial and gardening wayside. Over 80 cultivars and hybrids have been derived from *Cytisus scoparius*. A few mail order firms in the United States offer 4 or 5 broom selections but to my knowledge no one carries an extensive list and what is listed below is nothing more than a futuristic shopping list.

'Andreanus'—Brown crimson flowers.

'Burkwoodii'—Garnet red flowers (standard carmine red, wings red-brown with a narrow, gold border); vigorous, bushy.

'C.E. Pearson'—Rose, yellow, red flowers; reasonably common in commerce.

'Carla'—Flowers pink and crimson lined with white.

'Compact Crimson'—Deep crimson flowers, yellow centers, 3 to 4′ high.

'Cornish Cream'—Cream and yellow, bushy, open habit.

'Diana'—Standard ivory, wings gold, low habit.

'Donard Gem'—Pink flushed red, profuse.

'Donard Seedling'—Mauve-pink and flame red, loose habit.

'Dorothy Walpole'—Rose-pink with velvety crimson wings.

'Dragonfly'—Standard rich yellow, vibrant yellow keel, wings brown.

'Dukaat'—Clear yellow flowers, stiff upright habit, 20″ high.

'Enchantress'—Rose-pink and carmine, spreading bushy outline.

'Firefly'—Yellow and rich mahogany-crimson, bushy.

'Golden Sunlight'—Rich golden yellow, very free-flowering, vigorous arching habit.

'Goldfinch'—Crimson and yellow, pink and yellow wings.

'Hookstone'—Flowers lilac and orange.

'Johnson's Crimson'—Clear crimson, free-flowering, graceful arching habit.

'Killiney Red'—Flowers bright red, dwarf, compact habit.

'Knaphill Lemon'—Lemon yellow flowers.

'Lady Moore'—Pinkish yellow and orange flame, loose branching.

'Lena'—Ruby red standards and wings, pale yellow keels, freely borne, compact, comparatively dwarf, 3 to 4′ high; a *C.* × *dallimorei* form.

'Lilac Time'—Many conflicting descriptions; the plant in the trade is a compact grower with deep reddish purple flowers; certain literature ascribes a lilac color to the standard with lighter colored wings; the plant was obviously mislabeled in nursery circles; a *C.* × *dallimorei* form.

'Lord Lambourne'—Creamy yellow and maroon-crimson, branching and spreading.

'Luna'—Yellow flowers.

'Minstead'—Fuchsia-purple and white, slender arching habit; a *C.* × *dallimorei* form.

'Moonlight'—Glowing moonlight yellow (actually cream-white) flowers, nodding growth habit, 5 to 6′ high and wide.

'Nova Scotia'—An extra hardy form offered by Wayside Gardens with intense yellow flowers; tip injury and occasional severe branch kill at Orono, ME.

'Radiance'—Standard and keel white, wings brown.

'Red Favorite'—Showy red flowers on an upright-stemmed, compact mounding shrub.

'Red Wings'—Standard and wings crimson, keel lilac.

'Sulphureus'—Cream, tinged red in bud, wing and keel sulphur.

'Variegatus'—Leaves gray-tinged, edged in white.

'Windlesham Ruby'—Large ruby red flowers.

'Zeelandia'—Pale lilac-pink and red, long arching sprays.

PROPAGATION: Seeds should be soaked in hot water or acid soaked to break seed coat dormancy; for germination, it may require 30 minutes or more in acid and diurnally alternating temperatures of 68°F (night) and 86°F (day) for 28 days are recommended; apparently there is no embryo dormancy; seeds are usually produced in abundance. Two to 3″ long cuttings with a heel taken in August and September, placed in sand in cold frames, will develop roots by spring; various species and cultivars have been rooted anytime from June to December by treating the cuttings with a relatively high IBA level (8000 ppm); a loose medium is recommended since root systems are somewhat brittle.

ADDITIONAL NOTES: My general belief is that brooms should be viewed as temporary but beautiful garden plants. If one dies replace it for the floral display is worth the effort. Quite sandy soil and salt tolerant as many seedlings exist on Cape Cod, MA. In the Athens area, reasonably large masses have persisted over the years and appear to perpetuate themselves by seeding. Also, in the heat of the South, the plants appear better adapted to pine shade or the edges of woodlands. In northern California and much of the western park and range lands, this species has assumed weed-like proportions. Also out of control in Canada, Australia and New Zealand.

A final thought concerning performance in the South crossed my mind. Mr. Will Corley, Horticulturist, Griffin, GA, evaluated a tremendous number of *Cytisus* for adaptability. He was interested in persistence, flower quality, growth habit, hardiness, etc. The bottom line . . . he did not find a single taxon that was well-adapted. Will concluded that the best form was the one that seeded along Georgia highways.

NATIVE HABITAT: Central and southern Europe. Long cultivated.

RELATED SPECIES: It is beyond the scope of this book to treat extensively all the *Cytisus* species and related genera (*Genista*, *Ulex*). Approximately 33 species are known. I have included several that deserve a closer look.

Cytisus decumbens (Dur.) Spach., (sī'ti'sus dē-kum'benz), Prostrate Broom, smothers the ground in May–June with a sea of bright yellow. The species grows 4 to 12″ high. The leaves are simple, sessile, 1/4 to 3/4″ long, 1/8 to 1/6″ wide, oblong or obovate, pubescent, especially beneath. The 1/2 to 5/8″ long flowers occur singly, in two's or three's from the axils of previous season's wood. Pod is 3/4 to 1″ long, pubescent, 3- to 4-seeded. The 5-angled stems are sparsely pubescent. This species is confused with *C. procumbens* but is more pubescent. A fine choice as a low-growing ground cover in full sun or in the rock garden. Southern Europe. Introduced 1775. Zone 5 to 7.

Cytisus hirsutus L., (sī-ti'sus her-sūt'us), Hairy Broom, is a dwarf, 2 to 3′ high and wide shrub with rounded, slender, pubescent (not appressed) stems. The trifoliate leaves are composed of 3/8″ long, half as wide, oval to broadly obovate leaflets; their undersurface hairy. The 1″ long, yellow flowers occur 2 to 4 together in axillary clusters; the standard stained brown in the center. Pod is 1 to 1 1/2″ long, flattened, shaggily hairy. This species is not as showy as *C. scoparius* or *C.* × *praecox* but is considered the hardiest of the brooms. It is being successfully grown in Minnesota where some stem dieback occurs but flowering occurs heavily on the basal portion of the plant. This species can be distinguished from the other species treated herein by its rounded stems. Variety *hirsutissimus* is a sturdier, more erect form with more pubescent parts. Recent taxonomic treatment places this in *Chamaecytisus hirsutus* (L.) Link. Southeastern Europe. Cultivated 1739. Zone (4)5 to 6.

Cytisus* × *praecox Wheeler ex Bean, (sī-ti'sus prē'koks), Warminster Broom, is a hybrid complex resulting from crosses between *C. purgans* (yellow) and *C. multiflorus* (white). The typical and original clone should be known as *C.* × *praecox* 'Warminster'. It is a large shrub like *C. multiflorus*, but with denser and heavier masses of young branches. Plants grow 4 to 6′(10′) high and wide. Leaves mostly simple, about 1/2″ long and silky-pubescent like the long shoots. The sulfur yellow flowers are produced in abundance during May but are of a rather unpleasant odor. It first appeared among seedlings of *C. purgans* in Wheeler's nursery, Warminster, England, about 1867. It sets fertile seed but the resultant plants revert more or less to one or the other parents. Selections have been made and include: 'Albus'—white flowers; 'Allgold'—deep yellow flowers, mounded, 5 to 6′ high; 'Goldspeer' (also known as 'Canary Bird')—profuse, bright yellow flowers; 'Hollandia'—flowers salmon-pink to rosy pink on a robust 4′ shrub, flowers profusely borne, common in United States; 'Lucky'—peach-colored flowers, to 6′. Many other cultivars are included here, some of dubious parentage.

ADDITIONAL NOTES: The brooms literally light up a landscape. They are effective in mass and, like forsythia, can be blinding when used in this manner. *Ulex europaeus* L., Gorse, is a close relative but with extremely spiny branches; the gold-yellow flowers are equally attractive and I have seen it in abundance along English highways where it flowers at the same time as the broom. Gorse more or less flowers all season long in England, Wales, and Scotland and is found on sandy infertile soils and disturbed sites. Appears to be somewhat of a colonizer. It is a terrible weed in Europe and care should be exercised before unleashing its genetic fury on the American landscape. Raulston has grown the golden-foliaged form in Raleigh. The species could be likened to a green porcupine. Zone (6)7 to 8. Flint, *Horticulture* 65(6):46–52 (1987), presented an excellent overview of *Cytisus* and *Genista*.

Several other species that appear in European gardens include *Cytisus beanii* Dallim., a semi-procumbent form 16 to 20″ high, 5′ wide, with 1/2″ long, simple, hirsute, rich green leaves and rich yellow flowers borne 1 to 3 at the nodes. Zone 5. Have seen and admired at Kew Gardens. *Cytisus* × *kewensis* Bean (*C. ardoinii* × *C. multiflorus*) grows 12 to 18″ high and 4 to 6′ wide with usually trifoliate, pubescent, linear-oblong leaves and pale yellow to cream-white flowers borne 1 to 3 together from the axils. Beautiful in flower with ground cover possibilities. *Cytisus multiflorus* Sweet., White Spanish Broom, grows 6 to 10′ high with rather spindly branches, 1- to 3-foliate leaves, leaflets 1/3″ long, linear, silvery-pubescent. Flowers are white, 1 to 3 together. Several cultivars are known. All the above are best suited to Zone 6 and south.

Years past, I saw a single *Cytisus* of unknown identity in the Littlefield Garden, University of Maine, that had survived for a number of years. To my knowledge, the most cold hardy broom is *C. scoparius*. Anyone in northern gardens should start with this species and its cultivars. Cappiello listed *C. scoparius* and *C.* × *praecox* with regular tip dieback and occasional substantial dieback in Orono, ME (Zone 4).

Daboecia cantabrica (Huds.) K. Koch — Irish, Connemara or St. Daboec's Heath

FAMILY: Ericaceae
LEAVES: Alternate, simple, evergreen, 1/4 to 5/8″ long, 1/10 to 1/4″ wide, elliptic, revolute margins, silver tomentose beneath; at first glance appearing similar to heath, *Erica*.

Daboecia cantabrica, (dab-ē′shi-à kan′tà-bri-cà), Irish Heath, forms an evergreen ground cover mat much like *Erica* and *Calluna*. Plants grow 12 to 20″ high. In summer to fall, rose-purple, 1/3 to 1/2″ long, urn-shaped flowers appear in 3 to 5″ long, terminal racemes on new growth of the season. Each flower has four tiny reflexed corolla lobes and four glandular sepal divisions. Fruit is a 4-lobed, dehiscent, hairy, septicidal capsule. Requires moist, well-drained, acid soil. Ideally prepare the soil with copious amounts of organic matter. Prune in early spring to keep it in presentable condition. I have observed large plantings at Edinburgh Botanic Garden and Bells Cherrybank Gardens, Perth, Scotland, and simply fantasized about growing the plant in the southeastern United States. Many cultivars differing in flower color have been introduced. Forma or variety *alba* with rich green foliage and white flowers is well-known and represented. Another species, *Daboecia azorica* Tutin & E.F. Warb., with campanulate, ruby red, nodding, 1/4 to 3/8″ long flowers is found in the Azores. It grows one foot or less and has smaller leaves than *D. cantabrica*. It is also less winter hardy. Have observed hybrids between the two species with 'William Buchanan' a garnet red flowered form the most common. *Daboecia cantabrica* is native to western Europe, including Ireland. Cultivated 1800. Zone 6.

Danae racemosa (L.) Moench. — Alexandrian-laurel

FAMILY: Liliaceae
LEAVES: In this case, the "leaves" are modified stems (cladophylls) but serve the same function; alternate, oblong-lanceolate, 1 1/2 to 4″ long, 1/4 to 1 1/2″ wide, lustrous rich green on both surfaces, taper-pointed, abruptly narrowed at base and scarcely stalked.

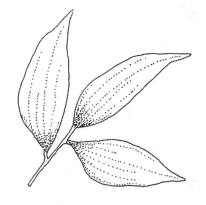

Danae racemosa, (da′nà-ē rà-se-mō′sà), Alexandrian-laurel, is an elegant, refined, evergreen shrub that grows 2 to 4′ high and wide. The habit is gracefully arching. The lustrous rich green leaves are handsome throughout the year. The greenish yellow flowers are rather inconspicuous but the fleshy, orange-red, 1/4 to 3/8″ diameter, rounded berry is quite attractive. Prefers a moist, well-drained soil in shade. "Foliage" discolors in sun and open, exposed situations. The "foliage" is excellent for use inside as the cut branches remain fresh a long time. Not common in the South but certainly worthy of cultivation. Has no serious insect or disease problems but have noticed some leaf spot on plants at Callaway Garden. Division of the parent plant will work. Spreads by rhizomes and is not a fast developer. Seed propagation has proven difficult and apparently seeds have an immature embryo and/or complex dormancy. The nearly emerging shoots in spring remind of asparagus. Certainly a worthy choice for a shady nook. Can be rejuvenated by pruning untidy shoots. Will regenerate from base. Tissue culture has proven successful. See *Acta Horticulturae* 226(1):212–222 (1988). Native to northern Iran and Asia Minor. Introduced 1713. Zone 7b to 9.

Daphne cneorum L. — Rose Daphne, Garland Flower
(daf′nē nē-ō′rum)

FAMILY: Thymelaeaceae
LEAVES: Alternate, simple, evergreen, 3/4 to 1″ long, 1/8 to 1/5″ wide, crowded, oblanceolate, usually obtuse and mucronulate, cuneate, lustrous dark green above, glaucescent and glaucous beneath.
BUDS: Sessile, usually solitary but sometimes superimposed or collaterally branched, ovoid, with 4 to 6 exposed scales.
STEM: Moderate, rounded or somewhat 4-sided; leaf scars crescent-shaped, small, exceptionally elevated; 1 bundle trace; pith—small, roundish, continuous.

SIZE: 6 to 12″(16″) high by 2′ or more in spread.

HARDINESS: Zone 4 to 7.

HABIT: A low-spreading evergreen shrub with long, trailing and ascending branches forming low, loose masses.

RATE: Slow.

TEXTURE: Medium-fine in all seasons although may look ragged in winter.

LEAF COLOR: Dark green throughout the year.

FLOWERS: Bright rosy-pink, 1/2″ across, delightfully fragrant; April and May and often flowering again in late summer; borne in 6- to 8-flowered umbels; often reminds one of the flower of Candytuft; literally smother the foliage and produce an ocean of rose-pink; sepals are showy part of flower.

FRUIT: Yellowish brown drupe; have not observed on cultivated plants.

CULTURE: Transplant as a container plant; does not move readily; should be accomplished in early spring or early fall; there is considerable incongruity in soil recommendations but the following composite was gleaned from several sources; prefer well-drained, moist, near neutral (pH 6 to 7) soil; shade—light to medium; snow-cover is beneficial; protect with pine boughs where winter sun and wind present a problem; mulch to maintain moist root zone; prune annually after the plants have become established, preferably after flowering and before mid-July; the plant resents disturbance and once located should be left there permanently; have grown many daphnes, some as many as three times, they die for no explicable reason; to date have lost *Daphne odora* and several cultivars, *Daphne* × *burkwoodii* and 'Carol Mackie', *Daphne caucasica*; interestingly when they decide to go it is usually with haste . . . one day green . . . the next day crinkled, dry looking leaves; the 1995 casualty was a magnificent 3 to 4′ high and 5′ wide *Daphne odora* 'Alba', Bonnie and I are still in mourning; upon removal I noted the sparse nature of the root system—stringy, minimally branched, no root hairs?; still in the first order of landscape plants; one or two branches in a vase will perfume a room.

DISEASES AND INSECTS: Leaf spots result in brown spots on both sides of the leaves, crown rot occurs more commonly on plants in shady areas; twig blight, canker, viruses, aphids, mealybug and scales present problems; virus may be the culprit when plants die for no logical reason; have seen virus-induced distortion of leaves of *D. odora*; excess moisture dooms the plant to failure so practice good husbandry when siting.

LANDSCAPE VALUE: Good small evergreen ground cover; works well in a rock garden or slightly shady spots; very fastidious as to culture and perhaps *Iberis sempervirens* is a decent substitute especially for southeastern and midwestern states; in my career I have come across many daphnes and can honestly say have not met one I do not like; this particular species is a real gem and my first significant exposure came when I visited the garden of the late Mr. Larry Newcomb, Sharon, MA, author of *Newcomb's Wildflower Guide*; Larry was showing me through his extensive wildflower garden and at the end of the tour as we were about to enter his house, by the stoop, was a tremendous bed of *D. cneorum* in full flower; he said that it received no special care and yet thrived; have seen time and again in rock gardens throughout Europe, absolutely stunning in flower; can never seem to get enough of this wonderful plant.

CULTIVARS:

'Alba'—White to ivory flowers and rather dwarfish habit.

'Eximia'—Larger leaves and flowers, the buds crimson opening rose-pink; have seen many times at Edinburgh Botanic Garden, a beautiful form.

'Pygmaea' (var. *pygmaea* Stoker)—A rose-pink, free-flowering form with prostrate branches, smaller leaves. Have seen 'Pygmaea Alba' with white fragrant flowers listed in northeast nurseries.

'Ruby Glow'—Dark pink flowers on a 6 to 12″ high framework of dark green foliage; Lake County Nursery Introduction, Perry, OH.

'Variegata'—A very beautiful, dainty, cream-edged leaf form of vigorous constitution; flowers like the species, I first saw this cultivar in Wisley Gardens, England and wanted to collect cuttings; a plant of delicate, quiet beauty; a model for other variegated plants to emulate, will revert and have observed fully green shoots among the variegated shoots. Also listed is 'Albomarginata'.

var. *verlotii* (Gren. & Gordon) Meissn.—Leaves up to an inch long and about 1/8″ wide, rose-pink flowers, the perianth tube 5/8″ long, resulting in larger flowers than the species; quite handsome.

PROPAGATION: Seed of most species requires a cold treatment of 2 to 3 months. Cuttings (December) of *D. cneorum* failed to root without treatment but rooted 56% after treatment with 100 ppm IAA/16 hour soak; July cuttings rooted 74% without treatment, and 93% with 1000 ppm IBA-talc; I have rooted *Daphne odora* with 100% efficiency in two separate tests; July cuttings from the Georgia campus and November cuttings from Longwood Gardens were treated with 3000 ppm IBA-quick dip, peat:perlite, mist, root systems were profuse; rooting takes about 8 weeks; cuttings of *D.* × *burkwoodii* and *D. cneorum* that I collected on August 24, treated with 8000 ppm IBA-quick dip failed to root.

At one time I thought *Daphne odora* propagation was as easy as cutting warm butter but have had up and down success; timing appears important and possibly best to take cuttings after growth flush hardens in June and July; I have watched cuttings "sit" in the rooting bench for months and never do anything; excess moisture is not conducive to good rooting and a covered frame using polyethylene and shade cloth might be beneficial; make sure the stock is clean, i.e., virus-free before collecting cuttings; virus infection may be the largest hindrance to good rooting. John and Tommy Alden, County Line Nursery, Byron, GA, one of the largest *Daphne odora* producers in the Southeast, root cuttings in June–July using an IBA-talc formulation. Rooting percentages are high.

Lamb and Nutty, *The Plantsman* 8(2):109–111 (1986), present interesting observations on propagation of daphnes. A summary follows. In Ireland (Kinsealy), June, July, August cuttings gave the most consistent results. Depending on species, percentages ranged from 28 to 96% with 50 to 70% being average. Treatment consisted of 8000 ppm IBA-talc, Captan, 2 peat moss:1 sand medium, mist; rooting time ranged from 7 to 11 weeks. Seeds should be collected before they change color, cleaned and sown; some, but not complete, germination will occur the first year; plants can also be grafted or layered.

ADDITIONAL NOTES: *Daphne* consists of some 50 small evergreen and deciduous shrubs distributed through Europe, North Africa into temperate and subtropical Asia. Indeed as garden subjects, they will prove frustrating. From my observations there are very few *old* daphnes in American gardens. A single, successful flowering season justifies their use. Heaven is truly a scent away.

NATIVE HABITAT: Europe, from Spain to southwest Russia. Introduced 1752.

RELATED SPECIES:

Daphne × burkwoodii Turrill, (daf'nē berk-wood'ē-ī), Burkwood Daphne, is a cross between *D. cneorum × D. caucasica*. The flowers are pinkish tinged, opening white, fragrant, and borne in dense, terminal, 2″ diameter umbels in May. Individual flowers are about 1/2″ wide while the red drupes are about 1/3″ wide. This species is performing quite well at the Morton Arboretum in Lisle, IL. The species will grow 3 to 4′ high. Zone 4 to 7(8). There are two clones, one termed 'Arthur Burkwood', the other 'Somerset', which have received considerable attention. Apparently, when the original cross was made only three seeds resulted but all germinated. Of the three plants, one died and the other two are the clones listed. Both forms make vigorous bushes to at least 3′, but of the two, 'Somerset' is larger and can grow to 4′ high and more in diameter. The foliage is semi-evergreen on both and, in this respect, intermediate between the parents. Wyman noted that a 20-year-old specimen was 4′ high and 6′ wide, very rounded and dense. This group is supposedly easily propagated by cuttings taken in summer and treated with IBA. Plants of *D. × burkwoodii* that I have seen maintain their foliage into late November–early December but finally lose all their leaves. They make superb garden plants and the dense, broad mounded form is particularly well-suited to the small garden. A most beautiful and unusual clone is 'Carol Mackie' with delicate cream-edged leaf margins and fragrant light pink flowers; it grows to about 3′ high and slightly wider; I have observed this clone in the University of Maine's display garden; it has withstood temperatures as low as −30°F without injury; in my mind this is a most lovely variegated cultivar. There are several forms with variegated foliage. All are fine garden plants. See *Amer. Nurseryman* 170(11):7–9 (1989) for a discussion of the variegated clones. Several clones mentioned in British literature include: 'G.K. Argles' with broad, gold-margined leaves; 'Lavenrii'—a spreading form with 1 1/4″ long, 1/3″ wide, narrow-oblanceolate leaves; 'Somerset Gold Edge'—leaves with a gold margin; and 'Somerset Variegated'. A new American introduction is 'Briggs Moonlight'—a reverse mutation of 'Carol Mackie' with pale yellow centers and narrow green margins, relatively strong growing. A few follow-up notes are in order. First this species and cultivars are no more or less persistent than *D. odora*. In my garden, *D. × burkwoodii* has disappeared faster than *D. odora*. In my travels, I will visit a garden and encounter a splendid specimen of *D. × burkwoodii* or 'Carol Mackie'. Several years later during follow-up visits, I ask the owners what happened to the daphnes. Oh, they died. Still, for gardeners in Zones 4 to 6(7), this is the preferred species because of quality attributes, slightly tougher garden constitution and commercial availability.

An absolute avalanche of *Daphne* information surfaced in 1989 when the 1990 edition was in publication. I xerox and file publications that add something to my knowledge base and can be integrated into teaching and writing. The immense debate in 1989 was about the differences in variegated forms of *D. × burkwoodii*. For daphneophiles I suggest reading *Horticulture* 66(4):16–22 (1988); *American Nurseryman* 170(4):62–68 (1989); *American Nurseryman* 169(10):45–46, 48–50 (1989) and 169(10):35,37,39–43 (1989)—over 20 species and their nuances are discussed by Milton Gaschk; and several *Daphne* (daffy) letters to the editor appear in *American Nurseryman* 170(4):7–9 (1989).

The gist of the articles and letters relative to the variegated clones from *D.* × *burkwoodii* and *D.* × *burkwoodii* 'Somerset' concerned their uniqueness. The consensus from the principals, Dr. Pellett and Mr. Bruckel, Vermont and Mr. Vrugtman, Royal Botanical Gardens, Ontario, was minimal difference. The late Jim Cross, Environmentals, Cutchogue, NY, noted that *D.* × *burkwoodii* and 'Somerset' are different in habit with the latter larger, therefore, the variegated forms should be different.

To my knowledge the issue has not been resolved. The 'Carol Mackie' that I know is mounded and broad-spreading. It originated in 1962, commercially introduced in 1968; name validly published in *Arnoldia* 30(6):253 (1970). 'Somerset Variegated', one form, originated at H.M. Eddie & Sons, Ltd., Vancouver, Canada in the summer of 1961. 'Silveredge', with a silver edge to the leaf is similar to 'Somerset' in habit and was listed in the Sheridan Nurseries, Canada, 1963 catalog. 'Silveredge' originated in Boskoop, Netherlands, at the F.J. Grootendorst Nursery in the 1950's. 'Astrid' is a small leaf, cream-margined form that I first witnessed at Powerscourt Garden Center in Ireland. The container-grown plants did not appear as vigorous as the typical 'Carol Mackie' type.

To truly bring closure to the discussions, someone needs to bring the clones together for side-by-side comparisons.

Daphne caucasica Pall. — Caucasian Daphne
LEAVES: Alternate, simple, oblanceolate to lanceolate, 1 to 1 3/4″ long, 1/3 to 1/2″ wide, obtuse, rarely acuminate, pale green above, glaucous beneath, glabrous, leaves appearing almost bluish green.

Daphne caucasica, (daf′nē kâ-kas′i-kà), Caucasian Daphne, is a deciduous, 4 to 5′ high and wide shrub that produces fragrant, white flowers in groups of 4 to 20 in May and June and sporadically thereafter. Fruits are black or red. The Scott Arboretum, Swarthmore College, is particularly high on this species and introduced me to the plant for the first time. The delightful fragrance and the long season of flower are desirable traits. A plant found its way to Georgia, was happily growing in a 3-gallon container, awaiting a new home in my garden. Unfortunately, the plant curled up the root apices, performed a Daphne Death, and withered away into oblivion. Early reports from the Philadelphia area noted the ease of culture. I have read some literature that states it is temperamental. Have seen respectable flowers as late as October in Boston area. Definitely temperamental like other daphnes and will implode for no explicable reason. The recurrent flower production and sweet fragrance justify use. One of the parents of *D.* × *burkwoodii*. Caucasus. Cultivated 1893. Zone (4)5 to 7(8). Paul Cappiello successfully grew this species in his Bangor, ME garden.

Daphne genkwa Sieb. & Zucc. — Lilac Daphne
LEAVES: Mostly opposite, occasionally alternate, lanceolate to ovate, 1 to 2 1/2″ long, 1/2 to 1″ wide, acute, rounded, entire, pubescent on veins beneath, dull green above, lighter beneath; petiole—1/6″ long.

Daphne genkwa, (daf′nē genk′wà), Lilac Daphne, grows 3 to 4′ high, is deciduous and composed of erect, slender, sparsely branched stems. Flowers are lilac-colored, produced during May in clusters of 2 to 5 at the nodes on naked wood of the previous year. Easily propagated by cuttings taken when the new growth is very soft. Very beautiful in flower but rather temperamental in the garden. It is unique among *Daphne* species because of the opposite leaves. Barnes Foundation, Merion, PA, has a specimen that I was fortunate to see in flower . . . beautiful but lacking fragrance. Have seen a reference that reported subtle fragrance. Mmm! I can smell a cheeseburger from three miles distant, but not this subtle fragrance with my nose pressed to the flowering branches. Have seen a plant or two that appeared quite prosperous in the Atlanta area. Native to China. Introduced 1843. Zone 5 to 7.

Daphne giraldii Nitsche. — Giraldi Daphne
LEAVES: Alternate, simple, crowded at end of branches in a whorled fashion, oblanceolate, 1 1/2 to 3″ long, 1/4 to 5/8″ wide, blunt or pointed and mucronate, cuneate, entire, glaucescent below, glabrous, rich green.

Daphne giraldii, (daf′nē ji-ral′dē-ī), Giraldi Daphne, is a deciduous, 2 to 3′(4′) high shrub of bushy habit. The flowers are fragrant, golden yellow, produced during May in umbels terminating the young shoots, 4 to 8 per inflorescence. The fruit is an egg-shaped, 1/4″ diameter, red drupe which matures in July–August. It is quite hardy (Zone 4) but difficult to culture successfully. Washington collector reported it easy to grow there. No damage in Orono, ME. Native of northwestern China. Introduced 1910. Zone 4 to 7.

Daphne mezereum L. — February Daphne, Mezereon
LEAVES: Alternate, simple, oblanceolate, 1 1/2 to 3 1/2″ long, 1/4 to 3/4″ wide, obtuse to acute, cuneate, entire, dull blue-green above and gray-green below, glabrous.

Daphne mezereum, (daf'nē me-zē'rē-um), February Daphne, is a semi-evergreen to deciduous, erect-branched shrub growing 3 to 5' high and as wide, usually becoming leggy at the base. The flowers are lilac to rosy purple, very fragrant, produced from the buds of the leafless stems in late March to early April, grouped in 2's and 3's, each flower 1/2" across. The fruit is a red, 1/3" diameter drupe which matures in June. Species must be self-fertile since I have observed heavy fruit set on an isolated plant at the Biltmore Gardens. In mid-July 1995, I noticed heavy fruit set on plants in Pacific Northwest. Several authorities have noted that the shrub will do well for years and then suddenly die. No one has a good explanation for the whims of *Daphne*, however, there is a lethal virus which affects *D. mezereum* and this could explain its sudden failings. The variety *alba* has dull white flowers and yellowish fruits; comes true-to-type from seed and is found in the wild. Selections called 'Paul's White' and 'Bowles White' have pure white flowers. 'Autumnalis' flowers in the fall and the flowers are larger than the species and equally fragrant and colored. 'Alba Plena'—double, white flowers; 'Grandiflora'—to 6' high with large dark flowers; 'Rubra'—deep red-purple flowers; 'Rubra Plena'—double red-purple flowers; 'Ruby Glow'—with broad, upright habit and abundant, large, red flowers; 'Rosea'—rose-pink flowers; and 'Variegata'—with white-variegated leaves, are also listed, none or which has crossed my garden path in the United States. *Daphne mezereum* and the clones can be propagated, although not very easily, by cuttings taken and planted in a mixture of peat moss, loam and sand. This is a most enchanting *Daphne* because of the deliciously fragrant flowers. It flowers before most shrubs and, cut branches, when brought into a house, provide a delightful spring perfume. Leaves may start to emerge from end of stem while flowers remain on previous season's growth. Have seen considerable scale injury on this species. Native of Europe and Siberia; found wild, although limitedly so in England; occasionally naturalized in northeastern states. Introduced in colonial times. Zone 4 to 7.

Daphne odora Thunb. — Fragrant or Winter Daphne
LEAVES: Alternate, simple, evergreen, leathery, elliptic-oblong, 1 1/2 to 3 1/2" long, 1/2 to 1" wide, glabrous, entire, pointed and tapered equally at both ends, deep shiny green.

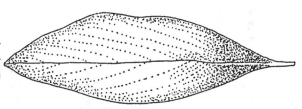

Daphne odora, (daf'nē ō-dō'rȧ), Winter Daphne, is a densely branched, mounded evergreen shrub that reaches 4'(6') in height and width. In the South I have seen plants in the 3 to 4' range. Reddell, *Horticulture* 66(4):16–22 (1980), reported *D. odora* over 10' tall and almost as wide. The fragrant, rosy purple flowers are borne in 1" diameter, terminal heads with up to 10 florets during February–March. The flowers last a long time and I have seen them showing color in January and persisting into March. The fragrance is wonderful. Fruits are red but I have never observed a single one on a cultivated specimen. This species performs well in shade and does not appear as fastidious about soil types as some *Daphne* species. The plant is usually offered in containers and presents no transplanting problems. What a wonderful plant! Temperamental, trying, but worth all the attention. I have charted flower times since the 1983 edition to indicate how flowering responses vary from year-to-year. I offer the following: full flower on February 28, 1983, March 9, 1984, March 1, 1986, February 14, 1989. Choice plant where people can sense its presence . . . i.e., by a walk, entrance. I know a great gardener, Mrs. Robert T. Segrest, in Athens, who puts it in a container by the entrance to her home so she can enjoy the fragrance. Native to China. Introduced 1790. Zone 7 to 9.

'Alba'—White flowers (actually off-white).

'Aureomarginata'—A handsome clone that is hardier than the species; the leaves are margined with yellow and the flowers are reddish purple on the outside and lighter (nearly white) within; survived –3°F with some leaf injury while the leaves of the species and 'Alba' were killed completely; also a form with similar leaf variegation and white flowers is known.

'Leucanthe'—Lustrous deep green foliage and abundant, fragrant, white blushed pink flowers on a 3' by 3' shrub.

'Mazelii'—Flowers are borne in terminal clusters and also out of the axils of the leaves subtending the cluster, the flowers are pinkish outside, whitish within.

'Rose Queen'—Dark carmine red flowers in dense heads.

'Rubra'—Dark red buds, open to reddish pink flowers; more compact than 'Leucanthe', perhaps 30" by 30" at maturity.

'Rubra Variegated'—As above but leaves with a creamy white margin.

'Variegata'—The yellow margins are more pronounced than those of 'Aureomarginata' and the flowers pale pink.

'Walberton'—Much akin to 'Aureomarginata', noticed at Wisley Garden.

Have grown about four cultivars over the gardening years and am unable to discern any significant differences in fragrance. Looked at my flower notes for the 1990's: full flower February 9, 1991, still heavy February 22, 1992, full flower February 12, 1993, full flower February 25, 1994.

ADDITIONAL NOTES: A choice group of plants for the garden but unfortunately fastidious as to cultural requirements. One can travel to private and public gardens without ever seeing a wealth of *Daphne*. English authorities speculated that most *Daphne* species do best in limestone soils; however, in the Arnold Arboretum several species are growing in a soil of pH 5 to 5.5 and in the Athens, GA area many plants of *D. odora* are growing well in soils of pH 4.5 to 5. Anyone interested in *Daphne* should read Brickell and Mathew, *Daphne*: *The genus in the wild and cultivation*, The Alpine Garden Society, 1976. Numerous other species beyond the scope of the *Manual* and the following are worth considering: *D. bholua* Buch.-Ham. ex D. Don, 'Gurkha' and 'Jacqueline Postill'; *D. blagayana* Freyer.; *D. collina* Dickson ex Sm.; *D. laureola* L.; *D. × mantensiana* ('Somerset' × *D. tangutica*); *D. pontica* L.; *D. retusa* Hemsl.; and *D. tangutica* Maxim. These have crossed my path in European gardens but their relative garden worthiness in the United States is unknown. Excellent down-to-earth *Daphne* article appeared in *Horticulture* 66(4):16–22 (1988).

Abundant virus research and one particular paper, *J. Environmental Hort.* 10:153–156 (1992), reported the daphne × potexvirus was literally universal in *D. cneorum*. Also, interesting nutritional research that demonstrated strong correlation of survival and flowering of *D. mezereum* with additional 3 grams $CaCo_3$ and pH of 6.5. *Daphne cneorum* achieved best growth and flowering with 3 grams $CaCo_3$ and pH of 5.0.

Daphniphyllum macropodum Miq.

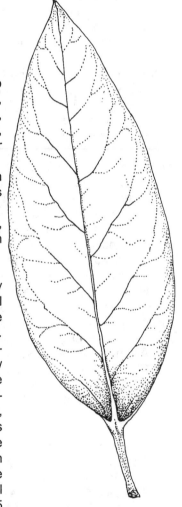

FAMILY: Daphniphyllaceae

LEAVES: Alternate, simple, evergreen, leathery, oblong or narrowly oval, 3 to 8″ long (5 to 6″ on samples from one plant), 1 to 3″ wide, taper-pointed, cuneate, lustrous polished dark green above, silver glaucous beneath, glabrous, 16 to 18 vein pairs, midvein yellow-green; petiole—1 to 2″ long, stout, red and color extending partially to midrib; usually red on upper part of petiole.

BUDS: Terminal or end buds—about 1/2″ long, imbricate, conical, greenish red, glabrous; lateral—1/8″ long, ovoid, imbricate, nestled tightly in axils of leaves.

STEM: Stout, glabrous, green initially, in winter tinged with red, glaucous, glabrous, with small, vertical, narrow-oval, gray-brown lenticels; when bruised—malodorous; pith—ample, white, prominently chambered.

Daphniphyllum macropodum, (daf-nē-fil′um mak-rō-pō′dum), was essentially unknown to me in 1990. I have observed the development of a wonderful haystack-shaped specimen at the University's Botanical Garden. The large, evergreen leaves remind of *Rhododendron catawbiense* or *R. maximum*. For textural effect this is a most effective substitute for large-leaved rhododendrons in Zone 7 and 8. The dark green leaves show minimal winter discoloration in Zone 7b. Leaves are closely spaced at the end of the shoots creating a pseudo-whorl. The undersides are silver-gray, not unlike those of *Magnolia virginiana*. The flowers are dioecious, pale green, pungent, and appear in May–June in about 1″ long racemes from the previous year's growth. Unless one knows when to look, the flowers sneak by. Fruits are 1/3″ long, bluish black drupes. Prefers high organic matter soils and light shade. Excessive shade results in more open, leggy habit. In full sun, the plant in the University's Botanical Garden has developed into a dense, oval-rounded haystack. Expect 15 to 25′ under cultivation, although plants are listed as reaching 40 to 50′ in the wild. A cream-white variegated form is known. Propagate by stratified seed and softwood/semi-hardwood cuttings. China, Japan, Korea. Introduced 1879. Zone (6)7 to 8(9). Hardiness is unknown but plants survived 4°F in January, 1994 without injury. Raulston reported no damage at 2°F in Raleigh, NC.

Also, in cultivation is *D. humile* Maxim., lower growing, 2 to 3′(6′) with a greater spread. The leaves average 2 to 5″ long, 1 to 2″ wide, lustrous dark green above and glaucous beneath. Flowers are small, numerous, greenish yellow; fruits blue-black. Japan, Korea. Introduced about 1879. Zone 7 to 9.

Davidia involucrata Baill. — Dove-tree, sometimes called Handkerchief Tree, Ghost Tree
(dā-vid′i-à in-vō-lū-krá′tà)

FAMILY: Nyssaceae

LEAVES: Alternate, simple, 2 to 5 1/2″ long, about 3/4's as wide, broad-ovate, acuminate, cordate, dentate-serrate with acuminate teeth, strongly veined, finally glabrous above, densely silky-pubescent beneath, vivid green, about 8 pairs of veins; petiole—1 1/2 to 3″ long.

BUDS: Solitary, sessile or the lateral developing into short spurs, rather large, with about half-a-dozen, blunt, pale-margined scales, lustrous, glabrous, reddish brown.

STEM: Moderately stout, terete, somewhat zig-zag; pith—moderate, rounded, pale, continuous with firmer plates at short intervals; leaf scars—moderate, half-elliptical or 3-lobed; little raised; 3 large bundle traces similar in appearance to those of *Nyssa sylvatica*.

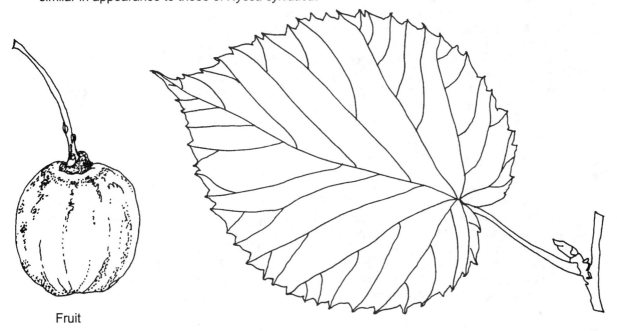

Fruit

SIZE: Under cultivation 20 to 40′ high and as wide; supposedly in the wild can roam from 40 to 65′ in height.

HARDINESS: Zone 6 to 7(8); probably not fully hardy as a young tree, once established performs well.

HABIT: Broad pyramidal tree, resembling a linden, especially in youth; loosening with age but still distinctly pyramidal in outline, have observed fully round-headed specimens in Europe.

TEXTURE: Medium in leaf; would also be medium in winter.

BARK: Orange, brown, scaly, handsome, adds winter interest to the plant.

LEAF COLOR: Bright green in summer; leaves supposedly strongly scented when unfolding, I have not noticed an objectionable odor; fall color of no consequence and dies off green or brown; leaves hold late and are often killed by a hard freeze with the majority of the leaves falling at the same time.

FLOWERS: Andro-monoecious, crowded in a 3/4″ diameter, rounded head at the end of a 3″ long, pendulous peduncle; staminate flowers composed of numerous long stamens with white filaments and red anthers, forming a brush-like mass; pistillate reduced to an egg-shaped ovary, with a short, 6-rayed style and a ring of abortive stamens at the top; the real beauty of the *Davidia* lies in two large bracts which subtend each flower; they are white or creamy white, of unequal size, the lower being the larger (7″ long by 4″ wide); the upper bract being 3 to 4″ long and 2″ wide; they are effective for 10 to 14 days in May; often the tree does not flower until about 10 years of age and even then some trees do not flower every year; tends to show alternate year patterns.

FRUIT: Solitary, ovoid, 1 1/2″ long drupe, green with a purplish bloom; becoming russet colored and speckled with red when ripe; contains a single, hard, ridged nut (endocarp) with 3 to 5(6) seeds; matures in fall.

CULTURE: Transplant balled-and-burlapped; prefers a well-drained, moist soil that has been amended with peat moss and the like; prefers light shade but will tolerate sun if the soil is kept moist; water during drought periods; prune in winter.

DISEASES AND INSECTS: None serious.

LANDSCAPE VALUE: Acclaimed by many gardening enthusiasts as the most handsome of flowering trees; that is quite an accolade when one thinks of all the beautiful flowering trees we have at our disposal; the obvious use is that of a specimen; any tree so grand should not be hidden in the shrubbery; Wyman noted that, for all its good features, it has the bad habits of being slow to flower, does not consistently flower every year and, even though stem and vegetative bud hardy, may not set flower buds in colder climates; during sabbatical at the Arnold Arboretum I was fortunate enough to witness the tree in full-flowering spectacle; when observed in flower there is an insatiable urge to secure a plant for one's garden; it should be mentioned that the tree will grow in the South; there are beautiful trees at Hills and Dales, LaGrange, GA and there was once a lovely specimen on the Georgia campus; the finest specimens I have seen are at the Arnold Arboretum, Swarthmore College and Hills and Dales; numerous specimens in European gardens.

CULTIVARS: Variety *vilmoriniana* (Dode) Wangerin. differs from the species in that the underside of the leaves are yellowish green or somewhat glaucous, slightly downy on the veins at first but otherwise glabrous; the variety is more common in cultivation than the species and is hardy in Zone 5.

PROPAGATION: According to Bean it is easily propagated by cuttings or by seed; one research report stated that hardwood cuttings taken in mid-January rooted 20 percent without treatment and there was no response to IBA; leaf-bud cuttings taken in September treated with 3000 ppm IBA-talc, placed in sand, shaded, and frequently syringed, rooted 85 percent in five weeks; I was able to root several cuttings from an old tree at the Arnold but was unable to keep the cuttings alive. A relatively recent cutting propagation account appeared in *The Plantsman*. Seeds are doubly-dormant and require a warm-cold treatment; they should be placed in moist medium and kept at 68 to 86°F until the radicle emerges, than transferred to cold for 3 months; after this they can be planted; nursery practice involves fall planting with germination taking place two springs later; often multiple seedlings result from a single fruit since each fruit may contain 3 to 5 seeds.

ADDITIONAL NOTES: Great story related to E.H. Wilson's introduction of the species. He traveled to a remote area where trees had been reported only to find them cut. He later discovered trees, collected seed and sent some to England around 1899–1901. The expedition to introduce the Dove-tree was largely underwritten by the Veitch Nursery of England. Mr. Veitch admonished Wilson to make the tree the focus of the expedition for most worthy garden plants in China had already been introduced. Apparently unknown to Veitch and Wilson was the 1870 introduction of *D. involucrata* into France via the de Vilmorin nursery by the French missionary Farges. Only one seed germinated and that not until 1899. The plant flowered in 1906. Wilson's introduction first flowered in Veitch's Coombe Wood Nursery in 1911.

NATIVE HABITAT: Native to China in West Szechuan and parts of West Hupeh. Introduced 1904.

Decaisnea fargesii Franch. — Blue-bean

FAMILY: Lardizabalaceae

LEAVES: Opposite, compound pinnate, 20 to 32″ long, 13 to 25 leaflets, each leaflet 2 to 6″ long, ovate to elliptic, slender-pointed, entire, rich blue-green, glaucous beneath, glabrous at maturity; petiole—swollen at base; rachis—often purplish brown.

BUDS: Appearing valvate with one scale actually engulfing (overlapping) the outer edges of the other scale, appressed, 1/3″ long, bloomy, reddish green.

STEM: Stout, slightly angled, green turning brown, bloomy, covered with numerous small rounded lenticels, glabrous; pith—solid, white, greater than one-half the diameter of one-year stems.

Decaisnea fargesii, (de-kās-nē-a̍ far-jēs′ē-ī), Blue-bean, is a 10 to 15′ high and wide, deciduous shrub with an almost tropical appearance. I have observed it repeatedly in European gardens where it begs to be identified. West Coast nurserymen have offered the species for a number of years but it is not common in gardens. The yellow-green, 6-sepaled, 1 to 1 1/4″ long flowers occur in 8 to 18″ long panicles in May–June. Bisexual and male flowers occur on separate parts of the inflorescence. The flowers mesh with the foliage and are not spectacular but certainly handsome on close inspection. Fruits are 2 to 4″ long, 3/4″ wide, cylindrical, bean-like, pendulous, metallic blue with the black seeds embedded in a whitish pulp. Ideally plant two seedlings to insure effective cross pollination and subsequent fruit set. The fruits are supposedly edible. Provide semi-shade to shade and moist, acid, high organic matter soils. Water in drought periods and protect from desiccating spring winds. Great adventure for the advanced gardener and also the one-of-a-kind plant with which to astonish your friends. Based on one year's observations of container-grown plants in Athens, the species dislikes (intensely) heat and drought. Introduced 1895. Western China. Zone 6 to 7. Has existed as root hardy, dieback shrub at the Morton Arboretum, Lisle, IL (Zone 5).

Decaisnea fargesii

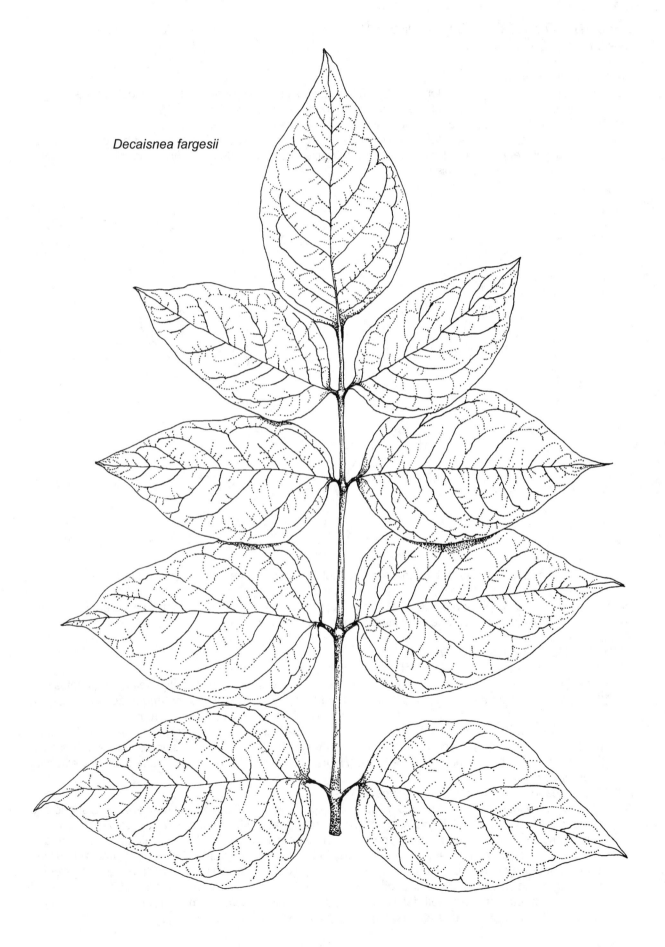

Decumaria barbara L. — Climbing Hydrangea, Wild Hydrangeavine, Wood Vamp
(dek-ū-mā′ri-à bär-bà′rà)

FAMILY: Hydrangeaceae
LEAVES: Opposite, simple, 3 to 5″ long, 1 1/2 to 3″ wide, oval or ovate, tapering at both ends, serrated at apex
   or entire, glabrous, leathery-textured, lustrous dark green; petiole—1 to 2″ long.
BUDS: Terminal—longer than laterals, reddish with short pubescence; laterals—1/16″ long, reddish, pubescent.
STEM: Terete, stout, light brown, glabrous; leaf scar—narrow, crescent-shaped, 3-distinct bundle traces, bud
   sits in slight depression in leaf scar; second year stem with epidermis exfoliating; aerial roots often
   abundant; pith—solid, greenish.

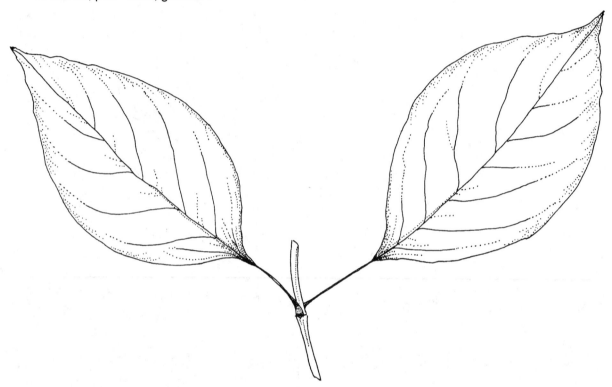

SIZE: 10 to 20′ and higher, climbs by aerial root-like holdfasts, have seen plants 30′ and higher in trees, 40′
   was reported.
HARDINESS: Zone 5 to 9; survived -20°F in Urbana, IL; grows successfully at the Morton Arboretum, Lisle, IL.
HABIT: True clinging deciduous vine remaining planar (flat) on the surface.
RATE: Fast.
TEXTURE: Medium in leaf and in winter.
BARK: Gray brown, developing aerial roots which anchor stems to structures.
LEAF COLOR: Lustrous dark green in summer, pale cream-yellow in autumn; beautiful foliage that holds well
   through the growing season; should be mentioned that new leaves of season and seedling leaves are
   often small and distinctly toothed, don't fret if the new plant does not appear normal.
FLOWERS: White, 1/4″ diameter, fragrant, with 7 to 10, narrow, oblong petals, similar number of calyx teeth,
   produced in a 2 to 3″ high and wide, terminal corymb in May–June; in Athens flowers peak in late May;
   the flowers do not have the showy sepals of *Hydrangea anomala* subsp. *petiolaris* or *Schizophragma
   hydrangeoides*.
FRUIT: Urn-shaped, 1/3″ long, dehiscent capsule.
CULTURE: Transplant from containers into moist, acid, high organic matter soils; almost always in shade and
   observations indicate partial shade, pine shade, north-east side of home would prove best; is not
   particularly fussy about soils but prospers with moisture; common in the wild along streams and is
   periodically flooded; many plants on our property in the flood plain; plant near a tree, structure and kind
   of aim it in the right direction, stand back, and enjoy; an easy to grow vine for North American gardens;
   returning home from a ten day vacation in Maine in late August–early September 1997, Bonnie and I
   discover a drought-stricken, half-defoliated *Decumaria* under a Sweetgum; no rain while away and the
   plant has the nerve to shed its leaves; moral—provide even moisture.

DISEASES AND INSECTS: None serious, to date has been amazingly free of pests, an enviro-friendly vine.

LANDSCAPE VALUE: Has a future in American gardens; typical vine uses but not as wild and unmanageable; self-clinging especially on trees, fences, etc.; beautiful foliage and subtle, attractive flowers.

CULTIVARS: Considerable interest by southern plantspeople and consequently at least two clones have been selected.

'Chatooga'—A form selected for small leaves and yellow-orange, perhaps with a tinge of red fall color, Head-Lee Nursery, Seneca, SC introduction.

'Vickie' ('Barber Creek')—Selected by author for large, lustrous dark green leaves; discovered by serendipity along my old jogging trail; the vine had climbed up an abandoned bridge support and finally surfaced on the old wood planks; in my jogging daze I look down and actually stop to admire this particular form; later I attempt to send Ms. Vickie Waters-Oldham, my loyal research technician, into snake-infested Barber Creek; she declined so I rolled up my pants and headed for the cuttings; the rest is history and is recounted in *Nursery Management and Production* 11(1):34–35 (1995).

PROPAGATION: Seeds germinate without pretreatment, sow on milled sphagnum or other suitable medium, 70°F, and maintain under mist until seedlings germinate and are large enough to transplant. Cuttings of 'Vickie' rooted 94% with 5000 ppm KIBA, 5-second dip, peat:perlite, May 27 collection (Athens). Untreated cuttings rooted 63%; 1000 ppm KIBA rooted 44%; 10000 ppm KIBA 25%. Rooted cuttings were shifted to one-gallon containers and by October were robust, salable plants. Loves moisture and nitrogen.

NATIVE HABITAT: Virginia to Florida and Louisiana. Introduced 1785.

Desfontainia spinosa Ruiz & Pav.

FAMILY: Loganiaceae or Potaliaceae. Does not appear to be a consensus.

LEAVES: Opposite, simple, evergreen, 1 to 2 1/2″ long, 3/4 to 1 1/2″ wide, oval to ovate, sharp triangular, 1/3 to 1/2″ long marginal spines, glabrous, lustrous dark green; petiole—1/3″ long.

Desfontainia spinosa, (des-fon′tȧ-nē-ȧ spī-nō′sȧ), is only included herein because of my inability to identify the species as separate from some esoteric *Osmanthus*. It develops into an upright shrub, 6 to 8′(10′) high with a greater spread. In my mind, I travel to Younger Botanic Garden, Scotland, where on a miserably cold and damp March day, I circled, stalked, mused and tried to identify a particularly fine specimen. Since no one was in sight, I had a pleasant conversation with the shrub. Holly, no, alternate leaves; *Osmanthus*, yes, has to be, opposite, spiny leaves; everything "looked" right, however, the label read *Desfontainia*. The bush won that particular day but I will not lose the next time. The leaves are hard (leathery) lustrous dark green. Flowers are unique, average 1 1/2″ long and 1/2″ wide, solitary on 1/2″ long pedicels, and develop from (June)July to fall. The funnel-shaped, waxy corolla is orange-scarlet with 5, rounded, yellow lobes. Also present is the 5-lobed, green calyx edged with fine pubescence. Doubtfully could the plant be successfully cultured in the United States anywhere but the Pacific Northwest. Requirements include well-drained, moist soil and relatively cool climate. Bean mentions a plant at Rowallane, County Down, Ireland, that was 10′ high, 32′ across, and 118′ in circumference. South America from Columbia to the area around the Straights of Magellan. Found in cool mountain cloud forests of the Andes south. Introduced 1799. Zone 7 to 9. Gossler reported hardy to 0°F in Oregon.

Deutzia gracilis Sieb. & Zucc. — Slender Deutzia
(dūt′si-ȧ gras′i-lis)

FAMILY: Saxifragaceae, sometimes places in Hydrangeaceae; in English literature have seen Philadelphaceae.

LEAVES: Opposite, simple, oblong-lanceolate, 1 to 3″ long, 3/8 to 5/8″ wide, long acuminate, broad-cuneate or rounded at the base, unequally serrate, with scattered stellate hairs above, flat bright to deep green, nearly glabrous beneath; petiole—1/3 to 1/2″ long.

BUDS: Ovoid, nearly sessile, with several pairs of outer scales, glabrate, brownish; this bud description is applicable to the species treated herein.

STEM: Yellowish gray-brown, glabrous; leaf scars—linear; pith—white, hollow after a time.

SIZE: 2 to 4' high by 3 to 4' in width; can grow to 6' high.

HARDINESS: Zone 4 to 8; occasional tip dieback in Orono, ME.

HABIT: A low, broad mound, graceful and free-flowering, with slender, ascending branches.

RATE: Slow to medium.

TEXTURE: Medium-fine in leaf; medium in winter.

LEAF COLOR: Flat bright deep green in summer; does not color effectively in fall, sometimes with a tinge of purple.

BARK: Older stems often develop exfoliating character.

FLOWERS: Perfect, weakly fragrant, pure white, 1/2 to 3/4" across; mid to late May (mid to late April, Athens); borne in erect racemes or panicles, 1 1/2 to 3" long; the plants are literally covered with flowers and are quite attractive at this time of year; effective for 10 to 14 days.

FRUIT: Dehiscent, brown capsule, not effective.

CULTURE: Transplants readily, usually container-grown, best moved in spring; any good, well-drained, garden soil is acceptable; pH adaptable; full sun or very light shade; prune after flowering; plants appear ratty and unkempt over time and should be renewal pruned, probably in late winter although flowers will be sacrificed for the year.

A Russian study reported that 6 species of *Deutzia* were drought resistant, winter hardy, immune to diseases and insects and to pollution by smoke, gases and dust.

DISEASES AND INSECTS: Leafspots, aphids, and leaf miner; basically problem-free plants.

LANDSCAPE VALUE: This is probably the best of the deutzias and makes a good mass, facer or shrub border plant; deutzias have lost favor over the years and, in my opinion, rightfully so; they offer only good flowers and the rest of the year are often bedraggled; I noticed that there was not one plant in the Arnold Arboretum's extensive collection that did not need considerable pruning after the winter of 1978–79 when the low temperature was –6°F; plants on the Illinois campus were less than well-dressed and usually possessed an allotment of dead branches; possibly the best way to handle the plant when it looks bedraggled is a rather complete pruning to within 6" of the ground; this will induce new shoot growth; some of the pink or rose-red flowered forms are beautiful but these are less hardy than *D. gracilis* or *D. × lemoinei*.

CULTIVARS: *D. gracilis* was used as a parent of several hybrid deutzias including *D. × rosea* (Lemoine) Rehd. [*D. g. × D. purpurascens* (Henry) Rehd.] with pink petals on the outside and paler within; 'Carminea' is a selection from the *D. × rosea* group with pale rosy pink petals within, darker pink outside and in bud, about 3/4" across, in large panicles; it is a rather spreading plant, with arching branches, to about 3' high; W.J. Bean calls it one of the most delightful of dwarf, deciduous shrubs.

'Nikko'—A compact, perhaps 2' high by 5' wide, small-leaved, graceful, almost ground cover shrub that offers good white flowers, rich green foliage and deep burgundy fall color; this plant has been kicked around in a taxonomic sense and may be listed as *Deutzia gracilis* var. *nakaiana*, 'Nana', or perhaps as a species; I have seen small plants and believe it has a place in a sunny rock or hillside garden; possibly a zone less hardy than *D. gracilis*; susceptible to late spring frosts.

PROPAGATION: All deutzias can be easily rooted from softwood cuttings collected any time in the growing season; ideally collect slightly firm softwoods, use 1000 ppm KIBA dip, peat:perlite, mist and root systems should be profuse in 3 to 4 weeks; have rooted 'Nikko' readily with this procedure; discovered that late season cuttings of *D. × rosea* with brown stems and hollow pith were more difficult to root; suspect that the maximum window of rooting opportunity is during May–June; have noticed that early season cuttings continue to grow after rooting; not necessarily true for later cuttings; seeds can be sown when collected as they have no dormancy.

ADDITIONAL NOTES: Deutzias, although usually dependable for flower display, rarely overwhelm one at any time of the year. In northern and southern areas they require annual pruning to remove the dead wood and to keep them looking acceptable. The summer foliage is a blasé green while fall color and fruits are not interesting. The crux of the matter is that if one has limited garden space he/she should look elsewhere for ornament; but in large landscapes, especially shrub borders, the excellent flower display provided by the deutzias is warranted. About 50 to 70 species are known worldwide (primarily Asia) and many hybrids have been produced over the years. The United States nurseries offer a small number of species compared to European establishments. In English gardens, deutzias are often woven into the fabric of the shrub border and after flowering blend in with the green woodwork. In the United States they are upstaged by viburnums, clethras, lilacs, potentillas and numerous other shrubs that offer multi-season attributes.

The identification of *Deutzia* species and particularly cultivars borders on impossible. My students have more trouble with this genus, especially in winter. One common thread that surfaces is the presence of setose (bristle) tipped serrations that appear to turn up toward the upper leaf surface. Holding the leaf flat at eye level and looking across the upper surface will confirm the configuration. I have not seen a *Deutzia* species that does not conform to this pattern. *Deutzia* species' leaves vary in size from about 1 to 4″(5″) long.

A few miscellaneous types that are encountered every so often in the United States include: *Deutzia* × *kalmiifolia* Lemoine (*D. parviflora* Bunge. × *D. purpurascens*) growing 4 to 5′ high with light green foliage that may turn plum-purple in fall, and good pink flowers, 5 to 12 in an umbellate panicle. Also, occasionally 'Mont Rose' with fuchsia purple flowers, crimped at the margin and 2 to 3 1/2″ long sharply toothed leaves; 'Contraste' has larger flowers similar to 'Mont Rose' but with a darker stripe on the back of the petals, habit is gracefully arching; 'Magician' ('Magicien') is similar to 'Contraste' but the petals are edged with white; from Glasnevin Botanic Garden comes *D. purpurascens* 'Alpine Magician' with an erect corona, formed by the dark purple filaments within the white petals; 'Perle Rose' has pale pink, freely borne flowers, slightly smaller than the others described here; and 'Pink Pompon' with deep carmine buds opening to strong double flowers, pink outside, and borne in dense, hemispherical corymbs. All of the above cultivars originated from unknown but suspected parentage of *D. longifolia*, *D. discolor*, *D. purpurascens* and/or *D.* × *elegantissima*. Often listed as *D.* × *hybrida* Lemoine, Pink-A-Boo™ ('Monzia') has thick-textured, pink flowers on a 6 to 8′ framework.

Deutzia × *rosea* (Lemoine) Rehd., a hybrid grex resulting from *D. gracilis* × *D. purpurascens*, produces compact shrubs with arching branches and campanulate-shaped, pink or white flowers. Lemoine, again, produced many garden forms and I have observed flowering specimens that appear to belong with this group. Nothing is clear cut in the world of *Deutzia* identification.

NATIVE HABITAT: Japan. Introduced 1880.

RELATED SPECIES:

Deutzia corymbosa R. Br.
LEAVES: Opposite, simple, 2 to 4″ long, 1 to 2″ wide, ovate, acuminate, sparse pubescence below, more prevalent above, dark green.

Deutzia corymbosa, (dūt′si-à kôr-imb-ō′sà), forms a 4 to 6′ high and wide, rounded shrub that produces 1/3 to 1/2″ diameter, white flowers in 4 to 7″ wide corymbs in June. My only exposure occurred at the Arnold Arboretum where I was most impressed by the flower display. Might prove worthy for massing like the summer flowering spireas or inclusion in perennial and shrub borders. Western Himalayas. Zone 6 to possibly 8.

Deutzia crenata Sieb. & Zucc., (dūt′si-à krĕ-nā′tà), is included herein because it umbrellas several cultivars that are more often associated with *D. gracilis*. Will grow 6 to 7′ high and the 1/2 to 3/4″ wide, white flowers are held in 4 to 6″ long racemes (occasionally panicles). 'Nakiana' is more correctly included here. 'Nikko', often considered synonymous with 'Nakiana', is listed by *New RHS Dictionary of Gardening* as having profuse, double, white flowers. 'Nakata' from Louisiana Nursery has small, single, white flowers (could this be the 'Nikko' of commerce?). 'Aureovariegata' produces irregular lemon yellow patches throughout foliage and white flowers. Forma *bicolor* bears a profusion of white-striped, pink flowers. 'Summer Snow' offers medium green leaves with white markings and white flowers. My observations of the variegated deutzias reflect their inclination to revert to green. Japan, southeastern China. Zone 5 to 8. Supposedly extremely close to *D. scabra* differing in the petioled leaves, those of *D. scabra* sessile to very short petioled. Further the panicle of *D. crenata* is elongated, that of *D. scabra* more rounded.

Deutzia × *elegantissima* (Lemoine) Rehd. — Elegant Deutzia

Deutzia × *elegantissima* (dūt′si-à el-e-gan-tis′i-mà), Elegant Deutzia is another Lemoine creation probably combining *D. purpurascens* and *D. crenata*. The typical form grows 4 to 6′ high with an upright branching habit. The oval-oblong leaves are 2 to 3″ long, short acuminate, irregularly serrate, rugose and dull green with stellate pubescence beneath. The individual pinkish (outside) white flowers average 3/4″ diameter and are carried in many-flowered, loose, erect cymes in June. 'Rosalind' has been popularized in the United States and, indeed, is a beautiful 4 to 5′ high form with deep carmine-pink flowers. It was found by Harry Bryce in the 1930's at the Slieve Donard Nursery in Newcastle, County Down, Northern Ireland. Other cultivars include: 'Arcuata'—pink buds, white flowers; 'Conspicua'—pink buds open to white flowers in rounded corymbs; 'Elegantissima'—the type described above; and 'Fasciculata'—dark pink buds open to lighter pink. Zone (5)6 to 8.

Deutzia × *lemoinei* Lemoine — Lemoine Deutzia

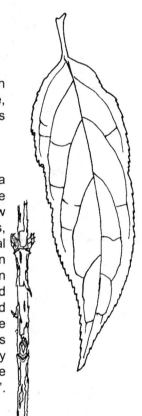

LEAVES: Opposite, simple, elliptic-lanceolate to lanceolate, 1 1/2 to 2 1/2″ long, on vigorous shoots to 4″ long, 1/2 to 1 1/4″ wide, long acuminate, cuneate at base, sharply serrulate, green on both surfaces, with scattered, 5- to 8-rayed hairs beneath.

STEM: Glabrous or nearly so, older with brown exfoliating bark; pith—white.

Deutzia × *lemoinei*, (dūt′si-à le-moi′nē-ī), Lemoine Deutzia, grows 5 to 7′ tall with a similar spread. It is a very twiggy, dense, round, erect-branched shrub. The medium green summer foliage does little to excite. Have observed good yellow fall color in Spring Grove, Cincinnati, OH. The flowers are pure white, 5/8″ across, after *D. gracilis* usually about late May; borne in 1 to 3″ long, erect, pyramidal corymbs. Some authorities say this species is more beautiful and effective than *D. gracilis*. It is considered one of the hardiest and is being successfully grown in Madison, WI and Chaska, MN (-30°F). Was never as impressed with the hybrid species compared to *D. gracilis*. The parentage is *D. gracilis* by *D. parviflora* and was raised by Lemoine of Nancy in 1891. Several cultivars of importance include 'Avalanche' and 'Compacta'. 'Avalanche'—bears white flowers in small clusters on arching branches, very dense and compact, about 4′ high; should be possibly placed under *D.* × *maliflora* Rehd. 'Compacta'—dwarf and compact in habit, pure white, large flowers in dense clusters, could be the same as 'Boule de Neige'. Zone (4)5 to 8.

Deutzia × *magnifica* (Lemoine) Rehd. — Showy Deutzia

Deutzia × *magnifica*, (dūt′si-à mag-nif′i-kà), Showy Deutzia, is the result of a cross between *D. scabra* × *D. vilmoriniae* Lemoine; raised by Lemoine of Nancy and put into commerce from 1909. This hybrid species is often listed as growing 6′ high but I have seen 8 to 10′ specimens. The plant is strongly multi-stemmed, usually leggy at the base, and clothed with foliage over the upper one-half. Medium green, sharp, fine-toothed leaves average 1 1/2 to 2 1/2″ long. The flowers are among the best of the deutzias. They are white, double, borne in dense 1 1/2 to 3″ long panicles in late May or early June (early to mid-May, Athens) and are extremely eye-catching. Originated before 1910. Zone 5 to 8. Several clones include:

'Eburnea'—Single, white flowers in loose panicles, each flower bell-shaped.

'Erecta'—Single, white flowers in large erect panicles.

'Latiflora'—Single, white flowers 1″ or more across with wide-spreading petals borne profusely in erect panicles.

'Longipetala'—Single, white flowers with long, narrow petals.

'Staphyleoides'—Single, white flowers with reflexed petals in drooping panicles.

Deutzia scabra Thunb. — Fuzzy Deutzia

LEAVES: Opposite, simple, ovate to oblong-lanceolate, 1 to 4″ long, up to 2″ wide, acute or obtusely acuminate, usually rounded at the base, crenate-denticulate, dull green, stellate-pubescent on both sides with 10- to 15-rayed hairs, sandpaper texture to upper surface.

STEM: Brown, rarely gray-brown, tardily exfoliating bark; stellate pubescent when young; pith—brown, excavated, finally hollow.

Deutzia scabra, (dūt′si-à skā′brà), Fuzzy Deutzia, grows 6 to 10′ tall with a spread of 4 to 8′. It is an oval or obovate, round-topped shrub, taller than broad, with spreading, somewhat arching branches with brown peeling bark; often straggly in appearance. Flowers pure white or tinged pink outside, 1/2 to 3/4″ long and wide, borne in upright, 3 to 6″ long, cylindrical panicles; flowers 10 to 14 days after *D. gracilis*, usually in early June in the Midwest and vicinity of Boston. Cultivars include:

'Candidissima'—Double, pure white.

'Flore-pleno'—Double, white, tinged with rosy purple on outside of corolla; same as 'Plena'?

'Godsall Pink'—Double, clear pink flowers in 3 to 6″ long panicles; also listed as 'Codsall Pink'.

'Pink Minor'—A 2 to 3′ tall, compact form with delicate light pink flowers and rich green foliage; from Duncan and Davies, New Zealand.

'Pride of Rochester'—Similar to 'Godsall Pink' but the rosy tinge is paler; put into commerce by Ellwanger and Barry; often seen in older Midwest and New England landscapes.

'Punctata'—Single, pure white flowers, with leaves strikingly marbled with white and 2 or 3 shades of green; will revert to the typical green state.

'Rosea'—Rose flowers.

'Variegata'—Leaves splashed with white variegation.

'Watereri'—Flowers 1″ across, single, petals rosy outside.

    I remember a specimen on the Illinois campus that resided next to the old faculty club which, alas, is now a parking lot. This was the coarsest of the three species I taught (*D. gracilis*, *D.* × *lemoinei*) but generally the most reliable for consistent year-to-year flower. Unfortunately, it is a coarse shrub and now outmoded by some of the newer green meatballs. Japan, China. Introduced 1822. Zone 5 to 7(8).

Diervilla sessilifolia Buckley — Southern Bush-honeysuckle

FAMILY: Caprifoliaceae

LEAVES: Opposite, ovate-lanceolate, 2 to 6″ long, half as wide, acuminate, cordate or rounded at base, sharply serrate, subsessile, glabrous except on the midrib above, new foliage with a bronze-purple cast changing to dark green, sometimes lustrous.

BUDS: Often superposed, sessile, oblong, appressed, with about 5 pairs of exposed scales.

STEM: Rounded, brownish, with 4 crisp-puberulent ridges decurrent from the nodes; pith—moderate, pale, continuous.

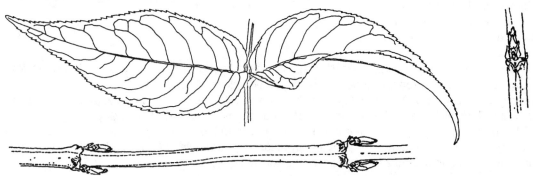

Diervilla sessilifolia,(dī-ēr-vil′ȧ ses-il-i-fō′li-ȧ), Southern Bush-honeysuckle, is a low-growing, suckering, 3 to 5′ high and 3 to 5′ wide or greater spreading, deciduous shrub. The foliage is glossy dark green and seldom colors in fall although European literature indicates good red-purple fall coloration. The flowers are sulfur yellow, 1/2″ long, June–July into August, borne in 2 to 3″ diameter, 3- to 7-flowered cymes on current season's growth. Fruit is a 2-chambered, many seeded, thin-walled capsule. Very adaptable and should be pruned back in early spring. Makes a good filler, possibly facer plant. A tremendously tough plant; this plant prospered in the evaluation tests at Illinois where it was exposed to −20°F and incessant winds. Would be a good choice for rough cuts and fills, banks, perhaps even planters or containers in outside areas. Foliage is not troubled by insects or diseases. I have seen this species in north Georgia and the Smoky Mountains where it forms a solid thicket on the side of mountains and stream banks. Will withstand shade but is best in full sun. Roots readily from cuttings. 'Butterfly' has deep yellow flowers and glossy dark green foliage that turns purple in fall, reaches 3 to 5′ in height. Native from North Carolina to Georgia and Alabama. Introduced 1844. Zone 4 to 7.

RELATED SPECIES:

Diervilla lonicera Mill.,(dī-ēr-vil′ȧ lon-iss′ēr-ȧ), Dwarf Bush-honeysuckle, is found from Newfoundland to Sasketchawan, south to Michigan and North Carolina but has not proven as vigorous as *D. sessilifolia* in Minnesota Landscape Arboretum tests. It differs in having short (1/8″ long) petioled leaves. 'Copper' was selected for the copper-colored new leaves that flush sporadically through the growing season. Introduced 1720. Zone 3 to 7.

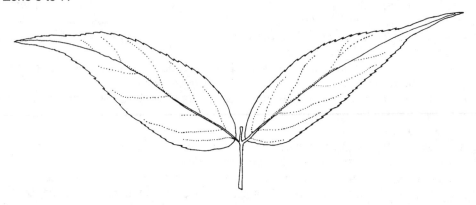

Diervilla rivularis Gatt.,(dī-ēr-vil′ȧ riv-ū-lā′ris), Georgia Bush-honeysuckle, occurs over a range similar to *D. sessilifolia* but the leaves are pubescent on both sides. The dark green leaves are 2 to 3″ long, ovate to oblong-lanceolate, acuminate, serrate, pubescent and color yellow-red in autumn. The lemon yellow flowers, often maturing yellow-red, occur in dense, cymose panicles in June. Summer Stars™ ('Morton') is a dwarf, 2 to 3′ high form with yellow trumpet-like flowers selected at the Morton Arboretum and introduced by the Chicagoland Grows® Program. Cultivated 1898. Zone (4)5 to 7.

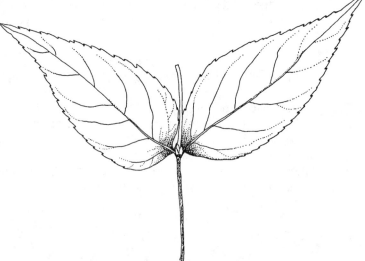

Diervilla × splendens (Carr.) Kirchn., (dī-ēr-vil′ȧ splen′dez), a hybrid between *D. sessilifolia* and *D. lonicera*, is known and listed in European literature and garden catalogs. Supposedly, it develops good purple-red autumn color. Dr. Wilbur Duncan told me that *D. sessilifolia* has glabrous leaves and stems or hairs in lines, while *D. rivularis* has hairy stems and leaf undersides. This is another group of deciduous shrubs that I have difficulty identifying. I see them in the wild from North Georgia to Maine and try as I do to convince myself the true identity of a given population, the truth lies in the middle. Does this mean the plants are hybrid populations? Originated 1850. Zone 5 to 7.

Diospyros virginiana L. — Common Persimmon
(dĭ-os′pi-ros vĕr-jin-i-ā′nȧ)

FAMILY: Ebenaceae

LEAVES: Alternate, simple, 2 1/4 to 5 1/2″ long, 3/4 to 2″ wide, ovate to elliptic, rounded at base, entire or irregularly serrate, lustrous dark green above, paler beneath, glabrous at maturity or with minimal pubescence on the midrib; petiole—1/3 to 1″ long, pubescent.

BUDS: Solitary, sessile, with 2 greatly overlapping scales, 1/4″ long, ovoid, acute, reddish black, glabrous, terminal bud lacking.

STEM: Slender, gray-red-brown, pubescent or glabrous.

FRUIT: Berry, globose, 1 to 1 1/2″ long, yellowish to pale orange, 1- to 8-seeded, edible, subtended by 4 persistent calyx lobes, persistent into winter.

BARK: Thick, hard, dark gray-black, in distinctive square, scaly blocks.

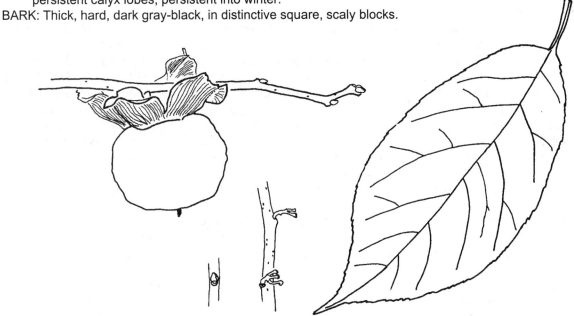

SIZE: 35 to 60′ in height with a spread of 20 to 35′, can grow to 90′ or larger but this rarely occurs; six national champions listed, five over 100′ high, the largest 132′ by 37′.

HARDINESS: Zone 4 to 9.

HABIT: Tree with slender oval-rounded crown, often very symmetrical in outline, will sucker and form colonies.

RATE: Slow to medium; one authority reported 15′ over a 20 year period in England; in the Southeast, growth is extremely vigorous.

TEXTURE: Medium in leaf and winter.

BARK: On old trunks the bark is thick, dark gray or brownish to almost black and is prominently broken into scaly, squarish blocks; handsome and easily recognizable.

LEAF COLOR: Dark green and often lustrous above, paler beneath in summer, changing to yellow-green, yellow, or reddish purple in fall; yellow-green was the usual fall color in central Illinois although the late Professor J.C. McDaniel, Department of Horticulture, University of Illinois, selected a clone that consistently colored a beautiful reddish purple; in the South the trees turn a consistent yellow to reddish purple every fall; the fall color is more pronounced and consistent than what I observed on trees in the North.

FLOWERS: Dioecious, although sometimes both sexes present on same tree; white or whitish to greenish white, delightfully fragrant, shaped like a blueberry flower; flowers constricted at their mouth, often tinged green on the end of the 4 corolla lobes, staminate usually in three's about 1/3″ long, with 16 stamens; pistillate short-stalked, solitary, 3/5″ long, borne in May–June; the pedicels and peduncles of the male flower persistent, woody.

FRUIT: An edible berry, yellowish to pale orange, 1 to 1 1/2″ long, subtended by 4, persistent calyx lobes; ripens after frost in late September through October and persisting into November–December; although cultivars are available which produce edible fruit without frost treatment; the fruits are palatable and frequented by wildlife such as racoon, opossum, skunk, foxes, white-tailed deer and other species; horses have died from eating the fruits; ten fruits eaten over a 2 hour period caused an obstruction in large intestine of a human being [see Letter to the editor, *HortScience* 17(2) (1982)].

CULTURE: Somewhat difficult to transplant and should be moved balled-and-burlapped as a small tree in early spring; prefers moist, well-drained, sandy soils but will do well on low fertility, dry soils; in southern Illinois the tree grows on coal stripped lands and often forms thickets on dry, eroding slopes; pH adaptable; full sun; prune in winter; does well in cities.

I have pedaled my bike many miles along local backroads and everywhere in evidence is persimmon. Apparently animals of all makes move the fruits around and act as "Johnny Persimmon Seeds." The plant is found in pastures, fence rows, roadside ditches and a hundred other less than hospitable sites. It also suckers rudely and can form thickets or naturalized type stands. Worthwhile leaving if in a naturalized situation.

DISEASES AND INSECTS: In years past, I would have said totally free, but have noticed, maybe I was not looking previously, a distinct, blackish leaf spot that affects the leaves and presents a measly appearance; plants can look pretty sick in the summer and fall months; lots of variability in susceptibility; fall webworm may develop.

LANDSCAPE VALUE: Interesting native tree, possibly for naturalizing, golf courses, parks; could be integrated into the home landscape but there are too many superior trees to justify extensive use.

CULTIVARS: I did not know how many cultivars existed but found an excellent article by Goodell, *Arnoldia* 42(4):102–133, that provides an excellent perspective of *D. virginiana* and *Actinidia arguta*. 'Early Golden' is the standard for early ripening. 'Garretson', 'Killen', 'John Rick', 'Florence', 'George', 'Mike', 'Wabash', 'Morris Burton', 'Juhl', 'Hick', 'Richards', 'Evelyn', 'Utter', 'Pieper', and 'William' are also mentioned in the article. Anyone interested in this or other native fruit and nut trees should consider joining North American Fruit Explorers, c/o Ray Walker, Box 711, St. Louis, MO 63188 and Northern Nut Growers Association, c/o John English, RR #3, Bloomington, IN 61701.

Several good home garden cultivars include:

'Early Golden'—Productive with medium-sized fruit, containing 3 to 8 seeds, excellent quality and firmness.

'John Rick'—Productive, excellent flavor and firmness, 2 to 8 seeds.

'Killen'—Good flavor and firm fruit, medium-sized and moderately productive.

'Miller'—Productive, flavor good with large, firm fruit.

'Woolbright'—Excellent flavor but soft and easily splits, productive.

PROPAGATION: Seed, stratify in sand or peat for 60 to 90 days at 41°F; cultivars are grafted on seedling understock; root cuttings will work.

ADDITIONAL NOTES: The wood of *D. virginiana* is heavy, hard, strong and close-grained. It is used for golf club heads, billiard cues, flooring and veneer.

Approximately 475 *Diospyros* species comprising deciduous and evergreen trees and shrubs are distributed in southern Europe, North and South America, Africa and Asia, particularly in the tropics. Several species are important sources of timber. *Diospyros ebenum* Koenig & Retz. is the ebony of commerce. Outside of the two species treated herein, I occasionally see *D. lotus* L., Date Plum, that can grow to 75' but is usually smaller. The leaves are dark polished green above, paler beneath. The 3/4 to 1″ diameter globose to ovoid fruit colors yellow, red, or purple and is covered with a waxy bloom.

NATIVE HABITAT: Connecticut to Florida west to Kansas and Texas. Introduced 1629. Frequently encountered in abandoned fields, in fence rows and along highways.

RELATED SPECIES:

Diospyros kaki L.— Japanese Persimmon, Kaki

LEAVES: Alternate, simple, elliptic-ovate to oblong-ovate or obovate, 2 1/2 to 7″ long, 1 1/2 to 3 1/2″ wide, acute to abruptly wide acuminate, broad cuneate to weakly cordate, glabrous, entire, lustrous dark green above, lighter and pubescent on veins beneath, leathery and strongly veined; petiole—1/2 to 1″ long, pubescent; easily distinguished from the above by larger leaves, buds and fruits.

BUDS: Imbricate, broad-ovoid, brownish with darker stripes on scales, pubescent particularly at tips, 3/16″ high by 1/4″ across, sets slightly oblique to half-ellipse leaf scars.

STEM: Stout, slightly angled to rounded, 1/4″ diameter, flat brown with abundant, large, vertical lenticels, glabrous or slightly pubescent at tip; second year stem light gray-brown; pith—green, solid, about 1/3 the diameter of the stem.

Diospyros kaki, (dī-os′pi-ros ka′kĭ), Japanese Persimmon, first came to my attention at the grocery store and most recently on a drive through south Georgia where I saw a most unusual mop-headed, small tree dripping with large, egg-shaped to rounded, 3 to 4″ diameter, yellow-orange fruits. In subsequent travels, I have seen trees distinctly upright. In fact, in Tulsa, OK I saw a Japanese Persimmon that had the upright habit of *Pyrus communis*, Common Pear. The fruit ripens after the leaves fall and considerable variation exists among cultivars as far as size, shape and quality. The lustrous dark green leaves turn a handsome yellow-orange-red in the fall. The species is dioecious with the male flowers in three's about 2/5″ long, with 16 to 24 stamens; the female 1/2 to 3/4″ long; both whitish. Flowers appear on current season's growth in May–June; the fruits ripen in October and later. The tree can grow 20 to 30′ high and wide but is usually smaller. The habit is low-branched and wide-spreading with semi-pendulous outer branches. Requires moist, well-drained soil and full sun. Could be used as a container or tub plant; integrated into the border. Summer foliage and fall color (orange-red on Athens trees) are exceptional. Leaf spot is not a problem. I believe male trees should be considered for use in difficult city sites. Propagation of *D. kaki* is primarily orchestrated through budding in summer and whip or cleft grafting in winter, *D. kaki* understocks are preferred because of incompatibility and other problems with *D. virginiana*. Work out of Israel [*Scientia Horticulturae* 48:1–2, 61–70 (1991)] reported decline of *D. kaki* on *D. virginiana*. Similar incompatibilities are showing up on cultivars grafted to *D. virginiana* in the Georgia Horticulture Farm plots.

CULTIVARS: Louisiana Nursery, Opelousas, Louisiana, 70570, offered 15 cultivars in its 1995 catalog. Many cultivars have been selected over the centuries.

'Chocolate'—Brown, sweet flesh; actually a group of selections with cocoa brown flesh that when ripe is moist and tasty.

'Eureka'—Bright orange-red, tomato-shaped fruits, must be fully ripe.

'Fuyu'—Golden orange-skinned fruit with firm, apple-like flesh, about the size of a handball but shaped like a tomato, non-astringent even before completely ripe, a most popular variety and ordinarily seedless.

'Fuyu Giant'—Similar but produces larger fruits, perhaps as much as 40% larger, non-astringent.

'Great Wall'—Vigorous trees with flat, small, orange-red fruit, astringent until ripe.

'Hachiya'—Handsome tree form with large (3 1/2 to 5″ long, 2 1/2″ broad), conical, essentially seedless fruits, needs to be soft before eaten, outside orange-red, flesh orange-yellow.

'Hana Fuyu'—Large, round-shaped, yellow-orange, non-astringent, good quality; moderately vigorous and productive trees.

'Sheng'—Moderately vigorous trees with large, flat, orange fruit, astringent until ripe.

'Tamopan'—Large, acorn-shaped fruit, often 5″ across, astringent unless fully ripe; very vigorous trees and moderately productive.

'Tanenashi'—Brilliant orange, cone-shaped fruits, heavy production, essentially seedless, must be fully ripe, otherwise astringent taste.

'Youhou'—Non-astringent hybrid between 'Fuyu' and 'Jirou', red-orange skin, deep orange flesh, weigh up to one-half pound.

Native to China. Long cultivated in China and Japan for its fruit; introduced into Europe 1796, but little known before 1870. Zone 7 although best in 8 and 9. Withstood 4°F during January 1994, flowered and produced prodigious quantities of fruit.

Dipteronia sinensis Oliv.

FAMILY: Aceraceae
LEAVES: Opposite, compound pinnate, 8 to 12″ long, (7)9 to 11(13) opposite leaflets, each 1 1/2 to 4″ long, one-third as wide, ovate or lanceolate, short-stalked, sharply and irregularly serrated, dark green, with tufts of pubescence in the axils of the veins, the lowest leaflet pair 3-parted or trifoliate.

Dipteronia sinensis, (dip-tĕr-ō′ni-à sĭ-nen′sis), is a small tree (20 to 30′) or large shrub that now appears in a few United States nursery catalogs. The plant is nowhere common in cultivation and the only place I have associated with the taxon was the Barnes Arboretum, Merion, PA. The foliage is pretty; the polygamous, smallish, greenish white flowers occur in 6 to 12″ long, terminal panicles and are followed by winged, 3/4 to 1″ wide, light brown samaras, borne together like schizocarp in maple. Plant in well-drained soil in partial shade, will possibly handle full sun if adequately watered. Central China. Introduced around 1900 by Wilson. Zone (5)6 to 8. Morton Arboretum, Lisle, IL grows the species.

Dirca palustris L. — Leatherwood, Wicopy

(dir′kà pa-lus′tris)

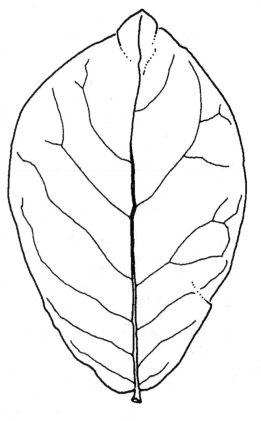

FAMILY: Thymelaeaceae
LEAVES: Alternate, simple, elliptic to obovate, 1 to 3″ long, about one-half as wide, obtuse, cuneate, entire, light green above, glaucescent beneath and pubescent when young; petiole—short, about 1/8″ long.
BUDS: Small, solitary, short conical, with about 4 indistinct, dark, silky scales; end bud lacking, buds are largely hidden by petiole bases, appear as gray rounded balls nestled about one-half way pressed into the raised leaf scar.
STEM: Slender, light brown becoming olive or darker, with conspicuous, small, white lenticels; first year stem develops vertical fissures and is deeper brown than second year and older wood; gradually enlarged upwards through the season's growth; bruised stems aromatic; pith—small, green, solid; called leatherwood because the bark is very leathery and it is quite difficult to remove a piece of broken stem.

SIZE: Variable over its native range; 3 to 6′ in height with a similar spread.
HARDINESS: Zone 4 to 9.
HABIT: Much-branched, rather dense, oval to rounded shrub in cultivation when sited in full sun; irregular, open and more spreading in the wild although still relatively dense.
RATE: Slow.
TEXTURE: Medium.
LEAF COLOR: Light green, by some authorities yellow-green; one of the first shrubs to leaf out in spring; may turn clear yellow in fall, can be very effective in fall color.
FLOWERS: Perfect, pale yellow, 3 to 4 in an inflorescence, from each node; not overwhelming but interesting by virtue of their March to April flowering date; has been in full flower in early March at the University's Botanical Garden; have also recorded full-flowering on February 22.
FRUIT: Oval drupe, 1/3″ long, pale green or reddish; containing one large, shining, brown seed; June–July; seldom seen as it is hidden among the leaves and falls soon after maturity.
CULTURE: Thrives in moist to wet, shady areas; prefers a deep soil supplied with organic matter; in Turkey Run State Park, IN, the plant appears to follow the water courses through the ravines and occurs in the alluvial soils.

DISEASES AND INSECTS: None serious, although I have observed scale infestations on selected plants; the two plants died at the Botanical Garden and I suspect borer infestation; several extremely dry growing seasons predisposed the plants to the insects.

LANDSCAPE VALUE: Interesting native shrub well-adapted to moist shady areas; if natural in an area it is worth leaving; the flowers are borne on leafless stems and are interesting; I have become very fond of this plant over the years; the rich green foliage is very distinct and the fall color can be an excellent yellow; in hot sun it does not have the handsome leaf color that occurs in a semi-shaded situation.

PROPAGATION: Seed can be sown as soon as ripe; seed requires a cold period of about 3 months to facilitate germination; the only definitive published information reported that cleaned fruits (pulp removed) sown immediately outside (Boston) germinated 54% in the spring; at the University's Botanical Garden, two side-by-side seedlings set prodigious quantities of fruits and numerous seedlings have germinated around the bases of these plants. Cuttings have proven difficult to root and I have had no success; layering offers a possible method of vegetative reproduction.

ADDITIONAL NOTES: The Indians used the bark for bow strings and fish lines and in the manufacture of baskets. *Dirca occidentalis* A. Gray is the other member of the genus and occurs in California. I can see no major vegetative differences between this and *D. palustris*. The flowers are sessile; those of *D. palustris* subsessile. Zone 6 to 8.

NATIVE HABITAT: New Brunswick and Ontario to Florida and Missouri. Introduced 1750.

Disanthus cercidifolius Maxim.

FAMILY: Hamamelidaceae

LEAVES: Alternate, simple, thickish, broad-ovate to rounded, 2 to 4 1/2″ long, about as wide, blunt and rounded at apex, cordate or truncate, entire, dark bluish green, glabrous, palmately veined; petiole—1 to 2″ long.

BUDS: End bud (no true terminal)—1/4 to 3/8″ long, ovoid-conical, tapering at both ends, acute at apex, 5- to 7-scaled, shining red tinged with brown at ends of bud scales, glabrous; lateral buds—smaller, 1/16 to 1/8″ long.

STEM: Rounded, medium, reddish brown, epidermis peels off like an onion skin on first year stems; lenticels small, gray, rounded; with slight odor not unlike cherry when bruised; pith—tan, solid.

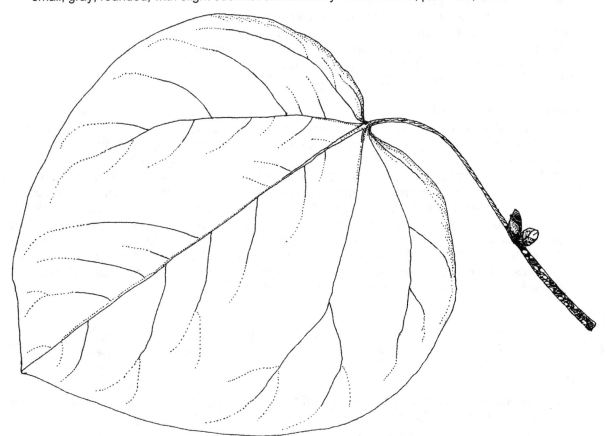

Disanthus cercidifolius, (diz-an'thus sẽr-si-di-fõ'li-us), is a magnificent, but rare, plant that is worthy of the discriminating gardener's attention. One of the purposes of this book is to introduce readers to unusual plants that are not common in the nursery trade. This is one such attempt. *Disanthus cercidifolius* becomes a broad-spreading shrub of slender branches. The ultimate height ranges between 6 and 10'(15'). The bluish green leaves turn combinations of claret red and purple, often suffused with orange. It is one of the most beautiful shrubs for fall color. The leaves resemble those of *Cercis* in shape and, hence, the specific epithet, *cercidifolius*. The perfect, paired, dark purple, 1/2" diameter, 5-petaled, non-showy flowers are borne in axillary pairs in October. The fruit is an obovoid, dehiscent capsule containing several glossy black seeds in each cell. The fruit ripens in October of the year following flowering. It is not the easiest plant to grow and requires a deep, moist, high organic matter soil in light to moderate shade and protection from strong wind. The Morris and Taylor Arboreta have fine specimens which I had the privilege of viewing. It is a knockout and certainly worth securing for one's garden. Someone, actually Roger Gossler, Gossler Farms Nursery, 1200 Weaver Road, Springfield, OR 97478-9663, heard my prayers and sent a plant that prospered for 11 years on the north side of our home in shade and a relatively moist soil. Unfortunately, it succumbed to the vagaries of Zone 7–8 conditions. Incidentally, for those looking for rare plants at reasonable prices, Gossler offers the créme de le créme. Cuttings have been rooted 100% using firm June cuttings, 10,000 ppm IBA, perlite:peat, mist; after rooting they are potted, lightly fertilized and continue to grow. Much easier to root than the literature indicates. A monotypic genus occurring in Japan. Introduced 1892. Zone 5 to 7(8). Hardy to at least -20°F.

Distylium racemosum Sieb. & Zucc. — Isu Tree

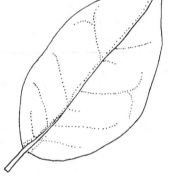

FAMILY: Hamamelidaceae
LEAVES: Alternate, simple, evergreen, leathery, 1 1/4 to 2 1/2" long, 1/2 to 1 1/4" wide, narrow-oblong to obovate, blunt, broadly tapering to almost rounded at base, entire, lustrous dark green, paler beneath, glabrous at maturity; petiole—1/4" long.
BUDS: Scales dusty pubescent, gray-brown, fused together in an ovoid shape, about 3/16" long, apparently mixed (floral and vegetative) buds.
STEM: Moderate, green, pubescent at end of first year's growth, later glabrous; second year stems shining brown, developing vertical fissures, small gray lenticels; pith—small, solid, greenish.

Distylium racemosum, (dis-til'ē-um ra-se-mō'sum), Isu Tree, is typically an upright-spreading, rather open, evergreen shrub in cultivation. An old specimen at the University's Savannah research station was about 10' high. A seven-year-old plant in my evaluation plots is 7' high, rather open and untidy. The literature describes specimens up to 60' high in the wild. The dark green, evergreen foliage is attractive. The apetalous, reddish maroon flowers consist of a pubescent, 5-parted calyx and purple stamens. The 2 to 3" long inflorescence stalks are covered with rust-colored pubescence. One almost has to fall into the plant to notice the flowers. Have seen in flower in early May at Biltmore Gardens, Asheville, NC. The pubescent, woody capsule is 2-beaked with one seed per cell. Should be sited in moist, acidic soils laden with organic matter in partial shade. Have seen and grown plants in full sun that were acceptable. More of a collector's item than a garden staple. More cold hardy that the literature credits. 'Guppy' is a compact form with smaller leaves, 3' high, from Brookside Gardens, Wheaton, MD. 'Variegatum' is blotched and margined with cream-white. Southern Japan. Suspect Zone 6b to 9.

Duranta erecta L. (formerly *D. repens* L.) — Pigeon Berry, Sky Flower, Golden Dewdrop

FAMILY: Verbenaceae
LEAVES: Opposite, simple, evergreen, to 3" long, 1 1/2" wide, ovate-elliptic to obovate, acuminate or obtuse, cuneate, serrate or entire, lustrous medium to dark green, glabrescent; petiole—1/2" long.
STEM: Gray-brown, may develop spines.

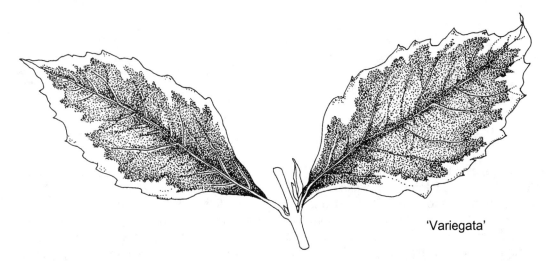

'Variegata'

Duranta erecta, (dū-ran′tà ē-rek′tà), Pigeon Berry, appears infrequently in gardens along the Georgia coast and into Florida. It is usually a dieback shrub and the largest specimens attain height and spread of 4 to 6′. Listed as growing to 18′ in central and southern Florida gardens. In Athens, Dr. Allan Armitage has successfully utilized it as an herbaceous perennial. The multi-colored, blue-white flowers develop on new growth of the season in up to 6″ long and wide racemes (look like panicles to me). The 3/8 to 1/2″ diameter, yellow, globose drupes are pretty and ripen in late summer–fall. Fruits are listed as poisonous. Any loose, well-drained soil in full sun is suitable. Nomenclature is really askew and names like *D. repens* and *D. grandiflora* are still in use. 'Alba' has white flowers. 'Variegata' has leaves margined and irregularly splashed with cream and white. Tropical America. Zone (8)9 to 10; 7 as an herbaceous perennial.

Edgeworthia papyrifera Sieb. & Zucc. — Paperbush

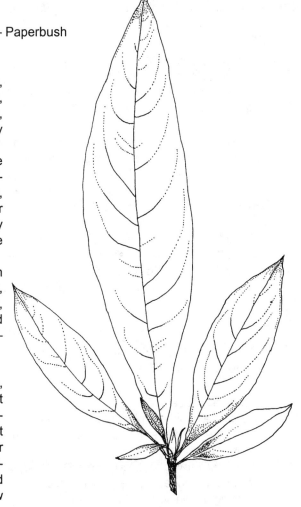

FAMILY: Thymelaeaceae

LEAVES: Alternate, simple, narrow oval to narrow ovate, 3 to 5 1/2″ long, 3/4 to 2″ wide, acute, cuneate, entire, dull dark green almost blue-green above, glabrous or pubescent, gray-green below with silky hairs when young; petiole—1/4 to 5/8″ long.

BUDS: Flower—terminal, visible from summer of the previous year, naked, 25 to 35 flowers in the head-like inflorescence, each covered with silky hairs, entire inflorescence 1/2 to 3/4″ across, each flower bud about 1/4 to 3/8″ long, curved 1/2″ long, silky pubescent peduncle; vegetative—naked, 2 visible scales, silky pubescent.

STEM: Slender, supple, can be tied in knots, reddish brown, pubescent near apex, glabrous later, unusual odor to bruised stem; leaf scars raised, half-elliptical, closely spaced; lenticels on 2nd and 3rd year stems, vertical, diamond-shaped; pith—green, solid.

Edgeworthia papyrifera, (edge-worth′ē-à pap-i-rif′ēr-à), Paperbush, has missed the previous editions but now makes a rather auspicious (suspicious) entrance. My first introduction to the plant occurred at Callaway Gardens in late February 1980. A rather large, suckering colony of 3 to 4′ high, naked-stemmed (except at end of stem) plants sported cream-yellow, slightly fragrant flowers. The show

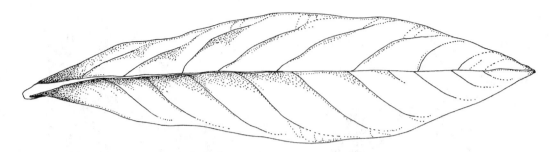

was not spectacular but unusual. The individual 1/2 to 3/4″ long flower is composed of a 4-lobed, silky calyx, yellow in the center, silky white on the outside of the tube, borne 25 to 35 (40 to 50) together in a globose, terminal, 1 to 2″ wide umbel during March–April (Athens). Fruit is a dry drupe but I have not seen any formed on cultivated plants. The dark blue-green leaves present a tropical look and die off in fall without coloring. Provide deep, moist, high organic matter soils in light to moderate shade. Makes a nifty woodland plant and is a great teaser for the visitor who knows everything. A lovely colony in the protection of the north side of our home simply died to its root tips at -3°F. A more recent planting has survived 4°F. Plants as large as 7′ are described. Propagate by division of the parent plant in mid to late winter. Forma *rubra* ('Rubra') with red flowers is available from a few United States nurseries. The red coloration appeared more orange on plants I observed. 'Red Dragon' ('Jitsu Red') may be a superior form. 'Grandiflora' produces larger flowers. China. Occurs in forest and streamside habitats. Used for paper and medicine in China. Nomenclature is not tidy and names like *E. chrysantha* and *E. gardenii* are cast about. Introduced 1845. Zone 7 to 8(9).

Ehretia acuminata R. Br. var. *serrata* (Roxb.) I.M. Johnst. [*E. thrysiflora* (Sieb. & Zucc.) Nak.] — Koko Wood

FAMILY: Boraginaceae
LEAVES: Alternate, simple, leathery, oval, ovate or obovate, 3 to 7″ long, 1 1/2 to 3″ wide, abruptly pointed, cuneate or rounded, serrated, lustrous dark green, paler, glabrous or pubescent in axils of veins below; petiole—1/2 to 3/4″ long.

Ehretia acuminata var. *serrata*, (e-rē'ti-à a-kū-mi-nā'tà ser-rā'tà), Koko Wood, is a small, deciduous, 20 to 25′ high, broad-spreading tree. The dark green summer leaves develop no fall coloration. The 1/4″ diameter, 5-lobed, white, fragrant flowers occur in 3 to 8″ long, terminal panicles in July–August. I have observed flowering specimens in England and indeed they are beautiful. The fruit is a 1/6″ diameter, blackish drupe. The bark is deeply ridged-and-furrowed. Provide well-drained soil and full sun. Young plants (seedlings) may be susceptible to cold injury. Raulston reported a plant surviving 5°F at Raleigh, NC after the 1983–84 winter. *Ehretia dicksonii* Hance has 4 to 8″ long, elliptic, downy-surfaced, leathery, shining green leaves. White flowers appear in 2 to 4″ wide, flattish, corymbose panicles in May–June. Probably not as cold hardy. China, Taiwan, Japan. *Erhetia acuminata* var. *serrata* is native to the Himalayas. Zone 7 to 9. The Morton Arboretum grows the plant as a dieback shrub.

Elaeagnus angustifolia L. — Russian-olive, Oleaster, Wild Olive, Silver Berry
(el-ē-ag'nus an-gus-ti-fō'li-à)

FAMILY: Elaeagnaceae
LEAVES: Alternate, simple, oblong-lanceolate to linear-lanceolate, 1 to 3″(4″) long, 3/8 to 5/8″ wide, dull green and scaly above, silvery-scaly beneath, acute to obtuse, usually broad-cuneate at base, entire; petiole—1/5 to 1/3″ long.
BUDS: Small, solitary, gray-brown, sessile, round, conical or oblong, with about 4 exposed silvery scales.
STEM: Young branches—silvery, sometimes thorny, covered with scales; older branches—assuming a glistening brown color; pith—brown.

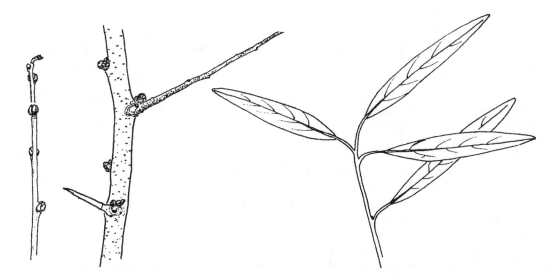

SIZE: 12 to 15'(20') tall and as wide, occasionally will grow 30 to 40'; national champion is 52' by 60' near Black Hills Speedway, SD.

HARDINESS: Zone 2 to 7.

HABIT: Large shrub or small tree of oval to rounded outline, often quite open and of light texture.

RATE: Medium to fast.

TEXTURE: Medium-fine in leaf; medium in winter.

LEAF COLOR: Silver-green to gray-green in summer and one of the most effective plants for gray foliage.

FLOWERS: Perfect, apetalous, calyx tube campanulate, with 4 spreading lobes as long as the tube, silvery or whitish outside, yellow inside, 3/8" long, fragrant, May, one to three together in each leaf axil, difficult to see among the foliage.

FRUIT: Drupe-like, most correctly considered an achene covered by a fleshy perianth, 1/2" long, yellow and coated with silvery scales, August–September, the flesh is sweet and mealy and in the Orient a sherbet is made from it.

CULTURE: Transplants readily, can be grown in any soil, but does best in light, sandy loams; withstands seacoast, highway conditions, drought and alkali soils; prefers sunny open exposure; can be pruned into a tight structure; the secret to keeping this plant looking good is to keep it vigorous; have seen in Colorado where it appeared more vigorous than in Midwest and East; displays high degree of salt tolerance, especially to soil salts; fixes atmosphere nitrogen making it amenable to poor soils, does not perform well in heat of the South.

DISEASES AND INSECTS: Leaf spots, cankers, rusts, *Verticillium* wilt, crown gall, oleaster-thistle aphid, and scales; *Verticillium* can wreak havoc on this species and for this reason it has lost favor as a highway plant in many parts of the Midwest and East.

LANDSCAPE VALUE: For grayish foliage effect it is difficult to beat; can be used for hedges, highways, seacoasts, about anywhere salt is a problem; possibly an accent plant in the shrub border; better in dry climates than moist.

CULTIVARS:
'Red King'—Rich rust-red fruits.

PROPAGATION: Seed should be stratified for 60 to 90 days at 41°F; cuttings collected in mid-October rooted after treatment with 40 ppm IBA for two hours but the percentage was poor; seed is the preferred method of propagation. Several successful tissue culture reports appear in *Acta Horticulturae* 227:363–368 (1988) and *Plant and Soil* 87:143–152 (1985).

NATIVE HABITAT: Southern Europe to western and central Asia, Altai and Himalayas. Long cultivated in Europe.

RELATED SPECIES:

Elaeagnus commutata Bernh. — Silverberry

LEAVES: Alternate, simple, ovate to oblong or ovate-lanceolate, 1 1/2 to 3 1/2" long, 3/4 to 1 1/4" wide, acute or obtuse, cuneate, both sides covered with glistening silvery white scales; petiole—1/8" long.

STEM: Silvery white like the leaves.

Elaeagnus commutata, (el-ē-ag′nus kom-mū-tā′tà), Silverberry, is a 6 to 12′ high and wide shrub of erect habit with rather slender branches. It suckers profusely and forms colonies. The silver-white leaves are the showiest of the *Elaeagnus* species treated here. The fragrant, silvery yellow, tubular, 1/2″ long flowers are produced in great numbers in the leaf axils during May. The fruit is a silvery, 1/3″ long, egg-shaped drupe that ripens in September–October. At Illinois, in our test plots, this species contracted scale and performed poorly. At the University of Maine, in their test area, it appeared more vigorous. It makes a rather striking shrub because of the silvery foliage but is rather untidy in growth habit. Have not seen in the Southeast and doubt whether it would survive in the humidity and heat. 'Coral Silver' with bright gray foliage and coral red fruits is described. Its taxonomic affinity is not clear. Roy Lancaster, the great British plantsman, describes the clone 'Quicksilver' in *The Garden* 118(2):76–77 (1993). He theorizes that it might be a hybrid between *E. angustifolia* × *E. commutata*. Years before the article appeared I had photographed the plant at Beth Chatto's garden and was puzzled over its identity. Eastern Canada to Northwest Territory, south to Minnesota, South Dakota and Utah. The only species native in North America. Introduced 1813. Lovely silver-leaved plant that might prove useful in Zone (3)4 to 6 gardens.

Elaeagnus multiflora Thunb. — Cherry Elaeagnus

LEAVES: Alternate, simple, elliptic or ovate to obovate-oblong, 1 1/2 to 2 1/2″ long, 3/4 to 1 1/2″ wide, short acuminate to obtusish, broad cuneate, green above with scattered, tufted hairs, silvery brown beneath with a mix of tiny, silver scales and larger, brown ones; petiole—1/4″ long.

Elaeagnus multiflora, (el-ē-ag′nus mul-ti-flō′rà), Cherry Elaeagnus, is a wide-spreading almost flat-topped shrub with rather stiff branches (grows 6 to 10′ high and as wide). Foliage is a silvery green (green above, silvery brown below). Fruits are red, scaly, 1/2″ long on a 1″ pedicel, oblong, of pleasant acid flavor, June–July; birds seem to like the fruits; as adaptable or more so than *E. angustifolia*. The 5/8″ long, 3/5″ wide flowers are fragrant and of the same color as the underside of the leaf. They occur in April and May from the axils of the leaves. This is a rather handsome species and the scaly, red fruits that hang from the underside of the branches are beautiful. The leaves are more green than the other deciduous species treated here. Easily cultured, fixes nitrogen and has been used as a nurse shrub in forestry plantings. A specimen at the Arnold Arboretum

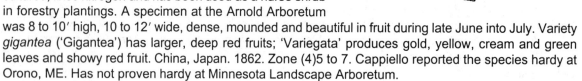

was 8 to 10′ high, 10 to 12′ wide, dense, mounded and beautiful in fruit during late June into July. Variety *gigantea* ('Gigantea') has larger, deep red fruits; 'Variegata' produces gold, yellow, cream and green leaves and showy red fruit. China, Japan. 1862. Zone (4)5 to 7. Cappiello reported the species hardy at Orono, ME. Has not proven hardy at Minnesota Landscape Arboretum.

Elaeagnus umbellata Thunb. — Autumn Elaeagnus, Autumn-olive

LEAVES: Alternate, simple, elliptic to ovate-oblong, 2 to 4″ long, 3/4 to 1 1/2″ wide, obtuse to short-acuminate, rounded to broad cuneate at the base, often with crisped margin, usually with silvery scales above when young, sometimes glabrous, bright green above at maturity, silvery beneath and usually mixed with brown scales; petiole—1/3″ long.

STEM: Silver-brown with many brownish scales which give a speckled appearance, spines may be present; pith—rich brown.

Elaeagnus umbellata, (el-ē-ag′nus um-bel-lā′tà), Autumn Elaeagnus or Autumn-olive, is a large (12 to 18′ tall by 12 to 18′ wide, sometimes 20 to 30′ across), spreading, often spiny-branched shrub. The foliage is bright green above, silver-green beneath. The 1/2″ long funnel-shaped, silvery white, fragrant flowers occur in May–June (early to mid-May, Athens). The globose fruits are silvery mixed with brown scales finally turning red, 1/4 to 1/3″ long, ripening in September to October. In Boston on July 11,

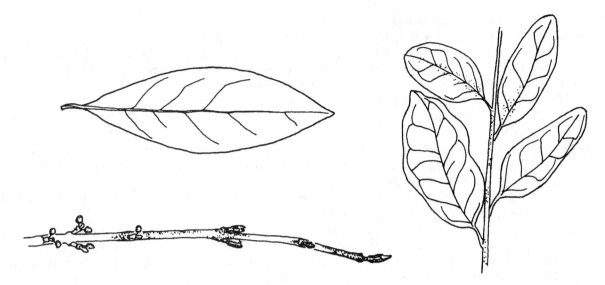

1991 fruits had ripened and were falling from the branches. Fruits are borne in great numbers on short (1/4″ long) stalks and appear to almost encircle the stem. Becomes a noxious weed with time for birds spread the seeds everywhere. 'Cardinal' is a Soil Conservation Service introduction that grows to 12′, fruits heavily and thrives in low-fertility, acid, loamy and sandy soils and displays excellent drought tolerance; sold for conservation purposes; not a plant for the home landscape. In the South, this species has escaped and can be found in abundance in almost any untended location. Appears to adapt quite well to light, shady pine and deciduous woods. The sweet fragrance is inescapable in early May, in fact, I can ride home from work (8 miles) and notice almost a continuum of fragrance. 'Titan' is an upright introduction that grows 12′ high and only 6′ wide with the other attributes of the species. Lake County Nursery introduction. China, Korea, Japan. 1830. Zone 4 to 8. Cappiello reported some tip dieback at Orono, ME.

ADDITIONAL NOTES: Forty-five species of *Elaeagnus* have been described. Most form nitrogen-fixing root nodules which assures their survival in inhospitable soils. The *Elaeagnus* species offer good foliage color, fragrant flowers and silvery to red fruits; unfortunately, several species are pestiferous and become weeds with time. I have seen numerous bird-planted *E. umbellata* in Georgia. At Illinois I conducted salt tolerance research with *E. angustifolia* and found that it was almost impossible to kill with soil applications. Apparently Russian-olive does not accumulate the Na or Cl ions and is able to survive in saline environments. Anyone interested in salt tolerant trees and shrubs should see Dirr, "Selection of trees for tolerance to salt," *J. Arboriculture*, 2:209–216 (1976).

Elaeagnus pungens Thunb. — Thorny Elaeagnus
(el-ē-ag′nus pun′jenz)

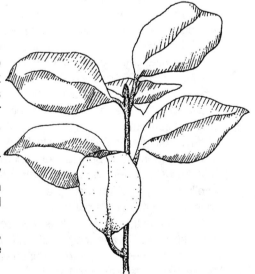

LEAVES: Alternate, simple, evergreen, margins as if ruffled (crisped), 2 to 4″ long, 1/4 to 1 3/4″ wide, linear-ovate to ovate, acute, cuneate, entire, glabrous and lustrous dark green above, prominently covered with punctate scales below, giving silver sheen to entire lower surface, major veins appearing brown; petiole—1/4 to 1/2″ long, brown, covered with brown scales.

BUDS: Four loosely aggregated, brownish scales give appearance of fingers glued together, 1/8 to 1/4″ long; apparently some buds are leaf buds, others develop into spines; both present at same node; spine continues to grow and produces leaves.

STEM: Moderate, terete, brown, densely covered with scales, will develop rather nasty 2 to 3″ long thorns that are covered with brown scales; pith—greenish white, solid.

SIZE: 10 to 15′ high, similar spread.

HARDINESS: Zone 6, succeeds in the Philadelphia area, to 9 (part of 10).

HABIT: In its natural form a genuine horror; long shoots wander in disarray from all areas of the plant; best described as a rather unkempt, dense, spreading, more or less thorny shrub; needs a good tailor.

RATE: Fast, does not adequately describe the speed with which it grows.

TEXTURE: Coarse, but some of the better cultivars fall in the medium category.

LEAF COLOR: Glossy dark green above; silvery with a hint of brown beneath, some leaves brown on underside.

FLOWERS: Perfect, silvery white, fragrant (similar to that of *Gardenia*), 1/2″ long, tubular but flaring above the ovary, usually in three's from the leaf axis, October–November, often lost among the leaves but the fine fragrance stimulates the olfactory senses.

FRUIT: Seldom seen, a 1/2 to 3/4″ long, scaly brown at first, finally red, oval drupe; fruits develop in April and May and attract birds; very similar to those of *E. multiflora*.

CULTURE: Easily grown, actually a weed in the South, adaptable to varied soils and withstands considerable drought; sun or shade, tends to become thin in shade but still makes an acceptable plant; tolerates salt spray and air pollutants; requires frequent pruning and regrowth of shoots following pruning is problematic.

DISEASES AND INSECTS: None serious, but spider mites do occur in dry weather.

LANDSCAPE VALUE: Not for the small property; has been used extensively for highway landscaping in the South; rest areas along interstates seem to abound with this plant; good for banks, hedges, screens, natural barriers; tends to sucker which makes it good for stabilizing soils; leaves were injured at -3°F in 1983–84 but did grow back as stems and buds were not hurt; used on a steep bank on the Georgia campus under *Quercus nigra*, Water Oak, and filled in within about three years, amazing tenacity in the face of adversity.

CULTIVARS: Many; names appear to be confused.

'Aurea'—Leaves bordered with bright yellow ('Aureopicta').

'Dicksonii'—Leaves bordered with a broad gold margin, with some leaves completely gold toward the apex.

'Frederici'—Small, narrow, 1 to 1 3/4″ long leaves, the cream-colored or pale yellow center bordered with a thin margin of green, have seen in England, not particularly striking and appears sick.

'Fruitlandii'—Supposedly symmetrical in outline; leaves slightly larger and more rounded than the species, wavy, silvery beneath.

'Golden Rim'—Apparently a branch sport of 'Maculata', leaves green in center with gold margins, originated in Holland, have not seen in the United States.

'Maculata' ('Aureovariegata')—Large leaves are marked with a deep yellow blotch of variable size in their center; often, between the yellow and green areas is an intermediate yellowish shade; this cultivar will revert back to the type and these branches must be cut out; I have seen plants that showed virtually complete reversion; common in the South but almost gauche; reversions to both yellow and green shoots occur.

'Marginata'—Leaves with silvery white margins.

'Simonii'—Larger (2 to 4 1/4″ long) leaves than the type with bright green upper surface, very silvery undersides, branches gray-brown, not thorny; similar to 'Fruitlandii'?

'Variegata'—Similar to 'Aurea' but border color yellowish white, very irregular and narrow. I have seen other variegated cultivars but do now know how different they are. Only so many variations can be selected with yellow on the inside or yellow on the outside.

The New RHS Dictionary of Gardening lists additional cultivars, however, I have never observed them in American or English gardens.

PROPAGATION: Not the easiest plant to root; use firm wood cuttings and some cold (October–November) may precondition cuttings to root better; 8000 ppm to 20,000 ppm IBA-talc have been used successfully; cuttings collected in February–March, 6″ long from previous season's growth, 8000 ppm IBA-talc, 2 peat: 1 sand, bottom heat, poly tent or mist rooted 90 to 100% in 8 weeks.

ADDITIONAL NOTES: *Elaeagnus pungens* develops long shoots almost devoid of leaves that give it a wild and woolly effect. The interesting aspect of these shoots is the spine development. The spines normally develop at a 45° angle to the terminal end of the shoot. However, if in contact with a structure such as a trellis or fence the spine angle is reversed and the spines act almost like hooks. If you ever attempted to pull a shoot out of a fence this effect is obvious. Plant literally "climbs" and I have observed 30′ high *E. pungens* snaking through tree branches.

NATIVE HABITAT: Japan. Introduced 1830.

RELATED SPECIES:

Elaeagnus* × *ebbingei Boom., (el-ē-ag′nus eb-bing′ē-ī), is a suspected hybrid between *E. macrophylla* and *E. pungens*. A batch of six seedlings was raised by S.G.A. Doorenboos in 1929; all six were propagated and two clones are still in commerce; supposedly more vigorous than either species. Based on observations, *E.* × *ebbingei* is not as wild and woolly as *E. pungens*; may show semi-evergreen tendencies but is evergreen in mild climates; grows 8 to 10′ high and wide. From the original seedlings, two were named: 'Albert Doorenbos' with large (3 to 5″ long, 2 to 2 1/4″ wide) leaves that more closely resemble *E. macrophylla*; and 'The Hague' with narrower leaves (3 to 4″ long, 2″ wide) that resembles *E. pungens*. More recently a particularly handsome form, 'Gilt Edge' with soft yellow-gold prominent margins and a light green center, has entered the marketplace. This is a particularly fine form that I have seen in many English gardens and has found its way into American commerce (Monrovia Nurseries). Raised by Waterer and Sons and Crisp Nursery, England. I have also seen a form called 'Clemson' which is somewhat similar but with lighter margins. It is probably not in the trade. 'Limelight' has leaves splashed pale gold to gold and is particularly striking in summer months, losing some of its intensity in cold weather. 'Salcombe Seedling' produces abundant, fragrant, white flowers. Probably Zone (6)7 to 9.

Elaeagnus macrophylla Thunb., (el-ē-ag′nus mak-rō-fil′à), as one of the parents of *E.* × *ebbingei* deserves mention. Grows 8 to 12′ high and generally wider at maturity. The 2 to 4 1/2″ long, 1 1/2 to 2 3/4″ wide leaves are gray-silver on both surfaces when young. Later, the upper surface becomes lustrous dark green and slightly scaly; lower surface silvery. Petiole is 1/2 to 3/4″ long. The 1/2″ long and wide, fuchsia-shaped, fragrant flowers occur in axillary clusters of 3 to 6. The 5/8″ long, scaly, red, ovoid fruits ripen in the spring. Culture is similar to that of *E. pungens* but it is not quite as cold hardy. I have seen plants in England and the new leaves appear coated with silver fur. Korea, Japan. Introduced 1879. Zone (7)8 to 9.

Elliottia racemosa Elliott — Georgia Plume, Elliottia

FAMILY: Ericaceae

LEAVES: Alternate, simple, narrowly oval or obovate, 2 to 5″ long, 3/4 to 1 3/4″ wide, tapering at both ends, dull dark green or blue-green and glabrous above, paler and slightly pubescent beneath; petiole—1/4 to 1/2″ long, pubescent.

BUDS: Terminal—1/4″ long, 2 distinct scales form a cone-like structure, glabrous, light brown; laterals—1/16″ long, ovoid, indistinctly scaled (2), rather stiff, almost mucronate; leaf scars—elliptical with one bundle trace.

STEM: Moderate, lustrous brown, glabrous, somewhat angled; in second year developing vertical fissures.

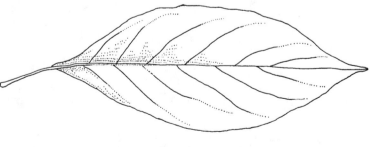

Elliottia racemosa, (el-i-ot′ti-à rā-se-mō′sà), Georgia Plume, is a beautiful large shrub or small tree found in isolated localities in Georgia and South Carolina. It tends to sucker from the roots and form colonies 8 to 12′ high, although larger trees are known. National champion is 48′ by 21′ in Tattnall County, GA. The real show occurs from mid-June to early July (in Georgia) when the pure white, slightly fragrant, 4-petaled flowers occur in 4 to 10″ long, terminal racemes or panicles. The fruit is a flattened-globose, 3/8″ diameter capsule that houses the small, winged seeds. The plant is magnificent in flower and would tantalize anyone's gardening palette. After flower it fades into relative obscurity and is quite difficult to identify unless one knows exactly what to look for. The foliage may develop bronze-red shades and on November

20, 1992, a notable specimen at Brookgreen Gardens, Murrell's Inlet, SC crossed my path. It has a historic past and many articles have been written of which I recommend Miller, "Wildfire's child," *American Forest* 84(2) (1978). It has not found its way into gardens owing to the difficulty of propagation but Al Fordham, former plant propagator of the Arnold Arboretum, worked out an excellent method from root cuttings. See *Proc. Intl. Plant Prop. Soc.* 29:284–287 (1979) for specifics. Interestingly, it is growing as far north as Boston, MA in the Arnold Arboretum where I have photographed it in full flower. Del Tredici, *Arnoldia* 47:2–8 (1987), discusses the species and mentions that it occurs in about 70 sites. A single tree at the Arnold produced viable seeds (1985) which were sown directly or stratified in 50 sand:50 peat medium at 36°F. Seeds were sown after 42 and 64 days of cold. Germination averaged 71 and 82% after 19 days, respectively. Untreated seeds did not germinate. Seedling growth was poor and it was surmised that mycorrhizae are essential for growth and development. South Carolina and Georgia. Cultivated 1813. Zone 6 (once established) to 8 (9).

Elsholtzia stauntonii Benth. — Staunton Elsholtzia, Mint Shrub

FAMILY: Lamiaceae
LEAVES: Opposite, simple, lanceolate, 2 to 6″ long, 1/2 to 1 1/2″ wide, slenderly tapered at both ends, acuminate, coarse triangular teeth except at ends, bright green above, pale and covered with minute dots beneath, glabrous on both surfaces, minutely downy on margins; when crushed emitting a mint-like odor.

Elsholtzia stauntonii, (el-shōlt′si-à stawn-tō′nē-ī), Staunton Elsholtzia, is a semi-woody, 3 to 5′ high and wide shrub that has no great merit other than the purplish pink flowers that occur in spikose panicles at the end of the stems in September and October. Each spike is normally 4 to 8″ long and about 1″ wide. It prefers a well-drained soil and a sunny site. It is probably best to prune the plant before new growth starts. Since it flowers on new wood of the season the flower effect is not impaired. Watched the plant at the Arnold Arboretum during sabbatical and never envisioned it as a major force in the garden. Should be treated almost like an herbaceous perennial in the North since it flowers on new growth of the season. Seed has no apparent dormancy and softwood cuttings can be rooted. 'Alba' produces white flowers. Northern China. 1905. Zone 5 to 8.

Emmenopterys henryi Oliv.

FAMILY: Rubiaceae
LEAVES: Opposite, simple, leathery, elliptic-ovate to oblong-ovate, variable in size, up to 4 to 6 to 9″ long, half as wide, acute, rounded or cuneate, entire, lustrous dark green above, glabrous, paler and pubescent on veins and midrib, 5 to 8 vein pairs; petiole—1/2 to 2″ long, red to purple, pubescent.
BUDS: Terminal with one scale, conical, pointed, red.

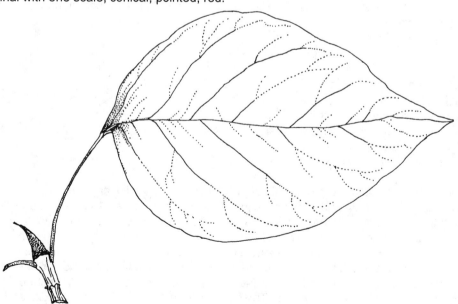

Emmenopterys henryi, (em-en-op'tĕr-is hen'ri-ī), is an enigmatic tree that incites the unfulfilled passions of the fanatical plant collector. In cultivation, it forms a rounded, spreading canopy and reaches 30 to 50' high. Supposedly, it can grow to 80' high. The individual flowers are 1" wide, long funnel-shaped, with 5 spreading, rounded lobes; the calyx is urn-shaped, 1/4" long with 5 rounded, hairy lobes, occasionally one lobe enlarging into a large (up to 2" by 1 1/2"), white "bract." Flowers appear in 6 to 8" high, up to 10" wide, terminal, corymbose panicles in June–July on the current season's growth. Fruit is a 1 to 1 1/2" long, 1/3 to 5/8" wide, ribbed, spindle-shaped capsule. The gray bark is ridged-and-furrowed and quite handsome. Provide deep, moist soil and full sun. Raulston reported no injury at 2°F in 1994 at Raleigh. English literature lists hardiness at -13°F. E.H. Wilson introduced it from Ichang, China where it grows at altitudes to 4000'. Wilson described it as one of the most strikingly beautiful trees of the Chinese forests. Flowered for the first time in the United States in Maryland in July, 1994 as reported by F. Meyer in *Arnoldia* 54(2):36 (1994). China. Introduced 1907. Zone (6)7 to 8. *Pinckneya bracteata* Michx., Feverbark, has similar floral characteristics.

Enkianthus campanulatus (Miq.) Nichols. — Redvein Enkianthus
(en-ki-an'thus kam-pan-ū-lā'tus)

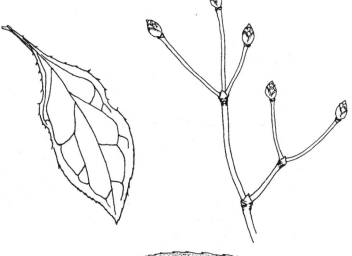

FAMILY: Ericaceae

LEAVES: Alternate, simple, mostly crowded at the end of branches, elliptic to rhombic-elliptic, 1 to 3" long, 1/2 to 1 1/4" wide, acute or acuminate, cuneate, appressed-serrulate with aristate teeth, dull dark green, with scattered bristly hairs above and on the veins beneath; petiole—1/3 to 5/8" long.

BUDS: Minute, sunken and in the notch of the leaf scar, solitary, sessile, indistinctly scaly; the flower buds large, ovoid, imbricate, about 1/3" long.

STEM: Slender, 3-sided or rounded, often reddish in youth, becoming brown, glabrous.

SIZE: 6 to 8' in cold climates but can grow from 15 to 30'; have seen 12 to 15' high specimens in the East, immense specimens in England fully 20' high and spectacular.

HARDINESS: Zone (4)5 to 7; large plant in Orono, ME.

HABIT: Narrow, upright shrub or small tree with layered branches and tufted foliage, becoming more rounded with age.

RATE: Slow.

TEXTURE: Medium in all seasons.

LEAF COLOR: Bright to medium green to almost dull blue-green to dark green in summer; brilliant yellow to orange and red in fall, often variable in quality of coloration, over the many autumns I have been privileged to roam gardens, an amazing range of vivid yellows, oranges and reds have crossed my trail, plants are most often seed-grown so variation is the norm.

FLOWERS: Perfect, creamy yellow or light orange, veined with red, 1/3 to 1/2" long; May–June, about the time the leaves are developing, in pendulous umbel-like racemes, from terminal bud of previous year's growth; very dainty and delicate; a rather unusual but harmless fragrance; corolla bell-shaped with 5 rounded lobes.

FRUIT: Dehiscent capsule, 5-valved, egg-shaped, 3/4" long, borne upright on a recurved pedicel.

CULTURE: Similar to rhododendrons, definitely acid soil requiring; in south requires moisture for will show drought stress; full sun or partial shade.

DISEASES AND INSECTS: None serious, scale has been reported.

LANDSCAPE VALUE: Excellent for flower and fall color, nice specimen, combines well with rhododendrons, lovely around a patio.

CULTIVARS:

    'Albiflorus'—White flowers with no veins, actually somewhat off-white (cream); fall color may approach orange-red; vigorous grower.

    'Hollandia'—Large red flowers; exceptional red fall coloration.

var. *palibinii* (Craib) Bean—Red flowers, each flower 1/3″ long, borne in a distinct raceme, leaves obovate to broad-ovate, pubescent on midrib.

'Red Bells'—Flowers redder toward tip than normal, basal 1/3 of corolla creamy yellow and lightly veined with red, red fall color, smaller growing than the species.

'Red Velvet'—Seedling selection with rich deep pink flowers, excellent fall color, upright habit.

'Renoir'—Named by Rob Nicholson, formerly of the Arnold Arboretum, this form offers subdued yellow flowers with pink lobes.

'Rubrum'—Intense red flowers and fiery red autumn foliage, small-growing.

'Showy Lantern'—Selected by the late Mr. Ed Mezitt, Weston Nurseries, for large solid pink flowers; dark green foliage turns rich scarlet, densely branched from the ground, less hardy than the species as it suffered regular tip kill and occasional severe dieback at Orono, ME.

'Sikokianus' (var. *sikokianus*)—Considered by Nicholson, *Amer. Nurseryman* 166(6):83 (1987), the darkest flowered *Enkianthus*; unopened flowers are maroon with violet undertones; when open the color is dark brick red with shrimp pink streaks.

'Variegata'—Green and white variegated leaves, bright red stems, pink and red fall color, have observed in a New England garden, not overwhelming.

'Weston Pink Strain'—One of the pioneer nurseries of New England, Weston at Hopkinton, MA, has selected forms for good pink corolla coloration; their 1988 catalog had a wrap-around color photo of the deep, almost rose-pink form; by growing seedlings from these superior types they have increased the opportunity for better pink coloration.

PROPAGATION: Seed, see under *Calluna*, very easy to grow from seed, almost like beans; cuttings collected in late May rooted 80% without treatment; have rooted the species from July softwoods using 1000 ppm IBA-quick dip; overwinter survival after rooting may be a problem; tissue culture is commercially practiced. Nicholson reported mid-June cuttings, 5000 to 8000 ppm IBA, sand:perlite, mist provided the best rooting. The exception being *E. perulatus* which is tricky.

ADDITIONAL NOTES: Not all *Enkianthus* are created equal. Their floral beauty is really evident only upon close inspection. The interesting growth habit and fall color make them valuable landscape plants. The consistent red fall color forms should be propagated vegetatively. I have observed leaves of *E. campanulatus* dying off green and those of other plants a brilliant red. Excellent practical article on the genus was authored by Nicholson, *Amer. Nurseryman* 166(6):82–89 (1987).

      The genus comprises about 10 species, all found in Asia. The Japanese species are the hardiest and most commonly grown.

NATIVE HABITAT: Japan. Cultivated 1870.

RELATED SPECIES:

Enkianthus cernuus (Sieb. & Zucc.) Mak.

LEAVES: Alternate, simple, elliptic to rhombic-obovate or obovate-oblong, 3/4 to 1 1/2″ long, 1/2 to 2/3's as wide, acute or obtusish, crenate-serrulate, bright green above, glabrous, or slightly pubescent on midrib below.

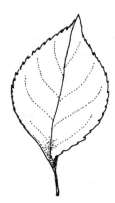

Enkianthus cernuus, (en-ki-an′thus sĕr′nū-us), is a rather pretty 5 to 10′ high, white-flowering shrub. Each flower is bell-shaped, 1/4″ long and borne in a nodding 10- to 12-flowered raceme in May. Variety *rubens* is a beautiful rich deep red-flowered form. Have seen in full flower at Biltmore Gardens in mid-May and was most impressed by the deep color. Not as large in habit, leaf or flower as the species. The red-flowered form is a plant of great beauty. Japan. Cultivated 1900. Zone 5 to 7.

Enkianthus deflexus (Griff.) Schneid. — Bent Enkianthus

LEAVES: Alternate, simple, oval, obovate or lanceolate, produced in a pseudo-whorled cluster at the end of the branch, 1 to 3″ long, 1/2 to 1 1/3″ wide, acute at apex, cuneate at base, serrulate, strigose on midrib beneath and sparingly hairy above and below.

Enkianthus deflexus, (en-ki-an′thus dē-fleks′us), Bent Enkianthus, is a narrow, upright shrub with layered, red branches reaching 10 to 20′ in height. Foliage is dark green in summer, scarlet in fall. Flowers are yellowish red with darker veins, 1/2″ diameter, May, borne in umbel-like racemes. Flowers are larger and showier than Redvein, however, not as hardy. Himalayas, western China. 1878. Zone 5 to 6.

Enkianthus perulatus (Miq.) Schneid. — White Enkianthus
LEAVES: Alternate, simple, narrow oval to obovate, clustered, 1 to 2″ long, 1/2 as wide, acute, sharply appressed-serrulate, glabrous and bright green above, pubescent on veins below; petiole—about 1/2″ long.

Enkianthus perulatus, (en-ki-an′thus per-ū-lā′tus), White Enkianthus, grows to 6′ high and about as wide. The foliage is bright green in summer, yellow to scarlet in fall. Flowers are white, urn-shaped, 1/3″ long, early May before the leaves in 3- to 10-flowered nodding umbel-like racemes. This is a neater shrub than the other species but hard to find in the trade. Koller, *Green Scene*, Sept. (1975), described a 60- to 70-year-old plant at the Morris Arboretum that was 9′ tall and 15′ wide. The branching pattern is somewhat tiered resulting in an oriental look. 'Compacta' is a dwarf cultivar only 18″ high and 25″ wide after 30 years; it only started to flower within the last few years. Japan. Introduced 1870. Zone 5 to 7.

Epigaea repens L. — Trailing Arbutus, Mayflower

LEAVES: Alternate, simple, evergreen, ovate or suborbicular to oblong-ovate, 1 to 3″ long, 3/4 to 2″ wide, rounded and mucronulate, rarely acute at apex, subcordate or rounded at base, ciliate, glossy dark green above, rough and covered with persistent stiff hairs on both surfaces; petiole—1/4 to 3/4″ long, pubescent.

Epigaea repens, (ep-i-jē′à rē′penz), Trailing Arbutus (Ericaceae), is, like *Andromeda polifolia*, one of the untamed members of Ericaceae. It resists cultivation but is deserving of every attempt that die-hard plantspeople make. The habit is one of a flat (4 to 6″ high by 2′ spread), evergreen mat which forms dense cover. In favorable locations it will carpet large areas but, alas, intrusion and disturbance by man puts it to rot. The foliage is leathery, of a rather dark glossy green, slightly bronzed by rusty hairs. The flowers are perfect, white to pink, 5/8″ long by 1/2″ wide, exceedingly fragrant, April, 4 to 6 together in a dense, terminal raceme. Fruit is a whitish, berry-like, 1/2″ diameter capsule. Extremely difficult to transplant and perpetuate; requires an acid, sandy or gravelly soil which has been mulched with decayed oak leaves or pine needles; best to move as a container-grown plant for the delicate roots are easily injured; shade or partial shade is advisable but freedom from man and his activities are even more necessary. This plant could be one where a mycorrhizal association plays a significant role in its survival. It could be transplanted specimens do not develop the fungal relationship that is necessary for their survival. A very dainty, delicate, evergreen ground cover that presents a challenge to every individual who considers him or herself a true plantperson. There is a cultivar termed 'Plena' which is a double-flowered type. 'Rosea' with pale pink flowers and 'Rubicunda' with dark pink flowers are reported. Asiatic species *E. asiatica* Maxim. and *E.* × *intertexta* Mullig. (*E. asiatica* × *E. repens*) are lesser known. Usually propagated from cuttings although large pieces of "sod" may be utilized. I am always on the lookout for the species during my forays into the "wilds." On the trail to Rabun Bald, Georgia, there are handsome colonies. Also, the memory lingers from my graduate days at UMASS, Amherst, where Bonnie and I discovered colonies during our walks. Native from Massachusetts to Florida west to Ohio and Tennessee. Introduced 1736. Zone 3 to 9. The state flower of Massachusetts.

Erica carnea L. (formerly *E. herbacea* L.) — Spring, Winter or Snow Heath
(ē-rī′kà kär′nē-à)

FAMILY: Ericaceae
LEAVES: Opposite (actually whorled), needle-like, evergreen, linear, 1/6 to 1/3″ long, acute to apiculate, in whorls of 4, margins revolute forming a channel beneath, lustrous bright to dark green above, needles forming a 90° angle with the stem.

SIZE: 6 to 10″ high, spreading to 20″; form cushion-like mounds that, when planted
    in mass, appear uniform like a ground cover.
HARDINESS: Zone 5 to 7.
HABIT: Neat, broad-spreading to trailing evergreen shrub.
RATE: Slow.
TEXTURE: Fine throughout the seasons.
LEAF COLOR: Bright to rich green, actually many shades of green; also cultivars
    with yellow, orange, and bronze foliage.
FLOWERS: Short of spectacular when maximized, perfect, cylindric, 4-lobed corolla,
    1/4″ long, anthers dark red, exserted, borne in 2 to 4″ long, leafy, one-sided
    racemes, winter–spring, colors from white to red, single and double; withers
    and persists enclosing the developing ovary; bees love them.
FRUIT: Dehiscent capsule with many seeds.
CULTURE: Most often available in small plastic cells, 3″ diameter to one-gallon
    containers; easily transplanted; requires moist, acid, high organic matter, low
    fertility, well-drained soils; full sun, semi-shade in hot climates; remove spent
    flowers; do not prune into leafless wood.
DISEASES AND INSECTS: None serious.
LANDSCAPE VALUE: Element in a rock garden, grouping, or ground cover use;
    absolutely beautiful and a March trip to Bells Cherrybank Gardens, Perth,
    Scotland, with great swaths of heath in rainbowrific colors turned me into a camera-crazed fanatic; alas
    I have numerous photographs and great memories, but can't grow the plant in our Georgia garden.
CULTIVARS: Over a hundred of varying sizes, foliage and floral colors; quite frightening what I don't know.
    Suggest locating a good nursery specializing in *Erica* and *Calluna* to determine availability. Rock Spray
    Nursery, Truro, MA has a handsome list. 'Springwood Pink' (with light pink flowers) and 'Springwood
    White' (white with brown anthers) are common in the United States.
PROPAGATION: Seeds like *Calluna* and *Rhododendron*; cuttings root readily when firm in mid to late summer,
    October through March; 1000 ppm IBA-quick dip, peat:perlite, mist, 100% rooting of *Erica* × *darleyensis*
    in late summer.
ADDITIONAL NOTES: With over 700 species of *Erica* any treatment is superficial. Even the taxonomists do not
    have the genus in good order. The needle-like leaves are almost always whorled (3 or 4, sometimes 5 or
    6) and pointing out from the stem. Over 90% of the species occur in South Africa. Wonderful collection
    in Edinburgh Botanic Garden and Bells Cherrybank Gardens, Perth, Scotland. Worthwhile article in *The
    Garden* 117(2):65–69 (1992) by John Battye describing the better cultivars of *Erica* and *Calluna* in the
    Wisley trials.
NATIVE HABITAT: Central and southern Europe. Introduced 1763.

RELATED SPECIES: This is a difficult genus to provide adequate coverage and readers of previous editions
    will note that I almost completely avoided the responsibility. Herein are presented those species that
    appear in United States nursery catalogs and gardens with some frequency.

Erica ciliaris L. — Dorset or Fringed Heath
LEAVES: In whorls of 3(4), evergreen, ovate, 1/8 to 1/6″ long, margin ciliate, revolute.

Erica ciliaris, (ē-rī′kȧ sil-i-ar′is), Dorset Heath, develops prostrate and ascending branches 24 to 32″ high. The
    young branches are densely pubescent. The rose-purple flowers occur in whorls of 3 on terminal, 2 to 5″
    long racemes. The corolla is urn-shaped, constricted at the mouth and 1/3 to 2/5″ long. Flowers in
    June–October. Culture as described for *E. carnea*. Plethora of cultivars with varying sizes, foliage and
    flower colors. Apparently not as hardy and easy to culture, at least in the United States, as *E. carnea* and
    E. × *darleyensis*. 'C.D. Eason' with reddish purple flowers is common. Common in European gardens.
    British Isles to Spain. Introduced 1773. Zone (6)7.

Erica cinerea L. — Twisted Heath
LEAVES: Usually in 3's, evergreen, 1/5 to 1/4″ long, linear, glabrous, margins revolute, lustrous green.

Erica cinerea, (ē-rī′kȧ sin-e′rē-ȧ), Twisted Heath, forms an evergreen, spreading shrub up to 2′ high. The
    young branches are minutely pubescent. The 1/4″ long, rose-purple flowers occur in 2 to 3″ long umbels
    or terminal racemes in June to September. Over 140 cultivars are known varying in growth habit, foliage
    and flower colors. Western Europe. Cultivated 1750. Zone 5 to 7.

Erica × *darleyensis* Bean, (ē-rī'kà där-lē-en'sis), has performed reasonably well in the Southeast. The habit is more shrub-like than *E. carnea* and plants grow 24″ high and form broad mounds. The leaves are up to 1/2″ long and white to rose-pink flowers appear in winter–early spring. A hybrid between *E. erigena* Ross., Irish Heath, and *E. carnea* that occurred around 1894. Over 20 cultivars have been selected. Zone 6 to 7. If one wants to grow a heath in the southeastern United States, this species represents a credible starting point.

Erica tetralix L. — Cross-leaved Heath
LEAVES: In whorls of 4, evergreen, 1/6 to 1/4″ long, lanceolate to linear-oblong, margins ciliate.

Erica tetralix, (ē-rī'kà tet'rà-liks), Cross-leaved Heath, grows 14 to 24″ high and forms a compact shrub. The 1/4″ long rosy flowers occur 4 to 12 together in umbel-like clusters in June–September. The stems are pubescent and glandular-hirsute. This is extremely cold hardy but not common in the United States. Over 30 cultivars are known. Rehder reported that it naturalized in Massachusetts. Northern and western Europe. Cultivated 1789. Zone 3 to 5.

Erica vagans L. — Cornish Heath
LEAVES: In whorls of 4 to 5, evergreen, 1/6 to 2/5″ long, spreading or deflexed, linear, dark green, glabrous.

Erica vagans, (ē-rī'kà vā'ganz), Cornish Heath, grows 20 to 30″ high and is more upright than *E. carnea*. The 1/4″ long, pinkish purple flowers occur in axillary pairs on slender, 1/3″ long pedicels on 3 to 6″ long, cylindric racemes in July to October. The yellowish gray stems are glabrous. Sometimes available through West Coast nurseries. Over 30 cultivars are known. 'Mrs. Maxwell' with red flowers is available. Western Europe from Ireland to Portugal. Cultivated 1811. Zone 5 to 7.

ADDITIONAL NOTES: Often it is extremely difficult to identify the various heath species. Hybrids are numerous and represent another source of new cultivars. The most common and horticulturally important crosses include: *E.* × *hiemalis* hort.; *E.* × *watsonii* Benth. (*E. ciliaris* × *E. tetralix*) with many cultivars; and *E.* × *williamsii* Druce. (*E. vagans* × *E. tetralix*) with several cultivars.

Most of the South African *Erica* species are probably not hardy below 25 to 28°F. *Sunset Western Garden Book* (1995) presents a valuable tabular treatment of West Coast adapted species and cultivars.

Eriobotrya japonica (Thunb.) Lindl. — Loquat,
Japanese Loquat
(ē-ri-ō-bot'ri-à jà-pon'i-kà)

FAMILY: Rosaceae
LEAVES: Alternate, simple, evergreen, broad oblanceolate to narrow obovate, variable in size, usually 6 to 9″(12″) long, 3 to 4″ wide, but up to 12″ long and 5″ wide, acuminate, cuneate, coarsely toothed, wrinkled, strongly set with parallel veins (ribs) about 1/4 to 1/2″ apart, lustrous dark green above and glabrous, lower surface covered with a grayish brown tomentum; petiole—short, 1/3″ long, woolly.
STEM: Stout, covered with a grayish woolly pubescence.
FLOWER: Inflorescences are formed the summer prior to flowering and provide a good identification feature.

SIZE: 15 to 25′ high and wide.
HARDINESS: Zone (7)8 to 10; leaves were severely injured in exposed locations after exposure to 0°F; killed at -3°F in Athens; plants that were well-hardened survived 4°F without injury; I keep reassessing the cold hardiness based on year-to-year performance; apparently, the species is slow to harden in fall, but if sufficient acclimatization takes place then a Zone 7 (0 to +10°F) designation is realistic.

HABIT: Small evergreen tree or more often a large, broad-spreading shrub forming a rounded outline; have observed it as an espalier on large expanses of brick.

RATE: Medium.

TEXTURE: Coarse.

LEAF COLOR: Lustrous dark green above; lower surface covered with a brownish tomentum.

FLOWERS: Perfect, off-white, fragrant, 1/2 to 3/4″ across, 5-petaled, borne in a 3 to 6″ long, stiff, terminal panicles, the entire structure covered with a dense, brown pubescence; flowers anytime from November to January; have seen it in flower during September in Savannah, GA.

FRUIT: Edible, pear-shaped, or oblong, 1 to 1 3/4″ long, yellow to orange pome with a large seed that ripens in April through June; in eastern Asia, southern Europe and the southern United States the plant is grown for its edible fruit; does not fruit in Athens–Atlanta area; farther south will set large quantities of fruit; have observed ripening fruit in late March on Georgia's Jekyll Island.

CULTURE: Easily grown, prefers moist, well-drained, loamy soil but will withstand coarse alkaline soils and a measure of drought; do not over fertilize as fireblight can be troublesome; withstands pruning quite well; site in full sun but will tolerate partial shade; probably should be grown in Zone 8 to 10.

DISEASES AND INSECTS: Fireblight.

LANDSCAPE VALUE: A beautiful evergreen shrub especially valued because of the lustrous dark green foliage; excellent for textural effects; has been utilized for street tree plantings in the South; makes a fine espalier against a wall; used as a lawn tree in Florida; displays good drought tolerance based on my observations during the summers of 1980 and 1981 in Athens, GA where one-inch of rain fell in four months and temperatures approached 90 to 100°F every day; have not seen fruit in middle South but does fruit heavily in lower South.

CULTIVARS:

'Advance'—More compact form with juicy fruits.

'Champagne'—Juicy, white-fleshed fruits, slightly astringent.

'Coppertone'—Copper new growth and retains leaf color into the season; 15′ high; listed as a hybrid of the species and *Rhaphiolepis*; could it be just a large growing *Rhaphiolepis*?

'Golden Nugget'—Large, abundant, pear-shaped, flavorful, yellow-orange fruit; this selection is commercially available.

'MacBeth'—Large fruit with yellow skin, creamy flesh.

'Thales'—Yellow-fleshed form, late ripening.

'Variegata'—Leaves variegated with white, rather attractive.

PROPAGATION: Seed requires no cold treatment; June–July cuttings have been rooted.

NATIVE HABITAT: China, Japan. Introduced 1784.

Erythrina crista-galli L. — Cockspur Coral-tree, Crybaby-tree

FAMILY: Fabaceae

LEAVES: Alternate, compound pinnate, 6″ by 3″ long leaflets, ovate-oblong to oblong-lanceolate, acute, rounded, glabrous above, sometimes with small prickles on lower midrib, bluish green.

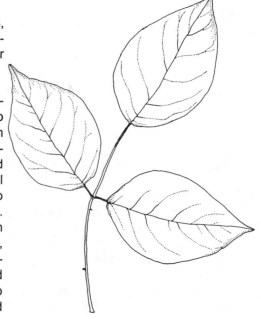

Erythrina crista-galli, (er-i-thrī′nȧ kris-tȧ gal′li), Cockspur Coral-tree, is noteworthy for its brilliant crimson (warm pink to wine red) flowers that appear on 16 to 24″ long racemes in summer–fall. Fruits average 2″ long by 3/5″ wide, constricted between seeds, each seed 1/2″ wide, rounded and brown. A dieback shrub along the Georgia coast; in central and southern Florida and the Gulf Coast, it grows 15 to 20′(25′) high. Prospers in any well-drained soil in full sun. South America. Root hardy in Zone 8. A southeastern United States, Mexican species, *E. herbacea* L., Cherokee-bean or Coral-bean, is hardier to Zone 7 (herbaceous), reaches 3 to 5′ in a single growing season, and produces 2 to 3′ long racemes laden with 2″ long, deep scarlet flowers. The woody pods average 8″ long and contain black-lined, scarlet seeds. A plant in a protected shady spot on the Georgia campus has survived −3°F and produces respectable flowers each late summer. 'Alba' with white flowers is known. *Erythrina × bidwillii* Lindl. a hybrid between the two species is also cultivated in southern gardens. Flowers are dark red, seemingly brighter red than either parent, in axillary clusters of 3 or in terminal racemes, each flower 2″ long by 1/2″ wide. I have always had trouble identifying the species but find the up to 5″ long, terminal, 3-lobed leaflets of *E. herbacea* a solid feature.

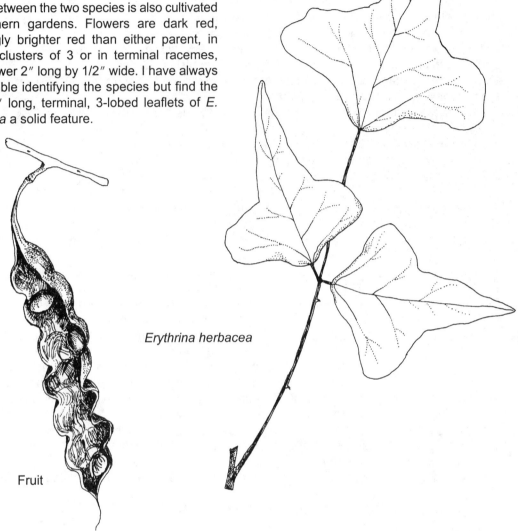

Fruit

Erythrina herbacea

Escallonia rubra (Ruiz. & Pav.) Pers.

FAMILY: Escalloniaceae or Grossulariaceae
LEAVES: Alternate, simple, evergreen, variable in shape, 1 to 2″ long, 5/8 to 1″ wide, acute or short acuminate, tapering at base, serrated, glossy dark green and glabrous above, speckled with resin glands beneath.
STEM: Young—hairy, often glandular and sticky.

Escallonia rubra, (es-ka-lō′ni-à rū′brà), is a large, evergreen shrub reaching 10 to 15′ high. The rose red to red flowers are produced in 1 to 4″ long, leafy panicles in June. This and the many *Escallonia* species (50 to 60) are common garden fixtures in English and European gardens. They prosper in full sun to partial shade in any well-drained soil. They are also extremely salt tolerant. I have seen numerous hedges fashioned from the various species and cultivars. My single attempt at cultivation in Athens resulted in defoliation, followed by releafing, followed by defoliation and death. Prefers a cooler, more even climate than that of the East Coast. *Escallonia × exoniensis* hort. 'Frades' with carmine-rose flowers is frequently listed by West Coast nurserymen. Also, 'Apple Blossom', 'Glory of Donard', 'Iveyi', 'Pink Princess' and 'Pride of Donard' are listed. *Escallonia rubra* is native to Chile. Introduced 1827. Zone 8 to 9(10). Best cultivated on the West Coast.

Eucalyptus L'Hérit — Eucalyptus
(ū-kȧ-lip′tus)
FAMILY: Myrtaceae

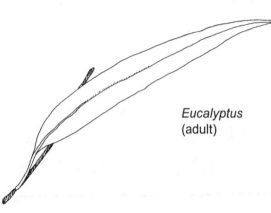

Eucalyptus
(juvenile)

Eucalyptus species have always fascinated me and their beautiful bark is one of the biological world's great treasures. Plant books from Australia and Tasmania present photographs of the species in the wild. For grandeur and size they remind of our Pacific Northwest rainforest trees. Over 500 species of trees and shrubs are found in Australia, Tasmania, Malaysia and the Phillippines. Plants show distinct juvenile and adult phases particularly in leaf development. The paired, perfoliate (rounded) leaves that are sold as dry materials represent the juvenile stage. Mature leaves are more often alternate with petioles, distinct midrib, forking veins from midrib or with parallel veins. Leaf colors are often gray, glaucous, blue to darker green. Additionally they are highly aromatic when bruised. Flowers are variable in shape, color, sex, and size. The few I have seen in flower were beautiful. The fruit is a capsule.

Eucalyptus
(adult)

Although some species are native to elevations of 6000 to 6500′, they are not cold hardy in the traditional sense of cool temperate angiosperms. Several species tolerate below zero temperatures in midwinter. Unfortunately, if the climate is mild like so in Zones 7b to 9, growth continues and plants do not acclimate. An early fall freeze or reciprocally late spring freeze will injure/kill plants. Every *Eucalyptus* species I have observed in Athens-Atlanta (Zone 7b) has been killed back. There are simply no large specimens. For the excellent juvenile, glaucous foliage, it is worth the effort. Simply don't expect large trees or shrubs.

All prefer full sun and well-drained soil. They are very drought tolerant when established. In California, I remember seeing them on the hillsides. Large specimens existed at Epcot Center, Orlando, FL, until the devastating cold of the early to mid-1980's. Large trees were rendered firewood. Propagation is primarily by seed that is provided cold, moist stratification for 1 to 2 months. Cuttings are difficult and demonstrate strong juvenile (rootable) and maturity (non-rootable) phases.

The most cold hardy species and those offered by a number of West Coast nurserymen include:

Scientific Name	Common Name	Zone
E. aggregata Deane & Maid.	Rodway Black Gum	8
E. archeri Maid. & Blakely	Alpine Cider Gum	7
E. camaldulensis Dehnh.	Red Gum	10
National champion is 132′ by 88′ in Boyce Thompson SW Arboretum, Arizona.		
E. camphora R. Bak.	Mountain Swamp Gum	7
E. cinerea F. Muell. ex Benth.	Corkscrew Eucalyptus, Silver Dollar Tree	8
E. citriodora Hook.	Lemon Scented Gum	10
E. coccifera Hook. f.**	Tasmanian Snow Gum	7
E. cordata Labill.**	Heartleaf Silver Gum	7
E. dalrympleana Maid.**	Mountain Gum	7
E. ficifolia F. Muell.	Red Flowering Gum	10
E. globulus Labill. 'Compacta'	Dwarf Blue Gum	9
National champion *E. globulus* is 165′ by 126′ at Fort Ross State Historical Park, Sonoma Co., California.		
E. gunnii Hook. f.*	Hardy Silver Gum, Cider Gum	(7)8
E. microtheca F. Muell.	Flouded Box	8
E. moorei 'Nana'		7
E. morrisbyi		8
E. neglecta Maid.	Omeo Round Leaved Gum	7
E. nicholii Maid. & Blakely	Willow-leaved Gum, Peppermint Gum	8

Scientific Name	Common Name	Zone
E. niphophila Maid. & Blakely* (*E. pauciflora* Sieber ex Spreng. subsp. *niphophila*)		
	Snow Gum	7
E. nortonii	Long-leaf Box	8
E. nova-angliae	New England Peppermint	7
E. oreades	Blue Mountain's Ash	7
E. parvifolia Cambage**	Small-leaf Gum	7
E. perriniana F. Muell. ex Rodway**	Spinning Gum	7
E. polyanthemos Schauer	Red Box Gum, Silver Dollar Tree	9
E. rudis Endl.	Desert Gum	
E. sideroxylon Cunn. ex Woolls	Ironbark	9
E. stellulata Sieber ex. DC.	Black Sally	8
E. subcrenulata Maid. & Blakely	Alpine Yellow Gum	7
E. torquata Luehm.	Coral Gum	9
E. urnigera Hook. f.*	Urn Gum	7
E. viminalis Labill.*	Ribbon Gum	8

Based on European literature and observations of the species in European gardens those plants marked with a single * could be considered the most hardy followed by the double **. The hardiness zones were assembled from West Coast nursery catalogs and *will not* reflect eastern or southeastern performance. In fact, *E. gunnii* is listed as hardy to +10°F, 0°F, and –10°F by three different nurseries. The difference translates to 20°F hardiness. I have serious doubts. My best advice is to give several of the hardier species a test.

Jim Gardiner, *The Garden* 121(1):15–17 (1996), presents a worthy synopsis of Wisley's *Eucalyptus* collection on Battleston Hill. I have walked the area on many occasions and am always enamored by the lovely barks and blue-green leaves. An Award of Garden Merit (AGM) is given by The Royal Horticultural Society to "plants of outstanding garden value." *Eucalyptus coccifera, E. dalrympleana, E. globulus, E. gunnii, E. parvifolia* and *E. niphophila* have received the AGM.

Eucommia ulmoides Oliv. — Hardy Rubber Tree
(ū-kom′i-à ul-moy′dēz)

FAMILY: Eucommiaceae
LEAVES: Alternate, simple, 3 to 6″ long, about 1/2 as wide, elliptic or ovate to oblong-ovate, acuminate, broad-cuneate or rounded, serrate, lustrous dark green and glabrous above and slightly rugose at maturity; leaf when torn exhibits rubbery substance.
BUDS: Imbricate, sessile, ovoid, chestnut brown, 1/4″ long, terminal lacking, ending in a leaf.
STEM: Stout, bloomy, olive-brown; pith—chambered; bark when stripped exhibiting elastic (rubbery) strings.

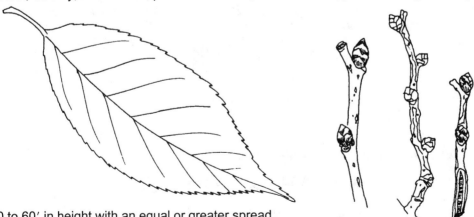

SIZE: 40 to 60′ in height with an equal or greater spread.
HARDINESS: Zone (4)5 to 7; has survived –20°F at the Secrest Arboretum.
HABIT: Rounded to broad-spreading tree of dapper outline at maturity; in youth somewhat pyramidal in outline.
RATE: Medium, 30′ over a 20 year period.
TEXTURE: Medium in all seasons.

BARK: On old trees, ridged-and-furrowed, of a gray-brown color and reasonably attractive; in China the bark is valued as a tonic and for its medicinal properties.

LEAF COLOR: Lustrous dark green in summer (very handsome); fall color is nonexistent as the leaves fall green or a poor yellowish green.

FLOWERS: Dioecious, inconspicuous and ornamentally unimportant, staminate clusters of brown stamens; female—consisting of a single pistil.

FRUIT: Capsule-like with compressed wings, 1 1/2″ long, oval-oblong, notched at apex, 1-seeded, like a large, waxy, fleshy elm fruit.

CULTURE: Transplants readily; very soil tolerant; resists drought; pH adaptable; full sun.

DISEASES AND INSECTS: None serious; this is debatable as I have observed, as have others, branch decline/dieback that has been attributed to disease; Morton Arboretum, Lisle, IL reported significant branch dieback in their collections.

LANDSCAPE VALUE: Excellent shade tree for many areas; outstanding summer foliage that is completely free of pests; excellent for Midwest; never has become popular and is doubtfully as urban tolerant as given credit.

PROPAGATION: Seeds require 2 to 3 months cold moist stratification; the only published report indicates that chloromone (1-naphthyl-acetamine) induced 57% rooting from a 50-year-old tree and 85% from an unspecified plant; cuttings should be taken just as the new growth is forming.

ADDITIONAL NOTES: Only rubber producing tree for the central and northern parts of the country. Rubber content is about 3% on a dry weight basis, however, the extraction is difficult. Ulmoides refers to the leaf shape which is similar to that of elm, *Ulmus*. Barker, *J. Arboriculture* 10(8):233–235 (1984), built an impressive case for the species in urban areas and reported that 34 trees planted in 6′ wide tree lawns in Cleveland, OH in 1952 were 25 to 30′ high with an average 14″ trunk diameter in 32 years. His data indicate that the tree will suffer some tip dieback at -20°F. Also tree is adaptable to soils ranging above pH 7 but intolerant to poor drainage. During my rather extensive travels, I have seen very few Hardy Rubber Trees that might be termed outstanding specimens.

NATIVE HABITAT: Central China. Introduced 1896.

Eucryphia glutinosa (Poepp. & Endl.) Baill. — Nirrhe

FAMILY: Eucryphiaceae

LEAVES: Opposite, compound pinnate, evergreen to deciduous, 3 to 5 leaflets, each 1 1/2 to 2 1/2″ long, ovate to oval, regularly serrated, lustrous dark green.

Eucryphia glutinosa, (ū-kriph′ē-à glū-ti-nō′sà), Nirrhe, is of importance in the Pacific Northwest and British Columbia. The habit is that of a small tree or large shrub 10 to 25′ high. The leaves may turn orange and red in autumn. The white, 4-petaled, 2 1/2″ diameter flowers with numerous yellow stamens occur singly or in pairs from the leaf axils in July–August. The fruit is a woody, 1/2 to 3/4″ long, pear-shaped capsule. Requires moist, well-drained, acid soil, mulch, no root disturbance. Site in partial shade and protect from desiccating winds. 'Flora Plena' has double, white flowers; 'Nana' is more compact than the species. *Eucryphia* × *nymansensis* Bausch (*E. cordifolia* × *E. glutinosa*) produces simple (from *E. cordifolia*) and compound pinnate, evergreen leaves. Flowers 2 to 3″ diameter, honey-scented, white. Upright habit to 20′. Specimens over 50′ are common in southwestern England. 'Nymansay' is the seedling selection from Nymans Garden, West Sussex that is described. 'Mt Usher' comes from Mt. Usher Garden, County Wicklow, Ireland. 'Rostrevor', representing *E.* × *intermedia* Bausch (*E. glutinosa* × *E. lucida*), has mixed leaf types, 1 1/2″ diameter flowers. *Eucryphia glutinosa* is native to central Chile. Zone 8. *Eucryphia cordifolia* Cav., central and southern Chile. Zone 9. *Eucryphia lucida* (Labill.) Baill., Tasmania. Zone 8. See Wright, *The Plantsman* 5:169–178 (1983), for a discussion of the species.

Euonymus alatus (Thunb.) Sieb. — Winged Euonymus
(ū-on′i-mus à-lā′tus)

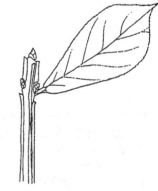

FAMILY: Celastraceae

LEAVES: Opposite to subopposite, simple, elliptic to obovate, 1 to 3″ long, 1/2 to 1 1/4″ wide, acute, cuneate, finely and sharply serrate, medium to dark green, glabrous or somewhat downy beneath; petiole—1/12″ long.

BUDS: Imbricate, green-brown-red, 6 to 8 pairs of bud scales, conical, ovoid, acute, glabrous, strongly divergent, actually breaking the continuous wing.

STEM: Green to brown with 2- to 4-armed, corky wings (prominent), wings 1/4 to 1/2″ broad, generally the more vigorous shoots have the biggest wings, glabrous.

SIZE: 15 to 20′ in height, similar in spread; here is a classic example of how the size descriptions given in the literature do not adequately estimate the actual landscape size; usually listed at 9 to 10′, this shrub defies description and develops into a 15 to 20′ well-preserved specimen.

HARDINESS: Zone 4 to 8(9), perhaps 9 on West Coast.

HABIT: Mounded to horizontal, spreading, flat-topped shrub, usually broader than high; extremely effective and architectural in the winter landscape; does not develop the "garbage can" look of many shrubs; always an aristocrat even under the most demanding of conditions; makes a rather handsome small tree if pruned properly.

RATE: Slow; produces one major growth flush in spring and shuts down; need to have plants primed with fertilizer so spring growth flush is maximized.

TEXTURE: Medium in leaf; medium in winter; the distinctive corky-winged branches are very effective in the winter landscape; beautiful when snow-capped as the flakes settle in the crevices of the wings.

LEAF COLOR: Flat medium to dark green, very clean looking foliage, fall color is usually a brilliant red; one of the most consistent fall coloring shrubs, seldom disappointing; colors as well in the Midwest and South as it does in the eastern states; over the years I have seen a million(?) plants in fall color; interestingly, although clonal (or is it), variation in degree of red coloration is evident; a few nurserymen have selected for superior fall color and growth habit; leafs out in early spring, lovely fresh green.

FLOWERS: Ornamentally unimportant, perfect, yellow-green, 3-flowered cyme, May to early June, early April in Athens; each flower 4-petaled, 1/4″ or larger, rounded petals.

FRUIT: A 1/4 to 1/3″ long capsule, red, September through late fall, not particularly showy for fruits are borne under the foliage; seed is actually the ornamental part of fruit as it possesses an orange-red seed coat (aril) which is exposed when the capsule dehisces; by the time the leaves have fallen many of the fruits have also abscised thus minimizing the ornamental quality; effect may vary from year-to-year; capsule normally 4-lobed, often only 1- to 2-lobed, one-seeded.

CULTURE: Easily transplanted balled-and-burlapped or from a container; very adaptable plant tolerating widely divergent soils; sun although performs well in heavy shade and still develops good fall color; not tolerant of water logged soils, best growth is achieved in well-drained soils; pH adaptable; withstands heavy pruning; shows stress in droughty soils; root system is quite fibrous and develops a mass of roots at the soil surface; ideally should be watered and/or mulched in hot, dry situations.

DISEASES AND INSECTS: None serious; does not contract scale; have seen a leaf anthracnose in the South especially on container-grown plants that were overhead watered; nematodes, two-spotted mites.

LANDSCAPE VALUE: Unlimited and, therefore, overused; excellent for hedging, in groups, as a specimen plant, borders, screening, massing; plants used near water are very effective in the fall where the brilliant red foliage color is reflected off the water; makes an excellent foundation plant because of horizontal lines, clean foliage, and interesting stem characters; still one of the finest landscape plants for American gardens and new selections add some diversity to the typical form; in early November I chanced upon a spectacular hedge in flaming fall color at Hershey Gardens, Hershey, PA; the air was cool, the sunlight rich, the bluegrass green, the sky blue and the hedge rich almost fluorescent red . . . a sight to behold.

CULTIVARS:

'Angelica'—Almost twice as dense and compact as the species with vibrant red fall color; also listed as 'Angelica Compactus', from Angelica Nurseries, Kennedyville, MD.

'Apterus' (var. *apterus* Reg.)—Not clear on the taxonomy but this is essentially a wingless form of the species; plant in the Arnold Arboretum produced abundant fruit; not common in commerce; there is a 10′ high, 18′ wide specimen at Wisley Gardens.

Chicago Fire® ('Timber Creek')—A more compact form (8 to 10′ by 6 to 8′ in 15 years) with reputed superior red (rich crimson red) fall color; it is difficult to beat 'Compactus' so this form is either outstanding or a biological figment of the introducer's imagination; introduced through the Chicagoland Grows® Program; one photo that I saw did not outdo a good 'Compactus'; selection by Scott Lindemann, Woodstock, IL, in 1979, described as producing abundant quantities of red-orange fruit.

'Compactus'—Corky wings not as pronounced, sometimes almost absent, appears to be a variable trait; branches more slender and more densely borne; overall rounded outline, 10′, definitely not a small diminutive form; makes an excellent hedge or screen without pruning; not as hardy as the species, will be injured in severe (–25°F) winters; also described is 'Compactus Coles Selection' with better branching, more compact, slower growth, 6 to 8′ high, Zone 4.

'Compactus'

Fire Ball™—Selection of 'Compactus' by Cole Nursery for tighter branching habit, superior hardiness compared to species, and rich fall color, 6'; is this the same as 'Compactus Coles Selection'?

'Microphyllus'—Smaller in all its parts, particularly leaves and stems, lower spreading growth habit, good fall color, saw at Hillier Nursery.

'Monstrosus'—Corkier wings, vigorous, not positive about the validity of this cultivar.

'Nordine Strain'—Named after Mr. Roy Nordine, former propagator, Morton Arboretum; selected from seedlings of the Korean strain; more compact than species and branches close to the ground; also more fruitful; considerably hardier than 'Compactus', possibly Zone 3b.

'October Glory'—A bushy, compact, 6 to 8' high form of *E. alatus* with brilliant red fall color; a Princeton introduction, possibly no longer in commerce.

'Rudy Haag'—A more compact form than 'Compactus' with pinkish rose to red fall color; 15-year-old plants being 4 to 5' high and wide; Bernheim Arboretum has a fine planting of this selection; no doubt will become extremely popular with exposure; in the last edition I commented about the potential for this plant and several nurserymen are starting to produce large numbers; Mr. Don Shadow, who is usually ahead of the pack with "new" plants has significant production of this form; my opinion has not changed about this cultivar; it will become a dominant plant in the market place.

PROPAGATION: Seeds should be cleaned and provided 1 to 3 months cold moist stratification; cuttings, anytime in leaf, 1000 ppm to 3000 ppm IBA-quick dip; I have had 100% success every time with 'Compactus' and 'Rudy Haag'; the plant develops a deep bud rest and cannot practically be induced to grow by anything but cold treatment; I have found 90 to 120 days at 40°F sufficient to induce bud break of terminal and lateral buds; any time period less than this has resulted in only terminal bud growth or no growth; would be a good plant to experiment with for inducing continuous growth as it grows slowly and in short flushes; interestingly, hardwood cuttings did not root, in fact, no callus was evident. I asked Hines Nursery, Houston, TX why the plant was not in their inventory. They said there was insufficient chilling to induce budbreak and sustain growth.

ADDITIONAL NOTES: Birds have seeded the plant in shady woods in some northern gardens. Although not wild like the honeysuckle it can move. Behnke and Ebinger, *Trans. Illinois State Acad. Science* 82:1–3 (1989), reported *E. alatus* being a dominant escaped shrub in their test plot. Recent correspondence indicated that the species and/or 'Compactus' were seeding freely in woodlands in the Midwest and East.

NATIVE HABITAT: Northeastern Asia to central China. Introduced about 1860.

Euonymus americanus L. — American Euonymus, Strawberry-bush

LEAVES: Opposite, simple, lance-ovate to lanceolate, 1 1/2 to 3 1/2″ long, 1/3 to 1 1/4″ wide, acuminate, cuneate, glabrous, crenate-serrate, flat medium green, turning yellow-green to shades of red in fall; petiole—1/12 to 1/8″ long.

BUDS: Imbricate, 3/16 to 1/4″ long, ovoid-conical, glabrous.

STEM: Slender, 4-sided with ridges running from side of leaf scar resulting in squarish stem, olive green, grainy; pith—white, solid.

Euonymus americanus, (ū-on'i-mus à-mer-i-kā'nus), Strawberry-bush, will never take the place of its aristocratic brother, *E. alatus*, but in fruit elicits tremendous interest and for that reason is given ink in this book. It is a most obscure plant until September–October when the warty, scarlet capsules open to display scarlet seeds. One of its common names, "Hearts-a-Burstin," is derived from this character. Strawberry-bush is a loose, suckering, 4 to 6' high, green-stemmed shrub that resides in the shadows of the forest giants. The 1/3″ diameter, greenish, 5-petaled (unusual for *Euonymus*, usually 4-petaled) flowers appear singly or in three's in May–June. The 1/2 to 3/4″ diameter, 3- to 5-lobed, warty, capsular, red fruits follow. The seed coat is bright red; the seeds white tinged yellow. Nice plant for naturalizing. A plant in heavy fruit is beautiful. I am amazed that a native plant tucked away in the recesses of a remote forest can be infected by *Euonymus* scale. This species is particularly susceptible and garden worthiness may be questionable. Have seen tree forms in north Florida with 2″ diameter trunks. Mr. Charles Webb, Superior

Trees, Lee, FL, has a 12 to 15′ high, obovate-crowned form with slender branches and narrow leaves. As I witnessed it in early October, 1997, the first impulse was to provide a cultivar name and go to market. Seeds are doubly dormant and 3 months warm:3 months cold are recommended. Cuttings will root or, for a few plants, simply divide the plant. Native from New York south to Florida and west to Texas. Introduced 1697. Zone (5)6 to 9.

Euonymus europaeus L. — European Euonymus, Common Spindle Tree
(ū-on′i-mus ū-rō-pē′us)

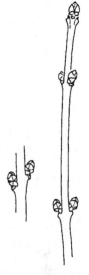

LEAVES: Opposite, simple, elliptic-ovate to lance-oblong to obovate, 1 to 3 1/2″ long, 1/3 to 1 1/4″ wide, acuminate, cuneate, crenate-serrate, dull dark green, glabrous; petiole—1/4 to 1/2″ long.

BUDS: Imbricate, plump, resembling Norway Maple bud, greenish often tinged with red.

STEM: Slender, green-red, glabrous the first year, usually becoming light gray-brown the second.

FRUIT: Capsule, 4-lobed, 1/2 to 3/4″ wide, pink to red, aril orange, seed white.

SIZE: 12 to 30′ high and 10 to 25′ wide.

HARDINESS: Zone 4 to 7, doubtfully suited for the South.

HABIT: Narrow upright shrub or tree when young, broadening with age, taller than broad at maturity, usually rounded in outline at maturity.

RATE: Medium to fast.

TEXTURE: Medium in leaf and winter.

LEAF COLOR: Dull dark green in summer; fall color varies from yellow-green to yellow to a good reddish purple; one of the first plants to leaf out in spring, early April in Urbana, IL.

FLOWERS: Perfect, 4-petaled, yellowish green, 1/2″ across, May, 3- to 5-flowered, 1 to 1 1/2″ long cyme, not showy.

FRUIT: Dehiscent capsule, smooth, 1/2 to 3/4″ across, of pink to red color, 4-lobed, opening to expose orange seeds; September into November; quite attractive in fruit.

CULTURE: Transplant balled-and-burlapped; tolerant of most soils as long as they are well-drained; pH adaptable; full sun or partial shade; very tough and tolerant.

DISEASES AND INSECTS: See under *E. fortunei*; the most significant problem is scale and all the tree species on the Illinois campus and virtually everywhere else I have encountered them were affected; timing of spray application is very important in the control of scale; should be applied when the young crawlers are moving about; fine oil (Sunspray GE at 2 or 3%) in May–August was effective; based on a great number of observations I do not believe there is a tree *Euonymus* that is not susceptible to scale; I have seen entire collections in arboreta and botanical gardens that were laden with the insects; the whitish scales infest the leaves, stems and older trunks and even the fruits; if not controlled they can devastate a planting; I hesitate to recommend these susceptible types because of the scale problem; virus has been reported. See *Phytopathology* 80:134–140 (1990).

LANDSCAPE VALUE: All of the tree *Euonymus* can be used in groupings, screens and massings; they do not make good specimens simply because of lack of ornamental characters; their flowers are not showy and the principle landscape value resides in the fruits; in the Morton Arboretum this species has been spread by birds and is something of a weed.

CULTIVARS:

‘Albus’ or var. *albus*—Fruit white; does not produce the rich effect of the species but is very striking in contrast with it.

‘Aldenhamensis’—Brilliant, large pink capsule borne on longer, more pendulous stalks than the species; more fruitful than the species; appeared sometime before 1922.

var. *intermedius*—A heavy fruiter with bright red capsules; supposedly enormous crops of fruits.

‘Nana’—Compact form, 2 1/2′ by 2′ after 8 years from a rooted cutting; more tender than the species; flowers and fruit have not been observed.

‘Red Ace’—Bears heavy crops of pink-red fruits; orange-red fall color; 15′.

'Red Cascade'—A free-fruiting form; there is a cultivar called 'Red Caps' which, according to several individuals in the Midwest, has proven the best of the tree *Euonymus*; rosy red capsules with orange seeds occur in abundance, whether 'Red Caps' ('Red Caps' was selected by University of Nebraska for persistent, bright red fruits) and 'Red Cascade' are synonyms for the same plant is not known by this author; Wyman noted that the color of the fruit may vary slightly, but when viewed from a distance there is little to choose among them, unless one is very particular about the exact shade of red or pink color in the fruits.

Other cultivars exist particularly in Europe where selections have been made over the centuries. Its garden merits are not outstanding and it does not belong in the upper ranks of small trees.

PROPAGATION: Seed should be stratified at 68 to 77°F for 60 to 90 days followed by 32 to 50°F for 60 to 120 days; cuttings should be taken in June and July and treated with IBA.

NATIVE HABITAT: Europe to western Asia. Escaped from cultivation in the United States.

RELATED SPECIES:

Euonymus atropurpureus Jacq. — Eastern Wahoo
(ū-on'i-mus at-rō-pĕr-pū'rē-us)

LEAVES: Opposite, simple, elliptic to ovate-elliptic, 1 1/2 to 5″ long, 3/4 to 2 1/4″ wide, acuminate, serrulate, dark green, pubescent beneath; petiole—1/3 to 2/3″ long.

BUDS: Small, green tinged red, appressed, with 5 to 6 scales.

STEM: Slender, greenish, glabrous, usually more or less (mostly less) 4-angled, often with slight, corky lines.

FLOWERS: Dark purple, 4-petaled, 1/3″ diameter, May–June, 7- to 15-flowered in 2- to 3-branched cymes.

FRUIT: Smooth, 3/5″ diameter capsule, deeply 4-lobed, crimson, glabrous, seed brown with scarlet aril; attractive in fruit.

GROWTH HABIT: Large shrub or small tree with wide, flat-topped, irregular crown, 12 to 24′ high; seldom seen in gardens; have observed reddish purple fall color in early November, Cincinnati.

NATIVE HABITAT: New York to Florida, west to Minnesota, Nebraska, Oklahoma and Texas. Introduced 1756. Zone 4 to 9.

Euonymus bungeanus Maxim. — Winterberry Euonymus
(ū-on'i-mus bun-jē-ā'nus)

LEAVES: Opposite to subopposite, simple, elliptic-ovate to elliptic-lanceolate, 2 to 4″ long, 3/4 to 1 3/4″ wide, long acuminate, broad-cuneate at base, serrulate, glabrous, light to medium green; petiole—1/3 to 1″ long.

BUDS: Terminal—unique arrangement, outer bud scales upright creating a stockade-like appearance around meristem; lateral—imbricate, appressed, green-red-brown.

STEM: Slender, often weeping, greenish, glabrous, almost round, often with slight corky lines.

FLOWERS: Yellowish (green), 1/4″ diameter, anthers purple, produced in 1 to 2″ long cymes, 4-petaled, May, not showy.

FRUIT: Smooth capsule, deeply 4-lobed, yellowish to pinkish white, usually pink, seeds white, seeds white or pinkish with orange aril, usually open at apex; is beautiful in fruit but unfortunately very susceptible to scale.

GROWTH HABIT: Rounded, small shrub or tree with pendulous branches to 18 to 24' in height. During my Illinois years, I watched a particularly fine specimen slowly deteriorate due to scale infestation. In rich pink fruit the tree was handsome.

ADDITIONAL NOTES: This species does not appear quite as susceptible to scale. Interestingly, Dr. Waddell Barnes, discovered a specimen tree that performed quite well over the years in Macon, GA. Cuttings have been rooted. Handsome specimens at Missouri Botanical Garden with deeply ridged-and-furrowed bark. Variety *semipersistens* has leaves and fruits which remain late in fall; var. *pendulus* has weeping branchlets.

NATIVE HABITAT: Northern China and Manchuria. Introduced 1883. Zone 4 to 7.

Euonymus hamiltonianus Wallich. var. *sieboldianus* (Bl.) Hara (*Euonymus yedoensis* Koehne) — Yeddo Euonymus
(ū-on′i-mus ham-il-tō-nē-ā′nus sē-bōl-dē-ā′nus)

LEAVES: Opposite, simple, obovate to obovate-oblong, sometimes elliptic, 2 to 5″ long and 1 3/4 to 2 1/2″ broad, abruptly acuminate, broad-cuneate, crenate-serrulate, dark green in summer, reddish purple in fall; petiole—1/4 to 3/4″ long.

BUDS: Similar to *E. europaeus*; terminal bud looks something like Norway Maple bud; greenish in summer, purplish in winter.

STEM: Stout, coarse compared to other shrub/tree species, greenish red, glabrous.

FLOWERS: Numerous, pale green, 1/3″ across, 4-merous.

FRUIT: Capsule, deeply 4-lobed, pinkish purple, aril orange, seed white, usually closed or with small opening; have read that seeds are blood red on var. *sieboldianus*.

GROWTH HABIT: Coarse-textured, small tree or shrub, much coarser than other species. Smaller than other shrub/tree species, 10 to 15' high. Tremendously susceptible to scale.

ADDITIONAL NOTES: *E. hamiltonianus* is confused and the available literature does not make things any more clear. Yeddo Euonymus appears as described above, as its own species, *E. yedoensis*, or the variety *yedoensis* under *E. hamiltonianus*. It can be rather attractive especially in fall but the scale susceptibility prevents any recommendation for garden use unless one is willing to spray at regular intervals.

NATIVE HABITAT: Japan, Korea. Introduced 1865. Zone 4 to 6(7).

Euonymus fortunei (Turcz.) Hand.-Mazz. — Wintercreeper Euonymus
(ū-on′i-mus fôr-tū′nē-ī)

LEAVES: This is a variable species because it sports (mutates) so readily and the range of leaf types produced is almost endless. The species has opposite, ever-green leaves, usually 1″ long or less, with crenate-serrate margins and leaves of dark green color prominently marked with silver veins. A non-fruiting form.

SIZE: 4 to 6 to 12″ if used as a ground cover, but can climb and scramble 40 to 70' when placed on a structure.

HARDINESS: Zone (4)5 to 8 and 9; not happy in Zone 4 unless provided snow cover or winter shade; Dr. Ed Hasselkus, University of Wisconsin, reported that none of the variegated forms are hardy in Madison, WI.

HABIT: Evergreen ground cover or high climbing, true clinging vine; many of the adult types make 1 1/2 to 3'(6'), mounding, woody, evergreen shrubs.

RATE: Fast.

TEXTURE: Medium-fine to medium depending on cultivar.

LEAF COLOR: Depends on cultivar but the species as I interpret it has small leaves less than 1″ long, the leaves are dark green almost bluish green with silver-nerved veins; the morphology changes considerably from the juvenile to the adult forms; very difficult to pinpoint exact leaf characteristics.

FLOWERS: Only on adult types; perfect, greenish white, 4-merous, 1/4″ diameter, June–July, axillary cymes; not particularly showy.

FRUIT: Dehiscent capsule, 1/3″ diameter, usually with a pinkish to reddish color which opens to expose the seeds which have an orange aril (fleshy seed coat), October–November and often persisting.

CULTURE: Extremely easy to culture, container-grown and transplants readily; tolerant of most soils except swampy, extremely wet conditions; tolerates full sun and heavy shade; pH adaptable.

DISEASES AND INSECTS: Anthracnose, crown gall (bacterial disease of considerable importance), leaf spots, powdery mildews, aphids, thrips, and scales (these have proved lethal on many plantings especially those containing 'Vegetus', 'Coloratus', and the tree species such as *E. europaeus*, *E. bungeanus* and *E. hamiltonianus* var. *sieboldianus*); many plantings have been ruined by scale (*Unaspis euonymi*).

LANDSCAPE VALUE: Multitudinous depending on cultivar; ground cover, vine, wall cover, low hedge, massing and groupings; tremendous variation occurs as a result of vegetative mutations; the number of variegated cultivars has exceeded the wildest imaginations of a rock star; yellow margins are thick, thin, yellow blotches occur on the inside and entire leaves are yellow; from 17' away they all look the same; whenever I think of yellow *E. fortunei* my mind drifts to a particularly oppressive and depressing mass planting at Lucent Technologies off I-85 heading to Atlanta; a yellow piece of plastic on the bank would have been as effective; an occasional plant for spot color in a border or rock garden is acceptable; landscapers are having second thoughts about wholesale use because of decline in heavy wet soils, leaf diseases and scale.

CULTIVARS:

'Acutus'—A rapidly growing, dark green-foliaged form that is relatively prostrate; may be more than one clone of this in the trade.

'Andy'—Described as a var. *carrieri* selection; slow-growing shrub with large, green leaves with white margins that turn rosy pink in cold weather; a Weston Nursery introduction.

'Azusa'—Ground cover type with prostrate branches, small dark green leaves with lighter colored veins; underside of foliage turns intense maroon in winter.

'Berryhillii'—Upright form with leaves 1 1/2 to 2" long; 5-year-old plants are 2 1/2' tall, definitely upright, and the leaves are evergreen; plant at Arnold was 7 to 8' high and 6' wide; looks like it might have some *E. kiautschovicus* blood based on leaf shape and growth habit.

'Canadale Gold'—Large, light green leaves are bordered with golden yellow, the color is deeper on new growth; forms a sturdy compact plant; variegation is substantial.

'Canadian Gold'—Low mounding shrub, 3 to 4' high, bright green foliage with gold edges; vigorous.

'Canadian Variegated'—Forms an 18" by 3', compact shrub with small, waxy green leaves strikingly edged in white; this is probably the same as 'Harlequin'.

'Carrierei'—Semi-shrub form or climbing if supported; leaves glossy deep green about 2" long; fruiting freely; adult state of var. *radicans*, may grow 6 to 8'; also listed as var. *carrierei*; flowers 4-parted, 5 or more at end of a slender stalk (cyme), fruit 1/3" across, green with red tinge, seed with a yellow-orange aril.

var. *coloratus* (Rehd.) Rehd., f. (often listed as 'Color-atus')—Vigorous ground cover form, foliage is a deep glossy green and turns plum-purple in the winter; there seem to be several clones in the nursery trade; some clones do not develop the good plum-purple to purple-red color on both leaf surfaces, while others show excellent color over the entire plant; have observed more scale on this, especially in South, in recent years.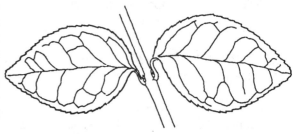

 Leaves: Without the prominent venation, usually lustrous dark green, 1 to 2" long, changing to reddish purple during the winter; this variety is variable for often the underside of the leaf is purple and the upper portion green; usually non-fruiting; supposedly introduced to the United States from Japan in 1914.

'Dart's Blanket'—A relative newcomer in America, found in Holland; thick, waxy, 1 to 2" long, dark green leaves; supposedly displays excellent salt tolerance; use as a ground cover near the ocean or where deicing salts present a problem; tends to be wide-spreading and grows to 16" in height; the leaves become bronzed in autumn and purplish red beneath; a juvenile form first distributed in 1969; considered an improvement on 'Coloratus'; also 'Dart's Carpet', 'Dart's Dab,' and 'Dart's Ideal' have been described.

'Duet'—Low-growing, vigorous form with pale yellow variegation.

'Dwarf Form'—A creeping selection with very fine foliage; from Camellia Forest Nursery, Chapel Hill, NC.

'Emerald Beauty'—Grows 6', spreads 8 to 10' and bears abundant pink capsules with orange seeds.

'Emerald Charm'—Shrub of erect habit to 3'; leaves broad elliptic, glossy green on both surfaces; fruits yellowish white with orange seed coats; adult form introduced by Corliss Brothers, Ipswich, MA.

'Emerald Cushion'—Dwarf, mounded form, dense branching habit, holds rich green foliage, 12" by 18".

'Emerald Delight'—Possesses the largest leaves of any of the Emerald series, and some of the richest foliage color on any broadleaf evergreen; leaves emerge light green edged with yellow; later becoming intense green with creamy borders; a vigorous spreading plant; distributed by Conard-Pyle.

'Emerald Gaiety'—Small, erect form of dense branching habit, distinguished by the pronounced irregular white margin on the deep green, 3/4 to 1 3/4″ diameter, rounded leaves, margin becomes pink-tinged in winter, 4 to 5′; will climb if planted next to a structure; 6′ high plant at Wisley was flowering in June, 1994.

'Emerald 'n Gold'—Low-growing, tight branching habit, 1 1/2 to 2′ high (have seen larger—3′); foliage glossy dark green with yellow margins, 1 to 1 1/2″ long, leaves turn pink-red in cold weather.

'Emerald Leader'—Similar to 'Emerald Beauty' in fruitfulness but grows to 5′ with a 30″ spread.

'Emerald Pride'—Small, erect form with lustrous dark green foliage and a close branching habit, 4 to 5′, spreading 42″.

'Emerald Surprise'—An unusual foliage mixture of green, gold and creamy white on an upright-branched shrub; introduced by Conard-Pyle, although have seen Corliss Nursery, Ipswich, MA associated with this introduction; also have seen the growth habit described as broad.

'Erecta'—Often a catchall term for upright, woody forms of the species.

'Gold Prince'—Vigorous, mounded form with new foliage tipped a bright gold; older leaves turn solid green; considered hardiest of all variegated *Euonymus fortunei* types; grows to 2′ and more; handsome foliage.

'Gold Splash'—Gold and green foliage, 3′ by 3′.

'Gold Spot'—Dark green foliage with bright gold centers; upright and stronger growing than most forms; could this be the same as 'Sun Spot', simply a rename?

'Gold Tip'—Leaves edged with gold, aging to creamy white; may also appear under the name 'Gold Prince'.

'Golden Pillar'—Small lanceolate leaves, yellow margins with a green center, relatively slow-growing, 3′ by 2 1/2′.

'Gracilis'—Used to designate a group of variable and inconstant forms which possess variegated white or yellow or pink foliage.

'Green Lane'—A better green foliage form and not as upright-growing as 'Sarcoxie', will mature about 4′ by 4 to 6′; thick, lustrous dark green leaves do not (supposedly) windburn and remain vibrant year-round; it develops pinkish fruits with orange seeds; considered superior to 'Sarcoxie' and 'Vegetus'.

'Harlequin'—Slow-growing, prostrate, with ivory variegation, unstable.

'Ivory Jade'—Large, rich green leaf with ivory margin; white portion develops pink color in cold weather; grows 2 to 3′ by 6′ and develops a low-spreading habit.

'Kewensis'—Dainty, prostrate form with leaves about 1/4 to 5/8″ long, 1/8 to 1/4″ in width; forms low mat only several inches high; if allowed to climb a tree it develops the var. *radicans* character and flowers and fruits; the basal portion however retains the 'Kewensis' characteristics.

'Longwood'—Another good, small-leaved form collected on Mt. Tsukuba, Japan; survived -25°F and 106°F; more vigorous and larger leaved than 'Kewensis' or 'Minimus'; rather handsome plantings at Longwood Gardens in the visitor parking lot.

'Microphylla Variegata'—Although described as being a form of *E. fortunei*, I suspect the nursery industry may have it confused with *E. japonicus*; small leaves edged silver-white, upright habit, slow-growing.

'Minimus'—Low-growing form with leaves 1/4 to 1/2″ long; a plant in my Georgia garden is performing well; shows excellent vigor and good heat tolerance; in overall effect a large-leaved form of 'Kewensis'; distributed by Simon-Louis Fréres in 1912.

'Minimus'

'Moonshadow'—Sport of 'Sunspot' from Dugan Nursery, OH; more yellow in middle, thinner green margin, wavy leaves, does not revert, lighter yellow leaves, internodes 1/4 to 1/2″ long, plant is short and dense, matures 1 to 2′ high, may grow larger and 3′ by 5′ is listed, plant patent 6177.

var. *radicans* (Miq.) Rehd.—Intermediate form trailing or climbing, fruiting, leaves ovate or broad-elliptic to elliptic, 1 1/2 to 2″ long, acute or obtusish, distinctly serrate, of thicker texture, veins obsolete; this variety represents an intermediate stage between the species and the 'Vegetus' type; trailing or climbing in habit; forming woody stems and exhibiting sporadic flowering and fruiting; leaves are shiny medium to dark green and wavy in appearance; very unstable and numerous variegated branch sports can be found on a large plant; nurseries will often use the var. *radicans* without any taxonomic basis; for example, var. *radicans* 'Argenteo-variegata' refers to a 6″ by 24″, low-spreading plant with silver to white variegation; 'Harlequin' (which see) has been included under var. *radicans*; 'Radicans Variegated' is listed.

var. *radicans*

'Raulston's Gold'—Evergreen ground cover, glossy green leaves with golden midsection; not subject to scale; similar to 'Sun Spot'; not stable and reverts, particularly to the green-leaved form; from the J.C. Raulston Arboretum.

'Rydholm's Gold'—A green center with gold margin, the leaf is larger than 'Emerald 'n Gold'.

'Sarcoxie'—Upright form to 4'(6') with glossy, 1" long leaves; polished dark green leaves are partially whitish-veined; genuinely confused in the nursery trade; I have seen many clones that were named 'Sarcoxie' but each differed in various characteristics; I have seen heavy fruit crops on this form (white tinged pink); raised by Sarcoxie Nursery, Missouri in 1950.

'Sarcoxie'

'Sheridan Gold'—Deep green foliage has sunshine yellow coloring in a full sun situation, color supposedly richer than most golden forms, leaves variable being greenish yellow, spotted yellow or completely yellow; forms a densely branched, mounded, 20" high shrub.

'Silver Gem'—Leaves like 'Silver Queen' but smaller with a white border and reddish speckles; strong climbing shrub to 6'.

'Silver Queen'—An old name attached to a low, shrubby type with metallic dark green leaves with creamy yellow margins on new growth, finally cream-white margins; again have seen several descriptions; probably a sport var. *radicans* or *carrierei*; may fruit.

'Silver Tip'—White-margined foliage; Louisiana Nursery.

'Sparkle 'n Gold'—Branch sport with large leaves with a dark green center and broad borders of brilliant gold; it is a mounded form growing 12 to 18"(36") tall and twice as wide; advertised as having the brightest gold of any *E. fortunei* type; somebody has to be fibbing because the hype that accompanies every new gold-leaved introduction says the same thing; Lake County Nursery introduction.

'Sun Spot' ('Sunspot')—Rounded, compact, shapely form (3' by 6') with good winter hardiness; thick green leaves with pronounced yellow centers; the leaves inside the plant being of the same variegated pattern as the leaves at the stem tips; margin is a dark green; will revert.

'Sunrise'—Sport of 'Emerald Charm' with yellow variegated foliage, the yellow averaging about 50% of total leaf surface; leaves 1 1/2 to 2" long, 4' high, 5' wide; to 16" shoot growth per year; tolerates heavy pruning; introduced by Erik Saeys, Oakville, Ontario, Canada.

'Sunshine'—The leaves are bordered with bold gold margins, the center is gray-green; reasonably fast grower.

'Thunderbolt'—Found as an entire plant growing among 2-year-old block of 'Sun Spot'; 2 to 2 1/2" long leaves, green with a ragged bolt of yellow among center vein, thick and glossy, 2 to 4" long internodes; light yellow-green flowers in May–June; bright orange fruit in September into late fall; grows 5 to 6' high and wide; survived –20°F; 50 to 70% rooting with 3000 ppm IBA-talc; introduced by Dugan Nursery, Ohio, plant patent 6178.

'Variegatus'—Perhaps another catchall term for variegated types of var. *radicans*; I have observed so many variegated sports on the adult form of *E. fortunei* that the reasons for the multitude of named color sports becomes immediately evident; I have collected variegated shoots from a plant in Spring Grove and rooted them; I also had the good sense not to name them; this form as well as some of the others are unstable and will revert to any number of color combinations (albino to green); is about the same taxonomic status as 'Gracilis'.

'Vegetus'—Somewhat similar to var. *radicans*; however, a heavy fruiting form; the leaves are medium green without the venation and of a more rounded, thick nature; actually the super-adult form; an upright shrub to 4 to 5' or a true clinging vine if trained; leaves are broad-elliptic to nearly suborbicular, 1 to 2" long, acute or obtusish, crenate-serrate, dull green to medium green; fruiting freely, however, this is a variable characteristic; tremendously susceptible to scale; one of the most cold hardy cultivars; 'Dart's Cardinal' is a selected form of 'Vegetus' that fruits heavily.

'Vegetus Cardinal'—More upright than 'Vegetus' with orange fruits; is this the same as 'Dart's Cardinal'?

'Woodland'—As I have observed it a selected form of 'Vegetus' with perhaps more lustrous and slightly smaller foliage; observed a plant at the Arnold Arboretum.

PROPAGATION: Seeds have dormant embryos and moist stratification at 41°F for 3 months is recommended; germination is more uniform if arils are removed; cuttings root easily almost any time of the year but especially when collected in June, July and August. It should be mentioned that many of the *E. fortunei* types will become sprawly if propagated from horizontal branches and more upright from vertical leaders; the term for this is topophysis.

ADDITIONAL NOTES: *Euonymus fortunei* behaves similar to *Hedera helix*; the juvenile form is non-flowering and of different leaf morphology; the adult form flowers and fruits and shows great variation in leaf morphology. In Spring Grove, I have noticed plants on trees that have every imaginable shape and some branches produce variegated sports; I have rooted cuttings of these variegated plants; someone needs to stop introducing new cultivars and straighten out the confusion that now exists; I recommend selecting the 5 or 6 best and leaving it go at those.

NATIVE HABITAT: China. Introduced 1907.

Euonymus japonicus Thunb. — Japanese Euonymus
(ū-on′i-mus jà-pon′i-kus)

LEAVES: Opposite, simple, evergreen, obovate to narrowly oval, 1 to 3″ long, 3/4 to 1 3/4″ wide, lustrous dark green, paler below, leathery, glabrous, tapered at base, acute, blunt or rounded at apex, serrated except at base; petiole—1/4 to 1/2″ long.

BUDS: Typically *Euonymus*; imbricate, conical, 6- to 8-scaled, green with edges of scales tinged red in winter, glabrous, 1/4″ long; terminal—similar but larger.

STEM: Stout, somewhat squarish, green, glabrous, appearing granular, decurrent ridges (slight) running from sides of leaf scar to next node, small brownish black glandular dot on either side of petiole at point of attachment to stem, nodes somewhat flattened; emit boxelder-like odor when bruised; pith—green.

SIZE: 10 to 15′ high, about 1/2 that in width; supposedly can grow to 25′ but I have seen nothing approaching that in the United States, 5 to 10′ is more common under landscape conditions; saw a particularly nice tree form at Inglenook Winery, California.

HARDINESS: Zone (6)7 to 9; severely injured at –3°F in Athens area; leaves killed but buds produced new leaves in spring; variegated types are more tender than the species; has survived up to –10°F at the U.S. National Arboretum.

HABIT: Very dense oval shrub when growing in full sun; more open in shade.

RATE: Medium to fast.

TEXTURE: Medium.

LEAF COLOR: Lustrous waxy dark green.

FLOWERS: Perfect, greenish white, 4-petaled, 1/3″ diameter, borne in 5- to 12-flowered, stalked cymes, June.

FRUIT: Four-valved, 1/3″ diameter, pinkish capsule, orange aril, late summer, early fall, not usually effective.

CULTURE: Easily transplanted from containers, adaptable to varied soils; appears to do well in Piedmont clays of Georgia; withstands salt spray; full sun to heavy shade; withstands heavy pruning; more widely used in Europe especially in coastal areas; over the years I have walked the cities of Hastings, Eastbourne, and Brighton in England and have observed the plant fully exposed to maritime conditions; appears about as salt tolerant as any broadleaf evergreen; have observed *old* plants in Georgia landscapes that border on relic status; once established appears to hold up well.

DISEASES AND INSECTS: Crown gall, anthracnose (*Colletrichum gloeosporioides*), mildew, leaf spots, aphids, euonymus scale.

LANDSCAPE VALUE: Has lost favor in the South where it is most at home; excessively stiff in habit and prone to significant insects and diseases; have not observed its use in many modern day landscapes; often a symbol of a hamburger establishment and used in great numbers in such locations; used as a houseplant; still large numbers being produced as evidenced by 3 to 7 different cultivars sitting side-by-side at larger retail green goods dealers; worth reiterating that the variegated forms will often revert to green and if the reversion shoots are not removed they will consume the shrub.

CULTIVARS: Numerous, have counted over 30 in the literature, probably 8 to 10 produced in the United States.

'Albomarginatus'—Leaves bordered with a slight margin of white.

'Aureomarginatus'—Yellow margins to the leaf, best color in sun, 5 to 10′, common in commerce.

'Aureus'—The bright yellow center bordered with green; 1 to 3″ long leaves; often reverts to the type; stems are yellow; common in South but not worthy of use; have seen plants being stocked at a local chain store with 1/3 of the branches already green; may also be listed as 'Aureovariegatus' and 'Aureopictus'; Hines Gold® is perhaps synonymous with 'Aureovariegatus'; grows 5 to 10′ high, 3 to 6′ wide.

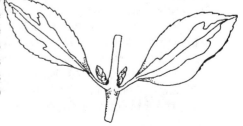

'Emerald Towers'—See 'Green Spire'.

'Grandifolius'—Large, shiny green leaves and a compact, tightly branched habit.

'Green Spire' ('Greenspire')—Interesting accent plant; columnar to 6′ high, 6 to 8″ wide; extremely dark green leaves; introduced by U.S. National Arboretum; I remember seeing a plant at the National but it was wider than the dimensions given above.

'Latifolius Albomarginatus'—Broad oval leaves with a wide margin of white; more vigorous and probably better than 'Albomarginatus'; center of leaf gray-green.

'Macrophyllus'—Larger leaves (green) than the type.

'Microphyllus'—A dwarf, small-leaved form with distinctly erect branches; leaves dark green, oval-lanceolate, 1/2 to 1″ long, 1/8 to 1/3″ wide; not as hardy as the type; grows 1 to 3′ high; has been used on the Georgia campus; is often a scale's best friend.

'Microphyllus Pulchellus'—Small leaves suffused with yellow.

'Microphyllus Variegatus'—Like 'Microphyllus' except the waxy, petite, deep green leaves have white margins; not a plant for every landscape; from a distance it is difficult to discern whether the plant is sick or variegated.

'Ovatus Aureus'—Leaves oval or ovate with a broad irregular margin of rich yellow that suffuses into the green center.

'Silver King'—Large, pale green leaves with creamy white margins; may be an American name for an older clone; upright grower.

Silver Princess™ ('Moness')—Large, dark green leaves with well-defined white margins, 3′ by 2′.

PROPAGATION: Cuttings root easily, June through August.

NATIVE HABITAT: Japan, Introduced 1804.

Euonymus kiautschovicus Loes. (formerly *E. patens* Rehd.) — Spreading Euonymus

LEAVES: Opposite, simple, evergreen, semi-evergreen or deciduous, broad-elliptic or obovate to oblong-obovate or elliptic-oblong, 2 to 3″ long, 3/4 to 1 3/4″ wide, acute or obtusish, cuneate, crenate-serrulate, lustrous dark green, subcoriaceous with obsolete veins beneath; petiole—1/6 to 1/3″ long.

BUDS: Imbricate, conical, sharp-pointed, greenish and often tinged with red in winter, perhaps becoming straw brown in winter.

STEM: Slender, green, rounded, not developing the straw brown color until the second or third year.

Euonymus kiautschovicus, (ū-on′i-mus kĭ-atch-ov′i-cus), Spreading Euonymus, is a semi-evergreen (also evergreen or deciduous) shrub of rounded habit reaching 8 to 10′ in height. The foliage is a good dark green in summer but usually burns in winter and looks quite unkempt. Flowers are greenish white, 4-parted, 1/3″ diameter, and borne in loose, erect, 1 1/2 to 4″ wide cymes in July–August. The flies and bees hover about this shrub when in flower and it is not a good plant for patio areas and the like. Fruit capsule is pink, seed coat is orange-red, matures in October–November. Decent plant for informal hedges, screens, and massing. Not as susceptible to scale as *E. fortunei* and tree types, but on the Georgia campus have seen heavy infestations on plants.

CULTIVARS: The cultivars are superior to the species.

'Dupont'—Hybrid form with large leaves (2 1/2″) and vigorous growth habit; 4-year-old plants are 4′ tall; quite hardy; a somewhat confusing clone.

'Hobbs'—Good-looking, dense-mounded form with lustrous dark green leaves; have seen at Bernheim Arboretum.

'Jewel'—Compact, low-growing form with bright green foliage.

'Manhattan'—Hybrid, excellent glossy dark green foliage form with leaves 2 1/2″ long and 1 1/4″ wide; has not proven particularly hardy and was killed to snowline in Illinois during rugged winters of 1976–77 and 77–78; will grow back rapidly; forms a rounded, 4 to 6′ high, evergreen shrub; easily rooted from cuttings; has a rather strange history and supposedly came out of Manhattan, KS from where the cultivar name is derived; have seen plants 8′ high and 12′ wide.

'Newport'—A form similar to 'Manhattan' but not as vigorous; flowers at same time as *E. kiautschovicus*; probably a hybrid.

'Paulii'—A glossy dark green-leaved form; more upright than 'Manhattan' with greater hardiness; 5′ by 5′ at maturity; leaves leathery, broad-ovate to rounded; flowers ahead of *E. kiautschovicus*.

'Sieboldiana'—Supposedly with good foliage and not as susceptible to scale as other types, do not know origin but have seen it listed in a nursery catalog.

Native to eastern and central China. Introduced 1860. Zone 5 to 8.

Euonymus nanus Bieb. var. *turkestanicus* (Dieck) Krishtofovich — Dwarf Euonymus

LEAVES: Alternate, whorled or occasionally opposite, simple, evergreen, semi-evergreen to deciduous, narrow to linear-oblong, sparsely toothed, 1 1/2 to 3″ long, 1/4 to 1/2″ broad, not revolute, bluish green.

Euonymus nanus var. *turkestanicus*, (ū-on′i-mus nā′nus tĕr-ke-stan′i-kus), Dwarf Euonymus, is a small (3′) shrub with erect, slender branches and leaves which may be alternate, opposite, or subopposite. The foliage is of a bluish green consistency in summer and changes to brilliant red tones in fall. The 4-petaled flowers are about 1/6″ across, brownish purple, and borne 1 to 3 on a slender stalk in May. The fruit is a 4-lobed, pink to rose red capsule; the seeds are brown and not wholly covered by the orange aril. The variety *turkestanicus* is the type in cultivation. The species is native from Caucasian Mountains to western China. Introduced 1830. Zone 2 to 6. This plant performed well in central Illinois and the fall color was brilliant. It is easily rooted from softwood cuttings treated with a quick-dip of 1000 ppm IBA. I doubt seriously whether anyone will take it into their hearts or gardens. Generally too straggly and unkempt to be given serious garden consideration.

ADDITIONAL NOTES: A good paper that anyone serious about *Euonymus* should read is "An account of *Euonymus* in cultivation and its availability in commerce," *The Plantsman* 3(3): 133–166 (1981) by Roy Lancaster.

As a curtain-closer, several other *Euonymus* species should be mentioned. None, I repeat none, will become mainstream items but for the collector and certain parts of the United States and Canada may prove useful. *Euonymus carnosus* was introduced to me in 1991 by Dr. Stephen Spongberg, Arnold Arboretum. The Arnold plant was a small tree, 10′ or greater in height, with leathery, lustrous dark green leaves, that turn rich red-purple in autumn. The capsules are pink. China. Zone 6. *Euonymus latifolius* (L.) Mill. is a large shrub or small tree to 10 to 15′ high by 8′ wide. The 3 to 5″ long, dark green leaves turn brilliant red in autumn. The rose red, winged fruits dehisce and expose the orange seeds. Southern Europe to Asia Minor. Zone (5)6 to 8. *Euonymus obovatus* Nutt., Running Euonymus, is a prostrate, deciduous shrub rarely more than 12″ high. The 1 1/2 to 2 1/2″ long, light green leaves, are followed by reddish green flowers and 3-lobed, 2/3″ wide, warty, red capsules that open to expose the red seeds. North America. Zone 3 to 7. *Euonymus oxyphyllus* Miq. is a small deciduous tree or large shrub with dull green leaves, green-brown flowers and 1/2″ wide, globose, 4- to 5-ribbed, dark red fruits and scarlet seeds. Plants I have seen in fruit were spectacular. China, Korea, Japan. Zone 5 to 7. Other species include: *E. phellomanus* Loes. with pink fruits and pink seeds, China, Zone 5; and *E. sachalinensis* (F. Schmidt) Maxim. with pendant, scarlet capsules and orange seeds, Asia, Zone 5.

Euscaphis japonicus (Thunb.) Kanitz — Euscaphis Tree, Sweetheart Tree

FAMILY: Staphyleaceae

LEAVES: Opposite, compound pinnate, 6 to 10″ long, 7 to 11 leaflets, each 2 to 4″ long, ovate to ovate-lanceolate, acuminate, rounded to broad cuneate, serrated, leathery lustrous dark green; petiole—short.

BUDS: Ovoid, 1/8 to 3/8″ long, appearing valvate with one scale slightly overlapping edges of the other, tapering to a sharp point, appearing keeled on outside, red, glabrous; at terminus of stem, due to shortened internodes, buds appear clustered akin to those of *Quercus*.

STEM: First year—stout, rounded, fatter at nodes, reddish brown, glabrous, few lenticels evident; 2nd year—similar in color but with elongated vertical fissures (lenticels) producing a snakeskin-like pattern, even more prominent on 3 year and older stems.

Euscaphis japonicus, (ū-skā′fis jà-pon′i-kus), Euscaphis Tree, Sweetheart Tree, has been popularized by the late J.C. Raulston and deserves mention because of its uniqueness. Early signals from the North Carolina trees indicate they will be compact-growing perhaps in the 15 to 25′(30′) range. Leaves turn mahogany purple in autumn. The deep reddish purple bark is striated and reminds of *Staphylea trifolia*. Yellowish white, 1/4″ diameter flowers occur in 4 to 9″(12″), broad, terminal panicles in May–June. The fruits are rose to ruby red, 1/2″ long pods, 3 together, opening to expose the shiny, steel blue to black, 1/5″ diameter seeds. Indeed the quality and quantity of the fruits make them eye-catching. I have observed the plants in October at Raleigh and they were in heavy fruit. I suspect the effect occurs over a long time frame. One reference said August–September. Raulston mentioned 3 to 4 months. Locate in well-drained soil in full sun. Kind of a novelty plant but worthwhile in the border, small garden. Raulston reported scarification and cold stratification required for seed germination which may take two years. China, Korea, Japan. Cultivated 1890. Zone (6)7 to 8. Survived 2°F at Raleigh, NC without injury. David Creech reported excellent performance in Zone 8, Nacogdoches, TX.

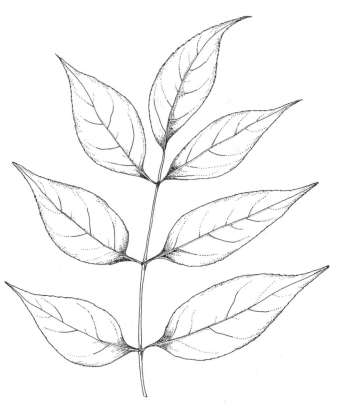

Evodia daniellii (Benn) Hemsl. [now listed as *Tetradium daniellii* (Benn) Hartley] — Korean Evodia
(ē-vō′di-à dan-i-el′ē-ī)

FAMILY: Rutaceae

LEAVES: Opposite, pinnately compound, 9 to 15″ long, leaflets (5)7 to 11, ovate to oblong-ovate, 2 to 5″ long, acuminate with obtusish point, rounded at base, sometimes broad-cuneate or subcordate, finely crenulate, lustrous dark green above and glabrous, pubescent below on the midrib and in the axils of the veins; petiole—1 1/2 to 2 1/2″ long.

BUDS: Solitary, sessile, ovoid, 1 pair of rather indistinct scales, terminal—puberulent, gray-brown; exposed and visible; differing from *Phellodendron* where the buds are hidden by the petiole base.

STEM: Round or somewhat 4-angled or wrinkled; leaf scars—broadly crescent-shaped, low; 3 bundle traces; pith—moderate, somewhat angular, firm, continuous.

SIZE: Will probably grow 25 to 30′ high under landscape conditions but can reach 50′; the spread is equal to or greater than the height.

HARDINESS: Zone (4)5 to 8; I have seen specimens at the Morton Arboretum, Lisle, IL, which showed good vigor and abundant fruit; recent reports from the Morton indicate dieback and decline possibly owing to disease; Cappiello reported tip injury in Orono, ME; Hayman reported 80% dieback at -24°F at Bernheim Arboretum during the January 1994 freeze; also a reasonably thrifty plant on the Georgia campus.

RATE: Medium to fast, especially in youth; seedlings which I grew in containers reached 5 to 6′ in a single growing season.

TEXTURE: Medium in leaf and in winter.

BARK: Older stems and branches develop a smooth gray appearance which is interrupted at irregular intervals by raised lenticels; reminds of beech bark.

LEAF COLOR: Lustrous dark green in summer; the foliage is quite free of pests and diseases and looks as good in August as it did when first maturing in May; fall color is of no consequence as the leaves usually drop green or yellowish green.

FLOWERS: Small, white, borne in 4 to 6″ broad, flattish corymbs on current season's growth in June, July–August; the flowers are borne in great quantities and provide quite a show when few other plants are in flower; bees love them; in full flower late July 1991 Boston.

FRUIT: Capsule, composed of 4 to 5 carpels which split from the top; red to black in color and effective in late August through November; the fruits are very effective from an ornamental standpoint; seeds are lustrous brownish black, about the size of buckshot.

CULTURE: Easy to transplant; seems to prefer a well-drained, moist, fertile soil; pH adaptable; full sun; may be a bit tender when young and should be well-sited and mulched; one authority noted that any soil is acceptable for culturing this plant; has performed reasonably well in the Georgia test plots.

DISEASES AND INSECTS: None of any consequence.

LANDSCAPE VALUE: A very interesting tree, but unfortunately little known and used; a lovely small tree which can be used in the small landscape; excellent summer foliage, flower, and fruit characteristics make this tree worthy of additional use; Wyman noted that the wood is comparatively weak and splits easily and the tree is short-lived (15 to 40 years); I have observed numerous Evodias throughout the Midwest, East and South and have not noticed any serious problems; this tree might warrant a close look especially for urban areas; old venerable specimens, possibly from Wilson collections, that I suspect are ±80-years-old reside in the Arnold Arboretum.

PROPAGATION: Seeds which were sent from the Morris Arboretum, Philadelphia, PA were direct sowed and germinated almost 100 percent.

NATIVE HABITAT: Northern China, Korea. Introduced by E.H. Wilson in 1905.

RELATED SPECIES:

Evodia hupehensis Dode, (ē-vō′di-à hū-pe-en′sis), Hupeh Evodia, is closely allied to *E. daniellii* and may be an ecotype. Supposedly it differs in larger stalked leaflets and the longer beak of the fruit, but according to W.J. Bean the characters are not reliable. *Evodia hupehensis* can grow to 60′ and may be slightly less hardy than *E. daniellii*. Native to central China. Introduced 1907. Zone 5 to 8. Current literature merges *E. hupehensis* with *E. daniellii*, the correct name being *Tetradium daniellii*. I suspect it will take a long time before the new name change is accepted. In fact, few everyday gardeners have heard of *Evodia*.

ADDITIONAL NOTES: The Evodias are closely allied to *Phellodendron* but differ in the buds which are exposed in the leaf axils rather than covered by the base of the petiole as in *Phellodendron*. *Evodia* is often written *Euodia* and this was the original spelling as rendered by the Forsters who founded the genus in 1776.

Evodia hupehensis (leaflet)

A few final thoughts concerning a rather handsome group of trees. More adaptable than given credit. Large trees at the Arnold provide inspiration and hope. A single seedling in my Georgia test plots has grown over 10′ in 3 years. No flowers yet, but it has persisted in the intense summer heat, particularly the summer of 1995.

Exochorda racemosa (Lindl.) Rehd. — Common Pearlbush
(ek-sō-kôr′dà ra-se-mō′sà)

FAMILY: Rosaceae

LEAVES: Alternate, simple, elliptic to elliptic-oblong or oblong-obovate, acute and mucronate, cuneate, 1 to 3″ long, about 1/2 as wide, entire or on vigorous shoots serrate above the middle, whitish beneath, glabrous, medium green; petiole—1/2″ long.

BUDS: Moderate, solitary, sessile, ovoid, with about 10 more or less pointed and fringed scales.

STEM: Round, slender, brown, glabrous, roughened by lenticels and longitudinal fissures; pith—small, continuous, pale.

SIZE: 10 to 15′ by 10 to 15′.

HARDINESS: Zone 4 to 8; does extremely well in Zone 8.

HABIT: An upright, slender-branched, loose, irregular shrub becoming floppy and often unkempt with age; often somewhat fountain-like in outline; easily rejuvenated by renewal pruning after flowering.

RATE: Medium.

TEXTURE: One of the earliest leafing shrubs and plants usually are in full leaf by early April (Athens, GA); medium in leaf, coarse in winter.

BARK: Old branches, 1 to 2″ diameter, develop a scaly bark of gray, brown and orange-brown combinations, rather attractive.

LEAF COLOR: Medium green in summer; no fall color of any consequence.

FLOWERS: Perfect, white, 5-petaled, 1 1/2″ across, odorless; (March, Athens) April–May for 7 to 14 days; borne in 6- to 10-flowered, 3 to 5″ long racemes at ends of short lateral stems from branches of previous year; each expanding bud reminds of a pearl; excellent for floral effect as the entire end of a branch appears in flower.

FRUIT: Broad turbinate, 5-valved, dehiscent, 1/3″ wide capsule ripening in October and persisting, green to yellow-brown and finally rich brown.

CULTURE: Transplant balled-and-burlapped or as a container plant in early spring; prefers well-drained, acid, loamy soil; full sun or partial shade; prune after flowering; pH adaptable.

DISEASES AND INSECTS: None serious.

LANDSCAPE VALUE: Good for flower effect; probably should be reserved for the shrub border; can be spectacular in flower but soon fades into oblivion; does quite well in Athens-Atlanta areas and is in flower by late March to early April; the plant thrives with neglect and is amazingly tough considering the heat and drought that it takes in stride in the Southeast.

PROPAGATION: Seeds will germinate sporadically when sown directly; a short stratification (30 to 60 days) improves germination; cuttings should be collected in June, July and August and treated with 3000 to 8000 ppm IBA talc or quick dip for best results; in general these recommendations apply to the other species treated here.

NATIVE HABITAT: Eastern China. Introduced 1849.

RELATED SPECIES:

Exochorda giraldii Hesse. — Redbud Pearlbush

LEAVES: Alternate, simple, oblong to obovate, 1 1/2 to 3″ long, entire, rarely toothed toward apex, pale green, veins tinged red; petiole—red.

Exochorda giraldii, (ek-sō-kôr′dȧ jir-al′dē-ī), Redbud Pearlbush, is closely allied and very similar to the above but less available. The young shoots are pinkish and the petioles and veins of mature leaves maintain this color through summer. Flowers white, 2″ across, 6 to 8 in a raceme. The variety *wilsonii* (Rehd.) Rehd. has flowers 2″ across, and is more upright and floriferous. A mature specimen at the Arnold was 15 to 18′ high and 25′ wide. 'Irish Pearl' is a hybrid between *E. racemosa* × *E. g.* var. *wilsonii* with greater vigor; almost 2″ diameter, pure white flowers, borne 8 to 10 per raceme; the entire flowering shoot 20 to 36″ long. Northwestern China. Introduced 1897. Zone 5 to 7.

Exochorda korolkowii Lav. — Turkestan Pearlbush

LEAVES: Alternate, simple, obovate, 1 1/2 to 3 1/2″ long, 3/4 to 1 1/2″ wide, acute or obtusish, mucronulate, toothed toward apex on vigorous shoots, olive to dark green above, gray to yellow-green beneath, glabrous; petiole—1/4 to 1/2″ long.

Exochorda korolkowii, (ek-sō-kôr′dȧ kôr-ōl-kōw′ē-ī), Turkestan Pearlbush, is a vigorous shrub (10 to 12′ high) much in the mold of *E. racemosa*. The pure white, 1 1/2″ diameter flowers occur in 3 to 4″ long, erect, 5- to 8-flowered racemes in April–May about the same time as the other Pearlbushes. In fact, I was evaluating the Pearlbush collection at the Arnold Arboretum on May 8, 1979 and could find few differences among the true species listed here. Early to leaf out. The only species that appeared inferior to the others was *E. serratifolia* which had poor flower quality. Turkestan. Introduced 1878. Zone 5 to 7.

Exochorda* × *macrantha (Lemoine) Schneid., (ek-sō-kôr′dȧ mȧ-kran′thȧ), is a hybrid between *E. racemosa* and *E. korolkowii* and a shrub of great beauty producing a raceme of flowers from every bud of the previous year's growth. 'The Bride' grows only 3 to 4′ tall and is quite bushy. I have seen the plant in several gardens, and it is indeed compact and refined compared to the parental species which grow 12 to 15′. It was raised by Messrs. Lemoine of Nancy about 1900. It produces a 3 to 4″ long, 6- to 10-flowered raceme, each flower 1 1/4″ diameter, from every bud of the previous year's growth. Herein, 'Irish Pearl' ('The Pearl') is treated under *E. giraldii*.

Exochorda serratifolia Moore

LEAVES: Alternate, simple, elliptic, 2 to 3″(4″) long, 1 1/4 to 2″ wide, sharply serrate particularly near apex, often entire below middle, medium green; petiole—1/3 to 4/5″ long.

Exochorda serratifolia, (ek-sō-kôr′dà ser-at-i-fō′li-à), was the least impressive in flower of the Pearlbushes at the Arnold Arboretum. Recently, the University of Minnesota Landscape Arboretum introduced 'Northern Pearls', a compact seedling selection, 6 to 8′ by 4 to 6′, which produces masses of 2″ diameter, white flowers in terminal racemes in mid-May (Chanhassen, MN); flowered prolifically after exposure to -34°F [see *J. Environ. Horticulture* 13:152–153 (1995)]. The species is native to Manchuria, Korea. Introduced 1918. Zone 4 to 7.

ADDITIONAL NOTES: Pearlbushes will never take over the horticultural world but they are rather pretty, trouble-free shrubs. The finest specimen I have observed was located at Mt. Auburn Cemetery, Cambridge, MA. It was about 18′ high and 22 to 25′ wide. The larger Pearlbushes might be trained as a small tree. In Illinois after a particularly devastating ice storm I noticed several large broken branches. It is amazing how many Pearlbushes are growing in southern gardens. The shrubs are nothing if not persistent. For about 50 weeks no one knows they exist, come March, usually mid-March in Athens, calls pour into the Horticulture Department wanting to know the identity of the white-flowered bush. I am secure in stating that *E. racemosa* (primary garden species) thrives with neglect.

Fagus grandifolia Ehrh. — American Beech
(fā′gus gran-di-fo′li-à)

FAMILY: Fagaceae

LEAVES: Alternate, simple, ovate-oblong, 2 to 5″ long, 3/4 to 2 1/2″ wide, acuminate, broad-cuneate at base, coarsely serrate, glossy dark green above, light green and usually glabrous below or with tufts of hairs in the axils of the veins and along the midrib, silky when unfolding; more veins than *F. sylvatica* (11 to 15 pairs); petiole—1/4″ or longer.

BUDS: Imbricate, slender, 3/4 to 1″ long, brown, shiny, apex sharp-pointed.

STEM: Slender, somewhat zig-zag, smooth, shining, silver-gray especially on older stems.

SIZE: 50 to 70′ in height with a maximum of 100 to 120′; spread is usually less than or equal to the height, although many specimens, especially those in forest stands, assume an upright-oval shape; national champion is 115′ by 138′ in Harwood, MD.

HARDINESS: Zone 4 to 9.

HABIT: A sturdy, imposing tree often with a short trunk and wide-spreading crown, a picture of character in a native situation; may sucker and form wide-ranging colonies.

RATE: Slow, possibly medium in youth, averaging 9 to 12′ over a 10 year period.

TEXTURE: Medium throughout the seasons.

BARK: Thin, smooth, light bluish gray almost silvery on young stems; similar on mature trees but darker.

LEAF COLOR: Silvery green when opening, gradually changing to dark green in summer; fall color is a beautiful golden bronze and the leaves (especially on the lower portion of the tree) often persist into winter.

FLOWERS: Monoecious; male and female separate on the same tree; male in globose heads; pistillate in 2- to 4-flowered spikes, however, sometimes at base of staminate inflorescence; usually flowers in April to early May with the emerging leaves.

FRUIT: Three-winged nut, solitary or 2 to 3, partly or wholly enclosed by a prickly involucre about 3/4″ long, the prickles recurved; nut is edible.

CULTURE: Transplant balled-and-burlapped in the dormant condition; container-grown trees are now more available; moist, well-drained, acid (pH 5.0 to 6.5) soil is preferable; will not withstand wet or compacted soils; soils with oxygen concentrations of less than 10 to 15% are not suitable; root system is shallow and it is difficult to grow grass under this tree; does best in full sun although withstands shade; prune in summer or early fall; abundant literature about the difficulty in transplanting; in my work have not lost a single tree; the first year after transplanting may not grow much but takes off during second; from a nursery production standpoint appears to require mycorrhizal inoculum (from local native beech stand) to facilitate reasonable growth under clean cultivation; at the 1996 Connecticut Nurseryman's Association meeting I asked one tree grower about this and he nodded in the affirmative; I purchased 200 bare-root seedlings of *F. grandifolia* and transplanted them into bark; *all survived* but did not jump out of the containers, perhaps beech forest inoculum is the answer.

DISEASES AND INSECTS: The following problems have been reported but are not particularly serious: leaf spots, powdery mildew, bleeding canker, leaf mottle, beech bark disease, cankers, aphids, brown wood borer, beech scale, beech mealybug, two-lined chestnut borer and caterpillars.

LANDSCAPE VALUE: Beautiful native tree; restricted to large area use; beautiful in parks, golf courses, and other large areas; a beech forest is worth viewing especially in early spring and again in fall; the boat has been missed as far as the use of this tree in the landscape; young trees can be moved successfully and will establish and prosper; I have seen examples in the southeast of American Beech and European Beech, planted at the same time, the American Beech outgrows and outperforms the European species; American Beech is more amenable to culture in Zones 7 to 9 than the European; unfortunately, no named selections of American Beech exist while the European has numerous; in a sense, a beech is planted for posterity and my children and yours will enjoy its grandeur; American Beech is a climax species and on hillsides in the Piedmont of Georgia it is the only species or is mixed with oak and hickory; the ash-brown to tan leaves, particularly on young trees or sucker growth, persist through the winter; a solid beech forest is indeed a magnificent spectacle.

PROPAGATION: Seed, 41°F for 90 days in moist sand; I have opened numerous prickly involucres only to be disappointed by shriveled and hollow seeds; according to several references large crops of seed may occur at 2 to 3 year or longer intervals; their germination rate is high, usually approaching 95%; American Beech shows a propensity to sucker from the roots and small trees often occur in the vicinity of mature specimens; beech would obviously seed naturally but the predominant number of small trees I have observed, especially in native stands, appear to be root sprouts.

ADDITIONAL NOTES: F.B. Robinson has termed the beech "the Beau Brummel of trees but clannish and fastidious as to soil and atmosphere, magnificent specimen casting a dense shade which does not permit undergrowth." J.U. Crockett noted, "If the word noble had to be applied to only one kind of tree, the honor would probably go to the beech." The nuts were once fed to swine and were a favorite food of the extinct passenger pigeon, squirrels, blue jays, titmice, grosbeaks, nuthatches and woodpecker. The American Beech is a variable species and there are at least three different races. The northern type is "Gray Beech" found from Nova Scotia to the Great Lakes, and on the higher mountains of North Carolina and Tennessee, mainly on neutral to alkaline soils. "White Beech" is found on the southern coastal plain and northward on poorly drained, acid sites. Between these two forms, mainly on well-drained, acid sites and mixing with them is "Red Beech." These races are anything but clear-cut and all types of intermediate forms occur. I like to think of American Beech as one contiguous population displaying the "typical" species characteristics that allow one to identify it in Minnesota as well as Florida. On the other hand, there are differences of a trivial nature much akin to the differences in accents of people from Boston and Atlanta.

NATIVE HABITAT: New Brunswick to Ontario, south to Florida and Texas. Introduced 1800.

Fagus sylvatica L. — European Beech, Common Beech
(fā′gus sil-vat′i-kȧ)

LEAVES: Alternate, simple, 2 to 4″ long, 1 1/2 to 2 1/2″ wide, may be 5″ by 3″, ovate or elliptic, acute, broad cuneate or rounded at base, undulate, entire or obscurely toothed, lustrous dark green above, light green beneath, glabrous at maturity, silky and ciliate when young; 5 to 9 vein pairs; petiole—1/4 to 1/2″ long, downy.

BUDS: Similar to *F. grandifolia*.

STEM: Similar, except olive-brown in color.

GROWTH HABIT: Tends to branch close to ground; dense, upright, oval character when young.

SIZE: 50 to 60′ in height with a spread of 35 to 45′; can reach 100′ in height.

HARDINESS: Zone 4 to 7; does not do well in extreme heat; trees in Athens, GA and Spartanburg, SC tell an interesting story; the purple-leaf types will survive but are quite slow-growing; if a European Beech is desired plant a green form; quite spectacular *F. s.* 'Pendula' on the grounds of Milliken & Co., Spartanburg, SC.

HABIT: Densely pyramidal to oval or rounded, branching to the ground; very formal (stately) in outline.

RATE: Slow to medium, 9 to 12′ over a 10 year period; an English reference noted 35′ in 20 years; much slower growing in the South.

TEXTURE: Actually fine when first leafing out, otherwise of medium texture in full foliage and winter.

BARK: Smooth, gray, usually darker than the American Beech; developing an elephant hide appearance on old trunks; a beauty unmatched by the bark of other trees.

LEAF COLOR: When unfolding a tender shimmering green unmatched by any other tree gradually changing to lustrous dark green in summer followed by rich russet and golden bronze colors in fall; the leaves are slow to emerge and do not fully develop until sometime in May (Boston).

FLOWERS: Essentially as described for American Beech.

FRUITS: Nuts triangular, 5/8″ long, usually 2 enclosed in 3/4 to 1″ long, hard, woody, 4-lobed husk covered with bristles, borne singly on an erect, pubescent pedicel.

CULTURE: More tolerant of soils than American Beech but otherwise requirements are comparable.

DISEASES AND INSECTS: Some bark disease problems; in Europe a bark feeding woolly aphid leaves punctures that are colonized by the coral spot fungus, which kills patches of bark and can girdle the whole tree.

LANDSCAPE VALUE: There is no finer specimen tree; so beautiful that it overwhelms one at first glance; excellent for public areas, also makes an excellent hedge for it withstands heavy pruning; the cultivars are especially beautiful and at least one will blend into every landscape; my favorites are 'Asplenifolia', 'Fastigiata', 'Pendula', and 'Riversii'.

CULTIVARS: There are a great number of cultivars which have developed in the wild and under cultivation. The European Beech is one of my great plant loves and in this edition I have expanded the list of cultivars based on the literature and my observations. Many of these are not available in this country and perhaps have even been lost to cultivation. It is interesting that no named cultivars have arisen from the American Beech considering the tremendous number that have occurred within the concept of the species, *Fagus sylvatica*. Had an opportunity to tromp around Germany with Dr. J.C. Raulston and made an attempt to look at every beech that crossed my path. Also at Trompenburg Arboretum in Rotterdam have seen a tremendous collection of unusual cultivars. In addition, the owner, Mr. J.R.P. van Hoey Smith, has numerous beech seedlings and new introductions waiting in the wings. This revised listing reflects my most recent observations.

'Albovariegata'—Leaves smaller than the type, margin coarser and irregularly undulate, streaked irregularly with yellowish white; the term f. *albovariegata* is used to represent leaves blotched and striped with white; saw several different forms of this, some apparently more stable than others; 'Albomarginata' is described; only for the collector.

'Ansorgei'—Leaves narrow lanceolate, only 1/2 to 1″ wide, of a dark brownish red; slow- growing, loose and open in outline, unusual and delicate; witnessed my first tree at Hamburg Botanic Garden and am still smitten 11 years later.

'Argenteomarmorata'—Leaves of the first spring flush are green, those in the second irregularly dotted with fine white specks or dotted and marbled.

'Asplenifolia'—A very beautiful but confused (with 'Laciniata') cultivar with gracefully cut leaves that offer a fern-like appearance; the lustrous dark green leaves turn excellent golden brown in fall; fine specimens occur at Smith College, Niagara Falls and Spring Grove, 60′ by 50′.

'Atropunicea' ('Purpurea')—The true or original purple leaf beech; the young leaves are a deep black-red and with time change to purple-green and often almost green; the purple leaf beech has been found on several occasions in the wild; the only authenticated source from which horticulturists have derived their stock occurred before 1772 in the Hanleiter Forest near Sonderhausen in Thuringia; it reproduces somewhat true-to-type from seed and has produced many named off-spring; the popular 'Cuprea', Copper Beech, designates trees whose leaves are paler than the true Purple Beech; I have seen so many trees labeled 'Cuprea' that I have no idea the correctness of any; 'Brocklesby' has deep purple leaves that are larger than the norm; 'Swat Magret' has dark purple leaves that supposedly retain their coloring until late summer, slower growing than 'Riversii'; other forms have arisen and are discussed below; apparently the name 'Atropunicea' may not be perfectly correct and names like 'Purpurea' and 'Purpurea Latifolia' are being used to designate the Purple Beech.

'Aurea Pendula'—A weeping beech with yellow leaves which become somewhat green in the summer months; usually trained with a leader and then permitted to weep; handsome and unusual, not common in gardens or commerce; originated as a branch sport in 1900; introduced 1904.

'Aureavariegata'—Leaves margined with yellow.

'Bornyensis' ('Borneyensis')—The trunk is upright and straight from which the branches hang down to form a green fountain or cone; found in Borny, France about 1870.

'Cockleshell'—A slow-growing, somewhat columnar form with lustrous leaves that are smaller than those of 'Rotundifolia'; discovered about 1960 in Hillier's Nursery; have seen this only once at the Holden Arboretum and identified it as 'Rotundifolia'; it is a rather handsome plant.

'Colcheata'—A dwarf, slow-growing, cone-shaped form; leaves about 1 1/2″ long, concave beneath, obovate and tapering to an acute base; margins toward apex with deep dentations (mini-lobes).

'Comptoniifolia'—Similar to 'Asplenifolia' except the linear-lanceolate leaves are more abundant; it is a weaker grower; cultivated before 1864 in Germany.

'Crarae'—Asymmetrically ovate and recurved leaves with oblique-cuneate and slightly auriculate bases, deeply lobed along the margins, sinuses are cut one-fourth to one-third the distance to the midrib; parent tree in Crarae Gardens, Inverary, Argyll, Scotland.

'Crispa'—Growth normal but upright; leaves narrowly elliptical with the edges deeply cut and a little frizzy (hairy).

'Cristata'—Leaves bunched at end of shoots, very short-petioled, coarsely triangular-toothed, the apex decurved, crumpled resembling a cockscomb flower.

'Dawyck' ('Dawyckii', 'Fastigiata')—There is considerable confusion about the upright beeches; 'Fastigiata' has been introduced but technically is different from 'Dawyckii' which is rigidly columnar to narrowly cone-shaped and maintains this condition without pruning; it can grow 80′ high or more while spreading only about 10′; it was found wild near the Scottish country estate Dawyck, Peeblesshire in 1864 and cultivated there; about 1907 the Hesse Nursery of Weener, Hanover, Germany, obtained scions and introduced it commercially in 1913; among the handsomest of all upright-columnar trees; in March 1994, my fellow plant colleague, Al Armitage and I visited Dawyck Arboretum and saw the original Dawyck beech which was discovered in the countryside, dug, and planted behind the manor house; its old gray bones are aching and a limb or two has been lost but to see this 130-year-old plant, the progenitor type, that has provided scions for gardens worldwide, was a great thrill.

'Dawyck Gold'—Introduced by J.R.P. van Hoey Smith in 1973; originated in 1968 as the result of a cross between 'Dawyck' and 'Zlatia'; it is narrow-columnar in habit with golden yellow leaves in spring that color similarly in the fall; see *The Garden* 105(7) (1980) for complete details on this and the next cultivar.

'Dawyck Purple'—As above but leaves of a deep purple color; the tops of the shoots turned slightly inward; narrower, more open growth habit than 'Dawyck Gold'; originated as did 'Dawyck Gold' from about 100 variable seeds collected in 1969 from a tree of Dawyck growing at Trompenburg Arboretum; of the seedlings, 63 were typical of the species, the others with the Dawyck habit—25 green leaf, 4 purple, and 8 golden; from these 'Dawyck Gold' and 'Dawyck Purple' were introduced; see *J. Royal Hort. Soc.* 98:206–207 (1973) for specifics.

'Foliis Variegatus'—The leaves variegated with white and yellow, with red and purple stains interspersed.

'Grandidentata'—Leaves broadly elliptical, margin coarse and evenly dentate, the teeth angular, cuneate at base; not as handsome as 'Asplenifolia'; possibly a branch sport; found in Germany around 1810.

'Interrupta'—Leaves irregular and deformed, often part of the blade is only connected by the venation.

'Laciniata'—A rather confusing group of serrated-leaf beeches; leaves ovate-lanceolate, with 7 to 9 deep and regular serrations on each side, the sinuses extending about one-third of the way to the midrib; known since 1792 and considerable variation in degree of serration occurs on any one tree; often listed as f. *laciniata* (Pers.) Domin.

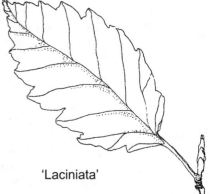

'Laciniata'

'Latifolia' (f. *latifolia* Kirchn.)—A form with larger, sturdier leaves than the type, often up to 6 and 7″ long, 5 1/2″ wide, on young trees.

'Luteovariegata'—Leaves marked with yellow blotches, margins yellow; stronger growing than 'Albovariegata'.

'Miltonensis'—A weeping form of great beauty; apparently quite confused; Bean has an excellent account of this cultivar.

'Pagnyensis'—A weeping form with a wide umbrella-shaped crown; has to be grafted on a standard or otherwise does not grow upright like typical 'Pendula'.

'Parkanaur'—Unique parasol appearance, extremely contorted older branches, 160-year-old parent tree is 10′ by 17′.

'Pendula' [f. *pendula* (Loud.) Schelle]—I have never seen one I didn't love and no two are exactly alike; a most beautiful weeping form, sometimes the branches are horizontal for a distance and then turn down forming a large tent-like mass; other trees have a central leader from which the branches hang down at various angles from 60 to 45° to almost "arms at one's side"; I can cite numerous examples of splendid Weeping Beeches but the finest is located at the Hunnewell Estate, Wellesley, MA; the center of the tree died out and the outer branches layered forming a copse; the entire tree (multiple trees) covers an area the size of a basketball court; a magnificent feeling to walk into this biologically domed coliseum; 50′ to 60′ high, wider at maturity.

'Purple Fountain'—This interesting form resulted as a seedling of 'Purpurea Pendula'; it differs in the narrow upright growth and the central stem from which the branches hang down in a loose cascading fashion; the purple foliage is not as dark as the parent's; like the parent's it fades in the summer heat; a plant was 12′ high and 3′ wide at the base, have read 25′ by 12 to 15′; introduced by Grootendorst in 1975.

'Purpurea Nana'—Compact, 10′ high, 6′ wide, oval form with small purple-brown leaves.

'Purpurea Pendula'—A broad mushroom-shaped, weeping, purple-leaved form that never becomes too large; the largest specimens I have seen were about 10′; the leaves fade to purple-green in summer; a slow grower; it does not develop a central leader and the branches develop in a broad arch; originated in Germany about 1865.

'Purpurea Tricolor'—Purplish leaves are edged and striped with rose and pinkish white, leaves narrower than usual; this may be the same as 'Roseomarginata'.

'Quercifolia'—Similar to 'Laciniata' types?; intermediate between 'Laciniata' and 'Grandidentata'.

'Red Obelisk'—Compact, pyramidal-columnar form with dark purple, dissected leaves, foliage similar to 'Rohanii'; 10 to 12′ high, 3′ wide in 12 years, to 50′.

'Remillyensis'—An umbrella-shaped form with tortuous branches.

'Riversii'—A deep purple form that supposedly holds this color into summer; trees I have seen turn purple-green like many of the Purple Beech cultivars; it was raised and distributed originally by Messrs. Rivers of Sawbridgeworth, England; the new spring leaves are perhaps the darkest (blackest) purple of any form and from my experience difficult to properly photograph; 50′ by 40′.

'Rohan Green'—Dark green leaves with undulating, lobed margins.

'Rohan Gold'—Another J.R.P. van Hoey Smith introduction; similar to 'Rohanii' but with yellowish foliage; originated in 1970 in the Trompenburg Arboretum.

'Rohanii'—A vigorous grower with brownish purple leaves, the margins of the leaves somewhat undulating, edged with rounded, shallow teeth, and almost crisped; the color fades with time; supposedly originated from a cross between a purple beech ('Brocklesby') and 'Quercifolia' in 1894.

'Roseomarginata' ('Tricolor', 'Purpurea Tricolor')—A purple leaf form with an irregular rose and pinkish white border; this form has been known since about 1883; there is considerable confusion between 'Roseomarginata' and 'Tricolor' with the leaves of the latter supposedly well marked with distinct cream and pink borders surrounding the purple center; I have seen many 'Roseomarginata' and must admit that there is sufficient white and pink in some to pass for the 'Tricolor' version; Bean suggests that the two are similar or identical; this cultivar is best provided some shade for the creamy pink areas often become scorched in hot, dry weather; 30′ by 20′; Bean supplement lists 'Tricolor' as a variegated green leaf form.

'Rohanii'

'Rotundifolia'—A beautiful tree, the leaves lustrous deep dark green, rounded, and 1/2 to 1 1/2″ in diameter, very closely set on the branches, usually with 4 vein pairs; it leafs out about two weeks later than the species; the habit is dense, pyramidal-oval to pyramidal-rounded; one of the most handsome forms of the European Beech; there is a splendid 50′ high specimen at the Arnold Arboretum.

'Rotundifolia'

'Spaethiana' ('Spathiana')—One of the most beautiful deep purple-leaf beeches, the veins of which are usually lighter than the interveinal areas; it holds the color well, probably better than any other purple form; leafs out about one week later than most other beeches; introduced by Späth Nursery about 1920; 50′ by 40′.

'Tortuosa' [f. *tortuosa* (Pepin) Hegi.]—A variable form with uniquely twisted trunk and branches; usually wide-spreading and mounded forming a dome of foliage and sometimes referred to as the Parasol Beech; occurs in the wild in several European countries; the foliage is normal; this is a beautiful form especially in winter when the branches are highlighted by snow; supposedly comes about 60% true-to-type from seed; seldom grows more than 10 to 15′ high; there are several magnificent specimens in the Arnold Arboretum; found for the first time about 1845 in France; at Trompenburg Arboretum, I saw a small purple-leaf, contorted branch form about 2 to 3′ high and 4 to 5′ wide; there was no name and whether Mr. van Hoey Smith introduced it is not known; the leaf color (May) was deep reddish purple.

'Viridivariegata'—The dark green leaves are marked with light green blotches; put into commerce about 1935.

'Zlatia'—Normal habit but slow-growing; new leaves yellow and fading to green in summer; discovered in 1890 near Vranje, Serbia; this form may belong to *F. moesiaca* since it was found in its range of distribution.

Other cultivars abstracted from various references include: 'Black Swan', 'Flagellaris', 'Friso', 'Greenwood', 'Horizontalis', 'Marmorata', 'Quercina', 'Quercoides', 'Rohan Pyramid', 'Rohan Trompenburg', 'Silverwood', and 'Tortuosa Purpurea'.

PROPAGATION: Seed should be stratified for 3 to 5 months at 41°F or fall sown; I have attempted to root soft and hardwood cuttings on several occasions but to no avail; cultivars are pot grafted usually in the winter months; tissue culture might prove extremely useful here; some interesting work by Dr. Bassuk and coworkers from Cornell on etiolation and banding relative to rooting cuttings; see *Proc. Intl. Plant Prop. Soc.* 34:543–550 (1984) for specifics.

ADDITIONAL NOTES: I have many "favorite" trees and this certainly ranks near the top. Unfortunately, it does not do well in the heat of the southern states (Zone 7–8) and was severely injured, especially on exposed sites in the Midwest during the difficult winter of 1976–77 (−20 to −25°F). It appears to reach its maximum size from Boston south to Washington, DC. Some of the most beautiful forms of European Beech can be found at Arnold Arboretum, Longwood Gardens, Mt. Auburn Cemetery, Swarthmore College, and the old estates in Newport, RI.

Ten species of beech are described and I considered including several such as *F. crenata* Bl., Japanese Beech; *F. engleriana* Seemen., Chinese Beech; and *F. orientalis* Lipsky, Oriental Beech. All have crossed my path but were largely undifferentiable from the two species treated herein. It took me until my second sabbatical (1991) at the Arnold Arboretum to realize that I had been walking under *F. engleriana* in the beech collection.

NATIVE HABITAT: Europe, Long cultivated.

Fatsia japonica (Thunb.) Decne. & Planch. — Japanese Fatsia
(fat′si-à jà-pon′i-kà)

FAMILY: Araliaceae

LEAVES: Alternate, simple, evergreen, deeply palmately, 7- to 9(11)-lobed, leathery, usually broader than high, 6 to 14″(16″) across, cordate, divided beyond the middle into oblong-ovate, acuminate, serrate lobes with rounded sinuses, lustrous dark green above, paler beneath, glabrous; petiole—4 to 12″ long, round, smooth.

STEM: Stout, coarse, usually unbranched, green, marked with large leaf scars.

SIZE: 6 to 10′ high by 6 to 10′ wide; can grow to 15′ but this is rare.

HARDINESS: Zone 8 to 10; Athens-Atlanta, GA areas (Zone 7b) are the upper limit; if not sited in a shady courtyard or against a wall it is doomed to failure in these areas; tolerant to about 10°F, literally blitzed at -3°F, no damage at 7°F in 1994.

HABIT: Rather rounded and open but I have seen plants that were quite full and dense.

RATE: Moderate.

TEXTURE: Coarse, tropical in effect, but exciting for the unique boldness it brings to a garden.

LEAF COLOR: Lustrous dark green through the seasons; will brown if sited in full sun and windy exposure.

FLOWERS: White, in 1 to 1 1/2″ diameter umbels which form a large, terminal, umbellose panicle to 20″ wide; October to November; flower stalks white like flowers; has flowered outdoors at Callaway Gardens, Pine Mountain and at Mrs. Robert Segrest's garden, Athens, GA; actually flowering times appear variable, have seen in full flower in early January in Savannah.

FRUIT: Subglobose, fleshy, black, 1/3″ diameter drupe, ripens in mid to late winter, early spring.

CULTURE: Transplants readily from containers; prefers moist, acid, high organic matter soils but tolerant of light sandy to heavy clay soils with less than adequate drainage; responds to fertility; moderate to full shade is preferable; excessive wind and winter sun may cause injury; tolerant of air pollution and salt spray.

DISEASES AND INSECTS: None serious.

LANDSCAPE VALUE: Excellent for bold textural effect but not exactly easy to blend with other plants; I have thought about combinations of *Aucuba*, *Danae racemosa*, and *Cyrtomium falcatum*; all require or love shade and would make for interesting foliage effects; used in courtyards and against brick walls to break up monotony; used in North as house and conservatory plant.

CULTIVARS:

'Aurea'—Golden variegated leaves.

'Manchu Fan'—Lacy-lobed form with attractive lobes on the 9 larger lobes forming an almost complete circle around the leaf petiole.

'Moseri'—More compact form with larger leaves; one of the parents of × *Fatshedera lizei*.

'Variegata'—White variegation patterns are dispersed over the leaf, but principally at end of lobes; have seen at Kew, very pretty form, leaf not as dark green.

ADDITIONAL NOTES: I learned these plants in a houseplant course at The Ohio State University and have found it difficult to accept them as outdoor hardy landscape plants. Their foliage is bold and handsome and, in a shady setting, they have much to offer. Head-Lee Nursery, Seneca, SC has selected a more cold hardy form from Sylva, NC. In addition, the nursery has several intriguing variegated forms that are being evaluated.

PROPAGATION: Cuttings should be taken after the wood is fairly firm and provided with bottom heat; cleaned seeds germinated 58% when sown directly.

NATIVE HABITAT: Japan. Introduced 1838.

RELATED SPECIES:

× **Fatshedera lizei** Guill., (fats-hed′ĕr-å liz-e′ī), is an intergeneric hybrid between *Fatsia japonica* 'Moseri' and *Hedera helix* 'Hibernica' raised in 1910 by Messrs. Lizè Fréres, nurserymen of Nantes, France. It forms a semi-climbing, evergreen shrub or vine, and is useful for shady situations. Grows 3 to 5′ if left to its own devices; can be trained on a wall to 10′ or more. The leathery, lustrous dark green leaves are 4 to 10″ across, and not quite as long, 5-lobed, palmate, with the lobes cut 1/3 to 1/2 the way to the base. The petiole is about as long as the blade and often purple. The pale green-white flowers are borne in an 8 to 10″ long and 4″ wide terminal panicle made up of 1″ diameter, 12- to 36-flowered, hemispherical umbels. Flowers in October in the Dirr garden. Can be

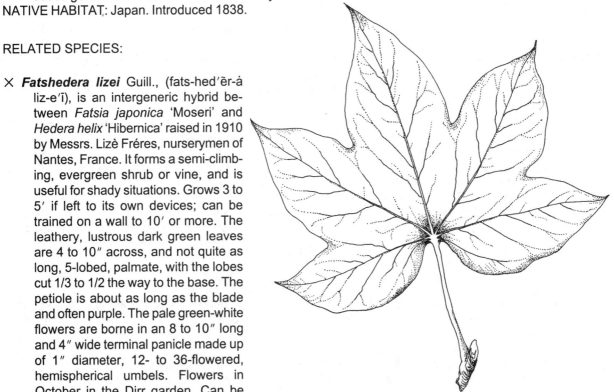

trained on a wall or trellis where the bold foliage makes a strong statement. Excellent as a house or conservatory plant. 'Variegata' has leaves that are splashed and bordered with white; this form does not appear as vigorous or stable as the yellow-variegated form. Also a form with irregular yellowish to yellow-green markings primarily in the center of the leaf; may be 'Anna Mikkels'. Can be successfully grown in Zone 8 and is hardier than *Fatsia japonica*. I have grown the plant for six years and watched it grow backward. In 1984, at −3°F, it died back to the ground but has regenerated. The variegated form is less cold hardy than the species. Easily rooted from cuttings. Develops weak, root-like holdfasts but needs support to stay affixed to walls and fences.

Feijoa sellowiana O. Berg — Guava, Pineapple Guava
(fē-jō′à or fē-hō′à sel-lōw-i-ā′nà)

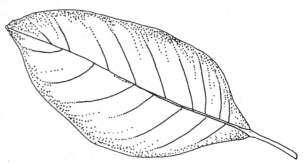

FAMILY: Myrtaceae

LEAVES: Opposite, simple, evergreen, oval or ovate, entire, blunt at apex, tapered or rounded at the base, 1 to 3″ long, 3/4 to 1 1/2″ wide, lustrous dark almost bluish green and glabrous above except when young, whitish, felted and conspicuously veined beneath; petiole—1/4″ or less, pubescent.

BUDS: Small, less than 1/16″ high, covered with gray-silver pubescence, appear partially embedded in stem, sit directly above half-elliptical leaf scar.

STEM: Somewhat squarish-rounded in cross-section, gray-brown, densely covered with pubescence on first year stems, fissured-exfoliating on second year and older stems, glabrous; pith—green-gold in young stem, light brown later.

SIZE: 10 to 15′ high, spread to 10′; at one time 8 to 10′ specimens at Callaway Gardens.

HARDINESS: Zone 8 to 10; considered hardy to 10°F; killed to ground at −3°F in Athens; 7°F in 1994 caused almost complete leaf drop, no stem damage.

HABIT: Evergreen shrub or small tree of bushy habit; plants I have seen were quite dense; apparently will spread if not pruned and can become rather loose and open; in Zone 7 probably best to treat as an herbaceous perennial or woody subshrub.

RATE: Fast.

TEXTURE: Medium.

LEAF COLOR: Dark green above, grayish beneath; gray-green effect due to whitish pubescence on underside of leaf; color is diminished in cold weather.

FLOWER: Perfect, solitary, produced in leaf axils of current year's shoots, 1 1/4 to 1 3/4″ long and borne on a pubescent, pendulous, 1 to 1 1/2″ long pedicel, 4 sepals are reflexed, 4 petals red in center, whitish at margin, stamens numerous, erect, 3/4 to 1″ long, rich crimson, May–June, opening early May 1995 (Athens), supposedly edible.

FRUIT: Green tinged red, maturing to yellow, 1 to 3″ long, egg-shaped berry, edible, with a rich aromatic flavor; ripen in late summer and early fall into January depending on climate; taste likened to pineapple with overtones of spearmint; sepals persist at distal end of fruit, remind of ears.

CULTURE: Transplant container-grown plants; prefers well-drained, light loamy soil; full sun, tolerant of partial shade if fruit is not a factor; tolerant of salt spray; prune after flowering.

DISEASES AND INSECTS: None serious.

LANDSCAPE VALUE: Excellent for foliage effect and flowers; suitable for screens and hedges; has been used at Callaway Gardens with good success; in colder areas of the South the tips of the shoots are killed and this has the effect of pruning; supposedly can grow 15 to 25′ but this is probably only realized under south Florida and West Coast conditions in the United States.

CULTIVARS:

'Coolidge'—Self-fruiting selection, small fruit with mild flavor.

'Mammoth'—Vigorous, evergreen shrub, self-fertile, large fruit of good quality ripening in mid-season.

'Nazemeta'—Large, excellent fruit, self-fruitful, no leaf drop at 7°F, appears more cold hardy than the species.

'Pineapple Gem'—Self-fruiting selection.

'Superba'—Self-sterile, round fruits, plant with 'Coolidge' to insure abundant fruiting.

'Trask'—Large fruit with deep green skin, skin is thicker and grittier than parent but pulp quality is good, productive and ripens early, self-fruitful.

'Unique'—Vigorous, upright-spreading, 8' or more, self-fruitful, high yielding, good tasting fruit at an early age.

'Variegata'—Leaves with white variegation.

PROPAGATION: Seeds can be sown when removed from the pulp; cuttings are the preferred method but published success is variable; I have not been able to root the plant; the parent plant influences rooting success, 15 clones that averaged 10 years of age rooted 4 to 76% when evaluated 7 months later; 3 to 4″ long, 2 leaf cuttings, August, rooted 75%; a rooting chemical has proven beneficial, possibly in the 3000 to 8000 ppm range.

ADDITIONAL NOTES: Beautiful shrub; flowers are delicate and spectacular; may require cross pollination to set fruit; plant on Georgia campus is now 6′ high after being killed to ground at -3°F in 1983–84 winter. New name is *Acca sellowiana* (O. Berg) Burret. Years will pass before this name gains acceptance.

NATIVE HABITAT: Southern Brazil and Uruguay; discovered by Friedrich Sellow in 1819.

Ficus carica L. — Common Fig

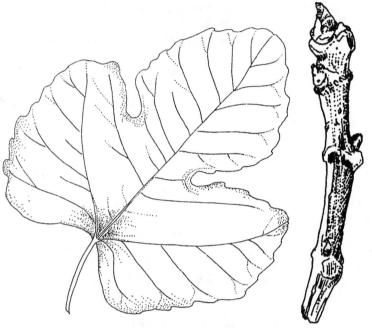

FAMILY: Moraceae

LEAVES: Alternate, simple, 3- to 5-lobed, 4 to 8″ long, and on occasion even larger in length and width, broadly ovate to orbicular, cordate, depth of sinuses variable, lobes usually scalloped into broad-rounded teeth, dark green, both surfaces scabrous with short stiff hairs; petiole—1 to 4″ long.

Ficus carica, (fī ′kus kar′i-kȧ), Common Fig, forms a rather coarse, broad-rounded shrub. Size varies from 10 to 15′(30′). The large, dark green leaves provide an interesting textural effect in the landscape. The flowers are produced on the inside of a concave receptacle which when mature is enlarged and fleshy and contains the true fruits (achenes). The tapering, top-shaped fruits average 2 to 4″ long, 1 to 2 1/2″ wide. The Common Fig is often seen around older homes in the South and at one time was widely planted. It prefers a moist, well-drained soil but appears to be adaptable to less-than-ideal conditions. Unfortunately, excessive cold will cause injury and it is best grown in Zone 7 and south. I have grown rather fond of this plant over the past 10 years, especially because of the large, rugged leaves. Unfortunately, -3°F killed most shrubs halfway to the ground. Most returned to a normal state. Several good cultivars include 'Brown Turkey' with purple-brown fruit and 'Comadria' a choice white fig blushed violet, thin-skinned with sweet white to red flesh. I have not noticed insects and diseases of any consequence. Have rooted leafless November hardwood cuttings utilizing 8000 ppm IBA-talc. Cuttings were placed in bark medium in 3-gallon containers with 1″ of stem above surface of medium. Cuttings rooted 80%. Western Asia and eastern Mediterranean region. Cultivated since early times.

Ficus pumila L. — Climbing Fig

FAMILY: Moraceae

LEAVES: *Juvenile* (more common), alternate, simple, evergreen, obliquely heart-shaped, pointed, 3/4 to 1 1/4″ long, 2/3's as wide, medium to dark green, usually glabrous above, warty/bumpy upper surface, pubescent below; petiole—very short; *Adult* (fruit-bearing state), more leathery, ovate, cordate, pointed, 2 to 4″ long, 1/2 as wide, rich dark green above, pale beneath, net-veined; petiole—pubescent, 1/2″ long.

Juvenile leaf

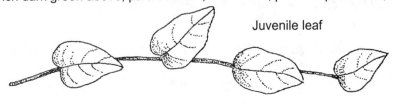

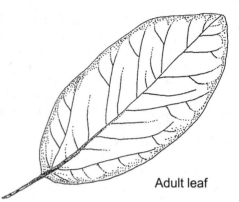

Adult leaf

Ficus pumila, (fĭ ′kus pū′mil-à), Climbing Fig, seems out of place in outdoor gardens since it usually covers the inside of conservatory walls in northern gardens. However in the South it is a regular feature on masonry structures. Grows like a pancake on walls and develops a woody structure in the adult state. Will grow 40 to 50′ high or more. The small medium to dark green juvenile leaves form an interesting mosaic and become dense and matted with time. Both juvenile (about 1″ long) and mature leaves (2 to 4″ long) develop. The vine climbs by aerial rootlets and can literally cement itself to porous materials. Prefers a moist, well-drained soil and high humidity; can be sited in full sun or partial shade; may need considerable pruning in deep South but cold controls growth in upper South. In many respects, the juvenile/mature stages parallel those of *Euonymus fortunei*. 'Gold Heart' has a gold center to each leaf; 'Minima' is a juvenile form with very small leaves; 'Snow Flake' has a thick white margin to the leaf; 'Variegata' has white- and green-mottled leaves. In 1982, 0°F defoliated the plant in the Athens area. In 1984, –3°F killed the same plant halfway to the ground but it has recovered and now blankets the wall completely. A few notes relative to performance since the 1990 edition might prove interesting: seven degrees in 1994 killed 80 to 90% of the leaves but did not damage the stems; in 1995, 13°F knocked off 50% of the leaves. Native of China, Formosa, and Japan. Introduced into cultivation in 1759. Zone (7)8 to 10.

Firmiana simplex (L.) W. Wight — Chinese Parasol Tree

FAMILY: Sterculiaceae
LEAVES: Alternate, simple, 6 to 8″ long and wide but often over 12″ especially on vigorous young plants, usually 3-lobed, but often 5-lobed, with the general appearance of a maple leaf, cordate at base, rich green, glabrous or pubescent beneath; petiole—2/3′s to about the length of the blade.

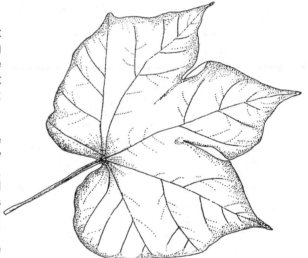

Firmiana simplex, (fir-me-ā′nà sim′pleks), Chinese Parasol Tree, is a round-headed tree that will grow 30 to 45′ high. Its chief interest resides in the large, rich green leaves which lend an almost tropical appearance. The stem and bark on young trees are smooth, gray-green and add winter interest. The yellowish green flowers occur in 10 to 20″ long, terminal panicles in June–July and are followed by pea-sized fruits that are attached to the edges of leaf-like carpels (follicle) that split open soon after flowering. The first time I saw the fruit I was intrigued by the pattern of seed development. Classically, angiosperms are hidden-seeded plants and the carpel walls usually enclose the seeds from view. I collected seeds that had dried and sowed them directly. Germination was sporadic but good. Seeds that were stratified for about 2 months did not germinate any better. Sow seed as soon as fruit appears ripe. A tree on the Georgia campus often develops reasonable yellow fall color. Numerous seedlings have germinated in the woods surrounding this tree. May grow 6 to 8′ as a young tree under reasonable water and nutrition. I doubt seriously whether the plant has a place in commerce. With some creative marketing, the species could gain a garden hold. A form with white-mottled leaves is known ('Variegata'). China, Japan. Introduced 1757. Zone (6)7 to 9.

Fontanesia fortunei Carr.— Fortune Fontanesia

FAMILY: Oleaceae
LEAVES: Opposite, simple, lanceolate or ovate-lanceolate, 1 to 4 1/2″ long, 1/3 to 1″ wide, acuminate, cuneate, entire, lustrous dark green, glabrous; petiole—1/2″ long.
BUDS: Small, 1/16″ long, imbricate, brown, glabrous, sitting directly on top of leaf scar.

STEM: Young—somewhat 4-sided, slender, purple, glabrous, with maturity shining light brown, glabrous, 4-decurrent ridges, 2 from edges of each leaf scar producing a squarish stem in cross-section; pith—white, solid.

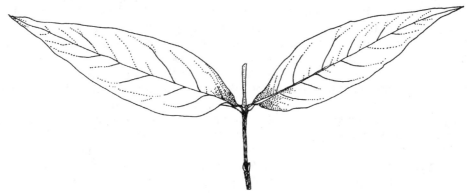

Fontanesia fortunei, (fon-tà-nē′zi-à fôr-tū′nē-ī), Fortune Fontanesia, is only included because one of my mentors, Dr. Ken Reisch, brought the plant to my attention many (now 35) years ago during my plant material courses at Ohio State. The plant has succumbed to progress, i.e., new construction, but I can picture this graceful 12′ high, multi-stemmed, almost bamboo-like, unperturbable shrub. Have seen it used as a screen in Clinton, OK where it appeared to thrive under harsh conditions. Morton Arboretum reported a >30′ high plant and noted that the trunks die unpredictably. The lustrous dark green foliage is what makes the plant run for the greenish white flowers, each 1/6″ long, occur in 1 to 2″ long panicles and do not overwhelm. The fruit is a 3/8″ long, flat, oblong samara with winged margins and a notched apex. For difficult sites and rough areas it would prove serviceable. In many respects, it has privet-like characteristics and is tougher to propagate so pales by commercial comparison. 'Titan' was selected by Cole Nursery Co., Circleville, OH (now out of business) for more upright habit and better foliage; 3″ high cuttings grew 76″ tall and 65″ wide in 3 growing seasons; this plant needs to be used in tough highway and urban sites. Have seen 'Nana' listed; is dwarf, slower and lower in habit. A single plant in the University's Botanical Garden has grown like topsy. Interestingly, no one has ever asked me its identity. Tells you something about its blandness. China. Introduced 1845. Zone 4 to 8.

Forsythia × intermedia Zab. — Border Forsythia
(fôr-sith′i-à in-tēr-mē′dē-à)

FAMILY: Oleaceae

LEAVES: Opposite, simple, toothed usually on the upper one-half, ovate-oblong to oblong-lanceolate, 3 to 5″ long, half as wide, medium to dark green above, lighter below, glabrous; petiole—1/2″ long.

BUDS: Imbricate, conical, light yellow-brown with a tinge of green, about 1/4″ long, borne several together in the axils, usually rather loosely scaled.

STEM: Often somewhat squarish or 4-sided, yellowish brown and strongly lenticellate; pith—chambered in the internodes, solid at the nodes, pith character does not always parallel the description because of age of stems.

SIZE: 8 to 10′ high by 10 to 12′ wide.

HARDINESS: Vegetatively hardy in zone 4, however, flower buds are often killed in Zone 5, acceptable in 6 to 8(9).

HABIT: Rank-growing, deciduous shrub, differentially developing upright and arching canes which give it the appearance that the roots were stuck in an electric socket; always needs grooming, one of the most overrated and over-used shrubs!; will sucker (slowly) to form large colonies.

RATE: Fast.

TEXTURE: Medium in leaf; wild in winter.

LEAF COLOR: Medium to dark green in summer; green or yellow-green in fall, sometimes with a tinge of purple; have seen respectable fall color on certain plants in the Athens area, leaves hold late (November) and may turn a deep burgundy; from year to year fall color is variable but on occasion the reddish purple is sufficient to incite me to *select* a new forsythia for this trait, alas, I resist the temptation; the fall of 1997 was such a year as seemingly every forsythia was reddish purple.

FLOWERS: Perfect, 1 1/4 to 1 1/2″ long, pale to deep yellow, 4-lobed corollas, scentless although I have detected a slight fragrance (privet odor) on occasion, usually March–April for 2 to 3 weeks; borne 1 to 6 together or often in 2's and 3's on old wood; the justifiable reason for using forsythia is the wonderful flower effect in early spring; in the Midwest one was easily frustrated waiting for a swaggering golden yellow shrub to appear in the spring landscape only to find that a significant portion of the flower buds was killed by cold; in Athens I have charted the flowering times with occasional flowering as early as late January but the peak normally early to mid-March.

FRUIT: Two-celled, dehiscent, brown capsule, 1/3″ long, often housing many winged seeds, not ornamental; have collected and germinated seeds of *F.* × *intermedia* but never kept the seedlings until flowering.

CULTURE: Fibrous, transplants readily bare root, container-grown or balled-and-burlapped; prefers a good, loose soil but will do well in about any soil; full sun to maximize flower; pH adaptable; withstands city conditions; air pollution tolerant; prune after flowering either by cutting plant to ground or removing the oldest stems.

DISEASES AND INSECTS: Crown gall, leaf spots, dieback, four-lined plant bug, Japanese weevil, northern root-knot nematode and spider mites; none of which are extremely troublesome.

LANDSCAPE VALUE: Chief value is in the early spring flower; forsythias do not belong in foundation plantings but are often used there; shrub border, massing, groupings, bank plantings are the most appropriate places; the early spring color is a strong selling point and when forsythia is in flower it is one of the hottest selling items at a garden center; often injured by late freezes and flower quality is reduced; I have seen forsythia flowers a beautiful golden yellow one day and with a hard freeze over night they are transformed to brown mush; temperatures about -10 to -15°F appear to coincide with flower bud kill; it is common in the North to see forsythia flowering only below the snowline; those flower buds above having been killed by low temperatures; Dr. Paul Cappiello, Orono, ME reports vegetative hardiness to -30°F, no flower bud survival; should be planted with other spring bulbs, hellebores, small evergreen shrubs to tie it to the landscape; I have seen the plant pruned into every imaginable shape from bubble gum machines to pink Cadillacs; this shrub was not made for extensive pruning.

CULTIVARS:

'Arnold Brilliant'—Not known by this author but Cappiello reported 50% dieback and flower bud kill in Orono, ME.

'Arnold Giant'—A colchicine induced tetraploid from a seedling of *F.* × *intermedia* 'Spectabilis'; the leaves are larger, thicker and darker green and the habit more erect; it is sparse in flower number and somewhat difficult to propagate from cuttings; Dr. Ed Hasselkus, retired, University of Wisconsin, has related to me that this cultivar is hardy in Madison where 'Beatrix Farrand' and other *F.* × *intermedia* types are not; it has never proved popular in commerce but has been used in crosses which resulted in some superior seedlings.

'Beatrix Farrand'—Whether this cultivar is still extant is a debatable point but there is a vivid golden yellow-flowered form with each flower about 1 1/2 to 2″ across; the flowers are borne in great numbers and each shoot is clothed with golden yellow; this cultivar resulted from crosses between 'Arnold Giant' and *F.* × *intermedia* 'Spectabilis'; it is supposedly a triploid and all subsequent clones identified as 'Beatrix Farrand' have been tetraploids; it (?) is a vigorous shrub easily growing 8 to 10′ high and wide; I chuckle somewhat at the thought of all the nutritional, propagation and hardiness experiments that have been conducted over the years with this cultivar(?); another plant with this name is vigorous, erect, with dull bluish green, coarsely serrated teeth; flowers are 3/4 to 1″ long, 3/8″ wide and soft yellow, more or less nodding, fruits are borne in abundance; foliage is considered ugly and habit is gaunt; during my 1991 sabbatical at the Arnold Arboretum I ferreted out and cross-checked 'Beatrix Farrand', 'Lynwood', and 'Spring Glory'; the Arnold's 'Beatrix Farrand' appears close to the prototype; it is later flowering than 'Spring Glory' (1st), 'Lynwood' (2nd) in Georgia.

'Densiflora'—Introduced by Späth Nurseries, Berlin, Germany in 1888; the result of seedling selection from *F.* × *intermedia*; the flowers are light yellow, the corolla lobes about 1 1/4″ long, spreading, not markedly revolute; borne singly, crowded along stem, its habit is spreading with pendulous branches like *F. suspensa*; not an outstanding form based on evaluations at the Arnold.

'Evergold'—Rich yellow-margined leaf, color holds in heat of summer, growth habit typical of species, introduced by Head-Lee Nursery, Seneca, SC.

'Fiesta'—Compact and densely branched, 3 to 4′ high, wide-growing, golden yellow flowers, rich green leaves with cream and gold centers; has performed well in our Georgia trials and examination of foliage on October 27, 1997 indicated good quality variegation and leaf retention; from Duncan and Davies, New Zealand.

'Fontanna'—Strong-growing up to 8′ high, large, broad-petaled, rich yellow flowers in profusion; flower buds very frost resistant; *F. ovata* × *F.* × *intermedia* 'Vitellina'.

'Gold Leaf' ('Goldleaf')—Golden foliage, actually more lime green then gold, uniform across leaf, witnessed May 26, 1990 at Arnold, best in partial shade.

Gold Tide™ ('Courtasol')—Compact grower, 1 1/2′ by 5′, heavy production of grapefruit yellow flowers, moss green foliage, graceful arching shoots cover the ground, from Europe.

'Golden Nugget'—Compact habit, 4 to 5′ by 4 to 5′, large bright yellow flowers.

'Golden Times' (selection of *F. giraldiana*)—Yellow foliage with sun tolerance, toothed leaf margins, more compact growth habit, possibly French origin.

'Goldzauber'—Flowers dark yellow resembling those of 'Lynwood', medium-sized, thin branched shrub, result of a cross between 'Lynwood' and 'Beatrix Farrand'.

'Karl Sax'—Of bushier habit and not as tall as 'Beatrix Farrand'; the deep yellow flowers are a shade darker than 'Beatrix Farrand'; the flowers may be 1 3/4″ across and are more or less horizontally disposed so their deep yellow to yellow-orange throats provide a golden glow to the entire shrub; it is a tetraploid and shows better flower bud hardiness than 'Beatrix Farrand'; this clone resulted from 'Arnold Giant' × *F.* × *intermedia* 'Spectabilis' and was named for Dr. Karl Sax, Director of the Arnold Arboretum, who with his students worked on improving the genus *Forsythia*; originated about 1944 as did 'Beatrix Farrand'.

'Lynwood' ('Lynwood Gold')—A branch sport of 'Spectabilis' which originated in the garden (Lynwood) of Miss Adair in Cookstown, County Tyrone, Northern Ireland; the owner noticed a branch that had flowers which were more open and better distributed along the stem than those on the rest of the plant; the Slieve Donard Nursery of Newcastle introduced it in 1935; the brilliant yellow flowers are slightly lighter than 'Spectabilis'; the habit of growth is upright; nurserymen in this country call it 'Lynwood Gold'; still one of the best and most reliable; not as loud as 'Beatrix Farrand', 'Karl Sax', and 'Spectabilis'; the flowering stems appear as yellow wands.

'Maluch'—Compact, slow-growing with regular shape, small yellow flowers densely placed on branches, very frost resistant, *F. ovata* × *F.* × *intermedia*.

'Minigold'—Described as growing one-half the size of the species with typical yellow flowers.

'Mr. K'—Amazing what the literature hides, according to Bob Ticknor, retired, Oregon State, a selection by Klehm Nursery, IL that Klehm's received as unnamed plants, much like 'Lynwood'.

'Nana'—Low, dwarf form, a 20-year-old plant being 5′ high and 8′ wide; leaves may be simple, lobed and sometimes compound, pith is solid at nodes, chambered in internodes; very slow to flower and may take 7 years from a cutting before the greenish yellow flowers appear; originated in the Midwest.

'Parkdekur'—Deep yellow flowers up to 2″ wide, abundant, on a semi-pendulous branched shrub, result of a cross between 'Beatrix Farrand' and 'Spectabilis'.

'Primulina'—A chance seedling discovered by Alfred Rehder of the Arnold Arboretum in 1912; the flowers are pale yellow and the growth habit similar to 'Spectabilis'; it has been largely superseded by 'Spring Glory'.

'Prostrate Form'—Heronswood describes a virtual ground cover form with 6″ high shoots . . . "walking low through our rock garden."

'Spectabilis'—Has been the standard by which all others are judged; called Showy Border Forsythia; a vigorous shrub that will grow 10′ high and wide; the leaves being ovate-lanceolate and 3 to 4 1/2″ long; the rich bright yellow flowers may be as much as 1 1/2″ across and contain the usual 4 corolla lobes as well as 5 and 6; the flowers occur profusely from the axils of the stems; this cultivar is also more flower bud hardy than 'Beatrix Farrand'; introduced by Späth Nurseries in 1906.

'Spring Glory'—A branch sport of 'Primulina' discovered in 1930 by M. Horvath of Mentor, OH; the 1 1/2″ wide, sulfur-yellow flowers are densely produced along the stems; it grows to 10′ in height; introduced into the trade by Wayside Gardens in 1942; lower chilling requirement and flowers earlier and more uniformly in Zone 7 and 8.

'Tremonia'—A rather curious form with deeply cut leaves and upright-spreading growth habit; the plants I have seen were not particularly vigorous; introduced into the Arnold Arboretum in 1966 from the Dortmund Botanic Garden, Dortmund, West Germany.

'Variegata'—Have seen more than one form with creamy variegated leaves; unfortunately, unstable and will revert to green, also weak-growing.

'Vitellina'—The deep yellow flowers are about the smallest (1 1/4 to 1 1/2″ diameter) of the *F.* × *intermedia* types; the habit is rather erect, finally arching; put into commerce by Späth in 1899.

Week-End® ('Courtalyn')—Upright-growing habit, flowers golden yellow, very abundant.

'Winterthur'—More compact-growing, 6' by 6', primrose yellow flowers and dark green foliage; *F. ovata* × 'Spring Glory'; introduced by Winterthur Gardens in 1987.

A corollary to the above is necessary to fully understand the background of these cultivars. In 1878 Hermann Zabel, Director of the Municipal Garden in Munden, found seedling forsythias in the Botanic Garden of Gottingen which were the result of crosses between *F. viridissima* and *F. suspensa* var. *fortunei*. In 1885 he described this as *F. × intermedia* which has been the source of the garden forms we utilize today. It is interesting to note that the introduction of these garden forms took place largely at the Späth Nurseries around 1900 and the Arnold Arboretum in the 1940's. It might be worth someone's time to produce new forms with better habit and greater flower bud hardiness. See "The story of *Forsythia*," *Arnoldia* 31:41–63 (1971).

PROPAGATION: Seeds will germinate without a pretreatment but one to two months at 41°F appears to improve and unify germination; seeds that were cold stratified for 3 months produced radicles in the bag; softwood cuttings are easy to root; I always give them 1000 to 3000 ppm KIBA quick dip and in 3 to 4 weeks the mass of white roots is so great it is difficult to remove them from the media; hardwood cuttings can also be rooted.

ADDITIONAL NOTES: All the *F. × intermedia* types tested at Orono, ME failed to flower. Vegetative wood was hardy. The most flower bud hardy based on Maine tests (see elsewhere in *Forsythia* treatment) included: 'Meadowlark', 'Northern Gold', 'Vermont Sun', 'Northern Sun', *F. ovata* 'Nakai', 'New Hampshire Gold', and 'Ottawa'.

Forsythia species and particularly cultivars are irretrievably confused in the trade. I know for certain that nurseries may grow only one cultivar. Whatever the buyer requests, the plant so becomes. Be leery and skeptical.

RELATED SPECIES:

Forsythia 'Arnold Dwarf' resulted from a cross between *F. × intermedia* and *F. japonica* var. *saxatilis*. It flowers (greenish yellow to pale yellow) sparsely and plants may not produce any flowers until they are 5- to 6-years-old. On occasion have seen reasonable flowering. Produces 1 to 2″ long, strongly serrated, bright green leaves. Principal landscape value is the comparatively low habit. Six-year-old plants may be 3' tall and 7' across. It makes an excellent bank or large area cover for wherever the branches touch the soil, roots invariably develop. I have watched plants form a solid mass of foliage with an entire planting a bright green, somewhat irregular mass of semi-arching and prostrate shoots. Does not produce the carpet effect of *Vinca*, *Pachysandra* and *Hedera*. Developed at the Arnold Arboretum in 1941 by Dr. Sax. Zone 5 to 8. Vegetatively hardy in Orono, ME, no flowers.

Forsythia europaea Deg. & Bald. — Albanian Forsythia
LEAVES: Alternate, simple, ovate to ovate-lanceolate, 2 to 3″ long, 3/4 to 1 1/2″ wide, acute, rounded or broad cuneate, usually entire or with a few teeth on leaves of vigorous shoots, thick-textured, dark green, glabrous; petiole—1/6 to 1/3″ long.
STEM: Green, more rounded than *F. × intermedia*, glabrous, dotted with lenticels; pith—chambered.

Forsythia europaea, (fôr-sith′i-à ū-rō-pē′à), Albanian Forsythia, is an upright shrub growing to about 6' in height. The pale yellow flowers are about 3/4 to 1″ long and occur singly or 2 to 3 together. Considered the least showy of the forsythias when in flower. Flowers tend to hang from the stems. The capsule is smooth with a long beak. It was discovered about 1897 in northern Albania and Yugoslavia. It is allied to *F. viridissima* but differs in the ovate leaves and lanky habit. Zone 5. About at hardy as *F. suspensa*. Report said hardy to -20°F.

Forsythia mandshurica Nak. 'Vermont Sun', (fôr-sith′i-à mand-shoor′i-kà), is an almost unknown entity in the United States but is one of the most flower bud hardy types for northern gardens. The species itself is essentially unknown for it does not appear in Rehder, *Hortus III*, Krüssmann or Bean. It was wild-collected only once in Manchuria. The habit is unique with stiff, upright branches. Flower buds are blackish and prominent. Leaves often color orange-yellow to wine red in autumn. Flowers are sulfur yellow and among the first of all forsythias to open. Flowers are not as abundant as *F. × intermedia* types. I will offer the history of this cultivar. In 1940 Montreal Botanical Gardens obtained cuttings of *F. mandshurica* from Mr.

L. Ptitsin of Harbin, Manchuria. The University of Vermont obtained cuttings from MBG in 1968. After extensive evaluation Drs. Pellett and Evert registered the name 'Vermont Sun' in August, 1978. Through field and laboratory testing, its flower bud hardiness is estimated between -25°F and -30°F. It flowers about one week earlier with larger, darker yellow flower buds than *F. ovata*. It is an upright, erect shrub that will grow 6 to 8′ high and slightly less in width. I have seen the plant in flower at the Vermont Horticultural Research Center and can recommend it for those climates that suffer harsh winters. It does not hold a candle to the *F. × intermedia* types so do not think of it in those terms. Softwood cuttings collected in June treated with 3000 ppm IBA-talc placed in vermiculite under mist rooted 85% in 3 months. See *HortScience* 19:313–314 (1984).

Forsythia ovata Nak. — Early Forsythia
LEAVES: Alternate, simple, ovate or broad-ovate, 1 1/2 to 3 1/2″ long, 1 1/4 to 2 1/2″ wide, abruptly acuminate, truncate, or sometimes subcordate or broad cuneate, nearly entire to coarsely toothed, dark green, glabrous; petiole—1/4 to 1/2″ long.
STEM: Rounded (terete), gray-brown, glabrous, covered with small darkish lenticels; pith—chambered.

Forsythia ovata, (fôr-sith′i-à ō-vā′tà), Early Forsythia, is a rather stiff, spreading shrub that will grow 4 to 6′ high and wide. A fine specimen at the Arnold is 6′ high and 8 to 10′ wide. The bright yellow (tinge of green), 1/2 to 3/4″ wide flowers are among the earliest of all forsythia to open, usually appearing in March–April. The flowers are usually solitary. This species is interesting because of its flower bud hardiness. It has survived -20°F temperatures and flowered satisfactorily in Vermont tests [see "*Forsythia* flower bud hardiness," *HortScience* 14:623–624 (1979)]. Hybrids have been produced between *F. suspensa* and *F. ovata* and a colchicine-induced tetraploid called 'Tetragold' was raised in Holland and distributed about 1963. It is a low-growing (5′), bushy shrub with large (1 1/4″ wide), deep yellow flowers. 'Ottawa' came out of Canada and is more flower bud hardy, more vigorous with heavy floral production, and flowers 7 to 10 days earlier than other cultivars. 'Ottawa' and 'Robusta' are not as flower bud hardy as 'Meadowlark', 'Northern Gold', 'Northern Sun', 'New Hampshire Gold', 'Sunrise', and 'Vermont Sun'. Ranged from about 4 to 8°F less hardy. 'French's Florence' is a 4 to 5′ high shrub with smaller and lighter yellow flowers than the species but with greater flower bud hardiness. Korea. Introduced 1917. Zone 4 to 7.

Forsythia suspensa (Thunb.) Vahl. var. *sieboldii* Zab. — Weeping Forsythia
LEAVES: Opposite, simple, sometimes 3-parted or 3-foliate, ovate to oblong-ovate, 2 to 4″ long, 1 to 2″ wide, acute, broad cuneate or rounded at base, coarsely toothed, medium to dark green; petiole—1/2″ long.
STEM: Pith—hollow in internodes and solid at the nodes, yellowish brown stem color; also stem appears more rounded than *F. × intermedia*.

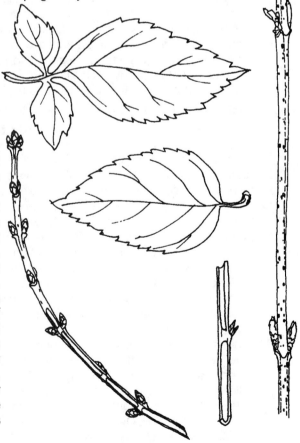

Forsythia suspensa var. *sieboldii*, (fôr-sith′i-à sus-pen-sà sē-bōl′dē-ī), Weeping Forsythia, grows 8 to 10′ tall and 10 to 15′ wide. The habit is upright, arching, almost fountain-like with slender, long, trailing, pendulous branches. The flowers are golden yellow, 1 to 1 1/4″ across, April, usually 1 to 3 together. This plant does not flower as heavily as *F. × intermedia*. Considerable confusion abounds as to the true name for "Weeping Forsythia." Variety *sieboldii* is the form with the long, trailing branches. I have seen the branches hanging over walls where they resemble brown ropes in winter. The branches can be trained on a wall or suitable structure and can grow 20 to 30′ high. In addition, if planted near a low-branched tree it will grow into and over the host plant. It is a most graceful shrub but lacks the strong floral display of *F. × intermedia* types. Variety *fortunei* (Lindl.) Rehd. is the upright version of *F. suspensa* with stiffer, erect or arching shoots. In variety *atrocaulis* the young shoots and unfolding leaves are dark purple, the older stems a rich brown. 'Nyman's Variety' is a selection from var. *atrocaulis* with soft yellow (ivory-yellow) flowers about 1 3/4″ across; it is of erect habit and one of the last forsythias to flower. Other cultivars include 'Decipiens' with single flowers and 'Pallida' with washed-out yellow flowers; both raised by Späth around 1905–06 and now scarce. Also listed is 'Volunteer' with dark colored young shoots and densely clustered, deep yellow flowers, medium-sized shrub, *F. ovata* × *F. suspensa*, originated at Clandon, Surrey, England. China. Zone 5 to 8.

Forsythia viridissima Lindl. — Greenstem Forsythia

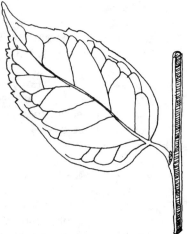

LEAVES: Opposite, simple, occasionally 3-parted, elliptic-oblong to lanceolate, 1 to 3″ long, 3/4 to 1 1/2″ wide, rarely obovate-oblong, broadest
about or above the middle, tapering at both ends, dark green, serrated
toward the apex or sometimes entire; petiole—1/4 to 1/2″ long.
STEM: Often greenish; pith—chambered through nodes and internodes on
young branches, or finally all excavated on old wood.

Forsythia viridissima, (fôr-sith′i-à vir-i-dis′si-mà), Greenstem Forsythia, grows
6 to 10′ high with a similar spread. The habit is stiff and upright, more or
less flat-topped. Flowers are bright yellow with a slight greenish tinge,
1″ long, April, 1 to 3 together. This species is rather pretty in flower and
usually flowers one or two weeks later than *F. suspensa*. Its chief claim
to fame is as one of the parents of the *F.* × *intermedia* group. A valuable
and interesting cultivar is 'Bronxensis'. This is a compact, flat-topped
form that grows about 12″ high and can spread 2 to 3′. The ovate leaves are serrated and about 3/4 to
1 3/4″ long. They are closely spaced along the stem and of a rich bright green. The primrose yellow
flowers occur in late March to April and are effective but not to the degree of the *F.* × *intermedia* types.
There is a myth or misstatement in the literature that 'Bronxensis' is difficult to root. This is absolutely false
for I have never failed to root softwood cuttings that were treated with 1000 ppm IBA-quick dip. In fact,
when at Illinois, I conducted a mini-experiment using softwood cuttings and 0, 1000, 5000 and 10,000 ppm
IBA-quick dip and 1000 ppm NAA quick dip. After 4 weeks the cuttings were evaluated and we found the
controls rooted as well as the hormone treatments. 'Bronxensis' grows extremely well in a container and
is often seen in landscapes throughout the Midwest and East. 'Klein' is a dwarf, 1 to 2′ high form that
flowers in the spring and again in fall, selected by Jules Klein, Crestwood, KY. Variety *koreana* Rehd.
grows to 8′ high, with larger leaves, pale yellow flowers, and often good maroonish fall color; var. *koreana*
'All Gold' is a selection from var. *koreana* 'Ilgwang' with uniform golden leaves; var. *koreana* 'Ilgwang' has
leaves that are edged and mottled with gold, introduced by Barry Yinger and Brookside Gardens,
Wheaton, MD; 'Robusta' is a vigorous form, has larger leaves to 5″ long and primrose yellow flowers,
leaves color mahogany red in fall. Also, in 'Variegata', the leaves are stippled white. *Forsythia viridissima*
is native to China. Introduced 1845. Zone 5 to 8.

COLD HARDY FORSYTHIA SELECTIONS

Apparently, many people have been working on forsythia for a literal yellow avalanche of new cold hardy
and other strange characteristic forsythias have been introduced. Here, they are presented in alphabetical order
or under the individual who introduced the plant(s). For rather complete histories and descriptions of the cold
hardy cultivars of *Forsythia*, see *Amer. Nurseryman* 159(9):167–173 (1984); also "Flower bud hardiness of
Forsythia cultivars," *J. Environ. Hort.* 11:35–38 (1993).

'Happy Centennial'—A free-flowering, dwarf, spreading shrub growing 2 to 2 1/2′ high and 3 to 5′ wide with
many short, secondary branches and an abundance of 1 3/4 to 2″ long, 1/2 to 1″ wide, leathery dark
green, ovate-lanceolate, entire leaves; the fragrant, golden yellow flowers are 1 1/4 to 1 3/4″ diameter,
3/4 to 1″ long, usually with several flowers per node; supposedly quite cold hardy and suspect -20°F
flower bud hardiness; derived from *F. ovata* 'Ottawa' × *F. europaea* crossed with an unknown seedling
found in the ornamental gardens at Central Experimental Farm, Ottawa, Canada; see *HortScience*
22(1):165 (1987) for more details.

'Meadowlark'—Introduction from North and South Dakota State Universities and the Arnold Arboretum; bright
yellow flowers in profusion on a 6 to 9′ high, rather unkempt, semi-arching shrub; leaves are dark green
and pest-free; flower buds hardy to -35°F; found by Dr. Harrison Flint at the Arnold Arboretum in heavy
flower while a mass planting of 'Spectabilis' surrounding the plant was nearly devoid of flowers after the
1966–67 winter; a cross between *F. ovata* and *F. europaea* and originated from the breeding work of Dr.
Karl Sax and Haig Derman at the Arnold; is being grown commercially in the Midwest; considered the
most flower bud hardy clone.

'New Hampshire Gold'—Drooping, single, cold hardy, yellow flowers on a 5′ high, mounded shrub; developed by Paul Joly, Windsor Road Nursery, Cornish, NH; result of a cross between 'Lynwood' and *F. ovata* 'Ottawa' and *F. europaea*; literature is not totally coherent on parentage and I have read *F.* 'Lynwood' × *F. ovata*; seed was collected in 1966, plant flowered in 1970; flowers are deeper yellow than *F. ovata* and more abundant; plants have flowered to the tops of the stems after -33°F.

'Northern Gold'—Golden yellow flowers and exceptional flower bud hardiness, greater than -30°F, result of crosses between *F. ovata* 'Ottawa' and *F. europaea*; 6 to 8′ high, upright habit; bred by F. Svejda, Agriculture Canada, and selected by D.R. Sampson.

'Northern Sun'—Has never failed to flower over a 12 year period at the Minnesota Landscape Arboretum where -30°F is common, 8 to 10′ high shrub, clear yellow flowers; possibly a hybrid between *F. ovata* and *F. europaea*, released in 1983; grown from seed collections in 1957 from open-pollinated plants of *F. ovata* growing in the Dominion Arboretum, Ottawa, Canada; selected, named, and registered by Dr. Harold Pellett and Laurie Malmquist; *Minn. Horticulturist* 120(4):22–23 (1992).

'Sunrise'—Bright yellow flowers, 2 to 3 per node, medium green leaves, squarish stems, full dense habit, 5 to 6′ high and wide, flower bud hardy to -20°F; offspring of *F. ovata* and a selected plant purchased as *F. ovata*; hardens later in fall; an Iowa State University introduction.

VAN DER WERKEN CULTIVARS

Van der Werken Irradiated 'Lynwood' Cultivars: A rather interesting story of irradiation-induced mutant forsythias is presented in *Amer. Nurseryman* 167(1):127–132 (1988) that resulted in the ultimate release of 5 (too many) cultivars. Abbreviated descriptions follow. All plants were released by Hendrick van der Werken, University of Tennessee, Knoxville, TN. Actual flower bud hardiness is unknown but suspect a Zone 6 to 8 distinction is safe.

'Fairy-Land'—A small, fine-textured shrub, 3 to 4′ high, 5 to 6′ wide, 2 to 4 flowers per node, each flower with 4 to 8 lobes, leaves 3″ long, 1/2″ wide.

'Lemon-Screen'—An upright fan-like habit, with lemon yellow, 1 1/2 to 1 3/4″ long flowers, 4 per node, and chartreuse foliage in spring; foliage turns green in summer and exhibits a golden glow where exposed to full sun; plant may grow 8 to 10′ in 5 years.

'Minikin'—Small, linear leaves, 1 1/2″ long, 1/4″ wide, on a 1/2″ long petiole; 1/2″ wide, yellow flowers with recurved petals, 2 per node, internodes short, only 1/4 to 3/4″ long; 2 to 2 1/2′ by 3 to 4′ in 5 years.

'Pygmy-Red'—The name reflects the high anthocyanin (red pigment) in the young shoots, also the leaves develop maroon fall color on their upper side; 3 1/2 to 4′ high and 5′ wide in 5 years; flowers 1 1/4 to 1 1/2″ wide with 4(5) lobes, 2 flowers per node; internodes 1/2 to 1 1/2″ long.

'Tinkle-Bells'—A rigid, upright, semi-dwarf, growing 4 to 5′ high, flowers young, 2 to 4 flowers per node, with 4 (5 to 6) petal lobes, internodes short, leaves 2 to 3″ long, 1/2″ wide.

POSTSCRIPT: The above five introductions never experienced the light of commercial horticulture. To my knowledge, plants were not distributed to other researchers for testing and evaluation. There is no better way to keep a "new" plant in abysmal obscurity than by preventing anyone from seeing it. My congratulations to Tennessee.

Fothergilla gardenii Murray — Dwarf Fothergilla
(foth-ĕr-gil′à găr-dē′nē-ī)

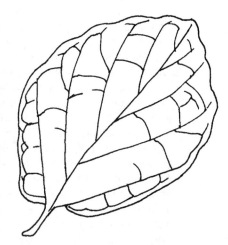

FAMILY: Hamamelidaceae

LEAVES: Alternate, simple, obovate to oblong, 1 to 2 1/2″ long, 3/4 to 1 3/4″ wide, rounded or broad cuneate, dentate above the middle, sometimes entire, blue-green to dark green above, pale or glaucous and tomentose beneath; petiole—1/4 to 1/3″ long, pubescent; leaves resemble those of *Hamamelis vernalis*.

BUDS: Vegetative—stalked, oblique, obovate or oblong, with 2 caducous scales, often collaterally branched, the end bud largest; flower buds—ovoid-rounded, 1/8 to 3/16″ diameter.

STEM: Rounded, light brown, zig-zag, slender, dingy stellate-tomentose; pith—small, somewhat angular, continuous, for a time greenish.

SIZE: 2 to 3′ in height, similar or greater in spread; many stories about the size of this plant; in the United States I have seen 5 to 6′ tall plants; Raulston reported 10′ tall plants in Europe, generally small, broad and rounded, however, I have 5 forms of the species and 2 are upright and have developed into 5 to 6′ high shrubs.

HARDINESS: Zone (4)5 to 8(9); Capiello reported the species hardy in Orono, ME, with 'Blue Mist' experiencing some tip kill.

HABIT: Small shrub with slender, crooked, often spreading branches, rounded in outline; forms a rather dense mound at maturity; suckers, some plants more so than others, and forms colonies.

RATE: Slow.

TEXTURE: Medium in foliage, medium in winter.

LEAF COLOR: Dark green, to a degree almost blue-green, summer foliage, quite attractive, somewhat leathery in texture; fall color is a brilliant yellow to orange to scarlet, often a combination of colors in same leaf; coloration develops late, often mid-November in Athens; *F. gardenii* has not fall colored with the brilliance of *F. major* types in Zone 7 and 8; this is generally the situation across the species' cultivated range.

FLOWER: White, fragrant, actually apetalous; showy parts are the stamens (white filaments, yellow anthers), borne in terminal, 1 to 2″ long by 1″ diameter spikes, April to early May, flowers appear before leaves, actually look like small bottlebrushes, honey-scented, lasting for 10 to 14 days; in some years the flowers and emerging leaves may appear together; usually flowers of *F. gardenii* open consistently ahead of those of *F. major* and on naked stems; in general, *true F. gardenii* flowers are smaller and not as showy as *F. major*.

FRUIT: Capsule, not showy, 2-valved with 2 shining black seeds.

CULTURE: Move balled-and-burlapped or as a container-grown plant; prospers in acid, peaty, sandy loam; does well in partial shade, flowers and colors best in full sun; requires good drainage; have read the exhortations of one author who noted that *Fothergilla* species in general will tolerate clay soils and pH of 6.8 to 7.5; admittedly, horticultural literature is not infallible but there are too many reports, especially out of England, where soils are often chalky (high pH) that list the plant as totally unsuitable for limey soils; my own experience, and I have grown countless fothergillas, is to maintain a moist, well-drained, acid soil and the plant will prosper.

DISEASES AND INSECTS: Trouble-free, making it worthy of wider landscape use.

LANDSCAPE VALUE: Foundation plantings, borders, masses, excellent for interesting flowers, good summer foliage and outstanding fall color; good in combination with rhododendrons and azaleas, and other ericaceous plants; among native plants I have many favorites but this and particularly *F. major* are near the top; the fothergillas ask so little from gardeners yet give so much; all friends should exhibit this kind of relationship; in our garden I count 17 fothergillas indiscriminately placed in every nook and cranny; those in more sun are denser in habit and more floriferous; amazingly *all* produce excellent fall color ranging from yellow, orange to red, often on the same branch or plant; it is one of the great American native shrubs for fall color.

CULTIVARS: Reasonable variation in summer foliage and fall colors as well as growth habit to warrant selection. For some inexplicable reason I discuss all the cultivars under *F. gardenii* even if they belong to *F. major*. Several new cultivars since the 1990 edition that deserve mention.

'Arkansas Beauty' (*F. major*)—White flowers before the leaves in April (Arkansas), thinner, lighter green leaves, virtually no pubescence on either surface and without the glaucous underside of *F. major*; yellow, orange, and red fall color; 6′ by 6′; introduced in 1995 by Larry Lowman, Wynne, AR, from a disjunct population of fothergilla identified about 11–12 years past in Cearcy County, AR by Dr. Gary Tucker; discovered in relatively dry natural habitat so Larry theorized may be more drought-tolerant than eastern cultivars; this cultivar is more difficult to root from cuttings than others.

'Black Mountain' (*F. major*)—An upright, compact form with smaller, more leathery dark green leaves than typical *F. major*; my single plant is handsome in summer foliage but somewhat disappointing in fall color with yellow-orange predominating; introduced by Head-Lee Nursery, Seneca, SC.

'Blue Mist' (*F. gardenii*)—A handsome glaucous blue foliage form with a rather wispy, delicate, mounded growth habit, the leaves hold late and do not fall color as spectacularly as some other forms, also may not be quite as cold hardy as the species; introduced by the Morris Arboretum; I like the plant and find the summer foliage color an interesting diversion from the typical green; roots easily from softwood cuttings, in fact, cuttings collected on September 13, 1988 from a container-grown plant, treated with 3000 ppm KIBA-quick dip, rooted 100% in six weeks; in 1989, the worst year for fall coloration in my 19 years in Georgia, 'Blue Mist' developed sickly yellow-green coloration while 'Mt. Airy' leaves were spectacular orange-red; is not as heat tolerant as 'Mt. Airy' and in Zone 7 and 8 should be sited in some shade; widely hyped, promoted and marketed but *far* from the best selection; in Zone 7b shows the effects of drought, also fall color is third-rate; in the Dirr garden 'Blue Mist' is 15′ distant from 'Mt. Airy' but might as well reside 1500 miles away for it is inferior in vigor, performance, flower and fall color.

'Eastern Form' (*F. gardenii*)—Listed by Gossler Farms Nursery as the typical form with small, oval foliage, dark green leaves that turn yellow-orange-red, and the normal white flowers.

'Epstein Form' (*F. gardenii*)—A small, 1 1/2″ long, oval-rounded leaf, almost ground cover type with excellent orange-red fall color; received my initial plant from the Arnold Arboretum; probably originated with Harold Epstein, Long Island; easy to propagate and grow; have heard this described as a *F. parvifolia* Kearney form but this species is merged with *F. gardenii*; interestingly, in our Georgia trials, which are in full sun, this form holds up much better than 'Blue Mist'; very diminutive form about 12″ high by 18″ wide, full and dense; certainly a good rock garden, small area plant.

'Feist Red' (*F. major*)—A large, dark green leaf form, robust stout stems, oval-rounded outline, large fragrant flowers, brilliant red fall color; fall color has not been spectacular in Athens; from Rich Feist, Burlington, KY; fall color in 1996 and 1997 has been inferior yellow.

'Huntsman' (*F. major*)—Thick, coarse dark green leaves, woolly pubescent on underside, fall color yellow to maroon, English references tout fall coloration, however, not as good as 'Mt. Airy', upright habit, taxonomically would fit under the old *F. monticola* designation.

'Jane Platt' (*F. gardenii*)—Selected from the Portland Garden of John and Jane Platt; the habit is more cascading than the 'Eastern Form', the leaves narrow rather than oval, and the fall color brilliant yellow-red, the flowers are slightly longer than 'Eastern Form', grows 3′ high, a Gossler introduction; not particularly outstanding on the East Coast, leaves are bluish green and fall color not as intense as described under West Coast conditions; Cappiello reported yellow-green with splotching of brown fall color in 1997 at Bernheim.

'Kelly's Select'—Upright selection, parent plant 12′ high, stoloniferous, yellow-orange fall color, introduced by Head-Lee Nursery, Seneca, SC.

'Mt. Airy' ('Mount Airy') (*F. major*)—A clone I selected from Mt. Airy Arboretum, Cincinnati, OH for good dark blue-green foliage, superb, consistent yellow-orange-red fall color, abundant flowers, vigorous constitution, more upright habit (5 to 6′), also shows a suckering tendency that is stronger than many plants; has survived –25°F and flowered; collected 189 cuttings on July 24, 1988, 3000 ppm KIBA with 100% rooting in 7 weeks and 100% overwinter survival; this form appears easy to grow in containers and even under high nutrition has developed spectacular fall color; it has been gratifying to watch this selection accelerate into the fast lane of nursery production and garden acceptance; I first observed the plant over 20 years ago; flowers are larger than typical often 1 1/2 to 2″ long, usually in full flower around mid-April and effective for 3 to 4 weeks; summer foliage is dark blue-green above, whitish beneath, and knockout yellow-orange-red in November; leaves are extremely frost resistant and are not damaged by early fall freezes; I have plants all over the Athens area and have given them to any individual who would accept them; the range of fall color expression has varied from yellow-orange in some years to brilliant red-purple in others; sun-shade siting, nutrition, water stress, and environmental preconditioning affect fall coloration; fall color is *always* significant even is Zone 7b; growers from Maine to Oregon to Georgia and Texas have embraced 'Mt. Airy'; Georgia Gold Medal Selection in 1994; see *Nursery Manager* 7(8):52, 54 (1991) for more specifics.

'Sea Spray' (*F. major*)—Medium-sized, blue-green leaves on a rather compact, oval-rounded framework; have seen at Bernheim Arboretum; do not know the origin but have rooted cuttings and look forward to evaluating this clone; the only plant I have observed appears similar to 'Mt. Airy' in habit and foliage; not much fall color in 1997 at Bernheim, only dark red-brown.

'September Morn' (*F. gardenii*)—A selection with "fuzzy" white flowers and intense orange to scarlet fall color; introduced by Eastern Plant Specialities, Georgetown, ME.

'Woodbridge Hybrids'—Dr. Darrel Apps, Woodbridge Farm, showed me a particularly fine form that was growing with 2 or 3 other seedlings from the same population; it was intermediate in size with perhaps the best red to purple, almost fluorescent color I have witnessed on any shrub; there is a chance it will be named and introduced; it is an improvement over both species; I talked to Darrel about the plant and he indicated it may be introduced through Conard-Pyle as 'Woodbridge Elite'; this and the other seedlings are probably hybrids.

Woodlanders Selections—The great Woodlanders Nursery, Aiken, SC has collected, particularly from the southeast Coastal Plain many new and worthy selections; included in my garden are three forms of *F. gardenii* known by the counties of collection; 'Berkeley County' is more compact, 'Colleton County' is an exceptionally tall form to 12′ in its native habitat, and 'Aiken County' is a very low-growing form with rounded leaves; all have blue-green leaves and, in our garden, minimal fall color.

PROPAGATION: The best seed information comes from Mr. Alfred Fordham, retired Propagator, Arnold Arboretum [see *Arnoldia* 31:256–259 (1971)]; seeds are somewhat difficult to germinate for they exhibit a double dormancy and pretreatment must be accomplished in two stages, seeds require warm fluctuating temperatures followed by a period of cold. *Fothergilla major* seeds have required exceptionally long warm periods with 12 months being optimum; after warm treatment they should be placed at 40°F for 3 months. *Fothergilla gardenii* has germinated well after 6 months of warm pretreatment followed by 3 months at

40°F. Cuttings, wood taken from suckers or root cuttings yielded good results, best with bottom heat; *F. major* untreated cuttings taken when shrubs were in flower rooted 67% in sandy soil in 60 days; June cuttings set in sand:peat rooted 67% without treatment, and 100% in 42 days after treatment with 200 ppm IAA/24 hours; for some reason the two species treated here have been listed as difficult to root; I have a "love affair" with these shrubs and would like to describe some of my propagation adventures [see Dirr, "Fothergillas: A garden aristocrat," *Horticulture* 40(12):38–39 (1977)]; softwood cuttings can be readily rooted when collected in June, July and as late as August; they should be treated with IBA-quick dip and placed in peat:perlite under mist; one experiment [see *The Plant Propagator* 24(1):8–9 (1978)] we conducted with *F. major* involved 0, 1000, 2500, 5000 and 10,000 ppm IBA-quick dip treatments and 1000 ppm NAA-quick dip; *all* cuttings, even the controls, rooted 80 to 100%; the greatest numbers of roots were produced with the highest IBA levels but surprisingly the NAA treatment resulted in the greatest number of roots; *F. gardenii* is also easily rooted; I have found that if the cuttings are still growing when rooted they can be transplanted, if not the following handling practice should apply; often after rooted cuttings are transplanted they enter a dormancy from which they never recover; the problem can be avoided if the cuttings, when rooted, are left in the flats and hardened off; the flats of dormant cuttings are transferred to cold storage, which is maintained at 34°F; in February or March the flats are returned to a warm greenhouse and when growth appears the cuttings are potted; over the years I have propagated thousands of both species and firmly believe I have made, along with my colleagues, a propagation mountain out of a molehill; standard procedure now includes 3000 ppm KIBA quick dip, 3 perlite:1 peat, in 3 by 3 by 3 1/2″ deep cells, mist, root in 4 to 7 weeks, remove from mist and leave be or apply 100 ppm nitrogen solution; rooted cuttings will often put out a flush of growth after the application; +90% of the cuttings overwinter regardless of the growth flush.

ADDITIONAL NOTES: Anyone interested in furthering their *Fothergilla* education should consult Dr. Richard Weaver's excellent article in *Arnoldia* 31:89–97 (1971), and Flint, Horticulture 43(9):12–16 (1984). As the reader can infer, I love this genus and have spent countless hours trying to understand the inherent variation. On a rainy day, I assessed herbarium sheets of both species. *Fothergilla gardenii* is usually smaller in all its parts and strongly suckering in habit. The leaves are often prominently coarsely toothed above the middle. In the University's Botanical Garden, the two species are planted side-by-side. *Fothergilla gardenii* has spread (suckered) into *F. major*. Although *F. major* will sucker, its tendency to do so is less than *F. gardenii*.

I have established a trial of *Fothergilla* taxa in our research plots and invite any and all additions. To date, 'Mt. Airy', along with 'Epstein Form', have held up the best in full sun. Will add about 6 new clones in 1998.

NATIVE HABITAT: Introduced 1765. All species are localized in the southeastern United States; *F. gardenii* is a Coastal Plain species and is often found in pine savannas, around the edges of ponds or boggy type depressions called pocasins, from North Carolina to southern Alabama and the Florida panhandle.

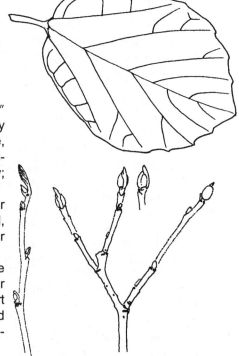

Fothergilla major Lodd. — Large Fothergilla
(foth-ĕr-gil′à mā′jôr)

LEAVES: Alternate, simple, suborbicular to oval or obovate, 2 to 4″ long, from 2/3's to as wide, cordate or truncate, coarsely crenate-dentate or sometimes denticulate above the middle, glabrous and dark green above, glaucous and stellate-pubescent beneath at least on the veins, sometimes leathery; petiole—1/3 to 1″ long, tomentose.

BUDS: Vegetative—moderate or small, stalked, oblique, obovate or oblong, with 2 caducous scales, often collaterally branched, terminal largest, appearing like a scalpel blade; flower buds—ovoid, about 1/4″ long, gray-brown, pubescent.

STEM: Rounded, zig-zag, slender, dingy stellate-tomentose or more or less glabrescent; leaf scars 2-ranked, half-rounded or deltoid, small, slightly raised; stipule scars unequal, one short the other elongated; 3 bundle traces, more or less compound or confluent; pith—rather small, somewhat angular, continuous, for a time greenish.

SIZE: 6 to 10′ in height; slightly less to a similar spread, greatly variable and the exceptions seem to outnumber the rule.

HARDINESS: Zone 4 to 8.

HABIT: A rounded, multi-stemmed shrub with mostly erect stems; very dense due to the leaves which are closely borne along the stems; have seen rounded and upright-oval versions, will sucker but not to the degree of *F. gardenii*.

RATE: Slow in the landscape, actually medium in youth with ample water and fertilizer.

TEXTURE: Medium in leaf and winter.

LEAF COLOR: Blue-green to dark green in summer, underside grayish to whitish; fall color ranges from yellow to orange and scarlet often with all colors present in the same leaf; one of our more handsome native fall coloring shrubs, peaking in November in the Dirr garden.

FLOWERS: Whitish, apetalous, the showy portion of the flower being the stamens, borne in 1 to 2″ long, 3/4 to 1 1/2″ wide bottlebrush-like spikes in April to early May lasting 3 to 4 weeks; the flowers are fragrant and remind one of the smell of honey; flowers open slightly ahead or with the leaves; in the Athens area, most *true F. gardenii* are in almost full leaf while *F. major* is in peak flower.

FRUIT: Two-valved, dehiscent capsule, 1/2″ long, splitting at the top, usually containing 2 shiny black seeds, generally not produced in great quantities.

CULTURE: Most plants are container-grown and easy to transplant; the need for acid soil conditions is of paramount importance; most authorities indicated that *Fothergilla* species are not suitable for limey soils; have observed a light green (yellow-green) margin around the leaf on stressed plants, see *F. gardenii* for further discussion.

DISEASES AND INSECTS: See under *F. gardenii*.

LANDSCAPE VALUE: Excellent shrub for the residential landscape; adds considerable color from April to October–November by virtue of flower and fall color; the summer foliage is a leathery dark blue-green and is not affected by diseases or insects; probably best used in the shrub border but could be employed in groupings, masses and foundation plantings; long-lived shrub and one plant at the Morton Arboretum has survived over 60 years.

CULTIVARS: Discussed under *F. gardenii*.

PROPAGATION: See under *F. gardenii*.

ADDITIONAL NOTES: This species and *F. monticola* Ashe., Alabama or Large Fothergilla, are quite similar and are now treated as one species, *F. major*. In the past, plants with more glabrous vegetative parts were listed as *F. monticola*. Also, *F. monticola* was supposedly smaller in size (6′) but these differences are not absolute; the current thinking is the lumping of the two species into the *F. major* category. This brief discussion has been left in the fifth edition in case people wonder what happened to *F. monticola*.

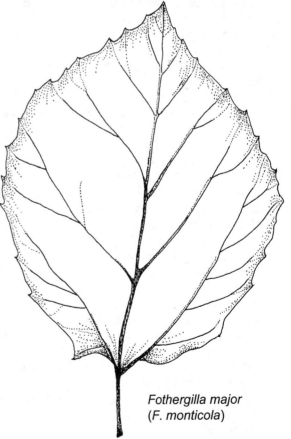

Fothergilla major
(*F. monticola*)

I have had many opportunities to propagate, grow and evaluate the two species treated here. I can say without equivocation that they are among the most beautiful shrubs for autumn coloration. No two are exactly alike which adds to their interest. In fact, often every leaf is colored differently. I do believe there is an opportunity for selection of superior flowering and fall coloring types by observant plantsmen. I have planted both species in my Georgia garden. Some shade and soil moisture in hot climates is a necessity.

The Arnold Arboretum has identified a hybrid between the two species which offers intermediate size and other characteristics. This could be a most valuable shrub for modern landscapes. Dr. Richard Weaver reported chromosome numbers of 24 and 36 for *F. gardenii* and *F. major*, respectively.

NATIVE HABITAT: Indigenous to the Allegheny Mountains from northern North Carolina and Tennessee to northern Alabama. Introduced late 1800's.

Franklinia alatamaha Bartr. ex Marshall — Franklinia, Franklin Tree
(frank-lin'i-à à-là-tà-mà'hà)

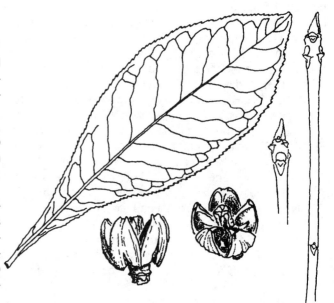

FAMILY: Theaceae

LEAVES: Alternate, simple, 5 to 6″ long, up to 3″ across, obovate-oblong, acute, cuneate and gradually narrowed into a short petiole, remotely serrate, shiny dark green above, pubescent below.

BUDS: Terminal—elongated, silky, pubescent, grayish brown, scales weakly overlap, 1/4 to 1/2″ long; laterals—conical-ovoid, brownish pubescence, 1/16″ long, sit above leaf scar, appearing partially imbedded.

STEM: Moderate, terete, young stems silky-pubescent, green to brown, dotted with numerous small lenticels; leaf scars half-round, or shield-shaped, scarcely raised; 1 bundle trace, transverse or V-shaped, compound; strange odor to bruised stems; pith rather large, coffee-colored, continuous.

SIZE: 10 to 20′(30′) in height by 6 to 15′ wide; national champion is 37′ by 42′ at Wyndmoor, PA.

HARDINESS: Zone 5 to 8(9).

HABIT: Small tree or shrub with upright-spreading branches, often leafless in their lower reaches, giving the plant an open, airy appearance; not unlike *Magnolia virginiana* in habit.

RATE: Medium, proper water and fertilizer induces excellent growth.

TEXTURE: Medium in all seasons.

BARK: Smooth, gray, broken by irregular vertical fissures; trunks assume a slight fluted condition; very attractive feature.

LEAF COLOR: Lustrous dark green in summer changing to orange and red in fall; very handsome foliage, leaves hold late, have recorded them present in early to mid-November, Boston; fall color can be spectacular red to purple.

FLOWERS: Perfect, white, 5-petaled, yellow center of stamens, very striking, 3 to 3 1/2″ across, fragrant, solitary, slightly cup-shaped; late July into August and weakly into September; in 1994 plants at a local nursery flowered heavily from mid-July to early August; in the Arnold Arboretum, maximum flowering occurs in mid-September.

FRUIT: Woody, 5-valved capsule, 1/2 to 3/4″ in diameter, splitting into 10 segments; a rather curious fruit on close inspection and one which is not easily forgotten; several flattened-angular seeds in each cell; develops the autumn after flowering.

CULTURE: Somewhat hard to transplant because of sparsely fibrous root system; best to move as a small container or balled-and-burlapped specimen; requires moist, acid, well-drained soil which has been supplied with ample organic matter; full sun or light shade but best flowering and fall coloration occur in full sun.

DISEASES AND INSECTS: Wilt caused by *Phytophthora cinnamoni* species is serious in propagating beds and container-grown plants [see *J. Arboriculture* 6(4):89–92 (1980) for details]; interestingly in the South this species does not perform as well as it does in the North; there is speculation that a disease associated with cotton infects *Franklinia*; since the organism is soil-borne and cotton once covered most of the Piedmont there is no "safe" place to culture the tree; some of the best specimens are located at the Arnold Arboretum, Heritage Plantation, and Longwood Gardens.

LANDSCAPE VALUE: A handsome small specimen tree or large shrub valued for the showy white flowers and good fall color; if one is so fortunate to procure this species he/she should provide it a place of prominence in the garden; an aristocrat because of its interesting history; somewhat akin to a fickle lover and may stay around and tease with its beauty, or simply leave . . . the garden that is; it is best not to become smitten with this plant.

PROPAGATION: Seeds should be sown as soon as the fruit has matured, it is important to prevent the seeds from drying out; best germination occurs after 30 days cold stratification; easily propagated from cuttings taken in summer; hormonal treatment results in increased rooting percentages. I have rooted cuttings with ease but the most difficult part is keeping them alive after they have rooted; Vermeulen, *Proc. Intl. Plant Prop. Soc.* 17:254–255 (1967), described his method which includes collecting 5 to 6″ long cuttings in mid-July before growth becomes woody, 5 or 6 leaves are left and these cut in half; cuttings are direct rooted in peat pots, roots appear in 3 to 4 weeks and mist should be cut off since roots rot easily; they are overwintered in an opaque poly-house. Mr. Mark Griffith, Griffith Propagation Nursery, Watkinsville, GA, successfully roots and overwinters cuttings with minimal fidgeting. The longer growing season in 7b allows cuttings to break bud after rooting and to develop extensive root systems.

ADDITIONAL NOTES: The story has been widely told how John Bartram found this plant in 1770 along the banks of the Altamaha River in Georgia and collected a few for his garden. Strangely, this plant has never been seen in the wild since 1790, and supposedly all plants in commerce today are derived from Bartram's original collection. The species may have been sighted again in 1803 in the wild, but this is not gospel.

I have read many articles and listened to theories on *Franklinia* and the suspected reasons for its disappearance from the wild. I offer *Franklinia* by Martha Prince, *Amer. Horticulturist* 56(4):39–41 (1977), as a good starting point.

NATIVE HABITAT: Once, the wilds of Georgia.

RELATED SPECIES:

Gordonia lasianthus (L.) Ellis — Loblolly-bay

LEAVES: Alternate, simple, evergreen, obovate-lanceolate, 4 to 6″ long, one half as wide, acute, cuneate, lightly serrate, glossy dark green above, lighter green below; petiole—1/2 to 1″ long.

BUDS: Extremely small, less than 1/16″ high, brown, glabrous, sitting directly above the leaf scar.

STEM: Stout, coarse, rich brown with onion-skin epidermis cracking and peeling on first year stem, glabrous, nodes closely spaced; leaf scar rounded-triangular with V-shaped marking in center; pith—light green-yellow, solid.

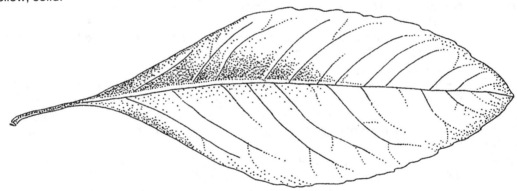

Gordonia lasianthus, (gôr-dō′ni-á lá-zi-an′thus), Loblolly-bay, is sometimes confused with *Franklinia* and at one time *Franklinia* was referred to as "The Lost Gordonia." Loblolly-bay is a wet soil species found throughout the Coastal Plain from Virginia to Florida to Louisiana. It has evergreen leaves, 2 1/2″ diameter, white flowers with yellow stamens (similar to *F. alatamaha*) which appear in May and continue to October on the Georgia campus. It is a slender, narrow-conical, open tree that grows about 30 to 40′ under cultivation. National champion is 95′ by 60′ in Ocala National Forest, FL. This species suffers under cultivation and I have seen too many young plants die from a wilt-type symptom. Perfectly drained soils are necessary under cultivation although the plant grows submerged, at least for a time, in the wild. Possibly the conditions in swamps result in such low pH that the causal organism does not grow. Also, young trees are usually open and rather unappealing. Dr. Orton produced hybrids between this and *Franklinia* in an attempt to trace the origin of the latter. His interesting work appeared in *Amer. Assoc. Bot. Gard. Arb. Bull.* 11(4):81–84 (1977). I vacillate on the true garden worth of the species and can say without equivocation that a full, dense, "good-looking" plant seldom crosses my path. Several were planted behind the Miller Plant Science Building on campus. One died and the 3 that remain just do not have the necessary garden pizzazz. Perhaps with selection, there is hope. The lack of ease-of-cultivation probably dooms it to novelty or collector status. In 1997, I witnessed several prosperous plantings in nurseries in central Florida. 'Variegata' has irregular creamy white margins that turn rose-pink with cold weather. Zone (7)8 to 9.

Fraxinus americana L. — White Ash
(frak'si-nus à-mer-i-kā'nà)

FAMILY: Oleaceae

LEAVES: Opposite, pinnately compound, 8 to 15″ long, 5 to 9 leaflets, usually 7, stalked, 2 to 6″ long, 1 to 3″ wide, ovate to ovate-lanceolate, acute to acuminate at apex, rounded or tapered at base, usually entire, or edged near the apex or the entire margin with remote serrations, dark green and glabrous above, glaucous beneath and usually glabrous; petiolules of lateral leaflets 1/3″ long, terminal 1/2 to 1″ long; petiole—yellowish, glabrous, round, with a slight groove above.

BUDS: Terminal present, 2 to 3 pairs of scales, semi-spherical to broadly ovate, scurfy, and more or less slightly downy, rusty to dark brown to sometimes almost black; terminal about 1/4″ long, usually broader than long; buds inset in the leaf scar.

STEM: Stout, rounded, smooth and shining, grayish or greenish brown often with a slight bloom, brittle, flattened at nodes at right angles to leaf scars; leaf scars U-shaped with deep to shallow notch; vascular bundles forming open "C" shape.

SIZE: 50 to 80′ in height with a spread of similar proportions, can grow to 120′; national champion is 95′ by 82′ in Palisades, NY.

HARDINESS: Zone 4 to 9.

HABIT: In youth weakly pyramidal to upright oval, and in old age developing an open and rather round-topped crown; unique in maintaining a central leader in youth with an even distribution of branches.

RATE: Medium, 1 to 2′ per year over a 10 to 15 year period.

TEXTURE: Medium in leaf; medium-coarse in winter.

BARK: Ash gray to gray-brown, furrowed into close diamond-shaped areas separated by narrow interlacing ridges; on very old trees slightly scaly along the ridges.

LEAF COLOR: Dark green above and paler beneath in summer changing to yellow to deep purple and maroon colors in fall; I have seen trees with yellow fall color as well as individuals of dark, intense, maroon color; colors early, often by late September, and most leaves abscised by mid to late October.

FLOWER: Dioecious (possibly polygamo-dioecious), usually unisexual, apetalous, both sexes appearing in panicles before the leaves, not ornamentally important, calyx minute, campanulate, corolla absent, green to purple, April.

FRUIT: Samara, 1 to 2″ long, 1/4″ wide, of no ornamental quality, body rounded in cross-section; wing extending about 1/3 of the way down the body, looks like a canoe paddle.

CULTURE: Easily transplanted; makes its best growth on deep, moist, well-drained soils but also withstands soils which are not excessively dry and rocky; seems to be pH adaptable; full sun; prune in fall; not as adaptable as the Green Ash but much superior to it as an ornamental.

DISEASES AND INSECTS: Ashes are susceptible to many problems and the following list is applicable to the plant types which follow as well White Ash. Leaf rust, leaf spots (many), cankers (many), dieback has been associated with White Ash (probably mycoplasms), ash borer (can be very destructive), lilac leaf miner, lilac borer, carpenter worm, brown-headed ash sawfly, fall webworm, ash flower gall (flowers develop abnormally and galls are evident on White Ash male flowers throughout the winter, caused by a mite), oyster shell scale, and scurfy scale. So termed "ash yellows" appears common in parts of East and Midwest, considerable literature indicates it is a significant problem.

LANDSCAPE VALUE: One would wonder if the ashes have any value after reading that impressive list of insects and diseases; vigorous-growing trees do not develop that many problems but homeowners should always be on the lookout and when something seems awry should call a tree specialist or seek help through their county extension office; the White Ash is a handsome native tree for parks and other large areas; I hesitate to recommend it for extensive homeowner use because of size and potential pest problems.

CULTIVARS: These selected clones are much preferable to seedling-grown trees and should be sought out if a White Ash is desired.

    'Autumn Applause'—Densely branched, oval form with close-knit branches, produces reliable maroon fall color, first to color in Zone 7b (October 15), narrower leaflet than typical White Ash, somewhat drooping appearance to the leaf, 40′ by 25′, male, Wandell introduction.

'Autumn Blaze'—First adapted White Ash for the prairie region of Dakotas and Canada, oval form with purple fall color, female but described as having light fruit set, Morden introduction, 50 to 60' by 25 to 30', original tree from Roseau, MN, Zone 3b.

Autumn Purple® ('Junginger')—A fine selection of pyramidal-rounded outline with deep green leaves and handsome reddish purple fall color, a male tree, I have seen the tree in fall color in the Midwest and East and the color was a more subdued reddish purple in the Midwest compared to a rich deep red on Maine's campus, reasonable fall color in Zone 7b, fall color may hold 2 to 4 weeks, the leaflets are glossy which also contributes to the beauty, 45' by 60', plants I have seen approach a rounded outline, subject to bark split at ground level on young trees.

'Champaign County'—Tight dense crown and lustrous bright green leaves that show no appreciable fall color (yellow to purple); the heavy trunk is so stout that whips supposedly do not need staking; strong central leader, 45' by 30', a male; at Spartanburg, SC trees have fruited.

'Chicago Regal'—Vigorous, upright growth habit, 18-year-old tree was 30' by 15', deep green foliage turns regal purple with earth tones, bark is resistant to frost cracking, 45' by 35' at landscape maturity, a Klehm introduction.

'Elk Grove'—Vigorous upright growth habit, lustrous dark green foliage that turns rich royal purple, bark resistant to frost cracking, a Klehm introduction.

'Empire'—Narrow pyramidal outline with strong central leader, medium green leaves turn rusty orange to purplish in autumn, 50' by 25', Zone 4.

'Greenspire'—A narrow upright form, eventually oval, 40' by 30', with dark green leaves that turn dark orange in autumn, a Princeton introduction.

'Manitou' ('Manitoo')—Noteworthy because of its narrow, upright growth habit, a Canadian introduction, does not develop good fall color.

'Rosehill'—Dark green summer foliage, bronze-red fall color, tolerant of poor, alkaline soils, may not be as hardy as 'Autumn Purple', seedless, 50' by 30', have seen in Raleigh, NC where fall color was yellow-bronze-red and not very effective.

'Royal Purple'—Royal purple autumn foliage, shapely upright growth habit, 30' by 25' in 24 years, resistant to frost cracking, a Klehm introduction.

Skyline® ('Skycole')—Oval form with central leader, symmetrical branching and good crotch angles, glossy medium green leaves turn orange-red, 50' by 40', seedless.

Windy City™ ('Tures')—Oval to rounded, good central leader, well-formed canopy, semi-glossy medium green foliage in summer, burgundy to reddish orange highlighted by copper, orange, gold and yellow accents in fall, male, recent reports indicate that fruits are produced, resists frost cracking, 50 to 60', selected in 1988 at Matt Tures Sons Nursery, Huntley, IL, promoted through Chicagoland Grows®.

PROPAGATION: Seeds germinate best with warm stratification at 68 to 86°F for 30 days followed by cold at 41°F for 60 days; cultivars are budded onto seedling understocks in summer.

ADDITIONAL NOTES: Truly a beautiful tree in fall color. In my travels through central and southern Indiana I have seen magnificent specimens 70 to 80' high and wide. Unfortunately, White Ash does not like harsh conditions. Much noise has been made about ash decline which results in dieback for no apparent reason. Appears to be a combination of factors impinging on the health of the tree plus mycoplasm-like organisms.

NATIVE HABITAT: Nova Scotia to Minnesota, south to Florida and Texas. Introduced 1724.

Fraxinus pennsylvanica Marsh. — Green Ash, Red Ash. Formerly listed as *F. p.* var. *lanceolata* while Red Ash was listed as *F. pennsylvanica*. Both Red and Green are now included in the same species.
(frak'si-nus pen-sil-vā'ni-kȧ)

LEAVES: Opposite, pinnately compound, up to 12" long, 5 to 9 leaflets, 2 to 5" long, 1 to 2" wide, ovate to oblong-lanceolate, acuminate, narrow to broad-cuneate, crenate serrate or entire, lustrous medium to dark green and essentially glabrous above, light green and pubescent beneath.

BUDS: Dark rusty brown, smaller and narrower than those of the White Ash, woolly, set above leaf scar, leaf scars nearly straight across at the top.

STEM: Rounded, rather stout, densely velvety downy or glabrous, leaf scar not notched, vascular bundles forming closed "C" shape.

SIZE: 50 to 60' in height by about 1/2 that in spread, although can grow to over 80'; national champion is 95' by 95' in Cass County, MI.

HARDINESS: Zone (2b)3 to 9.

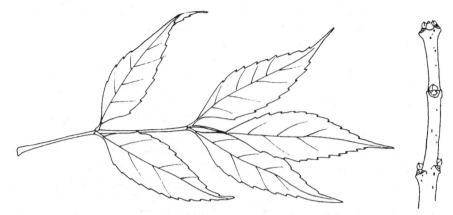

HABIT: Softly pyramidal when young, developing an upright-spreading habit at maturity with 3 to 5 main branches and many coarse, twiggy branchlets which bend down and then up at the ends; the crown is extremely irregular and the overall habit somewhat difficult to describe; sometimes rather unsightly.

RATE: Fast, 2 to 3′ per year in the landscape over a 10 year period; budded trees may grow 8 to 12′ in a single season; an ash evaluation at North Dakota State University showed that 73 ash accessions grew 1.63′ per year over a 10 year period; control Green Ash seedlings grew 1.6′; 'Marshall's Seedless' grew 1.4′; this is phenomenal growth for Zone 3 and 4 conditions.

TEXTURE: Medium in leaf; quite coarse in winter.

BARK: Similar to White Ash.

LEAF COLOR: Variable, but often a shiny medium to dark green in summer changing to yellow in the fall; fall coloration is inconsistent and seed-grown trees provide only disappointment; can be spectacular when right; almost in full fall color on October 16, 1993 in Athens.

FLOWER: See description for White Ash; produced on old wood just below new shoot, green to reddish purple, April.

FRUIT: Samara, 1 to 2″ long, 1/4″ or less wide, wing extending half-way or more down the cylindrical body.

CULTURE: Transplants readily and grows about anywhere; hence, its tremendous popularity; actually this is strange for it is found native in moist bottomlands or along stream banks; however, once established it tolerates high pH, salt, drought, wind, and sterile soils; requires full sun; prune in fall, tolerates 2,4-D better than many trees; interestingly, 'Marshall's Seedless' and 'Summit' averaged 1.7′ and 1.4′ per year, respectively, in Wichita, KS tests but both were attacked by borers.

DISEASES AND INSECTS: See White Ash; borers and scale are significant problems.

LANDSCAPE VALUE: In a way, this tree has been overplanted because of its adaptability; it has been used for streets, lawns, commercial areas, parks, golf courses and about any other area one can think of; best for plains states where few trees proliferate but somehow has become the favorite of many plantspeople; one of the real problems is the use of seedling-grown trees for they often fruit and in so doing become a significant nuisance; have observed a number of Green Ash in the South, some are performing reasonably well, others less so; for some odd reason a number were planted in Athens and on the Georgia campus; over a 12 year period most campus trees have declined, the Athens' trees are starting the descent; to my knowledge almost all cultivars were selected from northern provenances; someone in Zones 7 to 9 needs to select from the southern portion of the range.

CULTIVARS: Since the last edition, a number of selections have been introduced. In fact, I doubt if anyone could accurately list the top three cultivars. I have seen several of the variegated forms in England and Germany and find them virtually unredeeming. 'Aucubaefolia' and 'Variegata' continue to haunt me in my dreams.

Aerial™ ('Lednaw')—Tight, narrow crown, dense lustrous foliage, yellow fall color, branch sport of 'Summit', male, 45′ by 12′, have seen 30′ by 20′, a Wandell introduction, Zone 3b to 7b.

'Bergeson'—Upright-oval growth habit, straight trunk, vigorous, fast to caliper, long slender lustrous dark green leaves, yellow fall color, male, found by Melvin Bergeson, Fertile, MN; possibly along with 'Patmore' the most cold hardy of the cultivars, 50′ by 35′, Zone 3.

'Cardan'—A seed propagated cultivar that is supposedly quite borer resistant, released by USDA-SCS and SEA for farmstead and windbreak planting in the northern Great Plains.

Centerpoint™—Broad oval to rounded outline, glossy dark green foliage, yellowish fall color, male, 45′ by 35′, discovered in Iowa, released by Landscape Plant Development Center, University of Minnesota.

Cimmaron® ('Cimmzam')—Narrow in youth with upright branches forming an oval canopy, later leafing and holds leaves 7 to 10 days later in fall, rich dark green leaves turn brick red to orange-red in autumn, male, 60′ by 30′, Lake County Nursery introduction, Zone 4, resembles White Ash in morphological characteristics.

Dakota Centennial™ ('Wahpeton')—Male, seedless, fast-growing with a growth rate of 2.4′ annually over a ten year period, produces an elliptic pyramidal-shaped tree, widening with age, tends to maintain terminal dominance with uniform scaffold branch arrangement, bright glossy green foliage becomes dark green and semi-glossy as it hardens, fall color is deep yellow, 40 to 50′, introduced by Dr. Dale E. Herman, North Dakota State University, Zone 3.

'Emerald'—Round-headed form with glossy dark green leaves, yellow-green fall color, bark like Common Hackberry, 45′ by 40′, seedless, perhaps not as hardy as other selections, Zone 5, introduced by Marshall Nursery; in Milliken Arboretum, 'Emerald' set liberal quantities of fruit, round-headed tree in youth, dense foliage, handsome for a Green Ash, young trees reported subject to borers and/or low vertical cracks on trunks, looks more like a White Ash.

Fan-West™ ('Fanick')—Moderate globe-shape, symmetrical crown, olive green in summer, yellow in fall, male, 50′ by 40′, selected in the San Antonio, TX area, considered less hardy, Zone 7 to 8, possibly a *F. velutina* type.

'Harlequin'—Variegated foliage, discovered in Canada in 1987 as a branch sport (bud mutation) and propagated the same year, believed to be staminate (seedless), leaves with 5 to 9 ovate to lanceolate leaflets, green to gray-green with irregular white margins, Zone 3 and adaptable to a wide spectrum of edaphic conditions, see *HortScience* 29:971 (1994).

'Honeyshade'—Beautiful, glossy dark green leaflets, fast grower, seedless; unfortunately, seldom seen in commerce; does not look like it belongs to the Green Ash tribe, Klehm Nursery introduction.

'Jewell'—Shiny dark green leaves, well-branched form, fruitful.

'Kankakee'—Strong central leader, uniform straight trunk, lighter green foliage, 45′ by 35 to 40′, introduced by Kankakee Nursery, Aroma Park, IL.

'Kindred'—Maintains a central leader, fast-growing, good foliage, seedless, good hardiness, selected by Ben Gilbertson, Kindred, ND.

'King Richard'—Glossy deep green foliage, uniform upright growth habit, male, a Klehm introduction.

Leprechaun™ ('Johnson')—A newer introduction of rounded habit, described as a true genetic dwarf, probably 15 to 20′ by 15 to 20′, small, medium green leaves, yellow fall color, listed as Zone 3; discovered by Wayne Johnson Nursery, Menomomee Falls, WI; Schmidt Nursery is grafting it on a 6′ standard.

'Marshall's Seedless' (also listed as 'Marshall')—Male form with glossy dark green foliage; more vigorous and has less insect problems than the species; lustrous dark green foliage, yellow fall color; may be more than one clone originally introduced, 50′ by 40′, Zone 3, over the years I have observed 'Marshall's Seedless' with abundant fruits and assumed there was a mixup in production, or as mentioned, more than one clone, also the habit is not as neat and uniform as 'Patmore' or 'Summit'.

Newport™ ('Bailey', Bailey's Select Green Ash)—Straight trunk, good branching, foliage similar to 'Marshall's Seedless', male, 55′ by 40′, a Bailey Nursery introduction, Zone 3b to 8b.

'Patmore'—Upright-branching, oval head, more uniform and symmetrical than 'Marshall's Seedless', growth rate in nursery slower than 'Marshall's Seedless', equal to 'Summit', 5 to 7 glossy dark green, neatly serrated leaflets, male, hardier than 'Marshall's Seedless', discovered by the late Richard Patmore, Brandon, MN, as a native seedling in Vegreville, Alberta, near Edmonton, probably hardy to –40°F, 50 to 60′ by 35′; considered by the better shade tree growers to be one of the best selections, listed as Zone 2b/3a, see *American Nurseryman* 173(9):57–59 (1991) for a full description of 'Patmore'.

Prairie Dome™ ('Leeds')—Male, seedless, with a moderate growth rate of 1.44′ annually over a ten year period, very dense, distinctly oval form gradually becoming globose with age, terminal dominance is not as strong as Dakota Centennial™ and Prairie Spire™, thick, leathery, glossy green foliage becomes dark green and semi-glossy as it hardens, leaves are retained 6 to 9 days later in autumn than the other two cultivars, becoming yellow, Zone 3.

Prairie Spire™ ('Rugby')—Male, seedless, with an intermediate growth rate of 1.84′ annually over a ten year period, striking, narrowly erect growth habit with terminal dominance and dense lateral branches, becoming narrowly pyramidal-elliptical with age, bright glossy green foliage becomes dark green and semi-glossy as it hardens, changing to an intense golden yellow in autumn, Zone 3.

'Robinhood'—Lustrous, vibrant green foliage and vigorous, upright growth habit, male, a Klehm introduction.

Sherwood Glen™—Uniform upright tree with thick deep green foliage, a Klehm introduction.

Skyward™ ('Wandell')—Narrow constricted crown, good leaf texture, heavy rough bark, bronze-red to purple fall color, male, 35′ by 18′, a Wandell introduction.

'Summit'—Upright, pyramidal to moderate ovate, glossy foliage selection out of Minnesota tends to drop its leaves two weeks earlier in the fall than 'Marshall's Seedless'; straight central leader; foliage not as lustrous or dark green as 'Marshall's Seedless' but more refined; excellent golden yellow fall color; considerable confusion whether male or female although older trees I have seen did not fruit; 45′ by 25′, Zone 3b.

Urbanite®—Broad, pyramidal form with thick, leathery, lustrous dark green leaves and a deep bronze fall color, bark appears resistant to sun scald, seedless, again like 'Emerald', this form produced fruits at Milliken Arboretum, Spartanburg, SC; I know this may sound like heresy but evaluating 'Emerald' and Urbanite® I wondered if they were green ashes; safe to place them in the Red Ash category or move to White Ash, 50′ by 40′, Wandell introduction, Zone 5.

PROPAGATION: Seed requires warm (68°F), moist stratification for 60 days, followed by 120 days at 32 to 41°F; cultivars are budded onto seedling understocks.

NATIVE HABITAT: Nova Scotia to Manitoba, south to northern Florida and Texas. Introduced 1824.

RELATED SPECIES: Other *Fraxinus* of landscape importance but of significantly less concern than the previous species include:

Fraxinus angustifolia Vahl — Narrowleaf Ash

LEAVES: Opposite, compound pinnate, 6 to 10″ long, 7 to 13 leaflets, each 1 to 3″ long, 1/3 to 3/4″ wide, oblong-lanceolate to narrow-lanceolate, acuminate, cuneate, sharply and remotely serrate, dark green above, lighter beneath, glabrous.

BUDS: Brown, which separates it from the closely allied *F. excelsior*.

Fraxinus angustifolia, (frak′si-nus an-gus-ti-fō′li-à), Narrowleaf Ash, is a tree reaching 60 to 80′ in height. The specimens I have seen were upright-oval in habit with lustrous dark green leaflets of more refined nature than the two American species discussed above. At Kew Gardens, London, I saw a 60 to 70′ specimen of the species. It makes a good-looking tree where it can be properly grown. Native of the western Mediterranean and northern Africa. Cultivated 1800. Zone 5.

Fraxinus excelsior L. — Common or European Ash

LEAVES: Opposite, compound pinnate, 10 to 12″ long, leaflets 7 to 11, essentially sessile, ovate-oblong to ovate-lanceolate, 2 to 3 1/2″ long, 1 to 1 1/3″ wide, acuminate, cuneate, serrate, dark green above, lighter green beneath, glabrous except villous along the midrib beneath; rachis—usually pubescent.

BUDS: Black, pubescent, sessile, with 2 to 3 pairs of opposite scales.

STEM: Usually rounded, somewhat flattened at nodes, glabrous at maturity, grayish or grayish brown.

Fraxinus excelsior, (frak′si-nus ek-sel′si-or), Common or European Ash, grows 70 to 80′ with a 60 to 90′ spread, reaching on favored sites from 100 to 140′ in height. Forms a round-headed, broad-spreading outline, the lower branches upcurving. Foliage is dark green in summer and drops off green or develops a casual yellow. Prefers a deep, moist, loamy soil and thrives on limestone (calcareous) soils. One of the largest of European deciduous trees and much planted there. Has not had overwhelming acceptance in America because of borer susceptibility and the fact that our native ashes make better landscape plants. Many cultivars are available and the following are a few or the more popular. *Dendroflora* 26:6–30 (1989) discusses several ash species and cultivars with emphasis on *F. excelsior*.

'Aurea'—Young shoots yellow; older bark yellowish, quite noticeable in winter; fall color deep yellow; slow-growing.

'Aurea Pendula'—Branches weeping and forming a flat, umbrella-like head, young shoots yellow.

'Globosa'—A dense rounded head, 30′ in height with a 20′ spread; leaves smaller than the type.

'Gold Cloud'—Yellow leaves and stems, leaves turn yellow in fall; rapid-growing, seedless.

Golden Desert™—Round-headed, golden bark, gold spring new growth, yellow-green in summer, gold in fall, 30′ by 20′.

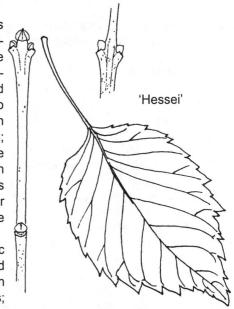

'Hessei'

'Hessei'—Leaves are simple and prominently toothed, lustrous dark green; very vigorous; upright oval to rounded; seedless; has shown good pest resistance compared to the species and other ashes; I had three in the Illinois evaluation plots and found them to be extremely hardy and vigorous; little fall color as the leaves stay green late into fall; trees form a straight sturdy trunk, well-filled with branches, and almost flat-topped at maturity, 60', Zone 4; one of the highest rated trees in the Ohio Shade Tree Evaluation Tests; unfortunately, this cultivar has proven almost as susceptible to borers as the species; shows great vigor and averaged 1.63' per year over a 9 year period in Wichita, KS tests; Dr. John Pair noted that despite the excellent vigor there was much borer damage.

'Jaspidea', 'Jaspidea Pendula'—Sometimes seen in botanic gardens; the former has yellow leaves when young with good yellow fall color; grows more vigorously, taller and open than 'Aurea'; the latter is a weeping form with similar leaf traits; arguably 'Aurea' and Golden Desert™ belong here.

'Kimberly' ('Kimberly Blue', also known as 'Rancho')—Santamour and McArdle in *J. Arboriculture* 9(10):271–279 (1983) and 10(1):21–32 (1984) published checklists of North American and European Ash cultivars. They straighten the confusion concerning this selection. It was selected by Kimberly Nursery, Kimberly, ID about 1936. Characteristics include attractive compact symmetrical form, 30' by 20', sturdy rapid growth, seedless. The authors noted that the tree has lost favor in recent years because of a "virus" or "decline." Not proven hardy at the Minnesota Landscape Arboretum and was also injured in the Chicago area during the harsh (–20 to –25°F) winter of 1976–77.

'Pendula'—Branches all weeping, forming a spreading umbrella-like head; this appears the most popular weeping tree in England and I have seen magnificent specimens throughout the cities and countryside; it does make a rather interesting tree and I will always remember a large, imposing specimen that reminded of a mop in Canterbury and a grizzled old specimen in Oxford Botanic Garden; the tree descends from the middle 1700's, female.

'Rancho'—Small (30') round-headed type, with dark green leaves and yellow fall color; same as 'Kimberly Blue'?

There are numerous other cultivars of Common Ash but their use is negligible or nonexistent in this country. Native of Europe and Asia Minor. Cultivated for centuries. Based on evaluations at arboreta in the East and Midwest I would estimate a Zone 5 to 7 adaptability range. A perusal of major tree producers in the United States echoes the paucity of this species in production. Perhaps, acceptable for the Pacific Northwest and I have seen trees in British Columbia coastal cities.

Fraxinus holotricha Koehne — Balkan Ash

LEAVES: Opposite, often whorled, compound pinnate, (5)9 to 13 leaflets, mostly 11, each leaflet elliptic or oblong-elliptic to lanceolate or broad elliptic, 1 1/2 to 2 3/4″ long, 1/2 to 3/4″ wide, acuminate, cuneate, serrate, most stalked on 1/3″ long petiolules, can be sessile, lustrous green, essentially glabrous above, with pubescence below.

BUDS: Often whorled, especially on young vigorous shoots, pubescent, brown-black.

Fraxinus holotricha 'Moraine', (frak'si-nus hol-ō-tri'kà), Moraine Balkan Ash, is a round-headed tree 30 to 40' in height with a similar spread. Very susceptible to borer injury. Has a finer texture than many ashes. Watched trees in Urbana, IL literally succumb to borer. Actually the tree was uniformly rounded, with a light foliage texture and rather handsome. Simply could not handle adversity. By some authorities 'Moraine' is placed with *F. angustifolia*. Balkans. Zone 5 to 6.

Fraxinus mandshurica Rupr. — Manchurian Ash

LEAVES: Opposite, compound pinnate, 8 to 14″ long, 9 to 11 leaflets, 2 to 4 1/2″ long, 1 to 2″ wide, oval to oblong-lanceolate, acuminate, sharply toothed, dull green with scattered bristles above, more so beneath, rachis winged above, wings forming a grove with tufts of brown pubescence where leaflets attach.

BUDS: Blackish, not unlike *F. excelsior*.

STEM: Dark green, squarish, glabrous.

Fraxinus mandshurica, (frak′si-nus mand-shoor′i-kà), Manchurian Ash, is a round-headed, 40 to 50′ tree, with mat green leaves. The only tree I have seen resides in the President's garden at the University of Illinois. It resembles *F. nigra* whose leaflets are basally rounded and the marginal teeth very shallow. The broad-rounded fruits are 1 to 1 1/2″ long. Susceptible to late spring frosts and not considered a satisfactory species for everyday culture. 'Mancana' grows 40 to 50′ by 20 to 25′ with a dense oval crown, yellow fall color, is easily transplanted, and tolerates drought and excess moisture. Introduced by Morden Station, Canada. The species is native to Japan and northeast China. Introduced 1882. Zone 3 to 5?

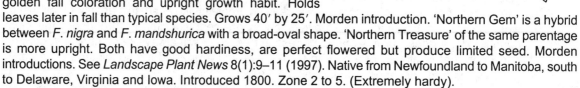

Fraxinus nigra Marsh. — Black Ash

LEAVES: Opposite, compound pinnate, 7 to 11 leaflets, oblong or oblong lance-shaped, 3 to 5″ long, 1 to 2″ wide, long acuminate, obliquely cuneate or rounded, serrate with small incurved teeth, dark green and glabrous above, lighter and hairy at base and on midrib below; all leaflets except terminal one are sessile.

BUDS: Black.

Fraxinus nigra, (frak′si-nus nī′grà), Black Ash, is a small to medium-sized tree reaching 40 to 50′ in height and developing a rather narrow, open crown. The national champion is 155′ by 108′ in Adrian, MI. The bark is scaly and flaky rather than ridged-and-furrowed. In the wild it occurs in wet places: low wet woods, cold swamps, and periodically inundated river bottoms. Does not have much to recommend it for ornamental use. 'Fallgold' is a seedless, clean, disease-free foliage form with long-persisting golden fall coloration and upright growth habit. Holds leaves later in fall than typical species. Grows 40′ by 25′. Morden introduction. 'Northern Gem' is a hybrid between *F. nigra* and *F. mandshurica* with a broad-oval shape. 'Northern Treasure' of the same parentage is more upright. Both have good hardiness, are perfect flowered but produce limited seed. Morden introductions. See *Landscape Plant News* 8(1):9–11 (1997). Native from Newfoundland to Manitoba, south to Delaware, Virginia and Iowa. Introduced 1800. Zone 2 to 5. (Extremely hardy).

Fraxinus ornus L. — Flowering Ash, Manna Ash

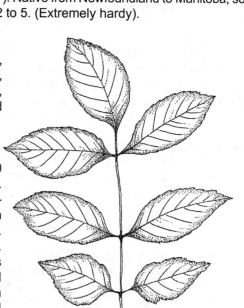

LEAVES: Opposite, compound pinnate, 5 to 8″ long, 5 to 9, usually 7 leaflets, each 2 to 4″ long, 3/4 to 1 3/4″ wide, oblong to ovate, terminal one obovate, abruptly pointed, broad cuneate, irregularly serrate, dull dark green and glabrous above, pubescent on base of midrib below.

BUDS: Pubescent, grayish brown.

Fraxinus ornus, (frak′si-nus ôr′nus), Flowering Ash, reaches 40 to 50′ in height and develops a rounded, spreading head. Hardy to –10°F (Zone 5 to 6). The flowers are showy, fragrant, and borne in 5″ long panicles in May. Full flower on May 26, 1990 in Mt. Auburn Cemetery, Cambridge, MA. This is one of the few ashes which has a corolla and calyx. This species has long been popular in European gardens and has been cultivated there for over 300 years. Beautiful specimen in Edinburgh Botanic Garden, Scotland that is in full flower in mid to late June. It makes a superb show and tempts one to at least try the tree. The bark is smooth and gray, not unlike that of European Beech. In July 1995, Bonnie and I traversed British Columbia and in Victoria this species was heavily utilized along streets. A trip to Van Dusen Botanical Garden, Vancouver, revealed 'Victoria', a seedless, dense-oval clone and 'Arie Peters', a female, broad-oval clone. 'Emerald Elegance' is pyramidal to rounded with large panicles of heavily scented, off-white flowers, male, medium green in summer, yellow in fall. Pair and Widrlechner, *Landscape Plant News* 5(4):1–3 (1994), reported on seed source trials and hardiness of *F. ornus*. The crux was no seedlings were reliably hardy in Zone 5. Native to southeastern Europe and western Asia. Introduced 1700. Zone 5 to 6, best in 6.

Fraxinus oxycarpa Bieb. ex Willd.
LEAVES: Very closely allied to *F. angustifolia* and often treated as a subspecies, often whorled, 3 to 7 leaflets, 1 1/2 to 2 1/2″ long, half this in width, lanceolate to narrow-elliptic, acute or acuminate, cuneate or long-cuneate, sessile, finely to coarsely serrate; the principal difference between this and *F. angustifolia* is a band of hairs on each side of the midrib at its base.

Fraxinus oxycarpa, (frak′si-nus ok-si-kär′pȧ), is closely allied to *F. angustifolia* and by some authorities is treated as a subspecies. Its chief distinction is a band of hairs on either side of midrib at the base. It also is less vigorous and smaller with a smoother bark. I only know this tree through its cultivar 'Raywood' which was raised in Australia about 1910. It is a handsome tree somewhat narrow in habit when young but opening up with age. The compound pinnate leaves are composed of 7 to 9, sharply serrated, lustrous dark green leaflets. The leaves are usually whorled or present in 4's immediately under the terminal bud. The leaves turn a rich plum purple in fall if sited in full sun and a somewhat dryish situation. It will probably average 40 to 50′ in height under cultivation but a 47-year-old tree has grown to 80′ in height. I have seen it at the Arnold Arboretum and in California. It might deserve a closer look from the nursery trade. In Spartanburg, SC trials, 'Raywood' looked like a world-beater for several years and then succumbed to borers. It was the latest ash to drop leaves with green leaves still present on November 6, 1992. Perhaps fine for Zone 8 and 9(10) in the West, certainly ephemeral in the East. 'Flame' has a symmetrical rounded outline and narrow, lustrous dark green leaflets that turn rich deep burgundy and then, to a flame color, 30′ by 25′, a Scanlon introduction, probably the same as 'Raywood'. Native to southeastern Europe, lower Danube, Asia Minor and the Caucasus. Zone 5 to 8(9).

Fraxinus quadrangulata Michx. — Blue Ash
LEAVES: Opposite, pinnately compound, 7 to 14″ long, (5)7 to 11 leaflets, 2 to 5″ long, 1 to 2″ wide, ovate to lanceolate, short-stalked, acuminate, broad-cuneate or rounded and unequal at base, sharply serrate, lustrous dark green, and glabrous above, pubescent along midrib near base beneath.
BUDS: Dark gray to reddish brown, slightly puberulous or often hairy-tomentose.
STEM: Stout, usually 4-angled and corky-winged, brown, glabrous at maturity; vascular bundles in a lunate arrangement.
BARK: Rather thin, gray, divided into plate-like scales, often shaggy; inner bark contains substance which turns blue on exposure.

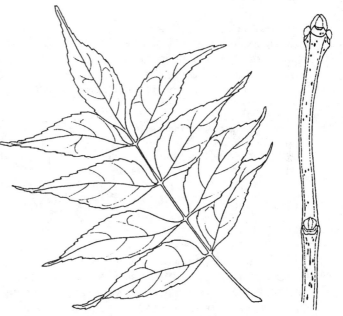

Fraxinus quadrangulata, (frak′si-nus kwa-drang-ū-lā′tȧ), Blue Ash, grows 50 to 70′ in height and develops a slender, straight, slightly tapered trunk which supports a narrow, rounded, often irregular crown of spreading branches. National champion is 86′ by 66′ in Danville, KY. The leaves are dark green in summer changing to pale yellow in fall. It frequents dry, limestone, upland soils. Does not seem to be a fast grower and is somewhat difficult to propagate. Bark is different from other ashes for on old trunks it is broken into scaly plates. The inner bark contains a mucilaginous substance which turns blue on exposure. 'True Blue' is an excellent, fairly fast-growing, square-twigged blue ash classified as a calciphyte capable of tolerating "sweet" soils. Usually found in limestone outcrop areas and sometimes in rich valleys of deciduous trees. Keeps green color throughout the growing season; does not "yellow out" like the species. Small, narrow leaves; full crown as it matures; 80′ by 40′. Minnesota Arboretum reports good success with the species. Grew 8.5″ per year over 9 years in Kansas. Showed good drought tolerance, did contract borer. Schmidt Nursery (1995) listed an unnamed budded strain, broad-oval symmetrical form, dark green leaves, yellow fall color, 40′ by 30′, Zone 4. Native from Michigan to Arkansas and Tennessee. Introduced 1823. Zone 4 to 7.

Fraxinus tomentosa Michx. f. [*F. profunda* (Bush) Bush] — Pumpkin Ash
LEAVES: Opposite, compound pinnate, 10 to 18″ long, 7
to 9 leaflets, 3 to 9″ long, 1 1/2 to 3 1/2″ wide, oblong-lanceolate or ovate, slender-pointed, rounded or
broad cuneate, entire or slightly toothed, dark green
and glabrous above, soft pubescent below especially
on midrib and veins, petiolules of lower leaflets 1/4″
long, rachis round not grooved or winged.
STEM: Young rounded, leaf scars deeply notched.

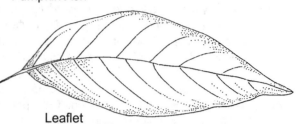
Leaflet

Fraxinus tomentosa, (frak′si-nus tō-men-tō′så), Pumpkin Ash, is strictly a tree of deep swamps and inundated
river bottoms which may grow 80 to 100′ or more. National champion is 133′ by 93′ in Big Oak State Park,
Missouri. The crown is open and narrow, with small, spreading branches. The leaflets are quite large
reaching 10″ in length. Interesting how taxonomy is never absolute. Southern authors refer to this species
as *F. profunda*; *The New Royal Horticultural Society Dictionary of Gardening* as *F. tomentosa*, a possible
hybrid between *F. americana* and *F. pennsylvanica*. Knowing the later two species intimately and having
collected *F. tomentosa* from a South Carolina Swamp, I see little resemblance. The leaves are lustrous
dark green, almost leathery and turn bronze-red to bronze-purple. Might be a worthy species for selection.
Native from western New York to southern Illinois, Louisiana, and northwestern Florida. Introduced 1913.
Zone 5 to 9.

Gardenia jasminoides Ellis — Cape Jasmine, Gardenia
(gär-dē′ni-å jas-min-oy′dēz)

FAMILY: Rubiaceae
LEAVES: Opposite or whorled, simple, evergreen, lanceolate to obovate, 2 to 4″ long, one-half as wide, short-
acuminate, cuneate, entire, thickish, lustrous dark green, leathery, dull and lighter green below, veins
impressed and rib-like below, glabrous; petiole—1/4″ long.
STEM: Green, moderate, turning brown, glabrous; pith—light green or whitish brown.

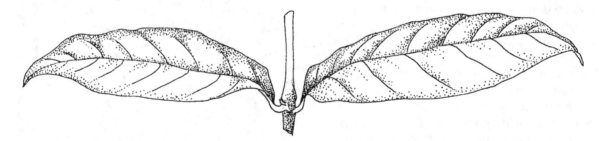

SIZE: 4 to 6′ by 4 to 6′; have observed 8′ high plants.
HARDINESS: Zone 7b to 10, marginal in Zone 7b but has survived –3°F; killed to ground but regenerated; after
the mid-1980's, every plantsman was searching for any gardenia with green leaves; several hardy single-
flowered forms (often listed as the daisy type) permit culture in Zone 6.
HABIT: Dense, rounded evergreen shrub with a sort of "blend into the woodwork constitution" after flowering;
outline sometimes oval-rounded; on occasion broad-rounded; have grown seedling populations with the
gamut of shapes and leaf sizes.
RATE: Medium.
TEXTURE: Medium.
LEAF COLOR: Very beautiful, lustrous dark green, quite leathery in texture; holds reasonable foliage color in
winter.
FLOWERS: Perfect, 6- to 7-petaled in single forms, multi-petaled in doubles, waxy white, aging to yellow,
solitary, exceedingly fragrant, 2 to 3″(4″) diameter, May, June, July.
FRUIT: Orange, fleshy, ovate, 1 to 1 1/2″ long berry, with 1/2 to 1″ long, strap-shaped sepals, carpel wall is 6-
winged, color develops in November in Athens.
CULTURE: Easily transplanted from containers; requires acid, moist, well-drained, high organic matter soils;
protect from winter winds and cold; full sun to partial shade; injured severely at –3°F; in 1994 and 1996,
temperature reached 4 and 7°F, respectively, in Athens and the only injury occurred on young shoots.

DISEASES AND INSECTS: Powdery mildew, canker (*Phomopsis gardeniae*), aphids, scale, mealybugs, white flies, thrips, mites, nematodes; requires a degree of attention to keep it looking thrifty; white flies are particularly troublesome.

LANDSCAPE VALUE: Excellent for fragrant flowers and handsome foliage; should be sited near patio or where people will notice the fragrance; flowers open over a long period of time; requires considerable maintenance; last statement is somewhat misleading for in a nursery setting white flies are a significant problem; in the garden, I have noticed less white flies, however, they are still present; my garden philosophy has always been to "live and let live" so chemical nuking is shunned; our gardenias, now numbering five, have prospered for over eight years.

CULTIVARS:

'Aimee Yoshida'—Large, fully double, fragrant, white flowers, one of first to flower, long flowering period, 5' high, 3' wide.

'August Beauty'—Large, double, white flowers, heavy-flowering, May–October, 4 to 6' high vigorous shrub.

'Belmont' ('Hadley')—Double, fragrant, cream-white flowers yellowing with maturity, glossy dark green leaves to 6" long, vigorous, uniformly branched shrub.

'Candle Light'—Double, fragrant, white flowers, dark green foliage, medium-sized shrub.

'Chuck Hayes'—Semi-double, ivory-white, fragrant flowers, May–June and then sporadically in September, hardier than doubles, possibly Zone 6b, from Virginia Polytechnic Institute and State University.

'Daisy'—Flat-faced, single, fragrant, white flowers, aging to yellowish, more compact habit, more cold hardy than the double forms.

'Daruma'—Dwarf form like 'Kleim's Hardy', single-flowered.

First Love™ ('Aimee')—Same as 'Aimee Yoshida'.

'Fortuniana'—Leaves larger than species, lustrous dark green, flowers to 4" diameter, double and carnation-like.

'Golden Magic'—Double, pure white flowers age to deep golden yellow, plant grows 3' by 2' in 3 years.

'Kleim's Hardy'—Single, fragrant, ivory, 2" diameter flowers, more cold hardy, listed as suffering only slight leaf burn at 0°F, considered by some the same as 'Daisy', small plant ±3' high and wide, lustrous black-green leaves, smaller flowers than the seedlings grown from Chinese seed, based on my evaluations not particularly cold hardy.

'Miami Supreme'—Double, large, fragrant, white flowers, dark green foliage.

'Michael'—Cold hardy form, excellent flower production, somewhat resistant to white fly, named after the son of Joe and Debbie Powell, Columbus, GA.

'Mystery'—Large, 4 to 5" diameter, double, white flowers on a large, 4 to 6'(8') rather upright-growing shrub.

'Radicans' ('Prostrata')—A handsome, small-leaved almost creeping version of the species; the small, lustrous leaves are especially handsome and coupled with the 1 to 2" diameter, double, fragrant flowers make this a better choice for many more landscapes than the species; grows 2 to 3' high and spreads 4', forms a graceful flowing evergreen shrub; good mass or facing plant; not particularly hardy; severely injured in exposed locations in Athens when low temperature was 12°F; no damage at 7°F in 1995 with ample preconditioning to induce increased cold hardiness.

'Radicans Variegata'—Like the above but with a creamy white leaf margin, same floral characteristics as 'Radicans'; may produce branch reversions which need to be removed.

'Shooting Star'—Single, 6-petaled, 3 1/2"(4") diameter, white, aging to yellow, exceedingly fragrant flowers, larger leaves and more upright grower than other singles, grown by author from seeds collected in China by Beijing Botanic Garden from northern portion of range, more cold hardy, and in laboratory tests as much as 12°F more cold hardy than 'Mystery', flowers over an extended period in May–June (Athens).

'Variegata'—A handsome cream-variegated leaf form that is doubtfully as hardy as the species; have seen at J.C. Raulston Arboretum and was impressed.

'Veitchii'—Grows 2 to 4' high, 2 to 3' wide, and produces 1 to 1 1/2" diameter, white flowers, flowers profusely.

'Veitchii Improved'—Grows taller than 'Veitchii' to 5' and produces slightly larger flowers in greater numbers.

'White Gem'—Single flowered form, supposedly growing 1 to 2' high and wide, listed in 1998 Monrovia Nursery catalog.

PROPAGATION: Tissue culture has been successful. Softwood cuttings root easily in June, July, August; have germinated seeds from wild collected material in China; simply sowed the seeds after removal from the berry and they germinated; flowers in 2 to 3 years from germination.

ADDITIONAL NOTES: Some 250 species of *Gardenia*; unfortunately, minimal hardiness.

The seedlings I raised were distributed to many individuals and I know that Mark Griffith has named and propagated one as 'Griffith's Select'. It is a robust, 3' by 4', evergreen shrub with abundant single white flowers. Should also be mentioned that the single forms are quickly becoming confused in the trade.

NATIVE HABITAT: China, Taiwan, Japan.

Gaultheria procumbens L. — Checkerberry or Creeping Wintergreen

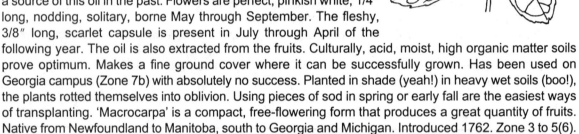

FAMILY: Ericaceae

LEAVES: Alternate, simple, evergreen, oval to obovate, rarely suborbicular, 3/4 to 1 1/2″ long, 1/2 to 7/8″ wide, obtuse and apiculate, crenate-serrate often with bristly teeth, lustrous dark green above, turn reddish with the onset of cold weather, strong aroma of wintergreen when bruised, glabrous; petiole—1/6″ long.

Gaultheria procumbens, (gâl-thē′ri-à   prō-kum′benz), Checkerberry or Creeping Wintergreen, is a low-growing (6″), creeping, evergreen ground cover. The leaves turn reddish with the advent of cold weather. When crushed they emit a wintergreen odor and have been a source of this oil in the past. Flowers are perfect, pinkish white, 1/4″ long, nodding, solitary, borne May through September. The fleshy, 3/8″ long, scarlet capsule is present in July through April of the following year. The oil is also extracted from the fruits. Culturally, acid, moist, high organic matter soils prove optimum. Makes a fine ground cover where it can be successfully grown. Has been used on Georgia campus (Zone 7b) with absolutely no success. Planted in shade (yeah!) in heavy wet soils (boo!), the plants rotted themselves into oblivion. Using pieces of sod in spring or early fall are the easiest ways of transplanting. 'Macrocarpa' is a compact, free-flowering form that produces a great quantity of fruits. Native from Newfoundland to Manitoba, south to Georgia and Michigan. Introduced 1762. Zone 3 to 5(6).

Gaylussacia brachycera (Michx.) Torr. & A. Gray — Box Huckleberry

(gà-lu-sā′shi-à bra-kis′e-rà)

FAMILY: Ericaceae

LEAVES: Alternate, simple, evergreen, 1/3 to 1″ long, about 1/2 as wide, elliptic, slightly revolute, toothed, glabrous, glossy dark green above, paler beneath; very short-petioled.

BUDS: Solitary, sessile, ovoid, small, with 2 or some 4 or 5 exposed scales; terminal lacking.

STEM: Slender, roundish; pith—small, 3-sided or rounded, continuous; leaf scars low, crescent-shaped or 3-sided; 1 bundle trace.

SIZE: 6 to 18″ high, spreading indefinitely.

HARDINESS: Zone 5 to 7; Cappiello, Orono, ME reported outright kill of the species but no damage to 'Margothy Creek'.

HABIT: Dwarf, evergreen shrub spreading by underground rootstocks and forming a solid mat or dense, broad mound.

RATE: Slow.

TEXTURE: Medium-fine in all seasons.

LEAF COLOR: Glossy dark green, although when grown in full sun often has reddish cast; becoming deep bronze to reddish purple in winter.

FLOWERS: Perfect, self-sterile but cross-fertile, white or pinkish, 1/4″ long, urn-shaped, May through early June; borne in short, axillary, few-flowered racemes near the end of the shoot.

FRUIT: Berry-like drupe, bluish, ripening in July–August.

CULTURE: Another ericaceous plant which requires considerable cultural manipulation if success is to be had; requires an *acid*, loose, well-drained soil supplied with organic matter; transplant from containers; preferably partial shade.

DISEASES AND INSECTS: None particularly serious.

LANDSCAPE VALUE: A very lovely, intriguing evergreen ground cover well-suited to areas underneath pine trees and rhododendrons where the soil is acid and well-drained.

PROPAGATION: Untreated seeds are slow to germinate; warm followed by cold stratification is recommended; fluctuating warm temperatures of 68 to 86°F for 30 days followed by 50°F for 27 days and 47 days resulted in 80 and 96% germination, respectively, of sound seeds; cuttings are variable based on my work; August cuttings treated with 8000 ppm IBA quick dip rooted only 20% while 'Amity Hall North' rooted 80% with the same treatment; other work reports excellent success with fall cuttings and 8000 ppm IBA talc.

ADDITIONAL NOTES: A rare American plant, lost to American gardens for a time, but was reintroduced through the efforts of the Arnold Arboretum. It has been theorized that one particular stand (colony) in the Amity-Hall area of central Pennsylvania covering an area of 300 acres and a mile long originated from one plant and is over 12,000-years-old; whether this is totally true is somewhat suspect but it does make for interesting reading.

NATIVE HABITAT: In the mountains and hills from Pennsylvania to Virginia, Kentucky and Tennessee. Introduced 1796.

Gelsemium sempervirens (L.) Ait. f. — Carolina Yellow Jessamine
(jel-sē′mi-um sem-pĕr-vī′renz)

FAMILY: Loganiaceae

LEAVES: Opposite, simple, evergreen, lanceolate or oblong-lanceolate, rarely ovate, 1 to 3 3/4″ long, 1/3 as wide, acute or acuminate, rounded, lustrous dark green and glabrous above, entire; short-petioled.

BUDS: Several pairs of scales rather loosely aggregated together.

STEM: Thin, wiry, greenish to brown, glabrous.

SIZE: 10 to 20′; will climb trees or scramble over fences, rock piles and other structures; can develop a 3 to 4′ mound of tangled stems if left to its own devices.

HARDINESS: Zone 6 to 9, probably to 10 and 11.

HABIT: Twining evergreen vine with thin, wiry stems; becomes more dense when sited in full sun; have used the species as a ground cover on the Georgia campus but plants twine around each other and ascend every which direction creating a rather wild and woolly aura, akin to my never combed hair.

RATE: Medium to fast; like most vines the better the soil the faster the growth.

TEXTURE: Fine.

LEAF COLOR: Lustrous dark green developing a slight yellow-green or purple-green cast in winter.

FLOWERS: Perfect, yellow, fragrant, solitary or in cymes, 1 1/2″ long, 1″ wide, funnelform with 5 short imbricate lobes; February into April; often flowers again in fall but sporadically; usually peaks in late March in the Athens area.

FRUIT: Compressed, 1 1/2″ long, short-beaked capsule, summer–fall, looks like an old water bottle.

CULTURE: Move as a container-grown plant; prefers moist, well-drained, organic matter laden soils but is quite adaptable; acid or slightly alkaline; best flowering in full sun but will grow and flower in shade; often found in shady situations in the wild; has a tenacious constitution; have observed it prospering in almost pure sand.

DISEASES AND INSECTS: None serious.

LANDSCAPE VALUE: Used in a multitude of ways in southern gardens; on fences, mailboxes, downspouts, trellises, structures, as a ground cover, in planters where it spills gracefully over the sides; quite beautiful in the wild where it scrambles into the crown of small trees (especially redbud and dogwood in the University's Botanical Garden) and lights them with bright yellow; especially noticeable along the highway when in flower; after flowering the vines become almost nondescript.

CULTIVARS:

'Margarita'—Cold hardy form, fragrant, flowers slightly larger than species, selected from seedlings sent by Tom Dodd, Jr. to Gene Cline, Canton, GA.

'Pride of Augusta' ('Plena')—Double-flowered form, from a distance scarcely discernible from the species, handsome on close inspection.

'Woodlanders Light Yellow'—Beautiful cream-yellow flowers, larger than species, vigorous, not as cold hardy as the species, best in Zone 8 and south, introduced by Woodlanders, Aiken, SC.

PROPAGATION: Seeds, semi-hardwood or hardwood cuttings; cuttings collected in August rooted 100% when treated with 3000 ppm IBA and placed in peat:perlite under mist; have seen many seedlings around parent plants; easy to root particularly after growth has hardened in spring.

ADDITIONAL NOTES: All parts of the plant are poisonous. Have grown both *G. sempervirens* and *G. rankinii* and find the latter not as invasive. Both are terrific, trouble-free plants for the southern garden.

NATIVE HABITAT: Virginia to Florida westward to Texas and Arkansas south to Central America. Introduced 1640.

RELATED SPECIES:

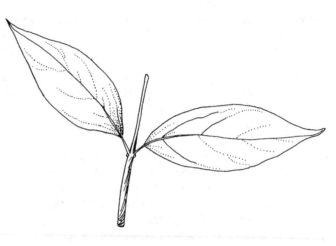

Gelsemium rankinii Small, (jel-sē'mi-um ran-ki'nē-ī), Swamp Jessamine, was popularized by the late J.C. Raulston at North Carolina State University and is certainly deserving of consideration by Zone 7 to 9 gardeners. In most characteristics it is like *G. sempervirens* except it flowers in October and November and waits for warm weather during the winter months to put forth an occasional yellow flower. Also flowers prolifically in March–April. In our garden, peaks in mid to late April but may spit flowers all winter. Godfrey noted that in Florida *G. sempervirens* flowers before *G. rankinii*. I have a single plant and have been delighted with its performance. This is certainly a plant for the future. The flowers are not fragrant and usually occur in 2- to 3-flowered cymes. The fruit is also smaller (1/2″ long) than that of *G. sempervirens*. 'Winter Purple' has the typical yellow, unscented flowers but offers purplish fall and winter leaf color. Head-Lee Nursery, Seneca, SC has a dwarf form. Found in swamps in North Carolina to Florida and Louisiana where it is rare in the wild. Grows where the soil may be water-logged for extensive periods of time. Need to consider this vine for wet areas in the garden. Zone 7 to 9.

Genista tinctoria L. — Common Woadwaxen or Dyer's Greenwood
(je-nis'tå tink-tō'ri-å)

FAMILY: Fabaceae

LEAVES: Alternate, simple, 1/2 to 1″ long, elliptic-oblong to oblong-lanceolate, nearly glabrous, apex pointed, base rounded, margin hairy-fringed, rich green.

BUDS: Small, solitary, sessile, ovoid, sometimes developing the first season or collaterally branched and producing a green grooved spine, with some half-dozen scales.

STEM: Green, more or less stripe-grooved, not spiny; stipules persistent; pith—small, rounded, continuous; leaf scars much raised, minute; 1 indistinct bundle trace.

SIZE: 2 to 3′ high and 2 to 3′ wide.

HARDINESS: Zone 3 according to Rehder; however, plants are killed back severely at the Minnesota Landscape Arboretum; probably best in Zone 4 to 7.

HABIT: Low shrub with almost vertical, slender, green, limitedly branched stems; spiky and twiggy in textural effect.

RATE: Slow, possibly medium.

TEXTURE: Fine to medium-fine in all seasons when well-maintained.

STEM COLOR: Green.

LEAF COLOR: Bright green in summer; no fall color.

FLOWERS: Yellow, 1/2 to 3/4″ long, produced on erect racemes, 1 to 3″ long, occurring on new growth from June to September although peak period is June and limited flowering may occur after that.

FRUIT: Pod, 1/2 to 3/4″ long, glabrous, 8- to 12-seeded.

CULTURE: Transplant from a container; somewhat difficult to transplant and once located should not be moved; prefers hot, sunny location in relatively infertile soils which are dry and loamy or sandy; succeeds in acid or neutral soils and thrives on limestone; can be pruned back after flowering and will flower sporadically again.

DISEASES AND INSECTS: None serious.

LANDSCAPE VALUE: Good low-growing plant for poor, dry soil areas; will add an element of color to the landscape; the few that I have seen were quite handsome and would make a nice addition to the landscape; might be used in Midwest and East.

CULTIVARS:

'Golden Dwarf'—Listed by Cappiello, Orono, ME, as suffering occasional tip dieback.

'Plena' ('Flore-Plena')—A dwarf, semi-prostrate shrub, with more numerous petals of a more brilliant yellow color.

'Royal Gold'—Stems erect, up to 2′ high; flowers golden yellow in terminal and axillary racemes, forming a narrow panicle.

There are numerous geographical varieties which differ in habit, leaf morphology and flower characteristics; Bean noted that *G. tinctoria* in its modern acceptation may be taken to cover a group of allied forms put under one variable species.

PROPAGATION: Seeds should be the preferred method of propagation; they germinate best when given a 30 minute acid scarification followed by a water soak; many hard seeded legumes can be handled this way; it is difficult to estimate the time of acid scarification and this needs to be worked out for each species and often each seed lot; late July, August and September appear to be ideal times for cuttings; they can be placed in sand in an outdoor frame and should be rooted by the following spring; good results can be obtained with 8000 ppm IBA and a sand:peat medium.

NATIVE HABITAT: Europe, western Asia. Cultivated 1789.

RELATED SPECIES:

Genista lydia Boiss., (je-nis′tà li′dē-à), has received attention in recent years because of the abundant, bright yellow, 3/8″ long flowers produced on 1 to 2′ high, lax, loose, arching shrub composed of slender 4- to 5-angled, glabrous green stems. Leaves are linear, 3/8″ long, 1/16″ wide, and spaced 1/2″ apart along the stem. Flowers explode in May–June and are extremely handsome. Requires well-drained soil and a full sun location. The common type in cultivation is procumbent. 'Lemon Spreader' produces bright lemon yellow flowers in late spring. Grows to 12″ high. Balkans, western Asia. Introduced 1927. Zone 6 to 7.

Genista pilosa L., (je-nis′tà pī-lō′sà), Silkyleaf Woadwaxen, is a low-growing (1 to 1 1/2′), procumbent shrub in youth, finally forming a low, tangled mass of slender, twiggy shoots. The 1/4 to 1/2″ long, narrow-obovate, margins folded upward, silvery haired leaves and stems are a grayish green and provide a nice contrast. The flowers are bright yellow, produced singly or in pairs from the leaf-axils, forming a crowded, 2 to 6″ long raceme. 'Goldilocks' produces abundant gold flowers and grows 2′ high and considerably wider. 'Vancouver Gold' grows 1′ high by 3′ wide and is covered with bright golden flowers in spring; promoted by University of British Columbia Botanical Garden in Vancouver; looks like a yellow blanket in flower. Demands sandy, gravelly, dry soils for best growth. Native to much of Europe. Cultivated 1789. Zone 5 to 7.

ADDITIONAL NOTES: The woadwaxens (there are numerous species) are not well-known in American gardens. They are popular in Europe where most are found wild. The Morton Arboretum has a small collection which I first saw in the summer of 1975; most were low-growing, spreading shrubs with handsome foliage colors. In Europe, *Genista* is everywhere in evidence. Several particularly outstanding species include the golden-yellow, spiny branched *Genista hispanica* L., Spanish Woadwaxen; the prostrate to 6″, winged, green-stemmed, golden yellow-flowered *G. sagittalis* L., Winged Genista; and the exquisite, virtually leafless, wispy green-stemmed, sweet yellow-flowered Mt. Etna Broom, *G. aetnensis* DC. The genus comprises some 90 species with most unsuitable for the southern United States. Best in East and West. When a plant with such beautiful flowers is no more common than a golden egg, then it is time to question general adaptability and performance. Flint, *American Nurseryman* 176(11):57–61 (1993), offers an overview of *Genista* that includes several additional species beyond my treatment. He essentially reiterated my assessment of the genus—not common in cultivation in the Midwest and East.

Ginkgo biloba L. — Ginkgo, often called Maidenhair Tree
(gingk′gō bī-lō′bȧ)

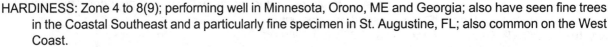

FAMILY: Ginkgoaceae

LEAVES: Alternate, simple, in clusters of 3 to 5 on spurs or single on long shoots, fan-shaped, dichotomously veined, more or less incised or divided at the broad summit, 2 to 3″ long, 2 to 3″ wide, bright green, glabrous; petiole—1 1/2 to 3 1/2″ long.

BUDS: Imbricate, mounded, often acute, brownish.

STEM: Stout, light brown 1st year, becoming gray with stringy peeling bark; prominent blackish spurs evident on older stems.

SIZE: 50 to 80′ in height with a tremendously variable spread ranging from 30 to 40′ to ultimately wider than high at maturity; the species can grow to 100′ or more.

HARDINESS: Zone 4 to 8(9); performing well in Minnesota, Orono, ME and Georgia; also have seen fine trees in the Coastal Southeast and a particularly fine specimen in St. Augustine, FL; also common on the West Coast.

HABIT: Usually pyramidal in outline when young; in old age often becoming wide-spreading with large, massive, picturesque branches; it is quite difficult to adequately describe the habit of this tree due to the tremendous variation in plants grown from seed; the male tree is supposedly more upright than the pistillate form; however, I have seen either side of the fence with male and female plants; young nursery trees are often gaunt and open without significant pruning in the production phase; Ginkgo gets better with age . . . be patient.

RATE: Slow to medium, probably 10 to 15′ over a 10 to 12 year period although with adequate water and fertilizer this tree will grow very fast; interesting Kansas study with 'Autumn Gold' producing 4.5″ of growth per year over a 9 year period; a famous old tree at Kew Gardens (one of the best I've seen) planted in 1762 was 56′ high 128 years later, tends to indicate that over time the species is slow-growing.

TEXTURE: Medium in leaf and coarse in winter but not objectionable.

BARK: Usually gray-brown ridges with darker furrows, actually quite handsome in the overall effect.

LEAF COLOR: Bright green on both surfaces in summer changing to an excellent yellow in fall; I would like to say that the yellow fall color is consistent from year-to-year but this is not the case; a freeze will cause the leaves to drop almost overnight whether they have colored or not; has colored spectacularly in the Athens area; I have been impressed with the performance of Ginkgo in the South; abundant myths about Ginkgo fall color and this manual has been responsible for some of the lore; in general, fall color rivals birches; in Zone 7 and 8, color initiates in early November and trees linger into December before shedding the yellow mantle; one seedling tree on campus colors consistently in early December.

FLOWERS: Dioecious, male flowers (green) are borne on the short shoots in cylindrical, 1″ long catkins during March–April; the female on a 1 1/2 to 2″ long pedicel bearing 1 or 2 greenish ovules.

FRUIT: Actually not a true fruit but simply a naked seed; tan to orangish in color, plum-like in shape, (3/4″)1 to 1 1/2″ long; the fleshy covering on the seed (female gametophyte) is extremely messy and malodorous and, for this reason, only male trees should be planted; the sperm which fertilize the egg are motile (swimming) and depend on water for accomplishing their mission; the seed is eaten by the Japanese and Chinese and is reported to be well-flavored; may take 20 years or more before a seedling *Ginkgo* flowers.

CULTURE: Transplants easily and establishes without difficulty; prefers sandy, deep, moderately moist soil but grows in almost any situation; full sun; very pH adaptable; prune in spring; have been told that summer pruning of young nursery-grown Ginkgo is anathema for they simply do not grow; air pollutant tolerant; a durable tree for difficult landscape situations; displays good soil salt tolerance; quite heat tolerant, does well in Zones 8 and 9 of the Southeast.

DISEASES AND INSECTS: Extremely free of pests although several leaf spots of negligible importance have been reported.

LANDSCAPE VALUE: Excellent city tree, public areas, perhaps too large for street use but is used extensively for this purpose; a well-developed Ginkgo is an impressive sight; often looks out of place in the small residential landscape because of unique foliage and winter habit; tends to be somewhat gaunt and open in youth but with time becomes one of the most spectacular of all trees; fall color alone is sufficient reason to plant the tree.

CULTIVARS:

'Autumn Gold' (possibly a trademark name, i.e., Autumn Gold™)—A handsome symmetrical broad conical form, very regular in shape, 50' by 30', perhaps broader later, excellent golden yellow fall color, considered one of the best of the *Ginkgo* cultivars for this character, male, introduced by Saratoga Horticultural Foundation, California about 1955.

'Bon's Dwarf'—Compact, "witches' broom" type, very slow.

'Canopy'—Broad-spreading, male form from Wavecrest Nursery, Fenville, MI.

'Chase Manhattan'—Dwarf Ginkgo with uniform shape, from Bon Hartline, IL; I had a small plant; based on current growth rate it should be 3' high by my one-hundredth birthday; other compact and "witches' broom" selections are known.

'Chi-Chi'—Novelty, almost fan-shaped habit like the leaf, densely branched, nice specimen at J.C. Raulston Arboretum, Raleigh, NC.

'Fairmount'—Narrow upright pyramidal form with strong central leader, male, selected from a tree in Fairmount Park, Philadelphia, PA, tree still exists, 70 to 80' by 30'.

'Fastigiata' (f. *fastigiata*)—Arguably there is more than one clone of the upright columnar type and several have been given cultivar names, ideally the selection should be male, in Vine Street Cemetery in Cincinnati, OH there is a large avenue planting of a distinct columnar form, apparently male, that predates the newer named selections.

'Gresham'—A distinct, horizontally spreading plant, no ascending or descending branches, discovered in front of Gresham Union High School, Gresham, OR, relatively slow-growing, probably 8 to 16" a year.

'Jade Butterfly'—A dwarf, V-shaped plant, with leaves growing in clusters, dark green, overall appearance resembles *Acer palmatum* 'Shishigashira', grows 4.8" a year, new introduction from Duncan & Davies, New Zealand.

'Lakeview'—Compact conical form, deep gold fall color, male, 45' by 25', a Scanlon introduction.

'Liberty Splendor'—Wide pyramidal form with strong central leader, rivals *Tilia cordata* Greenspire® and *Pyrus calleryana* 'Bradford' for shape, introduced by Arborvillage, Holt, MO.

'Magyar'—Uniform upright-branching habit, male, apparently a Princeton Nursery introduction; have never seen this tree and do not know the details of its origin.

'Mayfield'—Narrow columnar habit like Lombardy Poplar, male, 30' by 8', Zone 4, selected around 1948 in Ohio.

'Mother Load'—An abundant fruiting form, supposedly lacks pungent smell of the typical fruiting trees, from Louisiana Nursery.

'Palo Alto'—Nicely formed specimen, broad-spreading, male, representative of the species, Scanlon.

'Pendula' (f. *pendula*)—Actually, like f. *fastigiata*, a gathering place for plants with various degrees of pendulosity; the few plants of 'Pendula' I have seen were anything but . . . for the branches are horizontal for a distance but show no distinct weeping character like a weeping European Beech; I suspect that *Ginkgo* exhibits topophytic growth and if budwood is taken from a lateral branch the resulting plants show the arm-extended growth character.

'The President'—Upright oval-rectangular form selected by author from in front of the University's Presidential residence on Prince Avenue; have shown tree to my tree (true) friends who oohed and aahed; Schmidt Nursery in Oregon is building stock; different from all cultivar Ginkgos in strongly ascending branches but wider framework, excellent yellow fall color, male.

Princeton Sentry® ('PNI 2720')—Probably the best of the upright types, not perfectly columnar, i.e., like a fat telephone pole, but slightly tapered to the apex and slightly fatter at the base, yellow fall color, male, a Princeton introduction, have observed a row of these at the old Princeton Nursery site in Princeton, NJ, although listed as male I witnessed seed production on one of the trees, 60' by 25'.

'Santa Cruz'—Male, gold fall coloring, umbrella form, low and spreading, Scanlon introduction, although described as male have noted a reference that reports seed production.

'Saratoga'—Similar to 'Autumn Glory' in habit with distinct central leader, rich yellow fall color, male, 40' by 30', introduced by Saratoga Horticultural Foundation.

Shangri-la®—Uniform compact crown with good dense branching habit, excellent yellow fall color, fast-growing, male, 40' by 30', a Wandell introduction.

Spring Grove Witches' Broom —A compact, mounded-rounded form, discovered as a "witches' broom" at Spring Grove, Cincinnati, OH.

'WB'—A little ball of light green leaves derived from a "witches' broom," grows 2 to 4″ a year, listed by Stanley & Sons Nursery, Boring, OR.

'Windover Gold'—Broad-pyramidal to oval, unusual fan-shaped, bright green leaves, bright golden yellow fall color, male, originated at Windover Nurseries in southern Indiana.

Other cultivars: 'Aurea', 'Canopy', 'Epiphylla', 'Golden Girl', 'Kew' (described above, available as a vegetatively propagated clone), 'Laciniata', 'Ohazuki' (female with leaf and fruit stalks fused), 'Old Gold' (symmetrical, upright, male), 'Princeton Gold', 'Sinclair', 'Sterile', 'Tit', 'Tremonia', 'Tubiforme' ('Tubeleaf', tubular foliage, smaller habit), 'Variegata', and 'Woodstock' have been listed. Of these, I have only seen 'Variegata' which is irregularly streaked with yellow but unstable and reverts to the green form unless carefully pruned. There are multiple clones under the 'Variegata' umbrella.

PROPAGATION: Collect in mid-fall, remove pulp, place seeds in moist sand for 10 weeks at 60 to 70°F to permit embryos to finish developing; then seeds are stratified for 60 to 90 days at 41°F; reports have also indicated that freshly cleaned seed will germinate if directly sown; apparently some cold (1 to 2 months) improves germination; nursery practice involves fall planting; I have had good success rooting June cuttings from mature trees with 8000 ppm IBA quick dip, mist; cuttings root in 7 to 8 weeks; it appears 8000 to 10,000 ppm IBA is about ideal for stimulating good rooting; the cultivars are budded on seedling understock.

ADDITIONAL NOTES: W.J. Bean considers the Ginkgo "undoubtedly one of the most distinct and beautiful of all deciduous trees." It is a true gymnosperm and differs significantly from the angiosperms in the reproduction process. Anyone interested in botanical sidelights will find the history of the Ginkgo fascinating reading. One of the oldest trees, growing on earth for 150 million years (200 million years has been mentioned) and was native in North America at one time. The problem in determining the sex of Ginkgo is that they do not "fruit" until they are quite old (20 to 50 years). Always be leery when buying unnamed clones for this reason alone.

Abundant papers on Ginkgo with Huh and Staba, "The Botany and Chemistry of *Ginkgo biloba* L." *J. Herbs, Spices and Medicinal Plants* 1(1/2):91–124 (1992); Del Tredici, *Conservation Biology* 6(2):202–209 (1992) on the existence of Ginkgo in the wild; *Biosystems* 22(4):327–339 (1982) on seed dispersal; and *American J. Botany* 79(5):522–530 (1992) on natural regeneration, providing text for thought.

The medicinal aspects of Ginkgo have been known for centuries and are now touted in television and magazine advertisements. If memory loss seems to be encroaching and you can no longer differentiate a Ginkgo from Godzilla, I suggest reading Balch and Balch, 1997, *Prescription for Nutritional Healing*, Avery Publishing Group, Garden City Park, NY. The Ginkgo extracts improve brain functioning by increasing cerebral and peripheral blood flow, circulation and oxygenation. Also, good for depression, headaches, memory loss and tinnitis.

NATIVE HABITAT: Eastern China. Now known wild in Guizhou and Anhui/Zhejiang border. Introduced 1784.

Gleditsia triacanthos L. var. *inermis* (L.) Zab. — Thornless Common Honeylocust
(gle-dit'si-à trī-à-kan'thos in-ēr'mis)

FAMILY: Fabaceae

LEAVES: Alternate, pinnately or bipinnately compound, 6 to 8″ long, rachis pubescent all around, grooved, pinnate leaves with 20 to 30 oblong-lanceolate leaflets, 1/3 to 1 1/2″ long, 3/16 to 5/8″ wide, remotely crenate-serrulate, pubescent on midribs beneath; bipinnate leaves with 8 to 14 pinnae, the leaflets 1/3 to 1″ long, glossy bright green; base of petiole swollen and enclosing bud.

BUDS: Terminal—absent; laterals—small, about 5 more or less distinct at a node, some scaly, others naked.

STEM: Shining, smooth, reddish to greenish brown, often mottled or streaked, zig-zag with enlarged nodes.

SIZE: Tremendously variable in the cultivated types but usually in the range of 30 to 70' in height with a comparable spread; in the wild often grows to over 100'; tri-national champions (var. *inermis*) are 104' by 84', 116' by 104', and 90' by 88'; the species champion is 78' by 74'.

HARDINESS: Zone 4 to 9; most cultivars do not perform well in heat, humidity and heavy soils of the Southeast; most (all) cultivars were selected from northern seed sources and are not prosperous in the South; over my 19 years in Georgia I have watched every honeylocust on campus decline and/or die; a few Georgia nurserymen have tried to grow the tree without any great success; on an October 1997 visit to Waynesville, NC, I witnessed several trees in the city and all were disheveled while the Sugar Maples were in full fall regalia.

HABIT: Usually a tree with a short trunk and a rather open-spreading crown; light-shaded and consequently grass will grow up to the trunk; a very delicate and sophisticated silhouette which, unfortunately, has led to abuse by landscape planners.

RATE: Fast, as a young tree will grow 2′ or more per year over a 10 year period.

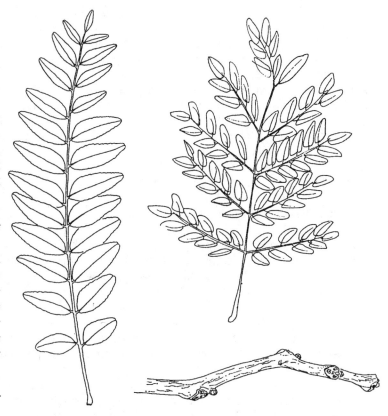

TEXTURE: Medium-fine in leaf (almost fine); medium in winter.

BARK: On old trees grayish brown, broken up into long, narrow, longitudinal and superficially scaly ridges which are separated by deep furrows.

LEAF COLOR: Bright green in summer, may be glossy above; clear yellow to yellow green in fall; leaves fall early.

FLOWERS: Polygamo-dioecious, perfect and imperfect flowers on same tree, greenish yellow, May–June, fragrant and nectar laden, not showy, male in clustered, downy, 2″ long racemes; females in few-flowered racemes.

FRUIT: Pod, reddish brown, brownish to blackish, strap-shaped, 7 to 8″ long up to 18″, about 1″ wide; seeds oval, shining dark brown and hard as a bullet; entire pod often irregularly twisted, the thickened margins contract during maturation causing the curving and coiling.

CULTURE: Readily transplanted; withstands a wide range of conditions although reaches maximum development on rich, moist bottomlands or on soils of a limestone origin; tolerant of drought conditions; high pH; salt tolerant (in fact has proven to be the most salt-tolerant tree growing along Chicago freeways); full sun; prune in fall; one of our most adaptable native trees but overused.

DISEASES AND INSECTS: Leaf spot, cankers, witches' broom, powdery mildew, rust, honeylocust borer, midge pod gall, webworm and spider mites; webworm can literally defoliate the tree; after the decline of the American Elm, honeylocust and the many cultivars were extensively used as a substitute; unfortunately, the insects and diseases have caught up with this tree in the urban landscapes and let us hope its fate is not similar to that of the predecessor; monogamous planting can lead to problems and for that reason I would strongly recommend using a diversity of trees and shrubs. In 1980 I returned to the Illinois campus to visit friends and as we walked the campus it became evident that the hundreds (thousands) of honeylocusts planted on the campus in the 1950's and 1960's were in trouble. Large trees were being removed from the Quadrangle for fear they might fall over and hurt students (perhaps faculty also), since one had already fallen over. The threat of liability will do wonders for campus beautification. The trees over the years had been subjected to every scourge mentioned above and apparently tremendous root rot had put the trees in a precarious way. Interestingly, the entire population was gradually removed and planted with four different species (no honeylocust).

The tree is beautiful but is not without problems. An aggressive canker, *Thyronectria austro-americana*, causes wilt, cankers or both. In Colorado, the most diseased trees were between 12- and 20-years-old, 20 to 30′ high and 6 to 12″ diameter. 'Sunburst' is the most susceptible cultivar. See *Amer. Nurseryman* 156(8):52–53 (1982) for details.

LANDSCAPE VALUE: At one time I would have said an excellent lawn tree for providing filtered shade but no more; it is overused and consequently the novelty has worn off; we might be looking for a replacement for this tree if serious insect and disease problems continue; I am not sure where the species is heading in turns of everyday commerce, certainly it has taken a back seat to *Acer rubrum* cultivars; at Quincy Market, Boston the honeylocusts have persisted against all odds.

CULTIVARS: Haserodt and Sydnor, *J. Arbor.* 9(7):186–189 (1983), reported on the growth characteristics of 5 cultivars after 15 years in the Ohio Shade Tree Evaluation Tests at Wooster, OH. Height/width of 'Imperial' was 25'/24'; 'Moraine'—32'/28'; 'Shademaster'—32'/25'; 'Skyline'—35'/26'; 'Sunburst'—32'/24'. Many cultivars with about 40 found in recent literature.

'Bujotii' ('Pendula')—A very elegant, pendulous tree; branches and branchlets very slender; leaflets narrower than the species, often mottled with white.

'Continental'—Vigorous narrow crown of stout branches, large leaves, fine leaflets, dark blue-green color, virtually seedless, 60 to 70', a Princeton introduction.

'Elegantissima'—Dense, shrubby habit, with elegant foliage; original plant grew 13' in 25 years; should be grafted on *G. t.* var. *inermis* understock; might be suitable under low wires and other structures.

'Emerald Kascade'—Irregular, weeping form with handsome dark green leaves, butter yellow in autumn; left to genetic regulation, it is a flopper, perhaps grafted on a standard or staked and then allowed to cascade, it would make a respectable small weeping tree, grows 16' by 16' if left to itself, apparently a male.

'Fairview'—Strong, sturdy growth habit, habit is similar to 'Moraine', produces one grade larger than most cultivars, 50' by 40', seedless or essentially so, a McGill introduction.

'Green Glory'—(50 to 75') Vigorous grower with strong central leader, pyramidal when young; retains foliage later than other types; shows some resistance to webworm damage; essentially fruitless.

'Halka'—Strong-growing, 40' by 40', large oval-rounded to round-headed with greater fullness and less pendulous branching than typical form, forms thicker trunk at an earlier age than most seedlings, essentially fruitless, although I have observed abundant fruits on occasion.

'Imperial'—(30 to 35') Graceful, spreading branches at right angles to main trunk, rounded outline; produces a few pods; Minnesota reports some dieback in severe winters; 1'7.9" per year over a 10 year period in Wichita, KS tests; a tree over 50' was reported.

'Majestic'—(60 to 65') Spreading but more upright-branched than above; excellent dark green foliage; one of the more popular clones; 1'10.8" per year over a 10 year period in Wichita, KS tests.

'Marando' (also listed as 'Weeping Marando' or 'Marando Weeping')—New form with semi-weeping habit, dark green leaves, dark brown bark, seedless.

'Maxwell'—Somewhat irregular grower, horizontally spreading branches; reputed hardy to low temperature, male.

'Moraine'—The first of the thornless honeylocusts to be patented (1949); broad, graceful in outline; 40 to 50'; fruitless; good dark green changing to golden yellow in fall; shows greater resistance to webworm than some of the new introductions; possibly should be considered the standard by which the others are judged.

'Perfection'—An excellent, well-scaffolded tree developing an early crown, slightly broader than 'Skyline' but not as spreading as 'Imperial', dark green foliage, 50' by 35', fruitless.

'Pin Cushion'—Interesting novelty form; foliage is borne in bunches along the stem; I have seen three planted together and the shade produced was not dense enough to protect an ant.

'Prairie Sky'—Cold hardy form from Sasketchewan, upright, symmetrical, see *HortScience* 28:280 (1993).

'Ruby Lace' ('Rubylace')—Ruby red when first unfolding, purplish bronze later and finally green, a poor specimen, ungainly, as bad as a cultivar can be, webworms love it, fruitless.

'Shademaster'—Ascending branches, dark green leaves, strong-growing, essentially podless; several horticulturists consider this the best, 45' by 35', 1'10.7" per year over a 10 year period in Wichita, KS tests.

'Skyline'—(45' by 35') Pyramidal form with ascending branches (60 to 90° angle), compact, dark green leaves, bright golden yellow fall color; another good form; Cole introduction; more upright than most forms; 1'9" per year over 10 years in Wichita, KS tests, essentially fruitless, one of the most cold hardy forms.

'Summer Lace' ('Summerlace')—Strong-growing, graceful appearance, light green foliage turns dark green, dark shiny bark, 60 to 70', broad-rounded with maturity.

'Summergold'—Open, elegant, lazy appearance, bright golden new growth turning to yellow-green, 40 to 50'.

'Sunburst'—(30 to 35') Broad pyramidal head, golden leaves on new growth changing eventually to bright green, somewhat hard to digest, fruitless, susceptible to Nectria canker.

'True Shade'—(40′ by 35′) Broad oval form, fine-textured medium green foliage turns yellow in fall, fast-growing; branch angles approximate 45°, fruitless under most conditions.

PROPAGATION: Seeds should be scarified in concentrated sulfuric acid for 1 to 2 hours; they will then germinate readily; cultivars are budded on seedling understock.

ADDITIONAL NOTES: The pods contain a sweetish, gummy substance from which the name honeylocust is derived. The species, *Gleditsia triacanthos*, is laden with multi-branched thorns, from 3 to 6″(16″) long, and should not be considered for landscape situations. It should be mentioned that very few of the clones are completely fruitless. The polygamous nature of the flowers usually allows for some perfect flowers and, hence, fruit will occur.

NATIVE HABITAT: Pennsylvania to Nebraska and south to Texas and Mississippi. Introduced 1700.

Gymnocladus dioicus (L.) K. Koch — Kentucky Coffeetree
(jim-nok′là-dus dī-ō-ī′kus)

FAMILY: Fabaceae

LEAVES: Alternate, bipinnately compound, to 36″ long and 24″ wide, with 3 to 7 pairs of pinnae, the lower usually reduced to simple leaflets, the upper with 6 to 14 leaflets; leaflets ovate or elliptic-ovate, entire, 1 1/2 to 3″ long, acute, rounded or cuneate at base, dark green, almost bluish green, pubescent beneath when young; short-petioled, swollen at base.

BUDS: Terminal —absent; laterals —small, bronze, pubescent, partially sunken, scarcely projecting beyond surface of twig, surrounded by an incurved downy rim of bark, axillary bud in depression at top of leaf scar, one or sometimes 2 or more superposed buds present; sometimes 2 lateral scales visible.

STEM: Very stout, more or less contorted, brown or slightly greenish, glabrous or often velvety downy; pith—wide, salmon-pink to brown, solid.

BARK: Dark brown, characteristically roughened with tortuous, recurved, scale-like ridges which are distinct even upon comparatively young branches.

SIZE: 60 to 75′ in height by 40 to 50′ in spread although can grow to 90′; national champion is 90′ by 89′ in West Liberty, KY.

HARDINESS: Zone 3b to 8.

HABIT: Usually develops vertically ascending branches which form a narrow, obovate crown; picturesque; bare-limbed and somewhat clumsy looking in winter; the finest specimen I know exists on the Illinois campus; I love this species for its unique habit; certainly no two exactly alike, some with very irregular branching, others with pseudo-pendulous lower branches; several nurserymen have started to notice the tree and selections for good habit and maleness are being made.

RATE: Slow to medium, growing 12 to 14′ over a 10 year period.

TEXTURE: Medium in leaf; coarse, but not offensively so, in winter.

BARK: Rough, with hard, thin, firm and scaly ridges curling outward (recurving) along their edges; very unique and interesting bark pattern which develops on 1 to 2″ diameter branches; grayish brown to dark brown.

LEAF COLOR: One of the latest trees to leaf out in spring, usually emerging about May 5 to May 20 in Midwest; new leaves are pinkish to purplish tinged gradually changing to dark green, almost dark bluish green in summer; fall color is often ineffective (some yellow) but on some trees is excellent.

FLOWERS: Dioecious or polygamo-dioecious, greenish white, 4 to 5 petals, spreading, each 1/3″ long, late May to early June, each flower 3/4 to 1″ long, pubescent, borne in large, 8 to 12″ long, 3 to 4″ wide, pyramidal panicles (female); on the male tree the panicle is about 1/3 the length of the female; interesting on close inspection; female fragrant like the best rose; males may be also but I have never noticed.

FRUIT: Reddish brown to brownish black, leathery pod, 5 to 10″ long, 1 1/2 to 2″ wide, containing a few, large, blackish brown, hard-shelled, rounded seeds imbedded in a sweet, sticky pulp; ripens in October, but hang on tree through winter; good crops produced alternately or on three year cycles; takes 4 to 8 years from seed before trees fruit.

CULTURE: Transplant balled-and-burlapped into deep, rich, moist soil for best growth; however, adaptable to a wide range of conditions such as chalk (limestone), drought, and city conditions; full sun; prune in winter or early spring; wood may be somewhat brittle.

DISEASES AND INSECTS: None serious.

LANDSCAPE VALUE: A choice tree for parks, golf courses and other large areas; at times somewhat dirty for the pods, leaflets and rachises are falling at different times; the tree has interesting characters especially the bold winter habit and handsome bark; essentially unknown in South but a young 5 to 6′ high tree grew 30′ high in 11 years on the Georgia campus; the tree is absolutely beautiful and results in a number of "What is it?" questions; the yellowish rachises have persisted until February.

CULTIVARS:

'Espresso'—Upward arching branches resulting in an almost elm-like vase form, 50′ by 30′, fruitless, introduced by J. Frank Schmidt, Boring, OR.

Prairie Titan® ('J.C. McDaniel')—Derived from the magnificent male tree that grew next to Davenport Hall on the University of Illinois campus, upright-spreading, clean-branching, parent tree 60 to 70′ high, 30 to 40′ wide, beautiful blue-green summer foliage, in all my travels surveying the Coffeetree kingdom, the Illinois tree is the best, particularly for striking winter architecture. Introduced by Heritage Trees, Inc., Jacksonville, IL.

'Stately Manor'—Narrow, upright form, 50′ by 20′, male, should make a good street tree, from Minnesota Landscape Arboretum.

'Variegata'—Is virtually unknown and I saw for the first time a small tree in Kew Gardens, the gray-green foliage was irregularly peppered and streaked with creamy white variegation; from a distance the variegation pattern was not pronounced but on close inspection is lovely; the combination of pinkish to purplish new growth and variegation is quite handsome, not as strong-growing as the species.

PROPAGATION: Seed should be scarified in concentrated sulfuric acid for 4 to 6 hours; I have left seeds in the acid for 24 hours and still got 90% germination; Frett and Dirr, *The Plant Propagator* 25(2):4–6 (1979), reported that 0, 2, 4, 8, 16, 32 hours of acid scarification resulted in 7, 93, 100, 95, 83, and 87% germination, respectively; root cuttings, 3/8″ diameter, 1 1/2″ long, December, can be used to vegetatively propagate the tree. Tom Tracz, former student, when he was with Synnesvedt Nursery, propagated three clones from root cuttings; interestingly one grew 50 to 100% faster than the other two clones; there is room for a good male tree and Tom's work indicated root cuttings will work. Deb McCown, Knight Hollow Nursery, Madison, WI has successfully propagated a male form in tissue culture. Deb informed me that rooting was difficult but that she had solved the problem. Geneve et al., *HortScience* 25:578 (1990), describe tissue culture shoot initiation from seedling explants.

ADDITIONAL NOTES: The seeds are great fun to throw and hit with a baseball bat. The seeds were used by the early settlers to Kentucky as a coffee substitute; hence, the tree's common name. Selections should be made for good male forms and these, in turn, propagated vegetatively. This tree has been slighted in the landscape industry and, considering its cultural tolerances, would make a valuable addition to the list of "tough" trees. Ford, *Secrest Arboretum Notes* Autumn (1975), reported that the leaves and seeds are poisonous to man and the seed and fruit contain the alkaloid cytisine. Cattle have been poisoned by drinking from pools of water into which seed pods have fallen. He speculated that roasting the seed may destroy its toxic principal(s). I mention this because in my youth I ate the sweetish gummy substance that lined the inside of the pod. Maybe that's what is wrong with me today.

NATIVE HABITAT: New York and Pennsylvania to Minnesota, Nebraska, Oklahoma and Tennessee where it occurs in deep, rich soils in bottomlands, deep ravines and moist slopes. Introduced before 1748.

Halesia tetraptera Ellis (formerly *H. carolina* L.) — Carolina Silverbell
(ha-lē′zhi-à te-trap′tēr-à)

FAMILY: Styracaceae

LEAVES: Alternate, simple, ovate or elliptic to ovate-oblong, 2 to 5″ long, about 1/3 to 1/2 as wide, acuminate, cuneate or rounded at base, serrulate to almost entire, tomentose at first, dark green and soon glabrous above, pubescent beneath; petiole—1/4 to 1/2″ long.

BUDS: Terminal—absent; laterals— ellipsoid to ovoid, superposed, 1/8 to 1/4″ long, with thick, broad-ovate, dark brown to red-black, acute puberulous scales, rounded on the back, slightly stalked.

STEM: Slender, glabrous or densely pubescent becoming slightly pubescent or remaining glabrous, brown; pith—white, chambered, 1 bundle trace; stem becoming stringy on 2nd year wood.

SIZE: 30 to 40′ in height with a spread of 20 to 35′; may grow up to 80′; tri-national champions are 104′ by 40′, 103′ by 45′, 96′ by 39′, all in the Great Smoky Mountains National Park, TN.

HARDINESS: Zone 4 to 8(9); respectable specimen on the Maine campus, Orono.

HABIT: Low-branched tree with a comparatively narrow head and ascending branches or often with several spreading branches forming a broad, rounded crown.

RATE: Medium, 9 to 12′ over a 6 to 8 year period; faster under nursery conditions.

TEXTURE: Medium in all seasons.

BARK: Gray to brown to black combination, ridged-and-furrowed with flat somewhat lustrous ridges which develop into scaly plates; intermediate branches are gray and streaked with darker vertical fissures.

LEAF COLOR: Dark yellowish green in summer; changing to yellow or yellow green in fall; usually dropping very early in fall.

FLOWERS: White, rarely pale rose, bell-shaped, 1/2 to 3/4″(1″) long, shallowly 4-lobed, styles about as long as carolla, perfect, flowering on year-old wood; borne on pendulous 1/2 to 1″ long stalks in axillary (cymose) 2- to 5-flowered clusters in April to early May; flowers early to mid-April in Athens and effective for 10 to 14 days, flowers emerge before or with the leaves; a subtle beauty not appreciated by most people.

FRUIT: Oblong or obovoid, 4-winged, dry drupe, 1 to 1 1/2″ long, green changing to light brown, effective in September into late fall, containing 2 to 3 seeds.

CULTURE: Transplants readily balled-and-burlapped; I wish this transplant statement was unilaterally true; container-grown plants are easily transplanted, however, field-grown nursery material has given our southern growers fits; I have recommended the species in some of my consulting work only to become dismayed when as many as 11 of 11 plants died within three years of transplanting; the root system is stringy and typical balled-and-burlapped handling does not facilitate a high degree of success; prefers rich, well-drained, moist, acid (pH 5 to 6), high organic matter soils; sun or semi-shade; in the wild often occurs as an understory tree on the slopes of hills, ridges and mountains, particularly along the streams; will become chlorotic in high pH soils.

DISEASES AND INSECTS: Exceptionally pest resistant; on occasion in the South have noticed leaf damage with sections of the blade removed, does not hurt the tree but is unsightly; necrotic spot virus was reported.

LANDSCAPE VALUE: One of my favorite small native trees; often neglected in this country but definitely with a place in shrub and woodland borders; handsome lawn tree; set off best with an evergreen background; rhododendrons grow well beneath silverbells; native on our Georgia property and always occurring in the understory where it flowers profusely; perhaps one of the best native trees for shady habitats; common in the southern Appalachians and I never tire of chancing upon a specimen.

CULTIVARS:

'Arnold Pink'—Rose pink flowers, up to 3/4″ long, introduced by Arnold Arboretum.

'Meehanii'—This interesting form was found in Meehan's nursery at Germantown, PA as a solitary plant in a bed of seedling-grown *Halesia tetraptera*; it forms a rounded shrub to 12'; the flowers are smaller than those of the species and apparently borne in great quantities; leaves coarser and more coarsely wrinkled.

'Rosea' (var. *rosea*)—I read a great deal about different plants but like to confirm the literature by actually seeing the plant; I have read that 'Rosea' is a pink form whose color is dependent on climate and soil; I have seen at least two pink forms, one with rich pink color and rather delicate flowers; the other pink-blushed and large-flowered; the first is worthy of distribution for it is a tree of great beauty; I have rooted both the clones mentioned above from August cuttings using 3000 ppm IBA quick dip, peat:perlite, mist; the pink corolla color is expressed regardless of climate but hot weather may reduce intensity of coloration; have walked nursery rows and assessed variation in corolla size and color; in almost any population some pink flowers develop; the pink must be under genetic control but like the expression of fall color, environmental conditions affect the degree of expression.

'Silver Splash'—Leaves are green, randomly interspersed with a silver-white and yellow variegation, discovered as a branch sport in 1992 at the Tyler Arboretum, Media, PA.

'Variegata'—Photographs of various cream-yellow streaked foliage forms have been presented at conferences; I am not sure a variegated silverbell has a great deal of appeal; the key to the variegation is the degree of stability; Clarence Towe, Walhalla, SC has seen a yellow-sectored variegated form. Fairweather Gardens, Greenwich, NJ, offers an olive green leaf form with brilliant greenish yellow edges.

'Wedding Bells' ('Uconn Wedding Bells')—Small tree, to 20', flowers significantly larger than the species, discovered in Ohio, introduced by Mark Brand through the University of Connecticut, Zone 5.

PROPAGATION: Seed must be moist stratified at 56° to 86°F for 60 to 120 days, followed by 60 to 90 days at 33 to 41°F; I have germinated seed but it was no easy task; I provided warm and cold as mentioned above and sowed the seeds in the greenhouse with no resultant germination; back into the cooler for another 60 days of cold and finally the seedlings came up; nursery production involves fall planting and two years of patience; student at Tennessee excised embryos from green or brown fruits and found they grew normally, embryo from stratified fruits germinated in 4 days; this work indicates that the dormancy may be related solely to physical factors, i.e., thick fruit wall; see Gersbach and Barton, "Germination of seeds of the silverbell, *Halesia carolina*," *Contributions Boyce Thompson Institute* 4:27–37 (1932). I have collected softwood cuttings from a tree on the Illinois campus, treated with 1000 ppm IBA/50% alcohol, placed in peat:perlite under mist and received 80 to 90% rooting; after this initial success one of my graduate students, Ms. Sue Burd (now Sue Brogden), undertook a detailed study; she sampled *Halesia* in May, June, July and August; cuttings rooted 80 to 100% when treated with IBA in the range of 2500 to 10,000 ppm; cuttings are easy to overwinter; for best results handle rooted cuttings like *Hamamelis* × *intermedia*, i.e., place under extended photoperiod (75 watt bulbs) until new growth ensues, fertilize, harden off and overwinter in a polyhouse, root cuttings in pots or cells so that root disturbance is minimized.

For tissue culture specifics see Brand and Lineberger, *Plant, Cell, Tissue and Organ Culture* 7:103–113 (1986); also see Brand, same journal 33:129–133 (1993).

ADDITIONAL NOTES: The largest specimens of *H. tetraptera* and *H. monticola* I witnessed were located on the campus of Purdue University, West Lafayette, IN. *Halesia tetraptera* was about 40 to 50' in height while *H. monticola* approximated 50 to 60'. No doubt much larger now since I saw them over 20 years past. *Halesia monticola* is now included with *H. tetraptera* by some authorities and this thinking is probably justified since it is extremely difficult to distinguish between the two species. If anyone is interested in the logic behind the merger of *H. monticola* with *H. tetraptera*, I recommend Spongberg, "Styracaceae hardy in temperate North America," *J. Arnold Arboretum* 57(1):54–73. Little did I know that the piece of property upon which my home rests is inundated by silverbells. They grace the slope above the creek and some extend their branches over the water.

NATIVE HABITAT: West Virginia, Ohio, Illinois to Florida and eastern Oklahoma, on wooded slopes and along streambanks. Introduced 1756.

RELATED SPECIES:

Halesia diptera Ellis — Two-winged Silverbell

LEAVES: Alternate, simple, obovate to nearly orbicular, 3 to 5 1/2" long, 1 1/2 to 3"(4") wide, abruptly long acuminate, cuneate or rounded, remotely sinuate-serrulate with minute callous teeth, dark green and glabrous above, pubescent at least on veins below; petiole—1/2 to 3/4" long.

Halesia diptera, (ha-lē'zhi-à dip'tēr-à), Two-winged Silverbell, is a beautiful, small (20 to 30'), rounded tree, usually multi-stemmed or low-branched. The national champion is 42' by 40' in Spring Grove, Cincinnati, OH. It is, unfortunately, not well-known in gardens. The 4-lobed, white, 3/4" long (1/2 to 1 1/4" long), bell-shaped flowers occur on 1/2 to 3/4" long pendulous slender pedicels in May. The corolla is deeply cut and the petals appear separate. The flowers are more refined than those of *H. tetraptera*. The flowers arrive 7 to 14 days later than *H. tetraptera*. The 1 1/2 to 2" long, 3/4" wide, dry drupes have two longitudinal, 1/4 to 3/8" wide wings. The common name is derived from the shape of the fruit. I have changed my mind on this species and recommend it highly. It makes a rather pretty small tree with leaves and bark not unlike that of *H. tetraptera*. Have not been able to root this from cuttings. Variety *magniflora* Godfrey has larger flowers ranging from 3/4 to 1 1/3" long. Several Georgia nurserymen have grown this under field conditions. Three- to five-year-old plants flower heavily. Again it has been difficult to transplant balled-and-burlapped but is being produced in containers and should be handled this way. Found in moist sites from South Carolina and Tennessee to Florida and Texas. Introduced 1758. It has withstood –25°F in Cincinnati and flowered profusely. Zone (4)5 to 8b.

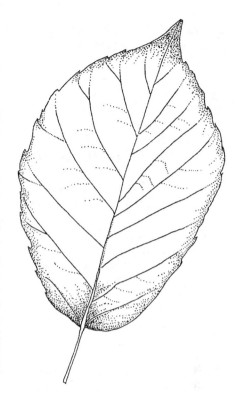

Halesia monticola (Rehd.) Sarg., (ha-lē'zhi-à mon-tik'ō-là), Mountain Silverbell, is similar to *H. tetraptera* but differs in having larger flowers, larger fruits and larger habit often reaching 60 to 80' with well-developed single or double leaders and a conical habit; some trees develop bushy crowns. Cultivar termed 'Rosea' has pale pink flowers. There is a variety *vestita* with more pubescent leaves that are often rounded at the base. It is a large tree that appears to maintain a central leader. Although now included in *H. tetraptera* (*H. carolina*) by most authorities, there are still pockets of resistance who treat it as a separate species (*The New RHS Dictionary of Gardening*). Native from North Carolina to Tennessee and Georgia in the mountains at altitudes not less than 3,000'. Introduced 1897. Zone 5 to 8.

Halesia parviflora Michx. — Little Silverbell
LEAVES: Alternate, simple, ovate, 2 to 4" long, 1 to 2" wide, irregularly wavy along margin, fine-toothed, dark green.

Halesia parviflora, (ha-lē'zhi-à pär-vi-flō'rà), Little Silverbell, is a large shrub or small tree that supposedly grows 25 to 30' high. Plants I have seen are about 8 to 12' and somewhat shrubby. The white flowers are the smallest of the group being only 1/4 to 1/2" long, while the fruits range from 1 to 1 1/2" long, with 4 narrow, essentially equal wings. This species is now placed under *H. tetraptera* or given separate species status as *H. carolina* L., the defining characteristics being smaller flowers and fruit and the style longer than the corolla. In February, I traveled to North Florida to visit Superior Trees where *H. parviflora* and *H. tetraptera* were present in containers and the owner's garden. Container-grown plants of the two had been mixed and we were unable to tell the difference by winter bud and stem characteristics. Although the *H. parviflora* is different in size, I believe reduction to a variety or the merging into *H. tetraptera*, akin to the fate of *H. monticola*, is the logical approach. Also, the use of DNA-techniques for determining taxonomic relationships would be a worthy study. Native in the woods and hillsides of the Coastal Plain of northern Florida and Mississippi. Zone 6 to 9.

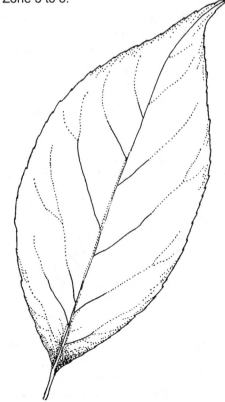

Hamamelis vernalis Sarg. — Vernal Witchhazel
(ham-à-mē′lis vĕr-nā′lis)

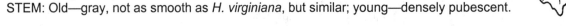
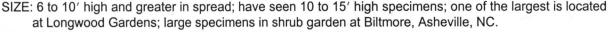

FAMILY: Hamamelidaceae

LEAVES: Alternate, simple, obovate to oblong-ovate, 2 to 5″ long, 1/2 to 2/3's as wide, obtusely pointed, narrowed toward the broad cuneate or truncate, rarely subcordate base, often unequal, coarsely sinuate dentate above the middle, medium to dark green above, green or glaucescent beneath, glabrous or nearly so, with 4 to 6 pairs of veins; petiole—1/4 to 1/2″ long, pubescent; leaves—thickish.

BUDS: Vegetative—naked, foliose, grayish brown, tomentose; flower—stalked, rounded, tan, pubescent, usually 3 or 4 per stalk.

STEM: Old—gray, not as smooth as *H. virginiana*, but similar; young—densely pubescent.

SIZE: 6 to 10′ high and greater in spread; have seen 10 to 15′ high specimens; one of the largest is located at Longwood Gardens; large specimens in shrub garden at Biltmore, Asheville, NC.

HARDINESS: Zone 4 to 8; second hardiest witchhazel after *H. virginiana*.

HABIT: Multi-stemmed, dense, rounded shrub, quite neat in appearance but variable in form; branches are often low and serpentine bending up at their extremities to form a broad-rounded outline; will sucker and form large colonies.

RATE: Medium.

TEXTURE: Medium in leaf and in winter.

STEM COLOR: Older stems, 3 year or greater, assume a gray to grayish brown color; quite attractive.

LEAF COLOR: New growth bronze to reddish purple, medium to dark green in summer, changing yellow to golden yellow in fall, fall color persists for 2 to 3 weeks and is often outstanding, fall color develops late; old leaves often persist particularly on young plants, can appear pretty forlorn in winter.

FLOWERS: Yellow to red, variable, 1/2 to 3/4″ across, 4-petaled, each about 1/2″ long, usually the inner surface of the calyx lobe is red and the petals are yellow, some plants exhibit solid yellow, orange, or red; pungently fragrant, January through February–March and effective for 3 to 4 weeks, borne in few-flowered (3 to 4) cymes; petals roll up on very cold days and in a protective sense, avoid freeze damage; this "adaptive" mechanism extends the flowering period; just to provide an idea of the differences in flowering times, my colleague in plant materials crime, Paul Cappiello, UMaine now Bernheim Arboretum, reported *H. vernalis* starting to open on March 6, 1991 and that was early; in the Dirr garden, first flowers opened on December 31, 1994; full flower January 17, 1993; when I am asked the inevitable question relative to flowering times, my stock answer/question is "Where do you live?"

FRUITS: Capsule, dehiscent, 2-valved, splitting in September–October, expelling the black seeds; green-yellow to brown and interestingly attractive in a quiet manner.

CULTURE: Supposedly somewhat difficult to transplant; my experience indicated no problem if handled as a container or balled-and-burlapped specimen; root pruning has been advocated for increasing root development; native on gravelly, often inundated banks of streams, performs best in moist situations; has grown admirably in poorly drained, clay soils; does well in full sun or 3/4's shade; pH adaptable; much more tolerant of high pH than *H. virginiana*.

DISEASES AND INSECTS: None serious; gall on leaves caused by leaf gall aphid (*Hormaphis hamamelidis*) can become rather ugly, at its worst reminds of Hackberry nipple gall; mildew. Mildew ratings in Athens, GA, July 26, 1996 (0 = clean, 1 = light, 2 = moderate, 3 = heavy): 'Lombart's Weeping'—1, Red Form—3+, 'Red Imp'—0.

LANDSCAPE VALUE: Durable plant for East, Midwest, and upper South; used effectively on University of Illinois campus in groupings near large buildings, also in planter boxes, would make a good screen, unpruned hedge; unusual because of the early flower date; selections should be made for good floriferous character, dense habit and excellent fall color; will often hold old leaves and they compete with flowers.

CULTIVARS:

'Autumn Embers'—Excellent red-purple fall color, orangish flowers; a plant in the Dirr garden produced yellow-orange fall color in 1994, weaker yellow-orange in 1995, about the same in 1996, even worse in 1997; selected by Roy Klehm and I listened to a lecture in which he showed photographs and the fall color rivaled the best *Fothergilla*; looks like a superb selection for the northern states; cannot compete with *Fothergilla* 'Mt. Airy' in Zones 7 and 8.

'Carnea'—Petals red at base grading to orange at tip, calyx red, 1/2″ long, 1/12″ wide, kinked, slightly twisted; deep flower color and worth growing for that reason alone.

'Christmas Cheer'—Professor McDaniel showed me this selection over 20 years ago and its presence in commerce by Gossler Farms Nursery provides impetus to mention the characteristics; selected from the garden of Dr. James Gerdemann for flowering around Christmas in Urbana, IL; was in flower on November 2, 1993 at the J.C. Raulston Arboretum.

'Lombarts Weeping'—Petals orange-red at base, orange toward the end, 1/3″ long, kinked, calyx red-pink; is not weeping just low-growing; tends to hold its old leaves; a form called 'Pendula' has crossed my path at Van Dusen Botanical Garden, Vancouver, BC; the plant was about the same as an octopus: high in the middle and a million leaders radiating in all directions; this may in fact be 'Lombarts Weeping'; this clone has caused considerable heartache in my garden life for every time someone provided a plant it turned out the be anything but; Bonnie and I, during a July 1995 foray to the Pacific Northwest, visited Van Dusen, found the plant, and marveled at its *unique* habit; could be grafted on a suitable understock, perhaps *Parrotia*, to produce a rather handsome small weeping tree.

'Red Imp'—Hillier selection with claret red petals at base, grading to copper at tips, calyx claret red.

'Sandra'—When I first read about this in *The Garden* I wrote to England asking how to procure plants and was told that a large mail order firm would be selling them in the United States; unfolding leaves are suffused with plum-purple, changing to green and lightly flushed with purple on the underside, in fall turning orange and red; the flowers are cadmium yellow; although my prayers were answered by Gossler the plant has not lived up to its billing; at the Arnold Arboretum the fall color was at best suffused with orange, the same in my garden and not as vibrant as some seedlings; also the new growth is a far cry from plum-purple, at best bronze-green; flowers are not outstanding, and open yellow tinged orange, fragrant, and later than typical for the species, usually in February (Athens). Excellent orange-red fall color in early November 1997 at Bernheim Arboretum.

'Sashay—Is a selection from Klyn Nursery, Ohio; not particularly showy in flower; fragrance is excellent.

'Squib'—Petals cadmium yellow with a green calyx.

PROPAGATION: Seed, difficult due to double dormancy but results have been obtained by stratifying seed for 60 days at 68°F plus 90 days at 41°F. Seeds germinate more readily than *H. virginiana*. Cuttings, collected in early June, wounded, 10 sec. 1000 ppm IBA/50% alcohol dip, placed in sand under mist rooted 70 to 80% in 3 months; this species is generally easy to root. Although described as easy, cuttings of this and the other witchhazels have peculiar quirks. Rooting is easy but their overwinter survival difficult. Ideally, to insure survival, induce a flush of growth *after* rooting. For complete details on the witchhazel rooting story see Dirr and Heuser, 1987. Another good reference is Lamb and Nutty, *The Plantsman* 6(1):45–48 (1984).

ADDITIONAL NOTES: Fall color on seedling material has been consistent brilliant yellow in Zone 7/8a and is sufficient reason to utilize the plant. Unfortunately, the retention of old leaves into spring is both unsightly and hides the flowers. I walk nursery rows looking for leafless plants. I have not found many and those that drop leaves cleanly have mediocre flowers.

NATIVE HABITAT: Missouri to Louisiana and Oklahoma. Found on gravelly, often inundated banks of streams. Introduced 1908.

Hamamelis virginiana L. — Common Witchhazel

(ham-à-mē′lis vĕr-jin-i-ā′ná)

LEAVES: Alternate, simple, obovate or elliptic, 3 to 6″ long, 2 to 3 1/2″ wide, obtusely short-acuminate or obtusish, narrowed toward the base and subcordate, rarely broad-cuneate, coarsely crenate-dentate, medium to dark green, nearly glabrous or pubescent on the veins beneath, with 5 to 7 pairs of veins; petiole—1/4 to 1/2″ long, pubescent; leaves—thinnish.

BUDS: Naked, brownish, tomentose; terminal—1/4 to 1/2″ long; flower buds—stalked, globose, opening in the fall, usually 3 or 4 on a bent stalk.

STEM: Young stems—zig-zag, slender, brownish, pubescent; older stems—glabrous, smooth, gray to brown; pith—small, green, continuous.

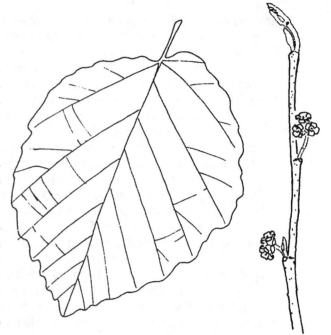

SIZE: 20 to 30′ in height by 20 to 25′ in spread; 15 to 20′ is more appropriate under landscape conditions; national champion is 35′ by 30′ in Bedford, VA.

HARDINESS: Zone 3b to 8(9).

HABIT: Small tree or large shrub with several large, crooked, spreading branches forming an irregular, rounded, open crown; architecturally the branches are beautiful.

RATE: Medium.

TEXTURE: Probably would be considered medium-coarse in leaf as well as winter habit, tends toward openness and gangliness but still makes an attractive shrub.

BARK: Smooth gray to grayish brown on 2-year-old stems to 80-year-old trunks.

LEAF COLOR: Medium green in summer yielding to good yellow in the fall, can be spectacular.

FLOWERS: Perfect, yellow, fragrant, four strap-like crumpled petals, each 1/2 to 2/3″ long, calyx lobes are yellowish to reddish brown inside, November; I have observed specimens in full flower in mid-October and others as late as early December; flowers are borne in 2- to 4-flowered cymes, effective for about 2 to 4 weeks depending on weather; often in full fall color at the time of flower thus reducing the quality and effectiveness of the flowers.

FRUIT: Capsule, 1/2″ long, pubescent, dehiscing at the distal end, with 4 sharp curved points; do not discharge the seeds until 12 months after flowering.

CULTURE: Similar to *H. vernalis*; full sun or shade; somewhat tolerant of city conditions; prefers a moist soil; avoid extremely dry situations.

DISEASES AND INSECTS: None serious, although when planted near birch trees an aphid makes small galls on the underside of the foliage, like hackberry nipple gall. See under *H. vernalis*.

LANDSCAPE VALUE: Native shrub covering much of eastern United States and therefore valuable in a naturalized situation, best reserved for the shrub border, near large buildings in shaded areas; probably too large for the small residential landscape; considerable selections could be made for quality and abundance of flower and the absence of foliage during the flowering period; when open-grown this makes a wonderful shrub especially in fall as the leaves turn a gorgeous yellow and the fragrance of the flowers permeates the cool autumn air; Kalmthout Arboretum, Belgium, has selected forms that drop their leaves ahead of flowering.

PROPAGATION: Seed, same as described for *H. vernalis*; cuttings, I have had little success rooting this species; cuttings taken and handled as described for *H. vernalis* yielded 2 to 5% rooting; an Illinois nurseryman told me this was easy to root; softwood cuttings from young plants (3- to 5-years-old) have been rooted using 10,000 ppm IBA; have read published reports of 80% and higher rooting but cuttings must be collected early; mature cuttings from old plants do not root as easily.

ADDITIONAL NOTES: The extract witchhazel is distilled from the bark of young stems and roots. It is found in moist, shady areas along streambanks throughout its range. Plants in the wild are often rather ragged but if placed in full sun make a large rounded shrub of great stability.

 Two additional species, *H. macrophylla* (see below) and *H. mexicana*, are lumped with *H. virginiana*. I have seen *H. macrophylla* in flower (usually cream-yellow) and it is not much different than the species. *Hamamelis mexicana* has white flowers that open during the dry dormant period of summer. Found in the Sierre Madre Orientale of Tamaulipas province, Mexico.

NATIVE HABITAT: Canada to Georgia, west to Nebraska and Arkansas. Introduced 1736.

RELATED SPECIES:

Hamamelis macrophylla Pursh., (ham-à-mē′lis mak-rō-fil′à), Southern Witchhazel, is closely related and for the previous editions I chose to ignore it until actually seeing the plant in flower with leaves present in early

December at Aiken, SC. The epithet *macrophylla* is certainly unjustified for the leaves are small, one half to two third's the size of *H. virginiana*. Also, the undersides are distinctly pubescent. It is smaller in all characteristics and flowers on the plant I saw were small and disappointing. Cream-yellow flowers in early November, Raleigh, NC. As previously mentioned, probably does not deserve species status. For the collector. South Carolina to Florida, Arkansas and Texas. Introduced 1928. Zone 6 to 9.

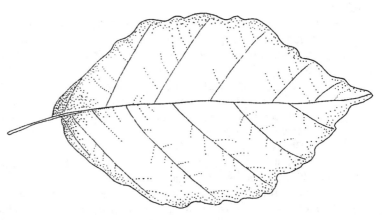

Hamamelis mollis Oliv. — Chinese Witchhazel
(ham-à-mē′lis mol′lis)

LEAVES: Alternate, simple, obovate to orbicular-obovate (appearing roundish), 3 to 6″ long, 3/4's as wide, short acuminate, obliquely cordate to sub-cordate at base, sinuately denticulate, dull green and pubescent above, grayish tomentose beneath; petiole—about 1/4″ long, stout and densely pubescent.

BUDS: Vegetative—1/2″ long, stalked, scales (2 to 3) tightly fitted together, densely pubescent, grayish brown; laterals smaller; one smaller outer scale appears to partially envelop the darker brown part; flower—on a crooked stalk, 2 to 4 together, egg-shaped, gray-brown, densely pubescent.

STEM: Slender, terete, grayish pubescence on first year stem, partially remaining on second, becoming gray to gray-brown and glabrous.

SIZE: 10 to 15′ high and wide, potential to 20′ and greater.

HARDINESS: Zone 5 to 8.

HABIT: Large shrub or small tree of oval to rounded outline, branches often spreading; usually more compact than *H. × intermedia* and *H. virginiana*.

RATE: Slow.

TEXTURE: Medium.

BARK: Smooth, gray to gray-brown on older branches.

LEAF COLOR: Medium green in summer, somewhat dull, can be a spectacular yellow to yellow-orange in fall, coloring late October–early November in the Dirr garden.

FLOWERS: Perfect, yellow with rich red-brown calyx cups, fragrant, 4-petaled, each petal strap-shaped, 5/8″ long, not wavy as in *H. japonica*, February to March, lasting for a long time, usually full flower in early to mid-February in Athens.

FRUIT: Two-valved, dehiscent capsule splitting at maturity and ejecting two jet black seeds.

CULTURE: Transplant balled-and-burlapped or container-grown material; prefers moist, acid, well-drained, organic soils; full sun or partial shade; the least hardy of the species treated here.

DISEASES AND INSECTS: None serious, although Japanese Beetles have been described as eating foliage of *H. × intermedia*; does not develop galls like the American species; mildew. Mildew ratings in Athens, GA, July 26, 1996 (0 = clean, 1 = light, 2 = moderate, 3 = heavy): 'Boskoop'—1, 'Early Bright'—3, 'James Wells'—2, 'Goldcrest'—1, 'Kort's Select'—1, 'Superba'—3.

LANDSCAPE VALUE: This is a fine species and is probably the most fragrant of the group; makes a beautiful show in February–March and the finest planting I have seen in this country is located at Swarthmore College; to my mind a much finer shrub than forsythia; unfortunately, the least hardy and temperatures in the range of -10 to -15°F can injure flower buds.

CULTIVARS:

'Brevipetala'—I have my doubts whether this is true *H. mollis* or a hybrid; flowers deep yellow, with red blush at base of petals, each petal 3/5" long, 1/12" wide, kinked, slightly twisted, heavy-flowering, fragrant; tends to hold old leaves into winter; the pubescence on the lower surface is thin compared to the species; upright-growing; put into commerce by Chenault's nurseries around 1935; seedlings of 'Brevipetala' display little *H. mollis* affinity; in this author's opinion not a good form.

'Coombe Wood'—Branches more spreading than the type with slightly larger golden yellow flowers that are strongly and sweetly scented, base of petals suffused red, large leaves, to 6" long by 5" wide, yellow autumn color.

'Donny Brook'—A golden yellow heavy-flowering form, apparently introduced by Brian Mulligan, University of Washington Arboretum.

'Early Bright'—Brighter yellow flowers that open 3 to 4 weeks ahead of the species, flowers in mid-January at Swarthmore, PA; original 37-year-old plant is 15' by 15'.

'Goldcrest'—Large flowers of a rich golden yellow suffused claret at base, strong and sweet scent, often later than other *H. mollis* cultivars; has been consistently spectacular in Athens-Atlanta; habit is upright, vase-shaped; petals are fatter than those of species; flowered early February in 1991, 92, 93, 94, 95, and 96 in the Dirr garden.

'Pallida'—Soft sulfur yellow flowers, each petal about 3/4" long, narrower than 'Goldcrest', reddish purple calyx cup, flowers profusely borne, sweetly fragrant, broad-spreading habit, often early to flower but have seen presentable flowers as late as February 26 in 1993, as early as February 9 and 10, 1991 and 1996, respectively; raised in the garden of the Royal Horticultural Society; leaves do not resemble those of *H. mollis* as they are somewhat lustrous above with sparse stellate hairs beneath; may be *H. × intermedia* type; left with *H. mollis* since many references associate it with *H. mollis*; one of the best.

PROPAGATION: Seed—3 months warm followed by 3 months cold has resulted in good germination; June cuttings treated with high IBA (1%) rooted well. See cuttings under *H. vernalis*.

NATIVE HABITAT: Central China. Introduced 1879.

RELATED SPECIES:

Hamamelis japonica Sieb. & Zucc. — Japanese Witchhazel

LEAVES: Alternate, simple, suborbicular to broad-ovate, or elliptic, 2 to 4" long, 1 1/4 to 2 1/2" wide, acute or rounded at apex, rounded or subcordate, rarely broad-cuneate at base, margins wavy, 5 to 8 vein pairs that run forward at an acute angle from the midrib, lower surface densely pubescent when young, essentially glabrous by late summer, medium to dark green; petiole—1/4 to 3/4" long, downy.

BUDS: Terminal—2 to 3 scales clumped together, naked, 1/4" long, dusty pubescent; flower—1 to 3, ovoid, 1/4" long, deep dusty brown, pubescent, borne on a crooked stalk.

STEM: Slender, gray-brown, scattered orangish brown lenticels, glabrous except near tip where slight pubescence remains.

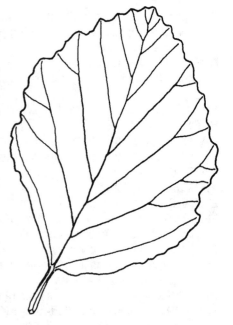

Hamamelis japonica, (ham-à-mē'lis jà-pon'i-kà), Japanese Witchhazel, is a spreading, at times almost flat-topped, sparsely branched shrub or small tree growing 10 to 15' high. Most of the plants I have seen in cultivation were wide-spreading shrubs. The leaves often have a sheen and in fall turn rich combinations of yellow, red, and purple. The yellow, 2/3" long, very narrow, strap-shaped, wrinkled and crinkled (akin to crepe paper), 4-petaled flowers occur 2 to 3 together on the leafless branches in February–March. Flowers are slightly behind those of *H. mollis*. Safe to state that flowers are less showy than *H. mollis* and *H. × intermedia*. The calyx lobes vary from green to reddish brown to red on the inside. The fragrance is not as strong as *H. mollis*. Several varieties and cultivars of note include:

var. *arborea*—A tall-growing form to 15 to 18', with horizontally disposed branches, flowers yellow, small, faint, sweet scent, produced in abundance, brown calyx, fall color yellow, a beautiful plant; introduced 1862; have seen at Edinburgh and others gardens where in flower it does not measure up to the *H. × intermedia* types.

var. *flavopurpurascens* (Mak.) Rehd.—Yellow petals suffused with red, overall effect is not staggering, calyx cup dark purple, reddish yellow fall color, a rather wide-spreading shrub; Japan; introduced 1919.

'Sulphurea'—Petals yellow, 3/8″ long, crimped, calyx cup red on inside, faint sweet odor, large shrub with spreading, ascending branches.

'Zuccariniana'—Petals good butter yellow with no tinge of red, greenish inside the calyx, 3/5″ long, 1/12″ wide, kinked and twisted, flowering late February into March, erect in youth, spreading with age, to 15′ high, yellow fall color.

Although not common in this country it is a handsome shrub especially in its loose, wide-spreading branching pattern. Japan. Introduced 1862. Zone 5 to 8.

Hamamelis × intermedia Rehd., (ham-à-mē′lis in-tēr-mē′di-à), represents a group of hybrids between *H. japonica × H. mollis* with intermediate characteristics. Originally described by Alfred Rehder in 1945 from plants growing in the Arnold Arboretum. Plants display hybrid vigor and may grow 15 to 20′ high. They are usually upright-spreading and rather loosely branched if not pruned. Some types display wide-spreading habits. They flower from late January into mid-March (North) depending on the cultivar. Their flower colors range from yellow to red. The red-flowered types may show more red fall coloration than the yellow-flowered types but this is not absolute. Cultivars have been raised in several countries (England, Germany, Belgium) but the greatest concentration has come from Kalmthout Arboretum. Mr. de Belder, owner of the Arboretum, provides an account of some of the Kalmthout introductions in *J. Royal Hort. Soc.* 94:85 (1969). Lancaster also provides a valuable account of the *Hamamelis* species and cultivars in *Gardeners Chronicle* 167 (1970). Also, I offered a reasonably complete account in *Amer. Nurseryman*, 157(5): 53–62 (1983). See Sanders, *Proc. Intl. Plant Prop. Soc.* 40:308–314 (1990) and Hohn, *Amer. Nurseryman* 177(2):64–73 (1993). Most are adaptable in Zones 5 to 8. Flower bud hardiness is less than wood hardiness. In 1994, after exposure to -22 to -24°F in vicinity of Louisville, KY, *H. × intermedia* cultivars did not flower above the snow line; 'Arnold Promise' and 'Jelena' had 20% dieback. Mildew ratings in Athens, GA, July 26, 1996 (0 = clean, 1 = light, 2 = moderate, 3 = heavy): 'Advent'—1, 'Allgold'—2, 'Aphrodite'—0, 'Arnold Promise'—1, 'Aurora'—1, 'Barmstedt Gold'—0, 'Carmine Red'—1, 'Diane'—2, 'Feuerzauber'—1, 'Hiltingbury'—3, 'Iwado'—0, 'Jelena'—1, 'Limelight'—2, 'Luna'—0, 'Moonlight'—1, 'Nina'—1, 'Orange Beauty'—0, 'Pallida'—2, 'Primavera'—0, 'Sunburst'—2, 'Vesna'—2, 'Westerstede'—3, 'Winter Beauty'—0, 'Tim's Purple'—3.

CULTIVARS: The number is now staggering and without a scorecard it is difficult to separate the best. I have included a reasonably complete list and would be pleased to hear of cultivars not appearing here. Personal favorites include 'Arnold Promise', 'Jelena', and 'Pallida' (see under *H. mollis*).

Tim Brotzman, Brotzman's Nurseries, Inc., Madison, OH, is an avid collector of *H. × intermedia* cultivars. He related that during a 1996 visit to Europe he witnessed 50 cultivars in flower at a horticulture exposition. Tim also related that an English friend (Chris Lane) has 170 clones of witchhazel of which 47 are named *H. × intermedia* forms. The cultivars presented herein represent those that I know intimately or from respectable literature. A list of other named clones is presented at the end of the cultivars. A recent article by Coombes, *The Garden* 121(1):28–33 (1996), provides color photos of 24 clones in flower. As I view the photographs, minimal differences are evident between and among many of the clones.

'Advent'—Bright clear yellow, faint fragrance, each petal 3/5 to 3/4″ long, 0.06 to 0.08″ wide, calyx maroon red, early December–January, do not open flat and straight, remain slightly curved with crimpled edges, yellow fall color, medium to large upright shrub, Hillier introduction.

'Allgold'—Deep buttercup yellow, sweet but faint fragrance, 3/5″ long, 0.05″ wide, crimped, purple-red calyx, January–February, yellow fall color, medium to large shrub with ascending branches, Hillier introduction.

'Angelly'—Clear light yellow, faint fragrance, 4/5 to 7/8″ long petals, 0.08 to 0.1″ wide, light green calyx, late February–March, yellow fall color, vigorous upright-spreading habit; Van Heijningen, Breda, Netherlands introduction; considered up and comer by the Europeans.

'Arnold Promise'—Raised and introduced by the Arnold Arboretum, clear yellow flowers with a reddish calyx cup, each petal almost an inch long, fragrant, large shrub, the original plant about 20′ high and wide; during by sabbatical I monitored the flowering progression of the original plant; it showed significant color in late February 1979 and still had a measure of color in mid-March; this cultivar is being grown by American nurserymen; still my favorite among the yellow types; flowers are definitely later than the others and my field notes indicate that flowers were still present on April 12, 1986; in 1984, flowers were just opening on February 4 and losing their effect on March 9; in 1989 full flower occurred on March 24; time of optimum effectiveness truly varies from year-to-year; looking at my

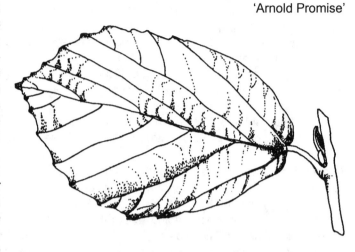

'Arnold Promise'

field notes since the 1990 edition, I see early to mid-March the dominant full flower period in Athens; based on our propagation and cultural research this is an easy form to root using 5000 to 10,000 ppm KIBA quick dip; in 1988, cuttings collected on April 27, May 26, June 1, June 10, and July 19 and treated with 5000 ppm KIBA rooted 100, 78, 61, 77 and 83%, respectively; rooted cuttings will set a greater number of flower buds their second year; this form appears to produce heavy crops of flowers every year; anyone who has listened to me chat about the withchhazels knows my abhorrence of grafted plants, time and again I have observed suckering and incompatibility; in our garden all the 'Arnold Promise' are on their own roots so if suckering occurs it presents no problem.

'Barmstedt Gold'—Rich golden yellow, suffused with red at base, sweet fragrance, each petal almost an inch long, 0.06 to 0.08″ wide, claret calyx cup, late January–February, yellow fall color, vigorous shrub with narrowly ascending branches; Hachmann, Germany introduction; considered by Ruth Dix, U.S. National Arboretum, to be one of the best yellows.

'Carmine Red'—Red-orange flower (red at base becoming coppery bronze at tips), sweet but faint, each petal about 4/5″ long, 0.04 to 0.06″ wide, claret red calyx, kinked, twisted and rolled, January–February, strong grower of spreading habit, yellow fall color, Hillier introduction.

'Diane'—One of the best red-flowering forms, better than 'Ruby Glow' but still more copper-red than red; rich yellow-orange-red fall color; each petal 3/5 to 4/5″ long, 1/15″ wide, calyx purple-red, faintly fragrant, petals bronze colored red, shiny, lighter at ends, turning bronze with age, February; have seen in flower on several occasions and was not as impressed as I hoped to be, flowers *are not* red, also old leaves persist more so on this form than some and must be removed to maximize flower effect; medium to large shrub with wide-spreading branches; Kalmthout introduction.

'Feuerzauber' ('Magic Fire', 'Fire Charm')—Excellent coppery orange-red flowers, each petal about 3/4″ long, 0.06″ wide, kinked, twisted, fragrant, purplish red calyx cup, late January–February, orange-yellow fall color, moderately spreading habit; excellent performer in Dirr garden; large flowers are produced in abundance; in Zone 7–8 has been superior to 'Diane' and 'Ruby Glow'; drops leaves; Hesse, Germany introduction.

'Gimborn's Perfume'—Clear bright yellow, sweet fragrance, 3/5 to 4/5″ long, 0.06 to 0.08″ wide petals, glossy bright red calyx cup, late January–February, yellow fall color, moderate vigor, upright branching; van Gimborn Arboretum, Netherlands introduction.

'Golden'—Good clear yellow with deep pink blush at base of petal, 5/8″ long, extremely kinked, slightly twisted.

'Hiltingbury'—Pale copper flowers of medium size, 3/5″ long, 0.045″ wide, faint but sweet odor, purple-red calyx, mid-January to mid-February, large shrub of spreading habit with large leaves that turn orange, scarlet and red in fall; have witnessed full coloration on October 23, 1993 and it rivals (beats) my beloved Fothergillas for intensity of coloration; seedling of *H. japonica* var. *flavopurpurascens*; Hillier introduction.

'Improved Winter Beauty'—A second generation seedling from 'Winter Beauty' and more floriferous than the parent.

'James Wells'—Abundant golden yellow flowers; have one plant that flowered so profusely that the branches were almost hidden by the flowers; probably *H. mollis* type.

'Jelena' ('Copper Beauty')—Excellent in flower and from a distance glows like copper; each 1″ long petal is red toward base, orange in middle and yellow at the tip, 0.06 to 0.08″ wide, kinked, twisted, sweet but faint, claret red calyx cup; rich orange-red fall color; beautiful shrub; becoming wide-spreading with age; Kalmthout introduction.

'Luna'—Each petal burgundy at base, light yellow to the tip, 4/5″ long, kinked, twisted.

'Moonlight'—Pale sulfur yellow, claret red at base, 3/5 to 4/5″ long, 0.04 to 0.06″ wide, strong, sweet fragrance, kinked and twisted petals, deep claret red calyx, early January to early February, large shrub with ascending branches, yellow fall color, Hillier introduction.

'New Red'—Starts deep red, eventually turning orange-brown.

'Nina'—Deep yellow flowers, each petal 1″ long, heavily produced; apparently not common in cultivation.

'Orange Beauty'—Deep yellow flowers verging on orange-yellow, 3/5″ long, 0.06″ wide, abundant, faint fragrance, glossy claret red calyx, late January–February, yellow fall color; literature says upright to spreading; at Missouri Botanic Garden, plants were wide-spreading and almost similar to *H. mollis* in flower color; Bruns, Germany introduction.

'Primavera'—Primrose-yellow, stained purple-red at base, each petal 3/5″ long, 1/16″ wide, glossy wine red calyx, sweet scent, exceedingly floriferous, late January–February, yellow fall color, wide-spreading shrub; Kalmthout introduction; at Don Shadow's, February 22, 1994, I savored the fragrance of 'Primavera' and 'Westerstede' growing side-by-side; 'Westerstede' as my notes reflect had a wonderful fragrance with 'Primavera' good but not as potent; the literature says the reverse, who does one believe?

'Rubra'—Good red until anthesis, afterward orange, 4/5″ long petals, kinked and twisted.

'Ruby Glow' (also listed as 'Adonis' and 'Rubra Superba')—Coppery red flowers maturing to reddish brown, 3/5″ long petals, 0.04″ wide, kinked and twisted, dark purple calyx, weak fragrance, late January–February, fall color combinations of orange and red; original plant over 20′ high and 20′ wide; erect vase-shaped, particularly in youth; Kalmthout introduction.

'Sunburst'—Listed under *H. mollis* but more properly belongs in the hybrid category; its lemon yellow, scentless flowers are produced in abundance during January and early February, the petals may be almost 1″ long by 1/12″ wide, wine red calyx cup; may hold some of its leaves through winter, obscuring the flowers; vigorous, vase-shaped; considered superior in flower to 'Pallida'; Veerman, Boskoop introduction.

'Vesna'—Dark yellow petals stained red at the base, 4/5 to 1″ long, 1/16 to 1/12″ wide and more twisted and crumpled than other *H. × intermedia* forms, with a strong, sweet scent, the calyx is claret red, which imparts an overall orange effect intermediate between 'Winter Beauty' and 'Jelena', January–February, yellow fall color, moderate vigor, upright shrub; Kalmthout introduction.

'Westerstede'—Probably a *H. × intermedia* form, although it is often listed as a cultivar of *H. mollis*; primrose yellow petals average 3/5″ long and are straight, 0.07″ wide, greenish brown calyx, faint fragrance, flowers appear in late February and last into March, yellow fall color, vigorous upright; Helmers, Germany introduction.

'Winter Beauty'—Dark yellow, grading to brownish red at base, similar to 'Orange Beauty' but petals are slightly longer, 3/5 to 4/5″ long, 0.04 to 0.06″ wide, dark red calyx, and more twisted with more red staining on the basal third, little or no fragrance, late December–January, moderate vigor, broad upright habit; raised by Hokaneya Nurseries, Yokohama, Japan and is said to be a cross between *H. mollis* and *H. japonica* 'Zuccariniana'; English literature reports this form difficult to grow.

There are additional cultivars but information is scant on their specifics. In early March at Longwood Gardens I saw 'Jelena', 'Ruby Glow' and *H. mollis* 'Brevipetala' in full flower and they were spectacular. November 2, 1981, I witnessed them in gorgeous fall color. Why these plants are not in greater use is beyond me. They are lovely, maintenance-free plants. The *H. × intermedia* types set good seed and no doubt many new seedlings will be selected and introduced over the years. Hopefully, evaluation and screening will be rigorous for a glut of rather indistinguishable cultivars is not needed. Compactness would be a good trait for which to select. Seed requires about 3 months warm followed by 3 months cold. A key to good rooting success is taking cuttings as early as obtainable. Our work (Athens) indicates late April to end of May is the best time.

Some of our work relative to cutting propagation appears in *North American Plant Propagator* 1(2):9–10 (1989); April 27 and May 28 cuttings, 10000 ppm KIBA rooted 100 and 78%, respectively, and overwintered 95 and 87%, respectively.

I have literature, lists, notes, observations relative to *H. × intermedia* that reflect my incomplete knowledge of the cultivar diversity. Other cultivars that may surface in the reader's garden travels include: 'Adieu', 'Aphrodite', 'August Lamken', 'Aureolin', 'Aurora', 'Birgit', 'Boskoop' (probably *H. mollis*), 'Brandes', 'Copper Cascade', 'Docrah', 'Early Bird', 'Friesia', 'Harry', 'Iwado', 'Kurt's Select', 'Lansing', 'Limelight', 'Molly Brooks' ('Bonny Brook'), 'Orange Peel', 'Sarah', 'Strawberry and Cream', 'Wiltonii', 'Wiro', and 'Zitronenjette'.

ADDITIONAL NOTES:

HAMAMELIS EVALUATION ON DECEMBER 29, 1996, ATHENS, GA

Cultivar	Flowers open (% of total)	Color	Leaf retention (% of total shrub)
Hamamelis × intermedia			
'Advent'	40	Yellow/maroon	3
'Allgold'	tight bud	6 to 8 bud tips yellow	20
'Aphrodite'	tight buds		5
'Arnold Promise'	tight buds		0
'Aurora'	tight buds		0
'Barmstedt Gold'	tight buds	several yellow-tipped	15
'Boskoop'	100	cadmium yellow	0
'Carmine Red'	no flower buds		15
'Diane'	5, red in bud	yellow-bronze-maroon	60
'Early Bright'	100	bright yellow-maroon	<2
'Feuerzauber'	tight bud		20
'Hiltingbury'	tight buds		0
'Iwado'	70	golden-yellow-maroon	15
'James Wells'	50	yellow-maroon	20
'Jelena'	50	coppery	30
'Limelight'	tight buds		0
'Luna'	10	soft yellow-maroon	15
'Moonlight'	one flower	soft yellow-maroon	40
'Nina'		yellow or red	15
'Orange Beauty'	tight buds	1 yellow-tipped bud	<1, 6 leaves
'Pallida'	no distinct flr. buds		<1, 6 leaves
'Primavera'	2	bright yellow-maroon	<1,4 leaves
'Sunburst'	tight buds		7
'Vesna'	tight buds	3 yellow-red-tipped	0
'Westerstede'		buds just showing color	0
'Winter Beauty'	5	yellow-maroon	3
Hamamelis japonica			
'Arborea'	tight buds	4 or 5 yellow-tipped	<2
'Flavo-purpurascens'	tight buds		0
'Rubra'	tight buds		<1, 6 leaves
Hamamelis mollis			
'Early Yellow'	100	yellow-maroon	15
'Goldcrest'	no flower buds		0
'Korts Select'	10	yellow-maroon	5
'Superba'	30	yellow-copper -maroon, small flrs.	5
Hamamelis vernalis			
'Autumn Embers'	tight buds		50
'Lombarts Weeping'		orange	<1
Red Form	5	copper-red-maroon	<2
'Red Imp'	25	golden-red-brown	3
'Sandra'	tight buds		0
'Tim's Purple'	100	purple-red	30

Hedera helix L. — English Ivy
(hed′ĕr-å he′liks)

FAMILY: Araliaceae

LEAVES: Alternate, simple, evergreen; on juvenile shoots—3- to 5-lobed, 1 1/2 to 4″ long, about as wide, lustrous dark green above, often with whitish or yellowish green veins, pale or yellowish green beneath; on mature (flowering branches)—ovate to rhombic and often lighter green in color, entire, rounded to cuneate at base; some cultivars with leaves to 6″ long.

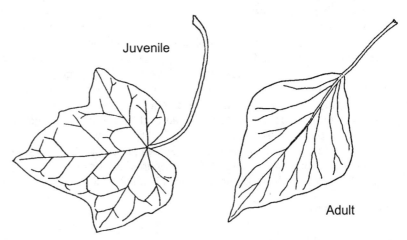

Juvenile

Adult

SIZE: 6 to 8″ high when used as a ground cover; can climb to 90′ as a vine.

HARDINESS: Zone 4 to 9, largely depends on cultivar selection.

HABIT: Low evergreen ground cover, rooting at the nodes, or a high-climbing, true-clinging vine attaching itself to structures with root-like holdfasts.

RATE: Fast.

TEXTURE: Medium in all seasons.

LEAF COLOR: Dark green and often lustrous above, often with whitish veins on juvenile leaves; on mature plants foliage is a bright, lustrous green, often without the prominent whitish veins, usually not as prominent.

FLOWERS: Perfect, only occurring on the "Adult" form, greenish white, borne in globose umbels, September–October.

FRUIT: Berry-like, black drupe, 1/4″ across, containing 2 to 5 seeds, April or May following flowering, apparently the fruits are poisonous.

CULTURE: Transplants readily; growth is maximized in rich, fairly moist, organic, well-drained soil; full sun or heavy shade; not a bad idea to protect from winter sun and wind as the leaves develop necrotic areas; may require considerable pruning to keep it in bounds; tolerates acid and alkaline soil; shows a fair degree of salt tolerance.

DISEASES AND INSECTS: Bacterial leaf spot (*Xanthomonas*) and canker, leaf spots, powdery mildews, aphids, caterpillars, mealybugs, scales, and two-spotted mite; mites and leaf spots can be serious.

LANDSCAPE VALUE: Ground cover with many uses; good in heavy shade, can look especially nice when given proper cultural conditions; has a nice effect when grown on trees or buildings; the adult form develops high up in trees or on buildings; the leaf morphology of the adult form is different from the vigorous normal type and the plant becomes quite woody; invasive at times and may smother an entire woodland floor, also can cover tree trunks and larger limbs, usually does not extend beyond the canopy.

CULTIVARS: A staggering number of ivy cultivars exist. There is an ivy society and an ivy handbook for those who are so inclined. I have included only a handful of the hardy forms. As one moves further south the number of selections that can be successfully grown increases. Ivy identification is fraught with difficulty.

'Baltica'—A hardy form with smaller leaves; introduced by Missouri Botanical Garden, selected from the wild in Latvia; unfortunately, not as hardy as advertised and 'Bulgaria' and 'Hebron' have proven hardier.

'Bulgaria'—One of the hardiest forms based on Wisconsin tests; a Missouri Botanical Garden introduction.

'Hebron'—Hardy form.

'Hibernica'—Large shiny leaf form, supposedly quite popular in cultivation; I cannot tell it from the others; *H. hibernica* (Kirchn.) Bean, Atlantic Ivy, is listed; occurs along the European Atlantic coast; more pubescent than *H. helix*.

'Rochester'—Hardy form.

'Rumania'—Similar to 'Bulgaria'.

'Thorndale'—Hardy form with larger leaves than the species; proved itself during the winter of 1976–77.

'Treetop'—Adult form; see *HortScience* 27:279–280 (1992).

'Wilson'—Hardy form.

'238th Street'—Supposedly a hardy form with adult characteristics, not subject to winter burn.

The adult form when rooted from cuttings makes a handsome broadleaf evergreen shrub. American Ivy Society recommended 'Harrison', 'Woerner', 'Tom Boy', 'Galaxy', 'Lustrous Carpet', and 'Buttercup' as notably winter hardy.

PROPAGATION: Seed, the pericarp must be removed and the seeds stratified; I tried an experiment using whole fruits and those with fruit walls removed; the germination only took place with the seeds which were extracted from the fruit; all seedlings were similar to the juvenile form. Cuttings can be rooted anytime of the year; it is best to use 1000 to 3000 ppm IBA-quick dip.

ADDITIONAL NOTES: I believe every individual knows ivy. It is used as a house plant and for outdoor purposes. Its shade tolerance is legendary and on the Georgia campus superb beds of English Ivy proliferate under the shade of water and willow oaks. It effectively covers trees and other structures. Old plants often develop a 4 to 6″ diameter, light brown, slightly ridged-and-furrowed trunk. For ivy aficionados consider joining the American Ivy Society, P.O. Box 2123, Naples, FL. Some salt tolerance work with ivies and *HortScience* 27:249–252 (1992) provides details.

NATIVE HABITAT: Europe, Scandinavia, Russia. Cultivated since ancient times.

RELATED SPECIES:

Hedera canariensis Willd. — Algerian Ivy
LEAVES: Alternate, simple, evergreen, 2 to 6″(8″) long, shallowly 3- to 7-lobed in the juvenile state, heart-shaped at base, leathery, glossy dark green; petiole and stems burgundy-red.

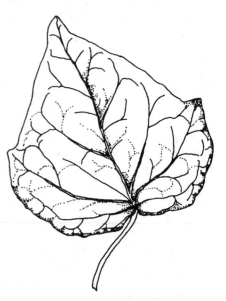

Hedera canariensis, (hed′ĕr-á ká-nâr-i-en′sis), Algerian Ivy, is not common in southern gardens but can be successfully grown in Zones 9 and 10. The large leaves and rampant growth provide solid cover. Used at Sea Island, GA, and during 1983–84 at 11°F was essentially eliminated. Best above 20°F. Grows well in coastal areas and is obviously quite salt tolerant. The stems and undersides of the leaves are covered with small, red, 15-rayed, stellate or scale-like pubescence. Was told by an English nurseryman that this does not fill in as well as *H. colchica*. Native of the Canary Islands, Madeira, the Azores, Portugal and northwestern Africa as far east as Algeria.

Hedera colchica (K. Koch) Hibb. — Colchis Ivy, Persian Ivy
LEAVES: Alternate, simple, evergreen, ovate or heart-shaped, leathery, dark green, 3 to 7″(10″) across, entire or slightly lobed with a few sharp teeth, fragrant when crushed, smelling like celery.

Hedera colchica, (hed′ĕr-á kol′chi-ká), Colchis Ivy, compares to English Ivy in most respects except it is often larger leaved and presents a slightly coarser texture. Have seen it in test planting at the Griffin, Georgia Experiment Station in full sun and dry soil performing magnificently. Very fast-growing. 'Dentata Variegata' offers a creamy white border and has proven adaptable in my Georgia garden. Native to the region south of the Caspian and westward through the Caucasus to the Pontic ranges of Asiatic Turkey. Zone (6)7 to 9.

Heptacodium miconioides Rehd. — Seven-son Flower
(hep-tá-cō-di′um mī-co-nē-oy′dēz or mī-co-noy′dēz)

FAMILY: Caprifoliaceae
LEAVES: Opposite, simple, 3 to 6″ long, 2 to 2 1/4″ wide, ovate-lanceolate, acute, rounded to truncate, entire with wavy margin, strongly 3-nerved, dark green at maturity, glabrous; petiole—1″ long.
BUDS: Imbricate, light brown, glabrous, ovoid, 3/16 to 1/4″ long, forming 45° angle with the stem.
STEM: Moderate, squarish with 4 more or less ridges, glabrous, whitish (grayish) on young stems due to an exfoliating epidermal layer, rich brown on young stems after exfoliating; pith—tan, solid.

SIZE: 15 to 20′(25′) high, one half to three quarter's this in spread; I doubt if mature size is known at least in the United States; Arnold Arboretum has plants over 10′ high.
HARDINESS: Zone 5 to 8; in South benefits from pine shade; slight tip dieback after -22 to -24°F.

HABIT: Upright, irregular, loose, open, almost artistic; grows to its own beat, not as neat as *Lagerstroemia* species, is a good candidate for pruning aficionados.

RATE: Medium; a five-year-old plant in the Dirr garden is 8′ high; in 5 seasons seedlings grew 6 to 10′.

TEXTURE: Medium in leaf, medium coarse in winter.

BARK: Gray brown, exfoliating on 1/2 to 1″ diameter stems to reveal a lighter inner bark, rather handsome, akin to a northern crapemyrtle.

LEAF: The most beautiful part of the plant, emerging early (by late March, Athens), soft green maturing to dark green, holding late into November with no memorable fall color, yellow at best.

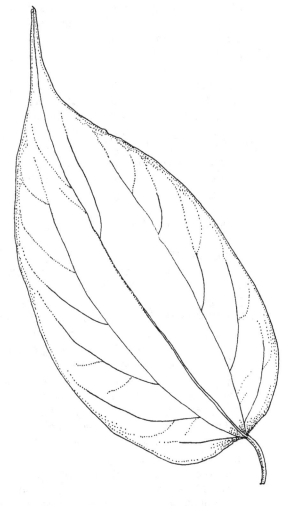

FLOWERS: Buds appear early in summer, tantalize, but do not open until August and linger into September, individual flowers are creamy white, fragrant and are borne in 6″ long terminal panicles. Koller describes the flowers thusly . . . "Single flowers are quite small but are borne in a tiered, six-flowered whorl that is terminated by a flower, hence the name *Heptacodium*, in allusion to the seven-flowered thryselike inflorescences." I have noticed butterflies visiting the plant in our garden.

FRUIT: Capsule with sepals that persist and change green to rose-purple, the effect is much more effective than the flower and lasts for 2 to 3 weeks, have noticed variation in sepal quantity and color quality among seedlings.

CULTURE: Transplants readily from containers and is probably the best way to handle the plant; moist, well-drained, acid, organic laden soils are best; plant appears adaptable; our plant is in clay loam under pine shade and has performed admirably; have seen several full sun, drought stressed plants that toward the end of summer looked tired; the Dirr garden plant suffered severe leaf necrosis in the September–October, 1997 drought.

DISEASES AND INSECTS: Dieback has occurred, possibly canker-related.

LANDSCAPE VALUE: Unusual plant that is best known in New England states because of the Arnold's efforts; best in a border; great foliage, interesting flower and fruit characteristics; will never replace a crapemyrtle in Zone 7 through 9.

PROPAGATION: Seeds—5 months warm, 3 months cold; variable reports on cuttings—my success has been miserable on firm wood summer cuttings, Raulston stated that softwood and semi-hardwood were easy; July 8 cuttings (Boston), 4 to 6″ long, 10000 ppm IBA-5 sec, 81% rooting (excellent root systems) by October 1. Lee and Bilderback, *J. Environmental Horticulture* 8:121–123 (1990), reported best rooting from containerized stock in May (softwood) and August (semi-hardwood) of 68% and 76%, respectively, with 5000 ppm KIBA.

ADDITIONAL NOTES: For superb first hand information see Koller, *Arnoldia* 46(4):2–14 (1986). The plant was reintroduced in 1980 into the United States through the Sino-American Botanical Expedition in which the Arnold Arboretum participated. For elucidation of the taxonomic situation see Spongberg, *Arnoldia* 50(3):29–32 (1990). The initial name was *Heptacodium jasminoides* Airy Shaw but the correct name is *H. miconioides* Rehder.

NATIVE HABITAT: China. Zhejiang Province. Introduced 1980, originally 1907 by E.H. Wilson.

Hibiscus syriacus L. — Shrub Althea, also called Rose-of-Sharon
(hī-bis′kus si-ri-ā′kus)

FAMILY: Malvaceae

LEAVES: Alternate, simple, palmately veined and 3-lobed, ovate or rhombic-ovate, 2 to 4″ long, often coarsely toothed with rounded or acutish teeth, broad-cuneate or rounded at base, medium to dark green, often lustrous, glabrous except a few hairs on the veins beneath; petiole—1/4 to 1″ long.

BUDS: Not evident, their position usually occupied by the scars of fallen inflorescences or branch vestiges.

STEM: Rounded, fluted near the dilated tip, glabrescent, gray; pith—small, white, continuous with green border; leaf scars crowded at tip, half round or transversely elliptical, raised, shortly decurrent in more or less evident ridges.

FRUIT: A dehiscent, 5-valved, upright, brown capsule which persists through winter and offers a valid identification character.

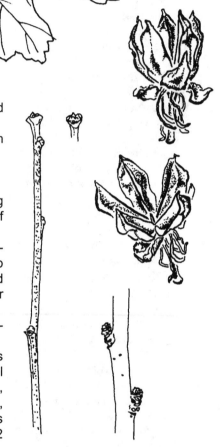

SIZE: 8 to 12′ in height by 6 to 10′ wide.

HARDINESS: Zone 5 to 8(9); have observed severe injury at -20°F; killed in Orono, ME.

HABIT: Shrub or small tree, very erect but occasionally spreading, with numerous upright branches.

RATE: Medium.

TEXTURE: Medium in leaf; medium to medium-coarse in winter.

LEAF COLOR: Medium to dark green in summer, holding late or changing to a poor yellow in fall; late leafing out in spring, have seen leaf emergence in late May in Boston.

FLOWERS: Perfect, 5-petaled, white to red or purple or violet, or combinations, single and double, short-stalked, broad campanulate, 2 to 4″ across, July, August through September; normally flowers in mid to late June in Athens; solitary on new year's growth; even if winter damage occurs flowers are produced on new growth.

FRUIT: Dehiscent capsule, 3/4″ long and wide when open, brown, 5-valved and persisting through winter.

CULTURE: Move container-grown, balled-and-burlapped or bare root as a small plant (5′ or less); transplants well; grows in about any soil except those which are extremely wet or dry; does best in moist, well-drained soils which have been supplemented with peat moss, leaf mold or compost; pH adaptable; full sun or partial shade; prefers hot weather; prune back heavily in early spring, or prune back to 2 or 3 buds in spring to get large flowers.

DISEASES AND INSECTS: Leaf spots, bacterial leaf spot, blights, canker, rust, aphids, Japanese beetle, mining scale, foliar nematodes and white-fly.

LANDSCAPE VALUE: Valuable for the late season flowers, groupings, masses, shrub borders but does not deserve specimen use; has and can be used for screening and hedges; not one of my favorite plants but has certainly been accepted by the gardening public; in recent years has experienced a resurgence of sorts and many more cultivars are now available.

CULTIVARS: Several cultivars have been introduced by the U.S. National Arboretum and include:

‘Aphrodite’—Erect-growing, multi-stemmed, low-branched shrub, 9 1/2′ high and 8′ wide in 14 years; solitary, short-stalked flowers are dark pink with a prominent dark red eye spot, 4 1/2 to 5″ in diameter, blooming from June to September; heavy-textured foliage; reliably hardy to Zone 5; triploid; has fruited heavily in the Dirr garden; see *HortScience* 23:223–224 (1988); I have not been overwhelmed with this cultivar.

‘Diana’—A triploid with large pure white flowers that remain open at night, the foliage is a waxy dark green; it sets very little fruit and flowers over a long period in summer; Dr. Egolf bred this cultivar; see *Baileya* 17:75–78 (1970) for specifics.

‘Helene’—Essentially white with a reddish purple blush at the base; heavy-flowering in August in the Dirr garden; a triploid and does not set much fruit, if any; see *American Nurseryman* 154(6):11, 66–67 (1981).

‘Minerva’—Erect-growing, multi-stemmed, low-branched shrub, 8 1/2′ high and 7′ wide in 14 years; solitary, short-stalked flowers are lavender with traces of pink overcast and a prominent dark red eye spot, 4 to 5″ in diameter, profuse blooming from June to September; lustrous foliage, reliably hardy to Zone 5; triploid; see *HortScience* 21:1463–1464 (1986).

Other cultivars that were assimilated from the literature and current nursery catalogs:

'Agnes'—Double, large, flat, mauve-purple flowers.

'Amplissimus'—Double, red.

'Ardens'—Double, rose-purple.

'Banner'—Single, white with red eye.

'Blue Bird' ('Bluebird')—Single, sky blue with small red center, 5″ diameter flowers, erect habit; an old French variety.

'Blushing Bride'—Double, rich pink fading to white.

'Bride'—Double, violet-blue, magnificent blue, azure blue.

'Collie Mullens' (seen as 'Connie Mullens')—Double, purple-lavender.

'Double Pink'—Double, pink.

'Double Red'—Double, red.

'Edna Frances'—Compact habit, 2 1/2 to 3″ diameter, red-purple flowers with crimson throats.

'Gussie'—Double, rich pink, large flowers.

'Hamabo'—Single, pale pink with red spot.

'Jeanne D'Arc'—Double, white.

'Ms. Julenne'—Double, pink, creamy leaf variegation.

'Lady Stanley'—Double, pink.

'Lucy'—Double, red flowers, on a strong-growing, vigorous shrub.

'Meehanii'—Lilac-mauve with darker eye, leaves margined in cream-yellow, lower growing.

'Peoniflora'—Double, pink.

'Paeonyflorus'—Double, violet-pink.

'Pink Giant'—Clear rose-pink, rich burgundy blotch, yellow stamens, 4 to 5″ diameter, 8 to 10′ by 6 to 8′.

'Red Heart'—Single, white with red center.

'Rubis'—Single, red.

'Sky Blue'—Single, clear blue flowers from July until frost.

'Tri-color'—Double, pink, red, and purple flowers over the entire plant.

'Woodbridge'—Single, rose-pink with red eye.

'W.R. Smith'—Single, white.

PROPAGATION: Seeds require no pretreatment and self-sown seedlings can be a nuisance in the landscape; softwood cuttings, June–July, root readily when treated with 1000 ppm IBA.

ADDITIONAL NOTES: Have grown 'Diana' and 'Helene' without becoming attached. They do not show great vigor but flowers are excellent. 'Diana', particularly, is a weak, humpy, rather wimpy form.

NATIVE HABITAT: China, India. Introduced before 1600.

RELATED SPECIES:

Hibiscus rosa-sinensis L. — Chinese Hibiscus

LEAVES: Alternate, simple, to 6″ long by 4″ wide, ovate to broad lanceolate, acute, serrate, lustrous waxy rich to dark green.

Hibiscus rosa-sinensis, (hī-bis′kus rō-zà-sī-nen′sis), Chinese Hibiscus, is at best a root hardy perennial in Zone 8, a subshrub in parts of Zone 9, and a small tree in Key West (Zone 11). Typically an upright shrub or small tree (if trained) to 8′, in the wild to 15′. The flowers are magnificent, single and double, white, yellow, pink, red to infinity, to 5 to 8″ across. All flower on new growth and are often utilized in conservatories. The species and cultivars make great container plants and any well-drained, moist soil in full sun suits them well. White flies are problematic. Over 120 cultivars are known. Native to Tropical Asia. Interesting cold hardiness work by Hummel and associates at the University of Florida. See *Plant, Cell and Environment* 12:495–509 (1989), *HortScience* 23:915 (1988), and *HortScience* 25:365 (1990) for specifics. In brief, of 22 *Hibiscus* species tested, only *H. syriacus* developed significant cold hardiness (to –11°F and –17°F). *Hibiscus rosa-sinensis* failed to survive 28.4°F. In Gainsville, FL (Zone 9) plants only survived when planted near buildings and then only as dieback shrubs. Controlled experiments using short days and cool day/night temperatures failed to induce cold hardiness.

Cultivars:

'Agnes Gault'—Single, rose-pink flowers, 8 to 10′ high, 4 to 6′ wide,

'All Aglow'—Single, large, orange with deep yellow blotches and pink blush ringing throat.

'Amour'—Single, large, light pink, flowers to 10″ wide, heavy bloomer, early spring, 10′ high.

'Big Red'—Single, red, large, late-flowering.

'Black Beauty'—Single, red, large, mid-season flowering, pretty foliage.

Bridal Veil™ ('Monora')—Single, large, white, crepe-textured petals, flowers last 3 to 4 days, 6 to 8′ high, 5 to 6′ wide.

'Bride'—Single, large, crepe-textured, ruffled petals, white blushed with pale pink, slow-growing to 6′ high, 4 to 5′ wide.

'Brilliant'—Single, bright red, heavy-flowering early spring and summer, 15′ high, 4 to 6′ wide.

'Brilliantissima'—Single, red.

'Butterball'—Double, lemon yellow, 8′ high.

'Butterfly'—Single, bright yellow flowers in profusion, slow-growing to 6′ high, 3 to 4′ wide.

'California Gold'—Single, yellow with red throat, 6′ high.

'Cecelia'—Double, red.

'Cherie'—Single, yellow-orange with maroon throat, flowers in profusion, 6 to 8′ high, 3 to 4′ wide.

'Classic Double'—Double, rose-pink.

'Classic Single'—Single, rose-pink.

'Cooperi Variegated'—Large-growing broad-leaf shrub with green-, pink- and white-variegated leaves, red flowers in summer.

'Crown of Bohemia'—Double, golden yellow with deep orange-red throat, 8 to 10′ high, 4 to 6′ wide.

'Diamond Head'—Double, large, dark red.

'Double Psyche'—Double, small, red, late bloomer.

'Dr. Jack Borge'—Double, red, late bloomer, attractive foliage.

'Dwarf Red'—Single, red.

'Dynamite Red'—Double, red, evergreen shrub in tropical climates.

'El Capitolio'—Pendulous, red flowers, spring through summer, rapid-growing medium-sized shrub, good hanging basket.

'El Capitolio Sport'—Pendulous, crested peach flowers, flowers heavily late in season.

'Empire'—Single, orange-red flowers in profusion, 6 to 8′ high, 5 to 6′ wide.

'Fiesta'—Single, large, bright orange with blush red eye zone over a white background, crinkled edges, 6 to 8′ high, 5 to 6′ wide.

'Fullmoon'™ ('Monoon')—Double, lemon yellow petals, widespread with the perfect symmetry of a full moon, 4 to 6′ high, 3 to 4′ wide.

'Golden Dust'—Single, large, intense orange with soft orange-yellow centers, crepe-like petals have an exquisite silky luster, 4 to 6′ high, 3 to 4′ wide.

'Hula Girl'—Single, large, vivid yellow with bright red throat, profuse, 6 to 8′ high, 3 to 4′ wide.

Itsy Bitsy™ Kona Princess ('Monria')—Double, miniature, bright pink, 6 to 7′ high, 5′ wide.

Itsy Bitsy™ Red ('Moned')—Small, bright red, profuse, 6 to 8′ high, 5 to 6′ wide.

'Jason Okumoto'—Semi-double, deep golden orange petals with deep scarlet throat surrounded by a hot pink collar, petaloids surround the pistil creating the "cup and saucer effect," 6′ high, 3′ wide.

'Kona Improved'—Double, rich pink, 8 to 10′ high, 4 to 6′ wide.

'Mary Morgan'—Single, large, pink, spring through summer, rapid-growing medium-sized shrub.

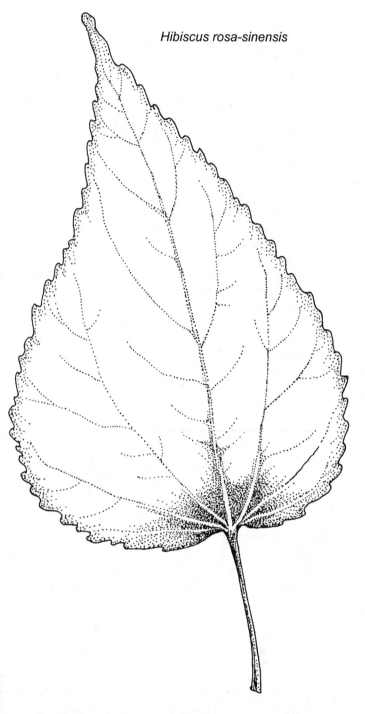

Hibiscus rosa-sinensis

'Morning Glory'—Single, bluish pink flower with magenta-pink rising from the throat to cover the petals nearly to the edge, creamy white coloring tips of the petal edges, 8 to 10' high, 4 to 6' wide.

'Mrs. James Hendrey'—Double, yellow.

'Mrs. Jimmy Spangler'—Single, red with yellow edges, spring through summer, medium-sized shrub.

'Niobe'—Single, large, burnt-orange with a dark red throat, spring through summer.

'The Path'—Buttercup yellow, 7″ diameter flowers with a bright pink center, large, heavy-textured, dark green leaves.

Powder Puff™ ('Monsa')—Double, creamy white, puff ball shape, pinkish tinge with cooler weather, 8 to 10' high, 4 to 6' wide.

'President'—Single, red, spring through summer.

Red Dragon™ ('Mongon')—Double, scarlet red, profuse during warm months, 6 to 8' high, 3 to 4' wide.

'Red Parasol'—Red with white edges, summer-flowering.

'Ross Estey'—Single, large, orange edges shading to glowing rose center, looks like paper mâché, ruffled and tufted flowers that last 3 to 4 days, heavy-flowering, 6 to 8' high, 3 to 4' wide.

'Ruby Brown'—Single, brown-orange with deep red throat, 6' high, 3' wide.

'Seminole'—Single, vibrant pink, each flower 6 to 8″ across.

'Yellow Moon'—Double, yellow.

Hippophae rhamnoides L. — Common Seabuckthorn
(hi-pof′ā-ē ram-noy′dēz)

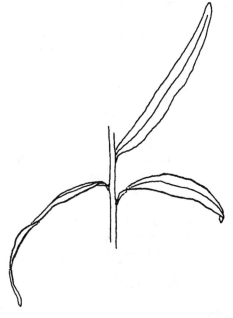

FAMILY: Elaeagnaceae

LEAVES: Alternate, simple, linear to linear-lanceolate, 1 to 3″ long, 1/8 to 1/4″ wide, acutish, cuneate, entire, upper surface dark gray-green and not as scaly as the silvery gray undersurface, willow-like in form and texture.

BUDS: Shrivelled and ragged with 2 thin, very loose scales, end bud lacking; on male plants flower buds are conical and conspicuous; on female—smaller and rounded.

STEM: Commonly with terminal and axillary twig-spines, stellately pubescent and with silvery or brownish small peltate scales, slender, subterete; pith—small, brown, round, continuous.

SIZE: 8 to 12 to 30' tall with a spread of 10 to 40'.

HARDINESS: Zone 4 to 7.

HABIT: Large shrub or small tree, spreading and irregularly rounded, loose and open; staminate trees are more erect than the spreading pistillate trees; tends to sucker and form large colonies; more common in Europe than United States and I have observed plants with shrub-like habit and also very upright tree forms; since plant is grown from seed variation is to be expected.

RATE: Medium.

TEXTURE: Medium-fine in leaf; medium-coarse in winter.

LEAF COLOR: Silver-green in summer, grayish green in fall.

FLOWERS: Essentially dioecious, yellowish before leaves in March or April, borne in axillary racemes on previous season's branches, male in short catkins, female in short racemes, flowers open with the first leaves, not showy.

FRUIT: Bright orange, drupe-like, globose to egg-shaped , short-stalked, 1/4 to 1/3″ long, September, persisting through April of the following year, apparently very acid and birds do not bother it, contains a single brown seed; Don Shadow told me that the eastern Europeans have made many selections for fruit size and quality, apparently juice is made from the fruits.

CULTURE: A bit difficult to get established; seems to do better in sandy, relatively infertile soil than in rich soil; prefers sand with a moist subsoil; sunny open area; withstands salt spray; supposedly a ratio of 6 females to 1 male is sufficient for pollination; pollen is carried by the wind; nitrogen fixing.

DISEASES AND INSECTS: None serious.

LANDSCAPE VALUE: One of the best plants available for winter fruit color; good for color contrast because of summer foliage and fruit; works well in masses, borders, and along the seashore for stabilizing sand; could be an effective plant for highway use where salt-spray is a problem; seldom available in commerce and since there is no way to determine the sex of seedling-grown plants, there is a chance that one will end up with non-fruiting plants.

CULTIVARS:
   'Sprite'—Dense compact gray leaf form, 15″ by 24″ in 3 years, reasonable cutting success if kept dry.
PROPAGATION: I have grown many seedlings but have had a tough time growing them on; seeds should be
   stratified for 90 days at 41°F and they will then germinate like beans; in the rich Illinois prairie soils the
   plant languished; shoot cuttings are apparently difficult but root cuttings will work, also layering and
   division of the suckers that occur around the parent plant; 1988 report noted high rooting of the species
   from early July semi-lignified cuttings in peat:polystyrene:sand, mist, plastic house; tissue culture has also
   been successful; see *Plant, Cell, Tissue and Organ Culture* 15:189–199 (1988).
ADDITIONAL NOTES: Abundant in Europe. Widely planted in the Netherlands and parts of Germany and
   France as a roadside cover. The fruit is handsome as is the soft grayish green foliage.
NATIVE HABITAT: Europe to Altai Mountains, western and northern China and northwestern Himalayas. Long
   cultivated.

Hovenia dulcis Thunb. — Japanese Raisintree
(hō-vē′ni-à dul′sis)

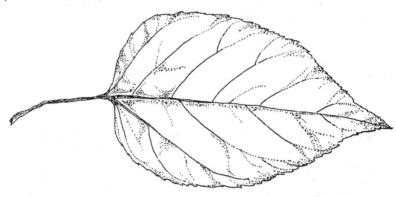

FAMILY: Rhamnaceae
LEAVES: Alternate, simple, broad-
   ovate to elliptic, 4 to 6″(8″)
   long, 3 to 5″ wide, acuminate,
   subcordate or rounded and
   usually unequal at base,
   coarsely serrate, glabrous or
   pubescent on veins beneath,
   prominently 3-veined, lustrous
   dark green; petiole—1 1/4 to 2″
   long.
BUDS: Dark brown, hairy, rather small, superposed, sessile, ovoid, with 1 or 2 exposed scales; no terminal.
STEM: Villous to glabrous, terete, slender, zig-zag, rich brown, small dot-like lenticels; pith—relatively large,
   pale, continuous, pale or white, round; leaf scars round heart-shaped, somewhat elevated; buds sit in
   notch formed by leaf scar.

SIZE: Usually reaching 30′ under cultivation; the spread would be about 2/3's to equal the height; can grow 40
   to 45′.
HARDINESS: Zone 5, probably safest in the southern areas of Zone 5 to 7.
HABIT: Small, handsome tree of upright-oval to rounded outline with clean, ascending main branches and a
   paucity of lateral branches.
RATE: Medium.
TEXTURE: Medium in all seasons.
BARK: Flat gray to gray-brown, rather wide ridges with shallow, darker furrows, very nice effect, especially
   pleasing bark, very soft gray and recognizable from a distance, large trees at the Arnold Arboretum and
   Swarthmore College have superb trunks and bark, although not widely recognized this is one of the tree's
   most handsome attributes.
LEAF COLOR: Handsome lustrous dark green in summer, no appreciable fall color, perhaps yellow under ideal
   conditions.
FLOWERS: Perfect, greenish white, 1/3″ diameter, borne in many-flowered, 2 to 3″ diameter cymes, June and
   July, fragrant, not overwhelming but attractive particularly with minimal competition at this time of year.
FRUIT: Fleshy drupe, 1/3″ diameter, light grayish or brown; the fleshy branches of the infructescence are
   reddish; the fleshy branches are sweet and are chewed by the Japanese and Chinese; mature in
   September–October; actually not bad tasting.
CULTURE: Not too difficult to culture; limited information is available on this species but I have seen the plant
   performing admirably in a planter on the Southern Illinois Campus at Edwardsville, at the Missouri Botanic
   Garden, St. Louis, U.S. National Arboretum, Washington, DC, Swarthmore College, and at the Arnold
   Arboretum; in all cases the soils, exposures, and maintenance levels were different yet the trees were
   vigorous and healthy; supposedly thrives in sandy loams.
DISEASES AND INSECTS: Nothing serious.
LANDSCAPE VALUE: A small lawn or street tree; hardiness may be a problem; could be used in planters.

PROPAGATION: Seed requires a considerable acid scarification period and somewhere between 1 and 2 hours is sufficient; paper by Frett, *HortScience* 24:152 (1989), indicates best germination 93.8% with 45 minutes acid followed by 90 days cold stratification, 45 minutes acid produced 36% germination, non-scarified and non-stratified seed gave 1.9% germination; apparently there is a type of embryo dormancy.

ADDITIONAL NOTES: The Dawes Arboretum, Newark, OH, had a rather sizable tree that was killed during the 1976–77 winter when temperatures dipped to -22°F in that area. Morton Arboretum, Lisle, IL reported the species as only root hardy and in severe winters even the roots are killed. This species may not acclimate fast enough to avoid fall freezes. I suspect temperature below -10 to -15°F will result in injury. Killed outright in Orono, ME.

NATIVE HABITAT: China; cultivated in Japan and India. Cultivated 1820.

Hydrangea anomala D. Don subsp. *petiolaris* (Sieb. & Zucc.) McClint. (formerly *H. petiolaris* Sieb. & Zucc.) — Climbing Hydrangea
(hī-dran'jē-ȧ ȧ-nom'a-lȧ pet-i-ō-lā'ris)

FAMILY: Hydrangeaceae (Also included in Saxifragaceae by some authorities.)

LEAVES: Opposite, simple, broad-ovate to ovate-oval, 2 to 4" long, nearly as wide, acute or acuminate, cordate or rounded at base, serrate, nearly glabrous, dark green and lustrous above, paler and often with tufts of down in the vein-axils beneath; petiole— ranging from 1/2 to 4" long.

BUDS: Imbricate, greenish brown, sometimes tinged red, shiny, 2 loosely overlapping scales visible, essentially glabrous.

STEM: Brown, with peeling, exfoliating shaggy bark (handsome), developing root-like holdfasts along the internodes.

SIZE: Almost unlimited in ability to climb tall trees, perhaps 60 to 80' in height; obviously can be maintained at lower heights but the inherent ability to cover large structures is present; has been used as a shrub in the open, will cover rock piles, walls and other structures.

HARDINESS: Zone 4 to 7(8), not as vigorous in South.

HABIT: True clinging vine and climbing by root-like holdfasts; interesting in that it develops in more than one plane and gives depth to the structure it is covering; the branches protrude out from the structure to which the vine is attached creating interesting shadows unlike that obtainable with *Parthenocissus* and juvenile *Hedera helix*.

Sepals

RATE: Slow in the establishment process, but quite vigorous after roots are established.

TEXTURE: Medium-fine in leaf; medium in winter habit.

STEM COLOR: Older stems (3 years or more) develop an exfoliating character much like *Acer griseum* (Paperbark Maple); the bark color is a rich cinnamon brown and unparalleled by any other hardy vine.

LEAF COLOR: Glossy dark green in summer foliage, exquisitely handsome, a rare jewel in the crown of vines; the leaves stay green late into fall and essentially abscise green, occasionally reasonable yellow fall color; November 7, 1997, Bernheim Arboretum, a magnificent bright yellow fall colored vine looked me in the eye and questioned why I had not given proper credence to the taxon's fall color; the clicking of the camera was the reply.

FLOWERS: White, late June to early July, effective for 2 weeks or longer, borne in 6 to 10" diameter, flat-topped corymbs with the outer flowers (sepals, in 3 to 5's) sterile and showy (1 to 1 3/4" across) and the inner flowers fertile, dull white, and weakly attractive, sweet fragrance; overall flower effect is magnificent; inflorescence borne on 1 to 1 1/2" long peduncle (stalk).

FRUIT: Capsule, dehiscent, small, not ornamentally important.

CULTURE: Somewhat slow to develop after transplanting, requires rich, well-drained, moist soil; full sun or shade; best used on east or north exposure in adverse climates; should be grown and handled as a container plant to avoid excessive abuse in transplanting.

DISEASES AND INSECTS: None serious compared to those listed for *H. arborescens*.

LANDSCAPE VALUE: The best vine! As Wyman so succinctly stated, "There is no better clinging vine." Excellent for massive effect on brick or stone walls, arbors, trees and any free structure; becomes quite woody, so needs ample support; the extra cultural care required in establishment is rewarded many times over in ornamental assets for the excellent foliage, flowers and winter bark effect make this species a four-season plant.

PROPAGATION: Somewhat difficult to root; I have collected cuttings in July, treated with 1000 ppm IBA and received 5% rooting; supposedly the optimum time to secure cutting wood is late spring or early summer before the stems turn brown; July cuttings have been rooted using 8000 to 10000 ppm IBA; see Dirr and Heuser, 1987, for detailed procedures; seed needs no pretreatment and can be directly sown; cold period of 1 to 2 months will hasten and unify germination.

NATIVE HABITAT: Japan, China. Introduced 1865.

RELATED SPECIES: Unfortunately, an enterprising taxonomist reduced the above to subspecies classification. *Hydrangea petiolaris* Sieb. & Zucc. has been around for a long time and is still not well-known. With the name change it will take another 50 years before the garden public catches up with the new name. My good friend, the late Professor Emeritus Clarence E. Lewis, once noted that *H. petiolaris* has been listed as such for 100 plus years so why change the name when it has been universally accepted. Elizabeth McClintock, "A Monograph of the Genus Hydrangea", *Calif. Acad. Science* 29:197–256 (1957) is the basis for this change. The real kicker in this change is that not all taxonomists agree. For example, Bean and *The New RHS Dictionary of Gardening* (1992) treat *H. petiolaris* as a species. Alas, if I had nothing better to do with my time than split taxonomic hairs I would have myself bound and shelved in the archives.

Hydrangea anomala D. Don., (hī-dran′jē-à à-nom′a-là), differs from the above in the elliptic-ovate, 3 to 6″ long, 1 to 3″ wide, pointed, rounded, triangular- or round-toothed, lustrous dark green leaves. Corymbs are smaller (6 to 8″ across), with fewer sterile sepals (2/3 to 1 1/2″ diameter) and 9 to 15 stamens instead of 15 to 22 as in *H. anomala* subsp. *petiolaris*. The inflorescence tends to be more lax and floppy than subsp. *petiolaris*. The Arnold Arboretum had both vines on the north wall of the Administration Building and in June–July they were magnificent. The elliptic-ovate leaves of *H. anomala* permit easy separation from the more rounded leaves of the subspecies. Probably not as hardy as the subspecies. Himalaya, China. Introduced 1839. Zone 5 to 7(8).

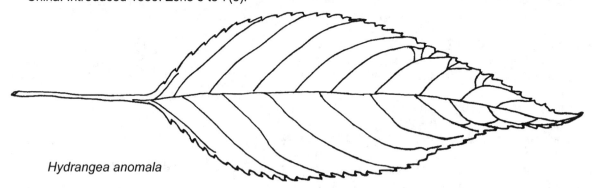

Hydrangea anomala

Hydrangea quelpartii, (hī-dran′jē-à kel-pär-tē-ī), is a small leaf form that I have read about and recently observed on a March 1996 visit to the southwest of England. It is less vigorous than the typical form and may be worthy of use in restricted growing areas. Authenticity of taxonomic status is dubious. Native to Quelpart Island, Korea. Hardiness unknown.

Schizophragma hydrangeoides Sieb. & Zucc. — Japanese Hydrangea-vine

LEAVES: Opposite, simple, suborbicular or broad-ovate, 2 to 4″(5″) long, about as wide, short acuminate, rounded to cordate at base, coarsely dentate, lustrous dark green, essentially glabrous; petiole—1 to 3″ long, reddish.

BUDS: Imbricate, 1/8″ long, reddish brown, 20 to 30° divergent from stem, pubescent, on 2nd year and older, developing from short side spurs, nodes compressed and constricted.

STEM: First year—reddish brown, pubescent; second year—light brown, vertically fissured, glabrous, developing root-like holdfasts; leaf scar large, inverted, triangular; pith—green.

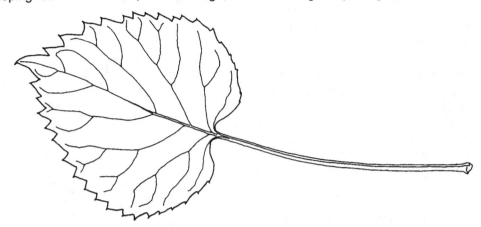

Schizophragma hydrangeoides, (skiz-ō-frag′mȧ hī-dran′jē-oy′dēz), Japanese Hydrangea-vine, is an allied but quite distinct climber. The vine stays flat and does not develop the protruding woody framework of *H. a.* subsp. *petiolaris*. Does not appear as vigorous or large as *H. a.* subsp. *petiolaris* and I suspect 20 to 30′ is a reasonable estimate of landscape size. The leaves are much more coarsely toothed and the sterile flowers are composed of a single, large 1 to 1 1/3″ long, ovate, entire sepal compared to the 3- to 5-parted sepals of *H. a.* subsp. *petiolaris*. The inflorescences are flat-topped and 8 to 10″ wide, showing a slight drooping tendency compared to the rather rigid inflorescence of *H. a.* subsp. *petiolaris*. It is in full flower just after *H. a.* subsp. *petiolaris*. Flowers late June–early July at the Arnold Arboretum. Requires about the same cultural manipulations as *H. a.* subsp. *petiolaris*. Found in woods and forests in the mountains of Japan where it often grows in association with *H. a.* subsp. *petiolaris*. This is a true clinging vine and cements itself by root-like holdfasts. Bark develops an exfoliating condition with age, but I have not noticed it being as prominent as Climbing Hydrangea. I have rooted late July cuttings with 3000 ppm IBA. Has been easier to root than *H. a.* subsp. *petiolaris*. 'Brookside Littleleaf' is a small leaf form introduced by Brookside Gardens, Wheaton, MD; leaves about 1/5 size of species; perhaps a juvenile trait as the size of the leaf gradually increases as the plant becomes larger. 'Iwa-garami' was listed by Surry Gardens, Maine, but I have been unable to locate details. 'Moonlight' has light gray-silver shading/mottling over the upper leaf surface. 'Roseum' is a lovely form with rose-flushed bracts; it is in this country and hopefully will find its way into cultivation. 'Strawberry Leaf' has leaves shaped like strawberry leaves; bark and stem quite attractive; listed by Gossler Farms, Oregon. Japan. Cultivated 1880. Zone 5 to 7(8).

Schizophragma integrifolium Oliv., (skiz-ō-frag′mȧ in-teg-ri-fō′li-um), Chinese Hydrangea-vine, differs from the above in its entire or sparingly denticulate, 4 to 6″(7 to 8″) long leaves, the immense 10 to 12″ wide inflorescences, and the 2 to 3″ long, single, ovate sepal. Have observed at Kew Gardens and the flowers are indeed immense. The lustrous dark green, ovate, narrow acuminate, rounded or cordate, entire or sparsely toothed leaves are beautiful. One of those plants that as a gardener you lust after. Central and western China. Introduced 1901 by Wilson. Zone 7(?).

ADDITIONAL NOTES: All of the above are lovely vines and make excellent choices on brick and stone buildings. As I write this, I recall beautiful plants of subsp. *petiolaris* at Spring Grove, Smith College and the Arnold Arboretum that would make believers of every gardener. Bonnie and I have included *H. anomala* subsp. *petiolaris* and *Schizophragma hydrangeoides* 'Moonlight' in our garden. After two years, the latter is outgrowing the former, but neither will win the Boston Marathon.

Hydrangea arborescens L. — Smooth Hydrangea
(hī-dran′jē-ȧ är-bō-res′enz)

LEAVES: Opposite, simple, ovate to elliptic, 2 to 8″ long, 2 to 6″ wide, acuminate, rounded or cordate at base, serrate, dark green, glabrous or sometimes puberulous beneath; petiole—1 to 3″ long.
BUDS: Imbricate, 4- to 6-scaled, greenish brown, divergent, 1/8 to 1/4″ long, glabrous, much longer than *H. paniculata* buds.

STEM: Stout, gray-tan-brown, shiny, young branches essentially glabrous, smooth, without gray streaks; older stems—exfoliating; pith—relatively large, roundish, continuous, whitish, second year pith brown, hollow.

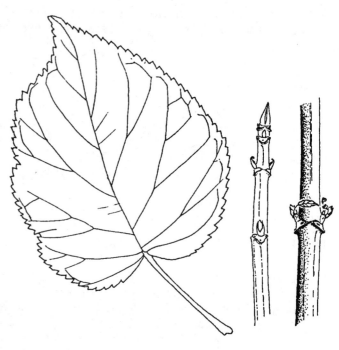

SIZE: 3 to 5′ in height by 3 to 5′ and larger in spread; suckers freely from roots and will cover large areas if not restrained.

HARDINESS: Zone (3)4 to 9.

HABIT: Usually low-growing, clumpy, rounded shrub with many weak, shreddy barked, non-branched canes; often broader than high at maturity.

RATE: Fast.

TEXTURE: Coarse in leaf, flower and winter habit; actually almost frightening in the winter landscape.

LEAF COLOR: Dark green in summer, fall color is green to brown, although leaves may die off a pleasing lemon yellow in certain years, generally nondescript; as I proof this text, on November 10, 1997, the plants in the Dirr garden have developed a soft lemon yellow fall coloration.

FLOWERS: Fertile flowers, dull white, June through September, borne in 4 to 6″ diameter, much-branched, flattish corymbs with few or no large, white, sterile flowers; actually the flowers pass from apple green to white to brown; probably best to cut off flowers at the early brown stage as they are ornamentally valueless after this time; flowers open one month or more before those of *H. paniculata*; open early to mid-June, Athens; 'Annabelle' flowers have been effective for 6 to 8 weeks in our garden.

FRUIT: Capsule, dehiscent, 8- to 10-ribbed, of no ornamental consequence, the infructescences persist into winter and depending on preference can be removed or left, seeds are like dust and entire fruiting structure should be collected in fall, brought inside and allowed to dry on newspaper, shake gently to remove seeds; seeds can be sown directly and will germinate or simply stored in glass vials under refrigeration until planting on seedling medium in spring.

CULTURE: Utilize container-grown plants; fibrous-rooted, transplants well; very adaptable; however, proliferates in rich, well-drained, moist soil; pH adaptable; prefers partial shade, however, does well in full sun if soil moisture is sufficient; often requires supplemental watering in hot dry summers; probably should mow it off with a lawnmower in late fall or early spring; flowers on new wood; leaves appear "dog-earred" under drought conditions; in South shade is a necessity.

DISEASES AND INSECTS: Bacterial wilt, bud blight, leaf spot, powdery mildew, rust, aphids, leaf tier, rose chafer, oystershell scale, two-spotted mite, and nematodes have been reported on this and other species. I have grown 'Annabelle' for 15 years and have never had a single problem. Hydrangeas in general are trouble-free and reward the gardener manyfold.

LANDSCAPE VALUE: Consider this species as an herbaceous perennial in colder climates; some flowers are so heavy as to weight the stem to the ground thus creating a very unkempt and unruly specimen; perhaps in the shrub border or massing in some shady, out-of-the-way area; in the 1983 edition I beat the plants into verbal submission, but after growing and loving 'Annabelle', I have tempered my earlier remarks; if cut to the ground in late winter and lightly fertilized, by June or July the regrowth will produce stunning flowers that are effective for a month or more in the South, two months in Zone 5; as flowers fade cut them at the base, strip the leaves, tie by their bases and hang to dry; we have done this for years and the sepals do not shatter and make excellent dried bouquets; in fact they could be dyed or painted for more colorful effects; I usually get two flushes of flower, the first in June, and after pruning, the second in August–September.

CULTIVARS:

'Annabelle'—Selected and largely promoted by J.C. McDaniel of the University of Illinois for its extremely large corymbs (up to 1′ across) and the fact it flowers 10 to 14 days later than 'Grandiflora'; flowers about mid-June in the Dirr garden; heads are more erect on the stem with a more nearly symmetrical radius, and are usually larger in total diameter than those of 'Grandiflora' grown under the same conditions; have seen it growing from Orono, ME to Clermont, KY to Athens, GA; has become one of the most popular hydrangeas and is widely available from nurserymen; this is definitely a superior plant and was introduced by a true plantsman and gentleman; the history of this selection is presented in *Proc. Intl. Plant Prop. Soc.* 12:110 (1962); selected for the 1995 Georgia Gold Medal Award; I have heard garden cognoscenti say the flowers are too large, gauche, obtrusive; one person's favorite garden plant is another's bane, life is great.

'Eco Pink Puff'—A light pink sepaled form, from Don Jacobs, Eco Gardens, Decatur, GA.

'Grandiflora'—This is the type commonly available from nurseries, often referred to as the Hills of Snow Hydrangea; the corymbs are 6 to 8″ across with primarily sterile white flowers; the individual "sterile" showy sepals are larger than 'Annabelle', but the total number of flowers in a head is fewer; the heads are not so radially symmetrical, looking like four parts loosely pushed together, and soon becoming floppy in appearance.

'Green Knight'—Described as unique and exciting with pure white, mophead inflorescences which turn a rich dark green as they age, from Louisiana Nursery.

'Highland Lace'—Imagine finding a million dollar bill by the side of the road, yes, dream; well, Bonnie and I found a sterile form at about 4000′ in the southern Appalachians intermixed with the species; lacey, sterile flowers on strong stems, not as large or heavy as 'Annabelle'; Bonnie selected the name; yes, dreams come true.

'Sterilis'—Often confused with 'Grandiflora', flatter topped head, showing some areas of small perfect flowers not covered by the persisting sepals of the showy flowers; Paul Cappiello and I identified a planting on the Maine campus as 'Sterilis'; the flower corymbs appeared more uniform, i.e., not as lumpy.

Current nomenclature, according to Kartesz, allows for subsp. *discolor* (Ser.) McClintock and subsp. *radiata* (Walter) McClintock. Based on countless observations in the southern Appalachians particularly in Georgia, Tennessee and North Carolina, I see no consistent difference. Subspecies *radiata* has silver-backed leaves and is sufficiently different at least in horticultural characteristics to warrant distinction. The silver-backed leaves are beautiful, particularly on a breezy day. The sepals appear reasonably abundant and result in a more pronounced floral effect. Also, cuttings have been more difficult to root than the other types. The plant is particularly abundant around Highlands, NC. Additionally two "sterile" forms of subsp. *radiata* have been found, one with double, clear white, larger than 'Annabelle', sterile flowers; the other single and sterile. I have seen photographs of both and believe that the double form will have a prominent place in American gardens. Subspecies *radiata* is quite drought susceptible. Subspecies *discolor* has gray tomentose undersides.

PROPAGATION: Seed—collect as described under *Hydrangea anomala* subsp. *petiolaris*; sow on milled sphagnum under mist, seeds germinate in 14 to 21 days, pick off seedlings and transplant after 6 weeks, will flower 2nd or 3rd year. Perhaps the easiest plant on earth to root; softwood cuttings, May–June, 1000 ppm KIBA, root 100% in 10 to 14 days; rooted cuttings continue to grow after removal from mist; have used 10,000 ppm KIBA and did not "burn" the cuttings.

ADDITIONAL NOTES: Interesting plant in its native haunts, ɪd often found growing out of rock crevices in deeply shaded woods. I have seen it growing out of tɪ e sandstone cliffs in Turkey Run State Park, Indiana, in shade so deep that one could not take an effective photograph.

NATIVE HABITAT: New York to Iowa, south to Florida and Louisiana. Introduced 1736.

Hydrangea heteromalla D. Don

LEAVES: Opposite, simple, ovate to broad-ovate, 3 1/2 to 8″ long, 1 1/4 to 5 1/2″ wide, cuneate, rounded to cordate at base, serrate, dark green above, whitish below, glabrous or with scattered pubescence above, densely hairy below or with hairs only in vein axils; petiole—3/4 to 2 1/4″ long, red.

STEM: Second year—olive brown with prominent lenticels.

Hydrangea heteromalla, (hī-dran′jē-à   het-ēr-ō-mal′à), is a rather coarse shrub that is seldom grown in American gardens. The habit is upright, not unlike *H. paniculata*, with ultimate garden height between 10 and 15′. At Hillier Arboretum I witnessed a particularly heavy flowering form that was easily 15′ high. Flowers occur in broad, semi-flat-topped corymbs, with showy elliptic or obovate sepals on the periphery of the inflorescence. Inflorescences are 5 to 8″(10″) across and open in May–June. Flowers develop on new growth of the season. Appears quite adaptable and plants at the Arnold and Morton Arboreta attest to cold hardiness. Maximum flowering occurs in full sun although plants I have witnessed produce respectable flowers in partial shade. Have also grown seedlings in Athens, transplanted them to containers but did not keep them until flowering. Plants were not pristine in the heat of Zone 7b. This is a highly variable species that ranges from the Himalayas into western and northern China. McClintock, in her revision of *Hydrangea*, lumped all the variation into *H. heteromalla*. *Hydrangea bretschneideri* Dipp. is now placed as 'Bretschneideri'. I have observed it in England and thought I was looking at *H. arborescens*. Grows 8 to 10' high, leaves 3 to 5" long, 1 to 2 1/4" wide, scarcely pubescent below, second year stems chestnut brown and peeling, flowers in flattened 4 to 6" diameter corymbs. Another handsome selection is 'Snowcap', a large stately shrub, with 8 to 10" wide, flattened corymbs. Introduced by Hillier Nursery and this is the plant referred to at the beginning of this treatise. *Hydrangea dumicola* W.W. Sm. and *H. xanthoneura* Diels are included within *H. heteromalla*. Introduced 1821. In its widest embodiment adaptable from Zone (4)5 to 7.

Hydrangea macrophylla (Thunb. ex J.A. Murr.) Ser. — Bigleaf Hydrangea
(hī-dran′jē-à mak-rō-fil′à)

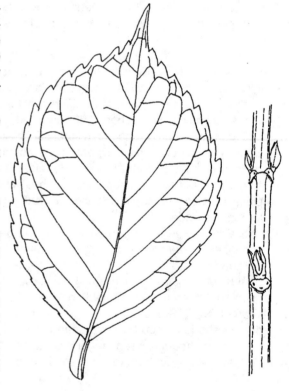

LEAVES: Opposite, simple, obovate to elliptic or broad-ovate, 4 to 8" long, two third's as wide, short-acuminate, broad cuneate at base, coarsely serrate with triangular obtusish teeth, lustrous medium to dark green above, rather fleshy texture and greasy to the touch, reminds of a cabbage leaf, glabrous or slightly puberulous beneath; petiole—stout, 1/2 to 1 1/4" long, leaving large scars, the opposite one contiguous.

STEM: Light brown, scarcely branched, often dying back in winter; pith—large, white.

SIZE: 3 to 6' in height but can grow to 10'; spread would be equal to or greater than the height.

HARDINESS: Zone 6 to 9, does not do well in Zone 5 unless extremely well-sited, as one goes south and east this becomes a very common plant; however, in the northern states it is rare to see it in full flower; qualification is necessary for I have seen the plant in Urbana, IL withstand –20°F; it never flowered, but did come back from the crown to produce a respectable mound of foliage; since flowers are set (largely) on last year's growth, if the shoots are killed then flowering is history; I have seen the most magnificent flowering specimens on Cape Cod; in Zone 7b, Athens, where the plant should prosper, 2 flowering years out of 3 might be considered good; the plant is soft and succulent and does not harden and the tops of the plant are killed; also have had problems with late spring frosts injuring and/or killing developing leaves and flowers; in July 1995, Bonnie and I journeyed to the Pacific Northwest to hike and visit gardens, the *H. macrophylla* cultivars were in their element and a terrific collection at Van Dusen Botanical Garden, Vancouver, led me to believe that a cool, even climate makes the difference; certainly this holds true in the British Isles and continental Europe where the plants are everywhere in evidence.

HABIT: Rounded shrub of many erect, usually unbranched, thick stems.

RATE: Fast.

TEXTURE: Medium-coarse in leaf although coarse is a definite possibility; coarse in winter, in fact, irreparably so.

STEM COLOR: Of a light, shiny, gray- or straw-brown color.

LEAF COLOR: Leaves are quite large (4 to 8″ long) and are lustrous medium to dark green in summer; the leaves are quite fleshy (succulent) with a waxy, greasy consistency; have on occasion seen the leaves die off yellow.

FLOWERS: Very difficult to adequately describe the typical species flower because of the numerous selections; the sterile, outer flowers are pink, bluish, purple, entire or toothed, up to 2″ or more in diameter, the fertile flowers are usually blue or pink; both are borne in large, broad, flat-topped, much-branched, cymose corymbs; July through August; June–July in Athens; flowers in early June in Athens, early July on Cape Cod, MA; prune after flowering since buds are formed on previous season's growth

FRUIT: Capsule, 1/4 to 5/16″ long, not showy.

CULTURE: Transplant as a container plant into moist, well-drained soil which has been amended with peat moss, leaf mold and the like; will withstand seashore conditions and actually flourish near the shore; full sun or partial shade, shade more imperative in Zones 7 to 9; moisture is a necessity or plants wilt and die; pruning is an art with the *Hydrangea* species and one must know the requirements of each type; this species flowers from buds formed on previous season's growth and any pruning should be done right after flowering; often winter killed in North and no flowering occurs. The flower color on some cultivars is strongly affected by the pH of the soil in which they are growing. The ray flowers (sepals) are often the most affected. The color changes depend on the concentration of aluminum ions in the soil. This depends in turn on the acidity of the soil, being highest on very acid soils and lowest where the soil is alkaline. The color range depends on the cultivar, but the bluest shades are always produced on the most acid soils. A pH range of 5.0 to 5.5 is listed as satisfactory for inducing blue coloration while pH 6.0 to 6.5 and probably slightly higher is best for pink coloration. I read color descriptions for various cultivars and then see the plant and color is opposite. Aluminum can really mess with one's horticultural mind-set; be leery of any absolute color description.

The rationale for blue-pink flowers correlates with free aluminum (Al^{+++}) that complexes with the pigment to produce blue coloration. Takeda et al., *Phytochemistry* 24:2251–2254 (1985), reported that the blueing of hydrangea sepals was primarily due to the delphinidin-3-glucoside-aluminum-3-caffeoylquinic acid complex, with aluminum serving as the stabilizer. I see some cultivars that do not turn blue even under ideal conditions for aluminum availability and suspect that those clones lack or have reduced concentrations of the anthocyanin, delphinidin-3-monoglucoside.

Blom and Piott, *HortScience* 27:1084–1087 (1992), showed that aluminum sulfate applications to greenhouse forcing hydrangeas induced blue coloration. There was a positive correlation between blueness ranking and Al^{+++} foliar concentration. They recommended an average 13.35 grams (~0.5 ounce) per 6″ diameter pot.

DISEASES AND INSECTS: See under *H. arborescens*, have observed leaf spot under nursery production conditions, 'Annabelle' has been infected by a bacterial wilt under container culture.

LANDSCAPE VALUE: Probably a good plant for the shrub border in southern areas; not adequately winter hardy in the northern states and is often killed back to the ground, the only benefit then is the foliage; this plant and the numerous cultivars are widely planted in the East and South; makes a good flower display; good choice for coastal areas; have incorporated several cultivars into our Georgia garden and have been rewarded with superb flowers on occasion; one of the great garden plants and with the 500 or so extant cultivars surely there is at least one for every gardener.

CULTIVARS: Unbelievably large number of cultivars many of which are not hardy. W.J. Bean's *Trees and Shrubs Hardy in the British Isles*, Vol. II (1973); *The Hillier Manual of Trees and Shrubs* (1991); Krüssmann's *Manual of Cultivated Broad-leaved Trees and Shrubs* Vol. II (1985); and Haworth-Booth's *The Hydrangeas* (1984), offer a wealth of cultivars and the technical information concerning them. Wyman has a list in his book based on his observations. Quite an interesting species with many lovely garden forms. The cultivars are divided into two groups: the *hortensias* and the *lacecaps*. The *hortensias* have essentially sterile flowers that are borne in large globose corymbs. These usually form solid masses of white, pink, red, blue, and/or purple which are often so heavy they cause the stem to bend. The *lacecaps* have a center of fertile, relatively non-showy flowers and an outer ring of showy, sterile flowers which together afford a pinwheel effect. Often the *lacecaps* have showy sterile flowers mixed with the fertile flowers as well as along the outer periphery of the inflorescence.

The cultivar treatment is essentially the same as the last edition with the addition of a checklist of types listed in commerce in the United States. No doubt some have been missed but this is a good starting point. With something like 500 cultivars, it is folly to pretend to know them in detail. In fact, as I photographed and studied the collection in Van Dusen Botanic Garden my thoughts centered on how *similar* they appeared, particularly when viewed from a distance.

Checklist of commercially listed cultivars:

HORTENSIAS
'Alpenglow'
'Alpengluhen'
'Altona'
'Amethyst'
'Anderson 1'
Angel's Blush™ ('Ruby')
'Ayesha'
'Blue Danube'
'Blushing Pink'
'Bottstein'
Buttons 'N Bows™ ('Monrey')
'Cardinal'
'Cardinal Red' } probably the same
'Charm'
'Charm Red' } probably the same
'Enziandon'
'Europa'
'Frillibet'
'Garten-Baudirecktor Kuhnert'
'Gen. Vic. Vibraye'
'Gertrude Glahn'
'Glory Blue'
'Glowing Embers'
'Goliath'
'Hamburg'
'Harlequin'—white-edged petal
'Heinrich Seidel'
'Holstein'
'Kluis Superba'
'La France'
'La Marne'
'Leuchtfeur'
'Masja'
'Mathilda Gutges'
'Merritt's Beauty'
'Merritt's Pink'
'Merritt's Pride'
'Merritt's Supreme'
'Miss. Belgium'
'Mme. Emile Mouillere'
'Mousseline'
'Niedersachen'
'Nigra'
'Nikko'
'Paris'
'Parzival' ('Parsival', 'Parzifal')
'Pink Beauty'
Pink 'N Pretty™ ('Monink')
Red 'N Pretty™ ('Monred')
'Schenkenburg'
'Sister Theresa'
'Souv. Pres. Doumer'
'Trophy'
'White'

LACECAPS
'Aureovariegata'
'Beaute Vendomoise'— immense sepals
'Blue Bird'
'Coerulea Lace'
'Geoffrey Chadbud'
'Lemon Wave'
'Libelle' ('Lybelle')
'Lilacina'
'Mariesii Variegata'
'Mousmee'
'Seafoam'
'Silver Variegated Mariesii'
'Teller White'
'Tokyo Delight'
'Veitchii'
'White Wave'

TELLER SERIES
'Bachstelze' (Wagtail)
'Bergfink' (Mountain Finch)
'Blaukehlchen' (Blue Throat)
'Blauling' (Bluebird)
'Blaumiese' (Titmouse)
'Buchfink' (Finch)
'Buntspecht' (Woodpecker)
'Eisvogel' (King Fisher)
'Elster' (Magpie)
'Fasan' (Pheasant)
'Flamingo' (Flamingo)
'Gimpel' (Bull Finch)
'Grasmucke' (White Throat)
'Libelle' (Dragonfly)
'Mowe' (Sea Gull)
'Mucke' (Mosquito)
'Nachtigall' (Nightingale)
'Papagei' (Parrot)
'Pfau' (Peacock)
'Rotdrossel' (Red Wing)
'Rotkehlchen' (Red Breast)
'Rotschwanz' (Red Tail)
'Taube' (Pigeon, Teller Red or Teller Pink)
'Zaunkonig' (Wren)
'Zeisig' (Finch)

The most commonly offered cultivars include: 'Nikko Blue' (12), 'Pia' (8), 'Sister Theresa' (7), 'Mariesii Variegata' (7), 'Merritt's Supreme' (6), 'Blue Wave' (5), 'Goliath' (5), 'Variegata' (5). The numbers in parenthesis are based on a survey of 13 commercial nursery catalogs and represent number of times listed.

HORTENSIAS

'All Summer Beauty'—Small plant with rich blue flowers in acid soil, prolific-flowering, will be different shade of pink/blue in near neutral soil, 3 to 4', will supposedly flower on the new growth of the season.

'Badger Hill Select'—Exceptionally hardy form introduced by Badger Hill Farms, Fennville, MI, grows 5 to 8' high with an equal spread, large rich blue, globe-shaped inflorescences.

'Blue Prince' ('Blauer Prinz')—Pink or purplish, medium blue in acid soil, dense corymbs, moderate height, one of the hardiest.

'Compacta'—Supposedly more compact than 'Nikko Blue' with darker green leaves, blue in acid soil.

'Domotoi'—Individual flowers large and doubled, pale pink or blue, in an attractive regular shaped head; literature is confusing as it reports the form as being both vigorous and weak-growing, may become fasciated and distorted if too well-fed, about 3' high.

'Dooley'—Reliable rich blue flower production in Zone 7b when others are killed to ground or seriously injured, flowers produced on lateral buds up and down the stem, late freezes in March 1996 and 1998 decimated many hydrangeas in Athens–Atlanta, this selection flowered heavily, discovered in Coach Vince Dooley's garden and named after him.

'Forever Pink'—Good compact, 3' high form with 3"(4") diameter pink flower heads that become rose-red in cool weather, flowers earlier than other types often in June, keeps good foliage color until frost, flowers on current season's growth.

'Nikko Blue'—An old form that is quite vigorous, 6', with large rounded medium blue inflorescences in acid soil; probably confused in the trade.

'Otaksa'—Pink or blue flowers, red leaf stalks, rather weak stems which bend down under the weight of wet flower heads, 3' high, an old Chinese variety.

'Pia'—Compact, 2 to 3' form with 3 to 4" diameter pink flowers as I have seen it in the Southeast, renamed Pink Elf™ by Monrovia Nursery, California, has become quite popular, young plants flower heavily.

'Westfalen'—Pure vivid crimson or deep purple-blue, free- and perpetual-flowering, richest colored of all, 2 1/2' high.

LACECAPS

'Blue Billows'—Rich blue ray flowers, bluish purple fertile flowers, about 3 1/2" across, supposedly more cold hardy, often ruined by late spring frosts in 7b.

'Blue Wave'—Ray flowers with 4 wavy-edged sepals, rich blue in acid soils, otherwise pink or lilac, a vigorous shrub 6' high and as wide with bold foliage, grows best in light shade, a seedling of 'Mariesii'.

'Coerulea'—Perfect flowers a deep blue, ray flowers blue or white, one of the hardier forms, Zone 6, cultivated 1846.

'Lanarth White'—Fertile flowers blue or pink, ray florets pure white, starting in July and lasting into August, a hardy form, 3' high and wide, very good old form.

'Mariesii'—A few sterile flowers are scattered among the fertile ones and are similar in shape to the normal ray flowers that edge the inflorescence, flowers are nearly always pink or mauve-pink (pale blue on very acid soils), grows 4 to 5' high.

'Quadricolor'—Supposedly the best of the variegated leaf types with shades of white, cream, lime and green in each leaf, more variegation than 'Variegata'.

'Variegata'—Leaves edged with creamy white, very attractive, flowers blue in acid soil; 3' high, nice accent plant, not a particularly strong grower, shoots revert to all green or cream on occasion.

PROPAGATION: Best to propagate from softwood cuttings of May, June, July growth; also semi-hardwood and hardwood cuttings will root; rooting is hastened with IBA treatment although the rooting percentage will approach 100 without any treatment; cultivars are rooted regularly in our shop with 1000 ppm KIBA, 3 perlite:1 peat, intermittent mist, cuttings are rooted in 10 to 20 days, removed from mist, fertilized and grow like topsy. See *Advances in Plant Sciences* 5:619–622 (1992) where 1,2 and 3 node cuttings all rooted in high percentages (88% and greater) when treated with 500 to 1500 ppm IBA-5 second dip.

ADDITIONAL NOTES: Considerable taxonomic confusion and this taxon and the next are often mixed. The Japanese botanist Hara concluded that the two taxa should exist as *H. macrophylla* subsp. *macrophylla* and *H. macrophylla* subsp. *serrata*. McClintock concurred with this analysis. True subsp. *macrophylla* has a limited distribution on the east coast of Honshu Island, on Izu and Boso peninsulas, and Oshima and Hachijo Islands. Subspecies *serrata*, a woodland plant, is widely distributed from the coast to 5000' elevation in the mountains of Kyushu, Honshu and Hokkaido. The botanical differences: subsp. *serrata* has slender stems, 2 to 6″ long ovate leaves, 1.5 to 4 times their width, more or less pubescent, with thin texture and dull upper surface, petals 1/12 to 1/8″ long, capsules 1/12 to 1/4″ long; subsp. *macrophylla* has stout stems, ovate, 3 to 8″ long leaves, length 1.5 times width, glabrous, shining upper surface, thick texture, 1/8 to 1/4″ long petals, 1/4 to 1/3″ long capsules.

Art and Terri Bee, *American Nurseryman* 186(12):86–91(1997), discuss the nomenclature of the Teller Series from Switzerland. Forty years of breeding produced 26 lacecap hydrangeas. Their names are included in the above checklist with the English translation name. Bonnie and I have grown 'Teller's White' in our garden and the flowers were spectacular. Unfortunately, this one representative is susceptible to late spring frosts and may suffer dieback. The foliage is glossy dark green.

Since the last 1990 edition, hydrangea in the literature and garden has increased exponentially, nurseries either devoted to or specializing in hydrangea have developed. For the best current literature particularly weighted toward *H. macrophylla* and *H. serrata* I recommend:

> Lawson-Hall, Tony and Brian Rothera. 1995. *Hydrangeas: A Gardener's Guide*. Timber Press, Portland, OR.
> Mallet, Corinne, Robert Mallet and Harry van Trier. 1992. *Hydrangeas*. Center D'art Floral, France.
> Mallet, Corinne. 1994. *Hydrangeas*. Center D'art Floral, France.

Nurseries include:

> Heronswood Nursery, LTD. 7530 NE 288th Street, Kingston, WA, 98346-9502.
>   phone (206) 297-4172, fax (206) 297-8321
> Hydrangeas Plus, 6543 South Zimmerman Road, Aurora, OR, 97002.
>   phone (503) 651-2887, fax (503) 651-2648
> Nurseries Caroliniana, Inc., 100 East Hugh St., North Augusta, SC, 29841
>   phone (803) 279-2707
> Wilkerson Mill Gardens, 9595 Wilkerson Mill Road, Palmetto, GA, 30268.
>   phone/fax (770) 463-9717, mail order customers call (770) 463-2400

Also, The American Hydrangea Society, P.O. Box 11645, Atlanta, GA, 30365 was started by Mrs. Penny McHenry and offers programs, newsletters, and garden tours for members.
NATIVE HABITAT: Japan.

RELATED SPECIES:

Hydrangea serrata (Thunb. ex J.A. Murr.) Ser.
LEAVES: Opposite, simple, lanceolate, ovate-elliptic, 2 to 6″ long, 1 to 2 1/2″ wide, acuminate, cuneate, finely or coarsely serrate, dark green and usually glabrous above, veins beneath often with short appressed or curled hairs.

Hydrangea serrata, (hĭ-dran′jē-à sĕr-rā′tà), is allied to the above but is not as robust, has slender stems, relatively narrow leaves and smaller flowers and seed capsules. It is found in mountain woodlands and is considerably hardier than *H. macrophylla*. Mildew is more problematic on *H. serrata* than *H. macrophylla*. Several beautiful cultivars include 'Bluebird' with pale pink or blue ray flowers, early-flowering, and a vigorous (5′), drought-resistant constitution; 'Nigra' has purple-red-black stems, smaller leaves and small pink flowers; 'Preziosa' has a hortensia type inflorescence that is rather small (3 to 4″) but the flowers start pink with a deeper shade at the edge and later change to crimson with deeper shades of the same color. This is a hardy and free-flowering form that does well in sun or half shade, 4′ high. I saw this in England and was genuinely impressed by the rich flower color. 'Preziosa' is now in the Dirr garden and in 1997 was exceptional. Japan, Korea. Cultivated 1870. Zone (5)6 to 7.

Hydrangea paniculata Sieb. — Panicle Hydrangea
(hĭ-dran′jē-à pan-ik-ū-lā′tà)

LEAVES: Opposite, sometimes whorled, especially on flowering and vigorous shoots, simple, 3 to 6″ long, 1 1/2 to 3″ wide, elliptic or ovate, acuminate, rounded or cuneate at base, serrate, dark green and sparingly pubescent or nearly glabrous above, setose pubescent beneath, particularly on the veins; petiole—1/2 to 1″ long.

BUDS: Imbricate, rounded, globose, 4- to 6-scaled, glabrous, brownish in color, sometimes with whorled character.

STEM: Stout, reddish brown, bark showing gray vertically streaked areas; older bark often peeling and more gray in color.

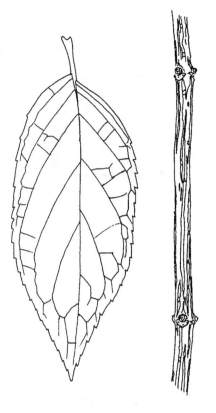

SIZE: 10 to 20′ in height by 10 to 20′ in spread; quite variable in size, often less than 10′.

HARDINESS: Zone 3 to 8, probably the most cold hardy hydrangea species.

HABIT: Upright, coarsely spreading, low-branched tree or large shrub, the branches assuming a semi-arching condition under the weight of the flowers; often rather straggly and unkempt with age.

RATE: Fast.

TEXTURE: Coarse the year round but peaking when denuded of leaves yet possessed with browned remains of the inflorescence; actually spent flowers should be removed in September or earlier.

STEM COLOR: Older wood, 1 to 2″ or greater, assumes a gray-brown, ridged-and-furrowed look; often quite handsome especially when lower branches are removed and the sun shadows are allowed to develop; especially handsome is the bark on cultivar 'Praecox' when treated in this fashion.

LEAF COLOR: Dark green, possibly a tinge of luster to the summer foliage, fall color is green with a hint of yellow, sometimes a tinge of reddish purple appears, never spectacular.

FLOWERS: White changing to purplish pink, mid-July into September, borne in pyramidal panicles approximately 6 to 8″ long, two third's as wide at base, the bulk of the flowers are fertile, yellowish white, not showy; a few flowers are sterile and showy; individual sterile florets composed of 4, sometimes 5, usually toothed sepals, flowers last for long periods while going through the color transformation.

FRUIT: Capsule, ornamentally without appeal.

CULTURE: Similar to *H. arborescens*; prefers good loamy, moist, well-drained soil; sun or partial shade; remove inflorescences in September as they are then turning brown; flowers on new wood as does *H. arborescens* and can be pruned in winter or early spring; very hardy plant; the most adaptable and most urban tolerant, difficult to kill.

DISEASES AND INSECTS: Same as previously described for *H. arborescens*.

LANDSCAPE VALUE: Several astute plantsmen have termed this species a "Monstrosity in the Landscape"; difficult to blend into the modern landscape because of extreme coarseness; totally disgusting in late fall and winter with inflorescences still evident; over planted in the past but little used in modern landscapes; grows very fast and will provide a large splash of white at a time when few plants are in flower; possibly should be reserved for the shrub border or the neighbor's yard; I have observed this plant through the seasons and always came to the same conclusion—a "loner" in the landscape; making somewhat of a comeback in recent years; good pruning can do a great deal to make this a better plant. The above tirade is directed at 'Grandiflora' which is used to excess. In the Midwest, Maine, and around Highlands-Cashiers, NC, it appears there were fire sales on the plant. Today there are many new cultivars entering the market particularly from the de Belder's Kalmthout Arboretum. The combined sterile-fertile flowered forms do not flop like 'Grandiflora' and can be fashioned into small trees and large shrubs.

CULTIVARS:

'Bridal Veil'—A supple plant with thin hanging branches, inflorescences are small with sterile florets up to 1 1/2″ wide, sepals very broad and sharply cut, flowers produced in succession throughout the season, flowers early August until first frost, possible to use in dried flower arrangements although very fragile, selection made from a seedling of 'White Moth' by Jelena and Robert de Belder in 1990.

'Brussels Lace'—Dense, ball-shaped, branchy shrub, inflorescence composed of a cushion of large numbers of yellowish beige fertile flowers on which are scattered the off-white sterile florets, which are very small, flowers in late July, grows to 6.5′, and is thus a less cumbersome size than 'Unique', foliage is healthy, sterile florets become unevenly spotted with pink at the end of the season, produces abundant, dependable flowers from early August until the first frosts, bred from a seedling of 'Unique' by Jelena and Robert de Belder in 1975.

'Burgundy Lace'—When grown in full sun, sterile flowers are beautiful pink, and mature to mauve to light violet, individual sterile florets are 1.2–1.6″ wide, inflorescences have an average length of 10″ long and 6″ wide, plant grows 10–13′ high, the photograph I saw was spectacular and sufficient reason to at least test this form, suspect high summer heat may reduce the intensity of the pink coloration, not sure how different this selection is from 'Pink Diamond', de Belder, Kalmthout Arboretum selection from seedlings of 'Unique'.

'Everest'—Produces large, dense panicles of showy sepals, the sepals are white and age to pink, foliage is dark green.

'Floribunda'—An older (1967) Japanese cultivar that was introduced to the St. Petersburg Botanical Garden in Russia by Maximowicz; the conical inflorescence is a mixture of primarily fertile flowers with a sprinkling of showy sepals; sterile flowers are more numerous but not sufficiently so to conceal the fertile flowers; the inflorescence may grow 18″ long and 6″ wide at the base; sepals are about 5/8 to 3/4″ long, broad, elliptic to rounded, 4 to 5 in number, overlapping; white sepals age to pink; flowers late July into September; cultivated specimens can reach a height of 16.5′, so this shrub should be kept for large spaces; the dark green leaves are about 6″ long, narrow, and tapering, slightly pubescent, with finely denticulate edges; the older woody parts become thick, but young shoots and the flower heads are fine and flexible.

'Grandiflora'—Almost all flowers are sterile and large; forming a tight panicle of white then purplish pink and finally brown; the inflorescences (normally 6 to 8″ long) can reach sizes of 12 to 18″ in length and 6 to 12″ wide at the base; this is the most common form and still widely available from nurseries; size of the inflorescence depends on pruning and plant vigor, plants left to their own devices have smaller flowers; to produce the large panicles mentioned it is necessary to thin the plant to 5 or 10 primary shoots; these, if properly fertilized and watered, will produce immense heads that literally weight the branches down; I have seen plants handled like this at Bernheim Arboretum and it is a welcome change from the normal shrub-tree type; this form was introduced from Japan in 1862; goes under the name PeeGee Hydrangea; I monitored flowering times of this and 'Praecox' during sabbatical at the Arnold; on July 10, 1978, 'Praecox' was in flower while 'Grandiflora' showed nothing.

'Greenspire'—A shrub with very light paniculate inflorescences of a greenish white color that become pink-tinged, growing clear of the foliage on shoots 12″ long by 8″ wide, made up of sterile and fertile flowers, with many leaves growing mixed in, growth is rapid and flowering is dependable, should be planted in partial shade to protect the flowers from excessive bright sunlight, flowers turn green towards the end of the flowering season, flowering from late July to late September, bred from a seedling of 'Unique' by Jelena and Robert de Belder in 1975; supposedly similar to 'Kyushu'.

'Kyushu'—Vigorous, upright selection, bright green, lush foliage, numerous white panicles of sterile and fertile flowers, more fertile than sterile as I saw the plant in flower on July 2 at the Arnold; produces abundant flowers from early years; originated from seeds collected by Capt. Collingwood Ingram in Kyushu, Japan and distributed by Jelena and Robert de Belder who received the explorer's cuttings which were labeled "*Hydrangea paniculata*, medium form, from Kyushu"; selection actually made at Kalmthout Arboretum, Belgium; I saw it for the first time at the Arnold Arboretum and, though beautiful in flower, it had suffered from the drought of 1991.

'Melody'—A majestic 13′ high shrub, with a soaring flight of inflorescences on thrusting, slender branches, inflorescences exceptionally long, to 14″, compared to a width of 7″, the panicles are "S" shaped, very delicate and light, with spare numbers of sterile florets, starting very early in the season and continuously opening to give a beautiful off-white color, tending towards pure white, flowers from mid-July to late September, bred from a seedling of 'Unique' by Jelena and Robert de Belder in 1985.

'Mont Aso'—Late-flowering, even later than 'Tardiva', can grow to a great width in a suitable environment, collected at the summit of the volcano Aso on the island of Kyushu, Japan, found growing where one might have expected the volcanic smoke, gases and ash to prevent the growth of plants, introduced by Jelena and Robert de Belder in 1970.

'Mount Everest'—Sturdy shrub with large, luxuriant paniculate inflorescences, pale pink fertile flowers and creamy white turning pale pink sterile florets, can grow taller than 10′, flowers late in the season, from mid-August to frost, Hillier introduction, probably 1989.

'Papillon'—A graceful plant growing up to 10′ tall, the inflorescences which grow on strong branches, are both long and wide, and are produced in large numbers in August, they have a profusion of sterile florets with raised sepals, giving the impression of a cloud of butterflies, flowers from late August to frost, bred from a seedling of 'Unique' by Jelena and Robert de Belder in 1985.

'Pee Wee'—A smaller flowered version of 'Grandiflora' that has picked up steam in American commerce, have seen in Orono, ME, grows over 10′ high.

'Pink Diamond'—At least from the photographs I have seen, is sufficient cause for any plantsperson to salivate, large inflorescences (12″ long by 8″ wide) are composed of fertile and showy flowers with the showy sepals turning rich pink, selected from a seedling of 'Unique' by Jelena and Robert de Belder; in late October 1997, I observed a plant with rose-purple sepals.

'Pink Wave'—An 8′ high shrub, very long branches with sparse numbers of leaves, inflorescences 8″ long by 8″ wide, many greenish white fertile flowers with scattered dish-shaped sterile florets up to 1.5″ wide, sterile florets pure white turning to greenish white, then late in the season to pink, when the fertile flowers also change to a reddish pink, very free-flowering from late July to late September, introduced by Edouard d'Avdeew around 1980.

'Praecox'—Possesses a smattering of sterile, showy flowers integrated with the fertile, non-showy ones, majority of the showy flowers are located at the base of the inflorescence; inflorescences are smaller (perhaps 6″ long) than some other forms; interestingly attractive; flowers three to six weeks earlier than 'Grandiflora' about late June in Zone 7; this is a vigorous form that will grow between 10 and 15′ in height; the sepals are grouped 4 together, about one inch long, scarcely overlap, and are prominently toothed, an obvious difference from those of the species; hardier than 'Grandiflora'; flowers on old wood; leaf is larger and stems coarser than other forms. Raised at Arnold Arboretum from seeds collected by Sargent from Hokkaido in 1893. Original plant still grows at the Arnold Arboretum and is more than 100-years-old, a testimonial to its inherent landscape adaptability. The parent plant is about 12 to 15′ tall and 18 to 20′ wide.

'Ruby'—Inflorescences with abundant sterile florets, early-flowering from late July until frost, takes on a carmine pink tint from August onwards, this color deepens gradually, becoming dark pink at the end of the season, bred from a seedling of 'Pink Diamond' by Jelena and Robert de Belder in 1990.

'Tardiva'—This cultivar is appearing in more and more American nurseries; it is somewhat similar to 'Floribunda' but the sepals are mostly in 4's compared to 5's; the inflorescence about 6″ long, the ray flowers are less numerous and smaller (1/2 to 3/4″ long); it flowers quite late (September); have raised seedlings from this with some flowering in October; origin unknown, possibly Hillier.

'Unique'—Large, pure-white, sterile florets (about 2″ across) and rounded sepals, the showy sepals completely conceal the fertile flowers, inflorescence may reach 16″ long by 10″ wide, the plant will grow 10 to 13′ high; this selection resulted from seedlings of 'Floribunda'; the seedlings were uprooted by birds and only one plant remained and was properly termed 'Unique'; Jelena and Robert de Belder, Kalmthout Arboretum introduction, 1968.

'Utsuri Beni'—Reputed to turn rich pink with age.

f. *velutina*—Prostrate habit, small inflorescences and leaves, felt-like covering of downy hairs on its leaves, stalks, branches, and inflorescences, flower in mid-August or early September until frost.

'Vera'—A shrub with a light and airy form. As the plant's origin is unknown, the question arises whether 'Vera' really is the name of a horticultural cultivar or the breeder simply wished to say that it conforms to the species type (vera = true, in Latin). The light green foliage acts as a good background for large numbers of small flowers.

'Webb's'—Most aptly described as an improvement of 'Grandiflora' with primarily sterile flowers and uniform, broad-conical head, sepals are pure white and age to a purplish pink; photos I took in mid-October at Byers Nursery, Inc., Huntsville, AL, attest to its staying power; would make a good cut and/or dried flower; selected by J.A. Webb of Huntsville.

'White Moth'—Flowers over longer period than 'Unique' and produces new flowers that are intermingled with the faded inflorescences; the inflorescences are irregular spheres, average 14 to 16″ in diameter, and develop green color in autumn, the sepals are ovate to ovate-rounded and occur in 4's and 5's, essentially covering the fertile flowers; average height is only 6 to 7′; a seedling selection from 'Unique' that was raised by the de Belders at Kalmthout.

PROPAGATION: Seed requires no pretreatment; see under *H. anomala* subsp. *petiolaris* for details; seeds sown in February, 1993 produced 12″ seedlings by 6-26-93, same plants flowered in August–September of 1994; obviously a very short juvenile period before flowering commences. Cuttings, May, June and July, softwood, root readily in sand:peat medium, with 1000 ppm KIBA quickdip in 4 to 5 weeks.

NATIVE HABITAT: Japan, Sakhalin, and eastern and southern China. Introduced 1861.

Hydrangea quercifolia Bartr. — Oakleaf Hydrangea
(hī-dran′jē-ȧ kwĕr-si-fō′li-ȧ)

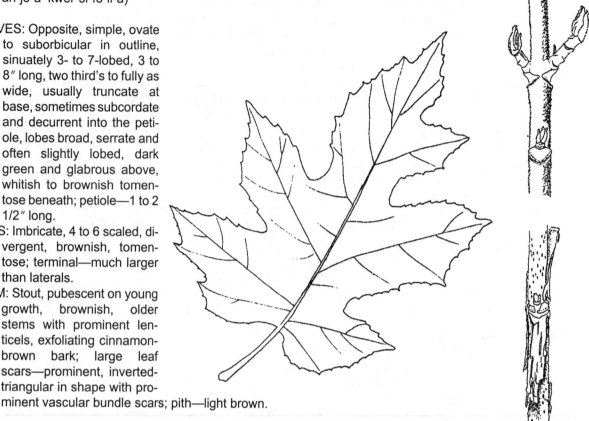

LEAVES: Opposite, simple, ovate to suborbicular in outline, sinuately 3- to 7-lobed, 3 to 8″ long, two third's to fully as wide, usually truncate at base, sometimes subcordate and decurrent into the petiole, lobes broad, serrate and often slightly lobed, dark green and glabrous above, whitish to brownish tomentose beneath; petiole—1 to 2 1/2″ long.

BUDS: Imbricate, 4 to 6 scaled, divergent, brownish, tomentose; terminal—much larger than laterals.

STEM: Stout, pubescent on young growth, brownish, older stems with prominent lenticels, exfoliating cinnamon-brown bark; large leaf scars—prominent, inverted-triangular in shape with prominent vascular bundle scars; pith—light brown.

SIZE: 4 to 6′(8′) in height; spread as wide and wider as it suckers from roots; the more I look the larger the plants that surface, the above size range is realistic in the typical landscape but old specimens in the South reach 10 to 12′ and never look back; 'Alice', one of my introductions, is now over 12′ high and wide, obviously there is need for smaller selections and certainly 'Sikes Dwarf' and 'Pee Wee' fit this criterion.

HARDINESS: Zone 5 to 9. I have entertained abundant discussion relative to cold hardiness ratings and am not sure there is an absolute answer. In the Morton Arboretum, –20 to –25°F is not unreasonable, and they report it not fully hardy killing back to some degree each winter, but flowering *every* summer from late June to mid-July. Spring Grove, Cincinnati has experienced –25°F and the extensive plantings of Oakleaf have not been seriously injured. Have observed the plant in Charleston, SC, Savannah, GA, and Lee, FL doing well when sited in shade and provided supplemental water.

HABIT: Upright, little-branched, irregular, stoloniferous shrub forming mounded colonies.

RATE: Slow to medium.

TEXTURE: Pleasantly coarse in leaf; coarse in winter, but handsome by virtue of exfoliating bark.

STEM COLOR: Young stems intensely brownish tomentose; older stems (3 years and more) exfoliating to expose a rich brown inner bark, quite attractive but often overlooked; on a March 1996 day I took a break from the text you are reading and toured our garden; with rain on the branches the rich cinnamon brown bark was almost vibrant.

LEAF COLOR: Deep green, sometimes glossy in summer, changing to shades of red, orangish brown and purple in fall; quite spectacular in fall color; seems to be great variability in the fall color among progeny of this species; selections should be made for this feature alone; new growth grayish green, leaves emerge folded in prayer and open to their 180° angle position from surface to surface, handsome in early spring; usually emerging by mid-March in Athens; leaves hold late, often into late November–early December and in winter of 1988–89 when lowest temperature was 21°F until February 22, many fall (winter?) colored leaves were still on the plants.

FLOWERS: White, changing to purplish pink and finally brown, outer flowers (sepals) sterile, 1 to 1 1/2″ diameter; fertile flowers numerous, creamy, fragrant; late June through July and persisting; in Athens, flowers invariably at their best in late May–early June; borne in 4 to 12″ long, 3 to 4″ wide, erect panicles; the cultivars are considerably more showy in flower than the straight species.

FRUIT: Capsule, not showy; old infructesences persist through winter.

CULTURE: Somewhat tender as a young plant and should be protected in Zone 5; stems and buds may be injured when winter temperatures go much below $-10°F$; requires moist, fertile, well-drained soil; sun or partial (1/2) shade; wise to mulch to maintain a cool, moist root environment; if terminal buds are lost during winter, no flowers will be produced; in the North it is possibly best to consider this plant for its excellent foliage and if flowering occurs accept it as an added bonus; prune after flowering; pruned in late August with full flower bud development and normal flowering the following spring in Zone 7b; excellent plant for southern gardens.

DISEASES AND INSECTS: Observations have led me to believe this species is quite trouble-free; leaf blight has been listed as a problem; not easy to grow in containers and nurserymen are constantly striving to produce a worthy plant; once in the ground problems are virtually nonexistent.

LANDSCAPE VALUE: Somewhat difficult to use in the residential landscape because of coarseness; the shrub border, massing or shady situations offer possibilities; excellent foliage makes it worthy of consideration; in common use at the University's Botanical Garden and those plants which have a moist root run and a modicum of shade do better than plants in exposed, dry, full sun situations; plants may show premature fall coloring as early as August if stressed; saw a wonderful combination planting with *Oxydendrum arboreum* surrounded by a planting of *H. quercifolia*; in late October both were in fall color and the effect was striking; have become enamored with this species and the cultivars; phenomenal variation in virtually all traits, have seen 4″ long and 14″ long inflorescences, minimal fall color to the most magnificent red-burgundy ('Alison'), compact ('Pee Wee') and gigantic ('Alice') habits; many selections have been made since the last edition and most are included herein.

CULTIVARS:

'Alice'—Last edition I was reticent to say much about this form but the industry, particularly McCorkle Nurseries, Dearing, GA, brought this selection into commercial production; the parent plant is now over 12′ high by 12′ wide, 10 to 14″ long inflorescences on vigorous shoots, about 8 to 10″ long on less active growth; cream-white sepals are large, almost 50 cent size, and cover the fertile flowers, age to pink-rose as they mature; the dark green summer foliage turns burgundy-red in autumn; has proven easier to grow in containers, quite vigorous; selected by the author from a seedling plant on the Georgia campus.

'Alison'—This clone was discovered and named at the same time as 'Alice'; again found by the author on the Georgia campus; flowers 10″ long plus or minus, some up to 12″ long, equal distribution of fertile flowers and showy sepals, pyramidal inflorescence held more upright than 'Alice'; again will grow 8 to 10′ high, broader spreading than 'Alice'; foliage lustrous dark green with stunning almost flourescent red-burgundy fall color; I told most people to grow 'Alice' after the feedback from McCorkle but am now enthusiastic about both cultivars; in November, Bonnie and I were touring the garden and commented on how spectacular the fall color appeared; both clones flower in late May–early June in Athens; easy to root from cuttings.

'Dayspring'—Improved form with large, white flowers, deep green foliage turns deep red bronze in fall, Flowerwood Nursery introduction.

'Harmony'—Mostly sterile, large paniculate inflorescences, 12″ long, white, will weigh down the branches; interesting and unusual but not as elegant as 'Snowflake' and 'Snow Queen'; large shrub to 10′; one of the best plantings is housed at Cedar Lane Farms.

'Lynn Lowrey'—Superior form introduced by Tom Dodd, III and named after the late Lynn Lowrey.

'Pee Wee'—Compact form, probably 2 to 3′ by 2 to 3′ with leaves and flowers more refined; has received rave notices from Atlanta gardeners who have observed it; have heard sizes to 3 1/2 to 4 1/2′ high by 6′ wide, in 3 years in the Dirr garden it has reached 2′ by 3 1/2′ wide; the inflorescence is about 4″ maybe 5″ long, somewhat broad-pyramidal shaped, almost appearing 4-sided, sepals are delicate, small, abundant and almost hide the fertile flowers; looks like an excellent form for small gardens; rose to red-purple fall color has occurred on plants in the Dirr garden; suffered slight tip dieback in Orono, ME, of course it may have had snow cover.

'Roanoke'—Loose and more open inflorescence than 'Harmony'; actually the differences are minimal; flowers will weigh down the branches; a massive planting at Bernheim Arboretum is 10′ high, 30′ wide and spectacular as I viewed it on June 24, 1997.

'Snowflake'—Multiple bracts or sepals emerge on tops of older ones creating a double-flowered appearance; 12 to 15″ long panicles, actually the most beautiful of the sterile-flowered forms; about 7 to 8′ at maturity; as is true with 'Harmony' and 'Roanoke', the heads are heavy and the branches may be weighed down, but never to the degree of those two; prefers moist soil and partial shade; have grown in the Dirr garden for years; flowers slightly later than the single types and flowers age more gracefully; the inflorescences on our plant average 8″ while colleague Allan Armitage's are fully 12″ and longer; is it possible that an "herbaceous person" can grow a better woody than a "woody person?"

'Snow Giant'—Leaves crimson red in fall; large, lightly fragrant, snow white flowers in early to mid-summer.

'Snow Queen'—An improvement of the species with larger and more numerous sterile florets that provide a more dense solid appearance, the 6 to 8″ long inflorescences are held upright and do not "flag" like many seedling plants, leaves are dark green and seem to hold up in the sun better than seedlings, leaves turn deep red-bronze in fall, flowers turn a good pink as they mature, more compact grower possibly 6′ high at landscape maturity, nurserymen have been impressed with this plant, a Princeton Nursery introduction, no damage at -22°F.

LOUISIANA NURSERY CULTIVARS: Louisiana Nursery, Opelousas, LA, has introduced several cultivars; a brief description of each per their catalog is provided.

'Back Porch'—Early-flowering, vigorous, with pretty, large white flowers that mature pink.

'Camelot'—Vigorous, large, upright conical inflorescences, deep red fall color.

'Cloud Nine'—Handsome large showy white flowers.

'Gloster Form'—Vigorous, with 5 petals (probably means sepals on each flower), does exceptionally well in the South.

'Joe McDaniel'—Vigorous with large showy white flowers, collected in the South by Professor McDaniel.

'John Wayne'—Selected from Florida, large white showy flowers, does well all over the South, excellent reddish purple fall color in the Dirr garden.

'Late Hand'—Choice late-flowering clone with large "hand-like" lobed leaves and pretty white flowers; extends flowering season about one month.

'Luverne Pink'—An attractive bushy medium-sized clone with pretty white flowers aging to a deep pink.

'Patio Pink'—Vigorous early-flowering, white flowers age pink, large leaves, good fall color.

'Picnic Hill'—A vigorous bushy form with short internodes and handsome flowers.

'Sikes Dwarf'—A dwarf clone, 2 to 2 1/2′ high, up to 4′ across, pretty white flowers and attractive leaves, considered a good form; plant in Dirr garden is 3 to 4′ high and will no doubt supersede published sizes.

'Tennessee Clone'—Attractive leaves and bold white flowers.

'Wade Mahlke'—Compact flowers of sterile constitution intermediate between those of 'Harmony' and 'Roanoke'.

PROPAGATION: Seed can be sown directly and will germinate; should be relatively fresh; layers and division of the parent plant provide a means of vegetative propagation; over the years I have had real problems with rooting; currently successes are 90% plus; too much moisture is a problem; our standard procedure is firm wood cuttings in May, June, and into September, 5000 ppm KIBA dip, well-drained medium, either all perlite or 3 perlite:1 peat, intermittent mist, 4 to 6 weeks rooting time; have taken cuttings in late April and had a salable one-gallon by fall; this plant is easy to root provided the few guidelines discussed above are followed; rooting time is 2 to 3 weeks and plants can be up-canned, fertilized, and will grow off quickly; tissue culture has been successful; see *Scientia Horticulturae* 31:303–309 (1987); commercial labs are supplying plants to the industry; recent research at the Center for Applied Nursery Research, Dearing, GA showed that early April, direct-stuck cuttings in 3-gallon containers, 3 per container, produced marketable plants by late July.

ADDITIONAL NOTES: Spring Grove, Cincinnati, OH, has mass-planted the species throughout the grounds and in June and July it makes a spectacular show. In my mind, should always be afforded some shade even in northern areas. One of our most beautiful native flowering shrubs particularly for the handsome flowers and bold foliage.

NATIVE HABITAT: Georgia, Florida, Alabama and Mississippi. Introduced 1803.

Hydrangea sargentiana Rehd. — Sargent Hydrangea

LEAVES: Opposite, simple, ovate, 4 to 5″ long, 2 to 3″ wide on flowering shoots, 6 to 10″ by 4 to 7″ on non-flowering shoots, short-acuminate, rounded or subcordate, crenate-serrate, dull dark green and hairy above, reticulate and densely hairy beneath; petiole—1 to 3″ long, bristly.

STEM: Stout, ribbed, clothed with stiff bristles and small erect hairs.

Hygrangea sargentiana, (hī-dran′jē-à sär-jen-tē-ā′nà), Sargent's Hydrangea, is not well-known in the United States, except in gardens in the Pacific Northwest. It is probably inferior to the species mentioned above for the Midwest, East and South. However, after observing the mixture of pinkish white sterile florets and deep rose-lilac fertile flowers it is difficult to at least not mention the plant. If it never flowered, there would be interest from the large hairy leaves and bristly-hairy stems. Flowers occur during July and August in a 6 to 9″ wide flat corymb with the 1 1/4″ diameter sterile flowers on the outside. The entire inflorescence is bristly. Develops into a large 6 to 10′ high mounded shrub with thick stems that develop an exfoliating character; would require moisture and shade along the eastern corridor. Have seen in shade and moist soils in English gardens, most notably at Hidcote. In Europe, I see this species often listed as a subspecies of *H. aspera* D. Don. which has somewhat similar characteristics. Also included by virtue of morphological similarities are *H. involucrata* Sieb. and *H. villosa* Rehd., the latter now merged into *H. aspera*. As often as I have studied these plants in European gardens, I still cannot identify them on-sight. Also, the labeling is *never* consistent. *Hydrangea sargentiana* is native to central China. Introduced 1907. Zone 7 to 9.

Hypericum prolificum L. — Shrubby St. Johnswort
(hī-per′i-kum pro-lif′i-kum)

FAMILY: Guttiferae, Hypericaceae

LEAVES: Opposite, simple, narrow-oblong to oblanceolate, 1 to 3″ long, 1/4 to 1/2″ wide, obtuse, dark lustrous green or bluish green above and pellucid-punctate; short-petioled.

STEM: Two-angled, light brown, glabrous; older stems with exfoliating bark.

SIZE: 1 to 4′ high by 1 to 4′ spread (up to 5′ high).

HARDINESS: Zone 4 to 8.

HABIT: A small, dense little shrub with stout, stiff, erect stems, rounded, variable in size.

RATE: Slow.

TEXTURE: Medium-fine in leaf; medium in winter.

BARK: On older stems light brown and exfoliating.

LEAF COLOR: Dark lustrous green in summer, perhaps could be considered bluish green; no fall color of consequence.

FLOWERS: Perfect, 3/4 to 1″ diameter, bright yellow, late June through July and August, borne in axillary and terminal few-flowered cymes, quite lovely in flower.

FRUIT: A dry, dehiscent, 3-valved capsule; persists all winter and could be used for dried arrangements, offers a good identification feature.

CULTURE: Best transplanted from a container; does extremely well in dry, rocky soils; full sun or partial shade; pH adaptable, does extremely well in calcareous soils; observations lead me to believe this is an excellent plant for dry, heavy soil areas; prune in early spring.

DISEASES AND INSECTS: In the past I mentioned that the genus was little troubled by insects and diseases. I have changed my mind. Over the years I have grown 'Hidcote', *H. androsaemum*, *H. olympicum* and a host of other species that were obtained in a seed exchange with The Royal Horticultural Society. Seeds germinated without any treatment and produced handsome plants. Once in the garden they developed a wilt or melting out that obliterated all. The only species that has handled the heat, humidity, and poorly drained soils, is *H. calycinum* and its performance has been less than satisfactory. In fact, extensive use on the Georgia campus, followed by slow demise, makes me question this species. I would estimate 2 to 3 years of landscape usefulness in the South, and this may be generous. As a final note, I had 'Hidcote' all over the garden and lost every one. Our campus has experienced the same phenomenon with 'Hidcote'.

LANDSCAPE VALUE: Nice plant for summer colors because of excellent yellow (buttercup-colored) flowers; would work well in the shrub border; possibly in groupings or in mass; I do not believe the Hypericums have been adequately explored and developed as landscape plants in the United States.

PROPAGATION: Cuttings root readily, softwood collected in June–July treated with 1000 ppm IBA and placed in sand under mist gave good rooting; seeds of most species will germinate without any pretreatment.

ADDITIONAL NOTES: As a garden plant the genus appears more content in European gardens (read cool, moist, even climate) and the Pacific Northwest. With something like 400 species, their identification is difficult. In my 19 years in Georgia, many were planted and subsequently died. *Hypericum calycinum* seldom flowers well in our area but is magnificent in Europe. *Hypericum frondosum* 'Sunburst' has held up in full sun, heat and drought better than any others. In winter of 1996, a February low of 7°F, followed by warm late February days and then record low of 17°F on March 10–11, reduced 'Hidcote' to rich Kraft bag status. *Hypericum kalmianum* and *H. prolificum* have staying power and if groomed are handsome shrubs.

NATIVE HABITAT: New Jersey and Iowa to Georgia. Introduced about 1750.

RELATED SPECIES:

Hypericum androsaemum L. — Tutsan
LEAVES: Opposite, simple, ovate, up to 3 1/2 to 4″ long, 2 to 2 1/4″ wide, blunt, cordate, dark blue green, sessile, slightly aromatic when bruised, about the largest leaved of the hardy hypericums.
STEM: Brown, 2-angled.

Hypericum androsaemum, (hī-per′i-kum an-drō-sē′mum), Tutsan, is doubtfully in cultivation to any degree in the United States but in Europe is found in abundance. This makes a vigorous, spreading, bushy shrub 2 to 3′ high. The leaves are among the largest of the hardy hypericums. The light yellow, 3/4″ diameter flowers occur 3 to 9 together in cymose clusters at the terminus of the stem and lateral branches. The fruit is a totally different berry-like capsule that transgresses from red to purple to almost black at maturity and is filled with a wine-colored juice. I saw it in fruit during September in Amsterdam and could not properly identify the species. In fruit, at least, it presents a genuine curve ball for a plantsman who is use to the American species. Appears to tolerate shady situations and is somewhat of a weed in European gardens. Allen Bush, former owner of Holbrook Farms, gave me 'Albury Purple' which stayed alive for 3 years in the Dirr garden and produced burgundy-suffused leaves on the young growth that faded with maturity and heat. Produces yellow flowers and red to purple-black fleshy capsules. Grows 1 1/2′ or more. 'Autumn Blaze' is similar to the species except fruits ripen pink to black and leaves develop shades of yellow-green, orange and red. My success with the species is nil since a large population of seedlings all perished in the garden. Western Europe, northern Africa, northwest Yugoslavia. Cultivated before 1600. Zone 6 to 8.

Hypericum buckleyi M.A. Curtis — Blueridge St. Johnswort
LEAVES: Opposite, simple, obovate to elliptic, 1/4 to 1″ long, rounded at apex, cuneate, rich green.
STEM: Brown, slender, 4-angled.

Hypericum buckleyi, (hī-per′i-kum buk′lē-ī), Blueridge St. Johnswort, is a low-growing (1′), spreading, decumbent, yellow-flowering shrub. Flowers range from 3/4 to 1″ diameter, 1, 3 to 5 in terminal clusters. Requires well-drained soil. North Carolina to Georgia. Introduced 1889. Zone 5 to 8.

Hypericum calycinum L. — Aaronsbeard St. Johnswort
LEAVES: Opposite, simple, ovate-oblong to ovate, 2 to 4″ long, 1/2 to 1 3/4″ wide, obtuse, slightly odorous, dark blue-green above, glaucous beneath, subcoriaceous, sessile.
STEM: Brown, obscurely 4-angled.

Hypericum calycinum, (hī-per′i-kum kal-ē-sī′num), Aaronsbeard St. Johnswort, is a stoloniferous semi-evergreen shrub with procumbent or ascending stems growing 12 to 18″ high and spreading 18 to 24″. The tops of the plant often winter-kill in severe cold but since it flowers on new wood little damage is done. The leaves are dark blue-green above and glaucous beneath. The flowers are a screaming bright yellow, 3″ across, borne singly or rarely 2 to 3 together on new wood in June through September. Easily transplanted in spring; does well in poor sandy soil; full sun or partial shade; best mowed to the ground to induce new growth each spring. Makes a rather handsome ground cover plant as it grows fast and effectively covers an area in a short time. Quite stoloniferous and can prove invasive under proper cultural conditions. Over the past 19 years this has become common in the Southeast but seldom flowers like I have seen it in the Pacific Northwest and Europe. Apparently flowers are not set prolifically on new growth of the season since regrowth after winter injury has produced minimal flowers, at least in the South. Roots easily from softwood cuttings (84% when taken in early summer and set in sand without hormone treatment in 42 days). In my 19 years at Georgia, the species has been utilized in large numbers starting with plantings on North Campus, and progressing in 1997–1998 to a lone, demented, tormented, bedraggled bed on South Campus. The campus horticulturist, Dave Berle, said that it was not being used anymore. Lousy performance over time doomed it to the scrap heap. Native to southeastern Europe, Asia Minor. Introduced 1676. Zone 5 to 8.

Hypericum densiflorum Pursh. — Dense Hypericum

LEAVES: Opposite, simple, linear-oblong to linear, 1 to 2″ long, 1/4 to 3/4″ wide, revolute, rich blue-green.
STEM: Brown, 2-edged.

Hypericum densiflorum, (hī-per′i-kum den-si-flō′rum), Dense Hypericum, grows to 4 to 6′ in height with a 3 to 4′ spread. The habit is upright oval, taller than broad and densely twiggy and leafy. The foliage is deep green in summer; flowers are golden yellow, 1/2″ across, July through September, borne in 5- to 15-flowered corymbs. It is an ally of *H. prolificum* but has smaller flowers and leaves. 'Creel's Gold Star' is a small shrub, dense and compact, linear leaves, small golden flowers. New Jersey to Florida, Missouri and Texas. Introduced 1889. Zone 5 to 8.

Hypericum frondosum Michx. — Golden St. Johnswort

LEAVES: Opposite, simple, ovate-oblong to oblong, 1 to 2 1/4″ long, 1/3 to 7/8″ wide, mucronate, entire, pellucid-dotted, rich bluish green.
STEM: With thin exfoliating reddish to rich brown bark on older branches, branches 2-edged.

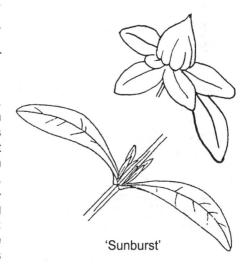

'Sunburst'

Hypericum frondosum, (hī-per′i-kum fron-dō′sum), Golden St. Johnswort, grows 3 to 4′ high with a similar spread. Often an upright rounded shrub with rather stout branches; bark is brown and exfoliating; foliage is a very handsome, distinct bluish green; flowers are bright yellow, 1 to 2″ diameter, with the stamens forming a dense, central mass, 3/4″ across, June–July, solitary. Fruit is a 1/2″ high, broad-based, 3-celled, reddish brown capsule. 'Sunburst' is lower growing (3′ by 4′) than the species and makes a lovely mass plant; this cultivar has proven superior in midwestern tests. The British consider it the handsomest of the American species in cultivation in their country. South Carolina and Tennessee to Georgia and Texas. 1747. Zone 5 to 8.

Hypericum 'Hidcote'

For the past four editions and now this I have attempted to find the correct place for this lovely cultivar. Current thinking (?) has it a hybrid of *H. × cyathiflorum* 'Gold Cup' and *H. calycinum,* where previously it was placed with *H. patulum.* No doubt, it grows taller than I gave it credit, although in the United States I never saw it above 3′ high. Invariably the shoots would be killed in winter but the vigorous regrowth and splendid, profusely borne 2 1/2 to 3″ wide waxy golden yellow flowers overcame the dieback deficiency. Peak flowering in my garden was late May to late June with sporadic flowers into fall. The old flowers became brown and looked messy. Unfortunately, I watched the complete decline of all Hidcotes in my garden and have largely given up on this. Mention is made in European literature of a virus or virus-like disease which causes the flowers to become malformed. Where it can be grown, the shrub is first rate. The dark blue-green, lanceolate, 2″ long leaves are a fine backdrop to the flowers. Grows 3′(5′) high and wide. Zone (5)6 to 8. Dies to ground at Morton Arboretum (Zone 5) and sends up new shoots that flower around mid-July.

Hypericum kalmianum L. — Kalm St. Johnswort

LEAVES: Opposite, simple, linear-oblong to oblanceolate, 1 to 2″ long, 1/8 to 1/3″ wide, bluish green above, glaucous beneath, and dotted with transparent glands.
STEM: Brown, 4-angled.

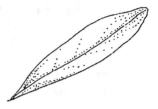

Hypericum kalmianum, (hī-per′i-kum kal-mē-ā′num), Kalm St. Johnswort, grows 2 to 3′ and has bluish green summer foliage. The flowers are bright yellow, 1 to 1 1/2″ diameter, July, borne in 3-flowered cymes; fruit is 5(4)-celled ovate capsule. A handsome hardy species, confined to cliffs or rivers and lakes. 'Ames' is a perfect mounded form, 2 to 3′ high and wide with improved hardiness, listed to Zone 4. Quebec and Ontario to Michigan and Illinois. 1760. Zone 4 to 7.

Hypericum × *moseranum* André, (hī-per′i-kum mō-sĕr-ā′num), Moser's St. Johnswort, is a hybrid between *H. patulum* and *H. calycinum* that was raised in Moser's nursery at Versailles in 1887. It is a compact plant of tufted habit and sends up reddish tinted, arching, 1 to 1 1/2′ long shoots each season. The blue-green leaves are intermediate, about 2″ long. Flowers occur from July to October, 1 to 5 at the end of the shoot with only one flower opening at a time. Each flower is 2 to 2 1/2″ across with broad overlapping golden-yellow petals and stamens whose anthers are pinkish purple. It should be treated like an herbaceous perennial and cut back to the ground in winter. It is considered more hardy than *H. patulum*, which died back in my Athens, GA garden. The cultivar 'Tricolor' will always stick in my mind for as I walked through Wisley Gardens I came upon this handsome white- and rose-variegated plant that looked like a hypericum. I found the label which confirmed my suspicions. This is not as hardy as the species and is not as vigorous. Zone 7(?).

Hypericum *patulum* Thunb. — Goldencup St. Johnswort
LEAVES: Opposite, simple, semi-evergreen to evergreen, 1 to 2 1/2″ long, ovate, ovate-oblong to lanceolate-oblong, obtuse and usually mucronulate, dark green above, glaucous beneath.

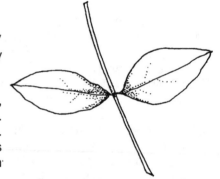

Hypericum patulum, (hī-per′i-kum pat′ū-lum), Goldencup St. Johnswort, grows to 3′ and is a semi-evergreen to evergreen spreading shrub. Flowers are golden yellow, 2″ diameter, July, solitary or in cymes. Quite close to *H. henryi* var. *henryi* which in some literature is listed as a variety of *H. patulum*. 'Variegata' with whitish veination is known. Japan. 1862. Zone 6 to 7.

ADDITIONAL NOTES: As previously mentioned there are numerous *Hypericum* species and to me they are universally attractive when well-grown. It is difficult to locate many in commerce. *Hypericum galioides* Lam., Bedstraw St. Johnswort, an evergreen species, with extremely narrow leaves; and *Hypericum olympicum* L., Olympic St. Johnswort, a procumbent, handsome gray-green leaved species, with large 1 1/2 to 2″ diameter bright yellow flowers, are definitely worthy of consideration. A selection of *H. galioides* called 'Brodie' grows 8 to 12′ high with lustrous foliage and 3/4″ diameter flowers. I turn around and find a species or cultivar that should be included. It is difficult to draw the *Hypericum* line. *Hypericum × inodorum* Mill. 'Elstead', a hybrid between *H. androsaemum* and *H. hircinum*, looks more like the former but is more compact and the fruits are orange-scarlet. Supposedly quite susceptible to a rust disease which weakens the plant. There is a golden-leaved form and suspect that 'Ysella' is this plant. 'Summergold' produces yellow foliage marbled with lime green. 'Gold Pansy' is also listed and appears to be a *H. androsaemum* selection with golden yellow flowers and red to black fruits, often all present at the same time. Also visible is *H. kouytchense* A. Lév., a 2 to 4′ high, semi-evergreen shrub with 2 1/2″ diameter golden yellow flowers. An old cultivar that I have seen at the Arnold Arboretum and other places is 'Sungold' which appears mired in synonymy with *H. kouytchense*. In many respects, it reminded of 'Hidcote', except not as large or deep yellow flowered. 'Sungold' is more cold hardy than 'Hidcote'. A new species in the Dirr garden is *H. lancasteri* N. Robson, already 3′ high and wide, with handsome blue-green 1 to 2″ long leaves and numerous 1 to 2″ diameter golden yellow flowers in June–July. The sepals are reddish in the bud stage. Has been semi-evergreen, withstood 4°F with no damage. Has deported itself more assertively than many hypericums in my garden. Time is the arbiter of excellence. Collected by the great British plantsman, Roy Lancaster. *Hypericum beanii* N. Robson, a 3 to 5′ semi-evergreen shrub with 2″ diameter golden yellow flowers was impressive as I viewed it in Europe. Several West Coast and southern nurseries offer the species. The hybrid 'Rowallane', from the garden with a similar name in Northern Ireland, is larger growing with 3 to 4″ diameter, cup-shaped, yellow flowers.

   An excellent review article, "Bowles of Beauty," by Roy Lancaster appeared in *The Garden* 122(8):566–571 (1997). The article includes most of the woody or semi-woody forms in cultivation. There are over 425 species of *Hypericum* comprising perennial and annual herbs, shrubs and trees. The

Lancaster article provides a wonderful base-line of garden information concerning this most taxonomically confused genus.

Additional *Hypericum* species that do not appear in the *Manual* but are included in the Lancaster article are: *H. acmosephalum, H. addingtonii, H. augustinii, H. beanii, H. bellum* subsp. *bellum, H. choisyanum, H. henryi, H. hircinum, H. hookerianum, H. × inodorum, H. lagarocladum, H. maclarenii, H. monogynum, H. pseudohenryi* (has performed admirably at the J.C. Raulston Arboretum), *H. stellatum, H. subsessile, H. tenicaule, H. uralum,* and *H. wilsonii*.

Iberis sempervirens L. — Candytuft
(ī-bē′ris sem-pĕr-vī′renz)

FAMILY: Brassicaceae

LEAVES: Alternate, simple, evergreen, linear-oblong, 1/2 to 2″ long, 1/8 to 3/16″ wide, obtuse, entire, dark green.

SIZE: 6 to 12″ high, spreading with time and forming handsome evergreen mats.

HARDINESS: Zone 4 to 8(9).

HABIT: Dwarf evergreen ground cover of sprawling habit.

RATE: Slow to medium; under good cultural conditions will fill an area reasonably fast.

TEXTURE: Fine in summer; possibly medium in winter as it looks a bit rough.

LEAF COLOR: Dark green and handsome.

FLOWERS: Perfect, white, borne in terminal 1 to 1 1/2″ diameter racemes which engulf the plant and give the appearance of a drift of snow; April–May and lasting for several weeks; spent flowers should be removed; flowers in late March in Athens, GA.

FRUIT: A silique, orbicular-elliptic, 1/4″ long, not showy.

CULTURE: Easy to transplant; I have moved seedlings and container plants with great success; prefer loose, loamy, average fertility soil; if fertility levels are excessive the plants become loose, leggy and open; full sun or partial shade; pH adaptable, prune heavily after flowering.

DISEASES AND INSECTS: Club root, damping off, downy and powdery mildews, and white rust.

LANDSCAPE VALUE: Excellent plant for early color; contrasts well with tulips and other bulbs; I have used it as drifts interplanted with woody shrubs; even after flowering it can look quite good if it is maintained as described under culture.

CULTIVARS:

    'Christmas Snow' ('Snowflake')—Flowers twice, early in season and again in fall, may grow 1′ high and 2′ wide, leaves dark green; flowers in 2″ diameter trusses.

    'Little Gem'—More dwarf than the type, only 6″ tall and quite hardy; leaves are smaller and finer in texture.

    'Purity'—Similar to 'Little Gem' in habit with large inflorescences.

    I counted 12 cultivars in one reference and after reading the descriptions reflected on whether it was one plant with 12 names.

PROPAGATION: Seed represents an easy method, sow as soon as mature; softwood cuttings root easily and I have used this method to reproduce seed grown plants which were especially floriferous.

NATIVE HABITAT: Southern Europe, western Asia. Introduced 1731.

Idesia polycarpa Maxim. — Igiri Tree
(ī-dē′zē-á pol-i-kär′pà)

FAMILY: Flacourtiaceae

LEAVES: Alternate, simple, ovate to oblong-ovate, 5 to 10″ long, 2/3's as wide, acuminate, cordate or subcordate, remotely crenate-serrate, deep green above, glaucous below, glabrous except in leaf axils; petiole—2 1/2 to 6″ long, with 1 to 3 obvious concave glands toward the middle, reddish particularly on upper surface.

BUDS: Terminal—1/4 to 1/3″ high, broadly dome-shaped with reddish brown scales, free at tips and narrowly pointed, glabrous; laterals —smaller, 1/16″ high, sit in a narrow notch on top of leaf scar.

STEM: Stout, dark brown with tinge of red, glabrous, numerous raised vertical lip-like orange-brown lenticels; leaf scar—broad crescent-shaped with three vascular bundle traces makes it resemble a giraffe face; strange odor to bruised stem; pith—solid, white, ample.

SIZE: 40 to 60′ high and as wide.
HARDINESS: Zone 6 to 9.
HABIT: In youth pyramidal, with age becoming rounded.
RATE: Fast.
TEXTURE: Coarse
BARK: Relatively smooth, grayish, almost grayish white, quite
    effective.
LEAF COLOR: Dark green, no appreciable fall color.
FLOWERS: Dioecious, yellow-green, apetalous, fragrant, in
    terminal panicles in June; male 5 to 6″ long, each flower
    1/3″ wide, sepals covered with brownish pubescence;
    female individual smaller but in a larger panicle, often to 8″.
FRUIT: Multiple seeded, pea-sized red berry, borne in 4 to 8″
    long pendulous panicles and swaying with the fall breezes;
    beautiful in fruit; unfortunately, it takes a male and female to
    guarantee fruit set and very few gardeners can afford the
    space necessary for the trees; have observed trees on
    November 20 at Brookgreen Gardens, Murrells Inlet, SC,
    with leaves and abundant fruit.
CULTURE: Transplant as a young container-grown specimen or
    balled-and-burlapped material; prefers loose, moist, well-
    drained soil and with proper fertility grows like a weed; full
    sun and frost protection as a young tree.
DISEASES AND INSECTS: None serious.
LANDSCAPE VALUE: Only for large areas where multiple trees can be grouped for success; beautiful in fruit
    and the tree provides a Catalpa-like texture, i.e., coarse; interesting about hardiness for in Boston (Arnold
    Arboretum) it is a stump sprout, in Brooklyn Botanic Garden a 60′ tree and in Washington, DC (U.S.
    National Arboretum) a rather handsome grove of fruiting 25 to 30′ high trees; two trees in the Georgia
    Botanical Garden are 25′ and as wide after 6 years, both are made up of 5 to 7 large stems and the bark
    has proven more stimulating than expected.
PROPAGATION: On many occasions I have raised seedlings by simply cleaning fruits and sowing cleaned
    seed; within 2 weeks germination was rampant; have also sown entire fruits and been successful; in
    October 1997, sowed cleaned seed and by November 25 seedlings were one inch high.
NATIVE HABITAT: Southern Japan, central and western China. Introduced 1864.

Ilex cornuta Lindl. & Paxt. — Chinese Holly
(ī′leks kôr-nū′tà)

FAMILY: Aquifoliaceae
LEAVES: Alternate, simple, evergreen, short-stalked, oblong-
    rectangular, 1 1/2 to 4″ long, 1 to 3″ wide with 3 strong
    almost equal spines at the broad apex and 1 or 2 spines
    on each side at the base, spines can vary from 5 to 9, or
    on older plants rounded at the base, lustrous dark green
    above, yellow-green below, leaves of old specimens show
    fewer spines, almost plastic in texture, extremely lethal to
    work around; petiole—1/6″ long.

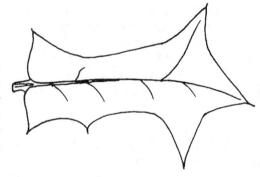

SIZE: 8 to 10′(15′) and perhaps to 25′, often wider than high at maturity.
HARDINESS: Zone 7 to 9, possibly 6 if protected.
HABIT: Bushy, dense rounded evergreen shrub, can be trained into a small tree.
TEXTURE: Medium to medium-coarse.
BARK: Stems and trunks become a lovely relatively smooth gray; some plants are grown as small trees and
    are limbed up to show off the bark.
FLOWERS: Small, dull white, 4-petaled, 1/4 to 1/3″ wide, male with 4 stamens, female with large green
    rounded ovary, produced in prodigious quantities in the axils of the leaves; male flowers have a sickenly
    sweet fragrance that is much more potent than the female's; late March–early April in Athens, GA; great

for bee pasture for the wonderful critters are buzzing about in droves savoring some of the season's first sweet nectar.

FRUIT: Variable, from bright red to almost blood-red at least on some plants I have observed, 1/4 to 1/3″ diameter, round, borne on 1/3 to 5/8″ long stalk, 4 pyrenes, abundant, persisting through winter, handsome, discoloring and falling in cold winters about February.

CULTURE: Transplant balled-and-burlapped or from a container; many *Ilex cornuta* types are container-grown; very adaptable, withstands drought; pH adaptable; extremely heat tolerant; an amazingly durable holly that displays tremendous heat and drought tolerance, has survived the worst droughts on record in the southeastern United States; a good parental species for introducing heat tolerance into the progeny; based on observations any hybrid ('Nellie R. Stevens', 'China Boy', 'China Girl', 'John T. Morris', 'Lydia Morris') with *I. cornuta* as one parent performs reasonably well in the heat; withstands considerable shade and still fruits respectably; tolerant of "chain saw" pruning; overgrown specimens have been cut back to 12 to 24″ of the ground in late winter and produced new shoots that covered the old trunk and stems by May–June; interesting study relating to flooding tolerance of selected *Ilex* taxa, *Landscape Plant News* 8(2):7–10 (1997), reported that 'Burfordii', 'Nellie R. Stevens', *I. cassine*, China Girl®, *I. glabra*, 'Winter Red', 'Warren Red', 'Stokes', 'Satyr Hill', and 'Convexa' survived 90% and above after 8 weeks of flooding; 'Blue Princess', *I. rugosa*, and *I. aquifolium* Sparkler™ survived 40, 15, and 6%, respectively.

DISEASES AND INSECTS: Scale can be a problem; many heavily fruited hollies need an application of nitrogen to green them up; numerous diseases, many related to nursery production of hollies and Lambe, *Proc. Intl. Plant Prop. Soc.* 29:536–544 (1979), presents an excellent overview; beyond the scope of this book to summarize but leaf spots, cankers, die-back, root rots and nematodes; these problems vary in severity with species and cultivars; my own ranking of resistant species and cultivars in the South (Zone 7 to 9) would start with *I. vomitoria*, *I. cornuta*, *I.* × *attenuata*, *I. opaca*, *I.* × *koehneana*, *I. latifolia*, *I. cassine*, *I.* × *meserveae* and *I. crenata*; lots of room to maneuver and add species but for the evergreen species this is a good attempt.

Ruter and Braman, *Landscape Plant News* 7(4):3–5 (1996), present ratings of holly resistance and susceptibility to two lined spittlebug. Two generations occur in Georgia (June, August–September). Spittlebugs feed (suck) on the leaves and stems and cause speckling and discoloration that leads to defoliation and death. I have observed *I. opaca* and *I.* × *attenuata* 'Foster's #2' with almost complete defoliation. In short, the study did not tell us (me) anything that was not already documented. *Ilex opaca*, *I. cassine* and their hybrids were most susceptible. *Ilex cornuta*, *I. vomitoria*, *I. verticillata*, *I. glabra* and a host of other taxa had none to slight damage.

Holly looper, *Thysanopyga intractata*, feeds on foliage of *I. aquifolium*, *I. crenata*, *I. cornuta*, *I. opaca*, and *I. vomitoria*.

LANDSCAPE VALUE: The species is seldom used in contemporary landscaping but the cultivars are abused to the point of boredom; the uses are numerous depending on the cultivar; certain situations warrant iron-clad, bullet-proof plants and *I. cornuta* and cultivars are the plants of choice.

CULTIVARS: Numerous selections of *I. cornuta* and the other holly species discussed in the *Manual*. I do not pretend or intend to know them. Most presented herein are in the trade or have crossed my observational path. A wonderful new reference, *Hollies* by Fred Galle, Timber Press (1997), is *the reference* to consult for the best in-depth information. Under *I. cornuta* Fred described 73 cultivars and listed another 15 without complete descriptions.

'Anicet Delcambre'—Two to 2 1/2″ long, narrow, slightly twisted lustrous dark green leaves and a single terminal spine, female, have seen abundant fruit on this clone, same as 'Needlepoint' and 'Willowleaf'.

'Autumn Fire'—Early maturing, red fruits, often by early September in Raleigh, NC area, grown from seed collected in Korea, J.C. Raulston Arboretum introduction.

'Avery Island'—Large, 1/4″ diameter, yellow fruits and lustrous dark green foliage, leaves entire to 7-spined.

Berries Jubilee™—Medium-sized, 6 to 10′ high form with 2 to 3″ long, squarish-rectangular leaves and large red fruit clusters inside the foliage canopy.

'Burfordii'—Considered a dense rounded shrub about 10′ in height but when left unchecked it makes a large, rather dense tree or shrub 20 to 25′ high; the lustrous dark green, 2 to 3″ long leaves usually have a single terminal spine but on occasion two lateral spines may develop; the fruit set is heavy and will occur without pollination (parthenocarpically); plants at Callaway Gardens were fully 20′ high and, in fruit, are beautiful; it is not a bad idea to prune away the lower branches thus making a small tree; have seen it killed to the ground at Bernheim Arboretum when temperatures reached −18°F; easily rooted; one of the most popular *I. cornuta*

forms; discovered in the early 1900's in West View Cemetery, Atlanta, GA, named after Thomas H. Burford, Superintendent; occurred as a branch sport on *I. cornuta* seedling received from U.S. Department of Agriculture.

'Cajun Gold'—A large shrub on the order of 'Burfordii' with gold-margined leaves, red fruits; chimera of 'Burfordii'.

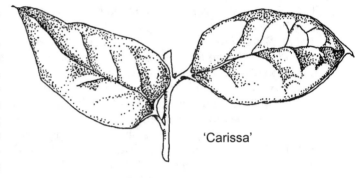

'Carissa'

'Carissa'—Leaves are alternate, simple, evergreen, ovate, 2 to 3″ long, 1 to 1 1/2″ wide, single terminal spine, entire, cuneate or slightly rounded, leathery to the point of plasticity, transparent rim around margin, glabrous, lustrous, waxy dark green above, flat olive green beneath; petiole—1/4″ long; some leaves develop a bullate or puckered condition; dense, dwarf form 3 to 4′ high and 4 to 6′ wide at maturity; it is a branch sport of 'Rotunda' and will revert to the 'Rotunda' form on occasion; older plants are more prone to this than young ones; I have not seen it fruit; definitely less cold hardy than 'Dwarf Burford'.

'Clarendon Bat Wing'—6′ high, 4′ wide, at 15 to 20 years of age, upright-spreading lax habit, variable leaf shape to 3″ long and wide, red, 2/5″ diameter globose fruits, Zone 7, see *Holly Soc. J.* 10:18–21 (1992).

'D' Or'—A yellow-fruited form that is quite similar to 'Burfordii', leaves lustrous dark green and with only a terminal spine; as I understand the origin it was found as a branch sport on the normal 'Burfordii' in Columbus, GA; quite a handsome plant; Callaway Gardens had some nice specimens; first observed in 1954 by Fred Galle.

'Dazzler'—Upright, somewhat irregular selection that grows to 10′ and more; heavy-fruiting, rich red, 1/2″ diameter fruits, 5-spined leaf; Dr. John Pair, Horticulture Research Center, Wichita, KS, noted it was the most fruitful of *I. cornuta* types in his tests.

'Dwarf Burford' ('Burfordii Nana', 'Burfordii Compacta')—Compact form, 5 to 6′(8′) high, with smaller and usually single-spined, 1 1/2 to 2″ long, 3/4 to 1″ wide leaves, does not fruit as heavily as Burford, fruits smaller and darker red, leaves show a blistered or bullate condition; much faster growing than given credit, there is an 18′ high plant on the Georgia campus; also, where open-grown in full sun becomes broader than high and looks like a giant puff ball mushroom; preferable to 'Burfordii' for small landscapes and is easily maintained with the proper pruning equipment; the new emerging bright green leaves are particularly outstanding when framed by the lustrous dark green mature leaves; one of the best *I. cornuta* selections for "no brainer" landscapes.

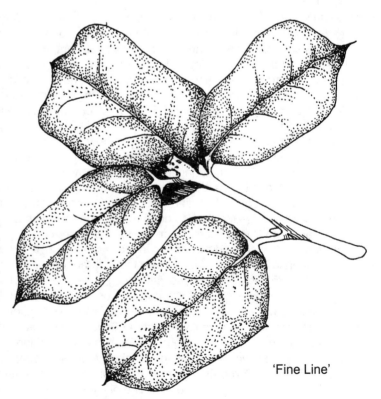

'Fine Line'

'E.A. McIlhenny'—Shield-shaped, mostly flat, 5-spined, up to 3″ long leaves and scarlet, 3/8″ diameter fruits.

'Fine Line' ('Fineline')—Upright bushy pyramidal-conical form with lustrous dark green, 1 1/2 to 2 1/2″ long leaves outlined with yellow-green, translucent rim, 1/4″ diameter red fruits, small plants appear handsome and southern growers are starting to produce significant numbers, mother plant was 12′ high and 5′ wide, popularized by Magnolia Gardens and Nursery, Chinchula, AL.

'Gable #76'—Exceptional tight compact pyramidal habit, glossy dark green leaves, male, withstood -12°F without damage, 6' in 10 years.

'Grandview'—Dense compact bushy form with smaller leaves than the species, male, good pollinator.

'Hody Wilson'—Produces abundant, large, vivid red fruits.

'Ira S. Nelson'—Large lustrous green leaves, bright red fruits.

'Jungle Gardens'—Excellent nearly flat dark green leaves with variable spines from 1 to 7, scarlet, 1/4" diameter fruits.

'Lib's Favorite'—*I. cornuta* × *I. latifolia*, handsome dark green foliage, large red fruits, that persist into winter, Tom Dodd, Jr. introduction.

'Lottie Moon'—Compact form intermediate between 'Burfordii' and 'Rotunda', 1 1/2 to 2" long, 2 marginal apical or 2 basal spines, deep red, 1/4" diameter fruits.

'Merry Berry'—Large bright red fruits in profusion, 5-spined leaf.

'Needlepoint'—The same as 'Anicet Delcambre'; this is a good fruiter, vivid red, 1/4" diameter, with a more delicate leaf than 'Burfordii' types; excellent upright slightly bulbous conical form in youth, becoming broader with age; have observed a 15' high, 10' wide specimen; becoming more popular in Southeast; one of the best for screening, massing, grouping.

'O. Spring'—Irregular, upright form with cream-yellow colored leaves, new foliage with a purple tinge, does best in partial shade, male, leaf shape like the species, grows 10' high.

'Rotunda'—A compact, dense, mounded form with (5)7-spined, 1 1/2 to 3 1/2" long leaves that make an impenetrable thicket; it grows 3 to 4' high and 6 to 8' across; widely used in South; a female clone and I have observed occasional fruit set; very tough, durable plant, akin to a living pin cushion; selected in 1930's by E.A. McIlhenny, Avery Island, LA.

'Rotunda'

'September Beauty'—Early coloring red fruit, from J.C. Raulston Arboretum, Raleigh, NC.

'Shangri La'—Fast-growing female clone with vermillion red, 1/2" diameter fruit that matures in June and remains until the following March.

'Slacks'—A large leaf form.

'Sunrise'—Leaves greenish yellow near tips, often blotchy, 1 1/2 to 2" long, akin to 'Burfordii' leaf, 1/4" diameter deep red fruit; see *Holly Society Journal* 9:15 (1991).

'Tall Stallion'—Male tree type for pollination, 25' by 15', introduced by Ken Durio, Louisiana Nursery.

PROPAGATION: In general there are a lot of different stories about holly seed germination. Take the following for its net worth and then heed what Mr. Gene Eisenbeiss, U.S. National Arboretum, has to say about germinating seeds. In general, *Ilex* seeds exhibit a deep dormancy that is caused partly by the endocarp surrounding the seed coat and partly to conditions in the embryo. According to J. Bon Hartline, an Illinois holly grower, the best way to handle holly seed is as follows. The fruits should be collected in fall, the pulp crushed and washed away. Seeds which float should be discarded, since they are usually not viable. Seeds of *I. crenata*, *I. vomitoria*, *I. glabra*, and of some *I. opaca* of southern origin will germinate in a very short time after being properly handled. *Ilex aquifolium*, *I. cornuta*, *I. verticillata*, *I. serrata*, *I. decidua*, and most *I. opaca* seeds require a longer period—up to 18 months before all seeds germinate. Patience is probably the necessary ingredient in holly seed propagation for it is the length of time rather than the cold treatment which aids germination. I visited Gene Eisenbeiss at the U.S. National Arboretum and asked him about the secrets of success. He showed me his operation and basically it consists of patience. The nutlets (pyrenes) are removed from the mealy part of the fruit and sown in a suitable medium, placed in a plastic bag; as I remember in a room where temperature is about 70 to 75°F. When the seeds start to germinate they are moved to the greenhouse. Cuttings of most evergreen types root about anytime of year. There are, no doubt, differences among species and cultivars but I have had excellent success with 1000 to 3000 ppm IBA-quick dip, peat:perlite, mist. Bottom heat is often helpful. Thousands of hollies have been rooted in our research work. For most species and cultivars, we take the cuttings when the first flush of growth has hardened and treat with a rooting compound like IBA. We have used 1000 to 5000 ppm KIBA depending on taxon. Rooting of the deciduous types is discussed under *Ilex verticillata*. June, July, August and September cuttings rooted in extremely high percentages.

NATIVE HABITAT: Eastern China, Korea. Introduced 1846.

Ilex crenata Thunb. — Japanese Holly, also called Box-leaved Holly
(ī'leks krē-nā'tà)

LEAVES: Alternate, simple, evergreen, crowded, short-stalked, elliptic or obovate to oblong-lanceolate, 1/2 to 1 1/4″ long, 1/4 to 5/8″ wide, acute, cuneate or broad-cuneate, crenate-serrulate or serrulate, with 6 to 10 teeth per margin, dull flat to lustrous dark green above, glabrous, of hard texture, dotted beneath with blackish pellucid glands; petiole—short, 1/16 to 1/8″ long.

STEM: Normally green on current season's growth turning gray-green to gray-brown in 2nd or 3rd year, often densely pubescent on young stems.

GROWTH HABIT: Except for the species, usually a much-branched shrub of dense, rigid, compact habit.

SIZE: Very difficult to ascertain from the literature the actual size of the species, listed as reaching 20′ by various authorities; in actuality a shrub 5 to 10′ high with a similar or greater spread.

HARDINESS: Zone 5 to 6 depending on cultivar to 8, does not do as well in the deep South as in Zone 5 to 7.

HABIT: Usually a dense, multi-branched evergreen shrub of rounded or broad rounded outline; apparently quite variable in the wild.

RATE: Slow.

TEXTURE: Medium-fine in all seasons.

LEAF COLOR: Lustrous dark green in summer and winter, foliage color dependent on cultivar with some flat green.

FLOWERS: Dioecious, unisexual, dull greenish white, with 4-petals, staminate in 3- to 7-flowered cymes; pistillate solitary (rarely 2- to 3-flowered cymes) in leaf-axils of current season's growth, May–June, not at all showy but if one is interested in determining the sex of any particular holly, inspection of the flowers is the only logical way.

FRUIT: Berry-like black drupe, globose, 1/4″(1/3″) diameter, containing 4 pyrenes, September–October, and persistent into spring in Zone 7b, borne under the foliage and, therefore, somewhat inconspicuous, only female plants have fruits.

CULTURE: Transplants readily balled-and-burlapped or from a container; most plants are container-grown; prefers light, moist, well-drained, slightly acid soils; sun or shade adaptable; seems to do well in city gardens; prune after new growth hardens off; will withstand severe pruning; have seen chlorosis in high pH soils.

DISEASES AND INSECTS: Spider mites can be serious, nematodes in South and black knot (*Thielaviopsis basicola*) disease; *I. crenata* is quite susceptible to *Thielaviopsis*.

LANDSCAPE VALUE: Excellent for textural differences in foundation plantings, hedges, and masses; hedges in Japan have been maintained for so long that they can be walked on; very handsome and worthwhile landscape plant; often overused and abused; used in masses, along walks and on gradual slopes on virtually every college campus; often massacred with a pruning shears to produce "handsome" pieces of geometric sculpture; actually nicer if left to their own genetic control; perhaps remove an odd branch here or there for shaping, but otherwise stand back and enjoy.

CULTIVARS: The Japanese Holly is prone to cultivarism and over the centuries numerous forms have been selected. There are at least 60 cultivars being offered by the trade. Their identification is fraught with difficulty and a reasonable list is presented here. A recent publication, *International Checklist of Cultivated Ilex. Part 2. Ilex crenata* by T.R. Dudley and G.K. Eisenbeiss, USDA-ARS, U.S. National Arboretum Contribution No. 6 (1992), provides species information as well as a checklist of cultivars with 170 legitimate named clones, 266 illegitimate or controversial. Also, see Galle, *Hollies* (1997), for more intense descriptions. Galle reported that more than 500 cultivars were introduced.

'Alan Seay'—Broad upright pyramidal form with lustrous dark green leaves similar in shape to 'Microphylla', holds good color during the winter; withstood -23°F with minimal damage, introduced about 1970.

'Angelica'—Low-spreading form with long narrow leaves, quite hardy.

'Beehive'—Dense, compact mounded form, slightly wider than high, 3 to 4′ by 5 to 6′, excellent lustrous dark green foliage, 1/2″ long, 1/4″ wide, good hardiness, male; selected by Dr. Elwin Orton, Rutgers from 21,000 seedlings; originated as a cross of 'Convexa' × 'Stokes'; in Georgia trials the leaves are light olive green, next to Dr. Orton's 'Jersey Pinnacle' in the same test row, it is like day ('Beehive') and night as far as lustrous dark green foliage color; cross-checking other references I read the same dark green leaf description; having seen the plant at Rutgers and growing it in Georgia, the color is not dark green.

Bennett Hybrid Group—I see 'Bennett's Compact' (see 'Compacta') in the trade, it is 3 to 4' high, 4 to 5' wide, leathery lustrous dark green, 3/5 to 1" long leaves and purplish stemmed; I suspect there are multiple clones residing under the above name. Also, Galle mentioned the work by E.L. Bennett, Greenbriar Farms, who grew approximately 250,000 seedlings in 1946–47, with the winter of 1947–48 reducing the number to 3000 to 4000. Fifty seedlings were selected with 20 named.

'Black Beauty'—Selected by Girard Nursery, Geneva, OH, for lustrous dark green foliage, compact habit, and extreme hardiness, Zone 5, grew this in our Illinois garden.

'Border Gem'—Dense, low-growing type with lustrous dark green, 1/2" long foliage and good hardiness, Zone 5b, has survived winters of −8°F in Illinois and looked fantastic, 'Hetzii', on the other hand, was winter killed at this temperature; male.

'Buxifolia'—A compact pyramidal form that grows to 15' in height; the leaves are oblong-lanceolate; a 10-year-old plant may be 6 to 8'.

'Cherokee'—Columnar form (upright pyramidal) with small rounded leaves, grows to 10', male, Zone 5.

'Chesapeake'—Dense, 6 to 7', upright pyramidal form with lustrous dark green, convex, 1/2 to 3/4" long leaves, plant in Dirr garden has prospered, good form for hedging.

'Compacta'—Compact, globose outline to 6'; leaves lustrous dark green, obovate, flat, 3/4" long; young stems are purple; little pruning is required to produce a compact, heavy plant; over the years I have seen a number of 'Compacta' forms and they are not all the same; probably a catch-all term, see Bennett Hybrid Group.

'Convexa'—One of the hardiest forms, 40-year-old plant somewhat vase-shaped in habit but extremely dense is 9' tall and 24' wide, takes pruning for hedging; leaves 1/2" long, convex above, concave beneath, somewhat bullate; of Japanese origin, Zone 5; a female clone that is often heavy with black fruits; severely injured at −20°F; susceptible to iron and nitrogen deficiency and spider mites; many seedling selections have been derived from this clone.

'Dwarf Pagoda'—Selected by Dr. Orton from his holly breeding program at Rutgers University in 1972; female with tiny leaves 5/16 to 7/16" long by 1/4" wide, short internodes, branching irregular; result is an extremely heavy foliage effect and artistic form; grows 2" per year, hardy to 0°F, from seedling population of 'Mariesii' × 'John Nosal', have seen 2 to 3' high plants.

'Elfin'—Dwarf, congested, 12" by 20" in 12 years, small dark green leaves, male, useful for rock garden, bonsai and other minutia; correct name is 'Delaware Diamond'.

'Excelsa'—Vigorous form to 12' with narrow glossy dark green leaves, considered hardy to Zone 5a.

'Fastigiata'—A narrow fastigiate form with thick, slightly convex, dark green leaves, good choice as an accent plant, E.L. Bennett introduction, Greenbriar Farms, VA; more than one clone with this name.

'Foster No. 1'—A cold hardy form that survived −23°F with minimal injury, minimal damage at −24°F in 1994, low compact-spreading outline, small flat leaves.

'Geisha'—Small shrub with spreading habit, 2 1/2' high and wide in 10 years, probably the smallest leaves of any *I. crenata* selection, leaves lustrous dark green, fruits yellow and contrast nicely with the foliage.

'Glass'—Male clone of *Ilex crenata* 'Microphylla' with compact upright habit and slightly smaller (1/2" long), dark green leaves; frozen to ground after exposure to −20°F.

'Glory'—Small compact globe form with 1/4 to 4/5" long, 1/8 to 3/8" wide, flat lustrous dark green leaves, male, after 12 growing seasons at Bernheim Arboretum, Clermont, KY, the plant was over 5' high and about 8' wide; the most impressive trait is cold hardiness, Flint and Hubbuch, *Amer. Nurseryman* 169(3):154 (1989), reported 'Glory' survived −23°F with minimal injury; in September 1994, Mike Hayman, Buddy Hubbuch and I surveyed these same plants that had been subjected to −24°F in January, 1994; there was no shoot kill and this plant continues to rate as the most cold hardy taxon; interestingly 'Hetzii' growing close by was not injured while in previous winters it was severely damaged at higher temperatures.

'Golden Gem'—Leaves golden, habit low and spreading, the color is best developed in sunny location, female, similar to 'Convexa'.

'Green Dragon'—Male clone, otherwise similar to 'Dwarf Pagoda'.

'Green Island'—Loose and open shrub form, usually growing twice as broad as tall; 11-year-old plant is 3' by 6', matures less than 5', lustrous medium green foliage, male, Zone 5

'Green Lustre' ('Green Luster')—Similar to above with leaves darker and more lustrous; injured by −20°F; good-looking foliage; grows about twice as wide as tall, somewhat flat-topped, female, seedling of 'Stokes'.

'Green Splendor'—Broad pyramidal form with lustrous leaves that are slightly larger than 'Microphylla'; survived winters of 1977–78 and 83–84 with limited leaf damage.

'Helleri'—Dwarf, mounded, compact form; 26-year-old plant is 4′ by 5′ with flat leaves about 1/2″ long, Zone 5b; supposedly a female but I have seen neither flowers nor fruits; leaves less lustrous than most; good form, does well in Zone 7b, one of the most widely planted cultivars, many better forms now available but 'Helleri' has name recognition; introduced in late 1930's; more than one 'Helleri' in trade; 'Helleri Dwarf Golden' (correctly 'Golden Helleri') is a low-spreading, 1′ by 2 to 3′, bright gold foliage form found by Centerton Nursery, New Jersey, needs full sun and winter wind protection for best expression of color; have also noticed reference to 'Golden Heller' from Lancaster Farms.

'Hetzii'—Larger form of 'Convexa' with bigger (1/2 to 1″ long) convex leaves of lustrous dark green, grows 6 to 8′ and several plants on the Georgia campus are easily 10′, appears quite adaptable to Zone 7b conditions, not as cold hardy as 'Convexa', a female and the fruits are larger than those of 'Convexa'; cold hardiness evaluations vary considerably; hybrid of 'Convexa' × 'Rotundifolia', selected about 1940, named by C. Hetz, Fairview Nursery; Zone 5b.

'High Light' ('Highlight')—Branch sport from 'Microphylla' with 1″ by 3/8″ wide leaves, 15-year-old plant 13′ by 11′, discovered by W.F. Kosar around 1956, extremely lustrous dark green leaves, more difficult to propagate than the other forms.

'Highlander'—Tall, pyramidal, rather loose form that grows to 6′ and greater, dark green leaves; interestingly this cultivar has shown good cold tolerance; has performed well at Bernheim Arboretum and at Wichita, KS, male, originated in a block of 'Convexa' seedlings, introduced in 1960's.

'Hoogendorn'—Lost among the 'Compacta' grex in previous editions but definitely worthy of distinction, low, dense, compact, wider than tall, 2 to 2 1/2′ high, excellent dark green foliage, 3/4 to 1″ long, leaves are flat, more handsome than 'Helleri', male, reasonably common in northeastern nurseries, becoming more popular in South, from Hoogendorn Nursery, RI, named by Tom Dodd, Jr.

'Howard'—Spreading form maturing at about 6′ high, the obovate-oblong, dark green leaves are slightly convex, male, Bennett Hybrid Group.

'Imperial'—Tight upright habit, good vigor and hardiness, glossy deep green foliage, 8′ high, female, introduced by Imperial Nursery.

'Ivory Tower'—Broad erect outline, fast-growing, with greenish yellow to yellowish white fruits.

'Jersey Pinnacle'—Dense, compact, upright in habit, 6′ by 4′, but not overly formal, glossy dark green, about 1″ long leaves, male, might serve as a standard upright type like 'Helleri' does for spreading, Orton introduction, result of a cross between 'Green Lustre' × 'John Nosal' made in 1974, have grown in our Georgia test plots, handsome selection.

'Kingsville Green Cushion'—Dense, low-growing form, small, very dark green leaves, male, 10-year-old plant is 8″ by 32″.

'Lemon Gem'—Lemon new growth, fading to lime green on a dwarf mounded plant.

'Major'—Similar to 'Rotundifolia', flat dark green, 1/2 to 1 1/2″ long leaves, grows thicker without extensive pruning, female, more than one clone.

'Mariesii'—Stiffly erect female clone with one or several upright stems and small, 1/8 to 5/8″ long and wide, rounded leaves.

'Maxwell'—Mounded habit and small leaves reminiscent of 'Microphylla', supposedly more gray-green than dark green, similar to 'Convexa' but faster growing, Bennett Hybrid Group.

'Microphylla' (f. *microphylla*)—Leaves smaller than the species, upright shrub or small tree in habit, confused taxonomic entity.

'Midas Touch'—Variegated male form with yellow green foliage, a branch sport of a seedling from a 1968 cross of a yellow-fruited clone × *I. crenata* (male); most leaves exhibit yellow sectors and light green areas in addition to normal pigmentation, occasional green shoots develop that must be pruned out; original plant 2 1/2′ high and 2 3/4′ wide; Orton introduction.

'Noble Upright'—Somewhat pyramidal form with excellent cold hardiness, survived -23°F with minimal injury, 1/2 to 1″ long, dark green leaves, male.

'Northern Beauty'—Similar to 'Hetzii' but more compact and hardy, good lustrous dark green foliage, male.

'Oconee River'—Lustrous dark green convex leaf form, rounded habit, dark purple winter stem color, male.

'Petite Pointe'—Upright growth habit, somewhat pyramidal, good in South, difficult to propagate, female.

'Piccolo'—Miniature cushion, good bonsai subject, female, grows about 1″ per year.

'Recurvifolia'—Spreading growth habit, elongated flat leaf and light green foliage, male, probably confused in the trade.

'Repandens'—Spreading form of compact habit with narrow flat lustrous dark green leaves; quite handsome, usually 2 to 3′ high and 4 to 6′ wide, male, originated about 1940.

'Rocky Creek'—Upright, 6 to 8′ high by 3 to 4′ wide, foliage similar but smaller than 'Hetzii', habit is twisted and contorted, mutation of 'Bennett's Compact'.

'Rotundifolia'—A somewhat confusing cultivar, but the ones I have seen have large, 1/2 to 1″ long leaves, 11 to 16 teeth per margin, and tend to grow upright-rounded to about 8 to 12′; called Bigleaf Japanese Holly; completely defoliated after exposure to -18°F; a male form; not accepted as a valid name by Dudley and Eisenbeiss, more than one clone with this name, 1 1/2 pages in their checklist are devoted to telling the reader why 'Rotundifolia' is an illegitimate name.

'Schworbel's Upright'—Pyramidal form, 6 to 8′ high, glossy green flat leaf, described as extremely hardy; also listed is 'Schworbel's Compacta' a mid-sized spreading form with excellent hardiness, small, light green, slightly convex leaves, female, both derived from open-pollinated seed of 'Convexa' × 'Microphylla'.

'Sentinel'—Tall upright form with glossy, convex foliage; male, have seen it listed as heavy fruiting, good cold hardiness, 7′ by 5′ in 30 years.

'Sky Pencil' (also trademarked in Canada as Sky Sentry™)—I thought I would hate this rather slender, densely branched, telephone pole oriented selection, lustrous dark green leaves, slightly convex to 1 3/8″ long, 4/5″ wide, grows 6 to 8′ high, female, Bonnie and I utilized it in a large container where it makes a pleasant formal appearance especially when underplanted with white impatiens, introduced into the United States in 1985 by U.S. National Arboretum, becoming more popular in the trade.

'Snowflake'—White- and green-variegated leaf, over one-half of the leaf is white.

'Soft Touch'—Dense, compact, 2′ by 3′, lustrous dark green, 3/4 to 1″ long, 5/16 to 3/8″ wide leaves with silver midvein, flexible branches and soft foliage, has become popular in South, female, pliable branches, will serve as a 'Helleri' substitute, surfaced in 1980's, from Magnolia Garden and Nursery, Chinchula, AL.

'Steeds'—Lustrous dark green flat leaves, upright pyramidal habit, might be a good choice for hedging.

'Stokes'—Compact in habit; low, dense rounded habit, glossy leaves; no injury after exposure to -18°F, male.

'Tiny Tim' (correctly 'Pride's Tiny')—A low-spreading form to 3′, similar to 'Helleri' but supposedly more hardy, female, 1/2 to 11/16″ long leaves.

'Variegata'—Leaves spotted or blotched with yellow, several clones included here.

'Wayne'—Low-growing, spreading form similar to 'Helleri'; 3′ by 6′ and more, female, dark green, 1/2″ long leaves.

'William Jackson'—Horizontally branched form, twice as wide as tall, vigorous, 3′ by 5′, male.

'Xanthocarpa'—Catch all to describe yellow-fruited forms, have seen color descriptions from pale lime green, creamy yellow ('Watanabe') to yellow ('Xanthocarpa'); 'Watanabe' is listed as growing to 10′, Galle treats as Watanabeana Group.

PROPAGATION: See under *I. cornuta*.

NATIVE HABITAT: Japan, Korea, Fujian Province, China, Kuril, Sakhalin Islands, Taiwan, Philippines, and the Himalayas. Introduced into Russia from Japan in 1864. Into the United States by C.S. Sargent, Arnold Arboretum, in 1898.

Ilex glabra (L.) A. Gray — Inkberry
(ī′leks glā′brà)

LEAVES: Alternate, simple, evergreen, obovate to ob-lanceolate, 3/4 to 2″ long, 1/3 to 5/8″(3/4″) wide, acute or obtusish, cuneate, with few obtuse teeth near apex or entire, dark green and often lustrous above, lighter beneath, glabrous, leaves are very thin compared to *I. crenata* forms with which it is often confused; petiole—1/8 to 1/4″ long.

STEM: Slender, green, powdery, pubescent at first, finally glabrous, lenticels roundish with vertical slits, normally holds green color longer than *I. crenata* types.

SIZE: 6 to 8′ in height by 8 to 10′ in spread; however, variable depending on growing conditions.

HARDINESS: Zone (4)5 to 9(10); more hardy than *I. crenata* but leaves will burn or discolor in severe winters (-15 to -20°F).

HABIT: Upright, much-branched, erect-rounded evergreen shrub, somewhat open with age and often losing the lower leaves; tends to sucker and form colonies.

RATE: Slow, fast from sucker shoots.

TEXTURE: Medium in all seasons.

LEAF COLOR: Dark green and often lustrous in summer, sometimes becoming light yellow-green in summer, have observed severe foliage burn in Midwest after −20°F temperatures.

FLOWERS: Similar to *I. crenata*; male borne 3 or more together on a slender stalk, female solitary, each with 6(8) creamy petals, flowers open late, usually late May in Athens, major nectar source for bees, producing a light clear honey.

FRUIT: Berry-like, black drupe, 1/4″(1/6 to 1/3″) diameter, with 5 to 7 pyrenes, September through May of the following year, often hidden by the foliage but usually more showy than *I. crenata* fruits, often purplish red changing to black.

CULTURE: Somewhat similar to *I. crenata* except prefers moist, acid soils and in the wild is common in swamps where it forms large colonies; withstands heavy pruning quite well and renewal of old plants is suggested; avoid extremely high pH soils, quite shade tolerant, best in full sun with ample root moisture; now universally available in containers and readily transplanted from same; red mites are problematic in South, particularly with warm days of late winter, "critters" can cause partial defoliation, southern growers should be vigilant, have not noticed problem in North.

DISEASES AND INSECTS: Seems to be quite free of problems, have observed leaf spot.

LANDSCAPE VALUE: Excellent (especially the cultivars) for foundation, hedges, masses, accent plant; always one of my favorite native plants that has taken a back seat to *I. crenata*; over the past 8 years, I assembled germplasm encompassing wild-collected and cultivated material, with over 20 taxa in the collection the differences become obvious; from a commercial standpoint the best forms must have dark green foliage that does not discolor significantly in winter, reasonably compact habit, and not drop the lower leaves early in the production or landscape phases; most fail on the later account; 'Nigra', 'Ivory Queen', Nordic®, 'Nova Scotia', and 'UGA' have maintained dense foliage to the ground; 'Nigra' has proven the best in our Georgia trials at Athens and Tifton; see Dirr and Alexander, *Arnoldia* 51(2):16–22 (1991), for additional information; I have observed many straggly, open seedlings that have minimal use in contemporary landscapes, however, a seedling population in a naturalized planting by the University of Georgia's Ecology building provides pause for reflection; what if a selection (selections) with the natural upright-suckering habit and heavy foliage complement was targeted and propagated; several ~5-year-old plants are 8′ high with handsome foliage and screening or massing potential; perhaps we (me) need to move outside the box and think about *I. glabra* as more than simply a replacement for *I. crenata* 'Helleri' and *I. vomitoria* 'Schillings'.

CULTIVARS:

'Alba'—Ivory white fruit, glossy deep green foliage, suspect a rename and probably belongs under f. *leucocarpa*.

'Bronze'—According to Hume (1953), this form has closely spaced, coriaceous, bright green leaves, 1 to 1.5″ long, 1/3 to 1/2″ wide, that assume a pleasing bronze color in winter, glossy black globose fruits are produced abundantly on compact plants, 5 to 6′ tall, selected by Elizabeth C. White of Whitesbog, NJ, no idea whether this cultivar remains in cultivation.

'Compacta'—A dwarf, female clone with tighter branching and foliage than the species; introduced by Princeton Nursery; found in a group of seedlings; grows 4 to 6′ high, will become leggy at base, survived −24°F. Notable for its compact, oval-rounded habit, fine-textured branches, dark green leaves, 1 1/4 to 1 1/2″ long, 1/3″ wide, lustrous, jet black fruits that persist through the winter, matures between 5 to 6′ tall, have encountered a 10′ tall and 15′ wide plant on Swarthmore campus. So much for plants reading their press releases! This form, like the species, becomes leggy at the base and loses a portion of the lower foliage, but if pruned in a timely and artistic manner, it will remain a handsome plant. The original plant grows next to the Princeton Nursery office and was described by William Flemer III in recent correspondence:

> The Princeton clone of *Ilex glabra* 'Compacta' was selected in 1937 by William Flemer II from a block of seedlings on our nursery. These seedlings came from seed collected in the New Jersey pine barrens near Whiting, New Jersey. The parent plant was planted near the nursery office for further observation. It proved to be of interest as a compact, very hardy, broadleaf evergreen shrub and was first listed for sale in the Princeton Nursery's wholesale price list for the fall of 1948. Some plants may have been sold a couple of seasons earlier than this, but no record of such sales survives. It has been

successfully grown in northern Vermont and Maine. It has also been shown to be somewhat more resistant to winter feeding of deer than regular seedling-grown *Ilex glabra*, as well as being much more resistant than *Ilex crenata* plants. However, it is by no means totally immune to deer damage in areas with a very high deer population.

More than one clone is included under 'Compacta'. Ideally the Princeton form should be called 'Princeton Compact'.

'Cape Cod'—Observed a 8 to 10′ high seedling in a large planting in Eastham, MA; plant was full to the ground with lustrous dark green foliage closely spaced along the stems, female, two males were collected in the area but both were inferior to female, am currently observing all in our tests.

'Densa'—Develops an oval-rounded uniform outline with upright branches, leathery dark green leaves, 1 1/2″ long, 1/2″ wide, sparse fruit set observed on Arnold Arboretum plants, 8 to 10′ high, becomes leggy with age.

'Dilatush'—Exceedingly large lustrous dark green leaf form collected in the New Jersey Pine Barrens by Tom Dilatush, Robbinsville, NJ, quite vigorous in our trials but open and rank, leaves somewhat concave.

'Dodd Compact'—Upright form with small and densely set leaves, has become quite leggy at an early age (3 years) in Georgia trials, plant now 4 1/2′ high.

'Georgia Wine'—Lustrous dark green, 1 1/2″ long by 3/4″ wide leaves, develop burgundy winter foliage coloration, female, produces abundant fruit, parent colony ranges from 2 1/2 to 3 1/4′ tall and 6 to 7′ wide, discovered by Mr. Bill Craven, Twisted Oaks Nursery, Waynesboro, GA, have tested the plant and it is somewhat leggy and open, winter coloration is variable.

'Green Billow'—Branch sport of 'Nigra' discovered by Mark Griffith, Griffith Propagation Nursery, Watkinsville, GA; smaller in all aspects, probably no more than 12 to 18″ high, leaves about 1/3 the size of 'Nigra', billowy growth habit, will make a handsome mass or ground cover, patent pending.

'Hawksridge'—Reasonably compact lustrous dark green leaf form, has looked good in our trials, still not the best in terms of compactness, from Hawksridge Farms, Inc., Hickory, NC.

f. *leucocarpa* ('Leucocarpa') F.W. Woods—White-fruited form, distinctly broad-rounded, lustrous medium to dark green foliage, 1 3/4″ long by 1/2″ wide, a plant at Georgia's Experiment Station in Griffin is 8′ tall by 12′ wide, displays good cold tolerance, discovered by Frank W. Woods in Jackson County, FL in 1955, distributed by the USDA as #275847 and the U.S. National Arboretum as #14278, cultivated at the Arnold Arboretum since 1961.

f. *leucocarpa* 'Ivory Queen'—Fruit ivory white with a black dot at the apex due to stylar scar, leaves are 2″ long by 1/2″ wide, originally considered same as f. *leucocarpa*, but they are distinct, 'Ivory Queen' has leaves that are more leathery, darker green, and more densely set, discovered by C.R. Wolf of New Jersey Silica Sand Co., Millville, NJ from a branch sport, grows 6 to 8′ high and wide, relatively dense in youth, opening with time.

'Nigra'—Although this selection is described as having purple foliage in winter, this is not the case on the specimen of 'Nigra' at the Arnold Arboretum. Indeed, its foliage color is a lustrous dark green, and the plants, relatively compact, do not appear to be as leggy as other clones. Wayne Mezitt of Weston Nurseries mentioned that 'Nigra' was not as cold hardy as 'Compacta' or 'Viridis'. The leaves are 1 1/4 to 1 1/2″ long by 1/3 to 3/4″ wide. In Georgia trials, this has surfaced as the best clone because of compact growth habit, increased lower leaf retention, thick, lustrous dark green leaves, female.

Nordic® ('Chamzin')—Compact rounded form with lustrous deep green leaves, grows 3 to 4′(5′) by 3 to 4′, has proven quite cold hardy; described as a male and I have not checked the plants in our tests to determine sex, as yet no fruit production; unfortunately, like 'Compacta' will drop lower leaves and probably needs to be pruned back to make it dense, survived -24°F. Selected by James Zampini of Lake County Nursery, Perry, OH. Mr. Zampini relates that while surveying a field of more than two thousand inkberry seedlings in early March, he noticed one plant in the middle of the field that was distinct from the others. This plant had the best foliage color and a distinct broad, pyramidal growth habit. The leaves, slightly larger than those of the species, maintain their dark green color through the winter.

'Nova Scotia'—Lustrous dark green leaves, dense, compact habit, female, no inclination toward legginess after 3 years in the field, collected from the wild in Nova Scotia by Raymond Fielding, Pleasantville, Nova Scotia, in 1994; continues to impress, however, I noticed some lower leaf drop.

'Shamrock'—Handsome compact form with lustrous dark green leaves, is slower growing than 'Compacta' and 'Nordic', plants in the University's Botanical Garden have performed well, leaves smaller, flat,

3 to 5' high in time, holds color, better branching. This cultivar is receiving considerable attention from gardeners, designers, and producers. It was selected in 1977 form a block of approximately five hundred seedlings by John Tankard, Tankard Nursery, Exmore, VA. Distinguishing characteristics include compact habit and bright, glistening new green foliage that overlays the previous year's mature dark green foliage, the leaves averaging 1 1/2" long by 1/2" wide, mature plants 5' tall and wide. Mr. Tankard feels that 'Shamrock' holds its lower leaves better than other forms. Now widely used and is showing leaf drop in the lower portions of the plant.

'Squat'—Like 'Steed', a compact form but I do not know the origin, have seen this listed as 'Princeton's Compact'.

'Steed' ('Stead')—Another compact form that I have not seen.

'Tin Mine'—Grows 4' high and 8' wide, a selection from Tom Dilatush, offered by Summer Hill Nursery, Madison, CT.

'UGA'—Relatively compact broad mound with dark green foliage, found by the author in a large planting of seedlings on the Georgia campus, seedlings were 6' high, 'UGA' about 2' by 3', have shown it to several nursery friends and all say "Wow"; selected in 1994.

'UMASS'—Lustrous rich green young leaves mature dark green, leaves smaller than typical, upright grower with leaves to the ground on young plants, lower leaf drop observed on older plants, female, selected from the University of Massachusetts campus by the author in 1991.

'Viridis'—This plant has a distinct pyramidal form, 3 to 6' high, with upright branches and dense foliage, leaves 1 1/2" long by 1/3" wide, distinctly lighter green than those of 'Compacta' and 'Densa', estimate a maximum height of 3 1/4 to 4 1/4', slightly less in spread, at Weston Nurseries and the Arnold Arboretum plants held their lower branches better than 'Compacta', but did develop slight legginess.

Four other forms currently under test at Georgia are not included here since none appear commercially worthy. Over the years I have corresponded with many plant friends about the merits of the species. Many feel as I do, that the species is ripe for selection. As you may infer from the above cultivar list, exciting garden days lie ahead.

PROPAGATION: Same as for *I. crenata*: 1000 ppm IBA or KIBA quick dip, 100% rooting in 4 to 6 weeks; cuttings have arrived at our shop in every imaginable package and condition, some were so flat that revival was virtually impossible; we have always rooted at least several cuttings with 1000 to 3000 ppm KIBA, peat:perlite, mist, within 4 to 6(8) weeks.

ADDITIONAL NOTES: Spreads by underground stems (stolons or rhizomes) and is the only holly to sucker in this manner. Amazingly adaptable and should be the plant of choice instead of *I. crenata*. The newer cultivars offer great promise. Two recent articles by the author discuss various facets of *I. glabra* that are beyond the scope of this treatment. See *Nursery Manager* 7(11):28, 30 (1991), and *Arnoldia* 51:16–22 (1991). See Polly Hill's article, Holly Letter #40 (June, 1971), wherein she discusses the many selections on Martha's Vineyard.

NATIVE HABITAT: Nova Scotia to Florida, west to Missouri, Mississippi, Texas. Introduced 1759.

RELATED SPECIES:

Ilex coriacea (Pursh) Chapman, (ī'leks kō-ri-ā'sē-ȧ), Large or Sweet Gallberry, is a large version of *I. glabra* that is not as handsome. Leaves average 1 1/2 to 2 1/2" (2 to 4") long, and 1/2 to 1 1/2" wide. Serrations are generally more numerous than *I. glabra*. The lustrous reddish brown to black fruits are globose and average about 1/3" wide. Grows 10 to 15' high and is found in pocosins and wet areas throughout Coastal Plain from southern Virginia to Florida, Texas and Mexico. Found intermixed with *I. glabra* where it flowers several weeks earlier. Stems are dark brown, short pubescent, older stems gray to tan, lenticels circular with longitudinal orientation. 'Brookgreen' with large multi-stemmed habit, dark green leaves and 1/3" diameter black fruit is described. 'Georgia Wine' is sometimes placed under *I. coriacea*. Zone 7 to 9.

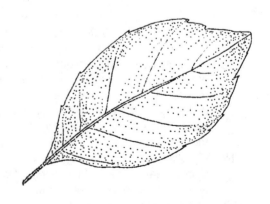

Ilex opaca Ait. — American Holly
(ī'leks ō-pā'kȧ)

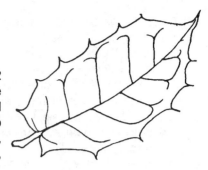

LEAVES: Alternate, simple, evergreen, elliptic to elliptic-lanceolate, 1 1/2 to 3 1/2″(4″) long, half to three-quarter's as wide, with large remote spiny teeth, teeth may be minimal on older plants, especially toward the tips of the plant, rarely nearly entire, from a single spine to 7 to 8 at most per side, dull to dark green above, occasionally lustrous, yellowish green beneath, glabrous; petiole—1/4 to 1/2″ long, grooved, minutely downy.

BUDS: Imbricate, ovoid, about 1/8 to 1/6″ long, greenish brown, slightly pubescent to glabrous, buds sit directly above leaf scar; leaf scar—half-moon shaped, one seemingly prominent vascular bundle trace in center of leaf scar.

STEM: Moderate, green when young, sparsely pubescent in youth, finally glabrous, older stems brown, rough, with circular raised lenticels; pith—solid, watery green.

SIZE: 40 to 50′ in height with a spread of 18 to 40′; usually smaller, 15 to 30′ in height is more reasonable under normal landscape conditions; takes a long time to get where it is going; co-national champions are 74′ by 48′ in Chambers County, AL and 55′ by 51′ in Buckingham County, VA.

HARDINESS: Zone 5 to 9.

HABIT: Densely pyramidal in youth with branches to the ground, many trees maintaining a symmetrically conical to cylindric crown at maturity, also becoming in age open, irregular, and picturesque, high branching, the branches at a wide angle and contorted.

RATE: Slow to moderate, less than 12″ per year on 5 cultivars in our Georgia trials.

TEXTURE: Medium in all seasons.

LEAF COLOR: Dull to dark yellow or olive green; great variation among trees but, in general, not a particularly handsome leaf; use superior lustrous dark green-leaved cultivars.

FLOWERS: Staminate in cymes, pistillate single to 3 on a peduncle, dull white, 4-lobed, about the latest evergreen holly to flower, May in Athens.

FRUIT: Berry-like, dull red rounded drupe, 1/4 to 1/2″ diameter, 4 pyrenes, borne singly on 1/4″ long stalk, maturing in October and persisting into winter; fruit display can be spectacular on good selections.

CULTURE: Transplant balled-and-burlapped or from a container in spring into moderately fertile, moist, loose, acid, well-drained soil; partial shade or full sun; avoid extremely dry, windy, unprotected places; does not tolerate poor drainage under cultivation; use 1 male for every 2 to 3 females; prune in winter; air pollution tolerant; have seen chlorosis in high pH soils; American Holly is more cold hardy than given credit but is not wind tolerant; if protected from winter sun and desiccating winds, cold hardy selections should withstand -20 to -25°F; in Illinois I have seen winters where virtually all the leaves were removed from plants *yet* the stem and bud tissue survived and a new flush of growth covered the scars of winter; Ford, *Secrest Arboretum Notes*, Spring 1983, reported that 48 cultivars of *I. opaca* were outplanted at Wooster, OH; there were striking differences among cultivars with 'Kildare' averaging 15″ per year, 9 averaged 11″ per year, average growth is 6″ per year; 'Christmas Carol' which averaged 15″ per year over a 6 year period in the protected test garden was moved to an exposed site and averaged 2″ per year in 8 growing seasons; the moral is that microclimate can make a big difference in plant performance.

DISEASES AND INSECTS: This species is affected by many problems including holly leaf miner, bud moth, scales, beetles, whitefly, berry midge, southern red mite, tar spot, leaf spots, cankers, bacterial blight, twig die back, spot anthracnose, leaf rot, leaf drop, powdery mildews, spine spot (nonparasitic) and leaf scorch (physiological); leaf miner and scale are particularly troublesome, spittlebug, particularly in wet springs cause yellowing, distortion and death of leaves and branches; recent evaluation paper by Braman and Ruter, *J. Environ. Hort.* 15:211–214 (1997) assessed preference of two-lined spittlebug for 137 *Ilex* taxa; although there was nothing new that has not been observed by others, the data did reaffirm in a quantitative sense the high susceptibility of *I. cassine*, *I. opaca* and *I.* × *attenuata* and the resistance of *I. cornuta*, *I. glabra*, *I. verticillata* and *I. vomitoria*.

LANDSCAPE VALUE: Specimen plant, grouping; requires male and female for fruit set; I feel there are too many superior hollies to justify extensive use of this species but the list of cultivars is endless; on the East Coast and South this is a favored plant; again, do not use seedlings; use one of many superior cultivars; I never fully appreciated the merits of this species as well as its overall geographic adaptability; one of the reasons it is not often available in large landscape sizes in commerce is the slowness of growth compared to *Ilex* × *attenuata*, *I.* 'Nellie R. Stevens' and others.

CULTIVARS: There are more than 1000 cultivar names and if one is extremely interested *The International Checklist of Cultivated Ilex*, put out by the U.S. National Arboretum, is a must. Desirable characteristics in holly cultivars should include annual bearing, large and bright-colored fruits, good foliage, and dense habit. American Holly appears to be regionally adapted and it is best to check with a local nurseryman for the best varieties in a given area.

Many great plantsmen have honed their introduction skills on this species. I had the good fortune to visit Mr. Theodore Klein, Crestwood, KY, and see his extensive *I. opaca* collection. Cave Hill Cemetery, Louisville, KY, Bernheim Arboretum, Clermont, KY, and Spring Grove, Cincinnati, OH, have extensive *I. opaca* plantings. Holly Ridge Nursery, 5125 South Ridge Rd., Geneva, OH 44041 (800-465-5901), offers an excellent litany of cultivars at reasonable prices. The 1996 catalog listed 42 *Ilex opaca* selections.

'Amy'—Large, spiny, lustrous dark olive green leaves and abundant 3/8″ diameter red fruit, large specimen tree.

'Angelica'—Fast-growing large form with large dark green leaves and red fruit, 5/16 to 3/8″ diameter.

'Canary'—Yellow-fruited form, heavy producer, leaves light green with small spines.

'Cardinal'—Compact, slow-growing form with small dark green leaves and abundant small, light red fruit, heavy fruiting at an early age.

'Carolina #2'—Good dark green form with heavy bright red fruit production, fairly common in Southeast; looks a little open in youth, becoming fuller with maturity.

'Croonenburg'—Compact, pyramidal, columnar tree with glossy deep green, wavy leaves that are less spiny than the species; fruits heavily every year, the plant is monoecious bearing flowers in the ratio of 10 female:1 male; good fruiter.

'Dan Fenton'—Broad pyramid, dark green, spiny leaves, and lustrous red, 1/4″ diameter fruit, 20′ by 15′ in 26 years, Orton considers it among the best, maintained healthy dark green foliage in Georgia trials but not as lustrous dark green or heavy red-fruited as 'Jersey Princess' and 'William Paca'.

'Farage'—An excellent form with large dark green, deeply spined leaves and lustrous persistent red fruits, broad conical habit.

'Goldie'—Heavy yellow-fruiting form, each fruit 3/8″ long, dull green leaves.

'Greenleaf'—Becoming more popular in Southeast, strong-growing pyramidal form with glossy medium green, spiny foliage, margin is somewhat undulating, bright red fruits at an early age, in cold hardiness tests leaves and stems were hardy to -22°F, an *I. × attenuata* form, defoliated with wood damage at Louisville, -20°F.

'Howard'—Dark green leaves, almost spineless, abundant bright red, medium-sized berries, good-looking clone that fruits heavily every year on the Georgia campus, probably an *I. × attenuata* form.

'Jersey Delight'—Exceptionally shiny foliage, reddish orange, 3/8″ diameter fruits, dense symmetrical upright-conical shape, hardy to -10°F, 19′ by 13′ at 30 years, Orton introduction.

'Jersey Knight'—A male with lustrous dark green leaves, a handsome form, foliage good but no match for 'Jersey Princess', male parent of 'Jersey Princess', Orton introduction.

'Jersey Princess'—Female version of above, good lustrous dark green foliage, abundant red fruits, has been sensational in my Georgia trials, holds foliage color and fruits through winter, has been the darkest green form, Orton introduction.

'Judy Evans'—Excellent glossy dark green foliage, red, 5/16″ diameter fruits, compact broad pyramid, hardy to -24°F, Theodore Klein introduction in 1940, selected from Cave Hill Cemetery.

'Manig'—Large dark green closely spaced leaves with large spines, large, glossy dark orange-red fruits, from New Jersey in mid to late 1930's.

'Merry Christmas'—Lustrous dark green, small to medium-sized, short-spined leaves on a fast-growing, densely foliaged and branched tree, lustrous ellipsoidal bright red, 1/3″ long fruits.

'Miss Helen'—Thick dark green leaves, glossy dark red, 3/8″ long, oblong fruits ripen early, dense conical tree.

'Old Heavy Berry'—Vigorous, large dark green-leaved selection that produces heavy crops of large red fruits, excellent winter hardiness.

'Steward's Silver Crown'—The leaf margins are edged in cream, glossy deep red, 1/3″ diameter fruits; the parent tree is 25′ high and wide.

'William Paca'—Dark green leaves, bright red fruit, tight pyramidal habit, excellent performer in the Georgia trials.

f. *xanthocarpa*—The yellow- to orange-fruited form that occurs sporadically throughout the range of *I. opaca*, Galle mentioned that over 50 yellow-fruited selections have been made.

PROPAGATION: Although I have rooted *I. opaca* many times from cuttings my experiences with 'Jersey Knight' and 'Jersey Princess' might prove valuable to other propagators. Dr. Orton sent cuttings in late December which I wounded, treated with 3000 ppm IBA-quick dip, placed in peat:perlite under mist and provided bottom heat (75°F). In 6 weeks a number of cuttings had rooted and the bulk of the roots originated from the wounded area. The cuttings were wounded (1″) on only one side and this is where the root systems were formed with the unwounded side showing essentially no root development. As discussed under *I. cornuta*, cuttings collected after the first growth flush hardens are often the easiest to root.

NATIVE HABITAT: Massachusetts to Florida, west to Missouri and Texas. Introduced 1744. *Ilex opaca* is frequently encountered in shady woods throughout the Southeast. Apparently birds disseminate the seeds. In these situations the plants are rather thin and open. They become much denser in full sun.

Ilex pedunculosa Miq. — Longstalk Holly
(ī′leks pe-dunk-ū-lō′sȧ)

LEAVES: Alternate, simple, evergreen, ovate or elliptic, 1 to 3″ long, 3/4 to 1 1/4″ wide, acuminate to abruptly acute, rounded or broad-cuneate at base, entire, persistent for 3 years, glabrous, lustrous dark green; petiole—1/2 to 3/4″ long.
STEM: Slender, somewhat flattened, brownish green, glabrous.

SIZE: 20 to 30′ in height but usually smaller under cultivation, perhaps 15′, often as wide as high.
HARDINESS: Zone 5; survived in Illinois field plots under the most adverse conditions: heavy soils, dry, sweeping winds, and intense summer heat.
HABIT: Large shrub or small tree of dense habit and handsome foliage, often irregular in outline.
RATE: Slow to medium.
TEXTURE: Medium in all seasons.
LEAF COLOR: Very beautiful lustrous dark green in summer; in exposed areas develops a yellow-green cast during winter; remind of *Kalmia latifolia* leaves.
FLOWERS: Male in clusters; female usually solitary, 4- to 5-merous, white, borne on current season's growth.
FRUIT: Berry-like, bright red, rounded drupe, with 5 pyrenes, 1/4 to 1/3″ diameter, borne singly on 1 to 2″ long pedicels, October and persisting into November.
CULTURE: Similar to *I. opaca*; from my observations perhaps not as fastidious as to soils.
DISEASES AND INSECTS: None serious; at least I have not seen any serious problems.
LANDSCAPE VALUE: One of the hardiest evergreen red-fruiting hollies; should be used more than it is; apparently not well-known; to me this is the most handsome of the evergreen hollies that can be grown in northern gardens; at its best, the habit is dense but still loose enough to show some grace; the beautiful fruits hang down on long pedicels and seem to be relished by birds; the Arnold Arboretum had several specimens by the corner of the Administration Building that rival any holly in cultivation; have seen it after the 1976–77 winter at Bernheim where temperatures dropped to -18°F and *no* injury was evident when all around other hollies dropped like flies; have not seen in Zone 7 and 8, suspect like other holly species may not be very heat tolerant; Fred Galle, formerly of Callaway Gardens, Pine Mountain, GA, said the plant never performed well there.
CULTIVARS:
    'Vleck'—Described as a particularly hardy form, performing well in Cleveland, OH, Zone 5.
PROPAGATION: I have had good success with cuttings, in fact, cuttings taken in February rooted 80% with 1000 ppm IBA/50% alcohol; have also rooted them in July and August with equal success.
NATIVE HABITAT: Japan, Korea, China. 1892.

Ilex verticillata (L.) A. Gray — Common Winterberry, Black Alder, Coralberry, Michigan Holly
(ī′leks vĕr-ti-si-lā′tȧ)

LEAVES: Alternate, simple, 1 1/2 to 3″(4″) long, 1/2 to 1″(2″) wide, elliptic or obovate to oblanceolate or oblong-lanceolate, acute or acuminate, cuneate, serrate or double serrate, dark green above, usually pubescent beneath, at least on the veins; petiole—1/4 to 1/2″ long.

BUDS: Imbricate, small, 1/16″ long, globose, brownish, buds smaller then leaf scar.

STEM: Slender, angled, olive-brown to purplish brown, glabrous or finely pubescent, lenticelled; second year stem developing an onion-skin effect; leaf scar half-elliptical, somewhat raised, with two small blackish projections at either side; pith—white, excavated, appearing chambered.

SIZE: 6 to 10′ in height with a similar spread, can grow to 15′ but this is rare under landscape conditions; co-national champions, both 13′ by 16′ are in Virginia Beach, VA.

HARDINESS: Zone 3 to 9.

HABIT: Oval-rounded to broad-rounded, deciduous shrub with dense complement of fine twiggy branches; tends to sucker and form large multi-stemmed clumps.

RATE: Slow, in youth can be induced into medium growth with adequate fertilizer and water.

TEXTURE: Medium in summer and winter.

BARK: Dark gray to dark brown or black on old stems, interesting architectural twist to the branches.

LEAF COLOR: Deep dark green in summer; no significant fall color; although occasionally yellow- to purple-tinged; considerable variation in summer leaf color with some cultivars lustrous dark green, others lighter.

FLOWERS: Male in clusters of 6 or more in the leaf axils; female flowers fewer, usually singly or in three's on short peduncles, 4- to 7-merous, white.

FRUIT: Berry-like rounded drupe, 2 to 7 pyrenes, bright red, 1/4 to 1/2″ across and often in pairs, ripening in late August–September and persisting into December–January in the North, March–April in Zone 7 and 8; depending on temperatures and bird populations, make a magnificent show, often spectacular and without rival in the winter landscape; over the past 8 years I have learned a great deal about fruit persistence, perhaps most important is the choice of cultivar(s) with local or regional adaptability, fruit abundance, size and persistence; consistently in our deciduous holly trials, Winter Red® has outperformed the rest; the fruits of all the hybrid *I. serrata* × *I. verticillata* cultivars bleach to yellow-white on the side of the fruit facing the southern-western, fall-winter sun, the *I. verticillata* cultivars do not; a seemingly universal pollinator for all the female hollies has been 'Raritan Chief' from Dr. Orton's Rutgers program; the late, great Mr. Robert Simpson introduced the males 'Jim Dandy' and 'Southern Gentleman' (see under CULTIVARS).

CULTURE: Transplant balled-and-burlapped or as a container plant; adaptable to wet conditions (native to swampy areas) and does well in light and heavy soils; prefers moist, acid (pH 4.5 to 6.5), high organic matter soils; full sun or partial shade; best fruit set in full sun; will develop chlorosis in high pH soils.

DISEASES AND INSECTS: Tar spots, leaf spots, and powdery mildew, nothing serious.

LANDSCAPE VALUE: Excellent for mass effect, shrub borders, water side and wet soils; requires male and female for fruit set; I have seen several mass plantings which were outstanding; superior when the red fruits are framed by snow; have observed in the wild in Maine on Cadillac Mountain in humus-rich, moist fissures and crevices, in moist low depressions in Tipton, MI, in kettle holes (fresh water pond edges) on Cape Cod, and in a bone fide swamp near Winder, GA; in wet areas of residential and commercial landscapes this is a first class choice.

CULTIVARS: Many great gardeners, nurserymen, and scientists have provided our gardens with superior selections. Mr. Robert Simpson, Simpson Nurseries, Vincennes, IN gave so much and asked so little in return; Mrs. Polly Hill, Bernard's Farm Inn, Martha's Vineyard, MA selected and named a number of excellent cultivars for the New England area; Professor O.M. Neal, University of West Virginia, Morgantown, WV was an early pioneer with 'Cacapon', 'Fairfax', 'Shaver', and others; Mr. David Jenkins, Mitchellville, MD selected forms for cut branches; Dr. Elwin Orton, Rutgers University bred and introduced several large *I. verticillata* × *I. serrata* hybrids; and Mr. Gene Eisenbeiss, U.S. National Arboretum, has provided 'Appollo', 'Sparkleberry', and the newest addition 'Sundrops'. Still others like Mr. Mike Johnson, Summer Hill Nursery, Madison, CT, Mr. Tom Dilatush, Robbinsville, NJ, and Mr. Ray Fielding, Pleasantville, Nova Scotia have selected and introduced new forms.

Their contributions are much appreciated by the author. There is a need to delineate the BEST types for the nursery producers and gardeners. Three articles that address this issue are Dirr, *American Nurseryman* 168(3):23–28, 32–41 (1988); Eggers and Hasselkus, *American Nurseryman* 176(12): 115–125; Andrews, *The Garden* 119:580–583 (1994). The cultivar descriptions that follow are distillations of literature, observation, and emotion. The introducer when known is listed in parenthesis or the text.

'Afterglow'—Seedling selection by Simpson Nursery in 1960, introduced in 1976, 30-year-old plant is multi-stemmed, slow-growing, compact globe-shaped, 10′ high and wide, glossy green leaves are smaller than average, fruits are globose or subglobose, 5/16″ long and 11/32″ diameter, borne singly or in 3's, on short pedicels, orange to orange-red, hardy to Zone 4, good in Minnesota, early flowering.

'Alfred Anderson'—20′ high and wide, 1/4″ diameter red fruits ripen in October and persist past September, large leaves 3 1/2″ by 1 1/4″, discovered in 1963 in Gettysburg, PA, zone 5a, female, see Peters, *Holly Soc. Jour.* 9(2):16 (1991).

'Aurantiaca' (Gulf Stream) [f. *aurantiaca* (Mold.) Rehd. is botanically correct]—Abundant orange fruits about 1/4 to 1/3″ in diameter; fruits do not persist as well as several of the red forms; they may start orange-red and fade to orange-yellow; early flowering; birds do not seem to bother the fruits; observations in Boston and Athens indicate fruit quality, color, and retention diminish more rapidly than most red types; fruits discolor terribly in Zone 7 to 8; about 6 to 8′ high and wide at maturity.

Berry Nice™ ('Spriber')—A new introduction from Spring Meadow Nursery, original fruit display was so vivid plant was spied a quarter of a mile away, 6 to 8′ high and wide, excellent bright red fruit coloration, good foliage mildew resistance, 'Southern Gentleman' is recommended as a pollinator, considered hardy to Zone 4.

Bright Horizon® (Hill)—Bright red, 1/2″ diameter fruits; small plants show a bushy habit; vigorous, wide, upright-growing, mid to late season flowering.

'Cacapon' (Neal)—Compact type similar to 'Afterglow' but more upright; abundant true red fruits; glossy dark green crinkled leaves; intermediate in height (6 to 8′); excellent performer in Athens area, second to Winter Red® for fruit retention, early flowering.

'Christmas Cheer' (Gulf Stream)—Smaller growing type with abundant red, 1/4″ diameter fruits; early flowering; dark green leaves; originally listed as 'Xmas Cheer'; may be a hybrid with *I. serrata*.

'Christmas Gem' (Jenkins)—Red-fruited; has not performed well in Wichita, KS; not much known about this clone; selected for cut-branch quality and named in 1970; original plant 6′ by 8′.

'Chrysocarpa' (f. *chrysocarpa* Robinson is botanically correct)—A yellow-fruited form that does not fruit as heavily as many of the red selections; fruits are handsome, especially before harsh weather; birds do not bother it as much as red forms; found several times in the wild in Massachusetts; this form exhibits early leaf drop compared to the red-fruited types.

'Earlibright' (Hill)—An early-ripening, orange-red fruited form from Martha's Vineyard; columnar fastigiate branching; original plant 7′ by 4′; sibling of 'Bright Horizon' but fruits ripen earlier.

'Fairfax' (Neal)—Heavy red fruit on a fairly compact plant; large leathery dark green leaves; fruit still present in late February at Swarthmore College, Swarthmore, PA; will grow 8 to 10′ high, early-flowering.

'Hoogendorn'—Dark green foliage, heavy dark red fruits, compact selection, 4′, 'Jim Dandy' pollinates.

'Jackson' (Neal)—A male form to accompany 'Cacapon', 'Fairfax', and 'Shaver'; grows to 10′.

'Jim Dandy' (Simpson)—Early-flowering male, slow-growing, 10′ by 7′, compact densely branched, Zone 4, pollinator for the northern types like 'Afterglow', 'Aurantiaca', 'Autumn Glow', 'Cacapon', 'Harvest Red', 'Red Sprite', 'Shaver', 'Stop Light', and others; originally distributed as 'Dwarf Male'.

'Jolly Red' (Hoffman, Bloomfield, CT)—Old clone discovered over 40 years ago; parent plant 10′ by 8′; large, red, 1/4 to 1/3″ diameter fruits in abundance; have seen in New England nurseries.

'Kennebago' (Johnson)—Dwarf, female form, selected by Mike Johnson, Summer Hill Nursery, Madison, CT, found growing by Kennebago Lake, Maine.

'Maryland Beauty' (Jenkins)—Shiny dark red fruit, large, tightly clustered around full length of stems, colors early, developed for commercial cutting, deep green foliage, compact, 6′.

'Millcreek'—I first observed this cultivar at Swarthmore College, Swarthmore, PA; 12′ by 10′, ascending habit, dense branching, red, 1/3″ diameter fruits, leaves up to 3″ by 1 1/8″ wide, Zone 4, introduced by Millcreek Nursery, Newark, DE; could this be the same as 'Scarlett O'Hara'?

'Quansoo' (Hill)—A male plant named after a swimming beach on Martha's Vineyard, 12′ by 10′.

'Quitsa' (have seen spelling as 'Quista') (Hill)—A female selection (red fruit) from Martha's Vineyard, 7′ by 6′.

'Red Sprite' (same as 'Compacta', 'Macrocarpa', 'Nana') (Hampden Nurseries)—Grows 3 to 5' high, compact, rounded, persistent, bright red, 3/8 to almost 1/2" diameter fruit, larger than typical *I. verticillata*, lustrous dark green leaves, 'Jim Dandy' and 'Appollo' will pollinate.

'Ruby Red' (Simpson)—Large red fruit, dark green foliage.

'Scarlett O'Hara' (Frederick)—Another New England type that I have seen with respectable fruit into southeastern Pennsylvania, red fruits that are not as large or abundant as the better types; 12' by 10'; 'Rhett Butler' (Frederick) is the male; 12' by 10'; these two selections are not in the mainstream of deciduous hollies; seedlings from Millcreek Nursery; selected and named by Bill Frederick, DE.

'Shaver' (Neal)—An excellent large, to 1/2" diameter, orange-red fruiting form; upright compact growth habit; gossy leaves; northern type; slow-growing, 5' by 3' in 15 years; early-flowering.

'Shortcake' (Hill)—More compact form, 5' by 3 1/2' in 28 years; leaves similar to the species; rich red, 1/4" diameter fruits.

'Southern Gentleman' (Simpson)—Male pollinator for the southern type, fast-growing cultivars such as 'Cacapon', 'Shaver', 'Sparkleberry', 'Sunset', Winter Red®, and 'Winter Gold'; hardy to Zone 3.

'Stoplight' (Simpson)—Formerly listed as 'Hopperton'; large, glossy dark red, 5/16 to 1/2" diameter fruits, colors early; dark green foliage; 'Jim Dandy' will pollinate; 8 to 10' by 6 to 8'.

'Sunset'—Seedling selection by Simpson Nursery in 1960, named in 1983, 30-year-old original plant was 8' by 9'; fruits are reddish orange to red, 7/16" diameter, borne singly on 1/8" long pedicels or in 3 short branched peduncles; original selection was based on dark olive-brown stem color, vigor, spreading habit, longer fruit than Winter Red® and heavy-fruiting characteristic; late-flowering.

'Tiasquam' (Hill)—Red fruits, 1/3" diameter, have seen plants in late February with abundant red fruits, large shrub 10' or more, lustrous dark green leaves, from Martha's Vineyard.

'Winter Gold'—Branch sport of Winter Red® discovered in 1984 at Simpson Nursery, Vincennes, IN; habit is multi-stemmed, rounded, 7' by 7'; leaf color is lighter green than Winter Red®; fruits are yellowish tinged pinkish orange, 3/8" diameter, borne singly on a 1/16" pedicel or 3 together; considered hardy in Zone 4.

Winter Red®—Introduced by Simpson Nursery, multi-stemmed, erect, deciduous rounded shrub, 9' by 8' after 30 years, lustrous dark green leaves, bright red, 3/8" diameter fruits are borne in tremendous profusion, intense color is maintained throughout the winter; have seen in a local nursery in early February with bright red fruit still persisting in good condition; truly one of the best introductions and now widely available; as mentioned early in this discussion by far the best in most of Midwest, East and South; fruits contain more pigment in the skin; cut stems keep for months indoors if *not in water*.

Other cultivar names that have crossed my path include: 'Aquinnah' (Hill)—glossy dark red fruits, depressed-globose, 5/32" high, 5/16" diameter, glossy foliage, 6' by 5' after 20 or more years, from Martha's Vineyard; 'Fire Storm'—female, from New England; 'Golden Verboom'—yellow-fruited form from Holland; 'Jimmy Peters' (Peters)—low compact shrub, 5' by 3' in 8 years, vivid red fruits, abundant, early, northern type; 'Johnny Come Lately'—male form; 'Peter's Fireworks' (Peters)—brilliant red, 1/3" diameter fruit persist from October to March, 8 to 10' high, northern type; 'Oosterwijk'—a Dutch cultivar with dark green leaves and large rich red fruit, was grown by a Georgia nurseryman but not superior to Winter Red®, see *Dendroflora* 25:35–36 (1988); 'Ralph E. Lincoln' (Seligmann)—medium-sized, globose, strong red, heavy-fruiting, ascending branches, 10' by 10' in 15 years.

HYBRIDS (*Ilex verticillata × Ilex serrata*): Seemingly with hybrid vigor, faster growing than true *I. verticillata* cultivars in Georgia trials. In fact over a 7 year period 'Autumn Glow' (7' by 6'), 'Bonfire' (8 to 9' by 8 to 9'), 'Harvest Red' (8' by 9'), and 'Sparkleberry' (7 to 8' by 6 to 7') produced phenomenal growth considering the heavy fruit production. These hybrids can usually be separated from *I. verticillata* clones by the plum purple new growth and the discolored winter fruit. The fruits ripen earlier than *I. verticillata* and color on 'Autumn Glow' is evident by September in Athens.

'Apollo' (U.S. National Arboretum)—Male form to accompany 'Bonfire', 'Harvest Red', and 'Sparkleberry'. Upright, ascending branches, 10 to 12' high and wide. New growth distinctly reddish maturing to dark green.

'Autumn Glow' (Orton)—Bushy form, slightly more erect than 'Harvest Red'. Landscape size approximates 6 to 8' high and slightly wider. Orton mentioned that a 20-year-old plant was 10' by 12'. Red fruits are retained until Christmas but bleach out earlier. Originally described as developing fiery orange fall color with bright flashes of yellow, but this has not held up for mature plants; generally yellow-green at best.

'Bonfire' (Simpson)—Originally listed as an *I. serrata* selection but belongs here. Masses of small red fruits ripen early in the fall while leaves are still green. Slender branches droop from the weight of the fruit.

Fruits are globose to ovoid, red, 5/16″ diameter, either singly or 2 to 4 on branched peduncles. Small plants fruit heavily. Grows 8 to 10′ high; 30-year-old plant is 12′ high with a spreading habit and mound-shaped crown. Large planting at Bernheim Arboretum consists of 12′ by 12′ shrubs. Witnessed them on November 7, 1997 and fruit display was outstanding. This may be the best of the hybrid cultivars. Originated from a group of 150 seedlings at Simpson Nursery in 1957, introduced in 1983. Selection was based on vigorous growth, spreading habit, fruiting at a young age, and persistence. Hardy at least to the Chicago area, Zone 5 to 8.

'Carolina Cardinal' (Raulston)—Although originally introduced as an *I. verticillata* form, appears to be a hybrid, low-growing, long-lasting red fruits, has not performed well in Georgia tests, foliage is dull green and unattractive, fruit production has been sparse in our trials while Winter Red® is heavily fruited, this is not a good selection and is inferior to 'Red Sprite' in foliage and fruit.

'Christmas Cheer' (Gulf Stream Nursery)—At one time considered an *I. serrata* form but probably a hybrid; see description under *I. verticillata*.

'Harvest Red' (Orton)—Slightly deeper and larger red fruits than 'Autumn Glow'. Lustrous, dark green summer foliage that supposedly turns deep red-purple in fall, but plants I have observed were yellow-green. Fruits (1/4″ diameter) are not as large as the best *I. verticillata* forms. An 18-year-old plant was 9′ by 16′.

'Hopewell Grenadier'—10′ tall in 10 years and more fastigiate than female parent 'Sparkleberry', bright red, 1/3″ diameter fruit, bears fruits closer to apical ends of stems, Zone 5, originated from 1979 cross by Dr. R.B. Rypma.

'Hopewell Myte' [(*I. serrata* × *I. verticillata*) 'Sparkleberry' × *I. serrata*] — Originated as a controlled cross made in 1980 by Dr. R.B. Rypma at Ohio University Botanic Garden, Athens, OH. Original plant is a low-spreading dwarf shrub, 2′ by 4′, fruits are small, 1/4″ diameter, red, borne singly or in fascicles of 2 to 3, -15 to -20°F hardiness.

'Raritan Chief' (Orton)—A male to accompany 'Autumn Glow' and 'Harvest Red'. Resulted from crossing a hybrid of *I. serrata* × *I. verticillata* with an unrelated female *I. verticillata*. Low, dense, spreading habit with handsome, lustrous, medium green foliage. Branches are rather brittle, so care should be exercised in handling. Grew 6 1/2′ by 12′ in 15 years. In our Georgia trials, this has been the slowest growing clone. Flowers over a long time period and will serve as a pollinator for most female selections.

'Sparkleberry' (U.S. National Arboretum)—The 3/8″ diameter brilliant red fruits persist into winter, often into March. Distinctly upright, becoming somewhat leggy with age. Original plant was 12′ high after 16 years; will grow over 15′ high. Polly Hill noted that if she were restricted to a single pair of deciduous hollies, 'Sparkleberry' and 'Apollo' would be her first choices. 'Sparkleberry' received the prestigious Styer Award from the Pennsylvania Horticultural Society in 1987.

PROPAGATION: Cuttings, softwood, root readily. June or July cuttings treated with 1000 to 3000 ppm IBA-quick dip, peat:perlite, mist will root 90 to 100% in 6 to 8 weeks. On one occasion, I stratified fruits for 3 months at 41°F and had about 70 germinate out of 300; I tried the same thing again and did not have a single one germinate; see propagation under *I. cornuta*.

ADDITIONAL NOTES: *Ilex verticillata* is an amazing plant. I have seen it growing in fresh water ponds on Cape Cod, the entire root system completely submerged. Some stems on these plants were 4″ in diameter. The fruit will often stay showy into winter. It makes a choice plant along lakes and ponds especially in fall when the fruit-laden branches are reflected off the water. Robert Simpson discusses two types, one called the Northern, which is native to New England, slower growing, with light brown bark, small broad oval leaves, 1 to 3″ long, often glossy, flowers earlier, may be more drought tolerant; the other, the Southern type, is more vigorous, taller, fewer and heavier stems with dark bark, leaves more leathery, longer 4″ or more, 10 to 15′ high, used by commercial growers for cut branches.

Bonnie and I spend a week or two in Maine, usually Deer Isle, at the end of summer. The occasion has become a spiritual renewal with time to walk, talk, delight in each other's company, appreciate the earth and try to understand our small part in preserving same. The wonderful walks provide the opportunity to identify the local vegetation and *I. verticillata* is a leading component. The plant is everywhere, usually in moist to wet areas, with fruits still green. I see so many potential introductions, yet resist the temptation, because I have yet to witness any that rival Winter Red®.

NATIVE HABITAT: Native in swamps from Nova Scotia to western Ontario, west to Wisconsin, south to Florida and west to Missouri; the most northerly distributed of the hollies native in America. Introduced 1736.

RELATED SPECIES:

Ilex amelanchier M.A. Curtis, (ī′leks am-e-lang′ki-ĕr), Serviceberry or Swamp Holly, has beautiful bloomy velvet-red to cerise-red, almost fluorescent, 1/4 to 1/3″ diameter persistent fruits with 4 pyrenes. Pedicels range to 3/4″ long. The 4-merous, white flowers occur solitary or in pairs. The 2 to 4″ long, 1/2 to 1 3/4″ wide leaves are ovate-lanceolate. The leaf margins are entire or finely serrated, with an elongated bristle tip to each serration. Leaves are pubescent beneath. Have seen plants at Spring Grove, Cincinnati, OH, Henry Foundation, Gladwyne, PA and the University's Botanical Garden. Somewhat open habit, 6 to 10′ high, fruiting is generally sparse. The species occurs in sandy swamps and wet woods on the Coastal Plain from southeastern Virginia to northern Florida, west to Alabama, Mississippi, and eastern Louisiana. Zone 6 to 9.

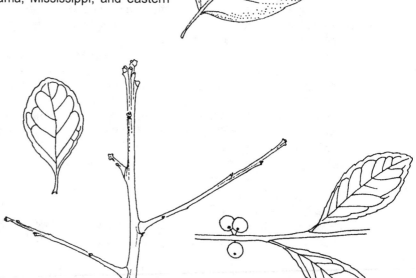

Ilex decidua Walter — Possumhaw

LEAVES: Alternate, simple, obovate to obovate-oblong, 1 1/2 to 3″ long, 1/3 to 3/4″ wide, usually obtusish, cuneate, obtusely serrate, dark green and lustrous above and with impressed veins, pale and pubescent on the midrib beneath, thickish; petiole—1/6 to 1/3″ long, pubescent.

BUDS: Small, imbricate, reddish brown, globular, glabrous, 1/16″ long.

STEM: Grayish, variable, on some plants a very soft gray, on others a grayish brown; the lateral branches are produced in great quantities and result in a very bushy main stem; short laterals sometimes appearing spur-like.

Ilex decidua, (ī′leks dē-sid′ū-à), Possumhaw, will grow 20 to 30′ in the wild but 7 to 15′ in height with 3/4's to equal that in spread is more reasonable under cultivation. Co-national champions are 42′ by 43′ in Richland County, SC and 47′ by 31′ in Gadsden County, FL. Habit is that of a shrub or small tree, much branched with horizontal and ascending branches. Often suckers develop at the base of the plant and produce lateral thickets. Foliage is glossy dark green in summer, yellow in fall; flowers white, 4-merous; fruits are orange to scarlet, singly to 3 together, 1/4 to 1/3″ diameter with 4 pyrenes, and ripen in September, often persisting until the following April. Better adapted to alkaline soils than *I. verticillata*. The stems are usually very light gray and stand out against an evergreen background. Knockout specimens (20′ high) at Missouri Botanic Garden, Bernheim Arboretum and Brookgreen Gardens. The gray bark even on large stems is effective. For everyday gardens this species is too large. Large masses are particularly outstanding. Has fruited heavily in pine shade in Zone 7b. *Ilex opaca* can serve as a suitable pollinator. Native from Maryland, Virginia to Florida, west to Texas, Mexico. Found in fencerows, open woodlands and along water courses. Cultivated 1760. Zone 5 to 9.

CULTIVARS:

'Byers Golden' (Byers)—Excellent yellow-fruited form. Fruits 1/4″ diameter. I have seen fruits in good condition in February. Large plant. Has been difficult to propagate and is not readily available.

'Council Fire' (Hartline)—Bushy, upright, oval-rounded in outline. Fruit remains orange after others turn dark. Plants grown in a North Alabama nursery and a Tennessee nursery still had abundant, colorful fruits in mid-March. Fruits are borne in dense clusters along the stem. Grew 6 1/2′ by 5 1/2′ in nine years at Wichita, KS. Mature size approximates 15′; 18′ by 10′ in 25 years. Some damage at -24°F in Bernheim.

'Finch's Golden' ('Gold Finch')—Yellow-fruited form that is easier to root than 'Byers Golden', seedling selection from Hale County, AL by Bill Finch in 1980's.

'Pocahontas' (Hartline)—Larger growing and more upright than 'Council Fire' and 'Sundance', very glossy bright red fruits, not as persistent as those of 'Council Fire', 15 to 18′ by 12′, leaves fall early.

'Red Cascade'—Simpson Nursery introduction selected in 1965 and named in 1987; 30-year-old plant is 20′ by 20′ with a rounded habit with horizontal undulating branches which produce a weeping appearance, stems are an intense gray color, leaves glossy dark green, fruits are 5/16″ diameter, glossy bright red, abundant, borne singly on 3/16″ long dark purplish pedicels; fruiting spurs with up to 7 closely spaced fruits, Zone 6 hardiness.

'Red Escort'—Simpson Nursery introduction named and introduced in 1987; 30-year-old parent is 25′ by 20′ with a globe-shaped crown, leaves are glossy dark green, considered one of the best males for habit and foliage, possibly the first named male clone, Zone 6 hardiness.

'Reed'—An older, red-fruited form that is probably not in commercial production. I have seen it at Simpson Nursery and was impressed by the bright red fruit. Leaves abscise early.

'Sentry'—A Simpson Nursery introduction in 1987; 25-year-old plant is 20′ by 10′ with a columnar habit; leaves are less glossy green than typical *I. decidua*, leaves abscise early; fruits are 1/4″ long and 5/16″ diameter, orange-red, subglobose, borne singly on dark purplish 1/4″ long pedicels, fruits also occur 6 to 7 on each spur, fruit is more firm than typical *I. decidua*, Zone 6 hardiness.

'Sundance' ('Hartline')—Broad-spreading bushy habit, very vigorous, abundant orange-red fruits that color early and persist late into winter, grew 7′ by 6′ in nine years at Wichita.

'Warren's Red' ('Warren Red')—Originated as a branch sport by Otis Warren and Son Nursery, Oklahoma City, OK; purchased before 1955 by Simpson Nursery and named by Robert Simpson, original plant is 25′ by 20′, more upright branching, lustrous dark green leaves, leaves are about the latest to drop of the cultivars described, bright glossy red 5/16″ diameter, globose fruits occur singly or 2 to 6 per fruiting spur, fruiting is heavy and fruits are long persistent, a particularly handsome form and probably a zone hardier than the typical species.

Ilex laevigata (Pursh) A. Gray, (ī′leks lev-i-gā′tà), Smooth Winterberry, is closely allied to *I. verticillata* except the fruits are borne singly, are slightly larger, and the leaf petioles are shorter. The plant grows to about 10′, usually with upright branches. The leaves are somewhat glossy, elliptic, oval, or sometimes lanceolate, 1 to 3 1/2″ long, the margins finely serrulate. The fruits are orange-red, 1/3″ diameter, 4 to 8 pyrenes, and supposedly can be set without pollination. There is a yellow-fruited cultivar called 'Hervey Robinson', also listed as f. *herveyi*, found along the Taunton River in Massachusetts. Native in swamps and low woods from Maine to New Hampshire, south to northern Georgia. Introduced 1812. Zone 4 to 7. The leaves turn yellow in the fall.

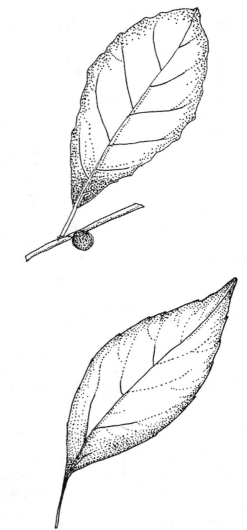

Ilex longipes Chapm. ex Trel., (ī′leks lon′ji-pēz), Georgia Holly, is another deciduous holly nurserymen might want to consider. It is akin to *I. decidua*. Grows 10 to 20′ high. The shiny, bright red, persistent fruits of *I. longipes* measure 1/4 to 1/2″ in diameter and occur on 1 to 1 1/2″ long stalks. Each fruit contains 4 pyrenes. The shiny light green, 1 3/4 to 2 1/2″ long, 4/5 to 1 1/4″ wide leaves are oblanceolate (widest above the middle) and serrate (spine-like bristle) toward the apex. Louisiana Nursery has designated male and female clones. Also, Galle lists 'Lagniappe', 'Natchez Belle', and 'Seven Sisters' in *Hollies*, none of which I have observed in the trade. It is native to Florida, west to Louisiana. I suspect temperatures between −10 and −15°F will result in some stem injury, although the species is growing in the Arnold Arboretum. This species, like *I. decidua*, develops fruit on side spurs up and down its stems. *Ilex longipes* in a taxonomic sense is allied to *I. decidua*.

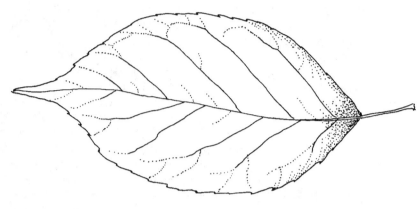

Ilex montana Torr. & A. Gray (*I. monticola* A. Gray), (ī′leks mon-tā′nȧ), Mountain Holly, can actually achieve tree status, reaching as high as 30 to 40′, with a trunk that measures 10 to 12″ in diameter, but usually it is more shrubby, growing about a third to half this size. National champion is 30′ by 30′ in Brooklyn Botanic Garden, NY. I first chanced upon the species in North Georgia at 4,700′ above sea level on Brasstown Bald. Since the first meeting, it has appeared with frequency in my southern Appalachian forays. The flowers are white and 4-merous. The 1/3 to 1/2″ diameter rich red fruits with 4 pyrenes do not persist like those of the other species and cultivars discussed. The species is usually found on well-drained, wooded slopes from New York to Tennessee, Georgia and eastern Alabama. The 2 1/2 to 6″ long leaves are the largest of the species treated herein. In the tests at Wichita, KS, this species grew slowly (3′ in 9 years), developed severe leaf scorch and produced few tiny red fruits. Zone 5 to 7.

Ilex serrata Thunb. — Finetooth Holly, Japanese Winterberry
LEAVES: Alternate, simple, elliptic or ovate, 1 to 3″ long, 1/3 to 1″ wide, acute or acuminate, serrulate, dull green above, pubescent beneath; petiole—1/3″ long or less, downy.

Ilex serrata, (ī′leks ser-rā′tȧ), Finetooth Holly, is similar to *I. verticillata* except the fruits are smaller (about 1/5 to 1/4″ diameter) and not as bright, and the leaves are more finely toothed. The new growth is plum-purple. The species may grow 12 to 15′ high with spreading branches; however, under landscape conditions 4 to 8′ is more logical. Flowers are pale lavender-purple to white, 4- to 6-merous. The 1/5″ diameter, red fruits (4 to 6 pyrenes) are abundantly borne and extremely showy after the leaves fall. The fruits ripen early, often in late August and persist for a long period and cut branches make excellent indoor decorations. Native to Japan and China. Found in moist sites in the wild. Introduced 1866. Zone 5 to 7(8).
CULTIVARS:
'Koshobai'—A dwarf from Japan with abundant, tiny, 1/18″ wide, red, persistent fruits. Habit is twisted and twiggy, new growth rich purple. Japanese name means "plum of youth." Very slow-growing and probably not a good garden plant but suitable for bonsai.
'Leucocarpa' (f. *leucocarpa* Beissner)—A white-fruited form that is quite striking. The U.S. National Arboretum has a handsome specimen that was heavily laden with fruit in early December. A 'Fructoalba' is known in Japan.
'Sundrops'—Fruits pale yellow, 1/4″ long and wide, original plant 8′ by 16′ in about 30 years, grown from open-pollinated seed of a yellow-fruited accession, U.S. National Arboretum introduction in 1991, have small plants that do not appear pleased with 7b heat, foliage is light green and wispy compared to *I. verticillata*, have seen photographs of 'Sundrops' in fruit and the plants were beautiful.
'White Profusion'—Described by Susyn Andrews as a white-fruited form that may be lost to cultivation.
'Xanthocarpa' (f. *xanthocarpa* Rehd.)—A yellow-fruited form.

OTHER HOLLIES OF LANDSCAPE IMPORTANCE

Ilex × altaclerensis Dallim. (*I. aquifolium* × *I. perado*), (ī′leks al-tȧ-klȧr-en′sis), Altaclera Holly, has evolved over the years to include a group of hollies that have larger, 2 1/2 to 5 1/2″ long, 2 to 2 3/4″ wide, evergreen leaves, flowers, fruits, and greater vigor than the parents. May grow 40′ high and greater. Numerous cultivars (50 and more) that are beyond the range of this Manual. Have observed several of the common cultivars like 'Camelliifolia' and 'James G. Esson' performing acceptably in the middle Atlantic states. The ones I have seen look more like *I. aquifolium*. Several notable cultivars include:

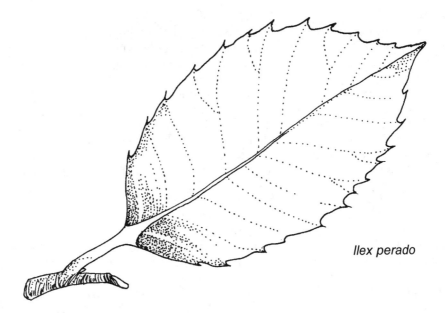

Ilex perado

'Camelliifolia'—A fine form with lustrous dark green leaves up to 5″ long and 3″ wide; the leaves are essentially entire but some leaves develop 1 to 8 spines; the long stems, petioles, and base of midrib are purplish; it is a female with rather large, dark red berries. 'Camelliifolia Variegata' is a branch sport with gray-green center and yellow-green margin.

'Camelliifolia'
'Camelliifolia Variegata'

'James G. Esson'—A beautiful, undulating, spiny-leaved form, the leaves being dark green; it makes a splendid specimen especially when the lustrous red fruits are present; the name does not fit the plant's sex; Longwood Gardens has a fine plant; leaves smaller than 'Camelliifolia' and habit is more open.

'J.C. Van Tol'—Fast-growing form with regular crops of red fruits, although listed here more accurately an *I. aquifolium* form.

'Indigo Knight' ('Wight's Selection')—Rather loose pyramidal form with soft spiny-margined leaves, new growth purplish red maturing to lustrous dark green, 20 to 30′ high, PP 6978 by Wight Nurseries, Cairo, GA, a plant in the Dirr garden is somewhat loose and open, will have a difficult time competing with 'Nellie R. Stevens', Zone 6 to 7.

'Scepter'—Rapid-growing, tree form, with a pyramidal habit, compact without pruning, 19 1/2′ high, 14′ wide in 16 years, leathery glossy dark green leaves that are thinner and more flexible than either parental species (*I. integra* × *I.* × *altaclerensis*), fruit is bright red, 2 to 10 fruits per infructescence, persistent through the winter, pollinated by *I. cornuta*, *I.* × *meserveae*, *I. pernyi*, *I. rugosa*, and *I. latifolia*, hardy to Zone 7.

'Wilsonii'—Leaves broad-elliptic or obovate, spiny, up to 5″ long, 3″ wide, glossy green, red fruits, grows 30′ high or more, a vigorous form; best grown in Zone 7 and south.

Common in Europe particularly the variegated forms. Witnessed a large collection at Van Dusen Botanical Gardens in Vancouver. Best suited to Pacific Northwest. On East Coast, adaptable in Zone 6b–7b.

Ilex aquifolium L., (ī′leks à-kwi-fō′li-um), English Holly, has a lustrous dark green, undulating, spiny-margined leaf that is quite distinct from other hollies. The leaves vary considerably in size ranging from 1 to 3″(4″) long and 3/4 to 2 1/2″ wide. Seed-grown trees tend to have extremely spiny leaves but as the trees

mature the spines decrease progressively with age and entire-margined leaves may be found in the tops of old plants. The dull white, occasionally pink-tinged, 4-petaled, fragrant flowers occur during May from the leaf axils and give rise to 1/4 to 7/8″ diameter, round, red drupes with 2 to 4 pyrenes. There are numerous cultivars of this species and published estimates approach 200. In a survey of hollies grown by United States nurseries, Klingaman, *American Nurseryman* 154(12): 10–11, 106–119 (1981), reported only 24 types. English Holly makes a dense, 30 to 50′ high (to 80′), evergreen tree that is well-clothed with branches even in old age. National champion silver-variegated form is 55′ by 30′ in Tillamouk County, OR. In Europe, immense specimens dot the landscape and mesh as an understory tree with oaks and beeches. It is everywhere in evidence in the famed hedgerows of the British Isles. Displays considerable salt tolerance for it is commonly planted in seaside cities, towns, and villages in England. In the United States, best growth occurs on the West Coast. Long Island and Cape Cod are the best refuges for superior culture on the East Coast. Tolerant of the most severe pruning and hedges and topiary forms in Europe have been maintained as such through the centuries. At Kew behind the Temperate House, a semi-circular walk is lined with tightly pruned *Ilex aquifolium*. Truly, an Alice in Wonderland ambience. It is especially attractive in fruit. In addition, many of finest holly hybrids (*I.* × *meserveae*, 'Nellie R. Stevens') have the species as one parent. Supposedly for best fruit set a male English Holly needs to serve as pollinator. The following list is derived from Klingaman's Survey.

'Argenteomarginata'—Dark green leaves marked with whitish margins, female.

'Aureomarginata'—A designation for yellow-margined types of which many have been named; in the common form the leaf is spiny-margined and with a bright yellow border; shows up with some regularity in Zone 7b.

'Balkans'—Noted for cold hardiness, survived Kansas tests, both male and female forms are offered, glossy dark green leaves, upright habit, considered about the hardiest *I.* × *altaclerensis* type.

'Boulder Creek'—Female with 1/3″ diameter, red fruits and large, glossy black-green, wavy leaves, with 4 to 7 spines per margin; did reasonably well in Wichita, KS tests; upright-growing.

'Ciliata Major'—Vigorous female with flat, ovate-elliptic leaves on which the spines point forward in the plane of the leaf, some leaves entire.

'Ferox' (Hedgehog Holly)—To me not a particularly lovely plant, the leaves are smaller than the species and have marginal spines as well as stiff, erect, silvery spines on the surface, male; 'Ferox Argentea' has white-margined leaves; in 'Ferox Aurea' the margin is green, the center yellow.

Gold Coast™ ('Monvila')—Small, dark green leaves, bright golden yellow margins, male form, relatively slow-growing, 4 to 6′ high and wide, Monrovia introduction.

'San Gabriel'—Female form with glossy foliage, prominent spines and red, 3/8″ diameter fruits.

Siberia™ ('Limsi')—Leathery, dark green single to multiple spined leaves, large crimson fruits, 15′ by 6′, −10°F hardiness, introduced by Conard-Pyle.

Sparkler® ('Monler')—Fast-growing, upright, free-fruiting form that sets heavy crops earlier than most cultivars, red, 1/3″ diameter fruits.

'Zero' ('Teufel's Weeping')—Erect form with long, thin, graceful branches, female, reasonably hardy, survived Kansas tests.

Native to Europe, northern Africa and western Asia. Best grown in lower part of Zone 6 to 7b, to 10 on West Coast.

Ilex × **aquipernyi** Gable, (ī′leks à-kwi-pĕr′nē-ī), is the result of crosses between *I. aquifolium* × *I. pernyi*. The habit is densely narrow pyramidal while the evergreen foliage is lustrous dark green. Leaves are nearer *I. pernyi*, 1 to 1 1/2″ long, 1 to 1 1/2″ wide, apex extended, spines undulate. 'Aquipern' is a male clone and 'San Jose' a female. 'San Jose' is hardy but best success is achieved under Zone 6 to 8 conditions. Proved extremely hardy in Kansas tests. The globose, slightly ribbed fruits are bright red and of good size. I have rooted cuttings of 'San Jose' with 100% success. This hybrid species grows 15 to 20′ high. 'Brilliant' (*I. aquifolium* × *I. ciliospinosa*) is cone-shaped, 10 to 20′ high, dense-foliaged, twice as large as *I. pernyi* with a few pronounced teeth, sets abundant red fruits supposedly without pollination. 'Carolina Sentinel' is a narrow, upright form, with showy red fruits, to 18′ high, J.C. Raulston Arboretum introduction. Dragon Lady™ is narrow, upright-pyramidal with perhaps the most spiny, glossy dark green leaves of any *I.* × *aquipernyi*, fruits are bright red, adaptable from Zone 6b to 8a. 'Dorothy Lawton' is more rounded and shrublike with dark green slightly rounded foliage and red fruits. 'Patricia Varner' is a broad upright columnar form with softer dark green foliage and large red fruits. The latter three cultivars have performed well in my Georgia trials. 'Patricia Varner' has grown the fastest and produced the heaviest fruit crops. 'San Jose' is popular on the West Coast. Recent literature mentions 'Wieman's Pacific Queen', a dense pyramidal form with curved, stiff, spiny, lustrous dark green leaves and red, globose fruits. 'September Gem' (*I. ciliospinosa* × *I.* × *aquipernyi*) forms a broad 6′ high (now 15′ in the University's Botanical Garden) pyramid of leathery dark green foliage and early-ripening, red fruits.

Ilex × attenuata Ashe. 'Fosteri' — Foster's Hybrid Hollies; species is often called Topel Holly.
LEAVES: Evergreen, alternate, simple, elliptic to oblong-ovate, 1 1/2 to 3″ long, about 1/2 as wide, spiny-pointed and with 1 to 4 spreading spiny teeth on each side, glossy dark green.

Ilex × *attenuata* 'Fosteri', (ī′leks à-ten-ū-ā′tà), represents a group of interspecific hybrids between *Ilex cassine* × *I. opaca*. There are selected clones known as Foster #1 through #5 made by E.E. Foster of Bessemer, AL. Foster #2 and #3, the most popular of this group in the South and the ones most often sold as Foster Holly, are used in general landscape work as foundation plants, hedges, and specimen plants. Both #2 and #3 are typically small-leaved, glossy green, with a spiny margin and have a compact, pyramidal growth habit. They are heavily fruited as is *I. cassine*. Foster #4 is a male plant while #1 and #5 are more like inferior forms of *I. opaca* and have been discarded. They make dense, narrow-conical, 20 to 30′ high trees of great beauty. The red fruits persist through winter. Zone 6 to 9. Easily rooted from cuttings. Foster #2 is the most popular form and is offered widely in the nursery trade. It makes a splendid 25′ high slender conical tree with rich deep red fruit. Several other selections, either from the wild or controlled crosses, have been made. They are correctly *Ilex* × *attenuata* selections. *Ilex opaca* and *I. cassine* overlap in the Southeast and many natural hybrids occur. Plants are fast-growing and intermediate in characteristics. The hybrids, as is true with the parents, are terribly susceptible to spittlebugs. Also, considerable pruning is necessary to produce dense compact plants under nursery production.

'Alagold'—A yellow-fruited form, possibly more orange-yellow, a seedling of 'Foster's #2', introduced in 1979.

'Attakapa'—Upright cone-shaped, vigorous, red fruits, larger leaves than 'East Palatka'.

'Bienville Gold'—Vivid lustrous yellow fruits, abundant, persistent on a narrow pyramidal tree with lustrous dark green foliage, beautiful selection, introduced in 1995 by Mr. Tom Dodd, Semmes, AL, name honors the French founder of New Orleans.

'Big John'—Pyramidal, glossy dark green foliage, male.

'Blazer'—Compact, slower growing with greater fruit production (red) than 'Foster's #2', seedling of 'Foster's #2', 1/3″ diameter fruits, 6′ by 3′ in 15 years.

'Eagleson'—Upright almost shrubby form without the defined terminal leader of 'Foster's #2', foliage medium to dark green, entire or with some spines toward the apex, red fruits, vigorous grower, has not been a good doer, 12′ by 9′ in 8 years.

'East Palatka'—Discovered in the wild near East Palatka, FL in 1927, it produces 1/4″ diameter bright red fruits in abundance, the dark green leaves may be entire or only toothed near the apex, this is looser and more airy than 'Foster's #2'; in the University's Botanical Garden, plants of this, 'Foster's #2' and 'Savannah' are planted in the Entrance Court Garden, all are quite different in habit, foliage and fruiting characteristics; in hardiness tests 'East Palatka' is less cold hardy than 'Foster's #2' and 'Savannah'.

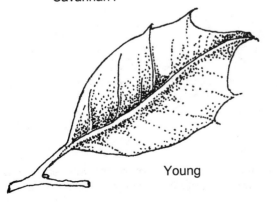

Young

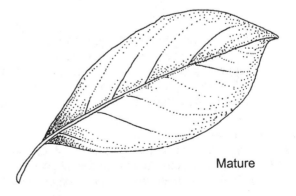

Mature

'Gato'—Bright green foliage and red fruits, upright pyramidal habit.

'Greenleaf'—see under *I. opaca*.

'Hoosier Waif'—Originated as a "wild" seedling in Monroe County, IN, introduced by Dr. R.B. Rypma, Ohio University, 14-year-old plant is a dwarf spreading evergreen shrub, 2 1/2' by 6' with drooping branches, fruit is deep red, globose, 1/4" diameter, borne singly on 3/16" long pedicels or 2 to 3 per branched peduncle, supposedly hardy to −20°F.

'Hume #2'—A tall 30 to 35' high loosely conical tree with lighter green leaves than 'East Palatka' and 'Foster's #2', the fruits are almost fluorescent red, small and reflect the *I. cassine* parentage, the leaves are somewhat rounded like 'East Palatka' but essentially spineless except at apex.

'Hume #4'—Supposedly has more spines than 'Hume #2'; I have rooted cuttings of 'Hume #4' and the leaves and fruits are larger, rather open grower in Dirr garden.

'Longwood Gold'—Excellent habit, dark green foliage and golden yellow fruits, observed in Longwood's nursery in February, 1998, appears more cold tolerant and maintains excellent winter foliage color, easy to root from cuttings.

'Nasa'—Resembles a compact 'Foster's #2', probably grows 8 to 10' high, 4 to 6' wide, dark green leaves, about 1 1/2" long, 1/3" wide, red 1/4" diameter fruits; I thought this form had something to offer in the commercial sector but it has not grown off quickly and is at best a novelty.

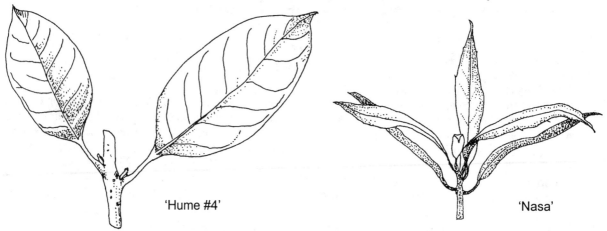

'Hume #4'   'Nasa'

'Oriole' (*I. myrtifolia* × *I. opaca*)—A slow-growing, compact form with large exposed red fruit; after 25 years the original plant was 6' high and 6' wide; I have not been impressed with this form or 'Tanager' of the same parentage and compact, slow-growing, was 6' by 7' after 25 years.

'Savannah'—A tremendously popular form in the Southeast because of large fluorescent red, 1/3" diameter, globose fruits that are borne in great abundance; the habit is loosely pyramidal and the foliage light green, in summer and fall when the fruits are ripening, a tremendous movement of nitrogen (I assume) from the leaves to the maturing fruits results in chlorotic foliage subtending the fruits, the leaves remind of *I. opaca* and are generally spiny from the middle to the apex and larger than those of 'Foster's #2', 'East Palatka' and 'Hume #2'; will grow 25 to 30' high.

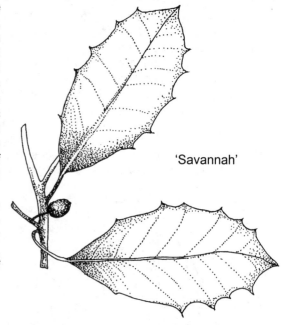

'Savannah'

'Sunny Foster'—New foliage yellow, fades to green with maturity, only for those who need something to remind them of their youthful Friday nights, discovered in 1964 by William F. Kosar, U.S. National Arboretum, as a branch sport of 'Foster's #2', produces red fruits.

Ilex cassine L. — Dahoon

LEAVES: Alternate, simple, evergreen, 2 to 4"(6") long, 3/4 to 1 1/2" wide, oblong or oblanceolate, acute or rounded, cuneate, glossy medium green, entire or with a few sharp mucronate teeth near apex, essentially glabrous at maturity; petiole—1/16 to 1/2" long.

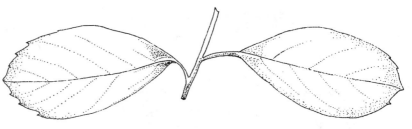

Ilex cassine, (ī′leks kȧ-sēn), Dahoon, is seldom seen in American gardens but deserves mention because of the garden hybrids between it and *Ilex opaca*. Typically it forms a small evergreen tree 20 to 30′ high and 8 to 15′ wide in the wild. Tri-national champions are 40′ by 60′ at Ft. Pierce, FL, 68′ by 31′ at Ft. Myers, FL and 42′ by 36′ at Immo Kalee, FL. Zone 7 to 9. Many native plant aficionados lament the paucity of this species in contemporary landscapes. In reality, the summer and winter foliage is not as dark green as 'Nellie R. Stevens' and other popular cultivars. Additionally, the plant tends to be open and somewhat scraggly and is terrifically susceptible to spittle bug feeding. Flowers are yellow-white, 4-merous. The 1/4″ diameter, globose fruits (4 pyrenes) range from red to almost yellow. The variety *myrtifolia* (*I. myrtifolia* Walter) is closely allied but differs in smaller leaves, 3/8 to 1″(2″) long by 3/8 to 3/4″ wide, with the midrib very prominent beneath and by the smaller fruits. All plants I have seen in cultivation are smaller than *I. cassine* and often shrubby, however, national champion is 40′ by 35′ at Lawtey, FL. 'Lowei' is yellow-fruited with dark green leaves. Several nurserymen have made selections for improved fruiting characteristics. Although the fruits are smaller than *I. opaca* and *I. cornuta* they are borne in great quantities. In addition, the color is much brighter. The fruits occur 1 to 3 at a node on 3/4″ long pedicels. The species is native in moist woods of the Coastal Plain region south and west to Texas. Introduced by Mark Catesby in 1726. The variety has a more coastal distribution than the species. Hybrids between the species and *I. opaca* occur naturally in the wild. Selections and hybrids have also been made, the most notable of which include *I. × attenuata* 'East Palatka', 'Hume #2', 'Savannah' and the Fosteri hybrids. Have observed many times since the 1990 edition and have not seen a true dark green leaf form. Significant variation in fruit size and color. Louisiana Nursery, Opelousas, LA lists two selections of the species and two of var. *myrtifolia*, red- and yellow-fruited in each taxon. Saw a number of interesting forms in the gardens and nursery of Charles and Allen Webb in February 1996 and October 1997. Even in North Florida foliage color was off-green. Fruits on some of the Webb seedlings were red, rose-red, and vermillion-red.

Ilex × 'Clusterberry' ('Nellie R. Stevens' × *I. leucoclada*) is a spreading shrub that grows 6 to 10′ high. The large, leathery, dull green evergreen leaves and large clusters of brick red fruits are the principal assets. Hardy to Zone 7. Released in 1978.

Ilex × 'Dr. Kassab' (*I. cornuta* × *I. pernyi*) is a beautiful dark green-leaved, broad pyramidal evergreen form that grows 15 to 20′ high. It is a female and offers excellent red fruits. I had the good fortune of meeting Dr. Kassab who showed me around his Philadelphia area garden. He showed a deep love of plants and his fine garden was a testimony to his enthusiasm. Like so many visits, there is never enough time to ask all the questions and sort out the pertinent details. There is no better fraternity than that bound by the love of plants.

Ilex × Ebony Magic™ is an upright pyramidal form with excellent leathery lustrous dark green spiny leaves and brilliant large orange-red fruits. Fruits persist through spring. The parentage appears *I. rugosa* and *I. aquifolium* but I have not been able to document this. Conflicting reports on hardiness are given with Zone 4 and Zone 6 designations. One nurseryman reported it was hardier than the Blue Hybrids. 'Ebony Male' can be used to pollinate 'Ebony Magic'. Name is derived from the dark color of the stem and leaves. Originated as an open-pollinated seedling discovered in Ohio. Will form a strong pyramidal upright tree 20′ by 10′ with heavy crop of deep orange-red fruits that persist into spring. Plants I have observed were more shrubby with size approaching 12 to 15′ high by 8 to 10′ wide.

Ilex × 'Emily Bruner' (*I. cornuta* 'Burfordii' × *I. latifolia*) is a fine broad, dense pyramidal female form that grows to 20′ high. The large evergreen leaves are a good dark green. Zone 7 to 9. It was introduced by Mr. Don Shadow, Winchester, TN. Don tells the story how a lady brought a plant into the greenhouse when he was an undergraduate at Tennessee. Don knew this plant was special and acquired the plant. It is a good choice for southern gardens. 'James Swan' is the male pollinator for 'Emily Bruner'. Several plants of 'Emily Bruner' have fruited abundantly on the Georgia campus. The large red fruits essentially encircle the stems. Temperatures around −3°F injured many leaves but did not kill stem tissue. Has become popular in the past 6 to 8 years and in many Zone 7 and 8a nurseries is third to 'Nellie R. Stevens' and *I. × attenuata* 'Foster's #2' in quantity produced. The fruits persisted in good condition (red not black) in

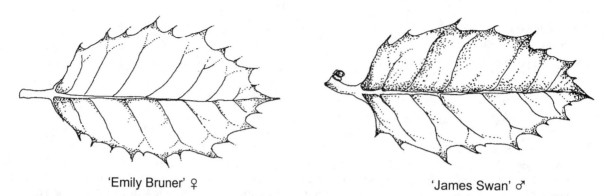

'Emily Bruner' ♀   'James Swan' ♂

the consistently cold 1995–96 winter. Requires a degree more fertilizer (nitrogen), than for example 'Nellie R. Stevens', to maintain consistent dark green foliage. Large plants at Milliken Arboretum, Spartanburg, SC that are superb. 'Ginny Bruner' has smaller leaves than 'Emily Bruner' and fruits ripen earlier. 'Lib's Favorite' is of similar parentage.

Ilex integra Thunb., (ī′leks in-te′grà), Nepal Holly, is a 20 to 30′ high evergreen tree with lustrous, almost black-green leaves and abundant subglobose, 1/3 to 1/2″ diameter, dark red fruits (4 pyrenes) on 1/4″ long stalks. The leaves average 2 to 4″ long, 3/4 to 1 1/4″ wide, and are essentially entire or toothed toward apex. Flowers are 4-merous and creamy yellow. This is more vigorous than *I. rotunda*, at least plants I have seen, and produces handsome fruit crops. 'Ban Croft' produces attractive red fruits while 'Bisexual' is a self-pollinating form. Japan. Introduced 1864. Zone 6b to 9. Has performed well in Savannah, GA area for many years. Reported hardy in Memphis, TN. Allied to *I. aquifolium*.

Ilex × 'John Morris' and 'Lydia Morris' represent male and female, respectively, hybrid hollies selected from seedlings which resulted from crosses between *I. cornuta* 'Burfordii' × *I. pernyi*. They exhibit a dense pyramidal shrub-type habit and possess lustrous dark green, almost black-green evergreen foliage. The leaves are tightly borne along the stems and are extremely spiny. Very handsome in foliage and the female form produces cardinal red fruits. The plants were named after the individuals who donated land for the establishment of the Morris Arboretum, Philadelphia, PA. Hardy in Zone 6, shakily so in Zone 5. These plants were killed after exposure to -20°F during 1976–77 winter. After 30 years, the original 'John T. Morris' was 15′ high and 12′ across. 'Lydia Morris' forms a pyramidal shrub to 12′ high and wide. Both were released in 1961 by Henry Skinner. Plants have performed well at the University's Botanical Garden and are 18′ high and 12′ wide; in outline they look like dark green haystacks.

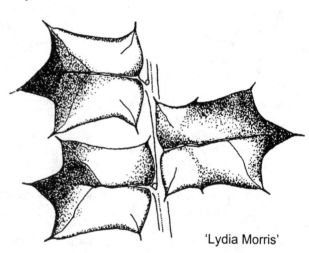

'Lydia Morris'

Ilex × koehneana Loes. — Koehne Holly
LEAVES: Alternate, simple, elliptic-ovate, 2 to 3 1/2″(5″) long, 1 1/2 to 3″ wide, leathery, with 8 to 12, 1/16″ long, spiny teeth on each margin, lustrous dark green above, light green beneath, glabrous; petiole—3/8 to 1/2″ long.

BUDS: Imbricate, 1/8″ long, ovoid, acute at tip, glabrous, purple.
STEM: Stout, glabrous, glossy, purplish above, green below.

Ilex × *koehneana*, (ī′leks kō-nē-ā′ná), Koehne Holly, is the grex
name for hybrids between *I. aquifolium* and *I. latifolia*. 'Ruby'
(female) and 'Jade' (male) are two rather non-descript hybrids,
the former languishing as a shrub at the U.S. National Arboretum. The only clone I see with regularity is 'Wirt L. Winn', a
beautiful glossy moderately spiny-margined dark green leaf
form that bears handsome large red fruits in abundance. The
habit is distinctly pyramidal and landscape size approximates
20 to 25′ in height. Interestingly, this plant has withstood the
heat and drought of the Southeast and prospered while its *I.
aquifolium* parent languished. At –3°F leaves were slightly
injured. Cuttings of 'Wirt L. Winn' collected June 29 and August
17, 10,000 ppm KIBA, peat:perlite, mist, rooted 100%. This
hybrid is much easier to root than *I. latifolia*. In my travels,
cultivars continue to surface with 'Chestnut Leaf', 'Chieftan', 'Lassie', 'Hohman', 'Martha Berry', 'San Jose',
'Watumpka', and two new U.S. National Arboretum releases 'Agena' (female), and 'Ajax' (male). The latter
two grew 30′ in 30 years, have glossy dark green leaves, and red fruits on 'Agena'. 'Hohman' bore
tremendous crops of red fruits in the U.S. National Arboretum and looked like the class of the group. A
plant next to 'Wirt L. Winn' in my Georgia evaluation tests looks and performs the same. Several 20-year-
old specimens of 'Wirt L. Winn' growing next to similar aged 'Nellie R. Stevens' at the University's Griffin
Station are bedraggled, thin, and yellow-green while the 'Nellie R. Stevens' are darker green and denser.
Zone (6b)7 to 9.

Ilex latifolia Thunb. — Lusterleaf Holly

LEAVES: Alternate, simple, evergreen, leathery, oblong to ovate-oblong, 4 to 6 1/2″(8″) long, 1 1/2 to 3″ wide,
apex obtuse to short acuminate, rounded at base, marginal teeth coarse and not spiny, lustrous dark
green above, lower surface yellow green, glabrous; petiole—1/2 to 1″ long.

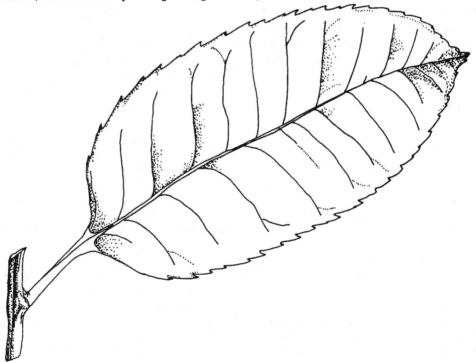

Ilex latifolia, (ī′leks lat-i-fō′li-á), Lusterleaf Holly, is a large, pyramidal evergreen tree. Although not common in
the South, it certainly ranks among the best of the broadleaf evergreens. Specimens on the University of
Georgia campus growing in one-half shade are quite dense. Landscape size approximates 20 to 25′. The
large lustrous dark green leaves hold their color throughout the year. Flowers are 4-merous and yellow
green. The deep dull red, 1/3″ diameter, globose fruits, with 4, rarely 6, pyrenes are borne in dense

axillary clusters and almost completely encircle the stems. Fruits hold into February–March but lose color and become dull, washed out red. Given a well-drained soil it appears to thrive. Holds up under drought conditions at least based on my Georgia observations. Offers the texture of *Magnolia grandiflora* yet without the inherent messiness. Louisiana Nurseries lists 'Gulino Gardens' with long glossy green leaves and abundant bright red fruits; 'Mike Richard' with smaller lustrous leaves with larger spines and bright red fruits, apparently also produces male flowers; 'Male' is compact with lustrous dark green leaves; and '69-135' which is a superior female selection from Tom Dodd Nurseries. Japan, China. Introduced 1840. Zone (6b)7 to 9. A relatively new hybrid selected in 1981, named 'Mary Nell' after the wife of former University of Illinois professor J.C. McDaniel, is starting to make waves in the Southeast. The habit is pyramidal and the leaves spiny, lustrous dark green. It sets great quantities of bright red fruits. Beautiful foliage but requires persistent pruning to keep it full and dense. The parentage is (*I. cornuta* 'Burfordii' × *I. pernyi* 'Red Delight') × *I. latifolia*. Hardiness should approximate Zone (6b)7 to 9. A selection called 'Mary Nell Sibling' with 3 1/2″ long, glossy deep green spiny leaves and bright red fruits was selected from the same cross. The form I have seen in cultivation is the first mentioned.

'Mary Nell'

Ilex × meserveae S.Y. Hu — Meserve Hybrid Hollies
(ī′leks me-sĕrv′ī-ē)

LEAVES: Alternate, simple, evergreen, leathery, spiny, 4 to 8 spines per margin, lustrous dark green with slightly impressed veins (above) that give the impression of ancient stoneware (fissured, cracked, reticulate pattern), size varies depending on cultivar from 1 to 2 1/2″ long, 3/4 to 1 1/4″ wide.
STEMS: Stout, often with slight ridges, reddish purple.

Mrs. F. Leighton Meserve (hence, × *meserveae*) of St. James, NY made crosses in early 1950's between the cold hardy *I. rugosa*, Prostrate Holly, and *I. aquifolium*, English Holly, that resulted in this magnificent series of introductions. Subsequent introductions were not always of the same parentage as above. Mrs. Meserve was honored for her work and received the American Horticultural Society's Citation for Outstanding Contributions to Amateur Horticulture. Conard Pyle, West Grove, PA, purchased rights to introduce, grow, and market the plants and has been highly successful with them. Cultivars include:

Berri-Magic™—Marketing ploy by Monrovia Nursery in which 'Blue Girl' and 'Blue Boy' are grown in the same container to facilitate cross-pollination and heavy fruit set. The same technique has been applied to 'China Girl' and 'China Boy' under the same trademark name.

Blue Angel®—Offers crinkled, glossy dark green foliage, large shiny deep red drupes, and a full dense habit, 8′ by 8′, slowest growing of the females and also the least cold hardy; at −17°F (Cincinnati, OH) every leaf was killed (browned); interestingly I have seen the plant since and it has recovered so stems and buds were not injured; definitely the "dumpiest" of the group, introduced in 1973, PP 3662.

'Blue Boy'—A 1964 introduction that was considered inferior to 'Blue Prince' and later introductions, but actually is an acceptable plant; the habit is shrubby, 10 to 15′ high, and I have observed older plants (15′ high) with a full compliment of lustrous dark green foliage; the patent (2435) has expired and this cultivar is starting to appear more commonly in the trade.

'Blue Girl'—A 1964 introduction like the above except a female with bright red fruits; this appears faster growing and more open than 'Blue Princess' but I have no absolute data to substantiate the statement; forms a shrubby upright, pyramidal outline, 8 to 10′(15′) by 6 to 8′; patent (2434) has expired on this cultivar; in Kansas tests this was the most cold hardy female form.

Blue Maid® ('Mesid')—Considered one of the hardiest of the group, fast-growing, forms a broad 15′ high pyramid and produces a good crop of red fruits similar to 'Blue Princess' in size; Conard Pyle promoted this as one of the hardiest, but 'Blue Princess' and 'Blue Girl' are hardier; PP 4685.

Blue Prince®—A lustrous, leathery dark green male form that produces abundant pollen, habit is dense and somewhat broad pyramidal but again tends toward a shrubby nature, can easily be pruned into any shape, will grow 8 to 12′ high; essentially no discoloration of foliage at –17°F, one of the hardiest along with 'Blue Princess'; introduced 1972; PP 3517.

Blue Princess®—An improved 'Blue Girl' (some will argue this) with more abundant darker red fruit, lustrous darker bluish green foliage, the habit is broad and shrubby and size approximates 15′ high by 10′ wide, considered by many who have grown and evaluated this plant as the best fruit producer, PP 3675.

Blue Stallion® ('Mesan')—A male form with purplish stems and lustrous dark green "snag-free" foliage (i.e., not spiny-margined), is listed as having 5 to 7 small spines per margin, grows faster than 'Blue Prince', a good pollinator for 'Blue Princess' and the other female forms for it supposedly flowers over a long time frame in spring, grows 16′ by 12′, PP 4804.

Other Meserve Hybrids:

Centennial Girl®—Hybrid between *I. centrochinensis* × *I. aquifolium*, the newest introduction from Conard-Pyle, foliage is deep matte green, produces abundant red fruits that persist into March, grows 12 to 15′ high, 5 to 8′ wide, forming a pyramidal outline, introduced 1997.

China Boy® ('Mesdob')—A compact mounded form that is stated to mature at 10′ by 8′; plants I have seen were rounded, compact with glossy green foliage; this cultivar is a pollinator for 'China Girl'; excellent cold hardiness, probably in the range of –20°F; based on observations this is more cold hardy than the Blue series and shows increased heat tolerance compared to Blue series; result of a cross between *I. rugosa* and *I. cornuta*, introduced 1979, PP 4803.

China Girl® ('Mesog')—A handsome female form with abundant, large, 1/3″ diameter, red fruits, foliage is a lustrous green but not as dark as the Blue series, also the leaves tend to cup, i.e., the margins turn down and in, a trait that easily separates it from the Blue series, habit is rounded, 10′ by 10′ at maturity, but all plants I have seen to date were 3 to 5′ by 3 to 5′; my first introduction came at Longwood Gardens, in the Idea Garden, where a number had been planted in a hedge arrangement, interspersed with several 'China Boy' for pollination, the foliage and fruiting effects were fabulous considering the December time frame; same parentage as 'China Boy'; excellent heat tolerance; Pair showed unequivocally that 'China Girl' was more heat tolerant than the true Blue hybrids and reported that 'China Girl' survived record high temperatures in 1983 that killed the Blue hybrids growing next to them; PP 4878.

Several footnotes to the above 'China Boy' and 'China Girl' discussion are in order. In Athens, GA these survive while the true blues disappear. Leaves have a tendency to fold under (cup), a type of revolute margin, and appear slightly abnormal. Interestingly, in my field plots, the leaves turn off-green in winter and do not have the same foliage appeal as the typical *I. cornuta* cultivars.

Dragon Lady® ('Meschick')—(*I. pernyi* × *I. aquifolium*) is more correctly listed as an *I.* × *aquipernyi* (which see) form; habit is distinctly pyramidal-columnar with lustrous dark green, spiny-margined leaves and large red fruits; have seen it used as a backdrop for the perennial border at Longwood, makes an excellent barrier plant; definitely less cold hardy than the Blue or China series, I suspect –5 to –10°F will cause some leaf damage; probably mature at 15 to 20′ by 4 to 6′; has not performed well in our Georgia trials; PP 4996; 'Blue Stallion' can serve as an effective pollinator.

Golden Girl® ('Mesgolg')—Broad pyramidal habit, dense satiny foliage, brilliant yellow (orange) fruits, the first yellow-fruited introduction, 1989, PP 7652.

A few final thoughts relative to the Meserve Hybrids: In a sense, they have been warmly embraced by northern gardeners. In the South, the true Blue (*I. rugosa* and *I. aquifolium*) do not perform well in the heat of Zone 7b to 9. If shade and well-drained soil is provided, the plants are acceptable, but still do not measure up to plants I have seen in Boston MA, Hershey PA, Columbus OH, Manchester NH, and Philadelphia PA. I tried to grow *I. rugosa* in Georgia but the heat reduced it to rubble. Also, *I. aquifolium* is not well-adapted to the Southeast, possibly because of the high summer night temperatures and poorly drained soils. They are worth a try but use should be tempered. Buddy Hubbuch, retired Horticulturist, Bernheim Arboretum, reported that various blue cultivars survived –24°F, however, the heavy wet clay soils predisposed the plants to decline and *Phytophthora* infection over time.

All the Meserve Hybrids can suffer from winter desiccation and in the Burlington, VT area, I witnessed extensive leaf kill above the snowline with stems, for the most part, still alive; the low temperature was about –20°F; the bottom line for any broadleaf evergreen in northern latitudes if the ground is frozen, the wind blowing, the sun bright, some water loss from the leaves is inevitable. No replacement water is available since the ground is frozen and eventually, especially over time, some or all exposed leaves may desiccate and/or die.

Drs. John Pair and Steve Still conducted outstanding practical research showing the effect of exposure on the blue hollies. They built a structure that offered various sun/shade exposures during winter and planted 'Blue Angel', 'Blue Maid', 'Blue Prince' and 'Blue Princess'. Air temperatures on south and southwest sides were as high as 109°F and 118°F, respectively; low temperature was –10°F. All cultivars survived with 'Blue Angel' most seriously injured. 'Blue Princess' was the hardiest and most fruitful. Shoot growth was greatest on 'Blue Prince' and 'Blue Maid'. Plants grew best on north, northeast, and northwest exposures where summer temperatures were relatively cool and foliage temperature fluctuations in summer were reduced. See *HortScience* 17(5):823–825 (1982); *HortScience* 22(2):268–270 (1987); and *Amer. Nurseryman* 159(9):51–52 (1984).

Ilex × 'Nellie R. Stevens'
LEAVES: Alternate, simple, evergreen, ovoid, 2 to 3″(4″) long, one-half as wide, slight twist to long axis of leaf, 2 to 3 spines per margin, lustrous dark green above, lighter beneath, veins impressed; petiole—1/2″ long.

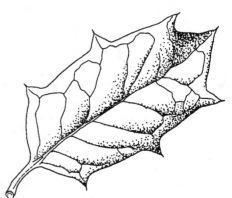

Ilex × 'Nellie R. Stevens' is a putative hybrid between *I. cornuta* × *I. aquifolium*. The habit is that of a large evergreen shrub or small broad pyramidal tree 15 to 25′ high. The leaves are lustrous dark green, slightly bullate, with 2 or 3 teeth on each side. The fruit is red, rounded, 1/4 to 1/3″ wide, and the female flowers can be effectively pollinated by male *I. cornuta* which flower at a similar time. Heavily fruitful and fruit develops parthenocarpically. Fruits often not persistent and do not provide the long term effect of an 'Emily Bruner'. Hardy in Zone 6 to 9. Very vigorous plant and relatively fast-growing. One of the best hollies for the southern states and is one of the most commonly used hollies. It was released by G.A. Van Lennep, Jr., St. Michael, MD, in 1954. It is named for the owner, Nellie R. Stevens, Oxford, MD. 'Edward J. Stevens' is a large male clone that is useful for pollinating 'Nellie R. Stevens'. Ms. Stevens obtained seed from *I. cornuta* at the U.S. National Arboretum around 1900. Apparently, three seedlings were named, 'Nellie R. Stevens' being the most important. 'Hefcup' is a yellow-variegated foliage form, with golden marginal markings and a deep green center, fruits are yellow when ripening in summer, maturing to red, forms a pyramidal growth habit, similar to 'Nellie R. Stevens' and should reach 18 to 20′ high by 18′ wide, branch sport of 'Nellie R. Stevens' found by Randy Hefner, Conover, NC, introduced by Wight Nursery, Cairo, GA, plant patent #8537.

Ilex pernyi Franch. — Perny Holly
LEAVES: Alternate, simple, evergreen, 5/8 to 1″ long, 3/8 to 5/8″ wide, rhombic or quadrangular-ovate, 1 to 3 spines on each side, the upper pair the longest, but shorter than the terminal spine, generally 5-spined, glabrous, glossy dark green above, leaves crowded together in more or less one plane; petiole—1/12″ long, puberulous; leaves persistent on 4- to 5-year-old growth.

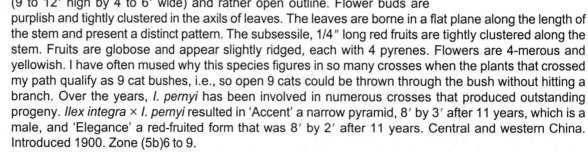

Ilex pernyi, (ī′leks pĕr′nē-ī), Perny Holly, is not common in American gardens but has been used for breeding purposes. Easily distinguished by its upright habit (9 to 12′ high by 4 to 6′ wide) and rather open outline. Flower buds are purplish and tightly clustered in the axils of leaves. The leaves are borne in a flat plane along the length of the stem and present a distinct pattern. The subsessile, 1/4″ long red fruits are tightly clustered along the stem. Fruits are globose and appear slightly ridged, each with 4 pyrenes. Flowers are 4-merous and yellowish. I have often mused why this species figures in so many crosses when the plants that crossed my path qualify as 9 cat bushes, i.e., so open 9 cats could be thrown through the bush without hitting a branch. Over the years, *I. pernyi* has been involved in numerous crosses that produced outstanding progeny. *Ilex integra* × *I. pernyi* resulted in 'Accent' a narrow pyramid, 8′ by 3′ after 11 years, which is a male, and 'Elegance' a red-fruited form that was 8′ by 2′ after 11 years. Central and western China. Introduced 1900. Zone (5b)6 to 9.

Ilex purpurea Hassk. (*I. chinensis* Sims), (ī′leks pĕr-pū′rē-à), Kashi Holly, is a beautiful evergreen 20 to 30′ high tree for Zones 7b to 9. In Athens and Aiken, SC trees have withstood –3°F and the hottest, driest summers on record. The oblong-elliptic, 3 to 5″ long, 1 to 2″ wide, lustrous dark green leaves have acuminate apices and crenate serrations. The new leaves are bronze. The 4- to 5-merous, lavender

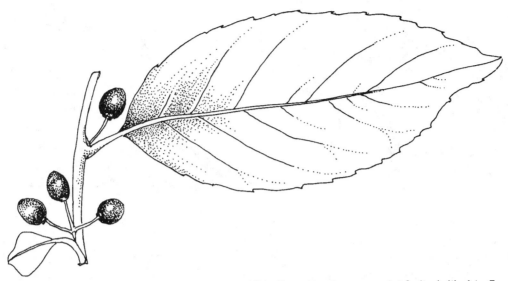

flowers open in May and are followed by 1/4 to 1/3″ diameter glossy scarlet fruits (with 4 to 5 pyrenes) in fall. Good and worthy holly for the Coastal Plain of the Southeastern United States. Introduced 1810 to England. Japan, China.

Ilex Red Hybrid Hollies

Newly introduced in the mid-1990's, these five hybrids are upright-pyramidal growers with glossy dark green foliage, the leaves prominently spined. The five cultivars, Cardinal™, Festive™, Little Red™, Oak Leaf™, and Robin™, were planted in Athens. Early observations (after 3 years) indicate that none will replace 'Nellie R. Stevens' for quality of foliage, growth rate and habit. The "Red" comes from the new growth which emerges reddish purple. Origin is purported to be open-pollinated seedlings of 'Mary Nell' selected by Mitch Magee, Poplarville, MS in the 1980's. Cardinal™ produces foliage similar to 'Mary Nell', new growth reddish, pyramidal habit, 14′ high and 8′ wide, female. Festive™ has the most spiny leaf of the group, extremely lustrous dark green, broad pyramidal and more compact, 12′ by 8′, female. Little Red™ is more rounded in habit, reddish new growth, 10′ by 6′, female. Oak Leaf™ has large leaves, more elongated and somewhat oak leaf-shaped, tall pyramidal habit, 14′ by 8′, fastest growing form, female. Robin™ produces leaves similar to 'Nellie R. Stevens', reddish when emerging, 14′ by 8′, female. None have fruited in our Georgia trials, so it is difficult to rate this most important trait. Their introduction is a joint venture between Evergreen and Flowerwood Nurseries.

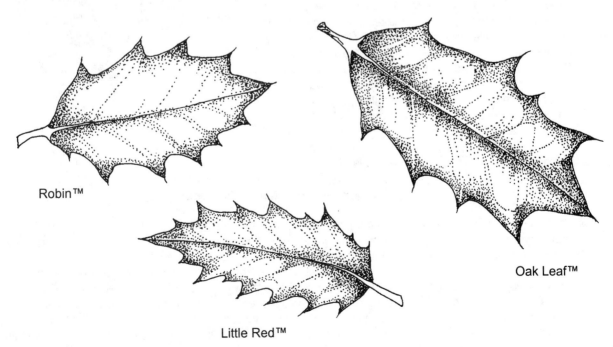

Robin™

Little Red™

Oak Leaf™

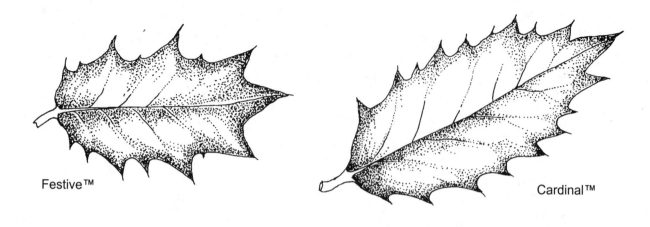

Festive™   Cardinal™

Ilex rotunda Thunb., (ī'leks rō-tun'dȧ), Lord's Holly, is occasionally cultivated in Zone 8 and 9 where it makes a small evergreen tree. The dark green ovate or elliptic, obtuse or acute, rounded or cuneate, entire leaves average 1 1/2 to 4″ long, 3/4 to 1 3/4″ wide, with 1/2 to 1″ long petioles. Flowers are 4- to 6-merous and white. The 1/4″ diameter bright red fruits with 4 to 6 pyrenes are borne in umbels on 1/4″ pedicels and look like a red shower in fall and winter. Fruits hold into winter in the Savannah,

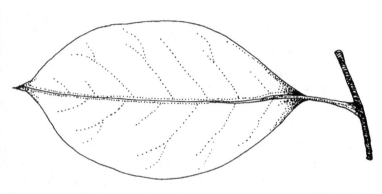

GA area. Difficult to propagate from cuttings and mid-January cuttings did not root at all under our typical procedure. Have noted references that stated the species could grow 75′ high. Japan and Korea. Introduced about 1850. Zone 8 to 9. Injury coincides with 5°F, killed outright at -9°F.

Ilex rugosa F. Schmidt, (ī'leks rū-gōs'ȧ), Prostrate Holly, has ovate, 1 to 1 1/2″ long, 5/8 to 3/4″ wide, obtuse, rounded to cuneate, serrate, glabrous, wrinkled, leathery lustrous dark green leaves. It is a low-growing (1 to 1 1/2′ high), almost prostrate evergreen shrub that, although paling to a degree with the larger types, makes a rather handsome shrub. The white flowers are 4-merous. The solitary, roundish, red, 1/4″ diameter fruits with 4 pyrenes ripen in September. I have seen it at Longwood Gardens in a shady location performing quite well. It is one of the parents of the Meserve hybrids. Quite hardy and a good parent for breeding cold tolerant hollies. Not at all heat tolerant and not recommended for Zone 7 to 8. 'Goliath' is a male with rich green soft-textured leaves. Japan, Sakhalin. Introduced 1895. Zone 3 to 6(7).

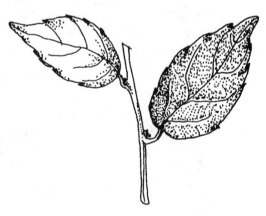

U.S. National Arboretum Introductions

Ilex 'Adonis', ('Nellie R. Stevens' × *I. latifolia*), is a large, rapidly growing, compact evergreen shrub, habit is broad pyramidal, listed as growing 18′ tall. Leaves exceptionally dark green, broad ovate, 5″ long, 2 1/2″ wide, with numerous short, blunt, uniform spines on margins, but with fewer spines than 'Venus', leaf tips twisted. A male pollinator for 'Venus'. Originated from a cross made in 1963 by E.F. Kosar at the U.S. National Arboretum, selected and named by F.S. Santamour, Jr. and G.K. Eisenbeiss. Zone 7.

Ilex 'Agena', (*Ilex* × *koehneana*), is a fast-growing pyramidal evergreen tree, listed as growing 35′ tall. Leaves ovate, 5″ long, margins continuous with small uniform spines. Red, elongated, 5/8″ long, 5/16″ wide fruits borne in fascicles of 11. Original plant grown from a seedling of unknown and disputed botanical status sent to U.S. National Arboretum for identification in 1962 and selected and named by F.S. Santamour, Jr. and G.K. Eisenbeiss. Zone 7.

Ilex 'Ajax', (*Ilex* × *koehneana*), is a fast-growing, pyramidal, evergreen tree, listed as growing 35′ tall. Leaves broadly lanceolate, 5″ long, margins continuous with small uniform spines. Male pollinator for 'Agena'. Original plant grown from a seedling of unknown and disputed botanical status sent to U.S. National Arboretum for identification in 1960 and selected and named by F.S. Santamour, Jr. and G.K. Eisenbeiss. Zone 7.

Ilex 'Coronet', ['Nellie R. Stevens' × (*I. ciliospinosa* × *I.* × *aquipernyi*)], is a compact, columnar evergreen shrub, listed as growing to 10′. Leaves are ovate-lanceolate, 2 5/8″ long, 1 1/2″ wide, twisted, soft and flexible, with 4 to 5 large spines on each side. Bright red, subglobose, 7/16″ long, 1/2″ wide fruits that set parthenocarpically (without pollination). Originated from a cross made by W.F. Kosar at the U.S. National Arboretum, selected by W.F. Kosar, and named by G.K. Eisenbeiss. Zone 7.

Ilex 'Miniature', ('Nellie R. Stevens' × *I. pernyi*), is a compact, narrow pyramidal, evergreen shrub, listed as growing to 8′ tall. Leaves are glossy dark green, broadly ovate, 1 3/4″ long, 3/8″ wide with 2 stout spines on each side and a strong reflexed tip spine. Red, rounded, 3/8″ diameter fruits. The habit and leaf shape is very similar to *Ilex* 'Lydia Morris' and 'John T. Morris' but the growth rate and leaf size is only half of these. Originated from a cross made in 1961 by E.F. Kosar at the U.S. National Arboretum.

Ilex 'Venus', ('Nellie R. Stevens' × *I. latifolia*), is a large, rapidly growing, compact evergreen shrub, habit is broad pyramidal, listed as growing 18′ tall. Leaves broadly ovate, 5″ long, 2 1/2″ wide, with numerous short, blunt, uniform spines on margins. Veins distinctly impressed on upper surface. Bright red, slightly elongate, 7/16″ long, 3/8″ wide, persistent (sometimes lasting more than 1 year) fruits borne in clusters of 14 or more. Originated from a cross made in 1963 by E.F. Kosar at the U.S. National Arboretum, selected and named by F.S. Santamour, Jr. and G.K. Eisenbeiss. Zone 7.

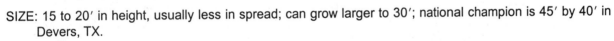

Ilex vomitoria Ait. — Yaupon
(ī′leks vom-i-tō′ri-à)

LEAVES: Alternate, simple, evergreen, narrowly oval to ovate, 1/2 to 1 1/2″ long, 1/4 to 3/4″ wide, tapered at base, blunt at apex, margin shallowly toothed usually to the base which separates it from *I. crenata*, glabrous, lustrous dark green; no blackish glands evident on underside; petiole—1/8″ long.

STEM: Young stems quite downy, purplish initially, finally whitish gray and glabrous.

SIZE: 15 to 20′ in height, usually less in spread; can grow larger to 30′; national champion is 45′ by 40′ in Devers, TX.

HARDINESS: 7 to 10.

HABIT: Very picturesque, upright, irregularly branched shrub or small tree, will sucker to form thickets.

RATE: Medium to fast, responds well to high fertility; 2 to 3′ of new growth occurred in a single season on plants at the University's Botanical Garden.

TEXTURE: Medium-fine.

BARK: White to gray, quite striking; good idea to limb up older specimens to expose and highlight the handsome bark.

LEAF COLOR: New growth with a purplish tinge but soon lost and turning a lustrous dark green.

FLOWERS: Dioecious, greenish white, 4 petals, produced in axillary clusters on year-old wood, males numerous on 1/8″ long peduncles, females solitary or in pairs mid-April, later than *I. cornuta* types.

FRUIT: Translucent, 1/4″ diameter scarlet drupe, 4 pyrenes, usually borne in prodigious quantities and persisting into spring; fruit is truly beautiful.

CULTURE: Easily transplanted, adaptable to varied soils from quite dry to extremely wet; found native in both popcorn dry and wet swampy areas; tolerant of salt spray; perhaps the most adaptable small-leaved evergreen holly for southern gardens.

DISEASES AND INSECTS: None serious although a leaf miner has been listed; shows much greater propensity to succeed under southern conditions compared to *Ilex crenata* and cultivars.

LANDSCAPE VALUE: Multitudinous uses including informal screens, hedges, specimens, barriers, espaliers; takes pruning well; the cultivars are widely used for mass and foundation plantings; also makes a good topiary plant; more adaptable and resistant to insects and diseases than *I. crenata*; where cold hardy it should be the small leaf holly of choice.

CULTIVARS: Difficult to track all the cultivars; other forms exist.

Bordeaux™ ('Condeaux')—Branch sport of 'Schillings' with smaller leaves and burgundy winter foliage color; winter color is not as wine red as advertised; not significantly more compact than 'Schillings'; Flowerwood Nursery introduction; PP 8779 in 1994.

'Dodd's Cranberry'—Upright, dense-foliaged form, leaves lustrous dark green, heavy cranberry red fruit set, from Tom Dodd Nurseries, attractive form.

'Dodd's Yellow'—A yellow-fruited form from Tom Dodd Nurseries, Semmes, AL.

'Fencerow'—Habit similar to species, dark green leaves, red fruits, found in a fencerow, hence the name.

'Folsom's Weeping'—A selection similar to 'Pendula', female, narrow in habit, introduced by Tom Dodd, Jr.

'Gold Top'—New growth yellow to golden maturing green, red fruits, introduced by Woodlanders, Aiken, SC, nice in late spring–summer, off-color in cold weather in Athens.

'Goodyear'—Semi-weeping form, red fruits, female, found near the Goodyear Blimp Hanger, Houston, TX, found by Lynn Lowery.

'Gray's Green Leaf'—Superior dark green foliage, red fruits, grows slower than the species.

'Gray's Little Leaf'—A cute diminutive small leaf form, foliage about 1/3 as wide as the species, new growth reddish purple, have seen only once and wondered why the plant is not more common, nice delicate, fine-textured plant, male.

'Hightower'—Upright form of the species, excellent for topiary work, beautiful scarlet fruits persisting into spring.

'Jewel'—Female form selected for its heavy fruit production, rounded compact outline.

'Katherine'—Golden yellow, long-persistent, abundant fruit that literally smothers the branches; March 27, 1996 fruits still heavy and with good color after a particularly difficult winter; fruits remain golden yellow and do not discolor or develop orange-red overtones; selected from a block of seedlings at Select Trees, Bishop, GA and named after my oldest daughter; vigorous grower like the species, parent plant was 15′ in 1997; Jim Berry, Flowerwood Nursery, AL visited and saw the plant in full fruit in late December, he commented that it was one of the best yellow-fruited forms he had observed.

'Kathy Ann'—Upright spreading habit, 20′ by 15′; 1″ by 1/2″, glossy dark green leaves; dark red fruit; chance seedling from a pine plantation, discovered in Stone County, MS in 1985 by D. Batson and named for his wife.

'Lynn Lowrey'—Large-growing like the species with large, 3/4 to 1 1/2″ long leaves and dark red fruit.

'Nana' ('Dwarf' in Galle's *Hollies*)—Dwarf, compact form with slightly smaller leaves than the species, new growth rich yellow-green without the purplish tinge associated with 'Schillings' ('Stokes Dwarf'), grows 3 to 5′ high and slightly wider after many years, a female based on my observations but fruit is usually hidden by the close-knit branches, branches are quite brittle and I have noticed a few branches dying at random on shrubs in the University's Botanical Garden and on campus; close examination indicated the branches had been broken; very fine cultivar but over used; a 25-year-old plant may be 5′ high and 8 to 10′ wide; makes a gigantic mounded cushion if not pruned; old specimen in Founder's Garden on campus is 10′ by 12′.

'Pendula' (f. *pendula* Foret & Solymosy)—I have decided this is a convenient holding area for any weeping form of the species; on the Georgia Campus there are male and female forms, one particular grouping of male plants was 20 to 25′ high; interestingly they had to be relocated due to construction, the plants were cut back, dug, and transplanted successfully, the basal trunk diameter was about 10″; apparently will come partially true-to-type from seed.

'Poole's Best'—A heavily fruited, strong-growing, compact selection, named and introduced by Ken Durio.

'Pride of Houston'—Medium-sized shrub with heavy fruit set, have seen at Hines Nursery in Houston, superior to the row-run seedlings in quality of foliage and red fruits.

'Sandy Hook'—Yellow-fruited form.

'Saratoga Gold'—Brilliant yellow-fruited form, vigorous upright-spreading, discovered in Saratoga, TX in 1951.

'Schillings' ('Stokes Dwarf')—One and the same, a more compact form than 'Nana' with smaller leaves, purplish new shoot extension, I have difficulty separating 'Nana' from this clone when plants are isolated; together the differences are more evident; 3 to 4′ by 3 to 4′; male; based on side-by-side comparisons in Georgia landscapes this cultivar does not grow as fast as 'Nana'; have seen 'Stokes Dwarf' listed as female, flowers examined by this author were consistently male; originated at Sam Stokes Nursery, LeCompte, LA; only 9″ by 12″ after 4 years; I am starting to doubt the validity of the form I see in everyday commerce; Galle lists it as one of 3 dwarf yaupon seedlings.

'Shadow's Female' (now trademarked as Hoskin Shadow™)—An excellent large dark green, almost oval-rounded leaf female form, with bright red translucent fruits, makes a large shrub or small tree and have seen it pruned into topiary form, probably several degrees hardier than the typical forms in cultivation, suspect about -5 to -10°F; possibly the best of the red-fruited forms, foliage is lustrous dark green, more abundant, resulting in a thicker, richer plant, named for the owner of Tennessee Valley Nursery, Winchester, TN and the father of Don and Fred Shadow, selected by Mr. Hoskins Shadow at Howard Nursery in late 1970's.

'Slim's Select'—Dwarf, female, pendulous to prostrate growth habit, introduced by Ken Durio, Louisiana Nursery.

Stephens Compact—Chance seedling that occurred at Nurseries Caroliniana, North Augusta, SC, plant is compact, probably 2′ tall, 4′ wide at maturity, large, lustrous dark green leaves, abundant red fruits, not yet named but I wanted to alert the reader about this potential introduction.

Stephens Weeping—Stiffly, broad, weeping, female form selected by Ted Stephens, Nurseries Caroliniana, has appeal as a container plant, terrific lustrous dark green foliage.

'Straughan's' ('Straughan's Dwarf')—A relative newcomer that appeared most promising as a boxwood substitute because of its billowy, rounded habit, supposedly less susceptible to breakage than 'Nana' but plants will often open up in the center almost like they have been pulled apart, will grow as large as 'Nana' perhaps more so, when I first saw the plant, I had great hopes; hopes are now tempered with the problem mentioned; stems are quite brittle and break readily in handling; supposedly a sport of 'Schillings'.

'Tricolor'—Foliage marked white, cream, and green and sometimes tinged pink, upright-spreading habit.

'Virginia Dare' ('Dare County' according to Galle)—Orange-fruited form from Woodlanders, pretty and long persistent fruits, large-growing, handsome dark green foliage.

'Wiggins' ('Wiggins Yellow')—Yellow-fruited form, upright-spreading habit, found near Wiggins, MS, introduced by Tom Dodd, Jr.

'Will Fleming'—Distinctly upright form, almost columnar in outline, unfortunately with time will pull apart particularly with ice and snow, a 12′ high plant in my trials has splayed and become disoriented, suspect this is a large-growing (15′ by 15 to 18″) cultivar, male, found by Will Fleming near Hempstead, TX.

'Yawkey'—A vivid orange-yellow fruited selection, upright-spreading habit, from South Island Plantation, Georgetown, SC, discovered in 1939 by F.G. Tarbox, originally named var. *yawkeyi*.

PROPAGATION: I had not worked with this species until moving to Georgia and learned quickly that it is difficult to root. My successes(?) range from 0 to about 50%. Nurserymen have reported similar percentages to 100%. Early March cuttings of 'Nana', 'Pendula', 'Schillings' and a heavily pruned plant of the species rooted 30, 20, 30, and 100%, respectively, in 9 weeks after 8000 ppm IBA quick-dip, peat:perlite, mist. An Alabama report mentioned 100% success with October cuttings of 'Pendula' rooted in poly houses. Possibly the use of KIBA would be beneficial.

ADDITIONAL NOTES: Easily separated from *Ilex crenata* by virtue of red fruits compared to black fruits, gray stems compared to green stems, red-purple veined new leaves compared to all green leaves and lack of dots or glands on the lower surface. The epithet *vomitoria* refers to the use the leaves were put by the Indians. They made an infusion of the leaves (high caffeine content) and drank freely until vomiting was induced. This cleansed them of any impurities of body and soul. A book titled *Black Drink, A Native American Tea*, University of Georgia Press, tells the fascinating story of *Ilex vomitoria*.

Terrific variation in seed grown material and the cultivar treatment above missed many that remain in the domain of selected nursery producers. Tom Dodd Nurseries, Inc., Semmes, AL has enthusiastically promoted and introduced new cultivars. I marvel at the variation in nature within the concept of the term species and certainly *I. vomitoria* fits this concept.

NATIVE HABITAT: Southeastern Virginia to central Florida and west to Texas, Southeastern Arkansas and Oklahoma. Introduced 1700.

Illicium floridanum Ellis — Florida Anise-tree
(i-liss′i-um flôr-i-dā′num)

FAMILY: Illiciaceae

LEAVES: Alternate, simple, evergreen, elliptic to elliptic-lanceolate, 2 to 6″ long, half as wide, acute, cuneate, entire, glabrous, lustrous to dull dark green above, pale beneath, leaves in pseudo-whorls at end of stem; petiole—1/2 to 3/4″ long, reddish purple which separates it from *I. parviflorum*; leaves highly aromatic when bruised or crushed, odor is more offensive than the other species discussed herein, several students described odor as resembling a gin-and-tonic, how would they know this?

BUDS: Flower—large, imbricate, reddish green, in upper leaves of pseudo-whorl; vegetative—small, 1/16″ long, imbricate, greenish red.

STEM: Stout, rounded, shiny, glabrous, gray-brown, dotted with small lenticels; pith—green, solid.

SIZE: 6 to 10′ high, slightly less in spread, can grow larger; national champion is 29′ by 20′ in Perry County, AL.

HARDINESS: Zone 6 to 9, survived –9°F in landscape plantings, in laboratory hardiness tests survived –15°F.

HABIT: Much branched, upright shrub usually compact in outline; requires pruning in early years to maintain shape; variable in habit; even in shade habit is relatively dense.

RATE: Medium, easy to induce several growth flushes per season by providing uniform moisture and fertilizer.

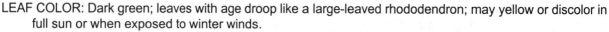

TEXTURE: Medium.

LEAF COLOR: Dark green; leaves with age droop like a large-leaved rhododendron; may yellow or discolor in full sun or when exposed to winter winds.

FLOWERS: Perfect, 1 to 2″ diameter, borne singly on a 1/2 to 2″ long pedicel, maroon-purple, odor is rather strange, composed of 20 to 30 strap-shaped petals, April–May; rather interesting but not overwhelming, has started to flower in late March in Athens and continued until late April, peak times have been mid-April in the Dirr garden; self incompatible, pollinated by flies and to lesser degree by beetles, minimal fruit production in gardens because of clonal production.

FRUIT: One-seeded, dehiscent follicles, 11 to 15 arranged in a whorl, one-inch diameter, at first green then yellow and finally brown, maturing in August–September (November in Athens), have a star-like configuration, distinct, seeds BB-like, brown, shiny.

CULTURE: Best transplanted from containers; prefers moist, well-drained, high organic matter soils; partial to heavy shade; have actually waded into swamp-like areas to photograph the plant; appears to thrive under moist to almost wet conditions; in full sun leaves are lighter green and not as handsome as those on shade-grown plants; have observed plants that were virtually yellow when grown in full sun and stress conditions; reports indicate considerable deer resistance.

DISEASES AND INSECTS: None serious; from nursery production and garden use aspects, the genus is one of the easiest to grow requiring minimal to no chemicals . . . truly a no maintenance plant.

LANDSCAPE VALUE: The entire shrub has a strong pungent odor and is simply wonderful to have in the garden; the flowers are beautiful but malodorous (April in the Piedmont area of Georgia); could be utilized in shrub borders, in shady, moist corners; Callaway Gardens has a planting in their wildflower garden area and the plant blends quite nicely into a naturalistic type setting; a new planting on campus has thrived under a large *Magnolia grandiflora*, performance has been amazing.

CULTIVARS: Several new cultivars since the last edition as well as a few older ones that I unearthed.

'Alba' (possibly f. *alba*)—White- to cream-colored flowers with same size, texture, odor, and petal number of species, leaves are slightly lighter green and petioles are green, plant in my garden is more restrained and compact than species, plant for shady nooks, probably 6 to 8′ high at maturity, found in the wild in Mississippi in 1982 by Chris Early.

Compact Forms—No cultivar designation but less vigorous than the species, the J.C. Raulston Arboretum plant appears more dense and broad-spreading but some of this may be due to the many cuttings that have been taken; also my Georgia colleague, Dr. John Ruter, discovered a compact form ('Peeblebrook') in South Georgia, a small plant in the Dirr garden is compact, John reported and I have seen on my plant, a fungal leaf spot that induces brownish lesions; the plant at J.C. Raulston Arboretum may be the same as 'Head-Lee Compact' which I observed at Head-Lee Nursery, Seneca, SC nursery, the plant was in a large container and not as dense as the one witnessed at J.C. Raulston Arboretum.

'Halley's Comet'—Heavier flower production, deep red petals that are slightly reflexed, vigorous grower, handsome dark green foliage, flowers over a longer period of time, often into fall, excellent performer in Dirr garden, discovered near De Funiak Springs, FL by John Allen Smith, Magnolia Nursery, Chunchula, AL.

'Jo's Variegated'—See under Variegated Form.

Pink Form—An unnamed light rose-pink flowered form sold by Woodlanders, Aiken, SC; discovered by Chuck Salter in the wild of Northwest Florida in 1987; in the Dirr garden it is less robust than the white-flowered forms and 'Halley's Comet'; have seen seedlings that fall into this category; Superior Trees, Lee, FL, gave me a pink-flowered form with an upright growth habit.

'Semmes'—White-flowered form from Semmes, AL area, introduced by Tom Dodd Nurseries, have given it a place of prominence by the entrance to our home, more restrained than the species, heavy-flowering; as I view 'Alba' and 'Semmes' in our garden there are not any major landscape differences, although the Semmes form is more restrained.

'Shady Lady' ('Thayer' may be the correct name; named after Tom Dodd's lovely wife who indeed is a shady lady)—Wavy leaf, gray-green with gray-white marginal variegation, pink flowers, variegated sport of 'Semmes', from Tom Dodd, III.

Variegated Form—Several in cultivation, the form I have is cream-yellow in the center with an irregular green border; also Woodlanders has a more irregular streaked and mottled cream-variegated form; this is possibly the selection from Green Images Nursery, Christmas, FL; 'Jo's Variegated' was introduced in 1995 by Ridgecrest Nursery and Gardens, Wynne, AR, originated as a branch sport of 'Alba' from Jo Levy's garden in Memphis, TN, rounded shrub, 10' high, 6 to 8' wide in 10 years, foliage shows more pronounced variegation (described as light and dark green) on young foliage with leaves slightly puckered, smaller and narrower than typical, flowers are not pure white but suffused with pale rose-pink, the dark green occurs irregularly in the center of the leaf, while 50 to 70% of the leaf is lighter creamy green or chartreuse.

Godfrey (1988) reported that white- and pink-flowered forms were intermixed with the red-flowered type in the wild.

PROPAGATION: Seeds germinate readily and according to Fred Galle, Callaway Gardens, have self-sown there to the point of weediness. I collected cuttings in late August, treated them with 3000 ppm IBA and had 100% rooting in 4 to 6 weeks; firm-wooded cuttings of all species described here root easily. In our shop cuttings are consistently rooted from firm-wooded summer cuttings (June–July) with 3000 to 5000 ppm KIBA, peat:perlite, mist. Rooting at times can be slow, up to 8 weeks, and patience is the key. Percentages are consistently high and average 90% or greater. Possible to take cuttings anytime into February–March with reasonable success.

ADDITIONAL NOTES: The *Illicium* species have become important elements of the southern garden matrix. Their attractive foliage and flowers, insect and disease resistances and general adaptability have elevated them to the forefront of broadleaf evergreens particularly for shady locations. A recent graduate student, Ms. Andrea Southworth, determined that *Illicium* leaves contain high levels of linolool, safrole, methyl eugenol ether, caryophyllene, and other compounds that are toxic to and/or repel insects. The reader is encouraged to crush the leaf and in doing will notice the highly aromatic scent. See Fantz, Raulston and McCartney, *Proc. Southern Nurseryman's Research Conf.* 36:300–304 (1991), for an evaluation of *Illicium* species.

NATIVE HABITAT: Florida to Louisiana. Found in moist wooded ravines, along or even in the small streams or seepage areas. Discovered by Bartram in western Florida in 1766. Introduced into cultivation in 1771.

RELATED SPECIES:

Illicium anisatum L. — Japanese Anise-tree, Star Anise

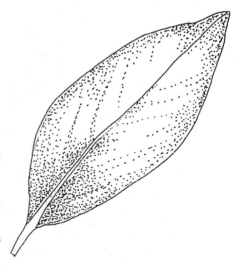

LEAVES: Alternate, simple, evergreen, 2 to 4″ long, 3/4 to 1 1/2″ wide, lustrous dark green, narrowly oval, blunt at apex, cuneate at base, glabrous, tapering to a 1/2 to 3/4″ long, glabrous, green petiole; confused in the Southeast with hardier *I. parviflorum* (which see), the leaves of *I. anisatum* are borne more perpendicular to the stem and are often slightly dog-eared compared to upright leaves on upper stems (at 45° angle) of *I. parviflorum*; also the margins are undulating creating a wavy-texture; this leaf, along with *I. henryi*, are the handsomest of the frequently cultivated species.

BUDS: Flower—large, imbricate, glabrous, green with reddish tipped scales; vegetative—extremely small, reddish green.

STEM: Stout, rounded, glabrous, green (into 2-year-old wood), lenticels scarce; pith—green, solid.

Illicium anisatum, (i-liss'i-um an-iss-ā'tum), Japanese Anise-tree, makes a rather dense medium to broad, pyramidal broadleaf evergreen shrub or small tree 6 to 10'(15') high. The habit is more formal than *I. parviflorum* and the plants I have seen do not form large suckering colonies like *I. parviflorum*. Plants maintain a central leader and give the appearance of a tree-type holly. The creamy (pale greenish yellow), up to 30-petaled, 1″ diameter, non-fragrant (perhaps slight fragrance) flowers normally occur in March–April, however, at Callaway Gardens, flowers have opened in late February. Flowers have opened from late February to early March in the Dirr garden. Flowers develop on 1″ long pedicels from the leaf axils. Fruit is a 1″ diameter, star-shaped, aggregate of follicles. At one time considered hardier than *I. floridanum* and *I. parviflorum* but the freeze of 1983–84 (-3°F) eliminated this species while the others were not affected. In the Dirr garden, 4 and 7°F did not injure leaves. If sufficiently acclimated going into winter, the species will survive in Zone 7. Requires moist, well-drained, reasonably rich soil and partial shade for best performance. Cultivars include: 'Pink Stars', named by J.C. Raulston because of the pink cast to the newly emerging flowers, new leaves emerge crimson and fade to green, this is a rather pretty form and the pink coloration real; also seen by this author was a cream-variegated leaf form that in the shade garden would prove handsome. Several variegated leaf forms are known from Japan. I recently was informed about a purple leaf form that bears apricot orange flowers. This selection will be introduced by a major southern nursery in the next few years. Native to China and Japan. Introduced 1790. Zone 7 to 9.

Illicium henryi Diels. — Henry Anise-tree

LEAVES: Alternate, simple, evergreen, 4 to 5″(6″) long, 1 to 1 1/2″ wide, elliptic ovate to elliptic obovate, acuminate and extended to a narrow point, narrow cuneate, entire, glabrous, flat in plane, lustrous dark green above, dull gray-green below; petiole—1/2 to 3/4″ long, green, glabrous.

BUDS: Flower—akin to *I. floridanum*; vegetative—imbricate, plumper, more strongly tinged with red.

STEM: Stout, rounded, green, glabrous, no evident lenticels; pith—solid, light green.

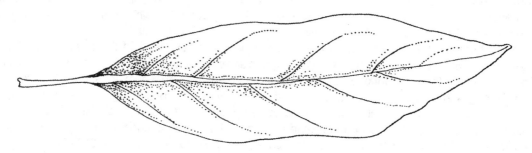

Illicium henryi, (i-liss'i-um hen'ri-ī), Henry Anise-tree, is a 6 to 8' (to 15') high, densely pyramidal broadleaf evergreen shrub with leathery, glossy dark green leaves. The 1/2 to 1″ diameter, 10- to 14- up to 20-petaled flowers vary from pink to deep crimson. The flowers develop from the leaf axils on 1 to 1 1/2″ long arching pedicels. This is a virtual unknown in American gardens but might prove a genuine gem with greater exposure. I have seen plants at Strybing Arboretum, San Francisco, CA, Woodlanders, Aiken, SC, and SFAU Arboretum, Nacogdoches, TX. The 1/2 to 1″ flowers open in April–May (late April, Athens) and are more colorful and aesthetic than those of *I. floridanum*, *I. anisatum*, and *I. parviflorum*. Will make a good shade tolerant plant and could be effectively mixed with winter flowering plants like *Camellia*. This has become my favorite among the *Illicium* species primarily because of the lustrous dark green foliage that is disposed in a pseudo-whorl at the end of the stem. The overall texture is reminiscent of rhododendron. Shade tolerance is exemplary and the potential for this species in Zone 7 and I suspect lower Zone 6 has not been tapped. Have been asked about sun tolerance and had no ready answer until late June 1997 when at Niche Gardens, NC I witnessed several plants in full sun that were performing magnificently. Might want to use this information cautiously but it does indicate the possibility. The original plant in cultivation in the United States came from Hillier's Nursery in 1972 via Bob McCartney. I believe there is significant opportunity to select for different flower colors and other traits. Easily rooted from firmwooded cuttings. I received *Illicium lanceolatum* from Camellia Forest Nursery, Chapel Hill, NC and initially placed it with *I. parviflorum* based on leaf shape. However, odor and flower color are similar to *I. henryi*. A plant in the Dirr garden will start talking in a few years. Western China. Hardiness is unknown, but Zone 7 to 9 is possible.

Illicium mexicanum A.C. Sm. — Mexican Anise-tree

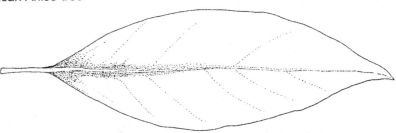

LEAVES: Alternate, simple, evergreen, narrowly elliptic-ovate, 4
to 5"(6"), 3/4 to 1 1/4" wide,
acuminate to acute, cuneate,
entire, glabrous, lustrous dark
green above, dull green below;
petiole—1/4 to 3/4" long, green.

BUDS: Flower—similar to *I. floridanum* but redder; vegetative—
small, reddish.

STEM: First year—moderate, rounded, red, more prominently so than *I. floridanum*, glabrous, lustrous, without
evident lenticels; older stems—maturing to gray-brown; pith—solid, green.

Illicium mexicanum, (i-liss′i-um mek-si-kā′num), Mexican Anise-tree, is another unknown broadleaf evergreen
that will possibly grow in stature with exposure. Leaves are lustrous dark green. The habit is pyramidal.
Flowers are reddish and 1 1/2 to 2" across. Raulston mentioned that flowers appeared in autumn in Raleigh,
NC, however, a small plant at Georgia has flowered in spring. The plant has proved hardy in Raleigh, NC
and should grow in Zone 7 to 9. In the 8 years since the last edition, I have grown the species in our garden.
It is not as robust, handsome, and garden worthy compared to the other species mentioned. The plant is
similar to *I. floridanum* in flower and leaf, except leaves have more pointed apices and redder petioles and
stems especially early in the season. Andrea's work showed distinct differences in leaf chemicals with 85%
of the total being elemicin compared to none in *I. floridanum*. I have observed other forms of the species with
better foliage and habit. Have seen the species listed as a variety of *I. floridanum*. Woodlanders has a hybrid
between *I. mexicanum* and *I. floridanum*; I observed it at the J.C. Raulston Arboretum, Raleigh, NC without
experiencing heart palpitations; perhaps for the collector. 'Aztec Fire' has larger flowers, borne on longer
peduncles and is overall more showy in flower; discovered on an expedition to northeastern Mexico; the
plant in our shop is loose, open and splaying; flowers not as large as *I. floridanum*.

Illicium parviflorum Michx. ex Vent. — Small Anise-tree

LEAVES: Alternate, simple, evergreen, oval to oval-elliptic, 2 to 4" long, 1/2 as wide,
abrupt to almost blunt or emarginate, cuneate, entire, olive green above and below,
glabrous; petiole—1/4 to 1/2" long, green; leaves have the most pleasant "anise"
odor of the species listed here; leaves borne at 45° angle to upper stems.

BUDS: Flower—large, imbricate, green; vegetative—smaller, imbricate, plump, green.

STEM: Stout, rounded, green, glabrous, lenticels barely apparent; pith—solid, green.

Illicium parviflorum, (i-liss′i-um pär-vi-flō′rum), Small Anise or Anise-tree, has surfaced
as the most rugged landscape performer among the *Illicium* species. Although
thoroughly confused with *I. floridanum* and *I. anisatum* the differences are manifest.
Habit is upright pyramidal to prominently suckering unless restrained. I have seen
plants in Savannah and Pine Mountain, GA about 15 to 20′ tall. National champion
is 18′ by 13′ in Ocala National Forest, FL. On our campus, 8 to 10′ high masses
have drifted along for many years. The olive green foliage is handsome and
provides a slightly different color than the lustrous dark green of many broadleaf
evergreens. Will tolerate extremely moist soils and does well in dry situations. The
best *Illicium* for sun and shade. Flowers are small, no bigger than 1/2" wide, 6- to
12(15)-petaled and yellow-green in color. Flowers appear in May–June, sporadically
into fall and go virtually unnoticed. There is no noticeable odor. Easily rooted from
cuttings. A most vigorous and worthwhile plant for southern gardens. Excellent large
foliage mass or screen. Have utilized the species extensively in the Dirr garden and
it must be pruned to keep it in bounds. The foliage color is a beautiful soft yellow-
green on new growth to olive green at maturity and contrasts handsomely with dark
green foliage plants. To date I have noticed little variation within this species except for a more lustrous,
darker green, more rounded leaf form now named 'Forest Green'. The habit is also more compact and
not quite as dense in foliage. Several growers have tried the plant and feel it offers no great advantages
over the typical species. Interestingly, the plants grow almost side-by-side in the University's Botanical
Garden and in the Dirr garden and are *night and day different*. Found in wet areas in southern Georgia
and Florida. Zone 6 to 9.

Indigofera kirilowii Maxim. ex Palib. — Kirilow Indigo

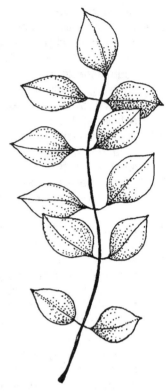

LEAVES: Alternate, compound pinnate, 7 to 11(13) leaflets, entire leaf—4 to 6″
long, each leaflet—sub-orbicular to obovate or elliptic, 1/2 to 1 1/4″ long,
mucronate, rounded at apex, broad cuneate or rounded at base, bright
green above, sparingly appressed-pubescent on both sides.

Indigofera kirilowii, (in-di-gof′ēr-à kir-il-ōw′ēī), Kirilow Indigo, is a low, dense
suckering shrub with erect stems that grows 2 to 3′ in height. The foliage
is bright green in summer. The flowers are rose-colored, 3/4″ long, borne
in June and July in dense 4 to 5″ long erect racemes on current season's
growth. Twenty to 30 individual flowers are densely packed in a raceme.
Extremely adaptable species which does well in calcareous soils.
Branches may be killed to the ground in severe winters but new shoots
quickly develop from the roots. Flowers on new growth of the season.
Might be used as a ground cover for difficult areas. The flowers are
somewhat masked by the foliage. Probably should be treated as an
herbaceous perennial in northern areas. Variety *alba* has white flowers and
is considerably hardier. The leaves appear somewhat bleached green. The
variety forms a 1 to 1 1/2′ high tangled meshwork of stems. Have seen the
variety used effectively as a ground cover. Native of Northern China, Korea
and southern Japan. Introduced 1899. Zone 5 to 7 (8). Cappiello listed it
as killed outright in Maine.

RELATED SPECIES:

Indigofera heterantha Wallich ex Brandis (*I. gerardiana* Graham), (in-di-gof′ēr-à het-ēr-an′thà), Himalayan
Indigo, has succeeded at the Arnold Arboretum. It grows about 2 to 4′(6′) high and has 13 to 21 leaflets.
The rosy purple, 1/2″ long flowers occur in a 3 to 5″ long raceme with 24 or more clustered along the axis
of the raceme. The racemes are produced from the leaf axils in succession from the base upwards, on
the terminal portion of the shoot. Has flowered from
second week in July to second week in September, in
Boston. This species has performed admirably in our
Georgia tests and in 6 years is 4′ high and 6′ wide. Also,
the largest specimen observed by this author resided on
a terrace at Knightshayes Garden in Somerset, England.
Most people who see it for the first time have no earthly
idea of its identity.

Indigofera decora Lindl., [*I. incarnata* (Willd.) Nak.], (in-di-
gof′ēr-à de-côr′à), Chinese Indigo, is encountered now
and again in American gardens. The 3 to 8″ long leaves
are composed of 7 to 13, 1 to 2 1/2″ long, dark green
leaflets. The 3/4″ long, pink flowers, 20 to 40, occur in 4
to 8″ long slender racemes in May (Athens), June, July
and August. I discovered a planting of *I. decora* at an old
antebellum home in Athens and spent about an hour
keying it out. The plant was about 12″ high with blue-
green leaflets and arching pinkish white racemes. The
unusual cultural aspect was the heavy flowering and
pinkish appearance in moderate shade. Most cultural
recommendations emphasize the need for full sun.
However, in south, species requires some shade or
foliage bleaches to off color. 'Alba' (f. *alba* Sarg.) has
white flowers. A plant in our garden has thrived under the
shade of Southern Red Oak, *Quercus falcata*. It suckers
and forms colonies and, as long as new growth is produced, flowers will develop. Easy to root from cuttings.
China, Japan. Introduced about 1878. Zone (5)6 to 7.

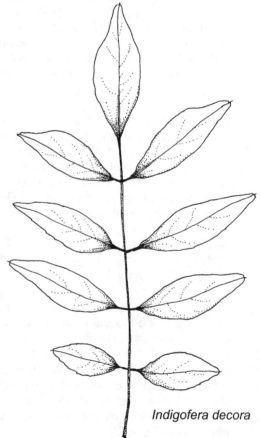

Indigofera decora

Indigofera amblyantha Craib., (in-di-gof'ĕr-à amb-lē-ān'thà), grows 4 to 6' high, has 4 to 6" long leaves with 7 to 11, 1/2 to 1 1/3" long, gray-green leaflets and pale rose to deep pink flowers borne in 2 1/4 to 5" long narrow racemes. This is a pretty form that occasionally surfaces in European gardens and in my American travels at the Arnold Arboretum where a planting was in full flower on May 30, 1991. China. Introduced 1908. Considered less cold hardy than *I. kirilowii*, probably Zone 6.

ADDITIONAL NOTES: A relative newcomer is *I. pseudotinctoria* Matsum. with small stature and leaves, and pink flowers. At best in our Zone 7b garden it is a low-spreading ground cover but the flowers appear for extended periods in June–July. *Indigofera* × 'Rose Carpet', of unknown parentage, from Scott Arboretum, Swarthmore College, grows 12 to 18" high with equal spread, more or less continuous rosy flowers in summer.

Not a whole lot of information available on propagation, however, shoot cuttings of *I. decora* taken in June, 1000 ppm KIBA, 3 perlite:1 peat, mist, rooted 100% and grew and flowered after removal from mist, transplanting, and fertilization. Seeds of *I. heterantha* (*I. gerardiana*), germinated best (70%) after 90 minutes acid scarification, untreated seed germinated 12%.

Indigofera pseudotinctoria
(leaflets)

Itea virginica L. — Virginia Sweetspire, Virginia-willow
(ī-tē'à vĕr-jin'i-kà)

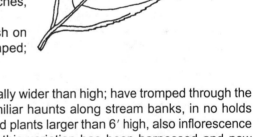

FAMILY: Saxifragaceae, Iteaceae or Escalloniaceae depending on the authority; although Grossulariaceae is considered in vogue.

LEAVES: Alternate, simple, deciduous, semi-evergreen or evergreen, elliptic or obovate to oblong, acute or short acuminate, usually cuneate at the base, 1 1/2 to 4" long, 3/4 to 1 1/4" wide, serrulate, glabrous and lustrous medium to dark green above, often sparingly pubescent beneath; petiole—1/8 to 1/4" long, pubescent, grooved on upper side.

BUDS: Superposed, upper larger than basal, forming short branches, imbricate, reddish green.

STEM: Fine to moderate, green to reddish purple, often reddish on side exposed to sun, glabrous, leaf scars crescent-shaped; pith—white, chambered irregularly.

SIZE: 3 to 5' in height, possibly to 10', spread variable but normally wider than high; have tromped through the Piedmont of Georgia and observed the species in its familiar haunts along stream banks, in no holds barred fashion it is safe to state that plants 3' high occur and plants larger than 6' high, also inflorescence sizes from 3" to greater than 6" were evident, some of this variation has been harnessed and new cultivars have been introduced, the 1990 edition listed only 'Henry's Garnet', this edition seven.

HARDINESS: Zone 5 to 9.

HABIT: Shrub with erect, clustered branches, often branched only near the top; have seen plants in full sun that were densely branched and wider than high; will form rather large colonies particularly in moist soils if left unchecked; much fuller in sun exposures, becomes rounded, arching in habit.

RATE: Medium, fast with adequate nutrition and moisture.

TEXTURE: Medium.

LEAF COLOR: Medium to dark green in summer changing to yellow, orange, reddish purple, scarlet and crimson with the advent of fall; often persisting quite long in fall; fall color can be a spectacular fluorescent red; at -3°F leaves were essentially removed from the plant, at 15 to 20°F virtually an evergreen to semi-evergreen shrub.

FLOWERS: Perfect, white, lightly fragrant, 1/3 to 1/2" diameter, borne in upright, dense, pubescent, 2 to 6" long and 5/8" wide racemes, terminating short, leafy twigs; flowers are formed on previous season's wood and pruning should be executed *after* flowering; June; sufficiently abundant to make the shrub very attractive; flowers in May in the Piedmont of Georgia; my description of the flowers as sufficiently abundant should be amended to slightly short of spectacular particularly when grown in full sun and provided adequate moisture and nutrition; this species is now utilized in the South for massing and large groupings the way junipers have been forever; the effect is staggeringly beautiful (someone asked me what this means . . . translation, the observer is so mesmerized that he/she is bedazzled to the degree of limpness and consequently staggers.)

FRUIT: Five-valved capsule, 1/4 to 1/3″ long, narrow, pubescent, persistent into the following year, seeds extremely small, like dust.

CULTURE: Easily transplanted from a container; however, pieces of the plant can be divided and successfully transplanted; prefers moist, fertile soils and in the wild exists in wet places; full sun or shade; amazingly adaptable and has displayed drought tolerance; appears pH adaptable.

DISEASES AND INSECTS: None serious; leaf spot, *Phyllosticta* spp., occurs in the landscape and production situations, does not hurt the plant.

LANDSCAPE VALUE: An interesting native shrub valued for fragrant flowers at a time when few plants are in flower; best situated in moist or wet areas in the garden; on some specimens the fall color is fantastic; not utilized enough in American gardens; it would make a good choice for naturalizing in moist areas of the garden; not given sufficient credit for drought tolerance which is considerable; I have collected it in the Piedmont area of Georgia along streams where it literally grows at the water's edge in moist, cool soil; it is rather straggly, thin, and open in the wild but becomes more dense under cultivation; holds its leaves into December in the Athens area and some leaves, in a mild winter, will persist until spring; coming into its own as an everyday garden plant, nurseries are producing the newer cultivars and gardeners are buying into the merits of the plant; Bonnie and I have all the cultivars/clones in our garden and believe that 'Henry's Garnet' is still the most spectacular although the new compact forms from Richard Feist, Burlington, KY show great promise, these compact clones will be marketed through Spring Meadow Nursery.

CULTIVARS: The most exciting aspect of the species is the movement toward cultivar selection. Before 1982, there were no named clones. That year, I discovered a beautiful burgundy-red, fall coloring form on the Swarthmore College campus in Pennsylvania. I mentioned the plant to Judy Zuk, at the time educational coordinator at Scott Arboretum. She put the machinery in motion to correctly name and introduce the plant. Josephine Henry of Gladwyne, PA brought several seeds/seedlings from Georgia to her garden. Plants were distributed and Swarthmore was the recipient of several seedlings. To recognize the Swarthmore connection, the school's color was meshed with Henry to produce 'Henry's Garnet'. Interesting how names evolve!

'Henry's Garnet'—A superb selection from the Swarthmore College campus with brilliant reddish purple fall color and up to 6″ long flowers; both fall color and flowers are superior to the species; grows 3 to 4′(6′) high and 1 1/2 times as wide; has proven cold hardy to -20°F and thrives in the heat of Zone 8; easily rooted from softwood cuttings; I have grown this for a number of years and believe it has a great future in American gardens; received prestigious Styer award; laboratory hardiness tests indicate tolerance to -20°F, killed to snow-line after -22 to -24°F in Louisville, KY area in 1994.

Little Henry™ ('Sprich')—More compact form with 3 to 4″ long flowers and excellent red-purple fall color; original plant in Feist's garden was round-mounded; I suspect with good water and fertility this will grow 3 to 4′ high.

'Long Spire'—Vigorous selection with lustrous dark green leaves, up to 8″ long racemes, fall color yellow-orange with a hint of red; nice, but not as spectacular as 'Henry's Garnet; discovered by Robert and Julia MacIntosh in the early 1990's during a canoe trip along the Augusta canal and introduced by Woodlanders, Aiken, SC

'Merlot'—Introduction by Mark Griffith for more compact habit and red fall color; handsome selection; will probably mature at 3 to 3 1/2′ high; dense twiggy growth.

'Sarah Eve'—Sepals and pedicels of flowers are pink (almost purple-pink), unfortunately, the petals are white. The effect is not spectacular and a single plant in the Dirr garden has never impacted my aesthetic consciousness. Leaves hold late, without significant color, and inflorescences are shorter. A 6- to 7-year-old plant at Woodlanders is 4′ tall. Discovered by Nancy Bissett, The Natives, Davenport, FL and introduced by Woodlanders. Bisset, who named the plant after her daughter, raised a large seedling population hoping for a pink-petaled form but found nothing better. 'Sarah Eve' is slower growing than 'Henry's Garnet', 'Long Spire', and 'Saturnalia'. I suspect this is one of the least hardy cultivars. Killed outright at Spring Grove in winter of 1994 after exposure to -25°F.

'Saturnalia'—Has a more restrained habit and excellent yellow-orange-red fall color. To date, in Athens, it has failed to impress on either attribute, for it grows as fast as 'Henry's Garnet' and seemingly will be as large at maturity. Have observed older landscape plants that are more compact than 'Henry's Garnet'. Also, fall color has been less than advertised. In 1994 and 1996, 'Long Spire', which isn't touted for fall coloration, proved superior to 'Saturnalia'. Leaf spot (*Phyllosticta* spp.) has not been as prevalent on this clone as 'Little Henry', 'Henry's Garnet', and 'Long Spire'. Introduced by Larry Lowman, Wynne, AR.

'Shirley's Compact'—Extreme dwarf from Biltmore House and Gardens; have only observed one small plant; extremely small leaves and habit, more a curiosity than a commercial item; I understand that another, possibly more, relatively compact form(s) may be forthcoming.

PROPAGATION: Although I have never germinated seeds, the process requires only direct sowing on a suitable medium, no pregermination treatments are required; softwood cuttings root easily in four weeks with or without IBA treatment; I have collected cuttings from wild plants in late August, treated them with 3000 ppm IBA quick-dip and they have rooted 100%; this success applies to the related species. The standard recipe includes May to September cuttings (even leafless cuttings have rooted), 1000 ppm KIBA, 3 perlite:1 peat, mist. *Itea virginica* like *Clethra alnifolia* will continue to grow under mist. A rooted cutting taken early in the season should make a salable 1-gallon plant by fall.

NATIVE HABITAT: Consistently found in swamps, wet woodlands and along wooded streams. Pine barrens of New Jersey to Florida, west to Missouri, Louisiana, and East Texas. Introduced 1744.

RELATED SPECIES:

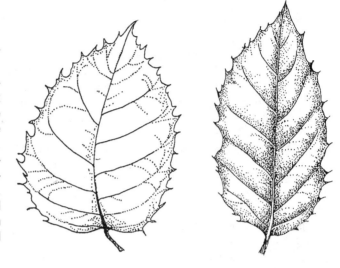

Itea ilicifolia Oliver, (ī-tē′à i-lis-i-fō′li-à), Holly Sweetspire, is a true evergreen, 6 to 12′ high shrub with lustrous dark green, spiny-jagged margined, 2 to 4″ long, 1 1/2 to 2 3/4″ wide leaves. The greenish white flowers occur in 6 to 12″ long, 1/2″ wide racemes in July–August. Prefers moist, well-drained soil, partial shade and protection from desiccating winds. Used in English gardens and is a most elegant shrub. Should prove hardy in Zone 8 to 9 and Raulston has successfully grown it in Raleigh. Easily rooted from softwood cuttings. Western China.

Itea japonica Oliver, (ī-tē′à jà-pon′i-kà), 'Beppu' ('Nana'), was introduced by the U.S. National Arboretum. It makes a rather handsome, 2 to 2 1/2′ high, spreading mound of rich green summer foliage that turns reddish purple in fall and persists into winter. The flowers are smaller than those of *I. virginica* but similar in color and fragrance. It is very fast growing and because of its suckering nature would make a good ground cover. Easily rooted from softwood cuttings. Twenty years ago I brought a rooted cutting to Athens and planted it in the University's Botanical Garden. The plant, with numerous cuttings removed, grew 4 to 5′ high and considerably wider due to its suckering nature. The 'Nana' epithet is actually a misnomer since the plant grows as tall or taller than *I. virginica*. Fall color, on occasion, has been a bright red and other times red-purple. Leaves will persist into winter at 15 to 20°F. The plant is not as hardy as *I. virginica* and some stem injury is possible at 0 to –10°F. Current thinking by me and others is that this is a form of *Itea virginica* that although collected in Japan represented nothing more than an early introduction of *I. virginica*. At times the fall color has been outstanding and, in fact, more true red than the species and cultivars. Probably deserves cultivar status. *The New Royal Horticultural Society Dictionary of Gardening* lists 'Beppu' as a form of *I. virginica*. A recent article in *Arnoldia* 56(3):21–25 (1996) alludes to the mix-up and relegates 'Beppu' to *I. virginica* status. Ohwi, *Flora of Japan*, describes *I. japonica* as a large, deciduous shrub with 3 to 5″ long leaves and 3 to 8″ long, many-flowered racemes.

 Two additional species that surface in the Southeast and West are *I. chinensis* Hook. & Arn., Chinese Sweetspire, with glossy foliage and multi-branched, pendulous, white inflorescences, is evergreen in Zone 8 to 9, and in flower is quite spectacular. Again, this species is not well defined in the literature. The other rather inadequately defined species is *I. oldhamii*, an evergreen with holly-like leaves, compact growth habit, and short racemes of white flowers in late spring. Taiwan. Zone 8 to 9.

Jasminum nudiflorum Lindl. — Winter Jasmine
(jas′mi-num nū-di-flō′rum)

FAMILY: Oleaceae

LEAVES: Opposite, pinnately compound, 3 leaflets, each leaflet ovate to oblong-ovate, 1/2 to 1 1/4″ long, one third to half as wide, narrowed at ends, mucronulate, entire, ciliolate, lustrous deep green; petiole—1/3″ long.

BUDS: Imbricate, 6- to 8-scaled, green-red-brown, glabrous.

STEM: First year—slender, trailing, green, glabrous, angled, 4-sided; 2nd year and older—brown; pith—solid white.

SIZE: 3 to 4′ high, 4 to 7′ wide; can grow 12 to 15′ if trained on a wall or trellis.

HARDINESS: Zone 6 to 10, perhaps hardy in Zone 5, at least wood hardy.

HABIT: A broad-spreading mounded mass of trailing branches arising from a central crown; can consume large areas with time for the trailing branches root in contact with moist soil and form new plants.

RATE: Fast.

TEXTURE: Fine.

BARK: Stems are fairly effective in the winter landscape; the green stands out in contrast to the grays and browns.

LEAF COLOR: Deep lustrous green in summer; no fall color of any consequence.

FLOWERS: Perfect, solitary and axillary along the previous season's growth, salver-shaped, with slender corolla tube, about 1 1/2 to 2″ long and 3/4 to 1″ across, usually 5 to 6 wavy lobes, bright yellow, waxy maroon-red in bud, non-fragrant, opening from January to March but peaking in February; never as potent as forsythia because the flowers open over a long period; responds to the slightest degree of warm weather; –3°F killed all flower buds.

FRUIT: Two-lobed, black berry; I have not observed the fruit on cultivated plants, scant literature indicates the species is self-sterile and requires out-crossing by another clone or seedling for fruit set.

CULTURE: Transplants readily; almost approaches weed status because of its widespread adaptability; prefers well-drained soil but does well in poor soils and is moderately drought resistant; full sun or shade (flowering is reduced); probably should be rejuvenated every 3 to 5 years by cutting plant to within 6″ of ground; roots where branches touch soil and tends to colonize an area; actually difficult to remove once it is established.

DISEASES AND INSECTS: None serious.

LANDSCAPE VALUE: A good plant for banks and poor soil areas where a cover is desired; often used for massing and works well along walls where the trailing branches flow over the side; often used to face down leggy shrubs; flower is lovely but foliage and tenacity may be the best assets.

CULTIVARS:

'Aureum'—Leaves blotched with yellow.

'Nanum'—Compact, slow-growing form.

'Variegatum'—Similar to species but not as vigorous, leaves with white margin and more gray-green cental color.

PROPAGATION: Cuttings root readily; I have had good success in July with 3000 ppm IBA quick dip, peat:perlite and mist; root systems were fantastic; probably could root the plant anytime of year and without a rooting hormone.

ADDITIONAL NOTES: Good article on the genus in *The Plantsman* 10(3):148–159 (1988). Over 200 species in the genus but only a few are cultivated.

NATIVE HABITAT: China. Introduced 1844.

RELATED SPECIES:

Jasminum floridum Bunge., (jas′mi-num flôr′i-dum), Showy Jasmine, is a half-evergreen to evergreen, 3 to 5′ high shrub that produces a mass of slender, arching, quadrangular, glabrous, green stems. This species is easily separated from the previous because the leaves are alternate. The oval to ovate, acuminate, glabrous, dark green leaves are composed of 3 to 5 leaflets, each leaflet 1/2 to 1 1/2″ long and 1/4 to 5/8″ wide. The yellow, 1/2 to 3/4″ long, 5-lobed flowers occur in cymes and open over a long time period from April into June and sporadically into the fall. At no time is the display really outstanding. It is extremely easy to root and the 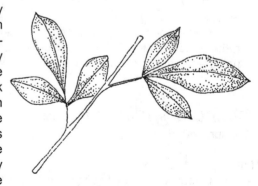 procedure described under *J. nudiflorum* applies here. In my opinion, the fine foliage is more valuable than the flowers. Plants were injured after exposure to 0°F during the 1982 winter. All leaves had abscised and considerable stem dieback occurred. I estimate that 5 to 10°F is about the break point. China. Introduced 1850. Zone 8 to 10.

Jasminum humile L., (jas′mi-num hū′mi-lē), Italian Yellow Jasmine, is allied to *J. floridum* with alternate, evergreen to semi-evergreen leaves, 3 to 7(13) leaflets, each to 1 1/2″ long, ovate-lanceolate. Leaflets are dark green and not as lustrous as those of *J. floridum*. The habit is more upright

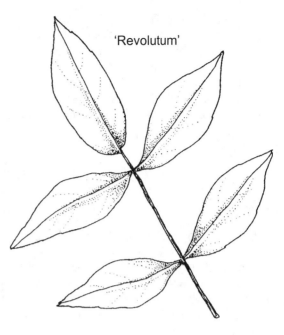

'Revolutum'

with ultimate height in the 5 to 7′ range. The minimally fragrant, yellow flowers appear in June (Athens) and are not particularly showy. The glossy black berries have developed on cultivated plants in England. Several old specimens have limped along on the Georgia campus for all of my 19 years in Athens. There has never been a year when someone did not bring the plant in for identification. 'Revolutum' is larger, more cold hardy and often with more leaflets. Middle East, Burma, China. Zone 7b to 9.

Jasminum mesnyi Hance., (jas′mi-num mes′nē-ī), Primrose Jasmine, is better adapted to the lower South. The species will grow 5 to 6′(9′) high and develops the mounded habit and long trailing branches common to *J. nudiflorum*. The oppositely arranged, pinnately compound, lustrous dark green leaves are composed of 3 leaflets, each from 1 to 3″ long and 1/3 to 3/4″ wide. The bright yellow, 1 1/2 to 1 3/4″ diameter flowers are produced singly on 1/2 to 1 1/2″ long pedicels in early spring through mid-summer (sporadically). Have observed flowers as early as early to mid-February in Athens. The

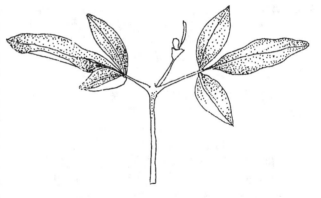

corolla is often semi-double, composed of 6 to 10 divisions, each 1/3 to 1/2″ wide and rounded at the end. Closely allied to *J. nudiflorum* but is larger in all its parts and flowers later, usually about late March into April in the Athens area. In 1996, a March freeze (15°F), after an extended earlier warm period, defoliated and killed many stems. Plants were cut back to the ground and as of April 20 were producing new shoots. Never reliable for flower in Athens-Atlanta (Zone 7b). China. Introduced 1900. Zone 8 to 9.

Jasminum officinale L., (jas′mi-num ō-fis-i-nā′lē), Common White Jasmine, is a deciduous or semi-evergreen climbing or spreading shrub growing 10 to 15′ and if trained on a wall 30 to 40′. The oppositely arranged, pinnately compound, rich green leaves have 5 to 9 leaflets, each 1/2 to 2 1/2″ long and 1/6 to 1″ wide. The 3/4 to 1″ long and wide, 4- to 5-lobed corolla is white and appears in June through October. The flowers are deliciously fragrant. One of the cherished plants in English gardens and has been cultivated there since time immemorial. 'Affine' has flowers tinged pink on the outside and broader calyx lobes. In 'Aureovariegatum' ('Aureum') the leaves are blotched yellow. 'Grandiflorum' has larger, more showy flowers, up to 1 1/3″ across. 'Inverleith' produces red flower buds and the backs of the outer petals contrast with the pure white inner surface [see *Kew Magazine* 9(2):63–67 (1992)]. Native to the Caucasus, northern Iran, Afghanistan, the Himalayas and China. Cultivated since ancient times. Zone 8 to 10, doubtfully hardy in Zone 8 of the Southeast.

Jasminum parkeri Dunn., (jas′mi-num pär-kēr′ī), is a compact, 12″(24″) high, 30″ wide, alternate-leaved, evergreen shrub. The 1/2 to 1″ long leaves are alternate and composed of 3 to 5, 1/8 to 3/8″ long, dark

green leaflets. The 1/2 to 3/4″ long, 1/2″ wide, 6-lobed, yellow flowers occur singly, rarely in pairs, from the axils or terminally. Fruit is a 2-lobed, greenish white, translucent, globose, 1/6″ wide berry. This is a cute, diminutive form with excellent foliage. I remember asking Don Shadow about the adaptability of a particularly handsome specimen at his Winchester, TN nursery. Recollection indicates Don just smiled, which translated to "What do you think?" Northwest India. Found in a limited area of the province of Himachal Pradesh. Introduced 1923. Zone (8)9 to 10.

Juglans L. — Walnut
FAMILY: Juglandaceae

The walnuts (about 15 species) are treated in this text as a group similar to the format under *Carya*. The flowers are monoecious; male catkins preformed, appearing as small, scaly, cone-like buds, unbranched; female in 2- to 8-flowered spikes. Fruit is a nut with the outer ovary wall (exocarp and mesocarp) semi-fleshy; the endocarp is hard and thick-walled, while the seeds are sweet and quite oily. Many references list fruit as a drupe. The flowers are wind pollinated. Walnuts are important timber trees and the Black Walnut, *Juglans nigra*, is a prime timber tree. The following are the more important species. An excellent paper by Edward Goodell, "Walnuts for the Northeast," appeared in *Arnoldia* 44:1–19 (1984). He traces history, commercial production, biology, culture, cultivars and myriad additional facts. What is abundantly evident is the volume of information available on nut culture. Goodell mentions that over 500 *J. nigra* cultivars have been selected and named. 'Thomas' is the only one I see with any regularity in nursery catalogs.

ADDITIONAL NOTES: Seed of most *Juglans* species have a dormant embryo and the native species also have a hard outer wall. Dormancy can be broken by stratification at 41°F. The cultivars are grafted or budded on seedling understocks.

Juglans cinerea L. — Butternut

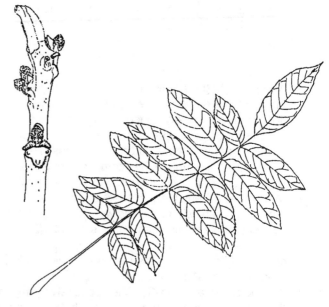

LEAVES: Alternate, pinnately compound, 10 to 20″ long, (7)11 to 19 leaflets, each leaflet 2 to 5″ long, 3/4 to 2 1/4″ wide, oblong-lanceolate, acuminate, obliquely rounded, appressed-serrate, dark green and finely pubescent above, pubescent and glandular beneath; petiole and rachis covered with gland-type sticky hairs.

BUDS: Densely pale downy; terminal bud—large 1/2 to 1″ long, flattened, oblong to conical, obliquely blunt-pointed; lateral buds—smaller, ovate, rounded at apex, 1 to 3 superposed buds generally present above axillary bud.

STEM: Stout, reddish buff to greenish gray, pubescent or smooth, bitter to taste, coloring saliva yellow when chewed; pith—chocolate brown, chambered; leaf scar—large, conspicuous, 3-lobed, inversely triangular, upper margin generally convex, seldom slightly notched, surmounted by a raised, downy pad.

BARK: Ridged-and-furrowed, ridges whitish, furrows grayish black, inner bark becoming yellow on exposure to air, bitter.

Juglans cinerea, (jū′glanz sin-ĕr′ē-ā), Butternut, reaches 40 to 60′ in height with a spread of 30 to 50′, although it can grow to 100′. Co-national champions are 80′ by 76′ in Chester, CT and 88′ by 103′ in Eugene, OR. The tree is usually round-topped with a short, usually forked or crooked trunk and somewhat open, wide-spreading crown of large horizontal branches and stout, stiff branches. Relatively slow-growing as is true for most walnuts and hickories (excluding *J. nigra*). Prefers moist, rich, deep soils of bottomlands although it grows quite well in drier, rocky soils, especially of limestone origin. The 1 1/2 to 2 1/2″ long, tapered, oblong fruit is covered with gland-tipped, sticky hairs; the actual endocarp (hard portion) is 1 to 1 1/2″ long with a sharp point; the seeds are sweet, edible, and very oily. The inner bark has mild cathartic properties and was used in older times as an orange or yellow dye. The species has been devastated by canker (*Sirococcus clavigignenti-juglandacearum*) over a 21 state area. Native from New Brunswick to Georgia, and west to the Dakotas and Arkansas. Cultivated 1633. Zone 3 to 7. Ranges much further north and occurs at higher elevations than *J. nigra*.

Juglans nigra L. — Black Walnut

'Laciniata'

LEAVES: Alternate, pinnately compound, 12 to 24″ long, (11)15 to 23 leaflets, the terminal one often missing, each leaflet 2 to 5″ long, 3/4 to 2″ wide, ovate-oblong to ovate-lanceolate, acuminate, rounded at base, irregularly serrate, at first minutely pubescent above, finally nearly glabrous and somewhat lustrous dark green, pubescent and glandular beneath, leaves fragrant when crushed; petiole and rachis minutely downy.

BUDS: Pale silky-downy; terminal buds—ovate, 1/3″ long, scarcely longer than broad; lateral buds—smaller, often superposed, grayish.

STEM: Stout, densely gray-downy to smooth and reddish buff, bitter to taste and coloring saliva yellow when chewed; pith—buff, paler than that of Butternut, chambered; leaf scar—upper margin distinctly notched, no downy pad above leaf scar.

BARK: Dark brown to grayish black, divided by deep, narrow furrows into thin ridges, forming a roughly diamond-shaped pattern.

Juglans nigra, (jŭ′glanz nī′grȧ), Black Walnut, is a large tree to 50 to 75′ in height and often a similar spread when open-grown. The species may reach a maximum height of 125 to 150′. National champion is 130′ by 140′ in Sauvie Island, OR. Usually develops a full, well-formed trunk which is devoid of branches a considerable distance (1/2 to 2/3's) from the ground. The crown is oval to rounded and somewhat open. Prefers deep, rich, moist soils and here maximum growth occurs; tolerates drier soils but grows much more slowly under these conditions. Develops an extensive taproot and is difficult to transplant. The globose, glabrous light green nuts average 1 1/2 to 2″ thick and are grainy surfaced; the sculptured wall (endocarp) is blackish and 1 to 1 1/2″ across. The wood is highly prized and has been used for cabinets, gunstocks and many furniture pieces. The wood is so valuable that "Walnut Rustlers" have developed sophisticated techniques to remove trees such as midnight operations and the use of helicopters. Tremendous call for walnut veneer; hence, the high value placed on the tree. Abundant provenance and genetic improvement research focusing on improved timber production. 'Laciniata' has leaflets that are finely dissected; makes a rather pretty tree. In early June 1997, Bonnie and I roamed the western side of the Great Smoky Mountains National Park. The soils are clay or clay loam around Maryville and Townsend, TN, apparently higher pH, and producing Black Walnut in abundance. I observed more seedling Black Walnuts in this area than any that I have visited. Native from Massachusetts to Florida and west to Minnesota and Texas. Cultivated 1686. Zone 4 to 9.

Juglans regia L. — Persian, Common, English Walnut

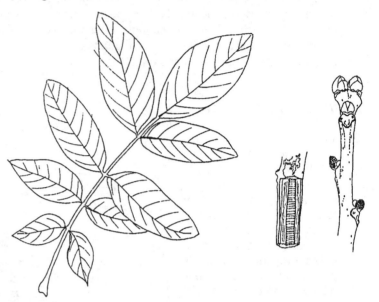

LEAVES: Alternate, pinnately compound, 5 to 9 leaflets, rarely to 13, 2 to 5″ long, elliptic to obovate, to oblong-ovate, acute or acuminate, entire, rarely and chiefly on young plants obscurely serrate, medium to dark green, glabrous except small axillary tufts of hairs beneath.

BUDS: Terminal—2- to 3-fold larger than lateral, 1/4 to 1/3″ long, valvate with scales barely overlapping, pubescent, brownish.

STEM: Stout, olive-brown when young, grayish on old branches; pith—uniformly chambered, brownish in color.

BARK: Smooth, silver-gray with large flat ridges; distinct from other species described herein.

Juglans regia, (jū'glanz rē'ji-à), Persian, Common, or English Walnut, is a tree which develops a rounded, often spreading and open crown, ultimately reaching 40 to 60′ in height with a comparable or greater spread. Prefers a deep, dry, light loamy soil; does not do well in wet or poor subsoil areas. Like most walnuts, should be pruned in summer or fall. The 1 1/2 to 2″ diameter nuts are edible, thin-shelled and widely available in stores; actual seeds (with hard covering) abscise or are released from fleshy outer covering unlike the other walnuts mentioned here; they do not have the wild, nutty taste of *J. nigra* but are much easier to shell. There are many cultivars of this tree but two which are well-adapted to cold conditions are 'Carpathian' which was brought to Canada from the mountains of Poland and supposedly bears heavy crops even when winter temperatures drop to –40°F; and 'Hansen', an annual bearer, shells are very thick, easily shelled and the nut meats (seeds) are classed as excellent with the highest percent of kernel reported; the tree is located at Clay Center, OH, southeast of Toledo. This particular cultivar ('Hansen') might make a respectable ornamental because of the quality characteristics. In addition, several lobed or cut-leaf forms ('Heterophylla' and 'Laciniata'), as well as a pendulous form ('Pendula'), are in cultivation. Native to southeastern Europe to Himalayas and China. Long cultivated. Zone (5)6 to 9, 10 in West.

Juniperus L. — Juniper
FAMILY: Cupressaceae

Junipers would have to rank as the toughest of evergreen landscape plants for they will grow and are used in all parts of the United States and, for that matter, the world. They include 50 to 70 (45 to 60) species widely distributed throughout the temperate and subtropical regions of the Northern Hemisphere and south of the equator in Africa. Thirteen species are native to the United States. The majority of types used in landscape plantings are found in the species *J. chinensis*, *J. communis*, *J. horizontalis*, *J. sabina*, *J. scopulorum*, and *J. virginiana*, with a few important cultivars found in *J. conferta*, *J. davurica*, *J. procumbens*, and *J. squamata*. For some strange reason the common name of *J. virginiana* is Eastern Redcedar with all other species known as junipers. The wood of the tree species is used for furniture (cedar chests), paneling, novelties, posts, poles, fuel, and pencils. The fleshy cones ("fruits") are used in medicine, varnish and for flavoring an alcoholic beverage known as gin.

MORPHOLOGICAL CHARACTERISTICS

Trees or shrubs; bark of trunk and main branches usually thin, shredding, rarely scaling; buds conspicuous, 1/8″ long, scales small, sharply pointed or buds inconspicuous and naked; leaves opposite or ternate, needle-like or scale-like, on young plants always needle-like, older plants have both forms, upperside of needle-like leaves with white or blue stomatic bands; male flowers united into an ovoid or oblong catkin, female flowers composed of 3 to 8 valvate scales, some or all bearing 1 to 2 ovules; the scales becoming fleshy and united into a berry-like cone; cones variously shaped, brown when young and covered with a thick mealy bloom, afterwards dark blue or blackish blue, ripening the second or third year; seeds elliptic to oblong, obtuse-ended, sometimes somewhat 3-angled in section, glossy brown; cotyledons 2 or 4 to 6.

GROWTH CHARACTERISTICS

It is impossible to stereotype the junipers as to habit because the species vary from low-growing, ground cover types to larger conical to pyramidal trees (*J. scopulorum* and *J. virginiana*). Among the species and cultivars are narrow, broad, columnar, conical and pyramidal; small and large spreading; globe, slow- and fast-growing ground cover types. Foliage color varies from lustrous dark green to light green, blue, silver-blue, yellow and shades in between.

CULTURE

Junipers are most successfully moved as container plants or balled-and-burlapped. In fact, most junipers are now grown in containers, especially the ground cover and shrubby types. They prefer open, sunny locations and light, sandy, low or high pH, moderately moist soils but will grow in about any situation. They are very tolerant of dry, clay soils and some types will grow in sand. They exhibit good air pollution tolerance and will withstand the dirt and grime of cities as well as any conifer. They have been used as windbreaks with good success. Some types (*J. chinensis* var. *sargentii*, *J. conferta*, and cultivars) show good salt tolerance. When junipers are located in heavy shade they become open, thin and ratty. Junipers withstand heavy pruning and for this reason make good hedges. A good rule of thumb is "if you cannot grow junipers, then do not bother planting anything else." In recent years (the 90's) a distinct shift away from junipers in American landscapes has occurred. Often, junipers, especially the ground cover types, decline over a 5 to 10 year period. Also, consumer tastes have shifted and carpets and mounds of green are no longer perfectly acceptable.

DISEASES AND INSECTS

Twig blights (*Phomopsis juniperovora*, *Kabatina juniperi*, *Seiridium cardinale*), cedar-apple rust, wilt, rocky mountain juniper aphid, bagworm, juniper midge, scale, webworm, redcedar bark beetle, and mites. Junipers have a number of very serious problems including blight (usually manifested in a tip dieback and sometimes whole plants are killed) and bagworm (so bad that plants are often completely stripped of foliage). *Juniperus horizontalis* and cultivars (especially 'Plumosa'), *J. procumbens*, and *J. chinensis* 'San Jose' are especially susceptible to blight. An excellent reference that takes the reader far beyond the *Manual* is *Diseases of Trees and Shrubs* by W.A. Sinclair, H.H. Lyon, and W.T. Johnson. 1987. Cornell University Press.

PROPAGATION

Seed and cutting propagation are adequately discussed under *J. chinensis*. Some cultivars are grafted on understocks of *J. virginiana*, *J. chinensis*, or *J. chinensis* 'Hetzii'. They are pot grafted using a side graft in February or March in the greenhouse.

LANDSCAPE VALUE

There is no limit to the use of junipers in landscape situations. They make excellent screens, hedges, windbreaks, ground covers, foundation plants, rock garden plants, groupings, and specimens. Because of their ease of culture and ubiquitous landscape value they are often overused almost to the point of monotony. Whole foundation plantings are often composed of nothing but junipers. Another problem is that consideration is seldom given to ultimate landscape size and in a few years plants have overgrown their boundaries. Many of the newer, smaller, better-foliaged types should be used in place of the cumbersome *J. chinensis* 'Pfitzeriana' and 'Hetzii'. Also it is important to consider the degree of shade in which the junipers will be grown. They can become "ratty" looking in a short time period if sited in heavy shade.

Junipers are an essential part of the North American and worldwide landscapes. In the 1990's, their production has decreased, albeit not greatly, and other plants have moved into production. A notable example on the Georgia campus is the use of *Itea virginica*, *Jasminum nudiflorum*, *Fothergilla* species, and grasses for massing and ground cover use where once junipers were the only plant considered. The introduction of new juniper cultivars has also abated in recent years. Growers, instead of increasing their number of cultivars, are paring down the list to the best and easier to grow forms.

ADDITIONAL NOTES

A strong diuretic, oil of juniper, is extracted from juniper berries and these are also used in flavoring gin. The utilization of juniper berries in the making of gin dates back many centuries. British gin is prepared by distilling a fermenting mixture of maize, rye and malt. Then the resulting liquid is redistilled after juniper and sometimes coriander have been added.

Juniperus chinensis L. — Chinese Juniper
(jö-nip′ēr-us chi-nen′sis)

LEAVES: Of two kinds, adult branches with the ultimate divisions about 1/25″ in diameter, clothed with 4 ranks
of leaves in opposite pairs which are closely pressed, overlapping and rhombic in outline, 1/16″ long, blunt
or bluntly pointed, the outer surface convex, green with a paler margin marked with a glandular depression
on the back; juvenile leaves awl-shaped, 1/3″ long, spreading, in whorls of 3, or in opposite pairs, with a
green midrib and 2 glaucous bands above, convex beneath, ending in a spiny point.

CONES: Dioecious, male is yellowish or brownish, numerous, usually borne on adult branchlets, occasionally
on branchlets bearing juvenile foliage; female, ripening the second year, at first whitish blue, bloomy, when
ripe brown, sub-globose or top-shaped, 1/3″ to on some forms 1/2″ in diameter, composed of 4 to 8
scales, seeds 2 to 5.

SIZE: Tree to 50 or 60′ in height, averages 15 to 20′ in spread, rarely represented in this country.

HARDINESS: Zone 4 to 9 depending on cultivar.

HABIT: Tree or shrub; most typically an erect, narrow, conical tree; sometimes very slender, sometimes bushy;
cultivars variable from ground covers to large, wide-spreading shrubs.

RATES: Slow to medium.

TEXTURE: Medium.

BARK: Gray-brown lightly ridged-and-furrowed, coming off in thin strips.

LEAF COLOR: Green to blue-green to grayish green.

FLOWERS: Dioecious, staminate flowers yellow-brown to orange-yellow, start to show color and shed pollen
in March (Athens, GA), pistillate greenish, trees with flowers of both sexes occasionally occur.

FRUIT: Cones globose or oblong irregularly globose, 1/3 to 1/2″ across, at first whitish blue bloomy, when ripe
dark brown; seeds oblong-obtuse or nearly 3-angled, glossy brown.

CULTURE: Transplant balled-and-burlapped or from a container; prefers moist, well-drained conditions; full sun;
pH adaptable, quite tolerant of calcareous soils; tolerates dry soils once established.

DISEASES AND INSECTS: *Phomopsis* and *Kabatina* blights (kill young shoots, prevalent in early spring and
wet weather); relatively trouble-free juniper.

LANDSCAPE VALUE: Depending on cultivar they can be used as a ground cover, foundation plant, hedge,
screen, specimen, and mass planting.

CULTIVARS:

‘Ames’—Initially grows as dwarf, spreading shrub; with time develops a broad-pyramidal shape 8 to 10′
high, steel blue foliage initially, turning green when mature, leaves needle-like; raised and introduced
by T.J. Maney, Iowa State, Ames, IA, in 1948; other forms introduced by Professor Maney include
‘Iowa’, ‘Maney’ and ‘Story’; a 14-year-old plant was 9′ high and 4′ wide at the base; this is a female
and I have seen a few cones, does not appear to cone heavily; originated from seed of *J. chinensis*
var. *sargentii*.

‘Angelica Blue’—Finer, brighter blue foliage than Blue Pfitzer, impressive glaucous blue needles, more
horizontal than Blue Pfitzer or Hetz, easier to propagate, introduced by Angelica Nurseries.

‘Aquarius’—A branch sport of ‘Hetzii’ with blue-green foliage, compact habit, fills out more readily than
‘Pfitzeriana Compacta’, 4′ by 6′ after 19 years, Lake County Nursery introduction.

‘Arctic’—Bluish green needles cover this wide-spreading form that grows 18 to 20″ high and 5 to 6′
across, considered to be hardier than most of the Pfitzeriana types.

‘Armstrong’—Dwarf form to 3 to 4′ high with an equal or greater spread, branches horizontally spreading,
leaves are primarily scale-like and soft to the touch except at the base; bright green (sage green),
holds color in cold weather; a branch sport of Pfitzer introduced by Armstrong Nurseries in 1932.

‘Aurea’—Upright type with golden foliage, has a mixture of needle and scale-type foliage.

‘Blaauw’—Foliage is a rich blue-green, dense-growing, upright form, reminds me of a number of wide V’s
stacked upon each other, 4 to 6′ high and wide (?); introduced from Japan by J. Blaauw and
Company of Holland about 1924.

‘Blaauw Golden’—Upright, vase-shaped form, compact habit, branches turn up at their tips, forming the
irregular vase shape, golden needles, 4 to 6′ by 4 to 6′.

‘Blue and Gold’—A strong upright vase-shaped form with blue and cream foliage intermixed, resembling
‘Hetzii’ in outline; probably 8 to 10′ high and slightly less in spread, Raulston reports growth at 1 1/2′
per year.

‘Blue Cloud’—Large-spreading ground cover type with dense blue-gray foliage.

‘Blue Point’—Pyramidal form with a teardrop outline, extremely dense branching, blue-green, needle and
scale-like foliage; listed as 7 to 8′ tall but will grow larger.

'Blue Vase'—Vase-shaped form with good summer and winter foliage; supposedly intermediate between upright and spreading type; dense steel blue primarily scale-like foliage; moderate growth rate, 4 to 5′ high, 3 to 4′ wide; have seen 10 to 15′ high plants in Georgia.

'Bordiers'—Gold tips, looks like 'Pfitzeriana Aurea'.

'Columnaris Glauca'—Narrowly columnar, 24′, loose in branching habit, needles awl-shaped, silvery-gray; 'Columnaris' is similar but has deep green foliage.

'Daub's Frosted'—Low-spreading form with pendulous branch tips, gold-frosted foliage with bluish green undertones, 2′ by 4′.

'Dropmore'—An extremely slow-growing form with a dense habit; extremely small (1/8″ long) leaves, collected by F.L. Skinner, Dropmore, Manitoba.

'Fairview'—Narrow-pyramidal, vigorous-growing, leaves mostly subulate, on some branches scale-like, bright green, silver berry-like structures (cones) during late summer and fall; rather handsome upright form.

'Fruitlandii'—Spreading form of vigorous growth, compact, dense with bright green foliage; actually an improved form of 'Pfitzeriana Compacta'; 3′ by 6′.

'Globosa'—Apparently rare in cultivation; three forms, gray, green and gold, were imported from a Japanese nursery; true 'Globosa' is dense, rounded, symmetrical, light green, male, a 24-year-old plant was 6′ by 7′.

'Globosa Cinerea'—Similar to 'Blaauw' but broader and less ragged; foliage in winter is gray-green rather than the blue-gray of 'Blaauw'.

'Gold Coast'—Graceful, compact, spreading form with golden yellow new growth that persists and deepens in cold weather, could be considered a refined, compact version of 'Pfitzeriana Aurea'; introduced by Monrovia Nursery, supposedly holds color better in winter than 'Old Gold'.

'Gold Lace'—Most golden of all junipers, golden color from center of plant outward, compact Pfitzer habit, 3 to 4′ by 5 to 6′, Zone 4 to 9.

'Gold Sovereign'—A branch sport of 'Old Gold' with bright yellow foliage color year round, more compact and slower growing than 'Old Gold' (rate estimated as one-half), 16 to 20″ by 24″, a Bressingham Nursery introduction.

Gold Star® ('Bakaurea')—Compact form with light blue-green foliage accented by golden yellow branches, resistant to root problems, 4′ by 6′, Conard-Pyle introduction.

'Golden Glow'—Compact growth habit, 2 1/2′ high, greater spread, bright gold foliage.

'Hetz Glauca Pyramid'—Listed as conical, 10 to 12′ by 5 to 6′ with blue-green foliage, how unique this is I am unsure, could be typical 'Hetzii' pruned to the above dimensions.

'Hetzii'—Large, rapid-growing, upright-spreading form, branches in all directions, 15′ by 15′ but usually *female* less, leaves scale-like, glaucous, a few leaves awl-shaped; bears liberal quantities of small glaucous cones; typical landscape size approximates 5 to 10′ high, found in a batch of seedlings from the West Coast before 1948; considered a hybrid between *J. virginiana* 'Glauca' and *J. chinensis* 'Pfitzeriana'; introduced by Hetz Nursery, Fairview, PA; roots easily from cuttings, transplants readily and is often used as an understock for grafting upright junipers.

'Hetzii Columnaris'—Upright pyramidal form, similar to 'Keteleeri' with scale and awl-shaped leaves; needles are bright green, 10 to 15′ high, female with heavy cone production; has performed well in Southeast; will grow larger, probably 20 to 25′ high in 15 to 20 years.

'Hetzii Glauca'—Semi-erect form with light blue foliage; intermediate between the previous two, grows 5 to 7′ high, wider than high at maturity.

'Hills Blue'—Similar to 'Pfitzeriana Glauca' but making a lower, flatter plant.

'Holbert'—Low-spreading, bluish green-needled shrub, long extended shoots that develop almost parallel to the ground, would make an excellent massing evergreen, 2 to 3′ by 8 to 10′, foliage color has held quite well in Georgia trials, very similar to 'Grey Owl' and growing side-by-side they are difficult to discern, 'Holbert' is a male, 'Grey Owl' a female.

'Hooks'—Tight pyramid, 12 to 15′ high and 2 to 3′ wide, green foliage, requires minimal pruning, from Midwest and also listed as Hooks #6 juniper.

'Iowa'—Forms a rather loose pyramid of blue-green foliage, it is more spreading and less compact than 'Ames' and more green in color; some fruiting; leaves awl-shaped and scale-like; 13-year-old plant was 10′ by 4′.

'Kaizuka' ('Torulosa')—Hollywood Juniper; this form is appropriately named for it belongs in California and I have seen it used in abundance in that state; leaves scale-like, vivid green, female, branches slightly twisted resulting in a Japanese effect; can be grown as a shrub or tree; will grow 20 to 30′ high; excellent heat and salt tolerance, used widely in the Southeast; a blue-green foliage form and a variegated form with rather bold creamy white markings are available in commerce.

'Kaizuka Variegated'—See above.

'Kallays Compacta' ('Pfitzeriana Kallay')—Another compact form of Pfitzer; deep green leaves and a preponderance of juvenile foliage; a rather flat-topped form growing 2 to 3′ high and up to 6′ wide; originated at Kallay Nursery, Painesville, OH.

'Keteleeri'—Broadly pyramidal tree with a stiff trunk and loose, light to medium green foliage, leaves scale-like, very pointed, cones with a recurved stalk, globose, 1/2 to 3/5″ across, initially grayish green, finally glossy light green; has been a popular form over the years and is common in midwestern landscapes, 15 to 20′.

'Kohankies Compact'—A dense, globose sport of Pfitzer that originated at the old Kohankie Nursery, Painesville, OH; not common in cultivation.

'Kuriwao Gold'—Upright reasonably thick branched, bright green needles with golden midrib, foliage effect from a distance is gold-green, forms an upright, fat, teardrop-shaped, airy texture, 4 to 5′ high and 3′ wide.

'Kuriwao Mist'—Open pyramidal form with creamy silver to golden gray-green foliage.

'Kuriwao Sunburst'—Open pyramidal shape, soft green foliage, tipped bright green to yellow.

'Lemon Hill'—Blue foliage, flat-planar habit, grows no more than 3″ high, slow-growing, good bonsai form.

'Mac's Golden'—Dense, pyramidal shrub with needle and scale foliage, shoots are soft yellow, slow-growing, from Alexander Nursery, Mt. Clemens, MI.

'Maney'—Bushy, semi-erect form, as broad as high, leaves acicular, bluish, bloomy, reports from Minnesota indicate it grows about 6′ high and wide, one of the best for cold climates, female, 7′ high by 12′ wide after 13 years.

'Mathot'—Similar to 'Kallays Compacta' in habit, but dense, juvenile leaves in pairs about 1/3″ long with bluish green band above, green below, the upper surface is turned out giving a general glaucous appearance; originated at Mathot Nursery, Holland 1940.

'Matthew's Blue'—Extremely blue-needled form with Pfitzer-like habit; small plants in my Georgia holding area, under 55% shade cloth, are rich blue, received from Mitch Nursery, Oregon.

'Milky Way'—Fast-growing, low-spreading form, 3 to 4′ high, dark green foliage with stippled markings of cream.

Mint Julep™ ('Monlep')—Compact grower with arching branches creating a low fountain-like form, foliage is a brilliant mint green; actually looks like a very green, compact Pfitzer; introduced by Monrovia around 1971; 4 to 6′ high, greater spread; looks similar to and is probably the same as 'Sea Green'.

'Mordigan'—Dark green foliage, taller and more blocky than Pfitzer, 7′ by 5′; a golden foliage form, 'Mordigan Aurea', is known.

'Mountbatten'—Dense, pyramidal, narrow form to 12′, similar to *J. communis* 'Hibernica'; foliage grayish green, most acicular.

'Nick's Compact' ('Pfitzeriana Nick's Compacta')—A relatively flat-topped, wide-spreading form with green, slight blue overcast foliage, more needle than scale-like foliage, grew 2 1/2′ by 6′ in eight years, a male, same as 'Pfitzeriana Compacta'?, *Phomopsis* susceptible.

'Obelisk'—Forms a narrow pyramid about 8 to 10′ high, leaves juvenile with sharp apices, glaucous gray foliage; introduced by F.J. Grootendorst and Sons.

'Old Gold'—Similar to Pfitzer only more compact, foliage bronze-gold, permeating the plant; color is retained through winter; a branch sport of 'Armstrong'?; Grootendorst introduction; 3′ by 4′; same growth habit as 'Armstrong', occasionally listed as 'Armstrong Aurea'; in Houston, TX, Hines mentioned this cultivar loses its color in summer; a branch sport, 'Improved Old Gold' holds the color.

'Pfitzeriana' ('Pfitzerana' in *Hortus III*)—The granddaddy of juniper cultivars; probably the most widely planted juniper, wide-spreading, variable form, usually listed as growing about 5′ high and 10′ wide, actually can grow larger than these values; foliage scale-like and awl-shaped, bright green (sage green), original plant was a male; main branches emerge at a 45° angle and the young shoots show a slight pendulous tendency; much more handsome in youth, often becoming ragged with age; interestingly this cultivar does well in the North (-25°F) and in the mid to deep South; named by Späth for his friend W. Pfitzer. As I travel through Europe, specimens of Pfitzer approaching 10′ high and 20 to 25′ wide appear, the Morton Arboretum listed a 26-year-old plant that was 5′ by 20′; Nordine, *Proc. Intl. Plant Prop. Soc.* 12:122 (1962), listed 12 clones (branch sports) of 'Pfitzeriana'.

'Pfitzeriana Aurea'—Similar to Pfitzer in growth but flatter and not as large, branchlets and leaves tinged golden yellow in summer, becoming yellowish green in winter; only the young shoots are gold-tinged, the body of the plant is green; I find this a rather attractive form that is not as obtrusive as some of the flagrantly yellow forms; branches emerge at a 30° angle compared to the 45° angle of Pfitzer.

'Pfitzeriana Compacta'—Bushy, compact, with greater proportion of awl-shaped leaves, grows 12 to 18″ high and up to 6′ across, the white upper surface of the needles gives an overall gray-green cast to the plant; grew 4′ by 4′ in 12 years, introduced by Bobbink and Atkins Nursery, Rutherford, NJ.

'Pfitzeriana Glauca' ('Blue Pfitzer')—Possibly more dense than Pfitzer with mixed leaves, markedly blue in older plants, becoming slightly purplish blue in winter; more prickly than 'Hetzii'; a male, handsome bluish foliage through the seasons in warmer climates, similar to Pfitzer in general growth characteristics.

'Pfitzeriana Gold Lace'—Broad-spreading, fine-textured, golden Pfitzer, color is clean yellow and persists throughout the year; gold leaves hold on the plant's center creating a more overall golden appearance, 4′ by 6′.

'Pfitzeriana Moraine'—Green with blue cast, sharp-needled form, 1 1/2′ by 5 to 6′ in 8 years, male.

'Pfitzeriana Nelson's Compact'—Dusty blue-green foliage, grew 3′ by 5′ in 5 years.

'Pfitzeriana Owens'—Compact, low-growing, 3 to 4′ high, mixture of juvenile and adult foliage, similar to 'Ozark Compact' but slightly hardier.

'Pfitzeriana Plumosa'—Spreading type with bluish green needles, 4′ by 8′ in 4 years, male.

'Plumosa'—Leaves mainly scale-like, deep green, male, however 'Hasselkus' noted it was female, 3 to 4′ high, broad-spreading with short dense drooping branches; 'Plumosa Albovariegata' is peppered with creamy white markings; 'Plumosa Aurea' has yellow-green growth that becomes more pronounced through the season and culminates in golden bronze during winter, more upright and stiff in outline; 'Plumosa Aureovariegata' is marked with deep yellow among the deep green foliage, another report indicated a mixture of scale and needle-like foliage that turns from light green to yellow to bronze-green in winter, habit is open and irregular with some branches completely needle-like; plant tends to have a one-sided development.

'Prostrata Variegata'—Low-growing, 18″ by 4 to 5′, creamy white variegation interspersed among blue-green foliage, will "burn" in extreme sun, may be the same as *J. davurica* 'Expansa Variegata'.

'Pyramidalis'—Dense columnar form with ascending branches, leaves acicular, bluish green, very pungent, often sold as *J. excelsa* 'Stricta'; not particularly handsome; there appear to be several clones with this designation; male, 10 to 20′ by 8 to 12′.

'Ramlosa'—Spreading vase shape, similar to Pfitzer with feathery dark green foliage.

'Robusta Green'—Upright form with tufted brilliant green foliage; actually a rather handsome, somewhat irregular form; have seen plants about 15′ high, 5 to 7′ wide; female; sets abundant cones.

'San Jose'—Creeping form, 12 to 18″(24″) high and 6 to 8′ wide, spreads irregularly; foliage sage green, young plants tend to be acicular but with maturity there is a mixture of scale and needle-like foliage, quite susceptible to juniper blight but in the University's Botanical Garden it has thrived on a dry bank; introduced by W.B. Clarke, San Jose, CA in 1935; sometimes confused with *J. davurica* 'Parsoni' but that form has more scale-like foliage; female.

'Sarcoxie'—Dense compact, low-spreading form of Pfitzer, listed as Ozark Compact Pfitzer Juniper by Greenleaf Nursery.

var. *sargentii* Henry—One of the best and by some treated as a species. I am in no position to argue and will stay with the format of the previous edition; low-growing (18″ to 2′ high), wide-spreading (7.5 to 9′ wide), branchlets 4-angled, leaves mostly scale-like in 3's, small, slightly grooved on back, blue-green, bloomy; cones blue, scarcely bloomy; seeds 3; resistant to juniper blight; branches have a whip-like appearance; discovered by C.S. Sargent on the coast of the North Island of Japan (Hokkaido) in 1892; found on seashores throughout Japan and on rocky cliffs in the mountains.

var. *sargentii* 'Compacta'—More compact than above with scale-like leaves light green, acicular leaves dark green, with very glaucous green top (surface), margins bounded by a dark green edge.

var. *sargentii* 'Glauca'—Dwarf, much better in growth than 'Compacta'; branchlets thin, feathery, leaves blue-green, 1 1/2′ by 6′.

var. *sargentii* 'Variegata'—Spreading, flat-topped, 2′ by 4 to 5′, steel blue foliage with cream-white young shoots.

var. *sargentii* 'Viridis'—Similar to var. *sargentii* but leaves light green year round.

'Saybrook Gold'—Considered the brightest gold foliaged *J. chinensis* type, primarily needle-like foliage, foliage bright yellow in summer, more bronze-yellow in winter, horizontally spreading type probably 2 to 3′ high by 6′ wide, Girard Nursery introduction.

'Sea Green'—Compact spreader with fountain-like, arching branches, and dark green (mint green) foliage; 4 to 6′ high, 6 to 8′ wide; good-looking form, more upright than 'Pfitzeriana', foliage darkens in cold weather, *Phomopsis* susceptible especially when overhead watered, female.

'Sea Spray'—According to Hines Nursery who introduced the shrub it is a better ground cover than 'Blue Rug', 'Bar Harbor', or var. *tamariscifolia*; grows 12 to 15″ high and 6′ wide, blue-green relatively soft-textured foliage; center branches stay full and dense; resistant to water molds, root rot and juniper blight; hardy to -20°F; a sport of 'Pfitzeriana Glauca', introduced in 1972; I like what I have seen to date.

'Shimpaku'—Low, irregular vase-shaped form, gray-green needles, flaking bark, widely utilized for bonsai, have never observed a plant in an everyday landscape.

'Shoosmith'—A dwarf, compact, globose or pyramidal form.

'Spartan'—A fast, dense grower of tall, pyramidal or columnar habit, of rich green color and very handsome appearance, a Monrovia introduction, may grow to 20' high by 3 to 4' wide, have also read size descriptions 10 to 15' by 6 to 8', *Phomopsis* susceptible.

'Spearmint'—Dense columnar-pyramidal habit to 15', 3 to 4' wide, foliage bright green, soft, predominantly scale-like.

'Story'—Upright and slender symmetrical small tree with horizontal branching and dark green foliage; a Maney introduction; 12' by 3' after 13 years; male.

'Stricta'—In youth somewhat flattened and conical with all juvenile blue-gray foliage, distinctly prickly; has the untidy habit of holding onto its foliage for several years, not a good plant.

'Sulphur Spray'—Semi-prostrate habit, soft light green foliage with white tips giving silvery appearance overall.

'Tokasu'—Loosely conical with unevenly spaced lateral branches at right angles to central leader, side branches turn upright at their ends in a thin taper, bright green in summer, slight golden brown cast in winter, 20 to 30' high.

'Variegata'—Conical form, slow-growing, juvenile and adult blue-green leaves, irregularly splashed with creamy white.

'Viridis'—Pyramidal, teardrop-shaped in outline, dense branching, gray-green foliage.

'Wintergreen'—Pyramidal, dense, rich green foliage, 15 to 20' by 5 to 6'.

PROPAGATION: Invaluable needle evergreens displaying cosmopolitan personalities that allow them to survive where other landscape plants succumb. Most are dioecious or occasionally monoecious trees, shrubs, or ground covers that "flower" in spring with the berry-like cones ripening the first or second (occasionally third) season. Each cone contains 1 to 4, to 12 seeds. Collect ripened fruits in late fall or winter, clean by maceration, dry seeds and store in sealed containers under refrigeration.

An expanded discussion of juniper propagation is necessary because of their importance to the nursery industry and the tremendous volume of literature. Simply stated, there is no ubiquitous recipe for all junipers. Some root easily; others with difficulty. Many upright types must be grafted. Cutting propagation is broken down by category.

FACILITIES (ROOTING ENVIRONMENT): Since the 1990 edition appeared I have visited countless nurseries particularly in Zone 7 to 9. The aspect of juniper cutting propagation that was most difficult to reconcile was the simplicity of the rooting facilities yet the high degree of success. Three major Georgia container nurseries, Dudley, Thomson; McCorkle, Dearing; and Wight, Cairo, direct stick juniper cuttings from January through March (April) into bark:sand media in cells, outside, with only wind baffles to keep the mist from being blown off coverage. Growth regulator is a standard EPA registered formulation like Hormodin, Wood's, or Dip N' Grow. Cuttings root by May–June. In Tennessee, cuttings are often rooted in hoop covered outdoor beds. As one moves further north traditional polyhouses and greenhouses are used. The point is to not over-capitalize for structures because success is still assured. In juniper rooting lingo, "less is more".

CONDITION OF STOCK PLANT: A vigorous, healthy plant is superior to an overgrown plant that has been sitting for 10 years unattended in a corner of the nursery. Major growers stress that cuttings taken from their container-grown plants are superior. They root in higher percentages and have better root systems.

TIMING: Generally, cuttings should be taken after several hard frosts or freezes. Major container juniper growers take cuttings in December to March. References point to any time from July through April. The data presented for summer rooting indicated that percentages were not as high as for late fall–winter rooting. It is truly a mixed bag as far as timing is concerned. November through February is considered optimum. Cuttings of *J. horizontalis* 'Plumosa' rooted 65% in August, 52% in September, 91% in October, 100% in December, 96% in February, 33% in April and 2% in June. A large grower noted that the best time to take cuttings from a physiological standpoint was when they had stopped growing. In one study, junipers were rooted year-round but best rooting occurred between November and December with 4000 ppm IBA-dip. *Juniperus chinensis*, *J. communis*, *J. horizontalis*, *J. sabina*, and *J. squamata* were easier to root than *J. scopulorum* and *J. virginiana*.

HORMONE: The standard recommendation throughout the literature is 3000 ppm IBA-solution or talc for easy-to-root types, 8000 IBA-solution or no hormone to 4.5% IBA-talc. Based on published data, a hormone definitely serves to improve rooting. The following hormones and concentrations are used by the largest and most successful juniper growers in the world; 600 to 5000 ppm IBA-solution; 3000, 8000, 3.0%, 4.5% IBA talc or 2000 ppm IBA + 1000 ppm NAA-solution; 5000 ppm IBA-solution; 1870 ppm to 1.0% IBA-solution; 1.6% IBA-talc; 3000 to 8000 ppm IBA-talc; 3.0 to 4.5% IBA-talc. About all this indicates is that everyone does it differently. Virtually all nurserymen/researchers agree that a hormone is beneficial. The reason for the disparity of rates is that easy-to-root types like *J. horizontalis* would be treated with a low hormone concentration, difficult-to-root types like 'Maneyi', 'Blaauw', *J. virginiana* cultivars, etc., with higher levels. There are several reports that indicate greener cuttings (July–August) require greater hormone concentrations than those taken later.

Author has observed alcohol burn on juniper cuttings, especially those taken in summer or early fall, although damage (basal burn) has occurred on *J. conferta* (one of the most susceptible) in January through March. A study [*The Plant Propagator* 29(2):8–10 (1983)] with *J. chinensis* 'Hetzii' confirmed and quantified this observation, 5000 ppm to 2.0% IBA in 50% ethanol or prolonged exposure to 50% ethanol (2 minutes) caused basal end necrosis (burning) and reduced rooting. KIBA (water soluble formulation) at similar IBA concentrations and exposure times did not damage cuttings and resulted in slight increases in percent and number of roots. Rooting ranged from a low of 18% (1250 ppm IBA in 50% ethanol-2 minute dip) to 86% (5000 ppm KIBA-water-2 minute dip).

CUTTINGS: SIZE, CONDITION, WOUNDING, BOTTOM HEAT, ROOTING TIME: Four to 6″ long cuttings with a tinge of brown (mature) wood seem to be preferred. If actively growing July–August cuttings are taken this type of wood is not possible. Cuttings are stripped one-third to one-half. This, in effect, provides a wound which appears to assist in juniper rooting. In general, stockier, larger cuttings root better than small spindly ones. Bottom heat (66 to 68°F) is used by some growers and not by others. It should be advantageous if cuttings are rooted outside in cold frames or poly houses in ground beds where the air temperature is rather cool. Rooting time varies from 6 to 8 weeks to 12 weeks and possibly longer. I have noticed that *J. conferta* (January, February, March) rooted quickly and appeared to require less heat than other conifers including junipers. In a controlled study using outdoor ground beds with and without bottom heat with two media (bark or peat: perlite), *J. conferta* rooted under all conditions (better and faster with bottom heat) while Leyland Cypress in the non-heated frames did nothing (not even callus). It may be that junipers have a lower heat requirement for the root initiation process to proceed.

I worked for a nurseryman during college who took all his juniper cuttings in the late summer, provided IBA-talc treatment, sand, on a shaded greenhouse bench, syringed when needed and waited patiently for 3 to 5 months for rooting. He had good success with a wide range of junipers.

MEDIUM: The choice of media is about like the hormone rate . . . variable. Sand, sand:peat, bark, sandy soil, peat:perlite, vermiculite, etc., have been used successfully. In a comparative study, vermiculite, sand: peat, soil: peat:perlite proved better than sand or German peat.

WATER AND SANITATION: Mist in summer months with hand syringing or controlled mist in fall–winter months. Observations indicate junipers do not require a great amount of water during the rooting process. Keep medium moist, but not wet. Do not leave a continual film of moisture on cuttings. Water tends to bead in axils of the needles and the opportunity for fungal invasion (*Phomopsis*) is excellent. Some growers dip all the cuttings in a fungicide solution before preparing them for rooting. Again, it is a mixed bag as far as those that do and don't. The large growers practice preventative medicine.

AFTERCARE: Cuttings can be rooted in place and allowed to go through the winter and transplanted into containers in spring. The better the root system, the more successful the transplanting. Junipers present no special problems as far as aftercare. Proper cultivation and fertility practices yield a high quality juniper.

GRAFTING: Many upright forms of *J. chinensis*, *J. virginiana*, and *J. scopulorum* are grafted because they do not root easily. Choice of understock has been argued for 40 years in the *Proceedings International Plant Propagator's Society* with *Juniperus chinensis* 'Hetzii' the clear leader followed by seedling *J. virginiana*, the cultivar 'Skyrocket' and a strange juniper called *J. pseudocupressus*. A large nursery noted 'Sky Rocket' was an excellent understock because it is straighter and more graftable and resists fungal diseases better than 'Hetzii' and *J. virginiana*. 'Hetzii' or 'Hetz Columnaris', however, are the most popular. Understocks should be 1/4 to 1/3″ diameter, cleaned 3 to 4″ from soil of needles, etc., tops evened up. Process can run from December–February. The potted understock is brought inside and evidence of root growth is a signal to start. Understocks are sprayed with a fungicide prior to grafting. Scionwood is collected (like cutting wood) from vigorous stock plants, is 5 to 6″ long with 1 to 2″ brown wood at base, lower 2″ are cleaned, soft growth at top is removed, scions dipped in fungicidal solution, side-grafted, wrapped and allowed to heal in greenhouse bench. Twenty-five percent of grafts are healed in 2 weeks, most are healed after 5 to 6 weeks. Watch for new growth on scion as an index to successful healing. Grafts can be placed under shade or moved to containers for growing on.

ADDITIONAL NOTES: The species is almost an unknown entity under cultivation but is adequately represented by the numerous cultivars which vary in size from prostrate, spreading types to upright tree forms. P.J. Van Melle, an American nurseryman, had an interesting hypothesis concerning the numerous cultivars of *J. chinensis*. He says that the original species *J. chinensis* L. was inadequately defined by Linnaeus and that certain true varieties within *J. chinensis* should have been listed as species. He also noted that numerous natural and garden hybrids have occurred between *J. chinensis* and *J. sabina* all of which are listed under *J. chinensis*. Mr. Van Melle stated that the name *J. chinensis* has come to include "everything but the kitchen stove—a loose aggregate, incapable of definition in terms of a species." He proposed to limit the use of *J. chinensis*, to resuscitate *J. sphaerica* and to raise *J. sheppardii* to specific status. He also proposed a new hybrid species, *J. × media*, to contain all the more or less bush-like forms in which *J. sabina* was discernible by the characteristic savin odor of the bruised foliage. He relegated *J. chinensis* var. *sargentii* to species level, *J. sargentii*. Van Melle did a considerable amount of study but his work has not been fully accepted by the botanical world. One taxonomist said that "Van Melle is probably right, but a lot more work will have to be done on these junipers before we can accept all he says—it will mean scrapping so much in all the books."

Anyone who has taken a close look and smell of the *J. c.* cultivars will see some truth in Van Melle's hypothesis. In recent years, more literature is including many of the spreading cultivars in the *J. × media* category. I have had fun watching and reading the move away from *J. chinensis* to *J. × media* van Melle. In fact, the *New RHS Dictionary of Gardening* (1992) adapted van Melle's *J. × media* grex and includes many of the cultivars listed herein as *J. chinensis* under *J. × media*.

NATIVE HABITAT: China, Mongolia and Japan. Introduced 1767.

Juniperus communis L. — Common Juniper
(jö-nip′ĕr-us kom-mū′nis)

LEAVES: Awl-shaped, persisting for 3 years, tapering from the base to a spiny point, sessile, spreading at a wide angle from stem, about 3/5″ long, concave above with a broad white band, sometimes divided by a green midrib at the base, bluntly keeled below, needles consistently ternate.

BRANCHLETS: Triangular with projecting ridges, the leaves in whorls of 3.

CONES: Usually dioecious, male solitary, cylindrical, 1/3″ long, yellow stamens in 5 to 6 whorls; female, solitary, ripening the second or third year, green when young, bluish or black when ripe, covered with a waxy bloom, globose or slightly longer than broad, 1/3 to 1/2″ diameter with 3 minute points at the top, the 3 scales of which the fruit is composed usually gaping and exposing the seeds; seeds, 2 to 3, elongated, ovoid, 3-cornered, with depressions between.

SIZE: 5 to 10′ (rarely to 15′, known to 40′) by 8 to 12′ spread; also many low-growing forms; national champion is 46′ by 28′ in Washtenaw County, MI.

HARDINESS: Zone 2 to 6(7); does not do well in deep South; have not observed a single *J. communis*, except 'Hibernica', in commercial production or gardens in Zone 7b to 9.

HABIT: A medium-sized tree with ascending and spreading branches or more often a much-branched, sprawling shrub; prostrate in some forms.

RATE: Slow.

TEXTURE: Medium.

BARK: Reddish brown, scaling off in papery sheets.

LEAF COLOR: Green-gray to blue-green in summer; often assuming a yellow or brownish green in winter, often discolors worse than *J. chinensis* forms.

FLOWERS: Dioecious; staminate yellow.

FRUIT: Cones sessile or short-stalked, globose or broadly ovoid, 1/3 to 1/2″ across, bluish black or black, glaucous bloomy, ripening the second or third season; seeds usually 3, elongated ovoid, tri-cornered with depressions between; fruits used as diuretic and for flavoring gin.

CULTURE: Transplants readily; grows on the worst possible land, common on dry, sterile soils, rock outcroppings and waste lands; withstands wind; tolerant of calcareous soils, will tolerate neutral or acid soils; extremely hardy; full sun; amazing in its adaptability to diverse soil and climatic conditions; not as heat tolerant as *J. chinensis*, *J. conferta*, *J. davurica*, *J. horizontalis*, and *J. virginiana*.

DISEASES AND INSECTS: Susceptible to juniper blight and other problems mentioned on the culture sheet.

LANDSCAPE VALUE: Can be handsome ground cover for sandy soils and waste places, useful for undergrowth and naturalized plantings; best represented in the landscape by the cultivars; used in European gardens to some degree and the northern United States, is adaptable to heat and possibly heavy clay and poorly drained soils; also the competition from the major landscape species is intense and under aesthetic scrutinization, *J. communis* often does not measure up; Bonnie and I traveled to the Pacific Northwest in July 1996 and while hiking in the Mt. Rainier area tripped over *J. communis* on the sides of the various ridges; plants were always flat as pancakes, probably because of natural selection due to the tremendous snow accumulation that would break branches of the upright forms.

CULTIVARS:

'Berkshire'—Slow-growing, compact form, small, blue-green (steel blue), awl-shaped needles with silver markings, bronze winter color, 12″ high, recommended for rock garden use because of its compact, slow growth.

'Compressa'—Dwarf, cone-shaped form, dense, very slow-growing, 2 to 3′ tall, leaves awl-shaped, thin, with a conspicuous silvery band above, margin narrow, green, dark green beneath.

'Depressa'—Dwarf, broad, low, vase-shaped, essentially prostrate shrub, rarely above 4′ high, glaucous band on upper surface with green margin; although listed as a cultivar in many collections it should properly be variety *depressa*; as such it represents the eastern North American segment of *J. communis*; it occurs in the most inhospitable soils including dry, sandy, stony or gravelly; extremely vigorous and hardy; tends to discolor (brown) in winter months.

'Depressa Aurea'—Yellow-foliaged form, new shoots strongly colored, fading with time, otherwise similar to above, rather depressing especially in winter.

'Echiniformis'—For the collector, prickly green needles on a bowling ball structured bush, slow-growing.

'Effusa'—A wide-spreading, low ground cover with rich green color on the lower needle surface, silvery band above, holds color during winter, 9 to 12″(18″) by 4 to 6′, similar to 'Repanda' but winter color is inferior and habit is more open.

'Gold Beach'—Excellent dwarf form with green foliage, 5-year-old plants are 5″ tall and 2′ across; in early spring, new growth is yellow, later turning green.

'Gold Cone'—Upright, columnar, compact habit, bright yellow-tipped foliage, extremely vibrant, from New Zealand.

'Golden Shower'—Upright bushy pyramidal form with bright golden yellow new shoots; foliage becomes bronze-yellow during cold weather.

'Green Carpet'—Ground cover form with bright green new growth that matures to dark green, 4 to 6″ high by 2 1/2 to 3′ wide.

'Hibernica'—Dense, upright in habit, can grow 10 to 15′ high, foliage bluish white to near the apex above, margin narrow, green, bluish green beneath; a poor plant in American gardens; called Irish Juniper; interestingly still grown and sold, distinct columnar habit lends formality to the landscape; over time, however, it travels the way of the Dodo bird.

'Hills Vaseyi'—Upright vase-shaped habit, 4 to 5′ high and wide, green and pale blue needle-like foliage.

'Hornibrooki'—Low-growing (12 to 20″) ground cover with short (1/4″ long), sharp needles, silver-white, broad band above, green and keeled below, appears rich silver-green in summer, losing its luster in winter and becoming brownish; branches lie flat on ground in youth, discovered in 1923 by Murray Hornibrook in County Galway, West Ireland.

'Pencil Point'—Columnar, resembling a pencil in outline, green needle foliage with silvery bands, 4 to 5′(6′) high, 10″ wide.

'Repanda'—A low-growing form that maintains the best foliage color of the low-growing types; medium green foliage turning yellowish green in winter, grows to 15″ high, the soft, coarse-textured foliage is densely set on slightly ascending branches, nodding at the tips, plants form nearly uniform circles.

'Saxatilis' (var. *saxatilis*)—Although not given taxonomic credence as a distinct variety, the plant is offered in American commerce; typically low-growing to semi-prostrate, with short blue-green needles, have observed enough discrepancies to know that one 'Saxatilis' is not the same as another.

'Sentinel'—A narrow columnar form with rich green foliage that will mature between 5 and 10′.

'Silver Mile'—Graceful pendant branchlets and rich foliage, tight-growing, from Hines (1995), Vacaville, CA.

'Suecica'—Similar to 'Hibernica' except the tops of the branchlets droop; leaves bluish green, about as lousy as above; listed as Swedish Juniper.

'Windsor Gem'—Like 'Effusa' with darker green needles, less densely arranged along the branches, and are more procumbent.

PROPAGATION: Refer to *J. chinensis*.

ADDITIONAL NOTES: The oil distilled from the fleshy cones ("berries") is used for medicinal and flavoring purposes (gin). There are numerous varieties and cultivars of this species none of which compete effectively with the *J. chinensis*, *J. horizontalis*, and *J. virginiana* types. For those who want in depth information see Den Ouden and Boom, Jackson and Dallimore and Welch (1979). I was wandering around on a 6600′ high mountain a short distance from Lucerne, Switzerland when what do I see but patches of *Juniperus communis*. Two things in life are inescapable: taxes and *J. communis*. Variety *montana* (var. *nana*, var. *saxatilis*) is the prostrate, often mat-forming type from which numerous selections have been made. Also listed are var. *alpina* (Suter) Celak., var. *depressa* (Pursh) Franco, and var. *hemispherica* (Presl & C. Presl) Nyman.

NATIVE HABITAT: *Juniperus communis* has a wider distribution than any other tree or shrub. Common in north and central Europe and also occurs in the mountains of the countries bordering on the Mediterranean. It is also found in Asia Minor, the Caucasus, Iran, Afghanistan, the western Himalaya, the United States, and Canada. In the eastern United States it occurs from New England to Pennsylvania and North Carolina. I have seen old farmland in Massachusetts completely overgrown with this species and the range of forms seemed infinite. One could select cultivars until the cows come home.

Juniperus conferta Parl. — Shore Juniper
(jö-nip′ĕr-us kon-fĕr′tà)

LEAVES: Crowded, overlapping, awl-shaped, 1/4 to 5/8″(1″) long, 1/16″ wide, ternate, glaucous green, tapering to a prickly point, deeply grooved above with one band of stomata, convex below and green.

CONES: Produced in abundance, globose, 1/3 to 1/2″ diameter, dark blue or bluish black, bloomy at maturity and appearing silvery; 3 seeds, 3-angled, ovate, with longitudinal grooves on back, acuminate.

SIZE: 1 to 1 1/2′(2′) in height by 6 to 9′ spread.

HARDINESS: Zone (5)6 to 9; widely planted in southern states; temperature below –10°F may result in injury; Schneider and Hasselkus, *Amer. Nurseryman* 158(2):38–59 (1983), reported severe burn and dieback at the University of Minnesota Landscape Arboretum.

HABIT: Dense, bushy, procumbent, evergreen shrub.

RATE: Slow.

TEXTURE: Medium.

LEAF COLOR: Bright bluish green in summer; often bronze-green or somewhat yellow-green in winter.

FLOWERS: Dioecious, inconspicuous.

FRUIT: Cones subglobose, flat at base, 1/3 to 1/2″ across, dark blue or bluish black, bloomy at maturity; seeds, 3, 3-angled, ovate, with longitudinal grooves on back, acuminate.

CULTURE: Tolerant of poor soils, especially adapted to plantings in sandy soils of the seashore; full sun; does not tolerate excess soil moisture, will develop dieback in exceedingly moist situations.

DISEASES AND INSECTS: I have noticed a fair amount of dieback in large scale plantings in the South; there are numerous ground cover plantings on the Georgia campus and some have been removed because of the persistent dieback; plants in extremely heavy, water-logged soils seem to languish.

LANDSCAPE VALUE: A low ground cover, especially adapted for planting on sand dunes in the seashore area; actually one of the handsomest of the ground cover type junipers; good in mass, on banks, in planter boxes, around tall shrubs or trees; lovely draped over a wall; my years in the southern states have brought me a greater appreciation of the species and particularly the cultivars; on Jekyll Island, GA plants grow on a barrier sand mound exposed to the Atlantic Ocean yet have increased in size and actually prospered over the 19 years I have observed them; the species and cultivars grow quite well in clay soils *as long as* drainage is adequate but thrive in well-drained situations; a landscape architect mentioned to me that the species and 'Blue Pacific' are more shade tolerant than the other junipers.

CULTIVARS:

'Akebono'—Cream-yellow new growth, maturing to medium green, irregular grower, introduced by Brookside Gardens, apparently the variegation is irregularly dispersed throughout the plant.

'Blue Lagoon'—A low-growing, blue-green foliage form that maintains a relatively uniform blanket of foliage, U.S. National Arboretum introduction.

'Blue Mist'—Bluish needles, ground cover habit, 1′by 8′, could this be the same as 'Silver Mist'?; have seen 'Blue Mist' listed by several United States nurseries.

'Blue Pacific'—Low trailing habit and ocean blue-green foliage color; distinctly different than the species and making a better ground cover; probably never grows more than 1′ high; appears to be hardier than the species; literature describes it as growing 2′ high but I have never seen plants this tall; needles shorter and more densely borne (spaced) along the stem than with the species or 'Emerald Sea'; the foliage color is superior to species or any other cultivar that I know; does not discolor as badly as the species in cold weather but loses some of the bluish sheen, considered hardier than the species but less hardy than 'Emerald Sea'; has become the most widely grown selection and is assuming monoculture proportions in many areas of the South; Tommy Foster, Dudley Nursery, told me that they are growing a more root rot resistant form.

'Blue Tosho' ('Blue Tosh', 'Tosho')—A silver-green foliage form growing 1 1/2′ by 4′, probably the same as 'Silver Mist'.

'Boulevard'—Glaucous green foliage, a prostrate grower with all the main branches growing horizontally.

'Compacta'—Young plants prostrate, needles and branches closely spaced, needle color light green; stomatal band not so apparent on older growth because of needle color and horizontal growth pattern; have seen in Tampa, FL.

'Emerald Sea'—A U.S. National Arboretum introduction with good salt tolerance and a dense, low prostrate habit; abundant confusion about this plant but with a plant in my garden the differences are evident; the foliage is akin to the species and not as blue as 'Blue Pacific', habit is larger and ultimate size will exceed 1', reports indicate 1 to 2' by 8 to 10' is possible; foliage color dulls slightly in winter but not to the degree of the species, needles are more loosely borne than 'Blue Pacific', considered hardier than the species or 'Blue Pacific' and without snow cover at least to −10°F or lower; will grow faster than 'Blue Pacific'.

'Hilary'—A green needle form that has performed well in the coastal Connecticut and Rhode Island areas, original cuttings from Portsmouth Abbey, Portsmouth, RI, named in honor of Father Hilary Martin by Robert van Hof.

'Luchuensis'—Dwarf, slow-growing, prostrate selection with grass green needles, grows 2 to 4″ per year, Zone 6 and higher.

'Silver Mist'—J.C. Raulston promoted this handsome silver-blue-green foliaged form that is more compact and dense than the species, summer foliage color is outstanding with needles developing a slight purplish cast in winter, could be the next major ground cover juniper cultivar in the Southeast if adaptable; have grown this in the Dirr garden and it now represents the only juniper in my garden; tight and compact, growing 12 to 16″ high with distinctly silver-blue-green new growth that ages to blue-green; has been a handsome plant over the past 6 years in the Dirr garden but is now in excessive shade and starting to thin out; I might add that it appears to persist in shade better than other junipers; hardy to at least −10°F; discovered and introduced from Japan by Mr. Barry Yinger under the name 'Shiro Toshio' through Brookside Gardens, Wheaton, MD.

'Variegata'—Listed by Iseli Nursery as having yellow-splashed foliage interspersed with the bluish green normal needle color, ground-hugging habit introduced originally by Brookside Gardens; this may be the same as 'Akebono' or 'Sunsplash'.

PROPAGATION: Refer to *J. chinensis*.

ADDITIONAL NOTES: A fine juniper but like many good plants overused and abused, especially in the southern states; has been widely used on the Georgia campus to the point of monotony; interesting to visit container nurseries in summer and assess root growth on this species and the cultivars; high container heat shuts down/kills roots and shoot growth is slowed/arrested; with the advent of cooler temperatures in early fall, the plants return to normal growth.

NATIVE HABITAT: Found on the sea costs of Japan, especially on the sand dunes of Hakodate Bay in Hokkaido. Introduced 1915.

Juniperus davurica Pall. — Dahurian Juniper

LEAVES: Opposite, gray-sage green; juvenile—acicular, spreading, 1/5 to 2/5″ long, crescent-shaped in cross section, pointed; mature—scale-like, appressed, diamond-shaped, acuminate, glandular on inner face, to 1/8″ long.

CONES: Globose, 1/4″ diameter, purple-brown, covered with grayish bloom, 2 years maturity, seeds 2 to 6.

Juniperus davurica, (jö-nip′ĕr-us dā-vūr′i-kà), Dahurian Juniper, is another confusing species that is apparently not common in cultivation. An 11-year-old plant was 2′ high and 8 to 9′ wide. 'Expansa' ('Parsoni'), which does well in the southern states and may have several names, develops stout, rigid, horizontally spreading primary branches which do not lay on the ground but extend themselves slightly above. It builds upon itself and forms a dome-shaped mound about 2 to 3′ high and 9′ across. It carries a mixture of adult and juvenile gray-sage green foliage. An attractive feature is the long, slender, filiform adult branches arranged in dense, rich looking sprays. It is a female. 'Expansa Variegata' is boldly splashed with creamy white over the plant on both adult and juvenile foliage. 'Expansa Aureospicata' is less vigorous than the above with primarily juvenile foliage and butter yellow variegation. The species is widely distributed in eastern Asia. 'Parsoni' is one of the best junipers in the Southeast and displays excellent heat and some shade tolerance. It is vigorous and adaptable. Eastern Mongolia, China, southeastern Siberia to Pacific Coast. Introduced 1862 from Japan by Parsons Nursery, New York. Zone 6 to 9.

Juniperus horizontalis Moench. — Creeping Juniper
(jö-nip′ĕr-us hôr-i-zon-tā′lis)

LEAVES: Conspicuously glaucous, soft-textured, almost feathery, of 2 kinds, mostly scale-like, about 1/6″ long, closely appressed, in 4 ranks, ovate to oblong, shortly pointed, each with a glandular depression on the back, the awl-shaped leaves in opposite pairs; foliage usually turning a plum-purple color in winter; foliage has a plume-like texture.
CONES: On recurved stalks, bluish or greenish black, 1/4 to 1/3″ long, seeds, 2 to 3.

SIZE: 1 to 2′ high by 4 to 8′ spread, variable but definitely low-growing, spreading type.
HARDINESS: Zone 4 to 9.
HABIT: Low-growing, procumbent shrub with long, trailing branches forming large mats.
RATE: Slow to medium may grow to a diameter of 10′ over a 10 year period.
TEXTURE: Medium-fine.
LEAF COLOR: Green, glaucous, bluish green or steel-blue turning plum-purple in winter.
FLOWERS: Dioecious, inconspicuous.
FRUITS: Cones on recurved stalks, 1/4 to 1/3″ across, blue, slightly glaucous; seeds 2 to 3; seldom produced on cultivated plants.
CULTURE: Adaptable, withstands hot dry situations and slightly alkaline soils; container-grown and transplants readily; tolerant of heavy soils; native to sandy and rocky soils and exposed situations; found on sea cliffs, gravelly slopes and in swamps.
DISEASES AND INSECTS: *Phomopsis* blight (Juniper blight) can be extremely serious, spider mites.
LANDSCAPE VALUE: A low ground cover valued for its adaptability in sandy and rocky soils as well as tolerating hot, dry, sunny locations; used for slope plantings and facer evergreens, ground covers, masses, foundations and in containers; probably the most popular ground cover type across the United States.
CULTIVARS:
‘Admirabilis’—A bluish green needle form that grows about 8″ to 1′ high and 8 to 10′ wide, the main branches are prostrate with the secondary branches and branchlets borne at a steep angle, primarily juvenile foliage but some scale-like, male, introduced by Plumfield Nurseries in 1953, turns darker green with purplish tips in winter.
‘Adpressa’—Another Plumfield introduction, very dense and prostrate, seldom growing more than 10″ high, foliage green with tips glaucous green.
‘Alberta’—Looks like ‘Prince of Wales’, 6″ high, medium green foliage turns bronzy green in summer, prostrate and dense habit.
‘Alpina’—Dwarf creeping form, 2′ by 5′, leaves exclusively awl-shaped, bluish or gray-blue, changing to dull purple in autumn; highly susceptible to twig blight.
‘Argenteus’—Blue foliage with whip-cord branches, 18″ high.
‘Banff’—Bright silver-blue-green foliage, grows 6″ by 2 to 3′, not as vigorous as some types.
‘Bar Harbor’—Low-growing, spreading form, 1′ by 6 to 8′, leaves chiefly awl-shaped, loosely appressed, bluish green, turning more purple in the winter; probably a number of clones have been introduced under this name; comes from Mt. Desert Island, ME, where it grows in crevices on the rocky coast and is frequently found within reach of the salt spray; in the best form(s), it makes a fine ground cover usually less than 12″ high; sometimes confused with ‘Blue Rug’ but ‘Blue Rug’ is female with more scale-like foliage, typical ‘Bar Harbor’ is male and turns more reddish purple than ‘Blue Rug’; apparently more than one clone in cultivation since male and female forms are known.
‘Blue Acres’—New foliage blue, blue-green with age, prostrate spreader, Sheridan Nursery introduction, 4″, female.
‘Blue Chip’—Selected by Hill Nursery Co. for low prostrate habit and excellent blue foliage color in summer, tipped purplish in winter, 8 to 10″ high and 8 to 10′ wide with vertical branchlets arranged in rows; Welch mentions that it was raised from seed by the Jensen Nursery, Denmark in 1940; whether Hill’s received it from Jensen is unknown; it is a tremendously handsome blue-foliaged form; I have seen it as late as August in Kentucky and the foliage was still a good blue. I rooted cuttings and brought a plant to Georgia where, unfortunately, it did not perform as well as in more northerly areas; not as prosperous in Zone 7 to 9 as further north; *Phomopsis* is problematic.
‘Blue Horizon’—Similar to ‘Wiltonii’ except it remains low and open, never mounding up in the center, male, blue-green turning bronze-green in winter.
‘Blue Mat’—Dense, slow-growing, 6″ high, prostrate type, with blue-green foliage, turns dark purplish green in winter.
‘Blue Rug’—See ‘Wiltoni’.

'Coast of Maine'—Scaly, blue-green foliage turns light purple in winter, male, vigorous, plant appears to open in center.

'Douglasii' ('Waukegan')—Trailing form, 1 to 1 1/2' by 6 to 9', steel blue foliage turning grayish purple through the winter; rapid-growing form, introduced by Douglas Nursery, Waukegan, IL about 1855; good choice for sandy soils.

'Dunvegan Blue'—Low-spreading form with a bright bluish green color that turns light purple in winter; also described as having silvery blue color; introduced by Beaver Lodge Nursery, Alberta, Canada; texture and habit like 'Plumosa'.

'Emerald Isle'—Slow-growing, compact form of low habit, rich green foliage, branchlets fern-like.

'Emerald Spreader'—Exceedingly low (7″), ground-hugging spreader is heavily set with emerald green branchlets giving it a full, feathery appearance; lacks density, mounds in center, grading off toward the perimeter; a Monrovia introduction in 1967.

'Emerson'—Low-growing form, 1' by 9 to 15', leaves acicular and scale-like, blue-green foliage turns dark purplish green in winter, slow-growing, drought resistant, female, found in Black Hills of South Dakota and originally distributed as Black Hills Creeper.

'Filicina'—Blue-green foliage turns pleasing bronze in winter, 4″ high, stays dense and low but has a few long scaly branches that overtop others, female and sparse fruiter; Schneider and Hasselkus consider it similar but superior to 'Admirabilis' and 'Prince of Wales' because of finer texture and greater density; 'Livida' is similar to 'Filicina' but superior because it is denser and lacks the long overtopping branches; 'Felicina Minima' resembles 'Wiltoni' but is more dwarf, greener, and finer textured.

'Fountain' ('Plumosa Fountain')—Gray-green foliage turns bright purple in winter, 15″ high, male, plant was selected for compact growth habit, similar habit and color to 'Plumosa'; selection from 'Plumosa' by D. Hill Nursery Co.

'Glenmore'—Light green needle foliage turns dark brown in winter, low-growing, extremely dense, flat branches overtop the plants, sparse cone producer, ugly in winter.

'Glomerata'—Extremely dwarf, 6″ high, leaves scale-like, green assuming dull plum purple color in winter, male, short nearly vertical branchlets with needles arranged like *Chamaecyparis*.

'Green Acres'—A dark green form that is similar to 'Blue Acres' in other features.

'Grey Carpet'—Creeping form with long, trailing branches forming low cushions, foliage more green than that of 'Bar Harbor', female, turns bronzy in winter.

'Grey Pearl'—Bright blue feathery foliage, branches more erect, compact form, 8″ by 16″ or more.

'Heidi'—Good blue-green foliage color, slow-growing, 3' wide in 8 years.

'Hermit'—Rather interesting shrubby type with blue-green foliage, somewhat similar to Pfitzer in habit; selected by Dr. R.B. Livingston, University of Massachusetts on Hermit Island, ME; thought to be a hybrid between *J. virginiana* and *J. horizontalis*.

'Hughes'—Low-growing, 1' by 9', foliage silvery blue, distinct radial branching habit, good ground cover, holds blue-green color in winter with only a tinge of purple.

'Huntington Blue'—Wide-spreading, dense branching habit, covered by intense blue-gray foliage, becomes slightly plum-colored in winter, first saw at Cottage Hill Nursery in Alabama and misidentified it as 'Blue Chip', similar in growth habit.

Icee Blue™ ('Monber')—Sport of 'Wiltonii' with silver-blue foliage, 4″ tall, 8' wide, tight compressed foliage, mature growth has purple-tinged tips, Monrovia introduction.

'Jade River'—Silver-blue foliage, 8″ high ground cover form, mixture of scale and needle foliage, turns light purple in winter, male.

'Jade Spreader'—Very low, wide-spreading form with dense jade green foliage which creates a heavy mat-like appearance, turns dark brownish purple in winter, male.

'Lime Glow'—A branch sport with lime green foliage, habit reminds of 'Plumosa', foliage as I observed it in late October 1997 at Head-Lee Nursery was chartreuse shading toward yellow, color persists in heat of Zone 7, found by Larry Hatch, NC State University.

'Livida'—Juvenile foliage, deep grass green with a grayish bloom giving the plant an overall blue-green appearance, turns bronzy purple in winter, dense mat-forming type, forms a 6″ high, ground-hugging circle.

'Livingston'—Procumbent type, generally 12 to 15″ high, steel blue summer foliage, bluish green in winter, mostly scale-like foliage, female, from Hermit Island, ME; introduced by University of Vermont, 1972.

'Maiden Gold'—Selection by Maiden Nursery, Newton, NC for golden foliage, found as a branch sport of 'Wiltoni', quite similar to Iseli Nursery's 'Mother Lode', color is actually a cream-yellow in summer, becoming copper-orange with cold weather.

'Marcella'—Ground-hugging type seldom more than 6″ high, bluish green juvenile foliage, female, open and lacks foliage density.

'Mother Lode'—Gold-variegated form introduced by Iseli Nursery, OR, sport of 'Wiltonii' supposedly induced by lightning, 2 to 3″ by 2 to 3′, does not hold up in South compared to 'Lime Green'.

'Petraea'—An early selection of ground cover inclination that grows 8 to 10″ high, bluish green juvenile foliage turning dull mauve in winter, female.

'Plenifolia' (may by spelled 'Planifolia')—Silvery blue-needled foliage turns slight bronze-green during winter, grows 18″ high with branches borne at a 45° angle to ground, habit is open, highly susceptible to blight, introduced by Plumfield Nurseries around 1940.

'Plumosa'—Wide-spreading, dense, compact form, 2′ by 10′, leaves awl-shaped and scale-like, blue-green to gray-green, purplish in winter, branches arise at a 45° angle to ground, introduced by Andorra Nurseries of Philadelphia in 1907; over the years this has proven to be one of the most popular junipers; can be seriously afflicted with blight; male.

'Plumosa Aunt Jemima'—Low-spreading, blue-green form growing about 8″ high and 4 to 5′ wide, supposedly reminds of a pancake; introduced by Hill's in 1957, male.

'Plumosa Compacta'—Compact form of 'Plumosa', dense branching, flat-spreading, 18″ high; stays full in center, gray-green summer foliage, light purple in winter; reports from a Canadian reference indicate it does not stay full in center.

'Plumosa Compacta Youngstown'—Similar to above but stays green all winter according to literature; this is not true for the plant will assume a purplish to bronze tinge in cold weather; however, this and the above are probably the same plant, male.

'Plumosa Fountain'—Flat-growing form, 16″ by 6′, rapid-growing, similar to 'Aunt Jemima'.

'Prince of Wales'—Very procumbent, 4 to 6″ high, bright green with a bluish tinge caused by a waxy bloom, purple-tinged in winter months; acicular and scale-like foliage; introduced by Morden Experiment Station in 1967; collected in southern Alberta, Canada, considered cold hardy to -40°F; plant opens up in center with age.

'Procumbens'—Spreading, prostrate form, 6″ by 12 to 15′, leaves awl-shaped, soft, glaucous green, becoming bluish green with age; name may be incorrect but plants are encountered with this name.

'Prostrata'—Dark silvery green foliage, grows 6″ high but lacks density with many long branches overtopping the plant, female.

'Prostrata Glauca'—Good blue-green foliage, maintains low-growing habit.

'Prostrata Variegata'—Similar to the species with foliage variegated yellow, cream, or white.

'Pulchella'—A very slow-growing, dense, compact type, forming a symmetrical, 4 to 6″ high mat that may spread to 3′ and more, greenish gray, bronzy in winter, acicular leaves, male.

'Repans'—Blue-gray, cord-like texture to foliage, to 20″ high.

'Slow Blue'—Blue foliage form.

'Sun Spot'—Similar to 'Waukegan' but spotted yellow throughout the branches.

'Turquoise Spreader'—Wide-spreading form, 12″ high, densely covered with soft and feathery branchlets of turquoise green foliage, turns bronzy green with lavender tips in winter; vigorous grower, remains quite flat; juvenile foliage; a Monrovia introduction.

'Variegata'—Vigorous, 15″ high form with creamy white variegation, turns dark purple in winter, branches at 45° angle to ground, lacks density, female.

'Venusta'—Darker blue-green than species, grows less than 12″.

'Wapiti'—Low-growing, 10 to 12″ high, with sharply ascending laterals, green foliage turning dull purple with cold weather.

'Watnong'—Bead-like texture, blue-green foliage.

'Webberi'—Extremely low, mat-like, spreading form of fine texture, bluish green foliage, 6″ to 1′ by 6 to 8′, male, bronze-green in winter.

'Wilms'—Silvery green foliage in summer, turns brownish purple in winter, lower and more compact than 'Plumosa', considered a new and improved 'Plumosa', grows 12″ high.

'Wiltoni' ('Wiltonii', 'Blue Rug')—Very flat-growing form with trailing branches, 4 to 6″ by 6 to 8′, foliage intense silver-blue, assumes light purplish tinge in winter, fairly fast-growing; a female with 1/4″ diameter, silvery blue cones; found on Vinalhaven, an island off the coast of Maine in 1914; introduced by South Wilton Nurseries, Wilton, CT; has become one of the most popular ground cover junipers in the United States and Europe; does quite well in the heat of the South; there are many beautiful established plants in the Athens area that are growing in soil with the consistency of blacktop.

'Winter Blue'—Similar to 'Plumosa' in habit with a pleasing light green summer foliage that becomes rich blue in winter.

'Wisconsin'—Selected in 1964 by Ed Hasselkus, University of Wisconsin near Brocks, WI, mixture of scale and needle blue-green foliage, turns dark purplish green in fall and winter, 8″ high, mounds slightly with good radial habit, fast-growing, no twig blight, male.

'Yukon Belle'—Bright silvery blue foliage, turns dark purplish green in winter, foliage is dense and fine-textured; winter foliage color like 'Wisconsin', ground-hugging, broad-spreading, Zone 2.

PROPAGATION: Refer to *J. chinensis*.

NATIVE HABITAT: North America where it inhabits sea cliffs, gravelly slopes, even swamps (Nova Scotia to British Columbia, south to Massachusetts, New York, Minnesota, and Montana). Introduced 1836.

Juniperus procumbens (Endl.) Miq. — Japgarden Juniper (Listed as a variety of *J. chinensis* by *Hortus III*).

(jö-nip′ēr-us prō-kum′benz)

LEAVES: In three's, linear-lanceolate, spiny-pointed, about 1/3″ long, concave above and glaucous with a green midrib toward the apex, lower surface convex, bluish with 2 white spots near the base below from which 2 glaucous lines run down the edges of the pulvini.

SIZE: 8 to 12″ to 2′ high by 10 to 15′ spread; plants 3′ high and over 22′ wide are known.

HARDINESS: Zone 4 to 8(9).

HABIT: A dwarf, procumbent plant with long, wide-spreading, stiff branches; a beautiful ground cover in its finest form, tips of branches ascend often at a 20 to 30° angle to the ground.

RATE: Slow, may cover 10′ diameter area in 10 years.

TEXTURE: Medium.

LEAF COLOR: Bluish green or gray-green.

FLOWERS: Dioecious, staminate yellow, pistillate greenish.

FRUIT: Cones subglobose, 1/3″ across; seeds 3, ovoid; cones not seen on cultivated plants.

CULTURE: Needs full sun; tolerant of many soils, thrives under adverse conditions, needs open situations, thrives will on calcareous soils.

DISEASES AND INSECTS: *Phomopsis* can be a problem.

LANDSCAPE VALUE: A handsome ground cover for beds, low borders, terraces, hillsides; can be pruned to retain size; in the third edition I really beat on the species relative to *Phomopsis* susceptibility but since moving south have seen minimal problem on a great number of plants; foliage is beautiful and when properly grown both the species and 'Nana' make superb ground covers for full sun.

CULTIVARS:

'Bonin Islands'—Similar to 'Nana' but smaller and shorter blue-green needles.

'Greenmound'—Attractive light green foliage that does not brown-out, grows with slight mounding habit, 8″ high and 6′ wide, a Hines introduction.

'Nana'—Dwarf, similar to species, forms a compact mat with branches one on top of the other, branchlets vary in length, spreading out as a compact mass of sprays, foliage bluish green, slightly purplish in winter, male; one of the best!; can become quite wide-spreading with time; have seen a 10 to 12′ wide plant at Longwood Gardens; may mound upon itself and become 2 to 2 1/2′ high after many years.

'Nana Californica'—Similar to 'Nana' but finer textured and with more pronounced blue-green color; slow-growing, ground-hugging, cushion-like form, 8″ high and spreading to 4′ or more; probably the same as 'Greenmound'.

'Variegata'—The bluish green foliage is streaked with creamy white coloring; variegated forms by some authorities have been relegated to *J. davurica*, but the foliage is always needle-like on *J. procumbens* and predominantly scale-like with some needle-like on *J. davurica*.

PROPAGATION: Refer to *J. chinensis*.

NATIVE HABITAT: Mountains of Japan. Also listed as southern Japan (Kyushu, coastal areas; Bonin Island). I have doubts about the latter nativity because of the excellent cold hardiness. Introduced 1843.

Juniperus sabina L. — Savin Juniper

(jö-nip′ēr-us så-bī′nå)

LEAVES: Scale-like, 4-ranked, in opposite pairs which are overlapping, ovate, shortly pointed or blunt at the apex, about 1/20″ long, rounded on back, which usually bears a resin gland, leaves on young plants and older branchlets awl-shaped, spreading, straight, 1/6″ long, apex sharply pointed; green or bluish green and with a conspicuous midrib above; foliage when crushed emits a disagreeable odor and has a bitter taste; quite distinct among the junipers.

CONES: Dioecious usually; may have both sexes on one plant; female cones ripening in the autumn of the first year or the following spring, on recurved stalks, globose to ovoid, about 1/5″ diameter, brownish or bluish black, bloomy, composed of 4 to 6 scales; seeds 2 to 3, ovoid, furrowed.

SIZE: 4 to 6′ high by 5 to 10′ spread; supposedly can grow to 15′.

HARDINESS: Zone 3 to 7.

HABIT: A spreading shrub, upright in habit, stiff, somewhat vase-shaped; distinctly stiff branches borne at a 45° angle to the ground; extremely variable from ground cover to distinctly upright; photos of plants in their native habitat reflect almost consistent ground cover habits, and indeed most of the cultivars are low-growing.

RATE: Slow.

TEXTURE: Medium.

LEAF COLOR: Dark green in summer, often a dingy green in winter showing a tinge of yellow, no purplish color in winter which allows easy separation, especially from the cultivars of *J. horizontalis*.

FLOWERS: Usually dioecious, occasionally monoecious.

FRUIT: Cones on recurved stalks, ripening in the first season or in the spring of the second season; seeds 1 to 3, ovoid, furrowed.

CULTURE: Does well on limestone soil, well-drained and dry soils, and open, sunny exposures; withstands city conditions; best suited to colder climates.

DISEASES AND INSECTS: Juniper blight (see LANDSCAPE VALUE).

LANDSCAPE VALUE: The species does not have a great deal to offer because of poor foliage and ragged nature; the cultivars are quite handsome especially the low-growing types; they make excellent ground covers, mass plants or foundation plants; I noticed that in many reports the var. *tamariscifolia* is listed as moderately to severely susceptible to juniper blight; I saw several handsome specimens of var. *tamariscifolia* at Purdue University's Horticultural Park, West Lafayette, IN, that showed no signs of blight while *J. procumbens*, *J. procumbens* 'Nana', and *J. horizontalis* and cultivars were heavily infested; apparently there are different clones in the trade with varying degrees of resistance; an excellent paper evaluating juniper susceptibility to *Phomopsis* appeared in the *J. Amer. Soc. Hort. Sci.* 94: 609–611 (1969).

CULTIVARS:

'Arcadia'—Growth habit dense and layered, 1 to 1 1/2′ high by 6 to 8′ wide, leaves predominantly scale-like, grass green; resistant to juniper blight; hardy in Zone 3, darker green than 'Skandia', less compact.

'Arcadia Compact Form'—Soft green lacy foliage, lower growing than above; 'Mini Acadia' is listed and is probably the same biological entity, 12″ by 5 to 8′, keeps soft green foliage in winter.

'Blue Danube'—Semi-upright yet more horizontal than the species, foliage bluish green, scale-like, awl-shaped inside the plant, 1 1/2′ by 5′, Zone 4.

'Blue Forest'—Blue foliage, spreading growth habit with upturned sprays, 18″ high and wide, blight-free, hardy to -20°F, have seen *Phomopsis* injury.

'Broadmoor'—A dwarf, low-spreading, staminate form which looks like a neat form of var. *tamariscifolia* when young, but the plant tends to build up at the center with age, the main branches are strong and horizontally spreading; the branchlets short and reaching upwards; the sprays very short, occurring mainly on the upper side of the branches; the foliage is a soft grayish green and is resistant to juniper blight; this clone as well as 'Arcadia' and 'Skandia' were selected from many thousands of seedlings raised by D. Hill Nursery Co., Dundee, IL from seed imported from near Petersburgh, Russia in 1933; all have proved resistant to juniper blight; Zone 4; will grow 2 to 3′ high and 10′ wide or more; I have been really impressed with this selection.

'Buffalo'—Similar to var. *tamariscifolia* with feathery branches and bright green foliage, 12″ high by 8′ wide in 10 years, female, retains good color in winter, Zone 2 to 3.

Calgary Carpet™ ('Monna')—A selection from 'Arcadia' with lower and more spreading growth habit, 6 to 9″ by 10′, soft green foliage, Monrovia introduction.

'Hicksii'—Upright tendency in youth yields to procumbent habit with age, dark bluish green needles.

'Hoar Frost'—Tufted, with *J. virginiana* 'Canaertii'-like tufts of foliage on a compact, spreading plant, new growth is light yellow aging to green.

Moor-Dense™ ('Monard')—A form with foliage color similar to 'Broadmoor', but flatter growing, more tiered branching habit, 8 to 12″ high by 5 to 6′ wide, a Monrovia introduction.

'Pepin'—Upright form with blue-green foliage, supposedly with greater blight resistance than typical *J. sabina*.

'Sierra Spreader'—Low-growing, 12″ by 5 to 8′, green foliage throughout the year.

'Skandia' ('Scandia')—Similar to 'Arcadia' with foliage mostly acicular and pale grayish green, 1 to 1 1/2′ by 10′ and more, Zone 3, female, blight resistant.

var. *tamariscifolia* Ait.—Low-spreading, mounded form, branches horizontal, branchlets crowded, leaves awl-shaped, very short, nearly appressed, bluish green; grows 18″ tall and 10 to 15′ across in 15 to 20 years; susceptible to blight; often listed as 'Tamariscifolia'; found in the wild on the mountains of southern Europe and, hence, may deserve botanical categorization, i.e., variety or forma; apparently more than one clone in the nursery trade; a blue-green form is listed as 'Tamariscifolia New Blue'; also have seen 'Tam No Blight' which is described as blight resistant.

'Thomsen'—Handsome, broad-mounded spreading form with tips free and extended, needles green with tinge of blue, blight resistant, probably 2 to 3′ by 10′.

'Variegata'—Dwarf form, 2 to 3′ by 3 to 4 1/2′, leaves scale-like, sprays streaked white.

'Von Ehren' ('Von Ehron')—Vase-shaped grower, 5′ by 5′, leaves awl-shaped, light to dark green, resistant to juniper blight; may grow 6 to 8′ high and 18 to 20′ wide.

PROPAGATION: Refer to *J. chinensis*.

ADDITIONAL NOTES: A very variable, spreading or procumbent shrub and one in which the numerous named selections are superior to the species types. Some of the cultivars are quite beautiful but do not seem to have the popular appeal of the *J. horizontalis* types.

NATIVE HABITAT: Mountains of central and southern Europe, western Asia, Siberia and Caucasus. Cultivated before 1580.

Juniperus scopulorum Sarg. — Rocky Mountain Juniper, Colorado Redcedar
(jö-nip′ĕr-us skop-ū-lôr′um)

LEAVES: Scale-like, tightly appressed, rhombic-ovate, apex acute or acuminate, entire, back varying in color, dark or light bluish green, glaucous or light green and obscurely glandular.

CONES: Ripening the second year, globose, 1/4 to 1/3″ diameter, dark blue, glaucous bloomy, seeds 2, reddish brown, triangular, prominently angled and grooved, pulp sweetish.

SIZE: 30 to 40′ high by 3 to 15′ wide; national champion is 40′ by 21′ in Cache National Forest, UT.

HARDINESS: Zone 3b to 7.

HABIT: A narrow, pyramidal tree often with several main stems, opening with age.

RATE: Slow, most of the cultivars will average 6 to 12″ per year.

TEXTURE: Medium.

BARK: Reddish brown or gray, shredding but persistent.

LEAF COLOR: Varying in color from dark green or bluish green, glaucous or light green.

FLOWERS: Monoecious or dioecious; male has 6 stamens compared to 10 or 12 of *J. virginiana*.

FRUIT: Cones nearly globular, to 1/3″ across, dark blue, glaucous bloomy, ripening in the second year, pulp sweetish; seeds 2, triangular, reddish brown, prominently angled, grooved.

CULTURE: Withstands drought conditions very well; same requirements as other *Juniperus*, not well-adapted to humidity and high night temperatures of the Southeast.

DISEASES AND INSECTS: *Phomopsis* blight, also serves as an alternate host for cedar apple rust. Canker caused by *Botryosphaeria stevensii* has attacked *J. scopulorum* in windbreak and ornamental plantings in Kansas. Proved pathogenic and caused cankers on *J. virginiana* and *J. chinensis* in greenhouse and field inoculation studies [see *Plant Disease* 72:699–701 (1988)]. *Seridium unicorne* (*S. cardinale*) likewise induced cankers on the same taxa [see *Plant Disease* 75:138–140 (1991)].

LANDSCAPE VALUE: Valued for use as screens, hedges, backgrounds and foundation plants, very nice blue cast to the foliage, more popular in upper Midwest, plains and Rocky Mountain states.

CULTIVARS:

'Blue Arrow'—Akin to 'Skyrocket' but foliage is more intense blue, very narrow-conical in youth.

Blue Creeper™ ('Monam')—Low-spreading habit, 2′ by 6 to 8′, bright blue foliage color that becomes more intense in cold weather, a Monrovia introduction.

'Blue Heaven' ('Blue Haven')—Neat pyramidal form, foliage strikingly blue in all seasons, heavy cone bearer, 20′ in 15 to 20 years, more open than 'Blue Arrow'.

'Chandler's Silver'—A broad-pyramidal form with bluish green foliage; may require pruning to keep it attractive.

'Cologreen'—Forest green-foliaged form that is susceptible to rust, forms a compact, upright, cone-like outline, 15 to 20′ by 5 to 7′, selected in 1930's.

'Cupressifolia Erecta'—Dense, pyramidal, rich green, with undertones of silvery blue, needle-like foliage, to 20′.

'Dewdrop'—A broad-pyramidal form with bluish green foliage, more needle-like foliage, slower growing than species.

'Erecta Glauca'—Upright bluish-needled form, supposedly a good grower; is this the same as 'Glauca Compacta'?

'Fairview'—Blue-green foliage and supposedly resistant to cedar apple rust.

'Glauca Pendula'—Extreme weeping form not unlike 'Tolleson's Weeping', bluish foliage, on stringy shoots; Hillier introduction.

'Gray Gleam'—Pyramidal, slow-growing, male, foliage distinct silvery gray, becoming more brilliant in the winter, grows 15 to 20' by 5 to 7' in 30 to 40 years.

Green Ice™ ('Monwade')—Broad-pyramidal, tight-branched form, new growth is ice-green, mature foliage gray-green, color is best in colder climates, 15' by 7 to 10', a Monrovia introduction.

'Grizzly Bear'—Broad-pyramidal, dense, uniform growth pattern, blue-green.

'Hillborn's Silver Globe'—A medium-sized more or less globe-shaped form with bluish green foliage, susceptible to rust.

'Lakewood Globe'—Compact form with excellent blue-green foliage, 4 to 6' in 10 years; several leaders may develop.

'March Frost'—Vigorous, upright selection with good blue-green foliage.

'McFarland'—Narrow columnar form with gray-green foliage, substitute for 'Skyrocket'.

'Medora'—Slender, columnar-pyramidal, compact form with good blue-green foliage, slow-growing, selection from Badlands of North Dakota, male, named in 1954, 10' by 2 to 3'.

'Moffettii'—Pyramidal and dense, foliage heavy, silvery green, abundant cones.

'Montana Green'—Pyramidal, dense, compact, green foliage color.

'Moonglow'—A dense, pyramidal conical selection, intense bluish gray-green foliage, 20' by 5'.

'North Star'—An upright, green form that may suffer slight windburn.

'Pathfinder'—Narrow, pyramidal tree, regular in outline, leaves in flat sprays, distinctly bluish gray, 20' high by 6 to 8' wide in 15 to 20 years.

'Pendula'—Listed and photos I observed reflect similarity to 'Tolleson's Weeping', suspect the latter may be the rename.

'Platinum'—A dense, slow-growing, narrow pyramidal, silvery blue needle form, 8 to 12' by 6 to 8', Zone 3 to 7.

'Silver King'—Essentially ground cover type that grows 24" high with a wide-spreading, loosely layered habit, scaly silvery green foliage holds color well in winter; although listed as male, some plants have male and female cones which is not unusual for *J. scopulorum* types.

'Skyrocket'—Probably the most narrow columnar juniper available, bluish green mostly acicular needles, has done well in Midwest, reminds a blue rocket sitting on the launching pad, actually this might be the best place for it in the landscape; if you want your landscape to have that third dimensional, outer space feeling, plant a couple hundred Skyrockets; formerly listed as a *J. virginiana* selection, 15' plant may be only 2' wide at base, roots readily from cuttings; 'Silver Star' has minimal cream-white variegated shoots otherwise similar to 'Skyrocket'.

'Sparkling Skyrocket'—Sport of 'Skyrocket' with gold streaking among the blue-green foliage.

'Springbank'—Slightly more loose, feathery pyramidal-columnar form, silvery blue foliage, have seen in Canada, a handsome form, appears to discolor more in winter and lose the strong blue coloration.

'Sterling Silver'—Compact pyramidal habit, with interesting tight-twisting, silver-blue foliage.

'Sutherland'—Strong-growing, silver-green foliaged form, broad pyramidal to 20'.

'Tabletop' ('Table Top')—Flat-topped form with silvery blue foliage, grows 5 to 6' high and 8' across in 10 years, female, formerly listed as 'Table Top Blue', semi-upright in habit.

'Tolleson's Weeping Juniper'—Silver-blue foliage hangs string-like from arching branches; supposedly cold hardy anywhere in the country; interesting form; has been grown in the South with some success, have seen as far south as Orlando, FL; there is also a form with soft green foliage ('Tolleson's Green Weeping'); both 20' high, 8 to 12' wide.

'Welchii'—Narrow, columnar, compact growth habit, to 8' tall, silvery new growth, changing to bluish green, handsome foliage.

'Wichita Blue'—Brilliant bright blue-foliaged, pyramidal form, 18' or greater, 5 to 8' wide.

'Winter Blue'—Semi-prostrate, spreading form, brilliant silver-blue foliage retains blue color in winter, grows 24 to 30" high, found by Clayton Berg, Valley Nursery, Helena, MT.

PROPAGATION: See under *J. chinensis*.

NATIVE HABITAT: Found wild on dry, rocky ridges, usually above 5,000', on the eastern foothills of the Rocky Mountains from Alberta to Texas, westward to the coast of British Columbia and Washington, and to eastern Oregon, Nevada, and northern Arizona. Introduced 1836.

Juniperus squamata Buch.-Ham ex D. Don — Singleseed Juniper, Flaky Juniper
(jö-nip′ĕr-us ska-mā′ta)

LEAVES: Awl-shaped, overlapping, in whorls of 3, pressed together or slightly spreading, the upper part free and 1/8 to 1/6″ long, curved, tapering to a sharp point, grayish green with 2 grayish white bands, green beneath, convex, furrowed; old leaves persisting on the shoots and branchlets as dry brown scales.

CONES: Ellipsoidal, 1/4 to 1/3″ long, reddish brown becoming black when ripe in the second year; scales 3 to 6, pointed; seeds solitary, ovoid, ridged, with 3 to 4 depressions below the middle.

SIZE: Extremely variable and is difficult to ascertain the exact nature of the species; the cultivars are used in landscaping but the species is not cultivated; 6 to 12″ to 25′ high.

HARDINESS: Zone 4 to 7(8); heat and humidity of Southeast have not been kind to the cultivars.

HABIT: Dwarf, decumbent, ascending or erect shrub; very variable over its wide geographical range; usually low to prostrate shrub, but in some forms capable of being trained as a small tree.

RATE: Slow.

TEXTURE: Medium.

BARK: Rusty brown, exfoliating in papery flakes.

LEAF COLOR: Grayish green to bright steely blue-green with two gray white bands; becoming bronze- or purple-tinted blue-green in winter.

FLOWERS: Dioecious (also monoecious); staminate yellow, pistillate green.

FRUIT: Cones elliptic, 1/4 to 1/3″ across, reddish brown, changing to purplish black; scales with a triangular mucro; seeds solitary, ovoid, keeled.

CULTURE: Adaptable, tolerates dry soils; not well-suited to the heat and humidity of the Southeast.

DISEASES AND INSECTS: Susceptible to bagworms.

LANDSCAPE VALUE: Cultivars are handsome, especially blue-foliaged forms; 'Blue Star' was promoted and sold with a frenzy in the Atlanta-Athens market; I witnessed many plants in pristine blue foliage that started to decline and die in the heat, humidity, and excessively wet soils; plants are spectacular in cool temperate climates, unsatisfactory otherwise.

CULTIVARS: Many forms have been selected in Europe and are common in gardens. They appear to prosper in the cooler European climate and would be suitable for the northern and West Coast states. Many are not commercially available but are now being produced in United States nurseries for eventual release. 'Blue Star' was essentially unknown and now is common. Some of the new ground cover types are particularly attractive. Many of the descriptions have been extracted from European nursery catalogs and horticultural literature as well as synthesized from face-to-plant confrontations.

'Blue Alps'—Upright branching with arching, slightly nodding branch tips, bright silver-blue needles, 5 to 6′ high by 2 to 2 1/2′ wide.

'Blue Carpet'—Handsome ground cover form with rich blue-gray-green foliage, 8 to 12″ by 4 to 5′ wide after 19 years, a mutation of 'Meyeri'.

'Blue Spider'—Appears similar to 'Blue Carpet' perhaps with more elongated shoots, becomes higher mounded in center than 'Blue Carpet'

'Blue Star'—A branch sport of 'Meyeri' found in about 1950; it is a slow-growing, low, rounded, squat plant, about as broad as high; the juvenile foliage is the same rich blue of 'Meyeri' but is more crowded on the branches; the plant does not develop the strong leaders of 'Meyeri' so it remains dense; it has remained stable under cultivation; I first saw the plant at Amstel Park, Amsterdam and it truly shone like a silver-blue star; rich foliage color is attractive; may decline under high humidity and high night temperatures; 3′ by 3 to 4′.

'Blue Swede'—Particularly attractive, almost Pfitzer-like growth habit, with rich blue-green foliage in summer turning metallic bluish gray in winter, 4′ by 4 to 5′.

'Chinese Silver'—Branches develop at a 45° angle to the ground and the tips develop a semi-pendulous character, handsome, blue-silver-green foliage in summer, 4 to 5′ high, 5 to 6′ wide.

'Golden Flash'—Creamy yellow-variegated sport of 'Meyeri', originated in New Zealand; 'Gold Tip' is similar.

'Holger'—Semi-spreading form with sulfur yellow new growth that becomes gray-blue-green in summer and later, foliage does not resemble typical *J. squamata*, considered a possible hybrid between *J. squamata* and *J. chinensis* 'Pfitzeriana Aurea'; eventually grows 2 to 3′ high, 3 to 4′ wide, plants I saw were small but some literature indicates 6′ by 6′ at maturity.

'Hunnetorp'—Sister plant (seedling?) of 'Holger' with blue-green foliage.

'Loderi'—Columnar form, branches dense, upright, tips nodding, rich blue-green foliage, grows 3 to 5′ high, possibly to 10′.

'Meyeri'—Bushy, dense form, 5' by 4', foliage striking blue-white above, needle-like, quite exotic when young but the old, dead needles persist and after a time the plant becomes a liability, often called the Fishtail Juniper; reported to grow as much as 6 to 8' high and 2 to 3' wide in 15 years; known to 20' high; one of the largest I have observed resides at Rowallane, Northern Ireland, a robust 20' by 25'; female; introduced in 1910 (have seen 1914 also) by F.N. Meyer; many branch sports have arisen from 'Meyeri' resulting in cultivars 'Blue Star' and 'Blue Carpet'.

'Prostrata'—Prostrate, slow-growing form, branchlets erect, short, green, leaves awl-shaped with bluish white bands above, margin broad, green; green and slightly keeled beneath, tips of leading shoots nod, 12", mounding in center, trailing off at edges, differs from 'Nana' in that the branch tips nod instead of turning up.

'Pygmaea'—Dwarf form; 3' by 3', upright branches with short blue-green needles turning purplish in winter.

'Variegata'—Prostrate, spreading form, 10" by 4 to 5', new growth is cream colored.

PROPAGATION: Refer to *J. chinensis*.

ADDITIONAL NOTES: Often difficult to distinguish this species and the cultivars from *Juniperus procumbens* and its kin. 'Prostrata' is a particularly confusing form that is apparently quite confused in gardens and the nursery trade.

NATIVE HABITAT: Afghanistan, Himalayas, western China. Introduced 1836.

Juniperus virginiana L. — Eastern Redcedar
(jö-nip′ĕr-us vĕr-jin-i-ā′nà)

LEAVES: Scale-like leaves arranged in 4 ranks closely pressed and overlapping, about 1/16″ long, short- or long-pointed, free at the apex, often with a small, oval, glandular depression on the back, shorter than the distance from the gland to the leaf-tip; leaves on older branchlets broader, about 1/12″ long becoming brown and withered, juvenile leaves often present on adult trees, spreading, in pairs 1/5 to 1/4″ long, ending in a spiny point, concave and glaucous above, green and convex beneath; bruised needles smell like a cedar chest or closet.

CONES: Dioecious, female cones ripening in one year, sub-globose, ovoid, up to 1/4″ across, often glaucous; seeds 1 to 2, ovoid, furrowed, shining brown, cones can be quite handsome and some appear almost blue, and with the waxy bloom almost as if frosted.

SIZE: 40 to 50' high by 8 to 20' spread; extremely variable over its extensive native range; co-national champions are 55' by 68' in Lone Hill Church Cemetery, Coffee County, GA and 90' by 45' in Coleman Cemetery, Angelina National Forest, TX.

HARDINESS: Zone 3b to 9.

HABIT: Densely pyramidal when young and slightly pendulous in old age; variable in the wild from almost columnar to broadly pyramidal.

RATE: Medium.

TEXTURE: Medium.

BARK: A handsome grayish to reddish brown, exfoliating in long strips.

LEAF COLOR: Medium green, sage-green to blue-green in summer often becoming bronze to yellow-brown in winter, variable from tree to tree.

FLOWERS: Usually dioecious, may have monoecious flowers on occasion; staminate yellow, pistillate green; interesting in late winter, February into March, when the staminate yellow-brown cones are swelling and starting to release pollen; male trees take on a rather ugly yellow-brown color and are easily distinguished from female trees at this time of year, in actuality the male cones are noticeable in fall and beyond; female trees are lovely with the various colored cones, some greenish blue to frosted blue, often the female cones are so abundant that the tree literally glows; to my knowledge no one has ever selected for this trait.

FRUIT: Cones globular or ovoid, up to 1/4″ across, brownish violet, glaucous bloomy, ripening in the first season; seeds 1 to 2, ovoid, small, apex blunt-angular, deeply pitted, shining brown.

CULTURE: Transplant balled-and-burlapped if root pruned or as a container-grown plant; tolerant of adverse conditions, poor gravelly soils; acid and high pH soils; prefers a sunny, airy location, and a deep moist loam on well-drained subsoil; will tolerate shade only in extreme youth; observations indicate this species thrives in limestone based soils; in Kentucky and Tennessee along I-75, I-64, I-24, and I-71, the species is weed-like in the limestone cuts, fills, and outcroppings; Wright and Hinesley, *HortScience* 26:143–145 (1991), almost killed themselves trying to prove that *J. virginiana* could not grow without calcium and magnesium in container media; yes, limestone was beneficial.

DISEASES AND INSECTS: Cedar apple rust and bagworms.

LANDSCAPE VALUE: An excellent specimen, grouping, and screening plant if used with care as to color combinations; useful for windbreaks, shelter belts, hedges, and topiary work; the cultivars are the truly ornamental plants of this species; in recent years significant attention has been afforded this species by Dr. Raulston, NC State, Mike Hayman, Louisville and others who believe that with selection, *J. virginiana* would prove a dominant contributor to our everyday landscape, I suspect the best days are ahead; the wood is used for cedar chests, closet linings, pencils, carving, and small ornamental work.

CULTIVARS:

'Baker's Blue'—Foliage with a defined blue cast.

'Blue Cloud'—Supposedly a hybrid between *J. v.* 'Glauca' and *J. chinensis* 'Pfitzeriana' that forms a large shrub with glaucous gray-green foliage; long feathery young shoots emerge from all over the plant providing a rather aesthetic, but unkempt appearance; 4' by 6'.

'Blue Mountain'—Spreading form with horizontal branches, blue-green foliage, abundant blue fruits, 3' high, have seen a 10' by 10' specimen.

'Brodie' (*J. silicicola* form)—Handsome upright columnar form with predominantly scale-like, rich green (grass green) foliage in summer becoming more sage-green and slightly off-color in winter, excellent tight form, probably 20 to 25' by 4 to 6' at maturity, good screen or hedge, rooted from cuttings and may lodge in heavy wind, ice, etc.; problem with this and *J. virginiana* types is root system development may be inadequate, i.e., 1 or 2 roots; these cuttings when grown on do not have a strong root system and suffer anchorage problems later in life.

'Burkii'—Narrow to broad pyramidal, 10 to 25' high, leaves acicular and scale-like, dull blue band above, narrow green margin, green beneath, steel blue with a slight purplish cast in winter, male, grew up with this cultivar in Cincinnati, OH.

'Canaertii'—Compact pyramidal form, leaves on young branchlets scale-like, on old ones awl-shaped, dark green; foliage tufted at ends of branches; cones small, grape-like, whitish blue bloomy, usually profusely produced, 20' tall in 15 years, very susceptible to rust, known to 35'; opens up with age becoming picturesque.

'Cupressifolia'—Pyramidal, loose, leaves cypress-like, soft yellow-green, female form, actually nomenclature is confused on this cultivar, probably should be called 'Hillspire', performed well in Zone 7b.

'Emerald Sentinel'—Pyramidal columnar form with dark green foliage, female, 15 to 20' by 6 to 8', excellent performer in my Georgia trials, grew 10' high and 6' wide after 4 years, foliage is largely scale-like, somewhat tufted but with a measure of needle-like foliage, holds color in winter better than typical seedlings, my field notes from 2-20-94 state "looks good at Bold Spring Nursery, Monroe, GA, dense foliage, dark green foliage, a winner," abundant blue-green cones; with exposure will become a popular screen, hedge, grouping type plant; not as stiff and dense as the typical seedling; patented by Conard-Pyle, West Grove, PA.

'Glauca'—Narrow, columnar form to 25', leaves scale-like, appressed, some awl-shaped leaves inside the plant; silver-blue foliage is best in spring as it turns blue-green in summer, more than one clone is grown under this name.

'Globosa'—Dense, compact form; branchlets crowded, thin, green mostly adult scale-like foliage; bronze-brown in winter, 50-year-old plant is about 15' tall.

'Greenspire'—Excellent rich green foliage, fastigiate-columnar habit, from Lincoln Nurseries, Michigan.

'Grey Orchard'—Found in Orchard, TX, keeps good gray-green foliage in winter, Hines introduction.

'Grey Owl'—Similar to Pfitzer in habit with small, appressed, soft silvery gray foliage; originated in 1938 in a batch of 'Glauca' seedlings; lower growing and wider spreading than 'Blue Cloud'; handsome, spreading, relatively compact, 3' by 6' form, female, sets abundant cones, possibly hybrid between *J. virginiana* 'Glauca' and 'Pfitzeriana'; excellent in Georgia tests, horizontal, wide-spreading branches, foliage attractive year-round, many visitors ask its identity and remark about the growth habit and foliage.

'Hillii'—Dense, columnar, slow-growing form, 6 to 16' high, leaves awl-shaped with a rather broad, bluish white band above, greenish blue beneath, conspicuously purple during winter, 8 to 12' in about 10 years.

'Hillspire'—Symmetrical conical-pyramidal habit with bright green foliage that is essentially maintained in winter, male, named 'Cupressifolia' in 1964 but that name was taken, renamed 'Hillspire' about 1963, introduced by D. Hill Nursery Co., Dundee, IL, cuttings taken in January, treated with 1% KIBA, rooted in high percentages.

'Idyllwild'—Broad-based pyramidal form, informal rugged upright branching, handsome dark green foliage, 15' by 5 to 7'.

'Kosteri'—Bushy form, 3 to 4' by 25 to 30', leaves loosely appressed, grayish blue, assuming a purplish cast, often confused with Pfitzer, but lower and wider spreading.

'Manhattan Blue'—Compact, pyramidal form, differing from 'Glauca' by the bluish green foliage; male; 10 to 12' by 6 to 8'.

'Nova'—Narrow, upright, symmetrical form, extremely hardy, 10 to 12'.

'O'Connor'— Globe-shaped with steel-blue foliage; developed from a "witches' broom" on *J. virginiana* 'Glauca' in former Donaldson Nursery, Sparta, KY.

'Pendula'—Form with spreading branches and pendulous branchlets; leaves mostly acicular, light green, 36 to 45' tall, female with bloomy blue-white cones; this could be designated f. *pendula* for several weeping clones have been selected and, in specific cases, introduced; Woodlanders has a handsome weeper.

'Platte River'—Tall, upright form with plume-like foliage, soft green in summer, purple in winter.

'Princeton Sentry'—A compact, narrow form with soft-textured dark green foliage that turns attractive purple-green in winter, a Princeton Nursery introduction.

'Pseudocupressus'—Narrow, columnar form with gray-green mostly scale-like foliage, 38' high plants are known; this name appears in propagation literature as an understock, first described about 1932, originated at the Morton Arboretum, Lisle, IL.

'Pyramidalis'—Unfortunately, a collective name for pyramidal-growing forms; Hill Nursery Co. has a form named 'Dundee' which falls into the 'Pyramidalis' group; it has soft foliage which turns a purple-green in winter; 'Pyramidiformis' is described as more compact and upright than 'Canaertii' but with similar foliage.

'Silver Spreader'—Wide-spreading, low-growing, branches rise at 30° angle to ground, silver-gray foliaged form introduced by Monrovia about 1955; somewhat similar to 'Grey Owl' but foliage is more silvery, a male, will probably grow (1 1/2') 2 to 3' by 4 to 6'.

'Stover'—A narrow symmetrical upright form with intense blue-gray foliage.

'Taylor'—Outstanding upright conical-columnar form that Steve Bieberich, Clinton, OK believes is one of the best forms for the Plains States; at least one nurseryman in Tennessee is testing this selection; may have originated or been tested through Nebraska Statewide Arboretum, terrible winter browning in Wichita, KS in January.

'Tripartita'—Dwarf, dense form, 4' by 7.5', branches stout, spreading, irregular, branchlets short; leaves acicular, fine, pale green or slightly glaucous, similar in habit to Pfitzer but does not grow as large and is a bit stiffer; assumes a slight purplish winter color.

PROPAGATION: Refer to *J. chinensis*. January cuttings from 4-year-old trees (NC), 5000 ppm IBA, rooted 87%; 30-year-old trees, cuttings rooted 67% (from lower third of tree). See *HortScience* 27:1272–1274 (1992). Seeds treated with 10000 ppm citric acid soak for 96 hours followed by warm moist stratification for 6 weeks and cold moist stratification for 10 weeks germinated best out of 22 treatments.

ADDITIONAL NOTES: Closely related to *J. scopulorum* but differing in floral characteristics and in its habit of ripening seeds the first year. It can be distinguished from *J. chinensis* by its juvenile leaves being in pairs (rarely 3's) and by the adult leaves which are pointed and from *J. sabina* by the absence of true savin odor or bitter taste. Apparently this species can hybridize with *J. horizontalis*. One of the late J.C. Raulston's favorite natives and his article in *Fine Gardening* 2(3):10–15 (1989) is required reading. J.C. loved *J. virginiana* and expanded on the *Fine Gardening* information in *The Chronicles of the NCSU Arboretum* (1993). He reported that 77 cultivars (taxa) were unearthed in the literature search and presented information on each. A series of papers by Henry et al. examined nitrogen nutrition [*J. Amer. Soc. Hort. Sci.* 117:563–567 (1992)], stock plant fertility and rooting [*J. Amer. Soc. Hort. Soc.* 117:568–570 (1992)], and vegetative propagation by stem cuttings [*HortScience* 27:1272–1274 (1992)]. In brief, citation one reported that nitrogen strongly affected growth and nutrient status of containerized *J. virginiana* seedlings. Height and stem diameter and root dry weight were optimized at 105 to 155 ppm N. Paper two showed no significant relationship between foliar N levels and measures of rooting response. In fact, a 20 ppm N level maximized rooting, higher concentrations decreased the response. Boron and potassium significantly correlated with rooting percentage. The third paper showed that 4-year-old trees rooted best (87%) when collected in January and treated with 5000 ppm IBA. Older (30 years) trees rooted in lower percentages (67%). Genotype strongly impacted rooting of cuttings from young and old trees.

NATIVE HABITAT: East and central North America, east of the Rocky Mountains. Introduced before 1664.

OTHER SPECIES:

Juniperus deppeana Steud. 'McFetters' (*J. pachyphlaea* Torr.), (jö-nip′ĕr-us dep-pē-ā′nå), McFetters Alligator Juniper, was mentioned by Raulston as a genuine surprise in the NCSU Arboretum (now J.C. Raulston Arboretum) because of rich blue foliage color, ease of propagation and 1 1/2' growth per year. He received the plant from Mr. Tom Dilatush. The color is better than any *J. scopulorum* or *Cupressus* taxa in the J.C. Raulston Arboretum. 'McFetters' was found in the mountains of Arizona. If like the parent, it should form a broad pyramidal or round-topped tree. The characteristic brown bark is broken into small, closely appressed "alligator hide" scales. Foliage is primarily scale-like, opposite, 4-ranked, diamond-shaped, appressed, obtuse to acute, gray-green with juvenile leaves in whorls of 2 to 3, acicular, acute. Cones 1/2 to 3/5″ diameter, globose, reddish brown with violet bloom, 2 years to mature; seeds 2 to 4. Had the opportunity to hike around Mt. Lemon, outside of Tucson in fall of 1990 and witnessed the species everywhere at the lower elevations growing in dry, rocky soil. Most plants I witnessed were bushy, 10 to 20′ high and as wide. National champion is 46′ by 49′ in Granite Mountain, Prescott National Forest, AZ. Foliage color range was extremely variable and the bark did indeed appear alligatorish. Bark is cross-hatched and presents itself in small squares which produce exfoliating patches. Certainly beautiful but I have doubts about species from low rainfall, hot, dry climates of the Southwest ever gaining a long term foothold in the East. Arizona, New Mexico, southwest Texas and Mexico. Cultivated 1873. Zone (6)7 to 9.

Juniperus rigida Sieb. & Zucc. — Needle or Temple Juniper
LEAVES: Always needle-like, spreading, linear-subulate, 1/3 to 3/4″(1″) long, tapering from the middle into a spiny, extremely sharp point, triangular in cross-section, in whorls of 3 (ternate), upper surface grooved with a glaucous stomatic band, rest of needle bright green and keeled below.
CONES: Globose, 1/4 to 1/3″ wide, brownish black, bloomy, ripening the second year, 3 to 6 scales; seeds 1 to 3 in each scale.

Juniperus rigida, (jŏ-nip′ĕr-us   rij′i-dà), Needle Juniper, has crossed the author's horticultural path on sufficient occasions to deserve inclusion. In fact, several nurseries are starting to grow it. My most lasting impression came from a 20′ tall specimen at the Arnold Arboretum with a central leader, horizontal secondary branches and weeping tertiary branchlets. The habit is most elegant and lends itself to specimen or accent use in the garden. Is successfully growing in Raleigh, NC. Raulston noted that 'Pendula', which is probably the same as the species, grew about 3′ per year at the NCSU Arboretum (now J.C. Raulston Arboretum). The plant is female with attractive bluish black fruits. December–January cuttings with reddish coloration at the base, 8000 ppm IBA-talc, mist, rooted 90 to 95%. This could become a popular plant in the future. The habit is somewhat open and plants do not make good screens. Raulston described 'Akebono', with sparkling white-tipped shoots, as growing 15 to 20′ high. Native to Japan, Korea, North China and apparently quite variable in the wild. Introduced by Veitch in 1861. Zones 6 to 7.

Juniperus silicicola (Small) Bail., (jŏ-nip′ĕr-us si-lis-i-kō′là), Southern Redcedar, is considered a separate species by some, but in most recognizable characteristics is simply *J. virginiana* with a southern coastal/ Florida distribution. The trees are abundant on the Georgia coast and literally grow on the sand dunes, coastal marsh edges, and sandy soils. Handsome tree where native and often with a more open and wide spreading habit than typical *J. virginiana*. Have observed 30 to 40′ high trees in the Orlando, FL area. National champion is 75′ by 52′ in Alachua County, FL. Recent taxonomic literature treats *J. virginiana* as consisting of two inadequately defined varieties, var. *virginiana* and var. *silicicola*. Selections could be made from var. *silicicola* that would enhance use in everyday nursery commerce. 'Brodie' (see *J. virginiana*) is one such selection. Zones (6)7 to 9.

Kadsura japonica (L.) Dunal.

FAMILY: Schisandraceae
LEAVES: Alternate, simple, evergreen, elliptic to ovate-lanceolate, 1 3/4 to 4 1/4″ long, 1 to 2 1/2″ wide, entire to remotely toothed, dark green, glabrous; petiole—reddish, glabrous, grooved above with slight wings running from base of blade along top (flat side of petiole) to point of attachment to stem, 1/4 to 3/8″ long.
BUDS: Imbricate, conical, 3/16 to 1/4″ long, diverge from stem at 60° angle, reddish brown, glabrous.
STEM: Young reddish, glabrous, maturing to brown, glabrous, decurrent ridges from sides of leaf scar, leaf scar elliptical; pith—solid, white.

Kadsura japonica, (kad′sēr-à jà-pon′i-kà), is a twining, evergreen vine with handsome dark green leaves. Leaves remind of *Hoya carnosa*, the common houseplant. The species is not as rampant as *Wisteria*,

Campsis, and *Lonicera*, growing 12 to 15′. The 1/2″ wide, cream-ivory (yellowish white), fragrant flowers occur from the leaf axils and are followed by 1 1/4″ long, fleshy, scarlet berries. As I have observed the vine in Zones 7 and 8, it is best sited in shade and moist, deep soil. Exposed plantings are at the mercy of winter sun, wind, and cold and have suffered (defoliated and/or died). One report noted defoliation at 0°F, but stem and bud survived. This is a vine for the collector and connoisseur and will never become a commercial, user-friendly item. 'Alba' produces white fruits. 'Chirimen' has cream-white marbling and streaking throughout leaf, somewhat unstable, not as showy as 'Fukurin'. 'Fukurin' ('Variegata', also incorrectly 'Fukurim') has leaves edged to various degrees with cream and yellow, striking variegation compared to 'Chirimen'. 'Tricolor' produces yellow and cream specks throughout the leaf. All are easy to propagate by cuttings. Japan, Korea. Introduced to western cultivation in 1846. Zone (7)8.

Kalmia latifolia L. — Mountain-laurel Kalmia or Mountain-laurel
(kal′mi-à lat-i-fō′li-à)

FAMILY: Ericaceae
LEAVES: Alternate, occasional leaves opposite or whorled, simple, evergreen, appearing irregularly whorled, elliptic to elliptic-lanceolate, 2 to 5″ long, 3/4 to 1 1/2″ wide, leathery, entire, acute or short acuminate, cuneate, dark green above, yellowish green beneath, glabrous; petiole—1/4 to 1″ long.
BUDS: Terminal or pseudo-terminal bearing the elongated inflorescences, visible in early March in Athens, lateral buds hidden behind petiole and virtually imbedded in stem, smallish.

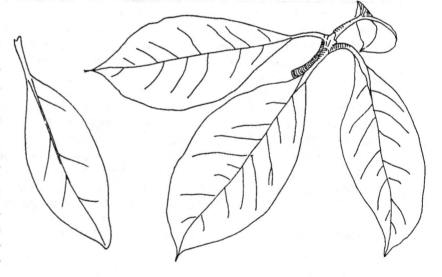

STEM: Moderate, bronze initially, sticky when young, green, red to brown at maturity, pubescent, older stems become brown, epidermis and bark cracking to expose lighter colors; pith—solid, light green.

SIZE: Variable, 7 to 15′ in height with a similar spread, can grow to 30 to 36′; I always apologize to my students about the above sizes (too large) and then proceed to tell them about walking through thickets of Mountain-laurel in the southern Appalachians that barely allowed light to penetrate; for sure, under cultivation, the plant is more compact, dense, haystack to rounded in outline; also many compact cultivars; Bonnie and I have traveled the Blue Ridge Parkway in North Carolina and observed *Kalmia latifolia* in every possible roadside habitat with no two exactly alike; national champion is 25′ by 28′ at the North Carolina Arboretum, Ashville, NC.
HARDINESS: Zone 4 to 9.
HABIT: Large, robust shrub which, if not crowded, is symmetrical and dense in youth; in old age becomes, open, straggly, loose, with picturesque gnarly trunks and limbs.

RATE: Slow, 4 to 8′ over a 10 year period.

TEXTURE: Medium in all seasons.

BARK: Gray-brown, striated to lightly ridged-and-furrowed; gnarly and crooked branches used for rustic mountain furniture.

LEAF COLOR: New growth a light yellow-green to bronze changing to glossy dark green at maturity; winter foliage color is usually a good dark green but in sun will become a yellowish green; have noticed heavy leaf spot on wild populations, much more prevalent than I ever imagined.

FLOWERS: Individually the most beautiful flower I know, especially as the buds are opening; variable from white to pink-rose to deep rose with purple markings within, 3/4 to 1″ across, broad-campanulate, May to June, borne in 4 to 6″ diameter, terminal corymbs, each flower has 10 stamens which on first expanding are held in little cavities in the corolla; the "knee" (bend) formed by the filament is sensitive, and when the pollen is ripe, if touched, the anther is released; obviously insect pollination is facilitated in this manner; traveling from 700′ to 4100′ elevation on May 16, 1996, *Kalmia latifolia* completed flowering in Athens (700′), was in full flower for 20 to 30 miles along Highway 441 (1500 to 2000′) and then disappeared into tight bud at 2500 to 4100′; was on the Blue Ridge Parkway July 12, 1997 when the plant was in full flower.

FRUIT: Brown, 5-valved, dehiscent capsule, 1/4″ across, persistent through winter.

CULTURE: Easy to transplant because of fibrous root system; requires acid, cool, moist, well-drained soil; full sun or deep shade but flowers best in sunnier locations; remove flowers immediately after fading; mulch to keep soil moist and to reduce cultivation; my observations indicate that many of the new cultivars introduced from Connecticut will not compete favorably in Zone 7 and 8 for soils are often heavy and inadequately drained; like *Rhododendron catawbiense* and cultivars, plants would best be served by planting on top of the ground and covering with pine bark; interesting production study showed best shoot and root growth occurred with 3 cultivars given 60% of the nitrogen in the nitrate form [see *J. Environ. Hort.* 8:10–13 (1990)].

A rather finicky garden and nursery plant and I suggest growers review Knuttel, "*Kalmia latifolia*—Tissue culture vs. cuttings," *Proc. Intl. Plant Prop. Soc.* 39:470–471 (1989), and Bir and Bilderback, "Growing better Mountain-laurel in containers," *Proc. Intl. Plant Prop. Soc.* 39:442–447 (1989). Also, Bir and Bilderback in an NC State Extension release reported that optimum growth and survival of *Kalmia latifolia* resulted from incorporation of pine bark, peat, or a combination and rototilled 8 inches deep compared to no amendment.

DISEASES AND INSECTS: Leaf spot, blight, flower blight, whitefly, scale, lace bug, azalea stem borer and rhododendron borer.

LANDSCAPE VALUE: Excellent broadleaf evergreen for shady borders; exquisite in mass; magnificent in flower; one of our best and most loved native shrubs; excellent plant for naturalizing; again requires attention to cultural details; I tried, unsuccessfully, to grow the plant in my Illinois garden where it simply languished and died.

CULTIVARS: Information presented below was distilled from many references; the best checklist is Jaynes, *Bull. Amer. Assoc. Bot. Gard. Arbor.* 17(4): 99-106 (1983); also Dr. Jaynes, *Kalmia-The Laurel Book II*, Timber Press (1988) lists 48 cultivars and several formae. Dr. Jaynes 3rd edition, *Kalmia, Mountain Laurel and Related Species*, Timber Press (1997) lists over 30 new cultivars; I have not included them in this edition.

'Alba'— Pure white flowers, Eichelser introduction.

'Alpine Pink'—Rich pink in bud opening to a medium pink with a white throat, good growth habit and foliage.

'Bay State'—Unusual coral-colored flower.

'Bettina'— Reduced corolla, deep purplish pink when grown in full sun, faint in shade.

'Bravo'— Flower buds and open flowers are dark pink, leaves are large and glossy dark green, new shoots have red stems, 3rd or 4th generation seedling from the late Ed Mezitt, Weston Nursery.

'Bridesmaid'— Rich deep pink in bud and heavily banded pink with a white center when open, low-spreading habit.

'Bullseye'—Deep purplish cinnamon-colored buds open to a creamy blossom with a broad purple band around the inside with a white throat and edge, new growth reddish bronze.

'Candy'—Buds and flowers deep pink, broad thick wavy leaves, petioles and young stems purplish red, a Weston Nursery introduction.

'Carol'—Bright red buds open to almost pure white; broad, thick, lustrous dark green leaves, wavy and twisted.

'Carousel'—Intricate pattern (starburst) of bright purplish cinnamon pigmentation inside the corolla, good grower, relatively easy to root.

'Clementine Churchill'—Tyrian rose outside, inside rose-red, good foliage and habit.

'Den Window'—Large flowers open light pink becoming deeper pink as they age, foliage is bluish green, purplish red new stems, robust grower.

'Elf'—Compact dwarf form with light pink buds, flowers white, habit 1/3 to 1/2 normal size, but flowers only slightly smaller than species.

'Emerald Sheen'—Medium pink buds open nearly white and mature to medium pink; outstanding feature is the thick-textured, glossy, rounded, convex, dark green foliage borne on a compact plant.

'Freckles'—Buds light pink, opening to a creamy white flower with purple spots just above the 10 anther pouches.

'Fresca'—Flowers white banded with burgundy, selection of f. *fuscata*.

'Fuscata' (f. *fuscata* Rehd.)—Flowers with a broad, brownish, purple or cinnamon band inside the corolla, called Banded Laurel.

'Galaxy'—Full-banded flower, white buds open like azalea, f. *fuscata* × 'Shooting Star'.

'Good Show'—Rich red buds open to pink flowers, broad dark green leaves, named by Wright's Nursery, Canby, OR.

'Goodrich'—Buds deep red, flowers with continuous cinnamon purple band when open, one of the darkest cultivars, difficult to propagate by cuttings, foliage susceptible to leaf spot.

'Heart of Fire'—Buds red, flowers deep pink, selected from 'Ostbo Red' seedling population for better foliage and habit; introduced by Melrose Nursery, Olympia, WA.

'Hearts Desire'—Buds dark red, flowers burgundy (cinnamon-red) with narrow white lip; better habit than 'Kaleidoscope'.

'Kaleidoscope'—Similar to 'Hearts Desire' but with larger white lip and brighter color to the bloom, giving more of a bicolor effect.

'Keepsake'—Raspberry red buds, open to purplish burgundy flowers with white edges, new growth reddish bronze, maturing to glossy deep bluish green, dense rounded habit, 4 1/2' by 4 1/2', discovered by Richard Jaynes, Broken Arrow Nursery, Hamden, CT.

'Little Linda'—Miniature form with red buds and deep pink flowers, 3' by 3' in ten years, Dr. Jaynes introduction, leaves are glossy dark green, somewhat rounded.

'Minuet'—Miniature form similar to 'Elf' but with broad maroon band inside corolla, buds light pink, leaves glossy dark green and narrow.

'Myrtifolia' (f. *myrtifolia* Jaeg.)—Compact-growing type less than 6' tall, one-third to one-half normal size, common name is Miniature Laurel, also listed as f. *minor* and f. *nana*.

'Nancy'—Buds pinkish red, opening to clear bright pink.

'Nathan Hale'—Red in bud open pink, symmetrical compact habit, thick shiny dark green foliage, petioles and stems of new growth purplish red.

'Nipmuck'—Intense red buds open creamy white to light pink, back of opened corolla is dark pink, rooted 91% over 9 year test period, light yellow-green foliage, upper foliage turns unattractive purplish color in fall.

'Obtusata' (f. *obtusata* Rehd.)—Dwarf, dense form with thick, leathery almost rounded leaves.

'Olympic Fire'—Large deep red buds open to pink flowers, seedling of 'Ostbo Red', good habit and foliage color, easier to root than 'Ostbo Red'.

'Olympic Wedding'—Flower buds pink, opening to pink flowers with a broken cinnamon-colored band, flat dark green broad leaves.

'Ostbo Red'—Buds bright red, flowers soft deep pink, introduced by Melrose Nursery, Olympia, WA; first red-budded selection named.

'Pequot'—Dark red buds open to rich pink, excellent glossy dark green foliage.

'Pink Charm'—Deep red-pink buds open to uniform rich pink, more deeply pigmented than 'Pink Surprise', a narrow and deeply red-pigmented ring occurs on the inside and near the base of the corolla, October cuttings rooted 82% in a poly tent, peat:perlite, bottom heat with no auxin; annual bloomer.

'Pink Frost'—Large pink buds open to silvery pink flowers, then deeper pink, excellent wide lustrous foliage; cuttings root better than the species.

'Pink Star'—Flowers deep pink, star-shaped, a seedling of 'Ostbo Red'.

'Pink Surprise'—Deep pink buds open to pink flowers, corolla has a crisp inner ring and 10 pigment flecks where the anthers are held, cuttings surprisingly easy to root, hence, the common name.

'Pinwheel'—Flowers maroon and edged in white, cinnamon-maroon band almost fills center of corolla, white on edges and center.

'Polypetala' (f. *polypetala* Nichols.)—Corolla cut to form five strap-like feathery petals, selection often lacks vigor.

'Pristine'—Compact habit, pure white flowers, found in Aiken County, SC by Mrs. Ernestine Law, introduced by Woodlanders, much more adaptable to the South than the Dr. Jaynes hybrids.

'Quinnipiac'—Intense red buds open to soft light pink, rich dark green foliage, somewhat similar to 'Nipmuck' but a more compact plant with darker green foliage, prone to purple leaf spot especially if container-grown, sister seedling of 'Nipmuck', rooted 77% over 9 year period.

'Raspberry Glow'—Deep burgundy buds open to deep raspberry pink flowers, foliage dark green.

'Richard Jaynes'—Red to raspberry red buds open to pink with silvery white sheen on the inside, heavy annual flowering, good glossy foliage, named after the famous *Kalmia* hybridizer.

'Royal Dwarf'—Compact, 2' high, blue-green foliage, rose-pink flowers in late spring and again in fall, Richard Jaynes introduction.

'Sarah'—Vivid red buds open to bright pink-red, flowers for a long time, foliage and habit excellent.

'Sharon Rose'—Deep red buds, fading to pink, much like 'Ostbo Red', good habit, thick broad flat leaves, cuttings are relatively easy to root.

'Shooting Star'—White flowers with five distinct lobes that reflex, selected from the wild in North Carolina, flowers one week later than species and less hardy.

'Silver Dollar'—Pale pink buds, large (1 1/2″ diameter), white flowers twice the size of the species, leaves large, leathery dark green; selected in 1952 by Weston Nurseries.

'Snowdrift'—Compact mound-shaped plant with pure white flowers, broad dark green leaves.

'Splendens'—Flowers deeper pink than the type, described in 1896 in England and is the oldest named cultivar.

'Star Cluster'—Similar to 'Fresca', flowers with white edge and center maroon slightly interrupted band, may tolerate heavy soils better than most mountain-laurels.

'Stillwood'—Flower buds and flowers clear white when growing in full sun, essentially lacking pink pigment, selected from wild population in New Hampshire.

'Sunset'—Bright red buds and near red open, leaves narrow and twisted with thick blades, purplish red new petioles and stems, low-spreading growth habit.

'Tiddlywinks'—A selection from forma *myrtifolia* (f. *myrtifolia* × 'Pink Charm'), much like 'Elf' in growth rate and form but with a broader, multi-branching habit and deeper colored flowers, medium to rich pink in bud and a soft or light pink when open; 10-year-old plant was 20″ by 30″.

'Tightwad'—Buds are pink if grown in full sun and remain in good condition for a month beyond the normal flowering period but never open.

'Tinkerbell'—Is a miniature laurel that is quite similar to 'Tiddlywinks', flower color is generally a deeper pink, the stems of new growth are green compared to red of 'Tiddlywinks'; 10-year-old plant was 30″ by 40″.

'Twenty'—Dark pink in bud opening to medium pink, glossy dark green leaves, low compact habit twice as wide as high.

'Wedding Band'—Pink buds open to reveal a 1/4″ diameter, solid maroon band, broad flat dark green leaves, good habit.

Weston Pink and Red-budded Selections—Long before the "Kalmia Kraze" this nursery envisioned a future for the species and over the years selected outstanding color forms. Seeds from the superior types are used to produce even better types and the evolution continues. A visit in late May–June will make a convert out of any non-believer.

'Willowcrest'—Willow-leaved foliage, light pink flowers.

'Yankee Doodle'—Red buds open to irregular maroon-banded blossom with large white throat, yellow-green foliage, a f. *fuscata* selection.

PROPAGATION: Seed should be directly sown on peat with lights to stimulate growth after germination; the seedlings are extremely small and hard to work with so it is necessary to get some size to them; detailed study, *J. Environ. Hort.* 7:161–162 (1989), showed that increasing the length of light exposure (continuous illumination) resulted in 90% germination at 77°F in 18 days; cuttings are extremely difficult to root but there are differences in rootability of various clones. Days could be spent discussing *Kalmia latifolia* cutting propagation. Some investigators have said a hormone treatment is a must while others say it does not make any difference. The mountain-laurel is inherently difficult to root from cuttings. I refer the reader to Fordham, "Propagation of *Kalmia latifolia* by cuttings," *Proc. Intl. Plant Prop. Soc.* 27:479-483 (1977). Taking vegetative propagation a step further, the interested reader should see Lloyd and McCown, "Commercially-feasible micropropagation of mountain-laurel, *Kalmia latifolia*, by use of shoot-tip culture," *Proc. Intl. Plant Prop. Soc.* 30:421-427 (1980). Kalmia is now being produced commercially through tissue culture which has literally opened the floodgate for the many new cultivars. See Dirr and Heuser, *Reference Manual of Woody Plant Propagation*, for a discussion.

ADDITIONAL NOTES: Alfred Rehder called it "one of the most beautiful native American shrubs." Interestingly, *Kalmia latifolia* is found south to Florida. I think most gardeners consider this a cool climate plant. In the South it follows the water courses and is found scattered and in large thickets on the slopes above streams and rivers. By March, in the Athens, GA area, the buds are already starting to elongate. There have been some interesting crosses between *K. hirsuta* and *K. latifolia*.
NATIVE HABITAT: Quebec and New Brunswick to Florida, west to Ohio and Tennessee. Introduced 1734.

RELATED SPECIES:

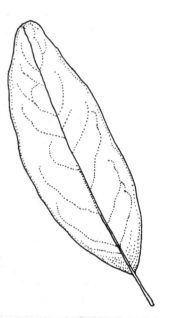

Kalmia angustifolia L. — Lambkill Kalmia, Sheep Laurel
LEAVES: Opposite or whorled, simple, evergreen, oblong to elliptic, 1 to 2 1/2″ long, 1/4 to 3/4″ wide, obtuse or subacute, entire, blue-green above, red-brown beneath when young, later paler; petiole—1/6 to 1/3″ long.
STEM: Rounded, glabrous.

Kalmia angustifolia, (kal′mi-à an-gus-ti-fō ′li-à), Lambkill Kalmia, is a low-growing (1 to 3′), blue-green foliaged, evergreen shrub of rounded, spreading habit with 2 forms; one a compact, tufted grower; the other thin and open. Flowers are usually rose-pink to purplish crimson, 1/2″ across, in up to 2″ diameter corymbs, June to July. Foliage may be poisonous if eaten in large amounts. 'Candida' with white flowers; 'Rosea' with pink-red flowers; and 'Rubra' with dark purple flowers are listed. Terrific variation in the wild and all the above are more or less discernable in a population. 'Kennebago' has shiny leaves and dark pink flowers, more vigorous than 'Hammonasset', from Kennebago Lake, Maine. 'Hammonasset' is a compact, stoloniferous form with rich blue-rose flowers; discovered in 1961 in a population of 300 plants within a few hundred feet of the Hammonasset River, Connecticut. 'Poke Logan' has a pleasing luster to leaf, light pink flowers, from Maine. The species is found on a variety of sites including rocky barrens, old pastures, wet sterile soils, often in semi-shade. Considered a weed species in forestry plantations [see *Canadian J. Botany* 71:161–166 (1993)]. Native from Newfoundland and Hudson Bay to Michigan and Georgia. Introduced 1736. Zone 1 to 6(7).

Kalmia cuneata Michx., (kal′mi-à kū-nē-ā′tà), White Wicky, with white, rarely pink, flowers and rounded corolla lobes occurs in North and South Carolina. Zone 7. Also, **Kalmia hirsuta** Walter, (kal′mi-à her-sūt′à), Sandhill Laurel, a rather straggly, 10 to 24″ high, evergreen shrub with 1/3 to 4/5″ diameter, pink flowers, grows from Virginia to Florida and has been hybridized with *K. latifolia* to produce more heat tolerant plants with larger flowers and small foliage and growth habit. Zone (6)7 to 9. Last is **Kalmia polifolia** Wangenh., (kal′mi-à pol-i-fō′li-à), Bog Kalmia, Swamp Laurel, Bog Laurel, a small, 4 to 30″ high, loose, evergreen shrub with 1/4 to 1 1/2″ long, 1/12 to 1/2″ wide, blue-green, opposite or whorled leaves. Flowers are vivid pink to purple-pink, 1/3 to 4/5″ across, in 1 to 1 1/2″ terminal corymbs in May–June. Grows on hummocks in bogs. Northern United States, Canada. Zone 2 to 5.

Kalmia cuneata

Kalmia hirsuta

Kalmia polifolia

Kalopanax pictus (Thunb.) Nak. [now *K. septemlobus* (Thunb. ex A. Murray) Koidz.] — Castor-aralia
(kal-ō-pan′aks pik′tus)

FAMILY: Araliaceae

LEAVES: Alternate, simple, palmately 5- to 7-lobed, 10 to 14″ wide on young trees, 7 to 10″ wide on mature trees, lobes shallow, triangular-ovate, long-pointed, uniformly toothed, reaching 1/3 or less toward the center, lustrous dark green above, glabrous, paler beneath except with hairs in the axils of the veins; petiole—often longer than the blade.

STEM: Coarse, stout, almost club-like, yellowish brown, glabrous, armed with numerous, prominent, broad-based prickles.

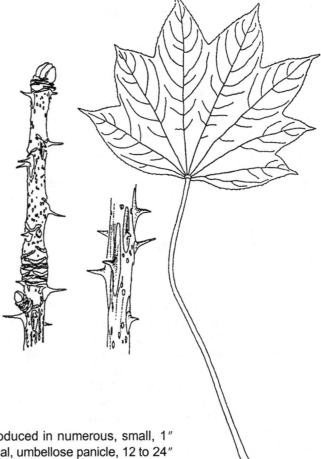

SIZE: 40 to 60′ high under cultivation with comparable spread; 80 to 90′ in the wild.

HARDINESS: Zone 4 to 7, possibly 8 with cultural coddling.

HABIT: In youth upright-oval, coarse, gaunt and not particularly attractive; rather impressive at maturity, with massive oval-rounded outline.

TEXTURE: Coarse in leaf and in winter.

BARK: Armed with stout, broad-based, yellowish prickles on young stems; mature trunks blackish, deeply ridged-and-furrowed.

LEAF COLOR: Glossy dark green above, lighter green beneath, somewhat similar in shape to Sweetgum, *Liquidambar styraciflua*; changing to yellow or red in the fall, usually not good; have only observed yellow fall color.

FLOWERS: Perfect, white, July to early August, produced in numerous, small, 1″ diameter umbels, forming a large, flattish, terminal, umbellose panicle, 12 to 24″ across, each individual flower is small, however they are borne in great quantity at the end of the shoots of the season, bees appear to love them.

FRUIT: Small, 1/6″ wide, black, globose drupe, late September–October, relished and soon devoured by birds.

CULTURE: Transplant balled-and-burlapped as a young specimen into deep, rich, moist soil; full sun exposure; prune during spring; supposedly tolerant of alkaline conditions; long lived and trouble-free.

DISEASES AND INSECTS: None serious.

LANDSCAPE VALUE: Excellent large shade tree yielding a tropical effect because of the large leaves; nowhere common in commerce; in youth it is extremely coarse but given time makes an impressive tree; has proven hardy at the University of Wisconsin Arboretum and University of Maine; survived -22°F during the rugged 1976–77 winter; will never surpass Sugar Maple in popularity; in the Arnold Arboretum small seedlings can be found in abundance.

CULTIVARS: There is a variety termed *maximowiczii* (van Houtte) Hand-Mazz. with deeply lobed leaves reaching 2/3's the way to the center; experienced this taxon for the first time in June 1995 at Dundonnell Garden, Scotland; leaves are deeply lobed and give the impression of a prehistoric 7-toed dinosaur; to find this plant in the highlands of Scotland in a garden that was truly off the trodden path was a unique experience. Other varieties are listed but their taxonomic status is questionable.

PROPAGATION: Dormancy of the seed is related to embryo condition (probably immature) and an impermeable seed coat; warm plus cold (41°F) stratification for 60 to 90 days may give reasonably prompt germination; soaking the seeds in sulfuric acid for 30 minutes will substitute for the warm period; recent study recommended 3 months at 59 to 68°F, followed by greater than 2 months at 32 to 41°F.

NATIVE HABITAT: Japan, Sakhalin, the Russian Far East, Korea and China. Introduced 1865.

Kerria japonica (L.) DC. — Japanese Kerria, Japanese Rose
(ker'i-à jà-pon'i-kà)

FAMILY: Rosaceae

LEAVES: Alternate, simple, ovate-lanceolate, 1 1/2 to 4″ long, about 1/2 as wide, acuminate, cuneate, double serrate, bright green and glabrous above, paler and slightly pubescent below on veins; petiole—1/4 to 1/2″ long.

BUDS: Imbricate, greenish brown, vari-colored, usually 5 exposed scales, glabrous.

STEM: Slender, green throughout winter, zig-zag, glabrous, glossy, supple.

SIZE: 3 to 6′ in height; spreading, with time, to 6 to 9′.

HARDINESS: Zone 4b to 9; flowered only below snow-line after −20°F; killed at Orono, ME; flowers at the Morton Arboretum, Lisle, IL.

HABIT: Stems distinctly upright-arching forming a low, broad-rounded, dense, twiggy mass becoming loose with age; stems are slender and refined in overall textural quality; have noticed the tendency to sucker and thus produce large colonies; the looser the soil the faster the colonization.

RATE: Somewhat slow in establishment, fast with time.

TEXTURE: Fine in foliage and winter.

STEM COLOR: Distinct yellowish green to bright green in winter, very noticeable and actually not objectionable, adds color to the winter landscape especially when used in mass.

LEAF COLOR: Leafs out early with young shoots emerging in March (Athens), bright green in summer usually exhibiting little change in fall and holding late, often late November (Athens), some yellow; the fall of 1997 brought soft lemon yellow coloration in late November that was beautiful; leaves of flowering shoots smaller than those on barren shoots of the season.

FLOWERS: Bright yellow, 5-petaled, 1 1/4 to 1 3/4″ across, April to early May (very effective) for 2 to 3 weeks, borne solitary at the terminal of short, leafy stems originating from previous year's growth; starts in late March to early April in Athens; sporadically flowers through the season; prune after flowering; in full sun, flowers tend to bleach out and look sickly, ideally site plant in partial shade or at least out of the afternoon sun.

FRUIT: Achene, seldom seen, not showy.

CULTURE: Transplant balled-and-burlapped or from a container; requires loamy, well-drained soil of moderate fertility; does well in full shade; actually best removed from full sun (flowers fade rapidly) in exposed locations; requires considerable pruning for dead branches are constantly evident; avoid winter damage by planting in a well-drained situation; if fertility levels are too high, the plant becomes weed-like and grows excessively with a resultant reduction in flowers; in spite of the cultural precautions, I find it an easy plant to grow; Creech, *American Nurseryman* 160(12):70–71 (1984), reported *K. japonica* growing on sunny, moist banks in Japan.

DISEASES AND INSECTS: Leaf and twig blight, twig blight, canker, leaf spot, and root rot; the above are possibilities but I have not noticed serious problems.

LANDSCAPE VALUE: Interesting free-flowering shrub; could be used more extensively; borders, masses, facer plant to hide leggy specimens; possibly on highways or other large public areas where extensive masses of foliage and flowers are welcome and needed; tough plant, seems to withstand considerable abuse; does extremely well in South and flowers in late March in Athens, GA, and sporadically into early summer.

CULTIVARS:

'Albescens'—Off-white flowered (creamy yellow) form with petals somewhat misshapen compared to those of the species, initially was excited about the possibilities but it does not measure up to the species, probably will grow 5′ high, has been listed as *Kerria albiflora*, fall color is creamy yellow, not quite as bright as the species.

'Aureovariegata'—Leaves edged with yellow, 2″ long.

'Aureovittata'—Branches striped green and yellow, will revert, tried to track a plant in the Arnold Arboretum but by the time I found it, green stems predominated, have seen 'Kin Kan' offered by one northeastern nursery, description read like that of 'Aureovittata' although stems are described as yellow and a pale yellow stripe bisects each leaf.

'Golden Guinea'—Flowers larger than the species and freely borne over a long period, rich green foliage, graceful delicate shrub, flowers on occasion reach 1 3/4 to 2″ diameter, will grow 4 to 5′ high.

'Kin Kan'—Yellow, actually soft yellow winter stems with green stripe, almost like a delicate racing stripe, good yellow-stemmed dogwood substitute in Zone 7, typical flowers and foliage.

'Picta'—Leaves edged white, handsome, not obnoxious like many variegated plants; good choice for massing; needs some shade in hot climates; single yellow flowers; a superb foliage shrub that with adequate moisture does not cook in the heat of the summer even in Zone 7b; the central leaf color is a soft gray-green, flowers are profuse, will occasionally produce green shoots which must be removed; easy to propagate and grows sufficiently fast to have impact; my exuberance is perhaps misdirected for I have grown and abandoned this form twice and now cultivate it again, branch reversions are common and the flowers are misshapen and bleach out worse than other taxa, less vigorous than the species and probably no larger than 3 to 4′ at maturity; the above reads as if two people authored the text; even in the plant world there are Jekyll and Hyde personalities.

'Pleniflora' ('Flora Pleno')—Flowers double, almost golden yellow, nearly ball-shaped, 1 to 2″ in diameter; flowers are more effective than those of species and longer lasting; it is quite different in habit from the species being more erect, gaunt and rather lanky; I have seen plants 6 to 8′ high and plants to 12′ have been reported; this form is quite common in southern gardens but is not as dainty as the species, opens in late March and still effective in late April, suckers freely; sent to Kew in 1805 by a British collector, Kerr; originally named *Corchorus* until De Candolle in 1817 named the genus *Kerria* after its collector.

'Shannon'—Vigorous form with larger flowers than typical species type, reaches the large side of the species range, 5 to 6′ high; leafs out and flowers earlier than the species, at least in the Dirr garden; an all around better doer than the run-of-the-mill species types.

'Splendens'—Large, buttercup yellow flowers.

'Superba'—Large, single flowers, to 6′ high, listed by Heronswood, how different from 'Golden Guinea' and 'Shannon', I do not know.

'Variegata'—Listed by several nurseries and I suspect nothing more or less than 'Picta'. Bonnie discovered a variegated sport on the species in our garden. It looked just like 'Picta'.

PROPAGATION: Easily rooted using untreated cuttings collected in summer and fall; I have never had a problem rooting the species or the cultivars, division in late winter also produces sufficient plants to share with friends.

NATIVE HABITAT: Central and western China. Also occurs in the mountains of all the main Japanese islands. Introduced 1834.

Koelreuteria paniculata Laxm. — Panicled

Goldenraintree, Varnish Tree, Pride of India
(kol-rö-tē′ri-à pan-ik-ū -lā′tà)

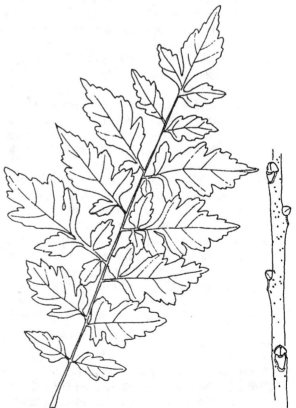

FAMILY: Sapindaceae

LEAVES: Alternate, pinnate or bipinnately compound, 6 to 18″ long, 7 to 15 leaflets, each leaflet ovate to ovate-oblong, 1 to 4″ long, coarsely and irregularly crenate-serrate, at base often incisely lobed, rich green and glabrous above, pubescent on the veins beneath or nearly glabrous.

BUDS: Terminal—absent; laterals—half-ellipsoid, sessile, with 2 exposed scales, brownish, 1/4″ long.

STEM: Stout, olive-buff to light brown, glabrous; leaf scars—raised, rather large, shield-shaped, glabrescent; lenticels—raised, prominent, orange-brown; pith—solid, white.

SIZE: 30 to 40′ in height with an equal or greater spread.

HARDINESS: Zone 5, possibly lower part of 4, to 8, has not been reliably hardy in Madison, WI; young plants much more susceptible to winter damage; suspect -20 to -25°F will result in some stem injury; killed at Orono, ME (-30°F).

HABIT: Beautiful dense tree of regular rounded outline, sparingly branched, the branches spreading and ascending.

RATE: Medium to fast, 10 to 12′ over a 5 to 7 year period.

TEXTURE: Medium in foliage, medium-coarse in winter.

BARK: Light gray-brown, ridged-and-furrowed on older trunks.

LEAF COLOR: Purplish red when unfolding, bright green at maturity changing to yellow and golden almost orange-yellow in fall but not coloring consistently; have had good yellow fall color on a tree in my garden, new leaves may be injured by late spring frosts.

FLOWERS: Perfect, yellow, each about 1/2″ wide, borne in a 12 to 15″ long and wide loose panicle in July, very showy; flowers early June in Athens and early July in Urbana, IL.

FRUIT: Dehiscent, papery, 3-valved capsule, 1 1/2 to 2″ long (changing from green to yellow and finally brown); seeds are black, hard, about the size of small peas, August to October for complete color transformation, earlier in Zone 7 and 8.

CULTURE: Transplants well but best moved balled-and-burlapped or container-grown as a small tree; adaptable to a wide range of soils; withstands drought, heat, wind and alkaline soils; tolerates air pollutants; prefers full sun; prune during winter; averaged 1′5″ per year over a 9 year period in Wichita, KS tests.

DISEASES AND INSECTS: None particularly serious, although coral-spot fungus, leaf spot, canker, wilt, root rot, and nematodes have been reported.

LANDSCAPE VALUE: Excellent and unrivaled for yellow flowers in summer; one of the very few yellow-flowering trees; excellent as a small lawn tree, for shading a patio; suggested as a street tree although supposedly somewhat weak-wooded; very lovely to look upon and lay under on a hot July day; choice specimen tree where space is limited; shows tremendous adaptability to extremes of soil; can look untidy in late summer when brown fruits mature.

CULTIVARS:

'Fastigiata'—I have seen this clone at several gardens and found it to be extremely upright; 25′ high tree with 4 to 6′ spread; raised at Kew Gardens, England, from seeds received in 1888 from Shanghai; it flowers sparsely; I received seeds of this clone from Dr. S.M. Still when he was at Kansas State; unfortunately they were never planted so their ability to produce fastigiate types will never be known at least by this author; averaged 1′4″ per year over a 10 year period in KS test but was killed to ground in 78–79 winter; not as cold hardy as the species.

'September'—Selection by J.C. McDaniel from a group of three trees on the Bloomington campus of the University of Indiana, two of which were in full flower on August 25, 1958; flowers first two weeks in September at the Arnold Arboretum; seedlings raised from the mother plant also exhibit the late-flowering habit; is not as hardy as the species; probably does not harden off early enough in fall to avoid early freezes; possibly a hybrid between *K. paniculata* and *K. bipinnata*; have included this in the Georgia evaluation plots, flowered the third year from seed, plant was 6′ high, flowers developed in late August–early September, full flower August 28, 1997; worthwhile plant for late season color where *K. bipinnata* is not cold hardy; a 1997 Pennsylvania Horticulture Society Styer Award Winner; see Dirr, *Nursery Manager* 7(9):36 (1991) for in-depth discussion of this cultivar; the Arnold trees are 40′ by 34′ at 30 years of age; the younger tree is 28′ by 35′; both flower at the end of August and into early September. The Arnold tree is apparently different from 'September' and a complete discussion on its parentage is offered by Santamour and Spongberg, *Arnoldia* 56:2, 32–37 (1996). The proposed name for the tree is 'Rose Lantern'.

'Stadher's Hill'—Listed as a hybrid with deep reddish fruits; see Louisiana Nursery, Opelousas, LA for availability.

PROPAGATION: Seed has an impermeable seed coat and internal dormancy; scarification for 60 minutes in concentrated sulfuric acid followed by moist stratification at 41°F for 90 days is recommended; very easy to grow from seed, I have raised many seedlings; root cuttings collected in December represent a vegetative means of propagation.

ADDITIONAL NOTES: Although several authors mention the tree is weak-wooded I have never observed anything in the field that supports this. I have witnessed horrendous ice storms in Illinois and Georgia but absolutely no damage to *K. paniculata*. There are numerous plants in the Athens area from 8′ to 35 to 40′. Damage to Siberian Elm, Water Oak, and Loblollybay from ice has been tremendous but I have not noticed a single broken limb on a Goldenraintree.

NATIVE HABITAT: China, Japan, Korea. Introduced 1763.

RELATED SPECIES:

Koelreuteria bipinnata Franch. — Bougainvillea Goldenraintree, Chinese Flametree, Southern Goldenraintree

LEAVES: Alternate, bipinnately compound, 20″ long or longer and as wide, 8 to 11 pinnae, leaflets 2 to 3″ long, oval-oblong, acute to acuminate, rounded to cuneate, entire to finely serrate, lustrous dark green.

BUDS: Similar to *K. paniculata*, 1/8 to 3/16″ long, dark brown, glabrous, sitting
   slightly above 3-lobed to shield-shaped leaf scar.
STEM: First year—coarse, 3 times the diameter of *K. paniculata*, dark brown,
   glabrous, heavily lenticelled, lenticels orange-brown rounded; 2nd year—
   more gray-brown, otherwise similar; pith—solid, cream-colored, about one-
   half the diameter of the stem.

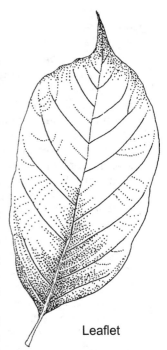

Koelreuteria bipinnata, (kol-rö-tē′ri-à bī-pin-ā′tà), Bougainvillea Goldenraintree,
   was not given its just due in the third edition but has emerged in the past 15
   years as a worthwhile, handsome, late summer flowering tree. Habit is
   distinctly upright-spreading with large, coarse, thick stems that must be
   pruned in youth to induce a full, dense crown. Height will approximate 20 to
   30′(40′) and 2/3′s this in width. The flowers occur in 12 to 24″ high, 8 to 18″
   wide, upright panicles in late August to mid-September in Athens. The effect
   is outstanding and since competition is nil the plant shines like a yellow star.
   The 3-valved, 1 to 2″ long, pink to rose capsules develop shortly after
   flowering and hold color for 3 to 5 weeks. If the fruits are collected in the pink
   stage and dried the color will persist. A fine bouquet in our home is still
   colorful 13 years after collecting. Like *K. paniculata*, any well-drained soil is
   suitable. Will withstand acid or alkaline conditions but requires full sun.
   Nurserymen indicate root systems may be sparse and trees should be root
   pruned or moved as a young container-grown plant. Two-year-old seedlings
   will flower. Interestingly, of all the plants in my garden, this produces the

Leaflet

most stray seedlings. Am concerned with the extraordinary number of surviving seedlings I see in the
woods and waste areas. Could this become another Chinaberry, Mulberry, et al.? As gardeners and
stewards, we need to be cognizant of the potential devastation from an introduced plant. Even if some cold
injury occurs on the tips of the branches, flowering will still occur since buds are set on the new growth of
the season. Possibly 0 to -5°F(-10°F) will induce some tip injury. Seeds sown in fall germinate the
following spring. Have heard of a variegated leaf form. China. Introduced 1888. Zone 6 to 8. *Koelreuteria
integrifolia* Merrill is occasionally listed but is nothing more than an old name for *K. bipinnata*.

Koelreuteria elegans (Seem.) A.C. Small (*K. formosana* Hayata), (kol-rö-tē′ri-à el′e-ganz), Flamegold,
   Chinese Raintree, appears in Florida landscapes and forms a small, 20 to 30′ high, rounded tree with the
   yellow flowers and rose fruits of *K. bipinnata*. Habit is more dense-rounded than *K. bipinnata*. The drive
   to Disney World has groupings of this species. Flowers in late summer—fall and the fruits are evident into
   December. At Jungle Gardens, Avery Island, LA, fruits were rich rose-pink in mid-October, 1996. Leaves
   are lustrous dark green, bipinnate to 18″ long with 9 to 16 pinnae, leaflets 4″ by 1 to 1 1/2″ wide, narrow
   ovate, entire to irregular serrate leaflets. Taiwan, Fiji. Introduced about 1916 into North America. It is
   distinctly less cold hardy and is reserved for Zone 9 to 10(11).

Kolkwitzia amabilis Gräbn. — Beautybush
(kolk-wit′zi-à à-mab′à-lis)

FAMILY: Caprifoliaceae
LEAVES: Opposite, simple, broad-ovate, 1 to 3″ long, 3/4 to 2″ wide, acuminate,
   rounded at base, remotely and shallowly toothed or nearly entire, ciliate, dull
   dark green above and sparingly hairy, pilose on the netted veins beneath;
   petiole—pilose, about 1/8″ long.
BUDS: Solitary, sessile, ovoid, with 3 to 4 pairs of scales.
STEM: Slender, round, villous at first, often purplish, later glabrous and developing
   an exfoliating, brownish bark.

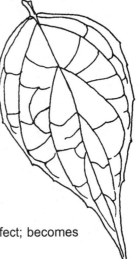

SIZE: 6 to 10′ in height and usually slightly smaller in spread, can grow to 15′.
HARDINESS: Zone 4 to 8.
HABIT: Upright arching, vase-shaped shrub, somewhat fountain-like in overall effect; becomes
   leggy with age and most of the foliage is in upper one-half of the plant.
RATE: Fast.
TEXTURE: Medium in leaf; coarse in winter.
BARK: Light grayish brown and often exfoliating on older stems.

LEAF COLOR: Dull dark green in summer; slightly yellowish to reddish in fall.

FLOWERS: Perfect, pink, yellow in throat, flaring bell-shaped, two-together, 1/2″ long, about as wide at the mouth, May–early June, borne in 2 to 3″ diameter corymbs; the principal attribute of this plant is the flower; full flower mid to late April on the Georgia campus.

FRUIT: Bristly, ovoid, 1/4″ long, dehiscent capsule with one seed, often long persistent, good identification feature.

CULTURE: Easily transplanted balled-and-burlapped; prefers well-drained soil; pH adaptable; full sun for best flowering; older stems should be pruned out every year; to renew plant simply cut it to the ground after flowering; flowers on old wood.

DISEASES AND INSECTS: None serious.

LANDSCAPE VALUE: Probably belongs where it can develop alone, but hardly falls into the category of a specimen plant; rather pretty in flower but too coarse and cumbersome for many landscapes; rather common in England but seldom encountered in modern day United States landscapes; at Mt. Congreve, Ireland, I witnessed the deepest pink form (possibly 'Rosea') in late June 1996, indeed this one time experience will persist for a lifetime.

CULTIVARS:

'Pink Cloud'—Clear strong pink flowers of good size and very floriferous, raised at Wisley in 1946.

'Rosea'—More reddish pink flower.

'Ruys Pink'—Listed by Dr. Cappiello in the Maine collection at Orono.

Variegated Form—Recently discovered a pinkish yellow-variegated leaf form, the margins of the leaf pinkish yellow when young maturing to cream-yellow, stems a deep purple-red.

PROPAGATION: Seeds can be sown as soon as ripe or stored in air tight containers in a cool place for up to a year; plants grown from seeds will often show inferior, washed out, pink flower color; it is best to use softwood cuttings, as they root readily, and select wood from floriferous, good pink-colored plants.

ADDITIONAL NOTES: I have a difficult time acclimating myself to this shrub. In flower it is singularly effective; however, the rest of the year it gives one a headache. Also not the easiest plant to identify unless the fruits are present. E.H. Wilson considered it one of the finest plants he introduced to cultivation.

NATIVE HABITAT: Central China. 1901.

RELATED SPECIES:

Dipelta floribunda Maxim. — Rosy Dipelta

FAMILY: Caprifoliaceae

LEAVES: Opposite, simple, ovate to oval-lanceolate, 2 to 4″(5″) long, 5/8 to 1 1/2″ wide, acuminate, rounded or cuneate, entire, or on vigorous shoots slightly denticulate, glabrous, dark green; petiole—1/4″ long.

Dipelta floribunda, (dī-pel′tà flôr-i-bun′dà), Rosy Dipelta, is a large, oval-rounded, 10 to 15′ high shrub. A 20′ high specimen was growing at the Hillier Nursery in England. The fragrant flowers are 1 to 1 1/4″ long, 1″ wide with 5 rounded, funnel-shaped, spreading lobes, pale pink and yellow in the throat. It is a rather pretty shrub and essentially unknown outside of arboreta. There is a fine specimen at the Arnold Arboretum. For several editions I had the bracts that subtend the ovary confused with the fruits. The four bracts, each 3/4″ long, 1/2″ wide, are greenish white, shield-like and unequal. The fruit is a dry capsule. Also, with time, the ash-brown to brown bark exfoliates in long strips but the entire matrix still assumes the presence of a pile of sticks. In truth the shrub is oafy and offers essentially single season interest. This is not the easiest plant to identify and in leaf alone can resemble honeysuckle and weigela. *Dipelta ventricosa* Hemsl. has larger leaves (to 6″) and 1 1/4″ long by 3/4″ wide, broad tubular flowers, pink to lilac on the exterior, pale rose to white, with yellow in the throat. In June 1995 I saw for the first time at Crathes Castle Garden, Scotland, *D. yunnanensis* Franch., a 6 to 12′ high shrub, with 2 to 3″ long, to 2″ wide, lustrous green leaves and cream to white, blushed shell pink, 1″ long flowers. *Dipelta floribunda* is quite tolerant of acid or alkaline soil and requires full sun. Some debate about hardiness but anything below −20°F will result in some injury. The Morton Arboretum, Lisle, IL (Zone 5) has maintained the species as a dieback shrub. May–June cuttings will root but I have had no success in my attempts. Central and western China. Introduced 1902. Zone 5 to 7.

Laburnum × *watereri* (Kirchn.) Dipp. (Hybrid between *L. alpinum* and *L. anagyroides*) — Waterer Laburnum, Goldenchain Tree

(là-bĕr′num wa-ter′er-ī)

FAMILY: Fabaceae

LEAVES: Alternate, trifoliate, each leaflet elliptic to elliptic-oblong or elliptic-obovate, 1 1/4 to 3″ long, usually obtuse and mucronulate, broad cuneate, glabrous at maturity, bright green.

BUDS: Ovoid, small, 1/16 to 1/8″ long, with 2 to 4, exposed silvery haired scales.

STEM: Slender to stout, olive, without prominent lenticels, green stem color is maintained into old wood, glabrous.

SIZE: 12 to 15′ in height with a spread of 9 to 12′.

HARDINESS: Zone 5 to 7; not a plant for deep South conditions.

HABIT: Distinctly upright oval to round-headed small tree or shrub which usually loses the lower branches and is in need of a facer plant after a period of years.

RATE: Medium, 12 to 18″ per year over a 5 to 8 year period.

TEXTURE: Medium-fine in leaf; somewhat coarse in winter condition.

BARK: Olive green in color on young and old branches; eventually developing fissured areas, brown.

LEAF COLOR: Bright green in summer with a bluish tinge; fall color is nondescript.

FLOWERS: Perfect, yellow, fragrant, 3/4″ long, borne on 6 to 10″(20″) long, pendulous racemes in May (early May, Spartanburg, SC), extremely beautiful in flower.

FRUIT: Pod, slightly pubescent, October, not ornamentally effective.

CULTURE: Transplant balled-and-burlapped or container-grown in spring as a small tree into moist, well-drained soil; the plant is adaptable to many situations but prefers light shade in the hot part of the day; will not withstand standing water; also cold injury can be a problem; withstands high pH conditions; prune after flowering; should be looked upon as a short-lived tree in the Midwest and probably East; not at all heat tolerant, possibly excessively high night temperatures, and therefore not suitable for the South, although a tree in Spartanburg, SC persists; several newly planted trees in the Milliken Arboretum have died and the remaining plant persists by a thread.

DISEASES AND INSECTS: Leaf spot, twig blight, laburnum vein mosaic, aphids and grape mealy-bug can affect this plant; the twig blight is often a serious problem.

LANDSCAPE VALUE: Good in the shrub border, near buildings, corners of houses; plant in a protected spot; very effective when grouped in three's and five's; makes a tremendous show in flower; truly a beautiful plant in flower and the German popular name, Goldregen (Golden Rain), is most appropriate; widely planted in Europe but not so common in the United States; at Bodnant Gardens, Wales, there is the famous "Laburnum Arch" with the plants trained across a structure about 50 to 75 yards long; the flowers cascade and the visitors can walk through this feature; my visit coincided with full flower and the effect was just overwhelming.

CULTIVARS:

'Alford's Weeping'—Pendulous in habit, discovered at Hillier's Nursery, England.

'Aureum' (*L. anagyroides*)—Leaves golden yellow; Bean considered it one of the prettiest of yellow-leaved trees; in commerce at least since 1874; in the 1990 edition I mentioned that the plant had not crossed my path, well all things in proper time for in late June, 1995 at Crathes Castle Garden, Scotland, 'Aureum' was front and center, glowing yellow; always rewarding to catch up with the elusive cultivar that one only reads about.

'Pendulum' (*L. anagyroides* and *L. alpinum*)—Branches slender and weeping, considered a very graceful form; during my graduate student days at the University of Massachusetts I found a small weeping form on campus; it displayed distinctly weeping branches and was rather pretty in all of its parts; I assume the weeping forms flower but have not seen them; described as producing lemon yellow, pendulous racemes.

'Vossii'—Often used as the specific epithet for *L.* × *watereri*, i.e., *L.* × *vossii*, when actually 'Vossii' is a superior clone selected for more dense habit and racemes which are up to 2′ long; raised in Holland late in the 19th century; the young stems are appressed hairy, not glabrous as in the typical form of the hybrid; a virus is known that causes a rosetting of foliage; in Wichita KS tests rarely bloomed and over a 7 year period averaged 4″ per year, finally dying; have read details of a virus that is inherent in 'Vossii', if true might be a worthy project for clean-up through micropropagation.

PROPAGATION: Seed should be scarified in sulfuric acid for 15 to 30 minutes; leaf bud cuttings taken in early summer rooted 80%; cuttings from root sprouts rooted 100%; apparently seeds have no internal dormancy and will germinate without difficulty when properly scarified.

ADDITIONAL NOTES: Seeds of *Laburnum* contain an alkaloid called cytisine, which can be fatal to children and adults. This compound is contained in all parts of the plant. Supposedly, one small seed can prove toxic to a small child. Extreme care should be exercised when using this plant in a public area.

RELATED SPECIES:

Laburnum alpinum (Mill.) Bercht. & Presl. — Scotch Laburnum
LEAVES: Alternate, trifoliate, leaflets oval or slightly obovate, 1 1/2 to 3″ long, acute, rounded, ciliate, deep green above, light green, glabrous or slightly pilose below; petiole —1 to 2″ long.
STEM: Green, glabrous.

Laburnum alpinum, (là-bĕr′num al-pī′num), Scotch Laburnum, is a 20′ tree with a short sturdy trunk and flat to round-topped crown. The deep green leaflets are not as hairy as in *L. anagyroides*. The golden yellow flowers occur in slender, pendulous, 10 to 15″ long racemes in May; pod is 2 to 3″ long, flat, glabrous, upper suture winged and forming a knife-like edge. Seeds are brown. This is considered the superior garden species. Throughout Scotland, but most impressively in Dawyck Arboretum, resided significant numbers of 20 to 25′ high specimens. Although viewed in March and again in mid-June (no flowers) the plants were larger than any reference provides credence. This and *L. anagyroides* are taxonomically quite similar—the first with glabrous stems, the latter pubescent. 'Macrostachys' has longer racemes and 'Pyramidale' is erect. Southern Alps, also occurring wild in the northern Apennines, northwest Yugoslavia (formerly) and southern Czechoslovakia (formerly). Found in moister situations than *L. anagyroides*. Cultivated 1596. Zone 4 to 7.

Laburnum anagyroides Medik. — Common Laburnum
LEAVES: Alternate, trifoliate, leaflets elliptic to elliptic-oblong or elliptic-obovate, 1 to 3″ long, obtuse and mucronate, broad cuneate, rich green above, grayish green and silky pubescent below; petiole—2 to 3″ long.
STEM: Gray-green, weakly pubescent.

Laburnum anagyroides, (là-bĕr′num an-a-jē-roy′dēz), Common Laburnum, tends to be a low branched, bushy, wide-spreading, 20 to 30′ high tree. The lemon to golden yellow flowers occur in cylindrical, pendulous, 6 to 10″ long downy racemes. Pods 2 to 3″ long, upper suture thickened and not winged as in *L. alpinum*. Seeds are black. 'Quercifolium' is only mentioned because the leaflets are slightly lobed, the effect not striking from more than 18″ away, but the plant was growing in the wonderful garden of the late Mr. Alan Rogers, Dundonnell, Scotland. Also, 'Columnaris' is described as slow-growing, forming a dense column and producing golden yellow flowers. Central and southern Europe. Cultivated 1650. Zone 5 to 7.

+ **Laburnocytisus adamii** (Poit.) C. Schneid., (là-bĕr-nō-sīt′i-sus a-dam′ē-ī), is a curious anomaly of great interest with considerable garden value. It is a graft hybrid between *Chamaecytisus purpureus* (Scop.) Link. (formerly *Cytisus purpureus* Scop.) and *L. anagyroides* that appeared in the nursery of Jean Louis Adam near Paris in 1825. On the grafted plant a branch appeared with purplish yellow flowers intermediate between the parents. Further, when outplanted it was found to revert back and produce yellow, pinkish purple and the combination colored flowers. The vegetative portions of the plant show pure as well as intermediate characteristics of the two parents. I have seen this plant at Kew Gardens in flower and it is genuinely fascinating. They have a high quality educational exhibit showing the parents and the resultant + *L. adamii*. It makes a small 20 to 25′ high tree. The Arnold Arboretum has a plant. Zone 5 to 7.

Lagerstroemia indica L. — Common Crapemyrtle
(là-gĕr-strō′mē-à in′di-kà)

FAMILY: Lythraceae
LEAVES: Opposite or the upper alternate or in whorls of three, very much privet-like, simple, 1 to 2 3/4″ long, 3/4 to 1 1/2″ wide, entire, subsessile, elliptic or obovate to oblong, acute or obtuse, broad-cuneate or rounded at base, dark green and often lustrous, glabrous or pilose along the midrib beneath, very small conical and deciduous stipules; petiole—very short.

BUDS: Small, solitary, sessile, oblong, somewhat elbowed above base, closely appressed, with 2 acute ciliate scales.

STEM: Rather slender, angled often almost squarish with rather prominent wings, glabrous, greenish, red, or combinations, maturing to brown; older stems becoming smooth, sinewy, and with age exfoliating.

SIZE: Variable but based on numerous observations a range of 15 to 25′ in height seems reasonable; saw a 40 to 45′ plant in Savannah; the range of sizes is astronomical from 18″ up.

HARDINESS: Zone (6)7 to 9; –5 to –10°F is about the break point between a woody plant and herbaceous perennial.

HABIT: Small to medium size shrub or small tree of variable habit; often seen in multi-stemmed form with a cloud of foliage reserved for the upper portion of the plant while the basal portion is leafless and only the handsome bark is evident.

RATE: Fast.

TEXTURE: Medium, possibly medium-fine in all seasons.

BARK COLOR: Smooth, gray, exfoliating and exposing vari-colored underbark which ranges from many handsome shades of brown to gray; the beautiful bark is a real landscape asset; about 8 years past Bonnie and I planted a curvilinear row (is this an oxymoron?) of 'Natchez', now 20′ high, with the cinnamon brown bark fully developed; if crapemyrtles never produced flowers and leaves, it would not be a bad thing.

LEAF COLOR: New emerging leaves are yellowish green, bronze to reddish purple yielding to lustrous medium to dark green at maturity; fall coloration ranges from yellow, orange and red with all colors interspersed on the same tree; white-flowered types often have yellow fall color (not always); pink and red types show yellow, orange, and red fall color.

FLOWERS: Perfect, 6-petaled, each flower 1 to 1 1/2″ wide, color varying from white, pink, purple to deep red on different plants; produced in 6 to 8″ long and 3 to 5″ wide panicles which terminate the current year's growth; (June)July through September; in Athens flowers appear in mid to late June on some of the early-flowering cultivars like 'Hopi', 'Sioux', 'Pecos', and 'Yuma'; petals crinkled; this rather generic description does not do justice to flower size and quality, generally the more vigorous the shoot growth the larger the flower, I remove spent flower panicles after the first flush in July and another is initiated by August–September, prune back to stems no larger than one's small finger, the brutal massacre of crapemyrtles to fist size and larger trunks looks terrible and results in long, supple, weak shoots which arch and cascade like a pendulous tree, the architectural framework and bark of crapemyrtles are exquisite and deserve to be preserved by proper pruning.

FRUIT: A broad-ellipsoidal 6-valved dehiscent capsule, brown, about 1/2″ wide and persisting through winter, seeds 3/8″ long and winged.

CULTURE: Transplant as a balled-and-burlapped or container-grown plant into moist, well-drained soil; prefers full sun; prune by removal of the deadwood or by judicious pruning as described under flowers; a former graduate student, Dr. Cindy Haynes, investigated timing of pruning and cold hardiness effects; pruning in late summer (August) through early winter (October–December) significantly reduced cold hardiness compared to unpruned controls; ideally try to complete pruning by early August, see *HortScience* 26:1381–1383 (1991) for details; the species prefers hot, sunny climates and, obviously, is best suited for southern and southwestern gardens; trunk shoots have been controlled via NAA applied as a directed trunk spray or lanolin paste, see *J. Environ. Hort.* 8:179–181 (1990).

DISEASES AND INSECTS: Powdery mildew, black spot, sooty mold, tip blight, leaf spot (*Cercospora* spp. are the causal agents), *Botryosphaeria* canker, root rot, aphid, Japanese beetle, Asian ambrosia beetle and Florida wax scale are problems; have observed more fungal leaf spot in recent years, starts with older leaves progressing to most recently formed, can cause serious defoliation; a study evaluating 37 cultivars of crapemyrtle to the crapemyrtle aphid, *J. Entomological Science* 28:1–7 (1993), showed that peak aphid numbers occurred in last week of July (northern Florida); cultivars with *L. fauriei* parentage, and cultivars susceptible or resistant to powdery mildew had significantly higher numbers of aphids per leaf than cultivars considered tolerant; mean number varied from a low of 6.2±1.7 on 'Centennial Spirit' to 84.8±19.1 on 'Biloxi'.

LANDSCAPE VALUE: Handsome and very beautiful specimen shrub or tree; often used in groups and underplanted with a ground cover; the dark green ground cover acts as a foil for the handsome bark; some of the smaller types are used as hedges, screens, masses; many of the new introductions from the U.S. National Arboretum are superior to the run-of-the-mill cultivars; crape myrtles are often given credit only for flower but many have superb fall color and excellent bark.

CULTIVARS: Flower colors range from white, pink, orchid to dark red. The U.S. National Arboretum, Washington, DC has an extensive breeding program with *Lagerstroemia*. The number of cultivars is staggering and I recommend *The Lagerstroemia Handbook/Checklist* by Egolf and Andrick, 1978. Descriptions of U.S. National Arboretum and other important cultivars are presented. A new checklist has been produced by the U.S. National Arboretum. The number of cultivars has exploded especially with the advent of the dwarf groups.

Dr. Don Egolf was one of the greatest woody plant breeders that history will ever recognize. He was a scientist, breeder, horticulturist, plantsman, and gardener—traits that allowed him to introduce only the best. His plants will withstand the test of time. Like the masterpieces of great artists, writers, and musicians, Dr. Egolf's plants stand out from those of mere mortals. As a young assistant professor at Illinois, I met and shook his hand, was able to attend several lectures, and voraciously read his cultivar releases in *Baileya* and *HortScience*. All young scientists and aspiring plantsmen should read his detailed descriptions of the new introductions. The plants leapt from the page into the reader's garden. Don Shadow told me that Dr. Egolf was endowed with the great eye for quality plants. With *Hibiscus*, *Lagerstroemia*, *Malus*, *Pyracantha*, and *Viburnum*—Dr. Egolf produced magic. Our gardens are richer due to one man's vision and persistence. His woody plant legacy is without parallel.

RAPID REFERENCE TO 20 *LAGERSTROEMIA INDICA* × *L. FAURIEI* CULTIVARS INTRODUCED BY THE U.S. NATIONAL ARBORETUM

SEMI-DWARF (5 to 12')

Cultivar	Flower color	Trunk color	Fall color
'Acoma'	Pure white	Light gray	Red-purple
'Caddo'	Bright pink	Light cinnamon brown	Orange-red
'Hopi'	Clear light pink	Gray-brown	Orange-red
'Pecos'	Clear medium pink	Dark brown	Maroon
'Tonto'	Fuchsia	Cream to taupe	Maroon
'Zuni'	Medium lavender	Light brown-gray	Dark red

INTERMEDIATE (13 to 20')

Cultivar	Flower color	Trunk color	Fall color
'Apalachee'	Light lavender	Cinnamon to chestnut brown	Orange-russet
'Comanche'	Dark coral pink	Light sandalwood	Purple-red
'Lipan'	Medium lavender	Near white to beige	Orange-russet
'Osage'	Clear light pink	Chestnut brown	Red
'Sioux'	Dark pink	Medium gray-brown	Red-purple
'Yuma'	Bicolored lavender	Light gray	Yellow-orange

TREE-TYPE (23 to 33')

Cultivar	Flower color	Trunk color	Fall color
'Biloxi'	Pale pink	Dark brown	Orange-red
'Choctaw'	Clear bright pink	Light to darker cinnamon brown	Bronze-maroon
'Miami'	Dark coral pink	Dark chestnut brown	Red-orange
'Muskogee'	Light lavender	Light gray-brown	Red
'Natchez'	White	Cinnamon brown	Orange to red
'Tuscarora'	Dark coral pink	Light brown	Red-orange
'Tuskegee'	Dark pink to red	Light gray-tan	Orange-red
'Wichita'	Light magenta	Russet brown to mahogany	Russet to mahogany

'Acoma'—Low-spreading, semi-pendulous, semi-dwarf, multi-stemmed growth habit, 10′ high and 11′ wide in 15 years. Panicles are pure white with pronounced golden anthers, 6 to 7 1/2″ long and 3 1/2 to 5″ wide, blooming from late June to September. Young leaves are dark bronze-tinged, becoming dark green, turning to dark purple-red in fall. Mildew resistant. Young branches are red-purple, becoming gray-brown, at maturity light gray that is exposed by exfoliating bark of older branches and trunk. Mildew has been reported. Appears more cold hardy than typical. See *HortScience* 21:250–251 (1987).

'Apalachee'—Upright, multi-stemmed large shrub or small tree, 12 1/2′ high by 8 1/2′ wide in 12 years. Panicles are light lavender, 5 1/2 by 9 1/2″ long and 5 1/2 to 7″ wide, blooming from mid-July to September. Young leaves are glossy, glabrous and bronze-tinged, later dark green, becoming dull orange to russet in autumn. Mildew resistant. Excellent foliage retention. New shoots are glabrous, dull red, becoming gray-brown as the branches mature, later sinuous, mottled exfoliating branches and trunk reveal cinnamon to chestnut brown bark coloration. See *HortScience* 22:674–677 (1987).

'Basham's Party Pink'—Larger form to 20′ and more, rapid-growing and somewhat resistant to mildew and aphids, soft lavender-pink.

'Biloxi'—Upright, multi-stemmed, arched-crown, small tree, 20′ high and 12′ wide in 12 years. Panicles are pale pink, 5 1/2 to 7 1/2″ long, 4 1/2 to 7 1/2″ wide, blooming from July to late September. Young leaves are glabrous, light bronze becoming lighter tinged, glossy, slightly leathery, becoming dark green, turning dark yellow-orange to orange-red to dark red in autumn. Mildew resistant. Young branches are glabrous, light brown becoming gray-brown, later sinuous, mottled, exfoliating bark of older branches and trunk reveals dark brown bark coloration. See *HortScience* 22:336–338 (1987).

'Byers Standard Red'—Upright tall-growing form reaching 25′ in height, flowers soft red in mid-July, fall color orange, good mildew resistance.

'Byers Wonderful White'—Upright form reaching 20′ and greater in height, flowers clear white blooming in July, fall color yellow, although listed as possessing good mildew resistance, I have observed considerable mildew on occasion.

'Caddo'—Low-spreading, semi-dwarf, multi-stemmed shrub, 8.25′ by 8.25′ in 18 years; bright pink flowers occur in 4 to 10″ long, 3 to 9″ wide panicles with 50 to 200 flowers per inflorescence in mid-July to September; young leaves are faintly tinged red, semi-glossy dark green, and bright orange-red in fall; young branches are gray-brown, finally light cinnamon brown; see *HortScience* 25:585–587 (1990) for additional information.

'Carolina Beauty'—Upright form reaching 20′ and greater in height, flowers dark red blooming in mid-July and later; fall color orange, poor mildew resistance, one of the worst for mildew susceptibility but among the best for intensity of red flower coloration, also adorned with bright yellow stamens, bark is gray-brown and quite handsome on mature specimens.

'Catawba'—Globose medium habit, glossy dark green foliage, abundant compact inflorescences of dark purple florets, mildew resistant, flowers late July to September, 10 1/2′ by 11′ in 11 years, has been outstanding in my garden and on campus with reddish fall color.

'Centennial'—Dwarf compact globular shrub reaching approximately 3 to 5′ in height, flowers bright lavender, blooming mid-June and later; fall color orange, sister to 'Victor', with similar habit and good mildew resistance.

'Centennial Spirit'—Upright shrub or small tree with generally 3 to 5 major stems with few secondary branches or suckers from base. Panicles are dark wine red, with very little discoloration before falling, 8 to 12″ long and 4 to 8″ wide, blooming from late June through early October. Leaves are smaller and thicker than the species average, dark green turning red-orange in autumn. Mildew resistant. Strong stems keep inflorescences from drooping after summer rains. Has withstood –4°F without damage but was killed to soil line at –22°F, regrowing and flowering by July.

'Cherokee'—Compact, medium growth habit, 8′ by 7 1/2′ in 11 years, glossy heavy dark green foliage, numerous pyramidal inflorescences of brilliant red florets, mildew resistant, late July with good recurrent flowering through September, this cultivar has been confused since the introduction and plants I have grown were light red and infested with mildew. However, I have seen slides of the original introduction and the flowers were indeed brilliant red. Doubtfully in modern cultivation. Introduced 1970.

'Chickasaw'—True genetic dwarf introduced by U.S. National Arboretum in 1997, result of Dr. Egolf's work, actually initial crosses were made in 1967 with final crosses in 1989 producing 'Chickasaw', compact mounded habit, 2′ by 3 to 3 1/2′, pink-lavender flowers, glossy dark green leaves turn bronze-red in fall, slow growth may limit extensive commercial use, in our trials, the various Egolf dwarf forms have proven spectacular.

'Choctaw'—Large multi-stemmed shrub to small tree, vase-shaped habit, 18.8′ by 20.1′ in 19 years, bright pink flowers in 7 to 17.3″ long, 5 to 14″ wide panicles, with 100 to 500 florets per inflorescence, sub-coriaceous glossy dark green leaves turn bronze to maroon in autumn, young branches gray-tan, cinnamon brown on older trunks; a beautiful crapemyrtle that was lost in the shadows of Dr. Egolf's earlier introductions, worthy of cultivation; mildew resistant; see *HortScience* 25:997–998 (1990).

'Christiana'—Vivid red flowers with yellow stamens, small to medium-sized shrub.

'Comanche'—Upright, multi-stemmed, broad-spreading crown, large shrub or small tree, 11 1/2′ high and 12 1/2′ wide in 15 years. Panicles are coral-pink, 5 1/2 to 9 1/2″ long and 5 1/2 to 7″ wide, blooming from late July to mid-September. Young leaves are glossy, glabrous, light bronze, maturing to dark green and turning dark orange-red to dark purple-red in autumn. Young branches are brown-maroon becoming medium gray-brown; later sinuous, mottled, sandalwood as bark exfoliates on older branches and trunk. See *HortScience* 22:674–677 (1987).

'Conestoga'—Open growth habit, flowers open, medium lavender, change to pale lavender, early flowers starting in mid-July and opening over a period of a month, slightly susceptible to mildew, 10′ by 14′ in 11 years, not impressive in my garden because of washed out lavender-pink color, flowers occur at the ends of long shoots and cause the stems to arch. Introduced 1967.

'Dallas Red'—Of interest because of excellent hardiness and Raulston noted it was the best of the *L. indica* cultivars at NCSU Arboretum (now J.C. Raulston Arboretum); he mentioned that the winters of 1984 and 1985 killed or severely injured 20′ tall mature plants without touching 'Dallas Red'; grows fast and produces large deep "red" panicles; mildew resistance is not known by this author.

Dynamite™ ('Whit II')—Flower buds crimson, cherry red flowers, 6 to 14″ long panicles, new leaves emerge crimson, mature to dark green, moderately leathery, highly resistant to powdery mildew, vigorous upright grower to 20′, PPAF, Whitcomb introduction.

'Glendora White'—Snow white flowers, 25′ by 20′, offered by Monrovia.

'Hardy Lavender'—Upright form reaching 20′ in height, flowers medium lavender, blooming late July; fall color red, good mildew resistance.

'Hope'—Open-growing dwarf form reaching 4′ in height, flowers white, blooming mid-June; fall color yellow, good mildew resistance.

'Hopi'—Spreading, semi-dwarf, multi-stemmed, 7 1/2′ high and 10′ wide in 12 years. Panicles are medium pink, 4 to 5 1/2″ long and 2 1/2 to 7″ wide, blooming from late June to late September. Young leaves are glabrous, slightly pink overcast, becoming dark green, turning bright orange-red to dark red in autumn. Mildew resistant. Young branches are dark red-purple becoming gray-brown prior to light gray-brown at maturity. Original information relative to extreme cold hardiness of this cultivar was incorrect. This is one of the first to flower in the Georgia trials, often by mid-June and repeat flowers into fall. See *HortScience* 21:256–257 (1986).

'Kiowa'—A large shrub or small tree, the original plant at the U.S. National Arboretum is about 30′ high and 25′ wide, white flowers, lustrous dark green foliage, beautiful cinnamon brown bark and good cold hardiness are the principal attributes, received as unnamed *L. fauriei* cuttings from Botanical Garden of Osaka, Japan, a Dr. Egolf selection, named and introduced in 1994 by Dr. Randy Johnson, U.S. National Arboretum.

'Lipan'—Upright, multi-stemmed, large shrub or small tree, 13′ high and 13′ wide in 12 years. Panicles are medium lavender, 5 1/2 to 7″ long and 6 to 8 1/2″ wide, blooming from mid-July to mid-September. Young leaves are glabrous, slightly leathery, slightly bronze-tinged, becoming dark green, turning light orange to dull red in autumn. Mildew resistant. Young branches are red-purple, becoming medium gray-green, later sinuous, mottled near white to beige as the bark exfoliates from the older branches and trunk. See *HortScience* 22:674–677 (1987).

Majestic Orchid™ ('Monia')—20′ by 15′, vivid orchid flowers, Monrovia introduction.

'Miami'—Upright, multi-stemmed small tree, 16′ high and 8 1/2′ wide in 12 years. Panicles are dark pink, 5 1/2 to 9 1/2″ long and 4 to 9 1/2″ wide, blooming from early July to September. Young leaves are burgundy, becoming dark green, turning orange to dull russet in autumn. Mildew resistant. Young maroon shoots become gray-brown, later sinuous, mottled, dark chestnut brown as older branches exfoliate. See *HortScience* 22:336–338 (1987).

'Muskogee'—Large shrub or small tree, 21′ high and 15′ wide after 14 years, medium brown bark, glossy green leaves turn good red in autumn, prolific light lavender-pink flowers, each inflorescence 4 to 10″ long, 4 to 5″ wide, July to September, mildew resistant, produces landscape plant in 3 years, hybrid between *L. indica* × *L. fauriei*, had a 20′ plant in our garden and was quite impressed by vigor and flower production, unfortunately, aphids are much more fond of this than 'Natchez' and sooty mold can really disfigure the plant; bark is a shiny light gray to tan and rather attractive but again does not measure up to 'Natchez'. See *HortScience* 16:576–577 (1981).

'Natchez'—Large shrub or small tree, 21′ high and 21′ wide after 14 years, dark cinnamon-brown, sinuous, mottled, exfoliating trunk bark that remains spectacular throughout the year, glossy dark green leaves that turn orange and red in fall, pure white flowers, 6 to 12″ long, 4 to 7 1/2″ wide panicle, late June–July into September, cinnamon brown bark develops after about 5 years, *L. indica*

× *L. fauriei*, widely planted in the Southeast and is probably the dominant white-flowering large tree type cultivar, cinnamon brown bark is outstanding, good aphid resistance compared to 'Muskogee', fall color some years is nil since an early freeze will kill the leaves, others a pretty bronze-orange but never red at least in the South. See *HortScience* 16:576–577 (1981).

'Near East'—Open spreading form with semi-pendulous tendencies, reaching 18′ in height, flowers light pink, blooming mid- July and later; fall color yellow-orange, moderately mildew resistant, excellent on Georgia campus.

'Ocmulgee'—Small 3′ by 3′, dark green foliage form with glistening red-maroon buds that open to "red" flowers and literally smother the foliage in July–August, have grown this for a number of years along with 'Victor' and can tell very little difference; at times I think they are one and the same. Aphids and sooty mold can prove troublesome.

'Osage'—Semi-pendulous, arched crown, open-branched, multiple-stemmed, large shrub or small tree, 12′ high and 10′ wide in 12 years. Panicles are clear light pink, 6 to 8″ long and 4 to 6″ wide. Young leaves are glossy, glabrous, bronze-tinged, becoming dark green, slightly leathery, turning red to dark red in autumn. Mildew resistant. Young shoots are red-purple, becoming gray-brown, later sinuous, mottled, exfoliating bark of older branches and trunk reveal chestnut brown bark coloration. See *HortScience* 22:674–677 (1987).

'Ozark Spring'—Compact dwarf, 3 to 5′, lavender flowers, good mildew resistance, yellow fall color, flowers become white with maturity.

'Pecos'—Globose, semi-dwarf, multi-stemmed shrub, 8′ high and 6′ wide in 12 years. Panicles are medium pink, 6 to 8″ long and 5 to 7 1/2″ wide, blooming from early July to September. Young leaves are glossy, glabrous, heavily tinged bronze, becoming dark green, turning maroon to dark purple-red in autumn. Mildew resistant. Young branches are red-purple becoming gray prior to dark brown at maturity. See *HortScience* 21:250–251 (1986).

'Peppermint Lace'—Deep pink, edged white, picotee flowers, producing candy striped effect, can grow 15 to 20′ high and wide, can be maintained as a smaller shrub in the 7′ by 6′ range, Monrovia introduction.

'Pink'—Upright form to 18′ tall, flowers bubblegum pink, blooming mid-July, fall color yellow-orange, moderate mildew resistance.

'Pink Lace'—Clear pink flowers that are produced over an extended period in summer, medium-sized shrub, 10 to 12′ high, named and introduced in 1958 by Texas Nursery, Sherman, TX.

'Potomac'—Upright growth habit, 10′ by 7 1/2′, dense dark green foliage, large terminal inflorescences of clear medium pink, mid-July to October, grew this for a number of years but it suffered significant dieback and was removed, flower color is as close to bright pink as any, mildew susceptible. Not particularly cold hardy. Introduced 1967.

'Powhatan'—Compact, medium growth habit, 10 1/2′ by 10 1/2′ in 11 years, glossy heavy foliage, abundant compact inflorescences of medium purple open in late July until late September, mildew resistant. Introduced 1967.

'Prairie Lace'—Compact, upright semi-dwarf shrub, 4 to 6′ in height in 6 years, panicle 4 1/2 to 10″ long, 3 to 8″ wide, individual petals medium pink banded with pure white on the outer margin, blooming mid-June through late September; leaves are smaller and thicker than the species. New leaves emerge wine-red, gradually turning very dark green, fall color red to red-orange, supposedly resistant to mildew but a small plant in our lath area contracted significant mildew. Have seen significant mildew on this clone.

'Prostrata Griffin'—20′ by 25′, watermelon red flowers.

'Purple'—Upright form to 20′ tall, flowers light purple, blooming mid-July; fall color orange, moderate resistance to mildew.

'Queen's Lace'—Upright, 12 to 14′(20′) high, frilly watermelon pink flowers, reddish new growth, similar to 'Peppermint Lace' but hardier.

Raspberry Sundae™ ('Whit I')—Crimson buds open cardinal red to pink, similar to red raspberry, upright growing with few spreading side branches, to 15′ high, new leaves crimson, then dull dark green, uniform bright orange in fall, hardy to −5 to −8°F, killed to ground at −15°F, PPAF, Whitcomb introduction.

'Regal Red'—Broad upright form reaching 16′ in height, flowers red, blooming mid-July; fall color red-orange, mildew resistance good.

Royal Velvet™ ('Whit III')—Crimson buds, bright pink flowers, shrub habit, 10 to 12′ high, burgundy wine foliage turns purple green or green at maturity, thick, leathery, mildew free foliage, hardy to −5 to −8°F, killed to ground at −15°F.

'Royalty'—Rich lavender flowers, medium size, survived -3°F with no dieback.

'Sarah's Favorite'—Large shrub or small tree to 20′ or more, akin to 'Natchez' but more cold hardy; white flowers are produced over a longer period of time, lustrous dark green foliage, cinnamon brown bark, originally an unnamed U.S. National Arboretum seedling, given a handle by Tom Dodd Nurseries.

'Seminole'—Compact medium growth habit, 7 to 8' (10 to 12') high and 6 to 7' wide, glossy medium green heavy foliage, numerous large globose inflorescences of clear medium pink from July to September, florets open over a 6 to 8 week period with recurrent bloom, high mildew resistance; in my mind one of the best for intensity of vivid pink and quality of flower, as soon as first flowers fade I cut them off and a second heavy bloom occurs about 3 to 4 weeks later, aphids can be heavy. Introduced 1970.

'Sioux'—Upright multiple-stemmed, large shrub or small tree, 14' high and 12' wide after 10 years, panicles dark pink, 5 to 9" long, 4 1/2 to 6 1/2" wide, maintains intense flower color, blooming late July to mid-September; young foliage glabrous, early bronze, leaves become glossy, slightly leathery, dark green turning light maroon to bright red in autumn, mildew resistant; young branches glabrous, dull red, maturing to gray brown, later sinuous, mottled, exfoliating bark of older branches and trunk reveals light medium gray-brown coloration. One of the best for summer foliage. See *HortScience* 22:674–677 (1987).

'Tonto'—Semi-dwarf, multi-stemmed shrub, 8.25' by 8.25' after 15 years at the U.S. National Arboretum, in Georgia trials, 10' by 8' after 5 years; fuchsia red flowers in 4 to 8" long, 3 to 5" wide panicles with 50 to 300 florets per inflorescence in July–September; young leaves dark bronze, semi-glossy dark green, bright maroon in autumn; red-purple young branches, cream to gray-brown bark at maturity; See *HortScience* 25:585–587 (1990) for details; have seen slight mildew but nothing serious.

'Tuscarora'—Large shrub or small tree, 15' high and wide after 12 years, red-tinged immature leaves turn dark green and then orange-red in fall, the dark coral-pink flowers appear in 5 to 12" long and 4 to 8" wide panicles from early July with recurrent bloom until late September, the mottled, light brown bark is spectacular, mildew resistant; have not been as impressed with this because of lack of hardiness at least in the Athens area. Open-grown plants are more upright with strongly ascending branches. See *HortScience* 16:788–789 (1981).

'Tuskegee'—Multi-stemmed small tree with distinct horizontal branching, 14' high by 18' wide in 17 years, long tapered panicles dark pink to near red (coral), 6 to 8 1/2" long and 4 1/2 to 7" wide, blooming early July to September; young foliage red tinged becoming glossy, subcoriaceous, dark green, turning orange-red in autumn, mildew resistant; young branches bright red, glabrous, becoming gray-tan, then sinuous, exfoliating, mottled light gray-tan. See *HortScience* 21:1078–1080 (1986).

Twilight®—Dark purple flowers, large shrub or small tree, Hines introduction.

'Velma's Royal Delight'—Superb magenta flowers occur in mid-summer, 5' by 4', possibly the most cold hardy clone, survived -18°F on December 22, 1989 in Wichita, KS, top was injured but plants flowered heavily in summer of 1990, selected by Mrs. Velma McDaniel as a chance seedling from the Otto Spring Nursery, Okmulgee, OK, introduced by Dr. John Pair, Kansas State in 1991.

'Victor'—Dwarf compact form reaching 3 to 5' in height, flowers dark red, blooming July–August; fall color reddish yellow, good mildew resistance, aphids and sooty mold occur.

'Watermelon Red'—Watermelon red flowers on a 15' or greater in height large shrub to small tree, not absolute on taxonomic authenticity, common in the South but could be more than one clone sold as such, flower colors have been described as rosy pink, reddish pink, and dark pink watermelon, mildew susceptible and should be replaced by the U.S. National Arboretum selections.

'Wichita'—Upright multi-stemmed small tree, 16' high and 9' wide in 12 years, long tapered panicles light magenta to lavender, 4 1/2 to 14" long, 3 1/2 to 19" wide, blooming early July to October; young foliage glossy, glabrous, bronze-tinged, becoming slightly leathery, dark green and turning russet to mahogany in autumn, mildew resistant; young branches glabrous, red-purple, becoming light gray, later sinuous, mottled, dark russet brown to dark mahogany and exfoliating, has proven difficult to root. See *HortScience* 22:336–338 (1987).

'William Toovey'—Vase-shaped form, 15' tall, flowers pink-red, blooming July–August; fall color red-orange, good mildew resistance.

'World's Fair'—Watermelon Red.

'Yuma'—Upright multi-stemmed large shrub or small tree, 13' high and 12' wide in 12 years; long-tapered panicles, medium lavender bicolored, 6 1/2 to 14" long, 5 to 8 1/2" wide, blooming in late July to late September; young foliage glabrous, dull bronze-tinged, later dark green, turning dull yellow-orange to russet to lighter mahogany in autumn, mildew resistant; young branches glabrous, red-purple becoming gray, later sinuous, mottled, light gray as the bark exfoliates on older branches and trunk. See *HortScience* 22:674–677 (1987).

'Zuni'—Globose, semi-dwarf, multi-stemmed shrub, 9' high by 8' wide in 12 years, panicles medium lavender, 3 to 5 1/2" long, 3 to 5" wide, blooming mid-July to late September; young foliage glossy, glabrous, leathery, red-tinged with heavier pigmentation on leaf margins, becoming dark green and turning orange-red to dark red in autumn, mildew resistant, young branches glabrous, heavily pigmented red, becoming gray prior to light brown and gray on older branches and trunk. See *HortScience* 21:250–251 (1986).

DWARF/MINIATURE CULTIVARS: In previous editions I avoided the "true" dwarf types but keep running into them in everyday commerce. They can be used almost like bedding plants but look pretty forlorn and abused in winter (like a small brush pile that needs burning). They have been utilized on the Georgia campus but only for a season as flowering was not as intense as advertised. Also, mildew and general untidiness contribute to lack of acceptance. With that stated, in drier areas (less humidity), the plants have a place. Hines Nursery, Chopin and Wright Nurseries, and Monrovia Nursery Co. are the largest purveyors of the dwarf forms.

DIXIE SERIES: From Hines, Chopin and Wright, 2 to 3′ high, called miniature weeping crapemyrtles, flower mid-May to October. The following are patented: 'Baton Rouge'—deep red; 'Bayou Marie'—bicolor pink; 'Bourbon Street'—watermelon red; 'Cordon Bleu'—lavender; 'Delta Blush'—pink; 'Lafayette'—delicate light lavender; 'New Orleans'—purple.

CHICA SERIES: From Monrovia.

   Chica™ Pink ('Monink')—Dwarf, 3 to 3 1/2′ high and wide, bright pink flowers.

   Chica™ Red ('Moned')—Dwarf, 3 to 4′ high and wide, rose red flowers.

PETITE SERIES: From Monrovia, 5′ by 4′, rich bronze foliage when young, dark green at maturity: Petite Embers™ ('Moners')—rose red; Petite Orchid™ ('Monhid')—dark orchid; Petite Pinkie™ ('Monkie')—clear pink; Petite Plum™ ('Monum')—deep plum purple; Petite Red Imp™ ('Monimp')—deep crimson red flowers; Petite Snow™ ('Monow')—snow white flowers.

PIXIE SERIES: Listed by Greenleaf Nursery; just how different from Dixie Series is unknown.

   From Greenleaf Nursery and Hines Nursery, listed as 3 to 6′ by first nursery, 6 to 12′ by second are: 'Low Flame'—red; 'Mandi'—dark red; 'Pink Ruffles'—pink; 'Royalty'—purple; 'Snow'—white. Possible synonyms: 'Dwarf Pink' ('Pink Ruffles'); 'Dwarf Purple' ('Royalty'); 'Dwarf Red' ('Low Flame'); 'Dwarf White' ('Snow').

PROPAGATION: Interestingly, seeds supposedly germinate best if given a 30 to 45 day cold treatment before sowing; however, I have collected seeds in January and sown them immediately with excellent germination taking place in 2 to 3 weeks. Softwood cuttings of young growth taken in May, June, July or semi-hardwood cuttings will root; I have had great success with 1000 ppm IBA-quick dip on softwood cuttings in July–August; rooting takes place in about 3 to 4 weeks; if rooted early in season will continue to grow. I am convinced that soft cuttings, especially from the first flush of growth which coincides with mid-May in Athens make ideal cuttings. They root quickly and can either be maintained as liners or shifted to one-gallon containers.

ADDITIONAL NOTES: Another plant I dreamed about growing when living in the deep freeze zone. Rooted cuttings in 4″ pots planted in May grew 3′ the first season and flowered. Plants respond to good fertility and moisture. There are so many wonderful cultivars available that I doubt if there is anyone who knows or grows the best of the lot. We need to refine the list to the best 10 in order to keep from confusing the gardening public. Some of the new U.S. National Arboretum introductions are worth considering since they have been bred for disease resistance, good flowering, and highly ornamental bark.

   A new publication, *Crapemyrtle: A Grower's Thoughts*, by David Byers, 1997, Owl Bay Publishers, Inc., Auburn, AL, is a wonderful pragmatic contribution to the history, culture, and aesthetics of the genus. It is a must for crapemyrtle enthusiasts and everyday gardeners. Available from the author at Byers Nursery, P.O. Box 560, Meridianville, AL 35759.

NATIVE HABITAT: China and Korea. Introduced 1747.

RELATED SPECIES:

Lagerstroemia fauriei Koehne, (lā-gĕr-strō′mē-à fàr′ē-ī), was unknown in the United States until Dr. John Creech, U.S. National Arboretum, brought it back from Japan in the 1950's. Has been the basis of mildew resistance in many of Dr. Egolf's U.S. National Arboretum hybrids. Also, the rusty brown bark character has proven aesthetically exceptional. Some of the original seedlings found their way to North Carolina State University and what is now J.C. Raulston Arboretum. In October, 1987, I first witnessed these most magnificent 30′ and greater in height, multi-stemmed, dark red-brown barked specimens. Flowers are white and not exceptional. Ohwi lists them as occurring in 2 to 4″ long panicles. Supposedly more difficult to root than *L. indica* with softwoods yielding 70% in 6 to 8 weeks. Plants grow 2 to 4′ per year and the excellent bark develops after three years from a cutting. This is hardier than *L. indica* and probably should be considered Zone 6 since plants have survived -10°F in Raleigh. 'Fantasy' was released by the J.C. Raulston Arboretum. It has outstanding bark and will make a handsome small tree. 'Fantasy' has become somewhat of a staple in the large balled-and-burlapped southern nurseries. I have included one in our garden and field tests and will provide several observations. Growth is fast. The small 4″ long paniculate flowers open before those of the hybrids or *L. indica*, usually by early June (Athens). They are moderately

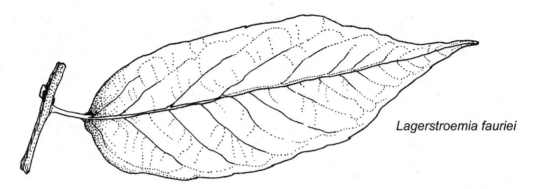

Lagerstroemia fauriei

fragrant, more so than *L. indica* types. Also, flowers are produced once and remittent flowering is uncommon. Growers reported cold injury while the hybrids were not affected. Perhaps 'Fantasy' does not shut down in fall as fast as the types with *L. indica* genes. Another introduction from the J.C. Raulston Arboretum is 'Townhouse', a darker barked form than 'Fantasy'. This is an exceptional form and would make a handsome small tree.

Lagerstroemia limii Merr., **L. speciosa** (L.) Pers., Queen's Crapemyrtle, and **L. subcostata** Koehne, Chinese Crapemyrtle, occasionally surface in botanical gardens and landscapes. The first is a rather ugly shrub with large blue-green leaves and lavender-purple flowers. Zone 6 to 9. The second is a tree form to 75', with purple to white flowers and minimal cold hardiness. Zone 9 to 11. The last produces pink-white flowers on a moderate shrub. Zone 7 to 9. I have grown all three and find minimal redeeming qualities. Seedlings of *L. speciosa* grew 8' high in a single season and all froze out the following winter. Several cultivars of *L. speciosa* are listed including: 'Doris Straub'—saffron pink flowers; 'Pastel Pink'—light pink flowers; and 'Pretty Purple'—purple flowers.

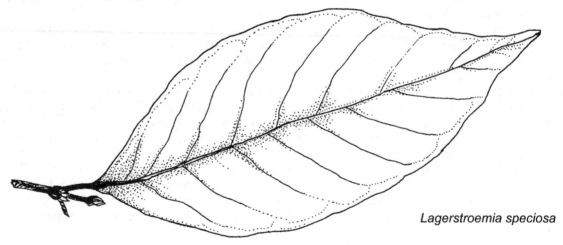

Lagerstroemia speciosa

Larix decidua Mill. — European or Common Larch
(lar′iks dē-sid′ū-à)

FAMILY: Pinaceae

LEAVES: Of long shoots up to 1 1/4″ long, narrow, pointed or blunt, those of short shoots (spurs) 30 to 40 together, 1/2 to 1 1/2″ long, narrower and blunter than those of the long shoots, both kinds keeled below, bright green when young, eventually soft deep green, turning yellow in autumn.

BUDS: Terminal of long shoots globose, short-pointed, with many brown pointed scales; lateral buds shorter, blunter, buds of short shoots small, rounded.

STEM: Young—gray or yellowish, furrowed, without pubescence; those of the second year roughened by cushion-like leaf bases of the previous year; short shoots dark brown or almost black, marked with as many rings as they are years old, the younger rings downy.

CONES: Ovoid, 1 to 1 1/2″ long, 3/4 to 1″ wide, scales rounded and entire above, striated, margin sometimes wavy.

SIZE: 70 to 75′ in height by 25 to 30′ in width; can grow 100 to 140′ high.

HARDINESS: Zone 3a to 6, struggles in Zone 7(8).

HABIT: Pyramidal, with horizontal branches and drooping branchlets, slender and supple in youth but irregular and lacking in dignity with age; this is a deciduous conifer, i.e., the needles abscise in the fall.

RATE: Medium to fast, 2 1/2′ a year in youth, slowing with time.

TEXTURE: Medium-fine in leaf; medium-coarse in winter.

BARK: On young trees thin, scaly; on old trees, thick, deeply fissured at the base exposing a reddish brown inner bark which contrasts with the grayish brown outer bark.

LEAF COLOR: Bright green in spring becoming a deeper green in summer and finally turning an ochre yellow in the fall; fall color can be spectacular.

FLOWERS: Monoecious, in early spring the attractive red, pink, yellow or green, 1/2″ long, egg-shaped female strobili and the smaller yellow male strobili cover the branchlets.

FRUIT: Cone, scales pubescent on the backside, 1 to 1 1/2″ long, changing from red to yellow-brown to brown at maturity, scales overlapping and *not* reflexed.

CULTURE: Readily transplanted when dormant; should have sufficient moisture, well-drained and sunny conditions although *L. laricina* often grows in wet or even boggy conditions in the wild; intolerant of shade, dry, shallow, chalky soils and polluted areas; prune in mid-summer.

DISEASES AND INSECTS: The larch case-bearer is a serious pest; this small insect appears in early May and eventually eats its way into the needles, causing them to turn brown for the remainder of the season; early and timely spring spraying will control them; also cankers, leaf cast, needle rusts, wood decay, larch sawfly, woolly larch aphid, gypsy moth, tussock moth and Japanese beetle can be serious problems; canker has been a problem in European forest plantings.

LANDSCAPE VALUE: Very effective for park and large area use as a specimen or grouping; fall colors can be excellent, new spring growth is as elegant as that of any tree.

CULTIVARS: About 20 described, dwarf, weeping, contorted, and other permutations.

'Fastigiata'—Columnar, similar to Lombardy Poplar with short ascending branches.

'Pendula'—Represents those trees with branches of a distinct pendulous nature; no doubt, more than one form is in cultivation; the common form is usually grafted on a standard and allowed to cascade; some plants are as "elegant" as mop heads; others rather graceful and attractive.

'Varied Directions'—Spreading, then arching branches, wider than tall at maturity, not as graceful as 'Pendula', probably a form of *L. × marschlinsii* Coaz non hort. (formerly *L. × eurolepis* Henry).

PROPAGATION: Seeds of most species germinate fairly well without pre-treatment; there seems to be a mild dormancy, however, that varies somewhat among species and lots within species; it can be overcome by cold stratification in a moist medium for 30 to 60 days at 30° to 41°F; cuttings are difficult to root although low percentages can be achieved with proper timing; the cultivars are grafted.

NATIVE HABITAT: Northern and central Europe. Introduced in colonial times. The main home of this species lies in the mountains of central Europe from southeastern France through the main chain of the Alps eastward to the neighborhood of Vienna. Here it forms beautiful forests, often in association with *Pinus cembra*. Subspecies *polonica* (Racib.) Domin., Polish Larch, is slender-crowned with drooping branchlets and smaller cones, 1/2 to 1″ long. Found in western Poland and the Ukraine.

Larix kaempferi (Lamb.) Carr. [formerly *L. leptolepis* (Sieb. & Zucc.) Gordon] — Japanese Larch
(lar′iks kem′fēr-ī)

LEAVES: 1 to 1 1/2″ long and 1/25″ wide; on short spurs 40 or more together, 1 1/2″ or longer; upper side of both kinds flat, glaucous, underside keeled and with 2 white bands, deep green.

BUDS: Small, oblong or conical, pointed, resinous with bright brown fringed scales.

STEM: Glaucous, covered in varying density with soft brownish hairs or sometimes without hairs, furrowed; short spurs stout, dark brown.

CONES: 1 to 1 1/2″ long and slightly narrower in width; scales about 1/2″ long and wide, rounded, with the upper edge rolled back giving the extended cones a rosette-like appearance.

SIZE: 70 to 90′ in height by 25 to 40′ in spread, can reach 150′ or more.

HARDINESS: Zone 4 to 7.

HABIT: Very open and pyramidal in habit with beautiful slender pendulous branchlets.

RATE: Medium to fast.

TEXTURE: Fine in foliage, coarse in winter.

BARK: Similar to *L. decidua*.

LEAF COLOR: Green, underside keeled with two white glaucous bands, turning yellowish gold in autumn.

FLOWERS: See *Larix decidua*.

FRUIT: Cones stalked, 1 to 1 1/2″ long and almost as wide, scales keeled forming a rosette appearance.

CULTURE: Readily transplanted when dormant; should have sufficient moisture, well-drained, sunny situations; susceptible to drought but tolerant of shallow, acid soils; intolerant of shade, chalk soils and polluted areas.

DISEASES AND INSECTS: Similar to other larches but more resistant to canker than *L. decidua*.

LANDSCAPE VALUE: Best ornamental among the larches but reserved for large areas such as a park, golf course, campus.

CULTIVARS: Over 20 cultivars described.

'Blue Rabbit'—A narrow, pyramidal form with conspicuously glaucous foliage, not common.

'Dervaes'—Branches horizontal, branchlets drooping, leaves fresh green, handsome but uncommon.

'Diana'—Contorted, twisted branches.

'Pendula' ('Inversa')—A weeping form with glaucous needles; I see various specimens labeled as either *L. decidua* 'Pendula' or this form and am really not sure how to differentiate between them; I have seen distinct, mop-headed forms with long trailing branches that look alike but are labeled differently; without cones it is difficult to tell; although the mature stems of *L. kaempferi* are reddish brown this does not seem to hold for the weeping form unless some are *L. decidua* forms labeled incorrectly.

PROPAGATION: As previously described.

ADDITIONAL NOTES: *Larix kaempferi* is difficult to distinguish from *Larix decidua* except shoots of the former are rich reddish brown, leaves blue-green to glaucous and wider, and broader cones with reflexed scales.

NATIVE HABITAT: Japan. Introduced 1861.

Larix laricina (Du Roi) K. Koch — Eastern or American Larch, Tamarack
(lar′iks lar-i-sī′na)

LEAVES: Light bluish green (pale green with 2 stomatal bands beneath), 3/4 to 1 1/4″ long, 1/50″ wide, 3-sided, strongly keeled beneath, on short spurs 12 to 30 in a bundle.

BUDS: Rounded, glossy dark red, slightly resinous.

STEM: Thin, at first glabrous, bloomy, later dull yellowish brown or reddish brown.

CONES: Egg-shaped, small, 1/2 to 1″ long, 1/4 to 1/2″ wide, with 15 to 20 scales, green to purple, maturing to straw brown.

SIZE: 40 to 80′ high by 15 to 30′ spread, usually smaller in cultivation.

HARDINESS: Zone (1)2 to 4 or 5; hates the heat.

HABIT: Open and pyramidal with a slender trunk, horizontal branches and drooping branchlets.

RATE: Slow-medium.

TEXTURE: Medium-fine in foliage; coarse in winter.

BARK: Thin and smooth on young stems, later becoming 1/2 to 3/4″ thick, gray to reddish brown, scaly.

LEAF COLOR: Bright blue-green foliage turning yellowish in the fall; often showy in fall color.

FLOWERS: Monoecious, sessile; staminate yellow, pistillate rosy colored.

FRUIT: Cones are small, oval, 1/3 to 2/3″ long, 1/4 to 1/2″ broad, pendulous, glabrous, green or violet becoming brown when mature.

CULTURE: Moist soils, less tolerant of cultivation then *Larix decidua*; intolerant of shade and pollution; makes best growth in moist, well-drained, acid soils.

DISEASES AND INSECTS: Subject to Larch case-bearer, Larch sawfly, wood rot and several rust fungi.

LANDSCAPE VALUE: Excellent in groves and in moist soil; less tolerant of cultivation than *L. decidua*, best left in its native confines; have seen in Maine and Michigan in boggy areas.

CULTIVARS: None important. 'Arethusa Bog', 'Aurea', 'Glauca', 'Newport Beauty #7', 'Newport Beauty #9' (both Newport forms derived from "witches' brooms," Sid Waxman introductions), and 'Ossorio Broom' are listed.

PROPAGATION: See previous entry.

ADDITIONAL NOTES: Seemingly everywhere in Maine. Bonnie and I vacation on Deer Isle and our walks take us through all types of habitats—one constant is *L. laricina*, particularly in moist soils. Appears quite salt tolerant.

NATIVE HABITAT: Northern North America, from the Arctic Circle in Alaska and Canada southwards to northern Pennsylvania, Minnesota and Illinois. Introduced 1737.

Laurus nobilis L. — True Laurel, Bay Laurel

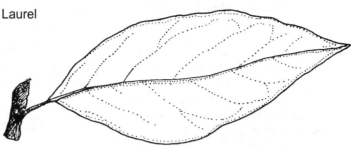

FAMILY: Lauraceae

LEAVES: Alternate, simple, evergreen, narrowly elliptic to ovate, 2 to 4″ long, 3/4 to 1 3/4″ wide, acute, cuneate, margin often undulate, appearing crimped, lustrous dark green above, glabrous; petiole—1/3″ long.

Laurus nobilis, (lâ′rus nō′bil-is), True Laurel, has been a part of gardens and cuisine since the beginning of recorded history. The habit is dense, pyramidal-oval to haystack-shaped. Variable in size but 8 to 12′ represents a fine specimen. Literature notes specimens over 60′ high. The dark green leaves are highly aromatic when bruised or cut. The yellow-green flowers are followed by lustrous black, 1/2″ diameter berries. Species is dioecious, the males with larger flowers. Requires semi-shade and moisture retentive soils under cultivation. Many gardeners in the South talk about cold hardy forms but I have yet to see a mature specimen (over 20′) as most exist as defoliated or dieback shrubs. Often utilized for formal gardens, and maintained in a taut geometric shape. Makes a wonderful container plant and is ideal in large terra-cotta containers on the patio and deck. Easily rooted from summer (July–August) cuttings. 'Aurea' with yellow-gold new growth loses most of the color with the heat of summer. 'Sunspot' with pale yellow mottled gray-green leaves was introduced by Brookside Gardens in 1982. Mediterranean. Probably best in Zone 8b to 9, 10 on West Coast.

Lavandula angustifolia Mill. — Common or English Lavender

(là-van′dū-là an-gus-ti-fō′li-à)

FAMILY: Lamiaceae

LEAVES: Opposite, entire, evergreen, linear to lanceolate, 1 to 1 3/4″ long, up to 3/16″ wide, obtuse, revolute, green to gray-green above, white tomentose below.

SIZE: 1 to 2′ high, wider at maturity; plants as tall as 3 to 5′ have been reported.

HARDINESS: Zone 5 to 8(9).

HABIT: Evergreen subshrub with a well-developed woody base forming a broad cushion-like mound, refined and aristocratic.

RATE: Slow, although I have grown it from seed and in 2 years had bushy 10 to 12″ diameter plants.

TEXTURE: Fine.

LEAF COLOR: Grayish to bluish green throughout seasons, develops an off-color during winter; at its best in spring and summer when the new foliage is present, foliage is fragrant.

FLOWERS: Lavender-purple in the typical form but numerous selections have been made that vary from white and pink, through blue, violet to lilac and beyond; flowers borne in 1 1/2 to 2 1/2″ long spikes on extended, 2 to 6″ long peduncles; have read references to inflorescences as long as 45″ and in travels through Europe have experienced large growing and flowering types but nothing approaching 45″; abundant flowers appear in June, July or August; dried flowers can be used for sachets.

FRUIT: Nutlet, not ornamental.

CULTURE: Readily transplanted from containers; prefers well-drained soil on the dry side; neutral to alkaline soil is best; full sun; stalks should be removed after flowers fade; excessive moisture will literally do the plant in.

DISEASES AND INSECTS: None serious.

LANDSCAPE VALUE: An essential ingredient in herb gardens, can be used as a border or pruned to form a low hedge; often used in mass where both foliage and flowers produce a striking effect; a fine plant with many uses in the home landscape; the textural quality and foliage color can be used to great advantage to soften the effect of excessive broadleaf evergreens; the leaves, flowers, and dried seed heads are very fragrant; this is the English Lavender that has been cultivated in England since the early 16th century; it is the source of the true oil of lavender.

CULTIVARS: Many, probably hybrids of the above and *L. latifolia* Medik., Spike Lavender; most are distinguished by flower and foliage color as well as time of flower and growth habit.

'Alba'—Pinkish white flowers, spikes 2 to 3″ long, stems about 20″ long.

'Hidcote'—Considered a cultivar of *L. angustifolia*, rich purple flowers born on 10 to 15″ long stalks, foliage is silvery, habit more compact; truly a handsome form that was selected at Hidcote Garden before 1950.

'Munstead'—Associated with Gertrude Jekyll and Munstead House and Garden, flowering plants grow 16 to 18″ high, foliage 10 to 12″, greenish gray 1 to 1 1/2″ long, 1/24″ wide leaves, flowering spikes blue-lilac, 1 3/4 to 2 1/2″ long, 6 to 10 flowers per whorl, June–July; synonymous with 'Munstead Dwarf', 'Munstead Variety', 'Munstead Blue', and 'Nana Compacta'.

PROPAGATION: Seeds can be directly sown; a fine 10 to 12″ diameter plant can be expected in two growing seasons from seed. Cuttings can also be rooted and should be collected in August or September and placed in a cold frame or suitable structure; I have attempted to root the species but with minimal success primarily because of excessive moisture in the rooting beds (mist). *Lavandula latifolia* has been reproduced from hypocotyl explants in tissue culture. See *HortScience* 24:375–376 (1989) for specifics.

ADDITIONAL NOTES: I have always loved this plant and believe it is worthy of cultivation in every garden. The wonderful flowers and fragrant plant parts are sufficient reason for using it.

Lavandula stoechas L., French Lavender, has persisted and flowered in our hodge-podge herb garden. Plants grow 2 to 3′ high, gray-green foliage, with purplish flowers and bracts (remind of butterflies). Spectacular in English gardens. Native to southwest Europe to Greece, north Africa. Zone 7b to 8.

NATIVE HABITAT: Southern Europe, northern Africa; cultivated since ancient times.

Ledum groenlandicum Oeder. — Labrador Tea
(lē′dum green-land′i-kum)

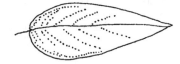

FAMILY: Ericaceae

LEAVES: Alternate, simple, evergreen, 3/4 to 2″ long, 1/4 to 1/2″ wide, elliptic or ovate to oblong, obtuse, margins recurved, glaucous and resinous, dark green above, covered with dark brown rust beneath, fragrant when crushed; petiole—1/6 to 1/4″ long.

BUDS: Solitary, sessile, somewhat compressed, small with about 3 exposed scales; the terminal flower buds large, round or ovoid, with some 10 broad mucronate, glandular-dotted scales.

STEM: Slender, rounded, young shoots densely covered with rusty tomentum; older branches reddish brown or copper-colored; pith—small, somewhat 3-sided, spongy, brownish; leaf scars—mostly low, half-elliptical or bluntly cordate, the lowest transversely linear; 1 bundle trace.

SIZE: 2 to 4′ in height by 2 to 4′ in spread.

HARDINESS: Zone 2 to 5.

HABIT: Dwarf evergreen shrub with erect branches forming a rounded mass, sometimes procumbent.

RATE: Slow.

TEXTURE: Medium-fine in all seasons.

LEAF COLOR: Deep dark green above, undersides covered with whitish or rusty brown hairs.

FLOWERS: Perfect, white, each flower 1/2 to 3/4″ across, borne in 2″ diameter corymbs from May through June.

FRUIT: Capsule, about 1/5″ long, not showy, 5-valved, opening from base to apex.

CULTURE: Transplants readily, fibrous rooted; prefers moist, sandy, peaty soils; found in swampy moors of northern latitudes; full sun or partial shade.

DISEASES AND INSECTS: Anthracnose, leaf galls caused by fungi, rusts and leaf spots.

LANDSCAPE VALUE: Another interesting and little known ericaceous plant which is good for cool, moist, swampy areas; the plants I have seen were attractive in flower.

CULTIVARS:

'Compactum'—Dense, neat shrub to 1′ in height with short branches, very woolly stems, short broad leaves, and small flower clusters.

PROPAGATION: Seeds can be grown as described for *Calluna*; layers and cuttings can also be used; cuttings collected in October rooted 66 to 100% when treated with 8000 ppm IBA-talc.

NATIVE HABITAT: Greenland to Alberta and Washington, south to Pennsylvania and Wisconsin. Introduced 1763.

RELATED SPECIES:

Ledum glandulosum Nutt., (lē′dum glan-dū-lō′sum), Trapper's Tea, Mt. Labrador Tea, grows 20 to 60″ high with dark green, 1/2 to 2 1/4″ long leaves and white flowers in 2″ diameter corymbs. Western North

America. Zone 5. Also found in the northern United States and Europe is **Ledum palustre** L., (lē′dum palus′trĕ), Crystal Tea, Wild Rosemary, which grows 1 to 4′ high with 1/2 to 2″ long, 1/16 to 1/2″ wide, linear to elliptic-oblong, revolute, dull dark green leaves that are rusty pubescent beneath. Both species require cold moist soils for successful culture.

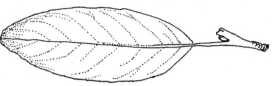

Ledum glandulosum

Leiophyllum buxifolium (Berg) Elliott — Box Sandmyrtle
(lī-ō-fil′um buk-si-fō′li-um)

FAMILY: Ericaceae

LEAVES: Usually alternate (may also be opposite), simple, 1/8 to 1/2″ long, 1/16 to 3/16″ wide, oblong or obovate-oblong, to almost orbicular, lustrous dark green above, paler beneath, entire, glabrous; petiole—short.

BUDS: Sessile, solitary, ovoid, appressed, with about 2 exposed scales.

STEM: Very slender, subterete; pith—minute, continuous; leaf scars—more or less broken and then 4-ranked, minute, crescent-shaped or 3 sided, raised; 1 bundle trace.

SIZE: 1 1/2 to 3′ high and spreading 4 to 5′; most that I have seen in the Southeast were almost prostrate, 2 to 12″ high and wider.

HARDINESS: Zone 5 to high elevations of the Southeast.

HABIT: Small evergreen shrub of great variability in the wild; erect, prostrate or decumbent according to location and altitude; in cultivation usually a dense bush up to 1 1/2′ high.

RATE: Slow.

TEXTURE: Fine in all seasons.

LEAF COLOR: Lustrous dark green in summer becoming bronzy with cold weather.

FLOWERS: Perfect, rosy in bud opening to white tipped with pink, each flower about 1/4″ diameter, 5-petals, sepals narrow lance-shaped, half as long as petals, 10 stamens; May through June; borne in terminal 3/4 to 1″ diameter corymbs.

FRUIT: Capsule, glabrous, 1/8″ long, 2- to 5-valved, numerous seeds.

CULTURE: Transplant balled-and-burlapped or container-grown plants; prefer moist, sandy, acid soil supplied with peat and leaf mold; full sun or partial shade; will not tolerate drought, not an easy plant to establish but like *Ledum* and *Epigaea* is well worth the effort.

DISEASES AND INSECTS: None serious.

LANDSCAPE VALUE: Dainty and unusual plant for the rock garden; blends well with other broadleaf evergreens; in flower makes a solid froth of white; handsome garden plant; added a plant to the garden with placement in a well-drained bed in full sun and the Zone 7b summer eliminated it; have observed plants growing at edges of duff extensions on rocky mountainsides in the southern Appalachians at 4000′; cool night temperatures might be more important than drainage.

CULTIVARS:

‘Nanum’—Compact, dense branching, pink flowers.

‘Pinecake’—Low, dense, creeping plant, described as flowing over the ground "glacier-like," 5″ high and 27″ wide, discovered in the wild by Dr. Richard Lighty, near Chatham, Morris Co., NJ, will be a good ground cover for acid, sunny sites, Zone 5 to ?

‘Prostratum’—Low trailing form with smallish, opposite, lustrous dark green leaves, pink buds and white flowers. From the var. *prostratum* (Loud.) A. Gray complex, Don Jacobs has named ‘Eco Red Stem’ with red branchlets and stems.

PROPAGATION: Seed as described for *Calluna*; root cuttings, layering and stem cuttings also work; one authority noted the best method is by cuttings made of shoots 1 to 1 1/2″ long in July or August, placed in peat:sand and provided bottom heat; October cuttings, 3000 ppm IBA-talc, rooted 100% in 8 weeks.

ADDITIONAL NOTES: The only species within the genus; resembles *Ledum* but can be distinguished by the small, quite glabrous, short-stalked to almost sessile leaves; the species is usually divided into three varieties.

NATIVE HABITAT: New Jersey southward, westward into the mountains of the Carolinas, Tennessee, and eastern Kentucky. Introduced 1736.

Leitneria floridana Chapm. — Florida Corkwood

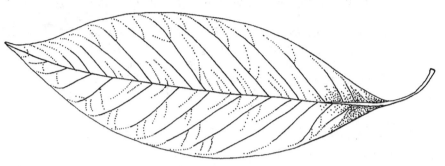

FAMILY: Leitneriaceae

LEAVES: Alternate, simple, elliptic-lanceolate to lanceolate, 3 to 6″ long, half as wide, acuminate, cuneate, entire, lustrous dark green above, paler, reticulate and silky pubescent below; petiole—1 to 2″ long, tomentose.

BUDS: Terminal the largest, pubescent, laterals small, grayish brown, sitting on top and in middle of large leaf scar.

STEM: Stout, rounded, pubescent at first, finally shiny dark brown, glabrous, covered with large and numerous vertical, elliptical, grayish lenticels, wood extremely light, malodor to bruised stems; pith—white, solid, half the diameter of stem.

Leitneria floridana, (light-neer′i-à flōr-i-dā′nà), Florida Corkwood, is a suckering 6 to 12′ high shrubby mass but in the wild can grow to 20′. Although ornamentally not particularly attractive it is rather interesting planted in moist soil along a brook or moist depression where it forms a large thicket of grove-like proportions. Flowers are dioecious and most plants I have observed in cultivation are male and the flowers occur in 1 to 1 3/4″ long catkins before the leaves in March–April. The flowers are more curious than attractive. Fruit is an oblong 1/2 to 3/4″ long, 1/4″ wide light olive-brown drupe. The wood is extremely light, with a specific gravity less than cork. In the wild has been reported growing under water. A tough durable plant that is cold hardy well north of its range probably withstanding –20°F. Morton Arboretum has grown it for over 50 years on a dry hillside. The gaps in my knowledge are gradually being filled and it was a great pleasure to visit Mr. Charles Webb and his son Allen at Superior Trees, Inc., Lee, FL in late February 1996. Both are passionate plantsmen and particularly fond of the natives. Their seedlings (needle and broadleaf trees/shrubs) are first class but it is their gardens/arboreta that really set them apart. Mr. Webb has collected and grown every *Quercus* species south of the Mason-Dixon line. He has collected seeds and plants from the Southeast and appreciates and understands provenance and seedling variation as well as anyone I have talked with. His stand of *Leitneria* got me so excited that our relationship was cemented from that point. I asked about availability, did he have male and female plants, could I possibly obtain both? He answered those prayers and numerous others. Now male and female plants reside among the Dirr holdings. True plantsmen, if they have two, share one. I am grateful for the Webb's kindness. Southern Missouri to Texas and Florida. Introduced 1894. Zone 5 to 9. Apparently not common in the wild.

Leptospermum scoparium Forst. & Forst. f. — Broom Teatree
(lep-tō-spĕr′mum skō-pā′ri-um)

FAMILY: Myrtaceae

LEAVES: Alternate, simple, evergreen, linear-oblong, 1/3 to 1/2″(3/4″) long, 1/12 to 1/4″ wide, sharply acuminate, dark green, fragrant when bruised, dotted with transparent oil glands.

SIZE: 6 to 10′(15′) high and slightly less in spread.

HARDINESS: Zone (8)9 to 10.

HABIT: Reasonably compact-rounded evergreen shrub with dense branching structure, quite refined because of small leaves; in wild found from coastal to mountain habitats and exhibits growth habits from prostrate to small tree status.

RATE: Medium.

TEXTURE: Fine through the seasons.

LEAF COLOR: Medium green often with a purplish tinge.

FLOWERS: Perfect, white, pink, or red, 1/2″ diameter produced singly from the leaf axils in June–July, spectacular on the best cultivars.

FRUIT: Pea sized and shaped, many seeded woody capsule.

CULTURE: Transplant container-grown material; moist, fertile, acid, well-drained soil; full sun to light shade, protect from sweeping winds, root rot may be a problem in poorly drained soils; shows good salt tolerance, necessary to site in a micro-climate for optimum growth, have seen used as a container plant in Southeast which means it must be overwintered in a cool greenhouse or room.

DISEASES AND INSECTS: None serious.

LANDSCAPE VALUE: In San Francisco, CA, a handsome plant; in Athens, GA of dubious value because of humidity and possibly high night temperatures; superb in the shrub border or in a container for excellent flower effect.

CULTIVARS: Many have been named but few are grown in the United States.

'Blossom'—Coral pink, double flowers, bright green foliage, bushy upright habit to 6' high.

'Burgundy Queen'—Deep burgundy red, double flowers, dark reddish bronze foliage, to 6' high.

'Charmer'—Pastel pink and white single flower with rose pink and dark eye, olive green leaves, vigorous bushy habit to 4' high.

'Cherry Brandy'—Blushed rose pink single flowers, deep bronze foliage, semi-dwarf habit to 2' high.

'Crimson Glory'—Bright crimson double flowers, bronze-red leaves, compact habit, 3 to 3 1/2' high.

'Fascination'—Light and deep candy pink, frilly, double flowers, green foliage, 4 to 5' high.

'Helen Strybling'—Gray-green foliage and large dark pink flowers.

'Jubilee'—Pink double flowers deepen to rose red, reddish foliage, upright bushy habit, 6' high.

'Martinii'—Pink double flowers, 6' high.

'Nanum Kea'—Pale pink, single flowers, smallish olive green foliage, dwarf compact habit to 12" high.

'Nanum Ruru'—Deep pink flowers at an early age, very dwarf, tightly branched shrub, tiny dark green foliage, 2' by 2'.

'Nanum Tui'—A compact, 2' high form with dark green foliage and white to pale pink flowers, darker at center.

'Red Damask'—Fully double, over 1/2" diameter deep cherry-red flowers, exceptionally free-flowering, dense habit, grows to about 6 to 8' high, raised in 1940's by W.E. Lamments, University of California.

'Ruby Glow'—The old standard and the plant most common in cultivation, the flowers are deep red, fully double and 1/2" across with bronzy foliage and red stems and a reasonably compact habit, 6 to 8' high.

'Snow White'—White double flowers, compact, spreading habit, 2 to 4' high.

PROPAGATION: Cuttings of firm wood will root, collect in early to mid-summer.

NATIVE HABITAT: New Zealand, Australia, Tasmania.

Lespedeza bicolor Turcz. — Shrub Bushclover
(les-pe-dē'zà bī'kul-ĕr)

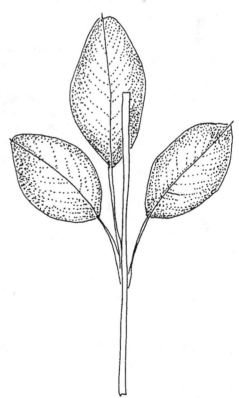

FAMILY: Fabaceae

LEAVES: Alternate, trifoliate, each leaflet 3/4 to 2"(3") long and two-third's to as much in width, broadly oval or obovate, midrib terminating in a small bristle, middle leaflet larger and longer petioluled than others, dark green (rich green) above, pale below, glabrous or sparsely covered with appressed pubescence on both sides.

SIZE: 6 to 9'(12') high and wide.

HARDINESS: Zone 4 to 7 or 8; may die back in cold climates and is best treated as an herbaceous perennial.

HABIT: Upright, open, loosely branched shrub that can become wonderfully unkempt and disorderly if not properly pruned.

RATE: Medium to fast.

TEXTURE: Medium.

LEAF COLOR: Dark green (rich green) usually with no appreciable fall color; leaves may turn yellow.

FLOWERS: Perfect, rosy-purple, 1/2" long, produced in 2 to 5" long racemes on current season's growth and are borne from the leaf axils of the uppermost 2' of the shoot; July–August; not really overwhelming.

FRUIT: Downy, ovate, 1/3" long, one-seeded pod.

CULTURE: Of the easiest culture given a well-drained soil; excess fertility should be avoided; pH adaptable; full sun; prune in winter or before new growth ensues in spring.

DISEASES AND INSECTS: None serious.

LANDSCAPE VALUE: Best utilized in the border; could serve as an herbaceous perennial in the North; a specimen in the Arnold Arboretum was about 10 to 12′ but had no great beauty being rather open and mediocre in flower.

CULTIVARS:

'Li'l Buddy'—A compact form with narrow leaflets, rose-purple flowers, graceful arching habit, 3′high after 4 years in a Chapel Hill, NC garden; offered by Niche Gardens, Chapel Hill, NC.

'Summer Beauty'—Flowers occur over an extended period from July through September on a 5′ high, spreading shrub; cut back to 6 to 12″ from the ground in late winter.

'Yakushima'—Grows about 12″ and forms a tight mound of foliage with smaller flowers and leaves than the species.

PROPAGATION: Seeds can be directly sown; when dry they might benefit from a slight acid treatment or hot water soak; softwood cuttings root easily.

NATIVE HABITAT: North China to Manchuria, Korea and Japan. Introduced 1856.

RELATED SPECIES:

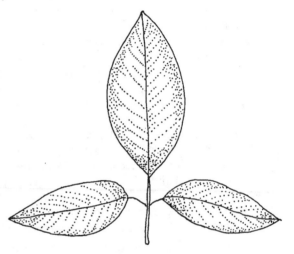

Lespedeza thunbergii (DC.) Nak., (les-pe-dē′zà thun-bĕr′je-ī), Thunberg Lespedeza, is really the beauty among the beasts of this genus. It exists as a semi-woody plant that is usually killed back in cold weather. In terms of height, it can grow 3 to 6′ in a single season. The flowering stems are so heavy they arch over producing a rather handsome fountain-like effect. The trifoliate, 1 to 2″ long, 1/2 to 1″ wide leaves are bluish green. The real beauty of the plant lies in the rosy purple, 1/2 to 5/8″ long, pea-shaped flower. They are produced in up to 6″ long racemes from the upper portion of the shoot, the whole constituting a 2 to 2 1/2′ long, loose panicle. Prune plant in late winter to induce new shoots and large flowers. In Zone 7b, it dies almost to ground level and it is easiest to remove old stems to within 6″ of the soil. The flowers peak in late August through September. I saw a beautiful plant at the Parc Floral, Orleans, France sited by water that provided a reflective surface and acted to enhance the floral beauty. This same body of water was traversed by a small arching bridge which from the opposite side provided the perfect frame for photographing the plant. This plant will stick in my mind forever. After my initial introduction, I knew the plant must find a home in the Dirr garden. A friend in Swarthmore, PA provided a clump which has been multiplied a thousand-fold and given to those who ask and those who do not. The plant has the curious habit of flowering in June in Zone 7b and again more heavily in late August–September. Growth habit is a large arching gracefully mounded shrub by the middle of summer. I have used the plant with *Sedum* 'Autumn Joy', *Miscanthus* 'Gracillimus', *Buddleia davidii* (white-flowered form) and the effect has been outstanding. Does extremely well under hot dry conditions. A white-flowered form, 'Alba', possibly more correctly 'Albiflora', is rather handsome but more upright in habit and not as graceful as the species. In the Dirr garden this form reaches 6 to 7′ by summer's end, leaflets are larger and greener than the typical species. In 1988, a pinkish white branch sport developed that might prove valuable. Also a white-variegated leaf form is in cultivation. The variegated pattern is rather subdued but handsome on close inspection. 'Gibraltar' produces deep rose-purple flowers. Arguably, I have trouble telling this form from the species. Some days I see differences; other days not. See *HortScience* 26:475 (1991) for specifics. 'Pink Cascade' has pinkish flowers and is more compact. I observed flowering in our garden during the summer of 1997. Will become popular with exposure. Have also propagated a form from Spring Grove, Cincinnati, OH that is more floriferous and deeper rose-purple than 'Gibraltar'. China, Japan. Introduced 1837. Zone 5 to 8.

Leucophyllum frutescens (Berl.) I.M. Johnst. — Texas Sage or Silverleaf

FAMILY: Scrophulariaceae

LEAVES: Opposite, simple, evergreen, elliptic to obovate, 1″ long, silvery pubescent on both surfaces, subsessile.

Leucophyllum frutescens, (lū-kō-fil′um frŭ-tes′enz), Texas Sage or Silverleaf, has become popular in recent years and is moving into southeastern markets. I have seen plants performing quite well; others dying. The species is typically a compact shrub probably 5 to 8′ high and 4 to 6′ wide but most of the new introductions will probably not grow as large. The evergreen, silvery pubescent on both surfaces, 1/2 to 1″ long leaves provide a handsome contrast to dark green shrubs. The 1″ wide rose-purple bell-shaped flowers appear in summer. Prefers low humidity environments and perfectly drained, acid or higher pH soil. Salt tolerant and amenable to pruning. Avoid excessive fertility and root zone moisture. Again, like other Southwest native plants, the humidity and high night temperatures of the eastern seaboard and southeastern states often prove lethal. Plant should be used in shrub border or possibly filler in herbaceous perennial borders. The cultivars include: 'Alba' with white flowers; 'Compactum' of smaller habit with orchid-pink flowers; 'Green Cloud' is a compact form with dark green foliage and violet-purple flowers; 'Rain Cloud' (*L. minus* A. Gray × *L. frutescens*)—violet-blue flowers, large and inflated, 5′ by 3′ in 5 years, does well in calcareous soil where rainfall is less than 35″, Zone 8; 'San Jose'—dwarf, ever-blooming selection from *L. frutescens*; Silver Cloud™—dense, rounded form, 3′ by 3′, with silver-white foliage and violet-purple flowers; 'Thundercloud' (*L. candidum* I.M. Johnston)—abundant dark purple flowers and dense globular habit, more floriferous than typical and has pleasing gray foliage, 30″ by 20″ in 3 years, superior to Silver Cloud™, drought tolerant, Zone 8; 'White Cloud'—produces gray foliage and white flowers on a 6 to 12″ high by 4 to 6′ wide shrub. Other species include: *L. langmanae* L.D. Flyr—upright, dense habit, small narrow leaf, 1/4 to 1/2″, deep blue-violet flowers, hardy to 4°F; 'Lynn's Ever-blooming' has light green foliage, pale blue-lavender flowers on a perpetual-flowering, compact shrub; and *L. zygophyllum* I.M. Johnston 'Desert Dazzler'— compact and low-growing, with silver-green foliage and bright blue-lavender flowers. Although *L. frutescens* and various cultivars have been distributed and sold in large numbers throughout the Southeast, the plants have not persisted. No doubt, the various taxa are better suited to the southwestern United States. Native to Texas and Mexico. Zone 8 to 9(?).

Leucothoe fontanesiana (Steud.) Sleumer [*L. catesbaei* (Walter) A. Gray] — Drooping Leucothoe, Fetterbush, Dog-hobble
(lū-koth′ō-ē fon-tȧ-nē-zē-ā′nȧ)

FAMILY: Ericaceae

LEAVES: Alternate, simple, evergreen, leathery, ovate-lanceolate to lanceolate, 2 to 5″ long, 1 to 1 1/2″ wide, long-acuminate, rounded or broad-cuneate at base, appressed ciliate-serrulate on margins, lustrous dark green above, lighter beneath, glabrous or with scattered hairs; petiole—1/3 to 2/3″ long.

STEM: Long, slender, with little or no lateral branch development, greenish, reddish, to purplish in color, glabrous, shiny, pith—solid, brown.

SIZE: 3 to 6′ by 3 to 6′, may be taller in native habitat, 5 to 6′ high specimens at Heritage Plantations, Cape Cod; have observed thousands of plants throughout the southern Appalachians and see no deviations from the 3 to 6′ height range.

HARDINESS: Zone (4)5 to 8, only in the coolest, shadiest locations in the southern (Zone 7 to 8) landscape; survived at Orono, ME.

HABIT: Very graceful evergreen shrub with long, spreading, arching branches clothed with long pointed leaves and cream-white flowers; almost fountain-like in habit.

RATE: Slow to medium, 3 to 5′ in 4 to 5 years.

TEXTURE: Medium in all seasons.

LEAF COLOR: New growth of bright green, bronze to purple color eventually changing to lustrous dark green, at maturity develops a bronze to purplish coloration in winter, my travels throughout the southern Appalachians indicate winter leaf color is genetically controlled, with some plants bronze, reddish purple, others green; in November 1996, Bonnie and I hiked the High Hampton golf course, Cashiers, NC and along the stream banks, green foliage forms were growing next to deep wine red forms.

FLOWERS: Perfect, white, fragrant, arguably somewhat ill-scented, slenderly urn-shaped, 1/4 to 1/3″ long, April to May, borne in 2 to 3″ long axillary racemes from the leaf axils and hanging down; somewhat masked by the foliage.

FRUIT: Capsule, dehiscent, 5-valved, 1/6″ diameter, not showy.

CULTURE: Transplants readily, best moved as a container plant in spring; prefers acid, moist, well-drained, organic soil; will not withstand drought or sweeping, drying winds; prefers partial to full shade but will grow in full sun if not too dry; rejuvenate by pruning to ground after flowering; fickle in the everyday landscape and virtually any stress serves as an open invitation to the fungal leafspots; careful siting (shade), moisture (uniform and adequate), and good drainage serve the species well.

DISEASES AND INSECTS: Leaf spots can be troublesome as at least 8 species of fungi infect *Leucothoe*; based on numerous observations over the years, this plant should only be used in ideal situations because any stress appears to predispose the plant to leaf spot which produces ugly lesions that often coalesce and consume the entire leaf, resulting in abscission of leaves and death of plants; the literature ascribes greater resistance to *L. axillaris* but it, too, is susceptible; also the hybrids like 'Scarletta' are quite susceptible; root rot problems can also be serious; have seen tremendous thickets in the southern Appalachians but always along streams in shade.

LANDSCAPE VALUE: Good facer plant, hides leggy plants, nice cover for a shady bank, massing, grouping or shrub borders; contrasts nicely with dull rhododendron foliage, good as undergrowth plant; leaf spot can render a plant unfit for any landscape; looks attractive in the container at the retail garden center, don't let first impressions hold sway; attention to cultural detail is a must.

CULTIVARS:

'Girard's Rainbow'—Selected by Girard Nursery, Ohio for its striking new growth which may emerge white, pinkish, coppery and other combinations; with time the effect is reduced but it is a showy evergreen shrub when the new leaves are emerging; cuttings collected on March 11, treated with 3000 ppm IBA-quick dip, peat:perlite, mist, had rooted by April 12.

'Lovita'—Mounded compact habit and dense deep bronze foliage in winter, probably 2' by 4', a hybrid between *L. f.* 'Nana' and *L. f.*?

'Mary Elizabeth'—Slow-growing, compact form with delicate appearance, thin strap-like leaves, bronze in winter.

'Nana'—Lustrous dark green foliage compliments a dense 2' high, 6' wide plant; this is a fine selection but is not widely available in the trade; I noticed a fine old plant in the Arnold Arboretum that was compact and handsome, there was no leaf spot but the plant was in a shady environment; unfortunately, leaf spot does occur on 'Nana'; have observed a 4' high plant at Longwood Gardens.

'Rollisoni' ('Rollissonii' may be correct spelling)—Rather obscure form with smaller leaves, 2 to 4" long by about 1/2 to 3/4" wide, relatively compact habit, 3' by 6', foliage lustrous dark green; several nurseries grow this form and consider it hardier than the species.

'Scarletta'—The first time I saw the plant I was impressed, several years later during a visit, the plants were gone . . . victims of leaf spot; my reason for excitement was the rich glossy scarlet (hint of purple) new growth that matures to dark green, foliage develops burgundy tones in fall and winter, will be more compact than the species, probably in the same range as 'Lovita'; I believe this is from the same parentage as 'Lovita'.

'Silver Run'—Creamy white variegated leaf form, pink tinge to white areas in winter, hardier than 'Girard's Rainbow', found on Silver Creek, Cashiers, NC, offered by Summer Hill Nursery, Madison, CT.

'Trivar'—Considered stronger growing than 'Girard's Rainbow' but not common in cultivation, red young leaves with cream-yellow-green variegation, developed around 1947 in New Jersey.

PROPAGATION: Direct sow the seed as described for *Calluna*; firm cuttings root readily when treated with 1000 ppm IBA/50% alcohol in peat:perlite under mist; actually cuttings collected in winter root readily when treated with 3000 to 8000 ppm IBA-talc or liquid.

ADDITIONAL NOTES: *Leucothoe fontanesiana* makes a magnificent evergreen shrub in the cool, moist, shady environment along streams in North Georgia. It forms large thickets that are almost impenetrable. It is usually not as beautiful under cultivation especially in stressed situations.

NATIVE HABITAT: Virginia to Georgia and Tennessee in the mountains. Introduced 1793.

RELATED SPECIES:

Leucothoe axillaris (Lam.) D. Don — Dog-hobble

LEAVES: Alternate, simple, evergreen, ovate, elliptic, elliptic-oblong or oval, 2 to 4"(6") long, 3/4 to 2" wide, short acute, short acuminate to abruptly mucronate, base tapering, variously serrate to entire, lustrous dark green above, paler beneath, glabrous with age; petiole—1/12 to 2/5" long.

Leucothoe axillaris, (lū-koth'ō-ē ak-sil-lā'ris), Coast Leucothoe, is receiving wide favor in the nursery trade as a potential replacement or substitute for *L. fontanesiana*. Grows 2 to 4' high (6') and 1 1/2 times that in width, with spreading branches, zig-zagged towards the end. The leaves are leathery, glossy dark green.

Flowers develop in axillary racemes, 1 to 2 1/2″ long, white, in April and May. This species is not particularly common in cultivation and in many respects resembles *L. fontanesiana*. It differs in comparatively shorter and broader, abruptly pointed leaves and fewer flowers (8 to 30) per inflorescence. Native from Virginia to Florida and Mississippi in lowland areas. Introduced 1765. Supposedly hardy in Zone 6, but based on observation of plants at Millcreek Valley Park, Youngstown, OH and in Lake County, OH, nursery area, I would place it in Zone 5. Occasional tip dieback in Zone 4, Orono, ME. Has survived at Morton Arboretum, Lisle, IL. This species will also contract the leaf spot disease and I have seen plants that were not in the best of condition. *Cylindrocladium leucothoeae* was described on leaves of plants from Florida. This species is similar to *L. fontanesiana* and much confused with it. From my observations I would say the differences, except for native range, are meager at best. Like *L. fontanesiana* it should be provided ideal cultural conditions. On casual inspection it is often difficult to separate this species from *L. fontanesiana*. In general, *L. axillaris* is smaller in all its parts, particularly growth habit. The new growth (leaves and stem) is somewhat twisted and curved. Pith is solid and brown.

CULTIVARS:

'Augusta Evans Wilson'—Compact form from Tom Dodd Nurseries, Semmes, AL.

'Beulah'—Compact form from Tom Dodd Nurseries.

'Compacta'—Listed as a 2′ by 6′, compact form, could be the same as *L. f.* 'Nana' although it is listed as an unique cultivar.

'Dodd's Variegated'—Cream variegated leaf.

'Florida'—Margie Jenkins, Jenkins Nursery, LA exhibited this compact form with normal size leaves.

'Greensprite'—Stiffly arching canes, leaves narrow, resembling those of willow, with long, thin apices, margins wavy, and each leaf is slightly twisted, is partially susceptible to leaf spot, leaves remain green year-round, 5 to 6′ by 10′, propagates readily and reaches salable size in 3 to 4 years, from Mt. Cuba Center for the Conservation of Piedmont Flora, received from an unknown source before 1965.

'Holly'—Listed as a pink variegated leaf form, from Tom Dodd, III.

'Macaria'—Compact form from Tom Dodd Nurseries, larger than 'Augusta Evans Wilson'.

Red Lips™ ('Lipsbolwi')—Rounded, compact, 10″ high, 12″ wide, glossy dark green leaves turn reddish purple in winter, a selection (branch sport?) of 'Scarletta' from A. Bolwijn, Netherlands.

'Redsprite'—Refined, twiggy growth, young growth reddish and winter color is coppery bronze, leaves flat and borne in herringbone pattern, 4′ by 5 to 6′, selected by James Plyler, Jr., Natural Landscapes.

'Sarah's Choice'—Low mounding evergreen shrub with long, arching branches, 4′ high and wide, striking red new leaves in spring shade to burgundy in autumn, slender branches are weighed down by the white flowers in April and May.

Leucothoe keiskei Miq., (lū-koth′ō-ē kēsk′ē-ī), Keisks Leucothoe, is a dwarf, rather compact, graceful evergreen shrub with 1 1/2 to 3 1/2″ long, 1/2 to 1 1/2″ wide, inconspicuously toothed, glossy dark green leaves. The young shoots are a shining red and the leaves become deep red in fall. The real beauty lies in the pure white, cylindrical, 1/2 to 5/8″ long, 1/4″ wide, nodding flowers that occur in short racemes during July. The flowers are the largest of the cultivated leucothoe. I was told that it is a rather temperamental garden plant. Have only seen once in the United States and that particular plant was in a container. Grows on wet shaded cliff faces in its native habitat. Japan. Introduced 1915. Zone 5.

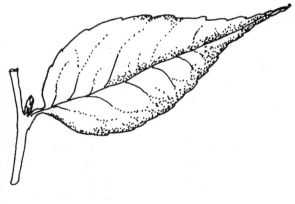

Leucothoe populifolia (Lam.) Dipp. [now correctly *Agarista populifolia* (Lam.) Judd.]
LEAVES: Alternate, simple, evergreen, ovate-lanceolate,
1 1/2 to 4″ long, one half as wide, acute to
acuminate, rounded, irregularly serrate or entire,
glossy rich green, new growth is tinged red or
purplish, stays green in winter, glabrous except for
hairs on midvein; petiole—1/4″ long, moderate
pubescence.

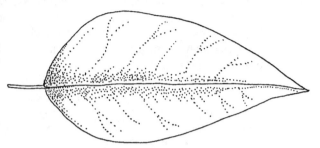

BUDS: About 1/16″ long, brown, angular-conical.
STEM: Fine, reddish above in sun, green below, usually
green throughout, shiny, pubescent on new growth,
brown at maturity; pith—lamellate, hollow at maturity.

Leucothoe populifolia, (lū-koth′ō-ē pop-ū-li-fō′li-á), Florida Leucothoe, is becoming more popular in cultivation
and is superior to *L. axillaris* and *L. fontanesiana* at least for southern gardens. The habit is lax, arching,
and multi-stemmed. The plant tends to sucker and can be used to great advantage along moist stream
banks in shady situations. The glossy rich green foliage is not as susceptible to leaf spot as *L.
fontanesiana*. In fact, I have seen no signs of infestation on cultivated plants. Cream-colored fragrant
flowers are born in axillary racemes in profusion during May–June. It makes a great companion with
large-leaved rhododendrons, mountain-laurel and similar shrubs. It grows 8 to 12′ high but can be
maintained at any height with proper pruning. A large planting at Brookgreen Gardens, Murrells Inlet, SC
was 15 to 18′ high. Given the correct landscape setting, it blends in beautifully. Wonderful textural
addition to a shade garden. One of the most handsome choices for understory plantings or creating a
naturalistic effect along streams. Must be in shade and cool, moist, acid, high organic matter soils. Easily
rooted from cuttings collected in late summer or fall. In the wild, found in moist to wet hummocks and wet
woodlands. This is an amazing broadleaf evergreen for much more difficult sites than I ever imagined.
Since the last edition, the plant has become more popular and is appearing in southern landscapes. In
1989, a large planting was installed for screening purposes at the University's Botanical Garden. Plants
are full, dense with arching branches, about 8′ tall and reside in competitive deciduous shade. Supplemental water is provided during droughty summers. The plants have exceeded my wildest expectations.
In the Dirr garden, two plants on the north side of our home continue to excel after 11 years. In fact, one
had grown 12′ and was pruned back to 12 to 18″. Regrowth even from naked trunks has been
phenomenal. Fred Galle, retired Horticulturist, Callaway Gardens, utilized the species under pine trees
to frame views, direct traffic and create green swatches throughout the garden. Has withstood -3°F with
no damage. May languish if sited in full sun and excessively dry soils. South Carolina to Florida.
Introduced 1765. Zone (6)7 to 9.

Leucothoe racemosa (L.) A. Gray — Sweetbells Leucothoe
LEAVES: Alternate, simple, elliptic to oval, 1/2
to 2 1/2″ long, 1/2 to 1 1/4″ wide, acute
to short acuminate, cuneate to rounded,
shallowly and obscurely crenate-serrate,
rich green, pubescent; petiole—short,
pubescent.

Leucothoe racemosa, (lū-koth′ō-ē ra-se-
mō′sá), Sweetbells Leucothoe, is a
rather handsome deciduous to tardily
deciduous shrub growing 4 to 6′(12′)
high and wide. It tends to sucker, producing a thicket effect. The bright green,
1 to 2 1/2″ long, 1/2 to 1 1/4″ wide, shal-
low-toothed, bright green leaves often
turn red in fall. The pretty white (some-

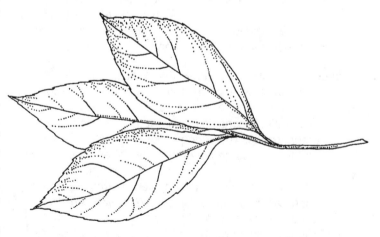

times pink), 1/3″ long, cylindric flowers are produced in 1 to 4″ long racemes during May–June (mid-April,
Athens). I have only seen a few plants but feel, as a native shrub, it has great landscape possibilities.
Grows in moist to wet areas throughout the native range and exists primarily as an understory shrub.
Massachusetts to Florida and Louisiana. Introduced 1736. Zone 5 to 9.

Leycesteria formosa Wallich — Pheasant-eye, Himalaya Honeysuckle

FAMILY: Caprifoliaceae
LEAVES: Opposite, simple, ovate, 3 to 8″ long, 1 1/2 to 4″ wide, acuminate, cordate, entire or serrulate, deep green above, paler and pubescent below; petiole—to 1″ long.
STEM: Bloomy, purple, later shiny glabrous.

Leycesteria formosa, (lī-ses-tē′-ri-à or lī-kes-tē′-ri-à fôr-mō′sà), Pheasant-eye, forms a 3 to 5′ high, multi-caned subshrub that looks the worst for wear after a time and should be rejuvenated by late winter pruning. The deep purplish red leaf and stem colors are richest on new growth and since flowers appear on current season's growth nothing is lost by annual rejuvenation. The sessile, purple flowers occur from the axils of the leaves in 3 to 4″ long, pendulous racemes. Each flower is subtended by an ovate, claret, 1 to 1 3/4″ long, persistent bract. The purple corolla averages 3/4″ by 3/4″. The bead-like, berry fruit ripens from glossy sea-green to maroon then purple-black with all colors present in the infructescence. Provide a moist soil and partial shade. Abundant in Europe and has escaped from cultivation. Planted as a source of food for game birds, particularly pheasants. Often seen in shrub borders and to a lesser degree in herbaceous borders. 'Rosea' with pink flowers is known. Himalayas, Western China, eastern Tibet. Zone 7. A related species is *L. crocothyrsos* Airy-Shaw, Golden Pheasant-eye, with yellow flowers in whorls of 6 on arching terminal racemes to 7″ long. Plant reaches 3′ high. Himalayas, Burma. Zone 7b to 9. Neither species has been seen by this author on the East Coast. Both are available from West Coast nurseries.

Ligustrum amurense Carr. — Amur Privet
(li-gus′trum a-moor-en′sē)

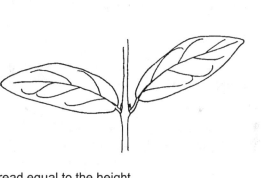

FAMILY: Oleaceae
LEAVES: Opposite, simple, elliptic to oblong, 1 to 2″ long, acute to obtuse, rounded or broad cuneate at base, ciliolate, entire, glabrous except on midrib beneath, dull green.
BUDS: Sessile, ovoid, small, with 2 or 3 pairs of exposed scales, brownish; typical for most privets.
STEM: New growth purplish, pubescent, older stems gray with some pubescence, glabrous at maturity.

SIZE: 12 to 15′ high and 2/3's that in width or with a spread equal to the height.
HARDINESS: Zone 4 to 7, I have not seen the plant in Zone 8.
HABIT: Dense, upright, multi-stemmed shrub with a weak pyramidal outline.
RATE: Fast, all privets are fast-growing shrubs.
TEXTURE: Medium-fine in leaf and in winter condition.
LEAF COLOR: Dull medium to dark green in summer; no fall coloration of any consequence.
FLOWERS: Perfect, creamy white, unpleasantly fragrant, May–June, 2 to 3 weeks, borne in axillary 1 to 2″ long panicles; each flower 4-lobed, with two stamens; flower effect is often lost because of use in hedges and flowers are cut off.
FRUIT: Berry-like rounded drupe, black, slightly gray-dusty with bloom, 1/4 to 1/3″ long, September–October, not particularly showy, persistent.
CULTURE: Transplants readily bare root or from containers, adaptable to any soil except those which are extremely wet; pH adaptable; full sun up to 1/2 shade; tolerant of smoke and grime of cities; does well in dry soils; prune after flowering.
DISEASES AND INSECTS: Anthracnose, twig-blight (affects *L. vulgare* more so than this species), leaf spots, galls, powdery mildew, root rots, privet aphid, leaf miners, scales, privet thrips, mealybugs, Japanese weevil, mites, whitefly and nematodes; in spite of this impressive array of problems, privets, in general, do well and rarely require spraying; the key is selecting the most reliable and hardy species.
LANDSCAPE VALUE: Hedging purposes, withstands pruning about as well as any plant; tends to be overused; there are many better hedging plants.
PROPAGATION: As a graduate student at the University of Massachusetts I was always attempting to propagate plants which were growing on campus. In winter I collected a quantity of *L. amurense* fruits and directly sowed one lot white removing the pericarp and cleaning the seed before sowing the second lot.

The first batch did not germinate while batch two came up like beans. Apparently there is a chemical or physical barrier to germination which resides in the fruit wall. The usual recommendation for seed is 3 months at 41°F in a moist medium. Softwood cuttings root readily, in fact, I do not know why people would bother to propagate this group of plants any other way unless they are into breeding.

ADDITIONAL NOTES: This species has disappeared from *The New Royal Horticultural Society Dictionary of Gardening* and several other modern references. In my mind, it is a distinct taxonomic unit that is (was) pervasive throughout the Midwest and East. No other species I know has the morphological characteristics to correctly umbrella *L. amurense* as a variety or cultivar.

NATIVE HABITAT: Northern China. Introduced 1860.

RELATED SPECIES:

Ligustrum × ibolium Coe, (li-gus′trum ī-bō′li-um), Ibolium Privet, is a cross between *L. ovalifolium* and *L. obtusifolium*. It is more handsome than *L. amurense* for the foliage is a glossy dark green. Foliage is semi-evergreen to deciduous and ultimate landscape size ranges between 8 to 12′. Similar to *L. ovalifolium* but with pubescent stems and leaf undersides. Actually a rather handsome privet seldom available in commerce. 'Variegatum' with soft cream margined leaves is known. Originated in Connecticut about 1910. Zone 4b to 7(8).

Ligustrum obtusifolium Sieb. & Zucc. — Border Privet

LEAVES: Opposite, simple, elliptic to oblong or oblong-obovate, 1 to 2″ long, 1/3 to 1″ wide, acute or obtuse, cuneate or broad-cuneate, entire, medium to dark green and glabrous above, pubescent beneath or only on midrib.

STEM: Green when young, possibly with a slight purplish tinge, pubescent; older stems gray, somewhat pubescent.

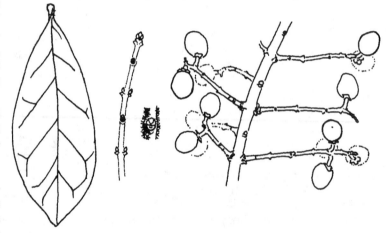

Ligustrum obtusifolium, (li-gus′trum ob-tö-si-fō′li-um), Border Privet, grows 10 to 12′ tall with a spread of 12 to 15′. Usually a multi-stemmed shrub of broad horizontal outline, broadest at the top, much branched and twiggy with wide-spreading branches. The foliage is medium to dark green in summer, sometimes turning russet to purplish in fall. Flowers are white, unpleasantly fragrant, early to mid-June and later, borne in 3/4 to 1 1/2″ long nodding panicles, usually numerous on short axillary branches. Fruit is a black to blue-black (dark gray), slightly bloomy, 1/4″ long, berry-like drupe which ripens in September and persists. Probably the best growth habit of the *Ligustrum* species and makes a good screen, background or hedge plant. The variety *regelianum* (Koehne) Rehd. is low (4 to 5′) with horizontally spreading branches and leaves regularly spaced in a flat plane (distichously) to give this plant a unique appearance. Extensively used for highway plantings, works well in mass, especially on banks and other large areas. Its leaves and stems are more pilose than the species. The species and variety are my favorite privets for northern climates. They rarely appear in southern gardens. 'Constitution' is a compact, dense form, 6 to 8′ high and 8 to 10′ wide in 10 years, leaves slightly twisted and smaller than normal, 1 to 1 1/4″ long by 1/3″ wide, hardy to –20°F, occurred as a chance seedling at the University of Tennessee, Knoxville. Japan. Introduced 1860. Zone 4 to 7.

Ligustrum ovalifolium Hassk. — California Privet

LEAVES: Opposite, simple, evergreen, semi-evergreen to deciduous, 1 to 2 1/2″ long, elliptic-ovate to elliptic-oblong, acute, broad-cuneate, entire, lustrous dark green above, yellowish green below, glabrous; petiole—1/6″ long.

STEM: Glabrous.

Ligustrum ovalifolium, (li-gus′trum ō-val-i-fō′li-um), California Privet, is a large, vigorous shrub forming a dense thicket of erect stems 10 to 15′ high. It varies from deciduous to semi-evergreen (evergreen) depending on the severity of the climate. In Zone 7b, the plant was evergreen to semi-evergreen every year except when temperatures dropped to -3°F. This was over a 10 year period. The dull white, heavy scented flowers are produced in 2 to 4″ long and wide, crowded, stiff, erect, terminal panicles during June–July. The fruits are globose, shining black. Actually, this is a handsome privet and in moderate climates makes a fine screen or hedge. It is hardy at the Arnold Arboretum and deserves at least a Zone 5 designation. Severely injured at Orono, ME, Zone 4. Like all privets, it thrives with neglect. 'Argenteum' has leaves that are bordered with creamy white. 'Aureum' has only a green spot in the center, being bordered with golden yellow. It will revert to the type and several plants I have seen in collections were more green than yellow. Used extensively in English cities and it is common to see gold, green and mixed combinations in large hedge plantings. Extremely tough, durable plant. Other cultivars include: 'Albo-marginatum', 'Globosum', 'Nanum', 'Lemon and Lime', 'Multiflorum', 'Tricolor', and 'Variegatum'. Japan. Cultivated 1847. Zone 5 to 7(8).

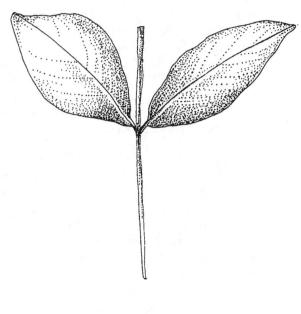

Ligustrum japonicum Thunb. — Japanese Privet
(li-gus′trum jà-pon′i-kum)

LEAVES: Opposite, simple, evergreen, broad-ovate to ovate-oblong, 1 1/2 to 4″ long, 3/4 to 2″ wide, obtusely short acuminate or acute to obtusish, usually rounded at base, entire, 4 to 5 pairs of indistinct veins raised below, margin and midrib often reddish, lustrous dark green, almost black-green, leathery, glabrous; petiole—1/4″ long.

BUDS: Imbricate, more or less 4-sided, 1/8 to 1/4″ long or less, brownish, glabrous.

STEM: Moderate, squarish, glabrous, green near apex finally gray-brown, profusely dotted with large, raised, light gray lenticels, nodes distinctly flattened; pith—green, solid.

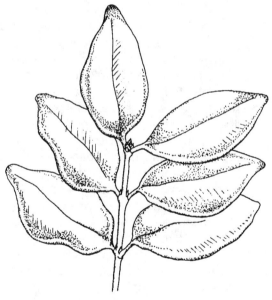

SIZE: 6 to 12′ high, 6 to 8′(12′) wide; may grow 15 to 18′ high and wide.

HARDINESS: Zone 7 to 10; in laboratory freeze tests was about 15°F more cold hardy than *L. lucidum*.

HABIT: Dense evergreen shrub of upright habit; can be grown as a small tree; frequently disfigured by pruning shears and assumes the geometric shape of a green meatball.

RATE: Medium.

TEXTURE: Medium.

BARK: Relatively smooth, gray, covered with large lenticels.

LEAF COLOR: Lustrous dark green.

FLOWERS: Perfect, creamy white, fragrant, borne in 2 to 6″ high and wide, relatively tightly branched, terminal, pyramidal panicles in mid to late May (Athens); odor is typically privet and is offensive to many people; flowers are effective for a long time; corolla tube is two times the length of the calyx; in *L. lucidum* corolla length and calyx length are the same.

FRUIT: Flat black with degrees of wax (bloom), 1/4″ diameter oval-rounded drupe, maturing in September–October and often persisting through winter; have not observed great fruit set on the species in

Georgia, possibly because of heavy pruning; planted 'Davidson Hardy', 'Nobilis' and 'Recurvifolium' in my evaluation plots; all set abundant fruits in fall 1997; all are dull black with slight grayish bloom.

CULTURE: Container-grown and easily transplanted; adaptable to varied soils; quite salt tolerant; sun or shade; withstands heavy pruning and is often fashioned into topiary subjects; probably the only soils this species will not grow in are those that are permanently wet.

DISEASES AND INSECTS: None serious, actually thrives with neglect.

LANDSCAPE VALUE: A favorite landscape plant in the South; has been used for everything imaginable: single specimen, foundations, screens, hedges, topiary, containers; very handsome when limbed up; almost has a sculptural quality about it.

CULTIVARS:

'Davidson Hardy'—Listed under *L. lucidum* in last edition but definitely a *L. japonicum* derivative; described as more cold hardy than typical (to -15°F); discovered on the Davidson College campus, Davidson, NC; larger and coarser than 'Nobilis' and 'Recurvifolium' and the leaves are flat dark green rather than lustrous; in side-by-side evaluations at the University of Georgia evaluation plots, this one pales by comparison; possibly for colder climates.

'Gold Spot'—Golden yellow blotch in center of leaf, green margin.

'Gold Tip'—New foliage is tipped with golden yellow until leaves mature; could be the same as 'Howard'.

'Green Meatball'—Compact, rounded form named by J.C. Raulston Arboretum, derived from seed collected by Dr. Raulston on the 1985 Korean Expedition, the globe-shaped habit and slightly smaller leaves than 'Recurvifolium' are distinguishing characteristics.

'Howard' ('Frazieri')—New leaves yellow turning green with maturity, usually some color present even late in the growing season that gives it away; plant is somewhat two-toned since emerging leaves are yellow, previous season's leaves green; not for the faint-of-heart.

'Jack Frost'—Leaves with irregular thin cream-white margins; 6 to 12' high by 6 to 8' wide.

'Korea Dwarf'—Collected by U.S. National Arboretum expedition in South Korea in 1985; team discovered a population of genetically dwarf plants on Taehuksen Island off the south coast; foliage and growth rate are 1/3 to 1/2 the species; Raulston believes it may have possibilities in the green meatball market; as I understand the taxonomy, this is the same as 'Green Meatball'.

'Nanum'—Dense compact form with closely spaced, smaller leaves.

'Nobilis'—More cold hardy form; upright habit with large lustrous dark green foliage; although largely indifferent about the Japanese Privets this form looks superior because of the above attributes; also has grown slightly faster than 'Recurvifolium' in Georgia tests.

'Recurvifolium'—A slightly smaller leaved form with wavy leaf margin, leaves twisted at tip; perhaps more open than the species in growth habit; hardier than the typical species but the exact taxonomic status is unknown; lustrous dark green leaf is more undulating than 'Nobilis'; plant actually grows slower than 'Nobilis' and is more compact.

'Rotundifolium' ('Coriaceum')—Called Curlyleaf Privet; distinctly upright in habit, exceedingly stiff, 4 to 6' high (usually less), leaves crowded (appear whorled), 1 to 2 1/2" long, almost as wide, broadly oval or rounded, blunt or notched at apex, lustrous dark green, thick and leathery; flowers are white in 2 to 3" long pyramidal panicles; fruits black, globose, 1/4" wide; introduced by Fortune from Japanese gardens in 1860; some references have described it as a piece of living sculpture; I cannot print my impression; defoliated at -3°F, less hardy than species.

'Silver Star'—Deep green center with gray-green mottling and creamy-silver edges; slow-growing, compact, erect habit, probably 6 to 8' high, 4 to 6' wide.

'Suwanee River'—Leathery, somewhat twisted, lustrous dark green leaves, compact habit, relatively slow-growing to 3 to 5'; may be a hybrid between *L. j.* 'Rotundifolium' and *L. lucidum*; have seen 8 to 10' established plants in a garden in Dearing, GA, definitely not compact growing.

'Texanum'—Somewhat ambiguous from a taxonomic standpoint, sometimes listed as *Ligustrum texanum*; leaves are large, glossy dark green, compact upright-growing to 10'; often offered by southwestern and California nurseries.

'Texanum Aureomarginata'—Deep green centers are bordered with yellow; new foliage in full sun has bright yellow variegation that fades to green as leaves mature and are shaded by later growth.

'Variegatum'—Leaves margined and blotched with creamy white.

PROPAGATION: Cuttings root readily, 3000 ppm KIBA, peat:perlite, 6 to 8 weeks, 80 to 90% rooting; seeds can be planted in fall and will germinate the following spring.

NATIVE HABITAT: Japan, Korea. Introduced 1845.

RELATED SPECIES:

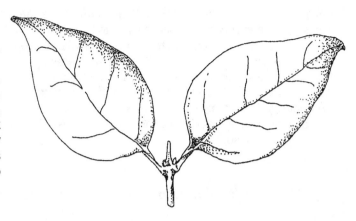

Ligustrum lucidum Ait. f. — Waxleaf,
    Glossy, or Chinese Privet
LEAVES: Opposite, simple, evergreen,
    ovate to ovate-lanceolate, 3 to 6″ long,
    1 to 2 1/2″ wide, acuminate or acute,
    broad-cuneate, entire, glossy dark
    green, with 6 to 8 pairs of veins usually
    distinct above and below, veinlets
    often impressed below; petiole—1/2 to
    3/4″ long.
STEM: Glabrous.

Ligustrum lucidum, (li-gus′trum lū′si-dum), Waxleaf Privet, is thoroughly confused with *L.
    japonicum* but need not be. In short, *L. lucidum* is larger (20 to 25′) and more loose in
    outline, the leaves are larger, not as lustrous dark green, have an opaque rim around
    the margin, and have 6 to 8 pairs of veins often sunken on the underside whereas the
    4 to 6 pairs of veins of *L. japonicum* are raised. Hold the leaves of the two species up
    to light (sky is suitable), if solid green than leaf belongs to *L. japonicum*, if veins are
    translucent then it is *L. lucidum*. In addition, the flower and fruit panicles are larger (5
    to 8″ long and wide), the 1/3 to 1/2″ long, oblong fruit is a dull blue-black and it flowers
    about 2 to 3 weeks later than Japanese Privet. Both species are common characters
    in southern landscapes. *Ligustrum lucidum* grows as tall as 40 to 50′ feet and
    becomes quite open in the process. 'Excelsum Superbum' is a fine creamy yellow
    margined form that is a strong grower; have seen at Kew Gardens and was reasonably
    impressed. 'Tricolor' ('Variegatus') has young leaves with an irregular broad border
    turning white with maturity, supposedly a handsome form, a tree 35′ high has been
    reported. Many cultivars have been selected over the millennia but few are offered
    through everyday commerce. *Ligustrum lucidum* is as tolerant to soil conditions as *L.
    japonicum* and both can be expected to do well under a variety of conditions.
    Temperatures dropped to -3°F in Athens during the 1983–84 winter and *L. lucidum*
    was severely injured or killed while *L. japonicum* survived. Native to China, Korea,
    Japan. Introduced 1794. Zone (7)8 to 10.

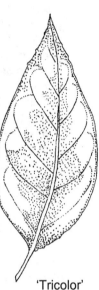

'Tricolor'

Ligustrum sinense Lour. — Chinese Privet

LEAVES: Opposite, simple, evergreen to semi-evergreen
    (deciduous in cold climates), elliptic to elliptic-oblong, 1
    to 3″ long, 1/2 to 1″ broad, acute to obtuse, broad
    cuneate, entire, dull dark green above, pubescent on
    midrib below; petiole—1/8″ long.
STEM: Pubescent with gray-yellow coloration.

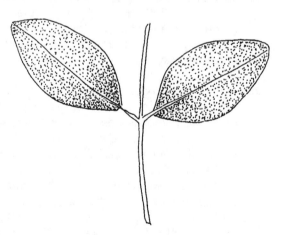

Ligustrum sinense, (li-gus′trum sī-nen′sē), Chinese Privet,
    is considered by the great British plantsman, W.J.
    Bean, the best and most ornamental of deciduous
    privets. I challenge that contention and would rank it as
    a noxious weed, especially in the southern states. In addition, the flowers are not better than those of *L.
    amurense*, *L. obtusifolium*, and others. In the southern states, it has escaped and is found about
    everywhere that birds fly. It has a tenacious constitution that allows it to thrive in concrete crevices, in back
    alleys, and flood plains along rivers. It thrives in heavy shade and full sun and forms impenetrable thickets.
    The species grows 10 to 15′(20′) high and like most privets can be fashioned into innumerable forms. The
    species is not available in commerce but 'Variegatum' is offered. This cultivar has leaves that are bordered
    gray to creamy white. In cold weather the leaves loose the pronounced variegation pattern and turn more
    or less uniform sickly yellowish to grayish green. May revert to the species and odd branches need to be
    removed. The cultivar grows about 6 to 8′ high and wide under typical landscape conditions, however,

have seen 15′ high plants of virtual tree stature. It is reasonably manageable but does flower and fruit. The seeds when they germinate give rise to the green form (species). There are apparently two variegated forms: one creamy-yellowish green; the other with a true white variegation pattern. The variegated form is used extensively throughout the South. 'Pendulum' with arching branches is described. Mr. Don Shadow discovered and is growing a selection, 'Green Cascade', with gracefully arching branches. 'Wimbei' ('Wimbish' by some) is an upright somewhat columnar grower with closely spaced nodes and exceedingly dark green 1/4″ long leaves. Grew 8′ high at J.C. Raulston Arboretum and many years past saw a plant that large at Gene Cline's, Canton, GA. Worthwhile for fooling your friends. China. Introduced 1852. Zone (6)7 south.

Ligustrum × vicaryi Rehd. — Golden Vicary Privet or Golden Privet

Ligustrum × vicaryi, (li-gus′trum vi-kâr′ē-ī), Golden Vicary Privet or Golden Privet, goes under many names in the trade. Result of a cross between *L. ovalifolium* 'Aureum' and *L. vulgare*. The habit is somewhat vase-shaped (oval-rounded) and the leaves are golden yellow the entire growing season especially if the plant is used in a sunny location. I do not find this shrub palatable but nurserymen claim they cannot grow enough of it. To each his own! If one must have golden foliage this plant is probably as good as any. Can grow 10 to 12′ high so should be afforded adequate garden space. If grown in the shade the foliage turns a sickly yellow-green (more green than yellow) and the only medicine which cures this malady is full sun. In the heat of Zone 7 and 8, even in full sun, some color is lost especially on leaves in the interior of the canopy. Reports from the Minnesota Landscape Arboretum indicate that Vicary is not hardy with them, however, they have a form called the 'Storzinger Strain' which looks similar but does not winter kill as bad. I would guess this strain has significant *L. vulgare* blood based on leaf characteristics. Also from Minnesota is 'Hillside' which is a quite cold hardy yellow foliage strain. Interestingly, seedlings of Vicaryi show the yellow foliage condition. This could open the way for better selections. Golden Vicary originated in the garden of Vicary Gibbs, Middlesex, England, before 1920. Vicaryi is rated Zone 5 to 8 and 'Storzinger Strain' Zone 4 to 9.

Ligustrum vulgare L. — European or Common Privet

LEAVES: Opposite, simple, oblong-ovate to lanceolate, 1 to 2 1/2″ long, 1/4 to 5/8″ wide, obtuse to acute, entire, glabrous, dark green; petiole—1/8 to 2/3″ long.
STEM: Young branches green and minutely pubescent, finally glabrous, gray.

Ligustrum vulgare, (li-gus′trum vul-gā′rē), European or Common Privet, is a stout, much branched shrub with irregularly spreading branches growing 12 to 15′ high with a similar spread. The foliage is a distinct dark green in summer; flowers are white, of heavy, objectionable odor, mid-June, borne in dense, terminal, 1 to 3″ long panicles; the fruit is lustrous black, 1/3″ long, berry-like drupe which ripens in September and persists through March and later of the following year. This used to be the favored privet species but has lost some of its appeal and perhaps should be entirely omitted because of the better species. The anthracnose twig blight (*Glomerella cingulata*) which causes drying out of the leaves, blighting of stems and development of cankers is serious on this species. Cultivars include:
'Cheyenne'—A hardy form but still not capable of sustaining itself at the Minnesota Landscape Arboretum; grown from seed collected in Yugoslavia by E. Anderson; introduced by Cheyenne Field Station, U.S.D.A.; holds leaves late, often into December.
'Densiflorum'—Upright form with dense habit; maintaining this, if unpruned, for at least 20 years.
var. *italicum*—Holds the leaves longer than any variety, found in the southern range of the species.
'Lodense'—Low, dense, compact form; 22-year-old plant was only 4 1/2′ tall; susceptible to a blight for which there is no cure, holds leaves late, existed on Illinois campus for a number of years.
'Pyramidale'—Excellent hedge plant, somewhat pyramidal in habit.
Other cultivars with green, white, and yellow fruits as well as variegated foliage are known, probably 20 or more cultivars. Native to Europe, northern Africa, naturalized in eastern North America. Zone (4)5 to 7. Cappiello, University of Maine, reported some winter injury to the 6 accessions tested at Orono.

Lindera benzoin (L.) Bl. — Spicebush
(lin-der′à ben′zō-in)

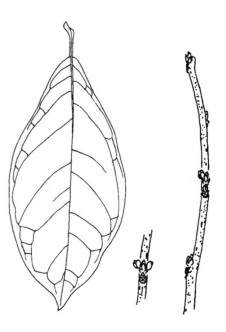

FAMILY: Lauraceae

LEAVES: Alternate, simple, oblong-obovate, 3 to 5″ long, 1 to 2 1/2″ wide, acute or short acuminate, cuneate at base, entire, light green above, pale beneath, margins ciliate; petiole—1/4 to 1/2″ long.

BUDS: Small, superposed, upper collaterally arranged producing green, ovoid, stalked flower buds, vegetative buds with 3 scales, end bud lacking.

STEM: Rounded, slender, green or olive-brown with pale lenticels; pith—large, round, white, continuous; all parts of the plant are aromatic when broken.

SIZE: 6 to 12′ high with a similar spread; national champion is 20′ by 20′ in Jefferson National Forest, VA.

HARDINESS: Zone 4 to 9.

HABIT: Usually rounded shrub in outline, somewhat loose and open in the wild; dense, full, and broad-rounded in full sun.

RATE: Slow to medium.

TEXTURE: Medium in all seasons.

LEAF COLOR: Light green in summer changing to yellow in fall, often excellent yellow to golden yellow.

FLOWERS: Dioecious, yellow, 1/5″ diameter, early to mid-April before the leaves, in axillary clusters, not overwhelming but attractive; will open about mid-March in Athens, GA.

FRUIT: Oval drupe, 1/3 to 1/2″ long, bright scarlet, September, seldom seen since it is showy only after the leaves fall and is borne only on pistillate plants, nevertheless, very ornamental.

CULTURE: Difficult to transplant because of coarsely fibrous root system and somewhat slow to reestablish; does best in moist, well-drained soils, full sun or 1/2 shade, does adequately in dry soils; have grown a plant in our garden and it appears worn out by late summer, requires more moisture and shade than I am able to supply.

DISEASES AND INSECTS: None serious.

LANDSCAPE VALUE: Good shrub for the border or naturalizing; I have seen it growing in deep woods where it is often rather thin and open; excellent for moist soil areas and semi-shady spots; in full sun it makes a splendid plant in flower and fall color; a harbinger of spring.

CULTIVARS:

'Green Gold'—Exceptionally showy large yellow flowers, male clone, introduced by Tom Clark, Fern Valley Farms.

'Rubra' (f. *rubra*)—A brick-red, male-flowered selection from Hopkinton, R.I.; the winter buds are a darker, red-brown color.

'Xanthocarpa' (f. *xanthocarpa*)—An orange-yellow fruited form that was discovered as a spontaneous plant at the Arnold Arboretum in 1967 by Alfred Fordham, the former propagator.

PROPAGATION: Seed should be stratified for 30 days at 77°F, followed by 90 days in peat at 34 to 41°F or 105 days in sand at 41°F. Have had good success with 90 days cold moist stratification. Cuttings of half-ripe (greenwood) shoots will root but percentages are usually not high. I have had poor success and have had only an occasional cutting root.

ADDITIONAL NOTES: The fruits are lovely and remind one of the fruits of *Cornus mas*. They are a brilliant scarlet and singularly eye-catching in the autumn landscape on close inspection.

NATIVE HABITAT: Maine to Ontario and Kansas, south to Florida and Texas. Introduced 1863.

RELATED SPECIES:

Lindera obtusiloba Bl. — Japanese Spicebush

LEAVES: Alternate, simple, variable in shape (see below), but distinctly 3-veined, 2 1/2 to 5″ long, 1 1/4 to 4″ wide, lustrous dark green and glabrous above, pale and pubescent on the veins below; petiole—1/2 to 1″ long, pubescent.

Lindera obtusiloba, (lin-der′à ob-tö-si-lō′bà), Japanese Spicebush, is a beautiful, large, multi-stemmed shrub or small tree that ranges from 10 to 20′ in height. Fourteen-year-old plants average 8 to 10′ in height and

slightly less in width. The rather leathery, lustrous dark green leaves are variable in shape ranging from 3-lobed, left-hand mitten, right hand mitten, to no lobes. In October the leaves turn brilliant golden yellow, color uniformly and remain effective for two weeks or longer. Surprisingly, it colors well in partial shade. I know of no other woody shrub that rivals it for intensity of yellow coloration. The flowers are similar to those of *L. benzoin* and appear 1 to 2 weeks earlier. The fruits are globose, 1/4″ wide, changing from red to shining black. The buds are plump, angular-ovoid and reddish in color, with one per node. Seeds will germinate after a 3 month cold period. July cuttings rooted 55 percent when treated with 8000 ppm IBA and placed under mist. This is a fine plant and is worthy of wider use. Japan, Korea, China. Introduced 1880. Hardy in Zone 6 to 7, although laboratory hardiness tests indicate it being hardy to −17°F (Zone 5).

OTHER MINOR RELATED SPECIES: There are 80 species of *Lindera*, some evergreen, others tardily deciduous, and others like *L. benzoin* cleanly and early deciduous. Their praises have been touted by plantsmen such as J.C. Raulston. Many species appear adaptable in the Southeast and Woodlanders, Aiken, SC and the Atlanta Botanical Garden have notable collections. *Lindera angustifolia*; *L. aggregata*; *L. chienii* (green-yellow flowers January 24, 1997, Atlanta Botanical Garden); *L. erythrocarpa*; *L. fragrans* Bl.; *L. glauca* (Sieb. & Zucc.) Bl.; *L. megaphylla* Hemsl.; *L. praecox* (Sieb. & Zucc.) Bl.; *L. reflexa*; *L. strychnifolia* (Sieb. & Zucc.) Vilm., Japanese Evergreen Spicebush; *L. subcoriacea*, Bog Spicebush; and *L. umbellata* Thunb. are commercially available or present in southeastern collections. My observations indicate *L. erythrocarpa* with outstanding yellow fall color; *L. glauca* (considered same as *L. angustifolia*) with narrow elliptic leaves, whitish beneath, orange, red, and purple in fall, holding late; and *L. strychnifolia* with prominently 3-veined, 2″ long by 1″ wide, ovate evergreen leaves are worth considering for the garden. For the best analysis of the unusual *Lindera* taxa see Raulston, *Proc. Southern Nurs. Assoc. Res. Conf.* 38:359–362 (1993). The J.C. Raulston Arboretum held 12 taxa in 1993.

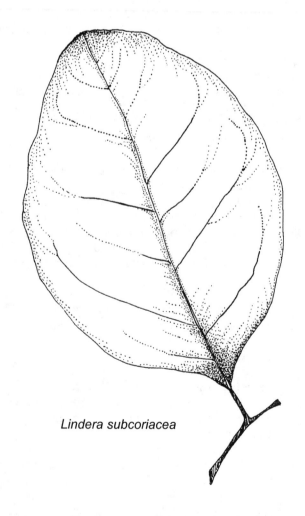

Lindera subcoriacea

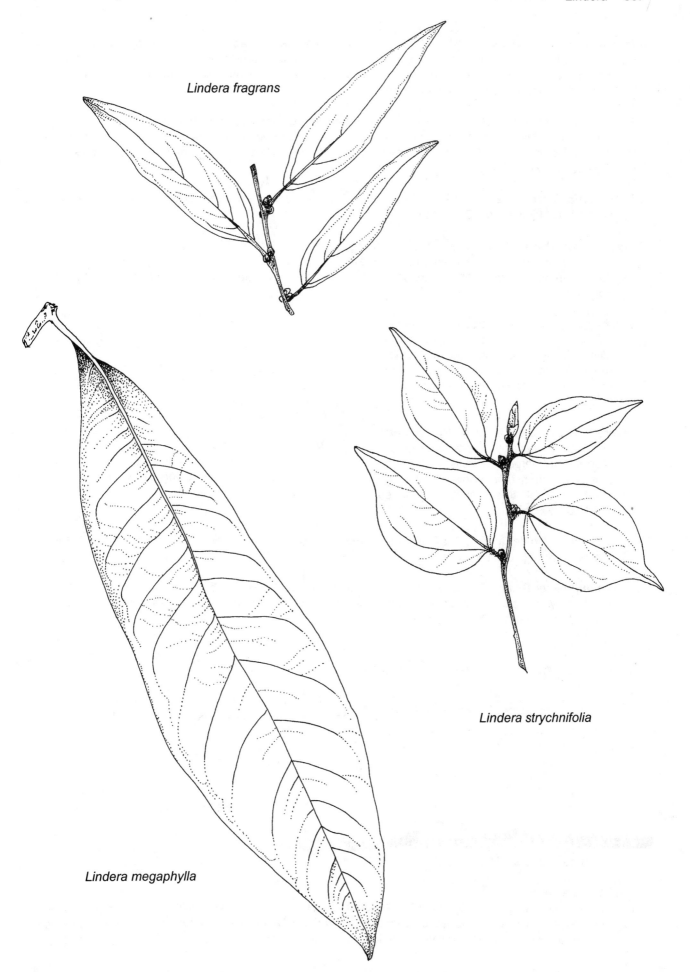

Lindera fragrans

Lindera megaphylla

Lindera strychnifolia

Lindera aggregata, (lin-der′à a-gre-gä′tà), ovate to orbicular, heart-shaped, leathery evergreen leaves, 1 to 2 1/2″ long, dark green above, gray-white below, small yellow flowers in umbellose clusters in March–April, 1/4 to 1/3″ long, rounded black fruit in October–November, large shrub or small tree to 15′, best in full sun, grayish green bark, Zone 7.

Lindera angustifolia W.C. Cheng, (lin-der′à an-gus-ti-fõ′li-à), Oriental Spicebush, is a 6 to 8′ high shrub with 3 to 4″ long, glossy green leaves, bluish green to silvery below, yellow flowers, black fruits, yellow, orange, to red fall color, foliage dies off gray-brown and persists into winter, site in partial shade and moist, well-drained soil, Zone 6 to 8.

Lindera chienii, (lin-der′à chi-ē′nē-ĭ), produces greenish yellow flowers in late January (Atlanta), yellow fall color, to 15′ high. China. Zone 7 to 8.

Lindera erythrocarpa, (lin-der′à er-i-thrõ′kär-pà), has developed into an 18′ by 20′ shrub in the University's Botanic Garden. The dark green, oblong leaves, 2 1/2 to 5″ long, turn stunning yellow in fall, yellow flowers appear in March–April, fruits are red, tolerates dryness better than *L. benzoin* in Zone 7b. China. Zone 6 to 8.

Lindera glauca (Sieb. & Zucc.) Bl., (lin-der′à glâ′kà), Grayblue Spicebush, has narrow-elliptic leaves, glaucous below, orange, red, purple in autumn. Similar to *L. angustifolia*? Japan, China, Korea, Taiwan. Zone 6 to 8.

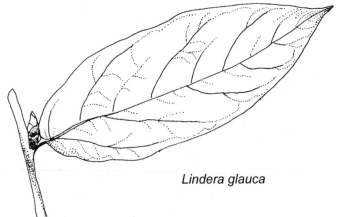

Lindera glauca

Lindera praecox (Sieb. & Zucc.) Bl., (lin-der′à prē′koks), produces yellow-green flowers in March–April, large red fruits, light green leaves that turn rich yellow in fall, large shrub or small tree. Japan. Introduced 1891. Zone 6 to 7.

Lindera reflexa, (lin-der′à rē-fleks′à), has handsome blue-green leaves, yellow flowers and red fruits, this is most similar to *L. benzoin*. China. Zone 7.

Lindera umbellata Thunb., (lin-der′à um-bel-lā′tà), bears thin textured, 3 to 6″ long leaves, glaucous below, good yellow fall color, yellow flowers; semi-erect medium sized shrub. Japan, Korea, central and western China. Introduced 1892. Zone 6 to 7.

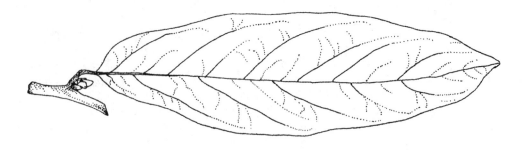

Liquidambar styraciflua L. — American Sweetgum
(lik-wid-am′bär stī-ra-se-flö′à)

FAMILY: Hamamelidaceae

LEAVES: Alternate, simple, 4 to 7 1/2″ wide and about as high, 5- to 7-lobed with oblong-triangular, acuminate, star-shaped, finely serrate lobes, cordate at base, dark green and lustrous above, paler beneath except axillary tufts in axils of principal veins; petiole—2 1/2 to 4″ long.

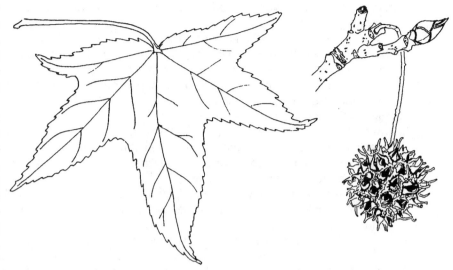

BUDS: Terminal imbricate, 6- to 8-scaled, ovate to conical, 1/4 to 1/2″ long, laterals smaller, reddish green-brown, sometimes fragrant when crushed, divergent.

STEM: Slender to stout, light to dark reddish or yellowish brown, aromatic, rounded or somewhat angled, frequently developing corky wings during the second year, on occasion extremely winged; pith—star-shaped, solid, white or brownish.

SIZE: 60 to 75′ in height with a spread of 2/3's to equal the height; can reach 80 to 120′ in the wild; national champion is 96′ by 66′ in Craven County, NC.

HARDINESS: Zone 5 to 9; consistently injured by cold at the Morton Arboretum, Lisle, IL.

HABIT: Decidedly pyramidal when young, of very neat outline; often with an oblong to rounded crown at maturity.

RATE: Medium to fast, 2 to 3′ per year in moist soil; 1 to 2′ per year in dry soil; 20.3′ high and 14.5′ wide after 10 years.

TEXTURE: Medium in leaf; medium in winter.

BARK: Grayish brown, deeply furrowed into narrow, somewhat rounded ridges.

LEAF COLOR: Very beautiful, glossy deep green above in summer, changing to rich yellow-purple-red tones in the fall; there is great variability in fall colors; I have seen sweetgums which were totally disappointing and others which should be propagated vegetatively for their fall color alone; holds leaves very late in fall; on young (juvenile) trees have seen leaves persist into February in Athens area.

FLOWERS: Monoecious, female, on a slender stalk terminated by a 1/2″ diameter globose head consisting of 2-beaked ovaries subtended by minute scales; the ovaries coalescing at maturity to form a solid structure; male flowers in a terminal upright 3 to 4″ long panicle; neither are showy; late April–May as the leaves are emerging and expanding.

FRUIT: Syncarp of dehiscent capsules, 1 to 1 1/2″ diameter, persisting into winter, the seeds are brownish and winged; the fruit can be quite messy; good identification feature; fruits fall over an extended period from November, December to April and beyond; definitely a maintenance liability as a street or general lawn tree; in our garden several large sweetgums drop prodigious quantities of fruits that carpet the ground; I have slipped, fallen, and taken offense; not the neatest lawn tree.

CULTURE: Transplant balled-and-burlapped in spring into deep, moist, slightly acid soil; full sun; the root system is fleshy and consequently is not greatly fibrous and takes a while to reestablish; have seen newly transplanted trees, even small trees, literally sit still for a year or so until root systems developed, leaves may be somewhat smaller the first growing season after winter or early spring transplanting; in the wild the tree occurs as a bottomland species on rich, moist, alluvial soils but is found on a great variety of sites; prune during the winter; not a good plant for city plantings and small areas where roots are limited in their development; avoid polluted areas; averaged 1′10″ per year over a 10 year period in Kansas tests, most vigorous on moist sites.

DISEASES AND INSECTS: Bleeding necrosis, leaf spots, sweetgum webworm, caterpillars, cottony-cushion scale, sweetgum scale, walnut scale; iron chlorosis can be a problem on high pH soils.

LANDSCAPE VALUE: Lawn, park, or street tree but needs large area for root development; used extensively on West Coast; there was tremendous injury during the winter of 1976–77 when temperatures reached −20°F; a tree in my Illinois garden did not leaf out until June; apparently the normal buds were killed and latent or adventitious buds developed from stems that had not been killed back; the tree recovered; trees that were newly planted in fall were essentially killed by the cold.

CULTIVARS:

'Albomarginata'—White edged leaves.

'Aurea'—Leaves blotched and striped yellow, the same as 'Variegata'.

'Aurora'—Bright yellow variegated foliage, yellow, orange and red fall color on a small pyramidal tree, growing in my Georgia test plots, fall color has been yellow-orange at best, not as good as the native trees on the periphery of the Horticulture farm.

'Brotzman #1'—A cold hardy, thick corky bark selection by Brotzman Nursery, Inc., Madison, OH.

'Brotzman #2'—A cold hardy, vigorous, good fall coloring form.

Burgundy™—Leaves turn wine-red to deep purple red in fall, may persist into winter, a selection by Saratoga Horticultural Foundation.

'Carnival'—Similar to 'Oconee' with excellent fall color.

Cherokee™ ('Ward')—Hardy, almost fruitless sweetgum tested for over 30 years by Earl Cully, Jacksonville, IL, vigorous grower, produces corky bark at a young age, fall color ranges from deep burgundy to red with some yellow, has withstood -28°F without injury, medium pyramidal habit in youth, more rounded with maturity.

'Corky'—Strong upright narrow pyramidal form, 34' by 18' in 25 years, corky-winged branches, good rose red fall color, original tree came to Longwood Gardens' Arboretum in 1965 from Kingsville Nursery, Maryland.

Festival™—Supposedly more narrow and upright than the species to 60'; fall color has been yellow in the Midwest; in West may color yellow, peach, pink, orange and red, Saratoga introduction.

Gold Dust® ('Goduzam')—Gold and green variegated leaf form, pyramidal in youth, oval-rounded with maturity, 60' by 35', supposedly quite winter hardy, Lake County introduction, suspect it is the same as 'Variegata'.

'Gold Star'—Wedges of gold variegation on the foliage.

'Golden Treasure'—Golden yellow margined leaves on a small tree framework, slow-growing, have seen in England where it was vivid; fall color described as dark burgundy in the deeper areas, orange to pink in the lighter zones; possibly cook in the heat of an United States summer.

'Gumball'—I like this rather strange, small, diminutive form that is supposedly shaped like a gumball machine; in actuality it is a multi-stemmed shrub rounded at the top and gradually tapering to a rather wide base, leaves are normal size and I have not observed flowers or fruits; fall color is not particularly good; in Cincinnati and Boston I have seen it severely frozen back by temperatures of -6°F; it did recover from the injury; I estimate that anything below 0°F will result in some injury; I have rooted it from softwood cuttings collected in late August, 8000 ppm IBA-quick dip, mist, at a 100% rate; introduced by Hiram Stubblefield, McMinnville, TN.

'Kia'—Orange-red turning deep purplish in fall, pyramidal habit; supposedly narrow, spire-like outline.

'Lane Roberts'—An English introduction with rich black crimson-red fall color; have not seen it in the United States.

'Levis'—Branches show no corky bark and leaves color brilliantly in autumn.

'Lollipop'—Globose growth habit.

'Moonbeam'—Green and cream in summer, turning pink and magenta in autumn, Duncan and Davies, New Zealand.

'Moraine'—More uniform and faster growing than the species; upright-oval habit with a medium branch texture and brilliant red fall color; I have seen this cultivar at the Ohio Agricultural Research and Development Shade Tree Evaluation Plots, Wooster, OH, and was impressed by the excellent glossy dark green foliage, as well as the good habit; has proven to be the most cold hardy cultivar surviving temperatures in the range of -20° to -25°F.

'Oconee'—A plant has grown on the Georgia campus for years, the habit is akin to 'Gumball' but more rounded and perhaps not as large at maturity; I estimate 8 to 10'(15') and 6 to 8' wide; makes a multi-stemmed tight shrub; fall color is superior to 'Gumball' and turns deep reddish purple in fall and holds for 3 to 4 weeks; hardiness is unknown but suspect more cold hardy than 'Gumball'; always fun to look back on one's estimates, this plant is now 15 to 18' high, 12' wide and has fruited; fall color over the years has been consistently excellent, rich reddish purple in mid-November.

Palo Alto™—A more uniform growth habit than the species and the leaves turn orange-red in fall, Saratoga introduction.

'Pendula'—Upright-columnar form with distinctly pendulous branches.

'Plattsburg'—Pyramidal form, with deeply furrowed bark.

'Rotundiloba'—In the 1983 edition I had listed this form as 'Obtusiloba' which is incorrect; my knowledge about this tree was scanty in that edition but have seen enough to believe it could have an impact on tree planting in Zone 6 to 9; a large tree on NC State campus is more narrow pyramidal than the typical species type; leaves are lustrous dark green and turn, at least based on observations in 1987 and 1988, rich reddish purple fall color; on a previous visit to NC State, I remembered yellow fall color; Raulston reported color varies from year-to-year with a range of yellow to dark burgundy; the

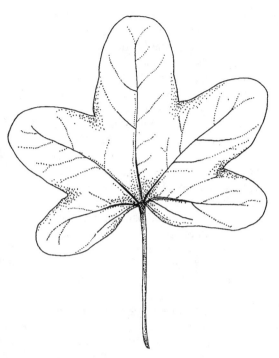

plant sets no fruit which is sufficient reason to grow it; probably hardy to -10°F; I have seen a branch reversion to the typical leaf shape and this should be kept in mind when growing the tree; was discovered in the wild in North Carolina in 1930; since the 1990 edition this cultivar has become more popular in commerce; trees are more open than typical aged seedlings under nursery production; one of my students, Kari Whitley, in fall 1996 brought me a xerox of a fruiting branch of 'Rotundiloba', the leaves were round lobed like the drawing but fruit was present; like any chimeral plant, from whence it came, it can return; no injury after -24°F in the Louisville area, true for Gold Dust®, 'Moraine', and 'Worplesdon'; Burns, *Proc. Intl. Plant Prop. Soc.* 39:320–324 (1989), discusses evaluation and propagation of 'Rotundiloba'; bench grafting in February–early March yielded 95% success; also chip-budding in mid-June into late August produced good results; cuttings rooted in low percentages, were difficult to overwinter and inferior to grafted and budded plants in growth form and vigor.

Shadow Columnar Form—An unbelievably columnar-conical form, appeared fruitless initially, but has now produced a few fruits, will be a great addition to the palette of columnar trees, I have only seen photographs of the tree and it may prove a plant of significant commercial worth, introduced by the great Don Shadow, who appears in this *Manual* more than the author.

'Starlight'—Variegated form with white speckles over the entire leaf surface, variegation does not appear to burn in sunlight and full sun, found as a chance seedling in the Raleigh, NC area, may be the same as 'Frosty', a selection found and named by Tony Avent.

'Variegata'—Leaves spotted, blotched and streaked with yellow; an unusual and interesting variegated type that displays reasonable hardiness; the same as 'Aurea' and Gold Dust®.

'Worplesdon'—Unique narrow lobed leaves and apricot-orange fall color.

PROPAGATION: Seeds exhibit only a shallow dormancy, but germination rate is considerably increased by cold, moist stratification at 41°F for 15 to 90 days; leafy cuttings taken with a heel can be rooted under mist in summer; have tried to root a variegated seedling clone but without success; cultivars are normally budded or grafted.

ADDITIONAL NOTES: Wood is used for plywood, furniture, cabinet making, and other uses. The name Sweetgum is derived from the sap which has a sweet taste and gummy consistency. Sweetgum, in the South, is a primary invader of abandoned fields as well as flood plain areas. It makes its best growth on the rich, moist, alluvial clay and loam soils of river bottoms. The species has tremendous potential for landscape use and selections from the southern states need to be made for superior habit and fall color. The variation in fall color is truly astounding and on the Georgia campus there are trees that remain green into November and seldom color well while others literally appear to be on fire. A good fruitless form would be welcome; perhaps 'Rotundiloba' is the answer to the problem.

NATIVE HABITAT: Connecticut, south to New York to Florida, southern Ohio, Indiana, Illinois, Missouri to Texas and Mexico. Introduced 1681.

RELATED SPECIES:

Liquidambar acalycina H.T. Chang, (lik-wid-am′bär ā-kal-i-sī′nȧ), sports rich reddish maroon new growth that matures to dark green and turns burgundy in autumn. The 3-lobed leaves remind of *L. formosana*. The largest plants I have observed are growing at the Arnold Arboretum. Growth habit is similar to *L. styraciflua*. Displays excellent vigor and has been cold hardy to -10°F. China. Zone 6 to 7.

Liquidambar formosana Hance. — Formosan Sweetgum

LEAVES: Alternate, simple, 3-lobed, middle triangular, laterals spreading, 2 to 4″(5″) high, 3 to 6″ wide, apex long acuminate, base truncate to cordate, sharply serrate from apex to base, glabrous and lustrous dark green above, medium green and pubescent on veins below; petiole—2 to 3″ long, glabrous.

BUDS: Imbricate, dark brown, 3/8 to 5/8″ long, scales covered with silky brown pubescence; flower buds larger than vegetative, elongated conical and tapering at base.

STEM: Stout, terete, dark gray-brown, prominently lenticelled, glabrous; stem when bruised emits a slight sweet-spicy odor; pith—greenish, solid.

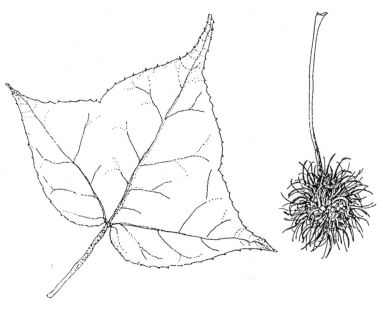

Liquidambar formosana, (lik-wid-am′bär fôr-mō-sā′nȧ), Formosan Sweetgum, will always place second to our native *L. styraciflua* in landscape use. It is a handsome species with distinct 3-lobed, lustrous dark green leaves that turn an excellent yellow in fall. Tree colors late, usually November 20 or so into early December. The tree becomes quite large with time and one stately specimen on the University of Georgia campus is fully 50′ tall and wide. A report from Mississippi State indicated that superior types were being selected for brilliant red fall coloration. A variety *monticola* Rehd. & Wils. is described as having plum purple new foliage, finally dull green, and changing to crimson in the autumn; whether this is a true variety has been questioned. Listed as Monticola Group and characterized by glabrous, large, 3-lobed, rich fall coloring leaves and greater cold hardiness. The species flowers 2 to 3 weeks ahead of *L. styraciflua* and the beaks of the capsules are not as stiff and rigid. Interestingly, the species (perhaps all sweetgums) is self-sterile and the lone tree on the Georgia campus has never produced a stray seedling. Apparently its earlier flowering date prevents any potential cross-pollination with *L. styraciflua*. Have seen hybrids listed for sale by Louisiana Nursery. The fruits do form and fall like the native species but are not as objectionable because of their less woody nature. 'Afterglow' appears in the California literature and is described as having lavender-purple new growth and rose-red fall color, the habit is broad asymmetrical. Native to Formosa, southern and central China from the coast to Szechuan and Hupeh, south to Kwantung province, and also occurs in Indochina. Introduced 1884. Zone 7 to 9. Wilson introduced the variety *monticola* from W. Hupeh in 1907. Zone 6 to 9.

Liriodendron tulipifera L. — Tuliptree, also called Tulip Magnolia, Tulip Poplar, Yellow Poplar, and Whitewood
(lir-i-ō-den′dron tū-li-pif′ēr-ȧ)

FAMILY: Magnoliaceae

LEAVES: Alternate, simple, 3 to 8″ across and as long, broad truncate apex, with a short acuminate lobe on each side and usually 3 to 4, acute or short-acuminate lobes on each side near the rounded or truncate base, bright green above, paler beneath; petiole—2 to 4″ long.

BUDS: Valvate; terminal—1/2″ long, greenish to reddish brown, covered with a bloom, white dotted, entire bud resembling a duck's bill; laterals—similar but considerably smaller.

STEM: Slender to stout, lustrous greenish to red-brown, sometimes bloomy, aromatic when broken but with intensely bitter taste, distinct stipular scars surrounding stem at nodes; pith—chambered.

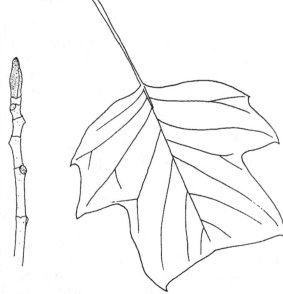

SIZE: 70 to 90′ in height with a spread of 35 to 50′; can grow to 150′ and greater, 198′ and 200′ high trees were recorded.

HARDINESS: Zone 4 to 9, is being grown in Minnesota Landscape Arboretum but will never attain the size there that it does further south; it has withstood temperatures as low as -25°F without injury.

HABIT: In open-grown situations somewhat pyramidal in youth maturing to oval-rounded with several large sinuous branches constituting the framework; in the wild often free of branches for 70 to 80 percent of its height with only a narrow conical ovoid canopy at the upper reaches.

RATE: Fast, 15 to 20′ over a 6 to 8 year period; rapid-growing especially when provided ample fertilizer and moisture; grows too fast for some field nursery producers, becomes so large (height and caliper) that field digging becomes cumbersome.

TEXTURE: Medium in leaf and winter.

BARK: Grayish brown, more gray than brown, furrowed into close, interlacing, rounded to flattened ridges which are separated by grayish crevices; easily recognizable in the deciduous forest community.

LEAF COLOR: Leaves emerge folded in flag-like outline, mature to bright green in summer, changing to golden yellow or yellow in fall, often superb during October and into early November; I have never given the species sufficient credit for fall coloration; truly an aristocratic tree.

FLOWERS: Perfect, with 6 greenish yellow petals in 2 rows, 3 reflexed sepals, interior of the corolla an orangish color; 2 to 3″ high, 1 1/2 to 2 1/2″ wide; somewhat reminiscent of the tulip flower; although described as delicately scented, I cannot sense much (any) odor; May to early June (often flowers by late April in Athens and continues for an extended period); solitary; may be slow to flower from seed although 6- to 10-year-old trees have flowered in the Athens area; flowers are often borne high in the tree and are missed by the uninitiated; a beautiful flower.

FRUIT: Cone-like aggregate of samaras, 2 to 3″ long, 3/4″ wide, eventually turning brown in October and persisting through winter, good identification feature, individual samaras are shed from the aggregate by November in Athens, fruit dispersal continues through winter.

CULTURE: Transplant balled-and-burlapped in spring into deep, moist, well-drained loam; the root system is fleshy and often poorly branched; full sun; pH adaptable although prefers a slightly acid soil; prune in winter; has been used for street tree plantings in narrow tree lawns and usually develops leaf scorch or simply dies after a time; one tree grew 1′8″ per year over a 10 year period in KS tests, but 2 of 3 trees died because of drought and sunscald.

DISEASES AND INSECTS: Cankers, leaf spots, powdery mildews, root and stem rot, *Verticillium* wilt, leaf yellowing (physiological disorder), aphid, scale, and tuliptree spot gall; aphids are a real problem; the insect secretes liberal quantities of "honeydew" and the leaves of the plants are often coated with this substance which is then overrun with the sooty mold fungus, which causes a blackening and unsightliness of the leaves; the leaf yellowing problem can be a headache with newly planted as well as established trees which do not receive adequate water; the leaves abscise prematurely and create a mess that requires constant attention.

LANDSCAPE VALUE: Not a tree for the small residential property or streets; should be restricted to large areas and this type of situation only; a very large and magnificent plant when fully grown and developed; somewhat weak-wooded, although variation occurs among individuals, and may break up in ice and severe storms; as a specimen on a large property it has great beauty and in fall can be spectacular; perhaps most handsome in large groupings or groves where trees develop a spire-like habit; on November 2, 1996, Bonnie and I traveled to Highlands, NC and on the ascent from Dilliard, GA on Highway 106, at the Sky Valley turn off was the most beautiful yellow patchwork-mottle of tuliptrees, most trees had dropped their leaves, oaks were brownish or russet red, the yellow of the tuliptrees simply spellbinding.

CULTIVARS:

'Ardis'—Compact-growing, smaller leaf form that grew in the small garden of the late Professor J.C. McDaniel, Urbana, IL; I am not sure why this was omitted from the last edition, might be the tuliptree of choice for smaller landscapes; short internodes and leaves about 1/3 the size of the species.

'Arnold'—Is actually the same as 'Fastigiatum', put into commerce by Monrovia Nursery and named after the Arnold Arboretum, where the scion wood was obtained.

'Aureomarginatum'—Leaves margined with yellow or greenish yellow; quite handsome and is the most common and best of the variegated types; Majestic Beauty™ by Monrovia is included here; gigantic, 70 to 80′ high specimen at Stourhead, England.

'Compactum'—Dwarf form, leaves about 1/2 the size of the species; the term possibly includes any form with reduced growth characteristics, Professor J.C. McDaniel had the plant described above ('Ardis') in his Urbana, IL garden; it was a rather cute diminutive form that could have commercial possibilities where a reduced version of the species is required.

'Fastigiatum'—Narrow, with upright lateral branches that almost parallel the center leader; the more I see this form the more I question why it is not being grown commercially; there are magnificent old specimens at the Arnold Arboretum and I have seen it used in several European gardens; grows 50 to 60′ high by 15 to 20′(25′) wide; a handsome, useful form; larger plants become fat at the base and lose some of the fastigiate character.

'Florida Strain'—Fast-growing, rounded lobes, large flowers at a young age, from Louisiana Nursery.

'Glen Gold'—Soft yellowish foliage, selection from Australia.

'Integrifolium' (f. *integrifolium* Kirch.)—Rather curious form, the lateral or lower lobes missing resulting in an almost rectangular leaf, have seen on occasion in gardens, not common.

'Mediopictum' ('Aureopictum')—Leaves with yellow blotch in middle, the margin typical bright green, rather handsome but have only seen in botanical gardens; the exact name is unknown and the two listed have been used in the literature and on botanical garden labels to describe what appears to be the same plant.

'Ramapoo' ('Ramapo'?)—Almost lobeless with rounded leaves, possibly f. *integrifolium* form.

'Tortuosum'—Supposedly with contorted stems but as I have seen it the leaves are distinctly tortuous, undulated and, rather innocuous; there is a form called 'Contortum' which resembles the 'Tortuosum' I have seen; 'Crispum' might be synonymous with both(?). Santamour and McArdle, *J. Arboriculture* 10(11):309– 312 (1984), report that 'Contortum' is the correct name for this form.

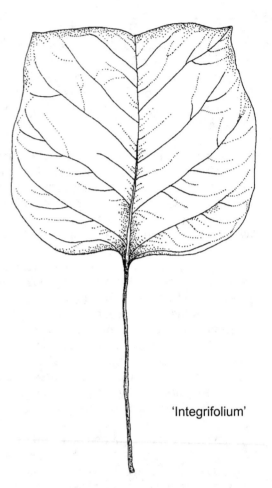

'Integrifolium'

Head-Lee Nursery, Seneca, SC told me about a variegated leaf form like *Cercis canadensis* 'Silver Cloud', i.e., leaves splashed and speckled with cream variegation.

PROPAGATION: Seeds should be stratified in bags of peat moss or sand for 60 to 90 days at 41°F; percentage of sound seed is usually quite low. Cuttings, July collected, made with basal cut 1/2″ below node, rooted 52%; have rooted cuttings from stump sprouts with success. Cultivars must be grafted.

ADDITIONAL NOTES: Wood is used for furniture and other products; one of our tallest native eastern American deciduous species and can grow to 190′. The showy flowers depend on honeybees for cross-pollination and the honey is supposedly of excellent quality. I was amazed at the percentage of great specimens in Europe. In fact, they appear as well-suited there as in their homeland. In Joyce Kilmer National Forest, near Robbinsville, NC, reside gigantic virgin tuliptrees. Visitors can hike around and under these venerable denizens of the southern Appalachian forest. Truly inspiring, humbling and also a reflection of what might have been had not the southern forests been decimated by the timber industries. My understanding is that the loggers stood in awe of the magnificent trees in Joyce Kilmer and with tears in their eyes were simply unable to cut these gentle giants.

NATIVE HABITAT: Massachusetts to Wisconsin, south to Florida and Mississippi. Cultivated 1663.

RELATED SPECIES:

Liriodendron chinense (Hemsl.) Sarg., (lir-i-ō-den′dron chi-nen′sē), Chinese Tuliptree, although listed in most references as smaller in habit (50′), the plants I have observed were terrifically fast-growing, and trees over 80′ high are recorded. One plant in our evaluation tests grew 25′ high and 15′ wide in seven years from a 3.2′ high seedling. The leaves are larger and more deeply cut (sinused) above the lower lobes, i.e., akin to a narrow waist. The rich green leaves turn brilliant yellow in Georgia. The buds are larger than those of *L. tulipifera*. Growing at Arnold Arboretum. A hybrid between *L. chinense* and *L. tulipifera* is known. I have observed plants at the Arnold Arboretum. Essentially intermediate in characteristics. China, Indochina. Introduced 1901. Estimate Zone 6 to 9 adaptability.

Lithocarpus henryi (Seem.) Rehd. & Wils. — Henry Tanbark Oak

FAMILY: Fagaceae

LEAVES: Alternate, simple, evergreen, narrow-oblong, 4 to 8″(10″) long, 1 1/2 to 2″ wide, acute, cuneate, entire, leathery, lustrous medium to dark green above, lighter green below, with 10 to 14 vein pairs, glabrous; petiole—1″ long.

Lithocarpus henryi, (lith-ō-kär′pus hen′ri-ī), Henry Tanbark Oak, is an oval to rounded evergreen tree with good heat and drought tolerance. Plants have been growing in the Southeast for years and appear adaptable. In winter, leaves turn yellow-green and appear to need fertilization. Fruits (acorns) are closely set on a 4 to 8″ long spike that occurs at the end of the shoot. Each acorn is globose, flattened at the top, 3/4″ wide and covered with a 1/8″ deep, shallow cap (involucre). A few Georgia nurserymen have offered this but acceptance has been slow. In youth the tree is somewhat open and no one is quite sure what it is or where to use it. In general the *Lithocarpus* differ from *Quercus* by erect spike flowers borne at the end of the shoots and spikes often with male and female flowers on the same structure. Central China. Introduced 1901. Zone 6b to 8(9).

RELATED SPECIES:

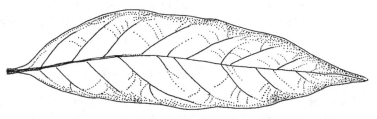

Lithocarpus edulis (Mak.) Nakai, (lith-ō-kär′pus ed′ū-lis), Japanese Tanbark Oak, tends toward a shrubby nature although I have seen small 20 to 25′ trees in Savannah, GA. Leaves are 3 1/2 to 6″ long, 1 to 2 1/4″ wide, entire, blunt at apex, hard leathery texture, lustrous and darker green than above with a slight silvery sheen below, 9 to 11 vein pairs, petiole—1/3 to 1″ long. Leaves are darker green and do not discolor to the degree of *L. henryi*. Japan. Introduced about 1842. Zone 7 to 8. Survived -3°F in Athens.

Have also grown **L. densiflorus** (Hook. & Arn.) Rehd. in my Georgia garden. Makes a handsome dense lustrous dark evergreen shrub/tree. Leaves are toothed. Flowered in late October on Georgia campus. Sapsuckers and canker killed the tree. National Champion is 92′ by 84′ in Six Rivers National Forest, CA. Southwestern Oregon and California. Zone 7 to 9.

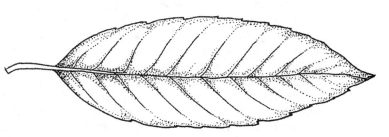

Lithocarpus densiflorus

ADDITIONAL NOTES: The *Lithocarpus* species are largely absent in North American landscapes. Possibly the best specimen of *L. henryi* grew at the U.S. National Arboretum. The Arnold Arboretum nursed a small specimen in the Chinese walk area. Lack of cold hardiness, sapsucker injury and general unfamiliarity insure minimal landscape use. About 300 species are described. The fruits take two years to mature and the acorn wall is hard shelled and enclosed in a calyx cupule, the scales of which are arranged in unique patterns.

Lonicera alpigena L. — Alps Honeysuckle

FAMILY: Caprifoliaceae

LEAVES: Opposite, simple, elliptic to oblong-ovate or oblong, 2 to 4″ long, 1 to 2″ wide, acuminate, rounded to cuneate, entire, dark green and glabrous above, lighter beneath and glabrous at maturity; petiole—1/2″ long.

Lonicera alpigena, (lon-iss′ēr-à al-pi-jē′nà), Alps Honeysuckle, grows 4 to 8′ high, developing an erect, much branched habit. Like many honeysuckles, the winter habit is less than appealing and the only appropriate way to alleviate the situation is to hide the plant in the shrub border. Leaves are dark green and somewhat lustrous in summer; fall color is of no consequence. Flowers are yellow or greenish yellow, tinged dull red or brown-red; effective in May (North); borne in axillary peduncled pairs; each flower about 1/2″ long. The fruits are red, up to 1/2″ long, cherry-like, often united for a portion of their length. This is a rather distinct species because of the long flower stalks, large leaves and large fruits. The cultivar 'Nana' is a low, slow-growing form; a 63-year-old plant being only 3′ high. This makes a rather handsome broad-mounded dark green foliaged form. The leaves are large (up to 4″ long) and slightly crinkled. The leaves are pubescent on the lower surface, particularly the veins. The gray-brown bark shows a slight exfoliating characteristic. Native to the mountains of central and southern Europe. Introduced 1600. Zone 5 to 7.

Lonicera alseuosmoides Gräbn.

LEAVES: Opposite, simple, evergreen, narrow oblong, 1 1/2 to 2 1/2″ long, 3/4″ wide, acuminate, cuneate, entire with recurved margins, lustrous dark green above, lower surface with appressed pubescence.

Lonicera alseuosmoides, (lon-iss′ĕr-à al-sŭs-moi′dēz), is a handsome evergreen vine for covering structures, trellises, and fences. The foliage is the principal asset. Flowers appear in short broad panicles, 1/2″ long, funnelform, yellow and glabrous outside, purple and pubescent inside. Fruit is globose, black-purple, and bloomy. Recently acquired a plant from Dr. Raulston and Ted Stephens, Nurseries Caroliniana and I admire the beautiful foliage. Like all new plants, testing and consumer education will determine success. This species is relegated to the minor vine category. Western China. Introduced 1908. Zone 6 to 8.

Lonicera × *bella* Zab. — Belle Honeysuckle

Lonicera × *bella*, (lon-iss′ĕr-à bel′la), Belle Honeysuckle, is the result of crosses between *L. morrowii* and *L. tatarica*. The hybrids were first raised in the Münden Botanic Garden from seeds received from the St. Petersburg (Russia) Botanic Garden before 1889. The plants will grow 8 to 10′ high and 8 to 12′ wide. The shrub develops a dense, rounded habit with spreading, somewhat arching branches. The foliage is bluish green in summer. Flowers vary in degrees of white to pink and usually fade to yellow. They are evident in early to mid-May (North). The fruit is a red, 1/4″ diameter berry which becomes effective in late June and July often persisting into fall but does not rival *L. tatarica* for abundance or showiness. A large mass was present on the Illinois campus but offered little in the way of aesthetics. Large foliage mass at best. Several selections have been made from the seedling populations and the best include: 'Albida'—flowers initially white, fading to creamy yellow; 'Atrorosea'—dark rose with a lighter edge; 'Candida'—pure white flowers; 'Dropmore'—white flowers; and 'Rosea'—flowers deep pink. Based on my travels and reading, this species has all but disappeared from the nurseries and arboreta of the United States. Several immense specimens on the Illinois campus were the last I have seen. Zone 4 to 7.

Lonicera × *brownii* (Reg.) Carr. — Brown's Honeysuckle, Scarlet Trumpet Honeysuckle

Lonicera × *brownii*, (lon-iss′ĕr-à brow′nē-ī), Brown's Honeysuckle, Scarlet Trumpet Honeysuckle, is a group of hybrids between *L. sempervirens* and *L. hirsuta* Eaton. with the habit and general foliage characteristics of the former but somewhat hardier and with the corolla more or less two-lipped and glandular-pubescent on the outside. The typical form of the cross arose before 1853. Unfortunately, it shows the first parent's susceptibility to aphids. 'Dropmore Scarlet' was raised by F.L. Skinner, Dropmore, Manitoba. The red flowers appear in June and continue into October–November. Flowered in May in the Athens area but the flowers are more orange-red than red. Flowers are not as large as those of *L. sempervirens*. This is considered to be the hardiest vine honeysuckle in the North. 'Fuchsioides' is used occasionally in European gardens but is less vigorous than 'Dropmore Scarlet' or *L. sempervirens*. The flowers are orangish red and not as large as the two mentioned above. 'Mandarin' with dark reddish orange outside, paler yellow-orange on inside, 2 1/2 to 2 3/4″ long, heavy flowers in May–June, sporadically thereafter, non-fragrant, non-fruiting, young leaves dark coppery brown, glossy dark green when mature, stems dark purplish brown, may grow 6 to 7′ per year; hybrid of *L. tragophylla* × 'Dropmore Scarlet'; controlled cross made by Dr. Wilf Nicholls in 1989 at UBC Botanical Garden, Vancouver; introduced 1997; see *Landscape Plant News* 8(4):8 (1997). Other cultivars are reported in the literature but I have not witnessed them in cultivation. Zone (4)5 to 7.

Lonicera caerulea L. — Bearberry Honeysuckle

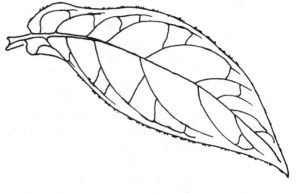

LEAVES: Opposite, simple, ovate, obovate or oblong, 1 1/2 to 3″ long, 1/4 to 1″ wide, acute to obtusish, rounded, entire, bright green, pubescent on midrib and veins below; petiole—1/8″ long, pubescent.

Lonicera caerulea, (lon-iss′ēr-á se-rū′lē-á), Bearberry Honeysuckle, is a rather dense, sturdy shrub that grows 4 to 5′ high. The yellowish white flowers give rise to bloomy bluish fruits. This is a highly variable species and occurs in the higher altitudes and latitudes of three northern continents. I grew it in the Illinois test plots and it never really proved superior to *L. tatarica*, *L. morrowii*, and *L. × bella*, which, in essence, provides reason for a strong inferiority complex. The blue fruits are interesting and var. *edulis* has sweetish edible fruits. Zone 2 to 5.

Lonicera fragrantissima Lindl. & Paxt. — Winter Honeysuckle
(lon-iss′ēr-á frā-gran-tis′i-má)

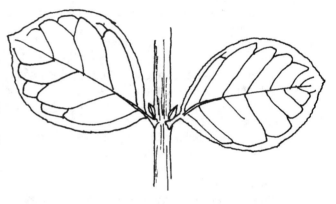

LEAVES: Opposite, simple, elliptic to broad-ovate, 1 to 3″ long, two-third's to almost as wide, acute, broad cuneate at base, setose-ciliate, dull blue-green to dark green and glabrous above, setose on the midrib; petiole—1/3″ long.

BUDS: Imbricate, sessile, with numerous 4-ranked scales, slightly pubescent.

STEM: Slender, glabrous, light, often lustrous brown; pith—white, solid or slightly excavated.

SIZE: 6 to 10′(15′) high by 6 to 10′(15′) in spread.

HARDINESS: Zone 4 to 8(9).

HABIT: Wide-spreading, irregularly rounded, deciduous shrub with tangled mass of slender recurving branches; holds foliage very late in fall and in southern states into winter.

RATE: Fast.

TEXTURE: Medium in leaf, medium-coarse in winter; this is true for most of the larger honeysuckles.

LEAF COLOR: Dull dark bluish green in summer; foliage holds late and falls green or brown; leafs out early in spring.

FLOWERS: Creamy white, tinged pink or red, 2-lipped, lemon-scented and extremely fragrant, relatively small, 1/2″ long, March–early April (Urbana, IL) for a 3 to 4 week period; opens in January, peaks in February, still flowering in mid-March (Athens), borne in axillary peduncled pairs before the leaves; not very showy but certainly among the most fragrant of woody flowering shrubs, the sweet lemon fragrance is about the first of all woody shrubs, tremendous plant for pulling one out of the winter doldrums.

FRUIT: Berry, two-ovaries fuse, 1/4 to 1/3″ diameter, dark red, late May–early June, seldom seen for it is borne under foliage.

CULTURE: The following discussion applies to the honeysuckles; transplant readily, adapted to many soils and pH levels; prefer good loamy, moist, well-drained soil; abhor extremely wet situations; full sun to partial shade; pruning should be accomplished after flowering and, in fact, when honeysuckles become overgrown the best treatment is to cut them back to the ground as they readily develop new shoots; I have given much thought to the aggressive nature of *Lonicera* species and have watched extensive understory acreage literally consumed by *L. japonica*, *L. maackii*, and *L. tatarica*; reminiscences take me to Peoria, IL, Concord, MA, Cincinnati, OH, and Athens, GA where woodlands were consumed; a point to emphasize is the tremendous shade tolerance of the above mentioned honeysuckles—much more so than horticulture literature indicates—thus permitting survival in understory habitats; I have observed an occasional stray seedling of *L. fragrantissima* but it falls in the welcome, not despised, category. These honeysuckles are extremely early to leaf and may benefit from an increased photosynthetic advantage before overstory plants emerge.

DISEASES AND INSECTS: Leaf blight, leaf spots, powdery mildews, aphids, Russian aphid (causes brooming), woolly honeysuckle sawfly, four-lined plant bug, planthopper, green house whitefly, flea beetle, looper caterpillar, long-tailed mealybug, fall webworm, a few scale species.

LANDSCAPE VALUE: Makes a good hedge, screen, mass, background; could be integrated into the shrub border; lovely for fragrance; worthwhile to force branches inside in winter; utilized in large shrub masses on the Georgia campus, effective for winter garden fragrance.

PROPAGATION: Most species show some embryo dormancy and stratification in moist media for 30 to 60 days at 41°F is recommended; some species have hard seed coats and warm followed by cold stratification is recommended. Cuttings of most species (softwood collected in June) root with ease under mist. Have rooted this species many times and discovered that one has to work to get less than 100%.

ADDITIONAL NOTES: The range and scope of *Lonicera* species supersedes 150 with numerous cultivars. A magnificent evaluation of honeysuckle apid susceptibility, cold hardiness and use was published in *J. Environ. Hort.* 15:177–182 (1997). In short, 135 taxa were evaluated in North Dakota, Manitoba or reviewed in the literature. Only three taxa, 'Dropmore Scarlet', 'Miniglobe' and 'Emerald Mound', were accorded the highest recommendation for landscape planting in Zones 2 to 5.

NATIVE HABITAT: Eastern China. Introduced 1845.

RELATED SPECIES:

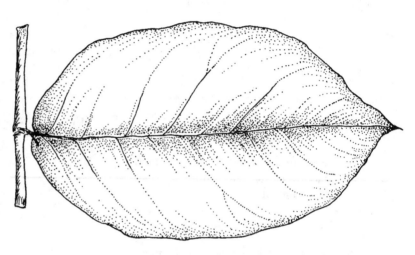

Lonicera standishii Jacq., (lon-iss'ĕr-à stan-dish'ē-ī), Standish Honeysuckle, is quite similar but not as good an ornamental. *Lonicera fragrantissima* differs by the absence of bristles on the young shoots, flower-stalks, and corolla; the leaf is shorter and the apex is not drawn out. Leaves of *L. standishii* are 2 to 4 1/2″ long, 3/4 to 2″ wide, oblong-lanceolate, acuminate, rounded with distinct pubescence below. Is listed as semi-evergreen but in South seems no more so than *L. fragrantissima*. Have seen a 9 to 10′ high plant in the Coastal Plain. China. Introduced about 1845. A hybrid between the two species, *L. × purpusii* Rehd., has the fine fragrance of the parents. 'Winter Beauty' has extremely fragrant, creamy white flowers. *Lonicera standishii* and *L. × purpusii* are growing at the Morton Arboretum, Lisle, IL. Zone 5 to 8(9) for both.

Lonicera × heckrottii Rehd. — Goldflame Honeysuckle

LEAVES: Opposite, simple, oblong or oval, 1 1/2 to 2 1/2″ long, two-third's as wide, glabrous, lustrous dark bluish green, firm, glaucous beneath, glabrous; scarcely petioled; upper leaves are fused at the base (connate) and form a disk that subtends the flower; new growth has a handsome purplish red tinge that becomes blue-green with maturity.

STEM: Purplish red and glabrous.

Lonicera × heckrottii, (lon-iss'ĕr-à hek-rot'ē-ī), often called the Everblooming or Goldflame (name used by Willis Nursery, Ottawa, KS for marketing) Honeysuckle, is a vine of unknown origin although the parentage is purported to be *L. sempervirens × L. × americana*. I would consider it the most handsome of the climbing honeysuckles. The flower buds are carmine and, as they open, the cream to yellow inside the corolla is exposed. The outside gradually changes to a pink color and the total flower effect is strikingly handsome. The slightly fragrant flowers are borne in elongated peduncled spikes, with several remote whorls; in the Dirr garden flowers are evident in March–April into summer with sporadic recurrent bloom in fall. As long as new growth occurs flowers continue to develop. Leaves are emerging in early March. Foliage is essentially evergreen to 15 to 20°F. Fruit is described as red but I have never observed a single berry; 10 to 20′ high. The actual hybrid species is something of an enigma. I see no *L. sempervirens* because of the distinct bilabiate (4 finger-like petals up, 1 down) flowers. Hold 4 fingers together and move thumb directly below 2nd and 3rd fingers. This configuration represents a *L.* × *heckrottii* flower form. Now consider the more or less even, 5-corolla lobes at the mouth of *L. sempervirens.* 'Goldflame' is considered a deeper red-purple flowered selection of this cross. My observations and instincts tell me that there is only one form (clone) of the species in cultivation. Mardi Gras™ (Flowerwood Nursery), Pink Lemonade™ (Hines Nursery), and 'Summer King' represent 'Goldflame' with more marketable names. Introduced before 1895. Zone 4 but best in Zone 5 and south (9).

Lonicera japonica Thunb. — Japanese Honeysuckle

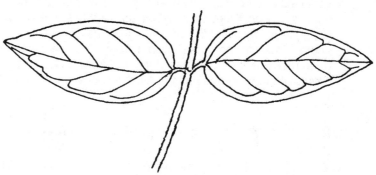

LEAVES: Opposite, simple, evergreen, semi-evergreen to deciduous, ovate to oblong-ovate, 1 1/4 to 3 1/4″ long, one half as wide, acute to short-acuminate, rounded to subcordate at base, entire, dark green to lustrous dark green, pubescent on both sides when young, later glabrate above; petiole—1/4″ long.

BUDS: Small, solitary, covered with 2 pubescent scales, superposed, sessile.

STEM: Reddish brown to light brown, covered with soft pubescence, twining; pith—excavated, eventually hollow.

Lonicera japonica, (lon-iss′ĕr-à jà-pon′i-kà), Japanese Honeysuckle, is a weedy, twining vine growing from 15 to 30′. The dark green foliage is evergreen to semi-evergreen to deciduous depending on the severity of cold. First leaves of the season often show a lobed condition. They must abscise because I cannot find them later in the growing season. Flowers are white (may be tinged pink or purple) turning yellow, fragrant; (early May in Athens) June through November, borne in peduncled pairs; usually a mass of white and yellow in full flower; fruit is a black, 1/4″ diameter berry ripening in August through October; a good, quick, ground, bank, or support cover but has escaped from cultivation and has become a noxious weed in many areas of the country. 'Aureoreticulata' is an interesting cultivar with yellow netted markings throughout the leaf, the overall effect is that of reverse chlorosis, best grown in full sun, an interesting novelty plant; 'Dart's World' is more spreading and bushy, 10″ high, 4′ wide, dark green leaves, flowers to 1 1/2″ long, exterior rose, interior white; 'Halliana' has pure white flowers which change to yellow, very fragrant, vigorous grower; 'Halliana Prolific' ('Hall's Prolific') is strong climbing to 20′ or more, profuse, strongly scented, white maturing to yellow flowers; 'Purpurea' (might be same as f. *chinensis*) is a vigorous grower with rich purple tinted dark green foliage, purple-red flowers on outside, white inside, and coral red fruit; 'Tricolor' produces pink, white, cream, yellow, and green foliage, Louisiana Nursery introduction. I am never sure whether to praise or curse this species for it has ruined many acres of native woodland understory by essentially out-competing and shading the native woodland flowers. It is vigorous to a fault and scarcely a fencerow in Georgia is free of the plant. The fragrance is quite appealing and can be sensed from the car at 65 miles per hour. A handsome and little-known taxon is forma *chinensis* (var. *repens*) that I have seen intermixed with the species in Georgia fence rows. It is slightly less vigorous, flatter growing with glabrous leaves. The flowers are more colorful being reddish purple on the outside. Stems and leaves also show the purplish red coloration. Might be a better garden plant. Japan, China, Manchuria, and Korea. Introduced 1806. Zone 4 to 9.

Lonicera korolkowii Stapf. — Blueleaf Honeysuckle

LEAVES: Opposite, simple, ovate to elliptic, 3/4 to 1 1/4″ long, 1/2 to 1″ wide, acute, cuneate to rounded, entire, pale bluish green, pubescent on both surfaces, petiole—about 1/4″ long; true *L. korolkowii* is distinct because of small leaves and glaucous blue foliage.

Lonicera korolkowii, (lon-iss′ĕr-à kôr-ōl-kōw′ē-ī), Blueleaf Honeysuckle, is a loose, open, irregular shrub with slender, spreading and arching branches growing 6 to 10′ high and as wide although one authority listed mature size between 12 and 15′ high with an equal spread. The largest true example (Barnes Foundation) I have seen was 6′ high and wide. The downy shoots and pale, sea green, pubescent leaves give the shrub a striking gray-blue hue and hence the name Blueleaf Honeysuckle. The flowers are rose-colored (pinkish), each flower about 2/3″ long (corolla), borne in peduncled pairs from the leaf axils of short lateral branchlets in May. The fruit is a bright red berry which matures in July and August. Culturally this species is more difficult to establish than other honeysuckles and should be transplanted balled-and-burlapped. This is one reason why Blueleaf Honeysuckle is seldom seen in the trade. The cultivars include 'Aurora' with moderate purplish pink flowers and a profuse flowering nature, and 'Floribunda' which supposedly is more floriferous than the species. There is a variety *zabelii* which has deeper rose-pink flowers and glabrous leaves broader than the species. This variety is often confused with the cultivar 'Zabelii' which is purported to belong to *L. tatarica*. The University of Minnesota has introduced 'Freedom' which resembles *L. korolkowii* with blue-green foliage, white with pink tinged flowers, red fruits, and freedom from the Russian aphid. 'Freedom' will grow 8′ by 6 to 8′. 'Honey Rose' is another Russian aphid resistant form from the University of Minnesota. Forms a compact shrub 6 to 8′ high, deep rose red flowers in May–June, red fruits develop in summer, foliage is rich green. Native to Soviet Central Asia, bordering parts of Afghanistan and Pakistan. Introduced 1880. Zone 4 to 7.

Lonicera maackii (Rupr.) Maxim. — Amur Honeysuckle

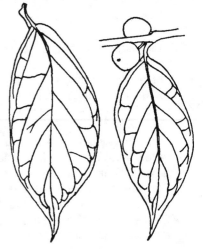

LEAVES: Opposite, simple, ovate-elliptic to ovate-lanceolate, 2 to 3″ long, 1/2 to 1 1/2″ wide, acuminate, broad-cuneate, rarely rounded at base, entire, dark green above, lighter beneath, usually pubescent only on the veins on both sides; petiole—1/8 to 1/5″ long, glandular-pubescent.

BUDS: Gray, pubescent, oblong or acute.

STEM: Grayish brown, short pubescence on current year's growth, finally glabrous; pith—brown, excavated in internodes, solid at nodes.

Lonicera maackii, (lon-iss′ēr-à mak′ē-ī), Amur Honeysuckle, is a large, upright-spreading, leggy, deciduous shrub reaching 12 to 15′ in height with a similar spread. The foliage is medium to dark green in summer and the fall color is ineffective. The flowers are white changing to yellow, 1″ long, May creeping into early June, borne in axillary peduncled pairs. The fruit is a red, 1/4″ diameter berry which ripens in October and is eaten by the birds. Variety *podocarpa* flowers in early June, Zone 4 hardiness, and is a better flowerer. 'Rem Red' is a Soil Conservation Service, U.S.D.A. introduction that grows 8 to 12′ tall, produces abundant white maturing to yellow flowers and red fruits. It is a seed-produced cultivar. In my mind, I am doubtful about how different this is from the species. Described as resistant to Honeysuckle Aphid. In the southern states, the species has escaped and the red fruits will be present into February and March. It appears that if other food is present, birds will pass over Amur Honeysuckle. The birds deposit the seeds in old shrub borders, hedges, wasteland and before one knows it, Amur Honeysuckle has taken over. Starts to leaf out in late February–early March with flowers by mid to late April in Athens. Shows amazing shade tolerance and exists as an understory plant in some woodlands. Truly a noxious weed. Manchuria and Korea. Introduced 1855–1860. Zone 3 to 8.

Lonicera maximowiczii (Rupr.) Maxim. var. *sachalinensis* F. Schmidt
(lon-iss′ēr-à max-im-ō-wix′ē-ī sa-ka-len-en′sis)

Sakhalin Honeysuckle, as my field notes say "was the most beautiful honeysuckle" in the Arnold's collection. It makes a dense, rounded to mounded, 6 to 8′ high shrub. The dark green, ovate, 1 1/2 to 3″ long, 3/4 to 1 1/2″ wide leaves may turn a golden yellow in fall. The 1 1/2″ long flowers are deep red, produced on a 1″ peduncle and the fruit is red. This is a handsome honeysuckle which is not well-known. Probably too many honeysuckles are already in commerce to allow this a toe-hold, however, for foliage effect it is superior to the run-of-the-mill offerings. Northern Japan, Sakhalin, Korea and the Ussuri region. Introduced 1917. Zone 4 to 6(7)?

Lonicera morrowii A. Gray — Morrow Honeysuckle

LEAVES: Opposite, simple, elliptic to ovate-oblong or obovate-oblong, 1 to 2 1/2″ long, 1/2 as wide, acute or obtusish and mucronulate, rounded at base, sparingly pubescent above at least when young, gray to blue-green, soft-pubescent beneath; petiole—1/12 to 1/8″ long.

BUDS: Small, somewhat puberulent, blunt.

STEM: Grayish to light brown, pubescent when young, older stems a distinct gray, hollow.

Lonicera morrowii, (lon-iss′ĕr-à môr-ōw′ē-ī), Morrow Honeysuckle, grows 6 to 8′ high and 6 to 10′ wide forming a broad, rounded, dense, tangled mound with branches and foliage to the ground. Foliage is grayish to bluish green in summer. Flowers are creamy-white changing to yellow, 3/4″ long, mid to late May, in peduncled pairs. Fruit is a blood-red, 1/4″ diameter berry ripening in July and August. Better than most honeysuckles as the foliage hugs the ground. Seldom seen in cultivation. 'Xanthocarpa' has white flowers and yellow fruits. Japan. Introduced 1975. Zone (3)4 to 6.

Lonicera nitida Wils. — Boxleaf Honeysuckle

LEAVES: Opposite, simple, evergreen, ovate to roundish, 1/4 to 5/8″ long, blunt, subcordate to broad-cuneate, entire, glossy dark green, glabrous; petiole—1/20″ long, minutely bristly.

STEM: Young shoots thin, purple, pubescent.

Lonicera nitida, (lon-iss′ĕr-à nit′i-dà), Boxleaf Honeysuckle, is often confused with *L. pileata*. Boxleaf Honeysuckle is a dense, leafy shrub that grows to 5′ and higher. Have seen 6 to 8′ high plants in Europe. European literature lists size between 10 and 12 feet. It is valued chiefly for the foliage. The creamy white, fragrant, 1/4 to 1/2″ long flowers are produced in axillary, short-stalked pairs. Based on actual smelling tests I can sense essentially no odor. The globular, bluish purple, translucent, 1/4″ diameter fruits appear in late summer. Have seen fruits on plants in Europe but never in America. Used extensively in Europe for hedges and masses; appears to tolerate more shade than many honeysuckles. It is quite difficult to ascertain the exact nature of *L. nitida* for the plants in cultivation in the United States do not adhere to the species description. A key difference between this and *L. pileata* is the more rounded, smaller leaf. Several cultivars have been introduced and may, in fact, represent the species in cultivation.

'Baggesen's Gold'—A form with golden leaves and mounded almost haystack habit, color fades but not completely with time; have seen 4 to 6′ high plants in England, better color under cool conditions.

'Elegant'—This form grows to about 3′ with horizontal or rather attractive slightly pendulous branches, leaves mat green, ovate to roundish ovate, 1/2″ long.

'Ernest Wilson'—Lateral branches drooping; leaves glossy bright green, mostly lanceolate-ovate or triangular ovate, less than 1/2″ long; have not noticed it in flower or fruit; probably offered as *L. nitida* in trade.

'Fertilis'—Branches arching or erect, to 8′ high, leaves dark green and slightly more than 1/2″ long; flowers and fruits well.

'Graciosa'—A dense, spreading shrub with small leaves, seedling of 'Elegant'.

'Hokenkrummer'—Groundcover-like habit, arching horizontal branches.

'Maigrun' ('Maigruen')—A new ground cover or low-growing hedge brought from France (where it is one of the top ground covers and is replacing cotoneaster, which is prone to fire blight) by the Saratoga Horticultural Research Foundation in San Martin, CA; it has small, round, boxwood-like leaves, like boxwood it makes an outstanding formal landscape element when clipped, unlike boxwood it also looks great unmanicured with its graceful, fountain-like growth habit that blends well into informal designs, plants have been found immune to major pests and diseases, grows in sun or shade, tolerant of drought and many soil types.

'Yunnan'—Similar to 'Ernest Wilson' but differs by virtue of more erect lateral branches and slightly larger leaves not arranged in two ranks; also flowers more freely; has been distributed as *L. pileata* var. *yunnanensis*; have seen as *L. yunnanensis* in the South which is apparently this clone or 'Ernest Wilson'.

   Other cultivars exist and are more important in European gardening. 'Silver Beauty' with cream margined leaves is being circulated in southeastern commerce. Performance in my garden is less than satisfactory. In fact many of these and the *L. pileata* types are promoted on a cyclical basis but none withstand the test of garden time.

ADDITIONAL NOTES: I first came in contact with the shrub on The Ohio State University campus. I collected cuttings, rooted them easily, and attempted to grow the plant in Urbana, IL. The –20°F winter effectively removed it from my landscape. Plants may display semi-evergreen tendencies in Zone 7 and 8. Native of western Szechuan and Yunnan, China. Introduced by Wilson in 1908. Zone 7 to 9.

Lonicera pileata Oliv. — Privet Honeysuckle

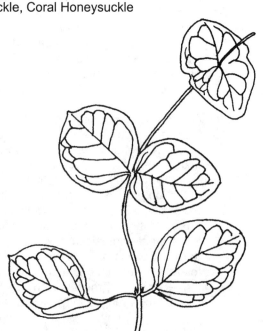

LEAVES: Opposite, simple, evergreen or semi-evergreen, ovate to oblong-lanceolate, 1/2 to 1 1/4″ long, 1/3 to 1/2″ wide, obtusish, cuneate, entire, lustrous dark green above, pale green and sparingly pubescent on midrib beneath or glabrous, sparingly ciliate; petiole—short.
STEM: Young shoots purple, thickly pubescent.

Lonicera pileata, (lon-iss′ĕr-à pī-lē-ā′tà), Privet Honeysuckle, is closely allied to *L. nitida* but differs in the larger, more elongated, lustrous dark green leaves. Yellowish white, 1/2″ long flowers occur in pairs during May and are not very effective. The translucent, rounded, amethyst fruit is about 1/5 to 1/4″ wide and handsome, but, again, is not common on United States plants. The habit is different being more spreading with horizontal branches that tend to build up on each other forming a rather graceful elegant 2 to 3′ high ground cover shrub. In Europe the plant is outstanding and appears to reach its aesthetic potential. In the eastern and southern United States, it struggles for identity. The habit is never as full or graceful and the leaves, especially in the heat of the South, do not have the lustrous dark green character. Ideally, locate in well-drained soil in shade or partial shade. At –3°F in Athens, plants were defoliated but developed new growth. *Lonicera pileata* is about 5 to 10°F more cold hardy than *L. nitida*. 'Moss Green' is low-spreading, compact, not vigorous, with bright green leaves; 'Royal Carpet' is 18″ high, 5′ wide, straight-spreading branches, glossy green leaves, purple fruit. The Georgia campus horticulturist, Dave Berle, and I were discussing how terrific this species could be if it performed to the level of the press clippings. Unfortunately, numerous plantings have been trialed on campus with none persisting. China. Introduced 1900. Zone 6 to 8.

Lonicera sempervirens L. — Trumpet Honeysuckle, Coral Honeysuckle
(lon-iss′ĕr-à sem-pĕr-vī′renz)

LEAVES: Opposite, simple, elliptic or ovate to oblong, 1 to 3″ long, 3/4 to 2″ wide, obtuse or acutish, usually cuneate, dark bluish green above, glaucous beneath and sometimes pubescent, 1 or 2 pairs below the inflorescence connate into an oblong disk, rounded or mucronate at ends; petiole—1/4″ long.
STEM: Twining, straw-colored, glabrous; pith—excavated.

SIZE: 10 to 20′ and higher depending on structure.
HARDINESS: Zone (3)4 to 9.
HABIT: Twining vine, not as vigorous or rampant as *L. japonica*, *Akebia*, and *Wisteria*.
RATE: Fast.
TEXTURE: Medium, looks ragged during the summer months in the Southeast but for 3 months from April to June is exceptionally handsome.
LEAF COLOR: New growth reddish purple or tinged some shade thereof turning bluish green at maturity; one of the earliest woody vines (plants) to leaf out, starting in late

February–early March in Athens; the earliest leaves of the season often linear and strap-like and nothing like the later leaves, significant variation in leaf shapes over the course of the growing season; essentially deciduous but in Zone 8 to 9 will show semi-evergreen tendency in mild winters.

FLOWERS: Perfect, non-fragrant, variable in color from orange-red to red on the outside of the tubular corolla, generally yellow to yellow-orange inside, 1 1/2 to 2″ long, produced in a 3- to 4-whorled spike, each whorl with 4 to 6 flowers, borne at the end of the shoot, never axillary as in *L. japonica*, the corolla mouth with 4 upper lobes of equal proportions, the lower almost the same, resulting in a more or less 5-lobed corolla, not two-lipped as in the majority of honeysuckles; flowers on shoots produced from last year's wood but also sporadically on new growth of the season; exceptional full flower effect in April in Athens, especially when grown in full sun on a structure.

FRUIT: Red, 1/4″ diameter rounded berry, September–November, that at times is produced in abundance, other times sparingly or not at all; have seen heavy fruit set on isolated specimens so assume plant is self fertile.

CULTURE: Transplant as a small container-grown plant into moist well-drained, acid or near neutral soil, full sun but also tolerates dense shade, however, does not flower as profusely in the latter, provide support otherwise plant forms tangles on the ground, prune after flowering to shape and control, if pruned in late winter most of the flowers will be removed.

DISEASES AND INSECTS: None serious although a leaf spot has occurred on occasion; in recent years have observed heavy defoliation particularly on 'Sulphurea'; perhaps was excessively kind to this species in previous editions as aphids are common and a *Pseudomonas syringae* disease can defoliate the species and particularly 'Sulphurea' by mid-summer; have noticed that foliage looks better in North than South; in fact early September observations of plants in Maine brought this to clear focus.

LANDSCAPE VALUE: Great twining vine for the imaginative gardener, flowers and foliage (when right) are superb, should be placed on a trellis, picket fence, old shrub framework; I planted it next to a fence and trained it to grow along the top where it has formed a billowy cloud of foliage and flowers, also have permitted it to scramble along the ground almost ground cover fashion, where it looks slightly lumpy; one of our most colorful native vines; great for hummingbirds.

CULTIVARS:

'Alabama Scarlet'—Darker red (scarlet) than 'Magnifica', perpetual-flowering, listed by Fairweather Nursery, Greenwich, NJ.

'Blanche Sandman'–Orange-red reblooming form, originally offered by Holbrook Farm and Nursery, NC, good leaf disease resistance.

'Bonneau'—Red, tubular flowers like the species, cuttings collected from a plant in South Carolina, lower leaf surface is silvery, flowers spring through fall, Dodd and Dodd Nursery introduction.

'Cedar Lane'—Excellent, profuse, remontant flowering form with deep vermillion red flowers, is less prone to aphids and leaf disease (drop) than the species but is still susceptible, from Cedar Lane Farms, Madison, GA.

'John Clayton'—Compact growing, repeat flowering, yellow-flowered form, good red fruit production, found in Abington Church, VA, offered by Woodlanders, possibly more leaf spot resistant than 'Sulphurea'.

'Leo'—Reddish on inside and outside, although plants in full sun at J.C. Raulston Arboretum produced orange-red flowers; remontant flowering pattern; more leaf disease resistant, however, as I witnessed the plant in August, about one-half the leaves remained.

'Magnifica'—Bright red, 2″ long flowers, interior yellowish; based on my observations of southeastern native populations 'Magnifica' could be f. *magnifica* since large bright red-flowered forms are reasonably common; literature says one thing, observation indicates another; many large growers produce this cultivar but flowers are orange-red on the outside, yellowish on the interior; tends to repeat flower all summer if provided adequate moisture and fertilizer; certainly a worthy selection, just does not correlate to the literature description.

'Major Wheeler'—Scarlet-crimson corolla, ever-blooming characteristic.

'Navasota'—Two-lipped, reddish pink and white flowers are produced in abundance in spring and sporadically through summer, foliage blue-green above with bluish white undersides, dark purple stems, possibly a hybrid of *L. sempervirens* and *L. periclymenum*, discovered in the Texas town of Navasota, introduced by the J.C. Raulston Arboretum.

'Manifich'—Lighter orange on the outside with a clear yellow inside, see Cresson, *Horticulture* 65(8):12–17 (1987).

'Sulphurea' ('Flava')—Beautiful pure yellow-flowered form with the wonderful attributes of the species, new leaves emerge without reddish purple coloration of the species; a literal shower of yellow flowers and bright green foliage in April; a must for every garden; each year I become more antsy waiting for the first flower; in recent years has defoliated to various degrees by mid to late summer, see comments under DISEASES AND INSECTS; interestingly except for the youngest leaves the plant is often void of foliage by mid-summer, the following April foliage and flowers appear in abundance.

'Superba'—Have seen it listed as orange-scarlet to bright scarlet, leaves are supposedly more broad-oval; I suspect the comments made under 'Magnifica' apply here, in fact Meyer, Mazzeo and Ross indicate 'Superba' is the correct name for 'Magnifica', however Griffiths treats 'Superba' as a distinct cultivar and includes 'Red Coral', 'Red Trumpet', 'Rubra', and 'Dreer's Everlasting' as synonyms.

PROPAGATION: Clean seed from the pulp and provide 3 months cold moist stratification; cuttings when firm root easily, use 1000 ppm KIBA quick dip; after rooting, cuttings will produce new growth and make a salable plant in a single growing season; cuttings can be taken as early as April.

NATIVE HABITAT: Connecticut to Florida, west to Nebraska and Texas.

RELATED SPECIES: In the past I have resisted the temptation to include many of the vining species which are so common in European gardens but in this edition have opened the floodgates. Many are beautiful and serve the same landscape functions as *L. sempervirens*. An excellent article on Climbing Honeysuckles appeared in *The Plantsman* 4(4):236–252 (1983).

Lonicera caprifolium L. — Italian Honeysuckle

LEAVES: Opposite, simple, obovate or oval, 2 to 4″ long, half as wide, rounded, cuneate, entire, dark green above and glaucous blue-green beneath; upper 2 to 3 pairs of leaves connate into acute disks subtending the flower.

STEM: Glabrous.

Lonicera caprifolium, (lon-iss′ēr-à cap-ri-fō′li-um), Italian Honeysuckle, is a twining vine with fragrant, yellowish white often tinged purplish on outside of the corolla, 1 3/4 to 2″ long, tubular flower borne in 4- to 10-flowered whorls from the axils of the terminal 3 pairs of leaves. Grows 10 to 20′. Flowers open in May–June and by this author have been confused with *L. periclymenum* which does not have the connately fused, disk-type leaves subtending the flower. Was able to photograph this at Pitmeddin, Scotland in 1995 and reconciled the foliar differences between this and *L. periclymenum*. Fruits are orange-red. 'Pauciflora' has flowers tinted rose on the outside of the corolla. 'Praecox' is an early-flowering form, cream tinted light red, turning yellow, with gray-green leaves. Europe and western Asia. Cultivated for centuries. Zone 5 to 7(8).

Lonicera flava Sims., (lon-iss′ēr-à flā′va), Yellow Honeysuckle, was introduced to me many years ago by Mr. Gene Cline of Canton, GA. He pointed out the difference between this and *L. sempervirens* 'Sulphurea'. The habit is weakly twining and not as robust as *L. sempervirens*. Will grow 6 to 10′. Leaves are bright green above, bluish green beneath, 1 3/4 to 3 1/4″ long, broad elliptic to elliptic, obtuse or acutish, the upper pairs connate at the base into a suborbicular or oval disk and usually mucronulate at tips. The orange-yellow, 1 1/4″ long, distinctly two-lipped (bilabiate) flower occurs in whorls of 1 to 3 at the end of the shoot. Have seen almost pure yellow forms to those with yellow-orange flowers stained red in bud. Authors have ascribed a slight fragrance to no fragrance. I cannot sense any distinct fragrance. Fruits are orange to red, 1/4″ diameter, and apparently not produced in great numbers. Flowers sometimes occur on a 1/2″ long peduncle. Quite difficult to locate in cultivation but a handsome vine well-suited to semi-shady conditions and probably equally at home in sun if the soil is moist. North Carolina to Missouri, Arkansas and Oklahoma. Cultivated 1810. Zone 5 to 8.

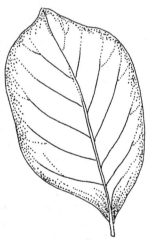

Lonicera periclymenum L. — Woodbine Honeysuckle, often simply called Woodbine.

LEAVES: Opposite, simple, ovate or elliptic to ovate-oblong, 1 1/2 to 2 1/2″ long, 1 to 1 1/2″ wide, acute to obtuse, cuneate, entire, dark green above, bluish green below, essentially glabrous at maturity; petiole—present on lower leaves, upper almost sessile but *never fused at the base* like *L. caprifolium*.

STEM: Often reddish purple, seemingly more so on red flowered forms, some glabrous, others with degrees of short pubescence; pith—hollow.

Lonicera periclymenum, (lon-iss′ēr-à per-i-klī′men-um), Woodbine Honeysuckle, is akin to *L. caprifolium* and *L. sempervirens* and serves a similar landscape function. Will grow 10 to 20′ and twine around structures and itself. Flowers are fragrant, 1 1/2 to 2″ long, glandular-glutinous on outside of corolla, two lipped (unlike *L. sempervirens*), occurring in a peduncled spike in 3 to 5 whorls at the end of the shoots. Flower color is typically yellowish white with a purplish tinge but many of the cultivated forms have deeper red to reddish purple outer corolla color. Fruits are red. 'Belgica' (Dutch) is a handsome form with purplish red outer color, whitish to yellowish within; the stems and leaves are purplish tinged; tends to be more bushy although plants I have seen were distinctly vine-like. Berries Jubilee™ ('Manul') is listed by Monrovia under this species but described as having lovely yellow flowers in summer and fall followed by attractive red fruits; foliage is blue-green above and glaucous gray beneath. The general characters do not fit true *L. periclymenum*. 'Graham Thomas' is a soft cream-yellow form, named after the great English plantsman, beautiful in flower. 'Serotina' (Late Dutch) has dark purple-red flowers (outside), yellowish inside, becoming paler with maturity; flowers open over a long period and occur later than the species. Apparently true 'Serotina' has been usurped by an imposter clone and is not common in cultivation; the plant is evident in English gardens and at least in flower color fits the above description. Other cultivars include: 'Belgica Select', 'Cream Cloud', 'La Gasnérie', 'Red Gables', and 'Winchester'. The species is not common in American gardens but will perform quite admirably. A lone plant on the Georgia campus ('Serotina') has flowered consistently in late April–May. Europe, North Africa, Asia Minor. Long cultivated. Zone 4 to 8.

Lonicera × *tellmanniana* hort., (lon-iss′ĕr-à tel-man-i-ā′nà), Tellman Honeysuckle, is a hybrid between *L. tragophylla* and *L. sempervirens* 'Superba' that was raised around 1920 in Budapest, Hungary. The elliptical-ovate leaves are 2 to 3 1/2″ long, much larger than the previous mentioned species, bright green and densely borne. The growth is vigorous and it appears to have acquired the best characteristics of both parents. Flowers, in my opinion, are the showiest of the vining honeysuckles presented here. Slender tubed to about 2″ long with a diameter of 1″ across the two lips at the mouth of the corolla; the yellow, almost fluorescent, perhaps yellow-orange flowers are flushed in the bud stage at their tips with a red cast. About 6 to 12 flowers are borne at the end of the shoots. Brought the species and 'Joan Sayers' to Georgia and their performance does not warrant great dialogue. Some plants are inherently better from afar, perhaps *L. × tellmanniana* is such a species. Zone 5 to 7.

Lonicera tatarica L. — Tatarian Honeysuckle

LEAVES: Opposite, simple, ovate to ovate-lanceolate, 1 1/2 to 2 1/2″ long, 1 to 1 1/2″ wide, acute to acuminate, rarely obtusish, rounded or subcordate at base, entire, bluish green, glabrous and glaucous beneath; petiole— 1/12 to 1/4″ long.
BUDS: Flattened, closely appressed, elongated, with valvate lower scales, glabrous.
STEM: Green at first, finally brownish, glabrous; pith—brown, excavated.

Lonicera tatarica, (lon-iss′ĕr-à tà-tār′i-kà), Tatarian Honeysuckle, grows 10 to 12′ in height with a 10′ spread. The general habit is upright, strongly multi-stemmed with the upper branches arching and the overall effect one of a dense, twiggy mass. Foliage is bluish green in summer; flowers are pink to white (profusely borne), 3/4 to 1″ long, May, soon after the leaves develop, borne in peduncled pairs on a 1/2 to 1″ long stalk in the axils of the leaves. Fruit is a red, 1/4″ diameter berry which colors in late June into July and August. Has become a weed in many areas. Leafs out very early in spring. Often considered the "best" of the honeysuckles because of the many cultivars which include:
'Alba'—Flowers pure white.
'Arnold Red'—Darkest red flowers of any honeysuckle, supposedly resistant to Russian aphid.
'Freedom'—Vigorous open grower, 8 to 10′ high, bluish green leaves, white flowers tinged pink, red fruit, resistant to Russian aphid, introduced by Minnesota Landscape Arboretum, see also under *L. korolkowii*.
'Grandiflora'—Large white flowers; sometimes called 'Bride'.
'Hack's Red'—Flowers deep purplish red.
'LeRoyana'—Dwarf variety, 3′ tall, poor flowerer, valued solely for dwarf character.
'Lutea'—Pink flowers, yellow fruit.
'Morden Orange'—Pale pink flowers and good orange fruits.
'Nana'—Flowers pink, dwarf habit, 3′ high at 9 years; apparently several different clones with this name.
'Parvifolia'—One of the best for white flowers.

'Rosea'—Flowers rosy pink outside, light pink inside.

'Sibirica'—Flowers deep rose.

'Valencia'—Upright, more compact, orange-fruited.

'Virginalis'—Buds and flowers are rose-pink; largest flowers of any *L. tatarica* form.

'Zabelii'—Dark red flowers similar to 'Arnold Red'; supposedly very susceptible to Russian aphid which causes "witches brooming."

In modern landscapes this is essentially an outmoded plant. Akin to the Edsel of deciduous shrubs. The Russian aphid has rendered the plant a liability in the Midwest and East. With wonderful viburnums to fill almost every nook and cranny of a garden this plant is headed for the recycling factory. Around Minuteman National Park, Concord, MA, this species has flagrantly escaped and overwhelmed the understory vegetation. Many summers past I noted the yellow, orange, and red fruited escapes. This, in my opinion, is a terrible weed and should be avoided. Central Asia to southern Russia. Introduced 1752. Zone 3 to 8.

Lonicera xylosteum L. — European Fly Honeysuckle

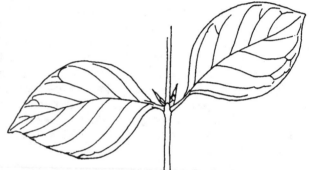

LEAVES: Opposite, simple, broad-ovate or elliptic-ovate to obovate, 1 to 2 1/2″ long, half or more than half as wide, acute, broad-cuneate to rounded at base, margins entire and sometimes fringed with pubescence, dark or grayish green and sparingly pubescent or glabrous above, paler and pubescent, rarely glabrate beneath; petiole—1/8 to 1/3″ long, pubescent.

BUDS: Brownish, woolly pubescent.

STEM: Pubescent, gray; pith—brown, excavated.

Lonicera xylosteum, (lon-iss′ĕr-à zi-los′tē-um), European Fly Honeysuckle, develops into a rounded mound with spreading, arching branches; grows 8 to 10′ with a spread of 10 to 12′. Foliage is a grayish green (has somewhat of a blue effect). The flowers are white or yellowish white, 5/8″ long, often tinged reddish; May; borne in peduncled pairs. Fruit is a dark red berry ripening in July and August. 'Claveyi' is a 3 to 6′ dwarf form recommended for hedges; however, I have seen plants that were 8 to 10′ high. 'Hedge King' is another selection by Clavey Nurseries and is a distinct narrow, upright grower which would be suitable for hedges. 'Emerald Mound' or 'Nana' is one of the very finest low-growing, mounded honeysuckles with rich bluish green foliage. I have seen this cultivar used in mass at the Minnesota Landscape Arboretum and was impressed. Roots easily from cuttings. Ultimate landscape size should run 3′ with a 4 1/2 to 6′ spread; does not move well in leaf, yellowish white flowers and dark red berries. 'Miniglobe' is a 1981 introduction from Morden Research Station that resembles 'Emerald Mound' but is hardier and more compact with dense green foliage. Flowers and fruits are not conspicuous. Grows 3 to 4′ high and wide. Zone 3 to 6. Considered a *L. × xylosteoides* Tausch. (*L. tatarica × L. xylosteum*) selection. Europe to Altai. Long cultivated. Zone 4 to 6.

Loropetalum chinense (R. Br.) Oliv. — Chinese Fringe-flower
(lō-rō-pet′à-lum chi-nen′sē)

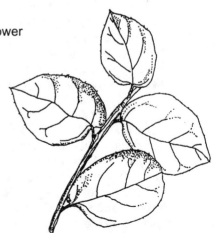

FAMILY: Hamamelidaceae

LEAVES: Alternate, simple, evergreen, ovate-rounded, 1 to 2 1/2″ long, 3/4 to 1 1/4″ wide, apex pointed, oblique leaf base, finely toothed to essentially entire, dark green and rough above, paler (grayish) beneath, pubescent; petiole—1/8″ long, pubescent.

BUDS: Imbricate, small, brown.

STEM: Slender, brown, densely pubescent; pith—solid, small, greenish.

SIZE: 6 to 10′ high with a similar spread; have seen plants 15′ high and wide; Creech reported 30′ high trees in the Ise Grand Shrine Forest, Japan; Lee's *Flora of China* noted 10 to 30′ high plants.

HARDINESS: Zone 7 to 9, injured at below 0°F temperatures.

HABIT: Irregularly rounded evergreen shrub often developing whip-like branches; leaves are borne in a single plane along the stem, artistic branches and can be limbed up to produce a handsome specimen; large specimens are upright, vase-shaped.

RATE: Fast.

TEXTURE: Medium-fine.

BARK: On old stems exfoliates in large strips, very rich brown; actually handsome but seldom seen.

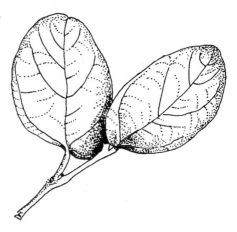

LEAF COLOR: Lustrous dark green throughout the seasons; underside of leaf is grayish green due to the dense pubescence but this is seldom seen because of the way the leaves are arranged.

FLOWERS: Perfect, fragrant, four, cream to white, strap-shaped, 3/4″ long, 1/16″ wide petals open in April (Athens), 3 to 6 flowers crowded together in each leaf axil; pedicel and outside of calyx clothed with whitish pubescence; magnificent in full flower, a fleecy cloud of creamy white and green, flowers are effective for 2 to 3 weeks, has flowered in late March in Athens, with flowers still effective in late April.

FRUIT: Woody, ovoid, nut-like, 3/8 to 1/2″ long capsule, not common in cultivation.

CULTURE: Easily transplanted from containers; prefers acid, moist, well-drained, high organic matter soils; does not do well in high pH soils: sun or medium shade; withstands any amount of pruning; does not perform well in extremely dry soils, although once established displays a tenacity just short of *Ilex cornuta*.

DISEASES AND INSECTS: None serious.

LANDSCAPE VALUE: Excellent for borders, screens, foundations; loses something when pruned; has a certain naturalness that is lost by turning it into a green meatball; one of the first plants I used for landscaping my Georgia home; can be effective as a single specimen or in groupings; have seen it thriving in heavy shade; could be easily espaliered; −3°F seriously damaged or killed many plants in the Athens area, the plant in my garden was killed to about 6 to 12″ from ground but produced new shoots, this plant is now 15′ high; leaves will probably show injury at 0 to 5°F; Creech mentions a plant as far north as Merion, PA, housed at the Barnes Foundation but it is less than satisfactory.

CULTIVARS: The most significant happening in Zone 7 to 9 gardening was the introduction of the reddish purple, to maroon red leaf and pink flowered forms from China. I alluded to 'Roseum' in the 1990 edition of the *Manual*. This was incorrect because this form is considered a variety (var. *rubrum*) and will produce relatively true-to-type from seed. The plant appeared in 1989 through the efforts of many people and institutions and is traced by Johnson in *Amer. Nurseryman* 178(6):7, 12–13 (1993). The Arnold Arboretum, during my 1991 sabbatical, gave me several plants of 'Burgundy' which were distributed to Georgia nurserymen. 'Blush' followed soon thereafter. Our Georgia program has doggedly pursued the various cultivars with the belief that they would become industry standards. That this has proven true is borne out by the everyday presence of the plants in retail outlets. See *Nursery Management and Production* 11(4):30–31 (1995) for additional information. Also, *J. Environ. Hort.* 14:38–41 (1996) for taxonomic status. Worthwhile garden information has come to light as I continue to grow and evaluate these wonderful plants, sun and shade are acceptable, protect from open, wind-swept locations, foliage color is enhanced and maintained under high nutrition, new soft growth is susceptible to cold damage, *prune* to maintain size, one 'Burgundy' in our garden is 14′ high, another is 3 to 4′ and dense, do not resist the pruning urge if plants are growing too fast, most are cold hardy to 0 to 5°F, lower than this expect some injury.

GREEN LEAF, WHITE FLOWERED CLONES:

Hillier Form—Acquired in late 1996, typical leaves and flowers but spreading, ground cover growth habit, vigorous grower, would make a handsome mass planting, several southern plantsmen questioned if the Hillier Form was not dwarfed because of the English climate; in containers it has maintained dense foliage and horizontally spreading branches.

Snow Dance™—Compact, shrubby form with smaller leaves than the species, has been slow-growing in our trials, from Piroche Plants, Pitt Meadows, B.C., via China; if the Hillier form maintains the growth habit, it will prove a more realistic commercial and garden form; Snow Dance™ also has possibilities because it is the most refined of the cultivars.

'Snow Muffin'—As yet unreleased, Bob Head describes it as 18″ high, almost groundcover-type, leaves are smaller than typical, observed plant in fall 1997 and was smitten by the commercial potential for this plant, large leathery dark green leaves cover the ground cover framework, saw parent plant in a large container, measured 15″ by 53″, adaptability to sun and shade will allow this plant to succeed on a major scale.

Variegated Form—Described to me as having leaves with creamy margins and green centers, it is in the hands of southern nurserymen, I await cuttings.

REDDISH PURPLE LEAF, FUCHSIA-PINK, PINK, OR WHITE WITH PINK-STRIPED FLOWERS:

var. *rubrum* 'Bicolor'—Possibly the most unique form because the leaves are deep maroon initially, finally turning dark olive green like 'Blush'; the flowers are white with a light pink streak, the contrast between foliage and flower is spectacular, most plants in the United States are too small to provide an index of size, however, young plants are vigorous.

var. *rubrum* 'Blush'—A more compact evergreen shrub than 'Burgundy'; without pruning or shaping, it is denser and fuller; new leaves are bronze-red and age to dark olive-green; leaves are 1 1/2 to 2 1/4″ long, thick and rough textured; flowers are rich fuchsia-pink and occur sporadically throughout the growing season, peaking in April; Monrovia Nursery Co. lists this form as Razzleberri™ ('Monraz') and describes it as growing 4 to 6′ high and 4 to 5′ wide; arrived in the United States from Nihon Kaki Nursery, Japan through several introducers; plants that we evaluated from three different vendors, all claiming uniqueness, were in fact the same as 'Blush'; after 3 years 'Blush' is 8′ by 8′ and will grow larger than my and others' early estimates.

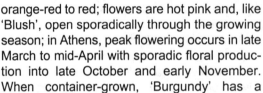

'Blush'

var. *rubrum* 'Burgundy'—Produces rich, reddish purple new foliage that matures to purple-green; in October and November, older leaves turn brilliant orange-red to red; flowers are hot pink and, like 'Blush', open sporadically through the growing season; in Athens, peak flowering occurs in late March to mid-April with sporadic floral production into late October and early November. When container-grown, 'Burgundy' has a groundcover-like constitution but starts to produce upright arching shoots by the end of the first growing season; a rooted cutting brought back from the Arnold Arboretum in September 1991 was 5′ high, strongly multi-stemmed and spectacular by fall 1993; growth rate is phenomenal and mature landscape size will range from 6 to 10′ high and wide; leaves average 1 1/4 to 1 3/4″ long, 5/8 to 1″ wide; pruning will be required to maintain a dense, full plant; a plant left to its own biological devices in the Dirr garden is 14′ high, strongly ascending, open, with relatively thin foliage, in flower it is spectacular; my feelings are that any red loropetalum is better than the average flowering shrub.

'Burgundy'

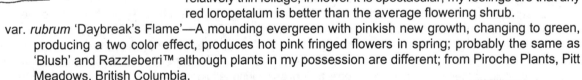

var. *rubrum* 'Daybreak's Flame'—A mounding evergreen with pinkish new growth, changing to green, producing a two color effect, produces hot pink fringed flowers in spring; probably the same as 'Blush' and Razzleberri™ although plants in my possession are different; from Piroche Plants, Pitt Meadows, British Columbia.

var. *rubrum* Fire Dance™—A new selection from China; discovered and introduced by Piroche Plants of Pitt Meadows, British Columbia; the initial plant we received, from which the leaf descriptions were made, developed an upright arching habit; Piroche stated that Fire Dance™ is a rapid grower to 3 to 6′ high. The ultimate habit is upright-arching, rounded to vase-shaped. New growth is a rich ruby red and leaves change to lustrous reddish-purple; ultimately the leaves change to green with only traces of reddish pigment in the lower veins and petiole; young leaves enlarge quickly and seemingly reach maturity faster than the other cultivars and clones; the flowers are dark pink; if kept in active state of growth Fire Dance™ provides exceptional foliage color; the original plants that came to Georgia contained more than one clone, plants varied in growth habits and foliage color, in discussions with Bruce Rutherford, Piroche, he acknowledged same and noted that the company selected the best red foliage form and named it 'Pipa's Red'.

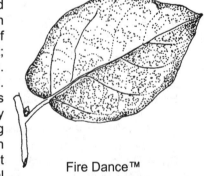

Fire Dance™

var. *rubrum* 'Pink Pearl'—Have only observed one small plant and am waiting for flower in spring 1998, simply wanted to alert the reader to the reality (possibility?) of another clone.

var. *rubrum* 'Pipa's Red'—Mounding shrub, like Dirr's tummy, with long narrow burgundy leaves and hot pink flowers, foliage color is more intense and persistent than the original Fire Dance™ from which it was selected, plants in Dearing, GA appear to hold their foliage color better than many of the purple leaf types, from Piroche Plants, Pitt Meadows, British Columbia.

var. *rubrum* Piroche Form—Similar to 'Blush' and Razzleberri™, in Georgia trials appears to be the same plant; have 'Blush' and Piroche Form in Dirr garden and am unable to detect worthy distinctions; believe Piroche has named this form, possibly 'Daybreak's Flame'.

var. *rubrum* Plum Delight™ (also listed as 'Hines Purpleleaf', 'Hines Burgundy' and Pizzazz™)—More compact with excellent reddish purple color under high nutrition and even moisture; has been the weakest grower in the Dirr garden and does not compete in foliage color or growth rate with 'Blush', 'Burgundy', Fire Dance™, and 'Zhuzhou Fuchsia'; originally trademarked by Hines Nurseries.

var. *rubrum* 'Ruby'—Has a more compact, rounded appearance with shiny, ruby red young leaves; leaves are more rounded and undulating than 'Burgundy', 'Blush', Fire Dance™, Small Leaf Form, and 'Zhuzhou Fuchsia'; 'Ruby' will probably be the smallest of the above introductions. Ying Qiang Huo, Oriental Trees and Plants, Inc., Athens, GA, germinated seeds of var. *rubrum* with five out of 500 seeds persisting into the seedling stage and subsequent maturity. He increased the quantity of these five plants by means of tissue culture and conventional cutting propagation. 'Ruby' and Variegated Form he considered worthy of introduction. I believe 'Ruby' has great commercial promise and can be utilized like red leaf barberries and dwarf nandinas.

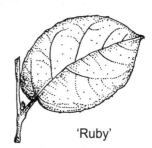

'Ruby'

var. *rubrum* 'Sizzlin' Pink'—Introduced by Mark Krautmann, Heritage Seedlings, Salem, OR and tissue cultured by Microplant Tissue Laboratory, Gervais, OR; my initial reaction was that this was no different than 'Burgundy', however, branches are more horizontal, layering one upon the other, producing a wide-spreading shrub, foliage color similar to 'Burgundy', flowers perhaps slightly lighter, although not much, tends to repeat bloom especially when maintained under high nutrition in container culture, a 4-year-old plant has become wider than high, about 4' by 6' without pruning, to date has not developed the wild splaying shoots of 'Burgundy', reddish purple foliage color is best under high nutrition and even moisture.

var. *rubrum* Small Leaf Form—Introduced by Huo from China where it is grown in the same provinces as 'Zhuzhou Fuchsia'; leaves are 1 to 1 3/4″ long, greenish purple; flowers light pink and produced abundantly, much more so than 'Zhuzhou Fuchsia', and appear sporadically throughout the growing season.

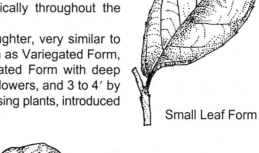

Small Leaf Form

var. *rubrum* 'Suzanne'—Named after my youngest daughter, very similar to 'Ruby' which came from the same seed population as Variegated Form, 'Suzanne' is a branch sport (chimera) of Variegated Form with deep reddish maroon, almost rounded leaves, rich pink flowers, and 3 to 4' by 3 to 4' outline, this and 'Ruby' will prove worthy massing plants, introduced in 1995 by the author.

var. *rubrum* Variegated Form—Comparable to 'Ruby' in growth and leaf characteristics; the difference is apparent in the green and maroon splashed leaves; unfortunately, this variegation pattern is not stable and most branch reversions to date have been reddish purple; this form will not be introduced commercially unless the chimera can be stabilized.

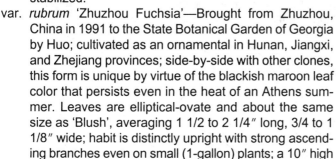

Variegated Form

var. *rubrum* 'Zhuzhou Fuchsia'—Brought from Zhuzhou, China in 1991 to the State Botanical Garden of Georgia by Huo; cultivated as an ornamental in Hunan, Jiangxi, and Zhejiang provinces; side-by-side with other clones, this form is unique by virtue of the blackish maroon leaf color that persists even in the heat of an Athens summer. Leaves are elliptical-ovate and about the same size as 'Blush', averaging 1 1/2 to 2 1/4″ long, 3/4 to 1 1/8″ wide; habit is distinctly upright with strong ascending branches even on small (1-gallon) plants; a 10″ high plant was 4' high in a single growing season; this form

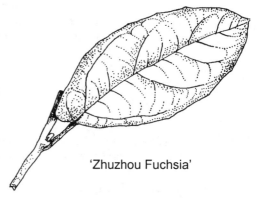

'Zhuzhou Fuchsia'

could be trained as a standard or espaliered on trellises and walls; flowers are deep pink; estimate mature landscape height around 10′ and possibly larger, early evaluations indicate this cultivar is the most cold hardy of the pink flowered forms treated herein.

PROPAGATION: Cuttings collected on July 28, treated with 3000 ppm IBA, alcohol quick dip, placed in peat:perlite under mist rooted about 80%. Based on my observations, the rooting medium should not hold too much moisture or the cuttings will rot; plants grown in containers were almost prostrate for a season and developed height later. Since the previous was written, we have rooted thousands. The keys are soft- or firm-wooded cuttings, 1000 ppm KIBA, 3 perlite:1 peat, mist, with rooting in 4 to 6 weeks; wean from mist as soon as rooted, fertilize lightly and growth ensues; indeed an easy plant to propagate by cuttings.

ADDITIONAL NOTES: Frequently misidentified; looks a bit like some of the honeysuckles and cotoneasters; looks nothing like a member of the witch-hazel family; definitely deserves to be more widely planted in southern gardens. Venerable specimens are abundant in the South and Aiken, SC and Orangeburg, SC house their share of large plants. Some nurserymen are field growing the reddish purple leaf types as standards or large, multi-stemmed shrubs. 'Zhuzhou Fuchsia', the most upright form and among the most cold hardy, is the preferred cultivar.

NATIVE HABITAT: China, one locality in Japan. Introduced 1880.

Lyonia lucida (Lam.) K. Koch — Fetterbush Lyonia

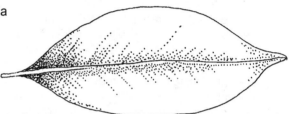

LEAVES: Alternate, simple, evergreen, broad elliptic to obovate to oblong, 1 to 3″ long, half as wide, abruptly acuminate, cuneate, entire, revolute, leathery, lustrous dark green above, lighter beneath, glabrous.
STEM: Glabrous, 3-angled.

Lyonia lucida, (li-ō′ni-à lū′si-dà), Fetterbush Lyonia, is a 3 to 5′ high suckering, open, arching evergreen shrub that I have never seen in good condition under cultivation. I grew it for a number of years in my Georgia garden and gave up because of weak growth and susceptibility to leaf spot. The pinkish white, up to 1/3″ long flowers occur in racemes from the axils of the leaves and are rather pretty. Prefers a moist, well-drained soil and at least partial shade under cultivation. Probably best only in a naturalized situation. The foliage is quite handsome but does not hold up under even mild stress. 'Morris Minor' is a compact, small leaf form offered by Woodlanders Nursery. Virginia to Florida and Louisiana. Introduced 1765. Zone 7 to 9.

Lyonia mariana (L.) D. Don — Stagger-bush

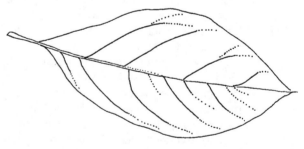

LEAVES: Alternate, simple, oblong, elliptic or narrowly obovate, 3/4 to 3″ long, acute or obtuse, cuneate, entire, medium to dark green, glabrous except for the pubescence on veins beneath.

Lyonia mariana, (li-ō′ni-à   mar-i-a′nà), Staggerbush Lyonia, is a rather handsome deciduous cousin of *L. lucida*. The white or pinkish, 3/8 to 1/2″ long ovoid to tubular flower occurs in May–June on leafless racemes. The flowers are almost as handsome unopened because the calyx is tinged red. The foliage colors a good red in autumn. A worthy shrub for a moist well-drained soil in a shrub border. Rhode Island to Florida, west to Tennessee and Arkansas. Introduced 1736. Zone 5 to 9.

Maackia amurensis Rupr. & Maxim. — Amur Maackia
(mak′ē-à a-moor-en′sis)

FAMILY: Fabaceae
LEAVES: Alternate, compound, odd-pinnate, 8 to 12″ long, leaflets opposite or nearly so, short-stalked, 7 to 11, elliptic to oblong-ovate, 1 1/2 to 3 1/2″ long, abrupt at apex, rounded at base, glabrous, grayish green when unfolding finally turning a dark almost olive-green, paler and glabrous below.

BUDS: Two large exposed pale-margined scales, 1/4″ high, 1/4″ wide, dark brown, tips of scales membranous, somewhat ovoid, plumpish, glabrous, shiny, similar in shape to the buds of *Koelreuteria*.

STEM: Stout, terete, grayish brown to black, usually glabrous, somewhat dingy in color and texture in winter, abundant and irregularly spaced lenticels, lenticels on second year and older stems distinctly diamond-shaped; leaf scar—raised, half ellipse, bud sits on top of flat leaf scar; pith—solid, white.

SIZE: Probably 20 to 30′ under cultivation but can grow to 45′ in the wild, usually as wide or wider than tall.

HARDINESS: Zone 4 to 7(8), have found several trees in Zone 7b, however, not as vigorous as further north; high night temperatures slow growth.

HABIT: Small, round-headed tree, branches upright-arching-spreading, quite dapper in outline when properly grown.

RATE: Slow, 12′ over a 20 year period according to an English source, faster under United States conditions.

TEXTURE: Medium in all seasons.

BARK: Peeling with maturity, rich shining amber to brown to copper, developing a curly consistency; bark is handsomest on 1 to 5″ diameter branches when the coloration and exfoliation are most pronounced; significant variation in bark from tree to tree.

LEAF COLOR: Initially grayish green finally dark green; fall color is nonexistent.

FLOWERS: Perfect, dull white, 1/2″ long, standard obovate-cuneate, notched, wings elliptic-oblong, closely set on stiff erect racemes, 4 to 6″ long, sometimes branched at the base, June–July, smell like new mown grass or alfalfa.

FRUIT: Pod, 2 to 3″ long, 1/3 to 1/2″ wide, flat, brown.

CULTURE: Easily transplanted, performs best in loose, well-drained, acid or alkaline soil; preferably sunny exposures; appears to be quite adaptable; fixes atmospheric nitrogen; Batzli et al., *J. Amer. Soc. Hort. Sci.* 117:612–616 (1992), reported that *M. amurensis* has the capacity to form N-fixing symbioses with rhizobial bacterium (*Bradyrhizobium* sp.).

DISEASES AND INSECTS: Nothing particularly serious.

LANDSCAPE VALUE: Of interest for the late summer flowers; the specimens I have seen had very clean foliage and appeared quite vigorous; the more I see of this tree the more impressed I am by its durability and general adaptation; has survived at Minnesota Landscape Arboretum and performed spectacularly at Bernheim Arboretum, Swarthmore College and Mt. Auburn Cemetery; the foliage has a certain richness and the bronze-colored bark is quite attractive; I believe it would be a good candidate for street tree and container planting; not perfectly adapted in the South (Zone 7 and 8) for plants at the Atlanta Botanical Garden, a local nursery and our garden are somewhat ragged and unkempt.

CULTIVARS:

var. *buergeri* (Maxim) Schneid.—Leaflets are pubescent below.

PROPAGATION: Seeds may be soaked in hot water overnight, then sown; 60 minutes acid will alleviate the seed coat dormancy and seeds will germinate readily; have sown green seeds and they germinated; considerable cutting work in Midwest with June–July cuttings, 2500 ppm IBA proving optimum, see *Landscape Plant News* 4(1): March (1993); cuttings from 20 mature trees of *M. amurensis* were treated with 0 or 2500 ppm KIBA, placed under mist with bottom heat, rooting ranged from 19 to 92% depending on genotype, collection date; KIBA treatment had little effect, see *J. Environ. Hort.* 12:147–149 (1994).

ADDITIONAL NOTES: A little-known genus which is closely related to *Cladrastis* and may have by some authorities been put in that genus. It differs from *Cladrastis* in that the leaf-buds are solitary and not hidden

by the base of the petiole (actually rachis); the leaflets are opposite and the flowers are densely packed in more or less erect racemes. Genus commemorates a Russian naturalist, Richard Maack.
NATIVE HABITAT: Manchuria. Introduced 1864.

RELATED SPECIES:

Maackia chinensis Tak., (mak′ē-à chi-nen′sis), Chinese Maackia, is closely related to the above but is not quite as hardy. There are 11 to 13 leaflets which are covered by a silvery gray pubescence as they emerge and give the effect of a Russian-olive during this period. Leaflets smaller than above, 3/4 to 1″ long. Tends to be a small, 20 to 30′ high, shrub-tree. Central China. Introduced 1908. Zone 4(5) to 7?

Maackia fauriei (Lév.) Tax., (mak′ē-à fàr′ē-ī), as I observed the species was similar to *M. amurensis*. During my 1991 sabbatical at the Arnold, I cross-examined the *Maackia* collection and was still confused about the differences among the species and variety described herein. *Maackia fauriei* has 9 to 13 leaflets, to 2″ long, ovate, obtuse, finely pubescent, finally glabrous. The pod is 1 3/4″ long, semi-elliptic to short rectangular with lower margin winged. Korea, central China. Zone 5 to 7.

Maclura pomifera (Raf.) Schneid. — Osage-orange, also called Hedge-apple and "bois d'arc"
(mà-klū′rà pō-mif′ĕr-à)

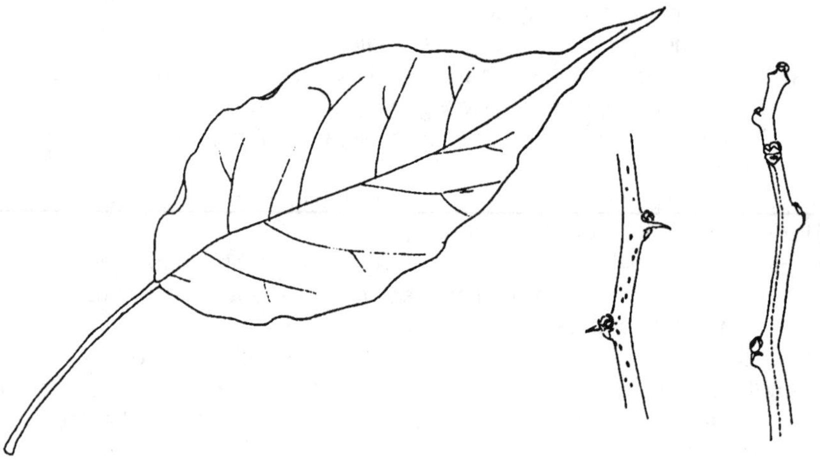

FAMILY: Moraceae
LEAVES: Alternate, simple, ovate to oblong-lanceolate, 2 to 5″(6″) long, about one-half as wide, acuminate, broad-cuneate to subcordate at base, entire, glabrous, lustrous bright to dark green and glabrous above, lighter and pubescent on veins beneath; petiole—1/2 to 1 1/2″ long, milky sap.
BUDS: Terminal—absent, laterals—small, globular, brown, depressed and partially imbedded in the bark, 5-scaled.
STEM: Stout, buff or orange-brown, glabrous, armed with straight, stout axillary spines, 1/2″ long, variable in degree of thorniness, exudes milky juice when cut.

SIZE: 20 to 40′ in height with a comparable spread, can grow to 60′; national champion is 60′ by 85′ in Charlotte County, VA.
HARDINESS: Zone 4 to 9.
HABIT: Usually develops a short trunk and low, rounded, irregular crown composed of stiff, spiny, interlacing branches; some of the branches show a pendulous tendency.
RATE: Fast, 9 to 12′ over a 3 to 5 year period.
TEXTURE: Medium in leaf; coarse in fruit and winter.
BARK: On old trunks, the bark develops ashy brown or dark orange-brown with irregular longitudinal fissures and scaly ridges; the wood itself is of a characteristic orange color.
LEAF COLOR: Bright, shiny medium to dark green in summer; fall color varies from yellow-green to a good yellow and on occasion approaches fantastic.
FLOWERS: Dioecious, inconspicuous; female borne in June in dense globose heads on short peduncles; male in subglobose or sometimes elongated racemes.
FRUIT: A large (3)4 to 6″ wide globose syncarp of drupes covered with a mamillate rind, yellow-green in color, becoming effective in September and lethal in October if one is sitting under the tree; usually fall after ripening, a real mess.
CULTURE: One of our very tough and durable native trees; transplants readily; the poorer the site the better; withstands wetness, dryness, wind, extreme heat, acid and high pH conditions once established; full sun;

male thornless selections could be made for inner city areas and other impossible sites where few plants will grow; 'Park' grew 1'7" per year over a 5 year period in Kansas tests.

DISEASES AND INSECTS: None serious—although a few leaf spots have been reported.

LANDSCAPE VALUE: Has been used for hedgerows in the plains states; not worth recommending for the residential landscape; has potential for rugged, polluted areas; wood is valuable for making bows and is amazingly rot resistant; I have seen patios made out of Osage-orange logs (rounds) which were quite handsome; the wood contains about 1% 2, 3, 4, 5-tetrahydroxystilbene, which is toxic to a number of fungi which may explain the decay resistance.

CULTIVARS:

'Double O'—Male form with pleasing upright crown, thornless except on juvenile stems, a Wandell introduction.

var. *inermis* (André) Schneid.—A thornless type; also many people (nurserymen) are interested in selecting superior clones and, no doubt, the future will yield several cultivars; a true thornless form has proved elusive and to date there is no cultivar that is completely thorn-free; it seems that budwood or cuttings taken from thornless branches are not stable and will produce thorns at some period in the growth cycle.

The late John Pair, Kansas State, Wichita, KS, was the leading advocate of this species and selected a number of desirable, almost thornless, male clones. In the last edition, I confused some numbers relative to thorniness of various cultivars. John sent me the correct data which are now included. Three-year-old budded trees produced the following number of thorns per node: 'Altamont'—0.39, 'Bois D'Arc Supreme'—0.25, 'Fan D'Arc'—0.36, 'Park'—0.47, 'Pawhuska'—0.42, and 'Wichita'—0.04. One-year-old softwood and/or hardwood cuttings produced the following number of thorns per plant: 'Park'—softwood 6.96, 'Pawhuska'—softwood 0.40, hardwood 2.22, 'Wichita'—softwood 0, hardwood 0.05. Based on his work, 'Wichita' appears the most thornless of the group.

Since the last edition new information on cultivars has come to light. 'White Shield' was discovered near White Shield Creek in western Oklahoma. It is the most thorn-free clone to date and has beautiful leathery lustrous dark green leaves. Budded trees display unbelievable vigor. A tree at the J.C. Raulston Arboretum, Raleigh, NC is over 20' high in about 4 years.

Was able to observe 'Wichita', a John Pair selection, in Clinton, OK in 1992. The trees were upright-spreading with a full, dense canopy. In actuality, better than Bradford Pears but the public will never believe it. Registered in 1990.

Other listed cultivars include: 'Denmark', 'Graham' and 'Smolan #1'.

PROPAGATION: Seeds exhibit a slight dormancy which can be overcome by stratification for 30 days at 41°F or by soaking in water for 48 hours. Softwood cuttings taken in July rooted 32% without treatment and 100% in 42 days after treatment with IAA; Dr. Pair has found that softwood cuttings from 3-year-old stock plants root readily with 5000 to 10000 ppm IBA; hardwood cuttings collected in January, given bottom heat, rooted in 6 weeks; these hardwood cuttings produced about 30" of growth in a single season which is about twice as much as a 2-year-old rooted softwood. Plants have been bench grafted in winter with 60 to 80% success depending on cultivar. For complete details see *The Plant Propagator* 30(1): 6 (1984). Has also been tissue cultured. See *HortScience* 23: 613–615 (1988).

ADDITIONAL NOTES: Select male trees; the large fruits are a nuisance and a problem around public areas as people will invariably use them for ammunition. The wood is used for fence posts, bow-wood, and rustic furniture. A bright yellow dye can be extracted from the wood. Squirrels often eat the seeds during the winter months and it is not unusual to see a small pile of pulp under the trees. An inter-generic hybrid between

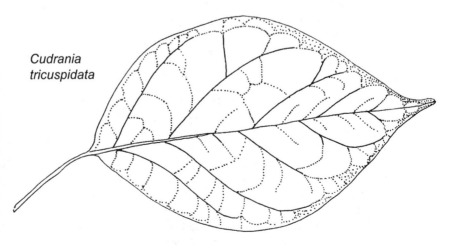

Cudrania tricuspidata

Cudrania and *Maclura*, × *Macludrania hybrida* André, exists. An excellent reference on Osage-orange, its history and economic uses appeared in *Economic Botany* 35(1): 24–41, 1981, and should be consulted by anyone who seeks additional information. See also Pair, *Arnoldia* 52:14–19 (1992) for an excellent discussion of history and the future.

NATIVE HABITAT: Arkansas to Oklahoma and Texas but grown far out of its native range. Introduced 1818.

Magnolia acuminata L. — Cucumbertree Magnolia
(mag-nō′li-à a-kū-mi-nā′tà)

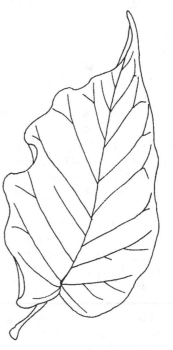
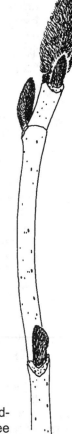

FAMILY: Magnoliaceae

LEAVES: Alternate, simple, elliptic or ovate to oblong-ovate, 4 to 10″ long, about half as wide, short acuminate, cordate, rounded or acute at base, entire, dark green above, soft pubescent and light green beneath; petiole—1 to 1 1/2″ long.

BUDS: Whitish, silvery, silky pubescent, covered (as is true for all magnolias) with a single keeled scale which on abscising leaves a distinct scar which appears as a fine line encircling the stem, terminal 1/2 to 3/4″ long, slight crook to long axis, lateral buds greenish silky pubescent, 1/4 to 3/8″ long, sit in depression of leaf scar and are slightly crooked, touching (often) their tips to the stem (appressed).

STEM: Moderate, brownish or reddish brown, glabrous, small gray vertical lenticels; the leaf scars U-shaped; emits a spicy odor when bruised.

SIZE: 50 to 80′ in height with a comparable spread at maturity; in youth a distinctly pyramidal tree and the spread is always considerably less than the height; national champion is 75′ by 83′ in Waukon, IA.

HARDINESS: Zone (3)4 to 8, performs well in Orono, ME and Athens, GA.

HABIT: Pyramidal when young (20 to 30 years of age), in old age developing a rounded to broad-rounded outline with massive wide-spreading branches; an open grown Cucumbertree Magnolia is a beautiful tree.

RATE: Medium to fast, 10 to 15′ over a 4 to 6 year period.

TEXTURE: Medium-coarse in leaf, coarse in winter.

BARK: Relatively smooth gray-brown in youth becoming ridged and furrowed with flat gray ridges and relatively narrow vertical fissures, some scaling occurs on the flat gray ridges.

LEAF COLOR: Dark green in summer, abscising green or brown in fall; some trees develop a soft ashy-brown fall color which is actually quite attractive.

FLOWERS: Perfect, often self-sterile, however, some trees are self-fertile, greenish yellow petals, 2 1/2 to 3″ long, in two sets of 3, sepals 1 to 1 1/2″ long, slightly fragrant, May to early June, borne solitarily, not particularly showy for the flowers are borne high in the tree and often are masked by foliage; seedling-grown trees may not flower until 20′ or more in height; one seedling from Arnold Arboretum trees outplanted in Athens in 1993 flowered in 1996, seedling was 5-years-old and 8 to 10′ high, other similar age seedlings did not flower.

FRUIT: Aggregate of follicles, pinkish red, October, briefly persisting, 2 to 3″ long, looks (more or less) like a small cucumber; hence, the name Cucumbertree.

CULTURE: Transplant balled-and-burlapped or from a container in early spring into loamy, deep, moist, well-drained, slightly acid soil; performs well in calcareous soils of Midwest; does not tolerate extreme drought or wetness; full sun or partial shade; does not withstand polluted conditions; do not plant too deep; prune after flowering; another of the fleshy rooted type trees which have a minimum of lateral roots and practically no root hairs; trees which fall into this category are often difficult to transplant and care should be taken in the planting process.

DISEASES AND INSECTS: Basically free from problems; scale can occur now and then.

LANDSCAPE VALUE: Excellent tree for the large property; parks, estates, golf courses, naturalized areas; the trees appear pyramidal and compact in youth but this is misleading for with maturity 60 to 70′ specimens with a spread of 70 to 85′ and large, massive, spreading branches often develop; great character tree.

CULTIVARS: Many selections have been introduced but are scarce, perhaps absent in commerce. One of my mentors, the late J.C. McDaniel, University of Illinois, introduced at least five with names of the homes or towns in which they were growing. 'Busey', 'Dunlap', 'Philo', 'Urbana', et al., have special meaning to me.

There is no logical way to keep up with the flood of cultivars. I suggest reading *Magnolia*, c/o Dorothy Callaway, P.O. Box 3131, Thomasville, GA 31799. Cultivar registrations are included in the journal.

The quest among the *Magnolia* elite for yellow-flowered selections resulted in a great number of hybrids involving *M. acuminata*, var. *subcordata*, and *M. denudata*. 'Butterflies', 'Sundance', 'Yellow Fever', and 'Yellow Garland' and some of following comprise the most common commercially available forms. No doubt others are on the way. It should be mentioned that heat reduces the intensity of yellow to the degree of cream.

'Butterflies'—Superior by all accounts to any of the other yellows which are often more cream; however have read a report that alludes to lightening of yellow in heat; deep yellow flowers, 3 to 4″(5″) across, 10 to 16 tepals, precocious, upright pyramidal grower, 18 to 20′, *M. acuminata* × *M. denudata* 'Sawada's Cream', Phil Savage hybrid, Plant Patent #7456, have seen photographs and the yellow borders on canary bird, a small plant in our garden is yet to flower . . . please hurry; supposedly tepals drop before leaves emerge.

'DC-4'—Larger and darker yellow than those of 'Elizabeth'.

'Elba' (var. *subcordata*)—Yellow flowers, Dick Figlar introduction.

'Elizabeth'—Result of a cross between *M. acuminata* and *M. denudata*. The habit is neat and pyramidal but the genuine beauty resides in the finely tapering buds that open to display flowers of the clearest primrose yellow that open to transparent yellow; at the Brooklyn Botanic Garden it opens from late April to mid-May; patented in 1977; a 3-year-old, 3′ high plant produced 3 flowers after -30°F at Orono, ME; also, has flowered heavily in Zone 7b; I have fallen in love with this plant, beautiful flowers, more yellow in cool weather, fragrant, open before leaves and after leaf development, extremely vigorous, probably maturing between 30 to 50′ high, 20 to 35′ wide; also, was able to root 'Elizabeth' at 50% which is surprising since the parental species are neigh impossible.

'Ellen'—Yellow-variegated leaf form, probably a var. *subcordata* selection, named after the daughter of Alfred Fordham, former propagator, Arnold Arboretum.

'Evamaria' (*M. acuminata* × *M. liliiflora*)—Unopened flower buds are purple, suffused with yellow shadings; open flower consists of 6 broadly rounded petals in two whorls of 3, the distinctive and unusual flower color is due to the contrasting shade of magenta-rose, suffused with a pale orange and yellow; patented in 1968, a Brooklyn Botanic Garden introduction.

'Fertile Myrtle'—Narrow grower produces abundant seed from its own pollen (self-fertile) and foreign pollen; seedlings flower young; from Phil Savage

'Gold Crown'—Flowers as yellow as or more so than 'Elizabeth' yet open later than most deciduous magnolias, 8 to 9 tepals, 9 to 10″ wide; *M.* × *brooklynensis* 'Woodsman' × 'Sundance'; Dr. August Kehr hybrid.

'Golden Girl'—Flowers similar to 'Evamaria' but virtually all yellow with only basal purple staining, from August Kehr.

'Golden Glow'—Flowers yellow, selected from a tree in the wild in Sevier County, TN.

'Golden Pond'—Yellow flowers, large tree type, from Phil Savage.

'Goldfinch'—Light yellow flowers, precocious, tall, upright form, *M. acuminata* var. *subcordata* 'Miss Honeybee' × *M. denudata* 'Sawada's Cream'; Phil Savage hybrid; one of the hardiest yellows.

'Goldstar' ('Gold Star')—Star-shaped, yellow flowers, actually pale yellow to creamy white, bronze new growth, densely branched symmetrical shrub, *M. acuminata* var. *subcordata* 'Miss Honeybee' × *M. stellata* 'Rubra', original name was 'Bronze Leaf Baby Shoes'.

'Green Beret'—New green-yellow hybrid, holds yellow color in Deep South, Louisiana Nursery introduction.

'Hattie Carthan'—Bright yellow flowers with magenta-purple basal flush and stripe on the back of the tepals.

'Ivory Chalice'—Yellow to yellow green tepals mature to ivory, to 6″ diameter flowers, hardy to -22°F, *M. acuminata* × *M. denudata*, David Leach hybrid, have seen it described as a carbon copy of 'Elizabeth'.

'Klassen'—Vigorous, large-flowered, heavy-fruiting, J.C. McDaniel introduction.

'Koban Dori'—Has soft canary yellow, cup-shaped flowers that open in late April–May, flowers are held upright and occur as the new leaves are emerging, 15 to 20′, from Nakamura, Japan, listed as an *M. acuminata* form, however the smaller size indicates a var. *subcordata* type.

'Large Yellow'—Exceptional large, yellow flowers, Louisiana Nursery.

'Laser'—Polyploid (16 N) seedling of 'Fertile Myrtle' with larger leaves and thicker stems; from Dr. August Kehr.

'Legend'—Soft pastel yellow flowers before the leaves, vigorous grower, small pyramidal tree, *M. acuminata* × *M. denudata*, from David Leach.

'Limelight'—Green-yellow to chartreuse flower buds, yellow to cream flowers, var. *subcordata* × 'Alexandrina', a Phil Savage introduction.

'Moegi Dori'—Deep yellow flowers reminiscent of *M. acuminata* var. *subcordata* 'Miss Honeybee', a Nakamura selection.

'Ontario'—From northern part of range, possible increased hardiness, selected by Richard Figlar, 'Syracuse' was selected for similar reasons.

'Patriot'—Polyploid (8 N) of 'Fertile Myrtle' with larger leaves and stems, yellow flowers, from Dr. August Kehr.

'Peachy'—Hybrid between *M. acuminata* × *M. sprengeri* 'Diva', flowers with the color and mottling of a peach, over color apricot, large, floppy flowers, fragrant, borne before the leaves in spring, large pyramidal tree in youth, spreading with age.

'Seiju'—Iridescent blue-green flowers, Nakamura selection.

'Sundance'—Yellow flowers, actually medium yellow, to 8″ wide, vigorous grower, flowers when young, extremely cold hardy, Zone 4 to 8, *M. acuminata* × *M. denudata*, hybridized by J.C. McDaniel, introduced by Dr. August Kehr.

'Sunray'—Yellow-flowered decaploid, flowers larger in size and possibly deeper yellow than those of 'Sundance', larger leaves and thicker stems.

'Ultimate Yellow'—Six inch wide, well-formed, distinctly yellow flowers with basal green coloration, from Harry Heineman, MA.

'Variegata'—Leaves blotched in a rather attractive manner with golden yellow, 'Ellen' is a named clone.

'Woodsman'—J.C. McDaniel selected this from a cross between *M. acuminata* 'Klassen' and *M. liliiflora* 'O'Neill'; the flowers are light purple-tinged and larger than the normal Cucumbertree type; technically, the cross is listed as *M.* × *brooklynensis* 'Woodsman'; registered in 1974.

'Yellow Bird'—Yellow with slight greenish tinge at base of outer tepals, held upright, tepals 3 to 3 1/2″(4″) long, about 2″ wide, later flowering, pyramidal habit like *M. acuminata*, good growth habit, fast growing to 40′, leaves 4 to 8″ long and akin to *M. acuminata*, hybrid of *M. acuminata* var. *subcordata* × *M.* × *brooklynensis* 'Eva Maria' from Brooklyn Botanic Garden, introduced 1981.

'Yellow Fever'—Offers 6 to 8″ wide, lemon yellow, fragrant flowers that are tinged light pink at the base of the tepals, flowers open before leaves appear and supposedly open late enough to avoid spring frosts, late-flowering, vigorous, *M. acuminata* × *M.* × *soulangiana*, Phil Savage introduction.

'Yellow Garland'—Yellow with yellow-green midribs, yellow anthers with maroon bases, 6 tepals, flowers to 8″ across, deeper yellow than 'Elizabeth', *M. acuminata* × *M. denudata*, David Leach introduction in 1985.

'Yellow-Green #1'—Sister seedling of 'Green Beret', Louisiana Nursery introduction.

'Yellow Lantern'—Lemon yellow, closer to cream than true yellow, cup-shaped flower, precocious, upright single-stemmed tree eventually urn-shaped to 25′, *M. acuminata* var. *subcordata* 'Miss Honeybee' × *M.* × *soulangiana* 'Alexandrina', Phil Savage hybrid, Zone 5 to 9, registered in 1985.

PROPAGATION: Seeds exhibit embryo dormancy which can be overcome by 3 to 6 months of stratification in moist peat at 32° to 41°F; I have had excellent success with this species by removing the fleshy seed coat, stratifying for 90 days at 41°F and directly planting; magnolia seeds are quite oily and deteriorate rapidly if not properly handled; it is best to collect the fruits, extract the seed, remove their fleshy seed coats and either direct sow or provide a cold period as mentioned above; in 1991 seeds were collected in September from Arnold Arboretum trees of *Magnolia acuminata*, *M. ashei*, *M. kobus*, *M. macrophylla*, *M.* × *soulangiana* 'Andre Le Roi', *M. salicifolia*, *M. virginiana* and *M. zenii*, fleshy seed coat removed, float-tested, stratified in moist peat for 90 days at 41°F, sown in flats in the greenhouse in January with uniform germination of all taxa within 4 to 6 weeks, plants were shifted to cells, grown for a year and then outplanted to the field; all except *M. macrophylla* flowered by 1997; *M. ashei* produced magnificent flowers on a 3′ high plant.

Merkle and Wiecko, *J. Amer. Soc. Hort. Sci.* 115:858–860 (1990), through somatic embryogenesis (using immature seeds as explants) reproduced whole *ex vitro* plants of *M. acuminata* var. *subcordata*, *M. fraseri* and *M. virginiana*. This system worked with *M. macrophylla*, *M. pyramidata*, *Liriodendron tulipifera* and hybrids of *L. t.* and *L. chinense*.

Mr. Don Shadow relates an interesting story relative to cutting propagation of this species. He collected from young trees and stuck something approaching 6000 cuttings. Not a single one rooted which indicated rapid loss of juvenility even though the species does not flower until much older.

ADDITIONAL NOTES: The magnolias are a difficult group to treat. There are numerous species but the great confusion arises in the almost overwhelming plethora of cultivars. I have attempted to include the more important landscape species and cultivars. I recommend an outstanding book, *Magnolias*, by Neil G. Treseder, Faber and Faber, Boston (1978) for anyone interested in advancing their knowledge of magnolias. The Magnolia Society Inc. publishes a newsletter that offers new information. Spongberg has an outstanding presentation of "Magnoliaceae Hardy in Temperate North America," *J. Arnold Arboretum* 57: 250–312 (1976).

Recent new *Magnolia* literature that includes Dorothy J. Callaway's *The World of Magnolias*, Timber Press (1994) and James M. Gardiner's *Magnolia's*, The Globe Pequot Press, Chester, CT (1989) are more horticultural and garden oriented. Both offer excellent photographs and cultivar treatments that transcend this Manual. Dorothy is a Horticulture graduate of our Georgia program.

NATIVE HABITAT: New York to Georgia, west to Illinois and Arkansas. Introduced 1736.

RELATED SPECIES:

Magnolia acuminata L. var. ***subcordata*** (Spach) Dandy, (sub-kôr-dā′tà), Yellow Cucumbertree, is a large shrub or small bushy tree, 20 to 30′ high, allied to *M. acuminata*. The leaves are smaller and comparatively broader being 4 to 6″ long, 2 1/2 to 3 1/2″ wide. They are more lustrous dark green and are covered with matted pubescence below. Stems are also quite pubescent compared to glabrous stems of *M. acuminata*. The flowers vary in size and color and resemble those of *M. acuminata* differing in their smaller size and yellow color. I have seen enough true *M. a.* var. *subcordata* to present a reasonably intelligent discussion. The tree is usually small, upright and at times shrubby. One exception is a giant +100′ high tree at Longwood Gardens which is labeled as this taxon. Eye to tree observation says otherwise. Flowers are more tulip-shaped, fuller, and closer to yellow. It flowers with the emerging leaves and can never compete with the early types, but is still a handsome plant. In the Dirr garden, flowers open in mid-April and continue until the end of the month. 'Lexwood' is a selection from Woodland Park in Lexington, KY. 'Miss Honeybee' is a good hardy yellow selection, that is used in hybridizing. 'Mister Yellowjacket' has brilliant canary yellow flowers, rounded habit, 25 to 30′, selected by Dick Figlar. 'Skyland's Best' is a compact grower with dark green leaves and well-formed, yellow, fragrant flowers up to 6″ across, discovered by Richard Figlar. Compact yellow-flowered forms as well as a variegated form ('Ellen') are known. Difficult to wade through the volumes of literature and not be able to adequately define this variety. Other varieties have been distinguished but Callaway in *The World of Magnolias* recognizes only var. *subcordata*. Interestingly, the co-national champion trees are 102′ by 63′ at Longwood Garden and 89′ by 90′, Virginia Beach, VA. Does this shoot a hole in the author's smaller is var. *subcordata* theory? A small 8 to 10′ high shrub form flowers profusely in the author's garden. North Carolina and Georgia. Introduced 1801. Zone 5 to 8(9). Has withstood -25°F in Cincinnati, OH.

Magnolia cylindrica Wils.

LEAVES: Alternate, simple, obovate-elliptic, 4 to 6″ long, 2 to 2 1/2″ wide, acute, cuneate, entire, dark green with distinct reticulate venation above, paler beneath, appressed pubescence on veins; petiole—3/4 to 1″ long.

Magnolia cylindrica, (mag-nō′li-à si-lin′dri-kà), is a difficult species to define and I am still not sure the real plant has crossed my path. Specimens at Long Hill, Beverly, MA and the Arnold Arboretum were more *M. kobus*-like. A plant at Trengwainton in Penzance, England was the real item. In late March, white, fragrant, 9-tepaled flowers, stamens stained violet, smothered a 15′ by 20′ shrub. The overall appearance was reflective of *M. denudata*, perhaps without the strong fragrance. In 1998, I witnessed the species at Killerton, The Garden House, again at Trengwainton, with all specimens similar in flower. At the base of each tepal is a triangular, pinkish blotch, widest at the base. Flowers, unlike *M. denudata*, are shaped somewhat like a lily, being trumpet-shaped at base and flaring below or at the middle. All trees were low-branched and broad-spreading. With some imagination one can see *M. denudata* × *M. kobus* producing *M. cylindrica* off-spring. China. Zone (5)6 to 8.

Magnolia denudata Desr. [formerly *M. heptapeta* (Buc'hoz) Dandy] — Yulan Magnolia

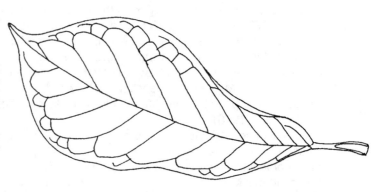

LEAVES: Alternate, simple, obovate to obovate-oblong, 4 to 6″ long, 2 to 3 1/2″ wide, short acuminate, tapering at base, entire, dark green and sparingly pubescent above, light green beneath and minutely pubescent chiefly on the nerves and slightly reticulate; petiole—about 1″ long.

BUDS: Flower—about 1″ long, ovoid-conical, grayish, woolly pubescent; leaf—smaller, flatter, pubescent.

STEM: Stout, pubescent initially, glabrous, gray-brown.

Magnolia denudata, (mag-nō′li-à de-nū-dā′tà), Yulan Magnolia, is a small, broad pyramidal (eventually rounded) tree growing 30 to 40′ high with a similar spread. Two 30′ high trees at Longwood Gardens and a 35′ high tree at Planting Fields reflect the large size. The flowers (9, 10–12 petals) are white to ivory, fragrant, 5 to 6″ across, goblet-shaped initially, spreading with time, borne singly and open before *M.* × *soulangiana*. Unfortunately, this species responds to early warm spells and the flowers are often injured by late freezes. Very beautiful when unadulterated by the weather. Fruits (I have observed them only once) are 4 to 6″ long, cylindrical aggregates of follicles that turn rose red with maturity. Has been difficult to root from cuttings and is often budded and grafted on *M.* × *soulangiana*. The variety *purpurascens* has rose red flowers outside, pink inside. Several other commercially available cultivars include: 'Caerhays' with pure white tepals; 'Gere' a large, hardy, ivory white-flowered form growing in Mt. Hope Cemetery, Urbana, IL, selected by J.C. McDaniel; 'Purple Eye' with white flowers and a purple blush at the base of the tepals, habit is broader than typical species form; 'Sawada' ('Sawada's Cream') has perfectly formed, creamy white flowers on a smaller plant, highly fertile and produces bright crimson fruit; and 'Wada' has smaller white flowers and is later flowering. I consider this one of the most beautiful of all the early flowering magnolias. Magnificent in flower and three 20′ high trees in the University's Botanical Garden flower consistently around early March. These plants are in partial shade and set prodigious quantities of flower buds. White was peeking through the bud scale on February 10, 1997. Young plants are distinctly upright and only with maturity does the plant become more open. Amazingly adaptable from Newburgh, ME to Tallahassee, FL west to Seattle and Los Angeles. Still one of the best. Central China. Introduced 1789. Zone 5 to 8. I suspect break point for wood hardiness is -25°F.

Magnolia grandiflora L. — Southern Magnolia, also called Evergreen Magnolia or Bull Bay.
(mag-nō′li-à gran-di-flō′rà)

LEAVES: Alternate, simple, evergreen, obovate-oblong or elliptic, 5 to 10″ long, usually less than half as wide, obtusely short-acuminate or obtusish, cuneate at base, entire, lustrous dark green and glabrous above, often ferrugineous-pubescent beneath, firmly coriaceous, surface often undulating; petiole—stout, about 1 to 2″ long, densely pubescent to almost glabrous.

BUDS: Terminal (flower)—3/4 to 1 1/4″ long, often brown woolly pubescent, tapering at apex and less so at base, slightly bulbous in lower middle; lateral—small, ±1/4″ long, in axils of leaves, appressed and almost shrouded by the indumentum.

STEM: First year—coarse, often 1/4″ diameter and greater even at apex of shoot, the woolly pubescence, often brown, completely covers the stem, on less pubescent types, like Greenback™, color is usually green, lenticels vertical, small, gray-brown, lemon fragrance to bruised stems; pith—large, white, appearing building block-like, with one segment laying upon the next.

SIZE: 60 to 80′ in height with a spread of 30 to 50′; national champion is 98′ by 90′ in Jones City, MS.

HARDINESS: Zone (6)7 to 9(10), supposedly the brown back type is hardier than the green form but no quantitative evidence supports this; have seen magnolias in Pittsburgh, Wichita, Cincinnati, Vincennes, IN, Louisville, Long Island, and Boston that have survived; realistically the great trees are in the South.

HABIT: Densely pyramidal, low-branching, stately evergreen tree; generally distinctly columnar-pyramidal but some trees become as wide as tall; terrific variation in growth habit from dwarf 'Pygmaea' to almost columnar 'Hasse' to wide-open and robust 'Majestic Beauty'.

RATE: Slow to medium; with water and fertilizer a fast grower.

TEXTURE: The overall textural effect is coarse.

BARK: Smooth gray on young and older trees although older trees may develop large scaly plates.

LEAF COLOR: Lustrous dark green above, lighter green below and often ferrugineous (rusty) pubescent beneath; leaves are messy and never seem to decompose, drop in spring and fall; dried leaves sound like a bowl of rice crispies when walked upon.

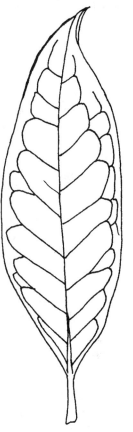

FLOWERS: Perfect, creamy white, beautifully fragrant (better than the best perfume), 8 to 12″ in diameter, solitary, in May–June, sporadically thereafter, usually with 6, 9 to 15 petals, each petal thick, concave, broadly obovate and 4 to 6″ long; may take as long as 15 to 20 years for trees to flower which have been grown from seed; the literature is so full of burbles that one does not often know who or what to believe; over the years I have read statements about the slowness to flower from seed; a one-gallon container plant (1-year-old) flowered 3 years later in my garden; after 13 growing seasons the plant was 30′ high and produced heavy crops of flowers; there is a great deal of difference among seedlings and cultivars in earliness to, and degree of, flower; buy seedling-grown plants in flower if possible or select a reliable cultivar; cultivars are now dominant in commerce and should be utilized ahead of seedling material; 'Little Gem' will flower as a one-gallon plant and continue to do so into October–November; why not enjoy the plant's most magnificent feature.

FRUIT: Rose-red, aggregate of follicles, 3 to 5″ long, splitting open to expose the red seeds; usually ripen in September–October–November; fruit heavily in the South; old "cone-like" structure falls in November–December and makes a mess; collect seeds as they emerge on funicular stalks (threads) from the follicles; seeds are beautiful.

CULTURE: Transplant balled-and-burlapped or from a container in winter or early spring; soil should be rich, porous, acidulous and well-drained; full sun or partial shade; some authorities indicate it does best in partial shade, supposedly will tolerate as little as 3 hours of sunlight per day; must be protected from winter winds and sun in northern area; tolerates high soil moisture levels; often shocks, i.e., drops many interior leaves when transplanted, try to move young plants or those that have been root pruned; southern growers identified August as the best time to transplant Southern Magnolia, less shock and reduced leaf drop were observed; even when trees drop leaves they recover and the new growth covers the sins of transplanting; this species and virtually all magnolias can be pruned into large wood and will regenerate new shoots; I saw large stumps that were left after cleanup from Hurricane Hugo send forth new shoots that resulted in bushy new Southern Magnolias; *Magnolia grandiflora* and all magnolias are surface rooted and competitive for water and nutrients; ground covers are few that will survive and include *Liriope*, *Ophiopogon*, *Sarcococca*, and *Pachysandra*.

DISEASES AND INSECTS: Essentially problem free; a paper in *J. Arboriculture* 11(9) (1985) presents information on the decline and death of Southern Magnolia that might be linked to a mycoplasma or bacterium; in recent years noticed weevil damage (puncture holes) on young leaves; interesting study by Santamour and Riedel, *J. Environ. Hort.* 19:257–259 (1993), showed *M. grandiflora* exhibited a tolerant or resistant response to all nematodes; leaf spot caused by *Pseudomonas cichorii* was reported on newly unfolded leaves, see *Plant Disease* 68:1013–1015 (1984).

LANDSCAPE VALUE: Specimen, widely used and planted in the southern states; needs room to develop; a very worthwhile and handsome tree; have seen it used as a screen, grouping and hedge; an almost indispensable part of the southern garden heritage; Yankees would kill to be able to grow this tree; the Freeman hybrids (*M. grandiflora* × *M. virginiana*) have survived but certainly not thrived in northern arboreta; have seen 'Edith Bogue' in Philadelphia that was handsome; the newer cultivars offer greater hope for the landscape and, to my way of thinking, seedling material is now outmoded; great strides have been made in cultivar selection and many (too) are searching for the best cold hardy forms; I have observed plants in Boston ('Winchester' at Arnold), Lexington, Louisville, Cincinnati, and Pittsburgh that survived and in some cases made worthy specimens; three clones from Spring Grove in Cincinnati were rooted by the author and are still growing in the Georgia test plots, unfortunately, none hold an aesthetic candle to the *best* Zone 7 to 9 types; the most cold hardy cultivars are 'Bracken's Brown Beauty', 'Edith Bogue', and 'Select #3'.

CULTIVARS: I did a literature search for a talk on this species and found something approaching 125 cultivars and that did not include the past 10 years. For many years, the biggest hindrance to growing the cultivars was propagation. Most had to be grafted which is almost a lost art in the United States. Most cultivars assembled here are historically noteworthy, and/or available in commerce. Louisiana Nursery (1998 catalog), Route 7, Box 43, Opelousas, LA 70570 lists about 67 cultivars. Wow!

We conducted cutting propagation research in the mid-1980's that many people have refined and improved. Many individuals selected, propagated and introduced their own cultivars.

Alta™ ('TIIMG')—Strongly upright form, resembling 'Hasse' in outline, leaves lustrous dark green, medium brown indumentum, foliage not quite as lustrous or dark green as 'Hasse', easier to propagate and transplant, will make an excellent screening, evergreen magnolia, parent tree 21′ by 8′, introduced by Tree Introductions, Inc., Athens, GA.

'Baby Doll'—Small, glossy green leaves, small flowers, semi-rounded, 22′ by 22′ in 25 years, Mary Shadow's favorite plant and for that reason included, Mary mentioned that it was great for indoor arrangements because of smaller foliage.

'Baldwin'—Upright growth habit, lustrous dark green leaves covered with brown indumentum on the lower surface, young stems carry the richly colored pubescence, flowers larger than normal, found by Tom Dodd, Jr. in Baldwin County, AL.

'Black Stem'—Strap-shaped leaves and unique pubescence on the stems, from Bob Island, Charmwood Nursery.

'Blackwell'—Compact form with glossy deep green leaves with undulating margins, flowers when young.

'Bracken's Brown Beauty'—Certainly one of the best selections; relatively compact and dense even in youth, forms multiple breaks from each shoot and thus makes a fuller specimen; leaves small, about 6″ long, leathery lustrous dark green above, rusty brown below with an undulating surface; flowers about 5 to 6″ diameter with 2 to 3″ long fruits; transplants better than many and does not drop as many leaves; possibly mature at 30 to 50′ by 15 to 30′; patented and introduced by Ray Bracken, Easley, SC; has become the dominant cultivar in the Southeast along side 'Little Gem'; also, one of the most cold hardy.

'Cairo'—Narrow, columnar, glossy leaves, early and long flowering, found in Cairo, IL, introduced by J.C. McDaniel.

'Charles Dickens'—Large broad leaves, 10″ diameter fragrant flowers, bright red fruits, tetraploid, on site of former Britton's Nursery, Winchester, TN.

'Chloe'—Good form with large leaves, fast growing, requires pruning, named after the daughter of the owner of Cherry Lake Tree Farm, Florida.

'Cinnamon Twist'—Large, shiny green leaves, rusty brown undersides, slight twist to long axis of leaf, 8″ diameter, fragrant, white flowers, 60′ by 25′, introduced by Plantation Tree Co., Selma, AL.

'Claudia Wannamaker'—A fine form with dark green foliage and medium rusty brown undersides; flowers at an early age; medium-broad pyramid, vigorous and more open than 'Bracken's'; relatively easy to root; widely planted in the Southeast; truly one of the best of the larger types, 50′ and greater; gets better with age in terms of density and uniformity of habit; Brailsford introduction, Orangeburg, SC.

'Coco'—Quality pyramidal habit, lustrous dark green leaves, heavy flowering over a long time period, handsome form, 50′ by 25′, Head-Lee Nursery, Seneca, SC introduction.

'D.D. Blanchard'—A pyramidal selection with lustrous dark green leaves and rich orangish brown undersides; relatively easy to root; exceptionally handsome form; selected over 30 years ago by Robbins Nursery, Willard, NC; tends to loosen with maturity and is more open than 'Claudia Wannamaker'; leaves are possibly the darkest green and the undersides spectacular orangish brown; 50′ and greater.

'Dauber'—Early flowering form from Stewartstown, PA, cold hardy.

'David Kirchhoff'—Compact tree with small leaves similar to those of *M. virginiana*, could be a hybrid.

'Dr. Henry Orr' ('Henry Orr')—Lustrous medium green leaves, prominent veins, typical flowers, dense habit without pruning, widening with age, considered a hybrid of 'Satin Leaf' and 'Charles Dickens'.

'Edith Bogue'—Lustrous dark green and narrow leaves, light tomentum on underside; possibly the most cold hardy clone; a large tree in the Morris Arboretum, Philadelphia, has withstood the test of cold, ice, and snow; Roger Gossler reports the branches less susceptible to breakage in heavy wet snows; 30′(40′) by 15′ (20′); originated from Florida as a tree sent to Miss E.A. Bogue, Montclair, NJ; since the 1990 edition, I have observed numerous Edith Bogues outside of the Morris Arboretum (my original dense pyramid) and have lost enthusiasm because of open framework of branches and rather lackluster foliage; the inclusion of a plant in my test plots confirmed continued observations; if in North utilize it, in South (Zone 7 to 9) opt for 'Bracken's Brown Beauty', Greenback™, 'Hasse', and 'Claudia Wannamaker'.

'Emory'—Fastigiate-columnar, 90′ by 12′, rich dark pubescence, fragrant white flowers.

'Fairhope I'—Rounded crown, wavy leaves, almost rounded, blunt tips, large flowers, short internodes, Magnolia Nursery.

'Fairhope II'—Small-flowered clone, lanceolate leaves with brown underside, fall flowering tree, Magnolia Nursery.

'Ferruginea'—Rounded habit, reasonably compact; large, globe-shaped, fragrant, cream-white flowers; dark green leaves with rust red pubescence below.

'Florida Giant'—Large glossy deep green leaves, larger flowers than typical.

'Gloriosa'—Flowers of great size and substance, very broad leaves, considered one of the finest, cultivated since 1860.

'Gold Strike'—Narrow, 12″ long leaves are splashed with golden yellow variegation, Louisiana Nursery introduction.

'Goliath'—Superior flowering form with large flowers up to 12″ across, the leaves are broad, rounded and blunt at the end and glossy green, up to 8″ long, with a trace of pubescence on midrib below; reasonably compact habit.

'Green Giant'—Robust grower, large, lustrous dark green leaves, up to 9″ long by 5″ wide, young leaves are golden green in color and contrast handsomely with the older leaves, leaves are green-backed, estimated size 60′ by 30′, introduced by Plantation Tree Co., Selma, AL.

Greenback™ ('Mgtig')—A bright star in the world of new *M. grandiflora* introductions; selected by John Barbour, Bold Spring Nursery, Monroe, GA; parent plant 30′ by 12′, dense, tightly branched, leaves to 4″(5″) long, lustrous waxy dark green above, minimal pubescence below, finally green; leaves cupped (convex) reflecting like a thousand points of light on a sunny day; great container plant as it forms many breaks from each shoot and fills in as a young plant; will prove a worthy screening plant; also, excellent sales appeal as a container-grown plant.

'Griffin'—Probably a hybrid between *M. grandiflora* × *M. virginiana*, discovered in Griffin, GA, not the most aesthetic selection.

'Harold Poole'—Unique, dwarf, bushy clone with dark green, strap-shaped leaves, up to 1 1/2″ wide, to 1′ long, medium-sized flowers.

'Harwell'—Leaves resemble a green calla lily due to fused margins.

'Hasse'—Rather unusual form with more upright growth habit, leaves smaller than species, extremely lustrous dark green, light rusty pubescence below; Mr. Johnny Brailsford, Sr., had a great eye for quality magnolias and 'Hasse' is no exception; he showed me the parent plant which is down the highway from his Shady Grove Nursery; parent tree 40 to 45′ high, 15 to 18′ wide, long tapering, dense conical crown; a wonderful magnolia for restricted spaces; not the easiest to propagate and transplant, but worth the effort.

'Isenberg'—Hardy form from Stewartstown, PA.

'Jubilee'—Selection from Tom Dodd with excellent flowers.

'Lakeside'—Fast-growing form with large, wavy leaves, easy to propagate from cuttings, Magnolia Nursery.

'Lanceolata' ('Exoniensis', 'Exmouth')—Narrow pyramidal form, leaves narrower than species, rusty tomentose beneath; flowers particularly handsome often with another set of tepals in the center of the flower; one of the first selections, has existed for over 200 years.

'Little Gem'—Definitely the smallest of the truly commercial forms presented here; wants to grow as a large dense shrub rather than with a single leader; leaves are small (4″), lustrous dark green and covered with a bronzy brown pubescence below; flowers smaller (3 to 4″ diameter, 6″ when fully open) but borne at a young age and continually, production slackens in summer heat, through October–November in Zone 7 and 8; rooted cuttings have produced flowers in their first year in a one-gallon container; actually makes a good medium-sized screen or hedge plant; one of the best for smaller properties, possibly 20′ high, 10′ wide in 20 years; have utilized this cultivar at Milliken & Co., Spartanburg, SC as a lightly pruned hedge separating the allée and parking lot, it has proven outstanding; one of the more recalcitrant rooters with 42% the highest ever achieved by this author; some propagators have recited higher percentages, others lower; Monrovia introduction, selected by Warren Steed Nursery, Candor, NC; new study in 1996–97 yielded 83% rooting, see data under propagation.

'Madison'—Hardy, compact, everblooming cultivar with neat growth habit, from Joe McDaniel.

'Main Street'—More columnar or fastigiate growth habit with oval, brown-backed leaves, Cedar Lane Farm, Madison, GA selection.

'Majestic Beauty'—Extravagantly large, lustrous dark green leaves, profuse flowering, up to 12″ wide, and broad pyramidal outline; young plants are open; foliage is immense and somewhat coarse, veins appear as ribs; not particularly handsome, almost too coarse-textured; in nursery production and landscapes in the South, open and rather ugly, 50′ by 30′, too many better choices; Monrovia introduction.

'Margaret Davis'—Dark green brown back foliage, broad flame-shaped, tight branching structure; flowers large, up to 14″ across; actually a respectable clone but simply outdistanced by Mr. Brailsford's other introductions.

'Meyers'—From Tifton, GA, second largest *M. grandiflora* in United States.

'Millais Variety'—Glossy, almost black-green leaves, from Fota Garden, Cork, Ireland.

'Milton's Wavy'—Attractive growth habit, wavy-edged leaves.

'Nannetensis'—Produces immense, fragrant, single to double flowers.

'Orbit'—Dwarf form of rounded outline, J.C. McDaniel introduction.

'Parris Selection'—Seedling of 'Little Gem', narrow pyramidal habit, self branching, lustrous dark green leaves with brown back, early-flowering, produced 4 flowers in second year from seed, reasonably easy to propagate from cuttings, from Gilbert's Nursery, Chesnee, SC.

'Pearl'—Somewhat like 'Coco', flowers in abundance, from Head-Lee Nursery.

'Phil Marino'—Upright conical tree with showy flowers.

'Pioneer'—Hardy, compact grower with 8″ diameter, creamy white flowers, found by Will Curtis, Oregon.

'Plantation #5'—Pyramidal grower, 60′ by 30′, tends to be broader than 'Claudia Wannamaker', lustrous dark green leaves with rusty brown undersides, introduced by Plantation Tree Co., Selma, AL.

'Poconos'—Glossy leaves, dark green and narrow, light brown indumentum on underside, found in Poconos of Pennsylvania, listed as -10°F cold hardy, as hardy or hardier than 'Edith Bogue'.

'Red Tip'—New growth bronzy red.

'Riegel'—Compact habit like 'Little Gem', denser, not as fastigiate, may be *M. grandiflora* × *M. virginiana* hybrid, leaves are 6″ long, 2″ wide, flowers are almost the size of *M. grandiflora*, introduced by Tom Dodd, Jr. from seedling population.

'Ripples'—Extremely wavy leaf margin.

'Robert Reich'—Broad, dark green leaves up to 17″ long and large, fragrant, white flowers.

'Ruff'—Large dark green leaves with red-brown indumentum, superior under Oregon conditions according to Gossler Nursery.

'Russet'—Tight dense columnar-pyramidal form with small narrow dark green leaves covered with orangish brown indumentum below; appears to be more cold hardy; in my tests this has been less than satisfactory, growth habit as mentioned but leaves not orangish brown, almost gray-brown; not worthy of extensive use in Zone 7 to 9; I have had a difficult time rooting this clone; Saratoga Horticultural Foundation introduction.

'Saint Mary' ('Glen St. Mary')—Lustrous dark green leaves, undulating surface, the underside of the leaf is bronzed by the felty pubescence; flowers at a younger age than most *M. grandiflora* forms; compact bushy pyramidal form, 20′ by 20′; flowers in 2 to 3 years from a cutting; as I witnessed the plant in a Louisiana nursery it was pyramidal, 2 to 3 times as tall as wide at maturity, probably much larger than the 20′ by 20′ reported above; introduced about 1905.

'Samuel Sommer'—Form of rapid growth, strong ascending habit and large, 10 to 14″ diameter, 12-tepaled, creamy white flowers, lustrous dark green foliage with heavy rusty pubescence below, becomes a handsome tree, 30 to 40′ by 30′, looser and more open than one would like but still a handsome form.

'Santa Cruz'—Dark green foliage, abundant brown indumentum, up to 7″ by 3″, 9″ wide, ivory white, fragrant, up to 22-tepaled flowers.

'Sasquatch'—Twice as wide as high.

'Satin Beauty'—Large, glossy foliage, J.C. McDaniel hybrid between 'Satin Leaf' and 'Empire State'.

'Satin Leaf'—Large, glossy dark green leaves, red-brown indumentum below, large flowers.

'Select #3'—Vigorous, intermediate pyramidal form with lustrous dark green leaves, medium brown pubescence, not as dark green as 'D.D. Blanchard' or 'Little Gem'; excellent cold hardiness; consistent quality from this clone; introduced by Select Trees, Oconee County, GA; I have walked rows of this clone and although it never overwhelms the sum total of its attributes equals a worthy tree.

'Silver Savage'—Good evergreen foliage, cold tolerant, Head-Lee introduction.

'Silver Tip'—Upright grower with huge, lustrous dark green leaves, silver-gray pubescence below.

'Simpson's Hardy'—Glossy dark green leaves, hardy to -25°F, from the late Robert Simpson, Vincennes, IN.

'Smith Fogle'—Large, elongated, almost acuminate leaf with a slight twist, lustrous dark green, brown below, 8 to 10″ diameter flowers, broad pyramidal, reasonably dense in youth, Brailsford introduction.

'Southern Lights'—Improved selection with beautiful creamy white flowers in May–June, sporadic flowering through summer, powerful fragrance.

Southern Pride™—Large, wide-spreading form, 60 to 80' high, from Hines Nursery.

'Spring Hill' ('Springhill')—Broad, dark green leaves with golden reddish brown pubescence below, columnar habit.

'Springfield'—Fused margin, leaves resemble flowers of calla lily.

'Symmes Select'—Full and branched to the ground, vigorous, broad pyramid, large lustrous dark green leaves with dark brown backs, large white flowers occur on young trees, Cedar Lane Farm introduction.

'Teddy Bear'—Dense, compact, upright-pyramidal form, wavy leaves.

'Topaz'—Pyramidal form, 50' high, 20' wide, listed by Moon's Tree Farm, Inc., Loganville, GA.

'Twenty-four Below' ('24 Below')—Uninjured by -24°F, Frank Galyon introduction.

'U.S.L. Variegated'—Glossy green leaves with showy yellow-gold variegation.

'Variegata'—Catchall term for types with cream to yellow foliar variegation, have seen my share of these, most are not stable.

'Victoria'—Considered among the hardiest of all *M. grandiflora* introductions; was selected in Victoria, B.C. for its lustrous foliage with brown pubescent undersides; used extensively in Pacific Northwest, seldom seen in Southeast; several southeastern growers have tried this with ambivalent feelings; in my trials it is wild and open-growing, does not compete with the upper echelon southern magnolias.

'Winchester' ('Tulsa')—A cold hardy form that grew by the Arnold Arboretum's greenhouse for many years, seed collected in Tulsa, OK, plant grown in Winchester, MA; flowers 6 to 8″ wide; definitely one of the more cold hardy forms; have observed significant burn on foliage.

'Workman'—Compact, semi-dwarf clone, small leaves with undulating margin, flowers over a long period, 20' by 15', 10- to 11-tepaled flowers appear over long time frame.

Cultivars and clones that have been tested by this author include: 'Phyllis Barrow', Spring Grove #16, #19, #43, Dawes Arboretum Clone, Tifton Clone, and Bob Simpson Clone. The Spring Grove, Dawes, and Simpson clones are cold hardy. 'Phyllis Barrow' is one of my introductions (originally 'Dearing Street') with lustrous dark green leaves and orangish brown indumentum. Unfortunately, it is open under cultivation. Use discretion before introducing another *M. grandiflora* clone.

PROPAGATION: Seeds exhibit embryo dormancy and should be stratified for 3 to 6 months at 32 to 41°F; after working with this plant over the past 13 years I have created and found enough information to fill several pages; suggest the reader see Dirr and Heuser, 1987, or Dirr and Brinson, *Amer. Nurseryman* 162(9): 38–51 (1985); our recipe for cutting success involves firm wooded cuttings July–early September, 5000 to 10,000 ppm NAA-50% alcohol, IBA will also work, perlite, mist, with rooting taking place in 6 to 10 weeks; if by fourth week no swelling of the stem has taken place the cuttings will probably not root. Many other successful recipes depending on propagator. Use the most juvenile material possible for stock plants. A 1996–97 rooting study with 'Claudia Wannamaker', 'Little Gem' and Greenback™ proved interesting. KNAA or a combination of KNAA plus 0.8% IBA in talc (double dip) resulted in the highest percentages and root quality. For the three taxa rooting percentages were 23, 23, and 50 for 1% KNAA, respectively, and 58, 83, 58 for the double-dip combination, respectively. Although many nurserymen and researchers show the effectiveness of IBA, our long-term experimental results point to KNAA as the most efficacious. Also, grafting and budding are practiced, particularly on West Coast. Tissue culture has proven effective with certain cultivars.

ADDITIONAL NOTES: Truly an aristocratic broadleaf evergreen and many old southern homes are graced with this tree. During the rugged winter of 1976–77 (-20°F) almost every tree in Champaign-Urbana was killed outright or at least to the ground. Similar response on trees in Spring Grove, Cincinnati, OH. Several survived and may represent the most cold-hardy clones available. Conducted laboratory cold hardiness tests on these clones. Articles on cold hardiness include Lindstrom and Dirr, *J. Environ. Hort.* 9:116–118 (1991), where laboratory tests paralleled observed field cold tolerance of seven cultivars. Also, a popular article by Dirr, *Horticulture* 70(3):54–60 (1992), presents this cold hardiness information in everyday garden terms. See also Lindstrom, *HortScience* 27:247–249 (1992), for use of leaf parts to estimate cold hardiness of *M. grandiflora*. Often found in the wild in moist areas and in alluvial soils under the shade of large trees. Birds move the plant throughout the cultivated landscape.

NATIVE HABITAT: North Carolina to Florida, Arkansas and Texas. Cultivated 1734.

Magnolia kobus DC. — Kobus Magnolia

LEAVES: Alternate, simple, broad-obovate to obovate, 3 to 6″(8″) long, half as wide, abruptly pointed, tapering to the cuneate base, dark green above, light green beneath and pubescent on the veins, finally glabrous or nearly so; petiole—1/2 to 3/4″ long.

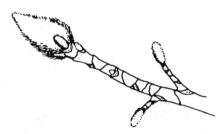

BUDS: Flower—1 to 1 1/2″ long, silky gray pubescent, bulbous base tapering to acuminate apex; vegetative—gray-green, valvate, silky pubescent, 1/8 to 1/4″(3/8″) long.

STEM: Slender, green, splashed with brownish splotches not unlike the spotting on a Holstein cow, glabrous except toward end, spotted with vertical grayish lenticels, strong pungent odor when bruised, more offensive than sweet or lemony like *M. salicifolia*.

Magnolia kobus, (mag-nō′li-à kō′bus), Kobus Magnolia, in youth develops a pyramidal crown and eventually becomes round-headed. The tree grows 30 to 40′ high and often develops a multi-stemmed character. The foliage is medium to dark green in summer and does not develop good fall color, although on occasion leaves die off yellow to golden brown. The flowers are white, slightly fragrant, 4″ across or less, 6(9) petals, with a faint purple line at the base outside, petals soon falling, March–April. Does not flower well when young and may take as long as 30 years to reach full flowering potential although there is variation in this respect among progeny. Easily propagated from cuttings. I have seen several mature specimens (35′) in flower at Cave Hill Cemetery, Louisville, KY, Arnold Arboretum, Winterthur, DE, Cold Spring Harbor Laboratory, Long Island, NY, and most recently 60′ trees outside of Amherst, MA (full flower mid-April); all were like white clouds. The floral effect borders on spectacular and it is unfortunate that the species is tardy to flower from seed. Seedlings that I grew from Arnold plants are now 7-years-old with no signs of flower buds. Plants in the University's Botanical Garden flowered in about 10 years from seed. These plants are now 20 to 25′ high. Flowering occurs around the first week in March with amazing consistency. This, *M. salicifolia* and *M. stellata* are among the earliest magnolias to flower. Variety *borealis* Sarg. represents a more vigorous, robust, larger (70 to 80′ high), pyramidal tree than the species. The leaves are 6 to 7″ long and the flowers average up to 5″ across. A seedling of variety *borealis* grown by C.S. Sargent of the Arnold Arboretum was still sparse flowering when almost 30-years-old, but 15 years later was making a fine display and bore more flowers in succeeding years. 'Janaki Ammal' is a hardy tetraploid clone with broad, white tepals that lie flat. Listed as *M. stellata* form at Wisley but definitively *M. kobus* and not a good form at that. 'Kehr 7-1' is a polyploid with both diploid and tetraploid growth on same plant. 'Nippon' has flowers almost as large as *M. denudata*. 'Parson's Clone' has good growth habit, flowers larger than typical. 'Pink' has pink flowers, attractive foliage. 'Wada's Memory' has 6″ diameter, fragrant, white flowers before the leaves, fast, large-growing, bronze foliage in spring, dark green in summer, butter yellow in fall; hybrid between *M. kobus* and *M. salicifolia*. A few worthy anecdotes: var. *borealis* flowered after 23 years from seed (1876–1899) in C.S. Sargent's Brookline Garden; Roger Luce, Newburgh, ME waited 18 years for it to flower; Roger considers it the most cold hardy of all magnolias; flowers at the Morton Arboretum, Lisle, IL in early to mid-April. Supposedly excellent for all types of soil, including limestone. Has grown amazingly fast in Georgia silty clay loams. Native to Japan. Introduced 1865. The species is hardy in Zone 4, the variety in Zone 3, grows well in Zone 7(8).

Magnolia liliiflora Desr. [formerly *M. quinquepeta* (Buc'hoz) Dandy] — Lily Magnolia

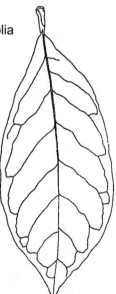

LEAVES: Alternate, simple, entire, obovate or elliptic-ovate, 4 to 7″ long, 2 to 5″ wide, short-acuminate, tapering at base, dark green and sparingly pubescent above, light green beneath and finely pubescent on the nerves; petiole—about 1/2″ long.

BUDS: Flower, large, 1/2 to 1″ long, hairy.

STEM: Glabrous except near the tip.

Magnolia liliiflora, (mag-nō′li-à li-lē-ī-flô′rà), Lily Magnolia, is a rounded, shrubby plant reaching 8 to 12′ in height with a similar spread. Often looks ragged in late summer to early fall when the leaves appear tattered, torn and mildewed. The 3 to 4″ wide flowers are vinous-purple outside and usually white inside, 6 petals [Callaway lists 9(18)], late April to early May, just before or as leaves are developing, borne singly. I have always admired this species for handsome flower but it does become somewhat ratty in habit and the foliage can look tired and worn by late summer. Has served as a good parent in several hybrids. Flowers about late March in Athens-Atlanta area and is beautiful in flower. Often growing around older residences; now largely superseded by Saucer, Star and Loebner magnolias. Seldom offered in everyday commerce and on occasion one or two of the better cultivars are available. Leaves often infected with mildew and my field notes list the species as defoliated by 9-25-92 at the University's Botanical Garden, while 'O'Neill' exhibited terrible mildew at Swarthmore College in early September 1992. Considered to be a native of China, although, according to Wilson, not found in the wild state in China. Zone 5 to 8.

CULTIVARS: Many more than presented here are described by Callaway.

'Al's Dwarf'—Diminutive size, dense habit, improvement over 'Mini Mouse', found by Albert Durio.

'Darkest Purple'—One of the best forms for large, dark purple-red flowers, repeat flowering, from Overlook Nurseries, Mobile, AL.

'Doris'—Large purple-pink flowered clone, long flowering season.

'Gracilis'—More narrow, fastigiate habit, with narrower, deeper purple petals, leaves narrower, paler green.

'Holland Red'—Large, deep reddish purple flowers over a long period.

'Lyons'—Deep reddish purple flowers, tepals twisted, later in season, may escape late spring frosts.

'Mini Mouse'—Dwarf shrub with 2″ leaves and 3″ flowers.

'Nigra'—Larger flowers, 5″ across, petals 5″ long, dark purple outside and light purple inside, makes a less straggly bush than the species, flowers later than species, have observed this in Dutch and English gardens where it appears relatively compact with dark green foliage and continued flowering after the leaves are fully expanded, tepals are extremely dark reddish purple.

'O'Neill'—Clone was selected by Professor J.C. McDaniel in 1973 for good vigorous compact habit and very dark purple flowers, 10 to 13 tepals, larger and darker than 'Nigra', flowers heavily as a young plant, possibly the best clone, but does contract mildew, listed as fully cold hardy in Orono, ME.

'Purple Prince'—Supposedly better than the species and 'Nigra' because of mildew resistance, from Frank Galyon, Tennessee.

THE LITTLE GIRL HYBRIDS

For lack of a better name I will advance this. This is a group of hybrids that resulted from crosses between *M. liliiflora* 'Nigra' and *M. stellata* 'Rosea' or the reciprocal. The original crosses were made in 1955 and 1956 at the U.S. National Arboretum. The idea was to produce a group with good floral characteristics that would flower later than the star magnolia and thus avoid frost damage. They are all rather erect, shrubby growers and will probably mature between 10 to 15′(20′). The flowers open before the leaves and make a magnificent display. Again in summer, sporadic flowers occur but are lighter colored owing to the heat. They root easily from softwood cuttings and have been successfully flowered at the Minnesota Landscape Arboretum (Zone 3b) and Athens, GA [Zone 7b(8)]. Flowers normally peak around mid-March in Athens. The girls' names are 'Ann', 'Betty', 'Jane', 'Judy', 'Pinkie', 'Randy', 'Ricki', and 'Susan'. 'Ann' is my favorite. See *Horticulture* 58(5):66 (1980) for additional details. Descriptions are provided in *Bulletin of the Morris Arboretum* 19(2):26–29 (1968). They are terribly confused in the trade and it is anybody's guess as to what is being offered, regardless of name.

'Ann'—8 to 10′ high, 10′ wide, more open than 'Betty', deep purple-red, 7- to 9-petaled, slightly earlier than 'Betty', mid to late March in the Dirr garden, good grower.

'Betty'—Deep purple-red outside to white inside, 12 to 15 tepals, copper-red new growth, large broad-rounded habit, 10 to 15′ high.

'Jane'—Reddish purple outside and white inside.

'Judy'—Deep red-purple outside, whiter inside, erect growth habit.

'Pinkie'—Pale red-purple fading to pink on the outside to almost white at the apex, lightest of all hybrids, white on inside, 9 to 12 tepals, 5 to 7″ diameter, mildew ridden, large growing.

'Randy'—Purple outside, white inside, nothing exceptional, mildew susceptible, broad-spreading, smallest of hybrids.

'Ricki'—Deep purple flower, white to purple-shaded inside, nicer shrub than 'Randy', upright.

'Susan'—Red-purple long slender buds, essentially same color inside as out, 6 tepals opening to 5″ wide flowers, the tepals slightly twisted, mildew susceptible, largest of group, broad haystack.

Probably best reserved for Zone 4 to 6b, although growing successfully in Zone 7. At one time, I was exuberant about the Little Girl Hybrids' landscape possibilities. Southern growers planted fields of them and bulldozed goodly numbers. Foliage is often tattered and mildew ridden, a genetically inherited trait from *M. liliiflora*. All Little Girls were mildew ridden and tattered at Arnold Arboretum (9-2-91). Also, they tend to develop water sprout-like growths when stressed. Size, which should be small considering the parents, is quite large. The collections at Swarthmore College and U.S. National Arboretum belie their stated smallness.

Magnolia × *loebneri* Kache. — Loebner Magnolia

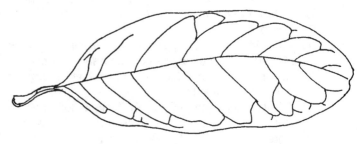

LEAVES: Alternate, simple, narrow obovate, 4 to 6″ by 1 to 2 1/4″, abruptly acute, rounded, entire, dark green.

BUDS: Flower—ovoid, tapering to obtuse apex, fattest at the base, silky-furry pubescent, 1 to 1 1/2″ long; vegetative—silky-hairy, fattest in middle, tapering at ends, 1/4 to 3/8″ long.

STEM: Much more slender than *M.* × *soulangiana* or *M. denudata*, about 1/8″ diameter, brown-purple-green, dotted with elliptical-oval, gray, vertical lenticels, sweet fragrance to bruised stems, older trunks gray and sculptural.

Magnolia × *loebneri*, (mag-nō′li-à lēb′nĕr-ī), is the result of a cross between *M. kobus* and *M. stellata* made by Max Löbner of Pillnitz, Germany, shortly before World War I. In 41 years one of the original plants was 25′ high and 28′ wide. In general, the hybrid can be expected to mature between 20 and 30′ with a slightly greater spread. The habit is rounded to broad-rounded. A 35′ high, oval haystack-shaped, 12-tepaled form resides in an Athens garden. Have seen in full flower by mid-February. The flowers typically have (9)12(15) tepals, entire flower 4 to 6″ diameter, are fragrant and open in early to mid-March in Athens, mid to late April in Boston. The hybrids are among the most beautiful of all magnolias and as I pen this (March 19, 1989) the 'Leonard Messel' in the garden is in full flower. The hybrids are quite vigorous and flower well in the second or third year from a cutting. In Athens, 'Leonard Messel' has always flowered later than *M.* × *soulangiana* and *M. stellata*, but in Zone 5 to 6 has opened 7 to 10 days earlier than *M.* × *soulangiana*. Cuttings are easy to root and grow off rapidly. I have not observed every deciduous Magnolia known to man but have watched with great satisfaction the superb flowering sequence of 'Ballerina', 'Leonard Messel', 'Merrill' and 'Spring Snow'. I have observed many new deciduous magnolia introductions that purport to greatness. This hybrid species is bypassed and unjustifiably so. Consistent performance in Maine and Georgia. Excellent foliage that emerges bronzy green, maturing to dark green and yellow-bronze in fall. Mildew has never been observed. I rate this hybrid grex in the top five early flowering deciduous magnolias. I have added a few cultivars in this edition that might be worthy of use.

'Ballerina'—A J.C. McDaniel introduction with up to 30 petals, fragrant, more than either 'Merrill' or 'Leonard Messel', pinkish in center, pure white over most of the flower, tends to escape late spring frosts, emerging buds almost cream-yellow; an F_2 seedling from 'Spring Snow' raised in 1963; have had good success (88%) rooting this clone from June softwoods treated with 10000 ppm IBA-quick dip, sand, mist in 8 weeks. Slightly smaller than 'Merrill' and 'Spring Snow', 15 to 20′.

'Donna'—Flat, fragrant, pure white, 8″ diameter flowers, from Harry Heineman, Massachusetts.

'Encore'—More compact grower, 18 to 25 tepals, white with tepal bases pink-tinged, 10 to 12′ high, introduced by August Kehr.

'Leonard Messel'—A chance hybrid between *M. kobus* and *M. stellata* 'Rosea' raised in Colonel Messel's garden at Nymans, Sussex, England; the 12 to 15 petals, 4 to 6″ across, are flushed with a purple-pink line along their center; fuchsia pink on the back of the strap-shaped, undulating, crinkled tepals, white on the inside; this is a beautiful hybrid that peaked between April 22–30, 1979 at the Arnold Arboretum; in the Dirr garden typically early to mid-March; 15 to 20′; it roots easily from softwood cuttings; truly one of the great magnolias, lovely fragrance, cannot resist picking a flower and savoring the fragrance when I return from work; interestingly, the plant espaliered on my garage has grown beyond the roof; those buds in the sun have opened as early as February 13 to 22; there is a deeper colored seedling of 'Leonard Messel' called 'Raspberry Fun'.

'Merrill'—A free-flowering, fragrant form raised from seed sown in 1939 at the Arnold Arboretum; there are 15(10 to 17) white tepals, each flower about 3 to 3 1/2″ across, grows about twice as fast as *M. stellata* and the parent plant is 25 to 30′ high and slightly wider; it peaks in late April (Boston) and is magnificent in flower, resembling a white cloud; roots readily from cuttings; has performed well at the Minnesota Landscape Arboretum (Zone 3b); outstanding performer in Zone 7 and 8; grows about 1 1/2 to 2 times as fast as *M.* × *soulangiana* which is faster than *M. stellata*; flowers open in early February to early March in Athens-Atlanta area; reportedly flowered after −45°F at Presque Isle, ME.

'Neal McEacharn' ('Neil McEachern')—Large shrub to small tree, pink buds open white, smaller flowers, grows 30′ high, from Great Windsor Park, England.

'Norman Gould'—A large-flowered, perhaps colchicine induced, 6- to 9-tepaled form, have seen in flower, not impressive, more probably a tetraploid *M. kobus*, counted 6 to 7 tepals on a plant at Hillier Arboretum that were larger than what I witnessed on the Swarthmore plant.

'Powder Puff'—Listed as having 18 to 25 tepals of purest white that give the appearance of a powder puff, have only seen it described in Beaver Creek Nursery catalog, Knoxville, TN.

'Raspberry Fun'—A seedling of 'Leonard Messel' from Ferris Miller, Chollipo Arboretum, Korea with deeper colored and better formed tepals, 16 to 18 tepals that appear to be clustered on the branches.

'Snowdrift'—Witnessed at Hillier in March 1998 in flower, smaller and fewer white tepals, not impressive.

'Spring Joy'—White flowers flushed pink, 5 to 6″ across, narrow tepals and double the number of 'Spring Snow', bushy grower.

'Spring Snow'—A J.C. McDaniel introduction; the parent tree is in the President's garden on the University of Illinois campus; the pure white tepals (15) hold their color well, I count 11 to 12(15) tepals; fragrant; it forms a 25 to 30′ high tree with a rounded outline; flowers a degree later and may escape late spring frosts; many magnolia experts consider this the best of the white *M.* × *loebneri* types, however, I do not.

'Star Bright'—Fragrant, pure white flowers, described as an arborescent *M. stellata*.

'Super Star' ('Bracken's Super Star')—Parentage is debatable, possibly *M. kobus*; pink-budded, white flowers, 6 tepals, minimal fragrance, excellent foliage, tremendous vigor, 30′ high plants at Milliken & Co., Spartanburg, SC; Ray Bracken introduction; worthy *tree* magnolia for the South; green stems like *M. kobus*.

'Vegetable Garden'—Compact habit, flowers resemble *M. stellata*, named after location in the vegetable garden, introduced by Camellia Forest Nursery, Chapel Hill, NC.

'White Rose'—White, heavy-textured tepals, up to 22; have only seen listed in Fairweather (1997) catalog; undamaged and flowered after −28°F in Wisconsin; open-pollinated seedling of 'Ballerina'.

'White Stardust'—Listed at one time as *M. stellata* but resoundingly *M.* × *loebneri*, impressive because of vigor (like 'Merrill') but without bark split, 14 to 15 tepals, good white, in full flower March 4, 1994 (Athens), excellent dark green foliage, about 60% of full flower on February 10, 1997, full flower February 20, 1998.

Magnolia macrophylla Michx. — Bigleaf Magnolia

LEAVES: Alternate, simple, entire, oblong-obovate, 12 to 32″ long, 7 to 12″ wide, obtuse, subcordate-auriculate at base, bright green and glabrous above, silvery gray and downy below, leaves borne in dense pseudo-whorls; petiole—2 to 4″ long.

BUDS: Large, tomentose, 1/2 to 1″ long.

STEM: Stout, pubescent at first, finally glabrous, coarse-textured, large leaf scars.

Magnolia macrophylla, (mag-nō′li-á mak-rō-fil′á), Bigleaf Magnolia, is a round-headed, cumbersome giant reaching 30 to 40′(60′) in height. National champion was 108′ by 42′ in Tight Hollow, KY. The flowers are creamy-white, 8 to 10″ and sometimes 14″ across, 6(9) tepals, fragrant, solitary, June. Inner 3 petals stained purple toward their base. The roundish, egg-shaped, rose-colored fruits are about 3″ long. The leaves are extremely large (12 to 32″ long) and give an overall coarse appearance which makes it difficult to use the tree in the landscape. It is an interesting sight when the leaves have fallen for the ground appears to be littered with large pieces of green and gray paper. This tree is not meant for the residential landscape and, along with the species treated herein, is reserved for parks, campuses and more fittingly the insatiable magnolia collector. The tree is particularly imposing and stately as an open-grown tree in a broad expanse of lawn. 'Sara Gladney' flowers over a long period, no purple stains at base of tepals, i.e., pure white. 'Whopper' has three foot leaves and 19″ diameter, white flowers with purple spots. *Magnolia macrophylla* is an interesting native tree which occurs limitedly from Ohio to Florida west to Arkansas and Louisiana. 1800. Zone 5 to 8. Some tip damage in Zone 4 at Orono, ME.

RELATED SPECIES:

Magnolia ashei Weatherby, (mag-nō′li-à ash′ē-ī), Ashe Magnolia, is very similar to *M. macrophylla* with
smaller leaves and a distinctly shrubby habit at least as I have seen plants in cultivation. Flowers (6 to 12″
across) as a young plant and have seen 4 to 6′ high plants with flowers and fruits. Seeds germinated in
1992 and outplanted as seedlings in 1993, flowered in our garden in 1996 with larger flowers than
literature generally states (~12″ diameter), purple-stained at base and pleasing fragrance, all on a 3′ high
plant. Most accurately in the 10 to 20′ height range, less in spread, at least cultivated specimens. National
champion is 52′ by 37′ in Gladwyne, PA. There is a fine plant at Biltmore House, Asheville, NC. Florida,
Texas. Introduced 1933. It is rated less cold hardy (Zone 6 to 9) than *M. macrophylla*. Cappiello, however,
reported the species as completely cold hardy in Orono, ME. Louisiana Nursery offers 'Florida' and
'Northern' strains.

Magnolia dealbata Zucc., (mag-nō′li-à dē-al-bā′tà), is the Mexican sister of *M. macrophylla* and is reportedly
growing in California and Texas. May grow to 60′ high with 2′ long leaves and 15″ wide, white flowers.
Flowers at 4 years of age, grew 23′ after 6 years at Chyverton, England. Zone 8 to 10.

Magnolia fraseri Walter, (mag-nō′li-à frā′zēr-ī), Fraser Magnolia, is another closely allied species. The general
shape of the leaves is similar but they are smaller, being about 8 to 15″ long, with glaucous green
undersides and a 2 to 4″ long petiole. The buds are glabrous and purple-green which distinguishes this
species from the pubescent, silky buds of the above species. Flowers are white, stinkily fragrant, 8 to 10″
across, 6- to 9-tepaled, tepals elongated tapering to narrow point. Tree is extremely common in the four
state mountain areas of Tennessee, North Carolina, Georgia, and South Carolina. Sixty-foot specimens
are not uncommon, although plants are usually smaller. Co-national champions are 107′ by 55′ and 110′
by 59′ in Great Smoky Mountains National Park. Virginia to Georgia and Alabama. Introduced 1787. Zone
5 to 8(9).

Magnolia pyramidata Bartr. ex Pursh, (mag-nō′li-à pi-ram-i-dā′tà), Pyramid Magnolia, although uncommon
in cultivation completes the true native North American "bigleaf clan." Plants are generally small, 10 to 20′
high, with glabrous greenish purple buds and stems, leaves 6 to 9″ long with a distinct auriculate base.
Leaves are green on the underside. Flowers are 3 to 5″ across, white and with a strong "turpentine" scent.
Co-national champions are 65′ by 32′ in Tallahassee, FL and 98′ by 90′ in Jones Co., MS. 'Neva Black'
is a choice clone with very fragrant flowers from Louisiana Nursery. 'Texas Strain' comes from a native
stand in Texas, has attractive leaves and fragrant, white flowers. Found in Georgia, Florida, Alabama to
Texas. Cultivated 1825. Zone 6 to 9.

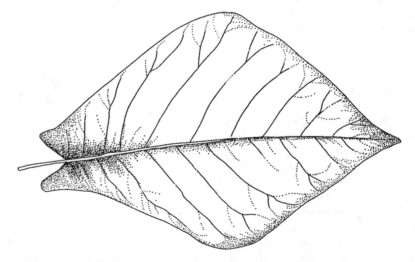

ADDITIONAL NOTES: All species are botanically interesting and horticulturally worthy. They will simply never
become mainstream plants. Bonnie and I have accumulated all the native Bigleaf Clan and situated them
in moderate to heavy woodland shade. The foliage texture is hauntingly exotic and possibly not for
everyone. The leaves of all often die-off a yellow to ash-brown in fall. Johnson, *Baileya* 23(1):55–56
(1989), reduced *M. ashei* and *M. dealbata* to varieties of *M. macrophylla*. Her interpretation is not wholly
accepted.

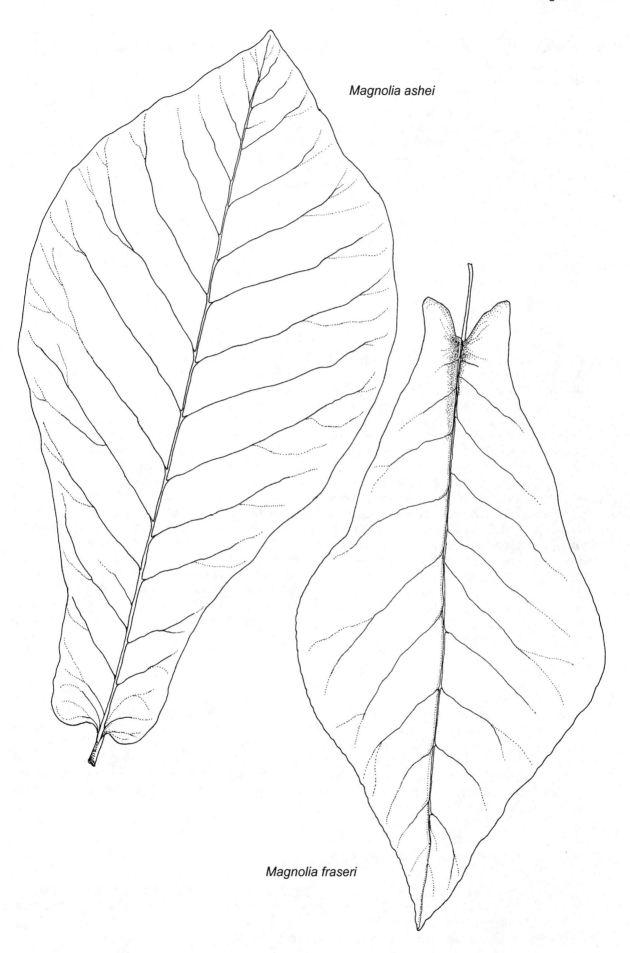

Magnolia ashei

Magnolia fraseri

Magnolia salicifolia (Sieb. & Zucc.) Maxim. — Anise Magnolia, Willowleaf Magnolia

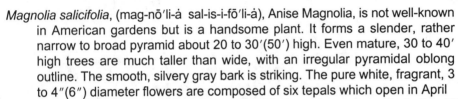

LEAVES: Alternate, simple, narrowly oval to lanceolate, 1 1/2 to 5″ long, 5/8 to 2″ wide, tapered at both ends, blunt or pointed at apex, dull dark green and glabrous above, slightly glaucous and covered with minute down below; petiole—1/4 to 5/8″ long, slender.

BUDS: Flower—1 to 1 1/4″(1 1/2″) long, ovoid-elliptical, covered with gray-brown pubescence; vegetative—1/8 to 1/4″ long, darker gray-brown, pubescent; buds are overall somewhat blackish which separates them from *M. kobus*.

STEM: Slender, first year 1/8 to 1/4″ diameter, shiny brown on top, green below, colors often mixed, glabrous, covered with small gray lenticels, sweet lemon odor to bruised stems.

Magnolia salicifolia, (mag-nō′li-à sal-is-i-fō′li-à), Anise Magnolia, is not well-known in American gardens but is a handsome plant. It forms a slender, rather narrow to broad pyramid about 20 to 30′(50′) high. Even mature, 30 to 40′ high trees are much taller than wide, with an irregular pyramidal oblong outline. The smooth, silvery gray bark is striking. The pure white, fragrant, 3 to 4″(6″) diameter flowers are composed of six tepals which open in April before the leaves. Tepals taper at their ends to narrow apices. Fruits 2 to 3″ long, rose-pink with scarlet seeds. The stems when bruised emit a pleasant lemon scent. It can be rooted from June–July cuttings by wounding and treating with 10000 ppm IBA. One of the more difficult magnolias to root. For sheer beauty of habit, this is one of the best. Tightly conical to pyramidal in youth, spreading and becoming broad-pyramidal with age, it makes an impressive specimen in and out of leaf. Seedlings of the species that I grew from Arnold Arboretum seed flowered in March 1997. I noticed that by the end of summer the foliage was somewhat tattered. The cultivars most often listed include: 'Else Frye' with 6″ diameter, white flowers, tinted pink at their base; 'Iufer' ('Iufer Clone') with pure white, star-shaped flowers with red tips on the creamy stamens; 'Kochanakee' a pyramidal form with large, fragrant flowers; 'Memorial Garden' has attractive white flowers, choice pyramidal habit; 'Miss Jack' is faster growing than 'Iufer', large tree with thousands of white flowers stained pink; 'Savage Selection' has flowers with prominent pink staining on the tepal backs; 'Van Veen Form' with exceptional fragrant flowers; I believe 'Wada's Memory' (discussed under *M. kobus*) belongs here; 'W.B. Clarke' with larger flowers and heavily veined, thicker textured foliage; and 'Willowwood' with white flowers, 20′ by 20′. Japan. Native in rocky granite soil by the side of forest streams. Introduced 1892. Zone 4 to 7.

RELATED SPECIES:

Magnolia* × *proctoriana Rehd. (*M. salicifolia* × *M. stellata*), (mag-nō′li-à proc-tōr-ē-ā′nà), the legitimacy of which was debated by Steve Spongberg and myself during the 1991 sabbatical, appears a legitimate hybrid. Plants at Wisley Gardens, England, and Mt. Congreve, Ireland are different than either parent. Habit is compact, broad-spreading, flowers with about 9 tepals. 'Slavin's Showy' with 6 to 9 tepals, up to 6″ diameter open flowers, white with a pink tinge should be included herein. Seedling from *M. salicifolia* that was growing in the Arboretum of T.E. Proctor. The original selection made at the Arnold Arboretum in 1928. Have seen reference to 'Gloster Form' with thick, pyramidal growth; 'Morris Arboretum' represents true clone. Zone 5 to 7.

Magnolia sieboldii K. Koch. — Oyama Magnolia

LEAVES: Alternate, simple, oblong or obovate-oblong, 3 to 6″ long, 3 to 4″ wide, obtusely pointed, cuneate to rounded, medium to dark green and glabrous above, glaucous and pubescent below, 7 to 9 impressed vein pairs; petiole—3/4 to 1″(2″) long.

STEM: Greenish, yellowish to grayish tan, pubescent, eventually glabrous.

Magnolia sieboldii, (mag-nō′li-à sē-bōl′dē-ī), Oyama Magnolia, is a superb, handsome, large shrub (10 to 15′) or small tree with cup-shaped flowers that are borne either horizontally or slightly nodding on a 1 to 2 1/2″ long pedicel. The stamens form a pinkish to rose-crimson to deep maroon-crimson center. Flowers egg-shaped in bud, 9 to 12 tepals, 3 to 4″(5″) diameter when open, fragrant. The carmine fruit is about 2″ long and houses scarlet seeds. Flowers appear from May–June and perhaps sporadically thereafter. Ideally provide a semi-shaded exposure in moist, fertile, well-drained soil. Have seen very few specimens in the eastern corridor, but enough to know the plant will grow. Cultivars include: 'Michiko Renge' a double-flowered form, photograph of this form makes one drool; 'Tetraploid Seedling' has larger flowers; 'White Flounces' with semi-double, up to 24 tepals, 4″ across, flower almost flat rather than cup-shaped. *Magnolia sieboldii* is native to southern China, Manchuria, Japan and Korea. Introduced about 1865. Zone 6 to 8. Hardy in Orono, ME.

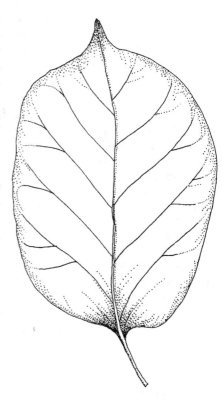

Two related species, **Magnolia sinensis** (Rehd. & Wils.) Stapf., Chinese Magnolia, and **Magnolia wilsonii** (Finet & Gagnep.) Rehd., Wilson Magnolia, as I have observed them are large (20′), more tree-like, with 3 to 4″ diameter, slightly cup-shaped, pendulous flowers with crimson-purple stamens. To view the flowers at their best, one must walk under the tree and literally look up at the flowers. Flowers occur with the leaves and are usually at their best in May–June. Gossler mentioned that *M. sinensis* is more shrub-like than *M. sieboldii*. In fact, I have seen *M. sinensis* listed as a subspecies of *M. sieboldii*. The taxonomy is not totally clear-cut among the 3 species. All are first rate garden plants where adaptable. Best used in a mixed shady border with hostas, ferns, and wildflowers planted underfoot. Have observed all in European gardens, most recently in Ireland (late June 1996). All were in flower and indeed are almost ethereal in flower effect. Several cultivars of *M. wilsonii* available in the United States include: 'Bovee' with up to 6″ diameter flowers and 'Phetteplace' with larger flowers. *Magnolia sinensis* is native to western China. Introduced 1908. Zone 7 to 8? *Magnolia wilsonii* is native to western China. Introduced 1908. Zone 6 to 8. In relative hardiness, *M. sieboldii* is greatest followed by *M. wilsonii* and *M. sinensis*, the latter two to - 10°F, although the Korean form of *M. wilsonii* is listed as hardier.

Magnolia × *soulangiana* Soul.-Bod. — Saucer Magnolia
(mag-nō′li-à sū-lan-gē-ā′nà)

LEAVES: Alternate, simple, 3 to 6″(7″) long, half as wide, obovate to broad-oblong, apex narrow and more or less abruptly short-pointed, base taper-pointed, dark green above, pubescent below.

BUDS: Terminal–flower, pubescent, silky to the touch, 1/2 to 3/4″ long, laterals smaller.

STEM: Brown, glabrous, with grayish lenticels, fragrant when crushed, with prominent stipular scars.

SIZE: 20 to 30′ in height with a variable spread, often about the same as height; witnessed a 40′ high specimen at Chyverton, England.

HARDINESS: Zone 4 to 9; hardy at Williamstown, MA. Abundant observations under my belt and coupled with comments from my plant material friends and a detailed letter dated August 19, 1997 from Larry Lowman, Wynne, AK, I offer the following:

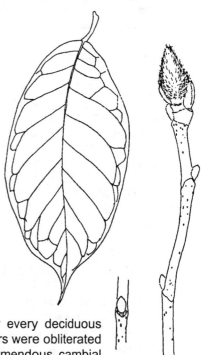

On March 9, 1996 after a warm February and with virtually every deciduous magnolia in flower, temperatures dropped to 12 to 15°F. Flowers were obliterated but what was painfully evident in April and May was the tremendous cambial damage and kill on *M.* × *soulangiana*. Plants in containers and in established landscapes were killed 30 to 80%.

Athens had a similar scenario, however, the majority of the damaged plants recovered and grew normally. At the University's Botanical Garden, no damage occurred on *M. denudata* or *M. liliiflora*, the parents of *M. × soulangiana*. Also, *M. kobus*, *M. × loebneri*, *M. stellata*, *M. salicifolia* and *M. zenii* were not injured. I did notice that *M. × soulangiana* 'Alexandrina', a dark purple-red flowered, upright form, showed no damage. Larry Lowman's notes reflect April 12, 1989 when temperatures dropped to 25°F for 4 hours. Most deciduous trees had partially or completely leafed out. His report: no damage to *M. × loebneri* 'Ballerina', 'Merrill', and 'Spring Snow', *M.* 'Pristine', *M. salicifolia*, *M. stellata* (several clones), and *M. virginiana*; severe damage to *M. denudata*, *M. sieboldii*, *M. × soulangiana*, Gresham Hybrids (6 clones), and 'Spectrum'.

HABIT: Distinctly upright in youth and often grown as a multi-stemmed shrub under nursery production; usually a large spreading shrub or small, low-branched tree with wide-spreading branches forming a pyramidal to rounded outline at maturity.

RATE: Medium, 10 to 15′ over a 10 year period.

TEXTURE: Medium-coarse in leaf; perhaps medium to medium-coarse in winter.

BARK COLOR: A handsome gray on older trunks, usually smooth, often with sapsucker damage.

LEAF COLOR: Medium to deep flat green in summer; sometimes (but not usually) an attractive yellow-brown in fall.

FLOWERS: Perfect, white to pink to purplish (variable when seed grown), often with 9 tepals, usually the outside of the tepals are flushed pinkish purple while the inside is whitish, 5 to 10″ diameter, campanulate, before the leaves in March–April, solitary; over the years, I have recorded the flowering dates of this tree more often than any other; in Athens flowers show color by late February and usually peak from March 1 to 15, in Savannah, GA plants have been in full flower on February 19, so a 200 mile trip slightly Southeast from Athens makes a two-week difference in full flower expression; no flowers out on March 10, 1991 while all *M. stellata*, *M. × loebneri*, *M. kobus*, and *M. denudata* are in full flower; flowers will persist and leaves follow quickly in some years so both are present; also the plant has the curious habit of flowering sporadically on new growth of the season but the flowers are never as brightly pigmented because of the heat and are often slightly twisted and misshapen; from rooted cuttings, 2- to 3-year-old plants will set flower buds which makes it a choice plant for nursery and garden center sales; a fine old 20 to 25′ high by 25 to 30′ wide specimen consumes a corner property on two heavily trafficked streets in Athens; when in perfect full flower, garden centers can't stock enough, when blitzed by the cold weather which happens 1(2) out of 3 to 4 years, demand is lower; amazingly the tree can look stunning one bright late winter or early spring afternoon and with an overnight temperature drop to 25 to 28°F, become a mass of limp brown tepals the next day.

FRUIT: Aggregate of follicles to 4″ long, asymmetric, August–September, seldom produced in significant numbers; in fact, I rarely see fruit; when produced often irregular with few fertile follicles; have grown seedlings from 'Andre LeRoy' that flowered in 5 years, colors were muddy purple and did not match the rich reddish purple of the maternal parent.

CULTURE: The following discussion applies to the other magnolias in this section with one notable exception; magnolias have a fleshy root system with minimal lateral roots and root hairs and should be transplanted balled and burlapped or from a container; soil should be moist, deep, preferably acid (pH 5.0 to 6.5), and supplemented with leaf mold or peat moss; prefer full sun but will withstand light shade; do not plant too deep; prune after flowering; *M. denudata* and *M. × soulangiana* display good pollution tolerance; if pruning is necessary perform the task after flowering, ideally in mid to late spring before all the flower buds are set for next year; try to avoid frost pockets and site in full sun with good air movement; in 1996, a March 9 temperature drop to 12 to 15°F simply devastated this species, plants were in full flower, sap was ascending, and plants were killed 30 to 70%; nurserymen experienced the same thing with container-grown material; *M. stellata* and *M. × loebneri* were not affected.

DISEASES AND INSECTS: Black mildews, leaf blight, leaf spots (at least 15 different ones), dieback, *Nectria* canker, leaf scab, wood decay, algal spot, magnolia scale, Tuliptree scale, and other scales; although this list is quite impressive I have not witnessed many problems. Perhaps the most unpleasant sight is the numerous circles of sapsucker holes that often ring the trees; apparently no permanent damage is done.

LANDSCAPE VALUE: Small specimen tree, often over-used but with ample justification; flowers when 2 to 4′ tall; could be used in groupings, near large buildings or in large tree lawns; roots need ample room to develop; one serious problem is that late spring frosts and freezes often nip the emerging flower buds; in fact, 1(2) out of every 3 or 4 years would be a conservative estimate for almost total flower loss in many areas; unbelievable (almost unjustifiable) variation in flower size, color, form, growth habit, and cold hardiness; Paul Cappiello and Roger Luce, Maine, have the best guide to cold hardy clones; also, the species is heat tolerant into northern Florida and Louisiana where it flowers in January; also, common on the West Coast.

CULTIVARS: Numerous selections have been made over the years and there is much confusion concerning their correct identity. The original hybrid was raised in the garden of Soulange-Bodin at Fromont, France from seed borne by *M. denudata* fertilized by pollen of *M. liliiflora*. The plant first flowered in 1826 and the cultivars have become the most popular of all magnolias in American gardens. During my 1991 sabbatical, I left Athens in early April and followed the ontogeny of spring into Boston, taking copious notes on the early flowering magnolias. My goal was to photograph and crystallize my opinions relative to the exact nature of the various cultivars. One of the most devious discrepancies in my evaluations were the multiple clones under one name. 'Alexandrina' was represented by three different flowered types. Ideally, buy this plant in flower. Three of my favorite cultivars are 'Brozzonii', 'Lennei Alba', and 'Verbanica'. Good article by Jim Gardiner, Curator of Royal Horticultural Society Garden at Wisley, *The Garden* 122(4):256–261 (1997), on *M. × soulangiana* that discusses the history, growth characteristics and cultivars. Author mentions that 50 published cultivar names are known with only 15 offered in 1996–97 edition of *The RHS Plant Finder*.

'Alba Superba' (Syn: 'Superba' or 'Alba')—Flowers white, outside of tepals colored very light purplish, fragrant, flower tepals 4″ long, cup and saucer shape; the true 'Alba Superba' is of dense, erect habit, early flowering, raised in Belgium in middle of 19th century.

'Alexandrina'—Flowers flushed rose-purple outside, inside of petals pure white, 9 tepals, 4″ long, one of the larger and earlier flowering varieties; more than one clone, some lighter, others darker rose-purple ('Alexandrina Dark Clone'); easily rooted from June cuttings; widely grown in the nursery trades; as mentioned above multiple clones are offered under this name, the common form is described above, however, a light pink, evenly colored outside of tepal form was labeled as such at the Arnold; have observed the typical species or 'Norbertii' type labeled as 'Alexandrina'; the typical clone is quite upright in habit as a young plant; deep red-purple color was evident on a 20′, distinctly upright oval plant on February 10, 1997 in the University's Botanical Garden; Louisiana Nursery lists this as 'Alexandrina Dark Clone'; has good late season foliage; full flower February 22, 1992 in Athens.

'Amabilis'—Missing from last edition but worthy of inclusion; large cream-white flowers with minimal pink blush on backside of tepals, tepals 3 1/2″ long; one of the prettier forms in the Arnold's collection; an old cultivar dating from 1860's; one of the most flower bud hardy forms, having survived -28°F in Newburgh, ME.

'Andre LeRoy' ('Andre LeRoi')—Flowers are dark pink to purplish on the outside, petals are white inside and flowers decidedly cup-shaped, immense reddish maroon flowers, spectacular in flower, habit is rough, coarse, sprawly, foliage tatty by late summer (Arnold observations), grew seedlings to flowering with none rivaling the cultivar.

'Big Pink'—Vigorous, upright, almost tree form that is becoming more common in southern nurseries, 9 tepals with bar on back, flowers deep rose, larger than typical and flowers slightly later, grown by Overlook Nurseries, Mobile, AL for years, recently marketed as 'Big Pink', older Japanese selection, have read that some magnolia experts consider this the same as 'Alexandrina'; my question . . . which 'Alexandrina'?

'Brozzonii' ('Brozzoni')—Essentially white, flowers 10″ across when fully open; outside of tepals tinged a pale purplish rose at the base; tepals about 5″ long, cup and saucer-shaped flower; beautiful floriferous form that is about the last to flower, perhaps 2 weeks later than the others, perhaps not as fragrant; makes a large plant 25 to 30′ high; might be a good choice where late spring frosts are a common occurrence; easily rooted; originated in Italy in the garden of Camillo Brozzoni about 1873; foliage still respectable in late summer; leaf much like *M. denudata*; flower bud hardy at -28°F in Newburgh, ME.

'Burgundy'—Flowers are a deep purple color of burgundy wine, flowers earlier than most varieties; easily rooted.

'Candolleana'—Excellent white flowers, clean foliage in late summer, 20′ plant at the Arnold that was magnificent, slightly later than the early *M. × soulangiana* forms.

'Deep Purple Dream'—Dark red-purple, bowl-shaped flowers, later than 'Lennei' which is one of its parents.

'Eleanor Coates'—Flowers lighter pink-purple than 'Rustica Rubra', tepals 4″ long, fast grower, seedling of 'Rustica Rubra'.

'Eleanor May'—Pink-purple flowers, a newer introduction.

'Etienne Soulange-Bodin'—Gardiner mentions this is the most common form (possibly in England), flowers cup and saucer-shaped, tepals to 4″ long, warm pink in bud, opening white inside, flushed pink on outside which deepens to purplish pink at the base, mid-season flowering.

'Forrest Pink' ('Forest Pink')—Often listed as *M. denudata* but more correctly *M. × soulangiana*, deep pink, broad-tepaled flowers, perhaps greater frost tolerance, Gossler reported only minor damage after -26 to -28°F, to 30′ high, spelled 'Forest Pink' in England where I experienced a wonderful specimen in flower on March 22, 1998 at Killerton, beautiful cultivar.

'Grace McDade'—Flowers (to 9″ diameter) are white with pink at the base of the tepals; growth habit like 'Lennei'; the actual flower color apart from textual description is purplish magenta but lighter than 'Lennei'; wild and broader spreading than typical, does approximate growth habit of 'Lennei'; have observed at Longwood Gardens, flowers smaller than 'Lennei'; named by Clint McDade, Semmes, AL in 1945; Callaway says hardier than most but killed outright in Maine; have read flower size of 12 to 14″ across, perhaps, but not on the plants I witnessed.

'Lennei'—Dark purplish magenta tepals (6), white inside, each tepal often 4″ long and wide, broad-obovate, concave; flowers later than the type and usually sporadically into summer; leaves are dark green and larger (8″ by 5″); the habit is that of a stiff broad shrub (15 to 20′ by 15 to 20′); many plants I have seen were more or less flat across the top; raised by Conte Guiseppe Salvi, Florence, Italy, introduced by Albert Topf to Germany about 1854; suffers regular tip dieback and occasional substantial dieback in Maine.

'Lennei Alba'—A pure white (ivory white) form of the above with goblet-shaped flowers (9 tepals) that appear about the same time or slightly later than 'Lennei'; magnificent in flower; seedling of 'Lennei'; raised by Froebel of Zurich in 1905, introduced by Kerssen, Aalsmer, Holland in 1931; killed to ground in Newburgh, ME at -28°F; used extensively in breeding work by D. Todd Gresham and Felix Jury.

'Lilliputian'—Smaller, light pink flowers and habit than species, slow grower, tight upright habit, probably one-half the size of *M. × soulangiana* at maturity, however, color not much different than species ('Norbertii'); have observed small plants just loaded with flower buds; killed to ground in Newburgh, ME at -28°F; introduced by Semmes Nursery, Semmes, AL in 1946.

'Lombardy Rose'—Lower surface of the petals is dark rose, upper surface white, flowers for several weeks, seedling of 'Rustica Rubra', free-flowering and more upright in habit, much like 'Lennei' and 'Andre LeRoy' in flower show.

'Momoju'—Large, pink-flowered hybrid from Nakamura, Japan.

'Nakamura #3'—Rich royal red, ivory white centers, cup-shaped flowers, offered via the Internet by Klehm Nursery, Roy Klehm obtained this form from a friend in Japan.

'Norbertii'—This looks suspiciously like the run-of-the-mill *M. × soulangiana*, somewhat dirty pinkish purple flowers, white inside, tepals narrower than most, to 4″ long, large tree (±30′), Swarthmore has a significant specimen, more than one clone has been named this, Loudon and Treseder described different flower colors for this clone.

'Picture' ('Wada's Picture')—Vigorous, upright grower, red-purple buds open to pink-white inside, heavy red-purple staining outside, larger flowers than typical *M. × soulangiana*, up to 10 to 12″ across, tepals 6 to 7″ long, possibly *M. sprengeri* 'Diva' as one parent; read much about this form and observed same at Trelissick Garden in southwest England in 1992, not as impressed as I had hoped to be; witnessed in several English gardens in late March 1998, flowers *are* larger than typical *M. × soulangiana*, and tepals are thickish and substantive; named by K. Wada, Yokohama, Japan about 1925; Pickard's Magnolia Gardens, Canterbury, Kent raised open-pollinated seedlings that are named 'Pickard's Opal', etc. and are discussed under Pickard Hybrids.

'Picture Superba'—Large, milk white flowers, from K. Wada.

'Purple and White'—'Lennei'-like flowers, purple outside, white inside.

'Purpliana' ('Purpleana')—Reddish purple outside, early-flowering, from Overlook Nurseries in 1950, more like Kosar-De Vos hybrids, some dieback in Maine.

'Red Head'—Large, red, cup-shaped flowers with the form of 'Lennei'.

'Ruby'—Although parentage is suspect, this appears to be a *M. × soulangiana* clone, ruby red, fragrant, goblet-shaped flowers are produced on young trees, the heavy textured tepals are enhance by a fine, white, picotee edge.

'Rustica Rubra' (also listed as 'Rubra')—Rose-red flowers, 5 1/2″ diameter, 9 tepals, 3 1/2″ long, inside of petals is white, this is purported to be a seedling of 'Lennei' but the flowers have more rose and it makes a larger, looser growing shrub; it is beautiful in flower; tatty foliage in late summer; killed to ground at -28°F in Newburgh, ME.

'San Jose'—Large flowers, rosy-purple (rose-pink with milky white interior), fragrant, and a vigorous grower, tatty late summer foliage, from W.B. Clarke, CA in 1940, true clone does not appear in commerce on East Coast, what I have observed is lighter rose-pink.

'Speciosa'—A late-flowered white form, the petals flushed purple at the base; the outer whorl of petals reflexed at their midpoint; makes a rather dense tree; excellent late summer foliage; there was a beautiful conical-pyramidal tree at Arnold.

'Striped Spice'—Typical flowers but the 9 tepals with a red-purple stripe, strong spicy fragrance, Richard Figlar introduction.

'Suishoreu'—Fine pink-flowered form from Nakamura, Japan.

'Superba Rosea'—Bright pink, late-flowering selection.

'Toju'—Clear pink-flowered form.

'Triumphans'—Beautiful goblet-shaped flowers, burgundy rose on outside of tepals, not unlike 'Rustica Rubra' in shape and color, habit as wide as tall at maturity.

'Veitchii Rubra'—Wine red in bud, fading as the flowers open.

'Verbanica'—Late-flowering form opening about the same time as 'Brozzonii'; the tepals rose on the outside but fading to white at the apex, the inner and medium tepals are strap-shaped and usually tinted rose on the outside; leathery, clean, lustrous dark green, late season foliage, 20 to 25' high and wide, outstanding specimen at Swarthmore, cold hardy in Maine.

'White Giant'—Large, milky white flowers open to a goblet form, splay on second day of opening, 5" long tepals, seedling of 'Picture', named by K. Wada, Japan.

CULTIVAR POSTSCRIPT: Thirty-seven cultivars are treated herein, most have been observed by the author. Callaway (1994) describes over 40. From my own experiences, a handful of open-pollinated seed can yield countless variants. Before naming another, judge the potential introduction against the best of the best and then ask if it is that much better and will it ever see the light of commercial day.

Worth mentioning that the Morton Arboretum, Lisle, IL reported 'Alexandrina' flowering April 20 to May 20, 'Lennei' in early to mid-May, and 'Lilliputian' on May 6. As I write this on February 9, 1997, an early-flowering form propagated from a campus plant is showing complete deep purple-red bud coloration; same stage on February 20, 1998.

PROPAGATION: Seed should be stratified for 3 to 6 months in moist media at 32 to 41°F to overcome embryo dormancy. My work indicates 3 months is sufficient with plants flowering 4 to 6 years later. In general it is best to collect cuttings when the terminal (flower bud) is formed, cuttings should be wounded and dipped in 10,000 to perhaps 20,000 ppm IBA, peat:perlite, mist; rooting generally occurs in high percentages; this approach is much preferable to grafting. *Magnolia* × *soulangiana* is more difficult to root than *M. stellata* or *M.* × *loebneri* but easier than *M. denudata*; for a thorough discussion of *Magnolia* propagation see Dirr and Heuser, 1987. Our experiences emphasize the firm wood, i.e., some brown coloration and end bud set; soft cuttings have not responded well.

Magnolia sprengeri Pamp. — Sprenger Magnolia

LEAVES: Alternate, simple, obovate to lanceolate-elliptic, 4 to 7" long, 2 to 4" wide, short acuminate, rounded or cuneate, entire, glabrous, dark green above, pale beneath, glabrous to villous below; petiole—about 1" long.

BUDS: Flower—covered with yellowish pubescence.

STEM: Yellow-green, glabrous.

Magnolia sprengeri, (mag-nō'li-à spreng'ēr-ī), Sprenger Magnolia, has eluded this *Manual* for the past four editions. The late J.C. McDaniel grew it in Urbana, IL and I am ashamed to admit the first time I witnessed flowers was at Wisley Garden in late March of 1992. Habit is rounded. Size approximates 30 to 50' high. What I have seen in cultivation is generally smaller. Over 50' specimen at Chyverton, England. Flowers range from 6 to 8" wide, with 12 to 14 tepals, each tepal 2 to 4" long, fragrant. Tepals are reddish purple outside, pale pink to whitish inside. Considerable taxonomic dismay about the exact status of the various varieties and Callaway should be consulted for more detail. Variety *sprengeri* Pamp. encompasses pink flowers and leaves less than twice as long as wide; var. *elongata* (Rehd. & Wils.) Johnstone produces smaller white flowers and leaves twice as long as broad. Plants prefer woodsy, organic, moist soils with wind protection. The species and 'Diva' have been widely utilized in hybridizing. Cultivars include: 'Burncoose Purple' with deep rose-purple flowers; 'Claret Cup' produces 10" wide, 12-tepaled, rose-purple outside, pale pink to white inside flowers; 'Copeland Court' has bright crimson pink, outside and inside the tepals, on a compact, symmetrical, erect, densely branched plant; 'Dark Diva' is a dark pink-flowered selection from Phil Savage'; 'Diva' with rose-pink, 8" wide, cereal bowl-shaped flowers, Gossler reported 30' high, 25-year-old tree in their Oregon garden; 'Diva #711' is listed by Louisiana Nursery as a hardy clone from J.C. McDaniel that survived cold in Opelousas, LA that killed other *M. sprengeri* selections; 'Double Form' has extra tepals; 'Eric Savill' produces large, showy, fragrant, deep red-purple, 12-tepaled flowers; 'Lanhydrock' has deeper cyclamen purple flower color than 'Diva', 35' high, 12 tepals, registered by Peter Borlase, Lanhydrock Gardens, Bodmin, England; 'Mary Slankard' is a hardy selection with clear pink and white flowers from Phil Savage. On the late March 1998 plant expedition to the southwest of England, was privileged to experience 'Diva', 'Burncoose Purple', 'Eric Savill', and 'Lanhydrock' in full flower. Absolutely magnificent! Zone (6)7 to 9. China.

Magnolia stellata Maxim. — Star Magnolia
(mag-nō′li-à ste-lā′tà)

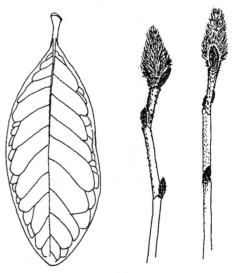

LEAVES: Alternate, simple, obovate or narrow elliptic to oblong-obovate, 2 to 4″ long, half as wide, obtusely pointed or obtusish, gradually tapering at base, entire, glabrous and dark green above, light green and reticulate beneath and glabrous or appressed-pubescent on the nerves; petiole—1/4 to 1/3″ long.

BUDS: Densely pubescent, flower buds 1/3 to 1/2″ long; vegetative—smaller, pubescent.

STEM: Slender, brown, glabrous, more densely borne than in *M. × soulangiana*.

SIZE: 15 to 20′ in height with a spread of 10 to 15′(20′).

HARDINESS: Zone 4 to 8(9).

HABIT: Dense oval to rounded shrub or small tree usually of thick constitution from the close-set leaves and stems.

RATE: Slow, 3 to 6′ over a 5 to 6 year period, with adequate water and fertilizer 10′ in 5 to 6 years; 'Pink Stardust' grew 10′ high and 8′ wide in 6 years in our trials.

TEXTURE: Medium in all seasons; possibly medium-fine.

BARK: Smooth, gray, handsome on mature plants.

LEAF COLOR: Dark green in summer, often yellow to bronze in fall.

FLOWERS: White, fragrant, 3 to 4″ in diameter, 12 to 18 petals, each petal 1 1/2 to 2″ long, narrowly oblong or strap-shaped, often wavy, at first spreading, finally reflexed, late February–early March in Athens and usually ahead of *M. × soulangiana* but at times in full flower at the same time, interestingly in the North seems to flower ahead of *M. × soulangiana*, flowers solitary opening before leaves, often flowering when less than one foot tall; flowers are delicate and since they open early are often at the mercy of the weather; late freezes and wind can severely damage the petals (tepals); peak flower mid to late April at Morton Arboretum, Lisle, IL.

FRUIT: Aggregate of follicles, 2″ long, twisted, and usually with only a few fertile carpels.

CULTURE: As discussed under *M. × soulangiana* this species should be protected as much as possible; try to avoid southern exposures since the buds will tend to open fastest in this location; prefers a peaty, organic-based soil; does quite well in heat of South; full sun for best flowering.

DISEASES AND INSECTS: Basically trouble-free; have noticed scale on a campus plant.

LANDSCAPE VALUE: Attractive single specimen or accent plant; I have seen it used against red brick walls and the effect is outstanding; very popular plant and with justifiable reason, could be, and often is, integrated into foundation plantings; often bushy and branched to the ground giving appearance of a giant meatball; multi-stemmed (3 to 7), limbed-up plants are attractive; I see more growers producing limbed up specimens; many excellent cultivars that are preferable to the species.

CULTIVARS: Many cultivars have been introduced although nothing resembling the *M. × soulangiana* complex. Request the better cultivars.

'Alexeed'—Light pink tepals are held upright, do not reflex (flop), single leader to 15′ in 12 years, chance seedling from William Brincka, Indiana.

'Centennial'—Originated at Arnold Arboretum; 28 to 32 white tepals [1 1/2 to 2″(2 1/2″) long], more open flower (5 1/2″ across), and tepals are blushed with slight pink tinge on the outside; commemorates the 100 year anniversary of the Arnold Arboretum (1872–1972); seedling of 'Rosea'; certainly the lead sled dog among *M. stellata* cultivars, more vigorous, more upright conical-pyramidal with easily maintained central leader; magnificent specimen in the Littlefield Garden on the UMaine campus, Orono and at Swarthmore College; probably mature around 25′ high; at Milliken Arboretum, 3 random flower counts produced 41, 29 and 39 tepals; 1997 Pennsylvania Horticulture Society Gold Medal Winner.

'Chollipo'—Pink form with 45 tepals, Don Shadow told me about this form, from Ferris Miller, Korea.

'Chrysanthemumiflora'—Clear pink fading to white flowers, appear similar to a football mum when opening, ±40 tepals, a K. Wada selection from Yokohama, Japan.

'Cody'—Fine deep pink-flowered form.

'Dawn'—White flower with pink stripe that runs length of tepal, pink color persists, 25 tepals, pink color supposedly holds, discovered in Bethesda, MD.

'G.H. Kern'—Rose-colored tepals, counted 9 on plant at Lanhydrock, weak grower, not very impressive.

'Jane Platt'—Light pink tepals open to white, 20 to 30 tepals, from the garden of the late Jane Platt, Portland, OR, in my opinion not as good as 'Pink Stardust' or 'Waterlily', size listed as 10' by 20', hardy in Maine.

'Kikuzaki'—In Maine and Georgia the growth habit is more compact and restrained, flowers heavily as a young plant, light pink in bud fading to white, have counted 25 tepals per 4″ diameter flower, later than 'Royal Star' and 'Waterlily', opens early to mid-March in Athens, Gossler reported 2' high in 10 years in Oregon, much faster than this in South, hardy in Maine.

'King Rose'—Buds develop pink, blush pink on the outside when open, essentially white, each flower about 5″ across, 22(20 to 25) tepals, forms a large spreading shrub of dense twiggy growth, plant at the U.S. National Arboretum was white-flowered.

'Persian Plum'—Beautiful, deep purple-pink, 32-tepaled flowers.

'Pink Stardust'—Outstanding pyramidal-haystack form from Tom Dodd Nurseries, Semmes, AL, 40 to 50 rich pink tepals lighten as they open to 4 to 5″ diameter flowers, nicely fragrant, heavy bud set up and down the stems, vigorous grower with 6-year-old plant 10' high and 8' wide, a good commercial cultivar.

'Pink Waterlily'—Clear pink, up to 32 tepals, rounded shrub, 6 to 8' high.

'Rosea'—Flower buds pink, fading white at maturity, handsome form at the Arnold dating I believe from 1899, in 1991 when last seen by the author it was true light pink, hardy in Maine, more than one clone with this name, 12' by 18' specimen with deep pink flowers at Hillier Arboretum.

'Rosea Fine Variety'—Good pink selection with up to 32 tepals, Louisiana Nursery describes it as one of the best *M. stellata*.

'Rosea Massey'—Witnessed at Cotehele, England, March 1998, pink but not impressive.

'Royal Star'—Possibly the most common in commerce; pink buds open to 25 to 30 nearly pure white tepals, 3 to 4″ diameter, fragrant, slightly later than typical *M. stellata*, clean dark green foliage, upright densely branched shrub in youth, more rounded with age; I have observed this plant year-in, year-out at the University's Botanical Garden and it is always the first to flower, again in variance with the literature, flowers sometimes 4 to 5″ across, recorded dates of February 1, 1992, February 9, 1997 indicated earliness, also have March 3, 1995 for full flower; a 12-year-old plant is 10' high and 12' wide; seedling of 'Waterlily' from Vermeulen Nursery, Neshanic Station, NJ, selected in 1950's; hardy in Maine, 15' by 20' at Lanhydrock.

'Rubra'—Flowers are purplish rose, fading to pink, 16 tepals, slightly twisted, compact shrub with yellow-green foliage, from K. Wada, Japan.

'Scented Silver'—Exceptionally fragrant, white flowers, taller than wide, to 15', from Frank Galyon.

'Select Pink'—Similar to 'Chrysanthemumiflora' with abundant deep pink flowers.

'Starlite'—Pink in bud, open pure white, handsomely formed.

'Two Stones'—Dr. Kehr introduction of a polyploid *M. stellata*, larger in all characteristics, registered in 1991, have seen it offered in commerce.

'Waterlily'—Buds rich pink, eventually white, 14 tepals according to literature (have counted 24 to 35), slightly narrower than those of the species, highly fragrant; upright, bushy grower, late-flowering; more than one clone under this name; Callaway mentions three clones with this name, perhaps?; I continue to count tepals on 3 plants in the University's Botanical Garden with 24 to 35 tepals representative of the range; flowers opening 3-10-91, 3-4-94, 3-3-95 and consistently later than 'Royal Star', also much pinker in bud than that cultivar; not a small plant and may grow 15' in 20 years; on February 10, 1997 assessed flowering, and was still in tight bud with 'Royal Star' in full flower; hardy in Maine.

'White Star'—White tepals, large flower.

'White Waterlily'—White, fragrant waterlily flowers on a small, bushy shrub.

PROPAGATION: See *M.* × *soulangiana*.

ADDITIONAL NOTES: I am frustrated with name changes and have watched this species with names such as *M. kobus* var. *stellata* (Sieb. & Zucc.) Blackburn and *M. tomentosa* Thunb. The genuine problem resides in the authorities who do not agree. Callaway lists *M. kobus* var. *stellata* as correct, while Meyer, Mazzeo and Ross use *M. stellata*.

NATIVE HABITAT: Japan. Introduced 1862.

Magnolia tripetala L. — Umbrella Magnolia

LEAVES: Alternate, simple, oblong-obovate, 10 to 24″ long, 6 to 10″ wide, acute or short acuminate, cuneate at base, entire, dark green above, pale green and pubescent beneath, at least while young; petiole—1 to 2″ long.

BUDS: Long, tapering, glaucous, greenish to purplish, glabrous.
STEM: Stout, glabrous, greenish, leaf scar-large, oval, very coarse-textured stems.

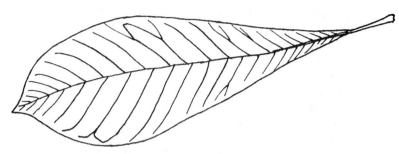

Magnolia tripetala, (mag-nō′li-à trĭ-pet′à-là), Umbrella Magnolia, reaches 15 to 30′ but can grow to 40′. National champion is 50′ by 50′ in Bucks Co., PA. It is similar to *M. macrophylla* in many respects but the 6- to 9(12)-tepaled flowers are 6 to 10″ across, creamy white, and unpleasantly fragrant, May to early June (before *M. macrophylla*), solitary. The elongated, cone-shaped, 4″ long, rosy red fruits mature in September–October. The leaves reach 10 to 24″ in length and are clustered near the ends of the branches and thus create an umbrella effect. Somewhat difficult to utilize in the home landscape because of cumbersome characteristics. Grows in deep, moist, woodsy soils along streams and swamp margins. In our garden, it is reasonably vigorous in an understory setting. Cultivars include: 'Bloomfield' with attractive large leaves and creamy white, 6-tepaled, showy, 12″ diameter flowers, from Phil Savage; 'Charles Coates' a tree-like form with white flowers and reddish stamens, fragrant, *M. sieboldii* × *M. tripetala*; and 'Woodlawn' with larger flowers and fruits, J.C. McDaniel introduction. Ranges from southern Pennsylvania to northern Georgia and Alabama and west to central Kentucky and southwestern Arkansas. Have observed in moist coves on the western side of the Great Smoky Mountains National Park. Introduced 1752. Zone (4)5 to 8. Has suffered some tip dieback in Maine.

A hybrid between this and *M. virginiana* is called *M.* × *thompsoniana* (Loud.) Vos. The leaves are a lustrous green, the flowers creamy white, about 3 to 5″ across, fragrant, and open over a long period from late May through June. This hybrid was first noticed around 1808 when Mr. Thompson found a distinct plant among seedlings of *M. virginiana*. It is, unfortunately, a shrub-tree of vigorous, unkempt habit and makes great long shoots in a single season. It will never replace *M.* × *soulangiana* or *M. stellata* in residential landscapes. Professor J.C. McDaniel selected a clone of *M.* × *thompsoniana* and named it 'Urbana'.

RELATED SPECIES:

Magnolia hypoleuca Sieb. & Zucc. (*M. obovata* Thunb.), (mag-nō′li-à hī-pō-loo′kà), White Bark or White Leaf Magnolia, always greeted my eye as I rounded the corner on the Arborway in Jamaica Plain heading for the Arnold Arboretum's main gate. I only studied the 30 to 40′ specimen on one occasion and then to simply admire the handsome gray bark. Observed 30′ high specimen at Killerton, England. Leaves (8 to 18″ long) remind of *M. tripetala* except with a glaucous underside. The creamy-white, 8″ diameter strong scented flowers open in May–June with a conspicuous central mass of purplish red stamens in the center. The red fruit is cone-shaped, 5 to 8″ long, 2 1/2″ wide aggregate of follicles. Habit is open and gaunt and with leaves in a pseudo-whorl at the tips of the branches; the appearance resembles *M. tripetala*. *Magnolia hypoleuca* × *M. tripetala* resulted in 'Silver Parasol' a vigorous, silver-barked introduction from the Arnold Arboretum. *Magnolia hypoleuca* has grown faster than any other large leaf magnolia in the Dirr garden. 'Lydia' is an upright form with handsome flowers. 'Pink Flush' has a noticeable pink flush on the outside of the tepals. Japan. Introduced 1865. Zone 5 to 7(8).

Magnolia × wiesneri Carr. (*M.* × *watsonii* Hook. f.), (mag-nō′li-à wĭz′nĕr-ī), has crossed my path several times. The flowers are quite fragrant. The ivory-colored tepals with red stamens average 6 to 8″ across. The habit is somewhat ungainly. Possibly hardy to 10°F. A hybrid between *M. hypoleuca* and *M. sieboldii*. Probably 15 to 25′ high. Leaves are 4 to 8″ long and taper to a 1/4 to 1″ long petiole. Have experienced many times in European gardens where it flowers during June. Offered by several West Coast nurserymen. Best reserved for the collector. Zone (6)7 to 9.

Magnolia virginiana L. — Sweetbay Magnolia, also called Laurel or Swamp Magnolia
(mag-nō′li-à vĕr-jin-ē-ā′nà)

LEAVES: Alternate, simple, evergreen, semi-evergreen to deciduous, elliptic to oblong-lanceolate, 3 to 5″(8″) long, about one-half as wide, acute or obtuse, broad cuneate at base, rarely rounded, entire, lustrous dark green (sometimes lighter green) above and glaucous (silvery) beneath; petiole—about 1/2″ long.

BUDS: Sparsely pubescent, somewhat silky.

STEM: Green, slender, pubescent or glabrous, glaucous; pith with prominent diaphragms.

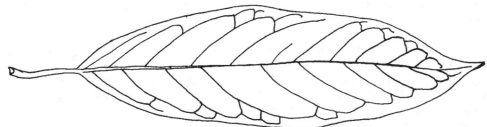

SIZE: In the North 10 to 20′ by 10 to 20′; in the southern part of its range can grow to 60′ or more; national champion is 92′ by 52′ in Union County, AR.

HARDINESS: Zone 5 to 9; killed outright in Orono and Newburgh, ME; interestingly has survived low temperatures in the range of -20 to -25°F in the lower Midwest.

HABIT: Small, multi-stemmed, deciduous shrub of loose, open, upright spreading habit in the North; deciduous, semi-evergreen to evergreen in the South and forming a large pyramidal tree.

RATE: Medium to fast.

TEXTURE: Medium in all seasons.

LEAF COLOR: Dark green (sometimes light) and often lustrous above, distinctly glaucous (silvery) beneath in summer, have observed respectable yellow to yellow-brown fall color on trees in Athens.

FLOWERS: Creamy white, lemon-scented, 2 to 3″ diameter, 9 to 12 petals, May–June, solitary; usually not produced in great abundance, often continuously on leafy shoots from May–June to September; may be slow to flower in youth; have observed flowers on April 23, 1995 in Athens.

FRUIT: Aggregate of follicles, 2″ long, dark red, very handsome where the bright red seeds are exposed, ripen in August (Athens).

CULTURE: Different than most magnolias in that it does well in wet and even swampy soils; also tolerates shade; seems to grow best in warm climates; requires acid soil.

DISEASES AND INSECTS: None serious, leaf miner on occasion, chlorosis is the worst malady I have seen.

LANDSCAPE VALUE: I have always considered this a lovely, graceful, small patio or specimen tree; the foliage is handsome especially as the wind buffets the leaves exposing the silvery underside; winter damage is a distinct possibility in the northern part of Zone 5; excellent for the sweet fragrance of its flowers, never overwhelming in flower.

CULTIVARS:

var. *australis* Sarg.—The southern representative with more pubescent branches and petioles, and often larger, more tree-like and evergreen; rejected by one authority as a true variety but accepted by others; see Treseder's *Magnolias* for an interesting discussion; in my opinion, really difficult to quantify; many *M. virginiana* in Athens-Atlanta area, in a mild winter some are evergreen to semi-evergreen; in harsh winters evergreen becomes semi-evergreen and semi-evergreen becomes deciduous; pubescence and leaf retention are always dubious characters; Meyer, Mazzeo and Ross lump everything into *M. virginiana*.

Dodd Small Leaf Forms—I asked Tom Dodd, III, and in his inimitable phraseology tells me about four with small leaves, less than 2″ long, 3/4″ wide, pubescent stems and upright habit; have observed several times; neat collector's item; 'Appalachi', 'Cahaba', 'Coosa', 'Perdido' and 'Tensaw' are the named forms.

'Dwarf'—Notched apices to the broad leaves, compact grower, from Don Shadow.

'Greenbay'—Evergreen, conical-oval habit, flowers over a long period, evergreen after -20°F, selected by Don Shadow from J.C. McDaniel seedlings.

'Havener'—Flowers with more tepals, 12 to 20, up to 4 1/2″ wide, slightly larger than normal, 30′ high, introduced by J.C. McDaniel, original tree found in Mt. Pulaski, IL, comes true-to-type from seed.

'Henry Hicks'—A tree that was given to the Arthur Hoyt Scott Horticultural Foundation at Swarthmore College and has remained evergreen even at temperatures as low as -17°F; I have seen the parent tree and it does offer evergreen foliage; good looking 25′ high plant at Bernheim Arboretum that has weathered -24°F; several in Dirr garden retain handsome evergreen foliage; somewhat difficult to propagate and therefore not common in commerce.

'Large Flowered Strain'—Large leaves and 6″ diameter, fragrant, white flowers, from Louisiana Nurseries.

'Louisiana Evergreen'—Compact, evergreen selection with rounded leaves, fragrant flowers produced spring until fall.

var. *ludoviciana*—According to Yucca Do Nursery a unique Texas variety that grows into a tree, large 8″ by 3″ leaves, silver beneath, larger flowers than typical; this author has been unable to document the taxonomic authenticity of this variety through standard references.

'Mayer'—Vigorous, multi-stemmed selection of pyramidal habit that flowers when young, J.C. McDaniel introduction from Champaign, IL.

Milton Clones—Multiple plants in Arnold Arboretum with different leaf shapes, evergreen to -10°F, have seen single clone described in literature but feel this is a seed derived cultivar; by virtue of northern provenance (Milton, MA), should be more cold hardy, but has not survived in Maine.

Moonglow® ('Wilson')—Distinct upright growth habit, dark green semi-evergreen foliage, survived -28°F without damage, matures at 35 to 40′ high, 15 to 18′ spread, Heritage Tree Introduction by Earl Cully, Jacksonville, IL.

'Nimbus'—Vigorous small tree to 30′ with partially evergreen foliage, 6″ diameter, 8-tepaled, ivory white, fragrant flowers, smooth gray bark; considered hardy to -10°F; hybrid between *M. hypoleuca* and *M. virginiana*; product of the U.S. National Arboretum.

'Santa Rosa'—Large, lustrous dark green, evergreen leaf form from Woodlanders, vigorous grower, more robust than most, leaves to 8″ long, worthwhile for commercial production because of handsome foliage.

'Satellite'—Dark green, evergreen leaves, blue-gray below, cream white, 3″ diameter, fragrant flowers, central leader, introduced by U.S. National Arboretum.

'Opelousas'—Tall, pyramidal tree with broad oval leaves and large (to 5″ across), fragrant, 11-tepaled, white flowers.

'Porcelain Dove'—Had for a time in our trials but not heat/cold tolerant, hybrid of *M. virginiana* × *M. globosa* Hook. & Thoms., beautiful milk white flowers with great fragrance, unfortunately, weak grower in Zone 7b, have seen reference to -22°F but doubt this, Todd Gresham hybrid, named in honor of his home, Hill of Doves.

'Ravenswood'—From northernmost native stand of *M. virginiana*, probably not totally accurate since the Essex County, MA population is the most northerly.

'Variegata'—Cream and yellow mottling throughout the leaves.

'Virginia Watson'—Similar to *M. virginiana* in habit but more spreading, 8-tepaled, cup-shaped, white flowers, strong pleasant fragrance, crimson stamens.

'Willowleaf Bay'—Reliable evergreen selection with narrower leaves densely clustered near ends of branches; selected by Larry P. Lowman, Wynne, AK from seedlings supplied by Tom Dodd Nurseries; original tree 20′ high, 6′ wide at 20 years of age; survived -12°F in 1989 without injury; juvenile cuttings resulting from stooling rooted 40 to 60% when treated with one-half strength Dip 'N Grow; cuttings from original tree rooted less than 20%.

'Freeman', 'Griffin', 'Maryland', 'Sweet Summer', and 'Timeless Beauty' represent hybrids between *M. virginiana* and *M. grandiflora* that appear more like *M. grandiflora* with larger foliage and flowers. 'Freeman' is hardy at the Arnold Arboretum; 'Griffin' was found in Griffin, GA and named by J.C. McDaniel; 'Timeless Beauty' from Monrovia Nursery, Azusa, CA, has an irregular habit with remontant flowers. Doubtfully are any worthy where good clones of *M. grandiflora* will grow.

PROPAGATION: Seed requires 41°F for best results although the literature is not absolutely clear on the best time period; seeds are remarkably sound and easily germinated; produced 1000's of seedlings from September collected seed (Arnold), 3 months cold, with germination like green beans within 3 weeks of sowing; cuttings can be rooted and I have taken softwood material from 2- to 3-year-old plants, treated with 1000 ppm IBA-quick dip, placed in sand under mist with 100% rooting; mature wood should be collected in June–July and treated with about 10,000 ppm IBA for best results; I have had a difficult time rooting cuttings from mature trees.

ADDITIONAL NOTES: Really a beautiful plant, especially when the sweet-scented flowers are opening. As one drives through coastal and southern Georgia and Florida, the species is quite evident along streams and moist areas. It makes a large tree and is seen growing in a mixed association with sweetgum and other wet soil plants. I have seen tremendous chlorosis in the calcareous soils of the Midwest.

NATIVE HABITAT: Massachusetts to Florida, Oklahoma, Arkansas and Texas, near the coast in swampy soils. Introduced 1688.

Magnolia zenii Cheng

LEAVES: Alternate, simple, oblong to oblong-obovate, 2 1/2 to 6″ long, 1 1/2 to 3″ wide, abruptly acuminate, cuneate to rounded, entire, medium to dark green above, lighter beneath, 10 to 12 lateral veins on each side, villous pubescent below; petiole—1/4 to 3/4″ long.

BUDS: Terminal—flower, ovoid-conical, silvery silky pubescent, 1/2 to 1"(1 1/2") long; laterals—valvate, 1/8 to 1/4" long, silvery silky pubescent, somewhat thumb-like in shape.

STEM: Slender, terete, dark purple-brown above, green below, glabrous except at end, pungently sweet, but not as much as *M. kobus*; stems somewhat blotched dark purple-brown that overlays the green, lenticels elliptical, vertical, gray; leaf scars like Calvin's mouth—a wide V-shaped ellipse; second year stems more even brown-purple, lenticels and vertical fissuring more pronounced.

Magnolia zenii, (mag-nō'li-à zē'nē-ī), was introduced by the Sino-American Expedition in the early 1980's and a seedling flowered at the Arnold Arboretum about 6 years later. Habit is strongly pyramidal with estimated ultimate size 20 to 25'. Based on the tremendous growth of two seedlings in the Athens area, I suspect 30 to 40' is more realistic. In fact, in 10 years, a plant is now 24' high and 10' wide. Leaves are medium to dark green, with an undulating surface. Bark is pleasing light gray. Flowers are the earliest of all species (including *M. kobus*, *M. stellata*) to open, with full flower in late January 1997; full flower on February 14, 1998. Tepals are streaked purple-pink (fuchsia pink) on outside basal half with a narrow purple-pink line ascending to apex of tepal, white inside, excellent fragrance, with generally 9 tepals. Tepals are reflexed outward at about one-half their length. Flowers average 3 1/2 to 4 1/2" diameter but tend to be more cup-shaped. Fruit occurs in 2 to 3" long, 1/2 to 1" wide, cylindrical aggregate of follicles, the seeds with a scarlet aril. A seedling I grew from Arnold Arboretum seed is 10' high, 6' wide in five growing seasons and flowered for the first time in early February 1997. It produced 5" diameter flowers with richer pigmentation on outside of the tepals. The outside of the stamens were deep fuchsia rose. Fragrance is also outstanding. Have noticed considerable water sprout development from the lower branches. Worth mentioning that while *M. kobus* showed no flower color, *M. zenii* had finished flowering on February 10, 1997. Have rooted June cuttings with 10000 KIBA, 1 peat:3 perlite, mist, in about 10 weeks. China. The newer reference books list hardiness as Zone 9 but successful culture in the United States indicates Zone 6 to 8. One reference reported flower bud hardy to ‑28°F.

OTHER LANDSCAPE MAGNOLIAS

In putting together this 5th edition I reflected on the astronomical number of hybrids that have been introduced in the decades of the 80's and 90's. The numbers exceed even the fondest dreams of the obsessed plantsperson. Often only the degree of shading on the outside of the tepals was justification for a new cultivar. Unfortunately, mainstream gardening America cannot absorb the many new magnolias. However, the days should be past when nurserymen offer only *M. × soulangiana* or *M. stellata*. The gardeners deserve the better cultivars.

The new yellow-flowered hybrids (see under *M. acuminata*) from Phil Savage and others have the magnolia world in a tizzy. 'Elizabeth' started the ball rolling and I wish I could tell the reader which is the best. By the next edition, I might know.

Three times since the last edition, travels have taken me to the southwest of England where in late March I was privileged to experience the magnificent Sino-Himalayan magnolias. They require a cooler, more even climate where temperatures seldom drop below 30°F. Their flowers, particularly the ***Magnolia campbellii*** Hook. & Thoms. and ***M. c.*** var. ***mollicomata*** (W.W. Sm.) Johnstone, a slightly hardier taxon, are 8 to 10" across, with 12 to 15 tepals, the outer opening and splaying, the inner in a clustered dome shape, producing a waterlily effect. Their beauty cannot be described, it must be experienced. A supposed reliable taxonomic criterion for separation of the above two taxa is the silky (pubescent) peduncle of var. *mollicomata* compared to the glabrous peduncle of *M. campbellii*. 'Lanarth' with deep purple-red flowers is possibly a var. *mollicomata* form. Unbelievably intense color and one of the breeding partners in the Jury Hybrids.

In the United States, successful culture is relegated to the West Coast from California (Strybing Arboretum in San Francisco) to British Columbia along the coast. All are large trees of pyramidal-oval outline as seen in England. At Lanhydrock, Caerhays, Trewithen, and Trengwainton gardens some trees were over 60' high *and* in full flower. The garden group that was with me stood mesmerized by a noble 50' high *M. campbellii* at Trengwainton. First *M. campbellii* to flower in the United States did so at Strybing Arboretum in 1940, 16 years after arriving from the English nursery of Stuart Lau & Co. Flowers January–February in San Francisco area.

Other species in this mold include: ***Magnolia dawsoniana*** Rehd. & Wils. with 9 white to pink-rose, recurving, finally drooping tepals. Flowers are not as "perfect" as *M. campbellii* and var. *mollicomata*, being somewhat "floppy." Large, rounded shrub or small tree to ±30'. This size is contradicted by 50 to 60' high trees in Lanhydrock and other English gardens. During a February 10, 1998 visit to Planting Fields Arboretum, Oyster Bay, Long Island, my former student Vinnie Simeone, now Assistant Director, showed me a *M. dawsoniana* 25 to 30' high and absolutely loaded with plump, ovoid, 2 to 2 1/2" long, dirty, furry flower buds. This was the first time I observed a member of this large-flowered group in such pristine condition in the East. Native to China. Zone 7 to 9.

   Magnolia sargentiana Rehd. & Wils. is more tree-like (60 to 80′) and does not possess the reticulate leaf venation. Flowers with 10 to 14 tepals, fragrant, white to purple-pink, pendant, similar to above in shape. Variety *robusta* Rehd. & Wils. has up to 12″ diameter, deeper rose-purple flowers and is hardier to 0 to −10°F. Could not detect fragrance on plants at Lanhydrock. Western China. Zone 8 and 9 for species.

   Magnolia × veitchii Bean embodies hybrids between *M. denudata* × *M. campbellii* which have an increased opportunity for success in the United States. The cultivars develop into large trees (50′ and greater) with off-white to wine red in bud flowers that lighten upon opening. Clocked 60′ high tree with rose-purple flowers at Killerton. Over 70′ high at Caerhays, reminded of a beech. Flowers average 8 to 10″ across. Most specimens observed by this author have flowers closer to *M. × soulangiana* size. Typical *M. × veitchii* has soft white flowers flushed with pink. 'Columbus' has creamy white flowers with purple blush, pyramidal tree 35′ by 20′, from U.S. National Arboretum. 'Isea' produces satiny white flowers flushed with pink. 'Peter Veitch' has pink flowers. Zone 7 to 9.

   The great reference books on *Magnolia* include Treseder, Millais, Johnstone, and more recently Callaway and Gardiner. I have purchased and read all. I leave their pages realizing how little I know. To be sure, the great literature can never replace the act of seeing, touching, and smelling this wonderful group of plants. Allan Armitage and I, on our initial visit to the southwest of England, when first viewing the Sino-Himalayan magnolias, thought we had ascended to heaven. Upon returning to reality, we realized that it was *only* a garden. Perhaps the two are equatable.

   Magnolia campbellii, M. c. var. *mollicomata, M. dawsoniana, M. sargentiana* taxa listed in 1995–97 United States magnolia nurseries' catalogs:

var. *alba* (*M. campbellii*)—Ivory white, 10 to 12″.
var. *alba* 'Caerhays Clone'—Large leaves, well-formed, ivory white flowers, 12 tepals.
var. *alba* 'Chyverton Clone'—Fine white-flowered selection.
var. *alba* 'Ethel Hillier'—Large white flowers, light pink at base.
var. *alba* 'Strybing White'—Ivory white flowers with drooping outer tepals, flowers to 12″ diameter.
'Albatross' (*M. cylindrica* × *M. × veitchii*)—Beautiful, large, white, 12-tepaled flowers, 25′ by 35′ at
   Lanhydrock, small plant at Trewithen bore respectable flowers.
'Betty Jessel'—Late flowering, bright pink to crimson.
'Blood Moon'—Very rich pink, darker than normal var. *robusta* types and 'Caerhays Belle', 40 to 50′, hardy
   to 0°F, as I witnessed at Trewithen, faint purplish pink on outside, white inside.
'Burncoose'—Deeper pink than 'Caerhays Belle', 10 to 12″ across.
'Caerhays Belle' (*M. s.* var. *robusta* × *M. sprengeri* 'Diva')—Salmon pink, 12 tepals, up to 12″ diameter,
   −10°F.
'Caerhays Surprise'—Reddish violet to lilac pink, 9 tepals, 8″ diameter, *M. c.* var. *mollicomata* × *M. liliiflora*
   'Nigra'.
'Charles Raffill' (*M. c.* × *M. c.* var. *m.*)—Bright rose-pink outside, inside pure white, flowers 10″ across,
   12 tepals, 40′ by 20′, witnessed at Lanhydrock in late March 1996, again in 1998, spectacular.
'Chyverton' (*M. dawsoniana*)—Crimson fading to carmine-pink, 50′ high.
'Clarke' (*M. dawsoniana*)—Rich pink, abundant, 8″ diameter flowers, 30′ high, 20′ wide in 30 years.
'Darjeeling' (*M. campbellii*)—Dark rose.
'Hendrick's Park' (*M. campbellii*)—Deep rich pink, 10 to 12″ diameter, 40 to 50′ tree.
'Lanarth' (*M. campbellii*)—Unbelievable dark reddish purple (cyclamen purple), 8 to 10″(12″) across, more
   tender than typical *M. campbellii*, a stunner; if only I could grow it . . . but then would I cherish it to
   the same degree?
'Landicla'—Deep purple-pink flowers.
'Marjory Gossler'—Flowers open off-white, 6″ diameter, eventually pure white with a pink flush and 12″
   across, vigorous, hardy, 30′ in 15 years, *M. denudata* × *M. sargentiana* 'Robusta Blood Moon'.
'Milky Way'—Large, white-flowered form with a rich pink flush, 12″ diameter, from New Zealand, flowers
   at a young age.
'Multipetal' (*M. s.* var. *robusta*)—Pink tepals, 19 to 27 in number, discovered by Ambrose Congreve, Mt.
   Congreve, Ireland.
'NY' ('New York') (*M. campbellii*)—Supposedly alive in Pomona, NY which is difficult to accept for *M.
   campbellii*.
'Ruby Rose' (*M. dawsoniana*)—Rose pink to 11″ wide, 12 tepals.
'Sir Harold Hillier' (*M. campbellii*)—Magnificent white-flowered form derived from the understock of the
   scion that died at Chyverton; Mr. Nigel Holman, owner of Chyverton, related the origin of this plant
   for our 7-person March 1998 exploration team; he mentioned that when his father was building the

garden he contacted Hillier's for assistance and the young Sir Harold Hillier was sent to assist; Mr. Holman called him The Great Man and I have heard similar accolades from former Hillier employees as well as American nurserymen who met Mr. Hillier.

'Star Wars' (*M. c.* × *M. liliiflora*)—Bright pink, as witnessed by author in England almost cyclamen rose, Blumhardt of New Zealand introduction, hardier than *M. campbellii*, have seen listed as Zone 5 but doubt this.

M. sargentiana var. *robusta*—Fragrant, pink-purple flowers, 12 to 14″ diameter, Gossler reported hardier than *M. campbellii* in Springfield, OR.

'Strybing Clone' (*M. dawsoniana*)—Pink flowers, long tepals.

'Strybing Pink' (*M. campbellii*)—Pink flowers.

'Strybing White'—White flowers, grown from seed received in Golden Gate Park in 1934.

'Washington Park Clone' (*M. campbellii*)—Large pink flowers, Louisiana Nursery reports it the best *M. campbellii* for the Gulf Coast.

FELIX M. JURY AND OTHER HYBRIDS

'Appollo'—Rose-red, bowl-shaped, 8 to 10″ diameter flowers, rich fruity fragrance, sister seedling of 'Iolanthe', to 20′, *M. campbellii* 'Lanarth' × *M. liliiflora* 'Nigra', hardy to 0°F(?), flowers at an early age.

'Athene'—White with violet-pink flush at base of each tepal, 8 to 10″ diameter, cup and saucer type flowers, to 5°F, similar to 'Iolanthe' with darker reddish pink flush at base, fragrant, upright tree in youth, rounded at maturity, 20 to 25′.

'Atlas'—Lilac-pink outside, cream-white interior, up to 12 to 14″ diameter, cup and saucer flowers, fragrant, rounded outline, to 30′, to 5°F, *M.* 'Mark Jury' × *M.* × *soulangiana* 'Lennei Alba'.

'Emma Cook' (Galyon hybrid)—Lavender-pink aging to white flowers, 12 tepals, 6″ across, to 30′, *M. denudata* × *M. stellata* 'Waterlily', Frank Galyon hybrid.

'Iolanthe'—Clear pink outside, white inside, cup and saucer type flower, to 10″ wide, vigorous erect grower, may repeat flower, flowers at an early age, witnessed several spectacular flowering specimens in England.

'Legacy' (Leach hybrid)—Tepals red-purple to pink, white satin inside, flowers to 11″ across, floriferous, 20′ tree in 20 years, *M. sprengeri* 'Diva' × *M. denudata* 'Rosea', a David Leach introduction, hardy to -20°F.

'Mark Jury'—Medium pink, cup-shaped, to 10″ diameter flowers, darker pink shadings, lavender tinge at edges, tall narrow tree, 'Lanarth' × *M. dawsoniana* var. *robusta*.

'Milky Way'—Fragrant, heavy-textured, ice white tepals with soft rose-pink basal coloration, open flowers up to 12″ across, floriferous, rounded tree 15 to 20′ tall.

'Paul Cook' (Galyon hybrid)—Light to medium pink on outside of broad, 6 to 9 tepals, white inside, up to 12″ across, like huge flat saucers, single-trunked tree, vigorous, *M. sprengeri* 'Diva' × pink 'Lennei' seedling, from Frank Galyon, Knoxville, TN, hardy to at least -10°F, witnessed at Lanhydrock and was less than impressed.

'Pristine' (McDaniel hybrid)—Pink in bud, ivory white, 12 to 15 tepals, goblet-shaped, opening to 5 to 6″ across, wonderful fragrance, tree type, pyramidal, 20 to 30′, vigorous, easy to root, *M. denudata* × *M. stellata* 'Waterlily', one seedling from the cross, J.C. McDaniel introduction in 1979.

'Serene'—Deep rose-purple, bowl-shaped flowers, precocious, flowers over a long period, vigorous.

'Vulcan'—Brilliant ruby red, 10 to 12″ diameter flowers of great substance and heavy texture, erect tree form, open-branched, rounded at maturity, 25′, 'Lanarth' × *M. liliiflora*, impressive as experienced at Chyverton.

GRESHAM HYBRIDS

Cultivars of mixed parentage with *M. campbellii*, *M. liliiflora*, *M. sargentiana* var. *robusta*, *M.* × *soulangiana*, *M. sprengeri* 'Diva', *M.* × *veitchii*. The history of the Gresham Hybrids shows that cultivarism can exceed rational boundaries. Something approximating 15,500 hybrids were produced by D. Todd Gresham. Many crosses were sent to Gloster Arboretum, MS and Tom Dodd Nurseries, Semmes, AL. Subsequently, numerous forms were named by magnolia experts. The *M.* × *veitchii* (*M. denudata* × *M. campbellii*) parentage means plants will be open and large. Flowers are beautiful but habit is somewhat ragged. Expect 20 to 30′ and larger. Several cultivars ('Jon Jon', 'Royal Crown') have been field grown in Zone 7b but were either so irreparably damaged or killed outright by late freezes in March 1996 that their big-time commercial worth is questionable. Under similar conditions, *M. kobus*, *M. stellata*, and *M.* × *loebneri* were untouched. Jim Gardiner presents an excellent overview of the Gresham Hybrids as well as the Blumhardt and Jury New Zealand Hybrids in *The Garden* 123(4):260–265 (1998). Zone (6)7 to 9.

'Candy Cane'—Six inch diameter flowers, thin deep rose stripes arise from base.

'Columbus'—White flowers similar to *M.* × *veitchii*, U.S. National Arboretum hybrid, *M.* × *veitchii* × *M. denudata*.

'Crimson Stipple'—White flowers with crimson suffusion on back of 9-tepaled flowers, fragrant, to 12″ across.

'Dark Shadow'—Deep red-purple, 4 to 5″ diameter, 9-tepaled flowers similar to 'Royal Crown', supposedly compact habit, 25 to 30′ high.

'Darrell Dean'—Wine-red flowers, 12″ across, 9 to 12 broad tepals, rounded vigorous tree, has been described as the best Gresham.

'David Clulow'—Large, white, cup and saucer-shaped flowers, 12 tepals, more recent introduction.

'Deep Purple Dream'—Darkest red-purple, slow-growing, small habit.

'Delicatissima'—White, 9-tepaled, fragrant flowers with faint rose-pink, basal staining.

'Dog Cage'—Bright pink, large flower, vigorous, tree type.

'Elisa Odenwald'—Cream and white, medium to large, 10 to 12″, fragrant, upright flaring growth habit.

'14 Karat'—Porcelain white flowers.

'Frank Gladney'—Deep pink cup and saucer-type flower, 10 to 12″ across, 12 tepals, creamy white inside, vigorous upright plants with broad green leaves.

'Full Eclipse'—Early flowering, red-purple outside, white inside, 9 tepals, columnar growth habit.

'Gresham Giant'—Large white flowers, largest and most vigorous of the Gresham Hybrids, from Gloster Arboretum.

'Heaven Scent'—Reddish pink flowers fading to white at tips, white inside, fragrant, vase-shaped, prolific flowering.

'Isca' (*M.* × *veitchii*)—White flowers flushed pink, spreading habit.

'Joe McDaniel'—Dark red-violet, opening to well formed bowls, darkest colored of all, large upright habit.

'Jon Jon'—White with slight rose at base, lighter at the tip upon opening, tepals 5 to 6″ long, 10 to 12″ across when open, rapid grower, later flowering, rounded habit.

'Lagniappe'—Purple outside, white inside, each tepal notched, new release by Bill Dodd, Alabama.

'Leather Leaf'—Cream-white, fragrant flowers, large thick-textured leaves, tree form.

'Manchu Fan'—Huge, white, bowl-shaped flowers, lightly stained pink on the outside.

'Mary Nell'—10″ diameter cup-shaped flowers, 9 tepals tinged purple-red at the base, inside pure white, vigorous bushy grower.

'Moondance'—Near white Gresham Hybrid from Gloster Arboretum.

'Peppermint Stick'—Large, white flowers marked purple at the base, longitudinal stripe on outside of each tepal.

'Peter Veitch' (*M.* × *veitchii*)—White flowers with pale garnet blush at base, vigorous grower.

'Peter Smithers'—Deep pink, 10″ diameter, white inner surface, 9 tepals, fast vigorous upright grower.

'Pink Goblet'—Solid pink (rose-pink on outside, white inside), goblet-shaped, 10 to 11″ diameter, mid-season flowering.

'Prince Charming'—Tree type, large, tasseled, white flowers, selected by Sara Gladney, Gloster Arboretum.

'Raspberry Ice'—Luminous, lavender-pink (purple-pink) tepals with violet shading at base, 12-tepaled, 9″ wide, upright growth habit, 25 to 30′ tree, sister seedling of 'Royal Crown', considered one of Gresham's best.

'Rouged Alabaster'—Vigorous, with cup-shaped, white flowers flushed pink at the base, 9 tepals, to 12″ wide, fragrant.

'Royal Crown'—Vigorous tree with 12-tepaled, red-purple flowers that open before the leaves with occasional flowering later, hardy to −10°F.

'Royal Flush'—White flowers with soft purple blush, to 12″ diameter, fast growing.

'Sangreal'—Dark red-purple flowers, 9 tepals, cup-shaped, to 8″ wide, floriferous, vigorous.

'Sayonara'—White, globular flowers, 7 to 12″ across, hint of purple at the base, bushy upright habit, 30′, FCC from Royal Horticultural Society (AM 1990).

'Spring Rite'—White flowers with faint rose-pink staining, 9 tepals, to 12″ wide, fast growing.

'Sulphur Cockatoo'—Large, 10″, creamy white, violet-pink staining at base, bowl-shaped flowers, 9 tepals.

'Sweet Sixteen'—White, candle-like, 5″ long buds open into fragrant, tulip-shaped, white flowers, later flowering, oval-rounded habit.

'Tiffany'—White flowers with a pink basal flush.

'Tina Durio'—White with slight pink tinge at base, 10 to 12″ diameter flowers, 9 to 12 tepals, profuse, flower late, fast grower.

'Todd Gresham'—Violet-rose outside, white inside flowers, 10 to 12″ across, 9 tepals, fast growing and vigorous, loose and open, also produces abundant red fruits.

'Winelight'—Blush pink at base covering 1/3 of tepal fading to white at tips, 9 thick tepals, flower to 8″ across, later flowering.

PICKARD HYBRIDS

Raised by Amos Pickard of Canterbury, England. Hybrid seedlings of *M.* ✕ *soulangiana* 'Picture' with pollen parent not known. All are fast-growing and do not set heavy flower buds in youth as does *M.* ✕ *soulangiana*. Witnessed these for the first time in late March 1996, and again in 1998, at Trewithen Garden in England. Colors were intense, well-shaped vase to goblet flowers, too many clones with at least 14 named. A closer evaluation in March 1998 indicated that the clones are excessively similar. Probably adaptable in Zone 5 to 8. In United States commerce the following cultivars have been offered:

'Pickard's Firefly' ('Fire Fly')—Deep purplish wine red, goblet-shaped flowers, upright, vigorous tree.

'Pickard's Garnet'—Garnet base streaked similarly to apex, meshing with white.

'Pickard's Glow'—Fragrant, wine red flowers fading to white, upright, vigorous tree.

'Pickard's Opal'—White flowers with faint purple-pink blush at base of tepals, goblet-shaped.

'Pickard's Ruby'—Deep purplish wine red, fragrant, goblet-shaped flowers up to 11″ across, almost fastigiate habit.

'Pickard's Schmetterling'—Elongated to 14″ across, wine red, fragrant flowers with narrow tepals.

'Pickard's Snow Queen'—Large, pure white flowers with 6 spatulate tepals.

'Pickard's Stardust'—Very fragrant, snow white flowers.

'Pickard's Sundew'—Creamy white flowers with a pink basal blush, fragrant, fast-growing, as I witnessed the cultivar in flower at Trewithen the color approximated muddy, off-white.

U.S. NATIONAL ARBORETUM HYBRIDS

'Galaxy'—Pyramidal, single-trunked, upright tree in youth, probably 20 to 30′ high; 12 tepals, 6 to 10″ across, red-purple to pink and open late enough to avoid spring frost damage, as late as 2 to 3 weeks after the frost sensitive magnolias, considered hardy in Zone 5 to 9; hybrid from a 1963 cross between *M. liliiflora* ✕ *M. sprengeri* 'Diva'; introduced by U.S. National Arboretum; may grow 30′ high by 10′ wide in 10 years; parent plant as I saw it was 25 to 30′ high and wide at the U.S. National Arboretum.

'Spectrum'—A sister seedling of 'Galaxy' with wider habit, flowers are larger and deeper colored and not as profuse, probably inferior to 'Galaxy', the parent plant is wide-spreading, about 25′ by 25′.

I thought the above two might make unique and much needed small urban and garden trees but am not satisfied with either because of the watersprout development and rather unkempt late summer foliage (inherited from *M. liliiflora*). Also, size is bigger than ideal and the parent plants are both over 25′ high and as wide.

✕ *Mahoberberis* Schneid.
FAMILY: Berberidaceae

✕ *Mahoberberis* is the result of intergeneric crosses between *Mahonia* and *Berberis*. The foliage varies from evergreen to semi-evergreen and from simple to compound on the same plant. Flowers and fruits are sparse or nonexistent. Having seen the following hybrids I would have to rate them poor quality ornamentals. They do have some interest for the plant collector and are chiefly found in arboreta although, to my surprise, I discovered several plants in Cave Hill Cemetery, Louisville, KY.

✕ *Mahoberberis aquicandidula* Krüssm., (ma-hō-bĕr′-bĕr-is a-kwi-kan-did′ū-là), resulted from a cross between *M. aquifolium* and *B. candidula*. The leaves are a leathery, glossy dark green, 1 to 1 1/2″ long, with 3 to 5 sharp spines on each margin of the leaf. The foliage turns brilliant scarlet, claret and other red-purple combinations in the winter. The habit is somewhat open and stiff and not attractive. Will probably grow 3 to 6′ at maturity. Zone 6, possibly 5. Lost most of its leaves after exposure to −6°F. ✕ *M. miethkeana* Meland. & Eade. is occasionally offered in commerce.

✕ *Mahoberberis aquisargentii* Krüssm., (ma-hō-bĕr′-bĕr-is a-qwi-sâr-jen′tē-ī), is a hybrid between *M. aquifolium* ✕ *B. sargentiana*. In general it is more vigorous than the previous species (6′). The glossy evergreen to semi-evergreen foliage may be simple or compound pinnate on the same plant. Leaves will turn bronze to reddish purple in winter especially if sited in full sun. First introduced from Sweden in 1948. Zone 6. Foliage injured at −6°F.

× *Mahoberberis neubertii* (Lem.) Schneid., (ma-hō-bĕr′-bĕr-is new-bĕr′tē-ĭ), is the first *Mahoberberis* I had ever witnessed. It was growing in the shrub collection at the Arnold Arboretum and probably represents the worst of the lot. It is leggy, open, and the leaves are of a dull, semi-evergreen nature. Result of crosses between *Mahonia aquifolium* and *Berberis vulgaris*. Grows 4 to 6′ high. Zone 6. Dropped *all* leaves after exposure to –6°F. Originated in France in 1854.

Mahonia aquifolium (Pursh) Nutt. — Oregongrapeholly, Oregon Grapeholly, Oregon Hollygrape, Oregon Grape depending on who or what is writing the common name.
(ma-hō′ni-à a-kwi-fō′li-um)

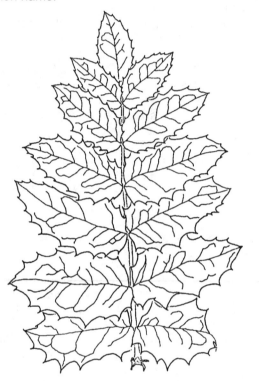

FAMILY: Berberidaceae
LEAVES: Alternate, compound pinnate, evergreen, 6 to 12″ long, 5 to 9(13) leaflets, sessile, ovate to oblong-ovate, 1 1/2 to 3 1/2″ long, spine-tipped, rounded or truncate at base, sinuately spiny-dentate, up to 12 per side, lustrous dark green above, rarely dull, extremely stiff and leathery, usually turning purplish in winter.
BUDS: Rather small, except for the terminal which is ovoid with half-a-dozen exposed scales.
STEM: Roundish, stout, becoming gray-brown at maturity; leaf scars—narrow, low, half encircling the stem; pith—large, pale, continuous.

SIZE: 3 to 6′, will grow to 9′ in height; spread of 3 to 5′; suckers and will form colonies.
HARDINESS: Zone (4)5 to 7(8); Cappiello reported occasional tip dieback in Orono, ME.
HABIT: Limited branching evergreen shrub with upright, heavy stems, often stoloniferous in habit, actually there seem to be two forms, one low and broad, dense and rounded; the other taller with upright branches, irregular and open, with lustrous foliage.
RATE: Slow, 2 to 3′ over a 3 to 4 year period.
TEXTURE: Medium in summer, medium-coarse in winter.
LEAF COLOR: Reddish bronze when unfolding, changing to light, glossy yellow-green and finally lustrous dark green in summer; purplish bronze in fall and winter, depending on genotype (clone) and exposure.
FLOWERS: Perfect, bright yellow, borne in fascicled, erect, 2 to 3″ long and wide terminal racemes in April (early to mid-March, Athens), very handsome in flower; has slightly fragrant flowers but not to the degree of *Mahonia bealei*.
FRUIT: True berry, rounded, blue-black, bloomy, 1/3 to 1/2″ diameter, July, August–September, about a month earlier in Zone 7b, look like grapes and, therefore, the common name grapeholly, may persist into December, observed plants in July in British Columbia that were much more heavily fruited than plants I have witnessed in eastern United States.
CULTURE: Transplant balled-and-burlapped or container-grown into moist, well-drained, acid soil; avoid hot, dry soils and desiccating winds; prefers shade (will tolerate sun); tends to brown up very badly unless sited in a protected location; will develop chlorosis in high pH soils.
DISEASES AND INSECTS: Leaf rusts, leaf spots, leaf scorch (physiological problem caused by desiccating wind and winter sun), barberry aphid, scale, and whitefly.
LANDSCAPE VALUE: Foundation plant, shrub border, specimen, shady area; not the best of the broadleaves but certainly not the worst; has a place in the landscape but should be used with discretion; severely injured at –20°F in central Illinois.
CULTIVARS: Reasonable confusion about the exact taxonomic status of many of the cultivars since they might represent hybrids or intergrades of *M. aquifolium*, *M. nervosa*, *M. pinnata* and *M. repens*. I see significant variation in foliage color and density. Discovered a plant in a local garden with *M. aquifolium* characteristics yet with flowers at every node that resulted in a golden wand.
  'Apollo'—Low-growing variety with conspicuous golden orange flowers in dense heads, makes a good ground cover, deep green leaves with reddish stalks, ±2′ high.
  'Atropurpureum'—Leaves dark reddish purple in winter.

'Compactum'—Dwarf form with very glossy leaves and a bronze winter color; grows about 24 to 36″ in height, hardy to -10°F, a handsome form.

'Donewell'—Broad-arching to 3′ high, leaflets long-spined, tinted blue below, red rachis.

'Forescate'—Leaves blue-white below, spring, winter leaves tinted red, 3′ high.

'Golden Abundance'—Heavy yellow flowers are born against bright green foliage; plants are vigorous, erect and dense, and covered with blue berries (Zone 5).

'King's Ransom'—A rather upright, dark green, closer to blue green leaf form that is being utilized in greater numbers every year, turns bronze-red-purple in winter, probably a hybrid of *M. aquifolium* × *M. pinnata*, 5′ high.

'Mayhan Strain'—A dwarf form with glossy foliage and fewer leaflets per leaf and the leaflets arranged more closely on the rachis. The Mayhan Nursery who introduced this cultivar claims it is the result of 25 years of selection and the form can be maintained by seed propagation. Plant should grow between 30 to 42″ high.

'Moseri'—Bronze-red or orange new leaves, in spring the young growth is rich apricot; leaves turn to apple green and finally dark green, 32″ high, *M.* × *wagneri* type.

'Orange Flame'—Blazing bronze-orange new foliage, contrasts with wine red or deep green older leaves, erect grower, stout stems, needs full sun.

'Smaragd' ('Emerald')—Handsome glossy emerald green leaves, assumes bronzy purple hue with advent of cold weather, deep yellow flowers occur in terminal and axillary racemes/panicles, habit is intermediate between 'Compacta' and larger growing types; this selection has spectacular foliage; in late March at Hillier Arboretum I witnessed the plant without any discoloration, i.e., bronze to red-purple; this and 'Appollo' have the loveliest foliage.

PROPAGATION: Seed should be stratified for 90 days as 41°F and should not be allowed to dry out after it is collected; best time to take cuttings is in November or after some exposure to cold, treat with 8000 to 10000 ppm IBA. If only a few plants are needed, simple division of the parent plant works well. Daguin et al., *Acta Hortic.* 320:193–197 (1992), reported regeneration of *M. japonica*, 'Appollo' and 'Winter Sun' from bud explants.

NATIVE HABITAT: British Columbia to Oregon. Introduced 1823.

RELATED SPECIES:

Mahonia 'Arthur Menzies' is a seedling that was selected in 1961 at Washington Park Arboretum, Seattle. Yeilow flowers occur in 5 to 10″ long, 8 to 10″ wide inflorescences in December–January. Withstood 11°F, however, at Callaway Gardens was defoliated with stem damage at 0 to -5°F. Tends toward a leggy upright cumbersome shrub but has the larger leaf of the *M.* × *media* hybrids. Zone (7)8 to 9. A *M. bealei* × *M. lomariifolia* hybrid.

Mahonia bealei (Fort.) Carr. — Leatherleaf Mahonia

LEAVES: Alternate, compound pinnate, evergreen, 9 to 13(15) leaflets, rigid, ovate, each leaflet 1 to 4″ long, 1 to 2″ wide, terminal leaflet larger than laterals, 3- to 5-nerved, endowed with 5 to 7 prominent spines, glabrous, sessile on rachis, leathery, dull dark to blue green above, pale green below; petiole—1 to 1 1/2″ long.

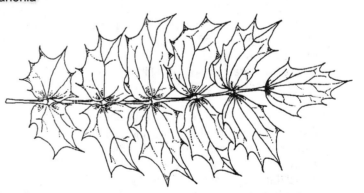

Mahonia bealei, (ma-hō′ni-à bēl′ē-ī), Leatherleaf Mahonia, is a clumsy, upright, coarse, evergreen shrub growing 6 to 10′(12′) high. The foliage is dull dark to blue-green and very coriaceous; texture is coarse; flowers are lemon yellow and extremely fragrant, March–April, has flowered as early as mid-January in Athens and is normally in full flower by late February; 3 to 6″ high and 6 to 12″ wide inflorescence; fruit is a bluish, 1/3 to 1/2″ long berry maturing in July–August. On the Georgia campus the fruits mature in late April, May–June. The fruits assume a bloomy, almost "robin's egg" blue color as they pass toward maturation. Seeds will germinate without cold stratification and can be sown as extracted from the fruits. Used in great numbers in the Southeast and is attractive in a shady corner of the garden where the fragrant flowers are particularly welcome. The fruits are especially attractive and occur in great numbers. Apparently the birds love the fruits since they are often removed shortly after ripening.

Also, numerous seedlings develop in out-of-the-way places where only birds could disseminate the seeds. Flowers open from the base to the apex and are not as vivid in color or as showy from a distance as *M. aquifolium*. A hybrid between *M. gracilipes* and *M. bealei* with lustrous green foliage and 12 to 15″ high framework has been successful in our garden. From Tom Dodd Nurseries, Semmes, AL. Coombes in the 1991 *Hillier Manual* reduced *M. bealei* to a cultivar of *M. japonica*. Griffiths and Meyer, Mazzeo and Ross in later works maintain species integrity. See comments under *M. japonica* for my interpretation. *Mahonia bealei* is native to China. Introduced 1845. Zone (6)7 to 9. Hardiness has never been adequately documented but plants in Cincinnati were killed to the ground at –17°F. In 1983–84, at –3°F, Athens, there was leaf browning but nothing particularly severe. Possibly hardy in the –5 to –10°F range.

Mahonia fortunei (Lindl.) Fedde. — Chinese Mahonia

LEAVES: Alternate, evergreen, pinnately compound, 6 to 10″ long, 5 to 9(13) leaflets, lanceolate to linear-lanceolate, long acuminate, cuneate, 2 to 5″ long, 1/2 to 3/4″ wide, 5 to 15 forward pointing spiny teeth on each margin, apex spine-tipped, sessile, flat dark green above, paler beneath, glabrous and marked with prominent netted veins.

STEM: Stout, generally 1/4″ or more in diameter, brown, rough, typically yellow when cut.

Mahonia fortunei, (ma-hō′ni-à fôr-tū′nē-ī), Chinese Mahonia, is perhaps the most beautiful mahonia because of its rather ferny foliage and, when properly grown, compact, dense stature. It grows 5 to 6′ high but in Zone 7 seldom reaches more than 3′ unless well protected. The yellow flowers occur in 2 to 3″ long, erect, cylindrical racemes in late summer–early fall (Georgia). The purple-black fruits are seldom developed. It is a rather graceful shrub and not as lethal to the touch as *M. bealei*. Temperatures of 0 to 5°F will take the leaves off and –3°F killed the plant to the ground. It resprouted but was only 18″ tall after 4 growing seasons. In Savannah, GA (Zone 8), this species is tucked away in a shady nook in a park by the Savannah River and makes a stunning filler. Plants are vigorous and quite full. For warmer regions, this might be the *Mahonia* of choice. A recent mass planting in the northeast alcove of a large Georgia campus building was handsome for a time but recently mildew and leaf browning have become prevalent. It survives in Athens because of the building protection, however, lack of air movement and any direct light may have induced the problems. China. Introduced 1846. Zone (7)8 to 9.

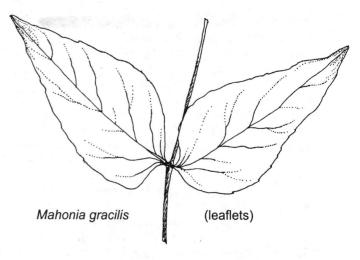

Mahonia gracilis (Hartw.) Fedde. (ma-hō′ni-à gras′i-lis), has fragrant, yellow flowers in December and glaucous blue, 1/2″ diameter fruit. Five to 13, often overlapping, light green, closely spiny serrate leaflets. Requires well-drained soil and filtered light. Mexico. Zone 7 to 9.

Mahonia gracilis   (leaflets)

Mahonia japonica (Thunb.) DC., (ma-hō′ni-à jà-pon′i-ká), Japanese Mahonia, is quite similar to *M. bealei* and for landscape purposes serves the same function. Principal difference resides in the lax, loose spreading inflorescence with the flowers more distantly spaced and individual flowers subtended by bracts as long as the flower stalks. Based on the few plants I have seen, the differences are not manifest and, in fact, hybrids are probably common in cultivation. The lone "true" plant in the Dirr garden was provided by the Scott Arboretum, Swarthmore College. The 7 to 19 leaflets are glossy dark green and do not display the strong nerves (veins) of *M. bealei*. Flowers occur in the same time frame. Each flower is larger and brighter yellow than *M. bealei*. Grows 6 to 7′ high. Handsome garden plant that as yet has not produced the 1/3 to 1/2″ long, ovoid, glaucous gray-mauve fruits. Japan. Zone 6 to 8.

Mahonia × media C.D. Brickell (*M. japonica × M. lomariifolia* Tak.), (ma-hō′ni-à mē′di-à). The progeny of this cross resemble, at least the plants I have seen, *M. lomariifolia*, a rather tender species with a 10 to 24″ long leaf composed of 19 to 37 leaflets. Plants of *M. × media* are upright branched becoming rounded with time and grow larger than typical *M. japonica*, between 8 and 15′. Leaflets number 17 to 21, each averaging 2 1/2 to 4 1/2″ long, 1 to 1 1/2″ wide, handsome, somewhat glossy green. Flowers (lemon yellow) occur at the ends of the branches in 10 to 14″ long, erect or spreading racemes. Flowers, at least on 'Winter Sun' and 'Charity', were not very fragrant. Plants are striking in flower. I have seen plants in flower ('Charity') in early January in England. They make great winter flowering shrubs where hardy, which is at best in Zone (6)7 to 9 in the southeastern states. Cultivars include:

'Buckland'—Inflorescence up to 27″ across, composed of 13 to 14 primary racemes, pale yellow, slightly fragrant.

'Charity'—Yellow flowers, excellent shrub, to 15′, leaves with up to 21 leaflets.

'Faith'—Closer to *M. lomariifolia* in habit and foliage but with soft-colored yellow flowers.

'Hope'—Soft bright yellow flowers, densely set.

'Lionel Fortescue'—Fragrant yellow flowers occur in racemes that may reach 16″ long.

'Underway'—Bushy shrub, flowers in late fall in Athens.

'Winter Sun'—More erect racemes than 'Charity', bright yellow, not wildly fragrant flowers, flowered in December in Athens.

'Winter Sun' and 'Underway' are growing in Athens and it is delightful to experience the rich yellow flowers in late fall. The mahonias, particularly the *M. × media* forms, were favorites of the late great J.C. Raulston. These plants carry great memories.

Mahonia nervosa (Pursh) Nutt., (ma-hō′ni-à něr-vō′sà), Cascades Mahonia, is a low, suckering, evergreen (11 to 23, thick, gray green, closely serrate, up to 3″ long leaflets) shrub rarely reaching more than 12 to 18″(36″). Flowers are yellow and borne in 8″ long racemes. Fruit is glaucous purplish blue, 1/4 to 1/3″ diameter. British Columbia to California. Introduced 1822. Zone 5 to 7.

Mahonia pinnata (Lagasca) Fedde., (ma-hō′ni-à pin-nā′tà), is confused (by me) with *M. aquifolium* but is more erect, regular in habit, leaflets more finely serrate, dull green above, glaucous gray below, tinted maroon to red-purple in winter. Flowers (spring) in terminal and axillary, 1 1/2 to 2 1/2″ long racemes, to 5-fascicled. Fruit is an ovoid, 1/4″ wide, glaucous blue berry. California. Zone 7.

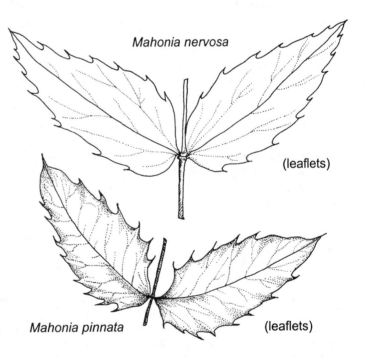

Mahonia nervosa

(leaflets)

Mahonia pinnata

(leaflets)

Mahonia repens G. Don., (ma-hō′ni-à rē′penz), Creeping Mahonia, is a low (10 to 18″), stoloniferous, evergreen ground cover plant of stiff habit. Pinnately compound leaves (3 to 7 leaflets, 1 to 2 1/2″ long, spine-toothed) are dull blue-green in summer; rich purple in winter. Flowers are deep yellow, April, borne in small racemes, 1 to 3″ long. Fruit is black, grape-like, covered with a blue bloom, 1/4″ diameter, August–September. 'Rotundifolia' has almost rounded, entire to serrulate leaflets. British Columbia to northern Mexico and California. Introduced 1822. Zone (4)5 to 7. Cappiello reported occasional tip dieback in Orono, ME.

Mahonia × wagneri (Jouin) Rehd., (ma-hō′ni-à wag′něr-ī), is a grex for plants resulting from crosses of *M. pinnata* and *M. aquifolium*. I first came across this name in 1978 during the initial sabbatical at the Arnold Arboretum. The Arnold's plant was compact and mounded. Most hybrids have the dull green summer foliage. 'King's Ransom' (see *M. aquifolium*) shows strong *M. pinnata* influence and turns rich red-purple in winter. It is more upright and open. Zone 6 to 8.

Malus Mill. — Flowering Crabapple
FAMILY: Rosaceae

I doubt if any treatment of flowering crabapples will ever be complete for as I write this someone is ready to introduce a new clone into the trade. The actual number of crabapple types is open to debate but across the country one could probably find 400 to 600 types, perhaps more. Crabapples tend to be cross fertile and freely hybridize. If one checked the parentage of many clones he or she would find that it was an open pollinated seedling, meaning that any number of trees within proximity of the fruiting tree could be the parent(s). There is a nice collection of crabapples on the University of Illinois campus and I collected fruits from many types and enjoyed watching the potpourri of seedlings which resulted. The diversity of foliage colors (light green, dark green, various tints of purple); leaf morphology (serrate, lobed, incised); and vigor (some seedlings grow 3 to 4 times faster than others) can be attributed to the heterogeneous genetic pool contributed by the many different parents. I was told a particular mass planting on campus was *M. hupehensis*, Tea Crabapple, a triploid which comes true-to-type from seed. The plants did not have the typical vase-shaped habit of the species and I found out why when the first group of seedlings developed. The leaves were different colors, shapes and sizes indicating anything but a species which breeds true from seed. I have attempted to assemble a fairly representative list of crabapples which are often grown and available from nurseries. The salient characteristics of flower, fruit, size and diseases are included. Many crabapples are almost worthless because of extreme susceptibility to apple scab, rust, fire blight, leaf spot and powdery mildew. Unfortunately, the most susceptible types seem to be the most popular (i.e., 'Almey', 'Hopa', 'Eleyi', 'Bechtels', 'Red Silver'). Considering the tremendous number of crabapples available only a handful or so meet the stringent requirements of excellent flower, fruit, habit and disease resistance. Many types are slightly susceptible to certain disease(s) and are perfectly acceptable provided their limitations are understood. I have used the late Dr. Lester Nichols, Pennsylvania State University, Dr. Ed Hasselkus, retired, University of Wisconsin, Dr. Elton Smith, retired, The Ohio State University, Dr. Malcolm Shurtliff, Univ. of Illinois, Eric A. Draper and James Chatfield, *Ornamental Plants*, Special Circular 154, Ohio State Univ. Extension (1997), and Dr. Norman Pellett and David Heleba, Univ. of Vermont disease ratings based on their many years of collecting data regarding disease susceptibility. In certain instances no data were available and no evaluation is given. I have cross-checked many references in regard to the flower and fruit characters and strongly recommend the following references for further reading: *Trees for American Gardens* by Donald Wyman; *Trees and Shrubs Hardy in the British Isles*, Vol. II by W.J. Bean; *Crabapples of Documented Authentic Origin*, U.S. National Arboretum Contribution No. 2 by Roland Jefferson; *Flowering Crabapples* by Arie den Boer; and *Flowering Crabapples* by John L. Fiala, Timber Press (1994). I recommend that anyone interested in staying current on crabapple join the International Ornamental Crabapple Society.

The fifth edition listing of crabapples has been enlarged and the data collated from many sources to reflect performance and disease susceptibility. The information was gleaned from the publications of Dr. Ed Hasselkus, Wisconsin, Dr. Elton Smith, Ohio State, Dr. Tom Green, formerly Morton Arboretum, now Western Illinois University, Dr. Tom Ranney, North Carolina State, the late Dr. John Pair, Kansas State, Dr. Karel Jacobs, Morton Arboretum [see Karel Jacobs and Michael Sprauka, *HortTechnology* 6(2):140 (1996)], Dr. Curt Peterson, Michigan State University and my personal observations. The Michigan State University Extension Bulletin E-2177 *Crabapples*: *A Selection Guide*, summarizes data on 85 crabapple taxa in easy-to-use chart form. It is available from MSU Bulletin Office, MSU, 10-B Agriculture Hall, East Lansing, MI 48824-1039 for 0.50¢. The authors categorized scab susceptibility by location where data were collected which results in very susceptible, susceptible and tolerant ratings for the same taxon. Yearly weather conditions affect incidence and degree of disease. So all ratings are correct for that report. If a crabapple is moderately to highly susceptible to scab, choose another. There are many new and some older cultivars that are essentially disease-free even in the worst climatic years. It makes no sense to spray or have half to fully defoliated trees in the garden when smart selection mitigates the above. Jacobs and Sprauka (see above) reported that in rainy 1995 in Morton Arboretum 102 *Malus* taxa were evaluated with 'Adirondack', 'Beverly', 'Bob White', *M. halliana* var. *spontanea*, 'Jackii', 'Mary Potter', 'Midwest', Molten Lava™, 'Prairie Maid', 'Prairifire', 'Purple Prince', Red Jewel™, 'Silver Moon', 'Tom's Pink', *M. tschonoskii*, 'White Angel', and 'Wooster' were most resistant.

In "A Malus Medley," *Amer. Nurseryman* 184(4):46–48, 50, 52–55 (1996), rated 'Bob White', 'Donald Wyman', 'Jackii', Red Jewel™, 'Mary Potter', Molten Lava™, 'Ormiston Roy', 'Prairifire', 'Sentinel', 'Strawberry Parfait', and Sugar Tyme® among the best based on fruit, foliage, and flower attributes. These ratings are from Ohio researchers. Tom Green, the guru of crabapples, listed 10 best taxa based on results of National Crabapple Evaluation research in *American Horticulturist* 75(2):18–23. The best include: 'Adams', 'Bob White', 'David', 'Donald Wyman', *M. floribunda*, 'Prairifire', 'Professor Sprenger', 'Snowdrift', Sugar Tyme®, and *M.* × *zumi* 'Calocarpa'. The following crabapples are my current favorites (note the selection is not necessarily based on complete disease resistance as was strongly suggested in the above discussion). It is important for the reader to notice that my list and the other two do not totally coincide, but that several cultivars appear on all lists.

M. 'Adirondack'
M. 'Callaway'
M. 'Donald Wyman'
M. floribunda — Japanese Crabapple
M. 'Harvest Gold' ('Winter Gold')

M. hupehensis — Tea Crabapple
M. Red Jewel™
M. sargentii — Sargent Crabapple
M. 'Snowdrift'
M. 'Sugar Tyme'

The late John Pair and Linda Parsons, Wichita, KS, *1994 Woody Ornamental Evaluations*, Kansas State University, evaluated fruiting of crabapples and noted most productive were 'Indian Magic', 'Indian Summer', 'Jewelberry', 'Sentinel', Sugar Tyme®, 'Christmas Holly', 'Beverly', 'Centurion', 'David', 'Donald Wyman', 'Manbeck Weeper', 'Mary Potter', 'Midwest', and 'Ormiston Roy'. More persistent into March were 'Centurion', 'Donald Wyman', 'Indian Summer', 'Indian Magic', 'Sentinel', and Sugar Tyme®.

There are few other trees or shrubs which approach the beauty of a crabapple tree in full flower. Ornamental crabapples are an outstanding group of small flowering trees for landscape planting. They are valued for foliage, flowers, fruit, and variations in habit or size. By using different species and cultivars, the flowering period can be extended from late April to late May and early June (late March to late April in Zone 7b) with colors ranging from white through purplish red. An interesting paper on crabapple flower sequence and length of effectiveness appeared in *Landscape Plant News* 8(2):4–6 (1997). Using the earliest crabapple to flower as zero-time ('Pink Spires'), the authors presented number of days to first flower for the others; the largest difference was 10 days for 'Silver Moon', with most in the 6 to 8 day range. Also, days from first open flower to 50% petal drop was highest in early flowering varieties to 9.4 days, with the majority in the (4)5 to 7 day category. Indeed the flowers are fleeting, but beautiful.

The small fruits, borne in the fall, are also effective, with colors of red, yellow, and green. Other features of this group are the small size (rounded, horizontal, pendulous, fastigiate, and vase-shaped). Crabapples are suited for home grounds, schools, parks, commercial and public buildings, and highway plantings.

CHARACTERISTICS

Deciduous trees and shrubs, rarely half evergreen; most are between 15 and 25′ in height at maturity; offer tremendous winter architecture because of unique branching.

Shape: Range from low mound-like plants to narrow upright or pendulous types.

Branches: Alternate, upright, horizontal, or drooping, rarely with spinescent branches.

Buds: Ovoid, with several imbricate scales, usually reddish brown with hairs protruding from the underside of the bud scales.

Bark: On old trunks, shiny gray-brown, scaly.

Flowers: White to pink or carmine to red to rose. Single flowers have 5 petals. Flowers occur in umbel or corymb-like racemes. Petals are small, suborbicular to obovate. Stamens 15 to 20, usually with yellow anthers. Ovary is inferior, 3 to 5 celled, styles present vary from 2 to 5, connate at base, perfect.

Fruit: A pome with persistent or deciduous calyx; colors range from red to yellow to green. If fruit is 2″ in diameter or less, it is a crabapple. If the fruit is larger than 2″, then it is classified as an apple.

HABITAT

Twenty to 30 species of crabapples are scattered in the temperate regions of North America, Europe, and Asia. Currently, at least 100 to 200 types of crabapples are grown in North American nurseries, with at least 300 to 400 additional types in arboretums and botanical gardens. Dr. Nichols crabapple printout listed approximately 700 types.

GENERAL CULTURE

Crabapples are quite adaptable to varying soil conditions, but have been observed to do best in a heavy loam. The soil, regardless of type, should be well-drained, moist and acid (pH 5.0 to 6.5). Most crabapples are hardy (Zone 4 to 7) and should be planted in full sun for best development of flowers and fruits. McNamara and Pellett, *J. Environ. Hort.* 14:111–114 (1996), determined stem hardiness of 38 crabapple taxa on 6 dates throughout the dormant period in 1992–93. All were amazingly cold hardy in midwinter from -26°F for 'Jewelberry' to -44°F for *M. baccata* 'Jackii'. 'Dolgo', 'Red Jade', 'Red Splendor', and 'Selkirk' were hardy to at least -40°F in midwinter and also exhibited early and late season hardiness.

Generally crabapples require little pruning, but if any is done, it should be completed before early June. Most crabapples initiate flower buds for the next season in mid-June to early July and pruning at this time or later would result in decreased flower production the following year. Pruning may be done, however, to remove sucker growth, open up the center of the plant to light and air, to cut off out-of-place branches, and shape the tree.

PROPAGATION

Practically all flowering crabs are self-sterile and are propagated by budding, grafting, from softwood cuttings or tissue culture. Two crabapples are, however, commonly propagated from seed and come true-to-type; *M. hupehensis* and *M. toringoides*. The Sargent Crabapple is also frequently propagated from seed, but considerable variation in size occurs. Although the literature is conflicting on seed treatment I have found that a 2 to 3 month cold period will induce good germination.

Crabapples are often grafted, using a whip graft, or are budded in summer. Understocks, include the common apple; *M. × robusta* and *M. sieboldii* seedlings have proven acceptable as has *M. baccata* where hardiness is a factor. The Malling rootstocks are now used routinely to reduce suckering and provide a better root system. In addition to grafting and budding, a few crabapples such as Arnold, Carmine, Sargent, or Japanese Flowering are propagated from softwood cuttings taken from mid-June through July. Anyone interested in cutting propagation should see Brown and Dirr, "Cutting propagation of selected flowering crabapple types," *The Plant Propagator* 22(4):4–5 (1976) and Burd and Dirr, *Proc. Intl. Plant Prop. Soc.* 27:427–432 (1977). See Dirr and Heuser, 1987, for a more in depth discussion.

DISEASES AND INSECTS

The Asiatic forms are much more resistant to insects and diseases than are the forms native to North America. In the southern states, crabapples are not as widely planted but, in general, types like *M.* 'Callaway', *M. floribunda*, *M. sargentii* and *M. × zumi* do well. Fireblight and woolly aphids are more prevalent in the southern states.

> *Fireblight.* The diseased plants have the appearance of being scorched by fire. The first visible signs of infection are often a drying up of the tips of young shoots and bud-clusters. The disease is caused by bacteria which are spread by aphids, leaf hoppers, and bees. Carelessness in handling diseased leaves and branches, and failure to adequately disinfect pruning equipment contribute to the spread of the disease. Control of this disease is difficult. Cultural control practices such as pruning out diseased branches and avoiding excessive nitrogen fertilization should be employed. Use resistant cultivars when possible.

> *Cedar Apple Rust* (Asiatic varieties are resistant). The disease appears on apple leaves in May as yellow (orange) leaf spots which subsequently enlarge, resulting in heavy leaf drop. The disease has as an alternative host (*Juniperus virginiana, J. horizontalis*, and *J. scopulorum*). Galls appear on junipers in early April and spores produced by these galls later infect apple trees.

> Cultural control is possible by keeping a minimum distance of 500′ between apple and juniper plants. The disease can be prevented from spreading to apples by spraying the galls when they form in early April with a suitable fungicide. Crabapples can be sprayed with a fungicide when the galls appear on junipers (about mid-April to mid-May). Make 4 to 5 applications at 7 to 10 day intervals.

> *Apple Scab.* The native North American species, Asiatic species, and hybrids and the fruiting apple (*Malus pumila*) are quite susceptible to this disease. Fruits show darkened, leathery spots with many small cracks. The leaves also have darkened spots which may look black or velvety. For control of scab use a suitable fungicide in late March before flowers show any color, and repeat the application at weekly or ten day intervals until petals have dropped and the fruits have set.

> *Canker.* Several species of fungi cause canker on the trunks of crabapples. They often gain entrance through wounds made by lawn mowers and other maintenance equipment.

> *Scale.* Three main types: San Jose, Oyster Shell, or Putman. Adequate control can be obtained by either using a dormant oil as a spray before bud break or with a suitable insecticide when the scales are in the crawling stage.

> *Borers* (may be a serious problem). For cultural control, keep the plants growing well with adequate fertilization and watering practices.

> *Aphids.* A serious problem generally only on native species. Adequate control can be obtained by spraying the trees with an insecticide.

> *Japanese Beetles.* These insects can feed on and defoliate trees. In recent years several studies rating crabapple resistance to feeding by beetles have been published. Spicer et al., *J. Economic Entomology* 88:979–985 (1995), reported consistent levels of resistance over two growing seasons. Defoliation ranged from 100% to <10% among cultivars at the same location. Red- and purple-leaved types and those with reddish leaves that turned to green were most heavily fed upon. *Malus baccata* 'Jackii', 'Harvest Gold', and 'Jewelberry' were highly resistant, while 'Liset', 'Radiant', 'Red Splendor', 'Royalty', and 'Ruby Luster' were severely damaged. The 1997 *Ornamental Plants*, Special Circular 154, from Ohio State University Extension presents evaluations of Japanese beetle and Apple-and-thorn skeletonizer.

Malus 'Adams' — Adams Nursery, Westfield, MA 1947 introduction.
FLOWERS: Single, 1 1/2″ diameter, carmine in bud, flowers fading to dull pink, annual.
FRUIT: Dark glossy red, 5/8″ diameter, persistent.
HABIT: Rounded and dense, 24′, reddish foliage in youth, tinge of purple when mature, i.e., reddish green.
DISEASES: Very resistant, proving to be a superior crabapple although slight fireblight, scab and mildew have
    been reported, poor resistance to Japanese beetle, outstanding at Milliken Arboretum, Spartanburg, SC.

Malus 'Adirondack' — *Malus halliana* form, introduced by U.S. National Arboretum, bred by Dr. Egolf.
FLOWERS: Red buds, flowers large waxy white with red tinge.
FRUIT: Red to orange-red, 1/2″ diameter, holding into December, Zone 7.
HABIT: Columnar, obovate, 10′ by 6′ (larger, 1 1/2 to 2 times initial reported size), dark green summer foliage.
DISEASES: Highly resistant to scab, fireblight, rust and mildew, selected from 500 seedlings, see *HortScience*
    22:269–270 (1987).

Malus 'Albright'
FLOWERS: Single, deep pink.
FRUIT: Purplish red, 3/4″ diameter.
HABIT: Upright spreading.
DISEASES: Slight susceptibility to fireblight, frogeye leaf spot.

Malus 'Aldenham' ('Aldenhamensis') — *M.* × *purpurea* (Barbier) Rehd. type
FLOWERS: Single and semi-double, expanding buds maroon-red, open purplish red fading to deep purplish
    pink, 1 3/4 to 2″ across.
FRUIT: Dark maroon-red to maroon-purple, shaded side green to bronze, 3/4 to 1″ diameter.
HABIT: Resembles 'Eleyi', 25′.

Malus 'Almey'
FLOWERS: Single, expanding buds deep maroon or purple-red, open purple-red with claw and base of petals
    and center vein pale lavender to nearly white, 1 4/5″ diameter.
FRUIT: Maroon, approximately 1″ across.
HABIT: Upright spreading tree to 24′.
DISEASES: Very susceptible to diseases, especially scab.

Malus 'Amberina'
FLOWERS: Deep red buds open to creamy white flowers.
FRUIT: Abundant, brilliant orange-red, excellent, persistent.
HABIT: Strongly upright, semi-dwarf reaching 10′, clean, deep green summer foliage, turning bright gold in fall.
DISEASES: Susceptible to scab.

Malus 'American Beauty'
FLOWERS: Deep red, double, exceptionally large.
FRUIT: Apparently does not set fruit.
HABIT: 20 to 25′ tall, foliage with bronze cast.
DISEASES: Extremely scab susceptible.

Malus 'American Masterpiece'
FLOWERS: Bright red, single, no bleaching.
FRUIT: Pumpkin orange, medium-sized fruit.
HABIT: 25′ by 18 to 20′, upright, midnight maroon foliage.
DISEASES: Resistant.

Malus American Spirit™ ('Amerspirzam')
FLOWERS: Deep rose.
FRUIT: Red, 1/2″ diameter.
HABIT: Rounded, 15 to 18′, red-purple foliage.
DISEASES: Highly resistant to scab.

Malus 'Ames White'
FLOWERS: Single, pink to white.

FRUIT: Yellow.
DISEASES: Highly resistant.

Malus 'Angel Choir'
FLOWERS: Buds pale pink, opening to double white flowers, flowers heavily on spur branches.
FRUIT: Red, reaching 3/8″ diameter.
HABIT: Small upright tree reaching about 12′ in height.
DISEASES: Highly disease resistant.

Malus 'Ann E.'
FLOWERS: Cardinal red buds, open white with crimson margins that quickly fade, 1 1/2″ diameter, single.
FRUIT: Bright red, 3/8″ diameter, persistent.
HABIT: Weeping, 10′ by 10′, cupped glossy green leaves turn handsome yellow in fall.
DISEASES: Highly resistant to scab.

Malus angustifolia (Ait.) Michx. — Southern Crabapple
(mā′lus an-gus-ti-fō′li-à)
FLOWERS: Single, pink to deep pink in bud, opening pinkish to white, extremely fragrant, 1 to 1 1/4″ diameter.
FRUIT: Yellowish green, 3/4″ diameter.
HABIT: Rounded small tree to 20′, usually deciduous but may remain semi-evergreen in mild winters.
DISEASES: Rust susceptible like most native crabapples.
NOTES: Quite an attractive crabapple in native setting; have seen it flowering as early as late February at Tifton, GA, normally mid-April in Athens, later than the Asiatic crabapples.

Malus × *arnoldiana* (Rehd.) Sarg. (*M. floribunda* × *M. baccata*) — originated at the Arnold Arboretum.
(mā′lus är-nōl-di-ā′nà)
FLOWERS: Single, buds rose red, flower phlox pink outside fading to white inside, 1 1/4 to 2″ diameter, fragrant, annual or alternate.
FRUIT: Yellow and red, 5/8″ diameter.
HABIT: Mounded, dense-branching, 25′ by 25′.
DISEASES: Susceptible to scab and fireblight; a handsome tree in flower but highly susceptible to scab.

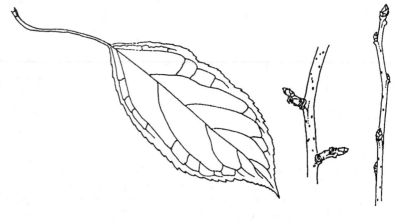

Malus × *atrosanguinea* (Späth) Schneid. (*M. halliana* × *M. sieboldii*) — Carmine Crabapple
(mā′lus a-trō-san-gwin′ē-à)
FLOWERS: Bud crimson, single, flower rose madder (pink) and 1 1/4″ diameter, annual; 'Shakespeare' is listed as a form that retains pink color without fading.
FRUIT: Dark red, 3/8″ diameter, not ornamental.
HABIT: Mounded, almost shrub-like, dense branching, 15 to 20′, very lovely small crabapple, good lustrous dark green foliage, usually partially lobed.
DISEASES: Very resistant to scab, have seen it listed as very susceptible to scab, variable to fireblight.

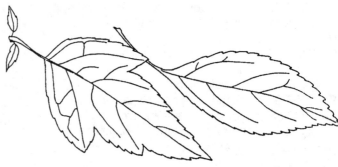

Malus 'Autumn Glory'
FLOWERS: Buds deep bright red, opening to blush white and full white; flowers heavily on spurs.
FRUIT: Glossy bright orange-red, oval, 1/4″ diameter, colors in August and remains firm into December–January.
HABIT: Upright to 12′, deep green, heavily textured leaves.
DISEASES: Highly resistant.

Malus 'Autumn Treasure'
FLOWERS: Single, buds red opening to white.
FRUIT: Gold, 1/4″ diameter, showy, colors early, persistent.
HABIT: Small weeper, refined form, 10′ high and wide; leaves medium to dark green.
DISEASES: Resistant.

Malus baccata (L.) Borkh. — Siberian Crabapple
(mā′lus ba-kā′tȧ)
FLOWERS: Single, pink in bud, opening white, 1 1/2″ diameter, very fragrant, annual.
FRUIT: Bright red or yellow, 3/8″ diameter.
HABIT: Tree, 20 to 50′ high, forming a rounded, wide-spreading head of branches.
DISEASES: Susceptible to scab; variable to fireblight.

M. baccata 'Columnaris'
FLOWERS: Single, buds creamy-white, open pure white, 1 1/2″ across.
FRUIT: Yellow with a red cheek, approximately 1/2″ diameter.
HABIT: Distinctly upright columnar tree probably 4 to 5 times as tall as wide; does not seem to flower and fruit
    well, at least this was true for few trees I have observed, 30′ by 8′.
DISEASES: Supposedly very susceptible to fireblight, resistant to scab.

M. baccata var. *gracilis* Rehd.
White flowers, 1 3/8″ diameter, gold fruit, more dense than the species with tips of the branches slightly
    pendulous and smaller leaves, highly resistant to scab.

M. baccata var. *himalaica* (Maxim.) Schneid.
FLOWERS: Buds pink opening to white.
FRUIT: Yellow.
DISEASES: Slightly susceptible to scab.

M. baccata 'Jackii'
FLOWERS: Single, expanding buds white with touch of pink, open pure white, approximately 1 3/5″ diameter.
FRUIT: Purplish or maroon-red, tan on shaded side, 1/2″ diameter.
HABIT: An upright type, finally rounded, with leaves of a remarkably deep green for a crabapple; probably grow
    30 to 40′.
DISEASES: Slightly susceptible to fireblight and powdery mildew, highly resistant to scab, excellent resistance
    to Japanese beetle.

M. baccata var. *mandschurica* (Maxim.) Schneid.
Flowers white, 1 1/2″ diameter, one of the first crabapples to flower, fruit bright red, 1/2″ diameter, moderately
    to very susceptible to scab and powdery mildew.

M. baccata 'Walters'
FLOWERS: White.
FRUIT: Small, yellow-red.
HABIT: Upright vase-shaped, 20 to 25′; glossy green, disease-free foliage.

Malus 'Ballerina'
FLOWERS: Single, white buds open to large, very cupped, showy white flowers.
FRUIT: Bright yellow, about 1/2″ diameter, persistent.
HABIT: Upright to fan-shaped, to 15′ high; dark green leaves.
DISEASES: Resistant.

Malus Ballerina Series
    Although technically fruiting apples, this series holds promise for ornamental purposes because of upright,
columnar habit. Most crabapples discussed herein are oval, rounded to wide-spreading. *Malus baccata*
'Columnaris', 'Sentinel', and 'Profusion' offer a degree of upright growth. The original germplasm was
discovered as a branch sport of 'Macintosh'. East Malling Research Station, England, initiated a breeding
program in the early 1970's. Over one-quarter million seedlings were raised and in 1984, 20 of the best were
evaluated in replicated trials. The four early introductions were 'Bolero' with pink-white flowers, 'Polka' with deep

purple to white flowers, 'Waltz' with purplish pink to white flowers, and 'Maypole' with carmine flowers. The first three produce large eating apples, the last large purple-red crabapples. Colonnade™ is the trademark umbrella used by Stark Brothers Nursery, Louisiana, MO to designate all the fastigiate apples grown under their license. Excellent article, "The Story of the Ballerina Apples," by D.N. Clark appeared in *Proc. Intl. Plant Prop. Soc.* 39:221–223 (1989).

Malus 'Barbara Ann' (A seedling of 'Dorothea').
FLOWERS: Double, deep purplish pink, fading to a light purplish pink, approximately 1 7/8″ diameter.
FRUIT: Purplish red, 1/2″ diameter.
HABIT: Rounded, 20′.
DISEASES: Severely susceptible to scab and slightly susceptible to frogeye leafspot.

Malus 'Baskatong'
FLOWERS: Single, expanding buds dark purplish red, open light purplish red with white claw, 1 3/4″ diameter.
FRUIT: Dark purplish red with many russet marks, 1″ diameter.
HABIT: Tree broad globose, 25 to 30′ by 25 to 30′; young leaves rich reddish purple-brown, finally bronze-green.
DISEASES: Very resistant, excellent Japanese beetle resistance.

Malus 'Beauty'
FLOWERS: Single, expanding buds pink to rose pink, open white and pinkish white, 2″ diameter, alternate.
FRUIT: Dark red, 1 3/5″ diameter, edible.
HABIT: Fastigiate, moderately columnar, 24′.
DISEASES: Very resistant.

Malus 'Beverly' — Originated at Morton Arboretum in 1940, one parent is *M. floribunda*.
FLOWERS: Single, buds red, opening to white, annual, one report noted biennial.
FRUIT: Excellent, bright red, 1/2 to 3/4″ across.
HABIT: Rounded, dense, 15 to 25′.
DISEASES: Fireblight can be severe under proper environmental conditions, have observed fireblight in Southeast, Shurtleff listed it as highly resistant to fireblight, highly resistant to scab.

Malus 'Blanche Ames'
FLOWERS: Semi-double, 1 1/2″ diameter, pink to white, petals narrow strap-shaped tapering at ends, annual.
FRUIT: Yellow then red, 1/4″ diameter.
HABIT: Rounded and dense (24′), slight weeping tendency, with purplish stems and gray trunk.
DISEASES: Resistant to scab.

Malus 'Bob White'
FLOWERS: Buds cherry-colored, flowers fade to white, 1″ diameter, fragrant, alternate.
FRUIT: Yellow to brownish yellow, 5/8″ diameter, persistent.
HABIT: Rounded, dense branching, 20′ by 20′.
DISEASES: Very susceptible to scab and fireblight, have seen listed as highly resistant to scab in Ohio and Vermont evaluations, prune to remove water sprouts.

Malus 'Bonfire'
FLOWERS: Single, red buds open to white.
FRUIT: Brilliant orange-red, abundant, 1/4″ diameter, colors early and persists until eaten by birds.
HABIT: Small, upright-rounded, 13 to 14′ high; medium to dark green leaves.

Malus 'Brandywine' (hybrid between 'Lemoinei' and 'Klehm's') — Simpson introduction.
FLOWERS: Double, fragrant, deep rose pink.
FRUIT: Yellow green, 1 to 1 1/2″ diameter.
HABIT: Vigorous, symmetrical, 15 to 20′ high and wide; leaves large, dark green with an overcase of wine-red.
DISEASES: Moderate scab, severe rust, high resistance to Japanese beetle.

Malus 'Bridal Bouquet' — Princeton introduction.
FLOWERS: Large, double, white.
FRUIT: Few fruits are formed.

HABIT: Small, rounded, 18 to 20′.
DISEASES: Good resistance to scab and fireblight.

Malus 'Bridal Crown'
FLOWERS: Pure white buds open to white, double flowers, resemble a bridal corsage.
FRUIT: Reddish, 1/2″ diameter.
HABIT: Upright tree reaching 12′ in height.

Malus 'Burgundy' (have seen 'Burgandy' spelling) — Simpson introduction.
FLOWERS: Abundant, dark red (one of the reddest flowered crabapples), fragrance like grapes.
FRUIT: Maroon, small.
HABIT: Vase-shaped, slender; dark green foliage.
DISEASES: Resistant to scab, also listed as highly susceptible.

Malus 'Burton'
FLOWERS: Single, buds pink opening to white
FRUIT: Yellow, 1 7/8″ diameter.
DISEASES: Highly resistant.

Malus 'Butterfly'
FLOWERS: Bright pink buds open to light pink flowers.
FRUIT: Bright red, 3/8″ diameter.
HABIT: Small tree reaching 10′ high.

Malus 'Callaway'
     Perhaps one of the best white-flowered crabapples for southern gardens because of excellent disease resistance as well as an apparently minimal flower bud chilling requirement. Mr. Fred Galle of Callaway Gardens made this selection from a number of *M. prunifolia* crabapples that he had ordered from a northern nursery. He noted that one was distinctly different from the others and thanks to his keen horticultural eye an excellent crabapple has become available and is in wholesale production.
FLOWERS: Single, expanding buds pink, open white, 1 to 1 1/2″ across, early April in the Piedmont area of
     Georgia; flowers later than rosy bloom types, about 7 to 10 days later.
FRUIT: Large, reddish maroon, 3/4 to 1 1/4″ diameter fruits that may persist for an extended time, good tasting.
HABIT: 15 to 25′ round-headed tree with graceful constitution.
DISEASES: Possibly the best crabapple for southern gardens; I have observed no scab on 'Callaway' in years
     when 'Almey' and 'Hopa' were almost leafless; Nichols 1980 survey lists it as slightly susceptible to mildew
     and fireblight, moderate to rust.
ADDITIONAL NOTES: With time trees become unkempt because of fruit retention and semi-pendulous form
     induced by heavy fruit set. Not a particularly handsome plant in the late fall–winter landscape.

Malus Camelot™ ('Camzam') — Lake County introduction.
FLOWERS: Red in bud, fuchsia pink on white when open.
FRUIT: Rich burgundy, 3/8″ diameter fruits.
HABIT: Compact, rounded, 10′ by 8′, dark green foliage with burgundy overcast.

Malus 'Canary' — Simpson introduction, chance seedling.
FLOWERS: Small, white flowers.
FRUIT: Tiny, canary yellow fruits on long stems late in fall.
HABIT: Vigorous with slender branches, spreading with age, somewhat open, medium size, to 18′.
DISEASES: Disease resistant.

Malus 'Candied Apple' (also 'Weeping Candied Apple') — Lake County introduction.
FLOWERS: Red buds opening to pink, single, 1 3/4″ diameter.
FRUIT: Bright oxblood red, 5/8″ diameter, persistent.
HABIT: Branches pendulous, not a particularly attractive habit, my field notes say unkempt, 10 to 15′ high;
     rather heavy-textured leaves with an overcast of red.
DISEASES: Slight to moderate scab susceptibility; was selected from a batch of 'Hopa' seedlings so its scab
     susceptibility is not surprising.

Malus 'Canterbury' — Lake County introduction.
FLOWERS: Light pink flower.
FRUIT: Red, 1/2″ diameter.
HABIT: Compact, rounded, 10′ by 15′.
DISEASES: Resistant to scab.

Malus 'Cardinal' — Princeton Nursery introduction.
FLOWERS: Bright red.
FRUIT: Few fruits are formed.
HABIT: Spreading, flat-topped with age, 15 to 20′; glossy red foliage.
DISEASES: According to Princeton it is the most disease resistant red-leaved crabapple.
ADDITIONAL NOTES: Listed as a *M. hupehensis* form which is doubtful considering the triploid nature of the tree.

Malus 'Cardinal's Robes'
FLOWERS: Single, bright orange-red buds open to bright red.
FRUIT: Bright red, about 1/2″ diameter.
HABIT: Medium-sized rounded tree to 15′; leaves dark green; bark like a cherry tree.
DISEASES: Resistant.

Malus 'Carnival'
FLOWERS: Single, pinkish red buds open to white.
FRUIT: Gold-orange-red, to 1/3″ diameter, distinctive and showy, remains firm and persistent until heavy freeze.
HABIT: Small, rounded tree, 10′; heavy-textured dark green leaves.

Malus 'Centennial'
FLOWERS: Single, white.
FRUIT: Red-yellow, 1 7/8″ diameter.
DISEASES: Highly resistant.

Malus 'Centurion' (*M.* × *zumi* × 'Almey') — A Bob Simpson introduction.
FLOWERS: Red buds open to rose red, flowers when young.
FRUIT: Glossy cherry red, 5/8″ across, attractive for several months, almost glowing.
HABIT: Upright branching, vigorous, becoming more oval-rounded with maturity, 25′ by 15 to 20′, at Milliken Arboretum it has developed wide-spreading growth habit; leaves reddish green.
DISEASES: Highly resistant; susceptible to highly susceptible to scab in 1989 Ohio State rating, also in 1997 report.

Malus 'Christmas Holly'
FLOWERS: Buds bright red, opening to white, single, 1 1/2 to 1 5/8″ diameter, annual.
FRUIT: Very bright red, 3/8″ across, stays hard and bright until after Christmas.
HABIT: Small, spreading tree, 10 to 15′ high; leaves in Zone 7b slightly cupped and not attractive, my comparative assessment at the Milliken Arboretum rated this quite low.
DISEASES: Slight scab susceptibility, fireblight.

Malus Cinderella™ ('Cinzam')
FLOWERS: Red in bud, opening white.
FRUIT: Gold, 1/4″ diameter, persisting into late autumn.
HABIT: Upright-oval to rounded at maturity, 8′ by 5′; dark green, deeply divided leaves.
DISEASES: Susceptible to scab.

Malus 'Color Parade'
FLOWERS: Single, bright red buds open to white.
FRUIT: Coral with red cheek, 1/2″ diameter, colors early and remains firm.
HABIT: Refined semi-weeper, 10 to 12′ high and wide; dark green leaves.
DISEASES: Very resistant.

Malus 'Copper King'
FLOWERS: Single, white buds open to large, spice fragrance flowers.

FRUIT: Reddish copper, 1/2″ diameter.
HABIT: Small, rounded tree, to 12′; leaves dark green, leathery, turning yellow to orange in fall.
DISEASES: Resistant.

Malus 'Coral Cascade' — Henry Ross introduction in 1989.
FLOWERS: Buds coral-red opening to blush white, annual.
FRUIT: Pink-coral-orange, 3/8 to 1/2″ diameter, oval, colors in September becoming deeper coral with frost and persisting into January.
HABIT: To 15′, medium weeper, leaves deep green.
DISEASES: Highly resistant.

Malus Coralburst™ — Developed at Gardenview Horticultural Park, Strongsville, OH.
FLOWERS: Coral pink buds open to double rose pink flowers.
FRUIT: Few, 1/2″ diameter, bronze, reddish orange.
HABIT: Dainty, dwarf type forming a rounded, bushy head, grows 10 to 15′ high, 8 to 10′ wide, grown both as a shrub and grafted on a standard; small dark green foliage.
DISEASES: Slight scab susceptibility, resistant in Vermont evaluations.

Malus 'Coralene'
FLOWERS: Single, red-pink buds open to white.
FRUIT: Coral pink and copper, firm, persistent, colors early.
HABIT: Small, refined semi-weeper, 12′ high; medium green leaves.
DISEASES: Resistant.

Malus coronaria (L.) Mill. — Wild Sweet Crabapple
(mā′lus kôr-o-nār-i-à)
FLOWERS: Single, white tinged with rose, fragrant like violets, 1 1/2 to 2″ diameter, pink in bud, essentially the last crabapple to flower along with *M. angustifolia* and *M. ioensis*.
FRUIT: Yellowish green, 1 to 1 1/2″ diameter, orange-shaped, very harsh and acid.
HABIT: A tree 20 to 30′ high with a short trunk and a wide-spreading head of gray branches.
DISEASES: Very susceptible to rust.

M. coronaria 'Charlottae'
FLOWERS: Double (12 to 18 petals), fragrant, expanding buds flesh pink, open pale pink, 1 1/2 to 2″ diameter, annual.
FRUIT: Dark green, 1 1/5″ diameter.
FOLIAGE: Leaves may turn excellent color in fall.
DISEASES: Susceptible to diseases, highly susceptible to scab.

M. coronaria 'Nieuwlandiana'
FLOWERS: Double, expanding buds rose red, open pink, 2 1/5″ diameter, annual, fragrant.
FRUIT: Yellowish green, 1 3/5″ diameter.
DISEASES: Susceptible to highly susceptible to scab.

Malus 'Cotton Candy'
FLOWERS: Annual, deep pink buds opening semi-double to fully double, 3-tiered blossoms of deep pink.
FRUIT: Deep yellow, 1/2″ across, browns and falls soon after ripening.
HABIT: Slow-growing, upright-rounded tree to 10′ with heavy-textured, deep green leaves.
DISEASES: Slight scab susceptibility.

Malus Crimson Spire™ has pink flushed white flowers and crisp, tangy, dark red fruit.

Malus 'David' — Named by Arie den Boer in 1957 after his grandson.
FLOWERS: Pink in bud, opening white, single, 1 1/2″ diameter.
FRUIT: Scarlet, 1/2″ diameter, fruits hold later than 'Beverly' which it resembles.
HABIT: Nice rounded habit, reminds of *M. floribunda* but more restrained, 12 to 15′ high and wide; dark green foliage tends to conceal flowers and fruit.
DISEASES: Slight fireblight susceptibility, good scab, mildew and Japanese beetle resistance, slight scab—less than 5% in 1997 Ohio report.

Malus 'Dolgo' — Introduced in 1917 by South Dakota Agr. Expt. Station.
FLOWERS: Pink in bud, opening white, 1 3/4″ diameter, fragrant, flowering well in alternate years.
FRUIT: Bright red, purple, almost fluorescent, 1 1/4″ diameter, ripening in July and falling by late August, can be used for jelly.
HABIT: Open, but vigorous, wide-spreading, 30 to 40′.
DISEASES: Resistant but with slight scab, fireblight, and frogeye leaf spot susceptibility, resistant to scab in Vermont.

Malus 'Donald Wyman'
FLOWERS: Single, expanding buds red to pink, opening to white, 1 3/4″ across, tends toward alternate year pattern, but even in "off" years, is still showy.
FRUIT: Glossy bright red, approximately 1/2″ diameter, abundant, persistent into winter.
HABIT: Large spreading form, 20′ high and 25′ wide; lustrous dark green foliage.
DISEASES: Slightly susceptible to powdery mildew and scab, although essentially without problems.
ADDITIONAL NOTES: Consistently one of the most highly touted and justifiably so, has performed magnificently in Zone 7, named after the late Dr. Donald Wyman, Horticulturist, Arnold Arboretum.

Malus 'Dorothea'
FLOWERS: Semi-double, 10 to 15 petals, expanding buds carmine, open rose pink, not fading to white, approximately 1 4/5″ diameter.
FRUIT: Yellow, approximately 1/2″ diameter.
HABIT: Rounded, dense branching, branches somewhat horizontal, 25′.
DISEASES: Severely susceptible to scab and fireblight, slightly susceptible to powdery mildew.

Malus 'Doubloons'
FLOWERS: Bright red buds, double white flowers.
FRUIT: Yellow-gold, 1/3″ diameter.
HABIT: Dense, rounded tree, 10 to 12′ high.
DISEASES: Susceptible to scab.

Malus 'Edna Mullins'
FLOWERS: Coral pink buds open to fragrant, double, white flowers.
FRUIT: Salmon, small.
HABIT: Upright with graceful pendulous branches and red stems.

Malus 'Egret'
FLOWERS: Deep pink buds open to semi-double or double pinkish white flowers.
FRUIT: Round, red, 3/8″ diameter.
HABIT: Weeping, 6′ high, very oriental in appearance; long, narrow, heavily-textured leaves.
DISEASES: Good resistance.

Malus 'Eleyi'
FLOWERS: Deep red in bud, opening reddish purple, 1 1/4″ across.
FRUIT: Reddish purple, conical.
HABIT: Broad-headed, rounded, 20 to 25′ high and wide; leaves reddish purple, later purple green.
DISEASES: Very susceptible to scab.

Malus 'Ellen Gerhart'
FLOWERS: Semi-double, pale pink, biennial.
FRUIT: Red, small, persistent, relished by birds.
DISEASES: Very susceptible to scab.

Malus 'Ellwangeriana'
FLOWERS: Single, pink and white, alternate.
FRUIT: Bright red, 5/8″ diameter.
DISEASES: Moderate fireblight susceptibility, slight rust and mildew.

Malus Emeraldspire™ has white tinged pink flowers and green apples with golden blush.

Malus 'Evelyn'
FLOWERS: Single, expanding buds deep rose red, open rose red to deep rose red, 1 2/5″ diameter, alternate.
FRUIT: Greenish yellow and red, 1 2/5″ diameter.
HABIT: Erect, 20′, foliage purplish initially, bronze-green at maturity; fall color listed as red-orange, purple.
DISEASES: Highly susceptible to scab, resistant in Vermont.

Malus Excalibur™
FLOWERS: Red buds open white.
FRUIT: Gold-green, 1/4″ diameter.
HABIT: Upright, 10′ by 8′.
DISEASES: Highly resistant to scab.

Malus 'Fiesta'
FLOWERS: Single, red in bud, open white.
FRUIT: Bright burnt coral to orange-gold, 1/3″ diameter, firm, persistent.
HABIT: Semi-weeper with slender, refined branches, 15′; dark green leaves.
DISEASES: Resistant.

Malus 'Firebelle'
FLOWERS: Single, red in bud, white at maturity, borne in heavy clusters.
FRUIT: Bright red, 1/3″ diameter, round, firm, persistent.
HABIT: Rounded tree, 12′; dark green foliage.
DISEASES: Resistant.

Malus 'Firebrand'
FLOWERS: Single, red in bud, open white.
FRUIT: Brilliant orange-red, 1/4″ diameter, abundant, extremely showy.
HABIT: Round headed tree, 14′; deep green leaves.
DISEASES: Resistant.

Malus 'Fireburst'
FLOWERS: Single, bright cherry red buds, white flowers.
FRUIT: Bright red, 1/4″ diameter, showy, persisting until hard freeze.
HABIT: Upright or slightly spreading, 15′; dark green leaves.
DISEASES: Resistant.

Malus 'Firedance'
FLOWERS: Red buds open to white flowers.
FRUIT: Abundant, red.
HABIT: Weeping, heavily branched, 5′ high.

Malus 'Flame' — University of Minnesota introduction.
FLOWERS: Single, expanding buds pink, open white, 1 1/2″ diameter, annual.
FRUIT: Bright red, 4/5″ across, persistent.
HABIT: Tree, 25′.
DISEASES: Extremely susceptible to diseases; one writer says highly resistant; I opt for the former.

Malus floribunda Van Houtte. — Japanese Flowering Crabapple. Introduced from Japan in 1862.
(mā′lus flō-ri-bun′dȧ)
FLOWERS: Buds deep pink to red, flowers gradually fading white, 1 to 1 1/2″ diameter, fragrant, annual.
FRUIT: Yellow and red, 3/8″ diameter, usually not persistent.
HABIT: Broad-rounded and densely branched, 15 to 25′, one of the best crabapples, one that all others are compared to, dark green leaves.
DISEASES: Slightly susceptible to scab and powdery mildew, moderately to fireblight, excellent Japanese beetle resistance.

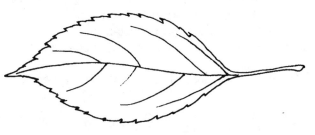

ADDITIONAL NOTES: Always one of my favorites, somewhat variable due to seed origin, although I suspect
    clones are now being offered. Wild and woolly in branch development when young, settling down with age.

Malus 'Fox Fire' — Lake County introduction.
FLOWERS: Pink buds open to white flowers.
FRUIT: Red with gold cheek, 1/2″ diameter.
HABIT: Broad-spreading, 15′ by 15′; dark green foliage.
DISEASES: Highly resistant.

Malus 'Garnet'
FLOWERS: Deep red buds open to blush white flowers.
FRUIT: Glossy deep red, persistent, remaining into winter.
HABIT: Small tree to about 8′ tall; narrow dark green leaves.
DISEASES: Resistant.

Malus 'Gibbs Golden Gage' — Originated in England in early 1920's.
FLOWERS: Single, buds pink, open white.
FRUIT: Yellow, 1″ diameter, waxy almost translucent.
HABIT: Small, rounded, 20′.
DISEASES: Highly resistant.

Malus 'Golden Dream'
FLOWERS: Single, red buds open white.
FRUIT: Bright yellow-gold, 1/4 to 1/3″ diameter, round, firm, persistent.
HABIT: Rounded tree, 12′; bright green foliage.
DISEASES: Resistant.

Malus 'Golden Galaxy'
FLOWERS: Single, pale pink buds, open white.
FRUIT: Bright gold, 1/2″ diameter, firm, persistent.
HABIT: Upright, fan-shaped, 16′; medium green leaves.
DISEASES: Resistant.

Malus 'Golden Gem'
FLOWERS: Single, white, 1 1/5″ diameter, pink buds.
FRUIT: Yellow, 1″ diameter, very freely borne and remaining long on the tree.
HABIT: Upright tree to 25′, spreads out with age.
DISEASES: Severely susceptible to fireblight, Shurtleff reports high resistance, high resistance to scab.

Malus 'Golden Hornet'
FLOWERS: Single, white, 1 1/5″ diameter, pink buds.
FRUIT: Yellow, 1″ diameter, very freely borne and remaining long on the tree.
HABIT: Upright tree to 25′, spreads out with age.
DISEASES: Severely susceptible to fireblight and scab, high resistance to scab in 1989 Ohio State report,
    resistant in 1996 Vermont evaluation.

Malus Golden Raindrops™ ('Schmidtcutleaf') — J. Frank Schmidt introduction.
FLOWERS: Pink in bud opening white.
FRUIT: Golden yellow, 1/4″ diameter.
HABIT: Small, rounded, horizontally spreading branches, 15 to 20′; fine-textured, deeply cut leaves; early
    evaluations in Zone 7 indicate this is a superior selection.
DISEASES: Excellent resistance to Japanese beetle.

Malus 'Goldilocks'
FLOWERS: Single, red buds open to white.
FRUIT: Golden copper, 1/4 to 1/3″ diameter, abundant, showy.
HABIT: Refined, semi-weeper, 15′; medium green leaves.

Malus 'Gorgeous'
FLOWERS: Single, 1 1/4″ diameter, pink buds followed by white flowers, annual.
FRUIT: Yellow, 1″ diameter, abundantly produced; have seen red listed for fruit color.
HABIT: Dense, rounded, 25 to 30′.
DISEASES: Moderate scab, slight fireblight and rust, severe mildew susceptibility.

Malus 'Guiding Star'
FLOWERS: Double, buds rose pink, open white, 2 1/4″ diameter.
FRUIT: Yellow, 5/8″ diameter.
DISEASES: Slightly susceptible to scab, moderate to powdery mildew, very to fireblight.

Malus Guinevere™ ('Guinzam') — Lake County introduction.
FLOWERS: Mauve buds open to white flowers.
FRUIT: Bright red, 3/8″ diameter.
HABIT: Rounded, 10′ by 10′; midnight green leaves with burgundy overtones.
DISEASES: Resistant.

Malus 'Gwendolyn' — Named after Gwendolyn Tobin, Des Moines, IA.
FLOWERS: Single, pink flowers.
FRUIT: Abundant, 1″ diameter, red.
DISEASES: Resistant.

Malus 'Gypsy Dancer'
FLOWERS: Single, bright red buds, open white.
FRUIT: Red-orange-yellow-coral, 1/2″ diameter, brilliant, persistent.
HABIT: Very graceful, somewhat spreading tree, 14′; dark green leaves.
DISEASES: Resistant.

Malus halliana Koehne var. *parkmanii* ('Parkmanii')
(mā′lus hâl-i-ā′nȧ pärk-man′ē-ī)
FLOWERS: Double (15 petals), deep rose in bud, finally shell pink, 1 1/4″ diameter, annual, late flowering.
FRUIT: Dull red, 1/4″ diameter, obovoid.
HABIT: Upright, almost vase-shaped, dense branching, 15 to 18′; foliage leathery lustrous dark green.
DISEASES: Moderate rust and fireblight susceptibility, high scab resistance, 1997 Ohio report moderate scab
    susceptibility.

Malus Hamlet™ ('Hamzam') — Lake County introduction.
FLOWERS: Deep scarlet buds open to rosy pink.
FRUIT: Red, 1/4 to 1/2″ diameter.
HABIT: Rounded, 10′ by 10′; dark green leaves with wine red suffusion.
DISEASES: Resistant to susceptible to scab.

Malus 'Harvest Gold'
FLOWERS: Single, red to pink in bud, white, flowers one week later than other crabs, leaves are full size so
    flower effect is reduced.
FRUIT: Gold, 3/5″ diameter, remaining colorful into December, and persisting until spring.
HABIT: Vigorous, moderately columnar to vase-shaped, 30′ by 15′(20′), large tree in Spring Grove, Cincinnati,
    OH that is probably 30′.
DISEASES: Highly resistant.
ADDITIONAL NOTES: Good in Michigan tests and at Milliken Arboretum, Spartanburg, SC, 1989 Ohio State
    report noted susceptible to highly susceptible to scab, small amount of fireblight in 1992, excellent
    resistance to Japanese beetle.

Malus 'Henningi' — Originated in Wrightsville, PA.
FLOWERS: Single, white.
FRUIT: Small, orange-red, 5/8″ diameter.
HABIT: Tree, upright-spreading, 25′ by 25′.
DISEASES: Highly resistant, susceptible to scab, moderate scab susceptibility in Ohio 1997 report.
ADDITIONAL NOTES: Excellent in Michigan evaluations.

Malus 'Henry F. Dupont'
FLOWERS: Single and semi-double (5 to 10 petals), expanding buds purplish red to deep rose red, open light
    purplish pink, fading to pale magenta, 1 1/2″ diameter, annual.
FRUIT: Brownish red, 1/3″ diameter.
HABIT: Rather open, low-spreading, 20 to 30′; new foliage is maroon-red.
DISEASES: Severely susceptible to scab and fireblight, slightly susceptible to powdery mildew.

Malus 'Henry Kohankie'
FLOWERS: Buds pink, opening pinkish white to white, single, 1 1/4 to 1 1/2″ diameter.
FRUIT: Glossy red, ellipsoidal, 1″ diameter, persistent.
HABIT: Rounded, 18′ tall, similar spread.
DISEASES: Slight scab susceptibility.

Malus 'Hollier' (a *Malus floribunda* selection)
FLOWERS: Red buds open pink, fade to white.
HABIT: Rounded, to 25′ high.

Malus honanensis Rehd.
FLOWERS: White, single, 3/4″ wide.
FRUIT: Yellow-green, 1/3″ diameter.
HABIT: Shrub or small tree, 10 to 15′ tall; deeply lobed foliage turns red in fall.
DISEASES: Unknown.

Malus 'Hopa'
FLOWERS: Single, ex-
    panding buds dark
    red to purplish red, open rose
    pink with almost white star in the center,
    approximately 1 1/2 to 2″ diameter.
FRUIT: Bright red to crimson, usually yellowish on
    shaded side, approximately 3/4 to 1″ diameter,
    ripen in August, drop by September.
HABIT: Spreading tree to 30′ high and wide.
DISEASES: This, along with the old standards 'Almey' and
    'Eleyi', should be on the discard list because of extreme
    disease susceptibility—especially to apple scab, in low rainfall
    areas probably acceptable, was told by a Brigham Young Univer-
    sity student that minimal scab occurs in Provo, UT because of low rainfall
    and humidity.

Malus hupehensis (Pamp.) Rehd. (triploid, comes true-to-type from seed) — Tea Crabapple
(mā′lus hū-pe-en′sis)
FLOWERS: Deep pink buds, gradually fading white, 1 1/2″ diameter, fragrant, alternate; also a 'Rosea' form
    with pinker flowers.
FRUIT: Greenish yellow to red, 3/8″ diameter.
HABIT: Vase-shaped, decidedly picturesque, 20 to 25′ and larger.
DISEASES: Severely susceptible to fireblight, never noticed any problems with trees on the Illinois campus,
    have also seen susceptibility listed as slight, highly resistant to scab, high resistance to Japanese beetle.
ADDITIONAL NOTES: Always a favorite of this author because
    of artistic growth habit, at its best in the top five.

Malus hupehensis 'Cornell' — registered in 1988.
FLOWERS: Single, light pink in bud, open to
    pinkish white.
FRUIT: Yellowish, turning red, 1/3″ diameter,
    persisting into winter.
HABIT: Vase-shaped.
DISEASES: Resistant to scab, cedar apple
    rust and leaf spot.

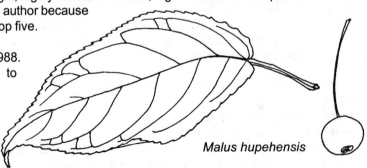

Malus hupehensis

Malus 'Indian Magic' — A Bob Simpson 1969 introduction.
FLOWERS: Single, red buds open rose red to deep pink, 1 1/2″ diameter.
FRUIT: Small glossy red, changing to orange, less than 1/2″ diameter, persisting.
HABIT: Rounded, 15 to 20′ by 15 to 20′; dark green leaves can develop orange-red fall color.
DISEASES: Moderately susceptible to scab although Nichols in his 1980 survey reported severely susceptible
to scab and slightly to rust; Shurtleff reported moderately susceptible to scab; Ohio State 1989 reported
high scab susceptibility, 1997 report likewise.
ADDITIONAL NOTES: Beautiful fruit coloration and retention at Milliken Arboretum.

Malus 'Indian Summer' — Sister seedling of 'Centurion'
FLOWERS: Red buds open rose red, fade to almost lavender.
FRUIT: Bright red, 5/8 to 3/4″ diameter, attractive over long period.
HABIT: Broad globe-shaped, 18′ by 25′; purple-green summer foliage, good fall color.
DISEASES: Good scab resistance, Ohio State (1989, 1997) reported moderate susceptibility to scab, excellent
fireblight, rust and mildew resistance.

Malus ioensis (Wood) Britt. — Prairie Crabapple
(mā′lus ī-ō-en′sis)
FLOWERS: Single, deep pink in bud, pink to white when open, fragrant, with the leaves, 1 1/2 to 2″ diameter.
FRUIT: Dull yellowish green, 1 1/4 to 1 1/2″ diameter.
HABIT: Small, rounded tree, 20 to 30′ high and quite similar to *M. coronaria* in appearance differing in the more
pubescent branches and undersides of the leaves.
DISEASES: Rust susceptible, highly resistant to scab.

Malus ioensis 'Klehm's'
FLOWERS: Double, pink, fragrant, 2″ diameter.
FRUIT: Sparse, green, 1″ diameter.
HABIT: Rounded, 20 to 25′ tall, strong grower.
DISEASES: Resistant, but have seen reports of susceptibility to cedar apple rust.

Malus ioensis 'Plena' — Bechtel Crabapple
FLOWERS: Double (33 petals), buds and flowers pink, 2″ diameter, fragrant.
FRUIT: Green, 1 1/8″ diameter, few produced.
HABIT: Rounded, open, 30′; supposedly a 'Dwarf Bechtel' that grows about 8′ and has highly fragrant double
pink flowers is known.
DISEASES: Extremely susceptible to diseases, especially rust which induces foliage abscission.

Malus Ivanhoe™ — Lake County introduction.
FLOWERS: Light scarlet.
FRUIT: Dark red, 1/2″ diameter.
HABIT: Rounded, 10′ by 10′; burgundy wine frosted foliage.

Malus 'Jewelberry'
FLOWERS: Hot pink buds and 1″ diameter, single, white flowers, biennial.
FRUIT: Glossy red, 3/8 to 1/2″ diameter, persistent into fall, fruits heavily as a young tree, excellent fruits.
HABIT: Dwarf, dense, shrubby tree, 8′ by 12′, will grow larger, noted at Milliken that growth is wide-spreading
and wild; dark green leaves.
DISEASES: Light scab (essentially resistant) and fireblight, 1997 Ohio report noted moderate scab.

Malus 'Katherine'
FLOWERS: Double (15 to 24 petals), expanding buds deep pink, open pink fading to white, 2″ diameter,
annual.
FRUIT: Yellow with a red cheek, 1/4″ diameter.
HABIT: Loose and open, 20′.
DISEASES: Susceptible to scab, 1989 Ohio report said highly susceptible.

Malus 'Kelsey'
FLOWERS: Semi-double, 10 to 16 petals, purplish red with a white marking at base of each petal.
FRUIT: 4/5″ diameter, shiny dark red-purple, persistent.
HABIT: Upright tree 18′ by 18′; bronze-green foliage.

Malus 'Kibele'
FLOWERS: Dark red buds open rose pink, single.
FRUIT: Dark burgundy red, 1/2″ diameter.
HABIT: Small, compact, spreading, maturing at 8′ and represents one of the smallest pink-flowered forms.
DISEASES: Slight to significant scab, moderate fireblight.

Malus King Arthur™ ('Kinarzam')
FLOWERS: Soft pink buds open to white.
FRUIT: Bright red, 1/2″ diameter.
HABIT: Upright rounded, 12′ by 10′; dark green leaves.
DISEASES: Highly resistant to scab.

Malus 'Kirk'
FLOWERS: Red buds open to white flowers.
FRUIT: Rich red, abundant, 7/8″ diameter.
HABIT: Upright rounded, 15′ in height.

Malus 'Koi'
FLOWERS: Single, red-pink buds, open white.
FRUIT: Bright orange-red, 1/2″ diameter, firm and persistent into February.
HABIT: Upright, fan-shaped tree, 14′; medium green leaves.
DISEASES: Resistant.

Malus 'Lady Northcliffe'
FLOWERS: Single, expanding buds rose red, open pale pink fading to white, 1″ diameter.
FRUIT: Yellow and red, 3/5″ diameter.
DISEASES: Resistant to scab.

Malus Lancelot™ ('Lanzam')
FLOWERS: Red buds open to white.
FRUIT: Gold, 3/8″ diameter, persistent into new year.
HABIT: Upright oval, 10′ by 8′; crisp green summer foliage turns golden yellow in fall.
DISEASES: Highly resistant to scab.

Malus 'Leprechaun'
FLOWERS: Red buds open to white flowers with red reverse.
FRUIT: Very heavy, round, 1/8 to 1/4″ diameter, persistent.
HABIT: Small tree to about 8′; thick, dark green leaves.
DISEASES: Resistant.

Malus 'Limelight'
FLOWERS: Single, light pinkish buds, open white.
FRUIT: Lime-chartreuse, 3/4″ long by 1/2″ wide, firm and persistent until frozen.
HABIT: Rounded tree, 16′; heavy-textured, leathery dark green leaves.
DISEASES: Resistant.

Malus 'Liset' — Originated in the Netherlands.
FLOWERS: Single, expanding buds dark crimson, open rose red to light crimson, approximately 1 1/2″ diameter.
FRUIT: Dark crimson to maroon-red, glossy, approximately 1/2″ diameter, persistent.
HABIT: Rounded, dense, 15 to 20′; deep purplish green leaves.
DISEASES: Moderately susceptible to powdery mildew, slightly susceptible to fireblight, high scab resistance.
ADDITIONAL NOTES: Excellent performance at Milliken Arboretum, flower color the deepest.

Malus 'Little Troll'
FLOWERS: Single, brilliant red buds, open white; numerous flowers form cascades along the branches.
FRUIT: Orange-red, 1/3″ wide, firm, persistent.
HABIT: Very refined, graceful weeper, 16′; dark green leaves.
DISEASES: Resistant.

Malus 'Louisa' — Polly Hill introduction, named after her daughter, selected in 1962.
FLOWERS: Red in bud opening true pink.
FRUIT: Yellow to amber with rose blush, 3/8″ diameter, persistent.
HABIT: Broad weeping, 15′ by 15′; glossy dark green foliage.
DISEASES: Susceptible to scab, rated having good resistance to big four in North Carolina tests, excellent Japanese beetle resistance.

Malus 'Lullaby'
FLOWERS: Red buds open to large, ruffled, coral-, rose- and white-tinted, candy-striped, semi-double flowers.
FRUIT: Golden orange.
HABIT: Low, weeping form, about 6′ in height; large deep green foliage; considered a smaller, finer, more disease resistant form of 'Red Jade'.
DISEASES: Highly resistant.

Malus 'Luwick'
FLOWERS: Deep pink buds open to pale pink, ruffled flowers.
FRUIT: Red, sparse.
HABIT: Weeping, reaching about 5′ with narrow leaves.

Malus Madonna™ — Lake County introduction.
FLOWERS: Double, buds pink opening to white, blooms early and holds a long time.
FRUIT: Golden with red blush, 1/2″ diameter.
HABIT: Compact upright, 20′ tall by 10′ wide; new growth bronze, mature dark green.
DISEASES: Susceptible to scab, excellent resistance to Japanese beetle.

Malus 'Makamik' — Developed about 1921 in Canada.
FLOWERS: Single, expanding buds dark red, open purplish red fading to a lighter tint, 2″ diameter.
FRUIT: Purplish red, 3/4″ diameter, good fruiter with fruits holding late.
HABIT: Rounded, 40′, bronze foliage.
DISEASES: Severely susceptible to mildew, slightly susceptible to fireblight, highly resistant to scab.

Malus 'Manbeck Weeper'
FLOWERS: Abundant pink and white blossoms.
FRUIT: Bright red.
HABIT: Strong central leader.
DISEASES: Resistant.

Malus 'Mandarin Magic'
FLOWERS: Single, buds reddish pink, open white.
FRUIT: Green-cheeked with red, turning orange-cheeked, bright red and yellow, 1/2″ wide by 3/4″ long, firm and persistent, colors late.
HABIT: Spreading, 17′; dark green leaves.
DISEASES: Resistant.

Malus 'Maria'
FLOWERS: Rose red buds open to fragrant reddish pink flowers which fade with age.
FRUIT: Shiny deep red, abundant, 1/2″ diameter.
HABIT: Moderately weeping, 12′ high; reddish bronze new growth.
DISEASES: Resistant.

Malus 'Marshall Oyama'
FLOWERS: Single, pink buds followed by white flowers, 1 5/8″ diameter, annual.
FRUIT: Yellow and red, 1″ diameter.
HABIT: Narrowly upright, 25′ high.
DISEASES: Resistant to scab and fireblight.

Malus 'Mary Potter' — Introduced by Arnold Arboretum in 1947; supposedly a triploid and will come true from seed.
FLOWERS: Single, expanding buds dark pink, open white, 1″ diameter, biennial.

FRUIT: Red, 1/2″ diameter, excellent fruit producer, good retention.
HABIT: Cross between *M.* × *atrosanguinea* × *M. sargentii* var. *rosea*, 10 to 15′ high, 15 to 20′ wide, dense, mounded, spreading, low-branched, a fine plant; lustrous dark green foliage, sometimes yellow and gold fall color.
DISEASES: Moderately susceptible to scab, resistant in 1996 Vermont evaluation, slight susceptibility to scab in 1997 Ohio report, powdery mildew, fireblight, and frogeye leaf spot; have not seen any serious problems, clean at Milliken Arboretum, excellent Japanese beetle resistance.

Malus 'Matador'
FLOWERS: Single, bright red buds, open white.
FRUIT: Brilliant red, 1/3″ diameter, firm and persistent.
HABIT: Wide spreading tree, 14′; dark green leaves.
DISEASES: Resistant.

Malus 'Maysong'
FLOWERS: Single, pinkish white buds, open white.
FRUIT: Medium red, about 1/2″ diameter.
HABIT: Upright, narrow tree, 20′, becoming more spreading to vase-shaped with age; deep green, heavily textured leaves.
DISEASES: Resistant.

Malus × *micromalus* Mak. (*M. baccata* × *M. spectabilis*) 'Midget' — Midget Crabapple
(mā′lus mi-krō-mā′lus)
FLOWERS: Single, deep red in bud, opening to pale pink at edge, deeper pink in center.
FRUIT: Red, 1/2″ diameter.
HABIT: Small, erect branched tree.
DISEASES: Very susceptible to diseases, Vermont (1996) reported resistant.
ADDITIONAL NOTES: 'Kaido' with non-fading deep pink, fragrant, 1 1/2″ diameter flowers, 1/2″ diameter, reddish yellow fruits, 12′ by 9′ habit is offered in commerce.

Malus 'Mollie Ann'
FLOWERS: Deep red buds open to five-petaled, feathery, white flowers, tetraploid.
FRUIT: Buff-gold, 1/2″ diameter.
HABIT: Semi-weeping, growing to 8′; deep green leaves.
DISEASES: Resistant.

Malus Molten Lava™ — Lake County introduction.
FLOWERS: Deep red in bud, opening to single white, 1 1/2″ diameter flowers, annual.
FRUIT: Red-orange, 3/8″ across, remaining firm into early December.
HABIT: Wide-spreading weeper, 15′ by 12′, with attractive yellow bark in winter, wild and woolly grower in Zone 7b.
DISEASES: Resistant, somewhat susceptible to fireblight at Milliken, rated good resistance to big four in North Carolina, excellent Japanese beetle resistance.

Malus 'Moonglow'
FLOWERS: Single, bright red buds, open white.
FRUIT: Lime-chartreuse with a rose cheek turning to pale lemon with a rose-coral cheek, 1/3″ diameter, firm and persistent.
HABIT: Rounded tree, 12′; dark green leaves.
DISEASES: Resistant.

Malus 'Mount Arbor Special'
FLOWERS: Carmine buds and flowers fade to dull pink.
FRUIT: Red, 3/4″ diameter, russet dotted, not persistent.
HABIT: Irregular.
DISEASES: Highly resistant.

Malus 'Narragansett' — U.S. National Arboretum introduction.
FLOWERS: Red buds open to white with pink tinge, annual.
FRUIT: Cherry red with light orange underside, 1/2″ diameter.

HABIT: Broad-crowned, small tree with wide crotch angles; leathery dark green leaves.
DISEASES: Resistant to scab, fireblight, rust and mildew.
ADDITIONAL NOTES: A superior form and more heat tolerant than many. Suggest use in containers, where
    urban heat is problematic.

Malus 'Oekonomierat Echtermeyer' (also listed as 'Echtermeyer')
FLOWERS: Single, expanding buds deep purplish red, open purplish pink, 1 3/5″ diameter.
FRUIT: Purplish red before ripening, later turning a dark reddish brown to greenish brown, 1″ diameter.
HABIT: Semi-weeping, 15′ by 15 to 18′; purplish foliage when young, maturing purplish green.
DISEASES: Extremely susceptible to diseases, especially scab, Vermont (1996) evaluation noted resistant, this
    is one of the worst.

Malus 'Ormiston Roy' — Arie den Boer 1954 introduction.
FLOWERS: Single, expanding buds rose red turning pale rose pink, open white, 1 3/5″ diameter, annual.
FRUIT: Orange-yellow with reddish blush, 3/8 to 1/2″ diameter, persistent.
HABIT: Upright in youth, assuming the shape of *M. floribunda* with age but not as dense, 20′ by 25′.
DISEASES: Slight scab and rust, moderate fireblight, Ohio State (1989, 1997) reported high scab resistance,
    excellent resistance to Japanese beetle.

Malus 'Pagoda'
FLOWERS: Single, bright carmine buds, open white.
FRUIT: Brilliant orange-red, 1/3″ diameter, firm and persistent.
HABIT: Small, rounded weeper, 12′; dark green leaves.
DISEASES: Resistant.

Malus 'Park Center'
FLOWERS: Light pink.
FRUIT: Golden, small.
HABIT: 25′, vigorous, vase-shaped.
DISEASES: High resistance.

Malus 'Peter Pan'
FLOWERS: Single, bright red buds, open white.
FRUIT: Bright red, 1/4″ diameter, firm, persistent, turning copper-red with heavy frosts.
HABIT: Rounded tree, 14′; medium green leaves.
DISEASES: High resistance.

Malus 'Pink Cascade'
FLOWERS: Deep rose pink buds open to soft pastel pink flowers.
FRUIT: Red, small.
HABIT: Semi-weeping, 20′, bronze spring foliage, maturing to green.
DISEASES: Resistant.

Malus 'Pink Dawn'
FLOWERS: Reddish pink flowers.
FRUIT: Purple fruit, 3/8″ diameter.
HABIT: Narrow upright form, 15 to 20′.
DISEASES: High resistance.

Malus 'Pink Pearl'
FLOWERS: Pink buds open to soft pink.
FRUIT: Green, firm, 3/4″ diameter, sparse.
HABIT: Broad, open habit with gracefully arching, gray branches, 8 to 10′ by 6 to 8′; new leaves silver-bronze
    maturing to leathery dark green.
DISEASES: May have *M. ioensis* parentage so rust is possible.

Malus 'Pink Perfection' — Seedling from 'Katherine' × 'Almey'.
FLOWERS: Red in bud, opening to large clear pink double flowers.

FRUIT: Sparse, yellow, 1/2″ diameter.
HABIT: 20′ by 20′, compact, semi-upright.
DISEASES: Extremely scab and fireblight susceptible.

Malus 'Pink Princess'
FLOWERS: Rose pink, single.
FRUIT: Deep red, 1/4″ diameter, persistent.
HABIT: Low spreading, 15′ by 12′; reddish spring foliage turns reddish green.
DISEASES: Slightly susceptible to scale.

Malus 'Pink Satin' — Simpson introduction.
FLOWERS: Clear pink, single, profuse on upright spurs.
FRUIT: Dark red, 3/8″ diameter, persistent.
HABIT: Upright rounded, medium green foliage.
DISEASES: Resistant to scab.

Malus 'Pink Spires'
FLOWERS: Full dark lavender buds open to lavender and fade to pale lavender, early.
FRUIT: Purplish red, persistent.
HABIT: Upright grower, 25′; copper-colored fall foliage, foliage reddish in spring.
DISEASES: Moderately to highly susceptible to scab, slightly to fireblight and leaf spot.

Malus 'Prairie Maid' — Simpson introduction.
FLOWERS: Deep pink, mid-season flowers.
FRUIT: Orange-red, small.
HABIT: Compact-rounded, medium-sized tree, to 15′; good dark green foliage.
DISEASES: Highly resistant to scab.

Malus 'Prairifire' — Dan Dayton 1982 introduction, University of Illinois
FLOWERS: Buds red opening to dark purplish red flowers, do not turn muddy like many so called red types.
FRUIT: Dark red-purple, 3/8 to 1/2″ diameter, somewhat cone-shaped, persistent.
HABIT: Upright when young, later rounded, 20′ high and wide, glossy dark red-brown bark with numerous prominent lenticels; new growth reddish maroon maturing to dark green.
DISEASES: Very resistant, excellent rating in North Carolina and Ohio 1989, 1997 tests.
ADDITIONAL NOTES: Clean and vigorous at Milliken Arboretum, not the neatest habit, somewhat irregular, open.

Malus 'Prince Georges'
FLOWERS: Double (50 to 61 petals), expanding buds deep rose pink, open light rose pink, 2″ diameter, annual, exceedingly fragrant, smells like a good rose.
FRUIT: Not known to produce fruit.
HABIT: Upright, dense, eventually rounded, 15 to 20′ by 15 to 20′.
DISEASES: Resistant although its parentage (*M. angustifolia* × *M. ioensis* 'Plena') suggests it should be rust susceptible, resistant to scab.

Malus 'Professor Sprenger' — Doorenbos introduction.
FLOWERS: Single, expanding buds red to pink, open white.
FRUIT: Orange-red, 1/2 to 5/8″ diameter, persistent into November–December, high ratings for fruit.
HABIT: Densely upright spreading, 20′ by 20 to 25′; dark green leaves.
DISEASES: Highly resistant.
ADDITIONAL NOTES: Excellent tree in Michigan and North Carolina tests.

Malus 'Profusion' — Doorenbos introduction in late 1930's.
FLOWERS: Single, expanding buds deep red, open purplish red fading to purplish pink, 1 3/5″ across.
FRUIT: Oxblood red, 1/2″ diameter, persistent.
HABIT: Small tree of excellent constitution, vase-shaped outline, vigorous, to 25′; new foliage purple fading to bronze-purple-green.

DISEASES: Moderately susceptible to powdery mildew, moderately to highly susceptible to scab and fireblight, clean at Milliken Arboretum.

Malus prunifolia (Willd.) Borkh. — Plumleaf Crabapple
(mā′lus prū-ni-fō′li-ȧ)
FLOWERS: Single, pink to red in bud, opening white, fragrant, 1 1/2″ diameter.
FRUIT: Round or ovoid, yellowish or red, 1″ diameter.
HABIT: Small tree.
DISEASES: Scab susceptible.
ADDITIONAL NOTES: *M. prunifolia* var. *rinkii* (Koidz.) Rehd. differs in being more downy and having pink flowers (usually); highly scab susceptible, Vermont (1996) listed *M. prunifolia* 'Xanthocarpa' as highly resistant.

Malus pumila Mill. 'Niedzwetzkyana' (*M. niedzwetzkyana* of some authors), (mā′lus pū′mil-ȧ), the young leaves, flowers, fruit (including the flesh), bark and wood of branches is purplish red. This form is a parent of many crabapples. Resistant to fireblight and variable resistance to scab. Often listed as highly susceptible to scab and from my observations this is the case. One of the parents of the rosy bloom group ('Almey', 'Chilko', 'Simcoe', 'Hopa', etc.)

Malus pumila 'Pink Joy' — Norman Stewart introduction.
FLOWERS: Pink- and white-variegated, lower surface more pink than the upper surface.
ORIGIN: Chance seedling, first observed in 1978, named and introduced by Norman Stewart, New Brunswick, Canada, see *HortScience* 30:446 (1995).

Malus 'Purple Prince'
FLOWERS: Single, carmine-red buds, open to bright red.
FRUIT: Bluish purple with a fine blue cast, about 1/2″ diameter.
HABIT: Rounded, 17′; deep purple-green leaves; bark like a cherry.
DISEASES: Resistant.

Malus × *purpurea* (Barbier) Rehd. 'Lemoine' (*M. pumila* 'Niedzwetzkyana' × *M.* × *atrosanguinea*)
(mā′lus pĕr-pū′rē-ȧ le-moyn)
FLOWERS: Single and semi-double, expanding buds dark red, open purple-red to crimson fading to lighter shades, 1 1/2″ diameter, annual.
FRUIT: Purplish red, 5/8″ diameter.
HABIT: Dense, wide-spreading outline, 25′; leaves purplish when unfolding and becoming deep green later.
DISEASES: Highly susceptible to scab and fireblight.

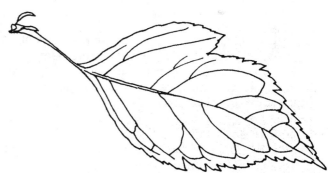

Malus 'Radiant' — A University of Minnesota introduction.
FLOWERS: Single, expanding buds deep red, open deep pink, annual, rose red buds fading to dark lavender.
FRUIT: Bright red, approximately 1/2″ diameter, persistent.
HABIT: Compact, round-headed, 25 to 30′; young leaves reddish changing to green.
DISEASES: Very susceptible to scab, one of the worst.

Malus 'Ralph Shay'
FLOWERS: Large pink buds opening white.
FRUIT: Brilliant red, rounded, 1 1/4″ diameter, colors mid-September and does not drop, excellent for jelly.
HABIT: Rounded, vigorous, 20′ by 20′.
DISEASES: Ohio State (1997) reported susceptibility to scab moderate, resistant at Milliken Arboretum, some scab in 1992.

Malus 'Red Baron' ('Red Barron' in some literature) — Simpson introduction, selected from Arnold Arboretum.
FLOWERS: Single, very deep red buds open to reddish to pink flowers.
FRUIT: Glossy dark red, 1/2″ across.

HABIT: Moderately columnar, 20′ by 12′, as broad as tall at maturity; dark green foliage with reddish tinge, one of the best for fall foliage color.
DISEASES: Susceptible to scab, resistant in Vermont (1996) evaluation, slightly susceptible to fireblight and rust.

Malus 'Red Jade' — Introduced by Brooklyn Botanic Garden.
FLOWERS: Single, expanding buds deep pink, open white, 1 3/5″ diameter, alternate.
FRUIT: Glossy red, 1/2″ diameter, birds like the fruits.
HABIT: Weeping, 15′, of a graceful pendulous nature; graft incompatibilities are a problem.
DISEASES: Moderately susceptible to scab and powdery mildew, have been reports of fireblight susceptibility.

Malus Red Jewel™ ('Jewelcole')
FLOWERS: White, single, abundant.
FRUIT: Bright cherry red, less than 1/2″ diameter, persisting with color until mid-December, color becomes darker in cold weather.
HABIT: Medium-sized, horizontally branched, rounded, 15′ by 12′; excellent dark green foliage.
DISEASES: Moderately susceptible to scab, Ohio State (1989, 1997) noted high resistance to scab, fireblight, slightly to mildew.
ADDITIONAL NOTES: Clean foliage, no scab, in Michigan and Spartanburg, SC trials.

Malus 'Red Peacock'
FLOWERS: Large, soft pink, ruffled.
FRUIT: Shiny red, 1/2″ diameter, persistent.
FOLIAGE: Clean dark green.

Malus 'Red Silver' — A South Dakota State University introduction.
FLOWERS: China rose color, 1 1/2″ diameter, single, alternate.
FRUIT: Purplish red, 3/4″ diameter.
HABIT: Dense, 30′; purplish red leaves turning reddish green.
DISEASES: Extremely susceptible to scab, the leaves fall off before your eyes in June or July.

Malus 'Red Snow'
FLOWERS: Orange-red buds open to creamy, slightly pinkish, 1 1/2″ diameter flowers.
FRUIT: Bright red, oblong, 5/16″ wide, persistent into December and January.
HABIT: Small tree 8 to 10′ high with long, graceful, arching branches and fine stems; leaves fine and narrow with a leathery texture, turn attractive gold in fall.
DISEASES: Highly resistant.

Malus 'Red Splendor'
FLOWERS: Single, expanding buds rose red, open pink to rose pink, 1 4/5″ diameter, alternate according to Dr. John Pair, Kansas State.
FRUIT: Red, 3/5″ diameter, persistent.
HABIT: Upright, more or less open tree, 20 to 30′; dark reddish green foliage turning reddish purple in fall.
DISEASES: Slightly to moderately susceptible to scab, moderate to fireblight, in 1980 survey Nichols found severe scab.

Malus 'Red Swan'
FLOWERS: Rose-opal buds open to bell-shaped flowers that turn white, 1 1/2″ diameter, described in some literature as deep orange-red.
FRUIT: Bright red, elliptical, 1/4 to 1/2″ diameter, mature in September, persist into December–January.
HABIT: Weeping, graceful, finely branched, to 10′; fine-textured, narrow, 2 1/2″ long leaves, are thick-textured and turn gold in autumn.
DISEASES: Highly resistant to scab.

Malus 'Redbird' ('Red Bird' in the 4th edition)
FLOWERS: Red buds open white, single.
FRUIT: Bright red, 3/8 to 5/8″ diameter, color early, often August, and persist.
HABIT: Rounded, 12 to 15′ high and wide.

Malus 'Robinson' — Introduced by C.M. Hobbs, Indianapolis.
FLOWERS: Single, crimson buds opening to deep pink flowers.
FRUIT: Dark red, 3/8″ diameter, not effective.
HABIT: Upright-spreading, dense branching, 25′ by 25′; reddish bronze-green leaves.
DISEASES: Some scab susceptibility, Ohio State (1997) noted high susceptibility to scab, fair Japanese beetle resistance.

Malus × *robusta* (Carr.) Rehd. (*M. baccata* × *M. prunifolia*)
(mā′lus rō-bus′tà)
FLOWERS: Single and semi-double, expanding buds white with trace of pink, open pure white.
FRUIT: Yellow and red to dark crimson, 1″ diameter.
HABIT: Oval-shaped, dense branching, 40′.
DISEASES: Resistant to scab, variable to fireblight.

M. × *robusta* 'Erecta' has an upright to moderate vase-shaped habit when young, with maturity opens up as side branches are often weighted down with fruits, 40′, same flowers as above, highly susceptible to scab.

M. × *robusta* 'Persicifolia' has single, white flowers; excellent red ornamental fruits, sometimes with a yellowish or brownish cheek, 3/4″ diameter; hang on late in season; slightly susceptible to scab and fireblight; leaves narrow, resembling a peach; 40′.

Malus 'Rockii'
FLOWERS: Single, pink buds opening to white flowers.
FRUIT: Bright red, approximately 1/2″ diameter.
DISEASES: Moderately susceptible to powdery mildew, slightly to scab.

Malus 'Rosseau'
FLOWERS: Single, expanding buds maroon-red, open purplish to rose red with white claw, 1 3/5″ diameter, annual.
FRUIT: Carmine to light jasper red, 1″ diameter.
HABIT: Rounded, dense, 40′; new foliage light bronzy red, becoming glossy green with red veins at maturity.
DISEASES: Resistant to scab and fireblight.

Malus Royal Fountain® ('Huber')
FLOWERS: Rose red.
FRUIT: Deep red, 3/8 to 1/2″ diameter.
HABIT: Weeping, 15′ by 15′; purple spring leaves, bronze-green with maturity.
DISEASES: Susceptible to scab, some fireblight susceptibility.

Malus 'Royal Ruby'
FLOWERS: Double, red-pink, 1 to 2″ across, annual flowers at an early age.
FRUIT: Red, 1/2″ across, limitedly produced, fruit shrivels.
HABIT: Vigorous, upright tree to 10 to 15′ with glossy dark green foliage.
DISEASES: Severely susceptible to scab.

Malus 'Royal Splendor'
FLOWERS: Single, red-pink buds, open white, produced in heavy cascades along the branches.
FRUIT: Brilliant red, about 1/2″ diameter, firm and persistent into mid-winter.
HABIT: Spreading weeper, 10′ by 11 to 12′; green leaves.
DISEASES: Resistant.

Malus 'Royalty'
FLOWERS: Single, crimson, almost purple, annual, sparsely produced.
FRUIT: Dark red-purple, 5/8″ diameter, sparse.
HABIT: 15 to 20′, upright; one of the best purple-foliaged forms, leaves are glossy purple in spring, purple-green in mid-summer, and brilliant purple in fall.
DISEASES: Severely susceptible to scab and fireblight.

Malus sargentii Rehd. — Sargent Crabapple
(mā′lus sär-jen′tē-ī)
FLOWERS: Single, red in bud opening white, 3/4 to 1″ diameter, fragrant, annual or alternate; this seems to be variable.
FRUIT: Bright red, 1/3 to 1/2″ diameter, birds like them.
HABIT: Mounded, dense branching, wide-spreading, 6 to 8′(10′) high, one and one-half to twice that in spread; dark green foliage.
DISEASES: Slightly susceptible to scab, Ohio (1997) and Vermont (1996) reported highly resistant, fireblight and leaf spot, excellent Japanese beetle resistance.
ADDITIONAL NOTES: Has fared quite well in Zone 7b, trees planted in 1979 were 12′ by 15′ in 1997.

M. sargentii 'Candymint Sargent' (PP 6606) — Simpson introduction.
FLOWERS: Deep carmine buds open to pink petals with red edging, effective for a long period.
FRUIT: Deep purple.
HABIT: Picturesque, horizontal growth habit, 10′ by 18′; shiny deep reddish brown bark; purplish green foliage.
DISEASES: Good resistance, although some scab susceptibility, excellent Japanese beetle resistance.

M. sargentii 'Rosea' is similar to species except flower buds darker pink in bud, 1 1/2″ across, taller growing and more susceptible to fireblight and scab, 8′ by 10′.

M. sargentii 'Roseglow' is a SCS, USDA, Rose Lake Plant Materials Center Release; 8′ high by 10′ wide, densely branched, white fragrant flowers, dark red, 1/4″ diameter fruit; seed produced cultivar, highly scab resistant.

Malus 'Satin Cloud' (octoploid from colchicine treatment)
FLOWERS: Buds pale white, open to pure white, cinnamon fragrant flowers, flowers abundant on spur shoots.
FRUIT: Amber yellow, 3/8″ diameter.
HABIT: Dwarf with dense, upright-rounded crown, 8′; deep green, thick-textured leaves turn yellow, orange and red in fall.
DISEASES: Highly resistant to scab.

Malus × *scheideckeri* Späth ex Zab. (*M. floribunda* × *M. prunifolia*)
(mā′lus shī-dek′ēr-ī)
FLOWERS: Double (10 petals), pale pink, 1 1/2″ diameter, annual.
FRUIT: Yellow to orange, 5/8″ diameter.
HABIT: Upright, dense, vase-shaped, 20 to 30′.
DISEASES: Extremely susceptible to diseases and not a good landscape plant.

Malus 'Sea Foam'
FLOWERS: Deep red buds open to pure white flowers.
FRUIT: Bright red, 3/8 to 1/2″ diameter.
HABIT: Low, strongly weeping, 5′ or less ultimate height.
DISEASES: Highly resistant.

Malus 'Selkirk' — A Morden introduction in 1962.
FLOWERS: Rose red, 1 1/2″ diameter, single to semi-double, annual or alternate, inconsistent.
FRUIT: Glossy purplish red, 4/5″ diameter; about the glossiest fruits of any crabapple.
HABIT: Open, upright, somewhat vase-shaped, 25′ by 25′; reddish green foliage.
DISEASES: Slightly susceptible to scab, fireblight and powdery mildew.

Malus 'Sensation'
FLOWERS: Single, carmine red in bud, open white.
FRUIT: Bright orange with red cheeks, 1/2″ wide, firm, persistent.
HABIT: Graceful, semi-weeper, 12′; dark green leaves.
DISEASES: Resistant.

Malus 'Sentinel' — A Bob Simpson introduction.
FLOWERS: Single, red buds open pale pink to white, profuse.
FRUIT: Small, red, 1/2″ diameter, persistent, attractive long after leaves have fallen.

HABIT: Moderately columnar oval, 18′ by 10 to 12′.
DISEASES: Slight scab and fireblight susceptibility, observed fireblight at Milliken Arboretum, poor Japanese beetle resistance, Pair noted high scab susceptibility at Wichita, KS.

Malus 'Serenade'
FLOWERS: Deep pink buds open to pale blush white flowers.
FRUIT: Pale yellow with orange-gold tinge, becoming burnt orange when mature, elliptical with rounded base.
HABIT: Graceful, semi-weeping, 12′ high, thick-textured leaves.
DISEASES: Resistant to scab.

Malus 'Shaker's Gold'
FLOWERS: Soft pink in bud, opening to white, 1 5/8″ across, single.
FRUIT: Light yellow then with frost to deeper yellow with orange cheeks touched with reddish, persistent and firm into January.
HABIT: Upright, spreading, to 16′.
DISEASES: Severely susceptible to fireblight.

Malus sieboldii (Reg.) Rehd.
(mā′lus sē-bōl′dē-ī)
FLOWERS: Pink buds, fading white, fragrant, 3/4″ diameter; may also range from pale pink to rose.
FRUIT: Yellow to red, 3/8″ diameter, bearing annually, long persistent.
HABIT: Mounded, dense branching, rarely more than 10 to 15′ high but known to 30′ in the wild.
DISEASES: Highly resistant to scab.

Malus sieboldii 'Fuji'
FLOWERS: Double, 13 to 15 petals, expanding buds purplish red, open greenish white with occasional traces of purplish red, approximately 1 1/2″ diameter.
FRUIT: Orange, approximately 1/2″ diameter, abundant.
HABIT: Large tree at maturity, original tree is 28′ high and 46′ wide, has ascending, declining and irregular branching.
DISEASES: Moderately susceptible to powdery mildew and scab, Ohio State (1989) said highly resistant.

Malus sikkimensis (Wenz.) Koehne — Sikkim Crabapple
(mā′lus sik-ki-men′sis)
FLOWERS: Single, rose in bud, opening white, 1″ across, annual.
FRUIT: Pear-shaped, dark red with pale dots, 5/8″ long and wide.
HABIT: Small tree of low, bushy habit; distinct among crabapples because of the excessive development of stout, rigid branching spurs on the trunk.
DISEASES: Resistant to scab, susceptible to fireblight.

Malus 'Silver Drift' — Simpson introduction.
FLOWERS: Red in bud open white.
FRUIT: Red, small, persist into December, good bird food.
HABIT: Rounded, to 20′ high.
DISEASES: Resistant.

Malus 'Silver Moon' — Simpson introduction.
FLOWERS: Pink in bud, opening to white, 1 1/2″ diameter, flowers at terminals after tree is in full leaf, alternate, one of last crabapples to flower.
FRUIT: Dark red, 3/8 to 1/2″ diameter, persistent.
HABIT: Compact, narrow-upright, eventually moderately ovate, 20′ by 12′.
DISEASES: Moderate scab [Ohio State (1989, 1997) said highly resistant as did Vermont (1996)] and frogeye leafspot, severe fireblight, fireblight in 1992 at Milliken Arboretum, clean foliage at Milliken Arboretum, excellent resistance to Japanese beetle.

Malus 'Sinai Fire'
FLOWERS: Single, brilliant red buds, open white.
FRUIT: Brilliant orange-red with a waxy sheen, 1/4 to 1/3″ diameter, firm, persistent.
HABIT: Upright weeper with very downward weeping branches, 12′ high and wide; rich dark green leaves.
DISEASES: Highly resistant to scab.

Malus Sir Galahad™
FLOWERS: Pink buds open white.
FRUIT: Gold turning red, 1/2″ diameter.
HABIT: Rounded, 10′ by 8′; leathery lustrous dark green foliage.

Malus 'Sissipuk'
FLOWERS: Single, expanding buds deep carmine, open rose pink fading to pale pink, 1 1/8″ diameter, annual.
FRUIT: Dark maroon-purple to oxblood red, 1″ diameter.
HABIT: Rounded, 40′.
DISEASES: Resistant to scab and fireblight.

Malus 'Snowcloud'
FLOWERS: Pink buds open to large, double, white flowers.
FRUIT: Yellow, 1/2″ diameter, not abundant.
HABIT: Upright, 22′ by 15′.
DISEASES: High susceptibility to scab.

Malus 'Snowdrift' — Cole Nursery introduction.
FLOWERS: Single, expanding buds pink, open white, 1 1/4″ diameter, annual, abundant.
FRUIT: Orange-red, 3/8″ diameter.
HABIT: Rounded, dense, good vigorous grower, 15 to 20′ by 15 to 20′, heavy-textured, lustrous dark green foliage.
DISEASES: Slight to moderate susceptibility to scab, 1980 evaluation lists it as severely susceptible to fireblight, high susceptibility in 1989 Ohio State report, have seen moderate listing, severe fireblight at Milliken Arboretum.

Malus 'Snow Magic'
FLOWERS: Pink buds open to white flowers.
FRUIT: Deep red.
HABIT: Compact pyramidal.
DISEASES: Susceptible to scab.

Malus 'Sparkler' — University of Minnesota introduction.
FLOWERS: Bright rose red, abundant.
FRUIT: 1/3″ diameter, dark red.
HABIT: A flat-topped, wide-spreading tree, 15′ high and 24′ wide; new foliage emerges reddish, matures to dark green.
DISEASES: Highly scab susceptible.

Malus spectabilis (Ait.) Borkh. — Chinese Crabapple
(mā′lus spek-tab′i-lis)
FLOWERS: Often double, deep rosy-red in bud, paling to blush-tint when fully open, 2″ diameter.
FRUIT: Yellow, 3/4 to 1″ diameter, poor fruiter.
HABIT: A tree to 30′ forming a rounded head of branches as wide as high.
DISEASES: Highly resistant to fireblight, variable to scab, listed as high susceptibility.

Malus spectabilis 'Riversii'
FLOWERS: Pink, double (up to 20 petals), 2″ diameter, alternate bearer.
FRUIT: Green, 1 1/4″ diameter, not effective.
HABIT: Open, 25′.
DISEASES: Highly resistant to fireblight, variable to scab.

Malus 'Spring Bride' — Introduction from Morden, Canada.
FLOWERS: White, double, short pedicels, produce garland effect as branches are clothed with color.
FRUIT: Yellow-orange, small, limited production.

Malus 'Spring Snow'
FLOWERS: White, considered sterile equivalent of 'Dolgo'.
FRUIT: Few to none.

HABIT: Dense, upright oval tree, 20 to 25′ tall.
DISEASES: Severely susceptible to scab; slightly susceptible to cedar apple rust and fireblight.

Malus 'Spring Song'
FLOWERS: Deep rose buds open to light pink fading to white, flowers about 2″ across.
FRUIT: Bright red, 1/2″ diameter.
HABIT: Small, upright compact rounded tree, 10′ high.
DISEASES: Resistant.

Malus 'Strathmore'
FLOWERS: Dark red.
FRUIT: Red-purple.
HABIT: Narrow vase-shaped, 20′ by 5 to 8′; reddish new foliage.
DISEASES: Highly susceptible to scab.

Malus 'Strawberry Parfait'
FLOWERS: Red buds open to large, pink flowers with red margins; heavy bloomer.
FRUIT: Yellow with red blush, 1/2″ diameter.
HABIT: Open, vase-shaped, 20′ by 25′; purple-tinged new leaves become leathery dark green.
DISEASES: Highly resistant, excellent resistance to Japanese beetle.

Malus Sugar Tyme™ ('Sutgzam') — Lake County introduction.
FLOWERS: Pale pink buds open to sugar white, fragrant flowers, annual.
FRUIT: Red, 1/2″ diameter, abundant, persistent.
HABIT: Upright oval, vigorous, 18′ by 15′; crisp dark green foliage.
DISEASES: Very resistant, slight scab in Ohio (1997) evaluations, great in Michigan, Minnesota, North Carolina, Spartanburg, SC, and Vermont tests, good Japanese beetle resistance, Green noted poor fireblight resistance.

Malus 'Sunset'
FLOWERS: Orange-red buds open to bright red to mauve flowers.
FRUIT: Deep red.
HABIT: Small, upright tree; leaves purple-red.

Malus 'Tanner'
FLOWERS: Single, white, 1 1/2″ diameter, alternate.
FRUIT: Red, 5/8″ diameter.
HABIT: Low, 20′.
DISEASES: Highly susceptible.

Malus 'Tea Time'
FLOWERS: Single, pale pink buds, open white.
FRUIT: Lime-chartreuse with a red cheek, 1/3″ diameter, firm and persistent.
HABIT: Upright, vase-shaped tree, 25′; dark green leaves.
DISEASES: Resistant.

Malus 'Thunderchild'
FLOWERS: Single, delicate pink to rose, turning white with age.
FRUIT: Dark red, purple, 1/2″ diameter.
HABIT: Compact upright spreading, broad oval to rounded; deep purple leaves.
DISEASES: Resistant.

Malus 'Tina'
FLOWERS: Red buds open to 3/4″ diameter, single, white flowers.
FRUIT: Red, 5/16″ diameter.
HABIT: Supposedly a dwarf Sargent type with low-spreading form, 12 to 18″ high plant was 3 to 3 1/2′ wide; will grow to 5′ in height; 20-year-old plant at University of Wisconsin was 4′ by 10′.
DISEASES: Highly resistant.

Malus toringoides (Rehd.) Hughes
(mā'lus tôr-in-goy'dēz)
FLOWERS: White, 3/4″ diameter, fragrant, alternate, expanding buds pink or pinkish white.
FRUIT: Pear-shaped, 1″ diameter, yellow on shaded side, red on sunny side.
HABIT: Upright-pyramidal, dense branching, 25′.
DISEASES: Resistant to scab and rust, Ohio State (1989) noted high scab susceptibility.

Malus tschonoskii (Maxim.) Schneid. — Tschonoski Crabapple
(mā'lus shō-nos'kē-ī)
FLOWERS: Slight pink finally white, not showy, 1 to 1 1/4″ diameter.
FRUIT: Yellow-green, somewhat russet-dotted, 1 to 1 1/4″ wide.
FOLIAGE: New leaves silver gray, changing to dark green and excellent apricot-red in fall, one of the best
    crabapples for fall color, impressive specimen at the Arnold that is spectacular in Autumn.
HABIT: Large tree, 30 to 40′ high.
DISEASES: Slight scab, severe fireblight.

Malus 'Van Eseltine' (a suspected hybrid between *M. spectabilis* and *M.* × *arnoldiana*)
FLOWERS: Double (13 to 19 petals), expanding buds deep rose to rose pink, often pink fading to pale pink,
    2″ diameter, alternate bearer.
FRUIT: Yellow, with brown or light carmine cheek, 3/4″ diameter.
HABIT: Narrowly upright, 20′ by 10′, vase-shaped crown; dense dark green foliage.
DISEASES: Severely susceptible to scab and fireblight.

Malus 'Vanguard'
FLOWERS: Single, rose red, 2″ diameter, annual.
FRUIT: Red, 5/8 to 3/4″ diameter, persistent, not persistent in Wichita, KS tests.
HABIT: Dense, somewhat vase-shaped, 18′ by 10′.
DISEASES: Highly susceptible to scab, Ohio State (1989) reported highly resistant.

Malus Velvet Pillar™
FLOWERS: Single, pink, sparse.
FRUIT: Red, 1/2″ diameter, sparse.
HABIT: Upright columnar, 20′ by 14′; dull purple foliage.
DISEASES: Highly scab susceptible.

Malus 'Victorian'
FLOWERS: Double white.
FRUIT: Bright gold-red.
HABIT: Upright-oval, to 12′ high.

Malus 'Volcano'
FLOWERS: Red buds open to white flowers, abundantly produced.
FRUIT: Orange-red, 3/8 to 1/2″ diameter, abundant.
HABIT: Small upright tree, 10′ in height; thick-textured leaves.
DISEASES: Highly resistant to scab.

Malus 'Walters'
FLOWERS: White.
FRUIT: Yellow, small, persistent.
HABIT: Upright vase-shaped.

Malus White Angel™ (also termed 'Inglis')
FLOWERS: Single, 1″ diameter, pure white, heavy flowerer, expanding buds pink.
FRUIT: Glossy red, 1/2 to 3/4″ diameter, heavy fruiter, almost overbears.
HABIT: Tends toward a rounded tree but often irregular because of heavy fruit loads, 20′ by 20′; lustrous dark
    green foliage.
DISEASES: Resistant to slight scab and rust susceptibility, slight to moderate fireblight.

Malus 'White Candle' — Introduced by Inter-State Nurseries, 1970.
FLOWERS: Semi-double, white, one reference said pale pink, 1 1/2″ diameter, borne in great quantity.
FRUIT: Red, 5/8″ diameter, limitedly produced.
HABIT: Good upright type, 12 to 15′ by 5 to 6′ wide; dark green foliage.
DISEASES: Susceptible to scab and fireblight.

Malus 'White Cascade' — Henry Ross introduction.
FLOWERS: Single, buds deep pink, 1 1/4″ across, white flowers uniformly from top to bottom, gives the appearance of a cascading waterfall.
FRUIT: Lemon yellow, small, 3/8″ diameter, pea-sized.
HABIT: Gracefully pendulous, 10 to 15′ by 10 to 15′.
DISEASES: Resistant, based on current data, new data from North Carolina indicates good scab, excellent fireblight, rust and mildew resistance, Ohio State (1989, 1997) reported moderate scab susceptibility.

Malus 'Wies'
FLOWERS: Single, pink.
FRUIT: Very dark red to purple, 1/2 to 5/8″ diameter.
HABIT: Upright, leaves purplish.
DISEASES: Highly resistant.

Malus 'Wildfire'
FLOWERS: Single, bright red buds, open pink.
FRUIT: Brilliant red, 1/4 to 1/2″ diameter, firm, persistent.
HABIT: Semi-weeper with attractive form, 16′; dark reddish green leaves.
DISEASES: Resistant.

Malus 'Winter Gold'
FLOWERS: Single, expanding buds deep carmine, open white, 1 1/5″ diameter, alternate.
FRUIT: Yellow, occasionally with orange to pink blush, 1/2″ diameter, abundant, persistent.
HABIT: Broadly pyramidal, 20′ by 20′.
DISEASES: Slightly susceptible to powdery mildew and scab, resistant in Vermont (1996) evaluation, Ohio State (1997) reported moderate, moderately susceptible to fireblight.
ADDITIONAL NOTES: Has performed exceptionally well at Milliken Arboretum, appears similar to 'Harvest Gold' and may be the same plant.

Malus 'Woven Gold'
FLOWERS: Single, carmine red buds, open white.
FRUIT: Yellow-gold, 1/3″ wide in spur clusters, firm, persistent.
HABIT: Semi-weeping tree, 12′; dark green leaves.
DISEASES: Resistant.

Malus yunnanensis (Franch.) Schneid.
(mā′lus yū-na-nen′sis)
FLOWERS: Single, white or with a faint pink tinge, 5/8″ diameter.
FRUIT: Red sprinkled with whitish dots, 1/2″ wide.
HABIT: Tree, 20 to 40′, leaves may turn orange and scarlet in fall; var. *veitchii* Rehd. is the common form in cultivation and is narrowly ovate in habit, 20′ by 10′, white flowers, heavy-textured foliage.
DISEASES: var. *veitchii*—slight scab, moderate powdery mildew and fireblight.

Malus × *zumi* (Matsum.) Rehd.
(mā′lus zū′mē)
FLOWERS: Single, pink in bud becoming white after opening, 1 to 1 1/4″ diameter, alternate.
FRUIT: Red, 3/8″ diameter, globose.
HABIT: Small tree of pyramidal habit, 20′, may become rounded, have seen considerable variation.
DISEASES: Slightly susceptible to scab.

Malus × *zumi* 'Calocarpa' — Arnold Arboretum introduction.
FLOWERS: Single, expanding buds deep red, open pinkish white to white, 1 2/5″ diameter, fragrant, annual, acts as a biennial bearer at times.

FRUIT: Bright red, 1/2″ diameter, abundant, persistent into December.
HABIT: Dense, rounded, 25′ by 25′; rich lustrous dark green foliage.
DISEASES: Slightly susceptible to scab, powdery mildew and severely susceptible to fireblight, has been disease-free at Milliken Arboretum.

Malus × *zumi* Winter Gem™
FLOWERS: White.
FRUIT: Bright red, abundant, persistent.
HABIT: Broad upright.

Malus × *zumi* 'Wooster'
FLOWERS: Salmon coral buds open to fragrant white flowers.
FRUIT: Abundant dark red fruits, 1/2″ diameter.
HABIT: Broadly ovate.
BARK: Tannish coral.

Malus 'Zumirang'
FLOWERS: White.
FRUIT: Red, 3/8″ diameter.
HABIT: Upright, broadly pyramidal to rounded.
DISEASES: Good resistance.

Malus × *zumi* 'Calocarpa'

Melia azedarach L. — Chinaberry, Pride of India, Persian Lilac, Bead Tree
(mē′li-à à-zēd′à-rak)

FAMILY: Meliaceae
LEAVES: Alternate, bipinnately compound, 12 to 24″(32″) long, half as wide, leaflets ovate to oval, slender-pointed, unequally serrate at base, toothed or lobed, 1 1/2 to 2″ long, 1/3 to 3/4″ wide, glabrous or slightly pubescent on midrib and petiolules when young, lustrous rich green.
BUDS: Small, 1/16″ high and wide, rounded, covered with brown pubescence, sits in a notch above leaf scar.
STEM: Stout, coarse, angled, olive-brown to brown, covered with light brown lenticels; leaf scar large, shield-shaped; malodorous when broken.

(leaflet)

SIZE: 30 to 40′ high with a similar spread.
HARDINESS: Zone 7 to 10; severely injured or killed at −3°F; 'Umbraculiformis' was more seriously injured than the species.
HABIT: Round-headed tree composed of stiff coarse branches; not very appealing in the winter months.
RATE: Fast.
TEXTURE: Medium in summer; coarse in winter.
BARK: Gray-brown, ridged-and-furrowed.
LEAF COLOR: Lustrous rich green in summer, yellow-green in fall; colors about mid-October into early November in Athens.
FLOWERS: Lavender-lilac to almost violet, 3/4″ across, perfect, fragrant, borne in large, loose, 8 to 16″ long panicles in May; foliage is present when flowers open and much of the effect is lost; rather pretty on close inspection; flowers occur on previous season's growth, i.e., buds are preformed, growth is so fast that emerging shoots effectively mask the delicate flowers.
FRUIT: Sub-globose, 3/8 to 1/2″ diameter, yellow to yellow-brown drupe with a hard, bony, seed that ripens in September–October and persists into the following spring; every flower must result in a fruit, actually somewhat attractive; fruits persist through winter and remind that this is a pestiferous species; fruit is significantly variable in size and literature points to a range from 2/5 to 2″ diameter.

CULTURE: A genuine weed tree; adaptable to about any situation; frequently seen along highways, fence rows and other waste areas; a rapid grower and very weak-wooded; interestingly trees that were killed to the ground in 1984 resprouted and by 1988 were producing abundant fruit crops; flowers as a small tree when seed-grown; 3- to 4-year-old trees produce flowers and fruits; considered one of the 16 most prevalent exotic trees in southern forests.

DISEASES AND INSECTS: None of any consequence.

LANDSCAPE USE: None, in my estimation much worse that Tree of Heaven or Silver Maple; a genuine nuisance; apparently birds and animals disseminate the fruits to waste areas; it is rare to see a fence row in the South without a Chinaberry.

CULTIVARS:

'Jade Snowflake'—Cream speckled and streaked variegated leaf form from J.C. Raulston Arboretum; unfortunately, not stable variegation and a plant in my possession reverted to almost complete green; have observed a rather handsome true-to-type specimen at Nurseries Caroliniana, North Augusta, SC; found in a farmyard near San Antonio, TX in 1989.

'Umbraculiformis'—Like the species a true biological vagrant; called the Texas Umbrellatree because of its multi-stemmed habit and dome or umbrella-like outline; it reproduces true-to-type from seed and can be seen in the waste areas as well as in the yards of older residences; at one time this form must have been fashionable because 2 and 3 trees are often seen in a single landscape; said to have appeared originally on the battlefield of San Jacinto, Texas; grows 20 to 25′ high, not as cold hardy as the species.

PROPAGATION: Seed is the logical and preferred method, root cuttings will work; Raulston reported softwood cuttings of 'Jade Snowflake' rooting easily; Indian literature reported that plants are rooted from cuttings and produced through tissue culture.

ADDITIONAL NOTES: Not too much good that can be said about the tree except that it does not grow north of Zone 7. Cultivated or naturalized in almost every warm temperate or subtropical country.

NATIVE HABITAT: Northern India, central and western China. Cultivated since the 16th century.

Menispermum canadense L. — Common Moonseed

FAMILY: Menispermaceae

LEAVES: Alternate, simple, orbicular-ovate, 4 to 10″ long, 4 to 7″ wide, acute or obtuse, rounded or truncate at base, entire or shallowly angulate-lobed, dark green above, slightly pubescent beneath or nearly glabrous at maturity; petiole—2 to 6″ long, attached to the blade near, but not at base (peltate).

BUDS: Small, hairy, superposed, with the uppermost developing the inflorescence and the lower covered by the leaf scar, about 3-scaled.

STEM: Round, fluted, green becoming buff to shiny brown, glabrescent, leaf scars raised, crater-like; sieve tubes prominent, visible to the naked eye; pith—white, solid.

Menispermum canadense, (men-i-spĕr′mum kan-a-den′sē), Common Moonseed, is a deciduous, twining vine growing 10 to 15′ and more. The stems are very slender and require support. The foliage is dark green in summer and the leaves are quite large (4 to 10″) which makes for effective screening; very adaptable; grows back quickly (6 to 10′ in a single season); flowers dioecious, greenish yellow to white, borne on a long stalked raceme, fruit bloomy purple-red to blue-black; seed resembles a half-moon, hence, the common name. Easily propagated by division. Almost a weed. The only cultivated plant I remember grew next to the Vegetable Crops Building at the University of Illinois. The building was a disaster and the plant did not help the appearance. Quebec and Manitoba to Georgia and Arkansas. 1646. Zone 4 to 8.

Mespilus germanica L. — Showy Mespilus

FAMILY: Rosaceae
LEAVES: Alternate, simple, oblong to oblong-lanceolate, 2 to 5″ long, short acuminate, minutely toothed, dull green and pubescent above, more so beneath, essentially sessile, may turn yellowish to red-brown in fall; petiole—very short.
STEM: Pubescent and armed with 1/2 to 1″ long, firm, straight spines, although cultivated trees I have seen in England were essentially thornless.

Mespilus germanica, (mes′pi-lus jĕr-man′i-kȧ), Showy Mespilus, is a small (20′), rounded to broad-rounded tree composed of tightly woven branches producing a rather picturesque habit. On past garden tours to Europe, I have always quizzed people about its identity which looks like nothing in the normal realm of the Rose family. Leaves develop golden orange tints in fall. The white to lightly blushed pink, 1 to 1 1/2″(2″) diameter, 5-petaled flowers occur at the end of short, leafy branches in May–June. The sepals provide a good identification feature for they are triangular at the base and extended into a long narrow point that reaches beyond the petals. Sepals are also woolly pubescent. Fruit is a brown, hard, apple to slightly pear-shaped (more top-shaped than anything), 1″ wide pome with the 5 sepals still present. Selections have been made for larger fruit size up to 2 to 2 1/2″ diameter. Fruits ripen late, require frost or cold weather or need to be stored cold until the fruit softens. One reference noted fruit should be kept until part rotten to enjoy maximum flavor, one which is an acquired taste. Jelly can be made from the fruits and I purchased my first vessel of same on a 1989 trip. The taste is perhaps similar to mayhaw (*Crataegus opaca*) jelly which is sold in the Southeast. Ideally, any well-drained soil and a sunny location suit it best. See Weiss, *The Garden* 117:538–539 (1992), for a discussion on history, uses, cultivars and characteristics. Cultivars most prevalent include: 'Dutch' with 2 1/2 to 2 3/4″ diameter fruit; 'Large Russian' and 'Monstrosus' with large fruit; and 'Nottingham' with smaller, 1 1/2″ diameter fruit of good flavor. 'Diekto' and 'Monetko' are relatively new graft chimeras of *Mespilus germanica* and *Crataegus laevigata* 'Paulii'. The outer envelop of 1 to 2 cell layers was *Mespilus*, red-flowering *Crataegus* formed the central core, taxonomically they are + *Crataegomespilus potsdamiensis* Simon-Louis ex Bellair. *Mespilus germanica* is native to southeastern Europe to Iran. Long cultivated. Zone (4)5 to 8. Morton Arboretum, Lisle, IL has successfully grown the plant over the decades. Probably hardier than thought.

Metasequoia glyptostroboides Hu. & Cheng. — Dawn Redwood
(met-a-sē-kwoy′ȧ glip-tō-strō-boy′dēz)

FAMILY: Taxodiaceae
LEAVES: Deciduous, opposite in arrangement, linear, flattened, straight or slightly curved, pectinately arranged, 1/2″ long and 1/16″ broad on mature trees; upper surface is bright green with a narrowly grooved mid-vein, lower surface bearing obscure lines of stomata, lighter green or slightly glaucous, the midrib slightly raised.

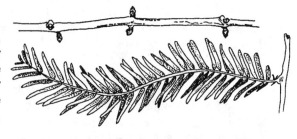

BUDS: Non-resinous (opposite), usually in pairs at the base of deciduous branchlets but sometimes solitary between the branchlets; ovoid or ellipsoid, about 1/4″ long, scales light reddish or yellowish brown with a linear keel, appearing stalked.
STEM: Branchlets of 2 kinds, persistent and deciduous; the persistent—bright reddish brown when young, shallowly ridged, carrying the deciduous branchlets, numerous vegetative buds and a few leaves; the green deciduous branchlets are up to about 3″ long, usually arranged distichously, more or less horizontal, ribbed with the long decurrent bases of up to 50 to 60 or more leaves.

SIZE: 70 to 100′ in height by 25′ spread, known to 120′ high; 40 to 50′ in 20 years under good growing conditions.
HARDINESS: Zone (4)5 to 8; species with tip dieback in Maine, 'National' killed outright.
HABIT: Pyramidal, conical, with a single straight trunk in youth; supposedly developing a broad-rounded crown with age; the Missouri Botanic Garden has a beautiful complement of trees which were grown from seed distributed to them by the Arnold Arboretum; have seen many large trees over the years and all maintain the feathery-pyramidal growth habit with a central leader.

RATE: Fast (50′ in 15 to 20 years); 30-year-old tree on William and Mary College campus was over 120′ high.

TEXTURE: Fine in leaf, less so when defoliated, but still with a feathery outline.

BARK: Reddish brown when young, becoming darker, fissured and exfoliating in long narrow strips; base buttressing and developing an irregular fluted character; directly below branch attachments to central leader are armpit-like depressions which serve as a good identification feature between this and *Taxodium distichum*.

LEAF COLOR: Bright green above changing to brown in fall; can be an excellent orange-brown to red-brown, coloration is as good in South as in the North.

FLOWERS: Monoecious; male flowers in racemes or panicles up to 12″ long; female solitary.

FRUIT: Cones pendulous, on 3/4 to 1 3/4″ long stalks, globose or cylindrical, female solitary, mature cones globose to ovoid, dark brown, reminiscent of *Sequoia* and *Sequoiadendron* cones, 3/4 to 1 1/4″ long, 3/5 to 3/4″ wide, with 14 to 28 scales, a scale bearing 5 to 8, 1/5″ diameter seed, each with 2 narrow surrounding wings, cones mature in 5 to 7 months and heavy crops occur on campus trees; *Metasequoia* appears to suffer from inbreeding depression so collect seeds from groves of seedling plants to insure outcrossing.

CULTURE: Easy to transplant; performs best in moist, deep, well-drained, slightly acid soils; is not well-adapted to chalky soils, although appears more tolerant than *Taxodium distichum*; full sun; may grow late into summer and early fall and is damaged by an early freeze; should be well-sited such as on a hill rather than a low area; seldom requires pruning due to neat, uniform, conical habit; a small grove at the Arnold Arboretum is growing in extremely wet soils and performing well, also the Morris Arboretum has a grove along the creek that flows through the property; English literature reported the species can be planted beside and even in standing water; Czechoslovakian research on forestry potential showed that at two lowland sites in Bohemia, shoot growth continued from May to September, culminating later on moister sites; vegetatively propagated plants grew as fast as seedlings; trees were susceptible to early fall frosts and occasional frost crack, but recovered.

DISEASES AND INSECTS: The U.S. National Arboretum has lost some trees through canker infestations; prior to this there was no known serious problem; usually if a tree is around long enough and has been planted in sufficient numbers some insect or disease catches up with it; Japanese beetles will feed on the foliage.

LANDSCAPE VALUE: I have changed my opinion of this tree since I first learned it in my plant materials courses at Ohio State in 1963; at that time the tree was . . . well . . . just another tree; but through closer association I find it a very lovely ornamental well suited to parks, golf courses and other large areas; would make a very effective screen, grouping or for use in lining long drives or streets; where it can be grown without problem of freeze damage it should be given adequate consideration; excellent in groves, along streams or lakes; Morris Arboretum has a beautiful grove along a stream; does well in Zone 7 and 8 and magnificent 50 to 60′ trees at Milliken Arboretum and the University of Georgia support this contention.

CULTIVARS:

'Emerald Feathers'—Luxuriant bright green foliage, vigorous constitution.

'National'—Habit conspicuously narrow-pyramidal, selection made in 1958 at U.S. National Arboretum, tree was 58′ high, 24′ wide and 23-years-old; see *Proc. Intl. Plant Prop. Soc.* 31:464 (1971).

'Nitschke Cream'—The new growth is cream-colored maturing to green.

'Ogon'—A golden leaf form, have only observed a small plant, significantly yellow on new growth, for a time kind of a rage in southern plantsmen circles, seems to have diminished.

'Rowena'—White-edged leaves (needles), variegation is not chimeral but due to genetically controlled mutation of green to white plastids, which is switched on and off during the annual growth cycle; see *New Plantsman* 2(1):54 (1995).

'Sheridan Spire'—More upright than typical for the species; several southern growers are producing this selection, more narrow-upright in youth, I am not sure of old age prospects.

Other cultivars include: 'Bailey', 'Clark', and 'Prospect' from Rutgers University; see *Arnoldia* 47(1):14–19 (1987).

PROPAGATION: Seeds, if viable, will germinate to a degree but one month cold stratification improves and unifies germination; abundant literature on cutting production, in general use firm-wooded softwoods, June–August, 8000 ppm IBA talc or solution, mist and rooting should approach 80% or greater. Monrovia Nursery uses 4″ long hardwood cuttings, soak in chlorine water and fungicide, place in plastic bags for 30 days at 45°F, 3000 ppm IBA dip, place in outdoor rooting beds with bottom heat, 90% rooting in 4 months.

ADDITIONAL NOTES: The genus was described by Miki in 1941 from fossils discovered in Japan in Lower Pliocene strata. Extant specimens were found growing at the edges of rice paddies by T. Kan in China in the same year. The natives of this area called the tree *shui-sa*, or "water fir." The Arnold Arboretum sponsored an expedition to the area in 1947 and collected seeds, which were shared with other arboreta and botanical gardens around the world. This species has been growing and reproducing itself for 100 million years. It is amazingly fast growing and has infatuated many good horticulturists and botanists. I have seen it as far north as the University of Maine, Orono, but there the top is often killed back. One hot summer day, I bicycled all over the campus of William and Mary looking for the 100′ plus high trees that Mitchell described in *J. Royal Hort. Soc.* See *Arnoldia* 28:113–123 for a full account of history, introduction and cultivation. Another detailed article by Sand, *Amer. Horticulturist* 7(10):40–44 (1992), is fact laden and provided a detailed account of the ontogeny of discovery. Some dates do not coincide with others I have read. At one time native to North America and after an absence of some 15 million years was returned in the 1940's. This tree provides a case history of perhaps how endangered species should be managed, i.e., propagate and share.

NATIVE HABITAT: Native of eastern Szechuan and western Hupeh, China. Introduced 1947–1948.

Michelia figo (Lour.) Spreng. — Banana Shrub

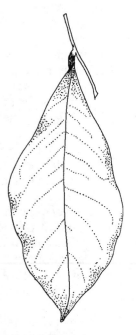

FAMILY: Magnoliaceae

LEAVES: Alternate, simple, evergreen, narrowly oval or slightly obovate, 1 1/2 to 4″ long, 1/2 to 2″ wide, initially covered with brownish pubescence, at maturity nearly glabrous, entire, lustrous and rich dark green; petiole—1/2″ long, brown pubescent.

BUDS: Flower—large, ovoid, 1/2 to 1″ long, covered with greenish to silky brown hairs, borne on a rusty brown peduncular stalk, diverge from stem at ±30° angle; vegetative—smaller, not as plump, 1/8 to 1/4″ long, covered with dark brown rusty pubescence.

STEM: Green, 1/16 to 1/8″ diameter, covered with short, rusty brown pubescence, pubescence maintained into older stems, mature stems gray-brown, glabrous; pith—white, divided into septa (chambers), ample, more than one-half the diameter of young stems.

Michelia figo, (mī-kē′li-à f ī′gō), Banana Shrub, is one of those plants that excites the plant lover but frustrates the individual when he/she attempts to locate it in commerce. It forms a dense, upright oval to rounded outline, 6 to 10′(15′) high and wide. The lustrous dark green foliage is truly magnificent. During winter, the leaves, at least in the Piedmont, become yellow-green, especially on plants sited in full sun. The extremely fragrant, 1 to 1 1/2″ long and wide, 6- to 9-tepaled, yellowish green, tinged purple, cup-shaped flowers are borne on a 1/2″ long, brown, downy peduncle in April through June. I recorded full flower from April 10 to 29 on a plant in our garden. The flowers are initially covered with brown, downy bracts. Prefers well-drained, fertile, acid, sandy loam with high organic matter content and full sun to partial shade. My observations indicate partial to one-half shade is best. Flower production is still excellent. It has no significant pest problems and is well-adapted to conditions in the Coastal Plain. The fragrance could be termed fruity—reminds of ripening cantaloupes and bananas. Has been used for foundations, single specimens, and groupings. A beautiful plant that was once widely planted in the Southeast, and should be brought back into commercial production. Unfortunately, the flowers are not explosive and do not "fit" the modern concept of a quality landscape plant. Summer cuttings root ±60 to 80% when treated with 3000 to 5000 KIBA. 'Stubbs Purple' has flowers that are more purple than the typical species form. 'Port Wine' is similar, if not the same; grows 10′. Several hybrids between *M. doltsopa* Buch.-Ham. ex DC. (a tender, Zone 9 to 10, 3 to 7″ long, 1 1/4 to 3″ wide, lustrous dark green-leaved form with soft creamy white, 3 to 4″ diameter, fragrant, 12- to 16-petaled flowers from the axils of the leaves in spring) and *M. figo* are known. Technically listed as *Michelia × foggii* selections, the cultivars include: 'Allspice' with exceedingly fragrant, white flowers and handsome lustrous dark green foliage on a vigorous plant; 'Belle Durio' with 3 to 4″ diameter, white flowers with purple styles; 'Jack Fogg' with white flowers with a pinkish purple edging to the petals, glossy dark green leaves, upright habit; and 'Picotee' with fragrant, 2 1/2″ wide, white flowers with red tips and edging. Have grown 'Allspice' and 'Jack Fogg' in trials at Georgia with no success. Plants were in full sun, wind exposed locations and lost all leaves every winter as well as fuzzy, rich brown promising buds. Perhaps with proper siting, i.e., shade and wind protection, some degree of success would have been experienced. The *M. × foggii* series includes: #2 with 2 1/2″ diameter, white flowers and red edging, #3 with 3 3/4″ diameter flowers, #4 with cup-shaped, 3 1/2″ diameter flowers. Other cultivars exist but probably represent overkill based on their descriptions. Hybrids are probably best in Zone (8b)9. *Michelia doltsopa* as I have seen it is a distinctly upright pyramidal tree and I suspect most hybrids will be quite upright in outline. It had only been observed by this author in the Strybing Arboretum, San Francisco, CA, however, on late March 1996 and 1998 trips to the southwest of England in Caerhays Garden resided a full-flowered, 30 to 40′ high and wide specimen. The opportunity to witness such a magnificent specimen was a significant high. 'Silver Cloud' flowers at a young age producing creamy white, fragrant flowers with up to 30 tepals, pyramidal form, 15′ by 8′, larger in frost-free San Francisco-type climates, this form is listed as hardy to 10°F. 'Strybing Strain' produces more open habit, flowers with wide tepals. *Michelia figo* is native to China. Introduced 1789. Zone 7 to 10; best in Zone 8 and warmer.

Microbiota decussata Komar. — Russian Arborvitae

FAMILY: Cupressaceae
LEAVES: Branchlets arranged in flattened sprays like *Thuja*, needles mostly scale-like and appressed, soft-textured; spreading and needle-like on young and seedling plants or those grown in shade, bright green in summer, bronzy purple to brown in winter.

Microbiota decussata, (mī-krō-bī-ō′tà dē-ku-sā′tà), Russian Arborvitae, has stirred considerable interest among gardeners since entering the marketplace. Abundant accolades have appeared in the literature and, indeed, when well grown the plant has few rivals among ground cover needle evergreens. In Europe, the plant appears more vigorous than in the hotter summers of the eastern, midwestern and southern states. Plants grow about 12″ high and spread almost indefinitely. The tips of the shoots nod gracefully. One report mentioned a 14-year-old plant that was 12″ high and 15′ in diameter. Literature reported sizes from 16 to 28″ high. I have not observed anything approaching the upper limits. Ideally, well-drained, moist soil is best but some shade is acceptable. I grew a plant under an oak tree for four years and it was miserable. The summer foliage is bright green and turns *Juniperus horizontalis* 'Plumosa' brownish purple in winter. Several clones are described with the Vancouver form supposedly better. A monoecious species with the female consisting of a single, naked, oval seed, surrounded at the base by spreading scales. Work from Russia reported the species forms, with *Pinus pumila*, extensive shrublands at the subalpine zone. Plants can grow 5 to 5 1/2′ high with a branch growing as wide as 23′ with stem diameter of 4.4 to 6.1″ and 230 years of age. Regeneration is after fire, the seed remaining dormant for up to 28 months. Discovered in 1921 near Vladivostock, Russia, growing above the tree line in the mountains. Southeastern Siberia. Considered hardy to –40°F and possibly lower. Zone 3 to 8? I left the zone designation as it appeared in the 4th edition to emphasize several points. I did not know how it would fare in the South. Also, what about soil tolerances, etc.? Well, the cultural facts are much clearer. Numerous plants were outplanted on the Georgia campus over the past 6 to 8 years. All are dead. Heat, heavy soils and root rot contributed to decline. Will require cooler climate and better drained soils for success.

Mitchella repens L. — Patridgeberry, also called Twinberry and Squawberry
(mi-chel′à rē′penz)

FAMILY: Rubiaceae
LEAVES: Opposite, simple, evergreen, 1/4 to 1″ long, of similar width, orbicular-ovate, obtuse, subcordate, truncate or rounded, lustrous dark green above, often variegated with whitish lines; petiole—1/8 to 1/4″ long, puberulent above.

SIZE: Two inches, usually a biological pancake; have seen reference to 12″ high but have looked at 1,000,000 natural populations and only seen the pancakes.
HARDINESS: Zone 3 to 9.
HABIT: Low-growing, ground-hugging, evergreen cover scarcely reaching above the ground.
RATE: Slow.
TEXTURE: Fine.
LEAF COLOR: Dark green and lustrous above, often with variegated whitish lines (veins).
FLOWERS: White or pinkish, possibly tinged with purple, 4-lobed at mouth, narrow trumpet-shaped, 1/2″ long, extremely fragrant; borne over an extended period in late spring and early summer in erect short peduncled pairs; have seen in flower late May–early June in North Georgia mountains.

FRUIT: Berry-like, globose drupe, red, 1/4 to 1/3″ diameter, fall into winter; somewhat irregular in shape due to fusion of two ovaries; in the wild it is not uncommon to see flowers and fruits appearing at the same time.

CULTURE: Best moved in sods being careful to maintain as much soil as possible; requires acid, moist, well-drained soil which has been abundantly supplied with acid leafmold or peat; requires shade; is sensitive to the encroachment of man.

DISEASES AND INSECTS: Several leaf diseases have been reported but none are serious.

LANDSCAPE VALUE: A worthwhile ground cover for the lover of plants; requires special attention and without it should not even be considered; the plants are collected from the wild and sold at Christmas time; there was a firm in Vermont which sold the Partridgeberry bowl, which consisted of Rattlesnake plantain, moss and the above; good rock garden plant; I delight in finding small patches of this in the woods; it has a delicate beauty and is usually found in combination with mosses and lichens under the shade of the forest canopy where it forms a most beautiful natural garden.

CULTIVARS:
f. *leucocarpa* Bissell—Listed as having white fruits; have never seen this but would like one for my garden.

PROPAGATION: Seed requires a 2 to 3 month cold period; cuttings can be rooted in November and through the winter months by using a poly tent and IBA treatment.

NATIVE HABITAT: Nova Scotia to Ontario and Minnesota, south to Florida, Arkansas and Texas. Introduced 1761.

Morus alba L. — White or Common Mulberry
(mō′rus al′bà)

FAMILY: Moraceae

LEAVES: Alternate, simple, polymorphic, undivided or lobed, serrate or dentate, ovate to broad-ovate, 2 to 7″ long, up to 6″ wide, acute or short acuminate, rounded or cordate at base, dark green and usually smooth above, pubescent on veins beneath or nearly glabrous; petiole—1/2 to 1″ long.

BUDS: Imbricate, terminal-absent, laterals-small, 1/8 to 1/4″ long, ovoid, 3 to 6 scales, appressed, sharp- or blunt-pointed, light brown to reddish brown, often set oblique to leaf scar, margins of bud scales somewhat finely hairy.

STEM: Slender, yellowish green to brownish gray, smooth, more or less shining, slightly sweetish if chewed, bark exuding a white juice if cut on warm days.

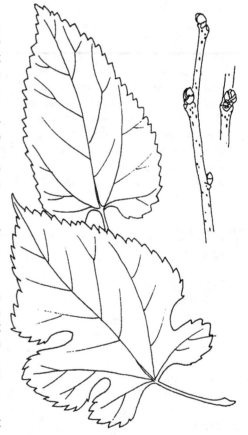

SIZE: 30 to 50′ in height with a comparable spread, usually smaller; national champion is 59′ by 73′ in Johnson Co., MO.

HARDINESS: Zone (4)5 to 8(9); some tip dieback at Orono, ME.

HABIT: Usually an extremely dense, round-topped tree with a profusion of tight-knit slender branches; often develops a "witches' broom" which gives the tree a messy, unkempt appearance; definitely one of the original garbage can trees; often seen as a shrub in fence rows and waste areas.

RATE: Fast, 10 to 12′ over a 4 to 6 year period; Pair reported 2′ of growth per year over a 10 year period in Wichita, KS tests.

TEXTURE: Coarse throughout the year; perhaps somewhat unfair assessment; medium in summer in the best forms.

BARK: On younger branches (1 to 4″) an ashy orange or light orangish brown, on larger trunks a brown color.

LEAF COLOR: Variable, dull yellow-green to lustrous dark green in summer; fall color ranges from green to yellow-green to yellow in the best forms; late coloring in Zone 7b, often mid to late November with some trees as notable as the best birch.

FLOWERS: Polygamo-dioecious (monoecious or dioecious according to Rehder), yellowish green, March–April, both sexes in stalked, axillary pendulous catkins, not showy, female 1/3 to 1/2″ long, male longer.

FRUIT: Multiple fruit of small, fleshy drupes, white, pinkish, red or purplish violet, sweet, but insipid, 1/2 to 1″ long, June to July somewhat similar in size and shape to blackberry; birds love them and create fantastic messes because of cathartic properties.

CULTURE: Transplants readily, adaptable, withstands drought, urban and seaside (quite salt tolerant) conditions; full sun to light shade; prune in winter; similar to *Maclura* in cultural adaptability, grows best in moist, well-drained, fertile soils; extremely pH adaptable; has become an out of control weed species in many parts of the country; in San Francisco Bay area, rated as second most notorious tree for damaging pavements and curbs, interestingly, sweetgum was first followed by mulberry, ash, Chinese Elm, and Southern Magnolia.

DISEASES AND INSECTS: Bacterial blight on leaves and shoots, leaf spots, cankers, powdery mildews, scales, two-spotted mites and other pests; in the southern states this species may be infested with many more problems.

LANDSCAPE VALUE: None; according to a landscape architect, whose name will remain anonymous, this tree has excellent color, texture, and form; possibly she and I are thinking of different trees; about the only beneficiaries are the birds and the silkworms; the tree was originally imported from China for the silkworm industry and unfortunately escaped and is now naturalized in Asia, Europe and America; the compact and weeping forms and the fruitless types offer the greatest hope for the landscape; widely used in Texas, Southwest and California; dry soil and alkaline as well as high pH tolerances make the species a prime candidate for the Southwest.

CULTIVARS: The European, Russian and Indian literature searches indicated numerous cultivars, unknown in the United States, selected for fruits, leaves (rolled blades, gold leaves), weeping, globose, pyramidal habits, et al.

'Bellaire'—A mature male selection, multiple trunk and distinctive form.

'Chaparral'—Non-fruiting, bright green-leaved, weeping type, usually grafted on a standard.

'Contorta'—Described by Gossler (1991) as a sharply twisted form, could this be 'Unryu'?

'Fan-San'—Glossy dark green leaves, deeply lobed, 30 to 50′ by 25 to 40′, could be the same as 'Mapleleaf'.

'Fegyvernekiana'—Have seen this bush-like, non-fruiting form that probably will never exceed 3 to 4′; makes a cute dense mound and every gardener needs at least one plant with such a name.

'Fruitless'—Male form, 30 to 50′, wide-spreading crown, deeply lobed, lustrous dark green leaves, I suspect this is similar to 'Mapleleaf', offered by several major Southeast nursery producers.

'Hampton'—Fruitless form selected from a 100-year-old specimen, wide spreading, picturesque habit, Pair introduction, Kansas State.

'Illinois Everbearing'—Produces several crops of flavorful fruits.

'Itoguwa'—Compact shrub form, 2 1/2′ by 2 1/2′, deeply dissected, dark green leaves, bright gold in fall.

'Lingan'—A type with leathery, lustrous foliage, fruitless, fast-growing, drought resistant and apparently somewhat salt resistant as it is often used for seashore plantings.

'Laciniata'—Leaves are deeply lobed, the lobes narrow, pointed and deeply serrated.

'Mapleleaf'—Dr. Pair calls this a standard in the trade but I am not sure where it belongs taxonomically; many years past I saw a plant like this in the Ohio Shade Tree Evaluation tests at Wooster with a large, lustrous dark green, lobed, "maple-like" leaf; a male form; see 'Fruitless'.

'Nuclear Blast'—An anomaly at best, ugly in its best form, uglier without divine intervention, compact, leaves shredded to ribbons, slivers and cheese wedges, also somewhat malformed, what a disaster!

'Pendula'—A form with slender, pendulous branches and gnarled, twisted growth habit; often in evidence in older landscapes; interesting but grotesque (also called Teas Weeping Mulberry), a fruiting clone, will grow 15 to 20′ high and wide.

'Pyramidalis'—Upright clone of conical habit, have not seen this.

'Silk Hope'—Large, sweet, 1 1/2″ long, black fruits, possibly a hybrid between *Morus alba* and *M. rubra*.

'Stribling'—Another fruitless, fast growing clone, have seen excellent yellow fall color on this clone, appears quite cold hardy, survived -25°F at Spring Grove, Cincinnati, OH, probably 40′ by 30′ at maturity.

var. *tatarica* (Pall.) Ser.—Called the Russian Mulberry, hardiest of all the mulberries.

'Urbana'—Weeping, fruitless clone named by J.C. McDaniel, otherwise like 'Pendula'.

'Widman Mitchell'—Dwarf form for bonsai use, see *HortScience* 26:475 (1991).

PROPAGATION: Seed, stratify for 60 days at 41°F to improve germination. Cuttings collected in late October rooted 30% without treatment and 87% in 13 weeks with IBA; have rooted August cuttings of 'Pendula' with 3000 ppm IBA-quick dip, peat:perlite, mist; over the years have rooted the various forms of *Morus alba* with excellent success; hardwood cuttings would root; tissue culture has been successful, see *Botanical Gazette* 146:335–340 (1985) and *Scientia Horticulturae* 42:307–320 (1990).

ADDITIONAL NOTES: A terrible weed species that survives under the most demanding cultural conditions. Should plant only male trees. Hybrids between this and *Morus rubra* might make worthy urban trees.

NATIVE HABITAT: China. Introduced into Jamestown, Virginia with the early settlers, cultivated since time immemorial in many European countries.

RELATED SPECIES:

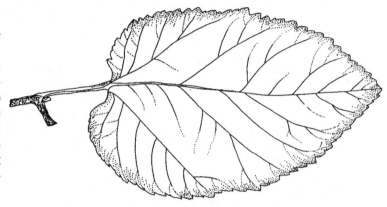

Morus australis Poir. (*M. bombycis* Koidz.), (mō′rus aw-strā′lis) 'Unryu' ('Tortuosa') was popularized by the late Dr. Raulston, NC State Arboretum (now J.C. Raulston Arboretum) and indeed this shrub or small tree has much to offer. I received a rooted cutting that in 5 years grew 12′ tall, 8 to 10′ wide with a 6″ diameter trunk at the base. One year it was killed almost to the ground by an April freeze, but returned to the size listed above. Raulston reported 6 to 10′ growth per year. Ultimate landscape size is probably 20 to 30′. Leaves are large, 6 to 7″ long, lustrous dark green and may turn a good bright yellow but have been killed off green on most occasions in our garden. The most interesting (curious) part of the plant's anatomy is the twisted, corkscrew-configured branches which serve as a poor man's *Corylus avellana* 'Contorta'. Branches are not quite as twisted as 'Contorta' but are sufficiently pronounced to make an effective accent. In Tripp and Raulston's *The Year in Trees* (Timber Press, 1995) the cultivar is termed 'Unryo' but in Raulston's *The Chronicles of the NCSU Arboretum* (1993) was published and distributed as *M. bombycis* 'Unryu'. The plant in our garden was removed in 1995 for it had exceeded soil and atmospheric boundaries. What a greedy plant! In January 1997, as I walked the NC State campus, a huge 20 to 25′ high by 30 to 35′ wide specimen caught my eye. My initial instincts were incorrect about this plant. Perhaps as a cut-back tree/shrub for the vigorous growth and contorted branches. Easily rooted from softwood and hardwood cuttings. It tends to leaf out early and may be injured by late freezes. Apparently a female. Native to China. Zone 6 to 9.

Morus nigra L., (mō′rus nī′grà), Black Mulberry, to 30′ with 1″ long, sweet, purple to black fruit. 'Wellington' was selected in New York for fruit quality and hardiness. 'Black Beauty' is a semi-dwarf, to 15′, with large, juicy, black fruit. Western Asia. Introduced 1548. Zone 5 to 9.

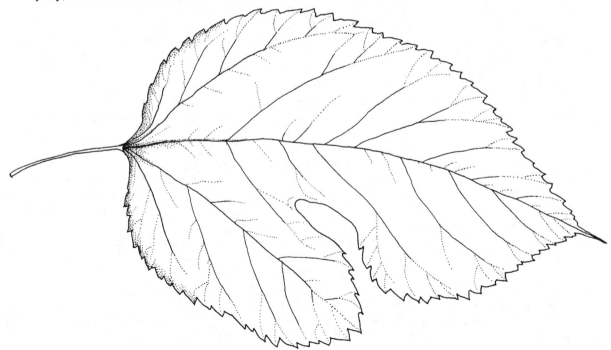

Morus rubra L. — Red Mulberry

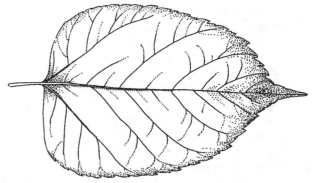

LEAVES: Alternate, simple, broad-ovate to oblong-ovate, 2- to 3-lobed on vigorous shoots, 3 to 5″(8″) long, abruptly long acuminate, truncate or subcordate at base, closely and sharply serrate, scabrous or sometimes smooth above, dark green, soft-pubescent below; petiole—1″ long, pubescent.

BUDS: Imbricate, brownish black, 1/4 to 1/3″ long, ovoid, glabrous, sits at slight angle on top of leaf scar.

STEM: Stout, brown, thinly pubescent.

Morus rubra, (mō′rus rū′brȧ), Red Mulberry, reaches 40 to 70′ in height with a 40 to 50′ spread and is taller, more open, and irregular than *M. alba*. National champion is 63′ by 78′ in Edmond, OK. The large dark green leaves are quite noticeable and tend to attract the eye of even casual biologists. Fall color is subdued yellow, however, in the Southeast trees develop, in good years, outstanding golden yellow fall color in early to mid-November (Athens). The 1″ long fruits are green ripening orange, red turning dark purple, juicy, edible and relished by birds. Bark is gray-brown, ridged-and-furrowed with flattened ridges. A better tree than *M. alba* and more fastidious as to soil requirements, preferring a rich, moist situation. I continue to evaluate this species and believe, with selection for handsome foliage, habit and maleness, it would make a worthy tree. On more than one occasion, I have made a 180 degree turn in the highway and back-tracked to the large, dark green, leafy tree thrusting its long shoots from the edge of the woodlands. To date, I have discovered terrific foliage, respectable habit but all were female. Perhaps by the next edition. *Xylella fastidiosa* has been isolated from trees with leaf scorch symptoms [see *Plant Disease* 75:200–203 (1991)]. Native from Massachusetts to Florida, west to Michigan, Nebraska, Kansas and Texas. Introduced 1629. Zone 5 to 9.

Myrica pensylvanica Lois. — Northern Bayberry, Candleberry
(mi-rī′kȧ pen-sil-vā′ni-kȧ)

FAMILY: Myricaceae

LEAVES: Alternate, simple, deciduous to semi-evergreen, almost always deciduous in the North, obovate to oblong-obovate or oblong, 1 1/2 to 4″ long, 1/2 to 1 1/2″ wide, obtuse or acutish, cuneate, shallowly toothed toward apex or entire, lustrous dark green and pubescent above, pubescent beneath, resin-dotted, leaves aromatic when bruised; petiole—short.

BUDS: Small, solitary, sessile, subglobose or ovoid, with 2 to 4 exposed, reddish brown scales, end bud absent.

STEM: Rounded or angular, stoutish, resin-dotted when young; pith—small, somewhat angled, continuous, green.

FRUIT: A small, gray, waxy-coated, rounded, 1/5″ wide drupe which persists throughout the winter; an excellent identification feature on female plants.

SIZE: Nine feet is a good average for height, however, quite variable ranging from 5 to 12′ in height and could equal that in spread; tends to sucker and therefore forms large colonies.

HARDINESS: Zone 3 to 6, suspect into Zone 7 since I am growing a few plants successfully; see comments under CULTURE.

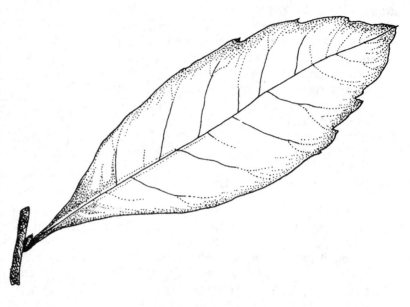

HABIT: Deciduous to semi-ever-green, upright-rounded, and fairly dense shrub; actually difficult to describe the habit of this plant; must be seen to be fully appreciated; suckers and forms large colonies; near the ocean a low, windswept shrub, further away a large, irregular, colonizing mass.

RATE: Medium from old wood, probably fast from shoots which develop from roots.

TEXTURE: Medium in foliage, possibly could be considered medium-fine; medium in winter habit; a very handsome specimen in winter because of interesting branch pattern and the gray, waxy fruits on female plants.

LEAF COLOR: Deep lustrous green, dotted with resin glands beneath, leaves have a leathery texture, very aromatic when crushed as are all parts of the plant; fall color is nonexistent.

FLOWERS: Monoecious or dioecious, tends toward the dioecious character; male and female plants are required for good fruit development, not showy, the flowers borne in catkins with male (yellowish green) consisting of varying number of stamens; the female of a one-celled ovary with two stalkless stigmas; sepals and petals are absent; flowering in late March to April before the leaves.

FRUIT: Drupe, 1/6 to 1/5″ across, grayish white, endocarp covered with resinous, waxy coating, effective from September through April and later of the following year, borne in great quantities and usually covering the stems of female plants.

CULTURE: Transplant balled-and-burlapped or as a container plant; thrives in poor, sterile, sandy soil; has performed well in heavy clay soils; appears to be extremely adaptable; full sun to one-half shade; withstands salt spray; chlorosis is a problem on high pH soils but can be corrected with soil treatments or iron sprays; displays excellent salt tolerance as evidenced by its natural proximity to the sea; tends to be low-growing along the coast where it is sculptured by the ocean spray and becomes larger inland; fixes atmospheric nitrogen; provenance may be extremely important for hardiness, although listed as Zone 2 to 3 hardy, plants have suffered damage at -20 to -25°F in Midwest; if plants are going to be used in northern areas make sure plants were grown from northern seed sources; Cappiello reported tip dieback in Orono, ME.

DISEASES AND INSECTS: None serious.

LANDSCAPE VALUE: Excellent plant for massing, border, combines well with broadleaf evergreens, could be integrated into the foundation plantings, possibly for highway plantings and other areas where salts present a cultural problem; could be used in many poor soil sites.

CULTIVARS: Two from Denmark: 'Myda' is a female clone that fruits well; 'Myriman' is a male clone to accompany above. For good fruit set at least 20% of plants should be male.

PROPAGATION: Seeds, collect in October, remove the wax, stratify in moist peat for 90 days and the germination approaches 100%; I have had excellent success with this procedure. Cuttings, I conducted an experiment using 0, 1000, 2500, 5000, and 10,000 ppm IBA treatments; the cutting wood was collected June 14, after 8 weeks rooting was evaluated; no roots were produced at 0 or 1000 ppm IBA; rooting was 36, 53, 46% for 2500, 5000, and 10,000 ppm IBA treatments, respectively; see Dirr and Heuser (1987) for additional information.

ADDITIONAL NOTES: The wax is used for making the finely aromatic bayberry candles. Certainly one of my favorite native plants, yet appears to be losing ground to other shrubs. Why no unique, particularly compact, cultivars have been selected is a mystery. See two described above. Considerable selection has been conducted with *Myrica cerifera*. On the outer banks of North Carolina in the Corolla area I have observed intergrades with some plants favoring *M. pensylvanica*, others *M. cerifera*, and some in between.

NATIVE HABITAT: Newfoundland to western New York, Maryland, and North Carolina. Primarily along the seashore. Introduced 1725.

RELATED SPECIES:

Myrica cerifera L., (mi-rī′kȧ sĕr-if′ĕr-ȧ), Southern Waxmyrtle, is best described as the southern evergreen extension of *Myrica pensylvanica*. However, it is distinctly different in leaf, fruit and growth habit. The leaves are narrowly obovate or oblance-olate and extremely variable in size ranging from 4 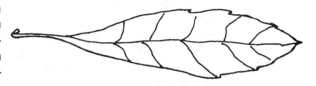 1/2″ long to 2″ wide, but more typically 1 1/2 to 3″ long, and 1/3 to 3/4″ wide. They are usually serrate at the apex, glossy olive green and glabrous above, dotted with yellowish resin glands above and beneath. The petiole is about 1/8 to 1/4″ long. In recent years, a leaf anthracnose that causes spotting and browning of the leaves has become evident. Also a "mosaic-type" leaf distortion was reported in Florida. Leaves developed pale green, blistered areas interspersed with dark green normal tissues. Actual culprit was a new species of eriophyid mite. See *HortScience* 22:258–260 (1987). *Fusarium oxysporum* has been isolated from stem lesions, roots and xylem tissues of Florida landscape plants. The gray, globose fruits are about 1/8″ wide and are massed in sessile clusters of 2 to 6 on the previous season's growth. This is a beautiful, rather wispy, broadleaf evergreen that will grow 10 to 15′(20′) high and wide. Four national champions are 28′ by 33′, 20′ by 38′, 25′ by 36′, 26′ by 37′. It makes an excellent pruned screen and may be limbed up to form an attractive small tree. At Sea Island, GA, it is limbed up to expose the handsome gray almost white bark. At the University's Botanical Garden, it has been used effectively to soften the vertical lines of the administration building and as a specimen plant. It tolerates infertile soils but responds tremendously to good watering and nutritional practices. Fixes atmospheric nitrogen which permits survival in miserable soils. I planted a small, container-grown plant by one side of the entrance to our house and in a single growing season it grew 5′ high and wide. In the spring when the new growth develops, the rich "bayberry candle" odor is evident. Its only limitation appears to be the sensitivity to cold for at 0°F plants were defoliated or the leaves severely browned. The stem tissue was not injured. Also, ice and snow loads effectively split several plants in the Athens area. It is tolerant of salt spray and will tolerate full sun or half shade. It has been reported as being used at Williamsburg in 1699. A significant number of selections have been introduced in the last 10 years and are here presented alphabetically for ease of assimilation:

'Club Med'—More dwarf than 'Fairfax', 3 to 4′, informal texture and appearance, Bill Craven introduction, Zone 7.

'Don's Dwarf'—Compact form (24″), bigger and deeper olive green leaf than 'Lynn's Dwarf', from Tom Dodd Nurseries.

'Emperor'—Unusual narrow serrated leaf form with lustrous rich green leaves, newly developed leaves produced on vigorous shoots have scalloped edge, results in a fine-texture, plant will grow as large as the species, introduced by Lane Bracken, Alabama.

'Fairfax'—Compact, 4 to 5′ high, spreading, colonizing form that was found by Mr. Bill Craven outside of Fairfax, SC; the leaves are slightly smaller than the species and lighter green; deer do not bother the plant at all; I have grown the selection in my garden and have been impressed with its performance; at the University's Botanical Garden, 8-year-old plants are 6 to 8′ high, slightly wider and densely foliaged; plants suffered slight foliage burn at 7°F in January 1994; this is a terrific form that I believe is currently the best of the compact forms.

'Georgia Gem'—Small-leaved, compact, mounded form for ground cover and massing; introduced by Bill Craven, Waynesboro, GA; will grow 12 to 18″ high, 30 to 36″ wide, with yellow-green to dark olive green leaves that are smaller than the species; unfortunately, significantly less cold hardy than 'Fairfax' or the species, a plant in our garden perished at 7°F.

'Hiwassee'—Hardier form that originated in University of Tennessee trial gardens in Knoxville, withstood –4°F with minor foliage burn.

'King's Dwarf'—Compact habit, smaller leaves, from Tom Dodd.

'Luray'—Dense form to 4′, introduced by Woodlanders, Aiken, SC.

'Lynn's Dwarf'—Dense, compact form made by Lynn Lowery, introduced by Tom Dodd Nurseries, smaller than 'Don's Dwarf' with smaller, brighter green leaves.

var. *pumila* Michx.—The dwarf, suckering form that by various authorities is merged with *M. cerifera* and treated as a separate species, *M. pusilla* Ref., by others; if accepted as a true species, I theorize that 'Don's Dwarf', 'Georgia Gem' and 'Lynn's Dwarf' are its cultivars; var. *pumila* grows 3 to 4′ high and colonizes; has remained evergreen at 0°F.

Variegated Form—Variegated sport discovered by NCSU horticulture student Richard Olsen, currently being propagated for future evaluation, information presented here based on Fall 1997 Newsletter of the J.C. Raulston Arboretum.

Best cutting propagation results occurred in May–August with or without a rooting hormone. Grows in diverse habitats including fresh to slightly brackish banks, shores, flats, interdune swales, wet hammocks, bogs, upland mixed woodlands, old fields, fence and hedgerows. Found in Coastal Plain from southern New Jersey to Florida Keys westward to east Texas, southeast Oklahoma into Central America. Zone (7)8 to 11.

Myrica gale L., (mi-rī′kȧ gāl), Sweetgale, is a low-growing, 2 to 4′ high, deciduous, bushy shrub with glossy, blue-green to dark green foliage. In gardens the Sweetgale is grown for its pleasing foliage fragrance. In England the branches were used to flavor a home-made beer known as "gale-beer." Plant is uncommon in cultivation but Garden in the Woods, Framingham, MA has a planting around the pond that is quite handsome. For foliage color and texture in wet soils in cold climates, it is meritorious. *Myrica gale* is an actinorhizal dinitrogen-fixing shrub common on wet soils. Seeds require 4, 16-hour photoperiods, one per day for maximum germination. Seeds were long-lived with no decrease in germination capacity after 6 years in dry storage at 41°F. Native to the higher latitudes of all the northern hemisphere. Cultivated 1750. Zone 1.

Myrica heterophylla Raf. — Swamp Bayberry
LEAVES: Alternate, simple, evergreen, oblanceolate, narrow obovate, sometimes elliptic, to 5″ long by 1 1/4″ wide, obtuse to rounded, cuneate, with one to few remote serrations on each side, occasionally entire, glossy dark green, glabrous or short pubescent along the midrib above, with amber or brownish punctate dots below, fragrant when bruised, sparse pubescence along midrib; petiole—short.
STEM: Dark brown to almost black, generally shaggy pubescence with most of it persistent the first year.

Myrica heterophylla, (mi-rī′kȧ het-ĕr-o-fil′ȧ), Swamp Bayberry, is a semi-evergreen to evergreen, 8 to 12′ high shrub that is receiving some attention from the nursery industry. The leaves are larger than *M. cerifera* and plants are fuller and denser. Fruits 1/12 to 1/5″ diameter, globose or short ovoid, coated with white or grayish wax, sometimes with little wax, and dark brown. Tolerant of moist to wet soils and grows in bogs and wet areas in the wild. Will tolerate sun and light shade. Coastal Plain from southern New Jersey to central Florida, west to east Texas. Zone (6)7 to 9.

Myrica inodora Bartr. — Odorless Bayberry
LEAVES: Alternate, simple, leathery, evergreen, elliptic or elliptic-oblanceolate, somewhat cupped, 1 1/2 to 3 1/4″ long, 3/4 to 1 1/4″ broad, obtuse or rounded, cuneate, dark green above, both surfaces with abundant punctate glands, not fragrant when bruised; petiole—short, pubescent.
STEM: Rust-colored, glabrous, scaly glandular; older stems smooth gray.

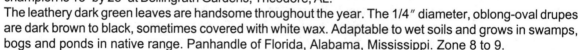

Myrica inodora, (mi-rī′kȧ in-ō-dō′rȧ), Odorless Bayberry, is a large, evergreen shrub or small tree growing 15 to 20′ high. National champion is 18′ by 23′ at Bellingrath Gardens, Theodore, AL.
The leathery dark green leaves are handsome throughout the year. The 1/4″ diameter, oblong-oval drupes are dark brown to black, sometimes covered with white wax. Adaptable to wet soils and grows in swamps, bogs and ponds in native range. Panhandle of Florida, Alabama, Mississippi. Zone 8 to 9.

Myrtus communis L. — Common Myrtle

FAMILY: Myrtaceae
LEAVES: Opposite, simple, evergreen, ovate or lanceolate, 1 to 2″ long, 1/3 to 3/4″ wide, pointed, entire, recurved, lustrous dark green above, paler beneath, glabrous, fragrant when bruised, covered with transparent dots; petiole—short or absent.

Myrtus communis, (mĕr′tus kom-mū′nis), Common Myrtle, is a dense, leafy shrub or small tree growing 10 to 12′ high and wide. The foliage is handsome throughout the seasons. Small, pinkish buds open to 3/4″ diameter, fragrant, white, 5-petaled flowers, each on a 3/4 to 1″ long pedicel arising from the leaf axils. The brushy mass of 1/3″ long stamens in the center of the flower is most conspicuous. Fruit is an ovoid-oblong, 1/2″ long, purplish black berry that is somewhat lost among the dark foliage. In Europe, I have experienced plants heavy in fruit yet did not notice same until on top of the plant. Good drainage is essential in full sun to partial shade. Can be pruned to any shape and is utilized for hedges and formal elements. A plant limbed up and allowed to develop a free-form canopy has merit. This allows the attractive branches and bark to show. Rated as deer resistant. Is occasionally utilized in Florida where mites and scale are listed as pests. Cultivars include: 'Boetica' with stiff, gnarled branches and upward-pointing, large, leathery dark green, noticeably fragrant leaves, grows 4 to 6′ high; 'Buxifolia' with small, elliptical leaves; 'Compacta' is slow-growing, compact, densely set with small leaves, good for low hedging; 'Compacta Variegata' has leaves edged in white; 'Flore Pleno' has double flowers; var. *leucocarpa* DC. produces white fruits; 'Microphylla' is dwarf with tiny, close-set leaves; 'Mr. Lain' is a compact form, 3 to 4′ high by 3 to 4′ wide, white flowers in summer, black fruit in winter, discovered by Bill Craven, Twisted Oaks Nursery, Waynesboro, GA, at the former USDA Plant Introduction Station, Savannah, GA; var. *tarentina* L. has 1/2 to 3/4″ long, 1/8 to 1/4″ wide leaves and whitish fruits; 'Variegata' grows like the species but has cream-margined leaves. Another species, **Myrtus luma** Mol., now more correctly *Luma apiculata* (DC.) Burret, has shorter leaves than the above, 3/4 to 1″ long, and one-half as wide. Although limitedly hardy (Zone 9 to 10), the spectacular cinnamon bark is a monumental attribute. In the South of England and in Ireland, most vividly at Mt. Usher Garden, a spectacular multi-stemmed plant rebounds into the brain cells. Grows 20 to 40′ high and plants in this range are reasonably common in the southwest of England. Native to temperate forests of Chile and Argentina. Introduced 1844. Zone 9 to 10. *Myrtus communis* is widely cultivated in the Mediterranean region. Origin lost to antiquity but Iran and Afghanistan often cited. Zone (8)9 to 10. During an Athens tour of gardens, I discovered a 5′ high, somewhat the worse-for-wear shrub. Indicates more cold hardy than I originally thought. Still, do not bet the nursery on this species.

Nandina domestica Thunb. — Nandina, Heavenly Bamboo

(nan-dē′nà dō-mes′ti-kà)

FAMILY: Berberidaceae

LEAVES: Alternate, bi- to tri-pinnately compound, evergreen, 12 to 24″(36″) long and wide, each leaflet subsessile, elliptic-lanceolate, 3/4 to 3″ long, half as wide, acuminate, cuneate, entire, leathery, rich metallic bluish green, various hues of red-green in winter, glabrous.

STEM: Stout, unbranched, erect, when young reddish purple and covered with a bloom; later ugly brown; petiole bases ensheathe stem; when cut shows yellow coloration typical of members of Berberidaceae.

SIZE: 6 to 8′ high, less in spread, can grow to 10′, tends to sucker (slowly) and colonies wider than high are often evident in the landscape.

HARDINESS: Zone 6 to 9; at -3°F during 1983–84 winter plants showed variable response with some completely defoliated, others not affected; in general stem tissue was not hurt; in southern Connecticut, Cape Cod, Cincinnati, and Louisville the plant is a dieback shrub; in September 1994, I witnessed 3′ regrowth on shrubs that were killed to the ground after -24°F in January 1994 at Bernheim Arboretum, Louisville, KY.

HABIT: Distinctly upright in outline, unless properly pruned becomes leggy at base with a flat-topped, spreading crown of foliage, spreads by rhizomes.

RATE: Medium.

TEXTURE: Medium, almost fine if not allowed to become leggy.

LEAF COLOR: New leaves coppery to purplish red becoming blue-green with age; tends to assume a reddish tint in winter especially when sited in full sun; this winter coloration trait is quite variable and there is no consistent rule of thumb; coloration depends on seedling or clone, some redder than others.

FLOWERS: Perfect, pinkish in bud finally white with yellow anthers, each flower 1/4 to 1/2″ across, 3 to 6 petals, borne in erect, terminal, 8 to 15″ long panicles, May–June, will flower in heavy shade, usually in full flower in Athens about late May, flowers not overwhelming but refreshingly elegant as they stand and arch ever so slightly, framed by the elegant foliage.

FRUITS: Spectacular, globular, 1/3″ diameter, two-seeded, bright red berry; ripening in September–October and persisting into and through winter; the large panicles are so heavy that the branches may bend; actually more showy than most hollies because the fruit is not hidden by the foliage.

CULTURE: Easily transplanted from containers; I doubt if anyone is growing *Nandina* in the field; adaptable to extremes of soil and exposure; prefers moist, fertile soil and here makes its best growth; full sun or shade; will grow in beds of ivy under the shade of large oaks and make a great showing; the canes do not branch and careful pruning must be practiced; best to thin out old stems every year or head back old canes at varying lengths to produce a dense plant; in our garden nandinas have been trampled, pruned and transplanted yet survive and thrive, in sun, shade, moist and dry conditions; once established they are forever, possibly one of the most durable broadleaf evergreens

DISEASES AND INSECTS: None serious; actually an amazingly trouble-free plant; powdery mildew caused extensive distortion and some defoliation on 'Wood's Dwarf', 'Firepower' and an unnamed clone, this is the first report of mildew on *Nandina domestica*, see *Plant Disease* 79:424 (1995).

LANDSCAPE VALUE: The species has fallen out of favor because of the competition from the compact-growing cultivars; nice in groups or drifts; softens the effect of coarse-textured shrubs; has been used for every imaginable purpose; possibly not given sufficient plaudits for the tremendous environmental toughness; large plants exist by old homes throughout the South *in situ* for 100 or more years; the species could be used effectively to hide (camouflage) unwanted structures; 'Harbour Dwarf' and 'San Gabriel were test marketed for indoor sales potential in 6 supermarket floral departments, plants captured 16% of 4″ pot sales, 60% of customers indicated newness was primary consideration for purchase.

CULTIVARS: The nursery industry has realized the great potential for this plant and, in recent years, selected and introduced a number of fine cultivars. Dr. Raulston assembled a large collection at the N.C. State Arboretum (now J.C. Raulston Arboretum) and published an excellent review in *Newsletter* 11, December (1984) which has been abstracted here. More easily obtained in Raulston, *The Chronicles of the NCSU Arboretum*, 1993. Raulston lists many small, unusual forms that are not discussed here but may have interest for the collector. I walked and studied J.C.'s wonderful *Nandina* collection many times, most recently January 20, 1997, the morning of his memorial service. It was heart wrenching and sobering to realize he would no longer walk the garden path with me.

'Alba'—White-berried form; the fruits are really off-white and not particularly attractive; apparently comes true-to-type from seed; a reference noted that it comes relatively true-to-type if self-pollinated; some almost yellowish white; foliage lighter green than red-fruited forms, new growth without red pigment; if lacking in reasonable nitrogen fertility, the foliage turns light yellow-green in winter; needs to be sited in some shade as berries will discolor in full sun; 4 to 6′ high; var. *leucocarpa* Mak. with dull white fruits is listed.

'Atropurpurea Nana' ('Nana Purpurea')—A rather upright, stiff, compact form that grows about 2′ high and 2 to 3′ wide; does not develop the graceful character of 'Harbour Dwarf'; usually yellow-green tinged with reddish purple throughout the growing season becoming uniformly red with the advent of cold weather; leaves do not have the gracefulness of the species or 'Harbour Dwarf', and are somewhat inrolled or cupped, probably from a virus infection; have never seen this form flower or fruit.

'Atropurpurea Nana'   (leaflets)

'Aurea'—Probably same as 'Alba', fruits and foliage have yellowish tinge depending on time of year, fertility, etc.

'Compacta'—Have seen offered but suspect a catchall term for more restrained types; Raulston reported 4 to 5′ high, he noted that a grower(s) was producing it from seed and *true* 'Compacta' next to seed-produced 'Compacta' were different entities; nurseries that grow the cultivar report 2 to 4′ high, red winter foliage, white flowers, red berries.

'Firepower' ('Fire Power')—Perhaps a virus-free 'Atropurpurea Nana', i.e., without the foliage distortion; I grew the plant and the winter color was fluorescent glowing red, the habit dense and compact and the foliage apparently virus free, at maturity 1 to 2' by 2'; somewhat similar to 'Wood's Dwarf'; originated in New Zealand.

Gulf Stream™ ('Compacta Nana')—Another good red winter foliage form that next to 'Moon Bay' in the University's Botanical Garden showed more intense red foliage color and more vigorous growth; leaves are flatter and larger than 'Moon Bay', will mature around 2 1/2 to 3 1/2' judging by early performance, good metallic blue-green summer foliage, forms a large compact mound, originated as branch sport of 'Compacta Nana' at Hines Nursery, Houston, TX; time has shed new light on this cultivar for it will grow 3 to 3 1/2' high, possibly slightly less in spread, extremely dense in habit and foliage; winter coloration is variable, some years intense red, others red-green; has flowered and fruited with inflorescence about 4" long; does not sucker (colonize) like 'Harbour Dwarf'; Post Properties, Atlanta, utilizes this clone because of its greater hardiness compared to other compact types.

'Harbour Dwarf'—Branches from the ground and forms a dense mound 2 to 3' high and slightly wider; one of the most widely used broadleaf evergreens in southern gardens; assumes reddish purple tinge of species in winter, extremely graceful form, flowers and fruits with age, inflorescence smaller than the species; the most rhizomatous (spreading) of the compact types, forms a wide mound with time; more graceful in foliage than 'Atropurpurea Nana', Gulf Stream™, 'Moon Bay', etc.

'Lanham'—A compact form with rich maroon purple new growth, reasonably compact 4 to 6' high, new leaves slightly twisted and artistic, mature leaves appear typical of the species.

'Lemon Hill'—Described as a true dwarf to 1' high with yellow fruit.

'Lowboy'—A more compact form, 4 to 5' high and wide, metallic blue-green foliage, red to red-green in winter, flower and fruit panicles about 2/3's those of species, growing in the Dirr garden for over 6 years, respectable selection, patented.

'Lutea'—Described as rare yellow-berried form; same as 'Alba' and 'Aurea'?

'Moon Bay' (Moon Bay™)—After observing this for one year in the University Botanical Garden I think it may have a great future; winter color was bright red, some years reddish green, depends on environmental conditions; leaves are smaller than the species with a slight cupping tendency; summer leaf color is lighter green than the species; will probably mature around 1 1/2 to 2 1/2' and form a broad mound; originated as a chance seedling in a population of the species at Hines Wholesale Nursery, Houston, TX.

'Moyer's Red'—May be a real winner for southern gardens as it is a tall growing form with good cold weather red pigment formation in the leaves; a local Georgia nursery has been growing this and the winter foliage color is a glossy reddish with a tinge of purple; Raulston reported flowers and fruits are pinker and redder, respectively, than other forms and fruits color 1 to 2 months ahead of the other; fruits are held in tighter panicles than the species; 2' high and 1 1/2' wide after 3 years, will grow 6' high; Post Properties reported 'Moyer's Red' as less cold hardy.

'Nana' ('Pygmaea', 'Compacta')—Probably several clones have been selected under this umbrella; 'Nana' grows about 2 to 4' and forms a dense, stiff, leafy mound, again not as graceful as 'Harbour Dwarf', also minimal berry production; 'Compacta' may be synonymous with 'Harbour Dwarf', also minimal berry production, it may represent a form that is a scaled down version of the species growing 3 to 4' high; see under 'Compacta' above.

'Okame'—Like 'Atropurpurea Nana' with virus-free foliage, excellent uniform bright red foliage color early in season, will be mounded and compact like 'Atropurpurea Nana'.

'Pink Daze'—Compact to 5', pink-fruited form found on Georgia campus and named by author.

Plum Passion™ ('Monum')—New growth deep purplish red, deep green in summer, reddish purple in winter, narrow leaflets, moderate grower, 4 to 5' high, 3 to 4' wide.

'Pygmaea' ('Minima')—A reasonably tight mounded foliage mass with smaller species-like foliage, supposedly will grow 3' high and produce bright red cold weather foliage.

'Richmond'—Vigorous form with bright red fall–winter foliage, large panicles of red fruit, Raulston reported as similar to species, virus-free, from Duncan and Davies, New Zealand.

'Royal Princess'—Individual leaflets narrower and reduced in size compared to species producing a finer textured effect; large fruit panicles; Raulston mentioned it may grow to sizes approximating the species, 6 to 8'.

'San Gabriel' ('Kurijusi', 'Orihime')—A fine-textured form with blades extremely narrow creating a fine ferny appearance; I had a plant in the garden and was impressed by the textural qualities; unfortunately, -3°F eliminated it; will be a compact possibly mounded form, 1 to 2' high at landscape maturity; new growth reddish, then light blue-green, turning red-purple with cold weather; have seen listed as var. *filamentosa*.

'Town and Country'—Akin to 'Harbour Dwarf'; witnessed at J.C. Raulston Arboretum, did not appear remarkable, mother plant 2' by 4', heavy berry set, supposedly increased winter hardiness; introduced by Wolf Branch Nursery.

'Umpqua Chief'—Medium-sized, typical foliage, 3' high by 2' wide after 3 years, mature 5 to 7'.

'Umpqua Princess'—Smallest of the Umpqua series, typical foliage, after 3 years 2 1/2' high and 2' wide, mature at 3 to 5'.

'Umpqua Warrior'—Largest in habit with the biggest flowers and fruits, foliage and fruit panicle more open than previous, 4' high and 3' wide in 3 years, will grow 6 to 9', I assessed the Umpqua Series in January 1997 at J.C. Raulston Arboretum and believe that any good East-South Coast seedling is as good if not better.

'Variegata'—White variegation, weak, unstable.

'Wood's Dwarf'—Have seen this on enough occasions to provide a reasonable assessment, much like 'Atropurpurea Nana' but the foliage appears virus-free and develops good red winter color, may be the most compact of the dwarf forms, developed by Ed Wood when he was a student at Oregon State University, supposedly a compact seedling from a normal population, probably 2 to 2 1/2' high and wide at maturity.

'Yellow Fruited'—A yellow-fruited form has been described; again, akin to 'Alba'.

PROPAGATION: Seed germination specifications are variable, generally conceded that two years are required if seeds are fall planted; have read information that noted direct sowing of clean seed resulted in 65% germination, also a Georgia horticulturist collected seeds in January, cleaned and sowed with successful germination; David Sandrock, former undergraduate student at Georgia, conducted an interesting seed germination study by collecting fruits in March, April, May, removing seeds and sowing, in all cases maximum (70 to 80%) germination occurred after 6 to 8 weeks; cuttings are rooted after the growth has hardened using a variety of rooting compounds, an Alabama nursery uses 2500 ppm IBA + 1500 ppm NAA with good success; the largest breakthroughs have occurred in tissue culture and, commercially, numerous plants are being produced by this means; see Dirr and Heuser, 1987, for details.

ADDITIONAL NOTES: The Japanese have selected and named numerous dwarf and variegated cultivars with over 50 described. To my knowledge, Dr. Raulston had the best United States collection, much of which has been shared with the Atlanta Botanical Garden. Other cultivars mentioned in British literature include: 'Flora', 'Little Princess', and 'Longifolia'. Unusual report of a puppy suffering seizures from chewing on *Nandina* foliage, toxic principal was cyanide.

NATIVE HABITAT: China. Introduced 1804.

Neillia sinensis Oliv. — Chinese Neillia

FAMILY: Rosaceae

LEAVES: Alternate, simple, ovate, 2 to 4" long, 1 1/4 to 2 1/2" wide, long acuminate, coarsely toothed, or with small lobes that are again sharply toothed, essentially glabrous at maturity, rich green; petiole—1/2" long.

STEM: Slender, zig-zag, angled, brown, glabrous, exfoliating with age.

Neillia sinensis, (nēl'i-à sī-nen'sis), Chinese Neillia, is rare outside of botanical gardens and arboreta. It is small, 5 to 6'(10') high, rounded in stature, with refined foliage and delicate pink flowers making it worthy of wider use. The flowers are produced in a slender, nodding, 1 to 2 1/2" long terminal raceme in May. There are 12 to 20 flowers per raceme. Flowers on previous season's wood so prune after flowering. The foliage is a rich green and is not troubled by any insect or disease problems. It prefers a well-drained, moist soil but appears to be adapted to less than ideal conditions. The glabrous brown stems develop a peeling characteristic with age. The plant could be used for massing and perhaps bank plantings or as a filler in the shrub border. Have grown the plant in my Georgia garden for a number of years and am less than excited about performance. High heat may reduce growth. Have seen excellent specimens in the North. Realistically, the plant will never become a force in the marketplace. Central China. Introduced 1901. Zone 5 to 7. Cappiello reported tip dieback in Orono, ME.

A closely related species is **Neillia thibetica** Bur. & Franch. (*N. longiracemosa* Hemsl.), Tibet Neillia, which ranges from 3 to 6′ in height and has 2 to 6″ long slender terminal racemes bearing up to 60 rosy-pink flowers in May–June. Flowers more emphatic than *N. sinensis*. A graceful, arching habit. Western China. Introduced 1910. Zone 5 to 7(8). Also, **Neillia affinis** Hemsl., as I have observed it, is similar to *N. sinensis* with the nodding rose-pink racemes in late spring carried on a 6′ shrub after the leaves have emerged. China. Introduced 1908. Zone 6 to 7(8).

New to the author's vocabulary was **Neillia uekii** Nak., a 3 to 4′ high, compact, suckering shrub with white flowers. The Arnold Arboretum has a handsome planting at the end of Meadow Road. Flowered in May. Korea. Introduced 1906. Zone 6 to 7. In the wild, *Neillia* species grow in scrub and rocky places by streams.

Nemopanthus mucronatus (L.) Trelease — Mountain Holly, Northern Mountain Holly

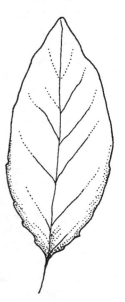

FAMILY: Aquifoliaceae
LEAVES: Alternate, simple, elliptic to oblong, 1 to 1 1/2″(2 1/2″) long, 3/4's as wide, mucronate, slightly toothed or entire, cuneate, dark blue-green above, gray-green beneath; petiole—1/4 to 1/2″ long.
BUDS: Ovoid, small, with about 3 outer scales.
STEM: Purplish when young, ash gray when old, glabrous.

Nemopanthus mucronatus, (nē-mō-pan′thus   mū-krō-na′tus), Mountain Holly, never found its way to the pages of the *Manual* until the current edition. Why? Familiarity breeds contempt or respect. The latter is the case. Through our many trips to Maine, the plant has become a friend. Walks, hikes, jogs . . . it shows up every-where, usually in quite moist areas, often forming thickets. Grows 6 to 10′ high. Flowers with 4 to 5 petals, about 1/5″ diameter, polygamo-dioecious, opening in May–June. The fluorescent, vermillion red, subglobose, 1/4 to 1/3″ diameter fruit is on a 1″ long pedicel. Fruits ripen in August–September (Maine) and although not overwhelming, like those of *Ilex verticillata*, are beautiful. In fact, I have observed *Nemopanthus* and *I. verticillata* growing side-by-side throughout Maine. The leaves turn yellow in autumn. For naturalizing in cold climate gardens, this is a worthwhile plant. Certainly not mainstream and not common in commerce even in New England nurseries. Nova Scotia to Ontario, Wisconsin and Virginia. Introduced 1802. Zone 4 to 6.

Nerium oleander L. — Oleander
(nē′ri-um ō-lē-an′dẽr)

FAMILY: Apocynaceae
LEAVES: Opposite or in whorls of 3 to 4, evergreen, simple, linear-lanceolate, 3 to 5″(8″) long, 1/2 to 3/4″ wide, apex acute, entire, leathery, dark green, with thick prominent midrib and short petiole.
STEM: Stout, green, glabrous, shining.

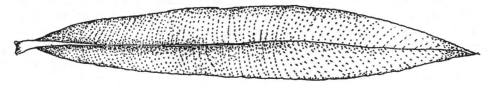

SIZE: 6 to 12′ high with a similar spread; often smaller in mid-South because of occasional freeze injury; to 20′ high in deep South; have seen 20′ specimens in Florida and along coast of Georgia.
HARDINESS: Zone 8 to 11, actually best in lower portion of Zone 8, below 15°F some foliar or stem damage is virtually guaranteed.
HABIT: Upright rounded bushy evergreen shrub; can be fashioned as a small tree in lower South; widely utilized in California, Arizona, New Mexico and coastal areas from South Carolina to Florida and Texas as massing plant, large shrub and small tree.

RATE: Medium to fast; actually quite weed-like in its growth pattern.

TEXTURE: Medium-fine.

LEAF COLOR: Dark green throughout seasons.

FLOWERS: Perfect, 5-petaled, each flower 1 to 1 1/2″(2″) across, borne in terminal cymes on new growth of the season from June–August and into mid-fall, fragrant or non-fragrant, single, hose-in-hose or true double, quite handsome in flower; colors range from white to cream, pink, lilac, red, carmine, purple, yellow, salmon, apricot, flesh, copper, and orange; have seen the plant in flower literally year-round, although summer is peak time, flowers on new growth of the season and after the 1983–84 winter numerous plants were killed to the ground along the Georgia coast yet came back and flowered the same year.

FRUIT: A 5 to 7″ long, slender pod (may be a follicle) that is present in various states of maturity through summer and into fall; not ornamental and probably should be removed; small fringed seeds remind of *Catalpa* seeds.

CULTURE: Easily transplanted, well-adapted to coastal areas; displays high salt and wind tolerance, prefers well-drained soil, withstands dry conditions, responds to fertility, used in Florida in sandy highway medium plant-ings which is an indication of its adaptability; needs protection in upper parts of Zone 8; sun or partial shade; tolerates polluted conditions; supposedly withstands marshy soils; killed to ground after exposure to 0°F.

DISEASES AND INSECTS: Scale, aphids, mealybug, oleander caterpillar, bacterial gall, nematodes.

LANDSCAPE VALUE: Excellent container or tub plant, foundations, borders, screens, groupings in coastal areas where wind and salt spray are problematic; displays good heat tolerance and could be used where there is a significant amount of reflected light; several years past I was traveling from San Francisco to Davis, CA and the highways were absolutely crammed with Oleander; it makes a great visual barrier and requires minimal maintenance.

CULTIVARS: Numerous, with 400 cultivars described; the following are representative of the color range and commercially available.

 ‘Algiers’—Single dark red, intermediate between Petite types and species, large shrub or small tree 10 to 12′ high.

 ‘Big Pink’—Hot pink, 3″ wide flowers.

 ‘Big Red’—Large, 2 1/2″ diameter, red flowers.

 ‘California Red’—Large red flowers, medium-sized shrub.

 ‘Calypso’—Showy, single cherry red flowers, a hardy form, to 10′ high.

 ‘Cardinal’—Single red flowers.

 Carnival™—Single, salmon-pink, burgundy edges, compact, 3 to 4′.

 ‘Casablanca’—Single, white, mounding shrub 4 to 6′ high.

 ‘Cherry Ripe’—Single, brilliant rose-red flowers.

 ‘Compte Barthelemy’—Double red flowers.

 ‘Double Pink’—Double pink flowers.

 ‘Double Red’—Double red flowers.

 ‘Double Yellow’—Double yellow flowers, to 10′.

 ‘Dwarf Red’—Single red flowers, semi-dwarf form, to 6′.

 ‘Eugenia Fowler’—Medium pink, hose-in-hose, fragrant flowers, to 10′.

 ‘Franklin D. Roosevelt’—Dark salmon with yellow throat, to 10′.

 ‘Garbing Mall’—Light pink flowers.

 ‘General Pershing’—Dark red flowers with light pink variegation.

 ‘Hardy Pink’—Single salmon-pink flowers; this is probably the cultivar that was planted on the University of Georgia campus; when I first arrived in Georgia this clone was growing somewhat successfully, i.e., it always suffered winter damage but regrew and flowered in summer; I received a true ‘Hardy Pink’ from Woodlanders, Aiken, SC and along with ‘Hardy White’ and Sugarland Red™, the supposed hardiest, trialed them at the University’s Botanical Garden; all suffer every year with ‘Hardy White’ the least cold adaptable followed by Sugarland™ and the hardiest being ‘Hardy Pink’, grows to 10′.

 ‘Hardy Red’—Single red flowers, to 10′, same as Sugarland Red™.

 ‘Hardy White’—Single, white flowers, to 10′.

 ‘Hawaii’—Single salmon-pink flowers with yellow throats, mounding shrub, 5 to 7′ high, frost sensitive.

 ‘Hot Pink’—Hot pink flowers.

 ‘Isle of Capri’—Single light yellow flowers, large mounding shrub, 5 to 7′ high.

 ‘Jannoch’—Deep red, single with long corolla teeth, to 10′.

 ‘Lady Kate’—Pinwheel-shaped light pink flowers with pale pink throats, to 10′.

 ‘Lane Taylor Sealy’—Large, light salmon with yellow throat, to 8′.

 ‘Little Red’—Dark red flowers, compact, 4 to 5′.

'Little White'—Single white, compact, 5'.

Marrakesh™ ('Moned')—Warm red flowers, grows 5 to 7' high and wide, from Monrovia.

'Matilda Ferrier'—Showy double yellow flowers, hardy, to 10'.

Morocco™ ('Monte')—Bright white flowers, grows 5 to 7' high and wide, from Monrovia.

'Mrs. Roeding'—Double salmon-pink flowers, grows 6 to 8' high, finer textured than species.

'Mrs. Runge'—Large, double, pink, fragrant flowers, variegated foliage, light green, yellow, cream, to 6'.

'North Carolina State Yellow'—Looked great on 1-20-97, accession #956567, yellow flowers.

'Peach Blossom'—Peach pink, fragrant flowers, medium-sized grower.

'Petite Pink'—Single, shell pink, dwarf, possibly 4 to 5' high.

'Petite Salmon'—Single, bright salmon-pink, dwarf, 4 to 5' high, both Petites Zone 9.

'Pink Beauty'—Large medium pink flowers, to 10'.

'Red Velvet'—Velvety dark red flowers.

'Ruby Lace'—Ruby red flowers, wavy-edged petals with a fringed lip, individual flowers large, up to 3",
     intermediate in growth habit, to 8'.

Shari D™—Buff yellow flowers with pink tinges, 6 to 8' high, Hines introduction.

'Shell Pink'—Light pink flowers.

'Sister Agnes'—Single, pure white flowers, vigorous, 10' in the garden, potential 15 to 20' at maturity, a
     hose-in-hose form is also listed.

'Snow Frost'—Cream flowers, survived −6°F.

'Sue Hawley Oakes'—Cream-yellow flowers with a yellow throat, to 8'.

Sugarland™ ('Sugarland Red')—Red, single, from Texas, supposedly more cold hardy, see notes under
     'Hardy Pink'.

'Tangier'—Single, soft medium pink flower, 4 to 6' high.

'Variegata'—Several forms, the one I know with pretty cream leaf variegation.

PROPAGATION: Seeds germinate without any pretreatment, the fringed seeds remind of catalpa; softwood
     cuttings root easily; cuttings collected in late July, given a 3000 ppm IBA dip, placed in peat:perlite under
     mist rooted well; hardwood cuttings treated with 2000 or 3000 ppm IBA rooted 100%, rooting in untreated
     controls was 93% for hardwood, 50% for softwood; work in Italy showed that May and September cuttings
     rooted better and faster (3 to 5 weeks) than those collected in February and November; plants can also
     be divided.

ADDITIONAL NOTES: Caution! All parts of the plant are poisonous. Green and dry wood contain the toxic
     principal. I continue to "look" for a true cold hardy clone whose foliage will not be injured until below 0°F.
     Observation tells me there is more to cold hardiness of this species than absolute low temperatures.
     Plants have looked in great health as late as February, a warm spell comes, sap moves, March cold snap
     and the foliage is obliterated. Leaf damage has occurred in Athens at 19°F in 1993, 7°F in 1994 and 13°F
     in 1995.

     See *The Garden* 122(7):488–491 (1997) for information on Pépinière Filippi Nursery in southeastern
     France at Mèze that holds the French National Collection of oleander cultivars with 120 extant. Also there
     is an International Oleander Society at P.O. Box 3431, Galveston, TX 77552-0431.

NATIVE HABITAT: Southern Asia, Mediterranean region.

Neviusia alabamensis A. Gray — Snow-wreath, Alabama Snow-wreath
(nev-i-ū′si-à al-a-bam-en′sis)

FAMILY: Rosaceae

LEAVES: Alternate, simple, ovate to ovate-oblong, 1 1/2 to 3 1/2" long, acute or acuminate,
     doubly serrate, those of shoots slightly lobed, nearly glabrous, medium green,
     pubescent on veins below; petiole—1/3" long, downy.

BUDS: Glabrate, rather small, solitary, sessile, ovoid, ascending, with about 6, somewhat
     keeled or striated scales.

STEM: Golden brown, puberulent, slender, long, somewhat zig-zag, decurrently ridged from
     the nodes; pith—relatively large, rounded, white, continuous.

SIZE: 3 to 6' high with an equal spread.

HARDINESS: Zone 4 to 8, growing at Morton Arboretum, Chicago, IL and Athens, GA.

HABIT: Upright deciduous shrub of somewhat straggly, open appearance with arching branches, eventually
     becoming rounded.

RATE: Slow to medium.

TEXTURE: Medium-fine in leaf; medium in winter.

FLOWERS: Perfect, apetalous, white, born in 3- to 8-flowered cymes in early to mid-May (early April, Athens); the stamens are the showy part of the flower and give a very feathery appearance to the plant, each 1″ diameter flower borne on a 3/4″ long pedicel with a mass of 1/4 to 1/3″ long stamens.

FRUIT: Achene, of no ornamental consequence.

CULTURE: Easily cultured; well-drained soil, ample moisture; full sun or partial shade; prune after flowering.

DISEASES AND INSECTS: None serious.

LANDSCAPE VALUE: A novelty item for the plantsman who wants something different; the flowers are quite showy and interesting; reminds of a petal-less spirea; I had this plant in my Illinois garden under the shade of a gross-feeding *Prunus serotina* and it performed reasonably well; it will show moisture stress if sited in an excessively dry location; otherwise it is a trouble-free shrub that could be used in the shrub border; it is a great plant with which to stump your plant material friends.

PROPAGATION: Roots easily from softwood cuttings; division of the plant works quite well; I have received dormant divisions from the Morton Arboretum and had good success by potting them and growing them on in the greenhouse.

ADDITIONAL NOTES: Anyone interested in additional information should refer to R.A. Howard, *Arnoldia* 36(2): 57–65 (1976). Also, Hinkley, *Pacific Horticulture* 51(3):43–46 (1990), discusses the plant.

    Neviusia cliftonii J.R. Shevock, B. Ertter & D.W. Taylor is a California native, extremely similar to *N. alabamensis* but supposedly has petals. As I observed a flowering plant at the Arnold, it had no petals.

NATIVE HABITAT: One species in Alabama. Found growing by W.S. Wyman in 1857 on cliff faces along the Black Warrior River. New populations have been discovered in Alabama, Arkansas, Tennessee, Mississippi and Georgia.

Nyssa sylvatica Marsh. — Black Tupelo, also known as Black Gum, Sour Gum, and Pepperidge.
(nis′à sil-vat′i-kà)

FAMILY: Nyssaceae

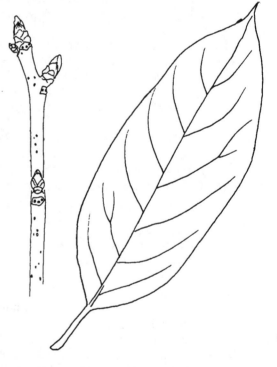

LEAVES: Alternate, simple, ovate, obovate or elliptic, 3 to 6″ long, 1 1/2 to 3″ wide, entire or remotely toothed, acute or obtusish, cuneate or sometimes rounded at base, lustrous dark green above, glaucescent beneath, pubescent on veins or glabrous at maturity; petiole—1/2 to 1″ long, often reddish.

BUDS: Imbricate, 1/8 to 1/4″ long, ovoid, vari-colored, yellow-brown to red-brown, smooth or slightly downy at tip, usually brownish on tip of scales.

STEM: Slender, glabrous or nearly so, grayish to light reddish brown, producing numerous short slow growing spurs; bundle traces 3, distinct, forming cavern-like entrance to stem; pith—chambered.

SIZE: 30 to 50′ in height with a spread of 20 to 30′ can grow to 100′ or more but this size is rare; national champion is 141′ by 93′ in Urania, LA.

HARDINESS: Zone 4 to 9.

HABIT: One of our most beautiful native trees; somewhat pyramidal when young with densely set branches, some of which are pendulous; in old age the numerous spreading and often horizontal branches form an irregularly rounded or flat-topped crown; I have seen 60′ specimens in Spring Grove, Cincinnati, OH which were distinctly upright-oval in outline; there is great variation in mature habit; the young trees take on the appearance of *Q. palustris*.

RATE: Slow to medium, 12 to 15′ over a 10 to 15 year period, easily accelerated with adequate water and fertility.

TEXTURE: Medium in leaf; medium in winter.

BARK: Dark gray, brown, brown-black, and at times almost black, broken into thick, irregular ridges which are checked across into short segments, giving it a block-like or alligator hide appearance; this trait is variable and some trees have an almost scaly bark, terrific variation in bark color, texture and form.

LEAF COLOR: Lustrous dark green in summer changing to fluorescent yellow to orange to scarlet to purple colors in the fall; one of our best, most consistent, and most beautiful trees in fall.

FLOWERS: Polygamo dioecious, appearing with the leaves, small, greenish yellow, female borne in 2- to 4-flowered axillary peduncled clusters; the male in many-flowered peduncled clusters, not ornamentally effective; the literature is not consistent on sexual characteristics and I have seen trees wholly male and wholly female; others with sporadic fruit set; polygamo-dioecious implies primarily dioecious but with the possibility of perfect (bisexual) flowers on the tree; this might explain limited fruit set sometimes observed on primarily male trees.

FRUIT: Oblong drupe, 3/8 to 1/2″ long, bluish black ripening late September through early October and eaten by many species of birds and mammals, on occasion fruits are present into November in the South.

CULTURE: Difficult to transplant because of taproot; move balled-and-burlapped in early spring; prefers moist, well-drained, acid (pH 5.5 to 6.5), deep soils; however, in the wild it is found on dry mountain ridges, burned over forest land, or abandoned fields, and in cold mountain swamps; does not tolerate high pH soils; full sun or semi-shade and sheltered locations from winds are preferred; prune in fall; Pair reported 4 to 6″ of growth per year over an 8 year period in Wichita, KS tests.

DISEASES AND INSECTS: Cankers, leaf spots, rust, tupelo leaf miner and scale; a summer leaf spotting results in irregular black lesions; most trees contract the disease which is quite disfiguring; selections need to be made for clean foliage; I had Georgia's former ornamental's pathologist isolate organisms from infected tissue, only secondary organisms *Pestalotia* sp. and *Triclodium* sp. were identified; Britton et al., *Plant Disease* 79:1187 (1995), reported anthracnose of *Nyssa sylvatica* was caused by *Colletotrichum acutatum*; *Botryosphaeria* sp. and *Phomopsis* sp. were occasionally isolated.

LANDSCAPE VALUE: Excellent specimen tree, acceptable street tree in residential areas, not for heavily polluted areas; outstanding summer and fall foliage and habit, lovely in a naturalized area; certainly one of the *best* and *most consistent* native trees for fall color.

CULTIVARS: None mentioned in last edition although several existed, primarily of European origin. Over the past 5 to 7 years, many individuals have made selections for improved form, summer and fall foliage. I selected a large, lustrous dark green leaf form with excellent red fall color, unfortunately, the leaf spotting is problematic. Still a respectable tree but not worthy of introduction. A few growers, however, offer it as the Dirr Clone, kind of poetic.

'Autumn Cascades'—A strongly weeping form with larger leaves and magnificent fall color, from Louisiana Nursery.

var. *biflora* (Walter) Sarg.—Swamp Tupelo is smaller, 40 to 50′, with smaller, leathery, oblanceolate leaves; female flowers are borne in pairs; national champion is 102′ by 57′ in Suffolk Co., VA.

Forum™ ('NXSXF')—Central dominant leader, conical shape, dense foliage, fast growth rate, lustrous dark green leaves, underside flat medium green, fall color is brilliant red with veins streaked with yellow, bark gray-brown with ridged-and-furrowed characters, parent tree 17′ by 8′, introduced by Tree Introductions, Inc., Athens, GA.

'Jermyns Flame'—Outstanding yellow, orange and red fall coloration, selected from plants in Hillier Arboretum in 1985.

'Miss Scarlet'—Selected for brilliant red fall color, summer leaves lustrous dark green, produces ornamental blue fruit, from Arborvillage, Holt, MO.

'Pendula'—Have one rather splaying irregular plant that was provided to me as 'Pendula'; have seen one other of similar stature.

'Red Jeanne'—Large, leathery lustrous dark green leaves with yellow orange fall color, sent to me by John Trexler for testing in Georgia, nice form as young tree, outstanding summer foliage but leaf spots and fall coloration is minimal in Zone 7b, in fact in early November 1996 I was evaluating the *Nyssa sylvatica* selections in my test plots and this along with the others did not compare in color with a seedling along the woods' edge.

'Sheffield Park'—Orange-red fall color, three weeks earlier than most tupelos, from Sheffield Park, England.

In the South, John Barbour, Bold Spring Nursery, has selected a dense, dark green-foliaged form with central leader. Mike Glenn, Select Trees, has three forms with similar attributes and Mike Hayman, Louisville, KY has a number of selections. They will not make it to market until 2000 or beyond.

PROPAGATION: Seeds exhibit moderate embryo dormancy and moist stratification for 60 to 90 days at 41°F is beneficial; I have raised numerous seedlings following this procedure. Generally not rooted from cuttings but a report in *The Plant Propagator* 14(4): 11–12 described a successful method. Shoots are forced in the greenhouse, 1 1/2″ long, 8000 ppm IBA talc, sand, 70°F bottom heat, mist, with rooting taking place in 2 to 3 weeks; cuttings are transplanted after 6 weeks and grow normally, rooting success of 95 to 100% was not unusual. Personally, I have had no success with the species from cuttings. Tissue culture has been successful, see *Proc. Florida State Hort. Soc.* 101:301–304 (1988). The newer selections are budded.

ADDITIONAL NOTES: I have a great love for *N. sylvatica* and do not adhere to the difficult transplanting philosophy. If container-grown and moved in small sizes it will reestablish quite well. Also, the knowledgeable nurserymen are root pruning ahead of transplanting to insure a proper root system. It responds well to water and fertilizer. I have seen it on rolling hills of southern Indiana, growing around fresh water ponds on Cape Cod and in a mixed forest association in the Piedmont of Georgia. Dunwiddie, *Rhodora* 93:347–360 (1991), reported several 300-year-old *Nyssa sylvatica* on Halfway Pond Island, MA. In all situations, the glory of its fall coloration always stands out above its other features. See Dirr, *Nursery Manager* 10(10):26, 28–29 (1994), for additional information on *Nyssa sylvatica*.

NATIVE HABITAT: Maine, Ontario, Michigan to Florida and Texas. Introduced before 1750.

RELATED SPECIES:

Nyssa aquatica L. — Water Tupelo

LEAVES: Alternate, simple, oblong-ovate or elliptic, 4 to 7″(12″) long, 2 to 4″ wide, acute or acuminate, rounded, subcordate or broadly tapered, entire or often serrated, dark green above, paler beneath and either glabrous or slightly pubescent; petiole—to 2″ long.

BUDS: Small and roundish.

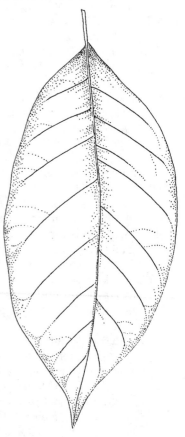

Nyssa aquatica, (nis'à à-kwat'i-kà), Water Tupelo, is one of the most characteristic of southern swamp trees and is found on sites which are periodically under water. The distinguishing differences from *N. sylvatica* include larger leaves to about 7″ long and larger fruit (about 1″ long) of reddish purple, finally dark blue or purple color with thin flesh and a deep, sharp, 8- to 10-ridged nutlet (endocarp). The trunk bulges conspicuously at the base but tapers rapidly to a long, clear trunk; the crown is rather narrow and open. The species grows 80 to 100′ high. National champion is 105′ by 56′ in Southampton Co., VA. The wood is commercially important, as is that of *N. sylvatica*. Grows in flood plain forests, swamps, ponds and lake margins, usually where bases are inundated for long periods. Growth rate of *N. aquatica* and *Taxodium distichum* in a permanently flooded area were higher than in areas with seasonal fluctuations, see *Amer. Midland Naturalist* 127:290–299 (1992) and *Can. J. For. Res.* 25:1084–1096 (1995). Native from Virginia to southern Illinois, Florida and Texas. Chiefly found in the Atlantic and Gulf Coastal Plains and Mississippi River Valley. Introduced before 1735. Zone 6 to 9.

Nyssa ogeche Marsh. — Ogeechee Tupelo, Ogeechee-lime

LEAVES: Alternate, simple, elliptic to obovate-oblong, 4 to 6″ long, acute to obtuse, entire, lustrous dark green and slightly pubescent above, pubescent or glabrous below, underside with pale grayish hue and soft to the touch; petiole—1/3 to 3/4″ long, sometimes 1 1/4″.

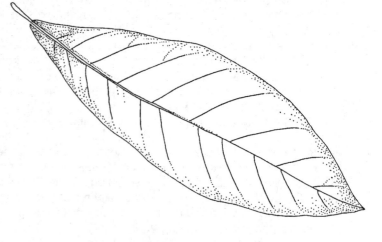

Nyssa ogeche, (nis'à ō-gē'chē), Ogeechee Tupelo, is a oval to round-headed, densely branched tree, 30 to 40′ high. Co-national champions are 93′ by 41′ and 81′ by 48′ in Apalachicola National Forest, FL. Most trees I experience in cultivation are smaller, 20 to 25′, with dense, dark green foliage. Fall color has been minimal in my experience. The 3/4 to 1 1/2″ long, 1/2 to 3/4″ wide, oblong to ovate drupes turn red at maturity, sometimes with only a red blush. The stone has paper wings extending through the pulp almost to the outer skin. Female trees are messy and fruit litters the ground. Several Georgia growers are growing this and it does not appear easy to manage under cultivation. Auburn University, in a 13 year study that evaluated over 200 trees, rated this in the top eight for superior performance, see *J. Arboriculture* 21:118–121 (1995). Although found in swamps, it tolerates dry soils. Serves as a major nectar source for bees. This, like *N. aquatica*, is a swamp species and follows the coastal plain from southeastern South Carolina, to Georgia and Florida. Introduced 1806. Zone 6 to 9.

Nyssa sinensis Oliv. — Chinese Tupelo
LEAVES: Alternate, simple, elliptic to oblong-lanceolate, 3 to 6″ long, tapering at both ends, dull dark green above, paler green and lustrous beneath; petiole—1/4″ long, hairy.

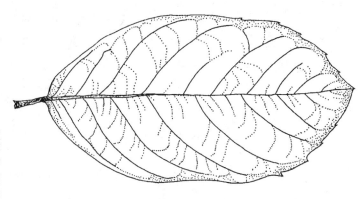

Nyssa sinensis, (nis′à sī-nen′sis), Chinese Tupelo, is a virtual recluse and, to my knowledge, is hidden in a select few gardens in the United States. A young plant at the J.C. Raulston Arboretum was gracefully pyramidal with a uniform branching habit. The Arnold Arboretum has successfully grown the plant. Foliage in late October was developing yellow and red hues. New growth bronze to plum purple turning flat dark green. Have seen good orange-red fall coloration. The species may grow 30 to 50′ high. A few Georgia nurseries are growing this. Leaves appear cleaner than *N. sylvatica* and do not contract the leaf spot. Difficult to guesstimate its possibilities in commerce. Perhaps best reserved for the collector. Central China. Introduced 1902. Zone 6 to 9.

Orixa japonica Thunb.

FAMILY: Oleaceae
LEAVES: Alternate, simple, obovate to oblanceolate, 2 to 5″ long, 1 to 2″ wide, obtuse, cuneate, finely crenulate or entire, lustrous bright green, with pellucid dots, glabrous, highly aromatic, almost sickenly so, when crushed; petiole—1/3″ long.

Orixa japonica, (ôr-ix′à jà-pon′i-kà), is a mounded, spreading, 6 to 8′ high shrub. Constitution is dense and the most familiar plants to me reside in the Arnold Arboretum. The plants have performed well over my years of observation. Leaves turn soft yellow in fall. Flowers are dioecious, 4-parted, males in short racemes from axils of previous season's wood, green, 1/4″ wide, on pubescent pedicels. Females are borne singly. Fruit is composed of 4 compressed, one-seeded (seed round and black) carpels, brown, about 3/4″ diameter. Performs best in well-drained, acid, organic-laden soil in partial shade. The Arnold's plant is growing in partial shade in dry soil. European literature indicated it was indifferent to soil type. Used in Japan as a hedge plant. 'Variegata' has cream-white margined leaves. Japan. Cultivated 1870. Zone (5)6 to 7. Successfully grown at Morton Arboretum, Lisle, IL.

Osmanthus heterophyllus (G. Don.) P.S. Green [formerly *O. ilicifolius* (Hassk.) Hort. ex Carr.]
— Holly Tea Olive, Holly Osmanthus, False-holly
(oz-man′thus het-ēr-ō-fil′us)

FAMILY: Oleaceae
LEAVES: Opposite, simple, evergreen, elliptic or ovate to elliptic-oblong, 1 to 2 1/2″ long, 1 to 1 1/2″ wide, spiny-pointed, cuneate or broad-cuneate, with 1 to 4 pairs of prominent spiny teeth, rarely entire, leathery, lustrous dark green above, yellowish green and veined (reticulate) beneath, glabrous; petiole—1/2″ long or less.
NOTE: In the adult stage the leaves at the top of the plant become oval or ovate and essentially entire; have noticed that mature specimens are largely entire.
BUDS: Multiple, brownish purple, small, 1/16 to 1/8″ long, stacked 2 to 3, one above the other, glabrous, borne at a 45° angle to stem.
STEM: More slender than *O.* × *fortunei* and *O. fragrans*, light ash to straw brown, compressed at nodes, glabrous, extremely small raised lenticels; pith—watery green, solid, ample.

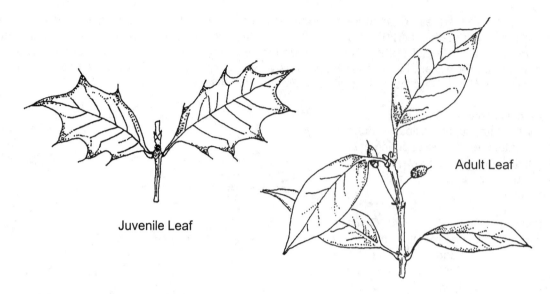

Juvenile Leaf

Adult Leaf

SIZE: 8 to 10′ (up to 20′) in height, spread slightly less; old plants on the Georgia campus are 12 to 15′ high and slightly wider; in youth the habit is distinctly upright; I continue to chase this species around the South and in Aiken, SC large +20′ specimens are common; discovered a 24′ high specimen in Athens; easily maintained at specific heights by proper pruning.

HARDINESS: Zone (6)7 to 9; more cold hardy than I or the literature gave credit, probably a respectable Zone 6; have observed excellent plants on University of Delaware campus at Newark; also a plant growing at F.W. Schumacher, Sandwich, MA.

HABIT: Dense, upright-oval to rounded evergreen shrub of impenetrable constitution.

RATE: Slow to medium.

TEXTURE: Medium throughout the seasons.

LEAF COLOR: Lustrous dark green above, yellow green beneath.

FLOWERS: In general, *Osmanthus* species may be perfect, polygamous, or dioecious; the flowers of this species are white, 4-petaled, 2 stamens, 1/4″ across with the petals reflexed, exceedingly fragrant, borne 4 to 5 together in axillary cymes during late September–October into early November. The flowers are largely hidden by the foliage but the fragrance is overpowering; this species is dioecious; flowers after *O.* × *fortunei*, generally mid to late October into November on the Georgia campus, my fascination with *Osmanthus* now borders on obsession and I chase about trying to better understand reproductive characteristics; examined flowers of this species have been bisexual and male on the same plant; the pistil reminds of a bowling pin so is easy to notice; yellow stamens are in two's on either side of pistil, absent or by themselves.

FRUIT: Seldom seen in cultivation; the fruit is a slender, ovoid, 3/8 to 1/2″ long, bluish purple-black to black drupe with stone scarcely ribbed; have seen fruits on campus plants, not showy; ripen in fall of the year following flowering.

CULTURE: Easily transplanted from containers; prefers fertile, moist, well-drained, acid soil but is adapted to higher pH soils; will withstand heavy pruning; seems to display a fair degree of urban tolerance, full sun (may discolor slightly) to medium shade; more shade tolerant than given credit.

DISEASES AND INSECTS: None serious.

LANDSCAPE VALUE: Borders, screens, hedge, formal specimen, by walks and entrances; this is the hardiest of the Asiatic *Osmanthus* and the best for the upper South and northern areas along the coast but is extremely spiny and not as handsome as *O.* × *fortunei*; makes an excellent screen or barrier planting.

CULTIVARS: In most cases, the variegated forms are less cold hardy than the species.

　　'Aureomarginatus'—Leaves margined with yellow, green in center, not as showy as above, leaves also smaller than 'Aureus', plant grows 10′ or more, was able to locate one for the Dirr garden.

　　'Aureus' ('Ogon')—Mixed this with 'Aureomarginatus' in the last edition, definitely two distinct plants, 'Aureus' has golden yellow leaves that fade to yellow-green and green, leaves strongly spiny in youth not unlike 'Gulftide', grows slower and smaller than species, kind of pretty in the right location.

　　'Fastigiata'—Upright form, somewhat open as a young plant, leaves like 'Gulftide', have only seen on one occasion and finally brought a plant to the Dirr garden that quickly passed away, this upright form may be the same as 'Head-Lee Fastigiate' which was derived from a "witches' broom," compact, upright habit, purple new growth, from Head-Lee Nursery, plants I observed at the nursery were impressive.

'Goshiki'—Offers green flecking on a gold, maturing to cream background, new growth is pink- to bronze-tinged and leaves mature to the green, gold and cream collage, mature leaves are striking and a plant in our shade house (55% saran shade) has held the excellent color all summer; in fact, plants growing in full sun at Brookside Gardens, Wheaton, MD appeared tired and bleached; some shade, particularly in Southeast, is warranted.

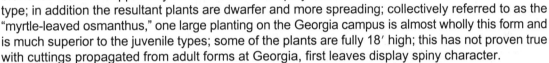

'Goshiki'

'Gulftide'—A compact, upright form of the species with extremely glossy green foliage and prominent spiny margins and a slight twist; introduced by Gulfstream Nursery; have seen plants 10 to 15′ high; leaves become progressively less spiny with maturity of the plant; more cold hardy than the species; I examined flowering specimens on October 26 at the University's Botanical Garden and recorded both male and bisexual flowers on the same plant; the preponderance of flowers are male.

'Kembu'—Leaves splashed, streaked and margined with cream.

'Latifolius Variegatus'—Leaves broader than 'Variegatus'.

'Myrtifolius'—Perhaps a misnomer for this represents plants that have been propagated from the adult portion with almost entire, narrowly-oval, 1 to 2″ long leaves; cuttings of the adult branches root and supposedly do not revert to the spiny-leaved type; in addition the resultant plants are dwarfer and more spreading; collectively referred to as the "myrtle-leaved osmanthus," one large planting on the Georgia campus is almost wholly this form and is much superior to the juvenile types; some of the plants are fully 18′ high; this has not proven true with cuttings propagated from adult forms at Georgia, first leaves display spiny character.

'Gulftide'

'Purpureus' ('Purpurascens')—Young leaves are black-purple and appear to have been dipped in tar; later green with purple tinge; considered the hardiest of all the forms of *O. heterophyllus*; raised at Kew in 1880; Raulston noted color was best in full sun in winter to early spring; rather striking but maturing to dark green.

'Rotundifolius'—A slow-growing, dwarf shrub with rigid, leathery, simple, evergreen, obovate, 1 1/2 to 2″ long, 1 to 1 1/4″ wide leaves, unique for margins are angled off to present a geometric pattern, lustrous dark green above, pale beneath, petiole 1/4″ long; grows 4 to 5′(8′) high, flowers are fragrant and often bisexual; slightly less cold hardy than the species

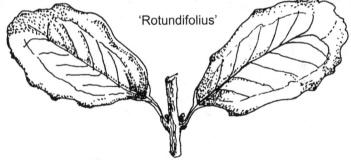

'Rotundifolius'

for leaves were browned on a protected plant while the species was not injured; seedlings grown from this cultivar were typical of the species with extremely spiny margins.

'Sasaba'—A plant handler's worst nightmare with deeply cut, incised, sharp, spiny, stiff, lustrous dark green leaves, will grow 3 to 5′ high, but is open and loose in outline, have seen plants flowering in early November.

'Variegatus'—Quite handsome shrub for color contrast; the leaves margined with creamy white; slower growing than the species and perhaps more upright in habit but equally dense; leaves not as stiffly spiny as the species; 8 to 10′ only after many years; have seen it in full sun where it showed no burning; interestingly, the leaves were completely killed at −8°F but the stem and buds were not injured; effective in a container for the patio and terrace.

'Sasaba'

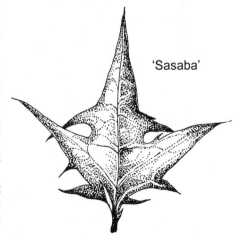

PROPAGATION: Cuttings root readily; a nurseryman told me that cuttings should be collected just as new growth hardens in late spring or early summer. Rooting times are generally quite long with 3 to 4 months the norm. A Georgia nursery roots *O. × fortunei* and *O. fragrans* in July–August, 8000 ppm IBA talc, bark-sand, mist with good success. Cuttings are taken from young container-grown plants. Blazich and Acedo, *J. Environ. Hort.* 7:133–135 (1989) rooted untreated *O. heterophyllus* 'Ilicifolius' in September and February at 92 and 81%, respectively.

In the pat 7 to 8 years, I have accumulated significant data relative to rooting *O. heterophyllus* and *O. × fortunei*. Ms. Andrea Southworth, former graduate student, conducted a timing study, with *O. × fortunei* and found that June to August cuttings, without IBA rooted 80% or greater in 3 perlite:1 peat under mist. *Osmanthus* are slow rooters and 12 to 15 weeks may be necessary. *Osmanthus heterophyllus* follows a similar trend. Korean work reported 93 to 90% rooting of young green wood of *O. fragrans* and *O. asiaticus*, respectively, *J. Korean For. Soc.* 75:19–24 (1986).

ADDITIONAL NOTES: Worthwhile paper, by the author, covering the *Osmanthus* species and cultivars appeared in *Nursery Management and Production* 11(7):14–15, 98–103 (1995).

NATIVE HABITAT: Japan, introduced 1856 by Thomas Lobb. Sargent describes *O. heterophyllus* as attaining the dimensions of a tree approaching 30′ in height and one foot or more in diameter.

RELATED SPECIES:

Osmanthus americanus (L.) A. Gray — Devilwood, Wild-olive

LEAVES: Opposite, simple, ever-green, elliptic, lanceolate-ovate, oblanceolate, 2 to 4 1/2″ long, 3/4 to 1 1/2″ wide, abruptly acute, cuneate, entire, leathery, lustrous dark olive green above, pale green beneath, prominent protruding midvein, laterals obscure, glabrous; petiole—1/4 to 3/4″ long.

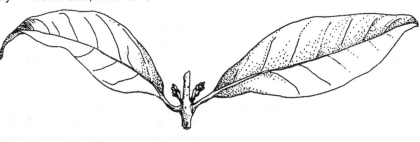

BUDS: Imbricate, 1/4″ long, greenish brown, in upper leaf axils flower buds are preformed and elongated.

STEM: Stout, squarish, glabrous, green finally gray-brown, dotted with numerous pale lenticels; pith—white, continuous, ample.

Osmanthus americanus, (oz-man′thus à-mer-i-kā′nus), Devilwood, is by no means a common landscape shrub but deserves consideration in southern and perhaps northern gardens. Most people would not recognize it as an *Osmanthus* because the leaves are entire. The habit is open and loose (15 to 25′ high), an attribute that separates it from other species. National champion is 46′ by 27′ in Putnam County, FL. The dark olive green leaves are handsome throughout the seasons but do lighten (yellow-green) in sun and exposed locations. In the axils of the upper leaves, paniculate inflorescences are present from fall until late March–April (Athens) when the white, fragrant, dioecious flowers open. Have recorded peak dates as early April, 1991; April 10–20, 1994; and April 13, 1996. The ovoid-rounded, 1/2″ long, dark blue-purple, single-stoned drupe matures in September and may persist into spring of the next year. Cultural requirements are similar to *O. heterophyllus*. Southern nurseries are producing this in containers and also in the field. Can be used in naturalized situations. Handsome grouping behind the first green at the Augusta National Golf Course that is in full flower during the Masters. North Carolina to Florida and Mississippi. Found along swamp margins, hammocks and borders of streams. Cultivated 1758. Listed as Zone 6 to 9(10) but have seen it as far north as Cincinnati, OH and Boston, MA. The most cold hardy *Osmanthus* species and some selections have withstood -20 to -25°F. A related species, **Osmanthus megacarpus** Small, Scrub Tea Olive, has larger fruits, up to 1 to 1 1/4″ long. It is native to the sand hills of Florida.

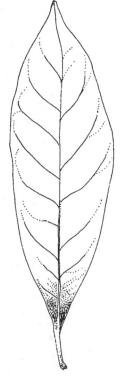

Osmanthus armatus Diels., (oz-man′thus är-mä′tus), is a species I have seen on rare occasions and have been impressed by the thick, rigid, lustrous dark green, 3 to 6″ long leaves edged with stout, often hooked, spiny teeth, up to 10 per margin. The spiny margins diminish or disappear as the plant matures. Veins are sunken into the leaf and appear as tributaries feeding into the midrib. The white flowers are sweetly fragrant and occur in small clusters from the leaf axils in autumn (late October, Athens). The two plants I examined were males. Fruits are egg-shaped, dark violet, 3/4″ long drupes. The plant develops into a large 8 to 15′ high, thickly branched shrub. A large, approximately 6 to 10′ high, specimen exists at the J.C. Raulston Arboretum, Raleigh, NC. Will prosper in dense shade or full sun. Native to western China where Wilson noted it growing on humus-clad cliffs and boulders, either in dense shade or full sun. Introduced by E.H. Wilson in 1902. Hardiness is unknown but Zone 7 to 8 is guaranteed with movement into Zone 6.

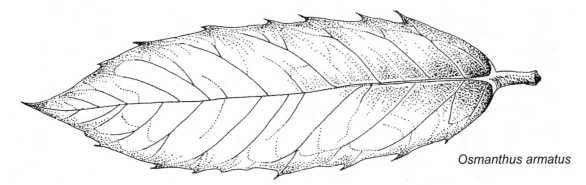

Osmanthus armatus

Osmanthus × **burkwoodii** (Burkw. & Skipw.) P. Green (formerly × *Osmarea burkwoodii* Burkw. & Skipw.)
LEAVES: Opposite, simple, evergreen, ovate to ovate-elliptic, 1 to 2″ long, narrow acute, cuneate-rounded, with serrulate marginal teeth, perhaps entire on mature plants, lustrous dark green above, paler beneath, glabrous; petiole—1/8″ long.
STEM: Slender, gray-brown, glabrous; pith—green.
FLOWERS: White, 3/8″ across, 4-lobed, corolla split half the length, fragrant, two yellow stamens, late February–March (Athens).

Osmanthus × *burkwoodii*, (oz-man′thus berk-wood′ē-ī), is a hybrid of *O. delavayi* × *O. decorus*, of compact habit, 6 to 10′ high, with lustrous dark green, finely toothed leaves. The base of the leaf is round and entire. The fragrant, white flowers appear in April–May. The foliage justifies use of the species. Probably hardy into Zone 6 to 8. The hybrid was raised by the English nurserymen Burkwood and Skipwith in the late 1920's. They are also responsible for two other notable garden shrubs: *Daphne* × *burkwoodii* and *Viburnum* × *burkwoodii*.

Osmanthus decorus (Boiss. & Bal.) Kasapl., (oz-man′thus de-côr′us), formerly *Phillyrea decorus* Boiss. & Bal., is a 5 to 10′ high, slightly wider, rigidly branched shrub that carries 2 to 5″ long, 1/2 to 1 3/4″ wide, oval, generally entire-margined leaves of firm, almost hard, texture. Leaves are flat to glossy dark green above, pale beneath, with short, 1/4 to 1/2″ long petioles. Veins are buried in leaf tissue like those of *O. armatus*. Foliage reminds of an evergreen privet. The pure white, fragrant, 1/3″ diameter flowers occur in dense axillary clusters in spring. The oval, 1/2″ long, reddish, finally purplish black fruits are borne on slender 1/2″ long stalks in September. The bold, thick-textured leaves are particularly attractive. Native to the southeastern coast of the Black Sea. Introduced in 1866. Zone (7)8 to 9?

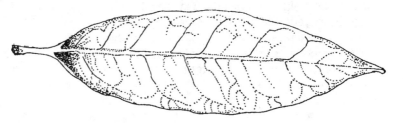

Osmanthus delavayi Franch., (oz-man′thus del-av′ā-ī), has many garden virtues that include 1/2 to 1″ long, lustrous dark green, ovate to oval, strongly toothed leaves, abundant fragrant, white flowers in April and a compact constitution, 6 to 10′ high and wide. Flowers are borne in terminal and axillary 4- to 8-flowered cymes; each flower about 1/2″ long and 1/2″ wide with 4 reflexed lobes. Fruits are roundish, egg-shaped, 1/2″ long, blue-black drupes. The more I see this handsome species, the more enamored I become. At Lanhydrock Gardens, Cornwall, England, I experienced 15′ high and wide shrubs in full flower during late March. Recently, one of my

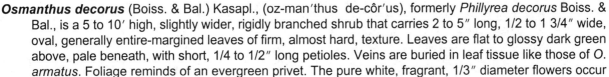

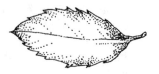

former students, Terry Tatum of Wildwood Farms in Madison, GA, showed me a specimen that was successful in her garden. This plant has potential for southeastern gardens and I estimate Zone 7 hardiness. Native to Yunnan and Szechuan provinces of China. Introduced through Abbé Delavay in 1890. Zone 7 to 10.

Osmanthus × *fortunei* Carr. — Fortune's Osmanthus

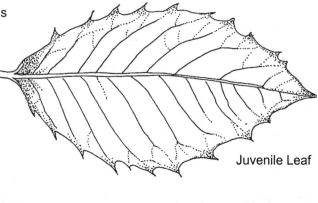

Juvenile Leaf

LEAVES: Opposite, simple, evergreen, 2 1/2 to 4″ long, 1 1/2 to 2″ wide, oval or slightly ovate, taper-pointed and spine-tipped, cuneate, margins with up to 10 or 12 triangular, 1/6″ long, spine-tipped teeth on each side, leathery, lustrous dark green; some leaves especially those in the upper reaches of the plant display an adult condition and have no marginal spines (teeth); petiole—1/4″ long.

I never believed leaf size in the literature and consistently measured leaves, buds, etc. for the *Manual*. Random sampling of leaves of *O.* × *fortunei* resulted in a range from 2.05 to 3.85″ by 0.85 to 2.175″.

BUDS: Imbricate, small, 1/8″ long, greenish brown, superposed, glabrous, emerge at 45° angle to stem.

STEM: Moderate, gray, glabrous, dotted with brown, vertical lenticels, compressed at nodes; pith—solid, green, ample.

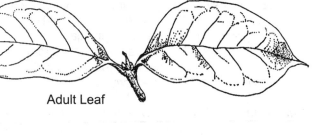

Adult Leaf

Osmanthus × *fortunei*, (oz-man′thus fôr-tū′nē-ī), Fortune's Osmanthus, is a hybrid between *O. heterophyllus* and *O. fragrans*. It tends to be intermediate between the two parents in most characteristics. It is a large, dense, oval-rounded shrub that matures between 15 to 20′. It can be easily restrained at about any height. Two massive specimens on the Georgia campus are 20 to 25′ high and wide and look like dark green haystacks. The 1/4 to 1/3″ diameter, 4-petaled, exceedingly fragrant, white flowers are produced in axillary cymes in October–November; mid to late October has been the normal flowering period in Athens. Have recorded peak flowering dates of October 16, 1993 and October 6, 1994 before those of *O. heterophyllus* show color. Quite hardy compared to *O. fragrans* and preferable to that species in the upper South. Introduced from Japan in 1856. According to Bean the early introduction into Britain was a male. This is true for the American introduction as all flowers examined have been male. Apparently this hybrid was reconstituted in California where a clone was given the name 'San

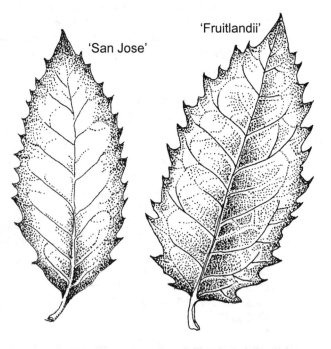

'San Jose'

'Fruitlandii'

Jose'. Over the past few years I have looked at sufficient 'San Jose' to know the form is different from typical *O.* × *fortunei*. The leaves are longer, slightly more narrow and the spines more abundant and longer. Another selection 'Fruitlandii', along with 'San Jose', now grows in the Dirr garden. Comparisons indicate they are similar but possibly not exact phenotypes. 'Fruitlandii' is described as more compact and cold hardy than *O.* × *fortunei*. I have doubts about both claims. Flowers of 'Fruitlandii' are pale cream-yellow compared to white of *O.* × *fortunei*. 'Variegatus' is described as having broad white marginal serrations. *Osmanthus* × *fortunei* is quite common in southern gardens. Displays greater vigor than *O. heterophyllus* and, in my mind, is a better landscape plant. Tolerates full sun and pine shade and remains dark green, full and dense.

Osmanthus fragrans Lour. — Fragrant Tea Olive

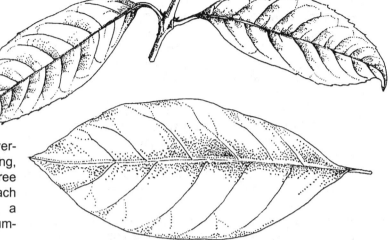

LEAVES: Opposite, simple, evergreen, oblong-lanceolate to
elliptic, 2 to 4″(5″) long, long
acuminate, cuneate, finely
dentate or entire, leathery,
lustrous dark green above,
lighter, glabrous and distinctly veined below; petiole—1/4 to 1/2″ long.

BUDS: Superposed in the axils of the evergreen leaves, usually 1/8″ long,
smaller on lower buds, often three
(sometimes 2) stacked on top of each
other, uppermost largest with a
crooked acuminate apex, small number of visible scales, perhaps two,
green, upper bud developing into a shoot, the new growth of which is reddish purple, buds positioned at
a 45° angle to central axis.

STEM: Green in youth, glabrous, gray-green to gray with age, often developing vertical fissures in outer
epidermal layer(s), small gray-brown lenticels, glabrous; pith—watery green, solid, ample.

Osmanthus fragrans, (oz-man′thus frã′granz), Fragrant Tea Olive, is the least cold hardy of the species
presented. In coastal areas it makes a large shrub or small tree, 20 to 30′ high; further inland it may be
damaged by low temperatures and thus reduced in size. The leaves which are larger than those of O.
× *fortunei* are not as coarsely serrated and may be entire. The small white flowers are the most fragrant
of the group and it has been stated that one or two of them will fill a fair-sized room with sweet perfume.
My first contact with the species came in September, 1979 at the American Camellia Society Head-
quarters in Fort Valley, GA where it was in flower. I have also observed flowers in the spring, around early
to mid-April in the Athens area. Probably grows too large for the average landscape but is certainly worth
considering where hardy and space permits. Would make a fine container plant for use on the patio or
near entrances. Was severely injured in Athens area after exposure to 0°F. Plants were generally
defoliated and young stems injured.

My affinity for this species has resulted in the collection of nine clones that are discussed in the
cultivar section. In the Athens-Atlanta area, the plant is more often multi-stemmed and shrubby with
potential to 10 to 15′. A cold winter may intercede and kill shoots to some degree. Flowers appear over
such a great time frame and are so fragrant that to not try the plant is to cheat one's garden. Bonnie
and I have them by the entrance to our porch and by every walking path through the garden. Flowers
have been clocked from September 13, 1994 and 1996 through October with sporadic flowers on warm
winter days into March. On February 21, 1997, numerous flowers were ready to burst forth on plants
in our garden.

CULTIVARS:

'Apricot Gold'—Produces fragrant, apricot-gold flowers.

f. *aurantiacus* (Mak.) P. Green—Pale orange-colored flowers, a beautiful form, open in fall, Zone 7.

'Butter Yellow'—Produces many fragrant, butter yellow flowers.

'Conger Yellow'—Offers fragrant, yellow flowers and showy green leaves.

'Fudingzhu'—Supposedly flowers continuously for nine months, flowers cream-white, abundant,
terrifically fragrant, a worthy commercial form, Zone 7.

'Hunter's Creek'—A large, well-formed, rounded, 20′ tall shrub with fragrant flowers.

var. *latifolia*—Light cream-yellow, fragrant flowers borne solitary or in clusters, June–September, 1/2″
long, bluish fruits, Zone 8, Piroche.

'Live Oak Gold'—Produces fragrant, golden-yellow flowers and attractive foliage.

'Nanjing's Beauty'—This is a new name for 'Fudingzhu'.

'Orange Supreme'—Showy, bright orange, fragrant flowers on a well-shaped, evergreen framework.

var. *semperflorens*—Continual flowers, hardiest of *O. fragrans* varieties, some surviving -15° F, see
J. Plant Resources Environ. 5:18–22 (1996).

var. *thunbergii*—Silver Osmanthus, is similar to var. *aurantiacus* except the flowers are light yellow.

'T-Tower'—A perfect, small, evergreen tree with white flowers.

China, Japan, Himalayas. Introduced in 1856. Zone 7 to 10.

Osmanthus serrulatus Rehd.

LEAVES: Opposite, simple, evergreen, elliptic-
    ovate, 1 3/4 to 3 1/4″ long, 1/2 to 1″ wide,
    acuminate, cuneate, with firm plastic saw-like
    teeth, 26 to 30 per margin on large leaves,
    lustrous dark green, paler and reticulate
    below, glabrous; petiole—1/4″ long.

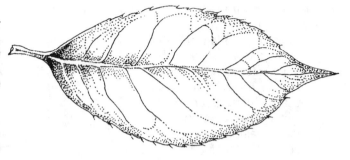

Osmantus serrulatus, (oz-man′thus ser-ū-lā′tus),
    is another rare shrub (6 to 12′) with lustrous
    dark green, leathery textured, strongly ser-
    rate leaves. Like *O. armatus*, leaves on mature plants may become entire. The fragrant, white flowers are
produced 4 to 9 per cluster from the leaf axils in spring. Fruits are oblong, blue-black drupes. The slow
growth would limit commercial use. Hardiness is unknown but I suspect Zone (7)8 to 9.

Osmanthus yunnanensis (Franch.) P. Green (*O. forrestii* Rehd.), (oz-man′thus yū-na-nen′sis), is, to my
    knowledge, the largest of the *Osmanthus* species with specimens 40′ tall in Cornwall, England. The dark
    green, firm-textured leaves range from 3 to 8″ long. Leaves may have up to 30 teeth per margin or be
    entire. The sweet flowers range from creamy white to pale yellow and appear in spring. Fruits are egg-
    shaped, 1/2 to 1″ long and deep bluish purple with a waxy bloom. My only exposure to the species has
    occured in English gardens, most notably Hidcote, where a 20 to 25′ tree begged for identification.
    Introduced from Yunnan, China in 1923 by George Forrest. Cold hardiness is minimal and a Zone 8 to 9
    designation is appropriate.

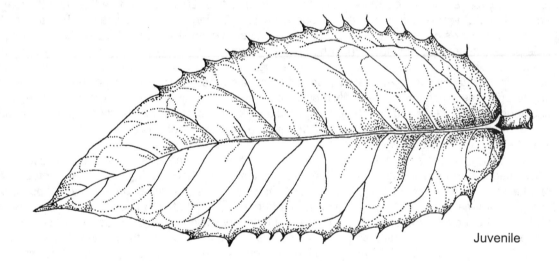

Juvenile

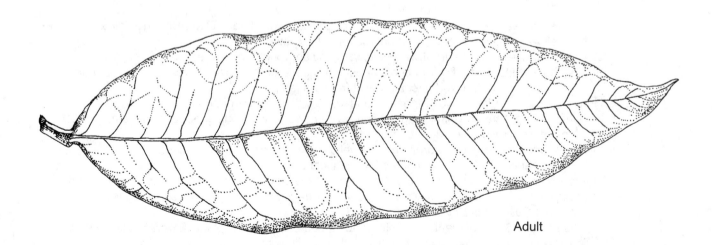

Adult

Ostrya virginiana (Mill.) K. Koch — American Hophornbeam, also known as Ironwood.
(os'tri-à vĕr-jin-ē-ā'nà)

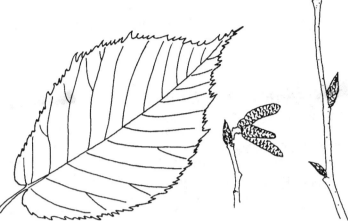

FAMILY: Betulaceae

LEAVES: Alternate, simple, oval-lanceolate, 2 to 5″ long, half as wide, acuminate, rounded or heart-shaped, dark green and hairy on midrib and between veins above, paler and more pubescent beneath, sharply and doubly serrate, veins forking at ends; petiole—1/4″ long, pubescent.

BUDS: Imbricate, small, 1/8 to 1/4″ long, narrowly ovate, pointed, glabrous or finely downy, green to brown, slightly gummy especially within, strongly divergent, terminal absent; scales longitudinally striate.

STEM: Slender, dark reddish brown, often zig-zag, for the most part smooth and shining.

FRUIT: Nutlet, enclosed in hop-like sac; staminate catkins, abundantly present, usually in 3's, good winter identification characteristics.

SIZE: A small tree averaging 25 to 40′ in height and 2/3's to equal that in spread; can reach 60′ but this is seldom attained; national champion is 74′ by 111′ in Grand Traverse Co., MI.

HARDINESS: Zone 3b to 9.

HABIT: Very graceful small tree with many horizontal or drooping branches usually forming a rounded outline, somewhat pyramidal in youth.

RATE: Slow, probably 10 to 15′ over a 15 year period.

TEXTURE: Medium-fine in leaf, medium in winter.

BARK: Grayish brown, often broken into narrow, longitudinal strips which are free at each end.

LEAF COLOR: Dark green in summer changing to yellow in the fall, seldom effective and falling early.

FLOWERS: Monoecious, male catkins usually grouped in 3's and visible throughout winter, each about 1″ long; female visible in April.

FRUIT: A 1/3″ long nut(let), enclosed in an inflated, membranous, hairy, ovate, 3/4 to 1″ long involucre and resembling the fruit of hops, hence, the name Hophornbeam; entire infructescence 1 1/2 to 2 1/2″ long, 2/3 to 1 1/2″ wide; hairs on fruits get stuck in fingers, skin, be careful when handling fruits.

CULTURE: Transplant balled-and-burlapped or from a container in early spring into a cool, moist, well-drained, slightly acid soil; often found in the wild growing in rather dry, gravelly or rocky soil; full sun or partial shade; prune in winter or early spring; somewhat slow to reestablish after transplanting.

DISEASES AND INSECTS: None serious, "witches' broom" occurs on occasion and results in broomy masses of small, bunchy, twiggy growths.

LANDSCAPE VALUE: Handsome medium-sized tree for lawns, parks, golf courses, naturalized areas, and possibly streets; the species has performed well in city plantings and very narrow tree lawns; once established it makes excellent growth; have seen it looking tired and tatty in late summer.

PROPAGATION: Seeds have an internal type of dormancy which is difficult to overcome; warm followed by cold seems to be the best treatment; one study reported that seeds collected fresh and sown immediately did not germinate, those given 3 months cold stratification germinated 2%, 3 months warm stratification followed by 3, 4, or 5 months cold produced 81, 92 and 92% germination, respectively.

ADDITIONAL NOTES: *Ostrya virginiana* is an attractive, small to medium-sized tree that the American nursery industry has never pursued. In the wild, it grows on the drier slopes of woodlands where it exists as an understory species. Interestingly, in the University's Botanical Garden it is abundant on the slopes above the Oconee River flood plain and is totally absent in the areas that are periodically flooded. At this sharp juncture, *Carpinus caroliniana*, American Hornbeam, becomes the dominant understory plant and even grows on the river banks where its roots literally dangle their apices in the cool water.

NATIVE HABITAT: Cape Breton, Ontario to Minnesota, south to Florida and Texas. Introduced 1690.

RELATED SPECIES: I would be hard pressed to separate ***Ostrya carpinifolia*** Scop., (os-tri'à kär-pi-ni-fo'li-à), European Hornbeam, and ***Ostrya japonica*** Sarg., (os-tri'à jà-pon'i-kà), Japanese Hornbeam, from the above species without close scrutiny. During sabbatical, I admired one particularly handsome specimen of *O. virginiana* only to find out that upon checking the label it was *O. japonica*. The first species differs from *O. virginiana* by virtue of never having any glands on the hairs of the stems. *Ostrya japonica* has fewer veins (9 to 12) compared to 12 to 15 of *O. virginiana* and more uniformly pubescent, velvety leaf surfaces. *Ostrya carpinifolia* has 15 to 20 vein pairs. **Ostrya knowltonii** Cov., (os-tri′á nōl-tōn′ē-ī), the western United States native, has smaller leaves to 2 1/2″ by 1 1/4″, 5 to 8 vein pairs and smaller, 1 1/4″ by 3/4″, fruiting clusters.

Oxydendrum arboreum (L.) DC. — Sourwood, also called Sorrel Tree or Lily-of-the-Valley Tree
(ok-si-den′drum âr-bō′rē-um)

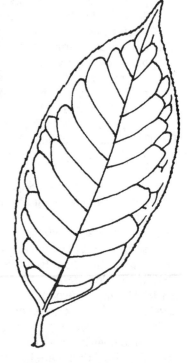

FAMILY: Ericaceae

LEAVES: Alternate, simple, elliptic-oblong to oblong-lanceolate, 3 to 8″ long, 1 1/2 to 3 1/2″ wide, acuminate, broad-cuneate, serrulate or entire, pale to lustrous dark green and glabrous above, lighter green and sparingly pubescent on veins beneath; petiole—1/2 to 1″ long.

BUDS: Small, 1/16″ long, conical-globose, solitary, sessile, with about 6 scales; terminal lacking.

STEM: Glabrous or sparingly pubescent, olive or bright red, slender.

SIZE: 25 to 30′ in height and approximately 20′ in spread; can grow 50 to 75′; national champion is 96′ by 28′ in Great Smoky Mountains National Park, near Cosby, TN; the landscape size is somewhat misleading for I regularly see 30 to 40′ trees in the piedmont of Georgia; in February 1997, Coach Vince Dooley and I were walking land in Madison County and discovered a 60′, possibly greater, tree.

HARDINESS: Zone 5, possibly 4, to 9; was an isolated tree on Maine campus that did flower and fruit.

HABIT: Pyramidal tree, with rounded top and drooping branches, very lovely outline, in youth, particularly nursery-grown trees, the habit is wild, woolly and somewhat misshapen, with time forms the pyramidal outline, often with regular distribution of branches, selections should be made for habit.

RATE: Slow, 14 to 15′ over a 12 to 15 year period.

TEXTURE: Medium in all seasons.

BARK: Grayish brown to brown, thick, deeply furrowed, and has rather scaly ridges that are often cut horizontally; resembling in its finest form the blocky bark of persimmon.

LEAF COLOR: Rich iridescent green in spring becoming lustrous dark green with maturity and turning yellow, red and purple in fall; often all colors on the same tree; I had a small tree in my Illinois garden that turned a brilliant red in fall; in the South this is one of the earliest and certainly best trees for fall coloration; fall color is quite variable and seedling material may not provide good reds.

FLOWERS: White, perfect, urn-shaped, 1/4″ long, fragrant, June to early July in 4 to 10″ long and wide, drooping, racemose-panicles, excellent flowering tree, literally smother the foliage, remind of a lacy veil, flowers open from base of each raceme toward apex and are effective for 3 to 4 weeks, the yellowish stalks of the inflorescence along with the yellowish green developing ovaries extend color season.

FRUIT: Dehiscent, 5-valved, 1/3″ long capsule, persistent, at first yellowish, finally brown, erect, good identification feature in winter months; pendulous in youth, upright at maturity.

CULTURE: Transplant as a young tree balled-and-burlapped or container grown into acid, peaty, moist, well-drained soil; full sun or partial shade although flowering and fall color are maximized in sun; does reasonably well in dry soils; not for polluted or urban areas.

DISEASES AND INSECTS: Leaf spots and twig blight, neither of which are serious.

LANDSCAPE VALUE: Truly an all season ornamental; excellent specimen plant; it has so many attributes that it should only be considered for specimen use; many gardeners feel, among native trees, this is second only to Flowering Dogwood; certainly one of my favorite trees and in Bernheim Arboretum, Clermont, KY, is a grouping, actually a grove, that is contrasted with a forest background; it is one of the handsomest uses imaginable; also in New England have seen the species in combination with *Hydrangea quercifolia* and in fall color at the same time, the pinkish red of the Sourwood and deep burgundy of Oakleaf Hydrangea were memorable.

CULTIVARS:
    'Albomarginatum'—White leaf margins plus white marbling on most, Louisiana Nursery.
    'Chaemeleon'—Upright conical habit, changing fall color from yellow, rose, red to purple, from Polly Hill, Martha's Vineyard, produced in tissue culture.
    'Mt. Charm'—Symmetrical grower with early fall color, introduced by West Virginia Association of Nurserymen.
PROPAGATION: I have attempted to root July cuttings using up to 10,000 ppm IBA-quick dip, peat:perlite, mist but have had no success; Dr. John Frett, currently University of Delaware, collected seeds from the wilds of Georgia and raised numerous seedlings by placing the seeds on a peat medium and placing the flats under mist until they germinated; he then moved the seedlings under fluorescent light where they proceeded to grow like weeds. Plants have been successfully produced through tissue culture. See Banko and Stefani, *HortScience* 24:683–685 (1989), for useful protocol that details micropropagation using mature trees; same authors, *HortScience* 26:1425 (1991), induced *in vitro* flower bud development with 16 to 24 hours of light per day.
    For producers not the easiest plant to grow. Takes staking, root pruning, and transplanting to produce quality plants. Mr. Keith Kilpatrick, Apalachee Nursery, Turtletown, TN 37391 is doing a terrific job. See Dirr, *Nursery Management and Production* 11(6):41, 45–46 (1995), for production techniques germane to Keith's nursery.
NATIVE HABITAT: Found on well-drained, gravelly soils on ridges rising above the banks of streams from the coast of Virginia to North Carolina and in southwestern Pennsylvania, southern Ohio, Indiana, western Kentucky, Tennessee; Appalachians to western Florida and the coasts of Mississippi and Louisiana. Introduced 1747.

Pachysandra procumbens Michx. — Allegheny Pachysandra
(pak-i-san′drå prō-kum′benz)

FAMILY: Buxaceae
LEAVES: Alternate, simple, evergreen, semi-evergreen to deciduous, ovate to rounded, much wider than those of *P. terminalis*, 2 to 4″ long, 2 to 3″ wide, prominently toothed especially above middle, gray to blue-green, often with a gray mottle above, slightly pubescent below; petiole—1/2 to 1 1/2″ long.
STEM: Brown-, pink-, and purple-tinted, glabrous.

SIZE: 6 to 10″(12″) high.
HARDINESS: Zone (4)5 to 9.
HABIT: Deciduous to semi-evergreen to evergreen ground cover spreading by rhizomes.
RATE: Slow, perhaps medium if soil is loose, moist and acid.
TEXTURE: Medium.
LEAF COLOR: Flat green to bluish green, often mottled, does not possess the luster of *P. terminalis*, very handsome foliage, some plants have a snake skin-like mosaic on the upper surface of the leaves, new growth emerges greenish turning blue-green with degrees of mottling.
FLOWERS: White or pinkish, fragrant, borne on 2 to 4″ long spikes in March–April, spikes arise from buds at the base of the stem, all seem to emerge from the center of a plant and make a rather attractive show.
FRUIT: Dehiscent, 3-pointed capsule, seeds lustrous blackish brown, seldom produced.
CULTURE: Appears adaptable, prefers moist, acid, organic, well-drained soil; partial to full shade; in cold climates some protection is necessary if plants are to maintain a smattering of evergreen leaves; a plant sited in an exposed location in my Illinois garden died to the ground and did not flower while in a protected area in a neighbor's garden it maintained green foliage and flowered profusely.
DISEASES AND INSECTS: Apparently this species is not troubled by dieback problems, scale, or leaf spot which sometimes ruin plantings of *P. terminalis*; the Cornell Plantations, Ithaca, NY, has maintained beds for 12 years and had no serious disease or dieback.
LANDSCAPE VALUE: Excellent and different ground cover for shade, forms a soft carpet of gray-green leaves; have seen superior plantings at the Morton Arboretum, Arnold Arboretum, Atlanta Historical Society,

Biltmore Gardens, and the University's Botanical Garden; plant has a great aura and deserves much wider use especially in naturalizing type situations; comparative plantings at University's Botanical Garden indicate this does not spread as fast as *P. terminalis*.

CULTIVARS:

'Eco Treasure'—More highly variegated form, from Don Jacobs, Eco Gardens, Decatur, GA.

'Forest Green'—Darker green form introduced by Dr. Richard Lighty, Mt. Cuba, Greenville, DE, acquired a plant and see minimal difference between this and the typical form, certainly not darker green.

Gary Lanham Form—Selected from wild populations in Kentucky for large leaves prominently marked with gray splotches, under evaluation at Center for Applied Nursery Research, Dearing, GA.

PROPAGATION: Cuttings of vigorous growth in June will root readily; Jack Alexander, propagator, Arnold Arboretum, and I found that 4000 and 8000 ppm IBA yielded excellent results; for a detailed discussion see Alexander and Dirr, *The Plant Propagator* 25(2):9–10 (1979).

ADDITIONAL NOTES: Plant is not widely available in commerce but is worth seeking out. I have observed enough excellent plantings to believe the plant should be more widely promoted and planted.

NATIVE HABITAT: Eastern Kentucky, West Virginia to Florida and Louisiana. Introduced 1800.

Pachysandra terminalis Sieb. & Zucc. — Japanese Pachysandra or Spurge
(pak-i-san′drà tĕr-mi-na′lis)

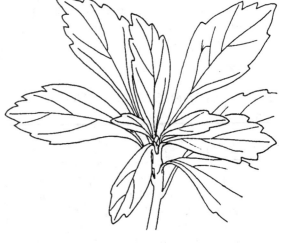

FAMILY: Buxaceae

LEAVES: Alternate, simple, evergreen, obovate to ovate, 2 to 4″ long, 1/2 to 1 1/2″ wide, dentate, cuneate, 3-nerved at base, lustrous dark green above, glabrous; petiole—1/2 to 1″ long; leaves appear whorled at top of stem.

STEM: Upright, greenish, glabrous.

SIZE: 6 to 12″ high.

HARDINESS: Zone 4 to 8, does not perform as well in the South as in northern areas; ideally requires year-round shade in Zone 7b and 8.

HABIT: Evergreen ground cover spreading by rhizomes and forming a solid mat if provided the proper soil conditions.

RATE: Slow.

TEXTURE: Medium, possibly medium-fine in all seasons.

LEAF COLOR: New growth is a lovely light green which gradually changes to lustrous dark green; foliage will yellow if plants are sited in full sun or exposed, windy situations.

FLOWERS: White, March to early April, borne in a 1 to 2″ long, upright spike at the end of the shoot in the center of the leaves, females at base, male toward apex.

FRUIT: Berry-like drupe, whitish, 1/2″ long, some plantings rarely produce fruits; this is probably because all the plants are of one clone; the plant is probably self-sterile and several clones are necessary along with bees to insure fruit set.

CULTURE: Easily transplanted; prefers moist, well-drained, acid soil abundantly supplied with organic matter (pH 5.5 to 6.5 is ideal); prefers shade and actually yellows in full sun; does extremely well under heavily shaded and shallow rooted trees; I have seen established plantings under the European Beech which provides one of the heaviest shades; space on 6″ to 12″ centers.

DISEASES AND INSECTS: Leaf blight, *Volutella pachysandricola*, causes both leaf blight and also stem cankers, *Pachysandra* leaf tier, scale, mites and northern root-knot nematode.

LANDSCAPE VALUE: Probably the best ground cover for deep shade; singularly beautiful when the new growth emerges; one of my favorites; siting is important and in exposed locations of sun and wind extensive foliar discoloration and damage occur; have observed plantings that qualify as perfect; unfortunately, in East and parts of Midwest the use has reached monoculture proportions; *Volutella* can be serious and can ruin a planting unless fungicides are employed.

CULTIVARS:

'Green Carpet'—A superior cultivar because the foliage is not trailing in habit but grows close to the ground, forming a low, neat ground cover; foliage is smaller and deeper, more waxy green than the species, many ground cover producers are growing this form, has been in our garden for over 10 years and appears more uniform and compact, although from a distance is difficult to distinguish from the species.

'Green Sheen'—High, mirror-like gloss to the leaves which is retained for at least 3 years in sun or shade, unbelievable glossy leaves, plants that I grew were not as vigorous as the species, selected by Dale Chapman of the University of Connecticut.

'Variegata' ('Silver Edge')—Leaves prominently mottled with white, is not as vigorous as the species and does not develop as fast; attractive in the right location.

PROPAGATION: Cuttings root readily with 1000 ppm IBA, peat:perlite, under mist; the best time to take cuttings (my experience) is after the spring flush of growth has hardened and leaves are fully mature; for my Illinois garden I rooted about 10 flats from campus cuttings; good rooting should take place in 6 to 8 weeks; freshly harvested seed germinated 20% in 30 days, scarified seeds germinated 90% in 34 days.

NATIVE HABITAT: Japan. Introduced 1882.

Parrotia persica C.A. Mey — Persian Parrotia, also called Persian Ironwood or Irontree
(par-rō′ti-à pĕr′si-kà)

FAMILY: Hamamelidaceae

LEAVES: Alternate, simple, oval to obovate-oblong, 2 1/2 to 5″ long, 1 to 2 1/2″ wide, with large lance-olate caducous stipules, obtuse, rounded to sub-cordate at base, coarsely crenate-dentate above the middle, almost glabrous above, with sparse pubescence below, undulate, lustrous medium to dark green, similar in shape to *Hamamelis* and *Fothergilla* leaves; petiole—1/12 to 1/4″ long.

BUDS: Vegetative—stalked, with 2 outer scales, to-mentulous, brownish; flower buds—globose, about 1/3″ diameter, quite pubescent, brownish black.

STEM: Slender, brownish, pubescent when young, finally becoming grayish brown and glabrous with maturity.

BARK: Exfoliating on old branches to expose gray, green, white, brown mosaic.

SIZE: 20 to 40′ in height with a spread of 15 to 30′; have seen many trees that were broader than tall.

HARDINESS: Zone (4)5 to 8; some twig dieback at Morton Arboretum, Lisle, IL.

HABIT: Small, single-stemmed tree or large, multi-stemmed shrub with an oval-rounded head of upright, ascending branches, also a form with wide-spreading branches, literature reported that plants in native stands are upright-strongly ascending, in Europe most plants I have observed were rounded, wide-spreading, often with arching, semi-pendent branches.

RATE: Medium, 10′ over a 6 to 8 year period, growth is much faster, 1 to 2 times this, with adequate water and nutrition.

TEXTURE: Medium in leaf; medium-fine in winter.

BARK: Older branches and trunks develop an exfoliating gray, green, white, brown color reminiscent of *Pinus bungeana*, Lacebark Pine; the bark is a welcome asset in the winter landscape; takes considerable time before exfoliating bark occurs, about 4 to 8″ diameter branches.

LEAF COLOR: Reddish purple when unfolding changing to lustrous medium to dark green during summer and developing brilliant yellow to orange to scarlet fall color, one of the most beautiful trees for foliage effect; leaves, like many members of the Hamamelidaceae, are freeze resistant into the low to mid-twenties; fall color (Athens) is yellow to yellow-orange from mid-November into early December; color is about the latest to develop among the deciduous trees/shrubs; selections for better oranges and reds could be made.

FLOWERS: Perfect, apetalous, before the leaves in March–April (early to mid-February, Athens), the showy parts of the flower are the crimson stamens, about 1/3 to 1/2″ across when fully open, pass from crimson-maroon to yellow (anthers shed their pollen); most people miss the flowers which are, at best, curiously effective.

FRUIT: A capsule, ornamentally ineffective, 2-valved, single seed per cell, about 3/8″ long, bright brown.

CULTURE: Transplant balled-and-burlapped or from a container; prefers well-drained, loamy, slightly acid (pH 6.0 to 6.5) soils; will tolerate chalky soils; full sun, but will do well in light shade; prune in spring; appears to be extremely tolerant once established; one of the unsung plants for stress tolerance as it withstands drought, heat, wind, cold; one of the most consistently beautiful plants in our garden; utilized on Georgia campus in traffic islands and planters surrounded by pavement/concrete/blacktop and never misses a beat.

DISEASES AND INSECTS: Very pest-free tree, noticed significant Japanese beetle damage in the South.

LANDSCAPE VALUE: One of the best small specimen trees that I know; the foliage, bark and pest resistance make it a tree worth considering; excellent small lawn or street tree, could be integrated into foundation plantings around large residences; is definitely a topic of conversation; a fine accent plant; since this is one of my favorite plants I am claiming eminent domain and reciting the following litany of institutions that have fine specimens, a pilgrimage would be worth the reader's time; Barnes Arboretum*, Bernheim, Brooklyn Botanic Garden, Rowe*, Arnold*, Morton, Dawes Arboreta; Cave Hill and Spring Grove Cemeteries; Biltmore* and Cantigny Gardens; Michigan State and Swarthmore* campuses; those marked with an asterisk have exceptional specimens; perhaps the most beautiful and definitely the largest (50 to 60′) specimen I have seen occurs at the Jardin des Plantes, Paris; also, notable specimens at Kew Gardens, Wisley Gardens*, and Westonbirt Arboretum in England.

CULTIVARS: In the last edition I mentioned the weeping form that had eluded my every attempt to locate . . . well, no more . . . for at Kew Gardens there is a 10 to 12′ high, 12 to 15′ wide, stiffly weeping form of superlative beauty, the habit is akin to a large umbrella with a long handle with the ribs extending to the ground. The trunk is 14 to 18″ in diameter and exfoliates like the species. I did receive a plant that was listed as 'Pendula' but appears nothing more than a side shoot, i.e., plagiotropic growth, with a more or less horizontal nature. My field notes also allude to pendulous forms that I observed in Boskoop, Edinburgh Botanic Garden, Hillier Arboretum, and Rowallane, Northern Ireland. All were semi-pendulous to horizontal, not as decidedly weeping as Kew form. Other selections have been brought to my attention or provided to me for evaluation.

'Biltmore'—Large, rounded habit, low-branched, with massive trunk and exfoliating bark, probably over 100-years-old, on outside of corner of walled garden at Biltmore House and Gardens, before entrance to Azalea dell.

New Zealand Form—Considerable nursery stock is imported from New Zealand and this form, could be others, has smaller leaves, is not as vigorous or winter hardy as the "typical" United States form(s); Don Shadow, Winchester, TN mentioned this form was not cold hardy at his nursery.

Purpleleaf Form—Noted this form in Greenbriar Farms, WV catalog, with bronzy purple new growth, how different this is from species which consistently produces bronze-purple new growth is unknown.

'Select'—Young leaves lime green with a purple edge, uniqueness of this form is unknown.

'Vanessa'—Upright form, distinctly columnar according to those people who have observed it, Bob McCartney, Woodlanders, Aiken, SC mentioned that there was a specimen at Colonial Williamsburg.

PROPAGATION: Seeds should be stratified for five months at warm, fluctuating temperatures and then 3 months at 41°F. European literature noted germination may take 18 months, sow seed in fall, germinates the second spring. Cuttings—I have had terrific success with June–July cuttings treated with 1000 to 3000 ppm KIBA and placed under mist. After the cuttings have rooted it is important to leave them in the medium where they can go dormant; after they have received an artificial or natural cold period and when new growth ensues they should be potted. I have had tremendous success with this approach and in cases where the cutting has rooted and the shoot is still growing have potted them directly with success. If cuttings are rooted in late May–June (Athens), they invariably produce a flush of growth especially if lightly fertilized after rooting. *Parrotia*, like *Fothergilla*, is not difficult to root or manage after rooting. Cutting propagation has become garden variety simple and, after rooting, cuttings are placed under extended photoperiod to induce growth and insure overwinter survival. Have had 6 to 12″ of new growth with this system the same year in which the cuttings were rooted.

Report in *The Plant Propagator* 30(4):9 (1984) describes the following success: 6-year-old tree, July (Boston), sand:perlite, mist, overwinter in flats and analyzed in March of 1984—100% rooting with 8000 ppm IBA talc plus thiram, 95% with 24 hour soak 400 ppm KIBA, and 65% rooting when untreated with poor root quality.

ADDITIONAL NOTES: In my mind, an outstanding ornamental tree that has few rivals. I have observed only limited fruit set and this was on a less-than-robust plant at William and Mary College. I had a nice small specimen in my Illinois garden which always evoked a "What is it?" from visitors. In Europe, I noticed the plants often tend to be more wide-spreading than plants in the United States. Worthwhile article by Nicholson, *Arnoldia* 49(4):34–39 (1989); essentially the same article in *American Nurseryman* 173(10):46–51 (1991).

NATIVE HABITAT: Iran, cultivated 1840, one species named after F.W. Parrot, German naturalist and traveler.

Parrotiopsis jacquemontiana (Decne.) Rehd.
(par-rō-ti-op′sis jak-mon-ti-ā′nȧ)

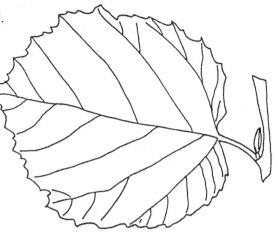

FAMILY: Hamamelidaceae
LEAVES: Alternate, simple, roundish or very broadly ovate, 2 to 3 1/2″ long and about as wide, margins with broad serrations, dark green and pubescent above to almost glabrous, dense stellate pubescence on veins beneath; petiole—1/4 to 1/2″ long.

SIZE: 8 to 12′ high, usually not as wide, can grow 15 to 20′.
HARDINESS: Zone 5 to 7; a dieback shrub at the Morton Arboretum, Lisle, IL.
HABIT: Usually an upright, oval to rounded shrub in this country although can become a small tree, the latter I have never observed.
RATE: Slow.
TEXTURE: Medium.
BARK: Smooth gray on older branches.
LEAF COLOR: Dark green, no fall color of consequence; leaves hold late and may turn yellow.
FLOWERS: Perfect, apetalous, white, 1/2 to 1″(2″) wide produced in a short-stalked cluster and open from April to May and intermittently through summer, 15 to 24 yellow stamens are showy, beneath the head of flowers are 4 to 6 petal-like bracts, white, 1/2 to 1″ long, that constitute the showy part of the inflorescence, 5 to 7 sepals.

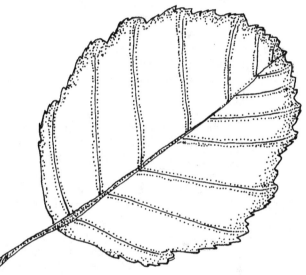

FRUIT: Ovoid, 2-beaked capsule containing shining brown, 1/6″ long, oblong seeds.
CULTURE: Similar to *Parrotia*.
DISEASES AND INSECTS: None serious.
LANDSCAPE VALUE: Interesting and unusual shrub; rather pretty in flower; not well-known and certainly not common; seldom seen in gardens and at best a collector's plant.
PROPAGATION: Apparently seed has a long warm-cold requirement; cuttings collected in August rooted 100% when treated with 8000 ppm IBA-talc; cuttings should probably be allowed to pass through a dormant period before being transplanted.
NATIVE HABITAT: Himalayas. Introduced 1879.

Parthenocissus quinquefolia (L.) Planch. — Virginia Creeper, also called Woodbine.
(pär-then-ō-sis′us kwin-kwe-fō′li-ȧ)

FAMILY: Vitaceae
LEAVES: Alternate, compound palmate, (3)5 leaflets, each stalked (1/3″ long), elliptic to obovate-oblong, 1 1/2 to 4″ long, 1/2 to 2 1/2″ wide, acuminate, usually cuneate, coarsely and often crenately serrate, lustrous dark green above, glaucescent beneath, young growth bright waxy bronze to red; petiole—1 to 4″ long.
BUDS: Often collateral, brownish, sessile, round-conical, with 2 to 3 exposed scales, end bud absent.
STEM: Round, light brown, prominently lenticelled, glabrous leaf scars distinctly concave; pith—white, tendrils with 5 to 8 branches ending in adhesive tips, longer than those of *P. tricuspidata*.

SIZE: 30 to 50′ and more; the structure upon which it climbs is the limiting factor.
HARDINESS: Zone (3)4 to 9.
HABIT: Deciduous vine with tendrils which have 5 to 8 branches, each ending in adhesive-like tips; has the ability to literally cement itself to the wall and therefore needs no support; good on trees, will also crawl along the ground; secretes calcium carbonate which serves as adhesive.

RATE: Fast, 6 to 10′ and beyond in a single season.

TEXTURE: Medium in leaf, somewhat coarse in winter.

LEAF COLOR: New growth bronzish to reddish, rich lustrous deep green in summer; usually a purple-red to crimson-red in fall; first of all woody plants to color effectively; often noticeable in the tops of tall trees.

FLOWERS: Greenish white (yellowish green), June–July, in cymes which usually form terminal panicles; totally ineffective as they are borne under the foliage.

FRUIT: Berry, 1/4″ diameter, bluish black, bloomy, 2- to 3-seeded, September–October, and only effective (actually noticeable) after the leaves have fallen, great bird food and is one of the most common weeds in our garden, I see bird-planted seedlings everywhere in my travels.

CULTURE: Supposedly coarsely fibrous and slow to reestablish but I have never had any problem rooting or growing it; best grown in containers and moved from them to the final growing area; tolerates just about any kind of soil; full sun or full shade; exposed, windy conditions; polluted situations, city conditions; actually difficult to kill; have seen it growing in the most inhospitable situations, even in pure sand on Cape Cod; quite salt tolerant; in a study of vines, their photosynthetic rates, et al., *P. quinquefolia* was the best adapted to shade, with a low compensation point, high photosynthetic rate under low light, see *Amer. J. Bot.* 75:1011–1018 (1988).

DISEASES AND INSECTS: Canker, downy mildew, leaf spots, powdery mildew, wilt, beetles, eight-spotted forester, leaf hoppers, scales and several other insects.

LANDSCAPE VALUE: Excellent, tough, low-maintenance cover for walls, trellises, rock piles; can be an asset if used properly; the ivy covered walls of most universities are not ivy covered but "creeper" covered; have seen the species growing on sand dunes in the company of *Rosa rugosa*, *Ammophila breviligulata*, *Myrica pensylvanica* and other salt tolerant species; if other vines fail this is a good choice; cements itself to structures and does not need support; may leave a residue on buildings that is difficult to remove; as emphasized under fruits, it can become a weed as birds "plant" the seeds with reckless abandon.

CULTIVARS: Three varieties of some note include var. *engelmannii* Rehd. with smaller leaflets than the species; var. *hirsuta* Planch. has leaves and young stems covered with soft, white pubescence; and var. *saint-paulii* (Koehne & Gräbn.) Rehd. with smaller leaflets but better clinging qualities because tendrils have 8 to 12 branches.

‘Dark Green Ice’—Glossy dark green foliage, does not turn red in the fall if grown in shady locations, selected from the wild in Canada by Jean-Pierre Devoyault, considered hardy to Zone 3, see *HortScience* 31(3):326 (1996).

Have seen a speckled, splashed cream-green leaf form, it is not stable and will revert to green.

PROPAGATION: Seed has a dormant embryo and stratification in cool moist sand or peat for 30 to 60 days at 41°F is recommended; softwood cuttings collected in August rooted 90% in 20 days without treatment; very easy to root from June, July or August cuttings, use 1000 ppm KIBA quick dip, peat:perlite, mist.

ADDITIONAL NOTES: Two related species that are not common or sufficiently different to warrant extended use include: *P. heptaphylla* (Buckl.) Britt. & Small, Seven-leaf Creeper, with coarsely serrate, waxy dark green, substantive leaves that turn rich crimson in fall; new leaves emerge delicate rose in spring; globose, blue-black, 1/3 to 1/2″ berry; grows 20 to 30′; native to Texas; Zone 7 to 9; and *P. inserta* (A. Kerner) Fritsch. is similar to *P. quinquefolia* but has 3- to 5-branched tendrils without adhesive disks; native from New England to Manitoba, south to Wyoming and Texas; Zone 3 to 7(8).

NATIVE HABITAT: New England to Florida and Mexico, west to Ohio, Illinois and Missouri. Introduced 1622.

RELATED SPECIES:

Parthenocissus henryana (Hemsl.) Diels. & Gilg. — Silvervein Creeper

LEAVES: Alternate, compound palmate, 3 to 5(7) leaflets, each 1 1/2 to 5″ long, about 1/2 as wide, obovate, oblanceolate, or narrowly oval, slender-pointed, tapered to a short petiolule, coarsely toothed except near base, glabrous above, downy on veins beneath, velvety dark green above, variegated with silvery white and pink along the midrib and primary veins, although this does not always appear to hold true; deep purple on underside especially on young leaves; petiole—1 1/2 to 4 1/2″ long.

STEM: Four angled, glabrous, tendrils with 5 to 7 branches, cementing itself to structures by disk-like cups.

Parthenocissus henryana, (pär-then-ō-sis′us hen-rē-ā′nȧ), Silvervein Creeper, is noteworthy for its distinct bluish green leaves which are veined with white in youth, and purple on their underside throughout the growing season. Fall color is also a good red to reddish purple. Colors around mid to late October in Athens, but not all leaves at same time. From a foliage standpoint this is the handsomest of the species treated here but the least hardy. Does reasonable in the South. Definitely more vigorous and handsome in European climates. Not as wild and invasive as *P. tricuspidata* and *P. quinquefolia*. Listed as growing to 15′ but have observed larger specimens in European gardens. Flowers in a leafy, terminal panicle 7 to 8″ long. Fruits dark blue with 3 seeds. The leaf coloration does not hold in the heat. Have also noted more leaf spot on this than the others treated here. Zone (6)7 to 8. Central China. Introduced about 1895.

Parthenocissus tricuspidata (Sieb. & Zucc.) Planch. — Japanese Creeper, Boston Ivy

LEAVES: Alternate, simple, slender-stalked, broad-ovate, 4 to 8″ wide, 3-lobed with acuminate coarsely serrate lobes; or chiefly on the young plants and basal shoots, smaller and partly 3-foliate with stalked leaflets, glossy dark green, glabrous above, finely pubescent on veins beneath.

BUDS: Brownish, similar to previous species.

STEM: Squarish, tendrils 5 to 12, shorter than those of *P. quinquefolia*, prominent, vertically arranged lenticels, usually glabrous.

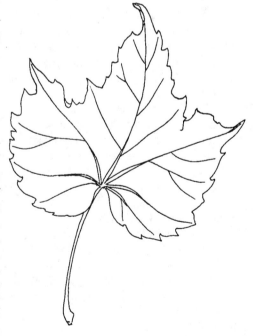

Parthenocissus tricuspidata, (pär-then-ō-sis′us trī-kus-pi-dā′tȧ), Japanese Creeper, is similar to *P. quinquefolia* in all respects except the foliage is usually more lustrous, the leaf is simple and 3-lobed and it is possibly not as hardy. It is excellent and can be used in the same situations as Virginia Creeper. Yellow-green, 1/8″ diameter, deflexed-petaled flowers occur in terminal thyrsoid panicles. Fruit is flattened-globose, 1/4 to 1/3″ long, bloomy dull dark blue with 1 to 2 seeds. More cultivars than I realized, particularly in Europe. 'Atropurpurea' is vigorous with green, tinged bluish, turning purple leaves, new spring growth and fall color are red. 'Aurata' has yellow leaves marbled green, red with rough margin. 'Beverley Brook' ('Beverley Brooks' of Jackman in England) has large leaves that turn brilliant shades of red and scarlet in fall. Have seen this described as having exceptionally small leaves, red fall color. 'Fenway Park' is a yellow-foliaged form that turns green in summer and brilliant scarlet in fall. Discovered by Dr. Peter del Tridici, Arnold Arboretum, during his trek to a baseball game at Boston's

Fenway Park. 'Green Showers' ('Green Spring' in European literature) has essentially fresh green foliage that is larger than typical, up to 10″ wide, fall color is rich burgundy. 'Lowii' has small, 3/4 to 1 1/4″, 3- to 7-lobed leaves when young and good red fall color. 'Purpurea' has reddish purple leaves throughout the summer. 'Robusta' offers thick, waxy, glossy green leaves and excellent orange to red fall color, vigorous grower and leaves are often trifoliate (3 leaflets) and 4 to 8″ wide. 'Veitchii' has small, simple or trifoliate leaves, coarsly serrated with blistered variegation, purple when young. Have seen described in 4 major United States nursery catalogs and may or may not be true 'Veitchii' based on the descriptions. Japan, Central China. 1862. Zone 4 to 8.

Paulownia tomentosa (Thunb.) Steud. — Royal Paulownia, also called Empress Tree or Princess Tree.
(paw-lō′ni-à tō-men-tō′sà)

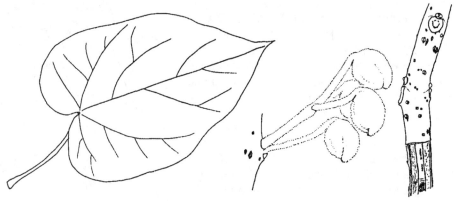

FAMILY: Scrophulariaceae, sometimes placed in Bignoniaceae.

LEAVES: Opposite, simple, broad-ovate to ovate, 5 to 10″(12″) long and wide, acuminate, cordate, entire or sometimes shallowly 3-lobed, dark green and sparsely pubescent above, tomentose beneath; petiole—about as long as blade; leaves on sucker growth may reach 2 to 2 1/2′ in diameter.

BUDS: Similar to *Catalpa speciosa*.

STEM: Stout, pubescent when young, heavily lenticelled, with vertical, lip-like shape, olive-brown color.

PITH: Chambered, *Catalpa* pith is continuous.

FLOWERS: Panicle, formed in summer; individual flower buds appear as light brown, pubescent spheres through winter, excellent identification feature.

SIZE: 30 to 40′ in height with an equal spread, may grow 50 to 60′ but this is rare; trees over 80′ high are known; national champion is 64′ by 67′ at Evansville, IN.

HARDINESS: Zone (5)6 to 9; often dies back to the ground at Morton Arboretum.

HABIT: Rounded, dense crown; resembles *C. bignonioides* in habit.

RATE: Fast, 14 to 17′ in 4 to 5 years and can grow as much as 8 to 10′ in a single year; the wood tends to be somewhat brittle.

TEXTURE: Coarse in all seasons.

LEAF COLOR: Medium to dark green in summer; fall color of no consequence as the leaves usually fall off green; watched leaves turn brown by a fall freeze when the temperature dropped to 24°F; new leaves are frost sensitive; leaves on suckers or seedlings may reach 24 to 36″ long and wide.

FLOWERS: Pale violet with darker spots and yellow stripes inside, reminds of a foxglove flower, 2″ long, vanilla-scented, borne in April (May in North) before the leaves in 8 to 12″ long, pyramidal panicles; flower buds are formed during the summer prior to flowering and are a brown color and very evident during the winter; unfortunately, the flower buds are often killed during the winter.

FRUIT: Ovoid, beaked, light brown aging to dirty brown, dehiscent capsule, 1 to 2″ long, not ornamentally overwhelming, persisting, containing up to 2000 small, winged seeds.

CULTURE: Transplant balled-and-burlapped in early spring into moist, deep, well-drained soil; will tolerate a wide range of soils but does best in the type mentioned; full sun or partial shade and sheltered from wind; withstands air pollutants and does well along coastal areas; prune in winter.

DISEASES AND INSECTS: Seldom troubled although leaf spots, mildew and twig canker have been reported.

LANDSCAPE VALUE: Falls in the same category as *Catalpa* except probably less desirable because of messiness and in northern climates the uncertainty of flowers; possibly for parks and other large areas; very dense shaded and therefore difficult to grow grass under; over the years have watched a grand avenue at Longwood Gardens and am always reluctant to criticize the tree after seeing them in flower; however, noticed, especially in fall, numerous leaves cascading at irregular intervals over the handsome lawn, there is always some "pick-up" necessary; old fruit capsules will persist and the tree can really look unkempt if they are not removed; I suspect Longwood Gardens spends considerable maintenance dollars; during a February 1998 visit to Longwood, I noticed large branches had been removed and the trees were declining; my question to Longwood was what will they be replaced with?; their answer: the same in the interest of preserving the historic landscape.

CULTIVARS:

'Coreana'—Yellow-tinted leaves, woolly beneath, and violet-speckled, yellow-throated flowers.

'Lilacina'—Pale lilac flowers.

'Somaclonal Snowstorm'—I would like to say good things about this cream-variegated leaf form, the variegation streaked, flecked and blotched throughout the leaf; unfortunately, the plant (now removed) in the University's Botanical Garden reverted to green, considerable vigilance is necessary to keep it variegated; resulted from hypocotyl explants in tissue culture and introduced by Dr. Marcotrigiano of the University of Massachusetts, see *HortScience* 23: 226–227 (1988) for details.

PROPAGATION: The seeds exhibit no dormancy but light is necessary for germination; fresh seed has a germination capacity of 90% in 19 days with alternating temperatures of 68° and 86°F; eight hours of light were supplied during the 86°F cycle; seeds will germinate like grass if placed on the surface of the medium under mist, never cover too deeply; I have grown many seedlings; red light and gibberellic acid (GA$_3$) promoted germination; root cuttings are successful, see *Tree Planters Notes* 45(3):101–103 (1994), also same journal 45(3):95–100 (1994); tissue culture has been successful with the species, see *HortScience* 20: 760 (1985).

ADDITIONAL NOTES: One of my former graduate students discovered a white form on the Georgia campus which we called 'Georgia Princess'. Unfortunately, the tree has never been propagated. The species has been used in strip mine reclamation in Kentucky. The wood is prized by the Japanese and is used for rice pots, bowls, spoons, furniture, coffins and air crates. There are 85,000 seeds per ounce and a large tree may produce 20 million seeds in a year. The tree was named after Anna Pavlovna, daughter of Czar Paul I and wife of Prince Willem of the Netherlands. It is tremendously fast-growing and a 22-year-old tree reached a height of 62' and averaged 3 growth rings per inch. This is the wonder that appears in Sunday supplements. It does amazing things like "soar to 23' in two seasons; flower continuously from spring to summer; withstand -25°F and produce leaves 2 1/2' across." The actual fact is that it does none of the above. Cold is its biggest enemy and flower buds are often seriously injured or killed between 0 and -5°F. Escaped from cultivation in Georgia and has found a home along highway cuts and fills. It is intolerant of competition and will give way to other species with time.

More literature than one would think necessary concerning the species. See *American Horticulturist* 71(6):27–29 (1992) for a worthy perspective on characteristics, use, history; and *J. Environ. Hort.* 8:205–207 (1990) for quantitative information that says *Paulownia* will grow in soil pH range of 4 to 7, with moderate fertility—50 to 100 ppm Nitrogen. Also, an Extension Service publication from the University of Kentucky, FOR-39, discusses establishment and cultivation.

Other species like: *Paulownia fargesii* Franch., *P. fortunei* Hemsl., and *P. kawakamii* Itô. are occasionally offered in American commerce, especially by Woodlanders, Aiken, SC. One of the proprietors, Mr. Robert McCartney, has a strong affinity for the genus and has planted many species in the Aiken area. Bob and I have divergent opinions about their net landscape worth. *Paulownia fortunei* has immense panicles with 2 to 3″ long individual fruits that looked as bedraggled as my old garden socks. The cream, flushed with lilac, foxglove-like flowers are 3 to 4″ long.

NATIVE HABITAT: China. Introduced 1834. Escaped from cultivation from southern New York to Georgia.

Paxistima canbyi A. Gray — Canby Paxistima (formerly spelled *Pachistima*), also called Rat-stripper, Cliff Green, Mountain Lover
(paks-iss′ti-mȧ kan′bē-ī)

FAMILY: Celastraceae

LEAVES: Opposite, simple, evergreen, linear-oblong or narrow-oblong, 1/4 to 1″ long, 3/16″ or less wide, revolute and usually serrulate above the middle, lustrous dark green, glabrous; petiole—short.

BUDS: Solitary, sessile, ovoid, appressed, very small, with about 2 pairs of exposed scales; the terminal somewhat larger with more visible scales.

STEM: Very slender, somewhat 4-sided, the bark becoming corky-thickened and transversely checked; pith—minute, rounded, brownish, and spongy; leaf scars minute, crescent-shaped, somewhat raised; 1 indistinct bundle trace.

SIZE: One foot in height by 3 to 5′ in spread at maturity.
HARDINESS: Zone 3 to 7, shows good cold hardiness; no damage in Orono, ME.
HABIT: Low-growing evergreen shrub with decumbent branches which often root when in contact with the soil; relatively neat and compact.
RATE: Slow, can grow 12″ high by 2 to 3′ wide in 3 to 4 years.
TEXTURE: Fine in all seasons.
LEAF COLOR: Lustrous dark green in summer becoming somewhat bronzish in cold weather.
FLOWERS: Perfect, greenish or reddish, 1/5″ across, 4 petals, 4 sepals, 4 stamens, early May, borne in few-flowered, 1/2″ diameter cymes, not particularly showy.
FRUIT: Leathery, 2-valved capsule, white, 1/6″ long, of no ornamental consequence.
CULTURE: Easily transplanted, but best moved as a container-grown plant; prefers moist, well-drained soil which has been well-supplied with organic matter; in the wild it is found on calcareous, rocky soils; full sun or partial shade although is denser and more compact in full sun; rarely requires fertilizer or pruning; will tolerate high pH soils.
DISEASES AND INSECTS: Leaf spot and scale have been reported.
LANDSCAPE VALUE: Good evergreen ground cover which once established requires little or no attention; excellent when used in combination with broadleaf evergreens; makes a good facer plant or low hedge; does not appear too often in midwestern or southern gardens but is occasionally used on the East Coast.
PROPAGATION: Plants can be divided; cuttings can be rooted easily; I have taken cuttings in late July, treated them with 1000 ppm IBA, placed them under mist and had good success. Another investigator collected softwood cuttings in summer, treated them with 3000 ppm IBA-talc and had 100% rooting in 6 weeks.
ADDITIONAL NOTES: *Paxistima mysinites* (Pursh) Raf., Oregon Boxwood, from western North America, grows to 3′, with finely serrated, 1″ long, glossy dark green leaves. Generally taller and more upright than *P. canbyi*.
NATIVE HABITAT: Mountains of Virginia and West Virginia, found chiefly on calcareous soils. Cultivated 1880.

Perovskia atriplicifolia Benth. — Russian-sage

Perovskia abrotanoides

FAMILY: Lamiaceae
LEAVES: Opposite, simple, rhomboidal or slightly obovate, 1 to 2″ long, 1/3 to 1″ wide, tapered at both ends, coarsely serrate, gray-green and slightly downy; petiole—1/12 to 1/3″ long.

Perovskia atriplicifolia, (pe-rof′ski-à at-ri-pli-si-fō′li-à), Russian-sage, is a beautiful plant when properly grown. It is semi-woody to herbaceous and reaches 3 to 5′. The foliage is a handsome gray-green. In August and September, violet-blue flowers occur in terminal, 9 to 12″ long panicles. In Athens, full flower has occurred as early as June 26. A mass planting, which is the only way to effectively utilize the plant, is without equal. The entire inflorescence, like the stems, is covered with a fine, whitish down which accentuates the color of the flowers. Locate in full sun in well-drained soil that is not excessively rich. It should be pruned back in spring to live wood as it generally winter kills in cold climates. I have propagated it from softwood cuttings but they should be removed from the mist bench soon after rooting for excess water is harmful. 'Blue Haze' has pale blue flowers and nearly entire leaves. 'Blue Spire' has deeply lobed leaves, is of upright habit to 3′ and bears the flowers in large panicles. One of the finest plantings in this country is located at Bernheim Arboretum. **Perovskia abrotanoides** Karel. is closely allied to *P. atriplicifolia* but differs in more deeply incised leaves, often almost to midrib; these segments are often again dissected (see line drawing). Afghanistan to western Himalayas and Tibet. Cultivated 1904. Zone 5 to 8.

Persea borbonia (L.) Spreng. — Redbay
(pĕr′sē-à bôr-bōn′ē-à)

FAMILY: Lauraceae
LEAVES: Alternate, simple, evergreen, oblong to lance-oblong, 2 to 4″(6″) long, 1/2 to 2 1/2″ wide, obtuse, acute to acuminate, cuneate, lustrous medium green above, glabrous above, with appressed glistening gold hairs below; petiole—1/2 to 1″ long, pubescent.

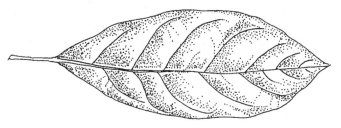

BUDS: Naked.
STEM: Stout, green, ridged, glabrous to the unaided eye but with golden appressed hairs, aromatic when bruised.

SIZE: 20 to 30'(40') high, two-third's to equal this in spread; co-national champions are 58' by 68' in Randolph City, GA and 77' by 52' in Hamilton Co., FL.
HARDINESS: Zone (7)8 to 9, defoliated or killed to ground at –3°F.
HABIT: Oval to rounded large shrub or reasonably robust tree; have seen 40' high single-trunked, round-headed trees along coastal Georgia and North Carolina.
RATE: Medium.
TEXTURE: Medium to coarse.
BARK: Gray-brown, shallowly ridged-and-furrowed on old trunks, the ridges becoming scaly.
LEAF COLOR: Lustrous medium green, in winter often yellowish green, especially noticeable on plants in the Athens area.
FLOWERS: Perfect, creamy, in peduncled, several-flowered cymes, not showy, June; did a double take with a plant on the Outer Banks of North Carolina; I thought I was looking at *Nyssa* flowers.
FRUIT: Subglobose, 1/2" long, dark blue to black drupe borne on a red pedicel; interestingly, have had heavy fruit set on campus plants; ripen in October.
CULTURE: Doubtfully available in commerce except from specialty growers; should be moved as a container-grown plant; prefers moist, acid, well-drained soil but in the wild occurs in swamps; I have seen plants growing submerged in North Carolina; interestingly appears to prosper under drier conditions as evidenced by performance on the Georgia campus; full sun or moderate shade.
DISEASES AND INSECTS: In the wild, the leaves are usually infected with a gall and appear swollen and watery, also rather ugly; on campus plants I have not noticed the problem.
LANDSCAPE VALUE: Coastal, native plant situations, appears quite salt-tolerant, best for naturalizing.
PROPAGATION: Seeds are the usual method and should be fall sown.
ADDITIONAL NOTES: Variety *pubescens* (Pursh) Little is described as more gall resistant and growing primarily in swamps. **Persea humilis** Nash, Silkbay, with 1 to 3" long, 1/2 to 1 1/4" wide leaves, the lower surface covered with silky, chestnut brown pubescence, develops into a medium-sized shrub or small tree, 10 to 20' high. Pretty in foliage. Inhabits sand pine-oak scrub in central peninsula of Florida. Zone 8 to 9.

Also, **Persea palustris** (Raf.) Sarg., Swamp Redbay, resembles *P. borbonia*, however, lower surface of leaves and stems are covered with shaggy brown pubescence, some of which is lost with maturity. Wet areas from eastern Virginia to Florida, west to southeast Texas. Zone 7 to 9.

Other obscure species include: *P. intermedia* Phil., *P. japonica* (Sieb. & Zucc.) Kosterm., *P. littoralis* Small, *P. thunbergii*, and *P. yunnanensis* (Lecomte) Kosterm. All are offered in American commerce.
NATIVE HABITAT: Southern Delaware to Florida, westward to southeastern Texas. Introduced 1739.

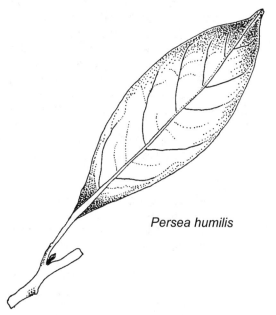

Persea humilis

Phellodendron amurense Rupr. — Amur Corktree
(fel-ō-den'dron a-moor-en'sē)

FAMILY: Rutaceae
LEAVES: Opposite, pinnately compound, 10 to 15" long, 5 to 11(13) leaflets, ovate to lance-ovate, 2 1/2 to 4 1/2" long, half as wide, entire, long-acuminate, rounded or narrowed at base, lustrous dark green above, glabrous beneath or with a few hairs along the base of the midrib, rachis tomentose.
BUDS: Solitary, half-ellipsoid, 1/8" long, compressed from the sides, silky with red or bronzed hairs so as to mask the overlapping of the two scales, enclosed by the base of petiole.

STEM: Stout, orange-yellow or yellowish gray, changing to brown, lenticels prominent, glabrous, leaf scars horseshoe-shaped, raised, rather large with bud setting in the "U" formed by the leaf scar; inner bark of young stems usually a bright yellowish green.

SIZE: 30 to 45′ in height with an equal or greater spread; trees 44′ by 60′, 39′ by 60′, 34′ by 60′ grew in the Morton Arboretum, Lisle, IL in late 1980's.

HARDINESS: Zone 3b to 7, will grow in Zone 8 but is slow; perfectly adapted in Orono, ME and Edmonton, Alberta, Canada.

HABIT: Broad-spreading tree with a short trunk and an open, rounded crown of a few large, often horizontally arranged branches; a tree of great beauty in its finest form.

RATE: Medium, 10 to 12′ over a 5 to 8 year period.

TEXTURE: Medium in leaf; would probably be considered coarse in winter habit.

BARK: On old trunks, ridged-and-furrowed into a cork-like pattern, gray-brown in color; very beautiful and unusual bark pattern but does not develop until old age.

LEAF COLOR: Deep, often lustrous green in summer, changing to yellow or bronzy yellow in fall and persisting briefly.

FLOWERS: Dioecious, yellowish green, 5 to 8 sepals and petals, 5 to 6 stamens, borne in 2 to 3 1/2″ long, 1 1/2 to 3″ wide panicles in late May to early June; not showy.

FRUIT: Subglobose, black, 1/2″ diameter drupe, 5-seeded stones, with strong odor when bruised; ripening in October and persisting into winter; borne only on female trees.

CULTURE: Transplants readily, has fibrous, shallow, wide-spreading root system; does well on many types of soils; withstands acid or alkaline conditions; drought and polluted air; full sun; prune in winter; Dr. John Pair's Wichita, KS tests provided data to support my long term observations that the tree is simply not as environmentally tough as given credit; authors, including me, have looked at the literature rather than the tree; over a 10 year period in Kansas tests the species averaged 4.7″ per year, developed severe leaf scorch and often defoliated by August; also, in nursery production trees produce a big trunk without much crown; interestingly, Raulston reported 3 to 5′ of growth per year on young plants.

DISEASES AND INSECTS: Unusually free of pests.

LANDSCAPE VALUE: Medium-headed shade tree of unique interest for bark; excellent in parks and other large areas, possibly for residential landscapes with lots of 20,000 square feet or more; not for streets although has been used for that purpose; from my observations not as urban tolerant as the literature would have us believe.

CULTIVARS:

'His Majesty'—Male selection with good foliage and habit, University of Minnesota Landscape Arboretum 1996 introduction.

'Macho'—The first selection of *P. amurense* with moderately spreading growth habit, thick leathery dark green leaves, handsome corky bark, high resistance to insects and diseases, a male, planted at Milliken Arboretum, Spartanburg, SC where performance is lack-luster, Bill Wandell introduction.

Shademaster® ('RNI 4551')—Strong-growing form, moderately spreading crown, improved branching structure, 35 to 40′ by 35 to 40′, lustrous dark green foliage, yellow in fall, male, Princeton introduction in 1991.

PROPAGATION: Seeds germinate like beans without any treatment; I have directly sowed seed and also stratified seed and then planted; the differences in germination percentage were negligible although the percent was slightly higher with stratification; have read research that intimated cold-moist stratification improved germination.

NATIVE HABITAT: Northern China, Manchuria and Japan. Introduced 1856.

RELATED SPECIES:

Phellodendron lavallei Dode., (fel-ō-den′dron la-val′ē-ī), Lavalle Corktree, tends to be more regular in outline than the above. The branches are more upright and the bark develops a corky characteristic but perhaps not as pronounced as *P. amurense*. The leaflets are duller green. I consider this a rather handsome tree and there are fine specimens in the Arnold Arboretum. Trees 44, 50, 50, 52, and 40' high grew in the Morton Arboretum in late 1980's. Central Japan. Introduced 1862. Zone 5 to 7.

Phellodendron sachalinense (F. Schmidt) Sarg., (fel-ō-den'dron sa-ka-len-en'sē), Sakhalin Corktree, tends to be more vase-shaped than the irregularly branched *P. amurense*. It also grows larger (50 to 60' high). Although the literature states the bark is non-corky, I do not find this to be true. There is a splendid specimen at the Arnold Arboretum. Minnesota Landscape Arboretum considers this species slightly hardier than *P. amurense* and has found it to be extremely fast-growing. Korea, northern Japan and western China. Introduced 1877. Zone 3b to 7.

ADDITIONAL NOTES: The Arnold and Morton Arboreta have beautiful specimens of these species. Their effect is strongly oriental and the trees must be seen in the mature state to be fully appreciated. Some authorities relegated the two related species to variety status. In spite of what the books say the species treated here are difficult to separate. I collected samples of the various *Phellodendron* species at the Arnold, took them home, spread them out on the kitchen table, and armed with reference books, a hand lens, and a degree of sanity attempted to separate them by leaf, bud and stem. If there were significant differences I did not locate them. *Phellodendron amurense* was once considered a good pollution tolerant tree but has not performed well as a city tree and almost languishes under hostile conditions. Given proper cultural conditions, it makes a fine tree.

About 10 species in Asia, six of which I assessed for differences and from day to day still got confused. My fondest memories of the species harken to the first sabbatical at the Arnold, when each day I would walk past the collection along Meadow Road, particularly the low-slung branching form (alas, now with trunk only remaining), and savor their architecture and bark characteristics.

Philadelphus coronarius L. — Sweet Mockorange
(fil-à-del'fus kôr-o-nā'ri-us)

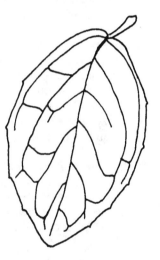

FAMILY: Saxifragaceae

LEAVES: Opposite, simple, ovate to ovate-oblong, 1 1/2 to 4″ long, 1/2 to 2″ wide, acuminate, broad cuneate or rounded at the base, remotely denticulate or dentate, dark green, glabrous except bearded in the axils of veins beneath and sometimes hairy on the veins; petiole—1/6 to 1/3″ long, hairy.

BUDS: Solitary, sessile, with 2 nearly valvate, mostly hairy scales, the terminal lacking.

STEM: Young branches glabrous or slightly pilose, dark reddish to chestnut-brown, exfoliating on old stems; pith—moderate, rounded, pale or white, continuous.

SIZE: 10 to 12' by 10 to 12'.

HARDINESS: Zone 4 to 8.

HABIT: Large rounded shrub with stiff, straight, ascending branches that arch with age; often leggy, straggly.

RATE: Fast.

TEXTURE: Somewhat coarse in all seasons.

BARK: Exfoliating, orangish to reddish brown.

LEAF COLOR: Medium, may be nondescript green in summer, although is often dark green, no change in fall.

FLOWERS: Perfect, 4-petaled, 4-sepaled, numerous stamens, white, 1 to 1 1/2″ across, very fragrant, May to early June, borne in 5- to 7-flowered racemes.

FRUIT: Four-valved dehiscent capsule, many seeded, persisting.

CULTURE: Transplants readily; not particular as to soil; full sun or light shade; prefers moist, well-drained soil supplied with organic matter and here make their best growth; should be pruned after flowering either by removing old wood or cutting to the ground; the root system on mockorange is more extensive and woody than the tops; I dug several large specimens out of our Illinois garden and simply could not believe the mass of roots.

DISEASES AND INSECTS: Canker, leaf spots, powdery mildews, rust, aphids, leaf miner and nematodes; none of these are serious.

LANDSCAPE VALUE: Old favorite for sweetly scented flowers; does not have much to recommend it for the modern landscape; some of the floriferous cultivars are much better than the species; much more common in European gardens than in United States.

CULTIVARS:
  'Aureus'—Yellow foliage with typical fragrant white flowers, a real lemon in any garden, becomes yellow-green to green with heat of summer; widely used in England where it appears to be more suitable; Mr. Gary Koller asked me to remove the real lemon comment, which was an attempt at subtle humor with "a peel"; in Orono, ME this was killed outright while the species survived without injury.
  'Nanus' ('Pumilus')—A rather handsome, compact (4'), haystack-shaped form with dark green foliage; it is rather sparse-flowering; there may be several dwarf types in cultivation.
  'Variegatus'—Leaves with an irregular border of creamy white, actually a weak grower but a rather dainty shrub when well-grown, flowers fragrant, supposedly no foliage burn in Raleigh, NC.
PROPAGATION: In general, seed of all species can be directly sown; softwood cuttings taken in June and July and treated with 1000 ppm IBA-quick dip or talc root readily.
NATIVE HABITAT: Southeastern Europe and Asia Minor. Cultivated 1560.

OTHER *PHILADELPHUS* TYPES OF SOME WORTH

Any treatment of *Philadelphus* species, hybrids and cultivars is superficial; for this I make minimal apology since the only redeeming character is fragrance and many cultivars do not offer this. New hybrids have been introduced from United States and Canadian programs and I have included most of these. A gardener's chances of locating, i.e., purchasing, more than 2 to 3 of those listed is quite dubious unless one locates a specialist *Philadelphus* grower who will be in business for about two weeks in May–June.

There are about 60 species of *Philadelphus* and I believe the numerous hybrids have blurred species integrity. At Edinburgh Botanic Garden many late Junes past, I attempted to assess the collection in full flower. Similarities of floral and foliage characteristics make the group hard to academically digest. Their fragrance (not all species) is heady and perhaps for those 7 to 14 days are deserving of the space in the garden. As yet, there are none in the Dirr garden. On a Scottish garden tour that Al Armitage and I lead in 1995, *P. delavayi* Henry with 1 to 1 1/2" long and wide, pure white, fragrant flowers subtended by purplish calyces excited our entire group. Also, *P. purpurascens* (Koehne) Rehd., with somewhat similar attributes, did likewise.

Philadelphus × cymosus Rehd., (fil-à-del'fus sī -mō'sus), and the cultivars:
  'Banniere'—Flowers semi-double, 1 1/2 to 2 1/2" diameter, fragrant.
  'Conquette'—Flowers single, 2" diameter, very fragrant, one of the best.
  'Norma'—Flowers single, 1 3/4" diameter.
  'Perle Blanche'—Flowers single, 1 1/2" diameter, one of the most fragrant.
    The plants in this group grow 6 to 8' high; tend to be rather open and lanky; hardy in Zone 4 to 5; result of crosses between *P. × lemoinei × P. grandiflorus*.

Philadelphus inodorus L., (fil-à-del'fus in-ō-do'rus), has non-fragrant, 1 3/4 to 2" diameter, cup-shaped flowers. The leaves are among the largest of the *Philadelphus*, up to 4" long, lustrous dark green and denticulate (sometimes entire). The habit is upright, arching, rounded and dense. Plants in Athens are 10' high. Has flowered heavily in partial to half shade. North Carolina to Georgia and Mississippi. Introduced 1738. Zone (5)6 to 8(9).

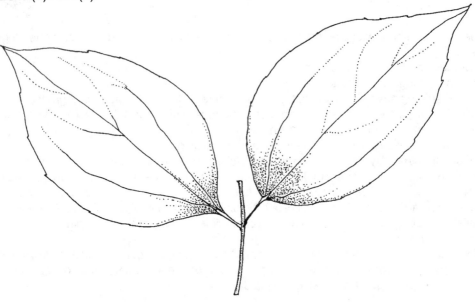

Philadelphus × ***lemoinei*** Lemoine (or *P.* × *purpureomaculatus* Lemoine), (fil-à-del′fus le-moy′nē-ī), and the cultivars:

'Avalanche'—Flowers single, 1″ diameter, 4′ high with arching branches and one of the most fragrant.

'Beauclerk'—Flowers single, up to 3″ across, white with pinkish tinge in center, fragrant, 8′ high, experienced at Edinburgh Botanic Garden.

'Belle Étoile'—Flowers single, 2 1/4″ diameter, 6′ high, fragrant, light maroon blotch at center.

'Boule d'Argent'—Flowers double, 2″ diameter, 5′ high, scarcely fragrant.

'Erectus'—Flowers single, 1″ diameter, 4′ high, good compact, upright habit, scarcely fragrant.

'Fleur de Neige'—Flowers single, 1 1/4″ diameter and very fragrant.

'Girandole'—Flowers double, 1 3/4″ diameter, 4′ high.

'Innocence'—Flowers single, 1 3/4″ diameter, 8′ high, one of the most fragrant forms, foliage sometimes with creamy white variegation.

'Manteau d'Hermine'—Flowers double, creamy, fragrant, small habit, 3 to 4′ high, small leaves to 1″.

'Mont Blanc'—Flowers single, 1 1/4″ diameter, 4′ high, one of the hardier forms.

'Silver Showers'—Graceful arching branches, 5 to 6′ high shrub, large flat-faced, fragrant, white flowers in early summer.

'Sybille'—Flower white, purple stained, highly fragrant, almost squarish, arching shrub, 4 to 5′ high, great plant.

'Sylvia'—Semi-dwarf with masses of double, white flowers.

Plants grow 4 to 8′, are very fragrant and hardy in Zone 5. Result of crosses between *P. microphyllus* × *P. coronarius*.

Philadelphus microphyllus A. Gray, (fil-à-del′fus mī-krō-fil′us), Littleleaf Mock-orange, grows about 3 to 4′ high with small, dark green leaves, 1/2 to 3/4″ long, 1/4 to 1/3″ wide. The pure white flowers, about 1″ across, are cross-shaped, exceedingly fragrant (pineapple-like) and beautiful. The shrub in full flower is exquisite. I first witnessed it in a German botanic garden. Native from Colorado to New Mexico and Arizona. Zone 6 to 9. Introduced 1883.

Philadelphus × ***virginalis*** Rehd., (fil-à-del′fus vĕr-ji-nā′lis), and the cultivars:

'Albatre'—Flowers double, 1 1/4″ diameter, 5′ high.

'Argentine'—Flowers very double, 2″ diameter, 4′ high.

'Bouquet Blanc'—Flowers single, 1″ diameter, 6′ high, mound-like habit and covered with flowers.

'Burford' ('Burfordiensis')—Flowers single to semi-double, 2 1/4 to 2 1/2″ diameter, not fragrant.

'Glacier'—Flowers double, 1 1/4″ diameter, 5′ high, hardy at Orono, ME.

'Minnesota Snowflake'—Fragrant, white, double, 2″ diameter flowers, 6 to 8′ in height, 5 to 6′ wide, and clothed with branches, supposedly withstanding temperatures as low as -30°F, some dieback in Orono, ME, G.D. Bush introduction.

'Snow Velvet'—Shrub to 6′, semi-double, sweetly scented, 2 to 3″ diameter flowers.

'Virginal'—Flowers double, 2″ diameter, very fragrant, 9′ high.

Plants grow 5 to 9′, are hardy in Zone 5. Result of crosses between *P.* × *lemoinei* × *P. nivalis* 'Plena'.

SEVERAL ADDITIONAL CULTIVARS THAT CANNOT BE CATEGORIZED AS TO GROUP INCLUDE:

'Audrey'—Large shrub to 8′ or greater; large, white, fragrant flowers, Morden introduction.

'Buckley's Quill'—Small, erect-branching shrub, 5 to 6′ high, 4′ wide, with compact clusters of fragrant, white, double flowers, petals are narrow with pointed tips, up to 30 petals per flower, result of cross between 'Frosty Morn' × 'Bouquet Blanc' made by D.F. Cameron in 1961, see *Canadian J. Plant Sci.* 59:879–882 (1976).

'Enchantment'—Large, semi-double, fragrant flowers, 6 to 7′ high and well-clothed with foliage to the ground.

'Frosty Morn'—Double, fragrant flowers on a 4 to 5′ high shrub; introduced in 1953 by G.D. Bush of Minneapolis.

'Galahad'—A new selection with single white fragrant flowers on a compact 4 to 5′ high rounded shrub, dieback shrub at Orono, ME.

'Janet Reidy'—Low compact shrub, very fragrant, semi-double, white flowers in May–June, clean foliage.

'Marjorie'—Single, large, fragrant flowers, 9 to 10′ high shrub, arching branches, introduced by Morden Experiment Station in 1962.

'Miniature Snowflake'—Double, fragrant flowers on a compact, 3 to 4′ high shrub, have seen listed as 2 to 3′ high, 1 to 2′ wide, prolific flower production, dark green, disease resistant foliage, branch sport of 'Minnesota Snowflake', Bailey Nursery introduction, no damage in Orono, ME.

'Natchez'—In flower perhaps the handsomest of all mockoranges with 1 1/2″(2″) diameter, slightly fragrant, pure white flowers that cover the leaves in May and produce an avalanche, some tendency toward petaloid stamens but the four major petals dominate, large upright form easily 8 to 10′ at maturity; have observed a great amount of *Cercospora* leaf spot in summer which disfigures foliage, good fertility and soil moisture reduce leaf spot incidence; killed at Orono, ME.

'Patricia'—Three to 4′ high shrub with cream-white flowers.

'Polar Star'—Semi-double, fragrant, white, 2 1/2″ wide, May–June, again in autumn, 10 to 12′ high, Zone 5 to 8, chance seedling from garden of late Herbert Fischer of Illinois.

'Purity'—Shrub to 5′ with porcelain white, fragrant flowers.

'Snow Velvet'—Semi-double, white, sweet fragrance, every branch covered with up to 3″ diameter flowers, 6′ high.

'Snowbelle'—Compact to 4′ high, double, white, fragrant flowers in compact clusters, from the Ottawa Canada breeding program.

'Snowdwarf'—A compact shrub, 1 1/2 to 2 1/2′ high and 1 1/2′ wide; flowers are pure white, 1 1/2 to 1 3/4″ wide, with 20 petals, 6 sepals and no stamens, occur in clusters of 5; leaves are dark green, about 2″ long, 1 1/4 to 1 3/4″ long; should be hardy to -25°F; only true dwarf besides 'Manteau d'Hermine' but it has a longer flowering season and is more productive; see *HortScience* 22:163 (1987) for other details.

'Snowgoose'—A free-flowering, winter hardy form with very fragrant, double (20 petals), pure white flowers; an upright shrub 4 to 5′ high and 2 to 3 1/2′ wide; foliage is dark green, 1 1/2 to 2 1/2″ long, 3/4 to 1 1/2″ wide; should be hardy to -25°F; a cross between 'Frosty Morn' and 'Bouquet Blanc' made in 1959; in Canada tests it was one of the most cold hardy cultivars, comparable to 'Galahad' and 'Siberregen' but more florally productive; *HortScience* 23: 785 (1988).

'Sylvia'—Upright, 6 to 7′ high shrub with semi-double, fragrant, white flowers.

All *Philadelphus* types require about the same care—none. They are vigorous, easy to grow plants but are strictly of single season quality. In flower they are attractive but the rest of the year (about 50 weeks) are real eyesores. My garden space and labor are too valuable to waste on shrubs which only return a small interest. Consider these factors before extensively planting shrubs of this type.

Am I weakening? In recent travels I started taking photographs and notes. Current favorites include: 'Belle Étoile', 'Manteau d'Hermine', and 'Sybille'. The latter I would *consider* placing in the Dirr garden. The purple-sepaled types, *P. purpurascens* and *P. delavayi*, also initiated pronounced heart palpitations.

Photinia serrulata Lindl. — Chinese Photinia, Oriental Photinia
(fō-tin′i-à ser-ū-lā′tà)

FAMILY: Rosaceae

LEAVES: Alternate, simple, evergreen, lanceolate to oblong, 4 to 8″ long, 1 1/2 to 3 1/2″ wide, firm and leathery, undulating, acute, cuneate, finely serrate from base to apex, midrib prominent, lustrous dark green above, flat medium green below, glabrous; petiole—about 1″ long, clothed on top with whitish aging to brownish hairs.

BUDS: Flower—imbricate, 3/4 to 1″ long, greenish red, conical with apex slightly crooked, 7- to 9-scaled, glabrous; laterals—small, obscure.

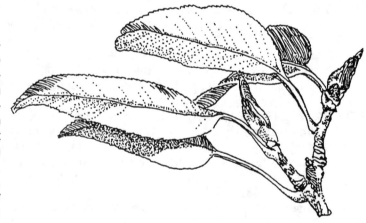

STEM: Stout, terete, glabrous, greenish brown, prominently dotted with brownish vertical lenticels; when bruised emits a prominent maraschino cherry odor; pith—solid, greenish white.

SIZE: 20 to 25′(30′) high, about two-third's that in spread, the largest of the commonly cultivated photinias; a 50 to 60′ high specimen resides at the Bath Botanic Garden.

HARDINESS: Zone 6 to 9; the most cold hardy of the three discussed herein.

HABIT: Small tree or enormous multi-stemmed evergreen shrub that tends to engulf every structure or plant in close proximity.

RATE: Medium to fast.

TEXTURE: Coarse.

BARK: Blackish often exfoliating in large scales, relatively attractive.

LEAF COLOR: Emerging leaves green to bronze to reddish purple soon turning lustrous dark green; very handsome for the new leaves coincide with the flower; start to emerge in early to mid-March (Athens) depending on weather; usually a few reddish leaves present during winter.

FLOWERS: White, perfect, 5-petaled, each flower 1/3″ across, borne in a 4 to 7″ wide, terminal, corymbose panicle, malodorous like many of the hawthorns; odor quite offensive; contrast handsomely with the young foliage; early to mid-April; flowers last a good two weeks; open ahead of those of *P.* × *fraseri* and *P. glabra*.

FRUIT: Globose, 1/4″ diameter, red pome which matures in late summer and persists through spring of the following year, the large panicles of red are quite effective in the winter landscape; may turn black with time but this has not been the situation with plants I have observed.

CULTURE: Easily transplanted, well-drained soil; pH adaptable; full sun or partial shade; does not tolerate extremely wet soils; responds well to fertilizer; tends to exhibit nitrogen deficiency in landscape situations; does not form a great number of lateral breaks when pruned thus making it difficult to make a dense shrub; interesting study on growth of *P.* × *fraseri* in shade—plants in full sun, 69, 47 or 29% sun showed no differences in growth 7 months after transplanting to field; while in production phase acceptable plants were produced in full, 69 and 47% sun which indicates terrific shade tolerances; this is further substantiated by observational data taken in the landscape; see *J. Amer. Soc. Hort. Sci.* 116:1046–1051 (1991); salt tolerance is discussed in *J. Environ. Hort.* 8:154–155 (1990).

DISEASES AND INSECTS: Mildew, leaf spots, fireblight, scales, and several other insects, resistant to *Entomosporium* leaf spot that is so troublesome to *P.* × *fraseri*.

LANDSCAPE VALUE: Large hedge or privacy screen; could be used as a small tree; often used erroneously on the corners of small buildings; have seen it used in groupings around large campus buildings and it tends to soften some of the harsh architectural lines; can be used in groupings, screens; flowers are really foul smelling.

CULTIVARS: Often wondered why no United States cultivars have been selected. Considerable variation in growth habit and color of emerging leaves. European literature notes 'Aculeata' with red stems and 'Rotundiloba' with smaller and more rounded leaves, and smaller habit. I have seen neither.

    'Green Giant'—Oval-rounded form more upright than most, extremely dense, lustrous dark green foliage, new leaves light apple green, 30 to 45′ high, 20 to 30′ wide, could be fashioned into a respectable single-stemmed tree, selected by author from the Georgia campus.

PROPAGATION: Seeds will germinate without cold treatment but 30 days of cold moist stratification unifies germination. Cutting information presented applies to *P.* × *fraseri* but is pertinent to *P. glabra* and *P. serrulata*. Many researchers have demonstrated the need for high IBA levels from 5000 to 10,000 ppm quick dip. Probably the best time to take cuttings is after the first flush of growth has firmed in late spring or early summer. However, cuttings can almost be rooted year-round. Use a well-drained medium and mist. Cuttings root in 4 to 6 weeks. May take 8 to 10 weeks depending on time of year. See Dirr, *J. Environ. Hort.* 8:83–85 (1990) for the discussion of P-ITB and its positive effect on rooting. Also, *J. Environ. Hort.* 7:158–160 (1989) for effects of carriers and IBA formulations on rooting.

NATIVE HABITAT: China. Introduced 1804.

RELATED SPECIES:

Photinia × ***fraseri*** Dress — Fraser Photinia

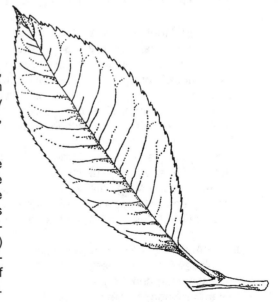

LEAVES: Alternate, simple, evergreen, elliptic-ovate to elliptic, 2 3/4 to 4″ long, half as wide, acute, cuneate, uniform small serrations, copper-red upon emerging, finally lustrous dark green, pale below; petiole—1/2 to 1″ long, slightly hairy.

Photinia × *fraseri*, (fō-tin′i-à frā′zēr-ī), Fraser Photinia, is the most popular photinia for southern gardens. In fact the words "red tip" mean only one thing: *P.* × *fraseri*. The name is derived from the red color of the new foliage. This plant is so overused that the term nauseous is not sufficiently applicable. Fraser Photinia grows 10 to 15′(20′) high and about one-half that in spread. At Hillier Arboretum, England, a 20′ to 20′ was thriving without the leaf spot. The outline is distinctly upright in youth and old age.

Young plants when first set in the landscape are relatively open but fill in with time. Ideally plants should be pruned when young to encourage basal branching. This plant shows nitrogen stresses quite vividly, with off-color (yellowish) foliage. Flowers and fruits are intermediate between the parents. The inflorescences range from 5 to 6″ across and open in mid-April, after *P. serrulata*. This plant is treated like privet and the flower buds are often removed in the pruning process. It is an undeniable fact that a hedge or screen fully clothed with the brilliant reddish foliage is an eye-catcher. The foliage does fade to deep green after 2 to 4 weeks, however, another flush of growth in summer or occasional spurious breaks will provide color. Basic problems and cultural requirements are the same as described under *P. serrulata*. This plant is a bread and butter item of many southern nurseries. *Photinia* × *fraseri* arose at the Fraser Nurseries, Birmingham, AL around 1940. All the seedlings agreed with the seed parent, *P. serrulata*, except one outstanding plant, which was propagated and put into commerce in 1955. The original selection was named 'Birmingham' and probably all plants grown in the South as *P.* × *fraseri* should be listed as *P.* × *fraseri* 'Birmingham' since it is a named cultivar and all plants are reproduced through vegetative means (cuttings). Undeniably tough plant except for leaf spot; I have observed it in almost impossible soil conditions and in heavy shade forming a respectable screen or hedge. The moist, humid weather in 1989 literally defoliated many plants in southern landscapes. A troublesome and often devastating leaf spot, *Entomosporium maculatum*, can wreak havoc on the species and complete defoliation may result. The disease is manifested by roundish lesions with purple halos that may coalesce and kill entire leaves. Spray schedules need to be vigorous to prevent the disease. Worthwhile discussion by Walker, *J. Environ. Hort.* 10:145–149 (1992) that traces factors affecting fungicidal control of *Entomosporium* leaf spot. Several relatively effective fungicides are available and it is best to check with the local extension agents. Several cultivars should be mentioned. 'Red Robin' is common in Europe but not in the United States. As I have seen it, the habit is more spreading than 'Birmingham' and the leaves are a rich ruby red but not as intense as 'Birmingham'. It was developed in New Zealand. Appears more compact than 'Birmingham', perhaps 8 to 10′. 'Robusta' has coppery red new leaves that become leathery dark green and resemble *P. serrulata*, also quite vigorous and grew 12′ in 6 years, originated in Hazlewood Nursery, Sydney, Australia. 'Indian Princess' is slower growing, dense branching with orange-coppery new foliage, leaves are about one-half the size of 'Birmingham', a branch sport discovered at Monrovia Nursery Co. 'Kentucky' was provided to me by a gentleman near Jellico, TN who called and reported a plant that withstood -17°F and had no leaf spot. Cuttings were sent, rooted and continue to be evaluated. A relatively clean form from campus was rooted, placed along with *P. glabra*, *P. serrulata*, and *P.* × *fraseri* in my test plots. After four years, *P. glabra* is dead, *P.* × *fraseri* from campus drops about one-half its leaves, *P. serrulata* and *P.* × *fraseri* 'Kentucky' remain clean. I theorize about the resistance in the discussion under *P. glabra*

ADDITIONAL NOTES. Zone 7 to 9. Less cold hardy than *P. serrulata*.

Photinia glabra (Thunb.) Maxim. — Japanese Photinia
LEAVES: Alternate, simple, evergreen, narrowly oval to slightly obovate, 1 1/2 to 3 1/2″ long, one-third to one-half as wide, pointed, cuneate, regularly and shallowly serrate, bronzy red when emerging, finally glossy dark green, glabrous; petiole—1/4 to 1/2″ long.

Photinia glabra, (fō-tin′i-à glā′brà), Japanese Photinia, is the smallest version of the 3 evergreen photinias presented here, topping out between 10 and 12′ high. The new growth is red, the leaves smaller, finer toothed, glabrous, and the flowers and fruits smaller than *P.* × *fraseri* or *P. serrulata*. The flowers also have the characteristic hawthorn odor and appear later and in smaller inflorescences. The petiole at maturity is glabrous compared to the pubescent petiole of *P. serrulata*. 'Rubens' has bright bronzy red leaves. 'Rosea Marginata' with green, gray, white and pink leaves and 'Variegata' with pink emerging leaves becoming green with white margins are described. Japan, China. Introduced 1914 by Wilson. Zone (7)8; definitely less cold hardy than previous two species, was killed to the ground or outright at -3°F.

ADDITIONAL NOTES: Photinias are ubiquitous throughout the South. When a customer asks a garden center employee for a good hedge plant these are recommended. Need I elaborate further. The flower odor is objectionable and the plant should not be located too close to entrances and walks. Over the past 19 years in Georgia I have learned the nuances of the species and hybrids. The following rankings are reasonably accurate. *Photinia serrulata* flowers before *P.* × *fraseri* before *P. glabra*. *Photinia serrulata* is more cold hardy (-5 to -10°F) than *P.* × *fraseri* (about -5°F) than *P. glabra* (0°F). *Photinia* × *fraseri* is more resistant to mildew than the other two species. *Photinia serrulata* is more resistant to *Entomosporium* than *P.* × *fraseri* and *P. glabra*. It is difficult to assess the actual degree of susceptibility of *P. glabra* since it is seldom grown in Zone 7 landscapes.

An interesting disease-screening methodology was published by Jacobs et al., *J. Environ. Hort.* 14: 154–157 (1996). Also, Dirr, *Nursery Management and Production* 13(7):14–15 (1997), waxes philosophically about the potential of breeding multiclonal red tips for disease resistance. In the *J. Environ. Hort.* study, *P. serrulata* was most resistant followed by 'Kentucky', with 'Birmingham' and *P. glabra* most susceptible on the mature leaves.

Photinia villosa (Thunb.) DC. — Oriental Photinia
(fō-tin'i-à vil-lō'sà)

LEAVES: Alternate, simple, obovate to oblong-obovate, 1 1/2 to 3 1/2″ long, 3/4 to 1 1/2″ wide, acuminate, cuneate, finely and sharply serrate, each serration gland-tipped, glabrous and dark green above, villous beneath with 5 to 7 pairs of veins, firm at maturity; petiole—1/25 to 1/5″ long.

BUDS: Sessile, solitary, ovoid, acute, with about 4, somewhat keeled and mucronate scales; terminal lacking.

STEM: Moderate or rather slender, rounded, with large lenticels; pith rather small, continuous; leaf scars 2-ranked, linear, crescent-shaped or somewhat 3-lobed, somewhat raised; 3 bundle traces.

SIZE: 10 to 15′ high, usually less in spread.
HARDINESS: Zone 4 to 7; hardy at Orono, ME.
HABIT: A large shrub, but can be trained as a tree, often with an irregular, obovoid crown, usually taller than broad, somewhat vase-shaped or broad-rounded and shrubby.
RATE: Medium.
TEXTURE: Medium throughout the year.
LEAF COLOR: Dark green above, villous beneath in summer changing to yellowish, reddish bronze and red in fall, fall color often approximates orange to orange-red.
FLOWERS: White, 1/3″ across, May into June; borne in 1 to 2″ diameter corymbs terminating short side branches; inflorescence conspicuously warty.
FRUIT: Pome, bright red, ellipsoidal, 1/3″ long; effective in October and persist for a time if not consumed by the birds.
CULTURE: Best to move balled-and-burlapped; prefers well-drained acid soil; full sun or light shade; pruning is rarely required.
DISEASES AND INSECTS: Leaf spots, powdery mildews, fireblight; fireblight can be a very serious problem and for this reason the plant is often not grown.
LANDSCAPE VALUE: Makes a good specimen or shrub border plant; the fruits and fall color are attractive; extensive use limited by fireblight susceptibility.
CULTIVARS:
var. *laevis* (Thunb.) Dipp. —Leaves longer pointed, glabrous or only slightly downy, red fruits are 1/2″ long, most plants grown as *P. villosa* are var. *laevis*. Japan.
forma *maximowicziana* (Lév.) Rehd.—Leaves almost sessile, rounded and abruptly acuminate, sometimes almost truncate at the apex, cuneate at base, veins deeply impressed, autumn color is described as yellow but as I observed it at the Arnold it was a good orange-red; the habit was that of a large, spreading shrub. Korean.
var. *sinica* Rehd. & Wils.—Downy young shoots, fruits egg-shaped, 1/2″ long, orange-scarlet, flowers borne in racemes, leaves color red in fall, 15 to 25′, leaves oval to oblong, finely serrated, bright green above, paler below, soon glabrous, represents species in central and western China.
The Arnold lists the additional varieties *longipes* and *zollingeri*. Their traits are unknown to me.
'Village Shade'—Vase-shaped habit, better form than the species with dark green foliage, heavy flower and fruit production, from J.C. Raulston Arboretum.
PROPAGATION: Softwood, semi-hardwood, or hardwood cuttings will root without great difficulty; I have rooted the species from softwood cuttings in July using 1000 ppm IBA, peat:perlite, mist. Reports from J.C. Raulston Arboretum noted that softwood cuttings are the easiest to root. Seed requires a 45 to 60 day cold treatment.

ADDITIONAL NOTES: I witnessed excessive fireblight on the species in Ohio and simply erased the plant from the mental palette. Occasionally, worthy plants appear at Swarthmore College, J.C. Raulston Arboretum, Biltmore Gardens and I think this is not such an inadequate plant. Often difficult to identify in leaf and bud and I have been stumped more than once. Flowers remind of a woodsy hawthorn while fruits, though colorful, are never overly abundant. At Biltmore the species has escaped from cultivation and many plants established along the exit road past the lower garden area.

I have experienced several other species primarily in arboreta that are worth the mention. ***Photinia parvifolia*** (Franch.) Schneid. is a small, vase-shaped shrub, 4 to 6′ high with 1 to 3″ long, 1/2 to 2″ wide, obovate to oval, finely serrated, dark green leaves that turn rich red to red-purple in fall. Fall color, as experienced at the Arnold, was brilliant. The species is still listed as extant in the collection. The white flowers occur in a 1 1/3″ wide panicle of 5 to 9, 1/3″ diameter flowers. Fruit is an oval, 1/3″ long, orange to bright red pome. China. Zone 6.

Other species listed in American commerce include: ***Photinia beauverdiana*** Schneid. with orange-red fall color, white flowers and red fruit to 15′, Zone 6; and ***Photinia davidsoniae*** Rehd. & Wils., an evergreen species with red spring leaves, 3 to 5″ long, lustrous green foliage, white flowers and sparsely produced, orange-red fruits, 15 to 30′ high, appears more resistant to leaf spot that affects *P.* × *fraseri*, central China, Zone 8.

NATIVE HABITAT: Japan, Korea, China. Introduced about 1865.

Physocarpus opulifolius (L.) Maxim. — Common Ninebark, also Eastern Ninebark
(fī-sō-kär′pus op-ū-li-fō′li-us)

FAMILY: Rosaceae

LEAVES: Alternate, simple, roundish ovate, 1 to 3″ long, one-half to as wide, usually 3- to 5-lobed, sometimes slightly so or not at all, with crenate-dentate obtuse or acutish lobes, cordate at base, medium green, glabrous or nearly so beneath; petiole—1/4 to 3/4″ long.

BUDS: Imbricate, appressed, basically glabrous, usually 5-scaled, brown.

STEM: Young—shiny red-brown, glabrous; old—brown, exfoliating in papery strips; stems distinctly angled from base of leaf scars; pith—brownish.

SIZE: 5 to 10′ in height, spread 6 to 10′.

HARDINESS: Zone 2 to 7.

HABIT: Upright-spreading shrub with stiffly recurved branches, rounded and dense in foliage but quite ragged in winter.

RATE: Medium to fast.

TEXTURE: Medium in leaf, definitely coarse in winter.

BARK: Peeling in long papery sheets on older stems.

LEAF COLOR: Flat green (medium) in summer; fall color yellowish to bronze; usually not effective.

FLOWERS: White or pinkish, each flower about 1/4 to 1/3″ diameter, May–June, borne in many-flowered, 1 to 2″ diameter corymbs, effective but not overwhelming, stamens purplish, numbering about 30.

FRUIT: Consist of 3 to 5 follicles, each 1/4″ long, inflated, glabrous, reddish, September–October, reasonably attractive; appears to be some variation in degree of red coloration.

CULTURE: Easily transplanted; adapted to difficult situations; full sun or partial shade; very tough individual resembling spirea in character; withstands acid and alkaline soils; dry situations; renew by cutting to ground in late winter.

LANDSCAPE VALUE: Quite coarse and therefore difficult to use in the small home landscape; massing, border, possibly a screen; limited in usefulness because of rather meager ornamental assets; bark on older stems (1/2″ diameter or larger) exfoliates into papery strips exposing a rich brown inner bark; unfortunately, this character is masked by the foliage and dense tangle of stems.

CULTIVARS:

'Dart's Gold'—A more compact (4 to 5′ by 4 to 5′) form than 'Luteus' with better yellow color; I have seen it in late June at Bernheim Arboretum and was quite impressed although the foliage color was yellow-green, it loses the yellow with time; possibly a good choice for spring and early summer foliage color but not superior to the golden foliaged forms of *Spiraea*, particularly 'Gold Mound' and 'Limemound'.

'Diablo'—A reddish purple foliage form that supposedly holds its color in the heat of the summer, however, plants at McCorkle Nurseries, Dearing, GA turned cucumber green in the Georgia summer heat; Dan Hinkley, *American Nurseryman* 186(2):56–61 (1997), noted that 'Diablo' may hold the reddish purple color where summers are hot and humid, so much for West Coast plantsmen evaluating plant performance in the Southeast.

var. *intermedius* Rydb.—A handsome, low-growing (4′), fine-textured form with darker green and smaller leaves than the species; preferable for modern gardens because of refined and humble character; found in Minnesota, Colorado and Black Hills of South Dakota.

'Luteus'—Leaves initially yellow gradually changing to yellowish green and finally almost green, large shrub, easily growing 8 to 10′ tall and as wide.

'Nanus'—Dwarf form with smaller, less deeply lobed, dark green leaves, red fruits, listed as growing 2 to 6′, useful as mounding bank cover.

'Nugget'—Superior dense, compact habit, 6′ by 5′, fine-textured foliage, emerges deep golden yellow, matures to lime green, then turns yellow in autumn, South Dakota State University introduction.

'Snowfall'—Neater, more compact than the species, 5 to 7′ by 6 to 10′, large flowers more showy than species, medium green summer foliage, at best yellowish bronze in autumn, selected from the wild on the north shore of Lake Superior.

PROPAGATION: Cuttings, easily propagated from softwood cuttings taken in summer; such cuttings rooted better in sand:peat than in sand, and better at 60°F than 70°F; November cuttings rooted 80% in 53 days without treatment. Probably better to not treat cuttings (best rooting) for IBA-treated cuttings rooted poorly; see *HortScience* 30:363–365 (1995). Seeds germinate readily without pretreatment.

ADDITIONAL NOTES: The Minnesota Landscape Arboretum has a large collection of ninebarks and after looking over the entire group, I still came away with the opinion that about anything is better than a *Physocarpus*.

NATIVE HABITAT: Quebec to Virginia, Tennessee, Michigan and Minnesota. Introduced 1687.

RELATED SPECIES:

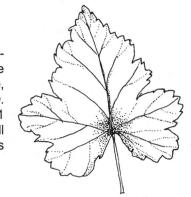

Physocarpus monogynus (Torr.) Coult., (fī-sō-kär′pus mon-ō′jī-nus), Mountain Ninebark, is an erect, much-branched, compact, 2 to 3′ high and wide shrub of refined proportions. The small, 3/4 to 1 1/2″ long, roundish ovate, 3-lobed, irregularly and doubly toothed leaves remind of *Ribes alpinum*. The small, 1/4″ diameter, white or rose-tinted flowers occur in 3/4 to 1 1/3″ diameter, few-flowered corymbs in May–June. Rather pretty small shrub for massing and low hedges. South Dakota and Wyoming to Texas and New Mexico. Introduced 1879. Zone 5 to 7.

Picea A. Dietr.— Spruce
FAMILY: Pinaceae

The spruces represent an interesting group of usually tall, symmetrical, conical trees. Numerous cultivars occur within selected species (*P. abies*, *P. glauca*, *P. pungens*) but are limitedly available in the everyday trade. The genus includes nearly 40 species which are largely restricted to the cooler regions of the Northern Hemisphere. No less than 18 of these are confined to China but some of the newer Chinese species are difficult to separate. *Picea* is the ancient Latin name of the spruces, derived from pix=pitch. The wood is strong for its weight and is of primary importance in the manufacture of pulp and paper. The resinous bark exudations of *P. abies* furnish the so-called Burgundy pitch which is the basic compound for a number of varnishes and medicinal compounds; while the new leafy shoots are used in brewing spruce beer. Sounding boards for musical instruments are made from the wood of *P. abies*. Healing salves from gums and aromatic distillations of *P. glauca* and *P. mariana* are made, as well as ropes from the roots of *P. abies* and *P. glauca*.

MORPHOLOGICAL CHARACTERISTICS
Monoecious trees, pyramidal or conical; bark usually thin, scaly on old trees, sometimes furrowed at base; branches whorled; branchlets with prominent leaf-cushions (pulveni), separated by incised grooves and produced at the apex into a peg-like stalk bearing the leaf and left when the leaves fall; winter buds ovoid or conical; scales imbricated, with or without resin; leaves spirally, often pectinately arranged, on underside of branchlets, usually 4-angled, stomatiferous on all 4 sides or compressed and stomatiferous only on the upper or ventral side which appears by twisting of leaves to be the lower one; usually with 2 marginal resin-ducts; male flowers axillary; female flowers terminal; cones mostly hanging, ovoid to oblong-cylindrical, not shattering at maturity; scales suborbicular to rhombic-oblong, subtended by small bracts; seeds 2 to each scale, compressed; wing large, thin, obovate or oblong.

GROWTH CHARACTERISTICS
Most spruces are large trees of pyramidal to conical outline of a very formal nature. This tends to limit their usefulness as they dominate a small landscape because of their size and strong vertical lines. Retention of foliage and branches results in dense, attractive trees even after many years. *Picea glauca* 'Conica' is the most common dwarf type available in the trade. *Picea abies* alone contains over 150 cultivars, only a few of which possess merit for landscape use, or are sufficiently different from each other that anyone could notice the differences.

CULTURE
Spruces should be transplanted balled-and-burlapped or from containers and, because of the shallow, spreading root system, large specimens can be transplanted successfully. Spruces prefer a moderately moist, well-drained soil although perform well in the clay soils of the Midwest and East. They do not grow well under hot, dry, polluted conditions. Spruces are not adapted to culture in the Southeast (Zone 8 to 11) although on occasion *P. abies* will show prosperity. *Picea omorika*, *P. orientalis* and *P. pungens* are more tolerant of dry conditions than other species. Usually little pruning is necessary but plants can be touched up in spring when the new growth is approximately one-half developed to create a denser plant. Selected species can be used for hedges as they tolerate heavy pruning.

DISEASES AND INSECTS
Canker (*Cytospora*), needle casts, rusts, wood decay, spruce gall aphid, cooley spruce gall aphid, other aphids, spruce budworm (serious in Maine on *Picea mariana*, *P. rubens*, and *Abies balsamea*), spruce bud scale, spruce needle miner, pine needle scale, spruce epizeuxis, sawflies, white pine weevil, spruce spider mite and bagworm. The three most prevalent pests appear to be mites, aphids and bagworms. A review of the forestry literature reveals an interminable number of studies on insect and disease problems.

PROPAGATION
Seeds of most *Picea* species germinate promptly without pretreatment, but cold stratification has been used for a few species. Cuttings have been used in isolated cases but percentages were usually low and this does not represent a practical method of propagation. Grafting is used on the cultivars of *P. abies* and especially the blue-foliaged forms of *P. pungens*. A side graft is used on seedlings of the species. Dirr and Heuser, 1987, present a detailed discussion of *Picea* propagation and should be consulted for specifics.

LANDSCAPE VALUE
Spruces are used extensively in large scale landscape plantings such as parks, golf courses, highways, and public buildings. The dense compact character of even older specimens provides attractive dependable evergreens which change little in effect over a long period of time. The symmetrical form results in plants with strong outlines and formal habit.
Textural variations are not great; however, some differences in branching habit can be used for different effect, i.e., the stiff branching of *P. pungens* contrasts with the pendulous branching of *P. abies*. Color contrasts are more distinctive and include light, dark, and yellow greens, and many shades of blue. Because of the conspicuous character of many of the so-called Blue Spruces, care and discretion should be used in

locating these plants in the landscape. One of the stigmas of our landscapes has been the placement of these plants in prominent places especially in the front of the property, which detracts from all other plantings as well as the house.

Selected forms are effective as hedges, screens, windbreaks, specimens, and plantings near large buildings.

SELECTED SPRUCE SPECIES
(the best spruces for general landscape use)

Picea abies
Picea glauca
Picea omorika
Picea orientalis
Picea pungens

Picea abies (L.) Karst. — Norway Spruce
(pī′sē-à ā′bēz)

LEAVES: Persistent for several years, those on the upper side of the stem more or less overlapping and pointing forwards, those on the lower side spreading right and left and exposing the stem; rhombic in cross-section, 1/2 to 1″ long, stiff, straight or curved, ending in a blunt, horny point; light or dark green with 2 or 3 stomatic lines on each side, often shining green.

BUDS: Reddish or light brown, not resinous, scales often with spreading tips, about 1/4″ long, rosette-shaped.

STEM: Reddish brown or orangish brown, glabrous or with minute scattered hairs.

CONES: Pendulous, cylindrical, 4 to 6″ long, brown when mature; cone scales without undulations, persisting through winter.

SIZE: 40 to 60′ in height by 25 to 30′ spread; can grow to 100′ and more; national champion is 120′ by 66′ at Hamilton College, Clinton, NY.

HARDINESS: Zone 3b to 7(8), survives but is not well-adapted to Zone 8 conditions.

HABIT: Pyramidal with pendulous branchlets; stiff when young, graceful at maturity.

RATE: Medium to fast especially in youth; may grow 75′ high after 50 years.

TEXTURE: Medium.

BARK: Usually thin on young trees; on old trees thick with small, thin, gray-brown, flaking surface scales.

LEAF COLOR: Bright green to purplish in youth changing to lustrous dark green with 2 to 3 stomatic lines on each side.

FLOWERS: Monoecious, male flowers are axillary and infrequent whereas female flowers are terminal, spread on the crowns of the trees and reddish pink in color.

FRUIT: Cones are cylindrical, 4 to 6″ long, 1 1/2 to 2″ wide, pendulous, purple or green in youth, light brown at maturity, seeds 1/6″ long, brownish black with a pale brown, 1/2″ wide wing.

CULTURE: The following applies to all spruces covered in this book unless other specifics are listed under a particular plant; transplant balled-and-burlapped in large sizes (3 to 4′ and greater); move readily because of shallow, spreading root system; performs best in moderately moist, sandy, acid, well-drained soils but can be planted in most average soils provided adequate moisture is available especially in the early years of establishment; prefers a cold climate; prune in early spring either by removing a selected branch or, if a hedge is desired, by pruning the young growth; full sun or perhaps very light shade in South but plants become thin and ragged in heavy shade.

DISEASES AND INSECTS: Susceptible to red spider, spruce gall aphid, budworm and borers.

LANDSCAPE VALUE: Much overplanted, with old age may lose its form and its usefulness; commonly used as a windbreak, shelters or as a temporary specimen; my judgements relative to *P. abies* have been jaded by countless early plantsmen who regarded it as little more than green trash; my evolving thoughts are perhaps not; certainly when utilized in small landscapes, by the house, near a walk, it becomes excessive, but does grow particularly well in the harsher climate of the Midwest and East; on a February 14, 1997 visit to Cincinnati it was everywhere, but green and rather soul-stirring under the dingy, dishwater gray winter sky; for reference I should add that compared to *P. orientalis* and *P. omorika*, particularly on Spring Grove's world-class grounds, *P. abies* will always be third tier; unfortunately, those earlier two species are not widely available and do not grow as fast.

CULTIVARS: For a complete list see Den Ouden and Boom, Dallimore and Jackson, and Welch. The following are some that I have observed and which are also available in the trade. Iseli Nursery, Boring, OR, lists 22 forms of *P. abies* in 1998 catalog. For fun, I counted over 120 forms in Krüssmann's *Manual of Cultivated Conifers. Conifers*, 1996, Timber Press, shows 76 forms in living color. Some are so ugly that they might be included in the garden simply to scare the deer.

'Argenteospica'—Really quite striking for the new shoots are creamy white and finally turn to dark green; the first time I saw this was at the Morton Arboretum where it stood out from the other species and cultivars.

'Clanbrassiliana'—The earliest dwarf form of the Norway Spruce to be discovered (1836); it forms a low, dense, flat-topped mound usually wider than high, a 30-year-old plant may be less than 3' high; the original plant after 120 years was only 16 3/4' high; this is a rather handsome form.

'Maxwellii'—Originated from a "witches' broom," the true form makes a low, rounded cushion with thick, short branches, needles radially arranged, 1/2" long, somewhat roundish; another form selected from "loose" growth of the broom is stronger growing and much larger.

'Nidiformis'—Bird's Nest Spruce, is a spreading, dense, broad plant of regular growth; usually a depression in center of plant that gives rise to the common name; quite common in commerce; after many years 3 to 6' high.

forma *pendula* (Jacq. & Herincq) Nash—A rather heterogenous group including plants with pendulous branches to some degree or another; included here are 'Aarburg', 'Farnsburg', 'Formanek', 'Frohburg', 'Inversa', 'Pendula', 'Pendula Major', 'Pendula Monstrosa', 'Pruhoniciana', 'Reflexa', and 'Wartburg'; 'Inversa' is particularly interesting because the main and secondary branches are pendulous, if not trained it simply becomes a prostrate or trailing form.

'Procumbens'—Strong-growing, flat-topped form with crowded, thin, stiff branchlets, 2 to 3' high.

'Pumila'—Dwarf, globular, flattened, compact, very broad, 3 to 4' high, lower branches spreading, upper ones nearly erect; branchlets dense, regularly set, directed slightly forward, stiff, flexible, light to reddish brown; several forms with various foliage colors, apparently quite a confused group.

'Repens'—A handsome, wide-spreading form which gradually builds up in the center, very uniform; there is a fine specimen at the Arnold Arboretum.

PROPAGATION: Seed does not require a stratification period and can be directly sown. Optimum period for rooting cuttings appears to be from November to February. Cuttings rooted better when taken in December. Cuttings root best when taken from the lower portion of old trees and should be made from the full length of the current year's growth. Cuttings generally rooted better if made with the basal cut at or slightly above the base of the current year's growth. Rooting was better in 1 sand:1 peat, than in sand. Hormonal treatments did not prove significantly beneficial for enhancing rooting.

NATIVE HABITAT: Northern and central Europe, growing in extended forests, in plains and in the mountains. Specifically from Ural Mountains to the Balkan Peninsula to Switzerland, Norway and northern Finland. Introduced in colonial times.

Picea glauca (Moench) Voss. — White Spruce
(pī′sē-à glaw′kà)   *Dwarf Alberta Spruce*

LEAVES: Persistent for several years, crowded on the upper side of the stem, pale green or dull blue-green, 1/2 to 3/4" long, incurved, ending in an acute or roundish horny point; quadrangular in cross-section; 2 to 5 bands of stomata on each surface; fetid when bruised.

BUDS: Up to 1/4" long with rounded chestnut brown scales, apex blunt, keeled, not resinous.

STEM: Slender, glabrous, often glaucous, becoming dark yellowish brown or pale brown in their second year.

CONES: Cylindric, blunt, 1 to 2 1/2" long and 1/2 to 3/4" in diameter, green initially, pale brown when ripe.

SIZE: 40 to 60' in height by 10 to 20' in spread; size descriptions for this species vary significantly with author; experienced many 50 to 70' high trees along the coast of Maine; national champion is 130' by 28' in Koochiching County, MN.

HARDINESS: Zone 2 to 6.

HABIT: A broad, dense pyramid in youth, becoming a tall, fairly narrow, dense spire, compact and regular, with horizontal to ascending branches.

RATE: Medium.

TEXTURE: Medium.

BARK: Thin, flaky or scaly, ashy brown; freshly exposed layer somewhat silvery.

LEAF COLOR: Glaucous green, variable dull blue-green to off-green.

FLOWERS: Monoecious; staminate, pale red becoming yellow; pistillate purple.

FRUIT: Pendulous, cylindrical cones, 1 to 2 1/2″ long, 1/2 to 3/4″ wide, green to purplish when young and light brown when mature, scales thin, flexible, broad, rounded, almost entire at margins.

DISEASES AND INSECTS: Susceptible to trunk and root rot, spruce bagworm, European sawfly and red spiders.

CULTURE: Transplants readily; makes its best growth on moist loam or alluvial soils, and although found on many different sites, it is typical of stream banks, lake shores and adjacent slopes; one of the most tolerant spruces as it withstands wind, heat, cold, drought and crowding; best in full sun, but tolerant of some shade.

LANDSCAPE VALUE: Useful as a specimen, mass, hedge, windbreak; widely used in the plains states because of its adaptability; probably should be relegated to secondary garden status in the eastern states because of superior evergreen alternatives; common in northern New England and where native simply leave it be; Bonnie and I spent several weeks in late August–early September 1996 on Deer Isle, ME with frequent excursions to the local islands, on Isle au Haut and many of the smaller islands near Stonington, it is the needle evergreen of commonality; grows in rocky crevices and on minimal organic substrate (duff); abundant variation in needle color from green to blue, selections have been made for the latter color; I suspect that the remarkable growth is particularly attributable to foggy, moist atmosphere conditions; definitely a high measure of air borne salt water tolerance.

CULTIVARS: Many more than I realized. Counted about 27 in *Conifers*, probably many additional. The few that I have experienced are described.

var. *albertiana* (S. Br.) Sarg.—Slow-growing, compact, narrow pyramidal tree; apparently there is considerable hybridization between *P. glauca* and *P. engelmannii* and this gives rise to numerous forms which have been classed as varieties by some authorities including *albertiana*, the northwestern North American representative of the species, leaves longer and cones larger.

'Cecilia'—Blue needles, globose, 18″ high.

'Coerulea'—Gray-blue needles, 6′ by 3′.

'Conica'—Often called the Dwarf Alberta Spruce and Dwarf White Spruce. This natural dwarf (could be listed as var. *conica*) was found by J.G. Jack and Alfred Rehder at Lake Laggan, Alberta, Canada in 1904 as they awaited the train to bring them back to the Arnold Arboretum; the plants become broadly conical with time; the foliage (needles 1/4 to 1/2″ long) is light green, densely set, and the needles radiate around the stem; growth is very slow (about 2 to 4″ per year); interesting specimen or novelty plant; will grow about 10 to 12′ in 25 to 30 years. This is one of the most common dwarf conifers and is widely available in commerce; it is easily propagated from cuttings; mites can sometimes be a problem and I have seen it revert to the species on occasion; many bud sports have arisen and these have given rise to forms with smaller needles and slower growth; 'Alberta Globe', 'Arneson Blue', 'Conica', 'Elegans Compacta', 'Gnome', 'Laurin', 'Pixie', 'Sander's Blue' are mutations.

'Densata'—This again could and often is listed correctly as var. *densata* Bailey; this is a slow-growing, conical type reaching 20 to 40′ after 40 to 80 years; the few trees on the Illinois campus were much denser and more ornamental than the species; often called Black Hills Spruce.

'Echiniformis'—Gray-blue, thin, short needles, low cushion habit, 12″.

'Ed Hirle'—Narrow form of 'Conica', 10-year-old plant 4′ by 1 1/2′.

'Elf'—Softball-sized dwarf.

'Jean's Dilly'—Smaller, shorter, thinner needles than 'Conica', shoot ends with twist, growth 3 to 4 weeks later, one-third slower.

'Little Globe'—Medium green needles, large buds, globose and compact, 2′ by 2′ in 10 years.

'Pendula'—Upright leader, weeping branches.

Rainbow's End™—Midsummer second growth flush is cream-yellow, sport of 'Conica', 5 to 10′ high, Iseli Nursery introduction.

'Sander's Blue'—Blue-green needles, sport of 'Conica'.

'Sander's Fastigiata'—Gray-green needles, tight, dwarf, dense cone.

PROPAGATION: Seed requires no pretreatment; cuttings collected in late July rooted 84 to 90% and better than cuttings taken earlier or later; treatment with IAA did not affect rooting; *P. g.* 'Conica' cuttings collected in December rooted better in sand:peat than sand, and the percentage was increased by 70 ppm IBA/24 hour soak; there are other reports which indicate this plant can be successfully rooted from cuttings.

NATIVE HABITAT: Labrador to Alaska, south to Montana, Wyoming, Arkansas, Minnesota, and New York. Introduced 1700.

RELATED SPECIES:

Picea breweriana Wats., (pī′sē-à brew-er-ē-ā′nà), Brewer's Spruce, forms a stiff pyramidal, often broad pyramidal, tree in youth but with age the secondary branches become pendulous and the tertiary branchlets are perpendicularly pendulous and often 7 to 8' long, hanging like curtains. It is truly one of the most striking spruces as it approaches maturity. It is limitedly represented in gardens. The 1 to 1 1/2" long, 1/20 to 1/12" wide needles point forward and radiate equally all around the stem. The needles are glossy dark green on one side and more or less gray-green on the other. The needles tend to be flattened or remotely 3-angled. The cylindrical-oval, 3 to 6" long, to 1 1/2" wide, purple cones, maturing red-brown, are composed of rounded, entire-margined scales. Seeds are blackish, 1/8" long. The tree in its finest form is beautiful, but I seldom see worthy specimens on the East Coast. My best remembrances are trees in European gardens. National champion is 176' by 55' at Trinity Alps Wilderness, Klamath National Forest, CA. Found at about 7,000' altitude in the Siskiyou Mountains of California and Oregon. Introduced 1893. Zone 5.

Picea engelmannii Parry ex Engelm., (pī'sē-à en-gel-man'ē-ī), Engelmann Spruce, is a large, narrow, almost spire-like, densely pyramidal tree with ascending branches. In the eastern states this species may grow 40 to 50' high in 40 to 60 years but in its native range can grow 100 to 120' tall. National champion is 179' by 43' at Payette Lake, ID. The needles are 4-sided, glaucous blue to blue-green, about 1" long and emit a rank odor when crushed. Cones are ovoid to cylindric, 1 to 3" long, 4/5 to 1" wide, pale yellow-brown to red-brown, with irregularly toothed, thin scales. The seeds are black, 1/12" diameter with 1/2" long wing. The bark is thin and broken into large, purplish brown to russet-red, thin, loosely attached scales. Maximum growth is made on deep, rich, loamy soils of high moisture content. Wyman considered this species one of the better spruces for ornamental planting. Several cultivars include: 'Argentea' which has silvery gray needles and 'Glauca' with needles bluish to steel blue. British Columbia and Alberta to Oregon, Arizona and New Mexico. Introduced 1862. Zone 3 to 5.

Picea mariana (Mill.) BSP, (pī'sē-à mar-ē-ā'nà), Black Spruce, is a small to medium-sized tree which grows 30 to 40' tall and develops a limited spread. National champion is 78' by 21' in Taylor County, WI. The habit is distinctly conical, spire-like. The needles are 4-sided, dull bluish green, more or less glaucous, 1/4 to 1/2" long. The cones are small, 3/4 to 1 1/2" long, ovoid, purplish and turn brown at maturity. Scales are woody, rounded at apex, finely toothed edges, with dark brown seeds. Cones persist on tree for several years. The bark is broken into thin, flaky, grayish brown to reddish brown scales, 1/4 to 1/2" thick; freshly exposed inner scales somewhat olive green. This is a cold climate tree and in the southern part of its range is commonly restricted to cold sphagnum bogs; in the far North it is found on dry slopes but makes its best growth on moist, well-drained alluvial bottoms. Have seen in Maine where it often grows around(in) bog edges, wet depressions, and swamps. The cultivar 'Doumettii' is a slow-growing, densely pyramidal, bluish green form which can be propagated by cuttings. It is a beautiful cultivar that appears to do quite well in the heat of Zone 6 and 7. 'Nana' is commonly seen in gardens and makes a dense mound of dull gray-green needles, 1 1/2 to 2' high, slightly wider. 'Ericoides' is a rounded mound, 18" by 30", of small almost heath-like stems, needles average 3/8" long and are bluish gray. 'Golden' has blue-gray needles that are frosted cream-yellow on their upper surface, broad upright, horizontally branched, large size. Labrador to Alaska, south to Wisconsin and Michigan and in the mountains of Virginia. Introduced 1700. Zone 3 to 5(6).

Picea rubens Sarg., (pī'sē-à rū'benz), Red Spruce, forms a broadly conical crown, 60 to 70' high under cultivation. National champion is 123' by 39' in Great Smoky Mountains National Park, NC. Maximum development occurs in the southern Appalachians where humidity and rainfall are high. The 1/2 to 5/8" long, 4-sided, lustrous bright or dark green needles are acute and mucronulate. The green or purplish green cones mature to reddish brown and range from 1 1/4 to 2" long. This is a beautiful tree and is abundant in the high mountains of the Great Smoky Mountains National Park along Route 441. I have photographed these trees several times and in the mountain mists, rich with reindeer moss (lichens), they are a ghostly presence. Not well-suited to cultivation. Nova Scotia to the high peaks of North Carolina. Introduced before 1750. Zone 3 to 5.

Picea omorika (Pančić) Purkyne. — Serbian Spruce
(pī'sē-à ō-môr-ē'kà)

LEAVES: Overlapping and directed forwards on upper side of branchlets, 1/2 to 1" long, 1/16 to 1/12" wide, apex short-pointed on young plants, rounded on older plants, compressed, flat, keeled on both sides, dark green, without stomata above; glaucous white with 4 to 6 distinct, stomatic bands on either side of the midrib beneath.

SIZE: 50 to 60' by 20 to 25' spread after 50 to 60 years, can grow to 100'.

HARDINESS: Zone 4 to 7, is being grown at Minnesota Landscape Arboretum where it may winter burn in exposed sites, no damage at Orono, ME.

HABIT: A tree with a remarkably slender trunk and short ascending or drooping branches forming a very narrow, pyramidal head; one of the most graceful and beautiful spruces; more variation in growth habit than I gave credence in previous editions, have observed broad pyramids to almost obelisk forms; the narrow to moderately conical types make beautiful accents.

RATE: Slow to medium.

TEXTURE: Medium.

BARK: Thin, scaling off in platelets, coffee brown in color.

LEAF COLOR: The upper surface is a glossy dark green in contrast to the lower with its two prominent white stomatic lines.

FLOWERS: Monoecious, male remind of strawberries in color and shape, 1/2 to 3/4" long, attractive.

FRUIT: Cones are oblong-ovoid, 1 1/4 to 1 3/4" long, 1/2 to 3/4" wide, pendent, purple when young, shining cinnamon brown when ripe, scales suborbicular, finely denticulate.

CULTURE: Prefers a deep rich soil that is both moist and well-drained; grows on limestone and acid peats, and will benefit from winter protection from strong winds; likes a dry atmosphere and semi-shade; my observations indicate terrific adaptability to full sun; supposedly tolerates city air; one of the most adaptable spruces.

DISEASES AND INSECTS: Subject to aphids, budworm and borers.

LANDSCAPE VALUE: Noted for its excellent foliage and narrow, pyramidal growth; excellent for the midwestern and northeastern states; would make an excellent evergreen street tree; I have seen many fine specimens of the species, from the University of Maine campus (-30°F) to Louisville, KY where summer temperatures and humidity can be horrendous; the species is much more adaptable than given credit; as a specimen or in groups it is an excellent choice; this and *P. orientalis* are my favorites among the spruces.

CULTIVARS: Have perused 13 cultivars of the species in *Conifers*, many nothing more than dwarf softballs, a few with commercial worth.

    'Expansa'—Interesting wide-spreading form with ascending branches and typical foliage; grows about 3' high; may revert to the type and throw a normal leader.

    'Machala'—Low-growing, spreading, mounded globe, needle colors white, gray-blue, and green; a hybrid, *P. × mariorika*, between *P. mariana* and *P. omorika*; from Czechoslovakia.

    'Nana'—A lovely conical to globose form of irregular outline eventually 8 to 10' high; needles closely set, 3/8" long, more or less radially arranged.

    'Pendula'—A very beautiful, slender tree with drooping, slightly twisted branches; needs staking when young to develop a leader; 'Pendula Bruns' from Bruns Nursery, Germany has more accentuated weeping branches.

    Also listed is a *P. omorika × P. breweriana* hybrid with broad pyramidal habit and drooping branchlets.

PROPAGATION: Seed requires no pretreatment. Cuttings taken in winter from 4-year-old trees rooted moderately well; rooting was improved by treatment with 200 ppm IBA/24 hour soak.

ADDITIONAL NOTES: Perhaps the most handsome of the spruces, although depending on the day, I still lean toward *P. orientalis*. The habit is more graceful and refined than most. Should be used in preference to other spruces when it can be located.

NATIVE HABITAT: Southeastern Europe (Yugoslavia). Confined to a few stands in the limestone mountains on either side of the upper Drina. Introduced about 1880.

Picea orientalis (L.) Link. — Oriental Spruce

(pǐ′sē-à ôr-i-en-tā′lis)

LEAVES: Very short, 1/4 to 1/2" long, 4-sided, lustrous dark green, blunt or rounded at the apex, quadrangular in cross-section with 1 to 4 lines of stomata on each surface; shortest needles of the spruce species, arranged at and above the horizontal plane, upper appressed and hiding the stem.

SIZE: 50 to 60' in height after about 60 years, can grow to 120'.

HARDINESS: Zone 4 to 7, performed well in Morton Arboretum, Lisle, IL.

HABIT: A dense, compact, narrow pyramid with horizontal branches that are often pendulous, usually full and dense from tip to bottom; more variation in cultivated material than I realized with some narrow, others broad pyramidal, all handsome.

RATE: Slow.

TEXTURE: Medium.

BARK: Brown, exfoliating in thin scales.

LEAF COLOR: Lustrous dark green with 1 to 4 stomatic lines on each side, needles very short and tightly set, holds dark green color better than other spruces during winter.

FLOWERS: Monoecious, male carmine-red and resembling strawberries in youth.

FRUIT: Cones short-stalked, nodding, ovoid-cylindrical, 2 to 4″ long by approximately 1″ wide, reddish purple when young turning brown when mature, scales entire at margin.

CULTURE: Will tolerate poor, gravelly soils; plant where winters are not excessively cold or dry; has done well in Midwest and Northeast as a young tree; protect from harsh winter winds.

LANDSCAPE VALUE: Because of its graceful and attractive habit it has value as a specimen spruce for small areas; much superior to Norway and White; may suffer browning of foliage in severe winters, although I have not observed this occurring, in fact, holds good foliage color in winter; there are many fine specimens in Spring Grove, Cincinnati and Cave Hill, Louisville, KY, also several magnificent 80′ high specimens at Biltmore Estate, Asheville, NC; once one sees this tree he or she wonders why Norway and White are ever planted.

CULTIVARS: Eighteen selections featured in *Conifers*.

　‘Atrovirens’—More open than typical species, elegant habit, to 60′, lustrous dark green needles.

　‘Aurea’—Young shoots golden yellow (creamy yellow) in spring, changing to green, often with a general golden sheen all over the leaves, colorful for a time and then regressing to normal, same as ‘Aureospicata’.

　‘Gowdy’—More narrow, columnar form with small, rich green leaves, slow-growing, possibly 8 to 10′, I have seen a few plants labeled as ‘Gowdy’ which were wider than the typical description.

　‘Gracilis’—A slow-growing, densely branched form developing into a small, conical tree, 15 to 20′ tall; needles radially set and bright grass green.

　‘Nana’—Dwarf, globular form, to 3′ high, short glossy dark green radiating needles.

　‘Pendula’ (now called ‘Weeping Dwarf’)—A compact, slow-growing form with pendulous branchlets, the foliage is normal; more than one clone with this name.

　‘Skylands’—Typical habit of the species but with golden needles that fade in the heat of the summer, may burn in hot climates, in cooler climates holds some of golden yellow through winter, sold as ‘Aurea Compacta’.

PROPAGATION: Seed requires no pretreatment.

ADDITIONAL NOTES: American nursery industry needs to grow this species. At Spring Grove there are many plants, some in the 70′ high range. One 40′ high, moderate pyramid is the darkest green and densely foliaged, a perfect candidate for grafting.

NATIVE HABITAT: Caucasus, Asia Minor. Introduced 1827.

Picea pungens Engelm. — Colorado Spruce
(pī′sē-å pun′jenz)

LEAVES: Spreading more or less all around the stem, but more crowded above than below, stout, rigid, incurved and very prickly, 3/4 to 1 1/4″ long, varying in color on different trees, dull green, bluish or silvery white, 4-sided with about 6 stomatic lines on each side, needles with acid taste when chewed.

BUDS: Broadly conical to nearly spherical, apex blunt, yellowish brown, not resinous; scales loosely appressed, apex often reflexed, the lowest ones keeled, long-pointed.

STEM: Stout, without pubescence, glaucous at first becoming orange-brown with age.

CONES: Cylindrical but slightly narrowed at each end, 2 to 4″(5″) long, 1 to 1 1/4″ wide, green with violet bloom, pale shining brown when mature, scales wavy, oval, blunt and jaggedly toothed at apex.

SIZE: 30 to 60′ in height with a 10 to 20′ spread under average landscape conditions; 90 to 135′ in height by 20 to 30′ spread in the wild; national champion is 122′ by 36′ in Ashley National Forest, UT.

HARDINESS: Zone 3 to 7(8).

HABIT: A dense, regular narrow to broad pyramid with horizontal stiff branches to the ground; often becoming open, poor and dingy in age.

RATE: Slow-medium, 30 to 50′ after 35 to 50 years; very stiff and formal in outline.

TEXTURE: Medium to coarse.

LEAF COLOR: Usually gray-green to blue-green, young growth soft, silvery blue-gray.

FLOWERS: Monoecious, staminate orange, pistillate greenish or purple.

FRUIT: Cones oblong, cylindrical, short-stalked, 2 to 4″(5″) long, 1 to 1 1/4″ wide, green with violet bloom when young, turning light or yellow-brown when ripe, scales wavy and toothed at apex.

CULTURE: It prefers rich, moist soil in full sunlight although is more drought tolerant than other *Picea*; very adaptable.

DISEASES AND INSECTS: Subject to spruce gall aphid, *Adelges cooleyi*, which causes tips of branches to die, spruce budworm and spider mite, *Cytospora* canker may infect lower branches, *Phomopsis occulta* caused branch dieback in Michigan nurseries.

LANDSCAPE VALUE: Overused; popular as a specimen but hard to combine well with other plants; acceptable in dry climates; can be used in groupings; one of the standard practices in past years has been the use of this plant or a blue-foliage type in the front yard where it immediately detracts from the rest of the landscape.

CULTIVARS: Over 45 cultivars are shown in *Conifers*; numerous odd blue, gold, compact, weeping forms offered via United States specialty nurseries.

'Argentea'—Foliage silvery white, a collective name for cultivars with silvery-colored needles, probably not a valid term.

'Bakeri'—Deeper blue than foliage of 'Argentea' and possibly better than 'Moerheimii', after 32 years a specimen in the Arnold Arboretum was only 12′ tall and 6′ across.

'Blue Kiss'—Selection from Brotzman's Nursery, Madison, OH, parent tree is an 8′ high by 10′ wide blue dome, parent plant 40 years of age.

'Fat Albert'—Dense upright pyramidal form with good blue needle color, considered semi-dwarf, about 15′ high, have seen a block of these at Iseli Nursery and the uniformity was astounding, produced by cuttings.

f. *glauca* (Reg.) Beissn. (var. *glauca* Reg.)—Foliage some variation of bluish green; in any population of seedlings variation in degree of blue or silver is evident; nurserymen often select these types and sell them at a higher price than the "normal" green types; it is from this forma or variety that the best cultivars have been selected and perpetuated by grafting; a nursery block of seed-grown trees is quite a sight for the foliage color often varies from green to silvery blue; Townsend and Davis, *J. Environ. Hort.* 8(2):64–67 (1990), tested 32 provenances of *P. pungens* for foliage color, height, and form; great variation occurred but trees from southern Colorado, northern New Mexico, and northern Arizona had the fastest growth, bluest color, and were most symmetrical in habit.

'Glauca Globosa'—A compact (3′ high), rounded, flat-topped bush that at maturity is wider than high; the needles are bluish white and more or less radially disposed, 'Globosa' is probably the same.

'Glauca Pendula' ('Glauca Procumbens', 'Glauca Prostrata')—I am a degree confused here for plants in this category more or less spread and sprawl over the ground becoming almost ground cover-like; the first listed has handsome silvery-blue needles, and makes a rather attractive, but somewhat gaudy, rock garden type plant; if lateral shoots of the species are propagated they tend to grow laterally or procumbently, so the production of these plants can be affected by selection of lateral growth from an otherwise normal tree; this type of growth response is termed topophysis.

'Golden Feathers'—Bright yellow new growth, changing to green, introduced by Brotzman's Nursery.

'Hoopsii'—Dense, pyramidal form with spreading branches, foliage extremely glaucous (blue-white); perhaps the most glaucous form and the best grower, the Dutch mention this form is difficult to graft and shape, my number one choice.

'Iseli Foxtail' ('Foxtail')—Bushy, blue, twisted new growth, distinct tight upright habit, appears more heat tolerant and has prospered in Raleigh, NC (Zone 7b), Raulston reported 40″ vertical growth in 2 years while other cultivars grew 2 to 6″, also propagated from cuttings, observed the plant at Raleigh in 1997, growth has slowed and the heat of the South is catching up with its "good looks," size has been listed as 10 to 15′ high, 7 to 8′ wide, appears to have even greater potential, partial explanation for Foxtail's southern adaptability is given in *Canad. J. For. Res.* 20:1871–1877 (1990), has the ability to respire slowly thus preserving carbon fixed in photosynthesis.

'Koster'—Plants I have observed never matched the quality of 'Thompsenii' and 'Hoopsii', plants were not uniform and dense, certainly this could have resulted from pruning and staking practices; selected as a group of blue seedling plants and so some variation is possible, at its best a regular conical form with silver-blue needles.

'Mission Blue'—Intense blue foliage color, compact, symmetrical grower with broad base, 40′, selected at Mission Gardens, Techny, IL.

'Moerheim'—Compact, dense-growing form with very blue foliage sometimes with longitudinal young shoots; retains blue color in winter; an irregular grower, ultimately 30′ or more.

'Montgomery'—A dwarf bush forming a broad cone; needles silver-blue and quite striking; given to the New York Botanical Garden by R.H. Montgomery of Coscob, CT; the original plant is still there.

'Omega'—Excellent silver-blue needles, typical habit, good grower, requiring little staking when young.

'Thompsenii' ('Thompsen')—Symmetrical pyramidal tree of a whitish silver-blue foliage color, more intense than the above varieties although somewhat similar to 'Hoopsii' with leaves at least twice as thick, one of the best.

'Thume'—Like 'Montgomery' but broad conical, 4′ by 3′, powder blue needles, faster than 'Montgomery'.

PROPAGATION: Seed requires no pretreatment. Most of the cultivars are grafted onto seedling understocks. This is usually done in January and February in the greenhouse and the grafted plants are placed under lath or lined out in the spring.

NATIVE HABITAT: Southwestern United States; Rocky Mountains from Colorado to Utah to New Mexico and Wyoming. Introduced about 1862.

Pieris japonica (Thunb.) D. Don ex G. Don — Japanese Pieris, also mistakenly called Andromeda
(pī ĕr′-is já-pon′i-kà)

FAMILY: Ericaceae

LEAVES: Alternate, simple, evergreen, obovate-oblong to oblanceolate, 1 1/4 to 3 1/2″ long, 1/3 to 3/4″ wide, crenate-serrate, lustrous dark green above, lighter green beneath, glabrous, new growth is a bronze-green to reddish color; petiole—1/4 to 3/8″ long.

STEM: Green to yellow-green, glabrous, terete to angled, older bark much like *Kalmia latifolia*, gray to gray-brown, vertically fissured.

FLOWERS: Buds form in summer prior to year of flowering and offer a valid identification characteristic.

SIZE: 9 to 12′ in height by 6 to 8′ in spread, size variable depending on cultivar with 3 to 4′ in height and up being realistic.

HARDINESS: Zone 4b to 7, does acceptably in Zone 4b with some protection.

HABIT: Upright evergreen shrub of neat habit with stiff, spreading branches and dense rosette-like foliage, often oval to haystack-shaped.

RATE: Slow, 4 to 6′ in 5 to 8 years.

TEXTURE: Medium in all seasons.

LEAF COLOR: New growth a rich bronze, changing to lustrous dark green at maturity; new foliage is almost the most aesthetic part of the plant and some of the cultivars like 'Mountain Fire' are spectacular.

FLOWER: Perfect, weakly fragrant, white, urn-shaped, 1/4″ long, March–April (early March, Athens), borne in 3 to 6″ long and wide, pendulous, racemose panicles, effective for 2 to 3 weeks.

FRUIT: Dehiscent, 5-valved, 1/4″ long capsule that persists into winter and is best removed after flowering.

CULTURE: Transplant as a container-grown plant into moist, acid, well-drained soil which has been supplemented with peat moss or organic matter; full sun or partial shade; in South some shade is a necessity; not as fastidious for acid soil as other ericaceous plants; prune after flowering; shelter from wind; well-drained soil is a must in the South and plants are short-lived if grown in wet soils; in Zones 6b to 7b, the plant does not grow old without struggle, plants often thin out, a branch or two may die, possibly the entire plant; provide maximum soil conditions.

DISEASES AND INSECTS: Leaf spots, die back (*Phytophthora*), lace bug (prevalent in eastern states where it has made the culture of *Pieris* very difficult, sucks juices from leaves and causes yellowing to browning of foliage), Florida wax scale, two-spotted mite, nematodes.

LANDSCAPE VALUE: Excellent large specimen broadleaf evergreen; works well in the shrub border, in mass, or blended with other broadleaf evergreens; does acceptably in South if sited in shade; have experienced large plants and/or collections at Savill Gardens and Trewithen in England where the plants appeared more prosperous than what I see in the Midwest, East and upper South; several Georgia nurserymen grow the plant under shade and sell it in the northern markets; goats and sheep have gotten sick and died from eating the foliage, see *Veterinary Record* 128:599–560.

CULTIVARS: It is becoming increasingly difficult to keep up with the number of cultivars that are flooding the literature. How far they will travel in the nursery trade is questionable. The list has been expanded since the fourth edition.

var. *amamiana*—Compact shrub, 5 to 6′, red young growth, at maturity dark green, offered by Hines Nursery.

'Bert Chandler'—Young leaves at first salmon pink, paling through cream and white and becoming normal green by summer; a seedling raised by the Australian nurseryman Bert Chandler around 1936.

'Bisbee Dwarf'—Leaves about 1/2 the size of the species, glossy dark green with a slight twist, reddish when young; compact, bushy plant.

'Blush'—Rose pink flowers that fade with maturity, open elegant habit, 5′ by 5′.

'Boltman's Pink'—Compact plant with bright red buds that open to blush pink flowers.

'Bonsai'—Small roundish leaves, dense, upright growing, bonsai and rock garden use, 12″ by 12″.

'Captain Blood'—Deep red flower buds hold color through winter, open white, long narrow leaves, compact growth habit.

'Cavatine'—Cold hardy, long lasting, white flowers, late developing, var. *yakushimanum* selection, looks like a dwarf rhododendron, from Esveldt, Holland.

'Christmas Cheer'—Flowers pink with the tips of the corolla a deeper pink creating a bicolor effect; good grower; imported from Japan; flowers early; a seedling of 'Daisen'.

'Coleman'—Pink-flowered form with red flower buds that maintain this color through the winter.

'Compacta'—Dense, compact form, to 6′, leaves small, heavy-flowering.

'Crispa'—Wavy-margined leaves, good white flowers.

'Crystal'—Large thick glossy dark green leaves and beautiful white flowers; heat tolerant and *Phytophthora* resistant, Verkade introduction.

'Daisen'—Flowers deep pink in bud paling as they open; leaves wider and smoother than those of 'Christmas Cheer', color is best in some shade, from Japan.

'Debutante'—Compact habit with dark green leaves, pure white flowers, dark green foliage.

'Deep Pink'—Bright red buds and flower stalks brighten the plant through winter, open to good pink in spring.

'Dorothy Wycoff'—Compact form but strong-growing, dark red flower buds opening to pale pink, excellent form.

'Firecrest'—New growth bright red.

'Flaming Silver'—Young leaves red, leaf margin pink at first, soon silver white, sport of 'Forest Flame', had this in the garden for a time, rather attractive but succumbed to the *Pieris* syndrome, more vigorous than 'Variegata'.

'Flamingo'—Deep rose red, non-fading flowers, new growth bronze-red, foliage lustrous dark green, vigorous grower, good form.

'Geisha'—Gracefully slender leaves, pure white flowers.

'Grayswood'—Bronzy green new shoots become dark green with maturity, white flowers in long arching racemes, freely borne, forms a dome-shaped outline, 4 to 5′ high.

'John's Select'—Compact, dark green leaves, red buds open to pure white flowers, grows about two-third's as tall as the species.

'Karenoma' (*P. floribunda* × *P. japonica*)—Has the foliage of the latter parent, the hardiness and flowers of *P. floribunda*, reasonably compact grower.

'La Rocaille'—Large plant, extremely floriferous, to 6′, white flowers in panicles to 12″ long, from Harold Epstein, Long Island.

'Little Heath'—Slow-growing, compact, leaves with yellowish green variegation, grows about 3′ high, will revert to the green form which has been propagated and offered as 'Little Heath Green'.

'Mountain Fire'—New growth fire red, exceptional, flowers white, common in commerce.

'Nana'—Low compact dwarf with small leaves.

'Nocturne'—Dwarf, slow-growing form with large, white, pendulous flowers, ideal rock garden plant.

'Pink Delight'—Pink buds, white flowers.

'Prelude'—Hardy rock garden plant, flowers white, 2 to 3 weeks later than typical, long lasting, var. *yakushimanum* selection, from Holland.

'Purity'—Unusually large, pure white flowers, flowers heavily as a young plant, grows 3 to 4′ high, foliage is light green, flowers and develops new shoots later in spring.

'Pygmaea' [f. *pygmaea* (Maxim.) Rehd.]—Leaves small, 1/2 to 1″ long and very narrow, feathery in effect, grows about 3 to 4′ high; white flowers.

'Red Bud'—Good vigorous form with showy red flower buds that open to light pink.

'Red Mill'—New leaves bright red turning mahogany then to lustrous dark green, leaves thick and leathery, maintains dense bushy habit in old age, supposedly quite insect and disease resistant, flowers white and last about 10 days longer than typical seed produced plants.

'Rosalinda'—Brownish red new shoots give way to glossy dark green leaves, flowers brown in bud due to colored calyx, pink in flower and holding the color, compact habit, about 4′ by 4′.

'Ryu Kuensis'—Compact form, rich green foliage, heavy budding, white flowers.

'Sarabonde'—Similar to 'Cavatine' and 'Prelude', deep pink buds open to pure white, long-lasting flowers.

'Scarlett O'Hara'—White-flowered form with tall slender habit, attractive red new growth, hardy.

'Shojo'—Black-red flower buds open to red; said to be the darkest red flowers of any *Pieris*, from Japan.

'Snowdrift' ('Snow Drift')—Slow-growing, dense habit, 4 to 6′ by 4 to 6′, bronze-red new growth, deep green foliage, abundant showy white flowers in long, upright panicles.

'Spring Snow' (*P. japonica* × *P. floribunda*)—Flowers like those of *P. floribunda* with snow white corollas; leaves are like *P. japonica*, selected by Del Brown, Marysville, WA; introduced by Briggs Nursery.

'Summer Hill'—Typical white flowers, thick, heavy, glossy dark green leaves, excellent branching, rapid growth, selected from a seedling population at Summer Hill Nursery, Madison, CT.

Sweetwater®—From Long Island, original plant is 35-years-old, long flowering period, 7 1/2 to 8 1/2 weeks, bright wine red buds open to white, sterile (no fruits are produced) flowers, energy goes into flower production.

'Temple Bells'—Slow-growing dwarf shrub with tiered branches, new foliage bronze-apricot maturing to lustrous dark green, large ivory white flowers are borne in dense, racemose panicles, a particularly fine form.

'Valentine's Day'—Early-flowering form.

'Valley Fire'—Vivid colored new growth, large white flowers, vigorous grower.

'Valley Rose'—Deep green foliage and pastel-pink flowers, introduced by Bob Tichnor of Willamette Valley Experiment Station, Oregon State University, tall shrub of open habit, flowers described as silvery rose passing to white.

'Valley Valentine'—From Dr. Robert Tichnor, Oregon State, considered best of his selections, rich maroon flower buds, long-lasting deep rose-pink flowers abundantly borne on dense upright plants that grow 4′ in 10 years; foliage is lustrous dark green.

'Variegata'—Leaves with white margins, will grow 10 to 12′ with age, usually one-half this in average garden setting, white flowers, actually rather pretty in a shady nook of the garden.

'Wada's Pink'—Deep pink buds, clear pink flowers, compact habit to 4′.

'White Caps'—Exceptionally long panicles of white flowers.

'White Cascade'—Long panicles of pure white flowers, effective for 5 weeks, very floriferous, seedling from Vermeulen Nursery in 1953, new leaves yellowish brown, glossy dark green later.

'White Pearl'—Distinct habit with erect branches and pure white flowers, dark green foliage.

'White Rim'—Compact habit, each leaf streaked light and dark green with uneven deep creamy white margins, young growth pinkish, flowers creamy white.

'White Water' ('Whitewater')—Floriferous white-flowered form, spreading habit.

var. *yakushimanum* T. Yamazaki—Low, slow-growing with dark green foliage and white flowers, integrity of variety is questionable but many new compact cultivars like 'Cavatine', 'Nocturne', 'Prelude' are derived from this seed origin, also listed as 'Yakushima'.

PROPAGATION: Seed, as discussed for *Calluna*. Cuttings root readily, see under *Leucothoe*. Seed was collected in November, 1975, and directly sown on peat and placed under mist; within 21 days excellent germination had occurred. A North Carolina State study, *J. Environ. Hort.* 10:121–124 (1992), showed that seeds of *P. floribunda* responded to light. Abundant treatments in the study but if seeds "see" light they will germinate in high percentages. Tissue culture was also successful, see *J. Environ. Hort.* 11:191–195 (1993).

NATIVE HABITAT: Japan, Taiwan, Eastern China. Cultivated 1870.

RELATED SPECIES:

Pieris floribunda (Pursh) Benth. & Hook. — Mountain Pieris, Fetter Bush

LEAVES: Alternate, simple, evergreen, elliptic-ovate to oblong-lanceolate, 1 to 3″ long, 1/2 to 1″ wide, acute or short acuminate, obtuse, crenate-serrulate, ciliate, glossy dark green above, paler beneath, with short black pubescence on each surface; petiole—1/4 to 3/8″long.

STEM: Green, rounded to slightly angled, downy, stiffly hirsute.

Pieris floribunda, (pī ĕr′-is flō-ri-bun′dà), Mountain Pieris, is a handsome evergreen shrub of neat, bushy habit, low and rounded, with rather stiff branches and dense, dark green, 1 to 3″ long leaves. Will grow 2 to 6′

high with a similar or greater spread. Flowers are white, fragrant, borne in 2 to 4″ long, dense, upright racemose panicles in April for 2 to 4 weeks. Very handsome small rounded shrub which has not been used enough in American gardens. Not afflicted by the lacebug like the Japanese Pieris. Also is tolerant of higher pH soils than most Ericaceae. Seed can be sown as soon as ripe, however, cuttings have proved somewhat difficult to root. 'Millstream' is a rather flat-topped, mounded, slow-growing form; it makes a splendid rock garden plant. Native from Virginia to Georgia. Introduced 1800. Zone 4 to 6.

An F_1 hybrid between the Japanese and Mountain Pieris has resulted in a clone called 'Brouwer's Beauty' which is dense and compact in habit. The leaves are dark green and shiny. The new foliage a distinct yellow-green. Panicles are horizontal but slightly arched. Flower buds are deep purplish red. Roots easier than *P. floribunda*. Cuttings should be taken in the fall and placed in plastic tents and a peat:perlite medium. Previously, this clone was thought to be resistant to the lace bug but recent controlled tests have shown that the hybrid is susceptible when exposed to large numbers of lace bugs. Less cold hardy than *P. floribunda*.

Other hybrids(?) between this and *P. japonica* include: 'Elongata' (flowers in long, terminal panicles, later flowering), 'Eco Snowball' (from Don Jacobs, Decatur, GA), 'Karemon' (see *P. japonica*) and 'Spring Snow' (see *P. japonica*).

Pieris formosa (Wallich) D. Don, (pī ēr′-is fôr-mō′sȧ), Himalaya Pieris, although doubtfully adaptable in the eastern and southeastern United States will grow in the western United States and is one of the most colorful shrubs in the spring. Abundant literature is available from English references, particularly Bean, and should be consulted for specifics. In general leaves are larger (1 to 4″ long) and the ultimate size is 10′ and up. 'Wakehurst' has brilliant red new leaves in March and April fading to pink-crimson and then a chlorotic, almost albino condition before developing normal deep green. I have seen the plant in England, particularly the fine old specimens at Wakehurst Place. It is difficult not to get excited about such a plant. 'Forest Flame' offers similar, perhaps not as brightly red-colored foliage as the above, and is more compact and symmetrical in habit. Possibly a hybrid between *P. japonica* and *P. formosa* var. *forrestii*. Other cultivars with related parentage are known but are primarily of European garden interest. Native to southeastern China, Vietnam, Himalayas, Nepal. Hardiness possibly to Zone 8 but a cool, even climate suits the plant best.

Pieris phillyreifolia (Hook.) DC. — Vine-wicky

LEAVES: Alternate, simple, evergreen, ovate to obovate, 3/4 to 2 1/2″ long, 1/5 to 3/4″ wide, apex serrate and sharp-pointed, cuneate to rounded, revolute, lustrous dark green, sparsely glandular hirsute; petiole—1/16 to 1/4″ long.

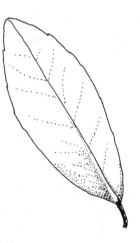

Pieris phillyreifolia, (pī ēr′is fil-ē-rē-i-fō′li-ȧ), Vine-wicky, grows as a vine with rhizomatous "fingers" that allow it to attach to Baldcypress, Atlantic Whitecedar, and Sabal Palmetto. Under cultivation, container-grown plants are rather handsome small shrubs. In late February 1996, I observed the plant in flower and asked Mr. Charles Webb, Superior Trees, Lee, FL about the anomalous shrubby growth. In cypress swamps it co-exists primarily as a vine on pond cypress. The 1/3″ long, urn-shaped, milk white flowers occur in 3- to 9-flowered racemes from the leaf axils of the shoot ends. I consider this species as a genetic resource to breed heat and wet soil tolerance into *P. japonica* and *P. floribunda*. South Carolina, Georgia, Florida and Alabama. Zone 7 to 9.

Pinckneya pubens Michx. [formerly *P. bracteata* (Bartr.) Raf.] — Pinckneya, Feverbark, Georgia Bark
(pink′nē-ȧ pū′benz)

FAMILY: Rubiaceae

LEAVES: Opposite, simple, elliptic to oblong-oval, 1 3/4 to 8″ long, 1 to 4 1/2″ wide, acute or short-acuminate, cuneate, entire, dark green and hairy above, pubescent below; petiole—1/2 to 1 1/4″ long.

BUDS: Terminal—red-brown to purple-brown, waxy, glabrous.

STEM: Gray-brown, pubescent, eventually reddish brown with raised, pale, corky lenticels, leaf scars heart-shaped, with narrow crescent-shaped vascular bundle trace; pith—continuous, white.

SIZE: 10 to 20′(30′) high; national champion is 21′ by 7′ in Marion County, FL.

HARDINESS: Zone (7)8 to 9.

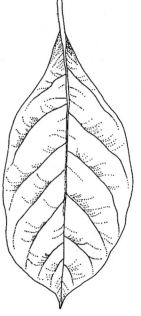

HABIT: Large shrub or small tree of rather open habit.

RATE: Slow to medium.

TEXTURE: Medium.

BARK: Gray-brown.

LEAF COLOR: Dark green in summer, no fall color.

FLOWERS: Perfect, yellowish green, mottled with brown or purple, tubular, 1/2 to 1″ long, with 5 reflexed corolla lobes resulting in distinct trumpet-shaped flower; actual showy parts are the white, pink to rose sepals that become petal-like and remind of the bracts of poinsettia; full flower in June in Athens, beautiful for flower effect, lasting for several weeks.

FRUIT: Dehiscent, brown, 2-valved capsule, 3/4″ diameter, containing many small flattish seeds.

CULTURE: Transplant from a container, prefers moist, acid, well-drained soil in partial shade.

DISEASES AND INSECTS: None serious. *Phoma macrostoma* causes leaf spot on the species, see *Plant Disease* 77:1168 (1993).

LANDSCAPE VALUE: Unusual for flower effect, nice effect along edge of stream or pond, unfortunately, not particularly hardy and −3°F killed the plant in my garden, but it did develop shoots from the roots.

CULTIVARS:

'Bostwick'—White-flowered form.

'Larry's Party Pinckneya'—Rich salmon-colored bracts, color holds for 4 to 6 weeks in June–July, habit typical for species, Larry Lowman introduction.

'Pink Fever'—Good pink-bracted form from Tom Dodd III, Alabama.

'White'—A white-bracted form.

PROPAGATION: Seeds require no pretreatment, I have grown many seedlings; cuttings at least from young plants root readily (June–July), 1000 ppm IBA, peat:perlite, mist.

ADDITIONAL NOTES: Have grown in Dirr garden with decreasing success. First plant reached 8′ or so, flowered and fruited but −3°F cold eliminated it. Second was placed in semi-shade with supplemental irrigation. After a 10 day vacation in August, I returned to a potato chip. Have observed in the wild in a low wet area at Ocmulgee State Park, GA, at which time (late June) plants were in flower and colors ranged from white to rose.

NATIVE HABITAT: Low woods in South Carolina to Florida. Introduced 1786.

Pinus L. — Pine
FAMILY: Pinaceae

Of all the needle-type evergreens, pines seem to show the greatest diversity of habit, distribution, and ornamental characteristics. Approximately 90 to 110 species are distributed throughout the Northern Hemisphere from the Arctic Circle to Guatemala, the West Indies, North Africa and Malayan Archipelago. Most are large trees, however, several species are dwarfish or shrubby and over their native range may vary from dense, compact, slow-growing types (3′) to large trees (75′, *Pinus mugo*). The pines are of primary importance in the production of timber, pulp, and paper manufacture. Turpentine, pine-wood oils, wood tars, and rosin are obtained from the wood of several species. The leaf oils of several species are used in the manufacture of medicines and the seeds of several others are suitable for food ("pine nuts"). Generally, pines are considered more tolerant of adverse soil and climatic conditions than species of *Picea* and *Abies*.

MORPHOLOGICAL CHARACTERISTICS

Evergreen, monoecious trees of various heights, tall, rarely shrubby; crowns of young to middle-aged trees pyramidal, older flat-topped or arched-umbelliformly branched; trunk of isolated trees usually large at base, rapidly tapering, that of forest-grown trees straight, lower branches shredding; bark usually thick, rough, furrowed or scaly; branches whorled; branchlets appearing as long shoots and as spurs; long shoots on seedling plants up to the third year with needle-like leaves, afterwards with dry-membranous (soon deciduous) scale-like leaves, in the axils of which arise the spurs; one year long shoots regularly grow from winter-buds producing a single internode, consisting of a leafless base, which often bears the male flowers, a longer upper part bearing foliage and ending in a terminal bud, surrounded by a whorl of smaller buds, one or more of which may be replaced by female flowers, or the shoot consisting of 2 internodes, each with a leafless base, a leaf-bearing portion, and a whorl of buds; some species produce occasional shoots that bear juvenile leaves until advanced in age; such often appear from adventitious buds; terminal buds varying in different species regarding the shape and character of their scales, resinous or not; leaves of three kinds: leaves borne on seedling-plants, solitary, spirally arranged, linear-lanceolate, entire or margin fringed, soon deciduous, except the basal portion; adult leaves, needle-like, borne in clusters of 2, 3 or 5, margin often minutely toothed, the section semi-circular in the 2-leaved species, triangular in the 3- to 5-leaved ones, persistent 2 or more years; sheaths of the leaf-bundles persistent, deciduous or partly so; cones variable in outline, symmetrical or oblique, opening upon ripening usually in second year or remaining on the tree unopened for many years; scales thin, or thick and woody, the exposed part of each scale (apophysis) thickened, showing a terminal or dorsal protuberance or scar, called the umbo, which is often pointed with a prickly point, boss or stout hook; seeds 2 to each scale, nut-like or ovoid, appressed, the kernel surrounded by a shell, winged or not; cotyledons 4 to 15.

GROWTH CHARACTERISTICS

It is difficult to stereotype the growth habits of pines but the majority are pyramidal, more or less symmetrical trees in youth becoming more round-topped, open and picturesque with age. There is considerable interest in the dwarf types and many selections have been made among species. One of the most beautiful of all upright types is *Pinus strobus* 'Fastigiata' which carries its plume-like foliage on strongly ascending branches and maintains a full complement of branches into old age.

CULTURE

Pines, with the exception of small seedlings or liners, should be moved balled-and-burlapped. If large plants have been properly root pruned, transplanting is accomplished with very little difficulty. Most pines will develop a tap root and therefore may be difficult to transplant from the wild.

Pines are more tolerant of adverse soil, exposure, and city conditions than *Abies* and *Picea*. The two needle types are considered more tolerant than the three which are greater than the five. *Pinus sylvestris*, *P. taeda*, and *P. nigra* are adapted to many soil types while *P. mugo*, *P. pungens*, *P. banksiana* and *P. thunbergii* are more satisfactory in sandy soils. *Pinus nigra*, *P. pungens*, *P. thunbergii* and *P. virginiana* exhibit salt spray tolerance. Several species such as *P. jeffreyi*, *P. thunbergii* and *P. wallichiana* are on the hardiness borderline in Zone 5.

Pines withstand pruning and can be maintained as hedges and screens. Removing one-half of the new candle growth (usually in June) will result in the formation of lateral buds below the cut. Christmas tree growers use machetes or power equipment for pruning.

DISEASES AND INSECTS

Late damping-off and root rot, dieback, tip blight, stem blister rust, Comandra blister rust, canker, *Cenangium* twig blight, leaf cast, needle blight, needle rust, shrub pine needle rust, littleleaf, white-pine aphid, European pine shoot moth, Nantucket pine moth, sawflies, pine webworm, pine false webworm, pine needle scale, pine needle miner, pine spittlebugs, pine tortoise scale, red pine scale, pales weevil, pine root collar weevil, white pine shoot borer, white pine tube moth, white pine weevil (causes severe deformity and growth losses to *Picea* species and pines in nearly all regions of United States and Canada), Zimmerman pine moth, bark beetles, pinewood nematode.

Physiological problems include:
White pine blight—browning of current season's needles especially in northeastern United States; primary cause is unknown.
Stunt—on *Pinus resinosa*; possibly from poor soil drainage.
Air pollutants—including sulfur dioxide and ozone, produce tip burn or speckling of leaves.
Salt—significant damage to trees located along highways which are heavily salted. Damage is usually evident only on side of tree facing the highway.

Good paper in *J. Arboriculture* 13:225–228 (1987) that reported *P. thunbergii*, *P. nigra*, and *P. ponderosa* most salt tolerant; most susceptible were *P. strobus*, *P. banksiana*, *P. cembra*, *P. peuce*, and *P. densiflora*.

PROPAGATION

All species are grown from seed and the stratification requirements vary significantly (see specific requirements which are listed under each species). Recently there has been considerable interest in producing seed-grown dwarf types. Cones are collected from "witches' broom" type growths and the resultant progeny are usually dwarfish in habit. Grafting is used on many of the cultivars. A side graft is usually used on seedlings of the species. Cuttings have also been rooted but the percentage was usually low. *Pinus radiata* is commercially rooted from cuttings in Australia.

LANDSCAPE USE

The tree species and cultivars of pine are used extensively in large scale landscape plantings such as parks, golf courses, estates, cemeteries, industrial grounds, shopping centers, and public buildings. More advantage is usually found in using a few or individual specimen plants, rather than mass planting, because of the interesting outlines and branching habits. Variations in color from blue to dark green and in texture from fine to coarse make possible the creation of many landscape effects.

Large dense specimens or groups should be used carefully, if at all, on small properties because of the massive and overpowering effects, unwanted shade in winter, and interference with air movement.

Selected forms can be used near the house or other small buildings, as hedges, screens, windbreaks, or specimens.

The continuing trend to large scale landscaping will increase the demand for high quality, landscape size pines in the future.

PINE LIST, ACCORDING TO NEEDLE NUMBER

FIVE NEEDLE TYPES
  PRIMARY

Pinus aristata	Bristlecone Pine
Pinus cembra	Swiss Stone Pine
Pinus flexilis	Limber Pine
Pinus koraiensis	Korean Pine
Pinus parviflora	Japanese White Pine
Pinus peuce	Balkan Pine
Pinus pumila	Japanese Stone Pine
Pinus strobus	Eastern White Pine
Pinus wallichiana	Himalayan Pine

  SECONDARY

Pinus balfouriana	Foxtail Pine

THREE NEEDLE TYPES
  PRIMARY

Pinus bungeana	Lacebark Pine
Pinus taeda	Loblolly Pine

  SECONDARY

Pinus ponderosa	Ponderosa Pine
Pinus rigida	Pitch Pine
Pinus serotina	Pond Pine

TWO NEEDLE TYPES
  PRIMARY

Pinus densiflora	Japanese Red Pine
Pinus mugo	Swiss Mountain Pine
Pinus nigra or *P. nigra* var. *nigra*	Austrian Pine
Pinus resinosa	Red Pine
Pinus sylvestris	Scotch Pine

  SECONDARY

Pinus banksiana	Jack Pine
Pinus echinata	Shortleaf Pine
Pinus pungens	Table Mountain Pine
Pinus thunbergii	Japanese Black Pine
Pinus virginiana	Scrub Pine

Pinus aristata Engelm. — Bristlecone Pine, also called Hickory Pine.
(pī′nus à-ris-tā′tà)

LEAVES: Borne 5 together, dark bluish green, persistent for 14 to 17 years, commonly dotted with white resinous exudations, 1 to 1 3/4″ long, leaf sheaths curling back into small rosettes, remaining 2 to 4 years at the base of the leaf.

SIZE: 8 to 20′ with an irregular spread; can grow to 40′ but this would take many years; co-national champions are 76′ by 39′ and 72′ by 33′, both in New Mexico.

HARDINESS: Zone 4 to 7, should be protected from desiccating winds in cold climates as foliage will burn.

HABIT: Dwarf, shrubby and picturesque in youth and in old age, tremendous character in a young plant.

RATE: Slow, in fact extremely so, 16-year-old plant being only 4′ high.

TEXTURE: Medium.

BARK: Gray, green and smooth when young, rust-colored and fissured with age.

LEAF COLOR: Dark bluish green with white, resinous exudations giving the leaf a bluish white cast.

FLOWERS: Monoecious.

FRUIT: Cones sessile, cylindrical-ovoid, brown, 2 to 4″ long by 1 1/2″ broad, apex blunt, a bristle-like prickle at the edge of each pine scale, seeds to 1/4″ long, gray-brown.

CULTURE: Will succeed in poor, dry, rocky soils whether alkaline or acid; dislikes shade and will not tolerate smoke-polluted air.

DISEASES AND INSECTS: See *Pinus* introduction.

LANDSCAPE VALUE: Suitable for rock garden or use as an accent plant; could possibly be used as a foundation plant because of its picturesque growth habit; makes a nice bonsai or patio plant.

CULTIVARS:

'Sherwood Compact'—Slow-growing (is this acceptable?) form of the species, said to be a show stopper, perhaps . . . for ants.

PROPAGATION: Seeds have no dormancy and will germinate immediately upon collection. I have raised many seedlings and the only requirement is that damping-off be controlled.

ADDITIONAL NOTES: Depending on what source you believe this species is one of the oldest living plants on earth. Estimates range from 2000 to 7000 years; however, several trees in the 4000- to 5000-year-old category have been adequately documented. One authority reported a 4900-year-old tree in eastern Nevada. Trees may attain only an inch diameter in a century. The literature often confuses me, just as this author confuses you. An article in *Arctic and Alpine Research* 24:253–256 (1992) reported that 12 trees in Colorado ranging from 1600 to 2100 years old were documented; one tree had an inner ring date of 442 B.C. Often referred to as a foxtail pine because of the length of needle retention and the bushy effect of the foliage. *Pinus balfouriana* A. Murray, Foxtail Pine, is a related type but does not develop the resinous exudations.

NATIVE HABITAT: Southwestern United States from the mountains along the Nevada-California border east through the highlands of Nevada, Utah, Colorado, northern Arizona and northern New Mexico. Introduced 1861.

Pinus banksiana Lamb. — Jack Pine
(pī′nus bank-sē-ā′nà)

LEAVES: In pairs, persisting 2 to 4 years, olive green, stiff, curved or slightly twisted, 3/4 to 2″ long, margin with minute or rudimentary teeth, apex short-pointed, stomata on each surface.

BUDS: Dark brown, 1/8 to 1/4″ long, cylindrical, resinous with closely pressed scales.

STEM: Smooth, glabrous, pale yellowish green, reddish or brown the second year.

SIZE: 35 to 50′ in height, known to 70′, irregularly spreading but usually less than height; national champion is 56′ by 61′ at Lake Bronson, MN.

HARDINESS: Zone 2 to 6 or 7.

HABIT: Pyramidal in youth, open, spreading, often shrubby and flat-topped at maturity.

RATE: Slow-medium.

TEXTURE: Medium; possibly coarse in winter as needles often color a sickly yellow-green.

BARK: Thin, reddish brown to gray on young stems, becoming dark brown and flaky; on old trunks furrowed into irregular thick plates.

LEAF COLOR: Young leaves light green to dull dark green; yellow-green in winter.

FLOWERS: Monoecious, staminate clustered, yellowish.

FRUIT: Pointing forward, slender, ovoid-conical, curved at the tapered point, 1 to 2 1/2″ long, 3/4″ wide, umbo unarmed or with small spine, yellowish brown on some trees, on some trees nearly all mature cones remain closed; on others most of them open; closed cones subjected to temperatures of 140°F will open.

CULTURE: Easily transplanted if root pruned; not good in limestone soils; but will survive in almost pure sand and extremely cold climates; full sun; dry, sandy and acid soils; grows in soils too poor for most plants.

DISEASES AND INSECTS: See *Pinus* introduction.

LANDSCAPE VALUE: Not especially ornamental but adaptable for windbreaks, shelterbelts and mass plantings in sand; also valued for its extreme hardiness and suitability to the colder regions; I have seen considerable plantings in poor soil regions of southern Indiana.

CULTIVARS:

Dwarf Forms—Many often derived from "witches' brooms."

'Uncle Fogy'—Weeping form, can be grafted to an upright standard and grown as a weeping tree or used as a ground cover; in 10 years, one plant had spread 15′ and was 2′ high.

PROPAGATION: Seeds have no dormancy, or only a slight one, and will germinate immediately upon collection after a light stratification.

ADDITIONAL NOTES: Species serves as a valuable pioneer tree on poor sandy soils, but, except on the very poorest, is eventually replaced by Red or White Pine. Parboiling the male flowers to remove excess resin supposedly makes them suitable for eating. I have doubts.

NATIVE HABITAT: Most northerly of North American species—grows near the Arctic Circle, south to northern New York and Minnesota. Introduced before 1783.

Pinus bungeana Zucc. ex Endl. — Lacebark Pine
(pī′nus bun-jē-ā′nȧ)

LEAVES: 3, remaining 3 to 4 years, stiff, apex sharp-pointed, 2 to 4″ long, 1/12″ wide, margins finely toothed, inside slightly rounded, made by the raised midrib, with stomatic lines on both sides, lustrous medium to dark green; needles are very stiff and rigid as well as sharp to the touch.

STEM: Grayish green, shining, glabrous.

SIZE: 30 to 50′ with a 20 to 35′ spread, can grow to 75′.

HARDINESS: Zone (4)5 to 7b, one plant on the Georgia campus is about 75-years-old, plant has been damaged at Orono, ME.

HABIT: Pyramidal to rounded, often with many trunks in youth; becoming open, picturesque, flat-topped and broad-spreading with age.

RATE: Slow, patience is a necessary virtue.

TEXTURE: Medium.

BARK: Exfoliating in patches like a planetree, young stems greenish with irregular whitish or brownish areas interspersed; one of the most handsome pines for bark character.

LEAF COLOR: Lustrous medium to dark green.

FLOWERS: Monoecious.

FRUIT: Cone, terminal or lateral, subsessile, ovoid, 2 to 3″ long, approximately 2″ across, light yellowish brown, scale-end broader than high, cross-keeled, with a reflexed, triangular spine.

CULTURE: Transplant balled-and-burlapped if root pruned; prefers well-drained soils and sunny conditions; supposedly tolerates limestone.

DISEASES AND INSECTS: See *Pinus* introduction.

LANDSCAPE VALUE: A good specimen tree valued for its striking, showy bark; excellent on corners of large buildings, and places where bark can be viewed; may break up under heavy snow and ice loads; surprising performance in Athens-Atlanta area with plants in John Barbour's Bold Spring Nursery in red Georgia clay and full sun growing 8 to 10′ in 10 years; bark starts to develop on 1 1/2 to 2″ diameter branches; have observed it as a container accent plant.

CULTIVARS:

'Compacta'—More compact uniform habit than the species, produces the wonderful exfoliating bark, grows about one-half the rate of the species.

ADDITIONAL NOTES: The U.S. National Arboretum, Washington, DC, has many handsome specimens. Has a place in almost every garden. One of the most beautiful of introduced pines. First observed by Dr. Bunge near Peking in 1831, cultivated in a temple garden.

NATIVE HABITAT: China. Introduced 1846.

Pinus cembra L. — Swiss Stone Pine (Arolla Pine)
(pī′nus sem′brȧ)

LEAVES: 5, remaining 4 to 5 years, densely set, rather stiff, straight, 2 to 3″(5″) long, scarcely 1/25″ wide, apex blunt-pointed, margins finely toothed, dark green outside, innersides with bluish white stomatic lines; leaf sheaths falling the first year, 3/4″ long.

STEM: Covered with dense, yellow-brown to orange-colored pubescence the first year, becoming grayish brown to brownish black the second year.

SIZE: 30 to 40′ in height, occasionally 70′ with a spread of 15 to 25′.

HARDINESS: Zone 3b to 7.

HABIT: A narrow, densely columnar pyramid in youth, becoming open and flat-topped with spreading, drooping branches when mature; extremely upright in youth.

RATE: Slow, rarely reaches 25′ after 25 to 30 years.

TEXTURE: Medium.

BARK: Gray-green, smooth, gray-brown, ridged-and-furrowed, with scaly ridges when mature.

LEAF COLOR: Lustrous dark green outside, innerside with bluish white stomatic lines.

FLOWERS: Monoecious, clustered and inconspicuous.

FRUIT: The cones are terminal, short-stalked, erect-ovoid, apex blunt, 2 to 3″ long by 1 1/2 to 2 1/4″ broad; greenish violet at first turning purplish brown when mature; cones never open but fall in the spring of the third year and seeds are released by birds or through decomposition of scales.

CULTURE: Requires a well-drained, loamy soil in full sun; transplants better than most other pines; soil must be well-drained and slightly acid; should be located in an open area with free air movement.

DISEASES AND INSECTS: See *Pinus* introduction.

LANDSCAPE VALUE: A picturesque and hardy tree; useful as a specimen or mass; very handsome pine but somewhat slow-growing.

CULTIVARS: Counted 10 cultivars being offered largely by northeastern United States nurseries.

‘Columnaris’—More narrow and columnar in habit than the species, at times seems to be the predominant form in cultivation, name used for more than one clone.

PROPAGATION: Seed should be stratified in moist medium for 90 to 270 days at 33 to 41°F; there is some indication that direct sowing will result in a good germination.

ADDITIONAL NOTES: I was studying plants on a 6600′ high mountain outside of Lucerne, Switzerland when I came across this species. It formed a much more loose, open, pyramidal outline than what I am accustomed to seeing in cultivation. On this same mountain, were large, shrubby colonies of *Pinus mugo*.

NATIVE HABITAT: Mountains of central Europe and southern Asia. Introduced 1875.

RELATED SPECIES:

Pinus pumila (Pall.) Reg., (pī′nus pū′mil-à), Japanese Stone Pine or Dwarf Siberian Pine, a rather shrubby species, was at one time regarded as a geographical form of the European species, *P. cembra*, with which it has much in common. Needles 5, densely bundled, slightly curved and directed forward, 1 1/2 to 3″(4″) long, apex blunt-pointed, margin sparsely toothed or entire, green on outer surface, inner glaucous, and entire leaf appearing bluish green, sheaths falling after the first year. The cones are subterminal, clustered, short-stalked, spreading, ovoid, 1 1/2″ long, 1″ wide, purplish when young, finally dull reddish or yellowish brown and remaining unopened until shedding seeds. In general, it is a dwarf, more or less, dense, prostrate, 1 to 7.5′ high shrub of great beauty. There are several plants at the Arnold and all appear different. One particularly handsome specimen in the dwarf conifer collection is a dense, spreading procumbent evergreen with rich bluish green needles. Plants cone at a young age. Many named selections of various shades of blue and growth habit. ‘Dwarf Blue’, ‘Glauca’, and ‘National Blue’ are listed in American commerce. The potential for the species is untapped. Occurs in large groves on the tops of the highest mountain in Japan, widely distributed in the province Shinano, north through Hondo and Hokkaido, and in the valleys down to sea-level on Saghalin, on the seashore of Ochotosk, in continental Manchuria and northern Korea. Read a discussion of *Microbiota decussata* that mentioned *P. pumila* was growing in the same vicinity. Introduced 1807. Zone 5 and perhaps lower. One European reference listed it as Zone 1 adaptable.

Pinus densiflora Sieb. & Zucc. — Japanese Red Pine
(pī′nus den-si-flō′rà)

LEAVES: 2, remaining 3 years, slender, twisted, soft, 3 to 5″ long, 1/25″ wide, apex acute, margins finely toothed, with inconspicuous stomatic lines on each side, lustrous bright to dark green, the needles appear as if tufted and are borne somewhat upright along the stems; sheath 1/4 to 3/8″ long, persistent, terminated by 1 or 2 slender threads.

BUDS: Cylindrical, resinous, reddish brown, to 1/2″ long.

STEM: Initially glaucous green, glabrous or minutely downy, eventually orangish, glabrous.

SIZE: 40 to 60' in height with a similar spread at maturity, can grow to 100'.

HARDINESS: Zone 3b to 7; some variation in hardiness but a strain introduced by the Forestry Experiment Station in Cloquet, MN has proven hardy, no injury at Orono, ME.

HABIT: The trunks are frequently crooked or leaning, branches horizontally spreading and the crown is rather broad and flat; very irregular even in youth as it is an open, floppy grower.

RATE: Slow to medium.

TEXTURE: Medium.

BARK: Orangish to orangish red when young, peeling off in thin scales; in old age grayish at the base, fissured into oblong plates.

LEAF COLOR: Lustrous bright to dark green.

FLOWERS: Monoecious.

FRUIT: Cones sub-terminal, short-stalked, solitary or in clusters, conical-ovoid to oblong, somewhat oblique at the base, 1 1/2 to 2" long by approximately 1" broad, umbo obtuse or with a short spine, dull tawny yellow opening the second year and remaining 2 to 3 years on the tree.

CULTURE: Prefers a well-drained, slightly acid soil and sunny conditions.

DISEASES AND INSECTS: See *Pinus* introduction.

LANDSCAPE VALUE: Used as a specimen because of its interesting form and decorative orange-red bark; also favorite subject for bonsai; in my mind one of the handsomest pines; I had this species planted alongside *Pinus thunbergii* in the Illinois test plots and after the 1976-77 winter (–20°F) the needles of the latter were completely brown (stem and buds not killed) while the former showed no injury.

CULTIVARS: Numerous forms have been selected in Japan. The following are a few that I have seen.

'Aurea'—Green in summer, bright golden yellow in winter.

'Globosa'—Rounded to hemispherical shrub, needles half as long as species, the trunk is semi-prostrate; slow-growing (15' in 50 years).

'Heavy Bud' ('Large Bud')—Dwarf, broad-rounded top, like 'Umbraculifera' with larger red buds and lighter green needles.

'Oculus Draconis'—Each leaf marked with two yellow lines (bands) and when viewed from above shows alternate yellow and green rings; can be rather attractive; especially in late summer and fall; I had a small plant in my Illinois garden and many people were fascinated by it; unfortunately, it discolors to a muddy yellow-brown in winter.

'Pendula'—A rather effective weeping form with rich green needles; it can be used to drape over rock walls and raised planters; needs to be top-worked on a standard to form a true weeping character, needles about 4" long.

'Tiny Temple' ('Temple')—Slow-growing, about 4" per year, 2 1/2" long, very thin needles are dark green outside, gray-blue inside; habit wide pyramid.

'Umbraculifera'—Dwarf, umbrella-like head, to 10' or more tall; branches densely borne, upright-spreading, very beautiful especially when the orange bark color is developed; a 42-year-old plant at the Secrest Arboretum was 25' high; unfortunately, heavy snow broke many of the branches; goes by name of 'Tanyosho' in Japan; there is also a compact form of this cultivar ('Umbraculifera Compacta'), grows 4 to 6' high and wide; have seen 'Jane Kluis' listed as a new form but more compact, 3 to 4' high, 5 to 6' wide.

PROPAGATION: Seeds require no stratification; I have grown many seedlings and with proper water and nutrition they grow quite rapidly.

NATIVE HABITAT: Japan, Korea, parts of China. Introduced 1854.

Pinus echinata Mill. — Shortleaf Pine
(pī'nus ek-i-nā'tà)

LEAVES: In fascicles of 2, but also in 3's on the same tree, 1 3/4 to 4 1/2" long, dark bluish green, slender, finely toothed, flexible, persistent 2nd through 4th season, resin ducts medial, 1 to 4.

BUDS: Oblong-ovoid, 1/4" long, apex acuminate, brown, slightly resinous or none, scales closely appressed.

STEM: First green and tinged with purple, glabrous, eventually reddish brown.

SIZE: 80 to 100' in height; less under landscape conditions, perhaps 50 to 60'; national champion 138' by 75' in Myrtle, MS.

HARDINESS: Zone 6 to 9.

HABIT: Pyramidal in youth, developing a well-formed trunk and a small, narrow pyramidal crown that opens with age, branches distinctly sinuous which permits easy separation from *P. taeda* which grows in a similar native range.

RATE: Fast.

TEXTURE: Medium-coarse.

BARK: Scaly, nearly black on young trees, with age reddish brown and broken into irregular flat plates, scaly on the surface, plates large, irregular-blocky and handsome.

LEAF COLOR: Dark bluish green.

FRUIT: Ovoid-oblong to conical, nearly sessile, 1 1/2 to 2 1/2″ long, 1 to 1 1/2″ wide, usually persistent for several years; umbo dorsal and armed with a small sharp, straight or curved, sometimes deciduous prickle.

CULTURE: Forms a deep taproot and therefore somewhat difficult to transplant, an 8-year-old tree may have a 14′ taproot; extremely adaptable and found on dry, upland soils; 8- to 10-year-old trees retain ability to sprout if stems are injured by fire or cutting.

DISEASES AND INSECTS: Nantucket pine-tip moth, southern pine beetle, littleleaf disease.

LANDSCAPE VALUE: Important timber species, inferior to Loblolly Pine for landscape use; tree of great character and beauty, several mature specimens on the Georgia campus are 70 to 80′ high, devoid of branches for 70% of their length; the quilt-work, puzzle-like, red-brown bark is beautiful and permits reliable separation from *P. taeda* with its gray, ridged-and-furrowed bark.

PROPAGATION: Seed requires no pretreatment.

NATIVE HABITAT: A colonizer of upland areas that are open, grassy or abandoned agriculture land. New Jersey, south to Georgia, Texas, Oklahoma. Introduced 1726.

Pinus flexilis James — Limber Pine
(pī′nus fleks′i-lis)

LEAVES: In fives, persisting 5 to 6 years, densely crowded on the ends of the branchlets, pointing forward, rigid, curved or slightly twisted, 2 1/2 to 3 1/2″ long, margins entire, apex sharp-pointed, 3 to 4 lines of stomata on each surface, dark green to a slight glaucous dark green.

BUDS: Ovoid, slender, sharply pointed, 3/8″ long.

STEM: Tough, flexible, glabrous or minutely tomentulous, actually can be tied in knots, shining green.

SIZE: 30 to 50′ in height by 15 to 35′ in spread; national champion is 58′ by 46′ at Uinta National Forest, UT.

HARDINESS: Zone 4 to 7.

HABIT: Dense, broad pyramid in youth; becoming a low, broad, flat-topped tree at maturity.

RATE: Slow.

TEXTURE: Medium.

BARK: In youth smooth, light gray or greenish gray, on old trunks grayish brown, separated by deep fissures into rectangular to nearly square, superficially scaled plates or blocks, looks similar to *P. strobus* bark.

LEAF COLOR: Dark bluish green, very attractive.

FLOWERS: Monoecious, staminate clustered, rose colored, female purple.

FRUIT: Cones subterminal, short-stalked, cylindric ovoid, 3 to 6″ long, 1 1/2 to 2 1/4″ wide, erect when young and pendulously spreading when mature, light brown, quite resinous.

CULTURE: Transplants well balled-and-burlapped if root pruned; does best in moist, well-drained soil and prefers sun or partial shade; adapted for planting on rocky slopes; very adaptable species and one of the best for midwestern and eastern states.

DISEASES AND INSECTS: White pine blister rust was reported on the species in a native stand at Cathedral Spires, Black Hills National Forest, see *Plant Disease* 76:538 (1992).

LANDSCAPE VALUE: A handsome specimen; this and *P. resinosa* were the only two pines that were not seriously wind-burned or injured in the Chicago region after the difficult winter of 1976–77; shows good adaptability and might be used more.

CULTIVARS:

'Columnaris'—Upright, good for areas where lateral space to spread is limited.

'Extra Blue'—Intense blue needles, forms an irregular pyramid, dense tufted branching.

'Glauca'—Foliage bluish green, much more so than the species, quite attractive; probably a catchall term for bluish green needled types.

'Glauca Pendula'—I grew this in my Illinois garden where it scampered along the ground forming a wide-spreading rather irregular shrub of bluish green color; actually rather attractive.

'Glenmore Dwarf'—Very slow-growing, forming a small, gray-blue, upright plant that becomes pyramidal with age; the main branches ascending or upswinging so that the growing tips are vertical or nearly so; needles are dense, about 1 1/2 to 1 3/4″ long, becoming shorter and tighter near the tips of the branches; averaged 5″ year, 6′ in 14 years at Longwood Gardens.

'Millcreek'—Excellent blue needle color, full pyramidal habit.

'Nana'—Dwarf bushy form, extremely slow-growing, needles about 1 1/4″ long.

'Pendula'—A wide-spreading, weeping tree becoming quite large with time.

'Vanderwolf's Pyramid'—Upright form with good vigor, averaged 25″ per year and 17′ in 8 years, handsome blue-green foliage, needles twisted, Vermeulen introduction.

PROPAGATION: Seed should be stratified for 21 to 90 days at 35 to 41°F.

NATIVE HABITAT: Rocky Mountains of western North America, Alberta to northern Mexico, east to Texas. Introduced 1861.

RELATED SPECIES:

Pinus albicaulis Engelm., (pī′nus al-bi-kaw′lis), White Bark Pine, differs in its smaller, 1 3/4 to 3″ long, entire needles and 2 1/2″ long, ovoid cones, and the fact they remain closed at maturity. Old specimens of *P. albicaulis* develop whitish bark. Experienced for the first time in 1995, when Bonnie and I hiked Mt. Rainier National Park. Beautiful, weather-beaten, ghostly, gray-white trunks. Plants at 6000 to 7000′ elevation were weathered like old cedar shingles. Rewarding to finally meet the plant. Largest trees were 20 to 30′ high. National champion is 69′ by 47′ in Sawtooth National Recreation Area, ID. In northern Rockies, species is rapidly declining for several reasons with white pine blister rust the most serious, see *Conservation Biology* 9:654–664 (1995). British Columbia to California and Wyoming. Introduced 1852. Zone 3 to 5.

Pinus koraiensis Sieb.& Zucc. — Korean Pine
(pī′nus kôr-ā-i-en′sis)

LEAVES: In 5's, persisting 3 years, 2 1/2 to 4 1/2″ long, lustrous dark green, with white stomatal lines on two inner surfaces giving an overall blue-green needle color, margins relatively coarse-toothed the entire length, apex bluntish; leaf sheaths 1/2″ long, soon falling.

STEM: Young shoots covered with a dense reddish brown pubescence which becomes dirty brown with age.

SIZE: 30 to 40′ under cultivation; may grow over 100′, a 38′ high plant was growing at the Morton Arboretum.

HARDINESS: Zone (3)4 to 7, surprisingly one of the hardiest pines but not well-known.

HABIT: Loose, pyramidal outline; rather refreshing compared to many of the stiff-habit types; feathered to the ground with branches; often rather broad and irregularly pyramidal.

RATE: Slow.

TEXTURE: Medium.

BARK: Thin, gray or grayish brown, peeling off in irregular flakes, reddish brown beneath.

LEAF COLOR: Lovely bluish green; actually dark green on outside; inner surfaces grayish.

FRUIT: Cone subterminal, solitary or few-together, short-stalked, cylindric-conical, apex blunt, 3 1/2 to 6″ long, 2 to 2 1/4″ wide, lurid-brown when mature, resinous, opening when mature, falling with the stalk.

CULTURE: Tremendously adaptable and also extremely cold hardy.

DISEASES AND INSECTS: None serious.

LANDSCAPE VALUE: Fine specimen plant, groupings or screens.

CULTIVARS:

'Glauca'—Long blue needles, soft-textured, extremely graceful.

'Morris Blue'—Two-tone bluish needle effect, to 35′, selection from Morris Arboretum.

'Silveray'—Upright columnar-pyramidal with rich blue-green needles.

'Winton'—Long, green needles with blue insides, wide-spreading bushy form, probably twice as wide as high.

PROPAGATION: Seeds will germinate without pretreatment although some cold may be valuable.

ADDITIONAL NOTES: I have real trouble separating this species from young *P. cembra* by needle characteristics. In general it is more openly branched and the needles are longer and are toothed to the apex. Cones are twice as long as those of *P. cembra*.

NATIVE HABITAT: Manchuria, Korea, mountainous areas on the main island of Japan. Introduced 1861.

Pinus mugo Turra. — Swiss Mountain Pine, Mugo Pine
(pī′nus mū′gō)

LEAVES: In pairs, persisting five or more years, rigid, curved, medium to dark green, 1 to 2″ (1 1/2 to 3″) long, margins finely toothed, apex short, blunt, horny point, stomatic lines on both surfaces, basal sheath up to about 3/5″ long.

BUDS: Oblong-ovoid, 1/4 to 1/2″ long, reddish brown scales encrusted with resin, scales closely appressed.

STEM: Young stems short, without down, green at first with prominent ridges, becoming brown to blackish brown.

SIZE: 15 to 20′ in height by 25 to 20′ spread; but can grow 30 to 80′ tall and as wide.

HARDINESS: Zone 3 to 7(8), have seen occasional plants in Zone 8 but they do not measure up to plants in the North.

HABIT: Very variable, prostrate or pyramidal; usually low, broad-spreading and bushy, at least the types available from nurseries.

RATE: Slow.

TEXTURE: Medium.

BARK: Brownish gray, scaly, split in irregular plates but not scaling off on old trunks; a good identification feature on 1/2″ to 2 to 3″ diameter stems are the regular bumpy protuberances which result when the leaves abscise.

LEAF COLOR: Medium green to dark green, often yellowish green in winter especially on the tips of the needles.

FLOWERS: Monoecious.

FRUIT: Cones, subterminal, sessile or short-stalked, erect, horizontal, or slightly pendulous, solitary or 2 to 3(4) together, ovoid or conical-ovoid, 1 to 2″ long by 1/2 to 1 1/2″ broad, apex surrounded by a darker ring, at maturity grayish black.

CULTURE: Moves well balled-and-burlapped if root pruned; many quality plants are being produced in containers, generally does not produce a tap root and is easy to transplant; prefers a deep, moist loam in sun or partial shade; can be pruned annually to thicken plant and keep dwarf habit; very calcareous soil tolerant.

DISEASES AND INSECTS: Subject to rusts, wood rots, borers, sawflies and especially scale (often very serious).

LANDSCAPE VALUE: The species is seldom used; valued chiefly for its dwarf cultivars which are useful in landscape plantings; especially for foundations, masses, groupings.

CULTIVARS: Over 40 dwarfish types shown in *Conifers*. Without a scorecard, they are anybody's guess. It is fun to walk through a block of seed-grown *Pinus mugo* where the variation in size is literally unbelievable. They range from the true dwarfs to rather large, spreading shrubs. Many newer selections than those presented. Have seen many in European gardens, particularly yellow to green needle forms. A perusal of conifer producer catalogs will yield untold treasures. See *American Nurseryman* 185(7):78–85 (1997) for "A Tale of Many Mugos." Discusses the dwarf Mugo Pines in commercial production and appears to emphasize how *slow* they grow. 'Mitsch Mini' is the slowest at a galloping rate of 1″ per year; the fastest cultivar is 'Big Tuna' at 3 to 5″ per year. Can the reader imagine naming a Mugo Pine BIG TUNA? Appetizing, ugh, only to Hobbes of Calvin and Hobbes fame.

'Amber Gold'—Compact, globose, slow-growing form with orange-yellow winter needles, green in summer, a chance seedling from Ferny Creek Nurseries, Australia, see *Plant Varieties Journal* 6(4):49–50 (1993).

'Aurea'—Semi-dwarf, light green needles turning bright gold in winter, 3′ by 3′, needs sun for best color.

'Gnom'—Twenty-five-year-old plant was 15″ high and 36″ wide, forms a dense, globular, dark green mound.

'Mops'—Dwarf globose form as tall as wide, dark green 1 to 1 3/4″ long needles, considered one of the better forms, grows about 3′ high, often wider at maturity.

var. *mugo* (var. *mughus*) (Scop.) Zenari—Low-growing form of the species usually less than 8′ tall and about twice that in width; variable due to seed source; found in eastern Alps and Balkans.

'Ophir'—Mounded, flat-topped form with good yellow winter color, chance seedling, from the Netherlands.

var. *pumilio* (Haenke) E. Murray—Usually prostrate grower up to 10′ wide, widely distributed in mountains of eastern and central Europe.

'Sherwood Compact'—Dwarf, flat-topped form with short, lustrous dark green needles year-round.

'Slavinii'—Forty-year-old plant is 3′ by 5′, dwarf, low, dense, needles crowded, dark green.

var. *uncinata* (Raymond) Domin.—Resembles *P. mugo* with usually a single stem and large size to 50 to 75′, Switzerland to western Alps, Cevennes, Pyrenees.

'Valley Cushion'—Slow-growing form, ~1 1/2″ per year, for the rock garden crowd and the nurseries that want to go out of business, 12″ by 12″.

PROPAGATION: Seeds have no dormancy and will germinate immediately upon collection.

ADDITIONAL NOTES: Perhaps one of the most confusing pines for the homeowner because of tremendous variability in size. The cute, diminutive, prostrate plant that comes from the garden center and is placed in the foundation planting often becomes 10 to 15′ tall and wide although it was advertised as a 2 to 4′ high, low-growing evergreen. One of the real problems with this and other plants is that they do not read the advertisements. This species includes a number of varieties or geographical forms which are difficult to classify, as the variations in habit are not always correlated with the character of the cones and appear to be due in many cases to soil, climate, and other growing conditions, or perhaps to hybridization with other species. Nomenclature is sometimes confused on this species as it is listed as *Pinus montana* var. *mugo* and other odd things. As I wandered atop a 6600′ high mountain outside Lucerne, Switzerland, I came across numerous patches of Mugo Pine. The habit was dense, shrubby and wide-spreading. I saw no colonies more than 3 to 5′ high. This could have been the geographical variety *pumilio*. I taught in Moline, IL and one of the local nurserymen showed me around an estate where a 35 to 45′ high Mugo Pine was growing. It took me awhile to accept the fact that the plant was, in fact, *Pinus mugo*.

NATIVE HABITAT: Mountains of central and southern Europe from Spain to the Balkans. Introduced 1779.

Pinus nigra Arn. (Also listed as *P. nigra* var. *nigra*, *P. nigra* var. *austriaca*) — Austrian Pine
(pī′nus nī′grà)

LEAVES: In pairs, persisting about 4(8) years, very dense on the branchlets, stiff, straight or curved, 3 to 5″(6″) long, 1/16 to 1/12″ wide, margins minutely toothed, apex a thickened horny point, sharp to the touch, 12 to 14 lines of stomata on each surface, dark green, sheath about 1/2″ long.

BUDS: Ovoid to oblong or cylindrical, 1/2 to 1″ long, abruptly contracted to a sharp point, scales light brown, resinous.

STEM: Young stems without down (pubescence), yellowish brown, ridged, the branchlets as they lose their leaves becoming roughened by the persistent leaf bases.

SIZE: 50 to 60′ in height by 20 to 40′ in spread but can grow to 100′ or more.

HARDINESS: Zone 3b to 7, survives in Zone 8, although seldom seen, not a reliable plant in Zones 7 and 8, best in colder climates.

HABIT: Densely pyramidal when young becoming a large, broad, flat-topped tree with a rough, short trunk and low, stout, spreading branches.

RATE: Medium, 35 to 50′ after 20 to 30 years; have seen 60 to 70′ trees under landscape conditions.

TEXTURE: Medium-coarse.

BARK: Dark brown furrows, usually with gray or gray-brown mottled, flattened ridges, quite attractive, one of the handsomest pines for bark.

LEAF COLOR: Lustrous dark green.

FLOWERS: Staminate clustered, yellow; pistillate yellow-green.

FRUIT: Solitary or in clusters, sub-sessile, ovoid, conical, 2 to 3″ long, 1 to 1 1/4″ wide before opening, tawny-yellow initially, becoming brown, scales about 1″ long, transversely keeled near the apex which often ends in a more or less persistent prickle.

CULTURE: A very hardy tree that withstands city conditions better than many other pines; very tolerant of soils, if moist; will stand some dryness and exposure; resists heat and drought; less fastidious in its soil requirements than most pines; will succeed in fairly heavy clay and alkaline soils; tolerates seaside conditions.

DISEASES AND INSECTS: In recent years this pine has exhibited severe dieback in midwestern and eastern states; some of the dieback as been attributed to *Diplodia* tip blight; however, whole trees have died in a single season so probably multiple factors are involved; recently a pine nematode has been reported; apparently the nematodes are transmitted by a beetle; they plug up the vascular system and an entire plant may die in a single season.

LANDSCAPE VALUE: An adaptable species with very stiff needles making a good specimen, screen or windbreak; can also be used for mass planting; develops its real character in old age when the branches become umbelliformly spreading and the bark colors develop fully.

CULTIVARS: Greatly variable over its native range with many varieties and cultivars. *Conifers* presents the essence of the variation in the wild and cultivation.

'Arnold Sentinel'—Columnar form, original plant 25′ by 7′ after 24 years, Arnold Arboretum introduction.

'ENCI'—Mounding habit, dark green needles, 5 to 6′ by 5 to 6′, from Evergreen Nursery.

'Hornibrookiana'—Originated as a "witches' broom," needles 2 1/2″ long, very compact, dwarf, shrubby and rounded, 30-year-old plant is 2′ tall and 6′ across, found in Seneca Park, Rochester, NY by B.H. Slavin.

'Pyramidalis'—A narrow, pyramidal plant with closely ascending branches and 4 to 5″ long bluish-green needles.

PROPAGATION: Seeds have no dormancy and will germinate immediately upon collection.

ADDITIONAL NOTES: A somewhat confusing pine often listed as *Pinus nigra* var. *nigra* or *P. nigra* var. *austriaca*. It is another species somewhat like *P. mugo* and has many geographical varieties and subspecies. Den Ouden and Boom noted that it is a fine tree for garden planting and a forest tree with good economic properties. On the other side of the ledger, Dallimore and Jackson stated that under cultivation it is usually a rough, heavily branched tree, too somber for ornamental planting and of little value as a timber tree as its wood is coarse and knotty. One wonders if these authorities are discussing the same plant. Variety *caramanica* (Loud.) Rehd., Crimean or Turkish Black Pine, is not clearly distinguished from *P. nigra* but usually has larger cones up to 4″ long. It occurs in Asia Minor, the Caucasus, the Crimea, the Balkans and the southern Carpathians. Variety *maritima* (Ait.) Melville, Corsican Pine, has a slender crown with horizontal branches. The needles are more slender and less rigid and may reach 6 to 7″ in length. Found in the southern part of the Italian peninsula, Sicily, Corsica and also Algeria. Excellent plant for afforesting sandy soils along coastal areas. Probably less hardy than the Austrian Pine, although it has grown quite fast at the Secrest Arboretum reaching 80 to 90′ in 67 years and withstood temperatures of –20 to –25°F. Variety *cebennensis* (Gron. & Godr.) Rehd. represents the western most race of *P. nigra*. It forms a small or medium-sized tree and is best distinguished by the orange stems and slender, 1/16″ diameter needles.

NATIVE HABITAT: It is a native of Europe, from Austria to central Italy, Greece and Yugoslavia. Introduced 1759.

RELATED SPECIES:

Pinus heldreichii Christ., (pī′nus hel-drēch′ē-ī), Bosnian Pine, particularly var. *leucodermis* is becoming more common in arboreta and gardens. The species has a conic-ovoid crown with ridged-and-furrowed, ash gray bark, the fissures exposing yellow-gray patches. Needles are in two's, 2 to 4″ long, 1/12″ wide, stiff, spine-tipped, lustrous dark green, dentate with stomatal lines on all surfaces, and 1/2″ long needle sheaths. The needles persist 5 to 6 years and remind of *P. nigra* (although generally shorter) in color and texture. Cones are solitary or 3-whorled, ovoid, 4 to 5″ long, yellow-brown with a short, acute umbo. Cones are listed as purple-blue in youth. Have only seen mature cones. Plants I have observed from New England to England are dense, compact and more appealing than *P. nigra*. Reported as resistant to *Diplodia* blight and salt tolerant. 'Satillit' is a handsome selection, narrow-conical, with dark green needles. 'Green Bun' is a slower growing, more compact form, introduced by Iseli Nursery. Variety *leucodermis* (Ant.) Markgraf ex Fitschen is slower growing than the species with smoother, more whitish bark. As a young plant, 5 to 10′ high, it is beautiful. Balkan Peninsula, southern Italy. Introduced 1865. Zone 5 to 6. The species cultivated 1891. Zone 5 to 6. The species was essentially irreparably injured at Orono, ME, while var. *leucodermis* has grown 31′ by 15′ at the Morton Arboretum, Lisle, IL. Have seen the complex reduced to *P. leucodermis* Ant. in much of the European literature. Reported as being particularly suitable for dry and chalky soils. A number of cultivars beyond 'Satillit' have been introduced.

Pinus parviflora Sieb. & Zucc. — Japanese White Pine
(pī′nus pär-vi-flō′rȧ)

LEAVES: 5, persisting 3 to 4 years, crowded, rather stiff, usually twisted, forming brush-like tufts at the ends of the branches, 1 1/4 to 2 1/2″ long, 1/25″ wide, apex usually blunt, margins finely toothed, without stomata outside, inner sides with 3 to 4 stomatic lines, leaf sheaths falling.

BUDS: Ovoid, non-resinous, 1/3″ long, yellow-brown.

STEM: Greenish brown, finally light gray, short, minutely downy, older stems glabrous.

SIZE: 25 to 50′ in height with a similar or greater spread at maturity; 50 to 70′ in the wild.

HARDINESS: Zone 4 to 7, has survived –24°F; growing in Orono, ME and Edmonton, Alberta, Canada.

HABIT: Dense, conical pyramid when young, developing wide-spreading branches, flat-topped head and picturesque character with age, primarily an accent or character plant.

RATE: Slow.

TEXTURE: Medium.

BARK: On young trees smooth, gray, eventually becoming darker gray and platy, scaly on old trunks.

LEAF COLOR: Bluish green, sometimes grass green with 3 to 4 stomatic bands on inner sides of needles.

FLOWERS: Monoecious.

FRUIT: Cones nearly terminal, almost sessile, horizontally spreading, straight, ovoid to nearly cylindrical, 1 1/2 to 4″ long, spreading widely when ripe, remaining 6 to 7 years on the tree, scales few, broad wedge-shaped, thick, leathery-woody, brownish red, scale-end undulated, slightly incurved, umbo inconspicuous; often abundant even on young trees.

CULTURE: Full sun, average moisture; good drainage essential; tolerant of most soils, even clay loam; salt tolerant.

DISEASES AND INSECTS: See *Pinus* introduction.

LANDSCAPE VALUE: A choice, extremely graceful small conifer whose low stature and fine-textured foliage make it a perfect tree for small places; good for the sea coast as it is salt tolerant; good accent or specimen conifer; artistic growth habit.

CULTIVARS: Many, particularly in European literature. Counted 38 in *Conifers*, mostly dwarf, irregular-shaped or with vari-colored needles. Will never become a household pine because it lacks everyday functionality, i.e., screening potential.

   'Adcock's Dwarf'—Slow-growing form with short, blue-green, twisted needles clustered at shoot ends, upright globe shape to 3′.

   'Bergman'—Wide-spreading, rounded shrub with many leaders of uniform length, leaves bluish green, a 15-year-old plant was 16″ high and 36″ wide.

   'Brevifolia'—An ascending narrow tree with few branches; branchlets with short, very thick, stiff, blue-green 1″ long needles in tight bundles.

   'Glauca' (f. *glauca* is more accurate)—Perhaps the most common form in cultivation; it forms a wide-spreading tree with glaucous green foliage, can grow 45′ and greater; cones heavily in youth, at least trees I have seen show this characteristic, many variations on the 'Glauca' theme with 'Glauca Brevifolia', 'Glauca Compacta', 'Glauca Early Cone', and 'Glauca Nana' listed in United States commerce.

PROPAGATION: Seed should be stratified for 90 days at 33 to 41°F in moist medium.

ADDITIONAL NOTES: Hybrids between this species and *P. pumila* are referred to as *P.* × *hakkodensis* with irregular spreading growth habit, soft blue-green needles.

NATIVE HABITAT: Japan. Introduced 1861.

Pinus peuce Griseb. — Balkan or Macedonian Pine
(pī′nus pū′cē)

LEAVES: 5, remaining 3 years, densely bundled, 3 to 4″ long, 1/36″ wide, apex pointed, straight, rather stiff, margin finely toothed, both inner sides with 3 to 5, stomatiferous lines, densely borne, pointing forward, dark green on upper side, grayish on inner surfaces, sheath to 3/4″ long, quickly falling.

BUDS: Ovate-acute, brown, resinous, 1/3″ long.

STEM: Thickish, glossy, greenish, in the 2nd year grayish green or brownish gray, glaucous.

SIZE: 30 to 60′ in height with a relatively narrow spread; can grow to 100′ and specimens of this size grow in Bulgaria.

HARDINESS: Zone 4 to 7; often listed as Zone 5 but no damage in Orono, ME.

HABIT: Narrow pyramid, sometimes columnar in form, very handsome and reminding of *P. cembra* in youth, becoming more open with age; branches ascending in youth, becoming more horizontal with age.

RATE: Slow.

TEXTURE: Medium.

BARK: Gray-brown, thin, on old trees develops a scaly character.

LEAF COLOR: Dark green, overall appearance is blue-green.

FLOWERS: Monoecious.

FRUIT: Cones terminal, short-stalked, solitary or 3 to 4 together, spreading or deflexed, nearly cylindrical, 3 to 6″ long, light brown and resinous.

CULTURE: Full sun; moist soils with good drainage; move balled-and-burlapped if root pruned; quite adaptable.

DISEASES AND INSECTS: See *Pinus* introduction.

LANDSCAPE VALUE: Specimen, handsome plant.

PROPAGATION: Seed may require no stratification or up to 60 days.

ADDITIONAL NOTES: Somewhat resembles *P. cembra* in outline, the green, glabrous shoots distinguish it from *P. cembra*. Closely allied to *P. wallichiana*, but differs in its narrow habit, smaller branches, and shorter, stiffer needles which are less spreading. Great and noble specimen at Stourhead, England that on first uneducated impulse could be misidentified as *P. strobus*. The few gardens, Arnold and Swarthmore, where I have observed the tree provided credence to the fact it is worthy of greater use.

NATIVE HABITAT: Balkans, confined to limited areas in Albania, Bulgaria, Greece and the former Yugoslavia. Introduced 1863.

Pinus ponderosa Douglas ex Lawson — Ponderosa Pine, Western Yellow Pine
(pī′nus pon-dĕr-ō′sȧ)

LEAVES: In three's, sometimes two's, remaining 3 years, densely crowded on the branchlets, rigid, curved, 5 to 10″ long, 1/20 to 1/12″ wide, margins minutely toothed, apex a sharp, horny point, stomatic lines on each surface, dark or yellowish green, sheath to 1″ long, persistent.

BUDS: Oblong, cylindrical, 4/5″ long, acute, resinous scales closely appressed, reddish brown.

STEM: Young stems stout, glabrous, orange-brown or greenish at first eventually becoming nearly black; with the odor of vanilla when bruised.

SIZE: Averages 60 to 100′ under cultivation, spread 25 to 30′; 150 to 230′ in height in the wild; co-national champions are 223′ by 68′ in Plumas, CA and 178′ by 45′ in Deschutes, OR.

HARDINESS: Zone 3 to 6 or 7.

HABIT: Narrow to broad pyramidal when young; with time develops an irregularly cylindrical and narrow crown, with numerous short stout branches, the lower ones often drooping; very old trees have short, conical or flat-topped crowns and are devoid of branches for one-half or more of their height.

RATE: Medium, 75′ after 40 to 50 years.

TEXTURE: Medium to coarse.

BARK: Brown-black and furrowed on vigorous or young trees; yellowish brown to cinnamon red and broken up into large, flat, superficially scaly plates separated by deep irregular fissures on slow-growing and old trunks.

LEAF COLOR: Dark or yellowish green.

FLOWERS: Monoecious, staminate clustered, yellow; pistillate red, in pairs.

FRUIT: Cones, terminal, solitary or 3 to 5 together, nearly sessile, spreading or slightly recurved, symmetrical, ovoid or oblong-ovoid, 3 to 6″ long, 1 1/2 to 2″ broad, light reddish brown, shining, after falling often leaving a few of the basal scales attached to the branchlet, umbo broad triangular, terminated by a stout usually recurved prickle.

CULTURE: Transplant balled-and-burlapped if root pruned; prefers a deep, moist, well-drained loam; sunny, open exposure; intolerant of shade; hurt by late frosts; resistant to drought; tolerates alkaline soils; has shown good salt tolerance in controlled studies.

DISEASES AND INSECTS: See *Pinus* introduction.

LANDSCAPE VALUE: Valuable forest tree but not recommended for areas outside of which it is native, useful for mass planting and shelter belts.

CULTIVARS: Several varieties are described and are distinguished by growth habit, needle and cone differences. To my knowledge none are important in commerce.

PROPAGATION: Seeds have no dormancy and will germinate immediately upon collection.

ADDITIONAL NOTES: The most important pine in western North America. Furnishes more timber than any other American pine and is second only to douglas fir in total annual production. Thrives under widely different conditions and in many kinds of soils with low elevations to a considerable altitude, on light and moist soils, on dry, arid land, on dried-up river beds and lakes where there is a deep and rich soil, and on almost bare rocks. The most abundant growth takes place on light, deep, moist, well-drained soils.

NATIVE HABITAT: Western North America. British Columbia to Mexico, east to South Dakota and Texas. Introduced 1827.

RELATED SPECIES:

Pinus cembroides Zucc., (pī′nus sem-broy′dēz), Pinyon or Mexican Nut Pine, is a rather bushy, small, 15 to 20′ high tree. National champion is 66′ by 44′ in Big Bend National Park, TX. I have seen it on the Kansas State and Colorado State campuses and was impressed by the good dark green needle color and attractive, but rather stiff growth habit. The needles occur in 3's (sometimes 2's), persist 4 to 5 years, are 1 to 2″ long, entire, the inner surfaces of the needles being pressed together. The cones are roundish, egg-shaped, 1 1/2 to 2″ long, 1 to 1 1/2″ wide with very few scales. The seeds are about 1/2″ long and edible. Southern Arizona to lower California and Mexico. Introduced 1830. Zone 5. Variety *edulis* (Engelm.) Voss has leaves chiefly in pairs instead of 3's and they are thicker; otherwise, it is similar to the above. National champion is 69′ by 52′ in Cuba, NM. Occurs in southern Wyoming to Arizona, Texas and northern Mexico. Introduced 1848. Zone 4. Variety *monophylla* (Torr. & Frém.) Voss has single needles (occasionally in pairs). National champion is 45′ by 40′ in Inyo County, CA. It has a more westerly distribution than var. *edulis*, primarily in Utah, Arizona, Nevada and southern California and often forms pure strands of considerable extent. Introduced 1848. Zone 5. All the above are good choices for dry soil areas.

Pinus contorta Douglas ex Loud., (pī′nus kon-tôr′tȧ), Lodgepole Pine, is widespread throughout western North America and from my limited observations more ornamentally attractive than *P. ponderosa*. It differs from *P. ponderosa* in that the needles are in fascicles of 2, 1 1/2″ long, yellowish green to dark green and twisted. The cones are about 1 1/2″ long, mostly remaining unopened and attached for many years. There are two distinct varieties: one termed *P. c.* var. *contorta* Dougl. ex Loud., Shore Pine (Zone 7), is a small tree, 25 to 30′ high characterized by a short, contorted trunk and a dense, irregular crown of twisted branches, many of which extend nearly to the ground, national champion is 101′ by 37′ in Bryant, WA; the other *P. c.* var. *latifolia* (Engelm.) Critchf., Lodgepole Pine (Zone 5), grows 70 to 80′ high and develops a long, clear, cylindrical trunk and short, narrow, open crown. National champion is 135′ by 41′ in Valley Co., ID. The Shore Pine tends to establish in wet, boggy areas and is seldom found far from tidewater while the Lodgepole Pine performs best in moist, well-drained, sandy or gravelly soils, although it grows on a variety of soils. Native habitat is western North America. Lodgepole is common in European gardens and makes an exceptionally handsome tree.

Pinus jeffreyi Balf. ex A. Murray, (pī′nus jef′rē-ī), Jeffrey Pine, differs from the previous two species in the blue-green, 7 to 9″ long, twisted needles (usually 3) and the 6 to 9″ long cones which open and fall at maturity. Similar to *P. ponderosa* in habit and other respects. Can endure great extremes of climate and is somewhat more frost hardy. The Morton Arboretum has several 60′ specimens which are rather attractive. Potentially can grow 90 to 100′ under favorable conditions. National champion is 197′ by 90′ in Stanislaus National Forest, CA. Native from southern Oregon to lower California. Introduced 1853. Zone 5.

Pinus resinosa Ait. — Red Pine
(pī′nus rez-in-ō′sȧ)

LEAVES: In two's, persisting 4 years, densely arranged on the branches, slender, snap when bent, 5 to 6″ long, margins finely and regularly toothed, apex sharp-pointed, stomata in ill-defined lines on each surface, medium to dark green; leaf sheaths 5/8 to 7/8″ long.
BUDS: Ovoid or narrow conical, about 1/2″ long, resinous, with some of the scales free at the tips.
STEM: Glabrous, stout, pale brown or yellowish green, roughened with the remains of the prominences on which each bundle was sealed.

SIZE: 50 to 80′ in height with a variable spread; can grow to 125′ and more; I have never seen a Red Pine larger than 60′ in the Midwest and East; national champion is 124′ by 60′ in Watersmeet, MI.
HARDINESS: Zone 2 to 5, can withstand seasonal variations of 40 to 60°F below zero to 90 to 105°F above; grows best in colder climates.
HABIT: When growing in the open the trunk is short and develops a heavily branched crown in youth; in old age the crown is somewhat symmetrically oval with the characteristic tufted foliage which separates it from the ragged, unkempt Jack Pines and the plume-like tops of the White Pine.
RATE: Medium, 50′ after 25 to 30 years.
TEXTURE: Medium.
BARK: On young trees scaly, orange-red; eventually breaking up into large, flat, reddish brown, superficially scaly plates, irregularly diamond-shaped in outline.
LEAF COLOR: Medium to dark green.
FLOWERS: Monoecious, clustered; staminate red, pistillate reddish.
FRUITS: Cones subterminal, solitary or two together, sessile, horizontally spreading, symmetrical, ovoid-conical, narrowing rapidly to the apex, approximately 2″ long by 1 to 2″ broad and light brown.

CULTURE: Transplant balled-and-burlapped if root pruned; does well on exposed, dry, acid, sandy or gravelly soils; full sun; susceptible to sweeping winds; extremely cold tolerant (-40 to -60°F); susceptible to salt damage.

DISEASES AND INSECTS: See *Pinus* introduction.

LANDSCAPE VALUE: A picturesque and desirable tree which survives under adversity; good on exposed and sterile soils; for groves and windbreaks; best in northern areas; unfortunately, with all the good press relative to environmental tolerances, it has not lived up to the clippings; in my travels, Red Pine has been as elusive as any for quality of presentation and the paucity of good slides is indicative of the plant's short-comings; in late August of 1996 at Fieldstone Perennials/Jones Tree Farm, Vassalboro, ME, witnessed a handsome plantation of *P. resinosa* that served as a backdrop to the herbaceous garden.

CULTIVARS:

'Don Smith'—Dwarf form with long, green needles, red-brown stems, and purple young cones, named for the late Don Smith, Watnong Nursery.

'Globosa'—A compact, globe-shaped selection with short needles; I have seen many compact types derived from "witches' brooms."

PROPAGATION: Seeds have no dormancy and will germinate immediately upon sowing.

ADDITIONAL NOTES: Sometimes termed Norway Pine. It is said that early settlers mistook it for Norway Spruce, and also that it grew in abundance near the town of Norway, ME. Very tolerant of sandy soils and ranks behind *P. banksiana* in its ability to invade cutover land.

NATIVE HABITAT: Newfoundland and Manitoba, south to the mountains of Pennsylvania, west to Michigan. Cultivated since 1756.

Pinus rigida Mill. — Pitch Pine, Northern Pitch Pine
(pī′nus rij′i-dȧ)

LEAVES: In three's, lasting 2 to 3 years, spreading, rigid, slightly curved and twisted, 3 to 5″ long, margins finely toothed, ending in a horny point, yellow to pale to occasionally dark green; leaf sheaths 1/3 to 1/2″ long.

BUDS: Cylindrical or conical, sharp-pointed, 1/4 to 3/4″ long, scales pressed together but often free at the tips, usually resinous.

STEM: Stout with many buds, green at first, becoming dull orange-brown in the second year, prominently ridged.

SIZE: Variable, 40 to 60′ in height by 30 to 50′ in spread although can grow to 100′; often dwarfed by its environment for on exposed sites it is very grotesque, often sprawling, spreading and unsavory, while in better situations a tall trunk and small open crown develop; national champion is 94′ by 43′ in Newberry, NH.

HARDINESS: Zone 4 to 7.

HABIT: Open, irregular pyramid in youth, becoming gnarled and more irregular with age.

RATE: Medium in youth becoming slower with age.

TEXTURE: Medium.

BARK: Initially dark and very scaly; eventually 1 to 2″ thick at the base of old trees and smoother with brownish yellow, flat plates separated by narrow irregular fissures.

LEAF COLOR: Yellowish green at first, becoming a dark green.

FLOWERS: Monoecious; staminate yellow, pistillate light green tinted rose.

FRUIT: Cones lateral, in whorls of 3 to 5, seldom solitary, 2 to 3″ long, 1 to 1 1/2″ wide, stalked or nearly sessile, deflexed when young, spreading at right angles when mature, rather symmetrical, ovoid-conical, light brown and remaining 2 or more years on the tree.

CULTURE: Prefers a light, sandy, acid, moist, well-drained soil; however, is found along the coast on peat soils of Atlantic Whitecedar, *Chamaecyparis thyoides*, swamps; my observations in the Atlantic White Cedar swamp on Cape Cod reflect almost a monoculture of scrub oak, black oak, and *P. rigida* in the sandy soils surrounding the peat bog; therein the dominant plant was *C. thyoides* with *Ilex glabra*, *I. verticillata*, *Clethra alnifolia*, and *Vaccinium corymbosum* in the understory; open, sunny exposure; susceptible to sweeping winds; salt tolerant; able to survive on the driest, sandiest, most unproductive sites.

DISEASES AND INSECTS: See *Pinus* introduction.

LANDSCAPE VALUE: Not highly ornamental but excellent for poor soils, wildernesses and solitary places.

CULTIVARS:

'Sherman Eddy' ('Little Giant')—A rather interesting compact 15′ high tree with pom-pom tufts of foliage; Weston Nurseries, Hopkinton, MA introduced this clone and named it after the discoverer of the plant.

PROPAGATION: Seed requires no stratification.

ADDITIONAL NOTES: A tree of great diversity in form, habit, and development. One of the few conifers that produces sprouts from cut stumps or when injured by fire. Produces anywhere from 1 to 3 whorls of branches in a single season which is unusual for a pine. Also produces cones very early as 12-year-old trees often bear quantities of seeds.

I have seen it all over Cape Cod in the sandiest of soils. In Maine, it grows on Cadillac Mountain out of rock crevices. On Isle au Haut, I discovered it on the highest points in the Park, almost always shrubby. On Whiteside Mountain between Cashiers and Highlands, NC it grew toward the top of the ±5000′ peak. It will never make a commercial item, but is still a worthy member of earth's biodiversity. Kind of like an old slipper.

NATIVE HABITAT: Eastern North America in sandy uplands. New Brunswick to Georgia, west to Ontario and Kentucky. Introduced before 1759.

RELATED SPECIES:

Pinus serotina Michx., (pī′nus ser-ot′i-nà), Pond Pine, is a coastal plain, largely southern relative of *P. rigida*. Needles in fascicles of 3, sometimes 2 or 4 intermixed, 2 to 8″ long, with 1/3″ long leaf sheaths. Mature cones are conic-ovoid, 2 to 3″ long, persistent, either open or unopen, with the umbo of each cone scale terminated by a straight or incurved sharp prickle. I have only seen once in a recreated wet habitat in a Florida garden. In the wild inhabits poorly drained, wet areas. Grows 30 to 50′ under cultivation. National champion is 89′ by 53′ in Thomas County, GA. Southern New Jersey, Delaware to central Florida, Florida panhandle, southeastern and central Alabama. Introduced 1713. Zone 7 to 9.

Pinus strobus L. — Eastern White Pine
(pī′nus strō′bus)

LEAVES: In five's, remaining 2 years, slender, 2 to 4″(5″) long, apex soft to touch, needles soft and pliable, margins finely toothed, white stomatic lines on the two inner surfaces, bluish green, sheath about 1/2″ long, falling away.

BUDS: Ovoid, with a sharp point, 1/4″ long, resinous, some scales free at the tips.

STEM: Slender with tufts of short hairs below the insertion of the leaf bundles, usually without down elsewhere, greenish to light greenish brown, most of the pubescence falls away with time.

SIZE: 50 to 80′ in height by 20 to 40′ in spread; can grow to 150′ and more; co-national champions are 201′ by 52′ and 181′ by 64′ in Marquette, MI.

HARDINESS: Zone 3 to 7(8), grows reasonably well in Piedmont of Georgia but for inexplicable reasons trees die out, possibly related to heat and drought stress.

HABIT: In youth a symmetrical pyramid of soft, pleasant appearance; in middle-age and on old trees the crown is composed of several horizontal and ascending branches; gracefully plume-like in outline and very distinctive when compared to other conifers.

RATE: Fast, one of the fastest growing landscape pines; becoming 50 to 75′ tall in 25 to 40 years.

TEXTURE: Medium-fine.

BARK: Thin, smooth, grayish green when young, becoming darker with age; dark grayish brown on old trunks and deeply furrowed longitudinally into broad scaly, 1 to 2″ thick ridges.

LEAF COLOR: Light to bluish green; however, greatly variable; needles generally fall the second year in late summer–early fall and the interior of the tree harbors yellow-brown needles.

FLOWERS: Monoecious; staminate clustered, yellow; pistillate pink.

FRUIT: Cones subterminal, pendent, 3 to 7″(8″) long by 1 1/2″ broad, stalked, cylindrical, often curved, apex pointed, resinous and light brown; mature in autumn of second year.

CULTURE: Easily transplanted because of wide-spreading and moderately deep root system with only a vestige of a taproot; makes its best growth on fertile, moist, well-drained soils, however, is found on such extremes as dry, rocky ridges and wet sphagnum bogs; light demanding but can tolerate some shade; humid atmosphere; quite susceptible to sweeping winds and branches are often lost in strong storms; is extremely intolerant of air pollutants (ozone, sulfur dioxide) and salts; may develop chlorosis in high pH soils.

DISEASES AND INSECTS: Two very serious pests include the White Pine blister rust, a bark disease, which eventually kills the tree; and the White Pine weevil which kills the terminal shoots thus seriously deforming the tree to the extent they become bushy and have been called "Cabbage Pines."

LANDSCAPE VALUE: A very handsome and ornamental specimen; valuable for parks, estates and large properties; also makes a beautiful sheared hedge; one of our most beautiful native pines; a well-grown, mature White Pine is without equal among the firs, spruces and other pines.

CULTIVARS: It is difficult to do even a half-baked job on the cultivars since there are so many and numerous others are waiting to be introduced. Mr. Al Fordham, former propagator, Arnold Arboretum, has conducted some fascinating research with "witches' brooms" of White Pine and the results of his work are many beautiful compact-growing types. Dr. Waxman, retired, University of Connecticut, had a sizeable program in the same area and has introduced a number of *Pinus strobus* variants. Vermeulen Nursery, NJ, lists 21 different cultivars. Our card file index of *P. strobus* cultivars totaled 33 from United States nurseries.

'Bennett's Fastigiate'—More columnar and tightly branched than 'Fastigiata', will grow 40 to 60' high, useful form for restricted spaces.

'Compacta'—A dense, rounded type, slow-growing, appears to be a catchall term for dwarfish clones.

'Contorta'—An open, irregular, pyramidal form with slightly twisted branchlets; 40-year-old plant is 18' high.

'Fastigiata'—Narrowly upright and columnar when young developing a wider character with age as the branches ascend at a 45° angle from the trunk; ultimately about three times as tall as wide; I have seen several large (70') specimens of this clone and they were beautifully formed and not at all harsh like many of the fastigiate plants, a beautiful cultivar.

'Glauca'—Leaves are a light bluish green and of beautiful color; a specimen in the Arnold Arboretum is 60' high and 60' wide, more than one 'Glauca' in cultivation, somewhat of a catchall term for blue-needled types.

'Minima'—Dense, low-spreading type, wider than high, 1″ per year, needles bluish green, 1″ long.

'Nana'—A catchall term and I have seen several different types listed, usually compact, mounded or rounded.

'Pendula'—Very interesting weeping type with long branches which sweep the ground; must be trained in youth to develop a leader; each plant is different, i.e., unique biological personality.

'Prostrata'—Another rounded, dwarf type; 20-year-old plant is 8' by 7'.

'Pumila'—Roundish plant with central shoot elongating.

PROPAGATION: Seed should be stratified for 60 days. Pines, in general, are difficult to root from cuttings; however, considerable work has been undertaken with White Pine. Cuttings can be rooted but the percentages were low averaging from 0 to 34% depending on the tree sampled. Several investigators have rooted fascicles with some success.

ADDITIONAL NOTES: Often produces cones at an early age, sometimes when not more than 10' high. Very aggressive and quickly seeds in abandoned fields so much so it received the name "Old Field Pine." Largest of the midwestern and northeastern conifers and a very valuable timber species. Great variation in needle color, resistance to salts and air pollutants. Some trees are beautiful and keep their good bluish green color through the winter while others turn yellowish green. Selections could be made for superior traits and adaptability to various climatic and environmental conditions. In Zone 7(8), particularly the latter, the species may be short-lived. To be sure, there are handsome specimens that appear to shake out of the genetic woodpile. A specimen will die and an even-aged tree in the same grouping remains prosperous.

NATIVE HABITAT: Newfoundland to Manitoba, south to Georgia, Illinois and Iowa. Introduced about 1705.

RELATED SPECIES: White Pine and the other 5-needled species are among the most beautiful of all pines for foliage color, texture and character of habit. Certainly where adapted, *P. strobus* is the standard. Several western United States and Mexican species may prove more adaptable in hot, dry climates than *P. strobus*. The following have crossed my horticultural path.

Pinus ayacahuite Ehrenb. ex Schldl., (pī'nus ī-ya-ca'hē-tē), Mexican White Pine, has beautiful 4 to 7″ long, 1/25″ wide, thinnish, arching, blue-green, finely toothed needles that persist 3 to 4 years. The 6 to 14″ long, 3 to 4″ wide, curved cylindric cones are extremely resinous, pendulous, borne singly or in groups. The species is beautiful and might serve as a White Pine substitute in Zone 7 to 9. Currently growing it in Athens and the Arnold has a plant. Estimate 30 to 50' under cultivation. Guatemala to southern Mexico. Introduced 1840.

Pinus lambertiana Dougl., (pī'nus lam-bĕrt-ī-ā'nȧ), Sugar Pine, which I misidentified as *P. flexilis* in the Arnold's collection, has 3 to 4″ long, blue-green, sharply pointed, twisted, serrulate needles, falling after 2 to 3 years. The lustrous light brown, cylindric cones range from 12 to 20″ long. Tree can grow over 100' and national champion is 232' by 29' at Dorrington, CA. Susceptible to blister rust. Oregon to lower California into Mexico. Introduced 1827. Zone 6 to 7.

Pinus monticola Douglas ex D. Don, (pī'nus mon-tĭk'ō-là), Western White Pine, grows over 100' in cultivation and the national champion is 151' by 52' in the El Dorado National Forest, CA. Needles are 3 to 4" long, persistent 3 to 4 years, densely serrate. Cones are 4 to 10" long, narrow conic to cylindric. Similar to *P. strobus* but denser and narrower. British Columbia to Idaho and California. Introduced 1851. Zone 5.

Pinus strobiformis Engelm., (pī'nus strob-i-form'is), Southwestern White Pine, will grow over 100' in the wild, but is smaller under cultivation. Plants I have observed in Kentucky and Massachusetts were pyramidal-conical in youth with dark blue-green needles. The national champion is 111' by 62' in Lincoln National Forest, NM. Needles are 3 to 6" long and finely serrated. Needles of labeled plants that I examined were not serrated and on those occasions I questioned whether the plants might be *P. flexilis*. Cones are cylindric, 7 to 14" long, and yellow-brown to rich brown. Northern Mexico. Zone (5)6 to 7.

Pinus sylvestris L. — Scotch Pine
(pī'nus sil-ves'tris)

LEAVES: In pairs, persisting about 2 to 4 years, variable in length, twisted, stiff, 1 to 3"(4") long, short-pointed, margins minutely toothed, glaucous with many well-defined lines of stomata on the outer side, blue-green in color; leaf sheaths 1/4 to 3/8" long, persistent.
BUDS: Oblong-ovate, 1/4 to 1/2" long, pointed, with lanceolate, fringed scales, the upper ones free at the tips, brown, resinous, reddish brown.
STEM: Green when young, dull grayish yellow or brown in the second year, marked with prominent bases of the scale leaves, glabrous.

SIZE: 30 to 60' in height with a spread of 30 to 40'; can grow 80 to 90' high.
HARDINESS: Zone 3a to 7, will grow in Zone 7b but is not well-adapted.
HABIT: In youth an irregular pyramid with short, spreading branches, the lower soon dying, becoming in age very picturesque, open, wide-spreading and flat- or round-topped, almost umbrella-shaped.
RATE: Medium when young, slow with age.
TEXTURE: Medium.
BARK: On the upper portion of the stems orangish or orangish brown, thin, smooth, peeling off in papery flakes, thick towards the base, grayish or reddish brown, fissured into irregular, longitudinal, scaly plates.
LEAF COLOR: Bluish green frequently changing to yellowish green in the winter; variable depending on seed source.
FLOWERS: Monoecious.
FRUIT: Cones mostly solitary to 2 to 3(6) together, short-stalked, ovoid-conic, 1 1/2 to 3" long, gray or dull brown, falling at maturity, umbo small, obtuse.
DISEASES AND INSECTS: From a landscape standpoint several that are debilitating including: *Diplodia*, nematodes and pine wilt fungus. Morton Arboretum does not recommend the species for contemporary landscapes.
CULTURE: Transplants easily balled-and-burlapped if root pruned; will grow on a variety of soils as long as they are well-drained; poor, dry sites will support this tree; full sun; preferably acid soils.
LANDSCAPE VALUE: Valued for its picturesque character; useful as a distorted specimen or in masses and on waste lands; not suitable for underplanting or shelter belts; for displaying unique form and color among the pines it is outstanding; makes a good Christmas tree when plantation-grown; have experienced magnificent 60 to 80' high, open-grown specimens in Scotland and Ireland and an unique irregular grove at Muckross House, Killarney, Ireland; the conical-ovoid-rounded crown, perhaps one-third of the total height, the rich orangish bark in the upper reaches, graduating to blocky rich brown toward the base, were the ingredients for the perfect pine.
CULTIVARS: *The New RHS Dictionary of Gardening* noted there were over 60 cultivars differentiated by needle color and growth habit. I have collided with many, particularly in the notable collections in Great Britain. Only 19 cultivars of endless shapes and needle colors listed in the card file of United States purveyors. Thirty-eight cultivars depicted in *Conifers*.
   'Aurea'—Rather striking with yellowish green new growth that turns green in summer and then golden in winter, have seen in European gardens, not for the faint hearted.
   'Beuvronensis'—Broad low dwarf bushy form that crops up in botanical gardens and commerce, needles bluish green, 3/4" long, extremely slow-growing about 1 to 2" per year in youth, about 20" in 25 years.

'Fastigiata'—Columnar, narrow in habit about the narrowest of any of the pines; often called Sentinel Pine, tends to break-up in heavy ice and snow, 25′ high and more if it lasts that long. Found in the wild in several European countries and correctly should be f. *fastigiata* Carr.

'Watereri'—A slow-growing, densely pyramidal to flat-topped form with steel-blue needles, usually about 10′ but original plant is 25′ high and wide. Handsome selection and available in commerce. Has held up well over the years in Midwest collections.

PROPAGATION: Seeds have no dormancy and will germinate without stratification.

ADDITIONAL NOTES: One of the most popular pines for Christmas tree use. The great problem with Scotch Pine is the tremendous variability in needle length and color, hardiness, habit, and adaptability due to geographic races or strains. Five major groups of variants are recognized by Dallimore and Jackson and one starts to realize why some Scotch Pines have bluish needles, others yellowish green, etc., after reading their interesting discussion.

I checked many references and came away with the feeling that no authority has a distinct idea of the variation in *P. sylvestris*. Krüssmann offers the best lists of geographical varieties and cultivars. Supposedly over 150 varieties (not cultivars) have been described and Krüssmann lists over 40 cultivars. In Zone 7 and 8, Scotch Pine, at least the race (geographical variety) commonly planted, is not heat tolerant. I have observed many trees that simply died for no explicable reason other than the heat and drought(s). Plantings on campus and the Athens area have died out completely over my 19 years in Georgia.

NATIVE HABITAT: One of the most widely distributed pines, ranging from Norway and Scotland to Spain, western Asia and northeastern Siberia; naturalized in some places in the New England states. Long cultivated.

Pinus taeda L. — Loblolly Pine
(pī′nus tē′dȧ)

LEAVES: In fascicles of 3, occasionally 2, 6 to 10″ long, 1/25 to 1/12″ wide, persistent until the second (3rd to 4th) autumn, slender, sometimes twisted, dark yellowish green, margins finely toothed, resin ducts usually 2, large, mostly medial, sheaths about 1″ long.

BUDS: Oblong-conical, apex long-pointed, 1/4 to 1/2″ long, light reddish brown, not resinous, scales fringed, often reflexed.

STEM: Yellowish to reddish brown, glaucous, glabrous, strongly ridged.

SIZE: 60 to 90′ in height, usually smaller under landscape conditions, 40 to 60′; national champion is 148′ by 83′ at Warren, AR.

HARDINESS: Zone 6 to 9; have seen it in central Illinois but it was barely surviving.

HABIT: Loosely pyramidal in youth losing its lower branches with age and forming a fairly open, oval-rounded crown at maturity, branches more or less horizontally spreading.

RATE: Fast, one of the fastest growing southern pines.

TEXTURE: As pines go this is medium-coarse.

BARK: Variable, scaly and gray on young trees, later with rounded ridges and deep furrows, gray-brown to red-brown.

LEAF COLOR: Dark green, becomes off-color in cold climates.

FRUIT: Cones, ovoid-cylindric to narrowly conical, sessile, 3 to 6″ long, buff rust brown, umbo dorsal and armed with a stout, sharp, recurved spine, grouped 2 to 5 together.

CULTURE: Easy to transplant, may develop a short taproot but it ceases growth in favor of an extensive lateral root system; grows on a wide variety of soils, prefers those with deep surface layers having abundant moisture and poor drainage; prefers acid soils.

DISEASES AND INSECTS: None particularly serious in normal context of the landscape; pine beetle can devastate plantings, fusiform rust, heart and butt rot.

LANDSCAPE VALUE: Not a graceful pine but very adaptable to extremes of soil and therefore valuable in South where the more graceful species do not thrive; good for fast screen in early years; one of the pioneer species along river bottoms; one particular abandoned bottomland agricultural field at the University's Botanical Garden was rapidly invaded by this species; is being used more frequently as a quick screen in southern landscapes, frequently container-grown and is easily transplanted.

CULTIVARS:

'Al's Dwarf'—Compact and dense, dark green needles, found by Albert Durio, offered by Louisiana Nursery.

'Nana'—Raulston described several 30-year-old dwarf loblollies that originated from "witches' brooms," 8 to 15' tall with dense rounded crowns; I have seen the plants and they are truly artistic and imbued with character.

PROPAGATION: Seeds germinate without pretreatment.

ADDITIONAL NOTES: One of the leading commercial timber species in the United States. On cutover areas in the South, the species has spread to a remarkable degree and is aggressive in forming pure stands in old fields. Have seen it growing in the reddest of red clay where few other species proliferate. I have come to appreciate the beauty of this species particularly in my travels through the Southeast. It is one ubiquitous pine, colonizing highway cuts, banks, ditches, open grassy fields, and abandoned agricultural land. In eroded, red clay, that resists other vegetation, *P. taeda* manages a toe-hold. Many landscapers utilize this species because of the fast growth and wholesale adaptability.

NATIVE HABITAT: Southern New Jersey to Florida, eastern Texas and Oklahoma. Introduced 1713.

RELATED SPECIES:

Pinus clausa (Champ.) Vasey., (pī'nus claw'sȧ), Sand Pine, is a 2-needled (sometimes 3), small tree, 30 to 40' high, with shiny rich green needles. I have only observed the tree in northern Florida at Superior Trees where it served as a windbreak. In late February, the color was exceptionally rich green. Needles range from 1 1/2 to 3 1/4″ long, are slender, straight or slightly twisted. Cones of two kinds: open and unopen (until fire), 2 to 3″ long, ovoid-oblong, scales hard and inflexible, umbo with prickle, scale darker brown at tip than remainder of the surface. Grows in deep, well-drained, infertile sands in the wild. Tri-national champion trees are 95' by 41', 100' by 42', and 94' by 38' at Starkey Wilderness Park, FL. Native to Florida, southwestern Alabama. Zone 8 and 9.

Pinus elliottii Engelm., (pī'nus el-i-ot'ē-ī), Slash Pine, is more coastal in distribution from South Carolina to Florida west to southeastern Mississippi and Louisiana and represents an important timber species in those areas. It is a tall tree with ovoid crown, reaching over 100' high. Not unusual on the Georgia coastal islands like St. Simons and Jekyll to see 80' high trees. Needles are variable, occur in 2's with a few 3's or 2 and 3 per fascicle well intermixed, 4 to 9″(12″) long and glossy dark green. The stalked (~1″) cones are lustrous chestnut brown, 3 1/2 to 6″ long, ovoid, with a short, stout prickle at the end of each cone scale. The bark is purple to red-brown at maturity, forming large, irregular blocks not unlike *P. echinata*, with scaly, flaking plates. Found in wet flat woods, interdune hollows and near coastal sands mixed with sand live oak, *Q. myrtifolia*. Zone 8 to 10.

Pinus glabra Walt., (pī'nus glā'brȧ), Spruce Pine, is a handsome 40 to 60' high, oval-rounded crowned species. Needles are dark green, 2 per fascicle, spirally twisted and 2 to 4″ long. The cones are brown, 1 3/4 to 3 3/4″ long, the scales with minute prickles. Cones may persist 2 to 4 years. Bark is dark gray and smooth at first, finally closely ridged-and-furrowed, producing small, thin, reddish brown plates suggestive of *Picea* bark. Found scattered on uplands, bluffs, slopes of ravines, in floodplain forests where flooding is shallow and brief. Have tested it in field plots in Athens and winter wind and sun induce yellow, off-color foliage. One of the more shade tolerant pines. South Carolina to northern Florida to Louisiana. Zone 8 and 9(10).

Pinus palustris Mill., (pī'nus pa-lus'tris), Longleaf Pine, is among the most unique of the southern pines because of the grass stage where seedlings produce dense, long, spreading needle fascicles, but minimal height extension. The tree grows 60' in landscape situations and the co-national champions are 134' by 38' and 110' by 50' in MS and TX, respectively. The dark green needles are in fascicles of 3, occasionally 2, 6 to 12″ long (up to 18″). The ovoid-oblong, brown, 6 to 8″(10″) long cones (up to 5″ wide at base) open promptly and abscise over the winter following maturation. Not a plant for everyday use but intriguing. On our trips to the coast, from Metter to Savannah, GA, the broomy-grassy stage of Longleaf Pine is common in the sandy or clay-sand ridges along with the scrub oaks. Southeastern Virginia to Florida, east to Texas. Zone 7 to 10. Introduced 1727.

Pinus thunbergii Parl. — Japanese Black Pine
(pī'nus thun-bērj'ē-ī)

LEAVES: Two, persisting 3 to 5 years, densely crowded, twisted, more or less spreading, 2 1/2 to 4 1/2″ long, 1/12″ wide, apex stiff, fine-pointed, rigid, margins finely toothed, with stomatic lines on each surface; very lustrous dark green; leaf sheaths 1/2″ long, ending in two long, thread-like segments, persistent.

BUDS: One of the few conifers in which the buds provide a good identification feature; the terminal buds characteristically ovoid-cylindrical, apex-pointed, 1/2 to 3/4″ long (may be longer), not resinous, scales appressed, tips free, gray or silvery white (very prominent), fimbriated.

STEM: Light brown, glabrous, ridged with the scale leaves persisting during the first year; in the second and third year blackish gray.

SIZE: 20 to 80′ in height with a greatly variable spread, usually 20 to 40′ under cultivation.

HARDINESS: Zone (5)6 to 8, -10 to -15°F will burn the needles.

HABIT: In youth artistically uneven but more or less pyramidal, in old age with spreading often pendulous branches, however, young trees can be pruned into a full dense specimen.

RATE: Medium.

TEXTURE: Medium.

BARK: On old trees blackish gray, soon becoming fissured into elongated irregular plates.

LEAF COLOR: Dark green, very handsome.

FLOWERS: Monoecious.

FRUIT: Cones subterminal, solitary or clustered, short-stalked, spreading, symmetrical, ovoid to conical, 1 1/2 to 3″ long, 1 1/4 to 1 3/4″ wide; scale end flattened, shiny light brown; umbo depressed, small, obtuse or with a minute prickle.

CULTURE: Transplants easily balled-and-burlapped if root pruned; makes its best growth on moist, fertile, well-drained soils; will grow on sandy soils and has been used for reclaiming sand dunes and other protective work near the shore; quite salt tolerant and has been used where foliar salts present a cultural problem; best in full sun; displays heat and drought tolerance.

DISEASES AND INSECTS: Abundant branch dieback (*Diplodia* ?) on plants in Zone 7 and 8. A nurseryman and I were discussing the merits of this species and asked whether the other had ever witnessed a robust old specimen, the answer was NO! Life span has been 5 to 10 years on the Georgia campus.

LANDSCAPE VALUE: Because of its tolerance to salt spray it is invaluable for seashore plantings and useful in stabilizing sand dunes; also a good accent or bonsai plant; in 1985 several 4 to 5′ plants were used as an irregular mass to screen a clay hillside at the University's Botanical Garden, by fall of 1989 the plants had grown 10 to 12′ high and filled in without any pruning, their habit is somewhat irregular, the lustrous deep green needles and white, candle-like buds are particularly handsome; these plants are now dead (1997), see the discussion under DISEASES AND INSECTS.

CULTIVARS:

'Compacta'—Dense irregular large shrub type.

'Globosa'—Large dense globe habit, dark green needles.

'Iseli' ('Aocha Matsu')—Gold-variegated, broad pyramidal form, 7′ by 3′.

'Kotobuki'—Small, pyramidal, with bright green, short needles.

'Majestic Beauty'—Habit like species, but more dense and compact, with lustrous dark green needles, resistant to smog, cutting propagated, Monrovia introduction.

'Mini Mounds'—Good name for this 2 to 4′ high, 7 to 9′ wide, 23-year-old selection, closely spaced, 3 to 5″(8″) long needles that are bunched to form mounds, Vermeulen introduction.

'Mt. Hood Prostrate'—Dramatic low sweeping habit, dark green needles, 6 to 8′ high, 8 to 12′ wide, Iseli.

'Oculus Draconis'—Needles are banded with yellow like *P. densiflora* 'Oculus Draconis', very stiff appearance and wide-spreading habit; for the collector.

'Pygmaea'—Compact form with rich green needles, 5′ to 4′, Iseli.

'Shioguro'—Compact, globose with bright green, long needles.

Thunderhead'—Heavy bud set, i.e., white, candle-like buds above heavy, dense, dark green needles, dwarf, broad habit, Angelica Nursery introduction.

PROPAGATION: Seeds have no dormancy and will germinate immediately upon planting.

ADDITIONAL NOTES: I conducted considerable salt tolerance research and in one comparative study between this species and *P. strobus* found that *P. thunbergii* was tremendously salt tolerant. Apparently, it is able to exclude the sodium and chloride ions and thus resist injury. White Pine accumulated chloride at levels greater than 2% of needle dry weight and died. For a rather complete listing of salt tolerant plants see Dirr, *Journal of Arboriculture* 2:209–216 (1976). See Townsend and Kwolek, *J. Arboriculture* 13(9): 225–228 (1987) for a discussion of the salt-tolerance of 13 pine species.

NATIVE HABITAT: Japan. Introduced 1855.

Pinus virginiana Mill. — Virginia (Scrub) Pine, Jersey Pine, Spruce Pine, Poverty Pine
(pī′nus vĕr-jin′ē-ā′nȧ)

LEAVES: In two's, remaining 3 to 4 years, twisted, spreading, stout, 1 1/2 to 3″ long, margins with minute, irregular teeth, apex sharp-pointed, yellow-green to dark green; sheath persistent, 3/16″ long.

BUDS: Ovoid with a short point, 1/3 to 1/2″ long, resinous with closely pressed scales.

STEM: Young-slender, reddish purple with a pale bloom; good way to separate it from *P. banksiana* and *P. sylvestris*.

SIZE: 15 to 40′ in height by 10 to 30′ spread; respectable 60′ plants at Bernheim Arboretum and Tyler Arboretum; co-national champions 103′ by 50′ and 114′ by 43′ at Madisonville, KY and Jefferson County, AL, respectively.

HARDINESS: Zone 4 to 8.

HABIT: A broad, open pyramid, becoming flat-topped, the branches springing irregularly from the stem; finally low, straggling, scrubby, with long outstretched limbs.

RATE: Slow.

TEXTURE: Medium.

BARK: Thin and smooth, eventually scaly-plated, reddish brown, 1/4 to 1/2″ thick.

LEAF COLOR: Yellow-green to dark green; often sickly yellowish green in winter.

FLOWERS: Monoecious; staminate orange-brown, pistillate pale green.

FRUIT: Cones 2 to 4 together or solitary, short-stalked or sessile, spreading or deflexed, oblong-conical, symmetrical, 1 1/2 to 3″ long by 1 to 1 1/4″ broad, apex blunt, dark brown; maturing in the second autumn but often persistent after that; cones sharp due to prickle-like appendage.

CULTURE: Does well in poor, dry soils where other pines will not grow; best on clay loam or sandy loam; dislikes shallow, chalky soils; open, sunny exposure.

DISEASES AND INSECTS: See *Pinus* introduction.

LANDSCAPE VALUE: Not very ornamental but valuable as a cover for dry and barren soils; serves as the basis for the Christmas tree industry in the southern states.

CULTIVARS:

'Wate's Golden'—Golden needles in winter, green in summer, start to change to yellow-gold in October–November.

ADDITIONAL NOTES: Chief merit lies in its ability to reproduce and grow on heavy, clay land where few other plants will grow, both on virgin soil and impoverished farm land.

NATIVE HABITAT: Long Island, New York, southwestward to central Alabama, in the Appalachian, Ohio Valley, Piedmont, and part of the Coastal Plain regions. Introduced before 1739.

Pinus wallichiana A.B. Jacks. — Himalayan Pine (Bhutan Pine); also called *P. griffithii* McClelland.
(pī′nus wâl-lik-ē-ā′nȧ)

LEAVES: Five, persisting 3 to 4 years, on young shoots more or less erect, the older ones spreading or drooping, slender, flaccid, creating a feathery effect, 5 to 8″ long, apex sharp pointed, grayish green to blue-green, margin minutely toothed, with glaucous, white stomatic lines inside, outside green, leaf sheaths about 3/4″ long, soon falling, needles often bent abruptly near base so greater part of needle is pendulous.

STEM: Stout, bluish green, glabrous, slightly ridged below each bundle of needles towards the apex.

SIZE: 30 to 50′ high under landscape conditions but can grow to 150′; spread is variable but the large specimens I have seen were 1/2 to 2/3's the height.

HARDINESS: Zone 5 to 7; shows considerable needle browning when temperatures drop below −15°F.

HABIT: Loosely and broadly pyramidal when young; graceful, of elegant habit and often feathered with branches to the ground in old age; tends to be more wide-spreading than many pines as it approaches maturity.

RATE: Slow-medium, in youth may grow 2 to 3′ per year.

TEXTURE: Medium.

LEAF COLOR: Gray-green to blue-green.

FLOWERS: Monoecious.

FRUIT: Cones subterminal, solitary, on a 1 to 2″ long stalk, erect when young; pendulous the second year, cylindrical, 6 to 10″ long by approximately 2″ broad, light brown when ripe and very resinous.

CULTURE: Listed as somewhat difficult to transplant and should be moved as a young plant to a permanent location; soil requirements are similar to those for White Pine and a sandy, well-drained, acid loam is best; full sun; not recommended for shallow, chalky soils; severe winter winds can result in needle browning; withstands atmospheric pollutants better than most conifers; in extremely exposed locations the top becomes thin and weak when the tree is 25 to 40′ high and, therefore, a sheltered position is desirable.

DISEASES AND INSECTS: See *Pinus* introduction.

LANDSCAPE VALUE: Excellent and beautiful pine for large areas, very graceful in effect; a lovely specimen tree; apparently there are differences in hardiness among nursery-grown trees (related to origin of seed) for some trees will do well in the Midwest and others succumb after a difficult winter; the Morton Arboretum has a lovely, well-formed specimen from which seed or scion wood should be collected for the midwestern states.

CULTIVARS: There is a yellow-banded clone which is listed as 'Oculus Draconis' by some authorities; however, Den Ouden and Boom categorize the clone as 'Zebrina' which they describe as having leaves barred, marked an inch below the apex with a cream-colored band, otherwise green and gold. I have seen this cultivar at the U.S. National Arboretum in the Gottelli Conifer Collection. Perhaps as striking and interesting a cultivar as one could hope to see among the pines. There are three 'Oculus Draconis' clones; one is *P. densiflora*, another is *P. thunbergii*, and the above. All are interesting but difficult to blend into the average landscape. For the hobby gardener they offer a worthwhile challenge. Other cultivars are known.

PROPAGATION: Seeds have no dormancy or a slight one and may require 15 days of stratification.

NATIVE HABITAT: Temperate Himalaya at 6,000 to 12,500′ elevation, extending westward to Afghanistan and eastward to Nepal. Introduced 1827.

RELATED SPECIES:

Pinus armandii Franch., (pī′nus är-man′dē-ī), David's Pine, Chinese White Pine, is closely allied to the above species and differs in its relatively broad, scarcely tapered, 4 to 8″ long, 2 1/2 to 3″ wide, thick-scaled cones. The needles occur in 5's, persistent for 2 to 3 years, 4 to 7″ long, glossy green on outside, glaucous on inner sides; pointed at apex and minutely toothed on the margin; the sheath soon falling away. It makes a graceful, broad pyramid in youth. It is as handsome as *P. wallichiana* but supposedly less hardy. I am not sure this is the case and degree of hardiness would no doubt reflect the provenance of the seed. It is a beautiful tree that certainly deserves consideration for landscape use. The large cones are quite resinous and my initial introduction to the species came at the expense of resin-coated hands when I plucked a beautiful, unripened cone from a tree at the Arnold Arboretum. The cones are so large and heavy as to partially weigh down the branches. Several varieties are described but I have not seen them in cultivation. Western and central China, Burma, Formosa and Korea. Introduced 1895. Zone 5 to 7?

Pistacia chinensis Bunge. — Chinese Pistache
(pis-tā′shi-à chī-nen′sis)

FAMILY: Anacardiaceae

LEAVES: Alternate, compound even pinnate, about 10″ long, 10 to 12(20) leaflets, each leaflet 2 to 4″ long, 3/4″ wide, terminal leaflets the shortest, lanceolate, short-stalked, acute or acuminate, mucronate to cuspidate, oblique, entire, glabrous at maturity, lustrous dark green; petiole—1 to 4″ long, puberulous.

BUDS: Terminal—1/4 to 3/8″ long, imbricate, brownish black, ovoid, composed of stout, mucronate keeled bud scales, glabrous to slightly pubescent; vegetative—1/8 to 1/4″ long, similar to above in color, directly centered over leaf scar.

STEM: Stout, light brown, prominently covered with orangish lenticels, glabrous with prominent odor when bruised; leaf scars raised, shield-shaped; pith—white, solid, ample.

SIZE: 30 to 35′ high, spread 25 to 35′, can reach 50′ by 40′.

HARDINESS: Zone 6 to 9.

HABIT: Oval-rounded to rounded in outline; main branches may be upright-arching; have seen many specimens of the tree in the Athens-Atlanta areas and most were oval-rounded with upswept branches; rather unorganized growth habit in youth, becoming more uniform and handsome with age.

RATE: Medium, however, may grow 2 to 3′ per year under good cultural conditions.

TEXTURE: Medium in leaf, coarse in winter.

BARK: Develops shallow furrows, the ridges becoming scaly, gray to gray-black in color; as the scales flake off they expose a salmon to orange inner bark.

LEAF COLOR: Dark green in summer, often lustrous; hold
    rather late in fall, becomes brilliant orange and orange-
    red; for the southern states this is the closest thing to
    rivaling Sugar Maple for fall color; over the past 19
    years I have monitored the quality and progression of
    fall color, color will vary from yellow-green to vivid
    orange-red and the best forms need to be propagated;
    in the Athens area color develops about mid-October
    and often extends into late November.
FLOWERS: Dioecious, small, greenish, male in dense, 2 to
    3″ long panicles; female in 7 to 9″ long, loose pani-
    cles, not showy, April before leaves; flowers occur on
    previous year's wood.
FRUIT: A globose to obovoid, 1/4″ diameter drupe, typically
    maturing to robin's egg blue or red in the same fruit
    cluster; fruits are reasonably showy but certainly not
    the reason for using the tree, old fruit stalks persist on
    some trees and are less than aesthetic; fruits ripen in
    October and either fall or are taken by birds before late
    November.
CULTURE: Transplants well balled-and-burlapped or from
    containers; very adaptable species, tolerates a wide
    range of conditions but makes its best growth on
    moist, well-drained soils; very drought resistant; full
    sun; needs pruning in youth to form a good crown; in
    Kansas tests it averaged 1′1″ per year over a 10 year
    period and prospered in dry sandy soils.
DISEASES AND INSECTS: None serious.
LANDSCAPE VALUE: Too long neglected in the southern states for lawn, park, and street use; selections
    should be made for good habit and excellent fall color; its ability to withstand poor, droughty soils holds
    it in good stead as an urban tree; trees in Athens, GA are thriving; I am most impressed by its complete
    freedom from insects and diseases; have observed great trees in Savannah and Tifton, GA and
    Woodward, OK where dryness and wind are ways of life; in fact, the Woodward tree was 25′ by 30′,
    broad-rounded, uniform, dense, and dark green on September 12, 1992; if superior clones are identified,
    propagated and marketed the tree will become commonplace; a truly tenacious species.
LANDSCAPE MAINTENANCE: As a young tree the habit is best described as gawky. Seedlings do not develop
    straight trunks and may produce multiple leaders. Some staking and pruning are necessary to produce a
    decent trunk. Once developed, the head seems to follow without a great deal of manicuring. My observa-
    tions indicate that male trees are much neater and uniformly branched than the females. 'Keith Davey' has
    been described in a California publication as a selected male form that is neater and easier to shape.
PROPAGATION: One report stated that the pulp should be removed from the seeds, the seeds soaked in water
    for 16 hours then sown. From actual experience I have found the following to be reasonably foolproof. First
    and most important is the collection of sound seed. Only collect the bluish fruits for these have solid seed.
    I tried cut tests on a great number of reddish fruits and they were invariably hollow. Clean pulp from the
    seeds, place seeds in a moist medium at 41°F and observe for radicle emergence. In our work, 54 days
    proved optimum, for many seeds had germinated in the bag. These were then sown and the germination
    percentages were in the 80 to 90% range. Seed was sown directly and not a single one germinated. Cut-
    tings: Morgan obtained 52% rooting of terminal cuttings with 1/3″ old wood attached, mid-May, 15000 ppm
    KIBA, mist, cuttings were collected from a mature, 45-year-old tree; with terminal new growth only, rooting
    was 20%; mid-June and August cuttings did not root as well. Grafting and budding have proven difficult.
    Mini-treatise on success with mounding in *North American Regions Plant Propagator* 8(2):20 (1996); more
    shoots were produced when plants were cut 2″ above soil line; rooting averaged 77% and 75% on wounded
    shoots plus 1.75% IBA; this might be a useful method for what is considered a recalcitrant rooter. Similar
    information, more detailed, in *J. Environ. Hort.* 13:109–112 (1995). Another study, same principal author,
    J. Amer. Soc. Hort. Sci. 121:269–273 (1996) assessed degree days and rooting; highest rooting was 44%,
    green softwood, 380 days after bud break, 8750 ppm IBA, from 34-year-old tree.
ADDITIONAL NOTES: Have seen the species as far north as Urbana, IL where it was far from happy but did
    survive. It is really a tree for Zone 7 through 9. Is used in California to a considerable degree. Used as an
    understock for the pistachio nut, *Pistacia vera* L., of commerce. In China, the young shoots and leaves are

eaten cooked as a vegetable. E.H. Wilson collected seeds of the species during his 1908 and 1910 expeditions to China. He noted that it turned a gorgeous crimson in the fall. Anyone interested in additional information should read Gary Koller's account in *Arnoldia* 38: 157–172 (1978). Also see McMillan Browse, *American Nurseryman* 167(1): 115–120 (1988), for excellent propagation and cultural discussion.

NATIVE HABITAT: Central and western China, Taiwan, Philippines. Introduced about 1890.

Pittosporum tobira Ait. — Japanese Pittosporum, Tobira
(pit-o-spō′rum to-bī′ra)

FAMILY: Pittosporaceae

LEAVES: Alternate, simple, evergreen, obovate, 1 1/2 to 4″ long, 3/4 to 1 1/2″ wide, blunt or rounded at apex, tapering to a short petiole, glabrous, entire, margins revolute, leathery, lustrous dark green, with a paler green midvein above.

SIZE: 10 to 12′ high, spread 1 1/2 to 2 times height; picturesque spreading plants 20 to 25′ high have been reported.

HARDINESS: Zone 8, preferably lower portion, to Zone 10; plant is often flattened in Athens-Atlanta by cold but in Macon and Augusta, GA prospers, distances of 100 to 120 miles south.

HABIT: Dense, compact, broad-spreading evergreen shrub of impenetrable proportions.

RATE: Slow.

TEXTURE: Medium.

LEAF COLOR: Lustrous dark green throughout seasons.

FLOWERS: Perfect, 5-petaled, fragrant (orange-blossom scent), creamy white becoming yellow with age, 1/2 to 1″ diameter, borne in terminal, 2 to 3″ diameter, umbellate clusters, April–May; somewhat inconspicuous but wonderfully fragrant.

FRUIT: Odd-looking, 3 valved, pear-shaped, 1/2″ diameter capsule, green changing to brown, September–October.

CULTURE: Easily transplanted from containers, adaptable, sandy soils to clays as long as well-drained; acid or alkaline; used extensively in Florida; seems to thrive in sandy soils and hot, dry locations; full sun or heavy shade; withstands heavy pruning; tolerates salt spray.

DISEASES AND INSECTS: Tough, durable plant but can contract leaf spot disease and mealy bugs.

LANDSCAPE VALUE: Overused in warmer areas of South; mass plantings are popular, foundation use, in drifts under trees; hedges, screens, buffer or barrier planting; handsome plant for containers, patio tubs.

CULTIVARS:

'Compacta'—Compact, dense, spreading.

'Compacta Green'—Listed in Florida literature, have been unable to track origin, mentioned in *HortScience* 27:1198 (1992).

Cream de Mint™ ('Shima')—Tightly mounded form, 2 to 2 1/2′ high and wide, soft mint green leaves with cream-white variegation.

'Laura Lee'—Compact form like 'Wheeler's Dwarf', with uniform white flecking throughout the leaves, experienced the plant for the first time (3-25-93) on St. Simons Island, GA, have not seen it since.

Louisiana Hardy Form ('Louisiana Compact')—Beautiful large, lustrous dark green leaves on compact framework, 6 to 8′ high and wide, McCorkle Nurseries, Dearing, GA is growing this form, might be suitable in Zone 7b.

'Tall 'N Tough'—Looser than typical species form as I viewed this J.C. Raulston introduction, may be more cold hardy as seedlings were grown from Korean seed, at best Zone 7 if sited away from wind and sun.

'Turner's Variegated Dwarf'—Green foliage edged in white, low and compact, 2 to 3′ high and wide, Zone 9.

'Variegata'—Leaf is edged with white, green areas take on a gray-green color, can be blended with green form for handsome effect, might not be as cold hardy as species; extremely popular and overused; grown as a house and conservatory plant in the North; flowers with same wonderful fragrance as species; 6′ or more at landscape maturity.

Variegata Winter Pride™—Grows 8 to 12′ high, like 'Variegata' but more cold hardy, Hines Nursery introduction.

'Wheeler's Dwarf'—Compact form of the species growing 3 to 4′ high and wide; forms a compact mound of dark green foliage, all parts smaller than the species, not as cold hardy as species and generally not as adaptable, can be used as a houseplant; at 0 to 5°F, bark split devastated this cultivar; in Savannah, GA a large mass planting was killed outright at 10°F; this cultivar is a Zone (8)9 plant at best; a friend gave me a plant for our garden and after two winters with nothing below 5°F, it is appearing the worst for wear.

'Winter Pride'—Green foliage, more cold hardy, otherwise like species; Hines Nursery introduction; how unique, I do not know.

PROPAGATION: Use firm wooded cuttings, 1000 to 3000 ppm IBA-talc or solution, well-drained medium, mist; have observed considerable "rot" under excessively moist propagation conditions. Wang, *J. Environ. Hort.* 9:199–203 (1991), reported the species easy to root, in fact, rooting was excellent in all months studied: February, April, June, October, and December. Lamb, *The Plantsman* 10(4):251–252 (1989), reported seed, cutting, and grafting procedures for *P. tenuifolium*.

ADDITIONAL NOTES: Something approaching 200 species have been documented. Most are tender and the genus as a whole is listed as Zone 9. In Scottish and Irish gardens, many species are grown but the most common is *P. tenuifolium* Banks & Sol. ex Gaertn., Tawhiwhi or Kohuho, a New Zealand native. It forms a 10 to 20′(30′), slender, conical, dense-foliaged, evergreen shrub or tree. Numerous cultivars with foliage of yellow, gray, cream-variegated, purple, almost black and dark green are known. At Mt. Congreve, Ireland, I still reflect on the kaleidoscopic variation in leaf coloration. Another species, *P. ralphii* T. Kirk, is an evergreen, 7 to 15′ high shrub with dark crimson flowers. It hybridizes with *P. tenuifolium*.

NATIVE HABITAT: Japan, the Ryukyus, Formosa, Korea and China. Introduced 1804.

Platanus × acerifolia (Ait.) Willd. (Result of a cross between *P. orientalis × P. occidentalis*, sometimes listed as *P. × hybrida* Brot.) — London Planetree
(plat′à-nus a-ser-e-fō′lē-à)

FAMILY: Platanaceae

LEAVES: Alternate, simple, 6 to 7″ long, (5)8 to 10″ wide, 3- to 5-lobed, with triangular-ovate or broad triangular, not or sparingly toothed lobes, with acute or rounded sinuses extending 1/3 the length of the blade, truncate to cordate at base, glabrous or nearly so at maturity, medium to dark green; petiole—2 to 4″ long.

BUDS: Similar to *P. occidentalis*.

STEM: Similar to *P. occidentalis*.

BARK: Olive-green to creamy, exfoliating; actually one of the best assets of the tree.

FRUIT: Rounded, syncarp of achenes, bristly, 1″ across, 2 per stalk, rarely 1 or 3.

SIZE: 70 to 100′ in height with a spread of 65 to 80′ although can grow to 120′ or more.

HARDINESS: Zone (4)5 to 8(9); not happy in central Florida.

HABIT: Pyramidal in youth, developing with age a large, open, wide-spreading outline with massive branches; does not spread as much as *P. occidentalis* but nonetheless is still not acceptable for small area use.

RATE: Medium, 35′ over a 20 year period, in Kansas tests grew 1′11″ per year over a 10 year period; under nursery production practices grows literally like a weed.

TEXTURE: Medium-coarse, but not particularly offensive; superb in winter when the bark is maximized.

BARK: Perhaps the handsomest of all large trees for winter character because of cream, olive, light brown bark; no two trees are exactly similar and as I write this large trees in Hyde Park, London;

Berne, Switzerland; Mainau, Germany; Cambridge, MA; Washington, DC; Vancouver, B.C. and the great allée at Jardin des Plantes, Paris flash into view; all are spectacular, all remembered because of noble habit and exquisite bark.

LEAF COLOR: Flat medium to dark green in summer, yellow-brown in fall.

FLOWERS: Monoecious, April, not showy, male and female similar in dense globose structures but on separate peduncles; develop with leaves.

FRUIT: Syncarp (multiple fruit) of elongated, obovoid achenes, 1″ diameter, ripening in October and persisting late into winter, usually borne 2 together although 3's and singles occur.

CULTURE: Easily transplanted; prefers deep, rich, moist, well-drained soils but will grow in about anything, withstands high pH conditions and pollutants; full sun or very light shade; prune in winter; withstands smoke and grime of cities and was so widely planted in London because of its adaptability that it acquired the name London Planetree; hardiness in Zone 4 and 5 is not guaranteed and individuals may or may not survive; Cappiello, Orono, ME, Zone 4, reported outright kill; Morton Arboretum, Lisle, IL, Zone (4)5, reported variation in hardiness but an 82′ by 55′ specimen is on the grounds.

DISEASES AND INSECTS: Cankerstain (very serious), anthracnose, *Xylella fastidiosa* [more serious than I knew with the literature replete with references to dieback of sycamores, see *J. Arboriculture* 18:57–63 (1992)], *Botryosphaeria* canker, powdery mildew, American plum borer, and Sycamore lace bug; the London Planetree was once touted as a "Super" tree by many people and was soon overplanted; many diseases have caught up with it and its use should be tempered, the cankerstain fungus is especially troublesome and I have seen trees badly infested with lace bug; frost cracking is common in the Midwest and anthracnose may occur on selected trees although the species generally shows degrees of resistance; considerable variation in anthracnose susceptibility among clones (see under CULTIVARS).

LANDSCAPE VALUE: Acceptable for open areas in parks, golf courses, campuses; use as a street tree should be restricted for it grows too large; in some respects its use has approached monoculture status; the influx of disease problems should be closely monitored; considering that the tree is seed-grown it shows good uniformity but some segregation occurs and types resembling either parent result.

CULTIVARS: Considerable interest in better selections with uniform characteristics. Several new cultivars *may be* superior to run-of-the-mill seedlings. In Europe, 'Augustine Henry', 'Cantabrigiensis', 'Hispanica', 'Kelseyana', 'Mirkovec', 'Pyramidalis', 'Sutternii', and 'Tremonia' are known. To my knowledge none are present in the United States.

'Bloodgood'—Greater resistance to anthracnose than the species and after 10 years was the 10th rated tree in the Shade Tree Evaluation Tests at Wooster, OH; tolerates soil compaction, heat, drought, as well as severe pruning and is rapid-growing; unfortunately, the severe winters of 1976–77, 77–78 caused considerable injury and laboratory tests have indicated it is very susceptible to 0.5 to 1.0 ppm ozone, still a good selection and is being produced in greater numbers, 50′ by 40′ after 20 to 30 years, good dark green summer foliage, yellow-brown in fall; at Milliken Arboretum, Spartanburg, SC, this was the most severely infected with anthracnose, followed by 'Columbia', with no symptoms on 'Yarwood', perhaps the fungus has caught up with and surpassed Bloodgood's early resistance.

'Columbia'—Original cross made by Dr. Santamour, U.S. National Arboretum in 1970 between *P. orientalis* (female) and *P. occidentalis* (male), pleasing pyramidal form in youth with dark green, mildew and anthracnose resistant foliage, compartmentalizes wounds well, grew 27′ in 12 years, 4″ diameter; 5-lobed leaves, length 80 to 90% of width; fruits in 2's and 3's; now being grown by American nurseries; see *HortScience* 19(6): 901–902 (1984) for more detailed information.

'Liberty'—*P. orientalis* × *P. occidentalis* (bottomland tree), remotely 5-lobed leaves, fruits 1 to 2 with less than 1/3″ between fruits, resistant to anthracnose and powdery mildew, readily compartmentalizes against decay organisms; tremendous growth at Milliken Arboretum with 6-year-old trees 20 to 24′ high and 12 to 14′ wide with a ±6″ trunk diameter, bark does not exfoliate as early as 'Yarwood'; some anthracnose; see *HortScience* 19(6): 901–902 (1984) for details.

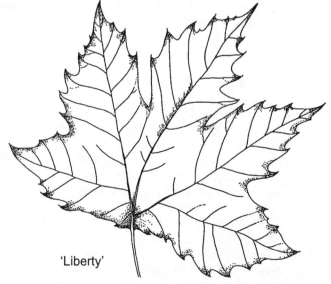

'Liberty'

'Mirkovec'—A shrubby form found in former Yugoslavia at the Mirkovec Nursery, introduced to western Europe via Belgium by the de Belder's at Kalmthout Arboretum, broad, finely lobed leaves are a mixture of pink, cream and bronze with prominent veins, have observed in England, unusual variant of a behemothic tree.

'Yarwood'—Appears promising, the last edition I listed it as mildew resistant; after seven years in the Milliken Arboretum, it appears the best of the improved selections; fast growth, tight pyramidal outline, disease-free, dark green leaves, early exfoliating, cream-colored aging to olive-brown bark; with 'Bloodgood' and 'Liberty' within a stone's roll, this exquisite form predominates; interestingly, fruits are borne singly suggesting *P. occidentalis* affinity; I am enamored with this cultivar's early performance.

Evaluation of anthracnose and mildew resistance of 'Bloodgood', 'Columbia', 'Liberty', 'Yarwood', and 'Saratoga 86-336-C' in *J. Arboriculture* 18:161–163 (1992) showed 'Bloodgood' significantly less affected by anthracnose, 'Yarwood' was most resistant to mildew. Study was conducted in an urban park in California.

PROPAGATION: Seed requires a cold treatment for 45 to 60 days; there is some indication that seeds will germinate without pretreatment. Softwood and hardwood cuttings can be rooted and this appears to be standard practice in European countries; best to use 8000 ppm IBA, bottom heat, open bench with hardwoods. Myers and Still, *The Plant Propagator*, September 1979, p. 9–11, present interesting data relative to rooting June softwood cuttings; they collected the cuttings from a 45-year-old and a 20-year-old tree, dipped them in 50% alcohol solution, 8000, 16,000, 32,000 ppm IBA; best rooting occurred with the control and was 100% for the 20-year tree and 95% for the 45-year tree; IBA at the 2 lowest concentrations was also effective but not better than control; NAA proved valueless. Winter hardwoods rooted 89–100% from 2- to 4-year-old trees.

ADDITIONAL NOTES: The history of the plant is interesting and I suggest the reader consult Bean for a fine account. The first record of the tree was in 1663 when the hybrid was found growing in London. It is widely planted in Europe and especially England where in London it is the dominant street and park tree. My wife and I walked through Hyde Park on a cool September day and admired the great beauty of the bark and massive trunks. I think it is safe to say I have changed my opinion of the species over the years. When properly grown, it is a fine tree. The tree withstands heavy pruning and is often pollarded and pleached to form hedges and allées. There is a magnificent allée at the Jardin des Plantes, Paris, that every visitor to that city should see and experience. Average life span of 39 years as street trees in Jersey City, NJ; see *J. Arboriculture* 17:303–305 (1991).

Platanus occidentalis L. — American Planetree, also known as Sycamore, Buttonwood, and Buttonball-tree
(plat′à-nus ok-si-den-tā′lis)

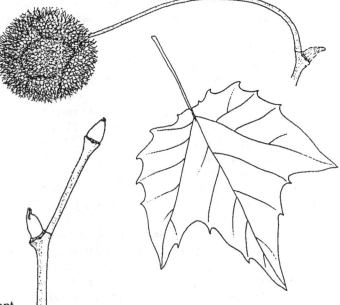

LEAVES: Alternate, simple, 4 to 9″ wide, often broader than long, 3- or sometimes 5-lobed with shallow sinuses and broad-triangular lobes, truncate or cordate, rarely cuneate, coarsely toothed or rarely entire, floccose-tomentulose when young, at maturity pubescent only along veins beneath, medium to dark green; petiole—3 to 5″ long, prominent stipules 1 to 1 1/2″ long, entire or toothed.

BUDS: Terminal—absent, laterals—large, 1/4 to 3/8″ long, conical, blunt-pointed, smooth, shiny dark reddish brown, with single visible scale formed within petiole base, second scale green, gummy, innermost scale covered with long rusty hairs; diverge at 45° angle.

STEM: Rather stout, round, smooth or pubescent, shiny yellow-orange-brown, generally zig-zag.

BARK: Red to gray-brown and scaly near base, exfoliating on upper trunk exposing lighter colored (white to creamy white) inner layers.

FRUIT: Multiple, globose fruit of achenes, 4/5 to 1 1/3″ diameter, borne singly on a 3 to 6″ long peduncle, occasionally 2 fruits per stalk.

SIZE: 75 to 100′ in height with a similar or greater spread; can grow to 150′ and next to *Liriodendron tulipifera* is one of our tallest eastern native deciduous broadleaf trees; national champion is 129′ by 105′ at Jeromesville, OH.

HARDINESS: Zone 4 to 9.

HABIT: Usually a tree with a large, massive trunk and a wide-spreading open crown of massive, crooked branches; a behemoth in the world of trees; a striking and impressive specimen especially in winter when the white, mottled bark stands out against the cold gray sky; the best description of habit would be irregular.

RATE: Medium to fast, in Kansas tests averaged 1′11″ per year over a 10 year period.

TEXTURE: Coarse, but humanely so.

BARK: Mostly smooth, very light grayish brown, flaking off in large, irregular, thin pieces and exposing the grayish to cream-colored inner bark which gradually becomes whitish and produces the impressive mottled appearance.

LEAF COLOR: Flat medium to dark green in summer; fall color is tan to brown and unrewarding; leaves emerge late in spring.

FLOWERS: Similar to *P.* × *acerifolia*.

FRUIT: Also similar except the fruits are borne singly, slightly larger.

CULTURE: Similar to, but not as tolerant as *P.* × *acerifolia*; found native in bottomlands and along the banks of rivers and streams; attains its greatest size in deep, moist, rich soils.

DISEASES AND INSECTS: Anthracnose, leafspots, aphids, Sycamore plant bug, Sycamore tussock moth, scales, bagworms, borers, ad infinitum; anthracnose (*Gnomonia veneta*, also listed as *G. platani*) is a serious problem as it affects developing leaves and stems; there is a dieback followed by a "witches' broom" type development beneath the dead area; cool temperatures and excessive moisture are ideal for the spread of this disease.

LANDSCAPE VALUE: If native to an area do not remove the tree(s); however, do not plant it; used for street tree planting in Urbana, IL; the tree is simply too large and is constantly dropping leaves, twigs and fruits; if people only considered all the factors regarding each tree they plant perhaps much maintenance and trouble could be avoided, but . . . !; the city forester and I had several bouts over the removal of a plant that happened to be located in the tree lawn (parkway) bordering my property; I wanted to remove the tree and he did not approve; I did end up removing the lower branches; the tree was forever dropping part of its anatomy but was truly at its "best" when anthracnose kept it devoid of leaves until mid to late June; in a native situation especially along water courses it is an impressive sight in the landscape.

CULTIVARS:

'Howard'—Never knew one existed until the 1989 Georgia-South Carolina nursery meeting when a gentleman approached me about rooting a yellow-foliaged form; the new growth is a bright yellow that fades with the heat of summer; it is spectacular when the leaves first emerge.

PROPAGATION: Supposedly no pregermination treatment is necessary, although 60 days at 41°F has proven beneficial.

ADDITIONAL NOTES: The wood is heavy, hard, tough and coarse grained, and is used for furniture, boxes, crates and butcher's blocks. A beautiful tree in its finest form and as a child growing up in Cincinnati, OH, much pleasure was derived from climbing and hiding in the hollow trunks of the magnificent specimens that occurred along the stream along the back of our property.

NATIVE HABITAT: Ranges from Maine to Ontario and Minnesota, south to Florida and Texas into northeastern Mexico. Introduced 1640.

RELATED SPECIES:

Platanus orientalis L., (plat′à-nus ôr-i-en-tā′lis), Oriental Planetree, is one of the parents of *P.* × *acerifolia* and mentioned here because of its resistance to anthracnose which was apparently transmitted to the London Planetree. Similar to other species except the 5- to 7-lobed, 4 to 8″ wide leaves are more deeply incised, the sinuses reaching nearly to the middle of the blade, the base long cuneate or truncate. The fruits are borne 3 to 6, rarely 2's. The bark is a cream color. I have seen a magnificent specimen at Kew Gardens and one can really appreciate the beauty of the tree in its mature state. It is not common in the United States. J.C. Raulston Arboretum promoted a clone called 'Digitata' with finger-like lobes. It proved susceptible to canker and leaf diseases. Definitely not superior to the better cultivars of *P.* × *acerifolia*. In China, hairs on fruits have been reported to cause extreme irritation to eyes, nose, ears, and throat; see *J. Arboriculture* 13:113–118 (1989). Southeastern Europe and western Asia. Zone 7 to 9. Not particularly hardy.

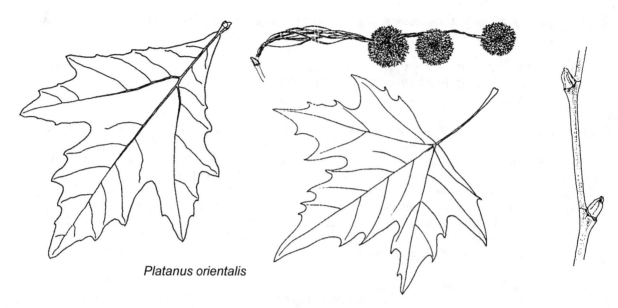

Platanus orientalis

Platanus racemosa Nutt., (plat′à-nus ra-se-mō′sà), California Sycamore, with 3- to 5-lobed, 6 to 12″ wide, leathery deep green above, tomentose below leaves and fruits grouped 3 to 7. National champion is 90′ by 64′ at Goleta, CA. Native to California. Cultivated 1870. Zone 7 to 9.

Platanus wrightii S. Wats., (plat′à-nus rīt′ē-ī), Arizona Sycamore, has deeply 5- to 7-lobed leaves and fruits grouped 2 to 4. On an expedition to Tucson, AZ, one of my former graduate students and the author were plant hunting on Mt. Lemon and witnessed handsome stands of the species in the ravines leading down from the mountain. National Champion is 114′ by 116′ in Sierra County, NM. Arizona, New Mexico to northwestern Mexico. Cultivated 1900. Zone 7 to 9.

Platanus wrightii

Platycarya strobilacea Sieb. & Zucc.

FAMILY: Juglandaceae
LEAVES: Alternate, compound pinnate, 7 to 15 leaflets, 6 to 12″ long, each leaflet 1 3/4 to 4″ long, sessile, ovate to oblong-lanceolate, acuminate, biserrate, dark green, glabrous.

Platycarya strobilacea, (plat-i-kā′ri-à strō-bil-ā′sē-à), is a small, 20 to 30′ high, round-headed tree with handsome dark green foliage and curious ovoid-oblong, 1 to 1 1/2″ long, upright, cone-like catkins that persist after maturation. The flowers are monoecious with the male in 2 to 3″ long, erect catkins in groups of 4 to 8. The fruit is a 1/5″ diameter, winged nutlet in a ±1 1/2″ long, ovoid, cone-like structure. Appears to prefer a moist, well-drained soil, but has grown vigorously at the Arnold and J.C. Raulston Arboretum. Certainly a tree for the collector. The fruits are unique. China. Introduced 1845. Zone 6 to 8.

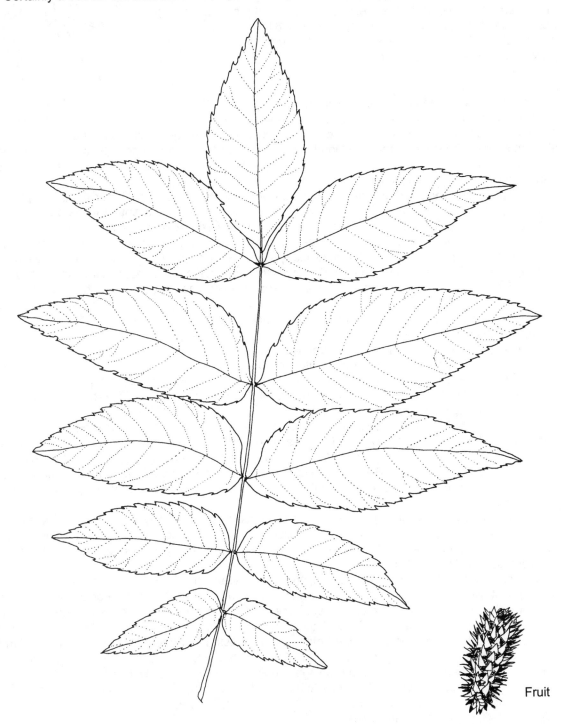

Fruit

Podocarpus macrophyllus (Thunb.) D. Don 'Maki' — Maki, Shrubby or Chinese Podocarpus
(pō-dō-kär′pus mak-rō-fil′us)

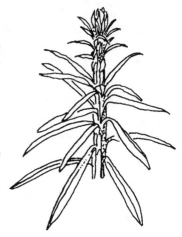

FAMILY: Podocarpaceae

LEAVES: Arranged spirally on stem, evergreen, needle-like, 1/2 to 2 3/4″ long, 1/4 to 3/8″ wide, sharply acute, leathery, lustrous waxy dark green above with two wide glaucous stomatiferous bands beneath, glabrous; needles give a bottlebrush-like effect.

STEMS: Stout, green, grooved, glabrous.

SIZE: 20 to 35′ high, one-half this in spread; smaller in Piedmont.

HARDINESS: Zone 8 to 10, severely injured at –3°F on Georgia campus, many plants burned at 11°F at Sea Island, GA, most probably because of cambial damage (bark split) during the 1983–84 freeze.

HABIT: Upright oval to columnar evergreen shrub or tree; quite stiff and rigid; useful for screening and hedging.

RATE: Slow.

TEXTURE: Medium-fine.

LEAF: Lustrous dark green throughout the seasons.

FLOWERS: Dioecious, male catkin-like, cylindrical, yellow brown, 1 to 1 1/2″ long in clusters, female consists of a short stalk bearing few scales of which only upper one or two are fertile; April–early May.

FRUIT: Naked seed, red to red-purple, 1/2″ long, have seen fruits with a pronounced bloom that gave them a bluish color, attached to a fleshy receptacle generally the same color as the seed; fruits are not poisonous and can be used to make preserves.

CULTURE: Transplants readily from containers; prefers well-drained, fertile soils; like *Taxus* does not tolerate wet feet; full sun or moderate shade; tolerant of salt spray; displays excellent heat tolerance.

DISEASES AND INSECTS: Root rot in wet situations, scale has been reported.

LANDSCAPE VALUE: Makes a good hedge, screen, or small specimen tree where adapted; in upper reaches of Zone 8 is more shrubby and not particularly vigorous; used in quantity along the Georgia coast, throughout Florida, Gulf Coast and California; at The Cloisters, Sea Island, GA it is appressed to and shaped to fit against the buildings, particularly in shady environments; considered deer resistant.

CULTIVARS:

'Brodie'—Spreading, compact form, 3′ high by 6′ wide.

'Nana'—Bushy, rounded, compact clone.

'Spreading'—Spreading form, ground cover-like habit.

'Variegatus'—Cream-white to white variegated foliage.

PROPAGATION: Seeds require 2 years to germinate. Hardwood cuttings root readily, handle like *Taxus*; also can be rooted in late summer and fall, 3000 to 8000 ppm IBA-talc, well-drained medium, mist. Tissue culture has succeeded; see *Scientia Horticulturae* 47:323–326 (1991).

ADDITIONAL NOTES: *Podocarpus* belongs to the gymnosperms and bears a naked seed that is referred to as a "fruit." The podocarps are warm climate trees and shrubs and in northern areas are utilized as house and conservatory plants. Approximately 100 species are known and many are superb ornamentals. Even in Zone 7b (5 to 10°F, Athens, GA) they do not perform well. *Podocarpus macrophyllus* 'Maki' was grown on the Georgia campus but suffered from the low winter temperatures and perhaps poorly drained clay soil of the Piedmont.

　　　'Maki' was listed as var. *maki* in the 1990 edition. As currently cataloged it represents more than one clone, although what I see in the trade is as described above. The species *P. macrophyllus* has larger, broad linear-lanceolate leaves, 3 to 4″ long, 2/5″ wide on mature trees, often longer to 7″ on young trees. It is coarser and less hardy than 'Maki'.

　　　Recently, the Atlanta Botanical Garden, under the leadership of Ron Determann, has assembled one of the best gymnosperm collections in the Southeast, with many *Podocarpus* species either growing in the outside collection or in the greenhouse. Time will tell if they have landscape merit. All are sited in raised beds in well-drained soil. Two of the hardiest are *P. alpinus* R. Br. ex Hook. f., Tasmanian Podocarp, and *P. nivalis* Hook., Alpine Totara. Both are listed as Zone 7 adaptable. In Ireland and the south of England, I made the acquaintance of *P. salignus* D. Don, Willowleaf Podocarp, with graceful, slender 3 to 5″ long, 1/4″ wide, lustrous foliage and *P. totara* G. Benn. ex D. Don, Totara, the largest and most robust species, with yew-like, 1/2 to 1″ long, 1/6″ wide, sharply spined needles. *Podocarpus salignus* is native to central Chile, Zone 8; *P. totara* to New Zealand, Zone 9.

NATIVE HABITAT: Japan, southern China.

RELATED SPECIES:

Podocarpus nagi (Thunb.) Mak., (pō-dō-kär′pus nā′jī), Broadleaf or Japanese Podocarpus, forms a loose
pyramidal outline of soft pendulous branches. Ultimate height ranges from 30 to 40′. The lustrous dark
green, elliptic leaves are 1 to 3″ long and 1/2 to 1 1/4″ wide, with numerous veins running lengthwise. This
species is distinct from all others in the width of the leaf as compared to its length. Fruits are about 1/2″
wide and covered with a plum-like bloom. Bark is quite attractive. Has been utilized at Disney
World with great success. Revisionary taxonomy affords the species the new name
of *Nageia nagi* (Thunb.) Kuntze. Native of southern Japan, Formosa, and China.
Introduced 1830. Only suited for Zones 9 and 10. Largely killed to the ground
at 11°F at Sea Island, GA.

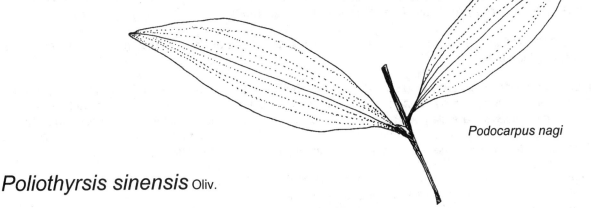

Podocarpus nagi

Poliothyrsis sinensis Oliv.

FAMILY: Flacourtiaceae
LEAVES: Alternate, simple, broad ovate, 3 to 6″ long, acuminate, rounded or truncate, medium green, dentate,
3 prominent veins, pubescent beneath; petiole—1 to 1 1/2″ long.

Poliothyrsis sinensis, (pōl-ē-ō-thĕr′sis sī-nen′sis), is not common and the only flowering plants I experienced
were at the Arnold Arboretum where in late July, large, white, fragrant panicles were dripping from the
ends of the shoots. This indicates that flowers are formed on the new growth of the season. Although
described as a tree, 40 to 45′, I envision a shrub-like constitution, 15 to 20′(25′) high and wide at maturity.
The foliage is rich green and turns yellow-burgundy in autumn. Flowers are monoecious, 1/3″ diameter,
with 5 sepals (apetalous) that initiate white and age to yellow. Fruit is a 3- to 4-valved, 1/2 to 3/4″ long
capsule with winged seeds. The flowers are borne in a (4″)6 to 8″ long, loose, terminal panicle. Does not
appear aloof about soils. The Arnold's plants were in full sun and in the 1991 summer I witnessed them,
the plants had persisted through an extended drought. Unusual accent, novelty, fool-your-friends plant.
Wonderful article by Spongberg, *Arnoldia* 54(3):32–34 (1994), provides history, characteristics, and
culture. Central China. Introduced 1908. Zone 6 to 7.

Polygonum aubertii L. Henry — Silvervine Fleeceflower, Silver Lace Vine, Russian Vine, China
Fleece Vine
(pō-lig′ō-num aw-ber′tē-ī)

FAMILY: Polygonaceae
LEAVES: Alternate, simple, ovate to oblong-ovate, 1 1/2 to 3 1/2″ long, acute, hastate at base, usually undulate
at margin, bright green; petiole—1 1/4 to 2″ long.

SIZE: 25 to 35′, seemingly to infinity.
HARDINESS: Zone 4 to 7(8).
HABIT: Twining deciduous vine of rampant growth.
RATE: Fast, as much as 10 to 15′ in one growing season is not unreasonable.
TEXTURE: Medium in foliage; rather coarse in winter.
LEAF COLOR: Reddish, bronze-red when emerging and developing bright green when mature.
FLOWERS: Perfect, white or greenish white, sometimes slightly pinkish, fragrant, about 1/5″ diameter; borne in
numerous, slender panicles along the upper part of the branches; July, August, and through September.
FRUIT: Three-angled achene, not showy, not setting freely, may turn pink.

CULTURE: Easily transplanted; rapidly spreads by underground stems (rhizomes); the smallest segment of which will produce a new plant; full sun or shade; does well in dry soils; almost a weed because of its ebullient, vigorous habit.

DISEASES AND INSECTS: Japanese beetle can be a problem.

LANDSCAPE VALUE: A vigorous, rapid-growing vine with good foliage; valued for its adaptability; makes a good, quick cover; this might be used where few other vines will grow.

PROPAGATION: Easily increased by stem cuttings or by division, seed requires no pretreatment.

ADDITIONAL NOTES: There were several *Polygonum* plantings on the University of Illinois campus which grew 1 to 2′ high and had pinkish flowers. They died back after a hard freeze and looked unsightly in the winter only to arise with reddish leaves in April. I noticed considerable variation in size, as some plants grew about a foot while others became almost vine-like and grew to 3′.

NATIVE HABITAT: Western China, Tibet, Russia. Introduced 1899.

RELATED SPECIES: The nomenclature is confused within this group of plants and some of the names almost appear "homemade."

Polygonum baldschuanicum Reg., (pō-lig′ō-num   bald-shwa′ni-kum), Mile-a-minute Vine, Bokaravine Fleeceflower, is similar to *P. aubertii* in virtually every character and probably cannot be reliably separated. The inflorescences are glabrous and crowded toward the end of the shoots forming compound panicles. I have seen the plant in England on many occasions and believe that from a landscape standpoint it is similar to *P. aubertii*. Russia, Afghanistan, Pakistan, Iran. Introduced 1883. Zone 4 to 8.

Polygonum japonicum Meissn. var. ***compactum*** (Hook. f.) Bail. — Low Japanese Fleeceflower
LEAVES: Alternate, simple, short-oval to orbicular-ovate, 3 to 6″ long, abruptly pointed, with an abrupt or truncate base, dark green, margins crimped; petiole—about 1″ long.

Polygonum japonicum var. *compactum*, (pō-lig′ō-num jà-pon′i-kum   kom-pak′tum), Low Japanese Fleeceflower, grows to 2′ and has greenish white flowers and small reddish fruits. Wyman reported that a few roots which were planted in a vacant spot in the perennial border developed into an eight foot square in a short period of time. Often offered in the trade as *P. reynoutria* hort. non Mak. Nomenclature (mine) is somewhat suspect and names like *P. cuspidatum* Sieb. & Zucc. have been superseded by *Fallopia japonica* (Houtt.) Ronse Decracne. A worthy article, "Japanese Knotweed: A reputation Lost," appeared in *Arnoldia* 57(3):13–19 (1997) and discussed the movement of the plant into the American landscape and its escapades away from cultivation. Eastern Asia. Zone 4 to 8.

ADDITIONAL NOTES: In southern gardens, I see a 5 to 7′ high and wide shrub that regenerates from the ground each year. In late summer–fall it is covered with sprays of red fruits and is quite attractive. This could be *P. japonicum* var. *compactum* but size is consistently larger than the literature purports. Also, *P. japonicum* is dioecious so male plants will not develop showy fruits.

From Maine to Georgia, *P. japonicum* has escaped and naturalized along roadways and vacant land. It is pernicious and will outcompete native vegetation. Be leery and careful when considering the above for the garden. All are thugs.

Poncirus trifoliata (L.) Raf. — Hardy-orange, Trifoliate-orange, Bitter-orange
(pon-sī′rus trī-fō-li-ā′tà)

FAMILY: Rutaceae

LEAVES: Alternate, trifoliate, terminal leaflet obovate to elliptic, 1 to 2 1/2″ long, 1/2 to 1″ wide, obtuse or emarginate, cuneate, crenulate, sub-coriaceous, the lateral ones similar, but smaller and usually elliptic-ovate, very oblique at base, lustrous dark green, glabrous; petiole—1/3 to 1″ long, often winged.

BUDS: Glabrous, rather small, solitary, sessile, subglobose, with about 3 exposed scales; terminal lacking.

STEM: Glabrous, glossy green, triangular, dilated into the thorns at nodes, rather stout; pith large, white, homogeneous; leaf scars very small, elliptical, scarcely raised; bundle trace 1, crescent-shaped; no stipule scars; single spine at node, 1 to 2″ long; green stem color and very prominent broad-based spines are good winter identification characters.

SIZE: 8 to 20′ high, 2/3's that in width.

HARDINESS: Zone 6 is more favorable; however, will grow in Zone 5 to Zone 9; have seen it killed to ground by -20°F.

HABIT: Small, oval shrub or tree with green spiny stems, usually low-branched and viciously spiny.

RATE: Slow to medium.

TEXTURE: Medium in leaf; medium to coarse in winter.

STEM COLOR: Young stems a distinct bright green with numerous spines, almost lethal to the touch.

LEAF COLOR: Lustrous dark green in summer changing to yellow or yellow-green in fall.

FLOWERS: Perfect, white, 5-petaled, axillary, subsessile on previous year's branches, 1 1/2 to 2″ across, supposedly very fragrant, borne singly usually in late April to early May; in spite of what the literature states I cannot sense the sweet odor.

FRUIT: A modified berry (hesperidium), yellow, 1 1/2″ across, covered with soft down or glabrous, containing numerous seeds, very sour, ripening in September or October; ripens an unbelievable quantity of fruits in the South.

CULTURE: Easy to transplant, prefers well-drained, acid soils; once established in the right situation it proves to be a vigorous grower; full sun; has escaped from cultivation near Wrightsville, GA and in the Houston, TX areas, fields have been colonized.

DISEASES AND INSECTS: None serious.

LANDSCAPE VALUE: More of a novelty plant than anything else in the North, used in the South for hedging because of its dense growth and thorny character; no sane person would attempt to penetrate this hedge! At one time I doubted its landscape usefulness but have seen plants in Longwood's Mediterranean garden with yucca, prickly pear, sedum, and blue sheep's fescue that appeared to belong; the plant has tremendous late fall and winter character because of yellow fruits and interesting green stems and spines; spines are lethal and, doubtfully, should be used in high traffic areas; visited Oklahoma State University campus and noticed the plant was used as a hedge; hedges were so tightly pruned that one could walk on top; could prove more effective than a good watch dog.

CULTIVARS:

'Flying Dragon'—Interesting twisted stems, a novelty at best; has been embraced for accent use; spines also have a slight twist; I never believed Don Shadow when he told me this cultivar had a future.

PROPAGATION: Seeds germinate like beans when stratified for 90 days at 41°F in a moist medium; one of my former students collected fruits from a tree in the Missouri Botanic Garden, St. Louis, and after stratification subsequent germination averaged 95% plus. I have also collected fruits in October from the University's Botanical Garden and sowed them directly, initial germination took 4 to 6 weeks and seeds were still coming up 3 months later; the cold period unifies and hastens germination more than anything else; also noted quite a number of albino seedlings, many more than occur in most seedling populations. Softwood cuttings taken in summer rooted after treatment with 50 ppm IBA/17 to 24 hour soak; cuttings taken in late October failed to root without treatment, but rooted 76% after treatment with 50 ppm NAA/24 hour soak. Species rooted 58% after treatment with 4000 ppm IBA; 'Flying Dragon' 100% with 2000 ppm IBA; 'Rubidoux' 44% with 6000 ppm IBA.

ADDITIONAL NOTES: Introduced into commerce in U.S. by William Saunders of the USDA and P.J. Berckmans of Augusta, GA. It was listed by the Prince Nursery in 1823. Ripe fruits set aside for several weeks become juicy and develop a sprightly, slightly acid flavor. Serves as a substitute for lemon, pulp can be made into marmalade, and peel can be candied. After removing the numerous seeds there is not a whole lot of pulp left over.

NATIVE HABITAT: Northern China, Korea. Introduced about 1850. Seems incongruous that Prince Nursery listed it in 1823 but its introduction date corresponds to about 1850. Such is the nature of the literature.

Populus alba L. — White Poplar, Silver-leaved Poplar
(pop′ū-lus âl′bá)

FAMILY: Salicaceae

LEAVES: Alternate, simple, on long shoots, palmately 3- to 5-lobed with triangular, coarsely toothed lobes, acute, subcordate or rounded at base, 2 to 5″ long, dark green above, white-tomentose beneath; on short branches, smaller, 1 to 2″ long, ovate to elliptic-oblong, sinuate-dentate, usually gray tomentose beneath; petiole—1/2 to 1 1/2″ long, tomentose.

BUDS: Imbricate, small, ovate to conical, light chestnut brown, appressed, shining or more or less covered especially toward base with cottony wool; laterals 1/5 to 1/4″ long, terminals larger.

STEM: Slender or sometimes stout, greenish gray, densely covered with thick whitish cottony wool which can be readily rubbed off; pith—5-pointed, star-shaped.

BARK: On young trunks characteristically light greenish gray or whitish, often with dark blotches; base of older trunk deeply furrowed into firm dark ridges.

SIZE: 40 to 70′ in height with a similar spread; can grow to 90′ or greater; national champion is 93′ by 86′ at St. Charles, IL.

HARDINESS: Zone 3 to 8(9).

HABIT: Usually a wide-spreading tree with an irregular, broad, round-topped crown; spreading abundantly by root suckers; tends to be weak-wooded and susceptible to breakage in storms.

TEXTURE: Medium-coarse in leaf; coarse in winter.

BARK: Greenish gray to whitish, marked with darker blotches, the bases of old trunks becoming fissured, with blackish ridges.

LEAF COLOR: Dark green above and silvery white beneath, the lower surface coated with a thick, matted tomentum; the leaves fall very early in the fall and usually show no coloration although yellowish and reddish have been listed by various authorities.

FLOWERS: Dioecious; male catkins 2 to 3″ long, 5 to 10 stamens per flower, anthers purple, female 3 to 4″ long.

FRUITS: Two-valved, dehiscent capsule.

CULTURE: Easy to grow, does well under any conditions but prefers moist, deep loam; pH adaptable; full sun; prune in summer or fall as it "bleeds" if pruned in winter and spring; air pollution tolerant; quite tolerant of salt spray.

DISEASES AND INSECTS: Poplars, in general, are affected by a whole host of diseases; they are poor ornamental trees and are continually dropping leaves, twigs and other debris; the following pests are the more common and include *Cytospora* canker, poplar canker, fusarium canker, hypoxylon canker, septoria canker, branch gall, leaf blister, leaf spots, leaf rusts, powdery mildew, dieback, aphids, bronze birch borer, poplar borer, red-humped caterpillar, poplar tent maker, scales and imported willow leaf beetle; if anyone plants poplars they deserve the disasters which automatically ensue.

LANDSCAPE VALUE: I hesitate to recommend this tree for anyone since it becomes a nuisance and liability after a time; wood is brittle, roots will clog drain tiles, sewers and water channels; avoid this pest.

CULTIVARS:

'Globosa'—Broad-rounded habit, large shrub-like constitution, young leaves pinkish, gray-tomentose below.

'Intertexta'—Leaves dull gray, developing yellow speckles with maturity.

'Nivea'—Stems, leaf undersides and petioles are white tomentose, leaves prominently lobed, considered a juvenile characteristic which is reduced as plant matures.

'Pyramidalis'—Columnar in habit; called Bolleana Poplar; better than Lombardy Poplar but still of negligible quality; slightly broader than Lombardy; several mature trees at the Morton Arboretum were 60′ by 9′ and 55′ by 5′, all diseased and declining.

'Richardii'—Upper surface of the leaves yellow, white beneath, slow-growing, effective from a distance, have seen a time or two and always wanted to fertilize the tree; sometimes treated as a cut-back shrub to encourage long shoots of better color and intensity; an old specimen at the Morton Arboretum is 72′ high.

PROPAGATION: Seed requires no pretreatment and germination will take place after dispersal. Cuttings root when treated with IBA but success may vary with timing; probably best in July–August.

ADDITIONAL NOTES: Some 30 to 35 species are known in the northern hemisphere with many hybrids occurring naturally. All are fast-growing, disease-ridden and with minimal redeeming everyday landscape value, particularly in American gardens. Ask yourself the last time a handsome poplar was seen in a cultivated situation. Possibly for naturalizing in rough areas. Few trees more impressive than *P. tremuloides* in yellow fall color. For windbreaks and quick screens, poplars might be considered. In Europe, *P.* × *jackii* 'Aurora' and *P. nigra* 'Italica' are as common as *Pyrus calleryana* 'Bradford' in the United States. For the average site in the United States, there are many superior tree selections.

NATIVE HABITAT: Central to southern Europe to western Siberia and central Asia. Long cultivated. Naturalized in North America. Introduced 1784.

RELATED SPECIES:

Populus nigra L. **'Italica'** — Lombardy Black Poplar, Italian Poplar

LEAVES: Alternate, simple, rhombic-ovate, triangular, 2 to 4″ long, about as wide, long-acuminate, broad cuneate to truncate, finely crenate-serrate, non-ciliate, dark green above, glabrous, light green beneath; petiole—3/4 to 2 1/4″ long, slender, flattened.

BUDS: Imbricate, small compared to other poplars, terminal 3/8″ long, laterals 1/3″ or less long, appressed, shiny, glutinous, reddish brown, glabrous.

STEM: Slender, round, lustrous brown.

GROWTH HABIT: Easily recognizable because of decidedly upright habit; often used for screens on old farm properties.

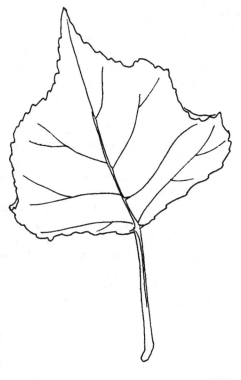

Populus nigra 'Italica', (pop′ū-lus nĭ′grà), Lombardy Black Poplar, is an upright, fast-growing cultivar that was introduced into this country in colonial times (1784). Can grow to 70 to 90′ with a spread of 10 to 15′ in 20 to 30 years but seldom attains this size because of a canker disease which develops in the upper branches and trunk for which there is no cure. In the Morton Arboretum trees are 50′ by 14′ and 44′ by 8′. Substitutes might include *Populus alba* 'Pyramidalis', *Alnus glutinosa* 'Fastigiata', although none will grow as fast as Lombardy. Lombardy is a male clone and is propagated by cuttings. The catkins are 1 to 2″ long, with 12 to 20 stamens per flower, the anthers crimson. It apparently arose in the Lombardy district of Italy in the 1600's and was spread to other parts of Europe in the early 1700's. *Cryptodiaporthe* (*Dothichiza*) *populea* canker is a devastating disease which starts in the upper branches of the tree. It also infects Balsam, Black, and Eastern Cottonwoods. A form often listed as 'Thevestina' ('Theves') and sold as an improved Lombardy does resemble Lombardy in habit but tends to be more broad, has a whitish bark that becomes dark and slightly furrowed on old trunks, and is a female clone. A more correct name is 'Afghanica' for this form arose by mutation from a race of *P. nigra* native to central Asia. A 60′ by 9′ tree grew in the Morton Arboretum. It is supposedly more resistant to the canker but I have seen no hard evidence to support this claim. 'Lombardy Gold', as I have seen it in Europe, is similar to Lombardy in growth habit but has yellow-gold leaves. 'Majestic' is a hybrid, fast-growing, pyramidal, male, with greater resistance to diseases, from University of Wisconsin. Other cultivars include: 'Charkowensis', 'Gigantea', 'Plantierensis', 'Vereeken', and 'Vert de Garonne', with variations on the upright growth habit of Lombardy are described in European literature. I have not observed them in the United States. See Wood, *Arnoldia* 54:24–30 (1994) for the history of 'Italica' in North America. Madsen, *Arnoldia* 54:31–34 (1994), offers fastigiate alternatives to the above. The species is native to western Europe, North Africa, Russia. Lombardy is adapted to Zones 3 to 9.

Populus deltoides Bartr. ex Marshall — Eastern Cottonwood, also called Eastern Poplar.
(pop′ū-lus del-toy′dēz)

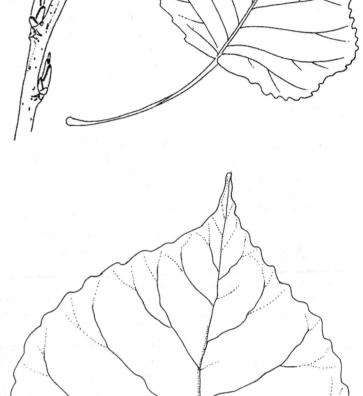

FAMILY: Salicaceae

LEAVES: Alternate, simple, deltoid-ovate or broad-ovate, 3 to 5″(6″) long, about as wide, acuminate, subcordate to truncate and with 2 or 3 glands at base, coarsely crenate-dentate with curved teeth, entire at base and apex, densely ciliate, medium green above, bright green below, glabrous; petiole—2 1/2 to 4″ long, flattened laterally.

BUDS: Imbricate, terminal—1/2 to 3/4″ long, 6 to 7 visible scales, conical, acute, shiny chestnut brown, resinous, balsam scented; laterals—more or less flattened, appressed, smaller.

STEM: Stout, yellowish to greenish yellow to brown, round or marked especially on vigorous trees with more or less prominent wings running down from the two sides and bases of the leaf scars; also quite ragged in appearance.

SIZE: 75 to 100′ in height spreading 50 to 75′; co-national champions are 96′ by 121′ and 92′ by 102′ at Cosper Co., NE and Gila Valley, NM, respectively.

HARDINESS: Zone 3a to 9.

HABIT: Pyramidal in youth but developing a broad vase-shaped habit in old age with the branching structure being somewhat open, irregular and ragged; often with massive, spreading branches.

RATE: Fast, 4 to 5′ a year in rich moist soil is not uncommon, in fact, in two years trees may attain heights of 30′ and diameters of nearly 5″.

TEXTURE: Medium-coarse in leaf, coarse in winter.

BARK: Ash-gray and divided into thick, flattened or rounded ridges separated by deep fissures on old trunks; young stems and trunks greenish yellow; impressive bark on mature trees.

LEAF COLOR: Lustrous light to medium green in summer, abscising early in fall and usually only with a trace of yellow; in some regions good yellow.

FLOWERS: Applies to most *Populus*; dioecious, anemophilous, in pendulous catkins appearing before the leaves, individual flowers (both sexes) solitary, inserted on a disk and subtended by a bract; male flowers with either 6 to 12, or 12 to many stamens; female with a single pistil; up to 60 stamens on *P. deltoides* with attractive red anthers; usually opening in March–April before the leaves.

FRUIT: Three- to 4-valved dehiscent capsule, 1/4 to 1/3″ long, the seeds are tufted and represent the "cottony" mass which is seen under and around the trees at dispersal time, June–July; hence, the name Cottonwood.

CULTURE: Easily transplanted and grown, prefers moist situations along waterways but tolerates dry soils; very common on moist alluvial soils through the plains and prairie states; tolerates saline conditions and pollutants; very pH adaptable; a short-lived species and trees over 70-years-old deteriorate rapidly.

DISEASES AND INSECTS: See under *P. alba*; serious canker problems with this species and the many hybrids, resistance has been illusive.

LANDSCAPE VALUE: Little, except in the difficult plains states; a messy tree often dropping leaves, flowers, fruits, twigs and branches; will break up in storms as the wood is light, soft and weak; impressive in river bottoms and should remain there; quite weed-like and stray seedlings are evident in fields alongside water courses where the tree grows naturally, quick to move into abandoned land.

CULTIVARS: Many cottonless (male) forms and hybrids between *P. deltoides* and *P. nigra* have been selected and named. Pair evaluated six different forms over a 10 year period.

'Colmar'—Resistant to leaf diseases, male, yellow fall color, from University of Illinois.

'Lydick'—Averaged 4′ per year, female clone.

'NE-355'—Averaged 3′ per year.

'Noreaster'—Averaged 4′ per year, hybrid, with thicker bark and canker resistance.

'Red Caudina'—Narrow pyramidal form 50 to 70′ by 8 to 12′, large deltoid leaves with red veins and petioles, young leaves are bronze-red, male.

'Robusta'—Averaged 4′1″ per year, vigorous, developed some canker, 40 to 60′ by 30 to 40′.

'Siouxland'—Averaged 2′10″ per year, rust resistant, male form, introduced by South Dakota State University, apparently is susceptible to canker after 18 to 20 years; have observed in Spring Grove where ~10-year-old trees averaged 30′ high and were quite pyramidal in outline, had dropped many interior leaves by late August and were not the most appealing specimens; included at Milliken Arboretum, Spartanburg, SC and leaves are essentially absent by September; estimated size 60 to 80′ by 30 to 40′.

Species Male Clone—Averaged 3′4″ per year, subject to breakage.

PROPAGATION: Seeds require no pretreatment; cuttings can also be used and apparently root with varying degrees of ease depending on the tree from which they were selected.

NATIVE HABITAT: Quebec to North Dakota, Kansas, Texas, Florida. Introduced 1750.

OTHER *POPULUS* OF GENERAL INTEREST

There are about 30 to 35 species of poplars widely distributed in North America, Europe, North Africa and in Asia south to the Himalayas. There are numerous hybrids and named cultivars. In European countries they are commonly used for streets, parks, fence row, windbreak and canal plantings. They are important sources of pulpwood and other wood products. Their growth rates are phenomenal and the following figures are derived from information put out by the Minnesota Landscape Arboretum. Bolleana Poplar grew about 30′ in 9 years; 'Siouxland' 40′ in 9 years; Japanese Poplar 30′ in 9 years; *Populus nigra* 'Afghanica' ('Thevestina') 30′ in 9 years; *P. tremula* 'Erecta' 30′ high and 4′ wide in 10 years; *P. tremuloides* 25′ in 10 years; *P. trichocarpa* 20′ high and 7′ wide in 9 years.

Poplars can be divided into four groups:

1. White and gray poplars, aspens.
   Young trunks and main branches at first smooth, eventually pitted with numerous diamond-shaped holes; leaves toothed or lobed; they can be further subdivided into:
      White or gray poplars—Leaves on long shoots woolly beneath, those of short shoots less woolly or almost glabrous, and of different shape; petioles usually not flattened; included here are: *P. alba*, *P. × canescens* (Ait.) Small, and *P. × tomentosa* Carr.
      Aspens—Leaves glabrous or almost so beneath; uniform in size and with laterally flattened petioles which allow them to flutter in the slightest breeze; included are: *P. grandidentata*, *P. tremula*, and *P. tremuloides*.

2. Leucoides
   The leaves are large and leathery, usually tomentose when young, and more or less the same size and shape; the bark is rough and scaly; *P. heterophylla* L., *P. lasiocarpa* Oliv., and *P. wilsonii* C. Schneid. belong here.

3. Balsam poplars
   The first to open in the spring, the buds and leaves very gummy, emit a pleasant balsam fragrance when expanding; usually whitish but not woolly beneath; petiole not compressed; *P. angustifolia* James, *P. balsamifera* L., *P. laurifolia* Ledeb., *P. maximowiczii* Henry, *P. simonii* Carr., *P. trichocarpa* Torr. & A. Gray, and others belong here.

4. Black poplars
   Leaves are green on both sides, petioles compressed, margins translucent and cartilaginous, trunks ridged-and-furrowed; *P. deltoides*, *P. nigra*, and others belong here.

Populus × canadensis Moench, (pop′ū-lus kan-à-den′sis), Carolina Poplar, represents a large group of hybrids between *P. deltoides* and *P. nigra*. They are more vigorous than either parent and propagate easily from cuttings. 'Eugenei' is of a columnar habit with comparatively short, spreading lateral branches. 'Prairie Sky' is a tall, narrow single-stemmed, male tree with short lateral branches, parent tree was 33′ high, 6 1/2′ wide, triangular-shaped leaves, approximately 4″ long and 4″ wide with a shiny green upper surface, exhibited high resistance to canker and only minor susceptibility to leaf rust diseases, from Morden, Manitoba, Canada. 'Florence Biondi', 'Gelrica', 'Marilandica', 'Noreaster' (only hybrid to show resistance in Dr. Pair's Wichita trials), 'Regenerata', 'Robusta' (small, vigorous, broad-oval), 'Serotina', 'Serotina Aurea', and 'Serotina de Selys' belong here. Considered adaptable to Zone 4 and south. For a complete description see Bean.

Populus grandidentata Michx. — Bigtooth Aspen

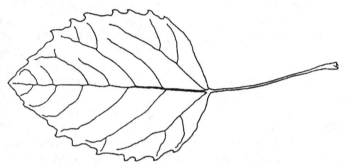

LEAVES: Alternate, simple, on long shoots, 3 to 4″ long, about as wide, acuminate, truncate to broad-cuneate at base, coarsely sinuate dentate with callous mucronate teeth, dark green above, gray tomentose beneath at first, soon glabrescent and glaucescent, those of short branches elliptic, with sharper teeth; petiole—glabrescent, 1 to 2 1/2″ long, slender, compressed toward the top.

BUDS: Imbricate, 1/8 to 1/4″ long, 6 to 7 visible scales, ovate to conical, pointed, generally divergent, dull, dusty-looking due to fine, close, pale pubescence especially at margin of scales.

STEM: Stout, round, reddish brown or somewhat yellowish brown, older stems greenish gray.

Populus grandidentata, (pop′ū-lus gran-di-den-tā′tà), Bigtooth Aspen, is normally a medium-sized tree reaching 50 to 70′, with a spread of 20 to 40′. Tri-national champions are 132′ by 67′, 74′ by 72′, and 66′ by 65′. Often pyramidal in youth with a central leader, developing an oval, open, irregular crown at maturity. Very fast-growing (65′ in 20 years). Reaches best development on moist, fertile soils but will grow on dry, sandy or gravelly soils. Ornamental assets are few but it is valuable for pulp wood and other wood uses. Have seen good yellow fall color. Native from Nova Scotia to Ontario and Minnesota south to North Carolina, Tennessee, Illinois and Iowa. Introduced 1772. Zone 3 to 5(6).

Populus × jackii Sarg., (pop′ū-lus jak′ē-ī), represents hybrids between *P. balsamifera* and *P. deltoides*. Leaves range from 1 to 5″ long, are deltoid-ovate, blue-green, with 1 to 2″ long petioles. Trees vary in size from 30 to 100′. Although not common in commerce in the United States, 'Aurora' is everywhere in Europe, particularly Ireland, where the bold variegated rose, pink, cream new shoots are striking. The tree is usually cut back to induce long, supple, brightly colored shoots. The hybrid occurs in central and eastern North America. Introduced 1900. Zone 2 to 5.

Populus maximowiczii Henry, (pop′ū-lus max-sim-ō-wix′ē-ī), Japanese Poplar, is a handsome, rather broad-spreading, large tree. The bark is smooth, light gray-green and attractive. It has proven to be one of the most promising and disease-free poplars in Minnesota's collection. The leaves open early in spring and persist late in fall. The leaves are slightly leathery, vivid green, pale green beneath, and about 3 to 5″ long and wide. It has hybridized with other species and produced named selections including 'Androscoggin', 'Geneva', 'Oxford' and 'Rochester'. Northeast Asia, Japan. Introduction before 1890. Zone 3 to ?

Populus simonii Carr. — Simon Poplar

LEAVES: Alternate, simple, rhombic-elliptic, 2 to 5″ long, 1 to 3″ wide, acute, broad-cuneate to narrowly rounded, crenate, bright green above, pale beneath; petiole—1/3 to 3/4″ long, red.

Populus simonii, (pop´ū-lus sī-mōn´ē-ī), Simon Poplar, is occasionally grown in the northern United States, with major sitings at the Chicago Botanic Garden and University of Maine. The species is a medium to large, 40 to 60´ high tree with vase-shaped habit. Unfortunately, the leaves, like many poplars, are susceptible to leaf spot and abscise prematurely. 'Fastigiata' has steeply ascending branches resulting in a rather columnar tree in youth, becoming fatter with age. Northern China. Introduced 1862. Zone 2 to 5.

Populus tremula L. 'Erecta' — Upright European Aspen

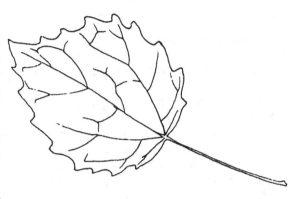

LEAVES: Alternate, simple, thin, suborbicular to ovate, 1 to 3″ long, rounded or acute at apex, truncate or subcordate at base, margins undulate, sinuately crenate-dentate, tomentose when emerging, quickly glabrous, dark green above, glaucescent beneath, gray-green; petiole—flattened, glabrous, often as long as the blade.

Populus tremula 'Erecta', (pop´ū-lus trem´ū-là), Upright European Aspen, is an excellent, narrowly fastigiate tree which was found in the forests of Sweden. It may prove to be a substitute for the canker-infested Lombardy Poplar. Based on evaluations of plants in the Illinois trials, the leaves contract a severe leaf spot and defoliated by early August. Specimens at the Minnesota Landscape Arboretum and Arnold Arboretum appeared in outstanding condition. 'Pendula' is a weeping form with stiffly pendulous branches and grayish purple catkins. The tree is best adapted to colder climates. *Populus* × *canescens* embodies hybrids between *P. alba* and *P. tremula*. 'Pyramidalis' and 'Tower' are upright forms, the latter almost columnar, resistant to stem cankers, and adapted to stresses of northern great plains, Morden introduction. The species is native to Europe, northern Africa, western Asia and Siberia. Zone 2 to 5.

Populus tremuloides Michx. — Quaking Aspen

LEAVES: Alternate, simple, thin, ovate to orbicular, short-acuminate, truncate to broad-cuneate at base, 1 1/2 to 3″ long and wide, finely glandular-serrate, lustrous dark green above, glabrous and glaucescent beneath, leaves of suckers ovate, large, glabrous; petiole—1 to 2 1/2″ long, slender, flattened.
BUDS: Terminal—imbricate, conical, sharp-pointed, sometimes very slightly resinous, 6- to 7-scaled, reddish brown; laterals—incurved, similar to terminal but smaller.
STEM: Slender, lustrous, reddish brown.
BARK: Smooth, greenish white to cream-colored; in old age furrowed, dark brown or gray, roughened by numerous wart-like excrescences.

Populus tremuloides, (pop´ū-lus trem-ū-loy´dēz), Quaking Aspen, is the most widely distributed tree of North America. It is fast-growing, relatively short-lived and attains heights of 40 to 50´ with a spread of 20 to 30´. National champion is 109´ by 59´ in Ontonagon Co., MI. Pyramidal and narrow when young, usually with a long trunk and narrow, rounded crown at maturity. Indifferent as to soil conditions and over its range can be found in moist, loamy sands to shallow rocky soils and clay. The leaves flutter in the slightest breeze; hence, the name Quaking Aspen. The fall color is a good yellow. Ornamentally not important because of disease and insect problems but, nonetheless, an interesting tree. The wood is important for pulpwood and other uses. Native from Labrador to Alaska, south to Pennsylvania, Missouri, northern Mexico and lower California. Introduced 1812. Zone 1 to 6(7). Have seen a population in the Piedmont of Georgia.

Potentilla fruticosa L. — Bush Cinquefoil
(pō-ten-til′á frö-ti-kō′sá)

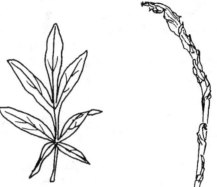

FAMILY: Rosaceae

LEAVES: Alternate, compound pinnate, elliptic to linear-oblong, 3 to 7 leaflets, usually 5, 1/2 to 1″ long, sessile, acute, with revolute margin, light medium blue to dark green, sometimes lustrous, more or less silky.

STEMS: Shiny brown, slender, wispy, exfoliating with age.

SIZE: 1 to 4′ in height and 2 to 4′ or larger in spread; dainty in size considerations.

HARDINESS: Zone 2 to 6(7), does not perform well in Zone 7; have tested several selections with no long term success.

HABIT: Very bushy shrub with upright slender stems forming a low, rounded to broad-rounded outline.

RATE: Slow.

TEXTURE: Fine in leaf, medium-fine in winter; refined, graceful appearance in foliage.

STEM COLOR: Interesting in winter if framed by a new snow; peeling, shredding, brown in color.

LEAF COLOR: Leafs out early in spring, silky gray-green when unfolding changing to bright to dark green in mature leaf; fall color is green to yellow-brown, not ornamental.

FLOWERS: Perfect, bright buttercup yellow, about 1 to 1 1/2″ across, June through until frost, borne singly or in few-flowered cymes, excellent color addition to any garden; numerous cultivars provide interesting color variation.

FRUIT: Achene, not showy, persistent.

CULTURE: Fibrous rooted, transplants well, of easy culture; withstands poor, dry soils and extreme cold; full sun for best flower although they seem to do well in partial shade; best in a fertile, moist, well-drained soil; most plants are container-grown; in the wild occasionally found in bogs but more common on wet or dry open ground especially that of calcareous origin; this is one of the reasons they perform so well in the midwestern states; remove one-third of the canes or renewal prune in late winter.

DISEASES AND INSECTS: Relatively free from insect and disease pests; there are several leaf spots and mildews which affect the plant but they are rarely serious; spider mites can be troublesome.

LANDSCAPE VALUE: Shrub border, massing, edging plant, low hedge, perennial border, facer plant, can be integrated into the foundation planting and will add a degree of color unattainable with most plants, dainty clean foliage, good flower color and length of flowering period justify wider landscape consideration; can become ragged with time and proper pruning practices should be employed; I tried to grow 'Goldfinger' in my Georgia garden but the plant lacked vigor and never measured up to performance in Zone 4 to 6; high night temperatures may be the limiting factor.

CULTIVARS: I am hedging on my responsibility by including all the cultivars together but for ease of presentation have chosen this approach. Cultivars have been selected from several species, *P. arbuscula* D. Don., *P. davurica* Nestl., *P. fruticosa*, and *P. parvifolia* (Lehm.) Th. as well as from hybrids between these. Excellent review of "The Shrubby Potentillas," appeared in *The Plantsman* 9(2):90–109 (1987). Article discusses culture, taxonomy, and cultivars. Since the 1983 edition, I have seen many new cultivars come onto the market, some good, others miserable. In addition, during sabbatical I carefully evaluated the entire collection at the Arnold Arboretum. Also, Bachtell and Hasselkus. *American Nurseryman* 153(3): 83–89 reported on their evaluations of *Potentilla* cultivars. Also used Bressingham Gardens catalog as a source for new introductions and consulted Krüssmann for more specifics. All of this information has been distilled and is presented here as a rather heterogeneous average that should serve as a reasonable guide to the selection of the best types.

Interestingly, *The New RHS Dictionary of Gardening* treats *P. fruticosa* as a polymorphic species and reduces the above species to varieties. In practice, it might be wise to consider all under the genetic umbrella of *P. fruticosa*. Cultivars exceed 130 and new additions, particularly from Europe and Canada, occur yearly. This edition discusses 81 cultivars.

'Abbottswood'—Dark bluish green foliage, spreading habit, large white flowers produced over a long period, considered one of the best whites, truly outstanding in flower, 3′ high, 3′ wide.

'Abbottswood Silver'—Leaves with creamy white margins, the entire shrub rather handsome on close inspection, does not appear to be a vigorous grower and is not preferable to 'Abbottswood'; flowers are white, probably only good in cooler climates, 24 to 30″ by 24 to 30″.

'Annette'—Orange-yellow flowers, compact dome shape, relatively new from Europe.

'Apricot Whisper'—Apricot flowers, light green foliage, oval-rounded habit, 2 to 3′ high, University of Manitoba introduction.

'Bann Bannoch'—Strong bushy constitution, a continuum of primrose yellow flowers, 30 to 36″ high.

'Beanii'—White flowers, shiny dark green leaves, medium height, irregular rounded form, severe dieback at –19°F.

'Beesii'—Buttercup yellow, 3/4″ diameter flowers, producing stamens only (should be fruitless), leaves rather silvery green, slow-growing to 2′ high.

'Boskoop Red'—Flame red flowers early in season becoming lighter later, bright green foliage on a semi-dwarf plant.

'Buttercup'—Deep yellow, 1″ wide flowers, pale green leaves, low, mounded, fine-textured form, severe dieback at –19°F.

'Coronation Triumph'—A large clone, 3 to 4′, with a softer green foliage cast compared to 'Jackmanii'; the habit is dense, full, and mounded, and the bright yellow 1″ diameter flowers are borne in great quantity; Drs. Jim Klett, Colorado State University and Dale Hermann, North Dakota State University voted it one of the best for their area; in my Illinois garden it outperformed 'Jackmanii'.

Dakota Goldrush™ ('Absaraka')—Comparable to 'Jackmanii', possibly more compact, golden yellow, 1 to 1 1/2″ wide flowers, flowers more profusely, especially late in season, 3 to 3 1/2′ by 4 to 5′, dark green foliage, North Dakota State University introduction.

'Dakota Sunrise'—Tends toward prostrate habit the first year, eventually dense and rounded, 1″ diameter, bright yellow flowers from June until frost, 2 to 3′, considered hardy to Zone 2, introduced in 1978.

Dakota Sunspot® ('Fargo')—Vivid yellow (deep golden), 1″ diameter flowers, spring to frost, compact-spreading habit, 2 to 3′ high, 3 to 4′ wide, North Dakota State University introduction.

'Dart's Golddigger'—A low-spreading form with large golden flowers, raised in Darthuizer Nurseries, Holland.

'Daydawn' ('Day Dawn')—Handsome form in a cool climate, peach pink, suffused with cream, flowers fade in heat to cream, tall mounded form with medium green leaves, 30″ high, sport of 'Tangerine'.

'Donard Gold'—Low-spreading form, perhaps 20″ high but much wider, green foliage, large golden yellow flowers.

'Elizabeth' ('Arbuscula')—Flowers rich, soft yellow and up to 1 1/2″ diameter, flowering over a long period, leaves somewhat grayish green, bushy shrub to 3′, I have always liked this form, 'Sutters Gold' is same plant, described in English literature as susceptible to mildew and mites.

'Farreri' ('Gold Drop')—Flowers deep yellow, 3/4 to 1″ diameter, leaves very small, 25-year-old plant—2′ tall and 3′ across, small bright green leaves, moderate flowering at Arnold.

'Farreri Prostrata'—Buttercup yellow, 1 1/4″ diameter flowers on a 1 1/2′ by 3′ shrub.

'Floppy Disc'—Deep pink, double flowers, long flower period, may fade in heat, low-spreading habit, 10 to 18″ high.

'Forrestii'—Medium yellow, large flowers, most abundant in late summer, gray-green leaves, coarse texture, low, mounded form, foliage may become bronzed and chlorotic in late summer.

'Friedrichsenii' ('Berlin Beauty')—Flowers creamy white to pale yellow, 1″ diameter, 58-year-old plant is 4 1/2′ high and 6′ across (hybrid origin), sparse flowered at Arnold, resembles 'Maanelys' but is more open, from a grex of several clones.

'Gold Carpet'—Improved form of 'Arbuscula', mildew-free with large deep yellow flowers.

'Gold Drop'—Often a common name for the yellow-flowered potentillas; in actuality a clone with 7/8″ diameter yellow flowers on a dwarf bushy framework, see 'Farreri'.

'Goldfinger'—Compact, mounded, 3′ by 4′ shrub with large, bright yellow, 1 3/4″ diameter flowers that occur into fall, dark green foliage, it has proven to be a superior clone in the Midwest.

'Goldstar' ('Gold Star')—This form keeps cropping up in my European travels and I believe it will become popular in the future; deep yellow-gold, 1 1/2 to 2″ diameter flowers are borne in abundance particularly in cool climates, mildew resistant and trouble-free, 3′ high, 2 to 2 1/2′ across, from West Germany.

'Goldteppich'—Somewhat similar to 'Dart's Golddigger' with smaller flowers and larger, deeper green leaves, golden yellow, 1 1/4 to 1 1/2″ diameter flowers are produced in great numbers.

'Grandiflora'—Flowers bright yellow, 1 3/8″ diameter, with large dark green leaves, ultimate height about 6′, abundant flowers, 3′ by 4′ at Arnold.

'Hollandia Gold'—Large, dark yellow flowers, medium green leaves, medium texture, low, mounded form, suffers chlorosis and leaf scorch under water stress.

'Hopley's Little Joker'—Seedling of 'Red Ace', very compact and low-growing, flowers are red but fade to white with a red margin, particularly in the heat.

'Hopley's Orange'—Rounded shrub, 2' by 2', warm deep orange flowers, flowers on-and-off for several months, color less intense in heat, Bressingham Nursery introduction, original plant from same nursery that produced 'Red Ace'.

'Hurstborne'—Bright yellow small flowers on a fine-textured, compact, globe form.

'Irving'—Golden yellow small flowers on a fine-textured, dense, 3' high shrub.

'Jackmanii' ('Jackman's Variety')—A larger form, 3 to 4' high, good dark green almost bluish green foliage color, and a profusion of bright yellow, 1 1/4 to 1 1/2" diameter flowers, has performed well in the Midwest, stops flowering before 'Goldfinger' and 'Coronation Triumph' at least in the Urbana, IL area, originated in the nursery of Messrs. Jackson, Woking, Surrey, England.

'Katherine Dykes'—A fine form with gracefully arching branches and seldom growing more than 2 to 3' high, the medium green foliage is glaucous-tinged and provides a framework for the lemon yellow, 1" or slightly wider flowers that are freely produced, 4 1/2' by 3 1/2' at Arnold, with age may become twiggy and unattractive, have read size estimates of greater than 6' high, arose in the garden of W.R. Dykes and named after his wife.

'Klondike' ('Klondyke')—A dwarf, compact shrub about 2' high is studded with 1 1/2" diameter, deep yellow flowers, foliage is bright green above, bluish green below, not performing well at Arnold.

'Knaphill'—Small, bright yellow flowers produced all season, medium green leaves, fine texture, dense low-mounded form, rated highly by Bachtell and Hasselkus, showed good tolerance to water stress but suffered slight dieback at -19°F.

'Kobold'—Low, compact, fresh green leaves, masses of small, yellow flowers from June into fall, 18" or greater.

'Lady Daresbury'—Large, bright yellow flowers, 1 1/2" diameter, sparsely produced after initial strong showing, blue-green leaves, medium height, to 3', and broad-spreading form, foliage chlorotic and bronzed under water stress.

'Logan'—Dark yellow flowers, pale green leaves, fine-textured, low, mounded form, may suffer from water stress.

'Longacre'—Similar to 'Elizabeth' but lower and more spreading, flowers large, bright sulfur-yellow, shiny dark green leaves, 3' by 4', heavy flowers at Arnold, self-sown seedling at Longacre Garden, Northern Ireland.

'Maanelys' ('Moonlight')—Soft yellow flowers about 1 1/4" diameter fading as they age but remaining darker at the center, foliage soft gray-green and silky above, whitish underneath, flowers from May to July–August, considered a low, mounded grower although may reach 4 to 5' by 8'; 4' by 4', 3/4" diameter yellow flowers at Arnold.

'Manchu' (var. *mandshurica*)—White flowers, 1" diameter, not prolific, a dense mounded shrub about 1 to 1 1/2' high, grayish green foliage, a rather wispy, shabby shrub at the Arnold.

'McKay's White'—Creamy white-flowering sport of 'Katherine Dykes' that occurred at McKay Nursery, WI, 2 to 3' high and 2 to 3' wide, no fruits, Zone 3.

'Mount Everest'—White, 1 to 1 1/2" diameter flowers in spring and summer on an upright branching shrub, 3' high, 5 leaflets, narrow, yellow-green.

'Mount Townsend'—Double to semi-double, yellow flowers, freely produced throughout summer (Washington), 18" high, discovered on Townsend Mountain in the Olympic Mountains in June 1994.

'Northman'—Rich yellow flowers, sage-green leaves and small habit.

'Ochroleuca'—A seedling of 'Friedrichsenii' with bright green leaves and small cream-colored flowers, small erect shrub to 6', may be confused in the trade for was described as spreading 4' by 6'.

'Pink Beauty'—Attractive pink flowers, free-flowering, 2' by 2 1/2', flower color holds reasonably well in heat, bred by Louis Lentz, University of Manitoba.

'Pink Pearl'—Large, mid-pink flowers on a neat, mounded, spreading shrub, 16 to 20" high.

'Pink Whisper'—Flowers blushed with deep pink, may fade to soft yellow in heat, small to medium size, 2 to 3', University of Manitoba introduction.

'Pixie Gold'—Smallish, 3/4", bright yellow flowers on 12 to 18" high and wide plant, small green leaves, Carroll Gardens introduction.

'Pretty Polly'—Small, salmon pink flowers on a compact shrub, 14 to 20" high.

'Primrose Beauty'—A small (3'), free-flowering shrub with 1 3/8" diameter, primrose with deeper center flowers that pale with age, grayish green foliage, may grow 4 to 5' high and 6' wide, allied to 'Vilmoriniana' but is better and is considered one of the finest of all the garden hybrids, moderate flowering at Arnold.

'Princess'—Delicate pink flowers, white on the reverse, May into October but become smaller and may fade to white in the heat of summer, robust shrub to 30", Bressingham Gardens introduction, beautiful as I have seen it in England, doubtfully as nice in the heat of the United States.

'Pyrenaica'—Perhaps a misnomer but plants with this name are dwarfish, 6 to 18″ high, and have 1″ diameter, bright yellow flowers.

'Red Ace'—I would like to relate that this is a superior red-flowering form but, unfortunately, that is not the case. It was introduced through Bressingham Gardens, England, and described as having 1″ diameter, flaming vermillion petals, undercoated with yellow on an ultra-hardy, 2 1/2′ by 2 1/2′ framework. In the United States it is a weak grower and the flowers in heat or drought bleach out to yellow or pale orange-red. It is also quite susceptible to mite damage and leaf scorch. I grew it in my Illinois garden and was woefully disappointed; handsome in England where I have seen it in June; will fade there also in summer. Arose as a chance seedling in 1973 in the nursery of Hopley's Plants, Much Hadham, England.

'Red Robin'—Single, red flowers on a 24″ by 28″ framework, small attractive green leaves, Hines introduction.

'Red Sunset'—Orange flowers fading to yellow, listed by Leo Gentry, possibly a rename.

'Rhodocalyx'—Low-growing, flowers nodding, corolla white, pedicel and calyx crimson.

'Royal Flush'—A seedling from 'Red Ace' with rosy pink, yellow-centered flowers on a compact shrub, 12 to 18″ high (twice as wide), leaves dark green, will lose its color and fade to soft pink or cream in hot weather.

'Ruth'—Small shrub, erect habit, with nodding, bell-shaped, cream flowers with red calyces.

'Sandra'—Ivory-white, 1 3/8″ diameter flowers on a 3′ high bushy shrub.

'Scarlet'—Red, from Leo Gentry, possibly a rename.

'Snowbird'—Cream-white, semi-double, 10 to 15 petals, dark green leaves, 2 to 3′ mounded habit, University of Manitoba introduction.

'Snowflake'—Flowers white, single to semi-double, 1″ diameter, not vigorous at Arnold.

'Sommerflor'—Listed in *Deutscher Gartenbau* 43:1282–1284 (1989) without description.

'Stocker's Variety'—White flowers, sparsely produced, glossy dark green leaves, almost leathery in appearance, medium texture, dense, globe form.

'Sundance'—Butter yellow, double flowers, light green foliage, 2 to 3′, University of Manitoba introduction.

'Sunset'—Pale yellow flowers tinged orange, retaining their unusual color but produced in small numbers, shiny medium green leaves, fine-texture, tall-mounded form, foliage may be chlorotic under water stress, has been noted that color may fade to yellow in hot weather.

'Sutter's Gold'—Bright yellow, silvery foliage, low-growing, 1 to 2′ by 3′.

'Tangerine'—Medium yellow, pale copper orange or flushed with orange-red (copper-red) under ideal conditions, in full sun, flowers are yellow, 1 1/4″ wide, gray-green leaves, 2′ by 4′, mounded, spreading shrub, raised by Slieve Donard Nurseries, Newcastle, Co. Down, Ireland.

'Tilford Cream'—White flowers on a compact plant, 12 to 18″ high, leaves bright green.

'Veitchii'—White flowers with dull red stamens, 1″ diameter, pale green leaves, to 5′ high.

'Vilmoriniana'—Flowers pale yellow to creamy white with a yellow center, up to 1 1/2″ diameter, silvery green leaves, stiffly erect shrub, 4 to 5′ high, flowers borne sparsely over a long period.

'Walton Park'—Golden yellow, 1 1/2 to 1 3/4″ diameter flowers, leaves deep green above, blue-green beneath, spreading shrub to 2′ high.

'White Gold'—Medium yellow, large flowers, gray-green leaves, coarse-textured, low, mounded form, chlorosis and foliage bronzing may occur under water stress.

'William Purdom' ('Purdomii')—Canary yellow flowers, with a deeper center, 1 1/8″ diameter, bright green leaves, fine-textured, large rounded, open, 4 to 6′ high.

'Woodbridge Gold'—Flowers buttercup-yellow, 1 1/4″ diameter, abundant over several months, leaves rich green and rather glossy, low-growing to about 2′ by 3′.

'Yellow Gem'—Bright yellow, 1 1/4″ diameter flowers, ruffled attractive petals, May until frost, gray-green leaves, 16″ high by 40″ wide, University of British Columbia Botanical Garden introduction.

'Yellowbird'—Double yellow flowers, 8 to 10 petals, may produce single flowers, new from Canada.

PROPAGATION: Seeds require no pretreatment. Softwood cuttings rooted 100% under mist in peat:perlite when treated with 1000 ppm IBA; very easy to root from softwood cuttings but reduce the water as soon as they root; tissue culture has been successful, see *Plant, Cell, Tissue Organ Culture* 32:235–240 (1993).

ADDITIONAL NOTES: Wyman noted that one cultivar grown in the Arnold Arboretum in the same location for 60 years was 3′ tall and had never required pruning or spraying. I have seen the Arnold and the Minnesota Landscape Arboreta's extensive collections of *Potentilla fruticosa* and wondered how anyone could separate them without labels. Many look similar in flower color, habit, and foliage characteristics. The logical approach would be to select the best 5 to 10 and use this as a guide. From what I understand continued breeding and selection is occurring so, no doubt, more clones will inundate an already confused group of plants. Their extreme hardiness and summer flowering sequence make them valuable landscape plants.

In June 1996, as I scurried through the National Botanical Garden of Ireland (Glasnevin) a *P. fruti-cosa* collection jumped in front of my camera and tape recorder. Madly I spat words into the machine with camera smoking and belching. After 20 minutes of this insaneness, I became totally confused by the similarity of habit, foliage, flower, et al., told myself it was time to quit and walked to the butterfly-bush collection, a much easier group to distinguish, particularly since they were only in leaf. There is a moral here. I will let the reader decide.
NATIVE HABITAT: Northern Hemisphere.

Prinsepia sinensis (Oliv.) Oliv. — Cherry Prinsepia
(prin-sē′pi-à sī-nen′sis)

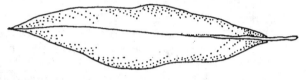

FAMILY: Rosaceae
LEAVES: Alternate on current season's growth, pro-duced in clusters on the year old shoots, simple, ovate-lanceolate to lanceolate, 2 to 3″ long, about 1/2″ wide, long acuminate, entire or sparingly serrulate, finely ciliate, otherwise glabrous, bright green; petiole—slender.
BUDS: Small, indistinctly scaly, concealed in brown hairs, buds may develop into spines.
STEM: Long and slender, round, spiny (1/4 to 1/2″ long), light gray-brown; pith—chambered; on older stems the bark exfoliates to varying degrees.

SIZE: 6 to 10′ in height and as wide; specimen at Arnold is 10′ high and wide.
HARDINESS: Zone 4 to 7; Cappiello reported as not cold hardy in Maine, however Minnesota Landscape and Morton Arboreta have grown for years.
HABIT: Haystack to rounded, dense, spiny shrub well-adapted for hedges and screens.
RATE: Medium.
TEXTURE: Medium in leaf, perhaps medium-coarse in winter.
BARK: On old stems brown and shredding off in long papery strips.
LEAF COLOR: Bright green in summer; fall color of little consequence, perhaps yellow-green; usually the first shrub to leaf out, have seen leaves in early to mid-March at the Arnold Arboretum; during 1991 sabbatical at Arnold leaves were one-third developed by March 25, also drops leaves early in fall.
FLOWERS: Perfect, small, light yellow, 5-petaled, 10-stamened, almost creamy yellow, borne in fascicles of 1 to 4 on previous year's wood in March–April, each flower about 3/5″ diameter, on a 1/2″ long pedicel, worthwhile but not overwhelming.
FRUIT: Red, cherry-like, 1/2″ long, subglobose or ovoid drupe which ripens in July, August and September and is effectively digested by birds; color is actually more orange to purple than red; supposedly edible; contains large amounts of ascorbic acid, dry matter content is 2.5 to 4 times that of currants, cherries, and apples; less sugar than most cultivated fruit plants; stone ovoid, flattened.
CULTURE: Easily transplanted, of undemanding culture, requiring only fertile, well-drained soil and open, sunny location; probably best to renewal prune when plants become overgrown; withstands pruning quite favorably.
DISEASES AND INSECTS: One of its principal merits is resistance to pests.
LANDSCAPE VALUE: Not a very common shrub but one certainly worth considering for hedges, screens or barriers; quite serviceable shrub and requires minimal maintenance; the endearing trait of being the first shrub to thrust its green leaves upon the spring landscape makes it worthwhile considering; no one characteristic is particularly outstanding but the sum of all the parts equals a good, serviceable shrub that could be utilized effectively on difficult sites.
PROPAGATION: Apparently seed germination is somewhat variable and the reports in the literature do not emphasize the best treatment; seeds will germinate when sown directly but a 2 to 3 month cold treatment definitely improves germination. Cuttings collected in June rooted 65 to 75% when treated with 3000 to 8000 ppm IBA; 100% rooting was obtained with August cuttings and 8000 ppm IBA, mist; a higher hormone concentration is advisable.
    Prinsepia uniflora appears more difficult to germinate and root; seeds will germinate if sown directly but cold treatments have produced variable results. Cuttings are difficult but can be rooted in July and August with high hormone and patience; during sabbatical I tried to root this species but was unable to induce a single root.
NATIVE HABITAT: Manchuria. Cultivated 1896.

RELATED SPECIES:

Prinsepia uniflora Batal. — Hedge Prinsepia

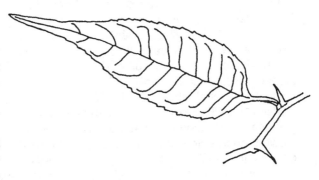

LEAVES: Alternate, simple, linear-oblong to narrow-oblong, 1 to 2″ long, 1/2 to 3/4″ wide, distinctly toothed, each serration terminated by a short bristle, lustrous dark green above, light green below, glabrous; petiole—1/4″ long.

BUDS: Small, indistinctly scaly, long, slender, scale-like appendages tend to mat together.

STEM: Slender, pale-gray to straw-brown, slight ridges, glabrous, small orangish bumps (lenticels); spines 1/2″ long, slender, sharp-pointed, borne singly above a node; pith—greenish white, finely chambered.

Prinsepia uniflora, (prin-sē′pi-á ū-ni-flō′rá), Hedge Prinsepia, is a rather thorny, moderately dense aggregate of light gray branches growing 4 to 5′ high with a similar spread. The Minnesota Landscape Arboretum has both species growing side-by-side and the growth habit and foliage characteristic differences become immediately evident. The leaves are very dark green, 1 to 2″ long and not as densely borne as those of *P. sinensis*. The flowers are white, 3/5″ wide, 5-petaled, 10-stamened, 1 to 3 together along with the leaves from nodes of the previous season's growth, on a 1/4″ long glabrous pedicel. The fruits are globose, about 1/2″ long, dark purplish red, bloomy, maturing in late summer. The stone is ovoid, flattened. The fruits are quite handsome and hang down from the branches in a rather pretty fashion. Interestingly, of two plants in the Arnold Arboretum, one fruited heavily, the other bore no fruits. This species would also make a good hedge or barrier and on the basis of foliage color is superior to *P. sinensis*. Rare in cultivation. Native to northwestern China. Introduced 1911. Zone 3 to 5(6).

Prunus L. — Cherries, Peaches, Plums, Apricots, Almonds
FAMILY: Rosaceae

The genus *Prunus* comprises over 400 species and numerous hybrids. The distinctions between species and cultivars are often difficult. Herein, I have presented an encapsulated treatment of the more popular ornamental types. The cherries provide a freshness to our gardens that is seldom achieved with any other plant. The delicate flowers pass quickly but in their finest hours are the equal of any ornamental tree. Unfortunately, *Prunus* as a group is beset with insect and disease problems and perhaps should not be looked upon as long term garden investments. Some, such as *Prunus subhirtella*, *P. sargentii* and selected *P. serrulata* types, can be expected to live for 30 to 50 years while *P. persica*, *P. cerasifera* 'Atropurpurea' and *P. glandulosa* may decline in 3 to 10 years.

Leaves are alternate, usually serrate with prominent, usually vestigial stipules. Flowers are white, pink to red, solitary, in clusters or racemes, 5-petaled, 5-lobed calyx, numerous stamens, solitary pistil, ovary superior. Fruit is a 1-seeded drupe of various shapes, usually bloomy; stone often compressed.

Since the 1990 edition, I have monitored flowering cherry performance from Maine to the coast of Georgia and northern Florida. For the colder climates, I would opt for *P. sargentii* and *P. subhirtella*, in the mid to deep South, *P. × yedoensis*, *P. campanulata* and *P.* 'Okame'.

ADDITIONAL NOTES: Two excellent books include Collingwood Ingram. 1948. *Ornamental Cherries*. Country Life, LTD, London; and Geoffrey Chadbund. 1972. *Flowering Cherries*. Collins, London. The first individual is considered the greatest force in ornamental cherry breeding and introduction. His 'Okame', correctly *P. × incamp* 'Okame', was introduced in 1947 and 50 some odd years later is receiving rave reviews from American gardeners. See discussion under *P. campanulata*. A trip through Ingram's book opens one's eyes to the beauty and diversity of flowering cherries.

Prunus americana Marsh. — American Red Plum, also known as Wild Plum, August Plum, Hog Plum

LEAVES: Alternate, simple, obovate to oblong-ovate, 2 to 4″ long, 1 1/4 to 1 3/4″ wide, acuminate, broad cuneate, sharply and doubly serrate, dark green and glabrous, or slightly pubescent on midrib below; petiole—1/3 to 3/4″ long, pubescent, without glands.

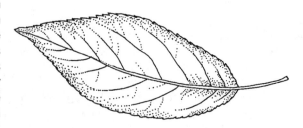

Prunus americana, (prö′nus à-mer-i-kā′nà), American Plum, is a common shrub or small tree, often forming large colonies along roadsides, in waste areas and other uncultivated habitats throughout its native range. I have seen the typical colonies which almost remind of sumacs the way they spread. Also, single-stemmed, 15 to 25′ trees are evident. National champion is 48′ by 36′ in Gadsden Co., FL. Flowers are pure white, about 1″ diameter, 2 to 5 together in sessile umbels, each flower on a slender, 2/3 to 1″ long, glabrous pedicel. Flowers open before the leaves in early to mid-March in Athens and depending on temperature are effective for 5 to 7 up to 14 days. A pronounced difference in flowering times is evident as one colony will be spent while another is in full splendor. Flowers have that sickly sweet typical plum species odor. Fruits are generally yellow to red, rounded, about 1″ long with yellow flesh that ripens in June–July. The fruits are utilized for jellies and jams. Cultivars have been selected for superior fruit quality. Obviously requires no special cultural requirements. Tends to thrive with neglect. Found from Massachusetts to Manitoba, south to Georgia, New Mexico and Utah. Cultivated 1768. Zone 3 to 8.

RELATED SPECIES:

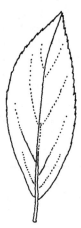

Prunus angustifolia Marsh., (prö′nus an-gus-ti-fō′li-à), Chickasaw Plum, is another suckering, colonizing shrub with comparable attributes. National champion is 32′ by 32′ in Henderson Co., NC. Branches are covered with thorn-like side branches. The leaves are 1 to 2″ long, one-third as wide, oval-lanceolate, strongly trough-shaped, acute, broad cuneate or rounded, fine glandular-serrate margined, lustrous dark green above. The white, 1/2″ diameter flowers occur 2 to 4 together before the leaves. Fruit is a 1/2″ diameter, rounded, lustrous red (yellow) drupe. This species is quite common in the Southeast and forms large, suckering colonies much like *Rhus glabra*. Flowers are evident in early March (Athens) and remind that spring is close at hand. Doubtfully useful in a contrived, cultivated situation but has merit for highway plantings and wildlife areas. Maryland and southern Delaware to Florida, west to Arkansas and Texas. Introduced around 1874. Zone 5 to 9.

Prunus avium L. — Mazzard or Sweet Cherry

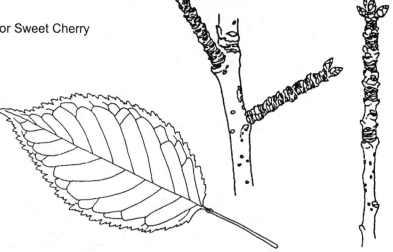

LEAVES: Alternate, simple, oblong-ovate, 2 to 6″ long, 1 1/2 to 2″ wide, acuminate, unequally serrate, dull dark green and often slightly rugose above, more or less pubescent beneath, of soft texture; petiole—1 to 1 3/4″ long with prominent often reddish glands near the blade.

Prunus avium, (prö′nus ā′vi-um), Mazzard or Sweet Cherry, is a large tree of conical shape growing to 70′ or more but usually under cultivation reaches 30 to 40′ with a similar spread. National champion is 80′ by 80′ in West Chester, PA. The emerging foliage is bronze, becoming deep green in summer and turns yellow to bronze in fall. Flowers are white, 1 to 1 1/2″ diameter, fragrant, mid to late April, in several flowered umbels. The fruit is a reddish black, rounded drupe about 1″ in diameter. This is the species from which most of our popular sweet cherry clones are derived. On a garden tour through Germany, the plant was everywhere in evidence on the slopes above the Rhine River. Also, at Mainau, the species was underplanted with tulips and daffodils, all flowering at the same time. Although not common as an ornamental in the Midwest and East, it is one of the longer lived cherries. 'Plena' has double, white, 1 1/2″ diameter flowers with as many as 30 petals and is superior to the species for flower effect. The Arnold Arboretum had a tree that was spectacular when in flower. An enterprising nurseryman could sell this form. There are other clones of limited importance. Europe, western Asia. Cultivated since ancient times. Zone 3 to 8. One of the hardiest cherries and might be used where the Oriental types are not hardy. Does reasonably well in Athens.

Prunus besseyi Bail. — Western Sand Cherry, Sand Cherry

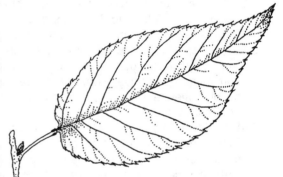

LEAVES: Alternate, simple, oval, oval-lanceolate, sometimes obovate, 1 to 2 1/2″ long, acute, cuneate, shallowly serrate on upper two-third's, glabrous, gray-green; petiole—1/4″ long.

Prunus besseyi, (prö′nus bes′sē-ī), Western Sand Cherry, is a suckering, spreading, 4 to 6′ high and wide shrub. The gray-green leaves are rather attractive and provide a different foliage color than most *Prunus* species. In late April–early May the shrub literally glows with pure white, 1/2″ diameter flowers that give way to sweet, purplish black, 3/4″ long fruits in July and August. I have only seen the plant in flower on one occasion and, indeed, it is attractive but cannot compete with the Oriental cherries. The species is found in the great plains and tolerates rather inhospitable, hot, dry conditions. It prefers a well-drained soil. Many cultivars have been selected for fruit quality with 'Black Beauty' (small, black, sweet) and 'Hansen's' (large, purple-black, flavorful) the most notable. Manitoba to Wyoming, south to Kansas and Colorado. Introduced 1892. Zone 3 to 6.

Prunus campanulata Maxim. — Bell-flowered, Taiwan or Formosan Cherry

LEAVES: Alternate, simple, ovate, oval or slightly obovate, 2 1/2 to 4 1/2″ long, 1 to 1 3/4″(2 1/2″) wide, slender-pointed, broadly wedge-shaped to slightly heart-shaped at the base, margins regularly set with fine forward-pointing or slightly incurved teeth, lustrous dark green, 6 to 8 vein pairs, glabrous; petiole—1/2 to 3/4″ long; stipules feathery, much divided.

Prunus campanulata, (prö′nus kam-pan-ū-lā′tà), Bell-flowered, Taiwan or Formosan Cherry, is a small, graceful tree ranging from 20 to 30′ in height. The young leaves emerge rich green and become dark green at maturity and develop bronzy red fall color. Before the leaves emerge, the deep rose, 3/4″ diameter flowers appear 2 to 6 together on 1/2 to 3/4″ long pedicels that arise from a 1 to 1 1/2″ long peduncle. The calyx tube is also deep rose and offers color after the petals have abscised. The red fruits are about 1/2″ long and about 3/8″ wide. In my mind, the flowers may be the most handsome of all ornamental cherries. I have seen flowers as early as late January in Athens, GA, but they usually open in February. I have been in Savannah on February 22 and the leaves were almost fully mature. In my garden the tree was in full leaf by mid-March. Several years past I received a seedling from the late Mr. Jack Jones, Savannah, GA after admiring flowering trees in his garden. The tree is now 15′ high and as wide with 3 strong, polished, reddish brown trunks. It ranks as one of my all time favorites simply because it is the first to flower and offers spectacular rose-carmine flowers. Because of the early flowering date, buds and/or flowers may be injured if they are too far open. Has flowered in early February along with *Hamamelis mollis*. This is a most effective combination, the bright yellow of the witchhazel and the rose-carmine of the cherry. Seeds will germinate in the spring following fall planting, I suspect a slight cold requirement is required. Early June cuttings, 5000 ppm KIBA, peat:perlite, mist, rooted 80%. It is probably best cultivated in the lower part of Zone 7 to 9. Temperatures of 0°F did not injure flower buds. The biological years have extracted their revenge on the Dirr garden specimen and the last vestiges were removed in 1996. Observations indicated that late spring freezes were more damaging than typical Zone 7b winter low temperatures. For best performance, Zone 8 to 9 is recommended. Native to Formosa, southern China, Ryukyu Islands of Japan. Cultivated 1899.

The late Dr. Don Egolf, U.S. National Arboretum, utilized *P. campanulata* in several innovative crosses including hybrids with *P. incisa* and *P. subhirtella* 'Autumnalis Rosea'. I have evaluated these hybrids since 1992 and am impressed by flower color, abundance, plant vigor and heat tolerance in the South.

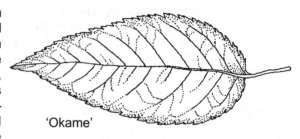

'Okame'

'Okame' with carmine-pink petals (March–April), a rose-red calyx, and reddish flower stalks is hardier and very striking. Flowers are fully open by late February in Athens. Leaves are fully developed by mid to late March. It has performed well in the Arnold Arboretum, Middle Atlantic States and on the Georgia campus. It is the result of a cross between *P. incisa* and *P. campanulata* raised by Collingwood Ingram. It definitely should be more widely planted for it also offers a good bronze to orange-red fall color. 'Okame' received the prestigious Styer Award from the Pennsylvania Horticultural Society and is now common in commerce. Will mature between 20 and 30' with a similar spread. 'Okame' has proven an outstanding cherry for Zone 6 to 8. The habit is almost broad-columnar in youth gradually feathering to a more rounded outline. A small rooted cutting in our garden is now 18' high in only 6 years. The shiny, reddish brown bark is ringed with grayish lenticels; quite handsome in the winter landscape.

A new selection, 'Dream Catcher', was released by the U.S. National Arboretum. It is an open-pollinated seedling of 'Okame' that grew 25' by 20' in 12 years. Bright pink flowers open one week after 'Okame'. Dark green leaves turn orange red in fall; foliage is relatively resistant to insects. Hardy in Zone 6 to 9.

Prunus caroliniana (Mill.) Ait. — Carolina Cherrylaurel
(prö′nus ka-ro-lin-i-ā′nà)

LEAVES: Alternate, simple, evergreen, oblong to oblong-lanceolate, 2 to 3″(4″) long, 1″ (1 1/2″) wide, sharp apex, cuneate margin entire or with several spiny teeth toward apex, leaves on seedlings or young plants more toothed than those from mature plants, glabrous, lustrous dark green; petiole—slender with 2 small glands, red in sun, green in shade.

STEM: Reddish on young stems, brownish on older, with a distinct maraschino cherry odor when bruised or broken, perhaps the most potent odor of the cherries and all have this odor or a modification to some degree.

SIZE: 20 to 30′(40′) high, 15 to 25′ spread; have seen large trees 40′ high with a 30 to 40′ spread; national champion is 47′ by 55′ in Lakeland, FL.

HARDINESS: Zone 7 to 10.

HABIT: Large evergreen shrub, or more often small tree of pyramidal-oval to rounded and irregular outline; usually dense and full but not always uniform in outline; often pruned into a hedge or screen.

RATE: Fast.

TEXTURE: Medium.

BARK: Dark gray to almost black.

LEAF COLOR: Lustrous dark green through the seasons, although will discolor in winter sun and wind; new growth rich yellow green or bronze.

FLOWERS: Perfect, 5-petaled, white, sickeningly fragrant, 1/4″ across, borne in 1 1/2 to 3″ long, 3/4 to 1″ wide racemes out of the leaf axils in March–April (usually late March to early April in Athens); flowers are not overwhelming but welcome by virtue of the early date.

FRUIT: Green maturing to lustrous dark black, 3/8 to 1/2″ diameter, top-shaped drupe, ripen in October, not particularly conspicuous as they are masked by the foliage; persist into winter and until flowering during the spring, abundant; birds deposit the seeds all over the landscape and consequently stray seedlings appear everywhere.

CULTURE: Easily transplanted, adaptable, prefers moist, well-drained soils and here grows like a weed; pH adaptable; withstands heavy pruning; full sun to partial shade.

DISEASES AND INSECTS: Leaf spot, some damage from chewing insects, have not noticed any serious problems, subject to ice, snow, wind damage, have seen what appears to be an *Entomosporium* leaf spot.

LANDSCAPE VALUE: Utilized widely for screens and hedges in the South; has been used to soften harsh vertical lines of large buildings; should not be planted too close to a residence, tends to overgrow its boundaries; used at Williamsburg by the early colonists; one of the few plants that can seed into a privet hedge and win; the weedy nature is something to be considered before making wholesale use of the plant; have seen it "everywhere" in the Coastal Plain of Georgia and South Carolina especially along fence rows and in waste areas, actually makes a pleasant small multi-stemmed tree or large shrub.

CULTIVARS:

Bright 'N Tight™—Compact, tightly branched, pyramidal form with smaller leaves than the species, leaves rarely have serrations, superior to the species for most situations; have seen 15- to 20-year-old plants at Disneyworld about 20′ tall; sold under the name 'Compacta' in much of the nursery trade to avoid the hassle of the trademarked name Bright 'N Tight™.

Cherry Ruffles™—Compact selection with a wavy leaf margin, introduced by Flowerwood Nursery.

PROPAGATION: Seeds can be fall sown and will germinate the following spring; seeds with pulp removed, sown in November, germinated immediately; if a cold requirement exists it is indeed brief, probably 30 days would be sufficient. Softwood and greenwood cuttings will root and I suspect November–January or later hardwoods; cuttings collected on August 23 (Athens), 2000 ppm KIBA, 2 perlite:1 peat, mist, rooted only 50%.

ADDITIONAL NOTES: Distinct cherry odor is evident when stems are bruised; leaves carry a high concentration of hydrocyanic acid which makes the plant unpalatable and dangerous to livestock.

NATIVE HABITAT: Coastal Virginia to northern Florida and west to Louisiana.

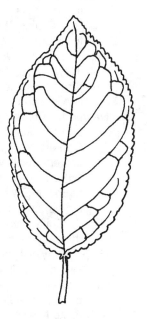

Prunus cerasifera Ehrh. — Cherry Plum or Myrobalan Plum
(prö′nus ser-à-sif′ĕr-à)

FAMILY: Rosaceae

LEAVES: Alternate, simple, ovate, elliptic or obovate, 1 1/2 to 2 1/2″ long, 1 to 1 1/4″ wide, apex pointed, broadly wedge-shaped or rounded, finely obtuse-serrate, glabrous above, bright green above, green beneath, usually less than 6 vein pairs, pubescent on midrib and major veins beneath, petiole—about 1/2″ long; if glands are present they usually occur at base of the blade near the point of petiole attachment.

SIZE: 15 to 30′ by 15 to 25′.

HARDINESS: Zone (4)5 to 8.

HABIT: Small, shrubby tree, twiggy and rounded, with ascending, spreading branches.

RATE: Fast.

TEXTURE: Medium in all seasons.

LEAF COLOR: Light green in summer, no significant fall color.

FLOWERS: Perfect, solitary, white, 3/4 to 1″ across, sickeningly fragrant, sometime in April before the leaves, open around early to mid-April (mid-March, Athens); usually borne solitary.

FRUIT: Reddish, slightly bloomy edible drupe, approximately 1″ across, June, July or August.

CULTURE: This discussion applies to the *Prunus* species. Transplant bare root, balled-and-burlapped or container-grown materials in spring; any average soil is acceptable but should be well-drained; pH adaptable; full sun; prune after flowering although potential fruits will be cut off; keep trees vigorous as there are numerous serious insects and diseases associated with *Prunus*; they are not particularly pollution tolerant and in most cases are short-lived (approximately 20 years) although certain species are much more durable than others; if the gardener would think in decades instead of lifetimes the pleasurable experience of growing some of the *Prunus* would be just that.

DISEASES AND INSECTS: Almost hopeless to list them all but some of the worst include aphids, borers, scale, tent caterpillars, canker, leaf spots.

LANDSCAPE VALUE: The species has no value and is only known in cultivation, but the following cultivars are extensively (over-used) used for specimens, groupings, and in foundation plantings; there is something about a purple-leaved beast that excites people to spend money.

CULTIVARS: For true collectors, the reference *Purpleleaf Plums*, Timber Press (1992) is must reading.

'Alfred'—An unknown to me but described as white-flowered, with 1 1/4″ wide fruit; upright-spreading habit, 20′ by 15′.

'Atropurpurea'—Upright, dense branching form with reddish purple foliage and 3/4″ diameter, light pink flowers, which open before the leaves (usually); often called Pissard Plum ('Pissardii'); introduced into France around 1880 from Persia (now Iran) through the efforts of Mr. Pissard, gardener to the Shah; for best foliage color the purple-leaved forms should be sited in full sun; in this particular form the new unfolding leaves are ruby red, later claret and finally dark reddish purple; the fruits are also purplish; it is shakily hardy in Zone 4 and a hard winter will produce some tip or branch dieback; found as a branch sport before 1880 and a number of selections have arisen from this selection either through hybridization or sports.

'Clark Hill Redleaf'—Tree form, leaves deep red, pink flowers in early March, fruits, 3/4 to 1 1/4″ diameter, red with yellow flesh, originated near Savannah River, collected in 1973/74, possibly of seedling origin, see *Fruit Varieties Journal* 43:58–59 (1989).

'Festeri'—Round-headed tree growing to 30′, pink flowers in spring, leaves red when young, turn purple with age, fruit 1″ long, edible.

'Hessei' ('Hessii')—Has narrow, irregular, reddish brown leaves with a yellowish margin and golden rim.

'Hollywood' (also called 'Trailblazer')—I have never been able to determine the exact nature of this selection and the literature is conflicting; flowers are light pink to white before the leaves, leaves dark green above, red purple below, distinct upright habit and may grow 30′ by 20′, red fruits 2 to 2 1/2″ wide, hybrid between *P. c.* 'Atropurpurea' and the 'Duarte' Japanese plum; have also seen the parentage listed as *P. cerasifera* 'Nigra' × 'Shiro' Japanese plum.

'Krauter Vesuvius'—Similar to 'Thundercloud' but more upright oval-rounded, light pink flowers before leaves, dark purple foliage, 30′ by 20′, supposedly quite heat tolerant; flowers were white-pink, 1/2 to 3/4″ diameter, on March 12 at the Milliken Arboretum, Spartanburg, SC; I compared this cultivar to 'Thundercloud' and simply could not find any tell-tale morphological differences between the two.

'Mt. St. Helens'—A branch sport of 'Newport' with a straighter, stronger trunk, faster growing than 'Newport', leafs out earlier in spring, has longer and wider leaves than the parent, richer purple color that holds later in summer, flowers light pink, round-headed tree, 20′ by 20′, a J. Frank Schmidt introduction.

'Newport'—Probably the hardiest of the purple-leaf types; a cross between *P. cerasifera* 'Atropurpurea' and the 'Omaha' Plum; introduced in 1923 by the University of Minnesota Horticultural Research Center; new growth light bronze-purple, finally changing to dark purple, pale pink to almost white flowers (full flower, mid-February, Athens) and dull purple, 1″ diameter fruits; a round-headed tree 15′(20′) high; best in Zone 5 but can be grown in 4; Cappiello reported occasional tip dieback at Orono, ME, while 'Thundercloud' was killed outright; appears to be the common form in the southern states, and has flowered before 'Atropurpurea' or *P. × cistena* even opened a single bud.

'Nigra'—Foliage very dark purple, color is retained through summer; flowers single, pink, 5/8″ diameter; this may be the same as 'Vesuvius'; also 'Woodii' is similar.

'Purple Pony'—Appears to hold up better in heat, good foliage color like *P. × cistena* but a tree form habit; single, pink flowers; 10 to 12′ high.

'Purpusii'—Have seen several descriptions for the plant: the first called it a delicate scrambled mixture of plum-red and creamy white; the other bronze with yellow and pink variegation along the midrib and white flowers.

'Thundercloud'—Single, pink flowers before the leaves, fragrant, retains its deep purple foliage through growing season; unfortunately, not hardy at Madison, WI and I have observed injury at Urbana, IL, 20′ by 20′, introduced in 1987, at Milliken Arboretum flowers opened later than 'Krauter Vesuvius'; in Michigan study, 30 to 70% defoliation each year by gypsy moth.

'Vesuvius'—See 'Krauter Vesuvius'.

PROPAGATION: *Prunus* seeds have an embryo dormancy and require a period of after-ripening to overcome it; generally 2 to 3 months at 40°F will suffice; seeds can also be cleaned and sown outdoors in fall with germination occurring the following spring. Cuttings show variable response depending on the species and cultivar; there is some indication that NAA may be more effective on *Prunus* than IBA but it is best to start with IBA and then experiment with NAA; in my own work, I have found the purple-leaf types easy to root with 1000 to 3000 ppm quick dip; this also applies to the evergreen *P. laurocerasus* and cultivars; *P.* 'Hally Jolivette' has proven easy; I know nurserymen who are producing 'Kwanzan', *P. × yedoensis* and others from softwood cuttings; from a practical standpoint it is better to establish many *Prunus* on their own roots to avoid possible graft incompatibilities; at Shadow Nursery, Winchester, TN, I have seen two-year-old rooted 'Kwanzan' cherries in the field that were 6 to 8′ high; tremendous movement to own-root cherry and plum; slightly firmer cuttings seem to root in higher percentages than extremely soft May–June material, rooted cuttings will grow if lightly fertilized, overwintering does not appear to be a problem.

NATIVE HABITAT: Western Asia, Caucasia. Introduced before or about the 16th century.

RELATED SPECIES:

Prunus* × *blireana André., (prö′nus blēr-ē-ā′nà), Blireana Plum, is a hybrid between *P. cerasifera* 'Atropurpurea' and a double form of *P. mume*. It is a rounded, dense branching tree with reddish purple foliage
that fades to green and double, 10- to 15-petaled, edges undulating, pleasantly fragrant, pink, 1 to 1 1/4″
diameter flowers in March–April, before the leaves. Fruits are purplish red and lost in the foliage so as not
to be effective. Grows 20′ by 20′. 'Moseri' has deeper purple leaves and smaller flowers, strong-growing,
observed at Hillier Arboretum and did not appear much different than *P.* × *blireana*. Put into commerce
by Lemoine in 1906. Zone 5 to 7.

Prunus* × *cistena (Hansen) Koehne, (prö′nus sis-tē′nà), Purple-
leaf Sand Cherry, is a cross between *P. pumila* and *P.
cerasifera* 'Atropurpurea' and grows 7 to 10′ tall usually with
a slightly smaller spread. The foliage is intensely reddish
purple and stays effective throughout summer. The flowers
are single, pinkish, fragrant, borne after the leaves have
developed in April–early May. Fruits are blackish purple.
Easily propagated from softwood cuttings. One of the hardiest
purple leaf plants. 'Minnesota Red' ('Minnesota Purpleleaf')
has deeper reddish purple leaf coloration that persists into
fall. 'Big Cis' is a branch sport of *P.* × *cistena* that grows twice
as fast producing a rounded, dense, 14′ by 12′, small tree,
the reddish purple leaves are larger, the trunk heavier, flowers
are pink like the parent. A J. Frank Schmidt introduction. All *P.* × *cistena* types in Zone 7b and 8 struggle
and are almost defoliated by late summer. They are much better adapted in the northern climes.
Introduced by Dr. N.E. Hansen of South Dakota State University in 1910. Zone 3b to 7.

Prunus glandulosa Thunb. — Dwarf Flowering Almond

LEAVES: Alternate, simple,
ovate-oblong or oblong to
oblong-lanceolate, 1 to 3
1/2″ long, 3/4 to 1″ wide,
acute, rarely acuminate,
broad-cuneate at base,
crenate-serrulate, medium
green, glabrous beneath
or slightly hairy on midrib;
petiole—1/4″ long; stip-
ules linear with gland-
tipped teeth.

Prunus glandulosa, (prö′nus
glan-dū-lō′sà), Dwarf
Flowering Almond, is the
bargain basement shrub
of many discount stores. It
grows 4 to 5′ tall and 3 to 4′ wide and is a spreading, weakly multi-stemmed, straggly shrub. The summer
foliage is light green. Flowers are pink or white, single or double, late April to early May, one or two
together. Fruits are dark pink-red, 1/2″ across and rarely produced. Chief value is in the flower. Basically
a very poor plant, single season quality, appearing distraught and alone in summer, fall and winter. Cannot
get over the hump with this plant when I consider all the wonderful viburnums that could be utilized.
Stands out in flower and then disappears, perhaps this is not all bad. Roots easily from cuttings. 'Alba' has
pure white, single flowers. 'Alba Plena' ('Alboplena') has double, white flowers and 'Rosea Plena'
('Sinensis') double, 1 to 1 1/4″ diameter, pink flowers. I saw a single, pink-white selection called
'Lawrence' in full flower in late March at Callaway Gardens, the double form nearby was still in tight bud.
Central and northern China, Japan. Introduced 1835. Zone 4 to 8. Some tip dieback at Orono, ME.

Prunus 'Hally Jolivette'

It is the result of a cross of *P. subhirtella* × *P. × yedoensis* backcrossed to *P. subhirtella* by Dr. Karl Sax of the Arnold Arboretum. It is a rounded, dense branching, shrubby tree growing 15′ and of relatively fine texture. The flowers are pink in bud, opening pinkish white, double, 1 1/4″ diameter and effective over a 10 to 20 day period in late April to early May as the flowers do not all open at once. I rooted a cutting and planted it in my Illinois garden. The plant grew 3′ or more a year and in the second year flowered. Still one of my favorite cherries and I have seen 20′ tall trees. Have heard about disease problems that may afflict the tree, but have not observed outright kill. The parentage indicates respectable adaptability. Easy to root from May, June, July cuttings; tissue culture was successful, see *HortScience* 18:182–185 (1983). Introduced 1940. Zone 5 to 7.

Prunus incisa Thunb. — Fuji Cherry

LEAVES: Alternate, simple, ovate to obovate, 1 to 2 1/4″ long, 2/3 to 1 1/4″ wide, acuminate, incisely double serrate, medium to dark green, pubescent above and below on veins; petiole—about 1/3″ long, pubescent with 2 purple glands near blade; leaves reddish when first emerging.

Prunus incisa, (prö′nus in-sī′så), Fuji Cherry, is a large shrub or low-branched tree, generally 15 to 20′(30′) high. In all my travels, I have only seen the species on three occasions. The small delicate leaves turn yellow, bronze, and red in autumn. The flowers are white to pale pink, campanulate, 3/4 to 1″ across, and open before the leaves in March. Petals are notched or jagged at their ends. The flowers are extremely delicate and are subtended by the vinous red calyx. The fruits are 1/4 to 1/3″ long, ovoid, purple-black drupes. This species does not appear long-lived in the midwestern and eastern United States. Served as a parent of 'Okame'. 'February Pink' with early, pale pink flowers; 'Moerheimii' is a spreading, weeping form with long, trailing branches, covered with pale pink flowers. 'Omoinoyama' with profuse, double, pale pink flowers; and 'Praecox' with pink-budded, open white, early flowers are described. Grows in great profusion on the slopes of Mt. Fuji. Wilson noted that no cherry is more hardy, more floriferous or more lovely. Japan. Cultivated 1910. Zone 5 to 6(7).

Prunus laurocerasus L. — Common Cherrylaurel, English Laurel
(prö′nus lâr-ō-sēr-ā′sus)

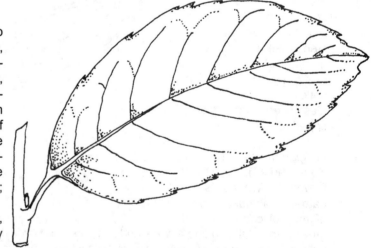

LEAVES: Alternate, simple, evergreen, 2 to 6″(10″) long, about 1/3 to 1/2 as wide, usually oblong or obovate-oblong, acuminate, cuneate to rounded at base, obscurely serrate to nearly entire, glabrous, lustrous medium to dark green above, 2 to 4 glands present on base of blade near point of attachment to petiole (seldom), or on underside of leaf at varying distances from point of petiole-blade on either side of midvein (commonly); petiole—1/2″ long.
BUDS: Solitary or collaterally multiple, sessile, subglobose or mostly ovoid with usually 6 exposed scales.
STEM: Slender or moderate, green, subterete or somewhat angled from the nodes, typical cherry odor when bruised; pith roundish or angled, pale or brown, continuous; leaf scars raised on a cushion flanked by the stipule vestiges or scars, half-round or half-elliptical, small; 3 bundle traces, usually minute.

SIZE: Species can grow 10 to 18′ high and under ideal conditions might become 25 to 30′ wide but is smaller under cultivation and principally represented by the cultivars; national champion is 32′ by 52′ in Seattle, WA.
HARDINESS: Zone 6 to 8.

HABIT: Large, wide-spreading, evergreen shrub of solid, dense constitution, extremely bold element because of large lustrous dark green leaves; have observed as low-branched tree.

RATE: Medium, 10′ in 5 to 6 years under good conditions.

TEXTURE: Medium in all seasons.

LEAF COLOR: Lustrous medium to dark green in summer; loses some of its sheen in cold climates.

FLOWERS: Perfect, white, each flower 1/4 to 1/3″ across, 20 stamens, April–May, (early April, Athens) born in 2 to 5″ long, 3/4″ wide racemes from the leaf axils, sickeningly fragrant.

FRUIT: Conical-rounded drupe, purple to black, 1/3 to 1/2″ long, summer, often lost among the leaves.

CULTURE: Transplant balled-and-burlapped or from a container; lately I have seen most being sold in containers; although a great number of large plants are offered balled-and-burlapped from the West Coast; performs best in moist, well-drained soil supplemented with organic matter; full sun or shade, salt spray tolerant; avoid excessive fertilization; withstands pruning very well; best in partial to heavy shade in well-drained soil.

DISEASES AND INSECTS: Not as susceptible to the problems which beset the tree *Prunus* but I have seen considerable foliage damage accomplished by insects, a shothole-type disease produces circular holes in the leaf that look like a shotgun was aimed at the plant; has become a significant problem in production nurseries where overhead watering is practiced, plants suffer from poorly drained soils and I have observed too many declining or dead plants because of this; several years past I was called to a large corporate site in Atlanta to assess the reason for many dying plants; 'Otto Luyken', a selection of the species was used in great numbers and bright brown plants were everywhere in evidence, plants were installed in January, I came in late May; I pulled one plant out of the ground and heard this slush, slosh, glush, glosh sound; obviously no drainage; moral: if the soil is not drained plant Baldcypress; root rot is also a problem that relates to inadequate drainage.

LANDSCAPE VALUE: Relatively handsome hedge plant; popular in the South; is not too successfully used north of Philadelphia; makes a good plant in the shade especially some of the cultivars, often used in groupings or masses; in fact, 'Otto Luyken' may be massed 50 to 100 in one location.

CULTIVARS: Numerous cultivars (over 40) have been described from Europe. The late J.C. Raulston, NCSU, assembled a fine collection of cultivars and produced an excellent cultivar checklist; see *Proc. Southern Nurseryman's Res. Conf.* 39:364–368 (1994). I have attempted to incorporate J.C.'s observations with mine to provide a wide angle view of the various taxa.

'Castlewellan'—See 'Marbled White'.

'Caucasica Nana'—Small, compact shrub with full, erect branching habit and thickly textured, rich green leaves.

'Forest Green'—Black-green foliage form, broader, darker green leaves than 'Schipkaensis', grows 4 to 6′ high, chance seedling from Bear Garden Nurseries, Silver Spring, MD, supposedly quite cold hardy.

'Magnoliifolia' ('Latifolia', 'Macrophylla', 'Magnifolia')—Large form with 10 to 12″ long, 3 to 4 1/2″ wide leaves; it may be trained into a tree; Dick Ammons, Florence, KY, mentioned that this was a shiny-leaved, hardy form; a massive 20 to 25′ high, 1 1/2 to 2 times as wide specimen has prospered at Kew Gardens, leaves remind of *Magnolia grandiflora* and are extremely lustrous, almost black-green; for textural effect this is a superb plant.

'Marbled Dragon'—Lustrous green leaves initially bronze variegated, maturing to cream and green, not uniform, large splotches and streaks of cream on some leaves, not much on others, an unstable chimera; 'Marbled White' is probably the same plant.

'Mischeana'—Compact, dense, flat-topped, wide-spreading, lustrous dark green leaves, collected in Balkans, apparently by Spath, Berlin in 1898, Hillier considers this one of the most beautiful forms, as I witnessed it a companion to 'Otto Luyken', only smaller, now have in our collection.

'Mt. Vernon'—Small, compact, 3′ high and wide form with large species type leaves; I got so excited the first time I saw the plant at Carlson Nursery in Oregon; Mr. Carlson gave me 5 cuttings and all rooted, 13 years later in my garden the plants are 2 to 3′ tall, grows very slowly and might be a good plant in a rock garden; Raulston suggests 3 to 5′ high and 5 to 8′ wide; introduced by Wells Nursery, Mount Vernon, WA.

'Nana'—Listed at 4 to 6′ high with foliage similar to species, from Monrovia.

'Otto Luyken'—Quite a fine form of compact habit, leaves dark green, 4″ long, about 1″ wide; very free-flowering; have seen it in heavy shade where it flowered profusely; grows 3 to 4′ high and may spread 6 to 8′; introduced about 1968 by Hesse Nurseries, Weiner, Hanover, Germany, have seen 6′ high by 10′ wide plants in England, easily

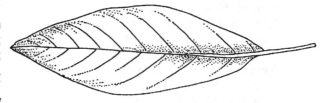

separated from 'Schipkaensis' and 'Zabeliana' because of the way the leaves are disposed at an upward, 60 to 45° angle to the stem. In the other two cultivars the leaves are more or less perpendicular to the stem or slightly drooping, usually the leaves of this form are not toothed toward the apex.

'Parkway'—Probably 'Magnoliifolia', named by Woodlanders, Aiken, SC.

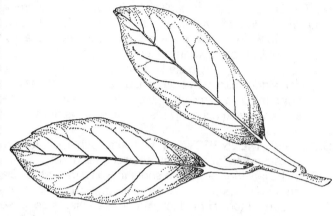

'Schipkaensis'—A dark green, narrow-leaved form found in 1889 near the Shipka Pass at 4000′ in Bulgaria; it is probably the hardiest of the cherrylaurels and I have observed plants with good foliage after a winter of –6°F; the leaves are 2 to 4 1/2″ long and 3/4 to 1 1/2″ wide; it is more refined than the species and forms a rather wide-spreading plant at maturity probably seldom growing more than 4 to 5′(10′) high; leaves may be entire or show only a few teeth toward the apex; Zone 5 to 8; at least 3 other 'Schipkaensis' forms are known and differ in growth habit, size and leaf characteristics.

'Variegata'—Leaves resembling those of the species and conspicuously mottled and variegated with creamy white, fairly robust and attractive, Zone 6 or 7, tends to revert; several white blotched and dotted forms are known.

'West Coast Schipkaensis'—Amazing how plants become mixed and this and 'Schipkaensis' are arriving in the Southeast, apparently on the same trucks, the West Coast version is much more upright and rapid-growing, I checked the leaf morphology and the West Coast form will be serrated for much of the leaf margin, the typical 'Schipkaensis' is toothed toward the apex, be careful because if mixed in landscape plantings the results will be *odd*, and clients will question you on the outcome.

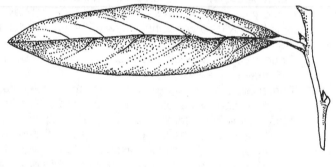

'Zabeliana'—Leaves dark green, narrow, entire, willow-like and, quite similar to 'Schipkaensis', very free-flowering, may grow to 3′ and spread 12′; plants 5′ high and 25′ wide are known; makes a good ground cover in dense shade; Zone 6 and does quite well in the South; put into commerce by Späth in 1898, along with 'Schipkaensis', the hardiest form, interestingly, laboratory hardiness tests indicated this was the most cold hardy cultivar, followed by 'Schipkaensis' and 'Otto Luyken'; see *J. Environ. Hort.* 8:71–73 (1990).

PROPAGATION: Seed requires a 2 to 3 month cold treatment, and radicles often emerge in the stratification medium. Cuttings taken in late summer rooted 90% in sand:peat in 7 weeks without treatment; have rooted this successfully many times; cuttings of the clone mentioned under additional notes were taken in early June and early July, 3000 and 5000 ppm IBA quick dip, respectively, peat:perlite, mist, with 100% rooting 4 weeks later. Tissue culture, *Acta Horticulturae* 300:177–180 (1992), was successful with 'Otto Luyken'.

ADDITIONAL NOTES: Collected seeds from 'Otto Luyken' in Oregon and grew 100 seedlings, saved the best four and planted them in my garden, only one proved superior with lustrous dark green foliage and tight upright-rounded habit with leaves like 'Schipkaensis'. Interestingly, none were similar to 'Otto Luyken'. Plant has been named 'Majestic Jade'.

NATIVE HABITAT: Southeastern Europe and Asia Minor. Introduced 1576.

RELATED SPECIES:

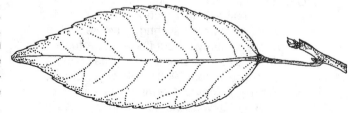

Prunus lusitanica L., (prö′nus lū-si-tan′i-kȧ), Portuguese Cherrylaurel, is a large, bushy, evergreen shrub or small tree 10 to 20′ high but occasionally larger. European literature reported tree-like stature to 60′. All my sightings correlate with shrub stature. The ovate or oval, 2 1/2 to 5″ long, 1 1/4 to 2″ wide, glabrous, toothed, glossy dark green leaves are handsome throughout the year. The white, 1/3 to 1/2″ diameter, fragrant flowers are produced in 6 to 10″ long, 1 to 1 1/4″ wide racemes in May–June from the ends of the previous season's growth and from the axils of their leaves. The 1/3″ long, cone-shaped fruits are dark purple. This is a rather handsome plant and surprisingly has survived on the campus of Reinhart College, Walesca, GA where winter temperatures may range from 0 to -10°F. One reference reported that *P. lusitanica* was hardier than *P. laurocerasus*. I believe the species has potential for southern gardens. Plants at the Atlanta Botanical and University's Botanical Garden have performed better than *P. laurocerasus*. Foliage is not affected by "shot hole." Performance in sun and shade is outstanding. Could be useful to breed resistance into *P. laurocerasus*. European forms of the species are different than what I see in the Southeast. Habit on the European type is larger, looser and leaves are more lustrous and elongated. What is common in the Southeast could be a cultivar for 'Angustifolia' with 3″ long, lanceolate leaves; 'Myrtifolia' with 2 to 2 1/2″ long, ovate leaves, and neat rounded habit; and 'Ormistonensis' with leathery dark green leaves and compact habit are described. 'Variegata' is quite common in European gardens, the leaves irregularly margined cream, but not overwhelmingly so. Spain, Portugal. Introduced 1648. Zone 7 to 9.

Prunus maackii Rupr. — Amur Chokecherry, Manchurian Cherry

LEAVES: Alternate, simple, elliptic to oblong-ovate, 2 to 4″ long, acuminate, rounded, finely serrate, medium green, gland dotted below, and slightly hairy on veins; petiole—1/2″ long.

Prunus maackii, (prö′nus mak′ē-ī), Amur Chokecherry, is an interesting, rounded, to almost mop-headed, dense branching tree that grows 35 to 45′ high. I have seen young trees that were pyramidal but with age the outline becomes more rounded. Although seldom credited with good flower characteristics, the white flowers occur in 2 to 3″ long, 20- to 30-flowered racemes in great profusion around early to mid-May. Numerous small, 1/4″ diameter, red maturing to black, ovoid-globose fruits ripen in August. The bark is beautiful and I have seen all kinds of combinations and permutations. My first exposure to this tree occurred at the Royal Botanical Garden, Hamilton, Ontario, and on that tree the bark was a rich cinnamon brown and actually exfoliated in shaggy masses. Other trees I have seen showed minimal exfoliation. The color varies from brownish yellow to reddish brown to the cinnamon brown mentioned above. There are several magnificent trees near the old shrub collection at the Arnold and these will make believers out of any gardener. The tree requires a well-drained soil and is best suited to cold climates. Seeds germinated best with 30 days warm, followed by 60 days cold stratification. It can be rooted from June–July softwoods. 'Amber Beauty' is uniform in habit with slightly ascending branches. Korea, Manchuria. Introduced 1878. Zone 3a to 6.

Prunus mandshurica (Maxim.) Koehne — Manchurian Apricot

LEAVES: Alternate, simple, broad-elliptic to ovate, 2 to 5″ long, half as wide, acuminate, rounded or broad-cuneate, sharply and doubly serrate, with narrow elongated teeth, deep green above, green beneath and glabrous except axillary tufts of hairs; petiole—1″ long, puberulous.

Prunus mandshurica, (prö′nus man-shūr′i-ká), Manchurian Apricot, is a small (15 to 20′), spreading, round-headed tree that is most noteworthy for the single, pinkish, 1 1/4″ diameter flowers that occur in April or early May before the leaves. It is rather handsome in flower and where peach and other *Prunus* cannot be relied upon for flower this species might be considered. Fruits are globose, 1″ diameter, and yellow. Old plants have an interesting gray, ridged-and-furrowed bark. Tree can grow larger than listed above, but I have not seen anything larger than 25′ high under cultivation. 'Manchu', 'Moongold', and 'Sungold' are hardy cultivars. Manchuria, Korea. Cultivated 1900. Zone 3 or 4 and south.

Prunus maritima Marsh. — Beach Plum

LEAVES: Alternate, simple, ovate or elliptic, 1 1/2 to 3″ long, 3/4 to 1 1/4″ wide, acute, cuneate, evenly and sharply serrate, dull green and glabrous above, paler and soft pubescent below; petiole—1/4″ long, pubescent, often glandular.

Prunus maritima, (prö′nus mȧ-rit′i-mȧ), Beach Plum, is a rounded, dense, suckering shrub growing to 6′ high and more. The flowers are white, single, 1/2″ across, May, 2 to 3 together. Fruits are dull purple, sometimes yellow to crimson, 1/2 to 1″ diameter, bloomy, ripening in August and relished for jams and jellies. A number of cultivars ('Eastham', 'Hancock', 'Squibnocket') have been selected for superior fruit qualities. Variety *flava* G.S. Torrey is a yellow-fruited form apparently found wild on the Cape. This species abounds on Cape Cod, MA and is one of the Cape Codder's cherished plants. A good salt tolerant species which grows in sandy, rocky soils along the coast from New Brunswick to Maine and Virginia. Introduced 1818. Zone 3 to 6.

Prunus mume Sieb. & Zucc. — Japanese Apricot

LEAVES: Alternate, simple, broad-ovate to ovate, 2 to 4″ long, long acuminate, broad cuneate, finely and sharply serrate, rich green above, pubescent on veins below; petiole—1/2 to 3/4″ long, glandular.
STEM: Polished, shining green, glabrous.

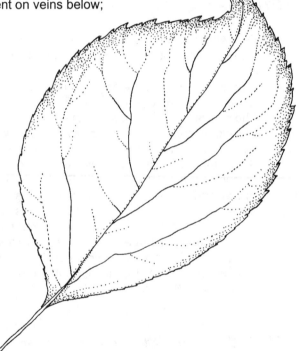

Prunus mume, (prö′nus mū′may), Japanese Apricot, was a favorite of the late Dr. J.C. Raulston and his continuous exhortations enthused me to the point that the plant was included. Prior to J.C.'s proselytizing, I had only seen the plant once at the Missouri Botanic Garden in summer and all I remember was the polished green stems. However, in February of 1989, my graduate student and I discovered a double pink form in flower in the University's Botanical Garden. I was converted. Since my non-believer days, the plant has shown up on the garden radar screen with increasing frequency. In fact, a handsome double pink form that I rooted from an unnamed clone at Milliken & Co., is now 12′ high and greets the early January–early February period with bulbous buds and fragrant, 1″ diameter flowers. Interestingly, this form has better summer foliage than many cultivars and does not develop the droopy, almost desiccated foliar appearance in the summer. The species' habit is rounded with long, supple, green stems that produce 1 to 1 1/4″ diameter, fragrant, pale rose flowers, singly or in pairs on naked stems in January–March. Chief attraction is the winter flowering character and the plant becomes obscure later. Have read several interesting thoughts on pruning the plant to obtain best flower. Cut back after flowering to produce long branches which will form next year's flower buds. From here, cut half the branches back every year so a guaranteed crop of flowers will be present while the other half (not cut back) will produce heavy bud set the following summer. Fruits are inedible, yellowish, globose, 1 to 1 1/4″ diameter drupes. A well-drained, reasonably fertile, acid soil in full sun suits it best. Raulston mentioned that the Japanese have over 250 named cultivars in white, pink, rose, red, in single and double forms, on plants up to 20′ high. Habit may be normal, fastigiate, corkscrew or pendulous. Interestingly, difficult to locate in commerce in the United States but a few nurserymen are now growing the species. W.B. Clarke of California apparently selected a number of forms. Cultivars include: 'Alba' with single, white flowers, strong-growing form; 'Alba Plena' with double, white flowers, to 20′, early-flowering; 'Alphandii' with semi-double, pink flowers; 'Andoh's White' with pale pink, semi-double flowers; 'Benishidare' with single, ruby crimson, cup-shaped, 3/8″ diameter, very fragrant flowers; 'Benishidori' with double, very fragrant, intense pink, fading later flowers, buds dark pink, late March–early April; 'Bonita' with double, pink, 1″ diameter flowers, semi-upright grower with rounded head, 25 to 30′ high; 'Dawn' with large, ruffled, double, pink flowers, one of the later flowering cultivars; 'Fragrant Snow' with white flowers; 'Kobai' with red, semi-double flowers; 'Matsurabara Red' ('Matsubara Red', 'Mitsubara Red') has double, dark red flowers, upright tree to 20′, flowers January–February in mild winter climates, February–March in colder areas;

'O-moi-no-wac' with semi-double, cup-shaped, white flowers, late March–early April; 'Peggy Clarke' bears double, deep rose flowers with extremely long stamens and red calyx; 'Pendula' with single or semi-double, pale pink flowers on a pendulous plant; 'Rose Bud' has large, semi-double, soft pink flowers; 'Rosemary Clarke' has large, double, fragrant, white flowers with red calyces, early to flower; 'Snow Cone' has deeper pink flowers; 'Trumpet' has early, pale pink, single flowers; 'Viridicalyx' with double, white flowers with a green calyx, upright tree to 20'; 'W.B. Clarke' offers double, pink flowers on a weeping plant; 'White Christmas' has very early, white, single flowers; and 'Winter Mist' has pale pink flowers. Easily rooted from softwood cuttings in June, 3000 ppm KIBA, mist. Cultivars are often grafted on peach ('Nemaguard') rootstocks. Have witnessed pronounced borer infestations on grafted plants. Seed requires a brief cold moist stratification. See Dirr, *Nursery Manager* 7(4):40–42 (1991), for an expanded discussion of the species. Japan, China. Introduced 1844. Zone 6 to 9, 10 in California.

Prunus nigra Ait. — Canada Plum, Canadian Plum

LEAVES: Alternate, simple, elliptic to obovate, 2 to 4"(5") long, half as wide, acuminate, broad-cuneate to subcordate, coarsely and doubly obtuse-serrate, dark green and glabrous above, pubescent or nearly glabrous beneath; petiole—1/2 to 1" long with two glands near point of attachment to blade.

Prunus nigra, (prö'nus n ĭ'grà), Canada Plum, is a small, 20 to 30' high, upright branched, narrow-headed tree. National champion is 51' by 48' in Macomb Co., MI. White, 1 1/4" diameter flowers occur 3 to 4 together in the leaf axils on 1/2" long, reddish pedicels before the leaves in April–May. The fruit is a 1 to 1 1/4" long, oval, yellowish red to red drupe. 'Princess Kay' is a double, white-flowered form that was found by Catherine Nylund in the wild in Itasca County, MN; the plant was introduced by the Minnesota Landscape Arboretum. It flowers heavily as a young plant and produces red fruit in August. The prominent lenticels, in combination with the black bark, add winter interest. Northeast and upper Midwest into Canada. Introduced 1773. Zone 2 to 5(6)

Prunus padus L. — European Birdcherry, Common Birdcherry

LEAVES: Alternate, simple, obovate to elliptic, 2 1/2 to 5" long, 1 1/2 to 2" wide, apex abruptly taper-pointed, base wedge-shaped, rounded or slightly cordate, teeth fine, very sharp, dull dark green above, grayish and hairless beneath or with axillary tufts; petiole—1/2 to 3/4" long, glabrous, with 2 or more glands.

Prunus padus, (prö'nus pā'dus), European Birdcherry, is a medium-sized (30 to 40'), rounded, low-branched tree with ascending branches. The foliage is a dull dark green in summer and may become yellow to bronze in fall. The flowers are white, fragrant, 1/3 to 1/2" across, mid-April to early May; borne in drooping, loose, 3 to 6" long racemes. The fruit is black, 1/4 to 1/3" diameter drupe, July to August. This is one of the first trees to leaf out and the new, lustrous light green leaves are a welcome sight after a difficult winter. Black knot disease has been serious in Minnesota and would be a limiting factor in the use of the species. A pretty tree that flowers after the leaves have matured, somewhat diminishing the overall effectiveness. Cultivars include:

'Albertii'—Pyramidal to rounded, 30' by 25' tree, supposedly good for street tree use, flowers profuse on long racemes, Zone 3.

'Berg'—Tight globe-headed form to 25' high, new growth green quickly turning to crimson all summer, white flowers in 5 to 8" long racemes, Zone 2.

'Colorata'—Offers bronze-colored new leaves that turn dark green above, purplish below, stems are dark purple, flowers light pink.

var. *commutata* Dipp.—Individual flowers 1/2" diameter in 6" long racemes, flowers 3 weeks before normal birdcherries.

'Plena'—Flowers large and double, remaining effective longer than any other form.

'Spaethii'—Racemes somewhat pendulous, flowers 3/4" across.

Summer Glow® ('DTR 117')—New leaves green, maturing to excellent red-purple leaf color through summer, turn purple-red in fall, white flowers in 4" long, pendent racemes, 1/4" diameter, red fruits, strong semi-spreading growth habit has not exhibited suckering that is common to Schubert or Canada Red Chokecherry, well-adapted to urban sites, oval to rounded habit, approximately 25′ high, Zone 3 to 7, a Wandell introduction.

'Watereri'—Racemes 8″ long, quite effective in flower, have seen at Niagara Falls and was taken by the long and rather beautiful flowers.

Reference to a fastigiate clone (no name given) that was reproduced in tissue culture; see *J. Hort. Science* 68:975–981 (1993).

ADDITIONAL NOTES: European literature describes at least 15 cultivars varying in foliage and flower colors. Certainly not common in American commerce and most plants I experienced were in the midwestern states.

NATIVE HABITAT: Europe, northern Asia, to Korea and Japan. Zone 3 to 6. Long cultivated.

Prunus pensylvanica L. f. — Pin or Wild Red Cherry

LEAVES: Alternate, simple, ovate, 3 to 4 1/2″ long, 3/4 to 1 1/4″ wide, long-pointed, cuneate to rounded, sharply serrate, teeth incurved and gland-tipped, lustrous dark green, glabrous; petiole—1/2″ long, with 1 or 2 glands.
STEM: Slender, shining, glabrous, reddish, aromatic when bruised.

Prunus pensylvanica, (prö′nus pen-sil-vā′ni-kȧ), Pin or Wild Red Cherry, is a small, slender, often shrubby tree with branches spreading at a broad angle forming a round-topped, oblong head. Size varies from 25 to 40′ in height by 18 to 25′ in spread. Co-national champions are 85′ by 30′ and 80′ by 35′. This is a very rapid grower and can quickly develop in abandoned areas. The leaves are a lustrous deep green in summer changing to yellow and red in fall. The flowers are white, 1/2″ across, May–June, borne in 2- to 5-flowered umbels or short racemes. Fruit is a light red, 1/4″ diameter, globose, sour drupe which ripens in July through August. Very adaptable species as it forms a pioneer association on cut-over or burned-over forest lands; intolerant of shade and soon yields to other species. A useful "nurse" type tree much in the mold of Gray Birch in this respect. 'Jumping Pond' is a form with drooping branches but it suffers from a leaf spot disease. 'Stockton' is a double-flowered, compact, round-headed form; the leaves turn red in fall. Native from Labrador west to British Columbia, south to North Carolina and Colorado. Introduced 1773. Zone 2 to 5(6).

Prunus persica (L.) Batsch. — Common Peach

LEAVES: Alternate, simple, elliptic-lanceolate or oblong-lanceolate, broadest about or slightly above the middle, 3 to 6″ long, 3/4 to 1 1/2″ wide, long-acuminate, cuneate, serrate or serrulate, glabrous, lustrous dark green; petiole—1/2″ long, glandular.
STEM: Offers a valid identification characteristic for the upper portion is often reddish while the lower part is greenish, has a somewhat grainy appearance, glabrous.

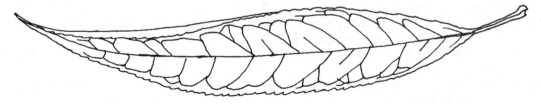

Prunus persica, (prö′nus pĕr′si-kȧ), Peach, as most people know, yields luscious, succulent, tasty fruit in summer. Yet the production of peaches is a highly specialized and technical art demanding considerable time, investment and luck. Peaches are notoriously susceptible to insect and disease pests. The Common

Peach grows from 15 to 25′ tall and usually develops a spread equal to or greater than its height. The habit is best described as one of ascending limbs and a low, broad, globular crown. The flowers are pink, 1 to 1 1/2″ across, solitary or paired, and develop in April (mid to late March, Athens) before the leaves. Actually, a mature peach orchard in flower is a magnificent experience. Flowers are often injured in cold winters or by late frosts. The fruit is a large, 3″ diameter, almost globular, yellow and/or reddish, pubescent drupe which matures in June–July into August. Peaches present many problems culturally and the homeowner should not be discouraged if they fail. The best approach is to avoid peaches altogether. There are many single, semi-double or double-flowered forms of the common peach which are beautiful in flower but almost impossible to keep in good condition. The colors range from white through pink to deep red to variegated. I watched a double pink peach flower spectacularly for several years but consistent munching by the borers resulted in the death of the tree. The temptation to buy these forms based on flower alone is overwhelming, but one's enthusiasm must be tempered with the knowledge that the peach is prone to insects and disease. Ideally provide well-drained, acid, moist soil and full sun. There are numerous cultivars of both the fruiting and double-flowered forms and it is wise to check with the local nurseryman for the best types for your area. The genetics of peach reproduction are unique for I know of double-flowering and weeping types that reproduce true-to-type from seed. In fact, in one Athens garden, white, pink, red, mottled, and double-flowered trees were all produced from seed. Over 40 ornamental cultivars are known, probably more. A few forms that I have observed and/or are offered through the nursery industry include:

'Alba Plena' ('Alboplena')—Rather handsome double, white form, flowers 2 to 2 1/2″ diameter and are effective 2 to 3 times as long as single forms, occasional fruits are set, comes partially true-to-type from seed; a fine form on the Georgia campus is 20′ by 20′, appears more resistant to insect and disease problems.

Dwarf Forms—Many genetic dwarfs of varying flower colors, often bear fruits, kind of cute; 'Bonanza' is common.

'Early Double Pink', 'Early Double Red', 'Early Double White'—All offer the respective colors and multiple petals early in the season.

'Helen Borchers'—Clear pink, 2 1/2″ wide flowers, late; have also seen this listed as semi-double with rose flowers.

'Peppermint Stick'—I remember trying to sell this form 35 years past at a garden center in Columbus, OH; flowers confused, being red- and white-striped, white or red often all on the same branch, double.

'Royal Red Leaf' ('Foliis Rubris')—Reddish purple young leaves deepening to maroon, flowers deep pink, fruit red-purple with a white flesh, edible; has been used as a rootstock to separate the scion growth more easily, if all red obviously the graft or bud did not take.

'Weeping Double Pink', 'Weeping Double Red', 'Weeping Double White'—Have seen a few of these types and generally they lack vigor or a strong constitution, perhaps in containers or as an accent but with limited long term value.

The peach is native to China and has been cultivated since ancient times. Zone 5 to 9.

Prunus sargentii Rehd. — Sargent Cherry

LEAVES: Alternate, simple, elliptic-obovate to oblong-obovate, 3 to 5″ long, about one-half as wide, long acuminate, rounded or sometimes subcordate at base, sharply serrate with acuminate teeth, purplish or bronzy when unfolding, dark green above, glabrous and glaucescent beneath; petiole—1/2 to 1″ long with 2 to 4 glands near the blade.

BUDS: Imbricate, conical-ovoid, reddish brown, sharply pointed, clustered at apex, often two buds at the nodes, one perhaps floral, the other vegetative.

STEM: Moderate, glabrous, reddish brown, marked with prominent lenticels, large gray-brown areas on stem.

BARK: Genuinely attractive, rich polished reddish to chestnut brown and marked with extended horizontal lenticels.

Prunus sargentii, (prö′nus sär-jen′tē-ī), Sargent Cherry, is one of the most useful cherries available. It grows 40 to 50′ in height with a spread approximately equal to height. Under cultivation 20 to 30′ high and wide would be more logical. The foliage is an excellent shiny dark green in summer and changes to bronze or red in the fall. The new leaves are reddish tinged as they emerge. The bark is rich, polished reddish to chestnut brown. The flowers are single pink, 1 1/4 to 1 1/2″ across; late April to early May, in full flower April 26, 1992 at Arnold Arboretum; borne in 2- to 6-flowered sessile umbels on 1″ long pedicels. Fruit is a 1/3″ long, ovoid, purple-black drupe which ripens in June and July. Both the species and 'Columnaris' (a narrow, columnar clone) have proved excellent in evaluations at the Shade Tree Evaluation Plots at Wooster, OH. I watched this most beautiful tree throughout the seasons at the Arnold Arboretum and decided it was the handsomest of the larger tree types for the northern states. The rich pink flowers open ahead of the leaves producing a frothy pink mass in the early spring landscape. Tremendous tree to work into a large border and perhaps underplant with bulbs and complimentary shrubs. Fall color as mentioned is superb for a cherry and often carries a mixture of yellow-bronze-red. Perhaps the best of the larger cherries for general landscape use. 'Columnaris' forms an upright columnar to narrow vase-shape, although most trees I have seen were more vase-shaped than true columnar. Will probably grow 25 to 35′ by 10 to 15′. Flowers and foliage are similar to the species. 'Rancho' is narrower than 'Columnaris', 20 to 30′ by 8 to 10′, with large deeper pink flowers than the species, and was introduced by Ed Scanlon. Recent literature tends to equate the two cultivars. I have observed that 'Columnaris' flowers latter than the species. Other selections with *P. sargentii* as one parent include:

'Accolade'—Semi-double, 12 to 15 petals, deep rose-pink in bud, opening blush pink, 1 1/2″ across, on 3/4 to 1″ long pedicels, dark green deeply serrated leaves, habit is open, spreading, 20 to 25′, *P. sargentii* × *P. subhirtella*; magnificent in flower, and the specimens that most incite passionate memories reside at Montecute House, Yeovil, England and Swarthmore College.

'Hillieri'—Single, blush pink, 1 1/4″ diameter flowers are borne on slender long hairy pedicels, leaves bronzy when emerging, later dark green, double toothed, hairy on veins below, developing good bronze-red fall color, broad-rounded tree, 25 to 30′ high and wide, probably *P. sargentii* × *P. × yedoensis*.

'Shosar'—Interesting hybrid from Collingwood Ingram, (*P. incisa* × *P. campanulata*) × *P. sargentii*, flowers several weeks ahead of *P. sargentii*, narrow-crowned tree, excellent bronze-red fall color, flowers single, 1 1/2″ diameter, rich vibrant pink, flower pedicel and calyx darker red, witnessed in full flower at Wisley on March 20, 1998, one of the most spectacular flowering cherries I have ever observed.

'Spire' ('Hillier Spire')—Soft pink flowers on a fastigiate tree, 27′ high, 10′ wide after 30 years, a sister seedling of 'Hillieri', yellow, orange, red fall color, originated around 1935.

This is one of the most beautiful cherries in flower but does not appear to relish the Zone 7 and 8 heat. Plants at Milliken Arboretum have not performed well while *P. subhirtella* and *P. × yedoensis* have thrived. Perhaps 'Accolade', with its *P. subhirtella* parentage, would prove better adapted. The late Dr. Don Egolf, U.S. National Arboretum, produced several clones that have grown and flowered (rich pink) well in my Georgia trials. They show no signs of borer or canker injury. Study by Jacobs and Johnson, *HortScience* 31:988–991 (1996), showed *P. sargentii* seedlings the most susceptible to flooding; eight taxa were studied over the 1, 4, or 5 day flooding period. Native to Japan. Introduced 1890. Zone 4 to 7. Not reliable in Minnesota; Cappiello reported no cold injury at Orono, ME.

Prunus serotina Ehrh. — Black Cherry

LEAVES: Alternate, simple, oblong-ovate to lance-oblong, 2 to 5″ long, 1 to 1 3/4″ wide, acuminate, cuneate, serrulate with small incurved callous teeth, lustrous medium to dark green above, light green beneath and often villous along the midrib; petiole—1/4 to 1″ long, glandular.

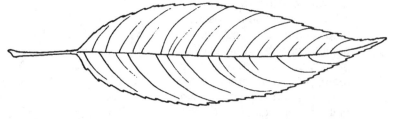

Prunus serotina, (prö′nus ser-ot′i-nà), Black Cherry, is a common sight over much of the eastern United States. Distinctly pyramidal to conical in youth becoming oval-headed with pendulous branches, commonly growing 50 to 60′ tall but occasionally reaching 100′. National champion is 136′ by 126′ in Washtenaw Co., MI. The leaves are a lustrous dark green in summer and often a good yellow to red in fall. Leaves emerge early, often by late March in the Athens area. Flowers are white, 1/3″ across, May (April, Athens), borne in pendulous, 4 to 6″ long, 3/4″ diameter racemes. Fruits are red, changing to black, 1/3″ across, ripening in August and September and have a bitter-sweet and wine-like flavor and are often used for making wine and jelly. Bark is gray-black and scaly on larger trunks. Valuable timber tree making its best growth on deep, moist, fertile soils but is also found growing on rather dry, gravelly, or sandy soils in the uplands. 'Spring Sparkle' has a dense growth habit with a decided weeping effect; abundance of white racemes in May–June, lustrous deep green leaves turn yellow to brilliant wine red in October, 35-year-old tree was 26′ high and 22′ wide, a Wandell introduction. Can be a troublesome pest in the garden because of weedy, aggressive nature. Ontario to North Dakota, Texas and Florida. Introduced 1629. Zone 3 to 9.

Prunus serrula Franch. — Paperbark Cherry

LEAVES: Alternate, simple, lanceolate, 2 to 4″ long, 1/2 to 1 1/4″ wide, long acuminate, rounded, finely and regularly serrated, lustrous dark green and glabrous above, pubescent along midrib or in vein axils below, 9 to 15 vein pairs; petiole—1/4 to 1/2″ long with 3 to 4 glands.

Prunus serrula, (prö′nus ser′ū-là), Paperbark Cherry, is a small, pyramidal to rounded tree growing 20 to 30′ high but seldom attains this size in the United States because of cankers, borers, etc. The main ornamental asset is the glistening surface of the red-brown, mahogany-like bark which ultimately peels. Flowers are white, 2/3″ diameter, produced in 2's and 3's, May, with the foliage. Fruit is a 1/2″ long red drupe. Very difficult to find commercially but worth seeking. Handsome in winter when the bark is maximally exposed. When properly grown it makes a tree of great beauty. Magnificent in its finest form and the venerable specimen in Beth Chatto's garden is unforgettable. Mike Hayman, a plantsman of the first magnitude, and I wax poetic over this tree during every social visit. Do you remember . . . ? Central China. Introduced 1908. Zone 5 to 6.

Prunus serrulata Lindl. — Japanese Flowering Cherry, Oriental Cherry

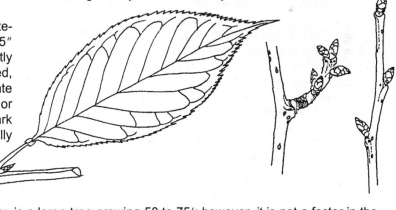

LEAVES: Alternate, simple, ovate to ovate-lanceolate, rarely obovate, 2 to 5″ long, 1 1/4 to 2 1/2″ wide, abruptly long acuminate, cuneate or rounded, serrate or often serrate with aristate teeth, glabrous, reddish brown or bronze when unfolding, lustrous dark green; petiole—1/2 to 1″ long, usually with 2 to 4 glands, glabrous.

Prunus serrulata, (prö′nus ser-ū-lā′tà), Japanese Flowering Cherry or Oriental Cherry, is a large tree growing 50 to 75′; however, it is not a factor in the modern landscape for the numerous cultivars are much preferable. Most cultivars grow 20 to 25′(35′) with a vase-shaped to rounded outline. The new foliage is often reddish tinged and eventually changes to lustrous dark green at maturity. Fall color is often a good bronze to subdued red. The flowers are greatly variable but range from single to doubles, white to pinks, and from 1/2 to 2 1/2″ diameter. They usually flower in April (mid-April, Athens) to early May and are borne profusely along the stems, usually before or with the leaves. They are usually grafted on *P. avium*, Mazzard Cherry, at heights of 4 to 6′. The origin of many of the cultivars is lost to antiquity. I suggest the reader consult Wyman, Bean, Wilson and Ingram for detailed discussions. Although the cultivars are not all true selections from *P. serrulata*, they are often treated that way for convenience. Roland Jefferson, "The Nomenclature of Cultivated Japanese Cherries (*Prunus*): The Sato-Zakura Group," details the complex parentage. Also, expanded treatment in *The New RHS Dictionary of Gardening* that discusses many cultivated taxa.

    'Amanogawa'—A form with the Lombardy Poplar type growth habit; flowers fragrant, pink, single to semi-double; sometimes developing the small black fruits; emerging leaves yellowish green, 20′ high, 4 to 5′ wide.

'Daikoku'—Double (+40 petals), deep pink, throat with light pink tinge, 2″ diameter, yellowish green new growth, open, spreading habit, 30′, Zone 5.

'Fugenzo'—2 1/2″ diameter, rosy pink flowers fading to light pink, double with about 30 to 35 petals; leaves finely toothed, rich coppery colored when young; habit spreading with a rounded crown.

'Hokusai'—Heavy semi-double (up to 12 petals), 2″ diameter, light pink to apricot, young leaves bronze, dark green and leathery at maturity, orange-red in fall; large rounded to spreading habit, 15 to 20′ by 30 to 35′.

'Kofugen'—Double, deep pink, more stiffly upright and dense than 'Kwanzan', 25 to 30′ by 15 to 18′, in essence similar to 'Kwanzan' but more upright in habit, Zone 5.

'Kwanzan' ('Kanzan', 'Sekiyama')—The most popular and probably hardiest of all the double types; deep pink, double (30 petals), 2 1/2″ diameter flowers; very free-flowering and utilized abundantly from Boston to Atlanta for every conceivable purpose; the new leaves are bronzy and may turn a good orange-bronze in fall; it is often grafted on *P. avium* about 4 to 6′ high and ends up looking like a manufactured tree; I have observed it on streets, along walks, etc., and it provides the uniformity (more or less) that every landscape architect dreams about; when grown on its own roots it makes a 30 to 40′ high and wide tree of great character and beauty; there is a splendid specimen on the Swarthmore campus; suffers from canker, virus and borers, often short lived; from recent literature I believe that 'Sekiyama' is the correct name with 'Kwanzan' sunk in synonymy.

'Royal Burgundy'—Appears to be a reddish purple leaf branch sport of 'Kwanzan', have observed in local nurseries, indeed, new leaves and flowers are deeper red-purple, upright vase-shaped in youth, rounded with age, 20 to 25′ by 15 to 20′, reasonable reddish orange fall color, discovered by Frank Parks, Speer and Sons, Oregon.

'Shirofugen'—Flowers pink in bud, white when open but aging to pink, 30 petals, leaves deep bronze when young; flat-topped, wide-spreading crown, vigorous grower, I rate this one of the best forms.

'Shirotae' ('Mt. Fuji')—Pink in bud, open to white, fragrant, semi-double, 2″ wide, produced early; leaves pale green with a slight bronze tinge in youth; spreading habit, often slightly pendulous, 15′ by 20′ or greater, Zone 5 to 7.

'Shogetsu' ('Shimidsu')—Double, 2″ diameter, blush pink flowers lighten to pure white, 30 petals, 3 to 6 flowers in long-stalked corymbs, new leaves bronze-brown, serrations ending in long, thread-like bristles, rounded habit, 18′.

'Snowgoose'—Upright oval-rounded in youth to 20′, white flowers before or with the bright green foliage, more pest resistant, has performed well in Zone 7.

'Taihaku' (Great White Cherry)—Single white, 2 to 2 1/2″ diameter flowers, reddish bronze leaves when unfolding, up to 8″ long, turning yellow-orange in fall, coarsely branched, broad inverted cone-shaped habit, 20 to 25′, potentially to 40′, slightly wider, Zone 5.

'Taoyame' ('Tao-yama')—Semi-double (up to 20 petals), soft shell pink, deep bronze emerging leaves, informal loose globe-like habit, 20′ high and wide-spreading, Zone 5.

'Ukon'—Semi-double to double, large, 1 3/4″ diameter, greenish yellow flowers, new growth supposedly reddish brown but photographs indicate more greenish than brown, 20′ by 30′.

No doubt the oriental cherries are among the most beautiful of all spring flowering trees. Unfortunately, 'Kwanzan' dominates the market when many other fine forms are available. In Japan, these cherries are called 'Sato Zakura', meaning "domestic cherries." The literature tells me that the wood of *P. serrulata* is used for smoke-drying ham and bacon; leaves are used in cake making; see *Acta Horticulturae* 228:541–548 (1988). Interestingly, I perused about 20 shade and ornamental tree nurseries and found only 'Amanogawa', 'Kwanzan', 'Shirofugen' and 'Shirotae' listed. Growers are now rooting cuttings with variable success but firm-wooded cuttings of 'Shirotae' collected in late June, 1000 ppm KIBA, peat:perlite, mist rooted 22%. Long-winded own-root protocol presented in *Amer. Nurseryman* 167(2):69–85 (1988). Japan, China, Korea. Zone 5 to 6 and south depending on the clone.

Prunus subhirtella Miq. — Higan Cherry, Spring Cherry, Rosebud Cherry

LEAVES: Alternate, simple, ovate to oblong-ovate, 1 to 4″ long, about 1/2 as wide, acuminate, cuneate, sharply and often doubly serrate, lustrous dark green above, pubescent on veins beneath, with about 10 pairs of veins; petiole—1/4″ long, pubescent, glandular.

Prunus subhirtella, (prö′nus sub-hĕr-tel′là), Higan Cherry, is seldom cultivated in the species form but is represented by the types var. *pendula* (Maxim.) Tanaka and var. *autumnalis* Mak. These types grow 20 to 40′ with a spread of 15 to 30′ or more. The variety *pendula*, Weeping Higan Cherry, is usually grafted

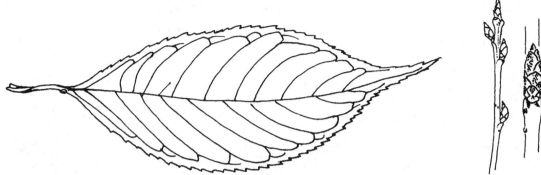

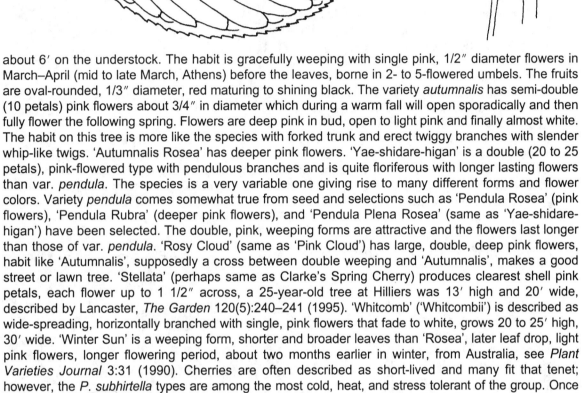

about 6′ on the understock. The habit is gracefully weeping with single pink, 1/2″ diameter flowers in March–April (mid to late March, Athens) before the leaves, borne in 2- to 5-flowered umbels. The fruits are oval-rounded, 1/3″ diameter, red maturing to shining black. The variety *autumnalis* has semi-double (10 petals) pink flowers about 3/4″ in diameter which during a warm fall will open sporadically and then fully flower the following spring. Flowers are deep pink in bud, open to light pink and finally almost white. The habit on this tree is more like the species with forked trunk and erect twiggy branches with slender whip-like twigs. 'Autumnalis Rosea' has deeper pink flowers. 'Yae-shidare-higan' is a double (20 to 25 petals), pink-flowered type with pendulous branches and is quite floriferous with longer lasting flowers than var. *pendula*. The species is a very variable one giving rise to many different forms and flower colors. Variety *pendula* comes somewhat true from seed and selections such as 'Pendula Rosea' (pink flowers), 'Pendula Rubra' (deeper pink flowers), and 'Pendula Plena Rosea' (same as 'Yae-shidare-higan') have been selected. The double, pink, weeping forms are attractive and the flowers last longer than those of var. *pendula*. 'Rosy Cloud' (same as 'Pink Cloud') has large, double, deep pink flowers, habit like 'Autumnalis', supposedly a cross between double weeping and 'Autumnalis', makes a good street or lawn tree. 'Stellata' (perhaps same as Clarke's Spring Cherry) produces clearest shell pink petals, each flower up to 1 1/2″ across, a 25-year-old tree at Hilliers was 13′ high and 20′ wide, described by Lancaster, *The Garden* 120(5):240–241 (1995). 'Whitcomb' ('Whitcombii') is described as wide-spreading, horizontally branched with single, pink flowers that fade to white, grows 20 to 25′ high, 30′ wide. 'Winter Sun' is a weeping form, shorter and broader leaves than 'Rosea', later leaf drop, light pink flowers, longer flowering period, about two months earlier in winter, from Australia, see *Plant Varieties Journal* 3:31 (1990). Cherries are often described as short-lived and many fit that tenet; however, the *P. subhirtella* types are among the most cold, heat, and stress tolerant of the group. Once establish, they are long-lived, and offer the garden a sublime quality unavailable from other ornamental trees. I can conjure visions of superb trees in the East, Midwest, and South, especially var. *pendula* which even if it never flowered would be garden worthy. Variety *pendula* might be likened to poor man's Weeping European Beech, with the artistically weeping gray-brown prominently horizontally lenticelled branches. Growth rate is extremely fast and one does not have to wait until retirement to appreciate the ornamental virtues. The various cultivars can be rooted from firm wood cuttings in June and July. Japan. Introduced 1894. Zone (4)5 to 8. In Orono, ME 'Autumnalis' suffered only tip injury while var. *pendula* was killed outright.

Prunus tenella Batsch — Dwarf Russian Almond

LEAVES: Alternate, simple, obovate or oblong, 1 1/2 to 3 1/2″ long, 1/2 to 1″ wide, acute, saw-toothed, lustrous dark green above, pale beneath, glabrous; petiole—1/6″ long.

Prunus tenella, (prö′nus te-nel′à), Dwarf Russian Almond, is a low, suckering shrub that may grow 2 to 5′ high. The principal value resides in the rosy red, 1/2″ wide flowers that occur singly or up to 3 from each bud of the previous year's growth. 'Alba' has white flowers and light green leaves; 'Gessleriana' has intensely red, almost 1″ diameter flowers; and 'Fire Hill', which has been offered commercially in the United States, has intense red flowers on a short-statured, 2 to 2 1/2′ high plant. These plants may be short-lived in American gardens. Have experienced 'Fire Hill' at Wisley just as it was coming into flower. Rather weak shrub but the petal color was intense red. 'Fire Hill' was killed outright in Maine. 'Ruth's 100' has a compact habit, profuse flowering, drought tolerant. Southeastern Europe, western Asia to eastern Siberia. Introduced 1683. Zone 2 to 6.

Prunus tomentosa Thunb. — Manchu Cherry, Nanking Cherry

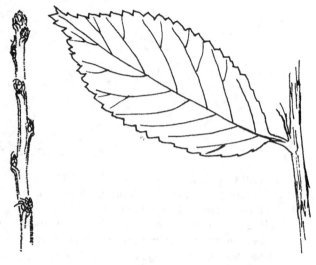

LEAVES: Alternate, simple, obovate to elliptic, 2 to 3″ long, 3/4 to 1 1/2″ wide, abruptly acuminate, cuneate, unequally serrate, rugose, dull dark green and pubescent above, densely villous beneath; petiole—1/12 to 1/6″ long, glandular.

STEM: Covered with a soft villous pubescence.

Prunus tomentosa, (prö′nus tō-men-tō′så), Manchu or Nanking Cherry, is a broad-spreading, densely twiggy shrub, becoming more open, irregular and picturesque with age. It grows 6 to 10′ high and spreads to 15′. The bark is shiny, reddish brown and exfoliating. Leaves are dark green in summer and extremely tomentose on the lower surface. The flowers are pinkish in bud changing to white, fragrant, 3/4″ across; early to mid-April; one of the earliest flowering *Prunus* species. The fruits are scarlet, 1/3″ across, edible, ripening in June through July. Could be used in mass plantings or the shrub border for the early flowers and fruits are valuable. 'Leucocarpa' has white fruits. 'Orient' has large orange-red fruits. Seeds require about 2 months cold. North and western China, Japan. Cultivated 1870. Zone 3 to 7?

Prunus triloba Lindl. var. *multiplex* (Bge.) Rehd., f. — Double Flowering Plum, Flowering Almond

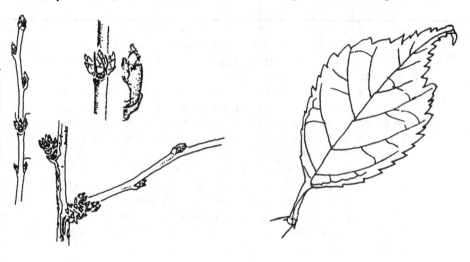

LEAVES: Alternate, simple, broad-elliptic to obovate, 1 to 2 1/2″ long, 3/4 to 1 1/4″ wide, acuminate or sometimes 3-lobed at apex, broad cuneate at base, coarsely and double serrate, medium green above, slightly pubescent beneath; petiole—1/2″ long, often with thread-like stipules.

Prunus triloba var. *multiplex*, (prö′nus trī-lō′ba mul′ ti-pleks), Double Flowering Plum, is a large (12 to 15′), cumbersome, clumsy shrub with tree-like qualities. The foliage is medium green in summer and turns yellow to bronze in fall. The flowers are double, pinkish, about 1 to 1 1/2″ across, borne in April. They are often nipped by a late freeze and severely injured. I have never seen any fruit on the plants. This species has always been somewhat confusing. Rehder listed the double-flowered type as *P. t.* var. *multiplex* and noted this was or is the original *P. triloba*. *Prunus t.* var. *simplex* (Bge.) Rehd., f. is the single-flowered type and bears 1/2″ diameter, downy, globose, red fruits. When right the flowers are rather impressive but it has nothing to recommend it beyond this. Variety *multiplex* was introduced from China in 1885. Zone 3 to 6(7).

Prunus virginiana L. — Common Chokecherry

LEAVES: Alternate, simple, broad-elliptic to obovate, 1 1/2 to 5″ long, two-third's as wide, abruptly acuminate, broad-cuneate to rounded at base, closely serrulate, dark green above, glaucescent or grayish green beneath, glabrous except axillary tufts of hair; petiole—1/2 to 3/4″ long, glandular.

Prunus virginiana, (prö′nus vĕr-jin-ē-ā′nȧ), Common Chokeberry, can grow 20 to 30′ tall with a spread of 18 to 25′.
National champion is 80′ by 45′ in Owings Mill, MD. It is a
small, suckering tree or large shrub with crooked branches
and slender twigs forming an oval-rounded crown. Flowers
are white, 1/3 to 2/5″ across; late April–May; in 3 to 6″
long, 1″ wide racemes. Fruit is red, finally dark purple,
round, 1/3″ across. The fruits have been used for making
jams, jellies, pies, sauces and wine. 'Schubert' is of
pyramidal habit with dense foliage, green at first, and
finally changing to reddish purple. 'Canada Red' is a
branch sport of 'Schubert' with faster growth rate,
straighter trunk, well-distributed branches, full-rounded
crown, brighter red leaves, Bailey Nursery introduction; I
always considered this a synonym of 'Schubert'. Also
listed are: 'Boughen's Chokeless' has non-astringent fruit;
'Boughen's Yellow' has large, yellow fruits; 'Copper
Schubert' is similar in size to 'Schubert' but produces
copper-green leaves and non-astringent, red fruits; 'Mini-
Schubert' with compact, upright-oval habit, interior branch-

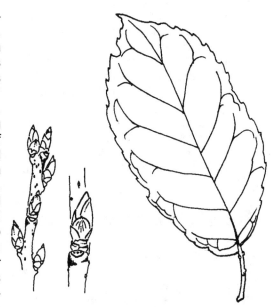

es small and upright, mature leaf color reddish purple; and 'Robert' is a large shrub with red-purple leaves,
compact inflorescences, large fruits, see *HortScience* 30:445 (1995). Newfoundland, to Sasketchewan,
North Dakota, Nebraska, south to North Carolina, Missouri and Kansas. Introduced 1724. Zone 2 to 6.

Prunus × *yedoensis* Matsum. — Yoshino Cherry

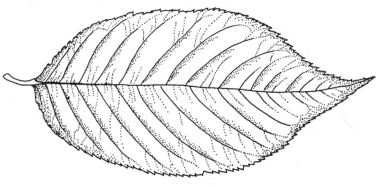

LEAVES: Alternate, simple, oval, broadly
ovate to obovate, 2 1/2 to 4 1/2″
long, 1 1/2 to 2 1/2″ wide, narrowed
to a slender point at apex, rounded
or broadly wedge-shaped at base,
doubly serrate, dark green and glabrous above, downy on midrib and
veins below.

Prunus × *yedoensis*, (prö′nus yed-ō-en′
sis), Yoshino Cherry, is rather difficult to pin down as to exact parent-
age and origin. I have seen it listed as a *P. serrulata* × *P. subhirtella* hybrid but also *P. speciosa* × *P.
subhirtella*. It is a plant of great beauty for the slightly fragrant, pink or white, 1 to 1 1/2″ diameter flowers
occur in racemes of 4 or more usually before, sometimes with, the leaves in March–April. The habit is
rounded, spreading, 20 to 30′ high, potentially 40 to 50′ high. Fruits are globose, 1/2″ diameter, shining
black drupes. 'Afterglow' is a handsome pink-flowered form that originated as a seedling from 'Akebono',
habit is upright-spreading, 25′ by 25′, glossy bright green summer foliage followed by yellowish fall color.
'Akebono' ('Daybreak') has soft pink, single flowers and forms a rounded, spreading, 25′ high and 25′
wide tree, put into commerce by W.B. Clarke of California. Has been outstanding at Milliken Arboretum,
with pink flowers fading to white, rapid growth and almost full leaf retention into early November. Cascade
Snow™ ('Berry') produces pure white flowers, followed by clean dark green foliage that changes yellowish
to bronze-orange in autumn, 25′ by 20′, this cultivar is more resistant to the common flower and foliage
diseases that plague ornamental cherries, Schmidt Nursery introduction. 'Ivensii' is a distinct weeping form
with white, slightly fragrant flowers, the habit is almost broad umbrella-shaped with the ribs (branches)
cascading to the ground to form a large mound. The first time I saw the plant in England I thought it was
a form of *P. subhirtella*. Later at Kew Gardens another specimen jumped in my path, a virtual carbon copy
of the first. Does not grow as large or wild as 'Shidare Yoshino' (f. *perpendens*). A seedling of *P.* × *yedoensis* raised by Hillier in 1925. 'Pink Shell' has shell pink petals that fade to a lighter shade. *Prunus*
× 'Snow Fountains' ('White Fountain' by Wayside) might be best included under *P.* × *yedoensis* although
I do not know the exact parentage. The habit is semi-weeping with snow white flowers on naked stems;
will grow 6 to 12′ high and wide at maturity, foliage is dark green and turns lovely gold and orange hues

in fall, may produce a few black fruits. 'Shidare Yoshino' (f. *perpendens*) is the weeping form and often called Weeping Yoshino Cherry. An 18-year-old plant in the University's Botanical Garden was 20′ tall and 30′ wide with wildly arching branches; the plant is beautiful when covered with masses of white flowers in late March. 'Washi-no-o' at the Arnold Arboretum was spectacular in white floral regalia. 'Yoshino Pink Form' has flowers of a charming pink shade that open later than 'Pink Shell'. Seeds require a 2 month cold period and softwood cuttings are being rooted in abundance. The weeping form is usually staked and at a certain height allowed to weep. Quite adaptable and although flowering is most profuse in full sun, a respectable display occurs in partial shade (pine shade). This is the species that graces the Tidal Basin in Washington, DC and allows Macon, GA to host the cherry blossom festival. It is terrifically fast-growing as a young tree and 3- to 4-year-old nursery trees might have 3 to 4″ diameter trunks. Found in Japan as a cultivated tree. Introduced 1902. Zone 5 to 8.

Pseudocydonia sinensis (Dum.-Cour.) Schneid. [*Cydonia sinensis* (Dum.-Cour.) Thouin.] — Chinese Quince
(sö-dō-sī-dō′ni-à sī-nen′sis)

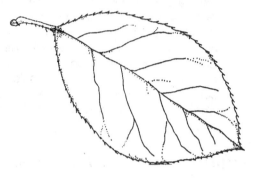

FAMILY: Rosaceae

LEAVES: Alternate, simple, obovate, ovate or oval, 2 1/2 to 4 1/2″ long, 1 1/2 to 2 1/2″ wide, acute, cuneate, covered with pale brown hairs beneath at least when young, margin regularly and minutely serrate, teeth gland-tipped, leathery lustrous dark green above, glabrous, pale green below, with spreading hairs on principal veins, midvein impressed; petiole—1/2″ long, grooved, with distinct raised bristly glands.

BUDS: Small, 1/8″ long, imbricate, 3-scaled, glabrous.

STEM: Slender, lustrous brown, glabrous, epidermal skin peeling off, few lenticels.

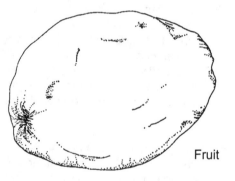

Fruit

SIZE: 10 to 20′(30 to 40′) high; one-half to two-third's that in spread.

HARDINESS: Zone 5 to 6 and into Zone 7; National, Tyler, and Morris Arboreta have notable specimens.

HABIT: Distinctly dense, upright-branching small tree or large shrub forming an oval to oval-rounded outline.

RATE: Slow-medium.

TEXTURE: Medium.

BARK: Quite beautiful, flaking off to produce a mosaic not unlike that of the Planetree and Chinese Elm; trees I have observed also developed a fluted trunk; the bark alone is sufficient justification for using this plant; colors range from gray, green to brown; bark exfoliates on 2 to 3″ diameter trunks.

LEAF COLOR: Leafs out early and I have observed emerging leaves in late February on the Georgia campus, turns lustrous dark green, yellow to red in fall.

FLOWERS: Perfect, soft pink, 1 to 1 1/2″ across, solitary, sessile, borne on year-old shoots, April–May.

FRUIT: A large, 5 to 7″ long, egg-shaped, citron-yellow pome, October, highly aromatic, fruits developed the third year after planting in the Horticultural Garden.

CULTURE: Moist, acid, well-drained soil; site in full sun; microclimatize as much as possible especially in North.

DISEASES AND INSECTS: Fireblight is a major problem; trees were devastated by fireblight and had to be removed from campus.

LANDSCAPE VALUE: Excellent plant for bark effect; not extensively cultivated in the United States; excellent for winter effect.

PROPAGATION: Seed required a cold period of 2 to 3 months, seeds extracted from fruits which had been kept in a cooler during winter germinated immediately upon planting.

ADDITIONAL NOTES: Branches spineless which separate it from *Chaenomeles* species. Not common in cultivation. Bark is very attractive. A red-fruited cultivar has been described. Best specimen I have seen is at Tyler Arboretum, Lima, PA. Not common in commerce but unique by virtue of foliage, fruit and bark. For the collector. Fruits can be utilized to make jelly.

NATIVE HABITAT: China. Introduced about 1800.

Pseudolarix amabilis (J. Nels.) Rehd. [*P. kaempferi* (Lamb.) Gordon] — Golden-larch
(sö-dō-lar'iks à-mab'à-lis)

FAMILY: Pinaceae

LEAVES: Scattered and spreading, often curved, 1 1/2 to 2 1/2″ long, 1/12 to 1/6″ wide, apex long-pointed, soft, light green and rounded above, keeled beneath, margins thin with 2 conspicuous gray bands of stomata, singly and spirally on long shoots, in a radiating cluster on spur-like branches.

BUDS: Of long shoots ovoid, pointed, surrounded by long-pointed, brown scales with free tips which fall away soon after the leaves develop in spring; of short shoots similar in shape with persistent scales; axillary buds rounded with short-pointed deciduous scales.

STEM: Two types: long shoots thin, smooth, bloomy, brown in the second year, roughened by permanent bases of fallen leaves; short spurs longer than those of *Larix*, with a distinct constriction between the annual rings, with 15 to 30 umbelliformly spreading leaves at the end.

SIZE: 30 to 50′ in height, spreading to 20 to 40′; can grow to 120′.

HARDINESS: Zone (4)5 to 7.

HABIT: Broad-pyramidal, deciduous conifer with wide-spreading horizontal branches and a rather open habit at maturity; I had a small (6′) specimen in my Illinois garden which was already quite open; Wyman noted that trees up to 30 to 40′ high may be almost as wide as tall; in some respects resemble a mature *Cedrus* in habit; wonderful venerable specimens of *Cedrus libani*-like habit at the Arnold Arboretum.

RATE: Slow, in fact a 100-year-old tree was only 45′ tall.

TEXTURE: Medium.

BARK: On old trunks grayish to reddish brown and lightly ridged-and-furrowed with rather broad ridges.

LEAF COLOR: Soft, light green above, bluish green beneath in summer turning a clear golden yellow (orange-yellow) in autumn; fall color is brief but it is fantastic; peaked on October 16, 1978 at Arnold and was essentially gone by October 24.

FLOWERS: Monoecious, borne on separate branches of the same tree, opening in May or June; male flowers yellow in densely clustered catkins; females solitary.

FRUIT: Cones solitary, ovoid, erect, 2 to 3″ long, 1 1/2 to 2″ wide, ripening in autumn of the first year; glaucous, bloomy, rich green to purplish during summer, ripening to golden brown, very beautiful but often borne in the upper reaches of the tree so as to be reduced in ornamental effectiveness; shattering soon after maturity.

CULTURE: Transplants readily balled-and-burlapped; requires a light, moist, acid, deep, well-drained soil; does not effectively tolerate high pH soils; prefers full sun although I have seen it in partially shaded situations; protect from wind; somewhat resistant to air pollutants.

DISEASES AND INSECTS: None serious.

LANDSCAPE VALUE: Truly a beautiful specimen in large areas; grows slowly enough that it can be integrated into the small landscape; the cones and fall color add seasonal interest; several magnificent trees along Bussey Brook in the Arnold Arboretum that are possibly the finest specimens in the country.

CULTIVARS:

'Annesleyana'—Dwarf, bushy; short, horizontal, pendent branches; leaves densely set; several other dwarf forms 'Dawsonii' and 'Nana' are described but I have not seen them.

PROPAGATION: Seeds are the usual method of reproduction; however, it is difficult to obtain fertile seeds. A specimen at the Missouri Botanic Garden has coned rather heavily but no viable seed has been produced. Den Ouden and Boom and Dallimore and Jackson noted that seeds were difficult to obtain from China in a fresh state, but fertile seeds were frequently produced on trees grown in Italy. On a 1976 trip to the Holden Arboretum, Dick Munson, the former propagator, now Director, showed me numerous seedlings he had grown from seed collected off a grove of trees in Mentor, OH. He was kind enough to show me the parent trees and needless to say I was impressed. We discussed the problems of seed propagation and theorized that the trees are self-sterile and the fact that several seedling-grown trees were in close proximity contributed to cross-pollination and viable seed production. Perhaps this is the reason the tree in the Missouri Botanic Garden does not develop viable seed. Seeds may germinate without pretreatment, but 60 days at 41°F will result in more uniform germination; trees in the Arnold Arboretum produce abundant viable seeds.

ADDITIONAL NOTES: Spectacular in fresh green spring foliage and in golden yellow fall color. The great trees at the Arnold Arboretum are the standards by which all other specimens are judged. Bonnie and I planted a small plant in 1995 in a shady part of the garden. If only I am able to watch it reach maturity!

NATIVE HABITAT: Eastern China at altitudes of 3000 to 4000′. Introduced 1854.

Pseudotsuga menziesii (Mirb.) Franco — Douglasfir [formerly listed as *P. douglasii* (Lindl.) Carr. and *P. taxifolia* (Lamb.) Britt. ex Sudw.]
(sö-dō-sö′gȧ men-zē′zē-ī)

FAMILY: Pinaceae

LEAVES: Pectinate with a V-shaped arrangement between the 2 lateral sets, straight, 1 to 1 1/2″ long, thin, shining green, gray-green, blue-green, to blue above, with 2 white bands of stomata beneath, smelling of camphor when bruised.

BUDS: Ovoid-conical, imbricate, apex pointed, 1/4 to 1/3″ long, shining chestnut brown, mostly resinous at base.

STEM: Yellowish green initially, becoming gray to brown, minutely pubescent or almost glabrous.

CONES: Three to 4″ long, 1 1/2 to 2″ wide, light brown, bracts are prominent and extend beyond the scales, persistent into winter.

SIZE: Under landscape conditions will grow 40 to 80′ in height with a 12 to 20′ spread; can grow to 200′ and greater in its native habitat; national champion var. *menziesii* is 329′ by 60′ in Coos County, OR.

HARDINESS: Zone (3b)4 to 6, depending on the seed source; there is a 30′ high tree on the Georgia campus (Zone 7) but it is not particularly vigorous.

HABIT: An open, spired pyramid with straight stiff branches; the lower drooping, upper ascending; dense in youth becoming loose with age.

RATE: Medium, will grow 12 to 15′ over a 10 year period; this rate based on observations taken with trees growing on University of Illinois campus; one authority noted that the tree might grow 40 to 100′ high after 50 to 75 years and 1 to 2′ a year when young; he leaves a pretty safe estimating range!

TEXTURE: Medium.

BARK: On young stems smooth except for resin blisters; on old trunks often divided into thick reddish brown ridges separated by deep irregular fissures; becoming 6 to 24″ thick.

LEAF COLOR: Depends largely on the seed source; the Rocky Mountain, Colorado type (var. *glauca*) is bluish green and hardy in Zone 4, this is the type which should be grown in the North; the other type (var. *menziesii*) is restricted to the Pacific slope where there is ample atmospheric moisture; this type has dark green foliage and is less hardy (Zone 6); this type is the largest growing and can grow to 300′ and more; types with yellow-green needles exist.

FLOWERS: Monoecious, on 2-year-old wood; staminate axillary, pendulous; pistillate terminal, with exerted, 3-pointed bracts, handsome rose-red when young.

FRUIT: Cones pendulous, oval-ovoid, 3 to 4″ long by 1 1/2 to 2″ broad, 3-pronged bracts, light brown.

CULTURE: Transplants well balled-and-burlapped; prefers neutral or slightly acid, well-drained, moist soils; fails on dry, poor soils; sunny, open, roomy conditions; injured by high winds; does best where there is an abundance of atmospheric moisture.

DISEASES AND INSECTS: Cankers (a number of species), leaf casts (similar to leaf spots), leaf and twig blight, needle blight, "witches' broom," aphids, Douglasfir bark beetle, scales, spruce budworm, pine butterfly, Zimmerman pine moth, tussock moth, gypsy moth, and strawberry root weevil.

LANDSCAPE VALUE: One of the noblest forest trees, very ornamental under cultivation; an excellent specimen, grouping or mass; not suited for underplanting or windbreaks; its use should be tempered in the dry windy areas of the Midwest; makes a nice short needle Christmas tree.

CULTIVARS: Probably 30 to 40 cultivars with very few available except from specialty growers. Thirty-one cultivars featured in *Conifers*. Worth a look as the variation is amazing.

'Fastigiata'—Distinctly ascending, spire-like, branches crowded, branchlets erect, needles green with a hint of gray, densely radial, short; good looking clone; Dawes Arboretum, Newark, OH has several beautiful specimens.

'Fletcheri'—I suspect the most popular dwarf form with blue-green, 1/2 to 3/4″ long needles and spreading, flat-topped, compact habit, 2 to 2 1/2′ by 2 1/2 to 3′, will grow 6′ high and slightly wider at maturity.

var. *glauca* (Beissn.) E. Murray—More compact with slightly more ascending branches than the species, leaves bluish green, hardy to Zone 4.

'Pendula'—Branches and branchlets held close to the stem and hanging like curtains, not particularly attractive.

PROPAGATION: Several papers on rooting Douglasfir discuss various factors related to successful rooting and would make interesting reading for propagators. See *J. Amer. Soc. Hort. Sci.* 99:551–555 (1974); *The Plant Propagator* 24(2):9 (1978); *Proc. Intl. Plant Prop. Soc.* 28:32 (1978); and *Proc. Intl. Plant Prop. Soc.* 43:284–288 (1993). Seeds will germinate without pretreatment although this may vary with seed source.

ADDITIONAL NOTES: There is considerable confusion related to the various types of Douglasfir and every individual tells a different story. The following information is based on the current thinking of the foresters and coincides pretty well with what most knowledgeable plantsmen relate. *Pseudotsuga menziesii* includes two geographic varieties: (1) the Coast Douglasfir (var. *menziesii*) is fast-growing, long-lived, and sometimes becomes over 300′ tall and attains a diameter of 8 to 10′. The foliage is typically of a yellow-green color, although some trees show bluish green, and the cones are often 4″ long and have straight, more or less appressed bracts; (2) the Rocky Mountain Douglasfir (var. *glauca*) is slower growing, shorter lived, and seldom exceeds 130′ in height. The national champion is 114′ by 62′ in Deschutes National Forest, OR. The foliage is bluish green but others with yellowish green needles are found standing together. The cones are smaller, barely 3″ in length, with much-exserted and strongly flexed bracts. Unfortunately, in certain areas the two varieties overlap and here intermediate forms are found. Variety *glauca* is widely grown and used for Christmas trees and ornamental plantings in the midwestern and northeastern United States.

At one time, the most important lumber producing tree in the United States. The wood has exceptional strength and is widely used for heavy structural timber; also used for plywood and pulp. One of the best short-needled Christmas trees because the needles do not easily fall off as is the case with *Abies* (fir) and *Picea* (spruce).

Had the opportunity to visit the Pacific Northwest on several occasions and upon reflection cannot remember witnessing anything but healthy, vigorous specimens. Took a cable car up a mountain outside Vancouver, British Columbia and the entire mountainside down to the Fraser River was seemingly nothing but *P. menziesii*. Also, in Van Dusen Garden, Vancouver, old isolated specimens and groupings provide stability to the fine garden. The old heads are often irregular-conical with long, slender boles.

Recommended reading for the taxonophile is "The Identity Crisis of the Douglasfir," in *The New Plantsman* 1(1):20–28 (1994). Before becoming *Pseudotsuga menziesii* (Mirb.) Franco in 1990, 20 other names were given since *Pinus taxifolia* Lamb. in 1803. Who said taxonomy was dead? The species has more aliases than the world's worst criminal.

NATIVE HABITAT: Rocky Mountains and Pacific coast (British Columbia to Mexico). Introduced 1827.

Ptelea trifoliata L. — Hoptree, also called Wafer-ash, Stinking-ash or Water-ash
(tē′lē-à trī-fō-li-ā′tà)

FAMILY: Rutaceae

LEAVES: Alternate, trifoliate, leaflets ovate to elliptic-oblong, 2 1/2 to 5″ long, narrowed at ends, sometimes acuminate, middle largest with a short petiolule, the lateral ones oblique at base, smaller, entire, or obscurely crenulate, sessile, lustrous dark green above and glabrous below; if viewed with a hand lens while back-lighted distinct oil-glands are evident; pungent when bruised; petiole—2 to 4″ long.

BUDS: Closely superposed in pairs, very low-conical, sessile, hidden beneath petiole bases, breaking through the leaf scars, not distinctly scaly, silvery silky; terminal lacking.

STEM: Glabrous, buff to reddish brown, moderate, warty and dotted, terete; pith rather large, roundish, continuous, white; leaf scars somewhat raised, rather long, horseshoe-shaped when torn by buds; 3 bundle traces.

SIZE: 15 to 20′ high and as wide, often 5 to 15′ high; national champion is 35′ by 40′ in Ada, MI.

HARDINESS: Zone 3 to 9.

HABIT: Large shrub or small tree of a bushy, rounded nature; if tree-like usually low-branched; has a tendency to sucker.

RATE: Slow to medium.

TEXTURE: Medium in leaf, medium-coarse in winter.

BARK: Dark gray, smooth, except for warty protuberances.

LEAF COLOR: Lustrous dark green in summer; yellow-green in fall; have observed good yellow on selected plants.

FLOWERS: Small, unisexual, greenish white, 1/3 to 1/2″ diameter, fragrant, borne in terminal, 2 to 3″ diameter corymbs (panicle?) on short lateral branches, late May–June, not particularly showy.

FRUIT: A compressed, broadly winged, suborbicular, 2-sided, 2/3 to 1″ diameter, indehiscent samara; brownish at maturity, rather conspicuous; effective August through September; the common name is derived from the shape and appearance of the parts; may persist into December and later.

CULTURE: Very adaptable species which performs maximally in well-drained soils; sun or shade; found in moist woodlands as an understory plant and for that reason makes a good choice for planting in heavy shade; I have seen plants in full sun and heavy shade and, in both situations, they made handsome specimens.

DISEASES AND INSECTS: Various leaf spots and a rust disease; none of which are serious.

LANDSCAPE VALUE: An interesting native plant covering much of the eastern United States; the cultivar 'Aurea' would be effective in the shrub border; this plant can grow on one after a while; I have developed a rather curious fondness for the species.

CULTIVARS:

'Aurea'—Quite a striking form with rich yellow young leaves fading to lime green by August; not as obtrusive as many yellow-foliaged plants because the color subsides with time; can be rooted from softwood cuttings treated with 8000 ppm IBA-talc; this form originated in the late 19th century on a nursery in Duerrgoy; Lancaster, *The Garden* 120(1):12–13 (1995), provides a great synopsis.

'Glauca'—Leaves blue-green and quite striking compared to the normal lustrous dark green leaves.

subsp. *polyadenia*—Mountain form that remains a small shrub but fruits heavily.

PROPAGATION: Seed requires a 3 to 4 month cold period; cuttings can be rooted with good success when collected in June–July and treated with 8000 ppm IBA-talc, mist; dug a plant from the wild for my garden and watched it grow like topsy in its new home. Moved it again and watched numerous shoots developing from remaining roots; this suggests root cuttings would work quite well.

ADDITIONAL NOTES: The fruits have been used as a substitute for hops; hence, the reason for the first common name. The bark has been utilized in medical preparations. The fruits and bark contain a bitter substance and the stems when bruised are rather pungent.

NATIVE HABITAT: Ontario and New York to Florida, west to Minnesota. Introduced 1724.

Pterocarya fraxinifolia (Lam.) Spach. — Caucasian Wingnut
(tēr-ō-kā′ri-à frak-si-ni-fō′li-à)

FAMILY: Juglandaceae

LEAVES: Alternate, pinnately compound, 8 to 18″ long, leaflets 7 to 27, ovate-oblong to oblong-lanceolate, acuminate, rounded, sharply serrate, 3 to 5″ long, thin, glabrous except stellate hairs in the axils and along the midrib beneath, shiny, handsome dark green; rachis terete, glabrous.

BUDS: Red-brown, rather large, superposed, the upper distinctly stalked or elongating the first year, naked with folded leaves.

STEM: Red-brown, moderate or rather stout, rounded, glabrous; pith moderate, angular, chambered with rather close thin light brown plates; leaf scars elliptical or 3-lobed, large, rather low; 3 bundle traces, crescent- or horseshoe-shaped, crenated or fragmented.

SIZE: 30 to 50′ in height with a similar spread, can grow to 90′, 115′ high specimen is known.

HARDINESS: Zone (5)6 to 8(9); none of the species are completely hardy at the Morton Arboretum which suggests that temperatures below -20°F will kill stems and branches.

HABIT: Broad-spreading, rounded, often with several stems near the base; can be a beautiful tree with wide-spreading branches; has a tendency to sucker.

RATE: Medium, 12 to 15′ over a 10 year period.

TEXTURE: Medium in leaf and winter habit.

LEAF COLOR: Dark glossy green in summer, excellent summer foliage and apparently quite free of insects and diseases; fall color is yellow-green; plants in Zone 7 have produced no fall coloration

FLOWERS: Monoecious; male in greenish catkins to 5″ long; female to 20″ long, catkin-like, May–June.

FRUIT: Winged nut(let), reminds of a wing nut, wings 3/4″ diameter, roundish, oblique, horned at the top, green changing to brown, ripening in September–October; interesting as they hang on a slender, pendent, 12 to 20″ long spike.

CULTURE: Transplant balled-and-burlapped into moist, well-drained soil deep enough to accommodate the extensive root system; full sun; pH adaptable; will tolerate wind, drought and hard soil if the roots are well-established; prune in summer; in the wild found in moist soil and there makes its best growth.

DISEASES AND INSECTS: None serious.

LANDSCAPE VALUE: Very handsome specimen plant which could be successfully used for large areas such as parks, schools, and golf courses; the largest specimen I have seen was very broad-spreading and made an excellent shade tree; much superior to ashes, honeylocusts and weak-wooded maples but little known; handsome foliage and interesting fruits that are not particularly messy; suspect suckering would limit landscape potential.

PROPAGATION: If seed is fresh some germination will take place upon sowing; as seed dries a period of cold (2 to 3 months) is probably necessary to insure uniform germination; I noticed that seeds from Arnold Arboretum trees were largely void while seeds from trees at the University's Botanical Garden were solid; this could be related to the length of the growing season and summer heat. Cuttings taken in summer and made from young shoots with a heel will sometimes root; probably best to collect cuttings in July and treat with high IBA concentration; the species shows a propensity to sucker which would indicate that root cuttings are a possibility.

ADDITIONAL NOTES: I first saw this at Vineland Station, Ontario, Canada, during a meeting of the American Society for Horticultural Science. No one could correctly identify the species until Dr. Lumis of the University of Guelph told us the identity. It was a massive, spreading specimen of great beauty. The root system is aggressive and the tree probably does not deserve consideration for residential or street use but in parks and large areas especially with abundant foot traffic, it might be utilized. I have observed the species or those treated under Related Species in European gardens, particularly in Germany where plants are quite common.

Wood is similar in appearance to walnut and mechanical properties are similar to those of Black Poplar. In southern Russia used in a wide range of interior furnishing, furniture, and packaging. Intergeneric hybrids between *Pterocarya* and *Juglans* were constituted, see *J. Amer. Soc. Hort. Sci.* 111:627–630 (1986).

NATIVE HABITAT: Caucasus to northern Iran. Introduced 1782.

RELATED SPECIES: I have some doubts as to the correct identity of many of the specimens I have seen labeled as *P. fraxinifolia*. Many appear to be *P.* × *rehderiana* or *P. stenoptera*.

Pterocarya* × *rehderiana C. Schneid., (tēr-ō-kā′ri-à rā-dēr-ē-ā′nà), Rehder Wingnut, is a hybrid between *P. stenoptera* and *P. fraxinifolia*. Leaflets number 11 to 21, 2 to 5″ long, narrow-oblong. Raised at the Arnold Arboretum from seeds received in 1879 from Lavallee's collection of Segrez. It is a rapid grower and tends to be prolific in its production of suckers. The rachis is winged but nowhere to the degree of *P. stenoptera* and not toothed. Apparently more vigorous and hardy than either parent. Zone (5) 6 to 8.

Pterocarya rhoifolia Sieb. & Zucc., (tēr-ō-kā′ri-à rō-i-fō′lē-à), Japanese Wingnut, carries 8 to 16″ long leaves with 11 to 21 leaflets, each 2 1/2 to 4″ long, 1 to 1 1/2″ wide, acuminate, rounded, finely and evenly toothed and dark green. The rachis is not winged. Differs from other species mentioned because buds have 2 to 3 large covering scales. Japan. Introduced 1888. Zone 6 to 8?

Pterocarya stenoptera DC., (tēr-ō-kā′ri-à sten-op′tēr-à), Chinese Wingnut, has 11 to 21(25) leaflets which are oblong or narrowly oval, finely and regularly toothed, 2 to 5″ long, and 1/3 to 2″ wide. The significant difference between this and *P. fraxinifolia* is the winged rachis with the wings sparsely toothed. Most Wingnuts I have seen show the winged character which indicates that they are not *P. fraxinifolia* although usually labeled as such. Considered the hardiest member of the genus. China. Introduced about 1860. Zone (5)6 to 8.

Fruit

Pterocarya stenoptera

Pteroceltis tartarinowii Maxim. — Tartar Wingceltis

FAMILY: Ulmaceae
LEAVES: Alternate, simple, ovate to ovate-oblong, 2 to 4″ long, 3/4 to 2″ wide, acuminate, broad cuneate, 3-nerved, irregularly and sharply serrate, upper medium to dark green, scabrous, lower with tufts of hairs in axils; petiole—1/4 to 1/3″ long.

Pteroceltis tartarinowii, (tēr-ō-sel′tis ta-tär-i-nō′ē-ī), Tartar Wingceltis, is a handsome 30 to 45′ high and wide tree with medium to dark green foliage. The species is closely allied to *Celtis* but differs in the winged, 1/2 to 3/4″ wide fruits. The gray-brown bark exfoliates in patches and is quite handsome. The only trees I have observed grew at the Morris and J.C. Raulston Arboreta. For the plant collector this is a treasure to be unearthed. Have attempted to root late June softwoods with little (6%) success. Northern and Central China. Introduced 1894. Zone 5 to 7. Freezes back regularly at the Morton Arboretum.

Pterostyrax hispida Sieb. & Zucc. — Fragrant Epaulettetree
(tēr-ō-stī′raks hiss′pi-dȧ)

FAMILY: Styracaceae
LEAVES: Alternate, simple, oblong to oblong-ovate, 3 to 7 1/2″ long, 1 1/2 to 4″ wide, acute or short-acuminate, rounded or cuneate at base, minutely denticulate, bright green and glabrous above, sparingly pubescent beneath at least on veins; petiole—1/2 to 1 1/2″ long.

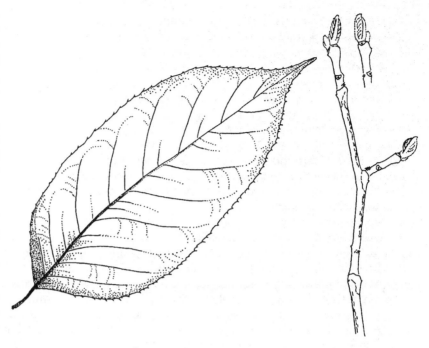

BUDS: Terminal elongated, hairy, and naked, 1/2″ long, yellowish brown, sits at oblique angle to leaf scar; one or two smaller, ovoid, 2-scaled, brown, 1/4″ long buds subtending terminal.

STEM: Quickly shedding gray bark, rounded, rather slender with distinct fetid odor when bruised; pith—off-white, continuous.

SIZE: 20 to 30′ tall with a similar or greater spread although can grow to 45′.

HARDINESS: Zone 4 to 8, has survived -22°F; best in Zone 5.

HABIT: A round-headed, small tree which develops an open crown, and slender, spreading branches.

RATE: Medium, 12 to 14′ in about 8 years.

TEXTURE: Medium-coarse in leaf; medium-coarse in winter.

LEAF COLOR: Bright green above, silvery green beneath in summer; yellow-green in fall and not effective; foliage is quite handsome and free of pest problems.

FLOWERS: White, perfect, fragrant, borne in large, 5 to 10″ long, 2 to 3″ wide, pendulous pubescent panicles which terminate short, lateral branches, May–June after the leaves have matured, trees start to flower when 8 to 10′ high, corolla 5-lobed, divided almost to base.

FRUIT: A 1/2″ long, cylindric, 10-ribbed, densely bristly, dry drupe.

CULTURE: Transplant balled-and-burlapped or from a container in spring into moist, well-drained, preferably acid soil; full sun, have seen respectable plants in partial shade; in northern areas protect from strong winds and extremes of temperature; prune in winter; prefers hot, sunny conditions if good flowering is to occur.

DISEASES AND INSECTS: None serious.

LANDSCAPE VALUE: Quite difficult to locate in commerce, but it does have possibilities for the small residential landscape; the flowers are extremely handsome and develop when a limited number of plants are offering color; makes a rather handsome and unusual tree; it is hardier than properly credited.

PROPAGATION: Seeds may germinate when directly sown but 3 months at 40°F is recommended to ensure more uniform germination. Softwood cuttings root easily and I have had 80 to 100% success with August cuttings treated with 3000 to 8000 ppm IBA-quick dip; the root systems were profuse and would serve as a model for any cutting one would ever hope to root.

NATIVE HABITAT: Japan. Introduced 1875.

RELATED SPECIES:

Pterostyrax corymbosa Sieb. & Zucc., (tēr-ō-st ĭ′raks kôr-im-bō′så), Little Epaulettetree, is distinguished from the above by the 1/2″ long, 3/8″ wide, 5-winged, ovoid fruits that are covered by a close down. Leaves are 2 to 4 1/2″ long, 1 1/2 to 2 1/2″ wide, serrulate with bristly teeth. Flowers occur in 3 to 6″ long, corymbose panicles. As I observed the two species there is not much ornamental difference. This species tends to be more shrub-like. This species also roots readily from softwood cuttings. Japan. Introduced 1850. Zone 5 to 7.

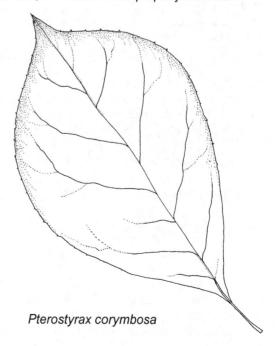

Pterostyrax corymbosa

Punica granatum L. — Pomegranate
(pū'ni-kȧ grȧ-nā'tum)

FAMILY: Punicaceae

LEAVES: Alternate, opposite, or whorled depending on growth rate of shoot, oval-lanceolate, 1 to 3″ long, 1/3 to 1″ wide, entire, glabrous, lustrous dark green; petiole—short.

STEM: Angled, light brown, glabrous.

SIZE: 12 to 20′ high, spread equal to or less than height.

HARDINESS: Zone (7b)8 to 10.

HABIT: Shrub or small tree of upright-oval to rounded outline; usually shrub-like in South.

RATE: Medium.

TEXTURE: Medium, perhaps almost fine.

LEAF COLOR: Lustrous dark green in summer, yellow-green fall color; leaves late to emerge in spring, also hold late in fall, tender spring foliage may be killed by late freeze.

FLOWERS: Perfect, 5- to 7-petaled, petals crumpled; calyx with 5 to 7 lobes and a funnel-shaped base to which the numerous stamens are attached; effect is similar to a carnation; red in type, orange-red, pink, white, yellow or variegated in the cultivars; each flower an inch or more across, borne singly or up to 5 at end of branches, May, June–July, usually starts to flower in late May–early June on the Georgia campus and may continue into fall, quite handsome; tubular portion of flower is fleshy.

FRUIT: A yellow, maturing to red (yellowish red), brown-yellow, purple-red, 2 to 3 1/2″(5″) diameter, globose, edible berry with a thick leathery rind crowned by the persistent calyx; central pulpy mass formed by the fleshy outer seed coats; ripens in September–October.

CULTURE: Easily transplanted; tolerates extremes of soil from sand to clay providing they are well-drained; pH adaptable; sun or partial shade (reduced flowering in shade); grows best in fertile, moist, well-drained soils; probably best to prune before flowering since it flowers on new growth.

DISEASES AND INSECTS: None serious.

LANDSCAPE VALUE: Truly a handsome shrub in flower; for some reason (cold hardiness) used sparingly in Piedmont area (Zone 7) of Georgia; good plant for shrub border, grouping, or perhaps screening; should not be used for hedges; really brightens a landscape in June and later; makes a fine container or tub plant, would be great on a patio during the summer months; flowers prolifically on Georgia campus; have successfully used 'Nana' on the Georgia campus where in groupings it is quite handsome; success in the Dirr garden with this and other cultivars has been nil for dieback almost always occurs; in the March freeze of 1996, the plants were killed to ground level but resprouted; at Byron, GA, the USDA facility has a large collection of fruiting types, all orange-red flowered that are easily 10 to 15′ high.

CULTIVARS: Several of the following may be found in commerce if one is tuned to treasure hunting. Numerous fruit-producing cultivars that are offered by specialty nurseries. Louisiana Nursery, Opelousas, LA 70570 offers the best selection.

'Alba Plena'—Double, creamy white or yellowish petals, waxy yellow calyx, new leaves bright green, 6 to 10′ high.

'Albescens'—White flowers.

'Chico'—Compact form with more refined branches, glossy leaves and double, bright orange-red flowers over the summer.

'Cloud'—Bright pink, medium- to large-sized fruit.

'Cranberry'—Red fruit, abundantly produced.

'Elf'—Dwarf type to 5′ with medium-sized, yellow-green fruit.

'Flavescens'—Yellow flowers, single, have seen it listed as double flowering.

'Granada'—Probably the hardiest flowering and fruiting clone, red flowers, red fruit with red flesh.

'Legrellei' ('Lagrelliae')—Double flowers with petals salmon-pink, variegated white (also described as red, striped yellowish white); apparently an unstable mutant from the double red, to which it reverts; has produced a branch sport with double white flowers; introduced before 1858 by Mme. Legrelle d'Hanis who obtained it from a friend, Mme. Parmentier, in Illinois; also listed as 'California Sunset'.

'Multiplex'—Double, white flowers.

var. *nana* (L.) Pers. ('Nana')—Red-orange, single flowers, smaller linear-lanceolate to linear leaves, smaller flowers and 2″ wide, orange-red fruit, may only grow 18″ high but 3 to 4′(6′) can be realized; apparently several (perhaps many) forms of this in cultivation; cultivated in 1723 in Kent, England; will come true when grown from seeds; makes a good glasshouse plant and will flower and fruit inside; has been described as hardier than the species; has flowered in October on Georgia campus and held leaves into mid-November, some tip dieback after exposure to 0°F.

'Nochi Shibari'—Fully double, dark orange-red flowers, introduced by Brookside Gardens, Wheaton, MD.

'Pleniflora' ('Plena')—Double, scarlet flowers, no fruit, 8 to 12' high.

'Scarlet Devil'—Compact, 4 to 6'; large, single, scarlet flowers; small, deep yellow, rounded fruits.

'Toyosho'—Double, light apricot to peach flowers.

'Wonderful'—A good fruit producer, burnished red fruit, juicy, wine-flavored; red-orange flowers; 8 to 12' high, fountain-like habit, vigorous grower.

PROPAGATION: Seeds germinate readily but progeny are extremely variable; this would be a good species to work with as far as flower color improvements and compactness. Softwood cuttings root readily; I have had good success with cuttings taken as late as September. The literature searches turned up numerous rooting studies, particularly prevalent in the Indian horticulture literature, 5000 ppm IBA was an effective concentration for rooting basal and sub-apical cuttings. Also numerous tissue culture research papers.

ADDITIONAL NOTES: An "old" plant. Grown for its fruits in southern Europe, northern Africa east to India from remote antiquity. Needs sunny situation and a long, warm growing season if fruits are to ripen. Have seen it fruit heavily in Madison, GA. Is used abundantly at Williamsburg in the Governor's Palace Garden where it is planted with figs and espaliered pears. Fruit was apparently a delicacy for the landed gentry.

NATIVE HABITAT: Lost to antiquity as far as origin; supposedly eastern Mediterranean to Himalayas. Cultivated since time immemorial.

Pyracantha coccinea Roem. — Scarlet Firethorn
(pī-rà-kan'thà kok-sin'ē-à)

FAMILY: Rosaceae

LEAVES: Alternate, simple, evergreen, narrow-elliptic to lanceolate or oblanceolate, rarely ovate-oblong, 1 to 2 1/2" long on long shoots, 1/2 to 1 1/2" long on flowering ones, range from 1/4 to 3/4" wide, acute, rarely obtusish, cuneate, closely crenulate-serrulate, lustrous dark green, slightly pubescent beneath at first; petiole—1/3" long, downy.

STEM: Woolly at first, becoming glossy brown with spines 1/2 to 3/4" long.

multi-stemmed

SIZE: 6 to 18' in height with an equal spread; this shrub can get out of hand and considerable pruning is necessary to keep it in bounds.

HARDINESS: Zone 6 to 9, Zone 5 if a hardy cultivar is used, the hardiest types will probably be killed at around -20°F.

HABIT: Semi-evergreen to evergreen shrub with stiff, thorny branches and an open habit if left unpruned; can become wild and woolly unless pruned properly throughout its lifespan.

RATE: Medium to fast.

TEXTURE: Medium throughout the seasons.

LEAF COLOR: Lustrous dark green in summer becoming brownish in winter in unprotected areas; if sited well, will maintain considerable green foliage.

FLOWERS: Perfect, whitish, 1/3" across, late April in Athens, late May–early June in Urbana, IL, borne in 1 to 2" diameter, 2 to 3" long, compound corymbs on spurs along the stem of last year's growth; quite showy in flower as the inflorescences literally shroud the plants; malodorous, subdued odor but still like a hawthorn.

FRUIT: Berry-like, rounded pome, 1/4" diameter, orange-red, ripening in September and persisting into winter; often spectacular.

CULTURE: Move as a container plant in spring into well-drained soil; does quite well where soil is dry in summer; full sun for best fruiting although will do well in partial shade; pH 5.5 to 7.5; pruning can be accomplished anytime; very difficult to transplant and once established should be left in that area; makes a good plant for container production.

DISEASES AND INSECTS: Fireblight can be serious, scab affects the fruits turning them a dark sooty color, twig blight, leaf blight, root rot, aphid, lace bug, and scales.

LANDSCAPE VALUE: Often used as an informal hedge or barrier plant, good for espaliers on walls, trellises and the like; fruit is the outstanding attribute; hardiness is a problem and selected cultivars must be used; The Ohio State University campus utilized large numbers of *Pyracantha* that were spectacular in the fall.

CULTIVARS: U.S. National Arboretum publication, *A Checklist of Pyracantha Cultivars* (1995), Contribution Number 8, is a wonderful guide. The number is colossal.

'Aurea'—Form with yellow fruits.

'Baker's Red'—Listed by Greenbriar Farms as their best red "berried" pyracantha for abundance of bright red fruit and cold hardiness.

'Chadwickii'—(Zone 5) Hardy form and a prolific fruiter, fruits are orange-red, 6′ high, spreading habit, one nursery noted it was hardier than 'Lalandei'.

'Forest Hills'—Compact habit, 5 to 6′ high and wide, orange-red fruits, Hines introduction.

'Government Red'—Red fruits, heavily produced, 6 to 10′, listed hardy to -5°F, I am not sure about nomenclatural integrity but then the name fits.

'Kasan'—(Zone 5) Orange-red fruits, originated in Russia, one of the hardier forms, quite scab susceptible, spreading growth habit, 10′.

'Lalandei'—(Zone 5) Probably the most widely grown and one of the hardiest, with orange-red fruits, originated about 1874, vigorous to 10 or 15′, scab susceptible.

'Lalandei Monrovia'—Orange-red fruits and slightly less hardy than 'Lalandei', also saw a report that notes significantly less hardy, also quite scab susceptible.

'Red Column'—Upright growth habit and bright red fruits, listed as Zone 5 to 6 by Angelica Nursery.

'Royal'—Hardy, upright-branched, orange-fruited form.

'Runyanii'—Another orange-fruited form, highly scab and fireblight susceptible.

'Thornless'—Red-fruiting, thornless form supposedly as hardy as 'Lalandei', highly susceptible to scab and fireblight.

'Wyattii'—Orange-red fruits prolifically produced, hardy to Zone 5, supposedly more cold hardy than 'Lalandei', 9 to 12′ high, tolerant of poor soil, highly susceptible to scab and fireblight.

OTHER CULTIVARS OF DIFFERENT PARENTAGE: The above were primarily derived from *Pyracantha coccinea* but the following come from different parentage. Dr. Donald Egolf, U.S. National Arboretum, and Dr. Elwin Orton, Rutgers University, have hybridized a number of fine cultivars many of which are included here.

'Apache'—A semi-evergreen to evergreen compact shrub with 1/3″ diameter, bright red fruits that ripen in September and persist until December and are not readily devoured by birds, resistant to pyracantha scab and fireblight, leaves are glossy dark green, grew 4 1/2 to 5′ high and 6′ wide after 14 years, a U.S. National Arboretum introduction; see *HortScience* 22:173–174 (1987), should be cold hardy in Zone 5/6.

'Cherri Berri' [*P. fortuneana* (Maxim.) Li]—Large, 3/8″ diameter, cherry red fruits which persist into winter; large, lustrous dark green leaves; 10′ by 8′; Zone 6 but I doubt this designation, probably less cold hardy.

'Fiery Cascade'—An upright grower to 8′ high and 9′ wide, small glossy dark green leaves, abundant small red fruit, first orange in September, red in October and persisting, good disease resistance, hardy to -10°F, Dr. Orton, Rutgers, introduced this clone.

'Gnome'—[Obviously I had the parentage wrong in the third edition for a number of reasons but John Sabuco straightened out the problem. 'Gnome' is a seedling of *P. coccinea* 'Lalandei' × 'Aurea'? The patent tag read *P. angustifolia* (Franch.) Schneid. 'Gnome' and in the disease update Oregon State listed it as *P. atalantioides* (Hance) Stapf. Got it!] Medium-sized shrub of compact, densely branched growth and somewhat spreading nature; 1/4 to 3/8″ diameter, orange fruits; quite hardy and successful in Zone 5; highly susceptible to scab on leaves and fruits, 6′ by 8′.

'Gold Rush'—Yellow-fruited hybrid of *P. angustifolia* × *P. fortuneana* selected by Washington Park Arboretum, University of Washington and registered in 1976 after 20 years of testing; described as an intricately branched shrub to 10′ high, persistent leaves and dense clusters of depressed-globular, orange-yellow, nearly 1/2″ diameter fruits that are so numerous the branches arch to the ground, resistant to scab and hardy to Zone 7.

'Golden Charmer' [*P. crenulata* (D. Don) Roem. var. *rogersiana* A.B. Jacks. × *P. coccinea*]—Orange-yellow fruits, good lustrous dark green foliage, scab resistant, bred in Germany.

'Graberi' (*P. fortuneana*)—Large, red fruits persisting into winter, 10 to 12′ by 8 to 10′, vigorous, upright branching, Zone 7.

'Harlequin'—Pinkish white variegated new shoots settle down to a life of green and white in summer, turn pinkish in cold weather, 6′ high and wide shrub; not as vigorous as the species, fruits are orange-red; as pyracanthas go this is at the bottom of the heap.

'Lowboy'—Vigorous, spreading, low-growing form, rich green foliage, orange fruit, extremely susceptible to scab, 2 to 3′ high and wider at maturity.

'Mohave' (*P. koidzumii* × *P. coccinea* 'Wyattii')—Heavy flowers and huge masses of bright orange-red berries on a medium-sized, densely branched, upright variety, grows 6 to 10' (9 to 12' high); based on tests in Illinois it is not hardy much below 0 to -5°F, quite resistant to scab and fireblight, lustrous dark green foliage, fruits exceptionally resistant to bird feeding, 8-year-old plant listed as 13 1/2' by 16'.

'Navaho' (*P. angustifolia* × *P.* 'Watereri')—Low-growing, 6' high and 7.5' wide, densely branched, mounded, rich orange-red fruits, resistant to scab and highly tolerant to fireblight.

'Orange Charmer' (*P. crenulata* var. *rogersiana* × *P. coccinea*)—Orange-red, 3/8" diameter fruits that color in September, scab resistant, bred in Germany.

'Orange Glow' (*P. crenatoserrata* (Hance) Rehd. × *P. coccinea*)—A popular form in England which has proven quite hardy, quite free-flowering with masses of orange-red, 3/8" diameter fruits which persist into winter, used frequently as an espalier on walls, 10' or more, scab resistant.

'Pauciflora'—Dense branching, low rounded form with small leaves and light crops of small, orange fruits, 4' by 4'; this may be a rename.

'Pueblo'—A semi-evergreen to evergreen, dark green leaved, 6 to 7' high, 12' wide shrub (after 16 years) with 1/3 to 1/2" diameter, depressed globose orange-red persistent fruit, resistant to fireblight and scab; vigorous-growing and heavy fruit producer, hardy to Zone 7, see *HortScience* 22:510–511 (1987).

'Red Elf'—Dwarf compact mounding habit; dark green foliage, bright red persistent fruits, low susceptibility to fireblight, Zone 7, Monrovia introduction.

'Ruby Mound'—Low mounding type with bright red fruits, Zone 7, Monrovia introduction.

'Rutgers'—A good, glossy dark green leaved form with abundant orange-red fruits and a spreading, sprawling growth habit, may reach 3' high and 9' wide, good disease resistance, roots easily from cuttings, shows good hardiness, much hardier that 'Mohave' and 'Navaho'; introduced by Dr. Elwin Orton, Rutgers University.

'Shawnee'—An F$_2$ seedling of *Pyracantha* 'San Jose', which is a spontaneous hybrid of *P. koidzumii* and *P. fortuneana*; clear yellow to light orange fruit, semi-persistent foliage, resistance to fire blight and scab, original plant was 9' by 10'.

'Soleil d'Or'—Another European garden form with golden yellow fruits, 8 to 10' high.

'Teton' ('Orange Glow' × *P. crenulata* var. *rogersiana* 'Flava')—Quite unusual for its upright growth habit and yellow-orange fruits; growth habit and fruit color are somewhat affected by where it is grown; in South fruits are yellow-orange and habit is upright-spreading but nowhere as upright as shown and described in original cultivar release [see *HortScience* 13(4): 483–484]; it is a strong grower and may become 16' high and 9' wide; resistant to scab and fireblight; reasonably hardy.

'Wonderberry'—Orange-red fruits, 10' by 10', good espalier form, Zone 7.

Yukon Belle™ ('Monon') (*P. angustifolia*)—Monrovia lists this form as the hardiest orange-berried form, medium-sized shrub with semi-evergreen tendencies, probably 6 to 10' high and wide, listed as Zone 4 but I doubt it.

PROPAGATION: Seed should be stratified for 90 days at 41°F. Softwood cuttings root readily under mist; treatment with 1000 to 3000 ppm IBA is recommended to hasten rooting.

ADDITIONAL NOTES: Pyracanthas make attractive fruiting shrubs but can become ratty with age. The disease ratings come from *Ornamentals Northwest*, December–January, 1977–78. A number of other cultivars were not included here because of their relative scarcity in commerce but are described in the publication. *Pyracantha*, in general, has lost its landscape pizzazz and, though commercially available, newer shrub introductions have reduced the plant's clout. In the South, the new *Loropetalum chinense* var. *rubrum* cultivars have competed favorably. Might mention that pyracantha spines can induce reactions in humans. Wear leather gloves when pruning and handling.

NATIVE HABITAT: Italy to Caucasus. Introduced 1629.

Pyracantha koidzumii (Hayata) Rehd. — Formosa Firethorn
(pī-rà-kan′thà koyd-zūm′ē-ī)

LEAVES: Alternate, simple, evergreen to semi-evergreen, oblanceolate, widest above the middle, 1 to 3" long, 1/2 to 3/4" wide, entire, or slightly serrate toward apex, apex often emarginate, lustrous dark green; easily separated from *P. coccinea* by the essentially entire leaf and emarginate apex; in clusters on old wood.

SIZE: 8 to 12'(20') high, 8 to 12'(20') wide.

HARDINESS: Zone 8 to 10; this species is not reliably hardy in Zone 7; severely injured and in exposed locations killed to ground during 1981–82 winter in Athens when temperatures dropped to 0°F, same occurrence in 1983–84 at -3°F, some plants killed, others developed new shoots from base.

HABIT: Large multi-stemmed, stiff, upright-branched shrub that becomes unkempt with time unless properly pruned; like *P. coccinea* this is a rank grower and rather unruly.

RATE: Fast.

TEXTURE: Medium.

LEAF COLOR: May start leafing out as early as late February in Athens; lustrous dark green; foliage may discolor in colder areas of South.

FLOWERS: Perfect, 5-petaled, malodorous, white, 1/4″ diameter, produced in small corymbose racemes in mid-April–early May (Athens); an entire plant in flower is quite attractive.

FRUIT: A globose, 1/4″ diameter, red pome that matures (colors) in September–October and persists through the ensuing winter; the entire shrub is a great mass of red; several plants on the Georgia campus are isolated specimens and they stand out like a sore thumb; birds apparently leave these until they are desperately hungry.

CULTURE: Transplant from a container; *Pyracantha* is inherently impossible to move from the field; prefers well-drained soil and full sun; responds vigorously to good growing conditions; an excellent choice for hot, dry areas; plants on the Georgia campus have survived numerous droughts during the 1980's and fruited heavily; prune selectively; there is no one best time to remove branches.

DISEASES AND INSECTS: Fireblight, lacebug, scab (affects fruit), mites in extremely dry situations, scale and leaf rollers.

LANDSCAPE VALUE: Excellent for fruit effect and widely used for every conceivable landscape purpose; single specimen, foundation plantings, hedges (a mistake), screens, masses, espaliers; requires a great amount of maintenance to keep it looking nice; where space permits it is worth using; the most widely used species in the Southeast.

CULTIVARS:

'Low-Dense' ('Lowdense')—Mounded habit of growth to 6′, large orange-red fruits may be masked by foliage, new growth light green, texture fine, severely injured or killed at 11°F during 1983–84 winter, true also for 'Red Elf' and 'Ruby Mound'.

'Rosedale'—Branches arching, large bright red fruit.

'Santa Anna'—Dark red fruits, shiny large lustrous green foliage, 10′ by 10′, Zone 7.

'San Jose'—Wide-spreading form, highly scab resistant.

'Santa Cruz'—Prostrate form with dark green leaves and red fruits, highly scab resistant; 2 1/2 to 3′ by 5 to 6′; Zone 7.

'Victory'—Vigorous form, upright arching growth habit, with dark red fruit, fruits among the last to color but are retained for many months, Zone 7, 10′ or more, good scab resistance.

'Walderi Prostrata'—Prostrate growth habit, 4′, large red fruits.

'Watereri'—Parentage is suspect but probably *P. atalantioides* × *P. crenulata* var. *rogersiana*; vigorous, dense shrub up to 8′ high and wide; dark red fruits on nearly thornless stems, leaves relatively small, 3/4 to 1 1/4″ long, 1/4 to 1/2″ wide, occasionally 2 1/2″ long.

PROPAGATION: Cuttings root readily especially from July to October when treated with 3000 ppm IBA-quick dip.

ADDITIONAL NOTES: Many cultivars available; I have updated disease susceptibilities based on evaluations made in the Pacific Northwest.

NATIVE HABITAT: Taiwan.

Pyrus calleryana Decne. 'Bradford' — Bradford Callery Pear. This discussion is concerned with the cultivar 'Bradford' and not the species.

(pī′rus kal-er-ē-ā′na)

FAMILY: Rosaceae

LEAVES: Alternate, simple, broad-ovate to ovate, 1 1/2 to 3″ long, about as wide, rarely elliptic-ovate, short acuminate, rounded, broad-cuneate, subcordate or truncate at base, crenate, usually quite glabrous, leathery, lustrous dark green; petiole—1 to 1 1/2″ long.

BUDS: Large, terminal and laterals of approximately same size, ovoid, elongated, 1/2″ long, intensely woolly, dirty gray to gray-brown.

STEM: Stout, brownish sometimes exhibiting ridges running from base of leaf scar, generally white woolly pubescent, especially below terminal, gradually changing to smooth, glossy brown at maturity, thornless.

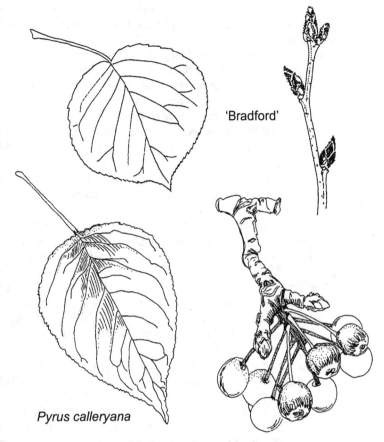

'Bradford'

Pyrus calleryana

SIZE: 30 to 50′ in height with a 20 to 35′ spread; 20-year-old trees were 50′ high and 40′ wide.

HARDINESS: Zone 5 to 8(9).

HABIT: Moderately conical (pyramidal) in youth, and broadening with time, densely branched and foliaged making it one of the great widget trees in American commerce.

RATE: Fast, 12 to 15′ over an 8 to 10 year period; a 12-year-old tree at the Secrest Arboretum was 24′ high, 22′ wide, and 7″ in diameter.

TEXTURE: Medium in leaf, medium in winter.

BARK: Lustrous brown in youth, lightly ridged-and-furrowed and grayish brown at maturity, often developing horizontal checks with age, creating a somewhat blocky appearance.

LEAF COLOR: Outstanding glossy dark green in summer changing to glossy scarlet and purple shades in fall; very spectacular in fall color but variable; I have observed a great number of Bradford Pears in fall coloration and some were spectacular reddish purple, others yellow to red reminding of a persimmon orange; the leaves hold late and in northern areas color may not develop properly depending on the earliness of cold weather; in the South fall color is often an excellent glistening yellow to red and peaks in mid to late November, with some leaves colorful into December.

FLOWERS: White, 3/8 to 3/4″ across, borne in 3″ diameter corymbs before or with the leaves, malodorous, in full flower in early to mid-March in Athens, GA, and late April–early May in Urbana, IL, the tree looks like a white cloud in full flower; beautiful flowering tree.

FRUIT: Small rounded pome, 1/2″ or less across, russet-dotted, hidden by the foliage; not ornamentally effective; may be present in great quantities; fruits can be eliminated by 1000 ppm Ethephon sprayed at full bloom, 95.3% of fruits removed in California study, see *California Agriculture* 48:21–24 (1994).

CULTURE: Easy to transplant balled-and-burlapped if moved in late winter or early spring; some nurserymen will not move them in leaf, very adaptable to many different soils; tolerates dryness, pollution, and should be sited in full sun; prune in winter or early spring.

DISEASES AND INSECTS: Resistant to fireblight which is so troublesome to the Common Pear, *Pyrus communis*; basically free of pests although I have seen tip dieback from fireblight in the South; many loose statements on fireblight susceptibility with one of the best documented studies (Alabama) in *J. Arboriculture* 17:257–260 (1991); in their study 'Aristocrat' and 'Autumn Blaze' were highly susceptible with 'Bradford' the least.

LANDSCAPE VALUE: In the second (1977) edition I commented that I hoped to see more Bradfords; little did I realize that this cultivar would literally inhabit almost every city and town to some degree or another; the tree has reached epidemic proportions and is over-planted similar to Green Ash, Silver Maple and Siberian Elm; 'Bradford' is beautiful but not a panacea for urban planting; to some extent problems are now starting to appear that should give reason to temper enthusiasm for the cultivar; incompatibility and severe splitting are occurring on older trees; Bradford tends to develop rather tight crotches and I have seen trees that were literally split in half; new cultivars have been introduced and several show promise; 'Bradford' is still popular but its limitations have been recognized by many knowledgeable plantsmen and nurserymen; unfortunately, the buying public has not yet caught up; for short term use perhaps 10 to 15 years, 20 with luck, the tree is magnificent; the plant will literally fall apart because of the development of many branches around a common length of the trunk, plants manifest the problem by losing the distinct pyramidal shape and eventually becoming wide fan-shaped; plants have literally split in half before even reaching the fan shape; a move toward better pruning in the nursery has been advocated but economically and practically this has not worked out; genetically the tree is programmed to grow the way it does; if liabilities are understood then the plant is acceptable for use. 'Bradford' was the first selection of *P. calleryana* and was selected at the USDA Plant Introduction Station, Glenn Dale, MD from seedlings of Chinese seed, named in 1963, at that time the original tree was 44-years-old, 50′ high and 30′ wide; I suggest that the reader refer to Dirr, "What do we know about cultivars?" *American Nurseryman* 154(6) (1981).

The above can be largely dittoed for this edition. Many nurserymen have stopped growing the tree and switched to 'Chanticleer' which, to date, is a longer lived, more stable selection. One thing is absolute, when a tree like 'Bradford' is known and accepted by the buying public, it is difficult to remove it from their consciousness. 'Bradford' will be a part of the North American landscape well into the 21st century.

Gerhold and McElroy, *J. Arboriculture* 20:259–261 (1994), evaluated eight *P. calleryana* cultivars, 2 of each cultivar in 10 communities in Pennsylvania; best were 'Aristocrat', 'Chanticleer', and 'Redspire'; 'Whitehouse' was the worst.

Bonnie and I comment about the overuse of the cultivar, particularly where native trees provide the architectural structure of a garden, street or neighborhood. The "cookie-cutter" Bradfords, lining drives and streets, are difficult to digest, particularly because I realize their time is finite.

OTHER CULTIVARS:

'Aristocrat'—Selection in 1969 by William T. Straw, Carlisle Nursery, Independence, KY; basically pyramidal to broad-pyramidal in outline, branches more horizontal and crotch angles wider, lustrous dark green leaves with a wavy edge and for that reason quite distinct from other *P. calleryana* selections; fall color is variable and ranges from yellow to red; trees I have seen were not as good as 'Bradford' although it is advertised as having better fall color; flowers are more sparsely borne but still quite attractive; tends to maintain a central leader and shows great vigor for 6-year-old trees may be 12′ high, 10′ wide with a 3″ trunk diameter; 36′ high and 16′ wide after 15 years; thornless; shows about the same cold and heat tolerance as 'Bradford'; is more fireblight susceptible than 'Bradford'; fireblight in the Southeast during 1988 and 1989 was devastating on this cultivar, many growers refuse to plant another 'Aristocrat'; in the North I have not noticed the problem to the degree it has occurred in the South; used along Broad Street, one of the main thoroughfares into Athens, and has performed respectably in spite of the fireblight infestations; flowers later than 'Bradford' and structurally has held together over time; on March 10, 1991 I noted that 'Aristocrat' was still in bud while 'Bradford' was in full flower; older specimens at Bernheim and Mt. Airy Arboreta, and Arlington Memorial Gardens, Cincinnati attest to this; with time the central leader is lost and trees are 40 to 45′ high by 20 to 25′ wide; Cappiello reported 'Aristocrat' hardy at Orono, ME while 'Bradford' was killed.

'Autumn Blaze'—An introduction by Dr. Westwood, Oregon State, for consistent reddish purple fall color; it is also more cold hardy than 'Bradford'; supposedly with upright, pyramidal crown with lateral branches at about right angles to the central leader, trees I have seen have been more pyramidal-rounded, also will develop a few thorns, appears highly susceptible to fireblight, selected in 1969 at Oregon State, patented in 1980, definitely more rounded than 'Bradford' in habit, successful in Orono, ME.

'Capital'—Introduction from the U.S. National Arboretum that is more upright than 'Whitehouse' and can be substituted for Lombardy Poplar; its leaves turn coppery in fall; see *HortScience* 16(6):799–800 (1981); early reports indicated it was a good selection; leaves are a lustrous dark green, show moderate to good fireblight resistance, grew 32′ high by 8′ wide after 15 years, possibly a good choice for narrow restricted growing areas, evaluations (1988 and 1989) reported tremendous fireblight susceptibility, in fact, so great that nurserymen are removing it from the fields in southern nurseries; when at its best, a respectable columnar form, particularly in foliage; pretty ragged in winter.

'Chanticleer' (same as 'Select', 'Cleveland Select' and 'Stone Hill')—A fine upright-pyramidal form that is much narrower than 'Bradford'; it flowers heavily and fall color may be a good reddish purple; the times I have seen it in fall color it did not measure up to 'Bradford'; the leaves are longer and more ovate (see drawing) than 'Bradford' and thinner in texture; thornless; a fine tree and probably a better choice where lateral space to spread is limited; interestingly 'Chanticleer' hardens off earlier than 'Bradford' and

'Chanticleer'

may be less susceptible to early freezes, will grow 35′ high, 16′ wide in 15 years, has shown good fireblight resistance, a 1965 Scanlon introduction, patented in 1965; I have always admired this cultivar and the last 8 years have not diminished the flame; in fact, it would be my first choice of the *P. calleryana* types; flowers later than 'Bradford', perhaps a week or more removed; also, almost as cold hardy as 'Autumn Blaze'; does not maintain a central leader and multiple leaders are common but the tree does not spread like 'Bradford'; the oldest tree I remember resides on the Peter's Hill side of the Arnold Arboretum and was still tightly columnar-pyramidal when last observed in 1991.

Dancer™ ('Southworth')—A selection of *P. betulaefolia*, new leaves gray-green on long flexible petioles, shimmer in the slightest breeze, prolific white flowers before the leaves emerge in spring, small russet 3/8″ diameter fruits, ovate growth habit, 30′ high, 20′ wide, introduced by Bill Wandell.

'Earlyred'—As I understand the introduction, a seedling of 'Bradford' with earlier developing red fall color and more compact habit, from the late, great Bob Simpson, Vincennes, IN who gave our garden world many great plants that have withstood the test of time, including: 'Winter King' hawthorn, 'Winter Red' Common Winterberry, Candymint Sargent Crabapple, ad infinitum; witnessed the plant at Bernheim Arboretum in early November 1997 among the other *P. calleryana* cultivars, 'Bradford' was in shambles, while this cultivar was densely branched and exhibited none of the fall-apart-at-the-seams traits of 'Bradford'; growers need to take a serious look at this clone as an alternative to 'Bradford'.

Edgewood™ ('Edgedell')—A hybrid between *P. calleryana* × *P. betulaefolia* Bunge, described as round-headed, small tree, 30′ by 25′, silvery green foliage turns reddish purple in the fall, emerging leaves with a purple tint, flowers white, Schmidt Nursery introduction.

'Fauriei' (*P. fauriei* Schneid.)—Often listed as a variety and by some authorities considered a species but because it is vegetatively propagated I will treat it as a cultivar; this is another tree that the literature said will be small (20′) and round-headed; unfortunately, the plant did not read the book and we know it will grow 30 to 40′ and develop a pleasing pyramidal outline; the ovate leaves are lustrous dark green and thin; it tends to fall color (yellow or red) earlier than 'Bradford' and drop the leaves earlier; tends to develop a nice crown even in youth; its crotch angles are wider than 'Bradford' and it makes a less stiff, formal appearance in the landscape; supposedly it shows good urban soil tolerance; the buds on this form are distinctly different than the other *P. calleryana* types for they are reddish brown and show only a minor amount of gray pubescence; thornless; a fine tree in Spring Grove was devastated by storm damage; grew 32′ by 25′ in 15 years; in Kansas, averaged 1′4″ per year over an 8 year period; Martin Meyer, retired, University of Illinois, grew a population of *P. fauriei* and the seedlings were smaller in leaf, 1 to 2″ long, the habit shrubby and smallish, the branches spiny, none equated with the 'Fauriei' that is described above; I suspect that a *P. calleryana* type was pinned with the 'Fauriei' name; true *P. fauriei* is inferior to true *P. calleryana* for ornamental purposes.

Korean Sun™ ('Westwood') (*P. fauriei*)—Compact, rounded habit, 12′ by 15′, fine-textured medium green foliage, red to red-purple fall color, white flowers, hardier than *P. calleryana*, Zone 4.

'Princess'—I have only seen the tree on one occasion and it reminded of a 'Bradford', considered a rounded form of 'Bradford' but hardier, the original tree (25-years-old) was 28′ high with an equal spread, fall color orange to red, a Scanlon introduction in 1976, found on a Cleveland, OH street.

Pzazz™—A smaller form than 'Bradford' with attractive bright green leaves and distinctive ruffled leaf margins, better branch structure than 'Bradford' or 'Redspire', 35′ by 25′, Zone 5 to 7, probably a *P. betulaefolia* selection, a Wandell introduction.

'Rancho'—Another Scanlon introduction with a columnar pyramidal form, fall color develops about 10 days earlier than 'Chanticleer', after 15 years averaged 32′ high and 15′ wide.

'Redspire'—A pyramidal form without the inherent stiffness of 'Bradford'; the ovate leaves are thick, shiny dark green and turn more yellow than red in fall; it colors ahead of 'Bradford'; and in my estimation makes a fine tree; thornless; slower growing and does not caliper as fast as 'Bradford'; unfortunately, quite susceptible to fire blight; originated as a seedling of 'Bradford'; ceases growth in early fall; patented in 1975 by Princeton Nursery.

'Stonehill' ('Stone Hill')—Apparently another name for 'Chanticleer', was informed by a Pennsylvania nurseryman that this is another rename.

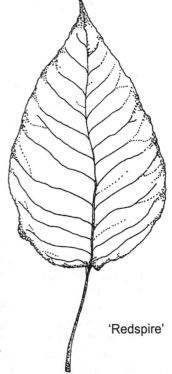

'Redspire'

'Trinity'—Tightly rounded head, profuse single white flowers, glossy light green leaves, orange-red fall color, negligible fruit, 30', introduced in early 70's by Handy Nursery, Oregon, not well-known but the few trees I observed were handsome, was patented #4530, original cultivar name was 'Sylvania'.

'Whitehouse'—A U.S. National Arboretum introduction selected in 1969 from a population of 2500 seedlings resulting from an open pollination of 'Bradford' and other *P. calleryana* seedlings; it develops a columnar-pyramidal form with a strong central leader and fine, profuse, upward arching branches, a tree may be 14' high and only 3 1/2' wide, 35' by 14' after 14 years; the leaves are glossy green, long pointed and narrower than 'Bradford'; fall color may range from red to reddish purple, colors earlier than other cultivars; in youth it is a faster grower than 'Bradford' because of the strong dominance of the central leader; thornless; see *HortScience* 12:591–592 (1977): flowers about 5 days later than 'Bradford'; leaf spot is terrible and disfigures leaves to the degree that trees are a liability; considerable hype has surrounded this tree and claims like "more urban tolerant and drought tolerant than 'Bradford'" have been made; unfortunately, this form is less than desirable and several southern nurserymen who started to grow the plant in the early 1980's have quit.

Santamour and McArdle, *J. Arboriculture* 9(4):114–116 (1983) provide excellent background information on the species and cultivars. Also Haserodt and Sydnor, *J. Arboriculture* 4(6):160–163 (1983) profile the growth habits of 5 cultivars of *P. calleryana*.

PROPAGATION: Seeds of the species require cold (32 to 36°F) for 60 to 90 days. Seeds collected on January 17 from trees at the Atlanta Botanical Garden germinated 7 days after planting. Apparently the seeds had received sufficient natural cold moist stratification while still in the fruit. Good paper on seed germination of 69 *Pyrus* crosses appeared in *Landscape Plant News* 3(2):13–14 (1992); in brief, germination was excellent for most crosses after cold-moist stratification for 90 days at 35°F. Much has been written about rooting cuttings and my graduate students and I have conducted considerable work. The best success I have seen was at Greenleaf Nursery, OK where the propagator Randy Davis took firm cuttings, treated them with 10,000 ppm IBA + 5000 ppm NAA quick dip, bark: sand, mist and achieved 70% rooting, with quality root systems. Also Gilliam et al., *J. Environ. Hort.* 6:81–83 (1988), reported 1 or 2% IBA in aqueous or ethanolic KOH solutions, or 2% KIBA promoted greatest rooting of terminal cuttings.

ADDITIONAL NOTES: The urban tolerance of this group makes them first choice when the questions are asked . . . what goes along the street? . . . in the planter? . . . in the parking lot? Have noticed numerous escapees and *P. calleryana* seedlings are forming monocultures in some areas of the South. Interestingly, I have walked these escapees and to date have seen nothing that supersedes the current cultivars in foliage, also most are thorny.

Worthwhile pear cold hardiness data in *North American Plant Propagator* 3(2):14–15 (1991) that points to 'Bradford' and other pear problems in northern climes. The data are presented in tabular form.

Lowest temperature tested (°F) that did not result in severe injury of stem tissue of *Pyrus* taxa:

	DATE TESTED		
TAXA	10-22-90	11-14-90	01-14-91
'Aristocrat'	+ 6.8	−4.0	−32.8
'Autumn Blaze'	+ 6.8	−4.0	−29.2
'Bradford'	+24.8	+3.2	−14.8
'Capital'	+21.2	−7.6	−18.4
'Chanticleer'	+ 3.2	−7.6	−22.0
'Redspire'	+17.6	+3.2	−25.6
'Whitehouse'	+21.2	+3.2	−22.0
'Fauriei' (*P. fauriei*)	+14.0	−4.0	−25.6

Interestingly, 'Bradford' was consistently killed at the University of Minnesota Landscape Arboretum. Additional information in *J. Environ. Hort.* 12:227–230 (1994). In the latter study, the data conclusively showed 'Autumn Blaze' was the most cold hardy followed by 'Chanticleer' in Minnesota, but both were killed after exposure to −33°F. *Pyrus fauriei*, *P. salicifolia* 'Silver Frost', and *P. ussuriensis* also survived −33°F.

NATIVE HABITAT: *Pyrus calleryana* is native to Korea and China. Introduced 1908. 'Bradford' was raised from seed purchased in 1919 from Nanjing, China. The original reason for introducing *P. calleryana* was to breed fireblight resistance into the fruiting pears. This never materialized but the original effort resulted in several ornamental trees.

RELATED SPECIES:

Pyrus communis L. — Common Pear

LEAVES: Alternate, simple, orbicular-ovate to elliptic, 3/4 to 3″(4″) long, up to 2″ wide, acute or short acuminate, subcordate to broad-cuneate, crenate-serrulate, glabrous or villous when young, lustrous dark green; petiole—1 to 2″ long.

BUDS: Imbricate, conical, sharp-pointed, smooth or slightly hairy, terminal about 1/3″ long, laterals—small, generally divergent and not flattened or at times on vigorous shoots both flattened and appressed.

STEM: Stout, glabrous or slightly downy, yellowish green or sometimes with tinge of brown; stubby-branched, slow-growing fruit spurs abundant.

BARK: Grayish brown, smooth on young branches, with age longitudinally fissured into flat-topped ridges which are further broken by transverse fissures into oblong scales.

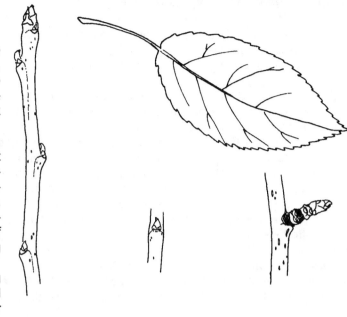

FRUIT: A large fleshy pome, top-shaped to rounded, green to yellowish green.

Pyrus communis, (pī′rus kom-mū′nis), Common Pear, is only mentioned here because it is sometimes trained as an espaliered plant. Tremendous fireblight susceptibility and not recommended for ornamental purposes although the white, 1 to 1 1/2″ diameter flowers are quite showy and malodorous. Very early-flowering and I have seen it in full flower on February 22 at Savannah, GA, usually March 1–15 in Athens, GA. Tends to seed and can form thickets. Fall color is sometimes excellent red to maroon and usually in mid-November (Athens). Europe, western Asia. Long cultivated. Escaped and naturalized. Zone 4 to 8(9).

Pyrus kawakamii Hayata. — Evergreen Pear

LEAVES: Alternate, simple, evergreen, ovate to obovate, 2 to 4″ long, finely and regularly serrate, leathery lustrous dark green; petiole—1 1/4″ long.

Pyrus kawakamii, (pī′rus kaw-a-cam′ē-ī), Evergreen Pear, is a small rounded evergreen tree that offers abundant white flowers in late winter or early spring. Tends toward a large shrub and the branches droop and sprawl. Used on the West Coast, particularly California. I have seen a few trees on the Georgia coast but they were decimated by fireblight. The branches may develop thorns. Fruit is globose, glabrous, about 1/2″ across and inedible. Native to China, Taiwan. Zone 8 to 10.

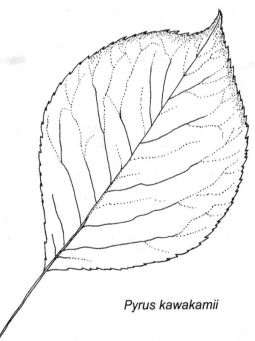

Pyrus kawakamii

Pyrus pyrifolia (Burm.) Nak. — Chinese Sand Pear

LEAVES: Alternate, simple, ovate-oblong, 2 3/4 to 4″(5″) long, about half as wide, acuminate, rounded or rarely subcordate, glabrous, margins conspicuously bristle-tipped, lustrous dark green above, petiole—1 1/4 to 1 3/4″ long.

Pyrus pyrifolia, (pī′rus pī-ri-fō′li-à), Chinese Sand Pear, is a rather large (40′), pyramidal-rounded tree that literally explodes into a white blanket in April. The tree reminds of a white cloud. Flowers are 1 to 1 1/2″ across in 6- to 9-flowered corymbs. The globular, 1 1/4″ long and wide fruits are brownish and spotted with white, quite hard and gritty. The lustrous dark green leaves turn excellent orange-red in fall. Wilson introduced it in 1909 when collecting for the Arnold and a magnificent specimen from his collection is located along the Chinese walk. Have read size descriptions of 15 to 40′. Central and western China. Zone 5 to 7.

Pyrus salicifolia Pall. — Willowleaf Pear
LEAVES: Alternate, simple, narrow-lanceolate, 1 1/2 to 3 1/2″ long, 1/3 to 2/3″ wide, tapering at both ends, entire or sparsely toothed, covered with gray down when young, later upper surface shining green, lower pubescent; petiole—1/2″ or less long.
STEM: Covered with a grayish white pubescence which falls away with age.

Pyrus salicifolia, (pī′rus sal-is-i-fō′li-à), Willowleaf Pear, reaches 15 to 25′ and possesses graceful, silvery gray, willow-like leaves. Unfortunately, it is very susceptible to fireblight and is seldom seen in cultivation in the United States. I learned this tree in my plant materials course at Ohio State in 1962 and did not see it again until 1981 at Bodnant Garden, Wales. Habit is oval rounded with graceful arching branches. 'Pendula' with elegant drooping branches is probably more common in cultivation than the species and, by some, is considered similar to the species. 'Silver Frost' is described as broadly weeping to pendulous, 12 to 15′ high, 10 to 12′ wide, with silver-gray foliage; I suspect it may be 'Pendula' with a fancy name. Flowers are cream to greenish white, 3/4″ diameter, and closely packed 6 to 8 in small, rounded corymbs. Fruits are typical pear shape and 1 to 1 1/4″ long and wide. Southeastern Europe, western Asia. Introduced 1780. Zone 4 to 7.

Pyrus ussuriensis Maxim. — Ussurian Pear
LEAVES: Alternate, simple, orbicular-ovate to ovate, 2 to 4″ long, acuminate, rounded or slightly cordate, finely and regularly bristle-toothed, glabrous, lustrous dark green; petiole—1 to 2 1/4″ long.

Pyrus ussuriensis, (pī′rus ū-sör-ē-en′sis), Ussurian Pear, is the hardiest of all pears. The habit is dense, rounded, 40 to 50′; the leaves are a handsome, glossy dark green in summer changing to red and reddish purple in the fall. Flowers may be faintly pink in bud, finally white, 1 1/3″ across, April–May. The fruit is a (5/8″)1 to 1 1/2″(2 1/2″) diameter, greenish yellow, subglobose pome. It, along with *P. calleryana*, is the least susceptible to fireblight. For colder climates it would prove a valuable ornamental. Truly a handsome ornamental tree but has never been developed like *P. calleryana*. 'McDermand' is a seed-produced cultivar useful for shelterbelts and wildlife food (1 to 1 1/2″ diameter fruits), released in 1990 by USDA-SCS-PMC, Bismarck, SD. Prairie Gem™ ('MorDak') is oval in youth, globose with age, to 25′ or greater, excellent lustrous dark green leaves turn golden yellow in autumn, the 1 1/4″ fruits only produced if cross-pollinated, from Dr. Dale Hansen, North Dakota State University. Northeastern Asia. Introduced 1855. Zone 3 to 6 or 7.

Quercus acutissima Carruth. — Sawtooth Oak
(kwĕr′kus a-kū-tis′i-mà)

FAMILY: Fagaceae
LEAVES: Alternate, simple, obovate-oblong to oblong, 3 1/2 to 7 1/2″ long, 1 to 2 1/4″ wide, acuminate, broad-cuneate or rounded at base, serrate with bristle-like teeth terminating the 12 to 16 parallel veins, lustrous dark green, glabrous above, glabrous beneath except axillary tufts of hairs, pubescent when unfolding; petiole—3/4 to 1″(2″) long; leaf looks like a *Castanea* leaf in many respects and is often confused with same.
BUDS: Imbricate, pubescent, almost woolly, grayish brown, 1/4 to 3/8″(1/2″) long, edges of scales membranous and gray pubescent, lower scale darker brown, creating two-toned effect; somewhat similar to *Q. velutina* in appearance, usually larger but not as angled.
STEM: Gray-brown, glabrous.

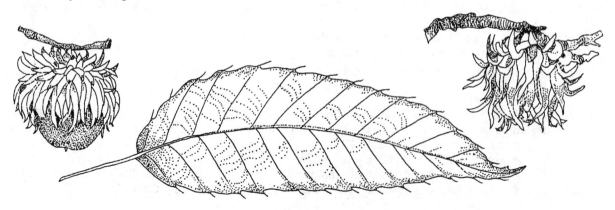

SIZE: 40 to 60′ in height; I have seen trees taller than wide and others wider than tall; probably great variation in seed-grown material although the trend is toward a broad, rounded outline; amazing 52′ high by 42′ wide specimen in Morton Arboretum.

HARDINESS: Zone (5)6 to 9.

HABIT: Dense, broad pyramidal in youth; varying in old age from oval-rounded to broad-rounded with low-slung, wide-spreading branches.

RATE: Initially medium, in 16 years grew 32′; in Wichita, KS tests averaged 2′3″ per year over a 7 year period; one of the fastest growing oaks particularly in youth; direct seeded into Mississippi floodplain, plants grew 28 to 34′ in 14 years; *Q. nuttallii* only 23′ on average; see *Tree Planters Notes* 36:3–5 (1985).

TEXTURE: Pleasantly medium in foliage, medium to medium-coarse in winter.

BARK: Deeply ridged-and-furrowed, on old trunks appearing almost corky, ash brown.

LEAF COLOR: Dark lustrous green in summer; often a good clear yellow to golden brown fall color, developing late, often in November; leaves open a brilliant yellow to golden yellow in spring, in late March–early April, Athens.

FLOWERS: Male, in 3 to 4″ long slender golden catkins in late March–early April with the emerging leaves.

FRUIT: Acorn, sessile, involucre with long, spreading and recurving scales, enclosing about 2/3's of the nut, about 1″ long, often heavy crops are borne, nut about 3/4″ long, lustrous rich brown, among the first acorns to ripen and fall; have clocked mature acorns on the ground on September 28, 1996; have read report that acorns take two years to develop but have not observed young acorns being carried through the winter.

CULTURE: Easily grown, transplants readily, grows off quickly; I have seen it over a wide geographic area and it prefers acid, well-drained soils but appears quite adaptable; may develop chlorosis on high pH soils; thrives in the heat of the South.

DISEASES AND INSECTS: None serious.

LANDSCAPE VALUE: Handsome, wide-spreading, clean-foliaged shade or lawn tree; could be used more than it is especially in South where it is fast-growing; Williams et al., *J. Arboriculture* 21:118–121 (1995), reported superior performance of *Q. acutissima*, and also *Q. prinus*, *Q. lyrata*, and *Q. shumardii* in Auburn University tests; hardiness reports are somewhat conflicting and I estimate it will withstand −20°F once established; at a conference in Lincoln, NE, where I lectured, a gentleman mentioned that the tree is growing in Blair, NE where winters can be extremely harsh; successfully growing at Morton Arboretum, Lisle, IL; in spring the tree is covered with pendent, golden, male catkins which are quite attractive; old leaves will persist on young trees throughout the winter; it also fruits heavily in the South showing an alternate year bearing tendency; considered a source of nutrition for wildlife; acorns are in certain years so abundant as to cover the ground in a solid mantle.

CULTIVARS:

var. *chenii* (Nak.) Camus—Similar to the above, although it has been listed as a separate species. The leaves are glabrous, the acorns smaller with more slender scales. Southern and central China.

'Gobbler'—The result of open-pollinated progeny that produce early and abundant acorns for wild turkey food.

PROPAGATION: Sow in fall, germination occurs in spring, root apparently emerges without cold treatment; shoot requires cold.

ADDITIONAL NOTES: Shows strong juvenility and young trees may hold the leaves all winter. New leaves emerge a light yellow and provide a golden glow to the entire tree. Two worthwhile references that describe cultivars of the various oaks are McArdle and Santamour, "Cultivar Checklist of White Oak Species (excl. *Quercus robur* L.)," *J. Arboriculture* 11(10):307–315 (1985) and same authors, "Cultivar Checklist of English Oak (*Quercus robur* L.)," *J. Arboriculture* 13(10):250–256 (1987).

Sternberg, *American Nurseryman* 172(2):33–45 (1990), presents a fine treatise on oak taxonomy and hybridity. Sternberg's premise is that there are many hybrid species with landscape potential. I believe oak vegetative propagation techniques will have to become mainstream to insure commercial success.

NATIVE HABITAT: Japan, Korea, China, Himalaya. Introduced 1862.

RELATED SPECIES:

Quercus variabilis Bl., (kwĕr′kus vãr-i-ab′-i-lis), Oriental Oak, Chinese Cork Oak, is a large (60 to 70′), fairly open tree with foliage similar to *Q. acutissima* except the upper surface is glossy dark green and the underside of the leaf is clothed with a distinct whitish tomentum and the teeth are shorter. Acorns are ovoid to subglobose, enclosed for most of their length by the cap made up of long, curled scales, 3/4″ long, ripen in second year. The bark is very corky, deeply ridged-and-furrowed and up to 4″ thick. Native to northern China, Korea, Japan. Introduced 1861. Zone 5 to 7.

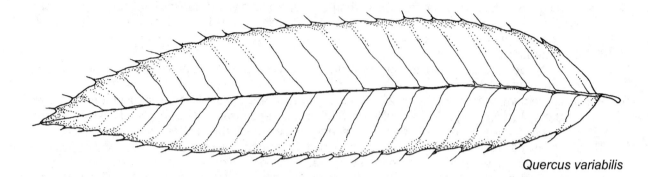

Quercus variabilis

Quercus alba L. — White Oak
(kwĕr′kus al′bȧ)

FAMILY: Fagaceae

LEAVES: Alternate, simple, obovate to oblong-obovate, 4 to 8 1/2″ long, about one-half as wide, apex abruptly acute, narrowed at cuneate base, with 5 to 9 oblong and obtuse, entire lobes, dark green to almost dark blue-green above, pale or glaucous beneath; petiole—1/2 to 1″ long, yellowish green.

BUDS: Imbricate, broadly ovate, blunt, reddish brown to brown in color, 1/8 to 1/4″ long, sometimes slightly hairy especially at ends of bud scales.

STEM: Stout, brown to purple, angled, sometimes covered with a waxy grayish bloom.

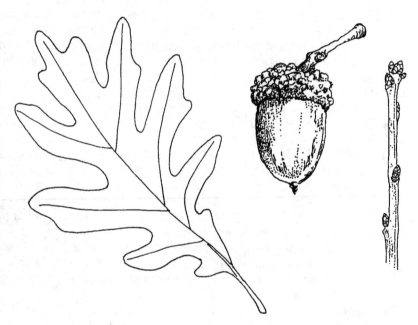

SIZE: 50 to 80′ high and wide; can grow over 100′ in the wild; national champion is 79′ by 102′ wide in Wye Mills State Park, MD.

HARDINESS: Zone 3b to 9.

HABIT: Pyramidal when young, upright-rounded to broad-rounded with wide-spreading branches at maturity; very imposing specimen when full grown; one of the most handsome oaks.

RATE: Slow to medium, 12 to 15′ over a 10 to 12 year period, very slow after first 20 to 30 years.

TEXTURE: Medium in leaf, medium to coarse in winter but with a strong, bold appearance.

BARK: On old trunks light ashy gray, variable in appearance, often broken into small, vertically arranged blocks and scales, scaly on the surface; later irregularly plated or deeply fissured, with narrow ridges; sometimes rather smooth and gray in spots; this is caused by a fungus.

LEAF COLOR: Grayish and pinkish when unfolding changing to dark green in summer, almost tends toward a blue-green; fall color varies from brown to a rich red to wine color and lasts for a long period of time; in falls of 1988 and 1996 I saw the best fall color, a rich reddish purple on many White Oaks in the South.

FLOWERS: The following discussion concerns the flowers of the genus *Quercus* and is applicable to most species covered in this text. Monoecious, appearing on the old or new growth; staminate catkins pendent, clustered; individual flowers comprising a 4- to 7-lobed calyx which encloses 6 stamens, rarely 6 to 12; pistillate flowers solitary or in few to many-flowered spikes from the axils of the new leaves; individual flowers consisting of a 6-lobed calyx surrounding a 3- (rarely 4- to 5-) celled ovary, the whole partly enclosed in an involucre.

FRUIT: Nut, solitary or paired, sessile or short-stalked, 3/4 to 1″ long, ovoid-oblong, enclosed for 1/4 to 1/3 of its length in a light chestnut brown, bowl-like cap (involucre), involucre with raised "bumpy" scales rather than smooth overlapping scales like *Q. rubra*, nut colors a deep chocolate brown, ripens the first year.

CULTURE: Transplant balled-and-burlapped as a small tree; found on many types of soil although performs maximally in deep, moist, well-drained soils; prefer acid soils, pH 5.5 to 6.5; full sun; prune in winter or early spring. There is a delicate balance in forest situations and when man encroaches and builds roads and houses in White Oak timber the trees often gradually decline and die. This is, in part, due to compaction, ruination of mycorrhizal associations and removal of the recycled organic matter from under the trees.

DISEASES AND INSECTS: The following is a list of problems reported occurring on oaks: anthracnose, bacterial leaf scorch caused by *Xylella fastidiosa* (*Q. alba*, *Q. imbricaria*, *Q. palustris*, and *Q. rubra*, also *Q. falcata*, *Q. laurifolia*, and *Q. nigra*), basal canker, canker, leaf blister, leaf spots, powdery mildew, rust, twig blights, wilt, wood decay, shoe-string root rot, various galls, scales, gypsy moth, yellow-necked caterpillar, pin oak sawfly, saddleback caterpillar, oak skeletonizer, asiatic oak weevil, two-lined chestnut borer, flatheaded borer, leaf miner, oak lace bug and oak mite; in spite of this inspiring list of pests, White Oak is a durable, long-lived tree.

LANDSCAPE VALUE: It is doubtful if this will ever become a popular ornamental tree unless it is native in a specific area; production is difficult, growth is slow, and transplanting can be a problem; a majestic and worthwhile tree for large areas; the state tree of Illinois; actually among the most handsome of oaks.

PROPAGATION: Seed requires no special treatment; direct sow after collection.

ADDITIONAL NOTES: The most important species of the White Oak group. The wood is used for furniture, flooring, interior finishing, boat building, wine and whiskey casks. The acorn is edible and is eaten by many kinds of birds and mammals. Best to boil in water to remove tannins. Difficult to pen my emotional ties to this species. A White Oak dominated forest is beautiful year round. From the south side (I believe) of Biltmore House, from the overlook, is a view to Mt. Pisgah and other mountains. In the foreground, dominating the rolling hills, are numerous open-grown White Oaks with unshaven gray fuzz in spring, dark green in summer, shades of bronze to red in fall, and gray in winter. If the reader has not observed this facet of the estate, take the time to savor the beauty during the next visit.

NATIVE HABITAT: Maine to Florida, west to Minnesota and Texas. Introduced 1724.

RELATED SPECIES:

Quercus bicolor Willd. — Swamp White Oak

LEAVES: Alternate, simple, oblong-obovate to obovate, 3 to 7″ long, 1 1/4 to 4″ wide, acute or rounded cuneate, coarsely sinuate-dentate with 6 to 10 pairs of coarse, obtuse teeth, or sometimes lobed halfway to the midrib, lustrous dark green above, whitish tomentose or grayish green and velvety beneath, midrib yellowish, leathery in texture; petiole—1/2 to 3/4″ long, yellowish.

BUDS: Imbricate, broadly ovate, light chestnut brown, 1/8 to 1/4″ long, coated with pale down above the middle; clustered buds often house needle- to strap-like appendages.

STEM: Stout to slender, yellowish brown to reddish brown, glabrous.

BARK: Flaky, grayish brown, divided by deep, longitudinal fissures into rather long, flat ridges; on old trunks rugged and handsome.

Quercus bicolor, (kwĕr′kus bī′kul-ĕr), Swamp White Oak, grows 50 to 60′ in height with an equal or greater spread forming a broad, open, round-topped crown and a short, limby trunk. The acorn is about 1″ long, usually paired, covered about 1/3 by the involucre, shining light brown nut, borne on slender 1 to 4″ long peduncles. Found in the wild in low lying and more or less swampy situations, often occurring in moist bottomlands and along the banks of streams. Requires acid soil. I have observed very severe chlorosis on this species. There are mixed answers as to the ease of transplanting; several nurserymen said easy, others difficult; generally considered easier than *Q. alba*. Many beautiful specimens at Mt. Airy, Cincinnati, OH, fully 60 to 80′ high and 60 to 70′ wide. On a rainy October day I walked Minutemen National Park, Concord, MA, and witnessed along the Concord River the largest *Q. bicolor* to date with coarse-textured, blackish, deeply ridged-and-furrowed bark and elephantine trunk (size), a tinge of yellow-bronze fall color, and no humans in sight, the tree was mine to savor, appreciate and respect. The national champion is 120′ by 92′ in Clearwater Nature Center, Clinton, MD. Excellent drought resistance is inherent in this species. Winter silhouette is more coarse than *Q. alba* because of the numerous short branches that develop from secondary branches. Normal fall color is yellow but have seen reasonable red-purple. Hybrids between this and *Q. alba* are termed *Q. × jackiana* hort. Oak rough bulletgall wasp is producing woody galls on the stems of *Q. bicolor* and *Q. macrocarpa* in Colorado where both species are utilized for shade trees. Native from Quebec to Georgia, west to Michigan and Arkansas. Introduced 1800. Zone 4 to 8.

Quercus cerris L. — Turkey Oak

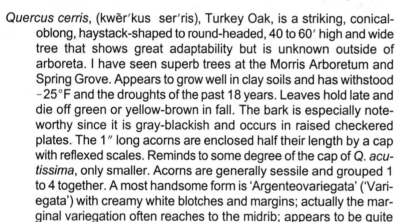

LEAVES: Alternate, simple, oval or oblong, 2 1/2 to 5″ long, 1 to 3″ wide, coarsely dentate to pinnately lobed, teeth triangular and acute, rounded to truncate, lustrous dark green above, dull light green and pubescent below, 6 to 10 vein pairs; petiole—variable, 1/8 to 3/4″ long.

Quercus cerris, (kwĕr′kus ser′ris), Turkey Oak, is a striking, conical-oblong, haystack-shaped to round-headed, 40 to 60′ high and wide tree that shows great adaptability but is unknown outside of arboreta. I have seen superb trees at the Morris Arboretum and Spring Grove. Appears to grow well in clay soils and has withstood -25°F and the droughts of the past 18 years. Leaves hold late and die off green or yellow-brown in fall. The bark is especially noteworthy since it is gray-blackish and occurs in raised checkered plates. The 1″ long acorns are enclosed half their length by a cap with reflexed scales. Reminds to some degree of the cap of *Q. acutissima*, only smaller. Acorns are generally sessile and grouped 1 to 4 together. A most handsome form is 'Argenteovariegata' ('Variegata') with creamy white blotches and margins; actually the marginal variegation often reaches to the midrib; appears to be quite vigorous. Beautiful specimens of the species at Knightshayes Garden in Devon, England, last experienced in the sullen light of late March, the massive trunk and muscular branches dominating the meadow that fronts the garden. Great trees are terrific! Southern Europe, western Asia. Introduced 1735. Zone 5 to 7(?).

Quercus falcata Michx. — Southern Red Oak, Spanish Oak

LEAVES: Alternate, simple, obovate to ovate, 5 to 9″(12″) long, 4 to 5″ wide, either shallowly 3-lobed at the apex or more or less deeply 5- to 7-lobed, often falcate, the terminal lobe sometimes much longer than the laterals, apex acuminate or falcate, base rounded to broadly cuneate, lustrous dark green above, grayish green and tomentose below turning brownish with time; petiole—1 to 2″ long, often pubescent, yellowish.
BUDS: Imbricate, 1/4″ long, ovoid, acute, dusty reddish brown, pubescent especially toward apex.
STEM: Reddish brown, angled, pubescent or nearly glabrous.

Quercus falcata, (kwĕr′kus fal-kā′tȧ), Southern Red Oak, is one of the most common upland southern oaks and is particularly characteristic of the drier, poorer soils of the Piedmont. There are a great number at the

University's Botanical Garden and several large specimens on the Georgia campus. The species will grow 70 to 80′ and with time forms a rounded outline. The national champion is 104′ by 135′ in Harwood, MD. The leaves hold late and fall color is at best brown, perhaps with a tinge of red. The 1/2″ long, subglobose nut is borne either singly or paired. The cap is shallow and sits on the top of the nut. The nut is distinctly striate with alternating, more or less parallel lines of light and dark brown to black. The variety *pagodifolia* Ellis., Cherrybark Oak, Swamp Spanish Oak, has leaves more uniformly 5- to 11-lobed than the species, with the margins of the ribs (lobes) at right angles to the midrib. The sinuses are not as deep as those of *Q. falcata*. Bark is cherry-like, blackish and scaly. National champion is 110′ by 108′ in Colonial Beach, VA. The variety is found in a number of bottomland habitats but develops best on loamy ridges. The species is native from New Jersey to Florida, west to Missouri and Texas. Introduced before 1763. Zone (6)7 to 9. The variety runs from Virginia to Florida west to southern Illinois and Arkansas. Introduced 1904. Zone 7 to 9. Neither are common in nursery commerce. Variety *pagodifolia* has possibilities.

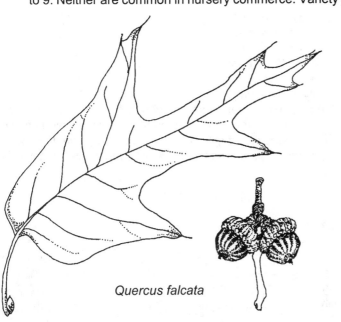

Quercus falcata

Quercus falcata
var. *pagodifolia*

RELATED SPECIES:

Quercus laevis Walt. — Turkey Oak
LEAVES: Alternate, simple, obovate, 4 to 14″ long, 3- to 7-lobed, lustrous dark green above, glabrous below except for hairs in axils of veins; petiole—less than 3/4″ long.
BUDS: Imbricate, long conical, to 1/2″ long, gray-brown, pubescent.

Quercus laevis, (kwĕr′kus lē′vis), Turkey Oak, is allied to *Q. falcata* but with petioles 1/2 to 3/4″ long and leaves at maturity lustrous and glabrous below. Leaves may develop red to red-brown fall coloration. The tree is common in the sand hills of the South. The leaves hang perpendicular to the ground. Tree grows 30 to 40′ high under cultivation, often limited by habitat extremes in the wild. National champion is 74′ by 42′ in Cockeysville, MD. Bark is thick and blackish with deep, irregular furrows and blocky ridges. Acorn caps 3/4 to 1 1/4″ wide, on 1/5″ long peduncles, covering about 1/3 of acorn. North Carolina to Florida and Louisiana. Introduced around 1834. Zone 7 to 9.

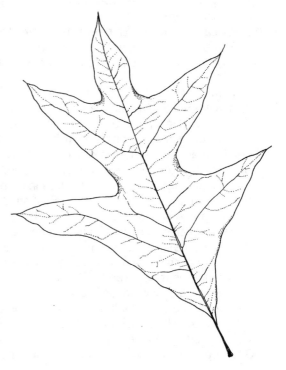

Quercus georgiana M.A. Curtis — Georgia Oak

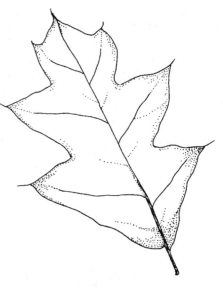

LEAVES: Alternate, simple, 1 1/4 to 4 1/2″ long, 1 to 3 3/4″ wide, 3- to 6(7)-lobed, usually with one bristle per lobe, acute with sharp bristle, cuneate, lustrous dark green above, glabrous, paler below with tufts of hairs on main vein axils; petiole—1/4 to 1/2″ long.

BUDS: Narrow ovoid to oval, dark brown, often with some luster, pubescent often at their tips, 1/8 to 1/4″ long.

STEM: First year—slender, shiny brown, glabrous; second year—gray-brown with numerous small lenticels.

Quercus georgiana, (kwĕr′kus jôrj-ē-ā′nȧ), Georgia Oak, is a small, 15 to 30′ high and wide tree that grows naturally on granitic outcrops in South Carolina, Georgia, and Alabama. It is often stunted in this habitat but under cultivation makes a rather handsome densely branched tree with beautiful lustrous dark green summer foliage and red to reddish purple fall color. The bark is dark gray, thin and smooth becoming scaly with maturity. Acorns (two years to mature) average 1/2″ long, the cap covering about 1/4 of the dark brown nut. The national champion is 47′ by 36′ at Pine Mountain, GA. Several 20′ trees on the Georgia campus make one believe that the species has possibilities as a small lawn, planter or park tree. Easily grown from seed planted in fall. Rehder places this as a species related to *Q. palustris*. Hybrids between the two might yield useful offspring. Introduced 1876. Zone (5)6 to 8.

Quercus hemisphaerica Bartr. — Laurel Oak

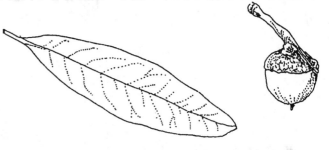

LEAVES: Alternate, simple, evergreen until February in Athens, lanceolate, elliptic to oblanceolate, obovate, or oblong-obovate, 1 1/4 to 4″ long, 1/2 to 1 1/4″(2″) wide, acute or obtuse, usually with a bristle-tip, cuneate or obtuse at base, entire or with a few shallow lobes or teeth, thick, leathery, often undulating, lustrous dark green, glabrous, lighter green below; petiole—1/4″ long, yellowish.

BUDS: Imbricate, shiny reddish brown, 1/8 to 1/4″ long, essentially glabrous, small for oak buds, similar to buds of *Q. phellos*, *Q. nigra*, and *Q. laurifolia*.

STEM: Gray-brown, glabrous, dotted with small lenticels.

Quercus hemisphaerica, (kwĕr′kus hem-i-sfer′ik-ȧ), Laurel Oak, is reasonably common throughout the coastal plain in the South. The habit is pyramidal-rounded with ultimate height ranging from 40 to 60′ and spread of 30 to 40′. National champion is 96′ by 95′ in Wrens, GA. Several trees on the Georgia campus are exceedingly handsome and are thriving in less than ideal locations. The lustrous dark green leaves persist into February and later, depending on the severity of winter. Acorns are short-stalked (virtually sessile), the nut subglobose to ovoid, about 1/2″ long, enclosed 1/4 to 1/3″ by the saucer-shaped cap.

It has found favor as a street tree in many cities of the South. It is not as long lived or sturdy as *Q. phellos* and *Q. virginiana* but because of smaller size is a good choice for residential landscapes. There are no special soil requirements or pests. 'Darlington' is more compact and the leaves more persistent than the species. I have observed the above cultivar (debatable as to cultivar status, name derived from proximity of trees to Darlington, S.C.) as far north as Cincinnati, OH where it was distinctly deciduous. In the wild occupies well-drained, sandy soil, established dune areas, scrub oak sandhills, stream banks, occasionally in mixed woods. The rapid growth makes it a worthwhile choice for landscape use.

Great confusion abounds concerning the existence of this oak and *Q. laurifolia* Michx., Swamp Laurel Oak or Diamondleaf Oak. Many authorities considered *Q. laurifolia* the major species with *Q. hemi-sphaerica* simply lumped thereunder. Current status (see R.K. Godfrey, 1988. *Trees, shrubs and woody vines of northern Florida and adjacent Georgia and Alabama*. The University of Georgia Press, Athens, GA.) separates the two and possibly with good reason. *Quercus laurifolia*, as I have observed it on the

Georgia campus, loses all the leaves by December–January and is more open in outline. Also, the leaves are larger and although many are similar to *Q. hemisphaerica*, others are almost diamond-shaped. The apices of the leaves are more obtuse, while those of *Q. hemisphaerica* are acute. Buds are 1/8 to 1/4″ long, ovoid, shiny rich brown, appearing 5-sided when viewed from apex down. Acorns are short-stalked, about 1/2″ long, much like *Q. hemisphaerica*. Probably about same landscape size as *Q. hemisphaerica*. An older specimen on the Georgia campus is 80′ high. Co-national champions are 93′ by 122′ and 131′ by 108′ in Marengo

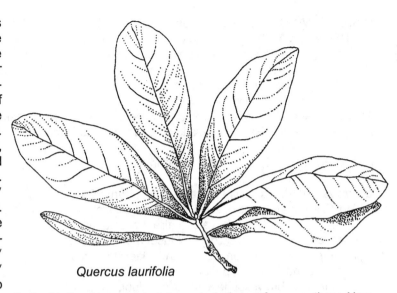

Quercus laurifolia

County, AL and Quitman, MS, respectively. Native to coastal plain and piedmont from southern New Jersey to Florida to east Texas and Southeast Arkansas. Zone 6 to 9.

Quercus imbricaria Michx. — Shingle Oak, also known as Laurel Oak
(kwĕr′kus im-bri-kā′ri-à)

LEAVES: Alternate, simple, oblong or lanceolate, 2 1/2 to 6″ long, 1 to 3″ wide, acute at apex with bristle-like tip, revolute margin, lustrous dark green and glabrous above, pale green or brownish and pubescent beneath; petiole—1/4 to 5/8″ long.

BUDS: Imbricate, ovoid, sharp-pointed, 1/8 to 1/4″ long, brownish, often slightly hairy.

STEM: Slender, green-brown, lustrous, glabrous, angled.

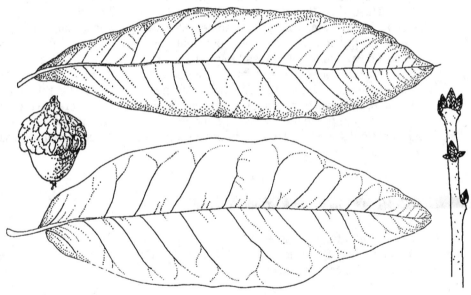

SIZE: 50 or 60′ in height, developing a comparable or slightly greater spread, can grow 80 to 100′ in height; national champion is 104′ by 68′ in Cincinnati, OH.

HARDINESS: Zone 4 to 8.

HABIT: Pyramidal to upright-oval in youth assuming a haystack-shaped to broad-rounded outline in old age, often with drooping, lower, lateral branches.

RATE: Slow to medium, 1 to 1 1/2′ per year over a 10 to 20 year period.

TEXTURE: Medium in leaf, medium-coarse in winter.

BARK: Gray-brown, close, eventually with broad, low ridges separated by shallow furrows.

LEAF COLOR: Reddish when first unfolding changing to a lustrous dark green in summer and assuming yellow-brown to russet-red colors in fall; old leaves often persisting through winter.

FRUIT: Nut, short-stalked, subglobose, about 5/8″ long, the nut enclosed 1/3 to 1/2 in a thin, bowl-shaped cap with appressed, red-brown scales, maturing second year.

CULTURE: Transplants with less difficulty than many oaks; prefers moist, rich, deep, well-drained, acid soil although is tolerant of drier soils; somewhat tolerant of city conditions; full sun.

DISEASES AND INSECTS: See under White Oak.

LANDSCAPE VALUE: Does quite well in the Midwest and has been used for lawn, street, park, golf course and other large areas; accepts pruning very well and can be used for hedges; the leaves persist into winter and aid in screening or breaking the wind; does not perform as well in Zone 7b(8) as further north.

PROPAGATION: Seed, stratify in moist sand or peat for 30 to 60 days at 41°F or directly sow outside and germination will take place in spring.

ADDITIONAL NOTES: The wood of Shingle Oak was used to make shingles; hence, the common name.

NATIVE HABITAT: Pennsylvania to Georgia, west to Nebraska and Arkansas. Introduced 1724.

RELATED SPECIES: At least in appearance.

Quercus oglethorpensis Duncan — Oglethorpe Oak

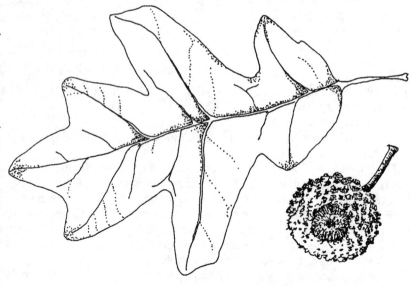

LEAVES: Alternate, simple, elliptic to narrow elliptic, seldom narrow obovate to obovate, entire, occasionally with several humps or shoulders, obtuse, with *no* bristle tip, cuneate, dark green above and glabrous, stalked, stellate hairs below; petiole—1/8 to 1/4″ long.

BUDS: Reddish brown, pubescent, ovoid-blunt, 1/8 to 3/16″ long, with numerous narrow stipular appendages subtending buds.

STEM: Reddish brown, lustrous, glabrous, dotted with small circular light gray lenticels.

Quercus oglethorpensis, (kwĕr′kus ō-gle-thôrp-en′sis), Oglethorpe Oak, is only mentioned because of the somewhat similar leaf shape. The apex of the leaf is *not* bristle-tipped like *Q. imbricaria*. The species is a White Oak group member with scaly, gray bark, stiff, coarse, twiggy branches and long-term leaf retention. Fall color is bronze-brown and brown leaves are retained through winter. Trees are irregular pyramidal when young, more rounded with age. Probably 30 to 40′ under landscape conditions. The national champion is 69′ by 69′ near Lexington, GA. Dark brown-black acorns average 1/2″ long and are covered 1/3 or more by the appressed scales. Found in the wild on poorly drained soils and adjacent slopes. Piedmont of eastern Georgia and western South Carolina, Mississippi and Louisiana. Zone 6 to 9.

Quercus lyrata Walt. — Overcup Oak

LEAVES: Alternate,   simple, obovate-oblong, 6 to 8″ long, 1 1/2 to 3″(5″) wide, acute or obtuse, cuneate at base, deeply lyrate-pinnatified, with 3 to 5 pairs of obtuse, acutish lobes, the 2 lower pairs smaller and triangular and separated from the upper pairs by wide sinuses, the large middle pair usually with a small lobe on the lower margin, the terminal lobe usually 3-lobed, dark green and glabrous above at maturity, white tomentose beneath or green and pubescent; petiole—1/2″ long, either glabrous or pubescent, orangish yellow.

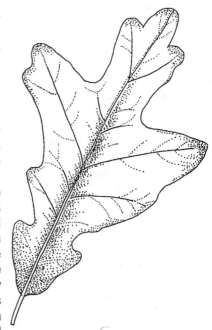

BUDS: Imbricate, brown, 1/8 to 1/4″ long, reminiscent of Swamp White Oak buds, gray-brown, stipular appendages nestled in cluster of terminal buds.

STEM: Stout, angled, gray-brown, small grayish lenticels, glabrous or slightly pubescent.

Quercus lyrata, (kwĕr′kus lĭ-rā′tȧ), Overcup Oak, is a relatively obscure species but certainly worthy of consideration. The habit in youth is pyramidal-oval and oval-rounded to rounded at maturity. The branching is very uniform and a row of seedling-grown, 45 to 50′ high trees on the Georgia campus are quite similar. The lower branches are upswept so minimal pruning is required compared to *Q. palustris*. These trees are growing in confined spaces on a slope and are thriving. Bark is reminiscent of White Oak from a distance, perhaps not as scaly, gray to brownish gray. The leaves are dark green and somewhat leathery. They turn a rich yellow-brown to tannin brown in fall and abscise earlier than those of other oaks. The common name is derived from the cap that almost completely encloses the nut. The nut is sub-globose to rounded, 3/4 to 1″ high and wide, usually covered by the cap except for a small window at the apex; other times the cap covers 3/4′s of the nut. Acorns mature in one year. It is a bottomland species in the wild where it is found in sloughs and backwater areas. Apparently it will withstand considerable flooding. The expected landscape size is 40 to 60′ high and wide. National champion is 156′ by 120′ in Bertie County, NC. It might be worth considering for especially difficult sites. With selection and propagation this could become an important landscape tree. I have been "pushing" this species to any nurseryman who would listen. Several have taken the lead and are producing it. Significantly easy to transplant compared to White Oak. Might add, do not remember an unworthy specimen. Shown superior in a 13 year evaluation of shade trees at Auburn; see *J. Arboriculture* 21:118–121 (1995). Also, Dirr, *Nursery Manager* 7(6):42 (1991) for a discussion of the species. New Jersey to Florida, west to Missouri and Texas. Introduced 1786. Zone 5 to 9.

Quercus macrocarpa Michx. — Bur Oak, also called Mossycup Oak

(kwĕr′kus ma-krō-câr′pȧ)

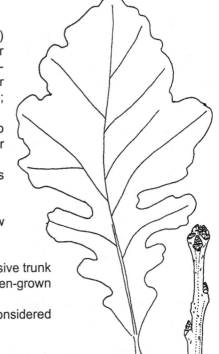

LEAVES: Alternate, simple, obovate to oblong-obovate, 4 to 10″(12″) long, about 1/2 as wide, cuneate or rarely rounded at base, lower portion of leaf with 2 to 3 pairs of lobes, upper 5 to 7 pairs of ovate-obtuse lobes, dark green and often lustrous above, grayish or whitish tomentulose beneath, leaf shaped like a base fiddle; petiole—1 1/4″ long, downy.

BUDS: Imbricate, conical to broadly ovate, sharp-pointed or blunt, 1/4 to 3/8″ long, pale pubescence covering entire bud, often with stipular structures arising out of clustered buds.

STEM: Stout, yellowish brown, smooth or downy, stems on some trees developing corky ridges after first year.

SIZE: 70 to 80′ in height with an equal or slightly greater spread, can grow to over 100′; national champion is 96′ by 103′ in Paris, KY.

HARDINESS: Zone 3 to 8.

HABIT: Weakly pyramidal to oval in youth gradually developing a massive trunk and a broad crown of stout branches; impressive as an open-grown specimen of the prairie.

RATE: Slow, over a 20 year period 15 to 20′ of growth could be considered average.

TEXTURE: Coarse in all seasons, but majestically so.

BARK: Rough, developing deep ridged-and-furrowed character, usually dark gray to gray-brown in color.

LEAF COLOR: Often lustrous dark green in summer, fall color is dull yellow-green, yellow, to yellow-brown.

FRUIT: Nut, solitary, usually stalked, 3/4 to 1 1/2″ long, broadly ovoid, downy at the apex, enclosed 1/2 or more in a deep cap which is conspicuously fringed on the margin, matures in a single season.

CULTURE: Difficult to transplant; very adaptable to various soils and is found on sandy plains to moist alluvial bottoms; on uplands, limestone soils are favored; succeeds well even in dry, clay soils; more tolerant of city conditions than most oaks; full sun.

DISEASES AND INSECTS: See under White Oak.

LANDSCAPE VALUE: Probably too large for the average home landscape; however, makes an excellent park or large area tree; very impressive and inspiring tree; there is a specimen in Urbana, IL over 90′ tall and estimated at 300 years of age.

PROPAGATION: No pretreatment is required although 30 to 60 days at 41°F in moist sand or peat is suggested.

ADDITIONAL NOTES: I have always been fascinated by variation within a species and when writing the identification features for many of the species in this book I literally cringe at the thought of presenting a stereotyped leaf, bud, stem, etc. I suggest the interested reader consult Dicke and Bagley, *Silvae Genetica* 29:171–196 (1980), for an interesting discussion of variation in Bur Oak. Professor Bagley told me that he has observed acorns on which the involucre is not fringed.

NATIVE HABITAT: Nova Scotia to Pennsylvania, west to Manitoba and Texas. Introduced 1811.

Quercus marilandica Muenchh. — Blackjack Oak

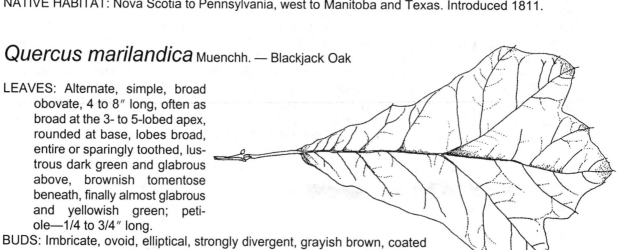

LEAVES: Alternate, simple, broad obovate, 4 to 8″ long, often as broad at the 3- to 5-lobed apex, rounded at base, lobes broad, entire or sparingly toothed, lustrous dark green and glabrous above, brownish tomentose beneath, finally almost glabrous and yellowish green; petiole—1/4 to 3/4″ long.

BUDS: Imbricate, ovoid, elliptical, strongly divergent, grayish brown, coated with rusty brown hairs, particularly from 2/3's to 1/2 the way from base to apex, 1/4 to 1/3″ long.

STEM: Stout, red-brown, pubescent initially, later brown to ash-gray, dotted with numerous small gray-brown lenticels.

Quercus marilandica, (kwĕr′kus mar-i-lan′di-kȧ), Blackjack Oak, is usually a scrubby tree with a Hounds-of-the-Baskervilles' gothic habit, the stout branches forming an irregular outline. Fall color is at best yellow-brown but not unattractive. Found in infertile, barren soils, often sandy veins, and is a good indicator of soil quality. I occasionally chance upon the species in Georgia and invariably the soils are quite sandy. The tree is often dwarfed by its environment and is somewhat shrub-like but can reach 30 to 40′. Tri-national champions are 90′ by 80′, 70′ by 80′ and 64′ by 87′ in South Carolina, Virginia, and Missouri, respectively. Acorns range from 3/4 to 1″ long, about half as wide, and are enclosed one-half in the yellow-brown cap. Mature in second year. Not a tree that will be found in nursery production but if native certainly worth treasuring. New York to Iowa south to Florida and Texas. Introduced before 1739. Zone 6 to 9.

Quercus muehlenbergii Engelm. — Chinkapin Oak, also called Yellow Chestnut Oak
(kwĕr′kus mū-len-bĕr′jē-ī)

LEAVES: Alternate, simple, oblong to oblong-lanceolate, 4 to 6 1/2″ long, 1/3 to 1/2 as wide, acute or acuminate, usually rounded at base, coarsely toothed, with about 8 to 13 pairs of acute and mucronate often incurved teeth, lustrous dark yellow-green above, whitish tomentulose beneath; petiole—3/4 to 1 1/2″ long.

BUDS: Light brown or pale margined, ovoid or conical-ovoid, 1/6 to 1/4″ long.
STEM: Glabrous, brown, rounded, slender.

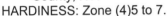

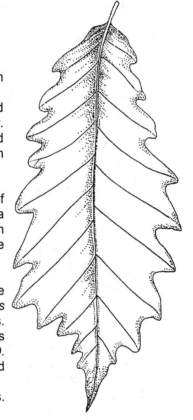

SIZE: 40 to 50′ under landscape con-
ditions but can, and often does,
grow 70 to 80′ tall in the wild,
spread is usually greater than
height at maturity; national
champion is 110′ by 92′ in Clark
County, KY.
HARDINESS: Zone (4)5 to 7.
HABIT: Weakly rounded in youth but of dapper outline; with
maturity developing an open, rounded crown.
RATE: Medium in youth, slowing down with age.
TEXTURE: Medium in leaf; medium-coarse in winter.
BARK: Ashy-gray, more or less rough and flaky.
LEAF COLOR: Lustrous dark yellowish green in summer; fall color varies from
yellow to orangish brown to brown.
FRUIT: Acorn, subsessile, globose-ovoid or ovoid, 3/4 to 1″ long, enclosed
about 1/2 by the thin cap, scales small, depressed, maturing the first year.
CULTURE: Like many oaks, somewhat difficult to transplant; in the wild is found
on dry limestone outcrops and soils with an alkaline reaction; prefers rich
bottomlands and there attains its greatest size.
DISEASES AND INSECTS: None particularly serious.
LANDSCAPE VALUE: Actually quite an attractive tree especially in old age; if
native in an area it is worthwhile saving; I doubt if it will ever become a
popular landscape tree; in Springfield, IL, I have seen 70 to 80′ mammoth
specimens with large, bold, scaly, gray trunks and branches; trees are
actually inspiring.
PROPAGATION: No seed pretreatment is necessary.
ADDITIONAL NOTES: Distinct species as I studied and understood its nature
in the Midwest. By some authorities the name was changed to *Q. prinoides*
Willd. I prefer the old name which is still used in some modern references.
The typical midwestern forms had narrow leaves with coarse teeth as
shown in drawings. Apparently some forms are similar to *Q. montana* (*Q.
prinus*) and *Q. michauxii*. Experienced many trees in western Kansas and
Oklahoma which provided an indication of drought tolerance.
NATIVE HABITAT: Vermont to Virginia, west to Nebraska, Mexico and Texas.
Introduced 1822.

Quercus myrsinifolia Bl. — Chinese Evergreen Oak
(kwĕr′kus mĕr-sin-i-fō′li-à)

LEAVES: Alternate, simple, evergreen, ovate to elliptic, 2 1/2 to 4″ long, 3/4 to 1 1/2″ wide, acuminate,
rounded, bristle-tipped serrations, 10 to 16 vein pairs, the midrib scarcely impressed above, lateral nerves
very slender, only slightly raised beneath, lustrous medium green above, glaucous green beneath;
petiole—1/2 to 3/4″ long.
BUDS: Imbricate, slender-conical, gray-brown, pubescent at top, 1/4 to 3/8″ long.
STEM: Slender for an oak, shining brown, glabrous, prominently covered with small lenticels.

SIZE: 20 to 30′, spread slightly less or similar; have seen mature trees and most were round headed; in
Savannah, GA observed many 40′ high, oval-rounded trees, also large (50′) specimens at U.S. National
Arboretum and North Carolina State University Campus.
HARDINESS: Zone 7 to 9, the most cold hardy evergreen oak.
HABIT: Small, densely foliaged, dapper, round-headed tree that deserves much greater use for streets, parking
islands, and containers; may develop oval-rounded outline.
RATE: Slow.
TEXTURE: Medium-fine throughout the seasons.

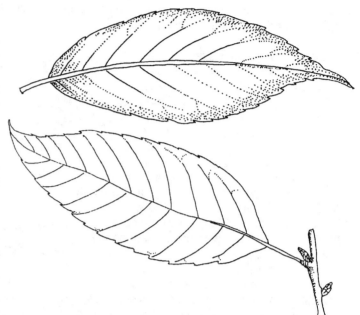

BARK: Smooth, gray, beech-like, actually smoother than a beech even in maturity.

LEAF COLOR: New foliage emerges purple-bronze, and changes to lustrous medium green with maturity; in sunny, exposed locations a slight discoloration may occur in winter months; persist for 2 years before falling.

FRUIT: Acorn, 2 to 4 together, 1/2 to 1″ long, oval-oblong, covered 1/3 to 1/2 by the glabrous cap which has 3 to 6 concentric rings, nut is brownish black, ripen in first year.

CULTURE: Transplant balled-and-burlapped before buds break in winter or early spring; unbelievable soil tolerance: sandy, clay, acid, alkaline or dry; withstands tremendous summer heat; full sun to partial shade.

DISEASES AND INSECTS: Sapsuckers can seriously injure trees; is probably the factor limiting use in some areas; am seeing "canker" on Dirr garden tree that is killing limbs; sapsuckers have wreaked havoc on this species in cultivated situations, however, I observe gigantic trees that have survived and prospered, an anomaly that I am unable to resolve.

LANDSCAPE VALUE: Superb small street or lawn tree, used in Greenville, SC to soften large office buildings, plants are in raised planters, beautiful throughout the seasons; trees at the old USDA Bamboo Station in Savannah are 30 to 40′ high and have withstood the test of time.

PROPAGATION: Collect seed in fall and sow immediately or store and provide 1 to 2 months cold moist stratification before spring planting. Have successfully rooted the species using June cuttings and 1.0% KIBA.

NATIVE HABITAT: Widely distributed in eastern Asia from Japan and Formosa through China and the Himalayas. Introduced 1807.

RELATED SPECIES: Upon arrival in Georgia, I was introduced to several new evergreen oaks, although *Q. myrsinifolia* I had previously seen at the U.S. National Arboretum. Unfortunately, the nursery industry has confused *Q. acuta*, *Q. glauca*, and *Q. myrsinifolia* which are listed in various catalogs as unique entities but in general describe the same oak, *Q. glauca*. The differences are adequately described under each species but for quick reference remember that the leaves of *Q. acuta* are entire, those of *Q. glauca* usually coarsely toothed one-third to one-half from the base to the apex. Also, *Q. myrsinifolia* is the most cold hardy, *Q. acuta* will grow only in Zone 8, if there, and *Q. glauca* was killed to the ground in Zone 7 at −3°F. Relative to hardiness, Dr. Randy Johnson, formerly U.S. National Arboretum, told me of a *Q. acuta* that was cold hardy there. U.S. National has experienced at least −10°F in the coldest winters of the past 20 years.

Quercus acuta Thunb. — Japanese Evergreen Oak

LEAVES: Alternate, simple, evergreen, elliptic to ovate, 2 1/2 to 5 1/2″ long, 1 to 2 1/4″ wide, long acuminate, rounded to broad cuneate, entire, somewhat undulate, lustrous dark green above, yellowish green below, glabrous, 8 to 10 vein pairs; petiole—about 1″ long.

Quercus acuta, (kwĕr′kus a-kū-tȧ), Japanese Evergreen Oak, is essentially non-existent in the Southeast and the first place I have turned up a specimen was in the Botany herbarium and it listed the location as a park in Albany, GA. For some unknown reason, this species has been listed in nursery catalogs instead of *Q. glauca* and *Q. myrsinifolia*, which are the principal trees in commerce. In Europe, where I have seen the tree, it is always small and shrubby to 20′ high and wide, the leaves are handsome and the new growth emerges a purplish brown. Acorns are clustered like *Q. myrsinifolia* and the concentric-ringed cap covers about 1/3 of the 3/4″ long nut. Woodlanders, Aiken, SC has a rather handsome specimen on the outside of their property. Bark is smooth and gray not unlike that of beech. Certainly beautiful in foliage but doubtfully competitive with the myriad broadleaf evergreens in Zone 8 and 9. Japan. Introduced 1878. Zone 8 to 9.

Quercus glauca Thunb. — Blue Japanese Oak, Ring-cupped Oak

LEAVES: Alternate, simple, evergreen, oblong, elliptic, to obovate-oblong, 2 1/2 to 5 1/2″ long, 1 to 2 1/2″ wide, strongly acuminate, slenderly tapered to rounded, strongly serrate in upper 1/2 to 2/3's, leathery, lustrous dark green above, gray-green beneath, pubescent, with 8 to 12 vein pairs, prominent beneath; petiole—1/2 to 1″ long, yellow.

BUDS: Imbricate, abundantly clustered (5 to 7) at ends of stem, conical-angular, 5-sided, 1/4 to 1/3″ long, brown, glabrous, laterals diverge from stem at 45° angle.

STEM: Stout, slightly angular, dark olive-green, eventually becoming brown or purplish brown, glabrous, covered with small grayish lenticels; pith—solid, off-white.

FRUIT: Acorn, 1 to 3 in a cluster, 3/4″ long, enclosed 1/3 in a downy cap with 6 to 7 raised concentric rings, ripens in one year.

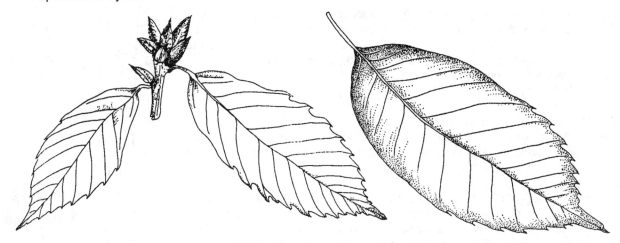

Quercus glauca, (kwĕr′kus glâ′kȧ), Blue Japanese Oak, makes a handsome, almost shrubby appearance in the landscape. The habit is distinctly upright-oval with ultimate size approximately 20 to 30′ and spread about one-half this. The overall appearance is quite formal and the plant is best utilized in groupings. New foliage is either a rich green or bronze to purple-green. Very handsome when the new foliage emerges which usually occurs in early April in the Piedmont. The emerging leaves may be injured by a late spring freeze. The leathery lustrous dark green leaves are handsome throughout the seasons. Tolerates heavy clay soils. Makes an excellent, large, screen plant and requires a minimum of maintenance. The 1983–84 winter (-3°F in Athens) devastated the species and fine old specimens in Athens-Atlanta were killed. Was used at Atlanta Historical Society as a large screen and was effective and functional. Cold rendered these plants rubble. Possibly the handsomest specimen in cultivation in the United States resides in Brookgreen Gardens, Murrells Inlet, SC. The tree is shaped like a giant mushroom, probably 30′ high and 40′ wide with low-slung, wide-spreading branches. Japan and China. Introduced 1978. Zone 8 to 9.

Quercus phillyraeoides Gray — Ubame Oak

LEAVES: Alternate, simple, evergreen, oval to obovate, 1 1/4 to 2 1/2″ long, at times almost as wide, acuminate to rounded, rounded to subcordate, entire on lower half, shallow dentate above, shining dark green, glabrous above, pale, shining and glabrous below; petiole—1/4″ long, pubescent.

Quercus phillyraeoides, (kwĕr′kus fil-ē-rē-oy′dēz), has been cold hardy at the J.C. Raulston Arboretum, Raleigh, NC where it forms an irregular, shrub-like habit. Landscape size approximates 15 to 25′. New growth emerges bronzy red. The leaves are quite handsome but beyond this has little to recommend it for everyday use. 'Emerald Sentinel' was introduced by J.C. Raulston Arboretum for its upright habit, fast growth (Raulston reported 5 to 6′ per year), showy catkins, and ease of rooting. China, Japan. Introduced 1862. Zone (6)7 to 8.

Quercus salicina Blume, (kwĕr′kus sal-is-ē′nà), is closely related to *Q. myrsinifolia* but the lanceolate leaves are lustrous dark green above, silvery below with acorns ripening the second year. The few trees I have seen were small, shrubby to 20′. Japan. Zone 8 to 9. Have read Zone 6b hardiness designation. Little in the better literature about this species.

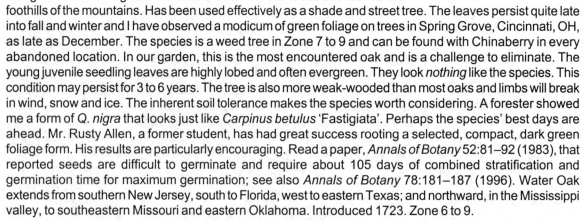

Quercus nigra L. — Water Oak, also called Possum Oak

LEAVES: Alternate, simple, exceedingly variable as to size and shape, obovate, 3-lobed at apex or sometimes entire, rarely pinnately lobed above the middle, 1 1/2 to 4″ long, 1/2 to 2″ wide, dull bluish green to lustrous dark green above, paler beneath, soon glabrous except for axillary tufts of brown hairs; petiole—1/10 to 1/4″ long.
BUDS: Imbricate, ovoid, pointed, prominently angled, smooth, brown, 1/8 to 1/4″ long.
STEM: Slender, smooth, dull red to brown.
FRUIT: Acorn, usually solitary, 1/2″ long and wide, enclosed 1/4 to 1/3 in a broad, shallow, short-stalked cap with appressed scales; nut with alternating striated bands of brown and black.

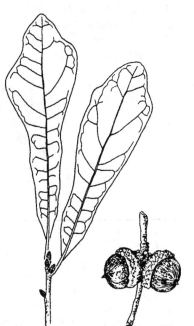

Quercus nigra, (kwĕr′kus nī′grà), Water Oak, is a conical to round-topped tree, 50 to 80′ high. National champion is 128′ by 79′ in Calhoun County, FL. It is popular in the South and has been used effectively on the University of Georgia campus. Transplants readily and is quite adaptable on moist to wet sites. Typically it is a bottomland species and is widespread and abundant along streams throughout the Southeast from the Coastal Plain to the foothills of the mountains. Has been used effectively as a shade and street tree. The leaves persist quite late into fall and winter and I have observed a modicum of green foliage on trees in Spring Grove, Cincinnati, OH, as late as December. The species is a weed tree in Zone 7 to 9 and can be found with Chinaberry in every abandoned location. In our garden, this is the most encountered oak and is a challenge to eliminate. The young juvenile seedling leaves are highly lobed and often evergreen. They look *nothing* like the species. This condition may persist for 3 to 6 years. The tree is also more weak-wooded than most oaks and limbs will break in wind, snow and ice. The inherent soil tolerance makes the species worth considering. A forester showed me a form of *Q. nigra* that looks just like *Carpinus betulus* ‘Fastigiata’. Perhaps the species’ best days are ahead. Mr. Rusty Allen, a former student, has had great success rooting a selected, compact, dark green foliage form. His results are particularly encouraging. Read a paper, *Annals of Botany* 52:81–92 (1983), that reported seeds are difficult to germinate and require about 105 days of combined stratification and germination time for maximum germination; see also *Annals of Botany* 78:181–187 (1996). Water Oak extends from southern New Jersey, south to Florida, west to eastern Texas; and northward, in the Mississippi valley, to southeastern Missouri and eastern Oklahoma. Introduced 1723. Zone 6 to 9.

Quercus palustris Muenchh. — Pin Oak, also called Swamp Oak
(kwĕr′kus pa-lus′tris)

LEAVES: Alternate, simple, elliptic or elliptic-oblong, 3 to 6″ long, at times almost as wide, terminal lobe long acuminate, cuneate at base, sometimes truncate, 5- to 7-lobed, lustrous dark green above, lighter green beneath with axillary tufts of hair; key feature—major lobes U-shaped in comparison with C-shaped lobes of *Q. coccinea*; petiole—up to 2″ long, slender.

BUDS: Imbricate, conical to ovate, sharp-pointed, 1/8 to 1/4″ long, gray-brown to chestnut brown.

STEM: First year stems slender, greenish to brown; second and third year often greenish.

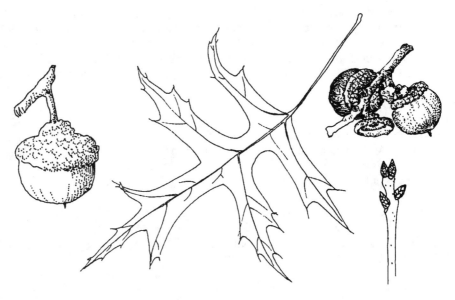

SIZE: 60 to 70′ in height with a spread of 25 to 40′, can attain a height of over 100′; national champion is 110′ by 112′ in Henderson County, TN.

HARDINESS: Zone 4 to 8.

HABIT: Strongly pyramidal, usually with a central leader; the lower branches pendulous, the middle horizontal, and the upper upright; in old age the tree assumes an oval-pyramidal form and loses many of the lower branches; very distinctive tree because of growth habit and widely planted as a lawn and street tree for this reason.

RATE: One of the faster growing oaks, 12 to 15′ over a 5 to 7 year period; 'Sovereign' averaged 2′5″ per year over a 10 year period in Kansas tests.

TEXTURE: Medium in leaf, medium-coarse in winter.

BARK: Grayish brown, thinnish, smooth and with age develops narrow, relatively shallow ridges and furrows.

LEAF COLOR: Glossy dark green in summer changing to russet, bronze or red in fall; fall coloration is variable; great opportunity for selection if vegetative propagation techniques could be developed.

FRUIT: Nut, solitary or clustered, sessile to short-stalked, 1/2″ high, 2/3 to 3/4″ wide, nearly hemispherical, light brown, often striate, enclosed only at basal 1/4 to 1/3 in a thin, saucer-like cap, mature in second year.

CULTURE: Readily transplanted because of shallow, fibrous root system; will tolerate wet soils and is found in the wild on wet clay flats where water may stand for several weeks; actually prefers moist, rich, acid, well-drained soil; very intolerant of high pH soils and iron chlorosis can be a significant and disastrous problem with this species; somewhat tolerant of city conditions; tolerant of sulfur dioxide; full sun.

DISEASES AND INSECTS: Galls are often a problem; iron chlorosis can be serious but can be corrected; the use of capsules (ferric ammonium citrate) placed in the tree has proven very effective and has worked over a 3 year period. Sinex, *American Nurseryman* 173(7):78–80, 82 (1991), discusses "Pin Oak Malady" and efforts to cure chlorosis. She utilized the iron-nutrient capsules to improve the appearance of the Pin Oaks but agonized over long-term damage from implanting and physical damage. The best advice is avoid Pin Oak when the pH is too high.

LANDSCAPE VALUE: Probably the most widely used native oak for landscaping; a 1989 published survey by *American Nurseryman* magazine listed this as the most popular shade tree; possesses interesting habit and has been used for lawn, park, golf courses, commercial landscapes and streets; personally I feel there are many other superior oaks and tree species but this oak has outstanding customer appeal; correcting the chlorosis problem can be painful for the homeowner.

CULTIVARS:

'Crownright' ('Crown Right')—More upright habit, branches occur at a 30 to 60° angle to central leader and do not sweep ground; introduced by Princeton Nursery.

'Green Pillar' ('Emerald Pillar')—Columnar form that will prove a significant addition to contemporary landscapes if graft incompatibility does not rear its ugly head, leaves lustrous dark green, red foliage in autumn, Princeton Nursery introduction.

'Sovereign'—The lower branches do not weep but are borne at a 90° to 45° angle to the main leader, former Cole Nursery Company introduction.

PROPAGATION: Seed, stratify at 32 to 41°F for 30 to 45 days; 'Sovereign' was originally grafted on Pin Oak seedlings; however, after several years a graft incompatability resulted; this was supposedly solved by grafting onto seedlings which had been produced from nuts collected from the original 'Sovereign' tree; from what I understand the incompatibility problem still occurs and this cultivar will probably be discontinued. Our early cutting propagation work indicated Pin Oak could be rooted, take cuttings when first growth flush hardens, 10000 ppm KIBA, 2 perlite:1 peat, mist, with rooting 4 to 8 weeks later; see

Drew and Dirr, *J. Environ. Hort.* 7:115-117 (1989); also Drew et al., *J. Environ. Hort.* 11:97–101 (1993). Another cutting paper discusses success with *Q. geminata*, *Q. hemisphaerica*, and *Q. nigra*, no success with *Q. laurifolia* and *Q. virginiana*. Rooting success coincided with 1st and 2nd flushes of growth and use of IBA and NAA; see *Proc. Florida State Hort. Soc.* 102:260–264 (1989)

NATIVE HABITAT: Massachusetts to Delaware, west to Wisconsin and Arkansas. Introduced before 1770.

RELATED SPECIES:

Quercus coccinea Muenchh. — Scarlet Oak
LEAVES: Alternate, simple, oblong or elliptic, 3 to 6″ long, 2 1/2 to 4 1/2″ wide, truncate or rarely broadly cuneate at base, with 7, rarely 9, bristle-tipped lobes, lustrous dark green above, shiny and glabrous beneath except tufts of hair sometimes occur in vein axils, major lobes C-shaped; petiole—1 1/2 to 2 1/2″ long, glabrous, yellow.
BUDS: Imbricate, broadly ovate, blunt apex, 1/4 to 3/8″ long, dark reddish brown and glabrous below, pale woolly pubescent above middle, bud is shaped like a rugby ball.
STEM: Light brown to red-brown, glabrous, dotted with small gray lenticels, angled, older stems green with a luster.

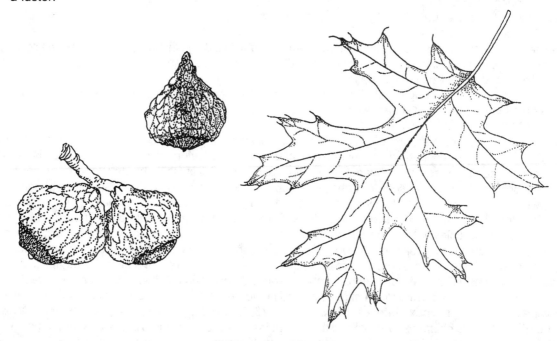

Quercus coccinea, (kwĕr′kus cok-sin′ē-à), Scarlet Oak, grows 70 to 75′ in height by 40 to 50′ in width under landscape conditions but can reach 100′ in the wild. On the Georgia campus 70 to 80′ high and wide trees have withstood the test of time. National champion is 120′ by 93′ in Powell County, KY. Habit in youth is somewhat similar to Pin Oak but becomes more rounded and open at maturity. Will grow 1 1/2 to 2′ per year over a 10 to 20 year period. Foliage is an excellent glossy dark green in summer changing to scarlet in the fall, unfortunately, some trees color russet red, if at all. Color develops in mid-November in the Athens area. One of the last species to develop fall color before the snow flies. Leaves, particularly on young trees, persist dry into winter. Fruit is solitary or paired, short-stalked, 1/2 to 1″ long and wide, oval to hemispherical, reddish brown, rarely striate, often with concentric rings near the apex, 1/3 to 1/2 enclosed in a deep, bowl-like cap. Less tolerant of adverse conditions than Pin Oak and Red Oak and not as available in the nursery trade. Interestingly, more nurseries are offering the species, although with difficulty in identification, it is tenuous to determine if true Scarlet Oak is being sold. Generally found on dry, sandy soils. Usually does not develop chlorosis problems to the degree of Pin Oak. Averaged 1′1″ per year over 10 years in Kansas tests. Native range extends from Maine to Florida, west to Minnesota and Missouri. Zone 4 to 9. Introduced 1691.

Quercus ellipsoidalis E.J. Hill — Northern Pin Oak, Hill's Oak
LEAVES: Alternate, simple, obovate or elliptic, 2 1/2 to 6″ long, 2 to 4 1/2″ wide, 5- to 7-lobed, truncate or cuneate, silky tomentose upon emergence, soon lustrous dark green, paler beneath with tufts of hair in vein axils; petiole—1 1/2 to 2″ long.

Quercus ellipsoidalis, (kwĕr′kus ē-lip-soy-da′lis), Northern Pin Oak, is a northern midwestern version of *Q. palustris* without the inherent chlorosis problems. The species is utilized in the Midwest. Will grow 50 to 60′ high and mature specimens in the Morton Arboretum are over 80′ high and wide. Acorn is 1/2 to 3/4″ long, ellipsoidal to subglobose, covered 1/3 to 1/2 by cap, nut brownish with striate lines. Southern Michigan, to Manitoba and Iowa. Introduced 1902. Zones 4 to 6.

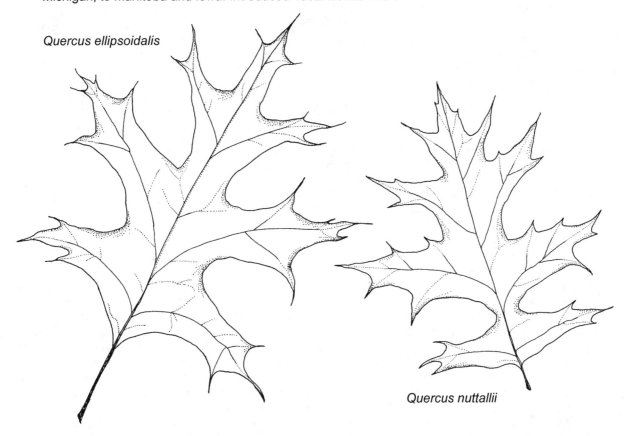

Quercus ellipsoidalis

Quercus nuttallii

Quercus nuttallii Palmer — Nuttall Oak
LEAVES: Alternate, simple, much like *Q. palustris*, perhaps *Q. shumardii*, deeply 5- to 9-lobed, with wide rounded sinuses and narrow lobes, 4 to 9″ long, 2 to 5″ wide, lustrous dark green above, paler beneath with tufts of hairs in axils of main veins.
BUDS: Imbricate, 1/8 to 1/4″ long, ash gray to brown-gray, pubescent, scale margins ciliate.
STEM: Brownish gray, glabrous.

Quercus nuttallii, (kwĕr′kus nū-tal′lē-ī), Nuttall Oak, is essentially an unknown landscape entity but is fast replacing *Q. palustris* and *Q. shumardii* in Zones (7)8 and 9 because of superior adaptability, rich reddish purple new growth, reddish fall color, rapid growth and clean leaf drop in autumn. Acorns are 3/4 to 1 1/4″ long, ovoid-oblong and covered 1/3 to 1/2 by the cap. The species is considered a southern version of *Q. palustris* and *Q. shumardii* by most taxonomists and is found in floodplains, bottomlands and river terraces. Landscape size will approximate 40 to 60′ high. National champion is 118′ by 85′ in Helena Meridian, LA. The better reference books cite similarities to *Q. coccinea*, *Q. palustris*, and *Q. shumardii*. Plants I have observed favor *Q. shumardii*. A 1991 article in *Nursery Manager* 7(10):14 presents an overview of grower thoughts about the species. I have summarized them here: does not stop growing in summer when it's hot like Shumard (Texas); grows faster, calipers quicker, doesn't fork (central leader), withstands greater diversity of pH; tolerates wet soils and early summer digging (Louisiana), develops a fuller canopy (head) at an early age. Western Alabama to east Texas and Oklahoma, north to southeastern Missouri and southern Illinois. Introduced 1923. Zone 5 to 9.

Quercus shumardii Buckl. — Shumard Oak
LEAVES: Alternate, simple, obovate to elliptic, 4 to 6″(8″) long, 3 to 4″ wide, usually with 7 lobes, occasionally 9, sinuses cut deeply to midrib, leathery, lustrous dark green above, glabrous except for axillary tufts of hairs below; petiole—1 1/2 to 2 1/4″ long.

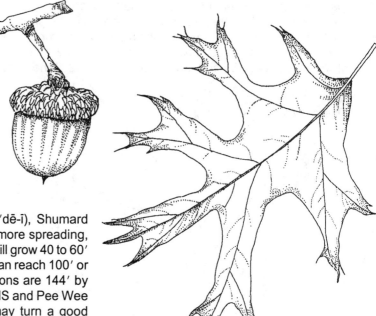

BUDS: Probably the only reliable aid to separate this species from *Q. palustris* and *Q. coccinea*; imbricate, angle-ovoid, 1/4 to 3/8″ long, glabrous, gray- or pale straw-colored, never reddish brown, scales appear waxed and often difficult to see the imbricate nature of the scales.

STEM: Gray-brown, glabrous, not as shiny as Pin Oak; older stems greenish brown with onion-like sheathing of epidermis.

Quercus shumardii, (kwĕr′kus shū-mar′dē-ī), Shumard Oak, is a pyramidal tree becoming more spreading, much like Scarlet Oak, at maturity. Will grow 40 to 60′ and wide at landscape maturity but can reach 100′ or more in nature. Co-national champions are 144′ by 112′ and 112′ by 111′ in Natchez, MS and Pee Wee Valley, KY, respectively. Leaves may turn a good russet-red to red in fall. Most of my observations reflect yellow-bronze to slight reddish fall coloration. Many trees on the Georgia campus and none develop outstanding reds. Acorns are ovate, 3/4 to 1″(1 1/2″) long, short-stalked and covered only at the base by a hemispherical-shaped involucral cap. Nut is striated with brown-black lines. Is relatively easy to transplant as I have seen no obvious transplant-related mortality in landscape settings. Considered a drought tolerant species and plantsmen in Florida, Oklahoma and Texas have extolled its virtues for use in those areas. Work in Mississippi showed that *Q. shumardii* had good survival and growth in three plantations, 10-, 11- and 25-years-old, on pH 7.8 to 8.0 alluvial soils along the Mississippi River. Interestingly, in the wild, is found along streams, near swamps, or bodies of water in well-drained soil. Grew 1′3.4″ per year over a 10 year period in Kansas tests. Proved superior in 13 year shade tree evaluations at Auburn University. 'Armistad' is listed as an evergreen form by Louisiana Nursery. Kansas to southern Michigan to North Carolina, Florida and Texas. Also known in 4 counties in southwestern Ontario. Introduced 1907. Zone 5 to 9.

Quercus phellos L. — Willow Oak
(kwĕr′kus fel′ōs)

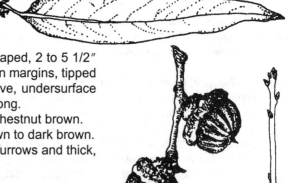

LEAVES: Alternate, simple, narrowly elliptical or lance-shaped, 2 to 5 1/2″ long, 1/3 to 1″ wide, acute, slightly wavy and entire on margins, tipped with a bristle, medium to dark green, glabrous above, undersurface glabrous or hairy along midrib; petiole—1/8 to 1/4″ long.

BUDS: Imbricate, 1/8 to 1/4″ long, ovoid, sharp-pointed, chestnut brown.

STEM: Slender, smooth, somewhat lustrous, reddish brown to dark brown.

BARK: Older, becoming gray and roughened by irregular furrows and thick, more or less scaly ridges.

SIZE: 40 to 60′ high, 30 to 40′ wide to a comparable spread, can grow 90 to 100′ in ideal situations; tri-national champions are 112′ by 114′ in Oxford, MD, 123′ by 100′ in Memphis, TN and 73′ by 132′ in Noxubee County, MS.

HARDINESS: 5 to 9, I still remember a handsome specimen on The Ohio State University Campus as well as older trees in Cincinnati that have been through –25°F, growing on Cape Cod, at the Public Garden in Boston, and in Newport, RI.

HABIT: Pyramidal in youth, developing a dense oblong-oval to rounded crown at maturity.

RATE: Medium, 1 to 2′ per year, may average 2′ per year over a 10 to 20 year period, difficult tree to train to a central leader and requires considerable pruning in early years to make a respectable crown.

TEXTURE: Medium-fine through the seasons.

BARK: On old trunks, lightly ridged-and-furrowed, gray-brown.

LEAF COLOR: Light to bright green in spring, dark green in summer, changing to yellow, bronze-orange, yellow-brown and russet-red in fall.

FRUIT: Acorn, solitary or paired, 1/2″ or less long and wide, subglobose, more or less stellate pubescent, enclosed at the base by a thin saucer-like cap, striated with alternating brown and blackish bands, maturing in second year.

CULTURE: Transplants more readily than most *Quercus* species because of more fibrous root system, should still be moved in dormant season, preferably during winter, prefers moist and well-drained soil but can adapt to virtually impossible habitats, many nurseries root prune the species to insure transplanting success.

DISEASES AND INSECTS: None serious.

LANDSCAPE VALUE: From Zone 7 to 9, still the best oak for overall texture and form; finer textured than most and makes a splendid avenue, street or boulevard tree, also excellent for large area use, i.e., commercial establishments, golf courses and parks; many years past Milliken Corporation planted either side of I-85 in Spartanburg, SC and the effect is outstanding; I have mentioned the planting to people and they immediately remember driving by the trees.

CULTIVARS:

'Pillow Oak'—An illegitimate name but one coined by Mr. Ray Bracken, Piedmont, SC to describe a suspected Pin/Willow hybrid; Ray discovered the plant in a seedling block of *Q. palustris* and noticed the rapid growth and different leaf shape; also it has been extremely easy to root from cuttings and overwinter; I worked with Ray in the early days on rooting protocol and he has grown trees to landscape size.

PROPAGATION: Stratify seed in moist sand or peat for 30 to 60 days at 40°F or directly sow outside and germination will take place in the spring. Mr. John Drew, a former graduate student, conducted interesting work on rooting *Quercus* species from cuttings. *Quercus phellos* was one of the easiest to root. He used firm cuttings after the first flush of growth hardened, 10,000 ppm KIBA-quick dip, 2 perlite:1 peat, mist, with 60 to 80% rooting in 10 weeks on *Q. phellos*, *Q. robur*, and *Q. lyrata*.

NATIVE HABITAT: Bottomlands, floodplains and adjacent slopes, rich uplands from New York to Florida, west to Missouri, Oklahoma and Texas. Introduced 1723.

Quercus prinus L. — Chestnut Oak, Basket Oak

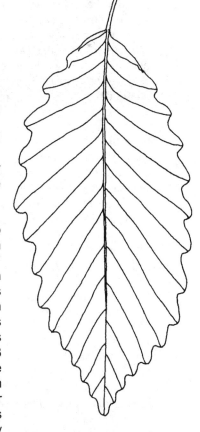

LEAVES: Alternate, simple, obovate to obovate-oblong, 4 to 6″(12″) long, 1 1/2 to 3 1/2″(4″) wide, acute or acuminate, cuneate or rounded at base, coarsely and regularly toothed, with 10 to 14 pairs of obtusish, often mucronate teeth, lustrous dark yellow-green, grayish tomentulose beneath; petiole—1/2 to 1″ long, yellow and color extends to midrib.

BUDS: Imbricate, 1/4 to 3/8″ long, conical, grayish, reddish brown, dusted with pubescence, resembling *Q. rubra* buds in shape and size.

STEM: Stout, glabrous, lustrous brown, dotted with numerous small gray lenticels, somewhat angled with decurrent ridges from sides and base of leaf scar.

Quercus prinus (*Q. montana* Willd.), (kwĕr′kus prī′nus), Chestnut Oak, is also called Rock Oak and Rock Chestnut Oak. This tree reaches 60 to 70′ in height with a comparable, but irregular spread. National champion is 95′ by 82′ in North Port, NY. The habit is pyramidal, oval to rounded in youth, eventually rounded and relatively dense. The leaves are lustrous dark yellowish green in summer changing to orange-yellow to yellowish brown in fall. One tree (the only) in the fair city of Watkinsville, GA turns a reasonable reddish brown. Acorns are borne 1 to 2 on peduncles shorter than the petioles, ovoid, 1 to 1 1/4″ high, 3/4″ wide, enclosed 1/3 to 1/2 by the tuberculate cap. The nut is a rich dark brown. This is a tree of rocky places and is found on poor, dry, upland sites where it may form pure stands. Maximum growth is made in well-drained soils and other moist sites. It is often found in association with Scarlet and Black Oaks on the rocky slopes of mountains. Have experienced the tree in quantity during my hikes through the southeastern Appalachian mountains. This species can grow 12 to 15′ over a 7 to 10 year period. The acorns are sweet tasting and are relished by the gray squirrel, black bear, white-tailed deer and many other forms of wildlife. The bark is brown to nearly black and, on older trees, very deeply and coarsely furrowed. The bark is valuable, being richer in tannin content (11%) than that of any other oak species. A very lovely tree which does exceedingly well in dry, rocky soil. No seed pretreatment is necessary. Have discovered that the species is relatively easy to transplant. Have observed trees in parking lot islands that have prospered. In my opinion a better landscape tree than ever considered. Auburn trials showed this to be a superior species in its 13 year test. Native from southern Maine and Ontario to South Carolina and Alabama. Cultivated 1688. Zone 4 to 8.

RELATED SPECIES:

Quercus michauxii Nutt., (kwĕr′kus mi-shō′ē-ī), Swamp Chestnut Oak, Basket Oak, is similar except it occurs in moister soils, grows larger and the involucral scales form a fringe around the rim. The silliness in plant taxonomic circles is evident when Q. *michauxii* has hairs solitary and in clusters of 2 to 8, Q. *prinus* in 2 to 5. Who can see them much less count them? For ease of identification it might be better lumped with Q. *prinus*. Leaves of Q. *michauxii* are, in general, more leathery-textured with greater pubescence on the lower surface. National champion is 200′ by 148′ in Fayette County, AL. This is a stately tree deserving of greater consideration in southern landscapes. The species is successful at the Morton Arboretum, Lisle, IL where over 40′ high specimens are growing. Small (4″ diameter) trees on the Georgia campus transplanted without difficulty. The bark on young trees is quite scaly. I have collected acorns from the great trees at Brookgreen Gardens, SC and found them easy to germinate and the resultant seedlings display great vigor, i.e., 3 to 4′ in a single season. The trees on the November 20th day I witnessed them developed bronze-red fall coloration. Common in low areas, river bottoms, swamp borders and ravines in New Jersey, Delaware to Florida, west to Indiana, Missouri and Texas. Angelor et al., *Tree Physiology* 16:477–484 (1996), showed that neither Q. *michauxii* nor Q. *falcata* var. *pagodifolia* seedlings survived one year of continuous flooding while *Nyssa sylvatica* var. *biflora* and *Liquidambar styraciflua* seedlings survived (~95%) more than two years of flooding. Introduced 1737. Zone 5 to 8(9).

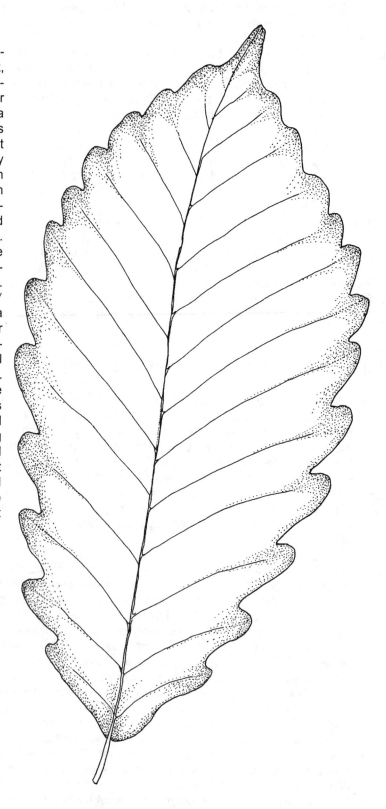

Quercus robur L. — English Oak, Truffle Oak, Pedunculate Oak
(kwĕr′kus rō′bĕr)

LEAVES: Alternate, simple, obovate to obovate-oblong, 2 to 5″ long, 3/4 to 2 1/2″ wide, apex rounded, auriculate to rounded base, 3 to 7 vein pairs of rounded lobes, glabrous, dark green to dark almost blue-green above, pale bluish green beneath; key feature, earlobe-like leaf base (auriculate); petiole—1/6 to 1/3″ long.

BUDS: Imbricate, rounded, plump, angled, 1/4 to 3/8″ long, chestnut to reddish brown, scales fringed with hairs.

STEM: Glabrous, reddish brown, often purplish, angled, similar to White Oak.

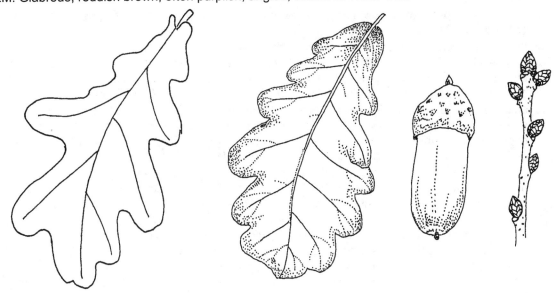

SIZE: The species can reach 75 to 100′ or more in height with a comparable spread; in the United States averages 40 to 60′ under landscape conditions.

HARDINESS: Zone 4 to 8.

HABIT: Large, massive, broadly rounded, open-headed tree with a short trunk; too large for the average landscape; in youth pyramidal to rounded; have seen magnificent specimens in England.

RATE: Slow to medium, averaged 1′4″ per year over a 10 year period in Kansas tests.

TEXTURE: Medium in leaf, probably would be considered coarse in winter.

BARK: Deeply furrowed, grayish black.

LEAF COLOR: Dark green to blue-green in summer; fall color is nil for the leaves either abscise green or persist and change to a nondescript brown.

FRUIT: Acorn, about 1″ long, narrow elongated-conical, enclosed 1/3 to 1/2 by the cap, one or several on a slender 1 to 4″ long peduncle, nut shiny brown, ripen the first year.

CULTURE: Transplant balled-and-burlapped; prefers well-drained soil; pH tolerant; full sun.

DISEASES AND INSECTS: Mildew is often a serious problem on the species and 'Fastigiata'.

LANDSCAPE VALUE: The species is widely used in Europe; good tree for parks and other large areas; too many better native oaks to justify extreme excitement over this introduced species although 'Fastigiata' (named clones) is a fine selection; does reasonably well in Zone 7 but cannot measure up to *Q. phellos*, *Q. lyrata*, and others; Dr. Dale Herman, North Dakota State University, mentioned that he had a good selection hardy to at least –35°F; also, I have observed a number of fastigiate hybrids involving 'Fastigiata' and *Q. bicolor*, *Q. prinus* and other species as parents; these hybrids are more mildew resistant and appear better suited to cultivation particularly in the plains states and Midwest; Earl Cully, Jacksonville, IL is introducing several that are listed under CULTIVARS.

CULTIVARS: Many selections are reported in the literature, most relegated to minor status. See *J. Arboriculture* 11(10):307–315 (1985) for the most up-to-date American checklist of *Q. robur* cultivars. Counted 117 valid cultivars tagged to this species. The following are forms that I have observed.

'Atropurpurea'—Since the 1983 edition this plant has jumped in my path many times in European gardens, the color is more brown-red than reddish purple and fades with time, leaves are slightly smaller than typical and the growth rate is slower, tree will probably mature between 20′ and 30′(40′) high and wide; I am often confused by f. *purpurescens* (DC.) A. DC. which supposedly has young leaves and stems reddish becoming green (almost) with maturity.

'Attention'—Superior tight columnar growth form, does not broaden with age, dark green foliage exhibits mildew resistance, 60 to 80′ by 15′, Zone 5 to 8, a Wandell introduction, selection from 'Fastigiata'; John Barbour, Bold Spring Nursery, Monroe, GA witnessed slight mildew susceptibility but this selection was much more resistant than typical 'Fastigiata' seedlings.

'Concordia'—Leaves are bright yellow when they first appear in the spring; should be sited in partial shade as the leaves will sun-scorch; there is a 25 to 30′ high specimen in Spring Grove which is rather striking when the leaves first emerge; leaves fade to green in summer; in fact, I tried to find the tree in summer and it looked so much like the species I was not sure if I had the real thing; old cultivar before 1843.

'Crimson Spire'—Upright oval growth habit, leaves turn reddish purple in fall, hybrid between *Q. alba* and *Q. robur*, Bill Wandell introduction.

'Cristata'—Small leaves clustered together and crinkled.

'Fastigiata'—Distinctly upright and columnar in habit; however, variation occurs because the cultivar is often grown from seed; it comes 80 to 90% true; a mature tree may be 50 to 60′ in height but only 10 to 15′ wide, also listed as var. *fastigiata* (Lam.) A. DC.; since it has been grown from seed various selections have been made; this is a beautiful tree and along with the Fastigiate European Beech should be more widely grown; definitely could use good mildew-free clones; as discussed earlier, hybrids between this and other oak species hold great promise for the future; counted 20 selections of 'Fastigiata' in McArdle and Santamour's *J. Arboriculture* checklist.

'Filicifolia'—In the 1983 edition, I reported this as 'Asplenifolia' as it was labeled at a particular arboretum, unfortunately, the name is correctly 'Filicifolia', a form with deeply cut sinuses and linear lobes that curve toward the apex creating a rather fern frond-like appearance; the tree was small, pyramidal-rounded and is probably not greatly vigorous but was indeed attractive.

Heritage® ('Clemons')—Selected from a row of F_2 hybrid seedlings for its outstanding vigor and superior form, maintains central leader and develops a dense, uniform pyramidal crown; leathery dark green, tattar-resistant foliage, highly resistant to mildew; with age develops broad rounded crown, Earl Cully introduction, *Q. robur* × *Q. macrocarpa*.

'Pendula'—Actually a handsome form of vigorous constitution with long growing shoots and widely arching weeping branches; have seen in Trompenburg Arboretum, Rotterdam, trained over a metal frame creating a vegetatively domed coliseum; worth seeking out, at least for the specialist; old cultivar possibly originated around 1816; reproduces from seed and multiple weeping clones are probably in commerce.

Regal Prince® ('Long')—Strong, upright oval silhouette similar to 'Bowhall' Red Maple, bold dark green, somewhat glossy, upper surface, glaucous on lower surface, highly resistant to powdery mildew, borers, wind, ice and low temperatures, Earl Cully introduction, *Q. robur* 'Fastigiata' × *Q. bicolor*.

Rosehill® ('Asjes')—Mildew-free selection, leaf color different than typical with glossy pure green rather than dull blue-green that is typical for species; is not as tight as typical 'Fastigiata'; looks like a hybrid with *Q. bicolor* but the acorns are typical *Q. robur*; has been mildew-free in the Southeast and disease pressure is terrific on typical English Oaks.

'Salicifolia'—Small, more compact, 20 to 30′ high, pyramidal-rounded form with entire, elliptic, dark green leaves, a plant at Spring Grove, Cincinnati, had me guessing for a long time, a novelty to be sure but another reflection of species variability.

Skymaster™ ('Pyramich')—Narrow when young, becoming pyramidal, strong central leader and excellent lateral branch development, branches diverge at wide crotch angles, dark green leaves, of the three Schmidt introductions this was by far the worst for foliage wear and tear in the Southeast, 50′ by 25′, Schmidt Nursery introduction, see Spongberg, *AABGA Bull.* 15(3):67–70 (1981).

Skyrocket™—A uniform, narrow, dark green-foliaged form with yellow-brown fall color, will grow 45′ by 15′; the most impressive of the three Schmidt introductions for southeastern conditions; leafs out early with leaves almost full size on March 30, 1997 in Oconee County, GA, the other two with buds only swelling; foliage highly mildew resistant; branches tight and columnar on 2-year-old trees; have hope for this columnar form; a 1989 Schmidt introduction.

Westminster Globe™ ('Michround')—A broad-spreading, round-headed, symmetrical form with sturdy branch development, dark green leaves, some mildew and leaf distress; probably, like Skymaster™, better suited in more northern climates; 45′ by 45′; Schmidt Nursery introduction.

There are variegated and other cut-leaf forms but none are particularly outstanding. Most white-variegated forms are rather weak growers and tend to produce reversion shoots. Amazingly, 55 variegated genotypes of *Q. robur* and *Q. petraea* were planted in Lisicine Arboretum, Zagreb, Croatia; see *Acta Horticulturae* 320:21–24 (1992). I visited a garden where the curator was proudly showing me a weeping White Oak.

I took one look and saw the auriculate leaf base and quietly explained that he had a weeping English Oak.
Sometimes it pays to learn these subtle identification characteristics.

PROPAGATION: Seed requires no pretreatment. Cultivars are grafted onto seedling understock.

NATIVE HABITAT: Europe, northern Africa, western Asia. Long cultivated.

RELATED SPECIES:

Quercus frainetto Ten. (kwĕr′kus fran-et′ō), Hungarian Oak, Italian Oak, is a large, 60 to 80′ high and wide,
boldly branched tree with large, heavily lobed, leathery dark green leaves, to 9″ by 5″. Have seen at
Spring Grove where leaf spot had rendered it miserable. At Anglesey Abbey near Cambridge England,
Magnificent trees were in evidence. 'Forest Green' has excellent foliage and was introduced by Schmidt
Nursery about 1989. Balkans, southern Italy. Cultivated 1838. Zone 5 to 7?

Quercus petraea (Mattusch.) Liebl. — Durmast Oak
LEAVES: Alternate, simple, ovate
to obovate, 3 to 5″(7″) long, 1
to 3 3/4″ wide, short- and
round-lobed, truncate, broadly cuneate to attenuate,
glossy dark green, almost
blue-green above; petiole—
3/8 to 3/4″ long, yellow.

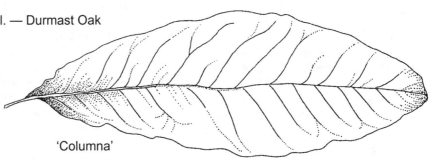

'Columna'

Quercus petraea, (kwĕr′kus pe-trē′à), Durmast Oak, is similar to and hybridizes with the above. It differs in the
comparatively long-stalked leaves, nearly stalkless acorns, and lack of an auriculate leaf base. The hybrid
(*Q. robur* × *Q. petraea*) is listed as *Q. × rosacea* Bechst. 'Columna', of fastigiate habit, like the Fastigiate
English Oak, is often confused with it but differs by the characteristics enumerated. Also, it is resistant to
powdery mildew. Leaves are more sparse and it is not as handsome as the better *Q. robur* 'Fastigiata'. The
species is a beautiful tree of rounded outline with bold, rugged branches. The most memorable tree for me,
and the first truly large specimen I had observed, resides by the lake in front of the Palm House at Kew. I
pulled a limb down to identify the tree and the sessile acorns spoke loudly—*Q. petraea*. Several cultivars
are described but rarely seen in cultivation. Europe, western Asia. Long cultivated. Zone 4 to 7.

Quercus rubra L. — Red Oak, Northern Red Oak
(kwĕr′kus rū′brà)

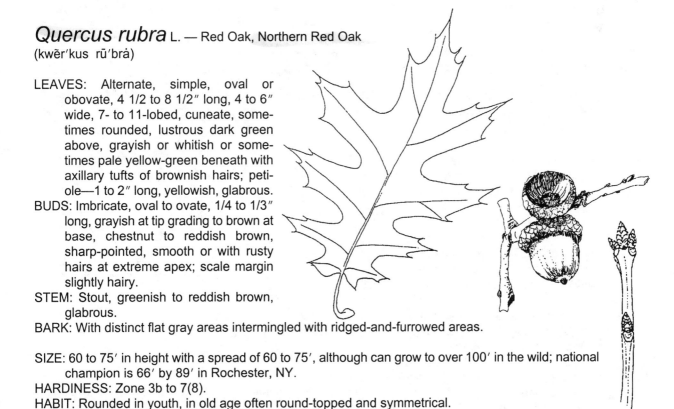

LEAVES: Alternate, simple, oval or
obovate, 4 1/2 to 8 1/2″ long, 4 to 6″
wide, 7- to 11-lobed, cuneate, sometimes rounded, lustrous dark green
above, grayish or whitish or sometimes pale yellow-green beneath with
axillary tufts of brownish hairs; petiole—1 to 2″ long, yellowish, glabrous.
BUDS: Imbricate, oval to ovate, 1/4 to 1/3″
long, grayish at tip grading to brown at
base, chestnut to reddish brown,
sharp-pointed, smooth or with rusty
hairs at extreme apex; scale margin
slightly hairy.
STEM: Stout, greenish to reddish brown,
glabrous.
BARK: With distinct flat gray areas intermingled with ridged-and-furrowed areas.

SIZE: 60 to 75′ in height with a spread of 60 to 75′, although can grow to over 100′ in the wild; national
champion is 66′ by 89′ in Rochester, NY.
HARDINESS: Zone 3b to 7(8).
HABIT: Rounded in youth, in old age often round-topped and symmetrical.

RATE: Another oak of fast growth, many individuals relegate the oaks to slow status; however, there are significant exceptions; Red Oak can grow 2′ per year over a 10 year period in moist, well-drained soil; however, in Wichita, KS tests averaged 11.5″ per year over a 9 year period.

TEXTURE: Medium in leaf and winter.

BARK: On old trunks brown to nearly black and broken up into wide, flat-topped, gray ridges, separated by shallow fissures; on very old trees often deeply ridged-and-furrowed.

LEAF COLOR: Pinkish to reddish when unfolding, lustrous dark green in summer changing to russet-red to bright red in fall; sometimes disappointing and never passing much beyond yellow-brown.

FRUIT: Nut, solitary or paired, 3/4 to 1″ long, variable in shape, but usually subglobose, enclosed at the base in a flat, thick, saucer-like cap, acorns mature and fall early, nut is medium brown with grayish streaks (hairs or wax?), mature in two years.

CULTURE: Transplants readily because of negligible taproot; prefers sandy loam soils which are well-drained and on the acid side; withstands the polluted air of cities; full sun; good performer although not as widely planted as Pin Oak; will develop chlorosis in high pH soils.

DISEASES AND INSECTS: Basically free of problems, although the problems listed under White Oak are limitedly applicable to this species.

LANDSCAPE VALUE: Valuable fast-growing oak for lawns, parks, golf courses and commercial areas; has been used as a street tree; excellent tree when properly grown; common street and urban tree throughout Midwest and East; on US-1 in Boston from Route 9 to Dedham, the trees line the street, amazing how well the plants have performed; not as well-adapted to Zone 7(8) because of heat and drought and although planted on the Georgia campus, it never attains the sizes that are common in the North.

CULTIVAR:

'Aurea'—A form with new leaves of a clear yellow to golden yellow; I have doubts about its success in intense summer heat in the United States; have seen it at Kew Gardens where it provides a golden glow during spring, supposedly comes partially true-to-type from seed.

'Splendens'—Excellent red fall color.

PROPAGATION: Seed requires 30 to 45 days at 41°F.

ADDITIONAL NOTES: Oaks hybridize freely and there are abundant hybrids evident in landscapes and the wild. Red and Black Oak are associated in the wild and hybrids frequently occur. The species is all over the coast of Maine, growing in rock and hardscrabble soil down to water's edge. Suspect there is a measure of salt tolerance.

NATIVE HABITAT: Nova Scotia to Pennsylvania, west to Minnesota and Iowa. Introduced 1800.

RELATED SPECIES:

Quercus velutina Lam. — Black Oak

LEAVES: Alternate, simple, oblong-ovate to obovate, 4 to 10″ long, 1/2 to 2/3's as wide, cuneate to truncate, 7 to 9 lobes, lustrous dark green above, glabrous below except in axils of veins; petiole—1 to 2 1/2″ long.

BUDS: Imbricate, ovate to conical, 1/4 to 1/2″ long, narrowed to a sharp point, generally 5-sided, strongly angled, covered with pale yellowish gray to dirty gray pubescence.

STEM: Stout, reddish brown or reddish, mottled with gray, tasting bitter if chewed and coloring saliva yellowish, downy when young, finally glabrous.

Quercus velutina, (kwĕr′kus ve-lū′ti-nȧ), Black Oak, reaches 50 to 60′ in height and the spread is variable, for the crown is often quite irregular and can be narrow or wide-spreading, elongated or rounded. Extensive tap root and for this reason is somewhat difficult to transplant. Makes best growth on moist, rich, well-drained, acid soils but is often found on poor, dry, sandy, or heavy clay hillsides.

Not an important tree in commerce. Fruit is solitary or paired, 1/2 to 3/4″ long, ovoid to hemispherical, often striate, light red-brown, 1/3 to 1/2 enclosed in a deep, bowl-like cap. Bark is nearly black on old trunks, deeply furrowed vertically, and with many horizontal breaks; inner bark bright orange or yellow. Have found several 30 to 40′ high trees on the Georgia campus which have prospered under the stresses of the southeastern summers. Co-national champions are 131′ by 137′ in St. Clair County, MI and 84′ by 95′ in East Granby, CT. Native from Maine to Florida, west to Minnesota and Texas. Introduced 1800. Zone 3 to 9.

Quercus stellata Wang. — Post Oak

LEAVES: Alternate, simple, obovate, lyrately pinnatifid, 4 to 8″ long, 3 to 4″ wide, cuneate at base, rarely rounded, with 2 to 3 broad, obtuse lobe pairs, the middle pair much larger and mostly with a lobe on the lower margin, separated from the lower lobes by wide, from the upper by narrow, sinuses, lustrous dark green and rough above, with grayish to brownish, rarely white tomentum beneath, finally glabrescent; petiole—1/2 to 1″ long, pubescent; entire leaf has a cruciform appearance.
BUDS: Imbricate, subglobose to broadly ovoid, 1/8 to 1/4″ long, reddish brown, pubescent or glabrous.
STEM: Stout, dirty gray-brown, tomentose, dotted with numerous lenticels.

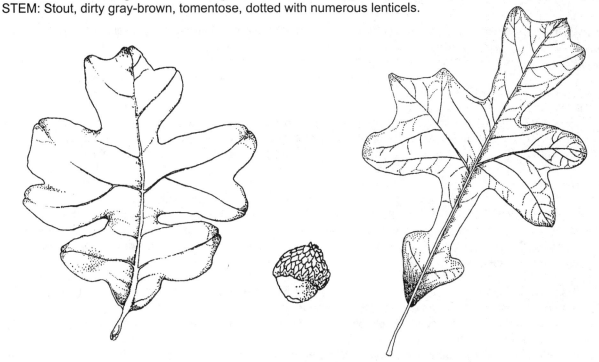

Quercus stellata, (kwĕr′kus stel-lā′tȧ), Post Oak, is seldom used in landscape situations but is frequently encountered in the wild throughout the southern states. Open-grown trees have a dense, round-topped crown with stout, spreading branches. Average height is 40 to 50′. In Georgia, 60 to 70′ high trees are common. National champion is 85′ by 88′ in Surry County, VA. Fall color has, on occasion, been reasonable golden brown. Most often the color is so nondescript that no one notices. The sessile nuts appear singly or in pairs, are egg-shaped, 3/4 to 1″ long and are covered about 1/3 to 1/2 by the top-shaped cap, the scales of which are pointed, downy and appressed. It is typically found on dry, gravelly or sandy soils and rocky ridges. In the lower Mississippi Valley, on silty loam soils, it attains its greatest size. Variety *margaretta* Ashe, Sand Post Oak, is common in the Coastal Plain from Virginia to Texas and is a small, scrubby tree. The lobes of the smaller leaves are more rounded and less cruciform than those of the species. Native from southern Massachusetts to Florida, west to Iowa and Texas. Introduced 1819. Zone 5 to 9.

Quercus virginiana Mill. — Live Oak
(kwĕr′kus vĕr-jin-ē-ā′nȧ)

LEAVES: Alternate, simple, evergreen, elliptic-obovate, 1 1/4 to 3″(5″) long, 3/8 to 1″(1 1/2″) wide, entire or spiny, young seedling trees have holly-like leaves, revolute, leathery, lustrous dark green above, glabrous, gray-green beneath, woolly pubescent, prominent yellowish brown midrib; petiole—1/4″ long, pubescent.

BUDS: Imbricate, slightly dome-shaped, reddish brown, glabrous or pubescent, 1/16 to 1/4″ long.

STEM: Slender, terete, gray, glabrous or pubescent toward tip.

SIZE: Massive, ranging from 40 to 80′ high and 60 to 100′ wide; national champion is 55′ by 132′ near Lewisburg, LA.

HARDINESS: Zone (7)8 to 10.

HABIT: Massive, picturesque, wide-spreading, evergreen tree with magnificent horizontal and arching branches that form a broad-rounded canopy; a single tree constitutes a garden; often imbued with Spanish moss which provides a mystical quality.

RATE: Moderate; slows down with age but in youth will respond to good fertility practices and produce 2 to 2 1/2′ of growth.

TEXTURE: Medium.

BARK: On old trees becomes exceedingly dark, almost black, and develops a blocky characteristic in the mold of an alligator hide.

LEAF COLOR: New spring growth is a bright olive green that matures to lustrous dark green; old leaves all drop in the spring.

FLOWERS: Typical oak; females 1 to 5 together in axils of leaves; male in catkins.

FRUIT: 1 to 5 on a common stalk, but I have only seen one per 1/2 to 3″(5″) long stalk on campus trees, 3/4 to 1″ long, 1/3 enclosed by an ellipsoidal cap, nut dark brown to black, mature in single season.

CULTURE: Transplant in small sizes; adapts to about any soil type and is found in its native haunts in sandhills and extremely moist soils; tolerant of compacted soils and has been used with great success as a street tree throughout the South; nursery trees need to be pruned to develop suitable leaders; tolerant of salt spray.

DISEASES AND INSECTS: A gall insect that is more unsightly than anything else and a root rot in the coastal areas; oak wilt reported in Texas, see *J. Arboriculture* 20:250–258 (1994); also bacterial leaf scorch reported, see *Plant Disease* 78:924 (1994).

LANDSCAPE VALUE: Magnificent shade and mansion tree, not for the small property; used extensively for street tree plantings in the South; Savannah and Thomasville, GA have notable plantings; makes a great park, golf course and campus tree; have seen beautiful specimens on the Louisiana State University campus; at the University of Georgia, trees do not make the growth they do further south, this is due in part to the colder temperatures.

CULTIVARS: Wonderful possibilities for selection particularly for central leader, dense foliage, and ease of production. Travel to southern cities and witness the almost monoculture of the species and the potential economics and practicalities of cultivars become manifest.

'Grandview Gold'—Gold-colored foliage, found by Earl Vallot, Grandview Nursery and offered by Louisiana Nursery.

Highrise™ ('QVTIA')—Upright pyramidal-columnar form that will revolutionize planting in narrow spaces, probably 2 1/2 to 3 times as high as wide at maturity, introduced by Tree Introductions, Inc., Athens, GA.

PROPAGATION: Seeds are the preferred method although Texas A&M has experimented with cutting propagation; see *HortScience* 24:1043 (1989) for cutting information; see *HortScience* 23:777 (1988) for seed work; Morgan used 10000 ppm KIBA with great success on younger trees; see Dirr and Heuser, 1987 for details.

ADDITIONAL NOTES: State tree of Georgia. May live 200 to 300 years. Considered a climax species in coastal Louisiana and along the east coast and outer banks of North Carolina. Tolerant of saline conditions. The wood is exceedingly strong and one of the heaviest of native woods; was used for ribs and other hull parts of wooden ships. The acorns are eaten by many songbirds as well as quail, turkey, squirrel and deer. Several geographical varieties have been noted. Variety *fusiformis* Sarg. is a small shrubby tree that occupies sandstone ridges in central Texas and Oklahoma. Variety *maritima* (Michx.) Sarg. integrates with the species and tends to be coastal from

Quercus virginiana
var. *maritima*

Virginia to Louisiana and Florida. Like many varieties, hairs are often being split in attempts to quantitatively separate them.

NATIVE HABITAT: Virginia to Florida, west to Oklahoma and Texas into Mexico. Introduced 1739.

RELATED SPECIES: Two smaller, often shrubby, versions of *Q. virginiana* are **Quercus geminata** Small, Sand Live Oak, and **Quercus myrtifolia** Willd., Myrtle Oak. The former grows 20 to 30′ high, is similar to *Q. virginiana* in growth form and acorns but flowers 2 to 3 weeks later, occurs on coastal dunes and inland sands from southern North Carolina to Mississippi, drought tolerant, Zone 7 to 9. The latter, *Q. myrtifolia*, grows 10 to 20′ high, with 3/4 to 2″(3″) long, obovate, dark green leaves. The acorns are sessile or stalked (1/5″ long), the caps covering 1/4 to 1/3 of the nut and mature the second season, rarely the first. Occurs in sandy pine or oak-pine scrub. Requires good drainage under cultivation. South Carolina to Mississippi. Zone 8 to 10.

Quercus myrtifolia

Also in this complex of evergreen (tardily deciduous) species resides **Quercus chapmanii** Sarg., Chapman Oak, with oblong to elliptic leaves unlobed or irregularly wavy margined to shallowly lobed toward apex. First year stems finely grayish hairy. Acorns 3/4 to 1″ long, cap covering 1/3 to 1/2. Grows to 30′. Sandy barrens and scrub, dunes, ridges. South Carolina to Alabama. Zone 8 to 9.

A nifty hybrid, **Quercus × comptoniae** Sarg., embodies *Q. virginiana* and *Q. lyrata*. Habit is pyramidal, fast growing, tardily deciduous leaves, a young tree on campus has produced heavy acorn crops, about 1″ long, ellipsoidal, dark brown-black, covered about 1/2 by cap, will grow to 60′. Introduced 1920. Listed as Zone 5 but best in (6)7 to 9.

Rhamnus cathartica L. — Common or European Buckthorn
(ram′nus kȧ-thar′ti-kȧ)

FAMILY: Rhamnaceae

LEAVES: Subopposite, simple, elliptic or ovate, 1 1/2 to 3″ long, half as wide, sometimes almost equal in width, acute or obtusish, rounded or subcordate at base, sometimes broad-cuneate, crenate-serrulate, dark glossy green above, light green and usually glabrous beneath, with 3 to 5 pairs of veins; petiole—1/4 to 1″ long.

BUDS: Imbricate, appressed, elongated, brownish black, glabrous, 1/4″ long.

STEM: Slender, somewhat grayish, gray-green or brown, glabrous, terminal bud a modified spine usually as long as or longer than the buds.

SIZE: 18 to 25′ in height with a comparable spread; national champion is 61′ by 65′ in Ann Arbor, MI.

HARDINESS: Zone 3 to 7.

HABIT: Large shrub or low-branched tree with a rounded, bushy crown of crooked, stoutish stems; may sucker from base to produce a thicket.

RATE: Medium to fast.

TEXTURE: Medium in leaf, coarse in winter.

LEAF COLOR: Dark glossy green in summer, very clean foliage throughout the growing season, excellent if foliage is the only ornamental asset desired; fall color is a disappointing green to yellowish green, leaves hold quite late.

FLOWERS: Usually dioecious, small, yellowish green, 4-petaled, May, borne in 2- to 5-flowered umbels and form a dense cluster at the base of the young shoot.

FRUIT: Berry-like drupe, 1/4″ diameter, glossy, black, not particularly effective, birds like them.

CULTURE: Easily transplanted, adapted to difficult conditions, withstands urban environments; a very tough, durable tree for areas where few other trees will survive; the fruits are eaten by the birds and the seeds deposited in hedgerows, shrub borders and other out-of-the-way places; can actually become a noxious weed.

DISEASES AND INSECTS: Leaf spots, rust, powdery mildew, aphids, scales; none are serious except the rust (*Puccinia coronata*) which can cause considerable damage to oats; eradication of buckthorn is the recommended control measure.

LANDSCAPE VALUE: Possibly as a background, screen or hedge under difficult growing conditions; has become a terrible weed in Midwest and I remember the infestations at the Morton Arboretum; be careful because one plant yields many, especially with the birds as planters.

PROPAGATION: Seed, 60 to 90 days in moist peat at 41°F; cuttings are apparently somewhat difficult although 1000 ppm IBA or higher may suffice.

NATIVE HABITAT: Europe and western and northern Asia, naturalized in eastern and midwestern United States.

RELATED SPECIES:

Rhamnus davurica Pall., (ram'nus dȧ-vur'i-kȧ), Dahurian Buckthorn, is a 25 to 30′ high (usually smaller under cultivation), spreading shrub or small tree with stout, often spinescent, stems. Foliage is lustrous dark green; differs only in longer and uniformly wedge-shaped leaves. Fruit is black with 2 large seeds much like *R. cathartica*. Extremely hardy and durable, well-adapted to difficult situations. Limitedly available in commerce. Have seen the plant literally consume waste areas; is a weed unless checked. Northern China, Manchuria, Korea, Japan. Introduced 1817. Zone 3 to 6(7).

Rhamnus frangula L. — Glossy Buckthorn, also called Alder Buckthorn
(ram'nus frang'ū-lȧ)

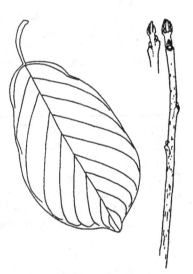

LEAVES: Alternate, simple, oval or obovate to obovate-oblong, 1 to 3″(4″) long, about half as wide, acute, rounded or broad-cuneate at base, entire, lustrous dark green above, lighter green and often slightly pubescent beneath, with 8 or 9 pairs of prominent, impressed veins; petiole—1/4 to 1/2″ long.

BUDS: Terminal—naked, pubescent, brownish, foliose, much larger than laterals; laterals—brownish, small.

STEM: Slender, pubescent on young stems, eventually becoming glabrous; prominently marked on young and old stems with gray, rectangular, vertical lenticels.

SIZE: 10 to 12′ possibly to 18′ in height and probably 8 to 12′ or greater in spread; national champion is 40′ by 25′ at Cranbrook Institute, Bloomfield Hills, MI.

HARDINESS: Zone 3 to 7.

HABIT: Upright, spreading, large shrub or small, low-branched tree with long arching branches yielding an upright-oval outline; quite gangly and open.

RATE: Medium to fast.

TEXTURE: Medium in leaf, medium-coarse in winter.

LEAF COLOR: Dark glossy green in summer changing to greenish yellow or yellow in fall; the fall color is usually a poor greenish yellow.

FLOWERS: Perfect, creamy-green, parts in fives, 2 to 10(10 to 20) together in leaf axils of new growth, not showy, bees love them, May.

FRUIT: Berry-like drupe, 1/4 to 1/3″ across, in maturation passes from red to purple-black, effective from July through September, 2 seeds.

CULTURE: Transplants well, adaptable, sun or partial shade, prefers well-drained soil; I noticed where Illinois students made paths through the hedges (*Rhamnus frangula* 'Columnaris'), a significant decrease in height is evident on either side of the path compared to non-trafficked areas.

DISEASES AND INSECTS: Until 1975 no serious problems had been reported. However, many of the hedge plants on the University of Illinois campus exhibited a dieback disorder typical of canker or wilt infestation. Don Schoeneweiss reported in the *Plant Disease Reporter* 58:937 that low temperature stresses predisposed Tallhedge to the fungus *Tubercularia ulmea*. He was consistently able to isolate the fungus from stem cankers that were girdling the shoots.

LANDSCAPE VALUE: Species is basically worthless for landscape considerations; falls into the weed character for the birds deposit the seeds everywhere and plants are found in unexpected places; cultivars offer some hope.

CULTIVARS:

'Asplenifolia'—Very fine texture, slow growing, but interesting, not common, will grow 10 to 12′ high and 6 to 10′ wide, leaves not cut but narrowed and with an irregular margin, offers an almost ferny texture to the landscape.

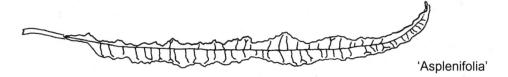

'Asplenifolia'

'Columnaris'—Narrow, upright deciduous shrub prized for hedges, has been overused in the Midwest; referred to as Tallhedge Glossy Buckthorn, will come partially true-to-type from seed; is usually produced from cuttings.

PROPAGATION: Seed, 60 days in moist peat at 41°F; softwood cuttings collected in June or July will root well when treated with 8000 ppm IBA.

ADDITIONAL NOTES: From a landscape viewpoint, difficult to become overly excited. Largely weedy, highly invasive plants. Need to keep use to a minimum. The genus contains 125 to 150 species with only a few of garden interest. Had the opportunity to catch up with *R. purshiana* DC, Cascara, in Oregon; amazing similarity in leaves with *R. frangula* and the others mentioned herein. Leaves turn rich yellow in autumn with red maturing to black fruits.

NATIVE HABITAT: Europe, western Asia, north Africa; naturalized in eastern and midwestern United States. Long cultivated.

RELATED SPECIES:

Rhamnus alaternus L., (ram′nus a̍-lā-ter′nus), Italian Buckthorn, is a medium-sized, evergreen shrub growing 10 to 12′ high. The oval to obovate, dark glossy green leaves average 3/4 to 2″ long and 1/2 to 1″ wide. Yellow-green, 5-merous, small flowers in a compact panicle; obovoid, black, 1/4″ diameter drupe with 3 seeds. The species is seldom seen in cultivation but 'Argenteovariegatus' ('Argentovariegatus') is a pretty creamy white-margined form that grows 6 to 8′(10′) high. I have seen it many times in Europe but never in the United States. Considered less cold hardy than the species. Mediterranean Region. Introduced about 1700. Zone 8 to 9?

Rhamnus caroliniana Walter — Carolina Buckthorn, Indian Cherry

LEAVES: Alternate, simple, elliptic-oblong or lance-oblong, 2 to 6″ long, acute or acuminate, rounded, serrulate or entire, lustrous dark green above, essentially glabrous, 8 to 10 impressed vein pairs; petiole—1/2″ long, pubescent.

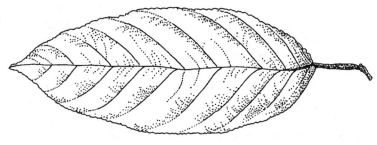

Rhamnus caroliniana, (ram′nus ka-rō-lin-i-ā′na̍), Carolina Buckthorn or Indian Cherry, is a handsome shrub or small tree with dark green, 8 to 10 vein-paired leaves. The real beauty resides in the 1/3″ diameter, globose, sweetish fruits (3 seeds) that change from red to black as they mature. I have grown the plant for several years and am most impressed with the handsome foliage and interesting fruits. Fruits ripen in August (red) and remain on the plant until October or later by which time they have turned black. It is quite attractive in fruit and is often brought in for positive identification. It can supposedly grow 30 to 40′ high but in the Piedmont of Georgia I have seen plants in the 10 to 15′ range. Co-national champions are 43′ by 18′ in Norris Dam State Park, TN and 27′ by 23′ in Middleburg, VA. New York to Florida, west to Nebraska and Texas. Introduced 1727. Zone 5 to 9.

Rhaphiolepis umbellata (Thunb.) Mak. — Yeddo (Yedda) Rhaphiolepis, Indian Hawthorn
(raf-i-ō-le′pis um-bel-lā′tà)

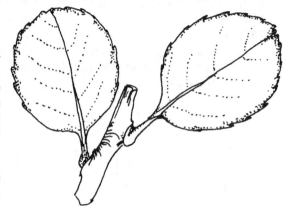

FAMILY: Rosaceae

LEAVES: Alternate, simple, evergreen, ovate to broad-ovate, 1 to 1 1/2″(3″) long, 3/4 to 1 1/4″(2″) wide, apex ranges from slightly acute to obtuse to emarginate, base rounded, leaves near end of stem entire, those lower on stem serrated to varying degrees, young leaves gray floccose above and below when emerging, finally extremely leathery, glabrous, lustrous dark green above, dull beneath, in winter assuming a slight purplish tinge especially on margin; petiole—1/4 to 1/2″ long, stout, with small blackish stipules.

BUDS: Flower—terminal, imbricate, scales loose at tips, 1/4″ high, reddish purple, pubescent; laterals—small, almost imbedded in bark.

STEM: Stout, pubescent at tip, finally glabrous, brown, streaked vertically with gray epidermal layer; pith—solid, green.

SIZE: 4 to 6′ by 4 to 6′, some forms growing 10 to 15′ high.

HARDINESS: Zone 7b to 10, actually shaky in Zone 7b; Mr. Will Corley, Georgia Experiment Station, evaluated 20 species and cultivars of *Rhaphiolepis* for hardiness and leaf spot resistance. In 1985, after −8°F, all were killed to the ground. At −3°F in 1983, the hardiest form was an unnamed, Plant Introduction (PI) accession from Japan. Interestingly, the PI showed near immunity to leaf spot while 'Majestic Beauty', 'Snow White', and 'Ovata' (var. *ovata*) showed good resistance; 'Enchantress', 'Fascination', and 'Pink Lady' the greatest susceptibility. Study in *J. Environ. Hort.* 10(1):1–3 (1992) showed that four new introductions were as cold hardy as the parent but maximum hardiness was still only 5 to 0°F.

HABIT: Dense, mounded-rounded evergreen shrub; leaves clustered at ends of branches like *Pittosporum*; some forms loose, open, making small trees if trained.

TEXTURE: Medium, rather stiff in appearance.

LEAF COLOR: New leaves almost gray-green, emerging in March (Athens), finally glossy dark green to blue-green in summer often assuming an off color during winter, somewhat of a subdued purple-green.

FLOWERS: Perfect, white, 5 petals, 5 sepals, 15 to 20 stamens, 2 to 3 styles, 3/4″ diameter, slightly fragrant, borne in dense, upright, tomentose, 2 to 3″ high and wide panicles or racemes; mid to late April into early May (Athens), makes a respectable show.

FRUIT: Subglobose, 3/8 to 1/2″ diameter, purple-black to bluish black, 1- to 2-seeded berry (possibly pome); ripen in early fall and persist attractively through winter.

CULTURE: Transplants readily from containers; prefers moist, well-drained soils, pH 6 to 7; will tolerate drought; adaptable to containers and above ground planters; tolerates restricted root space; good plant for coastal areas because of salt tolerance, injured at 0°F for many leaves were browned, probably best in Zone 8.

DISEASES AND INSECTS: Leaf spot in moist shady locations, have seen plants virtually defoliated, disease caused by *Entomosporium* species, symptoms are similar to those on *Photinia* × *fraseri*, red lesions develop on the leaf surface, may coalesce and kill entire leaf, disease more severe where moisture persists on leaves such as in semi-shaded locations.

LANDSCAPE VALUE: Have observed it in many landscape situations in the South; mass, unpruned hedge, containers, nice for textural effect; flowers and fruits are attractive; fruits tend to be lost in the dark green foliage especially when viewed at long distance; largely abandoned in late 1980's due to cold sensitivity and disease, memories are short and new cultivars have appeared with greater cold hardiness and disease resistance, am "seeing" the plant by the millions return to Zone 7b, Atlanta-Athens, widely used in large-scale masses; highly susceptible to deer browsing.

CULTIVARS: Could be cultivars of *R. indica* or *R. umbellata*. Have included all herein for ease of comparison. Corley's data on cold hardiness and disease resistance are worth monitoring.

    'Ballerina'—Vibrant rosy pink flowers with intermittent flowers in summer, foliage turns reddish color in winter, rounded habit 3 to 4′, *R. indica* form, killed at −3°F.

    'Bay Breeze'—Broad-mounded form, 2 1/2′ by 6′, new leaves bronze, finally lustrous dark black-green, rich deep pink flowers, in our trials more heavily browsed by deer, minimal leaf spot, Hines introduction.

'Betsy'—Selected for leaf spot resistance, introduced by Tom Dodd, Jr. and named for his daughter.

'Blueberry Muffin'—Has a dense rounded habit as I witnessed the plant in 1994, however, I believe the number of cuttings removed kept it compact; white flowers, blue-black fruit, leaves turn purple in winter; was free of leaf spot when viewed by the author; J.C. Raulston Arboretum introduction; J.C. gave me fruits that were cleaned, sown and produced many vigorous wild seedlings, none of which were small, seedlings are susceptible to leaf spot.

Cameo™ ('Ponto's Pink Clara')—Dense mounding shrub, 4' by 4', new foliage reddish colored, matures to rich dark green, bright pink single flowers in March–April, sporadic flowers in fall, bred at Ponto Nursery, Vista, CA, introduced by Hines Nurseries, Inc., Houston, TX.

'Charisma'—Double, soft pink flowers, rich green foliage, tight mounded growth habit, a Monrovia introduction, killed at -3°F.

'Clara'—White flowers cover plant in spring, red new growth maturing to dark green, low evergreen shrub, 4' high and 4' wide, killed at -3°F.

'Coates Crimson'—Crimson-pink flowers, compact spreading, slow-growing, 2 to 4' high and wide, killed at -3°F.

'Dwarf Pink'—Rose-pink flowers on a 4' high plant, bronze-red winter foliage.

Eleanor Taber™—Vigorous mounded form, large dark green leaves, pinkish flowers, good leaf spot resistance, has performed well in Georgia tests, Flowerwood Nursery introduction.

'Enchantress' ('Pinkie')—More compact than the species; rose-pink flowers in large panicles from late winter through early summer depending on geographic location, lustrous dark green leaves, moderate to severe injury at -3°F, 3' by 5'.

'Eskimo'—A plant introduction accession from the U.S. National Arboretum that Will Corley evaluated at the Griffin Experiment Station, was the hardiest and most leaf spot resistant in Will's trials, the progenitor parent for 'Georgia Charm' and 'Georgia Petite', parent plant 6' by 8', dark green leaves, white flowers, named 'Eskimo' and grown by Wight Nurseries, Cairo, GA.

'Fascination'—Compact, rounded form with large leaves and flowers; petals pink toward the edges, white in the center creating a star-like effect, moderate to severe injury at -3°F.

'Georgia Charm'—Compact, 4' by 3', dark green leaves, white flowers, more cold hardy to 5°F and leaf spot resistant, parentage supposedly 'Eskimo' × 'Ovata', patented, introduced by University of Georgia.

'Georgia Petite'—Compact mound, 2 1/2' by 3', light pink-white flowers, selected for cold and leaf spot tolerance, parentage as above, patented.

'Harbinger of Spring'—Deep pink flowers in loose panicles, 3″ long thick glossy green leaves, rounded habit, 5' by 5', moderate injury at -3°F.

'Hines Darkleaf'—Low-growing form, 2 to 2 1/2' high, 6' or greater in width, bronzy maroon to green new growth matures to glossy rich green, with foliage becoming dark purple in fall, leaves are somewhat recurved, flowers are single, bright pink with white center, sporadic flowers in fall, released by Hines Nurseries, Santa Ana, CA.

'Indian Princess'—Broad bright pink flowers, fade to white, heavily tomentose new leaves become glabrous and bright green, compact broad mounded form, 3' by 5', a Monrovia introduction.

'Jack Evans'—Vivid pink flowers in large panicles, strong upright habit, 4 to 5' by 4', killed at -3°F.

'Majestic Beauty'—Large form probably growing 8 to 10' and larger, often trained into a small tree, leaves up to 4″ long, bronze turning deep green, flowers are pinkish and fragrant, has shown good resistance to leaf spot, killed at -3°F, have observed in numerous plantings on Jekyll and St. Simons Islands, GA, this is the most robust growing of the common cultivars, have seen it listed as a *R. × delacourii* selection.

'Minor'—Smaller dark green leaves, white flowers, upright 3 to 4' high, definitely not minor except for the leaves, purple-black fruit, marketed as Gulf Green™ by Hines.

'Olivia'—Excellent large dark green leaves, white flowers, dense mounded habit, 4' by 4 to 5', high leaf spot resistance, has outgrown and outperformed 'Eleanor Taber', 'Bay Breeze', 'Georgia Charm', and 'Georgia Petite' in Georgia trials, every visitor who knows anything about *Rhaphiolepis* asks the identity of 'Olivia'.

'Pink Cloud'—Pink flowers and compact growth habit, 3' by 3 to 4', may be the same as 'Springtime'?

'Pink Dancer'—Compact, mounding habit, 16″ by 36″, lustrous leaves with undulating margins, become bronze or maroon in cold weather, deep pink flowers.

'Pink Flush' —Pink flowers in spring, intermittent flowering in summer, reddish foliage color in winter, rounded outline, 3 to 4' high, I believe this is the same as 'Ballerina'.

'Pink Lady'—Deep pink flowers, vigorous form, 4 to 5' by 4 to 6', resistant to leaf spot, the same as 'Enchantress'?, slight to moderate injury at -3°F.

'Pinkie'—Pink flowers on a 3' high, compact shrub.

'Rosalinda'—Large-growing form, bronzy red new foliage, changing to dark green, dark pink, fragrant flowers, Flowerwood introduction.

'Rosea'—Light pink flowers; loose, more graceful habit, 3 to 5' high and 5 to 6' wide; new growth bronze; also a compact form with similar attributes ('Rosea Dwarf'); 'Rosea Dwarf' was killed at -3°F.

'Snow White'—Dwarf form with a spreading habit; pure white flowers from early spring into early summer; foliage lighter green than other cultivars, good resistance to leaf spot, moderate to severe injury at -3°F.

'Spring Rapture'—Rose-red flowers cover a compact, mounding shrub, 3 to 4' high and wide, a Monrovia introduction, slight to moderate injury at -3°F.

'Springtime'—More vigorous grower; flowers pink, late winter to early spring; foliage bronzy green, thick and leathery; moderate to severe injury at -3°F; 4 to 6' high; same as 'Pink Lady'?; Monrovia introduction.

'White Enchantress'—Low-growing form with single white flowers, 3' by 5', hardy to 0°F, moderate to severe injury at -3°F, Monrovia introduction.

PROPAGATION: Seed collected in mid-February, pulp removed, direct down, germinated in high percentages. Cuttings: semi-hardwood to hardwood can be rooted, 2500 ppm IBA + 2500 ppm NAA, wound, has proved to be an effective treatment. I have had miserable success rooting this genus and cuttings have been taken in fall and winter. An interesting Florida study mentioned that best rooting occurred from June to August with 10,000 to 20,000 ppm IBA quick dip, wound, perlite:vermiculite medium, 47% shade and mist. Rooting ranged from 90 to 100%.

NATIVE HABITAT: Japan, Korea. Introduced before 1864.

RELATED SPECIES: Based on my explorations around the South the *Rhaphiolepis* species are somewhat confused. Although *R. indica* is listed as the plant most in cultivation the technical description favors either the above or a hybrid *R. × delacourii* André, (*R. umbellata × R. indica*). It showed slight to moderate injury at -3°F. The hybrid was raised by Delacour, gardener at the Villa Allerton, Cannes, France. Numerous forms varying in leaf and flower color were raised. It displays moderate to good resistance to leaf spot. I surmise some of the hybrids may have been named, renamed, and represent a few of the cultivars listed under *R. umbellata*. Louisiana Nurseries lists 'Belle' with deep pink flowers and tall growing; 'Elizabeth' with pink flowers over an extended season on a 4' by 5' shrub; 'Janice' with bright pink flowers and dwarf compact habit; 'Peggy' with white flowers, dark green foliage and compact habit; and 'Pink Charm' with deep rose-pink flowers on a low-growing framework.

Rhaphiolepis indica (L.) Lindl., (raf-i-ō-le'pis in'di-kà), Indian Hawthorn, is less hardy than *R. umbellata* and *R. × delacourii*. The 2 to 3" long leaves are thinner and narrower, lanceolate, acute or acuminate, more sharply serrate and the flowers either white or pinkish. From a landscape standpoint this species is probably similar. I have not observed a single plant of the species on the Georgia campus. Southern China. Introduced 1806. Zone 8 to 9(10).

Rhododendron L. — Rhododendrons and Azaleas
FAMILY: Ericaceae

The genus *Rhododendron* comprises over 900 species and infinite numbers of cultivars due to the ability of the species to freely hybridize. The continuing avalanche of cultivars has buried this author with considerable self-doubt relative to developing an effective presentation. My conclusion: no effective way exists. Individuals smarter and broader-versed have written monographs on the genus. I have checked and cross-checked articles, catalogs, books, living collections, and at best assembled a framework of descriptions that might assist the reader. Rest assured that even the experts do not know the rhododendron genus in its broadest sense.

The improvements in rhododendrons (foliage, flower color and quality, hardiness and growth habit) have come about through hybridization. There is a need for cold hardy forms with good flower color. Many of the hardy types available are endowed with the lavender-purple-magenta colors offensive to many people. Rhododendrons are indigenous to many parts of the world but the strongest concentrations of hardy, colorful, useful types exist in China, Japan, and the eastern United States. Greatest cultural success in the States is achieved in the Pacific Northwest and the eastern United States where soils and atmospheric conditions are close to optimum. The following list is not complete and was not intended to be. The types listed represent some of the hardier and more common forms. A good rhododendron display is without equal and a poll of gardeners (asking them their favorite shrub) indicated rhododendrons were *numero uno*. For additional information see Cox, Davidian, Greer, Bowers, Leach, Bean, Galle, Reilly, *The New RHS Dictionary of Gardening*, and join the American Rhododendron Society.

The truism is genuine that nurserymen B to Z will often grow the plants that nurseryman A offers. The large wholesale nurseries produce many of the standards like 'Nova Zembla', 'P.J.M.', 'Delaware Valley White', 'George Taber', 'Gibraltar', etc., because of ironclad performance and reasonable name recognition. The new hybrids and cultivars have a difficult time breaking the stranglehold of the few. I am not sure this will ever change. Small specialty nurseries offer the newer, perhaps better, azaleas and rhododendrons, and should be supported. I have observed our Georgia industry integrating the newer and better Girard, Robin Hill, and North Tisbury azaleas into production. Older varieties must be removed from production to make room for the new. At any time in the production cycle of the large nurseries a finite number of rhododendron members can be grown. With this stated, it is a sad commentary on the beautiful evergreen and deciduous azaleas that they are at the bottom of the economic container nursery food chain. Yes, azaleas, particularly the evergreen types, sell for less than almost all other container-produced plants of similar size.

Bonnie and I have "given up" on the large-leaf evergreen rhododendrons in our Georgia garden and grow only the deciduous native azaleas and a few small evergreen azaleas. The April–May flowering natives are exquisite with riotous colors of white, pink, rose, yellow, orange, and red and are often quite fragrant. We have tested the new Encore™ azaleas from Flowerwood Nursery and appreciate their August through November, subtle flowers. Unfortunately, they do not appear to be particularly cold hardy and cultivar by cultivar evaluation will be necessary. See this new section and discussion of the various cultivars. Bonnie and I spent several afternoons evaluating Encore™ performance.

Travels have taken me to the Highlands of Scotland, particularly Inverewe, Arduaine, and Crarae Gardens where I raised my eyes skyward to frame the large Himalayan rhododendrons. Magnificent leaves, *R. sinogrande* Balf. f. & W.W. Sm.; rich red-brown exfoliating bark, *R. barbatum* G. Don.; and yellow flowers so rich, *R. macabeanum* Balf. f.; were in full plumage. Realistically, only memories were carried home. However, with the great English plantsman, Roy Lancaster, I trekked Rabun Bald, second highest mountain in Georgia at 4696′, in late June 1997. We experienced *R. arborescens*, *R. calendulaceum*, and *R. catawbiense* in flower. The thrill was not too different for Roy from his adventures in China and the Himalayas. After all, rhododendrons and azaleas in the wild in any part of the world are magnificent experiences.

DIFFERENCES IN RHODODENDRONS AND AZALEAS

Actually, all azaleas are now included in the genus *Rhododendron*. There are no clear cut lines for distinguishing *all* azaleas from *all* rhododendrons but:

1. True rhododendrons are usually evergreen but there are exceptions such as *R. mucronulatum* and *R. dauricum*.
2. True rhododendrons have 10 or more stamens and leaves are often scaly or with small dots on their undersurface.
3. Azaleas are mostly deciduous.
4. Azalea flowers have mostly 5 stamens, leaves are never dotted with scales and are frequently pubescent.
5. Azalea flowers are largely funnel-form while rhododendron flowers tend to be bell-shaped.
6. Recent hybrids between true rhododendron and true azaleas have intermediate stamen numbers, Encore™ azaleas are an example.

Rhododendron carolinianum Rehd. — Carolina Rhododendron
(rō-dō-den′dron ka-rō-lin-i-ā′num)

LEAVES: Alternate, simple, evergreen, elliptic to narrow-elliptic, 2 to 3″ long, 1/2 to 1 3/4″ wide, acutish or abruptly short-acuminate, broad cuneate, dark green and glabrous above, entire, ferrugineous scaly often very densely so beneath, sometimes glaucescent; petiole 1/4 to 1/2″ long; leaves aromatic when bruised.

STEM: Glabrous, often deep red to purplish red.

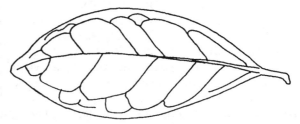

SIZE: 3 to 6′ in height with a similar or greater spread.

HARDINESS: Zone (4)5 to 8.

HABIT: Small, rounded evergreen shrub of rather gentle proportions; not as coarse as Catawba hybrids, often loose and open, particularly in the wild.

RATE: Slow, 3 to 5′ over a 10 year period.

TEXTURE: Medium in all seasons.

LEAF COLOR: Dark green in summer, usually assuming a purplish tinge in cold climates.

FLOWERS: Perfect, varies from pure white to pale rose, rose and lilac-rose in color; borne in a terminal, 4- to 10-flowered, umbel-like, 3″ diameter raceme (truss), May, corolla 5-lobed, about 1 1/2″ wide.

FRUIT: Dehiscent 5-valved capsule, best to remove after flowers have faded.

CULTURE: Having tracked rhododendrons and azaleas from the Midwest to East Coast to the southeastern United States, I can unequivocally state that inadequate drainage is the most prominent factor limiting growth. If poor drainage does not directly kill plants, it predisposes them to insects and diseases such as root rot. They have fine silk-like roots, generally without root hairs, and are easy to transplant balled and burlapped or from a container; the root mass is usually profuse, which allows for successful planting; numerous plants are container-grown and the roots form a web (almost fabric-like) at the interface of the medium/container; if plants are left in the containers too long the root mass is so thick and matted it must be cut; ideally make vertical slits with a knife; this will insure contact with the soil when planted and, hopefully, root penetration into the native soil; I have observed azaleas and rhododendrons newly transplanted into a landscape that were wilted or dead; a simple tug on the plant and removal from the ground showed the plant was removed from the container and planted as a solid mass; water uptake was severely limited as the planting hole became dry; I suspect more one gallon azaleas die this way than any other cause. Provide light shade in the North, even heavier shade in the South; have noticed tremendous lacebug infestations on plants exposed to full sun; the State Botanical Garden has a fine collection of ironclad *R. catawbiense* hybrids that were planted on a slope with the root balls above the soil and covered with pine bark; over the years they have prospered, but have received fertilizer and water as well as an occasional insect spray. Rhododendrons are extremely sensitive to salinity, high pH (chlorosis), and winter injury.

With emphasis, I recommend gardeners contact their local Extension offices for state or regional guides to the best rhododendrons and azaleas. Almost all states produce some type of guide. Recently, *Rhododendrons in Alabama*, Circular ANR-151, crossed my desk. Therein, 31 rhododendrons with hardiness, color, height, and characteristics are discussed. This is a logical starting point for those who simply want to test the *Rhododendron* waters. Be aware that many rhododendrons are grown in the Pacific Northwest and shipped East. The cultivars may or may not be adapted. Do your homework!

DISEASES AND INSECTS: Botryosphaeria canker, crown rot, dieback, dampening-off, azalea petal blight, azalea gall, leaf spots, leaf scorch, powdery mildew, rust, shoot blight, shoestring root rot, wilt, rhododendron aphid, azalea stem borer, azalea leaf tier, black vine and strawberry weevils, giant hornet, Japanese beetle, asiatic garden beetle, lace bugs (in the Southeast, lace bugs are terrific problems with the small leaf evergreen azaleas, although they appear to infest any plant with the generic name of *Rhododendron*; Dr. S. Kristine Braman, Entomology, University of Georgia, has an active program to determine resistance, et al.; *J. Environ. Hort.* 10(1):40–43 (1992) discusses resistance in deciduous azaleas); red-banded leafhopper, azalea leaf miner, rhododendron tip midge, mites, mealybugs, pitted ambrosia beetle, rhododendron borer, scales, thrips, rhododendron whitefly, nematodes, stem girdling caused by woodpeckers. Rhododendrons are troubled by many pests and their culture is often fraught with difficulty. Good cultural practices will reduce the incidence of disease and insect damage.

LANDSCAPE VALUE: Like all rhododendrons a nice plant for the shrub border, groupings, massing, foundations; should be sited in a slightly shaded area and out of strong winter sun and wind; survived -20°F in my Illinois garden and flowered nicely.

CULTIVARS:

‘Album’—White flowers.

‘Carolina Gold’—A new yellow flower color is brought to this species by Dr. August E. Kehr, dark shiny leaves, upright growing habit.

‘Luteum’—Mimosa yellow flowers.

‘White Perfection’—Compact habit, soft pink buds open to pure white flowers, shiny deep green foliage.

PROPAGATION: See under *Calluna*; I have raised many seedlings with a minimum of effort. Like most rhododendrons this species exhibits great variation when grown from seed. Cuttings are somewhat difficult to root but when taken in August and treated with a hormone and fungicide will give a reasonable percentage.

NATIVE HABITAT: Blue Ridge Mountains of Carolinas and Tennessee. Cultivated 1815.

Rhododendron catawbiense Michx. — Catawba Rhododendron
(rō-dō-den′dron ka-taw-bi-en′sē)

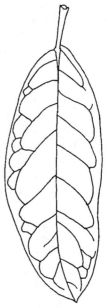

LEAVES: Alternate, simple, evergreen, elliptic to oblong, 3 to 6″ long, 1 to 2″ wide, obtuse and mucronulate, rounded at base, entire, dark green above, light green below, glabrous, leathery texture; petiole—1/2 to 1 1/4″ long.

FLOWER BUDS: Large—1/2″ long, scaly, pointed, yellowish green.

STEM: On new growth yellowish green changing to brown with age, glabrous.

SIZE: 6 to 10′ in height, rarely 15 to 20′, spread 5 to 8′ or more.

HARDINESS: Zone 4 to 8.

HABIT: Heavy evergreen shrub with large, dense foliage to the ground; often leggy in unfavorable locations; usually taller than wide although does assume a rounded outline.

RATE: Slow.

TEXTURE: Medium-coarse in all seasons.

LEAF COLOR: Dark green, very handsome; often in winter under exposed conditions will develop a yellow-green color.

FLOWERS: Lilac-purple, sometimes purplish rose, with green or yellow-brown markings on the inside of the corolla, 1 1/2″ long, 2 1/2″ broad; mid to late May in Urbana, IL (late April to late May in Athens, GA) depending on the cultivar, flowers borne in 5 to 6″ diameter umbel-like racemes (trusses), species as observed on Rabun Bald at ~4000′ in full flower late June 1997.

FRUIT: Capsule, dehiscent, 5-valved.

CULTURE: See under *R. carolinianum*.

DISEASES AND INSECTS: See under *R. carolinianum*.

LANDSCAPE VALUE: Very handsome and aesthetic broadleaf evergreen; the flowers are beautiful but the foliage is equally valuable; beautiful when used in mass; hardy to about -20°F with proper cultivar selection.

CULTIVARS: Several are not *R. catawbiense* hybrids but are included here for convenience.

    'A. Bedford'—Lavender-blue with dark blotch, -15°F.

    'Albert Schweitzer'—Award winner from Holland noted for its large, conical trusses of pink flowers enhanced by a striking red flare; upright, vigorous habit.

    'Album' (var. *album*)—A plant of great hardiness and vigor with buds flushed lilac, opening to pure white flowers with greenish yellow spotting, held in compact, rounded trusses; 6′ high, -25°F, excellent lustrous dark green foliage.

    'Album Elegans'—White, -15°F.

    'Alice'—Deep pink, -15°F.

    'America'—Brilliant deep red, very floriferous, forming a broad bush, not as hardy as 'Nova Zembla', -15 to -20°F.

    'Anah Kruschke' ('Purple Splendor' × *R. ponticum*)—Dense plant, glossy foliage, deep purple flowers form a tight truss, performed well in University's Botanical Garden, -15°F.

    'Anna Baldsiefen'—Star shaped ruffled flowers are light rose with darker midribs and edges, upright growing, to 3′.

    'Anna Rose Whitney' (*R. griersonianum* × 'Countess of Derby')—This huge plant is impressive with its large full truss of deep rose-pink flowers with very light spotting on the upper lobes, -15°F.

    'Antoon Van Welie'—Deep pink with a lighter blotch, -15°F.

    'Autumn Gold'—Apricot Salmon.

    'Baden Baden'—Red.

    'Betty Wormald'—Pink with light center.

    'Blue Diamond'—Lavender-blue.

    'Blue Ensign'—Lavender-blue with a prominent dark blotch held in a rounded truss, the leaves are large and dark matte green, smaller than 'Blue Peter', 4 to 5′ high, -15°F.

    'Blue Jay'—Lavender-blue with brown blotch, -15°F.

    'Blue Peter'—The flowers are a light lavender-blue with a striking purple flare, the leaves are dark green and glossy, 5 to 6′ high, -15°F.

    'Boursault'—Lavender flowers in a rounded truss, good sturdy habit, 5′ high, -25°F.

    'Bow Bells'—Bright pink, -15°F.

    'Butterfly'—Pale yellow, -15°F.

    'Calsap'—Pale lavender buds open to white with a dark red blotch, hardier than 'Sappho'; wider than high.

'Caractacus'—Red, -15°F.

'Caroline'—These pale lavender-pink flowers have a fragrance enhanced by the warmth of the sun; highly resistant to root disease, 6' high, -15°F.

'Cary Ann'—Coral-red, -15°F.

'Cheer' ('Cunningham's White' × red *R. catawbiense* hybrid)—Shell pink flowers have conspicuous red blotches in conical trusses, the plant is rounded and compact with glossy leaves, 5' high, -15°F, flowers early in University's Botanical Garden, often flowers in fall.

'Chionoides'—White flowers have the yellow centers and make numerous dome shaped trusses. The broad, dense plant is easy to grow and has attractive, narrow foliage, 4' high, -20°F.

'Christmas Cheer'—Light pink, -20°F.

'Cilpinense'—Apple blossom pink, -20°F.

'Compactum'—This form stays less than 3' tall.

'Cosmopolitan'—Pink with a red blotch, -20°F.

'Cunningham's Blush'—Blush pink petals with light pink blotch, dark green leaves on this small shrub with a compact habit, -20°F.

'Cunningham's White'—Pink blushed buds open to white flowers blotched with greenish yellow, excellent foliage, low compact growth, -20°F.

'Cynthia' (*R. catawbiense* × *R. griffithianum*)—Showy conical trusses of rosy crimson flowers with blackish crimson markings, large and vigorous, 6' tall, rather rank growing, -15°F.

'Daphnoides'—Purple.

'Dora Amateis'—Floriferous white flowers, lightly spotted with green, slightly aromatic, vigorous, 3' high, twice as wide as tall, deep green dense foliage, -15°F.

'Dr. V. H. Rutgers'—Aniline red, a compact grower with good flowering capabilities, -20°F.

'Edward S. Rand'—Crimson-red with a bronze eye, -20°F.

'Elisabeth Hobbie'—Red, semi-dwarf, -20°F.

'English Roseum'—Light rose, vigorous yet compact, upright plant, large foliage, good growing habit, heat tolerant, -25°F.

'Evening Glow'—Light yellow, -15°F.

'Everestianum'—Rosy lilac, -20°F.

'Fastuosum Flore Pleno' ('Fastuosum Plenum')—Lavender-blue, semi-double, -20°F.

'Fred Hamilton'—Yellow with pink bands, -15°F.

'Furnivall's Daughter'—Pink with a sienna blotch, -20°F.

'Gomer Waterer'—Buds are slightly rose tinged, opening to white, dark green glossy leaves, broad and upright, 6' high, -15°F.

'Good News'—Crimson-red, -15°F.

'Grandiflorum'—Lilac, -20°F.

'Grierosplendour'—Plum, -15°F.

'Halfden Lem'—Large, crimson trusses and heavy-textured, deep green foliage, a good grower and improvement over 'Jean Marie Montague', -5°F.

'Harvest Moon'—Pale yellow with red spots, -15°F.

'Henrietta Sargent'—Tall growing, hardy, deep rose-pink flowers.

'Ignatius Sargent'—Deep rose, -25°F.

'Jean Marie De Montague'—Bright scarlet flowers, dark green foliage, compact habit, -15°F.

'Jock'—Rosy pink, -15°F.

'Kluis Sensation'—Dark red, -15°F.

'Labar's White'—Pure white flowers with yellow-green spotting in the throat, from Labar's Nursery, exceptional heat and cold tolerance.

'Lady C. Mitford'—Peach pink, -15°F.

'Lavender Queen'—Lavender, -20°F.

'Lee's Best Purple'—Purple flowers in June, excellent, smooth, dark foliage, hardy to -20°F.

'Lee's Dark Purple'—Buds very dark purple, opening to dark purple, surrounded by wavy foliage, grows into a broad compact bush, common in the nursery trade, -20°F.

'Lemon Ice'—Yellow, -20°F.

'Loder's White'—White, -15°F.

'Lord Roberts'—Red with a dark blotch, -20°F.

'Madame Carvalho'—White with green spots, -20°F.

'Madame Cochet'—Purple with a white center, -15°F.

'Madame Masson'—White with a yellow blotch, -20°F.

'Marchioness of Lansdowne'—Rose, -20°F.

'Mary Belle'—Light salmon buds open to peach, -20°F.

'Michael Waterer'—Dark red, -20°F.

'Moonglow'—Extremely good grower with light pink flowers becoming white when fully opened; pink dots in throat with pink anther and stamens; an improved 'Pink Pearl' type, hardy to 0°F.

'Mother of Pearl'—White, -15°F.

'Mrs. Betty Robertson'—Creamy yellow with red spots, -15°F.

'Mrs. C.S. Sargent'—Rich carmine-rose flowers, spotted yellow, a worthy selection for cold areas.

'Mrs. E.C. Stirling'—Silvery pink, -15°F.

'Mrs. Lady de Rothschild'—White, flushed pink, -15°F.

'Mrs. T.H. Lowinsky'—White with a reddish brown blotch, -20°F.

'Myrtifolium'—Medium pink, small, -20°F.

'Nepal'—Pure white flowers, dark green wavy leaves, -25°F.

'Nova Zembla'—Red flowers, perhaps not as intense and with more lavender than 'America', quite cold tolerant and heat resistant, probably one of the best for the Midwest and does well in the South, -25°F.

'Old Port'—Medium purple with a dark blotch, -20°F.

'Parson's Gloriosum'—Compact, conical trusses of lavender flowers, compact yet tall growth habit, dense, dark green foliage, -25°F.

'Pearce's American Beauty'—Olive yellow spots on a dark rose red flower, mid-season, handsome dark foliage that resembles 'Scintillation', tight grower to 6'.

'Pink Pearl'—Soft rose-pink, -15°F.

'Pink Petticoats'—China rose, -15°F.

'Pink Twins'—Light shrimp pink, -20°F.

'Powell Glass'—White-flowering, wide, upright and vigorous.

'President Lincoln'—Lavender pink with a bronze blotch, -25°F.

'Prince Camille de Rohan'—Light pink, -20°F.

'Purple Lace'—Lacy purple with a light center, -15°F.

'Purple Splendour'—Dark purple with a black blotch.

'Purple Splendour Compacta'—A more compact sport of 'Purple Splendour', slightly smaller flower.

'Purpureum Elegans'—Bishop's violet, dark green foliage, fine compact shape and the flowers open a clear pure color, -25°F.

'Purpureum Grandiflorum'—Medium-dark purple flowers, somewhat later than typical large-leaf rhododendrons, slightly slower growing than average.

'Rosamundi'—Light pink flowers in profusion, showy, small mounded shrub, -15°F.

'Roseum Elegans'—The old stand-by, lavender-pink (rosy purple) flowers and reliability in flowering, withstanding temperature extremes without injury, more than one form under this name, -25°F, excellent heat tolerance.

'Roseum Pink'—Clear pale pink, similar to 'English Roseum', strong grower making a broad well filled plant, -25°F.

'Roseum Superbum'—Rose lilac, -25°F.

'Roseum Two'—Pink, a strong grower with excellent bud set capabilities, bud sport in Wells Nursery.

'Sappho'—Mauve buds open to pure white flowers with a conspicuous blotch of violet overlaid with blackish purple, the plant habit is open and rather leggy, good background plant, 6 to 10' high, -10°F.

'Scarlet Wonder'—Scarlet-red, -20°F.

'Shamrock'—Chartreuse flowers, extremely compact form, wider than high, -25°F.

'Sham's Candy'—Bright pink with yellow-green blotch, -25°F.

'Spitfire'—Deep red with brown blotch, -20°F.

'The General'—Crimson with dark red blotch, -25°F.

'Top Gun'—Compact habit, pinkish purple flowers, vigorous, sport of 'Anah Kruschke'.

'Trilby'—Deep crimson flowers with black blotches, small shrub with distinctive red stems, -20°F.

'Trude Webster'—Rich pink with dark spots, -15°F.

'Unique'—Reddish buds open to peach tinged yellow flowers, small, compact, mounded form, -15°F.

'Virginia Richards'—Large trusses open pale yellow with pink overtone, becoming deeper yellow with crimson blotch, small, compact shrub, -15°F.

'Vivacious'—Hardy, compact and clearer red than 'Nova Zembla', introduced by Vineland Experimental Station in Canada.

'Vulcan'—Heavy trusses of brick red flowers, small, compact shrub with excellent mounded form, -20°F.

'Vulcan's Flame'—Bright red, -20°F.

'Wilgen's Ruby'—Red with brown blotch, -20°F.

PROPAGATION: Seed, as previously described; cuttings show great variation in rootability. I have had good success rooting various Catawba types by collecting cuttings in mid-August, wounding for about 1 to 1 1/2″, cutting leaf surface in half, treating with 1000 to 10,000 ppm IBA/50% alcohol for 5 seconds and placing the cuttings in peat:perlite under mist; rooting takes place in 2 to 4 months. A protocol that produced outstanding results in our shop included firm July–August cuttings, two-sided wound, 10000 ppm KIBA quick dip, followed by 8000 ppm IBA-talc, 3 perlite:1 peat, mist, with excellent rooting in about 10 weeks. A respectable paper, *Proc. Intl. Plant Prop. Soc.* 43:178–182 (1993) discusses *Rhododendron* propagation in the Pacific Northwest. Brigg's Nursery, Olympia, WA produces 99% of the rhododendrons via tissue culture. In contrast, Van Veen Nursery produces over 400 cultivars from cuttings with 291,000 rooted in 1991–1992.

ADDITIONAL NOTES: One of the hardiest and best known of all the rhododendrons.

NATIVE HABITAT: Alleghenies, West Virginia, southwest to Georgia and Alabama. Introduced 1809.

Rhododendron mucronulatum Turcz. — Korean Rhododendron
(rō-dō-den′dron mū-kron-ū-lā′tum)

LEAVES: Alternate, simple, deciduous, elliptic to elliptic-lanceolate, 1 to 4″ long, 1/2 to 1 1/4″ wide, acute or obtusish, medium green, entire, very aromatic when crushed, thin textured; petiole 1/8 to 1/4″ long.

BUDS: Flower—rounded-ovoid, light brown, glabrous.

STEM: Slender, light straw-brown.

SIZE: 4 to 8′ in height with a similar spread.

HARDINESS: Zone 4 to 7.

HABIT: Deciduous shrub of upright-oval to rounded outline with clean branching and foliage characteristics.

RATE: Slow, perhaps medium in youth.

TEXTURE: Medium-fine in foliage, medium in winter.

LEAF COLOR: Soft green in summer changing to shades of yellow and bronzy crimson in fall.

FLOWERS: Bright rosy purple, 1 1/2″ long and 1 1/2″ wide, mid to late March to early April, 3 to 6 together at the ends of the branches; flowers well before the leaves and often as the buds are opening a freeze will kill or injure them; siting is very important and a protected location where the south and southwestern sun will not hit them in February and March is recommended.

CULTURE: Trouble free plant, one of the hardiest.

DISEASES AND INSECTS: See under *R. carolinianum*.

LANDSCAPE VALUE: First of all the hardy rhododendrons and azaleas to flower in northeastern United States; very lovely in a shrub border; I had 5 scattered around the northeast corner of our Illinois home and they made nice foundation plants because of compactness and good foliage as well as lovely early flower.

CULTIVARS:

'Album'—White form, with just a hint of pink, early-flowering.

'Bright Pink'—Pink flowers that are a bit brighter than 'Cornell Pink', late April.

'Cama'—Large soft flowers that fade to white, unusual semi-evergreen leaves.

'Cornell Pink'—Phlox pink flowers, unadulterated by the magenta present in the flowers of the species; raised by Henry T. Skinner, Cornell University; named and put in commerce in 1952.

'Crater('s) Edge'—A true dwarf, dark red buds open lavender-pink.

Dwarf Form—Intense lavender flowers, low and mounded to less than 3′, bright fall color.

'Easter Bunny'—Soft lavender with a light cream to light yellow flare, mid-April.

'Mahogany Red'—Bright red flowers; Dr. August Kehr selection.

'Nana'—Clear purple flowers, dwarf to 2′, mahogany fall color.

'Pink Mucronulatum'—Lovely shades of pink, occurs in seed produced populations.

'Pink Peignoir'—Soft pink clone, opens early April, at least two week earlier than 'P.J.M.', opens and remains an unusually soft shade of pink that blends particularly well with the typical lavender color of the species, more subtle in the landscape than brighter pink clones such as 'Salem Hill Pink' and 'Cornell Pink', should be hardy to -25°F, 6′ in 20 years.

'Radiant Pink'—Bright fluorescent pink flowers, warm, yellow-bronzy fall color; upright habit.

PROPAGATION: Seed, very easy; softwood cuttings collected in July rooted 50%. I have grown many seedlings of this species and also rooted many cuttings. One of the seedlings flowered in spring of 1975 and was a beautiful soft pink (apple blossom-like).

NATIVE HABITAT: Northern China, Manchuria, Korea and northern Japan. Introduced 1882.

Rhododendron schlippenbachii Maxim. — Royal Azalea

(rō-dō-den′dron shlip-en-bȧk′ē-ī)

LEAVES: Alternate, simple, usually 5 at ends of the branches, appear as if whorled, short-petioled, obovate or broad-obovate, 2 to 5 1/2″ long, 1 1/2 to 3″ wide, truncate or rounded to emarginate at apex, mucronate, cuneate, slightly undulate, sparingly pubescent when young, later glabrous except on veins beneath, dark green above, pale beneath.

SIZE: 6 to 8′ high and as wide at maturity, can grow larger but this seldom occurs in the United States.
HARDINESS: Zone 4 to 6, best in colder climates, I have tried it several times in Zone 7b with no success.
HABIT: Upright-rounded deciduous shrub.
RATE: Slow.
TEXTURE: Medium in all seasons.
LEAF COLOR: Dark green in summer, yellow, orange, crimson in fall.
FLOWERS: Pale to rose-pink, no trace of magenta, fragrant, early to mid-May; 3 to 6 together in a 2 1/4 to 3″ diameter inflorescence; one of the most delicate and beautiful of the azaleas for northern gardens; 10 stamens.
CULTURE: Seems to do better on high pH soils than other Ericaceae; pH 6.5 to 7 would be acceptable; may have a higher calcium requirement than other types.
LANDSCAPE VALUE: One of the finest azaleas, flowers open just as the leaves are expanding; no adequate way to do justice to the beauty of this plant by the written word.
CULTIVARS:
'Sid's Royal Pink'—Deeper pink, 3″ diameter flowers, 3 to 5′ high, brilliant fall color.
PROPAGATION: Seed as previously described. Cuttings taken in late May and treated with a hormone (IBA) will give a fair percentage.
ADDITIONAL NOTES: This species comes fairly true from seed as it fails to hybridize freely with other species.
NATIVE HABITAT: Korea, Manchuria. Introduced 1893.

Other Rhododendrons and Azaleas

Rhododendron alabamense Rehd., (rō-dō-den′dron al-ȧ-bam-en′sē), Alabama Azalea, is a deciduous shrub growing 5 to 6′(8′) high. It tends toward compactness and may sucker. Colonies of 5 to 6 acres are known. The white, yellow-blotched (not always present), exceedingly fragrant flowers appear with the new leaves in mid to late April (Athens). They occur 6 to 10 together in a terminal cluster. The 10 stamens are about twice as long as the 1″ long, tubular, funnel-shaped corolla. This is a beautiful plant in flower. Possibly the most fragrant of the native azaleas. An 8 to 10′ high and wide specimen at Biltmore House and Gardens is magnificent. Does not always appear true-to-type and should be purchased in flower. Great "doer" in the Dirr garden and flowers after *R. austrinum*, *R. canescens*, and *R. flammeum*. Possibly the most fragrant of the native azaleas. 'Caroline Dean' and 'Thomasville' have fragrant, white flowers, 10′ high. Found in dry open woodlands and rocky hill sites in north central Alabama and isolated areas in west central Georgia. Introduced 1922. Zone 7 to 8.

Rhododendron arborescens Torr., (rō-dō-den′dron är-bō-res′enz), Sweet Azalea, is a deciduous, erect-stemmed, loosely branched shrub growing from 8 to 20′ in height with an equal spread. Foliage is lustrous dark green in summer and may turn reddish in fall. Flowers are white to light pink with a reddish style and pinkish to rose filaments, 1 1/2 to 2″ long, after the leaves in May, June–July, fragrant odor like heliotrope. Best native white azalea that is hardy in the North. Prefers light, consistently moist, acid soil. Specialty growers offer pink, rose, smoky pink and yellow forms; also 'Hot Ginger' and 'Dynamite' selected for white flowers, pink stamens and intense fragrance; grew 6′ by 5′ in 18 years. 'White Lightning' is Clarence

Towe's vigorous, white-flowered clone. The more I study the native azaleas the more convinced I become of their similarities. Have observed this species on high mountains, 4000 to 5000′ altitude, in Georgia and North Carolina. Flower colors are rose, pink, white, and various shadings. Beautiful, delicate, and refined. Native from southern Pennsylvania to Georgia and Alabama; grows chiefly on the banks of mountain steams. Introduced before 1814. Zone 4 to 7.

Rhododendron atlanticum Rehd., (rō-dō-den′dron at-lan′ti-kum), Coast Azalea, makes a rather handsome 3 to 6′ high and wide shrub of suckering habit. The leaves are a distinct bluish green and offer a handsome color contrast. The fragrant pinkish white (white to pink) flowers occur with or slightly before the leaves in April. Each flower is 1 to 1 1/2″ long and about 1 1/4 to 1 1/2″ wide with the stamens twice the length of the corolla. Corolla is covered with sticky glands and can be easily identified by this trait coupled with distinct foliage and later flowering. This is a beautiful azalea but like many of the natives it does not have the blatant flair of the evergreen hybrids. I have had good success rooting it from softwood cuttings. Used as a parent along with *R. periclymenoides* in the Choptank Hybrids. They are natural hybrids found wild in the vicinity of the Choptank River, Maryland, by Mr. and Mrs. Julian Hill. Several selections are apparently seedlings from the original wild selected plants. A hybrid, *Rhododendron atlanticum* × *R. austrinum*, has fragrant, orange-yellow flowers, early season. Found in the Coastal Plain from Delaware to South Carolina often in open pine woods. Introduced about 1916. Zone 5 to 8 (9). Cultivars include:

'Choptank Blend'—A scrumptious blend of cream, rose and yellow makes a charming flower, full and tall.

'Choptank C-1'—Mrs. Julian Hill found this group of plants with delicate fragrant white flowers that perfume the garden, stoloniferous.

'Choptank Mellow'—Soft yellow flowers with lavender markings.

Choptank River'—Natural hybrid with *R. periclymenoides*, same intense lovely scent as *R. atlanticum* but usually a tad pinker, late May into June.

'Choptank River Belle'—Pink buds open to very fragrant white flowers flushed with pink, pink stamens, lovely blue-green foliage.

'Choptank Rose'—A fragrant rose and white flower with a golden blotch, plant is large and flowers are of good texture and fragrance.

'Choptank Yellow'—This offspring of 'C-1' is yellow with a slightly golden shading on the upper lobe, fragrant and hummingbirds flock to it.

'Choptank Yellow and Orange'—The yellow and orange colors mix and mingle in this huge ball truss, fragrant.

'Marydel'—Deep pink buds, white flowers with a touch of pink, very fragrant, Polly Hill's selected clone.

'Nacoochee'—A selected Choptank seedling that has a fragrant white flower with a touch of pale pink.

'Pink Choptank'—A clear pink flower adorns this large plant which is an offspring of a selfed cross made years ago by the late George Beasley, Transplant Nursery, Lavonia, GA.

'Twiggy'—A descriptive name for a small, almost miniature plant that has white, fragrant flowers, a Choptank seedling.

'Winterthur'—A superior compact white selection, not stoloniferous.

'Yellow Delight'—A choice seedling from an open pollinated *R. atlanticum*, large soft yellow with great fragrance and good growth habit.

Rhododendron austrinum Rehd., (rō-dō-den′dron aw-strī′num), Florida Azalea, grows 8 to 10′ high and forms a rather loose multi-stemmed shrub. The fragrant, clear yellow, cream, orange to almost pure red flowers occur 8 to 15 together, April–May. Flowers in our garden during mid-April; colors are variable as mentioned. Each flower is 3/4″ long and the tube somewhat cylindrical with 2″ long stamens. Again this is a most beautiful native plant that makes a splendid addition to the shrub border. Over the years, Bonnie and I have accumulated 15 different seedlings with a color range of soft yellow to orange, some trusses are almost ball-shaped and flowers are outstandingly fragrant. One of the easiest natives to grow; requires no pampering. Northern and western Florida to southwest Georgia, southern Alabama and southeastern Mississippi. Introduced 1914. Zone (6)7 to 9. Cultivars include:

'Adam's Orange'—Brightly colored deep orange selection.

'Alba'—A white-flowered form, selected by Steve Riefler in northwest Florida.

'Austrinum Gold'—Early opening, bright gold, fragrant flowers, plant grows as wide as tall.

'Clyde's Yellow'—Huge clusters of beautiful, large, bright yellow flowers in the spring.

'Coleman's Early Yellow'—Possibly a hybrid with *R. alabamense*, light yellow flowers that appear in April, 1 to 2 weeks earlier than the flowers of *R. austrinum*.

'Escatawpa'—Brilliant yellow-orange flowers, vigorous grower, terrific performer in Dirr garden, from the Escatawpa River area of Alabama.

'Harrison's Red'—A coral-colored (rosy red) selection found near Chipley, FL.

'Henry Foundation'—Fragrant yellow flowers, 12'.

'Millie Mac'—The yellow center of each flower is bordered with a distinct white margin, found in Escambia County, AL by Mr. and Mrs. Floyd T. McConnell of Mobile, AL.

'My Mary'—Fragrant, ball-shaped trusses of gleaming light yellow flowers with long stamens early in the season, compact growth, thickly textured foliage, named after Mary Beasley, Transplant Nursery.

'Pretty One'—Outstanding, large (2" long), salmon red, fragrant flowers with a yellow blotch, 8 to 10' in height.

'Rushin's Austrinum'—Bright yellow flowers with clear yellow tubes herald spring with their aroma.

Rhododendron bakeri (Lemmon & McKay) Hume, (rō-dō-den'dron bā'kĕr-ī), Cumberland Azalea, is allied to *R. calendulaceum* but is more compact and tends to flower 2 or more weeks later. The 1 1/4 to 1 3/4" long flowers are usually a good red but range from (yellow) orange to red. Have seen the species in flower on May 25 at Biltmore. Spectacular in flower. Does not tolerate excessive heat. Will grow 4 to 8' high; tends to be low-growing with somewhat horizontal branches. Similar to *R. calendulaceum* and by some authorities lumped with that species. 'Camp's Red' has red-orange flowers. 'Sunlight' has orange, deep rose, and gold flowers in early summer; dark green foliage; Polly Hill selection. A compact, double, red form is known. *Rhododendron bakeri* × *R. viscosum* has fragrant, pink flowers; late-flowering. Kentucky, Tennessee, mountains of North Carolina, Georgia, and Alabama. Introduced 1936. Zone 5 to 7.

Rhododendron 'Boule de Neige' is listed as a Caucasian hybrid and is one of the finest white flowering types. The evergreen foliage is a dark, lustrous green and the habit is compact and rounded. Zone 5, possibly 4. Usually described as flower bud hardy to -15°F. As a graduate student at the University of Massachusetts, I was introduced to this taxon by Professor Thompson, who literally considered this the best of all rhododendrons for habit (5' by 8'), dark green foliage and large white flower trusses. He considered this the standard by which others should be judged. Interestingly a 1988 article on rhododendrons by Peter Loewer, *Horticulture*, essentially reiterated Professor Thompson's beliefs; for as many rhododendrons that are introduced each year, it is amazing how few really measure up.

Rhododendron calendulaceum (Michx.) Torr., (rō-dō-den'dron ka-len-dū-lā'sē-um), Flame Azalea, is a deciduous, loosely branched shrub of upright habit, usually as wide as high (4 to 8' tall by a comparable spread to 10 to 15' high and wide). The summer foliage is medium green and the fall color subdued yellow to red. Flowers average 2" diameter, May–June, in loose trusses; colors range from lemon to dark yellows, tawny, apricot, salmon, deep flesh color, pinkish, brilliant shades of orange and scarlet, non-fragrant. Most showy and one of the most notable American azaleas (a parent of the Ghent hybrid race). Retains flowers for nearly two weeks. Excellent in naturalistic setting or mass planting. Abundant in southern Appalachians in every imaginable color. Native to mountains of Pennsylvania south to Georgia. Zone 5 to 7, does not prosper in high heat. Cultivated 1800. Cultivars include:

Abbott azaleas (*R. calendulaceum* × *R. prinophyllum*)—Super hardy hybrids created by Frank Abbott of Saxton's River, VT, withstood temperatures to -40°F.

'Carlsons Coral Flameboyant'—Large flowers in a bright shade of coral.

'Chattooga'—Pink, ruffled flowers with a yellow blotch gradually turn soft yellow, natural hybrid of *R. calendulaceum* × *R. periclymenoides*.

'Cherokee'—Soft apricot flowers with red stamens.

'Currahee'—Large shrub with orange flowers bordered with rosy pink, the buds are striped with red and yellow.

'Frank Lunsford'—Fuchsia pink with white coloration, long stamens.

'Golden Sunset Flame'—A blend of orange, gold and yellow colors.

'Golden Yellow Flame'—A large campanulate flower with crimped, pointed tips, the yellow background is accented with gold blotches.

'Lisa's Red Flame'—Large, ruffled, red flower with crimped edges.

'Scarlet Orange Flame'—Glows with its reddish orange flowers.

'Smokey Mountaineer'—Compact form with excellent orange-red flowers and red fall color, handsome planting at Arnold Arboretum.

'Soquee River'—Magnificent truss of orange, red and yellow at the same time, as wide as tall in habit.

'Wahsega'—Dark red form.

'Yellow Flame'—A large, clear bright yellow flower.

Rhododendron canadense (L.) Torr., (rō-dō-den′dron kan-à-den′sē), Rhodora, is often a rather scrawny, erect-branched, deciduous shrub that seldom grows more than 3 or 4′ high. The leaves are a distinct gray-green and appear after the flowers. The principal beauty lies in the bright rosy purple, 1 to 1 1/2″ wide flowers that occur about 6 together at the end of the stem in April. A white form is known. The corolla is quite distinct from other members of the genus in having the 3 upper lobes almost united to the end and erect, the lower 2 narrow-oblong, divided to the base and spreading. There are 10 stamens. It is seldom seen in gardens but makes a lovely splash of color in April. In the wild it is often found in swamps and should be provided moist, acid soil in cultivation. Emerson said of this species, "Beauty is its own excuse for being." Variety *albiflorum* is similar in all aspects to the more common lavender-pink form but with pure white flowers and yellowish fall foliage. Variety *album* has a compact, upright bushy habit to 2′ with pure white flowers in late spring. The species is native from Newfoundland and Labrador to central New York and Pennsylvania. Introduced before 1756. Zone 2 to ? Requires a cool climate.

Rhododendron canescens (Michx.) Sweet, (rō-dō-den′dron kà-nes′enz), Piedmont Azalea (also known as Florida Pinxter, Hoary Azalea), is a large shrub growing 10 to 15′ high. The fragrant white to pink to almost rose flowers open in March–mid-April. It is native in the Athens area along slopes and stream banks under high shade. There is tremendous variation in corolla color and I have seen forms with white to deep rose-pink flowers. It is stoloniferous and a 10 acre colony has been described. Hybridizes readily with other species. 'Brooke' has fragrant, pink flowers with creamy yellow overtones; vigorous growing and heavy branching. 'Spring Scene' has fragrant, pink flowers in spring; 12′. 'Varnadoes Phlox Pink' has fragrant, tubular, vivid pink flowers in April; medium-sized habit; somewhat more shade tolerant than other deciduous azaleas. 'Varnadoes Snow' has icy white, tubular, fragrant flowers; medium-sized habit. *Rhododendron canescens* × *R. flammeum* 'Clyo Red' has cherry red flowers. *Rhododendron canescens* is the most abundant species in the Southeast and the range extends from North Carolina, Tennessee to north Florida, Georgia, Alabama and Texas. Introduced around 1730. Zone 5 to 9.

Rhododendron chapmanii Gray, (rō-dō-den′dron chap-man′ē-ī), is an erect growing, evergreen, 6 to 10′ high shrub. The oblong to oval, 1 to 2″ long, dark green leaves have an obtuse apex and revolute margin with a 1/4″ long petiole. The rose-pink, funnelform flowers appear in late spring. Have observed plants in flower in October at Charles Webb's wonderful garden outside of Lee, FL. Would make sense to utilize the species for breeding heat tolerance. Allied to *R. carolinianum* and *R. minus*. Western Florida. Introduced 1936. Zone (6)7 to 9. Cultivars include:
White—White flowers in spring, 10′.
'Wonder'—Lavender-pink flowers, early to mid-season, rapid-growing, 4′, -15°F.
Rhododendron chapmanii × *R. dauricum* var. *album*—Bright lavender pink flowers, 4 to 5′, tolerates summer heat.

Rhododendron dauricum L., (rō-dō-den′dron dawr′i-kum), Dahurian Rhododendron, is a deciduous to semi-evergreen shrub that matures at about 5 to 6′. The small, 1/2 to 1 1/2″ long, 1/4 to 5/8″ wide, glossy dark green leaves are rather attractive and assume a purplish tinge in winter. The 1 to 1 1/2″ diameter, bright rose-purple flowers appear singly from a cluster of buds at the end of last season's growth in February–March. Variety *sempervirens* is noted for holding the very dark green leaves through the winter. It flowers in March–April and like the above is not particularly showy but does provide a breath of color. It is one of the parents of the P.J.M. rhododendron and has imparted its hardiness to that selection. Mountains of Korea, Manchuria and northern Japan. Cultivated 1780. Zone 4 to 5(6). Cultivars include:
'Adam'—Lavender form that consistently flowers first, a day or so earlier than 'Eve' in early April, colorful orange autumn foliage.
var. *album*—White flowers, used by Edmund Mezitt in some of the newer compact cold hardy rhododendrons.
'April Gem'—Compact, 4′ by 4′, evergreen plant covered by a profusion of lightly fragrant, double, white, long-lasting flowers, leaves bronze in winter.
'April Rose'—Hardy, dense, small-leaved plant, holding many of its deep bronze leaves in winter, bright magenta pink, double flowers, introduced by Dr. Mehlquist.
'Madison Snow'—Hardy, semi-evergreen, large, white flowers in early spring, fall color is bright golden, grows to 4′.
'Snowy Morning Blues'—With pure white flowers that open two weeks later than the species, holds most of the shiny green leaves all winter.

Rhododendron 'Exbury' and 'Knap Hill' Hybrids are deciduous, upright growing types, 8 to 12' high and 2/3's to as wide, with medium green summer foliage and yellow, orange, red fall colors. Flowers range from pink, creams, yellows, near whites or orange, rose and red, borne in 2 to 5″ diameter, 18- to 30-flowered trusses in May.

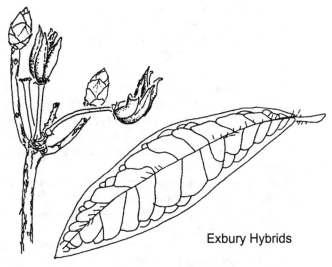

Exbury Hybrids

These hybrids are the result of crosses involving several species including *R. calendulaceum, R. arborescens, R. occidentale, R. molle*. Zone 5 to 7(8). The Exbury types do not display good heat tolerance but southern breeders are crossing them with native azaleas, particularly *R. austrinum*, and producing heat tolerant lines (see Aromi Hybrids). The Exbury Hybrids as well as the Knap Hill, Ilam, Windsor and Ghent types include a great number of selections. About the only way to find out if they will grow in a given region is to experiment with them. In general they are not suited for Zone 4 (considered flower bud hardy to -20°F, but depends on cultivar) and lower or Zone 8 and higher. Often imbued with mildew that renders them ugly.

EXBURY (EX) AND KNAP HILL (KN) HYBRIDS

'Altair'—Large creamy white with yellow flare, very fragrant. (KN)

'Anna Pavlova'—Beautiful, ruffled, double, white, fragrant flowers, smaller growing than many of the Knap Hill azaleas and has larger flowers than the well-known 'White Throat'. (KN)

'Annabella'—Very fragrant deep golden yellow with dark bronze foliage. (KN)

'Anquistas'—Translucent light yellow outlined in pink, lightly fragrant.

'Apple Tree Pink'—Large, rounded, pink flowers with subtle yellow markings, mid-season. (EX)

'Arneson Gem'—Large, warm golden flowers edged in bright glowing orange, free-flowering, compact, vigorous. (EX)

'Avocet'—Fragrant, white fringed with pink, large, ruffled flowers. (KN)

'Ballerina'—A beautiful white with a distinctive yellow center. (EX)

'Balzac'—Good red with flame markings on the many, star-shaped, fragrant flowers. (EX)

'Banana Split'—Vanilla white surrounding a banana yellow blotch with a cherry throat.

'Basilisk'—Pink buds open cream, edged in pink, golden flare. (KN)

'Beaulieu'—Salmon pink buds open to a paler shade of pink flowers with an orange flare. (EX)

'Berryrose'—Fragrant, orange-red. (KN)

'Big Punkin'—Fragrant, huge, round, multi-toned orange and golden trusses appear in mid to late May, lush green new growth, upright plant, -15°F. (EX)

'Brazil'—Brilliant tangerine-red, strong grower, buds early, flowers frilled. (KN)

'Bullfinch'—Deep red. (KN)

'Buzzard'—Fragrant pale yellow, tinged with pink, -24°F flower bud hardiness, vigorous growing, wide upright, resists mildew.

'Cannon's Double'—Double pink with light orange shading. (EX)

'Cecile'—Very large flowers in shades of salmon-pink and yellow, handsome form. (EX)?

'Cheerful Giant'—Double, yellow flowers, tips of the petals are slightly orange. (EX)

'Clarice'—Pale pink fading to almost white, vigorous upright growth. (EX)

'Cockatoo'—Fragrant peach-apricot. (KN)

'Colin Kendrick'—Fragrant, pale pink, hose-in-hose flower, truss appears like a beautiful rounded ball of soft cheery pink with a light touch of delicate yellow on the upper petal, good green coloring on the foliage. (KN)

'Coquille'—Vivid orange blotch in a bright yellow flower, tall and upright. (EX)

'Coronation Lady'—Orange-yellow blotch on the upper petal of the salmon pink flower, new foliage is bronze. (KN)

'Corringe'—Fluorescent red-orange with a hot orange flare on the upper petal. (EX)

'Crimson'—Crimson-red, robust, upright-growing. (EX)

'Dawn's Chorus'—Pink buds open white with rays of dawn's pink. (EX)

'Debutante'—Orange blotch on each of the very large, carmine-pink flowers. (KN)

'Desert Pink'—Pink. (KN)

'Doctor Rudolph Henny'—Buds of reddish orange, flower ages to a fantastic pink with a light touch of yellow on the upper petal, often has 6 petals instead of 5, flower is 4″ across, in large trusses of 6 to 10 flowers. (EX)

'Double Delight'—Buttercup yellow, very fragrant flowers, floriferous plant. (EX)

'Exbury Evening Glow'—Frilled, soft pink tinged with light yellow, golden throat.

'Exbury White'—Light cream-yellow buds open to white, star-shaped flowers with a hint of cream throughout, upper petal is graced with a bright bold splash of canary yellow.

'Fireball'—Bright shades of orange-red (scarlet), stronger growing plant than most red varieties, foliage is reddish bronze, then dark green when mature. (KN)

'Firefly'—Red. (EX)

'Fireglow'—Large orange-vermillion flowers, wine-red fall foliage. (KN)

'Flamingo'—Frilled fragrant deep pink with orange blotch, upright-growing. (KN)

'Fluffy'—Large, frilled flowers open light yellow changing to white with a showy yellow flare, petaloid double form.

'Fluorescent Orange'—Fluorescent, bright orange flower, superb rounded trusses.

'Frilly Lemon'—Glowing yellow, petaloid double, very frilly, full truss, broad-spreading upright plant, ‑25°F. (EX)

'Gallipoli Red'—Glorious frilled, deep watermelon orange-red flowers, strong growing. (EX)

'George Reynolds'—Enormous deep buttery yellow flowers with a deep golden throat. (KN)

'Gibraltar'—Spectacular flame-orange flower clusters with ruffled petals, by far the most heat tolerant and vigorous of the Knap Hill group, does well as far south as Zone 7b. (KN), often listed as (EX).

'Ginger'—Deep orange-carmine buds open to a brilliant orange with a pink flush, deeper pink lines down each petal, fragrant. (EX)

'Gold Dust'—Bright deep yellow fragrant flower. (EX)

'Golden Dream'—Large open-faced flowers of soft clear yellow. (KN)

'Golden Eagle'—Bright orange with a yellowish orange flare. (KN)

'Golden Flare'—Vivid yellow with reddish orange blotch, to 2 1/2″ diameter. (EX)

'Golden Oriole'—Brilliant yellow, deep orange blotch. (KN)

'Golden Sunset'—Vivid yellow, wide, upright habit. (KN)

'Goldfinch'—Light yellow flowers with a vivid yellow blotch and a hint of orange. (KN)

'Harvest Moon'—Pale yellow with a deeper blotch. (KN)

'Hawaiian Lei'—Flowers are a deep orange-rose-red with a lighter center punctuated by a showy golden orange flare on the upper petal, often has 6 petals instead of 5.

'High Fashion'—Flowers of dusty rose splashed with an orange blotch on the upper lobe. (KN)

'High Series'—Snow white flowers with a yellow blotch, kissed with soft pink, large, ball-shaped truss, fragrant. (KN)

'Homebush'—Unique rounded trusses of double, deep rose flowers, superb in full flower, vigorous upright shrub. (KN)

'Honeysuckle'—Fragrance similar to honeysuckle, pastel pink petals with a yellow-orange flare burning out from the throat, pink on the lower petals change to a soft white giving the whole plant a two-toned effect. (EX)

'Hotspur'—Rich red-orange. (EX)

'Hotspur Red'—Late flowering, nasturtium red flowers with golden orange throat. (KN)

'Hugh Wormald'—Vivid yellow with orange-yellow blotch, wide and upright-growing. (EX)

'Iora'—Flower starts out as a creamy peach bud opening to a blend of colors, five-petaled flower flaunts creamy tones which become more peach-pink toward the center of the flower, large yellow flare on the top petal. (KN)

'Irene Koster'—Sweetly scented, 2 1/2″ diameter, white flowers are flushed with strong pink coloring, medium size when mature. (Occidentale hybrid)

'J. Jennings'—Deep orange-red. (KN)

'Jackie Parton'—Double and triple buds opening to peach striped orange. (KN)

'King Red'—Vivid red, slightly ruffled in a ball-like truss. (EX)

'Klondyke'—Large golden orange, young foliage coppery red, wide upright, slow growing. (KN)

'Knap Hill Red'—Deep, intense red with bronze-tinted foliage, late May. (KN)

'Krakatoa'—Flame red flowers, medium-sized plant. (KN)

'Lace Valentine'—Light pink buds open to a brilliant white flower with a yellow blotch, fragrant. (KN)

'Lady Roseberry'—Developed by Waterer in 1944, flower is a vivid red. (KN)

'Lila'—True white with a large golden flare, buds and petal edges are peach. (KN)

'Mandarin Maid'—Large, warm salmon orange flowers with a solid orange-gold flare on the upper petal, wavy petals. (KN)

'Mandarin Spiced'—Large, showy trusses of hot orange flowers will often have 6 or more petals which are often twisted on the ends, upper petal has a slight warm orange flare, hardy and vigorous grower.

'Marina'—Large, pale creamy yellow flower with a deeper bright yellow blotch which is very showy. (EX)

'Marion Merriman'—Frilled chrome-yellow trusses, orange blotch. (KN)

'Mary Poppins'—Nasturtium red, dark green foliage. (KN)

'Mavis'—Large dusty pink flowers in ball-shaped trusses. (KN)

'Mazurka'—Pale orange buds open to very large, ruffled flowers of apricot yellow, with pink tones intermingled. (KN)

'Next to Hawaiian Lei'—Flowers are smaller in size, occur in large trusses with abundant flowers, pink buds turn a delicate light pastel pink on the lower petals contrasted by a very striking yellow gold flare on the upper petals. (EX)

'Old Gold'—Large, ball-shaped trusses of sunny orange gold, an even more orange flare on upper petal that merges into the solid gold of the lower petals. (EX)

'Orange Ball'—Solid orange, full ball-like trusses, medium green foliage. (EX)

'Orangeade'—Full and frilly, pure orange. (KN)

'Orient'—Hot orange-rose flowers with a yellow-orange flare, bronze green leaves in the fall turn a superb orange-red, vigorous, compact habit. (KN)

'Oxydol'—Large, white flowers with soft yellow blotch, bronze foliage. (KN)

'Peppermint'—Deep peppermint pink with lighter shades of pink and white on the midribs of the petals, creating a soft striped bi-color effect. (KN)

'Percil'—Flowers of white with a pale yellow blotch, fall foliage is outstanding brilliant reds and browns. (KN)

'Pink Delight'—Large flowers are deep rose pink with a marking of soft orange on upper petals. (EX)

'Princess Royal'—Flowers are creamy white, flushed pink with a superb yellow blotch, sweet fragrance. (EX)

'Royal Lodge'—Late-flowering, vermillion red, wide-growing.

'Renne'—Flower of rich flame red suffused with yellow appears to be an almost solid, rich hot red, shiny foliage, fall color is dark maroon red. (EX)

'Salmon Pink'—Pink flowers, brilliant purple-red to yellow fall foliage, wide upright, vigorous. (EX)

'Satan'—Scarlet red. (KN)

'Scarlet Pimpernel'—Hot, red-orange flowers. (EX)

'Seville'—Orange-red flowers, notable for excellent fall color.

'Strawberry Ice'—Peach-pink with yellow shadings. (EX)

'Sun Chariot'—Buttercup yellow, darker blotch.

'Sunset Pink'—Large trusses of vivid red with yellow blotch.

'Sunte Nectarine'—Brilliant orange flowers with a yellow blotch and a delightful fragrance.

'Sylphides'—Voluptuous pale pink and white with a touch of yellow in the throat, fragrant. (KN)

'Tangelo'—Soft, warm orange flowers, vigorous, easy to grow, withstands sun and heat. (EX)

'Toucan'—Pale cream with yellow blotch, very fragrant, tall growing. (KN)

'Tunis'—Deep crimson with orange flare, fast-growing, upright.

'Tutti Frutti'—Rose with large red blotch. (EX)

'Twinkle'—Yellow-orange, bi-color flowers, from the notable Arneson collection of Canby, OR. (KN)

'Twisted Leaf'—Orange buds and rich orange cream-colored flowers with a yellow flare, twisted leaves.

'Umpqua Queen'—Large, brilliant, sometimes double, sometimes single and sometimes semi-double, yellow trusses with vivid yellow blotches, profuse flowering, strong grower, hardy. (KN)

'Violet Gordon'—Bright orange beauty with bronze-tinted foliage. (KN)

'Wallowa Red'—Deep red flowers, mid-season, occasionally has 6 petals, open-round plant with arching branches reaching 4 to 8′ in height with about a 3 to 5′ spread. (KN)

'White Swan'—White with yellow blotch, very fragrant. (EX)

'White Throat'—Late-flowering, frilled, white flowers, red fall foliage, slow-growing, wide-spreading habit.

'Yachats'—Bright yellow flower sports a vivid orange flare, plants are taller and have larger leaves than most, named after the coastal Oregon Native American tribe. (EX)

Rhododendron fastigiatum Franch., (rō-dō-den′dron fas-tij-ē-ā′tum), Autumnpurple Rhododendron, is an excellent dwarf species for the rock garden with tiny leaves and small purple flowers. Western China. Introduced 1911. Zone 6 to 7.

Rhododendron flammeum (Michx.) Sarg. [*R. speciosum* (Willd.) Sweet], (rō-dō-den'dron flam'ē-um), Oconee Azalea, grows 6 to 8' high and wide and forms a rather attractive mounded shrub. The scarlet or bright red, funnel-shaped, 1 3/4" long, non-fragrant flowers appear in April after *R. canescens*. Flowers late April in the Dirr garden. The truss may contain up to 15 flowers. The stamens are about 2" long. It has been confused with *R. calendulaceum* but differs in the slender corolla tube. The flower color ranges from yellow, pink, salmon to orange-red. Georgia to South Carolina. Cultivated 1789. Zone 6 to 7. Cultivars include:

'Apricot Speciosum'—Lovely soft shade of apricot with tangerine stamens, late April.

'Double Pleasure'—Double flowers.

'Harry's Speciosum'—Beautiful scarlet-red flower on a medium-sized, stoloniferous plant.

'Hazel Hamilton'—Bright yellow, heat tolerant, from Al O'Rear in Georgia.

'Orange Speciosum'—Huge, round, orange balls, full dense truss, hardy and a good grower.

'Peach Parfait'—Pink flowers in spring, 8'.

'Red Speciosum'—A beautiful, well-clothed, mounded plant, brilliant red flowers.

'Scarlet Ibis'—Brilliant dark orange-red flowers.

'Varnadoe'—Good orange selected by Mr. Aaron Varnadoe of Colquitt, GA.

Rhododendron furbishi (Lemmon & McKay) Hume, (rō-dō-den'dron fẽr'bish-ī), is a very unusual native azalea, probably a hybrid between *R. bakeri* or a late *R. calendulaceum* type and *R. arborescens*, found in northern Georgia, mostly in orange and orange-red shades, a strong upright grower.

Rhododendron 'Gable Hybrids' are a mixed lot (azaleas and rhododendrons) but offer a quality range of colors and are considered among the hardiest evergreen azaleas for Zone 5 conditions. They were developed by the late Joseph Gable, a rhododendron hybridizer at Stewartstown, PA. These plants grow 2 to 4' high and as wide. The foliage is a shiny dark green, about 1" long, although there is considerable variation among clones. The flowers arrive in late April to early May and are about 2" across. The following cultivars were synthesized from the literature and observations. Hybridizer is listed when known.

'Ben Morrison'—(Gable) Red and white striped.

'Big Joe'—Reddish violet.

'Blaauw's Pink'—Shrimp pink, hose-in-hose, mid-season, 3/4" leaves, semi-upright with an abundance of flowers.

'Boudoir'—(Gable) Watermelon pink, darker blotch, compact plant, 5' by 4', did well in my Illinois garden.

'Cadis'—Deep pink buds are a lovely contrast to large fragrant light pink flowers in flat trusses, large growing (rhododendron).

'Cameo'—Hose-in-hose pink.

'Carol'—Hose-in-hose violet-red flowers, low-spreading habit.

'Caroline'—(Gable) Large heavy textured pale orchid flowers, large leaves with wavy margins, does well in hot climates but appreciates partial shade, medium height (rhododendron).

'Cherokee'—Orange-red flowers, upright growing, medium height.

'Conemaugh'—Lavender pink trusses of lovely star-shaped flowers, late April into early May, 4' (rhododendron).

'Corsage'—Fragrant, light lavender, 2 1/2" diameter, rounded dwarf plant, 4' by 4'.

'County of York'—Large, white flowers with pale green throat, pale lavender-pink buds, wide-growing, lustrous, long, convex, apple-green leaves.

'David Gable'—(Gable) Red-throated pink flowers in large, dome-shaped trusses, floriferous, medium height (rhododendron).

'Early Bird'—Vigorous plant, lavender-pink flowers in clusters early in the season, bright green, heavily textured leaves, upright plant.

'Elizabeth Gable'—Frilled, salmon pink flowers in June, upright-spreading, very hardy and evergreen.

'Forest Fire'—Hose-in-hose red.

'Gable's Pink Conewago'—(Gable) A tighter growing form of 'Conewago' with pinker flowers in early May, 4' (rhododendron).

'Gable's T-4-G'—(Gable) Double, salmon pink flowers, very dwarf and slow growing, late May.

'Herbert'—Possibly the hardiest of all Gable hybrids, vivid purple with darker blotch, hose-in-hose, 1 3/4" long, dense rounded habit, 4' by 4', flower bud hardy to -20°F, has performed well in Zone 7b, was the hardiest azalea in our Illinois garden.

'Jessie Coover'—Deep pink, double, hose-in-hose flowers, late May to early June.

'Karen'—Lavender pink, hose-in-hose, rounded habit, 4' by 4', excellent cold hardiness, similar to 'Herbert'.

'Katherine Dalton'—Light pink buds open to fragrant, blush pink flowers in mid-May, very hardy, tall.

'Keisrac Pink'—(Gable) Small leaves and flowers suggesting the pointed pink and white flower of Arbutus, compact.

'La Roche'—Single, magenta red flowers, early May, extremely bud hardy, 4 to 5'.

'Lorna'—(Gable) Masses of double, pink flowers resembling rosebuds, compact low-spreading habit.

'Louise Gable'—Double, deep salmon-pink, darker blotch, 2 1/2" across, rounded dense habit, 3 to 4' by 3 to 4'.

'Madame Greeley'—Single, large, white with green flecks in throat, 1" wide, rounded compact habit, 3' by 3'.

'Mary Dalton'—Orange-red.

'Maxecat'—Pink flowers, late flowering, hardy, vigorous form, 6'.

'Mildred Mae'—(Gable) Large, spotted lavender.

'Old Faithful'—Large, orchid pink flowers with a darker blotch, early May, very bud hardy, 6'.

'Olive'—Orchid-purple flowers, hardy, compact and spreading.

'Pink Rosette'—Bright rose red, double flowers, late May well into June, low growing.

'Purple Splendor'—(Gable) Purple, hose-in-hose.

'Robert Allison'—(Gable) Scented, pink flowers with golden throats, large waxy green leaves on a rugged upright shrub, medium height.

'Rose Greeley'—Large hose-in-hose white flowers with chartreuse blotch, dense low-spreading plant, 3' by 3'.

'Rosebud'—(Gable) Silvery rose-pink, double, hose-in-hose, 1 to 2" diameter, compact habit, 4' by 4', flowers resemble miniature roses, very popular cultivar.

'Springtime'—(Gable) Clear pink, early flowering.

'Stewartstown'—(Gable) Vivid, brick-red, small single flowers, foliage dark green and wine-red in winter, rounded habit, 5' by 4', flowers later, although listed as very cold hardy it is distinctly less so than 'Herbert' and 'Karen', grew this in our Illinois garden and it was ruined above snow line, in Manchester, NH I was told this is an adaptable cultivar, possibly due to winter snow cover because low temperatures hover in the -25 to -30°F range.

'Tryon Pink'—Medium pink, hose-in-hose flowers, mid-season, good compact habit, vigorous, with good foliage.

'White Rosebud'—A beautiful pure white, double flowers, resembles buds of a rose, 1 1/2 to 2" wide when open.

Rhododendron* × *gandavense Rehd., (rō-dō-den'dron gan-dà-ven'sē), Ghent Azaleas, are deciduous, 6 to 10' shrubby growers with flower colors ranging from pure white, pure yellow, to combinations of pink, orange and scarlet. Flowers are single or double, the doubles with numerous overlapping petals, 1 1/2 to 2" across. The hybrids were developed by crossing several species and some of the select clones are hardy to -20°F. Cultivars:

'Bouquet de Flore'—Orange-red flowers with yellow center, somewhat frilled, upright.

'Circus'—Yellow maturing to pink.

'Coccinea Speciosa'—Orange.

'Daviesi'—White to pale yellow, 2 1/4" diameter flowers, tall growing, reasonable heat tolerance, fragrant.

'Fanny'—Violet-red, yellow center.

'Gloria Mundi'—Orange-yellow-red combination.

'Magic'—Yellow, maturing to orange.

'Nancy Waterer'—Large golden yellow.

'Narcissiflora'—Double, yellow, hose-in-hose, fragrant, fine form, reasonable heat tolerance.

'Pallas'—Orange-red.

'Rainbow'—Yellow, maturing to orange-yellow.

Developed in Ghent, Belgium around 1820-1830 from *R. calendulaceum, R. molle, R. luteum, R. periclymenoides, R. viscosum,* and *R. flammeum.* In general the Ghent hybrids are best suited to cooler climates. 'Narcissiflora', as mentioned, is a fine form.

Rhododendron impeditum Franch., (rō-dō-den'dron im-ped-i'tum), Cloudland Rhododendron, forms a cushion of small dark green evergreen leaves upon which purple or bluish purple flowers are produced in April–May. It is an attractive, small rhododendron with good hardiness and for that reason should be considered in the colder regions of the country. 'Moerheim' is a *R. impeditum* hybrid from Holland with small violet flowers and tiny leaves on a tight, compact dwarf. 'Passionate Purple' has deep purple flowers and small leaves, summer foliage is olive green, winter foliage is reddish purple, 2'. Western China. Cultivated 1918. Zone 5 to 6.

Rhododendron japonicum (A. Gray) Sur., (rō-dō-den′dron jȧ-pon′i-kum), Japanese Azalea, is a bushy shrub of rounded outline that grows 4 to 8′ high. The flowers are beautiful and range from yellow, orange-yellow, soft rose, salmon-red, orange-red to brick-red in color. Each flower is 2 1/2 to 3 1/2″ wide, and produced in trusses of 6 to 10 during May at the end of leafless stems. It is one of the parents of the Ghent hybrids and also figures in the Mollis hybrids (*R. × kosteranum*). The species has proven a fairly reliable flowerer at Minnesota (best in Zone 5). Japan, where it is found in open grassland, never in woods or dense thickets. Introduced 1861. *Rhododendron molle* (Bl.) G. Don, Chinese Azalea, is similar but differs in the conspicuous pubescence on the underside of the leaf and buds. It grows 2 to 5′ high and although hardy (Zone 5) is not as vigorous as *R. japonicum*. Flowers are yellow.

Rhododendron kaempferi Planch., (rō-dō-den′dron kem′fēr-ī). The *kaempferi* hybrids can grow to 10′ high and 5 to 6′ wide after 5 to 10 years. The leaves are dark green, semi-evergreen to deciduous and turn reddish hues in fall and winter. The flowers range in color from salmon-red, orange-red, pink to rosy scarlet and white; each flower 1 3/4 to 2 1/2″ long and wide, funnel-shaped, 1 to 4 per truss. This is a very variable species and apparently has interbred with *R. obtusum* producing large hybrid swarms which dot the mountainsides of Japan. Usually found in sunny positions on hillsides, by the sea, on active volcanoes and also in thickets, pinewoods and deciduous forests. The species is found wild on the main islands of Japan from sea-level to the lower hills below 2600′. Introduced 1892. Zone 5 to 7. Several cultivars of merit include:
'Alice'—Salmon-red.
'Annamarie'—Pure white, small flowers, bright yellow autumn foliage, wide-spreading, upright outline, 6′ high, -13°F bud hardiness.
'Campfire'—Red, hose-in-hose.
'Carmen'—Red.
'Charlotte'—Dark orange-red.
'Christina'—Red, 2″ diameter, single, medium-sized shrub.
'Dorsett'—Bright salmon red flowers, upright selected form of *R. kaempferi*.
'Fedora'—Phlox-pink, with darker blotch, 2″ diameter, rounded habit, 6′ by 5 to 6′, reasonably common in commerce.
'Gretchen'—Reddish violet.
'Holland'—Single, large rich intense red, synonymous with 'Holland Red'.
'Johanna'—Red, 2″ diameter single flowers, medium-sized shrub.
'Juliana'—Deep pink.
'Kathleen'—Rosy red.
'Mary'—Violet-red.
'Mikado'—Dark red flowers, burgundy-red fall foliage, upright growth habit, synonymous with 'May King'.
'Norma'—Violet-red.
'Othello'—Red.
'Pride of Planting Fields'—Bright orange-red, double flowers, upright-mounded habit, semi-evergreen with bright green summer foliage, from Planting Fields Arboretum.
'Tachisene'—Small, very double, bright salmon-pink flowers in June, slow-growing, low-spreading, dwarf form.
'White Squall'—Pure white flowers with an accenting green flare which is the same color as the newly emerging leaves, foliage later darkens and is of larger size, compact and low branching.

Rhododendron keiskei Miq., (rō-dō-den′dron kīsk′ē-ī), Keisk Rhododendron, grows 4 to 5′ (1 to 10′ in some references) high and is of scraggly habit. Evergreen in foliage. Lemon-yellow flowers, early to mid-May, 3 to 5 flowers per cluster. It is one of the few evergreen rhododendrons with pale yellow flowers. Have observed it in flower in Urbana, IL, but it was less than inspirational. Much used in hybridizing. In fact, my survey of catalogs and literature uncovered interminable named hybrids. Japan. Zone 5.

Rhododendron kiusianum Mak., (rō-dō-den′dron kī-ö′sē-ā-num), is a dwarf evergreen or semi-evergreen shrub, occasionally up to 3′, dense spreading habit. Leaves are dark green, small and oval shaped. Flowers are funnel-shaped, produced in clusters of 2 to 5. Colors range from white, red to purple, hardy to 0°F, flowers late May–June. Cultivars include:
'Album'—Delicate white flower.
'Benichidori'—Small, bright reddish orange flowers.
'Benisuzume'—A reddish orange flower on a low-spreading plant.
'Betty Muir'—Vibrant pink, foliage is very dark green and covered with tiny hairs.

'Brick Red'—Tiny, dark orange-red flowers, dwarf.

'Chidori'—White flowers.

'Hanejiro'—White flowers.

'Hanekomachi'—Bright, pinkish red, Japanese selection.

'Harunokikari'—Lavender-blue flowers.

'Harunoumi'—Soft pink flowers early in the season.

'Harusame'—Bright pink flowers.

'Hinode'—Clearest red.

'Komo Kulshan' (also 'Komokulshan')—Small flower with a pale pink center and a rose margin.

'Mai Oghi'—Bright rose pink flowers.

'Mangetsu'—Delightful two-toned appearance with lavender-pink on the tips and light pink in the center.

'Murasaki Shikibu'—Reddish purple, hose-in-hose flowers.

'Myamo Katsura'—Vivid bright reddish purple flowers.

'Nu Moto'—Lovely purple form.

'Rose'—Rose flowers, small leaves and habit of the other Kiusianums but a slightly larger grower.

'Short Circuit'—Especially bright pink color.

'Ukon'—This Japanese diminutive has delicate pink flowers.

White Form—Rare albino form, flowers young and heavily.

'Yumbae'—Pinkish flowers.

Rhododendron × kosteranum Schneid. — Mollis Hybrid Azaleas

LEAVES: Alternate, simple, entire, 1 1/2 to 4″ long, obovate to oblong-ovate, apex bluntish, with a gland-like tip, base wedge-shaped, margin hairy on upper surface or becoming hairless, bristly-hairy on veins beneath.

BUDS: Flower—1/4 to 1/2″, imbricate, tip of scales tinged brown.

Rhododendron × kosteranum, (rō-dō-den′dron kos-tĕr-ā′num), Mollis Hybrid Azaleas, are somewhat similar to the Exbury group in flower characteristics but usually smaller (4 to 6′ high) and not as hardy, although from observations in the Midwest, I believe the hardiness is excellent. Foliage is deciduous. Generally yellow to orange flower color. Resulted from crosses between *R. japonicum × R. molle*. Originated in Holland and Belgium in the 1870's. Cultivars worth considering include:

'Chevalier de Reali'—Maize yellow, fading to cream, fragrant.

'Christopher Wren'—Yellow.

'Consul Ceresole'—Rose-pink.

'Dr. M. Oosthoek'—Darkest fire red-orange of the mollis group, hot orange color.

'Golden Sunrise'—Handsome yellow flowers in large trusses.

'Koster's Brilliant Red'—Flowers of brilliant orange-red.

'Lemon Twist'—A pleasing light yellow with uniquely twisted stems and branches, spreading growth.

'Queen Emma'—Large, light salmon-orange flowers, 10′ high, vigorous, synonymous with 'Koningin Emma'.

'Snowdrift'—White.

'Yellow Mollis'—Yellow flower, prolific.

Rhododendron × laetevirens Rehd., (rō-dō-den′dron lē-ti-vī′renz), Wilson Rhododendron, is a small (2 to 4′ by 2 to 6′), low growing, glossy leaved, evergreen shrub with pink to purplish flowers. Makes a good, neat, small evergreen plant in the rock garden or for foundation planting. Actually one of the finest evergreen foliaged rhododendrons, unfortunately the flowers are third rate. Zone 4 to 6. Result of a cross between *R. carolinianum × R. ferrugineum* L.

Rhododendron luteum (L.) Sweet, (rō-dō-den′dron lū′tē-um), Pontic Azalea, is a handsome 8 to 10′(12′) high shrub that produces fragrant, rich yellow, 1 1/2 to 2″ diameter flowers on naked stems in May. It is truly beautiful in flower and I will always remember a particular striking specimen in the border along Meadow Road at the Arnold Arboretum. It is a vigorous species and has been used in hybridizing. Common in

European gardens where it appears to thrive with neglect. 'Batumi Gold' has large, bright yellow flowers in a ball-shaped truss with long stamens; reliable heavy flowering. Asia Minor, Caucasus, eastern Europe. Introduced 1792. Zone 5 to 6.

Rhododendron maximum L., (rō-dō-den′dron maks′i-mum), Rosebay Rhododendron, grows 4 to 15′ in the North but can grow to 30′; habit is loose and open. Leaves are large (4 to 8″ long) and evergreen (dark green). Flowers are rose, purplish pink to white, spotted with olive-green to orange, 1 to 2″ across, June. Requires moist, acid soil and shade protection. Occurs in abundance throughout the southern Appalachian mountains along streams. Requires cool, moist, well-drained root run and is not ideally suited to "normal" landscape situations. Have observed many times in north Georgia where it often forms pure thickets. The trunks are brown, lightly ridged-and-furrowed, somewhat twisted and quite beautiful in syncopated composition. Native from Nova Scotia and Ontario to Georgia, Alabama and Ohio. Introduced 1736. Zone 3 to 7. Cultivars include:
var. *album* Pursh—White flowers.
'Leachii'—Recurved, curly and wider deep green leaves, slower growing and more compact, pinkish white flowers.
'Midsummer'—Rouge pink flowers with a glint of gold in the throat in compact trusses, deep forest green leaves, somewhat open habit.
'Pride's Pink'—Good-sized pink flowers, extremely hardy, upright-spreading.
var. *purpureum* Pursh—Deep pink to purple flowers.
var. *roseum* ('Roseum')—Flowers are reddish in bud, turning to pink, red stems and dark green leaves, vigorous, 8 to 12′.

Rhododendron minus Michx., (rō-dō-den′dron mī′nus), Piedmont Rhododendron, has funnel-shaped , rose-pink, spotted greenish flowers in large trusses, May–June. Grows 3 to 6′ by 3 to 6′, straggly to 10′ high. Have read *R. carolinianum* listed as *R. minus* var. *carolinianum*. Considerable inconsistency in botanical presentation of *R. minus*, *R. carolinianum*, and *R. chapmanii*. South Carolina, Georgia and Alabama. Introduced 1786. Zone 5 to 7(8).

Rhododendron nakahari Hayata, (rō-dō-den′dron nak-a-har′ī), is a dwarf, compact, spreading azalea. Great potential as a ground cover. Orange-red to red flowers. Northern Taiwan. Introduced 1960. Zone 6b to 9a.
Dwarf Form—Tiny buds that open red, smaller (1′ high) than the species, 1/2″ long, green, hairy leaves.
'Nakahari Mariko'—Red to red-orange flowers, 2 to 3 in a cluster, late-flowering, dwarf, minute, glossy green foliage.
'Nakahari Mini-pink'—Large, clear pink flowers, slow-growing dwarf.
'Nakahari Salmon Pink'—Salmon pink flowers, very prostrate ground cover with hairy leaves.

Rhododendron 'Northern Lights' resulted from crosses between *R.* × *kosteranum* and *R. prinophyllum*. The original crosses were made in 1957 by the late Albert G. Johnson. Originally they were produced from seed with resultant variations in flower color. Flowers range from white, light to deep pink, lilac, yellow, orange and have the pleasing fragrance of *R. prinophyllum*. Each flower is about 1 1/2″ long and occurs in trusses of up to 12. The plants are compact and grow 8 to 10′ high and wide. The flower buds occur on naked stems in May and are spectacular. I had one of the "culls" in my Illinois garden and it was fantastic. I realize fantastic is a relative term but when one lives in central Illinois and has an insatiable desire to grow flower bud hardy azaleas he/she has very few choices. 'Northern Lights' azaleas are flower bud hardy to -40°F. See *J. Environ. Hort.* 15(1):45–50 (1997) for 'Mandarin Lights', 'Spicy Lights', and 'White Lights' cold hardiness ratings. All were hardy to -30°F and below. Plants are now quite common in commerce with the success of tissue culture propagation. Original introductions were quite mildew susceptible Cultivars include:
'Apricot Surprise'—Bright yellow-apricot with orange shadings.
'Golden Lights'—Yellow, fragrant.
'Lemon Lights'—Lemon yellow flowers.
'Mandarin Lights'—Bright orange.
'Northern Hi-Lights'—Bi-colored, creamy white, yellow upper petals, mildew resistant foliage, red fall color.
'Northern Lights'—Pink flowers.
'Orchid Lights'—Semi-dwarf, bushy, lilac flowers.
'Rosy Lights'—Fragrant dark pink, rose-red shading.
'Spicy Lights'—Soft tangerine-orange, fragrant.
'White Lights'—Large, fragrant, floriferous white with yellow center.

Rhododendron oblongifolium (Small) Millais, (rō-dō-den'dron ob-long-i-fō'li-um), Texas Azalea, grows 6′ high and has distinct obovate to oblanceolate, 1 1/2 to 4″ long leaves. The slightly fragrant, funnel-shaped, pure white, 3/4 to 1″ long flowers occur in 7- to 12-flowered trusses after the leaves. Related to *R. viscosum* and *R. serrulatum* and some taxonomists would argue that it is not a distinct species. The species should be lumped with the above mentioned for the differences are within the purview of those species. '#3' is a medium-sized shrub with distinctive oblong leaves up to 4″ long; light pink flowers with a light fragrance of lemon and spice open in late May and June (Athens). Found in moist sandy woods or on the margins of sandy bogs and streams and even on limestone in Arkansas, Oklahoma and Texas. Introduced 1917. Zone 7(?).

Rhododendron obtusum Planch., (rō-dō-den'dron ob-tūs'um), Hiryu Azalea, is a spreading, dense evergreen shrub with glossy green leaves up to 1 1/4″ long. The flowers are reddish violet, but bright red, scarlet and crimson forms occur. Each flower may be 3/4 to 1″ across, funnel-shaped, 1 to 3 per truss. Nomenclature is somewhat confusing and is often referred to as 'Obtusum' group. Found wild in highly acid soil on three mountains in Kyushu, Japan. Introduced about 1844. Zone 6. There are a number of cultivars which have been derived from *R. obtusum*, *R. kaempferi*, *R. kiusianum*, and *R. satense*. This group has the name Kurume Azaleas (see Kurume Hybrid list) and while often considered dwarf they will develop into dense, 4 to 6′ high plants. Many of the cultivars have been used for greenhouse forcing and are simply not hardy in the northern areas. The range of colors travels from white to pink, lavender, scarlet, salmon and all shades in between. As hybridization continues new and better cultivars will appear in the trade. The real crux is being able to separate the good flowering, hardy (at least to -10°F) types from the rest of the lot. Callaway Gardens has an excellent collection of Kurumes and their famous Azalea bowl is primarily planted with this group. 'Amoena' has small, hose-in-hose, purplish red flowers, small shiny leaves, early to mid-May.

Rhododendron periclymenoides (Michx.) Shinn. (previously *R. nudiflorum* Torr.), (rō-dō-den'dron per-i-clī-men-oy'dēz), Pinxterbloom Azalea, is a low, much-branched, stoloniferous, deciduous shrub which averages 4 to 6′ in height but ranges from dwarfish (2′) to relatively large (10′) over the native habitat. The foliage is bright green in summer turning dull yellow in fall. The flowers vary in color from impure white or pale pink to deep violet and open in April or early May. Based on numerous visits to the azalea garden at Biltmore Estate, the flowers open with, or perhaps slightly later than *R. austrinum* and *R. canescens*. The flowers are fragrant (variable), each about 1 1/2″ across, borne 6 to 12 together before the leaves. This species is adapted to dry, sandy, rocky soils. Observed in flower in April at 4000′ elevation in north Georgia mountains. A useful plant for naturalizing, and along with *R. calendulaceum* and *R. viscosum* was used in the development of the Ghent hybrids. Native from Massachusetts to North Carolina and Ohio. Introduced 1730. Zone 4 to 8.

Rhododendron 'P.J.M.'
LEAVES: Small, 1 to 2 1/2″ long, usually elliptic, dark green above, changing to purple in winter, essentially hairless, rusty-scaly beneath, thick, leathery.
BUDS: Rounded and much smaller than those of *R. catawbiense*.

Rhododendron 'P.J.M.' hybrids resulted from crosses between *R. carolinianum* and *R. dauricum* var. *sempervirens*. The 'P.J.M.' Hybrids are a group of plants and, therefore, there may be differences in flower colors. The plant grows from 3 to 6′ in height and is of rounded outline. The foliage is evergreen, dark green in summer and turns plum purple in fall. The flowers are vivid, bright lavender pink and occur in mid to late April. The flowers occur heavily every year as the plant sets little or no seed. Zone 4 hardiness. Dr. Donald Wyman said the 'P.J.M.' Hybrids were the most promising rhododendrons that have originated in New England during the past 25 years. Originated in the Weston Nurseries, Hopkinton, MA, 1943. Many people do not like the "dirty, squalid lavender-pink flowers" but when the choice of rhododendrons is limited this is a bright element in the landscape. 'P.J.M.' grew in our Illinois garden and proved the hardiest broadleaf rhododendron. Minnesota Landscape Arboretum reported that it was the only flower bud hardy broadleaf rhododendron. Report from Calgary, Alberta, Canada that 'P.J.M' flowers there, see *Amer. Nurseryman* 180(6):106 (1994). It flowered in our garden along with daffodils and was a pleasant sight especially after a difficult midwestern winter.

MEZITT/WESTON HYBRIDS: The following is an attempt to assemble the fruits of the Mezitt's long tradition of breeding. Wayne Mezitt is continuing to breed garden-worthy rhododendrons and azaleas.

'Aglo'—Sister of 'Olga Mezitt', selected for its earlier flower and dark blotch, compact grower with light pink flowers.

'April Love'—Ruffled, double, light pink and yellow, some winter foliage retention, less than 50%, 6′ by 4′.

'April Snow'—Attractive small foliage becomes bronzy in winter, white flowers in mid-April, dense twiggy upright habit, stems yellow-green.

'April Song'—Large, frilly, double, light pink flowers at the end of April, inner set of petals are nearly white, imparting an unusual two-tone appearance, small, dark green leaves turn yellow and mahogany-red in autumn and are retained about fifty percent during winter, chunky, wide-growing upright shrub, 5′ by 4′.

'Balta' (*R. carolinianum* var. *album* × 'P.J.M.' Hybrid)—Small, glossy, partly convex evergreen leaves, compact and slow in growth, flowers a week after 'P.J.M.' hybrids, pale pink to almost white.

'Black Satin'—An F_3 hybrid of 'P.J.M.' hybrids, deep fall and winter foliage color, which is shiny coal-black, semi-upright in growth habit, flowers are a deep rose-pink.

'Bonfire'—Small, orange-red.

'Caronella'—Strongest pink.

'Checkmate'—Small, lavender-pink flowers, compact, mound-like bush, most "dwarf" form of *R.* 'P.J.M.'.

'Counterpoint'—Sister of 'Marathon', deciduous upright-spreading plant with semi-double, bright pink flowers along the entire length of the stems.

'Desmit'—A sister seedling of 'Waltham', selected for one week earlier flowering time and appears less susceptible to the sunscalding leaf spot problem.

'Elite'—A most vigorous selection of 'P.J.M.', tall growing, flowers are slightly pinker and open a few days later than 'Victor'.

'Frank Abbott'—Deciduous, vibrant, dark pink, spicy-scented flowers in late May, wide-growing, robust, upright, clusters of silvery, pointed buds, large, mildew-resistant foliage often turns reddish orange before dropping in autumn, hybrid between the rock-hardy *R. prinophyllum* and a red flowering *R.* × *kosteranum* selection, Ed Mezitt performed this cross in the 1960's.

'Golden Showers'—Lightly vanilla-scented, peach-yellow flowers, broad, upright growing, long, pointed, somewhat glossy green leaves, bronze in fall, -24°F.

'Henry's Red'—Very dark red, wide and upright with dark green foliage, have seen in Manchester, NH.

'Independence'—Upright growing, small green leaves with bluish undersides, red buds, small fragrant dark pink flowers in ball-like heads, maturing silvery-pink in July.

'Iridescent'—Spicy-scented, silvery pink in mid-June, wide-spreading, green foliage with a blue cast turns bronze-red in fall, -29°F.

'Jane Abbott Peach'—Large peach-pink fragrant flowers, vigorous, wide, upright-growing, -29°F.

'Jane Abbott Pink'—Cutting grown selections of *R.* × *kosteranum* × *R. prinophyllum* hybrid, large, fragrant flowers in shades of pink, wide, upright, robust, -29°F.

'Laurie' (*R. carolinianum* var. *album* × 'P.J.M.' hybrid)—Glossy green leaves turn red in fall and winter, compact and slow in growth, flowers pale pink to almost white with some branches exhibiting semi-double petaloid flowers just after 'P.J.M.'.

'Lavender Frost'—Profuse, ruffled, multi-petaled, light lavender to white flowers, small, dark green leaves turn bronze or mahogany in fall, 5′ by 4′.

'Lemon Drop'—A rare yellow form with spicy fragrant flowers in late June–July.

'Llenroc'—Dusty pale pink to almost white.

'Lollipop'—Pink flowers with yellow flare, maturing silvery pink, with a sweet fragrance, green leaves have silvery undersides and change to long-lasting red-orange in September.

'Low Red Frilled'—Medium red flowers with frilled edges, low-spreading and compact, dark green foliage.

'Lynne Robbins Steinman'—Clone of the Double Pink Hybrids, opening as early as the third week of April in Hopkinton, MA, ruffled, double flowers with yellowish centers, small foliage, nearly deciduous in winter.

'Marathon' (An F_2 hybrid of 'P.J.M.' × *R. mucronulatum* 'Cornell Pink')—Deciduous, semi-upright habit, bright magenta flowers early, usually the day (April 19) of the Boston Marathon, which starts in sight of Weston Nursery, Hopkinton, MA.

'Milestone'—Pink buds in mid to late April open to darker pink flowers, appear nearly red from a distance, small, green, slightly twisted and shiny foliage, few leaves that are retained on the branch tips in winter are mahogany colored, orange-red and yellow interior leaves in November, compact-growing shrub with a wide, upright, twiggy appearance, 3′ high and wide after 10 years, larger with age.

'Mindaura' (*R. minus* var. *compacta* × *R. dauricum* var. *sempervirens*)—Evergreen foliage, green in summer, deep purple in fall and winter, foliage is thinner in texture than 'P.J.M.', wide-spreading habit of growth, flowers a week after *R.* 'P.J.M.', discontinued and now used only for hybridizing.

'Molly Fordham'—Compact growing, white flowers, small glossy green foliage year-round, early May, named after Molly Fordham, wife of Alfred Fordham, the great propagator (now retired) at the Arnold Arboretum.

'New Patriot'—Violet-red flowers in mid-April, purplish-maroon winter foliage, 3 to 4', upright-spreading habit, some winter foliage retention.

'Northern Rose' (*R.* 'Waltham' × *R. mucronulatum* 'Cornell Pink', crossed by Dr. Robert Ticknor)—Narrow evergreen foliage on a semi-upright plant, small bright pink flowers in abundance at or slightly after 'P.J.M.', difficult to propagate but may become popular through tissue culture.

'Olga Mezitt' (*R. minus* var. *compacta* × *R. mucronulatum*)—Evergreen foliage turning light red in fall and winter, vigorous upright-spreading plant, bright peach-pink flowers about the time of *R. carolinianum*.

'Parade'—Sweet-scented dark pink flowers with orange eye, July, wide upright, -24°F.

'Pauline Bralit'—Mauve buds open to heavily textured, slightly fragrant white flowers in early May, large convex foliage, robust.

'Pillar'—Similar to *R.* 'P.J.M.', but more upright growing habit.

'Pillow Party'—See 'P.J.M. White Form'.

'Pink & Sweet'—Light pink flowers with a yellow flare in late June, rich spicy scent, bud hardy to -29°F, fall foliage is purple-red with tones of orange and yellow.

PJM Compact Form—Tetraploid form, flowers have greater substance and are much larger (2 to 3" diameter) than the diploid hybrid, trusses have 4 to 5 flowers and the truss is 4" wide by 2 1/2" high, leaves are broadly elliptic and are thicker and wider than the diploid form, stems are stout, erect, and thick, the plant habit is upright-spreading, and plants are bushy, hardy, flowers at the same time as 'P.J.M.'.

'P.J.M. Compact Briggs'—Lavender pink, smaller, tighter growth habit than 'Elite'.

'P.J.M. Lavender'—Hardy evergreen shrub, bright lavender pink flowers, early flowering, summer foliage green, winter leaves are reddish-brown to mahogany, semi-dwarf.

'P.J.M. Princess Susan'—Slow-growing, dwarf form, bright lavender purple flowers, deep mahogany-black winter foliage.

'P.J.M. White Form'—White-flowered counterpart to 'P.J.M.', small leaves turn rich mahogany red in winter, small clusters of white flowers in April, hardy, to 8' high and 5' wide.

'Popsicle'—Fragrant pink, -35°F.

'Regal'—A selection of 'P.J.M.', vigorous, wider spreading type of growth.

'Ribbon Candy'—Spicy scented, pink flowers with distinctive stripes in late June, medium green summer foliage turns burgundy red in autumn.

'Shrimp Pink Hybrids' (*R. carolinianum* var. *album* × *R. mucronulatum* 'Cornell Pink')—Green summer foliage turning light red in fall and retaining about 10% of the smaller leaves during the winter, upright-spreading habit of growth, flowers in abundance a week after *R. mucronulatum*, beautiful in flower at the Arnold Arboretum.

'Thunder'—Rich dark pink-purple flowers in late April, lustrous leaves are black-mahogany during winter, changing to green after flowering, slightly slower and more compact than 'P.J.M.'.

'Trumpeter'—Salmon-pink.

'Victor'—A selection of 'P.J.M.', a compact slow-growing type, earliest to flower.

'Wally' ('Vallya')—Soft pink flowers in mid-May, orange-red and yellow autumn tones color interior leaves before they drop in November, some of the long, leathery, dark green foliage is retained on the ends of the branches in winter, vigorous, wide-upright, growing to about 4' high and 2' wide in 8 years.

'Waltham' (*R. ferrugineum* × *R. carolinianum*, crossed by Dr. Robert Ticknor)—Deep green evergreen foliage on dense mound up to 3' high, flowers are pink *R. carolinianum* type, beautifully displayed about a week later, leaves develop spotting when the plant is growing in full sun.

'Weston's Innocence'—Small, white flowers on a vigorous but compact, mounding shrub, flowers are sweetly scented, bud hardy to -29°F.

'Weston's Mayflower'—Pink, slow growing and compact, small green foliage all year.

'Weston's Pink Diamond' (A petaloid 'P.J.M.' hybrid × *R. mucronulatum* 'Cornell Pink')—Semi-evergreen foliage and upright-spreading habit of growth, flowers early, at time of *R. mucronulatum*, with frilled pink heavily double flowers, 4' by 3' in 8 years.

'White Angel' (*R. carolinianum* var. *album* × *R. dauricum* var. *album*)—Semi-evergreen, upright plant, pale lavender buds opening white as they mature.

Rhododendron prinophyllum Millais (formerly *R. roseum* Rehd.), (rō-dō-den′dron prī-nō-fil′um), Roseshell Azalea, is a deciduous, 2 to 8', rarely to 15' tall, much branched shrub with numerous spreading branches. Spread is comparable to height. Foliage is bright green in summer; green to bronze in fall. Flowers are bright pink with clove-like scent, May, borne 5 to 9 per cluster before or with the leaves. In this author's opinion superior to *R. periclymenoides* and *R. canescens*. Extremely hardy, with marked tolerance to high pH. 'Album' has fragrant, white flowers in late spring, 4′ high and wide. 'Marie Hoffman' has larger flowers, clear true pink, extremely fragrant and cold hardy, 8′ by 8′, flowers late May. Native to New Hampshire and southern Quebec to Virginia, west to Illinois and Missouri. Introduced 1812. Zone 4 to 8.

Rhododendron prunifolium (Small) Millais, (rō-dō-den′dron prö′ni-fō′li-um), Plumleaf Azalea, grows 8 to 10′(15′) high and produces orange-red to red, funnel-shaped, 3/4 to 1″ long flowers in July–August. The stamens are 2 to 2 1/2″ long. The lateness of flower makes this a rather valuable addition to the garden. It is hardy to Boston but makes its best growth in the South and can be found in abundance at Callaway Gardens, Pine Mountain, GA. It is considered the most glabrous of all American azaleas and for that reason quite distinct. Found in sandy ravines along stream banks. Flowers in July in Dirr garden with flowers nestled among leaves. Tends to lose some of its pizzazz due to foliar competition but still beautiful. Southwestern Georgia and eastern Alabama. Introduced 1918. Zone 5 to 8. Cultivars include:
'Apricot Glow'—A selection of the plumleaf azalea with orange flowers in late July, wide and upright-growing, rounded dark green foliage.
'Cherry Bomb'—Orange-red, July.
'Coral Glow'—Pink-orange, July.
'Lewis Shortt'—Scarlet red flower on a plant with plum leaf foliage, found and introduced by Mr. Shortt.
'Peach Glow'—Orange-pink, July.
'Pine Prunifolium'—Bright red flowers open in mid summer.

Rhododendron 'Purple Gem' is a rounded, dwarf, evergreen type with small leaves and light purple flowers in mid-April. Hardy to -15°F. A cross between *R. fastigiatum* × *R. carolinianum*. 'Purple Imp' is similar to 'Purple Gem' but a truer blue; smaller and more alpine, low and dense.

Rhododendron racemosum Franch. 'Compactum', (rō-dō-den′dron ra-sem-ō′sum), compact form, 1 to 2′ high, apple blossom pink, a rock garden gem. Species is native to western China. Introduced 1889. Zone (5)6.

Rhododendron 'Ramapo' is another compact form with glaucous foliage, bright violet-pink flowers in early April and -25°F hardiness. 'Ramolet' has light lavender flowers, tidy upright habit, long slender leaves.

Rhododendron serrulatum (Small) Millais, (rō-dō-den′dron ser-ū-lāt′um), Sweet Azalea, is a medium to large-growing azalea, one of the latest flowering azaleas with flowers occurring after the foliage, from June through July. Flowers are 1 to 1 1/2″ long, from pale pink to white and exceptionally fragrant. In author's garden, not overwhelming. Does well in wooded swampy areas. Georgia to Florida and Louisiana. Introduced 1919. Zone 7 to 8.

Rhododendron smirnowii Trautv., (rō-dō-den′dron smēr-nōw′ē-ī), Smirnow Rhododendron, is an evergreen shrub growing 6 to 8′ high and as broad in 15 years. The foliage is dark green above with thick woolly tomentum beneath. The flowers are rose or rosy-pink and the corolla is frilled; each flower is 1 1/2″ long and 2″ across; May; in 5 to 6″ wide trusses. Very distinct and handsome rhododendron in flower. Has been used for breeding work because of good hardiness (Zone 4), flower and foliage. Will become increasingly evident in American gardens as its merits are extolled. Native to Caucasus at 5,000 to 8,000′ elevation. Introduced 1886.

Rhododendron vaseyi A. Gray, (rō-dō-den′dron vā′zē- ī), Pinkshell Azalea, grows 5 to 10′ in height. The habit is irregular upright. Foliage is deciduous, medium green in summer changing to light red in fall, may develop excellent fall color and have observed deep red on plants in Arnold Arboretum. Flowers are clear rose, bell-shaped with the two lower corolla lobes divided nearly at the base, before leaves, 1 1/2″ diameter, early to mid-May, 5 to 8 flowers per inflorescence, 5 to 7 stamens, no fragrance. One of the hardy American types. Makes a spectacular show when in flower. Apparently does not hybridize. Native to the Blue Ridge Mountains of North Carolina. Zone 4 to 7. Not as heat tolerant as *R. austrinum*, *R. canescens*, *R. alabamense*, and *R. prunifolium*.
Cultivars include:
var. *album*—White flowers.
'Pinkerbell'—Selected deep pink strain of the species.
'White Find'—A rare form, the white flowers have a greenish yellow blotch and are fragrant.

Rhododendron viscosum (L.) Torr., (rō-dō-den′dron vis-kō′sum), Swamp Azalea, grows 1 to 8′ (average 5′) by 3 to 8′ and is of loose, open habit with numerous spreading, very hispid branches. Flowers are white, rarely pink, clove-like scent, mid May to June, 4 to 9 flowers per inflorescence. Have seen it growing along fresh water ponds on Cape Cod. Leaves are lustrous green sometimes with a glaucous cast below. Maine to South Carolina, Georgia, Alabama, in swamps. Cultivated 1731. Zone 4 to 9.

'Antilope'—A cross of *R. viscosum* and Mollis, with excellent hardiness and strong fragrance, the clear pink flowers are marked with a darker pink median line and a faint yellow flare giving them a salmon glow.

'Arpege'—Warm yellow azalea with an even deeper yellow flare on the upper petal, superior fragrance, late flowering.

'Delaware Blue'—Blue-green leaves, fragrant flowers are pure white with a very narrow, tubular-shaped opening from softly pink-shaded buds.

'Jolie Madame'—Beautiful rose-pink, fragrant flowers with golden blotch in late May–June.

var. *montanum*—A low-growing form only waist high, is responsible for many of the natural hybrids as it flowers with other species in June.

'Pink Mist'—A fragrant, white tinged pink selection.

'Pink Rocket'—Red buds, slightly sweetly scented groups of small, pink flowers in late June, wide, upright-growing, small ascending blue-green foliage with silvery undersides, turns bronze-red in fall, -29°F.

'Rosata'—Fragrant carmine-rose flowers, wide, upright.

'Soir de Paris'—Fragrant, dark rose flowers with a brilliant orange blotch.

Rhododendron weyrichii Maxim., (rō-dō-den′dron wâr-ich′ē-ī), Weyrich Azalea, is a most unusual and beautiful deciduous azalea. Foliage is large, round and glossy with clusters of 2 to 3 leaves at end of the branches; turning vinous purple in autumn. Funnel-shaped flowers usually brick-red with purple blotch adorning the plant before leaves appear in early spring. Native of Quelpart Island, Korea, Japan. Introduced 1914. Zone 6.

Rhododendron 'Windbeam' is another very hardy (-25°F) evergreen type of low, semi-dwarf habit, with white flowers becoming suffused with pink. It is a cross between *R. carolinianum* and *R. racemosum* and will grow 4′ by 4′. Leaves are roundish, small and aromatic. In Zone 7b, foliage remains green in winter. In the 1983 Edition, I did not have much positive to say about performance in Zone 7b but over the past 15 years have altered my assessment. If given pine shade and a moist, well-drained root run, it makes a handsome plant. 'Manita(o)u' is more compact in growth habit, small, dark green, rough-textured leaves, light pink flowers, will withstand sun.

Rhododendron yakushimanum Nak. [now *R. degronianum* Carr. subsp. *yakushimanum* (Nak.) Hara], (rō-dō-den′dron ya-kösh-i-mā′num), is a dense, mounded, evergreen rhododendron growing about 3′ tall and 3′ wide. The foliage is dark green with a woolly indumentum beneath. The flowers are bright rose in bud opening to white in full flower (sort of an apple blossom effect), about 10 campanulate flowers in a truss; hardy from -5 to -15°F. Used extensively in hybridizing and superior clones are available. One reference indicated a 20-year-old plant may be only 3′ by 5′. The search of literature and nursery catalogs uncovered over 118 named selections or hybrids with *R. yakushimanum* as a parent.

Rhododendron yedoense Maxim. var. *poukhanense* Nak., (rō-dō-den′dron yed-ō-en′sē pök-hȧ-nen′sē), Korean Azalea, grows 3 to 6′ high and spreads that much or more. Develops into a broad mat on exposed locations. Foliage is dark green in summer; orange to red-purple in fall. Flowers are rose to lilac-purple, 2″ across, slightly fragrant, May, 2 to 3 flowers together. 'Pink Discovery' has clear pink flowers. *Rhododendron yedoense* (Yodogawa Azalea) has double flowers of a similar color. Native to Korea. Zone (4)5 to 7. Has performed well in Illinois and Athens, Georgia.

Azalea Cultivars and Hybrid Groups

In some respects, it is paralyzingly frightening to attempt to present the cultivars of azaleas. Numerous hybridizers using different progenitor species have produced hybrids that often bear their names. Mr. Fred Galle, in his great book *Azaleas* (1987), Timber Press, Portland, OR, presents the most comprehensive and up-to-date listing and description of azalea cultivars. I attempted to check the ones presented here (most derived from 1987–89 nursery catalogs for 1990 Edition, 1996–98 nursery catalogs for 1998 Edition) against Mr. Galle's list. Many did not appear in his book. About 30 catalogs plus current literature were used to assemble the following list. Anyone interested in azaleas, their history and development should consult Mr. Galle's book. It is the classic tome on the subject.

AICHELE HYBRIDS
'Laura'—Originally developed as a greenhouse forcing azalea, dense foliage and abundant, dark pink, 2″ diameter hose-in-hose flowers in early April, hardy in Zone 7 to 8.
'Posaman'—Medium-sized shrub with 3″ diameter, pink-white flowers.

AROMI HYBRIDS
Unable to grow Exbury Azaleas because of their intolerance of hot summers, but still determined to have Azaleas with incandescent flowers and large flower trusses, Dr. Eugene Aromi of Mobile, AL, embarked about 25 years ago on an undertaking to breed native heat tolerant species with Exbury Hybrid Azaleas, and his labors have produced Azaleas with lavish flowers as well as heat and cold hardiness. These hybrids flower in early May, but beyond that, they look good all season, and the foliage has never been disfigured by mildew at the end of the summer. Plant these azaleas in full sun or light shade. Dr. Aromi's original plants now measure about 12 to 15′ high and tend to be upright growing. Very heat tolerant.
'Aromi Sunny Side Up'—Rich golden yellow flowers carry an egg yolk yellow flare.
'Aromi Sunrise'—Numerous trusses of large flowers with orange-red buds that open light orange and gradually shade to darker orange in the center, the dark green foliage remains handsome all season.
'Carousel'—Scarlet buds open to delicate, ruffled flowers colored pale pink and marked with a prominent gold blotch, the large trusses bear several flowers, medium-green foliage, healthy foliage.
'Centerpiece'—Large, white flowers with a deep yellow blotch.
'Clear Creek'—Long, tubular flowers are a lovely translucent yellow with a discreet, darker yellow blotch.
'Frontier Gold'—Orange-scarlet buds open to rich gold flowers with scarlet shadings.
'High Tide'—Delicately colored, ivory flowers with a gold flare and a pale overlay of blush pink at the tips.
'Jane's Gold'—Frilly, creamy yellow flowers with tips lightly washed with rose.
'Liz Colbert'—This pastel-colored release extends the color range of these hybrids, brick-colored buds open to light peach flowers with a light orange flare.
LN—Beautiful light pinkish yellow flowers with a pronounced fragrance are displayed on a small to medium-sized shrub.
'Sun Struck'—Pale yellow buds open to lemon yellow flowers with a darker blotch.

BACK ACRE HYBRIDS
Plants are cold hardy to 0 to 5°F, flowers open in late April in Georgia, medium-sized shrubs.
'Marian Lee'—Flower has white center with reddish pink border, 3″ diameter with the appearance of butterflies, medium-sized upright grower, habit similar to the Kurumes.
'Orange Flair'—Low-growing plant with very unusual flower, orange-pink with a white center and double.
'Pat Kraft'—Single, 3″ diameter, scarlet red with a rose blotch, 6-lobed flower, low-spreading habit.
'Target'—Scarlet-pink, 3″ diameter flowers, upright grower.

BELTSVILLE (YERKES-PRYOR) HYBRIDS
'Casablanca'—Outstanding, single, white flowers, grows wider than high.
'Casablanca Improved'—Large, single, white flowers.
'Eureka'—Flowers pink, hose-in-hose, medium, spreading.
'Guy Yerkes'—Salmon-pink, hose-in-hose, low growing, semi-evergreen.
'H.H. Hume'—White, 2″ diameter, hose-in-hose flowers with faint yellow throat, flowers in clusters of 3 or 5, mid-season, 6′ by 6′.
'Placid'—White flowers with a slight green tinge, hose-in-hose, low, compact, spreading plant, hardy.
'Polar Bear'—White, with slight yellow-green throat, hose-in-hose, wide upright, slow-growing, green leaves in summer become yellow in autumn, flower buds tested hardy to −13°F, common in the trade.

BROOKS HYBRIDS
Developed to endure hot, dry summers, hardy to 20°F.
'Flamingo Variegata'—Variegated red, hose-in-hose, late.
'My Valentine'—Rose, double, mid to late season.
'Pinkie'—Pink, hose-in-hose, late.
'Red Bird'—Large, red, ruffled, semi-double to hose-in-hose.

CARLA HYBRIDS
Developed at North Carolina State University, Raleigh, NC, Zone 7b-8a (USDA) (5 to 15°F). Flowering dates are based on observations in the Raleigh area. In July 1976, 'Adelaide Pope', 'Carror', 'Elaine', 'Emily', 'Jane', 'Spalding', 'Pink Cloud', and 'Sunglow' were released. In 1982, 'Autumn Sun', 'Cochran's Lavender', 'Pink

Camellia', and 'Wolfpack Red' were released. Evergreen, bred for *Phytophthora* resistance. Grew several in Dirr garden, all have disappeared, terrible lace bug in Dirr garden.

'Adelaide Pope'—Flowers deep rose-pink, single, medium-large, 1 to 5 per bud, plant medium-large, vigorous, compact, April 15–April 25.

'Autumn Sun'—Flowers bronze-red, hose-in-hose, 2 to 3 per bud, plant small to medium, upright-spreading, dense, April 15–25.

'Carror'—Flowers rose-pink, semi-double, medium-sized, 1 to 4 per bud, plant medium-sized, compact, April 25–May 1.

'Cochran's Lavender'—Flowers purplish pink, single, medium-sized, 1 to 3 per bud, plant medium-sized, spreading, dense, April 15–25.

'Elaine'—Flowers light pink, fully double, medium sized rose-bud type opening full wide in later development, 1 to 3 flowers per bud, plant medium-sized, April 16–26.

'Emily'—Flowers deep rose-red, single, medium-small, 1 to 3 per bud, hose-in-hose, plant medium sized, compact, April 18–30.

'Fred D. Cochran'—Superior resistance to root rot.

'Greenthumb Peppermint'—Mid to late flowering, semi-double, hose-in-hose, 3″ diameter pinkish with white margins and a soft purplish pink inner pattern, typically plants develop sports of white and purplish pink, see *HortScience* 25: 236–237 (1990), not a Carla hybrid, but introduced through North Carolina State.

'Jan Cochran'—Compact shrub that resembles an English Boxwood in leaf, single rosy pink, 4/5 to 1″ long, 3/5 to 4/5″ wide, moderately resistant to *Phytophthora cinnamomi*, see *HortScience* 24: 717–718 (1989).

'Jane Spalding'—Flowers rose-pink, single, 1 to 3 per bud, medium-sized, plant is medium-sized, April 25–25.

'Pink Camellia'—Flowers light purplish pink, completely double, rosebud type, opening full in later development, 1 to 3 flowers per bud, plant medium-sized, April 15–25.

'Pink Cloud'—Flowers light pink, predominantly single, large-sized, 2 to 4 per bud, plants medium-sized, April 15–25.

'Rachel'—Compact shrub with ascending-spreading branches, wine-red flowers, single to semi-double, up to 2″ diameter, 40 to 50% of the flowers are semi-double, moderately resistant to *Phytophthora cinnamomi*, see *HortScience* 24: 717–718 (1989).

'Sunglow'—Flowers deep rose-pink, single, medium large, 1 to 4 per bud, plant medium-large sized, vigorous, April 20–30.

'Wolfpack Red'—Flowers strong red, single, small, 1 to 4 flowers per bud, plant semi-dwarf, spreading, April 15–25.

CONFEDERATE SERIES/TOM DODD, JR AND SON HYBRIDS

Alabama plantsmen Bob Schwindt, Tom Dodd, Jr. and Tom Dodd III have crossed the Exbury Azalea 'Hotspur Yellow' with *R. austrinum* to produce the following heat and cold tolerant hybrids. All of these azaleas also have a pleasant fragrance. Zone 6 to 9.

'Admiral Semmes'—Large inflorescences of big, fragrant, yellow flowers, named for Civil War Admiral and General Raphael Semmes for whom the town Semmes, AL was named.

'Col. Mosby'—Big inflorescences of large, fragrant flowers that start deep pink and fade to lighter pink with a yellow blotch.

'Robert E. Lee'—Fragrant, red flowers in spring.

'Stonewall Jackson'—Fragrant, orange flowers in spring.

011—Fragrant, pink flowers in spring.

TDN Selection #1—Fragrant, yellow-gold flowers, medium-sized grower.

TDN Selection #2—Abundant yellow-gold flowers.

COOLIDGE HYBRIDS

'American Beauty'—Double, holly berry red.

'Singing Fountain'—Single, rose-cerise.

ENCORE HYBRIDS: Unique for fall flowering, in the Dirr garden late August–September into November, again in April–May. Not particularly cold hardy as a group. Based on two complete growing seasons in the Dirr garden, Autumn Coral™, Autumn Embers™, Autumn Rouge™, and Autumn Royalty™ appear the most vigorous, cold hardy, and floriferous. Introduced by Flowerwood Nursery, Mobile, AL. The cultural conditions of the Encore

Azaleas are similar to Satsuki Azaleas. Should be planted in well-drained, slightly acidic soil, with light shade or afternoon shade.

  Autumn Amethyst™—*Rhododendron oldhamii* × *Rhododendron* 'Karens', the most cold hardy of the Autumn series, foliage is elongated, pointed and rough-textured, leaves take a beautiful dark cast in the winter, soft purple flowers, intermediately dense and spreading habit, flowering begins early fall.

  Autumn Cheer™—*Rhododendron oldhamii* × *Rhododendron* 'Pink Cheer', foliage, growth habit and flowers look like a Kurume type azalea, flowers are slightly larger than Kurume flowers and are deep pink, the most compact of the Autumn cultivars, flowering is from early August through the fall.

  Autumn Coral™—*Rhododendron oldhamii* × *Rhododendron* 'White Gumpo', mounding habit, flowers abundantly from July through the fall, flowers are salmon pink with prominent fuchsia flecking and medium in size.

  Autumn Embers™—*Rhododendron oldhamii* × *Rhododendron* 'Watchet', low, spreading and dense habit, foliage is dark green, flowering is from early July through the fall and very intense, single and semi-double, deep orange-red flowers, fall flowering is profuse.

  Autumn Rouge™—*Rhododendron oldhamii* × *Rhododendron* 'Double Beauty', the breeder's favorite, very prolific, flowering from early July through the fall, semi-double, strong pink almost red flowers, upright habit.

  Autumn Royalty™—*Rhododendron oldhamii* × *Rhododendron* 'Georgia Giant', robust, upright and globose, large, dark green foliage, flowers from late July to frost, flowers are large, single, rich purple.

GIRARD HYBRIDS

Excellent, large-flowered, show-stopping evergreen (also deciduous types) azaleas for colder climates. Flower bud hardiness ranges from -5 to -15°F. Grew many of these in our Illinois garden, need more attention from northern gardeners. Foliage is among the most handsome of the evergreen azaleas. Bred and introduced by Girard Nurseries, Geneva, OH.

Evergreen types:

  'Girard Arista'—Beautiful large deep pink flushed to light pink with a deep orange-yellow blotch, heavily ruffled, fragrant trusses up to 6″ across, dense habit with deep green foliage, mildew resistant, very early flowering.

  'Girard Better Letter'—Outstanding deep orange-red flowers and vigorous growth, hardy to -15°F.

  'Girard Border Gem'—Beautiful deep rose-pink flowers that completely cover the dwarf azalea, when in flower, the foliage and plant are completely hidden, leaves are glossy dark green only 1/4 to 3/4″ long, turning a glossy scarlet during winter months, an early flowering beautiful dwarf azalea.

  'Girard Caroline'—Solid rose-red, compact self-branching, prolific flowering, excellent dark green foliage that takes on a reddish cast in winter, longer flowering period than most.

  'Girard Clare Marie'—Large ruffled single white flowers up to 3″ in diameter, very vigorous upright grower, large light green foliage.

  'Girard Chiara'—Flowers are large, hose-in-hose, 2 1/2 to 3″ diameter, color is clear rose, pleasingly ruffled and very floriferous, foliage is glossy deep green type which holds very well, plant takes on a dense broad growing habit, ideal for borders, foundation planting and rock gardens, will withstand -15°F, ideal for forcing, originated in 1972.

  'Girard Crimson'—Large crimson flowers up to 2 1/2″ diameter, large glossy green leaves, good winter color, on a good compact plant.

  'Girard Dwarf Lavender'—Medium clear lavender flowers, one of the most uniform and compact growing of all the evergreen azaleas, excellent foliage, vigor and hardiness, needs little pruning, excellent for small gardens.

  'Girard Fireflash'—Large, 2 1/2″ diameter, beautiful deep orange-red flowers with an orange-yellow throat, hardy, flowers profusely mid to late season.

  'Girard Fuchsia'—A beautiful shade of reddish purple, flowers are beautifully waved and ruffled and heavy-textured, foliage dark green and glossy, -15°F.

  'Girard Hot Shot'—Fiery deep orange-red or scarlet flowers, 2 1/2 to 3″ diameter, heavily textured and completely covering the plants, foliage 3/4 to 1″ long, medium green during summer changing to brilliant orange-red in fall, more upright habit than 'Girard Scarlet'.

  'Girard Jeremiah'—Prolific, beautiful large hose-in-hose pink flowers, large dark green foliage turning red in winter, excellent compact self-branching habit.

  'Girard Joshua'—Beautiful dark red, ruffled flowers with white stamens and pistils, compact, medium height, wavy large green leaves, leaves similar to 'Nova Zembla' but darker and more heavily foliaged, later flowering than 'Girard Sandy Petruso', bud hardy -15°F, height 5 to 6′, named by Peter Girard, Sr. for his great grandson.

'Girard Kathy Ann'—Good 2″ diameter, single, white flowers on a medium-sized shrub.

'Girard Leslie's Purple'—Large hose-in-hose purplish red flowers with dark spotting, 2 1/2 to 3″ diameter, foliage deep glossy green, semi-dwarf, low compact rounded habit, 3′ by 3′.

'Girard Lucky Star(s)'—Buds pink opening to pure white with a light cream center, ruffled flower, compact growing.

'Girard National Beauty'—Beautiful ruffled rose-pink flowers, large dark green foliage and compact self-branching growth habit, matures to 24″ high, 3′ wide, hardy to -10°F.

'Girard Orange Jolly'—Large, double, bright orange flowers growing in large ball-like truss, sterile with no seed capsules, vigorous growing, to 6′, hardy to -25°F.

'Girard Peter Alan'—Rich orchid flowers with reddish shading to purplish black eye, strong upright habit, foliage is heavy rich green, hardy to -15°F.

'Girard Pink Dawn'—Large, hose-in-hose, rose-pink, foliage is dark green in summer and assumes red tints in fall and winter, compact and vigorous, one of the hardiest.

'Girard Pink Delight'—Fragrant, hose-in-hose, vivid pink with 20 to 24 flowers forming a nice compact truss, tall growing.

'Girard Pleasant White'—Large, 1 1/2 to 3″ diameter, white flowers with a cream center, late flowering and vigorous, 2 to 2 1/2′ by 3′, dark green foliage, hardy.

'Girard Purple'—Purple flowers, superior color and habit compared to 'Herbert' or other lavenders, extremely vigorous and compact growing.

'Gerard Remarkable Pink'—Bi-color pink with white center flowers, ball-shaped trusses, mid-season, medium habit, 4′.

'Girard Renee Michelle'—Clear pink flowers, 2 1/2 to 3″, foliage dark green, 1 1/2″ by 1/2″, plants are low, compact, a cross of 'Boudoir' and 'Gumpo Pink', beautiful flowers, flowered in my Illinois garden in a protected location, has withstood -10°F.

'Girard Roberta'—Double pink, ruffled petals, large to 3″ across.

'Girard Rose'—Rose, 2 1/2 to 3″ flowers, slightly wavy, foliage 1 1/2 to 2″ long by 3/4″ wide, glossy deep green during the summer, taking on brilliant deep red tints in early fall, stems turn deep red in winter, vigorous, upright growth habit.

'Girard Ruffled Red'—Rose-red, heavily ruffled flowers in tight trusses that sit flush to the foliage, leaves are heavy-textured and plant is vigorous upright growing, hardy.

'Girard Salmon'—Large, hose-in-hose, salmon flowers, compact habit, more upright and taller than most Girard selections, vigorous.

'Girard Sandra Ann'—Reddish purple, 3″ diameter flowers, bright green foliage, broad rounded habit, 5′ by 6′.

'Girard Sandy Petruso'—Gorgeous, bright fire-engine red, large trusses, semi-upright habit, large deep green leaves, sister seedling to 'Joshua', height to 7′, bud hardy to -10°F.

'Girard Saybrook Glory'—Large pink flowers, 2 1/2 to 3″ ruffled flowers, large dark green foliage, low compact plant.

'Girard's Scarlet'—Large flowers, strong red with deep orange-red glow, waxy textured, deep glossy green foliage, low compact plant, 1 1/2 to 2′ by 3′.

'Girard Unsurpassable'—Rose-pink flowers, compact with good dark green foliage, hardy.

'Girard Variegated Gem'— Bright rose-pink flowers, profuse flowering, a beautiful dwarf, 24″ by 30″ high, leaves are wavy, narrow, with a white margin along its edge, has more definition than other variegated azaleas.

'Girard Variegated Hotshot'—White- and green-variegated foliage and ruffled red flowers similar to 'Hotshot', a vigorous low compact plant.

'Girard Yellow Pom Pom'—Large, beautiful, double, fragrant, yellow flowers, forming a tight high truss approximately 5″ across and 3 1/2″ high, early May, long lasting, compact habit, some mildew resistance.

Deciduous types:

'Girard Crimson Tide'—Large double red flowers on a tight round head, vigorous grower and excellent flowerer.

'Girard Mount Saint Helens'—A blend of pink, salmon, with yellow and orange blotch exploding from all copper flower petals, very large trusses, 5″ by 6″, holding 12 to 15 large flowers of heavy texture, upright with good foliage that holds well until winter.

'Girard Red Pom Pom'—Fragrant, double red, forming a tight long-lasting truss, 3 1/2″ long and 4 1/2″ wide, compact, mildew resistant plant.

'Girard Salmon Delight'—Vivid rose flushed with yellow, flowers 2 to 1/2″ diameter with 25 to 30 flowers to each 5 to 5 1/2″ diameter truss, leaves medium green turning to yellow with orange tints, broad upright growth habit, appears mildew resistant.

'Girard The Robe'—Large, 2 1/2 to 3″, pink flowers, bright green foliage with white margin, dense, somewhat upright shrub, 3 to 5′ high.

'Girard Variegated'—Lipstick orange-red flowers, mid-spring, white-variegated foliage, low semi-deciduous shrub.

'Girard Wedding Bouquet'—Unique apple blossom pink hose-in-hose frilled flowers, 18 to 25 per truss, fragrant, medium growing.

'Girard White Clouds'—Seedling white, vigorous.

GLENN DALE HYBRIDS

Cold hardy for the Middle Atlantic States with flowers as large and as varied as those of the Southern Indica Azaleas! That was the aim of B.Y. Morrison, former head of the Plant Introduction Section at Glenn Dale, MD. The project began around 1929. To achieve that goal he selected and named 454 Glenn Dale Hybrids from 70,000 seedlings. Some of the hardiest will withstand –10°F, however, they are often listed as flower bud hardy to 0°F. Flower from (April in Zone 7b) May into June. Many have flecks or occasional stripes of a deeper complementary color that add considerable visual interest. Some will sport and produce branches with flowers that can be distinctively different in pattern and color.

'Alight'—Orange-pink.

'Amy'—Pink flowers in spring, vertical habit, 6′.

'Angela Place'—Pure white, wide open flowers with almost no blotch, late May into early June, dark glossy green leaves, spreading to 4′.

'Aphrodite'—Rose-pink, single, 2″ diameter flower.

'Artic'—White.

'Aztec'—White.

'Baroque'—White flowers with striping of phlox-purple, broad-spreading, to 5′ high, dark green leaves.

'Beacon'—Scarlet.

'Boldface'—White center with lavender margin.

'Bountiful'—Frilled, phlox purple flowers, early June, bushy habit to 4′.

'Bridal Veil'—Starry white flowers with a touch of green on the upper lobes, early May, to 5′.

'Buccaneer'—Orange-red.

'Burgundy'—Deep burgundy red, a little later than 'Carmel' in early May.

'Cadenza'—White with purple flecks, mid-season.

'Carmel'—Spinel red with a blotch of Indian red dots, carries in garden effect as a burgundy red, very effective as accents to masses of light colors, tall and spreading.

'Cascade'—White, spotted rose-pink, hose-in-hose, 1 1/2″ diameter, 4′ by 4 to 6′.

'Colleen'—Pink.

'Copperman'—Orange-red, single flowers on medium-size, spreading, dense plants.

'Dayspring'—Pink.

'Delaware Valley White'—White, single, 2″ diameter, one of the more common forms in commerce, mid-season.

'Delilah'—Begonia rose.

'Delos'—Rose-pink.

'Dimity'—Flowers are 2″ wide in combinations of reddish pink stripes and flecks on white, upright-spreading plant.

'Dragon'—Extremely floriferous, brilliant red with flowers 2″ across, dense and twiggy habit to 5′, mid-season.

'Driven Snow'—Pure white flowers, 6′ high.

'Eros'—Pink.

'Evensong'—Rose-pink.

'Everest'—White with pale chartreuse blotch, floriferous, 5′ high.

'F.C. Bradford'—Deep rose-pink with darker edges, blotch of purplish red dots, 5′ high.

'Fanfare'—Pink, hose-in-hose.

'Fashion'—Two inch diameter orange-red, hose-in-hose flower, medium-sized shrub, 6′ by 6′, 0°F.

'Fawn'—White center, pink margin.

'Festive'—White striped with red.

'Glacier'—White petals with faint green tone to the throat, to 3″ in diameter, vigorous grower to 6′, erect to spreading habit, handsome lustrous foliage, one of the best Glenn Dale's, used frequently in the South.

'Gladiator'—Orange-red.

'Glamour'—Rose-red flowers 2 to 3″ across, mid-April to early May, dark green leaves turn bronze in fall.

'Grace Freeman'—Pale pink.

'Greeting'—Ruffled coral-rose flowers, glossy dark green persistent leaves, erect-spreading, to 4′ high.

'Guerdon'—Light lavender with a lavender-rose blotch, low-spreading, to 2′ high.

'Helen Close'—Large, white flowers open with a very pale yellow blotch which fades to white, habit is dense and twiggy to 4′, mid-season.

'Helen Fox'—Light pink with irregular white margins, mid-June.

'H.H. Hume' (USDA, Beltsville hybrid)—White, with faint yellow throat, hose-in-hose, erect-spreading habit, 0 to 10°F.

'Illusions'—Lovely soft shades of pink, one of the hardiest, to 3′ high.

'Jessica'—Rose-pink.

'Joya'—Rose-pink.

'Jubilee'—A lovely coral pink in early June, low-spreading to 3′.

'Louise Dowdle'—Tyrian-pink.

'Manhattan'—Bold rose-pink flower, spreading to 4′, wider than high, hardy.

'Martha Hitchcock'—White flowers with purple edge.

'Mary Margaret'—Orange-red.

'Masquerade'—White, striped with pink.

'Melanie'—Rose pink, hose-in-hose with rose blotch, upright-spreading, 5′ high.

'Moonstone'—Profusion of cream-yellow flowers, compact mound, semi-dwarf.

'Morning Star'—Deep rose.

'Nectar'—Fragrant orange-pink.

'Niagara'—Exceptionally fine large, frilled, white flowers with a chartreuse blotch, dense growing, 3′ high.

'Nocturne'—Large, vivid purplish red with darker blotch flowers, early-flowering, broad-spreading, reaching 5′.

'Pearl Bradford'—Large, purple-pink flowers, broad-spreading.

'Pearl Bradford Sport'—Result of a "witches' broom" that occurred on a plant of 'Pearl Bradford', very petite and dense in foliage and habit, flowers are the same as 'Pearl Bradford'.

'Picotee'—White flowers with purple picotee edges, broad-spreading.

'Pink Ice'—Large, open-faced, double, light pink flowers with occasional spots and flecks of purple, spreading, 4′.

'Pinocchio'—White, striped red.

'Pixie'—White flowers with occasional stripes of bright pink, broad-spreading, 5′ high.

'Polar Sea'—Frilled white flowers with chartreuse blotch, low-spreading, 3′ high.

'Radiance'—Deep rose-pink.

'Refrain'—Rose-pink with white margin, hose-in-hose.

'Rosalie'—Bright rose flowers with dark green leaves, late May, spreading to 4′.

'Sagittarius'—Fine pink with salmon undertone, low-spreading, 2′ high.

'Sea Shell'—Deep rose-pink.

'Seafoam'—Frilled white flowers with chartreuse yellow throat, broad and low growing, 3′ high.

'Silverlace'—White with a green blotch, a few purple stripes, broad-spreading, 5′ high.

'Snowclad'—White with ruffled margins and a chartreuse blotch, low-spreading, 3′ high.

'Sterling'—Deep rose-pink.

'Suwanee'—Rose-pink.

'Swansong'—White with yellow blotch, early to mid-June, dwarf, dense and twiggy to 3′.

'Swashbuckler'—Red.

'Treasure'—White with very light pink edge, single flowers borne on spreading vigorous plants.

'Trophy'—Shell pink, very large, heavy informal double.

'Ursula'—Pink.

'Vespers'—Frilled white with chartreuse throat, broad-spreading, 5′ high.

'Vestal'—Large white flowers with chartreuse blotch, wide-spreading habit, 4′ high.

'Violetta'—Light mallow-purple.

'Wavelet'—Bowl-shaped, white flowers, yellow blotch, early June, 4′.

'Wildfire'—Red.

'Zulu'—Very large, purple flowers with a showy blotch of purple dots, mid-May, to 5′, colorful fall foliage.

GREENWOOD HYBRIDS

'Maria Elena'—Ideal for temperate, moist climates, double flower is a strong purplish pink and appears in late May, at maturity the plant is broad and rounded, approximately 3′ high and wide.

'Nancy'—Double, purplish red flowers are often over 2″ across, late-flowering, rounded habit.

'Popcorn'—Sweet-scented white.

'Red Beauty'—Astonishingly large, bright red flowers up to 5″ across, long lasting semi-double to double flowers.

'Su-Lin'—Large, deep red flowers which are waxy and beautiful, lovely green foliage all summer, easy to grow.

'Tina'—Rounded, very compact, dwarf plant, strong purplish-pink, hose-in-hose flowers in early April.

HARRIS HYBRIDS

'Bruce Hancock'—An azaleadendron with 'White Gumpo' and *R. keiskei* as parents, cascading branches, reaches a height of 4′, white, 3″ flowers bordered in pink, -10°F.

'Fascination'—Flowers red at the outer edges with a pink center, deep green, luscious foliage in summer.

'Joan Garrett'—Salmon-colored, 5″ flowers, rounded lobes, 3′ spreading plant.

'Miss Susie'—Bright red, hose-in-hose flowers, strong growing, very compact, 3′ plant, foliage shiny green in summer and reddish bronze in winter.

'Pink Cascade'—An unusual salmon-pink azalea with long cascading limbs that make this an unusual hanging basket plant, also makes an excellent ground cover when planted on 3′ centers.

'Rain Fire'—Large flowers, up to 3″ across, May, flowers are red towards orange, single, with broad lobes, plant is mounding and 2′ at 10 years, withstands sun.

'Sue Bell'—Two tone flower of light pink with a distinctive darker pink border, plant forms a 3′, upright-spreading mound, rounded leaves.

HINES HYBRIDS

Crosses of Belgian Indica with Southern Indica, evergreen, vigorous, supposedly sun and salt tolerant.

'Cinnamon Sugar'—Single cinnamon-rose.

'Heather Lynn'—Double rose-purple which changes into white blushed lavender-pink with darker edges.

'Ida Marnion'—Double magenta.

'Jessie May'—Single to semi-double, purple with mottled throat and frilled petals.

'Jessie Shirar'—Undulate hose-in-hose, rose-red to pink.

'Lois Hines'—Frilled double, clear orange-desert rose with faint mottling.

'Stella Hines'—Ruffled single, Persian rose flowers.

'Stella Sue'—Ruffled, hose-in-hose, blush rose.

ILAM HYBRIDS

A strain of deciduous azaleas developed in New Zealand. Rather large flowers completely cover plants in early spring, as hardy as the Exburys, Knaphills and Ghents. Many of the plants produce fragrant flowers, have seen them in Wooster, OH where they were performing well, suspect -10 to -20°F flower bud hardiness.

'Copper Cloud'—Fragrant, deeply frilled orange, heavy flowering, medium habit.

'Ilam Carmen'—Large trusses of warm salmon with a huge marking of gold on the upper petals.

'Ilam Cream'—Huge, fragrant flowers of satin cream, kissed with pink, 5′.

'Ilam Yellow Giant'—Large, over 3″, yellow flowers with darker flare.

'Louie Williams'—Trusses of lush pink flowers, two-toned pink, with darker pink buds and a slight yellow marking in the throat.

'Maori'—Vivid orange flowers borne in huge, 10″ trusses, plant grows 3 to 4′ tall in 10 years.

'Martie'—Frilled dusky red.

'Peach Sunset'—Orange-pink suffused, early, brilliant color.

'Peachy Keen'—Fragrant, with subtle shades of peach-pink, compact semi-dwarf growth habit.

'Persian Melon'—Orange yellow, large trussed like 'Gibraltar', vigorous habit.

'Pink Williams'—Clear silvery pink, large slightly fragrant flowers, slow, compact-growing.

'Primrose'—Fragrant clear light yellow with golden flare, vigorous but lax grower.

'Red Letter'—Brilliant red, vigorous grower.

'Red Velvet'—Deep rich red, vigorous-growing, wide upright, red-purple fall foliage.

'Rufus'—Deep blood-red, foliage deep bronze.

'Spring Salvo'—Dense foliage, deep, full-bodied, reddish-orange flowers with a bright orange blotch on the upper petals are 3″ diameter in size and bunch together to form 7″ diameter trusses.

'Supreme'—Deeply fringed, brilliant scarlet flowers, late May.

'Yellow Beauty'—Brilliant yellow-orange flowers with a faint blotch and frilly edges, mid to late season.

INDICA TYPES: Evergreen

'Balsaminaeflorum' ('Rosaeflora')—Very low growing, large flowered, double, salmon pink.

'Flame Creeper'—Flowers are orange-red, becoming very popular as a ground cover.

'Jennifer'—Red flowers in spring, shows remontant flowering characteristics, evergreen, 5', a little more cold hardy than Indica types.

'Kate Arendall'—Large heads of white flowers in spring, dark green foliage, evergreen, 5', sister plant to 'Jennifer' and 'Rebekah'.

'Kozan'—Shell pink flowers, late May into June, evergreen, low and mounding.

'Macrantha'—Low, compact, double red, spreading growth habit, 3' high.

'Macrantha Double'—Pretty double orange-pink flowers on compact plants.

'Macrantha Orange'—Bright orange-red flowers produced late on medium-sized plants with bright green foliage.

'Macrantha Pink'—Bright pink flowers produced late on medium size plants with bright green foliage.

'Macrantha Red' ('Osakazuki' or 'Red Macrantha')—Large, red flowers, repeat flowering.

'Macrantha Salmon'—Single, salmon-pink flowers on medium-sized plants.

'Mrs. L.C. Fischer'—Red with darker blotch, single, hose-in-hose.

'Primitive Beauty'—White flowers in spring, similar to "spider" azaleas, evergreen, 5'.

'Rebekah'—Pink flowers in spring, vigorous, evergreen, 5'.

BELGIAN INDICA TYPES

These evergreen azaleas grow best when not exposed to direct sun. Small bushy plants are covered with bright green, lush foliage, an excellent background for spectacular masses of large flowers. Best in Zone 10 to 11, coastal California type climate; primarily greenhouse forcing types.

'Ambrosia'—Double, very dark red, prolific flowerer.

'Avenir'—Double, deep salmon-pink, large flowers.

'California Peach'—Large, double salmon-peach coloring, sport of 'California Sunset'.

'California Snow'—Double, pure white, large flowers.

'California Sunset'—Double, variegated white and deep pink, extremely showy.

'Charles Encke'—Variegated pink and white.

'Chimes'—Semi-double, dark red flowers, same as 'Adventsclocke'.

'Dr. Glazer'—Large, double, deep cardinal red.

'Eri'—Large, semi-double, mottled pink and white.

'Freckles'—Semi-double, hose-in-hose, delicate white, red mottling, profuse.

'Jezebel'—Semi-double, deep cardinal red, hose-in-hose.

'Kathryn Aileen'—Huge, single red.

'Leuchtfeuer'—Single to semi-double, vibrant red.

'Marie-Louise'—Single, white sometimes splashed with pink, sport of 'Charles Encke'.

'Memoire John Hearrens'—Double, white edged with dark cerise.

'Mme. Alfred Sander'—Double, cherry red.

'Mme. Petrick'—Double, red.

'Orange Chimes'—Semi-double, bright orange.

'Orange Sanders'—Double, orange sport of 'Fred Sanders'.

'Paul Schaeme'—Double, light orange.

'Professor Wolters'—Single, variegated rose-red and white, ruffled edge.

'Red Poppy'—Very large, single to semi-double, bright deep red.

'Rose Glow'—Large, single, rose-red.

'Salmon Solomon'—Salmon flowers.

'Satellite'—Frilly, double to semi-double, 4", white with large rays and stripes of a vivid deep pink flowers, plant is vigorous, upright-spreading.

'Tickled Pink'—Single to hose-in-hose, rose-pink, edged in white.

'Triumph'—Double frilled red.

SOUTHERN INDICA TYPES

Best azaleas for high light areas, in coastal plain of the Southeast, vigorous, upright growers to 5 to 10' high, profuse spring flowers, hardy to 20°F.

'Albert-Elizabeth'—White with orange-red edges.

'Brilliant'—Single, watermelon red.

'Daphne Salmon'—Salmon flowers.

'Dixie Beauty' ('Formosa Red')—A deep red sport of 'Formosa'.

'Duc de Rohan'—Single, salmon-pink.

'Elegans'—Light pink.

'Fielders White'—Large, single, frosty white, 2 3/4" diameter.

'Fisher Pink'—Pink flowers.

'Formosa'—Magenta with deep blotch, single, 3″ diameter flowers, large upright habit.

'G.G. Gerbing'—Pure white, single, 3″ diameter, sport of 'George L. Taber', more cold hardy than the typical Southern Indica.

'George L. Taber'—Very large, single, light orchid-pink, variegated, 3″ diameter, more cold hardy than most.

'Gulf Pride'—Light lavender, tall upright, mid-season.

'Hexe de Saffelaere'—Red, hose-in-hose.

THE 'IMPERIAL' FAMILY (Monrovia Nursery hybrid introductions)

Splendid varieties in exciting rich colors. Handsome, rich green foliage creates a lush, full plant, a pleasing mounded form. Generously covered with flowers in season and occasionally spotted with color throughout the year.

Imperial Countess—Single, hose-in-hose, deep salmon-pink, petal edges are crinkled, needs partial shade.

Imperial Duchess—Later than above, rose bud-shaped flowers open to bright pink, then become soft pink, form is double, occasionally single, hose-in-hose, needs partial shade.

Imperial Princess—Lovely, long-lasting, large, single, rich pink flowers.

Imperial Queen—Double, pink flowers.

'Iveryana'—Single, white with orchid streaks, mid-season.

'Judge Solomon'—Pink, single, 3″ diameter flowers.

'Lady Formosa'—Large, single, violet-red, weeping habit.

'Lawsal'—Salmon-pink, same as 'Daphne Salmon'.

'Little Girl'—Light pink, with silver tips to petals, double.

'Little John'—Large, single, burgundy red flowers, symmetrical form accented by eye-catching reddish purple foliage.

'Moss Point Red'—Large red flowers, broad-spreading habit, same as 'Triumphe de Lederberg'.

'New White'—White.

'Orange Pride'—Bright orange, single, listed also as 'Orange Pride of Dorking'.

'Phoenicia'—Single, lavender-purple.

'Pink Formosa'—A pink-flowered sport of 'Formosa'.

'Pink Lace'—Petite, single, very compact, light rose-pink.

'Plum Crazy'—Large, deep mauve, single flowers have white and lilac-pink marbling with a blush of pale mauve overtone.

'President Clay'—Orange-red, single, 2 1/4 to 3″ diameter.

'Pride of Dorking'—Single, brilliant carmine-red.

'Pride of Mobile'—Deep rose-pink, single, 2 1/2″ diameter.

'Prince of Orange'—Heavy-textured, orange flowers.

'Red Formosa'—Deep violet-red flowers, large dark green foliage.

'Redwing'—Red, hose-in-hose, 3 to 4″ diameter flowers.

'Reverie'—Single, violet-pink, mid to late season.

'Rosa Belton'—Cream with bright lavender edges, large, single, profuse.

'Rosea'—Semi-double, rose-red flowers open from rose-like buds.

'Southern Charm'—Large, single, deep rose, a sport of 'Formosa'.

'Star Trek'—White, with very pale green throat, formal double.

'White April'—Large, single, pure white.

'White Grandeur'—Snow white, large, double flowers.

KURUME HYBRIDS

'Amoenum'—Flowers rich magenta, hose-in-hose, old cultivar, hardier than most, see under *R. obtusum*.

'Amoena Coccinea'—Small, hose-in-hose, red flowers, densely twiggy, compact and low-growing, -8°F.

'Appleblossom'—Light pink.

'Better Times'—Pink, hose-in-hose.

'Bridesmaid'—Salmon.

'Christmas Cheer'—Red, small, hose-in-hose flowers produced on dwarf, medium-spreading plants.

'Coral Bells'—Coral pink, small, 1 1/2″ diameter, hose-in-hose flowers produced on dwarf, low-spreading plants, 3′ by 3 to 4′, one of the most commonly available.

'Delicatissima'—White flowers are flushed a delicate pink, profuse, upright-spreading.

'Eileen'—Blush pink, semi-double to hose-in-hose.

'Eureka'—Pink.

'Flame'—Orange-red.

'Hahn's Red'—Low growing, bright red flowers.

'Heather'—Attractive rose-lavender.

'Hershey's Red'—Early, large, 2″ diameter, bright red, hardier than most, probably to -10°F, common in trade.

'Hexe Supreme'—Crimson, medium, hose-in-hose.

'Hino Orange Sport'—Sport from 'Hinodegiri', salmon orange flowers in profusion mid-season.

'Hino-Crimson'—Brilliant non-fading crimson flower, single, one of the hardiest, low growing compact with small, deep glossy green leaves turning bronze in winter.

'Hinodegiri'—Vivid red, 1 1/2″ diameter flowers, dark green summer foliage turns wine-red in fall and winter, 3′ by 3 to 4′, flower buds test hardy to -8°F.

'Hinomayo'—Soft pink flowers in profusion, wide upright, slow-growing.

'Hinoscarlet'—Hose-in-hose, red flowers, wide upright plant, bronze-red autumn foliage.

'Ho-Oden'—Light lilac pink flowers with white edges and violet red blotch measure 2 1/2″, low-spreading plant.

'Kermesina'—Fuchsia pink flowers, vigorous, small growing plant, small leaves.

'King's Luminous Pink'—Brilliant contrast of luminous purplish-pink margins surrounding a white throat and starry white rays, hardy, 4 to 5′ in 10 years.

'Konohana'—Deep coral pink flowers marked with a purple blotch.

'Koromo Shikibu'—Lavender flowers have very narrow separate petals and measure 2 1/2″, upright-spreading plant.

'Massasoit'—Single red flowers on dwarf, dense plants.

'Mauve Beauty'—Mauve, hose-in-hose.

'Mildred Mae'—Pale lavender, large, single.

'Mother's Day'—Large, red flowers, wide-growing.

'Peach Blossom'—Pale salmon-pink.

'Pink Pearl'—Pink, medium-sized, hose-in-hose flowers on dwarf, upright plants.

'Red Bordeaux'—Red-orange.

'Ruth May'—Single, bi-color flower in pink and white, medium grower.

'Salmon Beauty'—Salmon-pink, hose-in-hose.

'Sherwood Cerise'—Single, cerise.

'Sherwood Orange'—Early, vibrant orange flowers, compact growth habit, originated at Sherwood Nursery, Oregon.

'Sherwood Orchid'—Reddish violet with a darker blotch, single.

'Sherwood Pink'—Single, pink.

'Sherwood Red'—Orange-red, medium-sized, single flowers on dwarf, low plants.

'Snow'—Pure white, hose-in-hose, vigorous grower, common.

'Snowball'—White, hose-in-hose flowers, glossy medium green leaves, broad-spreading plant.

'Sweetbriar'—Hose-in-hose, pale pink flowers flushed red with a darker blotch, wide, upright.

'Tradition'—Clear light pink, double.

'Vesuvius'—Salmon-red.

'Ward's Ruby'—Brilliant ruby red, single.

'Yoro'—Very long stamens peering out from the clear white flowers.

LINWOOD HYBRIDS

'Hardy Gardenia'—Abundant, white flowers resemble *Gardenia*, especially when just unfurling, dense shrub, flowers in mid-spring, handsome green foliage in winter, 2′.

'Janet Rhea'—Semi-double, hose-in-hose flower in variegated colors of salmon, pink and rose with white edges, dwarf spreading plant.

'Linwood Blush'—Salmon-pink, semi-double.

'Linwood Lustre'—White, semi-double.

'Linwood Pink Giant'—Pink, hose-in-hose.

'Linwood White'—Double, hose-in-hose, white flowers with no stamens, tall, mid-May.

'Little Gardenia'—"Witches' broom" of 'Hardy Gardenia', white, double flowers, tight growing dwarf plant, heart-shaped dark green leaves, 1/4 to 1/3 normal size, ultimate height is probably 2′.

'Opal'—Hardy, low-growing plant, bright lavender pink, double flowers spotted with red in the throat, often will flower again in the fall.

'Salmon Pincushion'—Luscious double, salmon pink.

'Slim Jim'—Double, pink, an upright grower.

LOBLOLLY BAY HYBRIDS

'White Frills'—White with yellow-green blotch, hose-in-hose.

MAYO HYBRIDS

'Princess Augusta'—A large grower with light pink hose-in-hose, 2 1/2″ diameter flowers.

MISCELLANEOUS AZALEAS

No clear cut home so they are included here in alphabetical order.

'A Little Bit More'—Rounded, pure white petals with an occasional fleck of pink, a low spreader, June into July.

'Abigail Adams'—Evergreen, large, bright pink flowers, wide-spreading mound-shaped, vigorous, named in 1994 for the Abigail Adams Historical Society of Weymouth, MA.

'Alice de Steurs'—Flower changes in shading from yellow to salmon, bearing a strong deep orange blotch.

'Amelia Becales'—A more compact version of the lovely 'Martha Hitchcock' with white flowers bordered in rosy lavender.

'Ami Gasa'—Vivid red with wide overlapping lobes, large flowers

'Anna Kehr'—Evergreen shrub, 4′, strong purplish-pink double, 2″ diameter flowers.

'Anna's Smile'—Lightly sweet-scented flowers turn peach-pink as they mature, rounded shiny green foliage, wide and upright-growing hybrid of the Ghent and sweet azaleas.

'Atrosanguineum'—Low to medium in height, with growth habit like 'Ward's Ruby' or 'Hino Crimson', excellent red flowers.

'Baby It's You'—Bright coral pink, with a deeper coral rose flare on the upper 3 petals, narrow, dark green pointed leaves, a low spreader, June.

'Baby's Blush'—White, star-shaped flowers with a light rose speckling in the blotch, slightly whiter with a less prominent blotch than 'Sweet Maiden's Blush', mid-May.

'Baltic Amber'—Rounded heads of golden yellow flowers in early June, blue-green leaves appear dusted with silver, wide and upright with stout branches.

'Barbara'—Single, rich pink, a selection of *R. tasaense*, evergreen.

'Brianne'—Sport of 'Girard Rose', similar to 'Silver Sword', hardier, with a thinner, longer dark green leaf with a whole margin, leaf is tinged pink during winter.

'Burning Bush'—Late flowering, red as blazes from its parents 'Satan' × red *R. calendulaceum*, large growing plant hybridized by Olin Holsomback, Georgia.

'Camisole Fuchsia'—Rich fuchsia purple, hose-in-hose with a lovely second swirl of petals underneath the first, early to mid-May, 3′ by 3′ in 10 years.

'Camisole Rose'—Hose-in-hose rose red, early May, 3′ by 3′ in 10 years.

'Canby'—Bi-color with yellow-orange flowers.

'Cape Cod'—Low-growing, spreading form, covered with pure white hose-in-hose flowers.

'Cardinal'—Scarlet red sport of 'Mother's Day', burgundy fall foliage, compact, early May.

'Carlson's Dusty Pink'—Soft subdued, or dusted, light pink flowers, mid-May.

'Carlson's Itsy Bitsy'—Glowing coral orange hose-in-hose flowers, glossy foliage, 18″ tall by 2′ wide in 10 years, mid-May.

'Carlson's Pink Postscript'—Specially selected to add pink shades to the palette of orange, red, and white azalea species that flowers late in the season.

'Carlson's Postscript'—Mixed shades of pink, yellow, cream, and coral that haven't yet been tagged for color.

'Cherry Delight'—Compact plant reaches 2 to 3′ in 5 years, strong cherry-red, single flowers in abundance.

'Cherry Drop'—Flowers bright red, tiny leaves are dark green and deciduous, buds in early spring are bright red, plant is 3″ tall and 8″ across in 8 years.

'Chippewa'—Frilly, 2 1/2″ diameter flowers of lilac-rose have a deeper blotch, flowers late, dense, upright plant, medium height.

'Choice Cream'—Early flowering, fragrant, clear lemon yellow, yellow flare, touch of pink in the tube, 5′ high.

'Come To Baby Do'—Coral pink with a subtle deeper flare, a low spreader, June.

'Cookie'—Large flowers, rose spotted with maroon, wonderful fragrance, large leaves, upright plant, to 4′.

'Corneille'—Soft, double, pink flowers late mid-season.

'Daviesii'—Fragrant pale cream flower with a yellow flare in late May.

'Debbie'—Small dark forest green leaves, deep, bright, blood red flowers, 2' high.

'Donald Waldman'—Large, showy, semi-double flowers, red center surrounded by a pink flare on each petal and a contrasting white margin, low and compact plant.

'Double Pink'—Double flowering pink, outer petals of the buds are a dark pink which open to reveal the pale pink petals of the inner flower, and each is finally topped with a flare of yellow.

Double Pink Hybrids—Fully double, ruffled, clear pink flowers, late April and early May, small, dark green summer foliage, becomes coppery bronze in winter, slow-growing, wide and upright, ten-year-old plant is 4' tall and 2' wide, mature plant will be 6' or more tall.

Double White Hybrids—Multi-petaled, white flowers in late April and early May, compact, upright and wide-growing, small dark green leaves, interior foliage turns yellow before dropping in fall.

'Early Erroll'—Star-shaped, white flowers with dark tipped white stamens, a few lavender specks in the throat, carries in the garden as white, early to mid-May.

'Early On'—Bright glowing coral pink, one of our earliest evergreen azaleas, 5' by 6' in 20 years, dark burgundy fall color.

'Eleanor Allan'—Masses of soft pink flowers with a slightly deeper pink throat, low-spreading, heavy flowering, mid-May.

'Face 'Em Down Pink'—Selected soft pink forms that have not yet been named.

'Face 'Em Down White'—Selected white forms that have not yet been named.

'Fairfax'—Large, heavy-textured flowers marbled pink and white, dense, low growth habit.

'Firecracker'—Vivid red flecks burst and sparkle from the pure white flowers with distinctive rounded lobes late in the season, low-spreading mound.

'Firestar'—Clear scarlet red with pointed petals, hardy, upright with bright orange-red and orange-yellow fall foliage, mid-May.

'Florence Waldman'—Large, semi-double, hose-in-hose, white flowers are sanded and spotted with red flecks, upright-spreading.

'Galle's Choice'—Fragrant, light yellow flowers with white throats and light pink tips on wavy lobes, mid-season.

'Gordon'—Single, medium red flowers, hardy, early May.

'Great Expectations'—Double, orange-red flowers in spring, compact to 4' high.

'Green Glow'—Each ivory petal is suffused with an incandescent green glow, intensified by a yellow green eye, long lasting flowers, double hose-in-hose, low plant with rounded leaves.

'Hamlet'—Salmon-orange flowers are blotched on the upper petal with a huge, dark, red-orange flare.

'Happy Days'—Deep violet-purple, double flowers, heavy flowering in spring.

'Hill's Bright Red'—Vibrant red flowers on red stems, dark green leaves with deeper veining, 3' high.

'I'll Be Damned'—Broad, mounded, dense plant, huge (to 5 1/2" diameter) petaloid and deeply ruffled pink and white flowers.

'Il Taso'—Rose-red flower has a strong hint of salmon throughout, hose-in-hose flowers open a warm light salmon and darken to nearly a salmon-red.

'In A Mist'—Fragrant, star-shaped, white flowers with a faint watercolor wash of pale lavender pink, mid-May.

'In The Pink'—A hardier star-shaped, white flower with a light lavender flush, speckled red-purple blotch, mid-May.

'Ivan D. Wood'—Vigorous plant, large trusses of pinkish-cream blending toward the center into deep glowing yellow, large foliage is attractive, good grower, 3' high.

'Jack A. Sand'—Beautiful double flower which is bright pinkish red on the edges melting into a lighter yellowish-pink in the center, orange-yellow blotch on the upper petal, flowers are frilled and fragrant.

'Jane Elise'—Dark pink flowers in June, mounded plant.

'Janice Lynn'—Large, pink, semi-double, hose-in-hose flowers have a red flare and flecks of rosy red spread over its many petals, low-spreading habit.

'John Eichelser'—Large, ball-like trusses of candy pink flowers in spring.

'Joseph's Coat'—Flowers open yellow, turn orange and then red, cross of *R. bakeri* × *R. viscosum*, floriferous.

'Judie's Pink Angel'—Large partially petaloid flowers in rich shades of pink with a deeper pink flare, late May.

'Kagura'—Hose-in-hose, rose pink flower has blended white throat and dark blotch, stamens are longer than the petals, early season flowering, medium size.

'Kazan'—Showy orange-red flowers in June, small pointed shiny dark green leaves, a unique dwarf.

'Kennedy'—Superb red-orange flower highlighted with a slight yellow-orange blotch on the upper petal, frilled on the edge.

'Kennell's Gold'—Apricot buds open to large fragrant golden yellow flowers with a touch of red in large, ball-shaped trusses, upright-spreading habit, good fall color.

'Keowee Sunset'—Medium pink flowers with a yellow-orange flare on the upper petal, red pistils and filaments, flowers appear mid-season, upright-spreading plant, *R. calendulaceum* and *R. periclymenoides*.

'Konningen Emma'—Light orange yellow when young to strong orange yellow and finally to a suffused yellowish pink with a strong orange blotch, 2 1/2″ flowers, tall upright plant, mid to late season.

'Koromo Shikabu'—Strap-like petals are purplish pink with darker tips, hairy leaves, spreading, late May.

'Lady Jayne'—Vivid yellow suffused with reddish-orange and marked by an orange yellow flare, large, fragrant wavy textured flower, low growing, reaching about 3′.

'Lemonora'—Flowers yellow with a tinge of pink, tall and upright to a height of 8′ by 6′.

'Li'l Darlin'—Very large, lavender pink flowers, mid to late June, low-spreading.

'Little Frosted Orange'—White flowers with orange frosted border, compact, spreading mound.

'Little Gem'—Blood red flowers, prostrate plant, glossy, deep green leaves.

'Lorna X'—Late, hot pink with double flowers, more compact and lower growing than Gable's 'Lorna'.

'Luminosity'—Large, luminous clear rose pink, deeper speckling on the upper petal, mid-May.

'Mme. Butterfly'—Beautiful white flushed lavender, single flowers, low-spreading, mid to late May, especially hardy.

'Majesty'—Dark wine-red flowers in May, long, glossy, rounded, deep green, evergreen foliage turns burgundy in winter and is well-retained, low and compact-growing, mature plant is wider than high.

'Margaret Douglas'—Large, red-margined flowers have pink centers, low-spreading habit.

'Mary Lou Kehr'—Lovely, double pink camellia type flowers with the added bonus of fragrance, good form to 5′, and a lovely tribute to Dr. Kehr's wife.

'Matthew's Memory'—Bright golden yellow flowers in a petaloid double, long-lasting form, plant habit is upright, vigorous growth.

'Melford Lemon'—Glowing yellow flowers have an apricot flare.

'Mike Bullard'—Striking hot pink, early flowering, tall.

'Mildred'—Orchid purple, single, flowers early season.

'Miss Susie'—Strong hose-in-hose red flowers on compact, dark green plants, mid-season.

'Missy'—White flushed pink with a distinctly deeper rose blotch, colorful.

'M.L. Webb'—Rounded trusses of salmon pink flowers, bright green wavy leaves turning to a brilliant red fall foliage.

'Moonlight Rose'—Luscious, wavy, pale pink flowers enhanced with a bright yellow flare, upright growing.

'Mt. Ranier'—Large trusses of white flowers accented by a dark yellow flare, light fragrance, floriferous, upright-spreading plant.

'Mount Seven Stars'—A very late flowering, fire engine red that holds its color well, foliage is outstanding, small heavy-textured leaves with brown hairs.

'Nancy Plent'—Rich pink, large flowers, medium height, as wide as tall, mid-May.

'Nanticoke'—Double white flowers with many varied markings of pink to light purple, low cascading branches.

'Nico Red'—Sometimes called simply 'Nico', deep red flowers mid-season, compact plant.

'Nudiflora Pink'—Subtle old-fashioned pink with an antiqued look, mid-May, very hardy.

'Olympic Sunrise'—Peachy pink, hose-in-hose flowers with an orange throat, upright-spreading habit.

'Orange Splendor'—Funnel-shaped, frilly-edged, vivid red-orange flowers, mid to late May, upright-spreading, hardy.

'Otome-No-Mai'—Grows 2 to 4′ high spreading to 4′, violet flowers in spring repeating sporadically through the growing season.

'Peggy Ann'—Charming white hose-in-hose flowers edged in raspberry pink, compact, early May.

'Penna'—Deep rosy pink double flowers, upright-spreading to 5 to 6′.

'Pennsylvania'—Deciduous, delicate-pink flowers the third week of July, each flower has an orange eye and remains colorful with a touch of sweet, fruity fragrance into early August, wide-growing, slow and upright, small, rounded, apple-green foliage turns a distinctive coppery yellow before dropping in autumn.

'Pink Clusters'—Densely clustered, ruffled, bright pink flowers in mid-May, each flower is heavy-textured and has an orange coloration on one petal, low-growing, dwarf and spreading, a 10-year-old plant is 18″ by 3′, small, dark green leaves are wide, oval-shaped, foliage retained all winter is bronze-red until warm weather returns.

'Pin Cushion'—Lavender hose-in-hose flowers, mature plant is a dense, low-spreading mass.

'Pink Patootie'—Slightly rounded flowers in a delightful shade of antique pink, warm faint golden speckling in the throat, mid-May.

'Pink Pockets'—Dusty pink with tight fitting hose-in-hose flowers in early May, low growing.

'Pink Radiance'—Radiant pink, long lasting flowers with a white stripe down the reverse center of each lobe, vigorous upright plant, rich red fall color.

'Pocahontas'—Dark red flowers, evergreen, small foliage.

'Polypetalum'—Brilliant orange flowers, corolla is not fused, instead the petals are mere strips of scarlet orange, hardy, flowers late.

'Pride of Lindenhurst'—Large, white hose-in-hose flowers are bordered in pink, low and compact plant.

'Prominent'—Dusty orange brick-red with a dark speckling on the upper petal.

'Pure Perfection'—Clear white hose-in-hose flowers with wavy petals have a touch of light green in the throat, low mounded habit.

'Purple Pinwheel'—Low, almost prostrate plant, rich purple flowers late in the season with each individual strap-like petal whirling about the center, hairy attractive leaves, vigorous plant.

'Quiet Thoughts'—Fragrant, yellow-orange flowers in late May, deciduous.

'Radiant'—Deep reddish-orange to almost brick red flowers.

'Red Fuzzy'—Evergreen ground cover, 1′ by 5′, red flowers in spring.

'Red Planet'—Bright medium red flowers, dark green foliage with a bronzy tint, vigorous grower with a bushy plant habit.

'Rising Star'—Huge orange flare set on a background of white, edged with a tinge of salmon.

'Rosalie Nachman'—Large, light shrimp pink flowers with a vivid pink blotch, low-spreading plant.

'Rosy Ruffles'—Full truss of frilly rose pink flowers, upright plant habit reaching about 6′ by 4′ in sixteen years.

'St. James'—Orange-red with red blotch and white center, large, tall, spreading plant, mid-season.

'Salmon Queen'—Salmon bud opening to warm peach, accented by a golden flare, as the flower ages, colors become muted, apricot-goldens to paler peach-yellow.

'Sandy'—Violet-scented, apricot-pink flowers with a yellow flare on the top petal, late June, wide mound form, glossy, rounded, dark green leaves with blue-green undersides.

'Saturnus'—Large reddish-orange flowers.

'Secret Wish'—Frosty white petals on puffy, double camellia-like flowers, vigorous, upright plant reaching 5′.

'Short Sheet'—Clear white with a subtle hint of chartreuse deep in the throat, late June into July, spreading to 24″ in 10 years but less than a foot high.

'Silver Slipper'—Shimmering light pink to white flower with an orange patch, late May, upright plant.

'Siskin'—Bright yellow flowers, late May and early June, robust, wide and upright-growing plant with stout branches, prominent winter buds, dark green foliage, mildew-resistant.

'Snowball'—A hardy white from Ohio, 3′, mid-May.

'Snowbird'—Powerfully fragrant white flowers appear in spring with or before the first leaves, compact habit.

'Soft Echo'—Double pink flowers, darker on the margins and lighter in the center, forming a ball shaped truss, 4 to 5′ plant is upright-spreading.

'Soft Shimmer'—Hose-in-hose flower that opens from soft pink buds to a white flower, touched on the outer edges with pink, while the inner petals of the flower are pure white, gradually the whole flower becomes pinker, until it is a soft pink throughout.

'Sport of Easter Parade'—Double, rose red with creamy white blotches.

'Stadtman'—Gigantic, fully double, creamy yellow flowers have a gold flare and a touch of red or yellow coloring on the petal tips, colorful fall foliage shadings of yellow or red.

'Starry Eye'—Star-shaped, white flowers kissed with a distinctive pink tip at the end of each petal.

'Stolen Kiss'—Medium pink, semi-double flowers enhanced by a golden flare, long flowering period, burgundy fall color, 6′, upright-growing plant.

'Summer Gold'—Slightly fragrant, yellow flowers have a darker yellow flare, large, dark green foliage, upright growing and vigorous.

'Summer Lyric'—Soft pink, star-shaped flowers glow with a yellow throat in June and July in ball shaped trusses, bright green leaves, vigorous growing larger plant.

'Summer Rose'—Dark, rose-pink flowers in June, long leaves on reddish stems, wide growing.

'Supersuds'—Large star-shaped white flowers with soft green-gold speckled blotch, mid-May.

'Susan Oliver'—A prostrate low spreader with double, lavender-pink flowers in late June, exceptional.

'Sweet Maiden's Blush'—White star-shaped flowers with rose purple speckling in the blotch, lavender and white stamens, mid-May.

'Sweet September'—Clear pink flowers and red stamens in September, upright habit, *R. prunifolium* × *R. arborescens* hybrid.

'Texas Pink'—Dark pink flowers in May, small, rounded, dark green foliage becomes reddish orange in autumn and is partially retained, dwarf-growing and mound-shaped, growing less than two inches a year.

'Thomas Jefferson'—Large, fragrant flowers with ruffled petals form full trusses of a soft salmon tone, symmetrical 4' mound in six years.

'Totally Awesome'—Large-flowered, brilliant yellow combined with light yellow, vivid reddish orange shading to the edges of the flower, stamens are often petal-like.

'Toy'—Olin Holsomback from Chickamauga, GA, hybridized *R. arborescens* and *R. viscosum*, heat and cold tolerant, late flowering, apple blossom pink.

'Vida Brown'—Ruffled deep rose pink hose-in-hose flowers, compact and low, neat, tight foliage, late May.

'Vinecourt Duke'—Double, dark pink flowers with a heavy substance, soft fragrance, clusters of ball-shaped trusses have as many as 50 to 55 flowers, plant is upright and floriferous.

'Vinecourt Troubadour'—Strong red, softly fragrant, double flowers appear in domed trusses in mid-May, free-flowering, dense, upright habit.

'Vineland Dream'—Bright pink flowers with a slight orange flare appear in full trusses of 20 to 22 flowers, very floriferous, dense upright habit.

'Virginia Knight'—Large, hose-in-hose, pink flowers with light red blotch.

'Viscosepala'—Extremely fragrant creamy white flowers, late May into early June, 5', upright-growing, red-orange fall foliage.

'Vyking'—Dark rose red flowers in late May, glossy, rounded leaves turn purple-red in fall, some remaining on branches in winter, wide-spreading and compact-growing.

'Wachet'—Rich pink, large flat single flower, ruffled margins, mounded, broad and dwarf.

'Washington State Centennial'—Flowers open light orange-yellow and pale to white, with a blotch of vivid glowing yellow on the upper petal, petals are frilled and the flowers are fragrant, leaves are very shiny and resistant to mildew.

'Weird-O'—White, strap-like petals that are twisted or turned so that no two flowers are the same, resembles a Witchhazel flower, vigorous growing.

'Whitestone'—Double white flowers, plant is upright in habit.

'Whitney's White'—Scented, single white flowers on a upright growing plant, hardy, late May.

'Williamsburg'—Hose-in-hose flowers of white marked with strawberry pink and occasional solid pink flowers, broad, glossy green mound, 3'.

'Wombat'—Salmon-pink flowers, low-spreading, leaves having brown hairs over deep green base color.

'Yachiyo Red'—Not red, but white with pastel pink frosting, variable rose pink markings, tiny dark green leaves, low and compact, June.

NUCCIO HYBRIDS

'Garden Party'—Pink with peach flare.

'Nuccio's Carnival'—Large, single to semi-double, rose-red flowers, vigorous, 3' high and wide, long flowering season.

'Nuccio's Happy Days'—Deep violet-purple double flower, heavy spring flowers.

'Nuccio's Pink Champagne'—Light pink, double, hose-in-hose.

'Nuccio's Wild Cherry'—Large single flowers, round petals of cherry red, rapid upright grower, height 3 to 5'.

PENNINGTON HYBRIDS

The late Ralph Pennington of Covington, GA produced these outstanding plants. A collection was housed at the University's Botanical Garden.

'Beth Bullard'—Spreading plant with dark green foliage, 4" diameter reddish pink flowers, an excellent low-growing azalea, 2 1/2' tall with a spread of 4 to 5'.

'KJP'—Flowers light pink with dark pink stripes, 4" diameter, foliage is like the Southern Indica, plants grow 5 to 6' high.

'Mrs. Anne G. Pennington'—A very late, variable pink and white flower with blotches on a low growing plant, a late edition of 'KJP'.

'Mrs. R.W. Pennington'—A bright red flower on a low, bushy plant.

'Pennington Purple'—An early, fragrant, lavender flower on a well-formed plant.

'Pennington Red'—A striking, early, all red flower on a medium shrub.

'Pennington White'—An early, 2" diameter, frilled, white flower that is the best of the early whites.

PERICAT HYBRIDS

The Pericat Hybrids are similar to Kurume Hybrids, with larger flowers.

'China Seas'—Pink.

'Dawn'—Phlox-pink.

'Distinction'—Salmon-pink, semi-double.

'Flanders Field'—Red.

'Fortune'—Red.

'Hampton Beauty'—Rose-pink.

'Hiawatha'—Hose-in-hose, red.

'Miss Augusta'—Hose-in-hose, 2″ diameter, red flower, late mid-season, grows 4 to 6′ high, introduced by the late C.S. McCorkle.

'Pericat Pink'—Pink.

'Pericat Salmon'—Salmon.

'Pericat White'—White.

'Pinocchio'—Rose.

'Sensation'—Violet-red.

'Splendor'—Phlox-pink.

'Sweetheart Supreme'—Small, semi-double buds resemble delicate rosebuds, blush pink at maturity.

'Twenty Grand'—Violet-red, semi-double.

POLLY HILL'S NORTH TISBURY HYBRIDS

Since 1957, Mrs. Polly Hill, Martha's Vineyard, MA has been testing and selecting Japanese azaleas that she has grown from seed. Her objective was to produce prostrate, hardy, evergreen forms for ground cover use. Low growing azaleas with trailing branches that cascade over rocks or walls make suitable ground covers. Most are hybrids of *R. nakahari*, a prostrate evergreen species, that may reach 2 to 5″ in height in 10 years. As hybrids they are hardier than the species, benefitting from available snow cover. Flower in May–June.

'Alex'—A dwarf sport of 'Alexander', petite, prostrate and red.

'Alexander'—A low-growing spreading azalea eventually reaching 18″ high, flowers are salmon-red and open in late May and early June, excellent ground cover plant, cold hardy between 0 and ‑10°F.

'Andante'—A small to medium compact plant with salmon-pink flowers.

'Bartlett'—Covered with flowers most of June, the lightly ruffled flowers are medium pink, low, dwarf habit, ‑10°F.

'Cornia Borden'—Pale pink flowers with a slightly darker blotch, slow-growing, upright-spreading habit.

'Flat Out'—Vigorous late flowerer that blankets the ground with white, a ground hugging spreader, a perfect complement to the North Tisbury Azaleas.

'Fuzzy'—Brilliant orange flowers, prominent pubescence on stems and leaves.

'Gabrielle Hill'—Light pink with a rosy crimson blotch, plant habit is airy, irregular and not too dense, original plant is 15″ tall and 5′ across.

'Hill's Single Red'—Salmon-red flowers on a compact, spreading plant.

'Hotline'—Large ruffled flowers, hot purple-red, 1 1/2′ by 4′ after 16 years.

'Jeff Hill'—Deep pink flowers, plant is rounded, semi-dwarf and branching well, 17″ tall by 26″ wide in 13 years.

'Joseph Hill'—Bright red flowers, 12″ tall by 42″ wide in 13 years.

'Lady Locks'—Fragrant, lavender frilled flowers with large sepals.

'Late Love' ('Summertime')—Bright pink flowers, the latest of the North Tisbury Hybrids.

'Libby'—A gorgeous fresh cool pink.

'Marilee'—Rose-red flowers, smoky purple-green leaves are retained well, 16″ tall by 50″ wide in 12 years.

'Michael Hill'—Late soft pink frilled flowers with dark throat, very dwarf and spreading, an excellent ground cover, 17″ tall by 45″ wide in 13 years.

'Midori'—Large, snowy white, wavy flowers, low-spreading, compact habit.

'Mount Seven Star'—A vivid red with wavy lobes on a low, dense plant.

'Mrs. Hill's Flaming Mamie'—Red flowers.

'Pink Pancake'—Large, bright pink, wavy flowers on one of the fastest growing of all the North Tisbury Hybrids.

'Red Fountain'—Flowers are a strong red on branches that reach up at first, then arch down in a conspicuous fountain-like curve.

'Susannah Hill'—Deep red flowers with petaloid stamens, plant forms a vigorous low mound, 15″ tall by 52″ wide in 12 years.

'Trill'—Large, ruffled, medium red flowers, 14″ by 28″ in 12 years.

'Wintergreen'—Deep pink to light red flowers in late June, forms a circular mound 15″ by 39″ wide in 12 years.

'Wintergreen' ("witches' broom")—A smaller leaved, more compact sport of 'Wintergreen', deep pink flowers in late June.

'Yuka'—Another of Polly Hill's best 'Gumpo' seedlings, large flowers, most are pure white, some are striped with soft pink, others are nearly solid pink, low growing.

'Yukette'—A dwarf sport of 'Yuka', smaller and more consistently white, late May into June.

ROBIN HILL HYBRIDS

After some 50 years of hybridizing and selecting, Robert Gartrell succeeded in taking the flower characteristics of the Japanese Satsuki azaleas and producing a group of evergreens that are as lovely but more hardy and dependable. Their flowers are exceptionally large, open-faced and late flowering. Most are in soft, muted pastel tones. Their habits are low and prostrate. Considered hardy in the range of 0 to 10°F.

'Antoine'—Soft shades of coral, pink, and light pink, large, hose-in-hose wavy flowers, June.

'Barbara M. Humphreys'—Pure white single flower covers bright green glossy leaves, one of the best.

'Betty Ann Voss'—Lovely double, light pink flowers on a plant that has a weeping habit and beautiful dark green foliage.

'Blue Tip'—Large, lavender flower with a white center.

'Chanson'—Pink, semi-double to double flowers.

'Cherie'—Deep reddish orange flowers in late May, double, hardy and compact, burgundy winter leaves.

'Christie'—Broad trumpet-shaped, pink flowers, low mounding growth.

'Congo'—Vivid reddish purple flowers on a dwarf spreading plant.

'Conversation Piece'—Single, rich pink, 4″ diameter flowers with dots, blotches, sectors of pink, red and white, all at the same time, on a low to medium shrub, 25″ by 28″ in 10 years.

'Dorothy Hayden'—Single, open-faced, white flowers with a distinct green throat, broader than tall, 15″ by 34″ in 10 years.

'Dorothy Rees'—Large, single, pure white flower with a green throat has ruffled margins.

'Early Beni'—Gorgeous coral-red, hose-in-hose, semi-double with extra petals, 28″ by 36″ in 17 years.

'Eliza Scott'—Upright habit and pale pink-red single flowers.

'Eunice Updike'—Dwarf mounded, pale scarlet double flowers.

'Flame Dance'—A single, large, tubular, red flower, weeping habit.

'Frank Arsen'—Pink and white flowers with yellow overtones.

'Frosty'—The pink, single flower with a distinct dark blotch has a frosty overtone.

'George Harding'—Vivid red flower with a white throat.

'Gillie'—Single, rose-salmon.

'Givenda'—Single, light pink.

'Glamora'—Large semi-double white flowers tinted lavender, 18″ by 36″ in 10 years.

'Glencora'—A medium red, double, 2 1/2″ diameter flower on a dwarf plant.

'Gresham'—A very large, strong pink flower that has variable stripes and sectors on a compact, dwarf plant.

'Greta'—A low mound that is covered with dark pink, single flowers with wavy margins.

'Gwenda'—Pale pink, ruffled, 3″ diameter flowers, semi-dwarf growth habit, 21″ by 36″ in 10 years.

'Hilda Niblett'—Absolutely perfect mounded growth habit and large pink and white flowers.

'Jeanne Weeks'—Fully double flowers of lavender-pink, opening flowers resemble rosebuds, compact mounded growth habit.

'La Belle Helene'—Strong pink flower that develops a white throat.

'Lady Louise'—Single to semi-double pink flower with a darker blotch.

'Lady Robin'—Single white with variable stripes and sectors of bright pink, some will be white flushed pink or pink with white margins, with or without stripes or sectors, broad sprawling growth, 21″ by 36″ in 10 years.

'Laura Morland'—Soft warm pink semi-double flowers with occasional darker stripes, compact growth, 16″ by 23″ in 10 years.

'Little Louise'—"Witches' broom" sport of 'Lady Louise', large pink flowers, dense small leaf mound.

'Maria Derby'—Bright red, double flowers, dense compact growth.

'Mrs. Emil Hager'—Semi-double to double "hot" pink flower that is more vibrant than most Robin Hills, 12″ by 19″ in 10 years.

'Mrs. Villars'—A white, frilled, single flower with occasional pink splashing.

'Nancy of Robin Hill'—Light pink, hose-in-hose flowers, broad growing, 16″ by 36″ in 10 years.

'Octavian' (Formerly 'Rosenkavalier')—A light creamy pink flower.

'Olga Niblett'—The two Nibletts are the last two Robin Hills Mr. Gartrell named, Olga is white with a yellowish cast and a yellow throat and is one of the best.

'Ormsby'—Deep salmon pink, double, late May into June, dense and upright.

'Palmyra'—Delicate medium pink flowers, tall habit.

'Papineau'—White flower with a pale green throat stands out against the vigorous green foliage.

'Pat Erb'—Double, blush pink flowers (June) look like tiny rosebuds, compact plant with tiny, shiny dark green leaves.

'Peg Hugger'—Soft pink, double flowers on a compact plant.

'R-01-09'—This unnamed plant has a small, white flower that opens with the Glenn Dales and Backacres.

'Red Tip'—Single, white flower with margin of strong rose-red.

'Redmond'—Flat-faced, large, red, single flower.

'Robin Dale'—Wavy petaled, white flower with a greenish throat, pink splashing throughout.

'Robin Hill Gillie'—Very ruffled, flat-faced, scarlet flowers with dark blotch, dense foliage, 14″ by 36″ in 10 years.

'Robin Hill T-12-2'—Large, ruffled, white with occasional light pink stripes and a soft chartreuse blotch, June.

'Robin Hill T-51-1'—Large, bi-color white flowers splashed with soft pink, accented with bright rose speckling in the throat and occasional deeper pink stripes and sectors, June.

'Robin Hill U-10-8'—Frilled white with a chartreuse blotch, late May, low-spreading.

'Roseanne'—Large, ruffled, white flowers with bright pink margins, broad-spreading.

'Sarah Holden'—Huge, white, single flower with ruffled margins.

'Scott Gartrell'—Orchid pink, hose-in-hose flower with a striking dark blotch.

'Sherbrook'—Large, single, lavender flowers.

'Sir Robert'—Variable flower patterns that range from white to pink, flowers over a long period.

'Spink'—Delicate pink flower, the earliest of all the Robin Hill.

'Talbot'—Light lavender pink with a greenish white throat and an occasional white margin, June.

'Tan Dilly'—Strong pink often shading to tan at the tips of the petals, irregularly double, early June.

'Turks Cap'—A bright scarlet single flower on an upright plant.

'Verena'—Soft lavender, single flower, rounded habit.

'Watchet'—A rich pink, large, flat, single flower with ruffled margins, small leaves and mounded habit.

'Wee Willie'—Purplish pink, single flowers with ruffled edges.

'Welmet'—Single, lavender-pink flowers are large and flat-faced, as plants age they develop a white center.

'Wendy'—Tinted strong pink with dark pink sectors, wavy petals, mounding growth habit, late June.

'White Moon'—A lovely low mounded plant with huge flat wavy flowers that occasionally sport red specks or marks.

'Whitehead'—Large, 3″, single, white flowers of great variability in various patterns of pink and white, shiny evergreen foliage, early June.

RUSTICA FLORA PLENO HYBRIDS

'Norma'—Late flowering double rose-red with a salmon glow and vivid stamens.

RUTHERFORDIANA HYBRIDS

Medium-sized flowers, 2 to 4′ high, shrubby, evergreen plants with showy spring flowers, require mid-day shade, hardy to 20°F in protected location.

'Alaska'—Semi-double, pure white.

'Dorothy Gish'—Orange-salmon, semi-double, hose-in-hose.

'Gloria'—Variegated sport of 'Dorothy Gish'.

'L.J. Bobbink'—Hose-in-hose, white with pinkish-lavender blush, 6 to 8′ high and spreading, mid to late season.

'Pink Ruffles'—Flowers pink-violet, semi-double, 2″ diameter.

'Red Ruffles'—Large, deep red, ruffled flowers.

'Rose Queen'—Double, rose-pink.

'Southern Belle'—Green leaves have creamy white margins, strong pink, hose-in-hose flower with a dark blotch, medium-sized, sport of 'Pink Ruffles'.

'White Gish'—White sport of 'Dorothy Gish'.

SATSUKI HYBRIDS

Satsuki azaleas are lovely treasures from Japan, Satsuke meaning fifth month, the basic flowering period for most varieties. They are excellent evergreen spreading shrubs of dwarf size, featuring many flower forms and many color combinations on one plant. Large flowers appear in mid to late May to June in the Athens area.

'Amagasa'—Deep pink, 3 1/2″ diameter.

'Aozora'—Pale pink flowers flecked and striped with dark pink, plant habit is low-spreading.

'Azuma Kagami'—Single, 2 1/2″ diameter flowers are light pink with many variations from deeper pink at the edges to a delicate blush pink.

'Balsaminaeflorum'—Late, double, rose flowers with 40 petals or more and no pistil or stamens, low compact.

'Banka'—White flower with flecks of pink or a solid pink border on six rounded lobes.

'Beni-Kirishima'—Double, orange-red flowers on a broad-spreading plant.

'Bunkwa'—Flesh pink flowers, 2″ diameter, low grower.

'Chidori'—Deep pink, single, 3 1/2″ diameter flower with an inner light star, crinkled margins are intriguingly ringed with wide vivid reddish purple bands, early season.

'Chinsei'—Salmon pink flowers, small dark green, long, narrow leaves.

'Chinzan' ('Chinsayii')—Warm pink flowers, outstanding shiny, pointed, little leaves, quite dwarf and compact.

'Chojuho'—Single, 1 1/2″ diameter flowers are made of sepals instead of petals, first flowers are brilliant red, changing to orange and light brown, and remain until winter, upright-spreading habit.

'Coral Cascade'—Large, single, coral-pink flower with white blotches, spreading, cascading branches.

'Daisetsu-zan'—Extremely large, white flowers with yellow-green centers adorn this dark green, heavy-textured plant, collected by Dr. John Creech from the nursery of Mr. Yoshiyuki Shibahata in Japan.

'Eikan'—Extremely variable, white, ruffled, 4″ diameter flowers with all combinations of pink and rose, vigorous, spreading plant.

'Eiten'—Mallow purple.

'Flame Creeper'—Orange-red, low, dense.

'Fuku Ro Kuju'—Pristine white flowers with an occasional red fleck, shiny dark green leaves.

'Geisha'—White flowers often streaked with reddish purple, wide upright.

'Geisha Girl'—Deep rose and white.

'Getsutoku'—Large, single wavy petals are white with variegation of pink and salmon stripes or solid colors of shade mentioned.

'Gumpo Fancy'—Low growing, small, narrow leaves, large, bi-colored flowers have slightly wavy, white margins and a pink center, late flowering.

'Gumpo Pink'—Most common Satsuki in South, soft pink ruffled petals on a compact plant.

'Gumpo Red' (sometimes listed as Red Gumpo)—Red, low-spreading, compact, late flowering.

'Gumpo Rose'—Darker rose flower, otherwise like above.

'Gumpo White'—Large single white frilled flowers with occasional purple flecks, dense habit, late flowering.

'Gunbi'—A sport of 'Gumpo' that is white with reddish flecks and stripes, large 3″ diameter flowers have ruffled lobes, compact habit.

'Gunrei'—Frilled showy white with pink flecks, low growing.

'Hakusen-No-Mai'—Semi-double white flower with green blotch, has the appearance of snowflakes.

'Haru-No-Hikari'—Huge salmon-white, variable, single.

'Heiwa'—White with shadings of pink and rose.

'Higasa'—Extremely large, 4 1/2″ diameter flat flower, deep rose-pink with paler pink on margins.

'Hitoya-No-Haru'—Large, rose-mauve variable single.

'Ho Koku'—Low, mounding plant, deep pink flowers, often surrounded by a prominent white border in June.

'Issho No Haru'—A variable flower of lavender and white with many forms and combinations.

'Johga'—White to light pink or purple, 2 1/2 to 3″ diameter flowers with occasional flecks of purplish pink, reddish dots in blotch, low mound, 2 to 3′ high.

'Juko'—Medium-large, single, wide pointed petals of light orchid-pink, speckled or striped with deeper pink, some solid flowers of pink or rose, or edged with white, small foliage, tight habit.

'Kaempo'—Late flowering dwarf hot pink, particularly showy, *R. kaempferi* × *R.* 'Gumpo'.

'Kayo-No-Homare'—Flower has a white center, bordered orange-red, with an occasional sport of white with pink stripes and deep pink solids, has slightly pointed petals, slow growing round habit.

'Kazan'—Showy, salmon-orange flowers, dwarf, foliage is waxy deep green.

'Keigetsu'—Light pink flowers and a striking red margin, green leaves are variegated with flecks of white, low-spreading plant.

'Keisetsu'—Strong red, 3″ diameter flowers with a light pink to white center, unusual variegated leaves.

'Kimi-Maru'—A light pink flower with deeper pink edges may have many variations, single with medium round petals, small leaves and a slightly open form.

'Kinpai'—Early flowering, white-centered flowers with variations of coral, buff or reddish-orange border, some flowers are solid red or orange.

'Kisarazu'—Clear white sometimes blushed pale pink with deeper pink margin flowers, late May into early June, compact.

'Kobai'—Large red flowers with occasional circles of white on six, round, overlapping lobes, descriptively called 'Red Plum'.

'Kokan'—Small, growing plant with a 1 1/2″ long leaf that curls inward, making a tubed leaf.

'Ko-Kinsai'—Lacy, coral salmon, single flower with split spider like petals, foliage is small and the plant has a low, bushy habit.

'Komeno No Yuki'—White with variable flakes, sectors and selfs of deep pink, low-growing, June.

'Kozan'—Small, delicate shell pink flowers with individual rounded petals, slow growing plant.

'Linda R'—Sport of 'Eikan', large, soft shell-pink, flat-faced, ruffled flowers, dense plant habit.

'Mai-Hime'—Extremely variable flowers, rose pink to white, low grower.

'Matsu No Hikari'—White and orange-red with variable stripes and sectors on 3″ diameter, ruffled flowers with overlapping petals.

'Matsuyo'—White flowers with selfs, flushes and streaks of strong pink, late June.

'Miyuno no Tsuki'—Flowers white with heavy stripes of reddish pink and occasional all pink flowers.

'Mt. Baldy'—Single white flowers with a white throat and rose marking, unusual dense foliage with leaves curved inward for a tube-like effect.

'Myogi'—Flowers are light pink with dark pink stripes and flakes, 'Gumpo' type compact growth.

'Negligee'—Pale pink, 2″ diameter flowers with a scattering of darker pink dots on the upper petal, very low, rounded mound.

'Nyohozan'—Soft pink flowers have deep pink to red spotting in the center, leaves are small and covered with hairs, slow growing, flowers appear large in scale to the leaves, compact plant.

'Orchid Empress'—Large, deep orchid, double flowers, dark green foliage, compact habit, mid-season hybrid introduced by the late C.S. McCorkle, 3 to 4′ high.

'Otome'—White flowers with many light pink and yellowish pink variations, even occasional stripes of salmon pink, slow growing habit, low to medium height.

'Rinpu'—Means "long lasting wind", leaves are curled, twisted and contorted as if blown by the wind, flowers are medium pink, with a darker flare, slow growing dwarf, to 1′ in 10 years.

'Rukizon'—Small salmon-red flowers on a dense small plant with tiny 1/2″ long leaves, also known as 'Kazan'.

'Sakuragata'—White petals finely edged in purple, very low-spreading, late June into July.

'Shiko'—Large, wide, lavender-pink, variable, single.

'Shinkigen'—White flower with many variations of sectors and marks of pink and red with round overlapping petals.

'Shinnyo-No-Tsuki'—Large, white centers, rose border.

'Shinnyo-No-Tsuki' (Sport)—Large with crimson blotches in the flowers, foliage with creamy stripes longitudinally throughout.

'Shira Fuji'—Unusual white markings on green foliage, white flowers, sometimes with purple.

'Shugetsu' ('Autumn Moon')—Large, 3 to 4″ diameter flowers are white with deep purple border, or variations of completely white or purple, taller than wide in habit.

'Shumpow'—Rose pink flower with purple or white variegations, good dense growth habit.

'Summer Sun'—Orange-red flower with pointed lobes, related to *R. indicum* or *R. eriocarpum*.

'Tai Fuki'—White flower that may be one-half bright red.

'Tochi-No-Hikari'—Low growing plant with extremely deep red, 4 to 5″ diameter flowers.

'Tsuki-no-Hitomaru'—Flowers peach, pink, and white with stripes, flecks and borders and rounded, slightly separate petals, vigorous, full and upright grower.

'Uki Funei'—Foliage variegated with spots and speckles of yellow, funnel-shaped flowers are generally white, but also developing stripes and spots of pink, low-spreading plant.

'Un-Getsu-No-Hikari'—Flower is salmon-pink edged with a spotted coral red throat and has small, single, pointed petal, slow growing.

'Unzon Tao Tsigi'—Small leaves, low-spreading plant, small pinkish flowers.

'Wakaebisu'—Light salmon-pink flowers with deeper pink dots in the blotch.

'Yachiyo Red'—Flower is frosty white with a beautiful pastel pink blush, variable rose pink markings occur as streaks, spots and along the margins of the petals, plant is low and compact.

'Yaye'—Large ruffled white, chartreuse throat and occasional salmon stripes, late May into June.

SLONECKER HYBRIDS

'Chetco'—Bright yellow flowers, orange blotch.

VUYKIANA HYBRIDS

Several plants were growing in Mt. Airy Arboretum, Cincinnati, OH before -25°F obliterated them, probably -5 to -10°F at best.

'Double Beauty'—Large, double, deep rose flowers, fast grower, sport of 'Vuyk's Rosy Red'.

'Palestrina'—Super hardy, strong, upright, large specimen, single, white flowers have a large, yellow-green flare and a soft fragrance.

'Vuyk's Rosy Red'—Rosy pink, wavy margined flowers in May, dark leaves, tidy habit on a 2' mounded plant.

'Vuyk's Scarlet'—Bright scarlet-rose flowers, large, deep glossy green leaves, excellent plant habit.

'Wilhelmina Vuyk'—Ivory-white, tall growing.

WINDSOR HYBRIDS

Originally from Windsor Great Park/Savill Gardens in England. Introduced into the US by Wells Nursery, Penrose, NC.

'Burning Light'—The award form from Windsor bears stunning coral red flowers with an orange throat.

'Windsor Appleblossom'—An unusual multi-colored specimen that ranges from cream to deep pink, with a compact shape.

'Windsor Buttercup'—Brilliant clear yellow, heavy flowering, excellent shape.

'Windsor Daybreak'—A blend of dawn colors that is most fascinating, with a compact shape.

'Windsor Peach Glow'—A superb orange yellow, with an upright habit.

'Windsor Pink Souffle'—An extremely vigorous plant with soft pink flowers, trusses are large.

'Windsor Ruby'—A compact plant with large, deep red flowers.

'Windsor Sunbeam'—A darker yellow than 'Windsor Buttercup' with good shape and heavy flowering capabilities.

Rhododendron Hybrids

DEXTER HYBRIDS

Many of the rhododendrons that Charles O. Dexter of Sandwich, MA created from 1921 to 1943 were of a quality that had not previously been available. Noted for their fine, dense foliage, large stature and wonderful flowers and colors. Precise records of his crosses do not survive, but he appears to have used at least the following species: *R. decorum*, *R. discolor*, *R. griersonianum*, *R. haematodes*, and *R. fortunei*. The influence of *R. fortunei* is dominant in his plants, so much so that all widely distributed Dexter hybrids are referred to as Fortunei Hybrids. Hardy in the vicinity of -10°F and depending on cultivar has 5°F leeway from this number. Significant collection of Dexter hybrids at Heritage Plantation, Sandwich, MA which was the home of Mr. Dexter. Mid-May to mid-June is the optimum time for experiencing the rhododendrons in flower.

'Ben Moseley'—Slightly frilled, bright pink flowers with dark blotch.

'Betty Arrington'—Large, conical trusses of fragrant, pink flowers accented by ruby markings in the upper petals.

'Betty Hume'—Large, frilly, pink flowers, slight fragrance, large, bold foliage, compact, mounding plant to 6'.

'Brown Eyes'—Hardy pink with a brown blotch, introduced by Paul Bosley, Sr., Mentor, OH.

'Champaign'—Opulent creamy yellow, overlaid with pink, to 4' high.

'Dexter's Champagne'—Apricot flowers, spreading habit, olive green foliage.

'Dexter's Count Vitette'—Mound-like plant, multi-branched, spreading habit, pale lavender flowers, full trusses.

'Dexter's Giant Red'—Large, red-orange flowers fade to crimson with deep red and lighter red spots throughout, vigorous, upright habit.

'Dexter's Purple'—Lovely lilac-purple flowers of excellent substance.

'Dexter's Spice'—Extremely fragrant, large white flowers gently spotted with green on a full, lush plant.

'Dexter's Vanilla'—Delicate fragrance, multi-colored pink and white flowers, light bluish green foliage.

'Dexter's Victoria'—Frilly, deep pink with deeper throat flowers, mid to late May, 4' by 4' in 20 years.

'Dorothy Russell'—Rounded mounding habit, glossy foliage, rose-red flowers.

'Edgemont'—Large, rosy pink flowers, large growth habit.

'Frances Shannon Racoff'—Deep purplish pink shading to lighter pink in the throat, glossy dark green foliage, 8' by 10' in 25 years, from Winterthur, -15°F.

'Gi-Gi'—Rose-red flowers covered with deep red spotting.

'Gloxineum'—Prolific flowering with enormous pastel pink flowers.

'Governor's Mansion'—Found by Dexter at the governor's mansion in Asheville, NC, royal purple flowers have a bronze-yellow throat, glossy dark green foliage.

'Great Eastern'—Large light pink flowers, petals edged in light red, deeper red throat, floriferous, hardy.

'Hal Bruce'—Soft pink buds open to light cream-yellow with slight pink highlights, glossy dark green leaves, 8' by 5' in 25 years, named for former Winterthur garden curator, -15°F.

'Josephine Everitt'—Free-flowering, pure pink flowers, with a definite lighter center, well-shaped trusses, vigorous growing.

'Kelley'—Light red flowers with attractive dark spotting on all petals, medium growth habit.

'Lady of Belfield'—Late flowering, pink flowers with darker blotches adorn this tall pyramidal plant, magnificent foliage, 6' high.

'Merley Cream'—Large, creamy white flowers with a yellow flare, rounded, well-formed plant, medium green leaves.

'Mrs. W.R. Coe'—Intense pink.

'Parker's Pink'—Deep pink flowers shading darker at the margins and lighter near the center for a near bi-color effect.

'Paul R. Bosley'—Pink with a red blotch, mid-May, long, dark green, recurved foliage.

'Pink Satin'—Deep, rich pink flowers with a satiny finish, large trusses on a compact plant.

'Powder Puff'—Candelabra effect as rosy buds elongate and open to soft lilac-pink, outstanding in the garden.

'Sagamore Bayside'—Ball-shaped truss of lavender-pink flowers, wavy edges, yellow green spotting and stripe down the center, late May.

'Scintillation'—The best known of all Dexter rhododendrons and the most common in cultivation, luminous light pink flowers with an amber throat, good substance and heat resistance, lustrous dark green leaves on a compact plant, 6' high, excellent form and has performed magnificently in Zone 7b.

'Skyglow'—Peach-edged pink.

'Todmorden'—Strikingly intense rose-pink and white flowers giving nearly a bi-color effect, tall growing.

'Tom Everett'—Frilled soft sensuous pink with pale yellow throat, extremely floriferous, low-spreading growth.

'Warwick'—Mauve-pink.

'Wheatley'—Frilled vivid pink flower with yellow blotch.

'Wissahickon'—Bright rose.

'Wyandanch Pink'—Shiny bright pink flowers, handsome rugose and convex leaves on an upright plant, 6' high, quite hardy.

'Zoë Graves'—Mauve with deep red blotch, glossy dark green leaves, 10' by 6' in 25 years, Winterthur introduction, -15°F.

LEACH HYBRIDS (Rhododendrons and Azaleas)

Hybridized by the late Mr. David Leach, North Madison, OH, possibly the world's greatest authority on the subject. Mr. Leach was extremely discriminating and did not introduce a new cultivar unless it met rigid standards for quality of flower, foliage, habit, and hardiness.

'Anna H. Hall'—A semi-dwarf, apple blossom pink and white.

'Argentina'—Bright rosy red flowers, ball-shaped trusses of 25 flowers, well-shaped vigorous plant.

'Bali'—Soft pink flowers with a creamy yellow throat, 6 1/2' by 9' in 30 years.

'Bangkok'—Orange blended into pink, hardy to -15°F.

'Borneo'—Amber-colored flowers, unique blend of orange, yellow, and red.

'Bravo'—Hardy deep pink, described as "a huge, blowzy, Rubenesque sort of rhododendron with buxom trusses."

'Brittany'—Flowers open pale yellow, transform into two shades of pink, densely foliated, perfect mound, small, rounded leaves.

'Burma'—Cardinal red flowers, broad-spreading habit.

'Canary Islands'—Deepest yellow flowers to date, handsome foliage, mounded specimen.

'Casanova'—Pink buds, long lasting, yellow flowers, glossy leaves, extremely fertile, 4 to 5'.

'Dolly Madison'—Early flowering white, strong, tall grower, very hardy.

'Edmond Amateis'—Pure white with a bold red blotch emphasized by twin rays, glossy leaves, upright dense plant.

'Figi'—Claret rose-colored flowers with a yellow-orange tone to the throat, late-flowering, spreading habit, matte green leaves.

'Finlandia'—White flowers form ball-shaped trusses opening from pink buds, recurved, glossy leaves, well-branched, rounded plant, excellent hardiness.

'Golden Gala'—Creamy white flowers having a faint greenish throat, buds first show as magenta-rose, then open to a warm cream, deep forest green leaves, hardy, rounded shrub, to 3'.

'Hawaii'—Frilly, deep rose-pink flowers open in May with an almost iridescent glow, compact 4' plant, very good foliage.

'Hindustan'—Warm orange flowers are flushed with soft pink, dome-shaped trusses, wavy edges of the petals give a frilled effect, leaves twice as long as wide, deep fir green, plant grows as wide as tall, hardy to -10°F, 6'.

'Hong Kong'—Pale yellow.

'Ivory Coast'—White flowers with a warm ivory cast in April, small leaves that are chartreuse green in summer with a gold cast in winter, hardy, 3' by 3' in 10 years.

'Janet Blair'—A lovely lavender-pink flower with a greenish throat, 6' high, -10°F.

'Jeric(h)o'—P.J.M. type, small leaves, mounding habit to 3' by 5', soft yellow flowers in late April.

'July Jester'—Red, late flowering.

'July Jewel'—Blazing scarlet flowers in July, small plant, mildew-proof, matte green foliage, matures at 3'.

'July Jubilation'—Fragrant, bright red flowers with a light orange blotch, mid-July, branches well, matures at 3'.

'Last Hurrah'—Saucer-shaped, white flowers in September–October, complete trusses, habit is very low, growing three times wider than tall.

'Lodestar'—Large white flowers with a prominent flare of green-gold flecks, dense foliage.

'Madrid'—Dark pink with maroon blotch, 5' by 6' in 10 years.

'Malta'—Small leaved form with small semi-double rose-like pink flowers.

'Mist Maiden'—Rose-colored buds open apple blossom pink and fade to white, a slightly faster growing form with beautiful indumentum.

'Monaco'—Warm yellow flowers framed by a rosy red reverse and deepened by an olive-yellow flare, broad and rounded plant, narrow leaves.

'Montego'—Violet purple flowers deepen to darkest magenta with a green flare, ball-shaped trusses, dark green leaves, colorful reddish stems.

'Monterey'—Bright pink luminous flowers with a lighter center, broad and compact, free-flowering, hardy.

'Nepal'—White flowers emerge from rose pink buds, leaves are dark green with a slight wave, hardy, 6'.

'Nile'—Light yellow.

'Normandy'—Bright rose pink with deeper edges and tangerine spotting, broad to 4', late May.

'Nuance'—A pastel blend of yellow, orange and pink.

'Persia'—Reddish purple flowers have bold, yellow-green spotting, almost conical habit, hardy, 5'.

'Pink Flourish'—Large trusses of brilliant pink flowers shading to a lighter center and sporting a small, golden flare, vigorous grower.

'Pink Plush'—One of the smaller flowered, more dainty azaleas, flowers late, flowers of rose pink with deeper orange-rose on the upper petal.

'Pink Puff'—Small airy flowers of soft rose-pink with a showy golden yellow flare on the upper petal, late-flowering, deep green foliage.

'Red River'—Radiant red flowers with lighter centers in full pyramidal trusses appearing very late in the season, large leaves, vigorous growth habit.

'Rio'—Large, salmon pink flowers shading darker at the edges and enhanced by a golden yellow throat, in full trusses, glossy leaves, compact broad plant.

'Samoa'—Bright red flowers that are faintly spotted on the upper petal, compact plant, to 5'.

'Senegal'—Light yellow, open-faced flowers, small-leaved plant, rounded, mounding habit reaches 3' by 3' at maturity.

'Serenata'—Large trusses of light orange flowers with heavy substance, upright-spreading habit.

'Shanghai'—Vigorous, hardy hybrid, 6', large, pale pink flowers are edged with a deeper pink and a strong spot of orange yellow on the upper petal, up to 18 flowers in a tight round truss, narrow, good looking foliage.

'Small Wonder'—Compact, brilliant red.

'Spellbinder'—Tightly formed trusses of light pink, ruffled flowers marked with a spattering of red, heavily textured, unusually shiny leaves, free-flowering, well-rounded, tall grower.

'Spring Frolic'—White flowers emerging from pink buds, broad-rounded plant, dense, well-retained foliage.

'Sumatra'—Clear scarlet, dwarf, densely foliaged.

'Summer Glow'—Late-flowering, large trusses of incandescent pink flowers in summer, vigorous.

'Summer Snow'—Late-flowering with white, funnel-shaped flowers, large, vigorous grower.

'Summer Summit'—Large plant with a vigorous habit, large trusses of ruffled, white flowers in July, height to 8'.

'Tang'—Hardy, opens orange with a darker reddish orange margin, upright-growing.

'Tennessee'—Buds of strong purple-pink open to light purple-pink flowers that change to pale yellow-pink with a bold dorsal blotch of red, smooth, elliptic foliage.

'Tow Head'—Low-spreading and rounded to 2', smothered with creamy yellow clusters of flowers in early May.

'Trinidad'—An ivory center is surrounded by a bright cherry-red edging, showy but not strident, flowers open in mid-season in large trusses on a spreading shrub.

'Tuscany'—Sister of the well-known 'Party Pink', flowers of soft pink accented by a red blotch, good foliage and plant habit, 5'.

'Vernus'—Light pink flowers with darker centers, early May, 6'.

MEHLQUIST HYBRIDS

'April White'—Beautiful double, white flowers on a medium growing, upright plant with relatively small leaves, leaves hold 2 to 3 years, change to yellow when senescing, 3'.

'Connecticut Yankee'—Large, vigorous, deep purplish blue, greenish, yellow-splotched flowers, tight dome-shaped trusses, hardy, 5'.

'Dorothy Swift'—Compact habit, dark foliage with heavy beige indumentum, flowers are pink in bud and open a lovely soft pink, hardy, compact habit.

'Firestorm'—Scarlet red flowers, dark green foliage, early June, compact, 6', twice as wide as high, see *HortScience* 27(5):480–481 (1992).

'Gustav Mehlquist'—Clear red flowers, grows 3 to 4' tall by 4 to 6' across.

'Ingrid Mehlquist'—Exceptional foliage with light indumentum on the underside of the leaf, buds heavily, pink buds open to pristine white flowers with faint crimson spotting on the upper petal, 3'.

'Scarlet Romance'—Bright red flowers in early June, dense, low grower, 6', twice as wide as high.

'White Peter'—White with purple blotch, buds lavender-pink, grew 8.6' by 14.2' in 28 years, lustrous dark green foliage, see *HortScience* 27(5):480–481 (1992).

'Wojnar's Purple'—Dark purple with a reddish purple blotch, hardy, fir green foliage, 5'.

MISCELLANEOUS RHODODENDRONS

No clear cut home so they are included here in alphabetical order.

'Abe Arnot(t)'—Orchid purple flowers with a heavy blotch on the upper lobe spreading into the throat and adjacent lobes.

'Andrew Paton'—Early flowering, large shiny leaves, well-shaped habit, full trusses of white 3" diameter flowers contrast with their raspberry red markings.

'Arctic Pearl'—White flowers.

'Arsen's Pink'—Dense, compact dwarf with clouds of pink flowers, shading to white.

'Asia'—The dark orange buds open to large salmon-pink flowers with a lighter yellow center, a distinctive color for a hardy hybrid, mounded habit.

'Ben Foster'—Compact mound, deep pink flowers, reddish stems add colorful interest during the growing season.

'Big Red'—Large, upright trusses of bright red flowers, large dark green foliage, wide and upright-growing.

'Black Eye'—Deep red-purple flowers have distinct "black eye" on upper lobe, 5' high.

'Blue Boy'—Vibrant violet funnel-form flowers of good substance to 2 1/2" diameter.

'Blue Lagoon'—Mystical, smokey blue-purple flowers have a large and prominent deep purple eye, recurved, deep forest green foliage.

'Blue Rhapsody'—Large purple trusses, blotch of dark purple on the upper petal and throat, white stamens, 5' high.

'Bow Bells'—Deep pink buds open to light pink flowers, slow growing mounded small shrub, bronze-copper new growth.

'Carousel'—Low growing plant, full, wide mass of small lavender pink flowers, spotted in the throat, dark green leaves.

'Clement Bowers'—Deep rosy pink flowers in tight trusses, compact and vigorous, shiny fir-green foliage.

'Conestoga' (*R. minus* × *R. racemosum*)—Bright pink flowers, low growing twiggy small leaf plant.

'Damozel'—Brilliant red, hardy in the Atlanta area, it also grows well in Gainesville, FL, excellent foliage on spreading upright plant.

'Deming Brook'—Creamy white flowers kissed with a pink tinge at the edges, low dense mound.

'Dorothy Amateis'—Large trusses are deep purple with a deeper purple eye, foliage is an olive mat green and the leaves are held in an upright position, 5 to 6'.

'Edith Bosley'—Large, rich, royal purple flowers, darker blotch in the center, vigorous, 5 to 6'.

'Fairy Mary'—Densely foliaged mound, flowers are white to light yellow with pink and apricot.

'Floda'—White flowers marked with pink stripes radiating through each petal, and a suffusion of yellow-appearing in the garden as shrimp pink, semi-evergreen, fabulous red fall color, hardy and reliable.

'Friday'—Huge satin purple flowers, black-velvet blotch on the upper petal, each flower petal in the round trusses folds back, showing those delightful deep blotches, foliage is medium mat-green and leathery textured, good habit, 5'.

'Giganteum'—Spherical trusses of bright crimson flowers, hardy, rolled leaves, vigorous habit.

'Ginny Gee'—Flowers about an inch across, in groups of 11 buds, with 4 or 5 flowers each, party-pink, kissed with white, compact plant to 2' high.

'Goethe'—Large pastel lavender flowers enriched by brownish red spotting, rounded trusses.

'Hardgrove's April Snow'—Small rounded plant, pure white flowers, foliage is small, pointed and deep green.

'Hockessin'—Apricot flowers soften to white, hardy small-leafed dwarf.

'Honshu's Baby'—White flowers with pale purple-pink margins from buds that are a strong purplish-pink, conical trusses of 4, tight dense mounded plant, 1' high.

'Hortulanus H. White'—Orange yellow flower, moderate in size with a strong orange blotch.

'Hudson Bay'—White flowers, small leaves turn bronze in winter, branches freely, 3' by 4'.

'Humboldt'—Frilled trusses of mauve sport dusky brown-red eyes on the upper petals of each flower, foliage handsome kelly green, habit is upright.

'Hurricane'—Flowers are a beautiful pink with markings of deep pink, vigorous growing, compact plant, 5'.

'Hyperion'—White flowers with chocolate blotch, dark green foliage, 5'.

'Independence Day'—Red flowers with lighter centers and a deep ruby blotch on the upper lobe in June.

'Intaglio'—Miniature mound reaches only 8" high, spreads to 3', delicate flowers are white touched with clear pink, leaves are a brilliant green.

'Irresistible Impulse'—Large trusses of deep red purple, each flower has a large deep purple blotch on the upper lobe, deep green leaves have a leathery texture, 5'.

'Joe Paterno'—White truss splashed with yellow, extremely hardy.

'Joshua'—Large scarlet red flowers in a good sized truss, compact plant, slight twist to the dark green leaves.

'Juan de Fuca'—Deep rosy lilac flowers have an enriching red blotch and spotting, emerald green leaves, upright.

'June Magic'—Pastel pink flowers in June, excellent habit, glossy foliage.

'Ledikanense'—Attractively colored green leaves, wide-spreading and rounded, light lavender-pink with reddish spotting in the throat.

'Lemon Tea'—Delicate yellow and pink flowers.

'Matilda'—Great blue color, small-leaf, hardy variety, becomes more dense as it matures.

'Mini Brite'—Delicate mound, flowers are blended colors of yellow and pink with red spotting.

'Mrs. Charles E. Pearson'—Light pink flowers with brown spots, vigorous plant, to 6' high, lush foliage.

'Olin O. Dobbs'—Deep waxy red-purple flowers in large and compact trusses that are a perfect conical shape, much like 'Mars' in growth and plant habit, 4'.

'Orange Honey'—Unusual pink-orange flowers in each truss, vigorous growing with a slightly open habit.

'Party Pink'—Large round trusses of soft pink, hardy and strong growing to 5'.

'Patty Bee'—Dwarf, yellow flowers with outstanding small, fir green leaves, suitable for rock gardens or foreground.

'Paul Vossberg'—Bright red flowers enriched with a dark garnet flare in full, rounded trusses, low, well-branched and mounded plant, spinach green leaves.

'Peach Blend'—Pink flowers with a yellowish center in April, fast-growing when young, nearly deciduous.

'Peter Vermeulen'—Dark glossy 'Scintillation' foliage on strong stems, rosy pink flowers in full trusses, free-flowering and hardy, well-shaped, easily grown plant.

'Pikeland'—Puffs of pink flowers with darker pink wavy edges and spots, well rounded semi-dwarf.

'Pioneer'—Heavy flowering, flowers from clear pink to bluish tinged in early April, hardy, upright, 4 to 5' by 4 to 5'.

'Pioneer Silvery Pink'—Many silvery shades of pink, 4 to 5', more evergreen and later than 'Pioneer', early May.

'Princess Anne'—Beautiful yellow flowers on a compact plant, early May, bronze foliage in winter, 2'.

'Red Brave'—Compact, vigorous plant, dark red flowers in full trusses with white anthers.

'Red Eye'—Deep red-purple with a most interesting eye, when the flower first opens the eye is green gold, becoming red, foliage is shiny, medium sized, and dense, withstands heat well, 5'.

'Red Frilled'—Funnel-shaped, light red-purple flowers, glossy dark green leaves, broad-spreading growth habit, 3', hardy.

'Redder Yet'—Bright red flowers in a round truss.

'Rik'—Clusters of white flowers edged with pink, foliage in winter has red leaf and stem color.

'Rosemarie'—A very fine blue-violet with larger flowers than 'Purple Gem' or 'Ramapo' but not quite as hardy, compact to 3'.

'Roslyn'—Long leaves and violet purple flowers with lighter centers characterize this fine plant, the 2" diameter, ruffled flowers are held in a truss of twelve.

'Spring Song'—Soft yellow flowers changing to apricot on a small, compact mound.

'Staccato'—Silvery pink, semi-double, ruffled flowers, early spring.

'Swamp Beauty'—Magnolia purple buds which open to heavenly deep rose-pink with a maroon blotch which is solid in the throat, flaring to spots on the upper petal, foliage is medium fir green, vigorous, to 5'.

'Tapestry'—Trusses of purple flowers with a dark flare in late May, chunky, compact-growing plant, dark green foliage.

'Veronica Pfeiffer'—Shapely flowers with frilled lobes of an exquisite light purple shade, plant is well proportioned.

'Wee Bee'—Deep reddish pink flowers, dwarf plant, small flat leaves with scaly indumentum on a dense mound.

NEARING HYBRIDS

'Brandywine'—Ball-shaped trusses of 2" diameter, cream-colored flowers edged in rose, small, narrow hairy foliage, upright habit.

'Chesapeake'—Small leaves, long, willowy stems, small, light pink flowers appear in early April.

'Cliff Garland'—Petite trusses of shell pink flowers, small, rounded leaves, flowers early.

'Delaware'—Flowers apricot shading to white, small leaf.

'Elsmere'—Lemon yellow flowers, small-leaved plant.

'Flamingo'—Rich coral.

'Lenape'—Light yellow flowers, narrow leaves, upright habit.

'Mary Belle'—Ruffled flowers, mixed peach, coral and yellow.

'Mary Fleming'—Small-leaved variety, low-spreading to 3', flowers are pale yellow with blotches and streaks of salmon.

'Montchanin'—Graceful and willowy, adds diversity and interest, clusters of small white flowers near the ends of their slender branches make a welcome display.

'Purple Imp'—Bright bluish violet flowers in clusters early in the season, upright, vigorous, spreading plant, small shiny leaves, good heat tolerance.

'Wyanokie'—White.

SHAMMARELLO HYBRIDS (Rhododendrons and Azaleas)

For more than 40 years, A. M. "Tony" Shammarello hybridized and selected a group of large-leaved rhododendrons derived primarily from the standard ironclad cultivars. His goal was an extended season of flowers on compact bushy plants that are hardy around Lake Erie. He succeeded admirably. It is only a matter of time before they become more widely known and grown, not just as collectors items, but for their value as fine landscape plants.

'Belle Heller'—Enormous trusses of large glistening white flowers with throats flecked with gold, vigorous tall grower, tends toward loose open habit, has performed well in Zone 7b.

'Besse Howells'—Ruffled burgundy red flowers accented by a dark red blotch, compact like 'Boule de Neige', very floriferous and hardy.

'Elie'—Rounded trusses are cerise pink with a deeper pink flare, medium-sized, glossy green leaves.

'Elsie Lee'—Large frilled bluish lavender semi-double, 2 to 3" diameter flowers, upright and compact to 3 to 4', late May, orange-red and yellow fall leaves.

'Helen Curtis'—White, double flowers, broad-spreading, mid-sized plant.

'Hino-White Dwarf'—Sport of 'Hino-White', early-flowering, white, spreading with dwarf habit.

'Holden'—Rosy red flowers illuminated by a small dark red blotch, flowers fade to pink when fully open, one of the best for Zone 7b, buds consistently every year, medium height with lustrous dark green foliage.

'Ice Cube'—Ivory white flowers accented with a lemon blotch, dark green foliage, medium height.

'Pink Cameo'—Hardy compact plant to 5′, fresh pink flowers that have a deeper pink blotch.

'Red Red'—Flowers appear mid-season and are approximately 2″ in size, after 10 years this plant will be 2′ by 3′ in size.

'Rocket'—Slightly ruffled, deep, radiant, coral-pink with a scarlet-red blotch, lustrous dark green foliage.

'Sham's Yellow'—Golden buds open to large frilled lemon-yellow flowers.

'Sham's Juliet'—Compact grower, apple blossom pink flower with a rich chocolate blotch.

'Sham's Pink'—Light two-tone vivid pink flowers are darker at the edge with a light red blotch, low-spreading.

'Spring Dawn'—Rosy pink flowers with golden yellow blotch, mid-May, vigorous, 5 to 6′.

'Spring Glory'—Pink flowers that have a deeper pink marking, vigorous growing, compact habit.

'Spring Parade'—Glowing scarlet-red flowers cover a compact plant, dark green leaves, very hardy.

'Tony'—Bright cherry red, mid-May, attractive crinkled foliage, low growing, 4′ by 4′ in 10 years.

Rhodotypos scandens (Thunb.) Mak. — Black Jetbead
(rō-dō-tĭ′pōs skan′denz)

FAMILY: Rosaceae

LEAVES: Opposite, simple, ovate to ovate-oblong, 2 1/2 to 4″ long, half as wide, acuminate, rounded at base, sharply and doubly serrate, bright green and glabrous above, lighter green and silky beneath when young, prominently parallel-veined (ribbed); petiole—1/8 to 1/4″ long.

BUDS: Imbricate, brownish green, divergent, glabrous, slightly stalked, ovoid.

STEM: Young—green, glabrous, shiny, eventually turning brown; old—gray-streaked, reddish brown, orangish lenticels.

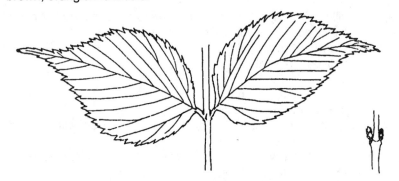

SIZE: 3 to 6′ in height by 4 to 9′ in spread, in native haunts may grow to 15′ but under cultivation I have never seen anything larger than 6′.

HARDINESS: Zone 4 to 8.

HABIT: Mounded, loosely branched shrub with ascending and somewhat arching branches, often of shabby appearance; perhaps unduly harsh for I have observed handsome (too strong) colonies and masses; the key is to not expect too much from the species.

RATE: Medium to fast.

TEXTURE: Medium in leaf; coarse in winter.

LEAF COLOR: Various authors report dark green as the typical summer foliage color; however, I feel the color tends toward a bright green; fall color is green with a slight tinge of yellow; one of the first shrubs to leaf out in spring.

FLOWERS: Perfect, white, 1 to 2″ diameter, 4-petaled (unusual for Rosaceae), 4-lobed calyx, May to early June (mid to late April, Athens), borne singly at the end of short twigs, not outstanding but interesting upon close inspection.

FRUIT: Drupe (have seen listed as a tumid berry), 1/3″ long, ellipsoidal, glabrous, hard, 3 to 4 in a group, shining black, October and persistent into the following spring and summer; neither flowers nor fruits are showy but do offer a degree of interest in the garden.

CULTURE: Readily transplanted; very tolerant of differing soil conditions; tolerates full sun or shade; crowding and polluted conditions; pH adaptable; one of the better shrubs for adverse conditions and heavy shade.

DISEASES AND INSECTS: Trouble free.

LANDSCAPE VALUE: Tough, durable plant for rugged conditions; good in shady areas, shrub borders, massing on banks and under shade trees; there are too many superior ornamental shrubs to justify extensive use of this species; in early November, 1997, I witnessed a planting in a parking lot island at Bernheim Arboretum, still green but thinking about blushing yellow, in full blazing exposure it was in terrific condition.

PROPAGATION: Softwood cuttings taken in late spring root readily; actually easy to root any time the plant is in leaf. Seed apparently requires acid scarification and a cold period; the best treatments have not been established.

NATIVE HABITAT: Japan and central China. Introduced 1866.

Rhus aromatica Ait. — Fragrant Sumac
(rös a-rō-mat′ik-à)

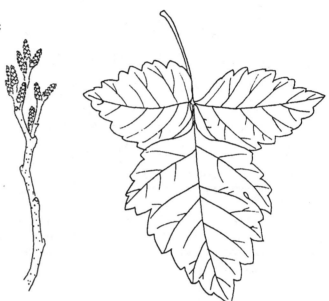

FAMILY: Anacardiaceae

LEAVES: Alternate, trifoliate, leaflets subsessile, ovate, the terminal 1 1/2 to 3″ long, acute or acuminate, cuneate and often obovate; the lateral ones oblique and rounded at the base, about one half as large, all coarsely toothed, lower surface pubescent becoming glabrous, variable in leaf coloration but often a glossy medium to dark green; petiole—1 to 1 1/2″ long.

BUDS: Small, yellow, pubescent, covered by leaf scar.

STEM: Slender, pubescent, aromatically fragrant when bruised, leaf scars circular, distinctly raised.

SIZE: 2 to 6′, possibly larger, with a spread of 6 to 10′, extremely variable in size over its native range; have seen 6′ high and wide mounded shrubs on occasion.

HARDINESS: Zone 3 to 9.

HABIT: Low, irregular spreading shrub with lower branches turning up at the tips; tend to sucker from the roots and produce a dense, tangled mass of stems and leaves.

RATE: Slow to medium.

TEXTURE: Medium in leaf, medium in winter habit.

LEAF COLOR: Medium green, almost blue-green effect, often glossy on the upper surface; fall color orange to red to reddish purple, coloring best on light soils.

FLOWERS: Polygamous or dioecious, yellowish, mid to late March–April, borne in approximately 1″ long catkins (male) or short panicles at ends of branches (female); male catkin persistent and exposed through late summer, fall and winter.

FRUIT: Red (female plants only), hairy drupe, 1/4″ diameter; August–September and may persist into winter but usually loses its good color.

CULTURE: Fibrous root system, easily transplanted from containers; adaptable, withstands 1/2 to 3/4 shade or full sun; prefers acid, well-drained soil, has not performed well in campus plantings at Georgia.

DISEASES AND INSECTS: None serious although various wilts, leaf spots, rusts, aphids, mites, and scales have been noted.

LANDSCAPE VALUE: Excellent fast cover for banks, cuts and fills, massing, facing; could be used as ground cover especially the low growing cultivars; this plant has the ability to develop roots as the stems touch the soil and is therefore useful for stabilizing banks or slightly sloping areas.

CULTIVARS:

‘Green Globe’—Grows to 6′, forms a rounded, dense shrub.

‘Gro-low’—Low, wide-spreading habit, excellent glossy foliage, 2′ high, 6 to 8′ wide, good looking plant; a female with yellow flowers and hairy red fruits, fall color is a good orange-red, introduced by Synnesvedt Nursery, Glenview, IL; has become extremely popular in the Midwest; utilized on

Georgia campus but consistently melted/died out, perhaps because of heavy, wet soils, replaced with dwarf *Myrica cerifera* and *Itea virginica* which have fared much better.

'Konza'—Dense grower, to 2' high, listed by Ferrucci Nursery.

Several varieties are listed by various authors but their botanical validity is questionable.

PROPAGATION: Seed, scarify for 60 minutes; and provide 1 to 3 months cold stratification or fall sow; softwood cuttings, July, 1000 ppm IBA gave 100% rooting in peat:perlite under mist; root cuttings will also work.

ADDITIONAL NOTES: In my mind this shrub is somewhat of a second class citizen but I have bumped into hundreds over the years and cannot remember any that were offensive. The bright yellowish flowers, especially on male plants, were always welcome after a difficult midwestern or eastern winter. The foliage has a certain sparkle and in fall, excellent reddish purple fall coloration may develop. When a planting becomes overgrown, it can be easily rejuvenated with a large mower, bush hog or other instrument of destruction.

NATIVE HABITAT: Vermont and Ontario to Minnesota, south to Florida and Louisiana. Introduced 1759.

RELATED SPECIES:

Rhus trilobata Nutt., (rös trī-lō-bā′tà), Skunkbush Sumac, is quite similar to *R. aromatica* and appears to be its western ally. It is an upright or ascending shrub, 3 to 6' high, with leaves and flowers smaller than *R. aromatica*. Flowers are more greenish and fruits slightly smaller than *R. aromatica*. The leaves are more unpleasantly scented. It makes a handsome and almost impenetrable mass which would lend itself to roadside and similar landscape sites. 'Autumn Amber' is low growing with prostrate branches, the plant tends to produce dense thickets, about 1 to 1 1/2' high, the dark green leaves brilliant yellow and red in fall, greenish yellow flowers appear in early spring, sex is unknown but no fruits have been produced; originated from seeds  collected near Littlefield, TX, found on limestone outcroppings and would be a good ground cover for high pH soils; hardy to Zone 4; see *HortScience* 21:1465–1466 (1986). Variety *malacophylla* Munz. with diffuse pubescent branches to 5' high, cuneate-obovate leaflets, yellow flowers, is found in California. Native from Illinois to Washington, California and Texas. Introduced 1877. Zone 4 to 6?

Rhus typhina L. — Staghorn Sumac
(rös tĭ-fē′nà)

LEAVES: Alternate, compound pinnate, entire leaf 1 to 2' long, 13 to 27 leaflets, often 19, each leaflet lance-oblong, 2 to 5″ long, 1 to 2″ wide, acuminate, serrate, bright green above, glaucous beneath, pubescent when young; petiole—about 2″ long, hairy; in fact, entire rachis maintains some pubescence.

BUDS: Hairy, leaf scars not elevated and somewhat C-shaped.

STEM: Stout, rounded, densely velvety hairy, concealing the lenticels, almost club-like; pith large, brownish, aromatic when broken.

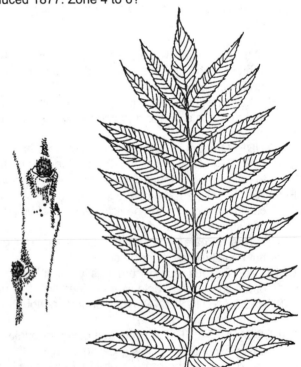

SIZE: 15 to 25' in a landscape situation; potential to 30 to 40' in the wild; spread is usually equal to or greater than height; national champion is 61' by 20' in Tallapoosa, AL.

HARDINESS: Zone 4 to 8.

HABIT: A large, loose, open, spreading shrub or a gaunt, scraggly tree with a flattish crown and rather picturesque branches resembling the horns on a male deer; hence, the name Staghorn; spreads by root suckers to form large colonies.

RATE: Fast when development occurs from root suckers; slow to medium on old wood.

TEXTURE: Species—medium in summer, coarse in winter; cultivars ('Laciniata' and 'Dissecta')—fine in foliage, coarse in winter.

STEM: Dense, velvety reddish brown pubescence persisting on 2- and 3-year-old branches; older stems gray and relatively smooth.

LEAF COLOR: Bright green in summer, yellow, orange and scarlet in fall; often spectacular; leafs out late in spring.

FLOWERS: Dioecious, greenish yellow, June to early July; female borne in dense, hairy panicles, 4 to 8″ long; male in a bigger, looser, wider panicle.

FRUIT: Crimson, late August through April, densely hairy drupe, closely packed in a pyramidal panicle; bright crimson in early fall, becoming duller and darker red with cold weather and often still colorful even into spring.

CULTURE: Easily transplanted, adapted to many soil types; however, prefers a well-drained soil, not a plant for poorly drained areas; tolerates very dry, sterile soil; often seen along railroad tracks and highways; suckers profusely and tends to form wide-spreading colonies; tolerates city conditions; can be rejuvenated by cutting to ground in later winter.

DISEASES AND INSECTS: Same as described under *R. aromatica* except *Verticillium* is often prevalent in Staghorn Sumac.

LANDSCAPE VALUE: Massing, naturalizing, waste areas, perhaps banks, cuts and fills; actually hard to kill this plant due to its ability to sucker freely from roots; should not be used as a specimen, foundation or container plant; the cutleaf forms offer superb texture and even better yellow-orange-red fall coloration, quite coarse in winter and considerable thought should go into proper siting.

CULTIVARS: Coombes, *The New Plantsman* 1(2):107–113 (1994), discusses the cut-leaved sumacs.

'Dissecta'—Similar to 'Laciniata' but leaflets more deeply divided; discovered in the late 1800's by a Massachusetts nurseryman; foliage is quite beautiful and colors handsomely in fall; a female.

'Laciniata'—Leaflets deeply divided creating a fine-textured, ferny appearance; a female, much like 'Dissecta' which is perhaps more finely divided, had both in Illinois and had a difficult time differentiating especially from more than 10′ away.

PROPAGATION: Seed, scarify for 50 to 80 minutes in sulfuric acid; cuttings, root pieces collected in December placed in moist sand:peat yielded plants in 2 months; the cultivars 'Dissecta' and 'Laciniata' are produced by root cuttings.

ADDITIONAL NOTES: Large genus comprising some 150 to 200 species of evergreen and deciduous shrubs and trees in temperate and subtropical climates worldwide. The best garden qualities reside in the North American species, *R. aromatica*, *R. copallina*, *R. glabra*, and *R. typhina*. The beautiful autumn color and rich red fruits are the principal attributes. Utilize with the knowledge that most will sucker and require maintenance. In 1987, while in West Berlin (the Wall still existed), I noticed *R. typhina* in the grassy medians. Photos from the bus window are still in my files. Also, in the great garden at Hidcote, *R. typhina* was growing in a large container. Europeans have long appreciated *R. glabra* and *R. typhina*. Perhaps, someday, Americans will become more introspective and appreciative of our rich woody plant heritage.

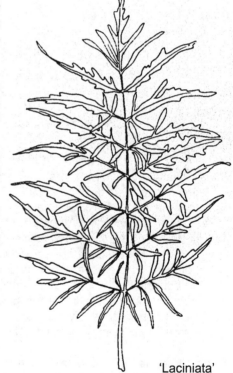

'Laciniata'

The only other *Rhus* [beyond *R. radicans* L., now *Toxicodendron radicans* (L.) Kuntz, Poison Ivy, with 3, rarely 5 or 7, leaflets, cream to yellow-green flowers, 1/4″ diameter cream to light brown drupes, vine-like to shrubby habit and *R. verniciflua* Stokes, now *Toxicodendron vernicifluum* (Stokes) F. Barkley, Varnish Tree, Chinese Lacquer, or Japanese Lacquer Tree, with 7 to 13 leaflets, 3 to 6″ long, 1 to 3″ wide, ovate-oblong, entire, dark green, 50 to 70′ high] are *R. potaninii* Maxim., a large shrub or small tree to 25′ with 7 to 11 leaflets, off-white flowers and red, densely pubescent fruits, Zone 6; and *R. virens* Lindh. ex A. Gray, Evergreen Sumac, a shrub to 10′ with 5 to 9, to 1″ long, lustrous dark green, evergreen leaflets, Zone 8 to 9. Have seen *R. potaninii* Maxim. at Hidcote and the Arnold Arboretum and *R. virens* at Stephen F. Austin Arboretum in Nacogdoches, TX.

NATIVE HABITAT: Quebec to Ontario, south to Georgia, Indiana and Iowa. Cultivated 1629.

RELATED SPECIES:

Rhus chinensis Mill. — Chinese Sumac
LEAVES: Alternate, compound pinnate, 8 to 15″ long, 7 to 13 leaflets, subsessile, ovate to ovate-oblong, 2 to
    5″ long, about half as wide, acute or short acuminate, coarsely crenate-serrate, lustrous bright green
    above, brownish pubescent beneath, rachis and often the petiole conspicuously winged, pubescent.
BUDS: Pubescent, almost woolly, gray-brown in color, leaf scars not elevated, C-shaped.
STEM: Yellowish brown, glabrous to minutely pubescent, lenticels prominent.

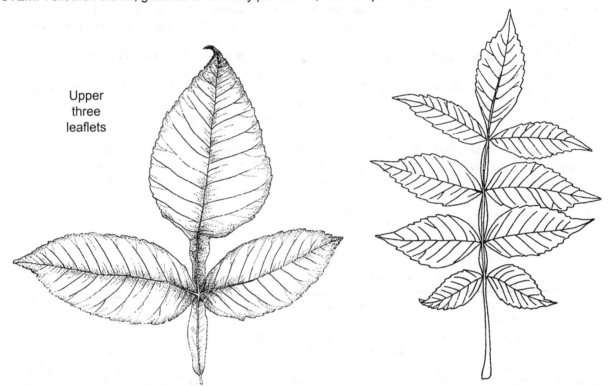

Upper
three
leaflets

Rhus chinensis, (rōs chi-nen′sis), Chinese Sumac, is a loose, spreading, suckering shrub or flat-headed tree
    growing to 24′ in height and width. The foliage is bright green in summer and can change to orangish red
    tones in fall but this color is seldom realized in the Midwest; however, I have seen excellent yellow-red fall
    color on a plant at the Arnold Arboretum. The flowers are yellowish white, August into September, borne
    in 6 to 10″ long and wide panicles. Panicles may be twice this size on vigorous specimens. The fruit is
    a densely pubescent, orange-red drupe that matures in October. Best used in large areas, naturalistic
    settings, possibly the shrub border; valued mainly for its late flower. Dr. Orton, Rutgers University,
    introduced 'September Beauty' which has immense panicles, and is superior to the species. Also offers
    good fall color which in the Dirr garden was apricot-yellow. Unfortunately, the species and 'September
    Beauty' are excessively aggressive and I was removing stray shoots three years after excavation of the
    parent plant. Utilize where lateral space is plentiful. China, Japan. Cultivated 1784. Zone 5 to 7(8).

Rhus copallina L. — Flameleaf (Shining) Sumac
LEAVES: Alternate, compound pinnate, 6 to 12″(16″) long leaf, 9 to 21 leaflets, oblong-ovate to lance-ovate,
    1 3/4 to 4″ long, usually acute, entire or sometimes with a few teeth near the apex, glabrous and lustrous
    dark green above, usually pubescent beneath, rachis winged, pubescent.
BUDS: Pubescent, reddish brown.
STEM: Terete, reddish, puberulous; leaf scars U-shaped, not as coarse as *R. chinensis*, *R. glabra*, and *R.
    typhina*.

Rhus copallina, (rōs ko-pal-lī′nȧ), Flameleaf or Shining Sumac, is compact and dense in extreme youth
    becoming more and more open, irregular and picturesque as it ages, with crooked, ascending and
    spreading branches; broader at the top. Grows 20 to 30′ high with a similar spread. National champion
    is 49′ by 19′ in Marion County, Texas. The foliage is lustrous dark green in summer changing to rich red,
    crimson, and scarlet in fall. Flowers (dioecious) are greenish yellow, July to August, borne in dense, 4 to

8″ long, 3 to 4″ wide panicles. The fruit is a pubescent, crimson drupe which ripens in September to October. One of the best sumacs; useful for dry, rocky places, banks, large areas, and naturalistic plantings. Probably the most ornamental of the sumacs but not commonly seen in gardens. Almost pestiferous in the South but certainly beautiful in the fall. A few disclaimers are needed to temper my exuberance. The species shows no penchant toward uniformity and usually forms large spreading colonies. For the small garden, it has no place. I have observed tremendous variation in fall color and believe the best form(s) should be vegetatively propagated. Use with discretion for the plant may turn on you tomorrow. 'Creel's Quintet' is a more 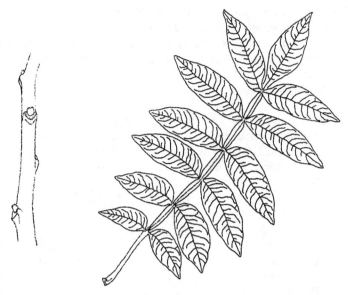 restrained form, 8 to 10′ high, suckering, with 5 lustrous dark green leaflets that turn burgundy in fall, female, a single plant in the Georgia trials has failed to impress but as of this publication date is only in the third year. Have also heard of another compact form. Gary Lanham, Lebanon, KY has discovered purple and yellow leaf summer foliage forms. Maine to Ontario and Minnesota south to Florida and Texas. Cultivated 1688. Zone 4 to 9.

Rhus glabra L. — Smooth Sumac
LEAVES: Alternate, compound pinnate, 12 to 18″ long, 11 to 31 leaflets, lance-oblong, 2 to 5″ long, 1/2 to 3/4″ wide, acuminate, serrate, medium to deep green, glaucous beneath, rachis normally red.
BUDS: Pubescent, round, ovoid, with leaf scar almost completely encircling bud.
STEM: Stout (thick), glabrous, somewhat 3-sided, green to reddish and covered with a waxy bloom; leaf scar horseshoe-shaped.

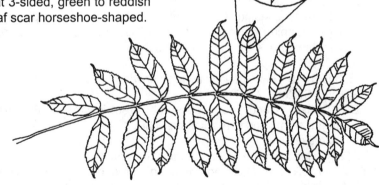

Rhus glabra, (rös glā′brá), Smooth Sumac, grows 10 to 15′ high with a comparable spread. Usually grows in colonies as it suckers and develops in all directions from the mother plant. This is very evident in plantings which occur along roadsides and other low maintenance areas. Co-national champions are 28′ by 27′ and 38′ by 19′ in Walla Walla, WA. The foliage is medium to dark green in summer changing to excellent yellow to orange-red-purple combinations in fall. Flowers are dioecious, greenish yellow, June–July, borne in 6 to 10″ long panicles. Fruit is a scarlet, hairy drupe which persists late into winter. Good plant for mass plantings, highways, dry, poor soil areas. The essential difference between this species and *R. typhina* is the lack of pubescence on the young stems. This is the more common species, compared to *R. typhina*, in the Piedmont of Georgia. 'Laciniata' has leaflets which are deeply cut and lobed. It is female and will produce the bright scarlet fruits. It was discovered in the mid 1800's near Philadelphia. In 1994, Allen Coombes, Botanist, Hillier Arboretum, named what I believe is the typical 'Laciniata', *R. × pulvinata* Greene 'Red Autumn Lace'. This is a hybrid between *R. glabra* and *R. typhina* and, indeed, 'Red Autumn Lace' has intermediate pubescence on leaves and stems. 'Morden's' ('Morden Selection') is a more restrained form to 6′ with bright red fruits. See Coombes, *The New Plantsman* 1(2):107–113 (1994), for the "Cut Leaved Sumacs." Also, Lancaster, *The Garden* pp. 531–533, October 1990, waxes poetic about *Rhus glabra*. Maine to British Columbia, south to Florida and Arizona. Found in all contiguous 48 states into northern Mexico. Cultivated 1620. Zone 3 to 9.

Rhus michauxii Sarg. — Michaux's Sumac
LEAVES: Alternate, compound pinnate, 9 to 15 leaflets, 2 to 4″ long, oval-
    oblong, acuminate, coarsely serrate, dark green and pubescent above,
    densely brown pubescent below, rachis winged below the terminal
    leaflets.
STEM: Densely hairy.

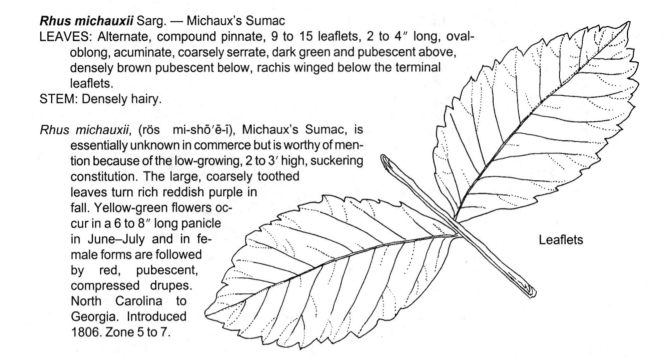

Leaflets

Rhus michauxii, (rös mi-shō′ē-ī), Michaux's Sumac, is
    essentially unknown in commerce but is worthy of men-
    tion because of the low-growing, 2 to 3′ high, suckering
    constitution. The large, coarsely toothed
    leaves turn rich reddish purple in
    fall. Yellow-green flowers oc-
    cur in a 6 to 8″ long panicle
    in June–July and in fe-
    male forms are followed
    by red, pubescent,
    compressed drupes.
    North Carolina to
    Georgia. Introduced
    1806. Zone 5 to 7.

Ribes alpinum L. — Alpine Currant
(rī′bēz al-pī′num)

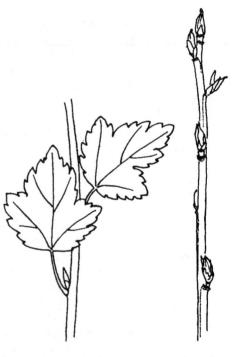

FAMILY: Saxifragaceae, more properly the Grossulariaceae(?).
LEAVES: Alternate, simple, roundish or ovate, 1 to 2″ long and wide, 3-
    rarely 5-lobed, with obtuse or acute dentate lobes, truncate or
    subcordate, bright green; petiole—about 1/2″ long, glandular
    hairy.
BUDS: Stalked, large, imbricate, distinctly gray-tan in winter.
STEM: Light to chestnut brown, often lustrous, with conspicuous
    ridges running down from edges of leaf scars, unarmed, as
    stems mature, exfoliation may occur.

SIZE: 3 to 6′(10′) high, usually as wide or wider.
HARDINESS: Zone 2 to 7.
HABIT: Densely twiggy, rounded shrub; erect in youth with stiffly
    upright stems and spreading branches.
RATE: Medium.
TEXTURE: Medium-fine in leaf; medium in winter.
STEM COLOR: Straw-colored on young stems; old becoming deep
    brown and shredding.
LEAF COLOR: Deep bright green in summer, poor yellow in fall; one
    of the first shrubs to leaf out in spring.
FLOWERS: Dioecious, greenish yellow, April, staminate with 20 to 30 flowers in 1 to 2″ long racemes; female
    smaller, with 10 to 15 flowers, not showy, on racemes one-half as long.
FRUIT: Juicy scarlet berry, 1/4 to 1/3″ diameter; June–July; attractive but seldom seen in cultivation as male
    clones seem to dominate; not edible.
CULTURE: Easily transplanted, best handled as a container plant; tolerant of any good soil; full sun or shade;
    prune anytime for flowers are not a factor; does well in calcareous soils.
DISEASES AND INSECTS: Anthracnose, cane blight, leaf spots, rust, currant aphid, imported currant worm,
    scales, and currant bud mite; during wet seasons leaf spot and anthracnose can be serious problems;
    male supposedly immune to rust diseases.
LANDSCAPE VALUE: Good hedge plant and is extensively used for that purpose, mass, good in semi-shady
    areas; male plants tend to dominate because of supposed rust resistance; occasionally plants with perfect
    flowers occur.

CULTIVARS:

'Aureum'—Dwarf type with yellowish leaves, colors best in full sun and supposedly maintains the color throughout summer, although have noted references that state yellow-green in summer; has been in cultivation since before 1881.

'Europa'—Good foliage, on a densely branched, 6 to 8′ high shrub, listed by Midwest Groundcovers, St. Charles, IL.

Green Jeans™—Selected for its superior summer leaf retention, foliage remains clean and persists, 3 to 5′(6′) high, Spring Meadow Nursery introduction.

'Green Mound'—Dwarf, dense, 2 to 3′ high and wide form; male; shows good resistance to leaf diseases; have also seen 'Nana', 'Pumila' and 'Compacta' listed, essentially more compact than species.

PROPAGATION: Softwood cuttings taken in June or July rooted well when treated with 1000 ppm IBA and placed in sand under mist; seeds may be fall sown or provided 3 months cold stratification.

ADDITIONAL NOTES: Great number (150) of species in the north temperate regions. Many species are thorny, and of no garden merit, others are important for fruit production with *R. alpinum* and *R. sanguineum* the most important garden species.

NATIVE HABITAT: Europe. Cultivated 1588.

RELATED SPECIES:

Ribes odoratum H.L. Wendl. — Clove, Buffalo, Missouri Currant

LEAVES: Alternate, simple, ovate or orbicular-reniform, 1 to 3″ wide and as long, deeply 3- to 5-lobed, cuneate or truncate, with coarsely dentate lobes, glabrate or puberulous beneath, bluish green, thinnish; petiole—1/2 to 2″ long.

STEM: Pubescent, grayish brown.

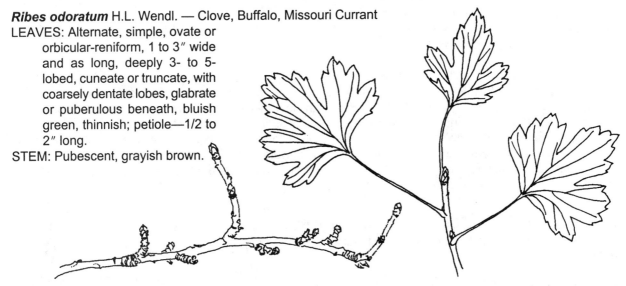

Ribes odoratum, (rī′bēz ō-dôr-ā′tum), Clove Currant, grows 6 to 8′ high and is an irregular shrub of ascending, arching stems, usually surrounded by a mass of young suckering growth, loose and open with age. It is not the neatest shrub and selection for dwarf attributes would be worthwhile. Foliage is bluish green in summer; briefly yellowish just before dropping in fall (may have reddish tones). Flowers (dioecious) are yellow, fragrant, odor of cloves; early to mid-April; borne in 5- to 10-flowered, usually nodding racemes. Fruit is a black berry, 1/3″ across, June or July. A yellow-fruited forma, *xanthocarpum* Rehd., is known. 'Crandall', with 3/5″ diameter, edible fruits and mildew resistant foliage, is listed. Good shrub for the border or where early spring color is desired. It is an alternate host for White Pine Blister Rust (*Cronartium ribicola*). *Ribes aureum* Pursh., Golden Currant, is similar with spicily fragrant, yellow flowers. Fruits are rounded, small, purple-black. Have seen on occasion and could not separate it from *R. odoratum*. Western United States to Mexico. *Ribes odoratum* is native from South Dakota to western Texas, east to Minnesota and Arkansas. Zone 4 to 6(7).

Ribes sanguineum Pursh. — Winter Currant

LEAVES: Alternate, simple, 3- to 5-lobed, 2 to 4″ wide, cordate, dark green above, whitish pubescent below; petiole—glandular pubescent.

Ribes sanguineum, (rī′bēz san-gwin′ē-um), Winter Currant, is a West Coast species that is seldom seen in eastern gardens. The habit is upright-arching to rounded, maturing between 6 to 10′(15′). The flowers of the better cultivars are exceptional. White, pink, rose-red flowers appear in pendulous, 3″ long racemes along the length of the stems during April-May. Fruits are bloomy, bluish black, slightly glandular, 1/3″ diameter berries. Plants prefer moist, well-drained soil in full sun or partial shade and will tolerate a

modicum of drought. As a shrub border plant, it is particularly attractive.
'King Edward VII' has red flowers and
is quite compact, about 5 to 6′ high,
while 'Brocklebankii' sports yellow
leaves that fade with the heat of summer. Also leaves may scorch in hot
sun. Flowers are pale pink. Common
in English and Scottish gardens, usually with buds expanding and showing
rich color in late March with full flower
development in April. A shrub in full
flower is spectacular. Another plant
that gardeners lust after. Have seen in
Dr. Richard Weaver's former garden
in the Boston area. Cultivars listed by
United States nurseries include: 'Apple Blossom' with deep pink buds, soft
white-pink flowers; 'Barrie Coate' with
pink-red flowers; 'Claremont' with soft
pink flowers; 'Elk River Red' with rich
red flowers; 'Emerson' with deep pink
flowers, upright growth habit; 'Han-
naman White' with white flowers in

long racemes; 'Mesa Red' with soft red flowers in 2 to 3″ long inflorescences; 'Montara Rose' with light
pink flowers on an 8′ high plant; 'Pokey's Pink' with clear medium pink flowers; 'Pulborough Scarlet' with
deep red flowers; 'Spring Snow' with white flowers; 'Spring Showers' with large pinkish red panicles;
'Tydermann's White' with deep green leaves and white flowers; 'Variegatum' with cream-splashed leaves
and rose-red flowers; and 'White Icicle' with white flowers in 2 to 3″ long inflorescences on an 8′ high
plant. British Columbia to northern California. Cultivated 1818. Zone 5 to 6(7).

Robinia pseudoacacia L. — Black Locust,
also Common Locust, Yellow or White Locust
(rōbin′ē-à sö-dō-à-kā′sē-à)

FAMILY: Fabaceae

LEAVES: Alternate, pinnately compound, 6 to 14″
long, 7 to 19 leaflets, elliptic or ovate, 1 or 2″
long, entire, mucronate at apex, rounded or
truncate, dark bluish green, glabrous beneath or slightly pubescent when young.

BUDS: Terminal—absent, laterals—minute, rusty-
downy, 3 to 4 superposed, generally close
together.

STEM: Slender, brittle, often zig-zag, light reddish
to greenish brown, smooth or nearly so,
more or less angled with decurrent ridges
from base and outer angles of leaf scars,
generally spiny with paired stipular prickles
at nodes, about 1/4 to 1/2″ long, prickles
larger and more prominent on sucker and
rapid shoot extensions.

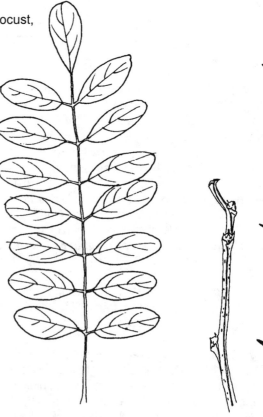

SIZE: Would average 30 to 50′ in height with a
spread of 20 to 35′ although can grow 70 to
80′ high; national champion is 96′ by 92′ in
Dansville, NY.

HARDINESS: Zone 4 to 8(9).

HABIT: Often an upright tree with a straight trunk and a narrow oblong crown, becoming ragged and scraggly with age; will develop thickets as it freely seeds, and develops shoots from roots; some forms are spreading in habit with several trunks.

RATE: Fast, will average 2′ or greater per year over a 10 year period.

BARK: Reddish brown to almost black, deeply furrowed into rounded, interlacing, fibrous, superficially scaly ridges; I see large deeply ridged-and-furrowed trunks that are gray-black, seldom red-brown.

LEAF COLOR: Dull, dark blue-green above, very strongly contrasting with the light and dark green of other trees; leaves show a slight yellow-green in fall and may abscise early; in Georgia, trees hold leaves late, often into mid-November.

FLOWERS: Perfect, 1″ across, white, extremely fragrant, borne in dense racemes, 4 to 8″ long in May to early June, flowers at a young age, effective for 7 to 10 days; flowers mid to late April in Athens.

FRUIT: Pod, flat, brown-black, 2 to 4″ long, smooth, 4- to 10-seeded, maturing in October and persisting for a time.

CULTURE: Transplants very easily, extremely adaptable to varied soils and climates; will grow in about any soil except those that are permanently wet; reaches maximum development on moist, rich, loamy soils or those of limestone origin; tolerant of dry conditions and saline environments; will grow on sandy, sterile soils; has the ability to fix atmospheric nitrogen and in this way partially creates its own nitrogen supply; this is true for many legumes as well as alders, bayberry, sweetfern and others; prune in late summer or fall for locusts "bleed" in spring.

DISEASES AND INSECTS: Canker, dampening-off, leaf spots, powdery mildews, wood decay, witches' broom, locust borer, carpenterworm, locust leaf miner, locust twig borer, and scales; the most destructive pest is the locust borer which can riddle whole trees or whole plantations; the wood is extremely hard and durable yet this borer can destroy it like balsa wood; tree vigor is the important factor, for fast-growing trees exhibit the greatest resistance; leaf miner also turns the tree brown.

LANDSCAPE VALUE: An "alley cat" type tree which can survive under the toughest of conditions; good for stripped-mined areas, highway cuts and fills, sandy, poor soils, shelter plantations and afforestation purposes; not recommended for the home landscape, but definitely has a place in difficult areas; the flowers are exceedingly fragrant from which bees produce a delicious honey; several cultivars offer attractive foliage and flowers.

CULTIVARS: The Europeans have grown, appreciated and selected superior forms of this tree while Americans treated it as some pedestrian weed. In truth, it often makes, in the best forms, a handsome tree. Several of the cultivars have crossed my path. There are many others that I may never see but it will not be for a lack of trying. I understand that the U.S. Forest Service has developed borer resistant clones. Use in cultivated situations must be tempered with the knowledge that borers and leaf miners can render trees unsightly or dead.

'Aurea'—New leaves emerge yellow and the color persists for a time but eventually becomes lime-green, plant at Arnold lost yellow color in early summer, cultivated since 1864, found in Germany around 1859.

'Bessoniana'—Ovoid crown, well-developed central leader, essentially unarmed stems, vigorous constitution and shy flowering characterize this form, in cultivation before 1871, have seen at Wisley Gardens.

'Dean Rossman'—A seedling selection with pale yellow leaves, color supposedly holds better than 'Frisia'.

'Decaisneana'—A vigorous tree with light rose flowers, first described in 1863, supposedly comes partially true-to-type from seed, considered more properly a hybrid and is listed under *R.* × *ambigua* Poir. (*R. pseudoacacia* × *R. viscosa* Vent.), branches slightly glutinous, stipular thorns small or absent.

Fibermaster™—Maintains a straight, controlled growth habit, compared to the irregular growth habit that is typical to the species.

'Frisia'—Leaves of a golden yellow color which hold (more or less) throughout the growing season, spines on young shoots red, discovered in an old nursery in 1935 at Zwollerkerspel, Holland; I noticed this form in abundance throughout Europe and it was a rather cheerful sight especially on some of the drab, dreary, rainy days; some older leaves become more yellow-green but overall it holds the yellow color as well as any colored foliage tree; displays excellent vigor; has become popular in Northeast and West but even in those cooler climates loses much (most) of the yellow leaf color.

'Purple Robe'—One of the prettiest forms with dark rose-pink flowers on a compact rounded tree that will probably never exceed 30 to 40′, the new growth emerges bronzy red, have seen this form only once in Spring Grove, Cincinnati, OH; flower color is much deeper than *R. hispida* and *R. fertilis*; this form flowers about 10 to 14 days earlier than 'Idaho' and over a longer period; may be the same as 'Rouge Cascade'; one nursery reference listed this form as seedless; have seen listed as a *R.* × *ambigua* form.

'Pyramidalis' ('Fastigiata')—A slender, medium-sized (40 to 50'), columnar tree with closely erect spineless branches, sparse flowers, shoots essentially unarmed, Lombardy Poplar-like in habit.

'Semperflorens'—A large, vigorous tree which produces a major flower flush in June and a second in September or may flower continuously from midsummer on, put into commerce in 1874.

'Tortuosa'—A small tree with slightly twisted and contorted branches; the greatest concentration I have seen in the United States was at Cantigny Gardens, Wheaton, IL, the racemes are small and thinly set with flowers.

Twisty Baby™ ('Lace Lady')—Lacy foliage, twisted shoots, does not flower, 8 to 10' high, wider at maturity, artistic form can be used for summer and winter interest in the garden.

'Umbraculifera'—Forms a dense, umbrella-like canopy, 20' high and 20' wide, but bears few or no flowers; susceptible to borers and ice; essentially spineless; may be confused with 'Inermis' but is not the same thing; prominent in European landscapes.

'Unifoliola'—The leaves are reduced to a single large leaflet or subtended by 1 or 2 normalized leaflets; I am almost positive that this form was used as a street tree in Paris but on a bus at 35 miles an hour it is hard to be absolutely sure; the single leaflet may be as long as 4″ and 1 1/2″ wide; it can grow 40 to 60' high.

PROPAGATION: Seed dormancy is caused by an impermeable seed coat and seeds should be scarified in sulfuric acid, soaked in hot water or mechanically scarified. Root cuttings, 1/4 to 1″ diameter, 3 to 8″ long, gave 25% plants; the younger the tree and roots the better.

NATIVE HABITAT: Pennsylvania to Georgia, west to Iowa, Missouri, and Oklahoma. Introduced 1635.

RELATED SPECIES AND CULTIVARS:

Robinia hispida L. — Bristly or Roseacacia Locust

LEAVES: Alternate, compound pinnate, to 9″ long, 9 to 15 leaflets, elliptic to oblong-ovate or oblong, 1 to 2″ long, acute to obtusish, mucronate, dark blue-green above, slightly pubescent beneath.

STEM: Rich brown, covered with hispid hairs creating a brush-like countenance.

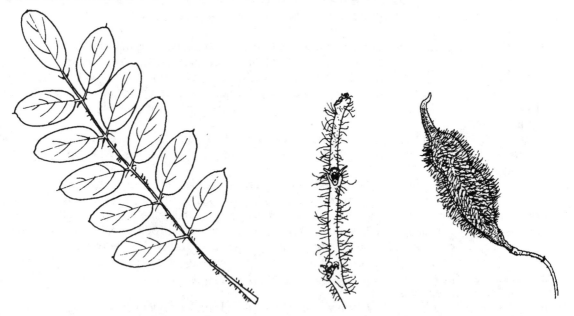

Robinia hispida, (rōbin′ē-à hiss′pi-dà), Bristly or Roseacacia Locust, and *R. fertilis* are closely related species. *Robinia fertilis* sets fruits and seeds while *R. hispida* does not or only sparingly so. Both are small, spreading, suckering shrubs in the 6 to 10' category with prominent hispid petioles and branches. The foliage is a blue-green and the flowers rose colored or pale purple, scentless; borne in 2 to 4″ long pendulous, hispid racemes; usually quite showy. Their cultural requirements are similar to *R. pseudoacacia*; both are good plants for stabilizing sandy banks and sterile, dry, impoverished soils. *Robinia hispida* is native from Virginia and Kentucky to Georgia and Alabama. 'Arnot' is a Soil Conservation Service selection that grows 3 to 8' high, forms dense thickets, has deep rose flowers, fixes nitrogen, and is good for stabilizing steep, sandy or gravelly slopes. 'Monument' is an old form of *R. fertilis* dating to the late 1940's when Wayside Gardens introduced it. The habit is small and compact with a narrow conical habit, flowers are rose colored, and the branches sparsely bristled, will grow 10 to 15' high, possibly a hybrid. 'Flowering Globe' is a supposed hybrid between *R. hispida* and *R. hispida* 'Macrophylla' with open, rather loose globe-headed outline, dark pink, 8 to 10″ long racemes and larger leaves than the species, will grow 15 to 18′ high and wide; no doubt grafted on *R. pseudoacacia* to produce a standard. *Robinia hispida* was introduced 1758. Zone 5 to 8. *Robinia fertilis* ranges from North Carolina to Georgia. Cultivated 1900. Zone 5 to 8. Current thinking merges *R. fertilis* into *R. hispida*. For all practical intents, *R. hispida* is the only species of taxonomic merit and appears in the most recent nomenclatural treatments as the correct species. In my mind, heart, and to a certain degree soul, as many "bristly" locusts as I have come across, with absolute certainty none could I positively acknowledge as *R. hispida* or *R. fertilis*. In June, 1996, Bonnie and I spied a deep rose-magenta flowered form along the highway in north Georgia. Small suckers were collected and have produced 4 to 5′ high plants in two growing seasons. The flower color is the deepest and most vibrant I have observed within the genetic boundaries of the species. Also, while hiking in the north Georgia mountains, I collected another flowering variation with light lavender flowers.

Robinia 'Idaho', Idaho Locust, will grow 25 to 40′ high with a spread of 15 to 30′, tends to be more open than *R. pseudoacacia* in habit. Flowers are rose-pink, fragrant, 1″ long, borne in 6 to 8″ long, pendent racemes in May to early June. The parentage is presumably *R. pseudoacacia* and *R. hispida*. Very popular in semi-arid parts of the West that suffer extremes of heat and cold (Zone 3 and 4). Supposedly meets the stringent requirements for street tree use. Medium in growth rate. Found a tree in Urbana, IL that fit the description and, in flower, was a rather pleasing experience. Listed currently as a *R. × ambigua* cultivar which means that *R. viscosa* and not *R. hispida* is the other parent.

ADDITIONAL NOTES: I am not a great fan of locust but there are situations where their use is warranted. I have observed miserable slopes along highways that were stabilized with *R. pseudoacacia* and it is doubtful that any other plant could have performed better. There are a number of southeastern United States species with pink to rose, glandular-hispid, sometimes sticky (glutinous) inflorescences that are difficult to positively identify. I attempted to make some sense of them from the Arnold Arboretum's collection during the 1991 sabbatical. Dr. Stephen Spongberg mentioned that, in essence, this is a highly confused group. The names most often listed include: *R. boyntonii* Ashe, *R. elliottii* (Chapm.) Ashe, *R. hartwegii* Koehne, *R. kelseyi* Kelsey ex Hutch., *R. luxurians* (Dieck) C. Schneid., *R. nana* Elliott, and *R. viscosa* Vent. Also hybrids: *R. × holdtii* Beissm. (*R. pseudoacacia* × *R. luxurians*), *R. × margaretta* Ashe (*R. hispida* × *R. pseudoacacia*), and *R. × slavinii* Rehd. (*R. kelseyi* × *R. pseudoacacia*).

The above species and hybrids are listed in *The New RHS Dictionary of Gardening*. However, one of the best field botanists in the Southeast, Dr. Wilbur Duncan, Emeritus Professor, University of Georgia, who has observed and collected in the wild, lists *R. pseudoacacia*, *R. hispida*, and *R. viscosa* (with sticky glands on stems, petioles, flower stalks, and fruits) as the legitimate southeastern species. See *Trees of the Southeastern United States*, University of Georgia Press (1988) for specifics. Further see *Castanea* 49(4):187–202 (1984) for additional *Robinia* taxonomic information.

Rosa L. — Rose
FAMILY: Rosaceae

With each new edition as I approach the rose revision my mind (cluttered) and heart tell me to eliminate the entire section. The rose is a magnificent garden plant and will remain an essential element in gardens as long as there are gardens. Unfortunately, to keep them prosperous, a spray, fertilizer, and pruning regime is essential. Over the years, I have observed the University's Botanical Garden attempt to properly care for a sizable collection of Hybrid Teas, Grandifloras, and Floribundas. Some years the results were excellent; others abysmal. Mildew, blackspot, and canker cause the greatest concerns but thrips, Japanese beetles, deer (yes deer), and cold contribute mightily to decline. In recent years there has been an approach to market certain roses as "carefree" and with the Meidiland group the word rose is not used. Most interesting is the advertising campaign that describes them as "all new . . . all season, 'hybrid' flowering shrubs," with the word ROSE obvious by its absence. In about 1995, the Flower Carpet™ ('Noatrum') roses, with rose pink and now white flowers, were foisted upon the gardening public via massive advertising and slick marketing campaigns. Outrageous shrill, even from major United States nurseries, touted a 2-year-old plant producing 2000 flowers in a season, flowering up to 10 months in mild climates, evergreen to 15°F, unprecedented resistance to black spot and mildew, hardy to −20°F with no stem dieback, to −45°F with snow cover, grows 2 to 2 1/2′ high and wide. Pink containers were utilized to market the rose and self-contained displays were installed in retail centers. Unfortunately, Flower Carpet™, at least in the Southeast, did not adhere to marketing hype. Blackspot, sporadic flowering, and somewhat sprawley growth habit reduced it to less-than-satisfactory. Many retailers ate the plants, wholesalers had a difficult time growing plants, gardeners were disappointed, and the ROSE once again suffered unnecessary lousy press.

The David Austin roses are immensely popular, widely advertised and promoted. I have not grown or evaluated them but do know they are susceptible to black spot and other rose maladies. Wayside Gardens, Hodges, SC and other nurseries offer extensive collections of Austin roses.

The movement toward lower maintenance roses created a frenzy of activity that could be termed "rose rustling." The plants are "rescued" from fencerows, pastures, cemeteries, and old gardens, with the concept that if they grow in such places over time then their adaptability is ironclad. Again, not so because they do contract black spot, mildew, beetles, etc., perhaps not to the degree of the modern hybrids. As I drive and jog through my beloved Georgia, I witness the roses in these habitats. At one time they were named, perhaps passed along with many name changes as they moved along the gardening path, the true name lost to antiquity. The Antique Rose Emporium, Dahlonega, GA and Brenham, TX, has attempted to assign the correct names to many of their offerings. In many cases a new name is assigned.

Roses tempt a gardener, not unlike candy to children (or adults). Years past I removed *all* species roses from our garden because of horrific Japanese beetle infestations and black spot. Well, a few years later in went Carefree Wonder™, Carefree Beauty™, and Carefree Delight™. Their promise was great but in Zone 7b, the problems of the past surfaced. Only the first two remain and they are defoliated by July–early August, cut back in winter, and flower with unrequited love in May–June.

The only rose that appears virtually immune to black spot and other diseases in Zone 7b climate is *Rosa banksiae* 'Lutea'. Unfortunately, even this evaluation is faulty as the spring of 1998 induced terrific powdery mildew infection. Whether the species displays resistance(s) is unknown. In northern climates, *Rosa rugosa* proves the stalwart. Bonnie and I love walking the beaches of New England, from Maine to Cape Cod we have traversed and experienced this wonderful, fragrant-flowered, bright orange to red-fruited species. Certainly for a rose it asks so little and offers so much.

Although the literature reports 100 to 150(200) rose species, the interminable hybrids and cultivars escalate the numbers into the tens of thousands. Bentham and Hooker recognized about 30 species; Gandoger 4266 species from Europe and western Asia. The great Alfred Rehder, in his *Manual of Cultivated Trees and Shrubs*, which I consider the best horticultural taxonomic reference ever published, stated, "Within the limited space of this book it has not been possible to describe all the spontaneous species which could be grown within our area nor to delve deeply into the numerous horticultural forms."

To visit Sissinghurst in June when the roses are in full force in the rose garden provides the bait to entice the gardener to at least test the shrub rose waters. Perhaps what makes the Sissinghurst rose garden so unique is the inclusion of other plants, herbaceous and woody, that complement rather than compete with the shrub roses.

Also, visited Mottisfont Abbey, a National Trust property, the garden of which is dedicated largely to roses and was orchestrated by Graham Stewart Thomas, the great English plantsman, author, and painter. June is peak time and the fragrances, colors, and planting schemes are magnificent. The Arnold Arboretum has a wonderful species rose collection, actually with many rosaceous relatives interspersed. This also is worthy of a visit from May to the end of June.

Rosa multiflora Thunb. ex Murray — Japanese Rose, also referred to as Multiflora Rose
(rō′zà mul-ti-flō′rà)

FAMILY: Rosaceae

LEAVES: Alternate, odd-pinnate, usually 9(5 to 11) leaflets, obovate to oblong, 1/2 to 1 1/4″(2″) long, acute or obtuse, serrate, pubescent, lustrous bright green, stipules with laciniate margins, glandular-bristly.

CANES: Usually with paired and occasionally scattered prickles; prickles short, recurved, more or less enlarged and flattened at base.

SIZE: 3 to 4 to 10′(15′) in height and may spread 10 to 15′.

HARDINESS: Zone 5 to 8.

HABIT: A fountain with long, slender, recurving branches; eventually forming an impenetrable tangle of brush suitable only for burning.

RATE: Fast; too fast for most farmers who have this species in their fields.

TEXTURE: Medium in leaf; somewhat repulsive in winter (medium-coarse).

LEAF COLOR: Very lustrous bright green in summer; fall color, at best, is a sickly yellow.

FLOWERS: White, single, about 1″ across, fragrant; June; borne in many-flowered corymbs.

FRUIT: Red, 1/4″ diameter, globular to egg-shaped hip which is effective in August and into winter.

CULTURE: Same as described under *R. rugosa* although this species is more invasive; tolerates dry, heavy soils very well.

DISEASES AND INSECTS: None serious.

LANDSCAPE VALUE: None in the residential landscape; has received a lot of attention for conservation purposes; makes a good place for all the "critters" to hide, yet can be a real nuisance for the birds deposit the seeds in fence rows and open areas, and soon one has a jungle; use this species with the knowledge that none of your gardening friends in the immediate vicinity will ever speak to you again.

CULTIVARS:

var. *cathayensis* Rehd. & Wils.—Pale pink, 1/2 to 1″(1 1/2″) diameter flowers which are borne in few- to many-flowered rather flat corymbs.

'Inermis'—A thornless type.

'Platyphylla'—Double form, flowers deep pink; according to Wyman, it is not a very vigorous grower.

PROPAGATION: Cuttings as described under *R. rugosa*. Seed should be stratified for 120 days.

ADDITIONAL NOTES: Utilized as an understock for budding the highly domesticated selections. Another species that appears resistant to blackspot and the typical rose diseases. I cannot overemphasize the invasive and greedy nature of this species. Have observed entire pastures/fields invaded and captured by the plant.

NATIVE HABITAT: Japan, Korea. Escaped from cultivation in the United States. Introduced 1868.

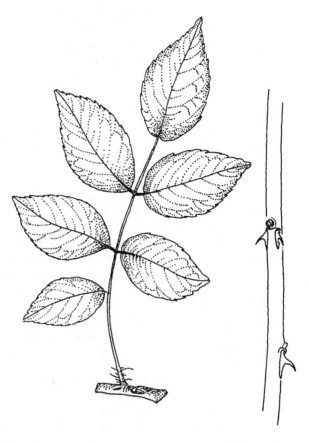

Rosa rugosa Thunb. — Rugosa Rose, also called Saltspray Rose, Beach Tomato, Japanese Rose
(rō′zà rū-gō′sà)

FAMILY: Rosaceae

LEAVES: Alternate, odd-pinnate, leaflets 5 to 9, elliptic to elliptic obovate, 1 to 2″ long, acute or obtusish, serrate, lustrous, rugose, wrinkled, dark green and glabrous above, glaucescent, reticulate, and pubescent beneath, thick and firm; petiole—tomentose and bristly.

CANES: Stout, densely bristly, prickly, downy.

SIZE: 4 to 6′ high by 4 to 6′ wide.

HARDINESS: Zone 2 to 7(8); has been seen 100 miles from Arctic Circle in Siberia where temperature regularly falls to -50°F.

HABIT: A sturdy shrub with stout, upright stems, filling the ground and forming a dense rounded outline; suckers and forms colonies.

RATE: Fast.

TEXTURE: Medium in leaf; medium-coarse when undressed.

LEAF COLOR: Lustrous, deep rugose green in summer then briefly yellowish to bronzish and in some forms excellent orange to red.

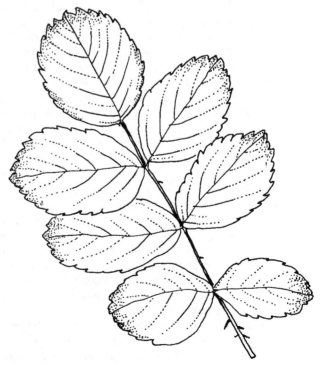

FLOWERS: Perfect, rose-purple to white, 2 1/2 to 3 1/2" across, deliciously fragrant; June through August, often found sporadically in September and October; solitary or few in clusters.

FRUIT: Hip (for lack of better terminology), actually an urn-shaped structure (receptacle) which encloses achenes, about 1" across, lustrous orange to brick-red; maturing in August through fall. The flowers and fruit are handsomely displayed against the dark green foliage.

CULTURE: Easy to grow, prefers well-drained soil which has been supplemented with organic matter; sunny and open; pH adaptable, however, a slightly acid soil is best; salt tolerant; possibly one of the most trouble-free roses. I have seen the species growing in pure sand not 100' from the Atlantic Ocean on Cape Cod, MA. The plant really stands out against the white sands, the dull green beach grass, and silvery wormwood (*Artemisia*). In Japan, confined to the beaches.

DISEASES AND INSECTS: Roses have about as many problems as *Prunus* and a complete listing is impossible. The most common include: blackspot (a leaf disease), powdery mildew, various cankers, rusts, virus diseases, aphids, beetles, borers, leafhopper, scales, rose-slug, thrips, mites, ad infinitum.

LANDSCAPE VALUE: Rugosa Rose is a valuable plant for difficult sites: banks, cuts, fills, sandy soils, and saline environments. Very beautiful in foliage, flower and fruit. Has escaped from cultivation in the northeastern United States and is often apparent along the sandy shores of the ocean. It is also called Saltspray Rose because of its tolerance. Withstands pruning and is often used in hedges. Has been used in hybridization work because of its extreme vigor and ease of culture which would be worthwhile traits to impart to offspring. Have great affinity for this species and grew it for several years in my Georgia garden until the Japanese beetles reduced it to fodder.

CULTIVARS: Epping and Hasselkus, *American Nurseryman* 170(2):29–39 (1989), presented an excellent evaluation of *R. rugosa* and other shrub roses. Their particular focus was *R. rugosa*, hybrids and cultivars. Herein I present their observations. With over 50 cultivars in existence, they evaluated 30 of the most commonly available.

Recommended *Rosa rugosa* selections:

'Alboplena' (*R. rugosa* var. *albo-plena* Rehd.)—A selected mutation of *R. rugosa* 'Alba'. 'Alboplena' has double, pure white, fragrant flowers, dark green foliage and a dense, low habit. It grows up to 4' tall. This cultivar does not produce hips, but it is highly resistant to blackspot and powdery mildew. 'Alboplena' has yellow to orange fall color and is winter hardy at -15 to -20°F. It is a good white-flowered cultivar; its only drawback is its lack of hip production.

'Belle Poitevine'—An old (1894), hybrid cultivar. It has slightly fragrant, large, semi-double, light mauve-pink flowers with showy yellow stamens. The hips are not showy, and the foliage is dull, medium green. It has yellow to orange fall color and a dense compact habit, reaching 3 1/2 to 4' tall and wide. This cultivar is highly resistant to blackspot and powdery mildew and is hardy to -20°F. 'Belle Poitevine' is a tough cultivar with attractive flowers, foliage and form. Hips abscise shortly after they form.

'Blanc Double de Coubert'—Very similar to 'Alboplena', differing only in flower form and ultimate height. This hybrid has semi-double to double, pure white, fragrant flowers and showy yellow stamens. This shrub is a vigorous grower with glossy, dark green foliage, and yellow fall color. It grows 4 to 6' tall. It is highly resistant to blackspot and powdery mildew and is hardy to -20°F. 'Blanc Double de Coubert' also produces fairly heavy suckers and can get somewhat leggy. References don't indicate that it is sterile, but if hips do form, they abort before becoming showy.

Rosa × *calocarpa* Willm.—A hybrid *R. rugosa* × *R. chinensis* with large, single, purplish crimson, fragrant flowers and showy stamens. This 4 to 5' tall cultivar has a dense, mounded habit and excellent burnt orange to red and maroon fall color. It produces attractive, orange-red hips that are somewhat oval and sparsely punctuated with tiny spines. The leaves are dull, medium green; they are more pointed, but less rugose, than those of the species. The twigs also have a finer texture than those of the species. *Rosa* × *calocarpa* is highly resistant to blackspot and powdery mildew and is hardy to -20°F. Plants were attacked by mites in the dry, hot summer of 1988.

'Frau Dagmar Hastrup' ('Frau Dagmar Hartopp')—A *R. rugosa* seedling that proved to be the best all-around performer of all cultivars evaluated. It is a prolific flowerer, with fragrant, light-pink, single flowers and showy yellow stamens. This cultivar produces very large red hips in great quantity that color as early as July. They appear along with the flowers and remain showy until November. 'Frau Dagmar Hastrup' has excellent yellow to orange fall color, rich dark green foliage, and a low, dense, mounded form growing 3 to 4' tall. It has the greatest resistance to blackspot and powdery mildew of any *R. rugosa* cultivar evaluated. It is very hardy with no winter injury at -21°F. This is one of my all time favorite roses. The flowers, fruits, and foliage are almost prescription perfect.

Acceptable cultivars:

'Delicata'—An old (1898), hybrid cultivar with large, semi-double, lilac-pink, slightly fragrant flowers and showy yellow stamens. The large orange-red hips are sparsely produced and sometimes occur with the flowers. The dark green foliage turns yellow in fall. 'Delicata' is a vigorous grower with a good, dense form (3 to 4′ tall) and is winter hardy at −21°F. It is not as disease-resistant as 'Belle Poitevine', but it is useful when a darker pink flower is preferred. 'Delicata' was moderately infected with blackspot in late August and September 1987 but was disease-free during the drier 1988 growing season.

'Hansa'—A hybrid cultivar with semi-double, large, purplish red, very fragrant flowers. It produces many orange-red hips, often along with the flowers. This cultivar has dark green, glossy, blackspot-resistant foliage and yellow to orange fall color. The upright habit is often tall and leggy, and this shrub grows to an ultimate height of 5 to 6′. Winter injury was not observed at −21°F and 'Hansa' is a good performer except for its leggy habit. This cultivar and 'Delicata' are rather similar, but 'Delicata' has lighter pink flowers and a better compact habit. 'Hansa' has a superior hip display and is more resistant to blackspot.

'Scabrosa'—A rather recent (1950) hybrid introduction. Its large, single, deep mauve-pink flowers have showy yellow stamens and usually appear in clusters of five. 'Scabrosa' produced attractive flowers and fruit, but not as freely as 'Frau Dagmar Hastrup'. The large, orange-red hips are abundant, and the bright green foliage is resistant to blackspot and powdery mildew. 'Scabrosa' has yellow to orange fall color and a dense, low, mounded form. It grows 3 to 4′ tall. This cultivar is very hardy.

'Schneezwerg' ('Snowdwarf')—A floriferous hybrid with semi-double, small, white flowers and showy yellow stamens. Small, orange-red, showy hips often appear with the flowers. The dark green foliage has a finer texture than that of *R. rugosa* but is somewhat susceptible to blackspot. 'Schneezwerg' has a mounded, dense habit and ultimately grows 4 to 5′ tall and wide. This cultivar is winter hardy to −20°F.

'Thérèse Bugnet'—A hybrid cultivar with large, double, medium pink, loosely clustered and very fragrant flowers. The red hips are rare, and the blue-green foliage is slightly susceptible to blackspot and turns yellow and orange in fall. The attractive, glossy red canes are somewhat susceptible to rose stem girdler attacks. The upright habit suckers to form dense thickets, and this shrub grows 5 to 6′ tall. 'Thérèse Bugnet' is very attractive in the winter landscape due to its shiny red canes and is winter hardy to −20°F. Its biggest drawback is its susceptibility to rose stem girdler. This is not surprising since *R. acicularis* Lindl., one of its parents, can be extremely susceptible to this insect.

Further Evaluation Needed:

'Dart's Dash'—Has large, semi-double, mauve flowers and large, orange-red hips. The foliage is bright green and showed no sign of disease.

'Roseraie de l'Hay'—A cultivar of a sport of *R. rugosa* 'Rosea'. It has large, double, crimson-purple and very fragrant flowers. The sparse hips are not showy. No blackspot, powdery mildew or other diseases on the light green foliage was evident. Krüssmann says this cultivar has a bushy form and reaches medium height. The cultivar is listed as hardy in Zone 2.

'Topaz Jewel'—A recent hybrid cultivar and one of the few yellow-flowered Rugosa Roses. It is a recurrent flowerer with semi-double, light yellow flowers and showy orange stamens. No hip production was noticed. The medium green foliage had no evidence of blackspot or other diseases. 'Topaz Jewel' is described as having a dense, bushy habit with arching canes. It grows up to 5′ high and 7′ wide.

Cultivars not recommended: Rather than describing attributes and liabilities, I chose to simply list those deemed unacceptable by Epping and Hasselkus. The reader may consult the original article for specifics. 'Agnes'; 'Alba'; 'Charles Albanel' (Explorer, Canada); 'David Thompson' (Explorer, Canada); 'Dr. Eckener'; 'F. J. Grootendorst'; 'Flamingo'; 'Grootendorst Supreme'; 'Henry Hudson' (Explorer, Canada); 'Jens Munk' (single, fragrant, medium pink, magnificent when viewed by this author, Explorer, Canada); 'Martin Frobisher' (Explorer, Canada); 'Mrs. Anthony Waterer'; 'Pink Grootendorst'; 'Rose a Parfume de l'Hay'; 'Sarah van Fleet'; 'Schneckoppe' (pink buds open to fragrant, double, white flowers with lavender suffusion, dwarf, bushy, 3′); 'Sir Thomas Lipton'; 'The Hunter' (Double, fragrant, brilliant red, repeat flowering); 'White Grootendorst'.

PROPAGATION: The seeds (actually achenes) of most species exhibit dormancy which is principally due to seedcoat conditions rather than embryo dormancy. Cold stratification at 40°F for 90 to 120 days is recommended for *R. rugosa*. Cuttings can be effective with the species roses. Hardwood cuttings should be taken from November through early March, stored in sand or peat at 35 to 40°F and planted outside in spring, with only about 1″ of the upper end of the cutting protruding. Softwood cuttings should be taken in July, August, and September with all but the top leaf removed. Rose cuttings respond to IBA and 1000 ppm IBA talc or quick dip is recommended.

ADDITIONAL NOTES: The species roses of which *R. rugosa* is a member, are not as prone to the diseases and insects as the hybrid types. They are more vigorous and less exacting as to culture. The fruits of *R. rugosa* are supposed to make the finest jelly.

NATIVE HABITAT: Northern China, Korea, Japan. Introduced 1845. Creech, *American Nurseryman* 160(6): 77–79 (1984), says introduced around 1770.

OTHER SPECIES ROSES

Rosa banksiae Ait. 'Lutea' — Lady Banks' Rose

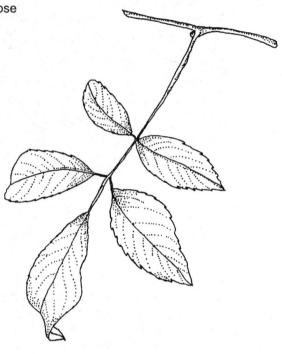

LEAVES: Alternate, compound pinnate, evergreen, elliptic-ovate to oblong-lanceolate, 3 to 5 leaflets, rarely 7, 1 to 2 1/2″ long, acute or obtusish, serrulate, glabrous except at base of midrib below, lustrous dark green; rachis pubescent.

STEM: Lustrous green, glabrous, thornless.

Rosa banksiae 'Lutea', (rō′zȧ bank′si-ȧ), Lady Banks' Rose, is a common occurrence in southern gardens especially those with period (1850 to 1900) connotations. The species is a sprawling climber (15 to 20′) that requires restraint to be kept in bounds. Have seen plants in England over 30′ high. The stems are nearly (in most cases completely) thornless. Used a great deal on fences, trellises, and also espaliered against walls. The flowers are white or yellow, 1″ across, slightly fragrant, on smooth stalks in many-flowered umbels from April into June. Flowering occurs in late March to mid-April in Athens and seldom disappoints. The double-flowered, slightly fragrant, yellow cultivar, 'Lutea', is the common representative of this species in southern gardens and is also called "Lady Banks' Rose." 'Alboplena' double, white, fragrant; 'Lutescens' single yellow; 'Normalis' has single, white flowers; 'Snowflake' bears single, white flowers, climbs to 20′, suspect it is a popular name for 'Normalis'. The plant requires no special insect and disease control measures and actually appears to thrive with neglect. Mildew was severe in spring of 1998. Tolerates a modicum of salt spray. Withstands full sun and partial shade. Roots readily from softwood cuttings. China. Zone 7 to 8.

Rosa blanda Ait. — Meadow Rose

(rō′zȧ blan′dȧ)

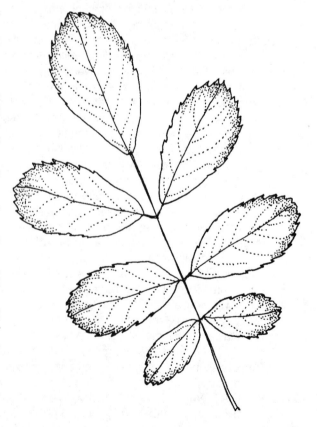

LEAVES: Alternate, compound pinnate, 5 to 7 leaflets, rarely 9, elliptic to obovate-oblong, 1 to 2 1/2″ long, acute, coarsely serrate, dull blue-green above, glabrous, paler and finely pubescent or glabrous below; stipules dilated.

CANES: Sparsely thorned or with scattered bristles to thornless with attractive red bark.

HABIT: Dense, mounded, strong growing, suckering, 4 to 5′ high.

FLOWERS: Single, light pink, fragrant, 2″ across, solitary or few together, May–June.

FRUIT: Subglobose to ellipsoidal, 1/2″ diameter, smooth bright red hips that color in late July and remain showy into winter.

ADDITIONAL NOTES: Epping and Hasselkus rated it one of the best roses for fruit display. Their only objection was late season blackspot susceptibility.

NATIVE HABITAT: Newfoundland to Pennsylvania, Missouri, North Dakota and Manitoba. Introduced 1773. Zone 2 to 6(7).

Rosa carolina L. — Carolina Rose, Pasture Rose
(rō′zà ka-rō-lī′nà)

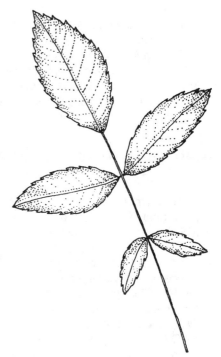

LEAVES: Alternate, pinnately compound, leaflets usually 5, rarely 7 to 9, elliptic to lance-elliptic, rarely oblanceolate, 1/2 to 1 1/4″ long, acute or obtuse, sharply serrate with ascending teeth, shiny rich green, glabrous beneath, pubescent on veins or nearly glabrous, stipules narrow; in autumn the leaves turn a dull red of varying shades.

CANES: Often covered with scattered and paired prickles and bristles when young, sometimes rather sparsely so later; prickles slender, usually not flattened except on vigorous branches, mostly straight.

HABIT: 3 to 6′ high, freely suckering shrub composed of erect branches forming dense thickets.

FLOWERS: Pink, single, 2 to 2 1/2″ across, solitary or 2 to 3 together, June into July (August). Variety *alba* Raf. has white flowers.

FRUIT: Red, 1/3″ diameter, urn- or pear-shaped, glandular-hairy, persisting into winter and maintaining good color.

ADDITIONAL NOTES: Encounter the species in Maine in late summer where a few flowers are still emerging. More petal color variation than literature affords from light to deep, almost rose, pink.

NATIVE HABITAT: Maine to Wisconsin, Kansas, Texas and Florida. Introduced 1826. Zone 4 to 9. Common in low wet grounds and borders of swamps and streams.

Rosa chinensis Jacq. — China Rose, Bengal Rose
(rō′zà chi-nen′sis)

LEAVES: Alternate, compound pinnate, 3 to 5 leaflets, 1 to 2 1/4″ long, lanceolate to broad-ovate, acuminate, serrate, glossy green, glabrous above, pubescent on midrib below.

CANES: Green-red, glabrous, with scattered, slightly hooked, extremely sharp prickles.

HABIT: Shrub 6 to 8′ high and as wide, semi-climbing to 20′; in cultivation ('Mutabilis') typically a 5 to 6′ tall shrub.

FLOWERS: Single or semi-double in species, usually fragrant, solitary or in multiples, 2″ diameter, flowering from April (Athens) to late summer (if foliage still present).

FRUIT: Ovoid to pear-shaped, 1/2 to 3/4″ long, green-brown to scarlet; I have not observed fruits on 'Mutabilis'.

CULTIVARS: Several but 'Mutabilis' (Seven-sisters Rose) grows 5 to 6′ high and wide, new leaves bronze-purple, finally blue-green, single, fragrant, 1 to 2 1/2″(3″) diameter, flowers change from yellow-orange (sulfur yellow), coppery salmon pink to deep pink, cultivated 1934, terrific plant for flower effect, unfortunately susceptible to blackspot, the more leaves the greater the flower production, still one of the better roses for unbridled use in Zones 7 and 8.

ADDITIONAL NOTES: Utilized to produce repeat flowering in European roses when it was introduced around 1800.

NATIVE HABITAT: China. Known only from gardens. Cultivated 1768.

Rosa foetida Herrm. — Austrian Brier Rose
(rō′zà fet′i-dà)

LEAVES: Alternate, pinnately compound, 5, 7, or 9 leaflets, oval or obovate, 3/4 to 1 1/2″ long, rounded or broad cuneate, edged with a few glandular teeth, brilliant parsley green and glabrous or with scattered hairs above, glandular and more or less downy below.

CANES: Grayish, furnished with many slender, straight or slightly curved prickles abruptly widened at base and up to 3/8″ long.

HABIT: Rather lax, with erect-arching canes, 6 to 7′ high.

FLOWERS: Deep yellow, 2 to 3″ across, usually solitary, or 2 to 4 together, May–June.

FRUIT: Rarely seen in cultivation, listed as globose to spherical, smooth or bristly, red, 1/2″ wide.

CULTIVARS:

'Bicolor' (Austrian Copper)—A magnificent rose with copper-red petals, yellow on the back side; often yellow or combination colored flowers occur on some branches; it is a tremendous experience to see it in full flower, perhaps no more handsome rose.

'Persiana'—Double, yellow flowers which are freely borne.

NATIVE HABITAT: Western Asia. Introduced before 1600. Have read before 1542. Zone 4 to 7. Has performed well in the University's Botanical Garden. Susceptible to black spot.

Rosa glauca Pourr. (*R. rubrifolia* Villars) — Redleaf Rose
(rō′zà glaw′kà)

LEAVES: Alternate, pinnately compound, 5 to 7(9) leaflets, ovate or elliptic, 1 to 1 1/2″ long, toothed, glabrous, of a beautiful coppery or purplish hue, and covered with a dull waxy bloom.

CANES: Covered with a purplish bloom, armed with small decurved prickles; strong canes clad with bristles and needles.

HABIT: A 5 to 7′(10′) high, erect-caned, eventually arching-spreading shrub of good density, with time will become leggy at the base.

FLOWERS: Clear pink, single, 1 1/2″ wide, solitary or in multiples, May–June, not effective especially against the reddish foliage backdrop.

FRUIT: Ovoid to subglobose, red to brown, 1/2″ long, usually smooth or with small bristles.

ADDITIONAL NOTES: A fine addition to any shrub border because of interesting foliage color. It can be used in groups where it makes a great show. Interestingly, I have read descriptions of the flowers which state bright red but the plants I have seen were pink flowered. Abundant variation in flower color from seed grown specimens. I have grown a number of seedlings to flowering size and witnessed light pink to very deep pink flowers. Susceptible to foliar diseases and I have observed plants with essentially no foliage in late summer; others heavily foliated.

NATIVE HABITAT: Mountains of central and southern Europe. Introduced 1814. Zone 2 to 7.

Rosa × harisonii Rivers. — Harrison's Yellow Rose
(rō′zà hăr-i-sō′nē-ī)

LEAVES: Alternate, pinnately compound, 5 to 9 leaflets, elliptic, glandular below, margins with compound, somewhat glandular teeth.

HABIT: Upright shrub growing 4 to 6′ high.

FLOWERS: Yellow, double, about 2″ diameter, borne over a two week period in early June; very dependable flowering shrub; has a somewhat unpleasant odor.

FRUIT: Nearly black, small, bristly, not ornamentally effective.

ADDITIONAL NOTES: The specific epithet is often spelled *harrisoni*. A hybrid between *R. pimpinellifolia* × *R. foetida*. Zone (4)5 to 7.

Rosa hugonis Hemsl. [now listed as *R. xanthina* Lindl. forma *hugonis* (Hemsl.) A.V. Roberts] — Father Hugo Rose
(rō′zà hŭ-gō′nis)

LEAVES: Alternate, pinnately compound, 5 to 13 leaflets, oval to obovate or elliptic, 1/4 to 1″ long, obtuse, sometimes acutish, finely serrate, glabrous, or slightly villose on the veins when unfolding.

CANES: Often reddish, with scattered prickles, usually also bristly at least at base of non-flowering young growth; prickles stout, straight, flattened, often red.

HABIT: Medium-sized (6 to 8′) shrub with upright arching canes and a twiggy rounded habit; often broader than high.

FLOWERS: Single, canary yellow, 2 to 2 1/2″ diameter, solitary, May–June.

FRUIT: Scarlet turning blackish red, nearly globular, about 1/2″ across, ripening in August.

ADDITIONAL NOTES: One of the more common species roses; often found in older gardens. Good, free flowering, bright yellow shrub. Looks a little ragged when not in flower.

NATIVE HABITAT: Central China. Introduced 1899. Zone 5 to 8.

Rosa laevigata Michx. — Cherokee Rose
(rō′zȧ lē-vi-gā′tȧ)

LEAVES: Alternate, pinnately compound, evergreen to semi-evergreen, trifoliate or with 5 leaflets, elliptic or ovate, 1 1/2 to 4″ long, half as wide, of thick, firm-texture, toothed, lustrous dark green, glabrous.

CANES: Armed with hooked, red-brown prickles, sometimes mixed with bristles on the branchlets.

HABIT: Spreading, arching, tangled, 8 to 10′ high shrub which will climb over and through trees; one plant on the Georgia campus was about 8 to 10′ high and 15 to 18′ wide and literally impenetrable; have seen plants on Georgia's Jekyll Island climbing over shrubs and through tree branches; canes may extend 30′ and greater.

FLOWERS: Pure white, fragrant, solitary, 3 to 4″ across, beautiful in flower, April–May.

FRUIT: Red, thickly set with bristles, pyriform, 1 1/2 to 1 3/4″ long, 3/4″ wide.

ADDITIONAL NOTES: The state flower of Georgia. It is a beautiful plant but with all the magnificent native plants in Georgia it seems strange that this would be chosen. Was cultivated about 1780 in Georgia. Not particularly cold hardy as –3°F in Athens killed the above described plant outright. A pink-flowered form ('Anemone') is available but is probably a hybrid. I grew it for a year and removed the plant because of rampant growth and vicious prickles. Flowers are beautiful.

NATIVE HABITAT: Southern China, Formosa, extending into Burma. Zone 7 to 9. Naturalized from Georgia to Florida to Texas.

Rosa moyesii Hemsl. & Wils. — Moyes Rose
(rō′zȧ moy-es′ē-ī)

LEAVES: Alternate, pinnately compound, 3 to 6″ long, 7 to 13 leaflets, ovate to roundish oval, 3/4 to 1 1/2″ long, singly or doubly toothed, glabrous except on midrib below which is downy and sometimes prickly, dark green above, pale or glaucous beneath; petiole—glandular, sticky.

CANES: Erect, armed with stout, pale, scattered, broad-based prickles, abundant on non-flowering shoots, the lower part being furnished with fine needle-like prickles; flowering shoots less prickly.

HABIT: Medium-size to large, erect branched shrub of sturdy habit; grows 6 to 10′ high and wide.

FLOWERS: Intense blood red, 2 to 2 1/2″ across, solitary or in pairs, June–July.

FRUIT: Red, 1 1/2 to 2 1/2″ long, bottle-shaped, crowned by the erect persistent sepals, glandular hairy.

ADDITIONAL NOTES: Popular species rose, and the parent of several hybrids. Beautiful in flower and fruit.

　　'Geranium'—A compact, bushy form with lighter green foliage and clear geranium red flowers; have seen frequently in English gardens, beautiful flower.

NATIVE HABITAT: Western China. Introduced 1894 and 1903. Zone 5 to 7.

Rosa omeiensis Rolfe [now listed as *R. sericea* Lindl. ssp. *omeiensis* (Rolfe) A.V. Roberts] — Omei Rose
(rō′zȧ ō-mī-en′sis)

LEAVES: Alternate, pinnately compound, usually 5 to 9(11) leaflets, oblong or elliptic-oblong, 1/2 to 1 1/2″ long, acutish, cuneate, serrate, rich green, glabrous, puberulous on midrib beneath; petiole—puberulous and prickly.

HABIT: Large spreading shrub with rich green, finely divided leaflets which give the plant a fern-like appearance. Can grow 10 to 15′ high and wide.

FLOWERS: White, single, 1 to 2 1/2″ across, June, not overwhelmingly effective.

FRUIT: Pear-shaped, 1/3 to 2/3″ long, glossy orange-red; borne on yellow stalks, maturing in July–August, falling soon after maturation.

ADDITIONAL NOTES: Fruits are especially beautiful as are the large, broad-based, translucent, ruby red prickles that provide winter interest and make for interesting flower arranging effects. Variety *chyrsocarpa* Rehd., f. Fr. has yellow fruits. Variety *pteracantha* (Franch.) Rehd. & Wils., f. has much enlarged reddish prickles often forming wide wings along the stem, reddish.

NATIVE HABITAT: Western China. Introduced 1901. Zone 4 to 7.

Rosa setigera Michx. — Prairie Rose, also called Michigan Rose or Climbing Rose
(rō′zȧ se-tij′ĕr-ȧ)

LEAVES: Alternate, pinnately compound, leaflets 3, rarely 5, ovate to oblong-ovate, 1 1/4 to 3 1/2″ long, short-acuminate, serrate, pubescent on veins beneath; lustrous dark green in summer; fall colors often a combination of bronze-purple, red, pink, orange and yellow.

CANES: With scattered or paired prickles; prickles strong, usually recurved, enlarged and flattened at base; stems, petioles and peduncles often glandular-pubescent; stems green or reddish, often dark purple with a bloom.

HABIT: A wide-spreading shrub with arching and spreading canes which may extend 15′ in a single season. May grow to 15′ but usually shorter; when climbing over flat ground grows 3 to 4′ in height.

FLOWERS: Deep pink fading to white, nearly scentless, single, about 2″ across; borne in few-flowered corymbs in late June through early July.

FRUIT: Red to greenish brown, globular, 1/3″ diameter, glandular bristly, maturing in fall.

ADDITIONAL NOTES: One of the latest flowering species roses. Quite hardy (Zone 4) and has been used in breeding work. Might be a good plant for difficult areas along highways; definitely not for the small garden.

NATIVE HABITAT: Ontario to Nebraska, Texas and Florida. Introduced 1810.

Rosa spinosissima L. — Scotch Rose (now listed as *Rosa pimpinellifolia* L.)
(rō′zȧ spī-nō-sis′i-mȧ)

LEAVES: Alternate, pinnately compound, 5 to 11 leaflets, usually 7 to 9, orbicular to oblong-ovate, 1/2 to 1″ long, simple serrate, or doubly glandular-serrate, lustrous bright green, glabrous, sometimes glandular beneath; stipules entire, rarely glandular-dentate.

CANES: Densely covered with straight, needle-like bristles and prickles.

HABIT: A dense, free-suckering shrub of mound-like, symmetrical habit, often forming thickets; may grow 3 to 4′ high.

FLOWERS: Pink, white, or yellow; solitary, single, but numerous on short branches along the stems, 1 to 2″ diameter; May–early June.

FRUIT: Black or dark brown, 1/2 to 3/4″ diameter, smooth, glabrous; effective in September.

ADDITIONAL NOTES: One of the most widely distributed rose species. Very variable and numerous cultivars are known. Assets include low habit, profuse flowering, variation in flower color, size, doubleness; also of easy culture. Is now used in commercial landscapes in the Southeast as a ground cover and mass planting. A named selection of unknown origin 'Petite Pink' was named by the J.C. Raulston Arboretum and heavily promoted. Many growers carried the banner and produced thousands. Unfortunately, in Zone 7, it is terrifically susceptible to mites and does not flower reliably; in actuality should be on the discard pile.

NATIVE HABITAT: Europe, western Asia, naturalized in northeastern United States. Cultivated before 1600. Zone 4 to 8.

Rosa virginiana Herrm. — Virginia Rose
(rō′zȧ vēr-jin-ē-ā′nȧ)

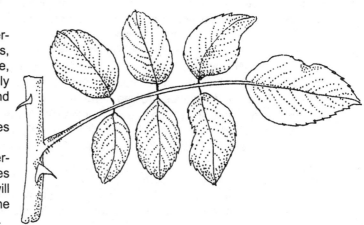

LEAVES: Alternate, pinnately compound, 7 to 9 leaflets, elliptic to obovate, 1 to 2 1/2″ long, usually acute at ends, serrate with ascending teeth, glossy dark green; upper stipules dilated.

CANES: Reddish, with mainly paired prickles, sometimes variously prickly or bristly; prickles thick-based, flattened, straight or often hooked.

HABIT: A low to medium-sized shrub which often forms a dense, suckering mass of erect stems. Will grow 4 to 6′ in height.

FLOWERS: Pink, single, fragrant, solitary or 2 to 3 together, 2 to 2 1/2″ across; June (May 25, 1991 at Arnold Arboretum).

FRUIT: Red, subglobose, about 1/2″ diameter, smooth or glandular bristly, ripening late and persistent through winter.

ADDITIONAL NOTES: One of the more handsome native roses. The summer foliage is excellent glossy dark green and changes first to purple then orange-red, crimson and yellow in autumn. The fruits are a bright glistening red and persist into winter. The canes are reddish with many paired prickles and are attractive in winter. Can be used as an effective barrier or low hedge, and when it has overstepped boundaries it can be cut to the ground and will develop quickly to excellent form. Excellent in sandy soils, particularly by the sea.

NATIVE HABITAT: Newfoundland to Virginia, Alabama and Missouri. Introduced before 1807. Zone 3 to 7(8).

Rosa wichuraiana Crépin. — Memorial Rose, Sunshine Rose
(rō′zȧ wi-shur-ē-ā′nȧ)

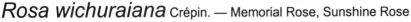

LEAVES: Alternate, evergreen to semi-evergreen, pinnately compound, 7 to 9 leaflets, suborbicular to broad-ovate or obovate, 1/2 to 1″ long, usually obtuse, coarsely serrate, lustrous dark green above and beneath, glabrous, stipules dentate.

CANES: With scattered prickles; prickles sparse, strong, and recurved.

HABIT: A procumbent shrub, of semi-evergreen nature, with long, green canes trailing over the ground and rooting; will climb if supported. Probably stays in the 8 to 16′ category from a height aspect.

FLOWERS: Pure white with rich yellow stamens in the center, fragrant, single, about 2″ across, borne in few- to many-flowered pyramidal corymbs in June and July.

FRUIT: Red, about 1/2″ long, egg-shaped; maturing in September–October.

ADDITIONAL NOTES: This species makes an excellent ground cover. I have seen it used on highway slopes where it does an excellent job of holding the soil as well as adding a touch of beauty. Has been used in breeding work and is a parent of many of the modern climbers. Good plant because of its ease of culture and freedom from insects and diseases.

NATIVE HABITAT: Japan, Korea, Taiwan, Eastern China. Found on beaches and low hills along the coast in southern parts of Japan. Introduced in 1891 into North America by the Arnold Arboretum. Zone 5 to 8.

LOWER MAINTENANCE ROSES

The name rose conjures maintenance and Conard-Pyle, West Grove, PA, the introducer of the Meidiland series in the United States wanted to avoid the connotation. The jury is still out on their absolute carefree nature but to date the reports have been favorable. They are definitely black spot and mildew resistant. However, early spring and midsummer fungicide applications are recommended. In my Georgia trials, Scarlet Meidiland™ and White Meidiland™ fared the best. All contracted some blackspot.

Alba Meidiland™ ('Meiflopan')—White, double flowers, red fruits, deep green foliage, yellow in fall, mounded-spreading, 2 1/2′ by 6′.

Bonica™ ('Meidomonac')—The first in the series with medium pink buds that open to pastel pink, fully double (50 petals), 3″ wide flowers; considered everflowering with cycle highest in spring and late summer-fall; produces bright orange-red hips (remained green in Madison, WI); upright, arching habit, 5′ by 4 1/2 to 5′; small glossy dark green leaves do not develop fall color; hardy to Zone 4 to 5; in Wisconsin tests -12°F caused tip die back of at least 12″; -21°F killed plants to the ground but they did resprout to 3′ and flower by mid-June.

Carefree Beauty™ ('Beubi')—Becoming more common in gardens; it is not a Meidiland selection; in Wisconsin tests, it produced semi-double, fragrant, medium pink flowers from June to frost; the hips remained green; foliage is thickish, glossy medium green and does not develop fall color; resistant to black spot and powdery mildew; habit is somewhat open, 3 to 4′ high and wide; hardiness response was akin to 'Bonica'; the cultivar has been included in the Dirr garden and is beautiful in flower but covered with black spot by summer.

Carefree Delight® ('Meipotal')—Single, deep pink flowers; glossy dark green foliage; low-mounding habit, 2 1/2′ by 4′; flowers on new growth, will flower to some degree into fall; tested in Dirr garden for one growing season and became so disease ridden it was removed, reported to have foliar resistance, possibly better in Zone 4 and 5 than 7b.

Carefree Wonder™—Upright shrubby vigorous form, not too different from Carefree Beauty™; produces rich pink, double (semi-double) flowers in great profusion in April and May, sporadically in summer into fall; have photographed the last "rose of summer" in late October; unfortunately, Carefree Wonder™ and Carefree Beauty™ side-by-side in the Dirr garden are often defoliated by late July–August; as temperatures cool new growth develops and flowers are produced; grows 3 to 5′ high in a single season; I cut the prominently prickled stems to 12 to 18″ of the ground in late winter; terrific bud and flower set on new growth flush of season.

'Chuckles'—Lovely mounded form with deep rose pink, 2″ diameter, single flowers, glossy green foliage, flowers continuously on new growth, 2 to 3′ by 2 to 3′, moderate disease resistance.

'The Fairy'—One of the roses I regret having never tested; abundant in New England, seemingly in gardens all along the coast; soft pink, double flowers are produced in profusion and literally enshroud the glossy green foliage during June–July; plant habit is spreading, almost ground cover-like, 2 to 3′(4′) by 2 to 3′(4′); foliage displays reasonable disease resistance.

Ferdy™ ('Keitoli')—Produces profuse coral-pink, 1 to 1 1/2″ diameter, double flowers over a 4 week period in spring; flowers so heavily that the glossy medium green foliage is almost obscured, in fall the leaves turn shades of red; grows 3 1/2 to 5′ by 3 to 4′ with a graceful cascading effect; Zone 4.

Fuchsia Meidiland™ ('Meipetala')—Mauve-pink, 2″ diameter, double flowers, red fruits, ground cover form, 2 1/2′ by 4 1/2′.

'Nearly Wild'—Excellent spreading shrub form, 2 1/2′ by 4′, often taller and wider, with 1 1/2 to 2″ diameter, rich pink, single flowers and grading to white at the petal base; excellent plant for massing; reasonable disease resistance based on my Arnold Arboretum observations.

Pearl Meidiland™ ('Meiplatin')—Ivory pink, double flowers, ground cover habit, deep green foliage, 2 1/2′ by 6′.

Pink Meidiland™ ('Meipoque')—Represents a more upright form, 3 to 4′ by 1 1/2 to 2 1/2′, that can be used as a buffer, mass or unpruned hedge; the single, 2 to 2 1/2″ diameter pink with white center flowers open from spring to frost and are followed by reddish fruits that provide winter interest; foliage is slightly glossy medium green and densely borne; Zone 4 to 5.

Red Meidiland™ ('Meinable')—Handsome low-growing form with single, red flowers, white center, yellow stamens; 1 to 1 1/2′ high, 4 to 5′ wide; produces orange-red fruits.

Scarlet Meidiland™ ('Meikrotal')—Double, 1 to 1 1/2″ diameter, scarlet flowers occur in profusion for 4 weeks in early summer and sporadically until frost; grows 3 to 4′ by 5 to 6′ and makes an excellent cover; abundant glossy rich green foliage adds to the plant's aesthetic qualities; Zone 4 to 5.

'Seafoam'—Another time-tested rose like 'The Fairy' and widely available in commerce; cream-white, fragrant, double flowers are borne in profusion during June; glossy foliage, reasonable disease resistance; vigorous, spreading habit, 2 to 3′ by 5 to 6′.

White Meidiland™ ('Meicoublan')—Was prospering in the University's Botanical Garden tests until the deer reduced it to rubble; a low-growing almost ground cover type with dense, lustrous, leathery dark green leaves and up to 4″ wide, double pure white flowers from June into fall; will grow 1 1/2 to 2′ high by 4 to 5′ wide; makes a good mass or ground cover; Zone 5.

A FINAL ROSE NOTE

For years Agricultural Canada has introduced cold hardy, disease-free roses for Canada and the northern United States. As long as I can remember Felicitas Svejda had her name attached to many (perhaps all?) of the new introductions. The introductions were tested at several locations in Canada and the northern United States over a number of years to assess floriferousness, hardiness and disease resistance. They are called the Explorer Series and are named accordingly. Many have *R. rugosa* in their parentage. I have added cultivars not included in the 1990 edition or designated them as Explorer types under *R. rugosa* (which see). May experience stem dieback in extremely cold winters, -25 to -35°F, but will flower on regrowth of season. Although these roses were bred for cold hardiness and disease resistance for the harsh climates of Canada and the northern United States, they did not prove particularly worthy in Epping and Hasselkus' trials in Madison, WI. See *Horticulture* 70(2):26–32 (1992) for "Roses from the North."

'Alexander MacKenzie'—Red, 10 petals, high disease resistance.

'Champlain'—Combines winter hardiness with the flowering habit and attractive flowers of Floribunda Roses; grows 3′ high with 2 to 2 3/4″ diameter, 30-petaled, dark red, fragrant flowers; leaves are abundant, lustrous and dark yellow-green, medium disease resistance.

'Charles Albanel'—Derived from 3 cycles of open pollination of *R. rugosa* 'Souvenir de Philemon Cochet'; grows 3′ by 3 1/2′; flowers are 3 to 4″ diameter, 20-petaled, fragrant, medium red; the leaves are rugose dark green and abundant; stems are prickly and bristly; high blackspot and mildew resistance; long flowering period, fragrance and vigor are principal attributes; interestingly, Epping and Hasselkus found this selection unacceptable.

'David Thompson'—Red, double, 32 petals, 2 3/4″ diameter, fragrant, recurrent flowers, 3 to 4′ high, derived from 'Schneezwerg' × 'Frau Dagmar Hastrup', high disease resistance.

'Henry Kelsey'—Red, 25 petals, climber, medium disease resistance.

'John Cabot'—Medium red, 30 petals, climber, high disease resistance.

'John Davis'—A trailing growth habit to 6 to 8′ long, medium pink, perfume fragrance, 3 to 4″ diameter, 40-petaled flowers occur in clusters of approximately 17; unopened bud is bright red and unfurls to pink; leaves are leathery, glossy dark green, resistant to black spot.

'John Franklin'—Red, 25 petals, fragrant, long flowering period, medium disease resistance.

'J.P. Connell'—A vigorous shrub, 3 to 5′ high and 2 1/2 to 3 1/2′ wide; flowers are yellow, 30- to 70-petaled, 3 to 4″ diameter, fragrant; foliage is dark green; this is the first yellow-flowered form introduced from the Plant Research Centre of Agricultural Canada; it is susceptible to black spot; interestingly, 24 parental types were used in breeding this selection, this represents a long term commitment to a breeding program; see *HortScience* 23:783–784, (1988) for additional information about this and 'John Davis'.'

'Rugosa Ottawa'—Introduced in 1984 as a source of insect and disease resistance for breeding roses; offers resistance to the 2-spotted spider mite, strawberry aphid, blackspot, and mildew; flowers are purple; habit is rounded-mounded, 5′ by 5′; cold hardy and flowers repeatedly but sparingly; see *HortScience* 19:896–897 (1984).

'William Baffin'—A cold hardy, disease resistant, strong climber; grows 9 to 10′ high; 2 1/2 to 3″ diameter, 20-petaled, deep pink flowers open in spring with a second flush in late summer; leaves are glossy dark green; see *HortScience* 18:962 (1983); probably Zone 4.

PARKLAND SERIES: Hybrids of native prairie roses from Morden Reseach Station, Canada. Introductions do freeze back but flowers on new growth of the season. Cultivars include:

'Adelaide Hoodless'—Bright red, 12 petals, medium disease resistance.
'Cuthbert Grant'—Velvety red, 18 petals, medium disease resistance.
'Morden Blush'—Light pink, 50 petals, medium disease resistance.
'Morden Centennial'—Pink, 50 petals, medium disease resistance.
'Morden Fireglow'—Red, 28 petals, medium disease resistance.
'Morden Ruby'—Ruby red, 70 petals, medium disease resistance.
'Prairie Dawn'—Pink.
'Winnipeg Parks'—Cherry red, double.

Rosmarinus officinalis L. — Rosemary

FAMILY: Lamiaceae
LEAVES: Opposite, simple, evergreen, 3/4 to 2″ long, 1/16 to 1/8″ wide, linear, narrow, entire, revolute margin, lustrous dark green above, white-tomentose beneath (gray-green effect), thick, aromatically fragrant when bruised, sessile.

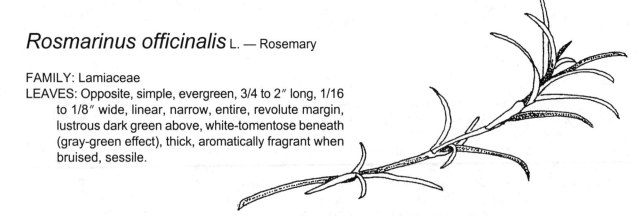

Rosmarinus officinalis, (rōs-mȧ-rī′nus o-fis-i-nā′lis), Rosemary, forms a 2 to 4′ high (to 6 to 7′ in favorable climates) and wide, irregular, evergreen shrub. The needle-like foliage is gray-green and contrasts nicely with other dark green foliage shrubs. The leaves when bruised emit a potent, unmistakable, aromatic odor. The pale to dark blue, 1/2″ long flowers are borne in the leaf axils from fall to spring. Flower effect is often reduced because flowers blend with foliage. Flowers are most pronounced during December, January, and February in Athens and colors are also the deepest. Flower color fades in the heat. Fruit is a nutlet. Easily cultured. Withstands drought and about any soil except those that are permanently wet. Full sun. Displays excellent salt tolerance. Deer resistant. Withstands pruning and can be fashioned into a low hedge. Has numerous uses in the garden but often kind of wild and woolly in appearance; this is not particularly bad because so many southern landscape plants look like they were dressed in tuxedos. I have become increasingly fond of this species over the years and offer the following cultivars for consideration:

'Arp'—Upright habit, vigorous growing, gray-green foliage, lemon-scented, sky-blue flowers; considered a Zone hardier (6) than typical.
'Beneden Blue' ('Collingwood Ingram')—Offers vivid blue, almost gentian blue flowers, narrow, dark green leaves and semi-erect habit.
'Blue Spire'—Light green, narrow leaves and clear blue flowers on an erect, compact shrub.
'Golden Rain'—Golden yellow-streaked leaves among the lush green foliage, blue flowers, 3 to 5′ high.
'Huntington Carpet'—Blue flowers, dark green leaves that are silvery beneath on a compact, semi-prostrate, dwarf, mounding shrub that grows less than 1′ tall; introduced by Huntington Botanical Garden, San Marino, CA.
'Lockwood de Forest'—Akin to 'Prostratus' in habit but has lighter green foliage and bluer flowers, 2′ by 4 to 8′.
'Majorca Pink'—Lilac-pink flowers, relatively broad leaves on an erect shrub.
'Miss Jessop's Upright'—Erect, robust form with broad, deep sea green leaves, considered one of the hardiest.
'Prostratus'—More trailing (12 to 18″) and irregular than the species and less hardy (Zone 8).
'Roseus'—Pink flowers.

'Severn Sea'—Fine blue flowers on a free-flowering, arching-spreading shrub.
'Tuscan Blue'—Clear blue flowers, light green rather broad leaves on an erect shrub.

I have grown the plant in my Georgia garden and no winter injury has been observed at 4°F. However, in Massachusetts the plant winter-killed at -5 to -10°F. Excellent garden plant because of foliage color and fragrance. Use the better blue-flowered forms. Have seen it used in containers and other places where it can cascade. The aromatic leaves are employed in cooking, sachets, etc. Easily rooted from cuttings about any time of year with a rooting hormone; the rooting medium should not be excessively moist. Southern Europe, Asia Minor. Cultivated for centuries. Zone (6)7 to 8(9).

Rubus L.
FAMILY: Rosaceae

The berries: black-, rasp-, dew-, wine-, thimble-, salmon-, cloud-, ad infinitum, have climbed up the fire escape and into the fifth edition. The cultivated, fruiting taxa are beyond the parameters of this *Manual* but several species and cultivars offer beautiful flowers, foliage, stem colors, and textures. Be leery, because they are prickly and lethal to work with and also invasive. Check local fields that are no longer in cultivation. The chances of finding the *Rubus* invasion are high.

Most *Rubus* flower on old growth so cut back canes after flowering. However, for best foliage and stem color and impact cut back stems in late winter.

Species are categorized by landscape attributes. With the exception of *R. calycinoides*, all are suckering shrubs growing 3 to 6'(10') tall.

GROUND COVER
Rubus calycinoides Hyata & Koidz. (also listed as *R. pentalobus* Hyata), is an evergreen spreading or prostrate shrub with 3- to 5-lobed, wrinkled, lustrous dark green leaves, brown pubescent, non-prickly stems, white flowers, and red fruits. 'Emerald Carpet' is a more compact clone with smaller leaves than the species, leaves turn burgundy in autumn, space 2 to 3' apart to achieve good coverage. Taiwan. Zone 7 to 9. Widely promoted but I have doubts about its staying power in heavy wet soils, high humidity and heat.

FLOWERS
Rubus amabilis Focke bears solitary, white, 2" diameter flowers on a 6' framework, western China; *R. coronarius* Sweet with double, white flowers; *R. deliciosus* Torr., Rocky Mountain Flowering Raspberry, produces pure white, 2" diameter flowers, western United States, Zone 5; *R. odoratus* L., Flowering Raspberry, offers rich pink-purple, fragrant, 1 to 2" diameter flowers in June–July, abundant in southern Appalachians into New England, Zone 5; *R.* 'Benenden', a hybrid between *R. deliciosus* and *R. trilobus* Ser., with 2 to 3" diameter, white flowers and golden-stamened centers, described as sterile, Zone 5.

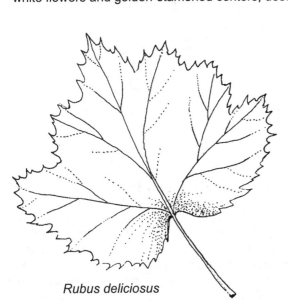

Rubus deliciosus

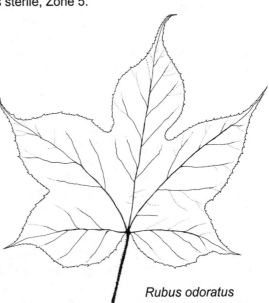

Rubus odoratus

FOLIAGE

Rubus idaeus L. 'Aureus' produces bright yellow foliage; *R. microphyllus* L. 'Variegatus' offers 3-lobed, to 3″ long leaves marbled pink and off-white, have photographed the plant in Europe but have not seen it in the United States, Zone 9; *R. thibetanus* Franch. bears large, 8 to 9″ long, 7 to 13 foliolate leaves, dark green above, white tomentose below; 'Silver Fern' has silver gray, attractively cut (dissected) leaves and waxy, bloomy, silver-white stems, Western China, Zone 6.

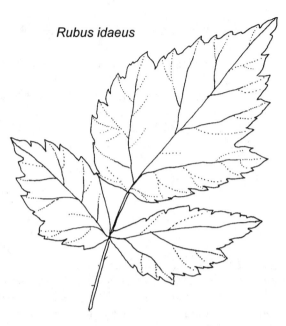

Rubus idaeus

STEMS

The following species have white-silver stems that are striking in winter. All have prickles or bristles. *Rubus biflorus* Buch.-Ham ex Sm., white flowers, Zone 9; *R. biflorus* var. *quinquiflorus* is described as having brilliant white stems in winter, vigorous, large; *R. cockburnianus* Hemsl., purple flowers, not as vigorous as above, Zone 6; *R. coreanus* Miq.; *R. koehneanus* Focke; *R. lasiostylus* Focke, maroon flowers, Zone 6; and *R. thibetanus* Franch., purple flowers, Zone 6. See *Arnoldia* 50(3):12–15 (1990) for a discussion of The Ghost Bramble, *R. lasiostylus* var. *hubeiensis*. Also, *The Garden* 117(12):578–579 (1992) for Roy Lancaster's account of *R. biflorus*.

Also, *R. phoenicolasius* Maxim., Wineberry, has dense, glandular-bristly, red stems that are sparsely prickly, white to pale pink flowers, Zone 5.

Ruscus aculeatus L. — Butcher's Broom

FAMILY: Liliaceae
LEAVES: Actually not really leaves but modified stems called cladophylls, evergreen, ovate, 3/4 to 1 1/2″ long,
    1/4 to 3/4″ wide, dark green, slightly glossy on both sides, tapering at the apex to a slender stiff spine.
STEMS: Grooved, dark olive-green, glabrous.

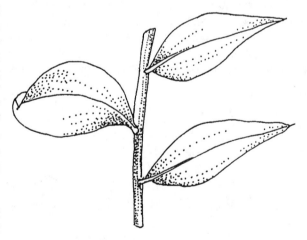

Ruscus aculeatus, (rus′kus ä-kū-lē-ā′tus), Butcher's Broom, is an unusual plant that can be used in deep shady corners of the garden where few plants will thrive. It forms a neat, 1 1/2 to 3′ high mound of rather erect, rigid stems. The plant tends to sucker and will gradually form a rather good-sized colony. The dull white, 1/4″ diameter flowers (March–April) are borne in the center of the cladophyll and make a curious sight. Plants are generally dioecious and male and female must be present if fruit set is to occur. The oblong fruits (berry) are glossy bright red, 1/3 to 1/2″ long and borne in the center of the cladophyll. They ripen in September–October and persist into the following spring. Fruits are genuinely handsome and appear as small, red cherries studding the branches. This species, although not spectacular, does quite well in Zone 7b. One particular plant on campus was literally smothered by shade but nonetheless maintained a rather dense and healthy constitution. The plant is quite prickly. It is frequently dried, dyed red (various colors), and sold for Christmas decorations. Bisexual forms are in commerce. Was given a hermaphrodite form from Kew Gardens in 1993 and carried it home in my back pack, the entire time being poked (jabbed) in the back. Plant has fruited in the Dirr garden in 1996 and 1997. 'Wheeler's Variety' grows to 2′ high and wide, produces brilliant scarlet berries without the presence of a male, obviously a perfect-flowered form. Europe, northern Africa and the Near East. Cultivated before 1750. Zone 7 to 9.

Salix alba L. — White Willow
(sā′liks al′bȧ)

FAMILY: Salicaceae

LEAVES: Alternate, simple, lanceolate, 1 1/2 to 4″ long, 1/4 to 5/8″ wide, acuminate, cuneate, serrulate, bright green above, glaucous and silky beneath; petiole—1/4 to 1/2″ long, with small glands; stipules—lanceolate.

BUDS: Terminal—absent, laterals about 1/4″ long, oblong, rounded at apex, smooth, more or less silky-downy, flattened and appressed against stem, a single bud scale visible, rounded on back, flattened toward the twig, yellow to yellowish brown.

STEM: Rather slender, light yellow-green to golden brown, smooth and shining or dull with more or less dense covering of fine silky hairs, bitter to taste.

SIZE: 75 to 100′ in height with a spread of 50 to 100′; national champion 'Tristis' is 133′ by 142′ in New Hudson, Oakland County, MI.

HARDINESS: Zone 2 to 8(9).

HABIT: Large, low-branching tree with long branches and flexible stems forming a broad, open, round-topped crown.

RATE: Extremely fast, 3 to 4′ a year over a 20 year period.

TEXTURE: Fine in leaf, medium in winter.

BARK: Yellowish brown to brown, somewhat corky, ridged-and-furrowed; there is a beautiful specimen at Smith College Botanic Garden, Northampton, MA, with a distinctly corky-textured bark, the correct identity of the Smith tree may be *S.* × *chrysocoma* ('Chrysocoma' = *S. alba* 'Vitellina' × *S. babylonica*).

LEAF COLOR: Bright green above, glaucous green beneath (silvery) in summer; may turn excellent golden yellow in fall, often variable; willows are one of the first plants to leaf out in spring and the last to drop their leaves in the fall; have seen new leaves by late February and old leaves into early January in Athens.

FLOWERS: Dioecious, entomophilous and also anemophilous; male and female borne in upright catkins; the males are quite showy and represent the "Pussy" willow character which is familiar to everyone; most are insect pollinated; on this species catkins 1 3/4 to 2 1/4″ long on leafy stalks, stamens 2, free, ovary sessile, conical and glabrous.

FRUIT: Two-valved capsule containing a number of cottony or silky hairy seeds.

CULTURE: Easily transplanted because of fibrous, spreading, suckering root system; prefers moist soils and are frequently found along streams, ponds, rivers and other moist areas; full sun; pH adaptable but do not like shallow, chalky soils; prune in summer or fall.

DISEASES AND INSECTS: Willows, like poplars, are afflicted by numerous problems such as bacterial twig blight, crown gall, leaf blight, black canker, cytospora canker, many other cankers, anthracnose, gray scab, leaf spots, powdery mildew, rust, tar spot, aphids, imported willow leaf beetle, pine cone gall, basket willow gall, willow lace bug, willow flea weevil, mottled willow borer, willow shoot sawfly, willow scurfy scale, nematodes, and other selected insects. Santamour and Batzli, *J. Arboriculture* 16:190–196 (1990), reported on the relative susceptibilities of *S. alba*, *S. babylonica* and 25 weeping willow clones to root-knot nematodes; most taxa were susceptible except for *S. babylonica* 'Babylon'.

LANDSCAPE VALUE: One of the best upright willows for landscape use; good for moist, wet places where little else will grow; wood is actually tougher than *Populus* but still very susceptible to ice and wind storms; tends to be a dirty street tree as do all willows because leaves, twigs, branches and the like are constantly dropping throughout the season; I am often mesmerized by the weeping willows, particularly when sited along water; on our campus several large weeping willows *always* have litter (leaves, small shoots, large shoots) under the canopy; additionally the surface root system out-competes other vegetation and man-made structures—be leery.

CULTIVARS:

f. *argentea* Wimm. ('Sericea', var. *sericea* Gandin.)—Leaves with an intense silvery hue; often called Silver Willow; I saw many willows in The Netherlands and Germany that had the silvery leaf color; apparently this form occurs occasionally in the wild where it is usually of dwarf habit; both surfaces are covered with silvery pubescence; saw 40 to 60′ high trees in Germany; beautiful for silver-gray foliage effect, not unlike Russian-olive, *Elaeagnus angustifolia*; could be cut back in winter to force new spring shoots.

'Britzensis' ('Chermesina')—Coral Bark Willow; first year stems reddish, must be cut back heavily for good stem color only occurs on young stems; male; the literature is really confusing and contradictory with one reference noting that 'Britzensis' is a distinct cultivar, another saying 'Chermesina' and 'Britzensis' are the same; 'Britzensis' as I have seen it has more orange-red stems and then only on the new growth of the season, it must be pruned or pollarded to encourage the extension shoots that color so vibrantly during winter; have evaluated 'Britzensis' in Georgia trials and stems are yellow-orange suffused red but still beautiful; grew 10′ in a single season, not a small plant; grown by the German nurseryman Späth at Britz, near Berlin.

'Caerulea' [var. *caerulea* (Sm.) Sm.]—Cricket Bat Willow; only mentioned because it is used for making cricket bats; the leaves are green above, bluish gray below, a female, will grow 80 to 100′, pyramidal and erect branching compared to the species.

'Cardinalis'—Described as producing sealing wax red stems, female, narrow conical tree, 15 to 20′ high.

'Tristis'—Called the Golden Weeping Willow and certainly one of the hardiest and most beautiful of the weeping types; sometimes listed as *S. vitellina* L. var. *pendula* and *S. alba* 'Niobe' in the trade; this form is also listed as *S.* × *chrysocoma* or *S.* 'Chrysocoma'; a hybrid between *S. alba*, *S. a.* 'Vitellina' and *S. babylonica*; this is essentially the standard weeping willow and has largely supplanted the other weeping types in gardens; will grow 50 to 70′(80′) and produce a broad canopy of graceful golden weeping branches. 'Tristis' is an enigmatic species with confusing botanical background. The typical tree, as I have seen it throughout the United States, is immense with large stout ascending (45 to 60° angle) branches with secondary branches steeply pendulous and often sweeping the ground, the whole tree rather dignified and majestic; for point of reference the flowers are male or female on the same or separate branches, or female flowers occupying the terminal part of the catkin, or with bisexual (perfect) flowers; the botanical uncertainties swept aside, it is a handsome tree but can suffer severe breakage and is likely to shed limbs at the drop of a hat or the wisp of a breeze. Have seen *S.* × *sepulcralis* Simonkai, Weeping Willow, utilized as a grex to house var. *chrysocoma* (Dode) Meikle, i.e., *S. a.* 'Tristis' and also var. *salamonii* Carr., a less prominent weeping form with dull green leaves and olive stems.

'Vitellina' [var. *vitellina* (L.) Stokes]—Bright yellow stems, almost egg-yoke yellow, must be cut back like 'Britzensis'; apparently several clones with the characteristics enumerated belong here; have observed this cultivar in Raleigh, NC in winter where it was distinctly yellow. Have read a reference to four male weeping clones of *S. babylonica* × *S. alba* 'Vitellina'; the grex name is *Salix* × *aureo-pendula*; clones are 'J841', 'J842', 'J1010', and 'J1011'; see *J. Jiangsu Forestry, Science and Technology* 23(4):1–5 (1996).

'Vitellina Tristis'—Semi-pendulous form of the above, in commerce before 1815, see 'Tristis' for accurate portrayal.

PROPAGATION: Seeds have no dormancy and germinate within 12 to 24 hours after falling on moist or wet sand; there is no dormancy known in any species; all willows are easily propagated by soft or hardwood cuttings at anytime of the year; just collect the cuttings and stick them; the stems have preformed root initials; a Czech Republic study noted best rooting of six *Salix* taxa occurred in June into early July; tissue culture has been successful with many *Salix* species.

A "willow rooting substance" that is quite effective in promoting rooting of difficult-to-root plants especially when used in combination with IBA has been described, see Kawase, *Physiol. Plantarum* 23:159–170 (1970) and same author *J. Amer. Soc. Hort. Sci.* 96:116–119 (1971); the young willow stems are cut into small pieces, steeped in water; the cuttings to be rooted are then placed in the extract and allowed to absorb for a period of time; IBA may also be applied in conjunction with the willow extract.

ADDITIONAL NOTES: The use of any willow should be tempered with the knowledge that serious problems do exist. Many are short-lived and require much maintenance to keep them presentable. All are fast-growing and somewhat weak-wooded. The weeping willows do add a light, graceful touch around ponds and streams. Extract of willow bark is one of the precursors of aspirin.

NATIVE HABITAT: Central to southern Europe to western Siberia and central Asia. Naturalized in North America. Long Cultivated.

RELATED SPECIES: The willows are not extensively treated in this text. There are about 250 (300) species generally confined to the northern hemisphere and about 75 species grow in North America. They hybridize freely and it is often difficult to distinguish hybrids from species. Bean, Krüssmann, *The New RHS Dictionary of Gardening* and Newsholme, *Willows, The Genus Salix*, Timber Press (1992) offer more advanced treatments of *Salix* and should be consulted. The latter is a terrific reference and the author mentions 400 species and more than 200 listed hybrids. In all the taxonomic literature I checked, no one cites the same number of species. Santamour and McArdle, *J. Arboriculture* 14(7):180–184 (1988) attempt to delineate the taxonomy of the various weeping types. I considered following their lead but am not convinced that anyone has a solid grasp on *Salix* nomenclature. Their paper is worth reading. The following are used in landscaping to one degree or another but are not enthusiastically recommended by this author.

Salix babylonica L. — Babylon Weeping Willow

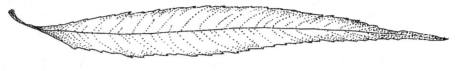

LEAVES: Alternate, simple, lanceolate to linear-lanceolate, 3 to 6″ long, 1/2 to 3/4″ wide, acuminate, cuneate, serrulate, light green above, grayish green beneath, with distinct venation, glabrous; petiole—1/5″ long; stipules—rarely developed, ovate-lanceolate, revolute.

STEM: Long, pendulous, glabrous except at nodes, brown, on upper surface reddish brown and never yellow as in *S. alba* 'Tristis'.

Salix babylonica, (sā′liks bab-i-lon′i-kȧ), Babylon Weeping Willow, grows 30 to 40′ with a comparable spread. A very graceful, refined tree with a short, stout trunk and a broad, rounded crown of weeping branches which sweep the ground. True *S. babylonica* is an enigma and appears almost to be a plant of the past. In European countries and the United States, it is almost nowhere to be found. In fact, trees that I have seen labeled as *S. babylonica* were usually something else. The normal form is a female. 'Blue Fan' with splashed blue-green foliage is described. 'Crispa' ('Annularis') is a cultivar with spirally curled leaves. I have read several historical renderings concerning this tree and am almost convinced it does not exist in gardens except in the minds of those who wish to associate it with the hanging gardens of Babylon and the tree described therein was *Populus euphratica*. Apparently, three different clones, maybe more, exist under this name. The bottom line translates to another weeping willow other than *S. babylonica*. 'Blue Fan' is a weeping clone with blue-green foliage. Santamour and McArdle, *J. Arboriculture* 14(7):180–184 (1988) propose the cultivar name 'Babylon' for the tree described above. Introduced 1730. China. Zone (5)6 to 8. In laboratory freezing tests, the species survived -76°F. See *Plant Physiology* 95:871–881 (1991).

Salix* × *blanda Anderss., (sā′liks blan′dȧ), perhaps more correctly listed as *S.* × *pendulina* Wender. 'Blanda', Wisconsin Weeping Willow, is a hybrid between *S. babylonica* and *S. fragilis* with increased hardiness (Zone 4). It is not truly weeping although the branches are somewhat pendulous. Grows to 40′ high. The leaves are glossy dark green, rather thick and bluntly toothed. Stems are olive-brown, glabrous. There is some indication this may be a hybrid between *S. babylonica* and *S. pentandra*. This is a female clone. First described around 1867. To my knowledge not available in commerce in the United States. 'Elegantissima', a more strongly weeping form, resides herein. Zones 4 to 7.

Salix caprea L. — Goat Willow, Pussy Willow

LEAVES: Alternate, simple, broad-elliptic to oblong, 2 to 4″(5″) long, 1 to 2 1/4″(3″) wide, acute, rarely rounded at base, irregularly and slightly toothed or nearly entire, pubescent at first, finally glabrate, rugulose and dark green above, gray-pubescent beneath and reticulate; petiole—1/3 to 2/3″ long; stipules—oblique-reniform, serrate.

BUDS: Stout at maturity, 1/4 to 1/2″ long, colored and clothed as the twigs, purplish brown; flower (catkin) buds larger than others.

STEM: Stout, yellowish brown to dark brown, purplish brown, pubescent to glabrescent.

Salix caprea, (sā′liks kap′rē-ȧ), Goat Willow, is an erect, small tree growing 15 to 25′(30′) with a 12 to 15′ spread. The major asset is the large (1 to 2″ long), male catkins which appear in March and early April and are affectionately referred to as Pussy Willows because of their silky softness. This species is often confused with *S. discolor* Muhl., the true Pussy Willow, which is native to wet areas over much of the eastern United States, but that species has deep brown branches and very glaucous (almost bluish white)

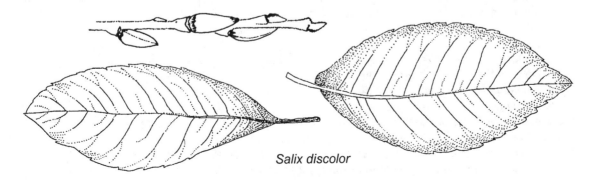

Salix discolor

lower leaf surface. *Salix discolor* is quite susceptible to canker and is considered inferior for landscape use although neither species is a plant of the first order. Co-national champions *S. discolor* are 47′ by 33′ in Clinton, MI and 25′ by 48′ in Jamestown, RI. *Salix caprea* 'Pendula' ('Kilmarnock') is a handsome weeping form (female) that can be used as a ground cover or raised on a standard to produce a small weeping tree. This clone was discovered on the banks of the River Ayr before 1853 and was put into commerce by Thomas Lang of Kilmarnock, Ayrshire, Scotland. There are two clones under the above name; one female, the other male. The female is the most common form in cultivation in the United States. Roy Lancaster named the female form 'Weeping Sally'. The cultivars are often grafted on a standard to produce a rather pretty small weeping tree. When not grafted or staked, the plant forms a large-trailing mound and serves almost a ground cover function. There is also a white-variegated leaf form that does not appear to be stable. Europe to northeast Asia and northern Iran. Long cultivated. Adapted from Zone 4 to 8.

Salix chaenomeloides Kimura — Japanese Pussy Willow
LEAVES: Alternate, simple, narrow elliptic to oblong or obovate, 2 to 5″ long, 1/2 to 2″ wide, short acuminate or acute, cuneate, serrate with incurved teeth, young leaves reddish brown, dark blue-green at maturity, glabrous, finely hairy beneath, 18 to 22 vein pairs; petiole—1/4 to 1/2″ long; stipules—lanceolate, persistent.
BUDS: Flower—large, 1/2 to 3/4″ long, plump, ovoid, irregular, lustrous reddish purple, glabrous to slightly pubescent at base; vegetative—smaller, 1/8 to 3/8″ long, appressed to stem, flattened, red-brown, pubescent.
STEM: Stout, hairy in youth, becoming glabrous, reddish purple on current year's growth, becoming shiny brown, glabrous, with small, lip-like lenticels; pith—solid, white on first year stems, brown on second.

Salix chaenomeloides, (sā′liks kē-nom-el-oy′dēz), Japanese Pussy Willow, was given to me by Don Shadow about 10 years past. The plant in our test plots was 12′ by 12′ in two seasons. Probably will mature between 15 to 20′ high. The large, red flower buds were almost more handsome than the 1 to 2″(3″) long, silky, pink- to rose-tinged, male catkins. The yellow-orange anthers follow and provide contrast. Extremely easy to grow and many individuals collected cuttings from my original plant. Probably better than *S. caprea* in Zone 7 and 8. Have observed a large plant in Mark Johnson's, Dearing, GA garden that is prospering. Japan. Zone 6 to 8.

Salix elaeagnos Scop. — Rosemary or Hoary Willow
LEAVES: Alternate, simple, linear to narrow lanceolate, 2 to 6″ long, 1/8 to 7/8″ wide, tapered at both ends, appearing narrower because of the revolute margins, finely serrate, rather lustrous dark green and glabrous above, covered with a white wool below; petiole—1/4″ long; stipules—absent.

Salix elaeagnos, (sā′liks el-ē-ag′nos), Rosemary or Hoary Willow, is a dense, medium-sized shrub, 15 to 20′ high, with long, linear, "Rosemary-like" leaves. The leaves are initially grayish and finally dark green above and whitish beneath. The mature stems are a distinct reddish brown. Catkins to 2″ long, 1/2″ wide, appearing before leaves. This is a handsome willow because of the pretty leaves and is recommended for wet areas where few other shrubs can be successfully grown. I first learned the plant as *S. rosmarinifolia* which is a respectable name when one takes into account the similarity of the leaves to Rosemary, *Rosmarinus officinalis*. This is a fine garden plant with wispy gray-green foliage and a delicate texture. Ideally the shrub is best pruned to the ground in late winter to promote the long shoot growth. If not occasionally renewal pruned, it will become leggy. Mountains of central and southern Europe, Asia Minor. Zone 4 to 7.

Salix × *elegantissima* Koch., (sā′liks el-e-gan-tis′i-mȧ), Thurlow Weeping Willow, is a hybrid between *S. babylonica* and *S. fragilis*. It is a rather confusing entity and may represent several clones. Grows to 50′. It is hardy to Zone 4. Doubtfully cultivated in the United States. See under *S.* × *blanda*.

Salix exigua Nutt., (sā′liks ex′i-gwa), Coyote Willow, of the western states offer intense silvery gray, narrow leaves that maintain color through the summer. Will

Salix exigua

grow 10′(30′) high. *Salix hastata* L. 'Wehrhahnii', (sā′liks has-tȧ′tȧ), presents silver-gray, male catkins that turn yellow when the stamens open, the leaves are fresh green, the habit bushy and spreading, 6′ by 12′. *Salix helvetica* Vill., (sā′liks hel-vet′i-kȧ), Swiss Willow, also offers silver-gray leaves and golden catkins on a 2′ high and 3′ wide shrub. *Salix integra* Thunb. 'Albomaculata' ('Alba Maculata' according to Newsholme), (sā'liks in-teg'rà), produces salmon-pink new shoots aging to white variegation that persists through summer. Will grow 10' high but is best cut back in late winter to encourage strong growth in spring and summer. All the willows listed above will require cool growing conditions for best foliage color/performance. I suspect most would develop the consistency of a soggy potato chip in Zone 7 to 8.

***Salix* 'Flame'**—Discovered by Melvin Bergeson of Fertile, MN. The habit is oval with a compact dense branching habit. Will grow 15 to 20' high. Bark is orange-red in winter. The tips of the branches curl upward and inward. Leaves turn a beautiful golden yellow in fall, long after those of other trees have fallen.

Salix gracilistyla Miq. — Rosegold Pussy Willow
LEAVES: Alternate, simple, oblong, oval, narrow ovate, 2 to 4″(5″) long, 1/2 to 1 1/4″ wide, acute at ends, serrulate, gray-green above, grayish and pubescent below; petiole—1/4″ long, pubescent; stipules—semicordate.

Salix gracilistyla, (sā'liks gras-il-is'tī-là), Rosegold Pussy Willow, is allied with *S. discolor* and *S. caprea* by virtue of being grown for its showy, 1 to 2″ long, male, pinkish or reddish tinged, silky villous catkins produced in March–April. The catkins are quite attractive and there is much variation in the degree of pinkish or reddish suffusion of the gray catkins. It is lower growing (6 to 10') than *S. caprea* and for this reason may be better suited to the small landscape. The leaves are grayish or bluish gray and offer a foliage contrast not available from many species. 'Variegata' is a rather pretty white-margined form that will revert to the species. Raulston mentioned that the variegation only appears on strong shoots exposed to full sun. Catkins are twice as long as the normal pussy willow grown in the nursery trade. I am unsure whether this variegated form mentioned here is akin to (same as) that listed under *S. caprea*. Japan, Korea, Manchuria. Cultivated 1900. Zone 5 to 8.

Salix lanata L. — Woolly Willow
LEAVES: Alternate, simple, oval, roundish or obovate, 1 to 2 1/2″ long, 3/4 to 1 1/2″ wide, undulating surface, abruptly pointed, cuneate, although sometimes rounded or heart-shaped, entire or essentially so, silvery gray pubescence on both surfaces; petiole—1/8 to 1/4″ long; stipules—1/3″ long, ovate, entire, prominently veined (5- to 6-paired).

Salix lanata, (sā'liks là-nā'tà), Woolly Willow, has *never* been seen by the author in a United States garden, but appears like privet in European gardens. It is a small, 2 to 4' high and slightly wider shrub that offers wonderful gray foliage. Among the traditional green-foliaged evergreens and deciduous shrubs it genuinely piques interest. The 1 to 2″ long, 1/2″ thick male catkins are bright golden and occur at the end of the previous season's growth. No doubt, it requires a cool climate and the heat and humidity of the Midwest and Southeast would prove disastrous. Another gray foliage type is 'Stuartii' which is probably a form of *S. lanata*. In my travels I have seen several handsome willows in Mr. Adrian Bloom's great garden at Bressingham that would be of interest to the intrepid willow-o-phile. ***Salix cinerea*** L. 'Tricolor', Gray Willow, has young leaves that are mottled pink, white and creamy yellow. Plants should be cut back in winter to encourage new growth. Apparently variegation is lost during summer and another pruning to induce new shoots is warranted. Will grow 6 to 10' high if not pruned. Northern Europe and Northern Asia. Cultivated 1789. Zone 3 to 5.

Salix matsudana Koidz. — Hankow Willow, Peking Willow
LEAVES: Alternate, simple, linear-lanceolate, 2 to 4″ long, 1/3 to 3/5″ wide, long acuminate, rounded or rarely cuneate, sharply glandular serrate, bright green above, glaucous and glabrous below; petiole—1/4″ long.
STEM: Yellowish in youth, later olive-green to greenish brown, glabrous.

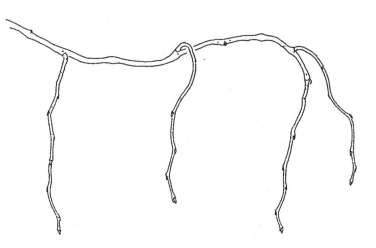

Salix matsudana, (sā'liks mat-sū-dā'nà), Hankow Willow, develops an oval-rounded head of fine-textured branches. The emerging leaves are bright green, turn darker green and yellow-green in fall. The species is seldom encountered in the United States. It is closely allied with *S. babylonica* and differences are based on 2 nectaries in the female flower of *S. matsudana* compared to a single of *S. babylonica*. It is more drought tolerant than most willows and for that reason might be worth considering. Australian study showed that the species was salt tolerant. The species matures between 40 and 50′. China, northeast Asia. Zone (4)5 to 7(8). 'Tortuosa' was killed in Orono, ME. Controlled study showed 'Tortuosa' hardy to −76°F. Laboratory and real world experiences are not always on the same field. Several cultivars include:

'Golden Curls'—A hybrid between *S. alba* 'Tristis' and *S. matsudana* 'Tortuosa' that tends toward a shrubby nature although I have seen small trees. The golden stems have a slight tortuosity and semi-pendulous nature while the leaves are somewhat curled. This is a possibility for cut branches. It might grow 40′ high and this is certainly possible considering the parentage. Have seen 30′ by 15′ size categorization. Probably correctly listed as *S.* × *erythroflexuosa* Rag. Apparently discovered in Argentina around 1971 and brought into the trade by Beardsley Nursery, Perry, OH. Zone 5 to 8.

'Navajo' (Globe Navajo Willow)—A large, 20′ high, round-topped tree that is tough and hardy. Apparently, this form is used in the southwestern United States. Same as 'Umbraculifera'?

'Pendula'—The branches are pendulous, the young branches green and the flowers female; a male pendulous form is also known.

'Scarlet Curls'—Probably has *S. matsudana* 'Tortuosa' as one parent and perhaps *S. alba* 'Britzensis' as the other. The stems are red (scarlet) in winter and the older branches golden brown. Stems more reddish brown in Zone 7. The leaves are curled somewhat like those of 'Golden Curls'. Will grow 30′ by 15 to 20′. Zone 5 to 8. In the *S.* × *erythroflexuosa* grex. Not as hardy as 'Golden Curls'.

'Snake'—A great plant name, sure to inspire confidence in the buying public. Not well-known but supposedly an improved form of *S. m.* 'Tortuosa' with perhaps greater branch contortions and canker resistance. Have observed and would be hard-pressed to quantify degree of contortion between this and 'Tortuosa'.

'Tortuosa' (Dragon's Claw Willow)—At one time I looked upon this contorted-stemmed tree with a habit similar to the species as a third class citizen but in recent years have come to appreciate the interesting architecture it brings to the winter landscape. The gray-brown branches are distinctly gnarled and contorted and make a great conversation piece. The tree may grow 50′ high but 20 to 30′ appears more typical. In a sense, the tree might be pruned heavily in youth like the Europeans pollard the bright red- and yellow-stemmed willows. The more vigorous shoots tend to have the greatest degree of contortions. Possibly this might be of use as a plant for the cut branch (florist) market. The fast growth is a distinct advantage over plants like *Corylus avellana* 'Contorta'. Unfortunately, in Zone 7b(8) the tree is short-lived. A female clone.

'Umbraculifera'—A bushy almost broad-rounded form without a central leader that will grow 25 to 35′ high; after 6 years in the Arnold Arboretum a plant was 20′ high and 30′ wide.

Salix melanostachys Mak., (sā′liks mel-an-ō-stā′kis), Black Pussy Willow, is a 6 to 10′ high shrub, the stems of which in winter assume a rich purple-black color. In spring the male catkins open a deep purple-black with brick red anthers and finally show yellow. It is an attractive and rather curious shrub. It is of Japanese origin and considered a hybrid. Should perhaps more correctly be listed as *Salix* 'Melanostachys', var. *melanostachys* (Mak.) C. Schneid., or *S. gracilistyla* 'Melanostachys'. Zone (4)5 to 7. Have not seen it in Zone 7b but suspect it would survive.

Salix pentandra L. — Laurel Willow, Bay Willow
LEAVES: Alternate, simple, elliptic to ovate to elliptic-lanceolate, 1 1/2 to 5″ long, 3/4 to 2″ wide, short-acuminate, rounded or subcordate at base, glandular-denticulate, lustrous dark green above, lighter beneath, glabrous, midrib yellow, aromatic when bruised; petiole—1/4 to 1/2″ long, glandular; stipules—oblong-ovate, often small.
BUDS: Yellow.
STEM: Lustrous, greenish brown, glabrous.

Salix pentandra, (sā′liks pen-tan′drȧ), Laurel Willow, has the most handsome foliage of all the willows. The leaves are a lustrous, polished, shimmering dark green in summer; grows 30 to 35′ high with a compact oval form. Catkins cylindric, 1 to 2″ long, 1/2″ wide, appearing with the foliage, stamens 5 to 12. The few I have seen in central Illinois were so infested with leaf disease that by August there were no leaves on the tree. Where leaf diseases do not present a problem it could be an interesting specimen. Native to

Europe. Naturalized in eastern United States. Often listed as hardy in Zone 2 and probably best in 2 to 5. Long cultivated.

Salix 'Prairie Cascade'—Introduced by the Morden Research Station in Canada. Apparently a hybrid between *S. pentandra* and *S.* 'Blanda' with hardiness and glossy green foliage of *S. pentandra* and weeping habit and stem color of the weeping willow. Will grow 35 to 45' high and wide. Zone 3 to 5(6).

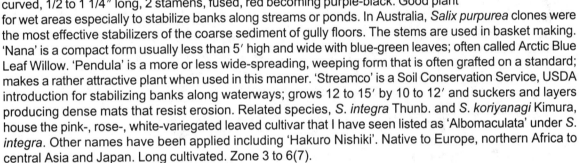

Salix purpurea L. — Purpleosier Willow, Basket Willow
LEAVES: Alternate or occasionally opposite, simple, oblanceolate, rarely oblong-obovate, 2 to 4″ long, 1/8 to 1/3″(1″) wide, acute or acuminate, cuneate, serrulate toward the apex, lustrous dark blue-green above, pale or glaucous beneath, glabrous or slightly pubescent at first, turning black upon drying; petiole—1/6 to 1/3″ long; stipules—small or wanting.
BUDS: Small, appressed, purplish, glabrous.
STEM: Slender, tough branches, purplish at first, finally light gray or olive-gray, glabrous.

Salix purpurea, (sā′liks   pĕr-pū′rē-à), Purpleosier Willow, is a rounded, dense, finely branched shrub, 8 to 10′(18′) high. National champion is 37′ by 49′ in Leelanua County, MI, however, I have doubts about authenticity. Can look horrendous unless properly maintained. When specimens become overgrown it is best to cut them to the ground. The long shoots are supple and with the fine-textured leaves can be rather attractive. The sessile catkins appear before the leaves, narrow-cylindrical, often curved, 1/2 to 1 1/4″ long, 2 stamens, fused, red becoming purple-black. Good plant for wet areas especially to stabilize banks along streams or ponds. In Australia, *Salix purpurea* clones were the most effective stabilizers of the coarse sediment of gully floors. The stems are used in basket making. 'Nana' is a compact form usually less than 5′ high and wide with blue-green leaves; often called Arctic Blue Leaf Willow. 'Pendula' is a more or less wide-spreading, weeping form that is often grafted on a standard; makes a rather attractive plant when used in this manner. 'Streamco' is a Soil Conservation Service, USDA introduction for stabilizing banks along waterways; grows 12 to 15′ by 10 to 12′ and suckers and layers producing dense mats that resist erosion. Related species, *S. integra* Thunb. and *S. koriyanagi* Kimura, house the pink-, rose-, white-variegated leaved cultivar that I have seen listed as 'Albomaculata' under *S. integra*. Other names have been applied including 'Hakuro Nishiki'. Native to Europe, northern Africa to central Asia and Japan. Long cultivated. Zone 3 to 6(7).

Salix 'Rubykins'—A small shrub, 6′ by 6′ in 5 years, with slender branches and narrow leaves. The catkins are small, ~1/2″ long, reddish. Given to me by Bill Wandell and I shared it with many people. Have seen it listed in Arborvillage, Woodlanders and Spring Meadow catalogs. Origin and taxonomy are shrouded in mystery. May be a form of *S. koriyanagi*. Zone 5 to 7.

Salix sachalinensis F. Schmidt 'Sekka'
LEAVES: Alternate, simple, lanceolate, 4 to 6″ long, 3/4″ wide, acuminate, cuneate, serrate, lustrous dark green above, glabrous; petiole—1/2 to 1″ long.
BUDS: Purplish red.
STEM: Reddish purple when exposed to the sun, lustrous, glabrous.

Salix sachalinensis 'Sekka', (sā′liks sa-kà-len-en′sis), Japanese Fantail Willow, is a large broad-rounded shrub or small tree with uniquely twisted branches that are sometimes flat. It grows 10 to 15′ high and forms a wide-spreading shrub. It is a male clone. The cylindric, gray, silky, 1″ long catkins are produced abundantly along the reddish purple stem. The branches are sometimes used for flower arranging. Have noted reference to *S. udensis* Trautv. & Meyen. as the correct species but my observations of 'Sekka' and the taxonomic description of *S. udensis* do not mesh. The species is native to Japan. Introduced 1905. Zone 4 to 7.

Sambucus canadensis L. — American Elder
(sam-bū′kus kan-à-den′sis)

FAMILY: Caprifoliaceae
LEAVES: Opposite, compound pinnate, 5 to 11, usually 7 leaflets, each 2 to 6″ long, 1/2 to 2 1/2″ wide, short-stalked, oval, oblong, rounded-ovate, acuminate, sharply serrate, dark green, slightly puberulous on the veins beneath or nearly glabrous; lowest pair of leaflets frequently 2- or 3-lobed.

BUDS: Solitary or multiple, terminal mostly lacking, brown, few-scaled, small, 1/8″ long.

STEM: Stout, pale yellowish gray to gray-brown, heavily lenticellate, glabrous; pith—white; leaf scars broadly crescent-shaped or 3- or 4-sided, large, more or less transversely connected.

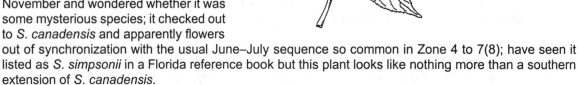

SIZE: 5 to 12′, quite variable in size, varies significantly with habitat; national champion is 16′ by 22′ in Jefferson National Forest, VA.

HARDINESS: Zone (3)4 to 9.

HABIT: Stoloniferous, multi-stemmed shrub, often broad and rounded with branches spreading and arching.

RATE: Fast.

TEXTURE: Medium in foliage (usually quite dense); coarse in winter.

LEAF COLOR: Dark green in summer, leafs out early in spring; fall color is generally an insignificant yellow-green.

FLOWERS: Perfect, white, actually more yellow-white due to stamens, June–July, borne in 5-rayed, slightly convex, 6 to 10″ wide, flat-topped cymes; usually quite profuse and covering the entire plant; flowers contain a volatile oil and are used to produce elderflower water for confectionery and cosmetics; in the Orlando, FL area I saw the plant in flower in March and November and wondered whether it was some mysterious species; it checked out to *S. canadensis* and apparently flowers out of synchronization with the usual June–July sequence so common in Zone 4 to 7(8); have seen it listed as *S. simpsonii* in a Florida reference book but this plant looks like nothing more than a southern extension of *S. canadensis*.

FRUIT: Purple-black, August–September, berry-like drupe with multiple pyrenes, about 1/4″ in diameter, rather pretty in late summer and certainly sustenance for birds, plant multiple clones for best fruit set.

CULTURE: Transplants well, does best in moist soils although will tolerate dry soils; thrives under acid or alkaline conditions; suckers profusely and requires constant attention if it is to be kept in presentable, decent condition.

DISEASES AND INSECTS: Borers, cankers, leaf spots, powdery mildew.

LANDSCAPE VALUE: Fruit is good for jellies, pies, juice, wine and attracting birds; Vitamin C content is 0.3 mg/g; difficult to utilize in home landscape situations because of its unkempt habit; potential near wet areas, naturalizing effect, roadside plantings; foliage forms are rather handsome.

CULTIVARS:

'Acutiloba' (also listed as 'Laciniata')—Leaflets very deeply divided, rather handsome plant, appears to be a weak grower, is nice for foliage effect, 6 to 8′ high.

'Adams'—Numerous fruits in large clusters, excellent for jams, pies and wine, 8 to 10′ by 8 to 12′, selected by William M. Adams of Union Springs, NY.

'Aurea'—Cherry red fruit, broad golden yellow leaves, grows vigorously and looks good throughout the growing season, 8 to 10′ by 8 to 12′.

'Maxima'—Flower clusters 10 to 18″ in diameter, leaves 12 to 18″ long, rose-purple flower stalks, vigorous, may have 11 leaflets instead of the normal 7.

'Rubra'—A red-fruited form, introduced before 1932 by A.P. Wezel, Smith College.

'York'—Larger fruits that mature later than those of 'Adams'; plant is also larger growing.

PROPAGATION: Seed, 60 days at 68°F plus 90 to 150 days at 41°F in moist sand. Cuttings, softwood root well; a report on *S. nigra* noted 92% rooting of semi-hardwood cuttings with 4000 ppm IBA; hardwood taken in late winter also root well; division is also effective.

ADDITIONAL NOTES: Approximately 25 species are distributed around the globe. To my way of defining a great garden plant, the *Sambucus* taxa come up short. However, the foliage when coppiced (cut back) proves effective in the border. This approach is common in Europe particularly with the golden, purple and cut leaf forms. The species appear to thrive with neglect and *S. canadensis* is weed-like over much of eastern North America.

Worthwhile article, "Mind Your Elders," by Ann Lovejoy in *Horticulture* 72(8):34–36, 38, 82 (1995). Also, "Elegant Elderberries" appeared in *Fine Gardening* 59:56–61 (1998). For a genus that receives no more than an askance from the casual gardener, it is receiving considerable column space.

NATIVE HABITAT: Nova Scotia and Manitoba to Florida and Texas. Found in damp, rich soil. Introduced 1761.

RELATED SPECIES:

Sambucus caerulea Raf. — Blueberry Elder, Blue Elder
LEAVES: Opposite, compound pinnate, 6 to 10″ long, 5 to 7(9) leaflets, 2 to 6″ long, 1/2 to 2″ wide, coarsely serrate, bright green to blue-green, glabrous.

Sambucus caerulea, (*S. glauca* Nutt.), (sam-bū′kus ser-ū′lē-å), Blueberry Elder, is a large shrub or small tree often growing 15 to 30′ high and larger. Several years past, while jogging on some back roads near Portland, OR, I noticed the plant in abundance. This was August and the dusty-coated, blue-black fruits were dripping from the plants. Fruits make good jam, jelly, pie and wine. The yellowish white flowers occur in convex, 5-rayed, 4 to 6″ wide cymes in May to July. Have not seen on East Coast but for an elder collector could be worthwhile. Morton Arboretum reported that the species had not performed well. British Columbia, east to Montana and Utah. Cultivated 1850. Zone 5 to 7.

Sambucus nigra L. — Common or European Elder
LEAVES: Opposite, compound pinnate, 4 to 12″ long, leaflets 3 to 9, usually 5, short-stalked, elliptic to elliptic-ovate, 1 1/2 to 5″ long, 3/4 to 2″ wide, acute, sharply serrate, dark green above, lighter and sparingly hairy on the veins beneath; of disagreeable odor when bruised.

Sambucus nigra, (sam-bū′kus nī′grà), European Elder, is a large, multi-stemmed shrub or tree ranging from 10 to 20′(30′) high. The foliage is dark green in summer and of a disagreeable odor when bruised. Flowers are yellowish white, of a heavy odor, and borne in 5 to 8″ diameter, 5-rayed, flat-topped cymes in June. The fruit is lustrous black, 1/4″ diameter, September. There are numerous cultivars associated with this species including white-variegated, yellow- and purple-leaved, cutleaf, yellow-fruited, and edible commercial clones. I counted 29 in *The New RHS Dictionary of Gardening*. The Strybing Arboretum, San Francisco had several cultivars that were quite handsome. I have observed the species all over the British Isles and continental Europe growing along roadsides, in ditches and in open fields. Have observed in shady environments in Europe. Appears more shade tolerant

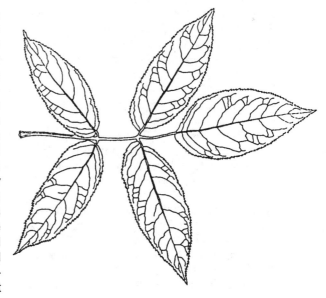

than *S. canadensis*. Apparently it deserves the same weed status as *S. canadensis*. A few of the cultivars are worth mentioning. 'Aurea' offers bright yellow new foliage that fades with time and heat. 'Laciniata' (f. *laciniata*) presents finely dissected, green leaflets not unlike those of *Acer palmatum* var. *dissectum* 'Filigree Lace'. A wonderfully fine-textured shrub that attracts considerable attention from members of our European garden tours. 'Guincho Purple' is supposedly more purple than 'Purpurea', however, I see little difference. 'Madonna' has bright and marbled golden yellow leaves on a 6 to 10′ shrub; in general leaves are bordered with a bright golden yellow margin. In 'Marginata' the leaflets are initially margined yellowish white, fading to creamy white. This is a most handsome form and probably requires heavy root moisture and partial shade in the eastern-southeastern United States. 'Aureomarginata' is akin to the above except the leaflets are bordered with a yellow-golden border. 'Pulverulenta' is splashed, marbled, speckled, and striped with white; certainly somewhat unstable and should be treated as a cut-back shrub in winter; about 4 to 5′ high. 'Purpurea' probably should be listed as f. *purpurea* since several purple leaf forms are known. The new shoots are bronze-purple and the flower petals are pinkish. The color does not hold well in heat but for spring effect is worthwhile. The purple-foliaged variant appears to have been reported only from the British Isles. According to Nelson, *The Plantsman* 8(3):189–190 (1986), the original cultivar names 'Foliis Purpureis' and 'Purpurea' are no longer valid and the name 'Guincho Purple' is proposed. 'Wildwood Snowtip' has white-edged leaves, 8′ high, Zone 3. All the above except 'Laciniata' are best cut back in late winter to encourage strong, highly colored shoots. For shrub borders, they offer a different touch. I have seen abundant aphids on the Black Elder, much more so than on *S. canadensis*. Spider mites and aphids are particularly troublesome in hot weather. East Malling Research Station, England, had a breeding program and made crosses among 'Aurea', 'Guincho Purple', and 'Laciniata'. The progeny showed characteristics of the parents but to my knowledge have not been introduced. See *Acta Horticulturae* 320:6–8 (1992). A hybrid between *S. nigra* and *S. racemosa* was discovered in southern Sweden. The plant was intermediate between the parents in inflorescence shape, flower size, flower color, pith, and fruit. Europe, northern Africa, western Asia. Cultivated since ancient times. Zone 5 to 6(7).

Sambucus pubens Michx. — Scarlet Elder, American Red Elder
LEAVES: Opposite, compound pinnate, 5 to 7 leaflets, ovate-oblong
    to oblong-lanceolate, 2 to 4″ long, stalked, serrate, lustrous dark
    green, pubescent or sometimes glabrous below.

Sambucus pubens, (sam-bū′kus pū′benz), Scarlet Elder, grows 12 to
    25′ high with a similar spread. The flowers are yellowish white,
    May, borne in a 5″ long, ovoid to pyramidal
    panicle. Have observed many times in the
    Great Smoky Mountains National Park, par-
    ticularly on the road and near the summit of
    Clingman's Dome. Actually quite respectable
    in flower. The fruit is a red or scarlet drupe,
    1/5 to 1/4″ diameter, ripening in late June
    into July, quite effective. Birds eat the fruits.
    Supposedly inedible for humans. White- and
    yellow-fruited forms are known. The buds are
solitary, 4-scaled, brown and the stems are light brown with a brown pith. 'Dissecta' has deeply divided leaflets. 'Leucocarpa' with white fruits and 'Xanthocarpa' with butterscotch-colored fruits are described. I have not yet made their acquaintance. Found in rocky woods from Newfoundland to Alaska, south to Georgia and Colorado. Appears to require a cooler climate for best performance. Handsome plant in fruit and certainly worth leaving if native. Introduced 1812. Zone 4 to 6. It is closely allied to *S. racemosa*.

Sambucus racemosa L. — European Red Elder
LEAVES: Opposite, compound pinnate, 6 to 9″ long, 5 to 7 leaflets, ovate or elliptic to ovate-lanceolate,
    subsessile, 2 to 4″ long, 3/4 to 1 3/4″ wide, acuminate, sharply, coarsely and regularly serrate, lustrous
    dark green, glabrous on both surfaces.

Sambucus racemosa, (sam-bū′kus ra-se-mō′sȧ), European Red Elder, grows 8 to 12′ high and has flowers
    and fruits similar to *S. pubens*, the fruits usually more tightly packed on the infructescence. 'Redman' is
    a heavy fruiting selection with finely dissected leaves. 'Sutherland Golden' ('Sutherland Gold') has golden
    yellow, finely cut leaflets. This appears to be a good plant for northern gardens. I have observed it at
    University of Minnesota Landscape Arboretum where it showed good vigor. 'Tenuifolia' forms a mound
    of arching branches with finely divided, fern-like leaves. This, too, is a beautiful form but I do not know its

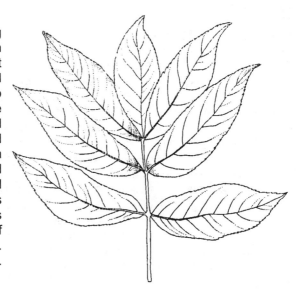

adaptability to hot, dry conditions. It is not a strong grower. 'Plumosa Aurea' is a handsome form with finely cut leaflets and bright yellow new leaves that mature to green. This form is common in Europe and is frequently cut to the ground in late winter to encourage vigorous shoots. Interestingly, I saw the plant in June at Sissinghurst and it literally jumped out and grabbed me. On a September visit, I had trouble locating the same plant; the yellow coloration had completely dissipated. 'Plumosa' is described with large leaflets up to 5″ long by 1 1/4″ wide and the serrations reaching halfway to the midvein. This is a green leaf form. A recent introduction is 'Goldenlocks' ('Golden Locks') from Canada, a dwarf form, to 30″, with golden, finely cut-leaved foliage. Native to Europe, western Asia. Cultivated 1596. Zone 4 to 6 or 7.

Santolina chamaecyparissus L. — Lavender Cotton
(san-tō-lī′nà kam-e-sip-à-ris′us)

FAMILY: Asteraceae

LEAVES: Alternate, pinnate, evergreen, 1/2 to 1 1/2″ long, 1/8″ or less wide, with short-oblong-obtuse, 1/24 to 1/12″ long segments, whitish tomentose; strong aromatic odor when bruised; easily identified by virtue of subshrub nature and silvery gray-green foliage.

SIZE: 1 to 2′ high, spread 2 to 4′.

HARDINESS: Zone 6 to 9.

HABIT: Evergreen subshrub forming a broad mound; almost cushion-like when properly grown.

RATE: Slow.

TEXTURE: Fine.

LEAF COLOR: Silvery gray-green through the seasons, a bit off-color in winter.

FLOWERS: Perfect, button-shaped, 1/2 to 3/4″ diameter, yellow heads cover the plant like lollipops; usually in June–August; borne on 4 to 6″ long stalks above the foliage; quite showy but should be removed after they fade; no ray florets present; apparently flowers set on new growth of season.

FRUIT: Achene, not important.

CULTURE: Transplants readily from containers; adaptable but prefers relatively dry, low fertility soils; will grow in pure sand; in excessively fertile soils becomes rank and open; full sun; prune after flowering or just about anytime during growing season to shape the plant; displays some salt tolerance.

LANDSCAPE VALUE: Quite a tough plant; have observed it used in a multiplicity of sites from pure sand on Cape Cod to heavy clay in Illinois; excellent in mass or for low hedge or border; works well in rock walls or rock gardens; have grown this along with *S. virens* in Urbana, IL and the Green Santolina did not prove as cold hardy; both are beautiful and elicit a positive response from the public.

CULTIVARS:

'Lambrook Silver'—Leaves silver-tinted.

'Lemon Queen'—Compact-mounded, gray foliage, 2′ by 2′.

'Little Ness'—Smaller, compact.

'Nana' (var. *nana*)—Perhaps catchall term for compact forms.

'Plumosus'—Lacy, silver-tinted foliage.

'Pretty Carol'—Compact, gray foliage, grows to 16″ high.

'Weston'—Dwarf, to 6″ high, leaves bright silver.

PROPAGATION: Seeds germinate readily; cuttings can be rooted about anytime; very important to keep medium on the dry side; too much moisture spells failure.

ADDITIONAL NOTES: Wonderful for foliage and flower effect. In our Zone 7b Georgia garden the two species tend to melt out over time. Still worthwhile cultivating. About 18 species are cataloged from the Mediterranean regions. Flower is used in folk medicine for its anti-spasmodic, -inflammatory, -septic, -microbial, and digestive properties. See *J. Natural Products* 49:1143–1144 (1986).

NATIVE HABITAT: Southern Europe. Cultivated 1596.

RELATED SPECIES:

Santolina virens Mill., (san-tō-lĭ′nȧ vī′renz), Green Santolina, is essentially a "dead ringer" for the above species except for the deep green, glabrous foliage and slightly more compact growth habit. Leaves are a degree longer (to 2″). The bright yellow, 3/4″ diameter flowers borne on 6 to 10″ long stalks are highlighted against the rich green foliage during July. In full flower on May 30 in the Dirr garden. Can be used in the same fashion as *S. chamaecyparissus*. Not as hardy as *S. chamaecyparissus*; requires same cultural manipulations. I have grown this a number of years and generally cut it back after flowering when it tends to open up and become floppy. 'Lemon Fizz' has consistent golden foliage with yellow flowers, from Pearce's Nurseries Pty Ltd., New South Wales, Australia; see *Plant Varieties Journal* 9(2):19–20 (1996). 'Primrose Gem' is listed with pale primrose yellow flowers, thread-like leaves, 12″ high. *The New RHS Dictionary of Gardening* lists the name as *S. rosmarinifolia* L. Southern Europe. Cultivated 1727. Zone 7 to 8(9).

Sapindus drummondii Hook. & Arn. — Western Soapberry
(sȧ-pin′dus drum-mon′dē-ī)

FAMILY: Sapindaceae

LEAVES: Alternate, compound and even pinnate, 10 to 15″ long, 8 to 18 leaflets, each short-stalked, obliquely lanceolate, 1 1/2 to 3 1/2″ long, 1/2 to 1″ wide, acuminate, off-set base, entire, lustrous medium green, glabrous above, pubescent beneath, each leaflet slightly curved or sickle-shaped not unlike pecan; rachis has no margin (wing).

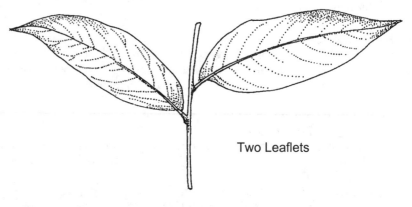

Two Leaflets

BUDS: Globose, gray, sometimes superposed, about 1/8″ high, 1/8″ wide, with 2 bud scales visible, pubescent.

STEM: Stout, angled due to decurrent ridges, dirty gray, covered with short pubescence, leaf scars orbicular to shield-shaped, large; pith—white, solid.

SIZE: 25 to 30′ high with a similar spread, have seen 40 to 50′ specimens; national champion is 62′ by 67′ in Corpus Christi, TX.

HARDINESS: Zone 5 but best in Zone 6 to 9.

HABIT: Single-stemmed or low-branched tree with a broad-oval to rounded crown similar to *Koelreuteria paniculata*; makes a rather graceful small shade tree.

RATE: Medium.

TEXTURE: Medium.

BARK: Shallowly furrowed, develops platy or scaly condition, as these fall they create a patchwork of gray-brown, orange-brown to reddish brown.

LEAF COLOR: Glossy medium green in summer, deep yellow-gold in fall; excellent fall color.

FLOWERS: Yellowish white, about 1/5″ across, borne in loose, 6 to 10″ long, pubescent, terminal, pyramidal panicles in May to June; apparently there is an initial growth flush and with increasing day length the terminal portion turns reproductive.

FRUIT: Subglobose, 1/2″ diameter, translucent, yellow-orange drupe that ripens in October; remains on tree through winter and into spring but the flesh may turn black; the seeds are black, rounded, 1/4 to 1/3″ wide, with one (sometimes 2 to 3) in each fruit; a single 30′ high, 40′ wide tree resides in Athens that sets prodigious quantities of fruit every year; *Sapindus drummondii* is supposedly unisexual and for argument's sake I know this one tree is female; the question then arises as to the source of pollen for effective fruit set unless fruiting is parthenocarpic; Rehder mentions that the genus, not this particular species, is polygamous, so it is possible that the Athens tree is polygamo-dioecious with sufficient pollen supplied by the polygamous flowers.

CULTURE: Easily transplanted, adaptable to varied soils and is native to infertile, dry soils throughout portions of the Southwest; extremely tolerant of urban sites and should be utilized more widely; wood is close-grained and strong, making the tree very wind resistant; seedlings may be objectionable.

DISEASES AND INSECTS: None serious, appears trouble-free as leaves are as clean in October as when first emerging in spring.

LANDSCAPE VALUE: Excellent choice for dry soil areas in South and Southwest; should be considered for use in urban situations; recommended as a shade and ornamental tree in dry areas of country; have reservations about recommending it for patio or street use because of the fruit litter; remember picking fruits off the ground in December at Missouri Botanical Garden; much better tree than *Melia azedarach*; observed as a thriving street tree in Wichita, KS; have witnessed numerous seedlings germinating in the vicinity of the Athens tree.

CULTIVARS:

'Narrow Leaf'—Described as having narrower foliage than typical for the species, offered by Louisiana Nursery.

PROPAGATION: The seeds have been described as doubly dormant and two hours scarification in sulfuric acid followed by 90 days at 40°F is recommended. I collected seed, removed the fleshy fruit wall by soaking, followed by extraction in a blender; the seeds were then placed in moist peat in poly bags at 41°F. After 54 days radicles had emerged in cold stratification. At this time the seeds were planted and about 95 out of 100 germinated. Seeds that received no cold treatment were also sown but only 2 to 3 seedlings emerged. Another test was conducted and it became evident that 30 days was sufficient time to induce some radicles to emerge. Based on the work I estimate 45 to 60 days cold to be sufficient. No scarification is necessary. Cuttings have also been rooted when collected in May–June, treated with 16,000 ppm IBA talc preparation; takes 5 to 6 weeks for rooting. In Kansas work, early June cuttings rooted equally well with a 10,000 to 30,000 ppm treatment.

ADDITIONAL NOTES: Generic name is derived from the nature of the fruits. When crushed in water they develop a lather. The West Indian natives used the saponin-rich fruits of *S. saponaria* L., Soapberry, as a soap substitute.

Occasional sightings of *S. mukorossi* Gaertn., Chinese Soapberry, with larger leaves, flowers and glossy orange-brown, 4/5″ diameter fruits; grows 40 to 50′ high; Eastern Asia, Himalaya; although listed as Zone 9 is growing in Raleigh, NC and Jungle Gardens, Avery Island, LA; will never become a commercial item.

Have experienced native stands of *S. drummondii* in western Oklahoma growing in a relatively dry, harsh environment. Holds up well to the heat. A fruitless form would prove a valuable urban tree.

NATIVE HABITAT: Southern Missouri, Kansas, New Mexico, and Arizona to Louisiana, Texas and northern Mexico. Cultivated 1900.

Sapium sebiferum (L.) Roxb. — Chinese Tallow Tree, Popcorn Tree

FAMILY: Euphorbiaceae

LEAVES: Alternate, simple, broadly rhombic-ovate or suborbicular, 1 1/2 to 3″ long and broad, abruptly acuminate, broad cuneate to truncate, entire, glabrous, medium green; petiole—1 to 2″ long, slender, with 2 glands on petiole at junction of blade.

BUDS: Small, appressed, brownish.

STEM: Wispy, green, finally brown, glabrous, glaucous, dotted with small brownish lenticels, milky sap.

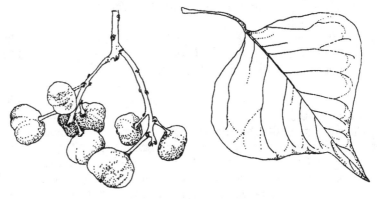

Sapium sebiferum, (sã′pi-um se-bif′er-um), Chinese Tallow Tree, is seldom seen in the Piedmont area of Georgia but becomes almost pestiferous in the Coastal Plain from South Carolina to Florida, Louisiana to Texas. Florida in 1997 listed it as a noxious weed. The medium green leaves are shaped much like a poplar and the first impulse is to relate this tree to that genus. The leaves emerge later in spring than most deciduous trees. The leaves turn reddish purple in the fall. Fall color in the Athens area has been disappointing for seldom do all the leaves color at the same time; leaves toward the interior color first with a progression toward the periphery; often yellow, orange-red and purple-red are intermingled on the same tree; some trees show limited coloration. Leaves fall by late October on the Georgia campus and are in full coloration in late December in Orlando, FL. The gray bark is ridged-and-furrowed with the ridges becoming flattened and scaly. The yellow-green, 2 to 4″ long, catkin-like flowers (male at apex, 1 to 5 females at base) are followed by brown, 1/2″ wide, 3-valved capsules which open to expose the white, oval, waxy seeds (October). The tree is known as "Popcorn Tree" because of the appearance of the seeds. The seeds are not messy but do persist into winter and eventually result in numerous seedlings where conditions permit. Chinese Tallow Tree is adaptable to moist, dry, acid, and alkaline soils but must be located in full sun. It is a *rapid* grower easily making 2 to 3′ and more a year especially in youth. The general shape is pyramidal-rounded and the canopy thin and airy. Grass can be grown up to the trunk. The ultimate height approximates 30 to 40′(60′). National champion is 51′ by 76′ in Polk County, TX. Makes a good, but not long-lived, tree for fall color in the southern states. The milky sap is poisonous. Orchard plantations occur in China. The waxy coat on the seeds is extracted by the Chinese for use in soaps and candles; hence, the name tallow. It has also been suggested as a source of oil and one estimate I read said it could supply 5% of the United States' oil needs. In our work, it became immediately evident that Chinese Tallow Tree was easy to propagate. I collected seeds with the white, waxy seed coat intact and directly sowed them. Within 4 weeks, most seeds had germinated. The seedlings exhibit tremendous vigor. I would speculate that because of the very rapid growth the species might have possibilities as a biomass source. Has been reproduced through tissue culture; see *Plant Cell Reports* 16:637–640 (1997). The tree was injured at 0°F and -3°F during the 1981–82 and 83–84 winters, respectively. Plants tend to harden late and early fall freezes may result in injury. A California reference listed 10 to 15°F as the breakpoint. Considerable deadwood was evident after the spring growth flush occurred. Will grow in Zone 7 but best in 8 to 10. Numerous studies with *S. sebiferum* that show its amazing tolerance to flooding by fresh and salt water, the ability to compete and prosper in low light and full sun. Has become a terrible weed in coastal plain of the South and is outcompeting the native vegetation; see *Castanea* 58:214–219 (1993), *Canadian J. Forest Research* 20:573–578 (1990); and *Bulletin Torrey Botanical Club* 116:371–377 (1989). China. Cultivated 1850. **Sapium japonicum** (Sieb. & Zucc.) Pax & Hoffm. is similar except the female flowers occur singly on 1/2″ long pedicels, rather than in the cymose clusters like those of *S. sebiferum*. I have only seen the plant once and the fall color was a handsome reddish purple. The true *S. japonicum* has 3 to 5″ long, 2 to 4″ wide, broad-ovate, abruptly acuminate, deep green leaves on about 1″ long petioles. Maybe a better tree than *S. sebiferum* for fall coloration but is probably less cold hardy. China, Japan, Korea. Zone 9, perhaps a Zone more cold hardy.

Sarcandra glabra (Thunb.) Nak.

FAMILY: Chloranthaceae
LEAVES: Opposite, simple, evergreen, 4 to 6″ long, 1 1/2 to 2 1/4″ wide, oblong or ovate-oblong, acuminate, sharply and coarsely serrate, serrations appearing gland-tipped, lustrous dark green, veins prominent, glabrous, flat green below; petiole—1/4 to 1/2″ long.
BUDS: Imbricate, green with red tinge, free at ends of scales, 1/4″ long.
STEM: Terete, green, brownish red in winter, glabrous, swollen and flattened at nodes; pith—large, excavated, green.

Sarcandra glabra, (sar-kan′drà glā′brà), has received considerable attention from southern plantsmen because of its lustrous evergreen foliage, mounded habit and bright red fruits that persist through winter. Habit is rounded-mounded, with size ranging from 1 to 3′ high and wide. The small, yellowish flowers occur in small, terminal, simple to few-branched spikes in May. The 1/4″ diameter, globose, fleshy, orange-scarlet drupes ripen in September–October and persist into spring of the following year. Container-grown plants are readily transplanted. Prefers moist, acid, organic, woodsy soil in partial shade. Will discolor/burn in excess sun and winter wind. I have grown the plant since 1996 and it suffered foliar burn at 15°F in the winter of 1996–97 yet flowered and fruited on new growth of the season. Raulston reported outright kill in Raleigh in the winter of 1993–94. Apparently an important plant in Chinese medicine. I have seen *Sarcandra glabra* offered at the health food store. An aside, I have yet to take any. 'Flava' is a yellow-fruited form. Common in Japan into Korea, Formosa, China, India and Malaysia. Occurs naturally as an understory plant, often near streams. Zone 8 to 9.

Sarcococca hookeriana Baill. — Himalayan Sarcococca, Sweetbox
(sar-kō-kōk'à hook-er-ē-ā'nà)

FAMILY: Buxaceae

LEAVES: Alternate, opposite, subopposite, simple, evergreen, coriaceous, lance-oblong to narrow-lanceolate, 2 to 3 1/2″ long, 1/2 to 3/4″ wide, slender-pointed, cuneate, lustrous dark green, glabrous, entire; petiole—1/3″ long.

STEM: Slender, green, slightly pubescent, foul smelling when bruised.

SIZE: 4 to 6′ high and wide, will spread by suckers to form a colony.

HARDINESS: Zone (5)6 to 8.

HABIT: Dense, evergreen shrub that forms a mounded outline, spreading by rhizomes to produce a colony.

RATE: Slow to medium.

TEXTURE: Medium-fine.

LEAF COLOR: Generally lustrous dark green although some plants have lighter green foliage; in English gardens especially on chalky or high pH soils, in a more exposed location, foliage is lighter green.

FLOWERS: Apetalous, unisexual, 1/2″ long, white, actually off-white, fragrant, in the leaf axils, the female flowers below the male flowers, male with pink anthers, female with 3 stigmas, may open in fall but usually in March–April (February–March, Athens), essentially unnoticed as they occur under the foliage, only the sweet fragrance advertises their arrival.

FRUIT: Have only seen on a few plantings and suspect the species may be self-sterile; globose, 1/4 to 1/3″ wide, shiny black drupe that persists into winter, not particularly showy and literally visible only then the leaves are parted.

CULTURE: Transplant from containers into loose, acid, high organic matter, moist, well-drained soils; will tolerate higher pH soils but does not appear as prosperous; partial shade to shade, will become off-color in full sun; appears to tolerate polluted atmospheric conditions; once established displays high drought tolerance.

DISEASES AND INSECTS: None serious.

LANDSCAPE VALUE: Nowhere common but at its best a worthy evergreen ground cover (var. *humilis*) that offers handsome foliage, and fragrant flowers; stoloniferous nature is not aggressive and can be kept in bounds; Longwood Gardens used it along a path above the rock garden with *Cornus florida* planted on either side, makes an excellent combination; the true species is rare and my first genuine introduction occurred at Wisley Gardens; the species is larger and more robust than var. *humilis* (the typical representative of the species in this country); in late March 1996, I visited Blackthorn Gardens, Kilmeston, England and met Robbie and Sue White the owners and noted breeders of *Helleborus*; I spied the true *S. hookeriana* and asked Mr. White if he would sell a plant; he noted that he only had two plants and was unable to part with any; when paying for other purchases at the checkout, the attendant handed me a plant of *S. hookeriana*, no charge; the mark of all true plantsmen—if there are two, then one is shared.

CULTIVARS:

var. *digyna* Franch.—More compact than *S. hookeriana*, perhaps 2 to 3′ high and wide, at least plants I have seen, with greenish shoots and narrow-elliptic to oblong-lanceolate lustrous green leaves about 1 3/4 to 3″ (4 1/2″) long, 1/2 to 1″ wide, petiole—1/8 to 2/5″ long. The key difference is the presence of two styles (i.e. *digyna*) compared to 3 for the species. Flowers are fragrant, plant is more hardy than *S. hookeriana* but less hardy than var. *humilis*. Produces black fruits. It is easily rooted from cuttings as described below. In 1996, I collected 'Purple Stem' with purple-tinted young stems; the flowers are extremely fragrant and were in full flower in late February 1998 in our garden. Western China. Introduced 1908.

var. *humilis* Rehd. & Wils.—Often treated as a separate species but current thinking provides varietal status. This is the best of the *Sarcococca* species for northern gardens because of cold hardiness; at -3°F this species was unfazed while *S. hookeriana*, var. *digyna* and *S. confusa* were virtually defoliated in the piedmont of Georgia. Variety *humilis* grows (12″)18 to 24″ high, is stoloniferous, smaller in all its parts than *S. hookeriana*, and is black-fruited. Native to western China. Introduced 1907. Zone (5)6 to 8.

Sarcococca hookeriana var. *humilis*

PROPAGATION: Seeds will germinate without pretreatment. Collected fruits of *S. confusa* in March 1997, removed pulp, sowed seeds with germination 8 to 10 weeks later; seedlings were planted in Dirr garden in fall 1997. Cuttings of all species root readily. Have collected cuttings of variety *humilis* in November and February, 3000 ppm IBA-quick dip, peat:perlite, mist with 100% success. The root systems were profuse. Suspect cuttings can be rooted year round if shoots are firm.

ADDITIONAL NOTES: Several years past I attempted to separate the various species and varieties, a feat which often distills to the fruit colors and number of styles. Enjoyed the academic chase but still am unable to separate the two varieties of *S. ruscifolia*. See Dirr, *Nursery Manager* 10(5):24, 26 (1994).

A revision of the genus appeared in *Botanical J. Linnean Soc.* 92:117–159 (1986). The genus comprises 11 species distributed in southeast Asia from Afghanistan through the Himalayas to southeast Tibet, Assam, Upper Burma, China southwards to India, Sri Lanka, Thailand, and beyond. Interestingly, the work does not recognize *S. orientalis* (which see), a species that is morphologically and garden-wise unique from the others.

NATIVE HABITAT: Western Himalayas and Afghanistan. Cultivated 1884.

RELATED SPECIES:

Sarcococca confusa Sealy

LEAVES: Alternate, simple, evergreen, leathery, 1 1/4 to 2 1/2″ long, 1/2 to 1″ wide, elliptic, elliptic-lanceolate to obovate, long obtuse to acute, obtuse to cuneate, lustrous green above, light green below, surface undulating; petiole—1/4″ long.

Sarcococca confusa, (sar-kō-kōk′à con-fū′sà), forms a 3 to 5′ high and wide, densely branched, evergreen shrub. The flowers are sweetly scented and based on olfactory comparisons, are more fragrant than *S. hookeriana*. They occur in late February–early March in Zone 7b. The female flowers have either 2 or 3 stigmas. Fruits turn red and finally glossy black at maturity. Where well-grown this is a handsome plant but is considerably less cold hardy than var. *humilis* and should only be grown in Zone (7)8. More cold hardy than given credit by this author as plants have withstood 7°F without foliar injury while leaves of *S. ruscifolia* in the same garden area were browned. Known only from cultivation and was apparently collected by Wilson in about 1908. Reproduces true-to-type from seed and every seedling I grew exhibited foliage identical to the maternal source. China. Introduced 1916. Zone 6b to 8.

Sarcococca orientalis C.Y. Wu
LEAVES: Alternate, simple, evergreen, leathery, 1 1/2 to 3″ long, 1/2 to 1 1/4″ wide, acuminate, cuneate, 3-veined at base, entire, glabrous, lustrous dark green; petiole—about 1/4″ long.
STEM: Flat olive green, covered with short pubescence, stouter stemmed than most *Sarcococca* species, malodorous when bruised; pith—green, solid, ample.

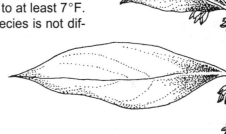

Sarcococca orientalis, (sar-kō-kōk′à ôr-i-en-tā′lis), has promise because of its larger, to 3″ long, lustrous dark green leaves and early winter flowering, late December to early February in Dirr garden. Flowers are larger than those of *S. hookeriana*. Flowers from the axils of the leaves with 2 to 5 buds on a short, crooked stalk. Males with pink-blushed anthers and sepals, females with 2 stigmas. Fruits are shining black at maturity. In the Dirr garden, plants have performed well and are cold hardy to at least 7°F. At least one reference (*RHS*) notes that the species is not different than *S. h.* var. *digyna*. Garden evaluations tell a different story. Probably will grow 2 to 4′ high and develop suckering colonies. See Lancaster, *The Garden* 119(1):16–17 (1994), for history of introduction and characteristics. Eastern China. Introduced 1980 by Roy Lancaster. Zone 6b to 8(9).

Sarcococca ruscifolia Stapf. — Fragrant Sarcococca
LEAVES: Alternate, simple, evergreen, broad ovate, 1 to 2 1/2″ long, half as wide, acuminate, rounded, perhaps cuneate, 3-nerved at base, glabrous, lustrous dark green above, lighter beneath; petiole—1/8 to 1/4″ long.

Sarcococca ruscifolia, (sar-kō-kōk′à rus-ki-fō′lē-à), Fragrant Sarcococca, is a 3′ high and wide shrub with handsome foliage and milk white, fragrant flowers in the axils of the terminal leaves. There are consistently 3 stigmas. Fruits are rounded, red, 1/4″ diameter. A handsome plant but not sufficiently cold hardy for inclusion in gardens below Zone (7)8. Variety *chinensis* (Franch.) Rehd. & Wils. has longer, narrower leaves and is the common form in cultivation. The fruits are dark red and the female flowers have 3 stigmas. Foliage shape reminds of *Ruscus aculeatus*. At 7°F, foliage of the species and so termed var. *chinensis* were injured. I see essentially no difference between the species and the variety. Species native to central and Western China. Introduced 1901. Zone 7 to 9.

Sarcococca saligna (D. Don) Muell.
LEAVES: Alternate, simple, evergreen, 3 to 5″ long, 1/2 to 3/4″ wide, linear lanceolate, pale green, glabrous.

Sarcococca saligna, (sar-kō-kōk′à sal-ig′nà), is a 2 to 4′ high, rhizomatous-spreading, evergreen shrub with non-fragrant, green, male flowers, with yellow anthers, female with 3 stigmas, in March. Fruit is dark purple to black. The most handsome planting I have observed grows at Caerhays Castle in Cornwall. About 3′ high, rather wide-spreading and located by a wall and inside a gate. In the Dirr garden, it is killed to the ground every year and recovers during the spring–summer. Himalayas. Introduced 1908. Zone 9.

Sassafras albidum (Nutt.) Nees. — Common Sassafras
(sas′à-fras al′bi-dum)

FAMILY: Lauraceae
LEAVES: Alternate, simple, ovate to elliptic, 3 to 7″ long, 2 to 4″ wide, acutish or obtuse, cuneate at base, bright to medium green above, glabrous and glaucous beneath, entire, mitten-shaped or 3-lobed; mittens occur in left and right hand models; petiole—1/2 to 1 1/2″ long.
BUDS: Terminal, solitary, ovoid, sessile, about 4 to 6 exposed scales, green-tinged with red toward tip, 1/3″ long; lateral buds small, divergent, green; terminal is the flower bud.
STEM: Bright yellowish green, often reddish where exposed to light, glabrous and glaucous; spicy-aromatic to both smell and taste; sympodial branching.

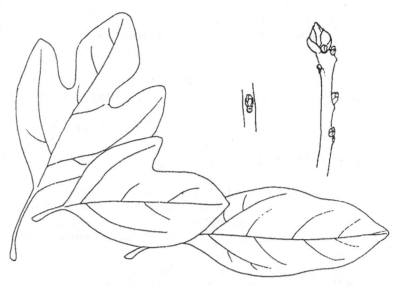

SIZE: 30 to 60′ in height with a spread of 25 to 40′, can grow larger; national champion is 78′ by 69′ in Owensboro, KY.

HARDINESS: Zone 4 to 9.

HABIT: Pyramidal, irregular tree or shrub in youth, with many short, stout, contorted branches which spread to form a flat-topped, irregular, round-oblong head at maturity; often sprouting from roots and forming extensive thickets.

RATE: Medium to fast, 10 to 12′ over a 5 to 8 year period.

TEXTURE: Medium in all seasons, very intriguing winter silhouette results from the sympodial branching habit.

BARK: Dark reddish brown, deeply ridged-and-furrowed, forming flat corky ridges that are easily cut across with a knife; bark almost a mahogany brown, handsome when mature.

LEAF COLOR: Bright to medium green in summer changing to shades of yellow to deep orange to scarlet and purple in fall; one of our most outstanding native trees for fall color; a sassafras thicket in October is unrivaled.

FLOWERS: Usually dioecious, yellow, weakly fragrant, developing before the leaves in April (late March, Athens), borne in terminal racemes, 1 to 2″ long, apetalous, calyx about 3/8″ long and wide, with 6 narrowly oblong lobes, 9 stamens in male; 6 and aborted in the female; flowers are actually quite handsome and can be readily distinguished in the early spring landscape.

FRUIT: Drupe, 1/2″ long, dark blue, ripening in September but quickly falling or devoured by birds; the fruit stalk (pedicel) is scarlet and very attractive at close range; many people think the pedicel is the fruit.

CULTURE: Move balled-and-burlapped in early spring into moist, loamy, acid, well-drained soil; have observed chlorosis in high pH soils; full sun or light shade; in the wild often found in acid, rocky soil; has a strong tendency to invade abandoned fields and form dense thickets; as a pioneer tree it is somewhat intolerant and gives way to other species after a time; prune in winter; it is difficult to establish (transplant) from the wild because of the deep tap root and the few spreading, lateral roots; could possibly be container-grown and thus many of the transplanting problems would be alleviated; if a single-trunked tree is desired be sure to remove the suckers (shoots) that develop.

DISEASES AND INSECTS: Cankers, leaf spots, mildew, wilt, root rot, Japanese beetle, promethea moth, sassafras weevil and scales have been reported. Sassafras has appeared remarkably free of problems except for occasional iron chlorosis.

LANDSCAPE VALUE: Excellent for naturalized plantings, roadsides, and home landscaping; with a little extra cultural effort one will be rewarded manyfold.

PROPAGATION: Seeds exhibit strong embryo dormancy which can be overcome with moist stratification at 41°F for 120 days. Root cuttings collected in December and placed in 2:1:1; peat:loam:sand, produced plants.

ADDITIONAL NOTES: The bark of the roots is used to make sassafras tea and the "oil of sassafras" is extracted from the roots. Some concern that the extract from *Sassafras* is carcinogenic, but then what isn't, since living can be construed as dangerous to one's health. Interestingly, many medicinal attributes were attributed to the species. In Rockville, IN, an October festival offers numerous concoctions of sassafras including candy, tea, bread, et al. Certainly a great native plant and on numerous back roads throughout the eastern United States there is no more inspiring sight than a sassafras thicket in full flaming fall color. See Dirr, *Nursery Management and Production* 9(4):26, 28 (1993), for commentary on root cutting success and SpinOut™ treated container culture.

NATIVE HABITAT: Distributed from Maine to Ontario and Michigan, south to Florida and Texas. Cultivated 1630.

Sciadopitys verticillata (Thunb.) Sieb. & Zucc. — Umbrella-pine or Japanese Umbrella-pine
(sī-à-dop′i-tis vĕr-ti-si-lā′tà)

FAMILY: Pinaceae, also listed as Taxodiaceae. Hart, *J. Arnold Arboretum* 68:269–307 (1987), suggested *Sciadopitys* should be in a separate family, Sciadopityaceae.

LEAVES: Of 2 kinds, some small and scale-like scattered on the shoot, but crowded at its end and bearing in their axils a whorl of (10)20 to 30 linear flat leaves, each 2 to 5″ long, 1/8″ wide, furrowed on each side, more deeply beneath with a glaucous-green groove, dark glossy green, thick, almost prehistoric in appearance; the way the needles radiate around the stem creates an "umbrella" effect.

STEM: At first green, later brown, glabrous, stout, flexible, striated, with prominent protuberances on stem.

BARK: Thin, nearly smooth, orangish to reddish brown, exfoliating in long strips, quite handsome but essentially hidden by the foliage.

SIZE: 20 to 30′ by 15 to 20′; can grow 60 to 90′ high; listed at over 120′ in the wild.

HARDINESS: Zone 5 to 7, not as prosperous in Zone 7 as further North, not quite hardy at the Morton Arboretum, Lisle, IL.

HABIT: Variable, from spire-like to broadly pyramidal tree in youth, with a straight stem and horizontal branches spreading in whorls, stiff and twiggy, the young branchlets with the leaves crowded at the ends; with age the branches become more pendulous and spreading and the whole habit loose; have also observed multi-stemmed versions.

RATE: Slow, extremely slow, perhaps 6″ a year.

TEXTURE: Medium-coarse, one of the most interesting conifers for textural effect.

BARK: Rich orangish to reddish brown and exfoliating in long shreds or strips; handsome but generally unnoticed since hidden by foliage.

LEAF COLOR: Dark green and glossy above throughout the year, persisting about 3 years.

FLOWERS: Monoecious; female solitary, terminal and subtended by a small bract, male flowers in 1″ long racemes.

FRUIT: Cones oblong-ovate, upright, 2 to 4″ long, 1 to 2″ wide, opening to 3″ wide, scales with broad reflexed margins; cones are green at first, ripening to brown the second year, each scale bears 5 to 9 narrowly 2-winged, 1/3 to 1/2″ long seeds.

CULTURE: Transplant balled-and-burlapped or container-grown plants, prefers rich, moist, acid soils and sunny, open locations; late afternoon shade is advantageous in hot areas; protection from wind is desirable; has not performed well in Zone 7b; certainly not a commodity evergreen; needs careful siting.

DISEASES AND INSECTS: None serious.

LANDSCAPE VALUE: F.B. Robinson called it "a queer tree of odd texture; can be used as an accent or specimen"; L.H. Bailey termed it "one of the most handsome and distinctive of conifers"; for foliage effect as well as texture this conifer ranks among the best; could be integrated into a foundation planting, rock garden or border; the plant will grow in Zone 7 but prefers light pine shade; its unusual texture makes it a valuable addition to the list of needled conifers; Tripp and Raulston, *The Year in Trees*, noted a +120-year-old, 35′ high specimen in the historic cemetery in Salisbury, NC.

CULTIVARS: Several forms are described in the literature but are not common in commerce, even from specialty producers. Featured in *Conifers* by van Gelderen and van Hoey Smith are: 'Ann Haddow'—yellow-variegated; 'Aurea'—entire needle yellow; 'Green Star'—dwarf with wider, dark green needles; 'Ossorio Gold'—much like 'Aurea'; 'Picola'—broad-conical with dark green, 2″ long needles, 16″ high in 10 years; 'Variegata'—with mixed green and yellow needles, offered by Gossler; and 'Wintergreen'—narrow conical, small tree with rich green (almost blue-green) needle color, Sid Waxman introduction.

'Jim Cross'—Dense, relatively compact form, with glossy dark green, slightly arching needles, foliage is densely borne and hides the stems and trunk from view, 10′ high, 8′ wide in 20 years, named after the late Jim Cross, Environmentals, Cutchogue, NY.

'Joe Kozey'—A columnar form, deep green needles, Sid Waxman introduction.

'Pendula'—Listed as a remarkable tree with pendulous branches; have not seen but would like to secure a plant.

'Richie's Cushion'—Low dense mound, 3′ by 6′, rich dark green needles, slow-growing.

PROPAGATION: Either warm stratification for 100 days in moist sand at 63 to 70°F or cold for 90 days in moist, acid peat at 32 to 50°F have been recommended for inducing prompt germination. A combination of the two may be more effective. Seedlings kind of sit there for a while and look at you before deciding to "grow up." Cuttings taken in January rooted 92% in sand:peat in 20 weeks after treatment with 100 ppm NAA for 24 hours. Cuttings from 7-year-old trees collected in January and treated with 20 ppm IBA rooted 70% in 8 months. In 32 weeks there was 43% rooting of untreated cuttings taken in August. See Waxman, *Proc. Intl. Plant Prop. Soc.* 28:546–550 (1978) for a detailed report on cutting propagation. In brief, Dr. Waxman noticed tremendous tree-to-tree rooting variability. The best rooting occurred when the cuttings were immersed in water and allowed to soak. There appeared to be a correlation between the amount of resin and rootability. Low resin correlated with high rooting. Hormones did not prove that critical. February–March and July–August were the best times. Interesting study, *HortScience* 30(1):133–134 (1995) that reported increased survival, callus development and rooting percentage when mycorrhizal fungi were added to a peat-based medium; rooting was 50% with fungi, 17% without.

NATIVE HABITAT: Restricted in a wild state to the Valley of the Kiso-gawa in central Hondo, and to Koya-san and its immediate neighborhood in east central Hondo; the best trees being found in steep, rocky, sheltered situations. Introduced 1861.

Securinega suffruticosa (Pall.) Rehd.

FAMILY: Euphorbiaceae
LEAVES: Alternate, simple, elliptic or ovate to lance-ovate, 3/4 to 2″ long, 1/3 to 1″ wide, acute or obtuse, cuneate, entire, bright yellowish green, glabrous, petiole—1/8″ long.

Securinega suffruticosa, (se-cūr-in-ē'gà su-frū-ti-kō'sà), is a virtual unknown in American gardening and probably will remain buried in anonymity. I first saw the plant at the Missouri Botanic Garden, St. Louis, and was taken by the fresh green foliage and upright arching branches and rather dense constitution. Grows 6 to 8′ high and wide. For use as a foliage mass, it has possibilities. The plant can be pruned in late winter to entice long shoot extensions. The greenish white flowers (July–August) and greenish capsules are not showy. Any well-drained soil and full sun suit it best. Will grow in partial shade. There was an 8′ high plant at the Arnold Arboretum that developed soft yellow fall color. Optimum seed germination occurred after 3 months of cold stratification. See Koller, *Arnoldia* 53(2):21–23 (1993) for detailed information. Northeast Asia to central China. Introduced 1783. Zone (4)5 to 7(8).

Sequoia sempervirens (D. Don) Endl. — Redwood, California Redwood, Coast Redwood
(sē-kwoi'à sem-pĕr-vī'renz)

FAMILY: Taxodiaceae
LEAVES: Evergreen, needles spirally arranged on the terminal leader, about 1/4″ long, slightly appressed to spreading, 2-ranked on the lateral shoots, 1/4 to 7/8″ long, 1/20 to 1/8″ wide, linear lanceolate or narrow oblong, sometimes falcate, with an abrupt point, lustrous dark green, almost bluish green above with two broad whitish stomatal bands below.

SIZE: Difficult to ascertain under landscape conditions on East Coast, perhaps 40 to 60′; in West 300′; 378′ is the tallest tree on record; current national champion is 313′ by 101′ in Prairie Creek Redwoods State Park, CA; trees may live 500 to 700 years, and trees over 2000-years-old were recorded; can the reader imagine counting the rings?
HARDINESS: Zone 7 to 9.
HABIT: Imposing conifer, densely branched and gracefully pyramidal in youth, with time losing the lower branches and devoid of branches 50 to 100′ from the ground with a still relatively narrow pyramidal crown.
RATE: Slow to medium in East, fast in West.
TEXTURE: Medium.
BARK: Exquisite on old trees being a rich red-brown and fibrous on the surface, with deep furrows and irregular ridges; I saw mature redwoods in Muir Woods, north of San Francisco, and walking in the shadows of these behemoths provided pause for reflection on man's coming and going; a living legacy that has held court over 30 generations of mankind and has never passed a negative verdict; yet man has attempted, albeit sometimes unintentionally, to destroy what is beyond his realm of comprehension, reasoning or appreciation.
LEAF COLOR: Dark green through the seasons, some forms show a distinct bluish green cast.
FLOWERS: Male flowers axillary and terminal with numerous spirally arranged stamens; female terminal with 15 to 20 peltate scales.

FRUIT: A 3/4 to 1 1/4″ long, 1/2 to 3/4″ wide, somewhat egg-shaped, dark brownish cone that ripens the first year; seeds reddish brown, 4 to 7 per scale, 1/6″ long with 2 narrow wings along the side.

CULTURE: Generally container-grown in West Coast nurseries and should be transplanted as such; prefers moist, acid, deep, well-drained soils in areas of high atmospheric moisture; will never perform in eastern states like it does in native habitat or British Isles.

DISEASES AND INSECTS: None serious.

LANDSCAPE VALUE: Only for specimen use as a noble conifer where room to ascend and spread is ample, a few of the compact cultivars are more suitable for smaller gardens.

CULTIVARS:

'Adpressa'—Has 1/4 to 3/8″ long, loosely appressed needles, the young shoots are tipped creamy white (gray-green), often listed as a dwarf conifer but will produce vertical shoots and unless removed will become tree-like, may also be listed under names like 'Albospica' and 'Albospicata', may grow 4′ by 4′ in ten years; however, a 73′ high tree has been described which indicates somebody forgot to prune; Raulston mentioned that this cultivar survived the -9°F winter while the species was killed; introduced before 1867 in France; was growing quite contently at Scott Arboretum, Swarthmore College; the 'Adpressa' that *Conifers* discusses is different from the above; my 'Adpressa' equates with *Conifers* 'Prostrata'.

'Aptos Blue'—Foliage is dark bluish green, secondary branches distinctly horizontal with tertiary branchlets pendulous.

'Cantab' ('Prostrata', 'Pendula Nana')—Arose as a branch sport of 'Adpressa' at the Cambridge Botanic Garden, semi-prostrate habit, distinct blue-green or gray-green, 1/2″ long needles, about one-half as wide, unstable and will send up vertical shoots with needles akin to 'Cantab'; abundant confusion caused by this author due to the above discussion; in Great Compton Garden, England, there is a 30 to 40′ high, compact pyramidal tree that is better suited to the small garden than the species; several authors described 'Cantab' as a reverted 'Prostrata'.

'Filoli' ('Woodside')—Foliage distinctly blue, akin to Blue Colorado Spruce, *Picea pungens* f. *glauca*.

'Glauca'—Foliage more blue-green than species, otherwise similar.

'Henderson Blue'—Makes a bushy, blue-foliaged tree.

'Los Altos'—Heavy-textured, deep green foliage on horizontal, arching branches.

'Majestic Beauty™ ('Monty')—Densely set, blue-green foliage, pyramidal form with denser branching.

'Prostrata'—Dwarf form with spreading branches clothed with 2-ranked leaves, originated as a branch sport at Cambridge University Botanic Garden about 1951; Gossler reported that a 25-year-old plant was 6″ high and 36″ across, also mentioned pruning out the branch reversions ('Cantab') that try to assume control each year.

'Santa Cruz'—Strong pyramidal, cone-shaped tree, soft-textured, pale green needles, distinct horizontal secondary branches.

'Simpson's Silver'—Silvery blue needles.

'Soquel'—Pyramidal habit, fine-textured dark green foliage, bluish on underside, holds good color in winter.

PROPAGATION: Seeds require no pretreatment. Cuttings of 'Santa Cruz' rooted 70% with 16,000 ppm IBA, 47% on 'Soquel' with 6000 ppm IBA + 6000 ppm NAA. Cuttings must be staked and pruned to develop a leader. Juvenility correlates strongly with rooting success; the younger the stock tree the higher the rooting percentage with or without hormone.

NATIVE HABITAT: Confined to the fog belt along the Pacific Ocean from southern Oregon to California around San Francisco. Introduced 1843.

RELATED SPECIES:

Sequoiadendron giganteum (Lindl.) Buchholz., (sē-kwoi′à-den′dron jĭ-gan′tē-um), Big Tree, Sierra Redwood, Wellingtonia, is another West Coast giant growing 250 to 300′ in the wild but much less, perhaps 60′, under cultivation in the East. National champion is 275′ by 107′ in Sequoia National Park, CA. In England, numerous +100′ high trees are common. The habit is dense and pyramidal-oval in youth, losing its lower branches with a narrow-pyramidal crown of foliage in the upper reaches at maturity. The bluish green needles vary in length from 1/8 to 1/2″ and are usually awl-shaped and triangular in cross section, tapering from the base to a fine point. Needles point forward toward the apex and completely cover the stem and spiral in 3 longitudinal rows. Needles persist 3 to 4 years. Cones are 1 1/2 to 3″ long, 1 1/4 to 2″ wide, reddish brown at maturity, upright the first year, pendulous the second, the flattened seeds shining pale to yellowish brown, 1/4″ long, with 2 broad wings, 5 to 9 per scale. The bark is spongy in texture and rich reddish brown. This species succeeds better in the eastern United States and

Longwood Gardens has a number of 30 to 40′ high trees. The species withstands drier conditions than *Sequoia sempervirens*. Tyler Arboretum, Lima, PA has a 100′ tall specimen. Also growing at Arnold Arboretum. Several cultivars are known but the most common is 'Pendulum' with an erratic leading stem that zigs, zags, arches, bends, dips and dives to form a piece of living sculpture. The secondary branches hang mop (mane)-like. The whole plant leaves much to the imagination. 'Hazel Smith' is a strong-growing, upright tree with bluish needles and greater hardiness; I have rooted it from winter cuttings with excellent success; received an Award of Merit from the Royal Boskoop Horticulture Society in 1993. 'Les Barres' is a better form than 'Glaucum' with bluer foliage, greater cold hardiness, and slower growing. 'Pygmaeum' is a compact, shrubby form, 2′ high, 9′ wide, may revert to the type. 'Requiem' is a more uniform, weeping form with a central leader and gracefully arching secondary branches. California in the Sierra Nevada Mountains at elevations of 4500 to 8000′. Introduced 1853. Zone 6 to 8. Have read that the species grows in Scandinavia and survived −22°F.

Serissa foetida (L. f.) Lam. — Yellow-rim

FAMILY: Rubiaceae
LEAVES: Opposite, simple, evergreen, semi-evergreen, deciduous, ovate to elliptic, 1 to 1 1/2″ long, to 1/2″ wide, acute, cuneate, entire, glabrous, deep green above, lighter below, with clusters of leaves in axils, virtually sessile.
STEM: Fine, gray, glabrous, malodorous when bruised.

Serissa foetida, (ser-ē′sȧ fet′i-dȧ), Yellow-rim, is a small, rounded, 3 to 4′ high, fine-textured, evergreen shrub with dark green leaves and 4- to 6-lobed, 1/3″ diameter, white, non-fragrant flowers in May–June. Peak flowering occurs in May; my notes say May 17, 1995 which was an "early" spring. The plant has been growing on the Georgia campus for numerous years without an identity. It has survived −3°F and droughts too numerous to recount, all in the shadow and root competition of a 30 to 40′ high *Quercus virginiana*. In Japan it is used as a hedging plant. Dr. Raulston succeeded with the plants at Raleigh and collected various cultivars for evaluation. Developed temporary insanity and tested the pink ('Rosea', 'Pink Swan'), double-flowered ('Flore-pleno'), more heavily variegated leaf ('Variegata') forms, and all were rendered objectionable by the cold. 'Cherry Blossom' has large, pink flowers and tiny, white-edged leaves. 'Kowloon' is a highly variegated form with 1/3 to 1/2 of leaf surface covered by a cream-yellow margin. 'Kyoto' is a compact clone with single, white flowers and tiny leaves. 'Mount Fuji' is compact with more heavily white-variegated leaves. 'Sapporo' is an upright form with smaller leaves that has proven cold hardy in our garden. 'White Swan' produces larger flowers and cream-edged leaves. The major species form still standing (~4′ high) in our garden is a propagule from the campus plant. In partial shade, it has prospered and is admired by visitors who want to know the identity. Bonnie and I have utilized the plant in containers where it provides handsome fine foliage texture and color (variegated margins). Adaptable and will withstand about any site conditions except permanently wet. Southeastern Asia. Introduced 1878. Zone (6)7 to 9.

Shepherdia canadensis (L.) Nutt. — Russet Buffaloberry
(she-pĕr′di-ȧ kan-a-den′sis)

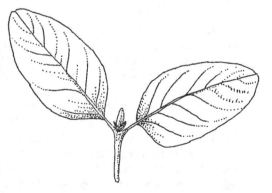

FAMILY: Elaeagnaceae
LEAVES: Opposite, simple, 1/2 to 2″ long, 1/4 to 1″ wide, elliptic to ovate, obtuse, dark green and sparingly scurfy above, silvery stellate pubescent below, often much of the pubescence is brown (brownish scales); petioles—1/8 to 1/6″ long, stellate pubescent.
BUDS: Rather small, solitary or multiple, stalked, oblong, with 2 or 4 valvate scales.
STEM: Red-brown, scurfy, scaly, not spiny, nearly terete, rather slender; leaf scars half-round, minute, slightly raised; 1 bundle trace; pith—small, round, continuous.

SIZE: 6 to 8′ high and as wide, varies from 3 to 9′ high.

HARDINESS: Zone 2 to 6.

HABIT: Small, loosely-branched shrub of rounded outline, not the most inspirational landscape shrub.

RATE: Slow to medium.

TEXTURE: Medium in all seasons.

LEAF COLOR: Silver-green to gray-green in summer; upper surface green, lower silvery mixed with brown scales, like most members of the Elaeagnaceae does not color well in the fall.

FLOWERS: Dioecious, small, apetalous, yellowish, 1/6″ across; in short axillary spikes or the pistillate often solitary, April to early May, not showy.

FRUIT: Drupe-like achene, yellowish red, insipid, ovoid, 1/6 to 1/4″ long; effective in June and July.

CULTURE: Easily grown and tolerates the poorest of soils; does well in dry or alkaline situations; prefers sunny open position; has the ability to fix atmospheric nitrogen.

DISEASES AND INSECTS: Several leaf spots, powdery mildew, and a rust have been reported but are not serious.

LANDSCAPE VALUE: Actually of no value where the soil is good and better shrubs can be grown; has possibilities along highways and other rough areas where poor soils, lousy maintenance, and salt are the rule, good plant for dry, high pH soils.

CULTIVARS:

'Rubra'—Red-fruited selection.

'Xanthocarpa'—Yellow-fruited type.

PROPAGATION: Seeds of both species have embryo dormancies and should be stratified for 60 to 90 days at 41°F; the seed coats are hard and an acid scarification for 20 to 30 minutes proves beneficial. July cuttings of the yellow-fruited form treated with 8000 ppm IBA-talc rooted 100%. Tissue culture and hardwood cuttings were successful with *S. canadensis* and *S. rotundifolia* Parry. Forty-seven percent rooting of *S. canadensis* occurred from May hardwood cuttings treated with 3000 ppm IBA. See *J. Environ. Hort.* 9:218–220 (1991).

ADDITIONAL NOTES: I have seen both species, but only in arboreta or on campuses and was not intrigued by either. They are extremely cold- and drought-tolerant as well as alkaline soil adaptable and should be used in areas where these conditions prevail. For fruit set both male and female plants are required. Fruits are the usual late summer food for bears in the Front Ranges of Banff National Park, Alberta, Canada.

NATIVE HABITAT: Newfoundland to Alaska, south to Maine, Ohio, northern Mexico and Oregon. Introduced 1759.

RELATED SPECIES:

Shepherdia argentea (Pursh) Nutt. — Silver Buffaloberry

LEAVES: Opposite, simple, elliptic, 1 to 2″ long, 1/8 to 5/8″ wide, obtuse, entire, covered with silver or silver-brown scales, densely pubescent; petiole—1/4 to 1/2″ long.

BUDS: Loosely scaly, 2-, 4- to 6-scaled, elongated, silvery to silvery brown, 1/4″ long, densely pubescent.

STEM: Young—terete, silver tomentose; old—brown, bark flaking and appearing like an onion skin; pith brown, excavated; spines 1 to 2″ long, terminating leafy branches.

Shepherdia argentea, (she-pĕr′di-à är-jen′tē-à), Silver Buffaloberry, is a thorny shrub, sometimes nearly tree-like, growing 6 to 10′ high, although it may reach 18′. National champion is 22′ by 20′ in Malheur County, OR. The foliage is silvery on both surfaces and much more gray in appearance than *S. canadensis*. The flowers and fruits (red or orange) are similar to the above species with only minor exceptions. The fruits of both species have been used for jellies. 'Xanthocarpa', a yellow-fruited form, is described in the literature. 'Goldeye' is a yellow-fruited type, could be a fancy name for 'Xanthocarpa'. Native to Minnesota and Manitoba to Saskatchewan, Kansas and Nevada. Introduced 1818. Zone 2 to 6.

Sinojackia rehderiana Hu — Jacktree

FAMILY: Styracaceae

LEAVES: Alternate, simple, elliptic to elliptic-obovate, 1 to 3″(4″) long, about 2/3's as wide, short acuminate, rounded, minutely serrate to entire, lustrous dark green and glabrous above, pubescent on veins below; petiole—1/4″ long.

BUDS: Terminal—naked, foliose, brown, pubescent, 1/8 to 1/4″ long, laterals—similar if not the same, stalked, another small bud sits above leaf scar at base of stalked foliose bud.

STEM: Slender, brown, pubescent, developing vertical fissures, becoming stringy; pith—green, solid.

Sinojackia rehderiana, (sī-nō-ja'kē-å red-ĕr-ē-ā'nȧ), Jacktree, offers potential as a large shrub or small tree, probably 15 to 20′ high at maturity. I have seen the plant at J.C. Raulston Arboretum in October and at that time the foliage was still dark green. The white, 1″ wide, 5- to 7-petaled flowers occur in 3- to 5-flowered cymes at the ends of lateral shoots in April–May. A plant at the Arnold Arboretum was abundant with flowers on May 13, 1991. This particular plant was growing in partial shade. I have also seen plants in full sun that appear robust. A small plant in a semi-shaded corner of our garden has performed well. The woody drupe is 3/4″ long and 1/2″ across with a broad conical obtuse apex. Appears to thrive in full sun and well-drained soil. Propagation by June cuttings has been successful. Seeds are difficult. May have to mechanically break the endocarp. A plant of the future? Also, *S. xylocarpa* Hu with smaller leaves, denticulate and rounded at the base, has crossed the author's path. Growth habit and size potential are similar. This species does not appear to have the same handsome foliage as *S. rehderiana*. *Sinojackia rehderiana* is native to eastern China. Introduced 1930. Zone 6 to 8.

Sinowilsonia henryi Helms.

FAMILY: Hamamelidaceae

LEAVES: Alternate, simple, broad ovate, 4 to 6″ long, to 4″ wide, acuminate, semi-cordate, bristle-toothed, dark green, stellate pubescent below; petiole—short.

STEM: Brown, stellate pubescent.

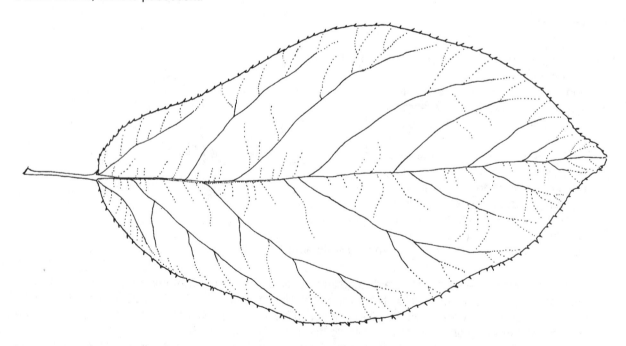

Sinowilsonia henryi, (sī-nō-wil-sō-nē'ȧ hen'ri-ī), is strictly a collector's tree, 15 to 20′ high, with large, handsome leaves and inconspicuous, apetalous flowers in terminal racemes. Monoecious with male flowers in 1 1/2

to 2″ long catkins; female in racemes 1/2 to 1 1/2″ long, extending to 6″ in fruit. The fruit is ovoid, 2-valved, 3/4″ long, woody capsule containing jet black seeds. This is a monotypic genus and I have seen the tree on just a few occasions, most indelibly etched from the Edinburgh Botanic Garden. Prefers woodland type soils. Named after the great plant explorer, E.H. Wilson. Central and western China. Introduced 1908. Zone 6 to 7.

Skimmia japonica Thunb. — Japanese Skimmia
(skim′i-à jà-pon′i-kà)

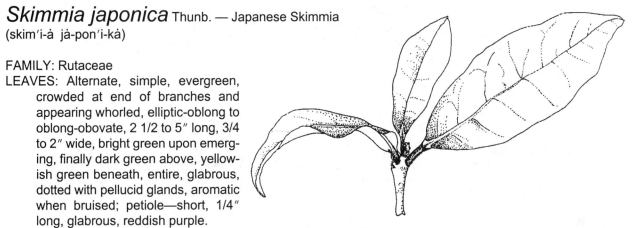

FAMILY: Rutaceae
LEAVES: Alternate, simple, evergreen, crowded at end of branches and appearing whorled, elliptic-oblong to oblong-obovate, 2 1/2 to 5″ long, 3/4 to 2″ wide, bright green upon emerging, finally dark green above, yellowish green beneath, entire, glabrous, dotted with pellucid glands, aromatic when bruised; petiole—short, 1/4″ long, glabrous, reddish purple.
BUDS: Imbricate, covered with red scales, glabrous, 1/16 to 1/8″ long.
STEM: Stout, green with an overcast of reddish purple, glabrous, spicy-fragrant when bruised; pith—ample, excavated, green.

SIZE: 3 to 4′ with a similar spread; have seen plants 6′ and larger.
HARDINESS: Zone (6)7 to 8(9).
HABIT: Dense, rounded to haystack-shaped (dome-shaped), evergreen shrub of rather gentle garden proportions.
RATE: Slow.
TEXTURE: Medium.
LEAF COLOR: Arguably dark green, although often stands out as a light green when compared to other broadleaf evergreens.
FLOWERS: Dioecious, glossy red-maroon in bud, creamy white when open, weakly fragrant, each flower 1/3″ across and borne in 2 to 3″ long, 1 to 2″ wide upright panicles; March–April (early April in Athens); flowers on male plants larger and more fragrant; selections have been made for this trait; peduncle and pedicels are glabrous and glossy reddish purple; almost more showy than flowers.
FRUIT: Only on female plant, bright red, 1/3″ wide, globose drupe that ripens in October and persists into the following spring; fruit is borne at end of shoots in panicles described above and is very effective; about one male to 6 females is necessary for good fruit set.
CULTURE: Transplant from containers; prefers moist, acid, high organic matter soils although will supposedly thrive in chalky (limestone) soils; partial shade or full shade is beneficial especially in winter when foliage is apt to discolor; in northern areas provide some winter protection.
DISEASES AND INSECTS: Mites can disfigure foliage.
LANDSCAPE VALUE: Beautiful evergreen shrub of dainty proportions for use in foundations, planter boxes, mixed broadleaf evergreen plantings; although sold and grown in Zone 7b, over my 19 years in Athens, I have yet to see a plant withstand the test of the southern landscape, simply languishes.
CULTIVARS: Many (25) are known but to my knowledge none are common in the United States.
  'Bronze Knight'—A male clone with flowers similar to 'Rubella', the leaves, however, more lustrous dark green and sharply pointed, leaves tinted red in winter
  'Foremanii' ('Veitchii')—Vigorous form with broad-obovate leaves and large clusters of brilliant red fruits; more properly *S. japonica* × *S. reevesiana* hybrid, flowers white; 2 to 3′ by 2 to 3′; flowers usually female although bisexual flowers occur.
  'Nymans'—Free-fruiting form with oblanceolate leaves and comparatively large red fruits; may be the best fruiting form but a male is required to insure fruit set.
  'Rubella'—A male clone with large, 3″ long, 2 1/2″ wide at base panicles of red buds through winter, peduncle and pedicels deep shiny bronze-red, opening to 4-petaled white with yellow anthers in spring, very fragrant; leaves dark green, 3 to 4″ long, petiole dark red; also listed as *S. reevesiana* clone.

'Ruby Dome'—Considered an improvement on 'Rubella' because it produces abundant pollen; have seen 'Ruby King' listed which sounds much like 'Ruby Dome'.

'Wakehurst White'—The proposed new name for the white-fruited cultivar previously termed 'Fructo-albo', see *Curtis's Botanical Magazine* 12(1):25–28 (1995).

PROPAGATION: Seeds when cleaned and sown germinate readily without treatment. Have collected fruits of *S. reevesiana* in fall, cleaned from pulp, sown, with germination in 3 to 4 weeks. Cuttings root quite readily when collected in fall and treated with 3000 to 8000 ppm IBA-talc; rooting should approach 100%.

ADDITIONAL NOTES: About four species are known along with a number of subspecies which at various times were elevated to species status. Beautiful plants in their forest incarnations but difficult to sustain in the East and South. Have observed terrific mite damage in the South. The best plants surface in the middle Atlantic States. The European literature is rich with cultivars and should be consulted. See *The New RHS Dictionary of Gardening*.

NATIVE HABITAT: Japan. Cultivated 1838.

RELATED SPECIES:

Skimmia laureola Sieb. & Zucc. — Skimmia

LEAVES: Alternate, simple, evergreen, 2 1/2 to 4 1/2″ long, 1 to 1 1/2″ wide, oblong-obovate or oblong-elliptic, acute to short acuminate, cuneate to rounded, entire, glabrous, rich green above, aromatic when bruised; petiole—1/4 to 3/8″ long, green.

Skimmia laureola, (skim′i-à lâ-rē-ō′là), Skimmia, forms a compact, low-growing, handsome-foliaged shrub about 2 to 3′ high and wide. The sweet-scented, creamy green flowers occur in lax, pyramidal, 4″ long, 3″ wide panicles in spring, although I saw plants in full flower in January in England. The fruit is purplish black but has not been seen on cultivated plants. Apparently all(?) forms in cultivation are male. 'Fragrant Cloud' is wide-spreading to 18″ high with bright green leaves and abundant flowers. 'Kew Green' is a handsome male form with large panicles of greenish flowers, larger than normal and quite unusual, no trace of reddish pigment in flowers; leaves are large dark green and densely set. 'Kew Green' is listed as a cultivar of *S.* × *confusa* N.P. Tayl. (*S. anquetilia* N.P. Taylor & Airy Shaw × *S. japonica*). Included in this grex are: 'Chelsea Physic' which is similar to 'Kew Green' but lower growing and with smaller leaves and smaller, 4″ diameter, pyramidal inflorescences of creamy white, male; and 'Isabella' with bright red fruits. See *Kew Magazine* 6(4):159–162 (1989) for specifics on 'Chelsea Physic'. Probably only adapted to Pacific Northwest and have never seen the species in the eastern corridor. Some speculation that *S. laureola* as described by Bean from plants in Kew Gardens are, in fact, hybrids. Best rooting on July–August, followed by September cuttings. Himalayas. Cultivated 1868. Zone 7(?) to 9.

Skimmia reevesiana Fort. — Reeves Skimmia

LEAVES: Alternate, simple, evergreen, lanceolate or oblong lanceolate, 1 to 4″ long, 3/4 to 1″ wide, acuminate, cuneate, entire, dark green above, light green beneath.

Skimmia reevesiana, (skim′i-à rēv′si-ā′nà), Reeves Skimmia, is a low-growing, 1 1/2 to 2′ high and 2 to 3′ wide, evergreen shrub. It tends to be more loose and open than *S. japonica*. The flowers are white, fragrant, bisexual, 1/2″ diameter, parts in 5's, and produced in 2 to 3″ long and wide terminal panicles. The oval to pear-shaped, 1/3″ long, rich crimson fruits persist into winter. Because of the bisexual nature of the flowers a lone plant will set fruit. It requires a rich, moist, acid soil. 'Chilan Choice' was introduced as a superior form by Wakehurst Place, England, grown from seed collected by Paul Meyer in 1979 in Taiwan. There is a variegated form with white-margined leaves. Also listed as *S. japonica* subsp. *reevesiana* (Fort.) N.P. Tayl. & Airy Shaw. China. Introduced 1849. Zone (6)7 and considered more cold hardy than *S. japonica*.

Smilax L. — Green-brier
FAMILY: Liliaceae

A large group, about 200 species, of deciduous or evergreen, woody or herbaceous climbers, stems often thorny (prickly), twining and high climbing, forming an impenetrable tangle of green to brown, armed stems. The flowers are dioecious, greenish, yellowish, whitish, in axillary umbels. The fruit is generally a rounded berry, about 1/4 to 1/3″ wide, blue, black or red.

The foliage, particularly on the evergreen types, is lustrous dark green; also leaves are often marked or splotched with lighter or darker markings. The evergreen types, particularly ***Smilax smallii*** Morong., (smī′laks smâl′ē-ī), Bamboo Vine, Jackson Vine, are used for their shiny foliage in Christmas decorations. This species grows wild in the Southeast. It is essentially thornless and therefore easier to handle than most species.

Smilax rotundifolia L., (smī′laks rō-tun-di-fō′li-à), Horse-brier, Common Green-brier, is the species that many gardeners, hikers and unsuspecting daydreamers most frequently encounter. It is deciduous (tardily) to semi-evergreen (South) with 1 1/2 to 6″ long, various shades of green with markings, ovate to sub-orbicular, acute or cuspidate, rounded or cordate, petiole—1/4 to 1/2″ long. The rounded green stems are armed with stout prickles. Fruits are 1/4″ long, 1- to 3-seeded, bluish black berries. Nova Scotia to Georgia, west to Minnesota, Illinois and Texas. Introduced about 1760. Zone 4 to 9.

The two species discussed grow in quantity around Athens and I have largely eliminated the latter, while preserving the former, on our property. Both form tubers or rhizomes which have unbelievable regenerative prowess. I have observed 4 to 6′ of growth in two weeks time from *S. rotundifolia*.

Smilax walteri Pursh., (smī′laks wâl′tēr-ī), Coral Green-brier, is similar to *S. rotundifolia* but produces red fruits. It also grows in wet soil areas and is distributed chiefly in the Coastal Plain from New Jersey to Florida and westward to Louisiana, central Arkansas and Tennessee.

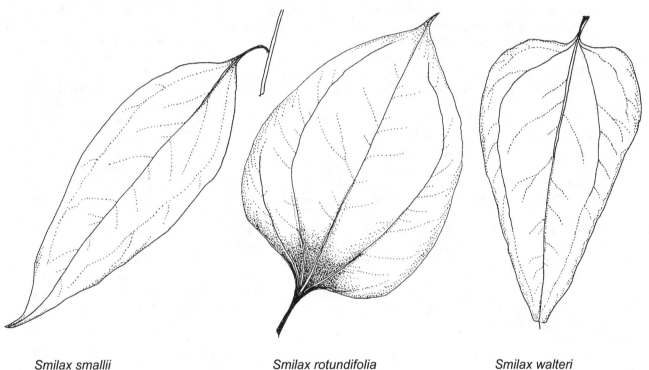

Smilax smallii   *Smilax rotundifolia*   *Smilax walteri*

Sophora japonica L. — Japanese Pagodatree, often called Scholar-tree
(so-fō′rà jà-pon′i-kà)

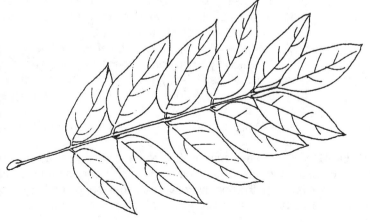

FAMILY: Fabaceae

LEAVES: Alternate, pinnately compound, 6 to 10″ long, 7 to 17 leaflets, ovate to lance-ovate, 1 to 2″ long, half as wide, acute, broad cuneate to rounded at base, entire, bright to medium green and lustrous above, glaucous beneath and closely appressed-pubescent.

BUDS: Blackish, woolly, sessile, indistinctly scaly, concealed by the leaf scar, end bud lacking; base of rachis swollen and enclosing bud.

STEM: Slender, essentially glabrous, green on 1- through 4- and 5-year-old wood, grayish lenticels, nodes prominently protruding; pith—solid, greenish.

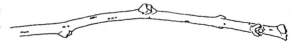

SIZE: 50 to 75′ in height with a comparable spread although great variation occurs.

HARDINESS: Zone 4 to 7, hardy in Orono, ME.

HABIT: Usually upright-spreading with a broadly rounded crown at maturity; casts a relatively light shade; many seedling trees have been planted on the Georgia campus and are rather open the first 2 to 3 years but form a decent canopy in the 4th and 5th years.

RATE: Medium to fast, 10 to 12′ in a 5 to 6 year period; has been faster than this in Zone 7b, probably 3′ per year the first 5 years.

TEXTURE: Medium-fine in leaf; medium in winter.

BARK: On old trunks somewhat Black Locust-like except pale grayish brown in color.

LEAF COLOR: Lustrous bright to medium green in summer; green color holds late and little fall color develops; on occasion soft yellow fall color; I have trouble with the shade of green, looks more bright green than anything.

FLOWERS: Perfect, creamy white, mildly fragrant; borne in 6 to 12″ long and wide terminal panicles (have measured them 12″ high and 14″ wide) in July through mid-August; each flower 1/2″ long, calyx 1/8″ long, green, bell-shaped, very showy in flower; flowered in July in Boston.

FRUIT: Pod, bright green changing to yellow and finally yellow brown, 3 to 8″ long, constricted between seeds, 3- to 6(10)-seeded; October, and may remain all winter; after the pods abscise the infructescence remains.

CULTURE: Transplant balled-and-burlapped as a young specimen; prefers loamy, well-drained soil; actually somewhat tender to cold when young but once over 1 1/2″ caliper seems to be fine; once established withstands heat and drought well; also tolerant of polluted conditions; prune in fall; tends to be a "floppy" grower and is somewhat difficult to train into a central leader with a nice head; the literature is full of comments about the lateness to flower, i.e., needs to grow 10 years or more; 3- to 5-year-old trees have produced *heavy* crops of flowers and fruits; perhaps most impressive has been the growth rate in the Southeast, probably 3′ per year during the first 5 years after transplanting; more urban tolerant than given credit; a number of plantspeople are taking a closer look at its attributes; with the 5th edition I bear somber news that the trees planted in the 1980's on the Georgia campus are suffering from canker, dieback, general malaise and simply have not performed well over time in Zone 7b.

DISEASES AND INSECTS: Canker, damping-off of seedlings, twig blight, powdery mildew and leaf hoppers; the potato leaf hopper can kill young stems and this in turn results in a "witches' broom."

LANDSCAPE VALUE: Good tree for city conditions, lawns, poor soil areas, parks, golf courses; probably best in Zone 5 and 6; excellent flower and good foliage are principal assets; could be considered messy for petals, fruits, leaves, rachises and pods drop differentially; flowers create a creamy carpet under the tree for a time in July–August; in Europe, the species is consistently rated among the highest for pollution and urban tolerances.

CULTIVARS:

'Columnaris' ('Fastigiata')—Upright growth habit, have never observed but young trees often show an upright outline.

'Pendula'—Weeping form, seldom flowers, quite interesting when used as an accent or formal specimen; comes relatively true-to-type from seed; I have collected seed from a plant at Bernheim Arboretum and a surprising number of the seedlings exhibited various degrees of pendulousness, about 1:1 ratio; my only regret is I gave them to my friends and did not save one for my garden; often grafted on a standard, will grow 15 to 25′ high.

'Princeton Upright'—All the good qualities of 'Regent' with a compact upright branching system, 40 to 50′.

'Regent'—Selection by Princeton Nurseries for fast growth rate, often twice the rate of seedling trees, straight growth habit, large oval-rounded crown, glossy deep green leaves, and earliness to flower (6- to 8-years-old); in Zone 7b this occurs after 1 to 3 years in the nursery; good plant and it flowers heavily in the Athens area.

'Variegata'—White speckled leaves; saw for the first time in Berlin Botanic Garden, for the dedicated collector.

PROPAGATION: Seeds supposedly require a weak scarification in acid to break down the impermeable seed coat, easy to grow from seed; I have grown numerous seedlings by sowing them as soon as they are removed from the pod; worthwhile to soak seeds overnight to prime for more even germination; cultivars are budded.

ADDITIONAL NOTES: Last of the large ornamental trees to flower in the North. Used around Buddhist temples. Yellow dye can be extracted from the flowers by baking them until brown and then boiling them in water. A very distinctive and aesthetically handsome tree in flower. Bean mentioned that the tree does not flower until 30 to 40 years of age. American references have stated 10 to 14 years. I have a sneaking suspicion that high summer heat, perhaps warm nights, foster early flowering. All authors, including this one, tend to pass along time-honored information without determining, first hand, the actual response in question.

NATIVE HABITAT: China, Korea. Introduced 1747.

RELATED SPECIES:

Sophora secundiflora (Ort.) Lag. ex DC. — Mescal Bean, Texas Mountain Laurel
LEAVES: Alternate, evergreen, compound pinnate, 4 to 6″ long, 6 to 10 leaflets, to 2″ long, oblong or obovate, notched at apex, pubescent below, rich green.

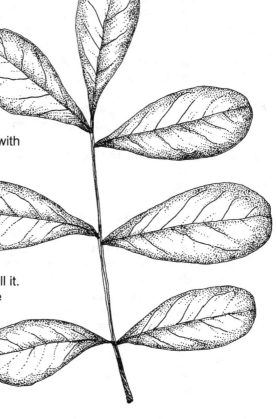

Sophora secundiflora, (so-fō′rȧ sē-kund-i-flō′rȧ), Mescal Bean, is a small, (15′)20 to 30′ high, evergreen tree with great foliage and branch character. The habit is irregular, upright-spreading, low-branched. The fragrant, 1″ long, violet-blue flowers occur in pendent racemes. Fruits are 6 to 8″ long, woody pods. Requires well-drained, drier soils and is best suited to the Southwest. I first saw the plant in a street side planting in San Antonio, TX. Holds up well under stress. Too much care (read water) will kill it. 'Alba', with white flowers, is described. Seeds germinate best after two hour concentrated sulfuric acid scarification. See *HortScience* 26:256–257 (1991). See *Nursery Manager* 11(12):14–15, 69 (1995) for a worthy discussion. Texas, New Mexico, northern Mexico. Zone 8 to 10.

Sorbaria sorbifolia (L.) A. Braun. — Ural Falsespirea
(sôr-bā′ri-ȧ sôr-bi-fō′li-ȧ)

FAMILY: Rosaceae
LEAVES: Alternate, pinnately compound, 8 to 12″ long, 13 to 25 leaflets, 2 to 4″ long, 1/2 to 1″ wide, lanceolate to ovate-lanceolate, long acuminate, double and sharply serrate, usually glabrous or nearly so beneath, deep green above, subsessile; resembles mountainash foliage.
STEM: Young—usually green or pink, often somewhat downy, gray-brown when old and glabrous; pith—large, brown, continuous.

SIZE: 5 to 10′ in height with a similar spread.
HARDINESS: Zone 2 to 7(8).
HABIT: Erect, rather coarse multi-stemmed shrub, with foliage similar to European Mountainash; spreads rapidly by suckers, forming colonies.
RATE: Fast.
TEXTURE: Many people say the texture is coarse but I feel if the shrub is properly pruned and maintained the texture is at worst medium in summer; tends toward coarseness in winter.

LEAF COLOR: Has a reddish tinge when unfolding gradually changing to deep green in summer; fall color is not effective; leafs out early and I have seen emerging leaves as early as late March in central Illinois.

FLOWERS: Perfect, white, 1/3″ across; late June into July; borne in large, terminal, fleecy, 4 to 10″ long, to 6″ wide panicles; very effective and, in fact, outstanding in flower, flowers turn brown upon senescing; flowers occur on new wood of the season; this is true for all species.

FRUIT: Dehiscent follicles.

CULTURE: Transplants readily, very fibrous rooted, suckers and spreads profusely; prefers moist, well-drained, organic soil; tends to become dwarfed in dry soils; full sun or light shade; pH adaptable; prune in early spring before growth starts as the flowers are produced on current season's growth; cut off old flowers; relatively easy plant to grow, however, it is not widely known.

DISEASES AND INSECTS: None serious.

LANDSCAPE VALUE: Excellent plant for the shrub border, for massing, grouping, might make a good bank cover as it freely suckers and spreads; is one of the first shrubs to leaf out in spring; needs considerable room to spread and is not suitable for small planting areas.

PROPAGATION: Easy to root from softwood, greenwood or hardwood cuttings, preferably in sand under mist; division is a good method; seeds can be sown as soon as ripe and will germinate.

ADDITIONAL NOTES: About four legitimate species although over the years I have seen many more listed. The Arnold Arboretum had a large collection in the rose garden, many appearing so similar as to be inseparable.

NATIVE HABITAT: Northern Asia from Ural to Japan. Cultivated 1759.

RELATED SPECIES:

Single leaflet

Sorbaria aitchisonii (Helms.) Rehd., (sôr-bā′ri-à atch′i-sō′nē-ī), Kashmir Falsespirea, is a rather graceful, 6 to 9′ (12′) high shrub with 11 to 23 sharply toothed and tapered, 2 to 4″ long, 1/4 to 5/8″ wide, single serrate, glabrous leaflets, in a 9 to 15″ long leaf. The young glabrous stems are usually a rich red. The white flowers occur in large, conical, 1 to 1 1/2′ long and 8 to 14″ wide panicles in (June)July and August. Handsome in full flower with the large billowy white panicles. Flowers age to brown and there always seems to be a transition between white and brown, never continuous white changing to brown. Possibly best to remove the old flower panicles. This is a handsome shrub which could be planted more than it is, especially in large masses along highways or in open spaces. Recent nomenclature treats the species as *S. tomentosa* (Lindl.) Rehd. var. *tomentosa* (leaflets pubescent below) and the plant discussed above as *S. tomentosa* var. *angustifolia* (Wenz.) Rahn. Afghanistan, Western Pakistan, Kashmir. Introduced 1895. Zone (5)6 to 7.

Sorbaria arborea Schneid., (sôr-bā′ri-à är-bō′rē-à), Tree Falsespirea, is a large, spreading shrub to 15′ with 13 to 17 slender-pointed leaflets. The white flowers are produced in large 12 to 15″ long and wide panicles similar to the previous species. Leaflets and stems are more pubescent than the previous species. As above, the nomenclature relegates *S. arborea* to pasture and treats *S. kirilowii* (Reg.) Maxim. as the correct entity. Central and western China. Introduced 1908 by Wilson. Zone 5 to 7, hardier than the above.

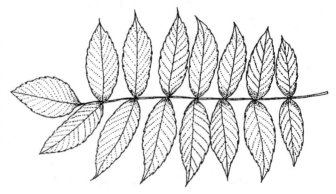

Sorbus alnifolia (Sieb. & Zucc.) K. Koch — Korean Mountainash
(sôr′bus al-ni-fō′li-à)

FAMILY: Rosaceae

LEAVES: Alternate, simple, 2 to 4″ long, 3/4 to 1 1/2″ wide, ovate to elliptic-ovate, short-acuminate, rounded at base, unequally serrate, glabrous above, glabrous or slightly pubescent beneath, on vigorous shoots sometimes pubescent, with 6 to 10 pairs of veins, leaf shape resembles *Fagus* to a degree, lustrous dark green; petiole—1/2 to 3/4″ long.

BUDS: Oblong, terminal bud scarcely larger than the lateral, solitary, sessile, with several dark margined scales, the inner of which are more or less pubescent with long hairs often matted in gum.

STEM: Moderate, lustrous reddish brown, prominent small gray lenticels; on older stems lenticels become distinctly diamond-shaped.

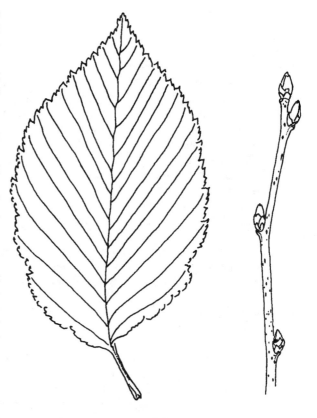

SIZE: 40 to 50′ in height by 20 to 30′(50′) in spread although can grow to 60′.

HARDINESS: Zone 4 to 7, growing successfully at Minnesota Landscape Arboretum.

HABIT: Pyramidal when young developing a weakly pyramidal-oval to almost rounded outline at maturity; have also seen broad rounded trees.

RATE: Medium to fast, 10 to 12′ over a 5 to 7 year period.

TEXTURE: Medium in all seasons.

BARK: Gray on old trunks, almost beech-like; the first time I witnessed Korean Mountainash was at the Arnold Arboretum and was instantly taken by the beautiful foliage, flowers, bark and habit; one of my favorite all around trees; unfortunately, not very well-known.

LEAF COLOR: New leaves a rich bright fresh spring green; lustrous dark green in summer changing to yellow, orange, and golden brown in fall; the leaves are simple and do not look anything like what we normally consider a mountainash leaf; look like beech or hornbeam leaves.

FLOWERS: Perfect, white, 1/2″ diameter, borne in 6- to 10-flowered, flat-topped, 2 to 3″ diameter corymbs in May, beautiful in flower but shows an alternate sequence, heavy one year, lighter the next.

FRUIT: Roundish or obovoid pome, pinkish red to orangish red to scarlet, bloomy, speckled with dark lenticels, 3/8 to 5/8″ long, September–October and persisting, spectacular, at its best perhaps the handsomest of all mountainash for fruit effect.

CULTURE: Transplant balled-and-burlapped into any well-drained soil; very pH adaptable; does not withstand polluted conditions; prune in winter or early spring; Donald Wyman noted that it was one of the most successful of the flowering trees introduced by the Arnold Arboretum from Japan and required little cultural attention.

DISEASES AND INSECTS: Discussed under *Sorbus aucuparia*, the least susceptible to borer injury; Hasselkus, Wisconsin, reported fireblight susceptibility; fireblight was reported on the species from trees growing in Washington, DC and Allentown, NJ, also reported on *S. folgneri* in same paper, see *Plant Diseases* 79(4):424 (1995).

LANDSCAPE VALUE: Specimen tree for lawns; not for streets or downtown city areas; the best of the mountainash; difficult to believe it is even related to the genus *Sorbus*, botanically placed in the section Micromeles.

CULTIVARS:

'Redbird'—Listed as having rosy red fruits that persist into winter and serve as a food source for birds, narrow upright columnar form, rich golden yellow fall color; possibly same as 'Skyline'.

PROPAGATION: Seeds require 3 months or more of cold stratification at 41°F in moist medium.

ADDITIONAL NOTES: Like most mountainash there is always the threat of fireblight and borer damage. Probably best not to utilize the tree in high stress environments (urban settings) where it would be predisposed to insect or disease infestations. I monitored the trees in the Arnold's collection during sabbatical and seldom a day would pass when I did not give them a caring inspection. The fruits can be spectacular and, during a heavy flowering year, it is the equal of any fruiting tree. The Arnold also has an upright form that is somewhat broad-columnar. To my knowledge it does not have a cultivar name although the name 'Skyline' appears in some literature. This selection was made by Alf Alford, Hillier Nursery, in 1962. I considered this a possibility for use in the South (Zone 7b) but remembered trees planted at the Biltmore Estate, Asheville, NC and even they died. Mountainash and heat, particularly high night temperatures, are diametrically opposed.

NATIVE HABITAT: Central China to Korea and Japan. Introduced 1892.

Sorbus aucuparia L. — European Mountainash, Rowan, Common Mountainash
(sôr′bus aw-kū-pā′ri-à)

LEAVES: Alternate, pinnately compound, 5 to 9″ long,
9 to 15(19) leaflets, 3/4 to 2 1/2″ long, oblong to
oblong-lanceolate, acute or obtusish, serrate,
usually entire in lower third, dull dark green above,
glaucescent beneath and pubescent, at least
when young, leaflet base asymmetric.

BUDS: Terminal—large, woolly, 1/2″ long, lateral often
reduced with several scales, the inner of which
are more or less pubescent, reddish brown.

STEM: Young branches pubescent, becoming glabrous, grayish brown and shiny when older.

SIZE: 20 to 40′(60′) in height with a spread of 2/3′s to
equal the height; national cham-
pion is 43′ by 42′ in Woodland
Park Zoo, Washington.

HARDINESS: Zone 3 to 6 or 7; excessive summer heat
induces problems.

HABIT: Erect and oval in youth forming an ovate or
spherical, gracefully open head at maturity; often
low-branched or multi-stemmed.

RATE: Medium, 25 to 30′ over a 20 year period.

TEXTURE: Medium-fine in leaf, medium or medium-coarse in winter.

BARK: Light grayish brown in color, usually smooth, both often somewhat slightly roughened on old trunks.

LEAF COLOR: Flat, dull dark green in summer; fall color ranges from green to yellow to reddish, often a fine
reddish purple.

FLOWERS: White, 1/3″ across, malodorous, borne in 3 to 5″ diameter, flat-topped corymbs in May; effective,
but not outstanding; not as showy as *S. alnifolia*.

FRUIT: Small, berry-like pome, 1/4 to 3/8″ diameter, orange-red; late August into September, very handsome,
frequented by birds and seldom persisting for any time; made into an alcoholic drink and also processed
into juice and vinegar, stewed, made into tea, and used medicinally.

CULTURE: Transplant balled-and-burlapped into well-drained loam; prefers acid soils and is often short-lived
on chalky soils; have seen far too many problems on the species especially where stress is common, does
not fare well in compacted soils, polluted atmospheres and the like; high summer temperatures appear
to limit growth; I have not seen a single European Mountainash in Zone 8 and generally those in Zone 7
are short-lived; stress apparently predisposes the species to canker and borer.

DISEASES AND INSECTS: Fireblight can be devastating, crown gall, canker, leaf rusts, scab, aphids, pear leaf
blister mite, Japanese leafhopper, roundheaded borer, mountainash sawfly, and scales; borers are serious
in weakened and poorly growing trees; the best line of defense is a vigorous, healthy, actively growing tree.

LANDSCAPE VALUE: Excellent for fruit effect but its use should be tempered by the knowledge that it is
susceptible to many pests; use in northern climates.

CULTIVARS: There are numerous cultivars, some of which were branch sports and others which came about
through hybridization. The following represent a small complement of the different types.

'Apricot Queen'—Apricot-colored fruit.

'Asplenifolia'—Leaflets doubly serrate and supposedly deeply divided; however, the one tree I saw was
just a degree more saw-toothed than the species.

'Beissneri'—A graceful variety with pinnately lobed leaflets; leaf petioles and branchlets bright red, stems
and trunk a rich copper-brown color.

'Black Hawk'—A strong columnar form with thick dark green leaves and large, orange fruits, appears to
be resistant to sun-scald, 30′ by 20′, reported to be the best for the Midwest.

'Brilliant Pink'—Pink fruit.

'Brilliant Yellow'—Golden yellow fruit in 3 to 5″ wide infructescences, 30′ by 20′, oval outline, offered by
Lake County Nursery.

'Cardinal Royal'—Vigorous grower with symmetrical upright narrow-oval habit, leaves dark green above,
silvery beneath, brilliant red fruits in August–September, introduced by Michigan State University,
35′ by 20′.

'Carpet of Gold'—Sulfur yellow to orange fruit, hybrid with *S. cashmiriana*.

'Charming Pink'—Pink fruit, 30' by 20', oval habit, Lake County Nursery offering.

Coral Fire™—Notable attributes include thick dark green leaves, bright red fall color, coral-red fruits, introduced by Pacific Coast Nursery, considered a *S. hupehensis* Schneid. selection and listed here for ease of presentation.

'Edulis'—Fruit larger (1/3 to 3/8″ diameter) than species and used for preserves in Europe.

'Fastigiata'—Upright with strongly ascending branches, dark green leaves, good large sealing wax red fruits; slow-growing, rather coarsely branched.

'Longwood Sunset'—Has showy orange fruits and burgundy fall foliage, 20' by 20', hardy to -30°F, Longwood Gardens introduction, listed as *S. rufoferruginea* Schneid. selection, species itself is very similar to *S. commixta*.

'Pendula'—Weeping in a rather irregular, unkempt manner and fruiting quite heavily, 15 to 20' high at landscape maturity, always remember a grouping on the UMass campus, pretty eye-catching.

'Red Cascade'—A small, compact oval tree with small orange-red fruits and yellow-orange fall color, size approximates 6' by 8', listed as a *S. tianschanica* Rupr. form in Schmidt Nursery 1988–89 catalog, 'Dwarfcrown' is cultivar name, Red Cascade is the trademark name.

'Red Copper Glow'—Bright scarlet fruits with coral and copper overtones, 30' by 20', Lake County Nursery offering.

'Scarlet King'—Scarlet fruit.

'Wilson'—Dense columnar form, red fruit, 30'.

'Xanthocarpa'—Yellow fruits, more properly amber-yellow to orange-yellow.

PROPAGATION: Seeds require 60 to 120 days of cold, moist stratification at 38°F. Cuttings have been rooted with some success. See *Scientia Horticulturae* 42:169–175 (1990). Cultivars are budded or grafted onto seedling understocks.

ADDITIONAL NOTES: My son Matt and I were hiking in the Lake District (Windemere) in England and growing from the rocky mountainsides were *S. aucuparia*. Based on native soil adaptability, the plant should withstand urban soils. Obviously, the cool, moist English climate is essential to long-term performance.

NATIVE HABITAT: Europe to western Asia and Siberia, and naturalized in North America. Long cultivated.

RELATED SPECIES:

Sorbus americana Marsh. — American Mountainash

LEAVES: Alternate, compound pinnate, 6 to 12″ long, 11 to 17 leaflets, 1 1/2 to 4″ long, 1/2 to 3/4″ wide, lance-oblong to lanceolate, acuminate, sharply serrate, dark green and glabrous above, paler beneath, pubescent or glabrous, generally serrated almost to the base, where on *S. aucuparia* the serrations start about 1/3 from the base.

Sorbus americana, (sôr′bus ȧ-mer-i-kā′nȧ), American Mountainash, is a northern species that grows from 10 to 30' high and is usually a small tree or shrub with a short trunk of spreading, slender branches that form a narrow, open, round-topped crown. National champion is 62' by 40' in West Virginia State Park. Flowers are white; fruit is a brilliant orange-red to scarlet-red. It frequents borders of cold swamps and bogs, or grows in a stunted form on relatively dry soils; grows slowly and is short-lived. Have observed on the top of the highest mountain (Brasstown Bald) in Georgia; attractive in the right situations. Bonnie and I see the species everywhere from Maine to the higher elevations of the southern Appalachians. The fall color can be beautiful, almost orange-yellow to reddish purple. Ranges from Newfoundland to Manitoba, south to Michigan, and North Carolina along the Appalachian Mountains. Cultivated 1811. Hardy to Zone 2 (-40 to -50°F).

Sorbus aria (L.) Crantz. — Whitebeam Mountainash

LEAVES: Alternate, simple, 2 to 4″(5″) long, one-half to two-third's as wide, elliptic to broad-elliptic or ovate, obtuse or acute, cuneate or rounded, double serrate except at base, dull green to lustrous dark green above, covered with whitish tomentum below, 8 to 13 parallel vein pairs; petiole—1/2 to 1″ long.

Sorbus aria, (sôr′bus är′ē-ȧ), Whitebeam Mountain-ash, is a tree which develops a broad-pyramidal or ovoid head. This species grows 35 to 45′ tall and has simple, leathery, gray-green to lustrous dark green leaves (upper surface) while the lower surface is white-tomentose in summer. Fall color varies from pale green to golden brown to reddish. Flowers are white, about 1/3″ across, borne in 2 to 3″ wide, terminal corymbs in May. Fruit is 1/2″ diameter, orange-red or scarlet, ovoid or rounded, berry-like pome that ripens in September through October. The leaves are quite different from what we associate with a "normal" mountainash leaf. There are several cultivars of note: 'Aurea' is a type with yellow foliage; 'Magnifica' with dense conical crown, large dark green leaves with snow white tomentum beneath, yellow fall color with leaves holding late; 'Majestica' with fruits as much as 5/8″ in diameter and the leaves reach 7″ in length; 'Ottery' is a hybrid between *S. aria* 'Lutescens' and 'Majestica', develops into a well-proportioned tree with uniform branch structure, leaves gray-silver and less prone to browning and abscission. Grows naturally on the chalky soils of the south of England and tolerates maritime as well as urban conditions. Native to Europe. Long cultivated. Zone 5.

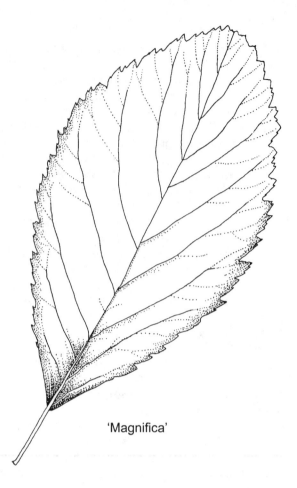

'Magnifica'

Sorbus cashmiriana Hedl. — Kashmir Mountainash

LEAVES: Alternate, compound pinnate, 3 1/2 to 7″ long, 13 to 19 leaflets, 1 to 2″ long, 3/8 to 5/8″ wide, lanceolate to oblong, acute, sharply serrate to base, rich green above and glabrous, gray-green below.

Sorbus cashmiriana, (sôr′bus kash-mēr-ē-ā′nȧ), Kashmir Mountainash, develops a conical crown and grows 20 to 40′ high with an equal spread. The flowers are pinkish white, 3/4″ diameter, and borne in mid to late May in 3 to 5″ wide, lax corymbs. In fall the leaves may change to a good red. The white fruits are about 3/8″ diameter and are often tinged pink; the fruit stalks are pink to red in color. This species has been used in hybridizing with *S. aucuparia* by European nurserymen. Some of the cultivars include: 'Carpet of Gold' with yellow fruits; 'Kirsten Pink' with dark pink fruits; and 'Maidenblush' with pale pink fruits. Wyman considered this species well worthy of a trial wherever mountainashes are grown. The exact taxonomic status is questionable; the trees I have seen are more loose and open than *S. aucuparia* types with smaller, fine-textured leaflets and bear large, loose, 5 to 7″ wide corymbs that are eventually laden with the handsome white to pinkish fruit. Native to Himalayas. Introduced 1949 into the Arnold Arboretum. Zone 4.

ADDITIONAL NOTES: *Sorbus* presents a real challenge to the taxonomist and horticulturist. There are numerous hybrids and cultivars and even intergeneric hybrids with *Aronia* (× *Sorbaronia* Schneid.), *Cotoneaster* (× *Sorbocotoneaster* Pojark.) and *Pyrus* (× *Sorbopyrus* Schneid.). The treatment I have presented is not extensive and I recommend the reader consult Bean, Hillier, Krüssmann, and *The New RHS Dictionary of Gardening* for additional information. I have observed so many European Mountainashes decimated by fireblight and borers in the Midwest and East that it became somewhat discouraging to recommend the tree to the gardener. The Arnold Arboretum had a significant collection and I delighted in the magnificent fruit displays that ranged in color from white, pink, yellow, orange to red and the excellent fall color on species like *S. commixta* and *S. esserteauiana* Koehne. In Europe, and especially England, they are planted in abundance. The cool, moist climate is more to their liking. In the United States, extreme heat and drought predispose them to many problems.

Unfortunately, since moving South, *Sorbus* has been removed from my gardening vocabulary simply because the plants do not prosper (survive) in Zones 7 to 9. In fruit, there are few trees that equal the mountainash especially some of the white, pink and coral-pink colored forms. In January 1989, I heard Dr. Hugh McAllister present a lecture on *Sorbus* at the Pershore Nursery Conference, Pershore, England. He provided an excellent overview of the garden attributes and discussed the confusion in identification.

There are 120 or so species and since *Sorbus* reproduces apomictically (without normal fertilization), numerous microspecies are known which further confound taxonomy. In brief, the best advice to gardeners is to enjoy the mountainash for their lovely fruit and fall color.

Other species of some interest but limited landscape acceptability include: **Sorbus commixta** Hedl., (sôr'bus com-miks'tà), Japanese Mountainash, with white flowers in 4 to 6″ wide inflorescences and globose, 3/8″ wide, lustrous bright red fruits, 20 to 30′, Zone 5; **Sorbus decora** Sarg. & Schneid., (sôr'bus de-ko'rà), Showy Mountainash, with white flowers and red fruit. Bailey Nursery considers it the hardiest of the mountainash grown in the United States, 20 to 25′, national champion is 58′ by 32′ in Mackinac County, MI, Zone 2 to 5; and **Sorbus discolor** (Maxim.) Maxim., (sôr'bus dis'kul-ēr), Snowberry Mountainash, with white flowers, 2 to 4(6″) wide, bright scarlet fruit clusters, 20 to 30′, Zone 2. Have seen red fruits on cultivated *S. discolor*, however, the literature lists fruit as white-yellow, occasionally pink. I have seen these species and was quite impressed by their fruit displays and fall color especially in the case of *S. commixta*. There is little doubt that *Sorbus* taxa are terribly confused.

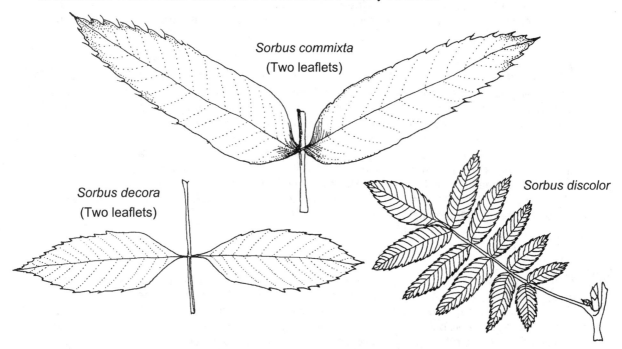

Sorbus commixta
(Two leaflets)

Sorbus decora
(Two leaflets)

Sorbus discolor

Two other *Sorbus* that appear in northern latitudes and are often listed by nurseries include: **Sorbus × hybrida** L. and **Sorbus × thuringiaca** (Ilse) Fritsch. Both are medium-sized, pyramidal oval trees about 25 to 35′ high and two third's as wide. *Sorbus × hybrida* (*S. aria × S. aucuparia*) is a tetraploid apomictic species and reproduces true-to-type from seed. The leaves are deeply lobed and essentially simple, but often cut to the midvein, the overall effect somewhat oak-like. Generally, they are lobed toward their end, lobes increasing in depth toward the base. Size ranges from 3 to 3 1/2″ long, 2 to 2 1/2″ wide, dull dark green above, white pubescent below, with a 1/2 to 1″ long petiole. White flowers occur in 2 to 5″ wide corymbs and are followed by globose, 1/2 to 5/8″ wide, deep red fruits. *Sorbus × thuringiaca* is often called the Oakleaf Mountainash and is a hybrid between *S. aucuparia* and *S. aria*. The habit is upright with numerous ascending branches forming with time a dense, rhombic crown, eventually 20 to 40′ high. White flowers occur in 3 to 5″ wide corymbs, followed by 3/8″ wide, globose or ellipsoidal, bright red fruits. The leaves are leathery dark green above covered with dull whitish tomentum below. Leaves average 3 to 6″ long and have the lobing pattern of *S. × hybrida*. Leaves are 2 to 2 1/2 times as long as wide. 'Fastigiata' is similar to the species but differs in more fastigiate form perhaps twice as tall as wide at maturity. Both species (hybrids) originated in or are native to Europe. Zone (3)4 to 5.

Spiraea albiflora (Miq.) Zab. — Japanese White Spirea

LEAVES: Alternate, simple, lanceolate, 2 1/2″ long, one third to half as wide, acuminate, cuneate, coarsely or sometimes double serrate, with callous-tipped teeth, rich bright green above, glabrous and bluish green beneath; petiole—short.

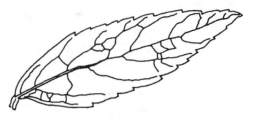

Spiraea albiflora, (spī-rē′à al-bi-flō′rà), Japanese White Spirea, could be equated with a white-flowered 'Anthony Waterer'. The habit is low (2 to 3′), rounded, dense and the white corymbs which appear in late June and July (late May–early June, Athens) are effectively foiled against the handsome foliage. I have observed leaves about half-size on February 27, 1991 in Athens. Makes an excellent facer plant, mass, or filler in the shrub border. Flowers on new wood so can be rejuvenated in early spring. Sometimes listed as *S. japonica* var. *alba* or 'Alba'. Roots very readily from cuttings and is infinitely superior to the large, cumbersome, unkempt, straggly spireas. Have seen tremendous chlorosis in some areas of the Midwest. Requires acid soil for best growth. It is probably more correctly listed as a cultivar ('Albiflora') of *S. japonica* but in this edition I have chosen to stay with the species treatment. Has performed well in Zone 7 and the overall foliage color is brighter green than *S.* × *bumalda* types. The pure white flowers are particularly handsome framed by the rich green leaves. 'Leucantha' is a seedling of *S. albiflora* with larger leaves and inflorescences. Cultivated in Japan. Introduced before 1868. Zone 4 to 8.

Spiraea × *billiardii* Hérincq., (spī-rē′à bil-yard′ē-ī), Billiard Spirea, resulted from crosses between

S. douglasii Hook. and *S. salicifolia* L. It is an upright (6′) shrub that shows a propensity to sucker. The chief beauty resides in rose-colored flowers which occur in narrow, dense-pyramidal, 4 to 8″ long panicles in June to August. The flowers fade to a rather ugly brown and should be removed. It is susceptible to iron chlorosis and should only be planted in acid soil. Other than the pretty flowers, there is little to recommend it. 'Alba' is white-flowered. 'Macrothyrsa' with bright pink flowers in 6 to 8″ long panicles is included here. 'Triumphans' has purplish rose flowers in dense, conical panicles and is considered among the finest of late-flowered spireas. These hybrids and West Coast species do not appear as well-adapted to the heat and humidity of the lower Midwest, East, and Southeast. Have seen in European gardens where they are perfectly content. Originated before 1854. Zone 3 to 6.

Spiraea bullata Maxim., (spī-rē′à bul-lā′tà), Crispleaf Spirea makes a rather intriguing, low (12 to 15″),

ground cover type plant. The foliage is thickish and bullate, dark almost bluish green above, grayish green beneath. Leaves average 1/2 to 1 1/4″ long, up to 3/4″ wide and are coarsely toothed. Flowers are deep rosy pink, borne in small, dense corymbs which form a terminal, 1 1/2 to 3″ diameter corymb; June–July. Valuable as a dwarf shrub, especially in a rock garden setting. Considered a selection from *S. japonica*. Often aphid infested and less than desirable in hot climates, best in colder areas. Japan. Cultivated 1880. Zone 4 to 7.

Spiraea × *bumalda* Burvénich — Bumald Spirea (result of a cross between

   S. albiflora and *S. japonica*)
(spī-rē′à bū-màl′dà)

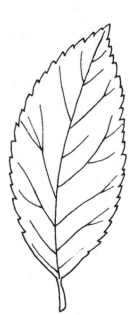

FAMILY: Rosaceae
LEAVES: Alternate, simple, 1 to 3″ long, ovate-lanceolate, apex pointed, base narrowed, teeth mostly double, sharp, pinkish-red-purple when young, finally dark green, almost bluish green.
STEM: Brown, slightly angled in cross section, somewhat lined or ridged, glabrous.

SIZE: 2 to 3′ (4 to 5′) high and 3 to 5′ wide.
HARDINESS: Zone 3 to 8, some tip kill on 'Anthony Waterer' and 'Froebelii' in Maine.
HABIT: A broad, flat-topped, low shrub, densely twiggy with erect branches, often mounded in habit, clean, relatively refined shrub.
RATE: Fast.
TEXTURE: Medium-fine in all seasons.
LEAF COLOR: Pinkish to reddish when unfolding changing to dark bluish green at maturity; leaves tend to show cream to yellow variegation patterns, particularly

'Anthony Waterer'; often turning bronzy red to purplish in fall; seldom spectacular; very early leafing as is true for many spireas, showing leaf color by early March in Athens.

FLOWERS: White to deep pink, June into August, borne in 4 to 6″ diameter, flat-topped corymbs; flowers on new growth; flowers mid to late May into early June in Athens, often sporadically thereafter.

FRUIT: Dry, brown follicle, not ornamental, maintained on large infructescence through winter, almost better to remove after flowering since fruits are rather ugly, this, in turn, induces new growth and resultant flowers.

CULTURE: Largely container-grown, easy to transplant; tolerant of many soils except those which are extremely wet; prefers full sun and open areas; pruning must be based on type of wood upon which flowers are produced; *S. × bumalda* and *S. japonica* should be pruned in early spring before growth starts if pruning is required, after flowers fade, remove them, and a second flush of growth is stimulated that will also produce additional flowers.

DISEASES AND INSECTS: Subject to many of the problems that afflict other members of the Rosaceae; fireblight, bacterial hairy root, leaf spot, powdery mildews, root rot, spirea aphid, oblique-banded leaf roller, scales, caterpillars and root-knot nematode; based on my experience it is difficult to kill a spirea.

LANDSCAPE VALUE: Good filler or facer plant, can be used as a low massing plant, possibly as a bank cover for it suckers from the roots; like most spireas has been overused.

CULTIVARS: *Spiraea × bumalda* is almost an enigma, and most European authorities place its cultivars (such as 'Anthony Waterer' and 'Froebelii') under *S. japonica*. In the hybrid form, *S. × bumalda* is considered a cross between *S. japonica* and *S. albiflora*. Since most American nursery catalogs and popular reference books call the plant *S. × bumalda*, I will maintain similar consistency.

   Spiraea × bumalda was described in 1891. England's Kew Gardens received it in 1885 from Karl Froebel of Zurich. (The original *S. × bumalda* was a dwarf plant, and a high proportion of the leaves were either marked with yellow or were totally yellow.) The emerging leaves of *S. × bumalda* are brownish red and essentially hairless and mature to a bluish green. The flowers are carmine-pink. Many authors have noted the instability of this clone, remarking that all the plants propagated throughout the world from this one plant are not the same due to the numerous branch sports.

'Anthony Waterer'—Originated from the original *S. × bumalda* described above. This cultivar also produces branch sports. The best form reaches 3 to 4′ high and 4 to 5′ wide at maturity. 'Anthony Waterer' has 4 to 6″ diameter, essentially flat-topped, carmine-pink inflorescences. The new leaves are brownish red changing to bluish green. They may turn wine-red to russet-red in fall. The leaves emerge in Georgia in early to mid-March. Flowers appear in late May and in June, and the reddish purple fall color is apparent by early November. The richly polished brown stems add a degree of winter interest. Based on many observations, I am convinced there are numerous (yes, numerous) forms floating around in the nursery trade. At the University's Botanical Garden, a so-called 'Anthony Waterer' planting develops puny, 2″ diameter inflorescences and the strangest yellow-green leaf patterns imaginable. Some shoots are completely yellow, others are yellow and green, and some are even completely green. Another form listed as 'Anthony Waterer' does not develop branch sports and has long-lasting deep cerise-red flowers. Flower color is another variable trait, with certain plants displaying flowers of a deep carmine-pink. In the heat of the South, the plants' pigmentation is not as vibrant as that of plants farther north.

'Candle Light'—Softer butter yellow foliage, not quite as loud as the other yellow leaf types, pink flowers, compact-mounded habit, 2 to 3′ high, from Liss Forest Nursery, England.

'Coccinea'—Is a bud mutation of 'Anthony Waterer' that has deep carmine-red flowers, decidedly more colorful than 'Anthony Waterer'; I first saw it at Bressingham Gardens in England and, although some literature says it differs very little in color, the plant I witnessed was much deeper red; maybe smaller than 'Anthony Waterer'; perhaps 2 to 3′ high; has developed branch sports; a plant in the University's Botanical Garden collection possessed the deep carmine red flowers; this is often listed as a *S. japonica* form.

'Crimson Glory'—In the Dirr garden, this appears to be nothing more than a deep crimson red-flowered form of 'Anthony Waterer'; has been stable with no shoot reversions; 3′ by 3′ in 3 years.

'Crispa'—Is not well-known, and my first introduction to the plant occurred at the Morton Arboretum in Lisle, IL. In most respects, 'Crispa' is similar to 'Anthony Waterer'. However, its leaves are slightly twisted and deeply incised, giving the plant a slightly finer-textured appearance than 'Anthony Waterer'. I grew 'Crispa' in my Illinois garden and gave a plant to my sister in Cincinnati but never brought it into my Georgia garden. The plant in Cincinnati is 3 1/2′ high and 4 to 5′ wide. It has shown the yellow-green variegation pattern typical of most 'Anthony Waterer' clones. I suspect 'Crispa' originated as a branch sport of *S. × bumalda* or 'Anthony Waterer' but cannot locate corroborating evidence in the literature. At Wakehurst Place, England, I observed a plant labeled *S. japonica* 'Walluff' that looked exactly like 'Crispa'. This plant is listed in the literature as *S. × bumalda* 'Wallufii' and 'Walluf'. 'Walluf' is described as having a compact growth habit, young leaves reddish without variegation, flowers bright pink-red but lighter than 'Anthony Waterer'. There is no mention of the finely cut leaves on 'Walluf' and I suspect the plant at Wakehurst was labeled incorrectly. 'Crispa' develops chlorosis in high pH soils.

'Dart's Red'—A branch sport of 'Anthony Waterer' with deep carmine-red flowers paling somewhat as they fade; 2 to 3′ by 4 to 5′; does not produce the albino shoots; introduced by Darthuizer Nursery, Holland.

'Dolchica'—Was sent to me by Michael Epp who had read an article that I published on the summer-flowering spireas [see *Amer. Nurseryman* 163(2):53–61 (1986)]. The plant, in most respects, has the same fine cutleaf character of 'Crispa' with deep purple-red (bronzy-purple) new growth and fine pink flowers; appears to be more stable, i.e., no variegated shoots and will mature between 1 1/2 and 2 1/2′ high, 2 to 4′ wide; the plant performed admirably, but contracted aphids more so than other cultivars.

'Fire Light'—Described as an improved 'Goldflame', with deeper orange new growth and fiery red fall color, does not turn completely green like 'Goldflame', pink flowers, compact, 1 1/2′ by 1 1/2′ in 5 years, although have seen 2 to 3′ high for mature plant.

'Froebelii'—Has the same characteristics as 'Anthony Waterer', but its habit is slightly taller, 3 to 3 1/2′ high, its leaves are slightly larger, its flowers are brighter (at least in the true form), and its inflorescences are smaller. New growth is brownish red and never develops variegated shoots. My observations of United States plants indicate that there is not a great deal of difference between the two, although the origin of 'Froebelii' is different from that of 'Anthony Waterer.' 'Froebelii' was distributed before 1894 by Froebel. Donald Wyman, author of *Shrubs and Vines for American Gardens*, noted that growth after flowering is vigorous enough to cover the dead flower heads. Dr. Harold Pellett, University of Minnesota Landscape Arboretum, believes that 'Froebelii' is probably the hardiest. He also believes that it is the best adapted to heat and drought. Wilson Nurseries Inc., Hampshire, IL, discovered a compact form of 'Froebelii' that is smaller and neater in habit. The selection has been called 'Dwarf Froebel' by this author, but more properly 'Gumball.' Grew this form in my Georgia garden, and the plant was 3′ high and 4′ wide; plants in the Botanic Garden are 3 1/2′ high and wide; the plant definitely grows larger than originally advertised. The flowers are light pink, but this could be due to the heat. Most 'Froebelii' types in cultivation do not have deep flower color compared to 'Anthony Waterer'.

'Goldflame'—Is one of the most popular forms and appears to be on fire when the leaves emerge in spring. Russet-orange to bronze-red leaves change to soft yellow, yellow-green and, finally, green. In Georgia, the summer leaf color is green; in England, it is yellowish. The spring leaf colors are often repeated in fall, making a rather handsome display. Leaves hold late, often into December in Athens. Will grow 2 to 3′(4′) high and slightly wider at maturity. Its flowers are smaller than those of 'Anthony Waterer' and 'Froebelii' and are a rather sickly pink. In England, I have observed the pink flowers in combination with the yellow-green leaves, and eyes and tummy became jaundiced and nauseous, respectively. The bright spot in the makeup of 'Goldflame' is its high heat tolerance. Leaf burn has not occurred on plants I have grown or observed in the Southeast. Like other selections, 'Goldflame' displays the propensity to produce variegated green-and-gold shoots and leaves. It also produces green shoots, which must be removed. This phenomenon seems to occur more frequently on European than on American plants. Perhaps climate affects the stability of this clone. 'Goldflame' flowers about a week later than 'Dwarf Froebel' ('Gumball') in our garden.

'Limemound'—Is an introduction from Monrovia Nursery Co., Azusa, CA, that arose as a branch sport of 'Goldflame'. In spring, dense, slender branches display lemon yellow leaves with a russet tinge. The leaf color becomes lime green when the leaves mature, and autumn foliage is orange-red on reddish stems. The branches form a uniform dwarf mounded outline. Supposedly, 'Limemound' is one zone more cold-hardy than 'Goldflame', which is hardy to Zone 4. Looks like a winner and will probably mature around 2′ by 3′. In actuality, difficult to separate from 'Gold Mound'.

'Magic Carpet'—Almost a ground cover variation of 'Goldflame', orange-red to reddish purple young shoots, yellow-gold at maturity, pinkish flowers, 10 to 18″ high, appears it will grow larger than this in Georgia.

'Norman'—Is another mystery selection, but both Wyman and Brian Mulligan (formerly of the University of Washington Arboretum) describe it as a small, 10 to 12″ high, compact plant with rosy pink flowers and raspberry-purple to red fall color that lasts for a month. It may be a form of *S. japonica*. Mrs. Wister has a plant in her Swarthmore, PA garden and indeed it fits the description to a "T". The fall foliage is particularly attractive. Leaves are much smaller than the typical *S.* × *bumalda* and *S. japonica*. Most plants labeled and sold as 'Norman' are something else.

'Superba'—Is not well-known but is listed in the literature. The only plant I observed was at the Arnold Arboretum in Jamaica Plain, MA. In general, it resembles 'Anthony Waterer', the only difference being that 'Superba' bears flowers of a lighter pink. Technically, it is a hybrid between *S. albiflora* and *S. corymbosa*, although I have seen it listed as a *S.* × *bumalda* type.

I have a great interest in the dwarf spireas and have grown 'Anthony Waterer', 'Crispa', 'Dolchica', 'Goldflame', 'Gumball', 'Nyewoods', *S. j.* var. *alpina*, *S. j.* var. *a.* 'Little Princess, *S. j.* 'Atrosanguinea', and others. They offered color (June–July) when other shrubs were in the green summer doldrums. Interestingly, 'Goldflame' became almost normal green in August in Athens while I observed the plant on Cape Cod in August and it was distinctly yellow-green. The summer heat has a great influence on whether yellow shrubs stay yellow, purple-purple and so forth. The compact spireas are excellent for modern landscapes where space is at a premium.

PROPAGATION: Seedlings have germinated in sidewalk cracks and edges from 'Froebelii' in our garden; I raised the seedlings to flowering and had golden forms and every growth habit imaginable; obviously from the staggering number of cultivars, it is apparent that the genetic shakeout from seed yields what you read in these *S.* × *bumalda* and *S. japonica* treatments; admonition—do not attempt this at home for another yellow cultivar could cause horticultural meltdown. All spireas root readily from softwood cuttings taken in May, June, July, August; IBA treatment usually improves rooting but is not necessary in most cases; I have had great success with all the *S.* × *bumalda* and *S. japonica* forms. Seed requires no special treatment and will germinate readily when directly sown although, if dried, a one-month cold stratification is beneficial.

Spiraea cantoniensis Lour. 'Lanceata' — Double Reeves Spirea

LEAVES: Alternate, simple, rhombic-oblong to rhombic-lanceolate, 1 to 2 1/2″ long, 1/2 to 3/4″ wide, cuneate, incised serrate, glabrous, bluish green above, pale bluish green beneath; petiole—1/3″ long.

Spiraea cantoniensis 'Lanceata', (spī-rē'á kan-tō-ni-en'sis), Double Reeves Spirea, is more prominent in the South than the species. The habit is mounded-rounded with graceful, wispy, arching branches. Height ranges from 4 to 6′ and the spread is similar. The leaves are bluish green and hold late in the fall without coloring. May be almost evergreen in deep South and part of California. The showy white, 1/2″ diameter, many-petaled flowers appear in abundance during early April (Athens) in upright terminal corymbs. The flowers open before those of *S.* × *vanhouttei* and often overlap those of Vanhoutte. Pruning should be accomplished after flowering. Often leaves and flowers emerge so early (March) that the tender flower buds are killed by a hard freeze. This species displays excellent heat tolerance and its only requirements are full sun and well-drained soil, although plants in half-shade are presentable. Have collected cuttings in July, treated them with 3000 ppm IBA quick dip, peat:perlite, mist and rooting was 100%. Grows extremely fast and would be a good filler in a shrub border. Should not be used for hedges. The species is one of the parents of the ubiquitous *S.* × *vanhouttei* and is seldom cultivated. The single-flowered form is also attractive but the flowers do not last as long as the doubles. 'Lanceata' has been growing in the Dirr garden for 19 years and has required *no* maintenance. Have observed bud swell and leaf emergence as early as February 15. China, Japan. Introduced 1824. Zone (4)5 to 9. Cappiello reported regular stem damage (dieback) in Orono, ME.

Spiraea × *cinerea* Zab. 'Grefsheim',

(spī-rē'á sin-e-rē'á), is about as handsome an early-flowering spirea as one could ever hope to find. The small, white flowers clothe the leafless branches in April presenting the entire shrub as a white cloud. Flowers occur about 10 days ahead of *S.* × *arguta*. In my opinion it is superior to *S.* × *arguta* and *S. thunbergii*. It forms a rather dense shrub with arching stems, 4 to 5′ high and wide. Leaves are narrow-elliptic or lanceolate, narrowed at both ends, almost entire, or with a few teeth at the apex; about 1″ long, 1/3″ wide, soft sea green, appressed silky hairs beneath. Result of a cross between *S. cana* Waldst. & Kit. and *S. hypericifolia* L. The hybrid originated before 1884 and the cultivar is of Norwegian origin. Zone 4 to 7(8).

Spiraea japonica L. f. — Japanese Spirea

LEAVES: Alternate, simple, ovate to ovate-oblong, 1 to 3″ long, 1/3 to 1 1/2″ wide, acute, lustrous dark green, glaucescent beneath and usually pubescent on the veins; petiole—about 1/8 to 1/5″ long.

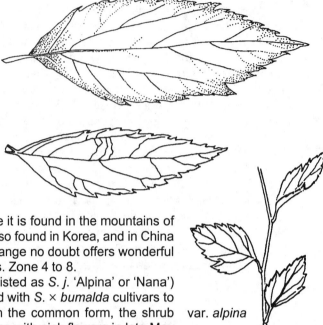

var. *alpina*

Spiraea japonica, (spī-rē′à jà-pon′i-kà), Japanese Spirea, is almost excessively variable and defies any reasonable description. It is most often considered a 4 to 5′ high shrub with rounded, flattened or angled, glabrous or hairy branches. The leaves range from 1 to 3″ long with distinct, sharp serrations. The plant has escaped and I have seen it in the north Georgia mountains most recently at Moccasin State Park along the hiking trail.

Normal flower color is rosy pink to carmine, rarely white, with inflorescences in some of the garden forms measuring as large as 12″ in diameter. Ohwi, in his *Flora of Japan*, noted that the species is common and variable where it is found in the mountains of Hokkaido, Honshu, Shikoku, and Kyushu. It is also found in Korea, and in China north to the Himalayas. This wide geographic range no doubt offers wonderful opportunities for the selection of different forms. Zone 4 to 8.

Spiraea japonica var. *alpina* (sometimes listed as *S. j.* 'Alpina' or 'Nana') is a rather handsome variety that has hybridized with *S.* × *bumalda* cultivars to produce several interesting new selections. In the common form, the shrub makes a dainty, fine-textured, low-growing mass with pink flowers in late May (in Athens), June or July. It leafs out and flowers later than the *S.* × *bumalda* types, usually 5 to 10 days later. The small, 5-veined, light blue-green leaves cover the plant thickly and provide a fine foil for the pink flowers. The leaves measure a half-inch or less but range to 1″ in some types. The plant ranges from 15 to 30″ high to as much as 6′ in diameter. Over the years, I have allowed it to cascade over walls and used it as a low facer and as a ground cover.

The origin of the plant is not clear. It was described in 1879 from a plant found wild on Mt. Hakone in the central island of Japan. It had procumbent or erect stems and grew a "hand-breadth" high. The general consensus is that the form of *S. j.* var. *alpina* in cultivation is of garden origin. The form in cultivation does not come true from seed, with seedlings being more lax and possessing larger leaves. Bean has treated var. *alpina* as a cultivar and listed it as 'Nana' ('Alpina').

One objection to *S. j.* var. *alpina* is posed by its retention of old seed heads, which give the plant a rather shabby appearance. In late summer, the plant can look pretty ragged.

'Atrosanguinea'—Is a beautiful, deep rose-red form with 4 to 5″ diameter inflorescences. I grew this plant in Illinois and found the flower color slightly deeper than the "best" 'Anthony Waterer'. The growth habit is more stiff and upright than that of 'Anthony Waterer'. Pellett also mentioned this spirea as one of the best for deep rose-red flower color. Will grow 3 to 4′ high and wide.

'Coccinea'—Is often listed, but I am not exactly sure how different it is from *S. j.* 'Atrosanguinea'. It is a compact bushy plant growing about 2′ tall and wide, and it has rich crimson flowers. It is described as being similar to 'Froebelii' by W.J. Bean in *Trees and Shrubs Hardy in the British Isles*. See *S.* × *bumalda* for a discussion of 'Coccinea'.

'Dakota Goldcharm® ('Mertyann')—Another yellow leaf, mounded spirea, bronze new shoots, pink flowers, have tested the plant in Georgia and it does not hold foliage color as well as 'Gold Mound', supposedly compact form, 12 to 15″ by 2 to 3′, but has grown rapidly and large, introduced via North Dakota State University, grown from open-pollinated seed of 'Little Princess'.

'Fortunei'—Was the first representative of *S. japonica* in Western gardens. It was sent from China to England by Robert Fortune in 1849. It was the commonest from in cultivation but has largely lost favor. I have not observed it in American gardens. The deep pink flowers occur in large inflorescences. *Spiraea japonica* 'Fortunei' is one of the largest garden forms, often growing to about 5′.

'Glabrata'—Is described as a vigorous form with rosy pink flowers in 12″ diameter (or larger) corymbs. The broad-ovate leaves can reach 4 to 5″ long and 2 1/2 to 3″ wide. The plant's origin is unknown.

'Gold Mound' ('Goldmound')—Is a hybrid between *S. j.* var. *alpina* and *S.* × *bumalda* 'Goldflame'. It was introduced by W.H. Perron Co. Ltd., Laval, Quebec, Canada. 'Gold Mound' is a low-mounded form reminiscent of *S. japonica*, with pink flowers in May and June and golden leaves throughout the growing season. The golden leaf color fades in summer to a yellow-green. One report noted that 'Gold Mound' burns badly in the heat of the South. From 1987 to 1998 this plant has been growing in the *Spiraea* test garden at the University's Botanical Garden and performing magnificently. The bright yellow coloration fades to yellow-green but even in August is still decidedly yellow and not green like 'Goldflame'. Develops reasonable orangish red fall color. Best of all, no foliage burn has been observed and 1987 and 1988 were two of the driest and hottest years on record in the Southeast. Might prove a great color addition to shrub and perennial borders, or any spot in full sun where some brightness is welcome, will mature around 2 1/2 to 3 1/2′ by 3 to 4′.

'Golden Dome'—Foliage golden yellow in spring and early summer, habit is compact, dome-shaped.

'Golden Princess'—Is an introduction from Bressingham Gardens, England, and is protected by United Kingdom Plant Breeders Rights. The new leaves are bronze-yellow and then change to yellow. I do not know how the plant fares in America but suspect some reduction in yellow coloration occurs. The flowers are pink. The habit of 'Golden Princess' is gently mounded with an ultimate height of about 30″. The leaves appear to be slightly smaller than those of 'Goldflame'; I have seen the plant many times in England and it appears to offer the same fine qualities as 'Gold Mound'. Apparently a seedling of 'Goldflame'.

'Lemon Princess'—Another yellow foliage form with pink flowers, compact mounded habit, 1 1/2 to 2′ high.

'Little Princess'—From Holland is one of several closely related forms. This selection has larger leaves and deeper pink flower color than *S. j.* var. *alpina*. After repeated observations it became evident that 'Little Princess' grew faster, larger, and had larger leaves, to 1″ long, than var. *alpina*. Ultimate size will approach 30″ or greater. Has become a popular commercial form.

'Macrophylla'—Has leaves as large as those of 'Glabrata' that display a distinctly inflated (bullate) condition. The leaves supposedly color well in autumn, but the flowers are small.

'Neon Flash'—An 'Anthony Waterer' type with rich red flowers, reddish new growth, dark green at maturity, and no branch reversions, 3′, introduced by Brookside Gardens, Wheaton, MD into the United States from Japan.

'Nyewoods'—Is considered to be the same as *S. j.* var. *alpina*, and, according to an article in *Dendroflora*, 1977, it is a synonym for *S. j.* var. *alpina*. I have observed 'Nyewoods' at several gardens in Ohio, and the proprietors insisted that 'Nyewoods' was different. The 'Nyewoods' I saw offered blue-green foliage, pink flowers and a compact habit. From a landscape viewpoint, the differences are probably not worth fighting over. The Holden Arboretum, Mentor, OH; Millcreek Valley Park, Youngstown, OH; and Wakehurst Place, England, display the plant as a distinct entity. If anything, 'Nyewoods' approximates 'Little Princess' more so than var. *alpina*.

A final note on *S. j.* var. *alpina* concerns the iron chlorosis that the plants often develop. In the Midwest, I have observed some wonderfully golden forms, and they were not meant to be that way. I have not noticed problems in the South and East on *S. japonica* or on 'Little Princess'. Of course, soil pH in the Athens area is 4.5 to 6.0.

'Ovalifolia'—Is sometimes listed as *S. j.* var. *ovalifolia*, offers white flowers in 3 to 5″ diameter corymbs.

'Ruberrima'—Has dark rose flowers in downy corymbs; the plant grows to 3′ and develops a mounded outline.

'Shirobana' ('Shibori')—Is an interesting selection that offers deep rose, pink and white flowers on the same plant. Individual inflorescences often have mixed colors. I first saw the plant at the University of British Columbia Botanical Garden, Vancouver, BC, Canada, in August 1985. The plant grows 2 to 3′ (4′) high and forms a handsome mound. I have grown the plant for several years and am most impressed by the recurrent flowering that continues through the summer sporadically even if the old inflorescences are not removed. The leaves are a lustrous deep green and probably the handsomest of any *S. japonica* form. The multi-colored flowers may not hold true depending on origin of propagation wood. The flowers are striking at their best. Often pink flowers dominate the color matrix. This has occurred on the five plants in the Dirr garden. In our garden, 'Shirobana' is combined with 'Annabelle' hydrangea which flowers at the same time in early to mid-June. Has been the latest flowering of the *S. japonica* and *S.* × *bumalda* types in our garden.

NOTE: Additional cultivars with *S.* × *bumalda*, *S. japonica* et al., parentage were introduced by W.H. Perron and Co., Laval, Quebec, Canada. Their descriptions were published in *HortScience* 3(3):455 (1988), and are presented here for reader awareness.

'Flaming Globe' (*S. japonica* 'Nana' and *S.* × *bumalda*)—Selected because of its rich, coppery pink young foliage, which turns bright yellow in summer and bright red in autumn; fast-growing, dense shrub that forms a 12″ globe in 3 years; flowers are rarely produced.

'Flaming Mound' (*S.* × *bumalda* 'Goldflame' with *S. japonica* 'Nana')—Selected because of flaming red foliage, red flower buds turning yellow, and small, dark pink flowers; has 3″ by 3/4″ leaves and forms a 24″ high and 24″ diameter mound.

'Flowering Mound'—Selected because of young, reddish leaves, which turn yellow, and abundant, dark pink flower clusters during June, July, and August; foliage turns pink-orange after frost; softwood cuttings grow into saleable plants in 17 months; forms a compact, bushy mound 28″ high by 36″ across in 7 years.

'Glowing Globe' (*S.* × *bumalda* 'Goldflame' with *S. japonica* 'Nana')—Selected because of reddish pink foliage, which turns salmon in the sun; becomes green-yellow in shade; forms a strong, bushy, globose plant 12″ in diameter in 3 years.

'Glowing Mound' (*S.* × *bumalda* with *S. japonica* 'Nana')—Selected because of yellow leaves with a pinkish glow; change to a coppery pink after the first frost; flowers sparingly, with small, pink flowers; forms a mound, 30″ high by 36″ across after 3 years; leaves are 2 1/2″ by 1/2 to 3/4″.

'Golden Carpet' (*S.* × *bumalda* 'Goldflame' with *S. japonica* 'Nana')—Selected because of creeping habit and golden leaves, which are 3/5″ long by 1/3″ broad; forms a carpet 3″ thick by 8″ in diameter in 3 years; in contact with soil, branches root easily.

'Golden Globe' (*S.* × *bumalda* 'Goldflame' with *S. japonica* 'Nana)—Chosen for salmon-pink new growth, which changes to golden yellow; color holds until fall, when it turns pink; in sunny, dry locations it forms a dense, globose shrub 10″ high by 10″ across.

'Green Globe' (*S.* × *bumalda* and *S. japonica* 'Nana')—Selected because of vigorous, compact habit and small, bright green leaves (1″ by 1/2″), which turn to brilliant purple-red in early fall; produces small, light pink flowers from June to September; forms a dense globe 7 to 8″ tall by 10″ in diameter in 4 years.

'Lightened Mound' (*S. japonica* 'Nana')—Selected because of creamy-lemon leaves, which turn to lime in summer; does best in partial shade, as it sunburns in hot summers; flowers rarely; forms dense mounds 18″ tall by 20″ in diameter in 2 years.

'Sparkling Carpet' (*S.* × *bumalda* 'Goldflame' and *S.* × *bumalda*)—Selected because of dense, prostrate habit and reddish pink leaves which turn yellow; the branches are stronger and denser than those of 'Golden Carpet' and the leaves are smaller (3/4″ long by 1/3″ broad); the plant forms a multi-colored carpet 4″ thick by 11″ across in 3 years; flowers are rare or nonexistent.

Spiraea nipponica Maxim. 'Snowmound' — Snowmound Nippon Spirea

LEAVES: Alternate, simple, narrowly oblong-obovate, 1 to 1 1/2″ long, 3/8 to 1/2″ wide, toothed at the rounded apex, rarely entire, cuneate, dark blue-green; petiole—1/6 to 1/8″ long.

Spiraea nipponica 'Snowmound', (spī-rē′à nip-pon′i-kà), Snowmound Nippon Spirea, has performed admirably and appears to be a superior replacement for *S.* × *vanhouttei*. The plant grows 3 to 5′(7′) high and as wide, with small, dark blue-green leaves and white flowers in small corymbs appearing in late May into June. It maintains a neater, denser outline than Vanhoutte. There have been reports of isolated branches dying out but I have not observed this. Have had reasonably good success with 'Snowmound' on the Georgia campus. 'Halward's Silver' is more compact than the species and densely branched, will grow 30 to 36″ in 3 to 5 years, covered with abundant white flowers, introduced by Royal Botanic Garden, Hamilton, Ontario. 'Rotundifolia' is considered the typical state of the species with broadly obovate or oval, sometimes nearly round, 1/2 to 1″ long, sometimes entire, but usually with a few broad teeth at the rounded apex. In variety *tosaensis* (Yatabe) Mak., which I believe is confused with 'Snowmound', the leaves are linear-oblong, tapered at the base, entire or with 2 or 3 teeth at the apex, 3/8 to 1″ long, 1/8 to 1/4″ wide. It is not a profuse flowerer. The species is native to the island of Shikoku, Japan. Zone (3)4 to 7(8).

Spiraea prunifolia Sieb. & Zucc. — Bridalwreath Spirea

LEAVES: Alternate, simple, elliptic to elliptic-oblong, 1 to 2″ long, 1/2 to 3/4″ wide, acute at ends, finely toothed, almost hacksaw-like, lustrous dark green and glabrous above, finely pubescent beneath; petiole—about 1/8″ long, with appressed pubescence.
STEM: Zig-zag, slender, shiny brown, glabrous.

Spiraea prunifolia, (spī-rē′à prū-ni-fō′li-à), Bridalwreath Spirea, is an old favorite (I do not know why) growing 4 to 9′ tall and 6 to 8′ wide. It is an open, coarse, straggly shrub, often leggy, upright and limitedly spreading with foliage on the upper 50% of the plant. The foliage is shiny dark green in summer and may turn yellow-orange to purplish bronze in fall but is never overwhelming. The flowers are white, double, 1/3″ diameter, 3 to 6 together and virtually cover the leafless stems in mid to late April; in Athens it starts to show color in February and is usually in full flower by early March. I really see no use for this plant in modern gardens; it belongs to the "Over the hill gang." The single-flowered form is listed as var. or forma *simpliciflora* Nak. and is rarely cultivated; 'Plena' is the form described here. Korea, China, Formosa. Cultivated 1864. Zone 4 to 8.

Spiraea thunbergii Sieb. — Thunberg Spirea

LEAVES: Alternate, simple, linear-lanceo-late, 1 to 1 1/2″ long, 1/8 to 1/4″ wide, acuminate to acute, narrow cuneate, finely serrate from apex to almost the base, glabrous, pale to yellow-green; petiole—extremely short.
STEM: Extremely slender and fine, slightly angled, zig-zag, light brown, downy to glabrous, primarily the latter on culti-vated plants.

Spiraea thunbergii, (spī-rē′à thun-bĕr′jē-ī), Thunberg Spirea, grows 3 to 5′ tall and 3 to 5′ wide, often wider than high at maturity. It is a bushy, slender-branched, tiny-leaved shrub, rather loosely spreading and arching and very twiggy. Foliage is yellowish green in summer and turns yellowish, tinged with orange and bronze in fall and holds late (not very effective). Flowers are white, 1/3″ across, March–April (early to mid-March, Athens) before the leaves; usually the first spirea to flower; borne in 3- to 5-flowered, sessile umbels. Definitely requires pruning to keep the plant in good condition as it becomes straggly and open. My fondness for the species has increased since coming to Georgia. The wispy, fine-textured foliage of light green contrasts with the darker greens of most shrubs. Have seen mass plantings and was impressed by the effect. 'Fujino Pink' has soft pink flowers and 'Ogon' offers soft yellow leaves that fade to green. A small plant of 'Fujino Pink' in our evaluation plots flowered pink; a branch I collected from a plant labeled as such in Ohio and forced in the greenhouse flowered white; perhaps the latter was incorrectly labeled or the greenhouse heat eliminated the pink. Also, 'Yat Sabusa' has double, white flowers. Another species, ***Spiraea × arguta*** Zab., Garland Spirea, is similar to the above but larger growing and, in fact, is a cross between *S. × multiflora* Zab. × *S. thunbergii*. I cannot see a great deal of difference in the two. The leaves of *S. thunbergii* appear to be serrated throughout their length while in *S. × arguta* the serrations are lacking or occur only above the middle. The oblanceolate leaves are 3/4 to 1 1/2″ long, 1/4 to 1/2″ wide, light green and glabrous above. *Spiraea × arguta* flowers later than *S. thunbergii*. It was raised sometime before 1884. 'Compacta' grows to 4′ tall and 'Graciosa' produces early white flowers. All flower on old wood and pruning should be accomplished after flowering. This is also true for *S. prunifolia* and *S. × vanhouttei*. Native to Japan, China. Introduced 1830. Zone 4 to 8.

Spiraea × arguta

Spiraea trilobata L. — Threelobe Spirea

LEAVES: Alternate, simple, roundish, 1/2 to 1″ long (1 to 1 1/2″ rarely), about as wide, coarsely toothed, sometimes obscurely 3- or 5-lobed, base rounded or sometimes slightly heart-shaped, glaucous green.
STEM: Zig-zag, round.

Spiraea trilobata, (spī-rē′à trī-lō-bā′tà), Threelobe Spirea, is a relatively small (4 to 5′) shrub of dense compact habit with slender, spreading branches. The small, usually rounded to 3-lobed leaves are bluish green.

The pure white flowers occur in 3/4 to 1 1/2″ diameter umbels at the ends of leafy shoots and appear in great profusion during May. Was magnificent in flower as I viewed it in the Arnold Arboretum in 1991. In many respects the flowers remind of *S. × vanhouttei*. One of the parents of Vanhoutte. Apparently withstands considerable shade and still flowers well. 'Fairy Queen' is a compact 3′ high and wide shrub with dark green, lobed leaves and frothy masses of white flowers in May–June. 'Swan Lake' is considered more floriferous than the species and a degree more compact. Based on photographs I've seen it might be an excellent alternative to Vanhoutte and the larger growing spireas; it will probably mature between 3 and 4′. Northern China to Siberia and Turkestan. Introduced 1801. Zone 3 to 7.

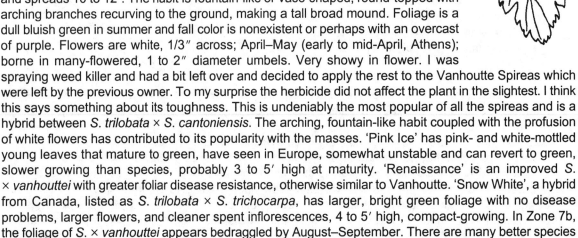

Spiraea × vanhouttei (Briot) Zab. — Vanhoutte Spirea

LEAVES: Alternate, simple, 3/4 to 1 3/4″ long, 1/2 to 1 1/4″ wide, rhombic-ovate or somewhat obovate, apex pointed, base tapering, teeth irregular, coarse, often incised,
obscurely to 3- to 5-lobed, dark blue-green above, glaucous below, glabrous.
STEM: Slender, brown, glabrous.

Spiraea × vanhouttei, (spī-rē′à van-hoot′ē-ī), Vanhoutte Spirea, grows 6 to 8′(10′) high
and spreads 10 to 12′. The habit is fountain-like or vase-shaped, round-topped with
arching branches recurving to the ground, making a tall broad mound. Foliage is a
dull bluish green in summer and fall color is nonexistent or perhaps with an overcast
of purple. Flowers are white, 1/3″ across; April–May (early to mid-April, Athens);
borne in many-flowered, 1 to 2″ diameter umbels. Very showy in flower. I was
spraying weed killer and had a bit left over and decided to apply the rest to the Vanhoutte Spireas which
were left by the previous owner. To my surprise the herbicide did not affect the plant in the slightest. I think
this says something about its toughness. This is undeniably the most popular of all the spireas and is a
hybrid between *S. trilobata × S. cantoniensis*. The arching, fountain-like habit coupled with the profusion
of white flowers has contributed to its popularity with the masses. 'Pink Ice' has pink- and white-mottled
young leaves that mature to green, have seen in Europe, somewhat unstable and can revert to green,
slower growing than species, probably 3 to 5′ high at maturity. 'Renaissance' is an improved *S.
× vanhouttei* with greater foliar disease resistance, otherwise similar to Vanhoutte. 'Snow White', a hybrid
from Canada, listed as *S. trilobata × S. trichocarpa*, has larger, bright green foliage with no disease
problems, larger flowers, and cleaner spent inflorescences, 4 to 5′ high, compact-growing. In Zone 7b,
the foliage of *S. × vanhouttei* appears bedraggled by August–September. There are many better species
and certainly for foliage quality and similar floral and habit characteristics, *S. cantoniensis* is superior. Leaf
spot caused by *Pleosporella filipendulae* can be serious and result in early defoliation. Appropriate
fungicides will control the disease. Zone 3 to 8(9). Raised by Billiard in about 1862.

OTHER *SPIRAEA* SPECIES

Spiraea betulifolia Pall. var. **aemiliana** (C. Schneid.) Koidz.,
(spī-rē′à bet-ū-li-fō′li-à à-mil′ē-ā′nà), Birchleaf Spirea,
is a compact mounded, rather dense shrub probably 2
to 2 1/2′ high at maturity. The white flowers occur in
flattish corymbs after the leaves have matured. The
principal ornamental characteristic is the long-persistent
gold, yellow and bronze fall color. I have obtained a
plant and look forward to evaluating its performance.
'Tor' has rich green leaves, yellow-gold, bronze and red
fall color, white flowers, 2 to 3′ high. True var. *aemiliana*
is generally smaller (8 to 12″ high) than the species,
however, the plant I have seen in cultivation listed as the
variety favors the above description. Japan, Kurile
Islands, Kamchatka. Introduced 1812, again in 1892.
Zone 4 to 6. A postscript relative to performance reads
like an epitaph. Not satisfied with Zone 7b conditions.
Probably best in the North.

Spiraea decumbens Koch., (spī-rē′à dē-kum′benz), literally jumped into my life during a June visit to Germany. The habit is compact-spreading, probably to 18″ high with prostrate branches. It was covered with frothy masses of white flowers. Might be an ideal ground cover species for full sun and certainly could be used in rock gardens. The flowers are only 1/4″ diameter but occur in 2″ wide, flat-topped corymbs. The mint green leaves are obovate or oval, tapered at both ends, and rather coarsely toothed toward the apex, glabrous with a 1/8″ long petiole. Found on limestone soil in the wild. Tested a plant in our Georgia garden but it was not vigorous and died. I suspect the heavy soils and high humidity were lethal. Southeastern Europe in the Alps. Cultivated 1830. Zone 5 to 7.

Spiraea fritschiana Schneid., (spī-rē′à frit-shē-ā′nà), Korean Spirea, is virtually unknown in the United States but offers dark green foliage and 1 to 3″ diameter, flat-topped, white flowers in May–June on a 2 to 3′ high, 4 to 5′ wide, compact mounded shrub. I have grown this in Illinois and Georgia with success and know that it grows in Fargo, ND which attests to hardiness. Worth a try in difficult climates. Leaves are elliptic or elliptic-ovate to elliptic-oblong, 1 to 3 1/2″ long, acute to acuminate, cuneate, simple serrate, with a 1/4″ long petiole. Fall color is often a good yellow. This species is closely related to *S. betulifolia*. Central China to Korea. Introduced 1919. Zone (3)4 to 7.

Spiraea latifolia L., (spī-rē′à lat-i-fō′li-à), Broad-leaved Meadowsweet, and ***Spiraea tomentosa*** L., (spī-rē′à tō-men-tō′sà), Hardhack, Steeplebush, are common, suckering, 2 to 4′ high shrubs along roadsides and in fields. I see them in lingering, flickering flower in Maine during August and September, colors ranging from pink to white. In the former, the leaves are 1 to 3″ long, broadly elliptic or obovate to oblong, blue-green and *glabrous* beneath. White to pink flowers occur in pyramidal, glabrous panicles on new growth of the season. Newfoundland and Canada to North Carolina. Cultivated 1789. Zone 3 to 5. The latter species with similar size leaves but yellowish or grayish *pubescence* below and on the angled stems; flowers deep rose to rose-purple in narrow, dense, brownish tomentose, 3 to 8″ long panicles. Flowers open from top to bottom. Grows in or near and requires moist soils. Nova Scotia to Georgia, west to Manitoba and Kansas. Introduced 1736. Zone 4 to 6. Neither will win *Spiraea* beauty contests but are reasonably attractive in a late summer sort of way.

Spiraea tomentosa

Stachyurus praecox Sieb. & Zucc.

FAMILY: Stachyuraceae

LEAVES: Alternate, simple, ovate-lanceolate, 3 to 7″ long, half as wide, acuminate, rounded, serrate with spreading teeth, lustrous dark green, glabrous or slightly pubescent on veins below.

BUDS: Flower at ends of stems, preformed and visible through winter, when taking cuttings use wood away from terminal since it possesses vegetative buds with the potential to produce new shoots; vegetative buds 1/8″ long, several-scaled, reddish brown, sitting directly above raised leaf scar.

STEM: Reddish brown to chestnut-brown, lustrous, glabrous, small oval-rounded, gray lenticels, leaf scars raised, crescent-shaped; pith—white, solid.

Stachyurus praecox, (sta-che-ū′rus prē′koks), is an enigmatic shrub with an element of mystery and beauty that few gardeners know anything about. In the 1990 edition, I commented that I had only seen the plant in leaf. No more, since traveling to the U.S. National Arboretum (early April) and Savill Gardens, England (late March) and capturing the elongated, off-yellow flowers. A form at the National had 6 to 8″ long flowers. The habit (4 to 6′ high) is upright, arching with an overall broad-rounded outline. The pale yellow, 1/3″ diameter flowers (15 to 24 per inflorescence, counted 20 on inflorescences in the Dirr garden) occur in 2 to 3″ long (6 to 8″ on some cultivated forms), pendulous racemes from each axil in March–April. It is considered one of the finest winter flowering shrubs. Soils should be acid, moist and well-drained. A sunny location is preferred but in the South, light shade is advisable. My observations indicate it is better in a woodland garden. 'Aurea Variegata' is listed by Heronswood as having leaves with green and gold, typical flowers, to 10′ high. 'Issai' is a earlier and more precocious flowering form with up to 6″ long, yellowish flowers, often each raceme multi-branched with up to 3 divisions. 'Magpie' is a creamy variegated form that is not particularly stable. I have seen it in Europe under *S. praecox* but understand it correctly belongs with *S. chinensis* Franch. Taxonomic affinity of 'Magpie' is not absolute and the vagaries are discussed in *New Plantsman* 2(1):50–53 (1995). *Stachyurus chinensis* flowers about 2 weeks later than *S. praecox* with long racemes of yellow flowers. The fruits are rounded, 1/3″ diameter, greenish, yellow-red cheeked and berry-like. Japan. Cultivated 1865. Zone 6 to 7(8). Plant dies to ground at Morton Arboretum but regenerates new shoots each summer. Other species have been promoted, particularly through the J.C. Raulston Arboretum, but are of dubious hardiness. The only one persisting in our garden is *S. praecox*.

Staphylea trifolia L. — American Bladdernut
(staf-i-lē′à trī-fō′li-à)

FAMILY: Staphyleaceae

LEAVES: Opposite, compound pinnate, 3 leaflets, ovate to broadly ovate, 2 to 4″ long, acuminate, sharply and unequally serrate, dark green above, pubescent beneath, sometimes glabrate at maturity, the middle leaflet long-stalked, the laterals shortly so.

BUDS: Solitary, ovoid, glabrous, terminal—usually lacking.

STEM: Moderate, rounded, glabrous, greenish to brown; pith—large, continuous, white.

Fruit

SIZE: 10 to 15′ in height, usually taller than wide at maturity; national champion is 36′ by 37′ in Macomb County, ME.

HARDINESS: Zone 4 to 8.

HABIT: Upright, heavily branched, suckering shrub with smooth striped bark forming a solid aggregate of brush; sometimes wide-spreading; actually a rather attractive shrub; have seen as a small tree.

RATE: Medium to fast.

TEXTURE: Medium in leaf; medium-coarse in winter.

BARK: Light, greenish gray with linear white fissures, branchlets at first pale green with white lenticels, downy, later brownish purple, finally ashen gray, glabrous.

LEAF COLOR: Bright green when emerging eventually turning dark green in summer; developing pale dull yellow in fall.

FLOWERS: Perfect, greenish white, bell-shaped, 1/3″ long, borne in nodding, 1 1/2 to 2″ long panicles, abundant, April–May.

FRUIT: A 3-lobed, 1 to 1 1/2″ long, inflated capsule, pale green changing to light brown, effective in September; usually containing several hard, yellowish brown, 3/16″ diameter, rounded seeds.

CULTURE: Prefers moist, well-drained soils; performs better under cultivation than in native haunts; in the wild is often loose and open, but under cultivation takes on a more dense, vigorous nature; have found it in heavy shade just above the flood plain in the University's Botanical Garden.

DISEASES AND INSECTS: None serious.

LANDSCAPE VALUE: Not a great deal; could be used in naturalizing; best reserved for parks and other low maintenance areas; rather nice for foliage effect.

PROPAGATION: Seed possesses a double dormancy; do not allow the seed to dry out before stratification; 3 months warm followed by 3 months at 40°F is recommended. Have germinated seeds by sowing in summer with germination the following spring and continuing into the next spring. Softwood and hardwood cuttings root easily. Also can be divided if a few plants are needed.

ADDITIONAL NOTES: The most curious aspect of bladdernuts is the inflated, balloon-like fruit.

NATIVE HABITAT: Quebec to Ontario and Minnesota, south to Georgia and Missouri. Cultivated 1640.

RELATED SPECIES:

Staphylea bumalda DC., (staf-i-lē'à bū-màl'dà), Bumald Bladdernut, and *Staphylea holocarpa* Hemsl., (staf-i-lē'à hol-ō-kär'pà), are occasionally encountered in gardens. The first is a 6' high, spreading shrub with 3 dark green leaflets and 1/3" wide, dull white flowers in 1 1/2 to 3" wide inflorescences in May–June. Was in full flower in early May at the Arnold Arboretum. Capsule is usually 2-lobed, to 1" long, with yellow-brown seeds. Japan, Korea, China, Manchuria. Introduced 1812. Zone 4 to 6. The second species is a large shrub or small tree to 30' high with 3 leaflets, pink flowers in slender-stalked, 2 to 4" long panicles, 1 1/2 to 2" long, pear-shaped capsule either acuminate or lobed at the end with 1/4" diameter, lustrous light gray-brown seeds. 'Rosea' has pink flowers and rose capsules. I first experienced 'Rosea' in fruit at Hidcote, in flower at the Arnold Arboretum and Forde Abbey, England. Central China. Also listed as growing in foothills of Japanese Alps. Introduced 1908. Zone 5 to 6.

Staphylea bumalda

Staphylea colchica Steven., (staf-i-lē'à kol'chi-kà), Colchis Bladdernut, is somewhat similar to the above but the leaflets are usually in 5's (3's) and the orange-blossom fragrant flowers are borne later, usually in May or June. It, too, is a suckering, upright shrub growing 6 to 10' high. The flowers occur in erect panicles, the largest up to 5" long and wide. The 2- to 3-lobed fruits are 2 1/2 to 3" long. The seeds are 1/3" long and pale brown. It is quite handsome in flower. 'Coulombieri' ('Colombieri') may be a hybrid between *S. colchica* and *S. pinnata*. The leaves are composed of 3 to 5 dark green leaflets. Flowers and fruits are intermediate between the parents. 'Hessei' has red-purple blushed flowers. I saw *S. colchica* in flower at Rockingham Castle, England, in mid-May. It was easily 10' high and 15 to 18' wide and made a fine display. Caucasus. Introduced 1850. Zone 6 to 7.

Staphylea pinnata L., (staf-i-lē'à pin-nā'tà), European Bladdernut, has (3)5 to 7 leaflets; white flowers, greenish at base, in 2 to 5" long, narrow, drooping panicles; rounded-subglobose, 1 to 1 1/4" diameter, 2- to 3-lobed capsule with 2/5" diameter, brownish yellow seeds. This is a vigorous, erect-growing shrub. Central and southern Europe. Cultivated 1596. Zone 5 to 7.

Stephanandra incisa (Thunb.) Zab. — Cutleaf Stephanandra
(stef-à-nan'drà in-sī'zà)

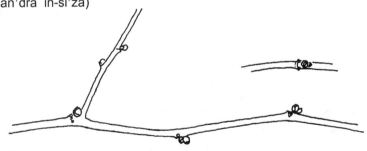

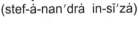

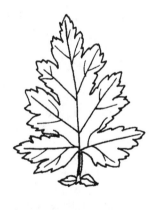

FAMILY: Rosaceae
LEAVES: Alternate, 2-ranked, simple, ovate, 1 to 2" long, or on shoots to 3" long, less in width, long-acuminate, cordate to truncate, incisely lobed and serrate, the lower incisions halfway to the midrib, bright green above, pubescent on the veins beneath; petiole—1/8 to 1/2" long; stipules—linear, toothed, 1/4" long.
BUDS: Small, superposed, ovoid, with about 4 scales.
STEM: Terete, or somewhat 5-lined from the nodes, slender, zig-zag, warm brown, glabrous.

SIZE: 4 to 7' high with an equal or greater spread.
HARDINESS: Zone 4 to 7(8).
HABIT: Graceful shrub with dense, fine to medium-textured foliage and wide-spreading, arching slender branches; tends to form a haystack-like mound; suckers freely from the base.

RATE: Fast.

TEXTURE: Medium to fine in leaf; medium in winter.

STEM COLOR: Warm brown.

LEAF COLOR: Tinged reddish bronze when unfolding, later bright green; red-purple or red-orange in fall, not particularly effective.

FLOWERS: Yellowish white, small, 1/6″ diameter; May–June; borne in loose, terminal panicles, 1 to 2 1/2″ long; not particularly showy, in fact, I did not know the two small plants in my garden were flowering, although I walked past them every day, until I was doing some hand weeding and inadvertently gazed upon the flowers.

FRUIT: Follicle, not showy.

CULTURE: Easy to transplant, best moved as a container plant; prefers moist, acid, well-drained soil that has been supplemented with peat moss or leaf mold, although tolerant of most soils; full sun or light shade; in exposed, windswept areas the very delicate young branches may be killed, at least near the tips, in winter; simply prune back to live tissue before new growth starts; tends to root wherever the stems touch the soil; will develop chlorosis in high pH soils.

DISEASES AND INSECTS: None serious.

LANDSCAPE VALUE: The species could be used for hedges, massing, screens, or in the shrub border while the low-growing cultivar 'Crispa' makes an excellent facer, bank cover, or ground cover plant.

CULTIVARS:

'Crispa'—Handsome form which grows 1 1/2 to 3′ tall and forms a low, thick tangle of stems; it makes an excellent mass or ground cover planting; more common than the species in cultivation.

PROPAGATION: Roots readily from cuttings taken at any time of the year. I have used softwood (June and July collected) cuttings and had 100% success; seeds appear to require a warm/cold period or perhaps light scarification followed by about 3 months cold; 3 months warm followed by 3 months cold produced 89% germination.

NATIVE HABITAT: Japan, Korea. Cultivated 1872.

RELATED SPECIES:

Stephanandra tanakae Franch., (stef-à-nan′drà tà-nà′kē), Tanaka Stephanandra, is larger (6′), more vigorous-growing than *S. incisa* with larger, 3 to 5″ long, 3- to 5-lobed and incisely toothed leaves. It is rather attractive but not preferable to *S. incisa*. Fall color is a warm golden yellow. Successfully growing at Morton and Arnold Arboreta. Japan. Introduced 1893. Zone 5 to 7.

Stewartia ovata (Cav.) Weatherby — Mountain Stewartia
(stū-är′ti-à ō-vā′tà)

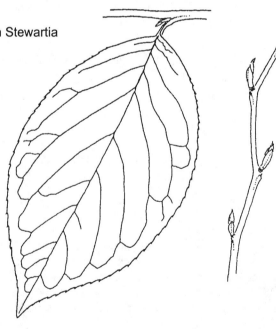

FAMILY: Theaceae

LEAVES: Alternate, simple, ovate or elliptic to ovate-oblong, 2 to 5″ long, about half as wide, acute, usually rounded at the base, serrulate almost to base, dark green above, sparingly pubescent and grayish green beneath, thickish with a rubbery texture; petiole—1/8 to 3/5″ long, winged.

BUDS: Solitary or superposed, sessile, compressed-fusiform, with 2 or 3 exposed scales, brown, covered with silky hairs.

STEM: Moderate, subterete, in youth tinged with red above, green or creamy below, distinctly zig-zag; pith—rounded, somewhat spongy.

SIZE: 10 to 15′ high and wide; national champion is 26′ by 17′ in Washington Park Arboretum, Seattle, WA.

HARDINESS: Zone 5 to 8.

HABIT: Large shrub or small tree with spreading branches and a bushy habit.

RATE: Slow.

TEXTURE: Medium in leaf and winter.

BARK: Not particularly handsome compared to the exfoliating species; gray-brown, slightly ridged-and-furrowed.

LEAF COLOR: Dark green in summer; beautiful orange to scarlet in fall, although this species is not as colorful as *S. pseudocamellia*; in fact, I have not observed good fall color on *S. ovata*.

FLOWERS: Perfect, white, 5, often 6, concave, obovate petals, each crimped and crenulated, pistils with 5 separate styles, filaments yellow-white, anthers white, orange to purple; each flower 2 1/2 to 3″ wide, up to 4″ on some plants, July to August; June–July in Athens; full flower on July 2, 1991 at Arnold Arboretum.

FRUIT: Woody, sharply pointed, strongly 5-angled, 1/2 to 1″ long, dehiscent capsule, each chamber containing up to 4 winged seeds, dull brown in color.

CULTURE: Applies to *Stewartia* in general, somewhat difficult to transplant and should be moved as a small (4 to 5′ or less) container or balled-and-burlapped plant in early spring; the soil should be moist, acid (pH 4.5 to 6.5), abundantly supplemented with leaf mold or peat moss; they do best where there is sun most of the day, but shade during the hottest periods; they seldom require pruning; *S. ovata* is found as an understory shrub along stream banks and occurs in the wild about 20 miles north of Athens, GA; I checked specimens in the Botany Department's herbarium and discovered that plants have been found in rocky, moist soils on the walls of a canyon.

DISEASES AND INSECTS: Basically free of problems.

LANDSCAPE VALUE: *Stewartia*, in general, make specimen plants and should not be hidden in some obscure corner of the landscape; the flowers, fall color and bark are among the best; I have seen plants used in shrub borders or on the edges of woodlands; some shade, at least in hot climates, is probably a necessity; observations in Zone 7b indicate *S. monadelpha*, *S. ovata* and *S. malacodendron* are the best, although the latter is subject to root rot; over the years, several *S. pseudocamellia* have been planted on the campus and in the University's Botanical Garden and none have lived; summer drought and high night temperatures contribute to decline; the beautiful exfoliating cream, tan, rich brown bark of *S. koreana* or *S. pseudocamellia* is unparalleled among *Stewartia* species.

CULTIVARS:

var. *grandiflora* (Bean) Weatherby—Has larger flowers than the species, up to 4″ diameter, and purple stamens; it is beautiful in flower, and may have up to 8 petals. I do not believe everyone is in agreement as to whether this is a true variety for people I have talked with say purple stamens occur in wild populations of the true species; it is best to use var. *grandiflora* as a name to distinguish purple-stamened types, or simply 'Grandiflora' to recognize seed-grown plants with purple stamens and larger flowers.

PROPAGATION: Seeds require a warm/cold treatment and 3 to 5 months warm followed by 3 months cold is probably best; personally I have not had much success with seed although a nurseryman friend, Mr. Don Shadow, Winchester, TN had tremendous success planting seeds in the fall with germination taking place the second spring following planting; the backyard gardener would do well to put the seeds in a clay flower pot, sink it in the ground, and practice the same patience as Mr. Shadow. Cuttings are, to say the least, a challenge; most species can be rooted from softwood cuttings at 70 to 90% using IBA, peat:perlite, mist; it is quite critical that the cuttings are not moved after rooting but allowed to go through a dormancy period; when new growth is initiated, they should be transplanted; this genus has driven me to the brink of propagation insanity; too many times cuttings have been successfully rooted only to lose them during the overwintering period; I have followed every precaution and have one *S. monadelpha* that has been successfully overwintered, probably out of 1000 rooted cuttings. Also seeds can be manipulated by warm/cold treatments to germinate but the resulting seedlings are reluctant to grow; many times I have had bags of seeds with root radicles evident yet have no plants to show; as far as I am concerned nurserymen deserve any price they charge.

Two recent research papers on tissue culture *J. Environ. Hort.* 15(2):65–68 (1997) and rooting and overwinter survival of stem cuttings *J. Environ. Hort.* 14(3):163–166 (1996) are worthy reading for anyone who has struggled with propagation. Mid-June cuttings treated with either 2000 or 4000 ppm IBA rooted in the highest percentages.

NATIVE HABITAT: North Carolina to Tennessee and Florida. Cultivated 1800. Found in rich soils under other broadleaf trees, sometimes in moist soils, steep slopes, bluffs.

RELATED SPECIES:

Stewartia koreana Rehd. — Korean Stewartia

LEAVES: Alternate, simple, elliptic to broad-elliptic, 1 1/4 to 4″ long, 3/4 to 3″ wide, abruptly acuminate, broad-cuneate or rounded, remotely serrate, dark green and glabrous above, slightly pubescent below.

Stewartia koreana, (stū-är′ti-à kôr-ē-ā′nà), Korean Stewartia, is a small (20 to 30′), dense, somewhat pyramidal tree that maintains an upright character into old age. The dark green leaves may turn excellent red to reddish purple in fall although I have seen trees with little color and others that were spectacular. The white, 3″ diameter, 5- to 6-petaled, yellow-stamened flowers occur on 3/4″ long, glabrous pedicels in June–July. The flowers tend to be flattened rather than cup-shaped and appear over a long time period. The best feature is the rich, flaky bark that, in spite of what the books say (reddish brown) ranges from soft grays and browns to orangish brown with often all colors intermingled on the same tree. In my mind this species is fairly similar to *S. pseudocamellia* and the differences are, at best, slight. The nomenclature is cloudy on a good day with *The New RHS Dictionary of Gardening* listing the taxon as *S. ptero-petiolata* Cheng. var. *koreana* (Rehd.) Sealy; Hillier's *Manual* lists it as *S. pseudocamellia* var. *koreana* (Rehd.) Sealy; the one plant of *S. ptero-petiolata* I observed was evergreen and looked nothing like *S. pseudocamellia* or *S. koreana*; Spongberg treated it as *S. pseudocamellia* 'Korean Splendor', a seedling cultivar (legitimate under rules of nomenclature for cultivated plants) with more saucer-shaped flowers, orangish fall color, pronounced flowers in June–July. This designation is somewhat difficult to accept based on plants of *S. koreana* that I have observed. Consistently, nurserymen, Bill Flemer and Don Shadow most notably, indicated *S. koreana* is more heat tolerant. Cappiello reported the plant hardy in Orono, ME. I have observed this particular plant in the Littlefield Garden during visits to Maine. Korean literature, *J. Korean Applied Ecology* 7(2):112–117 (1994) discusses its rarity in Korea while *J. Korean Soc. Hort. Sci.* 34(2):160–166 (1993) reports on seed (3000 ppm GA soak for 24 hours at 77°F in dark, followed by 3 months warm, then 3 months cold produced best germination) and cuttings (3000 ppm IBA, June 12 cuttings, 90% rooting; later collection dates correlated with decreased rooting). E.H. Wilson introduced this species from Korea in 1917. Zone 5 to 7. Trees from Mt. Sobaek, North Korea, survived -18°F. See *J. Korean Soc. Hort. Sci.* 33:413–424 (1992).

Stewartia malacodendron L. — Silky Stewartia
LEAVES: Alternate, simple, elliptic to elliptic-oblong, 2 to 4″ long, acute or short acuminate, cuneate, serrulate and ciliate, dark green and glabrous above, light green and pubescent beneath; petiole—1/4″ long, pubescent.

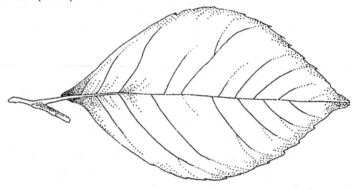

Stewart malacodendron, (stū-är′ti-à mal-à-kō-den′dron), Silky Stewartia, is a southeastern United States native found principally in the Coastal Plain. Herbarium sheets I checked noted that it is found on the side of streams but also in drier areas. The habit is that of a large shrub or small tree growing 10 to 15′(18′) high. Co-national champions are 15′ by 24′ in Chesapeake, VA and 19′ by 28′ in Ponce de Leon, FL. There was a fine specimen at Biltmore Estate, Asheville, NC; have seen the plant in Savannah, GA performing well. The 2 1/2 to 3 1/2″(4″) diameter, white-petaled, purple-filamented, blue-anthered flowers appear singly from the leaf axils in July and August (June, Asheville, NC). The fruit is a woody, egg-shaped, 1/2″ diameter, 5-valved, beaked capsule and the lustrous brown seeds are wingless. The bark is gray-brown, not effective compared to *S. koreana*, *S. pseudocamellia*, *S. monadelpha* and *S. sinensis*. Differs from *S. ovata* in leaf shape and the united styles. This is a finicky species to culture and I have failed on four occasions with the species. To witness the flowers, is to understand the quest. Dr. Wilbur Duncan, Emeritus Botanist, Georgia, brought a flowering branch from his garden plant to my office in May 1997. After composing myself and bringing the heart beat to normal, I grabbed the camera and captured the flowers. Apparently, tremendously susceptible to root rot, so plant high, mulch, provide even moisture and semi-shade (pine). Virginia and Arkansas to Florida, Louisiana and Texas. Cultivated 1752. Zone (6)7 to 9.

Stewartia monadelpha Sieb. & Zucc. —
   Tall Stewartia
LEAVES: Alternate, simple, elliptic to oblong-elliptic, 1 1/2 to 3″ long, 5/8 to 1 1/2″ wide, acute, rounded or broad cuneate, finely serrate, dark green above, somewhat lustrous, grayish green and pubescent below; petiole—1/2″ long.

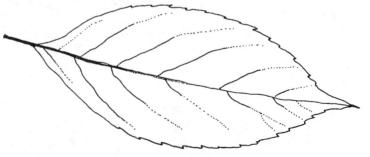

BUDS: Imbricate, brown, silky hairy, compressed, 1/4 to 3/8″ long, 3 to 4 scales visible, stalked or tapering to narrow base, broadest in middle, oblique to leaf scar, borne at 30 to 45° angle to stem.
STEM: Distinctly zig-zag, brown, pubescent, vertical fissures in epidermis; pith—green, solid.

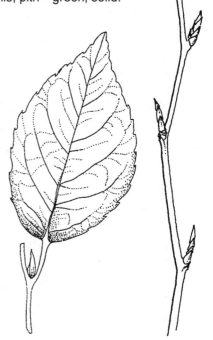

Stewartia monadelpha, (stū-är′ti-à mon-à-del′fà), Tall Stewartia, was little more than an afterthought in the last edition, but after observing it in the Middle Atlantic States and Southeast, I believe gardeners should consider growing this instead of *S. pseudo-camellia*. I have a 15′ high plant that has provided tremendous satisfaction over the last 18 years. The habit is pyramidal, rounded and almost shrubby although older trees at Callaway Gardens are more open and horizontally branched and about 20 to 25′ high after 30 plus years. Literature lists size in the wild as 75 to 80′ high. The dark green leaves have developed outstanding deep reddish, almost maroon fall color about 1 out of every 4 years in our garden. The leaves hold into early December and may be killed at 20 to 25°F. The bark is given short shrift in most references but in youth is rich brown and scaly. The scales are small and exfoliation is not as manifest as on *S. pseudocamellia*. However, with age, the older trunks become rich, almost cinnamon brown and smooth. I can focus in on this species more easily by bark than many of the other species. Interestingly, the species displays *excellent* heat tolerance and should be considered for northern and southern gardens. The flowers are the smallest of the species treated herein, being 1 to 1 1/2″ wide, white with yellowish stamens. Each flower is subtended by large leafy bracts.
Flowers tend to remain cupped and do not open as wide as *S. koreana* and *S. pseudocamellia*. Flowers open over 4 weeks starting in early June in our garden. Fruit is a small, 5-valved, 1/2″ long, woody, beaked capsule covered with appressed pubescence. Best in partial shade but will take full sun. Several Georgia field growers have tried *S. pseudocamellia*, *S. koreana* and *S. monadelpha* with only the last growing to the degree it was salable. Japan. Cultivated 1903. Zone (5)6 to 8.

Stewartia pseudocamellia Maxim. — Japanese Stewartia
LEAVES: Alternate, simple, elliptic or obovate-elliptic to elliptic-lanceolate, 2 to 3 1/2″ long, acuminate, cuneate, remotely crenate, serrulate, thickish, dark green and glabrous above, medium to dark green and glabrous or with scattered long hairs below; petiole—1/8 to 3/8″ long.

Stewartia pseudocamellia, (stū-är′ti-à sö-dō-kà-mēl′i-à), Japanese Stewartia, is a magnificent small to medium-sized, pyramidal-oval tree. The mature landscape size is 20 to 40′ but, in the wild, it will grow 60′ high. The medium to dark green leaves may turn yellow, red to dark reddish purple in fall. The 2 to 2 1/2″ diameter, broadly cup-shaped, white flowers with white filaments and orange anthers occur in July. Fruit is a broad-ovoid, 3/4 to 1″ long, hairy, 5-valved capsule. This is a worthy tree for the garden and is commercially available. Several fine specimens at the Dawes Arboretum have withstood –22°F. The plant pretty much speaks for itself with maturity. The bark is outstanding and develops a rather sinuous, muscled character with the wonderful exfoliating bark fragments painting a lovely portrait. The bark is much like that of *S. koreana* and provides excellent winter color. As I write this I reflect on beautiful specimens at the Arnold Arboretum, Hershey Gardens, Swarthmore . . . each an individual. As mentioned under *S. ovata*, I have reservations about its performance in Zone (7b)8. Japan. Introduced 1874. Zone (4)5 to 7.

Stewartia rostrata Spongb.
LEAVES: Alternate, simple, to 6″ long, to 2 1/2″ wide, serrated, lustrous dark green; petiole—short.

Stewartia rostrata, (stū-är′ti-à ros-trā′tà), is known by this author from the specimen that grows along the Chinese Walk at the Arnold Arboretum. A large, upright shrub to 15′ (40′ in the wild) with gray-brown, ridged-and-furrowed bark similar to *S. ovata*. The emerging flower buds are surrounded by large, reddish tinged bracts. The white flowers average 2 to 2 1/2″ diameter and flowered on May 30, 1991 at the Arnold. It was the first species to open. To my knowledge, not well-known in botanic gardens or commerce. The overall appearance and flower are more like the American species, but more easily cultured than them. A pink selection, i.e., pink markings on the flowers, has been offered by Camellia Forest Nursery. Eastern China. Introduced 1936. Zone 6 to 7.

Stewartia sinensis Rehd. & Wils. — Chinese Stewartia

LEAVES: Alternate, simple, elliptic-obovate to oblong-elliptic, 1 1/2 to 4″ long, 5/8 to 1 3/4″ wide, acuminate, cuneate or rarely rounded, remotely serrate or crenate-serrate, medium green and glabrous above, bright green below; petiole—1/8 to 1/4″ long, hairy.

BUDS: Imbricate, about 3 scales visible, reddish brown, covered with silky appressed pubescence, 1/4 to 3/8″ long, slightly crooked along the long axis, divergent but forming a 20° angle with the stem, imagination allows one (me) to equate the buds with *Carpinus betulus* in terms of shape, but never touching the stem as in that species.

STEM: Zig-zag, brown, densely pubescent, almost villous-hispid, the hairiest young stems of any *Stewartia*, cut stem bright lime green; pith of the same lime color, appearing excavated, bruised stem malodorous, older stem with epidermal fissuring and cracking.

Stewartia sinensis, (stū-är′ti-ȧ sĭ-nen′sis), Chinese Stewartia, is a small (15 to 25′) tree or large shrub with a rich, smooth, light tan-white bark. The medium green leaves may turn reddish in fall but the few trees I have observed were a subdued reddish and certainly not the rich crimson as described in some references. This is a delightful small landscape plant that should be more widely used. The white, fragrant, cup-shaped, 1 1/2 to 2″ diameter flowers are smaller than those of the other species treated here, with the exception of *S. monadelpha*. The ovoid to globose, 5-angled and 5-beaked, 3/4″ wide capsule is about the largest of the genus. Considerable travel was necessary before I was able to straighten the confusion between this and *S. monadelpha* and, indeed, hybrids between the two species are reported. The bark in the finest form is choice and a plant at Wakehurst Place, England, is my type specimen for comparing all others. Since my Wakehurst encounter of the first kind, the species was rekindled in Rowallane, Northern Ireland, and Trewithen, England. The Rowallane specimen was about 20′ by 25′, with low-slung branches, the bark exfoliating on 2 to 3″ diameter stems to reveal the polished underbark. Once observed, the image remains ingrained and for true gardeners the only hope is to secure a plant. Actually, it is akin to a quest. In 1996, small seedlings that I purchased as *S. sinensis* were actually as advertised. Plants grew 2′ in 3-gallon containers. More in the 6th edition. Bean terms the bark "as smooth as alabaster and the color of weathered sandstone" and, indeed, I have stroked the trunk and branches feeling I had touched polished marble. On young plants, the bark exfoliates in relatively long, shiny cinnamon brown sheets, not unlike that of *Acer griseum*. Hardy to Boston and should be pursued by discriminating gardeners. *Stewartia sinensis* is native to central China. Introduced 1901. Zone 5 to 7.

ADDITIONAL NOTES: All are wonderful garden plants and are worth seeking. I believe a moist, well-drained, high organic matter, acid soil is important. They have no serious pests and once established, offer many years of season-long beauty. Stewartias can easily be categorized among the crème de la crème of woody flowering shrubs/trees. Gossler Farms Nursery, 1200 Weaver Road, Springfield, OR 97478-9663 offers the finest assortment and most reasonable prices available.

Another species that the collector might want to track is ***Stewartia serrata*** Maxim. with dull green, incurved, serrated, 1 1/2 to 3″ long, 2 to 2 1/2″ wide leaves and 2 to 2 1/2″ diameter, creamy white flowers with yellow-anthered stamens, petals stained red on their outsides. Fruits are maroon-purple. Fall color is dusty reddish purple. Considered similar to *S. monadelpha* but with slightly larger leaves and flowers. Also among the earliest to flower in the spring. Bark is warm brown. I have not seen this species in flower but note that four United States nurseries offer it. Japan. Cultivated 1917. Zone 6.

As a final note, I recommend Spongberg's article on *Stewartia* in the *Journal of the Arnold Arboretum* 55:182–214 (1978) for the true aficionado. Also of more recent vintage is Nicholson's garden treatment of *Stewartia* in *Fine Gardening* 40:49–51 (1994).

STEWARTIA HYBRIDS AND CULTIVARS

With the taxonomy of *S. koreana* and *S. pseudocamellia* muddled, and the lineage of cultivars confounded, I chose to list in alphabetical order the taxa with reported (suspected) parentage.

'Ballet' (*S. pseudocamellia*)—Flowers to 3 1/2″ diameter, graceful, spreading branches, orange-brown fall color, Polly Hill introduction.

'Cascade' (*S. pseudocamellia*)—Arching, cascading branches, semi-pendent shoot-tips, 15′ by 12′ after 30 years, white flowers with golden yellow stamens, rich red-purple fall color.

'Milk and Honey' (*S. pseudocamellia*)—Numerous ~3″ diameter, cream flowers on a strong, upright-growing plant as witnessed at Windy Hill Nursery, Great Barrington, MA in late July 1994, beautiful, elegant, heavy-flowered plant; brighter reddish tan bark; literature reported habit as graceful and spreading with flowers to 4″ diameter; I have questions, with age possibly; a Polly Hill introduction.

Pink Form (*S. pseudocamellia*)—A light pink-budded form, opens to delicate pinkish white flowers, have observed in flower in mid-May at the Atlanta Botanical Garden, not particularly showy, particularly from a distance.

'Red Rose', 'Royal Purple', and 'White Satin'—Selections of *S. ovata* by Polly Hill with red stamens, yellow anthers; purple stamens, yellow anthers; and white stamens, yellow anthers, respectively.

'Skyrocket' (*S.* × *henryae*)—A vigorous form with 2″ diameter flowers and multi-colored bark, Polly Hill introduction.

Stewartia × *henryae* Li (*S. monadelpha* × *S. pseudocamellia*), is known; I suspect this is the *S. sinensis* that appears on occasion in gardens and arboreta, listed as more compact than *S. pseudocamellia*, large cream-white flowers, excellent fall color, exfoliating bark.

'Variegata'—Described for both *S. pseudocamellia* and *S. monadelpha*; I have yet to see.

Stranvaesia davidiana Decne. — Chinese Stranvaesia

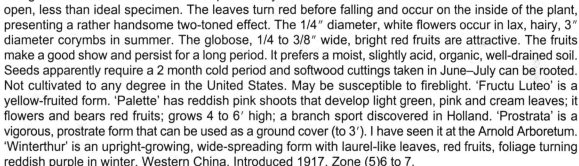

FAMILY: Rosaceae
LEAVES: Alternate, simple, semi-evergreen to evergreen, elliptic-ovate, 2 to 5″ long, 3/8 to 1″ (1 3/4″) wide, acute, rounded, entire, lustrous dark green above, pale beneath, glabrous or pubescent on veins; petiole—1/4 to 1/2″ long, grooved above, pubescent, 2 persistent stipules.
BUDS: 2- to 3-scaled, appressed, red, 1/4″ long, remind of willow buds; set directly above the leaf scar.
STEM: Stout, pubescent, red-purple, showing 3 decurrent ridges that run from base and sides of leaf scar; 2nd year stems brown; pith—green, solid.

Stranvaesia davidiana, (stran-vē′zi-à dã-vid-i-ā′nà), Chinese Stranvaesia, is a large shrub or small tree that may grow 30 to 35′ in height. In the United States it tends to be rather shrub-like and is doubtfully preferable to many evergreen shrubs. The leaves are not particularly dense which results in an open, less than ideal specimen. The leaves turn red before falling and occur on the inside of the plant, presenting a rather handsome two-toned effect. The 1/4″ diameter, white flowers occur in lax, hairy, 3″ diameter corymbs in summer. The globose, 1/4 to 3/8″ wide, bright red fruits are attractive. The fruits make a good show and persist for a long period. It prefers a moist, slightly acid, organic, well-drained soil. Seeds apparently require a 2 month cold period and softwood cuttings taken in June–July can be rooted. Not cultivated to any degree in the United States. May be susceptible to fireblight. 'Fructu Luteo' is a yellow-fruited form. 'Palette' has reddish pink shoots that develop light green, pink and cream leaves; it flowers and bears red fruits; grows 4 to 6′ high; a branch sport discovered in Holland. 'Prostrata' is a vigorous, prostrate form that can be used as a ground cover (to 3′). I have seen it at the Arnold Arboretum. 'Winterthur' is an upright-growing, wide-spreading form with laurel-like leaves, red fruits, foliage turning reddish purple in winter. Western China. Introduced 1917. Zone (5)6 to 7.

Bean describes 'Redstart' as a relatively new clone that may have promise in the United States. It is the result of a cross between *Stranvaesia davidiana* 'Fructu Luteo' and *Photinia* × *fraseri* 'Robusta'. 'Redstart' offers red new shoots, free-flowering (white) in May–June and pendent clusters of red, yellow-tinged fruits. Correctly it is listed as × *Stranvinia* (× *Stravinia*) 'Redstart'. Should mature 8 to 10′(15′). Raulston describes it as easy to root from stem cuttings. Am not bonded to this plant in any way and doubt long-term success in the United States. In the Pacific Northwest, England, and Ireland, numerous specimens have crossed my path. Actually quite handsome in flower and fruit. Nomenclature is a mess with *Photinia davidiana* (Decne.) Cordot listed as the correct name by some; as above by others. The name changes do not affect the plant characteristics. Two distinct morphological groups are described. Salicifolia—with narrow, lanceolate leaves and larger growing; Undulata—with wavy-margined leaves and shrubby habit (to 5′).

Styrax japonicus Sieb. & Zucc. — Japanese Snowbell
(stī′raks jà-pon′i-kus)

FAMILY: Styracaceae
LEAVES: Alternate, simple, broad-elliptic to elliptic-oblong, 1 to 3 1/2″ long, 1/2 to 1 1/2″ wide, acute to acuminate, cuneate, remotely denticulate to almost entire, medium to dark green and often lustrous above, glabrous, with axillary tufts below; petiole—1/3″ long.

BUDS: Small, sessile, naked, scurfy, superposed, 1/6 to 1/4″ long.
STEM: Rounded, zig-zag, rough-scurfy, light brown; pith small, rounded, continuous, green; leaf scars 2 ranked, at first torn, narrow, and shriveled, finally broadly crescent-shaped.

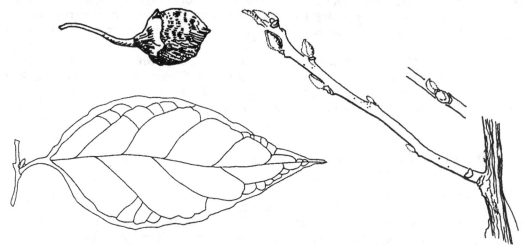

SIZE: 20 to 30′ in height and of a comparable or greater spread.
HARDINESS: Zone 5 to 8, injured at −20°F, very few flowers opened, wood was not killed; killed in Orono, ME.
HABIT: A lovely, small, low-branched tree which develops a rounded to broad-rounded crown and a distinct horizontal appearance because of the wide-spreading branches; a very dainty tree which will grace any landscape.
RATE: Medium, 9 to 10′ over a 7 to 10 year period; I have grown this at Illinois and with proper water and fertilizer it can easily grow 2 to 3′ per year in youth.
TEXTURE: Medium-fine in leaf; medium in winter.
BARK: Quite handsome gray-brown of smooth consistency but showing irregular, orangish brown, and interlacing fissures; excellent addition to winter landscape.
LEAF COLOR: Medium to dark green in summer, often lustrous, unusually pest-free; changing to yellowish or reddish in the fall; foliage is borne on the upper part of the branches and does not significantly detract from the flowers which are pendulous; I have not seen good fall color on this species; leaves hold late and are often killed by an early freeze.
FLOWERS: Perfect, 3/4″ wide, white, yellow-stamened, slightly fragrant, bell-shaped, corolla 5-lobed being united near base, each flower borne on a 1 to 1 1/2″ long pendulous stalk, occurring on short lateral shoots, each with 3 to 6 flowers, May–June and of great beauty. I have always considered this a most beautiful and delicate flowering tree yet is not well-known outside of arboreta and botanical gardens.
FRUIT: Dry drupe, ovoid, about 1/2″ long, grayish in color and somewhat attractive; effective in August and often falling by November; containing a single shiny brown hard seed.
CULTURE: Transplant balled-and-burlapped in early spring into a moist, acid, well-drained soil which has been abundantly supplemented with peat moss or organic matter; full sun or partial shade; prune in winter; site carefully in cold climates; probably best in partial shade in Zone 7 and 8.
DISEASES AND INSECTS: Dr. Darrel Apps mentioned a borer that had devastated plants in the Philadelphia area; have observed Ambrosia beetle damage and canker on field-grown nursery stock; Tubesing, *American Nurseryman* 172(4):145 (1990), reported serious damage to this and *S. obassia* from Ambrosia beetle, *Xylandras germanus*.
LANDSCAPE VALUE: A handsome small tree for any situation; excellent near the patio, in the lawn, or in the shrub border; it is another of the unknown trees that is worthy of extensive landscape use; Bean called it a tree of singular grace and beauty; can be planted on hillsides or slopes where the flowers are seen firsthand by passersby; the leaves are perched like butterflies on the upper part of the stem so the pendulous flowers are not masked; have utilized on the Georgia campus in significant numbers and plants in full sun without supplemental water have suffered, leaves abscise or at best crisp on their margins; in 19 years at Georgia, the species has been tried three times in our garden and perished unabashedly; the only survivor has been 'Emerald Pagoda'.
CULTIVARS: Several rather handsome and unusual cultivars have found their way into the United States and should be available to the gardening public in a few years.
　　'Angyo Dwarf'—8 to 10′, white, slightly fragrant flowers, collected by Barry Yinger in Japan in 1978, introduced by Brookside Gardens.

'Benibana'—Soft pink flowers, floriferous in youth, 4-year-old plants flowered, 10′ by 8′, also considered the umbrella name in Japan for all pink-flowered, seed-grown forms.

'Carillon'—See 'Pendula'.

'Crystal'—Dark green leaves, white flowers with purple pedicels and sepals, 2 to 9 petals, vigorous grower, somewhat upright fastigiate habit, from J.C. Raulston Arboretum, selected from seedlings of Korean origin.

'Emerald Pagoda' ('Sohuksan')—Introduced in 1985 by Dr. J.C. Raulston and U.S. National Arboretum collecting team from Korea; the plant and leaves are larger, more leathery and darker green than typical, flowers are also larger, this is a tremendous selection and is the only cultivar that displays significant heat tolerance, plant is upright, vase-shaped in youth, flowers have variable petal numbers (2 to 8) with great substance and are up to 1″ diameter, a wonderful specimen is starting to "strut its stuff" in our garden; I consider this one of J.C.'s best introductions.

'Fargesii'—Large leaves, flowers two weeks later than typical species, thick dark green leaves, green-purple pedicels that accent the pure white flowers, tree-like habit; I have seen this listed as variety *fargesii*.

'Issai'—Free-flowering selection, fast-growing, 20 to 30′ high, selected by Barry Yinger from Japan, distributed by Brookside Garden.

'Kusan'—A compact, globe-shaped form about 11′ high in 10 years, similar spread, flowers young, found by Bob Tichnor, retired, Oregon State University.

'Pendula'—A small (8 to 12′) weeping tree with foliage and flowers similar to the species; I have seen one of the early introductions and am quite impressed by the general refined nature and gracefulness; I believe 'Carillon' ('Carilon') is a rename of 'Pendula'; introduced by Brookside Gardens, Wheaton, MD.

'Pink Chimes'—Offers pink flowers on an upright shrub or small tree, lovely the one year it flowered in our garden, that winter I took the easy way out and burned the herbaceous plants in the same bed, the bark and a hot fire did not mix, to which I say never plant Armitage's herbaceous litter next to a good woody plant.

'Rosea'—A clear pink-flowered form that occurred as a bud sport, the parent plant was only 4′ high and the growth habit somewhat upright, perhaps same as 'Pink Chimes', although 'Pink Chimes' grows into a small tree; have observed a pink-flowered, weeping form at Atlanta Botanical Gardens.

'Snowfall'—More dense and rounded habit, prolific slightly fragrant flowers, selected from a superior plant on the NCSU campus, released via J.C. Raulston Arboretum.

I have also heard of double-flowered, variegated, dwarf, contorted and red-flowered forms.

PROPAGATION: Seeds exhibit a double dormancy and warm stratification for 5 months followed by cold for 3 months is recommended; I have germinated seeds of *S. obassia* but they proved to be doubly dormant and after several transfers from warm to cold to warm to cold to warm finally secured a modicum of seedlings. Seeds could be fall sown and germination will take place the second spring; if collected fresh and sown immediately they may come up the next spring. Softwood cuttings, treated with IBA will root readily under mist; *S. obassia* rooted well when collected in mid-July. *Styrax americanus, S. japonicus,* and *S. obassia* are extremely easy to root from softwood cuttings; about 1000 to 3000 ppm IBA-quick dip, peat:perlite, mist proved optimum. However, like *Stewartia*, the rooted cuttings are not easy to overwinter. Tissue culture was successful with *S. japonicus*.

ADDITIONAL NOTES: Meyer, *Arnoldia* 52(1):2–8 (1992), describes "The Snowbells of Korea."

NATIVE HABITAT: China, Korea, Japan, Philippines, Ryukyus, and Taiwan. Introduced 1862.

RELATED SPECIES:

Styrax americanus Lam. — American Snowbell

LEAVES: Alternate, simple, narrow oval to obovate, 1 1/2 to 3 1/2″ long, 1/2 to 1 1/4″ wide, acute or acuminate, cuneate, entire or serrulate, bright green, sparingly stellate-pubescent below; petiole—1/8″ long.

BUDS: Superposed, larger bud set at an oblique angle to stem, 1/16 to 1/8″ long, quite similar to *S. japonicus* in overall morphology.

STEM: Slender, light brown, glabrous or slightly scurfy, zig-zag, developing stringy condition; pith—green, solid.

Styrax americanus, (stī′raks à-mer-i-kā′nus), American Snowbell, is a small, slender-stemmed, rather wispy, 6 to 8′(10′) high rounded shrub. Co-national champions are 13′ by 15′ in Angelina County, TX and 15′ by 11′ in Pickens County, SC. The bright green leaves do not develop any significant fall color. The beautiful white, bell-shaped flowers with highly reflexed lobes hang from the leaf axils in May or June. Flowered late April–early May 1995 in Athens; May 30, 1991 in full flower at the Arnold Arboretum. Each 5-petaled flower is 1/2 to 3/4″ long, 3/4 to 1 1/4″ wide, produced 1 to 4 at the ends of short branches on 1/4 to 1/2″ long pedicels. The petals are quite narrow, usually about 1/4″ wide. The 1/3″ long, obovoid, grayish pubescent drupe develops in August–September. I consider this a beautiful shrub and if given a cool, moist, acid root run will reward the gardener many-fold. It is found in the wild in lowlands bordering streams. I have found it along a stream in Bishop, GA just south of Athens. In this situation it looks rather forlorn but when freed from competition it makes a fine garden shrub. Extremely easy to root from softwood cuttings in June–July. Seeds sown in fall will germinate the following spring. Variety *pulverulentus* (Michx.) Perk. (separate species according to some) has more pubescent leaves. Duncan, *Trees of the Southeastern United States*, reduces *S. pulverulentus* into synonymy. Virginia to Florida, west to Missouri, Arkansas and Louisiana. Introduced 1765. Zone 5 to 9, although some tip dieback may occur in severe winters.

Styrax grandifolius Ait. — Bigleaf Snowbell
LEAVES: Alternate, simple, elliptic to obovate to orbicular, 2 1/2 to 7″ long, 1 1/2 to 3 3/4″ wide, short acuminate, cuneate, denticulate or almost entire, dark green above, grayish tomentose below; petiole—1/4 to 1/2″ long.

Styrax grandifolius, (stī′raks gran-di-fō′li-us), Bigleaf Snowbell, is found along the banks of streams from Virginia to Georgia. I have discovered it mixed in the understory with *Kalmia* in the Piedmont of Georgia. The habit is shrub-like and it occurs as an understory plant. Size ranges from 8 to 12′(15′) in height. National champion is 22′ by 10′ in Chowan County, NC. The leaves remind of *S. obassia* and range from 2 1/2 to 7″ long. The beautiful white, fragrant, 3/4 to 1″ wide flowers occur in 7- to 12(20)-flowered, 4 to 8″ long, nodding racemes in May–June. This would be a good choice for southern gardens but is not commonly available from nurseries. Not as "tough" as *S. obassia* and for that reason tends to labor in obscurity. Have attempted to root May cuttings from a local native population but with no success. Introduced 1765. Zone 7 to 9.

Styrax obassia Sieb. & Zucc. — Fragrant Snowbell
LEAVES: Alternate, simple, suborbicular to broad-ovate, 3 to 8″ long, from 2/3's to as wide, abruptly acuminate, usually rounded at the base, remotely denticulate above the middle and sometimes tricuspidate at apex, glabrous and dark green above, densely pubescent beneath; petiole—1/3 to 1″ long, the base enclosing the bud.
BUDS: Scales enveloping rather than imbricate, tomentose, dirty gray-brown, usually 2 buds at a node, the larger 1/4 to 5/16″ long, ovoid and probably floral; the other smaller, 1/8 to 3/16″ long, appressed to the larger bud.
STEM: Stout, glabrous, lustrous reddish brown, exfoliating to expose greenish brown inner bark; pith—solid, green; second year smooth, lustrous brown; third year becoming gray-brown and developing prominent fissures.
BARK: Relatively smooth, gray to gray-brown, marked with shallow, vertical fissures; similar to bark of *S. japonicus*, very handsome.

Styrax obassia, (stī′raks ō-bās′ē-à), Fragrant Snowbell, is a small tree or shrub which develops dense, ascending branches and can grow 20 to 30′. Plants are distinctly pyramidal-oval in youth but become more open and rounded with age. 50′ high trees are known. The flowers are white, fragrant, borne in 4 to 8″(10″) long, arching-drooping racemes in May–June (mid-April in Athens). The leaves are dark green and quite large and detract slightly from the quality and intensity of the flowers. The leaves do not generally develop a good fall color, however, on occasion the small tree in our garden turned romantic yellow. The fruit is a 3/4″ long, ovoid, dry, pubescent drupe. This species is not considered as hardy as *S. japonicus* although I have observed them in the same collections where temperatures dropped as low as -25°F and both survived. I have noticed that it flowers ahead of *S. japonicus* opening its flowers in late May–early June at the Arnold while *S. japonicus* was in full flower around mid-June. Over the observational years, I have come to the conclusion that *S. obassia* is more cold hardy than *S. japonicus*. More stem damage is evident on *S. japonicus* than on *S. obassia* after a difficult winter. For the past 17 years, *S. obassia* has been a regular fixture in our garden and is one of my wife's and my favorite conversation pieces. Unfortunately, it leafs out early, about early April in Athens, and is injured 1 out of 3 years, the leaves

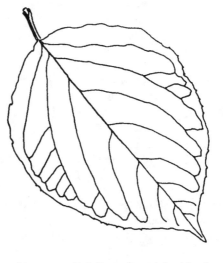

being rendered potato-chippy and the flowers useless. New growth follows from latent buds and full foliage is realized by June. Also, in fall an early freeze can render the leaves crispy gray-brown before their time. Architecturally, the smooth gray branches with numerous twists, turns and sinuations are handsome for winter effect. The flowers are also interesting as they appear to peek out from under the large leaves on slightly curve-shaped racemes that open from the base to the apex over a 2 to 3 week period. Ideally provide ample moisture and high organic matter soil in partial shade, although full sun is acceptable. The less stress the better for maximizing appearance through the summer months. Raulston reported root rot problems in heavy soils in Raleigh. Creech, *Amer. Nurseryman* 163(5):48–49 (1986), reported that *S. obassia* occurs widely in Northern Honshu and extends into Hokkaido, across the Sea of Japan into Korea and Manchuria. This indicates that *S. obassia* should be more cold hardy than *S. japonicus*. Native to Japan, Korea and Manchuria. Introduced 1879. Zone 5 to 8.

ADDITIONAL NOTES: I have observed the four species listed above and believe that *S. japonicus* is the most aesthetic; experiences with *S. americanus* and *S. japonicus* in my Georgia garden have been less than satisfactory. I had sited them in full sun and obviously partial shade and a cool, moist root run would have served better. At the Arnold Arboretum, *S. americanus* and *S. japonicus* make superb specimens. For additional information see Dirr, "The Exquisite Snowbells," *American Nurseryman* 147(2):7, 8, 87–90 (1978).

   Since 1980, numerous plant collectors have ventured into China, Korea, and Japan. *Styrax* species in the United States have increased in numbers with their efforts. About 100 species are known with the greatest concentration in Asia. Recently, **Styrax shiraianum** Mak. from Japan came into my possession. Also, **Styrax odoratissimus** Chapm. a small tree with sweetly scented, numerous, white flowers is offered in American commerce. **Styrax youngae** Cory is a small to medium-sized shrub from Texas and Mexico. Has been hardy in Raleigh, NC. J.C. Raulston was extremely interested in the genus and assembled about 21 taxa in Raleigh. See *Proc. Southern Nursery Assoc. Res. Conf.* 36:305–310 (1991) for excellent capsular treatment of over 30 species.

Sycopsis sinensis Oliv. — Chinese Fighazel

FAMILY: Hamamelidaceae
LEAVES: Alternate, simple, evergreen, elliptic-ovate to elliptic-lanceolate, 2 to 4″ long, 1/3 to 1/2 as wide, acuminate, broad cuneate, entire or remotely toothed above the middle, leathery, lustrous dark green and glabrous above, pale green and glabrous or with scattered pubescence below; petiole—1/3″ long, warty.

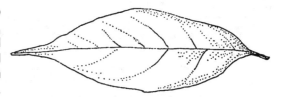

Sycopsis sinensis, (sī-cop′sis sī-nen′sis), is a pretty, glossy-leaved evergreen shrub that grows 10 to 15′ high and wide under cultivation. I have seen it used at Disney World, Orlando, FL in mass plantings and informal hedges. Apparently it is amenable to pruning and would make an excellent screen in warmer climates. The small, yellowish flowers have red anthers and are surrounded by dark reddish brown, tomentose bracts. Flowers open in February–March. Fruit is a 1/3″ long, 2-valved, dehiscent, pubescent capsule. Any well-drained soil is acceptable and I have observed plants in full sun in Zone 9. For southern gardens this plant might be worth a longer look. Hardiness is somewhat suspect but plants in Savannah, Ga have withstood 10°F with minimal injury. Also, a respectable specimen grows at the U.S. National Arboretum. This clone has experienced -10°F and survived. An interesting intergeneric hybrid, × *Sycoparrotia semidecidua* Endress & Aulinker, between *Sycopsis sinensis* and *Parrotia persica*, is known. It is a rather loose, arching, semi-evergreen (has been evergreen in my garden), 10 to 15′(20′) high shrub or tree with 1 to 5″ long, 2″ wide, lustrous dark green leaves that, although described as intermediate, tend toward the *Parrotia* parent. Flowers are particularly attractive and occur in February–March along the length of the stems. Full flower on February 20, 1994 in Dirr garden. The color effect is reddish brown eventually yellow as stamens develop. Have seen plants in Europe but only in Zone 8 and 9 in the United States. Certainly not a plant for every garden but does have botanical and horticultural interest. Partial shade and well-drained soil appear ideal. Developed from seed around 1950 in the nursery of P. Schonholzer, Basel, Switzerland. Zone (6)7 to 9. *Sycopsis sinensis* is native to central and western China. Introduced 1901. Zone 7 to 9.

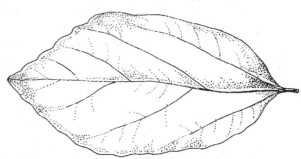

× *Sycoparrotia semidecidua*

Symphoricarpos albus (L.) Blake — Common Snowberry
(sim-fō-ri-kär′pos al′bus)

FAMILY: Caprifoliaceae

LEAVES: Opposite, simple, oval to elliptic-oblong, 3/4 to 2″ long, obtuse, roundish, on shoots often sinuately lobed, dark almost blue-green above, pubescent beneath; petiole—1/8 to 1/4″ long.

STEM: Slender, rounded, pubescent; pith—brownish, excavated.

SIZE: 3 to 6′ by 3 to 6′.

HARDINESS: Zone 3 to 7.

HABIT: Bushy, rounded to broad rounded shrub with numerous ascending shoots, densely fine and twiggy; tends to sucker and colonize.

RATE: Fast.

TEXTURE: Medium in leaf; however, in winter extremely sorrowful; needs a brush.

LEAF COLOR: Bluish green in summer; no effective fall color.

FLOWERS: Perfect, pinkish, 1/4″ long, June, borne in 1 1/2 to 1 3/4″ long, terminal spikes on current season's growth, basically inconspicuous.

FRUIT: Berry-like drupe, globose, ovoid to lumpy, white, 1/2″ diameter, September through November; most ornamental asset of this shrub; fruit can persist into winter but is often discolored by a fungus.

CULTURE: Transplants easily, very tolerant of any soil; native on limestone and clay; full sun to medium (heavy) shade; suckers profusely and tends to spread extensively; prune in early spring so current season's growth can produce flowers.

DISEASES AND INSECTS: Anthracnose (two genera affect the host; one causes a discoloration of the fruit, the other a spotting of the leaves), berry rot (fruits turn yellowish or brown and are affected by a soft, watery rot), leaf spots, powdery mildews, rusts, stem gall, aphids, snowberry clearwing, scale and glacial whitefly.

LANDSCAPE VALUE: Not a very valuable plant but fruit can be interesting; useful in shaded situations and for holding banks, cuts, fills; the hybrids and cultivars have greater landscape appeal.

CULTIVARS:

'Constance Spry'—With large, white fruit and 'Turesson' with nodding branches are listed in the English literature.

var. *laevigatus* (Fern.) Blake.—Taller (6′), leaves larger (to 3″ long) and broader, fruit larger and more abundant, vigorous grower; have seen *S. albus* var. *laevigatus* listed as *S. rivularis* Suksd.; the latter is now an invalid name; var. *laevigatus* is considered the western extension from Alaska to California.

'Variegatus'—Slow-growing, to 4' high shrub with small, white-margined leaves.

PROPAGATION: Immersion in sulfuric acid for 40 to 60 minutes followed by warm and then cold stratification will assist in breaking seed dormancy; cuttings are extremely easy to root, softwood taken in June, July, August, rooted readily; the entire group roots easily from softwood cuttings.

ADDITIONAL NOTES: The *Symphoricarpos* have limited ornamental value but fruit and shade tolerance are definite assets. Should be used sparingly; however, the cultivar 'Hancock' deserves further use as well as the *S.* × *doorenbosii* hybrids. Have observed *S. occidentalis* Hook., Wolfberry, at the Arnold Arboretum and in the Western United States where it is native. The bluish green, somewhat scalloped foliage and the white fruits are handsome. Fruits often discolor (brown) quickly after ripening.

NATIVE HABITAT: Nova Scotia to Alberta, south to Minnesota and Virginia. Introduced 1879.

RELATED SPECIES:

Symphoricarpos* × *chenaultii Rehd., (sim-fō-ri-kär'pos she-nō'ē-ī), Chenault Coralberry, is a cross between *S. microphyllus* × *S. orbiculatus*. The plant is a low-spreading, arching shrub growing about 3 to 6' high. Flowers are pink; fruit is pink or white and tinged pink. 'Hancock' is a beautiful low-growing type with small leaves and good ground cover possibilities, a 12-year-old plant may be 2' tall and 12' wide; have not seen mildew on this form; raised about 1940 at Hancock Nurseries, Cookville, Ontario, Canada. Chenault Coralberry fruits differ from those of Indiancurrant Coralberry in that the side away from the sun is white. Zone 4 to 7. The fruit is more rose-red than pinkish as mentioned above but variation exists. The leaves are quite small, dark blue-green, ovate, 1" long and pubescent below.

Symphoricarpos* × *doorenbosii Krüssm., (sim-fō-ri-kär'pos dôr-en-bo'sē-ī), are hybrids among *S. albus* var. *laevigatus*, *S. orbiculatus*, and *S.* × *chenaultii*. Plants were raised by G.A. Doorenbos, The Hague, before 1940. 'Erect' is a vigorous, compact, upright form with rose-lilac fruits. 'Magic Berry' is a compact-spreading shrub with abundant rose-pink (rose-lilac) fruits; I saw this clone in Amsterdam and was impressed by the fruit display. 'Mother of Pearl' is vigorous, semi-pendulous, 5 to 6' high shrub with broad elliptic or obovate leaves and dense clusters of 1/2" wide, white, pink-cheeked fruits. 'Pink Magic' with pink-tinged flowers and polished ivory blushed pink fruits was listed by Heronswood. 'White Hedge' grows 5' high, stiff and upright, and bears large, white fruits primarily in terminal clusters above the foliage. Their fruit effect justifies consideration for shady areas of the garden but availability is limited in the United States. All should be hardy to -30°F and will probably prove adaptable to Zone 7. Cappiello reported that 'Mother of Pearl' was killed outright in Orono, ME.

Symphoricarpos orbiculatus Moench. — Indiancurrant Coralberry or Buckbrush

LEAVES: Opposite, simple, elliptic or ovate, 1/2 to 1 1/4" long, 1/4 to 3/4" wide, obtuse or acutish, rounded at base, dull dark green above, glaucescent and pubescent beneath; petiole—1/12" long.

Symphoricarpos orbiculatus, (sim-fō-ri-kär'pos ôr-bi-kū-lā'tus), Indiancurrant Coralberry or Buckbrush, grows 2 to 5' high by 4 to 8' wide and develops into a spreading, arching shrub. The foliage is a dull green (possibly blue-green) in summer and hangs on late in fall. I observed this species loaded with mildew growing next to *S.* × *chenaultii* which had none. The flowers are yellowish white, flushed rose, borne in June or July, in dense and short, axillary clusters and terminal spikes. The fruit is a purplish red, 1/6 to 1/4" diameter, berry-like drupe, maturing in October and persisting late into winter. 'Hawkins' is a more compact form, 3' high, with dark green foliage tinted red in fall, coral red fruits. 'Leucocarpus' has white or whitish fruit. 'Variegatus' is a weak-growing, irregularly yellow-margined form, the leaves becoming creamy white-margined in full sun; I grew this for a number of years and was pleased with the performance; definitely more vigorous than given credit; now relegated to variegated plant heaven; also listed as 'Foliis Variegatus'. Also listed are: 'Albovariegatus' with rounded leaves with an irregular, white margin and 'Bowles Gold Variegated' with a wide, gold leaf margin. New Jersey to Georgia, Kansas and Texas, west to South Dakota. 1727. Zone 2 to 7(8).

Symplocos paniculata (Thunb.) Miq. — Sapphireberry or Asiatic Sweetleaf
(sim-plō′kos pan-ik-ū-lā′tà)

FAMILY: Symplocaceae

LEAVES: Alternate, simple, elliptic or obovate to oblong-obovate, 1 1/2 to 3 1/2″ long, 3/4 to 1 3/4″ wide, acute or acuminate, broad-cuneate, finely serrate, dark green and glabrous above, conspicuously veined beneath and usually pubescent, rarely glabrous; petiole—1/8 to 1/3″ long, hairy.

BUDS: Small, plump, broad-ovoid, imbricate, 1/16 to 1/8″ long, gray-brown, sitting directly above raised, half-circle leaf scar.

STEM: Stout, grayish, glabrous or pubescent, vertical fissuring of epidermis; pith—brown, spongy.

BARK: On older plants develops gray flat ridges and darker fissures, becomes slightly stringy; reminds of the bark of *Lonicera maackii*.

SIZE: 10 to 20′ high with a similar spread.

HARDINESS: Zone 4 to 8, has withstood -20 to -25°F and flowered normally.

HABIT: Large shrub or small, low-branched tree becoming wide-spreading at maturity; a particularly handsome specimen at the Arnold Arboretum was 20′ high and 30′ wide.

RATE: Slow.

TEXTURE: Medium.

BARK: Gray, ridged-and-furrowed, resembling that of *Lonicera maackii*.

LEAF COLOR: Dark green in summer; no appreciable fall color.

FLOWERS: Perfect or unisexual, 5-petaled, 30-stamened, filament white, anthers yellow, each flower about 1/2″ diameter, creamy white, fragrant, flowers are borne in 2 to 3″ long panicles in late May–early June on growth of previous season; the flower effect is much superior to honeysuckles.

FRUIT: Ellipsoidal, 1/3″ long, one-seeded drupe that color-wise can be categorized as ultramarine, sapphire, bright turquoise-blue and lapis-lazuli blue, September–October and often stripped by the birds; the color is unique among fruiting shrubs; fruit production may fluctuate from plant to plant because of the nature of the flowers, some being perfect, others male or female; several shrubs should be planted to insure adequate cross-pollination and the best solution is to vegetatively propagate; individual plants are almost always self-incompatible.

CULTURE: Easily transplanted from a container or as a balled-and-burlapped specimen; light or heavy, well-drained soil is acceptable; pH 5 to 7; full sun to partial shade in South; best to prune during winter although some flower buds will be lost.

DISEASES AND INSECTS: None serious, have never seen a scratch on this shrub.

LANDSCAPE VALUE: Probably best used in the back of the shrub border, as an unpruned screen or as a small specimen tree; this is an excellent plant for attracting birds; specimens are long-lived and require essentially no maintenance; plant several seedlings or different clones to insure cross-pollination; have a lone plant in my Georgia garden that flowers well but sets little fruit; another seedling is necessary for cross-pollination.

PROPAGATION: Softwood cuttings root readily and I have had 100% success with July cuttings, 1000 ppm IBA-quick dip, peat:perlite, mist; cuttings should root in 6 to 8 weeks and should be hardened off in a cooler or cold frame, and transplanted when new growth occurs; over the years have successfully rooted this plant numerous times, yet have been unable to overwinter the cuttings. Seeds appear to be double dormant and require 3 to 4 months warm, followed by 3 months cold. In Mt. Airy, Cincinnati, OH, numerous stray seedlings are evident around several large shrubs.

ADDITIONAL NOTES: Certainly one of the handsomest of fruiting shrubs and should be used in every park, bird sanctuary and the like. A plant in full fruit is truly spectacular. See Dirr, "Sapphireberry has true blue fruit," *American Nurseryman* 150(12):42, 44, 46, 48 (1979). About 250 species (have seen references to 380 species) of evergreen and deciduous trees and shrubs primarily in warm temperate and tropical regions. *Symplocos tinctoria* is the only United States representative.

NATIVE HABITAT: Himalayas to China and Japan. Introduced 1875.

RELATED SPECIES:

Symplocos tinctoria (L.) L'Her. — Horse-sugar
LEAVES: Alternate, simple, elliptic to oblong-lanceolate, 3 to 6″ long, half as wide, acute or acuminate, cuneate, entire or obscurely serrate, thickish, lustrous dark green above, paler and pubescent below, sweet taste is evident in old leaves.

STEM: Light gray-brown, pith chambered.

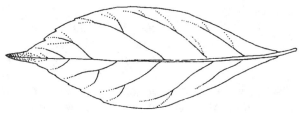

Symplocos tinctoria, (sim-plō´kos tink-tō´ri-à), Horse-sugar, is a semi-evergreen to deciduous shrub or small (15 to 25´ high) tree that occurs in woods, swamps and bottomlands from Delaware to Florida and Louisiana. The co-national champions are 54´ by 38´ and 70´ by 36´, both in southern Chesapeake, VA. The lustrous dark green leaves are attractive and to one degree or another may persist into spring. There are several colonies in the University's Botanical Garden that show a distinct suckering tendency. The 1/3˝ diameter, cream-yellow, fragrant flowers occur in dense, axillary clusters on the previous season's growth during April–May. The fruits, which I have not seen on the Georgia plants, are orange or brown, 1/3 to 1/2˝ long, ellipsoidal drupes. Rather interesting native plant, probably best in a naturalized landscape. In Charleston, SC the plant grows in sandy soils as an understory component. The foliage is often lustrous dark green and certainly selections could be made for foliage, growth habit and possibly floral characteristics. See Weaver, *Arnoldia* 44:34–35 (1984) for a good overview. Cultivated 1780. Zone 7 to 9.

Syringa meyeri Schneid. — Meyer Lilac, in the trade often referred to as *S. palibiniana* Nak. or possibly *S. velutina* Komar.

(si-ring´gà mī´ĕr-ī)

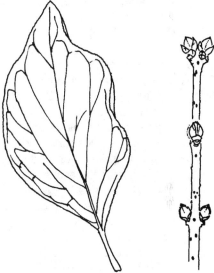

FAMILY: Oleaceae

LEAVES: Opposite, simple, 3/4 to 1 3/4˝ long, not quite as wide, elliptic-ovate to sometimes elliptic-obovate, acute or obtusish, entire, glabrous above, scarcely paler beneath and pubescent on the veins near base, with 2 to 3 pairs of veins from base nearly to apex, dark green, somewhat lustrous with a reddish purple rim around margin of young leaves; petiole—about 1/3˝ long.

SIZE: 4 to 8´ high and 1 1/2 times that in spread.

HARDINESS: Zone 3 to 7; I have seen it growing at Callaway Gardens, Pine Mountain, GA.

HABIT: Small, dense, neat, broad-rounded, mounded shrub; excellent clean branch structure, one of the best lilacs for uniform, pristine outline in summer and winter.

RATE: Slow.

TEXTURE: Medium-fine in leaf; medium in winter.

LEAF COLOR: New leaves rimmed with a purplish margin, finally turning dark green; fall color is nonexistent.

FLOWERS: Violet-purple (I see pink in them but most of the botanical descriptions do not); each 1/2˝ long, 1/4˝ wide, flowers are densely packed in 4˝ long and 2 1/2˝ wide panicles, May, effective for 10 to 14 days, fragrant but not the soft fragrance associated with Common Lilac; literally cover the entire plant and are spectacular; one of the best for flower effect if not adulterated by the vagaries of weather.

FRUIT: Capsule, warty, 1/2 to 3/4˝ long.

CULTURE: Does well in the Midwest and East, does not contract mildew like other species, requires little or no maintenance; possibly one of the easiest lilacs to grow, also suited to culture in the South; nifty study, *J. Environ. Hort.* 8(3):147–150 (1990), involving regeneration of 18 Syringa taxa by cutting all to 8˝ above ground, all regrew/regenerated at different rates, produced flowers and developed the typical form for each taxon; taxa included: *S.* × *chinensis*, Chinese Lilac; *S.* × *henryi* Schneid., Henry Lilac; *S.* × *hyacinthiflora*, Early Flowering Lilac; *S.* × *josiflexa*, Josiflexa Lilac; *S. josikaea*, Hungarian Lilac; *S. komarowii* Schneid., Komarof Lilac; *S. laciniata*, Feathered Persian Lilac; *S. meyeri*, Meyer Lilac; *S. microphylla*, Littleleaf Lilac; *S.* × *prestoniae*, Preston Lilac; *S. pubescens* Turcz., Hairy Lilac; *S. reflexa*, Nodding Lilac; *S. reticulata*, Japanese Tree Lilac; *S. reticulata* var. *mandschurica*, Amur Tree Lilac; *S.* × *skinneri* E. Skinner, Skinner Lilac; *S. sweginzowii*, Chengtu Lilac; *S. villosa*, Late Lilac; *S. vulgaris*, Common Lilac.

LANDSCAPE VALUE: Very handsome lilac, will start to flower when about one foot high; extremely floriferous; best used in shrub border with an evergreen background, flowers before leaves are fully developed; the flower buds emerge very early and can be injured by a late freeze.

CULTIVARS:

'Palibin'—The compact form of the species that is prevalent in the trade; will grow 4 to 5′ high, 5 to 7′ wide; reddish purple buds open whitish pink, since there was significant confusion as to what constituted true *S. meyeri*, Dr. Peter Green, *Curtis's Botanical Magazine*, 183. Part III. New Series 116–120, provided a degree of order by providing the above name.

PROPAGATION: Lilacs in general are not easy to root from cuttings and timing is critical; ideally softwood cuttings should be collected before end leaves mature, treat with 1000 to 5000 ppm IBA talc or quick dip, well-drained medium and mist; my successes with various *Syringa* species are minimal; Dirr and Heuser, 1987 offer a detailed discussion of the vagaries of lilac propagation. Seeds of most species should be provided 1 to 3 months cold, moist stratification.

ADDITIONAL NOTES: A good discussion of cultivated *Syringa* along with notes on introduction and identification was presented by Griffin and Maunder, *The Plantsman* 7(2): 90–113 (1985). Lilacs are overwhelming in sheer numbers, not necessarily quality attributes, and it is necessary to visit local gardens and survey the best. What grows in Boston, in all probability, has little opportunity for success in Atlanta. Also, Fiala's great reference on Lilacs by Timber Press is the best current reference. If passionate, join the Lilac Society.

Worthwhile discussion by Jane Taylor, *The Plantsman* 11(4):225–240 (1990), of *Syringa* hybrids developed by Lemoine. Also includes Lemoine's contributions in *Philadelphus*, *Deutzia*, and *Weigela*. One of the great plant breeders of all time and the plants stand as testimonials to his understanding and manipulation of plant genetics.

NATIVE HABITAT: Northern China. Introduced 1908 and known only in cultivation.

RELATED SPECIES:

Syringa microphylla Diels. — Littleleaf Lilac

LEAVES: Opposite, simple, orbicular-ovate to elliptic-ovate, 1/2 to 2″ long, 1/3 to 1 1/4″ wide, obtuse or abruptly acuminate, broad-cuneate to rounded at base, slightly pilose and medium green above, grayish green and pubescent beneath, at maturity only on the veins, ciliolate, or nearly glabrous; petiole—1/6 to 1/3″ long; quite distinct from the previous and following species by virtue of leaf color and pubescence but often confused with those species.

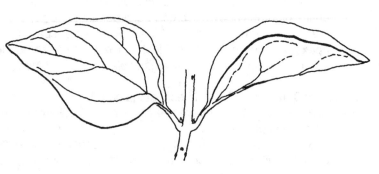

Syringa microphylla, (si-ring′gà mī-krō-fil′à), Littleleaf Lilac, is a very handsome, broad-spreading, dense shrub usually about 1 1/2 to 2 times as broad as tall, 6′ by 9 to 12′. The medium green leaves are about one-half the size of those of *S. vulgaris*. Flowers are rosy lilac, fragrant, borne in 2 to 4″ long, 1 1/2 to 2″ wide panicles in May into early June and often flowering sporadically again in September. Makes a nice plant for the shrub border, in groupings, possibly a free-standing hedge. 'Superba' has single, deep pink (pink-red) flowers, grows twice as broad as tall and is quite floriferous. Another versatile, adaptable, heat tolerant, mildew resistant species that is worthy of consideration. *The New RHS Dictionary of Gardening* places this under *S. meyeri*. Native to northern and western China. Introduced 1910. Zone 4 to 7(8).

Syringa patula (Palib.) Nak. — Manchurian Lilac (previously *S. velutina* Komar.)

LEAVES: Opposite, simple, elliptic to ovate-oblong, larger than those of *S. meyeri* or *S. microphylla*, 2 to 5″ long, 1/2 to 2″ wide, acuminate, broad-cuneate or rounded at base, entire, dull dark green and slightly pubescent to glabrous above, densely pubescent beneath or pilose only on midrib or veins; petiole—1/4 to 1/2″ long.

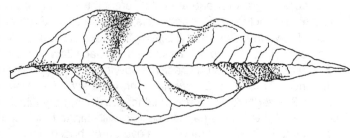

STEM: Purplish young shoots, slightly downy or glabrous at maturity.

Syringa patula, (si-ring'gȧ pat'ū-là), Manchurian Lilac, is frequently confused with the above two species. *Syringa patula* is a more upright, vigorous (9') shrub than *S. meyeri* and *S. microphylla*. Panicles often in pairs from the terminal pair of buds of the previous season's shoots, each 4 to 6″ long and rather thinly set with lilac-purple flowers of pleasing fragrance in May–June. 'Miss Kim' is listed as growing 3' high and 3' wide with 3″ long panicles of purple buds which open to fragrant icy blue flowers. I have seen this clone growing in the Holden Arboretum and, at that time, it was 6' high and 4 to 5' wide. I saw the parent plant at the Horticultural Farm at the University of New Hampshire and it was about 8 to 10' high and oval-rounded. It may develop a reasonably good reddish purple fall color. The so called *S. palibiniana* as used in the nursery trade does not really exist. One is buying either *S. meyeri* or *S. patula* or, perhaps, *S. microphylla*. Have seen the species at Callaway Gardens. Northern China, Korea. Cultivated 1902. Zone 4 to 7(8).

Syringa reticulata (Bl.) Hara [formerly *S. amurensis* Rupr. var. *japonica* (Maxim.) Franch. & Savat.] — Japanese Tree Lilac
(si-ring'gȧ re-tik-ū-lā'tȧ)

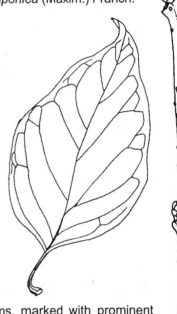

LEAVES: Opposite, simple, entire, broad-ovate to ovate, 2 to 5 1/2″ long, about half as wide, acuminate, rounded or subcordate, dark green above, grayish green and reticulate beneath and glabrous or slightly pubescent; petiole—1/2 to 1″ long.

BUDS: Sessile, subglobose, with 4 pairs of scales, end bud frequently absent, brownish.

STEM: Stout, shiny brown, heavily lenticelled resembling cherry bark, glabrous.

SIZE: 20 to 30' in height; 15 to 25' in spread.

HARDINESS: Zone 3 to 7, have not observed a plant in Zone 8.

HABIT: Large shrub or small tree with stiff, spreading branches developing a somewhat oval to rounded crown; with time branches and leaves become somewhat arching, the entire tree much more graceful.

RATE: Medium, 9 to 12' over a 6 to 8 year period.

TEXTURE: Medium in all seasons.

BARK: Cherry-like, reddish brown to brownish on young and old stems, marked with prominent horizontal lenticels, good feature to separate it from other lilacs; on old trunks gray, scaly.

LEAF COLOR: Dark green in summer; like most lilacs no good fall color; leafs out early, often by late March in Zone 7b.

FLOWERS: Perfect, creamy white, fragrant, early to mid-June, effective for 2 weeks, borne in large terminal 6 to 12″ long and 6 to 10″ wide panicles, extremely showy in flower, odor somewhat akin to that of privet, petals turn brown with age and appear rather untidy toward the end of their tenure; a long pole pruner does wonders for the tree's appearance.

FRUIT: Warty, glabrous, scimitar-shaped, dehiscent, 3/4″ long capsule, blunt at apex.

CULTURE: This discussion applies to the lilac species in general; transplant balled-and-burlapped or from a container, actually lilacs are easy to move; soil should be loose, well-drained and slightly acid although lilacs are pH adaptable; full sun for best flowering; pruning should be accomplished after flowering or if a plant is overgrown (applies to multi-stemmed clones) cut it to the ground for complete rejuvenation; should be good air movement; prefer cool summers.

DISEASES AND INSECTS: Bacterial blight, *Phytophthora* blight, leaf blights, leaf spots, powdery mildew (bad on Common Lilac, Persian Lilac), wilt, other minor pathological problems, ring spot virus, witches' broom, frost injury (in late spring the young leaves may be injured by near freezing temperatures), graft blight (occurs on lilacs grafted on privet), leaf roll necrosis (caused by various air pollutants), lilac borer, leopard moth borer, caterpillars, giant hornet, lilac leaf miner, scales and several other insects of negligible importance; it should be evident that lilacs require a certain degree of maintenance; I have seen the borer and scale insects decimate large shrubs and entire plantings.

LANDSCAPE VALUE: Possibly the most trouble-free lilac; excellent specimen tree, street tree, good in groups or near large buildings; one of my favorite lilacs; I believe there is a continued need for selection of superior flowering and foliage types within the species; have seen the species performing magnificently on the Nebraska campus at Lincoln as well as in Burlington, VT; I consider it the toughest of the lilacs but the flower fragrance is somewhat privet-like which turns many people off; is resistant to mildew, scale and borer, which is an unbridled recommendation; in the South, Zone 7b and higher, leaves emerge early and often desiccate or become necrotic by mid to late summer, not a good doer in the heat of a southern summer.

CULTIVARS:

'Chantilly Lace'—Margins on young leaves pale yellow, maturing to creamy yellow, margin width varying from 1/5 to 4/5″, central portion of leaf blotched dark green with light green halo, leaves may burn in hot sunny locations. Introduced by Herrmann Nursery, Limehouse, Ontario.

'China Gold'—Described as more upright and narrow habit than typical, young shoots reddish, young leaves light golden, turning pale yellow-green in summer, flower buds and open flowers more cream than pure white, 25-year-old parent tree was 25′ high, Zone (3)4, from the late Father Fiala, Falconskeape Gardens, Medina, OH, raised from colchicine-treated seed in 1955, first flowered in 1986, see *HortScience* 26:476–477 (1991).

'Ivory Silk'—A 1973 selection by Sheridan Nursery, Ontario, Canada, that flowers at a young age and is a rather sturdy and compact, rounded dense form, deep green leaves, heavy-flowering, 20 to 25′.

var. *mandschurica* (Maxim.) Hara—Tends toward a shrubby nature, 6 to 8′(12′) high, leaves and flowers smaller than those of the species, Manchuria, perhaps not as hardy.

'Regent'—An exceptionally vigorous upright form, Princeton Nursery introduction, utilized in Spartanburg, SC and it cooked in the heat.

'Summer Snow'—Offers compact rounded crown, profuse large panicles of fragrant, creamy white flowers, handsome glossy cherry-like bark, good small street or lawn tree, 20′ high, 15′ wide, a Schichtel Nursery introduction.

PROPAGATION: Seed dormancy is variable but cold stratification for 30 to 90 days at 34 to 41°F is recommended; I have attempted to grow this lilac from seed; however, all attempts met with failure; the seed, in all cases, was purchased and the origin was unknown. Cuttings which I collected in June rooted 90% when treated with 10,000 ppm (1%) IBA/50% alcohol and placed in sand under mist. Root formation was extremely profuse. Work in Canada indicated that early July, 8 to 10″ long cuttings rooted 87% after treatment with 8000 ppm IBA.

NATIVE HABITAT: Northern Japan. Introduced 1876.

RELATED SPECIES:

Syringa pekinensis Rupr. — Pekin Lilac

LEAVES: Opposite, simple, ovate to ovate-lanceolate, 2 to 4″ long, 1 to 2″ wide, acuminate, cuneate, dark green above, grayish green beneath and scarcely veined, quite glabrous; petiole—1/2 to 1″ long.

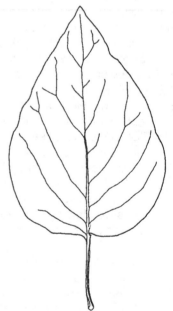

Syringa pekinensis, (si-ring′gà̇ pē-kin-en′sis), Pekin Lilac, is somewhat similar to the above but smaller (15 to 20′) with a more informal (multi-stemmed) habit and finer texture throughout. With only an exception or two, plants I've observed were multi-stemmed, upright arching, loose and open. Have seen good tree forms at Minnesota and Arnold Arboreta. The leaves and stems are smaller and finer. The flowers are yellowish white (creamy) and appear before *S. reticulata* in 3 to 6″ long panicles. I have seen plantings in various arboreta where the two plant types were flowering at about the same time. The bark is often quite handsome and adds significantly to the plant's landscape assets. Bark may be similar to *S. reticulata* or on some trees exfoliate in rich brown flakes or sheets. There is a clone named 'Pendula' with drooping branches. Summer Charm™ ('DTR 124') is a tree form with fine-textured foliage and impressive creamy white flowers that was introduced by Bill Wandell. Water Tower® ('Morton') has an upright habit with exfoliating, cherry-like bark. Northern China. Introduced 1881. Zone 4 to 7.

Syringa villosa Vahl. — Late Lilac
(si-ring′gà̇ vil-lō′sà̇)

LEAVES: Opposite, simple, broad-elliptic to oblong, 2 to 7″ long, 1 to 2 1/2″ wide, entire, acute at ends, dull dark green above, glaucescent beneath and usually pubescent near the midrib, rarely glabrous, veins impressed creating a pleated appearance; petiole—1/4 to 1 1/4″ long.

SIZE: 6 to 10′ high and 4 to 10′ wide.

HARDINESS: Zone 3 to 7.

HABIT: Bushy shrub of dense rounded habit with erect or ascending, stout, stiff branches.

RATE: Slow to medium.

TEXTURE: Medium in leaf and winter.

LEAF COLOR: Medium to dull dark green in summer.

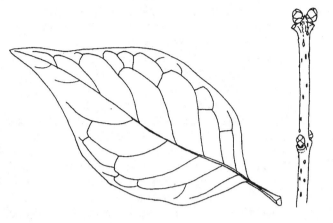

FLOWERS: Rosy lilac to white, not as fragrant as *S. vulgaris*, with a curious odor similar to privet; mid to late May possibly into early June; borne in dense, pyramidal, 4 to 8″ long panicles, forms a true terminal bud and 3 panicles often occur at the end of the shoot, flowers are borne on the current season's growth flush rather than last season's wood like *S. vulgaris*.

FRUIT: Capsule, 1/2″ long.

CULTURE: See under *S. reticulata*.

DISEASES AND INSECTS: See under *S. reticulata*.

LANDSCAPE VALUE: Nice lilac for the shrub border; performed well in Midwest and East, seldom used in contemporary gardens.

NATIVE HABITAT: China. Cultivated 1802.

CULTIVARS: The Preston Lilacs (*S.* × *prestoniae* McKelv.) are the result of crosses between *S. villosa* and *S. reflexa*. They are extremely hardy (Zone 3) and possess many of the morphological features of *S. villosa*. Developed by Isabella Preston of Ottawa in 1920's and later. Many new cultivars continue to be developed; however, somewhere along the line there needs to be a stopping point for the glut becomes mind-boggling. Krüssmann listed 43 cultivars.

'Alexander's Pink'—Large, pink flowers; later than *S. vulgaris*; 6 to 9′.

'Audrey'—Light magenta-pink outside, almost white within, in 9″ long, dense, conical panicles.

'Coral'—Single, light pink flowers, considered best pink, compact habit.

'Desdemona'—Single, purplish flowers.

'Donald Wyman'—Deepest pink to almost reddish flowers with buds and flowers the same color, 6″ by 4″ panicles, opening after *S. vulgaris* types; 8 to 10′.

'Elinor'—Dark purplish red in bud, opening to pale lavender, panicles erect.

'Hiawatha'—Single, red-purple opens to pink, good mildew resistance and foliage.

'Isabella'—Single, pinkish lilac flowers in large (1′ long, 8″ wide), pyramidal panicles.

'James MacFarlane'—Single, bright pink, light fragrance, June, vigorous, 8 to 10′ high, one of the more common commercial forms, introduced by University of New Hampshire.

'Jessica'—Single violet flowers, 7″ long, 5″ wide panicles.

'Minuet'—Light purple buds, light lavender flowers; large, dark green leaves; 6 to 8′ high, composite of *S. josikaea*, *S. reflexa*, and *S. villosa*.

'Miss Canada'—Deep reddish buds, bright rose-pink flowers, vigorous grower, late flowering, 6 to 8′ high.

'Nocturne'—Deep violet purple, opening to lilac pink, good mildew resistant foliage, ~6′ high.

'Patience'—Single lilac flowers.

'Redwine'—Single magenta flowers, considered darkest red form, probably more deep red in bud, opening pink, late-flowering, 8 to 10′.

'Royalty'—Violet-purple flowers, handsome deep green foliage, 8 to 10′.

'Virgilia'—Deep lilac magenta in bud, opening pale lilac, compact habit.

'W.T. Macoun'—Lilac pink, large panicles.

PROPAGATION: See *S. meyeri*.

RELATED SPECIES:

Syringa josikaea Jacq. f. ex Rchb. — Hungarian Lilac

LEAVES: Opposite, simple, broad-elliptic to elliptic oblong, 2 to 5″ long, acute to acuminate, broad cuneate to rounded, ciliolate, entire, lustrous dark green above, glaucescent (whitish) below, sparingly hairy on veins or glabrous; petiole—about 1/3″ long.

Syringa josikaea, (si-ring′gà jos-ik′ē-à), Hungarian Lilac, is a 8 to 10′ high, 8 to 12′ wide, spreading, arching, multi-stemmed shrub that offers slightly fragrant, lilac-violet flowers in 4 to 7″(8″) long, narrow panicles from late May into June. The leaves, habit and flowers remind of *S. villosa* but the color is usually deeper at least on plants I have seen. The loose panicles are handsome for late season effect. Has been used as a parent in the development of many late-flowering hybrids. Several selections including: 'Emerald' a medium-sized, compact shrub, 5 to 7' high, bright emerald green foliage, abundant dark lilac pink flowers; 'Eximia' with light red to pink flowers; 'H. Zabel' with red fading to white flowers; 'Pallida' with pale violet flowers; 'Rosea' with pink flowers; and 'Rubra' with violet, red-tinted flowers. Central and southern Europe. Introduced about 1830. Zone 5 to 7.

Syringa reflexa Schneid. — Nodding Lilac
LEAVES: Opposite, simple, oval-oblong to oblong-lanceolate, 3 to 6"(8") long, half as wide, acuminate, cuneate, entire, dark green and glabrous above, villous on veins beneath and paler; petiole—1/2" long.

Syringa reflexa, (si-ring′gȧ rē-flek′sȧ), Nodding Lilac, is a large 10 to 12' high and wide, stout-stemmed shrub with handsome foliage and 6 to 10" long, 1 1/2 to 4" wide, cylindrical or narrowly pyramidal panicles of purplish pink flowers that age pink with a white interior. Flowers are packed in a series of whorls along the length of the terminal, leafy, arching to pendulous panicle. I cannot pick up any fragrance of consequence. A parent of *S. × prestoniae* and other late-flowering hybrids. For the lilac collector a worthwhile addition; for the gardener with space for one lilac, forget it. Central China. Introduced 1901. Zone 5 to 7.

Syringa sweginzowii Koehne & Lingl. — Chengtu Lilac
LEAVES: Opposite, simple, oblong or ovate, 2 to 4" long, 1 to 2" wide, abruptly acuminate, broad-cuneate to rounded, thinnish, entire, dark green and glabrous above, light green below and pilose pubescent on veins; petiole—1/4 to 1/2" long.

Syringa sweginzowii, (si-ring′gȧ sweg-in-zō′ē-ĭ), Chengtu Lilac, is another of the late-flowering species that offers 6 to 8" long, fragrant panicles of rosy lilac, fading to flesh pink. The panicles occur at the end of the shoot with a few lateral ones developing further down the stem. The inflorescence is extremely loose and the flowers tend to hang and do not always present themselves in the most aesthetic manner. The habit is elegantly upright with landscape size approximately 10 to 12' by 10 to 12'. With *S. reflexa*, it resulted in the hybrid grex, *S. × swegiflexa* Hesse. 'Fountain' produces nodding pale pink panicles in June. Also, *S. × josiflexa* Preston (with *S. josikaea*) is a grex including such cultivars as 'Bellicent' (pink), 'Guinevere' (purple), and 'Lynette' (pink). Northwestern China. Introduced 1914. Zone 5 to 6.

ADDITIONAL NOTES: Despite the lack of overwhelming fragrance this group of lilacs deserves landscape consideration because of lateness and quantity of flowers. All are quickly recognizable by the impressed veins, rather loose inflorescences, late flowers, and inflorescences that appear at the terminus on the new growth of the season. All can be separated from each other by floral characteristics which, for example, come down to anthers not protruding from the corolla in *S. sweginzowii*, while those of *S. villosa* do. *Syringa wolfii* Schneid., Manchurian Lilac, is also included here as it is later than *S. vulgaris* with lavender flowers in up to 12" long panicles, on a large >10' high shrub, possibly more heat tolerant than *S. vulgaris* types. Manchuria, Korea. Cultivated 1910. Zone 4 to 7.

Syringa vulgaris L. — Common Lilac
(si-ring′gȧ vul-gā′ris)

LEAVES: Opposite, simple, ovate or broad-ovate, 2 to 5" long, 3/4's to as wide, acuminate, truncate or subcordate to broad-cuneate, entire, dark green almost bluish green, glabrous; petiole—3/4 to 1 1/4" long.
BUDS: Usually at end of stem, referred to by author as double terminal buds, 1/4 to 1/3" long, ovoid, plump, somewhat 4-sided, imbricate with 3 to 4 pairs of reddish brown scales; vegetative—smaller, 1/16 to 1/8" long, reddish brown, perhaps with only 2 pairs of visible scales.
STEM: Stout, angled, appearing 4-sided on first year stems, lustrous brown, glabrous, small raised lenticels, leaf scars raised, crescent-shaped; pith—solid, white.

SIZE: 8 to 15' in height (to 20') with a spread of 6 to 12'(15').
HARDINESS: Zone 3 to 7.
HABIT: Upright leggy shrub of irregular outline but usually devoid of lower branches after a time and forming a cloud-like head of foliage.

RATE: Medium.

TEXTURE: Medium to coarse in leaf depending on age and size of plant; coarse in winter.

FLOWERS: Lilac, extremely fragrant, early to mid-May (early April, Athens); borne in 4 to 8″ long panicles, usually in pairs from the terminal buds.

FRUIT: Smooth, 5/8″ long, beaked dehiscent capsule.

CULTURE: Best soil is one close to neutral and supplemented with peat or leaf mold; old flowers should be cut off as soon as flowers fade; I am continually astonished at the resiliency of the species and its cultivars as I travel throughout the Midwest and particularly Northeast; in cities, towns, farmsteads, old abandoned homes, the lilac resides, seemingly oblivious to the transgressions of mankind.

DISEASES AND INSECTS: See *S. reticulata*.

LANDSCAPE VALUE: Flowers of only value, probably best reserved for the shrub border or in groupings; considerable nostalgia attached to this shrub, often associated with Grandmother or Mom; my Mom would always pick large bouquets for the house and the fragrance literally permeated every room, I have tried to convince myself to plant one but in Zone 7 to 8 the plant is not prosperous, lacks vigor and does not flower reliably from year to year.

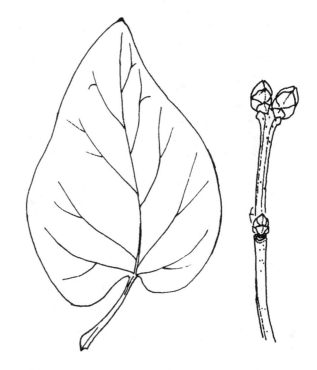

CULTIVARS: There are over 400, possibly 800 to 900 different clones (a 1990 publication, *American Horticulturist* 69(4):34–38, said 2,000 clones) and it is hopeless to attempt to list them. Donald Wyman has a valuable list in his *Shrubs and Vines for American Gardens* based on observations of the lilac collection at the Arnold Arboretum. Also Krüssmann, *Manual of Cultivated Broadleaved Trees and Shrubs III* and Bean present extensive lists of cultivars. A Timber Press (1988) book on lilacs by Father Fiala is another worthy reference. An interesting historical perspective is provided by Torer, *Horticulture* 61(5):25 (1983). The following list of the more popular types was gleaned from Rogers, *American Horticulturist* 57(2):13–17 (1978). This list resulted from a survey conducted by Mr. Frank Niedz in 1970 to determine the most popular types. Also, John H. Alexander, III, and the Arnold Arboretum permitted me to use a list of lilacs, "Fifty of the best lilacs for the gardens of New England", that appeared in *Arnoldia* 49(2):2–7 (1989).

Newer registrations include:

'Aino'—Single, fragrant, violet-blue, 4/5 to 1″ diameter, in 8 to 10″ long panicles, foliage dark green, disease resistant, 7 to 10′ high, moderate suckering, *HortScience* 26(5):476 (1991).

'Alvin R. Grant'—Single, red-purple in bud, opening purple, *HortScience* 31(3):327–328 (1996).

'Bernard Slavin'—Flowers single with some radial doubling, buds grayed yellow opening to white, fragrant, *HortScience* 32(4):587–588 (1997).

'Bishop McQuaid'—Flowers single with radial doubling, buds purple-violet opening to purple-violet, very fragrant, *HortScience* 32(4):587–588 (1997).

'Bridal Memories'—Shrub of globose habit, dense foliage, single, creamy white, cup-shaped, 3/4″ diameter flowers, flowers heavily in alternate years, lightly in off years, *HortScience* 29(9):972 (1994).

'Clyde Heard'—Single, medium red-purple in bud, purple when open, fading to pale red-purple.

'Comtesse d'Harcourt'—Single, pure white, *HortScience* 31(3):327–328 (1996).

'Elsa Maasik'—Single, fragrant, deeper purple, 3/4 to 7/8″ wide, in 6″ long panicles, dark green, disease resistant foliage, 7′ high shrub, moderate suckering, grown from open-pollinated seed of Ludwig Spaeth, *HortScience* 26(5):476 (1991).

'Frederick Douglass'—Flowers single with radial doubling, buds purple-violet opening to blue-violet, fragrant, *HortScience* 32(4):587–588 (1997).

'Independence'—Flowers single, buds gray-orange opening to yellow-white, slightly fragrant, *HortScience* 32(4):587–588 (1997).

'Martha Stewart'—Single, purple in bud, opening violet-blue, *HortScience* 31(3):327–328 (1996).

'McMaster Centennial'—A large, vigorous shrub, white double flowers, hybrid of 'Primrose' and 'St. Joan'.

'Prairie Petite'—Light pink, fades to lavender, parent plant was 3.25′ by 3.8′ after 25 years, *HortScience* 31(1):166 (1996).

'Prince Wolkonsky'—Double, red-purple in bud, pink-lilac when open, *HortScience* 31(3):327–328 (1996).

'Princesse Sturdza'—Single, dark pink in bud, pink-lilac when open, *HortScience* 31(3):327–328 (1996).

'Tiiana'—Single, pink, fragrant, 4/5″ wide, in up to 14″ long, 4″ wide panicles, dark green, disease resistant foliage, 10′ high shrub, suckering moderately, *HortScience* 26(5):476 (1991).

MR. FRANK NIEDZ'S LIST

Color	Double	Single
White	'Ellen Willmott' 'Edith Cavell' 'Mme. Lemoine' (vigorous)	'Aloise' 'Florence Stepman' 'Jan Van Tol' (fairly resistant to mildew) 'Mont Blanc' 'Rochester' (slow-growing) 'Vestale'
Violet	'Violetta' 'Maréchal Lannes'	'De Miribel' 'Cavour'
Blue	'Ami Schott' 'Nadezhda' 'Olivier De Serres' 'Prés. Grévy'	'Decaisne' 'Firmament' 'President Lincoln'
Lilac	'Alphonse Lavallée' 'Henri Martin' 'Léon Gambetta' 'Victor Lemoine'	'Christophe Columb' 'Jacques Callott'
Pink	'Belle De Nancy' 'Edward J. Gardner' 'Fantasy' 'Katherine Havemeyer' (mildew resistant, good season-long foliage) 'Mme. Antoine Buchner' 'Montaigne' 'William Robinson'	'Lucie Baltet' 'Macrostachya'
Magenta	'Charles Joly' (fairly resistant to mildew, good foliage) 'Paul Thirion' 'Prés. Poincairé'	'Capitaine Baltet' 'Clyde Heard' 'Congo' 'Mme F. Morel'
Purple	'Adelaide Dunbar' (fairly resistant to mildew, good foliage) 'Paul Hariot'	'Hulda' 'Ludwig Spaeth' 'Night' 'Monge' 'Mrs. W.E. Marshall'

JOHN ALEXANDER'S LIST

Color	Cultivar	Flower Type
Violet	Henri Robert	Double
	Louvois 0	Single
	Mieczta	Single
"Blue"	Dr. Chadwick 0	Single
	Laurentian + 0	Single
	Maurice Barres	Single
	Madame Charles Souchet	Single
	President Lincoln +	Single
Purple	Adelaide Dunbar +	Double
	Paul Hariot	Double
	President Roosevelt +	Single
	Sarah Sands	Single
	Sensation	Single (edged white)
	Zulu	Single
Magenta	Charles Joly +	Double
	Glory	Single
	Mme. F. Morel	Single
	Paul Thirion	Double
	Ruhm von Horstenstein +	Single
"Yellow"	Primrose	Single
"Pink"	Catinat + 0	Single
	Charm	Single
	Churchill 0	Single
	General Sherman +	Single
	Katherine Havemeyer +	Double
	Lucie Baltet	Single
	Mme. Antoine Buchner	Double
	Scotia 0	Single
	Vauban + 0	Double
	Virginite	Double
White	Jan Van Tol	Single
	Jeanne d'Arc	Double
	Joan Dunbar	Double
	Krasavitska Moskvy ('Beauty of Moscow', pink buds to white flowers)	Double
	Marie Legraye	Single
	Maude Notcutt	Single
	Miss Ellen Willmott	Double
	Mme. Lemoine	Double
	Saint Margaret	Double
	Sister Justena 0	Single
Lilac	Alphonse Lavallée	Double
	Assessippi + 0	Single
	Excel + 0	Single
	Hippolyte Maringer	Double
	Hugo Koster	Single
	Hyazinthenflieder	Single
	Michel Buchner	Double
	Nokomis 0	Single

+ indicates a high degree of fragrance
0 indicates an early-blooming hybrid

TEN FAVORITE UNCOMMON LILACS (from Alexander's Article)
The "best fifty" list includes only cultivars of *Syringa vulgaris* and the early-flowering *S.* × *hyacinthiflora* because they have the general appearance of the traditional or common lilac. Hybrids and selections of the species listed below have leaves, flowers and fragrance that are different, and offer adventurous gardeners the opportunity to break with tradition.

Syringa laciniata
S. meyeri
S. meyeri 'Palibin'
S. microphylla 'Superba'
S. patula 'Miss Kim'

S. pekinensis
S. × *prestoniae* 'Agnes Smith'
S. × *prestoniae* 'Miss Canada'
S. pubescens
S. reticulata

HEAT TOLERANT, LOW CHILL CULTIVARS
The Descanso hybrids were developed in Southern California for good flower production in mild winter environments. The following forms would be worth testing in Zone 8 and 9 of the Southeast.
'Angel White'—White, single, fragrant, compact grower.
'Blue Boy'—Blue flowers.
'Blue Skies'—Lavender-blue, single flowers, dark blue-green leaves, 8 to 10' high, low winter chill, not absolutely sure about Descanso origin.
'California Rose'—Pink-rose, fragrant.
'Chiffon'—Lavender flowers.
'Dark Knight'—Deep purple.
'Lavender Lady'—Lavender-purple, single, fragrant flowers, open growth habit, result of cross between *S. vulgaris* × *S. laciniata*; heat tolerance imparted by the latter parent.
'Mrs. Forrest K. Smith'—Light lavender flowers.
'Sylvan Beauty'—Rose-lavender flowers.

FATHER FIALA'S LILACS
The following cultivars were selected for color, size, form, fragrance, habit of growth and disease resistance. They are being produced through tissue culture by Knight Hollow Nursery, Madison, WI. Please see Fiala's *Lilacs: The Genus Syringa*, Timber Press, 1988 for additional details.
White
　　'Avalanche'—Large white, single flowers, fine lingering fragrance, rounded to upright habit, about 9' high, *S. vulgaris* type, 'Flora' × 'Carley'.
　　'Father John' ('Father John Fiala')—Yellow in bud, cream-white when open, double, large petals, named in memoriam for Father Fiala who produced a modern generation of lilacs.
Bicolor
　　'Albert F. Holden'—Deep violet flowers with a silvery blush on the reverse of the petals, good fragrance, large loose-open, somewhat reflexed panicles, dark green foliage, moderately rounded to 7', *S. vulgaris* type.
Blue
　　'Blanche Sweet'—Ethyl blue buds open to whitish blue petals tinged with pink, fine fragrance, good foliage, upright to 10', a *S.* × *hyacinthiflora* selection.
　　'Little Boy Blue' ['Wonder Blue', 'Wonderblue' in *HortScience* 24(3):435 (1988)]—Sky blue flowers of good fragrance on a compact rounded 4 to 5' high shrub, *S. vulgaris* type.
　　'Wedgewood Blue'—Lilac-pink buds open to the blue background of English Wedgewood pottery, excellent fragrance, large somewhat wisteria-like panicles, lower growing to 6', *S. vulgaris* type.
Pink
　　'Marie Francis'—True pink, almost 'Shrimp Pink', single, very fragrant, smallish in habit to 5' high.
Magenta and Purple
　　'Arch McKean'—Bright reddish purple, individual flowers, 4/5 to 1 1/5" wide, in large upright panicles, heavy-flowering, moderate fragrance, dark green leaves, practically non-suckering, 8' high, *S. vulgaris* type.
　　'Yankee Doodle'—Deepest and darkest purple, 1 to 1 1/5" diameter individual flowers in 8" long panicles, profuse-flowering, upright habit to 8', *S. vulgaris* type, 'Prodige' × 'Rochester'.
　　S. julianae Schneid. 'George Eastman'—Rich wine-red buds open to deep cerise-pink flowers, color is the same on inside and outside of the petals, a compact 5' high plant with horizontally spreading branches.

LATVIAN CULTIVARS

'Daudzpusīgais Zemzaris'—Single, purple in bud opening purple.

'Dobeles Sapņotājis'—Double, buds purple-violet opening purple-violet.

'Esības Prieks'—Single, buds purple opening violet, fading to red-purple.

'Gaistošais Sapnis'—Single, buds violet opening violet with silvery white markings.

'Gaiziņkalns'—Double, buds purple, opening purple, fading to red.

'Māte Ede Ūpītis'—Single, buds white opening white.

'Pērļu Zvejnieks'—Single, buds white opening white.

'TTT'—Single, buds violet opening purple-violet.

'Vēstule Solveigai'—Single, buds purple, opening purple, fading to violet.

The above are detailed more fully in *HortScience* 31(3):327–328 (1996).

PROPAGATION: If only a plant or two are needed simply divide and replant sucker(s); for commercial considerations see *S. meyeri*; tissue culture has been successful with this species. See McCulloch, *Proc. Intl. Plant Prop. Soc.* 39:105–108 (1989), for a good paper on tissue culture propagation of French hybrid lilacs and respectable literature citations on *Syringa* vegetative propagation.

NATIVE HABITAT: Southern Europe. Cultivated 1563.

RELATED SPECIES:

Syringa × *chinensis* Willd. — Chinese Lilac

LEAVES: Opposite, simple, ovate-lanceolate, 1 1/2 to 3″ long, to 1 1/4″ wide, acuminate, cuneate or rounded, entire, medium to dark green, glabrous; petiole—1/3 to 1/2″ long.

BUDS: Smaller and more refined than those of *S. vulgaris*.

Syringa × *chinensis*, (si-ring′gá chi-nen′ sis), Chinese or Rouen Lilac, also listed as *S. rothomagenesis* Hort., is a hybrid between *S.* × *persica* and *S. vulgaris*. The shrub is graceful, broad-spreading, round-topped, with arching branches, more delicate and more profuse in flower than *S. vulgaris*. Grows 8 to 15′ tall and as wide. Flowers are purple-lilac, fragrant, mid-May, borne in large and loose, 4 to 6″ long panicles from the upper nodes producing an elongated, arching, compound panicle that results in a shroud of color. Have seen excellent plantings in Midwest. One of the more handsome hybrid lilacs and often spoken of as the first hybrid lilac, originated as a chance seedling at Rouen, France, 1777. Midway in leaf size and habit between Persian and Common Lilac. Can become ratty looking like *S. vulgaris* and proper pruning techniques are a must. 'Alba' has light pink almost white flowers, and 'Saugeana' has lilac-red flowers and is more colorful than the species. The latter is also available in commerce. Zone 3 to 7. Variable mildew susceptibility.

Syringa × *hyacinthiflora* (Lemoine) Rehd., (si-ring′gá hī-à-sin-thi-flō′rà), Early Flowering Lilac, is the grex name for *S. oblata* and *S. vulgaris* hybrids. They were first raised by Lemoine in 1876 but have since been produced by Clarke of San Jose, CA, Dr. Frank Skinner of Dropmore, Manitoba and Elizabeth Preston at the Dominion Experiment Station, Ottawa. They are extremely hardy and flower before the *S. vulgaris* types. The leaves may turn reddish purple in fall. In general they grow to be large shrubs 8 to 10′ high and wide (approaching 10 to 12′ high and wide). Many cultivars including: 'Blanche Sweet' with blue buds opening to whitish blue petals tinged with pink; 'Arvid Williams' is single, fragrant, lilac, 1 1/4 to 1 1/2″ wide, lobes recurved, inflorescences large, dark green foliage, disease resistant, 10 to 12′ high, practically sucker-free, selected from seedlings grown from open-pollinated seed of 'Clarkes Giant'; 'Asessippi' with single lavender flowers; 'Dr. Chadwick' with single, blue, fragrant flowers, more compact to 8′; 'Esther Staley' with red buds opening to large, single, pink flowers; 'Ethel Webster' is coral pink, late, vigorous grower; 'Evangeline' with light purple, fragrant, double flowers, mildew resistant; 'Excel' with single, lilac-lavender (pink), fragrant flowers; 'Luo Lan-Zi' with red-purple buds opening to blue-purple, double flowers; 'Maiden's Blush' ('Maiden Blush') with pink to lavender-pink, fragrant flowers, excellent foliage turns burgundy in fall, 10 to 12′; 'Minnehaha' has single, bishop's purple flowers; 'Mt. Baker' with white, single, fragrant flowers, 10 to 12′ by 10 to 12′; 'Pocahontas' with deep maroon-purple buds open to deep violet, fragrant, single flowers, 10 to 12′; 'Sister Justena' with single, white flowers; 'Swarthmore' has lilac purple, fully double flowers, reliable flowering, extremely hardy; 'Vaiga' has single, pink to grayish white, fragrant, 1 to 1 1/4″ diameter, large panicles, good green disease resistant foliage, 7′ high, moderate suckering, from open-pollinated 'Esther Staley'; 'Xiang Xue' with double, white, fragrant flowers; and 'Zi Yun' with blue-purple buds opening to pink-purple flowers, corolla tube blue-purple. Suitable for Zone 3b to possibly 7; better in cold climates. Considered quite resistant to leaf curl necrosis.

Syringa laciniata Mill. — Cutleaf Lilac

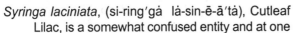

LEAVES: Opposite, simple, all or partly 3- to 9-lobed, 1 to 2 1/2″ long, 1/2 to 3/4″ as wide, blue-green, glabrous, very interesting and different leaf texture for a lilac; first leaves always lobed, later often not.

Syringa laciniata, (si-ring′gà là-sin-ē-ā′tà), Cutleaf Lilac, is a somewhat confused entity and at one time was listed as a variety of *S. × persica*. The habit is low, dense, rounded-mounded and 6 to 8′ high. With age, plants form colonies of a suckering nature. The small, pale lilac, fragrant flowers are often borne in 3″ long, loose panicles all along the stems in May. The lacy, fine-textured foliage is an unusual asset and quite striking when one considers the usual foliage complement of most *Syringa*. Hardy to at least Zone 4 as I have seen a thriving specimen in the Wisconsin Landscape Arboretum. It is one of the best lilacs for Zone 7(8) conditions and is frequently encountered in Athens and Atlanta, GA where it flowers in late March–early April. Displays excellent heat tolerance and will provide reliable flower in partial shade. Leaves are highly mildew resistant. Considered native to Turkestan and China. This form is largely sterile while another introduction, *S. protolaciniata* P.S. Green & M.C. Cheng, is fertile. See *Kew Magazine* 6(3):116–124 (1989). Also, Vrugtman lists *S. protolaciniata* 'Kabul' that was introduced to Kew Gardens from gardens in Kabul, Afghanistan and erroneously named *S. afghanica*. The corolla lobes are longer (~1/3″) than the original introduction from China.

Syringa oblata Lindl. — Early Lilac

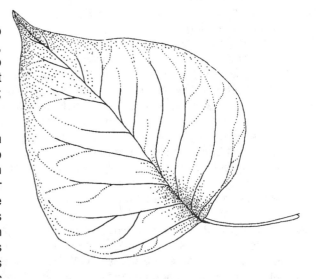

LEAVES: Opposite, simple, orbicular-ovate to reniform, often broader than long, 2 to 4″ broad, to 3″ long, abruptly acuminate, cordate to subcordate, entire, glabrous, dark green, almost bluish green, emerging leaves bronze-tinted; petiole—3/4 to 1″ long.

Syringa oblata, (si-ring′gà ob-lā′tà), Early Lilac, is a large (10 to 12′) shrub or small tree related to *Syringa vulgaris*. The young leaves are often bronzish and change to dark green in summer followed by muted reddish to reddish purple tones in fall. The pale to purple-lilac flowers occur in rather broad, 2 to 5″ long panicles from the upper-most nodes of the previous year's wood in April–May, usually opening 7 to 10 days ahead of *S. vulgaris*. This is a rather coarse lilac but is valuable for breeding work as well as the rather handsome fall color. Northern China. Introduced 1856. Zone 3 to 6. Variety *dilatata* (Nak.) Rehd. is more common and tends to be more shrubby with longer leaves and a longer, more slender corolla tube than the species. I had the variety in my Illinois garden and have seen it at the Arnold and University of Maine where the bronzy red to purple fall color was quite beautiful. Raulston mentioned that var. *dilatata* had proven reliable in Raleigh, NC with early and profuse-flowering every year. 'Wan Hua-zi' has single, purple-pink flowers about 15 days later than *S. oblata*, tolerant of summer heat and humidity as well as to winter cold and aridity; see *HortScience* 32(4):587–588 (1997). Korea. Introduced 1917. Zone 3 to 6.

Syringa × persica L. — Persian Lilac

LEAVES: Opposite, simple, lanceolate or ovate-lanceolate, (rarely 3-lobed), 1 to 2 1/2″ long, 1/3 to 1/2″(3/4″) wide, acuminate, cuneate, entire, dark green above, glabrous, often infested with mildew to a degree that the leaves assume a whitish cast; petiole—1/3″ long.

Syringa × *persica*, (si-ring′gȧ pĕr′si-kȧ),
    Persian Lilac, is a graceful shrub
    with upright, arching branches
    reaching 4 to 8′ in height and
    spreading 5 to 10′. The foliage is
    dark green. Flowers are pale lilac,
    fragrant, mid-May (has opened
    from early to late April, Athens),
    borne profusely in 2 to 3″ long and
    wide panicles from the upper
    nodes of the previous season's
    growth. A nice small lilac with a
    mass of flower when properly

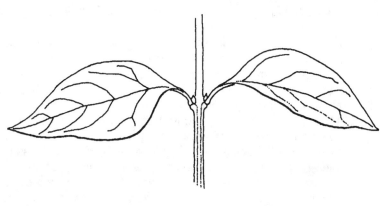

grown, good plant for the shrub border. Cultivated since time immemorial. Introduced 1614. Zone 3 to 7.
According to Wyman this may not be a true species and, in fact, may be a hybrid between *S. afghanica*
× *S. laciniata* since it is almost completely sterile and probably has not been found wild in any country.
'Alba' is a white-flowered form; 'Rosea' and 'Rubra' with light to dark pink flowers, respectively.

ADDITIONAL NOTES: Four of the nicest lilac collections I have seen are located at the Arnold Arboretum; Royal
    Botanic Garden, Hamilton, Ontario, Canada; Swarthmore College; and the Minnesota Landscape Arbor-
    etum. Species approach 20 or more and are not the easiest taxa to separate by vegetative characteristics.
    Great tirades in the literature discuss the need for near neutral to neutral (sweet) soils for best growth.
    Perhaps, but in the acidic soils of the Northeast, numerous specimens could attest to the opposite. Simply
    food for thought. You may read the literature, plants generally do not. Tremendous interest in heat tolerant
    lilacs. To my knowledge there is no such thing for Zone 8 and 9. Most *S. vulgaris* clones languish in Zone
    7b. I am not sure every plant has to grow everywhere! International Lilac Society, c/o Robert Gilbert,
    Assistant Treasurer, P.O. Box 83, Hyde Park, NY 12538 is a society for like-minded, fragrant people.

Tamarix ramosissima Ledeb. (formerly listed as *T. pentandra* Pall.) — Five-stamen Tamarix or
    Tamarisk
(tam′ȧ-riks ram-ō-sis′i-mȧ)

FAMILY: Tamaricaceae
LEAVES: Alternate, simple, lanceolate to ovate, 1/8″ long, acute, glaucous, small, usually scale-like, bright
    green, similar to juniper foliage.
BUDS: Small, sessile, rounded, compressed against twig, solitary or quickly becoming concentrically multiple,
    with about 3 exposed scales.
STEM: Slender, elongated, rounded; pith—small, rounded, continuous.

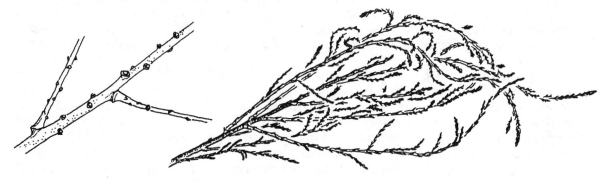

SIZE: 10 to 15′ high, usually less in spread, have observed 20 to 25′ high specimens along North Carolina and
    Georgia coasts.
HARDINESS: Zone 2 to 8; the hardiest species of *Tamarix*; Cappiello mentioned some tip dieback at Orono, ME.
HABIT: Usually a wild growing, very loose, open shrub; can be attractive with its fine-textured foliage, but
    definitely needs to be hidden when defoliated.
RATE: Fast.
TEXTURE: Fine in foliage; needs to be disguised in winter (coarse).

LEAF COLOR: Light green, scale-like; creating a feathery appearance; some forms and species are glaucous green, blue-green to bluish.

FLOWERS: Perfect, rosy pink, 5-petaled, 5-sepaled, borne in dense or slender, 1 to 3″ long racemes which form large, terminal panicles, June–July; quite attractive, the entire flowering shoot may approximate 3′ in length; normally in full flower by early to mid-April in Athens; flowering on May 1, 1998 at Biltmore Gardens, Asheville, NC.

FRUIT: Capsule, inconsequential.

CULTURE: Root systems are usually very sparse and, for this reason, care should be exercised in planting; container-grown plants are the best bet; prefer acid, well-drained, low fertility soil; full sun; not really particular as to soil and can grow in sand; ideal for seashore plantings as they are fantastically salt tolerant; prune back this species in early spring since it flowers on new growth; I have observed heavy flowering on plants that were pruned to the ground the previous winter; however, from the early flowering date in the South, it is obvious that flowers arose from previous years buds; apparently the plant can go both ways which is somewhat unusual; have observed 25′ high plants growing in pure sand less than 100 yards from the Atlantic Ocean on Georgia's St. Simons Island; indeed saline and dry soil tolerant.

DISEASES AND INSECTS: Cankers, powdery mildew, root rot, wood rot, and scales.

LANDSCAPE VALUE: Interesting for foliage effect as well as flowers but its uses are limited; perhaps best reserved for saline environments where it does amazingly well; have seen it used at Cantigny Gardens, Wheaton, IL where it had been treated like an herbaceous perennial to stimulate vegetative growth; for textural quality it is beautiful when handled this way; the flowers may last 4 to 6 weeks but show their age toward the end of the cycle; a particularly fine specimen resides at the Bridge of Flowers, Shelburne Falls, MA and flowers in mid to late July.

CULTIVARS:

'Cheyenne Red'—Deeper pink flowers than the species.

'Pink Cascade'—Slightly richer pink flowers than 'Rosea' and is quite vigorous.

'Rosea'—Rosy pink flowers, each 1/8″ across, arranged in slender, variable length (1 to 5″ long) racemes; flowers occur late and may develop in July–August in the North; considered one of the hardiest cultivars; ideally cut back in late winter and a 6 to 10′ tall plant will bear profuse flowers in mid to late summer.

'Rubra'—Deeper pink flowers than the species, a branch sport of 'Rosea'.

'Summer Glow'—Dense, feathery, blue-tinged foliage, bright pink flowers, 10′.

PROPAGATION: Fresh seeds usually germinate within 24 hours after imbibing water; no pretreatment is necessary; softwood cuttings, placed in peat:perlite under mist root easily; the rooting may be sparse and the roots coarse and somewhat difficult to handle; hardwood cuttings can also be rooted.

ADDITIONAL NOTES: This genus does not require high fertility soils, and I have noticed decline in container-grown specimens under high nutritional status. The plants also become more open and leggy than normal when grown under high fertility. This is a genus which has a distinct place when salt presents a cultural problem. The entire genus is rather taxonomically similar and from a landscape viewpoint there is little to differentiate the species, unless one considers the type of wood upon which the flowers are borne. In August, several students and I were hiking through Hidden Lake Gardens, Tipton, MI and came upon a 25′ high and 25′ wide, flowering specimen of *T. ramosissima*, or so I spouted until my graduate student read the label . . . *T. africanus* Poir., . . . as I said, not the easiest plants to separate . . . ahem! Indeed, my continued literature searches indicate the Hidden Lake Gardens species was not *T. africanus*.

Other species that appear in gardens and literature include: *T. chinensis* Lour., *T. gallica* L., and *T. hispida* Willd. Some indication that *T. chinensis* may be the most common form in cultivation, also in Southeast. I have read that *T. chinensis* is synonymous with *T. ramosissima*. Approximately 54 species are described from western Europe and the Mediterranean to eastern Asia and India. I suspect the ranges overlap and like our native deciduous eastern United States azaleas they are difficult to differentiate.

The deciduous, Asiatic *Tamarix* species have invaded and replaced most of the native vegetation on over 1,000,000 acres of wildlife and agricultural land in riparian ecosystems of the western United States. Numerous research papers on control strategies for eliminating *Tamarix* species in the western states have been published.

NATIVE HABITAT: Southeastern Europe to central Asia where it usually occurs on saline soils. Cultivated 1883.

RELATED SPECIES:

Tamarix parviflora DC., (tam′à-riks pär-vi-flō′rà), Small-flowered Tamarix, grows 12 to 15′ high, flowers on previous year's growth and should be pruned immediately after flowering. The 4-petaled, 4-sepaled flowers are light pink and usually develop in late May through early June. Considered the most easily recognized because of floral parts in 4's, rather than 5's in all other species. Native to southeastern Europe. Cultivated 1853. Zone 4 to 8.

Taxodium ascendens Brongn. — Pondcypress (Deciduous), also called Pond Baldcypress
(taks-ō'di-um ȧ-sen'denz)

FAMILY: Taxodiaceae
IDENTIFICATION CHARACTERISTICS: Similar to *T. distichum* except bark is light brown and deeply furrowed; deciduous branchlets erect; leaves appressed or incurved, awl-shaped, 3/8" long, bright green, rich brown in autumn.

SIZE: 70 to 80' in height, probably 15 to 20' wide; national champion is 135' by 79' in Newton, GA.
HARDINESS: Zone (4)5 to 9(10 and 11).
HABIT: Narrowly conical or columnar with spreading branches and erect branchlets; a deciduous conifer.
RATE: Slow to medium (18' in 20 years); sufficient evidence to indicate that with ample moisture and fertility, 2' of growth per year in the early years is possible.
TEXTURE: Fine in foliage; medium in winter.
LEAF COLOR: Bright green changing to rich brown (orangish brown) in autumn; late leafing, as late as late May–early June in the Midwest; fall color has also been described as fox red.
FLOWERS: Monoecious; male flowers ovoid, forming terminal and drooping panicles; female flowers scattered near the ends of branches of the previous year, sub-globose; male flowers appear as slender, pendulous catkins (4 to 5", branched, spikose panicle), often more prevalent in the upper reaches of the tree, March–April.
FRUIT: Cones short-stalked, globose or ovoid, 1/2 to 1 1/4" across, purplish and resinous when young, ripening the first year and turning brown.
CULTURE: Nurserymen mentioned that the tap root makes this and *T. distichum* difficult to transplant; however, suspect root pruning at an early age would alleviate the problem; have seen far too many successfully transplanted specimens; adaptable, prefers moist, acid soils; performs well on upland soils; full sun and open areas, extremely wind firm; have used this and the species in great quantities in my consulting work and have never lost a tree.
DISEASES AND INSECTS: Mites and gall, more problematic on *T. distichum*.
LANDSCAPE VALUE: Specimen for parks, large areas, wet and dry places; I used to look at this species as totally secondary to *T. distichum* but have questioned my conventional wisdom in recent years; have seen groves, groupings, isolated specimens and leave with strong positive impressions; tree is decidedly columnar compared to *T. distichum* with scaffold (secondary branches originating at right angles to central leader); also have not noticed the gall on this species which is so common on *T. distichum*.
CULTIVARS:
 'Nutans'—Branches short, horizontal, some ascending parallel with the trunk; branchlets crowded, closely set, more or less pendulous.
 'Prairie Sentinel'—An Earl Cully, Jacksonville, IL introduction; very tall in relation to width, 60' tall and 10' wide with very soft, fine-textured foliage; does well on upland soil and on very moist sites; Mr. Cully mentioned that the selection was not particularly cold hardy, but it has withstood -24°F at Bernheim Arboretum; Mr. Buddy Hubbuch, retired Horticulturist, Bernheim, planted this, 'Shawnee Brave' and 'Monarch of Illinois' in a large planting by the entrance side of the lake; I have observed it in winter, summer and fall . . . truly beautiful beyond words.
PROPAGATION: *Taxodium* seeds exhibit an apparent internal dormancy which can be overcome by 90 days of cold stratification; softwood cuttings have been rooted but success is variable and, doubtfully, commercially viable; hardwood cuttings have been used in England; grafting is the most reliable method for reproducing the cultivars, with bench grafting using 2- to 3-year-old seedlings, whip-and-tongue graft, and allow to heal at 55 to 60°F; see *The Plant Propagator* 9(1):11 (1962) and *Proc. Intl. Plant Prop. Soc.* 17:376 (1967).
ADDITIONAL NOTES: This species is now listed as a variety by several authors under the name *nutans* (Ait.) Sweet. I have treated it as a species, however, this may not be the case although everyone does not agree on the classification. The "knees" supposedly do not form to the degree they do on *T. distichum*.
NATIVE HABITAT: Virginia to Florida and Louisiana, on more upland areas, i.e., around ponds rather than in them, although the two species occur in mixed company. Cultivated 1789.

Taxodium distichum (L.) Rich. — Common Baldcypress (Deciduous)
(taks-ō′di-um dis′ti-kum)

LEAVES: Spirally arranged on the branchlets, 2-ranked on the deciduous shoots (branchlets), linear-lanceolate, apiculate, 1/3 to 3/4″ long, 1/16 to 1/12″ wide, bright yellow-green in spring, soft sage green in summer, rich orange to pumpkin brown in autumn.

BUDS: Alternate, near tip of stem rounded, with overlapping, sharp-pointed scales; smaller lateral buds also present, and from them leafy, budless branches (branchlets) arise which fall in autumn.

STEM: Of two kinds: later branchlets green, deciduous; young  branchlets green, becoming brown the first winter.

SIZE: 50 to 70′ high by 20 to 30′ wide, can grow to 100′ and more; national champion is 83′ by 85′ in Cat Island, LA, over 60′ high tree in Morton Arboretum.

HARDINESS: Zone 4 to 11; Baldcypress has been planted far north of its natural range; there are specimens in Minnesota, southern Canada and a few 75-year-old trees in Syracuse, NY; some of these trees have withstood temperatures of -20 to -30°F; Cappiello reported outright kill in Orono, ME.

HABIT: A lofty, deciduous conifer of slender, pyramidal habit, almost columnar in youth, with a stout, straight trunk buttressed at the base and short, horizontal branches, ascending at the ends, the lateral branchlets pendulous; sometimes becoming irregular, flat-topped and picturesque in old age.

RATE: Medium, 50 to 70′ high in 30 to 50 years; amazing growth rate in Wichita, KS tests where it averaged 2′7.4″ per year over a 9 year period.

TEXTURE: Medium-fine in leaf, medium in winter.

BARK: Rather attractive reddish brown, fibrous bark; the trunk becoming strongly buttressed especially in wet areas; I have observed specimens in the Coastal Plain of Georgia growing in wet areas that were magnificent; there is something hauntingly beautiful about a "grove" of Baldcypress; it should be mentioned that the "cypress knees" occur only near water or in exceedingly moist soils; I have not seen them on trees planted under normal conditions in cultivation; it has been shown that the "knees" are not necessary for gaseous exchange.

LEAF COLOR: Bright yellow-green in spring; it darkens in summer to a soft sage green; in autumn it becomes a russet, soft brown to a mellow orangish brown.

FLOWERS: Monoecious, staminate in drooping, 4 to 5″ long panicles; March–April; pistillate cones are subglobose, comprising several spirally arranged peltate scales, each bearing 2 erect, basal ovules.

FRUIT: Cones globular or obovoid, short-stalked, approximately 1/2 to 1″(1 1/2″) across, green to purple and resinous when young; brown at maturity, mature in one year; seed triangular, to 1/2″ long.

CULTURE: Transplants readily balled-and-burlapped as a small, root-pruned, nursery-grown plant; see comment under *T. ascendens*; makes it best growth on deep, fine, sandy loams with plenty of moisture in the surface layers and moderately good drainage; in the wild it is seldom found on such places and occurs primarily in permanent swamps where it forms pure stands; very adaptable tree to wet, dry and well-drained soil conditions; requires a sunny location; soils should be acid for chlorosis will occur on high pH soils; several trees on the Illinois campus were almost golden yellow and when treated with a trunk injection of ferric ammonium citrate they greened up within a month, however, treatments often have to be repeated; exceptionally wind firm and even winds of hurricane force rarely overturn them.

DISEASES AND INSECTS: Twig blight, small annual cankers caused by *Seiridium* were reported on landscape plants in Kansas, see *Plant Disease* 75(2):138–140 (1991), wood decay, cypress moth, fruit tree leafroller (*Archips argyrospilus*) reached outbreak densities in Louisiana, gypsy moth larvae feeding was reported in Maryland, spider mites, and a gall forming mite.

LANDSCAPE VALUE: A stately tree, a decided accent of texture and form; in parks or large estates it makes a distinctive specimen; good for wet areas; possibly a worthwhile highway plant or street tree; have seen used in groupings and groves around lakes and the effect is spectacular; interestingly the knees form in the shallow water at lake's edge and seldom on the land side; have planted extensively at the Milliken Arboretum, Spartanburg, SC in the water, on the shore and on upland sites, all have prospered; over a 13 year period, *T. distichum* was one of the most highly rated trees (out of 200) in the Auburn University test, see *J. Arboriculture* 21(3):118–121 (1995) for specifics; also, Nash and Graves, *J. Amer. Soc. Hort. Science* 118(6):845–850 (1993), showed *T. distichum* one of the most photosynthetically active species during flooding.

CULTIVARS:

'Apache Chief'—Wider, beautiful, from Klehm Nursery, Illinois.

'Fastigiata'—Columnar form, supposedly more fastigiate than the species, listed by Stanley & Sons Nursery, Boring, OR.

'Monarch of Illinois'—Truly a handsome specimen; wide-spreading, the parent tree has a limb spread of 65′ and a height of 85′; this type of growth habit is unusual for this species; my observations indicate this form is not as desirable as 'Shawnee Brave' because of squattier growth and greater mite susceptibility.

'Pendens'—Pyramidal form, branches nearly horizontal, nodding at the tips, branchlets drooping; have seen photos of this clone and the form represented was broad pyramidal with distinct semi-arching branches; available from Arborvillage, Holt, MO.

'Secrest'—A "witches' broom" of the species; discovered in the Secrest Arboretum, Wooster, OH; has golden fall color; grows 3 to 6″ a year.

'Shawnee Brave'—Form with narrow pyramidal habit; parent tree is 75′ tall and 18′ across; has street tree and single specimen possibilities; have seen 20′ high trees in Spring Grove that were beautiful; foliage deep sage green and mite resistant; an Earl Cully introduction.

PROPAGATION: As previously discussed under *T. ascendens*. I have rooted cuttings with 30 to 40% success using very soft growth, 1000 ppm IBA, peat:perlite, mist. Solid case for juvenility in *New Forests* 8(4):381–386 (1994) where cuttings of 1- or 25- to 50-year-old trees were untreated or treated with 1000 ppm IBA. Rooting was 75% for IBA-treated 1-year-old trees; 12% for 25- to 50-year-old trees. *Tree Planters Notes* 44(3):125–127 (1993) reported 58% rooting of 23-year-old clones.

ADDITIONAL NOTES: Several years past, I journeyed to Germany and visited gardens and parks with the denominator being *Taxodium distichum* in common use. Many trees were easily 50 to 60′ high and a match for plants in the wild. The Germans are great at reproducing habitat gardens and *T. distichum* was used with other plants of wet soil or geographical affinity. In fact, as I write this, the wonderful Planten und Blumen in Hamburg comes to mind with a tremendous number of *T. distichum* reflecting a southeastern habitat.

Interestingly, the plant is usually columnar to pyramidal without great variation but I have seen trees with broad-spreading canopies. Note the dimensions of the national champion. Many years past I walked the Kansas State University campus with Dr. Steve Still and could not reconcile the broad-spreading habit. Also, this is often the common habit in swamps along I-95 through coastal Georgia, the plants often draped with Spanish moss. Amazing plants in San Antonio, TX along the River Walk, some 100′ high. Common in Houston, TX and obviously growing with abandon.

NATIVE HABITAT: Delaware to Florida, west to southern Indiana, Illinois, Missouri, Arkansas, Louisiana, and Texas. Introduced 1640.

RELATED SPECIES:

Taxodium mucronatum Ten., (taks-ō′di-um mū-krō-nā′tum), Mexican Baldcypress, occasionally surfaces in southeastern gardens but is definitely inferior to the previous species. I have observed cold damage on the specimen at Raleigh, NC and suspect it does not shut down early in fall and/or initiates cambial activity too early in spring and is injured by late fall or early spring freezes, respectively. Technically evergreen to semi-evergreen, deciduous in Raleigh. Appears wider spreading at an early age, i.e., more bushy. National champion is 85′ by 87′ in San Benito, Cameron County, TX. Recent article in *Arnoldia* 57(4):2–11 (1998) discusses "The Ancient Giant of Oaxaca," the tree some 130′ high with 200′ trunk circumference. Mexico. Zone 8 to 10.

Taxus L. — Yew
FAMILY: Taxaceae

Taxus includes the highest quality needle type evergreens in landscape use. The quality characteristics include slow to medium growth rate, resistance to insects and diseases, excellent year-round color, wide variations in form, compact growth habit, winter hardiness, and ease of propagation. *Taxus canadensis* Marsh., *T. floridana* Chapm., and *T. brevifolia* Nutt. are native to this country, however, the important ornamental cultivars are found in the species *T. cuspidata* and *T.* × *media* with a few excellent types in the species *T. baccata*. Many of the *T. baccata* types are tender and may be damaged or discolor during winter in the Midwest. In addition to the factors mentioned above, the colorful red seed is an effective ornamental feature on some cultivars. Literature has it that Robin Hood made his bows from the yew tree.

Unfortunately, the nomenclature of *Taxus* is as confused as any genus. This has come about because of the lack of distinguishing features between cultivars, and the indiscriminate naming of cultivars by numerous plantsmen. This problem is particularly serious in the *T. cuspidata* and *T.* × *media* types, whereas the naming of *T. baccata* types, which have been under cultivation for hundreds of years, is less confused. A collection of

Taxus was begun at the Ohio Agricultural Research and Development Center in Wooster in 1942. This collection, containing over 100 cultivars, is the largest in the world and is intended to serve as a base for selecting outstanding forms which, after positive identification, are being disseminated throughout the world.

The various taxonomic treatments list 3 to 10 species worldwide and hint at the ambiguity in separating them into discrete phenotypic (and genetic) entities. Over the past 8 years, I have, along with my former graduate student, now Dr. Donglin Zhang, accumulated *T. chinensis* (Pilger) Rehd., Chinese Yew; *T. floridana* Chapm., Florida Yew; *T. globosa* Schldl., Mexican Yew; *T. mairei* (Lemée & Lév.) Hu ex Liu; and *T. sumatrana* (Miq.) Laub. with the hope of unearthing a heat tolerant species. Dr. Raulston showed that *T. chinensis* was well-adapted in Raleigh and this is also true in Athens. Small plants in the Morton Arboretum have been severely browsed by deer.

One of the looming problems for *Taxus* in the contemporary landscape is DEER susceptibility. My travels through the Midwest and East have provided endless evidence for the seriousness of deer browsing. Morton Arboretum noted that deer browse to the point of killing the plants with no harm to the deer. The Horticultural Research Institute has awarded significant money to the University of Rhode Island to develop methods to reduce deer feeding on landscape plants. See discussion under *Taxus baccata* ADDITIONAL NOTES.

MORPHOLOGICAL CHARACTERISTICS

Evergreen trees and shrubs with reddish to brown bark and spreading and ascending branches. Branchlets are green. Leaves are glossy or dull dark green above, lighter green below, flat and needle-like, abruptly pointed or tapering and acute. *Taxus baccata* types usually have sickle-shaped leaves. Leaves are arranged radially or in a flat plane. Winter buds are small and scaly. With rare exceptions, plants are dioecious with the *male flowers globose* and the *female flowers appearing as small stalked conical buds*. The seeds are brown and nut-like, covered by an attractive fleshy, red aril, ripening the first year; cotyledons 2. If one is interested in securing "fruiting" plants, the morphological differences italicized above are worth remembering.

GROWTH CHARACTERISTICS

Wide variation in habit, size, growth rate, and textural effects occurs. Practically all cultivars are compact and retain a dense character with age without extensive pruning. In addition to overall form, line and textural effects vary because of differences in branching habit and degree of compactness. Foliage color is essentially dark green with some variations to lighter greens and a few cultivars with yellow foliage. *Taxus* retain high quality characteristics indefinitely and, under good conditions, will continue to increase in value with age.

CULTURE

Taxus are most effectively moved balled-and-burlapped and can be planted in spring or fall with good success. Some growers are producing container yews and this represents an alternate choice to balled-and-burlapped specimens. However, most yews are field-grown, then dug and placed in containers for ease of handling during the marketing process. Yews require a fertile soil, sufficient moisture, and *excellent* drainage. Anything less than *excellent* drainage results in growth reductions or death of yews. Yews do equally well in sun or shade but should be kept out of sweeping winds. Often, in winter, the needles will brown or yellow because of desiccation. All, except some of the *T. baccata* cultivars, are reliably hardy in the Midwest and Northeast. Very few yews are used in Minnesota and areas with similar low temperatures. Conversely, yews are seldom used in the southern states for they do not tolerate the extreme heat. Several garden designers have reported success in the Atlanta area but for large scale corporate landscapes, the plant should not be used. One species, *Taxus floridana* Chapm., Florida Yew, occurs in a narrow area along the Apalachicola River in northwestern Florida. It becomes almost tree-like and may grow 20 to 24′ high. The national champion is 20′ by 26′ in Torreya State Park, FL. There is a fine specimen at the Biltmore Estate, Asheville, NC and the Atlanta Botanical Garden.

Many of the cultivars are naturally compact and symmetrical and relatively little corrective pruning is necessary. *Taxus* can be pruned severely and it is possible to maintain plants at determined sizes and shapes by frequent pruning or shearing. This is particularly advantageous in the culture of formal *Taxus* hedges or screens where early spring pruning followed by removal of "feather growth" in the summer will maintain the desired form. Although it is common practice to shear *Taxus* into tight, formally shaped plants, more interesting and attractive plants will result from pruning rather than shearing to retain the natural habit and appearance of the cultivar. The tight pruning results in the formation of green meatballs, cubes, rectangles, and other odd shapes. Overgrown plants have been pruned 12 to 24″ from ground and developed new shoots and filled in quite well. Plants have been pruned for over 1000 years.

DISEASES AND INSECTS

Needle blight, twig blight, *Phytophthora* root rot, other fungus diseases, twig browning, black vine weevil, strawberry root weevil, taxus mealybug, grape mealybug, scales, ants, termites, nematodes, and yew big bud mite on *T. brevifolia*.

PROPAGATION

Although *Taxus cuspidata* 'Capitata' is usually propagated from seed, all other cultivars are propagated by cuttings taken in the late summer through winter and rooted in cold frames and greenhouses. Specific recommendations are listed under *T. canadensis*. Many great recipes in *Proc. Intl. Plant Prop. Soc.* See Dirr and Heuser (1987) for detailed synopsis. With interest in Taxol production, tissue culture has entered the fray and *HortScience* 29(6):695–697 (1994) reported on success with in vitro culture of embryos of *Taxus* species.

LANDSCAPE VALUE

Probably the only negative comment one can apply to yews is that they are overused. Their ubiquitous landscape uses make them a favorite choice of designers. They appear, almost to the point of monotony, in hedges, foundations, groupings, broad masses, and as facer plants.

The moderate growth rate, uniform habit, high quality appearance, and maintenance-free aspect result in *Taxus* being classed as the best shrubby, needle type evergreen for landscape use. However, it should be emphasized that *T. baccata*, *T. cuspidata*, and *T. × media* can grow 40 to 50′ in height. Proper pruning does wonders to keep the plants in bounds.

Taxus baccata L. — English Yew (Common Yew)
(taks′us ba-kā′tà)

LEAVES: Spirally arranged, spreading all around in erect shoots but appearing more or less 2-ranked on horizontal shoots or on plants grown in shade, linear, 1/2 to 1 1/4″ long, 1/16 to 1/4″ wide, convex and shining dark, almost black-green on the upper surface, with recurved margins and a prominent midrib, paler and yellowish green beneath with ill-defined lines of stomata, gradually tapering at the apex to a horny point.

STEM: Branchlets surrounded at the base by brownish scales, greenish.

SIZE: 30 to 60′ high by 15 to 25′ spread; usually smaller; tremendous number of clones all varying in size and shape; large plants up to 85′ high and 8 1/4′ in girth have been recorded.

HARDINESS: Zone (5)6 to 7; hardiness dependant on genotype with 'Repandens' one of the hardiest.

HABIT: Tree or shrub-like, wide-spreading and densely branched; broad-rounded, or shrubby; indescribably beautiful in the best forms with a dense, dark, somber pyramidal outline and often a massive, fluted, rich reddish brown trunk; I have seen nothing in the States to match the splendid old trees in England; often church yards house the most magnificent specimens; the many cultivars offer a multitude of shapes from wide-spreading to distinctly columnar; wonderful collection at Bedgebury Pinetum, Kent.

RATE: Slow.

TEXTURE: Medium.

BARK: Reddish brown, furrowed, thin, scaly, flaky; often fluted on old trunks.

LEAF COLOR: Dark green and lustrous above.

FLOWERS: Usually dioecious, male strobili stalked, globose, arising from the axils of the leaves on the undersides of the branchlets of the previous year, each consisting of 6 to 14 stamens with short filaments; female strobili solitary, green, from the leaf axils, usually opening in March–April.

FRUIT: Seeds solitary, bi-, seldom tri-, or quadrangular, slightly compressed, 1/4″ long, 1/5″ broad, olive-brown; aril roundish, red.

CULTURE: Does well on calcareous soils as well as acid soils; prefers a moist, well-drained, sandy loam; see under culture in the introductory remarks.

DISEASES AND INSECTS: *Taxus* mealybug, black vine weevil, *Taxus* scale, yew-gall midge.

LANDSCAPE VALUE: Useful in gardens and parks, in shade, for undergrowth, hedges, screens and foundation plantings; used extensively for topiary work in England; not outstandingly hardy in Zone 5 and inferior to *T. × media* and *T. cuspidata* types for that reason.

CULTIVARS: Den Ouden and Boom list over 100 cultivars of this species. Apparently cultivated in England for over 1000 years and numerous selections have been made. The following might be considered among the best.

'Adpressa'—Wide-spreading, dense habit; dark green needles only 1/4 to 1/2″ long, 1/10″ wide, abruptly pointed at apex; will make a large shrub or small tree; plants as large as 30′ high are known; female; several 'Adpressa' variations are known including: 'Aurea', 'Erecta', 'Pyramidalis', and 'Variegata'.

'Adpressa Fowle' (Midget Boxleaf English Yew)—Handsome, compact form rather stiffly branched but clothed with short, heavy-textured, lustrous black green needles; grows slowly; introduced by Weston Nurseries, Hopkinton, MA; original plant 7 1/2′ high and 16′ wide.

'Aurea' (f. *aurea*)—Apparently several different yellow-foliaged types are included here; the few I have seen are golden in the new growth which eventually fades to green.

'Cheshuntensis'—Narrow columnar with small blue-green needles; faster and hardier than the Irish Yew; female; listed in 1988 Weston Nurseries catalog, not in 1989; raised from seed of 'Fastigiata' by R. Paul, Chestnut, England about 1857.

'Dovastoniana'—Tree form (may be shrub-like), usually short-trunked, widely spreading branches, pendulous branchlets, blackish green needles; apparently becomes immense with age for the original plant measured in 1929 was 56' wide and 12' in trunk circumference; a male but on occasion a branch produces seeds, have seen reference to this as a female; handsome specimen at Edinburgh Botanic Garden.

'Fastigiata' (Irish Yew)—This is one of the most fascinating of all yews and certainly one of the most common especially in European countries; it is fastigiate with all branches rigidly upright; needles blackish green above, streaked with dull green and a narrow shining midrib beneath; generally 15 to 30' high, 4 to 8' wide; have seen it used at Filoli Gardens, California where it is a fine biological accent to the formal architecture of the house; it is a female but male flowers may occur on isolated branches; several cultivars have been raised from seed of this form; 'Fastigiata' occurred (was discovered) sometime around 1780 in Ireland.

'Fastigiata Aurea'—Similar in habit but with golden foliage on the young shoots of the season; several selections have been made.

'Fructuluteo'—Arils are orange-red, otherwise similar to the species; first noted about 1817.

'Nana'—Dwarf form not exceeding 3'; pyramidal; needles smaller and darker green than species.

'Pygmaea'—Dwarf form to 15" high, wide, dense habit; needles less than 1/2" long, radially arranged.

'Repandens'—Dwarf, wide-spreading form with the tips of the branches pendulous; sickle-shaped needles shining dark green above, dull green below; probably the hardiest form of English Yew (Zone 5); widely used in the United States with some of the finest plants located at Longwood Gardens; may grow 2 to 4'(6') high and 12 to 15' across; I have seen plants considerably larger than this; excellent landscape plant; known before 1887; female.

'Standishii'—Somewhat similar to Irish Yew but slower growing and smaller in size; needles yellow, crowded; considered the best golden yew for small gardens; female.

'Summergold'—Foliage predominantly golden in summer, even in sun; semi-prostrate habit; raised from seed in Holland; looks like a golden 'Repandens'.

'Washingtonii'—Open, loose form; branchlets yellowish green, leaves tinted a rich gold, finally yellow-green; female; wide-spreading form, 5 to 6' high.

PROPAGATION: Most clonal selections of yews are propagated by cuttings, which root easily. Seedling propagation is little used, owing to the variation appearing in the progeny, the complicated seed dormancy conditions, and the slow growth of the seedlings. Polish work showed that seeds collected between August 20 to September 10, aril removed, stored at 41 to 47°F for an entire season germinated the best. Side or side-veneer grafting is practiced for those few cultivars which are especially difficult to start by cuttings.

ADDITIONAL NOTES: Yews are among the most toxic of plants. They appear to be poisonous all seasons of the year. The toxic principal is taxine. Foliage, bark, or seeds, whether dry or green, are toxic to people and to all classes of livestock. The fleshy red arils are not poisonous as the toxic principal is contained in the hard part of the seed. This is not digested and is passed so no harm is done. I had a veterinarian in one of my off-campus courses and while discussing yews he mentioned he had seen cows who had died from eating yew foliage and the amount removed from their stomach was very small in relation to their total body weight.

Yew has received notoriety in recent years as a source of taxol, a chemical used to treat ovarian cancer. Initially, the bark of the West Coast species, *T. brevifolia* Nutt., Pacific Yew, was utilized as the source. *American Forests* 102(3):28 (1996) discusses Pacific Yew and its emergence as a poster child for the conservation of biodiversity. The message is that every plant, no matter how seemingly insignificant, may hold the cure for one of the world's significant diseases. The national champion *T. brevifolia* is 54' high and 30' wide in Lewes County, WA. Foliage also produces the chemical and there is variation in concentration among cultivars with 'Nigra' and 'Hicksii' among the highest. See *J. Environ. Hort.* 10(4):187–191 (1992) for concentrations of taxol from the leaves of 14 *Taxus* taxa. I know one nurseryman, Bruce Vanicek, Rhode Island Nurseries, Inc., who is working with pharmaceutical companies to produce sufficient plants.

Yew is among the most ancient of trees with estimates of Scottish and English specimens in the 3000- to possibly greater than 4000-year-old range. A 4000-year-old tree was discovered in a churchyard in Llangernyw, Wales. The tree's circumference is 47'. At Dundonnell, Scotland in the garden of the late Mr. Alan Rogers, I experienced a plus 3000-year-old *T. baccata*. Our garden tour group huddled under its magnificent canopy on that bright sunny day in the West Highlands. For a brief moment one could imagine the gathering of the clans, the wailing of the bag pipes, and the call to battle. Actually sounds like a typical tour, only the call was, "Load the coach!"

Good article in *J. Arnold Arboretum* 71:69–91 (1990) that treats the genera of Taxaceae in the southeastern United States. *Torreya taxifolia*, *Taxus canadensis*, and *T. floridana* are discussed.

NATIVE HABITAT: Europe, northern Africa, western Asia. Cultivated since ancient times.

Taxus canadensis Marsh. — Canadian Yew
(taks′us kan-à-den′sis)

LEAVES: Densely set, in 2 ranks, 1/2 to 3/4″ long, 1/16 to 1/12″ wide, apex abruptly short-pointed, with a slightly raised midrib above and below, glossy dark green above, paler green beneath, needles with 2 blue-green stomatal bands below, assuming a reddish tint in winter, short-stalked.

SIZE: 3 to 6′ high by 6 to 8′ broad, often twice as wide as high at maturity.

HARDINESS: Zone 2 to 6.

HABIT: Often prostrate, loose, straggling; leaders prostrate and rooting in the ground; very straggly shrub compared to other yew types.

RATE: Slow.

TEXTURE: Medium.

LEAF COLOR: Glossy dark green assuming a reddish tint in winter, almost reddish brown not unlike the worst Andorra juniper color.

FLOWERS: Self fertility occurs in this species; also monoecious, as bagging studies showed both male and female stobiles present with 99% of male on current growth, greater than 33% of female on two year or older, see *Bulletin Torrey Botanical Club* 120(2):115–120 (1993); also, additional discussion of monoecy in same journal 123(1):7–15 (1996).

FRUIT: Seeds broader than high; aril light red.

CULTURE: Transplant balled-and-burlapped; moist, sandy loam; will not tolerate heat and drought; requires winter shade.

DISEASES AND INSECTS: None serious.

LANDSCAPE VALUE: Suitable as a ground cover but only for underplanting in cool, shaded situations; the hardiest of the yews; probably the least desirable of the yews for landscape purposes.

CULTIVARS:

'Stricta' ('Pyramidalis')—Branches stiffly upright yet the plant is wider than high at maturity; bronze-red-purple in winter.

PROPAGATION: Yew seeds are slow to germinate, natural germination not taking place until the second year. Seeds have a strong but variable dormancy that can be broken by warm plus cold stratification. One recommendation is to hold the seeds for 90 to 120 days at 60°F followed by 60 to 120 days at 36 to 41°F. Another recommendation specifies prechilling the seed for 270 days at 36 to 41°F. Vrablic and Shugert, *Proc. Intl. Plant Prop. Soc.* 43:467–468 (1993) discusses sexual propagation (seed) of *T. c.* 'Capitata'. Their summary reads as follows:

- seed shipped direct from Japan.
- seed stratified for 12 months in sand, outside.
- seed sown, ground beds, in poly houses covered from November to May, saran covered June to October, held for 3 years (3-0).
- seedlings transplanted for 3 years (3-3).
- transplants to the field for 4 to 7 years (10 to 13 years from seed).
- no top pruning as a seedling or transplant, field-grown plants pruned by hand annually during the first 2 weeks of August.

Most yews root readily from cuttings and the recommended practice is to procure wood from October through January. The cuttings are treated with a hormone dip or powder (IBA, 5000 to 10,000 ppm talc or quick dip) and placed in sand or sand:peat. Misting is used although I have placed flats of yew cuttings under the bench, watering them only when other plants needed water and had excellent success. Rooting time is rather long and 2 to 3 months would probably represent an average time span from sticking to rooting.

NATIVE HABITAT: Newfoundland to Virginia, Tennessee, Iowa and Manitoba. Introduced 1800. I have found it growing out of sandstone cliffs in deep shade in Turkey Run State Park, Marshall, Indiana. In the Midwest, this is probably its southernmost location.

Taxus cuspidata Sieb. & Zucc. — Japanese Yew
(taks′us kus-pi-dā′tà)

LEAVES: Short-stalked, mostly not distinctly 2-ranked, upright and irregularly V-shaped, straight or slightly curved, slightly leathery, apex rather abruptly sharp-pointed, 1/2 to 1″ long, 1/12 to 1/8″ wide, dull to dark lustrous green above, paler beneath with 2 yellowish green bands.

BUDS: Ovoid-oblong, chestnut brown, composed of overlapping, concave, ovate scales more or less keeled on the back.

SEEDS: Ovoid, about 1/3″ long, hard, aril red.

SIZE: 10 to 40′ with an equal or greater spread; usually smaller depending on cultivar; see cultivar list for specifics; in native haunts it may grow 40 to 50′ high.

HARDINESS: Zone 4 to 7; the hardiest and most adaptable species for the upper Midwest.

HABIT: Crown erect or flattened, broad or narrow, of irregular habit and spreading or upright-spreading branches; can be grown as a tree or multi-stemmed shrub.

RATE: Slow.

TEXTURE: Medium.

BARK: On old tree-like specimens is a handsome reddish brown, exfoliating in scales or longer strips.

LEAF COLOR: Dark lustrous green above, yellowish green beneath.

FLOWERS: Dioecious, see *T. baccata* for description.

FRUIT: Seeds ovoid, about 1/3″ long by 1/6″ broad, compressed, aril red.

CULTURE: Transplants well balled-and-burlapped; the roots of the yews are rather thick but abundant and a large mass of roots is normally present around the base of young plants which allows for successful transplanting; prefers a moist, sandy loam although adaptable, must be well-drained; shade or sun; superior to other conifers in shade; sun and wind may cause needles to turn yellowish brown; furthermore, it endures the dust and smoke of city atmospheres surprisingly well and withstands any amount of pruning.

DISEASES AND INSECTS: None serious.

LANDSCAPE VALUE: Excellent for many purposes: foundation plantings, hedges, topiary, screens, bonsai, masses, groupings, bank covers.

CULTIVARS:

‘Aurescens’—Low, compact, slow-growing form, 1′ by 3′; leaves of the current year’s growth deep yellow, after first season changing gradually to green; male.

‘Capitata’—Usually a pyramidal form, can be maintained in a tightly pruned form, however, will grow 40 to 50′; a common form in cultivation and certainly a functional landscape plant.

Captain™—Uniform, fast-growing; clone of ‘Capitata’ with improved winter foliage color.

‘Cross Spreading’—A form selected by Cross Nurseries, Lakeville, MN that is highly resistant to winter burn; grows 3 to 4′ high and 8 to 10′ wide.

‘Dark Green Spreader’—Compact habit, spreading, 4 to 5′ high; dark green needles; supposedly hardier and with less foliage discoloration in winter.

‘Densa’—Low shrub form, two times as broad as tall with extremely dark green leaves; 40-year-old specimen is 4′ by 8′; female; one of the best dwarf forms.

Emerald Spreader™ (‘Monloo’)—Low, flat-topped, wide-spreading habit, 30″ by 10′ in 20 years; lustrous dark green needles; some red-ariled seeds are produced; considered hardier than *Taxus baccata* ‘Repandens’, to Zone 4.

‘Expansa’—According to Wyman a name applied to many *Taxus cuspidata* seedlings with a vase-shaped habit; this form has an open center, loose foliage and branches at a 45 to 60° angle from the base; about 1 1/2 to 2 times as broad as high; male and female clones available.

‘F. & F. Compacta’—Rounded spreader, 4′ by 8 to 9′; offered by Angelica Nurseries, Kennedyville, MD.

‘Intermedia’—Dwarf, round, compact, slow-growing form; leaves densely set; resembles ‘Nana’ with the same heavy, plump, dark green leaves; starts growth earlier in the season and grows faster.

‘Jeffrey’s Pyramidal’—Heavy fruiting, pyramidal form.

‘Nana’—Slow-growing form with spreading branches; needles radially arranged; twice as wide as high; forty-year-old plant is 10 to 20′ high; excellent fruiting form; in Minnesota has shown some resistance to winter burn.

‘Pyramidalis’—Pyramidal form with dark green leaves; introduced by Hill’s, Dundee, IL.

‘Thayerae’—Slow-growing, wide-spreading form (8′ high, twice as wide) with branches at a 30° angle with ground and forming a flat-topped head, centers are full; some consider this a *T. × media* type; raised in Massachusetts around 1916–1917.

‘Winston Peters’—Lower, broader, faster growing than ‘Densiformis’ with lighter shiny green needles; supposedly with excellent root system and quite easy to transplant.

PROPAGATION: Cuttings of most clones will root readily. *Taxus cuspidata* var. *capitata* is often grown from seed as it comes fairly true-to-type. Cuttings from *capitata* should be collected from vertical terminal growth as laterally spreading cuttings will develop into spreading types.

ADDITIONAL NOTES: The new growth on *Taxus* is a lovely soft yellow-green which develops in May and is effective for about one month. The emphasis on well-drained soil cannot be stressed enough. *Taxus* does not tolerate "wet feet" for any period of time. Even if they do not die the growth is often reduced. About the best advice is to plant high if the soil is hopelessly wet and use raised beds. Pruning can be accomplished about any time but early in the growing season is often recommended. Hard, close pruning is not recommended as this results in the formation of a shell of foliage and a very formal appearance. The best way is to hand prune removing the longest growth every other year and thus creating an "unpruned" effect.

NATIVE HABITAT: Japan, Korea, Manchuria. Introduced 1853.

Taxus × media Rehd. (*T. cuspidata* × *T. baccata*) — Anglojap Yew
(taks′us mē′di-à)

Similar to *T. cuspidata* in many respects, however, differing in olive color of the branchlets which do not change to brown the second year, the blunt bud scales and the distinct two-ranked leaves.

SIZE: Variable, 2 to 3′ high to 20′ high; every cultivar is different.

HARDINESS: Zone 4 to 7.

HABIT: Broad-pyramidal, medium-sized tree to large shrub, of spreading habit often with a central leader. Actually, it is very difficult to ascertain the exact habit and size of the Anglojap types since they are hybrids and the growth characters they exhibit are variable. I have seen the excellent *Taxus* collection at Wooster, OH, and it is here that growth differences are very evident. The plants have not been pruned and have developed naturally. It is extremely difficult to identify *Taxus* by needle characteristics and when they have been pruned into little squares, balls and hedges in the landscape, there is no hope. Often nurserymen sell *Taxus* "spreaders" which could be about anything.

RATE: Slow.

TEXTURE: Medium.

LEAF COLOR: Similar to *T. cuspidata*; dark green, often lustrous above, lighter green beneath.

FLOWERS: Dioecious, see under *T. baccata*.

FRUIT: Fleshy, red aril covers hard, brown seed.

CULTURE: Transplants well balled-and-burlapped; prefers a moist, sandy, acid to neutral loam; must be well-drained; shade or sun.

DISEASES AND INSECTS: See culture sheet.

LANDSCAPE VALUE: Depending on the cultivar, may be used for hedges, screens, foundations, and mass plantings.

CULTIVARS:

'Amherst'—Slow-growing, dense, compact form; 12-year-old specimen is 6′ by 9′; male.

'Andersonii'—Spreading type to 4 to 5′ high; deep green foliage; excellent winter color; considered Zone 4 hardy.

'Angelica'—A slow, low-growing form, 3 to 4′ by 6 to 8′; good dark green needles; considered extremely hardy.

'Anthony Wayne'—Wild columnar form with light green new shoots; relatively fast growing; female; landscape effect is similar to 'Hatfield' but growth is faster.

'Beanpole'—Narrow columnar form, dwarf; Vermeulen Nursery introduction.

'Berryhillii'—A female clone; dense growing spreading type, 20-year-old plant is 5′ by 9′; resembles *T. cuspidata* 'Nana'.

'Brownii'—Male clone with a densely rounded habit; foliage dark green; 9′ by 12′ after 15 to 20 years; easily pruned and can be maintained at any height; common form in Midwest; have seen it listed as female but have not observed fruit set.

'Chadwickii'—Low-growing, compact spreader with handsome lustrous dark green foliage that holds up well in winter; 2 to 4′ by 4 to 6′; named after Dr. L.C. Chadwick, one of my mentors at The Ohio State University.

'Citation'—Compact, bushy upright form not unlike an intermediate between 'Hatfieldii' and 'Hicksii'.

'Deerfield'—Broad mound; dark green foliage, does not discolor significantly in winter, leafs out later; supposedly increased heat tolerance and better root system.

'Densiformis'—Dense, shrub-like form, twice as wide as high; needles bright green, first year branchlets greenish brown in winter; 3 to 4' high, 4 to 6' wide; Angelica Nurseries lists this as a female clone.

'Densi-Gem'—Spreading form; faster growing than 'Densiformis' with a fluffy fuller appearance; 4 to 6' high.

'Everlow'—A dark green-needled, low-growing spreader; resistant to wind desiccation; may be a good substitute for *T. baccata* 'Repandens' in colder climates; 1 1/2'(3 to 4') by 4 to 5'.

'Flemer'—Good dark green needles, color holds well in winter; similar to 'Sebian' but with full center, more dense and compact; female form; 6' by 10' in 20 years.

'Flushing'—Slender, stately form with thickish, lustrous dark green needles and red seeds.

'Green Wave'—Dark green foliage and low mounded spreading habit with distinctive, graceful, arching branches; considered a good substitute for *T. baccata* 'Repandens'; 3 to 4' by 6 to 8'; offered by Angelica Nurseries.

'Halloran'—Broad, compact form; branches erect, sprays erect; leaves densely set, dark green; 6' by 6' in 20 years.

'Hatfieldii'—Dense, broad pyramidal form; leaves dark green; 20-year-old plant is 12' by 10'; an excellent clone; predominantly male; I witnessed a 30' high, 20' wide specimen on the grounds of Chateau Sur Mer, Newport, RI; apparently this cultivar was in common use when many of the Newport mansions were being constructed.

'Hicksii'—Male and female clones; columnar in habit; needles lustrous dark green above, lighter green beneath; similar to the Irish Yew but more hardy; 20' high after 15 to 20 years; raised at former Parsons Nursery, Flushing, NY; selected and introduced by Henry Hicks; fairly narrow in youth becoming fatter with age.

'Kelseyi'—Erect, dense, compact form taller than broad; free-fruiting female form; very dark green needles; 20-year-old plant is 12' by 9'.

'L. C. Bobbink'—Fine-textured, glossy dark green needles, color holds well in winter; globe- to mound-shaped; 6' high, 6 to 8' wide; female.

'Meadowbrook'—Columnar growth habit and fine needle texture; 4' by 18" in 10 years; found on an estate on Long Island, NY.

'Moon'—Upright-rounded habit; branches and shoots ascending; shiny dark green needles, densely arranged; 10 to 12' by 10 to 12'.

'Old Westbury'—Handsome form with deep green needle color; narrow upright column; branches tight and compact.

'Runyan'—Handsome spreading form with lustrous dark green needles; popular in Ohio, lower Midwest; from Spring Grove, Cincinnati.

'Sebian'—Straight dark green needles; intermediate compact spreading form with flat top; good winter hardiness (Zone 4); 6' by 12' in 20 years; male.

'Sentinalis'—Very narrow form; female; 10-year-old plant is 8' by 2'.

'Stoveken'—Excellent columnar form; male; 20-year-old specimen is 12' by 6'.

'Tauntonii' ('Taunton')—Spreading form about 3 to 4' high; most interesting because it is about the only *T. × media* type to show resistance to winter burn; on the other side of the ledger, it is the only *T. × media* type performing well in the heat of Zone 7b.

'Vermeulen'—Slow-growing, rounded type; female; 20-year-old plant is 8' by 9'.

'Viridis'—Slow-growing narrow columnar form; foliage lighter green than typical, new growth bright yellow-green, needles twisted; 10 to 12' by 1 to 2'.

'Wardii'—Wide-spreading, flat topped, dense form; foliage dark green; female; 20-year-old plant is 6' by 19', range is 5 to 8' by 15 to 20'.

PROPAGATION: Propagate vegetatively (cuttings) to maintain trueness-to-type.

ADDITIONAL NOTES: A hybrid species first raised by T.D. Hatfield of the Hunnewell Pinetum, Wellesley, MA about 1900. Since that time numerous selections have been made and often it is difficult to tell if one is looking at a *T. cuspidata*, *T. baccata*, or *T. × media* type. Unfortunately, nurserymen have confounded the issue by indiscriminately naming and introducing clones which they thought were better. When one sees a whole nursery block of a certain yew next to another block, specific differences are noticeable such as foliage color, needle density, and habit, however, once they have been massacred in the landscape by the hedge shears (worst landscape tool ever invented), there is no effective way to distinguish between and among different clones.

"A Study of the Genus *Taxus*" is available from the OARDC, Wooster, OH, as Research Bulletin 1086. The publication contains a wealth of information on the *Taxus* collection at Wooster, early history of yews, the development of the Hatfield yews, morphology, sex and fruiting characteristics, propagation, culture, and an extensive treatment of *Taxus* species, clones, and cultivars. Written by Drs. R.A. Keen and L.C. Chadwick it should prove invaluable for anyone interested in this most important group of landscape evergreens. Anyone interested in hardiness evaluations should consult *Nursery Notes* Vol. II (4). July–August (1978). The Ohio State University. Drs. Chadwick and Smith performed a genuine service by evaluating the extensive *Taxus* collection after the devastating winters of 1976–77, 77–78.

Ternstroemia gymnanthera Thunb. (usually sold as *Cleyera japonica*) — Japanese Ternstroemia, formerly Japanese Cleyera
(tẽrn-strō′mi-à jim-nan′thẽr-à)

FAMILY: Theaceae

LEAVES: Alternate, simple, evergreen, leathery, narrow-oblong to ovate-oblong, 2 1/2 to 4″ long, 1/2 to 1 1/2″ wide, bluntly pointed at the apex, narrowly wedged-shaped at the base, entire, glabrous, lustrous deep green above, paler beneath; petioles—about 3/4″ long, stout, red or reddish purple in color; leaves appear whorled at end of stem.

SIZE: 8 to 10′ high, 5 to 6′ wide; may grow 15 to 20′ high; can be maintained at a 4 to 6′ height indefinitely with proper pruning.

HARDINESS: Zones 7 to 9 and into 10; severely injured at -3°F; many old 10 to 15′ high plants on the Georgia campus were killed to the ground; Raulston reported the loss of two 25-year-old specimens after -6 to -8°F in January 1985.

HABIT: Distinctly upright-oval to oval-rounded, densely branched evergreen shrub; may be grown as a small tree but most plants I have seen were shrub-like; open-grown specimens are quite artistic.

RATE: Slow.

TEXTURE: Medium.

LEAF COLOR: Emerging leaves bronze to red, changing to lustrous dark (midnight) green at maturity, and may develop a rich reddish bronze color in winter; leaves tend to be clustered at the end of the branch resulting in a whorled or tufted appearance; considerable variation in new leaf color since plants are most often seed-grown.

FLOWERS: Perfect, 5-petaled, white to yellowish white, 1/2″ across, borne 1 to 3 together from the leaf axils on the previous year's wood, or on short spurs, pedicels reflexed, about 1/2″ long, petals fleshy, May–June.

FRUIT: Egg-shaped, 1/2″ diameter, 1″ long, green to red berry that ripens in September.

CULTURE: Container-grown and easily transplanted; prefers moist, well-drained soils; appears to do best in shade or partial shade on east or north side of structures; acceptable in full sun but is prone to greater winter leaf discoloration; responds well to pruning; a pruning study of container-grown plants showed that pruning in late February (Mississippi) produced superior plants; essentially intolerant of wet, poorly drained soils.

DISEASES AND INSECTS: None serious.

LANDSCAPE VALUE: Good accent plant, can be used for screens and hedges; foliage is attractive; best used in shady situations, although sun is acceptable; a group of these plants sited in full sun on the Georgia campus is yellow-green, purple-green, and green in the winter; the plant is grown from seed and variation results.

CULTIVARS: Abundant interest in superior selections since the demise of *Photinia* × *fraseri*; Greenleaf Nurseries, Tallequah, OK and Wight Nurseries, Cairo, GA have introduced new selections.

'Burgundy'—Selection that has burgundy new growth, fall and winter color; selected by Tom Dodd, Jr.

'Burnished Gold'—A yellow-gold-bronze foliage form that is bright yellow-gold, almost yellow-bronze, in spring and summer; the foliage color diminishing with the heat of summer; plant habit akin to species; good vigor; introduced by the J.C. Raulston Arboretum.

Copper Crown™ ('Grewad')—Possesses a full, self-branching, regular growth habit; burgundy new foliage in spring; burgundy color in new growth is present on any new growth occurring during cool weather; this uniform, self branching variety is an improvement over the irregular growth rate and forms of seedling populations.

'Dodd Littleleaf'—A diminutive leaf form, about 1/4 to 1/3 those of the species; upright habit to 6′; relatively dense in branching and foliage; appears to have terrific commercial potential, yet not well-known; a plant in the Dirr garden is quite content; introduced by Tom Dodd, Jr.; the story goes that Mr. Dodd took seed of *T. gymnanthera* to Emory University and had them irradiated, four seedlings exhibited dwarf characteristics, one with smaller light green leaves and a smattering of variegation was named 'Emory'.

Jade Tiara® ('Grevan')—An improved selection with compact, uniform growth and full, self-branching habit; leaves are smaller and branching is denser than typical; symmetrical mound of dense semi-glossy foliage.

'Grimes'—Variegated leaf form, introduced by Tom Dodd, Jr., Semmes, AL.

'Phyllis Ann'—Small, deep green leaves; resistant to shot-hole fungus; selected by Jim Scoggins, Wight Nurseries.

Sovereign® ('Greyou')—Full uniform, self-branching habit; uniformity of growth is the real improvement over the typical seedling populations which are variable in growth and form.

'Variegata' ('Tricolor')—A very beautiful but perhaps excessively gaudy cultivar; the dark green leaves are marbled gray and possess a creamy white to yellowish margin that turns to rose-pink with the advent of cold weather; not as vigorous as the species.

PROPAGATION: Cuttings collected late in summer or fall can be rooted; seed collected in fall and planted germinates readily the following spring; seeds are the primary method of propagation; have seen whole nursery blocks in Mobile, AL and the variation was maddening.

ADDITIONAL NOTES: Totally confused in the nursery trade. What is called *Cleyera japonica* is actually *Ternstroemia gymnanthera*. The differences between the two species reside in various minute floral characters.

NATIVE HABITAT: Japan, Korea, Formosa, China, India, Borneo.

RELATED SPECIES:

Cleyera japonica Thunb. — Japanese Cleyera

LEAVES: Alternate, simple, evergreen, ovate, 1 to 3″ long, 3/4 to 1 1/4″ wide, twisted acuminate tip, cuneate, entire, lustrous dark green and glabrous above, veins scarcely evident, dull olive-green and glabrous below; petiole 1/4″ long.

BUDS: Terminal, 1/2″ long, red, twisted, and pointed, 2 visible scales; laterals 1/8″ long, reddish brown, borne at 45° to stem.

STEM: Green, slender, glabrous, becoming grayish brown with maturity; pith white, solid, small.

Cleyera japonica, (klē-ēr′à jà-pon′i-kà), Japanese Cleyera, is an upright, broadleaf evergreen shrub or small tree growing 10 to 15′ high. The new growth is often bronze or reddish (not to the degree of *Ternstroemia gymnanthera*) maturing to lustrous medium to dark green. Leaves do not discolor (stay green) in full sun during winter. Leaves range from 3 to 4″ long, 3/4 to 1 3/4″ wide, narrow-oblong to ovate-oblong with an extended, acute tip (rather than obtuse or emarginate like in *Ternstroemia*). The end bud is long-extended, pointed with a slight crook. The cream-white flowers occur 1 to 5 in the leaf axils and are followed by globose, indehiscent, black fruit. Although little known and almost totally confused in American horticulture, the plant has possibilities. Hardiness is greater than literature ascribes, at least to Zone 6b. It grows in sun or shade. Several variegated cultivars include: 'Fortunei' (often listed as *C. fortunei* Hook. f. 'Variegata') with thinner, bright green leaves variegated cream, golden yellow, and rose on margins; and 'Tricolor' with bronze-purple new growth, changing to cream-yellow margins with gray-green center, and in cold weather rose-pink. I have observed both. The latter is louder. Caution, wear your sun glasses. Approximately 17 *Cleyera* species are acknowledged with *C. japonica* the only cold hardy, garden worthy form. Native to Japan, Korea, China. Zone 6b to 8(9).

Eurya japonica Thunb., (ū′ri-à jà-pon′i-kà), and **Eurya emarginata** (Thunb.) Mak., (ū′rià ē-mär-ji-nā′tà), are the only two representatives of this rather large (about 70 species) genus that I encounter in gardens. The former has larger, lustrous dark green leaves, about 1 1/4 to 3 1/4″ long, 1/2 to 1 1/4″ wide; 1/4″ diameter, white, axillary flowers; and 1/5″ diameter, black, globose

Eurya emarginata

fruits. 'Winter Wine' was introduced by the U.S. National Arboretum. It is smaller, slower growing, more spreading, with burgundy winter foliage. The species can grow to 30′ high. The latter species is more common (still scarce) with small, 1 to 1 1/2″ long, 1/2″ wide, lustrous dark green, crenate-serrate leaves. Flowers are blackish, malodorous and fruits are 1/5″ diameter, glabrous, purple-black, globose. *Eurya emarginata* is at best hardy to Zone 7; *E. japonica* best in Zone 8 and higher. Neither species will make the horticultural hit parade. It has taken me almost a career to learn these two species and I still am tentative about identification. Both are native to Asia, Japan.

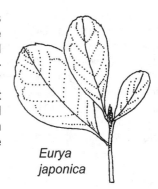

Eurya japonica

Tetracentron sinense Oliv.

FAMILY: Tetracentraceae
LEAVES: Alternate, simple, 3 to 5″ long, 1/2 to 3/4's as wide, ovate to elliptic-ovate, acuminate, subcordate or rounded, serrulate with obtuse teeth, 5 to 7 palmate veins, new growth bronze, dark green at maturity.
BUDS: Slender, pointed, with 2 outer scales.
STEM: Dark brown, glabrous, with light lenticels.

Tetracentron sinense, (tet-rȧ-sen′tron sī-nen′sē), is a small, round-headed tree not unlike *Cercidiphyllum* in leaf characteristics. It is essentially unknown in eastern gardens and probably best reserved for the Pacific Northwest. Garden size approximates 30′, although the species is listed to 100′ in the wild. There are worthy specimens at Edinburgh Botanic Garden and Mt. Stewart, Northern Ireland. Bark on the Edinburgh tree was gray-brown, with rounded mosaics. Difficult to describe, once observed, never forgotten. The perfect, yellowish flowers occur in 4 to 6″ long spikes in June–July. Fruit is a 4-celled, deeply lobed, dehiscent capsule. Probably best in light shade and a moist, woodland type soil. I have acquired several seedlings and look forward to evaluating them in Georgia. Central and western China. Found on moist slopes and bottomlands. Asian Ambrosia beetle has damaged trees at one nursery in the Atlanta area. Introduced 1901. Zone 6 to 7.

Teucrium chamaedrys L. — Wall Germander

FAMILY: Lamiaceae
LEAVES: Opposite, simple, evergreen, ovate to oblong-ovate, 1/4 to 1″ long, 1/2 as wide, acute, broad-cuneate, serrate or almost lobed, dark green and pubescent on both surfaces.

Teucrium chamaedrys, (tū′kri-um kam-ē′dris), Wall Germander, is best classified as an evergreen subshrub of mounded habit growing about 12 to 15″ high. The dark green leaves are present throughout the year. The rose-purple flowers (June–September) are borne in whorls of 4 from the axils of the uppermost leaves and form a 2 to 5″ long raceme. They are reasonably showy but are not the principal reason for growing the plant. The species is best used as edging material or a low hedge. It also fits nicely into a rock garden. I have grown the species in Illinois and Georgia with mixed success. In Urbana, IL the extreme cold killed it to the snowline but it did come back. In Georgia it performed more satisfactorily. Easily rooted from softwood cuttings in June provided there is not excessive moisture. 'Nanum' supposedly grows only 8″ high or less, spreads 2 to 3′, and flowers heavily. 'Variegatum' with cream-colored leaves is known. Central and southern Europe, northern Africa, western Asia. Cultivated 1750. Zone 5 to 8(9).

Thuja L. — Arborvitae
FAMILY: Cupressaceae

The genus *Thuja* constitutes a major group of small to medium size evergreens used extensively in landscape plantings, especially in the Midwest, East and West. Many cultivars of different form, size, and with varied foliage color are available. Five species in cultivation are native in North America and Eastern Asia. *Thuja orientalis* (*Platycladus orientalis*) is the least hardy (not totally accurate) of the species and is used extensively on the West Coast and in the South. Some cultivars of *T. occidentalis* are of good quality, however, many types have a tendency to discolor in the winter, with center foliage browning in the fall. *Thuja plicata* and *T. standishii* have the best foliage characteristics of the species. *Thuja koraiensis* is not common in cultivation, but had proven hardy in the lower Midwest. *Thuja occidentalis* and *T. plicata* are important timber trees, the wood being used extensively for shingles, shakes, siding, and poles. Some indication that *T. plicata* and hybrids with *T. occidentalis* and *T. standishii* may prove excellent for South, Midwest, and East, as well as West. Arborvitaes are not considered to be of the highest quality because of winter discoloration, loss of foliage, and a thin and "ratty" appearance with age. Because of this, many types tend to decrease rather than increase in value, especially in congested planting sites. *Thuja occidentalis* cultivars 'Emerald' ('Smaragd'), 'Nigra', and 'Techny' are very valuable for they maintain good green foliage color in all seasons.

MORPHOLOGICAL CHARACTERISTICS

Evergreen small trees and shrubs with thin, scaly bark and spreading or erect branches. Juvenile leaves are needle-like and the mature foliage scale-like and imbricate in four rows with glands sometimes on the back. The lateral leaves nearly cover the facial ones with branchlets flattened in one plane. Flowers are monoecious with male types yellow and female types rounded and forming a rounded cone. Cones solitary, ovoid or oblong; scales 8 to 12, with a thickened apical ridge or process, the 2 or 3 middle pairs fertile; seeds 2 to 3 beneath each scale, thick, wing broad or thick, or seeds wingless; cotyledons 2.

GROWTH CHARACTERISTICS

Arborvitaes are usually dense, pyramidal trees but vary from narrow- to broad-pyramidal. Numerous cultivars have been selected from *T. occidentalis* and *T. orientalis* and a selected few are available in the trade. Cultivars range from dwarf, round, globe, to narrow-upright types with foliage colors of yellow, bluish, and various shades of green. *American Conifer Society Journal* 14(4):146–151 (1997) reported 105 cultivars of *T. occidentalis*, 36 of *T. orientalis* and 17 of *T. plicata*. I know these numbers are low and in *Nursery Management and Production* 14(4):14–15, 71–73 (1998) I describe 36 cultivars of *T. plicata*.

CULTURE

Arborvitaes should be planted in fertile, moist, well-drained soils, although in the wild the species may be found on wet and dry soils; however, maximum growth is not realized on these sites. They are easily transplanted balled-and-burlapped or as container grown plants about any time of year. Arborvitaes perform best in full sun, although light shade is acceptable. In heavy shade plants become loose, open, and lose their dense constitution. *Thuja plicata* appears more shade tolerant than *T. occidentalis* or *T. orientalis*. The characteristic winter browning of *T. occidentalis* and cultivars results in an unsightly plant. *Thuja orientalis* also suffers from low temperature stresses and probably should be avoided in Zone 5 gardens although it is frequently sold in the local mass market outlets. Pruning can be accomplished prior to growth in the spring. Usually extensive pruning is not necessary and if heavy pruning is practiced the result is similar to that achieved with tightly pruned yews.

DISEASES AND INSECTS

Leaf blight, juniper blight, tip blight, canker (*Seiridium* spp.), arborvitae aphid, cedar tree canker, arborvitae leaf miner, mealybug, scales, bagworms, and other pests.
Physiological Diseases:
Leaf browning and shedding—inner leaves may drop in the fall.
Winter browning—caused by rapid temperature changes, desiccation of needles caused by sun and wind.
In general, arborvitaes exhibit few serious insect and disease problems.

PROPAGATION

Seeds do not usually require a stratification period although selected seed lots have exhibited dormancy. Stratification in a moist medium at 34 to 41°F for 40 to 60 days will stimulate prompt germination. Cuttings are taken in late summer through early winter. See specific recommendations under the species descriptions. Cultivars are also rooted from cuttings. Our standard procedure is December through March cuttings, 3000 to 5000 ppm KIBA, 3 perlite:1 peat, mist, 70°F bottom heat with superlative results.

LANDSCAPE USE

Arborvitaes have received wide acceptance in landscaping and are commonly used in foundations and as screens, windbreaks, accent plants, or hedges. They make excellent tall hedges and screens and, to a degree, have become stereotypes in these roles. The yellow-foliaged forms should be used with discretion for they detract from surrounding plantings. Arborvitaes will always be popular landscape plants but some of the new cultivars should be used in preference to the seedling-grown material.

Thuja occidentalis L. — Eastern Arborvitae, American Arborvitae, White Cedar
(thū′yȧ ok-si-den-tā′lis)

LEAVES: Scale-like, about 1/12″ long, abruptly pointed, those on the main axis conspicuously glandular; on the branchlets sometimes inconspicuously so, bright green above, pale green below, emitting a tansy-like odor when bruised. *vertical leaves*

BRANCHLETS: Alternate, compressed, flat; sprays horizontal, laterally compressed; 3 to 4 times divided.

CONES: Oblong, 1/3 to 1/2″ long, yellowish and erect when young, brown and pendent when mature at the end of the first summer, scales 8 to 10, usually 4 fertile, with a minute mucro at apex; differs from *T. orientalis* which has a distinct spine-like hook on the back of each cone scale near the apex.

SIZE: 40 to 60′ high, usually less, by 10 to 15′ spread; realistically under cultivation 20 to 30′ is more accurate.

HARDINESS: Zone 3 to 7, but not vigorous in the South.

HABIT: A dense, often broad-pyramidal tree with short, ascending branches to the ground which end in flat, spreading, horizontal sprays; usually there is one trunk but multiple trunks do occur; this is a good feature for separating this species from *T. orientalis* which develops many leaders and takes on a more dense, bushy appearance with the sprays borne in strong, vertical planes.

RATE: Slow to medium.

TEXTURE: Medium-fine.

BARK: Grayish brown to reddish brown; the native stands I examined were grayish brown, 1/4 to 1/3″ thick, fibrous, forming a more or less close network of connecting ridges and shallow furrows, grayish on the surface.

LEAF COLOR: Flat bright green in summer changing to yellow-brown-green in winter, at times terrifically ugly in winter.

FLOWERS: Monoecious, terminal, solitary.

FRUIT: Cones oblong, 1/3 to 1/2″ long, light brown; scales 8 to 10, usually 4 fertile, with a minute mucro at apex; seeds 1/8″ long, compressed; wing round the seed, narrow, emarginate.

CULTURE: Readily transplanted from containers or balled-and-burlapped if root pruned; should be grown in areas with considerable atmospheric moisture as well as soil moisture; requires a deep, well-drained soil; thrives in marshy loam; full sun; tolerant of pruning; susceptible to strong wind, snow, or ice damage; very tolerant of limestone soils; in spite of the absolute admonitions about this species and the cultivars, it will, once established, take considerable heat and drought; all over Cadillac Mountain, Maine, growing in rock crevices and exposed slopes.

DISEASES AND INSECTS: Subject to bagworm, heart rot, leaf miner, spider mites, and deer browsing; see culture sheet.

LANDSCAPE VALUE: Useful as a specimen or accent, good for hedges, shelter-belts, and commonly used as a foundation plant; at times over-used in landscape plantings; 'Emerald', 'Nigra', and 'Techny' are excellent for cold climates; several Februaries past, Dr. Harold Pellett, University of Minnesota, and I were walking around the Minnesota Landscape Arboretum, near the visitor's center, surrounded by snow, were several Techny arborvitaes that were still a good dark green color even with the reflected light from the snow, wind, and cold; interestingly, on the ride from the Minnesota airport I was thinking how ugly the yellow-brown arborvitaes looked in many of the home landscapes; moral: plant the superior cultivars.

CULTIVARS: Many, and I become confused trying to separate the various forms. I suspect there are 80 to 100 cultivars, some of worth, about 90% deserving of trash heap status. *American Conifer Society Journal* 14(4):146–151 (1997) reported 105 cultivars. I used the literature, nursery catalogs and my eyes in assembling this list. I counted 28 yellow, cream, or otherwise variegated cultivars in van Gelderen and van Hoey Smith's *Conifers*. Many of the smaller forms are collector's items or suitable for small scale landscapes or rock garden situations. Occasionally, I read the literature and see mention of shade tolerance. I don't believe it for a minute and neither does the plant for with time this species becomes thin, open, and generally ratty.

'Aurea'—Broad conical shrub with golden yellow leaves; 2 1/2 to 3′ by 2 1/2 to 3′.

'Boisbraind'—From W.H. Perron, Canada; dark green foliage; compact elliptical habit to 10′; listed as winter "burn" resistant.

'Boothii'—Dwarf, globular, dense; foliage bright green; broader than tall, flat-topped at maturity; 6 to 10′ high; named in 1874.

'Brabant'—Spire-like growth; medium green foliage; more resistant to winter discoloration; supposedly quite shade tolerant; 12 to 15′.

'Brandon'—Soft green foliage; resistant to winter burn; narrow cone, 12 to 15′.

'Canadian Green'—Good globose-rounded form with better bright green foliage color than the old standard 'Woodwardii'; listed as 3' high; Zone 3.

'Chalet'—Lime green foliage; similar to Techny; from W.H. Perron.

'Danica'—Dwarf form, 1 to 1 1/2' high; glossy emerald green foliage.

'Degroot's Spire'—Narrow columnar form with foliage like 'Spiralis'.

'Douglasii Aurea'—Pyramidal, slender, 30 to 45' tall, branchlets spreading; sprays yellow, grading to yellowish green at base; leaves golden yellow, bronzed in winter; developed by D. Hill Nursery Co., Dundee, IL before 1923.

'Elegantissima'—Narrow pyramidal form, broadening with age, with dark green foliage that is tipped yellow which turns bronze during winter; 10 to 15' high, 4 to 5' wide; old cultivar.

'Ellwangeriana'—Juvenile form; conical, sometimes broad-pyramidal; 6 to 9' tall; leaves on developed branches and branchlets scale-like, other leaves linear, spreading, acicular; a golden needled, slow-growing form is known ('Ellwangeriana Aurea').

'Emerald' ('Smaragd')—Out of Denmark; saw many years past at Iseli Nursery, Boring, OR and realized it had potential; many nurserymen are now growing it; narrow compact pyramidal form; 10 to 15' by 3 to 4'; bright lustrous emerald green foliage in more or less vertical sprays, does not discolor in winter like many forms; also displays excellent heat tolerance; cold hardy to at least -40°F; introduced in 1950; from Poulsen, Denmark; could this be a hybrid with *T. orientalis*? There is also a gold-marked variegated sport of 'Emerald'.

'Ericoides'—Juvenile form; dwarf, compact, rounded; 3' tall and wide; leaves linear, spreading in pairs, flat, apex sharp-pointed, yellowish green in summer, brownish in winter.

'Filiformis'—Weeping habit to the dense branches that hold loose tufts of long, thread-like, drooping branchlets, new growth bright green.

'Giganteoides'—Listed by Krüssmann as possibly a *T. occidentalis* × *T. plicata* form; found in a seedling bed by S. Poulsen of Kvistgaard, Denmark in 1935; I have three forms of this and all look, grow, and discolor the same; some thought the hybrid may be *T. plicata* × *T. standishii*; vigorous; rich mint green in summer; to 30 to 50' high; yellow-green tinge of brown in Georgia field tests in winter; in container studies, winter color was almost yellow-brown in February at Dearing, GA.

'Globosa'—Dwarf, globular; 4.5 to 6' high and wide; leaves green, slightly grayish green in winter.

'Golden Globe'—Golden yellow foliage; broad globe-shaped habit; supposedly non-burning; sport of 'Woodwardii'; 2 to 3' high and wide.

'Hetz Midget'—A dense, globe-shaped form that doubtfully will ever grow more than 3 to 4' high; it has a fine rich green foliage and is quite an attractive selection; originated about 1928 as a chance seedling at Fairview Nurseries.

'Holmstrup'—Compact, slow-growing, narrow pyramidal form with bright green, tight, bunchy, vertically arranged foliage; holds good foliage color in winter in Georgia; 5' by 2', eventually to 10' high; good for low hedges; have seen abundant cones on relatively young plants; has performed well in the University's Botanical Garden trials; introduced by A.M. Jensen, Holmstrup, Denmark; there is a yellow-foliaged sport.

'Little Gem'—Dwarf, globose, dense form; broader than tall, 3' high and 4.5 to 6' in diameter; leaves dark green, slightly brown in winter.

'Little Giant'—Slow-growing, globe-shaped, small form with rich green foliage.

'Lutea'—Pyramidal, narrow, 30 to 36' high; sprays and leaves golden yellow, light yellowish green on underside of branchlets; old name was 'George Peabody'; developed before 1873 in Geneva, NY; still one of the best yellow forms.

'Nigra'—Pyramidal form with good dark green foliage persisting through the winter; 20 to 30' high, 4 to 5' wide, possible to 10' wide.

'Ohlendorffii'—Juvenile foliage form; broad-mounded habit; 2 to 3' by 4'.

'Pendula'—An attractive small pyramidal form with rather open ascending-arching branches and pendulous branchlets; a first class plant for accent use; ±15' high; requires staking; developed before 1862 in the Standish Nursery, England.

'Pyramidalis'—Narrow pyramidal, formal in outline with bright green, soft-textured foliage, susceptible to winter burn; 20 to 30' by 5 to 8'; a catchall term?

'Rheingold'—A slow-growing, ovoid or conical shrub; 4 to 5' high by 3 to 4' wide; the foliage primarily adult and rich deep gold; it is quite similar to 'Ellwangeriana Aurea' except smaller in stature; no doubt propagated from the juvenile shoots of that form; turns copper to brownish yellow in winter.

'Rosenthalii'—Pyramidal, compact, slow-growing; 9 to 15' high, 2 to 3' wide; leaves shining dark green; good hedge form; one reference said no more than 6 to 9' in 50 years.

'Sherwood Forest'—According to Raulston, a variegated form, vigorous and fast-growing.

'Sherwood Moss'—Dwarf, cone-shaped; green juvenile foliage bronzing in winter; 4 to 6' high.

'Spiralis'—Narrow pyramidal, slender, 30 to 45' high; branches short; branchlets spirally arranged; sprays somewhat fernleaf-shaped; leaves dark green.

'Sudwelli'—Irregular outline with green, gold-tipped foliage, quite similar to 'Lutea'; has performed well in Zone 7b for over 10 years.

'Sunkist'—Good yellow foliage on a broad pyramidal plant, 5 to 8' high.

'Techny' ('Mission')—Broad-based, pyramidal form to 10 to 15'; excellent dark green foliage year-round; good hedge plant; slow-growing; probably the best form for northern gardens; extremely popular; discovered in Mission Gardens, Techny, IL.

'Umbraculifera'—Dwarf, globose, depressed, compact form, 2 to 2 1/2' high, 4 to 5' wide; foliage glaucous, bloomy.

'Wareana'—Pyramidal, low, dense; leaves bright green, developing thick, leathery green foliage, tinged blue, without a brown tinge; 35-year-old plant is 8' tall; good for northern areas.

'Wintergreen' ('Hetz Wintergreen')—Columnar pyramidal form holding good green winter color; coarser than other selections; 20 to 30' high, 5 to 10' wide; may display better shade tolerance.

'Woodwardii'—Globular form, wider than high; foliage dark green, turning brown in winter; 72-year-old plant is 8' by 18'; a popular form; not preferable to some of the smaller globose or rounded types; common in cemeteries in the Midwest, not the most appealing plant for placing by a loved one.

'Yellow Ribbon'—Young growth yellow-orange maturing to green, upright pyramidal selection, slow growth, 10' by 3' at maturity.

PROPAGATION: Cuttings made from current year's wood, taken with a heel, rooted well when taken each month in November through March. Cuttings taken in and after January rooted a little more quickly. In the past 5 years have collected cuttings of several clones and rooted all with 3000 to 5000 KIBA, 3 perlite:1 peat, mist, bottom heat (70°F). Tissue culture has been successful, see *In Vitro Cellular Developmental Biology–Plant* 29(2):65–71 (1993).

NATIVE HABITAT: Eastern North America (Nova Scotia to Manitoba, south to North Carolina, Tennessee and Illinois). Introduced about 1536.

RELATED SPECIES: I offer several additional species which may appear occasionally in arboreta and botanic gardens. They are inferior to the better forms of the three primary species.

Thuja koraiensis Nak., (thū′yà kôr-ē-en′sis), Korean Arborvitae, is usually a broad, rather irregular, 2 to 5' high, spreading shrub of no great beauty. I have seen it in the Midwest during the winter where it pales by comparison with 'Techny', 'Nigra', and others. The foliage is bright green above with distinct whitish markings below. The shoots are quite flattened and the branches procumbent-ascending. Wilson mentioned seeing the species in Korea from sprawling shrubs to slender, graceful, narrowly pyramidal trees reaching a maximum height of 25 to 30'. The plants I have recently observed and acquired are shrubby with distinct silver undersides to the foliage. Virtually every visitor asks the plant's identity. Korea. Introduced 1910. Zone 5 to 7.

Also worth mentioning is ***Thuja standishii*** (Gurd.) Carr., (thū′yà stan-dēsh′ē-ī), Japanese Arborvitae, with a broadly conical crown, slender trunk, and shaggy, deep red bark. The branch sprays arch, ultimate divisions are 1/16″ wide, sprays are bright green to dark on upper side, and glaucous with whitish spots beneath. Foliage is semi-weeping lending a shaggy appearance. Cones are oblong, about 10-scaled, and 3/8″ long. Probably 20 to 30' under cultivation, larger in the mountains of Honshu and Shikoku to 100'. The broad head may be the greatest difference from the other species. Actually a beautiful specimen but prone to winter discoloration. In March 1996, I visited the Missouri Botanic Garden, St. Louis and witnessed a handsome ±15' specimen that was dark green. Cuttings were granted, rooted, and small plants are growing in Georgia. Based on one year's evaluation in containers, the winter foliage color is a disappointing yellow-brown-green. Introduced 1860. Zone 5 to 6(7).

Thuja orientalis L. f. — Oriental Arborvitae (This plant has had its name changed to *Biota orientalis* L. and *Platycladus orientalis* (L.) Franco., the latter being more correct. I am staying with the old name because it keeps similar plants together.)

(thū′yà ôr-i-en-tā′lis)

LEAVES: Smaller than those of other species, distinctly grooved on the back, those on main axis about 1/12″ long, triangular, ending in a blunt point, not pressed close to the shoot, those on the finer spray about

1/16″ long, closely pressed, green on both surfaces, bearing minute stomata, giving off a slightly resinous odor when bruised. Branchlets arranged in a vertical plane.

CONES: Ovoid, fleshy, glaucous green before ripening, 3/4″ long, 6 to 8 scales, each with horn-like process or hook.

SIZE: 18 to 25′ high by 10 to 15′ in width; however, can grow 30 to 40′ high but this is seldom realized under cultivation; national champion is 41′ by 24′ in Baltimore County, MD.

HARDINESS: Zone (5)6 to 11; has performed poorly at the Morton Arboretum, Zone 5.

HABIT: A large shrub or small tree of dense, compact, conical, or columnar habit when young with the branchlets held vertically, becoming in age loose and open and not so markedly vertical; composed of many slender branches which tend to bend and break in ice and snow; quite difficult to "pin down" actual habit for some forms are loose, open, almost tree-like with stringy foliage rather than typical flattened sprays; Will Corley had several seedlings in his Griffin, GA tests and I have observed the same type of plants at Woodward, OK in the plant material center; these forms were 20 to 30′ high.

RATE: Slow to medium.

TEXTURE: Medium-fine.

LEAF COLOR: Bright yellow-green to grass green in youth changing to a darker green when older, often discolors in northern climates becoming yellow-green-brown.

FLOWERS: Monoecious, terminal, solitary.

FRUIT: Cones roundish egg-shaped, 3/4″ long, fleshy, bluish before ripening; scales usually 6, ovate, each with a horn-like projection, the uppermost sterile; seeds 2 to each scale, ovoid, about 1/8″ across, wingless; the wingless seeds distinguish it from the other *Thuja* species.

CULTURE: Transplant balled-and-burlapped or from a container; tolerant of most soils except those that are extremely wet; needs less moisture than *T. occidentalis*; best if the winter atmosphere is dry, protect from sweeping winds; pH adaptable; does quite well in Southeast and Southwest; in Key West, FL, yes, Key West, I saw the species on several occasions, robust, full-bodied and as obvious as a sore thumb; obviously it requires no significant chilling to satisfy any bud rest; also the plants were growing in/on coral/sand/sea shells and appeared to flourish; I have seen the plant all over Savannah, GA, particularly in cemeteries.

DISEASES AND INSECTS: Bagworm, spider mites, canker (*Seiridium* spp.); see list on general culture sheet.

LANDSCAPE VALUE: Useful for hedges and specimens but not of value in the north central states, although commonly sold; used extensively in the South and Southwest where it is more adaptable; several worthwhile cultivars that are a cut above the species; still remember a tour of the Aldrich Nursery, near San Antonio, TX and the 'Aurea Nana' was growing in the field.

CULTIVARS: Many cultivars (40 or more) are known but few are available in everyday commerce.

'Aurea Nana' (Berckman's Golden Arborvitae)—Dwarf, dense, globular to ovoid form; to 5′ tall, will eventually grow to 10′ and larger; foliage golden yellow and finally light yellow-green, slightly brownish in winter.

'Baker'—Bright green foliage, densely set needles and broad conical shape; does well in hot dry places; grows 5 to 8′ high in 8 to 10 years.

'Beverleyensis'—Upright cone-shaped to globe outline with time; soft golden yellow foliage turning bronzy gold in winter; may grow 10′ high and wide with age.

'Blue Cone'—Upright pyramidal form with compact sprays of flattened branchlets of dark green foliage with a bluish cast; my eyes see more green than blue and the habit is almost upright egg-shaped.

'Bonita'—Dwarf form, broadly conical; new growth yellow-green, later light green at tops, darker green below; 3′ high.

'Compacta'—Pyramidal, dense, formal, slow-growing form; foliage glaucous green, tips plum-colored in winter.

'Conspicua'—A medium-sized to large shrub of dense, compact, conical habit with the sprays strongly vertical; foliage golden yellow and holding longer than most yellow selections; probably the true "Berckman's Golden Biota."

'Elegantissima'—Narrow pyramidal; foliage in flat sprays, emerges bright golden yellow, maturing to yellow-green, brown in winter.

'Filiformis Aurea'—Similar to 'Filiformis Erecta' but having more yellow-green foliage in summer.

'Filiformis Erecta'—When young, plants have upright cord-like branching habit, eventually forming upright oval-shaped shrub with light green foliage, more brownish in winter.

'Fruitlandii'—Upright-conical shape; rich deep green foliage.

'Golden Ball'—Dwarf loosely rounded habit; soft golden foliage in summer, vivid orange-brown tints in winter.

'Green Cone'—Upright oval; bright green foliage produces abundant cones.

'Juniperoides'—Dense feathery blue-gray, needle-like juvenile foliage in summer changing to purplish plum in winter; rounded bushy habit, to 3′ high.

'Meldensis'—Tight globose to broad columnar; feathery, light green, needle-like foliage, purplish brown in winter; dwarf growing, juvenile form.

'Minima'—Dwarf globose habit, becoming 3 to 4′ high and nearly as wide at maturity; light yellow-green in spring, dark green in fall, brown in winter.

'Pyramidalis'—Over the years I have been confused by a large tree form with potential to grow 30 to 40′ and rather loose, open, stringy foliage compared to the typical form; at Griffin, GA, Mr. Will Corley has grown several seedlings of this form for 15 to 20 years, they appear to be related to anything but the species; open, loose, gangly with bright green foliage, the cones are typical.

'Sieboldii'—Bright green foliage on a dense mounded plant that rarely exceeds 6′ in height.

'Westmont'—Compact, globe-shaped, slow-growing type with rich dark green foliage tipped with yellow from spring to fall; 24 to 30″ high, 20″ wide in 10 years.

PROPAGATION: Seed germination is relatively easy but stratification of seeds for 60 days at about 40°F may be helpful. Cuttings of this species are more difficult to root than those of *T. occidentalis*. Based on grafted *Chamaecyparis* taxa received from the West Coast, this species is a popular rootstock. Also, scale leaf explants produced entire plants via tissue culture, see *Acta Horticulturae Sinica* 24(1):75–78 (1997).

ADDITIONAL NOTES: Always look ragged in Midwest and East, especially during the winter; best reserved for southern and western states.

NATIVE HABITAT: Korea, Manchuria and northern China. Introduced before 1737.

Thuja plicata D. Don. — Giant (Western) Arborvitae
(thū′yȧ plī-kā′tȧ)

LEAVES: On leading shoots, parallel to the axis, ovate, long-pointed, each with an inconspicuous resin gland on the back, up to 1/4″ long, the points free; those on the ultimate divisions smaller, about 1/8″ or less long, ovate, short and bluntly pointed, closely overlapping and often without glands, glossy dark green above, usually faintly streaked with white beneath but on some branches remaining green; emitting a tansy-like odor when bruised; similar to *T. occidentalis*, individual divisions not as wide and foliage more lustrous and dark green than *T. occidentalis*.

STEM: Branches horizontal, often pendent at the ends; branchlets in the same plane, much divided, the small lateral shoots falling after 2 or 3 years; often fern-like or stringy in appearance.

SIZE: 50 to 70′ high and 15 to 25′ wide; can grow in areas of the Northwest to 180 to 200′ high; co-national champions are 178′ by 54′ in Forks, WA and 159′ by 45′ in Olympic National Park, WA.

HARDINESS: Zone (4)5 to 7(8); performing well at Morton Arboretum.

HABIT: A narrow, pyramidal tree with a buttressed base and often with several leaders; usually maintaining the lower branches; have seen old 80 to 100′ high trees that were anything but narrow; still maintained branches and foliage to the ground.

RATE: Slow to medium, fast on some genotypes especially under nursery production.

TEXTURE: Medium.

BARK: Cinnamon-red on young stems; gray-brown to red-brown on old trunks, 1/2 to 1″ thick, fibrous, and forming a closely interlacing network.

LEAF COLOR: A good lustrous dark green in summer and winter, although have observed considerable yellowing and browning in windswept locations in full sun, selections are being made for improved winter color.

FLOWERS: Monoecious, small, inconspicuous; staminate yellowish, pistillate pinkish.

FRUIT: Cones erect, cylindric-ovoid, 1/2″ long, green in summer, brown in winter; scales 8 to 10, elliptic-oblong with usually the middle pair fertile; seeds winged, the wing notched apically.

CULTURE: Transplants readily balled-and-burlapped or from containers; prefers moist, well-drained, fertile soils and in the wild is found on moist flats, slopes, the banks of rivers and swamps, and is even found in bogs; occasionally found on dry soils but growth is usually stunted; moist atmosphere; full sun or partial shade; pH adaptable; have seen the species in the Vancouver, BC area and it grew everywhere from the steep slopes to the deep fertile valleys; truly an imposing evergreen if given optimum cultural conditions; handsome plants exist in the Midwest and East Coast and the species may be more adaptable than given credit; Raulston reported 2 to 4′ of growth per year at Raleigh, NC.

DISEASES AND INSECTS: Bagworm and heart rot.

LANDSCAPE VALUE: Useful as a specimen or for hedges in formal and semi-formal plantings, groupings, screens; a beautiful conifer when properly grown, some indication that the species may be deer resistant; common in France, Italy, Germany, Netherlands, and British Isles.

CULTIVARS: Many more selections in Europe. The following cultivar list is derived from an article published by the author in *Nursery Management and Production* 14(4):14–15, 71–73 (1998).

'Albospicata'—Darker green foliage background, cream splotches on new growth, fades to green with maturity; strong grower; ascending branches.

'Atrovirens'—One of better large, pyramidal arborvitae types; vigorous like the species; excellent shining dark green foliage, muddy brown in winter; excellent cold hardiness; an excellent hedge form.

'Aurea'—Large form like species but slower growing; yellow foliage more or less irregularly scattered over the tree.

'Canadian Gold'—Broad pyramidal; brilliant gold foliage, similar to 'Sunshine'; introduced by Mitsch Nursery, Aurora, OR about 1980.

'Clemson #1'—Slower growing; broad pyramidal; cream highlights in new growth.

'Clemson #2'—Larger than 'Clemson #1'; 30' by 8'; creamy highlights in new growth; cold hardy form with good green winter color; selected from Schoenike Arboretum, Clemson University, Clemson, SC; offered by Head-Lee Nursery, Seneca, SC and Nurseries Caroliniana, North Augusta, SC.

'Collyer's Gold' ('Colliers Gold')—Upright-columnar in youth, golden yellow foliage, has not performed well in Georgia trails.

'Cuprea'—Dwarf broad pyramidal form, 3 to 4' high, wider at maturity, copper to bronze-yellow shoots, more green in summer, a seedling of 'Aurea'.

'Doone Valley'—Listed in Hillier Arboretum database from Internet search but without description.

'Dura'—Pyramidal, more open with loose, deep green foliage on young plants, slower growing than species, introduced by Timm & Co., Elmshorn, West Germany, in 1925.

'Emerald Cone'—Grows 24 to 40' in height, excellent lustrous emerald green foliage, disease-free, used on West Coast as a substitute for Leyland Cypress and Monterey Pine, introduced and available from Saratoga Horticulture Foundation, 15185 Murphy Avenue, San Martin, CA 95046.

'Euchlora'—Narrow, conical, tall, soft rich green foliage, discovered in Bavaria in a private garden, excellent hardiness, excellent performance in Michigan.

'Excelsa'—Fast-growing, loose, pyramidal form, bright green foliage, discolors in winter, discovered in a cemetery in Berlin in 1962, introduced by Timm & Co. in 1941, named in 1947, excellent winter hardiness, apparently common in Pacific Northwest and British Columbia.

'Fastigiata'—A good columnar clone with a straight, slender outline and dense, rich green foliage; discolors in winter; somewhat firmer textured than species; over 40' high in Bedgbury Pinetum, Kent, England after 49 years.

'Gelderland'—Tight pyramidal-columnar form with lustrous medium green foliage, discovered about 1980 in the Netherlands.

'George Washington'—Bright green with hints of yellow during new growth, columnar, full specimen form, 15 to 20'.

Globose Form—Listed in Hillier Arboretum database from the Internet but without a description.

'Gracilis'—Loosely broad-conical, slow-growing, shoots finer and lighter than the species, needles small and light green.

'Gracilis Aurea'—Similar to above but shoots yellowish at their tips and nodding, not particularly attractive, can grow 20 to 25' high.

'Green Giant'—Somewhat of a genetic rover without a clear-cut taxonomic home; Martin and Tripp, *American Conifer Society Journal* 14(4):153–155 (1997), present "The Tale of *Thuja* 'Green Giant'"; I have collected three forms, one from the Arnold Arboretum, another from Manor View Nurseries, Monkton, MD, the last from Spring Grove, Cincinnati, OH; the Spring Grove form has been sold as *T. plicata* 'Spring Grove'; cuttings were rooted from the Spring Grove tree, plants grown side-by-side in the greenhouse and on a gravel pad, in two years "of watching," I see absolutely no difference among the clones; described as a hybrid(s) between *T. standishii* and *T. plicata*; excellent vigor in the field and containers in our trials, one field-grown plant was 5 1/2' high in two full growing seasons from a 12" high one-gallon container; habit is broad-pyramidal, lustrous rich medium green summer foliage, in winter foliage discolors to yellow-brown-green, literature days otherwise, I have seen too many plants North and South that were anything but winter green; on February 17, 1998, I evaluated the three clones(?) at the Center for Applied Nursery Research, Dearing, GA and all were bronze and significantly so, others who were with me concurred that the clones are so similar they cannot be dissimilar; plant greens with the advent of warm weather and is a terrific plant, simply not *green*, as promoted, through the seasons; certainly a worthy commercial item, 30 to 40′ and larger, found in a seedling bed by S. Poulsen, Kristgaard, Denmark in 1935.

'Green Sport'—Species type with good dark green color on February 5, 1998 at Longwood Gardens; Jeff Lynch graciously shared cuttings which rooted in 6 to 8 weeks; looked exceptionally good in the wind-swept nursery; have seen listed as synonymous with 'Watnong Green'; selected in 1960's by Watnong Nursery, Morris Plains, NJ.

'Green Survival'—Broad-conical habit, strong grower, bright green foliage summer and winter, originated as a seedling in the Darthuizer Nursery, Leersum, Holland.

'Grüne Kugel'—Small dwarf bushy form, dark green foliage, bronzes in winter, saw at February, 1998 Southeastern Flower Show, plant came from Larry Stanley, Sandy, OR.

'Hillier'—Compact form, 7 to 10′ high and wide with age, needle color described as blue-green, bronze-brown in winter, cultivated by Hillier Nursery since about 1900.

'Hogan'—Dense pyramidal-conical tree, rich lustrous medium green summer foliage, slight off-color in winter in Zone 7b, was told this is a grex including plants from a native population in Gresham, OR; Raulston distributed this as a clone; certainly a handsome plant; named after Hogan Road, Gresham, OR.

'Holly Turner'—Described as wide-spreading specimen, leaderless, producing lateral branches that arch gracefully downward, found on Whidbey Island, WA, introduced by Heronswood, discovered by Dana Moffett, named after Holly Turner.

'Irish Gold'—Loose, somewhat open, irregularly branched with golden yellow shoots, tree type habit, probably the most gold of all the "yellow" *T. plicata* types, awarded RHS Award of Garden Merit, see Lancaster, *The Garden* 121(12):760–761 (1996) for specifics.

'Pumila'—Dwarf, dense pyramidal form, considered one of the true slow-growing forms of the species that parallels it in growth habit.

'Pygmaea'—Dense, compact form, meant to be identical with 'Pumila' but, based on photo records, distinctly different; dwarf form; blue-green foliage; irregular branching; 2 to 2 1/2′ high, 2 to 3′ wide.

'Rogersii'—Dwarf, oval-rounded form; higher than wide; 3 to 4′(6′) after 25 years; golden yellow in summer, bronze-yellow in winter, dark green on the interior; same origin as *T. plicata* 'Cuprea'.

'Stoneham Gold'—Broad conical form, semi-dwarf; interior foliage dark green, bright yellow new growth; 6 to 10′ high, 2 to 3′ wide.

'Stribling'—Dense thick column that grows 10 to 12′ high, 2 to 3′ wide.

'Semperaurescens'—Upright tree, appearing extremely open in youth, with the foliage tinged yellow, not particularly striking, introduced about 1923 by Dallimore and Jackson, England, specimens greater than 70′ high are reported.

'Sunshine'—More even yellow suffusion over the foliage, grows like the species, respectable foliage color, has held yellow foliage color in heat of Zone 7.

'Virescens'—Species type with good green winter foliage color at the Longwood Gardens nursery on February 5, 1998; not much difference between this and 'Green Sport' as viewed by the author; will require time to assess net worth, introduced by Mitsch Nursery about 1990–91.

'Wansdyke Silver'—Although listed as a *T. occidentalis* form has greater affinity with *T. plicata* in this author's estimation; holds creamy variegation in Georgia trials; small pyramidal tree form.

'Watnong Green'—A wonderful lady introduced herself after a mid-February lecture on Long Island and told me about a good green form grown by the late Don and Hazel Smith, Watnong Nursery, NJ, she is tracking down plants/cuttings for my program, grows 40 to 50′, see under 'Green Sport', which appears to be a synonym.

'Winter Pink'—Dwarf, compact-mounded form with yellowish summer foliage, pinkish(?) in winter.

'Zebrina'—Kind of like an old friend, it tends to crop up in unexpected places; broad pyramidal outline with yellowish striped sprays (actually variable variegation pattern); have seen 30′ tall plants in England, plants 60 to 70′ (80′ at Stourhead) are known; the effect from a distance is a rather pleasing yellow-green; more than one 'Zebrina' resides in gardens and commerce; plant in my Georgia trials develops no yellowish markings but maintains good lustrous dark green color year-round.

'Zebrina Extra Gold'—Slower growing with even more gold foliage, witnessed a plant at Trengwainton Garden, Penzance in March 1996 and 1998 and was literally blinded, brought cuttings home and was completely disappointed, simply no variegation in the heat.

PROPAGATION: Dormant seed lots have been encountered occasionally on which stratification in a moist medium at 34 to 41°F for 30 to 60 days stimulated prompt germination (variation among seed lots). Cuttings rooted well when taken in January. Best to collect cuttings after cold weather has set in. Raulston mentioned 95% rooting on December–January cuttings with 8000 ppm IBA talc and mist. With 25 clones that I collected, rooting averaged 88% when treated with 5000 ppm KIBA, 3 perlite:1 peat, bottom heat (70°F), and mist.

ADDITIONAL NOTES: Extremely handsome conifer; probably better than *T. occidentalis* from an ornamental standpoint. Principal timber tree used for shingle manufacture in the United States and Canada. Is used for poles, posts, piling, boxwood, house-building, garden buildings, summerhouses, and green houses because of its durability. The Indians used the split trunks for totem poles and hollowed-out trunks for canoes. They used the inner bark for fiber which was woven into mats, baskets, and hats. The roots are so tough that they were used for fish hooks.

Tremendous interest for the species and the better cultivars because of the enthusiasm of the late J.C. Raulston who promoted the plant as a possible alternative to Leyland Cypress and its ilk. Little did any of us know that its adaptability to Zone 7 and 8 would prove so positively dramatic. There are numerous cultivars but most have little to offer. The types that are tree-like with lustrous dark green foliage that holds in winter have a significant future in Zone 5 through 8. I have been collecting clones as I lecture and travel to campuses, arboreta, and private gardens based on winter foliage color. Currently, there are three that appear promising but require field testing.

NATIVE HABITAT: Alaska to northern California and Montana. Introduced 1853.

Thujopsis dolobrata Sieb. & Zucc. — Hiba Arborvitae, False Arborvitae
(thū-yop′sis dol′ō-brā-tȧ)

FAMILY: Cupressaceae

LEAVES: Shining dark green above, flat ones glandless on the back, oblong-spatulate, with a green keel and a hollowed silvery white stripe of stomata on each side; the side leaves larger, hatchet-shaped, ovate or linear-oblong, bluntly keeled, the more appressed part on the underside of branchlets with a broad white stripe.

BRANCHLETS: Arranged in opposite rows, the ultimate divisions much flattened, about 1/4″ wide, sprays spreading in one plane.

SIZE: 30 to 50′ high, 10 to 20′ wide.

HARDINESS: Zone 5 to 7.

HABIT: Dense pyramidal evergreen of great beauty; the most magnificent specimen I have seen is located at the Isle of Mainau in Germany; in all appearances, at least from a distance, it resembles a fine *Thuja plicata*; fine plants at Anne's Grove Garden, Ireland.

RATE: Slow.

TEXTURE: Medium.

LEAF COLOR: Lustrous dark green on the upper surface and prominently marked with whitish streaks on the lower surface.

FRUITS: Subglobose, 1/2 to 3/4″ long cones with 6 to 8, thick, woody scales, each ending in a horn-shaped boss, seeds winged.

CULTURE: Readily transplanted from a container; prefers moist, acid, organic soil, and protection from sweeping winds; full sun but will tolerate considerable shade; found in moist forests in Japan; prefers high atmospheric moisture; the further south the plant is grown, ideally the more shade should be provided; has not been comfortable in Zone 7b but I keep trying.

DISEASES AND INSECTS: None serious.

LANDSCAPE VALUE: To my knowledge the species is seldom found in the United States; it is a beautiful plant but, from a practical standpoint, probably not worth the commercial effort when there are so many other conifers that offer similar landscape effects; a good plant for the collector.

CULTIVARS:

'Aurescens'—Beautiful yellow-gold form that I first experienced at Mt. Congreve, Ireland; certainly a collector's plant.

var. *hondai* Mak.—Branchlets densely arranged; larger cones; to 100′; northern Japan.

'Nana' ('Laetevirens')—Dwarf form of rounded-mounded outline to 3′ high; good dark green foliage, as I have seen and propagated it; several references say lighter green foliage than the species; perhaps there are several dwarf forms.

'Variegata'—The sprays marked with creamy white blotches; interesting plant but will revert rather readily to the green form; have seen compact and more tree-like forms under this grex.

PROPAGATION: Seeds are described as difficult. I have collected cuttings of 'Nana' in November, 3000 ppm IBA-quick dip, peat:perlite, mist and in 10 weeks had 100% rooting; the variegated form is also easy to root; apparently even large forest trees are easily propagated by cuttings; was able to secure cuttings from the finest specimen at Anne's Grove in June, treated them with 3000 ppm KIBA, 3 perlite:1 peat, mist and all rooted by the end of summer.

NATIVE HABITAT: Central Japan. Introduced 1861 to America.

Thymus serpyllum L. — Mother-of-Thyme, Wild Thyme
(thĭ′mus sĕr-pĭ′lum)

FAMILY: Lamiaceae

LEAVES: Opposite, simple, ovate or elliptic to oblong, 1/4 to 1/2″ long, about one-half as wide, obtuse, broad-cuneate, gray-green to medium green, glabrous beneath or pubescent and ciliate; petiole—short; dotted with oil glands.

SIZE: 1 to 4″ high.

HARDINESS: Zone 4 to 8.

HABIT: Prostrate, weak subshrub or nearly herbaceous perennial; spreading, trailing, with rooting stems which ascend at the ends.

RATE: Slow.

TEXTURE: Fine in leaf; hardly noticeable in winter.

LEAF COLOR: Medium green although the numerous cultivars and other species offer grayish, bluish, yellowish green, whitish margined, and yellowish colored foliage.

FLOWERS: On the species rosy purple, 1/4″ long; June through September; borne in dense terminal heads; the flowers are beautiful and one can walk by Thyme without ever noticing it underfoot but the bright flowers make it come alive; the bees appreciate the flowers and from same manufacture a delicious honey.

CULTURE: Easily moved as clumps or from containers in spring; prefers dry, calcareous, well-drained soil in a sunny location; if over-fertilized or the soil is too rich the stems become tall and weak and the plant loses its dainty character; plant 6 to 12″ apart and they will fill in adequately in one growing season; makes an excellent cover for gentle slopes, a filler among rocks, dry walks, and ledges, or a crevice plant for walls, terraces, sidewalk cracks, and the like.

DISEASES AND INSECTS: Apparently there are very few problems associated with the species although root rot and the ground mealybug have been noted.

LANDSCAPE VALUE: As discussed under culture this species and the many cultivars are well adapted for rocky, dry slopes, as an edging plant, ground cover, or among stepping stones; will endure a modicum of mowing and occasional tramping; in Stockbridge, MA, not far from Naumkeag, the species has naturalized in a dry, sandy field; actually provides swaths of color in June–July that would otherwise be dead grass.

CULTIVARS: Over 40 cultivars are known. I have had great difficulty locating specific names for many of the different flowering and foliage clones which exist.

'Albus'—Possesses white flowers.

'Citriodorus' (Lemon Thyme)—Lemon odor; will grow into a spreading, small shrub about 1′ high; considered a species, *T. × citriodorus* (Pers.) Schreb. ex Schweg. & Körte.

'Coccineus'—Has bright red flowers.

'Lanuginosus' (*T. lanuginosus* Mill. non Hort.)—A type with gray-pubescent leaves and the appropriate name, Woolly Mother-of-Thyme.

'Roseus'—A pink-flowering clone.

Other clones with lavender flowers, white leaf margins, and yellow coloring in the leaves are known.

PROPAGATION: Very easy to root from cuttings or simply divide the plant.

ADDITIONAL NOTES: *Thymus* contains 350 species and hybrids, most notably *T. × citriodorus* which embodies many cultivars. I have observed Thyme collections as far north as Minneapolis. In our garden, the thymes are lovely in spring and early summer and all but disappear by fall. Excess humidity, soil moisture, inadequate drainage, and heavy shade spell doom. Bonnie and I have tried about 12 different types and have none to recommend as good doers.

NATIVE HABITAT: Europe, western Asia, northern Africa. Cultivated for centuries.

Tilia americana L. — American Linden or Basswood
(til′i-á á-mer-i-kā′ná)

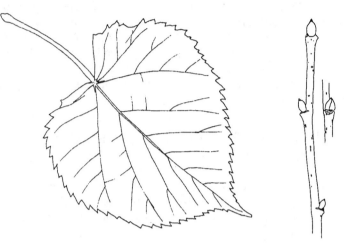

FAMILY: Tiliaceae

LEAVES: Alternate, simple, broad-ovate, 4 to 8″ long, almost as wide, abruptly acuminate, cordate to truncate at base, coarsely serrate with long-pointed teeth, lustrous dark green and glabrous above, light green beneath, 3 to 5 principal veins arising at the base, with tufts of hair in the axils of the lateral veins, wanting at base; petiole—1 to 3″ long, glabrous.

BUDS: Terminal—absent, laterals—1/4 to 1/3″ long, somewhat flattened, often lopsided, divergent, brown, reddish brown or greenish, smooth or slightly downy at apex, bud shaped like a teardrop, 2-scaled.

STEM: Moderate, smooth gray-brown, shining brown or greenish red, covered with a bloom, generally zig-zag, glabrous.

SIZE: 60 to 80′ in height with a spread of 1/2 to 2/3's the height, but can grow to 100′ or more; national champion is 78′ by 100′ in Montgomery County, PA.

HARDINESS: Zone 3b to 8(9).

HABIT: Tall, stately tree with numerous, slender, low hung, spreading branches; pyramidal in youth; at maturity the lower drooping down then up, forming a deep, ovate, oblong, or somewhat rounded crown.

RATE: Medium, 20 to 30′ over a 20 year period although some authorities indicate the tree may grow 2 to 3′ over a 10 to 20 year period; soil conditions largely govern the growth rate; in Minnesota tests both the species and 'Pyramidalis' ('Fastigiata') were 25′ high after 8 years from 1 1/4 to 1 3/4″ diameter whips.

TEXTURE: Coarse in all seasons, in this edition I bent a degree, perhaps medium-coarse.

BARK: Gray to brown, broken into many long, narrow, flat-topped, scaly ridges, very tough and fibrous.

LEAF COLOR: Dark green above, paler green beneath, sometimes changing to pale yellow in the fall; usually the leaves fall off green or yellow-green; leaves on some trees tend to develop a brownish cast in mid-September and actually become unsightly; this seems even more pronounced if the summer was extremely dry; common in the Great Smoky Mountains National Park on the banks above streams; easily identified by large leaves and particularly the silver-backed leaves (formally tied to *T. heterophylla*).

FLOWERS: Perfect, pale yellow, 1/2″ wide, fragrant, borne in 5- to 10(15)-flowered, 2 to 3″ wide, pendulous cymes in mid to late June; bees supposedly make the finest honey from these flowers; bracts spatulate, 3 to 4″ long.

FRUIT: Not clearly defined, but termed a nut-like structure, 1/3 to 1/2″ long, grayish tomentose, subglobose, of no ornamental value, thick-shelled, without ribs.

CULTURE: Transplants readily; prefers deep, moist, fertile soils and here reaches maximum size but will grow on drier, heavier soils and is often found in the wild on the slopes of hills, even in rocky places; pH adaptable; full sun or partial shade; not particularly air pollutant tolerant.

DISEASES AND INSECTS: Anthracnose occasionally occurs on the European lindens, leaf blight, canker, leaf spots, powdery mildew, *Verticillium* wilt, linden aphid, Japanese beetle, elm calligrapha, European linden bark borer, linden borer, walnut lace bug, caterpillars, basswood leaf miner, elm sawfly, thrips, galls caused by Eriophyid mite, scales and linden mite can be and often are serious problems; the foliage feeding insects can damage the trees as they strip them of almost all foliage.

LANDSCAPE VALUE: Limited because of size; too many superior European species which are more tolerant and ornamental; a handsome native tree which perhaps should be left in the woods; in the southern Appalachians, in rich coves, along streams, in floodplain soils, the species is relatively common, the large leaves, often silver- or gray-backed are prominent; definitely not for the small property; perhaps parks, golf courses, and other large areas.

CULTIVARS:

'Boulevard'—Narrow pyramidal; medium green summer foliage, yellow fall color; 50′ by 25′; Zone 3.

'Dakota'—A round-headed form introduced by Ben Gilbertson, Kindred, SD.

'Douglas'—Luxuriant deep green foliage; upright specimen tree growth with little staking or pruning; develops into broad pyramid; a Klehm introduction.

'Fastigiata'—A distinct pyramidal form which could be used in restricted growing areas; not a bad looking tree; spreads out a bit with age; selected in Rochester Parks about 1927.

Frontyard™ ('Bailyard')—Form with symmetrical branching; how different from 'Fastigiata' is unknown.

Legend™ ('Wandell')—Distinctly pyramidal with a central leader and excellent branching structure; thick dark green leaves are resistant to late season discoloration which often renders those of the species unsightly; winter stem and bud color is red; 55-year-old parent tree is 55′ high and 36′ wide; a Wandell introduction.

'Lincoln'—Slender-upright compact form with lighter green foliage; yellow in autumn; 27′ by 14′ after 24 years; a Klehm introduction.

'Redmond'—Originally listed as a *T.* × *euchlora* form but more properly included here; densely pyramidal with large leaves that are intermediate between *T. americana* and *T.* × *euchlora*; introduced by the Plumfield Nurseries of Fremont, NE in 1927; makes a handsome street or lawn tree; I have thoroughly examined this cultivar and find it to differ from *T.* × *euchlora* in stem color (gray-brown-maroon on top, underside often greenish brown) and buds (glossy, ovoid, 3/8″ long, reddish); the leaves approximate those of *T. americana* rather than *T.* × *euchlora* in size and color; in Kansas tests, this was slow to establish and averaged only 9.6″ per year over a 10 year period.

'Rosehill'—An improved selection, fast growing and developing an open crown.

'Sentry'—Uniform symmetrical habit; branches silver-gray in youth; McKay Nursery introduction, Waterloo, WI.

PROPAGATION: *Tilia* seed shows a delayed germination because of an impermeable seed coat, a dormant embryo, and a tough pericarp. Seed treatments that consistently result in good germination have not been developed. Recommendations include removing the pericarp, etching the seed coat in concentrated sulfuric acid for 10 to 15 minutes, and then stratifying in a moist medium for 3 months at 34 to 38°F. Seeds will germinate the following spring if picked before fruit wall and bract turn gray to brown. See *Seed Sci. Tech.* 16(1):273–280 (1988). Cuttings have been rooted using mid-May to late June softwoods (Kansas), wound, 20000 to 30000 ppm IBA quick-dip, perlite:peat, and mist. See *The Plant Propagator* 24(2):15 (1978) for details. Typically the cultivars are summer budded on seedling understock.

ADDITIONAL NOTES: The wood of these trees is used for many purposes including furniture, boxes, cooperage, wooden ware, veneer, and food containers. The tough inner bark is sometimes used for making rope. Since the 1983 edition several valuable papers concerning *Tilia* have been published. Some of the information is utilized herein but for in depth information, see Santamour and McArdle, *J. Arboriculture* 11:157–164 (1985); Muir, *The Plantsman* 5:206–242 (1985); and Muir, *The Plantsman* 10:104–127 (1988). Lancaster, *The Garden* 120(7):394–395 (1995), discusses *T. henryana* Szyszyl. and *T. oliveri* Szyszyl., two relatively unheralded species. The former is beautiful in new leaf, emerging pink to bronze-red, covered with silvery pubescence, the leaves maturing to lustrous dark green with long bristle-pointed teeth. *Tilia oliveri* is akin to *T. tomentosa*. I am unaware of large trees in the United States, although the Arnold Arboretum has accessioned *T. henryana*.

NATIVE HABITAT: Canada to Virginia and Alabama, west to North Dakota, Kansas and Texas. In the broadest interpretation ranging from Maine to Florida, west to eastern North Dakota, south to Oklahoma and Louisiana. Introduced 1752.

RELATED SPECIES: Somewhat crystal-ballish as to the exact taxonomic status of the closely related species and one reference, Duncan and Duncan, list *T. caroliniana* Mill., *T. floridana* (V. Engl.) Small, *T. georgiana* Sarg., *T. glabra* Vent., *T. heterophylla* Vent., and *T. monticola* Sarg. as synonyms. I attempted to teach both *T. americana* and *T. heterophylla* to my Illinois students and most simply raised their eyebrows or winced. Translation: who are you kidding, nobody can identify these things.

Tilia heterophylla Vent. — Beetree Linden, White Basswood
(Now merged with *T. americana*)

LEAVES: Alternate, simple, ovate, 3 to 6″ long, about as wide, gradually acuminate, obliquely truncate or rarely subcordate at base, finely serrate, with aristate teeth, lustrous dark green and glabrous above, beneath with close thick white tomentum or often brownish on the upper leaves, and with small tufts of reddish brown hairs; petiole—1 to 1 1/2″ long, glabrous.

BUDS: Terminal—absent, laterals—1/4 to 1/2″ long, prominently pointed, reddish maroon, glabrous.

STEM: Glabrous, relatively stout, reddish maroon.

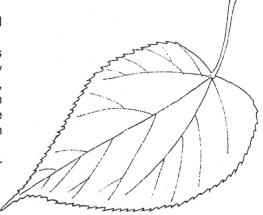

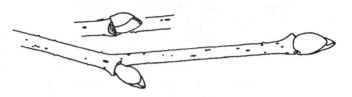

Tilia heterophylla, (til′i-à   het-ẽr-ō-fil′à), Beetree Linden, also called White Basswood, is similar to the preceding but is typically a southern species. Morphologically, very similar except for undersurface of leaf, which is densely whitish; flowers smaller (1/4″ long) and 10 to 25 per inflorescence. I have reason to suspect that many trees labeled *T. americana* are, in fact, *T. heterophylla* and possibly were bought from southern nurseries. At Illinois, I taught this and *T. americana* with students forever bringing me samples to identify. Many specimens were not clear-cut and apparently some forms of *T. heterophylla* are almost hairless below. Indeed, the tree is handsome but in my own mind probably does not deserve species rank. Mr. Bill Wandell introduced a handsome upright form, 'Continental Appeal', with a distinct oval form and a tremendous heavy crown, the large lustrous leaves being distinctly silvery on the underside, an excellent plant where lateral space to spread is limited, quite urban tolerant and transplants readily. Current thinking includes this species with *T. americana* which means 'Continental Appeal' would be a cultivar of *T. americana*. Native from West Virginia to northern Florida, Alabama and Indiana. Cultivated 1755. Zone 5 to 9.

Tilia cordata Mill. — Littleleaf Linden, Small-leaved Lime
(til′i-à   kôr-dā′tà)

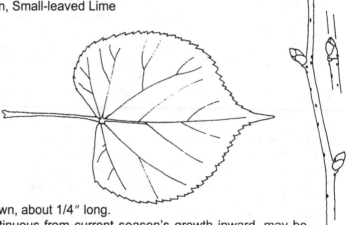

LEAVES: Alternate, simple, suborbicular, 1 1/2 to 3″(4″) long, almost as wide and sometimes broader than long, abruptly acuminate, cordate, sharply and rather finely serrate, dark green and glabrous and somewhat lustrous above, glaucous or glabrescent and glabrous beneath except axillary tufts of brown hairs; petiole—3/4 to 1 1/4″ long, slender, glabrous.

BUDS: Similar to *T. americana*—small, brown, about 1/4″ long.

STEM: Slender, lustrous brown, color continuous from current season's growth inward, may be greenish brown, glabrous.

SIZE: 60 to 70′ in height and 1/2 to 2/3's that in spread; can grow 80 to 90′ high.

HARDINESS: Zone 3b to 7; have observed a few trees in Athens and Atlanta, some have lived, others died; some shade in afternoon has allowed several trees on the Georgia campus to develop into respectable specimens.

HABIT: Pyramidal in youth; upright-oval to pyramidal-rounded and densely branched in old age.

RATE: Medium, 10 to 15′ over a 5 to 10 year period.

TEXTURE: Medium in all seasons.

BARK: Gray-brown, ridged-and-furrowed on older trunks.

LEAF COLOR: Dark shiny green in summer changing to yellow in fall; often, at best, only yellow-green, on occasion excellent soft yellow.

FLOWERS: Yellowish, fragrant, borne in 5- to 7-flowered, pendulous, 2 to 3″ wide cymes in late June or early July; flowers before *T. tomentosa*; floral bract 1 1/2 to 3 1/2″ long, 3/8 to 3/4″ wide.

FRUIT: Globose nutlet, thin-shelled, slightly or not ridged, covered with a gray pubescence, finally glabrous.

CULTURE: Readily transplanted; prefers moist, well-drained, fertile soil; full sun; pH adaptable; found on limestone in the wild; quite pollution tolerant; one of the best street and city trees and widely used for same.

DISEASES AND INSECTS: See under *T. americana*; aphids and Japanese beetles are often a problem; worthwhile study, *J. Arboriculture* 20(5):278–281 (1994), that reported the glabrous species had greater linden aphid populations than the pubescent species; I have noted these differences for *T. tomentosa* compared to *T. cordata* but the above is the first time it was quantified.

LANDSCAPE VALUE: Excellent shade tree for lawn, large areas, streets, planters, malls, and about any place a real quality tree is desired; can be pruned (and quite effectively) into hedges; the Europeans tend to use the tree much more as a hedge than do the Americans.

CULTIVARS:

'Bicentennial'—Tight pyramidal-conical form with acute branch angles; small typical dark green leaves; Ohio Shade Tree Tests mentioned an upright oval habit.

'Bohlje' ('Erecta')—Form of narrow, upright habit that supposedly is well-suited to street tree use in urban areas; leaves small, orbicular, coloring yellow and holding late in fall.

'Chancellor'—Fastigiate in youth becoming pyramidal with age; fast growing; has good crotch development.

'Corinthian'—Compact pyramid; formal shape created by uniform spacing of limbs around straight central leader; dense branching; lustrous dark green leaves; leaves smaller, thicker and more lustrous than species; 45′ by 15′; Lake County introduction.

'De Groot'—Sturdy, upright tree with compact head; glossy dark green foliage; slower growing than most lindens; 40′ by 25′.

'Fairview'—Strong, straight rapid growth; thick leathery dark green leaves are slightly larger than the species; well proportioned crown; matures as a liner about one grade larger than most *Tilia* of the same age; more informal habit than some cultivars.

'Firecracker'—Broad-pyramidal form; good branching character; leafs out about 2 weeks later than most cultivars.

'Glenleven'—Fast-growing selection with a straight trunk; more open than typical *T. cordata*; leaf 1 1/2 to 2 times size of 'Greenspire'; introduced by Sheridan Nurseries, Ontario, Canada; 50′ by 35′; possibly a *T. × flavescens* selection.

'Golden Cascade'—Similar to 'Norlin' but with cascading branches, globe-shaped crown, golden foliage in fall, introduced by Wilbert G. Ronald, Jeffries Nurseries, Portage la Prairie, Canada.

'Green Globe'—A bushy round-headed form that is top grafted at 6 to 7′ on *Tilia* understock; foliage is dark green; 15′ by 15′.

'Greenspire'—Maintains a single leader with a nice branching habit; widely used as a street tree; result of a cross between cultivar 'Euclid' and a selection from the Boston Parks; does well under difficult conditions; good dark green foliage; handsome tree; grew only 9.5″ per year over a 10 year period in Kansas tests; 40 to 50′ by 30′; have seen some of the early trees at Princeton Nursery which have maintained excellent form; listed as more susceptible to sunscald and mechanical damage, I am not sure this is the case, suspect that this being the most widely planted cultivar, the bark problems are more frequently associated with the clone.

'Handsworth'—Young stems are a light yellow-green; quite striking especially on young trees; also listed as *T. platyphyllos* form.

'June Bride'—According to the introducers, Manbeck Nurseries, Inc., New Knoxville, OH, this clone is distinguished from other clones by the "unique combination of substantially pyramidal habit of growth, maintaining an excellent straight central leader, the branches are evenly spaced around the leader; the small-sized leaves are more glossy than those of the species, and flowers more abundant with 3 to 4 times as many"; have seen in Spring Grove in flower, it is a handsome tree and absolutely dripping with flowers.

'Morden'—Dense pyramidal crown; quite hardy; introduced by Morden Research Station in 1968; slowest growing in Minnesota tests over an 8 year period.

'Norlin'—Broad pyramidal form with strong branches; listed as sun scald resistant; dark green leaves; selected for adaptability to northern plains; have tested in Georgia where it simply does not grow.

'Olympic'—Symmetrical form with better branching; glossy dark green leaves; 40′ by 30′.

'Pendula Nana'—Dwarf compact habit with pendent branches; strictly for the collector; Girard Nursery introduction.

'Prestige'—Excellent form, shape and limb structure; slightly broader than 'Greenspire' but with controlled shape; fast-growing; easily headed in nursery production; shiny bright green leaves; 60′ by 40′; Bill Wandell introduction.

'Rancho'—An upright-oval clone with small, glossy green leaves, good crotch development, and a medium-fine branch texture; has proven to be a good selection; flowers heavily with very fragrant, small, yellow flowers; 45′ by 20′.

'Salem'—Upsweeping branches form rounded head; brilliant deep green foliage; 35′ high.

Shamrock® ('Baileyi')—Supposedly stouter but more open crown than 'Greenspire'; strong broad-pyramidal outline; more vigorous; typical foliage; 40′ by 30′.

'Swedish Upright'—Narrow, upright in outline, old trees become pyramidal.

'Turesi' ('Turesii')—Strong-growing, pyramidal form.

PROPAGATION: See under *T. americana*; 49% germination after 7 months cold-moist stratification; successful tissue culture shoot proliferation utilizing thidiazuron, see *Biologia Plantarum* 29(6):425–429 (1987); cultivars are budded on seedling understocks.

ADDITIONAL NOTES: Pellett et al., *J. Environ. Hort.* 6(2):48–52 (1988) presented valuable growth data on *T. americana*, *T. cordata*, *T.* × *europaea*, and *T. platyphyllos* species and cultivars after 8 years. The information is difficult to compare because the liners were slightly different sizes at the time of planting. Perhaps the most striking aspect is the similarity in growth among the many *Tilia cordata* cultivars.

NATIVE HABITAT: *Tilia cordata* is native to Europe and has been planted as a shade tree since ancient times.

RELATED SPECIES:

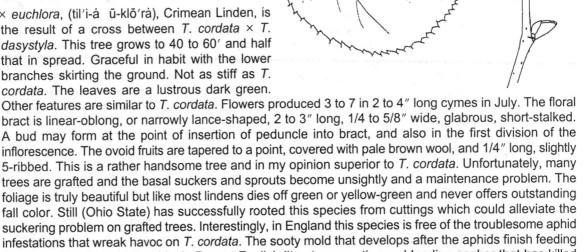

Tilia* × *euchlora K. Koch — Crimean or Caucasian Linden; more recently treated as *Tilia* 'Euchlora'.

LEAVES: Alternate, simple, roundish ovate, 2 to 4″ long and as wide, abruptly short-acuminate, obliquely cordate, finely and sharply serrate with mucronate teeth, lustrous dark green and glabrous above, pale green and glabrous beneath, except axillary tufts of brown hairs; petiole—1 to 2″ long, glabrous.

BUDS: Glabrous, 1/4″ long or greater, yellowish red to reddish above, green beneath.

STEM: Glabrous, slender, greenish yellow on bottom, light reddish brown on top, almost rose-brown.

Tilia × *euchlora*, (til′i-à ū-klō′rà), Crimean Linden, is the result of a cross between *T. cordata* × *T. dasystyla*. This tree grows to 40 to 60′ and half that in spread. Graceful in habit with the lower branches skirting the ground. Not as stiff as *T. cordata*. The leaves are a lustrous dark green. Other features are similar to *T. cordata*. Flowers produced 3 to 7 in 2 to 4″ long cymes in July. The floral bract is linear-oblong, or narrowly lance-shaped, 2 to 3″ long, 1/4 to 5/8″ wide, glabrous, short-stalked. A bud may form at the point of insertion of peduncle into bract, and also in the first division of the inflorescence. The ovoid fruits are tapered to a point, covered with pale brown wool, and 1/4″ long, slightly 5-ribbed. This is a rather handsome tree and in my opinion superior to *T. cordata*. Unfortunately, many trees are grafted and the basal suckers and sprouts become unsightly and a maintenance problem. The foliage is truly beautiful but like most lindens dies off green or yellow-green and never offers outstanding fall color. Still (Ohio State) has successfully rooted this species from cuttings which could alleviate the suckering problem on grafted trees. Interestingly, in England this species is free of the troublesome aphid infestations that wreak havoc on *T. cordata*. The sooty mold that develops after the aphids finish feeding colors the branches almost black. Recent English literature mentions a bleeding canker that has killed large trees. It is tolerant of air pollution and hot, dry conditions. 'Laurelhurst' is vigorous with straight, strong trunk, even, compact, broadly pyramidal crown, glossy dark green leaves. Zone 3 to 7. Originated about 1860 but its parentage is not clear cut.

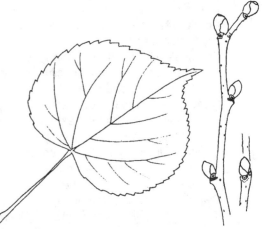

Tilia* × *europaea L. — Common or European Linden, also listed as *T.* × *vulgaris* Hayne. Former is correct according to *Kew Bulletin* 50(1):135–139 (1995).

LEAVES: Alternate, simple, broad-ovate, 2 to 4″ long, about as wide, short-acuminate, obliquely cordate or nearly truncate, sharply serrate, dark green and glabrous above, bright green beneath and glabrous except axillary tufts of hair; petiole—1 to 2″ long, glabrous.

Stems and buds glabrous, usually intensely red-maroon, buds and stems smaller, more refined than those of *T. heterophylla*. Occasionally stems are slightly pubescent, reflecting the *T. platyphyllos* parentage. Flowers earlier than *T. cordata* and *T.* × *euchlora*, usually around early June (Urbana, IL). Floral bract 3 to 4 1/2″ long, 1/2 to 7/8″ wide. Fruits tomentose, hard-shelled, faintly 5-ribbed.

Tilia × *europaea*, (til′i-à ū-rō-pē′à), European Linden, is another hybrid with *T. cordata* and *T. platyphyllos* the parents. Pyramidal in youth and develops a more rounded habit in old age than the previous species. Will grow over 100′ with time and a 150′ high specimen grows at Duncombe Park, Yorkshire. Tends to sucker from the base and also forms burls on the trunk. Probably not preferable to *T. cordata* and her cultivars. Widely used in Europe for allées, street, parks, formal areas. Susceptible to aphid and red spider mite attacks with subsequent sooty mold infestation. Produced by stooling and most trees in Europe have been derived from a single clone. In my estimation, it is inferior to *T. cordata* and *T.* × *euchlora*. Goldcrown® with bright golden yellow young leaves and reddish stems that mature to green was introduced by Lake County; I suspect it is a rename for 'Wratislaviensis'. 'Pallida' is a broadly conical form with reddish brown branchlets and leaves whose undersurface is yellowish green, highly rated in the Ohio Shade Tree Evaluation tests. 'Wratislaviensis' produces new growth of a yellow color which eventually becomes green; there is a plant at the Arnold Arboretum. In the United States, certainly not preferable to *T. americana*, *T.* × *euchlora* and certainly the best forms of *T. cordata*. Zone 3 to 7.

Tilia platyphyllos Scop. — Bigleaf Linden

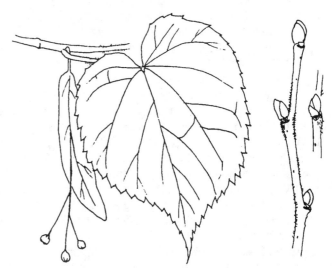

LEAVES: Alternate, simple, roundish ovate, 2 to 5″ long, about as wide, abruptly acuminate, obliquely cordate, sharply and regularly serrate, dark green and short pubescent or glabrous above, light green and pubescent beneath, especially on the veins, rarely nearly glabrous; petiole—1/2 to 2″ long, pubescent.

BUDS: Terminal—absent, laterals—1/4″ long, reddish green-brown.

STEM: Reddish green-brown, pilose on young stems, rarely glabrous.

FLOWERS: Borne about the same time as *T.* × *europaea*; generally the earliest flowering linden and soon followed by tomentose, 5-ribbed, hard-shelled, subglobose to pyriform, 1/3 to 1/2″ long fruits.

Tilia platyphyllos, (til′i-à plat-i-fil′ōs), Bigleaf Linden, grows 60 to 80′ high and larger. Not extensively planted in the United States although the few large specimens I have seen were extremely beautiful in foliage (dark green) and outline (similar to *T. cordata*). It has the largest leaves of the European species but in no way compares in size to our American species. Yellowish white flowers occur in 3-, sometimes 6-flowered, pendent, 3/4″ long cymes and are about the first to open. Floral bracts are 2 to 5″ long, 1/2 to 1 1/4″ wide. Very variable and numerous types have arisen. Cultivars include:

    'Aurea'—Young twigs and branches yellow; must be viewed close-up to be appreciated.

    'Fastigiata'—Upright-oval in habit; branches strongly ascending.

    'Laciniata'—Irregularly lobed leaves and considerably smaller tree than the species; not particularly handsome; several cut-leaf forms exist.

    'Rubra'—Young stems red in winter.

    'Tortuosa'—The branches are curiously curled and twisted; not a particularly handsome tree; Minnesota Landscape Arboretum has grown this for a number of years.

This species is supposedly easy to identify by the pubescent stems and leaves but this is not always true. The degree of pubescence varies tremendously from densely pubescent to almost glabrous. The ribbed nutlets may be the best feature when separating it from *T. cordata*, *T.* × *euchlora*, and *T.* × *europaea*. At the gardens of Fountainbleu, numerous *T. platyphyllos* form extended allées. Most of the trees I examined were densely pubescent. Planted in Europe for centuries. In Germany, the species is quite common. In my perusal of American nursery catalogs, I did not find a single listing of this or the cultivars. Santamour and McArdle, *J. Arboriculture* 11:157–164 (1985) listed 25 valid cultivars. Zone 4 to 6.

Tilia tomentosa Moench. — Silver Linden
(til′i-à tō-men-tō′sà)

LEAVES: Alternate, simple, suborbicular, 2 to 5″(6″) long, about as wide, abruptly acuminate, cordate to nearly truncate at base, sharply and sometimes doubly serrate or even slightly lobulate, dark green and slightly pubescent above at first, white tomentose beneath; petiole—1 to 1 1/2″ long, tomentose.

BUDS: Often partially covered with soft, short pubescence, green-red-brown in color, about 1/4″ long.

STEM: Covered with a soft, short pubescence; the dense, short pubescent stems separate this species and *T. petiolaris* (*T.* 'Petiolaris') from the other commonly grown lindens.

SIZE: 50 to 70′ high by 1/2 to 2/3's that in spread.

HARDINESS: Zone 4 to 7.

HABIT: Pyramidal when young, upright-oval to pyramidal-oval in old age; one of my favorite shade trees; can be effectively grown as a multi-stemmed specimen for in this way the light gray, smooth bark is maximally enjoyed; the largest tree I have seen is located in the Arnold Arboretum and grows next to an equally large and beautiful *T. cordata*; both are about 60′ in height with upright oval habits.

RATE: Medium, similar to *T. cordata*.

TEXTURE: Medium throughout the seasons.

BARK: Light gray and smooth, almost beech-like on trunks up to 8 to 10″ and eventually becoming gray-brown, ridged-and-furrowed.

LEAF COLOR: Lustrous, shimmering, glistening, gleaming dark green on the upper surface, silvery tomentose beneath; when the wind is blowing a nice effect is created as both leaf surfaces are exposed; have seen decent yellow fall color on occasion.

FLOWERS: Yellowish white, fragrant, supposedly narcotic to bees; late June to early July; borne in 7- to 10-flowered, pendulous cymes, generally the last *Tilia* to flower, bract 1 1/2 to 2 1/2″ long.

FRUIT: Egg-shaped with a short point, 1/3 to 3/8″ long, whitish pubescent, minutely warted, faintly 5-angled.

CULTURE: See under *T. cordata*.

DISEASES AND INSECTS: See under *T. cordata*.

LANDSCAPE VALUE: Good street tree as it tolerates heat and drought better than other lindens; overall less prone to insects and untidiness of the other species; I highly recommend this for residential plantings as it is an extremely beautiful ornamental shade tree.

CULTIVARS:

'Brabant'—Broad conical crown with a strong central leader; leaves dark green with yellow fall color; excellent street tree.

'Erecta' ('Fastigiata')—An upright clone; as I have seen it not too different from the species especially with age.

Green Mountain®—An improved rapid-growing form; develops a handsome, dense-headed tree that is heat and drought tolerant; dark green leaves with silvery undersides; 50 to 70′ by 40′; Princeton introduction.

'Satin Shadow'—Gilted green leaves with silver undersides; 50′ by 40′; Lake County introduction.

'Sterling'—Impressive, sculptured, broad pyramidal crown with lustrous dark green leaves, silvery on the underside; young leaves silvery; 30-year-old tree 45′ by 24′; handsome grayish bark and uniform winter silhouette; resistant to Japanese beetle and Gypsy moth; a Wandell introduction.

PROPAGATION: See under *T. americana*.

ADDITIONAL NOTES: Considerable German literature that points to honeybee and bumblebee death after sampling the nectar of *T. tomentosa*, *T. petiolaris*, *T. dasystyla*, *T.* × *euchlora* and others. One paper recommended that *T. cordata*, *T. platyphyllos*, and *T.* × *europaea* be no longer utilized in urban areas in Germany.

NATIVE HABITAT: Southeastern Europe, western Asia. Introduced 1767.

RELATED SPECIES:

Tilia mongolica Maxim. — Mongolian Linden

LEAVES: Alternate, simple, ovate to broadly ovate, 1 1/2 to 3″ long and as wide, acuminate, truncate or cordate, coarsely serrate, serrations triangular, with slender points, often 3- to 5-lobed especially on vigorous shoots, bronze-red when first emerging, lustrous dark green and glabrous above, paler and glabrous below except for tufts of pubescence in axils of veins; petiole—1″ long, glabrous, reddish.

Tilia mongolica, (til'i-à mon-gōl'i-kà), Mongolian Linden, is a small (30′), graceful, round-headed tree. The leaves are small and deeply cut (almost lobed), which makes the leaf unlike any linden leaf. The glabrous stems supposedly turn a good red in winter although most stems I have examined were reddish brown. Leaves may turn good yellow in autumn. Also is resistant to aphids. This tree received rave reviews early in its career but nurserymen and others have found it hard to grow, tends to flop, must be trained, grafted on *T. cordata*. In addition it is subject to storm damage, ice, and snow. I have changed my assessment of this species and recommend growers and home-owners temper their enthusiasm. Perhaps the most notable aspect is that the leaf does not look like a Linden. A leaf spot has also been reported. 'Harvest Gold' was selected for its upright habit, excurrent growth, exfoliating bark and consistent golden yellow fall color, introduced by Wilbert G. Ronald, Jeffries Nurseries, Portage la Prairie, Canada. Native to China, Mongolia. Introduced 1880. Zone 3 to 5(6).

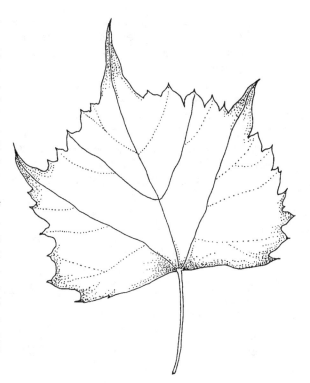

Tilia petiolaris DC. sensu Hooker (recent literature lists this as *T.* 'Petiolaris', a taxonomic change that was long overdue), (til'i-à pet-i-ō-lā'ris), Pendent Silver Linden, is closely allied to *T. tomentosa*, but differs chiefly in the pendulous, graceful branches. It makes a beautiful specimen tree and perhaps the finest in the country are located at Swarthmore College and the University of Illinois. Trees may reach 70 to 90′ high, perhaps one-half this in spread. Interestingly, this species exhibited the best fall color of all the lindens in the Arnold's extensive collection. It was a uniform golden yellow and extremely effective. I highly recommend the tree for the individual who wants something different and better than the standard *Tilia cordata* syndrome. The petioles are longer than those of *T. tomentosa* but this is not a black and white trait for separating the two taxa. I believe *T. petiolaris* is nothing more than a selection of *T. tomentosa* and should correctly be listed as a cultivar. Santamour and McArdle listed this as 'Pendula'. *The New RHS Dictionary of Gardening* reconciles it to *T.* 'Petiolaris'. Supposedly the bees find the flowers narcotic or poisonous and can be found in large numbers on the ground under such trees. I did not notice strange "bee-behavior" around the Illinois tree. It is interesting to note that although this tree is listed as a species, it is usually grafted. I would be interested in knowing what percentage of seed-grown trees exhibit the weeping tendency. 'Orbicularis' has somewhat more pendulous branches and a more conical crown; the petioles are shorter and undersides gray; may be a hybrid between *T. petiolaris* and *T.* × *euchlora*. There is a handsome specimen in Wisley Garden. Dr. Donald Wyman considered it the most beautiful of the lindens. Native to southeastern Europe and Western Asia. Introduced 1840. Zone 5 to 7.

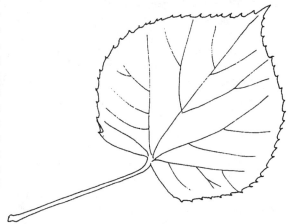

Toona sinensis (A. Juss.) M. Roem. (formerly *Cedrela sinensis* A. Juss.) — Chinese Cedrela or Chinese Toon
(tön'à sī-nen'sis)

FAMILY: Meliaceae

LEAVES: Alternate, pinnately compound, 10 to 20″ long, leaflets 10 to 22, short-stalked, oblong to lance-oblong, 3 to 6″ long, acuminate, base unequal on each side of midrib, remotely and slightly serrate or nearly entire, pubescent beneath on veins or finally glabrous; young leaves smell like onions when crushed; reddish bronze in color on newly emerging leaves, eventually medium to dark green; petiole—long.

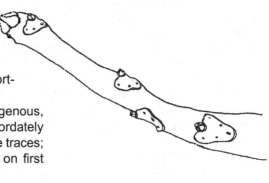

BUDS: Solitary, sessile, short-ovoid, with about 4 short-pointed, exposed scales; terminal much larger.

STEM: Coarse, terete, puberulent; pith—large, homogenous, roundish, white becoming colored; leaf scars cordately elliptical shield-shaped, slightly raised, large; 5 bundle traces; no stipular scars; could be mistaken for *Ailanthus* on first inspection.

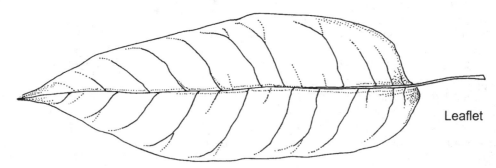

Leaflet

SIZE: 30 to 40′ tall under landscape conditions; can grow 60 to 70′ in the wild; often suckering and forming colonies.

HARDINESS: Zone 5 to 7; has survived –25°F, however, Morten Arboretum, Lisle, IL reported freeze injury almost every year.

HABIT: Upright-oval, single-stemmed and from a distance resembles *Carya ovata*, variable, may also be multi-stemmed or suckering.

RATE: Medium to fast.

TEXTURE: Medium-coarse in summer; coarse in winter.

BARK: Brown, peeling off in long strips similar to that of *Carya ovata* in appearance but on a reduced scale.

LEAF COLOR: Reddish purple when unfolding, gradually turning medium to dark green in summer; fall color is of no consequence, although yellow has been mentioned in the literature.

FLOWERS: Small, perfect, white, malodorous, campanulate, about 1/5″ long, borne in pendulous, 12″ long panicles in June.

FRUIT: Woody capsule, about 1″ long and wide, with winged seeds, fruit looks like a wood rose, discovered a tree outside the Nation's Capitol with fruits littering the ground, actually quite attractive but not sufficient reason to grow the tree.

CULTURE: Quite adaptable to different soils; grows under extreme stress; possibly should be given a longer look.

DISEASES AND INSECTS: None serious.

LANDSCAPE VALUE: Has been used as a street tree in Philadelphia, PA, Santa Barbara, CA, and Paris, France.

CULTIVARS:

    'Flamingo'—An interesting form with pink- to cream-colored new foliage that eventually changes to green; as I have observed it, the new foliage emerges hot purple-red and matures to green; originated in Australia around 1930 and the name was first published in 1981.

PROPAGATION: Seed apparently requires no pretreatment although reported success varies; a one-month cold stratification is suggested; root cuttings will produce shoots; collect in October and later.

ADDITIONAL NOTES: Resembles *Ailanthus altissima* in morphological features except it does not bear the glandular teeth near the base of the leaflet and the leaves have an oniony smell. The young shoots are boiled and eaten as a vegetable by the Chinese. The tree was known to botanists since 1743, but was not introduced to Europe until 1862. By some strange happenstance this species was included in a planting on the Georgia campus. At first I thought it was *Ailanthus* but the onion smell gave it away. Has not performed well in the heat of the Georgia summers. Probably the most complete landscape treatment of the species is offered by Koller, *Arnoldia* 38:158–161 (1978).

NATIVE HABITAT: Northern and eastern China. Introduced 1862.

Torreya taxifolia Arn. — Stinking Cedar, Florida Torreya

FAMILY: Cephalotaxaceae, Taxaceae
LEAVES: Evergreen, spirally arranged, needles spreading in one plane, needle-like, linear-acicular, 1 to 1 3/4″ long, flat, stiff, apices sharp to touch, lustrous dark green above, with gray-green stomatal lines below, short petioles; strongly malodorous when bruised.
BARK: Gray-brown, ridged-and-furrowed, forming almost woven pattern.

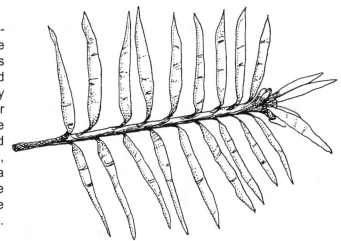

Torreya taxifolia, (tôr′i-à taks-i-fō′li-à), Stinking Cedar, is a small needle evergreen, usually loosely pyramidal in outline. Plants at the Biltmore Gardens are tree-like with somewhat open crowns while a large, 30 to 35′ high specimen in Lee, FL is dense and broad pyramidal. The national champion is listed as 45′ by 40′ in Norlina, NC. The species is on the Federal Endangered List and suffers from a twig (shoot) blight. Considerable effort to propagate and establish the species away from home base. Dioecious with the male cones borne singly in the axils of the needles of the previous year; the female in leaf axils of current season's growth. The olive-like seed is wholly enclosed by a leathery tissue, dark green with purplish stripes, bloomy, about 1 to 1 1/4″ long, 1/2 to 3/4″ wide. Seeds have been germinated and cuttings rooted. Certainly not a plant for the landscape but worth appreciating and preserving. Nicholson, *Natural History* 12/90, discusses "Chasing Ghosts" along the steep ravines of Florida's Apalachicola River. Florida, Georgia. Found in wooded slopes and bluffs east of the Apalachicola River and northward into Georgia. Introduced 1840. Zone 6 to 9.

RELATED SPECIES:

Torreya nucifera (L.) Sieb. & Zucc., (tôr′i-à nū-sif′ĕr-à), Japanese Torreya, forms a dense pyramid. The lustrous dark green needles are 3/4 to 1 1/4″ long, linear-lanceolate and taper to a sharp apex. Needles are highly aromatic when bruised. The second year stems are reddish brown compared to the greenish stems of *T. taxifolia*. The naked seed is ellipsoid-oblong, about 1″ long, green, faintly tinged purple. There is a handsome, ±40′ high specimen on the Swarthmore College campus. Possibly the hardiest of the *Torreya* species. Japan. Introduced before 1764. Zone 6 to 8.

Trachelospermum jasminoides (Lindl.) Lem. — Confederate or Star Jasmine
(trā-ke-lō-spĕr′mum jaz-min-oy′dēz)

FAMILY: Apocynaceae
LEAVES: Opposite, simple, evergreen, ovate-rounded, 1 1/2 to 3 1/2″ long, 1/2 to 1″ wide, abruptly acute, cuneate to rounded, entire, glabrous, leathery, new growth bronze-purple, lustrous dark green above, pale green beneath, with veins darker green creating a prominent mosaic; petiole—1/4″ long, pubescent.
BUDS: Imbricate, 1/32 to 1/16″ long, brown.
STEM: Slender, rounded, dark brown, pubescent, exuding a milky sap when cut.

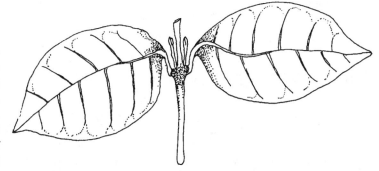

Trachelospermum jasminoides, Confederate or Star Jasmine, is a twining evergreen vine or ground cover (10 to 12′, possible to 20′) with lustrous dark green leaves and fragrant, 1″ diameter, 5-petaled, cream-white (tinge of yellow) flowers that occur in slender, stalked cymes. The flowers open from May to June (late April to early May in Athens) and sporadically thereafter and provide a delightful fragrance. Flowers are produced on short laterals from previous year's growth, although some flowers appear to develop on new growth of the season. For this reason, prune after flowering. The plant requires support and will make an effective cover on any type of latticework. Pruning is a necessary prerequisite every year if the plant is to be kept in bounds. Has been used on the Georgia campus in a courtyard area where the fragrant flowers hold court. Can also be used as a ground cover in shaded situations. Prefers partial or full shade and moist, well-drained soils but is adaptable to a wide range of conditions. 'Bruce Martin' is a large leaf, cold hardy form, has survived outside in containers at Seneca, SC; Head-Lee Nursery introduction. 'Bronze Beauty' has bronze-colored leaves that are more elongated and less lustrous. 'Madison' is more cold hardy and the underside of the leaf is densely pubescent compared to the glabrous undersides of the typical form, probably var. *pubescens*, introduced by the late Cedar Lane Farm, Madison, GA. 'Silver Mist' is spotted and blotched white. 'Yellow' has yellow flowers, otherwise as the species, offered by Louisiana Nurseries. Have observed a very pretty form on which the leaves are bordered and blotched with white ('Variegatum'), the interior of the leaf is gray-green, exterior creamy. In winter creamy areas turn pinkish red to carmine. Can be used for a multiplicity of purposes. Easily rooted from softwood cuttings in June or July and could probably be rooted about anytime of year. Often grown as a glasshouse plant in the north. Japan, China. Zone (7)8 to 10. Actually tender in the vicinity of Athens, GA and should be sited carefully. Leaves were killed at –3°F but stems and buds survived.

RELATED SPECIES

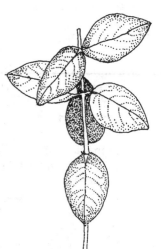

Trachelospermum asiaticum (Sieb. & Zucc.) Nak., (trã-ke-lō-spēr′mum ã-shi-at′i-kum), Japanese Star Jasmine, is a degree hardier but to my knowledge is not as common in the southern landscape. The leaves are smaller (3/4 to 2″ long, 3/8 to 3/4″ wide), elliptic or ovate, dark glossy green, glabrous, with a 1/8″ petiole and the main veins are almost white. It is apparently not as precocious as *T. jasminoides* and the flowers are yellowish white, 3/4″ across at their mouth and fragrant. Have seen it used effectively as a ground cover on the Louisiana State University campus and Coastal Plain gardens. The calyx lobes are erect; in *T. jasminoides* they are larger and reflexed. Can be used in similar landscape situations. Although the species is described as growing 15 to 20′, in the common landscape form it is a rather vigorous ground cover. I have not observed flowers on the typical ground cover forms. Also, the plant reacts to warm winter weather by deacclimating and subsequent late spring freezes kill the leaves. This happened numerous times to campus plantings, particularly those sited in full sun. 'Elegant' is a small leaf form with extremely lustrous dark green leaves. I believe this is the same as 'Asia Minor'. In 'Nortex' ('Nana'), the leaves are more lance-shaped. 'Oblanceolatum' has narrow, lustrous dark green leaves with gray veins and short internodes, makes a dense mat, hardy form from Clemson University test gardens offered by Nurseries Caroliniana. A creamy white-variegated form is known which has been utilized on the Georgia campus in a shady corner for ground cover purposes. The actual leaf color is similar to *T. jasminoides* 'Variegatum'. Japan, Korea. Cultivated 1880. Zone 7 to 9.

Tripterygium regelii Sprague & Tak. — Regels Threewingnut

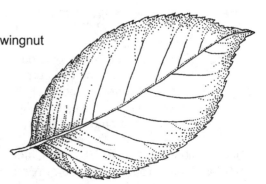

FAMILY: Celastraceae

LEAVES: Alternate, simple, oval or ovate, 2 1/2 to 6″ long, 1 1/2 to 4″ wide, acuminate at apex, broadly wedge-shaped to rounded at the base, blunt, incurved teeth, dark green and glabrous above except with minute down on the midrib when young; petiole—1/4 to 3/4″ long.

STEM: Angular, warty, brown.

Tripterygium regelii, (trip-te-rēg′i-um rē′jil′ē-ī), Regels Threewingnut, is a rather rank-climbing or rambling, deciduous shrub-vine (scandent shrub) to 30′ high. The yellowish white (green-white), 1/3″ diameter flowers are produced in large, terminal panicles and these in turn are supplemented by flowers in the axils of the terminal leaves, the entire inflorescence up to 8 or 9″ long and 2 to 3″ wide, July–August. It is an attractive plant in flower and appears to be adaptable to varied soils. The 3-angled, greenish white, winged fruits are 5/8″ long and 1/4″ wide. There was a fine plant at the Arnold Arboretum that served as my first and only field specimen. Obviously, it is not common in commerce. Relatively easy to root from firm wooded summer cuttings. Manchuria, Korea, Japan. Introduced 1904. Zone 4 to 7.

Trochodendron aralioides Sieb. & Zucc. — Wheel-tree

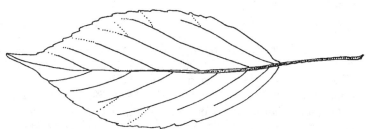

FAMILY: Trochodendraceae
LEAVES: Alternate, clustered, spiraled, simple, evergreen, rhombic-obovate to elliptic-lanceolate, 3 to 6″ long, 1 1/4 to 3″ wide, obtusely acuminate, cuneate, crenate-serrate at terminal end, leathery, lustrous dark green above, paler beneath; petiole—1 to 3″ long.
BUDS: Terminal about 1/4 to 1/3″ long, imbricate, pointed, reminding of a *Rhododendron catawbiense* flower bud.
STEM: Green year-round, glabrous, aromatic when bruised.

Trochodendron aralioides, (trō-kō-den′dron à-rā-li-oy′dēz), Wheel-tree, is a virtual unknown in American gardens but occasionally appears (like Brigadoon) in collections. The habit is distinctly shrub-like, probably no larger than 10 to 20′ high and half as wide. In the wild it supposedly reaches 60′ or greater. The branching is somewhat horizontal and almost sympodial like a sassafras. The most aesthetic aspect is the handsome foliage which although listed as dark green is a more vibrant rich green that appears to stand out from other evergreens. Flowers are a bright green and occur in 2 to 3″ long racemes in April–May. Each 3/4″ flower has a spoke-like arrangement of 40 to 70 stamens, each 1/8 to 1/4″ long, inserted on a broad disk. The fruit is a 3/4″ diameter follicle. The few plants I have seen in cultivation were in shady protected locations free from winter sun and desiccating winds. I suspect moist, well-drained, acid soil suits it best. Probably only use is a novelty or collector's item in a semi-shady area of the garden. Found in mountain forests in Japan and Korea. Seed germination was 92% at 82°F; seeds stored for 4 or 8 weeks also germinated in high percentages. Introduced 1894. Zone 6 to 7. Have tested the species in Zone 7b with no success. Heat is rate limiting factor.

Tsuga Carr. — Hemlock
FAMILY: Pinaceae

If I were forced to select one conifer for my garden it would certainly be *Tsuga canadensis*. The species has multitudinous uses and the infinite variation in seed-grown material has resulted in the selection of many excellent cultivars. The number of *Tsuga* species used in landscaping is small but they are considered among the most graceful and beautiful of large evergreen conifers. Nine to ten species have been reported, four occurring in the United States and the others in the Himalayas, China, Taiwan, and Japan. *Tsuga heterophylla* is the most important timber-producing species. Hemlock bark contains between 7 and 12% tannin, and in the United States that of *T. canadensis* was one of the principal commercial sources for many years.

MORPHOLOGICAL CHARACTERISTICS
Evergreen trees of graceful pyramidal habit with slender, horizontal to drooping branches. The bark is cinnamon-red color and furrowed. Buds are rounded and not resinous. Needles, borne on petioles, spirally arranged, more or less 2-ranked, flattened and grooved above, with 2 white stomatic bands below. Needle margin is toothed or entire and the apex is rounded, notched, or blunt-pointed. Male flowers are catkins and axillary on previous year's shoots. The greenish female flowers are terminal on previous year's lateral shoots with imbricated scales. Cones are pendulous and often produced in abundance.

According to Jenkins, *Arnoldia* 6:11–12 (1946), the name *Tsuga* is derived from a Japanese word, composed of the elements "tree" and "mother," meaning Tree-mother. Concerning the common name Hemlock, Sudworth states that the New York Indians use the descriptive name Oh-neh-tah, pronounced Hoe-o-na-dia or Hoe-na-dia, while the Indian name for the North Country (now Canada) was also Hoe-nadia, which means a land of the Hemlock.

GROWTH CHARACTERISTICS

Generally, the *Tsuga* species are stately, graceful, pyramidal trees and maintain their good characteristics in old age. The cultivars range from low ground cover types ('Coles Prostrate') to gracefully weeping ('Sargentii' or 'Pendula') to distinctly upright ('Fastigiata'). There are various globose types and the foliage colors may be whitish to yellow especially on the new growth. The Arnold Arboretum, Jamaica Plain, MA, assembled an excellent collection of hemlock variants. It is well worth the trip just to observe and study this one group of plants.

CULTURE

Hemlocks should be moved balled-and-burlapped in either spring or fall. Occasionally container-grown material is offered and this allows greater flexibility in planting schedules. They can be planted on many soil types; however, good drainage, cool, acid soils, and adequate moisture are necessary. They will not thrive under hot, extremely dry conditions. Sweeping winds may be detrimental. They will withstand full shade; however, partial shade is preferable and best growth is attained in full sunlight. They will not withstand air pollution and are susceptible to salt damage. Pruning can be accomplished in spring or summer. Hemlocks withstand heavy pruning and for this reason are often used for hedges.

DISEASES AND INSECTS

Leaf blight, cankers, blister rust, needle rust, sapwood rot, hemlock borer, hemlock looper, spruce leaf miner, hemlock fiorinia scale, grape scale, hemlock scale, spider mites and other pests. Woolly adelgid (*Adelges tsugae*) has wreaked havoc on the species in some New England and Middle Atlantic States; over time infestations lead to decline and death; any time I visit the upper East Coast the subject of woolly adelgid invariably surfaces; it has proven a bane to successful hemlock culture. Nitrogen fertilization increased hemlock susceptibility to woolly adelgid; see *J. Arboriculture* 17(8):227–230 (1991).

PHYSIOLOGICAL DISEASES

Sunscorch, drought injury—Hemlocks are more sensitive to drought than most other narrow leaf evergreens especially when sited in southern exposures and rocky slopes.

PROPAGATION

Seed dormancy is variable in hemlock, with some seed lots requiring pregermination treatment and other germinating satisfactorily without treatment. Cold stratification of mature seeds shortens incubation time and may substantially increase germinative energy, and is therefore recommended. General recommendation for *T. canadensis*, *T. caroliniana*, *T. heterophylla*, and *T. mertensiana* is 60 to 120 days at 41°F in moist sand. Some success has resulted from the use of cuttings but timing is critical and the rooting percentages are low. Most of the cultivars are grafted onto species understocks. For a detailed discussion of *Tsuga* propagation see Dirr and Heuser, 1987.

LANDSCAPE USE

Tsuga canadensis is used extensively for specimen, hedge, screen and grouping purposes. Often it is used in foundation plantings but care must be exercised in keep it in bounds over the years. This is quite simple for it can be maintained at a height of 3 to 5′ by judicious pruning. *Tsuga caroliniana* is less common in landscapes but, by some authorities, is considered a better plant because of greater pollution tolerance. The habit of Carolina Hemlock is a bit more stiff than Eastern Hemlock. I have observed it growing from the sides of rock mountain faces in the southern Appalachians. *Tsuga canadensis* makes one of the best evergreen hedges especially if pruned correctly. If individual shoots are removed every year (rather than shearing the entire plant) a more aesthetically pleasing effect is achieved.

Bean separated the two cultivars 'Pendula' and 'Sargentii', but according to Jenkins the nurseryman's stock has all been derived from the 4 original plants found near the summit of Fishkill Mountain (near Beacon City, on the Hudson River) by General Joseph Howland about 1870. The finder grew one in his own garden at Matteawan, NY, gave the second to Henry Winthrop Sargent (after whom the plant was named), of Fishkill; the third to H.H. Hunnewell, of Wellesley, MA, and the fourth to Prof. C.S. Sargent of the Arnold Arboretum. The second and third are dead but the first and fourth have made fine specimens. Most of the plants in cultivation have been grown from grafts; however, there are also seedlings, so some variation can be expected. The fascinating story of the Weeping Hemlock is told by Del Tredici, *Arnoldia* 40:202–223 (1980).

CULTIVARS

Amazing variety, simply too many to consider, counted 81 selections offered by various United States nurseries with 'Albospica', 'Aurea', 'Beehive', 'Bennett', 'Brandley', 'Cloud Prune', 'Cole's Prostrate', 'Curly', 'Everett Golden', 'Geneva', 'Gentsch White', 'Golden Splendor', 'Gracilis', 'Horsford Dwarf', 'Hussii', 'Jacqueline Verkade', 'Jeddeloh', 'Jervis', 'Lewisii', 'Minuta', 'Nana', 'Pendula', 'Rugg's Washington Dwarf', 'Stewart's Gem', 'Stockman's Dwarf', and 'Von Helm's Dwarf', each offered by at least three sources.

Tsuga canadensis (L.) Carr. — Canadian (Eastern) Hemlock
(tsū′gà kan-à-den′sis)

LEAVES: Almost regularly 2-ranked, linear, obtuse or acutish, 1/4 to 2/3″ long, 1/12 to 1/8″ wide, obscurely grooved, lustrous dark green above, with 2 whitish bands beneath, toothed, with a short petiole.
BUDS: Minute, ovoid, with hairy scales, light brown.
STEM: Young stems slender, grayish brown, hairy.
CONES: Small, ovoid, 1/2 to 1″ long on slender pendulous stalks, light to medium brown.

SIZE: 40 to 70′ in height by 25 to 35′ in spread; known to 100′ or more; national champion is 165′ by 38′ in Great Smoky Mountains National Park, TN.
HARDINESS: Zone 3b to 7(8); actually languishes in heat of Zone 7(8), although occasional good specimens occur.
HABIT: Softly and gracefully pyramidal in youth with tapering trunk becoming pendulously pyramidal with age; one of the most beautiful conifers.
RATE: Medium, 25 to 50′ in 15 to 30 years.
TEXTURE: Fine.
BARK: Flaky and scaly on young trees, brown, soon with wide, flat ridges; on old trees heavily and deeply furrowed; freshly cut surfaces showing purplish streaks.
LEAF COLOR: New spring growth light yellow-green changing to a glossy dark green, underside of needles with two glaucous bands.
FLOWERS: Monoecious; staminate light yellow, pistillate pale green.
FRUIT: Cones slender, stalked, ovoid, apex nearly blunt, 1/2 to 1″ long by approximately 1/4 to 1/2″ broad, brown at maturity; hang like small ornaments from the branches.
CULTURE: Transplants well balled-and-burlapped if root pruned; amenable to pruning; an excellent subject for moist, well-drained, acid soils, rocky bluffs or sandy soils; English literature lists this species as more lime tolerant than any other *Tsuga*; in Urbana, IL there were many handsome specimens growing in calcareous soils; unlike most conifers tolerates shade well; can grow in full sun as long as it has good drainage and organic matter in the soil and there is no strong, drying wind to contend with; heavy soil from which water is unable to drain is not suitable; does not tolerate wind or drought; plant in sheltered locations, avoid windswept sites and polluted conditions.
DISEASES AND INSECTS: Leaf blight, cankers, blister rust, needle rust, sapwood rot, hemlock borer, hemlock looper, spruce leaf miner, hemlock fiorinia scale, grape scale, hemlock scale, spider mites, hemlock rust mite causes emerging foliage to turn rusty or yellow in spring (mites feed openly sucking juices from the young needles, caused by a tiny Eriophyid mite), bagworm, fir flat headed borer, spruce budworm, gypsy moth, hemlock sawfly, and woolly adelgid. Two physiological problems include sunscorch which occurs when temperatures reach 95°F and above. The ends of the branches may be killed back for several inches. Another problem is drought injury for hemlocks are more sensitive to prolonged periods of dryness than most other narrowleaf evergreens. Plants may die during extended dry periods. For all the problems mentioned, hemlocks under landscape conditions can prove to be reliable, handsome ornamentals if given proper cultural care.

The most significant liability to successful culture is the woolly adelgid and this singular pest has limited the use of hemlock in the northeastern quadrant of the United States. Some indication that biological control of the adelgid may be possible from an arboreal oribated mite. Apparently maintains innocuous populations of the adelgid on *T. diversifolia* and *T. sieboldii* in Japan.
LANDSCAPE VALUE: Makes an extremely graceful evergreen hedge of value in almost any situation except city conditions; excellent for screening, groupings, accent plant and foundation planting; the most commonly planted of the hemlocks, popular over a wide area; one of our best evergreens.

CULTIVARS: At one time I considered including a long list of cultivars but decided against such a move when the long list looked end "list." There are prostrate, globose, mounded, weeping, fastigiate and variegated forms. I refer the reader to Welch and Den Ouden and Boom.

Since the last edition, more cultivars have been introduced and several new or revised books, including Del Tridici, Swartley, *Cultivated Hemlocks* (1984), Krüssmann, and van Gelderen and van Hoey Smith, offer greater coverage than this book. In the latter reference, 56 cultivars of *T. canadensis* were shown and I might add some are so ugly that they defy adjectives. In the summer of 1988, I had an opportunity to verify the collections in Mt. Airy Arboretum, Cincinnati, OH and the conifer collection, especially *Tsuga canadensis* cultivars, were neigh impossible to accurately verify. So many clones are virtually the same and when the differences are based on growth habit, i.e., compact, more compact, most compact, one is easily confused. Even 'Jeddeloh' in three or four areas did not look exactly similar. Iseli Nursery, Boring, OR listed 27 cultivars of *T. canadensis* while John Vermeulen and Son Nursery, Neshanic Station, NJ listed 38. Even a small specialty producer like Jordan Jack's Washington Evergreen Nursery, Leicester, NC listed 24 and one of the premier growers of hemlock in New England, Weston Nurseries, Hopkinton, MA described only four, but their 'Westonigra' strain which I have seen in the fields of Hopkinton, with extremely good dark green needle color in winter, may be the best around. The moral is that more is not necessarily better, only more.

'Sargentii' (f. *pendula* Beissn.)—A magnificent, broadly spreading, weeping form that is among the most handsome of all conifers; I have seen it used by water where it produced the effect of a green waterfall; as a single specimen or grouping it can be most effective; by no means a small plant although can be kept that way with judicious pruning; will grow 10 to 15′ high, twice as wide; the late Professor C.E. Lewis of Michigan State likened it to a ghost, gracefully sweeping across the landscape; really an eye-catching plant and one that is frequently available in commerce; see *Arnoldia* 40:202–223 (1980); many weeping forms have been introduced and named; several notable specimens reside at Longwood Gardens, Arnold Arboretum, Planting Fields Arboretum, and Biltmore Estate.

PROPAGATION: Seed dormancy is variable so to insure good germination it is advisable to stratify the seeds for 2 to 4 months at about 40°F. Layering has been used successfully. Cuttings have been successfully rooted but timing is important. Hormonal treatment is necessary. Percentages ranged from 60 to 90% depending on sampling time and hormonal strength.

NATIVE HABITAT: Nova Scotia to Minnesota, south along the mountains to Alabama and Georgia. Driving to the mountains from Athens (~700′ elevation), *T. canadensis* starts to appear about 1000 to 1200′ elevation and becomes common above 2000′. Abundant on slopes, mountain sides, almost anywhere drainage is reasonable. Introduced about 1736.

RELATED SPECIES:

Tsuga chinensis (Franch.) Pritz — Chinese Hemlock
LEAVES: Linear, 1/2 to 1″ long, 1/12 to 1/8″ wide, emarginate, glossy dark green above and slightly grooved, broad whitish bands below.
STEM: Yellow-brown, pubescent.

Tsuga chinensis, (tsū′gà chi-nen′sis), Chinese Hemlock, is a large tree growing over 100′ in the wild. The most inspiring news I have heard concerned the woolly adelgid resistance of the species. Considerable interest in the middle Atlantic and northeastern states as a potential alternative to *T. canadensis*. Several United States specialty nurseries offer the species. The ovoid cones are 1/2 to 1″ long, lustrous yellowish brown, scales orbicular with beveled margin. Western China. Introduced 1901. Zone 5 to 7.

Tsuga diversifolia (Maxim.) Mast. — Northern Japanese Hemlock
LEAVES: Densely arranged, generally shorter and more densely borne than *T. canadensis*, 1/4 to 5/8″ long, 1/10″ wide, distinctly notched at the apex, margins entire, glossy dark green and furrowed above, with two clearly defined chalk white bands of stomata below.

Tsuga diversifolia, (tsū′gà dī-vĕr-si-fō′li-à), Northern Japanese Hemlock, is a graceful, pyramidal tree that makes an excellent specimen in the landscape. Plant is broad pyramidal and gracefully branched. The branches are reddish brown, pubescent, while those of ***Tsuga sieboldii*** Carr., (tsū′gà sē-bōl′dē-ī), are glabrous, grayish to yellowish brown. *Tsuga sieboldii* is shrub-like and irregular as I know it in cultivation. The egg-shaped cones of *T. sieboldii* are 3/4 to 1″ long, shiny yellow buff brown with scales vertically ribbed and incurved. Cones of *T. diversifolia* are ovoid, 3/4 to 1″ long, dark brown, scales flat and striated. The finest plants of *T. diversifolia* I have seen were at Millcreek Valley Park, Youngstown, OH and based on their beauty and performance would have no trouble recommending the tree for general landscape use. Average landscape height would approximate 35 to 60'. On a recent tour of Ireland, experienced *T. diversifolia*, 30 to 40' high, gracefully arching, pyramidal habit, and lustrous dark green needles at Mt. Congreve. A specimen of *T. diversifolia* grows on the UMaine campus, Orono. Neither species are common in commerce and with so many excellent forms of *T. canadensis* it is difficult to compete. *Tsuga sieboldii* is native to Japan. Introduced 1850. Zone 5 to 6. *Tsuga diversifolia* is native to Japan. Introduced 1861. Zone (4)5 to 6.

Tsuga heterophylla (Raf.) Sarg. — Western Hemlock

LEAVES: More or less in 2 ranks (rows), although set all around the stems, 1/4 to 3/4″ long, 1/20 to 1/16″ wide, rounded at apex, entire, shining dark green and grooved above, broad white bands below.

STEM: With long pale pubescense when young, carrying pubescence into 5th and 6th years.

Tsuga heterophylla, (tsū′gȧ het-ĕr-ō-fil′ȧ), Western Hemlock, is a handsome tall tree with a narrow pyramidal crown, slightly semi-pendulous branchlets and fine-textured, dark green needles with two whitish bands below. Quad-national champions are 174' by 65'; 241' by 67'; 202' by 47'; and 227' by 49' in Olympic National Park. I have seen the tree in Washington, Vancouver, BC and all over Europe and it makes an imposing specimen. The 3/4 to 1″ long cones are sessile but hang from the branch tops. Best growth occurs in a moisture laden atmosphere and at cooler summer temperatures than are found in the eastern United States. The stems are yellow-brown, change to dark red-brown and remain pubescent for 5 to 6 years. 'Tharsen's Weeping' with emerald green foliage and procumbent branches is listed. Southern Alaska to Idaho and California. Introduced 1851. Zone 6 to ?

Tsuga mertensiana (Boug.) Carr. — Mountain Hemlock

LEAVES: Radially spreading, 1/3 to 3/4″(1″) long, 1/16″ wide, obtuse apex, convex above and often keeled, almost round in cross section, entire, stomatal lines on both surfaces resulting in a blue-green to gray-green color.

Tsuga mertensiana, (tsū′gȧ mĕr-ten′si-ā-nȧ), Mountain Hemlock, is possibly the least adaptable of the hemlocks treated herein. In the wild, a tree 50 to 90' high, but much less under cultivation. Co-national champions are 113' by 44' in Alpine County, CA and 152' by 41' in Olympic National Park. Forms a slender pyramidal outline with slender pendent branches. Prefers cool, moist root run and cooler air temperatures. Have seen plants in the Netherlands that appeared native they were so robust. Bonnie and I were hiking in the Mt. Rainer National Park and saw this species in its myriad colors. Almost always more narrow and slender than *T. heterophylla* which may be related to its ability to shed snow loads. Foliage color is distinctly different than other species and 'Argentea', 'Blue Star', 'Elizabeth', 'Glauca', and 'Mt. Hood Blue' are more silvery or blue-needled forms. 'Blue Star', as I witnessed, was as handsome as the blue forms of *Picea pungens* var. *glauca*. *Tsuga* × *jeffreyi* (Henry) Henry embodies hybrids between *T. mertensiana* and *T. heterophylla*. *Tsuga mertensiana* is, unfortunately, not a tree for the eastern United States. Highly susceptible to *Phytophthora* root rots in controlled studies; see *Tree Planters Notes* 40(1):15–18 (1989). Southern Alaska to northern Montana, Idaho and California. Introduced 1854. Zone 5 to ?

Tsuga caroliniana Engelm. — Carolina Hemlock
(tsū′gȧ ka-rō-lin-ē-ā′nȧ)

LEAVES: Radiating around the stem, linear, 1/4 to 3/4″ long, about 1/12″ wide, apex blunt or slightly notched, glossy green above, with 2 distinct white bands beneath, margins entire.

BUDS: Ovoid to roundish, apex blunt, pubescent.

STEM: Light orangish to reddish brown when young, finely pubescent or nearly glabrous.

SIZE: 45 to 60' in height by 20 to 25' spread; national champion is 88' by 54' in Burke Co., NC.

HARDINESS: Zone 4 to 7.

HABIT: Airy, spiry-topped tree with a tapering trunk and short, stout, often pendulous branches forming a handsome, evenly pyramidal head; often more compact and of darker green color than *T. canadensis*; handsome in the wild as it grows on the side of the mountains, tall and stately, surveying the valleys below.

RATE: Slow to medium, not as fast as *T. canadensis*.

TEXTURE: Medium.
BARK: Reddish brown, deeply fissured, scaly.
LEAF COLOR: Glossy green above, with two silvery bands below.
FLOWERS: Monoecious, inconspicuous.
FRUIT: Cones short-stalked to sessile, oblong-cylindrical, 1 to 1 1/2″ long, 1″ wide, scales radiating out from center.
CULTURE: Transplants well balled-and-burlapped if root pruned; needs moist, well-drained soils; partially shaded, sheltered exposure and will not tolerate droughty conditions.
DISEASES AND INSECTS: Ambrosia beetle has been reported on this species, also susceptible to woolly adelgid.
LANDSCAPE VALUE: Performs better than *T. canadensis* under city conditions, and probably as good a landscape plant but not as well-known; tends to be more stiff and rigid although I have seen plants that rival the best *T. canadensis*; qualities may be overstated for it has never found its way into the mainstream.
CULTIVARS: Several are noted in the literature.
    'Arnold Pyramid'—Pyramidal, dense, with a rounded top, 25 to 35′ high.
    'Compacta'—Dwarf, low growing and very dense, wider than high.
    'Greenbrier'—Weeping, 40-year-old tree is 5′ high, 20′ wide, good green needle color.
    'La Bar's Weeping'—Prostrate if allowed to its own devices, weeping if staked, handsome foliage.
PROPAGATION: Same as for *T. canadensis*.
ADDITIONAL NOTES: Easily separable from *T. canadensis* by the way the foliage radiates around the stem forming a bottlebrush-like effect, the larger cones and entire needles.
NATIVE HABITAT: Southeastern United States (southwestern Virginia to northern Georgia in the Blue Ridge Mountains). Introduced 1881.

Ulmus americana L. — American Elm, also known as White, Gray, Water, or Swamp Elm
(ul′mus à-mer-i-kā′nà)

FAMILY: Ulmaceae
LEAVES: Alternate, simple, ovate-oblong, 3 to 6″ long, 1 to 3″ wide, acuminate, unequal at base, doubly serrate, lustrous dark green, glabrous and rough or smooth above, pubescent or nearly glabrous beneath, lateral veins crowded, 13 to 18 pairs, straight, running out to teeth; petiole—1/4 to 1/3″ long.
BUDS: Terminal—absent; laterals—imbricate, ovate-conical, pointed, 1/4″ long, slightly flattened and more or less appressed against the stem, light reddish brown, smooth and shining or slightly pale-downy; flower buds stouter, obovate, appearing as if stalked, scales generally with darker and more or less hairy-edged margins.
STEM: Slender, round, red-brown, pubescent at first, becoming glabrous (sometimes maintaining pubescence); leaf scars with 3 distinct bundle traces that result in a "cat-face" configuration.

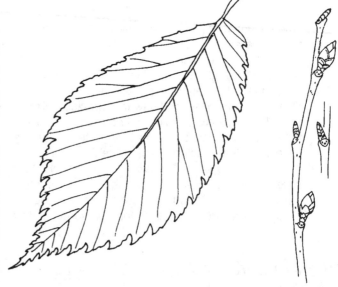

SIZE: 60 to 80′ with a spread of 1/2 to 2/3's the height, may grow larger; national champion is 112′ high in Copemish, MI.
HARDINESS: Zone 3 to 9.
HABIT: Three distinct habits are recognized and include the vase-shaped form in which the trunk divides into several erect limbs strongly arched above and terminating in numerous slender often pendulous branchlets, the whole tree a picture of great beauty and symmetry; a form with more widely spreading, less arching branches, often called the "oak-form"; and a narrow form with branchlets clothing the entire trunk.
RATE: Medium to fast, 10 to 12′ in 5 years; this rate of growth is common for many elms.
BARK: Dark gray with broad, deep, intersecting ridges, or often scaly; outer bark in cross section shows layers of a whitish-buff color alternating with thicker dark layers.
LEAF COLOR: Lustrous dark green in summer, yellow in fall; great variation in intensity of fall coloration.

FLOWERS: Perfect, greenish red, in fascicles of 3 or 4, March, usually late February in Athens, interesting but not showy.

FRUIT: Rounded, notched, disc-shaped samara, 1/2″ long, maturing in May through June, not ornamental, greenish, but may have reddish tinge, fringed with hairs.

CULTURE: Easily transplanted because of shallow, fibrous, wide-spreading, gross feeding root system; prefers rich, moist soils but grows well under a variety of conditions; in the wild the tree is a common inhabitant of wet flats where standing water may accumulate in the spring and fall; prune in fall; pH tolerant; shows good soil salt tolerance.

DISEASES AND INSECTS: The elms are, unfortunately, subject to many pests and I have often wondered why they have been treated as royalty when they are so fallible. Many of the pests are devastating and control measures are simply not effective or available. The following list should provide an idea of the potential problems which may beset "your" elm. Wetwood, *Erwinia mimipressuralis*, is a bacterial disease which appears as a wilt, branch dieback, and internal and external fluxing of elms. A pipe is often placed in the tree to relieve the tremendous gas pressure that builds up; no control known. Cankers (at least 8 species cause cankers and dieback of stems and branches), Dutch elm disease (*Ophiostoma ulmi*, devastating and essentially uncontrollable), bleeding canker, leaf curl, leaf spots (there are so many fungi that cause leaf spots that only an expert can distinguish one from another), bacterial leaf spot (*Pseudomonas syringae*), bacterial leaf scorch (*Xylella fastidiosa*), powdery mildews, *Cephalosporium* wilt, *Verticillium* wilt, woody decay, phloem necrosis (apparently caused by a mycoplasm), mosaic, scorch, woolly apple aphid, elm leaf curl aphid, Japanese beetle, smaller European elm bark beetle, elm borer, spring canker worms, fall cankerworms, elm cockscomb gall, dogwood twig borer, elm leaf miner, elm leaf beetle, gypsy moth, leopard moth borer, white marked tussock moth, elm calligrapha, mites and scales (many species infest elms). Many studies evaluating Dutch elm disease resistance in selected clones of American Elm and other species. *J. Environ. Hort.* 13(3):126–128 (1995) reported that 'American Liberty', 'Princeton' and 4 other clones showed relatively high Dutch elm disease resistance in controlled inoculations. Another study, *J. Environ. Hort.* 14(3):150–154 (1996), reported growth and response to Dutch elm disease among advanced generation progenies and clones of elms.

LANDSCAPE VALUE: At one time extensively used as a street and large lawn tree. The streets of the New England and Midwestern towns and cities were arched with this tree but the Dutch elm disease has killed many of the trees. People somehow have the notion that all the American Elms were destroyed. This is by no means true and many cities have extensive maintenance programs. Having gone to school in Massachusetts I can appreciate the legacy of these elms and the pride that people take in them. The elms, unfortunately, have not stopped dying and since the 1990 edition I have observed many old, venerable specimens succumb to Dutch elm disease. I can remember a fine planting of 'Ascendens' on the Amherst College campus which as a graduate student at the University of Massachusetts from 1969–1972 I photographed frequently. They are now gone. Urbana, IL was called the city of the elms and the Illinois campus was extensively planted. There may be no American Elms left for most of the remaining ones had died during my seven years on campus. In some respects it seems only a matter of time before Dutch elm disease wins. There are fine, established plantings on many campuses that are being maintained by systematic spray programs. Eventually because of age and/or disease these will pass and the search for a suitable substitute will continue. In my opinion, there is no substitute (presently) for the American Elm. See *Arnoldia* 42(2) (1982), for a good discussion of the American Elm.

CULTIVARS: Many cultivars were named, most succumbed to Dutch elm disease and are no longer extant.

    'Ascendens'—Upright form, 4 to 5 times as tall as wide, branches high up on trunk.

    'Augustine'—Fast growing, columnar form, branched to ground, 3 times as high as broad.

    'Delaware #2'—Highly resistant to Dutch elm disease, vigorous with a broad spreading crown, 70 to 80′ high, introduced by Nursery Crops Research Laboratory, Delaware, OH; Princeton is the only nursery I have seen offering this and the cultivar 'Washington'.

    'Independence'—One of the American Liberty elms that was patented.

    'Jackson'—Selection out of Wichita, KA, showing no Dutch elm disease damage at +50 years of age, this is the White Oak form covering over 1/2 acre.

    'Jefferson'—Vase-shaped with arching limbs, green summer foliage, changing to yellow in fall, 50′ by 50′, national park service introduction.

    'Lake City'—Upright form, wide at top and narrow at base, however, not the typical vase-shaped form.

    'Liberty' ('American Liberty')—Described as Dutch elm disease resistant by Elm Research Institute, Harrisville, NH 03450, however, the plants constitute a grex of 6 clones, probably 5 now extant, that were released via the University of Wisconsin; their Dutch elm disease resistance is not as high as that of 'Valley Forge' and 'New Harmony'; trees were noted as highly susceptible to elm yellows (phloem necrosis) in New York, see *J. Arboriculture* 20:176–189 (1994).

'Littleford'—Columnar, 3 times as high as wide.

'Moline'—Good, rugged, moderately vase-shaped form, one of the last of the American Elms to succumb to Dutch elm disease on the Illinois campus.

'New Harmony'—Broadly vase-shaped crown, main trunk divides nearly 30' from ground into a few erect and strongly arched limbs terminating in numerous, slender, often drooping branches, parent tree is 68' by 72', respectable tolerance to Dutch elm disease, reported tolerance one-fifth that of 'Valley Forge', discovered in Clark County, OH, U.S. National Arboretum introduction.

'Princeton'—Large leathery foliage, vigorous, and good resistance to elm leaf beetle (foliage feeder) and Dutch elm disease, became intrigued with this selection during my 1991 sabbatical at the Arnold, named in 1922 and introduced by Princeton Nursery, it has demonstrated moderate to high resistance to the disease, several nurseries have started to produce the tree, grows exceptionally fast under managed nursery care.

'Triploid Elm'—Natural hybrid found on National Mall, Washington, DC; highly resistant to Dutch elm disease, vase-shaped habit of American Elm but not as graceful, see *Can. J. Forest Res.* 24(4):647–653 (1994).

'Valley Forge'—Classic American Elm shape, upright-arching, broadly V-shaped branch structure with a full, dense canopy; 12-year-old propagules were 26' by 30'; controlled screenings for Dutch elm disease resistance showed 'Valley Forge' was the most tolerant; introduced by U.S. National Arboretum.

'Washington'—Selected for crown resistance to Dutch elm disease, good glossy foliage, 70 to 80' high, selected by Dr. Horace V. Webster, former plant pathologist, National Park Service, Washington, DC.

PROPAGATION: Seeds of some lots show dormancy and should be stratified at 41°F for 60 to 90 days in moist medium although some seeds do not require any treatment. In the long run it is probably safer to stratify. Cuttings can be rooted; those taken in early June rooted 94% with IBA treatment. Strong juvenility effect is evident with *U. americana* cuttings collected from stump sprouts (6 to 7 1/2' or 1' from ground) and a mature tree which rooted 64, 83, and 38%, respectively. See *HortScience* 10:615 (1975).

ADDITIONAL NOTES: The extensive use of one tree such as the American Elm is an example of foolhardy landscaping. The tree is tremendously ornamental and was overplanted. The diseases caught up with the tree and the results were disastrous. Unfortunately, people do not seem to learn by their mistakes and now Honeylocust, Bradford Pear, Green Ash, Red Maple, and Planetree are being used in wholesale fashion for cities, residences and about everywhere. I strongly urge a diversified tree planting program encompassing many different species and cultivars.

I receive many queries about what to substitute for the American Elm. Unfortunately, there is nothing but an American Elm. The *more resistant* clones that have hard disease resistant data ('Valley Forge', 'New Harmony') or longevity ('Princeton', 'Delaware #2') to support them are worthy of use. The American Liberty or Liberty series is not as resistant as the above and their use should be tempered. A few words of recognition are directed to Dr. Alden M. Townsend, Research Geneticist, U.S. National Arboretum, who has worked so diligently toward breeding and selection of elms, maples, and other treasures. Denny is a careful scientist and thoroughly tests the possible introductions. The new 'Valley Forge' and 'New Harmony' have been given tremendous press and represent the best Dutch elm disease germplasm for American landscapes.

My advocacy for *Ulmus parvifolia*, Chinese Elm, has resulted in new selections (Allée®, Athena®, 'Burgundy', 'Milliken') that will help to partially fill the American Elm void. Certainly the late John Pair, Kansas State University, made superior selections [see *Nursery Management and Production* 12(9):14–15, 65–67 (1996)]. In addition, Earl Cully, Heritage Trees, Jacksonville, IL is introducing a more cold hardy selection. The Morton Arboretum, largely through the work of Dr. George Ware, has introduced a number of Asiatic elm selections. These are detailed in *Nursery Manager* 9(5):32, 34–35 (1993), and 9(6):30–33 (1993). Santamour and Bentz, *J. Arboriculture* 21(3):122–131 (1995), provide a checklist of all elm cultivars introduced since 1964 and complete listings for *U. americana*, *U. japonica*, *U. parvifolia*, *U. pumila*, *U. wilsoniana*, and all cultivars of putative hybrids in which at least one parent was native to North America.

NATIVE HABITAT: Newfoundland to Florida, west to the foot of the Rockies. Naturally found in bottomlands, floodplains, swamp forests, ravines and rich woodlands. Introduced 1752.

RELATED SPECIES:

Ulmus rubra Muhl. — Slippery Elm, Red Elm

LEAVES: Alternate, simple, obovate to oblong, 4 to 8" long, about half as wide, long acuminate, very unequal at base, doubly serrate, tinged bronze-red when emerging, dark green and very rough above (scabrous), densely pubescent beneath; petiole—1/4 to 1/3" long.

BUDS: Terminal—absent, laterals about 1/4″ long, dark brown, nearly black at tips of scales, long rusty hairs at tip of bud; flower buds more or less spherical.

STEM: Rather stout, light grayish brown, pubescent, roughened by numerous raised lenticels, strongly and characteristically mucilaginous if chewed.

FRUIT: Orbicular or obovate, 1/3 to 3/4″ long samara, slightly notched at apex, center covered with red-brown hairs, glabrous elsewhere.

Ulmus rubra, (ul′mus rū′brȧ), Slippery Elm, is a close cousin of the American Elm and often goes under the names Red, Gras, or Moose Elm. The tree grows 40 to 60′ high with a somewhat vase-shaped habit but the branchlets are more ascending (upright) than those of American Elm. Co-national champions are 100′ by 119′ in Sugar Grove, OH and 100′ by 100′ in Monroeville, OH. The ornamental value is limited and this species actually becomes a weed as it tends to infest unkempt shrub borders, hedges, fence rows, and other idle ground. Prefers moist, rich, bottomland soils but also grows on dry, limestone soils. The name "Slippery" developed because of the mucilaginous inner bark which was chewed by the pioneers to quench thirst. It is susceptible to Dutch elm disease, but not to the degree of *U. americana*. Native from Quebec to Florida, west to the Dakotas and Texas covering much of the same range as *U. americana*. Cultivated 1830. Zone 3 to 9.

Two other native elm species worth mentioning include: **Ulmus thomasii** Sarg., (ul′mus tom-as′ē-ī), Rock or Cork Elm, and **Ulmus serotina** Sarg., (ul′mus ser-ot′i-nȧ), September or Red Elm. The former has an oblong crown and the trunk usually remains unbranched. It is found on dry gravelly uplands and rocky slopes but attains its best development in rich bottomland soils. The wood is heavy, hard and tough. The finest of all woods; hence the name Rock Elm. The wood was used in the construction of automobile bodies and refrigerators. It is now used for furniture, agricultural implements, hockey sticks, ax handles, and other items which require a wood which will withstand strains and shocks. Co-national champions are 117′ by 122′ in Cassopolis, MD and 97′ by 94′ in Gaithersburg, MD. Native from Quebec to Tennessee, west to Nebraska. Introduced 1875. Zone 3 to 7. The latter elm, *U. serotina*, is a southern species ranging from Kentucky to Alabama, to north Georgia, southern Illinois to eastern Oklahoma. National champion is 150′ by 64′ in Colbert County, AL. Cultivated 1903. Zone 5 to 8. Both are susceptible to Dutch elm disease.

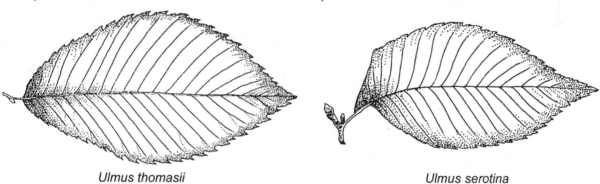

Ulmus thomasii   *Ulmus serotina*

OTHER ELMS

Ulmus alata Michx. — Winged Elm

LEAVES: Alternate, simple, ovate-oblong to oblong-lanceolate, 1 1/4 to 2 1/2″ long, half as wide, acute or acuminate, unequal, doubly serrate, leathery, dark green and glabrous above, with axillary tufts below; petiole—1/10″ long.

BUDS: Almost like miniature versions of *U. americana*—imbricate, reddish brown.

STEM: Gray to brown, glabrous, slender with two opposite corky wings but not always present; pronounced on young vigorous shoots.

Ulmus alata, (ul′mus ȧ-lā′tȧ), Winged Elm, is a medium-sized, 30 to 40′ (50 to 60′) high tree with spreading branches that form a round-topped, oblong head. National champion is 97′ by 78′ in Richmond County,

NC. It is common in the South and especially noticeable for the 2 broad, opposite, corky wings that develop on the branches. The dark green, 1 1/4 to 2 1/2″ long leaves may turn dull yellow in fall but are often infected with powdery mildew and remind of a Common Lilac in its best mildew condition. The species is much larger growing than I realized and trees 60 to 70′ are common in Athens and vicinity. In their finest forms, they approach American Elm in outline but are finer and more graceful in texture. Fall color has been beautiful yellow on occasion. Leaves abscise early. The mildew susceptibility is a variable trait for some trees approach whiteness while others are not affected. The greenish red flowers open in mid to late February (Athens) and are followed by oval, 1/3″ long, villous samaras with 2 inward curving beaks at apex. 'Lace Parasol' is a stiffly weeping form, 10′ by 15′, with handsome corky branches, leaves similar to species, one of the late J.C. Raulston's favorite plants, introduced through the J.C. Raulston Arboretum. Virginia to Florida, west to Illinois, Oklahoma and Texas. Introduced 1820. Zone 6 to 9.

Ulmus carpinifolia Rupp. ex Suckow. — Smoothleaf Elm

LEAVES: Alternate, simple, elliptic to ovate or obovate, 1 1/2 to 4″ long, 1 to 2″ wide, acuminate, very oblique at base, doubly serrate with about 12 pairs of veins, lustrous dark green and smooth above, glabrous when young, pubescent on veins beneath; petiole—1/4 to 1/2″ long, usually pubescent.
BUDS: Imbricate, terminal—absent, laterals—1/8 to 1/4″ long, deep brown to black, ovoid, bud scales covered with soft silky pubescence, edges of scales often finely ciliate.
STEM: Brown, slightly pubescent, older branches turning ashy gray.

Ulmus carpinifolia, (ul′mus kär-pĭ-ni-fō′li-à), Smoothleaf Elm, is native to Europe, North Africa and western Europe. The tree will grow 70 to 90′ with a straight trunk and slender, ascending branches forming a weakly pyramidal tree. Personally I find the tree attractive but again it is an elm and subject to all the pests although considered intermediate in resistance to Dutch elm disease. The foliage is a lustrous dark green in summer. Zone 5 to 7. The following cultivars are largely hybrids from various breeding programs and include mixed parentage. For lack of a better venue, I also included the Asiatic elm hybrids and selections (exclusive of *U. parvifolia*). Readers might want to read *Nursery Manager* 9(5):32, 34–35 (1993).
Accolade™ ('Morton') (*U. japonica* × *U. wilsoniana*)—American Elm-like exceedingly glossy dark green foliage, rich golden yellow fall color; very good Dutch elm disease resistance, good elm leaf beetle and leaf miner resistance, 80′ high in 68 years, a Morton Arboretum introduction, will be promoted through Chicagoland Grows program, grown from seed collected at the Arnold Arboretum in 1924, difficult to root from cuttings, Zone 4 to 5.
'Bea Schwarz'—Broad upright crown, 2 to 4″ long deep green leaves, 9 to 12 vein pairs, selected around 1935, resistant to Dutch elm disease, *U.* × *hollandica* type.
'Cathedral' (*U. pumila* × *U. japonica*)—Is more spreading than 'New Horizon' and is not as cold hardy; high resistance to Dutch elm disease, expect some elm leaf beetle damage, University of Wisconsin introduction that will be patented through the University's foundation, contact Ray Guries for more information.

'Christine Buisman'—Broadly erect form with central leader, 2 to 3 1/4″ long leaves, base very oblique, developed by Boskoop Experimental Station around 1945, 60′ by 45′, Zone 4, resistant to Dutch elm disease, a *U. × hollandica* type.

'Commendation™ ('Morton Stalwart')—Upright oval habit, 60′ by 50′, green summer foliage, changing to yellow in fall, rapid-growing.

'Dampieri'—Narrow conical form, leaves crisped, clustered on short shoots, broad-ovate, 2 to 2 1/2″ long, rough and deep green above, originated in Belgium around 1863, somewhat resistant to Dutch elm disease; 'Dampieri Aurea' ('Wredei') has yellow leaves and is slower growing; have seen both in English gardens, *U. × hollandica* type, Rehder lists it as a *U. carpinifolia* selection.

Danada Charm™ ('Danada', 'Morton Red Tip')—Marked American Elm shape at 30′ high, emerging leaves are red, glossy dark green at maturity, expect 60′ at maturity, very good Dutch elm disease resistance, grown from open-pollinated seed of *Ulmus japonica × Ulmus wilsoniana*, a Morton Arboretum introduction, Zone 4 to 5.

'Discovery' [*Ulmus davidiana* var. *japonica* (Rehd.) Nak.]—Has a distinctly upright, more compact, oval to vase-like habit, forming an arching vase-shaped canopy, 45′ by 35′, and its dark green leaves are 10% smaller than those of 'Freedom' and 'Jacan', yellow fall color, listed as Dutch elm disease, phloem necrosis, elm leaf beetle, and aphid resistant, low seed producer, selected in 1985 from open-pollinated seedlings grown from seeds collected from 20 mature Japanese Elms at the Morden Research Station, listed as hardy to Zone 2b.

'Groeneveld'—Like 'Commelin' but with tighter upright habit, dense crown, regular branching, 40 to 50′ high, averaged 2′1″ per year over a 10 year period in Kansas tests, resistant to wind and Dutch elm disease, from Boskoop Experiment Station, Holland, *U. × hollandica* type.

'Homestead'—Dutch elm disease and phloem necrosis resistant, symmetrical somewhat pyramidal crown to oval-arching, dense dark green foliage may turn straw yellow in fall, rapid growth rate, 12-year-old tree was 36′ high and 25′ wide, considered Zone 5 to 7, although will probably grow in Zone 8, result of complex parentage involving *U. pumila*, *U. × hollandica*, and *U. carpinifolia*; see *HortScience* 19:897–898 (1984) for all details; introduced by Nursery Crops Research Laboratory in 1984, have seen 25′ high plants in Cincinnati, has a pleasing form and good foliage, unfortunately, susceptible to elm leaf beetle, true for 'Pioneer' and 'Urban', this is a better cultivar than 'Pioneer' and 'Urban'.

'Jacan'—An *U. davidiana* var. *japonica* form with excellent hardiness (-30 to -40°F), vase-shaped outline with strong branches, tolerant to Dutch elm disease, 1977 introduction from Morden, Manitoba, Canada; see *Can. J. Plant Sci.* 59:267–268 (1979), Zone 3.

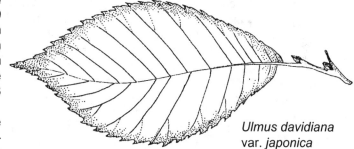

Ulmus davidiana var. *japonica*

'Jacqueline Hillier'—English literature lists this densely branched, slow-growing shrub form, 6′ high, as an *U. × hollandica* type, also listed as *U. × elegantissima*.

'Mitsui Centennial' (*U. japonica*)—Fast growth, exceptional hardiness, Dutch elm disease resistance, seedling from Morden.

'Morton Glossy' ('Charisma')—Upright oval to vase-shaped habit with arching branches, 55′ by 50′, glossy dark green summer foliage, changing to yellow in fall, hybrid between 'Accolade' and 'Vanguard'.

'New Horizon' (*U. pumila × U. japonica*)—Offers excellent Dutch elm disease resistance and vigor, upright habit, full crown, stress tolerance, and large, dark green leaves, expect some elm leaf beetle damage, University of Wisconsin introduction, Zone 3.

'Patriot' ('Urban' × selection of *U. wilsoniana*)—Upright, stiffly vase-shaped, dark green summer foliage, changing to yellow in fall, may stay narrower than most elms, 43′ by 25′ in 13 years from seed, high Dutch elm disease resistance, ARS, USDA introduction.

'Pioneer'—Dutch elm and phloem necrosis resistant, globe-shaped to rounded crown, large dark green leaves with empire yellow fall color, on occasion good yellow fall color in Spartanburg, SC, dense canopy, grows as rapidly as 'Homestead', result of *U. glabra × U. carpinifolia* cross, 11-year-old tree is 27′ high and 28′ wide, predicted 50 to 60′ by 50 to 60′, Zone 5 to 7(8); has survived in Minneapolis area as did 'Homestead', but was injured; see *HortScience* 19:900 (1984) for more details, introduced by Nursery Crops Research Laboratory; Delaware, OH in 1984.

'Prospector' (*U. wilsoniana*)—Offers American Elm-like habit, great vigor, 23′ by 21′ in 9 years, high resistance to Dutch elm disease and elm leaf beetle, large, 4 to 5″ long, dark green leaves that turn yellow in fall, see *HortScience* 26:81–82 (1991) for specifics, I have this cultivar in our evaluation plots where it displays tremendous vigor and dark green leaves, but is a wild grower, Zone 5 to 7.

'Regal'—Dutch elm disease resistant clone that resulted from a cross between 'Commelin' (*U. × hollandica* 'Vegeta' × *U. carpinifolia* #1) with N 215 (*U. pumila* × *U. carpinifolia* 'Hoersholmiensis'); develops strong central leader and rather open growth habit without the dignity or majesty of good American or Chinese Elms; will probably maintain a pyramidal-oval outline and mature about 50 to 60′ by 30′; mature leaves are a dusty spinach green; introduced by University of Wisconsin in 1983; see Smalley and Lester, *HortScience* 18:960–961 (1983) for additional details, should be hardy into Zone 4.

'Sapporo Autumn Gold'—Upright vase-shaped form resembling a densely branched American Elm; red tinge to new leaves, glossy dark green later and turn golden in fall, 50 to 60′, averaged 2′ per year over a 7 year period in Kansas tests, resistance to the aggressive strain of Dutch elm disease, so-so fall color in Kansas, Zone 3, University of Wisconsin introduction.

'Sarniensis'—Narrowly upright conical in habit; 1 3/4 to 2 1/2″ long, glossy dark green leaves, rather good looking form, susceptible to Dutch elm, still relatively common in areas of Middle Atlantic and New England States, 60 to 70′, *U. carpinifolia* form.

'Umbraculifera'—Usually grafted high on species, forms a single-trunked tree with a densely globose head; leaves smaller than the species, 1 to 2 1/2″ long, 20 to 30′, *U. carpinifolia* type.

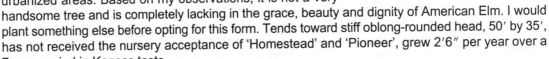

'Umbraculifera'

'Urban'—Result of crossing among *Ulmus × hollandica* var. *vegeta* × *Ulmus carpinifolia* × *Ulmus pumila*, resistant to Dutch elm disease. Developed by ARS Shade Tree Laboratory, Delaware, OH. Grows fast on various soil types, has dark green foliage, and is tolerant of drought, pollution, soil compaction and restricted root space. Should make a good tree for heavily urbanized areas. Based on my observations, it is not a very handsome tree and is completely lacking in the grace, beauty and dignity of American Elm. I would plant something else before opting for this form. Tends toward stiff oblong-rounded head, 50′ by 35′, has not received the nursery acceptance of 'Homestead' and 'Pioneer', grew 2′6″ per year over a 7 year period in Kansas tests.

Vanguard™ ('Morton Plainsman') (*U. japonica* × *U. pumila*)—Was grown from seed of *U. davidiana* var. *japonica* that came from northern China, American Elm shape, 50′ high, waxy lustrous leaves are slightly folded, grows into mid-summer, while Accolade™ and Danada Charm™ stop earlier, moderate resistance to elm leaf beetle, tough wood, moderate grower, grown at Morton Arboretum from seed provided by the Morden Experiment Station.

'Variegata'—Rather handsome form with white-streaked and -flecked leaves, 30′, appears to be an *U. carpinifolia* form.

ADDITIONAL NOTES: In Europe, particularly the Netherlands, elms are common throughout the cities and countryside. In Amsterdam, the canals are lined with elms that I suspect are of hybrid origin. Many were produced by Dutch breeding programs. In addition to those listed above, 'Dodoens', 'Lobel', and 'Plantyn' (all have *U. glabra* 'Exoniensis' as female parent, released in 1975) are at best moderately resistant to the aggressive strain of Dutch elm disease while 'Commelin' (1960 release, susceptible to aggressive strain of fungus) has no resistance. Interestingly, in Dr. Pair's Kansas field tests, 'Commelin' averaged 2′7″ per year over a 10 year period.

Ulmus glabra Huds. non Mill. — Scotch Elm, Wych Elm

LEAVES: Alternate, simple, oblong-ovate to elliptic or obovate, 3 to 7″ long, 1 1/2 to 4″ wide, abruptly acuminate, occasionally 3-lobed at apex, very unequal at base, sharply and double serrate, dark green and scabrous above, pubescent beneath, rarely nearly glabrous, 14 to 20 vein pairs; petiole—1/8 to 1/4″ long, pubescent.

BUDS: Imbricate, terminal-absent, laterals—1/4″ long, dark chestnut brown to brown-black with hispid bud scales.

STEM: Dark gray-brown with bristle-like pubescence, distinctly hairy.

Ulmus glabra, (ul′mus glā′brà), Scotch Elm, is a large, massive, rather open tree growing from 80 to 100′ with a spread of 50 to 70′. The foliage is dark green in summer and green to yellow to brown in fall. I would not recommend the species but the cultivars 'Camperdownii' and 'Pendula' are worthwhile. The former

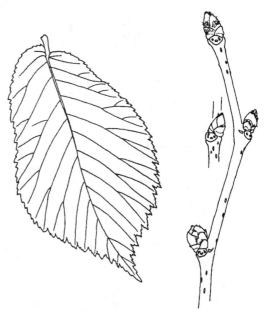

is a round-headed, pendulous-branched type that is usually grafted about 6 to 7′ high on the understock while the latter, although often confused with 'Camperdownii', is a flat-topped tree with horizontal branches and pendulous branchlets. The origin of 'Camperdownii' is interesting for it apparently originated as a seedling and was discovered creeping along the ground at Camperdown House, near Dundee, Scotland in the first half of the 19th century. On a scouting trip for our Scottish garden tour, Al Armitage and I took a side trip to Dundee to find the original tree. Find we did, the house in a park-like setting and one rather pathetic, snaggle-toothed, weeping elm that both of us said could not be the original. The mind conjures great expectations of what something should look like. When that something is found and is not up to concept, then it is easy to dismiss said object as not the original. In short, I was broken-hearted. Camperdown Elm will grow 15 to 25′ high, usually wider and is grafted on *U. americana* in the United States and what appears to be *U. carpinifolia* in Europe. The bark of Camperdown is somewhat blocky or cross-checked, almost scaly, while the understock is ridged-and-furrowed. I have seen plants of 'Horizontalis' (Tabletop Elm) that were 33′ across and no more than 15′ high. *Hortus III* lists 'Camperdownii' under *U. × vegeta* (*U. carpinifolia × U. glabra*). I am staying with the old nomenclature. I have seen tremendous crops of fruit on 'Horizontalis' but not on 'Camperdownii'. Most of the plants labeled as 'Camperdownii' are 'Horizontalis' at least as I have observed them in the United States. I saw the most magnificent planting of 'Horizontalis' near the Cathedral of Notre Dame, Paris. When used properly it makes a rather handsome and eye-catching plant. 'Exoniensis', an upright form with leaves folded along the midrib and clustered, grew 1′ per year over a 10 year period in Kansas tests. 'Nana' is a dense, broad-rounded mound, about 6′ high, that I fondly remember from its placement in the rock garden at Edinburgh. Native to northern and central Europe, western Asia. Zone 4 to 6.

Ulmus × hollandica Mill., (ul′mus hol-lan′di-kà), Dutch Elm,

includes a group of trees which resulted from crossing *U. carpinifolia × U. glabra* with the progeny supposedly intermediate between the two parents. Selections have been made from the group. Quite confused taxonomically and generally of little landscape interest in the United States. I have tried to make sense of the taxonomy of this grex but it is too complex to be presented in a condensed version. Bean simply lists the old hybrid or pure clones as 'Belgica' (Belgium or Holland); 'Dampieri' (also a golden form, see under *U. carpinifolia*); 'Hollandica' (Dutch); 'Smithii' ('Downton'); 'Vegeta' ('Huntingdon'); all, unfortunately, are susceptible to Dutch elm disease and many splendid specimens have been lost.

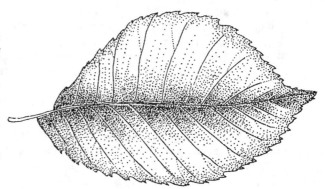

Ulmus parvifolia Jacq. — Chinese Elm, Lacebark Elm
(ul′mus pär-vi-fō′li-à)

LEAVES: Alternate, simple, elliptic to ovate or obovate, 3/4 to 2 1/2″ long, 1/3 to 1 1/3″ wide, acute or obtusish, unequally rounded at base, simply or nearly simply serrate, lustrous dark green and smooth above, pubescent beneath when young, subcoriaceous at maturity, 10 to 12 vein pairs; petiole—1/4 to 1/2″ long.
STEM: Gray-brown, glabrous to slightly pubescent, slender, very fine in texture.
BUDS: Small, 1/10 to 1/8″ (perhaps to 1/4″) long, brown, smallest buds of any elm, slightly pubescent.
FLOWERS: Easy to recognize because of late flower and fruit dates—August–September.
BARK: Mottled (rather than ridged-and-furrowed like other elms), exfoliating in irregular patches, exposing lighter bark beneath, trunks sometimes fluted.

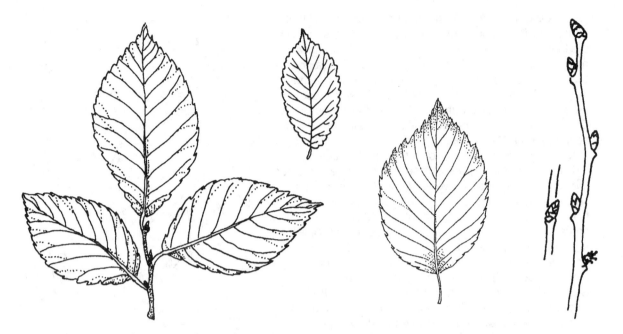

SIZE: 40 to 50′ high and wide; have seen a 70′ high tree that was about 59′ wide.

HARDINESS: Zone (4)5 to 9, hardiness greatly dependant on seed source; 40′ high trees in Morton Arboretum; Cappiello reported no injury on an accession at Orono, ME.

HABIT: Rather graceful round-headed tree often with pendulous branchlets; some forms are upright-spreading, almost American Elm-like; others broader than tall; much variation in habit with no two seedlings alike.

RATE: Medium to fast depending on moisture and fertility levels; grew 1′6″ per year over a 10 year period in Kansas tests.

TEXTURE: Medium-fine throughout the seasons.

BARK: Magnificent and often a beautiful mottled combination of gray, green, orange and brown; variable and selections could be made for superior traits.

LEAF COLOR: Lustrous dark green changing to yellowish and reddish purple in fall; fall color is usually not outstanding but appears to be better on southern grown trees than those I have observed in the north; leaves hold late and I have photographed trees in late November in fall color in Athens, GA.

FLOWERS: Inconspicuous, appearing in axillary clusters during August–September, essentially masked by the foliage.

FRUIT: Samara, elliptic-ovate, 1/3″ long, glabrous, notched at apex, seed in middle, ripens in September–October, collectable by November in Athens.

CULTURE: Easily transplanted, adaptable to extremes of pH and soil; best growth is achieved in moist, well drained, fertile soils; shows excellent urban soil tolerance and should be considered for urban areas.

DISEASES AND INSECTS: Shows considerable resistance to Dutch elm disease and also the elm leaf and Japanese beetle; in comparing Siberian Elm, Japanese Zelkova, and this species for elm leaf resistance I have found *U. parvifolia* the best followed by *Zelkova serrata* and *U. pumila* which did not even place.

LANDSCAPE VALUE: Excellent, tough, durable tree for about any situation; do not confuse it with the inferior *U. pumila*, Siberian Elm, which by the nursery trade is often offered as "Chinese" Elm; several authors have suggested the name Lacebark Elm to delineate it from *U. pumila* and provide a suitable description of its most beautiful morphological trait; some of the great gardens of the world consider this a superior tree and now we need to alert the nursery industry; Disney World, Orlando, FL., has used the tree extensively throughout the grounds; in my opinion, it has received a bad rap for supposed susceptibility to ice, snow and storm damage; I have never seen extensive damage and in February, 1979 a devastating ice storm hit Athens and caused extensive damage to pines, Water Oak, Siberian Elm, Silver Maple, and other trees; *U. parvifolia* was not damaged and the Georgia campus contains some of the largest, oldest and finest specimens in the country; since the 1990 edition the Chinese elm has risen from its biological grave and many new cultivars have been introduced; nurserymen, landscape architects and gardeners are taking a much closer look at the tree's attributes rather than treating it as another ELM; the gene pool is large and the variation in habit, leaf quality and hardiness almost unbelievable; some of this genetic variation is being exploited and I predict the species will provide some of our most beautiful shade trees in the years ahead; in fact I will crawl out on a limb and predict a bright future in the 21st century; kind of fun to peruse the above as it appeared in the 1990 edition; indeed, if prophecies do come true, this one has; so many plantsmen and growers assessing *Ulmus parvifolia* germplasm that it gives me the chills just to think about the possibilities; with this species the selection process is about the journey and not the destination.

CULTIVARS:

Allée® ('Emer II', 'Emerald Vase')—An upright-spreading tree with an outline similar to that of American Elm. It measures 70′ high and 59′ wide. At 4′ from the soil line the mature tree has a 35″ diameter trunk and a 110″ circumference. The bark exfoliates in a puzzle-like pattern exposing light gray, slate gray, gray-green and orangy brown colors; it is flecked with burnt orange corkish lenticels. The exfoliation begins at the base of the trunk and continues upward to include upper branches 1 to 2″ in diameter. Surface roots also exfoliate. Unlike the typically rounded trunk of the species, the trunk is irregularly fluted. The lustrous rich green foliage is densely borne at the ends of the fine branches, creating a dense canopy. Leaf color and texture are typical of the species. Fall color is subdued yellow. Despite the record drought conditions, no leaf scorch or dieback symptoms occurred. In addition, the parent tree is thriving in an 18′ by 18′ area surrounded by concrete. Allée® is also highly resistant to Dutch elm disease and elm leaf beetle. The leaves are alternate and simple, 3/4 to 2″ long and 3/8 to 3/4″ wide. They are ovate to slightly obovate, lustrous bright green on the top and gray-green on the bottom. They can be acute or obtuse, and they are oblique, with simple serrations that are slightly more pointed than those on Athena®. The leaves are glabrous on both sides and show 11 to 16 vein pairs. The petioles are 1/8 to 1/4″ long, light green and pubescent. The chestnut brown buds are ovoid, imbricate, slightly pubescent, 1/8″ long and slightly divergent. During the first year, the stems are fine textured, terete, brown and pubescent. In the second year they turn glabrous and gray brown, with small orangy lenticels. The pith is small, solid and brown.

Athena® ('Emer I', 'Emerald Isle')—A broad-spreading elm with a rounded crown resulting in a pleasing globe-shaped outline. It measures 40′ high and 55′ wide. At 3′ from the soil line, the mature tree has a 30″ diameter trunk and an 88″ circumference. The bark exfoliates 2′ from the ground in a puzzle-like pattern exposing light gray and gray-green to orangish brown colors. The bark is flecked with orangy brown, corky lenticels. The trunk's base develops a rough, blocky, gray-black bark. The leathery, lustrous dark green (almost black) foliage is densely borne at the ends of the fine branches, creating a dense canopy. The leaves are more leathery and a darker green than the typical phenotype. Fall coloration is bronze-brown and not really effective. Athena® showed no symptoms of leaf scorch during the 1986–88 summers, which were the driest on record in the Southeast. The tree is also highly resistant to Dutch elm disease and elm leaf beetle. The leaves are alternate and simple, measuring 1 to 2″ long and 1/2 to 7/8″ wide. They are ovate to slightly obovate and lustrous dark green, almost black-green on the top and gray-green on the bottom. They are oblique and have simple rounded serrations. They are glabrous on both sides and exhibit 10 to 16 vein pairs. The petioles are 1/8 to 1/4″ long, light green and often pubescent. The cultivar's chestnut brown buds are ovoid, imbricate, slightly pubescent, 1/8″ long and slightly divergent. In the first year, the stems are fine textured, terete, brown, and pubescent. By the second year, the stems turn gray-brown and glabrous with small orangy brown lenticels. The pith is small, solid and brown.

Bosque™ ('UPMTF')—Central dominant leader with strongly ascending secondary branches, pyramidal shape, and fast growth rate, lustrous dark green leaf, underside flat green, fall color yellow-orange, bark gray-orange to gray-brown, parent tree 18′ by 8′, introduced by Tree Introductions, Inc., Athens, GA.

'Brea'—Described as having an upright habit and larger leaves than 'Drake', 'True Green', and 'Sempervirens'. Apparently, Keeline-Wilcox Nurseries, Inc. in Brea, CA, originally listed 'Brea' in its 1982 winter catalog. According to Green [*Arnoldia* 24:41–80 (1964)] this selection is the same as 'Drake'. Also, Monrovia Nursery Co., Azusa, CA, described what seemed to be 'Brea' in its 1952–53 catalog but called the cultivar 'Drake'. Are 'Brea' and 'Drake', in fact, the same plant? I have not seen 'Brea' in commerce or at arboreta.

'Burgundy'—Selected from the University of Georgia campus as were Allée® ('Emerald Vase') and Athena® ('Emerald Isle') by Dirr and Richards for outstanding foliage and habit. This form has large, thick, dark green leaves that turn deep burgundy fall coloration. The habit is distinctly broad-rounded with uniform branch development and extremely fast growth. The parent tree was approximately 8-years-old and grew in a barren parking lot island. Tree was 18′ high and 20′ wide. Amazingly, the plant was removed after 12 years of biological existence. Fortunately, it has been reproduced and planted back on the Georgia campus. The bark has started to develop the exfoliating character and is a rich orangish brown. The characteristic flaking and mixed mottle are also apparent. Cuttings root readily and, in 1989, percentages averaged over 90 using 5000 ppm KIBA, 2 perlite: 1 peat medium, and mist. Many nurserymen have visited our campus and this tree piqued their aesthetic senses.

Central Park Splendor™ (formerly 'A. Ross Central Park', 'Aross/Central Park')—The parent tree was planted in New York's Central Park over 100 years ago. The tree is 59′ tall with a trunk that measures a little over 4 1/2′ in diameter at breast height. The branching habit is spreading, with strong angular branches that fan out from where the crown originates. The tree has strong wood; rarely do its stems or branches break in a storm. The bark of young trees is dark gray and smooth. The parent tree's bark is light gray to light brown fissured into irregular plates. The mature 1 to 1 3/5″ long, elliptical, round-serrated leaves are thick and leathery. They are a lustrous spinach green, turning mimosa yellow in fall. Hardy to Zone 5 and can be used as far north as the New York City area without suffering winter damage. Karnosky reported branch and twig dieback at -20°F; young trees were killed outright at -25°F. Softwood cuttings, 3 to 5″ long, root with high frequency in one month. Treat them with 3000 ppm IBA talc and place them in an equal mix of peat and perlite under mist. The plant grows 2 to 4′ high in two growing seasons or between 1 1/2 to 2′ per year under typical nursery conditions. Young trees head early in the nursery bed but require pruning to develop crowns at suitable heights. See *HortScience* 23:925–926 (1988).

'D.B. Cole'—Is a little-known selection, appears quite bushy in Georgia tests, may be rounded in outline, from an unknown provenance, selected over 30 years ago by Cole Nursery, Co., Circleville, OH, it has lustrous dark green leaves, tinge of red in fall, exfoliating bark on fluted trunks, found to be resistant to Dutch elm disease and phloem necrosis.

'Drake'—Used in the lower South and California and, according to one source, is probably not hardy below Zone 7. Whitcomb and Hickman reported that 'Drake' was severely injured during the 1983–84 winter in Stillwater, OK, when temperatures fell to -8°F on December 23 and -31°F on January 14. Although 'Drake' is listed as hardy in Zone 6, I find this extremely dubious. 'Drake' offers rich dark green foliage on spreading branches that grow more upright than those of regular evergreen cultivars ('Sempervirens') but still approach a weeping tendency. Leaves emerge early, often in March, and persist late into fall. Young trees in containers develop long arching branches. The tree is more or less evergreen in California and stays evergreen through most winters except when it loses its leaves during unusual cold snaps. This cultivar develops an attractive round-headed form of medium size for lawn and street tree use. Bark exfoliates early and is quite handsome. Trees in Athens are low-branched with bad crotches and several have split and required removal.

'Dynasty'—The result of a controlled cross between two trees of seedling origin at the U.S. National Arboretum. The parent trees were grown from seed from the 1929 introduction PI 92487 from the Forest Experiment Station, Keijo, Japan. 'Dynasty' is distinctly vase-shaped. After 16 years, it grew to 30′ high and 30′ wide with a 12″ trunk diameter at 39″ from the ground. Summer leaves and fruits are typical of the species. Fall color has been red in cooler climates, a notable trait since typical fall color is seldom effective. The bark is dark gray on young stems and starts to exfoliate when stem diameters approach 2″ or greater. Unfortunately, some say that the bark's patchiness does not approach a degree of color contrast that could be considered ornamental. One nurseryman told me that the cultivar's bark does not compare with the bark of Allée® and Athena®. 'Dynasty' is cold hardy in Zone 5 and perhaps lower, but it has not been thoroughly tested under Zone 4 conditions. The cultivar is easily propagated from softwood cuttings using an 8000 ppm IBA talc formulation, coarse medium, and mist. These factors are important since authors have reported great variation in rooting different clones. See *HortScience* 19:898–899 (1984). There are some gaps in this tree's pedigree and the published accounts do not concur with reality. The tree is rather ugly and certainly the bark is totally disappointing. A 20′ tree in the J.C. Raulston Arboretum is sufficient reason to convince people not to grow or buy this clone. Borders on a boondoggle.

'Elsmo'—Released by the USDA, Soil Conservation Service, Plant Materials Center, Elsberry, MO as an open-pollinated, seed-propagated cultivar, 'Zettler' and perhaps 'Matthew' are derived from this germplasm.

'Frontier'—Is an USDA introduction with lustrous dark green foliage, red fall color, moderate resistance to elm leaf beetle, handsome vase-shaped growth habit, 27′ by 16′ in 19 years, *U. carpinifolia* × *U. parvifolia*, see *HortScience* 26:80–81 (1991), has performed well in Georgia tests.

Garden City Clone—For lack of a better term I used this handle at the request of the late Dr. John Pair, Kansas champion tree, 60′ high, medium green foliage, good bark, no cankers, excellent cold hardiness, currently not in production and will receive another name.

'Glory'—Strong, upright growth habit, vase-shaped overall outline, withstood heavy ice loads with no damage, good street tree, from Arborvillage, Holt, MO.

'Golden Ray' ('Golden Rey' according to Santamour and Bentz, named by B. Rey)—Could be 'Aurea', there seem to be several names for the same tree, I saw the "parent" in Oklahoma, large, wide-spreading, dome-shaped habit, yellow foliage (in mid-September), excellent gray-orange-brown exfoliating bark, Steve Bieberich, Sunshine Farms, Clinton, OK is propagating this clone.

'Hallelujah'—Fast-growing selection with excellent foliage and bark detail, survived -35°F without damage, from Arborvillage, Holt, MO.

'Jade Empress'—Rounded habit, lustrous dark green leaves, described as easy to grow, from Head-Lee Nursery, Seneca, SC.

'King's Choice'—A gentleman walked into my office and introduced himself as Ben King. He said that he knew I liked Chinese Elm, and he wanted me to evaluate his new selection. After considerable discussion, he escorted me to his station wagon and handed me 18, strong, 4 to 6′ high liners. King selected the tree from 1,000 Chinese Elms seedlings that were planted at King's Men Tree Farm, Hampstead, MD, in April 1978. The tree had grown at twice the rate of the other seedlings and was saved for evaluation. It grew 22′ high and 16′ wide in seven years and developed an oval-rounded outline. The patent describes the branching pattern as "a single bole, which divides into laterals at angles greater than 90° above the horizon, which then droops to a canopy silhouette much like [that of] American Elm." A photograph that accompanies the patent description does not clearly show this trait. The leaves of this selection are up to 2 1/2″ long, leathery, semi-glossy and dark green and turn a dull yellow in autumn. After 8 years, the bark had not developed an exfoliating character but had regular vertical fissures. The bark's color is described as grayed orange, which means little until one looks at the Royal Horticultural Society Colour Chart. From the information given in the patent description, this tree may not develop the typical bark of a Chinese Elm until it is much older. Softwood cutting root 90% compared with 60 to 80% for the other Chinese Elms King tested. The hardiness is unknown, but a Zone 6 designation, possibly even 5, is probable. Laboratory hardiness testing indicates tolerance to at least –22°F. Had the opportunity to evaluate this under nursery conditions and several things went awry. First, more than one clone was circulated as 'King's Choice'. This appeared to be a result of a mixup in tissue culture. Second, the clones(?), although fast-growing, were weak-wooded and branches actually broke under nursery production via wind (storm damage). I do not know if it (they) is being produced on a commercial basis. PP# 5554, granted Sept. 10, 1985.

'Matthew'—Selection for extreme cold hardiness from Peter J. White, Earthscapes, Inc., Loveland, OH; upright vase-shaped growth habit, strong branches, early exfoliating bark, survived –30.4°F on January 19, 1994 and was the only elm in the nursery that did not suffer severe dieback, roots readily, named after Mr. White's youngest son, was sent photos of original tree, as described above, bark is early exfoliating and gray, green, orange and brown, good looking form, time will tell about ultimate performance.

'Milliken'—The parent tree resides in a grassy field in Spartanburg, SC and reminds of the outline of a White Oak from a distance; parent tree approximately 50′ by 40′ with dark green foliage; bark is superlative with brown, orange, tan mosaic on 2″ diameter branches and the mature trunk; has withstood ice, hurricane force winds, and the ravages of time; extremely uniform outer tracery of fine branches lends a well-tailored profile.

'Ohio'—Moderate vase-shaped habit, appears more loose and open than many of the newer clones, 40′ high in 28 years, small grass green leaves turn grayish red in fall, reddish purple fruit, exfoliating bark, see *American Nurseryman* 176(12):72 (1992), developed by A.M. Townsend, U.S. National Arboretum.

'Pathfinder'—Vase-shaped crown, 36′ high and 30′ wide after 27 years, glossy, yellow-green leaves, grayed red fall color, red-purple fruit, gray-orange exfoliating bark, see *American Nurseryman* 175(4):42 (1992), developed by A.M. Townsend, U.S. National Arboretum.

'Prairie Shade'—Selected from 800 seedlings planted in 1973. Researchers initially selected 13; only two of these exhibited good form and were easy to propagate from cuttings. Seven-year-old trees propagated from cuttings measure 30′ tall and 20′ wide, with 8″ diameter trunks 6″ above the soil line. The habit is upright-spreading. 'Prairie Shade' has leathery, dark green leaves that are smaller than typical for the species. The irregular bark character develops slowly, with only moderate flaking when branches are 2 to 3″ in diameter. The cultivar is resistant to anthracnose (*Gnomonia ulmea*) and elm leaf beetle. It survived the 1983–84 winter in Stillwater, OK, and no ice or wind damage has occurred. The tree has performed well in Lubbock, TX; Guymon, OK; and Dodge City and Manhattan, KS. See *HortScience* 21:162–163 (1986). Recent reports from Oklahoma indicate significant susceptibility to anthracnose. Pretty much died a commercial death due to fungal susceptibility. Interesting how it can be evaluated as disease resistant before release and susceptible after.

'Red Fall' ('Red')—Is a clone selected by Steve Bieberich for red fall color, dark green summer foliage, small trees are oval, have grown the tree in my Georgia trials, fall color is nonexistent and habit not particularly handsome, talked to originator and he is no longer enthused about this clone.

'Sempervirens'—Sometimes listed as a variety, but taxonomic references do not consider this valid. Generally the epithet refers to the semi-evergreen to evergreen nature of the foliage. The cultivar is described as a medium-sized, round-headed shade tree with graceful, broad-arching branches that assume a weeping tendency at the ends. The leaves are dark green. Older trees shed their bark in patches, somewhat like sycamores. This tree, or a reasonable facsimile, is widely grown in California and Florida but is listed as hardy in Zone 6. Hickman and Whitcomb reported severe injury at -8°F and -31°F during the 1983–84 winter in Stillwater, OK. Realistically, this tree is hardy in Zone 8 and possibly in Zone 7. Apparently 'Sempervirens' is extremely variable in form, which suggests it is seed-grown. The cultivar appears to have characteristics similar to those of 'Pendens' (forma *pendula*), which Rehder described in 1945 as having long, loosely pendulous branches.

'State Fair'—Globe-shaped crown with dense foliage and excellent exfoliating bark, selected by Steve Bieberich.

'The Thinker'—An introduction from University of Louisville campus, selected by Mike Hayman for rounded habit, good, dark green foliage and handsome exfoliating bark, probably will not become a commercial reality, named for proximity to statue by Rodin.

'True Green'—More evergreen then 'Sempervirens' or 'Drake' and also less hardy, although listed for Zone 7. At -4°F, the tree was severely injured in Stillwater, OK. 'True Green' develops a graceful, round-headed outline and has small, glossy, deep green leaves. Unfortunately, the bark characteristics of 'True Green' are unknown. I have observed older Chinese Elms in California and Florida with semi-evergreen tendencies that developed respectable exfoliating bark. However, there was no way to determine whether the trees were any of the above.

'Zettler'—Strong, upright growth habit, excellent branching structure, no damage after -28°F, parent tree has not suffered breakage from wind and ice, will be patented and given a trademark name, from Heritage Trees, Jacksonville, IL.

Numerous compact, dwarf, and variegated forms are known. The compact forms have long served as bonsai "fodder." Interestingly, 'Frosty' with white-tipped marginal serrations, grows over 20' high. 'Catlin' is semi-dwarf, smaller (1/4 to 1/2" long) leaves, may remain evergreen on containerized plants in California, exfoliating bark; 'Chessins' is shrubby to 3', small 1/3" long leaves, variegated; 'Cork Bark' ('Corticosa') has corky bark, ±20' high and wide; 'Ed Wood' is miniature with tiny leaves, good bonsai material; 'Geisha' has a low habit, creamy young leaves; 'Hokkaido' is slow-growing, small leaves, corky bark with age; 'Seiju' is compact, larger leaves than 'Hokkaido' of which it is a sport, corky bark, smaller than 'Catlin', faster than 'Hokkaido'; 'Stone's Dwarf' is a dwarf selection with rough but not corky bark; and 'Yatsubusa' with tiny leaves on corky branches (name also used as a grex to include small-leaved variants suitable for bonsai) are known.

PROPAGATION: If seed is collected fresh (green to greenish brown stage) it germinates in good quantities; however, if left to dry it requires about 2 months cold. I have experimented with the seed and found at least 30 days cold the best prescription for success. Cutting procedures vary with investigator; ideally take cuttings in May–June, 5000 to 10000 ppm K-IBA, peat:perlite, mist. See Dirr and Richards, "In search of the perfect Chinese Elm," *American Nurseryman* 169(3):37–49 (1989) for additional propagation information. Tissue culture has been successful, be leery of tissue culture plants for mixups and possible genetic changes have occurred.

ADDITIONAL NOTES: A fine tree whose use is limited only by the confusion the nursery industry has perpetuated. Superior selections can be made for a number of good features. I continue to view it as a tree of the future. See Dirr, *American Nurseryman* 155(4):75–79 for an in-depth analysis of this and *U. pumila*. The late John Pair, Kansas State, reported it is a good tree for Kansas. John championed this tree for the central Great Plains and had targeted 2 to 3 superior, cold hardy clones. I am hopeful that Kansas State will name one in John's honor. See Dirr and Richards, *Amer. Nurseryman* 169(3):37–49 (1989) for a detailed discussion. I remarked in the 1983 edition that *Ulmus parvifolia* had a great future. It is obvious from the new cultivars that others believed similarly.

NATIVE HABITAT: Northern and central China, Korea, Japan. Introduced 1794.

RELATED SPECIES:

Ulmus crassifolia Nutt., (ul'mus kras-i-fō'li-à), Cedar Elm, like the above, also flowers and fruits in the fall. It makes a large, 50 to 70' high, 40 to 60' wide tree of oval-rounded outline. The 1 to 2" long, 1/2 to 1 1/4" wide leaves are lustrous dark green, stiff and rough (scabrous) to the touch. Flowers in clusters in leaf axils. Fruits 1/3" long, ellipsoidal, tapering at ends, notched, pubescent. The tree may have possibilities for use from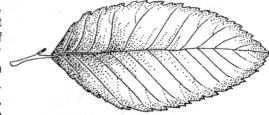
Zone 7 to 9 for it withstands drought and heavy, infertile soils. It is susceptible to Dutch elm disease, and elm leaf beetles may cause damage. It is probably not preferable to *U. parvifolia* but does offer a useful alternative. It is confused with *Ulmus alata*, Winged Elm, but does not have the pronounced corkiness on

the young branches and flowers in fall. Corky wings are often opposite each other along the stem. I saw numerous specimens in San Antonio, TX. Used as a street and shade tree throughout Southwest. Mississippi to Arkansas and Texas. Introduced 1876.

Ulmus procera Salis. — English Elm

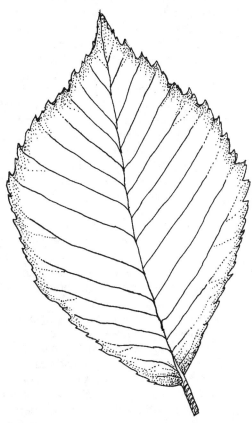

LEAVES: Alternate, simple, ovate or broad-elliptic, 2 to 3 1/2″ long, two-third's as wide, short acuminate, oblique, doubly serrate, dark green and scabrous or smooth above, soft pubescent beneath and with axillary tufts of white pubescence, 12 vein pairs; petiole—1/4″ long, pubescent.

Ulmus procera, (ul′mus prō-sē′rȧ), English Elm, has always been a mystery to me for what I was taught as English Elm never jibed with the published description. The answer to the problem is that plants do not read books and teachers should. I encountered a good guide to the elms commonly grown in England at the Chelsea Flower Show. It is entitled "Field Recognition of British Elms," by J. Jobling and A.F. Mitchell, Forestry Commission Booklet 42, available from HMSO, 49 High Holborn, London WCIV 6HB. The book describes the English Elm as broadest near the top, dense, either open umbrella in form or billowing hemispheres; the bark finely fissured into small rectangles, tissues seldom dominantly vertical, dark brown. There are creamy white-marked ('Argenteovariegata') and yellow leaf cultivars but they, like the species, have suffered the ravages of Dutch elm disease and I noticed in the *Hillier Colour Dictionary of Trees and Shrubs* that only one elm is presented with the comment that "the planting of elms has virtually ceased in England." One of the early introductions to America but difficult to locate. Interestingly, the tree is apparently wholly sterile and it is reproduced from suckers. The validity of this species has been questioned and it has been theorized it may be a hybrid between *U. carpinifolia* and *U. glabra* which should place it in the *U.* × *hollandica* group(?). Zone 4 to 6.

Ulmus pumila L. — Siberian Elm

LEAVES: Alternate, simple, elliptic to elliptic-lanceolate, 3/4 to 3″ long, 1/3 to 1″(1 1/2″) wide, acute or acuminate, usually nearly equal at base, nearly simply serrate, with the teeth entire or with only one minute tooth, dark green and smooth above, glabrous beneath or slightly pubescent when young, firm at maturity; petiole—1/12 to 1/4″ long, pubescent.
BUDS: Large, globose flower buds, 1/4″ long, blackish brown, with ciliate hairs along the edge of bud scales.
STEM: Slender, brittle, very light gray or gray-green, usually glabrous, can be slightly hairy, roughened by lenticellar projections.
FRUIT: Circular or rather obovate samara, 1/2″ across, seed almost centered, deeply notched at the top (apex).

Ulmus pumila, (ul′mus pū′mi-là), Siberian Elm, is a 50 to 70′ high tree with a spread 3/4's to equal the height. The habit is rather open, with several large ascending branches with flexible, breakable, pendulous branchlets. The growth is fast and the wood brittle. The tree grows under any kind of conditions. The foliage is dark green and loved by insects. Laboratory feeding study, *J. Environ. Hort.* 12(4):231–235 (1994), showed that *U. pumila* or any hybrid with it as a parent were fodder for the elm leaf beetle.

Resistant to Dutch elm disease and phloem necrosis. A poor ornamental tree that does not deserve to be planted anywhere! I have seen whole streets and cemeteries planted with this species. The initial growth is fast but the ensuing branch breakage, messiness, and lack of ornamental assets appalling. One of, if not, the world's worst trees. Several cultivars have been introduced which would seem to have preference over the species. They include:

'Chinkota'—A cold hardy, seed-propagated line introduced by South Dakota State University.

'Coolshade'—Resistant to breakage in ice storms compared to species, *U. pumila* × *U. rubra*, introduced by Sarcoxie Nursery, Sarcoxie, MO in 1951.

'Dropmore'—Fast-growing form with small neat foliage, hardy in Dropmore, Manitoba, Canada; original selection made by Dr. Frank Skinner; Santamour and Bentz propose name to encompass 'Chinkota', 'Harbin', 'Harbin Strain', and 'Manchu'.

'Hamburg Hybrid'—Stronger wooded than species, fast growing, 4 to 6′ per year, *U. americana* × *U. pumila*.

'Improved Coolshade'—Fast-growing, uniform habit, hardy, drought resistant and resistant to breakage from wind and ice, *U. pumila* × *U. rubra*.

'Lincoln'—Dark green leaves, hold into autumn, respectable branching, resistant to Dutch elm disease, 50′ by 40′, Zone 3, *U. pumila* × *U. rubra*.

'Mr. Buzz'—Selection by former Westerveldt Tree Co. (now Plantation Trees), Selma, AL for dense crown, dark green foliage, and vigorous growth, have seen photographs and looks too good to be true, probably is no longer in cultivation.

'Pendula'—Pendulous branches.

The principal attribute is for breeding Dutch elm disease resistance into hybrids like 'Regal', 'Urban', and others. I grew up with the species in the Midwest and fretted constantly about the potential for brain damage engineered by cascading branches. Upon arrival in Athens, I thought the blight was removed but, alas, the tree appeared with the same vengeance. Interestingly, in my 19 years in Athens, several large campus and city specimens have transpired. I have noticed tremendous elm leaf beetle damage; more than I remember from the Midwest. Some of the resistance is evident for a tree next to the University's agronomy greenhouses remains green into fall while others assume a skeletonized gray-brown. I may cut it (the good one) down before a breeder tunes in. How can I forget a September 1992 trip with Mike Glenn and John Barbour to Oklahoma where Steve Bieberich showed us the countryside? Most unforgettable was Woodward, OK where Siberian Elm was the tree of reckoning. The trip was in early September and by that time the elm leaf beetles had created a brown leafy haze. My question: can brown leaves photosynthesize? Native to eastern Siberia, northern China, Manchuria, Korea and, unfortunately, was not left there. Cultivated 1860. Zone 4 to 9.

Vaccinium corymbosum L. — Highbush Blueberry
(vak-sin′i-um kôr-im-bō′sum)

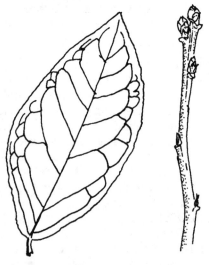

FAMILY: Ericaceae

LEAVES: Alternate, simple, ovate to elliptic-lanceolate, 1 to 3 1/2″ long, half as wide, acutish, cuneate, entire, dark green above, paler beneath, pubescent on midrib and veins; short petioled.

STEM: Slender, yellow-green to reddish in winter, granular; pith—solid, green; overall effect is quite handsome in winter.

SIZE: 6 to 12′ in height with a spread of 8 to 12′.

HARDINESS: Zone 3 to 7(8).

HABIT: Upright, multi-stemmed shrub with spreading branches forming a rounded, dense, compact outline, especially under cultivation.

RATE: Slow.

TEXTURE: Medium in all seasons.

LEAF COLOR: Dark green, almost dark blue-green in summer changing to yellow, bronze, orange or red combinations in fall; very excellent fall coloring shrub.

FLOWERS: White, possibly tinged pink or pinkish, urn-shaped, 1/3″ long, May, just before leaves completely unfold; borne in axillary racemes in great quantities.

FRUIT: Berry, blue-black, bloomy, rounded, 1/4 to 1/2″ across depending on the cultivar, edible but require a complement of sugar; July through August.

CULTURE: Transplant balled-and-burlapped or from a container into moist, acid, organic, well-drained soils (pH 4.5 to 5.5); native to somewhat swampy soils but does extremely well under acid, sandy conditions;

chlorosis is a significant problem and pH of the soils should be the first concern of anyone desiring to culture blueberries; actually they are very easy to grow if given the above conditions; mulch to reduce injury around roots and preserve moisture; prune after fruiting; full sun or partial shade.

DISEASES AND INSECTS: Actually the cultivated blueberries are subject to a number of insects and diseases; if the shrub is being grown for ornamental rather than commercial purposes no extensive control program is necessary and there are usually sufficient fruits for a few pies, jams, and the birds.

LANDSCAPE VALUE: Could blend well into the shrub border or small garden plot; two or three plants will provide many quarts of berries; it is wise to check with the local extension service or the state university to determine the best cultivars for a given area; Bonnie and I have sequestered a few bushes here and there in the garden, always some fruits for birds, Cheerios and gobbling on-the-go.

CULTIVARS: Numerous selections and hybrids have been named and are preferable to the wild types. When selecting cultivars for your garden, write or call your county extension service to find out which are best for your area. Note that the cultivars also vary in shape, vigor and productivity as well as size, color, and taste of the fruit. Although single cultivars can be planted, more than one cultivar should be planted for best pollination.

'Berkeley'—Mid-season, vigorous, spreading, and productive. Light-blue fruits of good quality are quite large. Berries store well and generally ripen one week after 'Blueray'.

'Blue Ridge'—Low chill, early mid-season form, field tolerance to stem blight, medium to large fruit, excellent color, firmness, pleasant high acid flavor, see *HortScience* 25(12):1668–1670 (1990).

'Bluecrop'—Midseason. Hardier and more drought resistant than most. Upright shrubs are unusually productive to the point of overbearing. Medium to large, light-blue fruit of good quality. Fruit flesh is firm, resistant to cracking, and flavor is good. Plants are vigorous, spreading and consistently productive. The ripening time is similar to 'Blueray'. 'Blueray' and 'Bluecrop' appear to be a good combination for cross-pollination.

'Blueray'—Midseason. Very hardy, upright, exceptionally vigorous bush produces large, light-blue, highly flavored tart fruit. It ripens 1 to 2 weeks after 'Bluetta', depending on vigor. 'Blueray' grows to heights of 4 to 5′, and its diameter is similar. Summer leaf color is a glossy, dark green, giving way to bright red in fall. Its very red stems stand out in the winter. It is a very neat, compact grower.

'Bluetta'—Medium vigor, productive bush which ripens in June.

'Bounty'—Produces high yields of large, good quality fruit, recommended for fresh fruit production, tolerant to *Botryosphaeria dithidea*, resistant to *B. corticis*, see *HortScience* 24(1):161–162 (1989).

'Burlington'—Late. Vigorous, upright, moderately productive shrub. Small to medium, light-blue fruit of fair dessert quality.

'Cape Fear'—Low chill, mid-early ripening, precocious, large fruit, fine color, firmness, average quality, see *HortScience* 25(12):1668–1670 (1990).

'Collins'—Ripens with 'Bluetta'. Fruit is light blue, sweet, and has an excellent flavor.

'Coville'—Late. Very vigorous, spreading bush with large, light-blue berries of good quality when fully ripe.

'Dixi'—Late. Vigorous, spreading bush that is not very hardy. Large, medium-blue berries are of excellent quality but subject to cracking.

'Earliblue'—Early. Vigorous, upright bush with large, good quality, sweet berries.

'Elliot'—More upright, reaching 6′ high and spreading as much as 4 to 5′ in diameter. Leaf color during summer is bluish green, turning to orange-red in fall.

'Herbert'—Late. Vigorous, upright bush. Medium-blue berries are among the largest and best quality. Fruit is resistant to cracking and does not shatter. Ripening time is late June.

'Jersey'—Late. An old favorite and perhaps the most widely grown. Vigorous, upright, very productive bush. Large, light-blue berries are acidic when picked early but sweet when fully ripe. 'Jersey' and 'Rubel' are the only cultivars to survive bad winter and late-spring frosts at Geneva, NY.

'Late Blue'—Large blue fruits maturing into September.

'Northland'—Can be used from the Canadian provinces through most of the southern states. It has bright green, oval leaves that turn orange in the fall. Its height exceeds 4′, and it spreads to a 5′ diameter.

'November Glo'—Developed by the late Dr. Arthur Elliott in Michigan, it was named for retaining the fiery red foliage throughout November and December. Plants reach heights of 4 or 5′ and can be used as accent plants and hedges. The foliage has good color on its graceful, lance-shaped leaves.

'Patriot'—Early. Sweet, large, about 25-cent size, resistant, upright grower, first witnessed at Wisley Garden and was amazed at the size of the fruits . . . gigantic.

'Pemberton'—Late. Unusually vigorous, erect bush that bears a year or two earlier than most. Productive, but medium-blue berries are difficult to pick and subject to cracking in wet weather.

'Rancocas'—Red stems, good foliage, heavy fruits.

'Rubel'—Good flavored fruits in midseason and red fall foliage.

'Sunrise'—Early-maturing tetraploid, large fruit, larger plant stature, 5-year-old plants grow 5 1/4 to 6' high, resistant to red ringspot virus, see *HortScience* 26(3):317–318 (1991).

'Weymouth'—Early. Erect bush of below average vigor with medium-size, dark-blue berries of poor dessert quality that fall off the plant.

SOUTHERN HIGHBUSH VARIETIES

These plants flower and ripen their berries before rabbiteye (*V. ashei*) blueberries.

'Avonblue'—Very early season, ripens one week after 'Sharpblue'. It is very prone to overbearing and pruning is necessary to balance the fruit load. Young plants must be defruited to obtain good growth. 'Avonblue' blooms a week after 'Sharpblue'. 400 chilling hours (45°F or below) required to satisfy bud rest and allow flowers to open and develop normally.

'Flordablue'—Very early season, it is difficult to propagate and grow. It ripens one week after 'Avonblue'. 300 chilling hours required.

'Sharpblue'—Very early season. Self-fertile, therefore, it may be planted in solid blocks. It does not grow as fast as rabbiteyes and the fruit must be stripped when the plants are young to obtain good growth. It is also necessary to prune off excess flowers on older plants. It must be grown on well-drained soil to prevent root rot. 'Sharpblue' is subject to early blooming and bird damage. The fruits have a wet scar when picked, but can be shipped with careful management. Grows as far south as Homestead, FL. It is slow growing, maturing at a height of 4 to 5'. It has the typical glossy green leaves that change to orange-red in fall. With its compact growth, large leaves and neat growing habit, it makes an altogether satisfactory landscape plant. 300 chilling hours required.

'Southland'—Moderately vigorous, dense, compact plant, light blue, medium to large fruits of good flavor.

PROPAGATION: Seed, some species germinate immediately, others germinate over a long period of time. Seeds of *V. corymbosum* do not require pretreatment. Cuttings, especially softwood, collected in June root readily under mist in peat:perlite when treated with 1000 ppm IBA; I have had good success this way; a rooting hormone may not be necessary but is always a good safeguard.

ADDITIONAL NOTES: There are about 150 species (have seen 450 species listed) of *Vaccinium* and it is quite difficult to separate many of the types without a road map. Many make great garden shrubs because of fruit and fall color. In general they prefer an acid soil and if provided this reward one for many years. I remember a retired professor in Urbana, IL who was determined to grow *V. corymbosum* at all costs in the calcareous, high pH soil of the area. He went so far as to use HCl (hydrochloric acid) to acidify the soil in his garden and still had chlorotic plants. The best way to handle the problem under conditions like his is the use of raised beds and a medium like pine-bark, peat moss or some other acid organic. On a magnificent October day I scouted a Maine bog with Professor Bill Mitchell of the University of Maine and saw *V. corymbosum* in fluorescent fall color growing in what appeared to be the wettest and most acid of soils. The photograph I took that day is included in my *Photo-Library* CD-ROM and *Hardy Trees and Shrubs*.

In the fall of 1997, the blueberries at the Horticulture Farm were as vibrant red as I remember during my 19 autumns in the South. In early January 1998, Bonnie and I hiked the White Cedar Swamp on Cape Cod and in the wet peat bog soils, primarily on hummocks, grew *V. corymbosum* .

NATIVE HABITAT: Maine to Minnesota, south to Florida and Louisiana. Introduced 1765.

RELATED SPECIES:

Vaccinium angustifolium Ait. — Lowbush Blueberry
LEAVES: Alternate, simple, lanceolate, 1/3 to 3/4″ long, acute at ends, serrulate with bristle-pointed teeth, lustrous dark green above essentially glabrous on both surfaces; var. *laevifolium* House has larger leaves about 3/4 to 1 1/2″ long and represents more southerly distributed members.

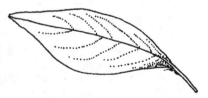

Vaccinium angustifolium, (vak-sin′i-um an-gus-ti-fō′li-um), Lowbush Blueberry, is a low, straggly, open-growing shrub reaching 6″ to 2′ in height and spreading 2′ and greater. The foliage is lustrous dark to blue-green in summer changing to bronze, scarlet and crimson in fall. The 5-lobed flowers are white, tinged pink to reddish, 1/4″ long, April–May. The fruit is a bluish black, bloomy, very sweet berry, 1/4 to 1/2″ across. Does extremely well in dry, acid, poor soils and is the main fruit crop in the state of Maine. Amazing plant that grows in the most sandy, rocky, impoverished soils imaginable. Wild blueberries are grown on 60,000 acres in Maine with only half this acreage available for harvesting each year. Most of the crop is frozen or canned with <1% sold fresh. Our annual late summer pilgrimage to Deer Isle, ME allows us to travel the route (15) not taken from US1. It snakes, curls, dips and dives heading toward the Atlantic when on Caterpillar Hill appears the most spectacular sight: Lowbush Blueberry fields, views of the ocean and islands. By late summer, the blueberries are initiating reddish foliage coloration, with residual glaucous blue berries remaining. We stop, photograph, sample, muse and appreciate. My vacation thoughts turn to blueberry cream pie, blueberry jelly, blueberry muffins . . . life on a late August day in Maine is wonderful. Interestingly, few, if any, commercial cultivars have been selected. The Lowbush Blueberry is a managed wild crop. The keys are weed management, burning, minimal to no fertility and mother nature. The value of the crop approximated 40 million dollars per year in the 1990's. For additional information write UMaine, Orono. University of Maine introduced six cultivars for ornamental rather than fruit value. All are prostrate, 5 to 7″ high, 'Burgundy', 'Claret', and 'Jonesboro' are notable for deep red autumn coloration of leaves and stems while 'Pretty Yellow', 'Spring', and 'Verde' have green to greenish yellow leaves in autumn. 'Cumberland' and 'Fundy' are sweet, large-fruited, fresh market cultivars, released by Agricultural Canada, see *Canad. J. Plant Sci.* 68(2):553–555 (1988). Newfoundland to Saskatchewan, south to the mountains of New Hampshire and New York. Introduced 1772. Zone 2 to 5(6).

Vaccinium arboreum Marsh. — Farkleberry
LEAVES: Alternate, simple, obovate to oblong, evergreen, semi-evergreen to deciduous depending on location, 1/2 to 2″ long, about half as wide, acute or obtuse, entire or obscurely denticulate, leathery, lustrous dark green and glabrous above, slightly pubescent beneath or downy.

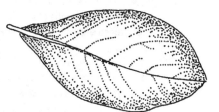

Vaccinium arboreum, (vak-sin′i-um är-bō′rē-um), Farkleberry, is abundant in the University's Botanical Garden as an understory plant in rather dry woods. It ranges from a spreading shrub to a 15 to 20′ small tree. Co-national champions are 24′ by 33′ in Aiken County, SC and 29′ by 45′ in Evergreen, AL. The 1/2 to 2″ long, leathery dark green leaves turn rich red to crimson in fall. The 1/4″ long, white, reflexed, 5-lobed flowers appear with the emerging fresh green spring leaves and are followed by 1/4″ diameter, shiny, black, inedible, persistent fruits with 8 to 10 seeds. The bark exfoliates and is composed of grays, rich browns, oranges and reddish brown. This is one of the most handsome native understory plants in deciduous woods. Heat and drought tolerances are legendary. Difficult (perhaps impossible) to root from cuttings and seeds represent the greatest hope. A pink-flowered form is in the process of being propagated and introduced into cultivation by Ted Stephens, Nurseries Caroliniana. Virginia to North Carolina to Florida, southern Illinois and Texas. Introduced 1765. Zone 7 to 9.

Vaccinium ashei Reade, (vak-sin′i-um ash′ē-ī), Rabbiteye Blueberry, is best described as the southern equivalent of *V. corymbosum* in modern taxonomy. In general, Rabbiteye is similar to Highbush but is better adapted to culture in the southern states. In general, habit is upright with landscape size approximating 8 to 10′ high. Many selections have been made for superior fruiting

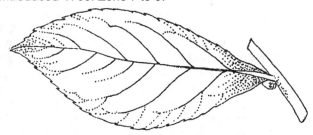

characteristics. The foliage of some selections is a glaucous blue-green and genuinely attractive. The plants color well in the fall and are enthusiastically recommended by this author for the home landscape. Because the rabbiteye blueberry requires cross-pollination for maximum fruit set, plant 3 or more cultivars with a minimum of 2 cultivars. Chill hours refer to the number of hours at 45°F or below necessary to satisfy bud rest and allow flowers to open and develop normally. Several good extension publications exist and those desirous of additional information should write the Horticulture Department, Coastal Plain Experiment Station, University of Georgia, Tifton, GA. Zone 8 to 9, possibly parts of 7. Cultivars include:
'Austin'—Early ripening, medium to large, high quality fruits for mechanical harvesting, 450 to 500 chill hours, named to recognize the contributions to blueberry industry of Max Austin, retired professor, Horticulture, University of Georgia, see *HortScience* 32(7):1295–1296 (1997).
'Baldwin'—Late season, vigorous and upright with fruit of medium size. The ripening season may extend into August and September and is an excellent choice for you-pick operations where late season fruit is desired. It is not recommended for mechanical, fresh market harvest. (450 to 500 chill hours).
'Beckyblue'—Early season, a University of Florida release for the fresh fruit trade. It blooms early. (300 chill hours).
'Bladen'—Upright vigorous grower, early ripening, medium-sized fruit, good flavor and productivity, easy propagation via softwood and hardwood cuttings, hybrid of *V. darrowi*, *V. corymbosum*, *V. tenellum*, and *V. ashei*, see *HortScience* 30(1):150–151 (1995).

'Bluebelle'—Mid-season, plants are moderately vigorous with upright growth. Berries are large, round, light blue, and have excellent flavor. Fruit ripening beginning in midseason and extends over a relatively long period. Under favorable conditions the berries size well throughout the season and production is high, thus being an excellent pick-your-own variety. Berries tend to tear when harvested. Therefore, this variety is not recommended for shipping. (450 to 500 chill hours).

'Bonita'—Early season, a new fresh fruit shipping variety from Florida. The shrubs are vigorous and ripen about three days after 'Climax.' It blooms early so it is best planted by 'Woodard' or 'Beckyblue'. (About 300 chill hours).

'Brightwell'—Early season, introduced by the University of Georgia Coastal Plain Experiment Station in 1982. Plants are vigorous and upright. The berries are medium in size, have small, dry stem scars and good flavor. 'Brightwell' ripens over a relatively short period beginning after 'Climax' and about the same season as 'Woodard.' It is suitable for mechanical harvest. (350 to 400 chill hours).

'Briteblue'—Mid-season, moderately vigorous and grows upright and open. Berries are light blue, large, and very firm with good flavor when fully ripe. The season of ripening is generally before 'Tifblue.' Berries are easily hand picked because they grow in clusters. Mature berries have a long retention on the plant and are an excellent choice for pick-your-own operations. (400 to 650 chill hours).

'Climax'—Early season, plants grow upright and open. Berries are medium in size and medium dark blue in color, have a small scar and good flavor. Fruit ripening begins 3 to 5 days before 'Woodard'. It has concentrated ripening with few shriveled or overripe fruit. This cultivar is excellent for mechanical harvesting. (450 to 550 chill hours).

'Cooper'—Upright grower, selected for fruit production in early June for the southeastern coastal plains, hybrid with 72% *V. corymbosum*, 25% *V. darrowi*, and 3% *V. angustifolium*, see *HortScience* 29(8):923–924 (1994).

'Delite'—Late season, moderately vigorous, producing an upright plant. Berries are light blue, sometimes being a reddish blue when ripe. They are large and firm, and have excellent flavor, not sharply acid before fully ripe. Its season is slightly later than 'Tifblue'. (500 chill hours).

'Georgiagem'—Moderately vigorous, semi-erect, produces moderate yields of medium-sized fruits of good flavor, color and firmness, ripens 15 days earlier than 'Climax', requires at least 350 hours of chilling below 45°F, see *HortScience* 22(4):682–683 (1987).

'Gulfcoast'—Similar to 'Cooper' but flowers and fruits earlier (mid-May), same pedigree as 'Cooper', see *HortScience* 29(8):923–924 (1994).

'Misty'—Low chill, 100 to 300 hours, selection for early season production, upright, vigorous growth habit, see *HortScience* 32(7):1297–1298 (1997).

'O'Neal'—Vigorous, semi-upright, early-flowering, self-fertile, low chilling (~400 hours) requirement, early-ripening, large fruits, good firmness and flavor, see *HortScience* 25(6):711–712 (1990).

'Powderblue'—Mid to late season, height averaging 6 to 10′, spreads to 5 or 6′ in diameter and does not sucker at the base. The leathery oval leaves are bluish, coloring from bright yellow to orange in fall. The stem color after leaf drop is green to yellow. It is similar enough to 'Tifblue' in appearance, quality, season and mechanical harvesting characteristics that the two can be harvested together and used as pollinators for each other.

'Premier'—Early season, a release from North Carolina State University. The shrubs are vigorous and productive, but the canes may be too limber to support the fruit load. It is similar in growth habit to 'Powderblue' except that its lanceolate leaves are a deeper green that turn to orange-red in the fall. The stem color varies from red to burgundy. (About 550 chill hours).

'Tifblue'—Mid to late season, plants make vigorous, upright growth. This has been the best commercial variety from the standpoint of appearance, productivity, and shipping qualities. However, most years the fruits ripen too late to receive high fresh market prices. The large, light blue berries are very firm and are highly flavored. Berries of this variety, like 'Woodard,' are very tart until fully ripe. Berries remain on the plant several days after fully ripe. (550 to 650 chill hours).

'Woodard'—Early season, plants are the shortest and most spreading of the rabbiteye varieties. The plant sprouts over an area of 3 to 4′ in 6 to 10 years. Plants do not grow as tall as 'Tifblue', so they may be hand picked more easily. Berries are light blue and are large early in the season. The quality of the berries is excellent when they are fully ripe but are very tart until ripe. 'Woodard' ripens 7 to 10 days before 'Tifblue'. It is a poor choice for fresh market sales, because it is too soft. (350 to 400 chill hours).

OTHER *VACCINIUM* (BLUEBERRY) HYBRIDS AND CULTIVARS:

'Ornablue'—According to a West Virginia University publication, it is a hybrid between *V. corymbosum* and *V. pallidum* collected from the wild in Alabama. During its 12th season in the field, it was about 3′ tall and 5 1/2′ in diameter, making it suitable for specimen planting. 'Ornablue' manifests all the attributes of the blueberry family in a pronounced manner. This plant was declared unfit for competition with commercial fruit varieties. However, someone fell in love with its beauty, and it was saved from being grubbed out.

'Top Hat'—A release from Michigan State University developed at the South Haven Experimental Station. Named for its neat, very dense growth, which is reminiscent of that of *Viburnum opulus* 'Nanum'. 'Top Hat' is a result of crosses between *V. corymbosum* and *V. angustifolium*. It has small leaves and matures at about 16″. This plant has glossy leaves, white bell-shaped flowers, delicious berries and fiery fall color. Besides being used in landscapes where a low plant is desired, it can also serve as a container plant for the patio and as an excellent bonsai subject.

The University of Minnesota and others introduced the half-high series, hybrids between *V. corymbosum* × *V. angustifolium* that survive -40°F, these cultivars may grow slightly taller in warmer areas. See HortScience 21(5):1240–1242 (1986) for full descriptions of the Minnesota half-high North series.

'Chippewa'—Half-high, with sweet, light blue berries, hardy, introduced in 1996.

'Friendship'—Similar in height and growth habit to 'Northcountry', fruits are mild, subacid, sweet, sky blue with waxy bloom, see *HortScience* 25(12):1667–1668 (1990).

'Northblue'—Half-high, taller than 'Northsky', growing to 25″(30″), large fruit, high yield, produces more fruit than 'Northsky', hardy, introduced in 1981.

'Northcountry'—Half-high, medium low-growing, grows 24″ high, 30 to 40″ wide, sweet, mild, sky blue fruits, excellent flavor, similar to 'Northblue', plant with other cultivars to improve fruit set, introduced in 1986.

'Northsky'—About 10 to 18″ tall, dense, with glossy, dark green summer foliage that turns dark red in the fall, introduced 1981.

'Polaris'—Half-high, with highly aromatic, firm berries, bright orange-red fall foliage, introduced 1996.

'St. Cloud'—Half-high, moderate growth habit, good yield, introduced 1990.

Vaccinium crassifolium Andrews, (vak-sin′i-um kras-i-fō′li-um), Creeping Blueberry, is scarcely a household name in American gardening circles but might deserve consideration for ground cover use. The lustrous dark green, finely serrate, 1/3 to 3/4″ long, 1/8 to 3/8″ wide, oval leaves are spaced about 1/4″ apart along the stem. The reddish petiole is only about 1/16″ long. The rosy red, 1/4″ diameter flowers occur in short lateral and terminal racemes in May. The evergreen nature makes it a good candidate for ground cover use in the southeastern United States. If provided a sandy, well-drained situation it might prove adaptable. Will probably grow 6″ (2′ is listed) high and has the potential to spread many times its height. 'Wells Delight' offers lustrous elliptic dark green leaves and outstanding disease tolerance; 'Bloodstone' is a *V. crassifolium* subsp. *sempervirens* form with reddish new growth that matures to lustrous dark green, will grow 6 to 8″ high and makes a rather pretty ground cover. In winter, the maturing foliage assumes an attractive reddish cast and the stems become distinctive dark red. Susceptible to *Phytophthora* and stem anthracnose. My observations indicate that these cultivars require a well-drained soil. 'Bloodstone' perished after several years on the Georgia campus. Simply never grew off and prospered. See *HortScience* 20:1138–1140 (1985) for specifics on both cultivars. North Carolina to Georgia. Introduced 1787. Zone 7 to 8.

Vaccinium elliottii Chapm.

LEAVES: Alternate, simple, tardily deciduous, elliptic-ovate, 1/2 to 1 1/4″ long, one-third to one-half as wide, acute to acuminate, finely serrate, rich green, shining, thin, glabrous or sparsely pubescent, particularly so on the lower surface; petiole—short.

STEM: Slender, green, almost grass green, turning reddish in autumn.

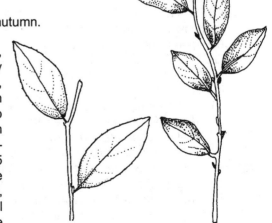

Vaccinium elliottii, (vak-sin′i-um el-i-ot′ē-ī), is a 6 to 12′ high, slender branched shrub that often occurs as an understory plant in deciduous woods. Habit is upright arching with long, slender, supple, green shoots. The small, handsome, green leaves turn rich red and reddish purple in fall. The white to pink, 1/4″ long, narrowly urceolate flowers often open before the leaves. Flowers occur in 2- to 6-flowered fascicles from the buds of the previous season's wood. The 1/5 to 2/5″ long, black berries ripen in summer. Grows in a wide variety of habitats from wet to well-drained, stream banks, wet thickets, bottomland woodlands. This is a wonderful understory plant that along a woodland edge would be superb. My observations of native populations indicate phenomenal resiliency. Southeastern Virginia to north Florida, westward to east Texas and Arkansas. Zone 6 to 9.

Vaccinium stamineum L. — Deerberry
LEAVES: Alternate, simple, elliptic, ovate, oblong, obovate, or sub-orbicular, 3/4 to 3″ long, 1/3 to 1 1/4″ wide, acute to short acuminate, cuneate to rounded to subcordate at base, entire, occasionally serrate, rich green to glaucous blue-green, pubescent to varying degrees above (less) and below (more); petiole—short.

Vaccinium stamineum, (vak-sin′i-um stam-in′ē-um), Deerberry, is a variable shrub from 3 to 15′, usually inhabiting well-drained soils, often sandy in nature. Foliage varies from green to glaucous blue-green. The white flowers appear with the leaves in April–May with the pistil-stamen complex about twice as long as the petals. The fruits range from 1/5 to 3/5″ diameter, are ovoid, globose to slightly pear-shaped and color from whitish to dark purple, bloomy or not, largely inedible. This is a terrifically variable species worthy of use for naturalizing. I have observed 2 to 3′ high shrubs in sandy woods and 10′ high shrubs in improved soil. Have seen blue foliage types that rival a Blue Colorado Spruce. Massachusetts to Minnesota, south to Florida and Louisiana. Introduced 1772. Zone 5 to 9.

Vaccinium macrocarpon Ait. — American Cranberry, Large Cranberry
(vak-sin′i-um mak-rō-kär′pon)

FAMILY: Ericaceae

LEAVES: Alternate, simple, evergreen, 1/4 to 3/4″ long, 1/8 to 1/3″ wide, elliptic-oblong, flat or slightly revolute, slightly whitened beneath, lustrous dark green in summer assuming reddish purplish hues in fall and winter; petiole—short.
BUDS: Small or minute, solitary, sessile, with 2 apparently valvate scales or the larger with some half-dozen scales.
STEM: Slender, very obscurely 3- or 5-sided or distinctly angled; pith small, nearly round, continuous; leaf scars small or minute, half-rounded or crescent-shaped, somewhat elevated; 1 bundle trace.

SIZE: 2 to 6″ in height, spread is indefinite.
HARDINESS: Zone 2 to 6.
HABIT: Low, dense, small-leaved evergreen ground cover.
RATE: Slow to medium; I have grown plants in containers with excellent success.
TEXTURE: Beautifully fine in all seasons.
LEAF COLOR: Glossy medium to dark green in summer; new growth is often bronzy; during cold weather the foliage takes on reddish bronze to reddish purple hues.
FLOWERS: Perfect, pinkish, 1/3″ across, corolla deeply 4-cleft with revolute linear-oblong lobes, borne solitary, axillary, nodding, jointed with pedicel; May–June; not showy but interesting from a morphological viewpoint.
FRUIT: Berry, red, globose, 1/2 to 3/4″ across, acid, ripening in September or October.
CULTURE: Transplant as a container-grown plant into a moist, high organic matter soil; in the wild is found growing in moist sphagnum bogs; full sun, possibly light shade; most important to keep the roots cool and moist.
DISEASES AND INSECTS: Many associated with commercial production but nothing of consequence for the homeowner to worry about; review of the literature indicated more problems than I realized with commercial production; not as easy as Ocean Spray makes it look.
LANDSCAPE VALUE: A novelty evergreen ground cover which is quite handsome. I have had good success with container-grown plants which were transplanted into a 1/2 soil:1/2 sphagnum peat mixture.
CULTIVARS:
    'Hamilton'—A compact form, non-vining, slow-growing, pink flowers.
    'Stevens'—A commercial variety that produces abundant fruit.
PROPAGATION: Seeds require 3 months cold stratification for best germination. Cuttings are easy to root. Softwood cuttings treated with 1000 ppm IBA, placed in peat:perlite under mist rooted 80% in 6 weeks.
ADDITIONAL NOTES: The American Cranberry is the source of the cranberries which we relish during the holidays and for that matter the rest of the year. My children have consumed vats of the tangy, tart juice. Like *V. angustifolium* and *V. corymbosum*, true American fruits. Massachusetts and Wisconsin are the leading states in cranberry production and a trip to Cape Cod at harvesting time (or for that matter any time) is well

worth the effort. In mid-January 1997, Bonnie and I spent a delightful sunny day on the Cape touring and hiking. In Sandwich, off Route 6A, a flat-surfaced reddish haze, acres in scope, caught our attention. Indeed, a cranberry bog, on such a fine sunny day, was the center of the plant universe. Very interesting crop as far as cultural and nutritional practices are concerned and anyone interested should consult a text on modern fruit production.

NATIVE HABITAT: Newfoundland to Sasketchewan, south to North Carolina, Michigan and Minnesota. Introduced 1760.

RELATED SPECIES:

Vaccinium oxycoccos L., (vak-sin′i-um ok-si-kōk′ōs), Small Cranberry, European Cranberry, has 1/6 to 1/3″ long, dark green, evergreen, strongly revolute, ovate to oblong-ovate, tinged blue beneath leaves on a creeping framework of filiform stems. Flowers and fruits smaller than those of *V. macrocarpon*. The red, 1/4 to 1/3″ diameter fruits are rounded to pear-shaped and may persist on plants through winter. Found in northern Europe, Asia and America. Cultivated 1789. Zone 2 to 5.

Vaccinium vitis-idaea L. — Cowberry, Foxberry
LEAVES: Alternate, simple, oval to obovate, 3/8 to 1″ long, half as wide, often notched at apex, leathery, lustrous dark green, lower surface sprinkled with black dots; short-stalked.

Vaccinium vitis-idaea, (vak-sin′i-um vī′tis ĭ-dē′à), Cowberry, may grow to 10″(4 to 12″). The evergreen foliage is lustrous dark green above and paler dotted beneath; turns metallic mahogany in winter. The flowers are white or pinkish, campanulate, 4-lobed, 1/4″ long; May through June; borne in short sub-terminal nodding racemes. The fruit is a dark red, 1/4 to 3/8″ diameter berry with an acid, bitter taste; ripens in August. Culturally it performs best on moist, peaty soil and in full sun. The variety *minus* Lodd., Mountain Cranberry, Lingonberry, is lower growing (4″ rarely 8″) and hardier (Zone 2) than the species. The variety ranges from Labrador to Massachusetts to Alaska and British Columbia (Cultivated 1825) while the species is native to Europe and northern Asia. Cultivated 1789. Zone 5. I have seen the variety *minus* in Maine and have come to cherish and appreciate it for the refined, dainty habit and the excellent evergreen foliage. Variety *majus* Lodd. is listed with larger fruits and leaves 1 to 1 1/2″ long. Many cultivars have been selected in Europe where the plant is more popularly known as Lingonberry and assumes fruit crop status. Supposedly famous for making tart jelly. Please send me a jar if you have multiples. Many cultivars of var. *majus* have been selected for fruiting qualities. 'Erntdank' produces heavy crops of medium-sized berries; 'Erntkrone' has large, dark red fruits; 'Koralle', one of the most widely grown forms, produces two harvests of fruits per year on a 12″ by 12″ framework; and 'Masovia' bears abundant fruits. University of Wisconsin released 'Splendor' and 'Regal' lingonberries for use in breeding or commercial production; see *Fruit Varieties J.* 48(3):182–184 (1994). Tissue culture propagation of cultivars is widely used; see *Fruit Varieties J.* 48(1):7–14 (1994).

Viburnum L. — Viburnum
FAMILY: Caprifoliaceae

A garden without a viburnum is akin to life without music and art. I have a special fondness for this great group of plants that numbers about 120 (150) species and contains numerous cultivars. They range in size from 2 to 3′ to 30′, in odor from the sweetest perfume to the stenchiest stink, in flower from white to pink (rose), and in fruit color from yellow, orange, pink, red, blue, and black. The late Dr. Donald Egolf, U.S. National Arboretum, introduced 18 superior types, all of which are presented here. For many years viburnums were slighted in the mid south region but I now see *Viburnum plicatum*, *V. p.* var. *tomentosum*, *V. macrocephalum*, *V.* × *pragense*, *V.* × *burkwoodii* and many of Dr. Egolf's excellent selections becoming almost commonplace. For additional information see Wyman, Krüssmann, Bean, and Dirr, *American Nurseryman* 150(9), (1979) and *Plants and Garden Handbook* 37(1):32–35 (1981). Also, Kathleen Fisher's article on Donald Egolf's Viburnums, *Amer. Horticulturist* 68(10):30–35 (1989) is required reading.

My Ohio State education had much to do with instilling this great love of viburnums. In the woody plants course we were required to learn about 22 different viburnums. The initial force-feeding energized my system and to this day I become excited when a flowering or fruiting specimen of a worthy viburnum species confronts my everyday life. In Rowallane, Northern Ireland, on a fine June day, I witnessed the cultivar 'Rowallane' in glorious flower. Having only read about this clone of *V. plicatum* var. *tomentosum*, it was exciting to experience the genuine article. Likewise, on the Blue Ridge Parkway in North Carolina, where in July *Viburnum cassinoides* grew on the mountainsides in profusion; that same species in late August to early September with glaucous pinkish to rose, maturing to blue-black and purple-black fruits.

I would like to collect and grow them all or, at the worst, at least see and touch them during my travels. Don Shadow, Paul Cappiello, Gene Griffin, and I plan to produce a singular tome on *Viburnum*. Timber Press has agreed to publish the work. Perhaps, five-years removed from this new edition of the *Manual*.

Viburnum acerifolium L. — Mapleleaf Viburnum, Dogmackie

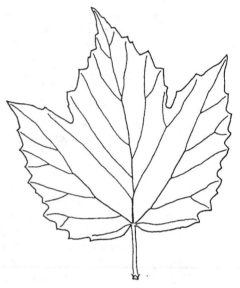

LEAVES: Opposite, simple, suborbicular to ovate, 3-lobed, sometimes slightly so, 2 to 4″(5″) long, about as wide, the lobes acute to acuminate, rounded to cordate at base, coarsely dentate, slightly pubescent above and dark green, more densely so and with black dots beneath; petiole—1/2 to 1″ long, pubescent.
BUDS: Remind of *V. dentatum*.
STEM: Pubescent in youth, brown, glabrous with maturity.

Viburnum acerifolium, (vĭ-bĕr′num ā-sĕr-i-fō′li-um), Mapleleaf Viburnum, is a low, sparsely branched shrub growing 4 to 6′ tall and 4′ wide. Clonal suckering thickets may extend forever. The foliage is bright to dark green in summer changing to reddish purple in fall. The flowers are yellowish white, all fertile, early June (early May, Athens), borne in 1 to 3″ diameter, long-stalked, flat-topped, terminal cymes. The fruit is a black, ellipsoidal, 1/3″ long drupe which ripens in September and often persists into winter. An extremely shade tolerant species reserved for naturalizing. The habit could best be described as suckering for it develops rather large, loose, open colonies in the wild. Is adapted to shade and rather dry soils as it occurs in the understory of the forest in southern locales. It is an excellent plant for use in heavily shaded situations and I find the range of fall colors (creamy pink, rose, red to grape-juice purple) intriguing. Roots well from June–July cuttings. New Brunswick to Minnesota, south to North Carolina and Georgia. Introduced 1736. Zone 4 to 8.

Viburnum alnifolium Marsh. — Hobblebush (Now *V. lantanoides* Michx. but I consider the name repulsive)

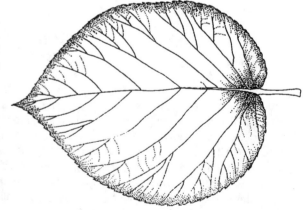

LEAVES: Opposite, simple, broad-ovate to suborbicular, 4 to 8″ long, nearly as wide, short acuminate, cordate, irregularly denticulate, stellate-pubescent above at first, later glabrous and dark green, more densely pubescent beneath, chiefly on the veins; petiole—1 to 2 1/2″ long, scurfy.

Viburnum alnifolium, (vĭ-bĕr′num al-ni-fō′li-um), Hobblebush, is a straggling shrub with pendulous outer branches; often develops a procumbent habit and roots develop where the branches touch the ground; reaches 9 to 12′ in height. The summer foliage is medium to dark green and develops reddish to deep claret in fall although I saw plants in Maine in rather deep shade that were beautiful rose-gold, green-gold to pinkish purple. Color or semblance of same develops early and it is not unusual to experience blushed red to red-purple leaves in mid to late summer. Easy plant to identify because of the large leaves, premature fall coloration and somewhat straggly habit. In the southern Appalachians, the plant grows in identifiable quantities above ±3000′ elevation. One of my favorite discoveries when hiking. The flowers are borne in flat-topped, 3 to 5″ diameter cymes, the outer flowers of which are sterile, white, about 1″ diameter and produced in mid-May. The fruit is a red, finally purple-black drupe about 1/3″ long which matures in September. Probably requires two seedlings to facilitate cross-pollination and heavy fruit set. This species is maximally adapted to shady, moist areas. This is a shrub that one has to adapt to for it lacks the symmetry of many viburnums. Probably best adapted to a naturalized situation. 'Serenity' is listed by Eastern Plant Specialties, Georgetown, ME, for more restrained habit. Native to New Brunswick and Michigan to North Carolina in the mountains. Introduced 1820. Zone 3 to 5(6).

Viburnum × *burkwoodii* Burkw. & Skipw. — Burkwood Viburnum
(vī-bĕr′num bĕrk-wood′ē-ī)

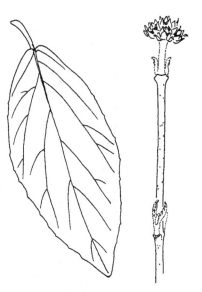

LEAVES: Opposite, simple, oblong, ovate to elliptic, 1 1/2 to 4″ long, 3/4 to 1 3/4″ wide, acute or obtuse, rounded or heart-shaped, indistinctly toothed, lustrous dark green above, a bit rough to the touch, much lighter (gray-green) beneath and tomentose, veins—often rusty brown in color; petiole—1/4 to 1/2″ long, scurfy-pubescent.
BUDS: Vegetative—foliose, naked, tomentose.
FLOWER BUDS: Clustered (cymose), 1/2″ across, grayish pubescent, remind of small cauliflowers.
STEM: Light tan in color, tomentose.

SIZE: 8 to 10′ with spread about 2/3's height.
HARDINESS: Zone (4)5 to 8; has been injured at Minnesota Landscape Arboretum but is about the hardiest of the semi-snowball fragrant types; also injured in Orono, ME; fine at Morton Arboretum, Lisle, IL.
HABIT: Upright, multi-stemmed, often tangled mass of stems yielding a somewhat straggly appearance; never as dense as *V.* × *juddii* and *V. carlesii* as the young growth extensions are elongated and seldom branched.
RATE: Slow to medium.
TEXTURE: Medium in foliage, medium in winter.
LEAF COLOR: Lustrous dark green above; light gray-brown beneath; holds green color late, tends toward a semi-evergreen character especially in southern states [Zone (7b)8]; fall color may be a sporadic wine-red.
FLOWERS: Pink in bud to white in flower, spicy, aromatic, almost *Daphne odora* fragrance, April, effective for 7 to 10 days, hemispherical, 5-rayed cyme approximately 2 to 3″(3 1/2″) across, each flower 1/3 to 1/2″ wide, with 5 spreading, rounded lobes, anthers pale yellow, often opens in late March in Athens, full flower April 9, 1993 and March 29, 1994.
FRUIT: Red changing to black, 1/3″ diameter, ellipsoidal-flattened drupe, July–August, usually sparsely produced and of insignificant ornamental importance; have seen respectable fruit when other plants of a similar nature (taxonomic affinity) were in close proximity thus facilitating good cross pollination.
CULTURE: Most viburnums require a slightly moist, well-drained soil, are pH adaptable but prefer a slightly acid situation; probably should be moved balled-and-burlapped or as a container specimen, small plants can be handled bare root; avoid sulfur sprays as many viburnums are defoliated by them; a very serviceable group of plants of easy culture provided the soil is well-drained; nematodes in the south can be problematic.
DISEASES AND INSECTS: Bacterial leaf spot, crown gall, shoot blight, leaf spots, powdery mildew, rusts, downy leaf spot, spot anthracnose, spray burn (caused by sulfur sprays), viburnum aphid, asiatic garden beetle, citrus flatid planthopper, tarnished plant bug, thrips, potato flea beetle, dogwood twig borer, and seven scale species; although the list is impressive the viburnums are relatively free of major problems.
LANDSCAPE VALUE: Excellent choice for the shrub border, works well with broadleaf evergreens, fragrance permeates the entire garden; thrives even in a polluted environment. The more I travel the more convinced I am that this is an excellent garden plant; it is often considered a second class citizen among fragrant viburnums but its heat and cold tolerance are notable assets; it is definitely one of the best viburnums in the Midwest and South; some pruning is necessary to keep it looking good; in the Dirr Georgia garden and has followed me through the horticultural years; asks little, gives much; still delight picking an emerging inflorescence and inhaling the fragrance.
CULTIVARS:
'Anne Russell'—Resulted from a back cross between *V. carlesii* with *V.* × *burkwoodii* made in 1951 at L.R. Russell Ltd., England. The habit is compact and will grow 6′ high and 8′ wide; the pink-budded, fragrant, 3″ wide flowers open several weeks before 'Fulbrook'.

'Chenaultii'—An extremely confused entity and in many respects resembles *V. × burkwoodii* except the leaves are smaller. I have seen specimens labeled as *Viburnum × chenaultii* but always thought they were *V. × burkwoodii*. Rehder does not list this species in his *Manual of Cultivated Trees and Shrubs* and *Hillier Manual of Trees and Shrubs* lists the plant as a cultivar and not a species. Several specimens I have seen were actually larger in size than the normal *V. × burkwoodii* but a bit more compact in the density of branching and leaves. The flowers are borne in great profusion and literally cover the shrub in late April or early May just slightly later than *V. × burkwoodii*. I have seen plants at Callaway Gardens, GA, that were still pink in bud while *V. × burkwoodii* was full and open white.

'Fulbrook'—Parentage supposedly as in 'Anne Russell' with comparatively large, sweet-scented, pink-budded flowers that open white, each flower 5/8″ wide, the cyme 3″ across; 8′ high and 10′ wide, leaves like *V. carlesii* with more luster, strongly serrated, 3 to 4″ long, 2 to 3″ wide, RHS Award of Merit 1957.

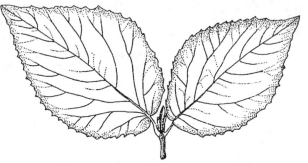

'Mohawk'—Resulted from a backcross of *V. × burkwoodii* × *V. carlesii* made in 1953. The cultivar was selected for the dark red flower buds which open to white petals with red-blotched reverse; abundant inflorescences; strong, spicy clove fragrance; compact growth habit; and foliage resistant to bacterial leaf spot and powdery mildew. The brilliant red flower buds appear several weeks before the flowers begin to open, and extend the effective ornamental period of the plant to several weeks rather than a few days as with *V. carlesii* types. The strong, spicy clove fragrance is very pleasant and a noteworthy attribute of 'Mohawk'. The glossy, dark green leaves, which turn a brilliant orange-red in autumn are highly resistant to bacterial leaf spot and powdery mildew. Fall color in Athens is subdued reddish purple, often at peak in mid-November with leaves dropping clean by late November. Leaves favor *V. carlesii* in shape and color. The original plant is a compact shrub, 7′ in height with spreading branches to 7 1/2′. 'Mohawk' has been hardy as far north as Ithaca, NY. In colder regions the plant may survive, but the naked flower buds may be frost damaged. I have seen the plant in flower in late April at the Strybing Arboretum, San Francisco. Has performed well in Zone 7b and is slightly later flowering than *V. × burkwoodii* although in some years peak times coincide. Plants have reached 7 to 8′ tall in 4 years after planting as 3′ high shrubs. It is every degree as handsome as the above description especially the glistening dark red buds; an Egolf introduction; 1992 Styer Award recipient from the Pennsylvania Horticulture Society.

'Park Farm Hybrid'—Similar to *V. × burkwoodii* but differing in its larger, 3 to 5″ diameter, pinker budded inflorescences and the wide-spreading habit; it may grow 4′ high and 7′ wide, some literature noted it as tall as typical *V. × burkwoodii*, have seen at Wisley and the specimen was more compact than typical *V. × burkwoodii*.

'Sarcoxie'—Listed in literature as *V. × burkwoodii* × *V. carlesii*, upright in youth, more rounded with age, fragrant flowers, 2 to 3″ across.

PROPAGATION: In general seeds of viburnums are not the easiest to germinate; they show a double dormancy and require warm/cold periods of different duration; 3 to 5 months warm followed by 3 months cold is sufficient for many; it is best to place the cleaned seeds in warm stratification and watch for radicle emergence; when this occurs the seeds should be transferred to the cold. I have rooted cuttings from June–July collected wood with 100% efficiency; cuttings were dipped in 1000 ppm IBA/50% alcohol solution; in general, cuttings of most viburnums are easy to root although some taxa, particularly the fragrant, semi-snowball types, experience overwinter survival problems. See Dirr and Heuser (1987) for a good discussion.

ADDITIONAL NOTES: The species was developed in England by Albert Burkwood and Geoffrey Skipwith in 1914 and introduced in 1924. It is a cross between *V. carlesii* and *V. utile*, the latter having proved to be of little worth as a garden shrub but a fine parent in breeding programs.

RELATED SPECIES:

Viburnum utile Hemsl. — Service Viburnum

LEAVES: Opposite, simple, ovate to oblong, 1 to 3″ long, 1/4 to 1 1/4″ wide, obtuse, rarely acutish, broad-cuneate or rounded, entire, leathery, lustrous dark green and glabrous above, prominently veined (5 to 6 pairs) and white beneath with a dense covering of stellate hairs; petiole—1/6 to 1/3″ long.

Viburnum utile, (vī-bĕr′num ū′ti-lē), Service Viburnum, is a small, 4 to 6′ high and wide, evergreen shrub of rather straggly habit. The leaves have a rather wavy and at times almost inrolled (revolute) appearance. The pink-budded, slightly fragrant, white flowers occur in mid-April (Athens) to May in 5-rayed, 2 to 3″ diameter, rounded cymes. The fruit is a 1/4″ long, bluish black drupe. This species has been most important in breeding work and has given our gardens *V. × burkwoodii* and its cultivars, along with *V. × pragense*, 'Chesapeake', 'Conoy', and 'Eskimo'. The species is seldom seen in gardens and is not the handsomest of plants owing to the open habit, small leaves and rather nondescript flowers. However, it carries genes for heat tolerance and old plants at Callaway Gardens and in Aiken, SC attest to this. Also, the fine glossy foliage character appears often in the off-spring. A small plant in our garden reminds one of the power of the *great* plant breeders. Our gardens are blessed because certain individuals see and seize the future. Central China. Introduced 1901. Zone 6 to 8.

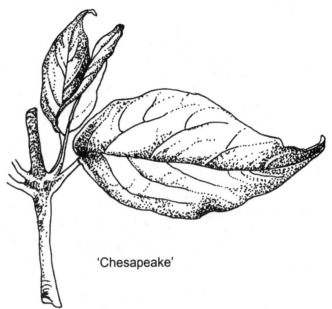

'Chesapeake'

'Chesapeake'—Compact, mounded, twice as wide as high, leathery lustrous dark green leaves, not as dark green as 'Eskimo', foliage long persistent; pink buds open to white, ever-so-slightly fragrant (almost undetectable) flowers, 2 to 3 1/2″ diameter cymes, dull red to black fruit; 6′ high and 10′ wide in 16 years, result of a cross between 'Cayuga' × *V. utile* made in 1962, introduced by U.S. National Arboretum, an Egolf selection; see *HortScience* 16:350 (1981); I had great hopes for this when it was first planted in our Horticulture Garden in 1982 but it has not measured up to expectations. The plant is 10′ by 10′, large, billowy and with medium density. Foliage tends toward a semi-evergreen nature with leaves at end of stems persistent. Leaves are undulating (wavy) with a slight twist to the long axis. Flowers are small, actually about 2″ diameter and ever-so-slightly fragrant. They peak in mid-April in Athens but have opened in early April and as I pen this are still effective on April 25. 'Chesapeake' has not been as hardy as 'Eskimo', a sister seedling, and I suspect -10 to -15°F is the break point. Actually, I have received mixed reports on hardiness and the plant supposedly survived -25°F in Cincinnati but in Winchester, TN was killed to the ground at -20°F. Branches are prone to breakage when tied or handled roughly.

'Conoy'—A spreading, dense-branched, evergreen shrub with glossy dark green, 1 1/2 to 2 1/2″ long leaves that may assume a dark maroon tinge in winter; the undersides of the leaves are pale blue-green and covered with stellate pubescence; the flowers occur in April with dark pink buds opening to creamy white, flowers are slightly fragrant (I cannot detect fragrance) and occur in 2 to 2 1/2″ diameter cymes, 70 to 75 florets per inflorescence; the 1/3″ long glossy ovoid drupes ripen in August changing from red to black at maturity and persist 5 to 8 weeks, 5′ by 8′ in 17 years; has been resistant to bacterial leaf spot; witnessed a 3′ by 5′ specimen on February 19, 1991 at U.S. National Arboretum with full complement of dark green leaves, has withstood -9°F without injury; in southern climates foliage remains green in winter; result of a backcross between *V. utile × V. × burkwoodii* 'Park Farm Hybrid', see *HortScience* 23:419–421 (1988) for additional information; a Don Egolf/U.S. National Arboretum introduction; one of Dr. Egolf's great plants and is particularly well-adapted for Zone 7 and 8; in our garden, it is a stalwart with pretty flowers, terrific lustrous dark green foliage that is somewhat undulating with margins recurved; visitors to whom I show the plant seldom know its identity, but are impressed by the ornamental virtues; has not fruited well, in fact, I can't remember a single fruit on our lone plant; requires, like many viburnums, a cross pollinator of related genetic parentage, but *not* the *same*.

'Eskimo'—Dense compact form, 4 to 5′ high and 5′ wide in 12 years, semi-evergreen at ends of stems, coriaceous, lustrous dark green leaves, pale cream buds have a touch of pink on edges, open to pure white, globose, snowball, 3 to 4″ diameter inflorescences composed of 80 to 175 tubular flowers, fruits dull red to black, resistant to bacterial leaf spot, a U.S. National Arboretum introduction, see *HortScience* 16:691 (1981); parentage is 'Cayuga' × *V. utile*; I believe this selection will win out over 'Chesapeake' with time for it is hardier, offers bigger, more abundant flowers on young plants and stays relatively compact. The leaves are flat without the waviness of 'Chesapeake'. Plants grown in containers appear prosperous and are show-stoppers in flower. Interestingly, the flowers are not in the least fragrant. Now have 6 to 8′ high plants in the University's Botanical Garden. Still in tight bud on April 9, 1993 while 'Chesapeake' and 'Mohawk' were in or had passed full flower stage.

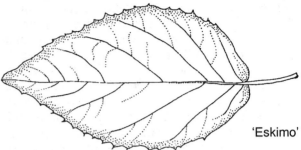

'Eskimo'

Viburnum carlesii Hemsl. — Koreanspice Viburnum
(vī-bĕr′num kär-lē′sē-ī)

LEAVES: Opposite, simple, broad-ovate to elliptic, 1 to 4″ long, 3/4 to 2 1/2″ wide, acute, usually rounded to subcordate at base, irregularly toothed, dull dark green and stellate pubescent above, densely so and paler beneath; petiole—1/4 to 1/2″ long.

BUDS: Vegetative—foliose, naked, hairy; flower buds large—1/4 to 1/2″ wide.

STEM: Light brown to gray, stellate pubescence on young stem; old stems are gray and exhibit a characteristic fissuring.

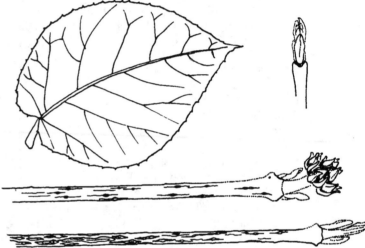

SIZE: 4 to 5′ possibly to 8′ in height, by 4 to 8′ in width, have seen plants 10′ high and wide, the more I travel the garden path the larger the specimens I see.

HARDINESS: Zone (4)5 to 7(8); injured in Orono, ME; fine at Morton Arboretum.

HABIT: Rounded, dense shrub with stiff, upright spreading branches.

RATE: Slow.

TEXTURE: Medium in summer and winter, clean in appearance.

LEAF COLOR: Dull dark green with a satiny sheen, very pubescent on the upper surface, more so on lower, reddish to wine-red in fall color, not consistent in coloration and usually disappointing, fall color on occasion is excellent prompting thoughts of clonal selection; Matt Vehr, horticulturist, Spring Grove, showed me slides of a rich red-purple fall-colored form.

FLOWERS: Perfect, pink to reddish in bud, opening white, each individual flower 1/2″ across; late April to early May; in dense hemispherical cymes, 2 to 3″ across, often termed semi-snowball type flowers; flowers are at their best when leaves are 1/2 to 2/3's mature size; fragrance almost like *Daphne odora*, truly outstanding.

FRUIT: Drupe, 1/3″ long, egg-shaped, flattened, red changing to black (not effective), August to September.

CULTURE: Transplant balled-and-burlapped or as a small bare root plant; best in well-drained, slightly acid soil with even moisture; full sun to partial shade; prune after flowering; plants used to be grafted on *V. lantana* and I have seen the scion consumed by the understock; be careful to buy own-root plants.

DISEASES AND INSECTS: Bacterial leaf spot can be troublesome; nematodes infect this species.

LANDSCAPE VALUE: A valuable shrub for fragrance; I used it in a foundation planting along a walk at my Illinois home and for ten days in late April–early May it was a joy; some of the newer cultivars and *V.* × *juddii* are superior and should be used in preference; not as adaptable as *V.* × *juddii* or *V.* × *burkwoodii*; just returned from Wichita, KS where the species is common and successfully cultured in high pH soils and wind-swept conditions.

CULTIVARS:

'Aurora'—In the last edition relegated to the other cultivars category but the extra terrestrial siting at the Arnold Arboretum during the 1991 sabbatical forced significant treatment in this edition; Arnold plant 6 to 8′ high and wide, rich deep pink-red buds open to pinkish white, spicily fragrant flowers; inflorescences larger to 5″ and more substantial than those of the species; starting to appear in United States nurseries; introduced by Slieve Donard Nursery, Newcastle, Northern Ireland; RHS Award of Merit, Wisley.

'Carlotta'—Improved form of *V. carlesii*; the leaves are larger than those of *V. carlesii* and broad-ovate in outline; introduced by W.B. Clarke Co., San Jose, CA.

'Cayuga'—Is the result of a backcross made in 1953 of *V. carlesii* × *V.* × *carlcephalum* (*V. carlesii* × *V. macrocephalum*). 'Cayuga' is distinct in producing abundant, 4 to 5″ diameter inflorescences with pink buds that open to white flowers in late April; compact, upright growth habit; and medium textured foliage, with tolerance to bacterial leaf spot and powdery mildew. The leaves, which are less susceptible to bacterial leaf spot and powdery mildew than those of *V. carlesii*, are a darker green, smaller and not as coarse as those of *V.* × *carlcephalum*, their greater numbers present a mass effect and a more ornamental plant. The flowers open from one side of the inflorescence in such a way that nearly all inflorescences have pink buds accenting the white, waxy flowers. Although 'Cayuga' is described as a compact spreading, deciduous shrub to 5′ high, plants in the University's Botanical Garden are distinctly upright oval and somewhat leggy at the base and 8′ high in January 1998. In full flower from late March to early April in Athens. Plants have been hardy as far north as Ithaca, NY. An Egolf introduction.

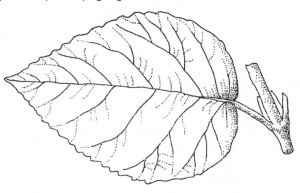

'Charis'—Vigorous form, probably larger than 'Aurora' at maturity, red-budded flowers open to pink and at maturity are white, highly fragrant, Slieve Donard Nursery introduction.

'Compactum'—One of the best dwarf clones available but is rarely found in modern landscapes; it grows 2 1/2 to 3 1/2′ high and wide and produces exceptionally dark green leaves and flowers about the same size as the species; shows greater resistance to leaf spot; introduced by Hoogendorn Nurseries, Inc., Newport, RI in 1953.

'Diana'—Vigorous clone of relatively compact habit, red in bud, opening same and finally turning pink, fragrant, purple-tinged young foliage, Slieve Donard introduction.

PROPAGATION: Generally considered difficult but June–July cuttings treated with 8000 ppm IBA-talc rooted 80% and all were successfully transplanted after going through a dormancy cycle; this is one of those plants that dislikes root disturbance after rooting. Several wide crosses with *V. lantana* were constructed at University of Wisconsin with embryo rescue being utilized to generate plants; see *J. Environ. Hort.* 13(4):193–195 (1995) for exciting possibilities.

NATIVE HABITAT: Korea. Introduced 1812.

RELATED SPECIES:

Viburnum bitchiuense Mak. — Bitchiu Viburnum
LEAVES: Opposite, simple, ovate to oblong, 1 to 3″ long, 1/? to 3/4″ wide, obtuse, subcordate to cordate, dentate especially toward apex, dark green above, pubescent on both surfaces, 6 to 7 vein pairs.

Viburnum bitchiuense, (vī-bĕr′num bitch-i-ū-en′sē), Bitchiu Viburnum, is somewhat similar to *V. carlesii* but with smaller leaves, more slender stems, looser habit and smaller pinkish white flowers [1 1/2 to 2″(3″) across] in looser clusters. Bitchiu is considered inferior to *V. carlesii* but selected forms may rival Koreanspice. Height varies from 8 to 10′. The dark bluish green foliage may turn dull reddish purple in fall but is usually not effective. The red, changing to black, fruit is produced sparsely. Bitchiu has imparted some of its good characteristics to *V.* × *juddii*. Keep looking for definitive ways to separate this from *V. carlesii*. The looser, laxer, more open inflorescence and stronger dentate serrations toward apex of the leaf are helpful. Have observed worthy, robust specimens of *V. bitchiuense* that rival *V. carlesii*. Japan, Korea. Cultivated 1909. Zone 5 to 7.

Viburnum × carlcephalum Burkw. & Skipwith ex V.V. Pike, (vī-bĕr′num kärl-sef′à-lum), Carlcephalum or Fragrant Viburnum, grows 6 to 10′ high with an equal spread. Habit is somewhat open and loose. Foliage is dark green with a slight luster in summer changing to reddish purple in fall. Leaves are the largest of the fragrant, semi-snowball group, often 4 to 5″ long. The flowers are pink in bud, finally white, fragrant, late April to early May, borne in 5 to 6″ diameter, up to 100-flowered, hemispherical cymes. In full flower from late March to early April in Athens. One of the best descriptions I read termed the inflorescences

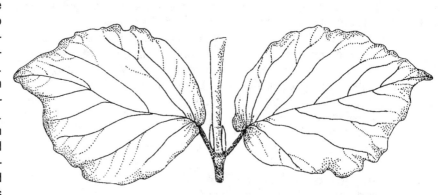

lumpy. Fruit is a drupe which changes from red to black; however, it is seldom effective. Reasonable plant for the garden. Result of a cross between *V. carlesii* × *V. macrocephalum* var. *keteleeri*. Originated in England in 1932 at the Burkwood and Skipwith Nursery and introduced into the United States about 1957. It is relatively easy to root from softwood cuttings. It is the latest of the semi-snowball types to flower. Usually somewhat coarse and in no way as fine a garden shrub as *V.* × *juddii*, 'Eskimo' or 'Mohawk'. Have seen on occasion in the South and was pleased with floral performance. 'Cayuga' is a superior alternative. Hardiness is somewhat suspect and a Zone (5)6 to 7(8) rating is safest. An 11′ high plant was reported at the Morton Arboretum (Zone 4b/5a).

Viburnum × juddii Rehd., (vī-bĕr′num jud′ē-ī), Judd Viburnum, is the result of a cross between *V. carlesii* and *V. bitchiuense* with the best features of both parents. I feel it is superior to run-of-the-mill *V. carlesii* and may eventually replace it in northern and southern areas. The habit is full and rounded with mature height approaching 6 to 8′. It is more resistant to bacterial leaf spot and roots much more readily from softwood cuttings. The inflorescence ranges from 2 1/2 to 3 1/4″ wide and when open is highly fragrant. I have heard people say that the fragrance of *V.* × *juddii* is not as pronounced as that of *V. carlesii* but am hard-pressed to distinguish between the two. This hybrid was raised at the Arnold Arboretum by William H. Judd, propagator, in 1920; flowered for the first time in 1929 when it was 6′ high and named in 1935. Nurserymen are selling this hybrid in greater numbers and someday it may replace *V. carlesii* as the dominant semi-snowball viburnum. Zone 4 to 8. Has proven an adaptable and floriferous shrub in the University's Botanical Garden. It is located by a walk that leads from the parking area and many people stop to sample its delicious perfume. The plants are now over 10′ high. Flowers in late March–early April in Athens.

Viburnum macrocephalum Fort. — Chinese Snowball Viburnum

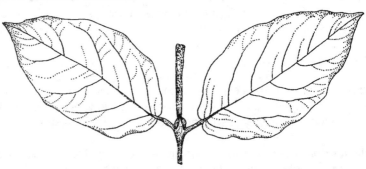

LEAVES: Opposite, simple, deciduous or semi-evergreen, ovate or elliptic to ovate-oblong, 2 to 4″ long, 1 1/4 to 2 1/2″ wide, acute or obtusish, rounded at base, denticulate or entire, dark green and nearly glabrous above, stellate-pubescent beneath; petiole—1/2 to 3/4″ long.

Viburnum macrocephalum, (vī-bĕr′num mak-rō-sef′à-lum), Chinese Snowball Viburnum, is a dense, rounded shrub growing 6 to 10′ high in more northerly climes. The flowers are white, non-fragrant, each individual floret 1 1/4″ across, May to early June, (mid-April in Athens), borne in 3 to 8″ diameter hemispherical cymes. Extremely showy in flower but requires a protected location and well-drained soil. I have seen it flowering in Columbus, OH, in a protected area. The foliage is semi-evergreen in the South. In the southern states the plant may grow 12 to 15′(20′) high and form a massive rounded shrub. It tends to flower in the fall during warm weather in the South. In full flower it is a spectacular shrub and certainly worthy of consideration in larger gardens. For 10 years, it has been a staple in the entrance planting to our home. Every 3 or 4 years I cut it 2 to 3′ from the ground because of its tendency to overgrow the surrounding vegetation. First year after cutting back, there are no flowers, subsequent years unbelievable profusion. Interestingly, the showy florets are apple green when emerging, finally white. People stop to ask the identity of the plant. Great for obtrusive show. It is relatively easy to root from June–July cuttings using 3000 to 5000 ppm IBA-quick dip but resents disturbance after rooting and should be left in place until the second year. Does not fruit as the flowers are sterile. The forma *keteleeri* (Carr.) Rehd. is the wild form and has sterile marginal flowers and fertile inner flowers in 4 to 5″ diameter, rather flat cymes. The forma was used in breeding *V.* × *carlcephalum*. Flowers are like those of *V. plicatum* var. *tomentosum* and are followed by shiny red, oblong fruits. China. Introduced 1844. Zone 6 to 9.

Viburnum cassinoides L. — Witherod Viburnum

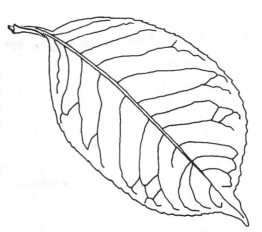

LEAVES: Opposite, simple, elliptic or ovate to oblong, 1 1/2 to 3 1/2″(4 1/2″) long, 3/4 to 2 1/4″ wide, acute or bluntly acuminate, rounded or wedge-shaped, obscurely dentate or denticulate, bronze- to chocolate-tinted in youth, dull dark green above, nearly glabrous, somewhat scurfy beneath; petiole—1/4 to 3/4″ long, scurfy.
BUDS: Valvate, flowers with a bulbous base terminating the shoots, similar to *V. lentago*; vegetative—long, narrow, without the fattened base.
STEM: Gray to brown, scurfy in youth, finally glabrous.

Viburnum cassinoides, (vī-bĕr′num kas-i-noy′dēz), Witherod Viburnum, grows 5 to 6′ tall with a similar spread but can reach 10′ or greater in height. It is a handsome dense shrub, compact and rounded, with spreading, finally slightly arching branches. The dull dark green foliage changes to orange-red, dull crimson, and purple in fall. The emerging leaves are often bronze- or purple-tinted. The flowers are creamy white, June to early July, borne in 2 to 5″ diameter, flat-topped, arching at extremities cymes. Each flower is about 1/5 to 1/4″ diameter and the yellowish stamens create a soft yellow patina over the entire inflorescence. The fruit is the most beautiful attribute as it changes from green to pink, then from red to blue before becoming black in September. Often all colors are present in the same infructescence (fruiting cluster). A very lovely but little used shrub which has a place in naturalizing, massing, and the shrub border. I have seen it used effectively in a mass planting at the Holden Arboretum, Mentor, OH. In Maine, I saw it growing along the roadside and while trekking the highest mountain in Georgia discovered it in full fruit all along the route. Many plants I have observed in the wild were in the 12 to 15′ range although most books do not allow the species to grow over 12′. This is a fine viburnum and in fruit is spectacular. Considerable variation would allow for selection of flower, fruit, foliage and habit. I am on patrol and by the 6th edition will have a worthy clone or three. Have three in the garden and none are as exciting as what I pass by in the wild or the current Dirr holdings of *V. nudum*. Variety *angustifolium* has more elongated-narrow leaves and grows slower and is more open than the typical species form. A plant in our garden has failed to impress. In fact, I don't remember seeing a plant so small and open that 10 cats could be hurled through the branches without striking a leaf. 'Deep Pink' is a deep pink-fruited form, found in Maine by Mike Johnson, Summer Hill Nursery, Madison, CT. Newfoundland to Manitoba and Minnesota south to Georgia. Introduced 1761. Zone 3 to 8.

A closely related species, **Viburnum nudum** L., (vī-bĕr′num nū′dum), Smooth Witherod, is equally beautiful and perhaps more so because the leaves are more lustrous. The leaves and stems may also be less pubescent but this appears to be somewhat variable. I grew this species in my Illinois garden where it survived -20°F. The red to reddish purple fall color is also attractive. 'Winterthur' is an improved form selected at Winterthur Gardens, Delaware. Killed the first one in Georgia, added another and it is growing well with lustrous, waxy foliage, compact, 6′ in 10 years.

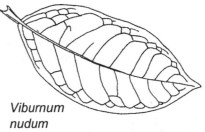

Viburnum nudum

'Count Pulaski' has a multi-stemmed, loosely structured form, rapid growth; larger leaf than typical, almost glossy; extremely floriferous, white, musky-scented flowers; fruit in 6 to 10″ diameter, flat-topped cymes; green, exotic salmon-pink, shades of lavender, to blue and purplish black fruits; original plant collected in Pulaski County, AR; Larry Lowman introduction. There is a 'Pink Beauty' listed. Dr. Darrell Apps, formerly Chadds Ford, PA had several *V. nudum* seedlings in his garden that developed outstanding fall color. With selection this could become a well-received garden plant. Current thinking merges *V. nudum* under *V. cassinoides*. For purposes of discussion, I have kept them separate. Those previous comments aside, I read Meyer, Mazzeo and Ross (1994) and *The New RHS Dictionary of Gardening* (1992) and both references maintain species status. As I grow wiser and more skeptical, I realize that almost everything in nomenclature comes full circle. The question remains whether I can outlast the taxonomists. See

Nursery Management and Production 14(1):14–15, 72 (1998) for an update on my emotional bonding with the above two species. Connecticut, Long Island to Florida, west to Kentucky and Louisiana. Introduced 1752. Zone 5 to 9.

Viburnum davidii Franch. — David Viburnum

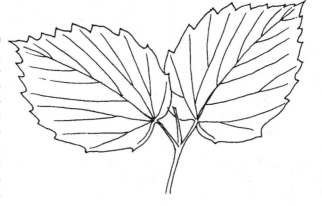

LEAVES: Opposite, simple, evergreen, narrowly oval or slightly obovate, 2 to 6″ long, 1 to 2 1/2″ wide, acuminate, cuneate, conspicuously 3-veined, toothed toward apex, leathery, dark green, almost dark bluish green above, pale beneath, glabrous except for axillary tufts of hair below; petiole—1/4 to 1″ long.

Viburnum davidii, (vī-bĕr′num dă-vid′ē-ī), David Viburnum, forms a low, compact, 3 to 5′ high mound of thick, dark blue-green evergreen foliage. It is a beautiful viburnum and if it never flowered or fruited it would still be a plant of the first order. I have seen it in abundance throughout Europe but seldom in the United States. In Athens, GA and Aiken, SC where I observed plantings, it is still subject to the vagaries of weather and the flowers and leaves may be injured. It appears to require a more moderate, even climate than can be offered in most parts of the United States. Ideally it is suited to the Pacific Northwest. The pink-budded, finally dull white flowers occur in dense, 2 to 3″ wide, 7-rayed cymes in April–May. The 1/4″ long, oval fruits are a beautiful shade of blue. Unfortunately, the plant is either functionally dioecious or requires cross pollination from another clone for fruit is not set unless the proper conditions are met. In England, clones have been designated "male" and "female." The plant in fruit is spectacular and the first impulse is to locate a source for one's own garden. I have seen the plant used in combination with other broadleaf evergreens and it was effective. The Isle of Mainau in Germany has several large specimens. 'Jermyn's Globe' is now considered a hybrid of *V. davidii* × *V. calvum* and the original plant is low, compact and rounded. Also, occasionally growing and seemingly more contentedly, is *V. cinnamonifolium* Rehd., that is larger, 6 to 10′(20′) high and apparently more cold hardy (Zone 7). There is a relatively respectable specimen at the Atlanta Botanical Garden. Woodlanders, Aiken, SC reported this a better doer than *V. davidii*. Shaky for all but the collector. China. *Viburnum davidii* is native to Western China. Introduced 1904. Zone (7)8 to 9.

Viburnum dentatum L. — Arrowwood Viburnum
(vī-bĕr′num den-tā′tum)

LEAVES: Opposite, simple, suborbicular to ovate, 2 to 4 1/2″ long, 1 to 4″ wide, short acuminate, rounded or subcordate, coarsely dentate, lustrous dark green and glabrous above, glabrous beneath or bearded in the axils of the veins, with 6 to 10 pairs of impressed veins; petiole—1/2 to 1″ long.

BUDS: Imbricate, usually appressed, green to brown, small, lower bud scale forming a V-shaped notch, glabrous, almost glossy.

STEM: Glabrous at maturity, gray to gray-brown, leaf scars with ciliate hairs around the margins.

SIZE: 6 to 8′ to 15′ in height in favorable locations, spread 6 to 15′.
HARDINESS: Zone (2)3 to 8.
HABIT: Multi-stemmed, dense, rounded shrub with spreading, finally arching branches, suckering tendency and will colonize.
RATE: Medium.
TEXTURE: Medium in leaf and winter habit; some specimens are so delicately branched as to appear medium-fine in winter.
LEAF COLOR: Lustrous dark green in summer, sometimes without the sheen, fall color ranges from yellow to glossy red to reddish purple; selections for superior clones both in habit and foliage could be made for

there is great variability within this species; I have seen poor fall-colored specimens growing next to brilliant glossy red forms; the differences were not attributable to soils or climate but genetics.

FLOWERS: White, actually yellow stamens create a creamy color rather than pure white, somewhat ill-scented, May to early June, early May (Athens), effective 10 to 14 days, borne in 2 to 4″(5″) diameter, flat-topped, 7-rayed cymes on 1 1/2 to 2 1/2″ high, raised peduncles.

FRUIT: Drupe, oval-rounded, 1/4″ long, blue or bluish black, late September through October; birds relish the fruits and seeds are found germinating in many out-of-the-way places; some plants have particularly striking blue fruits, actual seed (stone) has a narrow deep groove on one side.

CULTURE: Fibrous rooted, transplants well, adapted to varied soils (possibly most durable viburnum for East and Midwest), prefers well-drained conditions; sun or partial shade; suckers freely from the base and may have to be restricted from getting out of bounds.

DISEASES AND INSECTS: None serious, have not noticed any problems.

LANDSCAPE VALUE: Valued for durability and utility, the ornamental characters are secondary to other viburnums, good in hedges, groupings, masses, filler in shrub border; University of Illinois effectively employed this shrub for screening parking lots; its utilitarian and adaptable nature is readily evident for I have observed it growing in the sands of Cape Cod, not too far removed from the salt spray, but never forming the first or second line of defense; in Nebraska it withstands the high pH, heavy soils and the vagaries of that climate; without a doubt it is one of the most functional viburnums.

CULTIVARS: I read my 1990 comment under leaf color and chuckled since the words have now come true with several introductions, most of which I have observed and grown; still room for improvement.

Autumn Jazz® ('Ralph Senior')—Graceful vase-shaped habit, 8 to 10′ by 10 to 12′, glossy green summer foliage, yellow-orange-red-burgundy fall color, minimal fall color in Zone 7b, introduced through Chicagoland Grows.

'Cardinal'—Consistent brilliant red fall color, from Roy Klehm.

Chicago Lustre® ('Synnesvedt')—Glossy dark green foliage, reddish purple in fall according to literature but really not striking, rounded shrub, 10′ by 10′, no appreciable fall color in Zone 7b, our *V. bracteatum* 'Emerald Luster' is superior, Chicagoland Grows introduction.

'Deamii'—Listed by E.W. Coffman as one of the best forms of *V. dentatum*; this taxon has been afforded species status by previous authors, it is a midwestern representative of the terrific variation within *V. dentatum*, performing quite well in Iowa.

Dwarf Form—Described as a test selection that grew 5′ high while control plants grew 8′, heavy flowers and fruits are held above the foliage, Fairweather Gardens introduction.

Northern Burgundy® ('Morton')—Dark green summer foliage, burgundy in fall, 10 to 12′ high, more upright than Autumn Jazz®, same flowers and fruits as species, again nothing to get excited about in Zone 7b, Chicagoland grows introduction.

'Perle Bleu'—Described as producing heavy crops of blue fruits, 8 to 10′ high, otherwise like the species.

'Tree Form'—Listed by Louisiana Nurseries with small tree-like habit and large white flowers, followed by showy blue-black fruits.

Interesting story behind Autumn Jazz® and Northern Burgundy® that speaks to the current problems with introductions: two "superior" (questionable) viburnums growing in Chicago area, decided to release one, nurseries had quantities of both, to keep everybody at bay introduced both, no testing in Zone 6 or 7 to support "greatness," I acquired both and was not impressed, it is a responsibility to introduce *good* plants.

PROPAGATION: Seed, 180 to 510 days at fluctuating temperatures of 68 to 86°F, followed by 15 to 60 days at 41 to 50°F. Softwood cuttings are easy to root, 1000 to 8000 ppm IBA have given good results.

ADDITIONAL NOTES: Indians used the strong shoots which developed from the roots for the shafts of their arrows; hence, the name Arrowwood. There are a great number of closely related species that do not differ significantly at least from a landscape standpoint although there are those who will disagree with this contention. Godfrey (1988) calls *V. dentatum* a polymorphic species complex interpreted various ways by different authors. If the readers can envision this group as a north-south, east-west continuum showing slight differences in leaf characteristics, pubescence, habit and size but possessing similar creamy white flowers and blue to blue-black fruits then they have grasped the essence of a confusing group of species. The species include: *Viburnum bracteatum* Rehd., Bracted Viburnum; *V. molle* Michx. (see below), Kentucky Viburnum; *V. rafinesquianum* Schult., Rafinesque Viburnum; and *V. recognitum* Fern. Their landscape uses are somewhat similar. Except for *V. rafinesquianum*, if the leaves were confused, none of the readers or myself could straighten them out. The buds of *V. rafinesquianum* are reddish, pubescent and similar to *V. dentatum* in shape; stems are covered with tufted pubescence; habit is looser, more spreading 6 to 7′ high.

A form of *V. bracteatum* that grew in the University's Botanical Garden was named 'Emerald Luster' by this author. It will grow 10′ by 10′, has leathery, lustrous dark green, non-scorching leaves in full sun, 5″ diameter, cream-white inflorescences, abundant rich blue-purple-black fruits, and yellow-bronze fall color. I showed it to Don Shadow in early August, 1997 and he commented on the magnificent foliage. A large plant grows in the shade of *Quercus falcata* in our garden and has competed. Buds and stems are similar to *V. dentatum*. 'Emerald Luster' has pubescence on buds and stems. Terrific full sun, heat, drought and wind tolerances. Appears to be a serviceable, utilitarian viburnum for Zone 6 to 8.

NATIVE HABITAT: New Brunswick to Minnesota, south to Georgia, Introduced 1736.

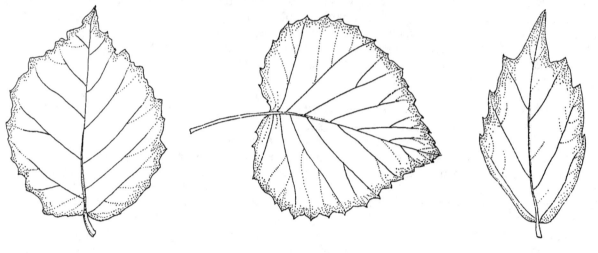

Viburnum bracteatum   *Viburnum recognitum*   *Viburnum rafinesquianum*

RELATED SPECIES:

Viburnum molle Michx. — Kentucky Viburnum
LEAVES: Opposite, simple, suborbicular to broad-ovate, 2 to 5″ long, 1 3/4 to 3 3/4″ wide, short acuminate, deeply cordate, coarsely dentate with 20 to 30 teeth per margin, lustrous dark green and glabrous above, paler and slightly pubescent below; petiole—1/2 to 2″ long.

Viburnum molle, (vī-bĕr′num mol′lē), Kentucky Viburnum, is a loose, open, multi-stemmed shrub reaching 10 to 12′ in height. The bark exfoliates in thin flakes exposing a brownish inner bark. The leaves are dark green in summer. The flowers are whitish, borne in long-stalked, 2 to 3″ diameter cymes in May–June. The fruit is a bluish black, 1/3″ long drupe that is effective in August through September. Much like *V. dentatum* except for the bark, the long-petioled leaves and often a pair of stipules on the petiole. Indiana to Kentucky and Missouri. Introduced 1923. Zone 5 to 7.

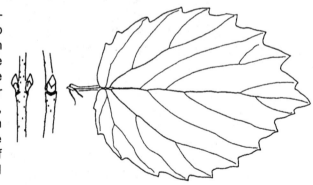

Viburnum dilatatum Thunb. — Linden Viburnum
(vī-bĕr′num dī-là-tā′tum)

LEAVES: Opposite, simple, suborbicular to broad-ovate to obovate, 2 to 5″ long, to about one-half to three-quarter's as wide, abruptly short acuminate, rounded or subcordate at base, coarsely toothed, dark green above, often lustrous, hairy on both sides, with 5 to 8 pairs of veins; petiole—1/4 to 3/4″ long.
BUDS: Imbricate, slightly pubescent, 4 to 6 bud scales, blunt, brownish, often with a tinge of red in the scales.
STEM: Young branches hispid, brown, lenticels—orange (prominent).

SIZE: 8 to 10′ in height, 2/3's to equal that in spread, actually have observed a few plants wider than tall.
HARDINESS: Zone (4)5 to 7, possibly in Zone 8 where some shade is helpful but does not appear well adapted, have seen in Zone 9 but the plants were languishing, seriously injured along with 'Catskill' and 'Erie' at Orono, ME.

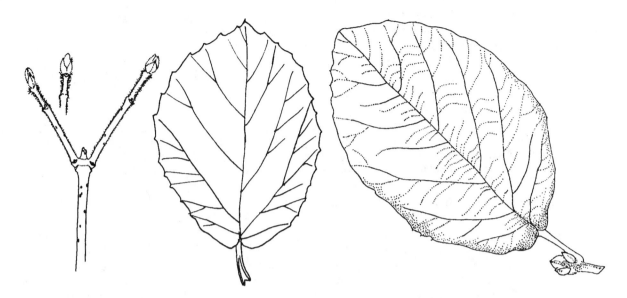

HABIT: Often upright, somewhat leggy and open; also dense and compact in other forms; selection is the key within this species; the newer cultivars are superior to run-of-the-mill seedlings.

RATE: Slow-medium.

TEXTURE: Medium in leaf, medium to coarse in winter.

LEAF COLOR: Dark green, often lustrous, changing to an inconsistent russet-red in fall, may range from bronze to burgundy, leaves hold late.

FLOWERS: White, 1/4″ diameter, May to early June, effective 7 to 10 days, borne in pubescent (pilose), flat-topped, 3 to 5″ diameter, mostly 5-rayed cymes; often profusely produced and literally smothering the plant in a veil of creamy white.

FRUIT: Drupe, 1/3″ long, ovoid, bright red, cherry red or scarlet (excellent color), September to October and often persisting into December (sometimes into spring) when fruits may take on the appearance of withered red raisins; I have seen fruiting cymes heavy enough to bend the branches; plant several clones for best fruiting; superior selections are available that hold their fruit color through winter; Don Shadow, Winchester, TN has a fine, somewhat upright selection ('Asian Beauty') that maintains the glossy rich red fruit color through winter while one of the outstanding U.S. National Arboretum selections, 'Erie', loses its rich red fruit color; I have compared these two forms as they grew side-by-side in the nursery in late January and the differences were quite striking.

CULTURE: Easily transplanted; best in moist, slightly acid, even-moistured soils but will do well in higher pH situations; full sun or partial shade; seems to prefer cooler climates but can be grown in Zone (7)8 if sited properly; ideally in Zone 8 provide moist soil and partial shade.

DISEASES AND INSECTS: None serious.

LANDSCAPE VALUE: Specimen, shrub border, all purpose shrub, ornamentally valuable in three seasons; out-standing for fruits, however, little used compared to the normal garden variety (forsythia, deutzia) shrubs; some of the new selections are outstanding and should be used in preference to seed-grown materials.

CULTIVARS:

'Asian Beauty'—As described under FRUIT, more upright as I saw it in Don's fields, dark green foliage, excellent cherry red fruit production and color retention.

'Catskill'—Is a dwarf *V. dilatatum* seedling selection made in 1958 from plants raised from seed obtained from Japan. 'Catskill' was selected for the compact growth habit; smaller and rounder leaves; and good autumn coloration. The compact, wide spreading growth habit has been constant. The smaller, dull, dark green leaves, which are more nearly rounded than on most *V. d.* plants, assume good yellow, orange, and red fall coloration.

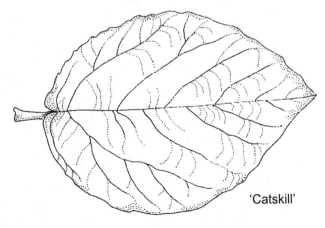

'Catskill'

The creamy white inflorescences are produced in May on new growth. The dark red fruit clusters, which are dispersed over the plant, ripen in mid-August and provide a display until mid-winter. The original plant, at 13 years old, was 5′ high and 8′ wide. This selection did not do well in the Illinois field tests; however, it has performed well in Tennessee, see *Baileya* 14:109–112 (1966). A planting in the University's Botanical Garden is now 6′ high, densely broad-rounded, and has produced red fruits although never as abundantly as its neighbor 'Erie'.

'Erie'—Rounded-mounded shrub, 6′ high and 10′ wide in 14 years, dark green leaves assume good yellow, orange and red fall color, white flowers in 4 to 6″ wide flat-topped cymes, prolific red fruits which after frost become coral and persist as coral to pink; highly resistant to diseases and insects. Excellent performer in Cincinnati and Athens, grows more upright than description above, in Athens now 10′ by 8′, excellent fruit set in Zone 7b if cross pollinator available. 1992 Styer Award recipient. See *HortScience* 10:430–431 (1957).

'Iroquois'—Resulted from a cross of two *V. d.* selections made in 1953. The cultivar was selected for large, thick-textured, dark green leaves; abundant inflorescences of creamy white flowers; large, glossy, dark scarlet fruits; and dense, globose growth habit. The heavy-textured foliage is ornamental in all seasons, glossy green in summer, and orange-red to maroon in autumn. In mid-May the inflorescences transform the plant into a mound of creamy white. The glossy red fruits are larger than those on *V. d.* plants. The flat, wide-spreading fruit clusters contrast well with the dark green leaves. The fruit, which ripens in late August, persists after the leaves have fallen, and often the dried fruits are in abundance in mid-winter if not eaten by birds earlier. The original specimen is 9′ high and 12 1/2′ wide. Excellent form based on my observations; have seen fruit so heavy it weighs the branches down. This is still one of the best forms and when well-fruited is the envy of *all* the fruiting shrubs. See *Baileya* 14:109–112 (1966).

'Michael Dodge'—New introduction with all the fine qualities of the species except the large fruits are yellow, reddish fall color, photographs that I have seen are sufficient force to induce one to purchase, named after the White Flower Farm horticulturist, discovered by the late Hal Bruce at Winterthur Gardens, supposedly matures smaller than most *V. dilatatum* types at 5′ by 6′.

'Mt. Airy'—While surveying the *Viburnum* collection at Mt. Airy Arboretum, Cincinnati, OH, I discovered a stray, misnamed seedling with lustrous leathery dark green foliage and abundant large bright red fruits; interestingly about 30′ away were plants of 'Erie' that were not close in fruit size and abundance; obviously ample opportunities existed for cross pollination so if good fruit were to occur, it should have; the new clone was 6 to 7′ high and wide with pleasing upright rounded outline; cuttings have been rooted and I look forward to this plant's competitive chances in the years to come; appears to be nothing more than a bird planted seedling, has all the characteristics of true *V. dilatatum*; Dudley Nursery, Thomson, GA has grown this for a number of years.

'Oneida'—Resulted from a cross of *V. dilatatum* × *V. lobophyllum* made in 1953. This deciduous shrub was selected for the abundance of flowers in May and sporadic flowers throughout the summer; the glossy, dark red fruit that persists until late winter; and the thin textured foliage that turns pale yellow and orange-red in autumn; and upright growth habit with wide spreading branches. Because of the two or three sporadic flowering periods, abundant fruit is produced that ripens in August and persists on the plant until mid-winter. The original plant has grown to a height of 10′ and a width of 9 1/2′. It has not proven as impressive as 'Erie' and 'Iroquois' but is still a good choice. My more recent field notes are more positive including comments about a 10′ high plant with excellent red fruit on September 27 at Brooklyn Botanic Garden and a Swarthmore plant with fruit as good as any typical *V. dilatatum*. Also, the leaves and stems are more glabrous than typical *V. dilatatum* due to *V. lobophyllum* parent.

'Vernon Morris'—Cream-, white- to pale yellow-colored fruits, large upright shrub, recently named after the Pottstown, PA doctor, introduced in 1993, have yet to see the plant, however, I met the namesake.

'Xanthocarpum'—Form with yellow to almost amber-yellow fruits which are not produced in great abundance and do not make the show of the better red-fruited types; as I have seen the fruits, scarcely yellow in the classical sense, more yellow-orange.

PROPAGATION: Seeds require about 5 months warm/3 months cold but even then germination is not guaranteed; softwood cuttings, 8000 ppm IBA, peat:perlite, mist equals high rooting; I have rooted this species without difficulty; on July 24 collected cuttings of 'Erie' and 'Mt. Airy' in Cincinnati, OH, 10000 ppm KIBA, 2 perlite:1 peat with 100 and 80% rooting, respectively, and 100% overwinter survival.

NATIVE HABITAT: Eastern Asia. Introduced before 1845.

RELATED SPECIES: A number of similar species have been observed by the author. Doubtfully, will any supersede *V. dilatatum* in every day commerce, and it is not as easily obtainable as should be the case. *Viburnum betulifolium* Batal. with abundant red fruits at Trewithen Garden; *V. burejaeticum* Reg. & Herd. with heavy red fruits, eventually black, at the Morton Arboretum; *V. corylifolium* Hook. f. & Thorn.; *V. cotinifolium* D. Don.; *V. erosum* Thunb.; *V. hupehense* Rehd.; *V. ichangense* (Hemsl.) Rehd.; *V. kansuense* Batal.; *V. lobophyllum* Gräbn.; *V. phlebotrichum* Sieb. & Zucc. and possibly others might be considered.

Viburnum wrightii Miq. — Wright Viburnum

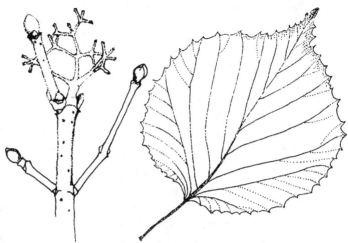

LEAVES: Opposite, simple, ovate or broad-ovate, 3 to 5″ long, 1 to 2 1/2″ wide, abruptly acuminate, rounded or broad-cuneate at base, coarsely dentate, dark green and glabrous above, essentially glabrous beneath, except tufts of hairs in axils of veins, 6 to 10 vein pairs; petiole—1/4 to 3/4″ long.

STEM: Essentially glabrous which permits easy separation from *V. dilatatum*.

Viburnum wrightii, (vī-bĕr′num rīt′ē-ī), Wright Viburnum, is similar to the above but differs in its larger leaves and the relative absence of pubescence on the stem and inflorescence. I have seen true *V. wrightii* enough times to be able to separate it from *V. dilatatum*. The habit is upright-rounded, 6 to 10′ high. The round-ovoid red fruits average about 1/3″ in length and are quite showy. The dark metallic green leaves may turn a good red in fall. Might add that what is sold or labeled as *V. wrightii* is most situations is *V. dilatatum*. Variety *hessei* (Koehne) Rehd. ('Hessei') is a compact form with attractive foliage and sealing-wax red fruits. Apparently many plants were grown from seed collected by C.S. Sargent, Arnold Arboretum, by Hesse Nurseries, Germany. 'Hessei' has occasionally been listed as superior, but one person's 'Hessei' may not be the same as another's. Japan and Korea. Introduced 1909. The species is native to Japan. Introduced 1892. Zone 5 to 7. Possibly, slightly more cold hardy than *V. dilatatum*.

Viburnum farreri Stearn. — Fragrant Viburnum

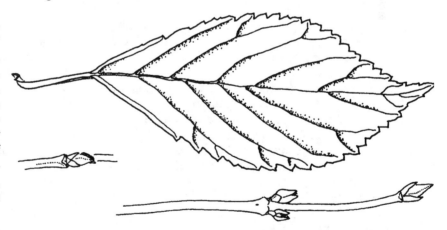

LEAVES: Opposite, simple, obovate or oval, 1 1/2 to 4″ long, 1 to 2 3/4″ wide, acute, broad-cuneate or cuneate, serrate with triangular teeth, sparingly pubescent above and pubescent on veins beneath, finally glabrous or nearly so, with 5 to 6 pairs of veins and the veinlets impressed above and below, dark green; petiole—1/3 to 3/4″ long, purplish.

Viburnum farreri (*V. fragrans*), (vī-bĕr′num făr′er-ī), Fragrant Viburnum, grows 8 to 12′ tall with a similar spread and is often rather loose, unkempt and unruly. The foliage emerges bronzy-green and matures to dark green in summer changing to reddish purple in fall. The fragrant flowers are pinkish red in bud opening to white tinged with pink, early to mid-April before the leaves, borne in a 1 to 2″ long and wide panicle; one of the earliest viburnums to flower. Fruit colors red, finally black and is effective in July to August but I have never seen a good display. 'Candidissimum' ('Album') has pure white flowers and the leaves do not show the reddish pigment of the species and are much lighter green. 'Farrer's Pink' has pink-budded flowers in open inflorescences. 'Nanum' is a dwarf type growing 2 to 3′ tall and 4 to 6′ across with pinkish buds and flowers that fade to pinkish white. The flowers often open in the fall on a rather sporadic basis and push forth full force in spring at the first sign of warm weather. Unfortunately, late frosts wreak havoc on the species and it is seldom that the flowers are not browned to one degree or another. I grew the species in my Illinois garden and enjoyed the foliage more than the flowers which suffered from the vagaries of the midwestern winters. I have had good success rooting the species and 'Candidissimum' from softwood cuttings. *Viburnum × bodnantense* Stearn. 'Dawn' is a hybrid of *V. f.* × *V. grandiflorum* Wallich. (*V. grandiflorum*, as I have witnessed it in Hillier Arboretum in late March 1996, is a large, coarse shrub, 10 to 15', with rich pink, fragrant flowers.) It is pink-flowered and suffers the same fate as *V. farreri* from the vagaries of weather. It was raised at Bodnant Gardens, Wales about 1935. 'Dawn' receives an unbelievable amount of press for the rather undistinguished but fragrant flowers. Even in England, where it flowers in January through March, although English literature states October to April depending on weather, the shrub is valued only for winter wake-up and fragrance value. A small plant in our garden flowered in February, 1989 and is worthwhile for cuts for a winter

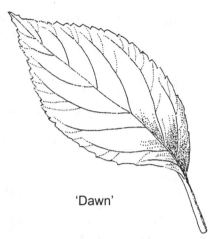

'Dawn'

bouquet. Plants in England were 8 to 10' high so it is by no means "dainty." 'Deben' and 'Charles Lamont' are of the same parentage, the former with shell pink buds opening white with a pink blush; the latter considered better than 'Dawn' with more abundant bright pink flowers that open later. 'Pink Dawn' produces rose-budded, pink, fragrant flowers and rich green, deeply veined leaves. Northern China. Introduced 1910. Zone (4)5 to 8. Has survived and performed reasonably well at the Morton Arboretum, Lisle, IL.

Viburnum japonicum Spreng. — Japanese Viburnum

LEAVES: Opposite, simple, evergreen, leathery, ovate to broad-ovate, 2 to 3″ long, 1 1/2 to 2 1/4″ wide, abruptly acuminate, cuneate to rounded, nearly entire with remote teeth toward apex, leathery lustrous dark green and glabrous above, lighter green and glabrous below with minute black dots, 3 to 5 vein pairs, veins impressed; petiole—1/2 to 3/4″ long, reddish green, channeled above; leaves with no distinct odor when crushed.
BUDS: Terminal—loosely scaled, reddish green, glabrous, 1/2″ long; laterals—with 3 visible scales, appressed, 1/4 to 1/3″ long.
STEM: Stout, angled, green initially, finally gray, with onion skin type of epidermis, remote small rounded orangish brown lenticels; pith—white, solid, ample.

Viburnum japonicum, (vī-bĕr′num jà-pon′i-kum), Japanese Viburnum, is an evergreen shrub that matures between 6 to 8′ in height. It is extremely dense in habit and would make a fine screen. The lustrous dark green foliage is attractive throughout the seasons. The fragrant, white, 3/8″ wide flowers are produced in 2 to 4″ diameter, rounded, short-stalked, 7-rayed cymes. The fruit is a 1/3″ long, oval-rounded, red drupe. Terribly confused with the next two species which are more prevalent in cultivation than true *V. japonicum*. Japan. Introduced 1859. Zone 7 to 9.

RELATED SPECIES:

Viburnum awabuki K. Koch.

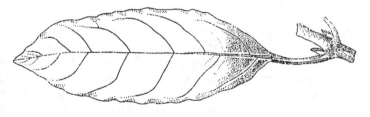

LEAVES: Opposite, simple, evergreen, ovate-lanceolate, 3 to 6 1/2″ long, 1 1/2 to 2 1/4″ wide, obtuse to acute, cuneate, remotely serrate (quite variable), leathery lustrous waxy dark green and glabrous above, dull olive green below and glabrous, 7 to 11 vein pairs; petiole—3/4 to 1″ long, stout, brown and rubbery; leaf with no discernable odor when crushed.
BUDS: Terminal—large, 1/2″ long, grayish brown, glabrous with long-pointed scales; laterals—smaller, otherwise similar.
STEM: Stout, angled, brown, glabrous, dotted with abundant grayish lenticels; pith—white, solid, ample.

Viburnum awabuki K. Koch., (vī-bĕr′num à-wà-bū′kē), a large lustrous dark green leaf form of great beauty was promoted by the late J.C. Raulston. He mentions observing "large pendulous masses (6 to 10″ diameter) of bright red fruits hanging in the 15′ tall plant like ornaments on a Christmas tree." There is a large 15 to 20′ high specimen at the Augusta National Golf Course. I have a gift plant from Dr. Raulston that above 10°F showed no injury. Most field growers have stopped growing the plant because of foliage burn and plant damage due to cold and heavy, wet soils. Much easier to produce in a container. Unfortunately, the nomenclature of this form is confusing, being a Japanese continuum of the widely distributed *V. odoratissimum*. *Hortus III* reduces it to variety *awabuki*. Perhaps the var. *awabuki* should be more properly classified under *V. odoratissimum*. *Viburnum awabuki* is also listed as *V. macrophyllum*, a name with no botanical credibility. It is often confused with *V. odoratissimum* but the young wood is not so warted, the secondary veins run to the margin, and the inflorescence is rounded-cymose rather than paniculate. 'Chindo' was introduced by J.C. Raulston, discovered in a schoolyard on Chindo Island, Korea, noted for producing large, pendulous, red fruit clusters, grows 15 to 20′ high, from my perspective not much different than typical *V. awabuki*, probably requires cross pollination for heavy fruit set, protect from wind, cold, winter sun. 'Variegatum' has white-blotched and marbled markings against the deep green leaves. Japan. Introduced 1879. This is a handsome viburnum and probably best suited to Zone 8 and into 9. In the South, this has been grown and cultivated as *V. japonicum*, *V. macrophyllum*, and *V. odoratissimum*.

Viburnum odoratissimum Ker.-Gawl.

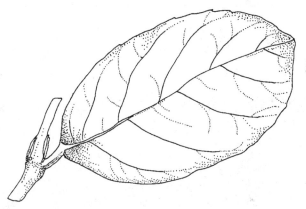

LEAVES: Opposite, simple, evergreen, elliptic-ovate to elliptic-oval, 2 to 4″ long, 1 to 2 1/4″ wide, obtuse, rounded, entire or with remote teeth toward apex, dull olive green and glabrous above, pale gray-green below with 4 to 6 vein pairs, with brownish tufts of hair in the vein axils, veins not as impressed as *V. japonicum*; petiole—1/4″ long, glabrous, brown; leaf when broken extremely fetid, similar to odor of *V. sieboldii* leaves.

BUDS: Laterals—valvate, with two loosely fitting scales, 1/3″ long, brownish green, glabrous.

STEM: Stout, brown, glabrous, dotted with numerous, small grayish lenticels; pith—white, ample.

Viburnum odoratissimum, (vī-bĕr′num ō-do-rà-tis′i-mum), has a dull dark green upper leaf surface, the leaf is wider, and with foul odor when broken. It grows 10 to 20′(30′) high and is relegated to Zone 7b, ideally 8 to 10. 'Red Tip' with young foliage reddish green is being offered by Wight Nurseries, Cairo, GA. Japan. 'Red Tip' and the species are less cold hardy than *V. awabuki*.

RELATED CULTIVARS: An arbitrary system since the following two clones have true *V. japonicum* as a common parent and are most logically included here. Now have both in our evaluation trials and will properly evaluate them. Seldom hear anything mentioned about the two cultivars even among the most ardent viburnum supporters. Reported that both cultivars need to be in close proximity for good fruit set.

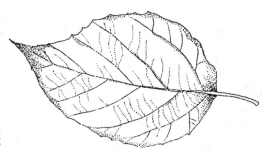

'Chippewa'—A hybrid between *V. japonicum* × *V. dilatatum* with semi-evergreen leaves and a dense branched, multi-stemmed nature; parent plant was 8′ high and 10′ wide after 10 years; leaves are leathery glossy dark green, 2 to 4 1/2″ long, 1 1/2 to 3″ wide, and turn dark maroon to bright red in autumn; the white flowers occur in 4 to 7 1/2″ wide, 5 to 7 rayed cymes containing 200 to 300 flowers per inflorescence; oblong dark red, 3/8″ long, 1/3″ wide fruits ripen in August and persist into winter, no winter damage has occurred at -10°F but foliage is deciduous; have seen young plants and still do not have a good fix on relative landscape worth. Have not been overly impressed.

'Huron' (*V. lobophyllum* Gräbn. × *V. japonicum*)—A semi-evergreen, dense-branched, multi-stemmed shrub that grew 7 1/4′ by 9 1/4′ after 17 years; leaves are leathery dull dark green turning rich purple in late autumn; white flowers occur in 4 to 6″ wide, 6- to 7-rayed cymes containing 250 to 400 florets per inflorescence; ovoid dark red, 1/4 to 1/3″ long, 1/3″ wide fruits ripen in August and persist into winter; hardy to at least −10°F at which temperature it will be deciduous; for additional information on both cultivars see *HortScience* 22:174–176 (1987).

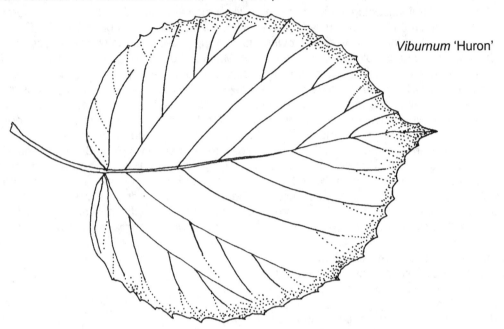

Viburnum 'Huron'

Viburnum lantana L. — Wayfaringtree Viburnum
(vī-bĕr′num lan-tā′nȧ)

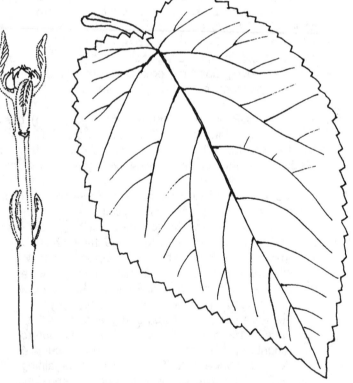

LEAVES: Opposite, simple, ovate to oblong-ovate, 2 to 5″ long, 1 1/2 to 4″ wide, acute or obtuse, cordate to rounded at base, rather closely denticulate, dark green and sparingly stellate-pubescent and wrinkled above, stellate-tomentose beneath; petiole—1/2 to 1 1/2″ long; very uniform serrations and a strong reticulate venation pattern are good identification features.

BUDS: Naked, foliose, grayish tomentose; flower buds similar to *V. carlesii* but larger and coarser.

STEM: Young branches light gray-brown, scurfy pubescent, older branches gray, usually heavily lenticelled, stout, coarse, thick.

SIZE: 10 to 15′ in height (possibly as large as 20′) by 10 to 15′ in spread.

HARDINESS: Zone (3)4 to 7(8), does not appear vigorous in Zone 7, in fact not well-suited in the mid and lower South.

HABIT: Multi-stemmed shrub with stout spreading branches, usually rounded in outline, often leggy.

RATE: Medium.

TEXTURE: Medium in leaf, often quite ragged in winter habit, appearing coarse.

LEAF COLOR: Dull dark green (almost a bluish green), leaves quite pubescent below and somewhat leathery in texture; fall color tends toward purplish red; however, very inconsistent in Midwest and East, often poor.

FLOWERS: White, no fragrance (somewhat stinky?), actually creamy due to numerous yellow stamens, early to mid-May, 10 to 14 days, borne in 3 to 5″ diameter, flat-topped, 7-rayed cymes; flowers profusely in Midwest and one of the better viburnums for that area.

FRUIT: Drupe, 1/3″ long, yellow changing to red and finally black, often all colors present in same infructescence, August to late September, outstanding attribute of this plant; I have noticed that fruit set is best when several different clones are in close proximity.

CULTURE: Fibrous rooted, readily transplanted; withstands calcareous and dry soils better than other viburnums; sun or 1/2 shade; prefers well-drained, loamy situation.

DISEASES AND INSECTS: None serious.

LANDSCAPE VALUE: Used for hedges, screens, massing, shrub border; foliage persists until November in parts of Midwest; winter coarseness should be considered before this species is used extensively; reports of it escaping and seeding in woodlands in northern Illinois and I suspect other midwestern locales.

CULTIVARS:

'Aureum'—The young shoots rather handsome golden yellow, later becoming green; have seen on occasion, not too offensive, reported to hold yellowish coloration when sited under some shade, not as large as the species, to 8′ high.

'Emerald Triumph'—More compact than *V. lantana*, probably 6 to 8′ by 6 to 8′; leathery lustrous dark green foliage; white flowers in 2 to 3″ diameter cymes; green-red-black, 3/8 to 5/8″ long fruit matures earlier than *V. lantana*; red coloration lasts for 3 to 4 weeks; have observed at UMaine, Orono, looks like an excellent viburnum for northern Zones 4 to 6(7); 'Alleghany' × *V. burejaeticum* hybrid, from Dr. Harold Pellett, University of Minnesota Landscape Arboretum, see *J. Environ. Hort.* 12(1):59–60 (1994).

'Mohican'—A seedling selected in 1956 from a population grown from *V. lantana* seed received from Poland. The plant, as a deciduous shrub, was selected for compact growth habit; thick dark green leaves; fruit that turns orange-red and maintains an effective display for 4 or more weeks; and resistance to bacterial leaf spot. The creamy white flowers and expanding pale green leaves appear together for a week in early May. The orange-red fruit begins to ripen in early July and remains effective for 4 or more weeks, whereas fruits on other *V. l.* plants pass rapidly from red to black. The original specimen in 15 years had grown 8 1/2′ high and 9′ wide. An Egolf introduction and has become extremely popular in the nursery trade.

'Rugosum'—Leathery leaf form with larger, darker green leaves which are more handsome than those of the species; tends to become open and rather ragged with age.

'Variegatum'—Has yellow-variegated leaves.

'Versicolor'—Has pale yellow young leaves, finally turning gold.

PROPAGATION: Cuttings, softwood, root easily. This species is often grown from seed.

NATIVE HABITAT: Europe, western Asia, occasionally escaped from cultivation in eastern United States. Long cultivated.

Viburnum lentago L. — Nannyberry Viburnum, Sheepberry
(vī-bĕr′num len-tā′gō)

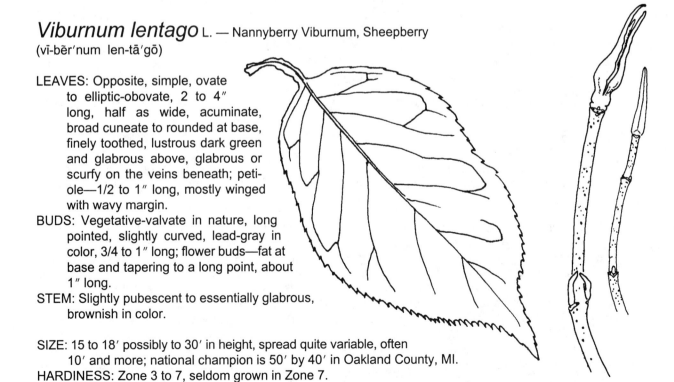

LEAVES: Opposite, simple, ovate to elliptic-obovate, 2 to 4″ long, half as wide, acuminate, broad cuneate to rounded at base, finely toothed, lustrous dark green and glabrous above, glabrous or scurfy on the veins beneath; petiole—1/2 to 1″ long, mostly winged with wavy margin.

BUDS: Vegetative-valvate in nature, long pointed, slightly curved, lead-gray in color, 3/4 to 1″ long; flower buds—fat at base and tapering to a long point, about 1″ long.

STEM: Slightly pubescent to essentially glabrous, brownish in color.

SIZE: 15 to 18′ possibly to 30′ in height, spread quite variable, often 10′ and more; national champion is 50′ by 40′ in Oakland County, MI.

HARDINESS: Zone 3 to 7, seldom grown in Zone 7.

HABIT: Shrub or small tree with slender finally arching branches, somewhat open at maturity, often suckering.

RATE: Medium.

TEXTURE: Medium in leaf, medium-coarse in winter.

LEAF COLOR: Soft yellow-green when unfolding, gradually changing to glossy dark green; fall color develops purplish red but is not guaranteed, often poor green and falls off as such.

BARK: Blackish, patterned scaly to blocky.

FLOWERS: White, appearing creamy due to yellow stamens, early to mid-May, 7 to 10 days, borne in 3 to 4 1/2″ diameter, flat-topped cymes; flower is good but color is typical of many viburnums.

FRUIT: Drupe, oval, 1/2″ long, bluish black, bloomy, September to October and often December; common name is derived from smell of the fruits; the color actually starts out green and in the coarse of maturation may show tinges of yellow, rose and pink before finally becoming bluish black; actually most handsome in the early stages of coloring.

CULTURE: Fibrous rooted, transplants readily, often suckers profusely forming a thicket; adaptable to a wide range of conditions; sun or shade; native species of great durability; moist or dry soils.

DISEASES AND INSECTS: Often covered with mildew especially when grown in shaded area; usually no serious problems are encountered.

LANDSCAPE VALUE: Ideal shrub for naturalizing, works well in shrub borders, as a background or screen plant and limitedly for specimen use; good winter food for the birds; large notable specimen at Biltmore Gardens, almost tree-like, 25′ high, flowers late April-early May.

CULTIVARS:

'Deep Green'—New selection with thick glossy leaves, white flowers and pink-rose to bluish black fruits, large shrub to 20′, from Fairweather Gardens.

'Pink Beauty'—Has pink fruits maturing to violet; I have never seen the cultivar but Krüssmann mentions that it is quite attractive.

PROPAGATION: Seed, 150 to 270 days at 68 to 86°F fluctuating temperatures followed by 60 to 120 days at 41°F. Cuttings, softwood; from personal experience this species roots easily from softwood cuttings.

ADDITIONAL NOTES: A hybrid, *Viburnum × jackii* Rehd., between *V. lentago* and *V. prunifolium* exists. If the identification characteristics do not fit one or the other species, blame it on hybridity.

NATIVE HABITAT: Hudson Bay to Manitoba, south to Georgia and Mississippi. Introduced 1761.

Viburnum obovatum Walt. — Small Viburnum

LEAVES: Opposite, simple, semi-evergreen to deciduous, oblanceolate to spatulate, some rounded-obovate, 3/4 to 2″ long, 1/3 to 1 1/4″ wide, obtuse or rounded, cuneate, entire or finely serrate midway to apex, dark green, often lustrous, glabrous, lower surface brown dotted; sessile or with petiole to 1/5″ long, red.

BUDS: Extremely small, 1/32 to 1/16″ long, rusty brown, pubescent, not unlike those of *V. rufidulum* only smaller and lighter colored.

STEM: Slender, pubescent, gray brown on first year stem; light gray-brown on second, glabrous; pith—solid, white, ample.

Viburnum obovatum, (vī-bēr′num ob-ō-vā′tum), Small Viburnum, is a densely twiggy, upright ascending, large shrub or small tree, the only thing small being the leaves. Habit is rather wild and splaying with a 10-year-old plant now 12′ high and wide. National champion is 23′ by 23′ in Gainesville, FL. The small leaves turn bronze-purple in fall–winter and persist into the New Year during mild winters, 15°F and above. Small, white flowers in 1 3/4 to 2 1/4″ diameter cymes open with the emerging leaves, April in Athens. Flowers are not in any sense spectacular. Fruits are 1/4 to 1/3″ diameter, ellipsoidal to spherical, red to shiny black drupes. Adapted to wet soils in the wild. Seemingly supportive of drier situations under cultivation. Semi-shade to full sun for best growth. Have seen in Tampa, FL landscapes. A more compact form is known. 'St. Paul' has rather pendulous branches, evergreen foliage, although as I learned with this species, the further north it is grown out of the range, the more (completely) deciduous it becomes, introduced by Woodlanders. South Carolina to Florida and Alabama. Zone 6 to 9.

Viburnum opulus L. — European Cranberrybush Viburnum
(vī-bĕr′num op′ū-lus)

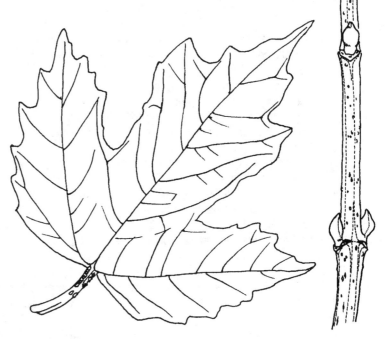

LEAVES: Opposite, simple, similar to *V. trilobum*, with rather shorter, more-toothed lobes, 2 to 4″ long, as wide or wider, lobes pointed, base truncate, dark green and glabrous above, pubescent beneath or sometimes glabrous; petiole—1/2 to 1″ long, with a narrow groove and a few large disk-like glands of a concave nature.

BUDS: Plump, 2-scaled, green-red-brown, 1/3 to 1/2″ long, glabrous, shiny, scales connate (fused at edges).

STEM: Light gray-brown, glabrous, smooth, ribbed, rather stout.

SIZE: 8 to 12′ possibly 15′ in height, spread 10 to 15′.

HARDINESS: Zone 3 to 8.

HABIT: Upright, spreading, multi-stemmed shrub, often with arching branches to the ground creating a rounded habit, thicket forming in its native habitat.

RATE: Medium.

TEXTURE: Medium in foliage; medium to coarse in winter, can look "ratty" in winter.

LEAF COLOR: Good glossy dark green in summer, changing to yellow-red and reddish purple in fall; not a consistent fall coloring shrub, often leaves show no change, simply falling off green.

FLOWERS: White, outer ring of 3/4″ diameter flowers sterile and showy, inner flowers fertile and inconspicuous, anthers yellow, creating a pin-wheel effect, May, borne in 2 to 3″(4″) diameter, flat-topped cymes, flowers are handsome and interesting because of unique combination of sterile and fertile flowers in same inflorescence.

FRUIT: Berry-like drupe, bright red, ripening in September–October and persisting into winter, each fruit is about 1/4 to 1/3″ diameter and globose in shape; the fruits often shrivel through the winter months and take on the appearance of dried red raisins.

CULTURE: Transplant balled-and-burlapped or from containers, one of the easiest viburnums to grow; adaptable to extremes of soil and in its native haunts is particularly rampant in wet or boggy situations; pH adaptable; large canes should be thinned out; fruits best in full sun but will stand partial shade.

DISEASES AND INSECTS: Often infested with aphids (plant lice) but this is more common on the cultivar 'Roseum'; can be easily controlled; borer has been a problem in the Midwest.

LANDSCAPE VALUE: Shrub border, screen, large areas, massing, excellent for its showy flower and fruit display; weed-like in Midwest and East as birds have planted it with abandon; the following cultivars may prove superior to the species.

CULTIVARS:

'Aureum'—New growth a reasonably good yellow but soon fading to rather sickly yellow-green, the color is either lost or the foliage may burn in hot climates, slower growing than the species, rather limited landscape appeal, flowers and fruits like the species, to 12′ high, needs some shade.

'Compactum'—Excellent plant where space is limited, 1/2 the size of the species in height and extremely dense in habit, excellent in flower and fruit, fruit makes a brilliant show; excellent in masses, probably should be considered over the species in the smaller, more restricted planting areas of the modern landscape; have been told that stem borers can be a problem, very fine plant when properly grown.

'Fructuluteo'—Pale yellow fruits turn rich yellow tinted pink.

'Harvest Gold'—Leaves richer yellow than 'Aureum', otherwise similar; 'Park Harvest' is akin to 'Harvest Gold'.

'Leonard's Dwarf'—Have only seen description in Forest Farm's 1997 fall catalog, reads like 'Compactum' and 'Nanum'.

'Nanum'—Dwarf form, much-branched and dense, 18 to 24" in height and 1 1/2 times that in spread; I have seen specimens between 4 and 5' high; supposedly never flowers or fruits but, again, I have seen several isolated flowering and fruiting specimens, makes a good filler or facer plant; can be used for low hedges; will not withstand wet, poorly drained conditions, and in wet weather contracts significant leaf spot; leaves range from 3/4 to 1 1/2" in width, E.W. Coffman reported a branch sport of 'Nanum' that is slower growing and more compact.

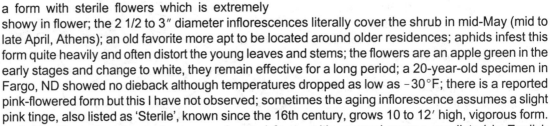

'Nanum'

'Notcutt'—More vigorous than the species with larger flowers, fruits and excellent maroon-red fall color.

'Roseum'—The European Snowball or Guelder-rose, a form with sterile flowers which is extremely showy in flower; the 2 1/2 to 3" diameter inflorescences literally cover the shrub in mid-May (mid to late April, Athens); an old favorite more apt to be located around older residences; aphids infest this form quite heavily and often distort the young leaves and stems; the flowers are an apple green in the early stages and change to white, they remain effective for a long period; a 20-year-old specimen in Fargo, ND showed no dieback although temperatures dropped as low as -30°F; there is a reported pink-flowered form but this I have not observed; sometimes the aging inflorescence assumes a slight pink tinge, also listed as 'Sterile', known since the 16th century, grows 10 to 12' high, vigorous form.

'Variegatum'—Several white- and cream-variegated forms with unusual names are listed in English literature.

'Xanthocarpum'—Form with yellowish gold fruits, quite attractive, and often persistent; a nice color compliment to the red-fruited type; have seen in England on several occasions, worth considering, will grow 8 to 10' high.

PROPAGATION: Seed, 60 to 90 days at fluctuating temperatures of 68 to 86°F followed by 30 to 60 days at 41°F. Russian work reported harvesting seeds in September, clean, wash, and stratify in peat at ~45°F, with germination the following June–July. Cuttings are easy to root. I have had 100% success with softwood and greenwood cuttings.

NATIVE HABITAT: Europe, northern Africa and northern Asia. Cultivated for centuries.

Viburnum plicatum Thunb. var. *tomentosum* (Thunb.) Rehd. — Doublefile Viburnum
(vĭ-bĕr'num plĭ-kā'tum tō-men-tō'sum)

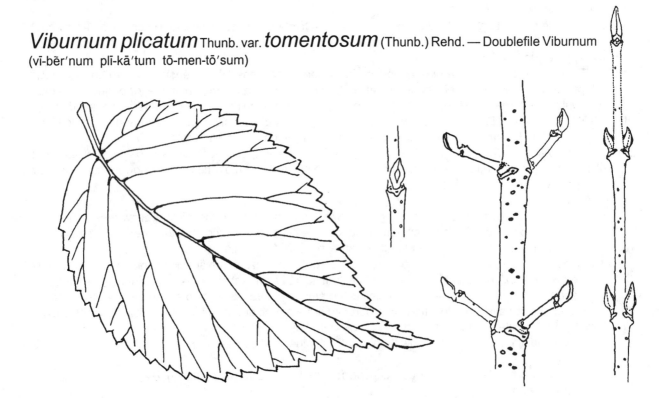

LEAVES: Opposite, simple, broad-ovate to oblong-ovate, sometimes elliptic-obovate, 2 to 4″(5″) long, 1 to 2 1/2″ wide, acute or abruptly acuminate, rounded to broad-cuneate to cordate, dentate-serrate, dark green and nearly glabrous above, stellate-pubescent beneath, with 8 to 12 pairs of nearly straight, impressed veins; petiole—1/2 to 1″ long.

BUDS: Vegetative buds—naked, foliose, pubescent; flower buds—valvate, angular, tan-brown, hairy, appressed to stem or divergent.

STEM: Young branches stellate tomentose; older branches dark gray or brownish, orangish lenticels, many small branches (2 at node) forming a fishbone effect.

SIZE: 8 to 10′ in height, usually slightly wider than tall at maturity (9 to 12′), one old plant at Bicton outside Bristol, England, was 10′ tall and 20′ wide; have seen this plant run the gamut in terms of size.

HARDINESS: Zone 5 to 7(8); Morton Arboretum reported *V. plicatum* and var. *tomentosum* are killed to the ground on a sporadic basis.

HABIT: Horizontal, tiered branching, creating a stratified effect, appearing rounded to broad-rounded at maturity.

RATE: Medium.

TEXTURE: Medium in foliage, medium in winter, can prove respectable in winter because of clean grayish brown branches and horizontal habit.

LEAF COLOR: Leaves emerge early, often by the first or second week of March in Athens, GA; dark green with maturity, veins are impressed creating a ridge-furrow effect; fall color is consistent reddish purple, leaves are borne opposite along the stems and tend to hang down creating a "dog-eared" effect.

FLOWERS: White, no fragrance, outer flowers sterile, 4 to 5 lobes, 3/4 to 1 1/2″ wide, pure snow white; inner flowers fertile, not showy, May (mid-April, Athens), borne in 2 to 4″ (up to 6″) diameter flat-topped cymes which are borne on 2″ long peduncles above the foliage creating a milky way effect along the horizontal branches; a choice specimen of Doublefile Viburnum is without equal; plants were in full flower on April 9, 1993 in Athens.

FRUIT: Drupe, egg-shaped, 1/3″ long, bright red changing to black, (June, Athens) July and August, usually devoured by birds before completely ripened; one of the earliest viburnums to display excellent fruit color.

CULTURE: Fibrous rooted, transplants well, demands moist, well-drained soil; from my own observations this plant will not tolerate heavy, clayey, poorly drained soils; I have grown well-branched, 3 to 4′ high specimens in two growing seasons from cuttings without special care; received several comments about stem dieback which does occasionally occur; old overgrown or ratty specimens on campus are cut back to 12″ from the ground and rejuvenate quite nicely; in Zone 7b the plant is spectacular in April and May but heat and drought of the summer often induce marginal leaf necrosis; some shade, supplemental water, and mulch are recommended in the South.

DISEASES AND INSECTS: None serious, although I have observed stem dieback in wet areas; I am not sure if the problem was of a pathological or physiological nature.

LANDSCAPE VALUE: Possibly the most elegant of flowering shrubs; easily the biggest resided at Swarthmore College, fully 15 to 18′ high and 20′ or more wide; a choice specimen when placed near red brick buildings where the snow white flowers are accentuated; massing, screen, shrub border; blends well into a border as the horizontal lines break up the monotony of upright growing shrubs; could be integrated into foundation plantings especially corner plantings where it would help to soften vertical lines and make the house appear longer; I witnessed tremendous winter kill during the difficult winters of 1976–77, 77–78 throughout the Midwest (-20 to -25°F); large, well-established, 8 to 10′ high plants in the President's Garden on the Illinois campus were killed; I am estimating the break point for injury in the -15°F or lower range; at Orono, ME, Cappiello reported moderate to severe dieback on var. *tomentosum* and 'Shasta'.

CULTIVARS: The species, *V. plicatum*, Japanese Snowball Viburnum, by all botanical standards, should not be considered as such since it possesses sterile, 2 to 3″ diameter, rounded, white flowers and, hence, cannot reproduce itself since fruits are not formed and therefore does not fit the definition of a species. Similar in all respects to Doublefile except for carnation-like, snowball flowers and upright growth habit to 15′ high. The flowers are borne in 2 ranks along the arching branches and make a spectacular show in May for 2 to 2 1/2 weeks. This has proven to be an excellent plant for Zone 7b conditions provided there is ample root moisture. Several plants on the Georgia campus grew 15′ high and wide and were spectacular in flower. Generally, *V. plicatum* flowers 2 to 3 weeks later than *V. p.* var. *tomentosum*.

Viburnum plicatum cultivars:

'Chyverton'—Low, wide-spreading habit, flowers all sterile as in typical *V. plicatum*, a mature plant grew 4′ high and 20′ wide in 24 years; at Stourhead, England, there is also a relatively low-growing, wide-spreading form with abundant flowers; this form might be welcome in American gardens since the principal form in cultivation is upright, large and coarse.

'Grandiflorum'—A fine form with abundant, slightly larger flower heads than *V. plicatum*, leaves wider, more rounded, veins tinted red below, white flowers occasionally tinted pink at petal edges, earlier flowering than most *V. plicatum* types, the plants I have seen showed an accentuated horizontal branching pattern; this form is worth seeking out.

'Kern's Pink'—See under 'Roseace'.

'Leach's Compacta'—A dwarf form that grows 4' by 3', with double, white flowers in snowball inflorescences, foliage is red-burgundy in fall.

'Magic Puff'—Listed but no specifics provided.

'Mary Milton' ('Mary Melton')—Akin to 'Kern's Pink'/'Roseace' with consistent pink, snowball flowers, starting to make the garden rounds but I have not observed a plant in flower, 8 to 10' high, have read descriptions that flowers open white and age to pink, know several gardeners who have purchased this cultivar and all have flowered white.

'Newport' ('Nanum Newport')—Have seen it a number of places in the Midwest; the habit is extremely dense, mounded, with smaller dark green leaves than the species that turn burgundy in fall, 5 to 6' by 5 to 6'; initially I did not think much of flower quality but reasonably mature plants at Spring Grove flowered profusely; flowers are a looser, snowball type and in the 1990 edition it was placed under var. *tomentosum*; flowers are nestled among the foliage and since the plant is so dense, their effect is reduced compared to *V. plicatum*, but still appreciable; Matt Vehr, Spring Grove, showed me plants that were severely killed back (not eliminated) at -25°F in January 1994, plants had grown back to 3 to 4' high by January 1998.

'Pink Dawn'—Described by Kinsey Gardens, Knoxville, TN as a hot pink, early-flowering type, flowers 2 1/2" across, new foliage bronzy purple and holding some of this color as the leaves mature, vigorous upright habit, although listed as *V. plicatum* may be a form of *V. farreri*.

'Roseace'—Selected and introduced around 1953 by Carl Kern of Wyoming Nursery, Cincinnati, OH for its medium-pink flower and bronze tinged foliage; I believe this is the same as 'Kern's Pink' and 'Pink Sensation', as I saw 'Kern's Pink' the color was on/off-pink with some inflorescences pink, others white and still others mixed; Don Shadow has grown this for years and tried to stabilize the chimera, i.e., pink flowers; the plants are beautiful in flower with pink being genetic and not environmentally or culturally regulated; in fact the mix of pink and white inflorescences on the same plant is beautiful; full flower April 25, 1994 at Winchester, TN; reasonable vigor and plants should mature between 6 to 10'.

'Rotundifolium'—A form with round leaves which are 1 to 2" long and 1 to 1 1/2" wide; it is more refined than *V. plicatum*; grows 7 to 8' high, wider at maturity.

'Sawtooth'—Like the species, large, coarsely toothed, dark green leaves, large, snowball flowers.

'Triumph'—More compact form, 3 to 4' high and 3 to 4' wide, white typical snowball flowers, few fruits, Lake County introduction; could this be a rename?; possibly the same as 'Newport'.

Viburnum plicatum var. tomentosum cultivars:

'Cascade'—A seedling of 'Rowallane' with wide-spreading branches, ultimately taller than 'Mariesii'; inflorescences umbrella-shaped, 2 1/2 to 4" across, with large sterile outer flowers; red fruits are produced in abundance; good burgundy fall color; witnessed in flower at Crathes Castle Garden in late June 1995, actually better than the text; a must have for serious Doublefile junkies.

'Dart's Red Robin'—Broad-spreading to 5', dark green leaves, profuse flowers in umbrella-shaped inflorescences, deep red fruits, profusely borne.

'Everblooming'—Listed but I have not observed, suspect may be the same as 'Summer Snowflake'.

'Fireworks'—Six inch, white flowers, 8' by 6', hardy to -23°F.

'Igloo'—Originated as a chance seedling at Winterthur Gardens, Delaware; the plant develops a wide-spreading, mounded habit, 6' by 12'; lacecap flowers occur in 4 to 5" diameter, flat-topped cymes in May and are followed by dark red fruit in July; Ken Day, of the Winterthur nursery, speculates that 'Mariesii' may be the parent.

'Lanarth'—Larger flowered from than typical Doublefile with strong horizontal branching habit; ray flowers up to 2" diameter and larger; is probably confused with 'Mariesii'; as I have observed it a very beautiful selection; 12 to 14' by 12 to 14'; wonderful plant at the Arnold Arboretum that was 8' by 10 to 12', flat-topped, distinctly horizontal in branch architecture; one of the best forms.

'Mariesii'—Ray flowers large, up to 1 3/4" diameter, raised on a 2 1/2" high peduncle that brings the flowers above the foliage; habit is distinctly horizontal and a plant in full flower is a magnificent sight; the leaves may turn reddish purple in fall; this form is available in commerce; introduced in the late 1870's; I have read accounts that state 'Mariesii' is the best fruiting form and also that fruit is sparsely set; I have not resolved this discrepancy in my own mind; like many viburnums lack of fruit set may be due to absence of cross pollinator; leaves perhaps lighter green in summer than other types; many plants offered as 'Mariesii' are, in fact, something else; lower growing than 'Lanarth'; 'Mariesii' bears leaves that have extended apices (long-acuminate) with a slight drooping tendency; have seen many plants labeled as such and they are not the same; also, plants over 10′ high in England are common.

'Nanum Semperflorens' ('Watanabei', 'Watanabe', 'Nanum')—A compact form introduced from Wada's Nursery in Japan; habit dense, flowers smaller than the type but making a good display; may grow 5 to 6′ high, flowers on and off through summer, sparse fruit set; I have been unable to convince myself that this is not the same as 'Summer Snowflake'; supposedly grows very dwarf and some literature states less than 2′ high, I don't buy the latter designation.

'Pink Beauty'—Handsome form with pink petals; specimens I have observed had leaves and flowers slightly smaller than doublefile but the deep pink petal color was outstanding; somewhat upright in habit, generally smaller in all its parts, flower color develops as petals age; this pink coloration is variable for over my traveling years, I observed a plant at Sissinghurst that one season was outstanding pink, later visits I was not sure if it was the same plant; have on occasion discovered heavily red-fruited specimens.

'Popcorn'—Six inch, white flowers, 8′ by 6′, red fruit, hardy to -23°F.

'Roseum'—The sterile flowers open white and gradually fade to an excellent deep pink, smaller leaf, less vigorous than the type; in several respects 'Pink Beauty' and 'Roseum' are similar and may be one and the same; from Brooklyn Botanic Garden.

'Rowallane'—Less vigorous than 'Lanarth' and 'Mariesii' with smaller, broadly ovate, short acuminate leaves; flowers not as wide but the ray-florets are still large and form a uniform circle around the sparse, fertile inner flowers; supposedly fruits heavier than 'Mariesii'; witnessed in flower in late June at Rowallane, best description is haystack-shaped, inflorescences smaller than typical but produced in wondrous quantities, amazing show, plant was 8 to 10′ high, 6 to 8′ wide; selected before 1942 in Rowallane Park, Northern Ireland.

'Shasta'—A tremendous 1979 introduction from the U.S. National Arboretum and Don Egolf's breeding program; it is a broad, horizontally branched shrub being 6′ high and about 10 to 12′ wide at maturity; the abundant, 4 to 6″ wide inflorescences have sterile, marginal, pure white florets about 1 1/4 to 2″ wide and 5 to 15, 1/2 to 1 1/2″ wide, inner florets dispersed among the fertile flowers; the flowers are followed in July by bright red, maturing to black fruits; this is an excellent plant and should become extremely popular as it becomes better advertised; see *HortScience* 14(1):78–79 (1979) for additional information; I nurtured a supposed specimen of 'Shasta' into a 7′ by 8′ specimen only to decide it was just the species or a cheap imitation; my garden heart was broken especially when I saw the real McCoy with wide-spreading, horizontally accentuated branches and immense inflorescences that literally smothered the leaves; in the South what is being passed as 'Shasta' is anything but; also, will become a large plant, easily 10′ or more high and wider at maturity; plants in University's Botanical Garden are over 12′ high.

'Shasta Variegated'—Leaves resemble 'Shasta' in shape and size, yellow-green marbling, some heavily yellow-marbled, branch sport found by George Krauth, Estill Springs, TN.

'Shoshoni'—A seedling of 'Shasta' with all the attributes of that form on a smaller scale; in 17 years the parent plant was 5′ high and 8′ wide; the dark green leaves are 2 1/2 to 6″ long, 1 1/4 to 2 1/2″ wide, and turn dull purplish red in fall; the flowers occur in 3 to 5″ wide flat topped cymes in April–May; the 5 to 7 outer, sterile, showy florets average 3/4 to 1 1/4″ long and 1 to 1 3/4″ wide with 50 to 130 greenish white perfect flowers in the center; the ovoid 1/3″ long, 1/5″ wide drupe ripens red and matures to black; will be hardy to at least -5°F; never really jumped out of the starting blocks, have seen at the National and, indeed, worthy of consideration for the smaller garden; a Don Egolf/National Arboretum introduction, see *HortScience* 21:1077–1078 (1986) for additional information.

'St. Keverne'—Large form like var. *tomentosum*, 10 to 12′ high and wide, inflorescences umbrella-shaped, seldom produces fruit; better than typical species.

'Summer Snowflake' ('Fujisanensis')—Also may be the same as 'Nanum Semperflorens' and 'Watanabei'; the University of British Columbia Botanical Garden has gone overboard renaming plants to suit marketing needs; I am thoroughly confused and have a hunch that all names may lead to the same plant; Tsk! Tsk! to such a fine institution; definitely more compact (4 to 6′ at maturity) than the type with a continuum of flowers from April into November in the South; have seen photographs and must admit it is a handsome plant deserving of garden consideration; supposedly sets good quantities of bright red fruits but has not done so with regularity in the South; widely promoted by J.C. Raulston Arboretum; have now observed 8′ high and greater plants, leaves smaller, more open and upright in habit, flattened to ground after -22°F in Louisville; had in Dirr garden and made the mistake of taking a summer vacation, upon returning 'Summer Snowflake' was a lovely potato chip brown; have read that 'Summer Snowflake' was a sibling of 'Nanum Semperflorens', a tale I do not believe.

'Watanabei'—See 'Nanum Semperflorens'.

PROPAGATION: Cuttings—I have taken cuttings throughout the growing season and achieved 100% success with 1000 ppm IBA, peat:perlite, mist; one of the easiest viburnums to root.

NATIVE HABITAT: China, Japan. Introduced 1865; the sterile form in 1844 by Robert Fortune.

Viburnum prunifolium L. — Blackhaw Viburnum
(vī-bĕr′num prö-ni-fō′li-um)

LEAVES: Opposite, simple, broad-elliptic, ovate, obovate, occasionally rounded, 1 1/2 to 3 1/2″ long, 1 to 2″ wide, acute or obtuse, rounded at base or broad-cuneate, serrulate, dull to lustrous dark green above, pale below, glabrous or nearly so; petiole—not narrowly winged, 1/3 to 3/4″ long, reddish.

BUDS: Vegetative and flower buds short-pointed, valvate, lead-colored, about 1/2″ long, flower buds with a bulbous base.

STEM: Glabrous, usually short and stiff in nature, gray-brown, side branches present a hawthorn-like appearance.

SIZE: 12 to 15′ in height by 8 to 12′ in width, can grow 20 to 30′ high, co-national champions are 24′ by 33′ in Wakefield, VA and 24′ by 28′ in Roanoke City, VA.

HARDINESS: Zone 3 to 9.

HABIT: Round headed tree or multi-stemmed shrub, stiffly branched, similar to *Crataegus* in growth habit; Robinson described this species as a "puritan with a rigidity of character similar to some of the hawthorns"; have seen 20 to 25′ high plants in tree form that were quite handsome.

RATE: Slow to medium.

TEXTURE: Medium in leaf; handsomely coarse in winter.

LEAF COLOR: Dark green, handsome, clean foliage in summer changing to purplish to reddish purple in the fall; various authorities have described the fall color as shining red, dull deep red to bronze; variable from plant to plant.

FLOWERS: White, actually creamy due to numerous yellow stamens, 1/4″ across, May, borne in 2 to 4″ diameter, flat-topped cymes; not overwhelming but certainly attractive.

FRUIT: Drupe, oval, up to 1/2″ long, pinkish, rose and at maturity bluish black, bloomy, September through fall, fruit is palatable and has been used for preserves since colonial days; at Bernheim Arboretum on a magnificent early November day, a wandering group of demented plantsmen, led by Don Shadow, snacked on the fruits of a particularly heavy-fruited specimen; to watch purple-black juices oozing from the mouths of supposedly civilized men, well, it ranked with the greatest experiences of my life, thankfully no photographs were taken and the entire group is in denial.

CULTURE: Transplants well, adaptable to many soil types; sun or shade; does well in dry soils.

DISEASES AND INSECTS: None serious.

LANDSCAPE VALUE: Interesting as a small specimen tree, massing, shrub border, groupings; habit is somewhat similar to hawthorns.

CULTIVARS:
  'Early Red'—New leaves open subdued red in spring, colors burgundy in autumn, Fairweather Gardens offering.

NATIVE HABITAT: Connecticut to Florida, west to Michigan and Texas. Introduced 1727.

RELATED SPECIES:

Viburnum rufidulum Raf. — Rusty Blackhaw Viburnum, Southern Blackhaw

LEAVES: Opposite, simple, oval, ovate to obovate, 2 to 4″ long, 1 to 1 1/2″ wide, sometimes almost as wide as long, obtuse, or short acuminate, broad cuneate to almost rounded, leathery, serrulate, lustrous dark green above, pubescent below initially, finally glabrous; petiole—1/4 to 1/2″ long, more or less winged, with rusty pubescence.

BUDS: Much like *Viburnum prunifolium* in shape and size but covered with short, dense, rusty brown hairs that set this species apart from the closely allied *V. prunifolium* and *V. lentago*.

Viburnum rufidulum, (vī-bēr′num rū-fid′ū-lum), Southern or Rusty Blackhaw, has handsome lustrous dark green leathery foliage, more pubescent plant parts, and is slightly less hardy than the above species. Worthwhile specimen where it can be grown. I have developed a real fondness for this species and found it wild in the Athens, GA environs. Flowers cream-white, early to mid-April (Athens), 1/3″ across, in up to 5″ diameter cymes. Fruit is a 1/2 to 2/3″ long, ellipsoidal, bloomy dark blue drupe. The buds are covered with a deep rich rusty brown pubescence which distinguishes it from any viburnum in this book. The habit can be shrubby or tree-like and larger branches develop a blocky, *Cornus florida*-like bark. The leaves may turn a rich burgundy in fall. Excellent plant and should be used more widely. Will grow 10 to 20′ high under typical landscape conditions but may reach 30 to 40′ in the wild. National champion is 25′ by 30′ in Hampstead City, AR. Occurs as an understory plant in the Piedmont of Georgia and tends toward an open habit in such locations. In full sun, it becomes more dense. An upland species in well-drained woodlands, hedgerows and fencerows. Displays excellent drought tolerance and has withstood -25°F in Midwest without damage. A compact form would be a tremendous garden addition. On the Georgia campus, a group of seedlings were planted in 1993. They are now 6 to 10′ high and each is different. I have propagated the most dense, lustrous dark green leaf form but it is the largest, now about 10′ high. 'Royal Guard' has excellent glossy dark green foliage that turns rich burgundy to deep maroon in autumn, supposedly grows 12′ by 6′ high, have read 10 to 20′, flowers and fruits similar to the species; hardiness is often debated but 15′ high specimens have withstood -20 to -25°F at the Morton Arboretum. Virginia to Florida, west to Illinois and Texas. Introduced 1883. Zone 5 to 9.

Viburnum × *rhytidophylloides* J. Sur. — Lantanaphyllum

Viburnum — A hybrid of *V. lantana* × *V. rhytidophyllum*.
(vī-bēr′num rī-ti-dō-fil-oy′dēz)

Similar to *V. rhytidophyllum* except leaves broader and less rugose, not as elongated and a degree less dark green and leathery. Leaves 4 to 8″ long. Another good trait is the flower bud which is tightly clustered like a cauliflower where *V. rhytidophyllum* is larger and looser. Usually deciduous in North; often semi-evergreen in Zone 7b.

SIZE: 8 to 10′, possibly 15′ in height, spread would probably equal height at maturity; robust shrub often exceeding the first mentioned size range.

HARDINESS: Zone (4)5 to 8 depending on cultivar.

HABIT: Upright, spreading shrub with slightly arching branches; eventually somewhat rounded in outline; large, robust and coarse.

RATE: Medium.

TEXTURE: Medium to coarse in summer and winter.

LEAF COLOR: Dark leathery green above, light gray to gray-brown and extremely tomentose beneath, the foliage has a bold coarseness which is quite attractive, leaves hold late often into November.

FLOWERS: White (creamy), borne in 3 to 4″ diameter, flat-topped cymes; flowers in early to mid-April in Athens; mid-May, Urbana, IL.

FRUIT: Drupe, reddish changing to black, late August through September into fall, can be excellent depending on cultivar and the presence of a pollinator; actually much like *V. lantana* in color transformations.

CULTURE: Transplants well, adaptable; sun or partial shade; best sited in a protected location; much hardier than *V. rhytidophyllum*; has performed well in the heat of Zone 7b; can be located in full sun with good success.

LANDSCAPE VALUE: Possibly should replace *V. lantana* because of excellent foliage; could be utilized for screen, foundation plant, blended with other broadleaf evergreens; I had never seen a good fruiting specimen prior to 1977; since that time I have observed some magnificent specimens with a fruit character not unlike that of *V. lantana*, i.e., yellow-red-black; I have noticed that if *V. lantana*, *V. rhytidophyllum* and other clones of *V.* × *rhytidophylloides* are close, fruit set is significantly better; many viburnums must be cross pollinated for good fruit set to occur; planting several plants of the same clone is not the answer.

CULTIVARS:

'Alleghany'—A selection from an F₂ *V. rhytidophyllum* × *V. lantana* 'Mohican' seedling population in 1958. Plants have very dark green, coriaceous leaves; abundant inflorescences; resistance to bacterial leaf spot; hardiness; and vigorous, dense, globose growth habit. The foliage, which tends to be deciduous to semi-persistent, is intermediate between the parental species. It is smaller than *V. r.*, and is more leathery than *V. l.* The rugose, coriaceous leaves are resistant to leaf spot and are highly ornamental. The abundant, yellowish white inflorescences in May are effectively displayed above the dark green foliage. For several weeks in September and October the fruit becomes brilliant red as ripening advances to black at maturity. In 13 years the original plant attained a height of 10 1/2' and a spread of 11'. This has proven to be an outstanding selection and is being successfully grown as far north as the University of Minnesota Landscape Arboretum although is not perfectly cold hardy. Has been a stalwart in Zone 7b but little known or grown. It is so superior to normal *V. lantana* that I do not understand the reasons for planting that species; a Don Egolf/U.S. National Arboretum introduction.

'Dart's Duke'—Large, leathery dark green foliage, 6 to 8″ diameter, white flowers, 8 to 10' high and wide.

'Holland'—Only presented here for historical purposes; it was apparently one of the first named hybrids between the two species; raised about 1925.

'Willowwood'—A form with excellent lustrous rugose foliage and arching habit. Has performed admirably in the Midwest. Has at times come through the winter with foliage in good condition. I have seen this cultivar flowering in October on the Purdue University campus at West Lafayette, IN. Result of a cross made by Henry Tubbs of Willowwood Farm, Gladstone, NJ. In Georgia, flowers in October–November and again in spring.

PROPAGATION: Cuttings, softwood and greenwood, 1000 ppm IBA solution, rooted 100%; the cultivars are extremely easy to root from cuttings.

ADDITIONAL NOTES: Used by Dr. Harold Pellett as one parent to produce 'Emerald Triumph'. Cappiello reported that 'Alleghany' was more cold hardy than 'Willowwood' in Orono, ME, although the former did suffer stem kill, the latter was killed outright.

Viburnum rhytidophyllum Hemsl. — Leatherleaf Viburnum

(vī-bĕr'num rī-ti-dō-fil'um)

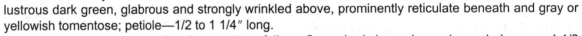

LEAVES: Opposite, simple, evergreen, ovate-oblong to ovate-lanceolate, 3 to 7″ long, 1 to 2 1/2″ wide, acute or obtuse, rounded or subcordate at base, entire or obscurely denticulate, lustrous dark green, glabrous and strongly wrinkled above, prominently reticulate beneath and gray or yellowish tomentose; petiole—1/2 to 1 1/4″ long.

BUDS: Vegetative—large, rusty colored, tomentose, foliose; flower buds borne in semi-rounded cymes, 1 1/2 to 2″ across, evident throughout winter and rather open compared to *V. × rhytidophylloides*.

STEM: Gray to brown in color with stellate pubescence on young stems, older stems glabrous.

SIZE: 10 to 15' in height with a similar spread.

HARDINESS: Zone 5 to 7, although in severe winters will be killed to the ground; usually develops new shoots the following spring as the roots are not injured; –10 to –15°F is about the break point.

HABIT: Upright, strongly multi-stemmed shrub, often somewhat open with age, usually upright-rounded in outline.

RATE: Medium.

TEXTURE: Coarse throughout the year.

LEAF COLOR: Dark lustrous leathery green above, gray to brownish tomentose beneath, essentially evergreen in the North and with proper siting (in a micro-climate) will maintain most of its foliage; evergreen in the South.

FLOWERS: Yellowish white, mid-May (mid-April, Athens), borne in 4 to 8″ diameter, 7- to 11-rayed, flat-topped cymes; the color is not outstanding but the quantity and size of the flowers are ornamental assets; the naked flower buds are formed in July–August–September of the year prior to flowering and are interesting because of large cymes on which they are borne; flowers are slightly fragrant.

FRUIT: Drupe, oval, 1/3″ long, red changing to black, September, October through December; prior to 1973 I had never observed good fruiting on this species; in 1973 I found three specimens on the north side of a house in Urbana, IL, literally weighted down with beautiful red fruits; often viburnums are self-sterile and do not fruit heavily unless different clones are present; perhaps what I stumbled upon are three clones (seedlings) of Leatherleaf.

CULTURE: Transplants well, well-drained soil aids hardiness; shelter from wind and winter sun, tolerates heavy shade (3/4's); -10°F will injure leaves; best where it is offered some protection; prune to ground to rejuvenate; not as content in heat of Zone 7b to 8, needs shade and moisture.

DISEASES AND INSECTS: None serious.

LANDSCAPE VALUE: Excellent specimen where it can be grown without coddling; blends well with other broadleaf evergreens; possibly massing or as a background plant; everything is relative in life and even my great emotional ties to viburnums have influenced me unfairly in appraising the merits of this shrub; in the North it was welcome for the reasons enumerated; in the South the competition is so ferocious from other broadleaf shrubs that it is second class; the 10′ high plant in our garden that my wife, Bonnie, loathed in the 1990 edition is now compost.

CULTIVARS:

'Cree'—More compact, oval-rounded, lustrous dark green leaves, 6″ by 2″, have observed at the U.S. National and was not overwhelmed, a small plant in my evaluation tests is traveling nowhere, better than run-of-the-mill *V. rhytidophyllum* but no reason to rejoice, grew 8 1/2′ by 8′ in 14 years, leaves in winter do not curl or roll as profoundly as the species, possibly more cold hardy, produces abundant white flowers and red, maturing to black fruits.

'Green Trump'—Darker green, more compact form from Holland.

'Roseum'—Has pink flower buds that open yellowish white; have seen this form in England and indeed the buds are an attractive pink, not overwhelming.

'Variegatum'—I had high hopes for this creamy white, irregularly variegated shrub but after seeing it in England a few times, came away disappointed; the plant reverts and it is often difficult to locate the variegated leaves; for the collector who has time to prune away the green shoots.

PROPAGATION: Cuttings, I have taken firm cuttings throughout the growing season and achieved 100% success; use 1000 to 3000 ppm IBA to improve rooting.

NATIVE HABITAT: Central and western China. Introduced 1900.

RELATED SPECIES:

Viburnum × ***pragense*** Vik., (vī-bĕr′ num prag-en′sē), Prague Viburnum, is the result of a cross between *V. rhytidophyllum* and *V. utile*. It is an attractive evergreen shrub with lustrous dark green, 2 to 4″ long, elliptic leaves. The flowers are pink in bud, opening creamy white, slightly fragrant and produced in terminal 3 to 6″ wide, essentially flat-topped 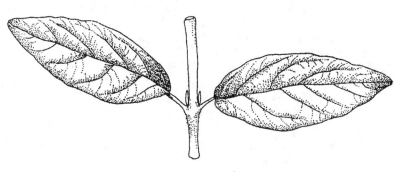 cymes in mid-April in Athens. This hybrid was raised in Prague in the 1950's and is extremely hardy. There was a plant in the woody plant test plots at the University of Illinois which held up well under the rigors of midwestern winters. It survived -6°F in the Arnold Arboretum without foliage discoloration. I observed severe leaf burn (no stem or bud damage) at Spring Grove after exposure to -17°F. It will grow 10′ or more and is suited to culture in Zone 5 to 8. It is easily propagated from softwood cuttings. The species has received considerable attention in the mid to lower South and is now grown by several major nurseries. The habit is upright oval to oval-rounded. The growth extensions are so vigorous that they must be pruned to achieve reasonable density. Extremely fast growing and makes a good screen, grouping or accent plant. Has much more ornamental charm than *V. rhytidophyllum* and based on my observations is hardier than either parent. In fact, in the Arnold Arboretum's viburnum collection, *V.* × *pragense* was 8 to 10′ high, *V. rhytidophyllum* a die-back shrub, and *V. utile* did not exist. 'Decker' was selected by Decker Nursery, Ohio for lustrous dark green leaves, pink-budded flowers that open white, supposed quite hardy; looks like typical *V.* × *pragense* to me.

Viburnum sargentii Koehne — Sargent Viburnum
(vī-bĕr′num sär-gen′tē-ī)

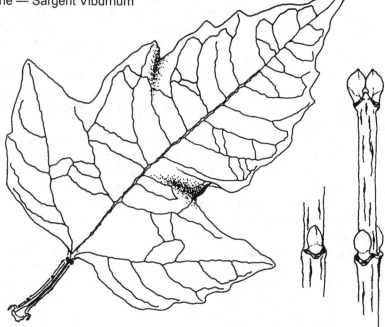

LEAVES: Opposite, simple, similar to
V. opulus but of thicker texture
and often larger, 2 to 5″ long,
the upper ones usually with
much elongated entire middle
lobe and short spreading lateral
lobes, sometimes oblong-lanceolate and without lobes, medium to dark green and glabrous above, lighter beneath
and slightly pubescent below;
petiole—3/4 to 1 3/4″ long with
large disk-like glands, pinkish or
reddish in color.

BUDS: Oblong or flask-shaped, 1/3″
long, mostly appressed, scurfy,
scales closely valvate or connate as a closed sac, green to
red in color.

STEM: Straw-colored to brownish, often of polished appearance, thickish for a viburnum stem, about
1/3″ diameter, glabrous, somewhat corky compared to *V. opulus* and *V. trilobum*.

SIZE: 12 to 15′ high and 12 to 15′ in width.

HARDINESS: Zone 3b to 7.

HABIT: Multi-stemmed upright-rounded to rounded shrub of relatively coarse texture; somewhat similar to *V. opulus* but not as handsome.

RATE: Medium, I noticed a specimen at Purdue's Horticultural Park which exhibited extreme vigor.

TEXTURE: Would have to be rated coarse in all seasons.

LEAF COLOR: New spring growth often bronze-purple; medium to dark green in summer; often assuming
yellowish to reddish tones in fall.

FLOWERS: White, borne in flat-topped, 3 to 4″ diameter cymes on 1 to 2″ long stalks; sterile outer flowers about
1″ or slightly greater in diameter; the anthers are purple and differ from the yellow anthers of *V. opulus*, May.

FRUIT: Scarlet, 1/3 to 1/2″ long, globose, berry-like drupe; effective in August through October.

CULTURE: Similar to other viburnums especially *V. opulus*; definitely not heat tolerant and is best suited to
colder climates.

DISEASES AND INSECTS: None particularly serious.

LANDSCAPE VALUE: More vigorous than *V. opulus* and more resistant to aphids; interesting species but a
degree too coarse in comparison to other viburnums with similar ornamental characters; the fruits are
excellent and of a bright, translucent red, lasting well into winter.

CULTIVARS:

var. *calvescens* Rehd.—Occasionally listed in commerce, 6 to 10′ high, 2 to 4″ diameter inflorescences,
long persisting red fruit, performed well in University of Wisconsin Arboretum.

'Flavum'—A type with yellow anthers and golden yellow translucent fruits; Wyman has an interesting
anecdote concerning a trial he conducted growing seedlings from the yellow-fruited form, he noted
that many seedlings showed yellowish leaf petioles and others reddish; the seedlings with yellowish
petioles fall colored yellowish green; those with reddish petioles fall colored red. Obviously the fruit
will also follow the same trends exhibited in petiole color.

'Onondaga'—A U.S. National introduction distinguished by the velvety, fine-textured, dark maroon young
foliage that maintains a maroon tinge when mature; flowers in 2 to 5″ diameter flat topped cymes,
buds red, opening creamy white with a trace of pink, with 10 to 17 outer, 1 1/4 to 1 3/4″ wide, sterile
florets; the red fruits are sparsely produced; forms a globose shrub 6′ high and wide; will grow larger
than original size description; have seen 8 to 10′ high specimens; introduced 1966.

'Susquehanna'—A U.S. National introduction best described as a select *V. sargentii* with a heavy-
branched, corky trunk; coriaceous, dark green foliage; abundant flowers and fruits; and upright
growth habit; appeared as a seedling in population of 209 raised from seed obtained from Province
Matsu, Hondo, Japan; it is a large shrub (12 to 15′ high) approximating the species in size; I have

seen it in fruit and the effect is striking; probably too large for the average landscape but good for parks, campuses and large areas.

PROPAGATION: Easily propagated by cuttings. Seed probably possesses a double dormancy similar to *V. opulus* and a warm stratification of 60 to 90 days followed by cold for 30 to 60 days should suffice.

ADDITIONAL NOTES: Interesting paper in *J. Japanese Bot.* 69(1):31–32 (1994), that proposes *V. sargentii* as the Asiatic variety of *V. opulus*, i.e., *V. opulus* var. *sargentii*; variety *opulus* is the typical form that occurs in the west of the distribution.

NATIVE HABITAT: Northeastern Asia. Introduced 1892.

Viburnum setigerum Hance. — Tea Viburnum
(vī-bĕr′num se-tij′ĕr-um)

LEAVES: Opposite, simple, ovate-lanceolate, 3 to 6″ long, 1 1/4 to 2 1/2″ wide, acuminate, rounded at base, remotely denticulate, flat, soft blue-green to dark green above, glabrous except silky hairs on the veins beneath with 6 to 9 pairs of veins; petiole—1/2 to 1″ long, glabrous or hairy like midrib.

BUDS: Imbricate, terminal—green with red; lateral—green with red tip, large and glabrous, very prominent, usually with 3 to 5 visible scales.

STEM: Glabrous, smooth, gray and usually stout.

SIZE: 8 to 12′ tall, 2/3's that in width.

HARDINESS: Zone 5 to 7b(8), have seen plants in Zone 8, essentially flattened at Orono, ME.

HABIT: Upright, multi-stemmed, often leggy at the base, but if used properly the leggy character is minimized, delicate foliage with slight nodding tendency.

RATE: Slow, possibly medium.

TEXTURE: Medium-coarse in foliage; coarse in winter.

LEAF COLOR: Flat, soft blue-green foliage in summer; fall color is inconsistent but can develop reddish purple.

FLOWERS: White, mid to late May, borne in 1 to 2″ diameter, 5-rayed, flat-topped cymes on 1/2 to 1″ long peduncles; limitedly ornamental.

FRUIT: Drupe, egg-shaped, 1/3 to 1/2″ long, bright red, September–October into late fall, very effective, possibly the most handsome fruiter among the viburnums, always one of my favorites for fruit effect.

CULTURE: Similar to other viburnums.

DISEASES AND INSECTS: None serious.

LANDSCAPE VALUE: Shrub border situations because of leggy habit, fruit is outstanding; derives its name from the fact that the leaves were used for making tea.

CULTIVARS:

‘Aurantiacum’—Orange-fruited form, handsome in fruit but like the species, often leggy.

PROPAGATION: I have rooted this species from leafy cuttings collected as late as September.

ADDITIONAL NOTES: I have seen branches so heavily laden with fruit that they literally arched and almost touched the ground. Unfortunately, this is not a very popular viburnum but when used correctly it can hold its own against any, especially in fall.

NATIVE HABITAT: Central and western China. Introduced 1901.

Viburnum sieboldii Miq. — Siebold Viburnum
(vī-bĕr′num sē-bōl′dē-ī)

LEAVES: Opposite, simple, elliptic or obovate to oblong, 2 to 5″(6″) long, 1 1/2 to 3″ wide, acute, broadcuneate, coarsely crenate-serrate, lustrous dark green and glabrous above, stellate pubescent chiefly on the veins beneath, with 7 to 10 pairs of prominent impressed veins; petiole—1/4 to 3/4″ long; leaves when crushed emitting a fetid odor.

BUDS: Flower large, valvate, angled, 4-sided, gray-green-brown, slightly pubescent.

STEM: Slightly pubescent, stout, leaf scars connecting around the stem, usually grayish in color.

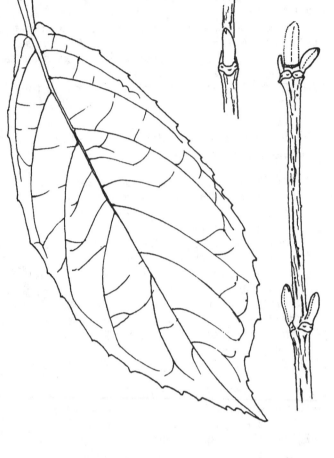

SIZE: 15 to 20′ in height, spread 10 to 15′, can reach 30′ in height.

HARDINESS: Zone 4 to 7(8); growing successfully at Minnesota Landscape Arboretum, also at Orono, ME.

HABIT: Large shrub or small tree of open habit with stiff, stout, rigid branches.

RATE: Medium, possibly fast under ideal growing conditions.

TEXTURE: A rugged, handsome coarseness in summer and winter.

LEAF COLOR: Lustrous dark green, extremely clean looking foliage, very fetid (green peppers) if crushed, fall color is usually nonexistent (green); however, various authors indicated red-purple a possibility and I saw one specimen at the University of Maine with an ashy purple color; tends to hold leaves late often into November.

FLOWERS: Creamy white, late May, borne in 3 to 6″ diameter, flat-topped, long-stalked, cymose-paniculate clusters; excellent effect because flowers are borne in great abundance literally masking the bright green foliage.

FRUIT: Drupe, oval, 1/3 to 1/2″ long, rose-red to red changing to black, effective for two weeks in August through early October, birds seem to devour the fruits; however, the inflorescences are handsome rose-red and remain effective for two to four weeks after the fruits are gone; the fruit must be seen to be fully appreciated and the result is usually love at first sight.

CULTURE: Transplants well, adaptable, prefers moist, well-drained soils; tolerates partially shaded situations; definitely needs sufficient moisture as leaf scorch will develop under dry soil conditions; pH adaptable.

DISEASES AND INSECTS: None serious.

LANDSCAPE VALUE: Specimen, against large buildings, blank walls, groupings; open habit, excellent foliage, flowers and fruits make it worthy of consideration for many landscape situations.

CULTIVARS:

'Roy's'—From Klehm Nursery, no additional information available.

'Seneca'—Resulted from a self-pollination of *V. sieboldii*. The plant was selected for the abundant, large, pendulant inflorescences of firm red fruit on red pedicels which persist on the plant up to 3 months before turning black and falling. The massive, creamy white panicles are produced in May to early June as the young foliage unfolds. The panicles are supported on stout, spreading branches that are picturesque at all seasons. The pendulant, multi-colored clusters of orange-red ripening to blood red fruits are spectacularly displayed above the coriaceous, green foliage. Birds normally eat the fruit of *V. s.* before it has matured, leaving only the red pedicels which provide an ornamental display. However, the fruit of 'Seneca' is very firm and is not devoured by birds even when the fruit becomes fully ripe. Although 'Seneca' is tree-like and has attained a height of 14′ and a width of 13 1/2′, the plant can be trained with several branches from the base and kept as a large spreading shrub. This cultivar will undoubtedly equal in size plants of the species and be as much as 30′ with a gnarled trunk.

'Wavecrest'—Brick to barn red fall color, large leaves and flowers, vigorous grower, from E.W. Coffman, Iowa.

PROPAGATION: Cuttings, softwood—root easily.

NATIVE HABITAT: Japan. Cultivated 1880.

Viburnum suspensum Lindl. — Sandankwa Viburnum

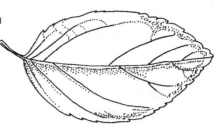

LEAVES: Opposite, simple, evergreen, ovate to oval, 2 to 5″ long, 1 1/2 to 3″ wide, pointed, rounded or broadly wedge-shaped, toothed in the upper two-third's or scarcely at all, leathery lustrous green, glabrous, 4 to 5 vein pairs; petiole—1/4 to 1/2″ long.

Viburnum suspensum, (vī-bĕr′num sus-pen′sum), Sandankwa Viburnum, is a 6 to 12′ high evergreen shrub that is used in the Coastal Plain and frequently seen in Florida gardens. The white, faintly tinged pink, fragrant flowers occur in a 2 1/2 to 4″ long and wide, corymbose panicle. The globose fruits are red maturing to black. I have seen it used for hedges in Florida. It appears to prefer a hot dry climate and also seems well-suited to sandy soils. I see the species everywhere in Florida all the way to Key West where it is used for screens, specimens and the ubiquitous hedge. Interestingly, sizeable plants were killed to the ground or outright on the Georgia coast at 11°F. Ryukyus. Introduced 1850. Zone (8)9 to 11.

Viburnum tinus L. — Laurustinus

LEAVES: Opposite, simple, evergreen, narrowly ovate to oblong, 1 1/2 to 4″ long, 3/4 to 1 1/2″ wide, entire, lustrous dark green above, paler beneath, axillary tufts below; petiole—1/3 to 3/4″ long, usually pubescent.

Viburnum tinus, (vī-bĕr′num tī′nus), Laurustinus, is a fine upright-rounded evergreen species that reaches 6 to 12′ in height and usually less in spread. The lustrous dark green leaves are handsome throughout the year. The pink-budded, 2 to 4″ diameter flowers open to white and often flower in January–February in the South. Species is reported to be self incompatible so another seedling or clone must be in proximity to induce good fruit set. The flowers are followed by ovoid, metallic blue fruits that mature blue-black to black. It is an excellent plant for screening, hedging and withstands considerable shade as well as salt spray. It is hardy to 0°F once established and appears to be insect and disease-free. 'Bewley's

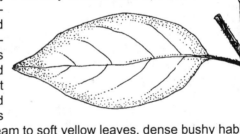

Variegated' has significantly variegated pale cream to soft yellow leaves, dense bushy habit, 6 to 7′ by 6 to 7′, a small plant in our shop has been impressive, flower buds pink, white when open. 'Clyne Castle' has large, glossy leaves and improved hardiness. 'Compactum' will grow one-half to three quarter's the size of the species and has slightly smaller leaves than the species. 'Eve Price' is a compact form with smaller leaves than the species and attractive buds and pink-tinged flowers. 'French White' is a strong-growing form with large, white flower heads. 'Froebelii' is compact with light green leaves and snow white flowers. 'Gwenllian' grows 10′ by 10′, leaves dull green, flowers rich pink in bud, opening blush. 'Isreal' has large leaves and waxy, clear white flowers. 'Lucidum' is larger in all its parts. 'Pink Prelude' produces white flowers that age pink. 'Purpureum' has purple young leaves that mature green tinted red. 'Spectrum' ('Pyramidale') is erect, narrow-conical in habit. 'Spring Bouquet' may be the same as 'Compactum' and offers dark red flower buds that open to white on a 5 to 6′ high and wide compact plant. 'Robustum' is larger in habit (15′) and leaf (4″), has deep green leaves, upright dense habit, blush white flowers. 'Variegata' is a handsome clone with conspicuous creamy yellow variegations. This is a variable species in degree of pubescence, leaf size, etc. It is not common in the South but does make a handsome evergreen shrub. It can be used for screening, hedging, and massing. I noticed the plant was frequently used in England. Since the 1990 edition, I have observed numerous plants, especially in English gardens. It is a serviceable evergreen shrub for Mediterranean climates or where winter temperatures seldom drop below 10°F. Over my 10 years in Athens, GA, I have watched a 7′ high specimen disappear to its root tips. The University grounds department tried several plants of 'Spring Bouquet' in a protected area only to have them succumb to the vagaries of a southern winter. I do not believe the plant hardens off early enough in fall to avoid the early fall freezes. In Washington, GA, 40 miles southeast of Athens, I discovered two 8 to 10′ specimens that survived the mid-1980's and 1994 cold. Perhaps 5°F difference between Athens and Washington. Southern Europe, primarily in the Mediterranean region, northern Africa. Cultivated since 16th century in England. Zone (8)9 to 10.

Viburnum trilobum Marsh. — American Cranberrybush Viburnum
(vī-bĕr′num trī-lō′bum)

LEAVES: Opposite, simple, 3-lobed, broad-ovate, 2 to 5″ long, lobes acuminate, rounded or truncate at base, coarsely dentate, sometimes the middle lobe elongated and entire, dark green and usually lustrous above, pilose on the veins beneath, or nearly glabrous; petiole—1/2 to 1″ long with shallow groove and small dome-shaped, usually stalked glands.

BUDS: Similar to *V. opulus*, sometimes sticky, green-reddish and smooth, with 2 connate outer scales.

STEM: Gray-brown, glabrous, with a waxy appearance.

SIZE: 8 to 12′ in height, spread 8 to 12′.

HARDINESS: Zone 2 to 7, can grown in 8 but not well-adapted to the heat.

HABIT: Similar to *V. opulus*, round-topped and fairly dense.

RATE: Medium.

TEXTURE: Medium in foliage; medium to coarse in winter.

LEAF COLOR: Lustrous medium to dark green changing to yellow through red-purple in fall; new growth has a reddish tinge.

FLOWERS: White, similar to *V. opulus*, mid to late May, 3 to 4 1/2″ diameter, flat-topped cymes; extremely handsome, possibly better than *V. opulus* but the plant is not as available through nurseries.

FRUIT: Drupe, nearly globose, 1/3″ long, bright red, early September through fall into February, holds better than *V. opulus*, edible, used for preserves and jellies.

CULTURE: Native species, transplants well; prefers good, well-drained, moist soil; sun or partial shade; should be more adaptable than *V. opulus* due to wide native range, however, limitedly planted; in Maine I see it growing along the roadsides in moist ditch banks.

DISEASES AND INSECTS: A stem blight can kill plant in warm humid states.

LANDSCAPE VALUE: Excellent plant for screening and informal hedging; like *V. opulus* it becomes too large for the small landscape; I have seen it used to define boundaries between houses in subdivisions and it really affords a good privacy screen and at the same time offers excellent flower, fruit and foliage; if subjected to excessive water stress it declines rapidly and makes a rather poor specimen.

CULTIVARS:

'Andrews', 'Hahs', 'Wentworth'—Have been selected for larger fruits; the story goes deeper than that for in early 1900's a Mr. Hahs and Mr. Andrews (there may have been others) selected the above three plants from over 3000 seedlings, cuttings and divisions in 1922; apparently the initial collections took place near the White Mountains of New Hampshire; they are early, mid, and late ripening, respectively, and were selected for edibility; I have observed 'Wentworth' and it is beautiful as the fruit passes from a yellow-red to bright red but, in my mind, is no better than other plants I have seen in various locations, may have best red fall color; 'Hahs' has large fruits and is popular in the Chicago region; 'Hahs' matures at a smaller size, 6 to 8′ by 6 to 8′, than the species; 'Wentworth', of the three, is the most available in commerce, grows 10 to 12′ by 10 to 12′.

'Compactum'—Excellent compact, dwarf form with good flowering and fruiting habit; the stems are much more slender and uniformly upright-spreading than its counterpart, *V. opulus* 'Compactum'; grows about one-half the size of the species (6′); fall color is not particularly good and is usually yellow at best. The entire taxonomy of this group is rather confusing and I am not sure I can "unconfuse" it. In my Illinois garden, 'Compactum' grew with passion and flowered and fruited without any significant fall color. Along comes . . . I think . . . several new forms, the one called 'Alfredo' which is similar to 'Compactum' but with a denser, broader habit, 5 to 6′ by 5 to 6′, good summer foliage and excellent red fall color. Supposedly quite aphid resistant. Selected by Alfredo Garcia, Bailey Nursery. Flower and fruit set are sparse. Unfortunately, I have read literature that said fruit set was good. Another form is 'Bailey Compact' (Bailey Nursery, St. Paul, MN) with compact habit, 5 to 6′ by 5 to 6′, deep red fall foliage, and moderate fruit.

Also, there is some confusion about true 'Compactum' which is alternately listed as virtually sterile and heavy flowering and fruiting. I have a suspicion that lack of fruit set on 'Compactum' may be the result of the lack of a suitable cross pollinator.

'Leonard's Dwarf'—Have seen this clone placed under *V. opulus*, vigorous, broom-like branches, compact, how different from other compact forms, I do not know.

'Red Wing'—Reddish new leaves and leaf petioles that remain so throughout growing season, excellent flowering and fruiting, 6 to 8' high, from McKay Nursery.

'Spring Green Compact'—More refined than the species in flower, foliage and fruit, excellent red fruit and orange-red fall color, 3 to 4' high.

'Spring Red Compact'—New reddish growth turns green at maturity, good orange-red fall color, limited fruit set, somewhat upright in growth habit, 3 to 5' high.

PROPAGATION: Seeds require the normal warm/cold routine but cuttings are easy to root; softwood cuttings in late July, 1000 ppm IBA-quick dip, peat:perlite, mist, rooted 100% in 6 weeks.

ADDITIONAL NOTES: I have refrained from giving recipes primarily because I like Snicker's bars better than ornamental plant concoctions. I relent here and present what sounds like a recipe for a fine jam. Simmer cleaned fruit for 10 minutes in 1/3 its weight of water; put through a sieve, use a little more water to remove pulp from seeds; add sugar to equal weight of cleaned fruit; boil to 222°F; pour into jars and immediately seal; yields beautiful ruby jam with distinctive flavor. Actually part of native fruit improvement program in Saskatchewan, see *HortScience* 27(8):866, 947 (1992).

NATIVE HABITAT: New Brunswick to British Columbia, south to New York, Michigan, South Dakota and Oregon. Introduced 1812.

Vinca minor L. — Common Periwinkle
(ving'kȧ mī'nôr)

FAMILY: Apocynaceae

LEAVES: Opposite, simple, evergreen, elliptic, oblong or elliptic-ovate, 1/2 to 1 1/2" long, 1/2 to 3/4" wide, acutish or obtuse, rounded or cuneate, entire, lustrous medium to perhaps dark green above, lighter green beneath; petiole—short, 1/2 to 1 1/4" long, exuding a milky juice when broken.

STEM: Shining green, glabrous.

SIZE: 3 to 6"(8") high, ground-hugging plant.

HARDINESS: Zone 4 to 8(9), can be grown further north when protected by snow.

HABIT: Low growing, prostrate, mat-forming evergreen ground cover, spreading indefinitely, flowers borne on erect shoots.

RATE: Medium to fast; in a loose, organic, well-drained soil will fill in very fast.

TEXTURE: Medium-fine in all seasons.

LEAF COLOR: New growth emerges early, often March in Athens and is a handsome yellow-green maturing to lustrous green in summer, often losing some of the sheen in winter.

FLOWERS: Perfect, lilac-blue, blue-violet, 1" diameter, March–April, borne solitary on 1/2 to 1 1/4" long pedicels; very attractive in flower and sporadically flowering over a long period, monitored flowering for the entire month of March, 1994.

FRUIT: Follicle, not ornamental, seldom set on cultivated plants.

CULTURE: Transplant from pots or as a bare root plant into moist, well-drained soil abundantly supplemented with organic matter; supposedly does equally well in full sun or shade, but I have seen considerable leaf discoloration (yellowing and browning) in winter and summer under full sun conditions; can tolerate poor soils but will not develop and fill in as fast.

DISEASES AND INSECTS: Blight, canker and dieback, *Colletrichum gloeosporioides* causes leaf spots and stem lesions [see *Plant Disease* 79(1):83 (1995)], leaf spots, cucumber mosaic virus, and root rot; the canker and dieback (*Phomopsis livella*) disease has been a significant problem; the shoots become dark brown, wilt, and die back to the surface of the soil; also, *Verticillium albo-atrum* was reported on *Vinca major* in California [see *Plant Disease* 72(12):1077 (1988)]; *HortScience* 30(3):554–557 (1995) discusses fungicidal control of foliar diseases caused by *Colletotrichum* sp. and *Phoma* sp.

LANDSCAPE VALUE: Excellent ground cover in spite of problems; the dainty blue flowers are handsome as is the lustrous foliage; plant on 1' centers; makes its best growth in shade and here can form large carpets under the leafy canopy; the new growth emerges a rich spring green and the flowers appear at the same time; flowers over a long period; never really spectacular unless viewed close up, too often large seas of the plant are used in dense shade; I have seen mixed plantings with daffodils and other bulbs that bring the carpet to life in spring; I suspect that *Colchicum* species would do nicely and perhaps even *Lycoris radiata* in more southerly locations.

CULTIVARS:

‘Alba’—White-flowering form representing a nice change from the lilac-blue of the species; ‘Alba Plena’ (‘Albo Plena’ is listed) with double, white flowers is known.

‘Alba Variegata’—White flowers and leaves edged with light yellow, old cultivar.

‘Argenteovariegata’—Blue flowers and leaves margined with white; leaves shorter and broader than typical species.

‘Atropurpurea’—Deep plum-purple flowers, rather handsome form, flowers are large and have good substance, first recorded in 1826.

‘Aureovariegata’—Blue flowers and leaves with yellow blotches and stripes.

‘Azurea Flore Pleno’—Sky-blue double flowers.

‘Blue & Gold’—Bright yellow-margined leaves, blue flowers.

‘Bowles White’—Flowers flushed pink in bud, white when open, large.

‘Bowlesii’—See ‘La Grave’.

‘Burgundy’—With burgundy flowers, saw at Van Dusen Botanical Garden, Vancouver.

‘Dart’s Blue’—Sport of Bowles with blue flowers, canker resistant.

‘Emily’—Large, white flowers.

‘Florepleno’—Double, purple-blue flowers.

‘Gertrude Jekyll’—A form with glistening white flowers, quite attractive, flowers freely borne; flowers and foliage smaller than typical.

‘Gold Heart’—Irregular splashes of golden yellow in the center of the leaves.

‘Golden’—Yellow-margined leaves and white flowers.

‘Golden Vein’—Bright green leaves with golden center radiating out along the veins.

‘Green Carpet’ (‘Grüner Teppich’)—Apparently a non-flowering form of *V. minor* with luxuriant rich green leaves that are larger than the type.

‘La Grave’—Large, up to 1 1/2″ diameter, lavender-blue (deep mauve) flowers; this is also the same, according to the literature, as ‘Bowles Variety’ which is listed as having larger azure-blue flowers, vigorous growth habit but more clumpy rather than spreading like the species; I received ‘La Grave’ from Dr. Raulston and indeed it is superior in size and color, the petals having more substance than the typical species type; the ‘Bowles Variety’ I have seen in commerce is not the same as ‘La Grave’ but the plant does not always match up with the name; true ‘La Grave’ is a more handsome plant and is worth pursuing; collected by E.A. Bowles in the 1920’s in the churchyard of La Grave in the Dauphine, France.

‘Multiplex’—Plum purple double flowers.

‘Onland Blue’—Form with large light violet-blue flowers, narrower in the petals than ‘La Grave’, see *The Garden* 109:426–429 (1984) for a Wisley Garden “Trial of *Vinca* cultivars.”

‘Ralph Shugert’—Uniform creamy white to white margins on dark green leaves; more regular marginal variegation and darker green, smaller leaves than ‘Argenteovariegata’, similar to ‘Bowlesii’ in floral characteristics, introduced by David MacKenzie, Spring Lake, MI.

‘Rosea’—Flowers violet-pink, smaller leaves.

‘Rosea Plena’—Flowers violet-pink, double.

‘Royal Blue’—Deeper blue flowers, witnessed at Van Dusen Botanical Garden.

‘Shademaster’—A dense, evergreen, ground cover with purple flowers, a Princeton Nursery introduction.

‘Sterling Silver’—Pretty, cream-variegated leaf form with pale violet-blue flowers, handsome selection, popular in New England.

‘Valley Glow’—New growth golden, white flowers.

‘Wine’—Wine red flowers.

PROPAGATION: Fresh seeds of ‘Gertrude Jekyll’ were give a 24 hour soak in Gibberellic acid (GA) at 0 or 1000 ppm and/or stratified for 0, 30, 60, 90 days; 1000 ppm GA, plus 90 days cold stratification resulted in 70% germination in 30 days; neither GA nor cold alone induced germination. Division, also extremely easy from cuttings.

NATIVE HABITAT: Europe and western Asia, cultivated since ancient times; escaped from cultivation.

RELATED SPECIES:

Vinca major L. — Large Periwinkle

LEAVES: Opposite, simple, evergreen, ovate to broad ovate to lanceolate, 1 to 3″(3 1/2″) long, half to two-third’s as wide, acute or obtusish, often nearly cordate, entire but often with marginal ciliate hairs, lustrous dark green and glabrous above, lighter beneath; petiole—1/3 to 1/2″ long.

Vinca major, (ving′kà mā′jôr), Large Periwinkle, is essentially a large carbon copy of
the *Vinca minor*. The plant averages
between 12 to 18″ high. It flowers well in
full sun and the flowers often occur sporadically over the growing season. Flowers in March–April in Athens. *Vinca major* prefers moist, well-drained soils and
shade. Makes a good ground cover in
dense shade. 'Variegata' ('Elegantissima') has leaves that are blotched and
margined irregularly with creamy white
markings. 'Variegata' is as hardy and
vigorous as the species and the flowers
are similar. Have seen 'Variegata' used
at a residence in Columbus, OH with

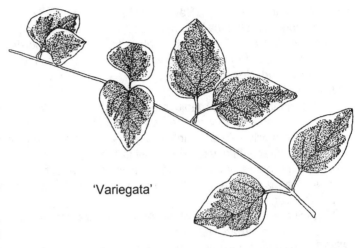

'Variegata'

some success. Near the foundation it overwintered in good condition but was obliterated 3 to 4′ from the
foundation. Should be cut back in spring. Used for window boxes, containers and urns; cascades
gracefully over their edges. In the 1983 edition, I commented that this species was more drought resistant
than *V. minor*. After observing both species during the two hottest and driest back-to-back summers on
record in the south, I give the adaptability nod to *V. minor*. *Vinca major* showed pronounced wilting. Have
also seen a narrow-petaled, deep purple form in England termed 'Oxyloba'. 'Aureomaculata' has a central
blotch of yellow-green and arose as a chimera on 'Variegata'. 'Jason Hill' has deeper violet-blue flowers.
'Major' has dark green leaves, blue-violet flowers. 'Reticulata', with yellow veining when young, later green
is known. France, Italy, former Yugoslavia. Cultivated 1789. Zone 6 to 9.

Vitex negundo L. — Chastetree
(vī′teks nē-gun′dō)

FAMILY: Verbenaceae

LEAVES: Opposite, compound palmate, leaflets usually 5, sometimes 3 to 7, 1 1/4 to 4″(5″) long, sessile or
short-petioled, elliptic-ovate to lanceolate, entire or serrate, grayish green, tomentulose beneath;
petiole—3/4 to 2″ long.

BUDS: Superposed, sessile or the upper commonly developing the first season, subglobose, the 1 or 2 pairs
of leaf rudiments or scales concealed in pubescence.

STEM: Compressed at nodes, quadrangular with obtuse or flattened angles, rather slender; pith relatively large,
more or less angled, white, continuous and homogeneous; leaf scars U-shaped, rather small, low; the
surface usually torn and the solitary bundle trace indistinct.

SIZE: Difficult to predict in the North since the plants are often frozen to the ground; the height in one growing
season might be 3 to 5′ but if no damage is done, over the years the plant may grow 10 to 15′; plants at
the J.C. Raulston Arboretum were over 20′ high.

HARDINESS: Zone 6, often listed as 5 but shakily so, does well in southern states, into Zone 8.

HABIT: Not a bad looking plant in leaf; develops a loosely branched, airy, open outline, vase-shaped habit with
cloud-like airy foliage canopy, can become ratty with time, requires pruning.

RATE: Fast.

TEXTURE: Medium-fine in leaf; medium-coarse in winter; leafs out late.

LEAF COLOR: Grayish green cast in summer; nothing to speak of in the way of fall color.

FLOWERS: Small, blue-purple, lilac or lavender, in loose clusters forming slender spikes collected into terminal
5 to 8″ long panicles; effective in July–August (early to mid June in Athens); flowers on new growth of the
season.

FRUIT: A small drupe of no consequence, persists, if removed new growth often ensues and additional flowers
are produced.

CULTURE: Transplant as a container plant into loose, moist, well-drained soil; full sun; prefer hot weather; well-
drained situation definitely aids in reducing winter injury; if pruning is necessary, cut the plant to within 6
to 12″ of the ground in spring or back to live wood on old plants.

DISEASES AND INSECTS: Several leaf spots and a root rot have been reported but are not serious; in nursery settings, particularly with overhead watering, leaf spot can disfigure and induce premature defoliation.

LANDSCAPE VALUE: Possibly a plant for the shrub border; should almost be treated as an herbaceous perennial in the North; interesting foliage texture and late season flowers; large shrub or small tree in South and West.

CULTIVARS:

'Heterophylla'

'Cannabifolia'—Has marijuana-like foliage, the leaflets lightly incised/cut along their margins, produces lilac to lavender flowers.

'Heterophylla'—The leaflets are gray-green and finely divided creating a graceful, airy texture especially when treated as an herbaceous perennial and grown primarily for its foliage; based on my evaluations at the Arnold, this form appears hardier than *V. agnus-castus* var. *latifolia*.

'Incisa'—As I viewed it at the Arnold Arboretum, with more deeply cut leaflets than 'Heterophylla'.

PROPAGATION: Softwood cuttings root like weeds but must not be left in the mist too long after rooting; this applies to *V. a.* var. *latifolia*; seeds can be directly sown.

ADDITIONAL NOTES: The *Vitex* species make attractive summer flowering garden plants but are not common. See Dirr, *American Nurseryman* 150(3):11, 75–78 (1979) for additional information. Good plant for hot climates and might even be grown as a small tree. Will flower recurrently during late summer as long as new growth develops. Not a bad idea to remove spent flowers since this may result in a late season flush of growth.

     Vitex negundo has been shown to have repellent, insecticidal, and juvenile hormone activity against several insect pests, including stored product pests and larvae of Lepidoptera.

     Some 250 species of trees and shrubs with opposite leaves, finger-like, 1 to 7 foliate leaflets, white, yellow to blue-violet flowers, found in tropics with a few temperate species. Occasionally see **Vitex trifolia** L. in Florida. It has 1 to 3 leaflets, to 10″ long, panicles of fragrant to blue-purple flowers. 'Variegata' with cream-edged leaves is available. Asia to Australia. Zone 9 to 10. **Vitex rotundifolia** L.f. taxonomically resembles *V. trifolia* but is a prostrate-sprawling shrub, growing 1 to 2′ high and spreading indefinitely. Leaves a bluish green, about 2″ long by 1 1/2″ wide, broad-oblong to suborbicular. Flowers are blue-purple in short inflorescences out of the leaf axils. Good beach plant, excellent salt tolerance. Asia to Australia. Zone 7 to 10.

NATIVE HABITAT: Actually rather wide-ranging from southeast Africa, Madagascar, eastern and southeastern Asia, Philippines. Introduced 1697.

RELATED SPECIES:

Vitex agnus-castus L. — Chastetree

LEAVES: Opposite, compound palmate, digitate (finger-like) in appearance, 5 to 7(9) radiating leaflets, each narrow elliptic to lanceolate, 2 to 4″(5″) long, 1/2 to 1″ wide, tapering at the apex and base, entire or toothed toward apex, dark gray-green above, grayish beneath with a fine pubescence, leaves aromatic when bruised; petiolule—1/4″ long or less.

Vitex agnus-castus, (vī′teks ag′nus-kās′tus), Chastetree, is not as hardy as the above species. The flowers are more prominent, lilac or pale violet, fragrant (although I can't detect much), and occur from June–July through September. Flowers occur in 3 to 6″ long racemes from the ends and leaf axils of the current season's growth resulting in 12 to 18″ long and slightly less in spread panicles. This species grows 8 to 10′ high. In the South, it makes a fine small, 15 to 20′ high and wide tree and is spectacular in flower. The bark on old plants is grayish and develops a blocky characteristic. There are many fine specimens on the Georgia campus The cultivars include: 'Abbeville Blue' produces deep blue flowers; 'Alba' with white flowers; 'Blushing Spires' has soft pink flowers, growth more restrained, from Niche Gardens, North Carolina; 'Fletcher Pink' is a lavender-pink flowered selection; 'Lilac Queen' with lavender flowers, broad-spreading, multi-stemmed shrub, 20′

by 18′, introduced by Plantation Tree Co., Selma, AL; 'Montrose Purple' produces rich violet flowers in large inflorescences, strong-growing form, 8 to 10′ by 8 to 10′, an introduction by Nancy Goodwin, Hillsborough, NC; 'Rosea' with pink flowers; 'Shoal Creek' with large, blue-violet flowers in 12 to 18″ long inflorescences and leaf spot resistance, although have observed leaf spots on plants under overhead water; 'Silver Spire' with white flowers and good vigor; and 'Snow Spire' with white flowers in panicles as large as the species. A variety *latifolia* is supposedly more vigorous and hardier than the species. I remember learning the variety in my plant material courses at Ohio State, for it was always necessary to hunt through the old Horticulture garden to see if there were a few live branches. Native to southern Europe and western Asia. Introduced 1570. Zone (6)7 to 8(9).

Vitis L. — Grape
FAMILY: Vitaceae

Through four editions, *Vitis* escaped the *Manual*, but the time has come for inclusion. With some 65 species worldwide anything I include is superficial. In European gardens several species and cultivars are used repeatedly. The species most common in the wild in the midwestern and eastern United States include: *V. aestivalis* Michx., Summer Grape; *V. cinerea* Engelm., Sweet Winter Grape; *V. labrusca* L., Fox Grape; *V. riparia* Michx., Frost Grape; and in the southeastern United States, *V. rotundifolia* Michx., Muscadine Grape, around which a small industry has evolved due to breeding efforts at the University of Georgia.

Childhood days were often spent with my buddies swinging from wild grapevines (identity not important). Our Tarzan impressions were feeble—the dreaming was important. I remember the rich brown, shreddy-barked stems and trunks that ascended the trees. If only I could climb those vines, then and now.

Suffice it to add that *Vitis* beyond the commercial production has not become an ornamental plant of significance in United States' gardens. Maintenance, primarily pruning, is necessary. I have grown *V. rotundifolia* and *V. coignetiae* in the Dirr garden. Both have long since been removed. The former too vigorous, the latter did not live up to the fall color expectations.

Vitis coignetiae Poll. ex Planch — Crimson Glory Vine
LEAVES: Alternate, simple, rounded, to 10 or 12″ long by 10″ wide, 3- to 5-lobed, acute, cordate, dentate, dark green above, tomentose below; petiole—2 to 6″ long.

Vitis coignetiae, (vī′tis kog-net′ē-ȧ), Crimson Glory Vine, is a rampant climber that scrambles to the tops of tall trees in its native Korea and Japan. The dark green leaves turn rich crimson and scarlet in fall. In Athens, newly tested plants developed excellent red fall color under 50% shade. The 1/3 to 1/2″ diameter, glaucous purple-black fruits are barely edible. Japan, Korea. Cultivated 1875. Zone 5, possibly into 7.

Vitis rotundifolia Michx. — Muscadine Grape
LEAVES: Alternate, simple, rounded to broad-ovate, 2 1/2 to 5″ high and wide, acute, cordate, occasionally slightly lobed, coarsely serrate, glossy dark green above, glossy yellow green below, glabrous except hairs in axils of veins; petiole—usually shorter than blade.

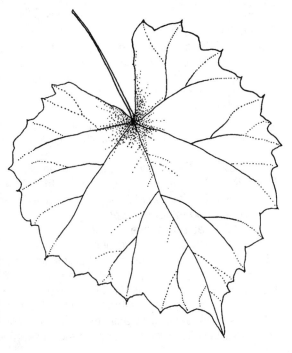

Vitis rotundifolia, (vī′tis rō-tun-di-fō′li-ȧ), Muscadine Grape, is a phenomenally vigorous (over 100′) and long-lived vine that permeates much of the Southeast. The leaves turn a pleasing yellow in fall. Fruits are rounded, greenish to purplish, 1/3 to 1″ diameter, with a thicker skin. As I have eaten them: pop in mouth, extract skin, savor sweet juice on outside of interior, remove rest. Used for jellies, jam, wine and ammunition. Many cultivars of outstanding merit bred and introduced by Griffin, GA scientists. As I walk the woodlands of the Southeast this plant is everywhere. Also, common in older southern gardens. Delaware to northern Florida, west to Missouri, Kansas, Texas and Mexico. Introduced 1806. Zone 5 to 9.

Vitis vinifera L. — Common Grape
LEAVES: Alternate, simple, 3- to 7-lobed, 2 to 6″ high and wide, cordate, irregularly dentate, dark green above,
variably pubescent, tomentose beneath.

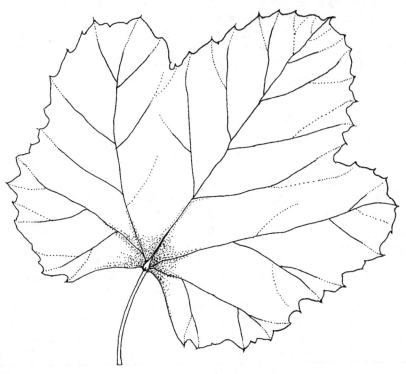

Vitis vinifera, (vī′tis vī-nif′ĕr-à), Common Grape, is the grape of commerce with hundreds of selections over the
centuries. Again, like the above it can reach tall trees and grow over 100′ long. Several ornamental cultivars
with deeply lobed leaves ('Apiifolia', 'Ciotat'), purple leaf types ('Madame Mathias Muscat', 'Purpurea') and
cream-variegated leaves ('Variegata') are known. The purple leaf types are utilized in European gardens,
less so in the United States. Southern and central Europe. Cultivated for centuries. Zone 6 to 9.

Weigela florida (Bunge.) A. DC. — Old Fashioned Weigela
(wī-gē′là flôr′i-dà)

FAMILY: Caprifoliaceae
LEAVES: Opposite, simple, elliptic to ovate-oblong, or obovate, 2 to 4 1/2″
long, 3/4 to 1 1/2″ wide, acuminate, rounded to cuneate at base,
serrate, medium green and glabrous above except on mid-rib,
pubescent or tomentose on veins beneath; petiole—short, about 1/8
to 1/4″ long.
STEM: With 2 rows of hairs running from node to node, gray-brown, scurfy,
with large circular lenticels; pith—moderate, pale brown, continuous.

SIZE: 6 to 9′ high by 9 to 12′ wide; smaller in exposed and harsh situations.
HARDINESS: Zone 5 to 8(9); most of the older cultivars are not cold
hardy in Orono, ME but the Dance (Canadian) hybrids have
performed extremely well.
HABIT: Spreading, dense, rounded shrub with coarse branches that
eventually arch to the ground.
TEXTURE: Medium in summer, at times almost offensive in winter.
LEAF COLOR: Nondescript medium green, no fall color of consequence.
FLOWERS: Perfect, funnelform-campanulate, 1 to 2″ long, abruptly narrowed below the middle, rosy
pink outside, paler within, with rounded spreading lobes, May–June (mid to late April, Athens),
singly or several in axillary cymes on short twigs from last year's branches, also flowering
sporadically on current season's growth, have seen flowers as late as mid-October.

FRUIT: Two-valved, glabrous capsule of no ornamental value, to 1″ long; seeds unwinged to slightly winged.

CULTURE: Transplant bare root or from a container; extremely adaptable but prefers a well-drained soil and full sun; often considerable dieback occurs and pruning (after flowering) is necessary to keep it in shape; quite pollution tolerant.

DISEASES AND INSECTS: None serious, viruses have been reported, *Plant Disease* 77(3):318 (1993).

LANDSCAPE VALUE: Best used in the shrub border, for grouping or massing; have seen it used frequently as a foundation planting in older sections of cities; really appears forlorn in the winter landscape; looks like it needs a place to hide.

CULTIVARS: One truly needs a score card to keep track of the many cultivars that have resulted from hybridization among the various species. A glance at the list is sufficient reason to throw the hands in the air and give up. Krüssmann mentions that there are 170 known hybrids that resulted from the work of van Houtte, Billard, Lemoine and Rathke. New cultivars are coming primarily from Holland and Canada. Svejda from Agriculture Canada has introduced several cold hardy, compact, free-flowering forms since the 1983 edition of the *Manual*. Pellett and McNamara, *Landscape Plant News* present acclimation data for 18 *Weigela* taxa; on December 2 'Centennial' was the hardiest (-40°F); followed by 'Java Red', 'Minuet', 'Polka', and 'Samba' at -36°F; 'Rumba' at -32°F; 'Pink Delight', 'Tango', and 'White Knight' at -29°F; 'Gustav Melquist', 'Pink Princess', 'Red Prince', 'Rosabella', and 'Vanicek' at -26°F. The cultivars listed here are not necessarily progeny of *W. florida*.

'Abel Carriere'—Large, rose-carmine flowers flecked gold in the throat, free-flowering, buds carmine-purple, 1876, Lemoine.

'Avalanche'—Vigorous, free-flowering, white form, the flowers with pink tinge, 1909, Lemoine.

'Boskoop Glory'—Large, trumpet-shaped, salmon pink flowers, about 7 to 8′ at maturity.

'Bristol Ruby'—Ruby red flowers, erect growth habit, free-flowering, a hybrid between *W. florida* and 'Eva Rathke,' 7′ high, good hardiness, 1954.

'Bristol Snowflake'—White, with some pink, more vigorous than 'Candida', 1955.

'Canary'—Yellow-flowered form, selected by Dick Lighty, Mt. Cuba Center, Greenville, DE, listed as a *W. subsessilis* selection, could be related to *W. coraeensis* Thunb., nomenclature is somewhat unclear, plants I have seen at the Arnold Arboretum open yellow, fading to pink, or have pink and yellow flowers mixed.

'Candida'—Pure white in bud stage and older flowers, foliage light green, 1879.

'Carnaval' ('Courtalor')—More compact and restrained growth habit, red, white and pink, thickish, substantive flowers occur in great profusion, tetraploid hybrid, French origin, 3 to 4′ high.

'Centennial'—Robust shrub to 9′ with erythrite red flowers to tips of branches, cold hardy form introduced in 1967, hybrid between 'Dropmore Pink' and 'Profusion'.

'Conquerant'—Very large, deep pink flowers almost 2″ long, spreading habit, 1904, Lemoine.

'Dame Blanche'—Almost pure white but with a pink tinge, large flowers, 1902, Lemoine.

'Dart's Colordream' ('Colourdream')—Cream and rose-red, while others are mixed, will be in the medium size category, probably 4 to 6′ high.

'Dropmore Pink'—Hardy pink form developed by Dr. Skinner using a Manchurian strain for hardiness, 1951.

'Eva Rathke'—A slow-growing cultivar of compact habit with bright crimson-red flowers with yellow anthers, opening over a long period, 1892, Rathke.

'Eva Supreme'—Vigorous grower with bright red flowers; hybrid of 'Eva Rathke' and 'Newport Red', supposedly only 5′ high, limited repeat flower, quite cold hardy, 1958, Holland.

'Evita'—Resembles 'Eva Rathke' in flower color, crimson red with yellow anthers, but is dense and spreading in habit, 2 to 3′ high, 4 to 5′ wide, flowers profuse in May–June, with recurrent bloom later, good looking form.

'Fairy'—Large trusses of bright salmon pink flowers, 4 to 5′ high.

'Floreal'—Clear rose-pink outside, deep carmine-pink throat, large-flowered, floriferous, 1901, Lemoine.

'Foliis Purpureis'—Pink flowers with purplish green foliage, dwarf, for a 20-year-old plant is purple-red, densely rounded and 4′ tall, a *W. florida* form; buds carmine red, same as 'Java Red'.

'Gracieux'—Erect, free-flowering, salmon-rose with sulfur yellow throat, large-flowered, floriferous, 1904, Lemoine.

'Java Red'—Somewhat confused in my mind, may be the same as 'Foliis Purpureis', carmine red buds open to deep pink (rose-pink) flowers, more compact-spreading, 3 to 4′ by 4 to 5′, foliage deep green with a purplish red overcast.

'Jean's Gold'—A golden-foliaged branch sport of 'Bristol Ruby', more resistant to sun-scorch, first noticed by Staffordshire England nurseryman Paul Zako in 1988.

'Looymansii Aurea'—Is a form that jumps in my path in many European gardens; the leaves are bright golden yellow with a narrow, red, marginal rim, foliage will fade with heat and probably scorch in the heat of the United States summers, flowers are pink and habit is more restrained than *W. florida* but still 4 to 6′ high at maturity.

'Lucifer'—A compact form, 3 to 5′ high with dark green foliage and large, 1 3/4″ long, deep red flowers.

'Minuet'—Very dwarf compact form with dark ruby red flowers profusely borne over the purple-tinged, dark green foliage, flowers slightly fragrant, 30″ high, has shown excellent cold hardiness, flowers are ruby red on outside of corolla, lobes lilac-purple, throat yellow, 1 1/2″ long, 1 1/4″ wide; released by Agricultural Canada, parentage 'Foliis Purpureis' × 'Dropmore Pink'; see *Canadian J. Plant. Sci.* 62:249–250 (1982); grew in Dirr garden, pretty tatty by end of summer, now removed.

'Mont Blanc'—Vigorous form with large, white, fragrant flowers; often considered the best white, 1898, Lemoine.

'Naine Rouge' ('Courtalor')—Bright orange-red flowers with creamy white stigma and style, rich green leaves turn red in fall, 2 to 3′ high, French introduction.

'Newport Red'—Similar to 'Eva Rathke', flowers not as bright and more purple-red, vigorous grower, winter stems green, the same as 'Vanicek' and, in fact, introduced by V.A. Vanicek, Newport, RI, 5 to 6′ high, good hardiness.

'Pink Delight'—Deep pink flowers that do not fade as blatantly as many forms, more compact habit, greater cold hardiness, 5 to 6′ by 5 to 6′, from Mission Gardens, IL.

'Pink Princess'—A pink-flowered (actually lavender-pink), hardy selection from Iowa, 5 to 6′ high, spreading, loose, open, from Iowa State University, does not flower as heavily as 'Polka'.

'Polka'—Develops into a 3 to 4′ high, 4 to 5′ wide shrub, foliage is thick and dark green, leaves 2 1/2 to 3″ long, 1 1/2 to 2″ wide, flowers are pink on outside of the corolla with a yellow inner throat and average 1 3/4″ long, 1 1/4 to 1 1/2″ wide, suffered 7% winter injury in Ottawa and flowered for 10 to 11 weeks from June to September, counted 12 progenitor taxa in this clone's makeup, Wow!; see *HortScience* 23:787–788 (1988) for additional details.

'Red Prince'—Good red flower that does not fade, recurrent flowering in late summer, 1 1/3″ long, 1″ wide, upright growing when young, 5 to 6′, hardier than 'Newport Red' ('Vanicek'), listed as adaptable to Zone 4a, introduced by Iowa State University, see *HortScience* 26(2):218–219 (1991).

'Rubidor'—Probably the same as 'Rubigold', same exact floral (red) and foliage (yellow) characteristics; until somebody tells me something different, I will stay with two name theory for one plant; 5 to 7′ high.

'Rubigold'—Have seen this at Bressingham Gardens in England and find the yellow or yellow-green splashed foliage and red flowers a degree indigestible but for those who want bright foliage and flowers it might be worth a shot; might cook in heat of South or at least fade quickly; a branch sport of 'Bristol Ruby'; actually grew in Dirr garden, hired a hit gardener to eliminate it.

'Rumba'—Vigorous, compact-spreading shrub, 3′ by 3 1/2′ wide, yellow-green leaves with purple edges, 3″ long by 1 1/2″ wide, flowers dark red with a yellow throat, 1 3/4″ long and 1 to 1 1/4″ wide, winter hardy and flowers for 8 weeks from June to September; see *HortScience* 20:149 (1985); result of cross between 'Foliis Purpureis' and 'Dropmore Scarlet'.

'Samba'—Compact, vigorous, well-formed shrub that grows about 3′ high and wide, leaves are dark green with purple tips and edges, 2 1/2 to 3″ long, 1 to 1 1/2″ wide, flowers are red with a yellow throat, 1 3/4″ long, 1″ wide, displays excellent winter hardiness, a hybrid between 'Rumba' and 'Eva Rathke', see *HortScience* 21:166 (1986) for details.

'Seduction'—Magenta-rose, buds dark red, heavy-flowering.

'Snowflake'—Profuse, white flowers, 3 to 4′ high, good cold hardiness.

'Styriaca'—Small, carmine-rose flowers freely borne on arching branches, smaller shrub, foliage light green.

'Sunny Princess'—Golden bands along the leaf margin, otherwise like 'Pink Princess' from which it sported.

'Tango'—Compact shrub, 2′ high by 2 1/2′ wide, leaves 2 1/2 to 5″ long, 3/4 to 2″ wide, purple on the upper surface, dark green below, purple is predominant and maintained throughout the growing season, flowers are red on the outside, yellowish in the throat, 1 1/4 to 1 1/2″ long, 3/4 to 1″ wide, has shown a maximum of 4% winter injury in Ottawa, Canada, and flowered for 3 to 4 weeks in June (Canada); see *HortScience* 23:787–788 (1988) for more details; interestingly, this clone resulted from four progenitor taxa.

'Vanicek'—Same as 'Newport Red'.

'Variegata'—Flowers deep rose, leaves edged pale yellow to creamy white, compact grower, about 4 to 6′ high although have seen 10′ tall plants.

'Variegata Nana'—Most dwarf of the variegated weigelas, 3′ tall, same foliage as above, again have seen larger specimens than the norm.

var. *venusta* (Rehd.) Nak.—Leaves smaller, flowers rosy pink, very hardy, free-flowering, listed as Zone (3)4.

'Versicolor'—Cream-colored flowers mixed with pink, rose, red flowers on the same plant, foliage green, 5 to 6′ high and wide.

'Victoria'—May be the same as Wine and Roses® which is trademarked and if sold under that name a royalty fee is assessed; from my literature searches, it appears 'Victoria' was being sold by a number of United States nurserymen *before* the trademarked version appeared; was told that 'Victoria' is different, i.e., larger growing.

'White Knight'—Smaller than species, 5 to 6′ high and wide, medium green foliage, large pure white flowers in our Georgia trials, flowers are lovely, Iowa State University introduction.

Wine and Roses® ('Alexandra')—Compact shrub, 4 to 5′ high and wide with dark burgundy-purple leaves and hot rose-pink flowers, have seen small plants and they do have customer appeal in a container.

PROPAGATION: Seeds can be directly sown; softwood cuttings in June, July, August root readily; one of the easiest plants to root; tissue culture has been successful, protoplasts have been regenerated into whole plants, see *Plant, Cell, Tissue and Organ Culture* 33(3):315–320 (1993).

ADDITIONAL NOTES: Cultivars, cultivars, and more cultivars. At Hillier Arboretum several years past I observed and photographed a number of *W. praecox* (Lemoine) L.H. Bail. French-named hybrids. Also, at Glasnevin, Ireland, an entire collection of cultivars confused me to the point where all looked the same. Without labels I am lost. Have also seen *W. japonica* Thunb. in flower without knowing it was different from *W. florida*.

Considering that some 10 species are recognized it might be easier to lump them together. The numerous hybrids preclude any type of sanity at taxonomic order. All are found in Japan (greatest number), China, Korea, and Manchuria.

NATIVE HABITAT: Japan. Introduced 1860.

RELATED SPECIES:

Weigela coraeensis Thunb., (wī-gē′là kôr-ē-en′sis), produces 1 1/2″ long, cream-yellow, pink, changing to carmine flowers in 2- to 8-flowered, axillary cymes. Quite handsome in flower, 5 to 6′ high and wide. Japan. Cultivated 1850. Zone 6 to 7. Also, **W. praecox** (Lemoine) L.H. Bail., (wī-gē′là prē′koks), produces pale yellow flowers that fade to soft pink, finally deep pink. Early flowering, often mid to late March in Zone 7. Japan, Korea, Manchuria. Cultivated 1894. Zone 5 to 7.

Weigela middendorffiana (Carr.) K. Koch, (wī-gē′là mid-en-dôr-fi-ā′nà), Middendorf Weigela, is a small (3 to 5′ high) shrub of note for the 1 to 1 1/2″ long, sulfur yellow flowers, dotted orange on the lower lobes. I have seen it at the Arnold Arboretum and, although interesting, cannot compete with the better hybrids. Manchuria, northern China, Japan. Introduced 1850. Zone (4)5 to 7.

Another soft yellow-green flowered species is **W. maximowiczii** (S. Moore) Rehd., (wī-gē′là max-im-ō-wix′ē-ī), a smaller shrub to 4′ that flowers early in spring. China. Introduced 1915. Zone 5.

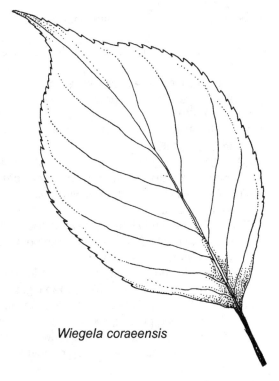

Wiegela coraeensis

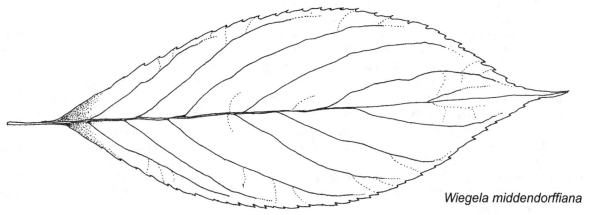

Wiegela middendorffiana

Weigela subsessilis (Nak.) Bailey, (wī-gē′là sub-ses′i-lis), is a 4 to 5′ by 4 to 6′, compact, twiggy shrub with yellowish green flowers changing to shades of pink and pale lavender. I first experienced this species in spring of 1991 at the Arnold Arboretum and indeed the flowers were spectacular. Looked a little tatty by the end of summer. See *Arnoldia* 53(4):331–333 (1993). China. Zone 6 to 7.

Wisteria floribunda (Willd.) DC. — Japanese Wisteria
(wis-tē′ri-à flôr-i-bun′dà)

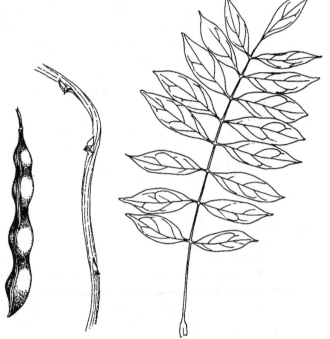

FAMILY: Fabaceae

LEAVES: Alternate, pinnately compound, 10 to 15″ long, (11)13 to 19 leaflets, ovate-elliptic to ovate-oblong, 1 1/2 to 3″ long, acuminate, rounded at base, rarely broad cuneate, entire, bright green above, appressed pubescent when young, soon nearly glabrous; petiole—flattened at base.

BUDS: Narrowly oblong and acute at the tip with 3 outer scales, one scale usually surrounding the entire bud, reddish brown, pubescent, appressed.

STEM: Twines clockwise, somewhat angled, light tan or brown changing to gray-brown, 2 spine-like projections at the top sides of the leaf scar.

SIZE: 30′ or more, essentially limited by structure on which it is allowed to grow; have seen plants 40 to 50′ (70 to 80′) high in trees.

HARDINESS: Zone (4)5 to 9, Cappiello reported kill in Orono, ME.

HABIT: Stout vine, climbing by twining stems which turn clockwise developing twisted woody trunks several inches in diameter and requiring considerable support.

RATE: Fast, as is true with most vines; will grow 10′ or more in a single season once established, especially in the South.

TEXTURE: Medium in leaf, somewhat coarse in winter.

BARK: On old trunks a grayish color, smooth and sometimes irregularly fluted; almost reminiscent of the bark of *Carpinus caroliniana*.

LEAF COLOR: Bright green, usually late to leaf out, no fall color of any consequence, a tad of yellow, have on rare occasions savored reasonably good yellow fall color, new growth often bronze or purplish.

FLOWERS: Perfect, violet or violet-blue, on old wood on short leafy shoots, each flower 1/2 to 3/4″ long, on a 1/2 to 1″ long pedicel, slightly fragrant, April–May (early to mid-April, Athens), borne in slender, 8 to 20″ (16 to 48″) long racemes, the flowers opening from the base to the apex; very lovely as the flowers open before or just as leaves emerge; not too many vines rival it for flower effect; flowers occasionally on new growth of the season.

FRUIT: Pod, brown, 4 to 6″, October, persisting into winter, velutinous.

CULTURE: Supposedly hard to transplant and slow to establish; however, I have grown many in containers and have had no difficulty establishing them; plant in deep, moist, well-drained loam; pH adaptable although supposedly does better at a higher pH; in order to insure successful culture it is wise to use nitrogen sparingly for this promotes excess vegetative growth, use superphosphate, root prune, cut back vigorous growth leaving only 3 to 4 buds, plant in full sun and use named cultivars rather than seedling grown material; if left to its own devices, the plant can consume fences, trellises, arbors and people; indeed it is one of the most beautiful of all flowering vines and deserves first consideration where it can be maintained; although all types of horticultural voodoo and folk art are recommended to keep it flowering, in the South it is unstoppable; for two or more weeks in April in Athens the plant appears as common as Japanese Honeysuckle.

DISEASES AND INSECTS: Crown gall, leaf spots, stem canker, powdery mildew, root rot, tobacco mosaic virus, sweet potato leaf beetle, Japanese mealybug, citrus flata planthopper, fall webworm, black vine weevil and scale.

LANDSCAPE VALUE: Excellent flowering vine, nice over patios, on large structures, or trained into a tree form; needs ample support and metal pipe is recommended for it will actually crush wood supports with time; not the easiest plant to keep flowering and cultural practices must be fairly precise.

CULTIVARS:

'Alba'—Racemes 11″ long, moderate fragrance, dense, white, 13 leaflets.

'Aunt Dee'—Light purple, slightly fragrant flowers in 7 to 12″ long racemes, succeeded in protected areas of Zone 4, Bailey introduction.

'Beni Fugi'—Slightly fragrant, light pink flowers, 19 leaflets.

'Geisha'—White flowers.

'Honko Fuji'—Pink flowers similar to 'Rosea'.

'Issai'—Racemes 12″ long, moderate fragrance, violet to bluish violet, 17 leaflets, have seen 'Issai' described as having 24 to 30″ long racemes.

'Ivory Tower'—White flowers, abundantly produced, heady fragrance.

'Kyushaku'—Racemes 26″ long, fragrance fair, reddish violet to violet.

'Lavender Lace'—Fragrant, lavender-mauve flowers, inflorescence 2 to 3′ long.

'Lawrence'—Flowers pale blue with white keels, original plant 20′ by 10′, discovered in Brantford, Ontario, 1970; selected because of exceptional hardiness and floriferousness.

'Longissima Alba' ('Shiro Noda')—Racemes 15″ long, good fragrance, 13 leaflets, white; plants I have observed had 24 to 36″ long racemes.

'Macrobotrys'—Racemes 18 to 36″ (48″) long, fragrance excellent, reddish violet to violet.

'Murasaki Naga Fuji'—Produces purple and white flowers in up to 3′ long racemes.

'Murasaki Noda'—Racemes 10″ long, fragrance fair, 15 leaflets, reddish violet to violet.

'Naga Noda'—Pale violet, very fragrant.

'Pink Ice'—Soft pink flowers.

'Rosea' ('Honbeni', 'Honey Bee Pink')—Pale rose, tipped purple, excellent fragrance, in long racemes to about 18″.

'Royal Purple' ('Black Dragon')—Violet-purple, 12 to 14″ long, slightly fragrant, 15 leaflets, bronze new growth.

'Sekine's Blue'—Flowers blue-violet, 6 to 7″ long racemes.

'Shiro Naga Fuji'—Produces long, narrow, white racemes.

'Snow Showers'—Offers fragrant, white flowers to 2′ long, RHS Award of Merit in 1931, Award of Garden Merit 1969.

'Texas Purple'—Violet-purple, precocious, a Monrovia offering.

'Variegata' ('Mon Nishiki')—Cream-flecked variegated foliage and pale blue-lavender racemes, in Zone 7 fades to green in the heat of the summer.

'Violacea Plena'—Double flowers, violet-blue, flowers rosetted, slightly fragrant, 13 leaflets, racemes 10 to 12″ long.

'White Blue Eye'—Has a blue-purple spot on each flower, pretty on close inspection, am not sure about the validity of this name.

PROPAGATION: Seeds germinate readily without treatment; I have collected seed in fall and direct sowed them with good results; if seed is quite dry and hard, a 24 hour soak in warm water is recommended; June to July cuttings rooted without treatment; hardwood cuttings taken in late January rooted 43%, 2000 ppm IBA produced greatest number of roots per cutting; cultivars are also grafted.

ADDITIONAL NOTES: No matter how many times I am asked to identify this and *W. sinensis*, the process is never easy. *Wisteria floribunda* leafs out perhaps two weeks earlier than *W. sinensis* and may be injured by late spring frosts. Also, there is a hybrid, *W.* × *formosa* Rehd., between the above species that was raised on Professor C.S. Sargent's estate, Holm Lea, Brookline, MA in 1905. Flowers open, or almost so, simultaneously along the length of the inflorescence.

The wisterias are lovely vines but do require considerable care. In the South (Zone 7 and higher) they are pernicious pests and *W. floribunda* can be found strangling everything in its grasp. Admittedly, it is quite pretty draped over and around trees especially during April. Must be used with a certain amount of discretion and a commitment to proper culture and pruning. Good articles on *Wisteria* selection and culture appeared in *Horticulture* 63(4):38–40 (1985), *The Plantsman* 6(2):109–122 (1984), *The Garden* 120(2):92–97(1995), and *Brooklyn Botanic Garden Plants and Garden News* 12(1):8–10 (1997).

Wisteria is not the easiest taxonomic genus to sort through. The newest and best reference is Peter Valder, *Wisterias, A Comprehensive Guide*, Timber Press (1995).

NATIVE HABITAT: Japan. Introduced 1830.

RELATED SPECIES:

Wisteria frutescens (L.) Poir — American Wisteria
LEAVES: Alternate, compound pinnate, 7 to 12″ long, 9 to 15
    leaflets of uniform size, elliptic-ovate to oblong or oblong-
    lanceolate, 1 1/2 to 2 1/2″ long, to 1 1/4″ wide, glabrous
    and bright green above, slightly pubescent below.

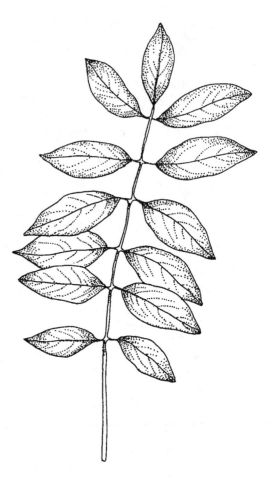

Wisteria frutescens, (wis-tē′ri-à frŭ-tes′enz), American Wis-
    teria, is a vigorous, climbing vine that grows 20 to 30′ or
    more. The fragrant, 3/4″ long, pale lilac-purple flowers
    have a yellow spot and are compressed into 4 to 6″ long,
    dense villous racemes in June–August on the current
    season's growth. Flowers are much later than those of *W.
    floribunda* and *W. sinensis* and, in Athens, open from late
    April into May with recurrent flowering during summer on
    new growth of the season. Flowers appear after the
    foliage has developed. Handsome plant in leaf and
    flower; much more restrained than the Asiatic bullies. The
    pods are compressed, 2 to 4″ long, and glabrous with the
    seeds more rounded than those of *W. floribunda* and *W.
    sinensis*. 'Amethyst Falls' produces beautiful, fragrant,
    lavender-blue flowers, introduced by Head-Lee Nursery,
    Seneca, SC. 'Magnifica' has lilac flowers with a large
    yellowish blotch on the standard. 'Nivea' is a white-
    flowered form. Occurs naturally along moist shores of
    streams, ponds, lakes, borders of wet woodlands and
    swamps, moist to wet thickets. Virginia to Florida and
    Texas. Introduced 1724. Zone 5 to 9.

Wisteria macrostachys Nutt. — Kentucky Wisteria
LEAVES: Alternate, compound pinnate, about 9 leaflets, 1 to 3″ long, ovate-elliptic to lanceolate, acuminate,
    bright green, pubescent above initially, finally glabrous, pubescent beneath.

Wisteria macrostachys, (wis-tē′ri-à mak-rō-sta′kēs), Kentucky Wisteria, is restrained, much like *W. frutescens*,
    and grows 15 to 25′ long. The lilac purple flowers are packed 70 to 90 to the 8 to 12″ long raceme and
    open in May–June and later. Flowers in June in Morton Arboretum. The 3 to 5″ long, glabrous pod is often
    twisted. Probably the hardiest wisteria. Also, more moist to wet soil tolerant. Considered by some a variety
    of *W. frutescens*. 'Abbeville Blue' is blue-flowered; 'Bayou Two O'Clock' has blue flowers in long-pointed
    racemes; 'Clara Mack' has white flowers in longer racemes, late flowering, introduced by Woodlanders,
    selected by Columbia, SC gardener Clara Mack; 'Pondside Blue' has light blue flowers in full racemes.
    Missouri to Tennessee and Texas. Cultivated 1855. Zone (4)5 to 8(9).

Wisteria sinensis (Sims.) Sweet — Chinese Wisteria
LEAVES: Alternate, pinnately compound, 10 to 12″ long, 7 to 13 leaflets,
    usually 11, ovate-oblong to ovate-lanceolate, 2 to 4″ long, 1/2 to 1
    1/2″ wide, abruptly acuminate, usually broad-cuneate at base,
    ciliate, densely appressed-pubescent at first, deep green and
    glabrous above, somewhat hairy beneath, especially on the midrib.

Wisteria sinensis, (wis-tē′ri-à sī-nen′sis), Chinese Wisteria, is similar to
    W. floribunda except the flower is blue-violet, about 1″ long, not as
    fragrant, May, borne in dense, 6 to 12″ long racemes, all flowers of
    one raceme opening at about the same time. Fruit is a pod, 4 to 6″
    long, densely velutinous with 1 to 3 seeds. Twines counter-clock-
    wise. The exact identity of this species has brought much hand

wringing to the author especially when confronted with a shoot and no flower. It would seem that leaflet numbers should be a good criterion for separation from *W. floribunda*. I have seen true *W. sinensis* in the Netherlands and England and, indeed, the flowers open more or less at the same time along the axis of the raceme compared to the differential opening of *W. floribunda* from base to apex. The clockwise (*W. floribunda*) and counter-clockwise (*W. sinensis*) turnings also leave room for interpretations. Most plants I see in cultivation and escaped into the wild are *W. floribunda*, not *W. sinensis*. *Wisteria sinensis*, according to Bean is more vigorous than *W. floribunda*. Perhaps this is true in England but is not the case in this country. Variety *alba* Lindl. has white flowers; 'Amethyst' has 12″ racemes of light rose-purple flowers; 'Augusta's Pride' is an early flowering, light lavender-lilac selection from the Augusta National Golf Course in Augusta, GA, the old vine still resides outside the clubhouse, no doubt planted by P.J. Berckmann in the 1950's; 'Black Dragon' has double, dark purple flowers; 'Blue Moon' is a bi-colored, blue-flowered form; 'Blue Sapphire' is an early-flowering form with fragrant, lilac to mauve flowers; 'Caroline' has very fragrant, deep blue-purple flowers; 'Cooke's Purple' offers large, fragrant, dark lavender-blue flowers; 'Fuji White' offers fragrant, white flowers; 'Jako' is a selected form of *alba* with extremely fragrant flowers in up to 12″ long racemes; 'Plena' has double, rosette-shaped, lilac flowers; 'Profilica' ('Oosthoeks Variety') is a vigorous Dutch clone with blue-violet flowers of the species, flowers before the leaves; 'Rosea' bears pink flowers in 12″ long racemes; 'Shiro Captain Fuji' produces abundant, broad racemes of fragrant, white flowers; 'Showa Beni Fuji' has broad dark pink inflorescences; 'Sierra Madre' with white standard and lavender-violet wing and keel, very fragrant; 'Texas White' has larger inflorescences of white flowers than typical for the species, may be a *W. floribunda* type; and 'Whowa Beni Fuji' has broad, dark pink inflorescences. Bacterial stem gall was caused by *Pantoea dispersa*, see *Plant Disease* 78(12):1217 (1994). Also, *Phyllosticta wistariae* causes leaf spots. China. 1916. Zone 5 to 8.

Wisteria venusta Rehd. & Wils. — Silky Wisteria
LEAVES: Alternate, compound pinnate, 8 to 14″ long, 9 to 13 leaflets, usually 11, elliptic to ovate, 1 1/2 to 3 1/2″ long, 1/2 to 1 1/2″ wide, short acuminate, rounded, pubescent on both surfaces, bright green above.

Wisteria venusta, (wis-tē′ri-à ve-nus′tà), Silky Wisteria, offers 1″ long, white, fragrant flowers that are borne in 4 to 6″ long, 3 to 4″ wide racemes; all flowers opening about the same time. The 6 to 8″ long pod is compressed and densely velutinous. Grows to 30′ long. Turns counter-clockwise akin to *W. sinensis* but shoots pubescent when young. Variety *violacea* Rehd. is the wild form with violet flowers. Japan, where it (white) was only known in cultivation; before 1900. Zone 5 to 8.

Xanthoceras sorbifolium Bunge — Yellowhorn

FAMILY: Sapindaceae
LEAVES: Alternate, compound pinnate, 5 to 9″ long, 9 to 17 leaflets, narrow elliptic to lanceolate, 1 1/2 to 2 1/2″ long, deeply and sharply serrate, lustrous dark green above, lighter beneath, persisting late in the fall.

Xanthoceras sorbifolium, (zan-thŏs′ĕr-as sôr-bi-fō′li-um), Yellowhorn, is a striking tree or more often large shrub, but virtually unknown in commerce and gardens. It tends to be upright in habit and the branching pattern is rather stiff and coarse. Size ranges from 18 to 24′. The beautiful, slender-stalked, 3/4 to 1″ diameter flowers occur in 6 to 10″ long racemes in May. Each fragrant flower is composed of 5, rather thin, white petals with a blotch at the base that changes from yellow to red. It is a striking tree in flower and one which any gardener would be proud to display. Adaptable to any good loamy soil even those of calcareous origin (high pH). Supposedly has the reputation for being difficult to transplant. Should be sited in full sun. The fruit is a 3-valved, thick-walled, 2 to 3″(4″) diameter, rounded capsule; each cell contains several globose, dark brown, large pea-sized seeds. The seeds, when roasted, supposedly taste a little like macadamia nuts. At a conference in Nebraska, I talked with a gentleman who said the tree was growing well in Blair, NE where winter lows reach -25 to -30°F. Does not prosper in the heat of the South. Seed requires no pretreatment although 2 to 3 months at 40°F may unify and hasten germination. Root cuttings offer a feasible means of vegetative propagation. The lustrous green leaves remain late in fall. Have seen the tree in flower around mid-May at the Wister Garden, Swarthmore, PA and Winterthur Gardens, DE. At the Arnold Arboretum, flowers peaked during late April–early May, 1991. It is striking and certainly the rival of any flowering tree. Northern China. Introduced 1866. Zone (3)4 to 6(7).

Xanthorhiza simplicissima Marsh. — Yellowroot
(zan-thō-rī′zȧ sim-pli-cis′i-mȧ)

FAMILY: Ranunculaceae

LEAVES: Alternate, compound pinnate, or appearing bipinnate, clustered at stem ends, leaflets usually 3 to 5, 1 1/2 to 2 3/4″ long, the basal pair 2- to 3-lobed, ovate to ovate-oblong, incisely toothed, sometimes serrate, lustrous bright green.

BUDS: Lateral buds solitary, sessile, ovoid-oblong, compressed and flattened against stem, with about 3 scales; terminal buds (flower) much larger, fusiform, terete, with about 5 scales, red-brown.

STEM: Outer bark yellowish brown, inner bark yellow, branchlets pale greenish gray; pith large, round, continuous; leaf scars low, slightly curved, more than half encircling twig; about 11 bundle traces.

ROOT: Long, slender, deep yellow; hence, the name Yellowroot.

SIZE: 2 to 3′ in height and spreading freely as it suckers from the roots, observed 5′ high plants in Savill Gardens, England.

HARDINESS: Zone 3 to 9, in laboratory tests survived –55°F.

HABIT: A flat-topped ground cover with erect stems and celery-like leaves, filling the ground as a thicket; magnificent plant for difficult as well as normal sites especially where shade is a problem.

RATE: Medium.

TEXTURE: Medium in all seasons.

STEM AND ROOT COLOR: The inner bark and roots are yellow.

LEAF COLOR: Lustrous bright green in summer; very handsome foliage; fall color may develop golden yellow and orange, sometimes develops a slight purple fall color; holds late, have seen foliage in early December in Boston.

FLOWERS: Brownish purple, 1/6 to 1/4″ across, star-shaped, usually occurring before the leaves in March–April, borne in 2 to 4″ long racemes, forming a racemose panicle, not showy but interesting.

FRUIT: Follicle, single-seeded, pale brown.

CULTURE: Transplant in spring or fall; utilize container-grown plants or divide old plants and space these 18 to 24″ apart; prefers moist, well-drained soils and here makes its best growth; will do well in heavy soils; does well under average conditions but is less invasive in dry soils; full sun or partial shade; thrives along streams and moist banks; avoid high pH soils for it will develop chlorosis.

DISEASES AND INSECTS: None serious.

LANDSCAPE VALUE: A very desirable ground cover for moist areas; little known and grown; makes a very solid mat; the more I see it the more I believe it has been slighted by American gardeners; had several clumps in my Illinois garden where it did quite well; did notice chlorosis in a high pH pocket of soil; have seen tremendous plantings at Arnold Arboretum, Smith College and Heritage Plantation that would be sufficient to entice anyone to find a place for it in their landscape; abundant in Southeast along water courses in the dense shade of large trees; appears to savor a cool, moist root run.

PROPAGATION: Most effective method is by division of the parent plant; root cuttings will also work and June shoot cuttings treated with 8000 ppm IBA rooted in high percentages.

ADDITIONAL NOTES: From the juice (sap) the Indians extracted a yellow dye. Just a beautiful native that is extremely common along water courses in the southern Appalachians. Obviously is able to withstand flooding for certain periods. Lancaster, The Garden 120(12):742–743 (1995), offers a worthy treatise on the species. Also discussed in Arnoldia 54(2):31–35 (1994).

NATIVE HABITAT: New York to Kentucky and Florida. Introduced 1776.

Yucca L.
FAMILY: Agavaceae

There is a certain reluctance on my part to include these sword-like members of the Agavaceae but their use in landscaping, especially in the Midwest, Southeast, Southwest and West, is an undeniable and often horrible fact. When I see them in a landscape a feeling of old Mexico or the desert Southwest arises. Several are native to the Southeast and they are treated here. Some 40 species of evergreen perennial herbs or trees, acaulescent or branched. Too many Yuccas are sufficient reason to cause one to YUK!

Yucca filamentosa L. — Adam's-needle Yucca

LEAVES: Sword-like and ready for battle, 1 to 2 1/2′ long, 1 1/2 to 4″ wide, abruptly narrowed at the apex where the margins are usually infolded (cusped); from the margins curly thread-like filaments, 2 to 3″ long break away and are especially numerous toward the base.

Yucca filamentosa, (yuk′à fil-à-men-tō′sà), Adam's-needle Yucca, is a low evergreen shrub with stiffly erect and spreading leaves, the stem of which does not rise above ground level. The real attraction occurs during May–June (Athens), July–August (Urbana) when the 3 to 6′ high, erect, conical panicles are covered with 2 to 3″ diameter, yellowish white, pendulous flowers. It is best used in mass and is not particular as to soil as long as it is not excessively wet. This is a very hardy species and can be grown as far north as Minnesota with some protection. It has long been confused with **Yucca smalliana** Fern. but that species has thinner, flatter, narrower leaves, 7/8 to 1 3/4″ wide, long-tapered at apex. The central axis of the panicle is pubescent and the flowers are smaller (2″ long). *Yucca filamentosa* 'Ivory Tower' ('Ivory') forms a mounded rosette of sword-like leaves 3 to 4′ high, tall panicles of ivory-white flowers occur in summer, from Monrovia. Also listed by Monrovia is *Y. f.* 'Starburst' with narrow, long, green leaves striped with creamy yellow, tinged with pink in cooler weather; flowers like the species.

   Another closely related species is **Yucca flaccida** Haw. (now *Y. filifera* Chabaud.), Weakleaf Yucca, but the leaves of this species are 1 to 1 3/4′ long and 1 to 1 1/2″ wide and bent downwards, above the middle, long-pointed, with straight marginal thread-like fibers. The flowers are similar to *Y. filamentosa* but occur in a downy, shorter panicle. 'Golden Sword' has a green margin and yellow center while in 'Bright Edge' the color patterns are reversed. As near as I can determine they are *Y. flaccida* selections, although plants I have grown appear more like *Y. filamentosa* in habit. There are many variegated forms and unfortunately their taxonomic affinities elude this author. 'Bright Edge' is included in the Dirr garden near a rock wall with lavender, rosemary and thyme. A handsome combination and Bonnie was the orchestrator. 'Colour Guard' has luminous cream-yellow central striped variegation against green, turns rose in cold weather. 'Garland Gold' has rich broad golden interior bands on the green leaves, grows about 2′ high, more intense than 'Golden Sword'. 'Hofer's Blue' is rich blue-green foliaged.

   Yucca filamentosa occurs from South Carolina to Mississippi and Florida. Cultivated 1675. Zone 4 to 9. *Yucca flaccida* tends to be more inland from North Carolina to Alabama. Introduced 1816. Zone 4 to 9. *Yucca smalliana* occurs from North Carolina, west to Louisiana and Tennessee. Zone 5 to 9.

Yucca glauca Nutt. ex J. Fraser — Small Soapweed

Yucca glauca, (yuk′à glâ′kà), Small Soapweed, is an evergreen shrub with a low, often prostrate stem that carries a hemispherical head of leaves 3 to 4′ in diameter. The glaucous green leaves are narrow linear, 1 to 2 1/2′ long and 1/2 to 3/4″ wide. They taper to a fine point with whitish margins beset with a few threads, the dull greenish white, 2 1/2 to 3″ long, pendulous flowers occur on an erect, 3 to 4 1/2′ high, rarely branched raceme. Flowers occur in July–August. Variety *stricta* (Sims) Trel. is a vigorous form with a more branched inflorescence; in 'Rosea' the flowers are tinted pink on the outside. South Dakota to New Mexico. Introduced about 1656. Zone 4 to 8. This is a rather attractive species especially for its foliage.

Yucca gloriosa L. — Spanish-dagger

Yucca gloriosa, (yuk′à glō-ri-ō′sà), Spanish-dagger, is often encountered in the Southeast where it forms an evergreen shrub 6 to 8′ high or more. I have seen it branched but it often produces a single, thick, fleshy stem that is crowned with stiff, straight, 1 1/2 to 2′ long, 2 to 3″ wide, glaucous green, spine-tipped leaves. The leaves are usually entire. The pendulous, creamy white, often tinged red or purple, 4″ diameter flowers occur on an erect, narrowly conical, 3 to 8′ high, 1′ wide panicle from July to September. **Yucca recurvifolia** Salisb., Curveleaf Yucca, is similar (to 6′) except the upper leaves, 1 1/2 to 3′ long, 1 1/3 to

2 1/4″ broad, are recurved rather than straight as in *Y. gloriosa* and the inflorescence is more loosely branched. It is found along the coast of Georgia and Mississippi. Introduced 1794. Zone 6 to 9. *Yucca gloriosa* occurs from South Carolina to northeast Florida often on sand-dunes. Introduced 1550. Zone 6 to 9. There are variegated forms of both but I have not seen them in cultivation in the Southeast.

Propagation of the various species and cultivars is best achieved by dividing the fleshy roots (stems) and placing them horizontally in a suitable medium; shoots and roots regenerate from these pieces. Pollination of most species is effected by the pronuba moth. The moths emerge from the pupae before the flowering of the species with which they are associated. The female gathers pollen and rolls it into a ball; she then lays her eggs in the ovary of another flower and places the pollen-ball in the stigmatic chamber of the ovary. The grubs feed on the ovules but leave enough to supply adequate seeds. The yucca is entirely dependent on the moth and vice-versa. The seeds are black, compressed and remind of little wafers. They usually occur in great numbers. Seeds germinate without pretreatment but may take several months.

Yucca identification is scarcely straight lined and I have a difficult time separating the various species. Dr. Wilbur Duncan, Professor Emeritus, Department of Botany, University of Georgia supplied the following key to southeastern *Yucca* species that might prove helpful to yuccaphiles.

Key to Southeastern *Yucca* Species

1. Leaves rigid, margin minutely but sharply serrate; mature fruits fleshy . . . . 1. *Y. aloifolia*

1. Leaves pliable, leathery, margin entire and often frayed into filamentous threads; mature fruits dry . . . 2

   2. Leaf margin set with a thin, very narrow light brown strip (eroding with age), usually lacking curved or curled fibers; fruits not splitting open when mature 3

      3. Leaves erect to spreading, often drooping at ends with age; fruits mostly pendent, seeds glossy . . . . 2. *Y. gloriosa*

      3. Leaves mostly recurved, only the upper younger ones erect to spreading; fruits erect, seeds dull . . . . 3. *Y. recurvifolia*

   2. Leaf margin green to whitish, not extremely thin, usually with filamentous curved or curly fibers; fruits splitting open when mature 4

      4. Inflorescence a raceme, rarely a panicle, reaching just below to a little above tip of upper leaves . . . . 4. *Y. arkansas* (*Y. glauca* var. *mollis*)

      4. Inflorescence a panicle, rarely a raceme, held prominently above tip of upper leaves 5

         5. Leaves stiffly pliable, minutely scabrous on both surfaces, the tips cusped . . . . 5. *Y. filamentosa* (*Y. concava*)

         5. Leaves quite pliable, sometimes rough but not scabrous, the tip long-tapering and not cusped 6

           6. Leaves 1/2 to 2 1/2″ wide; styles oblong, whitish . . . . 6. *Y. flaccida* (*Y. smalliana*)

           6. Leaves 3/8 to 1 1/4″ (1 1/2″) wide; styles swollen, greenish . . . . 7. *Y. louisiansis*

Zanthoxylum americanum Mill. — Prickly-ash, Toothache Tree

FAMILY: Rutaceae
LEAVES: Alternate, compound pinnate, 6 to 8″(12″) long, 5 to 11, sometimes 13 leaflets, often with 1 or 2 spines on the main stalk where the leaflets are attached, leaflets 1 1/2 to 2 1/2″ long, ovate to oval, lustrous dark green above, pubescent below, minutely or not serrated.

Zanthoxylum americanum, (zan-thŏ-zī′lum à-mĕr-i-kā′num), Prickly-ash, is a seldom cultivated shrub or small tree (15 to 25′) that is prominently armed with 1/3 to 1/2″ long prickles. National champion is 28′ by 38′ in Beverly Hills Rouge Park, MI. The dark green foliage is handsome and not susceptible to insect or disease problems. The yellowish green flowers occur in axillary clusters before the leaves on the previous season's wood. This is a dioecious species. The 2-valved, 1/5″ long, black capsule matures in July–August and contains small, lustrous black seeds. This species might be used in poor soil areas or where a barrier plant is needed. Supposedly the stems and fruits were chewed by the Indians to alleviate toothache for the acrid juice has a numbing effect. From a landscape standpoint this is possibly the least desirable of the species treated here. Quebec to Nebraska and Virginia. Introduced about 1740. Zone 3 to 7.

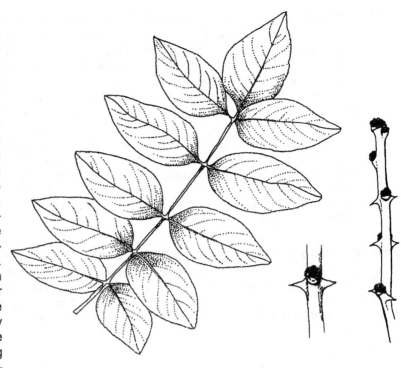

RELATED SPECIES:

Zanthoxylum clava-herculis L., (zan-thŏ-zī′lum clā′và-hĕr-kū′lis), Hercules-club, is a shrub or small tree, 25 to 30′ high, usually smaller, with glabrous leathery dark green, compound pinnate leaves with 7 to 9(19) leaflets. The leaves and stems are aromatic when bruised and an oil from the bark has medicinal qualities. Flowers are borne terminally. Important source of butterfly caterpillar food. Virginia along the coast to Texas and Oklahoma. Zone 7 to 9 (10).

Zanthoxylum piperitum DC., (zan-thō-zī'lum pī-pĕr'i-tum), Japanese Prickly-ash, is perhaps the most ornamental member of the genus. It forms a compact, dense shrub or small tree about 8 to 15' high and is clothed with handsome lustrous dark green leaves. Each 3 to 6" long leaf contains 11 to 23 sessile leaflets that average 3/4 to 1 1/2" long. The greenish yellow flowers occur in small 1 to 2" long corymbs in June. The fruits are reddish. The black seeds are ground and used as a pepper in Japan. The stems are armed with 1/3 to 1/2" long, flat spines that occur in pairs at each node. This is a rather handsome plant, the leaves of which may turn yellow in the fall. Northern China, Korea, Japan. Cultivated 1877. Zone 5 to 7.

Zanthoxylum schinifolium Sieb. & Zucc., (zan-thō-zī'lum skī-ni-fō'li-um), Peppertree, is a graceful medium-sized shrub growing 10' or more. The 3 to 7" long leaves are composed of 11 to 21, 3/4 to 1 1/2" long, deep green leaflets. The green-petaled flowers occur in 2 to 4" diameter, flattish corymbs in July–August and are followed by greenish or brownish (red) fruits. The 1/2" long spine is solitary at the node thus differentiating this species from *Z. piperitum* and *Z. americanum*. Japan, Korea, eastern China. Cultivated 1877. Zone 5 to 7.

Zanthoxylum simulans Hance., (zan-thō-zī'lum sim'ū-lanz), Flatspine Prickly-ash, is a graceful, spreading shrub growing 10' or greater in height, although I have seen plants almost tree-like and 15 to 20' high. The stems are armed with broad, flat, 1/4 to 3/4" long spines. The 3 to 5"(9") long leaves are composed of 7 to 11, 1/2 to 2" long, lustrous green leaflets. The greenish flowers occur in 2 to 2 1/2" wide panicles in July and are followed by reddish fruits. Northern and central China. Introduced 1869. Zone 5 to 7.

Zelkova serrata (Thunb.) Mak. — Japanese Zelkova
(zel-kō'và ser-rā'tà)

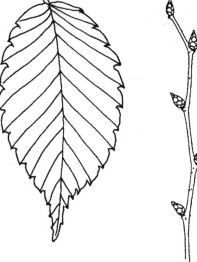

FAMILY: Ulmaceae
LEAVES: Alternate, simple, ovate to oblong-ovate, 1 1/4 to 2" long, or on vigorous shoots to 5" long, 3/4 to 2" wide, acuminate or apiculate, rounded or subcordate at base, sharply serrate with acuminate teeth, with 8 to 14 pairs of veins, dark green and somewhat rough above, glabrous or nearly so beneath; petiole—1/12 to 1/4" long.
BUDS: Ovoid, acutish, with many imbricate, shiny dark brown, broad scales, 1/4" long; diverge at 45° angle from stem.
STEM: Pubescent when young, glabrous at maturity, brown.
BARK: Beautiful, smooth-gray initially, lenticels cherry-like and prominent, finally resembling that of Chinese Elm but usually not as exfoliating.

SIZE: 50 to 80' in height, spread generally less than height; may grow over 120' high in native range.
HARDINESS: Zone (4)5 to 8; successful plants of 'Village Green' on UMaine campus, Orono; species was killed.
HABIT: In youth, a low-branched, vase-shaped tree; in old age maintaining a similar form with many ascending branches.
RATE: Medium, possibly fast in youth, 10 to 12' over a 4 to 6 year period, have seen 3 to 4' of growth on young trees.
TEXTURE: Medium-fine in leaf; medium in winter.
BARK: In youth cherry-like, reddish brown, heavily lenticelled; in old age gray-brown, often exfoliating with a character not unlike that of Chinese Elm, *Ulmus parvifolia*; not as exfoliating as *U. parvifolia*.
LEAF COLOR: Dark green in summer, may bronze or turn off-color in heat of Zone 7, variable from year to year; possibly the intensity and duration of the summer heat initiates the response; yellow-orange-brown in fall, possibly deep red to reddish purple; in Athens fall color is maximized from early to mid-November.
FLOWERS: Trimonoecious with male, bisexual, and female flowers in regular sequence on a short shoot; the average number of flowers was 22.6, 2.2, and 3.3, respectively, on each shoot; not showy, flowers in April with the leaves; in Athens have charted full flower as early as February 24 with some years the second week of March.
FRUIT: A small, kidney bean-shaped drupe, about 1/4" across, ripening in fall.

CULTURE: Transplants readily balled-and-burlapped; prefers moist, deep soil; pH adaptable; once established very wind and drought tolerant; young trees are susceptible to frost; prune in fall; displays reasonable pollution tolerance; in Kansas tests 'Village Green' averaged 11.6″ per year over a 9 year period.

DISEASES AND INSECTS: Susceptible to some of the problems which beset the elms; however, resistant to Dutch elm disease; the trees I have observed were much cleaner than the elms; shows good resistance to elm leaf beetle and Japanese beetle; English reference mentioned that it was proving susceptible to Dutch elm disease as well as bacterial canker.

LANDSCAPE VALUE: Very handsome tree because of good foliage, interesting growth habit and handsome bark; well suited to lawns, residential streets, parks, large areas; considered as a replacement for the American Elm but this has not, and will never, come about; there are beautiful specimens at the Arnold, Spring Grove, Cave Hill, Bristol, RI area; does quite well in the South and should be used more for streets and urban areas than it is; January 1998 trip to Wichita, KS confirmed good performance there where high pH soils are the norm.

CULTIVARS:

'Aurea'—Listed but with no technical description in *Biochemie Physiologie Pflanzen* 188(2):97–103 (1992), apparently a yellow leaf form.

'Autumn Glow'—Well-proportioned head, good leaf texture, deep purple fall color; John Barbour mentioned that fall color was zilch in his Monroe, GA nursery.

'Goblin'—Dwarf, rounded bush, 3 to 4′ high and wide.

'Goshiki'—Leaves are irregularly cream-marked, -speckled, -splashed, have seen the cultivar only once, leaf variegation pattern is akin to *Osmanthus heterophyllus* 'Goshiki'.

'Green Vase'—Vase-shaped with upright arching branches, very vigorous, producing a taller more graceful tree than 'Village Green', good dark green foliage, orange-brown to bronze-red fall color, 60 to 70′ by 40 to 50′, grows twice as fast as 'Village Green' as a young tree and 2-year-old trees are 2 to 3 times higher; in this author's opinion the best commercially available form; received the prestigious Styer Award in 1988 from the Pennsylvania Horticultural Society.

'Green Veil'—Upright narrow vase shape with gracefully arching shoots producing a soft pendulous effect, does not appear to grow as fast as the big three.

'Halka'—Have seen 'Green Vase', 'Village Green' and this form in the same nursery with 'Green Vase' and 'Halka' the fastest growing of the three and the most graceful; 50′ by 30′; nursery evaluations do not always ring true and plants of the three forms at the Milliken Arboretum, with 8 years of seasoning, reflect the greatness of 'Green Vase', followed by 'Village Green' and then 'Halka'; in Zone 7b 'Halka' is looser growing and open, the foliage never, summer and fall, a match for the other two, actually fall color is yellowish.

'Illinois Hardy'—Described by Princeton Nursery as surviving a particularly harsh northern Illinois winter that pummeled the other Zelkovas in the vicinity.

Korean Forms—Dense, broad-rounded, full-headed specimens from seed collected in Korea by Drs. Spongberg and Weaver, worthy germplasm for the nursery industry.

'Low Weeper'—Listed as a lovely weeping form, developing into a true specimen plant, offered by Arborvillage, Holt, MO.

'Parkview'—A selection with a good vase shape; size similar to species; Dr. Hasselkus reported that it winterkilled in Madison, WI.

'Spring Grove'—A handsome vase-shaped form with arching branches that appear slightly stiffer than 'Green Vase' and 'Halka'; the parent tree in Spring Grove, Cincinnati, OH puts other mature zelkovas to shame because of handsome dark green foliage, wine red fall color, excellent branch structure and bark; parent tree is probably 80′ with a 50 to 60′ spread; has been produced in limited quantities and young trees outplanted in Spring Grove show excellent form; January 1998 visit confirmed the superiority of 'Spring Grove' to 'Village Green'.

'Variegata'—Weak-growing, small-leaved (3/4 to 1 1/2″ long) form with a narrow, white rim around the margin of the leaf; might be a good bonsai subject.

'Village Green'—Selected by Princeton Nurseries, the tree grows more rapidly than ordinary seedlings and develops a smooth, straight trunk; the dark green foliage turns a rusty red in fall; much hardier than trees of Japanese origin and is highly resistant to Dutch elm disease and to leaf eating and bark beetles; I studied this selection closely during sabbatical and it is superior to the normal *Z. serrata*; it is vigorous and I recorded as much as 3′ of new growth in 1978; interestingly, the fall color was a reasonably good wine red while every other *Z. serrata* in the Arnold and Boston environs was a golden brown; in laboratory hardiness tests (Dr. Harold Pellett, University of Minnesota), we found that it was not as cold hardy as some seedling material in the Arnold's collections; probably could be grown in Chicago area without too much trouble; was killed at Madison, WI; listed in 1988

Princeton Nursery catalog as one zone hardier than 'Green Vase'; actually broad, broom head shape with age, denser in form that 'Green Vase', still a worthy selection.

PROPAGATION: Seeds germinate without pretreatment but percentage is better when stratified at 41°F for 60 days (this was my own personal experience). I have rooted cuttings taken from seedlings with 100% success when treated with 1000 ppm IBA. Cuttings from older trees root 50 to 60%(70%). Sprouts from 30- to 100-year-old trees rooted in the range of 46 to 83% with 68% average. P-ITB at 5000 ppm promoted excellent rooting, see *J. Environ. Hort.* 8(2):83–85 (1990). Cultivars are budded on seedling understock. Tissue culture has been successful.

ADDITIONAL NOTES: High quality timber, beautifully grained, used for expensive furniture; extreme durability and strength and used in construction. See *The Plantsman* 11(2):80–86 (1989) for detailed descriptions of *Z. serrata, Z. carpinifolia, Z. sinica, Z. abelicea,* and *Z. × verschaffeltii.*

NATIVE HABITAT: Found in rich colluvial soils at the foot of mountains and along the banks of rivers and streams. Japan, Korea, Taiwan, Manchuria. Introduced about 1860, 1862 to America.

RELATED SPECIES:

Zelkova carpinifolia (Pall.) K. Koch — Elm Zelkova, Caucasian Zelkova

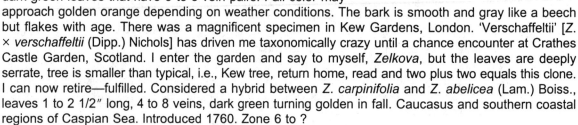

LEAVES: Alternate, simple, ovate or oval, 1 1/2 to 3″ long, 3/4 to 1 3/4″ wide, acute, rounded or subcordate, coarsely crenate-serrate, obtuse serrations, dark green with scattered hairs above, paler and more downy below, 6 to 8 vein pairs; petiole—about 1/8″ long.

Zelkova carpinifolia, (zel-ko′và kär-pĭ-ni-fō′li-à), Elm Zelkova, forms an ovoid or oblong head of rather upright branches, 50 to 75′ high, with a short, beech-like trunk. It is a beautiful tree with dark green leaves that have 6 to 8 vein pairs. Fall color may approach golden orange depending on weather conditions. The bark is smooth and gray like a beech but flakes with age. There was a magnificent specimen in Kew Gardens, London. 'Verschaffeltii' [*Z. × verschaffeltii* (Dipp.) Nichols] has driven me taxonomically crazy until a chance encounter at Crathes Castle Garden, Scotland. I enter the garden and say to myself, *Zelkova,* but the leaves are deeply serrate, tree is smaller than typical, i.e., Kew tree, return home, read and two plus two equals this clone. I can now retire—fulfilled. Considered a hybrid between *Z. carpinifolia* and *Z. abelicea* (Lam.) Boiss., leaves 1 to 2 1/2″ long, 4 to 8 veins, dark green turning golden in fall. Caucasus and southern coastal regions of Caspian Sea. Introduced 1760. Zone 6 to ?

Zelkova schneiderana Hand.-Mazz., (zel-kō′và shnī-dĕr-ā′nà), Schneider Zelkova, is a virtually unknown entity in the United States but may prove worthy of consideration. A tree in the Morris Arboretum developed excellent wine red fall color. At first, I thought the tree was *Z. serrata* 'Village Green', but the label said otherwise. The habit is akin to *Z. serrata.* The dark green, 1 3/4 to 4″ long, 3/4 to 2″ wide leaves have 7 to 14 indented vein pairs. Leaves are quite scabrous on their upper surface, much like sandpaper. Supposedly similar to *Z. sinica* and may grow to 100′. Have had correspondence with several individuals who commented on the outstanding fall color. Southwest, central, and eastern China. Introduced 1920. Zone 6 to 8.

Zelkova sinica Schneid. — Chinese Zelkova

LEAVES: Alternate, simple, elliptic to oblong, 1 to 2 1/2″ long, 2/3 to 1 1/8″ wide, acuminate or apiculate, rounded or broad cuneate, sharply serrate with acute or apiculate teeth, dull dark green and scabrous above, grayish green and pubescent below, 7 to 10 vein pairs; petiole—short, pubescent.

Zelkova sinica, (zel-kō′và sin′i-kà), Chinese Zelkova, is smaller (probably 20 to 40′ high under cultivation) than the other species and sometimes multi-trunked. The dark green leaves have 7 to 10(12) vein pairs. Leaves may turn orange-yellow in autumn. The bark is the handsomest of the genus and on old trunks assumes a rich mottle of gray, orange, and brown. One key difference I noted between this and *Z. serrata* is that the winter buds are more plump and rounded while those of *Z. serrata* are ovoid and pointed. There is a specimen at the Morton Arboretum that indicates the species may be hardier than the Zone 6 rating it was originally given. Cappiello reported cold hardy to Orono, ME. Also fine specimens at the Arnold Arboretum and the old USDA Bamboo farm, Savannah, GA. Central and eastern China at altitudes to 6500′. Introduced 1907–1908 by E.H. Wilson.

Zenobia pulverulenta (Bartr. ex Willd.) Pollard. — Dusty Zenobia

FAMILY: Ericaceae
LEAVES: Alternate, simple, semi-evergreen to deciduous, oval to oblong, 1 to 3″ long, obtuse or acutish, usually rounded at base, entire to serrulate-crenate, glabrous and covered more or less with a glaucous bloom on both surfaces, appearing green, gray-green to bluish green to glaucous blue.
STEM: Glabrous, glaucous, bloomy, often arching.

Zenobia pulverulenta, (zen-ō′bi-à pul-věr-ū-len′tà), Dusty Zenobia, is a 2 to 3′(6′) high, gracefully arching shrub. The leaves are particularly attractive and in fall may turn yellowish with a tinge of red. The 3/8″ broad, white, anise-scented, narrow bell-shaped flowers occur on slender, nodding, 3/4″ long stalks in axillary clusters during May–June. Cuttings are slow to root but it will come readily from seed. Requires acid, moist, well-drained soil for best growth. Full sun to partial shade. Often available from native plant nurseries. Some nurseries offer selected dusty blue foliage forms and appear to have no trouble rooting them. Great planting of green, blue-green, and bluish foliaged seedlings in a sweep by Bussey Brook in the Arnold Arboretum. Terrific native plant for wet soil areas. 'Raspberry Ripple' is a glaucous blue-foliaged form that develops good autumn color, flowers like the species, have only seen listed in Heronswood 1998 catalog. North Carolina to Florida. Introduced 1801. Zone 5 to 9. Injured, on occasions severely, in Orono, ME.

Ziziphus jujuba Mill. — Chinese Date (The generic name is also spelled *Zizyphus*)

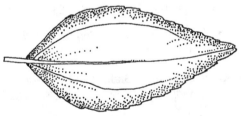

FAMILY: Rhamnaceae
LEAVES: Alternate, simple, oval, ovate to ovate-lanceolate, 1 to 2 1/2″ long, acutish or obtusish, oblique, 3-nerved at base, crenate-serrulate, lustrous dark green, glabrous, firm; petiole—1/8 to 1/4″ long.
STEM: Glabrous, flexuose, with paired spines at the nodes, the larger straighter ones to 1 1/4″, the shorter—decurved.

Ziziphus jujuba, (ziz′i-fus jö-jö′bà), Chinese Date, is a rather unique large shrub or small tree with handsome lustrous green foliage, rounded outline, and 15 to 20′(25′) ultimate size. Saw a 40′ high tree on United States capital grounds with blocky, persimmon-like bark. Leaves may turn good yellow in fall. The small, 1/4″ diameter, fragrant (grape soda), yellowish flowers occur 2 to 3 together from the leaf axils of the current season's growth. The edible fruits, which I have been fooled by on previous occasions, are plum-like to egg-shaped in outline, 1/2 to 1″ long and generally listed as dark red to black when ripe. Grown in China for over 4000 years and one of the five most popular fruits there. A former student's, Mr. Mark Callahan, greatest joy was trying to ruin my Monday by attacking me with some unusual plant from the vicinity of Hazelhurst, GA. The fruits he brought were more brownish than red or black. The species will grow in any well-drained, acid, alkaline, and droughty soil and based on observations at Tennessee Valley Nursery, Winchester, TN is hardy to -15°F. An old planting at Bernheim Arboretum is kind of limping along after exposure to -24°F in January 1994. Obviously this is a plant for the collector and will never find its way into the gardening mainstream. However, at least four individuals wanted to know why it was left out of the earlier editions. Well, I couldn't take the pressure and relented. Happy Chinese Dating. Seeds are the usual means of propagation and apparently require 3 months warm/3 months cold for best germination. June cuttings were rooted at 85% using 250 ppm IBA + 500 ppm NAA. Tissue culture has been successful. Cultivars are grafted to seedling understocks. 'Inermis' (var. *inermis* Rehd.) is thornless. 'Lang' is precocious and bears 1 1/2 to 2″ long, pear-shaped fruits while 'Li' has 2″ long, rounded fruits. 'Sherwood' produces large, sweet fruit that does well in the deep South. Southeastern Europe to southern and eastern Asia. Introduced about 1640. Zone 6 to 9.

BIBLIOGRAPHY

Adams, William D. 1976. *Trees for Southern Landscapes*. Pacesetter Press. Houston, TX. 85 p.

Adams, William D. 1979. *Shrubs and Vines for Southern Landscapes*. Pacesetter Press. Houston, TX. 70 p.

Agricultural Research Service. U.S.D.A. 1970. *Crabapples of Documented Authentic Origin*. Washington, D.C. 107 p.

Agricultural Research Service. U.S.D.A. 1973. *International Checklist of Cultivated Ilex*. Supt. of Doc., U.S. Gov. Printing Office. Washington, D.C. 84 p.

Alberta, University of. 1989. *Woody Ornamentals for the Prairies*. Faculty of Extension, University of Alberta. 279 p.

Allan, Mea. 1974. *Plants That Changed Our Gardens*. David and Charles. North Pomfret, VT.

Allen, Gertrude E. 1968. *Everyday Trees*. Houghton Mifflin. Boston, MA. 47 p.

American Horticultural Society. 1976. *Environmentally Tolerant Trees, Shrubs and Ground Covers*. AHS. Mt. Vernon, VA. 27 p.

Angelo, Ray. 1978. *Concord Area Shrubs*. Concord Field Station Museum of Comparative Zoology Harvard University. Cambridge, MA. 128 p.

Apgar, Austin C. 1892. *Trees of the Northern United States*. American Book Co. New York, NY. 224 p.

Apgar, Austin C. 1910. *Ornamental Shrubs of the United States*. American Book Co. NY. 352 p.

Arno, Stephen F. and Ramona P. Hammerly. 1977. *Northwest Trees*. Mountaineers. Seattle, WA. 161 p.

Arnold, Henry F. 1980. *Trees in Urban Design*. Van Nostrand Reinhold. New York, NY. 168 p.

Arthurs, Kathryn. 1979. *Sunset Lawns and Ground Covers*. Lane Publ. Co. Menlo Park, CA. 96 p.

Atkinson, Robert E. 1970. *The Complete Book of Groundcovers: Lawns You Don't Have to Mow*. McKay. New York, NY. 210 p.

Auburn University Staff. 1993. *Shade Trees for the Southeastern United States*. Alabama Agricultural Experiment Station. Auburn, AL. 132 p.

Baerg, Harry J. 1973. *How to Know the Western Trees*. W. C. Brown Co. Dubuque, IA. 179 p.

Bailey, Liberty Hyde. 1914. *The Standard Cyclopedia of Horticulture*. Vols. I, II, III. Macmillan Co. New York, NY. 3639 p.

Bailey, Liberty Hyde. 1923. *The Cultivated Evergreens*. Macmillan Co. New York, NY. 434 p.

Bailey, Liberty Hyde. 1933. *How Plants Get Their Names*. Macmillan Co. New York, NY. 209 p.

Bailey, Liberty Hyde. 1934. *Gardener's Handbook*. Macmillan Co. New York, NY. 292 p.

Bailey, Liberty Hyde. 1948. *The Cultivated Conifers in North America*. Macmillan Co. New York, NY. 404 p.

Bailey, Liberty Hyde. 1949. *Manual of Cultivated Plants*. Macmillan Co. New York, NY. 1116 p.

Bailey Hortorium. 1976. *Hortus III*. Macmillan Co. New York, NY. 1290 p.

Barber, Peter N. and C. E. Lucas Phillips. 1975. *The Trees Around Us*. Follett. Chicago, IL. 191 p.

Barnes, Burton V. 1981. *Michigan Trees: A Guide to the Trees of Michigan and the Great Lakes Region*. Univ. Michigan Press. Ann Arbor, MI. 383 p.

Bärtels, Andreas. 1986. *Gardening With Dwarf Trees and Shrubs*. Timber Press. Portland, OR. 294 p.

Bartrum, Douglas. 1957. *Rhododendrons and Magnolias*. Trinity Press. London. 176 p.

Bartrum, Douglas. 1959. *Lilac and Laburnum*. John Gifford, Ltd. London. 175 p.

Batdorf, Lynn R. 1995. *Boxwood Handbook: A Practical Guide to Knowing and Growing Boxwood*. The American Boxwood Society. Boyce, VA. 99 p.

Bawden, H. E. and J. E. G. Good. 1980. *Dwarf Shrubs: A Gardener's Guide*. Alpine Garden Society. Woking, Surrey, England. 121 p.

Bean, W. J. Variable dates. *Trees and Shrubs Hardy in the British Isles*, 8th Ed. Vols. I, II, III, IV and Supplement. John Murray Ltd. London.

Beckett, Kenneth A. 1975. *The Love of Trees*. Octopus Books. London. 96 p.

Beckett, Kenneth A. 1981. *The Complete Book of Evergreens*. Ward Lock Ltd. London. 160 p.

Benson, Lyman. 1959. *Plant Classification*. D. C. Heath and Co. Lexington, MA. 688 p.

Berg, Johann and Lothar Heft. 1969. *Rhododendron and Evergreen Deciduous Trees*. E. Ulmer. Stuttgart. 284 p.

Berns, E. R. 1967. *Native Trees of Newfoundland and Labrador*. St. John's. Newfoundland. 74 p.

Berry, James Berthold. 1966. *Western Forest Trees*. Dover. New York, NY. 238 p.

Bir, Richard E. 1992. *Growing and Propagating Showy Native Woody Plants*. The University of North Carolina Press. Chapel Hill, NC. 192 p.

Blackburn, Benjamin. 1952. *Trees and Shrubs in Eastern North America*. Oxford University Press. New York, NY. 358 p.

Blakeslee, Albert Francis and Chester Deacon Jarvis. 1972. *Northeastern Trees in Winter*. Dover. New York, NY. 264 p.

Blanchard, Robert O. and Terry A. Tattar. 1981. *Field and Laboratory Guide to Tree Pathology*. Academic Press, Inc. New York, NY. 285 p.

Bloom, Adrian. 1986. *Conifers and Heathers for a Year-Round Garden*. Aura Books and Floraprint Ltd. London. 78 p.

Bloom, Adrian. *Conifers for Your Garden*. American Garden Guild. 145 p.

Bloom, Adrian. 1996. *Summer Garden Glory*. HarperCollins. London. 144 p.

Bloom, Adrian. 1994. *Winter Garden Glory*. HarperCollins. London. 144 p.

Bloom, Alan. 1976. *Plantsman's Progress*. T. Dalton. Lavenham, England. 142 p.

Bloom, Alan and Adrian Bloom. 1992. *Blooms of Bressingham Garden Plants*. HarperCollins. London. 320 p.

Boddy, Frederick A. 1974. *Ground Cover and Other Ways to Weed Free Gardens*. David and Charles. North Pomfret, VT. 184 p.

Bonar, Ann. 1973. *Shrubs for All Seasons*. Hamlyn. London. 64 p.

Boom, Dr. B. K. and H. Kleijn. 1966. *The Glory of the Tree*. George G. Harrap and Co. Ltd. London. 128 p.

Britton, Nathaniel Lord and Addison Brown. 1912. *Illustrated Flora of the Northern United States, Canada and the British Possessions*, Vols. I, II, III. Charles Scribner's Sons. New York, NY.

Brooklyn Botanic Gardens' Plants and Gardens Handbooks covering a multitude of subjects. Book list available from Brooklyn Botanic Garden, 1000 Washington Avenue, Brooklyn, N.Y. 11225.

Brown, Clair Alan. 1966. *Mississippi Trees*. Mississippi Forestry Commission. Jackson, MS. 938 p.

Brown, Claud L. and L. Katherine Kirkman. 1990. *Trees of Georgia and Adjacent States*. Timber Press. Portland, OR. 292 p.

Brown, George E. 1972. *The Pruning of Trees, Shrubs & Conifers*. Faber and Faber. London. 351 p.

Brown, H. P. 1975. *Trees of New York State*. Dover Publications, Inc. New York, NY. 433 p.

Brown, H. P. 1938. *Trees of Northeastern United States*. Christopher Publishing House. Boston, MA. 488 p.

Brown, Russell G. and Melvin L. Brown. 1972. *Woody Plants of Maryland*. Univ. Maryland. College Park, MD. 347 p.

Buckley, A. R. 1980. *Trees and Shrubs of the Dominion Arboretum*. Agriculture Canada, Research Branch. 237 p.

Burns, George Plumer and Charles Herbert Otis. 1979. *The Handbook of Vermont Trees*. Tuttle. Portland, VT. 244 p.

Bush, Charles S. 1972. *Flowers, Shrubs and Trees for Florida Homes*. Florida Dept. Agr. and Consumer Services. Tallahassee, FL. 176 p.

Butcher, D. 1964. *Knowing Your Trees*. American Forestry Assoc. Washington, D.C. 349 p.

Byers, Marcus David, Jr. 1997. *Crapemyrtle: A Grower's Thoughts*. Owl Bay Publishers. Auburn, AL. 108 p.

Callaway, Dorothy. 1994. *The World of Magnolias*. Timber Press. Portland, OR. 322 p.

Campbell, Christopher S., Fay Hyland and Mary L. F. Campbell. 1977. *Winter Keys to Woody Plants of Maine*. University of Maine Press. Orono, ME. 52 p.

Cappiello, Paul E., and Lyle E. Littlefield. 1994. *Woody Landscape Plant Cold-Hardiness Ratings*. Maine Agricultural and Forest Experiment Station. Technical Bulletin 156. Orono, ME. 40 p.

Carpenter, Philip L., Theodore D. Walker, and Frederick O. Lanphear. 1975. *Plants in the Landscape*. W. H. Freeman. San Francisco, CA. 481 p.

Carter, Cedric J. 1964. *Illinois Trees: Their Diseases*. Ill. Nat. Hist. Survey. Urbana, IL. 96 p.

Carter, Cedric J. 1970. *Illinois Trees: Selection, Planting and Care*. Ill. Nat. Hist. Survey. Urbana, IL. 123 p.

Chadbund, Geoffrey. 1972. *Flowering Cherries*. Collins. London. 160 p.

Clapham, A. R., T. G. Tutin, and E. F. Warburg. 1962. *Flora of the British Isles*. University Press. Cambridge. 1269 p.

Clark, Ross C. 1962. *A Distributional Study of the Woody Plants of Alabama*. Univ. North Carolina Press. Chapel Hill, NC. 269 p.

Clark, Ross C. 1972. *The Woody Plants of Alabama*. Missouri Bot. Gar. Press. St. Louis, MO. 242 p.

Clouston, Brian (ed.) 1977. *Landscape Design and Plants*. Heinemann. London. 456 p.

Clovis, Jesse F. 1977. *The Woody Plants of the Core Arboretum*. West Virginia University. Morgantown, WV. 83 p.

Coats, Alice M. 1964. *Garden Shrubs and Their Histories*. E. P. Dutton & Co., Inc. New York, NY. 416 p.

Collingwood, George Harris. 1978. *Knowing Your Trees*. Amer. Forestry Assoc. Washington, D.C. 392 p.

Compton, James. 1987. *Success with Unusual Plants*. William Collins, Sons and Company Ltd. London. 192 p.

Coombes, Allen J. 1994. *Dictionary of Plant Names*. Timber Press. Portland, OR. 210 p.

Cope, Edward A. 1986. *Native and Cultivated Conifers of Northeastern North America*. Cornell University Press. Ithaca, NY. 231 p.

Core, Earl L. and Nelle P. Ammons. 1958. *Woody Plants in Winter*. Boxwood Press. California. 218 p.

Courtright, Gordon. 1988. *Trees and Shrubs for Temperate Climates*, 3rd Ed. Timber Press. Portland, OR. 250 p.

Cox, Peter A. 1973. *Dwarf Rhododendrons*. Macmillan Co. New York, NY. 296 p.

Cox, Peter A. and Kenneth N. E. Cox. 1988. *The Encyclopedia of Rhododendron Hybrids*. Timber Press. Portland, OR. 384 p.

Cox, Peter A. and Kenneth N. E. Cox. 1990. *Cox's Guide to Choosing Rhododendrons*. Timber Press. Portland, OR. 176 p.

Crittenden, Mabel and Jack Popovich. 1977. *Trees of the West*. Celestial Arts. Millbrae, CA. 212 p.

Crockett, James Underwood. 1972. *Evergreens*. Time-Life Series. Time-Life Books. New York, NY. 160 p.

Crockett, James Underwood. 1972. *Flowering Shrubs*. Time-Life Series. 160 p.

Crockett, James Underwood. 1972. *Lawns and Ground Covers*. Time-Life Series. 160 p.

Crockett, James Underwood. 1972. *Trees*. Time-Life Series. 160 p. (Numerous other books in Time-Life Series.)

Curtis, Carlton C. and S. C. Bausor. 1943. *The Complete Guide to North American Trees*. Collier Books. New York, NY. 342 p.

Curtis, Ralph W., John F. Cornman, and Robert G. Mower. 1962. *Vegetative Keys to Common Ornamental Woody Plants*. New York State College of Agriculture. Cornell University. Ithaca, NY. 83 p.

Dallimore, W. and Bruce A. Jackson. 1967. *A Handbook of Coniferae and and Ginkgoaceae*. St. Martin's Press.New York, NY. 700 p.

Dallimore, W. 1978. *Holly, Yew and Box*. John Lane Co., The Bodley Head. New York & London. 284 p.

Dame, Lorin L. and Henry Brooks. 1972. *Trees of New England*. Dover Publications, Inc. New York, NY. 196 p.

Daniels, Roland. 1975. *Street Trees*. Penn State Univ. State College, PA. 47 p.

Davis, Brian. 1987. *The Gardener's Illustrated Encyclopedia of Trees and Shrub*. Viking. Penguin Books Ltd. England. 256 p.

Davis, Donald E. and Norman D. Davis. 1975. *Guide and Key to Alabama Trees*. Kendall Hunt. Dubuque, IA. 136 p.

Dayton, William A. and Harlan P. Kelsey. 1942. *Standardized Plant Names*. J. Horace McFarland Co. Harrisburg, PA. 675 p.

Deam, Charles C. 1921. *Shrubs of Indiana*. State of Indiana Publication No. 44. Indiana. 350 p.

Dean, Blanche E. 1968. *Trees and Shrubs in the Heart of Dixie*. Southern University Press. Birmingham, AL. 246 p.

Dean, F. W. and L. C. Chadwick. *Ohio Trees*. Ohio State University. Columbus, OH. 127 p.

Degraaf, Richard M. and Gretchin M. Witman. 1979. *Trees, Shrubs, and Vines for Attracting Birds: A Manual for the Northeast*. Univ. Mass. Press. Amherst, MA. 194 p.

denBoer, Arie F. 1959. *Ornamental Crabapples*. American Association of Nurserymen. 226 p.

Dickerson, Brent C. 1992. *The Old Rose Advisor*. Timber Press. Portland, OR. 400 p.

Dirr, Michael A. 1978. *Photographic Manual of Woody Landscape Plants*. Stipes. Champaign, IL. 376 p.

Dirr, Michael. 1984. *All About Evergreens*. Ortho Books. San Francisco, CA. 96 p.

Dirr, Michael A. 1990. *Manual of Woody Landscape Plants*, 4th Ed. Stipes. Champaign, IL. 1007 p.

Dirr, Michael A. 1997. *Dirr's Hardy Trees and Shrubs*. Timber Press. Portland, OR. 494 p.

Dirr, Michael A. 1997. *Photo-Library of Woody Landscape Plants on CD-ROM*. PlantAmerica. Locust Valley, NY. 7,600 images.

Dirr, Michael A. and Charles W. Heuser, Jr. 1987. *The Reference Manual of Woody Plant Propagation*. Varsity Press, Inc. Athens, GA.

Duble, Richard and James C. Kell. 1977. *Southern Lawns and Groundcovers*. Pacesetter Press. Houston, TX. 91 p.

Duncan, Wilbur H. 1975. *Woody Vines of the Southeastern United States*. Univ. Georgia Press. Athens, GA. 75 p.

Duncan, Wilbur H. and Marion B. Duncan. 1987. *The Smithsonian Guide to Seaside Plants of the Gulf and the Atlantic Coasts*. Smithsonian Institution Press. Washington, D.C. 409 p.

Duncan, Wilbur H. and Marion B. Duncan. 1988. *Trees of the Southeastern United States*. University of Georgia Press. Athens, GA. 322 p.

Easterly, Nathan William. 1976. *Woody Plants of the Oak Openings*. Dept. of Biological Sciences, Bowling Green State University. Bowling Green, OH. 143 p.

Ebinger, J. E. and H. F. Thut. 1970. *Woody Plants of East Central Illinois*. Kendall Hunt. Dubuque, IA. 135 p.

Edlin, Herbert L. 1970. *Know Your Conifers*. Forestry Commission Booklet 15. HMSO. London. 64 p.

Edlin, Herbert L. 1976. *Trees and Man*. Columbia Univ. Press. New York, NY. 269 p.

Edlin, Herbert L. 1978. *The Illustrated Encyclopedia of Trees: Timbers and Forests of the World*. Harmony Books. New York, NY. 256 p.

Edlin, Herbert L. 1978. *The Tree Key: A Guide to Identification in Garden, Field, and Forest*. Scribner. New York, NY. 280 p.

Egolf, Donald R. and Anne O. Andrick. 1978. *The Lagerstroemia Handbook Checklist*. Amer. Assoc. Bot. Gardens and Arbor. 72 p.

Elias, Thomas S. 1980. *The Complete Trees of North America: Field Guide and Natural History*. Van Nostrand Reinhold. New York, NY. 948 p.

Elias, Thomas S. 1981. *Illustrated Guide to Street Trees*. The New York Botanical Garden. Bronx, NY. 107 p.

Elmore, Francis H. 1976. *Shrubs and Trees of the Southwest Uplands*. Southwest Parks and Monuments Association. Tucson, AZ. 214 p.

Els, David (ed.). 1994. *Dictionary of Horticulture*. Penguin Books. New York, NY. 830 p.

Elwes, Henry John and Augustine Henry. 1906–1913. *The Trees of Great Britain and Ireland*. VII volumes with index plus VII accompanying volumes of photographs. Magnificent Work. Privately printed.

English, L. L. 1970. *Illinois Trees and Shrubs: Their Insect Enemies*. Ill. Nat. Hist. Survey. Urbana, IL. 91 p.

Evelyn, John. 1979. *Silva: et. al.* Strobart and Son. London. 235 p.

Everett, Thomas H. 1980. *The New York Botanical Garden Illustrated Encyclopedia of Horticulture*. Garland STP. Press. New York, NY.

Evison, Raymond J. 1998. *The Gardener's Guide to Growing Clematis*. Timber Press. Portland, OR. 160 p.

Farrer, Reginald. 1938. *The English Rock-Garden*. Vol. 1 & 2. C. & E. C. Jack, Ltd. Edinburgh. 524 p. and 504 p.

Feathers, David L. and Milton H. Brown. 1978. *The Camellia (History, Culture, Genetics and a Look Into Its Future Development.)* R. L. Bryan Co. Columbia, SC. 476 p.

Ferguson, Barbara (ed.). 1982. *All About Trees*. Ortho Books. San Francisco, CA. 112 p.

Fernald, Merritt Lyndon. 1950. *Gray's Manual of Botany*, 8th Ed. American Book Co. New York, NY. 1632 p.

Fiala, John L. 1988. *Lilacs*. Timber Press. Portland, OR. 372 p.

Fiala, John L. 1995. *Flowering Crabapples*. Timber Press. Portland, OR. 340 p.

Finch, Irene. 1969. *Autumn Trees*. Longmans. London. 79 p.

Fish, Margery. 1970. *Ground Cover Plants*. David and Charles. North Pomfret, VT. 144 p.

Foley, Daniel J. 1969. *The Flowering World of "Chinese" Wilson*. Macmillan Co. New York, NY. 334 p.

Foley, Daniel J. 1972. *Ground Covers for Easier Gardening*. Dover Publ. Inc. New York, NY. 224 p.

Foley, Daniel J. 1974. *Gardening by the Sea*. Chilton Book Co. Radnor, PA. 295 p.

Forest Service, U.S.D.A. 1974. *Seeds of Woody Plants in the United States*, Agriculture Handbook No. 450. Supt. of Doc. U.S. Gov. Printing Office. Washington, D.C. 883 p.

Forsberg, Junius L. 1979. *Diseases of Ornamental Plants*. Univ. Illinois Press. Urbana-Champaign, IL. 222 p.

Frederick, William H., Jr. 1975. *100 Great Garden Plants*. Knopf. New York, NY. 207 p.

Galle, Fred C. 1985. *Azaleas*. Timber Press. Portland, OR. 486 p.

Galle, Fred C. 1997. *Hollies: The Genus Ilex*. Timber Press. Portland, OR. 621 p.

Garden and Landscape Staff, Southern Living Magazine. 1980. *Trees and Shrubs, Gound Covers, Vines*. Oxmoor House. Birmingham, AL. 260 p.

Gardiner, J.M. 1989. *Magnolias*. The Globe Pequot Press. Chester, CT. 144 p.

Gault, S. Millar. 1976. *The Color Dictionary of Shrubs*. Crown Publishing, Inc. New York, NY. 208 p.

Gerhold, Henry D., Willet N. Wandell, and Norman L. Lacasse. 1993. *Street Tree Fact Sheets*. Pennsylvania State University. University Park, PA.

Gilman, Edward F. 1997. *Trees for Urban and Suburban Landscapes*. Delmar Publishers. Albany, NY. 662 p.

Godfrey, Robert K. 1988. *Trees, Shrubs, and Woody Vines of Northern Florida and Adjacent Georgia and Alabama*. Univ. of Georgia Press. Athens, GA. 734 p.

Gorer, Richard. 1971. *Multi-season Trees and Shrubs*. Faber and Faber. London. 192 p.

Gorer, Richard. 1976. *Trees and Shrubs: A Complete Guide*. David and Charles. North Pomfret, VT. 264 p.

Graetz, Karl E. 1973. *Seacoast Plants of the Carolinas for Conservation and Beautification*. U.S.D.A. Soil Conservation Service. Raleigh, NC. 206 p.

Grant, John A. and Carol L. Grant. 1990. *Trees and Shrubs for Pacific Northwest Gardens*, 2nd Ed. Timber Press. Portland, OR. 456 p.

Graves, Arthur Harmount. 1956. *Illustrated Guide to Trees and Shrubs*. Harper and Row. New York, NY. 271 p.

Green, Charlotte Hilton. 1939. *Trees of the South*. The University of North Carolina Press. Chapel Hill, NC. 551 p.

Greene, Wilhelmina F. and Hugo L. Blomquist. 1953. *Flowers of the South*. The University of North Carolina Press. Chapel Hill, NC. 208 p.

Greuter, W., F. R. Barrie, H. M. Burdet, W. G. Chaloner, V. Demoulin, D. L. Hawksworth, P. M. Jørgensen, D. H. Nicolson, P. C. Silva, and P. Trehane (editorial committee). 1994. *International Code of Botanical Nomenclature*. Koeltz Scientific Books. Königstein, Germany.

Grey-Wilson, Christopher and Victoria Matthews. 1997. *Gardening with Climbers*. Timber Press. Portland, OR. 160 p.

Griffiths, Mark. 1994. *Index of Garden Plants*. Timber Press. Portland, OR. 1200 p.

Grimm, William Carey. 1962. *The Book of Trees*. Stackpole Co. Harrisburg, PA. 493 p.

Grimm, William Carey. 1966. *Recognizing Native Shrubs*. Stackpole Co. Harrisburg, PA. 319 p.

Grimm, William Carey. 1969. *Recognizing Flowering Wild Plants*. Stackpole Co. Harrisburg, PA. 319 p.

Grimm, William Carey. 1970. *Home Guide to Trees, Shrubs and Wildflowers*. Stackpole Co. Harrisburg, PA. 320 p.

Grounds, Roger. 1974. *Shrubs and Decorative Evergreens*. Ward Lock. London. 127 p.

Grounds, Roger. 1974. *Trees for Smaller Gardens*. Dent. London. 269 p.

Halfacre, R. Gordon and Anne R. Shawcroft. 1989. *Landscape Plants of the Southeast*. Sparks Press. Raleigh, NC. 426 p.

Hansell, Dorothy E. (ed.). 1970. *Handbook on Hollies*. The American Horticultural Magazine. Mt. Vernon, VA. 333 p.

Hardwicke, Denis, A. R. Toogood, and A. J. Huxley. 1973. *Evergreen Garden Trees and Shrubs*. Macmillan Co. New York, NY. 216 p.

Harlow, William M. 1942. *Trees of the Eastern United States and Canada*. Whittlesey House. New York, NY. 512 p.

Harlow, William M. 1946. *Fruit Key and Twig Key*. Dover Publications, Inc. New York, NY. 56 p.

Harlow, William M. and Ellwood S. Harrar. 1969. *Textbook of Dendrology*, 5th Ed. McGraw-Hill. New York, NY. 512 p.

Harrar, Ellwood S. and J. George Harrar. 1962. *Guide to Southern Trees*, 2nd Ed. Dover Publications, Inc. New York, NY. 709 p.

Harris, Cyril Charles (ed.). 1979. *An Illustrated Guide to Flowering Trees and Shrubs*. Orbis. London. 444 p.

Harris, Richard W. 1992. *Arboriculture: Care of Trees, Shrub, and Vines in the Landscape*. Prentice-Hall, Inc. Englewood Cliffs, NJ. 674 p.

Harrison, Charles R. 1975. *Ornamental Conifers*. Hafner Press. New York, NY. 224 p.

Harrison, Richmond E. 1974. *Handbook of Trees and Shrubs*. A.H. & A.W. Reed Ltd. Wellington, New Zealand. 409 p.

Harrison, Richmond E. and Charles R. Harrison. 1965. *Trees and Shrubs*. Charles E. Tuttle. Rutland, VT. 199 p.

Hartmann, Hudson T., Fred T. Davies, Jr., Robert L. Geneve and Dale E. Kester. 1997. *Plant Propagation: Principles and Practices*, 6th Ed. Prentice-Hall, Inc. Upper Saddle River, NJ. 770 p.

Haworth-Booth, Michael. 1984. *The Hydrangeas*. Constable Publishers. London. 217 p.

Hay, Roy and D. M. Synge. 1975. *The Color Dictionary of Flowers and Plants for Home and Garden*. Crown. New York, NY. 584 p.

Helmer, Jane Coleman and John L. Threlkeld. 1979. *Pictorial Library of Landscape Plants*. Merchants Publ. Co. Kalamazoo, MI. 335 p.

Helwig, Larry. 1975. *Native Shrubs of South Dakota*. 97 p.

Heptig, George H. 1971. *Diseases of Forest and Shade Trees of the United States*. Agricultural Handbook No. 386. U.S.D.A. Forest Service. Supt. of Doc. U.S. Gov. Printing Office. Washington, D.C. 658 p.

Hicks, Ray R. and Scott Swearingen. 1978. *Woody Plants of the Western Gulf Region*. Kendall/Hunt. Dubuque, IA. 339 p.

Hightshoe, Gary L. 1978. *Native Trees for Urban and Rural America: A Planting Design Manual for Environmental Designers*. Iowa State. Ames, IA. 370 p.

Hillier and Sons. 1981. *The Hillier Colour Dictionary of Trees and Shrubs*. David and Charles. North Pomfret, VT. 323 p.

Hillier and Sons. (Allen Coombes, editor). 1991. *The Hillier Manual of Trees and Shrubs*. David and Charles. North Pomfret, VT. 704 p.

Hoag, Donald, G. 1965. *Trees and Shrubs for the Northern Plains*. North Dakota Institute for Regional Studies. Fargo, ND. 376 p.

Hora, Bayard. 1981. *The Oxford Encyclopedia of Trees of the World*. Oxford Univ. Press. Oxford. 288 p.

Hosie, R. C. 1973. *Native Trees of Canada*. Queens Printer. Ottawa. 380 p.

Hudak, Joseph. 1980. *Trees for Every Purpose*. McGraw-Hill. New York, NY. 229 p.

Hume, H. Harold. 1954. *Gardening in the Lower South*. Macmillan Co. New York, NY. 377 p.

Huxley, Anthony (ed.). 1973. *Deciduous Garden Trees and Shrubs*. Macmillan Co. New York, NY. 216 p.

Huxley, Anthony (ed.). 1973. *Evergreen Garden Trees and Shrubs*. Macmillan Co. New York, NY. 181 p.

Hyams, Edward. 1965. *Ornamental Shrubs for Temperate Zone Gardens*. A.S. Barnes and Co. New York, NY. 315 p.

Hyland, Fay. 1977. *The Woody Plants of Sphagnous Bogs of Northern New England and Adjacent Canada*. Univ. Maine Press. Orono, ME. 110 p.

Ingram, Collingwood. 1948. *Ornamental Cherries*. Country Life Ltd. London. 259 p.

Jacobson, Arthur Lee.1996. *North American Landscape Trees*. Ten Speed Press. Berkeley, CA. 722 p.

Janick, Jules. 1986. *Horticultural Science*, 4th Ed. W. H. Freeman and Co. New York, NY. 746 p.

Jaynes, Richard A. 1997. *Kalmia*. Timber Press. Portland, OR. 360 p.

Jefferson, Roland M. and Alan E. Fusonie. 1977. *The Japanese Flowering Cherry Trees of Washington D.C.; A Living Symbol of Friendship*. U.S.D.A. Washington, D.C. 66 p.

Jefferson-Brown, M. J. 1957. *The Winter Garden*. Faber and Faber. London. 156 p.

Jennings, Neal A. 1978. *Broadleaf Trees for Nebraska*. Coop. Ext. Service, Univ. Nebraska. Lincoln, NE. 58 p.

Jobling, J. and A. F. Mitchell. 1974. *Field Recognition of British Elms*. Forestry Commission Booklet 42. HMSO. London. 24 p.

Johns, Leslie. 1973. *Garden Trees*. David and Charles. North Pomfret, VT. 172 p.

Johnson, Hugh and Paul Miles. 1981. *The Pocket Guide to Garden Plants*. Simon and Shuster. New York, NY. 192 p.

Johnson, Hugh. 1973. *The International Book of Trees*. Simon and Shuster. New York, NY. 286 p.

Johnson, Hugh. 1979. *The Principles of Gardening*. Simon and Shuster. New York, NY. 272 p.

Johnson, Warren T. and Howard H. Lyon. 1982. *Diseases of Trees and Shrubs*. Cornell University Press. Ithaca, NY. 575 p.

Johnson, Warren T. and Howard H. Lyon. 1991. *Insects That Feed on Trees and Shrubs*. Cornell University Press. Ithaca, NY 560 p.

Johnstone, G. H. 1955. *Asiatic Magnolias in Cultivation*. The Royal Horticultural Society. London. 160 p.

Jones, Almut G. and David T. Bell. 1976. *Guide to Common Woody Plants of Robert Allerton Park*. Stipes Publishing Company. Champaign, IL. 36 p.

Jones, George Neville. 1971. *Flora of Illinois*. University of Notre Dame. Notre Dame, IN. 401 p.

Jones, Ronald K. and Robert C. Lamb. *Diseases of Woody Ornamental Plants and Their Control in Nurseries*. Cooperative Extension Service, University of Georgia. Athens, GA. 130 p.

Jones, Samuel B. and Arlene E. Luchsinger. 1986. *Plant Systematics*. McGraw-Hill. New York, NY. 512 p.

Jones, Samuel B. and Leonard E. Foote. 1989. *Native Shrubs and Woody Vines of the Southeast*. Timber Press.Portland, OR. 199 p.

Kartesz, John. 1994. *A Synonymized Checklist of the Vascular Flora of the United States, Canada, and Greenland*. Volume I—Checklist. Timber Press. Portland, OR. 622 p.

Kartesz, John. 1994. *Synonymized Checklist of the Vascular Flora of the United States, Canada, and Greenland*. Volume II—Thesaurus. Timber Press. Portland, OR. 816 p.

Keator, Glenn. 1994. *Complete Garden Guide to the Native Shrubs of California*. Chronicle Books. San Francisco, CA. 314 p.

Keeler, Harriet L. 1916. *Our Northern Shrubs*. Charles Scribner's Sons. New York, NY. 519 p.

Keith, Rebecca McIntosh, and F.A. Giles. 1980. *Dwarf Shrubs for the Midwest*. University of Illinois at Urbana-Champaign, College of Agriculture Special Publication 60. 163 p.

Kelly, George W. 1979. *Shrubs for the Rocky Mountains: A Manual of the Use and Care of Shrubs in the Rocky Mountain Area*. Rocky Mountain Horticultural Publ. Co. Cortez, CO. 171 p.

Kelly, George W. 1970. *A Guide to the Woody Plants of Colorado*. Purett Publ. Co. Boulder, CO. 180 p.

Kelsey, Harlan P. and William A. Dayton. 1942. *Standardized Plant Names*, 2nd Ed. J. Horace McFarland Co. Harrisburg, PA. 675 p.

Kent, Adolphus H. 1900. *Veitch's Manual of the Coniferae*. James Veitch and Sons, Ltd. Chelsea, England. 562 p.

Knobel, Edward. 1972. *Identify Trees and Shrubs by Their Leaves*. Dover Publications, Inc. New York, NY. 47 p.

Koller, Gary L. and Michael A. Dirr. 1979. *Street Trees for Home and Municipal Landscapes*. Arnoldia 39:73–237.

Krüssmann, Gerd. 1982. *Pocket Guide to Choosing Woody Ornamentals*. Timber Press. Portland, OR. 140 p.

Krüssmann, Gerd. 1985. *Manual of Cultivated Broad-Leaved Trees and Shrub.* Vol. I–III. Timber Press. Portland, OR. 1923 p.

Krüssmann, Gerd. 1985. *Manual of Cultivated Conifers.* Timber Press. Portland, OR. 361 p.

Kumlier, Loraine L. 1946. *The Friendly Evergreens.* Rinehart. New York, NY. 237 p.

Labadie, Emile L. 1978. *Native Plants for Use in the California Landscape.* Sierra City Press. Sierra City, CA. 244 p.

Lamb, Samuel H. 1975. *Woody Plants of the Southwest.* Sunstone Press. Sante Fe, NM. 122 p.

Lancaster, Roy. 1974. *Trees for Your Garden.* Charles Scribner's Sons. New York, NY. 145 p.

Lancaster, Roy. 1989. *Travels in China.* Antique Collector's Club Ltd. Woodbridge, England. 520 p.

Lanzara, Paolo. 1978. *Simon and Shuster's Guide to Trees.* Simon and Shuster. New York, NY. 327 p.

Lawrence, George H. M. 1951. *Taxonomy of Vascular Plants.* Macmillan Co. New York, NY. 823 p.

Lawson-Hall, Toni and Brian Rothera. 1995. *Hydrangeas, A Gardeners' Guide.* Timber Press. Portland, OR. 160 p.

Leach, David G. 1961. *Rhododendrons of the World.* Charles Scribner's Sons. New York, NY. 544 p.

Lee, Frederic P. 1965. *The Azalea Book.* D. Van Nostrand Company, Inc. New York, NY. 435 p.

Lemmon, Robert S. 1952. *The Best Loved Trees of America.* The American Garden Guild. Garden City, NY. 254 p.

Lentz, A. N. *Common Forest Trees of New Jersey.* Ext. Bull. 396. Coop. Ext. Service Rutgers Univ. New Brunswick, NJ.

Leopold, Donald J., William C. McComb, and Robert N. Miller. 1998. *Trees of the Central Hardwood Forests of North America.* Timber Press. Portland, OR. 509 p.

Li, Hui-lin. 1963. *The Origin and Cultivation of Shade and Ornamental Trees.* Univ. of Pennsylvania Press. Philadelphia, PA. 282 p.

Li, Hui-lin. 1972. *Trees of Pennsylvania, The Atlantic States and the Lake States.* Univ. of Pennsylvania Press. Philadelphia, PA. 276 p.

Little, Elbert L. 1968. *Southwestern Trees—A Guide to the Native Species of New Mexico and Arizona.* U.S.D.A. Forest Service. Washington, D.C. 109 p.

Little, Elbert L. 1977. *Atlas of United States Trees.* U.S.D.A. Superintendent Documents. Washington, D.C.

Little, Elbert L. 1980. *The Audubon Society Field Guide to North American Trees, Eastern Region.* Knopf. New York, NY. 714 p.

Little, Elbert L. 1980. *The Audubon Society Field Guide to North American Trees, Western Region.* Knopf. New York, NY. 639 p.

Logan, Harry Britton. 1974. *A Traveler's Guide to North American Gardens.* Charles Scribner's Sons. New York., NY. 253 p.

Lord, Tony (ed.). 1997. *The RHS Plant Finder 1997–1998.* Dorling Kindersley. London. 918 p.

Loudon, John C. 1836. *Arboretum et Fruticetum Britannicum.* VII volumes plus index. A. Spottiswoode. London.

Lyons, Chester Peter. 1952. *Trees, Shrubs and Flowers to Know in British Columbia.* J. M. Dent & Sons Ltd. Canada. 194 p.

Lyons, Chester Peter. 1956. *Trees, Shrubs, and Flowers to Know in Washington.* Dent. Toronto. 211 p.

Macdonald, Bruce. 1986. *Practical Woody Plant Propagation for Nursery Growers*. Timber Press. Portland, OR. 669 p.

MacKenzie, David S. 1997. *Perennial Ground Covers*. Timber Press. Portland, OR. 379 p.

Maki, Mary M., P. Bischoff, E. H. Emerson, L. T. Grady, B. L. Hoadley, H. W. Lanphear, and M. A. Livingston. 1975. *Trees in Amherst*. Garden Club of Amherst. Amherst, MA. 116.

Makins, F. K. 1948. *The Identification of Trees and Shrubs*. E. P. Dutton and Co. New York, NY. 350 p.

Mallet, Corinne. 1994. *Hydrangeas*. Volume 2. Centre d'Art Floral. Varengeville, France. 112 p.

Mallet, Corinne, Robert Mallet, and Harry van Trier. 1992. *Hydrangeas*. Centre d'Art Floral. Varengeville, France. 112 p.

Maino, Evelyn and Frances Howard. 1955. *Ornamental Trees*. Univ. Calif. Press. Berkeley, CA. 219 p.

Marshall, Humphry. 1967. *Arbustum Americanum: The American Grove*. Hafner Publishing Co. New York, NY and London. 278 p.

Mayer, A. M. and A. Poljakoff-Mayber. 1982. *The Germination of Seeds*. Pergamon Press. New York, NY. 211 p.

McClintock, Elizabeth. 1957. "A Monograph of the Genus *Hydrangea*." *Proc. California Academy of Sciences* 29:147–256.

McClintock, Elizabeth and Andrew T. Leiser. 1979. *An Annotated Checklist of Woody Ornamental Plants of California, Oregon and Washington*. Univ. Calif. Berkeley. 134 p.

McMillan, Browse, P. D. A. 1979. *Hardy Woody Plants from Seeds*. Grower Books. London. 163 p.

Menninger, Edwin A. 1970. *Flowering Vines of the World: An Encyclopedia of Climbing Plants*. Hearthside Press. New York, NY. 410 p.

Meyer, Frederick G., Peter M. Mazzeo, and Donald H. Ross. 1994. *A Catalog of Cultivated Woody Plants of the Southeastern United States*. USDA-ARS National Arboretum Contribution Number 7. Washington, D.C. 330 p.

Miller, Howard A. and H. E. Jacques. 1978. *How to Know the Trees*. Wm. C. Brown. Dubuque, IA. 263 p.

Miller, Howard A. and Samuel H. Lamb. 1985. *Oaks of North America*. Naturegraph Publishers, Inc. Happy Camp, CA. 327 p.

Mitchell, A. F. 1972. *Conifers in the British Isles*. Forestry Commission Handbook 33. HMSO London. 322 p.

Mitchell, A. F. 1974. *A Field Guide of the Trees of Britain and Northern Europe*. Collins. London. 415 p.

Mitchell, A. F. 1981. *The Gardeners Book of Trees*. J.M. Dent. London. 216 p.

Mitchell, A. F. 1985. *The Complete Guide to Trees of Britain and Northern Europe*. Dragon's World Ltd. Surrey, England. 208 p.

Mohlenbrock, Robert H. 1972. *Forest Trees of Illinois*. State of Ill. Dept. of Conservation. Div. of Forestry. 178 p.

Montgomery, F. H. 1970. *Trees of Canada and the Northern United States*. Ryerson, Toronto. 144 p.

Moody, Mary (ed.). 1992. *The Illustrated Encyclopedia of Roses*. Timber Press. Portland, OR. 304 p.

Moore, Dwight M. 1972. *Trees of Arkansas*. Arkansas Forestry Commission. Little Rock, AR. 142 p.

Morrisey, Sharon Irwin and F. A. Giles. 1990. *Large Flowering Shrubs for the Midwest*. University of Illinois at Urbana-Champaign, College of Agriculture Special Publication 74. 240 p.

Morton Arboretum Staff. 1990. *Woody Plants of the Morton Arboretum*. Lisle, IL. 506 p.

Mulligan, Brian O. 1977. *Woody Plants in the University of Washington Arboretum, Washington Park*. Univ. Washington. 183 p.

Neelands, R. W. 1968. *Important Trees of Eastern Forests*. U.S.D.A.-Forest Service Southern Region. Atlanta, GA. 111 p.

Nelson, W. R., Jr. 1975. *Landscaping Your Home*. Circ. 111. U. of I. Coop. Ext. Service. Champaign, IL. 246 p.

Nelson, W. R., Jr. 1985. *Planting Design: A Manual of Theory and Practice*. Stipes. Champaign, IL. 271 p.

Newcomb, Lawrence. 1977. *Newcomb's Wildflower Guide*. Little, Brown. Boston, MA. 490 p.

Newsholme, Christopher. 1992. *Willows: The Genus Salix*. Timber Press. Portland, OR. 224 p.

Nicholson, Barbara E. and Arthur R. Clapham. 1975. *The Oxford Book of Trees*. Oxford University Press. London. 216 p.

Notcutt, R. C. 1926. *A Handbook of Flowering Trees and Shrubs for Gardeners*. Martin Hopkinson and Co. Ltd. Covent Garden. 245 p.

Notcutts Nurseries Ltd. 1981. *Notcutts Book of Plants*. The Thelford Press Ltd. London and Thelford. 328 p.

Novak, F. A. 1965. *The Pictorial Encyclopedia of Plants and Flowers*. Crown Publishers, Inc. New York, NY. 589 p.

Odenwald, Neil G., Charles F. Fryling, Jr., and Thomas E. Pope. 1996. *Plants for American Landscapes*. Louisiana State University Press. Baton Rouge, LA. 266 p.

Odenwald, Neil G. and James R. Turner. 1996. *Identification, Selection and Use of Southern Plants for Landscape Design*. Claitor's Publishing Division. Baton Rouge, LA. 684 p.

Ohwi, Jisaburo. 1965. *Flora of Japan*. Smithsonian Institution. Washington, D.C. 1067 p.

Osborne, Richard. 1975. *Garden Trees*. Lane Publ. Co. Menlo Park, CA. 96 p.

Osborne, Robert. 1996. *Hardy Trees and Shrubs*. Key Porter Books Ltd. Toronto, Canada. 113 p.

Otis, Charles Herbert. 1954. *Michigan Trees*. Univ. of Michigan Press. Ann Arbor, MI. 333 p.

Ouden, P. Den and B. K. Boom. 1965. *Manual of Cultivated Conifers*. M. Nijhoff. The Hague. Netherlands. 526 p.

Outdoor World. 1973. *Trees of America*. Outdoor World. Waukesha, WI. 192 p.

Partyka, R. E. 1980. *Woody Ornamentals: Plants and Problems*. Chemlawn Corp. Columbus, OH. 427 p.

Peattie, Donald Culross. 1950. *A Natural History of Trees*. Houghton Mifflin Co. Boston, MA. 606 p.

Peattie, Donald Culross. 1953. *A Natural History of Western Trees*. Houghton Mifflin Co. Boston, MA. 751 p.

Pellett, Harold, Nancy Ross, and Mervin Eisel. 1991. *The Right Tree Handbook*. Minnesota Landscape Arboretum. University of Minnesota. Chanhassen, MN.

Perry, Bob. 1992. *Landscape Plants for Western Regions*. Land Design Publishing. Claremont, CA. 318 p.

Peterson, Russell. 1980. *The Pine Tree Book*. The Brandywine Press. New York, NY. 144 p.

Petrides, George A. 1972. *A Field Guide to Trees and Shrubs*, 2nd Ed. Houghton Mifflin Co. Boston, MA. 428 p.

Philips, Roger. 1978. *Trees in Britain, Europe, and North America*. Ward Lock. London. 224 p.

Philips, R. and M. Rix. 1989. *Shrubs*. Random House. New York, NY. 288 p.

Pirone, Pascal P. 1978. *Diseases and Pests of Ornamental Plants*, 5th Ed. Wiley. New York, NY. 566 p.

Pirone, P. P., J. R. Hartman, M. A. Sall, and T. P. Pirone. 1988. *Tree Maintenance*. Oxford University Press. New York, NY. 514 p.

Platt, Rutherford. 1952. *A Pocket Guide to Trees*. Pocket Books. New York, NY. 256 p.

Plumridge, Jack. 1976. *How to Propagate Plants*. Lothian Publishing Co. Pty Ltd. Tattersalls Lane, Melbourne. 214 p.

Pokorny, Jaromír. 1973. *A Color Guide to Familiar Trees—Leaves, Bark and Fruit*. Octopus Books. London. 184 p.

Pokorny, Jaromír. 1974. *A Color Guide to Familiar Flowering Shrubs*. Octopus Books. London. 191 p.

Poor, Janet Meakin (ed.). 1984. *Plants That Merit Attention Vol. I—Trees*. Timber Press. Portland, OR. 400 p.

Poor, Janet Meakin (ed.). 1996. *Plants That Merit Attention Vol. II—Shrubs*. Timber Press. Portland, Oregon. 364 p.

Powell, A. Michael. 1988. *Trees and Shrubs of Trans-Pecos Texas*. Big Bend Natural History Association, Inc. Big Bend National Park, TX. 536 p.

Powell, Thomas and Betty. 1975. *The Avant Gardener*. Houghton Mifflin Co. Boston, MA. 263 p.

Preston, Richard J. 1940. *Rocky Mountain Trees*. Iowa State College Press. Ames, IA. 285 p.

Preston, Richard J. 1976. *North American Trees*, 3rd Ed. Iowa State University Press. Ames, IA. 399 p.

Preston, Richard J. and Valerie G. Wright. 1976. *Identification of Southeastern Trees in Winter*. North Carolina Agr. Ext. Serv. Raleigh, NC. 113 p.

Prime, Cecil T. and Richard John Deacock. 1970. *Trees and Shrubs: Their Identification in Summer or Winter*. Heffer. Cambridge. 131 p.

Radford, Albert E., Harry E. Ahles, and C. Ritchie Bell. 1978. *Manual of the Vascular Flora of the Carolinas*. The University of North Carolina Press. Chapel Hill, NC. 1183 p.

Randall, C. E. and H. Clepper. 1976. *Famous and Historic Trees*. Amer. For..Assoc. Washington, D.C. 90 p.

Raulston, J.C. 1993. *The Chronicles of the NCSU Arboretum*. NCSU Department of Horticultural Science. Raleigh, NC. 402 p.

Reader's Digest Editorial Staff. 1978. *Reader's Digest Encyclopedia of Garden Plants and Flowers*. Reader's Digest Assoc. Ltd. London. 800 p.

Rehder, Alfred. 1940. *Manual of Cultivated Trees and Shrubs*, 2nd Ed. Macmillan Co. New York, NY. 996 p.

Reiley, H. Edward. 1995. *Success with Rhododendrons and Azaleas*. Timber Press. Portland, OR. 314 p.

Reisch, Kenneth W., Philip C. Kozel, and Gayle A. Weinstein. 1975. *Woody Ornamentals for the Midwest*. Kendall/Hunt. Dubuque, IA. 293 p.

Reynolds, Phyllis C. and Elizabeth F. Dimon. 1993. *Trees of Greater Portland*. Timber Press. Portland, OR. 210 p.

Robinette, Gary. 1967. *The Design Characteristics of Plant Materials*. American Printing and Publishing, Inc. Madison, WI. 244 p.

Robinson, Florence B. 1941. *Tabular Keys for the Identification of Woody Plants*. Garrard Press. Champaign, IL. 156 p.

Robinson, Florence B. 1960. *Useful Trees and Shrubs*. Garrard Publishing Co. Champaign, IL.

Rogers, Matilda. 1966. *Trees of the West Identified at a Glance*. The Ward Ritchie Press. 126 p.

Rogers, Walter E. 1935. *Tree Flowers of Forest, Park, and Street*. Dover Publications, Inc. New York, NY. 499 p.

Rosendahl, Carl Otto. 1963. *Trees and Shrubs of the Upper Midwest*. University of Minnesota Press. Minneapolis, MN. 411 p.

Rosendahl, Carl Otto and Frederic K. Butters. 1928. *Trees and Shrubs of Minnesota*. University of Minnesota Press. Minneapolis, MN. 385 p.

Royal Horticultural Society. 1992. *The New Royal Horticultural Society Dictionary of Gardening*. Vols. I–IV. The Macmillan Press, Ltd. London. 3240 p.

Sabuco, John J. 1987. *The Best of the Hardiest*, 2nd Ed. Good Earth Publishing Ltd. Flossmoor, IL. 368 p.

Salley, Homer and Harold E. Greer. 1992. *Rhododendron Hybrids*, 2nd Ed. Timber Press. Portland, OR. 442 p.

Santamour, F. S., Jr., H. D. Gerhold, and S. Little. 1976. *Better Trees for Metropolitan Landscapes*. U.S.D.A. Forest Service General Technical Report NE-22. 256 p.

Sargent, Charles Sprague. 1947. *The Silva of North America*. 14 Vols. Peter Smith. New York, NY.

Sargent, Charles Sprague. 1965. *Manual of the Trees of North America*, Vols. I and II. Dover Publications, Inc. New York, NY. 934 p.

Schaffner, John H. 1950. *Field Manual of Trees*. Long's College Book Co. Columbus, OH. 160 p.

Schuler, Stanley. 1973. *The Gardener's Basic Book of Trees and Shrubs*. Simon and Schuster. New York, NY. 319 p.

Seabrook, Peter. 1975. *Shrubs for Your Garden*. Scribner. New York, NY. 144 p.

Settergren, Carl and R. E. McDermott. 1969. *Trees of Missouri*. Agr. Exp. Sta. Univ. of Missouri. Columbia, MO. 123 p.

Shosteck, Robert. 1974. *Flowers and Plants*. New York Times Book Co. New York, NY. 329 p.

Smith, Alice Upham. 1969. *Trees in a Winter Landscape*. Holt, Rinehart and Winston of Canada, Ltd. 107 p.

Snyder, Leon C. 1978. *Gardening in the Upper Midwest*. Univ. of Minnesota Press. Minneapolis, MN. 292 p.

Snyder, Leon C. 1980. *Trees and Shrubs for Northern Gardens*. Univ. of Minnesota Press. Minneapolis, MN. 411 p.

Sperry, Neil. 1991. *Texas Gardening*. Taylor Publishing Co. Dallas, TX. 388 p.

Spongberg, Stephen A. 1990. *A Reunion of Trees*. Harvard University Press. Cambridge, MA. 270 p.

Stearn, William T. 1992. *Botanical Latin*. Timber Press. Portland, OR. 560 p.

Steele, Frederic L. and Albion R. Hodgdon. 1975. *Trees and Shrubs of Northern New England*. Society for the Protection of New Hampshire Forests. Concord, NH. 127 p.

Stephens, H. A. 1967. *Trees, Shrubs and Woody Vines in Kansas*. Univ. Press of Kansas. Lawrence, KS. 250 p.

Stephens, H. A. 1973. *Woody Plants of the North Central Plains*. Univ. Press of Kansas. Lawrence, KS. 530 p.

Sternberg, Guy and Jim Wilson. 1995. *Landscaping with Native Trees*. Chapters Publishing Ltd. Shelburne, VT. 288 p.

Stresau, Frederic B. 1986. *Florida, My Eden*. Florida Classics Library. Port Salerno, FL. 299 p.

Stupka, Arthur. 1964. *Trees, Shrubs, and Woody Vines of Great Smokey Mountains National Park*. Univ. Tennessee Press. Knoxville, TN. 186 p.

Sudworth, George B. 1967. *Forest Trees of the Pacific Slope.* Dover Publications, Inc. New York, NY. 455 p.

Sunset Editorial Staff. 1995. *Sunset Western Garden Book.* Lane Publishing Co. Menlo Park, CA. 624 p.

Swain, Roger B. 1989. *The Practical Gardener: A Guide to Breaking New Ground.* Little, Brown and Co. Boston, MA. 268 p.

Swanson, Robert E. 1994. *A Field Guide to the Trees and Shrubs of the Southern Appalachians.* The Johns Hopkins University Press. Baltimore, MD. 288 p.

Symonds, George W. D. 1958. *The Tree Identification Book.* William Morrow and Co., Inc. New York, NY. 272 p.

Symonds, George W. D. 1963. *The Shrub Identification Book.* M. Barrows and Co. New York, NY. 379 p.

Tattar, Terry A. 1978. *Diseases of Shade Trees.* Academic Press. New York, NY. 361 p.

Taylor, Norman. 1961. *Taylor's Encyclopedia of Gardening.* Houghton Mifflin Co. Boston, MA.

Taylor, Norman. 1965. *The Guide to Garden Shrubs and Trees.* Houghton Mifflin Co. Boston, MA. 450 p.

Taylor, Norman. 1988. *Taylor's Guide to Trees.* Houghton Mifflin Co. Boston, MA. 479 p.

Taylor, Patrick. 1995. *Gardening with Roses.* Timber Press. Portland, OR. 256 p.

Taylor, Sally L. 1979. *Garden Guide to Woody Plants.* Connecticut College. New London, CT. 100 p.

Tehon, Leo R. 1942. *Field Book of Native Illinois Shrubs.* Nat. Hist. Survey Div. Urbana, IL. 300 p.

Thomas, Graham Stuart. 1983. *Trees in the Landscape.* Sagapress/Timber Press. Portland, OR. 224 p.

Thomas, Graham Stuart. 1990. *Plants for Ground-Cover.* Sagapress/Timber Press. Portland, OR. 380 p.

Thomas, Graham Stuart. 1992. *Ornamental Shrubs, Climbers, and Bamboos.* Sagapress/Timber Press. Portland, OR. 544 p.

Thomas, Graham Stuart. 1994. *The Graham Stuart Thomas Rose Book.* Timber Press. Portland, OR. 472 p.

Del Tredici, Peter. 1983. *A Giant Among the Dwarfs—The Mystery of Sargent's Weeping Hemlock.* Theophrastus. Little Compton, RI. 108 p.

Trehane, P., C. D. Brickell, B. R. Baum, W. L. A. Hetterscheid, A. C. Leslie, J. McNeill, S. A. Spongberg, and F. Vrugtman (editorial committee). 1995. *International Code of Nomenclature for Cultivated Plants.* Quarterjack Publ. Wimborne, UK. 175 p.

Trelease, William. 1931. *Winter Botany,* 3rd Ed. Dover Publications, Inc. New York, NY. 396 p.

Treseder, Neil G. 1978. *Magnolias.* Faber and Faber. London. 243 p.

Treshow, Michael, Stanley L. Welsh, and Glen Moore. 1970. *Guide to the Woody Plants of the Mountain States.* B.Y.U. Press. Provo, UT. 178 p.

Tripp, Kim and J.C. Raulston. 1995. *The Year in Trees.* Timber Press. Portland, OR. 204 p.

Trustees' Garden Club. 1991. *Garden Guide to Lower South.* Trustees' Garden Club. Savannah, GA. 248 p.

Valavanis, William N. 1976. *The Japanese Five-Needle Pine.* Symmes Systems. Atlanta, GA. 68 p.

Valdar, Peter. 1995. *Wisterias.* Timber Press. Portland, OR. 160 p.

van Gelderen, D. M. and J. R. P. van Hoey Smith. 1986. *Conifers.* Timber Press. Portland, OR. 385 p.

van Gelderen, D. M. and J. R. P. van Hoey Smith. 1992. *Rhododendron Portraits.* Timber Press. Portland, OR. 424 p.

van Gelderen, D. M. and J. R. P. van Hoey Smith. 1996. *Conifers*. Vols. I and II. Timber Press. Portland, OR. 706 p.

van Gelderen, D. M., P. C. de Jong, and H. J. Oterdoom. 1994. *Maples of the World*. Timber Press. Portland, OR. 458 p.

Van Melle, P. J. 1943. *Shrubs and Trees for the Small Place*. Charles Scribner's Sons. New York, NY. 298 p.

Verey, Rosemary. 1981. *The Scented Garden*. Van Nostrand Reinhold Co. New York, NY. 167 p.

Verey, Rosemary. 1988. *The Garden in Winter*. Timber Press. Portland, OR. 168 p.

Vertrees, J. D. 1987. *Japanese Maples*. Timber Press. Portland, OR. 189 p.

Viereck, Leslie A. and Elbert L. Little. 1972. *Alaska Trees and Shrubs*. Agricultural Handbook No. 410, U.S.D.A. Forest Service. Supt. of Doc. U.S. Gov. Printing Office. Washington, D.C. 265 p.

Vines, Robert A. 1960. *Trees, Shrubs, and Woody Vines of the Southwest*. Univ. Texas Press. Austin, TX. 1104 p.

Voigt, T. B., Betty R. Hamilton, and F. A. Giles. 1983. *Groundcovers for the Midwest*. Univ. of Illinois Printing Division. Champaign, IL. 184 p.

Wait, D. Dwight. 1977. *Ornamental Plants, Their Care, Use, Propagation, and Identification*. Kendall/Hunt. Dubuque, IA. 426 p.

Walheim, Lance (ed.). 1977. *The World of Trees*. Ortho Books. San Francisco, CA. 112 p.

Walker, Egbert H. 1976. *Flora of Okinawa and the Southern Ryukyu Islands*. Smithsonian Institution Press. Washington, D.C. 1159 p.

Walker, Mary C. and F. A. Giles. 1985. *Flowering Trees for the Midwest*. University of Illinois. Champaign, IL. 102p.

Walkins, John V. and Thomas J. Sheehan. 1975. *Florida Landscape Plants*. The University Presses of Florida. Gainesville, FL. 420 p.

Wandell, Willet N. 1994. *Handbook of Landscape Tree Cultivars*. East Prairie Publishing Co. Gladstone, IL. 394 p.

Wasowski, Sally. 1994. *Gardening with Native Plants of the South*. Taylor Publishing Co. Dallas, TX. 196 p.

Watkins, John V. and Herbert S. Wolfe. 1968. *Your Florida Garden*. Univ. of Florida Press. Gainesville, FL. 382 p.

Watkins, John V. and Thomas John Sheehan. 1975. *Florida Landscape Plants: Native and Exotic*. Univ. of Florida Press. Gainesville, FL. 520 p.

Weaver, Richard E. 1972. *A Guide to City Trees in The Boston Area*. The Arnold Arboretum. Jamaica Plain, MA. 97 p.

Weiner, Michael A. 1975. *Plant a Tree: A Working Guide to Regreening America*. Macmillan Co. New York, NY. 276 p.

Welch, H. J. 1966. *Dwarf Conifers*. Charles T. Branford Co. Boston, MA. 334 p.

Welch, H. J. 1979. *Manual of Dwarf Conifers*. Theophrastus. Little Compton, RI. 493 p.

Welles, J. C. 1985. *A Dictionary of the Flowering Plants and Ferns, Student Edition*. Cambridge University Press. England. 1245 p.

Wharton, Mary E. and Roger W. Barbour. 1973. *Trees and Shrubs of Kentucky*. Univ. Press of Kentucky. Lexington, KY. 582 p.

Whitcomb, Carl E. 1984. *Plant Production in Containers*. Lacebark Publications. Stillwater, OK. 638 p.

Whitcomb, Carl E. 1986. *Know It and Grow It*. Lacebark Publications. Stillwater, OK. 920 p.

Whitehead, Stanley B. 1956. *The Book of Flowering Trees and Shrubs*. Frederick Warne and Co. Ltd. New York, NY. 246 p.

Wigginton, Brooks E. 1963. *Trees and Shrubs for the Southeast*. University of Georgia Press. Athens, GA. 280 p.

Wilder, Louise Beebe. 1974. *The Fragrant Garden*. Dover Publications, Inc. New York, NY. 407 p.

Wilson, Ernest Henry. 1914. *A Naturalist in Western China*. Volume I. Doubleday, Page & Co. New York, NY. 251 p.

Wilson, Ernest Henry. 1914. *A Naturalist in Western China*. Volume II. Doubleday, Page & Co. New York, NY. 229 p.

Wilson, Ernest Henry. 1920. *The Romance of Our Trees*. Doubleday. Garden City, NJ. 278 p.

Wilson, Ernest Henry. 1925. *America's Greatest Garden: The Arnold Arboretum*. The Stratford Co. Boston, MA. 123 p.

Wilson, Ernest Henry. 1926. *Aristocrats of the Garden*. The Stratford Co. Boston, MA. 312 p.

Wilson, Ernest Henry. 1927. *Plant Hunting*. Vols. I and II. The Stratford Co. Boston, MA.

Wilson, Ernest Henry. 1928. *More Aristocrats of the Garden*. The Stratford Co. Boston, MA. 288 p.

Wilson, Ernest Henry. 1929. *China Mother of Gardens*. The Stratford Co. Boston, MA. 408 p.

Wilson, Ernest Henry. 1930. *Aristocrats of the Trees*. The Stratford Co. Boston, MA. 279 p.

Wilson, Ernest Henry. 1931. *If I Were to Make a Garden*. The Stratford Company. Boston, MA. 295 p.

Woodland, D. 1997. *Contemporary Plant Systematics*. Andrews Univ. Press. Berren Springs, MI.

Wyman, Donald. 1954. *The Arnold Arboretum Garden Book*. D. Van Nostrand Co., Inc. New York, NY. 354 p.

Wyman, Donald. 1956. *Ground Cover Plants*. Macmillan Co. New York, NY. 175 p.

Wyman, Donald. 1965. *Trees for American Gardens*. Macmillan Co. New York, NY. 502 p.

Wyman, Donald. 1969. *Shrubs and Vines for American Gardens*. Macmillan Co. New York, NY. 613 p.

Wyman, Donald. 1971. *Wyman's Gardening Encyclopedia*. Macmillan Co. New York, NY. 1221 p.

Wyman, Donald. 1975. *Dwarf Shrubs*. Macmillan Co. New York, NY. 137 p.

Young, James A. and Cheryl G. Young. 1992. *Seeds of Woody Plants in North America*. Dioscorides Press. Portland, OR. 407 p.

GLOSSARY OF TAXONOMIC TERMS COMMONLY EMPLOYED IN THE IDENTIFICATION OF WOODY PLANTS

a-: prefix indicating not or without.

abortive: defective, barren, not developed.

abruptly pinnate: without a terminal leaflet.

abscission: the separating of a leaf from a self healing, clean-cut scar.

acaulescent: stemless or apparently so. Ex: *Taraxacum, Dodecatheon, Primula*.

accessory buds: those found beside or above the true bud at a node.

accessory fruit: one whose conspicuous tissues have not been derived from those comprising the pistil of the fl. Ex: in strawberry, (*Fragaria*) the fleshy part of the fr. is of receptacular and not of pistillate origin. An accessory fr. may or may not also be an aggregate fr. (it is so in the strawberry and not so in the banana).

accessory parts of a flower: the petals and sepals.

achene: a dry indehiscent one-seeded fruit. Ex: fr. of members of the Compositae.

acicular: needle-shaped. Ex: lvs. of *Pinus*, spines of some cacti.

acorn: the fruit of oaks, a thick walled nut with a woody cup-like base.

actinomorphic: of regular symmetry, applied to perianth whorls, as opposed to zygomorphic.

aculeate: prickly.

acuminate: having an apex whose sides are gradually concave and tapering to a point.

acute: having an apex whose sides are straight and taper to a point.

adherent: a condition existing when two dissimilar organs touch each other (sometimes seemingly fused) but not grown together.

adnate: fused with unlike parts, as in the fusion of a filament to a petal.

adventitious: arising from an unusual or irregular position.

aerial rootlets: those produced above ground, especially as in climbing organs of a vine.

aestivation: the arrangement of floral parts (especially sepals and petals) in the bud.

aggregate flower: a flower heaped or crowded into a dense cluster.

aggregate fruit: one formed by the coherence or the connation of pistils that were distinct in the flower (as in *Rubus*) when the pistils of separate flowers (as in mulberry) make up the fr. it is designated as a multiple fruit.

akene: a small dry indehiscent fruit with one seed free inside the thin pericarp.

alternate: an arrangement of leaves or other parts not opposite or whorled; parts situated one at a node, as leaves on a stem: like parts succeeding each other singly with a common structure.

ament: *see catkin.*

amplexicaul: encircling the stem.

anastomosing: netted, applied to the veins of a lf.; the marginal reticulations closed.

androecium: stamens of a fl. as a unit.

anemophilous: describes flowers that are pollinated by wind.

angiospermous: having seeds borne within a pericarp.

angular: of pith; not rounded in cross section.

annual: maturing and living one season only.

annular: shaped like a ring.

anterior: on the front side, away from the axis, toward the subtending bract.

anther: pollen-bearing part of a stamen, borne at the top of a filament, or sessile.

anthesis (an-thee-sis): that period of fl. development when pollen is shed from the anther; also used to designate the act of flowering or the time of fl. expansion.

apetalous: without petals. Ex: fls. of grasses.

apex: the tip or terminal end.

apical: describes the apex or tip.

apiculate: ending abruptly in a short pointed tip.

apocarpous: having separate carpels; frequently applied to a gynoecium of several pistils.

apophysis: that part of the cone scale that is exposed when the cone is closed.

appressed: pressed close to the stem, not spreading.

arboreal, arboreous: treelike or pertaining to trees.

arching: curving gracefully.

arcuate venation: pinnate, with the secondary veins curving and running parallel to the margin.

areole: small pit or raised spot, often bearing a tuft of hairs, glochids, or spines.

aril: a fleshy appendage of the seed, usually a fleshy seedcoat.

aristate: bearing a stiff bristle-like awn or arista, or tapered to a very slender stiff tip. Ex: awns of many grasses, apices of many calyx-teeth.

armed: provided with a sharp defense such as thorns, spines, prickles or barbs.

aromatic: fragrantly scented, at least if broken or crushed.

articulate: having nodes or joints where separation may naturally occur.

ascending: curving indirectly or obliquely upward. Ex: branches of *Taxus canadensis*.

assurgent: rising at an angle, not straight upwards.

attenuate: showing a long gradual slender taper; usually applied to apices, but equally appropriate for bases of leaves, petals, etc.

auriculate: bearing ear-like appendages, as the projections of some leaf and petal bases.

awl-shaped: tapering to a slender stiff point.

awn: a bristle-like appendage.

axil: belonging to the axis. *See placentation.*

axillary: in the axil.

axis: the main stem or central support of a plant.

baccate: pulpy, fleshy.

barbed: bristles, awns, etc. provided with terminal or lateral spine-like hooks that are bent sharply backward. Ex: pappus on fruits of beggar's ticks.

bark: a dead outer protective tissue of woody plants, derived from the cortex. Varies greatly in appearance and texture; often including all tissue from the vascular cambium outward.

basal: pertaining to the extremity of an organ by which it is attached to its support; said of lvs. when at base of plant only. *See rosette.*

basifixed: attached basally as ovules or anthers.

beak: a long prominent point. Ex: on lettuce (*Lactuca*) or dandelion (*Taraxacum*) frs.

beaked: ending in a point, especially on fruits.

bearded: having long hairs.

berry: a fleshy indehiscent pulpy multi-seeded fr. resulting from a single pistil. Ex: tomato.

bi-: prefix indicating twice or doubly.

biennial: of two seasons duration, normally flowering, fruiting and dying the second growing season from time of seed germination.

bifid: two-cleft, as in apices of some petals and leaves. Ex: petals of some *Lychnis* or leaves of *Bauhinia*.

bifurcate: forked, as some Y-shaped hairs.

bilabiate: two-lipped, often applied to a corolla or calyx: each lip may or may not be lobed or toothed. Ex: corolla of snapdragon (*Antirrhinum*) and most members of the mint family (Labiatae).

bipinnate: twice pinnate.

bisexual: stamens and pistil present in the one fl.

biternate: twice ternate; a structure basically ternate, but whose primary divisions are again each ternate. Ex: lvs. of some columbines (*Aquilegia*) and meadow-rues (*Thalictrum*).

bladder-like: inflated, empty with thin walls.

blade: the expanded part of lf. or petal; lamina.

bloom: a waxy coating found on stems, leaves, flowers and fruits, usually of a grayish cast and easily removed.

bole: stem of a tree.

boss: a raised usually pointed projection.

bract: a much-reduced lf., often scale-like and usually associated with a fl. or infl.

branch: one of the coarser divisions of a trunk or main branch.

branchlet: smaller, a division of the branch.

bristle: a stiff hair.

broad-elliptic: wider than elliptic.

broad-ovate: wider than ovate.

bronzing: turning a metallic bronze or coppery color, especially of foliage after a winter.

bud: a structure of embryonic tissues, which will become a leaf, a flower, or both, or a new shoot. Especially the stage in which a growing point spends the winter or a dry season. May be naked or enclosed in scales.

bud scale: a modified leaf or stipule (there may be one, a few, or many) protective of the embryonic tissue of the bud.

bud scale scar: the mark left by the sloughing off of the bud scale.

bulb: a modified underground stem comprised of shortened central axis surrounded by fleshy scale-like lvs.

bulbil: small bulbs arising around parent bulb.

bulblet: small bulbs arising in leaf axils.

bullate: with the surface appearing as if blistered between the veins. Ex: Savoy cabbage.

bundle scar: seen in the leaf scar, the broken ends of the woody vascular strands that connected the leaf and the stem.

bur: any rough or prickly seed envelope.

burl: a knot or woody growth of very irregular grain.

bush: a low several stemmed shrub with no single trunk.

caducous: falling off early or prematurely.

calcarate: having a spur.

calcicole: a plant growing best on limey soils.

callus: a hard protuberance, or the new tissues formed in response to a wound.

calyx: the outer set of perianth segments or floral envelope of a flower, usually green in color and smaller than the inner set.

campanulate: bell-shaped.

cane: a long woody pliable stem rising from the ground.

canescent: having a gray hoary pubescence.

capillary: hair-like; very slender.

capitate: headlike, in a dense rounded cluster.

capsule: a dry dehiscent fruit produced from a compound pistil. Ex: fruit of a tobacco, *Catalpa*, *Dianthus*.

carinate: keeled; with longitudinal ridge or line.

carpel: one of the foliar units of gynoecium. *See pistil.*

carpophore: elongated axis bearing a gynoecium and projecting between the carpels.

caryopsis: the fruit of members of the grass family; not basically distinct from an achene.

castaneous: dark brown.

catkin: a spike-like infl. comprised of scaly bracts subtending unisexual fls., often somewhat flexuous and pendulous but not necessarily so. Ex: infl. of willows (*Salix*) and poplars (*Populus*).

caudate: bearing a tail-like appendage. Ex: spadices of some aroids.

caulescent: having an evident leaf-bearing stem above ground.

cauliflorous: flowering from the trunk or main branches directly or on short specialized spurs.

cauline: of or belonging to the stem.

ceriferous: waxy.

cernuous: drooping or nodding.

cespitose: growing in tufts or dense clumps.

chaff: dry, thin, membranous bract, particularly those subtending the fls. of the Compositae.

chaffy: covered with small thin dry scales or bracts.

chalaza: basal part of ovule, where it is attached to the funiculus.

chambered: of pith, divided into empty horizontal chambers by cross partitions.

channeled: grooved lengthwise.

chartaceous: of papery or tissue-like texture.

ciliate: marginally fringed with hairs, often minutely so and then termed "ciliolate."

cinereous: ash colored.

circinate: rolled coil-wise from top downward. Ex: unopened fern fronds.

circumscissile: opening or dehiscing by a line around the fr. or anther, the top (valve) coming off as a lid. Ex: fr. of *Portulaca* or *Plantago*.

cladophyll: a flattened, foliaceous stem having the form and function of a leaf, but arising in the axis of minute bract-like often caducous true leaf. Ex: the so-called leaves of *Ruscus* and *Asparagus*.

clasping: a stalkless leaf, with the base partly surrounding the stem.

clavate: club-shaped, as a baseball bat.

claw: the constricted petiole-like base of petals and sepals of some flowers. Ex: petals of flowers of mustard family, of *Cleome*.

cleft: divided to or about the middle into divisions.

cleistogamous: describes a small, closed self-fertilized flower, usually near the ground.

climbing plant: one which raises its foliage by supporting itself on surrounding objects, by twining stem or tendrils, grasping rootlets, or scrambling.

clone: a group of plants derived vegetatively from one parent plant, identical to each other and to the parent.

close bark: not broken up or scaly.

clustered: of leaves, crowded so as not to be clearly opposite or alternate, also said of whorled condition.

coalescent: two or more parts united.

coarse (texture): consisting of large or rough parts.

coherent: two or more similar parts or organs touching one another in very close proximity by the tissues not fused. Ex: the two ovaries of asclepiadaceous flowers. (By some the term treated as if synonymous with connate.)

collateral buds: accessory buds to either side of the true lateral bud at a node.

columella: the carpophores in umbellifer fruits.

column: the structure formed by union of filaments in a tube (as in mallows) or of the filaments and style of orchids.

commisure: the edge or face of two adjoining structures.

comose: tufted with hairs. Ex: milkweed seeds.

compact: arranged in a small amount of space, dense habit.

complete flower: one which has corolla, calyx, stamens and one or more pistils.

composite: compound.

compound leaf: a leaf of two or more leaflets, in some cases (Citrus) the lateral leaflets may have been lost and only the terminal lft. remain. *Ternately compound* when the lfts. are in 3's; *palmately compound* when three or more lfts. arise from a common point to be palmate (if only three are present they may be sessile); *pinnately compound* when arranged along a common rachis or if only three are present at least the terminal lft. is petioled; *odd-pinnate* if a terminal lft. is present and the total number of lfts., for the lf. is an odd-number; *even-pinnate* if no terminal lft. is present and the total is an even number.

compound pistil: a pistil comprised of two or more carpels. The number of cells or locules within the ovary may or may not indicate the number of carpels. An ovary having more than one complete cell or locule is always compound, but many one-celled ovaries are compound also. A pistil having a one-celled ovary, but more than one placenta or more than one style or more than one stigma, or any combination of these duplicities, may be presumed to be compound insofar as taxonomic considerations are concerned.

compressed: flattened from the sides.

concave: curved like the inner surface of a sphere.

conduplicate: folded together lengthwise.

cone: a coniferous fruit, having a number of woody, leathery, or fleshy scales, each bearing one or more seeds, and attached to a central axis.

conelet: a young, immature first season cone, in the pines.

conical: cone shaped, as the young form of many spruces.

confluent: blending together, not easily distinguishable as separate.

coniferous: cone bearing.

connate: like parts fused together into one, fused into a tube. Ex: filaments of a mallow androecium, or anthers of a Composite flower.

connective: the tissues between the two anthers of a stamen, often much elaborated when the anther cells are separated. Ex: *Salvia*.

connivent: a synonym of coherent.

constricted: squeezed or compressed as if by shrinking or tightening.

continuous pith: solid and without interruption.

convex: curved like the outer surface of a sphere.

convulate: rolled up lengthwise; in flower buds when overlapping of one edge of a perianth segment by the next while the other margin is overlapped by its preceding member.

coppice: growth arising from sprouts at the stump, bushy.

cordate: heart-shaped, with a sinus and rounded lobes; properly a term applied only to bases of leaves and bracts, but frequently employed to designate a structure of ovate outline and heart-shaped base.

coriaceous: of leathery texture. Ex: *Buxus* lf.

corky ridges: elongated warts or strips of soft springy wood.

corm: a solid bulb-like underground stem not differentiated into scales, often depressed-globose in form, bearing scale-like buds on surface, usually tunicated. Ex: *Gladiolus, Crocus*.

cormel: small corm arising from base of parent corm.

corolla: the usually petaloid, inner whorl or floral envelopes; when the parts are separate and distinct they are petals and the corolla is said to be *polypetalous*; when connate in whole or in part the distal parts are teeth, lobes, divisions, or segments and the corolla is said to be *gamopetalous*.

corona: a crown; an appendage or extrusion that stands between the corolla and stamens; an outgrowth of perianth tissue in the "cup" of *Narcissus*, or of the androecium in the milkweeds.

corymb: a more or less flat-topped indeterminate infl. whose outer fls. open first. Ex: *Viburnum*, some verbenas.

costate: having longitudinal ribs or veins.

cotyledon: the primary leaves of the embryo, present in the seed.

creeping: running along at or near the ground level and rooting occasionally.

cremocarp: a dry dehiscent 2 seeded fruit of the Umbelliferae, each half a mericarp.

crenate: rounded teeth on mgn. Ex: lvs. of some *Coleus*.

crenate-serrate: having a mixture of blunt and sharp teeth.

crenulate: having very small rounded teeth.

crested: with an elevated and irregular or toothed ridge; found on some seeds or some floral parts.

crisp-hairy: with kinky hair or tomentum.

crown: the upper mass or head of a tree, also a central point near the ground level of a perennial herb from which new shoots arise each year.

cruciform: cross shaped.

cucullate: hooded.

culm: stem of grasses and sedges.

cultigen: a plant arising through domestication and cultivation.

cultivar: a cultivated variety.

cultivated: maintained by man.

cuneate: wedge-shaped with essentially straight side, the structure attached at the narrow end.

cuspidate: with an apex somewhat abruptly and concavely constricted into an elongated sharp-pointed tip.

cuticle: an outer film of dead epidermal cells, often waxy.

cyathium: the infl. characteristic of *Euphorbia*, the fls. condensed and congested within a bracteate envelope, emerging at anthesis.

cymbiform: boat-shaped.

cyme: a more or less flat-topped determinate infl. whose outer fls. open last. Ex: elderberry (*Sambucus*).

cymose: of or arranged on cymes.

cymule: a diminutive cyme. Ex: *Armeria*.

deciduous: falling off, as lvs. of a tree.

decompound: more than one compound.

decumbent: reclining on ground with tip ascending.

decurrent: extending down the stem.

decussate: with alternating pairs at right angles to each other, as pairs of opposite lvs. on a stem.

deflexed: synonym of reflexed.

defoliation: casting off or falling off of leaves.

dehiscent: splitting open, the sides or segments of the splitting organ usually termed valves; *loculicidally* dehiscent when the split opens into a cavity or locule, *septicidally* dehiscent when at point of union of septum or partition to the side wall, *circumscissilely* when the top valve comes off as a lid. *Poricidally* when by means of pores whose valves are often flap-like. The term is commonly applied to anthers or seed pods.

deliquescent: the primary axis or stem much branched. Ex: branching of an elm tree.

deltoid: triangular.

dense: crowded together, thick, compact.

dentate: having marginal teeth whose apices are perpendicular to the margin and do not point forward.

denticulate: slightly or minutely dentate.

denuded: naked through loss of covering.

depressed: flattened, as if compressed somewhat.

determinate: said of an inflorescence when the terminal flower opens first and the prolongation of the axis is thereby arrested.

di-: prefix indicating two.

diadelphous: in two sets, applied to stamens. In many legumes the androecium is comprised of 10 stamens: 9 in one set, 1 in the other.

diandrous: having an androecium of two stamens.

diaphragmed pith: having horizontally elongated cells with thickened walls spaced throughout the pith like the rungs of a ladder.

dichlamydeous: having both a corolla and a calyx.

dichotomous: forked in pairs.

diclinous: with unisexual flowers.

dicot: angiospermous plant having two cotyledons.

didynamous: in two pairs of different length.

diffuse: loosely or widely spreading, an open form.

digitate: palmate.

dimorphic: having two forms.

dioecious: having unisexual fls., each sex confined to a separate plant, said of species.

disarticulate: to fall away leaving a clear cut scar.

discoid: having only disk fls. as an infl. of a member of the Compositae family.

disk: (1) a glandular elevation about the base of a superior ovary; (2) the flattened receptacle of the infl.; (3) a flattened extremity as a stigma or as on the tendrils of some climbing vines.

disk flower: the tubular fl. in the center of the usual Composite infl. Ex: daisy, aster.

disposed: arranged.

dissected: divided in narrow, slender segments.

distal: toward the apex, away from the base.

distichous: two-ranked, with lvs., lfts. or fls. on opposite sides of a stem in the same plant.

distinct: separate, not united with parts of like kind. Compare with "free".

diurnal: blossoms opening only during the day.

divaricate: spreading very wide apart.

divergent: spreading broadly.

divided: separated to the base into divisions.

dormant: in a restive or non vegetative state, especially a winter condition.

dorsal: the black or outer surface.

dorsiventral: referring to a front-to-back plane.

dotted: describes the underside of a leaf having a pattern of spots or hair glands visible.

double flower: one with more than the usual number of petals, colored sepals or bracts.

double serrate: serrations bearing minute teeth on margins.

doubly compound: bi-pinnate.

doubly crenate, dentate, or serrate: having small teeth of the given kind within the larger ones.

downy: pubescent with fine soft hairs.

drooping: hanging from the base, suggesting wilting.

drupaceous: drupe-like.

drupe: a fleshy indehiscent fr. whose seed is enclosed in a stony endocarp. Ex: date, cherry.

drupelet: a small drupe. Ex: raspberry.

duct: generally, a water conducting tube, also a canal through the wood carrying resin, latex or oil.

dwarf: an atypically small plant.

dwarf shoots: spur shoots.

ebracteate: without bracts.

echinate: with stout bluntish prickles.

eglandular: without glands.

ellipsoid: three dimensional shape of ellipse, football shaped.

elliptic-oblong: a shape between the two forms.

elliptical: having the outline of an ellipse, broadest at middle and narrower at each end.

elongate: lengthened.

emarginate: with a shallow notch at the apex.

emergences: appendages other than hairs.

endemic: confined to a small geographic area.

endocarp: the inner layer of the pericarp.

ensiform: sword-shaped.

entire: having a margin without teeth or crenations.

entomophilous: describes flowers that are pollinated by insects.

ephemeral: persisting for one day only, of short duration. Ex: fls. of *Tradescantia*.

epidermis: the outer superficial layer of cells.

epigynous: borne on the ovary; said of the fl. when the ovary is inferior, or of stamens when apparently borne on the gynoecium.

epitrophic: more nourished and developed on the upper side.

equitant: overlapping in two ranks. Ex: lvs. of *Iris*.

erect: upright habit of growth.

erose: having a margin appearing eroded or gnawed; of a jaggedness not sufficiently regular to be toothed. Ex: leaf apices of the fish-tail palm (*Caryota*).

espalier: any plant trained lattice fashion in one plane.

established: growing and reproducing without cultivation.

estipulate: without stipules.

evanescent: describes veins grown very faint near the margin.

even-pinnate: results in a lack of the terminal leaflet, since each one is paired.

evergreen: having green foliage throughout the year.

excavated: describes pith which is hollow between the nodes.

excurrent: extending beyond the margin or tip. Ex: awns of some grasses.

exfoliate: to peel off in shreds or thin layers, as bark from a tree.

exotic: foreign, not naturalized.

exserted: projecting beyond, as stamens beyond a corolla.

exstipulate: without stipules.

extrorse: facing outward from the center; in the case of anthers, dehiscing outward; a character most accurately determined by a cross-section of the anther.

falcate: sickle-shaped.

falls: outer whorl of perianth segments of an iridaceous fl., often broader than the inner and, in some *Iris*, drooping or flexuous.

farinaceous: with a powdery or mealy coating.

fasciated: abnormally much flattened, and seemingly several units fused together.

fascicle: a close cluster. Ex: lvs. of white pine.

fastigiate: branches erect and close together.

felty: having compressed matted fibers.

fenestrate: perforated with opening or with translucent areas. Ex: lvs. of *Monstera deliciosa*.

ferrugineous: rust colored.

fertile: capable of producing fruit and seed.

fibrous: having long narrow shreds or flakes.

filament: that portion of a stamen comprising the stalk.

filamentous: thread-like.

filiform: long and very slender; thread-like.

fimbriate: fringed.

fine texture: consisting of small rather delicate parts.

firm bark: close, not broken into loose or shaggy parts.

fissured bark: torn lengthwise, with vertical furrows.

fistulose: hollow and cylindrical.

fistulous: describes a hollow stem with excavated pith.

flabellate: fan-like.

flaccid: limp.

flaking: shreddy, with shorter fragments.

flat: a low horizontal habit of growth.

fleshy: applied to a fruit somewhat pulpy or juicy at maturity, as opposed to a dry hard or papery fruit.

flexous: waxy.

floccose: having surface with tufts of soft woolly hair, often rubbing off easily.

floret: technically a minute flower; applied to the flowers of grasses and Composites.

flower: an axis bearing one or more pistils or one or more stamens or both: when only the former, it is a *perfect flower* (i.e. bisexual or hermaphroditic). The androecium represents a series or whorls, derived from a spiral condition adjoining the pistil. When this perfect flower is surrounded by a perianth represented by two floral envelopes (the inner envelope comprising the corolla, the outer the calyx), it is a *complete flower*.

flower scar: marks remaining after the abscission of the flower parts.

fluted: having rounded lengthwise ridges.

foliaceous: leaf-like in color and form.

foliage: leaves.

-foliate: -leaved.

-foliolate: -leafleted.

follicle: a dry dehiscent fruit opening only along one suture and the product of a single carpel (simple ovary). Ex: peony, columbine, milkweed.

forma: a subdivision of a species which occurs occasionally in the wild, seldom breeds true, and does not develop a natural population or distribution.

foveola: a pit.

fragmented: not continuous, especially of vascular bundle scars.

free: separate in that it is not joined to other organs; as petals free from calyx or calyx tree from capsule. Contrast with "distinct".

free-central: *see placentation.*

fringed: ciliate with glands or scales rather than hairs.

frond: a leaf, once applied only to leaves of ferns but now to leaves of palms also.

fruit: technically a ripened ovary with its adnate parts, the seed-containing unit characteristic of all Angiosperms. The term is also employed loosely for all similar structures as the "fruit" of a Cycad which in reality is a naked seed or the "fruit" of the Blue Cohosh (an Angiosperm) which also is a naked seed: all are functionally fruiting structures.

fruticose: shrubby, in sense of stems being woody.

fugacious: falling or withering very early.

fulvous: tawny, a dull grayish yellow color.

funiculus: the stalk by which an ovule is attached to the ovary wall.

funnelform: the tube gradually widening. Ex: corolla of morning-glory.

furcate: forked.

furrowed: having longitudinal channels or grooves.

fuscous: grayish brown.

fusiform: spindle-shaped; tapering to each end from a smaller mid-section.

galea: a helmet. Ex: *Aconitum.*

gamopetalous: the petals united, at least at base, to form a corolla of one piece; the corolla coming off from the fl. as a single unit.

geniculate: bent like a knee.

genus: a group of species possessing fundamental traits in common but differing in other lesser characteristics.

gibbous: swollen on one side, usually basally. Ex: snapdragon corolla.

glabrate: becoming glabrous with maturity, but as seen under a lens is noted to be not quite so prior to maturity.

glabrous: not hairy. Note: a glabrous surface need not be smooth, for it may be bullate or rugose.

gland: a general term applied to oil-secreting organs, or sometimes an obtuse projection or a ring at base of a structure.

glandular: bearing glands.

glandular-pubescent: glands and hairs intermixed.

glandular-punctate: *see punctate.*

glaucescent: slightly glaucous.

glaucous: covered with a waxy bloom or whitish material that rubs off readily. Ex: the bloom on many sorts of grape.

globose: having a round or spherical shape.

globular: circular.

glochid: a minute barbed spine or bristle. Ex: the components of the tawny hair-like tufts on many species of *Opuntia.*

glomerate: in dense or compact clusters, usually applied to flowers.

glossy: shining, reflecting more light than if lustrous.

glume: a stiff chaff-like bract, usually applied to the two empty bracts at base of grass spikelets.

glutinous: sticky.

granular: minutely roughened.

grooved: marked with long narrow furrows or channels.

ground cover: a plant that grows near the ground densely, and spreads.

gum: a fluid sticky resin.

gymnospermous: plant bearing naked seeds without an ovary.

gynoecium: collectively the female element of a fl.; a collective term employed for the several pistils of a single fl. when referred to as a unit; when only one pistil is present the two terms are synonymous.

gynophore: a stalk bearing a pistil above point of stamen attachment. Ex: *Cleome*.

habit: the general aspect or mode of growth of a plant.

habitat: the type surrounding in which a plant grows.

hair: superficial outgrowth, trichome.

hairy: pubescent with longer hairs.

hardened: conditioned by various factors to withstand environmental stresses; contrast with succulent growth which is very vulnerable.

hardy: capable of enduring winter stresses.

hastate: having the shape of an arrow-head and the basal lobes pointed outwards at or nearly at right angles to the mid-rib.

head: a short dense infl. of variable form, as in Compositae (daisy) family, *Eryngium*, or many clovers.

helicoid: spiraling like a snail shell.

herb: a plant dying to the ground at the end of the season; one whose aerial stems are soft and succulent without appreciable parenchymatous xylem tissue; a plant not woody in texture.

herbaceous: having no persistent woody stem above ground.

herbage: vegetative parts of an herb.

hermaphrodite: bisexual.

hesperidium: a fleshy berry-like fr. with hard rind and definite longitudinal partitions. Ex: orange.

heterogamous: bearing two kinds of flowers.

heterogeneous: not uniform in kind of flowers.

hidden bud: bud covered by the petiole base and therefore inconspicuous.

hilum: the scar on a seed marking its point of attachment.

hip: fruit of the rose.

hippocrepiform: horseshoe-shaped.

hirsute: pubescent with coarse or stiff hairs.

hirtellous: minutely hirsute.

hispid: with stiff or bristly hairs.

hispidulous: minutely hispid.

hoary: with a close white or whitish pubescence.

hollow: describes pith with a central cavity.

homogamous: bearing only one kind of flower.

homogeneous: all of one kind and texture, continuous pith.

hooked: bent like a hook, having a hook.

horizontal: with broad faces parallel to the ground.

humifuse: spreading over the ground.

husk: outer covering of the seed or fruit.

hyaline: translucent when viewed in transmitted light.

hybrid: plant resulting from a cross between two or more other plants which are more or less alike.

hydrophyte: an aquatic plant.

hypanthium: the cup-like "receptacle" derived from the fusion of perianth parts and on which are seemingly borne the stamens, corolla, and calyx. Ex: fuchsia, plum.

hypocrateriform: *see salverform.*

hypogynous: borne on the torus or receptacle, beneath or at base of ovary; said of stamens, petals or calyx when the ovary is superior or above their point of attachment.

hypotrophic: more nourished and developed on the under side.

imbricated: overlapping, as shingles on a roof.

imperfect flower: one which lacks either stamens or pistils.

impressed: bent inward, furrowed as if by pressure.

incised: cut by sharp and irregular incisions more or less deeply, but intermediate between toothed and lobed.

included: not protruding as stamens not projecting beyond a corolla; opposed to exserted.

incomplete flower: one which lacks any one or more of these parts: calyx, corolla, stamens, and pistils.

incumbent: having cotyledons which within the seed lie face to face with the back of one lying against the hypocotyl; anthers are incumbent when turned inwards.

incurved: bent into an inward curve.

indehiscent: not opening regularly, as a capsule or anther.

indeterminate: said of those kinds of infl. whose terminal fls. open last, hence the growth or elongation of the main axis is not arrested by the opening of first flowers.

indigen: plant native and original to a region.

indumentum: with a generally heavy covering of hair: a general term without precise connotation.

indurate: hardened.

indusium: the epithelial excrescence that, when present, covers or contains the sporangia of a fern when the latter are in sori.

inferior: beneath, below; said of an ovary when situated below the apparent point of attachment of stamens and perianth; a fl. having such an ovary is said to be epigynous.

inflated: bladder like, loose and membraneous about the seed.

inflorescence: the method of flower-bearing; the disposition of flowers on the axis (or axes).

infundibular: funnel-shaped.

inner bark: cortical tissues inside the protective outer layers but outside the wood.

internode: the part of an axis between two nodes.

interrupted: not continuous, smaller parts or lack of parts between normal ones.

introduced: brought intentionally from another region for purposes of cultivation.

introrse: turned or faced inward, toward the central axis; said of stamens whose anthers dehisce on the side facing inward.

involucel: a secondary involucre.

involucral: of the involucre.

involucrate: having an involucre.

involucre: one or more whorls or series of small lvs. or bracts that are close underneath a fl. or infl.; the individual bracts termed phyllaries by some. Ex: subtending the heads of most members of the Compositae.

involute: a longitudinal curving or rolling upwards as opposed to revolute.

irregular flower: a flower that can be cut longitudinally into two equal halves at only one place; one having some parts different from other parts in the same series; a flower that is not symmetrical when in face view; a zygomorphic flower.

isodiametric: as broad as tall.

jointed: having nodes or points of real or apparent articulation.

jugum: a pair, as of leaflets.

junctures: winter nodes.

juvenile: an early phase of plant growth, usually characterized by non-flowering, vigorous increase in size, and often thorniness.

keel: of a papilionaceous corolla, the two front petals united along lower margin into a boat-shaped structure enveloping the pistil and stamens.

key: a small indehiscent fruit with a wing.

knees: pointed or domelike outgrowths from baldcypress roots, rising above the water.

labellum: a modified petal; the enlarged spreading or pouch-like lip of the orchid flower.

labiate: lipped, as in the corolla of most mints; as a proper noun, a member of the Labiatae family.

lacerate: irregularly torn or cleft.

laciniate: slashed into narrow pointed incisions.

lactiferous: milky.

lacuna: a cavity, hole or gap.

lageniform: gourd-shaped.

lamellae: thin flat plates or laterally flattened ridges.

lamellate: made up of thin plates.

lamina: a blade.

lanate: woolly; with long intertwined curly hairs.

lanceolate: much longer than wide, broadest below the middle and tapering to the apex.

lanuginose: cottony or woolly; downy, the hairs somewhat shorter than in lanate.

lanulose: very short woolly.

lateral: borne at or on the side, as flowers, buds or branches.

lateral bud: a bud borne in the axil of a previous season's leaf.

latex: milky sap.

lax: loose; the opposite of congested.

leader: the primary or terminal shoot, trunk of a tree.

leaf: the whole organ of photosynthesis, characterized by an axillary bud most of the year.

leaf ratio: the fraction obtained by dividing length by width.

leaf scar: the mark remaining after the leaf falls off a twig.

leaflet: a foliar element of a compound leaf.

legume: a dry fruit dehiscing along both sutures and the product of a single carpel (simple ovary). Ex: pea, most beans.

lemma: the outer or lowermost bract of the two immediately inclosing a grass flower.

lenticel: a small corky spot on young bark made of loosely packed cells, providing gaseous exchange between the inner tissues and the atmosphere.

lenticular: lens-shaped, the sides usually convex.

lepidote: covered with minute scurfy scales.

liana: a tropical woody vine.

lignified: woody, hardened.

ligulate: strap-shaped; a leaf blade with the sides essentially parallel and abruptly terminated.

ligule: (1) a strap-shaped organ; (2) (in grasses) a minute projection from the top of the leaf sheath; (3) the strap-shaped corolla in the ray flowers of Composites.

limb: the expanded, and usually terminal, part of a petal (as in *Dianthus*), or of a gamopetalous corolla as distinguished from the often constricted tube.

linear: long and very narrow, as in blades of grass.

lineate: lined; bearing thin parallel lines.

lined: lightly ridged or ribbed.

lingulate: tongue-shaped.

lip: one of the parts of an unequally divided corolla or calyx; these parts are usually two, the upper lip and the lower lip, although one lip is sometimes wanting; the seemingly lower lip of orchid fls. (the labellum) has this position because of a twisting of the pedicel or receptacle.

lobe: a projecting part or segment of an organ as in a lobed ovary or stigma; usually a division of a lf., calyx, or petals cut to about the middle (i.e. midway between margin and midrib).

locule: a cell or compartment of an ovary, anther or fruit.

loculicidal: *see dehiscent*.

lodicule: minute, gland-like structure at base of grass ovary.

loment: a legume constricted between the seeds (as in peanut) or which separates into one-seeded articulations (as in *Desmodium* or *Lespedeza*).

loose: not compact, irregularly formed.

lorate: strap-shaped.

lunate: crescent-shaped, as a quarter moon.

lustrous: having a slight metallic gloss, less reflective than glossy.

lyrate: having a pinnately compound leaf with the terminal lft. much larger than the lateral lfts. and the latter becoming progressively smaller basally.

macrospore: the larger of two spores (as in Selaginella) which on germination produces the female gametophyte; synonymous with megaspore.

marcescent: withering, but the remains persisting.

margin: the edge of a leaf.

marginal: pertaining to the margin.

matted: growing densely, forming a low close ground cover or compact tufts.

mature: a later phase of growth characterized by flowering, fruiting, and a reduced rate of size increase.

mealy: having a mottled, granular appearance.

membranaceous: of parchment-like texture.

meristem: nascent tissue, capable of developing into specialized tissues.

-merous: referring to the number of parts; as fls. 3-merous, in which the parts of each kind (as petals, sepals, stamens, etc.) are 3 each or in multiples of 3.

metamorphosed: changed from one state to a different one.

microsporangium: the microspore-containing case; an anther sac.

microspore: the smaller of two kinds of spores (as in *Selaginella*) which on germination produces the male gametophyte; sometimes applied to a pollen grain.

midrib: the primary-rib or mid-vein of a leaf or lft.

milky sap: whitish in color, often thicker than water.

monadelphous: said of stamens when united by their filaments. Ex: hollyhock.

moniliform: constricted laterally and appearing bead-like.

monocarpic: fruiting once and then dying. Ex: some palms and most bamboos.

monocot: angiospermous plant having only one cotyledon.

monoecious: a species with unisexual fls., having both sexes on the same plant. Ex: corn.

monogymous: having a gynoecium of one pistil.

monopodial: continuing growth from a terminal bud each year.

mossy: describes a matted growth habit, with small overlapping foliage.

mound: plant having a massive form, full to the ground.

mucilaginous: slimy.

mucro: a short, sharp, abrupt tip.

mucronate: abruptly terminated by a mucro.

mucronulate: minutely mucronate.

multiple buds: a terminal or lateral bud crowded by many accessory buds.

multiple fruit: one formed from several fls. into a single structure having a common axis, as in pineapple or mulberry.

mummy: a dried shrivelled fruit.

muricate: rough, due to presence of many minute spiculate excrescences on the epidermis.

muriform: with markings, pits, or reticulations arranged like bricks of a wall; as on some seed coats and achenes.

mutation: a sudden change in genetic material resulting in an altered individual. Generally disadvantageous to survival.

naked bud: one without scales.

naked flower: one having no floral envelopes (perianth).

nascent: in the act of being formed.

native: inherent and original to an area.

naturalized: thoroughly established, but originally from a foreign area.

navicular: coat-shaped, as glumes of most grasses.

nectary: a nectar-secreting gland; may be a protuberance, a scale, or a pit.

needle: the slender leaf of many conifers.

nerve: a slender rib or vein, especially unbranched.

netted venation: the veins reticulated and resembling a fish net; the interstices close.

neutral flower: a sterile fl. consisting of perianth without any essential organs.

nocturnal: opening at night and closing during the day.

nodding: drooping, bending over.

node: a joint on a stem, represented by point of origin of a leaf or bud; sometimes represented by a swollen or constricted ring, or by a distinct leaf scar.

nodulose: having small, swollen knobs; knot-like.

notched: with v-shaped indentations.

nut: a dry, indehiscent, 1-celled, 1-seeded fruit having a hard and bony mesocarp; the outermost endocarp may be fibrous or slightly fleshy.

nutlet: diminutive nut; applied to one of the four nucules of the fruit of the mint family.

ob-: prefix indicating the inverse.

obcordate: the apex being cordate.

oblanceolate: inversely lanceolate.

oblate: flattened at the poles.

oblique: lop-sided, as one side of a leaf base larger, wider or more rounded than the other.

oblong: longer than broad; rectangular; the sides nearly parallel.
oblong-lanceolate: a shape in between the two forms.
oblong-obovate: a shape in between the two forms.
obovate: inversely ovate, broadest above the middle.
obovoid: three dimensional shape of obovate, pear shaped.
obsolete: rudimentary.
obtuse: rounded, approaching the semi-circular.
ochrea: a nodal sheath formed by fusion of the two stipules. Ex: *Rumex, Polygonum.*
odd-pinnate: *see compound.*
odoriferous: aromatic but questionably pleasant.
oligo-: a prefix meaning few, as oligospermous-few-ovuled.
operculate: provided with a cap or lid (the operculum).
opposite: two at a node, as leaves.
orbiculate: circular or disk-shaped. Ex: leaf of common nasturtium.
orthotropous: said of an ovule or seed when straight and erect, the hilum at the base and micropyle at the apex.
osier: a long lithe stem.
oval: twice as long as broad, widest at the middle, both ends rounded.
ovary: the ovule-bearing part of a pistil; one borne above the point of attachment of perianth and stamens is a *superior ovary*; when below attachment of these floral envelopes it is an *inferior* or *hypogenous ovary*; when intermediate or surrounded by an hypanthium it is a *half-inferior* or *perigynous ovary.*
ovate: egg-shaped in outline, broadest below the middle, like an oval.
ovate-oblong: a combination of the two forms.
ovoid: said of a solid that is three-dimensionally egg-shaped.
ovulate: bearing ovules.
ovule: the egg-containing unit of an ovary, which after fertilization becomes the seed.

paired: occurring in twos.
palamatified: cut palmately about half-way down.
palate: the projecting part of the lower lip of a bilabiate corolla that closes the throat of the corolla or nearly does so. Ex: toad-flax, snapdragon.
palea (Palet): the inner of the two bracts immediately subtending a grass flower; the lower one is the lemma.
palmate: digitate, radiating, fan-like from a common point, as leaflets of a palmately compound lf. or veins of palmately-veined lf.
pandurate: fiddle-shaped.
panicle: an indeterminate infl. whose primary axis bears branches of pedicel led fls. (at least basally so); a branching raceme.
paniculate: bearing panicles.
papilionaceous: having a pea-like corolla that is comprised of standard, wings and keel.
papillate: bearing minute, pimple-like protuberances (Papillae).
pappillose: with small nipple-like projections.
pappus: the modified calyx of Composites, borne on the ovary (usually persisting on the achene) and represented by hairs, bristles, awns, scales, or others.
parallel: especially of veins, running side by side from base to tip.
parallel venation: the veins extending in more or less parallel fashion from base to apex.
parenchyma: unspecialized living cells, present in the pith.
parietal: borne on the side walls of an ovary (or capsule), or on invaginations of the wall that form incomplete partitions or septae within the ovary.
parted: cleft or cut not quite to the base.
pectinate: comb-like or pinnatifid with very close narrow divisions or parts; also used to describe spine conditions in cacti when small lateral spines radiate as comb-teeth from areole.
pedate: a palmately divided or compound lf. whose two lateral lobes are again cleft or divided.
pedicel: the stalk of a flower or fruit when in a cluster or when solitary.
peduncle: the stalk of a fl. cluster or a single fl. when that fl. is solitary, or the remaining member of a reduced infl. (as in *Euphorbia* where a constriction designates the "break" between peduncle and pedicel).
pellucid: clear or translucent, said of minute glandular dots that can nearly be seen through when viewed in transmitted light.

peltate: having the petiole attached inside the margin, such a lf. is typically shield-shaped.

pendulous: more or less hanging or declined.

penniveined: pinnately arranged.

percurrent: the main trunk continuing through to the top.

perennial: of three or more seasons duration.

perfect flower: having both functional stamens and pistils.

perfoliate: the leaf-blade surrounding the stem. Ex: *Uvularia perfoliatus.*

perianth: the two floral envelopes of a fl.; a collective term embracing both corolla and calyx as a unit; often used when it is not possible to distinguish one series from the other (as in most monocots) and the parts then called tepals.

pericarp: a term used by some to designate a fruit; technically, the ovary wall.

periderm: a protective layer of corky cells.

perigynous: borne around the ovary but not fused to it, as when calyx, corolla and stamens are borne on the edge of a cup-shaped hypanthium. Ex: coral-bells, fuchsia, evening-primrose.

persistent: adhering to position instead of falling, whether dead or live.

personate: concealed; a corolla whose tube is closed by a palate, as in snapdragon.

perulate: scale-bearing, as a scaly bud.

petal: one unit of the inner floral envelope or corolla of a polypetalous fl., usually colored and more or less showy.

petaloid: a structure not a petal (for example a sepal) that is of the color and shape of a petal; resembling a petal.

petiole: leaf-stalk.

petiolule: leaflet-stalk.

phylloclad: a branch, more or less flattened, functioning as a leaf. Ex: Christmas cactus.

phyllodium: a flattened, expanded petiole without blade and functioning as a lf. Ex: some spp. *Acacia.*

phyllotaxy: arrangement of lvs. or of floral parts on their axis.

picturesque: striking in an unusual way.

pilose: shaggy with soft hairs.

pinked: notched.

pinna: the lft. of a compound lf.; of ferns, the primary division attached to the main rachis; feather-like.

pinnate: compounded with the lfts. or segments along each side of a common axis or rachis; feather-like.

pinnatifid: pinnately cleft or parted.

pinnatisect: pinnately cut to midrib or almost to it.

pinnule: the lft. of a pinna; a secondary lft. of a pinnately decompound lf.

pistil: the unit of the gynoecium comprised of ovary, style and stigma: it may consist of 1 or more carpels; the former with a single placenta is a *simple pistil*, the latter with 2 or more carpels is a *compound pistil. See carpel* or *ovary.*

pistillate: having no functional stamens (staminodia may be present) in the flower.

pith: the central part of a twig, usually lighter or darker than the wood.

pitted: marked with small depressions.

placenta: that place in the ovary where ovules are attached. A location, not a structure.

placentation: the arrangement of ovules within the ovary. Several types are recognized, among them are: *parietal placentation* (see *parietal*), *axile placentation*, the ovules borne in the center of the ovary on the axis formed by the union and fusion of the septae (partitions) and usually in vertical rows; in 2-celled ovaries they are borne in the center and on the cross partition or on a proliferation of it often filling the loculi; *free central placentation*, the ovules borne on a central column with no septae present; *basal placentation*, the ovules few or reduced to one and borne at the base of the ovary, the solitary ovule often filling the cavity; *lamellate placentation*, the ovules completely sunken in spongy ovarian and receptacular tissues with only the discoid stigmas exserted.

plicate: folded, as in a folding fan, or approaching this condition.

plugged pith: having cross partitions at the nodes.

plumose: feather-like, plumy.

pod: a dry dehiscent fruit; a general term.

pollen: microspores contained within an anther; sometimes agglutinated into a mass.

pollinium: an agglutinated, coherent mass of pollen. Ex: milkweeds, orchids.

polycarpic: flowering and fruiting many times. *See monocarpic.*

polygamo-dioecious: having male and female fls. on separate plants, but these plants having perfect flowers as well.

polygamous: bearing unisexual and bisexual flowers on the same plant.

polypetalous: with a corolla of separate petals. *See corolla.*

polysepalous: having a calyx of separated sepals.

pome: a type of fleshy fruit represented by the apple, pear and related genera, resulting from a compound ovary.

poricidal: *see dehiscence.*

porrect: said of cactus spines when the laterals are at right angles to the central one of an areole.

posterior: at or toward the back; opposite the front; nearest the axis; away from the subtending bract.

preformed: already having definite structure, such as leaves within a bud.

prehensile: clasping or coiling in response to touch.

prickle: an excrescence of bark that is small, weak, and spine-like.

primocane: the first year's shoot or cane of a biennial woody stem. Ex: *Rubus.*

procumbent: lying flat on the ground but the stem not rooting at nodes or tip.

prominent: projecting outward, conspicuous.

prostrate: lying flat on the ground; a general term.

protandrous: with anthers maturing before the stigma.

protogynous: having stigma receptive to pollen before pollen is released from anthers of same fl.

proximal: toward the base, away from the apex.

pruinose: having a coarse, granular, dust-like, waxy bloom.

pseudo-terminal bud: seemingly the terminal bud of a twig, but actually the upper-most lateral bud with its subtending lf. scar on one side and the scar of the terminal bud often visible on opposite side.

puberulent: minutely pubescent as viewed with a lens.

pubescent: covered with short soft hairs; a general term.

pulvinate: cushion-shaped.

pulvinus: a minute gland or a swollen base of the petiole or petiolule responding to vibrations. Ex: sensitive-plant (*Mimosa*).

punctate: with translucent or covered dots, depressions, or pits.

pungent: terminated by a sharp stiff point; sharp and acid to taste or smell.

pustular: blistery, usually minutely so.

pyramidal: broadest at base, tapering apically; pyramid-shaped.

pyrene: the pit or "seed" of a drupelet.

pyriform: pear-shaped.

pyxidium: pyxis: a capsule dehiscing circumscissilely.

quadrangular: four angled, of pith or a twig.

raceme: a simple indeterminate inflorescence with pedicel led flowers.

racemose: having flowers in racemes.

rachilla: a diminutive or secondary axis; a branch of a rachis; the minute axis bearing the individual florets in grass and sedge spikelets; the secondary axes of decompound fern fronds.

rachis: axis bearing leaflets or the primary axis of an infl.; the axis bearing pinnae of a fern frond.

radial: arranged around and spreading from a common center.

radiate: (1) said of a Composite infl. when bearing ray fls.; (2) star-shaped or spreading from a common center.

radical: of or pertaining to the root.

radicle: the embryonic root of a seed.

ramified: branched.

ramiform: branching.

ranked: foliage is arranged in longitudinal planes around the stem.

raphides: needle-like crystals in plant tissues.

ray: (1) the ligulate or lorate corolla of some composite flower; (2) the fl. of a Composite having a ligulate or strap-shaped corolla; (3) the axes of an umbel or umbel-like inflorescence.

receptacle: a torus; the distal end of a flower-bearing axis, usually more or less enlarged, flattened, or cup-like on which some or all of the flower parts are borne. Ex: Compositae, Onagraceae.

reclining: having an axis that is falling back or bent down from the vertical.

recurved: bent or curved backward, usually roundly or obtusely so. *See reflexed.*

reduced: smaller or simpler than normal.

reduplicate: said of buds whose components have their edges rolled outward in aestivation.

reflexed: bent abruptly backward or downward.

regular flowers: (1) a flower that can be cut longitudinally into two equal halves along an indefinite number of radii; (2) one having the parts of any one series all alike and uniformly disposed about the axis, as petals all alike, sepals all alike, etc.; a symmetrical or actinomorphic fl.

remote: widely spaced.

reniform: kidney-shaped.

repandate: having a weakly sinuate margin, one slightly uneven.

repent: creeping along the ground and rooting at the nodes.

replum: the partition separating the two loculi or cells or cruciferous fruits.

resin duct: a lengthwise or transverse canal carrying resins.

resinous: secreting a viscid exudate.

reticulate: like a net, the interstices closed.

retrorse: turned back or downwards, usually applied to armament or vesture.

retuse: notched slightly at a usually obtuse apex.

revolute: rolled toward the back, as a margin tightly or laxly rolled along the lower side.

rhizome: an underground stem distinguishable from a root by presence of nodes, buds or scale-like lvs.

rhombic: with four nearly equal sides, but unequal angles, diamond shaped.

rhombic-ovate: somewhere between egg and diamond shaped.

rhomboidal: of the shape of a rhomboid.

rib: conspicuous vein of a lf.; a prominent ridge.

root: the descending axis of the plant, without nodes and internodes, usually underground.

rootlet: a subdivision of a root, also an aerial root.

rosette: a crown of lvs. radiating from a st. and at or close to the surface of the ground.

rostellum: a small beak: a projection from the distal edge of the stigma in many monandrial orchids.

rostrate: beaked.

rosulate: in rosettes, or rosette-like in form.

rotate: wheel-shaped, a corolla whose limb flares out at right angles to the fl. axis and with no conspicuous tube produced; a flat circular or disc-like limb.

rotund: orbicular and inclining to be oblong.

rudiment: the beginning of an undeveloped member.

rufous: reddish brown.

rugose: wrinkled, usually covered with wrinkles.

ruminate: mottled in appearance, in a surface or tissue due to dark and light zones or irregular outline.

runcinate: pinnatifidly incised, the incision sharp and pointing backward. Ex: some *Taraxacum* leaves.

runner: a slender trailing shoot that usually roots at the tip and some nodes.

saccate: bag-shaped, pouchy.

sagittate: shaped like an arrow-head with the basal lobes pointing directly downward (backward) or inward.

salverform: said of a corolla with a slender tube and an abruptly expanded flat limb extending at right angles to the tube. Ex: *Phlox, Galium*, most primulas.

samara: a dry indehiscent fruit bearing a wing (the wing may be limb-like or envelop the seed and be wafer-like). Ex: maple, ash, *Ptelea*.

sarmentose: producing long flexuous runners.

scabrous: rough or gritty to the touch; rough-pubescent.

scalariform: said of pits or pith partitions when arranged like ladder rungs.

scale: a small and usually dry bract or vestigial leaf or a structure resembling such.

scandent: climbing, usually without tendrils.

scape: a leafless peduncle arising from the basal rosette of a few or no basal leaves; sometimes a few scale-like lvs. or bracts may be borne on it; a scape may be one or many-flowered.

scapose: bearing its fls. on a scape.

scar: the mark left from a former attachment.

scarious: thin, dry, membranous and usually translucent margins or parts that are not green in color.

scattered: not in any patterned arrangement, especially of vascular bundle scars.

schizocarp: a dry dehiscent fr. that splits into two halves. Ex: maple.

scorpioid-cyme: a determinate infl. (often seemingly indeterminate) that is coiled with the fls. 2-ranked and borne alternately at the right and the left. Ex: forget-me-not, heliotrope.

scrambler: plant that climbs without twining or grasping in some way.

scurfy: describes a surface covered with bran-like particles.

scutate: like a small shield.

secund: one-sided, in that the fls. are seemingly borne in a one-sided infl.

seed: a fertilized ripened ovule that contains an embryo.

segment: a portion of a leaf or perianth that is divided but not compound.

semi-cordate: partly heartshaped.

semi-evergreen: green for only a part of the winter, or only part of the foliage fully evergreen.

sepal: one of the units comprising the calyx; a usually green foliaceous element subtending the corolla.

septate: divided by partitions.

septicidal: *see dehiscence*.

septum: a partition.

sericeous: *see silky*.

serotinous: produced late in the season, late to open; having cones that remain closed long after the seeds are ripe.

serrate: saw-toothed, the teeth pointing forward.

serrulate: minutely serrate.

sessile: without a stalk.

seta: a bristle.

setaceous: bristle-like.

setose: covered with bristles.

shaggy: covered with or resembling long rough woolly hair.

sheath: any elongated, more or less tubular structure enveloping an organ or part.

shrub: a woody plant that is never tree-like in habit and produces branches or shoots from or near the base.

silicle: the short fr. of some crucifers, which is usually not more than 1 1/2 times as long as wide.

silique: the elongated fr. of some crucifers, usually 3 times as long as wide or longer.

silky: covered with soft appressed fine straight hairs; sericeous.

simple: said of a lf. when not compound, of an infl. when unbranched.

sinuate: with a strongly wavy margin.

sinus: the space between two lobes, segments, or divisions; as of lvs. or perianth parts.

smooth: not roughened, not warty.

solitary: occurring alone, not paired or clustered.

sori: *see sorus*.

sorus: cluster of sporangia (of ferns), appearing usually as a dot on the dorsal surface of a frond.

spadix: a fleshy usually club-shaped axis on which are borne fls. and which is generally enveloped by a spathe; the infl. of most Araceae; sometimes employed for the branched infl. of palms.

spathe: the bract or modified leaf surrounding or subtending a flowering infl. (usually a spadix); it may be herbaceous, colored, and "flower-like" as in the calla-lily or the anthurium, or hard, dry and woody in many palms. By some the term is restricted to members of the Araceae.

spathe valves: one or more herbaceous or scarious bracts that subtend an inflorescence or a flower.

spatulate: spoon-shaped.

species: a natural group of plants composed of similar individuals which can produce similar offspring; usually including several minor variations.

spicate: with spikes.

spicula: a cymule or small cyme.

spike: (1) a usually unbranched, elongated, simple, indeterminate infl. whose fls. are sessile; the fls. may be congested or remote; (2) a seemingly simple infl. whose "fls." may actually be composite heads (Liatris).

spikelet: (1) a secondary spike; (2) one part of a compound infl. which of itself is spicate; (3) the floral unit, or ultimate cluster, of a grass infl. comprised of fls. and their subtending bracts.

spine: an excrescence of st., strong and sharp-pointed. Ex: spines of hawthorns.

spinescent: more or less spiny.

spinose: beset with spines.

spirally arranged: the actual pattern of alternate leaves.

spongy: porous, as parenchyma cells of the pith.

sporangium: a spore-containing case, as in ferns.

spore: a minute reproductive body comprised of a single gametophytic cell.

sporocarp: a body containing sporangia or spores.

sporophyll: a spore-bearing leaf.

spray: a branchlet with foliage.

spreading: growing outward or horizontally.

spur: a tubular or sac-like projection from a fl. and usually from a sepal or petal.

squamate: with small scab-like projection from a fl. and usually from a sepal or petal.

squamose: covered with small scales, more coarsely so than when lepidote.

squarrose: with branches spreading and recurved at the ends.

stalk: a supporting structure of a leaf, flower or fruit.

stalked bud: a bud whose outer scales are attached above the base of the bud axis.

stamen: the unit of the androecium and typically comprised of anther and filament, sometimes reduced to only an anther; the pollen-bearing organ of a seed plant.

staminate: describes an imperfect flower with only functional stamens, male.

staminate flower: *see flower.*

staminode (staminodium): a sterile stamen reduced to a non-functional filament-like stalk, a gland, or sometimes expanded and petal-like; borne in the same or adjacent whorl as the functional stamens.

standard: (1) of a papilionaceous fl., the upper usually expanded, more or less erect petal; (2) the erect petals of an iris fl. as opposed to the broader and often drooping falls.

stellate: star-like; stellate hairs having radiating branches or are separate hairs aggregated in star-like clusters; hairs once or twice forked often are treated as stellate.

stellate-pubescent: with hairs in small starlike tufts.

stem: the primary axis of a plant having foliage and flowers opposed to the root axis.

sterigma: the raised base from which some small evergreen leaves finally fall (spruces).

sterile: barren, not able to produce seed.

stigma: the usually distal end of the pistil that receives the pollen, of varied shapes and surfaces.

stipe: (1) a naked stalk; (2) the petiole of a fern frond.

stipel: a stipule of a lft.

stipellate: having stipels at the base of the leaflets.

stipular, stipulate: having stipules at the base of the leaves.

stipule: a basal appendage of a petiole, usually one at each side, often ear-like and sometimes caducous.

stipule scar: a pair of marks left after the stipules fall off, to either side of the leaf scar.

stolon: a horizontal stem that roots at its tip and there gives rise to a new plant.

stoloniferous: bearing slender stems just on or under the ground which roots at the tips.

stoma: a minute pore in the epidermis, especially in the lower surface on the leaf.

stomatiferous: bearing stomata.

stone: the hard usually one-seeded endocarp of a drupe.

stratified: arranged in horizontal layers.

striate: with fine longitudinal lines, channels or ridges.

strict: rigidly erect.

strigose: with sharp, stiff, straight and appressed hairs.

strobilus: a cone.

style: the more or less elongated part of a pistil between the stigma and the ovary.

stylopodium: a disk-like enlargement at the base of a style.

subcontinuous pith: with occasional but not regular gaps.

submerged bud: a bud hidden by the petiole or embedded in the callus of the leaf scar.

subopposite: pairs of leaves close but not exactly at the same level on the stem.

subpetiolar: under the base of the petiole.

subtend: to stand immediately beneath.

subulate: awl-shaped.

succulent: thickened, juicy, fleshy tissues that are more or less soft in texture.

sucker: a shoot arising from the roots or from beneath the surface of the ground; also the adhering discs of a vine.

suffrutescent: a plant whose stems are woody basally but herbaceous above, dying back to the woody portion at the close of each growing season. Ex: *Alyssum saxatile* (now *Aurinia saxatile*), rock rose, *Pachysandra.*

sulcate: deeply grooved lengthwise.

superficial: on the surface, not connected to inner tissues.

superior ovary: *see ovary*.

superposed bud: accessory bud above the true lateral bud.

supine: lying flat, face upwards.

suture: a line of dehiscence or groove marking a face of union.

syconium: the fruit of a fig.

symmetrical: actinomorphic or regular (flower) to the extent that the parts of the several series (calyx, corolla, stamens) are each of the same number.

symmetrical flower: one having the same number of parts in each envelope (calyx and corolla).

sympetalous: the petals united at least at the base; synonym for gamopetalous.

sympodial: continuing growth by the development of an axillary bud and not the terminal bud, season after season.

sympodial inflorescence: a determinate infl. that simulates an indeterminate infl., as if a scorpioid cyme were straight rather than circinate.

syncarp: a fleshy aggregate fruit.

syncarpous: having a gynoecium with all the carpels united.

syngenesious: stamens connate by their anthers in a cylinder about the style. Ex: Compositae family.

tailed: said of anthers having caudal appendages.

tapering: gradually decreasing towards an end.

taxonomy: the area of botany dealing with the classifying and naming of plants.

tendril: a modified stem or leaf, usually filiform, branched or simple, that twines about an object providing support.

tepal: a segment of perianth not differentiated into calyx or corolla. Ex: tulip, magnolia.

terete: cylindrical, or at least circular in cross section.

terminal: at the tip or distal end.

ternate: in threes.

testa: the outer coat of a seed.

tetradynamous: with an androecium of 6 stamens, four longer than the other two, as in Cruciferae.

texture: the effect of the surface structure.

thallus: a foliaceous organ, not differentiated into the stem and foliage and not bearing true roots.

thicket: a dense growth of shrubs, a copse.

thorn: a modified twig which has tiny leaf scars and buds; can be single or branched.

throat: the opening into the lower end of a gamopetalous corolla, the point where the limb joins the tube.

thyrse: compact panicle-like infl. whose distal end is indeterminate and the lateral branches determinate. Ex: lilac (*Syringe vulgaris*).

tomentose: densely woolly, the hairs soft and matted.

tomentulose: diminutive of tomentose; delicately tomentose.

tomentum: the dense matted hairs.

toothed: the margin broken up into small rather regular segments.

torose: cylindrical with constrictions at intervals, slightly moniliform.

torsion: twisting.

torulose: twisted or knobby; irregularly swollen at close intervals.

torus: *see receptacle*.

trailing: prostrate and not rooting.

translucent: transmitting light but diffuse enough to distort images.

transverse ridge: one which runs across the stem from one leaf scar to its pair on opposite twigs.

tree: a woody plant with one main stem at least 12 to 15 feet tall, and having a distinct head in most cases.

triangular-ovate: a flattened angular egg shape.

trichoma: a bristle.

trifid: three-cleft.

trifoliate: three-leaved. Ex: *Trillium*.

trifoliolate: with a leaf of three lfts.

tripinnate: with compounded pinnules.

triquetrous: three-angled.

triternate: a biternate lf. again divided in 3's. Ex: many spp. *Thalictrum*.

truncate: as if cut off at right angles to the primary axis; a term applicable to bases or apices.

tuber: a short, thickened organ, usually—but not necessarily—an underground stem.

tubercle: a miniature tuber, tuber-like body or projection.

tubular: having petals, sepals, or both united into a tube.

tuft: a clump of hairs growing close together.

tumid: swollen.

tunic: a coat about an organ, often fibrous or papery. Ex: about the crocus corm or tulip bulb.

tunicated: with concentric layers, often of fleshy scales. Ex: onion bulb.

turbinate: inversely conical, top-shaped.

turgid: swollen to firmness.

turion: a young shoot or sucker. Ex: asparagus stalk.

twig: the shoot of a woody plant representing the growth of the current season.

twig scar: mark left by the sloughing of a length of dead twig tissue.

twiggy: having many divergent twigs.

twining: the stem winding about a support.

umbel: an indeterminate infl., usually but not necessarily flat-topped with the pedicels and peduncles (termed rays) arising from a common point, resembling the stays of an umbrella.

umbellate: having umbels.

umbellet: a secondary umbel.

umbo: a conical projection arising from the surface.

unarmed: without a sharp defense such as spines or bristles.

uncinate: hooked at the tip.

undulate: wavy, as a leaf margin.

unguiculate: narrowed into a petiole-like base; clawed.

unijugate: a compound lf. reduced to a single pair of leaflets.

unilateral: one-sided.

unilocular: one-celled or with a single cavity.

unisexual flowers: of one sex only. *See flower.*

urceolate: urn-shaped; constricted at the throat.

utricle: a small dry thin-walled, usually dehiscent, 1-seeded fruit; an achene whose pericarp is loose and readily removed. Ex: *Amaranthus.*

vaginate: sheathed.

valvate: (1) dehiscing by valves; (2) meeting by the edges without overlapping, as lvs. or petals in the bud.

valve: a separable part of a dehiscent fruit or stamen; the unit into which a capsule splits or divides in dehiscing.

variegated: striped, margined or mottled with a color other than green, where green is normal.

variety: subdivision of a species having a distinct though often inconspicuous difference, and breeding true to that difference. More generally also refers to clones.

vascular bundle: a discrete group of conducting vessels.

vascular bundle scar: a minute spot within the leaf scar where the vessels were positioned.

vasiform: an elongated funnel-shaped object.

vein: a vascular rib of the leaf.

velutinous: clothed with a velvety indumentum comprised of erect straight dense moderately firm hairs.

venation: arrangement of veins.

ventral: relating to the anterior or inner face or part of an organ, the opposite of dorsal.

ventricose: a one-sided swelling or inflation, more pronounced than gibbous.

venulose: with very fine veins.

vernal: related to spring.

vernation: the arrangement of leaves within a bud.

verrucose: having a wart-like surface.

versatile: moving freely because of attachment near the middle, as an anther attached crosswise medianly to the filament.

vertical: having broad faces perpendicular to the earth.

verticil: a whorl.

verticillate: arranged in whorls.

verticillate inflorescence: one with the flowers in whorls about the axis, the whorls remote from one another (as in many salvias) or congested into head-like structures (catnip). Such whorls are false-whorls since they are actually sessile cymes arranged opposite one another in the axils of opposite bracts or leaves.

vesicle: a small bladdery sac or cavity filled with air or fluid.

vestige: the remains of an exhausted or dead member.

vesture: any substance on or arising from the surface rendering it other than glabrous.

vexillum: the petal of a papilionaceous corolla known also as the standard; the upper broad petal.

villous: having long, soft, shaggy hairs that are not matted.

vine: a slender-stemmed climbing or trailing plant.

virgate: wand-like; long straight and slender.

viscid: sticky or with appreciable viscosity.

vittatae: the oil tubes of Umbelliferae, especially of their fruits.

voluble: twining.

warty: marked with rounded tubercles, rougher than granules.

watery sap: thin and clear.

wavy: alternating concave and convex curves.

weeping: dropping conspicuously, pendent.

whorl: arrangement of three or more structures arising from a single node.

whorled: in a whorl, as leaves.

wilt: to become limp and lose turgor through a deficit of water.

wing: (1) the lateral petal of a papilionaceous flower; (2) a dry, thin, membranous appendage.

wither: to dry up and shrivel.

wood: a dead, hard xylem tissue.

woolly: having long, soft, more or less matted hairs; like wool.

×: indicates a hybrid.

zig-zag: bent back and forth at the nodes.

zone: an area restricted by a range of annual average minimum temperatures, used in describing hardiness.

zygomorphic: irregular, not symmetrical.

SCIENTIFIC NAME INDEX

(Main treatment is given in **bold**.)

COMMON NAME INDEX

Common Name	Scientific Name	Number
American Arborvitae	Thuja occidentalis	1009
Arizona Cypress	Cupressus arizona	307
Chinese Fir	Cunninghamia lanceolata	303
David Viburnum	Viburnum davidii	1064
Dwarf Alberta Spruce	Picea glauca	716
Hetz Juniper *blue female*	Juniperus chinensis "Hetzi"	504
Hinoki Cypress	Chamaecyparis obtusa	218
Japanese Andromeda	Pieris japonica	722
Japanese False Cypress	Chamaecyparis pisifera	220
Leatherleaf Mahonia	Mohonia bealei	627
Lusterleaf or Magnolialeaf Holly	Ilex latifolia	481
Mt. Laurel	Kalmia latifolia	526
Oriental Artorvitae	Thuja orientalis	1011
Pfitzer's Juniper *green male*	Juniperus chinensis "Pfitzeriana"	504
Scarlet Firethorn	Pyracantha coccinea	803
Western Arborvitae	Thuja pliccata	1013

sawa

Common Name	Scientific Name	Number
Hinoki Cypress	Chamaecyparis obtusa	218
Japanese False Cypress	Chamaecyparis pisifera 'Fillifera'	220
Chinese Fir	Cunninghamia lanceolata	303
Arizona Cypress	Cupressus arizona	307
Lusterleaf or Magnolialeaf Holly	Ilex latifolia	481
Hetz Juniper *blue female*	Juniperus chinensis "Hetzi"	504
Pfitzer's Juniper *green male*	Juniperus chinensis "Pfitzeriana"	504
Mt. Laurel	Kalmia latifolia	526
Leatherleaf Mahonia	Mohonia bealei	627
Dwarf Alberta Spruce	Picea glauca	716
Japanese Andromeda	Pieris japonica	722
Scarlet Firethorn	Pyracantha coccinea	803
American Arborvitae	Thuja occidentalis	1009
Oriental Artorvitae	Thuja orientalis	1011
Western Arborvitae	Thuja pliccata	1013
David Viburnum	Viburnum davidii	1064

Rhapidophyllum hystrix - Needle Palm ~ long hollow
needles near bottom (mulch)
- native to coast
- cold hard to 15 below 0
ora

foster   savannah

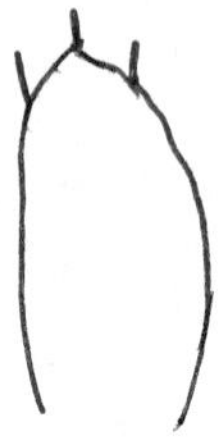

Hinoki - sculpted shapes
- clumps of fan
shaped needles

Sawara false cypress - graceful
mounding

① Arizona cypress - upright, pyramidal
evergreen
- Δ leaves
- grey green or blue green.

firethorn - thorny stiff upright shrub,
heavy berry set

~~Thu~~
American Arborvitae - narrow
upright, vertical leaves

Oriental Arborvitae - broader,
swirled foilage

Western Arborvitae - soft needle
foilage, replacement
for Leyland cypress

Leyland - more
handish than
Bald cypress

Japanese Andromeda
flowers: white! lots of them

- lacebug

leather leaf mahonia

David's viburnum
- fuzzy foilage
- usually only
green in zone 7

lusterleaf holly - magnolia leaf
holly - LARGE, sunburns, big as
opaca but shiny rounder leaves

Juniper chinensis - large & wide

Mt. Laurel - lots of white balloon flowers

Edible

- 1950's
- bad pesticides
- local produce good
- multicultural polyglot
- antioxidants
- less likely to gain weight
- fruit trees is Rosaceae
  - Pome fruits: apples, pears
  - stone fruit - peaches, plums
- persimmon Diospyros kaki
- mullberry Morus alba
- common fig Ficus carica
- pawpaw Asimina triloba
- strawberry tree Arbutus unendo
- Vitis - grapes
- Kiwi Actinidia deliciosa
- Ribes spp. - gooseberries
- highbush blueberry - vaccinium corymbosum (antioxidants)
- Rubus spp. - raspberry, blackberry
- Herbs - health + well being
- Camelia sinensis - tea camelic (potent antioxidant)

Climate

lobal warming - move plants north   origins: mediterranean, Africa,
one 8 + 9 - SE U.S. - humid   South America, North America
sabal palmetto - Palmetto

Parson's Nursery

1959
Louis P. Parsons

45. **Quercus myrsinifolia(Chinese evergreen)-** Long dark lustrous leaves, smooth gray bark, street tree, slow growth, poor soils, slightly scalloped leaf margins, behind p&a
46. **Quercus virginia-** you know this one
47. **Rhaphiolepsis umbellate(Indian Heather)-** Mounded shrub w/ round leaves, white spring flowers, black fall berries, Drought tolerance, red tip in shade, insect & disease
48. **Rhododendron catawbiense-** NATIVE w/ pest problems, very large flowers truss, small flowers all in one big bunch. Acid soils, shallow roots
49. **Rhododendron 'Encore'-** No wet feet, blooms twice a year, Big Flowers, all different colors.
50. **Rhododendron x indica (Southern indica)-** larger leaves, larger flowers than kurume, lacebugs & petal blight, whites pinks purples in Early Spring, Shallow Roots, traditional plants of Deep South.
51. **Rhododendron x obtusum (Kurume)-** acidic soils ; red, white, pink, salmon flowers in spring, shallow roots, brown scaly leaves. I DON'T KNOW!
52. **Taxus media (anglojap)-** Dark, green needle leaf, Flat in ranks of two, multi stemmed, flat top, rounded. No wet feet
53. **Ternstroemia gymnanthera(Cleyera)-**upright oval broadleaf, fragrant flowers in spring, red new growth, shade, no wet feet, round looking hangy things?
54. **Trachycarpus fortunei(windmill palm)-** Whorled Leaves, Most Cold hardy of tree types, really a grass, Exfoliating bark
55. **Tsuga Canadensis(Hemlock)- LITTLE PINE CONES hang off end** Large Flat needles in rows of 2, shade or sun, avoid heat, drained cool acid soils, Disease and insects, No urban sites, behind the sorority dorms.
56. **Viburnum awabucki-** Pyramidal Christmas tree shape, Large dark green leaves, bright red lustrous berries, winter burn, leaves look like a frito scoop shape ☺
57. **Viburnum tinus(Laurustinus)-**metallic blueberries, white flowers
58. **X Cupressocyparis leylandii(Leyland Cypress)-** pyramidal tree w/ fine foliage in bright green, short lived, fast growing, no wet feet, Oppressed needles, Beside P&A.

1. **Abelia x grandiflora-** tough tri-color screen, fast growth, caning shrub, shade & sun, Behind Brooks Center.
2. **Aucuba japonica-** Yellow Spotted Leaves, No direct Sun, Moist Soils
3. **Berberis julianae(Wintergreen)-** Large prickly leaves, Large Thorns, yellow spring flowers
4. **Buxus microphylla(Japanese boxwood)-** densely branched shrub, Opposite leaves, no extreme heat or cold, variety of forms available, no acid soils, well drained soils
5. **Camelia Japonica-** Bigger Leaves and Flowers than Sasanqua, some pests. Glossy Dark Leaves
6. **Cedrus deodara(deodar)-** True Cedar, blue whorled needles, long yellow cones pollen(males), Rose like pine cones(females), well drained soils, flat topped w/ die back problems, Next to Sirrine across from Fernow.
7. **Cephalotaxus harrintonia ' Prostrata'(plum yew)-** Spreading evergreen shrub, Large flat needles arrange in 2 ranks along stem, fine in sun but takes shade, needs water to establish, long shoots close to ground.
8. **Cryptomeria japonica (Japanese Cedar)-** Rounded Needles, Pyramidal Shape, Strong Wood
9. **Eriobotrya japonica(Loquat)-** P&A entrance, Large Green deeply veined leaves, Cream white fall flowers-Fragrant, Will fruit in warmer areas
10. **Fatsia japonica-** Large palmately lobed leaf, Brooks Center walkway
11. **Ilex x attenuata-** Most popular in South, Heavy Fruit set, Spiny slender leaves, fast growing, acid soils. 'Foster Holly'(narrow tree, small berries) and 'Savannah'(larger multi stemmed tree, larger berries, broader leaves)
12. **Ilex cornuta-** Fork looking leaves, looks as if you would die if you fell in
13. **Ilex cornuta 'Burfordi'-** Blue green leaves w/ single barb. Leaf looks thick with Heavy berry set, indented veins.. Used as Screen. Near ramp at P&A.
14. **Ilex cornuta 'Carissa'-** Broad leaf, single barb, not known for berries, thinner leaf
15. **Ilex crenata 'Compacta'-** Small round leaves, black fruit
16. **Ilex crenata 'Hetzi'-** bigger leaves than compacta. Near P&A
17. **Ilex glabra(inkberry)-** rounded leaves, black fruit, Pest Free, Wet Sites
18. **Ilex x 'Nellie R. Stevens'-** Large fruit heavy, Large dark leaf w/ 3 small terminal spikes, fast growing, Popular in South
19. **Ilex opaca(American)-** Pyramidal multi stemmed tree, large spiny leaves, red berries on females, NATIVE, slower than hybrids. Leaf minor & berry midge
20. **Ilex vomitoria-** Purple Petioles, small leaves, red berries, Dry soils, wet sites, Pest resistant NATIVE!
21. **Illicium floridanum(Florida anise shrub)-** Resembles sweetshrub, red thingys, wetter soils ok. Aromatic, Pest free NATIVE!
22. **Juniperus chinensis 'kaizuka'(Hollywood)-** Upright tree w/ twisted shape, can be blue green, full sun, no wet feet, Near McAdams
23. **Juniperus conferta(Shore)-** Bright blue green, no wet sites, very poor sites, very dry conditions, Dense pointed leaves w/ grooved blue stripe on back, In front of Daniel.

24. **Juniperus davurica 'Expansa' (Parsons)-** Juvenile and Mature foliage present, NO wet feet, stiff groundcover. Caboose at Botanical Garden
25. **Juniperus horizontalis(creeping)-** Low growing long stems & tapered leaves, green or blue, all soils, poor hot dry sites, 'Bar Harbor"-male, 'Blue rug'-Female(we saw this one) berries
26. **Juniperus procumbens(Japanese garden)-** Blue green leaves, long low branching w/ upward pointing tips, Rock garden plant, 'nana'(we saw- near library)-blue green & dense
27. **Juniperus virginiana(Eastern red cedar)-** NATIVE, Looks crappy in old age, yellow-green to blue, Beautiful bark in Maturity, poor soils, across from Fernow
28. **Loropetalum chinense(Chinese Fringe)-** White stringy things, Purple or white fragrant flowers in Spring, Small vase shaped tree or irregular shrub, Beside Daniel, and in corner at McAdams. Resembles tree shape of Crape Myrtle, peely bark
29. **Leucothoe axillaries(Coastal)-** Glossy leathery leaves, drooping arching branches, pest free NATIVE, wet sites, New growth is red, White flowers
30. **Ligustrum japonicum(Waxleaf)-** Dark matt green foliage, White Flower racemes in Spring, No wet feet, heat cold salt spray drought
31. **Magnolia grandiflora(Southern Magnolia)-** If you get this one wrong!
32. **Myrica cerifera(wax myrtle)-** Wet Sites, Pest Free NATIVE, little spiky looking thing, long lanceolate leaves, fragrant
33. **Nandina domestica(heavenly bamboo)-** Trifoliate leaf, berries, White flowers in spring, berries in fall/winter, Very hardy, Sterile.
34. **Osmanthus hetrophyllus-** Most Cold Hardy, Small Holly shaped leaves, Fragrant flowers in fall, white flowers, Opposite
35. **Osmanthus x fortunei-** Opposite leaves, Pest Free, most soils, White flowers.
36. **Osmanthus fragrans 'Aurantiacus'-** non serrated leaves, **Orange**(said it would be on slide if on test) or white flowers
37. **Photinia serrulata(Chinese)-** Massive Shrub or Small tree, White Flowers in Spring, Berries in Fall, Resistant to Leaf Spot, NO wet feet.
38. **Picea abies(Norway Spruce)-** Large pyramidal tree, well drained soils, insect problem, not used much in South, Near Hardin
39. **Pinus strobes(White)-** long soft needles in 5's, blue stripes, fast growing, insect and disease problem, acid and dry soils.
40. **Pinus taeda(Loblolly)-** Long green leaves, 3 in fascicle, Large open loosely pyramidal, poor acidic soils, Fast easy screen, Large pine cones, furrowed gray brown bark, pine beetles
41. **Pinus thunbergii(Japanese black)-** Twisted, long needles in 2's, twisted coarse branches, easy to transplant
42. **Podocarpus macrophyllus-** No wet feet, Red 'fleshy berry' naked seed, slow growth, saw between pillars at Botanical Gardens
43. **Prunus laurocerasus-** White bottlebrush flowers, dark green lanceolate leaves
44. **Quercus glauca(blue Japanese)-** I mean did we even do this one? Serrated leaves a lot of branches come out of the central trunk

American Holly	Ilex opaca	465
Anglojap yew	Taxus x media	1003
Bigleaf Viburnum	Viburnum awabuki	1070
Blue Rug Juniper	Juniperus horizontalis 'Wiltoni'	514
Camellia	Camellia japonica	169
Catawba Hybrid Rhododendron	Rhododendron catawbiense	847
Chinese Evergreen Oak	Quercus myrsinifolia	823
Chinese Horned Holly	Ilex cornuta	454
Chinese Photinia	Photinia serrulata	708
Chinesefringe	Loropetalum chinense	586
Cleyera	Ternstroemia gymnanthera	1005
Coastal Leucothoe	Leucothoe axillaris	556
Compact Japanese Holly	Ilex crenata 'Compacta'	458
Cryptomeria Jap. cedar	Cryptomeria japonica	301
Deodar Cedar	Cedrus deodara	197
Eastern Hemlock	Tsuga Canadensis	1031
Eastern Redcedar	Juniperus virginiana	522
Eastern White Pine	Pinus strobus	742
Encore hybrids	Rhododendron oldhami x R. spp.	870
English laurel	Prunus laurocerasus	780
Fatsia	Fatsia japonica	374
Florida Anise	Illicium floridanum	489
Fortune Tea Olive	Osmanthus x fortunei	688
Foster's No. 2 Holly	Ilex x attenuata 'Foster's No. 2'	477
Fragrant Tea Olive	Osmanthus fragrans	689
Glossy Abelia	Abelia x grandiflora	1
Holly-leaf Tea Olive	Osmanthus heterophyllus	683
Hollywood Juniper	Juniperus chinensis 'kaizuka'	504
Indian Hawthorne	Raphiolepis umbellata	842
Inkberry	Ilex glabra	461
Japanese Aucuba	Aucuba japonica	113
Japanese black pine	Pinus thunbergii	746
Japanese Boxwood	Buxus microphylla japonica	154
Japanese Garden Juniper	Juniperus procumbens 'Nana'	517
Japanese Yew	Podocarpus macrophyllus	758
Julian (wintergreen) Barberry	Berberis julianae	118
Kurume Azalea	Rhododendron (Azalea) x obtusumn	876
Laurustinus	Viburnum tinus	1087
Leyland Cypress	X Cupressocyparis leylandii	304
Live Oak	Quercus virginiana	837
Loblolly Pine	Pinus taeda	745
Loquat	Eriobotrya japonica	349
Nandina heavenly bamboo	Nandina domestica	673
Nellie Stevens Holly	Ilex x 'Nellie R. Stevens'	?
Norway spruce	Picea abies	715
Parson's Juniper	Juniperus davurica	513
Prostrate Plum Yew	Cephalotaxus harringtonia 'Prostrata'	204
Sasanqua	Camellia sasanqua	173
Savannah Holly	Ilex x attenuata 'Savannah'	477
Shore Juniper	Juniperus conferta	512
Southern Indica Azalea	Rhododendron (Azalea) x indica	875
Southern Magnolia	Magnolia grandiflora	598
Waxleaf Ligustrum	Ligustrum japonicum	561
Waxmyrtle	Myrica cerifera	671
Windmill Palm	Trachycarpus fortunei	?
Yaupon	Ilex vomitoria	487

(handwritten, top): list 3

(handwritten, right margin):

Jap. Plum Yew
- ground - small

Jap Yew
- bush, woody stem
- crazy forms

Anglo Jap Yew
- bigger
- flat top big bush

holly -
alternate
leaves

<u>Pest-Free Native</u>
American holly
Inkberry holly
Yaupon holly
Wax myrtle
Fortune tea olive
Catawba rhondendron (not pest free)
Florida anise shrub
Southern magnolia
Eastern red cedar
Coastal leucothoe

Camelia sasanqua- finer branching patterning than C. japonica
Japanese Ceder- large pyramidal shape

Japanese Holly- densely branches, round little leaves, black fruit
Chinese Holly- many barbed lethal leaves
Chinese Holly "Burfordi"- single barbed, heavy red berry set
Chinese Holly "Carissa"- single barbed, not known for berries
Inkberry Holly- rounded leaves, black fruit
Yaupon Holly (vomitoria)- tree like (crape myrtle like on one picture), red berries, small
            leaves, wet sites
Ilex x 'Nellie R. Stevens'- Putative hybrid of *I. aquifolium* and *I. cornuta.,* tree, orange
            Berries
American Holly- large pricks on leaves
Fortune tea olive- *O. heterophyllus x O. fragrans.*
Fragrant tea olive- triangle in picture, orange flowers
English laurel- white flower spikes
catawba rhododendron- truss of flowers
Encore azalea- Hybrids of *R. oldhami*
*Viburnum tinus (*Laurustinus)- lil bush w/ blue berries
Japanese aucuba- yellow spotted varigation
Wintergreen barberry- prickly serrated leaf, lil yellow flower clumps
Loquat- Large, dark green deeply veined leaves, whitish flower panicles, yellow berry
        fruit
Florida anise shrub- dark red sculpted berries, NOT densely branched
Hollywood juniper- upright branching, twisting shape
Shore juniper- 'Blue Pacific' very low,
Creeping juniper- "blue harber' 'blue rug', creeps on ground - will have snow/ice on it
Japanese garden juniper- 2 blue strips on leave 'nana'
Chinese fringe- irregular shrub, pink or white hairy flowers, var. rubrum clones popular
Heavenly bamboo- red berries, lil white flowers, tri leaf shape
Glossy abelia- pink trumpet flowers
Easter red ceder- ugly with age
Fatsia- beside brooks, tropical leaf, hybridize w/ English ivy
Coastal leucothoe- surfboard leaves, has glossy dark red leaf color
Norway spruce- pretty limbs, curls and points up
Chinese photinia- green cousin of red tip, massive shrub, large bundle of lil white flowers
Indian heather- mounded shrub w/ round leaves
Southern indica azalea- lacebugs and petal blight
Cleyera- Upright oval broadleaf glossy leafed evergreen, good in shade
Loblolly- 3 fascicle, harsh looking
White pine- 5 fascicle, soft looking

Japanese black cedar- twisted

- mulch + leaf litter retard weed growth
- OM may be most important factor for plant growth

slopes
North: less light
south: solar gain, winterburn
Eastern: sunny mornings
Western: hot afternoons, winter damage

- xeriscape: dry landscape 30-60% H2O reduction
- shade garden
- H2O garden - space + new textures
- courtyard garden - inside
- rock + alpine garden

smaller gardens better?
- use less resources (land + E)
- less labor, but more intensive
- wave of future?

Irrigation
overhead - 40% loss
precision - 5% loss

- topography - slopes and contours of land

Allergy
- glycoproteins -
- ragweed pollen
  - 99% falls w/in 20ft of tree
  - male clones are favored b/c less litter
  - CA leads in nation

red   ## white
pin   post
Northern   bur
southern   water
-

Allergy

-glycoproteins
-ragweed:
*99% falls w/in 20 feet of tree
*male clones are favored b/c less litter
*CA leads nation

>   -Mow grass before it flowers, or if in flower mow in
>   afternoon (grass pollen is released between 3 AM and 8 AM).

- Weed species in bloom can problematic.
- Hard pruning of plants that flower on 'next years' wood.
- Choose plants wisely with sexual characteristics in mind.
- Avoid specific allergenic pollen sources.

Best plants

- Females, without messy fruit.
- In theory, female only landscapes would never set fruit.
- Mutations with reduced numbers of anthers or reduced pollen production.
- Bi-sexual with anthers set deeply within flowers.

Worst plants

- Acer rubrum – 'Autumn Spire' and 'Tilford'
- Aspidistra eliator
- Camelia ssp. (doubles)
- Cephalotaxus males.
- Chionanthus males (seed propagated)
- Acer rubrum – 'October Glory' and 'Red Sunset'
- Callistemon ssp.
- Carya ssp. Pecan is allergenic.
- Cephalotaxus females.
- Chionanthus females (seed propagated)

Oaks-

- Can be the dominant, largest plant in environment.
- Produces the most pollen over longest season.

Weeds

- Ailanthus altissima (tree of heaven)
- Albizia julibrissin (mimosa)
- Paulownia tomentosa (empress tree)
- Melia azedarach (Chinaberry)
- Triadica sebifera (Chinese tallow tree)
- Euonymus fortunei (winter creeper)
- Hedera helix (English ivy)
- Lonicera japonica (Japanese honeysuckle)
- Pueraria montana (kudzu)
- Vinca major/minor (big and small periwinkle)
- **Wisteria sinensis/floribunda (Chinese/Japanese wisteria)**

10-20% Americans suffer
hay fever + asthma

2 functions: feed itself, reproduce

shoot functions: collect E, collect CO_2, storage, photosynthesis, functions as 1 organism
root functions: anchors plant, provide H_2O + nutrients

photosynthesis: $CO_2 + H_2O \xrightarrow{E} C_6H_{12}O_2$
     • low E sources +E → high E
• E is transported in sucrose, stored as starch or used for growth as cellulose

respiration:
     $(C_6H_{12}O_2)n$ 'burned' w/ O_2 to yield chem E for metabolism

Net Photosynthesis Rate (NPR) = Photosynthesis − Respiration
     − NPR positive - plant grows   −at night NPR is neg.

development - formation of new organs   growth - elongation of existing cells

leaf function - solar collector
leaf stomata - CO_2 fixed in C, H_2O diffuses out to cool leaf (transpiration)

stem - sugar moves down phloem   Root anatomy
     H_2O UP   xylem

                                      lateral root
-canopy architecture   root hairs — region of cell elongation
                                     meristem (undercap)
                                     root cap

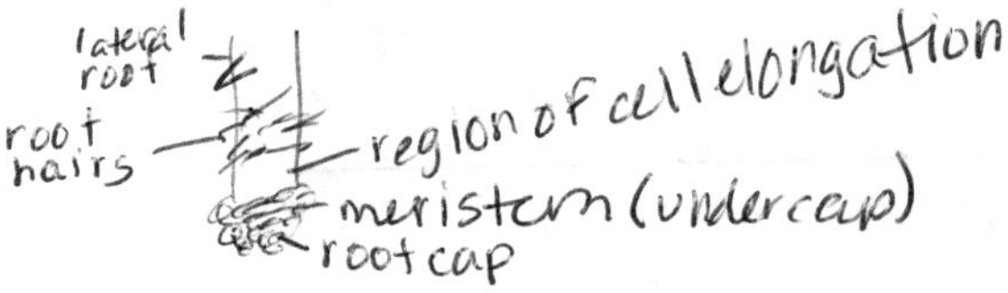

water absorption - no biological processes
nutrient   "   - lots of biological energy - sugars

Taproots   Fibrous   Fine feeder roots
                                     -short lived
                                     -grow where the resources are
- primary root   -no one root prominant
- deep soil   -close to surface
- pine tree   -grass, corn
                -easy to transplant

Planting too deep: reduce O_2, H_2O, nutrient; increase fungal infestation
     -best practice: plant where root flare is at surface + apply mulch

soil environment: air, water, minerals, OM
aerial   "   : wind, light, heat, humidity

loam are ideal: 50% solid
            25% water ⎫ 50% pores
            25% air ⎭

Native:

- Summersweet
- Flowering dogwood
- Virginia sweetspire
- Sweetshrub
- White fringe tree
- Loblolly bay (to marshes)
- Cross vine
- Carolina yellow Jessamine
-
-
-
-

Pest Free:
- japanese dogwood
- star magnolia
- sweetshrub
- cornelian cherry dogwood
- cross vine
- carolina yellow jessamine
- lily turf and creeping lilyturf
- monkeygrass
- bugle flower
- five leaf akebia
- cast iron plant
- holly fern

Armand's clematis- overhang at SCBG
Buckeye- opposite, palmately compound leaves
Bumald spirea- dense shrub; green leaves w/ hints of purple or yellowish leaves
Burning bush- flame red fall color, horizontal shrub
Confederate Jasmine- climbing vine with white flowers
Clematis- good for growing on evergreen for pretty flower color
Crossvine- yellow, orange, pink trumpet flowers
Creeping fig- flat on wall
Cornelian cherry dogwood- shrubbier, limbs all the way down stem
Dogwood:
 Flowering-disease problems
 Japanese- pest-free
XFatshedera- Inter-generic hybrid of *Fatsia* and *Hedera*;Cold hardy and variegated like *Hedera*; Flowers
and erect like *Fatsia*; Does not run like *Hedera*
Fringe tree:
    Chinese fringe tree: rounder, leathery, dark green leaves
    White fringe tree: more oblong leaves
Golden rain tree:
  Bougainvillea: larger tree, later bloom, salmon fruit, always bipinnatley lobed leaves
  Common: small tree; alternate compound leaves; both pinnate or bi-pinnate
Higan cherry- var. Pendula is weeping form
Holly fern- spore clusters make spotted pattern on back of leaves
Hydrangea- opposite leaves
Japanese spurge- spreads by rhizomes
Japanese spurge- spreads by rhizomes
Korean spice viburnum- looks like a hydrangea - white flower + pink buds, sandpaper texture
Lady Banks rose- thornless; resistant to black spot; yellow or white flowers
Lenten rose- roses nod upside down
Loblolly bay- sweet smell in crushed leaves
Marlberry- winter kill is problem
Paper bark maple- trifoliate leaves, opposite
Serviceberry- fruit is edible
Sweetshrub- red, fragrant flowers
Sargent's viburnum- lacecap flowers; related to cranberry bush
Tea crabapple- many insect and disease problems (resists jap. Beetles)
Winter jasmine- looks like thunbergii but has small trifoliate leaves; square stem
Winterberry holly-male is needed for berry
Winterberry and Amer. Beautyberry- large coarse shrub with winter interest in berries

forsythia- scragely

Scientific name	Common name	No.
Acer buergerianium	trident maple	13
Acer griseum	Paperbark maple	19
Acer palmatum	Japanese Maple	27
Aesculus parviflora	Bottlebrush Buckeye	75
Aesculus pavia	Red Buckeye	7
Ajuga reptans	Bugleflower	
Akebia quinata	Fiveleaf Akebia	8
Amelanchier sp.	Serviceberry	47
Ardisia japonica	Whitecap Marlberry	10
Aspidistra elatior	Cast-iron Plant	11
Bignonia capreolata	Crossvine	69
Buddleia davidii	Butterfly-bush	14
Callicarpa americana	American Beautyberry	159
Calycanthus floridus	Sweetshrub; carolina allspice	160
Cercis canadensis	Eastern Redbud	208
Chionanthus retusus	Chinese Graybeard	229
Chionanthus virginicus	Fringetree	227
Clematis armandii	Armand's clematis	236
Clematis virginiana	Virgin's Bower	238
Clethera alnifolia	Summersweet clethera	239
Cornus florida	Flowering Dogwood	253
Cornus kousa	Chinese Dogwood	260
Cornus mas	Cornelian Cherry Dogwood	268
Corylus avellana 'Contorta'	Henry Lauder's walking stick	279
Cyrtomium falcatum	Holly Fern	311
Euonymus alatus	Burning Bush	354
Euonymus fortunei	Wintercreeper	359
Ficus carica	Common fig	377
Ficus pumila	Climbing Fig	377
Forsythia x intermedia	Forsythia	379
Fothergilla gardenii	Dwarf Fothergilla	385
Gelsemium sempervirens	Carolina yellow Jessamine	403
Gordonia lasianthus	Loblolly Bay	391
Hamamelis mollis	Chinese Witchhazel	419
Hedera helix	English Ivy	425
Helleborus orientalis	Lenten Rose	107
Hemerocallis spp.	Daylilies	197
Hibiscus syriacus	Rose-of-Sharon	427
Hosta	Hosta	
Hydrangea arborescens	Smooth Hydrangea	435
Hydrangea paniculata	Panicle Hydrangea	442
Hydrangea quercifolia	Oakleaf Hydrangea	446
Ilex verticillata	Winterberry	467
Itea virginica	Virginia Sweetspire	495
Jasminum nudiflorum	Winter Jasmine	497
Koelreuteria bipinnata	Bougainvillea Goldenrain Tree	534
Koelreuteria paniculata	Goldenrain Tree	533
Lagerstroemia indica	Crape Myrtle	538
Liriope muscari	Lilyturf	
Liriope spicata	Creeping Lilyturf	599
Magnolia stellata	Star Magnolia	616
Magnolia virginiana	Sweetbay	618
Magnolia x soulangiana	Saucer Magnolia	611
Malus hupehensis	tea crabapple	644
Ophiopogon japonicus	Monkeygrass	
Pachysandra terminalis	Japanese Spurge	694
Prunus serrulata	Japanese Cherry	789
Prunus subhirtella	Higan Cherry	790
Prunus x yedoensis	Yoshino Cherry	793
Pyrus calleryana	Callery Bradford Pear	806
Rhododendron canescens	Piedmont Azalea	854
Rosa banksiae	Lady Banks Rose	910
Rosmarinus officianalis	Rosemary	918
Sarcococca hookeriana var. humilis	Sweetbox	935
Spiraea x bumalda	Bumald Spirea	956
Spirea thunbergii	Thunberg's spirea	963
Stewartia pseudocamelia	Japanese stewwartia	971
Styrax japonica	Japanese snowbell	973
Trachelospermum asiaticum	Yellow star jasmine	1028
Trachelospermum jasminoides	Confederate Jasmine	1027
Viburnum carlesii	Koreanspice Viburnum	1060
Viburnum sargentii	Sargent viburnum	1084
Vinca major	Big Periwinkle	1090
Vitex agnus-castus	Chastetree	1091
Wisteria floribunda	Japanese Wisteria	1098
X Fatshedera lizei	Bush Ivy	375

Common name	No.
trident maple	13
American Beautyberry	159
Armand's clematis	236
Big Periwinkle	1090
Bottlebrush Buckeye	75
Bougainvillea Goldenrain Tree	534
Bugleflower	
Bumald Spirea	956
Burning Bush	354
Bush Ivy	375
Butterfly-bush	144
Callery Bradford Pear	806
Carolina yellow Jessamine	403
Cast-iron Plant	112
Chastetree	1091
Chinese Dogwood	260
Chinese Graybeard	229
Chinese Witchhazel	419
Climbing Fig	377
Common fig	377
Confederate Jasmine	1027
Cornelian Cherry Dogwood	268
Crape Myrtle	538
Creeping Lilyturf	599
Crossvine	694
Daylilies	197
Dwarf Fothergilla	385
Eastern Redbud	208
English Ivy	425
Fiveleaf Akebia	81
Flowering Dogwood	253
Forsythia	379
Fringetree	227
Goldenrain Tree	533
Henry Lauder's walking stick	279
Higan Cherry	790
Holly Fern	311
Hosta	

Japanese Cherry	789
Japanese Maple	27
Japanese snowbell	973
Japanese Spurge	694
Japanese stewwartia	971
Japanese Wisteria	1098
Koreanspice Viburnum	1060
Lady Banks Rose	910
Lenten Rose	107
Lilyturf	
Loblolly Bay	391
Monkeygrass	
Oakleaf Hydrangea	446
Panicle Hydrangea	442
Paperbark maple	19
Piedmont Azalea	854
Red Buckeye	77
Rosemary	918
Rose-of-Sharon	427
Sargent viburnum	1084

Saucer Magnolia	611
Serviceberry	471
Smooth Hydrangea	435
Star Magnolia	616
Summersweet clethera	239
Sweetbay	618
Sweetbox	935
Sweetshrub; carolina allspice	166
tea crabapple	644
Thunberg's spirea	963
Virginia Sweetspire	495
Virgin's Bower	238
Whitecap Marlberry	107
Winter Jasmine	497
Winterberry	467
Wintercreeper	359
Yellow star jasmine	1028
Yoshino Cherry	793

American Beech	369
American Elm	1034
Bald Cypress	996
Bitternut Hickory	184
Black Gum	680
Bur Oak	821
Catalpa	193
Chinese Chestnut	190
Chinese Pistache	749
Dawn Redwood	662
Fraxinus pennsylvanica/ Green A	393
Freeman's maple	45
Ginkgo	406
Hackberry	203
Japanese Zelkova	1106
Katsura Tree	207
Lacebark/Chinese Elm	1041
Large leaf linden	1018
Little leaf linden	1020
London Plane Tree	752
Mimosa	83
Northern Red Oak	835
Norway Maple	40
Overcup Oak	820
Pecan	154
Persian Parrotia	695
Pin Oak	826
Post Oak	837
Red Maple	44
River Birch	126
Sawtooth Oak	812
Shumard Oak	829
Silver Maple	50
Sourwood	692
Southern red oak	816
Sugar Maple	53
Sweetgum	568
Thornless Honeylocust	408
Tulip Poplar	572
Umbrella Magnolia	617
Upright English Oak	833
Upright European Hornbeam	178
Water Oak	826
Weeping Willow	922
White Oak	814
Willow Oak	830
Winged Elm	1037

Drought tolerant

Pistacia Chinensis
Norway Maple
80 Shumard oak
  mimosa
bitternut hickory-
winged elm-
pecan
post oak
overcup oak-

_____ tolerant

river birch
weeping willow
bald cypress
- bitternut hickory
dawn redwood
- winged elm
silver maple
- overcup oak
Red maple

moist, organi soils

umbrella magnol
black gum
sourwood

Messy

Mimosa
Tulip Poplar
chinese chestnut
Pecan
sweetgum
water oak
weeping willow

Street tree

Pin Oak
Jap. zelkova
Green Ash
Ginkgo

chinese pistache 
persian parrotia 
Japanese zelkova

light canopy

thornless honey locust
southern red oak

white oak - whiskey
sourwood - best honey
green ash - base ball bats

willow oak - leaves acidic, kills weeds + grass.
american beech - elephant leg trunk; carving tree
catalpa - long bean pods
sugar maple - SC furthest S you can grow it
Ginkgo - no pest; only plant in family + order